P9-DXO-065

Cassell's French and English Dictionary

Other Cassell's Dictionaries available from Collier Books

Cassell's Spanish and English Dictionary

Cassell's German and English Dictionary

Cassell's

French and English Dictionary

Compiled by

J. H. DOUGLAS, B.A.

DENIS GIRARD

W. THOMPSON, M.A.

COLLIER BOOKS

MACMILLAN PUBLISHING COMPANY

New York

Macmillan Publishing Company
866 Third Avenue, New York, N.Y. 10022
Collier Macmillan Canada, Inc.

Library of Congress Cataloging-in-Publication Data
Douglas, J. H. (John Henry)
    Cassell's French and English dictionary.
    Originally published: Cassell's new compact
French-English, English-French dictionary. New York :
Funk & Wagnalls, 1978.
    1. French language—Dictionaries—English.
2. English language—Dictionaries—French. I. Girard,
Denis.   II. Thompson, W., M.A.   III. Title.
PC2640.D68   1986   443'.21   86-8814
ISBN 0-02-013680-3

First Collier Books Edition 1986

17 16

Printed in the United States of America

Contents

Contents

Preface

This new edition of a work which appeared for the first time in 1904 represents a departure from tradition in that it is not a revised version of its immediate predecessor, but an entirely new work based on 'Cassell's New French Dictionary' compiled by Denis Girard and first published in 1962.

The availability of such a recent publication, and one moreover which has been widely accepted as a reliable work, has made the editors' task much easier than it could ever have been otherwise. The dead wood had already been cut away and many new words had been introduced, but it will come as no surprise that there are entries in the 'Concise' which do not appear in the 'New', e.g. 'escalate', and that others which were included in the 'New' for the first time in 1962 have already been discarded as obsolete, e.g. 'teddy boy'.

It is, of course, the question of selection which poses the greatest problem for anyone concerned with the compilation of a dictionary of limited size. Many uncommon words inevitably fail to find a place, as do the less frequent uses of some which have been included. We have tried wherever possible to illustrate by examples, but we have not attempted to incorporate information which properly belongs to a grammar book rather than a dictionary. It is assumed that the user will have a knowledge not only of parts of speech but also of the essential basic grammar of both languages. Although personal preference may have played a part, we have always tried to regard suitability for this type of dictionary as the primary consideration for or against the inclusion of a word, and we hope that we have, if anything, erred on the safe side.

Several features in the general layout of the 'New French Dictionary' have been incorporated for the first time in the 'Concise'. These include the use of the symbols of the International Phonetic Association throughout, the detailed information given in the 'Advice to the User' and the tables of English and French verbs. Completely new features are the notes at the head of the verb tables and the increased use of French in the explanatory parentheses in the English–French section.

J. H. D.

Advice to the User

Grouping of Words
In both sections of the dictionary alphabetical order has been strictly observed for all entries, including proper nouns.

Numbering of Identical Words
Words which are spelt alike but which differ in origin or pronunciation are numbered separately.

Punctuation
When several translations are given for one word it can generally be assumed that those which are separated by commas have much the same meaning; semi-colons are used where there is a clear difference in meaning or usage.

Words or meanings marked with an asterisk (*) are obsolete.

Pronunciation
The phonetic transcription is given in square brackets immediately after the key-word and alternative pronunciations have been given where necessary. The mark (') precedes the syllable which carries the stress.

The symbols of the International Phonetic Association have been used throughout the dictionary, and the user who is unfamiliar with these should refer to the Key to Pronunciation.

Daniel Jones' *English Pronouncing Dictionary* has usually been followed in the English–French section.

Grammatical Information
It is assumed that the user will have a reasonable knowledge of the basic grammar of the two languages. For example, when a noun merely adds **-s** for the plural or an adjective **-e** for the feminine, it has not been considered necessary to show this. Parts of speech are indicated by an abbreviation in italics (*a.*, *n.m.*, *v.t.*, *adv.* etc.) except in the case of proper nouns where in English no indication has been given and in French only the gender. For the meanings of the abbreviations the user is referred to the list on page xiv.

Nouns and Adjectives
In the French–English section French nouns are classed as *n.m.* for the masculine, *n.f.* for the feminine or *n.* for a noun which may be masculine or feminine according to context. In the English–French section the gender of French nouns is shown by the abbreviations *m.* or *f.*; where a noun, without change of form, may be masculine or feminine both genders are given. In a list of nouns the gender is not given after each one and the user should therefore read on to the next gender mentioned, e.g. under **damage** he will find 'dommage; tort,

viii

Groupement des Mots

Dans les deux parties du dictionnaire l'ordre alphabétique a été strictement suivi pour tous les articles, y compris les noms propres.

Numérotage de Mots Identiques

Les mots qui ont la même orthographe sont numérotés séparément lorsqu'ils ont une racine ou une prononciation différente.

Ponctuation

Quand plusieurs traductions sont données pour un même mot, celles qui ne sont séparées que par des virgules ont en règle générale des sens à peu près identiques; le point-virgule est utilisé pour indiquer des différences très nettes de sens ou d'emploi.

Les mots précédés d'un astérisque (*) sont désuets.

Prononciation

La transcription phonétique est donnée entre crochets immédiatement après le mot principal. Lorsqu'il y a d'autres prononciations possibles, elles sont également indiquées. L'accent (') précède la syllabe qui porte l'accent tonique.

Les signes de l'Association Internationale de Phonétique sont utilisés dans les deux parties du dictionnaire et le lecteur qui n'est pas familiarisé avec ces signes devra consulter la Table de Prononciation.

Pour la section Anglais–Français, on a généralement suivi le dictionnaire de M. Daniel Jones, *An English Pronouncing Dictionary*.

Indications Grammaticales

Le lecteur est considéré comme ayant une connaissance suffisante de la grammaire de base des deux langues. Par exemple, quand un nom français forme son pluriel en -s et quand un adjectif forme son féminin en -e, il n'a pas paru nécessaire de l'indiquer. La nature des mots est indiquée par une abréviation en italique (*a.*, *n.m.*, *v.t.*, *adv.* etc.) excepté dans le cas des noms propres pour lesquels aucune indication n'a été donnée dans la partie Anglais–Français et seulement le genre dans la partie Français–Anglais. On trouvera la signification des abréviations à la page xiv.

Noms et adjectifs

Dans la partie Français–Anglais, les noms français sont classés en *n.m.* pour les noms masculins, en *n.f.* pour les noms féminins et *n.* pour ceux qui se modifient selon le contexte. Dans la partie Anglais–Français, le genre des noms français est indiqué par les abréviations *m.* ou *f.*; lorsqu'un nom peut, sans changer de forme, être soit du masculin soit du féminin, les deux genres sont donnés. Dans une

dégât; (*fig.*) préjudice, détriment, *m.*' and he will know from this that all these five nouns are masculine. In the English–French section the feminine forms of French adjectives and nouns (where applicable) are not normally given. The user should consult the relevant French word in the French–English section.

Where plurals or feminines of nouns or adjectives are given, abbreviated forms are used. For example the entry **cheval** (pl. **-aux**) means that the full plural word is **chevaux**. Similarly, **acteur** (*fem.* **-trice**) indicates that the feminine form is **actrice**.

Verbs

All Verbs, other than reflexive verbs, form their compound tenses with **avoir** unless there is an indication with the entry that they take **être**. For all further information on verb entries please consult notes on Verb Tables below.

Verb Tables

1. French verbs have been listed in the tables as follows:

   a. A pattern verb for each of the three regular conjugations.
   b. Pattern verbs which may best be described as 'anomalous', i.e. verbs which are basically regular but which, for one reason or another, show slight variations from the normal forms.
   c. An alphabetical list of irregular verbs, some of which are used as a reference for other verbs which show similar irregularities.

Full conjugations have been given for the regular verbs but elsewhere only where it is considered necessary or desirable.

2. An alphabetical list of all irregular English verbs included in this dictionary is given. The user is referred to the Verb Tables for a note on the following:

   a. Verbs ending in **-y** preceded by one or more consonants.
   b. Certain verbs ending in a consonant preceded by a vowel.

3. The following explanation of verb entries in the dictionary may be helpful:

   a. *irr.* See the verb in question in the list of irregular verbs.
   b. *irr.* (*conjug. like* . . . . . .) See the pattern verb in the list of irregular verbs.
   c. (*see Verb Tables*) See the verb in question in the list of anomalous verbs.
   d. (*conjug. like* . . . . . .) See the pattern verb in the list of anomalous verbs.

liste de noms, le genre n'est pas donné après chacun d'eux et le lecteur doit alors se référer au premier genre indiqué, e.g. pour **damage** il trouvera 'dommage; tort, dégât; (*fig.*) préjudice, détriment, *m.*' et il en déduira que ces cinq noms sont du masculin. Dans la partie Anglais–Français, le féminin des mots français, lorsqu'il existe, n'est en principe pas indiqué; on le trouvera dans la partie Français–Anglais.

Lorsque le pluriel ou le féminin des noms ou des adjectifs est indiqué, il est donné en abrégé. Par exemple, **cheval** (*pl.* -aux) signifie que la forme de ce mot au pluriel est **chevaux**. De même, **acteur** (*fem.* -**trice**) signifie que la forme du féminin est **actrice**.

Verbes
Tous les verbes, autres que les verbes réfléchis, forment leurs temps composés avec l'auxiliaire **avoir**, à moins qu'il soit indiqué qu'ils se conjuguent avec **être**. On trouvera ci-dessous des renseignements complémentaires sur les verbes.

Tables des Verbes

1. Les verbes français sont présentés de la façon suivante:

   a. un verbe-type pour chacune des trois conjugaisons régulières.
   b. des verbes-types 'anomaux', c'est-à-dire, des verbes qui sont fondamentalement réguliers mais qui comportent de légères variations par rapport aux formes normales.
   c. une liste alphabétique des verbes irréguliers dont certains servent de références à d'autres verbes présentant des irrégularités analogues.

La conjugaison des verbes réguliers a été donnée en entier, mais pour les autres verbes elle ne figure que lorsque cela paraît nécessaire.

2. On trouvera une liste alphabétique de tous les verbes irréguliers anglais qui sont donnés dans ce dictionnaire, précédée par des renseignements sur les groupes suivants:

   a. Verbes qui se terminent en **-y** précédé d'une ou plus d'une consonne.
   b. Certains verbes qui se terminent en une consonne précédée d'une voyelle.

3. Les renseignements suivants concernant la présentation des verbes dans le dictionnaire pourront s'avérer utiles:

   a. *irr.* Se reporter à la liste des verbes irréguliers.
   b. *irr.* (*conjug. like* . . . . . .) Voir le verbe-type dans la liste des verbes irréguliers.
   c. (*see Verb Tables*) Voir ce verbe dans la liste des verbes anomaux.
   d. (*conjug. like* . . . . . .) Voir le verbe-type dans la liste des verbes anomaux.

Key to Pronunciation

VOWELS

FRENCH (1)

i   as in cri [kri], difficile [difi'sil]
i: ,, ,, écrire [e'kri:r], finir [fi'ni:r]
e   ,, ,, thé [te], mélodie [melɔ'di]
ɛ   ,, ,, réel [re'ɛl], aile [ɛl]
ɛ: ,, ,, bête [bɛ:t], dentaire [dɑ̃'tɛ:r]
a   ,, ,, patte [pat], apparat [apa'ra]
a: ,, ,, tard [ta:r], barbare [bar'ba:r]
ɑ   ,, ,, pas [pɑ], tailler [tɑ'je]
ɑ: ,, ,, gaz [gɑ:z], pâte [pɑ:t]
ɔ   ,, ,, coter [kɔ'te], voler [vɔ'le]
ɔ: ,, ,, confort [kɔ̃'fɔ:r], porc [pɔ:r]
o   ,, ,, côté [ko'te], gros [gro], tôt [to]
o: ,, ,, dôme [do:m], rôle [ro:l]
u   ,, ,, coup [ku], tourner [tur'ne]
u: ,, ,, bourre [bu:r], cour [ku:r]
y   ,, ,, cru [kry], salut [sa'ly]
y: ,, ,, littérature [litera'ty:r]
ø   ,, ,, neveu [nə'vø], rocheux [rɔ'ʃø]
ø: ,, ,, mitrailleuse [mitrɑ'jø:z]
œ   ,, ,, feuillet [fœ'jɛ]
œ: ,, ,, faveur [fa'vœ:r]
ə   ,, ,, le [lə], refaire [rə'fɛ:r]

ENGLISH (1)

i: as in seat [si:t]
i   ,, ,, finish ['finiʃ], physics ['fiziks]
e   ,, ,, neck [nek], bread [bred]
æ   ,, ,, man [mæn], malefactor ['mælifæktə]
ɑ: ,, ,, father ['fɑ:ðə], task [tɑ:sk]
ɔ   ,, ,, block [blɔk], waddle [wɔdl]
ɔ: ,, ,, shawl [ʃɔ:l], tortoise ['tɔ:təs]
o   ,, ,, domain [do'mein]
u   ,, ,, good [gud], July [dʒu'lai]
u: ,, ,, moon [mu:n], tooth [tu:θ]
ʌ   ,, ,, cut [kʌt], somewhere ['sʌmwɛə]
ə: ,, ,, search [sə:tʃ], surgeon ['sə:dʒən]
ə   ,, ,, cathedral [kə'θi:drəl], never ['nevə]

NASAL VOWELS

ɛ̃   as in faim [fɛ̃], vingt [vɛ̃]
ɛ̃:   ,, ,, feindre [fɛ̃:dr], poindre [pwɛ̃:dr]
ɑ̃   ,, ,, ensemencement [ɑ̃smɑ̃s'mɑ̃]
ɑ̃:   ,, ,, défendre [de'fɑ̃:dr]
ɔ̃   ,, ,, son [sɔ̃], fonder [fɔ̃'de]
ɔ̃:   ,, ,, contre [kɔ̃:tr], trompe [trɔ̃:p]
œ̃   ,, ,, défunt [de'fœ̃], un [œ̃]
œ̃:   ,,   humble [œ̃:bl]

DIPHTHONGS

ei   as in great [greit]
ou   ,, ,, show [ʃou]
ai   ,, ,, high [hai]
au   ,, ,, crowd [kraud]
ɔi   ,, ,, boy [bɔi]
iə   ,, ,, steer [stiə]
ɛə   ,, ,, hair [hɛə]
uə   ,, ,, moor [muə]

CONSONANTS

FRENCH (1)

p as in peine [pɛn], papier [pa'pje]
b „ „ bon [bɔ̃]
t „ „ tâter [tɑ'te], thé [te]
d „ „ dinde [dɛ̃:d]
k „ „ coquelicot [kɔkli'ko]
ɡ „ „ gare [ɡa:r]
m „ „ maman [ma'mɑ̃], même [mɛ:m]
n „ „ nonne [nɔn]

ɲ „ „ agneau [a'ɲo], soigner [swa'ɲe]
f „ „ fier [fje:r]
v „ „ vivre [vi:vr]

s „ „ sucre [sykr]
z „ „ raser [rɑ'ze]
l „ „ lettre [lɛtr], valise [va'li:z]
ʃ „ „ charme [ʃarm]
ʒ „ „ ronger [rɔ̃'ʒe], joue [ʒu]
r „ „ arrière [a'rjɛ:r]

ENGLISH (1)

p as in paper ['peipə]
b „ „ ball [bɔ:l]
t „ „ tea [ti:], till [til]
d „ „ deed [di:d]
k „ „ cake [keik]
ɡ „ „ game [ɡeim]
m „ „ mammoth ['mæməθ]
n „ „ nose [nouz], nun [nʌn]
ŋ „ „ bring [briŋ], finger ['fiŋɡə]

f „ „ fair [fɛə], far [fɑ:]
v „ „ vine [vain]
θ „ „ thin [θin], bath [bɑ:θ]
ð „ „ this [ðis], bathe [beið]
s „ „ since [sins]
z „ „ busy ['bizi]
l „ „ land [lænd], hill [hil]
ʃ „ „ shield [ʃi:ld], sugar ['ʃuɡə]
ʒ „ „ visionary ['viʒənəri]
r „ „ rut [rʌt], brain [brein]
h „ „ here [hiə], horse [hɔ:ə]
x „ „ loch [lɔx]

SEMI-CONSONANTS

j as in rien [rjɛ̃]
w „ „ ouate [wat], oui [wi]
ɥ „ „ huile [ɥil]

j as in yellow ['jelou], yes [jes]
w „ „ wall [wɔ:l]

When the same symbol is used in both English and French it often represents a different sound in each language.

' denotes that the stress is on the following syllable.
: denotes that the preceding vowel is long.
~ placed over a vowel-symbol shows that the vowel has a nasal sound.

List of Abbreviations

a.	adjective
abbr.	abbreviation
Adm.	Administration
adv.	adverb
adv. phr.	adverbial phrase
affirm.	affirmative
Agric.	Agriculture
Alg.	Algebra
Am.	American
Anat.	Anatomy
Ant.	Antiquities
Arch.	Architecture
Archaeol.	Archaeology
Arith.	Arithmetic
art.	article
Artill.	Artillery
Astron.	Astronomy
aux.	auxiliary
Av.	Aviation
Bibl.	Bible, Biblical
Biol.	Biology
Bookb.	Bookbinding
Bot.	Botany
Box.	Boxing
Build.	Building
(C)	Canadian usage
Carp.	Carpentry
Ch.	Church
Chem.	Chemistry
Cine.	Cinema
Civ. Eng.	Civil Engineering
Coin.	Coinage
collect.	collective
colloq.	colloquially
comb.	combination
comb. form	combining form
Comm.	Commerce
comp.	comparative
Conch.	Conchology
cond.	conditional
conj.	conjunction
conjug.	conjugated
contr.	contraction
Cook.	Cookery
Cost.	Costume
Cycl.	Cycling
dat.	dative
def.	definite
dem.	demonstrative
Dent.	Dentistry
dial.	dialect
dim.	diminutive
Dress.	Dressmaking
Eccles.	Ecclesiastical
Econ.	Economics
Elec.	Electricity
ellipt.	elliptic
emphat.	emphatic
Eng.	Engineering
Engl.	English
Engr.	Engraving
Ent.	Entomology
esp.	especially
Exam.	Examination
f.	feminine
fam.	familiarly
facet.	facetiously
fem.	feminine
Fenc.	Fencing
Feud.	Feudal
fig.	figuratively
Fin.	Financial
foll.	the following
Fort.	Fortification
Fr.	French
Ftb.	Assoc. Football
fut.	future
Gard.	Gardening
Geog.	Geography
Geol.	Geology
Geom.	Geometry
Gr.	Greek
Gram.	Grammar
Gym.	Gymnastic
Her.	Heraldry
Hist.	History
Horol.	Horology
Hort.	Horticulture
Hunt.	Hunting
Hydr.	Hydrostatics
i.	intransitive
Ichth.	Ichthyology
imp.	imperfect
impers.	impersonal
Ind.	Industry
indec.	indecent
indef.	indefinite
indic.	indicative
inf.	infinitive
int.	interjection
inter.	interrogative
inv.	invariable
iron.	ironical
irr.	irregular (see table of Irregular Verbs, pp. 636–58)
It.	Italian
Jew.	Jewish
Journ.	Journalism
L.	Latin
Lit.	Literature
Log.	Logic
m.	masculine
Mach.	Machinery
Manuf.	Manufacturing
masc.	masculine
Math.	Mathematics
Mech.	Mechanics
Med.	Medicine
Metal.	Metallurgy
Meteor.	Meteorology
Mil.	Military
Min.	Mineralogy
Motor.	Motoring
Mount.	Mountaineering
Mus.	Music
Myth.	Mythology
n.	noun
Nat.	Natural
Naut.	Nautical
neg.	negative
obj.	object
obs.	obsolete
Opt.	Optics
Orn.	Ornithology
Paint.	Painting
Parl.	Parliamentary
part.	participle, participial
Path.	Pathology
pej.	pejorative
perf.	perfect
pers.	person, personal
Pharm.	Pharmacy
Phil.	Philosophy
Philol.	Philology
Phon.	Phonetics
Phot.	Photography
phr.	phrase
Phys.	Physics
Physiol.	Physiology
pl.	plural
poet.	poetical
Polit.	Politics
pop.	popular
poss.	possessive
p.p.	past participle
prec.	the preceding
pref.	prefix
prep.	preposition
pres.	present
pres. p.	present participle
Print.	Printing
pron.	pronoun
prop.	proper, properly
Pros.	Prosody
Psych.	Psychology
Pyro.	Pyrotechnics
r.	reflexive; reciprocal
Rad.	Radio
Rail.	Railway
R.C.	Roman Catholic
reg.	registered
rel.	relative
Relig.	Religion
rhet.	rhetoric
Rom.	Roman
Row.	Rowing
Sc.	Scottish
Sch.	Schools
Sci.	Science
Sculp.	Sculpture
sing.	singular
s.o.'s	someone's
Spt.	Sport
St. Exch.	Stock Exchange
subj.	subjunctive
superl.	superlative
Surg.	Surgery
Surv.	Surveying
Swim.	Swimming
t.	transitive
Tech.	Technical
Tel.	Television
Teleg.	Telegraphy
Teleph.	Telephone
Ten.	Tennis
Tex.	Textiles
Theat.	Theatrical
Theol.	Theological
Trig.	Trigonometry
Univ.	University
U.S.	United States
usu.	usually
v.	verb
Vet.	Veterinary
v.i.	intransitive verb
v.r.	reflexive or reciprocal verb
v.t.	transitive verb
vulg.	vulgar
Zool.	Zoology

A, a [a], *n.m.* in French *a* has two sounds: (1) as in *part*, shown in this dictionary by 'a'; (2) as in *pas*, shown by 'ɑ'.

à [a], *prep.* [*see also* AU, AUX] to, at, in, into, on, by, for, from, with.

abaisse [a'bɛːs], *n.f.* undercrust of pastry.

abaissement [abɛs'mã], *n.m.* lowering, falling, abatement, depression; humiliation, abasement.

abaisser [abɛ'se], *v.t.* to let down, to let fall, to lower; to diminish, to reduce; (*fig.*) to bring low, to humble, to depress; to roll out (*paste*). **s'abaisser**, *v.r.* to sink, to subside, to decrease, to abate, to decline; to humble oneself, to stoop, to cringe.

abajoue [aba'ʒu], *n.f.* (*Zool.*) cheek pouch.

abalourdir [abalur'diːr], *v.t.* to make dull *or* stupid.

abalourdissement [abalurdis'mã], *n.m.* dullness, stupidity.

abandon [abã'dɔ̃], *n.m.* relinquishment, surrender, cession; abandonment, forlornness, destitution; lack of restraint; *à l'abandon*, at random, in confusion, at sixes and sevens; (*Naut.*) adrift.

abandonné [abãdɔ'ne], *a.* abandoned, forsaken; lost to decency, shameless, profligate.

abandonnement [abãdɔn'mã], *n.m.* abandonment; desertion; (*fig.*) dissoluteness, profligacy.

abandonnément [abãdɔne'mã], *adv.* freely, unreservedly.

abandonner [abãdɔ'ne], *v.t.* to give up, to hand over, to surrender; to renounce; to forsake, to desert, to abandon; to leave, to quit; to neglect. **s'abandonner**, *v.r.* to give oneself up, to give way (*à*); to indulge (*à*); to neglect oneself.

abaque [a'bak], *n.m.* (*Arch.*) abacus; (*Arith.*) abacus.

abasourdir [abazur'diːr], *v.t.* to stun, to dumbfound; (*fig.*) to astound.

abasourdissant [abazurdi'sã], *a.* astounding, overwhelming.

abasourdissement [abazurdis'mã], *n.m.* stupefaction, bewilderment.

*****abat** [a'ba], *n.m.* killing, knocking down; heavy shower.

abâtardi [abatar'di], *a.* degenerate, corrupt, debased.

abâtardir [abatar'diːr], *v.t.* to render degenerate; to debase, to corrupt. **s'abâtardir**, *v.r.* to degenerate.

abâtardissement [abatardis'mã], *n.m.* degeneracy.

abatée *or* **abattée** [aba'te], *n.f.* swoop (*of plane*).

abat-jour [aba'ʒuːr], *n.m. inv.* sky-light; lamp shade; shade for the eyes.

abat-son [aba'sɔ̃], *n.m.* (*pl. unchanged or* **abat-sons**) a series of sloping louvres in the window of a bell tower for directing the sound downwards.

abattage [aba'taːʒ], *n.m.* cutting down, felling (*of trees*); slaughtering (*of animals*).

abattant [aba'tã], *n.m.* flap (*of a counter etc.*).

abattée [ABATÉE].

abattement [abat'mã], *n.m.* weakening; prostration; dejection, despondency, low spirits.

abatteur [aba'tœːr], *n.m.* one who fells (*trees etc.*); slaughterer.

abattis [aba'ti], *n.m.* things *or* materials brought down (*such as houses, walls, trees*); slaughtered animals, game etc.; killing of game; giblets (*of poultry*).

abattoir [aba'twaːr], *n.m.* slaughter-house.

abattre [a'batr], *v.t.* (*conjug. like* BATTRE) to throw *or* hurl down; to knock, beat *or* batter down; to pull down; to fell; to kill, to slaughter; to overthrow, to demolish; to dishearten, to discourage, to depress. **s'abattre**, *v.r.* to throw oneself down, to fall, to tumble down; to crash (down); to abate; to be cast down *or* dejected; to pounce upon; *le vent s'abat*, the wind is dropping.

abattu [aba'ty], *a.* cast down, depressed, dejected; humbled, crestfallen.

abat-vent [aba'vã], *n.m. inv.* louvre-boards (*of a window*); wind-cowl (*of a chimney*).

abat-voix [aba'vwa], *n.m. inv.* sounding board (*of a pulpit*).

abbaye [abe'ji], *n.f.* monastery, abbey.

abbé [a'be], *n.m.* abbot, abbé; *l'abbé Martin*, Father Martin.

abbesse [a'bɛs], *n.f.* abbess.

A.B.C. [abe'se], *n.m.* alphabet; primer, spelling-book.

abcéder [apse'de], *v.i.* (*conjug. like* CÉDER) to turn into an abscess, to gather.

abcès [ap'sɛ], *n.m.* abscess, gathering; *abcès aux gencives*, gumboil.

abdication [abdika'sjɔ̃], *n.f.* abdication; renunciation (*of property etc.*); surrender (*of authority*).

abdiquer [abdi'ke], *v.t.* to abdicate, to resign, to renounce.

abdomen [abdɔ'men], *n.m.* abdomen.

abdominal [abdɔmi'nal], *a.* abdominal.

abducteur [abdyk'tœːr], *a.* (*Anat.*) abducent. —*n.m.* (*Anat.*) abductor.

abduction [abdyk'sjɔ̃], *n.f.* abduction.

abécédaire [abese'dɛːr], *a.* alphabetical; *ordre abécédaire*, alphabetical order.— *n.m.* spelling book; elementary reading book; primer.

abecquer [abe'ke], *v.t.* to feed (*a bird*).

abeille [a'bɛːj], *n.f.* bee; *abeille mère*, queen bee.

aberration [abera'sjɔ̃], *n.f.* deviation from the normal *or* the correct course; (*Astron.*, *Opt. etc.*) aberration.

abêtir [abɛ'tiːr], *v.t.* to render stupid; to dull, to blunt.—*v.i.* to become dull *or* stupid. **s'abêtir**, *v.r.* to grow stupid.

abêtissement [abetis'mã], *n.m.* stultification.

abhorrer [abɔ're], *v.t.* to abhor, to hate, to loathe.

abîme [a'bi:m], *n.m.* abyss, the deep, chasm; hell.

abîmé [abi'me], *a.* swallowed up, engulfed; ruined; damaged.

abîmer [abi'me], *v.t.* *to engulf, to swallow up; to ruin; to damage. **s'abîmer**, *v.r.* to fall into ruin; to be spoiled.

abject [ab'ʒekt], *a.* abject, base.

abjectement [abʒɛktə'mã], *adv.* abjectly.

abjection [abʒɛk'sjɔ̃], *n.f.* abasement, humiliation; vileness.

abjuration [abʒyra'sjɔ̃], *n.f.* solemn renunciation, abjuration.

abjurer [abʒy're], *v.t.* to abjure, to renounce; to foreswear.

ablatif [abla'tif], *a.* (*fem.* **-tive**) ablative. —*n.m.* (*Gram.*) ablative (case).

ablation [abla'sjɔ̃], *n.f.* (*Surg.*) removal (*of a part*).

able [abl], *n.m.* any small freshwater fish of the bleak family [ABLETTE].

ablette [a'blɛt], *n.f.* bleak [ABLE].

ablution [ably'sjɔ̃], *n.f.* ablution, washing, purification.

abnégation [abnega'sjɔ̃], *n.f.* abnegation, renunciation, sacrifice, self-denial.

aboi [a'bwa], *n.m.* (*dog's*) bark, barking, baying; (*fig.*) desperate condition; **aux abois**, at bay.

aboiement [abwa'mã], *n.m.* barking, baying.

abolir [abɔ'li:r], *v.t.* to abolish, to repeal, to annul, to suppress.

abolissement [abɔlis'mã], *n.m.* abolition.

abolition [abɔli'sjɔ̃], *n.f.* abolition, repeal.

abominable [abɔmi'nabl], *a.* abominable, execrable; heinous.

abominablement [abɔminablə'mã], *adv.* abominably.

abomination [abɔmina'sjɔ̃], *n.f.* abomination, detestation, horror.

abominer [abɔmi'ne], *v.t.* to abominate, to detest.

abondamment [abɔ̃da'mã], *adv.* abundantly.

abondance [abɔ̃'dã:s], *n.f.* a great quantity, abundance, plenty; affluence.

abondant [abɔ̃'dã], *a.* abundant, plentiful, copious; exuberant, effusive.

abonder [abɔ̃'de], *v.i.* to abound, to be plentiful, to be in great quantity; **abonder dans le sens de quelqu'un**, to support somebody's views strongly.

abonné [abɔ'ne], *n.m.* (*fem.* **-ée**) subscriber (*to periodicals etc.*); season ticket holder.

abonnement [abɔn'mã], *n.m.* subscription (*to periodicals, theatres etc.*); agreement; season ticket; **carte d'abonnement**, season ticket.

abonner (s') [sabɔ'ne], *v.r.* to become a subscriber.

abonnir [abɔ'ni:r], *v.t.* to mend, to improve (*wine*).—*v.i.* to become good. **s'abonnir**, *v.r.* to mend, to grow better.

abonnissement [abɔnis'mã], *n.m.* improvement.

abord [a'bɔ:r], *n.m.* landing; arrival; access, approach, meeting; onset, attack; (*pl.*) approaches, surroundings; **d'abord**, at first.

abordable [abɔr'dabl], *a.* accessible, easily approached, affable.

abordage [abɔr'da:ʒ], *n.m.* (*Naut.*) boarding; fouling, colliding.

abordée [abɔr'de], *n.f.* the act of meeting, accosting *or* beginning.

aborder [abɔr'de], *v.t.* to arrive at; to approach, to accost; to enter upon (*a subject etc.*); to grapple (*a vessel*); to run foul of (*a ship*).—*v.i.* to arrive; to land. **s'aborder**, *v.r.* to accost each other; to run foul of each other.

aborigène [abɔri'ʒɛ:n], *a.* native, original.— *n.m.* aboriginal, aborigine.

aborner [abɔr'ne], *v.t.* to mark out, to delimit.

abortif [abɔr'tif], *a.* (*fem.* **-tive**) abortive.

abouchement [abuʃ'mã], *n.m.* interview, conference.

aboucher [abu'ʃe], *v.t.* to bring (*things or persons*) together. **s'aboucher**, *v.r.* to have an interview, to confer (*with*); to get in touch (*with*).

aboutement [abut'mã], *n.m.* abutment; placing *or* fitting end to end.

abouter [abu'te], *v.t.* to join end to end.

aboutir [abu'ti:r], *v.i.* to end at *or* in, to result (à); (*Surg.*) to come to a head (*with aux.* ÊTRE *or* AVOIR).

aboutissant [abuti'sã], *a.* bordering upon, abutting on, ending in.

aboutissement [abutis'mã], *n.m.* result, issue.

aboyer [abwa'je], *v.i.* (*conjug. like* EMPLOYER) to bark, to bay, to yelp.

abracadabra [abrakada'bra], *n.m.* abracadabra (*magic word*).

abracadabrant [abrakada'brã], *a.* stupendous, amazing, stunning.

abrasif [abra'zif], *n.m.* abrasive.

abrégé [abre'ʒe], *a.* short, summary.—*n.m.* abridgment, résumé, précis, abstract, summary.

abrégement [abreʒ'mã], *n.m.* abridging, abridgment.

abréger [abre'ʒe], *v.t.* (*conjug. like* ASSIÉGER) to abridge, to shorten; to abbreviate.

abreuvage [abrœ'va:ʒ], **abreuvement** [a brœv'mã], *n.m.* watering, soaking, steaming.

abreuver [abrœ've], *v.t.* to water (*animals*); to water (*the ground etc.*). **s'abreuver**, *v.r.* to drink, to be watered (*of animals*).

abreuvoir [abrœ'vwa:r], *n.m.* watering place, horse pond; drinking trough.

abréviation [abrevja'sjɔ̃], *n.f.* abbreviation, shortening.

abri [a'bri], *n.m.* shelter, cover, refuge, dugout.

abricot [abri'ko], *n.m.* apricot.

abricotier [abriko'tje], *n.m.* apricot tree.

abriter [abri'te], *v.t.* to shelter, to shade, to protect. **s'abriter**, *v.r.* to take refuge.

abrogation [abrɔga'sjɔ̃], *n.f.* abrogation, repeal, annulment.

abroger [abrɔ'ʒe], *v.t.* (*conjug. like* MANGER) to abrogate, to repeal, to annul. **s'abroger**, *v.r.* to fall into disuse.

abrupt [a'brypt], *a.* abrupt, steep, sheer; (*fig.*) blunt, rugged, rough (*of style etc.*).

abruptement [abrypta'mã], *adv.* abruptly.

abruti [abry'ti], *a. and n.m.* (*fem.* **-e**) brutalized, stupid (*person*).

abrutir [abry'ti:r], *v.t.* to stupefy, to brutalize. **s'abrutir**, *v.r.* to become brutalized *or* stupid.

abrutissant [abryti'sɑ̃], *a.* brutalizing, stupefying.

abrutissement [abrytis'mɑ̃], *n.m.* the act of brutalizing; brutishness, degradation.

absence [ap'sɑ̃:s], *n.f.* absence; want, lack; *absence d'esprit*, absence of mind.

absent [ap'sɑ̃], *a.* absent, away from home; wandering, woolgathering.—*n.m.* (*fem.* -e) absentee.

absentéisme [apsɑ̃te'ism], *n.m.* absenteeism.

absenter (s') [sapsɑ̃'te], *v.r.* to absent oneself, to be away; to play truant.

abside [ap'si:d], *n.f.* apse.

absinthe [ap'sɛ̃:t], *n.f.* absinth; wormwood.

absolu [apsɔ'ly], *a.* absolute; despotic, arbitrary; unrestricted; peremptory; positive.

absolument [apsɔly'mɑ̃], *adv.* absolutely; arbitrarily.

absolution [apsɔly'sjɔ̃], *n.f.* absolution, acquittal.

absolutisme [apsɔly'tism], *n.m.* absolutism.

absorbant [apsɔr'bɑ̃], *a.* absorptive, absorbent; engrossing.—*n.m.* absorbent.

absorber [apsɔr'be], *v.t.* to absorb, to imbibe; to eat *or* drink; (*fig.*) to engross. **s'absorber**, *v.r.* to be absorbed; (*fig.*) to be entirely taken up with (*dans*).

absorption [apsɔrp'sjɔ̃], *n.f.* absorption.

absoudre [ap'sudr], *v.t. irr.* to absolve, to acquit; to exonerate, to forgive.

abstenir (s') [apstə'ni:r], *v.r. irr.* (*conjug. like* TENIR) to abstain (*from voting*); to refrain, to forbear, to forgo.

abstention [apstɑ̃'sjɔ̃], *n.f.* abstention.

abstinence [apsti'nɑ̃:s], *n.f.* abstinence; temperance, sobriety; (*pl.*) fasts, fasting.

abstinent [apsti'nɑ̃], *a.* abstemious, sober.

abstraction [apstrak'sjɔ̃], *n.f.* abstraction, abstract question *or* idea.

abstraire [aps'trɛ:r], *v.t. irr.* (*conjug. like* TRAIRE) to abstract; to separate, to isolate.

abstrait [aps'trɛ], *a.* abstract, abstruse; absent-minded.

abstraitement [apstrɛt'mɑ̃], *adv.* abstractedly; separately; in the abstract.

abstrus [aps'try], *a.* abstruse; obscure.

absurde [ap'syrd], *a.* absurd, nonsensical, stupid, silly, preposterous.

absurdement [apsyrdə'mɑ̃], *adv.* absurdly, nonsensically.

absurdité [apsyrdi'te], *n.f.* absurdity, nonsense.

abus [a'by], *n.m.* abuse; grievance; misuse.

abuser [aby'ze], *v.t.* to deceive, to lead astray, to delude.—*v.i.* to misuse, to make ill use (*de*); to take advantage (*de*). **s'abuser**, *v.r.* to be mistaken, to deceive oneself.

abusif [aby'zif], *a.* (*fem.* -sive) irregular, improper.

abusivement [abyziv'mɑ̃], *adv.* irregularly, improperly.

abyssal [abi'sal], *a.* unfathomable.

abysse [a'bis], *n.m.* abyss, unfathomable gulf *or* depth.

Abyssinie [abisi'ni], **l'**, *f.* Abyssinia.

abyssinien [abisi'njɛ̃] (*fem.* -enne), **abyssin** [abi'sɛ̃], *a.* Abyssinian. — *n.m.* (**Abyssinien**, *fem.* -enne) Abyssinian (*person*).

acabit [aka'bi], *n.m.* quality (*of fruits, vegetables*); character, nature, stamp (*of persons*).

acacia [aka'sja], *n.m.* (*Bot.*) acacia.

académicien [akademi'sjɛ̃], *n.m.* academician.

académie [akade'mi], *n.f.* academy, society of learned men, *esp.* the Académie Française; school (*of dancing, fencing, riding etc.*).

académique [akade'mik], *a.* proper, appropriate *or* belonging to an academy, academic(al).

acagnarder [akaɲar'de], *v.t.* to make lazy. **s'acagnarder**, *v.r.* to drift into an idle, slothful life.

acajou [aka'ʒu], *n.m.* mahogany.

acanthe [a'kɑ̃:t], *n.f.* acanthus.

acariâtre [aka'rja:tr], *a.* contrary, crabbed, cross-grained, quarrelsome, shrewish.

acariâtreté [akarjɑtra'te], *n.f.* crabbedness, peevishness, shrewishness.

accablant [akɑ'blɑ̃], *a.* oppressive, overwhelming, crushing.

accablement [akablə'mɑ̃], *n.m.* prostration, oppression, extreme discouragement *or* dejection.

accabler [akɑ'ble], *v.t.* to crush, to overpower, to overcome; (*fig.*) to weigh down, to overload, to overwhelm.

accalmie [akal'mi], *n.f.* (*Naut.*) lull.

accaparant [akapa'rɑ̃], *a.* engrossing.

accaparement [akapar'mɑ̃], *n.m.* monopoly, monopolizing.

accaparer [akapa'rce:r], *v.t.* to monopolize, to hoard, to engross.

accapareur [akapa'rœ:r], *n.m.* (*fem.* -euse) monopolist, monopolizer, hoarder.

accéder [akse'de], *v.i.* (*conjug. like* CÉDER) to arrive, to reach, to have access; to accede, to comply with.

accélérateur [akselera'tœ:r], *a.* (*fem.* -trice) accelerative, with increasing speed.—*n.m.* (*Elec., Mech., Phot. etc.*) accelerator; (*fam.*) *appuyer sur l'accélérateur*, to step on the gas.

accélération [akselera'sjɔ̃], *n.f.* acceleration.

accéléré [aksele're], *a.* accelerated.

accélérer [aksele're], *v.t.* (*conjug. like* CÉDER) to accelerate, to quicken, to hasten, to press, to dispatch.

accent [ak'sɑ̃], *n.m.* pitch, accent, stress, tone; pronunciation; expression (*of the voice*).

accentuation [aksɑ̃tɥa'sjɔ̃], *n.f.* accentuation, stressing.

accentuer [aksɑ̃'tɥe], *v.t.* to accent, to accentuate, to stress.

acceptable [aksɛp'tabl], *a.* acceptable, worth accepting.

acceptation [aksɛpta'sjɔ̃], *n.f.* acceptance; acceptation.

accepter [aksɛp'te], *v.t.* to accept, to agree to, to welcome (*what is offered or proposed*).

acception [aksɛp'sjɔ̃], *n.f.* respect, regard, sense, meaning, acceptation.

accès [ak'sɛ], *n.m.* access, opportunity of approach, admittance; attack, fit, paroxysm.

accessibilité [aksɛsibili'te], *n.f.* accessibility.

accessible [aksɛ'sibl], *a.* accessible, approachable; within reach.

accession [aksɛ'sjɔ̃], *n.f.* accession; adhesion, union (*of a country, province etc. to another*).

accessit [aksɛ'sit], *n.m.* award of merit, honorable mention; 'proxime accessit'.

accessoire [aksɛ'swa:r], *a.* accessory, additional, subordinate.—*n.m.* an accessory; (*pl.*) (*Theat.*) properties.

accessoiriste [aksɛswa'rist], *n.m.* props man.

3

accident [aksi'dɑ̃], *n.m.* accident, fortuitous incident; casualty, mishap, mischance; unevenness, irregularity (*in the ground*).

accidenté [aksidɑ̃'te], *a.* varied, unequal (*of style etc.*); rough, uneven, broken, hilly (*of ground*); chequered (*of life, career etc.*).— *n.m.* (*fem.* -ée) one injured by an accident

accidentel [aksidɑ̃'tel], *a.* (*fem.* -elle) accidental, adventitious, fortuitous, unexpected; *signe accidentel,* (*Mus.*) accidental.

accidentellement [aksidɑ̃tel'mɑ̃,], *adv.* accidentally, casually, by chance.

accidenter [aksidɑ̃'te], *v.t.* to make irregular *or* uneven; to diversify, to chequer, to make picturesque.

accise [ak'si:z], *n.f.* (*Law*) inland duty, excise; *préposé à l'acoise,* exciseman.

acclamation [aklama'sjɔ̃], *n.f.* acclamation, cheering.

acclamer [akla'me], *v.t.* to acclaim, to applaud, to cheer.

acclimatable [aklima'tabl], *a.* that may be acclimatized.

acclimatation [aklimata'sjɔ̃], *n.f.* acclimatization.

acclimater [aklima'te], *v.t.* to acclimatize. **s'acclimater**, *v.r.* to become acclimatized.

accointance [akwɛ̃'tɑ̃:s], *n.f.* (*used generally in pl. and in a bad sense*) intimacy, familiarity; *avoir des accointances (avec),* to have dealings (*with*).

accointer [akwɛ̃'te], *v.t.* to make acquainted.

accolade [akɔ'lad], *n.f.* embrace; kiss; accolade (*in knighting*).

accolader (**s'**) [sakɔla'de], *v.r.* to embrace mutually.

accolage [akɔ'la:ʒ], *n.m.* tying up, training (*branches etc.*).

accolement [akɔl'mɑ̃], *n.m.* joining, uniting.

accoler [akɔ'le], *v.t.* to embrace; to tie up, to fasten, to place against; (*fig.*) to couple, to join together, to bracket.

accommodable [akɔmɔ'dabl], *a.* that may be arranged; adjustable.

accommodage [akɔmɔ'da:ʒ], *n.m.* preparation *or* dressing (*of meat*).

accommodant [akɔmɔ'dɑ̃], *a.* accommodating, easy-going, courteous.

accommodation [akɔmɔda'sjɔ̃], *n.f.* accommodation.

accommodement [akɔmɔd'mɑ̃], *n.m.* accommodation, arrangement, composition; settlement, reconciliation, compromise.

accommoder [akɔmɔ'de], *v.t.* to adapt, to accommodate, to fit, to adjust; to reconcile; to conciliate; to dress, to trim; to cook, to do up; to suit, to be convenient. **s'accommoder**, *v.r.* to agree, to come to terms; to accommodate oneself, to adapt oneself (*à*); to put up with (*de*).

accompagnateur [akɔ̃paɲa'tœ:r], *n.m.* (*fem.* -trice) accompanist (*with instrument or voice*); conductor (*of a tour*).

accompagnement [akɔ̃paɲ'mɑ̃], *n.m.* accompanying; attendance, retinue; an accompaniment, an accessory; (*Mus.*) accompaniment.

accompagner [akɔ̃pa'ɲe], *v.t.* to accompany, to attend on; to go with, to escort; (*Mus.*) to accompany.

accompli [akɔ̃'pli], *a.* accomplished, performed, fulfilled; complete, faultless, perfect, out and out.

accomplir [akɔ̃'pli:r], *v.t.* to fulfil, to effect, to perform; to realize, to carry out.

accomplissement [akɔ̃plis'mɑ̃], *n.m.* accomplishment, fulfilment, realization.

accon, acconier [ACON etc.].

accord [a'kɔ:r], *n.m.* accord, concurrence, unanimity, harmony; agreement, bargain; convention, settlement; (*Mus.*) chord; *être d'accord,* to agree; *d'accord,* granted, agreed.

accordable [akɔr'dabl], *a.* that may be accorded; reconcilable; (*Mus.*) tunable.

accordage [akɔr'da:ʒ], **accordement** [akɔrdə'mɑ̃], *n.m.* tuning (*of a musical instrument*).

accordailles [akɔr'da:j], *n.f.* (*used only in pl.*) betrothal.

accordant [akɔr'dɑ̃], *a.* accordant, harmonious.

accordé [akɔr'de], *n.m.* (*fem.* -ée) fiancé, fiancée; *les accordés,* the bride and bridegroom.

accordéon [akɔrde'ɔ̃], *n.m.* accordion.

accordéoniste [akɔrdeɔ'nist], *n.* accordionist.

accorder [akɔr'de], *v.t.* to bring into harmony *or* accord, to make agree, to reconcile; to concede, to grant; to admit, to avow; (*Mus.*) to tune, to harmonize; to bestow (*hand in marriage*). **s'accorder**, *v.r.* to agree, to concur; to correspond; to suit, to be suited.

accordeur [akɔr'dœ:r], *n.m.* tuner (*of musical instruments*).

accordoir [akɔr'dwa:r], *n.m.* tuning hammer, key *or* cone.

accore [a'kɔ:r], *a.* abrupt, sheer, vertical (*of a coast*).

accort [a'kɔ:r], *a.* gracious, courteous.

accostable [akɔs'tabl], *a.* easy of access, approachable.

accostage [akɔs'ta:ʒ], *n.m.* the act of accosting, approaching *or* drawing alongside.

accoster [akɔs'te], *v.t.* to accost, to go up to; (*Naut.*) to come alongside.

accotement [akɔt'mɑ̃], *n.m.* (*Civ. Eng.*) roadside; footpath.

accoter [akɔ'te], *v.t.* to prop up, to support, to stay. **s'accoter**, *v.r.* to lean (*contre*).

accotoir [akɔ'twa:r], *n.m.* prop, support, leaning post.

accouardir [akwar'di:r], *v.t.* to make a coward. **s'accouardir**, *v.r.* to turn coward.

accouchée [aku'ʃe], *n.f.* woman in childbirth, woman who has just had a child.

accouchement [akuʃ'mɑ̃], *n.m.* childbirth, delivery, confinement; *centre d'accouchement,* maternity home.

accoucher [aku'ʃe], *v.t.* to deliver (*a woman*). —*v.i.* to lie in, to be brought to bed, to be delivered.

accoucheur [aku'ʃœ:r], *n.m.* male midwife, accoucheur.

accoucheuse [aku'ʃø:z], *n.f.* midwife.

accoudement [akud'mɑ̃], *n.m.* the act of leaning (*on*).

accouder (**s'**) [saku'de], *v.r.* to lean on one's elbow.

accoudoir [aku'dwa:r], *n.m.* elbow rest; (*Arch.*) rail, balustrade.

accouple [a'kupl], *n.f.* leash (*for tying dogs in couples*).

accouplement [akuplə'mã], *n.m.* coupling; pairing.

accoupler [aku'ple], *v.t.* to couple; to join together in pairs; (*Elec.*) to connect, to group (*batteries etc.*).

accourci [akur'si], *n.m.* abridgement (*of a book*).

accourcir [akur'si:r], *v.t.* to shorten, to abridge, to curtail. **s'accourcir**, *v.r.* to become shorter, to decrease.

accourcissement [akursis'mã], *n.m.* shortening, diminution.

accourir [aku'ri:r], *v.i. irr.* (*conjug. like* COURIR) to run up to, to hasten, to flock.

accoutrement [akutrə'mã], *n.m.* garb, dress, *esp.* as an object of ridicule.

accoutrer [aku'tre], *v.t.* to rig out, to dress. **s'accoutrer**, *v.r.* to dress absurdly, to rig oneself out.

accoutumance [akuty'mã:s], *n.f.* habit, custom, wont, usage.

accoutumé [akuty'me], *a.* ordinary, accustomed, habitual.

accoutumer [akuty'me], *v.t.* to accustom, to habituate, to inure.—*v.i.* (*only in compound tenses*) to use, to be wont. **s'accoutumer**, *v.r.* to be accustomed, to be used (*à*).

accouvage [aku'va:ʒ], *n.m.* hatching (*esp. by artificial means*), incubation.

accouver [aku've], *v.t.* to set (*a hen etc.*).—*v.i.* to sit, to hatch.

accréditation [akredita'sjɔ̃], *n.f.* accreditation, accrediting (*of an ambassador*).

accréditer [akredi'te], *v.t.* to give credit, standing *or* sanction to; to authorize; to accredit (*an ambassador etc.*); to confirm, to spread (*rumors etc.*). **s'accréditer**, *v.r.* to gain credit *or* reputation; to ingratiate oneself; to spread (*of rumors etc.*).

accréditeur [akredi'tœ:r], *n.m.* guarantor, surety.

accroc [a'kro], *n.m.* impediment, hitch; hindrance; rent, tear.

accrochage [akro'ʃa:ʒ], *n.m.* hanging, hooking, hitching; catching, retarding, stopping; grazing (*vehicles*).

accroche-cœur [akroʃ'kœ:r], *n.m. inv.* spit curl.

accrochement [akroʃ'mã], *n.m.* hooking, catching (*in something*).

accrocher [akro'ʃe], *v.t.* to hang upon a hook; to hook, to catch, to hitch; to catch and tear; to get hold of; to pick up (*a radio station*). **s'accrocher**, *v.r.* to catch in, to be caught *or* hooked (*par*); to lay hold of, to cling (*à*).

accroire [a'krwa:r], *v.t. irr.* (*used only in the infinitive after faire*) to believe.

accroissement [akrwas'mã], *n.m.* increase, growth, enlargement, extension.

accroître [a'krwa:tr], *v.t. irr.* (*conjug. like* CROÎTRE *except for p.p.* accru) to increase, to augment, to enlarge, to amplify. **s'accroître**, *v.r.* to increase, to grow.

accroupi [akru'pi], *a.* crouched, crouching, cowering, squatting.

accroupir (s') [sakru'pi:r], *v.r.* to sit down on the hams *or* heels, to squat, to crouch.

accroupissement [akrupis'mã], *n.m.* cowering, squatting, crouching.

accru [a'kry], *n.m.* (*Gard.*) sucker, scion.

accrue [a'kry], *n.f.* increase of land through the retreat of waters; encroachment of a forest on adjoining land.

accu [a'ky], *n.m. abbr.* [ACCUMULATEUR].

accueil [a'kœ:j], *n.m.* reception, welcome, greeting.

accueillir [akœ'ji:r], *v.t. irr.* (*conjug. like* CUEILLIR) to receive (*well or ill*); to receive graciously, to welcome.

acculer [aky'le], *v.t.* to drive into a corner; to bring to a standstill. **s'acculer**, *v.r.* to set one's back against something.

accumulateur [akymyla'tœ:r], *a.* (*fem.* -trice) storing, heaping up, hoarding up.—*n.m.* accumulator (*person or thing*); (*Elec.*) storage cell *or* battery.

accumulation [akymyla'sjɔ̃], *n.f.* accumulation; mass, pile.

accumuler [akymy'le], *v.t.* to accumulate, to pile up, to amass. **s'accumuler**, *v.r.* to accumulate, to increase.

accusable [aky'zabl], *a.* accusable, chargeable.

accusateur [akyza'tœ:r], *a.* (*fem.* -trice) accusing, accusatory.—*n.m.* (*fem.* -trice) accuser, denouncer.

accusatif [akyza'tif], *a.* (*fem.* -tive) and *n.m.* (*Gram.*) accusative (case); *à l'accusatif*, in the accusative.

accusation [akyza'sjɔ̃], *n.f.* accusation, indictment, charge; (*fig.*) prosecution; *mise en accusation*, arraignment.

accusatoire [akyza'twa:r], *a.* accusatory.

accusé [aky'ze], *n.m.* (*fem.* -ée) the accused, prisoner, defendant; *accusé de réception*, acknowledgment of a letter, receipt.

accuser [aky'ze], *v.t.* to impute, to charge with; to reproach, to blame; to indict, to impeach, to prosecute. **s'accuser**, *v.r.* to admit, to avow, to confess.

acéphale [ase'fal], *a.* acephalous, headless.

acérain [ase'rɛ̃], *a.* like *or* pertaining to steel, steely.

acerbe [a'sɛrb], *a.* sour, harsh, sharp, astringent; (*fig.*) bitter, acrimonious.

acerbité [asɛrbi'te], *n.f.* acerbity, harshness; (*fig.*) bitterness, severity.

acéré [ase're], *a.* steely, steeled; sharp, keen; (*fig.*) mordant, trenchant, acute.

acérer [ase're], *v.t.* (*conjug. like* CÉDER) to steel; to sharpen, to render biting, incisive *or* mordant.

acétate [ase'tat], *n.m.* (*Chem.*) acetate.

acéteux [ase'tø], *a.* (*fem.* -euse) acetous, sour, tasting like vinegar.

acétique [ase'tik], *a.* acetic.

acétone [ase'ton], *n.m.* acetone.

acétoselle [aseto'sɛl], *n.f.* wood-sorrel.

acétylène [aseti'lɛ:n], *n.m.* acetylene.

achalandage [aʃalã'da:ʒ], *n.m.* custom, customers; goodwill (*of a shop*).

achalandé [aʃalã'de], *a.* having plenty of custom; *boutique bien achalandée*, a well-frequented shop.

achalander [aʃalã'de], *v.t.* to get custom, to attract customers, to draw trade.

acharné [aʃar'ne], *a.* fleshed, fierce, tenacious, implacable; stubborn, obstinate, intense.

acharnement [aʃarnə'mã], *n.m.* tenacity; rancor, animosity, fury; stubbornness, obstinacy, desperation.

5

acharner [aʃar'ne], v.t. to flesh; to set on; to excite, to madden; to embitter, to envenom. **s'acharner**, v.r. to be intent, bent or obstinately set upon; to set one's heart upon, to persist in; to be infuriated or implacable.

achat [a'ʃa], n.m. purchasing, buying; purchase; *faire des achats*, to go shopping; *pouvoir d'achat*, purchasing power.

acheminement [aʃmin'mã], n.m. progress, advance, conveying.

acheminer [aʃmi'ne], v.t. to send on (*towards a place* or *object*); to train (*a horse*). **s'acheminer**, v.r. to set out (*pour*), to make one's way towards.

achetable [aʃ'tabl], a. purchasable.

acheter [aʃ'te], v.t. (*conjug. like* AMENER) to buy, to purchase; (*fig.*) to bribe. **s'acheter**, v.r. to be bought; to be for sale, to be venal.

acheteur [aʃ'tœːr], n.m. (*fem.* -euse) buyer, purchaser.

achevage [aʃ'vaːʒ], n.m. completion, finishing; finish (*of a work of art*).

achevé [aʃ've], a. finished, accomplished, perfect, exquisite; absolute, downright, consummate, arrant.

achèvement [aʃɛv'mã], n.m. completion, conclusion.

achever [aʃ've], v.t. (*conjug. like* AMENER) to finish, to terminate; to put the finishing touch to; to complete, to achieve; to consummate, to perfect; (*fig.*) to do for completely, to ruin, to kill.

Achille [a'ʃil], m. Achilles.

achoppement [aʃɔp'mã], n.m. obstacle, impediment; unforeseen difficulty, embarrassment; *pierre d'achoppement*, stumbling block.

achopper [aʃɔ'pe], v.i. and **s'achopper**, v.r. to stumble, to knock against something; (*fig.*) to come to grief; to fail.

achromatopsie [akrɔmatɔp'si], n.f. achromatopsy, color blindness.

acide [a'sid], a. acid, sour, tart, sharp.—n.m. acid.

acidifier [asidi'fje], v.t. to acidify. **s'acidifier**, v.r. to become acidified.

acidité [asidi'te], n.f. acidity, sourness, sharpness, tartness.

acidule [asi'dyl], a. subacid, acidulous.

acidulé [asidy'le], a. acidulated; *bonbons acidulés*, acid drops, sour balls.

aciduler [asidy'le], v.t. to acidulate.

acier [a'sje], n.m. steel; *acier chromé*, chrome steel; *acier coulé* or *fondu*, cast steel; *acier doux*, mild steel; *acier inoxydable*, stainless steel.

aciération [asjera'sjõ], n.f. steeling, plating with steel.

aciérer [asje're], v.t. (*conjug. like* CÉDER) to convert into steel, to cover with steel; to acierate. **s'aciérer**, v.r. to steel oneself.

aciéreux [asje'rø], a. (*fem.* -euse) steely, like steel.

aciérie [asje'ri], n.f. steel factory, steelworks.

acné [ak'ne], n.f. (*Med.*) acne.

acolyte [akɔ'lit], n.m. (*Eccles.*) acolyte; (*fig.*) assistant, confederate, associate, accomplice.

acompte [a'kõːt], n.m. instalment, partial payment.

acon or **accon** [a'kõ], n.m. small lighter, punt.

aconier or **acconier** [akɔ'nje], n.m. lighterman.

aconit [akɔ'nit], n.m. aconite.

acoquinant [akɔki'nã], a. alluring, engaging, captivating.

acoquiner [akɔki'ne], v.t. to make fond, to allure, to bewitch, to captivate. **s'acoquiner**, v.r. (*fam.*) to be bewitched, to be greatly attached to.

Açores [a'sɔːr], les, f.pl. the Azores.

à-côté [ako'te], n.m. aside; (*pl.*) little extras.

à-coup [a'ku], n.m. jerk, jolt; sudden stop.

acousticien [akusti'sjɛ̃], n.m. (*fem.* -enne) acoustician.

acoustique [akus'tik], a. acoustic.—n.f. acoustics.

acquéreur [ake'rœːr], n.m. (*fem.* -euse) buyer, purchaser.

acquérir [ake'riːr], v.t. irr. to purchase, to buy, to get; to earn, to win, to gain; to acquire, to obtain. **s'acquérir**, v.r. to get or win for oneself; to be acquired, obtained or purchased.

acquiescement [akjɛs'mã], n.m. acquiescence, compliance, consent, willingness.

acquiescer [akjɛ'se], v.i. (*conjug. like* COMMENCER) to acquiesce, to agree, to assent, to yield, to comply.

acquis [a'ki], a. acquired, secured.—n.m. acquirements, attainments, experience.

acquisitif [akizi'tif], a. (*fem.* -tive) acquisitive.

acquisition [akizi'sjõ], n.f. acquisition, acquiring, attaining, acquirement, attainment; purchase, conquest.

acquisivité [akizivi'te], n.f. acquisitiveness.

acquit [a'ki], n.m. receipt, discharge, release, acquittance; (*Billiards*) break (*i.e. start*).

acquittement [akit'mã], n.m. payment, quittance; (*Law*) acquittal.

acquitter [aki'te], v.t. to pay; to discharge, to pay off (*a dependant*); to acquit. **s'acquitter**, v.r. to fulfil, to perform; to pay off one's debts, to be quits (*in gambling*); to acquit oneself (*well* or *ill*).

acre [akr], n.f. acre.

âcre [ɑːkr], a. sour, sharp, tart, acrid; (*fig.*) bitter, pungent, caustic.

âcrement [ɑːkrə'mã], adv. tartly, sourly.

âcreté [ɑːkrə'te], n.f. sourness, acridity, sharpness, tartness, acrimony.

acrimonie [akrimɔ'ni], n.f. bitterness, sharpness, keenness, acrimony.

acrimonieux [akrimɔ'njø], a. (*fem.* -euse) pungent, acrimonious, ill-natured, sharp.

acrobate [akrɔ'bat], n. acrobat, rope-dancer.

acrobatie [akrɔba'si], n.f. acrobatics; (*Av.*) stunt.

acrobatique [akrɔba'tik], a. acrobatic.

acrobatisme [akrɔba'tism], n.m. acrobatics.

acrocéphale [akrɔse'fal], a. having a pointed head, acrocephalic, acrocephalous.—n. a person with such a head.

acropole [akrɔ'pɔl], n.f. acropolis.

acrostiche [akrɔs'tiʃ], a. and n.m. acrostic.

acrotère [akrɔ'tɛːr], n.m. (*Arch.*) acroterium, ornamental summit (*of a pediment*).

acte [akt], n.m. action, deed; (*Law*) deed, indenture; instrument; document, charter; (*Theat.*) act; (*pl.*) records, public registers, rolls, transactions, proceedings; *acte de naissance*, birth certificate.

acteur [ak'tœːr], n.m. (*fem.* -trice) actor; actress; player.

actif [ak'tif], *a.* (*fem.* **-tive**) active, busy, energetic, assiduous; nimble, brisk, agile; (*Gram. etc.*) active.—*n.m.* (*Gram.*) active voice; assets, credit balance.

action [ak'sjɔ̃], *n.f.* action, operation, work; activity, motion; deed, feat, performance; fight, engagement, battle; (*Law*) action, law-suit; (*Theat.*) gesture; (*Lit.*) subject, action, plot; (*Comm.*) share, stock.

actionnaire [aksjɔ'nɛːr], *n.* shareholder.

actionnariat [aksjɔna'rja], *n.m.* shareholding; **actionnariat ouvrier**, industrial co-partnership.

actionner [aksjɔ'ne], *v.t.* to bring an action against, to sue at law; to bestir, to rouse up, to set going; to operate, to run, to drive. **s'actionner**, *v.r.* to bestir oneself.

activement [aktiv'mɑ̃], *adv.* actively, vigorously.

activer [akti've], *v.t.* to press, to accelerate, to forward, to expedite, to stir up (*a fire, people*).

activisme [akti'vism], *n.m.* (*Polit.*) militancy, activism.

activiste [akti'vist], *n.m.* activist.

activité [aktivi'te], *n.f.* activity, full swing; nimbleness, alacrity, promptitude, dispatch.

actrice [ak'tris], [ACTEUR].

actuaire [ak'tɥɛːr], *n.m.* actuary.

actualisation [aktɥaliza'sjɔ̃], *n.f.* actualization; realization.

actualiser [aktɥali'ze], *v.t.* to bring up to date. **s'actualiser**, *v.r.* to become real.

actualité [aktɥali'te], *n.f.* actuality; event of the moment, present interest; (*Ciné.*) **les actualités**, the newsreel.

actuel [ak'tɥel], *a.* (*fem.* **-elle**) present, of the present time.

actuellement [aktɥel'mɑ̃], *adv.* now, at the present time.

acuité [akɥi'te], *n.f.* sharpness, acuteness, keenness.

acutangle [aky'tɑ̃:ɡl], **acutangulaire** [akytɑ̃ɡy'lɛːr], *a.* acute-angled (*of triangles etc.*).

acutesse [aky'tɛs], *n.f.* acuteness, sharpness.

adage [a'daːʒ], *n.m.* adage, proverb, saying.

Adam [a'dɑ̃], *m.* Adam.

adamantin [adamɑ̃'tɛ̃], *a.* adamantine.

adaptable [adap'tabl], *a.* adaptable.

adaptateur [adapta'tœːr], *n.m.* adapter, converter.

adaptation [adapta'sjɔ̃], *n.f.* adaptation.

adapter [adap'te], *v.t.* to adapt, to adjust, to apply (*à*); to fit, to make suitable. **s'adapter**, *v.r.* to fit, to suit, to adapt oneself (*to*).

addition [adi'sjɔ̃], *n.f.* adding up, addition; an addition; bill, reckoning, check.

additionnel [adisjɔ'nɛl], *a.* (*fem.* **-elle**) additional.

additionner [adisjɔ'ne], *v.t.* to add up.

Adélaïde [adela'id], *f.* Adelaide.

Adèle [a'dɛl], *f.* Adela.

adénite [ade'nit], *n.f.* adenitis, inflammation of the glands.

adénoïde [adenɔ'id], *a.* adenoid; **végétations adénoïdes**, adcnoids.

adent [a'dɑ̃], *n.m.* dovetail, tenon.

adenter [adɑ̃'te], *v.t.* to dovetail, to join with mortise and tenon.

adepte [a'dɛpt], *n.m.* adept, initiate, follower.

adéquat [ade'kwa], *a.* adequate; (*Phil.*) equal in content; appropriate.

adhérence [ade'rɑ̃:s], *n.f.* adhesion, adherence; (*fig.*) attachment.

adhérent [ade'rɑ̃], *a.* adherent.—*n.m.* (*fem.* **-e**) adherent, follower, partisan.

adhérer [ade're], *v.i.* (*conjug. like* CÉDER) to adhere, to cling; (*fig.*) to hold (*à*), to cleave (*to a sect etc.*).

adhésif [ade'zif], *a.* (*fem.* **-sive**) adhesive.—*n.m.* (*Phot.*) dry-mounting tissue.

adhésion [ade'zjɔ̃], *n.f.* adhesion, adherence, union; compliance; joining (*a party*).

adhésivité [adezivi'te], *n.f.* adhesiveness.

adieu [a'djø], *int.* adieu, good-bye, farewell. —*n.m.* (*pl.* **-eux**) farewell, parting, leave; **faire ses adieux à**, to take leave of, to say good-bye to.

adipeux [adi'pø], *a.* (*fem.* **-euse**) adipose, fat.

adiposité [adipozi'te], *n.f.* adipose *or* fatty condition.

adjacence [adʒa'sɑ̃:s], *n.f.* adjacency

adjacent [adʒa'sɑ̃], *a.* adjacent, bordering upon, contiguous.

adjectif [adʒɛk'tif], *a.* (*fem.* **-tive**) (*Gram.*) adjectival.—*n.m.* adjective.

adjectivement [adʒɛktiv'mɑ̃], *adv.* adjectivally.

adjoindre [ad'ʒwɛ̃:dr], *v.t. irr.* (*conjug. like* CRAINDRE) to adjoin, to associate, to add as an assistant. **s'adjoindre**, *v.r.* to join as a partner *or* associate; to take on.

adjoint [ad'ʒwɛ̃], *a.* adjunct, associate.—*n.m.* (*fem.* **-e**) associate, assistant, deputy; **adjoint au maire**, deputy mayor.

adjonction [adʒɔ̃k'sjɔ̃], *n.f.* adjunction.

adjudant [adʒy'dɑ̃], *n.m.* company sergeant-major; warrant officer; **adjudant-major**, adjutant.

adjudicataire [adʒydika'tɛːr], *a.* and *n.* contracting party; successful tenderer, highest bidder.

adjudicateur [adʒydika'tœːr], *n.m.* (*fem.* **-trice**) adjudicator, awarder; auctioneer.

adjudication [adʒydika'sjɔ̃], *n.f.* auction; knocking down; adjudication.

adjuger [adʒy'ʒe], *v.t.* (*conjug. like* MANGER) to adjudge, to adjudicate, to knock down (*to the highest bidder*); to award; **adjugé!** (*at auctions*) gone!

adjuration [adʒyra'sjɔ̃], *n.f.* adjuration, imprecation.

adjurer [adʒy're], *v.t.* to adjure, to conjure; to call upon, to beseech.

admettre [ad'mɛtr], *v.t. irr.* (*conjug. like* METTRE) to admit, to let in; to concede, to allow; to acknowledge.

administrateur [administra'tœːr], *n.m.* (*fem.* **-trice**) manager, director; administrator, administratrix, trustee (*of an estate*).

administratif [administra'tif], *a.* (*fem.* **-tive**) administrative.

administration [administra'sjɔ̃], *n.f.* administration, management, direction, government; (*collect.*) the management, the administration.

administré [adminis'tre], *n.m.* (*fem.* **-ée**) person under one's administration *or* jurisdiction.

administrer [adminis'tre], *v.t.* to manage, to govern, to direct; to administer, to dispense.

admirable [admi'rabl], *a.* admirable; wonderful.

admirablement [admirablə'mã], *adv.* admirably; wonderfully.

admirateur [admira'tœːr], *n.m.* (*fem.* -**trice**) admirer, praiser.

admiratif [admira'tif], *a.* (*fem.* -**tive**) admiring, wondering.

admiration [admira'sjɔ̃], *n.f.* admiration.

admirer [admi're], *v.t.* to admire.

admissibilité [admisibili'te], *n.f.* admissibility.

admissible [admi'sibl], *a.* admittable, admissible.

admission [admi'sjɔ̃], *n.f.* admission, admittance; *soupape d'admission*, inlet valve.

admonestation [admɔnɛsta'sjɔ̃], *n.f.* admonishment, admonition.

admonester [admɔnɛs'te], *v.t.* to reprimand, to admonish.

admoniteur [admɔni'tœːr], *n.m.* (*fem.* -**trice**) admonisher.

admonitif [admɔni'tif], *a.* (*fem.* -**tive**) admonitory.

admonition [admɔni'sjɔ̃], *n.f.* (*chiefly R.-C. Ch.*) admonition, advice, reprimand.

adolescence [adɔlɛs'sãːs], *n.f.* adolescence.

adolescent [adɔlɛs'sã], *a.* adolescent.—*n.m.* (*fem.* -**e**) adolescent, youth, teenager.

Adonis [adɔ'niːs], *n.m.* Adonis, beau.

adonné [adɔ'ne], *a.* given to, addicted, devoted. **s'adonner**, *v.r.* to give, devote *or* addict oneself (à).

adopté [adɔp'te], *a.* adopted *or* adoptive (*child*).

adopter [adɔp'te], *v.t.* to adopt; to embrace, to espouse; to pass, to carry (*a bill*).

adoptif [adɔp'tif], *a.* (*fem.* -**tive**) adoptive, by adoption.

adoption [adɔp'sjɔ̃], *n.f.* adoption.

adorable [adɔ'rabl], *a.* adorable, charming, delightful, exquisite.

adorablement [adɔrablə'mã], *adv.* adorably, delightfully.

adorateur [adɔra'tœːr], *n.m.* (*fem.* -**trice**) adorer, worshipper.

adoration [adɔra'sjɔ̃], *n.f.* adoration, worship; admiration, respect, reverence.

adorer [adɔ're], *v.t.* to adore, to worship.

adossé [adɔ'se], *a.* with one's back against.

adosser [adɔ'se], *v.t.* to set *or* lean with the back against; to put back to back. **s'adosser**, *v.r.* to lean one's back (à, *contre*).

adoucir [adu'siːr], *v.t.* to soften; to sweeten; to mitigate, to alleviate, to smooth. **s'adoucir**, *v.r.* to grow mild *or* soft; to get milder (*of weather*).

adoucissement [adusis'mã], *n.m.* softening, sweetening; assuaging, appeasing; ease, mitigation, alleviation; consolation.

adrénaline [adrena'lin], *n.f.* adrenalin.

adresse [a'drɛs], *n.f.* address; memorial, a document addressed to an assembly *or* person in authority; skill, dexterity, cleverness.

adresser [adrɛ'se], *v.t.* to direct, to address; to turn, to direct (*one's steps etc.*). **s'adresser**, *v.r.* to be directed; to speak, to address oneself, to make application, to appeal (à); *s'adresser ici*, apply within.

Adriatique [adria'tik], **l'**, *f.* the Adriatic.

adroit [a'drwa], *a.* ingenious, clever, skilful; artful.

8

adroitement [adrwat'mã], *adv.* skilfully, artfully, cleverly.

adulateur [adyla'tœːr], *a.* (*fem.* -**trice**) flattering, adulatory.—*n.m.* (*fem.* -**trice**) adulator, flatterer, sycophant.

adulatif [adyla'tif], *a.* (*fem.* -**tive**) flattering, adulatory.

adulation [adyla'sjɔ̃], *n.f.* adulation, flattery, sycophancy.

aduler [ady'le], *v.t.* to flatter, to fawn upon.

adulte [a'dylt], *a.* adult, grown-up.—*n.* adult.

adultère [adyl'tɛːr], *a.* adulterous; *femme adultère*, adulteress.—*n.m.* adultery.—*n.* adulterer, adulteress.

adultérer [adylte're], *v.t.* (*conjug. like* CÉDER) (*Pharm.*) to adulterate; (*Law*) to falsify (*money*); (*fig.*) to corrupt, to pervert, to falsify.

adultérin [adylte'rɛ̃], *a.* adulterine.

advenir [advə'niːr], *v.i.* irr. (*used only in inf. and 3rd pers.*) to occur, to happen, to befall.

adventice [advã'tis], *a.* adventitious.

adventif [advã'tif], *a.* (*fem.* -**tive**) (*Bot.*) adventitious, casual.

adverbe [ad'vɛrb], *n.m.* adverb.

adverbial [adver'bjal], *a.* adverbial.

adverbialement [adverbjal'mã], *adv.* adverbially.

adversaire [adver'sɛːr], *n.* adversary, opponent.

adverse [ad'vɛrs], *a.* adverse, opposite, contrary; calamitous.

adversité [adversi'te], *n.f.* adversity, misfortune.

aérage [ae'raːʒ], *n.m.* ventilation, airing.

aérateur [aera'tœːr], *n.m.* ventilator.

aération [aera'sjɔ̃], *n.f.* ventilation, airing.

aéré [ae're], *p.p.* ventilated.—*a.* airy.

aérer [ae're], *v.t.* (*conjug. like* CÉDER) to ventilate, to air, to renew the air of; (*Chem.*) to aerate.

aérien [ae'rjɛ̃], *a.* (*fem.* -**enne**) aerial; living *or* occurring in the air, celestial; (*fig.*) light, airy; *base aérienne*, air base; *fil aérien*, overhead wire; *ligne aérienne*, airline; *pont aérien*, airlift; *raid aérien*, air raid.

aérifère [aeri'fɛːr], *a.* air-conducting.

aérification [aerifika'sjɔ̃], *n.f.* gasification.

aérifier [aeri'fje], *v.t.* to gasify.

aéro-club [aero'klœb], *n.m.* (*pl.* **aéro-clubs**) flying club.

aérodrome [aero'droːm], *n.m.* aerodrome, airfield.

aérodynamique [aerodina'mik], *a.* aerodynamic, streamlined.—*n.f.* aerodynamics.

aérogare [aero'gaːr], *n.f.* air terminal.

aérographe [aero'graf], *n.m.* aerograph.

aérographie [aerogra'fi], *n.f.* aerography.

aérolithe [aero'lit], *n.m.* aerolite.

aérolithique [aeroli'tik], *a.* aerolitic.

aérologie [aerolɔ'ʒi], *n.f.* aerology.

aéromètre [aero'mɛtr], *n.m.* aerometer, air-poise.

aéronaute [aero'noːt], *n.* aeronaut.

aéronautique [aerono'tik], *a.* aeronautic.—*n.f.* aeronautics, aerial navigation.

aéronef [aero'nɛf], *n.m.* airship.

aéroplane [aero'plan], *n.m.* airplane.

aéroport [aero'pɔːr], *n.m.* airport.

aéroporté [aeropor'te], *a.* airborne (*troops*).

aérosphère [aero'sfɛːr], *n.f.* the mass of air surrounding the globe, atmosphere.

aérostat [aeros'ta], *n.m.* acrostat, air-balloon.

aérostation [aerosta'sjɔ̃], *n.f.* aerostation, air navigation.

aérostatique [aerosta'tik], *a.* aerostatic.—*n.f.* aerostatics.

aérostier [aeros'tje], *n.m.* aeronaut, one directing an aerostat.

aérothérapie [aerotera'pi], *n.f.* aerotherapy.

affabilité [afabili'te], *n.f.* affability, kindness, courtesy.

affable [a'fabl], *a.* affable, courteous.

affadir [afa'diːr], *v.t.* to make unsavory or insipid; (*fig.*) to make flat or dull. **s'affadir**, *v.r.* to become insipid.

affadissement [afadis'mã], *n.m.* insipidity, nausea, sickliness.

affaiblir [afɛ'bliːr], *v.t.* to enfeeble, to weaken; to lessen. **s'affaiblir**, *v.r.* to grow weak; to abate.

affaiblissement [afɛblis'mã], *n.m.* weakening, allaying, abatement.

affaire [a'fɛːr], *n.f.* affair, business, concern, matter; trouble, scrape; lawsuit; transaction, bargain; **c'est mon affaire**, it is my own concern; **mêlez-vous de vos affaires!**, mind your own business!; **être dans les affaires**, to be in business; **homme d'affaires**, business man, legal adviser.

affairé [afɛ're], *a.* busy.

affairement [afɛr'mã], *n.m.* hurry, bustle, ado.

affaissement [afɛs'mã], *n.m.* depression, subsidence, giving way, collapse.

affaisser [afɛ'se], *v.t.* to cause to sink, to weigh down, to press down; to bear down, to overwhelm. **s'affaisser**, *v.r.* to sink, to subside; to give way; to be bent down (*by age*); to collapse.

affamé [afa'me], *a.* famished, hungry, starving; greedy, craving; **être affamé de**, to be greedy or eager for.

affamer [afa'me], *v.t.* to starve, to famish, to deprive of food.

affectation [afɛkta'sjɔ̃], *n.f.* appropriation, destination or attribution (*to a certain object*); simulation, show, pretence, affectation; preference; distinction; (*Mil.*) **recevoir une affectation**, to be posted.

affecté [afɛk'te], *a.* affected, assumed, simulated, put on; attributed, destined (*to a certain object*); (*Path.*) affected (*by a disease etc.*); (*Mil.*) posted to.

affecter [afɛk'te], *v.t.* to affect, to make frequent or habitual use of, to have a predilection for; to assume (*a certain shape etc.*); to feign, to pretend; to set apart, to earmark, to destine, to appropriate (*to a certain object*); to move, to touch, to impress emotionally. **s'affecter**, *v.r.* to be affected.

affection [afɛk'sjɔ̃], *n.f.* affection, love, attachment; (*Med.*) affection, ailment.

affectionné [afɛksjo'ne], *a.* affectionate, loving, attached, loved, liked.

affectionner [afɛksjo'ne], *v.t.* to love, to be fond of, to like.

affectueusement [afɛktɥøz'mã], *adv.* affectionately, fondly.

affectueux [afɛk'tɥø], *a.* (*fem.* **-euse**) affectionate, tender, warm-hearted.

afférent [afe'rã], *a.* reverting; relating to; assignable to; accruing to.

affermage [afɛr'maːʒ], *n.m.* farming, renting.

affermataire [afɛrma'tɛːr], *n.m.* tenant farmer.

affermateur [afɛrma'tœːr], *n.m.* (*fem.* **-trice**) lessor.

affermer [afɛr'me], *v.t.* to farm or let out by lease; to take a lease of, to rent.

affermir [afɛr'miːr], *v.t.* to strengthen, to make firm; to confirm, to establish, to consolidate. **s'affermir**, *v.r.* to become strong, firm, or fast; to become established.

affermissement [afɛrmis'mã], *n.m.* strengthening, consolidation, establishment; support, prop, stay.

affété [afe'te], *a.* affected, prim, finical; canting, mincing, pretty-pretty.

afféterie [afe'tri], *n.f.* affectation, mannerisms, primness.

affichage [afi'ʃaːʒ], *n.m.* bill-posting; placarding.

affiche [a'fiʃ], *n.f.* placard, bill, poster; **homme affiche**, sandwichman; **affiche électorale**, election poster.

afficher [afi'ʃe], *v.t.* to post up; to publish, to divulge, to proclaim; to make a show of, to parade; **défense d'afficher**, post no bills; billposting prohibited. **s'afficher**, *v.r.* to set up (*for*); to attract public notice.

afficheur [afi'ʃœːr], *n.m.* bill-poster.

affidavit [afida'vit], *n.m.* affidavit.

affidé [afi'de], *a.* trusty, trustworthy; in the know.—*n.m.* (*fem.* **-ée**) confederate, confidential agent; spy.

affilage [afi'laːʒ], **affilement** [afil'mã], *n.m.* whetting, sharpening, setting.

affilé [afi'le], *a.* sharp; nimble, glib (*of the tongue*).

affilée (d') [dafi'le], *adv. phr.* at a stretch; **trois heures d'affilée**, three hours at a stretch.

affiler [afi'le], *v.t.* to sharpen, to set, to put an edge on.

affiliation [afilja'sjɔ̃], *n.f.* affiliation (*to a society, company, plot etc.*).

affilié [afi'lje], *a.* affiliated, admitted a member or associate.—*n.m.* (*fem.* **-ée**) affiliated member, associate, confederate.

affilier [afi'lje], *v.t.* to admit, to affiliate, to receive. **s'affilier**, *v.r.* to become admitted or affiliated, to join.

affiloir [afi'lwaːr], *n.m.* hone, oilstone, steel, strop.

affinage [afi'naːʒ], **affinement** [afin'mã], *n.m.* refining, fining (*of metals, sugar etc.*); heckling (*of hemp*), maturing (*of a wine*), ripening (*of a cheese*).

affiner [afi'ne], *v.t.* to fine, to refine. **s'affiner**, *v.r.* to be refined, to be fined; to become finer, wittier etc. (*of the mind*).

affinerie [afin'ri], *n.f.* metal refinery.

affineur [afi'nœːr], *n.m.* metal refiner.

affinité [afini'te], *n.f.* affinity, relationship.

affinoir [afi'nwaːr], *n.m.* carding brush.

affiquet [afi'kɛ], *n.m.* knitting sheath; (*pl.*) gewgaws, trinkets.

affirmatif [afirma'tif], *a.* (*fem.* **-tive**) affirmative, asserting.—*n.f.* (**-tive**) affirmative statement, answer etc.; asseveration; **répondre par l'affirmative**, to answer in the affirmative.

affirmation [afirma'sjɔ̃], *n.f.* affirmation, assertion.

9

affirmativement [afirmativ'mã], *adv.* affirmatively.
affirmer [afir'me], *v.t.* to affirm, to assert, to vouch, to declare; to confirm by *or* on oath. **s'affirmer**, *v.r.* to grow stronger, to assert oneself.
affixe [a'fiks], *n.m.* affix.
affleurement [aflœr'mã], *n.m.* levelling, making flush; (*Mining*) outcrop.
affleurer [aflœ're], *v.t.* to make even, to level; (*Arch.*) to make flush.—*v.i.* to be level, to be flush (*with*); (*Mining*) to crop out.
affliction [aflik'sjõ], *n.f.* affliction, trouble, distress; trial, vexation.
affligé [afli'ʒe], *a.* afflicted, grieved, distressed.
affliger [afli'ʒe], *v.t.* (*conjug. like* MANGER) to afflict, to trouble, to distress, to grieve, to vex, to torment; to mortify, to chasten. **s'affliger**, *v.r.* to grieve, to be afflicted, troubled *or* cast down; to take something to heart.
afflouage [aflu'a:ʒ], *n.m.* (*Naut.*) refloating (*of a ship*).
afflouer [aflu'e], *v.t.* to refloat.
affluence [afly'ã:s], *n.f.* affluence, abundance; concourse, crowd; *heures d'affluence*, rush hour.
affluent [afly'ã], *a.* falling into, running into (*of rivers*).—*n.m.* tributary.
affluer [afly'e], *v.i.* to fall, run *or* flow into (*as a tributary*) (*dans*); to abound; to come in great quantity (*à, vers*).
affolant [afɔ'lã], *a.* distracting.
affolé [afɔ'le], *a.* distracted, panic-stricken; (*Mech.*) disconnected, defective.
affolement [afɔl'mã], *n.m.* distraction, panic.
affoler [afɔ'le], *v.t.* to distract; to infatuate; to bewitch; to madden, to drive crazy. **s'affoler**, *v.r.* to fall into a panic, to stampede.
afforestage [afores'ta:ʒ], *n.m.* right of cutting firewood, estovers.
afforestation [aforesta'sjõ], *n.f.* afforestation.
affouillable [afu'jabl], *a.* subject *or* liable to undermining.
affouillement [afuj'mã], *n.m.* undermining, washing away.
affouiller [afu'je], *v.t.* to undermine, to wash away.
affouragement *or* **affourragement** [afuraʒ 'mã], *n.m.* foraging, foddering.
affourager *or* **affourrager** [afura'ʒe], *v.t.* (*conjug. like* MANGER) to fodder, to give fodder to.
affourcher [afur'ʃe], *v.t.* to seat astride; (*Carp.*) to join in a tongue and groove.
affranchi [afrã'ʃi], *a.* set free, freed.—*n.m.* (*fem.* -e) freedman; freedwoman.
affranchir [afrã'ʃi:r], *v.t.* to free, to set free, to enfranchise; to absolve, to exempt; to frank (*a letter*); to stamp. **s'affranchir**, *v.r.* to free oneself; to rid oneself of (*de*), to shake off, to break away from.
affranchissement [afrãʃis'mã], *n.m.* enfranchisement; exemption, discharge; deliverance; payment of postage (*of a letter*).
affranchisseur [afrãʃi'sœ:r], *n.m.* emancipator, liberator.
affres [a:fr], *n.f.* (*used only in pl.*) dread, horror, agony; *les affres de la mort*, the pangs of death, death throes.

affrètement [afrɛt'mã], *n.m.* chartering, freighting.
affréter [afre'te], *v.t.* (*conjug. like* CÉDER) (*Naut.*) to charter, to freight (*a vessel*).
affréteur [afre'tœ:r], *n.m.* charterer, freighter.
affreusement [afrœz'mã], *adv.* frightfully, horribly, dreadfully.
affreux [a'frø], *a.* (*fem.* -euse) frightful, hideous, shocking, horrible, ghastly.
affriander [afriã'de], *v.t.* to allure, to entice to tempt.
affricher [afri'ʃe], *v.t.* to leave fallow.
affrioler [afriɔ'le], *v.t.* to allure, to entice.
affront [a'frõ], *n.m.* affront, insult; disgrace.
affronter [afrõ'te], *v.t.* to face, to confront, to brave; to attack boldly.
affruiter [afrɥi'te], *v.t.* to plant with fruit-trees.—*v.i.* to bear *or* supply fruit. **s'affruiter**, *v.r.* to come into fruit.
affublement [afyblə'mã], *n.m.* grotesque make-up *or* rig-out (*of dress*).
affubler [afy'ble], *v.t.* to dress up, to rig out (*grotesquely*). **s'affubler**, *v.r.* to dress up ridiculously.
affût [a'fy], *n.m.* stand *or* place for lying in wait, watch; gun carriage; *être à l'affût*, to lie in wait.
affûtage [afy'ta:ʒ], *n.m.* setting *or* sharpening (*of tools*).
affûter [afy'te], *v.t.* to grind, to sharpen.
affûteur [afy'tœ:r], *n.m.* sharpener, setter, grinder; stalker.—*n.f.* (-euse) sharpening machine.
afghan [af'gã], *a.* Afghan.—*n.m.* (**Afghan**, *fem.* -ane) Afghan (*person*).
Afghanistan [afganis'tã], *l'*, *m.* Afghanistan.
afin [a'fɛ̃], *conj.* afin de (*with inf.*) to, in order to, so as to; afin que (*with subj.*) to, in order that, so that.
africain [afri'kɛ̃], *a.* African.—*n.m.* (**Africain** *fem.* -aine) African (*person*).
Afrique [a'frik], *l'*, *f.* Africa.
agaçant [aga'sã], *a.* irritating, worrying; provoking, provocative; alluring, enticing.
agace *or* **agasse** [a'gas], *n.f.* magpie.
agacement [agas'mã], *n.m.* irritation, setting on edge.
agacer [aga'se], *v.t.* (*conjug. like* COMMENCER) to worry, to irritate, to set on edge; to excite, to provoke; to entice, to allure.
agacerie [aga'sri], *n.f.* allurement, coquetry, enticement.
agaillardir [agajar'di:r], *v.t.* to cheer up.
agate [a'gat], *n.f.* agate.
Agathe [a'gat], *f.* Agatha.
âge [ɑ:ʒ], *n.m.* age, years; period, epoch, era, (*pl.*) the ages, time; *Moyen Âge*, Middle Ages; *d'un certain âge*, elderly; *entre deux âges*, of uncertain age.
âgé [ɑ'ʒe], *a.* aged (*so many years*); old, elderly; *âgé de vingt ans*, twenty years old.
agence [a'ʒã:s], *n.f.* agency, bureau, branch office.
agencement [aʒãs'mã], *n.m.* arrangement, grouping, ordering; (*Arch.*) composition, layout.
agencer [aʒã'se], *v.t.* (*conjug. like* COMMENCER) to arrange, to dispose.
agenda [aʒɛ̃'da], *n.m.* notebook; diary; engagement book.

agenouiller (s') [aʒnu'je], v.r. to kneel down, to fall on one's knees; (fig.) to bow down (devant).

agenouilloir [aʒnuj'waːr], n.m. hassock.

agent [a'ʒɑ̃], n.m. agent; deputy; middleman; broker; **agent de change**, stockbroker; **agent électoral**, canvasser; **agent de liaison**, liaison officer; **agent de police**, policeman.

agglomération [aglɔmera'sjɔ̃], n.f. agglomeration, built-up area.

aggloméré [aglɔme're], n.m. compressed fuel, briquette.

agglomérer [aglɔme're], v.t. (conjug. like CÉDER) to agglomerate, to mass together, to pile up, to assemble.

s'agglomérer, v.r. to mass together, to assemble.

agglutinant [aglyti'nɑ̃], a. adhesive.

agglutiner [aglyti'ne], v.t. to bind, to cake.

s'agglutiner, v.r. to unite, to cohere; to heal over (wound).

aggravant [agra'vɑ̃], a. (Law) aggravating, making more heinous.

aggravation [agrava'sjɔ̃], n.f. aggravation, additional penalty; **aggravation de peine**, increase of punishment.

aggraver [agra've], v.t. to aggravate, to make worse. **s'aggraver**, v.r. to worsen (illness, situation).

agile [a'ʒil], a. agile, nimble.

agilement [aʒil'mɑ̃], adv. nimbly, with agility.

agilité [aʒili'te], n.f. agility, nimbleness, lightness.

agio [a'ʒjo], n.m. stock-jobbing, speculation.

agiotage [aʒjɔ'taːʒ], n.m. stockjobbing; **faire l'agiotage**, to deal in stocks.

agioter [aʒjɔ'te], v.i. to speculate, to job.

agioteur [aʒjɔ'tœːr], n.m. speculator, jobber.

agir [a'ʒiːr], v.i. to act, to do; to operate; to have an effect (sur); to negotiate, to manage a business; to sue, to prosecute, to proceed (contre); to behave. **s'agir**, v.r. (impers.) to be in question, to be the matter; **de quoi s'agit-il?** what is it about? **il s'agit de votre vie**, your life is at stake.

agissant [aʒi'sɑ̃], a. active, busy; efficacious, effective.

agitateur [aʒita'tœːr], n.m. (fem -trice) agitator.—n.m. stirring rod.

agitation [aʒita'sjɔ̃], n.f. agitation; disturbance, tossing, shaking, tumult; trouble, emotion, uneasiness, restlessness.

agité [aʒi'te], a. restless (sleep); rough (sea); fretful (child).

agiter [aʒi'te], v.t. to agitate, to put in motion, to shake, to stir; to disturb, to trouble; to excite, to perturb; to debate, to discuss. **s'agiter**, v.r. to be agitated or in movement; to get rough; to be restless, disturbed or uneasy; to toss, to wave, to flutter; to be debated.

agneau [a'ɲo], n.m. (fem. -elle, pl. -eaux) lamb.

agnelage [aɲə'laːʒ], **agnèlement** [aɲɛl'mɑ̃], n.m. lambing; lambing time.

agneler [aɲə'le], v.i. (conjug. like AMENER) to lamb, to yean.

Agnès [a'nɛːs], f. Agnes.

agnès [a'nɛːs], n.f. raw young girl.

agnosticisme [agnɔsti'sism], n.m. agnosticism.

agnosticiste [agnɔsti'sist], **agnostique** [agnɔs'tik], a. and n. agnostic.

agonie [agɔ'ni], n.f. agony, death pangs;

(fig.) trouble, anguish, torture; **être à l'agonie**, to be at the point of death.

agonir [agɔ'niːr], v.t. to insult grossly.

agonisant [agɔni'zɑ̃], a. dying, in a dying condition.—n.m. (fem. -e) dying person.

agoniser [agɔni'ze], v.i. to be at the point of death.

agoraphobie [agɔrafɔ'bi], n.f. agoraphobia.

agrafe [a'graf], n.f. fastener, clasp, clip, staple (for papers); **agrafe et porte**, hook and eye.

agrafer [agra'fe], v.t. to hook, to clasp, to fasten with a clasp; to staple.

agrafeuse [agra'føːz], n.f. stapler.

agraire [a'grɛːr], a. agrarian.

agrandir [agrɑ̃'diːr], v.t. to make greater, to enlarge, to augment; to widen; to exaggerate; to promote, to advance; (fig.) to elevate. **s'agrandir**, v.r. to become greater or larger.

agrandissement [agrɑ̃dis'mɑ̃], n.m. enlargement, increase; aggrandizement, elevation.

agrandisseur [agrɑ̃di'sœːr], n.m. (Phot.) enlarger.

agréable [agre'abl], a. agreeable, pleasing, pleasant, acceptable.

agréablement [agreablə'mɑ̃], adv. agreeably, pleasantly.

agréé [agre'e], n.m. solicitor, attorney.

agréer [agre'e], v.t. to accept, to approve, to allow, to receive kindly.—v.i. to please, to be agreeable; **veuillez agréer mes salutations**, yours truly.

agrégat [agre'ga], n.m. aggregate, composite mass.

agrégation [agrega'sjɔ̃], n.f. (Phys.) aggregation, aggregate; (**concours d'agrégation**) competitive examination for admission on the teaching staff of State secondary schools or of faculties of law, medicine, pharmacy.

agrégé [agre'ʒe], a. and n.m. **professeur agrégé**, one who has passed the **agrégation**.

agréger [agre'ʒe], v.t. (conjug. like ASSIÉGER) to admit into a society, to incorporate; (Phys.) to aggregate.

agrément [agre'mɑ̃], n.m. consent, approbation; pleasure, charm, gracefulness; amenity; (pl.) ornaments, embellishments, amenities (of life); **arts d'agrément**, accomplishments.

agrémenter [agremɑ̃'te], v.t. to set off, to ornament, to adorn.

agrès [a'grɛ], n.m. (used only in pl.) rigging (of a ship etc.); apparatus, gear (of a gymnasium etc.).

agresseur [agre'sœːr], n.m. aggressor.

agressif [agre'sif], a. (fem. -ive) aggressive.

agression [agre'sjɔ̃], n.f. aggression.

agressivité [agresivi'te], n.f. aggressiveness.

agreste [a'grɛst], a. rustic; countrified (manners).

agrestement [agrɛstə'mɑ̃], adv. rustically.

agricole [agri'kɔl], a. agricultural.

agriculteur [agrikyl'tœːr], n.m. agriculturist, husbandman, farmer.

agriculture [agrikyl'tyːr], n.f. agriculture, husbandry, tillage.

agriffer [agri'fe], v.t. to claw; to clutch, to grip. **s'agriffer**, v.r. to claw (at).

agrion [agri'ɔ̃], n.m. dragonfly.

agripper [agri'pe], v.t. to grip, to snatch. **s'agripper**, v.r. to cling (to).

agronome [agrɔ'nɔm], *n.m.* agriculturist.

aguerri [agɛ'ri], *a.* inured to war; disciplined.

aguerrir [agɛ'ri:r], *v.t.* to train *or* inure to the hardships of war; to accustom, to inure (*to hardships etc.*). **s'aguerrir**, *v.r.* to inure *or* accustom oneself (*to hardships, abstinence etc.*), to be inured.

aguerrissement [agɛris'mɑ̃], *n.m.* inuring to war, hardening.

aguets (s') [sacr'te], *v.r.* to persist (*in*).

aheurter (s') [sacr'te], *v.r.* to persist (*in*).

ahuri [ay'ri], *a.* bewildered, perplexed, flurried.

ahurir [ay'ri:r], *v.t.* to bewilder, to flurry, to stupefy.

ahurissant [ayri'sɑ̃], *a.* bewildering.

ahurissement [ayris'mɑ̃], *n.m.* bewilderment, confusion, perplexity.

aï [a'i], *n.m.* (*Zool.*) sloth.

aide [ɛːd], *n.f.* help, relief, assistance; succor, support, protection, rescue; relief (*of the poor etc.*); helper, female assistant, help; **à l'aide de**, with the help of.—*n.m.* a male assistant; **aide de camp** (*pl.* **aides de camp**), aide-de-camp.

aide-mémoire [edmɛ'mwaːr], *n.m.* *inv.* précis; memorandum.

aider [ɛ'de], *v.t.* to aid, to help, to relieve, to assist, to succor; to abet; to conduce to, to further.—*v.i.* to be helpful, to be of assistance (*à*). **s'aider**, *v.r.* to make use (*de*); to avail oneself.

aïe! [aj], *int.* oh! oh dear!

aïeul [a'jœl], *n.m.* (*fem.* **aïeule**, *pl.* **aïeuls**, **aïeules**) grandfather, grandsire; grandmother, grandam; (*pl.* **aïeux**) forebears, ancestors.

aigle [ɛːgl], *n.* eagle; (*fig.*) clever *or* brilliant person, genius.—*n.m.* reading desk, lectern (*with effigy of an eagle*).

aiglefin [ɛglə'fɛ̃], **aigrefin** (1) [ɛgrə'fɛ̃], *n.m.* haddock.

aiglon [ɛ'glɔ̃], *n.m.* (*fem.* **-onne**) eaglet.

aigre [ɛgr], *a.* sour, tart; (*fig.*) harsh, bitter, shrill.—*n.m.* sourness, mustiness.

aigre-doux [ɛgrə'du], *a.* (*fem.* **-douce**) sourish, bitter-sweet.

aigrefin (2) [ɛgrə'fɛ̃], *n.m.* sharper, swindler; adventurer; [AIGLEFIN].

aigrelet [ɛgrə'lɛ], *a.* (*fem.* **-ette**) sourish.

aigrement [ɛgrə'mɑ̃], *adv.* acrimoniously, sourly, bitterly; roughly, harshly.

aigret [ɛ'grɛ], *a.* (*fem.* **-ette** (1)) sourish.

aigrette [ɛ'grɛt], *n.f.* aigrette, tuft, cluster *or* plume (*of feathers, diamonds etc.*); horn (*of an owl*); crest (*of a peacock*); egret, tufted heron.

aigreur [ɛ'grœːr], *n.f.* sourness, sharpness, tartness; (*fig.*) harshness, bitterness, surliness, animosity, spite.

aigrir [ɛ'griːr], *v.t.* to make sour *or* sharp, to sour; (*fig.*) to irritate, to embitter, to make worse, to incense, to make ill-humoured. **s'aigrir**, *v.r.* to turn sour; (*fig.*) to grow worse, to be exasperated, to be irritated.

aigrissement [ɛgris'mɑ̃], *n.m.* souring, embittering.

aigu [ɛ'gy], *a.* (*fem.* **aiguë**) pointed, sharp, keen, acute; (*fig.*) shrill, piercing; **accent aigu**, acute accent.

aiguë [AIGU].

aigue-marine [ɛgma'rin], *n.f.* (*pl.* **aigues-marines**) aquamarine.

aiguière [ɛ'gjɛːr], *n.f.* ewer.

aiguillage [egɥi'ja:ʒ], *n.m.* (*Rail.*) shunting, switch.

aiguillat [egɥi'ja], *n.m.* dogfish.

aiguille [ɛ'gɥi:j], *n.f.* needle; index, pointer, hand (*of a dial, watch etc.*); spire (*steeple*); point (*of an obelisk, peak etc.*); rock pinnacle *or* needle-shaped peak; **trou d'une aiguille**, eye of a needle; (*pl., Rail.*) switch.

aiguiller [egɥi'je], *v.t.* (*Rail.*) to shunt.

aiguillette [egɥi'jɛt], *n.f.* aglet, point; (*Mil.*) ornamental shoulder-knot.

aiguilleur [egɥi'jœːr], *n.m.* (*Rail.*) switchman, shunter.

aiguillier [egɥi'je], *n.m.* (*fem.* **-ière**) needle-maker.

aiguillon [egɥi'jɔ̃], *n.m.* goad, sting; (*fig.*) spur, incentive; (*Bot.*) prickle.

aiguillonner [egɥijɔ'ne], *v.t.* to goad, to prick; (*fig.*) to incite, to spur on; to stimulate.

aiguisage [egi'za:ʒ], **aiguisement** [egiz'mɑ̃], *n.m.* whetting, sharpening.

aiguisé [egi'ze], *a.* whetted, sharpened.

aiguiser [egi'ze], *v.t.* to whet, to sharpen, to set an edge on; to point; (*fig.*) to make keen, acid, piquant etc.; to excite, to stimulate.

aiguiseur [egi'zœːr], *n.m.* knife-grinder, sharpener.

aiguisoir [egi'zwaːr], *n.m.* sharpening-tool, whetstone.

ail [a:j], *n.m.* (*pl.* (*Cook.*) **aulx** [o:], (*Bot.*) **ails**) garlic.

aile [ɛl], *n.f.* wing; brim (*of a hat*); flipper (*of a penguin*); blade (*of a propeller*), vane, sail (*of a windmill*); flank *or* wing (*of an army, building etc.*); fender, mudguard (*of a car*).

ailé [ɛ'le], *a.* winged.

aileron [ɛl'rɔ̃], *n.m.* pinion (*of a bird*); aileron, balancing flap (*of an aircraft*); fin (*of some fish*).

ailette [ɛ'lɛt], *n.f.* small wing; vane (*of a torpedo etc.*); (*Motor.*) rib, fin, flange.

ailier [ɛ'lje], *n.m.* (*Ftb.*) wing forward, wing three-quarter.

ailleurs [a'jœːr], *adv.* elsewhere, somewhere else; **d'ailleurs**, besides, moreover, in other respects.

aimable [ɛ'mabl], *a.* kind, amiable, obliging.

aimablement [ɛmablə'mɑ̃], *adv.* amiably, kindly.

aimant [ɛ'mɑ̃], *a.* loving, affectionate.—*n.m.* magnet; (*fig.*) attractiveness.

aimantation [ɛmɑ̃ta'sjɔ̃], *n.f.* magnetization.

aimanter [ɛmɑ̃'te], *v.t.* to magnetize.

Aimée [ɛ'me], *f.* Amy.

aimer [ɛ'me], *v.t.* to love, to be fond of, to be in love with; to like; **aimer mieux**, to prefer. **s'aimer**, *v.r.* to love oneself, to be vain; to love each other.

aine (1) [ɛːn], *n.f.* groin.

aine (2) [ɛːn], *n.f.* herring-stick; leather band on organ bellows.

aîné [ɛ'ne], *a.* (*fem.* **-ée**) eldest, elder, senior.—*n.m.* (*fem.* **-ée**) eldest son *or* daughter.

aînesse [ɛ'nɛs], *n.f.* seniority, priority by age, primogeniture; **droit d'aînesse**, birthright.

ainsi [ɛ̃'si], *adv.* thus, so, in this *or* that manner; *ainsi de suite*, and so on and so forth; *ainsi soit-il*, so be it, amen; *pour ainsi dire*, so to speak, as it were; *ainsi que*, in the same way (*as*).

air (1) [ɛːr], *n.m.* air; wind; (*Chem. etc.*) gas;—(*pl.*) atmosphere; *chambre à air*, inner tube; *courant d'air*, draught; *en plein air*, in the open air.

air (2) [ɛːr], *n.m.* mien, look, expression, air, manner, appearance.

air (3) [ɛːr], *n.m.* (*Mus.*) tune.

airain [ɛ'rɛ̃], *n.m.* bronze; (*Poet.*) cannon, bell.

aire [ɛːr], *n.f.* area, space; threshing floor; eyrie; *aire d'atterrissage*, (*Av.*) landing area, apron.

airelle [ɛ'rɛl], *n.f.* whortleberry, bilberry.

ais [ɛ], *n.m.* board, plank; stave (*of a barrel*).

aisance [ɛ'zɑ̃ːs], *n.f.* ease, facility; easiness, affluence; competency; (*Mach.*) play; freedom; the comforts *or* conveniences of life; *cabinet* (*or* *lieu*) *d'aisances*, public convenience.

aisceau [AISSETTE].

aise [ɛːz], *a.* glad, well pleased; *je suis bien aise de vous voir*, I am very glad to see you.—*n.f.* ease, comfort, convenience; (*pl.*) comforts, comfortable circumstances; *à l'aise*, at ease, comfortable; *être à son aise*, to be well off.

aisé [ɛ'ze], *a.* easy; convenient, comfortable; in easy circumstances.

aisément [ɛze'mɑ̃], *adv.* easily, readily, freely; comfortably.

aisseau [ɛ'so], *n.m.* (*pl.* **-eaux**) *aissante* [ɛ'sɑ̃ːt], *n.f.* (*Carp.*) shingle, wooden tile.

aisselier [ɛsə'lje], *n.m.* (*Carp.*) tie beam, brace, strut.

aisselle [ɛ'sɛl], *n.f.* armpit; (*Bot.*) axil.

aissette [ɛ'sɛt], *n.f.*, **aisceau** [ɛ'so] (*pl.* **-eaux**), *n.m.* adze (*of a cooper*); hooked hammer (*of a tiler*).

Aix-la-Chapelle [ɛkslaʃa'pɛl], *f.* Aachen.

ajointer [aʒwɛ̃'te], *v.t.* to join on to, to fit.

ajonc [a'ʒɔ̃], *n.m.* furze, gorse.

ajournement [aʒurnə'mɑ̃], *n.m.* adjournment, postponement; (*Law*) summons.

ajourner [aʒur'ne], *v.t.* to adjourn; to defer; (*Law*) to summon (*for a specified day*).

ajouter [aʒu'te], *v.t.* to add, to join, to subjoin, to interpolate. **s'ajouter**, *v.r.* to be joined, to attach oneself.

ajusté [aʒys'te], *a.* close-fitting (*clothes*).

ajustement [aʒystə'mɑ̃], *n.m.* adjustment, arranging, fitting, settlement; laying out; attire, apparel.

ajuster [aʒys'te], *v.t.* to adjust, to regulate, to square, to fit, to adapt (*one thing to another*); to take aim at; to set in order; (*Mus.*) to tune; to bedeck; to settle *or* arrange (*a dispute*). **s'ajuster**, *v.r.* to accommodate oneself, to be adapted; to dress, to deck oneself out.

ajusteur [aʒys'tœːr], *n.m.* fitter; weigher (*at the mint*).

alacrité [alakri'te], *n.f.* alacrity, cheerful briskness.

Aladin [ala'dɛ̃], *m.* Aladdin.

Alain [a'lɛ̃], *m.* Alan.

alaise [a'lɛːz], *n.f.* rubber sheet for pram *or* cot.

alambic [alɑ̃'bik], *n.m.* alembic, still.

alambiquer [alɑ̃bi'ke], *v.t.* to distil, to refine.

alangui [alɑ̃'gi], *a.* languid, downcast.

alanguir [alɑ̃'giːr], *v.t.* to enfeeble, to make languid. **s'alanguir**, *v.r.* to languish, to flag, to become languid.

alanguissement [alɑ̃gis'mɑ̃], *n.m.* languor.

alarmant [alar'mɑ̃], *a.* alarming, startling.

alarme [a'larm], *n.f.* alarm, affright, sudden fear, uneasiness.

alarmer [alar'me], *v.t.* to alarm; to startle, to render anxious *or* frightened. **s'alarmer**, *v.r.* to take alarm, to be alarmed.

alarmiste [alar'mist], *a.* and *n.* alarmist.

albanais [alba'nɛ], *a.* Albanian.—*n.m.* Albanian (*language*); (**Albanais**, *fem.* **-aise**) Albanian (*person*).

Albanie [alba'niː], l', *f.* Albania.

albâtre [al'bɑːtr], *n.m.* alabaster; (*fig.*) whiteness.

albatros [alba'trɔs], *n.m.* albatross.

albinisme [albi'nism], *n.m.* albinism.

albinos [albi'nɔs], *a.* and *n.* albino.

album [al'bɔm], *n.m.* album, scrapbook, sketch book.

albumine [alby'min], *n.f.* albumen.

alcaïque [alka'ik], *a.* alcaic (*verse*).

alcali [alka'li], *n.m.* alkali.

alcalin [alka'lɛ̃], *a.* alkaline.

alcalinité [alkalini'te], *n.f.* alkalinity.

alcaliser [alkali'ze], **alcaliniser** [alkalini'ze], *v.t.* to alkalify.

alchimie [alʃi'mi], *n.f.* alchemy.

alchimique [alʃi'mik], *a.* alchemical.

alchimiste [alʃi'mist], *n.m.* alchemist.

alcool [al'kɔl], *n.m.* alcohol; spirit(s); *alcool à brûler*, *alcool dénaturé*, methylated spirit.

alcoolique [alkɔ'lik], *a.* alcoholic.

alcoolisme [alkɔ'lism], *n.m.* alcoholism.

Alcoran [alkɔ'rɑ̃], [CORAN].

alcôve [al'koːv], *n.f.* alcove, recess.

alcyon [al'sjɔ̃], *n.m.* halcyon; (*Orn.*) kingfisher.

alcyonien [alsjɔ'njɛ̃], *a.* (*fem.* **-enne**) halcyon, peaceful.

aléa [ale'a], *n.m.* chance, hazard.

aléatoire [alea'nwaːr], *a.* hazardous, uncertain.

alène [a'lɛn], *n.f.* awl.

alentour *or* **à l'entour** [alɑ̃'tuːr], *adv.* about, around, round about.

alentours [alɑ̃'tuːr], *n.m.* (*used only in pl.*) environs, neighborhood.

Aléoutiennes [aleu'sjɛn], **les**, *f.pl.* the Aleutian Islands.

alerte [a'lɛrt], *a.* alert, vigilant; active, lively, agile.—*n.f.* alarm, warning; *alerte aérienne*, air-raid warning.

alerter [alɛr'te], *v.t.* to give the alarm to, to warn.

alésage [ale'zaːʒ], *n.m.* boring, drilling, bore (*of cylinder*).

aléser [ale'ze], *v.t.* (*conjug. like* CÉDER) to smooth *or* enlarge the bore of (*a tube, gun etc*); *aléser un canon*, to bore a cannon.

aléseuse [ale'zøːz], *n.f.* boring machine.

alésoir [ale'zwaːr], *n.m.* borer, boring tool.

alester [alɛs'te], **alestir** [alɛs'tiːr], *v.t.* (*Naut.*) to lighten *or* disencumber (*a vessel*).

alésure [ale'zyːr], *n.f.* metal turnings *or* filings.

alevin [al'vɛ̃], *n.m.* fry, young fish.

aleviner [alvi'ne], *v.t.* to stock with fry.

13

alevinier [alvi'nje], *n.m.* breeding pond.
Alexandre [alɛk'sɑ̃:dr], *m.* Alexander.
Alexandrie [alɛksɑ̃'dri], *f.* Alexandria.
alexandrin [alɛksɑ̃'drɛ̃], *a.* and *n.m.* (*Pros.*) Alexandrine.
alezan [al'zɑ̃], *a.* and *n.m.* chestnut (horse).
alèze or **alèse** [a'lɛ:z], [ALAISE.]
alfa [al'fa], *n.m.* esparto grass.
algarade [alga'rad], *n.f.* insult, affront; rating.
algèbre [al'ʒɛbr], *n.f.* algebra.
algébrique [alʒe'brik], *a.* algebraical.
algébriquement [alʒebrik'mɑ̃], *adv.* algebraically.
Alger [al'ʒe], *m.* Algiers.
Algérie [alʒe'ri], *l'*, *f.* Algeria.
algérien [alʒe'rjɛ̃], *a.* (*fem.* **-enne**) Algerian.—*n.m.* (**Algérien**, *fem.* **-enne**) Algerian (*person*).
algie [al'ʒi:], *n.f.* ache.
algue [alg], *n.f.* seaweed, alga.
alibi [ali'bi], *n.m.* (*Law*) alibi.
aliboron [alibo'rɔ̃], *n.m.* jackass, stupid or self-conceited fellow.
aliénable [alje'nabl], *a.* alienable, transferable.
aliénation [aljena'sjɔ̃], *n.f.* (*Law*) conveyance of property to another; (*fig.*) alienation, mental derangement; estrangement, aversion.
aliéné [alje'ne], *a.* lunatic, mad.—*n.m.* (*fem.* **-ée**) lunatic.
aliéner [alje'ne], *v.t.* (*conjug. like* CÉDER) to alienate, to give away (*property*), to transfer, to make over; to estrange, to make hostile; to derange (*the mind*). **s'aliéner**, *v.r.* to become estranged (*from*).
aliéniste [alje'nist], *n.m.* alienist.
alignée [ali'ne], *n.f.* line, row.
alignement [aliɲa'mɑ̃], *n.m.* alignment; laying out in line; (*Mil.*) dressing; (*Print.*) ranging.
aligner [ali'ɲe], *v.t.* to align, to lay out in line; to put in a straight line; (*Mil.*) to dress; (*Print.*) to range. **s'aligner**, *v.r.* (*Mil.*) to dress.
aliment [ali'mɑ̃], *n.m.* aliment, food, nourishment, nutriment; (*Law, pl.*) alimony, maintenance.
alimentaire [alimɑ̃'tɛ:r], *a.* alimental, alimentary; (*Mech.*) **pompe alimentaire**, feed pump, donkey engine.
alimentateur [alimɑ̃ta'tœ:r], *a.* (*fem.* **-trice**) alimentary.
alimentation [alimɑ̃ta'sjɔ̃], *n.f.* alimentation; nourishment, feeding; **rayon d'alimentation**, food department.
alimenter [alimɑ̃'te], *v.t.* to feed, to nourish; to maintain; to supply, to provision; to fuel, to keep up.
alimenteux [alimɑ̃'tø], *a.* (*fem.* **-euse**) nutritive.
alinéa [aline'a], *n.m.* indented line; new paragraph.
alisé [ali'ze], [ALIZÉ.]
aliter [ali'te], *v.t.* to confine to bed; **être alité**, to be bedridden. **s'aliter**, *v.r.* to take to one's bed.
alizé or **alisé** [ali'ze], *a.* soft (*said of the trade winds*); **vents alizés**, trade winds.—*n.m.* trade wind.
alkali etc. [ALCALI.]
Alkoran [alko'rɑ̃], [CORAN.]

Allah [a'la], *m.* Allah.
allaitement [alɛt'mɑ̃], *n.m.* lactation, nursing, suckling; **allaitement artificiel**, bottle feeding.
allaiter [alɛ'te], *v.t.* to suckle, to nurse.
alléchant [ale'ʃɑ̃], *a.* alluring, seductive.
allèchement [alɛʃ'mɑ̃], *n.m.* allurement, enticement, seduction, attraction.
allécher [ale'ʃe], *v.t.* (*conjug. like* CÉDER) to allure, to entice, to attract.
allée [a'le], *n.f.* passage, drive, alley, avenue, walk; (*pl.*) goings.
allégation [alega'sjɔ̃], *n.f.* allegation, assertion.
allège [a'lɛ:ʒ], *n.f.* lighter, hopper; (*Arch.*) window basement, sill of window.
allégeance [ale'ʒɑ̃:s], *n.f.* alleviation, relief; allegiance.
allégement [aleʒ'mɑ̃], *n.m.* alleviation, relief; reduction.
alléger [ale'ʒe], *v.t.* (*conjug. like* ASSIÉGER) to ease, to unburden, to lighten; to unload (*a boat*); to alleviate, to relieve, to assuage (*pain* or *grief*).
allégorie [alego'ri], *n.f.* allegory.
allégorique [alego'rik], *a.* allegorical.
allégoriquement [alegorik'mɑ̃], *adv.* allegorically.
allégoriser [alegori'ze], *v.t.* to allegorize.
allégoriste [alego'rist], *n.m.* allegorist.
allègre [al'lɛgr], *a.* lively, nimble, sprightly; jolly, cheerful.
allègrement [allegrə'mɑ̃], *adv.* briskly; joyfully, merrily, joyously.
allégresse [alle'grɛs], *n.f.* gaiety, joy, mirth, cheerfulness; sprightliness.
alléguer [alle'ge], *v.t.* (*conjug. like* CÉDER) to allege, to advance, to urge; (*Law*) to quote, to adduce, to cite, to plead.
alléluia [allelly'ja], *n.m.* and *int.* hallelujah.
Allemagne [al'maɲ], *l'*, *f.* Germany.
allemand [al'mɑ̃], *a.* German.—*n.m.* German (*language*); (**Allemand**, *fem.* **-ande**) German (*person*).
aller [a'le], *v.i. irr.* (*with aux.* ÊTRE) to go, to go on, to proceed, to progress (*well, ill etc.*); to be (*in good or ill health*); to act (*in a certain way*); to suit, to fit (*well or ill*); to be going to; **aller au pas**, to go at a walking pace; **aller et venir**, to go up and down; **je ne ferai qu'aller et venir**, I won't be a minute; **cela va tout seul**, it is plain sailing; **cet enfant ira loin**, this child will go far; **comment allez-vous?** how are you? **je vais bien**, I am well; (*fam.*) **ça va!** all right! **cet habit vous va mal**, this coat does not fit you; **allons!** come on! **allons donc!** surely not! **cela va sans dire**, it stands to reason; **il y va de sa vie**, his life is at stake; **se laisser aller**, to yield, to give way, to abandon oneself to a thing. **s'en aller**, *v.r.* to go away, to run away; to vanish, to disappear; to die, to wear out; **va-t-en! allez-vous-en!** go away! be off with you!—*n.m.* going, course, run; outward voyage, trip, journey; **billet d'aller et retour**, return ticket.
allergie [alɛr'ʒi], *n.f.* allergy.
allergique [alɛr'ʒik], *a.* allergic.
alliage [a'lja:ʒ], *n.m.* alloy, mixture; (*fig.*) impure mixture or combination.

alliance [a'ljɑ̃:s], *n.f.* alliance; marriage; union, league, coalition, confederacy; compact, covenant; mixture, blending; wedding ring.

allié [a'lje], *a.* allied; related *(by marriage)*; akin, kindred.—*n.m. (fem.* **-ée)** ally; connection *(by marriage).*

allier [a'lje], *v.t.* to mix; to combine; to join, to unite, to ally, to marry; to reconcile; to match. **s'allier,** *v.r.* to be incorporated *or* mixed; to become allied, to join forces *(avec)*; to combine *(of metals).*

alligator [aliga'tɔːr], *n.m.* alligator.

allitération [alitera'sjɔ̃], *n.f.* alliteration.

allo! [a'lo], *int. (Teleph.)* hello!

allocataire [aloka'tɛːr], *n.* recipient of an allowance.

allocation [aloka'sjɔ̃], *n.f.* allocation, allowance; *allocation de chômage,* unemployment benefit; *allocations familiales,* family allowances.

allocution [aloky'sjɔ̃], *n.f.* allocution, short address, speech.

allonge [a'lɔ̃:ʒ], *n.f.* leaf *(of a table)*; flyleaf, addendum; rider *(of a document)*; reach *(in boxing)*; *allonge de boucher,* meat hook.

allongé [alɔ̃'ʒe], *a.* lengthened, elongated, out-stretched; downcast, long *(of face).*

allongement [alɔ̃ʒ'mɑ̃], *n.m.* lengthening, elongation, protraction.

allonger [alɔ̃'ʒe], *v.t. (conjug. like* MANGER) to lengthen, to elongate, to eke out; to stretch; to drag out, to protract. **s'allonger,** *v.r.* to stretch out, to grow longer; to stretch, to lie down at full length.

allouer [a'lwe], *v.t.* to allow, to grant, to accord; to allocate.

alluchon [aly'ʃɔ̃], *n.m.* cog, tooth *(of a wheel).*

allumage [aly'ma:ʒ], *n.m.* lighting, kindling; ignition; *un raté d'allumage,* misfire; *mettre l'allumage,* to switch on; *couper l'allumage,* to switch off.

allumé [aly'me], *a.* lighted, ignited; *(colloq.)* excited; drunk, lit-up.

allume-feu [alym'fø], *n.m. inv.* firewood, firelighter, kindling.

allume-gaz [alym'ga:z], *n.m. inv.* gas lighter.

allumer [aly'me], *v.t.* to light; to kindle, to set on fire; *(fig.)* to inflame, to incite, to stir up. **s'allumer,** *v.r.* to light, to take *or* catch fire; to blaze, to sparkle, to glare; to flare up, to break out.

allumette [aly'mɛt], *n.f.* match.

allumeur [aly'mœːr], *n.m. (fem.* **-euse)** lighter.

allure [a'lyːr], *n.f.* carriage, gait, pace, way of walking; demeanor; aspect, look; speed; *(pl.)* ways *(of a person)*; *à toute allure,* at full speed.

allusion [aly'zjɔ̃], *n.f.* allusion, hint, innuendo.

alluvial [aly'vjal], *a. (m. pl.* **-aux)** alluvial.

alluvion [aly'vjɔ̃], *n.f.* alluvium.

almanach [alma'na], *n.m.* almanac, calendar.

aloès [alo'ɛːs], *n.m.* aloe; aloes.

aloi [a'lwa], *n.m.* the statutory degree of purity of gold and silver; *(fig.)* standard *(good or bad)*, quality, kind *(of persons etc.).*

alors [a'lɔːr], *adv.* then, that time; in that case; *d'alors,* of that time; *alors que,* while, whereas; *jusqu'alors,* up to then,

till that moment; *alors même que,* even though.

alose [a'loːz], *n.f.* shad.

alouette [a'lwɛt], *n.f. (Orn.)* lark.

alourdir [alur'diːr], *v.t.* to make heavy, dull *or* stupid. **s'alourdir,** *v.r.* to grow heavy *or* dull.

alourdissant [alurdi'sɑ̃], *a.* oppressive, burdensome.

alourdissement [alurdis'mɑ̃], *n.m.* heaviness, dullness.

aloyau [alwa'jo], *n.m. (pl.* **-aux)** sirloin.

alpaca [alpa'ka], **alpaga** [alpa'ga], *n.m.* alpaca.

alpenstock [alpɛn'stɔk], *n.m.* alpenstock.

Alpes [alp], **les,** *f.pl.* the Alps.

alpestre [al'pɛstr], *a.* Alpine *(scenery, flora).*

alpha [al'fa], *n.m.* alpha; *(fig.)* beginning.

alphabet [alfa'bɛ], *n.m.* alphabet.

alphabétique [alfabe'tik], *a.* alphabetical.

alphabétiquement [alfabetik'mɑ̃], *adv.* alphabetically.

alpin [al'pɛ̃], *a.* Alpine *(club etc.).*

alpinisme [alpi'nism], *n.m.* mountaineering.

alpiniste [alpi'nist], *n.m.* Alpinist, mountaineer.

Alsace [al'zas], **l',** *f.* Alsace.

alsacien [alza'sjɛ̃], *a. (fem.* **-enne)** Alsatian.—*n.m.* (**Alsacien,** *fem.* **-enne)** inhabitant of Alsace.

altérable [alte'rabl], *a.* alterable, corruptible, adulterable.

altérant [alte'rɑ̃], *a.* causing thirst.

altération [altera'sjɔ̃], *n.f.* deterioration; falsification, adulteration, debasing *(of money etc.)*; weakening, impairing.

altercation [altɛrka'sjɔ̃], *n.f.* altercation, wrangle, dispute, quarrel.

altérer [alte're], *v.t. (conjug. like* CÉDER) to alter for the worse; to impair, to adulterate, to corrupt; to pervert, to debase, to falsify; to disturb, to trouble, to upset; to make thirsty. **s'altérer,** *v.r.* to be impaired, to degenerate.

alternance [altɛr'nɑ̃:s], *n.f.* alternation, rotation.

alternant [altɛr'nɑ̃], *a.* alternating, rotating *(as crops).*

alternat [altɛr'na], *n.m.* rotation *(of crops etc).*

alternatif [altɛrna'tif], *a. (fem.* **-tive)** alternate, alternating, alternative.—*n.f.* **(-tive)** alternation; alternative, choice, option *(between two possible actions).*

alternativement [altɛrnativ'mɑ̃], *adv.* alternately, by turns.

alterne [al'tɛrn], *a. (Geom.)* alternate *(of angles)*; *(Bot.)* alternate.

alterner [altɛr'ne], *v.t.* to grow *(crops)* in rotation.—*v.i.* to alternate, to succeed each other alternately.

Altesse [al'tɛs], *n.f.* Highness.

altier [al'tje], *a. (fem.* **-ière)** haughty, proud, arrogant, lordly, lofty.

altimètre [alti'mɛtr], *n.m.* altimeter.

altitude [alti'tyd], *n.f.* altitude.

alto [al'to], *n.m.* alto; tenor violin; tenor saxhorn.

altruisme [altry'ism], *n.m.* altruism.

altruiste [altry'ist], *a.* altruistic.—*n.* altruist.

alumine [aly'min], *n.f.* alumina, oxide of aluminum.

aluminer [alymi′ne], *v.t.* to aluminate, to aluminize.

aluminium [alymi′njɔm], *n.m.* aluminum.

alun [a′lœ̃], *n.m.* alum.

alunage [aly′na:ʒ], *n.m.* (*Dyeing*) steeping in alum; (*Phot.*) hardening (*negatives etc.*) in an alum bath.

aluner [aly′ne], *v.t.* (*Dyeing*) to steep in alum water; (*Phot.*) to harden in an alum bath.

alunière [aly′njɛ:r], *n.f.* alum pit or mine, alum-works.

alunir [aly′ni:r], *v.i.* to land on the moon.

alvéole [alve′ɔl], *n.m.* alveolus, cell (*in a honey-comb*); socket (*of a tooth*).

amabilité [amabili′te], *n.f.* amiability, affability, kindness.

amadou [ama′du], *n.m.* amadou, (German) tinder; touchwood.

amadouer [ama′dwe], *v.t.* to coax, to wheedle, to cajole.

amaigrir [amɛ′gri:r], *v.t.* to make lean, meager or thin, to emaciate; to reduce, to lessen (*in bulk etc.*); to impoverish; to exhaust (*soil etc.*).—*v.i.* to fall away, to grow lean or thin. **s'amaigrir,** *v.r.* to grow thin, to fall away.

amaigrissant [amɛgri′sɑ̃], *a.* causing emaciation; *régime amaigrissant,* slimming diet.

amaigrissement [amɛgris′mɑ̃], *n.m.* emaciation, wasting away.

amalgamation [amalgamɑ′sjɔ̃], *n.f.* amalgamation.

amalgame [amal′gam], *n.m.* amalgam; (*fig.*) medley, heterogeneous mixture.

amalgamer [amalga′me], *v.t.* to amalgamate, to blend, to combine. **s'amalgamer,** *v.r.* to amalgamate, to blend, to combine.

amande [a′mɑ̃:d], *n.f.* almond; kernel; *amandes lissées,* sugar-plums.

amandier [amɑ̃′dje], *n.m.* almond tree.

amant [a′mɑ̃], *n.m.* (*fem.* **-e**) lover, suitor; sweetheart, mistress; gallant, paramour; passionate admirer.

amarante [ama′rɑ̃:t], *n.f.* amaranth.

amareilleur or **amareyeur** [amarɛ′jœːr], *n.m.* worker on an oyster bed.

amarinage [amari′na:ʒ], *n.m.* (*Naut.*) manning (*a prize*).

amariner [amari′ne], *v.t.* to man (*a prize*); to inure (*a crew etc.*) to sea. **s'amariner,** *v.r.* to become used to the sea.

amarrage [ama′ra:ʒ], *n.m.* (*Naut.*) mooring, anchorage; lashing.

amarre [a′ma:r], *n.f.* (*Naut.*) cable, rope, hawser.

amarrer [ama′re], *v.t.* to moor, to belay, to make fast.

amaryllis [amari′lis], *n.f.* amaryllis.

amas [a′mɑ], *n.m.* mass, heap, pile, accumulation.

amasser [amɑ′se], *v.t.* to accumulate, to heap up, to amass; to hoard; to collect, to get together. **s'amasser,** *v.r.* to gather, to get together, to accumulate, to be collected, to crowd, to assemble.

amassette [amɑ′sɛt], *n.f.* small palette knife.

amasseur [amɑ′sœːr], *n.m.* (*fem.* **-euse**) hoarder.

amateur [ama′tœːr], *n.m.* amateur; devotee; connoisseur.

amazone [ama′zo:n], *n.f.* Amazon, female warrior; horse-woman; riding habit; *habit d'amazone,* riding habit; *monter en amazone,* to ride side-saddle.

ambages [ɑ̃′ba:ʒ], *n.f.* (*pl.*) circumlocution; *sans ambages,* straight out.

ambassade [ɑ̃ba′sad], *n.f.* embassy, ambassador's staff.

ambassadeur [ɑ̃basa′dœːr], *n.m.* ambassador; (*fig.*) envoy, messenger.

ambassadrice [ɑ̃basa′dris], *n.f.* ambassadress.

ambiance [ɑ̃′bjɑ̃:s], *n.f.* surroundings, environment; atmosphere.

ambiant [ɑ̃′bjɑ̃], *a.* ambient, surrounding.

ambidextre [ɑ̃bi′dɛkstr], *a.* ambidextrous.—*n.* ambidexter.

ambigu [ɑ̃bi′gy], *a.* (*fem.* **-guë**) ambiguous, equivocal.—*n.m.* heterogeneous mixture, medley.

ambiguïté [ɑ̃bigɥi′te], *n.f.* ambiguity.

ambigument [ɑ̃bigy′mɑ̃], *adv.* ambiguously.

ambitieusement [ɑ̃bisjøz′mɑ̃], *adv.* ambitiously.

ambitieux [ɑ̃bi′sjø], *a.* (*fem.* **-euse**) ambitious.—*n.m.* (*fem.* **-euse**) ambitious person.

ambition [ɑ̃bi′sjɔ̃], *n.f.* ambition.

ambitionner [ɑ̃bisjɔ′ne], *v.t.* to desire earnestly; to be ambitious of, to aspire to.

ambivalence [ɑ̃biva′lɑ̃:s], *n.f.* ambivalence.

ambivalent [ɑ̃biva′lɑ̃], *a.* ambivalent.

amble [ɑ̃:bl], *n.m.* amble.

ambler [ɑ̃′ble], *v.i.* to amble.

ambleur [ɑ̃′blœːr], *a.* (*fem.* **-euse**) ambling.

amblyope [ɑ̃′bljɔp], *a.* amblyopic, weak-sighted.—*n.* weak-sighted person.

ambre [ɑ̃:br], *n.m.* amber; *ambre gris,* ambergris.

ambré [ɑ̃′bre], *a.* amber-colored.

ambrer [ɑ̃′bre], *v.t.* to perfume with amber.

ambrette [ɑ̃′brɛt], *n.f.* amber seed; musk seed.

ambroisie [ɑ̃brwa′zi], *n.f.* ambrosia.

ambulance [ɑ̃by′lɑ̃:s], *n.f.* ambulance; field hospital; peripatetic clerkship; *chirurgien d'ambulance,* field surgeon.

ambulancier [ɑ̃bylɑ̃′sje], *n.m.* (*fem.* **-lère**) ambulance man, stretcher-bearer, nurse.

ambulant [ɑ̃by′lɑ̃], *a.* ambulant, ambulatory, itinerant, peripatetic; travelling (*of a railway post office*); strolling (*players*).

ambulatoire [ɑ̃byla′twaːr], *a.* ambulatory; (*Law*) movable.

âme (1) [ɑ:m], *n.f.* soul, spirit; sentiment, sensibility; (*fig.*) inhabitant, person (*on a lost ship etc.*); core, pith, heart (*of a thing etc.*); *rendre l'âme,* to give up the ghost.

âme (2) [ɑ:m], *n.f.* sounding board (*of a violin etc.*); bore (*of gun*).

amélioration [ameljorɑ′sjɔ̃], *n.f.* amelioration, improvement; (*pl.*) repairs, decorations (*of a house etc.*).

améliorer [ameljo′re], *v.t.* to ameliorate, to improve, to better. **s'améliorer,** *v.r.* to get better, to mend, to improve.

amen [a′mɛn], *int.* and *n.m.* amen.

aménagement [amenaʒ′mɑ̃], *n.m.* arrangement; disposition (*of a house etc.*); management (*of a forest*).

aménager [amena'ʒe], *v.t.* (*conjug. like* MANGER) to dispose, to arrange, to lay out; to regulate the felling of (*a wood or forest*).

amendable [amã'dabl], *a.* improvable, mendable.

amende [a'mã:d], *n.f.* fine, penalty, forfeit, compensation, reparation; *faire amende honorable*, to make a full apology; *mettre* or *condamner à l'amende*, to fine.

amendement [amãd'mã], *n.m.* amendment; improvement; manuring (*of land*).

amender [amã'de], *v.t.* to amend, to better; to manure (*land*). **s'amender**, *v.r.* to mend, to grow better.

amène [a'mɛːn], *a.* agreeable, pleasant (*site*).

amener [am'ne], *v.t.* (*see Verb Tables*) to lead (*hither*), to bring; to induce, prevail upon; to introduce; to bring about; to occasion, to lead to; (*Naut.*) to lower, to strike (*colors, sails etc.*); *mandat d'amener*, warrant.

aménité [ameni'te], *n.f.* amenity, pleasant-ness, affability; grace, urbanity.

amenuiser [amənɥi'ze], *v.t.* to make thinner *or* smaller. **s'amenuiser**, *v.r.* to grow thinner *or* smaller.

amer (1) [a'mɛːr], *a.* (*fem.* **amère**) bitter, harsh; painful, grievous; biting, galling.—*n.m.* something bitter; gall; bitterness; (*pl.*) bitters.

amer (2) [a'mɛːr], *n.m.* (*Naut.*) any landmark *or* leading mark.

amèrement [amɛr'mã], *adv.* bitterly, grievously.

américain [ameri'kɛ̃], *a.* American.—*n.m.* (**Américain**, *fem.* **-aine**) American (*person*).

américanisme [amerika'nism], *n.m.* Americanism.

Amérique [ame'rik], l', *f.* America.

amérir or **amerrir** [ame'riːr], *v.i.* (*Av.*) to alight on the water.

amerrissage [ameri'saːʒ], *n.m.* alighting (*on the water*).

amertume [amɛr'tym], *n.f.* bitterness, grief; gall, venom.

améthyste [ame'tist], *n.f.* amethyst.

ameublement [amœblə'mã], *n.m.* furniture, suite of furniture.

ameublir [amœ'bliːr], *v.t.* (*Agric.*) to make (*soil*) more broken up *or* lighter.

ameublissement [amœblis'mã], *n.m.* (*Agric.*) loosening, mellowing.

ameulonner [amœlɔ'ne], *v.t.* to stack (*hay, corn etc.*).

ameuter [amœ'te], *v.t.* to train dogs as a pack; (*fig.*) to stir up, to rouse, to excite.

ami [a'mi], *n.m.* (*fem.* **amie**) friend; well-wisher, partisan; lover; *chambre d'ami*, spare room.—*a.* friendly; sympathetic, favorable, kindly-disposed; kind, propi-tious.

amiable [a'mjabl], *a.* friendly, courteous, amicable, conciliatory; *vente à l'amiable*, sale by private contract.

amiablement [amjablə'mã], *adv.* amicably.

amiante [a'mjãːt], *n.m.* asbestos.

amibe [a'mib], *n.f.* amoeba.

amical [ami'kal], *a.* (*m. pl.* **-aux**) amicable, friendly.

amicalement [amikal'mã], *adv.* amicably, in a friendly manner.

amidon [ami'dõ], *n.m.* starch.

amidonner [amidɔ'ne], *v.t.* to starch.

amincir [amɛ̃'siːr], *v.t.* to make thinner. **s'amincir**, *v.r.* to become thinner.

amincissement [amɛ̃sis'mã], *n.m.* thinning.

amiral [ami'ral], *n.m.* (*pl.* **-aux**) admiral; *contre-amiral*, rear admiral; *grand amiral*, high admiral; *vice-amiral*, vice admiral; *vaisseau amiral*, flagship.

Amirauté [amiro'te], **Îles de l'**, *f.* Admiralty Islands.

amirauté [amiro'te], *n.f.* admiralship; ad-miralty.

amitié [ami'tje], *n.f.* friendship, affection; favor, kindness; (*pl.*) kind regards, com-pliments; *mes amitiés à tout le monde*, love to all; *par amitié*, out of friendship.

ammoniac [amɔ'njak], *a.* (*fem.* **-iaque**) ammoniac; *sel ammoniac*, sal ammoniac. —*n.f.* (**-iaque**) ammonia.

ammonite [amɔ'nit], *n.f.* ammonite.

amnésie [amne'zi], *n.f.* amnesia.

amnistie [amnis'ti], *n.f.* amnesty, pardon.

amnistier [amnis'tje], *v.t.* to pardon by amnesty.

amoindrir [amwɛ̃'driːr], *v.t.* to lessen, to decrease, to diminish. **s'amoindrir**, *v.r.* to grow less.

amoindrissement [amwɛ̃dris'mã], *n.m.* lessening, decrease.

amollir [amɔ'liːr], *v.t.* to soften; (*fig.*) to mollify. **s'amollir**, *v.r.* to soften, to grow soft; to grow effeminate *or* weak.

amollissant [amɔli'sã], *a.* softening; enervat-ing.

amollissement [amɔlis'mã], *n.m.* softening, enervation, effeminacy.

amonceler [amõs'le], *v.t.* (*conjug. like* APPELER) to heap up, to lay in a heap; (*fig.*) to ac-cumulate. **s'amonceler**, *v.r.* to gather; to accumulate, to drift together.

amoncellement [amõsɛl'mã], *n.m.* accumu-lation; heap.

amont [a'mõ], *n.m.* upstream water (*used chiefly in en amont*, up-stream, up-river).

amoral [amɔ'ral], *a.* (*m. pl.* **-aux**) amoral.

amorçage [amɔr'saːʒ], *n.m.* priming (*of pumps, motors, guns etc.*); baiting (*of hook*).

amorce [a'mɔrs], *n.f.* bait; (*fig.*) allurement, charm; priming, percussion cap (*of guns etc.*); priming (*for a pump*).

amorcer [amɔr'se], *v.t.* (*conjug. like* COM-MENCER) to bait; (*fig.*) to allure, to entice, to decoy; (*Hydraulics*) to prime; (*Artill.*) to cap (*a shell*).

amorphe [a'mɔrf], *a.* amorphous.

amortir [amɔr'tiːr], *v.t.* to deaden, to allay, to moderate; to weaken, to break (*a fall, shock etc.*); to redeem, to pay off; to cool (*passions*).

amortissable [amɔrti'sabl], *a.* redeemable.

amortissement [amɔrtis'mã], *n.m.* redemp-tion, buying up; liquidation; deadening (*of a blow etc.*); *fonds d'amortissement*, sinking fund.

amortisseur [amɔrti'sœːr], *n.m.* shock absorber.

amour [a'muːr], *n.m.* (*usu. fem. in pl.*) love, affection, passion; the object of love, flame, fancy; *l'Amour*, (*Myth.*) Eros, Cupid.

amouracher (s') [samura'ʃe], *v.r.* to be smitten with; to become enamored (*de*).

amourette [amu'rɛt], *n.f.* passing amour, love affair.

amoureusement [amurøz'mã], adv. amorously, lovingly; tenderly.

amoureux [amu'rø], a. (fem. -euse) loving, in love, smitten, enamored (de); amorous. —n.m. (fem. -euse) lover, sweetheart; fiancé or fiancée.

amour-propre [amur'prɔpr], n.m. self-respect; vanity, conceit.

amovibilité [amɔvibili'te], n.f. removability, liability to removal; precariousness of tenure.

amovible [amɔ'vibl], a. removable, revocable.

ampère [ã'pɛːr], n.m. (Elec.) ampere.

amphibie [ãfi'bi], a. amphibious.—n.m. amphibian.

amphibiens [ãfi'bjɛ̃], n.m. pl. (Zool.) Amphibia.

amphigouri [ãfigu'ri], n.m. rigmarole, gibberish.

amphithéâtre [ãfite'aːtr], n.m. amphitheatre; the whole body of occupants of this; the gallery in a theatre rising above the boxes and facing the stage; lecture-room; en amphithéâtre, in semi-circular tiers.

Amphitryon [ãfitri'ɔ̃], n.m. Amphitryon; host, entertainer.

amphore [ã'fɔːr], n.f. amphora.

ample [ã:pl], a. ample, full; large, vast, spacious; copious.

amplement [ãpla'mã], adv. amply, fully; largely, plentifully.

ampleur [ã'plœːr], n.f. width, fullness (of clothes); abundance; profusion; dignity (of style etc.); volume (of voice).

amplifiant [ãpli'fjã], a. magnifying (of a lens etc.); amplifying.

amplificateur [ãplifika'tœːr], a. (fem. -trice) magnifying; amplifying.—n.m. (Phot.) enlarger.

amplification [ãplifika's̃ɔ̃], n.f. amplification; magnification, enlargement; (fig.) exaggeration.

amplifier [ãpli'fje], v.t. to amplify, to develop, to enlarge.

amplitude [ãpli'tyd], n.f. extent, amplitude.

ampoule [ã'pul], n.f. blister, swelling; (Elec.) bulb; (Med.) ampoule.

ampoulé [ãpu'le], a. bombastic, turgid.

amputation [ãpyta'sjɔ̃], n.f. amputation; (fig.) curtailment.

amputer [ãpy'te], v.t. to amputate, to cut off.

amulette [amy'lɛt], n.f. amulet, charm.

amusant [amy'zã], a. amusing, diverting, entertaining.

amusement [amyz'mã], n.m. amusement, entertainment, diversion; fooling, trifling.

amuser [amy'ze], v.t. to amuse, to divert, to entertain; to fool, to beguile, to dupe; to detain, to delay. s'amuser, v.r. to amuse oneself, to divert oneself; to trifle; to have a good time; s'amuser de quelqu'un, to make fun of someone; amusez-vous bien ! enjoy yourselves, have a good time.

amusette [amy'zɛt], n.f. petty amusement.

amuseur [amy'zœːr], n.m. (fem. -euse) amuser, entertainer.

amygdale [ami'dal], n.f. (Anat.) tonsil.

an [ã], n.m. year; (pl.) years, time, age; elle a quinze ans, she is fifteen; le jour de l'an, New Year's Day.

anacarde [ana'kard], n.m. cashew nut.

anachorète [anakɔ'rɛt], n. anchorite, hermit.

anachronisme [anakrɔ'nism], n.m. anachronism.

anaéroïde [ANÉROÏDE].

anagramme [ana'gram], n.f. anagram.

analgésie [analʒe'zi], analgie [anal'ʒi], n.f. (Med.) analgesia.

analgésique [analʒe'zik], analgique [anal'ʒik], a. and n.m. analgesic.

analogie [analɔ'ʒi], n.f. analogy.

analogique [analɔ'ʒik], a. analogous, analogical.

analogue [ana'lɔg], a. analogous, similar.

analyse [ana'liːz], n.f. analysis; outline, précis, abstract (of a book etc.); (Gram.) parsing, analysis.

analyser [anali'ze], v.t. to analyze.

analyste [ana'list], n.m. analyst.

analytique [anali'tik], a. analytic, analytical.

analytiquement [analitik'mã], adv. analytically.

ananas [ana'na], n.m. pineapple.

anarchie [anar'ʃi], n.f. anarchy; (fig.) disorder, confusion.

anarchique [anar'ʃik], a. anarchical.

anarchiste [anar'ʃist], n. anarchist.

anathème [ana'tɛːm], n.m. anathema; sentence of reprobation or excommunication, ban, curse.

anatomie [anatɔ'mi], n.f. anatomy; dissection; (fam.) body, figure.

anatomique [anatɔ'mik], a. anatomical.

anatomiquement [anatɔmik'mã], adv. anatomically.

anatomiser [anatɔmi'ze], v.t. to anatomize, to dissect.

anatomiste [anatɔ'mist], n. anatomist.

ancêtre [ã'sɛːtr], n. ancestor, ancestress.—n.m. pl. ancestors, forefathers.

anchois [ã'ʃwa], n.m. anchovy.

ancien [ã'sjɛ̃], a. (fem. -ienne) ancient, old; former, late, ex-; antique; un ancien élève, an old boy.—n.m. (fem. -ienne) senior; ancient; (Eccles.) elder; (Mil.) veteran; (pl.) the ancients; our forefathers.

anciennement [ãsjɛn'mã], adv. formerly; *of yore; in former times.

ancienneté [ãsjɛn'te], n.f. antiquity; seniority.

ancillaire [ãsil'lɛːr], a. ancillary.

ancrage [ã'kraːʒ], n.m. anchorage.

ancre [ã:kr], n.f. anchor; ancre de miséricorde (or de salut), sheet anchor; (fig.) last resource; cramp iron, tie plate (of a wall).

ancrer [ã'kre], v.t. to anchor; (fig.) to fix or establish firmly.—v.i. to anchor. s'ancrer, v.r. to establish oneself, to get a footing (in a place), to take deep root (in).

Andalousie [ãdalu'zi], l', f. Andalusia.

Andes [ã:d], les, f. pl. the Andes.

Andorre [ã'dɔːr], l', m. Andorra.

andouille [ã'duːj], n.f. pork sausage (made of chitterlings); (pop.) imbecile, duffer.

andouiller [ãdu'je], n.m. tine (of antler).

André [ã'dre], m. Andrew.

Andromède [ãdrɔ'mɛd], f. Andromeda.

âne [aːn], n.m. ass, donkey; blockhead, stupid, ignorant or foolish person, idiot.

anéantir [aneã'tiːr], v.t. to annihilate, to destroy utterly, to abolish; (fig.) to overwhelm.

anéantissement [aneɑ̃tis'mɑ̃], *n.m.* annihilation; destruction, ruin, overthrow; humiliation, prostration.

anecdote [aneg'dɔt], *n.f.* anecdote.

anecdotique [anegdɔ'tik], *a.* anecdotic.

anémie [ane'mi], *n.f.* anaemia.

anémique [ane'mik], *a.* anaemic.

anémone [ane'mon], *n.f.* anemone, windflower.

ânerie [ɑn'ri], *n.f.* stupidity; gross ignorance; gross blunder.

anéroïde [anero'id], **anaéroïde** [anaero'id], *a.* aneroid.—*n.m.* aneroid barometer.

ânesse [ɑ'nɛs], *n.f.* she-ass.

anesthésie [aneste'zi], *n.f.* (*Med.*) anaesthesia.

anesthésier [aneste'zje], *v.t.* to anaesthetize.

anesthésique [aneste'zik], *a.* and *n.m.* anaesthetic.

anesthésiste [aneste'zist], *n.m.* anaesthetist.

anévrisme [ane'vrism], *n.m.* aneurism.

anfractueux [ɑ̃frak tɥø], *a.* (*fem.* **-euse**) anfractuous, winding, sinuous, craggy.

anfractuosité [ɑ̃fraktɥozi'te], *n.f.* anfractuosity, cragginess, twist, jagged *or* rugged outlines.

ange [ɑ̃ʒ], *n.m.* angel; (*fig.*) an adorable *or* beloved person.

Angèle [ɑ̃'ʒɛl], *f.* Angela.

angélique [ɑ̃ʒe'lik], *a.* angelic, angelical.

angélus [ɑ̃ʒe'lyːs], *n.m.* angelus.

angevin [ɑ̃ʒə'vɛ̃], *a.* of Anjou.—*n.m.* (**Angevin,** *fem.* **-ine**) native of Anjou.

angine [ɑ̃'ʒin], *n.f.* angina, quinsy, sore throat.

anglais [ɑ̃'glɛ], *a.* English; British.—*n.m.* English (*language*); (**Anglais,** *fem.* **-aise**) Englishman, English girl *or* woman; (*pl.*) the English.

angle [ɑ̃:gl], *n.m.* angle, corner; (*Arch.*) quoin; *angle aigu,* acute angle; *angle droit,* right angle.

Angleterre [ɑ̃glə'tɛːr], **l'**, *f.* England.

anglican [ɑ̃gli'kɑ̃], *a.* and *n.m.* (*fem.* **-e**) Anglican.

angliciser [ɑ̃glisi'ze], *v.t.* to Anglicize. **s'angliciser,** *v.r.* to become Anglicized *or* English.

anglicisme [ɑ̃gli'sism], *n.m.* Anglicism.

anglomanie [ɑ̃glɔma'ni], *n.f.* Anglomania.

anglo-normand [ɑ̃glɔnɔr'mɑ̃], *a.* and *n.m.* (*fem.* **-e**) Anglo-Norman; *les Îles anglo-normandes,* the Channel Islands.

anglophile [ɑ̃glɔ'fil], *a.* and *n.* Anglophil.

anglo-saxon [ɑ̃glɔsak'sɔ̃], *a.* and *n.m.* (*fem.* **-saxonne**) Anglo-Saxon.

angoisse [ɑ̃'gwas], *n.f.* anguish, agony, great distress; (*Med.*) angor, anguish.

angora [ɑ̃gɔ'ra], *a.* Angora.—*n.m.* Angora cat.

anguille [ɑ̃'giːj], *n.f.* eel; (*pl., Naut.*) launching ways, slips; *il y a anguille sous roche,* I smell a rat.

angulaire [ɑ̃gy'lɛːr], *a.* angular.

angusture [ɑ̃gys'tyːr], *n.f.* (*Pharm.*) angostura.

anhélation [anelɑ'sjɔ̃], *n.f.* panting.

anhéler [ane'le], *v.i.* (*conjug. like* CÉDER) to pant.

anhydre [a'nidr], *a.* (*Chem.*) anhydrous.

anhydride [ani'drid], *n.m.* anhydride; *anhydride carbonique,* carbon dioxide.

anicroche [ani'krɔʃ], *n.f.* slight obstacle.

animadversion [animadver'sjɔ̃], *n.f.* animadversion, reproof, reprimand, censure.

animal [ani'mal], *n.m.* (*pl.* **-aux**) animal; beast, brute; *société protectrice des animaux,* Society for the Prevention of Cruelty to Animals.—*a.* (*m.pl.* **-aux**) animal; sensual, carnal.

animateur [anima'tœːr], *a.* (*fem.* **-trice**) animating.

animation [anima'sjɔ̃], *n.f.* animation, vitality, life; liveliness; excitement; irritation.

animé [ani'me], *a.* animated; spirited, gay, sprightly; *rue animée,* busy street.

animer [ani'me], *v.t.* to animate, to give life to; to arouse, to excite, to urge on; to enliven, to give force to (*style etc.*). **s'animer,** *v.r.* to become animated *or* lively; to cheer up; to become angry.

animosité [animozi'te], *n.f.* animosity, ill will, spite, rancor.

anis [a'ni], *n.m.* anise, aniseed.

aniser [ani'ze], *v.t.* to flavor with aniseed.

anisette [ani'zet], *n.f.* aniseed cordial.

ankylose [ɑ̃ki'loːz], *n.f.* (*Path.*) anchylosis, stiffness in the joints.

annales [a'nal], *n.f.* (*used only in pl.*) annals, public records.

annaliste [ana'list], *n.m.* annalist.

anneau [a'no], *n.m.* (*pl.* **anneaux**) ring; link (*of a chain*); ringlet (*of hair*).

année [a'ne], *n.f.* year, period of twelve months; *année bissextile,* leap year; *souhaiter la bonne année,* to wish a happy New Year.

année-lumière [anely'mjɛːr], *n.f.* (*pl.* **années-lumière**) light-year.

annelé [an'le], *a.* having *or* arranged in rings, ringed; (*Zool.*) annulated.

annelet [an'lɛ], *n.m.* ringlet, small ring.

annexe [a'nɛks], *n.f.* annex; appendage; appendix, schedule, rider; chapel of ease.

annexer [anɛk'se], *v.t.* to annex, to attach.

annexion [anɛk'sjɔ̃], *n.f.* annexation.

annihilation [aniila'sjɔ̃], *n.f.* annihilation; (*Law*) annulment.

annihiler [anii'le], *v.t.* to annihilate, to destroy; (*Law*) to annul.

anniversaire [aniver'sɛːr], *a.* and *n.m.* anniversary, birthday.

annonce [a'nɔ̃:s], *n.f.* announcement, notification; indication, sign, mark; advertisement; *annonce de mariage,* banns of marriage.

annoncer [anɔ̃'se], *v.t.* (*conjug. like* COMMENCER) to announce, to give notice of; to advertise; to announce (*a visitor*); to usher *or* show in; to proclaim; to foretell. **s'annoncer,** *v.r.* to present oneself; to manifest itself.

Annonciation [anɔ̃sja'sjɔ̃], *n.f.* Annunciation; Lady Day (March 25).

annoncier [anɔ̃'sje], *n.m.* publicity manager.

annotateur [anɔta'tœːr], *n.m.* (*fem.* **-trice**) annotator (*of a book etc.*).

annotation [anɔta'sjɔ̃], *n.f.* annotation.

annoter [anɔ'te], *v.t.* to annotate, to make notes on (*a text etc.*).

annuaire [a'nɥɛːr], *n.m.* annual, year-book; *l'Annuaire des Téléphones,* the telephone directory.

annuel [a'nɥɛl], *a.* (*fem.* **-elle**) annual, yearly.

annuellement [anɥɛl'mɑ̃], *adv.* annually, yearly.

annuité [anɥi'te], *n.f.* annuity.
annulable [any'labl], *a.* revocable.
annulaire [any'lɛ:r], *a.* annular, ring-shaped.
—*n.m.* ring finger, third finger.
annulation [anyla'sjɔ̃], *n.f.* annulment, cancellation, repeal, abolition.
annuler [any'le], *v.t.* to annul, to rescind, to cancel, to abolish, to set aside, to make void.
anobli [anɔ'bli], *a.* ennobled.—*n.m.* newly created nobleman.
anoblir [anɔ'bli:r], *v.t.* to ennoble, to raise to the rank of the nobility.
anoblissement [anɔblis'mɑ̃], *n.m.* ennoblement.
anode [a'nɔd], *n.f.* (*Elec.*) anode, positive pole.
anodin [anɔ'dɛ̃], *a.* (*Med.*) anodyne, soothing; (*fig.*) harmless, mild, inoffensive, insignificant.
anomal [anɔ'mal], *a.* (*m. pl.* **-aux**) (*Gram.*) anomalous, irregular.
anomalie [anɔma'li], *n.f.* anomaly, irregularity.
ânon [a'nɔ̃], *n.m.* ass's foal, young ass; (*fig.*) a little fool.
ânonnement [anɔn'mɑ̃], *n.m.* faltering, mumbling way of reading a text.
ânonner [anɔ'ne], *v.t.* to mumble and blunder through (*a lesson etc.*).—*v.i.* to read in a faltering way.
anonymat [anɔni'ma], *n.m.* anonymity.
anonyme [anɔ'nim], *a.* anonymous, nameless; *société anonyme*, joint-stock company. —*n.* anonymous person.
anonymement [anɔnim'mɑ̃], *adv.* anonymously.
anorak [anɔ'rak], *n.m.* (*reg. trade mark*) anorak.
anormal [anɔr'mal], *a.* (*m. pl.* **-aux**) abnormal, irregular, mentally deficient.
anormalement [anɔrmal'mɑ̃], *adv.* abnormally.
anse [ɑ̃:s], *n.f.* handle (*of a pot, basket etc.*); bay, cove.
antagonique [ɑ̃tago'nik], *a.* antagonistic.
antagonisme [ɑ̃tago'nism], *n.m.* antagonism.
antagoniste [ɑ̃tago'nist], *a.* antagonistic.— *n.m.* antagonist, adversary, opponent; competitor, rival.
*antan [ɑ̃'tɑ̃], *n.m.* yesteryear; *les neiges d'antan*, the snows of yesteryear.
antarctique [ɑ̃tark'tik], *a.* Antarctic.
antécédent [ɑ̃tese'dɑ̃], *a.* antecedent, preceding, foregoing, previous.—*n.m.* precedent; (*Gram.*) antecedent.
antéchrist [ɑ̃te'krist], *n.m.* Antichrist.
antédiluvien [ɑ̃tedily'vjɛ̃], *a.* (*fem.* **-ienne**) antediluvian.
antenne [ɑ̃'tɛn], *n.f.* (*Rad., Tel.*) aerial; (*Ent.*) antenna, (*pl.*) antennae.
antépénultième [ɑ̃tepenyl'tjɛm], *a.* antepenultimate.
antérieur [ɑ̃te'rjœ:r], *a.* anterior, earlier, antecedent, previous, former.
antérieurement [ɑ̃terjœr'mɑ̃], *adv.* previously, before.
antériorité [ɑ̃terjori'te], *n.f.* anteriority, priority, precedence.
anthologie [ɑ̃tɔlɔ'ʒi], *n.f.* anthology.
anthracite [ɑ̃tra'sit], *n.m.* anthracite.
anthrax [ɑ̃'traks], *n.m.* (*Med.*) anthrax.
anthropoïde [ɑ̃trɔpɔ'id], *a.* and *n.m.* (*Zool.*) anthropoid.

anthropologie [ɑ̃trɔpɔlɔ'ʒi], *n.f.* anthropology.
anthropologiste [ɑ̃trɔpɔlɔ'ʒist], **anthropologue** [ɑ̃trɔpɔ'lɔg], *n.* anthropologist.
anthropophage [ɑ̃trɔpɔ'fa:ʒ], *n.* cannibal.
anti-aérien [ɑ̃tiae'rjɛ̃], *a.* (*fem.* **-enne**) anti-aircraft.
antibiotique [ɑ̃tibiɔ'tik], *a.* and *n.m.* antibiotic.
anti-brouillard [ɑ̃tibru'ja:r], *n.m.* (*Motor.*) fog light.
anti-buée [ɑ̃ti'bye], *a.* (*Motor.*) demisting.— *n.m.* demister.
antichambre [ɑ̃ti'ʃɑ̃:br], *n.f.* (*formerly m.*) antechamber, anteroom.
anti-char [ɑ̃ti'ʃa:r], *a.* anti-tank.
antichrétien [ɑ̃tikre'tjɛ̃], *a.* and *n.m.* (*fem.* **-ienne**) antichristian.
anticipation [ɑ̃tisipa'sjɔ̃], *n.f.* anticipation; encroachment, trespass; *par anticipation*, in advance, beforehand.
anticipé [ɑ̃tisi'pe], *a.* done or occurring in advance.
anticiper [ɑ̃tisi'pe], *v.t.* to anticipate, to forestall.—*v.i.* to encroach or trespass (*sur*).
anticlimax [ɑ̃tikli'maks], *n.m.* anticlimax.
anticommunisme [ɑ̃tikɔmy'nism], *n.m.* anti-communism.
anticonstitutionnellement [ɑ̃tikɔ̃stitysjɔnɛl'mɑ̃], *adv.* (*the longest French word*) anticonstitutionally.
anticorps [ɑ̃ti'kɔ:r], *n.m.* (*Med.*) antibody.
anticyclone [ɑ̃tisi'klɔ:n], *n.m.* (*Meteor.*) anticyclone.
antidate [ɑ̃ti'dat], *n.f.* antedate.
antidater [ɑ̃tida'te], *v.t.* to antedate.
antidérapant [ɑ̃tidera'pɑ̃], *a.* non-skidding; *pneu antidérapant*, non-skid tire.
antidote [ɑ̃ti'dɔt], *n.m.* antidote, antitoxin; (*fig.*) cure.
anti-éblouissant [ɑ̃tieblui'sɑ̃], *a.* (*Motor.*) antidazzle.
antienne [ɑ̃'tjɛn], *n.f.* antiphon; anthem.
antigel [ɑ̃ti'ʒɛl], *n.m. inv.* anti-freeze.
antillais [ɑ̃ti'jɛ], *a.* West Indian.—*n.m.* (Antillais, *fem.* **-aise**) West Indian (*person*).
Antilles [ɑ̃'ti:j], les, *f.pl.* the West Indies; *la mer des Antilles*, the Caribbean Sea.
antilope [ɑ̃ti'lɔp], *n.f.* antelope.
anti-mite [ɑ̃ti'mit], *a.* moth-proof.
antimoine [ɑ̃ti'mwan], *n.m.* antimony.
Antioche [ɑ̃'tjɔʃ], *f.* Antioch.
antiparasite [ɑ̃tipara'zit], *n.m.* suppressor.
antiparlementaire [ɑ̃tiparləmɑ̃'tɛ:r], *a.* unparliamentary.
antipathie [ɑ̃tipa'ti], *n.f.* antipathy, aversion.
antipathique [ɑ̃tipa'tik], *a.* antipathetic, repugnant.
antiphonaire [ɑ̃tifɔ'nɛ:r], *n.m.* antiphonal.
antipode [ɑ̃ti'pɔd], *n.m.* the region of the globe diametrically opposite; (*pl.*) antipodes.
antiputride [ɑ̃tipy'trid], *a.* and *n.m.* antiseptic.
antiquaire [ɑ̃ti'kɛ:r], *n.m.* antiquary, antiquarian, antique dealer.
antique [ɑ̃'tik], *a.* antique, ancient; old-fashioned.—*n.f.* antique, ancient work of art.
antiquité [ɑ̃tiki'te], *n.f.* antiquity; old times; (*pl.*) antiquities; *magasin d'antiquités*, old curiosity shop.
antirouille [ɑ̃ti'ru:j], *n.m.* rust preventive.

antirrhine [ãti'rin], *n.f.* (*Bot.*) antirrhinum, snapdragon.
antisémite [ãtise'mit], *n.* anti-Semite.
antisémitique [ãtisemi'tik], *a.* anti-Semitic.
antisémitisme [ãtisemi'tism], *n.m.* anti-Semitism.
antiseptique [ãtisɛp'tik], *a.* and *n.m.* (*Med.*) antiseptic.
antisocial [ãtisɔ'sjal], *a.* (*m. pl.* **-aux**) antisocial.
antisportif [ãtispɔr'tif], *a.* (*fem.* **-ive**) unsportsmanlike; opposed to sports.
antithèse [ãti'tɛːz], *n.f.* antithesis.
antitoxine [ãtitɔk'sin], *n.f.* (*Med.*) antitoxin.
anti-vol [ãti'vɔl], *a. inv.* anti-theft.—*n.m.* burglar-proof device.
antivivisection [ãtivivisɛk'sjɔ̃], *n.f.* antivivisection.
Antoine [ã'twan], *m.* Anthony.
antre [ã:tr], *n.m.* den, lair; cavern.
anuiter (**s'**) [sanɥi'te], *v.r.* to be benighted.
anus [a'ny:s], *n.m.* anus.
Anvers [ã'vɛr], *m.* Antwerp.
anxiété [ãksje'te], *n.f.* anxiety; uneasiness; (*Med.*) pain in the heart.
anxieusement [ãksjøz'mã], *adv.* anxiously.
anxieux [ãk'sjø], *a.* (*fem.* **-euse**) anxious, uneasy, restless.
aorte [a'ɔrt], *n.f.* (*Anat.*) aorta.
août [u(t)], *n.m.* August; (*fig.*) harvest; *la mi-août*, the middle of August.
aoûté [u'te], *a.* ripened by the heat of August.
aoûter (**s'**) [su'te], *v.r.* to ripen (*in August*).
apache [a'paʃ], *n.m.* ruffian of the Paris streets, hooligan.
apaisement [apɛz'mã], *n.m.* appeasement; abatement, lull.
apaiser [apɛ'ze], *v.t.* to pacify, to calm, to appease; to quiet; to mitigate, to alleviate (*pain, sorrow etc.*); to stay (*hunger*); to quench (*thirst*). **s'apaiser**, *v.r.* to be appeased; to sober down; to grow quiet; to abate, to subside.
Apalaches [apa'laʃ], *m.pl.* Appalachians.
(*C*) **apalachien** [apala'jɛ̃], *a.* (*fem.* **-chienne**) Appalachian.
apanage [apa'naːʒ], *n.m.* apanage; (*fig.*) lot.
apanager [apana'ʒe], *v.t.* (*conjug. like* MANGER) to endow.
aparté [apar'te], *n.m.* aside.
apathie [apa'ti], *n.f.* apathy, indolence, listlessness.
apathique [apa'tik], *a.* apathetic, listless.
apatride [apa'trid], *a.* and *n.* stateless (person).
Apennins [apɛ'nɛ̃], *les*, *m.pl.* the Apennines.
apepsie [apɛp'si], *n.f.* (*Path.*) apepsy, indigestion.
apeptique [apɛp'tik], *a.* dyspeptic.
apercevable [apɛrsa'vabl], *a.* perceivable, perceptible.
apercevoir [apɛrsa'vwaːr], *v.t.* (*conjug. like* RECEVOIR) to catch sight of, to notice; to perceive, to understand, to comprehend. **s'apercevoir**, *v.r.* (*de quelque chose*) to remark, to notice, to be aware of; to find out, to discover; to be visible.
aperçu [apɛr'sy], *n.m.* rapid view, glance *or* survey; rough estimate *or* summary; judgment, idea.
apéritif [aperi'tif], *a.* (*fem.* **-ive**) aperient, appetizing.—*n.m.* (*Med.*) aperient, laxative; appetizer, aperitif (*e.g. vermouth, bitters*).

à peu près [apø'prɛ], *n.m.* approximation, approach; a word roughly standing for another.—*adv.* nearly, about.
apeuré [apø're], *a.* frightened, scared.
apex [a'pɛks], *n.m.* apex.
aphélie [afe'li], *n.m.* (*Astron.*) aphelion.
aphide [afi'de], **aphidien** [afi'djɛ̃], *n.m.* (*Ent.*) aphis, greenfly.
aphone [a'fɔn], *a.* voiceless.
aphonie [afɔ'ni], *n.f.* aphony, loss of voice.
aphorisme [afɔ'rism], *n.m.* aphorism.
à-pic [a'pik], *n.m.* steep hill, cliff.
apiculteur [apikyl'tœːr], *n.m.* bee-keeper.
apiculture [apikyl'ty:r], *n.f.* apiculture, bee-keeping.
apitoiement [apitwa'mã], *n.m.* pity, compassion.
apitoyant [apitwa'jã], *a.* piteous.
apitoyer [apitwa'je], *v.t.* (*conjug. like* EMPLOYER) to move to pity, to soften. **s'apitoyer**, *v.r.* to pity.
aplanir [apla'niːr], *v.t.* to smooth, to level, to make even; (*fig.*) to level down *or* remove (*obstacles, difficulties etc.*). **s'aplanir**, *v.r.* to grow easy, smooth etc.
aplanissement [aplanis'mã], *n.m.* smoothing, levelling, making even; smoothness, evenness.
aplat [a'pla], *n.m.* flat tint.
aplatir [apla'tiːr], *v.t.* to flatten, to beat flat; (*fig.*) to vanquish, to silence, to floor. **s'aplatir**, *v.r.* to become flat, to be flattened; (*fig.*) to crouch, to cringe.
aplatissement [aplatis'mã], **aplatissage** [aplati'saːʒ], *n.m.* flattening, flatness; (*fig.*) humiliation.
aplomb [a'plɔ̃], *n.m.* perpendicularity; equilibrium; (*fig.*) assurance, self-possession, steadiness, coolness; impudence, cheek; *d'aplomb*, perpendicularly, upright.
apocalypse [apɔka'lips], *n.f.* Apocalypse, the Book of Revelation.
apocalyptique [apɔkalip'tik], *a.* apocalyptic, obscure.
apocryphe [apɔ'krif], *a.* apocryphal, spurious.
apode [a'pɔd], *a* (*Zool.*) apodal, footless.
apogée [apɔ'ʒe], *n.m.* apogee; (*fig.*) acme, height, zenith.
apologétique [apɔlɔʒe'tik], *a.* by way of apology, apologetic.
apologie [apɔlɔ'ʒi], *n.f.* apology, vindication, justification.
apologue [apɔ'lɔg], *n.m.* apologue, fable.
apoplectique [apɔplɛk'tik], *a.* and *n.* apoplectic.
apoplexie [apɔplɛk'si], *n.f.* apoplexy.
apostasie [apɔsta'zi], *n.f.* apostasy.
apostat [apɔs'ta], *a.* and *n.m.* (*fem.* **-e**) apostate.
aposter [apɔs'te], *v.t.* to place in ambush, to station.
apostille [apɔs'ti:j], *n.f.* marginal note, postscript, footnote.
apostiller [apɔsti'je], *v.t.* to add a postscript *or* marginal recommendation.
apostolat [apɔstɔ'la], *n.m.* apostleship.
apostolique [apɔstɔ'lik], *a.* apostolic; papal.
apostrophe [apɔs'trɔf], *n.f.* (*Rhet. and Gram.*) apostrophe; address; (*fig.*) reprimand, attack.

apostropher [apɔstrɔ'fe], *v.t.* to apostrophize, to address; (*fig.*) to reprimand.
apothéose [apɔte'oːz], *n.f.* apotheosis.
apothicaire [apɔti'kɛːr], *n.m.* apothecary.
apôtre [a'poːtr], *n.m.* apostle; (*fig.*) leader of a cause.
apparaître [apa'rɛːtr], *v.i. irr.* (*conjug. like* CONNAÎTRE) to appear, to become visible; to be evident.
apparat [apa'ra], *n.m.* pomp, show, ostentation, parade.
apparaux [apa'ro], *n.m.* (*used only in pl.*) (*Naut.*) gear, tackle, outfit etc.
appareil [apa'rɛːj], *n.m.* formal preparation; pomp, display; appearance, show; apparatus, appliances, machinery, paraphernalia; (*Surg.*) dressing; *appareil (photographique)*, camera; *qui est à l'appareil?* who is speaking?
appareillage [aparɛ'jaːʒ], *n.m.* installation; (*Naut.*) act of getting under sail, weighing.
appareillement [aparɛj'mã], *n.m.* coupling, yoking; pairing (*for breeding*).
appareiller [aparɛ'je], *v.t.* to install equipment; to match; to pair (*animals*).—*v.i.* to get under way, to weigh anchor. **s'appareiller**, *v.r.* to pair (*of birds*).
appareilleur [aparɛ'jœːr], *n.m.* (*Building*) stone dresser; *appareilleur à gaz*, gas fitter.
apparemment [apara'mã], *adv.* apparently.
apparence [apa'rãːs], *n.f.* appearance, look, semblance, likelihood, probability; *en apparence*, seemingly, apparently.
apparent [apa'rã], *a.* visible, prominent.
apparenté [aparã'te], *a.* related; *bien apparenté*, well connected.
apparentement [aparãt'mã], *n.m.* political alliance.
apparenter [aparã'te], *v.t.* to ally, to connect by marriage. **s'apparenter**, *v.r.* to ally oneself (*by marriage*).
appariement or **appariment** [apari'mã], *n.m.* pairing, matching; coupling, mating; *appariement d'écoles*, school consolidation.
apparier [apa'rje], *v.t.* to assort by pairs, to pair (*birds etc.*), to match (*horses, gloves etc.*).
apparition [apari'sjɔ̃], *n.f.* apparition, sudden appearance; phantom, ghost; *apparition d'anges*, vision of angels.
appartement [apartə'mã], *n.m.* apartment.
appartenances [apartə'nãːs], *n.f.* (*used in pl.*) appurtenances.
appartenant [apartə'nã], *a.* belonging, appertaining.
appartenir [apartə'niːr], *v.i. irr.* (*conjug. like* TENIR) to belong, to appertain; to relate, to pertain, to concern; to behoove, to be the right, privilege, duty etc. of (*à*); *il appartient*, (*v. impers.*) it is meet *or* fit; it behooves, concerns. **s'appartenir**, *v.r.* to be master of one's own actions, to be free.
appas [a'pɑ], *n.m. pl.* feminine charms, attractions.
appât [a'pɑ], *n.m.* bait; lure, allurement, enticement.
appâter [apɑ'te] *v.t.* to attract with a bait, to allure; to fatten (*fowls etc.*).
appauvrir [apo'vriːr], *v.t.* to impoverish. **s'appauvrir**, *v.r.* to grow poor, to become impoverished.

appauvrissement [apovris'mã], *n.m.* impoverishment.
appel [a'pɛl], *n.m.* appeal, call, summons; (*Mil.*) roll call, muster; summoning of conscripts to the colors; (*Law*) appeal to a higher court; *battre* or *sonner l'appel*, (*Mil.*) to sound the fall-in.
appelé [ap'le], *a.* called up.—*n.m.* soldier called up for service.
appeler [ap'le], *v.t.* (*see Verb Tables*) to call, to send for; to call over; to call up, to call together; to summon, to cite, to invoke, to call upon, to invite; to name, to term; to challenge.—*v.i.* to appeal (*to a higher court*). **s'appeler**, *v.r.* to be called, to call oneself.
appellation [apɛlɑ'sjɔ̃], *n.f.* calling; appellation; trade name; *appellation contrôlée*, registered trade name.
appendice [apã'dis], *n.m.* appendix, appendage, addition.
appendicite [apãdi'sit], *n.f.* (*Path.*) appendicitis.
appendre [a'pãːdr], *v.t.* to hang up, to suspend; to attach.
appentis [apã'ti], *n.m.* shed, lean-to.
appesantir [apazã'tiːr], *v.t.* to make heavy, to weigh down; (*fig.*) to make dull. **s'appesantir**, *v.r.* to grow heavy and dull, to be weighed down; to dwell on, to expatiate (*sur*).
appesantissement [apazãtis'mã], *n.m.* heaviness, dullness.
appétissant [apeti'sã], *a.* desirable, appetizing, tempting; dainty, delicious.
appétit [ape'ti], *n.m.* appetite, relish; desire, sensuous craving (*usu. in pl.*); appetite (*for food*); (*fig.*) inclination, taste, stomach.
applaudir [aplo'diːr], *v.t., v.i.* to clap the hands, to applaud; to praise, to commend, to approve. **s'applaudir**, *v.r.* to boast, to glory (*in a thing*); to congratulate oneself (*de*); to rejoice (*de*).
applaudissement [aplodis'mã], *n.m.* (*usually pl.*) applause, public praise; cheering.
applicabilité [aplikabili'te], *n.f.* applicability, appositeness.
applicable [apli'kabl], *a.* applicable, apposite, relevant, suitable.
application [aplika'sjɔ̃], *n.f.* application, applying; employment (*of a sum of money*); infliction (*of a penalty*); attention, care, diligence; appliqué lace.
applique [a'plik], *n.f.* ornamental accessories, candelabrum *or* bracket fixed to a wall.
appliqué [apli'ke], *a.* studious; *sciences appliquées*, applied sciences.
appliquer [apli'ke], *v.t.* to apply (*à*), to stick; to apply (*one's mind*); to adapt, to employ; to inflict, to impose (*a penalty etc.*). **s'appliquer**, *v.r.* to apply oneself, to work hard.
appoint [a'pwɛ̃], *n.m.* money paying off an account, balance; change; contribution; *faire l'appoint*, to pay the exact sum.
appointé [apwɛ̃'te], *a.* receiving a salary.
appointements [apwɛt'mã], *n.m.* (*pl.*) salary (*of employee*); emoluments; (*Eccles.*) stipend.
appointer (1) [apwɛ̃'te], *v.t.* to give a salary to.
appointer (2) [apwɛ̃'te], *v.t.* to sharpen to a point, to point.
appontement [apɔ̃t'mã], *n.m.* (*Naut.*) bridge-

like structure for loading vessels; (*wooden*) wharf *or* pier.

apport [a'pɔːr], *n.m.* property brought by a husband or wife into the common stock; a shareholder's contribution to the assets of a company.

apporter [apɔr'te], *v.t.* to bring; to furnish, to supply; to bring to bear, to employ (*trouble, pains etc.*); to cause, to produce, to bring about.

apposer [apo'ze], *v.t.* to set, to put, to affix; to insert (*a clause etc.*).

apposition [apozi'sjɔ̃], *n.f.* setting, putting, affixing; (*Gram.*) apposition.

appréciable [apre'sjabl], *a.* appreciable, perceptible.

appréciateur [apresja'tœːr], *n.m.* (*fem.* -trice) valuer.

appréciatif [apresja'tif], *a.* (*fem.* -ive) denoting the value of; *état or devis appréciatif,* estimate.

appréciation [apresja'sjɔ̃], *n.f.* appreciation, valuation, estimation; rise in value.

apprécier [apre'sje], *v.t.* to value, to estimate, to appraise, to judge; to appreciate, to esteem.

appréhender [apreã'de], *v.t.* to arrest, to apprehend; to be apprehensive of, to fear, to dread.

appréhensible [apreã'sibl], *a.* apprehensible, comprehensible.

appréhensif [apreã'sif], *a.* (*fem.* -ive) apprehensive, timid.

appréhension [apreã'sjɔ̃], *n.f.* apprehension, fear, dread.

apprendre [a'prãːdr], *v.t. irr.* (*conjug. like* PRENDRE) to learn; to hear of, to be informed of; to acquire (*a habit etc.*); to tell, to inform; to teach, to impart knowledge of (*a subject*).

apprenti [aprã'ti], *a.* apprenticed, articled.—*n.m.* (*fem.* -e) apprentice; (*fig.*) novice.

apprentissage [aprãti'saːʒ], *n.m.* apprenticeship; trial, experiment.

apprêt [a'prɛ], *n.m.* preparation; cooking, dressing (*of food*); manner of preparing cloth, silk, lace etc.; the substance used in this process; (*pl.*) preparations.

apprêtage [apre'taːʒ], *n.m.* dressing, application of the preliminary preparation to cloth, silk etc.

apprêté [apre'te], *a.* studied, affected, stiff.

apprêter [apre'te], *v.t.* to prepare, to get ready; to dress, to cook; to apply the *apprêts* [q.v.] to. **s'apprêter**, *v.r.* to prepare oneself, to get ready (à).

apprêteur [apre'tœːr], *a.* and *n.m.* (*fem.* -euse) dresser, finisher.—*n.f.* (-euse) hat trimmer.

apprivoisé [aprivwa'ze], *a.* tame.

apprivoisement [aprivwaz'mã], *n.m.* taming.

apprivoiser [aprivwa'ze], *v.t.* to tame (*animals*); to win (*people*) over, to make sociable *or* tractable.

apprivoiseur [aprivwa'zœːr], *n.m.* (*fem.* -euse) tamer.

approbateur [aproba'tœːr], *a.* (*fem.* -trice) approving.

approbatif [aproba'tif], *a.* (*fem.* -tive) approbatory; *geste approbatif,* nod of approbation *or* approval.

approbation [aproba'sjɔ̃], *n.f.* approbation, consent, approval.

approbativement [aprobativ'mã], *adv.* approvingly.

approchable [aprɔ'ʃabl], *a.* approachable, easy of access.

approchant [aprɔ'ʃã], *a.* like, much the same, something like, approximate, bordering on.

approche [a'prɔʃ], *n.f.* approach, coming, advance, nearness; (*pl.*) approaches, access.

approcher [aprɔ'ʃe], *v.t.* to bring, put *or* draw near *or* nearer; to come near *or* nearer; to approach.—*v.i.* to approach, to draw near, to come near; to be something like, to be nearly. **s'approcher**, *v.r.* to approach, to advance.

approfondir [aprɔfɔ̃'diːr], *v.t.* to deepen, to make deeper; to examine thoroughly, to investigate. **s'approfondir**, *v.r.* to become deeper.

approfondissement [aprɔfɔ̃dis'mã], *n.m.* deepening; fathoming; thorough investigation.

appropriation [aprɔpria'sjɔ̃], *n.f.* adaptation, assimilation; appropriation.

approprier [aprɔpri'e], *v.t.* to make appropriate, to accommodate, to adapt; to clean, to tidy etc.; to suit, to fit, (*style to subject etc.*). **s'approprier**, *v.r.* to appropriate a thing to oneself; to conform, to adapt oneself.

approuver [apru've], *v.t.* to sanction, to consent to, to ratify, to authorize; to approve, to approve of; to pass (*accounts*).

approvisionnement [aprovizjɔn'mã], *n.m.* victualling, supply, stock.

approvisionner [aprovizjɔ'ne], *v.t.* to supply with necessaries, to victual, to stock. **s'approvisionner**, *v.r.* to supply oneself; to lay in supplies.

approvisionneur [aprovizjɔ'nœːr], *n.m.* (*fem.* -euse) caterer, purveyor.

approximatif [aproksima'tif], *a.* (*fem.* -tive) approximate.

approximation [aproksima'sjɔ̃], *n.f.* approximation, rough estimate.

approximativement [aproksimativ'mã], *adv.* approximately.

appui [a'pɥi], *n.m.* support, prop, stay; any kind of mechanical support, *as* buttress, rail, handrail, sill (*of windows*); (*Mech.*) fulcrum; (*fig.*) corroboration; (*Gram.*) stress.

appui-main [apɥi'mɛ̃], *n.m.* (*pl.* appuis-main) painter's maulstick *or* hand rest.

appuyer [apɥi'je], *v.t.* (*conjug. like* EMPLOYER) to prop up, to support; to lean (*something against a wall etc.*); (*fig.*) to second, to back up, to uphold, to stand by, to reinforce.—*v.i.* to weigh upon, to lay stress (*sur*); (*fig.*) to insist; *appuyer à droite,* to bear to the right. **s'appuyer**, *v.r.* to lean, to rest (*sur*); to rely upon, to depend (*sur*); to lay stress *or* a stress on, to dwell (*sur*).

âpre [ɑːpr], *a.* hard, rough, harsh, rugged; sharp, tart, sour; bitter, biting, bleak raw; grating (*of sound*); (*fig.*) austere; crabbed; violent, eager (*in pursuit of something*); *âpre à la curée,* out for the kill (*of animals*); (*fig.*) on the make (*of persons*).

âprement [ɑːprə'mã], *adv.* harshly, roughly; peevishly, crabbedly; violently, eagerly.

après [a'prɛ], *prep.* after, behind (*in time, order etc.*); next to; in pursuit of; *d'après,* after, according to.—*adv.* afterwards, later; *et après?* (*ellipt.*) what next? what then? so what?—*conj. après que,* after, when.

après-demain [aprɛd'mɛ̃], *adv.* the day after tomorrow.

après-midi [aprɛmi'di], *n.m. or f. inv.* afternoon.

âpreté [aprə'te], *n.f.* harshness, tartness, sharpness; roughness, ruggedness; (*fig.*) acrimony, asperity; eagerness; keenness; greediness.

à-propos [apro'po], *n.m.* aptness, suitability.

apside [ap'sid], *n.f.* (*Astron.*) apsis.

apte [apt]. *a.* apt, fit, proper, suitable.

aptitude [apti'tyd], *n.f.* aptitude, natural disposition *or* capacity (*for*).

apurement [apyr'mɑ̃], *n.m.* verification *or* audit (*of accounts*).

apurer [apy're], *v.t.* to verify, to audit.

aquaplane [akwa'plan], *n.f.* surf-board; *faire de l'aquaplane,* to go surf-riding.

aquarelle [akwa'rɛl], *n.f.* painting in water-colors, aquarelle.

aquarelliste [akwarɛ'list], *n.m.* painter in water-colors.

aquarium [akwa'rjɔm], *n.m.* aquarium.

aquatique [akwa'tik], *a.* aquatic.

aqueduc [aka'dyk], *n.m.* aqueduct, conduit; (*Anat.*) duct.

aqueux [a'kø], *a.* (*fem.* **-euse**) aqueous, watery.

aquilin [aki'lɛ̃], *a.* aquiline, curved, hooked, Roman (*of noses etc.*).

aquilon [aki'lɔ̃], *n.m.* north wind, cold blast.

ara [a'ra], *n.m.* (*Orn.*) ara, macaw.

arabe [a'rab], *a.* Arabic, Arabian.—*n.m.* Arabic (*language*).—*n.* (**Arabe**) Arab, Arabian.

arabesque [ara'bɛsk], *n.f.* arabesque.

Arabie [ara'bi], l', *f.* Arabia; *Arabie Séoudite,* Saudi Arabia.

arabique [ara'bik], *a.* Arabic, Arabian; *gomme arabique,* gum arabic.

arable [a'rabl], *a.* arable, tillable.

arachide [ara'ʃid], *n.f.* pea-nut, ground-nut.

araignée [arɛ'ɲe], *n.f.* spider; a spider-like implement etc.; (*Mil.*) a series of branching galleries in a mine; (*Naut.*) crowfoot; *toile d'araignée,* cobweb.

arasement [araz'mɑ̃], *n.m.* levelling, making even.

araser [ara'ze], *v.t.* to level (*a wall, a building etc.*).

aratoire [ara'twa:r], *a.* pertaining to farming.

arbalète [arba'lɛt], *n.f.* arbalest, cross-bow.

arbalétrier [arbale'trje], *n.m.* cross-bowman; (*Carp.*) principal rafters of a roof; strut (*of plane*); (*Orn.*) (black) swift.

arbitrage [arbi'tra:ʒ], *n.m.* arbitration; (*Banking*) arbitrage.

arbitraire [arbi'trɛ:r], *a.* arbitrary; absolute, despotic.

arbitrairement [arbitrɛr'mɑ̃], *adv.* arbitrarily; despotically.

arbitral [arbi'tral], *a.* (*m. pl.* **-aux**) by arbitration; composed of arbitrators (*of a tribunal etc.*).

arbitralement [arbitral'mɑ̃], *adv.* by arbitration.

arbitre [ar'bitr], *n.m.* arbitrator, umpire, referee; arbiter, disposer; will.

arbitrer [arbi'tre], *v.t.* to arbitrate, to judge, to settle (*a dispute etc.*), to referee *or* umpire (*a match*).

arborer [arbo're], *v.t.* to put up, to hoist, to unfurl (*a flag or as a flag*); (*fig.*) to put on.

arbre [arbr], *n.m.* tree; (*fig.*) anything resembling this (*e.g. a genealogical tree*); (*Mach.*) arbor, shaft, spindle, axle-tree; (*Naut.*) mast; (*Motor.*) **arbre moteur,** mainshaft; *arbre coudé,* crankshaft.

arbrisseau [arbri'so], *n.m.* (*pl.* **-eaux**) shrubby tree.

arbuste [ar'byst], *n.m.* bush, shrub.

arc [ark], *n.m.* bow, long-bow; (*Arch.*) arch; (*Geom., Phys. etc.*) arc.

arcade [ar'kad], *n.f.* arch-shaped opening; (*pl.*) arcade.

arcanes [ar'kan], *n.m. pl.* secrets, mysteries.

arc-boutant [arkbu'tɑ̃], *n.m.* (*pl.* **arcs-boutants**) (*fig.*) buttress, arched flying buttress; supporter, pillar.

arc-bouter [arkbu'te], *v.t.* to strengthen by a flying buttress; (*fig.*) to support, to buttress.

arceau [ar'so], *n.m.* (*pl.* **-eaux**) curved part of a vault *or* arch; anything shaped like an arch; (*croquet*) hoop.

arc-en-ciel [arkɑ̃'sjɛl], *n.m.* (*pl.* **arcs-en-ciel**) rainbow.

archaïque [arka'ik], *a.* archaic.

archaïsme [arka'ism], *n.m.* archaism, obsolete word etc.

archange [ar'kɑ̃:ʒ], *n.m.* archangel.

arche (1) [arʃ], *n.f.* arch (*of a bridge*).

arche (2) [arʃ], *n.f.* ark; *l'arche de Noé,* Noah's ark.

archéologie [arkeɔlɔ'ʒi], *n.f.* archaeology.

archéologique [arkeɔlɔ'ʒik], *a.* archaeological.

archéologue [arkeɔ'lɔg], *n.m.* archaeologist.

archer [ar'ʃe], *n.m.* archer, bowman.

archet [ar'ʃɛ], *n.m.* (*Mus.*) bow, fiddle-stick.

archevêché [arʃəvɛ'ʃe], *n.m.* archbishopric; archiepiscopal diocese; archbishop's residence.

archevêque [arʃə'vɛk], *n.m.* archbishop.

archi- [arʃi *or* ar'ki], *pref.* arch-, archi-, chief; extremely as *in archiriche etc.*

archidiacre [arʃi'djakr], *n.m.* archdeacon.

archiduc [arʃi'dyk], *n.m.* archduke.

archiduché [arʃidy'ʃe], *n.m.* archdukedom, archduchy.

archiduchesse [arʃidy'ʃɛs], *n.f.* archduchess.

archiépiscopal [arkiepiskɔ'pal], *a.* (*m. pl.* **-aux**) archiepiscopal.

archière [ar'ʃjɛ:r], *n.f.* loophole.

Archimède [arʃi'mɛd], *m.* Archimedes.

archipel [arʃi'pɛl], *n.m.* archipelago.

archiprêtre [arʃi'prɛ:tr], *n.m.* arch-priest, high priest.

architecte [arʃi'tɛkt], *n.m.* architect; *architecte paysagiste,* landscape gardener.

architectural [arʃitɛkty'ral], *a.* (*m.pl.* **-aux**) architectural.

architecture [arʃitɛk'ty:r], *n.f.* architecture.

architrave [arʃi'tra:v], *n.f.* (*Arch.*) architrave.

archives [ar'ʃi:v], *n.f.* (*used only in pl.*) archives; state, civic *or* family records; record office, muniment room.

archiviste [arʃi'vist], *n.m.* archivist, keeper of records, registrar; filing clerk.

arçon [ar'sɔ̃], *n.m.* saddle-bow; bow-shaped tool used by hat makers etc.

arcot [ar'ko], *n.m.* dross, slag.

arctique [ark'tik], *a.* Arctic.

ardemment [arda'mɑ̃], *adv.* ardently.

ardent [ar'dɑ̃], *a.* burning, hot, fiery, scorching; (*fig.*) violent, intense; ardent, vehement, fervent, earnest, energetic, active; red, reddish (*of hair*); *charbons ardents*, live coals; *buisson ardent*, the burning bush.

ardeur [ar'dœːr], *n.f.* intense heat; ardor, intense activity, fervor, earnestness; fire, spirit, mettle.

ardoise [ar'dwaːz], *n.f.* slate; (*colloq.*) score, account.

ardoisé [ardwa'ze], *a.* slate-colored.

ardoiser [ardwa'ze], *v.t.* to cover (*a roof*) with slates.

ardoisier [ardwa'zje], *n.m.* owner of or workman in a slate quarry.

ardoisière [ardwa'zjeːr], *n.f.* slate quarry.

ardu [ar'dy], *a.* steep, abrupt; (*fig.*) arduous, difficult.

are [aːr], *n.m.* 100 sq. metres (*approx. 120 sq. yds.*).

arène [a'rɛːn], *n.f.* (*poet.*) sand; arena; (*fig.*) cock-pit, battle ground, theatre, scene; (*pl.*) the ancient Roman amphitheatres.

arénière [are'njeːr], *n.f.* sand pit.

aréomètre [areo'mɛtr], *n.m.* areometer, hydrometer.

aréopage [areo'paːʒ], *n.m.* areopagus.

arête [a'rɛːt], *n.f.* fish-bone; awn or beard of wheat etc.; (*Geog. etc.*) ridge; *arête du nez*, bridge of the nose.

argent [ar'ʒɑ̃], *n.m.* silver; silver money; money, cash; (*fig.*) wealth, riches; (*Her.*) argent; *argent doré*, silver-gilt; *vif-argent*, quicksilver; *argent comptant*, ready money.

argentage [ARGENTURE].

argenté [arʒɑ̃'te], *a.* plated, silvered over; silvery.

argenter [arʒɑ̃'te], *v.t.* to silver over, to plate; to give the appearance of silver to.

argenterie [arʒɑ̃'tri], *n.f.* plate, silver plate.

argentin [arʒɑ̃'tɛ̃], *a.* silvery, argentine (*tint*); silver-toned (*ringing*); Argentinian, Argentine.—*n.m.* (**Argentin**, *fem.* -**ine** (1)) Argentinian (*person*).

Argentine (2) [arʒɑ̃'tin], **l'**, *f.* Argentina, the Argentine.

argenture [arʒɑ̃'tyːr], *n.f.*, **argentage** [arʒɑ̃'taːʒ], *n.m.* silvering, silver-plating.

argile [ar'ʒil], *n.f.* clay, potter's clay, argil; *argile à porcelaine*, china clay; *argile réfractaire*, fire clay.

argileux [arʒi'lø], *a.* (*fem.* -**euse**) clayey, clayish.

argilière [arʒi'ljeːr], *n.f.* clay pit.

argon [ar'gɔ̃], *n.m.* (*Chem.*) argon.

argonaute [argo'noːt], *n.m.* argonaut, nautilus.

argot [ar'go], *n.m.* slang, cant.

arguer [ar'gɥe], *v.t.* to infer, to deduce, to argue; (*j'argue*, nous arguons)

argument [argy'mɑ̃], *n.m.* argument, reasoning; proof, evidence; summary; theme, subject.

argumentateur [argymɑ̃ta'tœːr], *n.m.* (*fem.* -**trice**) habitual arguer or disputer.

argumentation, [argymɑ̃tɑ'sjɔ̃], *n.f.* argumentation, reasoning.

argumenter [argymɑ̃'te], *v.i.* to argue; to quibble.

argutie [argy'si], *n.f.* quibble, hair-splitting, cavil.

aria [a'rja], *n.m.* (*Mus.*) aria; (*pop.*) nuisance; fuss, bother.

arianisme [arja'nism], *n.m.* Arianism.

aride [a'rid], *a.* arid, dry; sterile.

aridité [aridi'te], *n.f.* aridity, dryness, barrenness, sterility.

arien [a'rjɛ̃] *a.* (*fem.* **arienne**) Arian.—*n.m.* (**Arien**, *fem.* **Arienne**) Arian (*person*).

aristocrate [aristo'krat], *a.* aristocratic.—*n.* aristocrat.

aristocratie [aristokra'si], *n.f.* aristocracy.

aristocratique [aristokra'tik], *a.* aristocratic.

aristocratiquement [aristokratik'mɑ̃], *adv.* aristocratically.

Aristote [aris'tɔt], *m.* Aristotle.

arithmétique [aritme'tik], *n.f.* arithmetic.—*a.* arithmetical.

arithmétiquement [aritmetik'mɑ̃], *adv.* arithmetically.

arlequin [arlə'kɛ̃], *n.m.* harlequin; (*fig.*) turn-coat; weathercock; *habit d'arlequin*, patchwork, motley.

arlequinade [arləki'nad], *n.f.* harlequinade.

armagnac [arma'nak], *n.m.* brandy (*made in Armagnac, S. of France*).

armateur [arma'tœːr], *n.m.* shipowner; captain of a privateer; privateer.

armature [arma'tyːr], *n.f.* armature, iron braces, stays, casing, gear etc.

arme [arm], *n.f.* arm, weapon; branch or arm (*of the service*); (*Her.*) armorial bearings; *arme blanche*, cold steel; *aux armes!* to arms! *un maître d'armes*, a fencing master.

armé [ar'me], *a.* armed, equipped; (*Her.*) armed (*with claws, horns, teeth etc.*); *béton armé*, reinforced concrete.

armée [ar'me], *n.f.* army; forces, troops, host; (*fig.*) body (*of officials etc.*); *l'Armée du Salut*, the Salvation Army.

armement [armə'mɑ̃], *n.m.* arming, raising of forces, warlike preparations; armament, equipment; (*Am.*) ordnance.

Arménie [arme'ni], **l'**, *f.* Armenia.

arménien [arme'njɛ̃], *a.* (*fem.* -**enne**) Armenian.—*n.m.* Armenian (*language*); (**Arménien**, *fem.* -**enne**) Armenian (*person*).

armer [ar'me], *v.t.* to equip, to arm; (*Artill.*) to load, to mount (*guns etc.*); to cock (*a gun etc.*); (*fig.*) to fortify; to strengthen; (*Naut.*) to fit out. **s'armer**, *v.r.* to arm oneself, to take up arms; to protect oneself (*against something*).

armistice [armis'tis], *n.m.* armistice.

armoire [ar'mwaːr], *n.f.* closet, cupboard; clothes-press, wardrobe.

armoiries [armwa'ri], *n.f.* (*used only in pl.*) arms, armorial bearings.

armorial [armo'rjal], *a.* (*m. pl.* -**aux**) armorial, pertaining to heraldry.—*n.m.* armorial, book of heraldry.

armoricain [armori'kɛ̃], *a.* Armorican (*of Brittany*).

armorier [armo'rje], *v.t.* to put or paint a coat of arms upon, to blazon.

Armorique [armɔ'rik], *l'*, *f.* Armorica.
armoriste [armɔ'rist], *n.m.* armorist, heraldic engraver.
armure [ar'my:r], *n.f.* armor, arms and armor; casing, wrapper; armature (*of a magnet, dynamo etc.*); (*Agric.*) tree-guard; (*Naut.*) fish (*of a mast, yard etc.*); (*fig.*) defence, protection.
armurerie [armyrə'ri], *n.f.* armory; manufacture of arms; arms factory.
armurier [army'rje], *n.m.* armorer, gunsmith.
arnica [arni'ka], *n.m.* (*Bot.*) arnica.
aromatique [arɔma'tik], *a.* aromatic, fragrant, spicy.
aromatiser [arɔmati'ze], *v.t.* to aromatize, to perfume, to flavor.
arome [a'ro:m], *n.m.* aroma, perfume, scent.
aronde [a'rõ:d], *n.f.* (*Carp.*) dovetail, tenon.
arpège [ar'pɛ:ʒ], *n.m.* arpeggio.
arpéger [arpe'ʒe], *v.i.* (*conjug. like* ASSIÉGER) to play arpeggios.
arpent [ar'pɑ̃], *n.m.* acre (*French; about one and a half English or American acres*).
arpentage [arpɑ̃'ta:ʒ], *n.m.* land measurement; survey, measurement.
arpenter [arpɑ̃'te], *v.t.* to survey, to measure (*land*); (*fig.*) to stride up and down.
arpenteur [arpɑ̃'tœ:r], *n.m.* land surveyor.
arpon [ar'põ], *n.m.* ripsaw, crosscut saw.
arqué [ar'ke], *a.* bent, curved, arched (*of horses*).
arquebuse [arkə'by:z], *n.f.* arquebus.
arquebusier [arkəby'zje], *n.m.* arquebusier; gunsmith, armorer.
arquer [ar'ke], *v.t.*, *v.i.* to bend, to curve, to arch.
arraché [ara'ʃe], *a.* uprooted.
arrachement [araʃ'mɑ̃], *n.m.* tearing up or away, pulling or rooting up or out; drawing, extraction.
arrache-pied (d') [daraʃ'pje], *adv. phr.* without interruption; *travailler d'arrache-pied*, to work with a will.
arracher [ara'ʃe], *v.t.* to pull or tear away, up or out; to extract, to uproot, to grub up; (*fig.*) to extort. **s'arracher**, *v.r.* to tear oneself away, to get away; to break away or off.
arraisonner [arezɔ'ne], *v.t.* (*Naut.*) to hail (*a ship*); to stop and examine (*a ship*).
arrangeant [arɑ̃'ʒɑ̃], *a.* accommodating, easy to deal with or get on with.
arrangement [arɑ̃ʒ'mɑ̃], *n.m.* arrangement, disposition, adjustment, setting in order; order, plan, method; agreement, settlement; (*pl.*) terms; measures; (*Math.*) permutations.
arranger [arɑ̃'ʒe], *v.t.* (*conjug. like* MANGER) to arrange, to put in order; to settle, to compromise, to compose (*a difference etc.*); to manage, to regulate; to make suitable; to fit up (*a house*); to trim up; *cela m'arrange*, that suits me; *comme vous voilà arrangé!* what a sight you look! **s'arranger**, *v.r.* to prepare oneself, to make arrangements (*pour*); to come to an agreement; to be satisfied (*de*); *arrangez-vous*, that is your lookout.
arrérages [are'ra:ʒ], *n.m.* (*used only in pl.*) arrears.

arrestation [arɛstɑ'sjõ], *n.f.* arrest, apprehension; custody.
arrêt [a'rɛ], *n.m.* stoppage, stop, check, pause, halt; suspension, cessation; (*Law*) award, judgment; arrest, apprehension; (*fig.*) decree; (*pl.*) imprisonment; *arrêt fixe*, regular (bus) stop; *arrêt facultatif*, request stop; *arrêt de mort*, sentence of death; *chien d'arrêt*, setter, pointer; *robinet d'arrêt*, stopcock.
arrêté (1) [are'te], *a.* stopped; decreed, agreed upon, resolved; arrested; fastened.
arrêté (2) [are'te], *n.m.* departmental minute, order, decree, decision; *arrêté ministériel*, order in council.
arrêter [are'te], *v.t.* to check, to stop the movement of, to throw out of gear; to delay, to detain, to hinder, to impede, to hold up; to arrest; to decide, to resolve; to settle (*an account*). **s'arrêter**, *v.r.* to stop, to pause, to hesitate; to remain, to loiter; to lag; to leave off; to be concluded, determined or resolved (*of bargains etc.*); to resolve upon; to dwell (*upon*), to insist (*sur*).
arrhes [ar], *n.f. pl.* earnest (*money*), deposit.
arrière [a'rjɛ:r], *adv.* behind (*of time and place*); backward; (*Naut.*) aft, abaft; *en arrière*, backward; behindhand, in arrears; at the back, at the rear (*of a train*); *en arrière de*, behind.—*int.* away!—*n.m.* back part, rear; (*Naut.*) stern (*of a vessel*); (*Ftb.*) back.
arriéré [arje're], *a.* in arrears; behindhand, backward, poorly developed.—*n.m.* arrears.

[In *pl.* of all the following compounds *arrière* is *inv.* The *n.* has its normal *pl.*]

arrière-boutique [arjɛrbu'tik], *n.f.* room at the back of a shop.
arrière-cour [arjɛr'ku:r], *n.f.* back yard.
arrière-cousin [arjɛrku'zɛ̃], *n.m.* (*fem. cousine*) distant cousin, cousin several times removed.
arrière-cuisine [arjɛrkɥi'zin], *n.f.* back kitchen, scullery.
arrière-garde [arjɛr'gard], *n.f.* rear guard.
arrière-goût [arjɛr'gu], *n.m.* after-taste.
arrière-grand-mère [arjɛrgrɑ̃'mɛ:r], *n.f.* (*pl.* -grand-mères) great-grandmother.
arrière-grand-père [arjɛrgrɑ̃'pɛ:r], *n.m.* (*pl.* -grands-pères) great-grandfather.
arrière-main [arjɛr'mɛ̃], *n.f.* back of the hand; (*Ten.*) backhand (stroke).—*n.m.* hindquarters (*of a horse*).
arrière-neveu [arjɛrnə'vø], *n.m.* (*pl.* -eux) grand-nephew.
arrière-nièce [arjɛr'njɛs], *n.f.* grand-niece.
arrière-pays [arjɛr'pei], *n.m. inv.* hinterland.
arrière-pensée [arjɛrpɑ̃'se], *n.f.* mental reservation, hidden motive, underlying design.
arrière-petite-fille [arjɛrpətit'fi:j], *n.f.* (*pl.* -petites-filles) great-granddaughter.
arrière-petit-fils [arjɛrpəti'fis], *n.m.* (*pl.* -petits-fils) great-grandson.
arrière-petits-enfants [arjɛrpətizɑ̃'fɑ̃], *n.m. pl.* great-grandchildren.
arrière-plan [arjɛr'plɑ̃], *n.m.* (*Paint.*, *Cine.*) background.
arrière-point [arjɛr'pwɛ̃], *n.m.* back-stitch.
arrière-port [arjɛr'pɔ:r], *n.m.* inner harbor.

arriérer [arje′re], *v.t.* (*conjug. like* CÉDER) to defer, to put off; to leave in arrears. **s'arriérer**, *v.r.* to stay behind; to be in arrears.

arrière-saison [arjɛrsɛ′zɔ̃], *n.f.* end of autumn.

arrière-train [arjɛr′trɛ̃], *n.m.* hindquarters (*of an animal*).

arrimage [ari′ma:ʒ], *n.m.* (*Naut.*) stowage.

arrimer [ari′me], *v.t.* (*Naut.*) to stow (*cargo etc.*).

arrimeur [ari′mœːr], *n.m.* stower, stevedore.

arrivée [ari′ve], *n.f.* arrival, moment of landing, coming etc., advent.

arriver [ari′ve], *v.i.* (*conjug. with* ÊTRE) to arrive, to come; to arrive at, to attain, to get to, to reach (*à*); to make one's way, to succeed; to happen, to occur, to take place; to veer; *quoi qu'il arrive*, come what may.

arrivisme [ari′vism], *n.m.* push, unscrupulous ambition.

arriviste [ari′vist], *n.m.* an unscrupulously ambitious person.

arrogamment [aroga′mɑ̃], *adv.* arrogantly, haughtily; insolently.

arrogance [aro′gɑ̃:s], *n.f.* arrogance, haughtiness, superciliousness.

arrogant [aro′gɑ̃], *a.* arrogant, haughty, supercilious, overbearing.

arroger (s') [saro′ʒe], *v.r.* (*conjug. like* MANGER) to assume *or* claim presumptuously.

arrondi [arɔ̃′di], *a.* rounded.—*n.m.* curve (*of shoulder, face etc.*).

arrondir [arɔ̃′diːr], *v.t.* to make round; to give a curved shape to, to round off; (*fig.*) to enlarge, to extend. **s'arrondir**, *v.r.* to grow *or* become round; to increase one's estate.

arrondissement [arɔ̃dis′mɑ̃], *n.m.* rounding, making round; roundness; division of a (*French*) department; (*in Paris*) one of the 20 wards.

arrosage [aro′za:ʒ], **arrosement** [aroz′mɑ̃], *n.m.* watering, sprinkling; irrigation.

arroser [aro′ze], *v.t.* to water, to wet, to sprinkle; to irrigate (*land*); to soak, to moisten; to flow through (*of a river*); to bathe (*with tears*).

arrosoir [aro′zwaːr], *n.m.* watering can.

arsenal [arsə′nal], *n.m.* arsenal; *arsenal maritime*, naval dockyard.

arsenic [arsə′nik], *n.m.* arsenic.

arsenical [arsəni′kal], *a.* (*m. pl.* **-aux**) arsenical.—*n.m. pl.* (**-aux**) arsenical compounds.

art [aːr], *n.m.* art; skill, dexterity, artifice; *arts d'agrément*, accomplishments; *les beaux-arts*, the fine arts.

artère [ar′tɛːr], *n.f.* artery; (*fig.*) thoroughfare (*in a town*).

artériel [arte′rjɛl], *a.* (*fem.* **-elle**) arterial; *tension artérielle*, blood pressure.

artériole [arte′rjɔl], *n.f.* small artery.

artésien [arte′zjɛ̃], *a.* (*fem.* **-enne**) artesian; *puits artésien*, artesian well.—*n.m.* (**Artésien**, *fem.* **-enne**) inhabitant *or* native of Artois.

arthrite [ar′trit], *n.f.* arthritis.

arthritique [artri′tik], *a.* arthritic.

artichaut [arti′ʃo], *n.m.* globe artichoke.

article [ar′tikl], *n.m.* article (*in all English senses*); clause, provision (*of a treaty etc.*); item; commodity; (*pl.*) goods; *article de fond*, leading article, éditorial.

articulaire [artiky′lɛːr], *a.* articular.

articulation [artikyla′sjɔ̃], *n.f.* articulation, pronunciation; (*Bot., Anat.*) joint, articulation; (*Law*) enumeration of facts.

articulé [artiky′le], *a.* articulate, clear, distinct; jointed, articulated.

articuler [artiky′le], *v.t.* to articulate, to put together by the joints; to pronounce distinctly; (*Law*) to enumerate. **s'articuler**, *v.r.* to be connected by joints.

artifice [arti′fis], *n.m.* artifice, contrivance, expedient; dodge, trick, stratagem; craft, ruse; *un feu d'artifice*, fireworks.

artificiel [artifi′sjɛl], *a.* (*fem.* **-elle**) artificial; fictitious, spurious.

artificiellement [artifisjɛl′mɑ̃], *adv.* artificially.

artificieusement [artifisjøz′mɑ̃], *adv.* cunningly, craftily, artfully, slyly.

artificieux [artifi′sjø], *a.* (*fem.* **-euse**) artful, cunning.

artillerie [artij′ri], *n.f.* artillery, ordnance.

artilleur [arti′jœːr], *n.m.* artilleryman, gunner.

artimon [arti′mɔ̃], *n.m.* mizen-mast *or* -sail.

artisan [arti′zɑ̃], *n.m.* artisan, operative, mechanic; (*fig.*) author, architect, contriver, maker.

artiste [ar′tist], *a.* artistic (*of persons*).—*n.* artist; player, performer.

artistement [artistə′mɑ̃], *adv.* in an artistic manner; skilfully, artistically.

artistique [artis′tik], *a.* artistic, pertaining to art.

as [ɑːs], *n.m.* ace (*at cards, dice*); as (*Roman coin and weight*).

asbeste [az′bɛst], *n.m.* asbestos.

ascendance [asɑ̃′dɑ̃:s], *n.f.* ascent; ancestry.

ascendant [asɑ̃′dɑ̃], *n.m.* ascendant; ascendency, influence; (*pl.*) ancestors.—*a.* ascending, ascendant; going upward, rising.

ascenseur [asɑ̃′sœːr], *n.m.* lift, (*Am.*) elevator.

ascension [asɑ̃′sjɔ̃], *n.f.* ascent, climbing, rising; upstroke (*of machinery*); (*Jour de*) *l'Ascension*, Ascension Day.

ascète [a′sɛt], *n.* ascetic.

ascétique [ase′tik], *a.* ascetic, rigid, severe.

ascétisme [ase′tism], *n.m.* asceticism.

asepsie [asɛp′si], *n.f.* (*Med.*) asepsis.

aseptique [asɛp′tik], *a.* and *n.m.* aseptic.

aseptiser [asɛpti′ze], *v.t.* to render aseptic.

asexué [asɛk′sɥe], **asexuel** [asɛk′sɥɛl] (*fem.* **-elle**), *a.* asexual.

asiatique [azja′tik], *a.* Asiatic; *grippe asiatique*, Asian flu.—*n.* (**Asiatique**) native of Asia.

Asie [a′zi], *f.* Asia; *Asie Mineure*, Asia Minor.

asile [a′zil], *n.m.* asylum, place of refuge, sanctuary, retreat, home (*for the aged etc.*); (*fig.*) protection, refuge; *asile d'aliénés*, mental hospital.

asine [a′zin], *a.* asinine.

aspect [as′pɛ], *n.m.* aspect, view, look; countenance; phase, bearing; point of view.

asperge [as′pɛrʒ], *n.f.* asparagus (*head of*).

aspergement [aspɛrʒə′mɑ̃], *n.m.* sprinkling.

asperger [aspɛr′ʒe], *v.t.* (*conjug. like* MANGER) to sprinkle.

aspergerie [aspɛrʒə′ri], **aspergière** [aspɛr′ʒɛːr], *n.f.* asparagus bed.

27

aspérité

aspérité [asperi'te], *n.f.* roughness, harshness; unevenness, ruggedness; (*fig.*) asperity.

aspersion [asper'sjɔ̃], *n.f.* aspersion, sprinkling.

aspersoir [asper'swa:r], *n.m.* holy water sprinkler; rose (*of a watering can*).

asphaltage [asfal'ta:ʒ], *n.m.* asphalting.

asphalte [as'falt], *n.m.* bitumen, asphalt.

asphalter [asfal'te], *v.t.* to asphalt.

asphodèle [asfɔ'dɛl], *n.m.* asphodel.

asphyxiant [asfik'sjɑ̃], *a.* asphyxiating, suffocating; **gaz asphyxiant**, poison gas.

aspyhxie [asfik'si], *n.f.* (*Med.*) asphyxia, suffocation.

asphyxié [asfik'sje], *a.* asphyxiated.—*n.m.* (*fem.* -ée) person in a state of asphyxia.

asphyxier [asfik'sje], *v.t.* to asphyxiate, to suffocate. **s'asphyxier**, *v.r.* to commit suicide by suffocation.

aspic [as'pik], *n.m.* asp, viper; (*Bot.*) spike lavender; (*Cook.*) cold meat *or* fish, in jelly.

aspidistra [aspidis'tra], *n.m.* aspidistra.

aspirail [aspi'ra:j], *n.m.* (*pl.* -aux) airhole (*in a stove, oven etc.*).

aspirant (1) [aspi'rɑ̃], *a.* suction, sucking (*of pumps*).

aspirant (2) [aspi'rɑ̃], *n.m.* aspirant, candidate; suitor; officer-cadet; midshipman.

aspirateur [aspira'tœ:r], *n.m.* ventilator; suction pump; vacuum cleaner.

aspiration [aspira'sjɔ̃], *n.f.* aspiration (*of the letter* h *etc.*); inhaling, inspiration; (*of pumps*) exhaustion, suction; (*fig.*) yearning, aspiration; (*Motor.*) suction, intake.

aspirer [aspi're], *v.t.* to inspire, to inhale; to draw in, to suck in; (*Gram.*) to aspirate. —*v.i.* to aspire, to aim at.

aspirine [aspi'rin], *n.f.* aspirin.

assagir [asa'ʒi:r], *v.t.* to make wiser, to impart wisdom to. **s'assagir**, *v.r.* to become wiser; to settle down.

assaillant [asa'jɑ̃], *a.* attacking, aggressive.— *n.m.* (*fem.* -e) aggressor, assailant, besieger.

assaillir [asa'ji:r], *v.t. irr.* to assault, to assail; to worry, to molest, to beset.

assainir [asɛ'ni:r], *v.t.* to render healthy; (*fig.*) to cleanse, to purify morally etc. **s'assainir**, *v.r.* to become healthy.

assainissement [asɛnis'mɑ̃], *n.m.* purification, sanitation salubrity; drainage.

assaisonnement [asɛzɔn'mɑ̃], *n.m.* condiment, seasoning, dressing.

assaisonner [asɛzɔ'ne], *v.t.* to season, to dress, to give a relish to.

assassin [asa'sɛ̃], *a.* killing, murderous.— *n.m.* (*fem.* -e) assassin, murderer; ruffian.

assassinat [asasi'na], *n.m.* assassination, wilful murder, homicide.

assassiner [asasi'ne], *v.t.* to assassinate, to murder; (*fig.*) to bore; to tease, to importune.

assaut [a'so], *n.m.* assault, onset, attack.

assèchement [asɛʃ'mɑ̃], *n.m.* drying up, drainage.

assécher [ase'ʃe], *v.t.* (*conjug. like* CÉDER) to drain (*a mine, pond etc.*).—*v.i.* to become dry, to be drained.

assemblage [asɑ̃'bla:ʒ], *n.m.* assemblage, collection, union, combination; (*Print.*)

gathering; (*Carp.*) joint, scarf; **chaîne d'assemblage**, assembly line.

assemblée [asɑ̃'ble], *n.f.* assembly, meeting, company, party; convocation, congregation (*of churches*); meet (*of hunters*).

assembler [asɑ̃'ble], *v.t.* to assemble, to call together; to collect, to gather; to bring together; (*Print.*) to gather; (*Carp.*) to trim, to scarf. **s'assembler**, *v.r.* to assemble, to meet, to congregate.

asséner [ase'ne], *v.t.* (*conjug. like* CÉDER) to strike *or* deal (*a blow*).

assentiment [asɑ̃ti'mɑ̃], *n.m.* assent, agreement.

asseoir [a'swa:r], *v.t. irr.* to seat, to put on a seat, to set, to place, to fix, to establish; to pitch (*a camp etc.*). **s'asseoir**, *v.r.* to sit, to sit down, to take a seat, to settle, to perch.

assermenté [asɛrmɑ̃'te], *a.* sworn in, attested.

assermenter [asɛrmɑ̃'te], *v.t.* to swear in.

assertif [asɛr'tif], *a.* (*fem.* -tive) assertive.

assertion [asɛr'sjɔ̃], *n.f.* assertion, affirmation.

asservir [asɛr'vi:r], *v.t.* to enslave, to reduce to servitude; to subdue, to conquer. **s'asservir**, *v.r.* to obey, to submit (*à*).

asservissant [asɛrvi'sɑ̃], *a.* enslaving, subjecting, coercive.

asservissement [asɛrvis'mɑ̃], *n.m.* bondage, servitude, slavery, subjection.

assez [a'se], *adv.* enough, sufficiently; tolerably, passably, rather.

assidu [asi'dy], *a.* assiduous, diligent, attentive; punctual; regular, constant.

assiduité [asidɥi'te], *n.f.* assiduity, application, diligence, attention.

assidûment [asidy'mɑ̃], *adv.* assiduously, diligently, constantly; punctually.

assiéger [asje'ʒe], *v.t.* (*see Verb Tables*) to besiege; to lay siege to; to surround; to importune.

assiette [a'sjɛt], *n.f.* plate; plateful; attitude *or* posture (*in sitting etc.*), pose, situation, bearing, basis; seat (*in the saddle*); position, site; tone, state, disposition (*of the mind etc.*).

assiettée [asje'te], *n.f.* plateful.

assignation [asiɲa'sjɔ̃], *n.f.* order to pay, transfer; (*Law*) summons, subpoena, writ; appointment, rendezvous, assignation.

assigner [asi'ne], *v.t.* to assign (*property in payment of a debt etc.*); to cite, to summon, to subpoena; to appoint, to make (*a rendezvous etc.*).

assimilation [asimila'sjɔ̃], *n.f.* assimilation.

assimiler [asimi'le], *v.t.* to make like; to liken, to compare, to assimilate.

assis [a'si], *a.* seated, sitting; situated; established.

assise [a'si:z], *n.f.* course (*of stones etc.*), foundation, basis; (*Geol.*) stratum; (*Mining*) measure (*of coal*); (*pl.*) assizes; **cour d'assises**, assize court.

assistance [asis'tɑ̃:s], *n.f.* audience, company, bystanders; congregation (*in a church*); assistance, help, aid; relief.

assistant [asis'tɑ̃], *n.m.* (*fem.* -ante) assistant (*priest, teacher etc.*); person present, bystander, witness etc.; **assistant(e) social(e)**, social welfare worker.

assisté [asis'te], *a.* receiving public assistance. —*n.m.* (*fem.* -ée) person in receipt of relief.

28

assister [asis'te], *v.t.* to assist, to help, to succor.— *v.i.* to be at, to be present (à), to look on, to be a witness (à).

association [asɔsja'sjɔ̃], *n.f.* association; union; partnership, fellowship, society, order.

associé [asɔ'sje], *a.* associated, admitted (*as a member*).—*n.m.* (*fem.* -ée) associate, fellow, member, partner.

associer [asɔ'sje], *v.t.* to associate, to take into partnership etc.; to divide *or* share something with someone; to link together, to connect (*ideas etc.*). **s'associer**, *v.r.* to enter into partnership, to associate oneself, to combine (*with*).

assoiffé [aswa'fe], *a.* thirsty; eager (*for*).

assolement [asɔl'mɑ̃], *n.m.* (*Agric.*) rotation (*of crops*).

assoler [asɔ'le], *v.t.* to vary or rotate (*crops*).

assombrir [asɔ̃'briːr], *v.t.* to darken, to throw a gloom over, to cloud. **s'assombrir**, *v.r.* to become dark *or* gloomy; to darken (*of the brow*).

assombrissement [asɔ̃bris'mɑ̃], *n.m.* darkening, gloom.

assommant [asɔ'mɑ̃], *a.* wearisome, tiresome, boring.

assommer [asɔ'me], *v.t.* to beat to death, to knock on the head; to overpower; to overwhelm, to stun; (*fig.*) to bore, to importune, to oppress.

assommeur [asɔ'mœːr], *n.m.* (*fem.* -euse) slaughterer (*of oxen etc.*).

assommoir [asɔ'mwaːr], *n.m.* poleaxe; bludgeon.

Assomption [asɔ̃p'sjɔ̃], *n.f.* (*Eccles.*) Assumption of the Blessed Virgin (August 15).

assomption [asɔ̃p'sjɔ̃], *n.f.* assumption.

assonance [asɔ'nɑ̃ːs], *n.f.* assonance.

assonant [asɔ'nɑ̃], *a.* assonant.

assorti [asɔr'ti], *a.* assorted, matched, paired.

assortiment [asɔrti'mɑ̃], *n.m.* suitability, match; assortment, set.

assortir [asɔr'tiːr], *v.t.* to assort, to match, to pair; to stock, to furnish (*with things that go together or match*).—*v.i.* to match, to suit, to go well together. **s'assortir**, *v.r.* to match, to agree, to go well together.

assortissant [asɔrti'sɑ̃], *a.* suitable, matching, going well (*with something else*).

assoupi [asu'pi], *a.* dozing; dormant (*volcano*).

assoupir [asu'piːr], *v.t.* to make drowsy, sleepy, heavy *or* dull; (*fig.*) to assuage, to allay, to deaden. **s'assoupir**, *v.r.* to grow drowsy, sleepy, dull *or* heavy; to doze; (*fig.*) to be assuaged; to be appeased, to be stilled.

assoupissant [asupi'sɑ̃], *a.* making drowsy *or* sleepy, soporific.

assoupissement [asupis'mɑ̃], *n.m.* drowsiness, sleepiness, heaviness; (*fig.*) carelessness, sloth; (*Med.*) coma.

assouplir [asu'pliːr], *v.t.* to make supple, flexible *or* tractable; to break in (*a horse*). **s'assouplir**, *v.r.* to become supple, tractable *or* manageable.

assouplissement [asuplis'mɑ̃], *n.m.* suppleness, tractability, docility.

assourdir [asur'diːr], *v.t.* to deafen, to stun; to muffle.

assourdissant [asurdi'sɑ̃], *a.* deafening.

assourdissement [asurdis'mɑ̃], *n.m.* deafening, muffling, deadening; deafening noise; temporary deafness.

assouvir [asu'viːr], *v.t.* to glut, to satiate, to surfeit; to gratify; to cloy. **s'assouvir**, *v.r.* to be satiated, gratified *or* cloyed.

assouvissement [asuvis'mɑ̃], *n.m.* glutting, satiating.

assujettir [asyʒe'tiːr], *v.t.* to subdue, to subjugate; to compel; to fix, to fasten. **s'assujettir**, *v.r.* to subject oneself, to submit.

assujettissant [asyʒeti'sɑ̃], *a.* binding, constraining, fettering, restrictive.

assujettissement [asyʒetis'mɑ̃], *n.m.* subjection, subjugation; obligation, fixing.

assumer [asy'me], *v.t.* to take upon oneself, to assume.

assurance [asy'rɑ̃ːs], *n.f.* confidence, security, assurance; certainty, conviction; warrant, pledge; insurance, underwriting; (*fig.*) boldness; (*les*) *assurances sociales*, the French equivalent of social security.

assuré [asy're], *a.* assured, confident; sure, secure, positive, certain; trusty; insured.— *n.m.* (*fem.* -ée) insured person.

assurément [asyre'mɑ̃], *adv.* assuredly, confidently; surely, undoubtedly; certainly.

assurer [asy're], *v.t.* to fix securely, to fasten, to steady; (*Naut.* and *Mount.*) to belay; to assure, to guarantee; to insure; to underwrite; to assert, to affirm. **s'assurer**, *v.r.* to make sure of, to ascertain.

assureur [asy'rœːr], *n.m.* underwriter, insurer, assurer.

Assyrie [asi'ri], *f.* Assyria.

assyrien [asi'rjɛ̃], *a.* (*fem.* -enne) Assyrian.— *n.m.* (**Assyrien**, *fem.* -enne) Assyrian (*person*).

aster [as'tɛːr], *n.m.* (*Bot.*) aster.

astérie [aste'ri], *n.f.* starfish.

astérisque [aste'risk], *n.m.* asterisk.

astéroïde [astero'id], *n.m.* asteroid.

asthmatique [asma'tik], *a.* asthmatic.

asthme [asm], *n.m.* asthma.

asticot [asti'ko], *n.m.* gentle (*bait for fishing*); maggot.

asticoter [astiko'te], *v.t.* (*colloq.*) to tease, to worry.

astigmate [astig'mat], *a.* astigmatic.

astigmatisme [astigma'tism], *n.m.* astigmatism.

astiquer [asti'ke], *v.t.* to polish, to furbish, to glaze.

astracan *or* **astrakan** [astra'kɑ̃], *n.m.* astrakhan, Persian lamb (*fur*).

astral [as'tral], *a.* (*m. pl.* -aux) astral.

astre [astr], *n.m.* star; (*fig.*) celebrity.

astreindre [as'trɛ̃ːdr], *v.t. irr.* (*conjug. like* CRAINDRE) to oblige, to compel, to subject. **s'astreindre**, *v.r.* to confine oneself, to tie oneself down (à).

astreinte [as'trɛ̃ːt], *n.f.* (*Law*) compulsion; fine for delay in the performance of a contract.

astringence [astrɛ̃'ʒɑ̃ːs], *n.f.* astringency.

astringent [astrɛ̃'ʒɑ̃], *a.* and *n.m.* astringent.

astroïde [astro'id], *a.* star-shaped.

astrologie [astrolɔ'ʒi], *n.f.* astrology.

astrologique [astrolɔ'ʒik], *a.* astrological.

astrologue [astro'log], *n.m.* astrologer.

astronaute [astro'noːt], *n.m.* astronaut.

astronautique [astrono'tik], *n.f.* astronautics.

astronome [astro'nom], *n.m.* astronomer.

astronomie [astrɔnɔ'mi], *n.f.* astronomy.
astronomique [astrɔnɔ'mik], *a.* astronomical, astronomic.
astrophysique [astrɔfi'zik], *a.* astrophysical. —*n.f.* astrophysics.
astuce [as'tys], *n.f.* craft, guile; cunning.
astucieusement [astysjøz'mɑ̃], *adv.* craftily, cunningly.
astucieux [asty'sjø], *a.* (*fem.* -euse) crafty, wily.
Asturies [asty'ri], les, *f. pl.* the Asturias.
asymétrie [asime'tri], *n.f.* asymmetry.
asymétrique [asime'trik], *a.* asymmetrical.
atelier [atə'lje], *n.m.* workshop, studio, atelier; (*collect.*) gang of workmen etc.; (*Freemasonry*) lodge, lodge meeting.
atermoyer [atɛrmwa'je], *v.t.* (*conjug. like* EMPLOYER) to put off, to delay (*a payment*). —*v.i.* (*fig.*) to put off, to make shifts. s'atermoyer, *v.r.* to compound with one's creditors.
athée [a'te], *a.* atheistic.—*n.* atheist.
athéisme [ate'ism], *n.m.* atheism.
Athènes [a'tɛːn], *f.* Athens.
athénien [ate'njɛ̃], *a.* (*fem.* -enne) Athenian. —*n.m.* (Athénien, *fem.* -enne) Athenian (*person*).
athlète [a'tlɛt], *n.m.* athlete.
athlétique [atle'tik], *a.* athletic.
athlétisme [atle'tism], *n.m.* athleticism; athletics.
Atlantide [atlɑ̃'tid], *f.* Atlantis.
atlantique [atlɑ̃'tik], *a.* Atlantic.—*n.m.* (L'Atlantique) the Atlantic (Ocean).
atlas [a'tlaːs], *n.m.* atlas.
atmosphère [atmɔs'fɛːr], *n.f.* atmosphere.
atmosphérique [atmɔsfe'rik], *a.* atmospheric; pression atmosphérique, atmospheric pressure.
atoll [a'tɔl], *n.m.* atoll.
atome [a'tɔːm], *n.m.* atom; corpuscle.
atomicité [atɔmisi'te], *n.f.* (*Chem.*) atomicity, valency.
atomique [atɔ'mik], *a.* atomic(al); commissariat à l'énergie atomique, atomic energy authority.
atomiser [atɔmi'ze], *v.t.* to pulverize.
atomiste [atɔ'mist], *n.m.* atomist.
atomistique [atɔmis'tik], *a.* atomic(al).
atone [a'tɔn], *a.* atonic, debilitated, dull; lacklustre, expressionless (*of eyes*); (*Gram.*) atonic, unaccentuated.
atonie [atɔ'ni], *n.f.* atony, debility.
atonique [atɔ'nik], *a.* atonic.
atours [a'tuːr], *n.m.* (*used only in pl.*) woman's attire, dress, ornament.
atout [a'tu], *n.m.* trump; trump card.
atoxique [atɔk'sik], *a.* non-poisonous.
atrabilaire [atrabi'lɛːr], *a.* morose, peevish.
âtre [ɑːtr], *n.m.* hearth; fireplace.
atroce [a'trɔs], *a.* atrocious, cruel, excruciating; heinous, odious, dreadful.
atrocement [atrɔs'mɑ̃], *adv.* atrociously, cruelly, outrageously.
atrocité [atrɔsi'te], *n.f.* atrociousness, heinousness; atrocity, cruelty.
atrophie [atrɔ'fi], *n.f.* (*Path.*) atrophy.
atrophié [atrɔ'fje], *a.* atrophied, wasted, withered, stunted.
atrophier [atrɔ'fje], *v.t.* to cause to waste or wither. s'atrophier, *v.r.* to waste away, to atrophy.

atrophique [atrɔ'fik], *a.* atrophic.
attablé [ata'ble], *a.* seated at table.
attabler (s') [sata'ble], *v.r.* to sit down to or take one's place at table.
attachant [ata'ʃɑ̃], *a.* engaging, winning, attractive.
attache [ata'ʃ], *n.f.* bond, cord, leash, strap; (*fig.*) attachment, affection for.
attaché [ata'ʃe], *n.m.* attaché (*of an embassy*).
attachement [ataʃ'mɑ̃], *n.m.* attachment; affection, liaison; eagerness, zeal.
attacher [ata'ʃe], *v.t.* to fasten, to tie, to attach, to fix; (*fig.*) to apply, to affix; to connect, to associate; to engage, to endear. —s'attacher, *v.r.* to take hold, to attach or fasten oneself; to cling, to adhere; to have an affection for; to apply oneself to.
attaquable [ata'kabl], *a.* assailable; of doubtful validity.
attaquant [ata'kɑ̃], *n.m.* assailant.
attaque [a'tak], *n.f.* attack, assault, aggression; fit, stroke.
attaquer [ata'ke], *v.t.* to attack, to assail, to assault; to seize suddenly (*of illness etc.*); to criticize; attaquer en justice, to sue for. s'attaquer, *v.r.* to make or conduct an attack (à); to set upon.
attaqueur [ata'kœːr], *n.m.* attacker.
attardé [atar'de], *a.* late, behindhand; mentally retarded (*child*).
attarder [atar'de], *v.t.* to make late, to delay. s'attarder, *v.r.* to be belated; to loiter, to linger.
atteindre [a'tɛ̃ːdr], *v.t. irr.* (*conjug. like* CRAINDRE) to reach, to hit, to attain; to arrive at; to overtake, to come up to.—*v.i.* to reach with difficulty, to attain (à); atteindre à la perfection, to attain to perfection.
atteint [a'tɛ̃], *a.* hit, struck; attacked, seized, affected; reached.
atteinte [a'tɛ̃ːt], *n.f.* reach, blow, stroke, touch; attack, fit, seizure (*of disease*); injury, damage, harm, wrong.
attelage [at'laːʒ], *n.m.* harnessing, yoking; team, yoke, set, pair; carriage, horses; (*Rail.*) coupling.
atteler [at'le], *v.t.* (*conjug. like* APPELER) to put horses etc. (*to*); to harness, to yoke; (*fig.*) to subjugate. s'atteler, *v.r.* to settle down to (à); (*fig.*) to apply oneself to, to hitch one's wagon to.
attelle [a'tɛl], *n.f.* hame; (*Surg.*) splint.
attenant [at'nɑ̃], *a.* contiguous, adjoining, next door to, close by (à).
attendre [a'tɑ̃ːdr], *v.t.* to await, to wait for, to stay for; to look forward to, to expect; to look for, to count upon. s'attendre, *v.r.* to rely upon, to count upon, to trust (à); to expect, to look forward (à).
attendrir [atɑ̃'driːr], *v.t.* to make tender, to soften; to touch, to move. s'attendrir, *v.r.* to grow tender; to be moved, to melt, to pity, to relent.
attendrissant [atɑ̃dri'sɑ̃], *a.* moving, touching.
attendrissement [atɑ̃dris'mɑ̃], *n.m.* compassion, pity; tears, sensibility; tenderness.
attendu [atɑ̃'dy], *prep.* considering, on account of, in consideration of.—*conj.* attendu que, seeing that, as, whereas, since.
attenir [at'niːr], *v.i. irr.* (*conjug. like* TENIR) to adjoin, to be contiguous (à); to be related.

attentat [atɑ̃'ta], *n.m.* attempt at crime; crime, attempt; outrage, violation.

attente [a'tɑ̃:t], *n.f.* waiting, expectation; hope; *salle d'attente*, waiting-room.

attenter [atɑ̃'te], *v.i.* to make a criminal attempt.

attentif [atɑ̃'tif], *a.* (*fem.* -tive) attentive, heedful; considerate.

attention [atɑ̃'sjɔ̃], *n.f.* attention, notice; heed, care, vigilance; regard, respect, consideration; *attention!* look out! stand by!

attentionné [atɑ̃sjo'ne], *a.* attentive, considerate.

attentivement [atɑ̃tiv'mɑ̃], *adv.* attentively, carefully.

atténuant [ate'nɥɑ̃], *a.* mitigating; (*Law*) extenuating.

atténuation [atenɥa'sjɔ̃], *n.f.* attenuation, extenuation, mitigation.

atténué [ate'nɥe], *a.* attenuated, wasted, emaciated.

atténuer [ate'nɥe], *v.t.* to make smaller, thinner, feebler etc.; to attenuate; to extenuate; to mitigate.

atterrant [ate'rɑ̃], *a.* astounding, startling, overwhelming.

atterrement [ater'mɑ̃], *n.m.* overthrow, prostration, amazement.

atterré [ate're], *a.* horror-stricken, dumb-founded.

atterrer [ate're], *v.t.* to overwhelm; to astound.

atterrir [ate'ri:r], *v.i.* to land, to make land.

atterrissage [ateri'sa:ʒ], *n.m.* landing; *terrain d'atterrissage*, landing-ground.

atterrissement [ateris'mɑ̃], *n.m.* alluvion, accretion, alluvium.

attestation [atesta'sjɔ̃], *n.f.* attestation, evidence; certificate, voucher, testimonial; *attestation sous serment*, affidavit.

attester [ates'te], *v.t.* to attest, to certify, to avouch, to witness, to testify.

attiédir [atje'di:r], *v.t.* to cool, to make luke-warm; to take the chill off. **s'attiédir**, *v.r.* to grow cool *or* lukewarm; to cool off.

attiédissement [atjedis'mɑ̃], *n.m.* lukewarm-ness, coolness; abatement.

attifage [ati'fa:ʒ], **attifement** [atif'mɑ̃], *n.m.* get-up, rig-out.

attifer [ati'fe] (*always in a bad sense*), *v.t.* to dress up. **s'attifer**, *v.r.* to dress up, to rig oneself out.

attique [a'tik], *a.* Attic; (*fig.*) witty, urbane.— *n.m.* (*Arch.*) attic.

attirail [ati'ra:j], *n.m.* (*collect.*) apparatus, implements, utensils, gear, tackle; baggage, paraphernalia; show, pomp.

attirance [ati'rɑ̃:s], *n.f.* attraction (*vers*).

attirant [ati'rɑ̃], *a.* attractive, alluring, enticing, engaging.

attirer [ati're], *v.t.* to attract, to draw; to win *or* gain over, to lure, to wheedle, to entice; to occasion. **s'attirer**, *v.r.* to draw to *or* down upon one, to bring upon one; to incur, to win.

attisage [ati'za:ʒ], **attisement** [atiz'mɑ̃], *n.m.* the act of stirring up, poking (*a fire*), fanning (*flame*).

(C) **attisée** [ati'ze], *n.f.* a good fire; armful (*of stove wood*).

attiser [ati'ze], *v.t.* to make *or* stir up (*a fire*); to poke; (*fig.*) to incense, to stir up.

attisoir [ati'zwa:r], **attisonnoir** [atizɔ'nwa:r], *n.m.* poker (*especially in foundries*), fire rake.

attitré [ati'tre], *a.* recognized, appointed, regular, ordinary; hired.

attitude [ati'tyd], *n.f.* attitude; (*Paint.*) posture; (*fig.*) attitude of mind etc.

attouchement [atuʃ'mɑ̃], *n.m.* touch, contact.

attracteur [atrak'tœ:r], *a.* (*fem.* -trice) attractile.

attractif [atrak'tif], *a.* (*fem.* -tive) attractive.

attraction [atrak'sjɔ̃], *n.f.* attraction; (*pl.*) cabaret show.

attractivement [atraktiv'mɑ̃], *adv.* attractively.

attrait [a'trɛ], *n.m.* allurement, attraction, charm; inclination, bent; (*pl.*) attractions, charms; bait.

attrape [a'trap], *n.f.* trap, gin; (*fig.*) trick, take-in, sell, hoax; (*Naut.*) hawser.

attrape mouche *or* **attrape-mouches** [atrap'muʃ], *n.m. inv.* flycatcher.

attrape-nigaud [atrapni'go], *n.m.* (*pl.* attrape-nigauds) booby trap.

attraper [atra'pe], *v.t.* to catch; to entrap, to ensnare; to take in, to trick, to bamboozle; to imitate; (*fam.*) to scold; to hit; to over-take, to catch up; to get accidentally (*a cold etc.*); *attrape!* take that! **s'attraper**, *v.r.* to hit (*against*); to be caught (*in*); to get hold of; to seize, to stick (*à*).

attrapeur [atra'pœ:r], *n.m.* (*fem.* -euse) deceiver, cheat, trickster.

attrayant [atre'jɑ̃], *a.* attractive, winning, engaging, charming.

attribuable [atri'bɥabl], *a.* attributable, due to.

attribuer [atri'bɥe], *v.t.* to assign, to confer; to attribute, to ascribe, to impute (*a thing to someone*). **s'attribuer**, *v.r.* to assume, to take upon oneself, to claim.

attribut [atri'by], *n.m.* attribute, prerogative; special symbol *or* emblem; (*Gram.*) predicate.

attributif [atriby'tif], *a.* (*fem.* -tive) (*Gram.*) attributive; predicative; (*Law*) conferring a right.

attribution [atriby'sjɔ̃], *n.f.* attribution, conferment, awarding (*of a grant*); (*usu. in pl.*) privilege, prerogative (*of a person*); province, department, jurisdiction.

attristant [atris'tɑ̃], *a.* saddening, sorrowful, melancholy, grievous.

attrister [atris'te], *v.t.* to grieve, to sadden, to trouble. **s'attrister**, *v.r.* to be sad, to become sorrowful.

attrition [atri'sjɔ̃], *n.f.* attrition, friction.

attroupement [atrup'mɑ̃], *n.m.* riotous assemblage, mob, crowd, gathering of people.

attrouper [atru'pe], *v.t.* to assemble, to gather together in troops *or* a mob. **s'at-trouper**, *v.r.* to flock together, to gather in crowds.

au [o], (*contraction of À LE*) to the.

aubade [o'bad], *n.f.* aubade, dawn song; (*iron.*) hot reception.

aubaine [o'bɛn], *n.f.* (*Law*) escheat; windfall, piece of good luck.

aube [o:b], *n.f.* the dawn; alb (*priest's vestment*).

aubépine [obe'pin], *n.f.* hawthorn, white-thorn, may.

aubère [o'bɛːr], *a.* red roan (*horse*).

auberge [o'bɛrʒ], *n.f.* inn, public-house, tavern; *auberge de (la) jeunesse*, youth hostel.

aubergine [ober'ʒin], *n.f.* aubergine, egg-plant.

aubergiste [ober'ʒist], *n.* innkeeper, publican, landlord, host.

aubour [o'buːr], *n.m.* laburnum; guelder-rose.

aucun [o'kœ̃], *a.* and *pron.* none, no one, not one; not any; anyone; any.

aucunement [okyn'mã], *adv.* in no wise, not at all, not in the least; at all.

audace [o'das], *n.f.* audacity, daring, bold-ness; impudence, insolence; *payer d'audace*, to brazen it out.

audacieusement [odasjøz'mã], *adv.* audaci-ously, daringly, boldly; rashly; impudently.

audacieux [oda'sjø], *a.* (*fem.* -euse) audaci-ous, bold, daring; impudent, presumptuous.

au deçà, au dedans, au dehors, au delà [DEÇÀ, DEDANS, DEHORS, DELÀ].

au-dessous [od'su], *prep.* below.

au-dessus [od'sy], *prep.* above.

au-devant [od'vã], *prep.* towards; *aller au-devant d'un danger*, to anticipate danger.

audibilité [odibili'te], *n.f.* audibility.

audible [o'dibl], *a.* audible.

audience [o'djãːs], *n.f.* audience, hearing; reception; sitting, session, court, tribunal.

audiomètre [odjo'mɛtr], **audimètre** [odi 'mɛtr], *n.m.* audiometer.

audiophone [odjo'fɔn], **audiphone** [odi'fɔn], *n.m.* audiphone.

audio-visuel [odjovi'zɥɛl], *a.* (*fem.* -elle) audio-visual; *moyens audio-visuels*, audio-visual aids.

auditeur [odi'tœːr], *n.m.* (*fem.* -trice) hearer, listener.

auditif [odi'tif], *a.* (*fem.* -tive) auditory.

audition [odi'sjɔ̃], *n.f.* hearing; (*Law*) hearing (*of a case etc.*); audition (*of a singer etc.*).

auditionner [odisjɔ'ne], *v.t.* to audition.

auditoire [odi'twaːr], *n.m.* auditory; congre-gation (*in church*), audience (*theatre etc.*).

auditrice [odi'tris], [AUDITEUR].

auge [oːʒ], *n.f.* trough (*for drinking etc.*); (*plasterer's*) hod; (*Elec.*) cell.

auget [o'ʒɛ], *n.m.* small trough; seed box.

augmentation [ogmãta'sjɔ̃], *n.f.* augmenta-tion, increase, addition, rise (*in salary*).

augmenter [ogmã'te], *v.t.* to augment, to increase; to enlarge; to raise the salary of.— *v.i.* to augment, to increase, to grow, to rise (*in price*), to multiply. **s'augmenter**, *v.r.* to increase, to enlarge, to improve.

augural [ogy'ral], *a.* (*m. pl.* -aux) augural.

augure [o'gyːr], *n.m.* augur, soothsayer; augury, omen, sign; *de mauvais augure*, ominous, portentous.

augurer [ogy're], *v.t.* to augur; (*fig.*) to con-jecture, to surmise.

Auguste [o'gyst], *m.* Augustus.

auguste [o'gyst], *a.* august, majestic.

augustin [ogys'tɛ̃], *n.m.* (*fem.* -ine) Augustin-ian *or* Austin friar *or* (*f.*) nun.

aujourd'hui [oʒur'dɥi], *adv.* today, during this day; nowadays, now, at present.

aulnaie [AUNAIE].

aulne [AUNE].

aulx [o:], [AIL].

aumône [o'moːn], *n.f.* alms, alms-giving; (*fig.*) charity, favor.

aumônerie [omon'ri], *n.f.* chaplaincy.

aumônier [omo'nje], *n.m.* (*Eccles.*) almoner, chaplain; *aumônier militaire*, army chap-lain, padre.

aunaie *or* **aulnaie** [o'nɛ], *n.f.* grove of alders.

aune (1) *or* **aulne** [oːn], *n.m.* alder tree.

aune (2) [oːn], *n.f.* ell; (*fig.*) measure, standard.

aunée [o'ne], *n.f.* length of an ell.

auparavant [opara'vã], *adv.* before, formerly previously.

auprès [o'prɛ], *adv.* near, by, close by.— *prep. auprès de*, near to, close to; in com-parison with; in the service of; in the opinion of.

auquel [o'kɛl], *contraction* of À LEQUEL (*fem.* à laquelle, *pl.* auxquels, auxquelles) to whom, to which.

auréole [ore'ɔl], *n.f.* aureole, halo, nimbus; (*fig.*) glory, prestige.

auréoler [oreɔ'le], *v.t.* to crown with a halo.

auriculaire [oriky'lɛːr], *a.* auricular.—*n.m.* the little finger.

auricule [ori'kyl], *n.f.* lower lobe of the ear, auricle; (*Bot.*) auricula.

auriculiste [oriky'list], *n.m.* ear specialist.

aurifère [ori'fɛːr], *a.* auriferous.

auriste [ɔ'rist], *n.m.* ear specialist.

aurore [ɔ'rɔːr], *n.f.* dawn, morn, daybreak; (*fig.*) promise, beginning, the East; (*Astron.*) aurora.

auscultation [oskylta'sjɔ̃], *n.f.* (*Med.*) auscul-tation.

ausculter [oskyl'te], *v.t.* to sound a patient.

auspice [os'pis], *n.m.* auspice, omen, presage; (*pl.*) protection, patronage.

aussi [o'si], *adv.* also, likewise, too, besides; as; so.—*conj.* and so, accordingly, therefore, consequently; but then.

aussière [o'sjɛːr], *n.f.* (*Naut.*) hawser.

aussitôt [osi'to], *adv.* immediately, forthwith. —*conj. aussitôt que*, as soon as.

austère [os'tɛːr], *a.* austere, severe, stern.

austèrement [oster'mã], *adv.* austerely.

austérité [osteri'te], *n.f.* austerity; severity; strictness.

austral [os'tral], *a.* (*m. pl.* -als *or* -aux) austral, southern.

Australasie [ostrala'zi], *l'*, *f.* Australasia.

australasien [ostrala'zjɛ̃], *a.* (*fem.* -enne) Australasian.

Australie [ostra'li], *l'*, *f.* Australia.

australien [ostra'ljɛ̃], *a.* (*fem.* -enne) Austra-lian.—*n.m.* (**Australien**, *fem.* -enne) Aus-tralian (*person*).

autant [o'tã], *adv.* as much, so much, as many, so many; *autant de têtes, autant d'avis*, there are as many opinions as there are men; *autant que*, as much as, as many as, as far as, in the same way as; *d'autant*, in the same proportion; *d'autant mieux* or *d'autant plus*, the more, so much the more.—*conj. d'autant que*, seeing that, since, more especially as.

autel [o'tɛl], *n.m.* altar; (*fig.*) ministry, Church, religious life.

auteur [o'tœːr], *n.m.* author, creator, maker; writer (*of a book etc.*); perpetrator; achiever, contriver, framer; composer, sculptor; informant, authority; *droit d'auteur*, royalty.

authenticité [otãtisi'te], *n.f.* authenticity, genuineness.

authentique [otã'tik], *a.* authenticated, genuine, incontestable, positive.

authentiquement [otãtik'mã], *adv.* authentically.

authentiquer [otãti'ke], *v.t.* to authenticate; (*Law*) to make legal and binding.

auto [o'to], *n.f. abbr.* [AUTOMOBILE].

auto-allumage [otoaly'maːʒ], *n.m.* knocking (*of a car*).

autobiographe [otɔbjo'graf], *n.m.* autobiographer.

autobiographie [otɔbjɔgra'fi], *n.f.* autobiography.

autobiographique [otɔbjɔgra'fik], *a.* autobiographical.

autobus [oto'bys], *n.m.* bus.

autocar [oto'kaːr], *n.m.* motor coach.

autochenille [oto'ʃniːj], *n.f.* caterpillar tractor; half-track vehicle.

autoclave [oto'klaːv], *a.* and *n.m.* vacuum pan, sterilizer; *marmite autoclave*, autoclave, digester; pressure cooker.

autocopie [otoko'pi], *n.f.* cyclostyling.

autocopier [otoko'pje], *v.t.* to cyclostyle.

autocopiste [otoko'pist], *n.m.* duplicator, cyclostyle.

autocrate [oto'krat], *n.m.* autocrat.

autocratie [otokra'si], *n.f.* autocracy.

autocratique [otɔkra'tik], *a.* autocratic.

autocratiquement [otokratik'mã], *adv.* autocratically.

autocritique [otokri'tik], *n.f.* self-criticism.

auto-cuiseur [otokɥi'zœːr], *n.m.* pressure cooker.

autodidacte [otodi'dakt], *n.* self-taught person.

autodrome [oto'droːm], *n.m.* race-track for motor cars.

auto-école [otoe'kɔl], *n.f.* school of motoring.

autogare [oto'gaːr], *n.f.* bus or coach station.

autographe [oto'graf], *a.* autographic.—*n.m.* autograph.

autographie [otogra'fi], *n.f.* autography.

autographier [otogra'fje], *v.t.* to autograph.

autogyre [oto'ʒiːr], *n.m.* autogyro.

automate [oto'mat], *n.m.* automaton, robot.

automation [otoma'sjɔ̃], *n.f.* automation.

automatique [otoma'tik], *a.* automatic; *distributeur automatique*, (penny-in-the-) slot machine; *machine à vente automatique*, vending machine.—*n.m.* l'*Automatique*, automatic telephone.

automatiquement [otomatik'mã], *adv.* automatically.

automatisme [otoma'tism], *n.m.* automatism, purely mechanical movement.

automitrailleuse [otomitra'jøːz], *n.f.* light armored car.

automnal [otɔ'nal], *a.* (*m. pl.* -aux) autumnal.

automne [o'tɔn], *n.m.* or *f.* autumn.

automobile [otomɔ'bil], *a.* self-moving, self-propelling; *canot automobile*, motor-boat.—*n.f.* motor car; *salon de l'automobile*, motor show.

automobilisme [otomɔbi'lism], *n.m.* automobilism, motoring.

automobiliste [otomɔbi'list], *n.* motorist.

automoteur [otomɔ'tœːr], *a.* (*fem.* -trice) self-acting, self-moving, self-propelling.

(C) **auto-neige** [oto'nɛːʒ], *n.f.* snowmobile.

autonome [oto'nɔm], *a.* autonomous.

autonomie [otono'mi], *n.f.* autonomy, self-government; cruising range.

autonomiste [otono'mist], *n.m.* autonomist.

autoplastie [otoplas'ti], *n.f.* (*Surg.*) plastic surgery.

auto-portrait [otopɔr'trɛ], *n.m.* self-portrait.

auto-propulsé [otoprɔpyl'se], *a.* self-propelled.

auto-propulsion [otoprɔpyl'sjɔ̃], *n.f.* self-propulsion.

autopsie [otop'si], *n.f.* autopsy; post-mortem examination.

autorail [oto'raːj], *n.m.* rail car.

autorisation [otorizɑ'sjɔ̃], *n.f.* authorization; authority, warrant; written consent or permission, license (*of a preacher*).

autoriser [otori'ze], *v.t.* to authorize, to empower, to commission; to license, to warrant, to permit, to sanction. **s'autoriser**, *v.r.* to have, get or assume authority; to act on the authority (*of*), to be warranted by (*de*).

autoritaire [otori'tɛːr], *a.* and *n.* authoritative, commanding, arbitrary (person).

autoritairement [otoritɛr'mã], *adv.* authoritatively.

autorité [otori'te], *n.f.* authority, legal or legitimate power; an authority; (*fig.*) control.

autoroute [oto'rut], *n.f.* motorway; (*Am.*) speedway.

auto-stop [oto'stɔp], *n.m.* hitch-hiking; *faire de l'auto-stop*, to hitch-hike.

autostrade [oto'strad], *n.f.* special road for motor cars, motorway.

autosuggestion [otosygʒɛs'tjɔ̃], *n.f.* auto-suggestion.

autour (1) [o'tuːr], *adv.* about, round about.—*prep. phr.* autour de, about, round, around.

autour (2) [o'tuːr], *n.m.* (*Orn.*) goshawk.

autre [o:tr], *a.* other; second; another different, distinct (*but of the same kind*).—*pron. indef.* another person, someone else; (*pl.*) the others, the rest.

autrefois [otrə'fwa], *adv.* formerly, in former times; of old; *d'autrefois*, former, bygone; *des mœurs d'autrefois*, bygone customs.

autrement [otrə'mã], *adv.* otherwise, after another manner; else; or else; *autrement dit*, in other words.

Autriche [o'triʃ], l', *f.* Austria.

autrichien [otri'ʃjɛ̃], *a.* (*fem.* -enne) Austrian.—*n.m.* (**Autrichien**, *fem.* -enne) Austrian (person).

autruche [o'tryʃ], *n.f.* ostrich.

autrucherie [otryʃ'ri], *n.f.* ostrich farm.

autrui [o'trɥi], *pron. indef. inv.* others, other people, one's or our neighbors.

auvent [o'vã], *n.m.* weather-board, porch roof; *auvent de capot*, hood louver.

aux [o], *pl.* [AU].

auxiliaire [oksi'ljɛːr], *a.* auxiliary, aiding, subsidiary.—*n.* auxiliary; helper, assistant.

auxquels [o'kɛl], *pl.* (*fem.* -elles) [AUQUEL].

avachi [ava'ʃi], *a.* out of shape, worn out; (*fam.*) flabby, floppy, downcast (*of a person*).

33

avachir (s') [ava'ʃiːr], *v.r.* to flag; to grow fat and flabby; to get out of shape *or* down at heel.

avachissement [avaʃis'mɑ̃], *n.m.* flabbiness; lack of energy.

aval (1) [a'val], *n.m.* (*pl.* **avals**) guarantee, endorsement.

aval (2) [a'val], *n.m.* down stream; *en aval de*, below.

avalaison [avalɛ'zɔ̃], **avalasse** [ava'las], *n.f.* sudden flood, spate; (*Naut.*) a long-continued wind from the sea.

avalanche [ava'lɑ̃ːʃ], *n.f.* avalanche.

avalasse (AVALAISON).

avalement [aval'mɑ̃], *n.m.* descent, lowering, letting down; swallowing.

avaler [ava'le], *v.t.* to swallow, to swallow down; to drink; to gulp down; to let down, to lower (*things into a cellar*); (*fig.*) to endure, to pocket (*an affront*); to believe.—*v.i.* to go down (*a river etc. with the stream*).

avaliser [avali'ze], *v.t.* to guarantee, to endorse (AVAL (1)).

avance [a'vɑ̃ːs], *n.f.* part of a building etc. projecting forwards; advance; start, distance in advance; payment of money in advance; (*fig., pl.*) attentions, first steps in an acquaintanceship.

avancé [avɑ̃'se], *a.* advanced, forward, early; late (*of the hour*); over-ripe, tainted, high; liberal, progressive (*of opinions etc.*); paid in advance; put forward, enunciated.

avancement [avɑ̃s'mɑ̃], *n.m.* projection; progress, advancement; preferment, promotion, rise.

avancer [avɑ̃'se], *v.t.* (*conjug. like* COMMENCER) to move, bring, put *or* hold forward, to advance; to pay beforehand *or* in advance; to assert, to bring forward, to urge; to promote, to give promotion to; to advantage, to profit; (*fig.*) to bring nearer, to hasten, to forward; to put on (*a clock*).—*v.i.* to advance, to proceed, to keep on; to project, to jut out; to make progress, to thrive, to get on, to gain ground; to go too fast; *l'horloge avance*, the clock is fast. **s'avancer**, *v.r.* to advance, to go on, to move forward; to get on, to improve; to get promoted, to be successful; to grow old; to project.

avanie [ava'ni], *n.f.* insult, affront; snub.

avant [a'vɑ̃], *prep.* before, in advance of (*of time and order*); *avant J.-C.*, B.C.—*adv.* before, previously; forward, in front; farther in advance.—*conj. avant que*, before; *en avant!* forward!—*n.m.* front; prow, head, bow (*of a ship*); (*Ftb.*) forward.

avantage [avɑ̃'taːʒ], *n.m.* advantage, benefit, profit, superiority, whip-hand; (*Ten.*) advantage, vantage.

avantager [avɑ̃ta'ʒe], *v.t.* (*conjug. like* MANGER) to advantage, to give an advantage to; to favor. **s'avantager**, *v.r.* to take advantage.

avantageusement [avɑ̃taʒøz'mɑ̃], *adv.* advantageously, to advantage; usefully, favorably.

avantageux [avɑ̃ta'ʒø], *a.* (*fem.* **-euse**) advantageous, profitable, favorable; conceited, presumptuous; (*of dress*) becoming.

[In *pl.* of the following compounds *avant* is *inv.* The *n.* has its normal *pl.*]

avant-bassin [avɑ̃ba'sɛ̃], *n.m.* outer dock.

avant-bras [avɑ̃'bra], *n.m. inv.* forearm.

avant-centre [avɑ̃'sɑ̃ːtr], *n.m.* (*Ftb.*) centre-forward.

avant-corps [avɑ̃'koːr], *n.m. inv.* (*Arch.*) forepart (*of a building*).

avant-cour [avɑ̃'kuːr], *n.f.* fore-court.

avant-coureur [avɑ̃ku'rœːr], *a.* going in front, preceding, presaging.—*n.m.* forerunner, precursor, harbinger.

avant-courrier [avɑ̃ku'rje], *n.m.* (*fem.* **-ière**) (*fig.*) herald, forerunner, harbinger.

avant-dernier [avɑ̃dɛr'nje], *a.* and *n.m.* (*fem.* **-ière**) the last but one.

avant-garde [avɑ̃'gard], *n.f.* vanguard, van.

avant-goût [avɑ̃'gu], *n.m.* foretaste; earnest; anticipation.

avant-guerre [avɑ̃'gɛːr], *n.m.* the pre-war period.

avant-hier [avɑ̃'tjɛːr], *adv.* and *n.m.* the day before yesterday.

avant-main [avɑ̃'mɛ̃], *n.m.* flat of the hand; forehand (*of a horse*); (*Ten.*) forehand (stroke); (*Cards*) lead.

avant-port [avɑ̃'poːr], *n.m.* outer harbor, tide dock.

avant-poste [avɑ̃'pɔst], *n.m.* (*Mil.*) advanced post, outpost; (*fig.*) outer defence.

avant-première [avɑ̃prə'mjɛːr], *n.f.* dress rehearsal; (*Cine.*) preview.

avant-projet [avɑ̃prɔ'ʒe], *n.m.* rough draft.

avant-propos [avɑ̃prɔ'po], *n.m. inv.* preface, preamble, introduction, foreword.

avant-scène [avɑ̃'sɛːn], *n.f.* front of the stage (*between curtain and orchestra*), proscenium.

avant-toit [avɑ̃'twa], *n.m.* eaves.

avant-train [avɑ̃'trɛ̃], *n.m.* fore-carriage, limber.

avant-veille [avɑ̃'vɛːj], *n.f.* two days before.

avare [a'vaːr], *a.* avaricious, miserly, covetous, stingy, close-fisted.—*n.m.* miser, niggard.

avarement [avar'mɑ̃], *adv.* stingily.

avariable [ava'rjabl], *a.* perishable, damageable.

avarice [ava'ris], *n.f.* avarice, greed, covetousness; niggardliness, stinginess.

avaricieusement [avarisjøz'mɑ̃], *adv.* avariciously.

avaricieux [avari'sjø], *a.* (*fem.* **-euse**) avaricious, covetous, stingy.

avarie [ava'ri], *n.f.* damage (*to a ship or cargo*); deterioration.

avarié [ava'rje], *a.* damaged, spoiled, deteriorated.

avarier [ava'rje], *v.t.* to damage, to spoil. **s'avarier**, *v.r.* to become damaged.

avec [a'vɛk], *prep.* with, at the same time as, along *or* together with; by means of, by; regarding; against, in spite of; *avec ça!* (*colloq.*) nonsense!

aveline [a'vlin], *n.f.* filbert, Kentish cob.

avelinier [avli'nje], *n.m.* filbert tree, hazel tree.

aven [a'vɛ̃], *n.m.* pothole, swallow, chasm (*in mountain limestone*).

avenant [av'nɑ̃], *a.* personable, prepossessing, comely, pleasing, taking.—*adv. phr. à l'avenant*, in keeping, in the same proportions, of a piece.—*n.m.* additional clause (*to an insurance policy*); rider (*to a verdict*); codicil (*to a treaty*).

avènement [avɛn'mã], *n.m.* coming, advent; accession, succession (*to a throne etc.*).

avenir [av'ni:r], *n.m.* future, future ages; posterity; (*fig.*) prospects; **à l'avenir**, in future, henceforth.

Avent [a'vã], *n.m.* (*Ch.*) Advent.

aventure [avã'ty:r], *n.f.* surprising *or* unexpected event *or* experience, chance, accident, luck; adventure, daring enterprise, hazardous exploit; love affair *or* intrigue; **à l'aventure**, at random; **d'aventure** or **par aventure**, by chance, perchance.

aventurer [avãty're], *v.t.* to venture, to hazard, to risk. **s'aventurer**, *v.r.* to venture, to take one's chance, to take risks.

aventureux [avãty'rø], *a.* (*fem.* **-euse**) venturesome, adventurous; left to chance.

aventurier [avãty'rje], *n.m.* (*fem.* **-ière**) adventurer, adventuress.

avenue [av'ny], *n.f.* approach; avenue.

avéré [ave'rе], *a.* authenticated, established by evidence.

avérer [ave're], *v.t.* (*conjug. like* CÉDER) to verify, to confirm, to establish. **s'avérer**, *v.r.* (*used only in inf. and p.p.*) to appear, to be distinctly, to turn out to be, to prove.

avers [a've:r], *n.m.* obverse (*of coins etc.*).

averse [a'vɛrs], *n.f.* sudden and heavy shower of rain, downpour; (*fig.*) flood (*of talk etc.*).

aversion [avɛr'sjõ], *n.f.* aversion, dislike, detestation.

averti [avɛr'ti], *a.* warned, informed; wide awake; well-informed, experienced.

avertir [avɛr'ti:r], *v.t.* to inform, to acquaint with, to give notice, to warn, to admonish (*de*).

avertissement [avɛrtis'mã], *n.m.* information, notification, advice, warning, caution; **avertissement au lecteur**, foreword (*of a book*).

avertisseur [avɛrti'sœ:r], *n.m.* look-out man; (*Theat.*) callboy; call bell, hooter; **avertisseur d'incendie**, fire-alarm.

aveu [a'vø], *n.m.* (*pl.* **-eux**) admission, avowal, confession; approbation, consent; **homme sans aveu**, vagrant, vagabond.

aveuglant [avœ'glã], *a.* blinding, dazzling; (*fig.*) distracting, misleading.

aveugle [a'vœgl], *a.* blind, sightless; blinded by passion etc., deluded.—*n.* blind person.

aveuglement [avœglə'mã], *n.m.* blindness; (*fig.*) infatuation, delusion.

aveuglément [avœglе'mã], *adv.* blindly, rashly; implicitly.

aveugle-né [avœglə'ne], *a.* and *n.m.* (*fem.* **-née**, *pl.* **aveugles-nés**) blind from birth.

aveugler [avœ'gle], *v.t.* to blind, to make blind; (*fig.*) to dazzle; to delude. **s'aveugler**, *v.r.* to shut one's eyes (*to*); (*fig.*) to be blinded, to be infatuated.

aveuglette [avœ'glɛt], *n.f.* (*only used in*) **à l'aveuglette**, blindly; **aller à l'aveuglette**, to go groping along, to go blindly *or* rashly; (*Av.*) **voler à l'aveuglette**, to fly blind.

aveulir [avœ'li:r], *v.t.* to render weak, to enfeeble, to enervate. **s'aveulir**, *v.r.* to sink into sloth.

aveulissant [avœli'sã], *a.* enfeebling, enervating.

aveulissement [avœlis'mã], *n.m.* enfeeblement, enervation.

aviateur [avja'tœ:r], *n.m.* (*fem.* **-trice**) aviator; air-man, air-woman; flyer.

aviation [avja'sjõ], *n.f.* aviation; **terrain d'aviation**, flying ground, airfield.

aviculteur [avikyl'tœ:r], *n.m.* one who raises birds *or* poultry; bird fancier.

aviculture [avikyl'ty:r], *n.f.* bird raising; poultry farming.

avide [a'vid], *a.* greedy, voracious, rapacious; eager for, grasping.

avidement [avid'mã], *adv.* greedily, voraciously; eagerly.

avidité [avidi'te], *n.f.* avidity, greediness, eagerness.

avilir [avi'li:r], *v.t.* to debase, to depreciate, to disparage; to lower; to degrade, to disgrace. **s'avilir**, *v.r.* to degrade oneself, to stoop to (*doing something*).

avilissant [avili'sã], *a.* debasing, degrading, humiliating.

avilissement [avilis'mã], *n.m.* debasement, degradation; depreciation, disparagement.

avilisseur [avili'sœ:r], *a.* (*fem.* **-euse**) debasing, degrading.—*n.m.* (*fem.* **-euse**) one who debases, disparages *or* degrades.

aviné [avi'ne], *a.* drunk, unsteady (*from drink*); wine-soaked (*of a cask*).

aviner [avi'ne], *v.t.* to soak *or* fill with wine. **s'aviner**, *v.r.* to get drunk.

avion [a'vjõ], *n.m.* airplane, aircraft; **avion de bombardement**, bomber; **avion de chasse**, fighter; **avion de ligne**, airliner; **avion à réaction**, jet-plane; **avion-fusée**, rocket-plane; **avion-taxi**, charter-plane; **par avion**, by air, by air mail.

aviron [avi'rõ], *n.m.* oar; (*Spt.*) rowing.

avis [a'vi], *n.m.* opinion, way of thinking, judgment; vote, motion; advice, counsel; information, notice, warning, caution, intelligence; **à mon avis**, in my opinion; **j'ai changé d'avis**, I have changed my mind; **avis au public**, notice.

avisé [avi'ze], *a.* shrewd, clear-sighted, wary, circumspect, prudent.

aviser [avi'ze], *v.t.* to perceive, to espy; to inform, to apprise; (*Comm.*) to advise by letter.—*v.i.* to consider, to think (*about*), to look (*to*). **s'aviser**, *v.r.* to think (*of*), to be minded (*to*); to venture to do.

avivage [avi'va:ʒ], *n.m.* brightening, reviving (*of colors*).

aviver [avi've], *v.t.* to revive, to brighten; to sharpen the edges of, to polish, to burnish; to irritate, to exacerbate (*a wound, resentment etc.*). **s'aviver**, *v.r.* to revive.

avocat (1) [avo'ka], *n.m.* (*fem.* **-e**) barrister, advocate, counsel; (*fig.*) pleader, intercessor, champion.

avocat (2) [avo'ka], *n.m.* avocado, alligator pear.

avoine [a'vwan], *n.f.* oats.

avoir [a'vwa:r], *v.t.* *irr.* to have, to possess; to experience, to feel (*pain, hunger etc.*); to obtain, to get, to buy etc.; to be aged (*so many years*); to have on, to wear; to ail; **avoir à**, to have to, to be under obligation to (*do etc.*); **y avoir** (*impers.*), to be; **avoir faim**, to be hungry; **combien y a-t-il de Paris à Londres?** how far is it from Paris to London? **il a quarante ans**, he is forty; **il n'y a pas de quoi**, don't mention it, no offence taken; **il y a deux mois que je**

suis ici, I have been here two months; *il est arrivé il y a trois semaines*, he arrived three weeks ago; *j'ai à vous parler*, I have something to tell you; *qu'avez-vous donc?* what's the matter? *quel âge avez-vous?* how old are you? *qu'est-ce que vous avez?* what is the matter with you? *la pièce a cinq mètres de large*, the room is fifteen feet wide.—*n.m.* possessions, property, what one is worth.

avoisinant [avwazi'nɑ̃], *a.* neighboring, adjoining, close by.

avoisiner [avwazi'ne], *v.t.* to border upon, to be contiguous to.

avortement [avɔrtə'mɑ̃], *n.m.* abortion, miscarriage; failure.

avorter [avɔr'te], *v.i.* to miscarry, to have a miscarriage; to fail to develop, ripen etc. (*of plants, fruit etc.*); to prove abortive, to fail.

avorton [avɔr'tɔ̃], *n.m.* abortion; abortive child; (*fig.*) a paltry *or* miserable person *or* thing, a miserable specimen.

avoué [a'vwe], *n.m.* attorney, solicitor; *une étude d'avoué*, a solicitor's office.

avouer [a'vwe], *v.t.* to own, to acknowledge, to confess; to approve; to recognize as one's own, to avow.

avril [a'vril], *n.m.* April.

avunculaire [avɔ̃ky'lɛːr], *a.* avuncular.

axe [aks], *n.m.* axis; axle, axle-tree, spindle, trunnion; (*Bot., Geol., Anat. etc.*) axis; (*fig.*) central support *or* main axis of a system of ideas etc.; (*Polit.*) the Nazi-Fascist Axis.

axiomatique [aksjɔma'tik], *a.* axiomatic.

axiome [ak'sjoːm], *n.m.* axiom; (*fig.*) an accepted proposition, truism.

ayant [ɛ'jɑ̃], *pres. p.* [AVOIR].

ayant cause [ɛjɑ̃'koːz], *n.m.* (*pl.* **ayants cause**) (*Law*) trustee, executor, assign.

ayant droit [ɛjɑ̃'drwa], *n.m.* (*pl.* **ayants droit**) beneficiary, rightful claimant.

azalée [aza'le], *n.f.* azalea.

azotate [azo'tat], *n.m.* nitrate.

azote [a'zɔt], *a.* nitric.—*n.m.* nitrogen.

azoté [azo'te], *a.* nitrogenized.

azoter [azo'te], *v.t.* to charge with nitrogen; to azotize.

azoteux [azo'tø], *a.* (*fem.* **-euse**) nitrous.

azotique [azo'tik], *a.* nitric.

azur [a'zyːr], *n.m.* azure, blue, sky-color; washing blue; *la Côte d'Azur*, the French Riviera.

azuré [azy're], *a.* azure, sky-colored; *la voûte azurée*, the azure skies.

azyme [a'zim], *a.* azymous, unleavened (*bread*).—*n.m.* azyme, unleavened bread; *fête des azymes*, feast of unleavened bread.

B

B, b [be], *n.m.* the second letter of the alphabet.

baba [ba'ba], *n.m.* a sponge cake, with sultanas, steeped in rum and syrup.

Babel [ba'bɛl], *n.f.* Babel; (*fig.*) uproar, disorder.

babeurre [ba'bœːr], *n.m.* buttermilk.

babil [ba'bi], *n.m.* babble, prattle; chit-chat, tattle; chattering, babbling.

babillage [babi'jaːʒ], **babillement** [babij'mɑ̃], *n.m.* prattle, babbling, twaddle; tittle-tattle.

babillard [babi'jaːr], *a.* babbling, prattling, talkative, garrulous; gossiping, tell-tale.—*n.m.* (*fem.* **-e**) chatterer, babbler; tattler, blabber, gossip, tell-tale.

babillement [BABILLAGE].

babiller [babi'je], *v.i.* to babble, to prattle, to chat; to gossip, to chatter; (*fig.*) to blab, to backbite.

babine [ba'bin], **babouine** [ba'bwin], *n.f.* the pendulous lip (*of certain animals*); (*colloq.*) chops.

babiole [ba'bjɔl], *n.f.* bauble, trinket, toy; (*fig.*) trifle, trumpery affair.

bâbord [bɑ'bɔːr], *n.m.* (*Naut.*) port (*side*).

babouche [ba'buʃ], *n.f.* Turkish heelless slipper, babouche.

babouin [ba'bwɛ̃], *n.m.* baboon, monkey.

Babylone [babi'lɔn], *f.* Babylon.

babylonien [babilɔ'njɛ̃], *a.* (*fem.* **-enne**) Babylonian.—*n.m.* (**Babylonien**, *fem.* **-enne**) Babylonian (*person*).

bac [bak], *n.m.* ferry, ferry-boat; vat; (*Elec.*) *bac d'accumulateurs*, accumulator-jar.

baccalauréat [bakalɔre'a], *n.m.* baccalaureate, bachelorship (*of arts, science etc.*), school-leaving certificate.

bacchanal [baka'nal], *n.m.* (*colloq.*) racket, uproar.

bacchante [ba'kɑ̃ːt], *n.f.* bacchante, lewd woman.

bâche [bɑːʃ], *n.f.* cart tilt; awning; tank, cistern; *bâche (goudronnée)*, tarpaulin.

bachelier [baʃə'lje], *n.m.* (*fem.* **-ière**) Bachelor (*ès Lettres, ès Sciences, of Arts, Science*).

bachique [ba'ʃik], *a.* bacchic, jovial, convivial; *chant bachique*, drinking song.

bachot [ba'ʃo], *n.m.* wherry, small ferry-boat; (*Univ. slang*) bachot.

bachoteur [baʃo'tœːr], *n.m.* ferryman.

bacille [ba'sil], *n.m.* (*Biol.*) bacillus; *porteur de bacilles*, germ carrier.

bacillose [basi'loːz], [TUBERCULOSE].

bâclage [bɑ'klaːʒ], *n.m.* closing of a port by means of chains, booms etc.; line of boats (*in a port*) for the discharge *or* loading of cargo; (*fig.*) hasty, scamped work.

bâcle [bɑːkl], *n.f.* bar (*for door or gate*).

bâcler [bɑ'kle], *v.t.* to bar, fasten *or* secure (*a door, window etc.*); to stop, obstruct *or* interrupt (*traffic, navigation etc.*); (*fig.*) to do hastily, to polish off, to scamp (*work*); to bungle.

bactérie [bakte'ri], *n.f.* bacterium, microbe.

bactérien [bakte'rjɛ̃], *a.* (*fem.* **-enne**) bacterial.

bactériologie [bakterjolɔ'ʒi], *n.f.* bacteriology.

bactériologique [bakterjolɔ'ʒik], *a.* bacteriological; *guerre bactériologique*, germ warfare.

bactériologiste [bakterjolɔ'ʒist], *n.m.* bacteriologist.

bactériothérapie [bakterjotera'pi], *n.f.* medical treatment by means of bacteria.

badaud [ba'do], *n.m.* (*fem.* -**e**) ninny, booby, star-gazer; lounger, idler, rubber-neck.

badaudage [bado'da:ʒ], *n.m.* star-gazing, lounging, loitering, idling.

badauder [bado'de], *v.i.* to go gaping about; to lounge, to saunter, to loiter.

badauderie [bado'dri], *n.f.* star-gazing, silliness; lounging, idling, sauntering.

Bade [bad], *f.* Baden.

badigeon [badi'ʒɔ̃], *n.m.* badigeon, filling paste; whitewash; calcimine.

badigeonnage [badiʒɔ'na:ʒ], *n.m.* filling up with badigeon, making up; daubing; whitewashing.

badigeonner [badiʒɔ'ne], *v.t.* to fill up (*stone-work, sculpture etc.*) with badigeon; to whitewash; (*fig.*) to disguise defects with varnish, rouge etc.; (*Med.*) to anoint.

badigeonneur [badiʒɔ'nœ:r], *n.m.* white-washer; (*pej.*) dauber.

badin [ba'dɛ̃], *a.* waggish, jocular, roguish, droll.—*n.m.* (*fem.* -**e** (1)) wag, joker; buffoon.

badinage [badi'na:ʒ], *n.m.* badinage, raillery, banter; playfulness, jocularity (*of style*); mere child's-play.

badine [ba'din], *n.f.* switch, light cane, wand; (*pl.*) small tongs.

badiner [badi'ne], *v.i.* to trifle, to dally, to toy; to speak *or* write banteringly *or* playfully.

badinerie [badin'ri], *n.f.* jesting, foolery, trifling; silliness, childishness.

(C) **bâdrant** [ba'drã], *a.* bothersome.

(C) **bâdrer** [ba'dre], *v.t.* to annoy, to bother.

bafouer [ba'fwe], *v.t.* to scoff at, to make game of.

bafouillage [bafu'ja:ʒ], *n.f.* gibberish, rigmarole; spluttering; bad running (*of engine*).

bafouiller [bafu'je], *v.i.* (*colloq.*) to stammer; to splutter; to miss, to chatter (*of engine*).

bafouilleur [bafu'jœ:r], *n.m.* (*fem.* -**euse**) stammerer.

bagages [ba'ga:ʒ], *n.m. pl.* luggage; *bagages enregistrés*, checked luggage.

bagarre [ba'ga:r], *n.f.* riot; uproar; crush, squabble, scuffle.

bagatelle [baga'tɛl], *n.f.* bauble, trinket, trifle, anything frivolous; trifling sum, mere nothing.

bagne [baɲ], *n.m.* penitentiary; penal servitude.

bagnole [ba'ɲɔl], *n.f.* (*fam.*) (old) motor car.

bague [bag], *n.f.* ring; ring band (*for birds*).

bague-agrafe [bags'graf], *n.f.* (*d'un stylo*) (fountain-pen) clip.

baguer [ba'ge], *v.t.* to baste, to tack, to stitch; to decorate or bind with rings; (*Hort.*) to ring (*trees*); to ring (*a bird*).

baguette [ba'gɛt], *n.f.* switch, rod, wand; pointer; clock (*of stockings*); glove-stretcher; long roll (*French bread*).

baguier [ba'gje], *n.m.* casket for rings, jewels etc., jewel box, ring stand.

bah! [ba], *int.* pooh! pshaw! nonsense! fudge!

bahut [ba'y], *n.m.* cabinet, trunk, chest; press, cupboard; (*Sch. slang*) grammar school.

bahutier [bay'tje], *n.m.* maker of trunks, chests, cabinets, etc.

bai [bɛ], *a.* bay; *une jument baie*, a bay mare.

baie (1) [bɛ], *n.f.* bay, gulf; (*Arch.*) bay, opening.

baie (2) [bɛ], *n.f.* berry.

baignade [bɛ'ɲad], *n.f.* bathing; bathing place.

baigner [bɛ'ɲe], *v.t.* to bathe, to give a bath to, to dip; (*fig.*) to wash, to water (*a coast etc.*); to wet, to suffuse.—*v.i.* to be plunged into; to welter (*in blood etc.*). **se baigner**, *v.r.* to bathe, to wash.

baigneur [bɛ'ɲœ:r], *n.m.* (*fem.* -**euse**) bather; bathkeeper *or* attendant, bathing attendant.

baignoire [bɛ'ɲwa:r], *n.f.* bathtub, bath; (*Theat.*) ground-floor box.

bail [ba:j], *n.m.* (*pl.* **baux** [bo]) lease.

bâillement [baj'mã], *n.m.* yawning, yawn.

bâiller [ba'je], *v.i.* to yawn, to gape; to open (*of fissures etc.*); to be ajar (*of doors*).

bailleur [ba'jœ:r], *n.m.* (*fem.* -**eresse**) one who leases, lessor.

bâilleur [ba'jœ:r], *n.m.* (*fem.* -**euse**) yawner; gaper.

bailli [ba'ji], *n.m.* (*Fr. Hist.*) bailiff.

bâillon [ba'jɔ̃], *n.m.* gag, muzzle.

bâillonnement [bajɔn'mã], *n.m.* gagging.

bâillonner [bajɔ'ne], *v.t.* to stop the mouth of, to gag, to muzzle; (*fig.*) to silence.

bain [bɛ̃], *n.m.* bath; bathing tub; (*pl.*) baths, bathing establishment, watering place, spa; *la salle de bain(s)*, the bathroom.

bain-douche [bɛ̃'duʃ], *n.m.* shower bath.

bain-marie [bɛma'ri], *n.m.* (*pl.* **bains-marie**) (*Cook.*) double saucepan for foods that burn easily; boiler (*in a kitchen range etc.*).

baïonnette [bajɔ'nɛt], *n.f.* bayonet.

baiser [bɛ'ze], *v.t.* (*of strictly literary use, no longer decent in conversation, practically replaced by* **embrasser**) to kiss.—*n.m.* kiss, kissing; salute.

baisse [bɛ:s], *n.f.* fall, abatement, decline; reduction or fall (*of prices etc.*); falling off (*of credit etc.*).

baisser [bɛ'se], *v.t.* to let down, to lower; to reduce the height of; to strike (*a flag etc.*); to bow (*the head etc.*).—*v.i.* (*with aux.* ÊTRE *or* AVOIR) to go down; to ebb; to be on the decline or the wane; to flag, to droop; to fail, to diminish. **se baisser**, *v.r.* to stoop, to bow down; to be lowered.

bajoue [ba'ʒu], *n.f.* jowl, chap (*of pigs etc.*); full and pendulous cheek.

bakélite [bake'lit], *n.f.* bakelite (*trade mark*)

bal [bal], *n.m.* ball, dance; *bal costumé*, fancy-dress ball.

baladeuse [bala'dø:z], *n.f.* street vendor's barrow; portable lamp; trailer (*for cycle or tram*).

baladin [bala'dɛ̃], *n.m.* (*fem.* -**e**) mountebank; buffoon.

balafre [ba'la:fr], *n.f.* gash, slash, cut; scar.

balafrer [bala'fre], *v.t.* to gash, to slash.

balai (1) [ba'lɛ], *n.m.* broom, besom; (*Elec.*) brush.

(C) **balai** (2) [ba'lɛ], *n.m.* cedar.

balalaïka [balalai'ka], *n.f.* balalaika.

balance [ba'lã:s], *n.f.* balance, scales, pair of scales; (*Comm.*) balance (*of an account*), balance sheet.

balancement [balãs'mã], *n.m.* balancing, poising; rocking, see-saw; (*fig.*) fluctuation, wavering, hesitation.

balancer

balancer [balɑ̃'se], *v.t.* (*conjug. like* COM-MENCER) to balance, to poise, to hold in equilibrium; to swing to and fro, to rock; (*fig.*) to weigh, to consider; to square (*accounts*); to counterbalance.—*v.i.* to hesitate, to be in suspense, to waver; to fluctuate, to oscillate, to remain undecided. **se balancer** *v.r.* to swing, to rock.

balancier [balɑ̃'sje], *n.m.* maker of weights and scales; pendulum, balance; balancing-pole.

balançoire [balɑ̃'swa:r], *n.f.* see-saw; swing.

balandre [ba'lɑ̃:dr], *n.f.* flat canal boat.

balayage [balɛ'ja:ʒ], **balayement** [balɛ'mɑ̃], *n.m.* sweeping; (*Tel.*) scanning.

balayer [balɛ'je], *v.t.* (*conjug. like* PAYER) to sweep, to clean with a broom; (*Tel.*) to scan.

balayette [balɛ'jɛt], *n.f.* small broom, whisk.

balayeur [balɛ'jœ:r], *n.m.* (*fem.* -**euse**) sweeper, scavenger.—*n.f.* (-**euse**) sweeping-machine.

balayures [balɛ'jy:r], *n.f.* (*used only in pl.*) sweepings.

balbutier [balby'sje], *v.t.* to pronounce indistinctly.—*v.i.* to stammer, to stutter; to mumble.

balbutieur [balby'sjœ:r], *n.m.* (*fem.* -**euse**) stutterer, stammerer.

balcon [bal'kɔ̃], *n.m.* balcony; (*Theat.*) dress circle.

baldaquin [balda'kɛ̃], *n.m.* baldachin, canopy; tester (*of bed*).

Bâle [ba:l], *f.* Basel, Basle.

Baléares [balɛ'a:r], **les**, *f. pl.* the Balearic Isles.

baleine [ba'lɛ:n], *n.f.* whale; whalebone; rib of an umbrella.

baleiné [balɛ'ne], *a.* stiffened with whalebone.

baleineau [balɛ'no], *n.m.* (*pl.* -**eaux**) young whale.

baleinier [balɛ'nje], *n.m.* (*fem.* -**ière**) whaler.—*n.f.* (-**ière**) whaleboat.

balisage [bali'za:ʒ], *n.m.* (*Naut.*) buoying, signalling; (*Av.*) ground lights.

balise [ba'li:z], *n.f.* sea mark, buoy, beacon; (*Av.*) ground light.

baliser [bali'ze], *v.t.* to buoy; to mark with beacons *or* ground lights.

balistique [balis'tik], *a.* ballistic.—*n.f.* ballistics.

balivage [bali'va:ʒ], *n.m.* *staddling.

baliveau [bali'vo], *n.m.* (*pl.* -**eaux**) *staddle; sapling.

baliverne [bali'vɛrn], *n.f.* nonsense, humbug.

baliverner [balivɛr'ne], *v.i.* to talk idly, to talk twaddle.

balkanique [balka'nik], *a.* Balkan.

ballade [ba'lad], *n.f.* ballade; ballad.

ballant [ba'lɑ̃], *a.* waving, swinging, dangling.

ballast [ba'last], *n.m.* (*Rail.*) ballast.

balle [bal], *n.f.* ball; bullet, shot; bale, pack.

ballerine [bal'rin], *n.f.* ballerina.

ballet [ba'lɛ], *n.m.* ballet.

ballon [ba'lɔ̃], *n.m.* hand-ball; football; balloon; air balloon (*child's*).

ballonné [balɔ'ne], *a.* distended, swollen.

ballonnier [balɔ'nje], *n.m.* maker *or* vendor of toy balloons.

ballon-sonde [balɔ̃'sɔ̃:d], *n.m.* sounding balloon.

ballot [ba'lo], *n.m.* small pack (*of wares for sale*).

ballottement [balɔt'mɑ̃], *n.m.* tossing, shaking.

ballotter [balɔ'te], *v.t.* to toss, to toss about; to bandy; to keep in suspense.—*v.i.* to shake, to rattle.

balnéaire [balne'ɛ:r], *a.* pertaining to baths etc.; *station balnéaire*, watering place; seaside resort.

balourd [ba'lu:r], *a.* dull, heavy, thick-headed.—*n.m.* (*fem.* -**e**) stupid *or* dull person, numskull, dunce.

balourdise [balur'di:z], *n.f.* gross blunder; stupidity.

balsamier [balza'mje], **baumier** [bo'mje], *n.m.* balsam tree.

balsamine [balza'min], *n.f.* balsamine.

Baltique [bal'tik], **la**, *f.* the Baltic (Sea).

balustrade [balys'trad], *n.f.* balustrade; low railing etc.

balustre [ba'lystr], *n.m.* baluster, hand rail.

balustrer [balys'tre], *v.t.* to rail in, to surround.

balzane [bal'zan], *n.f.* white stocking (*of a horse*).

bambin [bɑ̃'bɛ̃], *n.m.* (*fem.* -**e**) (*colloq.*) urchin, brat, tiny tot.

bambou [bɑ̃'bu], *n.m.* bamboo (*cane*).

ban [bɑ̃], *n.m.* ban, announcement, public order, edict *or* proclamation; banishment, proscription; (*pl.*) banns (*of matrimony*).

banal [ba'nal], *a.* (*m. pl.* -**aux**) common, commonplace, trite.

banalité [banali'te], *n.f.* vulgarity; banality, commonplace, trite expression.

banane [ba'nan], *n.f.* banana.

bananier [bana'nje], *n.m.* banana tree; banana boat.

banc [bɑ̃], *n.m.* bench, settle, form; reef, sand bank; shoal (*of fish*); (*Geol.*) layer, bed; dock, bar; *banc d'essai*, (*Motor.*) test bench; (*C*) *banc de neige*, heap of snow; *banc d'huîtres*, oyster bed.

bancal [bɑ̃'kal], *a.* (*m. pl.* -**als**) bandy-legged.—*n.m.* (*fem.* -**e**) bandy-legged person.

bandage [bɑ̃'da:ʒ], *n.m.* application of bandages; bandage; belt; truss; tire (*of wheels*).

bande (1) [bɑ̃:d], *n.f.* band, belt, strip; ribbon; bandage; *bande de papier*, slip of paper, wrapper.

bande (2) [bɑ̃:d], *n.f.* band, troop, company; gang, crew, set (*of brigands etc.*); flock, pack.

bandé [bɑ̃'de], *a.* bandaged, taut, stretched.

bandeau [bɑ̃'do], *n.m.* (*pl.* -**eaux**) headband, bandage (*for the eyes*).

bandelette [bɑ̃'dlɛt], *n.f.* little band, string fillet.

bander [bɑ̃'de], *v.t.* to bind *or* tie up; to bandage; to tighten, to bend (*a bow etc.*).—*v.i.* to be stretched, to be taut *or* too tight.

banderole [bɑ̃'drɔl], *n.f.* banderole, streamer.

bandit [bɑ̃'di], *n.m.* brigand, bandit; ruffian, blackguard; scamp.

bandoulière [bɑ̃du'ljɛ:r], *n.f.* shoulder strap, bandolier; *en bandoulière*, slung across the back.

banjo [bɑ̃'ʒo], *n.m.* banjo.

banlieue [bɑ̃'lj ø], *n.f.* suburbs, outskirts (*of a town*).

banne [ban], *n.f.* hamper; awning; tilt, tarpaulin.

banni [ba'ni], *a.* banished, outlawed; (*fig.*) banned, forbidden.—*n.m.* (*fem.* **-e**) exile, outlaw.

bannière [ba'njɛːr], *n.f.* banner, standard, flag.

bannir [ba'niːr], *v.t.* to banish; (*fig.*) to expel, to dismiss.

bannissement [banis'mã], *n.m.* banishment.

banque [bãːk], *n.f.* bank, banking.

banqueroute [bã'krut], *n.f.* bankruptcy; (*fig.*) failure, collapse.

banqueroutier [bãkru'tje], *n.m.* (*fem.* **-ière**) bankrupt.

banquet [bã'kɛ], *n.m.* banquet, feast.

banquette [bã'kɛt], *n.f.* bench; towing path; (*Fort.*) banquette.

banquier [bã'kje], *n.m.* banker.

banquise [bã'kiːz], *n.f.* ice floe, ice pack.

bantam [bã'tam], *n.m.* bantam.

baptême [ba'tɛːm], *n.m.* baptism, christening; *nom de baptême,* Christian name.

baptiser [bati'ze], *v.t.* to baptize; (*fig.*) to christen, to give a name *or* nickname to.

baptismal [batiz'mal], *a.* (*m. pl.* **-aux**) baptismal.

baptistaire [batis'tɛːr], *a.* of baptism; *registre baptistaire,* parish register.

Baptiste [ba'tist], *n.m.* Baptist.

baquet [ba'kɛ], *n.m.* tub; (*Av.*) cockpit.

bar (1) [baːr], *n.m.* (*Ichth.*) bass.

bar (2) [baːr], *n.m.* bar (*of a public-house etc.*).

baragouin [bara'gwɛ̃], *n.m.* gibberish, jargon, lingo.

baragouinage [baragwi'naːʒ], *n.m.* talking, gibberish, jargon etc.

baragouiner [baragwi'ne], *v.t.* to sputter out (*words*).—*v.i.* to talk gibberish; to gabble.

baraque [ba'rak], *n.f.* hut, shed, shanty; (*fam.*) hovel; booth (*at a fair*).

baraquement [barak'mã], *n.m.* (*Mil.*) hutting.

barattage [bara'taːʒ], *n.m.* churning.

baratte [ba'rat], *n.f.* churn.

baratter [bara'te], *v.t.* to churn.

barbacane [barba'kan], *n.f.* (*Fort.*) barbican.

Barbade [bar'bad], *f.* Barbados.

barbare [bar'baːr], *a.* barbarous, barbarian; cruel, inhuman; (*fig.*) uncouth, rude; incorrect, ungrammatical.—*n.m.* (*usu. in pl.*) barbarians.

barbarement [barbar'mã], *adv.* barbarously.

barbaresque [barba'rɛsk], *a.* of *or* pertaining to Barbary.

Barbarie [barba'ri], **la,** *f.* Barbary.

barbarie [barba'ri], *n.f.* barbarity, rudeness; (*fig.*) cruelty.

barbarisme [barba'rism], *n.m.* (*Gram.*) barbarism.

barbe (1) [barb], *n.f.* beard; whiskers (*of cats, dogs etc.*); beard (*of grain*); wattles (*of fowls*).

barbe (2) [barb], *n.m.* barb, barbary horse.

barbeau [bar'bo], *n.m.* (*pl.* **-eaux**) barbel; (*Bot.*) bluebottle, cornflower.

barbelé [barbə'le], *a.* barbed, spiked; (*fil de fer*) *barbelé,* barbed wire.

barbiche [bar'biʃ], **barbichette** [barbi'ʃɛt], *n.f.* beard growing only on the chin, goatee.

barbier [bar'bje], *n.m.* barber.

barbiturate [barbity'rat], **barbiturique** [barbity'rik], *n.m.* (*Chem.*) barbiturate.

barboter [barbɔ'te], *v.i.* to dabble about in mud *or* water (*with the beak, like a duck*); to paddle, to flounder about in the mud; (*fig.*) to mumble.

barboteuse [barbɔ'tøːz], *n.f.* rompers.

barbotière [barbɔ'tjɛːr], *n.f.* duck pond; trough.

barbouillage [barbu'jaːʒ], *n.m.* daubing; daub; scrawl; (*fig.*) twaddle.

barbouiller [barbu'je], *v.t.* to soil, to dirty, to blot; to daub, to besmear; to scrawl, to scribble; to splutter out, to mumble; to bungle.

barbouilleur [barbu'jœːr], *n.m.* (*fem.* **-euse**) dauber, scribbler; mumbler.

barbu [bar'by], *a.* bearded.

barbue [bar'by], *n.f.* brill.

barcarolle [barka'rɔl], *n.f.* (*Mus.*) barcarolle.

Barcelone [barsə'lon], *f.* Barcelona.

bardane [bar'dan], *n.f.* burr, burdock.

barde (1) [bard], *n.m.* bard.

barde (2) [bard], *n.f.* bard (*iron armor for horses*); thin rasher of bacon used for larding poultry etc.

bardé [bar'de], *a.* barded; larded.

barder [bar'de], *v.t.* to bard a horse; to cover with thin slices of bacon, to lard; (*slang*) *ça barde* or *ça va barder,* things are beginning to hum.

bardot or **bardeau** (*pl.* **-eaux**) [bar'do], *n.m.* hinny; pack mule.

barème [ba'rɛːm], *n.m.* ready-reckoner.

barguignage [bargi'naːʒ], *n.m.* (*colloq.*) hesitation, wavering, shilly-dallying.

barguigner [bargi'ne], *v.i.* to be irresolute, to waver, to shilly-shally.

barguigneur [bargi'nœːr], *n.m.* (*fem.* **-euse**) waverer, haggler.

baril [ba'ri], *n.m.* small barrel, cask, keg.

bariolage [barjɔ'laːʒ], *n.m.* variegation, odd medley of colors, motley.

bariolé [barjɔ'le], *a.* gaudy, motley, many-colored.

barioler [barjɔ'le], *v.t.* to streak with several colors, to variegate.

barnache [BERNACLE].

baromètre [barɔ'mɛtr], *n.m.* barometer.

barométrique [barɔme'trik], *a.* barometrical.

baron [ba'rɔ̃], *n.m.* (*fem.* **-onne**) baron, baroness.

baronnet [barɔ'nɛ], *n.m.* baronet.

baronnial [barɔ'njal], *a.* (*m. pl.* **-aux**) baronial.

baronnie [barɔ'ni], *n.f.* barony.

baroque [ba'rɔk], *a.* irregular, grotesque, odd; baroque.

barque [bark], *n.f.* bark, boat, small craft.

barquerolle [barkə'rɔl], *n.f.* small mastless barge.

barquette [bar'kɛt], *n.f.* small craft; light puff-biscuit.

barrage [ba'raːʒ], *n.m.* barrier; toll bar; dam, weir, barrage.

barre [baːr], *n.f.* bar (*of metal, wood etc.*); dash, cross, stroke (*of the pen etc.*); bar (*in courts*) of justice; (*Naut.*) helm, tiller, bar; (*Mus.*) bar; bore (*of river*).

barreau [ba'ro], *n.m.* (*pl.* **-eaux**) small bar (*of wood, metal etc.*); bench reserved for barristers; (*fig.*) lawyers, barristers; rung (*of a ladder*); *être reçu* or *admis au barreau,* to be admitted to the bar.

barrer [ba're], *v.t.* to bar up, to fence off; to obstruct, to thwart; to cross off, to erase.

barrette (1) or **barette** [ba'rɛt], *n.f.* square flat cap, biretta; cardinal's hat.

barrette (2) [ba'rɛt], *n.m.* axle, pin, bolt, etc. (*in watches, jewelry etc.*); bar (*of medal*).

barreur [ba'rœːr], *n.m.* helmsman, coxswain.

barricade [bari'kad], *n.f.* barricade.

barricader [barika'de], *v.t.* to barricade, to obstruct.

barrière [ba'rjɛːr], *n.f.* railing, barrier; gateway; farm gate.

barrique [ba'rik], *n.f.* large barrel *or* cask, hogshead.

baryton [bari'tɔ̃], *n.m.* baritone.

baryum [ba'rjɔm], *n.m.* barium.

bas (1) [ba], *a.* (*fem.* **basse** (1)) low; in a low situation; inferior; (*fig.*) vile, base, sordid; mean; subdued (*of sounds*); decadent; *la marée est basse*, it is low tide; *les Pays-Bas*, the Netherlands.—*adv.* low, down; in a subdued voice, tone, etc.; *ici bas*, here below; *là-bas*, over there, yonder.—*n.m.* the lower part, bottom *or* foot (*of something*); *en bas*, below, downstairs; *le bas de l'escalier*, the foot of the stairs.

bas (2) [ba], *n.m. inv.* stocking.

basalte [ba'zalt], *n.m.* basalt.

basane [ba'zan], *n.f.* sheepskin.

basané [baza'ne], *a.* sunburnt, bronzed, swarthy, tawny.

bascule [bas'kyl], *n.f.* see-saw; weighing machine.

basculer [basky'le], *v.i.* to see-saw; to rock, to swing.

base [baːz], *n.f.* base, foundation; lower part, bottom; basis.

base-ball [bes'bol], *n.m.* baseball.

baser [ba'ze], *v.t.* to found, to base, to ground. **se baser**, *v.r.* to be grounded; to depend, to rely.

bas-fond [ba'fɔ̃], *n.m.* (*pl.* **bas-fonds**) low-lying ground, hollow, bottom; shallow, shallow water; (*fig., pl.*) underworld.

basilic [bazi'lik], *n.m.* (*Bot.*) basil, sweet basil; (*Myth.*) basilisk, cockatrice.

basilique [bazi'lik], *n.f.* basilica.

basket-ball [basket'bol], *n.m.* basketball.

basketteur [baskɛ'tœːr], *n.m.* (*fem.* **-euse**) basketball player.

basque (1) [bask], *n.f.* flap, skirt, tail (*of a garment*).

basque (2) [bask], *a.* Basque.—*n.m.* Basque (*language*).—*n.* (**Basque**) Basque (*person*).

bas-relief [barə'ljɛf], *n.m.* (*pl.* **bas-reliefs**) bas-relief.

basse (1) [baːs], [BAS (1)].

basse (2) [baːs], *n.f.* bass; violoncello; saxhorn.

basse (3) [baːs], *n.f.* shallow, reef.

basse-contre [bas'kɔ̃tr], *n.f.* (*pl.* **basses-contre**) (*Mus.*) contra-bass, lower tenor.

basse-cour [bas'kuːr], *n.f.* (*pl.* **basses-cours**) farmyard, poultry yard.

bassement [bas'mɑ̃], *adv.* basely, meanly, vilely.

bassesse [ba'sɛs], *n.f.* baseness; lowness (*of station etc.*); meanness, vileness; mean *or* sordid action.

basset [ba'sɛ], *n.m.* basset hound; *basset allemand*, dachshund.

basse-taille [bas'taːj], *n.f.* (*pl.* **basses-tailles**) (*Mus.*) baritone; (*Sculp.*) bas-relief.

bassin [ba'sɛ̃], *n.m.* basin; pond; dock; (*Anat.*) pelvis.

bassine [ba'sin], *n.f.* deep, wide pan.

bassiner [basi'ne], *v.t.* to warm (*a bed etc.*); to bathe (*with warm lotions*), to foment, to steep; to water, to sprinkle (*crops etc.*).

bassinet [basi'nɛ], *n.m.* small basin, pan, bowl.

bassinoire [basi'nwaːr], *n.f.* warming pan; (*pop.*) bore.

bassiste [ba'sist], *n.m.* saxhorn player; 'cellist.

basson [ba'sɔ̃], *n.m.* bassoon; bassoonist.

bastide [bas'tid], *n.f.* (*Provence*) country cottage, villa.

bastille [bas'tiːj], *n.f.* bastille, fort.

bastion [bas'tjɔ̃], *n.m.* bastion.

bastionner [bastjɔ'ne], *v.t.* to bastion, to fortify with bastions.

bastonnade [bastɔ'nad], *n.f.* bastinado; caning.

bastringue [bas'trɛ̃ːg], *n.m.* (*pop.*) dance hall; (*slang*) noise.

bas-ventre [ba'vɑ̃ːtr], *n.m.* (*pl.* **bas-ventres**) lower part of the belly.

bât [ba], *n.m.* pack-saddle.

bataclan [bata'klɑ̃], *n.m.* (*fam.*) paraphernalia.

bataille [ba'taːj], *n.f.* battle, fight, engagement.

batailler [bata'je], *v.i.* to give battle; to be at war, to fight; to struggle hard, to strive.

batailleur [bata'jœːr], *a.* (*fem.* **-euse**) combative, pugnacious, quarrelsome; disputatious.

bataillon [bata'jɔ̃], *n.m.* battalion; (*fig.*) host; (*pl.*) troops.

bâtard [ba'taːr], *a.* and *n.m.* (*fem.* **-e**) bastard, illegitimate *or* natural (child).

bâté [ba'te], *a.* saddled with a pack; *c'est un âne bâté*, he is an ignorant lout.

bateau [ba'to], *n.m.* (*pl.* **-eaux**) boat; *bateau mouche*, pleasure steamer (*Paris and Lyons*).

batelage [ba'tlaːʒ], *n.m.* juggling, legerdemain; lighterage charges.

bateleur [ba'tlœːr], *n.m.* (*fem.* **-euse**) juggler, buffoon, mountebank.

batelier [batə'lje], *n.m.* (*fem.* **-ière**) boatman, boatwoman, ferryman, ferrywoman.

bâter [ba'te], *v.t.* to load with a pack-saddle.

bathyscaphe [batis'kaf], *n.m.* bathyscape.

bâti [ba'ti], *n.m.* framing, structure; basting, tacking (*of a garment*).

batifolage [batifɔ'laːʒ], *n.m.* romping; fondling.

batifoler [batifɔ'le], *v.i.* to play, to romp; to fondle.

bâtiment [bati'mɑ̃], *n.m.* building, structure, edifice; building trade; ship, vessel.

bâtir [ba'tiːr], *v.t.* to build, to erect, to construct; *faire bâtir*, to have built, to build; *terrain à bâtir*, building site.

bâtisse [ba'tis], *n.f.* masonry, ramshackle building.

batiste [ba'tist], *n.f.* cambric.

bâton [ba'tɔ̃], *n.m.* stick, staff, cudgel, cane.

bâtonner [batɔ'ne], *v.t.* to cudgel, to cane.

batracien [batra'sjɛ̃], *n.m.* (*Zool.*) batrachian.

battant (1) [ba'tɑ̃], *n.m.* clapper (*of a bell*); leaf (*of a table or door*); fly (*of a flag*); *porte à deux battants*, double door.

battant (2) [ba'tɑ̃], a. beating, pelting, falling heavily (of rain etc.); **mener tambour battant**, to hurry on (a business).

batte [bat], n.f. long wooden staff or beater; **batte de blanchisseuse**, washing board; **batte (de cricket)**, (cricket) bat.

battée [ba'te], n.f. jamb of door or window.

battement [bat'mɑ̃], n.m. beating; clapping (of hands), stamping (of feet), flapping (of wings); beating (of the heart); shuffling (of cards).

batterie [ba'tri], n.f. (Artill., Elec., Cook. etc.) battery; **batterie de cuisine**, complete set of kitchen utensils.

batteur [ba'tœːr], n.m. (fem. -euse) beater; (cricket etc.) batsman; (jazz) drummer.—n.f. (-euse) threshing machine.

battre [batr], v.t. (see Verb Tables) to strike upon, against etc.; to beat, to thrash, to whip (a horse etc.); to beat up, to mix; to de-feat, to shuffle (cards); **battre des mains**, to clap; **la fête battait son plein**, the party was in full swing.—v.i. to beat, to knock; to pant, to throb. **se battre**, v.r. to fight, to combat; to hit oneself (contre etc.).

battu [ba'ty], a. beaten (of a path, road etc.); frequented; (fig.) trite, commonplace.

battue [ba'ty], n.f. (Shooting) wholesale slaughter, battue.

baudet [bo'dɛ], n.m. ass; (fig.) dolt, donkey; sawyer's trestle.

bauge [boːʒ], n.f. lair of a wild boar; squirrel's nest; (fig.) a dirty hovel.

baume [boːm], n.m. balm; balsam; (fig.) consolation.

baumier [BALSAMIER].

baux [BAIL].

bauxite [bo'sit], n.f. bauxite.

bavard [ba'vaːr], a. prating, talkative, loquacious.—n.m. (fem. -e) prater, babbler, chatterer.

bavardage [bavar'daːʒ], n.m. babbling, prattling; (fig.) twaddle, nonsense.

bavarder [bavar'de], v.i. to babble, to prattle.

bavarois [bava'rwa], a. Bavarian.—n.m. (Bavarois, fem. -oise) Bavarian (person).

bave [baːv], n.f. slaver, dribble, foam; (fig.) slime.

baver [ba've], v.i. to slobber, to dribble.

bavette [ba'vɛt], n.f. bib.

baveux [ba'vø], a. (fem. -euse) dribbling, slobbering.

Bavière [ba'vjɛːr], la, f. Bavaria.

bavure [ba'vyːr], n.f. seam (left by a mold); smudge (of a pen).

bazar [ba'zaːr], n.m. bazaar; ill-kept, untidy house; (fam.) **mettre tout son bazar dans une malle**, to put all one's belongings in a trunk.

bazooka [bazu'ka], n.m. (Artill.) bazooka.

béant [be'ɑ̃], a. gaping, yawning, wide open.

béat [be'a], a. blessed; devout; sanctimonious.

béatement [beat'mɑ̃], adv. sanctimoniously.

béatification [beatifika'sjɔ̃], n.f. beatification.

béatifier [beati'fje], v.t. to beatify.

béatifique [beati'fik], a. beatific, blissful.

béatitude [beati'tyd], n.f. beatitude, blessedness.

beau [bo], **bel** [bɛl] (before nouns singular beginning with a vowel or h mute).—a. (fem. **belle**, pl. **beaux**, **belles**) beautiful, fine, handsome, fair; smart, spruce; glorious; lofty, noble;

seemly, becoming; (iron.) nice, precious; **au beau milieu**, in the very middle; **il fait beau**, it is a fine day; **il l'a échappé belle**, he has had a narrow escape.—adv. finely, promisingly; in vain; **avoir beau dire**, to speak in vain; **de plus belle**, with renewed ardor, worse than ever; **tout beau**, gently, not so fast.—n.m. that which is beautiful, fine, excellent etc.; beauty; beau.—n.f. (belle) belle; **la Belle et la Bête**, Beauty and the Beast.

beaucoup [bo'ku], adv. many, much; a great many, a great deal; **avoir beaucoup d'argent**, to have plenty of money.

beau-fils [bo'fis], n.m. (pl. beaux-fils) stepson.

beau-frère [bo'frɛːr], n.m. (pl. beaux-frères) brother-in-law.

beau-père [bo'pɛːr], n.m. (pl. beaux-pères) father-in-law; step-father.

beaupré [bo'pre], n.m. (Naut.) bowsprit.

beauté [bo'te], n.f. beauty; lineliness, loveliness, comeliness, elegance, agreeableness.

beaux-arts [bo'zaːr], n.m. pl. fine arts.

beaux-parents [bopa'rɑ̃], n.m. pl. father-in-law and mother-in-law.

bébé [be'be], n.m. baby; baby doll.

bec [bɛk], n.m. beak, bill; (fig.) mouth; snout (of some fishes); lip (of a jug), spout (of a kettle etc.); gas jet, burner; mouthpiece (of musical instrument); nib (pen); **avoir bon bec**, to have the gift of the gab.

bécane [be'kan], n.f. (pop.) bike.

bécarre [be'kaːr], a. and n.m. (Mus.) natural.

bécasse [be'kas], n.f. woodcock; (fam.) stupid woman.

bécassine [beka'sin], n.f. snipe.

bec-de-lièvre [bɛkdə'ljɛːvr], n.m. (pl. becs-de-lièvre) harelip; harelipped person.

bec-fin [bɛk'fɛ̃], n.m. (pl. becs-fins) warbler; pipit.

béchamel [beʃa'mɛl], n.f. cream sauce, béchamel sauce.

bêche [bɛːʃ], n.f. spade.

bêcher [be'ʃe], v.t. to dig.

becquée [be'ke], **béquée** [be'ke], n.f. billful; **donner la becquée**, to feed.

becqueter [bɛk'te], **béqueter** [bek'te], v.t. (conjug. like AMENER) to peck; (colloq.) to eat. **se becqueter**, **se béqueter**, v.r. to peck one another.

bedaine [bə'dɛn], n.f. (colloq.) paunch.

bedeau [bə'do], n.m. (pl. -eaux) beadle, verger.

bedonnant [bədɔ'nɑ̃], a. stout, pot-bellied.

bedonner [bədɔ'ne], v.i. to get or grow stout.

bédouin [be'dwɛ̃], a. Bedouin.—n.m. (Bédouin, fem. -e) Bedouin.

bée [be], a. only used in **bouche bée**, gaping, open-mouthed.

beffroi [be'frwa], n.m. belfry.

bégaiement [bege'mɑ̃], n.m., **bégayant** [bege'jɑ̃], a. stammering, faltering.

bégayer [bege'je], v.t. (conjug. like PAYER) to stammer out, to stutter, to lisp.—v.i. to stammer.

bégayeur [bege'jœːr], n.m. (fem. -euse) stammerer, stutterer.

bégonia [begɔ'nja], n.m. begonia.

bègue [bɛg], a. stammering, stuttering.—n. stammerer, stutterer.

bégueule [be'gœl], a. prudish, squeamish; straitlaced.—n.f. (fam.) prude.

bégueulerie [begœl'ri], *n.f.* prudery, prudish airs, squeamishness.

béguin [be'gɛ̃], *n.m.* hood, child's cap; *avoir un béguin pour*, to be sweet on; *c'est mon béguin*, he *or* she is my darling.

béguine [be'gin], *n.f.* beguine (*Flemish nun*); nun; bigoted person.

bégum [be'gɔm], *n.f.* begum.

beige [bɛ:ʒ], *a.* natural, undyed (*of wool*); beige.—*n.f.* unbleached serge.

beignet [bɛ'nɛ], *n.m.* fritter.

béjaune [be'ʒo:n], *n.m.* (*Falconry*) eyas, unfledged hawk; (*fig.*) ninny, novice; blunder, silliness, mistake.

bel [BEAU].

bêlant [bɛ'lɑ̃], *a.* bleating.

bêlement [bɛl'mɑ̃], *n.m.* bleating (*of sheep*).

bêler [bɛ'le], *v.i.* to bleat.

belette [bə'lɛt], *n.f.* weasel.

belge [bɛlʒ], *a.* Belgian.—*n.* (**Belge**) Belgian (*person*).

Belgique [bɛl'ʒik], **la,** *f.* Belgium.

bélier [be'lje], *n.m.* ram; battering-ram; Aries.

bélière [be'ljɛːr], *n.f.* sheep bell; clapper ring (*of a bell*); watch ring; sword sling.

bélitre [be'litr], *n.m.* rascal, cad.

belladone [bela'dɔn], *n.f.* belladonna, deadly nightshade

bellâtre [bɛ lɑːtr], *a.* having insipid beauty; foppish.—*n.m.* insipid beauty; fop, coxcomb.

belle-fille [bɛl'fi:j], *n.f.* (*pl.* **belles-filles**) daughter-in-law; stepdaughter.

belle-maman [bɛlma'mɑ̃], (*colloq.*) [BELLE-MÈRE].

bellement [bɛl'mɑ̃], *adv.* prettily, charmingly, softly, gently.

belle-mère [bɛl'mɛːr], *n.f.* (*pl.* **belles-mères**) mother-in-law; stepmother.

belles-lettres [bɛl'lɛtr], *n.f. pl.* polite literature, belles-lettres.

belle-sœur [bɛl'sœːr], *n.f.* (*pl.* **belles-sœurs**) sister-in-law; stepsister.

belligérance [bɛliʒe'rɑ̃:s], *n.f.* belligerence, belligerency.

belligérant [bɛliʒe'rɑ̃], *a.* and *n.m.* (*fem.* **-e**) belligerent.

belliqueux [bɛli'kø], *a.* (*fem.* **-euse**) warlike, martial; bellicose, quarrelsome.

belvédère [bɛlve'dɛːr], *n.m.* turret, terrace, belvedere, gazebo.

bémol [be'mɔl], *a.* and *n.m.* (*Mus.*) flat.

bémoliser [bemɔli'ze], *v.t.* (*Mus.*) to mark flat *or* with a flat.

bénédicité [benedisi'te], *n.m.* grace (*before meals*).

bénédictin [benedik'tɛ̃], *a.* and *n.m.* (*fem.* **-e**) Benedictine.

bénédiction [benedik'sjɔ̃], *n.f.* benediction, blessing, consecration; (*fig.*) expression of thanks.

bénéfice [bene'fis], *n.m.* benefit, gain, profit; privilege, advantage; (*Eccles.*) benefice, living.

bénéficiaire [benefi'sjɛːr], *a.* receiving a benefit *or* benefice.—*n.* beneficiary, recipient.

bénéficial [benefi'sjal], *n.m.* beneficiary (*of ecclesiastical livings*).

bénéficier [benefi'sje], *v.i.* to gain, to profit.—*n.m.* beneficed clergyman, incumbent.

benêt [bə'nɛ], *a.* silly, foolish, simple.—*n.m.* booby, fool, simpleton.

bénévole [bene'vɔl], *a.* well-disposed, kindly; unpaid.

bénévolement [benevɔl'mɑ̃], *adv.* out of good will; voluntarily, spontaneously.

Bengale [bɛ̃'gal], **le,** *m.* Bengal.

bengali [bɛ̃ga'li], *a.* Bengali.—*n.m.* Bengali (*language*).—*n.* (**Bengali**) Bengali (*person*).

Béni-oui-oui [beniwi'wi], *n.m. inv.* (*fam.*) yes-man.

bénignement [beniɲ'mɑ̃], *adv.* benignly, kindly, graciously.

bénignité [beniɲi'te], *n.f.* benignity, kindness; mildness (*of a disease*).

bénin [be'nɛ̃], *a.* (*fem.* **bénigne**) benign, good-natured, indulgent; mild (*of attacks of disease, remedies etc.*).

bénir [be'niːr], *v.t.* to bless, to hallow, to consecrate; to call down blessings on; to thank; to praise.

bénit [be'ni], *a.* hallowed, consecrated.

bénitier [beni'tje], *n.m.* holy-water basin; font.

benjamin [bɛ̃ʒa'mɛ̃], *n.m.* favorite (*especially the youngest child*).

benjoin [bɛ̃'ʒwɛ̃], *n.m.* benjamin, benzoin.

benne [bɛn], *n.f.* hamper, basket; (*Mining*) hopper, bucket.

benzine [bɛ̃'zin], *n.f.* benzine.

benzol [bɛ̃'zɔl], *n.m.* benzol.

béquillard [beki'jaːr], *a.* (*pop.*) crippled, going on crutches.—*n.m.* (*fem.* **-e**) cripple.

béquille [be'kiːj], *n.f.* crutch; (*Av.*) tail-skid.

béquiller [beki'je], *v.i.* to walk on crutches.

berbère [bɛr'bɛːr], *a.* Berber.—*n.* (**Berbère**) Berber (*person*).

berbéris [bɛrbe'ris], *n.m.* (*Bot.*) barberry, berberis.

bercail [bɛr'kaːj], *n.m.* (*used only in sing.*) sheepfold, fold.

berce [bɛrs], *n.f.* cow-parsnip.

berceau [bɛr'so], *n.m.* (*pl.* **-eaux**) cradle; (*fig.*) infancy; origin, source; (*Hort.*) arbor, bower.

bercement [bɛrsə'mɑ̃], *n.m.* rocking; lulling.

bercer [bɛr'se], *v.t.* (*conjug. like* COMMENCER) to rock, to lull asleep; to lull, to soothe; (*fig.*) to delude *or* flatter with vain hopes. **se bercer**, *v.r.* to rock; (*fig.*) to delude oneself (*de*).

berceuse [bɛr'søːz], *n.f.* woman who rocks an infant; rocking chair; cradle that rocks; (*Mus.*) lullaby.

béret [be'rɛ], *n.m.* beret, tam-o'-shanter (*worn by the French Alpine regiments*).

berge [bɛrʒ], *n.f.* steep bank (*of a river*); side (*of a canal, ditch, roadway etc.*).

berger [bɛr'ʒe], *n.m.* (*fem.* **-ère** (1)) shepherd, shepherdess; (*poet.*) swain; (*fig.*) pastor, guardian (*of the people etc.*); (*Chess*) *le coup du berger*, fool's mate.

bergère (2) [bɛr'ʒɛːr], *n.f.* large and deep armchair.

bergerie [bɛrʒə'ri], *n.f.* sheepfold, pen; (*Lit.*) (*chiefly used in the plural*) pastoral.

bergeronnette [bɛrʒərɔ'nɛt], *n.f.* (*Orn.*) wag-tail.

berlue [bɛr'ly], *n.f.* dimness of sight.

Bermudes [bɛr'myd], **les,** *f. pl.* the Bermudas.

bernacle [bɛr′nakl], **bernache** [bɛr′naʃ], **barnache** [bar′naʃ], n.f. barnacle goose; barnacle (shell-fish).
bernard-l'ermite [bɛrnarlɛr′mit], n.m. hermit-crab.
berne (1) [bɛrn], n.f. tossing in a blanket.
berne (2) [bɛrn], n.f. (Naut.) mettre le pavillon en berne, to fly the flag at half-mast.
berner [bɛr′ne], v.t. to toss in a blanket; (fig.) to ridicule, to make a fool of, to deride; to deceive, to hoax.
bernique [bɛr′nik], int. (pop.) no use; not a bit of it, no go.
berthon [bɛr′tɔ̃], n.m. a small collapsible boat.
béryl or **béril** [be′ril], n.m. beryl.
besace [bə′zas], n.f. beggar's wallet, scrip.
bésigue [be′zig], n.m. bezique (card game).
besogne [bə′zɔɲ], n.f. work, business, labor; job, piece of work.
besogner [bəzɔ′ne], v.i. to work, to labor.
besogneux [bəzɔ′nø], a. and n.m. (fem. -euse) necessitous, needy (person).
besoin [bə′zwɛ̃], n.m. need, want; necessity; poverty, distress, emergency; au besoin, at a pinch, if need be.
Bessarabie [besara′bi], la, f. Bessarabia.
bestial [bes′tjal], a. (m. pl. -aux (1)) bestial, brutish.
bestialement [bestjal′mã], adv. bestially, brutally, like a beast.
bestialité [bestjali′te], n.f. bestiality.
bestiaux [BESTIAL, BÉTAIL].
bestiole [bes′tjɔl], n.f. little animal.
bêta [be′ta], n.m. (fem. -asse) a bit of a blockhead, rather a simpleton.
bétail [be′taj], n.m. (pl. bestiaux (2) [bes′tjo]) cattle, livestock; gros bétail, oxen etc.; menu bétail, sheep, goats etc.
bêtasse [be′tɑːs], [BÊTA].
bête [bɛːt], a. silly, stupid, nonsensical.—n.f. animal, beast, brute; fool, blockhead, stupid creature; bête noire, pet aversion; bête sauvage, wild animal.
bêtement [bɛt′mã], adv. like a fool, foolishly, stupidly.
Bethléem [betle′ɛm], f. Bethlehem.
bêtise [be′tiːz], n.f. silliness, stupidity; tomfoolery, foolish act, suggestion etc., silly thing, absurdity.
béton [be′tɔ̃], n.m. (Masonry) beton (a kind of concrete); béton armé, reinforced concrete.
bétonnière [betɔ′njɛːr], **bétonneuse** [betɔ′nøːz], n.f. concrete mixer.
bette [bɛt], **blette** (2) [blɛt], n.f. beet.
betterave [be′traːv], n.f. beets; betterave à sucre, sugar beet; betterave fourragère, mangel-wurzel.
beuglement [bøglə′mã], n.m. bellowing, lowing (of cattle).
beugler [bø′gle], v.i. to bellow, to low.
beurre [bœːr], n.m. butter.
beurrée [bœ′re], n.f. slice of bread and butter.
beurrer [bœ′re], v.t. to butter (bread etc.).
beurrerie [bœr′ri], n.f. butter factory.
beurrier [bœ′rje], n.m. butter dish.
bévue [be′vy], n.f. blunder, oversight, mistake; (colloq.) howler.
bey [bɛ], n.m. bey.
biais [bjɛ], a. slanting, sloping, askew; oblique.—n.m. bias, obliquity, slope; (fig.) shift, subterfuge.

biaisement [bjɛz′mã], n.m. sloping, slanting, shift, evasion.
biaiser [bjɛ′ze], v.i. to be oblique, to go obliquely, to slope, to slant, to lean on one side; to use shifts or evasions.
bibelot [bi′blo], n.m. trinket, knick-knack.
biberon (1) [bi′brɔ̃], n.m. (Med.) feeding cup; feeding bottle (for infants).
biberon (2) [bi′brɔ̃], n.m. (fem. -onne) tippler, toper.
Bible [bibl], n.f. Bible.
bibliographe [biblio′graf], n.m. bibliographer.
bibliographie [bibliogra′fi], n.f. bibliography.
bibliographique [bibliogra′fik], a. bibliographical.
bibliomane [biblio′man], n.m. book collector.
bibliomanie [biblioma′ni], n.f. bibliomania.
bibliophile [biblio′fil], n.m. book lover.
bibliothécaire [bibliote′kɛːr], n.m. librarian.
bibliothèque [biblio′tɛk], n.f. library; book-case.
biblique [bi′blik], a. Biblical.
bicarbonate [bikarbɔ′nat], n.m. (Chem.) bicarbonate.
biceps [bi′sɛps], n.m. biceps.
biche [biʃ], n.f. hind, doe.
bichon [bi′ʃɔ̃], n.m. (fem. -onne) lap dog with long, silky hair.
bichonner [biʃɔ′ne], v.t. to curl; (fig.) to caress. se bichonner, v.r. to curl one's hair; to make oneself smart.
biconcave [bikɔ̃′kaːv], a. bi-concave.
biconvexe [bikɔ̃′vɛks], a. bi-convex.
bicoque [bi′kɔk], n.f. (colloq.) ramshackle house, shanty.
bicorne [bi′kɔrn], a. and n.m. cocked (hat).
bicyclette [bisi′klɛt], n.f. bicycle.
bidet [bi′dɛ], n.m. pony, small nag; bidet (bath).
bidon [bi′dɔ̃], n.m. tin, can (esp. gas can); camp kettle; soldier's water bottle.
bidonville [bidɔ̃′vil], n.m. shanty town.
bielle [bjɛl], n.f. (Mach.) connecting rod.
Biélorussie [bjelory′si], la, f. Byelorussia, White Russia.
bien [bjɛ̃], n.m. good; that which is pleasant, useful or advantageous; benefit; welfare, well-being, blessing; wealth, estate, property; gift, boon, mercy; (pl.) goods, chattels; fruits (of the soil etc.); biens de consommation, consumer goods; biens immobiliers, real estate.—adv. well; rightly, finely; much, very, far, entirely, completely; about, well-nigh; favorably, successfully; well off; on good terms, in favor; certainly, truly, indeed; formally, clearly, expressly; aussi bien, anyhow, in any case; bien de, plenty of, many; bien mieux, far better; bien plus, besides, moreover; bien que, although; c'est bien, that's right; cette femme est bien, that woman is good-looking; eh bien! well or well? je vous l'avais bien dit, I told you so; ou bien, or else; si bien que, so that; tant bien que mal, so-so.—int. (sometimes pronounced colloq. [bɛ̃]) well!
bien-aimé [bjɛne′me], a. beloved, well-beloved.—n.m. (fem. -ée) darling, dear.
bien-dire [bjɛ̃′diːr], n.m. (no pl.) fine speaking.

bien-être [bjɛ̃'nɛːtr], *n.m.* (*no pl.*) well-being, welfare, comfort.

bienfaisance [bjɛ̃fə'zɑ̃ːs], *n.f.* beneficence, charity, munificence.

bienfaisant [bjɛ̃fə'zɑ̃], *a.* charitable, beneficent, kind, gracious; beneficial, salutary.

bienfait [bjɛ̃'fɛ], *n.m.* good turn, kindness, benefit, favor, courtesy.

bienfaiteur [bjɛ̃fɛ'tœːr], *n.m.* (*fem.* **-trice**) benefactor, benefactress, patron.

bien-fonds [bjɛ̃'fɔ̃], *n.m.* (*pl.* **biens-fonds**) real estate.

bienheureux [bjɛ̃nœ'rø], *a.* (*fem.* **-euse**) happy, fortunate; (*Eccles.*) blessed.

biennal [bɪɛ'nal], *a.* (*m. pl.* **-aux**) biennial.

bienséance [bjɛ̃se'ɑ̃ːs], *n.f.* propriety, decency, decorum, seemliness.

bienséant [bjɛ̃se'ɑ̃], *a.* decent, becoming, seemly, decorous, fit.

bientôt [bjɛ̃'to], *adv.* soon, before long, shortly; *à bientôt!* see you soon!

bienveillance [bjɛ̃vɛ'jɑ̃ːs], *n.f.* benevolence, goodwill, favor, kindness.

bienveillant [bjɛ̃vɛ'jɑ̃], *a.* benevolent, kind, friendly, favorable.

bienvenu [bjɛ̃v'ny], *a.* welcome; *soyez le bienvenu,* it's nice to have you with us.

bienvenue [bjɛ̃v'ny], *n.f.* welcome; *souhaiter la bienvenue à quelqu'un,* to greet *or* welcome someone.

bière (1) [bjɛːr], *n.f.* beer.

bière (2) [bjɛːr], *n.f.* coffin.

biffer [bi'fe], *v.t.* to cancel, to blot out, to erase.

biflore [bi'flɔːr], *a.* (*Bot.*) biflorate.

bifocal [bifo'kal], *a.* (*m. pl.* **-aux**) bifocal.

bifolié [bifo'lje], *a.* (*Bot.*) bifoliate.

bifteck [bif'tɛk], *n.m.* beefsteak.

bifurcation [bifyrka'sjɔ̃], *n.f.* bifurcation; fork (*of a road*).

bigame [bi'gam], *a.* bigamous.—*n.* bigamist.

bigamie [biga'mi], *n.f.* bigamy.

bigarré [biga're], *a.* parti-colored, streaked.

bigarrer [biga're], *v.t.* to chequer, to streak, to variegate.

bigarrure [biga'ryːr], *n.f.* medley, mixture, motley, variegation.

bigot [bi'go], *a.* bigoted.—*n.m.* (*fem.* **-e**) bigot.

bigoterie [bigo'tri], *n.f.*, **bigotisme** [bigo'tism], *n.m.* bigotry.

bigoudi [bigu'di], *n.m.* curling pin *or* curler (*for the hair*).

bijou [bi'ʒu], *n.m.* (*pl.* **-oux**) jewel, gem; (*fig.*) darling.

bijouterie [biʒu'tri], *n.f.* jewelry.

bijoutier [biʒu'tje], *n.m.* (*fem.* **-ière**) jeweler.

bilan [bi'lɑ̃], *n.m.* balance sheet.

bilatéral [bilate'ral], *a.* (*m. pl.* **-aux**) bilateral.

bilboquet [bilbo'kɛ], *n.m.* cup-and-ball (*toy*); small weighted figure that balances itself.

bile [bil], *n.f.* bile, spleen, gall; (*fig.*) anger.

bilieux [bi'ljø], *a.* (*fem.* **-euse**) bilious; (*fig.*) choleric, passionate.

bilingue [bi'lɛ̃ːg], *a.* bilingual.

billard [bi'jaːr], *n.m.* billiards; billiard table; billiard room.

bille [biːj], *n.f.* billiard ball; marble, taw; log, unworked piece of timber; *roulement à billes,* ball bearings.

billet [bi'jɛ], *n.m.* note, missive; bill, handbill; ticket, lottery ticket; promissory note;

billet (*for quartering soldiers*); *billet de banque,* bank note; *billet d'aller et retour,* return ticket; *billet doux,* love letter.

billevesée [bilvə'ze], *n.f.* idle story, stuff, nonsense, bunkum.

billion [bi'ljɔ̃], *n.m.* (*since 1948 = 1 followed by 12 ciphers*), billion, one million million(s); (*Am.*) trillion.

billot [bi'jo], *n.m.* block; executioner's block.

bimbelot [bɛ̃'blo], *n.m.* plaything, toy, bauble.

bimensuel [bimɑ̃'sɥɛl], *a.* (*fem.* **-elle**) twice monthly, fortnightly.

bimoteur [bimɔ'tœːr], *a.* and *n.m.* twin-engined (plane).

binaire [bi'nɛːr], *a.* binary.

biner [bi'ne], *v.t.* (*Agric.*) to dig again; to hoe.

binette [bi'nɛt], *n.f.* hoe; (*colloq.*) face.

biniou [bi'nju], *n.m.* Breton bagpipe.

binôme [bi'no:m], *n.m.* (*Alg.*) binomial.

biochimie [bioʃi'mi], *n.f.* biochemistry.

biographe [bio'graf], *n.m.* biographer.

biographie [biogra'fi], *n.f.* biography.

biographique [biogra'fik], *a.* biographical.

biologie [biolo'ʒi], *n.f.* biology.

biologique [biolo'ʒik], *a.* biological.

biologiste [biolo'ʒist], **biologue** [bio'log], *n.m.* biologist.

bion [bjɔ̃], *n.m.* sucker, shoot.

bioxyde [biok'sid], *n.m.* dioxide.

biparti [bipar'ti], **bipartite** [bipar'tit], *a.* bipartite.

bipède [bi'pɛd], *a.* and *n.* (*Zool.*) biped.

biplan [bi'plɑ̃], *n.m.* biplane.

bipolaire [bipɔ'lɛːr], *a.* bipolar.

bique [bik], *n.f.* nanny goat.

biréacteur [bireak'tœːr], *n.m.* twin-engined jet plane.

birloir [bir'lwaːr], *n.m.* window catch.

birman [bir'mɑ̃], *a.* Burmese.—*n.m.* (**Birman,** *fem.* **-ane**) Burmese (*person*).

Birmanie [birma'ni], **la,** *f.* Burma.

bis (1) [bi], *a.* brown; tawny, swarthy; *du pain bis,* brown bread.

bis (2) [bis], *adv.* twice.—*int.* encore!

bisaïeul [biza'jœl], *n.m.* great-grandfather.

bisaïeule [biza'jœl], *n.f.* great-grandmother.

bisannuel [biza'nɥɛl], *a.* (*fem.* **-elle**) (*Bot.*) biennial.

bisbille [biz'biːj], *n.f.* (*fam.*) petty quarrel, tiff, bickering.

biscornu [biskɔr'ny], *a.* irregular, misshapen; (*fig.*) outlandish, odd, queer.

biscotte [bis'kɔt], *n.f.* rusk.

biscuit [bis'kɥi], *n.m.* biscuit; pastry made with flour, eggs, and sugar; (*Am.*) cracker; unglazed porcelain.

bise [biːz], *n.f.* dry and cold north wind; (*colloq.*) kiss.

biseau [bi'zo], *n.m.* (*pl.* **-eaux**) bevel, chamfer, bevelling tool.

biseauter [bizo'te], *v.t.* to bevel.

bismuth [biz'myt], *n.m.* bismuth.

bison [bi'zɔ̃], *n.m.* bison, buffalo.

bisque [bisk], *n.f.* soup made of crayfish, chicken *or* game, fish etc.; (*colloq.*) ill-humor, spite.

bisquer [bis'ke], *v.i.* (*colloq.*) to be vexed *or* riled.

bissac [bi'sak], *n.m.* double wallet, sack *or* bag, haversack.

bissecter [bisɛk'te], *v.t.* to bisect.

bisser [bi'se], *v.t.* to encore.
bissextile [bisɛks'til], *a.* **année bissextile**, leap year.
bissexué [bisɛk'sɥe], **bissexuel** [-sɥɛl] (*fem. -elle*), *a.* (*Bot.*) bisexual.
bistouri [bistu'ri], *n.m.* bistoury, lancet.
bistourner [bistur'ne], *v.t.* to twist, to distort; to castrate.
bistre [bistr], *n.m.* bistre, sepia.
bistro or **bistrot** [bis'tro], *n.m.* (*slang*) pub.
bitume [bi'tym], *n.m.* bitumen.
bituminer [bitymi'ne], *v.t.* to asphalt.
bitumineux [bitymi'nø], **bitumeux** [bity'mø], *a.* (*fem. -euse*) bituminous.
bivalent [biva'lɑ̃], *a.* divalent, bivalent.
bivalve [bi'valv], *a.* bivalvular.—*n.m.* bivalve.
bivouac [bi'vwak], *n.m.* bivouac.
bivouaquer [bivwa'ke], *v.i.* to bivouac.
bizarre [bi'za:r], *a.* queer, strange, whimsical, bizarre.
bizarrement [bizar'mɑ̃], *adv.* oddly, queerly, whimsically.
bizarrerie [bizar'ri], *n.f.* singularity, oddness; caprice, whim.
black-out [blak'aut], *n.m.* black-out.
blafard [bla'fa:r], *a.* pale, wan; livid.
blague [blag], *n.f.* tobacco pouch; (*slang*) chaff, humbug, hoax, fib; trick, practical joke; *sans blague!* you don't say!
blaguer [bla'ge], *v.i.* to chaff, to hoax, to humbug.
blagueur [bla'gœ:r], *n.m.* (*fem. -euse*) wag, hoaxer, humbug.
blaireau [blɛ'ro], *n.m.* (*pl. -eaux*) badger; shaving brush; badger-hair brush.
blâmable [blɑ'mabl], *a.* blameworthy.
blâme [blɑ:m], *n.m.* blame; reproach, reprimand.
blâmer [blɑ'me], *v.t.* to blame, to criticize; to censure, to reprimand.
blanc [blɑ̃], *a.* (*fem.* **blanche** (1) [blɑ̃:ʃ]) white; hoar, hoary; clean; blank; *gelée blanche*, hoar frost; *passer une nuit blanche*, to have a sleepless night; *vers blancs*, blank verse.—*n.m.* white; blank; target, mark; *blanc de chaux*, whitewash; *de but en blanc*, point-blank; *en blanc*, left blank.
blanc-bec [blɑ̃'bɛk], *n.m.* (*pl.* **blancs-becs**) beardless youth, youngster; greenhorn; sucker.
blanchaille [blɑ̃'ʃɑ:j], *n.f.* whitebait.
blanchâtre [blɑ̃'ʃɑ:tr], *a.* whitish.
blanche (1) [BLANC].
blanche (2) [blɑ̃:ʃ], *n.f.* (*Mus.*) minim.
blancheur [blɑ̃'ʃœ:r], *n.f.* whiteness; cleanliness; light; (*fig.*) purity, innocence.
blanchiment [blɑ̃ʃi'mɑ̃], *n.m.* whitening, bleaching; blanching.
blanchir [blɑ̃'ʃi:r], *v.t.* to whiten; to whitewash; to wash, to bleach, to clean; to blanch.—*v.i.* to whiten.
blanchissage [blɑ̃ʃi'sa:ʒ], *n.m.* washing; refining (*of sugar etc.*).
blanchissant [blɑ̃ʃi'sɑ̃], *a.* that whitens or grows white; foaming.
blanchisserie [blɑ̃ʃis'ri], *n.f.* laundry, washhouse.
blanchisseuse [blɑ̃ʃi'sø:z], *n.f.* washerwoman; laundress.
blanc-manger [blɑ̃mɑ̃'ʒe], *n.m.* (*pl.* **blancs-mangers**) blancmange.

blaser [blɑ'ze], *v.t.* to blunt, to cloy, to sicken, to surfeit.
blason [blɑ'zɔ̃], *n.m.* coat of arms; blazon; heraldry, blazonry.
blasonner [blɑzɔ'ne], *v.t.* to blazon; to interpret (*coats of arms*).
blasphémateur [blasfema'tœ:r], *n.m.* (*fem. -trice*) blasphemer.
blasphématoire [blasfema'twa:r], *a.* blasphemous.
blasphème [blas'fɛ:m], *n.m.* blasphemy.
blasphémer [blasfe'me], *v.t., v.i.* (*conjug. like* CÉDER) to blaspheme; to curse.
blatte [blat], *n.f.* cockroach, black beetle.
blé [ble], *n.m.* corn, wheat; *halle au blé*, corn exchange; *manger son blé en herbe*, to spend one's money before one has it.
blême [blɛ:m], *a.* sallow, pale, wan; ghastly.
blêmir [blɛ'mi:r], *v.i.* to turn or grow pale.
blèsement [blɛz'mɑ̃], *n.m.* lisping.
bléser [ble'ze], *v.i.* (*conjug. like* CÉDER) to lisp.
blessant [blɛ'sɑ̃], *a.* wounding; (*fig.*) offensive, mortifying.
blessé [blɛ'se], *a.* wounded; (*fig.*) offended.—*n.m.* (*fem. -ée*) (*Mil.*) casualty.
blesser [blɛ'se], *v.t.* to wound, to hurt; to offend, to injure; to shock. **se blesser**, *v.r.* to hurt oneself; (*fig.*) to take offence.
blessure [blɛ'sy:r], *n.f.* wound, hurt, injury; offence; *coups et blessures*, assault and battery.
blet [blɛ], *a.* (*fem. -ette* (1)) over-ripe, sleepy (*of fruit*).
blette (2) [BETTE].
bleu [blø], *a.* blue, black and blue (*as a bruise*); (*fig.*) amazed; *cordon bleu*, first-rate cook. —*n.m.* blue, blueness; blueprint; greenhorn, novice; (*C*) Conservative, Tory.
bleuâtre [blø'a:tr], *a.* bluish.
bleuet [BLUET].
bleuir [blø'i:r], *v.t.* to make blue, to blue (*in washing*).—*v.i.* to become blue.
blindage [blɛ̃'da:ʒ], *n.m.* iron-plating, armor-plating.
blindé [blɛ̃'de], *a.* armored, armor-plated; screened; (*slang*) drunk.
blinder [blɛ̃'de], *v.t.* to armor-plate (*a ship, fort etc.*).
bloc [blɔk], *n.m.* block, lump, the whole lot.
blocage (1) [blɔ'ka:ʒ], *n.m.* blockading; blocking; block (*of traffic*); obstruction; (*Fin.*) freezing.
blocage (2) [blɔ'ka:ʒ], *n.m.* rubble.
blockhaus [blɔ'ko:s], *n.m. inv.* blockhouse.
bloc-note(s) [blɔk'nɔt], *n.m.* writing pad.
blocus [blɔ'ky:s], *n.m. inv.* blockade.
blond [blɔ̃], *a.* blond, fair; light (*ale*); *blond ardent*, auburn; *blond cendré*, ash-blond. —*n.f.* (*-e*) (*C*) sweetheart.
blondin [blɔ̃'dɛ̃], *a.* fair-haired.—*n.m.* (*fem. -e*) fair-haired child.—*n.m.* spark, beau.
blondir [blɔ̃'di:r], *v.i.* to grow blond or fair.
blondissant [blɔ̃di'sɑ̃], *a.* growing yellow or golden (*of corn etc.*).
bloquer [blɔ'ke], *v.t.* to block up, to fill up (*cavities in walls*) with mortar; (*Mil.*) to blockade; (*Fin.*) to freeze; to jam on (*brakes*).
blottir (se) [sablɔ'ti:r], *v.r.* to curl up, to snuggle, to huddle; to cower, to crouch.
blouse [blu:z], *n.f.* smock, tunic; blouse; pinafore; overall.

blouser [blu'ze], *v.t.* to mislead, to cheat. **se blouser**, *v.r.* (*Billiards*) to pocket one's own ball; (*fig.*) to blunder; to bark up the wrong tree.

blouson [blu'zɔ̃], *n.m.* lumber-jacket, wind-cheater.

bluet [bly'ɛ], **bleuet** [blœ'ɛ], *n.m.* blue-bottle, corn-flower; (*C*) blueberry.

bluette [bly'ɛt], *n.f.* spark; (*fig.*) literary trifle, novelette.

bluff [blœf], *n.m.* bluff.

bluffer [blœ'fe], *v.t.* to bluff.

blutage [bly'ta:ʒ], *n.m.* bolting, sifting (*of flour*).

bluter [bly'te], *v.t.* to bolt, to sift (*flour etc.*).

boa [bɔ'a], *n.m.* boa (*snake*); boa (*of feathers*).

bobèche [bɔ'bɛʃ], *n.f.* socket (*of a candlestick*); sconce.

bobine [bɔ'bin], *n.f.* bobbin, spool, reel; (*Cine.*) reel; *bobine d'induction*, induction coil.

bobiner [bɔbi'ne], *v.t.* to wind on a bobbin, to spool.

bobineuse [bɔbi'nø:z], *n.f.* winder, winding machine.

bobo [bɔ'bo], *n.m.* (*Childish*) hurt, sore, bump; *avoir bobo* or *du bobo*, to have a slight pain, sore etc.; *faire bobo*, to hurt.

bocage [bɔ'ka:ʒ], *n.m.* copse, grove.

bocager [bɔka'ʒe], *a.* (*fem.* **-ère**) of groves or woodlands; shady.

bocal [bɔ'kal], *n.m.* (*pl.* **-aux**) druggist's short-necked bottle; carboy; glass jar, fish-bowl.

boche [bɔʃ] (*aphæresis of* **Alboche**), *n.* (*pej.*) German, Jerry.

bock [bɔk], *n.m.* bock or glass (*beer*).

bœuf [bœf], *n.m.* (*pl.* **bœufs** [bø]) ox; beef.

Bohême [bɔ'ɛ:m], **la**, *f.* Bohemia.

bohème [bɔ'ɛ:m], *a.* Bohemian.—*n.* Bohemian, person of careless, unconventional habits.

bohémien [bɔe'mjɛ̃], *a. and n.m.* (*fem.* **-enne**) Bohemian; gipsy.

boire [bwa:r], *v.t. irr.* to drink; to consume or waste on drink; to absorb; to swallow (*an insult etc.*).—*v.i.* to drink (*to someone's health*); to tipple; to blot (*of paper*).—*n.m.* drink; drinking.

bois [bwa], *n.m.* wood, forest; wood, timber; wooden part or object; horns (*of a deer etc.*).

boisage [bwa'za:ʒ], *n.m.* wood-work; timbering (*of mines etc.*); wainscotting.

(*C*) **bois-brûlé** [bwɑbry'le], *n.m.* half-breed.

(*C*) **bois-debout** [bwad'bu], *n.m.* standing timber.

boisé [bwa'ze], *a.* wooded, well-timbered.

boisement [bwaz'mã], *n.m.* planting land with trees.

boiser [bwa'ze], *v.t.* to put woodwork to; to timber (*a mine etc.*); to wainscot; to plant with woods.

boiserie [bwaz'ri], *n.f.* wainscot, wainscotting.

boisseau [bwa'so], *n.m.* (*pl.* **-eaux**) bushel.

boisson [bwa'sɔ̃], *n.f.* drink; beverage; (*fig.*) drinking, drunkenness; (*C*) hard liquor; *boisson forte*, strong drink, (*Am.*) liquor.

boîte [bwat], *n.f.* box; casket, caddy, chest; case (*of a watch, rudder etc.*); (*pop.*) mouth; *boîte à feu*, stoke-hole; (*Motor.*) *boîte de*

vitesses, gear box; *boîte de nuit*, night club; (*pop.*) *ta boîte!* shut your big mouth!

boitement [bwat'mã], *n.m.* halting, limping.

boiter [bwa'te], *v.i.* to limp; to be lame.

boiteux [bwa'tø], *a.* (*fem.* **-euse**) lame, halt, limping; rickety (*furniture*).—*n.m.* (*fem.* **-euse**) lame man or woman.

boîtier [bwa'tje], *n.m.* surgeon's case of instruments; case (*of a watch, an electric torch*).

bol [bɔl], *n.m.* bowl, basin.

bolchevik [bɔlʃə'vik], *n.m.* Bolshevik.

bolchevisme [bɔlʃə'vism], *n.m.* Bolshevism.

bolée [bɔ'le], *n.f.* bowlful.

boléro [bɔle'ro], *n.m.* bolero (*dance and garment*).

Bolivie [bɔli'vi], **la**, *f.* Bolivia.

bolivien [bɔli'vjɛ̃], *a.* (*fem.* **-enne**) Bolivian. —*n.m.* (**Bolivien**, *fem.* **-enne**) Bolivian (*person*).

bombance [bɔ̃'bã:s], *n.f.* feasting, junketing.

bombardement [bɔ̃bardə'mã], *n.m.* bombardment, shelling; *bombardement en piqué*, dive-bombing.

bombarder [bɔ̃bar'de], *v.t.* to bombard, to bomb; *quartier bombardé*, bombed site.

bombardier [bɔ̃bar'dje], *n.m.* bombardier.

bombe [bɔ̃:b], *n.f.* bomb; spray flask; *bombe atomique*, atom bomb; *bombe à hydrogène*, H-bomb; *bombe incendiaire*, incendiary bomb; (*colloq.*) *faire la bombe*, to be on a binge.

bombé [bɔ̃'be], *a.* convex, arched.

bombement [bɔ̃bə'mã], *n.m.* convexity, swelling, bulge.

bomber [bɔ̃'be], *v.t.* to cause (*something*) to bulge, jut, swell out, arch, curve or barrel.—*v.i.* to bulge, to jut out.

bombyx [bɔ̃'biks], *n.m.* (*Ent.*) bombyx; silk-worm.

bon (1) [bɔ̃], *a.* (*fem.* **bonne** (1)) good; kind, favorable; fine, convenient, advantageous, profitable, proper; well-executed, cleverly done etc.; easy, good-natured, (*iron.*) simple, credulous; *à quoi bon tant de peine?* what is the good of so much trouble? *il fait bon dans cette pièce*, this room is nice and warm; *pour de bon*, for good and all.—*n.m.* that which is good; the best.—*adv.* well, right, properly; *tout de bon*, seriously, truly.

bon (2) [bɔ̃], *n.m.* bond, coupon, voucher; *bon du trésor*, treasury bond; *bon d'essence*, gasoline coupon.

bonasse [bɔ'nas], *a.* simple-minded, credulous; soft.

bon-bec [bɔ̃'bɛk], *n.m.* (*pl.* **bons-becs**) chatterbox, gossip.

bonbon [bɔ̃'bɔ̃], *n.m.* sweet, (*Am.*) candy.

bond [bɔ̃], *n.m.* bound, leap, jump, caper; *faire faux bond*, to give (*someone*) the slip.

bonde [bɔ̃:d], *n.f.* bung-hole, bung; sluice, flood-gate.

bondé [bɔ̃'de], *a.* chock-full, packed, crammed.

bondir [bɔ̃'di:r], *v.i.* to bound, to leap, to bounce, to caper, to frisk.

bondissant [bɔ̃di'sã], *a.* bounding, skipping.

bondissement [bɔ̃dis'mã], *n.m.* bounding, skipping, frisking.

bonheur [bɔ'nœ:r], *n.m.* happiness, prosperity, welfare; good fortune, good luck, success.

bonhomie [bɔnɔ'mi], n.f. good nature; simplicity, credulity.

bonhomme [bɔ'nɔm], n.m. (pl. **bons-hommes** [bɔ'zɔm]) simple, good-natured man; foolish or credulous person; (fig.) rough drawing or effigy of a man; **bonhomme de neige**, snowman.

boni [bɔ'ni], n.m. bonus.

boniface [bɔni'fas], a. and n. (pop.) simple, artless (person).

bonification [bɔnifika'sjɔ̃], n.f. amelioration, improvement (of land); (Fin.) bonus, discount.

bonifier [bɔni'fje], v.t. to better, to improve; (Fin.) to pay, to transfer.

boniment [bɔni'mɑ̃], n.m. quack's show; (fig.) humbug.

bonjour [bɔ̃'ʒuːr], n.m. and int. good morning, good afternoon, good day.

bonne (1) [BON (1)].

bonne (1) [bɔn], n.f. servant maid; housemaid; **bonne d'enfants**, nursery-maid; **bonne à tout faire**, general maid.

bonnement [bɔn'mɑ̃], adv. plainly, simply, honestly; **tout bonnement**, quite frankly.

bonnet [bɔ'nɛ], n.m. cap; **c'est bonnet blanc et blanc bonnet**, it is six of one and half a dozen of the other.

bonneterie [bɔn'tri], n.f. hosiery business; hosiery.

bonnetier [bɔn'tje], n.m. (fem. **-ière**) hosier.

bon-prime [bɔ̃'prim], n.m. (Comm.) free-gift coupon.

bonsoir [bɔ̃'swaːr], n.m. and int. good evening, good night.

bonté [bɔ̃'te], n.f. goodness, kindness.

boom [bum], n.m. (Fin.) boom.

borax [bɔ'raks], n.m. borax.

bord [bɔːr], n.m. edge, margin, brink, brim, border, rim; shore, bank, side; **au bord de la mer**, at the seaside; **à bord**, on board; **par-dessus bord**, overboard.

bordage [bɔr'daːʒ], n.m. bordering, hemming etc.; (Naut.) planking, bulwarks.

bordé [bɔr'de], n.m. hem, edging, bordering (of a garment); (Naut.) planking.

bordeaux [bɔr'do], n.m. Bordeaux wine; **bordeaux rouge**, claret.

bordée [bɔr'de], n.f. (Naut.) broadside; volley, salvo; (C) **une bordée de neige**, a snow-fall.

bordelais [bɔrdə'lɛː], a. of Bordeaux.—n.m. (**Bordelais**, fem. **-aise**) native of Bordeaux.

border [bɔr'de], v.t. to border, to edge, to hem, to skirt, to bind; to tuck in (bedclothes); (Naut.) to haul (the sheets).

bordereau [bɔrdə'ro], n.m. (pl. **-eaux**) memorandum, note, schedule, account.

bordure [bɔr'dyːr], n.f. frame, edge, edging; margin, border, curb; rim.

boréal [bɔre'al], a. (m. pl. **-aux**) boreal, northern.

borée [bɔ're], n.m. Boreas, north wind (poet.).

borgne [bɔrɲ], a. one-eyed; **rue borgne**, blind alley.—n. one-eyed person.

borique [bɔ'rik], a. boric.

borne [bɔrn], n.f. landmark; boundary, limit, confine; milestone; (Elec.) terminal; **borne kilométrique**, milestone.

borné [bɔr'ne], a. bounded, limited, confined, narrow, mean, hide-bound.

borne-fontaine [bɔrnfɔ̃'tɛːn], n.f. (pl. **bornes-fontaines**) street fountain (like a boundary post).

borner [bɔr'ne], v.t. to set landmarks to; to bound, to limit, to confine.

Bosphore [bɔs'fɔːr], **le**, m. the Bosphorus.

bosquet [bɔs'kɛ], n.m. grove, thicket, arbor.

bosse [bɔs], n.f. hump, hunch; bump, bruise; knob, protuberance, lump, boss; (Arch.) embossment; (Sculp.) relief.

bosselage [bɔs'laːʒ], n.m. embossing.

bosseler [bɔs'le], v.t. (conjug. like APPELER) to dent; to emboss.

bossu [bɔ'sy], a. hunch-backed; deformed; crooked; pigeon-breasted.—n.m. (fem. **-e**) hunch-back; **rire comme un bossu**, to split one's sides with laughter.

bossuer [bɔ'sɥe], v.t. to dent, to batter.

boston [bɔs'tɔ̃], n.m. boston (card game, dance).

bot [bɔ], a. **pied bot**, club foot, club-footed.

botanique [bɔta'nik], a. botanical.—n.f. botany.

botaniser [bɔtani'ze], v.i. to botanize.

botaniste [bɔta'nist], n. botanist.

botte (1) [bɔt], n.f. wellington boot, jack-boot.

botte (2) [bɔt], n.f. bunch, truss, bale.

botte (3) [bɔt], n.f. (Fenc.) pass, thrust

bottelage [bɔt'laːʒ], n.m. tying up in bundles.

botteler [bɔt'le], v.t. (conjug. like APPELER) to put up in bundles, to truss.

botteloir [bɔt'lwaːr], n.m., **botteleuse** [bɔt'løːz], n.f. sheaf-binding machine, binder.

botter [bɔ'te], v.t. to put boots on (a person).

bottier [bɔ'tje], n.m. bootmaker.

bottin [bɔ'tɛ̃], n.m. a directory published by the firm of Didot Bottin.

bottine [bɔ'tin], n.f. (ankle) boot.

bouc [buk], n.m. billy goat; **bouc émissaire** scapegoat.

boucanage [buka'naːʒ], n.m. smoke-drying.

boucaner [buka'ne], v.t. to smoke (meat, hides etc.).

boucanier [buka'nje], n.m. buccaneer; freebooter.

(C) **boucanière** [buka'nɛːr], n.f. smokehouse (for fish).

bouchage [bu'ʃaːʒ], n.m. stopping, corking.

bouche [buʃ], n.f. mouth; lips; tongue; voice; victuals; muzzle (of a cannon); **bouche d'eau**, hydrant.

bouchée [bu'ʃe], n.f. mouthful.

boucher (1) [bu'ʃe], v.t. to stop, to choke.

boucher (2) [bu'ʃe], n.m. butcher.

bouchère [bu'ʃɛːr], n.f. butcher's wife; woman keeping a butcher's shop.

boucherie [buʃ'ri], n.f. butcher's shop; butchery, slaughter.

bouche-trou [buʃ'tru], n.m. (pl. **bouche-trous**) stopgap.

bouchon [bu'ʃɔ̃], n.m. stopper, cork; wisp (of straw etc.).

bouchonner [buʃɔ'ne], v.t. to rub down (a horse).

bouchonnier [buʃɔ'nje], n.m. one who cuts or sells corks.

boucle [bukl], n.f. buckle; curl; lock (of hair); loop (of a river etc.).

bouclé [bu'kle], a. buckled, curled.

boucler [buˈkle], *v.t.* to buckle; to put a ring to; to curl (*hair*); **boucler la boucle,** to loop the loop. **se boucler,** *v.r.* to curl one's hair.

bouclier [buˈklje], *n.m.* buckler, shield; (*fig.*) defense.

Bouddha [buˈda], *m.* Buddha.

bouddhisme [buˈdism], *n.m.* Buddhism.

bouddhiste [buˈdist], *n.* Buddhist.

bouder [buˈde], *v.i.* to sulk, to be sullen, to pout. **se bouder,** *v.r.* to be cool towards each other.

bouderie [buˈdri], *n.f.* pouting, sulkiness.

boudeur [buˈdœːr], *a.* (*fem.* -**euse**) sulky, sullen.

boudin [buˈdɛ̃], *n.m.* blood sausage; spring (*of a coach*).

boudoir [buˈdwaːr], *n.m.* boudoir, lady's private room.

boue [bu], *n.f.* mud, mire, dirt, filth.

bouée [buˈe], *n.f.* buoy.

boueux [buˈø], *a.* (*fem.* -**euse**) muddy, dirty, miry; foul.—*n.m.* scavenger; garbage man.

bouffant [buˈfɑ̃], *a.* a puffed (*sleeve*), baggy (*trousers*).

bouffe [buf], *a.* comic.—*n.m. pl.* **Les Bouffes,** the Italian opera (*in Paris*).

bouffée [buˈfe], *n.f.* puff, gust, blast, whiff.

bouffette [buˈfɛt], *n.f.* bow of ribbon; tassel.

bouffi [buˈfi], *a.* puffed up, swollen, inflated.

bouffir [buˈfiːr], *v.t.* to puff up, to swell, to bloat.—*v.i.* to swell.

bouffissure [bufiˈsyːr], *n.f.* swelling, puffing up.

bouffon [buˈfɔ̃], *a.* (*fem.* -**onne**) jocose, facetious, comical.—*n.m.* buffoon, clown, jester.

bouffonner [bufoˈne], *v.i.* to play the buffoon; to be jocose *or* full of jests.

bouffonnerie [bufonˈri], *n.f.* buffoonery, drollery, jesting.

bougainvillée [bugɛ̃viˈle], *n.f.*, **bougainvillier** [bugɛ̃viˈlje], *n.m.* bougainvillea.

bouge [buːʒ], *n.m.* den, dirty hole, hovel.

bougeoir [buˈʒwaːr], *n.m.* flat candlestick.

bouger [buˈʒe], *v.i.* (*conjug. like* MANGER) to stir, to budge, to fidget.

bougie [buˈʒi], *n.f.* wax candle; (*Elec.*) candlepower; **bougie d'allumage,** (*Motor.*) spark plug.

bougran [buˈgrɑ̃], *n.m.* buckram.

bouillabaisse [bujaˈbɛs], *n.f.* Provençal fish soup with saffron etc.

bouillant [buˈjɑ̃], *a.* boiling, hot, scalding.

bouilleur [buˈjœːr], *n.m.* brandy distiller; boiler tube (*of an engine*).

bouilli [buˈji], *n.m.* boiled beef.

bouillie [buˈji], *n.f.* pap (*for infants*), porridge; pulp.

bouillir [buˈjiːr], *v.t. irr.* to boil (*milk etc.*).—*v.i.* to boil.

bouilloire [bujˈwaːr], *n.f.* kettle.

bouillon [buˈjɔ̃], *n.m.* broth, beef tea; bubble; ebullition.

bouillonnement [bujonˈmɑ̃], *n.m.* bubbling up, spouting, gushing.

bouillonner [bujoˈne], *v.i.* to bubble, to boil; (*fig.*) to be in a state of excitement.

bouillotte [buˈjot], *n.f.* foot warmer; hot-water bottle; small kettle.

boulanger [bulɑ̃ˈʒe], *n.m.* (*fem.* -**ère**) baker, baker's wife.—*v.t.* (*conjug. like* MANGER) to make, knead *or* bake (*bread*).

boulangerie [bulɑ̃ˈʒri], *n.f.* baking, baker's business; baker's shop.

boule [bul], *n.f.* ball; bowl; (*pop.*) face, pate, head.

bouleau [buˈlo], *n.m.* (*pl.* -**eaux**) birch, birch tree.

bouledogue [bulˈdɔg], *n.m.* bulldog.

boulet [buˈlɛ], *n.m.* cannon *or* musket ball.

boulette [buˈlɛt], *n.f.* pellet; forcemeat ball.

boulevard [bulˈvaːr], *n.m.* rampart; (*fig.*) to agitate, to boulevard.

bouleversement [bulvɛrsəˈmɑ̃], *n.m.* overthrow; commotion, confusion; destruction, ruin.

bouleverser [bulvɛrˈse], *v.t.* to overthrow, to throw down; to upset.

boulier [buˈlje], *n.m.* (*Fishing*) bag net; scoring board (*at billiards*).

bouline [buˈlin], *n.f.* (*Naut.*) bowline.

boulon [buˈlɔ̃], *n.m.* bolt, large iron pin.

boulonner [buloˈne], *v.t.* to fasten with iron pins, to bolt.

boulot [buˈlo], *a.* (*fem.* -**otte**) fat, dumpy, squat.

bouquet [buˈkɛ], *n.m.* bunch (*of flowers*), nosegay, bouquet; aroma (*of wine*), perfume.

bouquetier [bukˈtje], *n.f.* flower vase.

bouquetière [bukˈtjeːr], *n.f.* flower girl.

bouquetin [bukˈtɛ̃], *n.m.* ibex.

bouquin (1) [buˈkɛ̃], *n.m.* (*Zool.*) old billy goat; old hare.

bouquin (2) [buˈkɛ̃], *n.m.* old book; second-hand book; (*colloq.*) book.

bouquiner [bukiˈne], *v.i.* to hunt after old books; (*colloq.*) to read.

bouquineur [bukiˈnœːr], *n.m.* (*colloq.*) lover of old books, book fancier.

bouquiniste [bukiˈnist], *n.m.* dealer in second-hand books.

bourbe [burb], *n.f.* mud, mire, slush.

bourbeux [burˈbø], *a.* (*fem.* -**euse**) miry, muddy, sloshy.

bourbier [burˈbje], *n.m.* slough, puddle, mire.

bourdaine [burˈdɛn], **bourgène** [burˈʒɛn], *n.f.* black alder.

bourdon (1) [burˈdɔ̃], *n.m.* pilgrim's staff.

bourdon (2) [burˈdɔ̃], *n.m.* bumblebee; great bell; (*Organ*) drone.

bourdonnant [burdɔˈnɑ̃], *a.* humming, buzzing.

bourdonnement [burdɔnˈmɑ̃], *n.m.* buzz, buzzing; humming.

bourdonner [burdɔˈne], *v.t.* to hum.—*v.i.* to buzz, to hum; to murmur.

bourdonneur [burdɔˈnœːr], *a.* humming.—*n.m.* hummingbird, colibri.

bourg [buːr], *n.m.* borough, market-town.

bourgade [burˈgad], *n.f.* small market-town.

bourgène [BOURDAINE].

bourgeois [burˈʒwa], *a.* middle-class; plain, common, ordinary.—*n.m.* (*fem.* -**e**) citizen, townsman, townswoman; commoner; middle-class person, bourgeois.

bourgeoisie [burʒwaˈzi], *n.f.* bourgeoisie, middle class.

bourgeon [burˈʒɔ̃], *n.m.* (*Bot.*) bud, shoot; pimple.

bourgeonnement [burʒɔnˈmɑ̃], *n.m.* budding.

bourgeonner [burʒɔ'ne], *v.i.* to bud; to break out in pimples.
bourgeron [burʒə'rɔ̃], *n.m.* workman's blouse, smock frock.
bourgmestre [burg'mɛstr], *n.m.* burgo-master.
Bourgogne [bur'gɔɲ], **la**, *f.* Burgundy.
bourguignon [burgi'ɲɔ̃], *a.* (*fem.* **-onne**) Burgundian, of Burgundy.—*n.m.* (**Bour-guignon**, *fem.* **-onne**) native *or* inhabitant of Burgundy.
bourrade [bu'rad], *n.f.* blow, thrust, buffet.
bourrasque [bu'rask], *n.f.* squall, gust; fit of anger.
bourre [bu:r], *n.f.* hair, fluff (*of animals*); flock (*of wool*); floss (*of silk*); (*fig.*) stuff, trash.
bourreau [bu'ro], *n.m.* (*pl.* **-eaux**) hangman, executioner; tyrant.
bourrée [bu're], *n.f.* brushwood, faggot; an Auvergne dance.
bourreler [bur'le], *v.t.* (*conjug. like* APPELER) to torment, to rack.
bourrelet [bur'le], *n.m.* pad, cushion.
bourrelier [burə'lje], *n.m.* harness maker.
bourrellerie [burɛl'ri], *n.f.* harness maker's shop.
bourrer [bu're], *v.t.* to tamp; to stuff, to cram; (*fig.*) to ill-treat, to thrash. **se bourrer**, *v.r.* to cram oneself; to thrash each other.
bourriche [bu'riʃ], *n.f.* game basket, basket of game.
bourrique [bu'rik], *n.f.* she-ass; (*fig.*) stupid person, dolt.
bourriquet [buri'kɛ], *n.m.* ass's colt *or* small ass; hand barrow.
bourru [bu'ry], *a.* cross, peevish, moody, surly.
Bourse [burs], *n.f.* Stock Exchange; *Bourse du travail,* labor exchange.
bourse [burs], *n.f.* purse, bag; scholarship, grant, bursary; rabbit net.
boursier [bur'sje], *a.* (*fem.* **-ière**) pertaining to the Stock Exchange.—*n.m.* (*fem.* **-ière**) speculator on the Stock Exchange, exchange broker; purse maker; scholarship holder.
boursouflage [bursu'fla:ʒ], *n.m.* bombast.
boursouflé [bursu'fle], *a.* bloated; bombastic, swollen.
boursouflement [bursuflə'mã], *n.m.* bloated-ness, puffiness; blister (*of paint*).
boursoufler [bursu'fle], *v.t.* to bloat, to puff up.
boursouflure [bursu'fly:r], *n.f.* bloatedness (*of face etc.*); (*fig.*) turgidity (*of style*).
bousculade [busky'lad], *n.f.* jostling, hustling; scrimmage.
bousculer [busky'le], *v.t.* to throw into disorder; to jostle, to hustle. **se bousculer**, *v.r.* to jostle each other.
boussole [bu'sɔl], *n.f.* compass.
bout [bu], *n.m.* end, tip, top, point; fragment, bit; *venir à bout de,* to succeed, to get through (*something*).
boutade [bu'tad], *n.f.* whim, fit, start, caprice; witticism.
boute-en-train [butã'trɛ̃], *n.m. inv.* one who promotes gayety in others, merry-maker; *être le boute-en-train,* to be the life and soul of the party.
boutefeu [but'fø], *n.m.* (*pl.* **-eux**) (*fig.*) incendiary, fire-brand.

bouteille [bu'tɛːj], *n.f.* bottle; bottleful.
bouteillerie [butɛj'ri], *n.f.* bottle-works.
boutique [bu'tik], *n.f.* shop; work-shop; (*collect.*) tools, implements.
boutiquier [buti'kje], *n.m.* (*fem.* **-ière**) shop-keeper.—*a.* (*fem.* **-ière**) shopkeeping.
bouton [bu'tɔ̃], *n.m.* bud; pimple; button, stud, knob; (*Elec. etc.*) switch.
bouton d'or [butɔ̃'dɔːr], *n.m.* (*pl.* **boutons d'or**) (*Bot.*) buttercup.
boutonné [butɔ'ne], *a.* buttoned; pimpled.
boutonner [butɔ'ne], *v.t.* to button; (*Fenc.*) to touch.—*v.i.* to bud; to button up. **se boutonner**, *v.r.* to button one's coat.
boutonnière [butɔ'njɛːr], *n.f.* buttonhole.
bouture [bu'ty:r], *n.f.* slip, cutting.
bouveau [bu'vo] (*pl.* **-eaux**), **bouvelet** [buv'lɛ], *n.m.* young ox.
bouverie [bu'vri], *n.f.* cattle shed, byre.
bouvet [bu've], *n.m.* joiner's grooving-plane.
bouvetage [buv'ta:ʒ], *n.m.* grooving and tonguing.
bouveter [buv'te], *v.t.* (*conjug. like* APPELER) to groove and tongue.
bouvier [bu'vje], *n.m.* (*fem.* **-ière**) cow-herd, ox-drover.
bouvillon [buvi'jɔ̃], *n.m.* young bullock, steer.
bouvreuil [bu'vrœːj], *n.m.* bullfinch.
bovin [bɔ'vɛ̃], *a.* bovine.
box [bɔks], *n.m.* (*pl.* **boxes**) horse box, loose box; lock-up garage; *le box des accusés,* the dock.
boxe [bɔks], *n.f.* boxing.
boxer [bɔk'se], *v.i.* to box, to spar.
boxeur [bɔk'sœːr], *n.m.* boxer, prize-fighter.
boy [bɔj], *n.m.* groom; native servant.
boyau [bwa'jo], *n.m.* (*pl.* **-aux**) bowel, gut; catgut; hose-pipe; (*Cycl.*) racing tire.
brabançon [brabã'sɔ̃], *a.* (*fem.* **-onne**) Brabantine, Belgian.—*n.m.* (**Brabançon**, *fem.* **-onne**) Brabantine, Belgian (*person*).
bracelet [bras'lɛ], *n.m.* bracelet, armlet, bangle.
bracelet-montre [braslɛ'mɔ̃:tr], *n.m.* (*pl.* **bracelets-montres**) wrist watch.
braconnage [brakɔ'na:ʒ], *n.m.* poaching.
braconner [brakɔ'ne], *v.i.* to poach, to steal game.
braconnier [brakɔ'nje], *n.m.* (*fem.* **-ière**) poacher.—*a.* (*fem.* **-ière**) poaching; pertaining to poaching.
braguette [bra'gɛt], *n.f.* fly (*of trousers*).
brahmane [bra'man], **brahme** [bram], *n.m.* Brahmin.
brahmanisme [brama'nism], *n.m.* Brahmin-ism.
brahme [BRAHMANE].
brai [brɛ], *n.m.* resin, rosin, pitch.
braillard [bra'ja:r], *a.* brawling, squalling; obstreperous.—*n.m.* (*fem.* **-e**) brawler, squaller.—*n.m.* small speaking-trumpet.
braille [braj], *n.m.* braille.
braillement [braj'mã], *n.m.* squalling.
brailler [bra'je], *v.i.* to bawl, to shout, to be noisy.
brailleur [bra'jœːr], *a.* and *n.m.* (*fem.* **-euse**) [BRAILLARD].
braiment [brɛ'mã], *n.m.* braying (*of an ass*).
braire [brɛːr], *v.i. irr.* to bray; (*fig.*) to cry, to whine.
braise [brɛːz], *n.f.* wood embers, live coals.

braiser [brɛ'ze], *v.t.* to braise.
braisier [brɛ'zje], *n.m.* brazier.
braisière [brɛ'zjɛːr], *n.f.* braising pan.
bramer [bra'me], *v.i.* to bell (*of deer*).
brancard [brɑ̃'kaːr], *n.m.* stretcher, litter; hand barrow; shaft (*of a cart*).
brancardier [brɑ̃kar'dje], *n.m.* stretcher bearer, ambulance man.
branchage [brɑ̃'ʃaːʒ], *n.m.* (*collect.*) branches, boughs.
branche [brɑ̃ːʃ], *n.f.* branch, bough; part, division.
brancher [brɑ̃'ʃe], *v.t.* to divide into branches; (*Elec.*) to connect, to plug in; to tap (*a gas or water pipe*).—*v.i.* to branch off.
branchu [brɑ̃'ʃy], *a.* forked, bifurcated, ramifying.
brande [brɑ̃ːd], *n.f.* heather; heath.
Brandebourg [brɑ̃d'buːr], *m.* Brandenburg.
brandebourgs [brɑ̃d'buːr], *n.m. pl.* braid; frogs and loops (*on a uniform*).
brandillement [brɑ̃dij'mɑ̃], *n.m.* tossing; swinging.
brandiller [brɑ̃di'je], *v.t.* to swing, to shake to and fro.—*v.i.* to swing, to move to and fro. **se brandiller,** *v.r.* to swing.
brandir [brɑ̃'diːr], *v.t.* to brandish, to flourish.
brandissement [brɑ̃dis'mɑ̃], *n.m.* brandishing, flourishing.
brandon [brɑ̃'dɔ̃], *n.m.* torch, fire-brand.
branlant [brɑ̃'lɑ̃], *a.* shaking, loose, tottering.
branle [brɑ̃ːl], *n.m.* oscillation, shaking or tossing motion; jog; an old-fashioned dance.
branle-bas [brɑ̃l'ba], *n.m. inv.* (*Naut.*) clearing for action; (*fig.*) commotion, disturbance.
branlement [brɑ̃l'mɑ̃], *n.m.* oscillation, shaking, swing.
branler [brɑ̃'le], *v.t.* to shake, to wag.—*v.i.* to shake, to stagger, to rock; to move; to waver.
braquage [bra'kaːʒ], *n.m.* aiming, steering, lock (*of a car*).
braque (1) [brak], *n.m.* French pointer.
braque (2) [brak], *a.* madcap, hare-brained.
braquer [bra'ke], *v.t.* to aim, to level, to point.
bras [brɑ], *n.m.* arm; bracket; branch (*of a stream etc.*); (*fig.*) power, action, assistance.
braser [bra'ze], *v.t.* to braze.
brasier [bra'zje], *n.m.* quick clear fire; brazier, furnace.
brasiller [brazi'je], *v.t.* to grill, to broil.—*v.i.* to glitter, to shine (*of the sea*).
brassage [bra'saːʒ], *n.m.* mashing, brewing.
brassard [bra'saːr], *n.m.* brace (*armor*); armlet.
brasse [brɑs], *n.f.* fathom, six feet; armful; stroke (*in swimming*).
brassée [bra'se], *n.f.* armful; stroke (*in swimming*).
brassement [bras'mɑ̃], *n.m.* brewing; mixing.
brasser [bra'se], *v.t.* to mix; to brew, to mash; to stir up.
brasserie [bras'ri], *n.f.* brewery; brewing; drinking-saloon, 'pub'.
brasseur [brɑ'sœːr], *n.m.* brewer.
brassière [bra'sjɛːr], *n.f.* shoulder strap (*of a knapsack etc.*); infant's undershirt.
brassin [bra'sɛ̃], *n.m.* brewing tub; mash tub; a boiling (*quantity boiled or brewed*).

bravache [bra'vaʃ], *n.m.* bully, swaggerer, blusterer.—*a.* blustering, bullying.
bravade [bra'vad], *n.f.* bravado, boast, bluster.
brave [braːv], *a.* brave, courageous, gallant; worthy, honest, good.—*n.m.* brave *or* courageous man; good fellow.
bravement [brav'mɑ̃], *adv.* bravely, stoutly, valiantly; skilfully, finely.
braver [bra've], *v.t.* to defy, to dare; to brave, to beard.
bravo [bra'vo], *n.m.* (*pl.* **bravos**) and *int.* bravo; hear, hear!
bravoure [bra'vuːr], *n.f.* bravery, courage, gallantry; (*pl.*) exploits.
break [brɛk], *n.m.* break (*carriage*).
brebis [brə'bi], *n.f.* ewe; (*fig.*) sheep; (*pl.*) flock.
brèche [brɛʃ], *n.f.* breach, flaw; notch, gap.
bréchet [bre'ʃɛ], *n.m.* (*Orn.*) breast-bone.
bredouillage [brədu'jaːʒ], *n.m.* bredouillement [brəduj'mɑ̃], *n.m.* stammering, stuttering, sputtering.
bredouille [brə'duːj], *n.f.*(*backgammon*)lurch. *a. inv.* empty-handed; *revenir bredouille,* to return with an empty bag (*of sportsmen*).
bredouillement [BREDOUILLAGE].
bredouiller [brədu'je], *v.t.*, *v.i.* to stammer, to stutter.
bredouilleur [brədu'jœːr], *a.* (*fem.* **-euse**) stammering, stuttering.—*n.m.* (*fem.* **-euse**) stammerer, stutterer.
bref [brɛf], *a.* (*fem.* **brève** (1)) short, brief, concise; brusque.—*adv.* in short, in fine, in a word.
brelan [brə'lɑ̃], *n.m.* brelan (*card game*); gaming house.
brêler, or breller [brɛ'le], *v.t.* to lash.
breller [BRÊLER].
breloque [brə'lɔk], *n.f.* trinket, gewgaw, charm.
Brême [brɛːm], *m.* Bremen.
brème [brɛːm], *n.f.* bream.
Brésil [bre'zil], **le,** *m.* Brazil.
brésil [bre'zil], *n.m.* Brazil-wood (*for dyeing*).
brésilien [brezi'ljɛ̃], *a.* (*fem.* **-enne**) Brazilian.—*n.m.* (**Brésilien,** *fem.* **-enne**) Brazilian (*person*).
Bretagne [brə'taɲ], **la,** *f.* Brittany; *la Grande-Bretagne,* Great Britain; *la Nouvelle-Bretagne,* New Britain.
bretelle [brə'tɛl], *n.f.* strap; brace; (*pl.*) pair of braces; (*Rail.*) switch; (*rifle*) sling.
breton [brə'tɔ̃], *a.* (*fem.* **-onne**) Breton.—*n.m.* Breton (*language*); (**Breton,** *fem.* **-onne**) Breton (*person*).
bretteur [brɛ'tœːr], *n.m.* swashbuckler, duellist.
bretzel [brɛt'sɛl], *n.m.* pretzel.
breuil [brœːj], *n.m.* enclosed coppice, covert.
breuvage [brœ'vaːʒ], *n.m.* beverage, drink, liquor.
brève (1) [brɛːv], [BREF].
brève (2) [brɛːv], *n.f.* short syllable; (*Mus.*) breve.
brevet [brə've], *n.m.* warrant, brevet, certificate (*school etc.*); diploma, license (*of printers*); patent; badge (*of boy scouts*); (*Mil.*) commission.
breveté [brəv'te], *a.* patented; (*Mil.*) certificated—*n.m.* (*fem.* **-ée**) patentee.

breveter [brəv'te], v.t. (conjug. like APPELER) to patent; to license; to certificate.

bréviaire [bre'vjɛːr], n.m. breviary.

brévité [brevi'te], n.f. shortness (of syllables).

bribes [brib], n.f. pl. scraps, bits; odds and ends.

bric-à-brac [brika'brak], n.m. inv. curios, bric-a-brac; curiosity shop.

brick [brik], n.m. brig.

bricolage [briko'la:ʒ], n.m. puttering.

bricoler [briko'le], v.i. to putter, to do odds and ends.

bricoleur [briko'lœːr], n.m. (fem. -euse) odd job man, handyman or woman.

bride [brid], n.f. bridle, bridle rein; check, curb; string (of a woman's cap, bonnet etc.).

brider [bri'de], v.t. to bridle; to restrain, to curb; to truss (a fowl); to tie; to check.

bridge [bridʒ], n.m. bridge (card game), bridge (in dentistry).

bridger [bri'dʒe], v.i. to play bridge.

bridgeur [bri'dʒœːr], n.m. (fem. -euse) bridge player.

bridon [bri'dõ], n.m. snaffle bridle.

brie [bri], n.m. Brie cheese.

brièvement [briɛv'mã], adv. briefly, succinctly, in short.

brièveté [briɛv'te], n.f. brevity, briefness, conciseness.

brigade [bri'gad], n.f. brigade; (fig.) troop, gang, body.

brigadier [briga'dje], n.m. corporal (in cavalry, artillery); sergeant (of police).

brigand [bri'gã], n.m. brigand; (fig.) robber, thief.

brigandage [brigã'da:ʒ], n.m. brigandage, plunder.

brigander [brigã'de], v.i. to rob, to plunder.

brigantin [brigã'tɛ̃], n.m. brigantine.

brigantine [brigã'tin], n.f. (Naut.) spanker; small vessel.

brigue [brig], n.f. intrigue, cabal, faction.

briguer [bri'ge], v.t. to canvass for, to solicit, to court.

brigueur [bri'gœːr], n.m. (fem. -euse) intriguer, canvasser.

brillamment [brija'mã], adv. brilliantly, in a brilliant manner.

brillance [bri'jã:s], n.f. (Opt.) brilliancy.

brillant [bri'jã], a. brilliant, sparkling, glittering; radiant.—n.m. brilliance, splendor; brilliant (diamond).

brillanter [brijã'te], v.t. to cut into a brilliant.

brillantine [brijã'tin], n.f. brilliantine (hair-oil); glossy cotton cloth.

briller [bri'je], v.i. to shine, to glitter, to sparkle; (fig.) to distinguish oneself, to stand out.

brimade [bri'mad], n.f. ragging; vexation, persecution.

brimborion [brɛ̃bo'rjõ], n.m. knick-knack, bauble.

brimer [bri'me], v.t. to rag, to bully.

brin [brɛ̃], n.m. blade, slender stalk, shoot (of corn etc.); (fig.) bit, jot.

brindille [brɛ̃'di:j], n.f. sprig, twig.

brio [bri'o] [It.], n.m. (Mus. etc.) dash, spirit, go.

brioche [bri'ɔʃ], n.f. brioche, bun; (fig.) blunder.

brique [brik], n.f. brick; brique anglaise, Bath brick.

briquet [bri'kɛ], n.m. tinder box; (cigarette) lighter.

briquetage [brik'ta:ʒ], n.m. brick work; imitation brick work.

briqueter [brik'te], v.t. (conjug. like APPELER) to brick, to pave with bricks.

briqueterie [brik'tri], n.f. brick field, brick making; brickworks.

briqueteur [brik'tœːr], n.m. bricklayer.

briquetier [brik'tje], n.m. brick maker.

briquette [bri'kɛt], n.f. briquette; compressed slack.

brisant [bri'zã], n.m. sand bank, reef, shoal; (pl.) breakers.

brise [bri:z], n.f. breeze; strong wind.

brisé [bri'ze], a. broken to pieces; (fig.) harassed.

brise-bise [briz'bi:z], n.m. inv. draft excluder; sash curtain.

brisées [bri'ze], n.f. (used only in pl.) footsteps, wake; aller or marcher sur les brisées de quelqu'un, to poach on someone's preserves.

brise-glace [briz'glas], n.m. (pl. brise-glace or -glaces) ice-breaker (ship).

brise-jet [briz'ʒɛ], n.m. inv. anti-splash tap nozzle.

brise-lames [briz'lam], n.m. inv. breakwater.

brisement [briz'mã], n.m. breaking, dashing (of waves); (fig.) trouble, contrition.

briser [bri'ze], v.t. to break to pieces, to smash, to break, to shatter; to burst; to crack; to destroy.—v.i. to break; to dash (of waves).

brise-tout [briz'tu], n.m. inv. person who breaks everything; rough, clumsy fellow.

briseur [bri'zœːr], n.m. (fem. -euse) one who breaks or likes to break anything; iconoclast.

brise-vent [briz'vã], n.m. (pl. brise-vent or brise-vents) wind-screen (for protecting plants).

brisque [brisk], n.f. a card game; (Mil.) stripe; war service chevron.

brisure [bri'zy:r], n.f. break; folding-point in a piece of joiner's work; small fragment.

britannique [brita'nik], a. British, Britannic; Les Iles Britanniques, the British Isles.

broc [bro], n.m. large jug or quart pot.

brocantage [brokã'ta:ʒ], n.m. dealing in second-hand goods, broker's business; bartering.

brocante [bro'kã:t], n.f. second-hand trade; article of trifling value.

brocanter [brokã'te], v.i. to deal in second-hand goods; to exchange, to barter.

brocanteur [brokã'tœːr], n.m. (fem. -euse) dealer in second-hand goods, junk-shop owner.

brocard [bro'ka:r], n.m. taunt, jeer; lampoon.

brocarder [brokar'de], v.t. to taunt, to ridicule.

brocardeur [brokar'dœːr], n.m. (fem. -euse) scoffer, jeerer.

brocart or **broquart** [bro'ka:r], n.m. brocade.

brochage [bro'ʃa:ʒ], n.m. stitching (of books).

broche [broʃ], n.f. spit; spindle; skewer; spigot; knitting needle; brooch; (pl.) tusks (of wild boars); (Elec.) fiche à deux broches, two-pin plug.

broché

broché [brɔ'ʃe], *a.* embossed (*of linen*); brocaded, figured (*of other materials*); *livre broché,* paper-bound book.

brocher [brɔ'ʃe], *v.t.* to stitch (*a book etc.*); to figure (*materials*); to emboss (*linen*).

brochet [brɔ'ʃe], *n.m.* pike (*fish*).

brocheter [brɔʃ'te], *v.t.* (*conjug. like* APPELER) to skewer.

brochette [brɔ'ʃɛt], *n.f.* (*Cook.*) small spit.

brocheur [brɔ'ʃœːr], *n.m.* (*fem.* **-euse**) stitcher, esp. book-stitcher.

brochure [brɔ'ʃyːr], *n.f.* stitching; booklet, brochure, pamphlet, tract; embroidery.

brocoli [brɔkɔ'li], *n.m.* broccoli.

brodequin [brɔd'kɛ̃], *n.m.* buskin, half-boot.

broder [brɔ'de], *v.t.* to embroider; to adorn, to embellish (*a story etc.*).—*v.i.* to romance.

broderie [brɔd'ri], *n.f.* embroidery; (*fig.*) embellishment.

brodeur [brɔ'dœːr], *n.m.* (*fem.* **-euse**) embroiderer.

broiement *or* **broîment** [brwa'mã], **broyage** [brwa'jaːʒ], *n.m.* grinding, powdering.

bromure [brɔ'myːr], *n.m.* bromide.

bronche [brɔ̃ːʃ], *n.f.* (*pl.*) (*Anat.*) bronchial tubes.

bronchement [brɔ̃ʃ'mã], *n.m.* stumbling; flinching.

broncher [brɔ̃'ʃe], *v.i.* to stumble, to trip, to reel; to falter.

bronchial [brɔ̃'ʃjal], *a.* (*m. pl.* **-aux**) (*Anat.*) bronchial.

bronchique [brɔ̃'ʃik], *a.* bronchial.

bronchite [brɔ̃'ʃit], *n.f.* (*Path.*) bronchitis.

broncho-pneumonie [brɔ̃kɔpnømɔ'ni], *n.f.* broncho-pneumonia.

bronze [brɔ̃ːz], *n.m.* bronze; bronze statue *or* medal.

bronzer [brɔ̃'ze], *v.t.* to bronze; to tan (*the face etc.*).

broquart [BROCART].

broquette [brɔ'kɛt], *n.f.* tack, carpet nail.

brosse [brɔs], *n.f.* brush; painter's brush *or* pencil; *cheveux en brosse,* crew-cut hair.

brosser [brɔ'se], *v.t.* to brush. **se brosser,** *v.r.* to brush oneself.

brosserie [brɔs'ri], *n.f.* brushmaking business; brush factory.

brou [bru], *n.m.* husk *or* peel (*of nuts, esp. walnuts*); **brou de noix,** walnut stain, walnut liquor.

brouet [bru'e], *n.m.* thin broth.

brouette [bru'ɛt], *n.f.* wheelbarrow.

brouettée [brue'te], *n.f.* barrow load.

brouetter [brue'te], *v.t.* to wheel in a barrow.

brouetteur [brue'tœːr], **brouettier** [brue'tje], *n.m.* barrowman.

brouhaha [brua'a], *n.m.* hubbub, uproar, hurly-burly.

brouillage [bruj'aːʒ], *n.m.* (*Rad.*) atmospherics, jamming.

brouillard [bru'jaːr], *n.m.* fog, mist, haze; (*Comm.*) daybook.

brouillasse [bru'jas], *n.f.* drizzle, Scotch mist.

brouillasser [bruja'se], *v.impers.* to drizzle.

brouille [bruːj], **brouillerie** [bruj'ri], *n.f.* quarrel, falling-out.

brouillé [bru'je], *a.* scrambled (*eggs*); blurred; on bad terms.

brouillement [bruj'mã], *n.m.* mixing together, jumbling.

brouiller [bru'je], *v.t.* to mix together, to jumble up, to shuffle; to embroil, to confuse; (*Rad.*) to jam. **se brouiller,** *v.r.* to fall out (*with someone*).

brouillerie [BROUILLE].

brouillon [bru'jɔ̃], *a.* (*fem.* **-onne**) mischief-making; blundering.—*n.m.* rough draft, rough copy; blunderer, bungler.

brouillonner [brujɔ'ne], *v.t.* to write in a blundering *or* confused way, to botch.

brouir [bru'iːr], *v.t.* to blight, to nip, to parch.

brouissure [brui'syːr], *n.f.* blight, scorching.

broussailles [bru'saːj], *n.f.* (*usu. in pl.*) bushes, brushwood, undergrowth.

broussailleux [brusa'jø], *a.* (*fem.* **-euse**) bushy, covered with bushes.

brousse [brus], *n.f.* brushwood, bush (*Australia etc.*).

brouter [bru'te], *v.t., v.i.* to browse, to graze.

broutilles [bru'tiːj], *n.f. pl.* sprigs; (*fig.*) trifles.

brownien [bro'nɛ̃], *a. mouvements browniens,* molecular motion.

browning [bro'niŋ], *n.m.* automatic pistol.

broyage [brwa'jaːʒ], *n.m.* crushing (*of ore*), grinding (*of colors*).

broyer [brwa'je], *v.t.* (*conjug. like* EMPLOYER) to grind, to pound, to pulverize.

broyeur [brwa'jœːr], *a.* (*fem.* **-euse**) grinding.—*n.m.* (*fem.* **-euse**) grinding; grinder, pounder.

bru [bry], *n.f.* daughter-in-law.

brucelles [bry'sɛl], *n.f. pl.* tweezers.

brugnon [bry'nɔ̃], *n.m.* nectarine.

bruine [bruin], *n.f.* light drizzling rain.

bruiner [brui'ne], *v.impers.* to drizzle.

bruineux [brui'nø], *a.* (*fem.* **-euse**) drizzly, drizzling.

bruire [bruiːr], *v.t. irr.* to make a noise; to rustle, to rattle; to roar, to sough (*of the wind*).

bruissant [brui'sã], *a.* rustling, rattling, roaring.

bruissement [bruis'mã], *n.m.* rustling noise, rattling, roaring.

bruit [brui], *n.m.* noise, din, uproar, clamor; fame, renown; report, talk, rumor.

bruitage [brui'taːʒ], *n.m.* sound effects.

bruiter [brui'te], *v.i.* to make sound effects.

bruiteur [brui'tœːr], *n.m.* sound-effects specialist.

brûlage [bry'laːʒ], *n.m.* burning (*of rubbish*); singeing (*of hair*); roasting (*of coffee*).

brûlant [bry'lã], *a.* burning, scorching, hot, torrid; (*fig.*) eager, ardent.

brûlé [bry'le], *n.m.* smell of burning; (*C*) burnt-out area *or* field.

brûle-gueule [bry'gœl], *n.m. inv.* (*colloq.*) short pipe, cutty.

brûle-pourpoint, à [abrylpur'pwɛ̃], *adv.* point-blank (*of shooting*).

brûler [bry'le], *v.t.* to burn; to cauterize; to scorch, to parch; to singe (*hair*).—*v.i.* to burn, to be on fire; (*fig.*) to be eager. **se brûler,** *v.r.* to burn oneself, to be burnt.

brûleur [bry'lœːr], *n.m.* (*fem.* **-euse**) burner; incendiary; *brûleur à gaz,* gas-ring, gas jet.

brûlis [bry'li], *n.m.* burnt part of a wood *or* field.

brûloir [bry'lwaːr], *n.m.* coffee burner *or* roaster.

52

brûlot [bry'lo], *n.m.* fire ship; (*fig.*) firebrand, incendiary; (*C*) kind of gnat *or* midge.

brûlure [bry'ly:r], *n.f.* burn, frost nip, scald.

brumaire [bry'mɛ:r], *n.m.* Brumaire (*second month of the calendar of the first French Republic, from Oct. 22nd to Nov. 20th*).

brume [brym], *n.f.* haze, mist.

brumeux [bry'mø], *a.* (*fem.* **-euse**) hazy, misty; (*fig.*) sombre.

brun [brœ̃], *a.* brown, dark, dusky.—*n.m.* brown (*color*); (*fem.* **-e** (1)) dark-complexioned person.

brunâtre [bry'nɑ:tr], *a.* brownish.

brune (2) [bryn], *n.f.* dusk (*of the evening*); dark woman, dark girl, brunette.

brunet [bry'nɛ], *a.* (*fem.* **-ette**) brownish.—*n.f.* (**-ette**) dark woman, dark girl.

brunir [bry'ni:r], *v.t.* to make brown; to burnish.—*v.i.* to turn brown. **se brunir**, *v.r.* to turn dark or brown.

brunissage [bryni'sa:ʒ], *n.m.* burnishing.

brunisseur [bryni'sœ:r], *n.m.* (*fem.* **-euse**) burnisher.

brunissoir [bryni'swa:r], *n.m.* burnisher (*tool*).

brunissure [bryni'sy:r], *n.f.* burnishing; polish.

brusque [brysk], *a.* blunt, abrupt, rough; unexpected.

brusquement [bryskə'mɑ̃], *adv.* bluntly, abruptly; uncivilly.

brusquer [brys'ke], *v.t.* to be sharp with (*someone*); to offend; (*fig.*) to precipitate.

brusquerie [bryskə'ri], *n.f.* abruptness, bluntness; hastiness.

brut [bryt], *a.* rough, raw, unhewn; uncultured.—*adv.* (*Comm.*) gross (*as opposed to net*).

brutal [bry'tal], *a.* (*m.pl.* **-aux**) brutal; surly, churlish.—*n.m.* (*fem.* **-e**) brute, brutal person.

brutalement [brytal'mɑ̃], *adv.* brutally.

brutaliser [brytali'ze], *v.t.* to bully; to brutalize.

brutalité [brytali'te], *n.f.* brutality, brutishness.

brute [bryt], *n.f.* brute, brutal person; boor.

Bruxelles [bry'sɛl], *f.* Brussels.

bruyamment [bryja'mɑ̃], *adv.* noisily.

bruyère [bry'jɛ:r], *n.f.* heath, heather.

buanderie [bɥɑ̃'dri], *n.f.* wash house, laundry.

buandier [bɥɑ̃'dje], *n.m.* (*fem.* **-ière**) bleacher; washerman, washerwoman.

bube [byb], *n.f.* pimple.

bubonique [bybo'nik], *a.* bubonic.

Bucarest [byka'rest], *m.* Bucharest.

buccin [byk'sɛ̃], *n.m.* (*Mus. Ant.*) long trumpet; (*Conch.*) whelk.

bûche [byʃ], *n.f.* log; (*fig.*) blockhead, dolt.

bûcher (1) [by'ʃe], *n.m.* wood house; funeral pile, pyre; stake.

bûcher (2) [by'ʃe], *v.t.* to roughhew.—*v.i.* to cram, to bone.

bûcheron [byʃ'rɔ̃], *n.m.* (*fem.* **-onne**) wood cutter.

bûchette [by'ʃɛt], *n.f.* stick of dry wood.

bucolique [byko'lik], *a.* bucolic.

budget [byd'ʒɛ], *n.m.* budget.

budgétaire [bydʒe'tɛ:r], *a.* budgetary.

buée [bɥe], *n.f.* steam (*on window panes*).

buffet [by'fɛ], *n.m.* sideboard; buffet; refreshment room.

buffetier [byf'tje], *n.m.* (*fem.* **-ière**) refreshment room manager.

buffle [byfl], *n.m.* buffalo; buffalo hide; buff leather.

buffleterie [byfla'tri], *n.f.* buff belts, straps etc. (*of a soldier*).

bugle [bygl], *n.m.* key bugle.

buis [bɥi], *n.m.* box; box tree, boxwood.

buissaie [bɥi'sɛ], **buissière** [bɥi'sjɛ:r], *n.f.* box grove.

buisson [bɥi'sɔ̃], *n.m.* bush; thicket.

buissoner [bɥiso'ne], *v.i.* to grow into a bush.

buissonnet [bɥiso'nɛ], *n.m.* little bush.

buissonneux [bɥiso'nø], *a.* (*fem.* **-euse**) bushy.

buissonnier [bɥiso'nje], *a.* (*fem.* **-ière**) retiring into the bushes; *faire l'école buissonnière*, to play truant; *lapins buissonniers*, thicket-rabbits.—*n.m.* shrubbery.

bulbe [bylb], *n.m.* bulb.

bulbeux [byl'bø], *a.* (*fem.* **-euse**) bulbous.

bulgare [byl'ga:r], *a.* Bulgarian.—*n.m.* Bulgarian (*language*).—*n.* (**Bulgare**) Bulgarian (*person*).

Bulgarie [bylga'ri], **la**, *f.* Bulgaria.

bulle [byl], *n.f.* bubble; blister; a papal bull.

bullé [by'le], *a.* authenticated with a seal; by papal bull.

bulletin [byl'tɛ̃], *n.m.* bulletin, official report (*school etc.*); certificate, receipt; ballot; ticket; *bulletin d'information* news bulletin; *bulletin météorologique*, weather forecast.

bulleux [by'lø], *a.* (*fem.* **-euse**) bubbly; blistery.

buraliste [byra'list], *n.* receiver of taxes; tobacco dealer.

bure [by:r], *n.f.* drugget; fustian, baize.

bureau [by'ro], *n.m.* (*pl.* **-eaux**) writing table, desk; office; board; committee; *Deuxième Bureau*, Intelligence Service, M.I.5.

bureaucrate [byro'krat], *n.m.* (*pej.*) bureaucrat.

bureaucratie [byrokra'si], *n.f.* bureaucracy; (*fig.*) red tape.

bureaucratique [byrokra'tik], *a.* bureaucratic; formal.

burette [by'rɛt], *n.f.* cruet; oil-can; (*Chem.*) burette.

burin [by'rɛ̃], *n.m.* graver, graving tool; (*fig.*) pen.

buriner [byri'ne], *v.t.* to engrave; to drill (*a tooth*).

burineur [byri'nœ:r], *n.m.* engraver.

burlesque [byr'lɛsk], *a.* burlesque, ludicrous.—*n.m.* burlesque.

burnous [byr'nus], *n.m.* burnous, hooded Arab cloak.

busard [by'za:r], *n.m.* buzzard.

buse (1) [by:z], *n.f.* buzzard; (*fig.*) blockhead.

buse (2) [by:z], *n.f.* channel, pipe; nozzle; (*Mining*) air shaft.

busqué [bys'ke], *a.* aquiline (*nose*).

buste [byst], *n.m.* bust, head and shoulders.

but [by(t)], *n.m.* mark; object, end; purpose, design, goal, objective; *de but en blanc* bluntly; (*Ftb.*) *marquer un but*, to score.

buté [by'te], *a.* stubborn, (*fam.*) dead set on.

buter or **butter** (1) [by'te], *v.t.* to support, to prop.—*v.i.* to rest *or* abut (*contre*); to stumble *or* hit (*contre*). **se buter**, *v.r.* to be bent on, to stick (*à*).

butin [by'tɛ̃], *n.m.* booty, spoils, prize, plunder.
butiner [byti'ne], *v.t.*, *v.i.* to pillage, to plunder.
butoir [by'twa:r], *n.m.* buffer, buffer-stop (*on railway*); tappet.
butor [by'tɔ:r], *n.m.* bittern; (*fig.*) churl, lout, booby.
butte [byt], *n.f.* rising ground; knoll, mound.
butter (1) [BUTER].
butter (2) [by'te], *v.t.* to earth up.
butteur [BUTTOIR].
buttoir [by'twa:r], **butteur** [by'tœ:r], *n.m.* ridging plough.
buvable [by'vabl], *a.* drinkable, fit to drink.
buvard [by'va:r], *a. papier buvard,* blotting paper.—*n.m.* blotting pad, blotter.
buvetier [byv'tje], *n.m.* (*fem.* **-ière**) inn-keeper, publican.
buvette [by'vɛt], *n.f.* refreshment room (*railway station*); pump room (*at spa*).
buveur [by'vœ:r], *n.m.* (*fem.* **-euse**) drinker; toper; *buveur d'eau,* teetotaller.
buvoter [byvɔ'te], *v.i.* to sip, to tipple.
Byzance [bi'zɑ̃:s], *f.* Byzantium.
byzantin [bizɑ̃'tɛ̃], *a.* Byzantine.—*n.m.* (**Byzantin,** *fem.* **-ine**) Byzantine (*person*).

C

C, c [se], *n.m.* the third letter of the alphabet.
ça [sa], *pron.* [*contraction of* cela] that; *comme ci comme ça,* only so-so; *donnez-moi ça,* give me that.
çà [sa], *adv.* here; *çà et là,* here and there.—*int.* now; *çà alors!* well, I never!
cabale [ka'bal], *n.f.* cabal, faction.
cabaler [kaba'le], *v.i.* to cabal, to plot.
cabaleur [kaba'lœ:r], *n.m.* (*fem.* **-euse**) caballer, intriguer.
caban [ka'bɑ̃], *n.m.* hooded cloak, oilskins.
cabane [ka'ban], *n.f.* hut, shed, cabin, shanty; central part (*of an airplane*).
cabanon [kaba'nɔ̃], *n.m.* small hut; prison cell; padded room.
cabaret [kaba'rɛ], *n.m.* inferior kind of wine shop, tavern; night club.
cabaretier [kabar'tje], *n.m.* (*fem.* **-ière**) publican, tavern keeper.
cabas [ka'bɑ], *n.m.* flat two-handled basket.
cabeliau [CABILLAUD].
cabestan [kabɛs'tɑ̃], *n.m.* capstan, windlass.
cabillaud [kabi'jo], **cabeliau** [kab'ljo] (*pl.* **-aux**), *n.m.* fresh cod.
cabine [ka'bin], *n.f.* cabin; (*Av.*) *cabine de pilotage,* cockpit; *cabine téléphonique,* telephone booth.
cabinet [kabi'nɛ], *n.m.* closet, study; practice (*of a professional man*); office (*of a lawyer, barrister etc.*); (*Polit.*) Cabinet; *cabinet d'aisances* or *les cabinets,* lavatory.
câblage [kɑ'bla:ʒ], *n.m.* (*Elec.*) wiring.
câble [kɑ:bl], *n.m.* cable.
câbler [kɑ'ble], *v.t.* to twist into a cord; to telegraph by cable.

câblogramme [kɑblɔ'gram], *n.m.* cablegram.
cabochon [kabɔ'ʃɔ̃], *n.m.* fancy brass nail; (*Cycl.*) *cabochon rouge,* red reflector.
cabosse [ka'bɔs], *n.f.* (*pop.*) bruise, bump.
cabosser [kabɔ'se], *v.t.* to bump, to bruise; to dent.
cabotage [kabɔ'ta:ʒ], *n.m.* coasting, coasting trade.
caboter [kabɔ'te], *v.i.* to coast.
caboteur [kabɔ'tœ:r], **cabotier** [kabɔ'tje], *n.m.* coasting vessel; coaster.
cabotin [kabɔ'tɛ̃], *n.m.* strolling player; bad actor, mummer.
cabotiner [kabɔti'ne], *v.i.* to act badly; (*fig.*) to strut.
cabré [ka'bre], *a.* rearing (*of a horse*); bucking (*of a plane*).
cabrer [ka'bre], *v.t.* to make (*a horse, a plane*) rear. **se cabrer,** *v.r.* to prance, to rear; (*fig.*) to revolt, to fly into a passion.
cabri [ka'bri], *n.m.* kid.
cabriole [kabri'ɔl], *n.f.* caper, leap.
cabrioler [kabriɔ'le], *v.i.* to caper, to cut capers.
cabriolet [kabriɔ'lɛ], *n.m.* cabriolet, cab.
cacahouète [kaka'wɛt], **cacahuète** [kaka'ɥɛt], *n.f.* peanut, monkey nut.
cacao [kaka'o], *n.m.* cacao, chocolate nut.
cacaoyer [kakaɔ'je], **cacaotier** [kakaɔ'tje], *n.m.* cacao tree.
cacaoyère [kakaɔ'jɛ:r], **cacaotière** [kakaɔ'tjɛ:r], *n.f.* cacao plantation.
cacatois [kaka'twa], **cacatoès** [kakatɔ'ɛ:s], *n.m.* cockatoo.
cachalot [kaʃa'lo], *n.m.* sperm whale.
cachalotier [kaʃalɔ'tje], *n.m.* whaler.
cache [kaʃ], *n.f.* hiding place.
cache-cache [kaʃ'kaʃ], *n.m.* hide-and-seek.
cachemire [kaʃ'mi:r], *n.m.* cashmere.
cache-nez [kaʃ'ne], *n.m.* muffler, comforter.
cacher [ka'ʃe], *v.t.* to hide, to conceal; to mask. **se cacher,** *v.r.* to hide, to lurk.
cache-sexe [kaʃ'sɛks], *n.m.* trunks; panties; (*colloq.*) G-string.
cachet [ka'ʃɛ], *n.m.* seal, stamp; signet ring; ticket; tablet (*of aspirin*); (*fig.*) character, stamp, mark.
cacheter [kaʃ'te], *v.t.* (*conjug. like* APPELER) to seal.
cachette [ka'ʃɛt], *n.f.* hiding place.
cachot [ka'ʃo], *n.m.* dungeon, prison.
cachotter [kaʃɔ'te], *v.t.* to make a mystery of, to conceal.
cachotterie [kaʃɔ'tri], *n.f.* mysterious ways; underhand work.
cachottier [kaʃɔ'tje], *a.* (*fem.* **-ière**) mysterious, sly.—*n.m.* (*fem.* **-ière**) one who makes a mystery of things.
cachou [ka'ʃu], *n.m.* cachou.
cacophonie [kakɔfɔ'ni], *n.f.* cacophony.
cacophonique [kakɔfɔ'nik], *a.* cacophonous.
cactier [kak'tje], **cactus** [kak'ty:s], *n.m.* cactus.
cadastral [kadas'tral], *a.* (*m. pl.* **-aux**) cadastral, referring to the register of lands.
cadastre [ka'dastr], *n.m.* cadastre, register of the survey of lands.
cadastrer [kadas'tre], *v.t.* to survey.
cadavéreux [kadave'rø], *a.* (*fem.* **-euse**) cadaverous, corpse-like, ghastly.
cadavérique [kadave'rik], *a.* of or pertaining to a corpse.

cadavre [ka'da:vr], n.m. corpse, dead body.
cadeau [ka'do], n.m. (pl. -eaux) present, gift.
cadenas [kad'na], n.m. padlock; clasp.
cadenasser [kadna'se], v.t. to padlock; to snap, clasp.
cadence [ka'dã:s], n.f. cadence, rhythm, time (in dancing).
cadencer [kadã'se], v.t. (conjug. like COM-MENCER) to cadence, to harmonize.
cadène [ka'dɛ:n], n.f. chain (for convicts); chain gang.
cadenette [kad'nɛt], n.f. tress (of hair).
cadet [ka'de], a. and n.m. (fem. -ette) younger, junior (of two).
Cadix [ka'diks], f. Cadiz.
cadmium [kad'mjom], n.m. cadmium.
cadrage [ka'dra:ʒ], n.m. (Phot., Cine.) centering.
cadran [ka'drã], n.m. dial plate, dial; cadran solaire, sundial.
cadre [kɑ:dr], n.m. frame, framework; (Mil.) the staff; (pl.) the higher staff (of an administration or a firm).
cadrer [ka'dre], v.t. (Phot., Cine.) to center.—v.i. to agree, to tally, to square (à or avec).
caduc [ka'dyk], a. (fem. -uque) decrepit, decayed; frail, tumble-down (for convicts); void (of legacies); (Bot.) deciduous.
caducité [kadysi'te], n.f. caducity, decrepitude.
cafard [ka'fa:r], a. hypocritical, sanctimonious.—n.m. (fem. -e) hypocrite, sanctimonious person; humbug; (Sch.) sneak.—n.m. cockroach.
cafarder [kafar'de], v.i. (fam.) to sneak, to tell tales (at school).
cafarderie [kafar'dri], n.f. cant, hypocrisy, sanctimoniousness.
café [ka'fe], n.m. coffee; café, coffee house; coffee berry.
caféière [kafe'jɛ:r], n.f. coffee plantation.
caféine [kafe'in], n.f. caffeine.
cafetan or caftan [kaf'tã], n.m. caftan.
cafetier [kaf'tje], n.m. (fem. cafetière (1)) coffee-house keeper.
cafetière (2) [kaf'tjɛ:r], n.f. coffee pot, percolator.
cafouillage [kafu'ja:ʒ], n.m. floundering.
cafre [kɑ:fr], a. and n. (Cafre) Kaffir, Bantu.
caftan [CAFETAN].
cage [ka:ʒ], n.f. cage; coop.
cageot [ka'ʒo], n.m. little cage, hamper, crate.
cagibi [kaʒi'bi], n.m. small hut or room.
cagneux [ka'nø], a. (fem. -euse) knock-kneed, pigeon-toed.
cagnotte [ka'nɔt], n.f. kitty, pool, jackpot.
cagot [ka'go], a. (fem. -otte) bigoted, hypocritical.—n.m. (fem. -otte) bigot, hypocrite.
cagoterie [kagɔ'tri], n.f. an act or word of hypocrisy or bigotry.
cagotisme [kagɔ'tism], n.m. hypocrisy, bigotry.
cagoule [ka'gul], n.f. monk's cloak; penitent's cowl; hood.
cahier [ka'je], n.m. stitched paper-book; exercise book; quarter of a quire of paper.
cahot [ka'o], n.m. jerk, jolt.
cahotage [kao'ta:ʒ], cahotement [kaot'mã], n.m. jolting, jerking.
cahotant [kao'tã], a. rough, jolting.
cahoter [kao'te], v.i. to jolt, to be jerked about.

cahute [ka'yt], n.f. hut, hovel.
caïd [ka'id], n.m. Arab chief or judge.
caïeu or cayeu [ka'jø], n.m. (pl. -eux) (Hort.) offshoot of a bulb, clove.
caillage [ka'ja:ʒ], n.m. curdling, congealing.
caille [kɑ:j], n.f. quail.—(C) a. piebald.
caillé [ka'je], n.m. curdled milk, curds.—a. curdled.
caillebottage [kajbo'ta:ʒ], n.m. curdling.
caillebotte [kaj'bɔt], n.f. curds.
caillebotter (se) [səkajbo'te], v.r. to curdle.
caille-lait [kaj'lɛ], n.m. inv. rennet.
caillement [kaj'mã], n.m. curdling, coagulating.
cailler [ka'je], v.t. to curdle, to clot. se cailler, v.r. to coagulate, to turn to curds.
cailleteau [kajto], n.m. (pl. -eaux) young quail.
caillette (1) [ka'jɛt], n.f. rennet.
caillette (2) [ka'jɛt], n.f. (Orn.) petrel; flirt.
caillot [ka'jo], n.m. clot of blood, coagulum.
caillou [ka'ju], n.m. (pl. -oux) pebble, small stone, flint, flint stone.
cailloutage [kaju'ta:ʒ], n.m. gravelling; ballasting; rough-cast, pebble-work.
caillouter [kaju'te], v.t. to gravel, to ballast.
caillouteux [kaju'tø], a. (fem. -euse) pebbly, flinty.
cailloutis [kaju'ti], n.m. broken stones, gravel; road metal.
caïman [kai'mã], n.m. American crocodile, cayman.
Caïn [ka'ɛ̃], m. Cain.
caïque or caïc [ka'ik], n.m. (Naut.) caique.
Caire [kɛ:r], Le, m. Cairo.
caisse [kɛ:s], n.f. chest, case, box, trunk; till; cash; cashier's office, pay desk; la grosse caisse, the (big) drum; caisse d'épargne, savings bank.
caissette [kɛ'sɛt], n.f. small box.
caissier [kɛ'sje], n.m. (fem. -ière) treasurer, cashier.
caisson [kɛ'sõ], n.m. ammunition wagon; (Naut.) locker.
cajoler [kaʒo'le], v.t. to cajole, to coax.
cajolerie [kaʒol'ri], n.f. cajolery, coaxing.
cajoleur [kaʒo'lœ:r], n.m. (fem. -euse) cajoler, coaxer.—a. cajoling, coaxing.
cal [kal], n.m. callosity, callus.
Calabre [ka'la:br], la, f. Calabria.
calage [ka'la:ʒ], n.m. lowering (of sails etc.) propping, wedging (of furniture).
calaison [kalɛ'zõ], n.f. load line, sea gauge.
calamine [kalami'na:ʒ], n.m. (Motor.) carbonizing.
calamine [kala'min], n.f. carbon (on plugs of a car etc.).
calamité [kalami'te], n.f. calamity, misfortune.
calamiteusement [kalamitøz'mã], adv. calamitously.
calamiteux [kalami'tø], a. (fem. -euse) calamitous.
calandrage [kalã'dra:ʒ], n.m. calendering, hot-pressing.
calandre [ka'lã:dr], n.f. mangle, calender; (Motor.) radiator grill.
calandrer [kalã'dre], v.t. to calender, to press, to smooth.
calandrette [kalã'drɛt], n.f. song-thrush.
calcaire [kal'kɛ:r], a. calcareous.—n.m. limestone.
calcéolaire [kalseo'lɛ:r], n.f. calceolaria.

calcination [kalsina'sjɔ̃], n.f. calcination.
calciner [kalsi'ne], v.t. to calcine, to burn. se calciner, v.r. to calcine.
calcium [kal'sjɔm], n.m. calcium.
calcul [kal'kyl], n.m. calculation; arithmetic; reckoning, counting; (Math.) calculus; (fig.) design, selfish motive; (Med.) calculus (stone).
calculable [kalky'labl], a. computable, calculable.
calculateur [kalkyla'tœːr], a. (fem. -trice) calculating, scheming.—n.m. (fem. -trice) calculator, reckoner; schemer.—n.f. (-trice) computer.
calculer [kalky'le], v.t. to calculate, to compute, to estimate; machine à calculer, computer.
cale (1) [kal], n.f. hold (of a ship); stocks, slip; ducking, keel-hauling (punishment); cale sèche, dry dock.
cale (2) [kal], n.f. wedge, block; prop, strut.
calebasse [kal'bas], n.f. calabash, gourd.
calèche [ka'lɛʃ], n.f. calash; barouche, open carriage.
caleçon [kal'sɔ̃], n.m. (men's) drawers, pants; caleçon de bain, bathing trunks.
Calédonie [kaledɔ'ni], la, f. Caledonia.
calédonien [kaledɔ'njɛ̃], a. (fem. -enne) Caledonian.—n.m. (Calédonien, fem. -enne) Caledonian (person).
caléfaction [kalefak'sjɔ̃], n.f. heating, calefaction.
calembour [kalɑ̃'buːr], n.m. pun.
calembourdiste [kalɑ̃bur'dist], n.m. punster.
calembredaine [kalɑ̃brə'dɛn], n.f. quibble, subterfuge, nonsense.
calendes [ka'lɑ̃ːd], n.f. pl. (Ant.) calends; convocation of the clergy of a diocese.
calendrier [kalɑ̃dri'e], n.m. calendar, almanac.
calendule [kalɑ̃'dyl], n.f. calendula.
cale-pied [kal'pje], n.m. toe clip.
calepin [kal'pɛ̃], n.m. notebook, memorandum book.
caler (1) [ka'le], v.t. (Naut.) to lower, to strike; to draw, to have a draft of.
caler (2) [ka'le], v.t. to prop up, to wedge; to steady; to jam; (Motor.) to stall.—v.i. (Motor.) to stall.
calfeutrage [kalfø'traːʒ], calfeutrement [kalføtr'mɑ̃], n.m. stopping of chinks.
calfeutrer [kalfø'tre], v.t. to stop up the chinks of, to make air-tight. se calfeutrer, v.r. to shut oneself up.
calibre [ka'libr], n.m. calibre, bore (of a gun); size (of a bullet); (fig.) kind, sort.
calibrer [kali'bre], v.t. to calibrate; to give the proper calibre to (bullets etc.).
calice (1) [ka'lis], n.m. chalice, communion cup; (fig.) grief, sacrifice.
calice (2) [ka'lis], n.m. (Bot.) calyx, flower, cup.
calicot [kali'ko], n.m. unbleached muslin; (slang) dry-goods store clerk.
calicule [kali'kyl], n.m. calicle, caliculus.
califat [kali'fa], n.m. caliphate.
calife [ka'lif] n.m. caliph.
Californie [kalifɔr'ni], la, f. California.
califourchon [kalifur'ʃɔ̃], n.m. à califourchon, astride.
câlin [kɑ'lɛ̃], a. wheedling, winning, coaxing.—n.m. (fem. -e) wheedler, cajoler.

câliner [kɑ'li'ne], v.t. to cajole, to wheedle. se câliner, v.r. to coddle oneself, to take one's ease.
câlinerie [kɑ'lin'ri], n.f. wheedling, cajolery, caressing.
calleux [ka'lø], a. (fem. -euse) callous, horny.
calligraphe [kali'graf], n.m. calligrapher, good penman.
calligraphie [kaligra'fi], n.f. calligraphy, penmanship.
callisthénie [kaliste'ni], n.f. callisthenics.
callosité [kalozi'te], n.f. callosity.
calmant [kal'mɑ̃], a. calming, soothing, sedative.—n.m. (Med.) anodyne, sedative.
calme [kalm], a. tranquil, quiet, serene, calm; composed, dispassionate.—n.m. calm, stillness, quiet; composure.
calmer [kal'me], v.t. to calm, to still, to quiet, to allay, to soothe.—v.i. (Naut.) to lull, to become calm. se calmer, v.r. to become calm, to compose oneself; to blow over.
calomel [kalɔ'mɛl], n.m. calomel.
calomniateur [kalɔmnja'tœːr], a. (fem. -trice) slanderous.—n.m. (fem. -trice) calumniator, slanderer.
calomnie [kalɔm'ni], n.f. calumny, slander.
calomnier [kalɔm'nje], v.t. to calumniate, to slander.
calomnieusement [kalɔmnjøz'mɑ̃], adv. calumniously, slanderously.
calomnieux [kalɔm'njø], a. (fem. -euse) calumnious, slanderous.
calorie [kalɔ'ri], n.f. calorie, unit of heat.
calorifère [kalɔri'fɛːr], n.m. hot-air stove or pipe; central heating.—a. heat-conveying.
calorifique [kalɔri'fik], a. calorific.
calorifuger [kalɔrify'ʒe], v.t. (conjug. like MANGER) to insulate, to lag (pipes).
calorique [kalɔ'rik], a. and n.m. caloric, heat.
calotte [ka'lɔt], n.f. skullcap (esp. that worn by priests); small dome; box on the ears.
calotter [kalɔ'te], v.t. to box the ears of.
calque [kalk], n.m. tracing; close copy.—a. papier calque, tracing paper.
calquer [kal'ke], v.t. to trace; to copy, to imitate closely. se calquer, v.r. (sur) to model oneself (on).
calumet [kaly'me], n.m. pipe, calumet.
calvados [kalva'dos], n.m. apple brandy, calvados.
calvaire [kal'vɛːr], n.m. calvary; (fig.) torture, suffering, tribulation.
calvinisme [kalvi'nism], n.m. Calvinism.
calviniste [kalvi'nist], a. Calvinistic.—n. (Calviniste) Calvinist.
calvitie [kalvi'si], n.f. baldness.
camaïeu [kama'jø], n.m. (pl. -eux) cameo (brooch etc.).
camail [ka'maːj], n.m. (pl. -ails) hood, capuchin; hackles (of poultry).
camarade [kama'rad], n. comrade, fellow, mate, chum, playmate.
camaraderie [kamara'dri], n.f. comradeship, intimacy.
camard [ka'maːr], a. snub-nosed, flat.—n.m. (fem. -e) snub-nosed person.
Cambodge [kɑ̃'bɔdʒ], le, m. Cambodia.
cambodgien [kɑ̃bɔ'dʒjɛ̃], a. (fem. -enne) Cambodian.—n.m. (Cambodgien, fem. -enne) Cambodian (person).
cambouis [kɑ̃'bwi], n.m. dirty cart-grease, dirty lubricating oil.

cambrage [kɑ̃'braːʒ], *n.m.* cambering, bending.

cambrai [kɑ̃'brɛ], *n.m.* machine-made lace; cambric.

cambré [kɑ̃'bre], *a.* bent, cambered.

cambrement [kɑ̃brə'mɑ̃], *n.m.* arching, curving.

cambrer [kɑ̃'bre], *v.t.* to arch, to bend, to curve. **se cambrer**, *v.r.* to be cambered; to warp; to draw oneself up.

cambriolage [kɑ̃brio'laːʒ], *n.m.* house-breaking, burglary.

cambrioler [kɑ̃brio'le], *v.t.* to break into (*a house*), to burgle.

cambrioleur [kɑ̃brio'lœːr], *n.m.* house-breaker, burglar.

cambrure [kɑ̃'bryːr], *n.f.* bend, curvature, arch; the arched part in a shoe.

cambuse [kɑ̃'byːz], *n.f.* (*Naut.*) storeroom, canteen.

came [kam], *n.f.* cam, wiper; *arbre à cames* camshaft.

camée [ka'me], *n.m.* cameo.

caméléon [kamele'ɔ̃], *n.m.* chameleon.

camélia [kame'lja], *n.m.* camellia.

camelot [kam'lo], *n.m.* camlet; cheap-jack, pedlar, hawker.

camelote [kam'lɔt], *n.f.* inferior merchandise, shoddy; (*fig.*) trash.

caméra [kame'ra], *n.f.* ciné camera.

camérier [kame'rje], *n.m.* chamberlain (*of the Pope etc.*).

Cameroun [kamə'run], **le,** *m.* Cameroon.

camion [ka'mjɔ̃], *n.m.* dray, low wagon, truck.

camionnage [kamjɔ'naːʒ], *n.m.* carting, carriage.

camionner [kamjɔ'ne], *v.t.* to convey on a dray, lorry, truck etc.

camionnette [kamjɔ'nɛt], *n.f.* light motor lorry; van.

camionneur [kamjɔ'nœːr], *n.m.* drayman; vanman; haulage contractor, trucker.

camisole [kami'zɔl], *n.f.* woman's morning jacket; *camisole de force*, strait jacket.

camomille [kamɔ'miːj], *n.f.* camomile.

camouflage [kamu'flaːʒ], **camouflement** [kamuflə'mɑ̃], *n.m.* disguise; camouflage.

camoufler [kamu'fle], *v.t.* to disguise; to camouflage. **se camoufler**, *v.r.* to disguise or camouflage oneself.

camouflet [kamu'flɛ], *n.m.* whiff of smoke (*in the face*); (*fig.*) affront, snub.

camp [kɑ̃], *n.m.* camp; (*fig.*) army; party; (*C*) country cottage.

campagnard [kɑ̃pa'naːr], *a.* rustic, countrified, rural.—*n.m.* (*fem.* **-e**) countryman *or* countrywoman, peasant; clodhopper.

campagne [kɑ̃'paɲ], *n.f.* the country, the fields, plain; seat, estate, country house; campaign; (*Naut.*) cruise.

campagnol [kɑ̃pa'nɔl], *n.m.* vole, field mouse.

campanile [kɑ̃pa'nil], *n.m.* campanile, bell tower.

campanule [kɑ̃pa'nyl], *n.f.* campanula, bellflower, bluebell.

campé [kɑ̃'pe], *a.* established, firmly planted, well set up.

campement [kɑ̃p'mɑ̃], *n.m.* encamping; encampment; camp party, billeting party.

camper [kɑ̃'pe], *v.t.* to encamp (*troops etc.*); to place, to seat, to clap down.—*v.i.* to live in camp, to encamp. **se camper**, *v.r.* to encamp; to plant oneself.

campeur [kɑ̃'pœːr], *n.m.* (*fem.* **-euse**) camper.

camphre [kɑ̃:fr], *n.m.* camphor.

camphré [kɑ̃'fre], *a.* camphorated.

camphrier [kɑ̃fri'e], *n.f.* camphor tree.

camus [ka'my], *a.* flat-nosed, snub-nosed.

Canada [kana'da], **le,** *m.* Canada.

canadien [kana'djɛ̃], *a.* (*fem.* **-enne**) Canadian.—*n.m.* (**Canadien,** *fem.* **-enne**) Canadian (*person*).

canaille [ka'naːj], *n.f.* rabble, riffraff, mob.

canaillerie [kanaː'jri], *n.f.* blackguardism; vulgarity.

canal [ka'nal], *n.m.* (*pl.* **-aux**) canal; conduit, drain; pipe, tube, spout; water-course.

canalisation [kanaliza'sjɔ̃], *n.f.* canalization; mains; *canalisation de gaz*, gas mains.

canaliser [kanali'ze], *v.t.* to canalize; to install pipes (*for gas etc.*).

canamelle [kana'mɛl], *n.f.* sugar cane.

canapé [kana'pe], *n.m.* sofa, couch.

canapé-lit [kanape'li], *n.m.* divan-bed.

canard [ka'naːr], *n.m.* duck; drake; (*fig.*) hoax.

canardeau [kanar'do], *n.m.* (*pl.* **-eaux**) young duck.

canarder [kanar'de], *v.t.* to shoot from behind a shelter; to snipe.—*v.i.* (*Naut.*) to pitch heavily.

canardière [kanar'djeːr], *n.f.* duck pond; duck gun.

canari [kana'ri], *n.m.* canary (*bird*).

Canaries [kana'ri], **les Îles,** *f. pl.* the Canary Islands.

canasta [kanas'ta], *n.f.* canasta.

cancan [kɑ̃'kɑ̃], *n.m.* tittle-tattle, scandal; French cancan.

cancaner [kɑ̃ka'ne], *v.i.* to tattle, to invent stories.

cancanier [kɑ̃ka'nje], *a.* (*fem.* **-ière**) addicted to gossip.—*n.m.* (*fem.* **-ière**) scandal-monger.

cancer [kɑ̃'seːr], *n.m.* (*Astron., Geol., Med.*) cancer.

cancéreux [kɑ̃se'rø], *a.* (*fem.* **-euse**) cancerous.

cancre [kɑ̃:kr], *n.m.* crab; (*fig.*) dunce (*at school*).

cancrelat *or* **cancrelas** [kɑ̃krə'la], *n.m.* cockroach.

candélabre [kɑ̃de'laːbr], *n.m.* candelabrum, sconce.

candeur [kɑ̃'dœːr], *n.f.* artlessness, guilelessness, ingenuousness.

candi [kɑ̃'di], *a.m.* candied; *fruits candis*, crystallized fruits.—*n.m.* sugar candy.

candidat [kɑ̃di'da], *n.m.* candidate.

candidature [kɑ̃dida'tyːr], *n.f.* candidature.

candide [kɑ̃'did], *a.* ingenuous, artless.

candidement [kɑ̃did'mɑ̃], *adv.* ingenuously.

candir [kɑ̃'diːr], *v.i.* *or* **se candir**, *v.r.* to candy, to crystallize.

cane [kan], *n.f.* (*female*) duck.

canebière [CANNEBIÈRE].

canepetière [kanpə'tjeːr], *n.f.* lesser bustard.

caneton [kan'tɔ̃], *n.m.* duckling.

canette (1) *or* **cannette** (1) [ka'nɛt], *n.f.* small duck, duckling; teal.

canette (2) *or* **cannette** (2) [ka'nɛt], *n.f.* measure for beer; spool (*inside shuttle*).

canevas [kan'va], *n.m.* canvas; sailcloth; outline sketch, rough draft.

caniche [ka'niʃ], *n.m.* poodle.

57

canichon [kani'ʃɔ̃], *n.m.* small poodle; duckling.

caniculaire [kaniky'lɛːr], *a.* canicular.

canicule [kani'kyl], *n.f.* dog-days; (*Astron.*) Dog Star.

canif [ka'nif], *n.m.* penknife.

canin [ka'nɛ̃], *a.* canine.—*n.f.* (*dent*) *canine*, canine (tooth).

canitie [kani'si], *n.f.* whiteness of the hair.

caniveau [kani'vo], *n.m.* (*pl.* -**eaux**) (*Arch.*) channel stone, gutter.

cannage [ka'naːʒ], *n.m.* cane work (*in chairs etc.*).

cannaie [ka'nɛ], *n.f.* cane plantation, cane field.

canne [kan], *n.f.* cane, reed; walking stick; glass-blower's pipe.

canneberge [kan'bɛrʒ], *n.f.* cranberry.

cannebière or **canebière** [kan'bjɛːr], *n.f.* (*S.-E. France*) [CHÈNEVIÈRE].

cannelé [kan'le], *a.* fluted (*column*); grooved (*tire*).—*n.m.* ribbed silk.

canneler [kan'le], *v.t.* (*conjug. like* APPELER) to flute, to channel, to groove.

cannelier [kanə'lje], *n.m.* cinnamon tree.

cannelle (1) [ka'nɛl], *n.f.* cinnamon bark, cinnamon.

cannelle (2) [ka'nɛl], **cannette** (3) [ka'nɛt], *n.f.* spigot, tap.

cannelure [kan'lyːr], *n.f.* fluting, channelling.

cannette (1) [CANNETTE (1).]

cannette (2) [CANETTE (2).]

cannette (3) [CANNELLE (2].

cannibale [kani'bal], *n.m.* cannibal.

cannibalisme [kaniba'lism], *n.m.* cannibalism; (*fig.*) ferocity.

canon (1) [ka'nɔ̃], *n.m.* cannon, gun; barrel (*of a gun*); cylinder, pipe, tube (*of lock*).

canon (2) [ka'nɔ̃], *n.m.* (*Eccles.*) canon; (*Mus.*) round, canon.

cañon [ka'nɔ̃], *n.m.* canyon.

canonial [kano'njal], *a.* (*m.pl.* -**aux**) canonical.

canonicat [kanoni'ka], *n.m.* canonry; (*fig.*) sinecure.

canonicité [kanonisi'te], *n.f.* canonicity.

canonique [kano'nik], *a.* canonical.

canonisation [kanoniza'sjɔ̃], *n.f.* canonization.

canoniser [kanoni'ze], *v.t.* to canonize.

canonnade [kano'nad], *n.f.* cannonading, cannonade.

canonner [kano'ne], *v.t.* to attack with heavy artillery, to cannonade.

canonnier [kano'nje], *n.m.* gunner.

canonnière [kano'njɛːr], *n.f.* pop-gun; gunboat.

canot [ka'no], *n.m.* small open boat, dinghy; (*C*) Canadian canoe; *canot automobile*, motor-boat; *canot de sauvetage*, lifeboat.

canotage [kano'taːʒ], *n.m.* boating, rowing.

cantate [kɑ̃'tat], *n.f.* (*Mus.*) cantata.

cantatrice [kɑ̃ta'tris], *n.f.* cantatrice, (*classical*) singer.

cantharide [kɑ̃ta'rid], *n.f.* (*Ent.*) cantharis, Spanish fly.

cantilène [kɑ̃ti'lɛːn], *n.f.* cantilena, ballad, popular song.

cantine [kɑ̃'tin], *n.f.* canteen; kit-case.

cantique [kɑ̃'tik], *n.m.* canticle, hymn.

canton [kɑ̃'tɔ̃], *n.m.* canton (*district*); (*C*) township.

cantonade [kɑ̃to'nad], *n.f.* (*Theat.*) either of the wings; *parler à la cantonade*, to speak to an actor off the stage.

cantonnement [kɑ̃tɔn'mɑ̃], *n.m.* (*Mil.*) cantonment, billet, quarters.

cantonner [kɑ̃to'ne], *v.t.* (*Mil.*) to billet (*troops*). **se cantonner**, *v.r.* to take up a position, quarters *or* abode; to fortify oneself.

cantonnier [kɑ̃to'nje], *n.m.* roadman; (*Rail.*) platelayer.

cantonnière [kɑ̃to'njɛːr], *n.f.* valance.

canule [ka'nyl], *n.f.* clyster pipe, injection tube, douche tube.

caoutchouc [kau'tʃu], *n.m.* (India-)rubber mackintosh; (*pl.*) galoshes.

cap [kap], *n.m.* head; bow (*of a ship*); cape, headland, promontory.

capable [ka'pabl], *a.* able, fit, capable; apt; competent.

capacité [kapasi'te], *n.f.* extent, size; ability.

caparaçon [kapara'sɔ̃], *n.m.* caparison, trappings.

caparaçonner [kaparaso'ne], *v.t.* to caparison (*a horse*).

cape [kap], *n.f.* cape, mantle *or* cloak with a hood.

capharnaüm [kafarna'ɔm], *n.m.* lumberroom, storeroom for odds and ends.

capillaire [kapi'lɛːr], *a.* capillary.—*n.m.* capillary; maidenhair fern.

capilotade [kapilo'tad], *n.f.* hash, ragoût; (*fig.*) thrashing.

capitaine [kapi'tɛn], *n.m.* captain; (*fig.*) eminent commander.

capital [kapi'tal], *a.* (*m.pl.* -**aux**) capital, main, chief, principal.—*n.m.* capital, principal; property stock.

capitale [kapi'tal], *n.f.* capital, chief city; capital letter.

capitaliser [kapitali'ze], *v.t.* to put at compound interest; to add to the capital; to realize, to capitalize.—*v.i.* to save, to lay by.

capitaliste [kapita'list], *n.* capitalist, moneyed man *or* woman.

capitan [kapi'tɑ̃], *n.m.* braggadocio, swaggerer.

capitation [kapita'sjɔ̃], *n.f.* capitation, poll tax.

capiteux [kapi'tø], *a.* (*fem.* -**euse**) heady, strong.

Capitole [kapi'tɔl], *n.m.* Capitol (*of Rome etc.*).

capitonner [kapito'ne], *v.t.* to stuff, to pad.

capitulaire [kapity'lɛːr], *a.* and *n.m.* capitulary.

capitulation [kapityla'sjɔ̃], *n.f.* capitulation; compromise.

capituler [kapity'le], *v.i.* to capitulate; to compound, to compromise.

capoc [ka'pɔk], *n.m.* kapok.

capon [ka'pɔ̃], *a.* (*fem.* -**onne**) cowardly.—*n.m.* (*fem.* -**onne**) mean fellow, sneak; coward.

caponner [kapo'ne], *v.i.* to cheat; to be cowardly; to rat.

caporal [kapo'ral], *n.m.* (*pl.* -**aux**) corporal; sort of 'shag' (*tobacco*).

capot (1) [ka'po], *n.m.* (*Motor.*) bonnet, (*Am.*) hood.

capot (2) [ka'po], *a. inv.* capot (*at piquet etc.*); flabbergasted.

capote [ka'pɔt], *n.f.* capote, large cloak with a hood; (*soldier's*) overcoat; baby's bonnet.

capoter [kapo'te], *v.i.* (*Naut. etc.*) to capsize; to turn turtle.

câpre [kɑ:pr], *n.f.* (*Bot.*) caper.

caprice [ka'pris], *n.m.* caprice, whim, humor; flight, sally.

capricieusement [kaprisjøz'mã], *adv.* capriciously, whimsically.

capricieux [kapri'sjø], *a.* (*fem.* **-euse**) capricious, whimsical, fickle.

capricorne [kapri'korn], *n.m.* (*Astron.*) Capricorn.

capsule [kap'syl], *n.f.* capsule; pod; percussion cap (*of firearms*).

captation [kapta'sjõ], *n.f.* captation, inveigling; intercepting.

captatoire [kapta'twa:r], *a.* inveigling.

capter [kap'te], *v.t.* to obtain by underhand methods; to win by bribery etc.

captieusement [kapsjøz'mã], *adv.* insidiously, cunningly, deceitfully.

captieux [kap'sjø], *a.* (*fem.* **-euse**) insidious, cunning, specious.

captif [kap'tif], *a.* and *n.m.* (*fem.* **-tive**) captive.

captivant [kapti'vã], *a.* captivating; enthralling.

captiver [kapti've], *v.t.* to captivate, to charm.

captivité [kaptivi'te], *n.f.* captivity, bondage.

capture [kap'ty:r], *n.f.* capture, prize, booty.

capturer [kapty're], *v.t.* to capture; to arrest.

capuchon [kapy'ʃõ], *n.m.* hood, cowl.

capuchonné [kapyʃo'ne], *a.* cowled; hooded.

capucin [kapy'sɛ̃], *n.m.* (*fem.* **capucine** (1) [kapy'sin]) Capuchin friar *or* nun.

capucine (1) [CAPUCIN].

capucine (2) [kapy'sin], *n.f.* nasturtium.

caque [kak], *n.f.* keg, barrel.

caquet [ka'ke], *n.m.* cackle (*of geese etc.*); tittle-tattle, gossip, scandal.

caquetage [kak'ta:ʒ], *n.m.*, **caqueterie** [kak(ə)'tri], *n.f.* babbling, prattling; tattling, gossiping.

caqueter [kak'te], *v.i.* (*conjug. like* APPELER) to cackle, to chatter; to gossip.

car (1) [ka:r], *conj.* for, because.

car (2) [ka:r], *n.m.* (*fam.*) coach, long-distance bus.

carabin [kara'bɛ̃], *n.m.* (*colloq.*) saw-bones, medical student.

carabine [kara'bin], *n.f.* carbine, rifle.

carabiné [karabi'ne], *a.* rifled; (*colloq.*) strong, violent.

carabiner [karabi'ne], *v.t.* to rifle (*a gun barrel*).

carabinier [karabi'nje], *n.m.* carabinier, rifleman.

caractère [karak'tɛ:r], *n.m.* character, letter; handwriting; nature, disposition; temper, spirit; stamp; quality.

caractériser [karakteri'ze], *v.t.* to characterize, to describe.

caractéristique [karakteris'tik], *a.* and *n.f.* characteristic.

carafe [ka'raf], *n.f.* carafe, decanter, water-bottle.

carafon [kara'fõ], *n.m.* small carafe *or* decanter.

Caraïbes [kara'ib], **les**, *f.pl.* the Caribbean Isles.

carambolage [karãbo'la:ʒ], *n.m.* (*Billiards*) carom; (*pop.*) affray, shindy; (*fig.*) rebound (*against*).

caramboler [karãbo'le], *v.i.* (*Billiards*) to carom.

caramel [kara'mɛl], *n.m.* caramel.

carapace [kara'pas], *n.f.* (*Zool.*) carapace, shell.

carat [ka'ra], *n.m.* (*Gold*) carat.

caravane [kara'van], *n.f.* caravan, convoy; trailer (*car*).

carbonate [karbo'nat], *n.m.* (*Chem.*) carbonate.

carbone [kar'bon], *n.m.* carbon.

carboné [karbo'ne], *a.* carbonated, carbonized.

carbonique [karbo'nik], *a.* carbonic.

carboniser [karboni'ze], *v.t.* to carbonize.

carburant [karby'rã], *a.* and *n.m.* motor fuel.

carburateur [karbyra'tœ:r], *n.m.* carburetor.

carbure [kar'by:r], *n.m.* (*Chem.*) carbide.

carburé [karby're], *a.* carburetted.

carcasse [kar'kas], *n.f.* carcass, skeleton.

cardage [kar'da:ʒ], *n.m.* carding.

cardan [kar'dã], *n.m.* (*Mech.*) universal joint.

carde [kard], *n.f.* (*Bot.*) cardoon.

carder [kar'de], *v.t.* to card, to comb.

cardialgie [kardjal'ʒi], *n.f.* cardialgy, heartburn.

cardiaque [kar'djak], *a.* and *n.* cardiac (*case*).

cardinal [kardi'nal], *a.* (*m. pl.* **-aux**) cardinal, chief, principal.—*n.m.* (*pl.* **-aux**) (*Eccles.*) cardinal.

cardinalat [kardina'la], *n.m.* cardinalate, cardinalship.

cardiogramme [kardio'gram], *n.m.* cardiogram.

cardiographe [kardio'graf], *n.m.* cardiograph.

cardon [kar'dõ], *n.m.* (*Bot.*) cardoon.

carême [ka'rɛ:m], *n.m.* Lent; Lent sermons.

carénage [kare'na:ʒ], *n.m.* careening.

carence [ka'rã:s], *n.f.* (*Law*) insolvency.

carène [ka'rɛ:n], *n.f.* (*Naut.*) bottom (*keel and sides up to water-mark*).

caréné [kare'ne], *a.* (*Bot.*) carinate; keeled; (*Motor.*) streamlined.

caréner [kare'ne], *v.t.* (*conjug. like* CÉDER) to careen; to streamline.

caressant [kare'sã], *a.* caressing, endearing; tender.

caresse [ka'rɛs], *n.f.* caress, endearment.

caresser [kare'se], *v.t.* to caress, to fondle, to stroke.

caret (1) [ka're], *n.m.* rope-maker's reel.

caret (2) [ka're], *n.m.* turtle.

cargaison [karge'zõ], *n.f.* cargo, freight.

cargo [kar'go], *n.m.* (*Naut.*) tramp, cargo boat.

carguer [kar'ge], *v.t.* to reef (*sails*).

cargueur [kar'gœ:r], *n.m.* (*Naut.*) reefer.

cari [ka'ri], *n.m.* curry powder.

cariatide [karja'tid], *n.f.* caryatid.

caribou [kari'bu], *n.m.* cariboo.

caricature [karika'ty:r], *n.f.* caricature; (*fam.*) fright (*person*).

caricaturer [karikaty're], *v.t.* to caricature.

caricaturiste [karikaty'rist], *n.* caricaturist.

carie [ka'ri], *n.f.* (*Path.*) caries, decay; (*Bot.*) brown rust; rot (*of timber*).

carier [ka'rje], *v.t.* to make carious, to rot.

carillon [kari'jõ], *n.m.* carillon; chime, peal.

carillonnement [karijon'mã], *n.m.* chiming, jingling.

carillonner [karijɔ'ne], v.i. to chime; to ring the changes; to jingle.

carillonneur [karijɔ'nœːr], n.m. bell ringer.

carlin [kar'lɛ̃], a. pug; turned-up (nose).

carlingue [kar'lɛ̃:g], n.f. (Av.) cockpit.

carmagnole [karma'ɲɔl], n.f. Piedmontese jacket; carmagnole.

carme [karm], n.m. Carmelite friar, White friar.

carmélite [karme'lit], n.f. Carmelite nun.—a. light brown.

carmin [kar'mɛ̃], a. and n.m. carmine.

carnage [kar'na:ʒ], n.m. carnage, slaughter.

carnassier [karna'sje], a. (fem. -ière) carnivorous, flesh-eating.—n.m. feline animal; flesh-eater.—n.f. (-ière) game bag.

carnation [karna'sjɔ̃], n.f. complexion; flesh color.

carnaval [karna'val], n.m. carnival; masquerade, festival; good fellow.

carné [kar'ne], a. flesh-colored; composed of meat.

carnet [kar'nɛ], n.m. notebook, log book.

carnier [kar'nje], n.m. game bag.

carnivore [karni'vɔːr], a. carnivorous.—n. carnivore.

carogne [ka'rɔɲ], n.f. hag, jade, impudent slut.

carotide [karɔ'tid], a. and n.f. carotid.

carotte [ka'rɔt], n.f. carrot; (slang) fake, ruse, hoax; sign outside a tobacconist's shop.—a. (inv.) ginger (hair).

carotter [karɔ'te], v.t. to cheat.

carotteur [karɔ'tœːr], **carottier** [karɔ'tje], n.m. (fem. -euse, -ière) cheat, trickster; wangler.

carpe (1) [karp], n.f. (Ichth.) carp.

carpe (2) [karp], n.m. (Anat.) wrist.

carquois [kar'kwa], n.m. quiver.

carrare [ka'raːr], n.m. Carrara marble.

carré [ka're], a. square; well-set; plain, straightforward.—n.m. square; landing, floor; (Hort.) plot.

carreau [ka'ro], n.m. (pl. -eaux) small square; square tile or brick, small flagstone; pane (of glass); diamond (at cards).

carrefour [kar'fuːr], n.m. crossroads.

carrelage [kar'la:ʒ], n.m. tile flooring, paving squares.

carreler [kar'le], v.t. (conjug. like APPELER) to pave (a floor) with square tiles, bricks, stones etc.; to cobble (shoes etc.).

carrelet [kar'lɛ], n.m. plaice.

carrelette [kar'lɛt], n.f. flat file.

carreleur [kar'lœːr], n.m. floor tiler.

carrément [kare'mɑ̃], adv. squarely; (fig.) bluntly, plainly.

carrer [ka're], v.t. to square. **se carrer**, v.r. to strut, to pose.

carrier [ka'rje], n.m. quarryman.

carrière (1) [ka'rjɛːr], n.f. career, course; scope, play, vent; profession, vocation; la Carrière, the diplomatic service.

carrière (2) [ka'rjɛːr], n.f. quarry.

carriole [ka'rjɔl], n.f. light covered cart.

carrossable [karɔ'sabl], a. practicable for vehicles (of roads).

carrosse [ka'rɔs], n.m. state-coach, four-wheeled carriage.

carrosserie [karɔ'sri], n.f. coach-building; body (of motors).

carrossier [karɔ'sje], n.m. coach maker, carriage builder.

carrousel [karu'zɛl], n.m. merry-go-round; tournament.

carrure [ka'ryːr], n.f. breadth of shoulders.

cartable [kar'tabl], n.m. school satchel.

carte [kart], n.f. pasteboard; card, playing card, postcard; ticket; bill of fare; map, chart; avoir carte blanche, to have full power; carte d'abonnement, season ticket; carte d'alimentation, ration card, ration book; un jeu de cartes, a pack of cards.

cartel [kar'tɛl], n.m. challenge; cartel; dial case; wall clock; frieze panel.

carte-lettre [karto'lɛtr], n.f. (pl. cartes-lettres) letter-card.

carter [kar'tɛr], n.m. gearcase (of bicycle); crankcase (of car).

cartésianisme [kartezja'nism], n.m. Cartesian philosophy.

cartésien [karte'zjɛ̃], a. and n.m. (fem. -ienne) Cartesian.

cartilage [karti'la:ʒ], n.m. cartilage, gristle.

cartilagineux [kartilaʒi'nø], a. (fem. -euse) cartilaginous, gristly.

cartographe [kartɔ'graf], n.m. cartographer.

cartographie [kartɔgra'fi], n.f. cartography.

carton [kar'tɔ̃], n.m. cardboard, pasteboard; cardboard box, hatbox; (Paint.) cartoon; (Phot.) mount.

cartonnage [kartɔ'na:ʒ], n.m. (Bookb.) boarding.

cartonneur [kartɔ'nœːr], n.m. (fem. -euse) binder (of books).

carton-pâte [kartɔ̃'pɑːt], n.m. millboard; papier mâché.

carton-pierre [kartɔ̃'pjɛːr], n.m. pasteboard for making ornaments.

cartothèque [kartɔ'tek], n.f. card index.

cartouche (1) [kar'tuʃ], n.m. escutcheon, scroll.

cartouche (2) [kar'tuʃ], n.f. cartridge.

cartouchier [kartu'ʃje], n.m., **cartouchière** [kartu'ʃjɛːr], n.f. cartridge pouch or box.

cas [kɑ], n.m. case; instance, circumstance, state of things, conjuncture; (Law) cause; c'est le cas ou jamais, it is now or never; en tout cas, at all events.

casanier [kaza'nje], a. (fem. -ière) domestic, stay-at-home, home-loving.

cascade [kas'kad], n.f. cascade, waterfall.

case [kɑːz], n.f. cabin, hut, small house; division, compartment; box (for animals); pigeonhole; square (of chess- or draught-board); (Naut.) berth.

casemate [kaz'mat], n.f. (Fort.) casemate.

caser [ka'ze], v.t. to put in order, to file (documents), (fam.) to provide for; to marry off.—v.i. (backgammon) to make a point. **se caser**, v.r. to take up one's abode, to settle.

caserne [ka'zern], n.f. barracks.

caserner [kazer'ne], v.t. to quarter in barracks.—v.i. to be in barracks.

casier [ka'zje], n.m. rack, card or music stand, set of pigeonholes; casier judiciaire, police record.

casilleux [kazi'jø], a. (fem. -euse) brittle.

casino [kazi'no], n.m. casino, club.

casque [kask], n.m. helmet, headpiece; (Nat. Hist.) crest; headphone (radio).

casquette [kas'kɛt], *n.f.* cap.

cassable [ka'sabl], *a.* breakable.

cassage [ka'saːʒ], *n.m.* breakage.

cassant [ka'sɑ̃], *a.* brittle; crisp; breakable; *(fig.)* abrupt, gruff.

cassation [kasa'sjɔ̃], *n.f.* (*Law*) cassation, annulment, repeal; *cour de cassation*, the highest court of appeal in France.

casse (1) [kɑːs], *n.f.* breakage(s); damage, losses.

casse (2) [kɑːs], *n.f.* (*Print.*) case; *bas de casse*, lower case.

casse-cou [kas'ku], *n.m. inv.* death trap; roughrider; daredevil.

casse-croûte [kas'krut], *n.m. inv.* quick meal, snack.

casse-noisette [kɑsnwa'zɛt], *n.m.* (*pl.* **casse-noisettes**) nutcracker; (*Orn.*) nuthatch.

casse-noix [kɑs'nwɑ], *n.m. inv.* nutcrackers.

casse-pipes [kas'pip], *n.m. inv.* shooting gallery; (*pop.*) war.

casser [ka'se], *v.t.* to break, to smash; to cashier (*an officer*), to reduce to the ranks; to dissolve (*Parliament etc.*); to annul, to rescind. **se casser**, *v.r.* to break, to snap; to break down.

casserole [kas'rol], *n.f.* saucepan, stewpan.

casse-tête [kas'tɛːt], *n.m. inv.* cudgel, club; *(fig.)* din; conundrum.

cassette [ka'sɛt], *n.f.* casket; cash box.

casseur [ka'sœːr], *n.m.* (*fem.* -euse) breaker, smasher.

cassis [ka'sis], *n.m.* black currant.

casson [ka'sɔ̃], *n.m.* piece of broken glass *or* pottery; rough lump (*of sugar*).

cassonade [kaso'nad], *n.f.* moist brown sugar.

cassoulet [kasu'le], *n.m.* stew of beans with mutton and pork.

cassure [ka'syːr], *n.f.* break, crack, fracture; broken piece.

castagnette [kasta'nɛt], *n.f.* castanet.

caste [kast], *n.f.* caste.

castillan [kasti'jɑ̃], *a.* Castilian —*n.m.* Castilian (*speech*); (**Castillan**, *fem.* -ane) Castilian (*person*).

castine [kas'tin], *n.f.* (*Metal.*) flux.

castor [kas'tɔːr], *n.m.* beaver.

casuel [ka'zɥɛl], *a.* (*fem.* -uelle) casual, fortuitous, accidental.—*n.m.* perquisites, fees.

casuiste [ka'zɥist], *n.m.* casuist.

cataclysme [kata'klism], *n.m.* cataclysm; *(fig.)* disaster.

catacombes [kata'kɔ̃b], *n.f. pl.* catacombs.

catafalque [kata'falk], *n.m.* catafalque.

cataire [ka'tɛːr], *n.f.* (*Bot.*) catmint.

catalan [kata'lɑ̃], *a.* Catalan.—*n.m.* Catalan (*language*); (**Catalan**, *fem.* -ane) Catalan (*person*).

catalepsie [katalɛp'si], *n.f.* catalepsy.

catalogue [kata'log], *n.m.* list, catalogue.

cataloguer [katalo'ge], *v.t.* to catalogue.

catalyse [kata'liːz], *n.f.* (*Chem.*) catalysis.

catalyseur [katali'zœːr], *n.m.* catalyst.

catalytique [katali'tik], *a.* catalytic.

cataphote [kata'fɔt], *n.m.* cat's eye (*reflector*).

cataplasme [kata'plasm], *n.m.* cataplasm, poultice.

cataracte [kata'rakt], *n.f.* cataract, waterfall; (*Path.*) cataract.

catarrhal [kata'ral], *a.* (*m.pl.* -aux) catarrhal.

catarrhe [ka'taːr], *n.m.* catarrh.

catastrophe [katas'trɔf], *n.f.* catastrophe, calamity.

catastrophique [katastrɔ'fik], *a.* catastrophic.

catéchiser [kateʃi'ze], *v.t.* to catechize; *(fig.)* to reason with; to lecture.

catéchisme [kate'ʃism], *n.m.* catechism.

catégorie [katego'ri], *n.f.* category.

catégorique [katego'rik], *a.* categorical, explicit.

catégoriquement [kategorik'mɑ̃], *adv.* categorically.

catharsis [katar'sis], *n.f.* (*Med.*) catharsis.

cathédral [kate'dral], *a.* (*m.pl.* -aux) cathedral.

cathédrale [kate'dral], *n.f.* cathedral.

cathode [ka'tɔd], *n.f.* cathode.

cathodique [katɔ'dik], *a.* cathode.

catholicisme [katɔli'sism], *n.m.* Catholicism.

catholique [katɔ'lik], *a.* catholic; moral, orthodox.—*n.* Catholic (*person*).

cati [ka'ti], *n.m.* gloss, luster.

catir [ka'tiːr], *v.t.* to give a gloss to.

catissage [kati'saːʒ], *n.m.* glossing, pressing.

catisseur [kati'sœːr], *a.* and *n.m.* (*fem.* -euse) presser.

Caucase [ko'kɑːz], **le**, *m.* the Caucasus.

caucasien [koka'zjɛ̃], *a.* (*fem.* -enne) Caucasian.—*n.m.* (**Caucasien**, *fem.* -enne) Caucasian (*person*).

cauchemar [koʃ'maːr], *n.m.* nightmare.

caudataire [koda'tɛːr], *n.m.* train-bearer.

cauri, **cauris** *or* **coris** [ko'ri], *n.m.* cowrie.

causal [ko'zal], *a.* causal.

causant [ko'zɑ̃], *a.* chatty, talkative.

causatif [koza'tif], *a.* (*fem.* -tive) (*Gram.*) causative, causal.

cause [koːz], *n.f.* cause; grounds, motive; interest; case, trial, suit, action; *à cause de*, because of; *mettre en cause*, to be the cause of.

causer (1) [ko'ze], *v.t.* to cause, to be the cause of.

causer (2) [ko'ze], *v.i.* to chat, to talk; to prate.

causerie [ko'zri], *n.f.* talk, chat, gossip; chatty essay, review etc.

causette [ko'zɛt], *n.f.* chit-chat, small talk.

causeur [ko'zœːr], *a.* (*fem.* -euse) talkative, chatty.—*n.m.* (*fem.* -euse) talker.—*n.f.* (-euse) small sofa, settee for two.

causticité [kostisi'te], *n.f.* causticity.

caustique [kos'tik], *a.* caustic, biting, cutting. —*n.m.* caustic.

caustiquement [kostik'mɑ̃], *adv.* caustically.

cauteleusement [kotløz'mɑ̃], *adv.* craftily, slyly.

cauteleux [kot'lø], *a.* (*fem.* -euse) cunning, crafty.

cautère [ko'tɛːr], *n.m.* (*Med.*) cautery; issue.

cautérisation [koteriza'sjɔ̃], *n.f.* cauterization.

cautériser [koteri'ze], *v.t.* to cauterize.

caution [ko'sjɔ̃], *n.f.* security, bail, surety; *(fig.)* pledge, guarantee; *verser une caution*, to pay a deposit.

cautionnement [kosjon'mɑ̃], *n.m.* bail; security.

cautionner [kosjo'ne], *v.t.* to stand bail for someone.

cavage [ka'vaːʒ], *n.m.* cellarage.

cavalcade [kaval'kad], *n.f.* procession; cavalcade.

cavale [ka'val], *n.f.* mare.

cavalerie [kaval'ri], *n.f.* cavalry.

cavalier

cavalier [kava'lje], *n.m.* horseman, rider, trooper; (*Dancing*) partner; (*C*) lover, sweetheart; (*Chess*) knight.—*a.* (*fem.* **-ière**) cavalier, unceremonious (*of manners etc.*); off-hand, flippant.

cavalièrement [kavaljɛr'mã], *adv.* cavalierly, bluntly.

cave (1) [ka:v], *a.* hollow.

cave (2) [ka:v], *n.f.* (*wine*) cellar, vault; cellarage.

caveau [ka'vo], *n.m.* (*pl.* **-eaux**) small cellar; burial vault.

caver [ka've], *v.t.* to hollow, to scoop out, to dig under; (*fig.*) to undermine; (*Fenc.*) to lunge. **se caver**, *v.r.* to become hollow *or* sunken.

caverne [ka'vɛrn], *n.f.* cavern, cave, hollow; (*fig.*) retreat, lair.

caverneux [kavɛr'nø], *a.* (*fem.* **-euse**) cavernous, hollow.

caviar [ka'vja:r], *n.m.* caviare.

cavillation [kavila'sjɔ̃], *n.f.* sophistry, cavil.

cavité [kavi'te], *n.f.* cavity, hollow.

ce (1) [sə], *dem. a.* (*before vowels* **cet**, *fem.* **cette**, *pl.* **ces**) this, that, (*pl.*) these, those.

ce (2) [sə], *dem. pron. inv.* it, that (*sometimes* — he, she, *or*, *with plural verb*, they); *c'en est fait*, it is all over, it is done; *c'est-à-dire*, that is to say; *c'est que*, the fact is that; *pour ce qui est de* . . . , as for . . . .

*****céans** [se'ã], *adv.* within, here within, in this house, at home.

ceci [sə'si], *dem. pron.* this, this thing.

cécité [sesi'te], *n.f.* blindness.

cédant [se'dã], *a.* that grants; (*Law*) that assigns, transfers.—*n.m.* (*fem.* **-e**) (*Law*) grantor, assignor, transferrer.

céder [se'de], *v.t.* (*see Verb Tables*) to give up, to yield, to surrender, to cede; to transfer, to make over.—*v.i.* to give way; to submit.

cédille [se'di:j], *n.f.* cedilla.

cédrat [se'dra], *n.m.* citron tree; citron.

cèdre [sɛ:dr], *n.m.* cedar.

cédule [se'dyl], *n.f.* schedule, memorandum; notice; (*Law*) notification.

cégétiste [seʒe'tist], *n.m.* a member of the C.G.T. (Confédération Générale du Travail.)

ceindre [sɛ̃:dr], *v.t. irr.* (*conjug. like* CRAINDRE) to gird, to encircle, to encompass, to surround; to bind *or* gird on. **se ceindre**, *v.r.* to bind round one, to put on (*a scarf etc.*).

ceinture [sɛ̃'ty:r], *n.f.* sash, girdle, belt, waistband; waist; enclosure, circle; *ceinture de sauvetage*, life belt.

ceinturer [sɛ̃ty're], *v.t.* to girdle, to surround.

ceinturon [sɛ̃ty'rɔ̃], *n.m.* belt, sword-belt.

cela [sə'la], *dem. pron.* that, that thing (*in opposition to this, of which we are speaking*); *c'est cela*, that's it. *In popular speech* cela *becomes* **ça**; *pas de ça*, none of that; *comme ci comme ça*, middling.

céladon [sela'dɔ̃], *a.* and *n.m.* sea-green (*color*).

célébrant [sele'brã], *n.m.* celebrant.

célébration [selebra'sjɔ̃], *n.f.* solemn performance, celebration.

célèbre [se'lɛbr], *a.* celebrated, famous, renowned.

célébrer [sele'bre], *v.t.* (*conjug. like* CÉDER) to celebrate, to praise, to extol; to solemnize.

célébrité [selebri'te], *n.f.* celebrity.

*****celer** [sə'le], *v.t.* (*conjug. like* AMENER) to conceal, to keep secret. *****se celer**, *v.r.* to conceal oneself, to hide.

céleri [sel'ri], *n.m.* celery; *un pied de céleri*, a stick of celery.

célerin [sel're], *n.m.* (*Ichth.*) pilchard.

célérité [seleri'te], *n.f.* celerity, rapidity.

céleste [se'lɛst], *a.* celestial, heavenly, divine.

célibat [seli'ba], *n.m.* celibacy, single life.

célibataire [seliba'tɛ:r], *a.* single.—*n.m.* bachelor.—*n.f.* spinster.

celle [sɛl], [CELUI].

cellérier [sele'rje], *n.m.* (*fem.* **-ière**) cellarer.

cellier [se'lje], *n.m.* cellar, storeroom.

cellophane [sɛlo'fan], *n.f.* cellophane.

cellulaire [sɛly'lɛ:r], *a.* cellular.

cellule [se'lyl], *n.f.* cell; *cellule photo-électrique*, electric eye.

celluleux [sɛly'lø], *a.* (*fem.* **-euse**) cellular.

celluloïd *or* **celluloïde** [sɛlylo'id], *n.m.* celluloid.

cellulose [sɛly'lo:z], *n.f.* cellulose.

Celte [sɛlt], *n.* Celt.

celtique [sɛl'tik], *a.* Celtic.—*n.m.* Celtic (*language*).

celui [sə'lɥi], *dem. pron. m.* (*fem.* **celle**, *pl.* **ceux**, **celles**) the one, that, those (*sometimes* — he *or* she). Followed by **-ci** *or* **-là** — this one, that one etc. *or* the latter *and* the former.

cément [se'mã], *n.m.* (*Metal.*) cement.

cémentation [semãta'sjɔ̃], *n.f.* (*Metal.*) cementation.

cémenter [semã'te], *v.t.* (*Metal.*) to cement.

cénacle [se'nakl], *n.m.* (*Ant.*) guest chamber; (*fig.*) literary society *or* coterie.

cendre [sã:dr], *n.f.* ashes, embers, cinders; dust, ashes (*of the dead*).

cendré [sã'dre], *a.* ashy, ashen.

cendrée [sã'dre], *n.f.* small shot; cinders (*for track*); *piste en cendrées*, dirt track, cinder track.

cendrer [sã'dre], *v.t.* to paint ash-grey; to mix *or* cover with ashes.

cendreux [sã'drø], *a.* (*fem.* **-euse**) ashy.

cendrier [sãdri'e], *n.m.* ash pan, ash pit; ash tray.

cendrière [sãdri'ɛ:r], *n.f.* peat.

Cendrillon [sãdri'jɔ̃], *n.f.* Cinderella, drudge.

Cène [sɛ:n], *n.f.* The Lord's Supper, Holy Communion.

cenelle [sə'nɛl], *n.f.* haw.

cénobite [seno'bit], *n.m.* coenobite.

cénotaphe [seno'taf], *n.m.* cenotaph.

cens [sã:s], *n.m.* census; rating.

censé [sã'se], *a.* accounted, reputed, supposed.

censeur [sã'sœ:r], *n.m.* censor; critic; proctor (*of Engl. Univ.*); assistant headmaster (*in French Lycée*).

censure [sã'sy:r], *n.f.* censorship; criticism, censure; audit (*of accounts*).

censurer [sãsy're], *v.t.* to find fault with, to criticize; to censure.

cent [sã], *a.* one hundred; *faire les cent pas*, to walk up and down.—*n.m.* a hundred; *cinq pour cent*, five per cent.

centaine [sã'tɛn], *n.f.* a hundred; a hundred or so.

centaure [sã'tɔ:r], *n.m.* centaur.

centenaire [sãt'nɛ:r], *a.* a hundred years old.—*n.* centenarian.—*n.m.* centenary.

centième [sɑ̃'tjɛm], *a.* hundredth.—*n.m.* hundredth part.

centigrade [sɑ̃ti'grad], *a.* centigrade.

centigramme [sɑ̃ti'gram], *n.m.* centigram, the hundredth part of a gram (.1543 grain).

centilitre [sɑ̃ti'litr], *n.m.* centiliter, hundredth part of a liter (.61028 cubic in.).

centime [sɑ̃'tim], *n.m.* centime, hundredth part of a franc.

centimètre [sɑ̃ti'mɛtr], *n.m.* centimeter, hundredth part of a meter (.39371 in.).

centipède [sɑ̃ti'pɛd], *n.m.* centipede.

central [sɑ̃'tral], *a.* (*m. pl.* **-aux**) central; chief, principal, head.—*n.m.* **central téléphonique**, telephone exchange.—*n.f.* **centrale électrique**, electric power station.

centralement [sɑ̃tral'mɑ̃], *adv.* centrally.

centralisateur [sɑ̃traliza'tœːr], *a.* (*fem.* **-trice**) centralizing.

centralisation [sɑ̃traliza'sjɔ̃], *n.f.* centralization.

centraliser [sɑ̃trali'ze], *v.t.* to centralize.

centre [sɑ̃tr], *n.m.* center, middle.

centrer [sɑ̃'tre], *v.t.* to center.

centrifuge [sɑ̃tri'fyːʒ], *a.* centrifugal.

centripète [sɑ̃tri'pɛt], *a.* centripetal.

centuple [sɑ̃'typl], *a.* and *n.m.* centuple, hundredfold.

centupler [sɑ̃ty'ple], *v.t.* to multiply a hundredfold.

centurion [sɑ̃ty'rjɔ̃], *n.m.* centurion.

cep [sɛp], *n.m.* vine stock.

cépage [se'paːʒ], *n.m.* vine plant.

cépée [se'pe], *n.f.* (*Agric.*) tuft of shoots from a pollarded stump; copse of one or two years' growth.

cependant [spɑ̃'dɑ̃], *adv.* in the meantime, meanwhile.—*conj.* yet, still, however, nevertheless.

céramique [sera'mik], *a.* ceramic.—*n.f.* ceramics.

Cerbère [sɛr'bɛːr], *m.* (*Myth.*) Cerberus.

cerceau [sɛr'so], *n.m.* (*pl.* **-eaux**) hoop, ring; hoop net.

cerclage [sɛr'klaːʒ], *n.m.* hooping (*of casks*).

cercle [sɛrkl], *n.m.* circle, ring; circumference; club, club-house.

cercler [sɛr'kle], *v.t.* to bind with hoops, to hoop.

cercueil [sɛr'kœːj], *n.m.* coffin; (*fig.*) the tomb.

céréale [sere'al], *n.f.* cereal, corn, grain.

cérébral [sere'bral], *a.* (*m.pl.* **-aux**) cerebral.

cérémonial [seremo'njal], *a.* (*m. pl.* **-aux**) ceremonial.—*n.m.* (*no pl.*) ceremonial, pomp.

cérémonie [seremo'ni], *n.f.* ceremony; pomp; fuss, ado.

cérémonieux [seremo'njø], *a.* (*fem.* **-euse**) ceremonious, formal.

cerf [sɛːr], *n.m.* stag, hart, deer.

cerfeuil [sɛr'fœːj], *n.m.* chervil.

cerf-volant [sɛrvo'lɑ̃], *n.m.* (*pl.* **cerfs-volants**) stag beetle; kite, paper kite.

cerisaie [səri'zɛ], *n.f.* cherry orchard.

cerise [sə'riːz], *n.f.* cherry.—*n.m.* cherry-color, cerise.—*a.* cherry-colored, cerise.

cerisier [səri'zje], *n.m.* cherry tree, cherry wood.

cerner [sɛr'ne], *v.t.* to cut *or* dig round (*a tree*), to ring (*a tree*); to surround, to encompass, to hem in.

certain [sɛr'tɛ̃], *a.* certain, sure, positive; fixed, determined; *d'un certain âge*, not so young.—*n.m.* certainty; a sure thing.

certainement [sɛrtɛn'mɑ̃], *adv.* certainly.

certes [sɛrt], *adv.* indeed, most certainly.

certificat [sɛrtifi'ka], *n.m.* certificate; testimonial; diploma.

certification [sɛrtifika'sjɔ̃], *n.f.* certification.

certifier [sɛrti'fje], *v.t.* to certify, to testify, to vouch for.

certitude [sɛrti'tyd], *n.f.* certitude, certainty.

cerveau [sɛr'vo], *n.m.* (*pl.* **-eaux**) brain; mind, intellect, intelligence.

cervelas [sɛrvə'la], *n.m.* saveloy.

cervelle [sɛr'vɛl], *n.f.* brains; mind, intelligence.

cervin [sɛr'vɛ̃], *a.* cervine; *le* (*Mont*) *Cervin*, the Matterhorn.

César [se'zaːr], *m.* Caesar.—*n.m.* Caesar, emperor.

césarien [sena'rjɛ̃], *a.* (*fem.* **ienne**) Caesarean.—*n.f.* (**-ienne**) Caesarean operation.

cessant [sɛ'sɑ̃], *a.* ceasing, suspended.

cessation [sɛsa'sjɔ̃], *n.f.* cessation, suspension, stoppage.

cesse [sɛs], *n.f.* ceasing, intermission, respite.

cesser [sɛ'se], *v.t.* to leave off, to break off, to stop.—*v.i.* to cease, to leave off, to stop.

cession [sɛ'sjɔ̃], *n.f.* transfer, assignment (*of property*).

cessionnaire [sɛsjo'nɛːr], *n.m.* grantee, assignee.

césure [se'zyːr], *n.f.* caesura.

cet, cette [sɛt], [CE].

cétacé [seta'se], *a.* cetaceous.—*n.m.* cetacean.

ceux [søː], [CELUI].

Ceylan [se'lɑ̃], *le*, *m.* Ceylon.

chablis (1) [ʃɑ'bli], *n.m.* deadwood.

chablis (2) [ʃɑ'bli], *n.m.* Chablis (*white wine*).

chacal [ʃa'kal], *n.m.* jackal.

chacun [ʃa'kœ̃], *pron. indef. sing.* each, each one, every one.

chafouin [ʃa'fwɛ̃], *a.* weasel-faced, mean-looking.

chagrin (1), [ʃa'grɛ̃], *n.m.* grief, chagrin, sorrow.—*a.* gloomy, melancholy, sad.

chagrin (2) [ʃa'grɛ̃], *n.m.* shagreen.

chagrinant [ʃagri'nɑ̃], *a.* distressing, sad.

chagriner [ʃagri'ne], *v.t.* to grieve, to afflict; to cross, to vex. **se chagriner**, *v.r.* to fret, to grieve.

chahut [ʃa'y], *n.m.* row, shindy.

chahuter [ʃay'te], *v.i.* to make a row, to kick up a shindy.

chaîne [ʃɛːn], *n.f.* chain; shackle, fetters; bonds, bondage; (*Naut.*) cable; (*fig.*) series, range; (*Ind.*) **chaîne de montage**, assembly line.

chaîner [ʃɛ'ne], *v.t.* (*Surveying*) to measure (*land*) with the chain.

chaînette [ʃɛ'nɛt], *n.f.* little chain; (*Arch.*) catenary arch.

chaînon [ʃɛ'nɔ̃], *n.m.* link.

chaintre [ʃɛ̃ːtr], *n.m.* (*Agric.*) balk, headland.

chair [ʃɛːr], *n.f.* flesh; meat; (*fig.*) the human body, the flesh; (*Paint.*, *pl.*) naked flesh.

chaire [ʃɛːr], *n.f.* pulpit; professorship; bishop's throne.

chaise [ʃɛːz], *n.f.* chair, seat; post chaise.

chaland (1) [ʃa'lɑ̃], *n.m.* lighter, barge.

chaland (2) [ʃa'lɑ̃], *n.m.* (*fem.* **-e**) customer, client.

chalandeau [ʃalɑ̃ˈdo], *n.m.* (*pl.* **-eaux**) lighterman, bargeman.

chalcographe [kalkoˈgraf], *n.m.* chalcographer, engraver on metal.

chalcographie [kalkograˈfi], *n.f.* chalcography; engraving establishment.

chaldaïque [kaldaˈik], *a.* Chaldaic.

Chaldée [kalˈde], *f.* Chaldea.

chaldéen [kaldeˈɛ̃], *a.* (*fem.* **-éenne**) Chaldean. —*n.m.* (**Chaldéen,** *fem.* **-éenne**) Chaldean (*person*).

châle [ʃɑːl], *n.m.* shawl.

chalet [ʃaˈlɛ], *n.m.* chalet, Swiss cottage.

chaleur [ʃaˈlœːr], *n.f.* heat; warmth, warm weather; (*fig.*) glow; zeal, ardor; '*craint la chaleur*', 'store in a cool place'.

chaleureusement [ʃalœrøzˈmɑ̃], *adv.* cordially, warmly.

chaleureux [ʃalœˈrø], *a.* (*fem.* **-euse**) warm, cordial.

chalicose [ʃaliˈkoːz], *n.f.* silicosis.

châlit [ʃaˈli], *n.m.* bedstead.

chaloupe [ʃaˈlup], *n.f.* ship's boat, launch.

chalumeau [ʃalyˈmo], *n.m.* (*pl.* **-eaux**) stalk of wheat; drinking-straw; flute, pipe.

chalut [ʃaˈly], *n.m.* dragnet, trawl.

chalutier [ʃalyˈtje], *n.m.* trawler.

chamaillard [ʃamaˈjaːr], *a.* squabbling, quarrelsome.

chamailler [ʃamaˈje], *v.i.* to bicker, to squabble. **se chamailler,** *v.r.* to squabble, to wrangle.

chamaillis [ʃamaˈji], *n.m.* fray; squabble; uproar.

chamarrer [ʃamaˈre], *v.t.* to bedizen, to bedeck.

chambellan [ʃɑ̃beˈlɑ̃], *n.m.* chamberlain.

chambranle [ʃɑ̃ˈbrɑːl], *n.m.* door frame, window frame.

chambre [ʃɑ̃ːbr], *n.f.* chamber, room; apartment; House (*of Parliament*); court (*of justice*); *chambre à air*, inner tube (*bicycle etc.*); *chambre à un (deux) lit(s)*, single (double) room; *chambre d'ami*, spare bedroom; *chambre d'écluse*, lock; *chambre noire*, camera obscura.

chambrée [ʃɑ̃ˈbre], *n.f.* barrack room; roomful (*Theat. etc.*) house.

chambrer [ʃɑ̃ˈbre], *v.t.* to keep (*someone*) confined; to bring wine to room temperature.—*v.i.* to lodge (*together*). **se chambrer,** *v.r.* to become pitted.

chambrette [ʃɑ̃ˈbrɛt], *n.f.* little room.

chameau [ʃaˈmo], *n.m.* (*pl.* **-eaux**) camel; (*pop.*) nasty, evil-minded person.

chamelier [ʃaməˈlje], *n.m.* camel driver.

chamelle [ʃaˈmɛl], *n.f.* female camel.

chamelon [ʃamˈlɔ̃], *n.m.* young camel.

chamois [ʃaˈmwa], *n.m.* chamois; chamois leather.—*a.* chamois-colored, buff.

chamoiseur [ʃamwaˈzœːr], *n.m.* chamois or leather dresser.

champ [ʃɑ̃], *n.m.* field, piece of ground; scope, range; (*poet.*) land; (*fig.*) space; *sur-le-champ*, at once, immediately.

champagne [ʃɑ̃ˈpaɲ], *n.m.* champagne; *champagne frappé*, iced champagne; *champagne mousseux*, sparkling champagne; *fine champagne*, liqueur brandy.

champenois [ʃɑ̃pəˈnwa], *a.* of Champagne. —*n.m.* (**Champenois,** *fem.* **-oise**) inhabitant of Champagne.

champêtre [ʃɑ̃ˈpɛːtr], *a.* rural, rustic; *garde champêtre*, village policeman.

champignon [ʃɑ̃piˈɲɔ̃], *n.m.* mushroom, fungus.

champion [ʃɑ̃ˈpjɔ̃], *n.m.* (*fem.* **-onne**) champion.

championnat [ʃɑ̃pjoˈna], *n.m.* championship.

chançard [ʃɑ̃ˈsaːr], *a.* and *n.m.* (*fem.* **-e**) (*fam.*) lucky (*person*).

chance [ʃɑ̃ːs], *n.f.* chance; luck, good luck, good fortune; (*pl.*) chances, (*fam.*) odds.

chancelant [ʃɑ̃sˈlɑ̃], *a.* staggering, tottering.

chanceler [ʃɑ̃sˈle], *v.i.* (*conjug. like* APPELER) to stagger, to totter; to reel.

chancelier [ʃɑ̃saˈlje], *n.m.* chancellor.

chancellement [ʃɑ̃selˈmɑ̃], *n.m.* tottering, staggering.

chancellerie [ʃɑ̃selˈri], *n.f.* chancellery.

chanceux [ʃɑ̃ˈsø], *a.* (*fem.* **-euse**) lucky, fortunate; risky, doubtful (*of things*).

chanci [ʃɑ̃ˈsi], *a.* moldy.

chancir [ʃɑ̃ˈsiːr], *v.i.* to grow musty or moldy.

chancissure [ʃɑ̃siˈsyːr], *n.f.* mustiness, moldiness.

chancre [ʃɑ̃ːkr], *n.m.* ulcer, tumor; canker.

chancreux [ʃɑ̃ˈkrø], *a.* (*fem.* **-euse**) ulcerous, cankered.

chandail [ʃɑ̃ˈdaːj], *n.m.* jersey, sweater.

Chandeleur [ʃɑ̃ˈdlœːr], *n.f.* Candlemas.

chandelier [ʃɑ̃dəˈlje], *n.m.* candlestick.

chandelle [ʃɑ̃ˈdɛl], *n.f.* (*tallow*) candle; (*fig.*) light; (*Tennis*) lob.

change [ʃɑ̃ːʒ], *n.m.* exchange; exchange of money; exchange office; agio; (*Hunt.*) wrong scent; *agent de change*, stockbroker; *cours du change*, rate of exchange.

changeant [ʃɑ̃ˈʒɑ̃], *a.* changeable, fickle, unstable; unsettled (*of the weather*).

changement [ʃɑ̃ʒˈmɑ̃], *n.m.* change, alteration; (*Law*) amendment.

changer [ʃɑ̃ˈʒe], *v.t., v.i.* (*conjug. like* MANGER) to change, to exchange; to alter.

changeur [ʃɑ̃ˈʒœːr], *n.m.* (*fem.* **-euse**) moneychanger.

chanoine [ʃaˈnwan], *n.m.* canon.

chanson [ʃɑ̃ˈsɔ̃], *n.f.* song, ballad; (*fig.*) idle story, stuff, trash; *chansons que tout cela!* humbug!

chansonner [ʃɑ̃soˈne], *v.t.* to lampoon.

chansonnette [ʃɑ̃soˈnɛt], *n.f.* little song, ditty.

chansonneur [ʃɑ̃soˈnœːr], *n.m.* lampooner.

chansonnier [ʃɑ̃soˈnje], *n.m.* (*fem.* **-ière**) song-writer, ballad writer; singer of satirical songs.

chant [ʃɑ̃], *n.m.* singing; song; air, tune; poem; canto; chant, hymn.

chantable [ʃɑ̃ˈtabl], *a.* fit to be sung, worth singing.

chantage [ʃɑ̃ˈtaːʒ], *n.m.* extortion of hush money, blackmail.

chantant [ʃɑ̃ˈtɑ̃], *a.* easily sung; tuneful, harmonious.

chanteau [ʃɑ̃ˈto], *n.m.* (*pl.* **-eaux**) hunk (*of bread*), bit (*of material etc.*), remnant; (*Dress.*) gore.

chantepleure [ʃɑ̃tˈplœːr], *n.f.* funnel pierced with holes; strainer.

chanter [ʃɑ̃'te], *v.t.* to extol, to praise, to celebrate; to sing.—*v.i.* to sing; to chirp, to warble, to crow; *cela vous chante-t-il?* how do you like the idea? **se chanter**, *v.r.* to be sung.

chanterelle [ʃɑ̃'trɛl], *n.f.* first string of a violin etc.; decoy bird.

chanteur [ʃɑ̃'tœ:r], *a.* (*fem.* **-euse**) singing.—*n.m.* (*fem.* **-euse**) singer, vocalist.

chantier [ʃɑ̃'tje], *n.m.* timber-yard, wood-yard; stone-yard; dockyard; site; (*C*) shanty, lumber camp.

chantonner [ʃɑ̃to'ne], *v.t.*, *v.i.* to hum.

chantourner [ʃɑ̃tur'ne], *v.t.* to cut in profile; *scie à chantourner*, bow saw.

chantre [ʃɑ̃:tr], *n.m.* singer, *esp.* a chorister; precentor, lay clerk; (*fig.*) songster (*of birds*).

chanvre [ʃɑ̃:vr], *n.m.* hemp.

chanvreux [ʃɑ̃'vrø], *a.* (*fem.* **-euse**) hempen.

chaos [ka'o], *n.m.* chaos; (*fig.*) confusion, disorder.

chaotique [kao'tik], *a.* chaotic.

chaparder [ʃapar'de], *v.t.* (*slang*) to steal, to scrounge.

chape [ʃap], *n.f.* cope (*ecclesiastical vestment*); tread (*of a tire*).

chapeau [ʃa'po], *n.m.* (*pl.* **-eaux**) hat; (*Mech. etc.*) cap; *un coup de chapeau*, a bow.

chapelain [ʃa'plɛ̃], *n.m.* chaplain.

chapelet [ʃa'plɛ], *n.m.* rosary, beads; (*Arch. etc.*) chaplet; *chapelet de bombes*, stick of bombs; *chapelet d'oignons*, string of onions.

chapelier [ʃapə'lje], *n.m.* (*fem.* **-ière**) hatter.

chapelle [ʃa'pɛl], *n.f.* chapel; coterie, school (*of literature etc.*); church plate; living.

chapellenie [ʃapel'ni], *n.f.* chaplaincy.

chapellerie [ʃapel'ri], *n.f.* hat-making; hat trade, shop *or* business.

chapelure [ʃa'ply:r], *n.f.* grated bread-crumbs.

chaperon [ʃa'prɔ̃], *n.m.* hood; (*fig.*) chaperon; *Le Petit Chaperon Rouge*, Little Red Riding Hood.

chaperonner [ʃapro'ne], *v.t.* to cope (*a wall*); (*fig.*) to chaperon.

chapiteau [ʃapi'to], *n.m.* (*pl.* **-eaux**) capital (*of column etc.*); cornice (*of a wardrobe etc.*); big top (*circus*).

chapitre [ʃa'pitr], *n.m.* chapter (*of a book, of knights, of a cathedral*); subject matter of discourse.

chapitrer [ʃapi'tre], *v.t.* to reprimand, to rebuke.

chapon [ʃa'pɔ̃], *n.m.* capon; sop in broth.

chaponner [ʃapo'ne], *v.t.* to caponize.

chaque [ʃak], *a.* each, every.

char [ʃa:r], *n.m.* chariot, carriage, vehicle; *char d'assaut*, (*Mil.*) tank.

charabia [ʃara'bja], *n.m.* gibberish.

charançon [ʃarɑ̃'sɔ̃], *n.m.* weevil.

charbon [ʃar'bɔ̃], *n.m.* coal, charcoal; (*pl.*) embers; (*Path.*) anthrax; (*Chem.*) carbon.

charbonnée [ʃarbɔ'ne], *n.f.* piece of grilled meat; charcoal drawing.

charbonner [ʃarbɔ'ne], *v.t.* to char; to black with coal. **se charbonner**, *v.r.* to be charred, to burn black.

charbonnerie [ʃarbɔn'ri], *n.f.* coal depot.

charbonneux [ʃarbɔ'nø], *a.* (*fem.* **-euse**) coaly; affected *or* infected with anthrax.

charbonnier [ʃarbɔ'nje], *n.m.* (*fem.* **-ière**) charcoal burner; coal man.—*n.m.* coal heaver; coal hole; (*Naut.*) collier.—*n.f.* (*-ière*) charcoal kiln; coal scuttle; (*Orn.*) great tit.

charcuter [ʃarky'te], *v.t.* to hack and hew (*meat*); to hack, to butcher (*of a surgeon*).

charcuterie [ʃarky'tri], *n.f.* pork-butcher's meat; pork-butcher's business *or* shop.

charcutier [ʃarky'tje], *n.m.* (*fem.* **-ière**) pork-butcher; (*colloq.*) sawbones.

chardon [ʃar'dɔ̃], *n.m.* thistle; spikes (*on a wall or railing*).

chardonneret [ʃardɔn're], *n.m.* goldfinch.

charge [ʃarʒ], *n.f.* pack; load; expense, cost; accusation; post, employment; care, custody; charge, onset; *à charge de revanche*, provided that I may return the favor.

chargé [ʃar'ʒe], *a.* loaded, burdened.

chargement [ʃarʒə'mɑ̃], *n.m.* cargo, freight; bill of lading; load; charging (*of a battery*).

charger [ʃar'ʒe], *v.t.* (*conjug. like* MANGER) to load, to charge; to burden; to charge with; to register (*a letter*). **se charger**, *v.r.* to take upon oneself, to saddle oneself with (*de*).

chargeur [ʃar'ʒœ:r], *n.m.* loader, shipper; stoker; (*Phot., Cine.*) cassette.

chariot [ʃa'rjo], *n.m.* wagon, go-cart; (*Mach.*) truck, trolley.

charitable [ʃari'tabl], *a.* charitable.

charitablement [ʃaritablə'mɑ̃], *adv.* charitably.

charité [ʃari'te], *n.f.* charity; benevolence, alms.

charivari [ʃariva'ri], *n.m.* rough music; hubbub, clatter.

charlatan [ʃarla'tɑ̃], *n.m.* charlatan, mountebank, quack.

charlatanisme [ʃarlata'nism], *n.m.* quackery, charlatanism.

charlot [ʃar'lo], *n.m.* (*Orn.*) curlew.

charmant [ʃar'mɑ̃], *a.* charming, delightful.

charme (1) [ʃarm], *n.m.* charm; spell, enchantment.

charme (2) [ʃarm], *n.m.* (*Bot.*) hornbeam.

charmer [ʃar'me], *v.t.* to charm, to enchant, to bewitch, to fascinate, to captivate, to delight.

charmeur [ʃar'mœ:r], *n.m.* (*fem.* **-euse**) charmer, enchanter; bewitching woman, enchantress.

charmille [ʃar'mi:j], *n.f.* hedge of young hornbeam; bower, arbor.

charnel [ʃar'nɛl], *a.* (*fem.* **-elle**) carnal; sensual (*person*).

charnellement [ʃarnɛl'mɑ̃], *adv.* carnally.

charnier [ʃar'nje], *n.m.* charnel house.

charnière [ʃar'njɛ:r], *n.f.* hinge; joint, articulation.

charnu [ʃar'ny], *a.* fleshy, plump; pulpy (*of fruits*).

charogne [ʃa'rɔɲ], *n.f.* carrion; (*pop.*) blackguard; slut.

charpente [ʃar'pɑ̃:t], *n.f.* frame, framework.

charpenter [ʃarpɑ̃'te], *v.t.* to square (*timber*); (*fig.*) to frame, to construct.

charpenterie [ʃarpɑ̃'tri], *n.f.* carpentry, carpenter's work *or* trade.

charpentier [ʃarpă'tje], *n.m.* carpenter.

charpie [ʃar'pi], *n.f.* lint.

charretée [ʃar'te], *n.f.* cartload.

charretier [ʃar'tje], *n.m.* (*fem.* **-ière**) carter, wagoner. —*a.* passable for carts etc.

charrette [ʃa'rɛt], *n.f.* cart; *charrette à bras*, hand cart.

charriage [ʃa'ria:ʒ], *n.m.* cartage; haulage.

charrier [ʃa'rje], *v.t.* to cart.—*v.i.* to drift (*of ice*).

charroi [ʃa'rwa], *n.m.* cartage.

charron [ʃa'rɔ̃], *n.m.* wheelwright.

charroyer [ʃarwa'je], *v.t.* (*conjug. like* EMPLOYER) to cart (*heavy things*).

charrue [ʃa'ry], *n.f.* plow.

charte [ʃart], *n.f.* charter.

chartreuse [ʃar'trøːz], *n.f.* Carthusian monastery *or* convent; Carthusian nun; isolated country house; chartreuse (*liqueur*).

chartreux [ʃar'trø], *n.m.* Carthusian friar; cat of a bluish-grey color.

chartrier [ʃartri'e], *n.m.* keeper of charters; archives; muniment room.

Charybde [ka'ribd], *n.m.* Charybdis.

chas [ʃa], *n.m.* eye (*of a needle*).

chasme [kasm], *n.m.* chasm.

châsse [ʃɑ:s], *n.f.* reliquary, shrine; frame.

chasse [ʃas], *n.f.* hunting, shooting, fowling; the hunt, the chase; game preserve; play (*of machinery etc.*); flush (*of lavatory*).

chassé [ʃa'se], *n.m.* chassé (*a step in dancing*).

chassé-croisé [ʃasekrwa'ze], *n.m.* (*pl.* **chassés-croisés**) (*Dancing*) a dance step; (*fig.*) *faire un chassé-croisé*, to exchange places.

chasselas [ʃas'la], *n.m.* table grapes.

[In the following compounds **chasse** is *inv.*]

chasse-marée [ʃasma're], *n.m.* fish cart.

chasse-mouches [ʃas'muʃ], *n.m.* a form of fan; fly swatter.

chasse-neige [ʃas'nɛːʒ], *n.m.* snow plow.

chasse-pierre(s) [ʃas'pjɛːr], *n.m.* (*Rail.*) guard-iron, cow-catcher.

chasser [ʃa'se], *v.t.* to hunt; to chase, to pursue; to drive in (*a nail etc.*); to expel, to turn out, to discharge; to propel.—*v.i.* to go shooting *or* hunting; to glide along; (*Motor.*) to skid.

chasseresse [ʃas'rɛs], *n.f.* huntress.

chasseur [ʃa'sœːr], *n.m.* (*fem.* **-euse**) hunter *or* huntress, sportsman *or* sportswoman.—*n.m.* page boy; light infantry soldier; (*Av.*) fighter.

chassie [ʃa'si], *n.f.* gum on the edge of the eyelids.

chassieux [ʃa'sjø], *a.* (*fem.* **-euse**) blear-eyed.

châssis [ʃa'si], *n.m.* case, frame; window sash; garden frame; printer's chase; (*Motor.*) chassis; (*Theat.*) flat for scenery.

chaste [ʃast], *a.* chaste; pure, virtuous.

chastement [ʃasta'mã], *adv.* chastely, purely, virtuously.

chasteté [ʃasta'te], *n.f.* chastity, purity.

chasuble [ʃa'zybl], *n.f.* chasuble.

chat [ʃa], *n.m.* (*fem.* **chatte**) cat; darling, dear little thing; *à bon chat bon rat*, set a thief to catch a thief; (*C*) *chat sauvage*, raccoon; *Le Chat Botté*, Puss in Boots.

châtaigne [ʃa'tɛɲ], *n.f.* chestnut.

châtaignier [ʃatɛ'ɲje], *n.m.* chestnut tree.

châtain [ʃa'tɛ̃], *a. inv.* chestnut, nut-brown, auburn.

chat-cervier [ʃaser'vje], *n.m.* (*pl.* **chats-cerviers**) lynx.

château [ʃa'to], *n.m.* (*pl.* **-eaux**) castle, fortress; country seat, mansion, hall, palace.

châteaubriand [ʃatobri'ã], *n.m.* large grilled rump steak.

châtelain [ʃa'tlɛ̃], *n.m.* (*fem.* **-aine**) lord *or* lady of a manor, squire *or* squire's wife.

chat-huant [ʃa'ɥã], *n.m.* (*pl.* **chats-huants**) tawny owl.

châtiable [ʃa'tjabl], *a.* chastisable, punishable.

châtier [ʃa'tje], *v.t.* to chastise, to punish; (*fig.*) to correct.

chatière [ʃa'tjɛːr], *n.f.* cat's hole (*in door etc.*).

châtiment [ʃati'mã], *n.m.* chastisement, punishment.

chatoiement *or* **chatoîment** [ʃatwa'mã], *n.m.* play of colors, changing luster (*as of shot silk, opals etc.*).

chaton (1) [ʃa'tɔ̃], *n.m.* kitten; catkin.

chaton (2) [ʃa'tɔ̃], *n.m.* setting of a gem; stone in a setting.

chatouillant [ʃatu'jã], *a.* tickling.

chatouillement [ʃatuj'mã], *n.m.* tickling, titillation.

chatouiller [ʃatu'je], *v.t.* to tickle, to titillate; (*fig.*) to please, to gratify, to flatter.

chatouilleux [ʃatu'jø], *a.* (*fem.* **-euse**) ticklish; (*fig.*) delicate, touchy.

chatoyant [ʃatwa'jã], *a.* shot, glistening (*of colors etc.*).

chatoyer [ʃatwa'je], *v.i.* (*conjug. like* EMPLOYER) to shimmer, to glisten.

châtrer [ʃa'tre], *v.t.* to castrate, to geld; (*Hort.*) to lop, to prune; (*fig.*) to expurgate.

chattée [ʃa'te], *n.f.* litter of kittens.

chatte [ʃat], [CHAT].

chatterie [ʃat'ri], *n.f.* playfulness, pretty *or* coaxing way; wheedling caress; (*pl.*) titbits.

chatterton [ʃater'tɔ̃], *n.m.* insulating tape.

chaud [ʃo], *a.* hot, warm, burning, glowing.—*n.m.* heat, warmth; *il fait chaud*, it is hot.—*adv.* hot, warm.

chaudeau [ʃo'do], *n.m.* (*pl.* **-eaux**) egg flip.

chaudement [ʃod'mã], *adv.* warmly; (*fig.*) quickly, eagerly, fiercely, hotly.

chaud-froid [ʃo'frwa], *n.m.* cold jellied chicken *or* game with mayonnaise.

chaudière [ʃo'djɛːr], *n.f.* copper; boiler (*of a steam engine etc.*); (*C*) pail.

chaudron [ʃo'drɔ̃], *n.m.* cauldron.

chaudronnerie [ʃodrɔn'ri], *n.f.* boiler works.

chaudronnier [ʃodrɔ'nje], *n.m.* brazier, coppersmith, tinker.

chauffage [ʃo'fa:ʒ], *n.m.* heating, warming; stoking; fuel, firewood; *chauffage central*, central heating.

chauffard [ʃo'faːr], *n.m.* (*pop.*) road hog.

chauffe [ʃo:f], *n.f.* furnace.

chauffe-bain [ʃof'bɛ̃], *n.m.* (*pl.* **chauffe-bains**) geyser.

chauffe-eau [ʃof'o], *n.m. inv.* water heater.

chauffelinge [ʃof'lɛ̃ːʒ], *n.m. inv.* clothes-horse, airing cupboard.

chauffer [ʃo'fe], *v.t.* to heat, to warm; (*fig.*) to excite.—*v.i.* to grow hot; to be heating; (*fig.*) to be urgent *or* pressing. **se chauffer**, *v.r.* to warm oneself.

chaufferette [ʃof'rɛt], *n.f.* foot warmer.

chauffeur [ʃoˈfœːr], *n.m.* fireman; (*fem.* -euse) (*Motor.*) driver, chauffeur, chauffeuse.
chaufour [ʃoˈfuːr], *n.m.* lime kiln.
chaulage [ʃoˈlaːʒ], *n.m.* (*Agric.*) liming.
chauler [ʃoˈle], *v.t.* to lime (*soil*).
chaume [ʃoːm], *n.m.* stubble; stubble field; thatch.
chaumer [ʃoˈme], *v.t.*, *v.i.* (*Agric.*) to cut stubble.
chaumière [ʃoˈmjɛːr], *n.f.* thatched house, cottage.
chausse [ʃoːs], *n.f.* shoulder band (*worn in universities etc.*); *(pl.)* hose (*covering the body from waist to foot*).
chaussée [ʃoˈse], *n.f.* embankment, dike; causeway; roadway, (*Am.*) pavement; *le rez-de-chaussée*, the ground floor.
chausse-pied [ʃoˈpje], *n.m.* (*pl.* **chaussepieds**) shoe-horn.
chausser [ʃoˈse], *v.t.* to put on (*footwear*); to shoe, to make (*the shoes etc.*) for; (*colloq.*) to fit, to suit.—*v.i. chausser du* 40, to take a 7 (*in shoes*). **se chausser**, *v.r.* to put on one's shoes etc.
chausse-trape [ʃoˈtrap], *n.f.* (*pl.* **chaussetrapes**) snare, trap.
chaussette [ʃoˈsɛt], *n.f.* sock.
chausseur [ʃoˈsœːr], *n.m.* footwear dealer.
chausson [ʃoˈsɔ̃], *n.m.* slipper; gym shoe; bootee (*for infants*).
chaussure [ʃoˈsyːr], *n.f.* footwear.
chauve [ʃoːv], *a.* bald.
chauve-souris [ʃovsuˈri], *n.f.* (*pl.* **chauvessouris**) bat, flittermouse.
chauvin [ʃoˈvɛ̃], *n.m.* fanatical patriot.—*a.* chauvinistic, jingoistic.
chaux [ʃo], *n.f.* lime; limestone.
chavirage [ʃaviˈraːʒ], *chavirement* [ʃavirˈmã], *n.m.* capsizing, upsetting.
chavirer [ʃaviˈre], *v.t.*, *v.i.* to capsize, to upset.
chef [ʃɛf], *n.m.* chief, commander, conductor, master, principal, ringleader; chef.
chef-d'œuvre [ʃeˈdœːvr], *n.m.* (*pl.* **chefsd'œuvre**) chef-d'œuvre, masterpiece.
chef-lieu [ʃeˈljø], *n.m.* (*pl.* **chefs-lieux**) chief town, county seat.
cheik [SCHEIK].
chelem or schelem [ʃlɛm], *n.m. inv.* slam (*at cards*).
chemin [ʃəˈmɛ̃], *n.m.* way, road, path, track; (*fig.*) means; course; *chemin de fer*, railway, (*Am.*) railroad.
chemineau [ʃəmiˈno], *n.m.* (*pl.* **-eaux**) tramp.
cheminée [ʃəmiˈne], *n.f.* chimney; funnel; fire-place; mantelpiece; nipple (*of a percussion gun*).
cheminer [ʃəmiˈne], *v.i.* to walk, to tramp; to proceed.
cheminot [ʃəmiˈno], *n.m.* railwayman; rail layer.
chemise [ʃəˈmiːz], *n.f.* shirt; wrapper, cover.
chemiserie [ʃəmiˈzri], *n.f.* shirt factory; shirt making.
chemisette [ʃəmiˈzɛt], *n.f.* short-sleeved shirt (*men*).
chemisier [ʃəmiˈzje], *n.m.* (*fem.* -ière) shirt maker or seller.
chênaie [ʃeˈne], *n.f.* oak plantation.
chenal [ʃəˈnal], *n.m.* channel, fairway.
chenapan [ʃənaˈpã], *n.m.* vagabond, goodfor-nothing, scamp.

chêne [ʃɛːn], *n.m.* oak.
chêneau [ʃɛˈno], *n.m.* (*pl.* **-eaux**) young oak.
chéneau [ʃɛˈno], *n.m.* (*pl.* **-eaux**) (eaves) gutter.
chenet [ʃəˈnɛ], *n.m.* fire-dog.
chènevière [ʃɛnˈvjɛːr], *n.f.* hemp-field.
chènevis [ʃɛnˈvi], *n.m.* hemp-seed.
chènevotte [ʃɛnˈvɔt], *n.f.* stalk (*of hemp*).
chenil [ʃəˈni], *n.m.* dog-kennel; kennels; dirty hovel.
chenille [ʃəˈniːj], *n.f.* caterpillar; kind of silk cord, chenille; *tracteur à chenille* (*reg. trade name*), caterpillar tractor.
chenillère [ʃəniˈjɛːr], *n.f.* nest of caterpillars.
chenillette [ʃəniˈjɛt], *n.f.* (*Mil.*) half-track.
chenu [ʃəˈny], *a.* hoary, grey-headed; snowcapped.
cheptel [ʃəˈtɛl, ʃɛpˈtɛl], *n.m.* live-stock (*of a country*).
chèque [ʃɛk], *n.m.* cheque, (*Am.*) check.
chéquier [ʃeˈkje], *n.m.* cheque-book.
cher [ʃɛːr], *a.* (*fem.* **chère** (1)) dear, beloved; precious; expensive.—*adv.* dear, dearly, expensively.
chercher [ʃɛrˈʃe], *v.t.* to seek, to look for, to search for; to endeavour, to try, to attempt; *aller chercher*, to go for; to fetch.
chercheur [ʃɛrˈʃœːr], *n.m.* (*fem.* -euse) seeker, searcher; research worker.
chère (1) [ʃɛːr], [CHER].
chère (2) [ʃɛːr], *n.f.* entertainment, fare; *bonne chère*, good cheer, good living.
chèrement [ʃɛrˈmã], *adv.* dearly, tenderly; dear, at a high price.
chéri [ʃeˈri], *a.* beloved; cherished.—*n.m.* (*fem.* -e) darling, dearest.
chérif [ʃeˈrif], *n.m.* shereef (*Arabian prince*).
chérir [ʃeˈriːr], *v.t.* to love dearly, to cherish.
cherté [ʃɛrˈte], *n.f.* dearness, high price.
chérubin [ʃeryˈbɛ̃], *n.m.* cherub.
chérubique [ʃeryˈbik], *a.* cherubic.
chester [ʃɛsˈter], *n.m.* Cheshire cheese.
chétif [ʃeˈtif], *a.* (*fem.* -**tive**) puny, pitiful, worthless.
chétivement [ʃetivˈmã], *adv.* meanly, pitifully, poorly, feebly.
chétiveté [ʃetivˈte], *n.f.* puniness, paltriness.
cheval [ʃəˈval], *n.m.* (*pl.* **-aux**) horse; nag, steed; *aller à cheval*, to ride; *cheval d'arçons*, **cheval de bois**, (*Gym.*) vaulting horse; *cheval à bascule*, rocking-horse; *chevaux de bois*, merry-go-round; *cheval marin*, sea horse; walrus.
chevaleresque [ʃəvalˈrɛsk], *a.* chivalrous, knightly.
chevaleresquement [ʃəvalrɛskˈmã], *adv.* chivalrously.
chevalerie [ʃəvalˈri], *n.f.* knighthood, chivalry.
chevalet [ʃəvaˈlɛ], *n.m.* easel; bridge (*of a stringed instrument*); sawing-trestle; buttress, prop; clothes-horse.
chevalier (1) [ʃəvaˈlje], *n.m.* knight.
chevalier (2) [ʃəvaˈlje], *n.m.* (*Orn.*) sandpiper; redshank.
chevalière [ʃəvaˈljɛːr], *n.f.* knight's lady; signet-ring.
chevalin [ʃəvaˈlɛ̃], *a.* equine; *boucherie chevaline*, horse butcher's shop.
cheval-vapeur [ʃəvalvaˈpœːr], *n.m.* (*pl.* **chevaux-vapeur**) horsepower.
chevauchant [ʃəvoˈʃã], *a.* overlapping.
chevauchée [ʃəvoˈʃe], *n.f.* ride, excursion on horseback; cavalcade.

chevauchement [ʃəvoʃ'mã], *n.m.* overlap *or* crossing (*tiles, wires*).

chevaucher [ʃəvo'ʃe], *v.i.* to ride on horse-back; to be astride; to overlap.

chevaucheur [ʃəvo'ʃœːr], *n.m.* rider, horse-man.

chevauchure [ʃəvo'ʃyːr], *n.f.* overlapping.

chevelu [ʃə'vly], *a.* hairy, long-haired; (*Bot.*) fibrous.

chevelure [ʃə'vlyːr], *n.f.* hair, head of hair.

chevesne [ʃə'vɛn], *n.m.* (*Ichth.*) chub.

chevet [ʃə've], *n.m.* head (*of a bed*); bolster; pillow; bedside.

cheveu [ʃə'vø], *n.m.* (*pl.* -**eux**) a single hair; *pl.* the hair (*of the head*).

chevillage [ʃəvi'jaːʒ], *n.m.* fastening, bolting, dowelling.

cheville [ʃə'viːj], *n.f.* ankle; peg, pin, dowel, bolt; plug.

cheviller [ʃəvi'je], *v.t.* to dowel, to peg, to bolt.

cheviotte [ʃə'vjɔt], *n.f.* cheviot (*tweed*).

chèvre [ʃɛːvr], *n.f.* goat, nanny goat.

chevreau [ʃə'vro], *n.m.* (*pl.* -**eaux**) kid (*animal or skin*).

chèvrefeuille [ʃɛvrə'fœːj], *n.m.* honeysuckle.

chèvrerie [ʃɛvrə'ri], *n.f.* goat pen.

chevrette [ʃə'vrɛt], *n.f.* small goat; young roe.

chevreuil [ʃə'vrœːj], *n.m.* roe, roe deer.

chevrier [ʃəvri'e], *n.m.* (*fem.* -**ière**) goat-herd.

chevron [ʃə'vrɔ̃], *n.m.* rafter; chevron, stripe.

chevronnage [ʃəvrɔ'naːʒ], *n.m.* rafters, raftering.

chevronné [ʃəvrɔ'ne], *a.* (*fam.*) experienced.

chevrotain *or* **chevrotin** [ʃəvrɔ'tɛ̃], *n.m.* chevrotain, musk deer.

chevrotant [ʃəvrɔ'tɑ̃], *a.* quavering, tremulous.

chevrotement [ʃəvrɔt'mã], *n.m.* tremulous motion, trembling (*of the voice etc.*).

chevroter [ʃəvrɔ'te], *v.i.* to sing *or* speak in a tremulous voice.

chevrotin (1) [CHEVROTAIN].

chevrotin (2) [ʃəvrɔ'tɛ̃], *n.m.* fawn of roe deer; kid (*leather*).

chevrotine [ʃəvrɔ'tin], *n.f.* buckshot.

chez [ʃe], *prep.* at, to, in (*the house, family or country of*); in, with, among; in the works of, (*on letters*) care of.

chiasse [ʃjas], *n.f.* dross, scum.

chibouque *or* **chibouk** [ʃi'buk], *n.f.* chibouk (*Turkish pipe*).

chic [ʃik], *n.m.* style, chic; aplomb, ease and elegance.—*a. inv.* stylish, smart.

chicane [ʃi'kan], *n.f.* cavil, evasion, quibble; chicanery.

chicaner [ʃika'ne], *v.t.* to quarrel *or* wrangle with.—*v.i.* to cavil, to quibble.

chicanerie [ʃikan'ri], *n.f.* chicanery, quibbling, cavilling.

chicaneur [ʃika'nœːr], *n.m.* (*fem.* -**euse**) *or* **chicanier** [ʃika'nje], *n.m.* (*fem.* -**ière**) caviller, pettifogger.—*a.* litigious, cavilling, wrangling.

chiche (1) [ʃiʃ], *a.* niggardly, stingy.

chiche (2) [ʃiʃ], *a.* **pois chiches**, chickpeas.

chichement [ʃiʃ'mã], *adv.* stingily.

chicorée [ʃikɔ're], *n.f.* endive; chicory.

chicot [ʃi'ko], *n.m.* stub *or* stump (*of tree or tooth*).

chicotin [ʃikɔ'tɛ̃], *n.m.* bitter juice of aloes.

chien [ʃjɛ̃], *n.m.* (*fem.* **chienne**) dog; hammer, cock (*of a gun* or *pistol*); **chien de mer**, dogfish.

chiendent [ʃjɛ̃'dɑ̃], *n.m.* couch grass.

chiennée [ʃjɛ'ne], *n.f.* litter of pups.

chiffe [ʃif], *n.f.* poor stuff, rag; (*fig.*) weakling; spineless person.

chiffon [ʃi'fɔ̃], *n.m.* rag, scrap, bit; frippery.

chiffonnage [ʃifɔ'naːʒ], *n.m.* rumpled drapery, rumpling, crumpling.

chiffonner [ʃifɔ'ne], *v.t.* to rumple, to crumple; (*collog.*) to ruffle, to tease, to vex.—*v.i.* to be a rag collector.

chiffonnier [ʃifɔ'nje], *n.m.* (*fem.* -**ière**) rag-picker; chiffonnier.

chiffrage [ʃi'fraːʒ], *n.m.*, **chiffrement** [ʃifr'mã], *n.m.* figuring, figures; calculation; writing in cipher, coding.

chiffre [ʃifr], *n.m.* figure, number; total amount; cipher; monogram.

chiffrer [ʃi'fre], *v.t.* to calculate, to tot up; to code.—*v.i.* to cipher.

chiffreur [ʃi'frœːr], *n.m.* (*fem.* -**euse**) reckoner, cipherer.

chignole [ʃi'nɔl], *n.f.* ratchet drill.

chignon [ʃi'nɔ̃], *n.m.* chignon, coil of hair.

Chili [ʃi'li], **le**, *m.* Chile.

chilien [ʃi'ljɛ̃], *a.* (*fem.* -**enne**) Chilean.—*n.m.* (**Chilien**, *fem.* -**enne**) Chilean (*person*).

chimère [ʃi'mɛːr], *n.f.* chimera; myth, idle fancy.

chimérique [ʃime'rik], *a.* chimerical, visionary.

chimériquement [ʃimerik'mã], *adv.* chimerically.

chimie [ʃi'mi], *n.f.* chemistry.

chimique [ʃi'mik], *a.* chemical.

chimiquement [ʃimik'mã], *adv.* chemically.

chimiste [ʃi'mist], *n.m.* chemist (*not pharmaceutical chemist*).

chimpanzé [ʃɛ̃pɑ̃'ze], *n.m.* chimpanzee.

chinchilla [ʃɛ̃ʃil'la], *n.m.* chinchilla.

Chine [ʃin], **la**, *f.* China.

chiner [ʃi'ne], *v.t.* to color differently; to figure (*stuffs*).

chinois [ʃi'nwa], *a.* Chinese.—*n.m.* Chinese (*language*); **un chinois**, a small green orange preserved in brandy; (**Chinois**, *fem.* -**oise**) Chinese (*person*).

chinoiserie [ʃinwa'zri], *n.f.* Chinese thing, curio; (*fig.*) trick; red tape.

chiot [ʃjo], *n.m.* puppy.

chiourme [ʃjurm], *n.f.* convict gang.

chipolata [ʃipɔla'ta], *n.f.* onion stew; small sausage.

chipotage [ʃipɔ'taːʒ], *n.m.* dawdling; haggling.

chipoter [ʃipɔ'te], *v.i.* to dally, to dawdle; to haggle; to peck at a dish.

chipotier [ʃipɔ'tje], *n.m.* (*fem.* -**ière**) trifler, dallier, shuffler.

chique [ʃik], *n.f.* quid of tobacco.

chiquement [ʃik'mã], *adv.* smartly.

chiquenaude [ʃik'noːd], *n.f.* flick.

chiquenauder [ʃikno'de], *v.t.* to flick.

chiquer [ʃi'ke], *v.i.* to chew tobacco.

chiquet [ʃi'ke], *n.m.*, **chiquette** [ʃi'kɛt], *n.f.* driblet, bit, shred.

chiqueur [ʃi'kœːr], *n.m.* chewer of tobacco; pretender.

chiromancie [kirəmɑ̃'si], *n.f.* chiromancy, palmistry.

chiromancien [kirəmɑ̃'sjɛ̃], *n.m.* (*fem.* **-ienne**) chiromancer, palmist.

chirurgical [ʃiryrʒi'kal], *a.* (*m. pl.* **-aux**) surgical.

chirurgicalement [ʃiryrʒikal'mɑ̃], *adv.* surgically.

chirurgie [ʃiryr'ʒi], *n.f.* surgery.

chirurgien [[ʃiryr'ʒjɛ̃], *n.m.* surgeon.

chirurgique [ʃiryr'ʒik], *a.* surgical.

chiure [ʃjy:r], *n.f.* flyspeck.

chlorate [klɔ'rat], *n.m.* chlorate.

chlore [klɔ:r], *n.m.* (*Chem.*) chlorine.

chloré [klɔ're], *a.* containing chlorine.

chlorhydrate [klɔri'drat], *n.m.* (*Chem.*) hydrochlorate.

chlorhydrique [klɔri'drik], *a.* hydrochloric.

chloroforme [klɔrɔ'farm], *n.m.* chloroform.

chloroformer [klɔrɔfɔr'me], *v.t.* to chloroform.

chlorure [klɔ'ry:r], *n.m.* (*Chem.*) chloride.

choc [ʃɔk], *n.m.* shock; impact; clash, encounter.

chocolat [ʃɔkɔ'la], *n.m.* chocolate.—*a.* chocolate-colored.

chocolaterie [ʃɔkɔla'tri], *n.f.* chocolate-making; chocolate factory.

chocolatier [ʃɔkɔla'tje], *n.m.* (*fem.* **-ière**) chocolate maker *or* seller.—*n.f.* (**-ière**) chocolate pot.

chœur [kœ:r], *n.m.* choir; chancel; (*Ant. and fig.*) chorus.

choir [ʃwa:r], *v.i. irr.* to fall, to drop.

choisir [ʃwa'zi:r], *v.t.* to choose, to single out, to select.

choix [ʃwa], *n.m.* choice, alternative; selection; distinction.

choléra [kole'ra], *n.m.* cholera.

cholérique [kole'rik], *a.* choleraic.—*n.* person affected with cholera.

chômable [ʃo'mabl], *a.* (*of days, fêtes etc.*) to be kept as a holiday.

chômage [ʃo'ma:ʒ], *n.m.* unemployment, enforced idleness; stoppage; *allocation de chômage*, unemployment benefit, 'dole'.

chômer [ʃo'me], *v.i.* to be doing nothing; to be unemployed.

chômeur [ʃo'mœ:r], *n.m.* (*fem.* **-euse**) idle *or* unemployed person.

chope [ʃɔp], *n.f.* large beer glass; mug of beer.

chopper [ʃɔ'pe], *v.i.* to stumble, to trip (*contre*).

choquant [ʃɔ'kɑ̃], *a.* offensive, unpleasant, improper.

choquer [ʃɔ'ke], *v.t.* to shock, to strike *or* dash against; to displease, to offend.—*v.i.* to clink glasses; to be offensive, to be shocking. **se choquer**, *v.r.* to take offence; to come into collision with each other.

choral [kɔ'ral], *a.* choral.—*n.m.* (*pl.* **-als**) choral(e).—*n.f.* (**chorale**) choir, choral society.

chorée [kɔ're], *n.f.* chorea, St. Vitus's dance.

chorégraphe [kɔre'graf], *n.m.* choreographer.

chorégraphie [kɔregra'fi], *n.f.* choreography.

choriste [kɔ'rist], *n.m.* chorister; (*Theat.*) member of the chorus.

chorus [kɔ'ry:s], *n.m.* chorus.

chose [ʃo:z], *n.f.* thing; matter, business, affair; (*Law*) chattel, property.

chou [ʃu], *n.m.* (*pl.* **choux**) cabbage, kale; (*colloq.*) puff paste; darling, dear; bow, rosette; *choux de Bruxelles*, Brussels sprouts.

chouan [ʃwɑ̃], *n.m.* Chouan, Breton royalist insurgent (*during the French Revolution*).

choucas [ʃu'kɑ], *n.m.*, **chouchette** [ʃu'ʃɛt] *n.f.* jackdaw.

choucroute [ʃu'krut], *n.f.* sauerkraut.

chouette (1) [ʃwɛt], *n.f.* owl.

chouette (2) [ʃwɛt], *int.* (*pop.*) fine, marvellous.—*a.* nice, fine, good of its kind.

chou-fleur [ʃu'flœ:r], *n.m.* (*pl.* **choux-fleurs**) cauliflower.

chou-rave [ʃu'ra:v], *n.m.* (*pl.* **choux-raves**) kohl rabi, turnip-cabbage.

choyer [ʃwa'je], *v.t.* (*conjug. like* EMPLOYER) to take great care of, to be fond of, to pamper, to pet. **se choyer**, *v.r.* to pamper oneself.

chrême [krɛ:m], *n.m.* chrism, holy oil.

chrémeau [kre'mo], *n.m.* (*pl.* **-eaux**) chrism cloth.

chrétien [kre'tjɛ̃], *a.* and *n.m.* (*fem.* **-enne**) Christian.

chrétiennement [kretjɛn'mɑ̃], *adv.* like a Christian.

chrétienté [kretjɛ̃'te], *n.f.* Christendom.

christ [krist], *n.m.* crucifix; representation of Christ crucified; *le Christ*, Jesus Christ.

christianisme [kristja'nism], *n.m.* Christianity.

Christophe [kris'tɔf], *n.m.* Christopher.

chromage [krɔ'ma:ʒ], *n.m.* chromium plating.

chromate [krɔ'mat] *n.m.* (*Chem.*) chromate.

chromatique [krɔma'tik], *a.* (*Chem., Mus.*) chromatic.—*n.f.* (*Mus., Paint.*) chromatics.

chrome [kro:m], *n.m.* chromium, chrome.

chromé [krɔ'me], *a.* chromium-plated.

chromer [krɔ'me], *v.t.* to chrome.

chromique [krɔ'mik], *a.* chromic.

chromosome [krɔmɔ'zo:m], *n.m.* chromosome.

chronique (1) [krɔ'nik], *n.f.* chronicle, history; news summary.

chronique (2) [krɔ'nik], *a.* (*Med.*) chronic.

chroniqueur [krɔni'kœ:r], *n.m.* (*fem.* **-euse**) chronicler; newswriter, columnist.

chronologie [krɔnɔlɔ'ʒi], *n.f.* chronology.

chronologique [krɔnɔlɔ'ʒik], *a.* chronological.

chronomètre [krɔnɔ'mɛ:tr], *n.m.* chronometer.

chronométrer [krɔnɔme'tre], *v.t.* (*conjug. like* CÉDER) to time.

chronométreur [krɔnɔme'trœ:r], *n.m.* timekeeper.

chrysalide [kriza'lid], *n.f.* chrysalis.

chrysanthème [krizɑ̃'tɛ:m], *n.m.* chrysanthemum.

chuchotement [ʃyʃɔt'mɑ̃], *n.m.* whispering, whisper, rustling.

chuchoter [ʃyʃɔ'te], *v.t., v.i.* to whisper.

chuchoterie [ʃyʃɔ'tri], *n.f.* whispering.

chuchoteur [ʃyʃɔ'tœ:r], *n.m.* (*fem.* **-euse**) whisperer.

chuinter [ʃɥɛ̃'te], *v.i.* to hoot (*of owls*); to hiss (*of gas*).

chut [ʃ:t], *int.* and *n.m.* hush!

chute

chute [ʃyt], *n.f.* fall, tumble; collapse, ruin; downfall; disaster.

chuter [ʃyˈte], *v.i.* (*fam.*) to fall, to fail.

Chypre [ʃipr], *f.* Cyprus.

ci [si], *adv.* here.

cible [sibl], *n.f.* target, mark; (*fig.*) purpose.

ciboire [siˈbwaːr], *n.m.* sacred vase, pyx.

ciboule [siˈbul], *n.f.* Welsh onion, scallion.

ciboulette [sibuˈlɛt], *n.f.* chive.

cicatrice [sikaˈtris], *n.f.* scar, seam, mark.

cicatrisant [sikatriˈzɑ̃], *a.* cicatrizing.

cicatrisation [sikatrizaˈsjɔ̃], *n.f.* cicatrization.

cicatriser [sikatriˈze], *v.t.* to cicatrize; to close, to heal up. **se cicatriser**, *v.r.* to skin over, to heal up.

Cicéron [siseˈrɔ̃], *m.* Cicero.

cicérone [siseˈron], *n.m.* cicerone, guide.

cicéronien [sisɛrɔˈnjɛ̃], *a.* (*fem.* **-enne**) Ciceronian.

cidre [sidr], *n.m.* cider.

cidrerie [sidrəˈri], *n.f.* cider making; cider factory.

ciel [sjɛl], *n.m.* (*pl.* **cieux**) the heavens, the firmament, the sky; heaven.

cierge [sjɛrʒ], *n.m.* taper, church candle.

cigale [siˈgal], *n.f.* cicada.

cigare [siˈgaːr], *n.m.* cigar.

cigarette [sigaˈret], *n.f.* cigarette.

cigogne [siˈgɔɲ], *n.f.* stork.

cigogneau [sigoˈɲo], *n.m.* (*pl.* **-eaux**) young stork.

ciguë [siˈgy], *n.f.* hemlock (*plant or poison*).

cil [sil], *n.m.* eyelash.

cilice [siˈlis], *n.m.* cilice, hair shirt.

cillement [sijˈmɑ̃], *n.m.* blink, winking.

ciller [siˈje], *v.t., v.i.* to wink, to blink (*the eyes*).

cimaise or **cymaise** [siˈmɛːz], *n.f.* cyma, ogee; dado rail, picture rail.

cime [sim], *n.f.* top, summit, peak.

ciment [siˈmɑ̃], *n.m.* cement.

cimenter [simɑ̃ˈte], *v.t.* to cement; to strengthen, to consolidate.

cimentier [simɑ̃ˈtje], *n.m.* cement maker.

cimeterre [simˈtɛːr], *n.m.* scimitar.

cimetière [simˈtjɛːr], *n.m.* cemetery, churchyard.

cimier [siˈmje], *n.m.* crest (*of a helmet*); rump (*of beef*).

cinéaste [sineˈast], *n.m.* film producer.

cinéma [sineˈma], *n.m.* cinema.

cinémascope [sinemasˈkop], *n.m.* cinemascope.

cinémathèque [sinemaˈtɛk], *n.f.* film library.

cinématographier [sinematograˈfje], *v.t.* to film.

cinérama [sineraˈma], *n.m.* cinerama.

cinétique [sineˈtik], *n.f.* kinetics.—*a.* kinetic, motive (*energy*).

cinétiquement [sinetikˈmɑ̃], *adv.* kinetically.

cingalais [sɛ̃gaˈlɛ], *a.* Sin(g)halese *or* Cingalese.—*n.m.* Sin(g)halese *or* Cingalese (*language*); (**Cingalais**, *fem.* **-aise**) Sin(g)halese *or* Cingalese (*person*).

cinglage [sɛ̃ˈglaːʒ], *n.m.* sailing, ship's course, run of a ship in twenty-four hours.

cinglement [sɛ̃glˈmɑ̃], *n.m.* lashing, slashing.

cingler (1) [sɛ̃ˈgle], *v.i.* to sail before the wind.

cingler (2) [sɛ̃ˈgle], *v.t.* to lash; (*fig.*) to chastize.

cinname [siˈnam], **cinnamome** [sinaˈmom], *n.m.* cinnamon.

70.

cinq [sɛ̃:k], *a.* five.—*n.m.* five.

cinquantaine [sɛ̃kɑ̃ˈtɛn], *n.f.* about fifty.

cinquante [sɛ̃ˈkɑ̃:t], *a.* fifty.

cinquantenaire [sɛ̃kɑ̃tˈnɛːr], *a.* and *n.* quinquagenarian.—*n.m.* fiftieth anniversary, jubilee.

cinquantième [sɛ̃kɑ̃ˈtjɛm], *a.* fiftieth.—*n.m.* fiftieth part.

cinquième [sɛ̃ˈkjɛm], *a.* fifth.—*n.m.* fifth part; fifth floor.

cintrage [sɛ̃ˈtraːʒ], *n.m.* arching, curving (*of arches etc.*).

cintre [sɛ̃:tr], *n.m.* curve of an arch; coathanger.

cintrer [sɛ̃ˈtre], *v.t.* to arch, to curve.

cipaye [siˈpaːj], **cipahi** [siˈpai], *n.m.* sepoy.

cipolin [sipɔˈlɛ̃], *n.m.* cipollino, cipolin marble.

cippe [sip], *n.m.* cippus (*half-column*).

cirage [siˈraːʒ], *n.m.* waxing; blacking (*composition or process*); shoe polish.

circoncire [sirkɔ̃ˈsiːr], *v.t. irr.* (*conjug. like* CONFIRE *except for p.p.* **circoncis**) to circumcise.

circoncis [sirkɔ̃ˈsi], *a.* circumcised.—*n.m.* one who is circumcised.

circoncision [sirkɔ̃siˈzjɔ̃], *n.f.* circumcision.

circonférence [sirkɔ̃feˈrɑ̃:s], *n.f.* circumference.

circonflexe [sirkɔ̃ˈflɛks], *a.* and *n.m.* circumflex.

circonlocution [sirkɔ̃lɔkyˈsjɔ̃], *n.f.* circumlocution.

circonscription [sirkɔ̃skripˈsjɔ̃], *n.f.* circumscription; district; constituency.

circonscrire [sirkɔ̃sˈkriːr], *v.t. irr.* (*conjug. like* ÉCRIRE) to circumscribe, to encircle; to limit.

circonspect [sirkɔ̃sˈpɛkt, -spɛ], *a.* circumspect, wary, discreet, reserved.

circonspection [sirkɔ̃spɛkˈsjɔ̃], *n.f.* circumspection, wariness, caution.

circonstance [sirkɔ̃sˈtɑ̃:s], *n.f.* circumstance; occurrence, event.

circonstanciel [sirkɔ̃stɑ̃ˈsjɛl], *a.* (*fem.* **-elle**) circumstantial.

circonstancier [sirkɔ̃stɑ̃ˈsje], *v.t.* to state circumstantially, to particularize.

circonvenir [sirkɔ̃vˈniːr], *v.t. irr.* (*conjug. like* TENIR) to circumvent, to outwit.

circonvention [sirkɔ̃vɑ̃ˈsjɔ̃], *n.f.* circumvention, fraud.

circonvoisin [sirkɔ̃vwaˈzɛ̃], *a.* circumjacent, neighboring, adjoining.

circonvolution [sirkɔ̃vɔlyˈsjɔ̃], *n.f.* circumvolution.

circuit [sirˈkɥi], *n.m.* circuit, circumference; detour; lap; (*Elec.*) **court circuit**, short circuit; **en circuit**, switched on.

circulaire [sirkyˈlɛːr], *a.* circular, round.—*n.f.* circular.

circulation [sirkylaˈsjɔ̃], *n.f.* circulation; currency; traffic.

circulatoire [sirkylaˈtwaːr], *a.* circulatory, circulating.

circuler [sirkyˈle], *v.i.* to circulate, to revolve, to move round; to be current.

cire [siːr], *n.f.* beeswax; wax; taper.

ciré [siˈre], *n.m.* (*Naut.*) (suit of) oilskins.

cirer [siˈre], *v.t.* to wax; to black *or* to polish (*boots*).

cireur [si'rœ:r], *n.m.* (*fem.* **cireuse** (1)) polisher; *cireuse électrique,* electric polisher.

cireux [si'rø], *a.* (*fem.* **cireuse** (2)) waxy.

ciron [si'rɔ̃], *n.m.* mite.

cirque [sirk], *n.m.* circus.

cirrus [sir'ry:s], *n.m.* cirrus (*cloud*).

cirure [si'ry:r], *n.f.* prepared wax.

cisaille [si'za:j], *n.f.* clipping *or* shearing of metals; (*pl.*) shears; (*Bookb.*) guillotine.

cisailler [siza'je], *v.t.* to pare, to clip (*coins etc.*); to cut with shears.

cisalpin [sizal'pɛ̃], *a.* cisalpine.

ciseau [si'zo], *n.m.* (*pl.* **-eaux**) chisel; (*pl.*) scissors.

ciseler [siz'le], *v.t.* (*conjug. like* AMENER) to chisel; to chase.

ciselet [siz'lɛ], *n.m.* small chisel, graver.

ciseleur [siz'lœ:r], *n.m.* chaser; carver, sculptor.

ciselure [siz'ly:r], *n.f.* chasing, sculpture, carving.

cisoires [si'zwa:r], *n.f.* (*used only in pl.*) big bench-shears (*to cut sheet iron*).

ciste [sist], *n.m.* cistus, rockrose.

citadelle [sita'dɛl], *n.f.* citadel; (*fig.*) stronghold.

citadin [sita'dɛ̃], *n.m.* (*fem.* **-e**) citizen, townsman *or* -woman.

citation [sita'sjɔ̃], *n.f.* citation, quotation; summons.

cité [si'te], *n.f.* city; town.

citer [si'te], *v.t.* to cite, to quote; to summon.

citérieur [site'rjœ:r], *a.* (*Geog.*) nearer, hithermost.

citerne [si'tɛrn], *n.f.* cistern, reservoir; (*Naut.*) tanker.

cithare [si'ta:r], *n.f.* zither.

citoyen [sitwa'jɛ̃], *n.m.* (*fem.* **-enne**) citizen, burgess; (*fig.*) patriot.

citrate [si'trat], *n.m.* citrate.

citrin [si'trɛ̃], *a.* citrine, lemon-colored.

citrique [si'trik], *a.* citric.

citron [si'trɔ̃], *a.* lemon-colored. —*n.m.* lemon, citron.

citronnade [sitrɔ'nad], *n.f.* lemon squash.

citronnat [sitrɔ'na], *n.m.* candied lemon peel.

citronné [sitrɔ'ne], *a.* lemon-flavored.

citronnier [sitrɔ'nje], *n.m.* citron tree.

citrouille [si'tru:j], *n.f.* pumpkin, gourd.

cive [si:v], **civette** (1) [si'vɛt], [CIBOULETTE].

civet [si've], *n.m.* wine stew (*of venison*); *civet de lièvre,* jugged hare.

civette (1) [CIVE].

civette (2) [si'vɛt], *n.f.* civet cat; civet.

civière [si'vjɛ:r], *n.f.* hand barrow; stretcher; bier.

civil [si'vil], *a.* civil; private; plain; polite.— *n.m.* civilian.

civilement [sivil'mɑ̃], *adv.* civilly; courteously.

civilisable [sivili'zabl], *a.* civilizable.

civilisateur [siviliza'tœ:r], *a.* (*fem.* **-trice**) civilizing.

civilisation [siviliza'sjɔ̃], *n.f.* civilization.

civiliser [sivili'ze], *v.t.* to civilize. **se civiliser,** *v.r.* to become civilized.

civilité [sivili'te], *n.f.* civility, good manners; (*pl.*) compliments.

civique [si'vik], *a.* civic.

civisme [si'vism], *n.m.* good citizenship.

clabaudage [klabo'da:ʒ], *n.m.* barking, bawling.

clabauder [klabo'de], *v.i.* to clamor, to bawl out.

clabaudeur [klabo'dœ:r], *n.m.* (*fem.* **-euse**) brawler, scandalmonger.

claie [klɛ], *n.f.* wattle, hurdle; screen (*of a sieve*).

clair [klɛ:r], *a.* clear, bright, luminous; light-colored, pure, cloudless; thin (*of liquids etc.*); plain, intelligible, obvious.—*adv.* clearly, distinctly, plainly.—*n.m.* light, clearness; (*Paint.*) highlight.

Claire [klɛ:r], *f.* Clara, Cla(i)re.

clairement [klɛr'mɑ̃], *adv.* clearly, plainly, distinctly.

clairet [klɛ'rɛ], *a.* (*fem.* **clairette** (1)) palish, lightish (*of wines*).—*n.m.* light-red wine.

clairette (2) [klɛ'rɛt], *n.f.* white grape.

claire-voie [klɛr'vwa], *n.f.* (*pl.* **claires-voies**) wooden fencing; opening (*in garden wall*); wicket; skylight.

clairière [klɛ'rjɛ:r], *n.f.* clearing, glade.

clair-obscur [klɛrɔps'ky:r], *n.m.* (*pl.* **clairs-obscurs**) chiaroscuro; light and shade.

clairon [klɛ'rɔ̃], *n.m.* clarion, bugle; bugler.

clairsemé [klɛrsə'me], *a.* thin, thinly sown, scattered.

clairvoyance [klɛrvwa'jɑ̃:s], *n.f.* sharpness, perspicacity; clairvoyance.

clairvoyant [klɛrvwa'jɑ̃], *a.* clear-sighted, discerning; clairvoyant.

clamer [kla'me], *v.t.* to cry out, to shout.

clameur [kla'mœ:r], *n.f.* clamor, outcry.

clan [klɑ̃], *n.m.* clan.

clandestin [klɑ̃des'tɛ̃], *a.* clandestine, secret.

clandestinement [klɑ̃destin'mɑ̃], *adv.* clandestinely, secretly.

clapement [CLAPPEMENT].

clapet [kla'pɛ], *n.m.* valve, clapper.

clapier [kla'pje], *n.m.* hutch (*for rabbits*).

clapir [kla'pi:r], *v.i.* to squeak (*of rabbits*). **se clapir,** *v.r.* to hide in a hole, to squat, to cower.

clapotage [klapɔ'ta:ʒ], *n.m.* rippling, plashing; lapping.

clapotement [klapɔt'mɑ̃], *n.m.* [CLAPOTAGE].

clapoter [klapɔ'te], *v.i.* to plash, to chop.

clapoteux [klapɔ'tø], *a.* (*fem.* **-euse**) plashing, choppy, rough.

clapotis [klapɔ'ti], *n.m.* [CLAPOTAGE].

clappement *or* **clapement** [klap'mɑ̃], *n.m.* clacking, smacking.

clapper [kla'pe], *v.i.* to clack, to smack (*of the tongue*).

claque (1) [klak], *n.f.* slap, smack; claque (*paid applauders at theatres*); (*pl.*) (C) clogs, galoshes.

claque (2) [klak], *n.m.* opera hat, crush hat.

claquebois [klak'bwa], *n.m.* xylophone.

claquement [klak'mɑ̃], *n.m.* clapping, clap; snapping; cracking; chattering; slamming.

claquemurer [klakmy're], *v.t.* to coop up, to imprison. **se claquemurer,** *v.r.* to shut oneself up.

claquer [kla'ke], *v.t.* to slap, to crack, to slam.—*v.i.* to snap, to crack, to clap, to click; to slam, to bang.

claqueter [klak'te], *v.i.* (*conjug. like* APPELER) to cackle (*of a hen*); to cry (*of the stork*).

claquette [kla'kɛt], *n.f.* clapper, rattle; *danseur à claquettes,* tap dancer.

claquoir [kla'kwaːr], n.m. [CLAQUETTE].
clarification [klarifika'sjɔ̃], n.f. clarification.
clarifier [klari'fje], v.t. to clarify; to purify, to fine. se clarifier, v.r. to clarify, to settle.
clarine [kla'rin], n.f. bell (attached to cattle).
clarinette [klari'net], n.f. clarinet.
clarinettiste [klarine'tist], n. clarinetist.
clarté [klar'te], n.f. light, splendor; clearness.
classe [klɑːs], n.f. class, order, rank; kind, tribe; class or grade (in a school); classroom; lesson; (pl.) school hours; school time.
classement [klɑs'mɑ̃], n.m. classing, classification, filing.
classer [klɑ'se], v.t. to class, to classify, to sort; to file.
classeur [klɑ'sœːr], n.m. card index; file.
classification [klasifika'sjɔ̃], n.f. classification.
classifier [klasi'fje], v.t. to classify.
classique [klɑ'sik], a. classic, classical; standard (of authors, books etc.); conventional.—n.m. classic (author, book etc.).
claudicant [klodi'kɑ̃], a. lame, limping.
claudication [klodika'sjɔ̃], n.f. lameness, limping, halting.
clause [kloːz], n.f. clause.
claustral [klos'tral], a. (m. pl. -aux) claustral; monastic.
claustration [klostra'sjɔ̃], n.f. claustration, confinement.
claustrer [klos'tre], v.t. to cloister, to confine.
claustrophobie [klostrofɔ'bi], n.f. claustrophobia.
clavecin [klav'sɛ̃], n.m. harpsichord, clavecin.
clavette [kla'vet], n.f. (Tech.) peg, pin; key, cotter.
claviculaire [klaviky'lɛːr], a. clavicular.
clavicule [klavi'kyl], n.f. clavicle, collarbone.
clavier [kla'vje], n.m. clavier, keyboard (piano, typewriter), key frame.
clayère [klɛ'jɛːr], n.f. oyster bed or breeding ground.
clayon [klɛ'jɔ̃], n.m. wattle; stand (for draining cheese).
clef or clé [kle], n.f. key; plug (of a cock); spanner; keystone (of arch); (Mus.) clef, tuning key.
clématite [klema'tit], n.f. (Bot.) clematis.
clémence [kle'mɑ̃ːs], n.f. clemency, mercy.
clément [kle'mɑ̃], a. clement, merciful, lenient; mild (of the weather).
Clémentine [klemɑ̃'tin], f. Clementine.
clenche [klɑ̃ːʃ], clenchette [klɑ̃'ʃet], n.f. catch or latch (of a lock).
cleptomane [kleptɔ'man], n. kleptomaniac.
cleptomanie [kleptɔma'ni], n.f. kleptomania.
clerc [klɛːr], n.m. clergyman; (fig.) scholar.
clergé [klɛr'ʒe], n.m. clergy.
clérical [kleri'kal], a. (m. pl. -aux) clerical.
cléricalisme [klerika'lism], n.m. clericalism.
cléricaliste [klerika'list], n. clericalist.
clic-clac [klik'klak], n.m. cracking (of a whip).
clichage [kli'ʃaːʒ], n.m. stereotyping, stereotype.
cliché [kli'ʃe], n.m. stereotype plate, cliché; (fig.) stereotyped phrase; (Phot.) negative; (Sculp.) cast.
clicher [kli'ʃe], v.t. to stereotype.
client [kli'ɑ̃], n.m. (fem. -e) client (of law-

yers etc.); patient (of physicians); customer (of tradesmen).
clientèle [kliɑ̃'tɛl], n.f. clientele; practice; connection; custom; goodwill (of a business).
clignement [kliɲ'mɑ̃], n.m. winking, blinking, wink.
cligner [kli'ɲe], v.t., v.i. to wink, to blink.
clignotant [kliɲɔ'tɑ̃], a. winking, blinking.—n.m. (Motor.) winker, flashing indicator.
clignotement [kliɲɔt'mɑ̃], n.m. winking, blinking.
clignoter [kliɲɔ'te], v.i. to wink, to blink.
climat [kli'ma], n.m. climate; region, country.
climatérique [klimate'rik], climatique [klima'tik], a. climatic.
climatisation [klimatiza'sjɔ̃], n.f. air conditioning.
climatisé [klimati'ze], a. air-conditioned.
climatiser [klimati'ze], v.t. to air-condition.
clin [klɛ̃], n.m. wink (of an eye).
clinicien [klini'sjɛ̃], a.m. clinical.—n.m. clinical physician.
clinique [kli'nik], a. clinical.—n.f. clinical surgery; clinic, nursing home.
clinquant [klɛ̃'kɑ̃], a. showy, gaudy, trumpery.—n.m. tinsel; (fig.) glitter, affectation.
clip [klip], n.m. clip-fastened jewel.
clipper [kli'pɛr], n.m. (Naut. and Av.) clipper.
clique [klik], n.f. set, coterie, party, clique.
cliquet [kli'ke], n.m. catch, pawl.
cliqueter [kli'kte], v.i. (conjug. like APPELER) to click or jingle; (Motor.) to knock.
cliquetis [klik'ti], n.m. clanking, clash.
cliquette [kli'ket], n.f. sinker (of net); (usu. pl.) bones (a kind of castanets).
clissage [kli'saːʒ], n.m. wickering.
clisse [klis], n.f. wicker mat for draining cheese; basket-work cover for a bottle; (Surg.) splint.
clisser [kli'se], v.t. to wicker, to cover with wicker-work etc.
clivage [kli'vaːʒ], n.m. (Min.) cleavage; cleaving.
cliver [kli've], v.t. to cleave (diamonds etc.). se cliver, v.r. to split, to be cleft.
cloaque [klɔ'ak], n.m. drain, sewer, sink, cesspool; (fig.) filthy hole.
clochage [klɔ'ʃaːʒ], n.m. cultivation under cloches.
clochard [klɔ'ʃaːr], n.m. (fam.) tramp, vagrant; (Am.) hobo.
cloche [klɔʃ], n.f. bell; dish cover; blister; stewpan; (Gard.) cloche.
clochement [klɔʃ'mɑ̃], n.m. hobbling, halting.
cloche-pied [klɔʃ'pje], n.m. hopping on one leg.
clocher (1) [klɔ'ʃe], n.m. steeple, belfry; (fig.) parish, native place.
clocher (2) [klɔ'ʃe], v.t. (Gard.) to cover with a cloche.
clocher (3) [klɔ'ʃe], v.i. to limp, to hobble; (fig., fam.) to go wrong somewhere, to be defective.
clocheton [klɔʃ'tɔ̃], n.m. bell turret.
clochette [klɔ'ʃet], n.f. small bell, hand bell; bellflower.
cloison [klwa'zɔ̃], n.f. partition, division; compartment; (Naut.) bulkhead.
cloisonnage [klwazɔ'naːʒ], cloisonnement [klwazɔn'mɑ̃], n.m. partition work, wainscoting.

cloisonner [klwazɔ'ne], *v.t.* to partition.
cloître [klwa:tr], *n.m.* cloister.
cloîtrer [klwa'tre], *v.t.* to shut up in a cloister, to immure. **se cloîtrer**, *v.r.* to enter a monastery *or* convent.
cloîtrier [klwa'trie], *n.m.* (*fem.* **-ière**) cloistered monk *or* nun.
clopin-clopant [klɔpɛ̃klɔ'pɑ̃], *adv.* limpingly, hobbling along.
clopiner [klɔpi'ne], *v.i.* to limp, to halt, to hobble.
cloporte [klɔ'pɔrt], *n.m.* woodlouse.
cloque [klɔk], *n.f.* blister (*on skin, paint etc.*); blight, rust (*of plants*).
cloquer [klɔ'ke], *v.i.* to blister (*of paint*).
clore [klɔ:r], *v.t. irr.* (*chiefly used in p.p.*) to close, to enclose; to end.—*v.i.* to close, to shut. **se clore**, *v.r.* to close, to be closed; to end.
clos [klo], *a.* closed, sealed; completed; **à huis clos**, in camera.—*n.m.* close; enclosure, field.
closeau [klo'zo], *n.m.* (*pl.* **-eaux**) small garden.
closerie [kloz'ri], *n.f.* small enclosed farm *or* garden.
clôture [klo'ty:r], *n.f.* enclosure, fence; closing, close; closure; (*Relig.*) enclosure (*of nuns etc.*).
clôturer [kloty're], *v.t.* to close.
clou [klu], *n.m.* nail, spike, stud; (*Path.*) carbuncle, boil; **clou de girofle**, clove.
clouage [klu'a:ʒ], **clouement** [klu'mɑ̃], *n.m.* nailing.
clouer [klu'e], *v.t.* to nail; to fix; (*fig.*) to detain.
clouter [klu'te], *v.t.* to adorn with nails, to stud; **passage clouté**, pedestrian crossing.
clouterie [klu'tri], *n.f.* nail factory; nail trade.
cloutier [klu'tje], *n.m.* nail maker, nail dealer.
cloutière [klu'tjɛ:r], *n.f.* nail box.
clovisse [klɔ'vis], *n.f.* winkle; cockle.
clown [klun], *n.m.* clown.
cloyère [klwa'jɛ:r], *n.f.* oyster basket.
club [klʌb, klœb], *n.m.* club (*sporting or political*).
clystère [klis'tɛ:r], *n.m.* clyster, injection, enema.
coaccusé [koaky'ze], *n.m.* (*fem.* **-ée**) fellow prisoner; co-defendant.
coacquéreur [koake'rœ:r], *n.m.* (*fem.* **-euse**) co-purchaser, joint buyer.
coacquisition [koakizi'sjɔ̃], *n.f.* joint purchase.
coactif [koak'tif], *a.* (*fem.* **-tive**) coactive.
coaction [koak'sjɔ̃], *n.f.* coercion, compulsion.
coadjuteur [koadʒy'tœ:r], *n.m.* coadjutor.
coadjutrice [koadʒy'tris], *n.f.* coadjutrix.
coagulant [koagy'lɑ̃], *a.* coagulant.
coagulation [koagyla'sjɔ̃], *n.f.* coagulation.
coaguler [koagy'le], *v.t.* to coagulate. **se coaguler**, *v.r.* to coagulate.
coaliser [koali'ze], *v.t.* to unite in a coalition. **se coaliser**, *v.r.* to coalesce, to league, to unite, to combine.
coalition [koali'sjɔ̃], *n.f.* coalition, union, league.
coassement [koas'mɑ̃], *n.m.* croaking (*of frogs*).
coasser [koa'se], *v.i.* to croak (*of frogs*).

coassocié [koasɔ'sje], *n.m.* (*fem.* **-ée**) co-partner.
coauteur [koo'tœ:r], *n.m.* co-author.
cobalt [kɔ'balt], *n.m.* cobalt.
cobaye [kɔ'ba:j], *n.m.* guinea pig.
cobra [kɔ'bra], *n.m.* cobra, hooded snake.
cocagne [kɔ'kaɲ], *n.f.* **mât de cocagne**, greasy pole; **pays de cocagne**, land of plenty.
cocaïne [kɔka'in], *n.f.* cocaine.
cocarde [kɔ'kard], *n.f.* cockade; rosette.
cocasse [kɔ'kas], *a.* (*fam.*) odd, laughable, comical.
cocasserie [kɔkas'ri], *n.f.* drollery, foolery, farce.
coccinelle [kɔksi'nɛl], *n.f.* ladybug.
coche (1) [kɔʃ], *n.m.* coach; **c'est la mouche du coche**, he is a busybody.
coche (2) [kɔʃ], *n.f.* notch, score.
coche (3) [kɔʃ], *n.f.* sow.
cochenille [kɔʃ'ni:j], *n.f.* cochineal.
cocher (1) [kɔ'ʃe], *n.m.* coachman, driver.
cocher (2) [kɔ'ʃe], *v.t.* to notch.
cochère [kɔ'ʃɛ:r], *a.f.* for carriages; **porte cochère**, carriage entrance, gateway.
cochet [kɔ'ʃe], *n.m.* young cock, cockerel.
cochon [kɔ'ʃɔ̃], *n.m.* hog, pig; pork; **cochon d'Inde**, guinea pig.
cochonnée [kɔʃɔ'ne], *n.f.* litter (*of pigs*).
cochonner [kɔʃɔ'ne], *v.i.* to farrow, to pig.
cochonnerie [kɔʃɔn'ri], *n.f.* nastiness, filth.
cochonnet [kɔʃɔ'ne], *n.m.* young pig; jack (*at bowls*).
cocktail [kɔk'tɛl], *n.m.* cocktail; cocktail party.
coco [kɔ'ko], *n.m.* coconut.
cocon [kɔ'kɔ̃], *n.m.* cocoon.
cocotier [kɔkɔ'tje], *n.m.* coconut palm.
coction [kɔk'sjɔ̃], *n.f.* coction, boiling; digestion (*of food*).
code [kɔd], *n.m.* code (*digest or collection of laws*); law, rule.
codemandeur [kɔdəmɑ̃'dœ:r], *n.m.* (*fem.* **-eresse**) co-plaintiff.
coder [kɔ'de], *v.t.* to code (*telegram*).
codétenteur [kɔdetɑ̃'tœ:r], *n.m.* (*fem.* **-trice**) joint holder.
codétenu [kɔdet'ny], *n.m.* (*fem.* **-e**) fellow prisoner.
codicillaire [kɔdisi'lɛ:r], *a.* contained in a codicil.
codicille [kɔdi'sil], *n.m.* codicil, rider.
codifier [kɔdi'fje], *v.t.* to codify.
codirecteur [kɔdirɛk'tœ:r], *n.m.* (*fem.* **-trice**) joint manager.
codonataire [kɔdɔna'tɛ:r], *n.* joint donee.
codonateur [kɔdɔna'tœ:r], *n.m.* (*fem.* **-trice**) joint donor.
coéquipier [kɔeki'pje], *n.m.* fellow member (*of a crew, team etc.*).
coercer [kɔɛr'se], *v.t.* to coerce.
coercition [kɔɛrsi'sjɔ̃], *n.f.* coercion.
cœur [kœ:r], *n.m.* heart; (*fig.*) bosom, mind, soul; courage; core, middle; love, affection; hearts (*cards*).
coexistant [kɔɛgzis'tɑ̃], *a.* coexistent.
coexistence [kɔɛgzis'tɑ̃:s], *n.f.* coexistence.
coexister [kɔɛgzis'te], *v.i.* to coexist.
coffre [kɔfr], *n.m.* chest, trunk; coffer; (*Naut.*) mooring buoy; boot (*of a car*).
coffre-fort [kɔfrə'fɔ:r], *n.m.* (*pl.* **coffres-forts**) strongbox, safe.

coffret [kɔ'frɛ], n.m. little chest, casket.
cogitation [kɔʒita'sjɔ̃], n.f. cogitation, reflection.
cognac [kɔ'nak], n.m. cognac, brandy.
cognasse [kɔ'nas], n.f. wild quince.
cognassier [kɔna'sje], n.m. quince tree.
cognée [kɔ'ne], n.f. axe, hatchet.
cogner [kɔ'ne], v.t. to knock in, to drive in; to thump.—v.i. to hit, to bump (contre); to knock (engine). **se cogner**, v.r. to knock (against).
cohabitant [koabi'tɑ̃], a. cohabiting (with).
cohabitation [koabita'sjɔ̃], n.f. cohabitation.
cohabiter [koabi'te], v.i. to cohabit.
cohérence [koe'rɑ̃s], n.f. coherence.
cohérent [koe'rɑ̃], a. coherent.
cohériter [koeri'te], v.i. to inherit conjointly.
cohéritier [koeri'tje], n.m. (fem. -ière) co-heir, co-heiress.
cohésif [koe'zif], a. (fem. -sive) cohesive.
cohésion [koe'zjɔ̃], n.f. cohesion.
cohorte [kɔ'ɔrt], n.f. cohort; (poet.) troop, host; (colloq.) crew, gang.
cohue [kɔ'y], n.f. throng, mob, crush.
coi [kwa], a. (fem. **coite** (1)) quiet, calm, still.
coiffe [kwaf], n.f. hood, headdress.
coiffer [kwa'fe], v.t. to put on the head of; to dress the hair of; (fig.) to infatuate.—v.i. to dress hair; to become; to suit. **se coiffer**, v.r. to put one's hat on; to do one's hair.
coiffeur [kwa'fœːr], n.m. (fem. -euse) hairdresser.—n.f. (-euse) lady's dressing-table.
coiffure [kwa'fyːr], n.f. headdress, hairstyle.
coin [kwɛ̃], n.m. corner, angle, nook; (Coin. etc.) stamp.
coincer [kwɛ̃'se], v.t. (conjug. like COMMENCER) to wedge. **se coincer**, v.r. to jam (of machines).
coïncidence [kɔɛ̃si'dɑ̃ːs], n.f. coincidence.
coïncident [kɔɛ̃si'dɑ̃], a. coincident.
coïncider [kɔɛ̃si'de], v.i. to coincide, to be coincident.
coing [kwɛ̃], n.m. quince.
cointéressé [kɔɛ̃tere'se], a. jointly interested.
—n.m. (fem. -ée) associate, partner.
coite (1) [kwat], [COI].
coite (2), **coitte** [COUETTE].
cojouissance [kɔʒwi'sɑ̃ːs], n.f. (Law) joint use.
coke [kɔk], n.m. coke.
cokéfier [kɔke'fje], v.t. to coke.
col [kɔl], n.m. neck (of a bottle, dress etc.); collar; pass, col (of mountain).
colback [kɔl'bak], n.m. busby.
colchique [kɔl'ʃik], n.m. (Bot.) meadow saffron, colchicum.
colégataire [kɔlega'tɛːr], n. co-legatee.
coléoptère [kɔleɔp'tɛːr], a. coleopterous.—n.m. beetle.
colère [kɔ'lɛːr], n.f. anger, wrath, rage, fury.
colérique [kɔle'rik], a. choleric, irascible.
colibri [kɔli'bri], n.m. hummingbird.
colifichet [kɔlifi'ʃɛ], n.m. trinket, knick-knack.
colimaçon [kɔlima'sɔ̃], n.m. snail; **escalier en colimaçon**, spiral staircase.
colin-maillard [kɔlɛ̃ma'jaːr], n.m. inv. blindman's-buff.
colique [kɔ'lik], n.f. colic, stomach ache.
colis [kɔ'li], n.m. package, parcel, case.
collaborateur [kɔlabɔra'tœːr], n.m. (fem. -trice) collaborator.

collaboration [kɔlabɔra'sjɔ̃], n.f. collaboration.
collaborer [kɔlabɔ're], v.i. to collaborate.
collage [kɔ'laːʒ], n.m. pasting, gluing; paper-hanging; (Art) collage.
collant [kɔ'lɑ̃], a. sticky; tight, close-fitting.
collatéral [kɔllate'ral], a. (m. pl. -aux) collateral.
collatéralement [kɔllateral'mɑ̃], adv. collaterally.
collation [kɔlla'sjɔ̃], n.f. light meal; comparison (of documents etc.).
collationnement [kɔllasjɔn'mɑ̃], n.m. collating, comparing.
collationner [kɔllasjɔ'ne], v.t. to collate, to compare.—v.i. to have a snack.
colle [kɔl], n.f. paste, gum; poser; sham, fib.
collecte [kɔ'lɛkt], n.f. collection (of money etc.); collect (prayer).
collecteur [kɔlɛk'tœːr], n.m. (fem. -trice) collector.
collectif [kɔlɛk'tif], a. (fem. -tive) collective.
collection [kɔlɛk'sjɔ̃], n.f. collection; set.
collectionner [kɔlɛksjɔ'ne], v.t. to collect, to make collections of things.
collectionneur [kɔlɛksjɔ'nœːr], n.m. (fem. -euse) collector.
collectivement [kɔlɛktiv'mɑ̃], adv. collectively.
collectivisme [kɔlɛkti'vism], n.m. collectivism.
collectiviste [kɔlɛkti'vist], n. collectivist.
collectivité [kɔlɛktivi'te], n.f. collectivity; common ownership.
collège [kɔ'lɛʒ], n.m. college; grammar school.
collégien [kɔle'ʒjɛ̃], n.m. (fem. -enne) high-school boy or girl.
collègue [kɔl'lɛg], n. colleague.
coller [kɔ'le], v.t. to paste, to glue; to stick together.—v.i. to stick, to adhere. **se coller**, v.r. to stick to.
collerette [kɔl'rɛt], n.f. collar (for ladies).
collet [kɔ'lɛ], n.m. collar (of gown etc.); cape; flange; snare.
colleter [kɔl'te], v.t. (conjug. like APPELER) to collar, to seize by the neck.—v.i. to set snares. **se colleter**, v.r. to come to grips (with someone).
colleur [kɔ'lœːr], n.m. (fem. -euse) gluer, paster, paperhanger; billposter.
collier [kɔ'lje], n.m. necklace; gold chain (of knightly orders etc.); collar (for animals).
colline [kɔ'lin], n.f. hill, hillock.
collision [kɔli'zjɔ̃], n.f. collision.
collocation [kɔlɔka'sjɔ̃], n.f. classification.
colloque [kɔl'lɔk], n.m. colloquy, conference.
collusion [kɔlly'zjɔ̃], n.f. collusion.
collusoire [kɔlly'zwaːr], a. collusory, collusive.
Colomb [kɔ'lɔ̃], m. Columbus.
colombe [kɔ'lɔ̃ːb], n.f. (poet.) pigeon, dove.
Colombie [kɔlɔ̃'bi], la, f. Colombia.
colombien [kɔlɔ̃'bjɛ̃], a. (fem. -enne) Colombian.—n.m. (Colombien, fem. -enne) Colombian (person).
colombier [kɔlɔ̃'bje], n.m. dovecot, pigeon house.
colombin [kɔlɔ̃'bɛ̃], a. columbine; dove-color.
colombophile [kɔlɔ̃bɔ'fil], a. and n. pigeon fancier.

colon [kɔ'lɔ̃], *n.m.* colonist, planter; settler.

côlon [ko'lɔ̃], *n.m.* (*Anat.*) colon.

colonel [kɔlɔ'nɛl], *n.m.* colonel; (*Av.*) group captain.

colonial [kɔlɔ'njal], *a.* (*m. pl.* **-aux**) colonial. —*n.m.* (*fem.* **-e**) colonial.

colonie [kɔlɔ'ni], *n.f.* colony, settlement; *colonie de vacances*, holiday camp.

colonisation [kɔlɔniza'sjɔ̃], *n.f.* colonization.

coloniser [kɔlɔni'ze], *v.t.* to colonize.

colonnade [kɔlɔ'nad], *n.f.* (*Arch.*) colonnade.

colonne [kɔ'lɔn], *n.f.* column, pillar; column (*of units, tens etc.*).

colonnette [kɔlɔ'nɛt], *n.f.* little column.

colorant [kɔlɔ'rɑ̃], *a.* coloring.—*n.m.* dye.

coloration [kɔlɔra'sjɔ̃], *n.f.* coloration, staining.

colorer [kɔlɔ're], *v.t.* to color, to dye; to varnish. **se colorer,** *v.r.* to color (*of a thing*).

coloriage [kɔlɔ'rja:ʒ], *n.m.* (*Paint.*) coloring.

colorier [kɔlɔ'rje], *v.t.* to color, to stain (*a drawing etc.*).

coloris [kɔlɔ'ri], *n.m.* coloring, art of coloring.

coloriste [kɔlɔ'rist], *n.* colorer; colorist.

colossal [kɔlɔ'sal], *a.* (*m. pl.* **-aux**) colossal.

colosse [kɔ'lɔs], *n.m.* colossus, giant.

colportage [kɔlpɔr'ta:ʒ], *n.m.* hawking, peddling.

colporter [kɔlpɔr'te], *v.t.* to hawk about; to spread.

colporteur [kɔlpɔr'tœ:r], *n.m.* hawker, pedlar.

coltiner [kɔlti'ne], *v.t.* to carry heavy loads (*on head and back*).

coltineur [kɔlti'nœ:r], *n.m.* coal heaver, loadporter.

colza [kɔl'za], *n.m.* colza, rape, rape seed.

coma [kɔ'ma], *n.m.* coma.

comateux [kɔma'tø], *a.* (*fem.* **-euse**) comatose.

combat [kɔ̃'ba], *n.m.* combat, fight, battle, contest; struggle; *hors de combat*, disabled.

combattant [kɔ̃ba'tɑ̃], *n.m.* combatant; champion; *anciens combattants*, ex-service men.

combattre [kɔ̃'batr], *v.t.* (*conjug. like* BATTRE) to fight, to combat, to wage war against, to strive against.—*v.i.* to fight, to vie, to struggle. **se combattre,** *v.r.* to combat; to contend with each other.

combien [kɔ̃'bjɛ̃], *adv.* how much, how many; how; how far; how long.

combinaison [kɔ̃binɛ'zɔ̃], *n.f.* combination; contrivance, scheme; overalls; slip (*woman's undergarment*).

combiné [kɔ̃bi'ne], *n.m.* (*Chem.*) compound; (*Rad.*) radiogram.

combiner [kɔ̃bi'ne], *v.t.* to combine; (*fig.*) to contrive.

comble [kɔ̃bl], *n.m.* heaping up above a full measure; summit; (*fig.*) zenith; (*pl.*) roof timbers.—*a.* full, heaped up, full to the top; *salle comble*, house full.

comblement [kɔ̃blə'mɑ̃], *n.m.* filling up, heaping up.

combler [kɔ̃'ble], *v.t.* to heap up, to fill up; to complete; to overwhelm.

comburant [kɔ̃by'rɑ̃], *a.* (*Chem.*) causing burning (*of oxygen etc.*).—*n.m.* fuel.

combustibilité [kɔ̃bystibili'te], *n.f.* combustibility.

combustible [kɔ̃bys'tibl], *a.* combustible.—*n.m.* combustible; fuel, firing.

combustion [kɔ̃bys'tjɔ̃], *n.f.* combustion, flame.

comédie [kɔme'di], *n.f.* comedy; theatre; players.

comédien [kɔme'djɛ̃], *n.m.* (*fem.* **-enne**) comedian, actor, actress, player; (*fig.*) hypocrite.

comestible [kɔmɛs'tibl], *a.* edible, eatable.—*n.m.* eatable; (*pl.*) eatables.

comète [kɔ'mɛt], *n.f.* comet.

comice [kɔ'mis], *n.m.* meeting; electoral meeting; *comice agricole*, agricultural show.

comique [kɔ'mik], *a.* comic; comical, ludicrous.—*n.m.* comic art, comedy.

comiquement [kɔmik'mɑ̃], *adv.* comically.

comité [kɔmi'te], *n.m.* committee, board.

commandant [kɔmɑ̃'dɑ̃], *a.* commanding.—*n.m.* (*fem.* **-e**) commander, commanding officer, commandant; major.

commande [kɔ'mɑ̃:d], *n.f.* order; (*Mach.*) driving wheel.

commandement [kɔmɑ̃d'mɑ̃], *n.m.* command; authority, control; order; commandment, law.

commander [kɔmɑ̃'de], *v.t.* to command, to order; to govern; to overlook.—*v.i.* to command, to have authority. **se commander,** *v.r.* to control oneself.

commandeur [kɔmɑ̃'dœ:r], *n.m.* commander (*in orders of knighthood*).

commanditaire [kɔmɑ̃di'tɛ:r], *n.* silent partner.

commandite [kɔmɑ̃'dit], *n.f.* limited partnership.

commanditer [kɔmɑ̃di'te], *v.t.* to finance (*a commercial undertaking*).

commando [kɔmɑ̃'do], *n.m.* commando.

comme [kɔm], *adv.* as; like, such as; almost, nearly, as if; how, in what way, to what extent.—*conj.* as, since, because.

commémoraison [kɔmemɔrɛ'zɔ̃], *n.f.* (*R.-C. Ch.*) commemoration, remembrance.

commémoratif [kɔmemɔra'tif], *a.* (*fem.* **-tive**) commemorative.

commémoration [kɔmemɔra'sjɔ̃], *n.f.* commemoration.

commémorer [kɔmemɔ're], *v.t.* to commemorate, to remember.

commençant [kɔmɑ̃'sɑ̃], *n.m.* (*fem.* **-e**) beginner, novice.

commencement [kɔmɑ̃s'mɑ̃], *n.m.* beginning, commencement.

commencer [kɔmɑ̃'se], *v.t., v.i.* (*see Verb Tables*) to begin, to commence; to initiate.

commensal [kɔmɑ̃'sal], *n.m.* (*m. pl.* **-aux**) habitual guest; fellow boarder, messmate.

commensurable [kɔmɑ̃sy'rabl], *a.* commensurable.

comment [kɔ'mɑ̃], *adv.* how, in what manner; why, wherefore.—*int.* what! indeed!—*n.m.* the why and wherefore.

commentaire [kɔmɑ̃'tɛ:r], *n.m.* commentary, exposition; (*fig.*) unfavorable comment.

commentateur [kɔmɑ̃ta'tœ:r], *n.m.* (*fem.* **-trice**) commentator, annotator.

commenter [kɔmɑ̃'te], *v.t.* to comment on, to explain, to annotate.—*v.i.* to criticize adversely.

commérage [kɔme'ra:ʒ], *n.m.* gossip, tittle-tattle.

commerçant [kɔmɛr'sɑ̃], *a.* commercial, mercantile, trading.—*n.m.* (*fem.* **-e**) merchant, tradesman, shopkeeper.

commerce [kɔ'mɛrs], *n.m.* commerce, trade, trading, traffic; intercourse, dealings.

commercer [kɔmɛr'se], *v.i.* (*conjug. like* COMMENCER) to trade, to deal.

commercial [kɔmɛr'sjal], *a.* (*m. pl.* **-aux**) commercial.

commercialement [kɔmɛrsjal'mɑ̃], *adv.* commercially.

commercialisation [kɔmɛrsjaliza'sjɔ̃], *n.f.* commercialization.

commercialiser [kɔmɛrsjali'ze], *v.t.* to commercialize.

commère [kɔ'mɛr], *n.f.* godmother; gossip.

commettre [kɔ'mɛtr], *v.t. irr.* (*conjug. like* METTRE) to commit, to perpetrate; to appoint, to empower; to entrust. **se commettre**, *v.r.* to commit oneself.

commis (1) [kɔ'mi], *n.m.* (*fem.* **commise**) clerk; *commis voyageur*, commercial traveller.

commis (2) [kɔ'mi], *a.* committed, appointed.

commisération [kɔmizera'sjɔ̃], *n.f.* commiseration, compassion, pity.

commissaire [kɔmi'sɛ:r], *n.m.* commissioner; manager, steward, trustee; purser (*of a vessel*).

commissaire-priseur [kɔmisɛrpri'zœ:r], *n.m.* auctioneer; valuer, appraiser.

commissariat [kɔmisa'rja], *n.m.* commissaryship, trusteeship; (*Mil., Navy*) commissariat; police station.

commission [kɔmi'sjɔ̃], *n.f.* commission, charge; errand; power; (*Comm.*) percentage; warrant.

commissionnaire [kɔmisjɔ'nɛ:r], *n.m.* commission agent, commissionnaire; messenger, porter.

commissionner [kɔmisjɔ'ne], *v.t.* to empower, to commission; to order (*goods*).

commode [kɔ'mɔd], *a.* convenient, commodious, handy; comfortable, suitable; easy.—*n.f.* chest of drawers, commode.

commodément [kɔmɔde'mɑ̃], *adv.* commodiously, conveniently; comfortably, suitably.

commodité [kɔmɔdi'te], *n.f.* convenience, accommodation.

commotion [kɔmo'sjɔ̃], *n.f.* commotion; shock; concussion.

commotionné [kɔmosjɔ'ne], *a.* suffering from concussion.

commuable [kɔ'mɥabl], *a.* commutable.

commun [kɔ'mœ̃], *a.* common; usual, ordinary; mean, vulgar; *le bien commun*, the common weal; *lieux communs*, commonplaces.—*n.m.* common people.

communal [kɔmy'nal], *a.* (*m. pl.* **-aux**) communal, parochial; common.—*n.m. pl.* (*biens*) *communaux*, communal property.

communauté [kɔmyno'te], *n.f.* community, society, corporation.

commune [kɔ'myn], *n.f.* commune (*parish, township, in France*).

communément [kɔmyne'mɑ̃], *adv.* commonly, usually.

communiant [kɔmy'njɑ̃], *n.m.* (*fem.* **-e**) communicant.

communicatif [kɔmynika'tif], *a.* (*fem.* **-tive**) communicative, open.

communication [kɔmynika'sjɔ̃], *n.f.* intercourse, communication; (*Teleph.*) call.

communicativement [kɔmynikativ'mɑ̃], *adv.* communicatively.

communier [kɔmy'nje], *v.i.* to communicate, to receive the sacrament.

communion [kɔmy'njɔ̃], *n.f.* communion, fellowship; persuasion; sacrament.

communiqué [kɔmyni'ke], *n.m.* statement, communiqué.

communiquer [kɔmyni'ke], *v.t.* to communicate, to impart; to tell, to acquaint.—*v.i.* to be in contact or correspondence (*with*).

communisant [kɔmyni'zɑ̃], *a.* communistic.—*n.m.* (*fem.* **-e**) fellow traveller.

communisme [kɔmy'nism], *n.m.* communism.

communiste [kɔmy'nist], *n.* communist.

commutable [kɔmy'tabl], [COMMUABLE].

commutateur [kɔmyta'tœ:r], *n.m.* (*Elec.*) switch.

compact [kɔ̃'pakt], *a.* compact, dense.

compagne [kɔ̃'paɲ], *n.f.* female companion, consort; playmate.

compagnie [kɔ̃pa'ɲi], *n.f.* society, companionship; company; (*Comm.*) company.

compagnon [kɔ̃pa'ɲɔ̃], *n.m.* companion, comrade; playmate; mate; (*Bot.*) campion.

comparable [kɔ̃pa'rabl], *a.* comparable.

comparablement [kɔ̃parablə'mɑ̃], *adv.* in comparison (*with*).

comparaison [kɔ̃parɛ'zɔ̃], *n.f.* comparison; similitude.

comparaître [kɔ̃pa'rɛ:tr], *v.i. irr.* (*conjug. like* CONNAÎTRE) to appear (*before a tribunal*).

comparant [kɔ̃pa'rɑ̃], *n.m.* (*fem.* **-e**) person appearing in court on a summons.

comparatif [kɔ̃para'tif], *a.* (*fem.* **-tive**) comparative.—*n.m.* comparative degree.

comparativement [kɔ̃parativ'mɑ̃], *adv.* comparatively.

comparer [kɔ̃pa're], *v.t.* to compare. **se comparer**, *v.r.* to be compared.

compartiment [kɔ̃parti'mɑ̃], *n.m.* compartment, division.

compas [kɔ̃'pa], *n.m.* pair of compasses; mariner's compass.

compassé [kɔ̃pa'se], *a.* formal, stiff, starchy.

compasser [kɔ̃pa'se], *v.t.* to measure, set out; to proportion, to regulate; (*fig.*) to weigh, to consider.

compassion [kɔ̃pa'sjɔ̃], *n.f.* compassion, pity, mercy.

compatibilité [kɔ̃patibili'te], *n.f.* compatibility.

compatible [kɔ̃pa'tibl], *a.* compatible, consistent.

compatir [kɔ̃pa'ti:r], *v.i.* to sympathize; to agree, to be compatible (*with*).

compatissant [kɔ̃pati'sɑ̃], *a.* compassionate, tender.

compatriote [kɔ̃patri'ɔt], *n.* compatriot, fellow countryman.

compendium [kɔ̃pɑ̃'djɔm], *n.m.* summary.

compensable [kɔ̃pɑ̃'sabl], *a.* that may be compensated.

compensation [kɔ̃pɑ̃sa'sjɔ̃], *n.f.* compensation, amends, reparation.

compensatoire [kɔ̃pɑ̃sa'twaːr], *a.* compensatory.

compenser [kɔ̃pɑ̃'se], *v.t.* to counterbalance, to compensate, to make up for. **se compenser**, *v.r.* to compensate each other; to be set off against.

compère [kɔ̃'pɛːr], *n.m.* godfather; (*fig.*) gossip, crony; confederate.

compétence [kɔ̃pe'tɑ̃ːs], *n.f.* competence, cognizance; (*fig.*) department, province; proficiency.

compétent [kɔ̃pe'tɑ̃], *a.* competent, qualified; (*fig.*) suitable, requisite.

compétiteur [kɔ̃peti'tœːr], *n.m.* (*fem.* **-trice**) competitor, candidate.

compétitif [kɔ̃peti'tif], *a.* (*fem.* **-tive**) competitive.

compétition [kɔ̃peti'sjɔ̃], *n.f.* competition, rivalry.

compilateur [kɔ̃pila'tœːr], *n.m.* compiler.

compilation [kɔ̃pila'sjɔ̃], *n.f.* compilation.

compiler [kɔ̃pi'le], *v.t.* to compile.

complainte [kɔ̃'plɛ̃ːt], *n.f.* tragic *or* plaintive ballad, lament; (*fig.*) lamentation.

complaire [kɔ̃'plɛːr], *v.i. irr.* (*conjug. like* PLAIRE) to be pleasing (*à*). **se complaire**, *v.r.* to delight (*dans* or *à*).

complaisamment [kɔ̃plɛza'mɑ̃], *adv* complaisantly, obligingly.

complaisance [kɔ̃plɛ'zɑ̃ːs], *n.f.* complaisance, good nature; complacency.

complaisant [kɔ̃plɛ'zɑ̃], *a.* affable, civil, obliging, kind.—*n.m.* (*fem.* **-e**) flatterer; gobetween.

complément [kɔ̃ple'mɑ̃], *n.m.* complement; (*Gram.*) object; extension (*of subject*).

complémentaire [kɔ̃plemɑ̃'tɛːr], *a.* complementary, completing.

complet [kɔ̃'plɛ], *a.* (*fem.* **-plète**) complete, whole; full, filled.—*n.m.* complement, full number; suit (*of clothes*).

complètement [kɔ̃plɛt'mɑ̃], *adv.* completely, entirely, thoroughly.

complètement [kɔ̃plɛt'mɑ̃], *n.m.* finishing, completion.

compléter [kɔ̃ple'te], *v.t.* (*conjug. like* CÉDER) to complete, to perfect; to fill up.

complexe [kɔ̃'plɛks], *a.* complex, complicated.—*n.m.* **complexe d'infériorité**, inferiority complex.

complexion [kɔ̃plɛk'sjɔ̃], *n.f.* constitution; disposition, humor, temper.

complexité [kɔ̃plɛksi'te], *n.f.* complexity.

complication [kɔ̃plika'sjɔ̃], *n.f.* complication, intricacy.

complice [kɔ̃'plis], *a.* accessory, privy to.—*n.* accomplice, accessory.

complicité [kɔ̃plisi'te], *n.f.* complicity, participation.

compliment [kɔ̃pli'mɑ̃], *n.m.* compliment; (*pl.*) regards, congratulations.

complimenter [kɔ̃plimɑ̃'te], *v.t.* to compliment, to congratulate.

complimenteur [kɔ̃plimɑ̃'tœːr], *a.* and *n.m.* (*fem.* **-euse**) over-complimentary; obsequious (person).

compliqué [kɔ̃pli'ke], *a.* complicated, intricate.

compliquer [kɔ̃pli'ke], *v.t.* to complicate, to entangle. **se compliquer**, *v.r.* to become complicated.

complot [kɔ̃'plo], *n.m.* plot, conspiracy; *chef du complot*, ringleader.

comploter [kɔ̃plɔ'te], *v.t.* to plot.

comploteur [kɔ̃plɔ'tœːr], *n.m.* plotter, schemer.

componction [kɔ̃pɔ̃k'sjɔ̃], *n.f.* compunction; solemn manners *or* expression.

comportement [kɔ̃pɔrtə'mɑ̃], *n.m.* demeanor, deportment, behavior.

comporter [kɔ̃pɔr'te], *v.t.* to permit, to allow; to require; to comprise. **se comporter**, *v.r.* to behave; to act, to manage.

composant [kɔ̃po'zɑ̃], *n.m.* (*Chem.*) component, constituent.

composé [kɔ̃po'ze], *a.* composed, compound. —*n.m.* compound.

composer [kɔ̃po'ze], *v.t.* to compose, to compound, to make up; to form, to create; to adjust, to regulate; *composer un numéro*, to dial a number.—*v.i.* to compound, to compromise, to make up.

composeuse [kɔ̃po'zøːz], *n.f.* type-setting machine.

composite [kɔ̃po'zit], *a.* composite.

compositeur [kɔ̃pozi'tœːr], *n.m.* (*fem.* **-trice**) composer (*of music*); (*Print.*) compositor.

composition [kɔ̃pozi'sjɔ̃], *n.f.* composition; chemical composition; settlement; (*fig.*) disposition; (*Print.*) composing.

compost [kɔ̃'post], *n.m.* (*Agric.*) compost.

composter [kɔ̃pos'te], *v.t.* to compost; to date *or* obliterate (*ticket etc.*).

compote [kɔ̃'pot], *n.f.* stewed fruit, compote.

compotier [kɔ̃pɔ'tje], *n.m.* fruit dish.

compréhensibilité [kɔ̃preɑ̃sibili'te], *n.f.* comprehensibility.

compréhensible [kɔ̃preɑ̃'sibl], *a.* understandable, intelligible.

compréhensif [kɔ̃preɑ̃'sif], *a.* (*fem.* **-sive**) comprehensive; broadminded.

compréhension [kɔ̃preɑ̃'sjɔ̃], *n.f.* comprehension; (*fig.*) understanding, intelligence.

compréhensivité [kɔ̃preɑ̃sivi'te], *n.f.* comprehensiveness, faculty of comprehending.

comprendre [kɔ̃'prɑ̃ːdr], *v.t. irr.* (*conjug. like* PRENDRE) to include, to comprise; to understand, to conceive, to realize.

compresse [kɔ̃'prɛːs], *n.f.* (*Surg.*) compress, pledget.

compresseur [kɔ̃prɛ'sœːr], *a.* compressive.— *n.m.* compressor, roller.

compressif [kɔ̃prɛ'sif], *a.* (*fem.* **-ssive**) compressive, repressive.

compression [kɔ̃prɛ'sjɔ̃], *n.f.* compression; (*fig.*) constraint.

comprimable [kɔ̃pri'mabl], *a.* compressible.

comprimé [kɔ̃pri'me], *a.* compressed, condensed; kept under.—*n.m.* (*Pharm.*) tabloid, tablet.

comprimer [kɔ̃pri'me], *v.t.* to compress, to condense; to repress, to restrain.

compris [kɔ̃'pri], *a.* understood; included.

compromettant [kɔ̃promɛ'tɑ̃], *a.* compromising; damaging.

compromettre [kɔ̃pro'mɛtr], *v.t. irr.* (*conjug. like* METTRE) to expose, to commit, to compromise, to jeopardize.—*v.i.* to compromise; to submit to arbitration. **se compromettre**, *v.r.* to compromise oneself.

compromis [kɔ̃pro'mi], *n.m.* mutual agreement, compromise.

comptabilité [kɔ̃tabili'te], *n.f.* accountancy, bookkeeping; accountant's department.

comptable [kɔ̃'tabl], *a.* responsible for accounts; accountable, responsible.—*n.m.* accountant, bookkeeper; (*Naut.*) purser.

comptant [kɔ̃'tɑ̃], *a.m.* (*of money*) ready; (*of payment*) in cash.—*n.m.* ready money, cash.

compte [kɔ̃t], *n.m.* reckoning; account, score, statement, report; (*fig.*) profit; esteem, value; *se rendre compte de*, to realize.

compte-gouttes [kɔ̃t'gut], *n.m. inv.* (*Med.*) drop-tube, dropper; filler; (*fig.*) *au compte-gouttes*, sparingly.

compte-pas [kɔ̃tə'pa], *n.m.* pedometer.

compter [kɔ̃'te], *v.t.* to count, to calculate, to compute; to pay down; to comprise.—*v.i.* to reckon, to count; to be reckoned; to expect; to intend; to rely (*sur*). **se compter**, *v.r.* to be reckoned *or* included.

compteur [kɔ̃'tœːr], *a.* and *n.m.* (*fem.* **-euse**) that counts; computer.—*n.m.* meter; (C) *compteur de stationnement*, parking meter.

comptoir [kɔ̃'twaːr], *n.m.* counter; cashier's desk; counting-house; branch bank; factory.

compulser [kɔ̃pyl'se], *v.t.* to inspect (*documents etc.*).

computation [kɔ̃pyta'sjɔ̃], *n.f.* computation.

computer [kɔ̃py'te], *v.t.* to compute.

comtal [kɔ̃'tal], *a.* (*m. pl.* **-aux**) pertaining to an earl *or* a countess.

comte [kɔ̃t], *n.m.* count; earl.

comté [kɔ̃'te], *n.m.* county, shire; earldom.

comtesse [kɔ̃'tɛs], *n.f.* countess.

concassage [kɔ̃kɑ'saːʒ], *n.m.* pounding, crushing.

concasser [kɔ̃kɑ'se], *v.t.* to pound, to crush.

concasseur [kɔ̃kɑ'sœːr], *n.m.* crushing-mill; steam roller.

concave [kɔ̃'kaːv], *a.* concave.

concavité [kɔ̃kavi'te], *n.f.* concave; concavity.

concéder [kɔ̃se'de], *v.t.* (*conjug. like* CÉDER) to grant, to concede, to allow.

concentration [kɔ̃sɑ̃tra'sjɔ̃], *n.f.* concentration; condensation; *camp de concentration*, concentration camp.

concentré [kɔ̃sɑ̃'tre], *a.* concentrated; (*fig.*) silent, reserved.—*n.m.* extract.

concentrer [kɔ̃sɑ̃'tre], *v.t.* to concentrate, to focus; (*fig.*) to repress, to smother (*anger etc.*). **se concentrer**, *v.r.* to concentrate; to withdraw within oneself.

concentrique [kɔ̃sɑ̃'trik], *a.* concentric.

concentriquement [kɔ̃sɑ̃trik'mɑ̃], *adv.* concentrically.

concept [kɔ̃'sɛpt], *n.m.* concept.

conceptibilité [kɔ̃sɛptibili'te], *n.f.* conceivability.

conceptible [kɔ̃sɛp'tibl], *a.* conceivable.

conceptif [kɔ̃sɛp'tif], *a.* (*fem.* **-tive**) conceptive.

conception [kɔ̃sɛp'sjɔ̃], *n.f.* conception; thought, notion; understanding.

concernant [kɔ̃sɛr'nɑ̃], *prep.* concerning, relating to.

concerner [kɔ̃sɛr'ne], *v.t.* to relate (*to*), to concern, to regard.

concert [kɔ̃'sɛːr], *n.m.* harmony; concert; (*fig.*) concord.

concertant [kɔ̃sɛr'tɑ̃], *a.* in concert (*of a*

piece of music).—*n.m.* (*fem.* **-e**) performer in a concert.

concerté [kɔ̃sɛr'te], *a.* concerted, united; studied, stiff.

concerter [kɔ̃sɛr'te], *v.t.* to contrive, to concert; to plan, to devise; to compose (*one's demeanor etc.*). **se concerter**, *v.r.* to plan together, to concert.

concertiste [kɔ̃sɛr'tist], *n.* performer (*at a concert*).

concerto [kɔ̃sɛr'to], *n.m.* concerto.

concession [kɔ̃sɛ'sjɔ̃], *n.f.* concession, privilege.

concessionnaire [kɔ̃sɛsjɔ'nɛːr], *a.* concessionary.—*n.* grantee.

concevable [kɔ̃sə'vabl], *a.* conceivable, imaginable.

concevoir [kɔ̃sə'vwaːr], *v.t. irr.* (*conjug. like* RECEVOIR) to become pregnant, to conceive; to imagine, to understand; to comprehend.

concierge [kɔ̃'sjɛrʒ], *n.* concierge, hall-porter, caretaker.

conciergerie [kɔ̃sjɛrʒə'ri], *n.f.* caretaker's lodge; *La Conciergerie*, a prison in Paris (*during French Revolution*).

concile [kɔ̃'sil], *n.m.* an assembly of prelates and doctors, council, synod.

conciliable [kɔ̃si'ljabl], *a.* reconcilable.

conciliabule [kɔ̃silja'byl], *n.m.* conventicle, secret meeting.

conciliaire [kɔ̃si'ljɛːr], *a.* of *or* belonging to a council.

conciliant [kɔ̃si'ljɑ̃], *a.* conciliating, reconciling.

conciliateur [kɔ̃silja'tœːr], *a.* (*fem.* **-trice**) conciliatory.—*n.m.* (*fem.* **-trice**) conciliator.

conciliation [kɔ̃silja'sjɔ̃], *n.f.* reconciliation.

conciliatoire [kɔ̃silja'twaːr], *a.* conciliatory.

concilier [kɔ̃si'lje], *v.t.* to conciliate, to reconcile; to gain, to win, to procure. **se concilier**, *v.r.* to gain, to win.

concis [kɔ̃'si], *a.* concise, brief, short.

concision [kɔ̃si'zjɔ̃], *n.f.* brevity, conciseness.

concitoyen [kɔ̃sitwa'jɛ̃], *n.m.* (*fem.* **-enne**) fellow citizen.

conclave [kɔ̃'klaːv], *n.m.* conclave, assembly of all the cardinals.

concluant [kɔ̃kly'ɑ̃], *a.* conclusive, decisive.

conclure [kɔ̃'klyːr], *v.t. irr.* to conclude; to infer; to judge.

conclusif [kɔ̃kly'zif], *a.* (*fem.* **-sive**) conclusive.

conclusion [kɔ̃kly'zjɔ̃], *n.f.* conclusion, upshot.

concombre [kɔ̃'kɔ̃ːbr], *n.m.* cucumber.

concomitance [kɔ̃kɔmi'tɑ̃ːs], *n.f.* concomitance.

concomitant [kɔ̃kɔmi'tɑ̃], *a.* concomitant.

concordance [kɔ̃kɔr'dɑ̃ːs], *n.f.* agreement; (*Bibl. etc.*) concordance.

concordant [kɔ̃kɔr'dɑ̃], *a.* concordant.

concordat [kɔ̃kɔr'da], *n.m.* concordat, agreement; bankrupt's certificate.

concordataire [kɔ̃kɔrda'tɛːr], *n.m.* certificated bankrupt.

concorde [kɔ̃'kɔrd], *n.f.* concord, agreement, harmony; good understanding.

concorder [kɔ̃kɔr'de], *v.i.* to be in accord, to agree, to concur.

concourir [kɔ̃ku'riːr], *v.i. irr.* (*conjug. like* COURIR) to concur; to contribute to; to co-operate; to compete; to converge.

concours [kɔ̃'ku:r], *n.m.* concourse, meeting; coincidence; competition; co-operation; competitive examination; assistance.

concret [kɔ̃'krɛ], *a.* (*fem.* **-crète**) concrete, solid.

concubine [kɔ̃ky'bin], *n.f.* concubine.

concupiscence [kɔ̃kypi'sɑ̃:s], *n.f.* concupiscence, lust.

concurremment [kɔ̃kyra'mɑ̃], *adv.* concurrently; jointly, together.

concurrence [kɔ̃ky'rɑ̃:s], *n.f.* competition; rivalry, opposition.

concurrent [kɔ̃ky'rɑ̃], *n.m.* (*fem.* **-e**) competitor, rival.

concussion [kɔ̃ky'sjɔ̃], *n.f.* extortion, embezzlement.

concussionnaire [kɔ̃kysjɔ'nɛ:r], *a.* guilty of peculation, of bribery *or* of extortion.—*n.m.* extortioner, peculator, embezzler.

condamnable [kɔ̃da'nabl], *a.* condemnable, blamable.

condamnation [kɔ̃dana'sjɔ̃], *n.f.* condemnation, judgment, sentence; penalty.

condamné [kɔ̃da'ne], *a.* condemned, convicted.—*n.m.* (*fem.* **-ée**) convict.

condamner [kɔ̃da'ne], *v.t.* to condemn, to sentence, to convict; (*fig.*) to blame, to censure.

condensateur [kɔ̃dɑ̃sa'tœ:r], *n.m.* (*Phys.*) condenser.

condensation [kɔ̃dɑ̃sa'sjɔ̃], *n.f.* condensation.

condensé [kɔ̃dɑ̃'se], *a.* condensed.—*n.m.* digest.

condenser [kɔ̃dɑ̃'se], *v.t.* to condense.

condenseur [kɔ̃dɑ̃'sœ:r], *n.m.* condenser.

condescendance [kɔ̃desɑ̃'dɑ̃:s], *n.f.* condescension.

condescendant [kɔ̃desɑ̃'dɑ̃], *a.* condescending, complying.

condescendre [kɔ̃de'sɑ̃:dr], *v.i.* to condescend, to comply.

condiment [kɔ̃di'mɑ̃], *n.m.* condiment, seasoning.

condisciple [kɔ̃di'sipl], *n.m.* schoolfellow.

condit [kɔ̃'di], *n.m.* candied fruit.

condition [kɔ̃di'sjɔ̃], *n.f.* condition; rank, station; domestic service; situation, circumstances; terms; *à condition or sous condition*, on condition, on approval.

conditionné [kɔ̃disjɔ'ne], *a.* conditioned (*bien* or *mal*); well-conditioned, sound.

conditionnel [kɔ̃disjɔ'nɛl], *a.* conditional.—*n.m.* (*Gram.*) conditional.

conditionnellement [kɔ̃disjɔnɛl'mɑ̃], *adv.* conditionally, on condition.

conditionner [kɔ̃disjɔ'ne], *v.t.* to condition; to dry (*silk*); to season (*wood*).

condoléance [kɔ̃dɔle'ɑ̃:s], *n.f.* condolence.

condominium [kɔ̃dɔmi'njɔm], *n.m.* condominium.

condor [kɔ̃'dɔ:r], *n.m.* condor.

conductance [kɔ̃dyk'tɑ̃:s], *n.f.* (*Elec.*) conductance.

conducteur [kɔ̃dyk'tœ:r], *n.m.* (*fem.* **-trice**) conductor, conductress, leader, guide; driver, drover.—*a.* (*Phys.*) conducting.

conductibilité [kɔ̃dyktibili'te], *n.f.* conductibility.

conductible [kɔ̃dyk'tibl], *a.* conductible.

conduction [kɔ̃dyk'sjɔ̃], *n.f.* (*Phys.*) conduction; (*Civic Law*) hiring.

conduire [kɔ̃'dɥi:r], *v.t. irr.* to conduct, to lead, to guide; to drive; to accompany; to bring, to take; to be at the head of.—*v.i.* to lead (*à*); to drive. **se conduire**, *v.r.* to conduct *or* behave oneself.

conduit [kɔ̃'dɥi], *n.m.* conduit, duct, pipe, passage, tube, canal.

conduite [kɔ̃'dɥit], *n.f.* conducting, leading, driving, steering; management, direction, administration; conveyance, distribution; scheme, plan; water-pipe, conduit; behavior, demeanor; prudence, discretion.

cône [ko:n], *n.m.* cone; *en cône*, conical.

confection [kɔ̃fɛk'sjɔ̃], *n.f.* preparation, making; making of ready-made clothes; (*Pharm.*) confection; *vêtements de confection*, ready-made clothes.

confectionner [kɔ̃fɛksjɔ'ne], *v.t.* to make, to manufacture, to finish.

confectionneur [kɔ̃fɛksjɔ'nœ:r], *n.m.* (*fem.* **-euse**) maker, finisher (*of wearing apparel*), clothier, outfitter.

confédération [kɔ̃federa'sjɔ̃], *n.f.* confederation, confederacy; *la Confédération Générale du Travail* (*abbr.* **C.G.T.**), the French equivalent of the c.i.o.

confédéré [kɔ̃fede're], *a.* and *n.m.* (*fem.* **-ée**) confederate, associate.

confédérer (se) [səkɔ̃fede're], *v.r.* (*conjug. like* CÉDER) to combine, to enter into confederation.

conférence [kɔ̃fe'rɑ̃:s], *n.f.* conference, lecture.

conférencier [kɔ̃ferɑ̃'sje], *n.m.* (*fem.* **-ière**) lecturer.

conférer [kɔ̃fe're], *v.t.* (*conjug. like* CÉDER) to confer, to bestow, to grant; to compare.—*v.i.* to consult together, to confer.

confesse [kɔ̃'fɛs], *n.f.* (*always used with à* or *de*) *aller à confesse*, to go to confession; *venir de confesse*, to come from confession.

confesser [kɔ̃fɛ'se], *v.t.* to confess; to acknowledge, to admit; to shrive. **se confesser**, *v.r.* to confess one's sins, to confess (*to a priest*).

confesseur [kɔ̃fɛ'sœ:r], *n.m.* (father) confessor.

confession [kɔ̃fɛ'sjɔ̃], *n.f.* confession, acknowledgment, avowal.

confessionnal [kɔ̃fɛsjɔ'nal], *n.m.* confessional.

confetti [kɔ̃fɛt'ti], *n.m. pl.* confetti.

confiance [kɔ̃'fjɑ̃:s], *n.f.* confidence, reliance, trust.

confiant [kɔ̃'fjɑ̃], *a.* confident, unsuspecting, sanguine; self-conceited.

confidemment [kɔ̃fida'mɑ̃], *adv.* confidentially.

confidence [kɔ̃fi'dɑ̃:s], *n.f.* confidence; secret.

confident [kɔ̃fi'dɑ̃], *n.m.* (*fem.* **-ente**) confidant, confidante.

confidentiel [kɔ̃fidɑ̃'sjɛl], *a.* confidential.

confidentiellement [kɔ̃fidɑ̃sjɛl'mɑ̃], *adv.* confidentially.

confier [kɔ̃'fje], *v.t.* to confide, to entrust, to commit (*à*). **se confier**, *v.r.* to trust in; to unbosom oneself (*à*).

configuration [kɔ̃figyra'sjɔ̃], *n.f.* configuration, form, shape, lay (*of the land*).

confinement [kɔ̃fin'mɑ̃], *n.m.* confinement; overcrowding.

confiner [kɔ̃fi'ne], *v.t.* to confine, to imprison; *air confiné*, stuffy atmosphere.—*v.i.* to border upon, to be adjoining. **se confiner**, *v.r.* to confine *or* to limit oneself.

confins [kɔ'fɛ̃], *n.m. (used only in pl.)* confines, borders, limits.

confire [kɔ'fi:r], *v.t.* irr. to preserve; to candy, to pickle.

confirmatif [kɔ̃firma'tif], *a. (fem -tive)* confirmative.

confirmation [kɔ̃firma'sjɔ̃], *n.f.* confirmation, ratification.

confirmer [kɔ̃fir'me], *v.t.* to strengthen, to corroborate; to confirm; to ratify. **se confirmer**, *v.r.* to be confirmed.

confiscable [kɔ̃fis'kabl], *a.* confiscable, forfeitable.

confiscation [kɔ̃fiska'sjɔ̃], *n.f.* confiscation, forfeiture.

confiserie [kɔ̃fiz'ri], *n.f.* confectionery; confectioner's shop.

confiseur [kɔ̃fi'zœ:r], *n.m. (fem. -euse)* confectioner.

confisquer [kɔ̃fis'ke], *v.t.* to confiscate, to forfeit, to impound; to seize.

confit (1) [kɔ'fi], *p.p.* [CONFIRE].

confit (2) [kɔ'fi], *n.m.* meat, poultry etc. preserved in fat; bran mash *(for pigs etc.)*.

confiture [kɔ̃fi'ty:r], *n.f.* preserve, jam.

conflagration [kɔ̃flagra'sjɔ̃], *n.f.* conflagration.

conflit [kɔ'fli], *n.m.* conflict, collision, encounter; contention, strife, contest, rivalry; jar, clash.

confluent [kɔ̃fly'ɑ̃], *n.m.* confluence, junction *(of rivers)*.

confluer [kɔ̃fly'e], *v.i.* to meet, to unite *(of streams etc.)*.

confondre [kɔ'fɔ:dr], *v.t.* to confound, to confuse; to mix, to mingle; *(fig.)* to amaze, to astound. **se confondre**, *v.r.* to mingle, to be lost in; to be confounded, to be abashed.

conformation [kɔ̃forma'sjɔ̃], *n.f.* conformation, structure.

conforme [kɔ'form], *a.* conformable; congenial, consistent; *pour copie conforme*, certified true copy.

conformé [kɔ̃for'me], *a.* formed, shaped *(bien or mal)*.

conformément [kɔ̃forme'mɑ̃], *adv.* suitably; according to.

conformer [kɔ̃for'me], *v.t.* to give form to. **se conformer**, *v.r.* to conform, to comply *(with)*.

conformisme [kɔ̃for'mism], *n.m.* conformity, orthodoxy.

conformité [kɔ̃formi'te], *n.f.* likeness, conformity, compliance.

confort [kɔ'fɔ:r], *n.m.* comfort, ease.

confortable [kɔ̃for'tabl], *a.* cosy, comfortable.

confortablement [kɔ̃fortablə'mɑ̃], *adv.* comfortably.

confraternité [kɔ̃fraterni'te], *n.f.* fraternity, brotherhood.

confrère [kɔ'fre:r], *n.m.* colleague; fellow member.

confrérie [kɔ̃fre'ri], *n.f.* brotherhood, fraternity.

confrontation [kɔ̃frɔ̃ta'sjɔ̃], *n.f.* confrontation; comparing.

confronter [kɔ̃frɔ̃'te], *v.t.* to confront; to compare.

confus [kɔ'fy], *a.* confused, muddled, vague, indistinct, obscure; abashed, crestfallen.

confusément [kɔ̃fyze'mɑ̃], *adv.* confusedly, vaguely, dimly.

confusion [kɔ̃fy'zjɔ̃], *n.f.* confusion, disorder; bewilderment; embarrassment, shame, blush; misunderstanding.

congé [kɔ'ʒe], *n.m.* leave, permission; leave of absence, holiday; discharge, dismissal; notice (to quit); permit.

congédier [kɔ̃ʒe'dje], *v.t.* to discharge, to dismiss, to pay off; to disband.

congélateur [kɔ̃ʒela'tœ:r], *n.m.* refrigerator.

congeler [kɔ̃ʒ'le], *v.t.*, **se congeler**, *v.r. (conjug. like* AMENER) to congeal, to freeze; to coagulate.

congénère [kɔ̃ʒe'ne:r], *a.* congeneric; of same species; *(Philol.)* cognate.

congénial [kɔ̃ʒe'njal], *a. (m. pl. -aux)* congenial, of the same nature.

congénital [kɔ̃ʒeni'tal], *a. (m. pl. -aux)* congenital, hereditary.

congère [kɔ̃'ʒe:r], *n.f.* snowdrift.

congestion [kɔ̃ʒes'tjɔ̃], *n.f.* congestion.

conglomération [kɔ̃glomera'sjɔ̃], *n.f.* conglomeration.

conglomérer [kɔ̃glome're], *v.t. (conjug. like* CÉDER) to conglomerate.

congolais [kɔ̃go'le], *a.* Congolese.— (**Congolais**, *fem. -aise*) Congolese *(person)*.

congratulation [kɔ̃gratyla'sjɔ̃], *n.f.* congratulation.

congratulatoire [kɔ̃gratyla'twa:r], *a.* congratulatory.

congratuler [kɔ̃graty'le], *v.t.* to congratulate.

congre [kɔ̃:gr], *n.m.* conger, conger eel.

congrégation [kɔ̃grega'sjɔ̃], *n.f.* fraternity, brotherhood, general body *(of an order etc.)*.

congrès [kɔ̃'grɛ], *n.m.* congress.

congressiste [kɔ̃grɛ'sist], *n.m. (Am.)* congressman.

congru [kɔ̃'gry], *a.* suitable, consistent, congruous, proper.

congruité [kɔ̃gryi'te], *n.f.* congruity, consistency, propriety.

congrûment [kɔ̃gry'mɑ̃], *adv.* congruously, properly.

conifère [kɔni'fe:r], *a.* coniferous.—*n.m.* conifer.

conique [kɔ'nik], *a.* conical.

conjecture [kɔ̃ʒɛk'ty:r], *n.f.* conjecture, surmise, guess.

conjecturer [kɔ̃ʒɛkty're], *v.t.* to conjecture, to guess, to surmise.

conjoindre [kɔ̃'ʒwɛ̃:dr], *v.t.* irr. *(conjug. like* CRAINDRE) to conjoin, to unite together; to marry.

conjoint [kɔ̃'ʒwɛ̃], *a.* conjoined, united, joint. —*n.m. (fem. -e)* spouse.

conjointement [kɔ̃ʒwɛ̃t'mɑ̃], *adv.* conjointly, unitedly.

conjoncteur [kɔ̃ʒɔ̃k'tœ:r], *n.m. (Elec.)* circuit breaker, switch key.

conjonctif [kɔ̃ʒɔ̃k'tif], *a. (fem. -tive)* conjunctive.

conjonction [kɔ̃ʒɔ̃k'sjɔ̃], *n.f.* conjunction; union, connection; coition.

conjoncture [kɔ̃ʒɔ̃k'ty:r], *n.f.* conjuncture, juncture.

conjugaison [kɔ̃ʒygɛ'zɔ̃], *n.f.* conjugation.

conjugal [kɔ̃ʒy'gal], a. (m. pl. -aux) conjugal.
conjugalement [kɔ̃ʒygal'mɑ̃], adv. conjugally.
conjugué [kɔ̃ʒy'ge], a. (Mech.) twin.
conjuguer [kɔ̃ʒy'ge], v.t. (Gram.) to conjugate.
conjuration [kɔ̃ʒyrɑ'sjɔ̃], n.f. conspiracy, plot.
conjuré [kɔ̃ʒy're], a. confederate, sworn.—n.m. (fem. -ée) conspirator, plotter.
conjurer [kɔ̃ʒy're], v.t. to implore; to conspire; to swear; to conjure up; to exorcize, to ward off.
connaissable [kɔnɛ'sabl], a. recognizable.
connaissance [kɔnɛ'sɑ̃:s], n.f. knowledge, learning; consciousness (de); acquaintance; intercourse; (Law) cognizance; (pl.) attainments.
connaisseur [kɔnɛ'sœ:r], a. (fem. -euse) expert, skilled.—n.m. connoisseur, expert.
connaître [kɔ'nɛ:tr], v.t. irr. to know, to perceive; to understand; to be acquainted with.—v.i. to have or take cognizance of; to deal with (a matter). se connaître, v.r. to know oneself; to know each other; to be a connoisseur.
connecter [kɔnɛk'te], v.t. to connect; (Elec.) to couple (up), to group.
connétable [kɔnɛ'tabl], n.m. high constable.
connexion [kɔnɛk'sjɔ̃], n.f. connection, affinity.
connexité [kɔnɛksi'te], n.f. connection.
connivence [kɔni'vɑ̃:s], n.f. connivance.
connotation [kɔnɔta'sjɔ̃], n.f. connotation.
connu [kɔ'ny], a. known, understood.—n.m. that which is known.
conque [kɔ̃:k], n.f. conch, sea-shell.
conquérant [kɔ̃ke'rɑ̃], a. conquering.—n.m. (fem. -e) conqueror.
conquérir [kɔ̃ke'ri:r], v.t. irr. (conjug. like ACQUÉRIR) to conquer; to subdue (a country); (fig.) to gain, to win over.
conquête [kɔ̃'kɛ:t], n.f. conquest, acquisition.
conquis [kɔ̃'ki], a. conquered.
consacrant [kɔ̃sa'krɑ̃], a. consecrating, officiating.—n.m. consecrator, officiant.
consacrer [kɔ̃sa'kre], v.t. to consecrate, to dedicate, to sanctify; to sanction; to authorize. se consacrer, v.r. to devote oneself.
consciemment [kɔ̃sja'mɑ̃], adv. consciously, knowingly.
conscience [kɔ̃'sjɑ̃:s], n.f. consciousness, perception; conscience, conscientiousness.
consciencieusement [kɔ̃sjɑ̃sjøz'mɑ̃], adv. conscientiously.
consciencieux [kɔ̃sjɑ̃'sjø], a. (fem. -euse) conscientious.
conscient [kɔ̃'sjɑ̃], a. conscious (de); self-conscious.
conscription [kɔ̃skrip'sjɔ̃], n.f. enlistment; conscription.
conscrit [kɔ̃'skri], a. conscript.—n.m. conscript; (raw) recruit.
consécrateur [kɔ̃sekra'tœ:r], [CONSACRANT].
consécration [kɔ̃sekra'sjɔ̃], n.f. consecration; ordination.
consécutif [kɔ̃seky'tif], a. (fem. -tive) consecutive, following.
consécutivement [kɔ̃sekytiv'mɑ̃], adv. consecutively.
conseil [kɔ̃'sɛ:j], n.m. counsel, advice; resolution; council, board; (Law) counsel;

conseil d'administration, board of directors; Conseil d'État, Council of State; Conseil de Sécurité (de l'O.N.U.), (U.N.) Security Council; conseil judiciaire, guardian; conseil de guerre, court-martial; council of war; conseil municipal, town council, corporation.
conseiller [kɔ̃sɛ'je], v.t. to advise, to counsel; to recommend.—n.m. (fem. -ère) counsellor, adviser, councillor.
consensus [kɔ̃sɑ̃'sy:s], n.m. consent, consensus.
consentant [kɔ̃sɑ̃'tɑ̃], a. consenting, willing.
consentement [kɔ̃sɑ̃t'mɑ̃], n.m. consent, assent.
consentir [kɔ̃sɑ̃'ti:r], v.i. irr. (conjug. like SENTIR) to consent, to agree, to acquiesce (à).
conséquemment [kɔ̃seka'mɑ̃], adv. consequently, accordingly.
conséquence [kɔ̃se'kɑ̃:s], n.f. consequence, sequel; issue, result; inference, conclusion.
conséquent [kɔ̃se'kɑ̃], a. rational, consistent.—n.m. (Log., Math.) consequent; par conséquent, consequently.
conservateur [kɔ̃sɛrva'tœ:r], a. (fem. -trice) preserving, conservative.—n.m. (fem. -trice) Conservative, Tory.—n.m. guardian, keeper, curator.
conservatif [kɔ̃sɛrva'tif], a. (fem. -tive) conservative, preservative.—n.m. preservative.
conservation [kɔ̃sɛrva'sjɔ̃], n.f. conservation, preservation; registration (of mortgages etc.).
conservatisme [kɔ̃sɛrva'tism], n.m. conservatism.
Conservatoire [kɔ̃sɛrva'twa:r], n.m. academy of music and school of elocution in Paris.
conserve [kɔ̃'sɛrv], n.f. preserve; tinned (Am. canned) food.
conserver [kɔ̃sɛr've], v.t. to preserve; to keep. se conserver, v.r. to be preserved; to bear one's age well; to keep (of meat, fruit etc.).
considérable [kɔ̃side'rabl], a. considerable, notable, eminent; peu considérable, of little importance.
considérablement [kɔ̃siderabla'mɑ̃], adv. considerably.
considérant [kɔ̃side'rɑ̃], conj. phr. considérant que, whereas.
considération [kɔ̃sidera'sjɔ̃], n.f. consideration, attention; motive, grounds; regard, respect.
considérément [kɔ̃sidere'mɑ̃], adv. considerately, prudently.
considérer [kɔ̃side're], v.t. (conjug. like CÉDER) to consider, to look at, to view; to ponder; to value, to esteem; to pay attention to. se considérer, v.r. to esteem oneself.
consignataire [kɔ̃siɲa'tɛ:r], n. trustee, depositary.
consignateur [kɔ̃siɲa'tœ:r], n.m. (fem. -trice) (Comm.) consignor, shipper.
consignation [kɔ̃siɲa'sjɔ̃], n.f. (Comm.) deposit, consignment.
consigne [kɔ̃'siɲ], n.f. (Mil.) order, password; (fig.) strict command, prohibition; (Rail.) baggage check room, cloak-room; (sch.) gating, detention.

consigner [kɔ̃si'ɲe], v.t. to deposit; to consign; to record, to register; to keep in; to refuse admittance to.

consistance [kɔ̃sis'tɑ̃:s], n.f. consistency; firmness, stability; (fig.) credit, consideration.

consistant [kɔ̃sis'tɑ̃], a. consisting of; consistent, firm, solid.

consister [kɔ̃sis'te], v.i. to consist; to be composed of.

consistoire [kɔ̃sis'twa:r], n.m. consistory.

consolable [kɔ̃sɔ'labl], a. consolable.

consolant [kɔ̃sɔ'lɑ̃], a. consoling, comforting.

consolateur [kɔ̃sɔla'tœ:r], a. (fem. -trice) consoling.—n.m. (fem. -trice) comforter, consoler.

consolation [kɔ̃sɔla'sjɔ̃], n.f. consolation, comfort, solace.

console [kɔ̃'sɔl], n.f. console, bracket.

consoler [kɔ̃sɔ'le], v.t. to console, to comfort. **se consoler**, v.r. to console oneself.

consolidation [kɔ̃sɔlida'sjɔ̃], n.f. consolidation; strengthening; funding (of interest).

consolidé [kɔ̃sɔli'de], a. funded.—n.m. (Fin., used only in pl.) consols.

consolider [kɔ̃sɔli'de], v.t. to consolidate; to strengthen. **se consolider**, v.r. to consolidate, to grow firm.

consommable [kɔ̃sɔ'mabl], a. consumable, edible.

consommateur [kɔ̃sɔma'tœ:r], n.m. (fem. -trice) consumer (as opposed to producer), eater, drinker.

consommation [kɔ̃sɔma'sjɔ̃], n.f. consumption; consummation; food, drinks, refreshments.

consommé [kɔ̃sɔ'me], a. consumed; consummated; consummate; accomplished.—n.m. clear soup.

consommer [kɔ̃sɔ'me], v.t. to consume, to use; (fig.) to consummate, to accomplish.—v.i. (pop.) to have a drink.

consomption [kɔ̃sɔp'sjɔ̃], n.f. consumption, using up; (Path.) phthisis, decline.

consonance [kɔ̃sɔ'nɑ̃:s], n.f. consonance; (fig.) concord.

consonant [kɔ̃sɔ'nɑ̃], a. consonant.

consonne [kɔ̃'sɔn], n.f. consonant.

consort [kɔ̃'sɔ:r], a. consort (of the husband or wife of a sovereign).—n.m. (used only in pl.) consorts, confederates; (Law) associates.

consortium [kɔ̃sɔr'sjɔm], n.m. consortium.

conspirateur [kɔ̃spira'tœ:r], n.m. (fem. -trice) conspirator.—a. conspiring.

conspiration [kɔ̃spira'sjɔ̃], n.f. conspiracy, plot.

conspirer [kɔ̃spi're], v.t. to plot.—v.i. to conspire, to concur; to plot.

conspuer [kɔ̃s'pɥe], v.t. to despise, to spurn; to boo, to barrack.

constamment [kɔ̃sta'mɑ̃] adv. steadily, continually, constantly.

constance [kɔ̃s'tɑ̃:s], n.f. constancy; perseverance.

constant [kɔ̃s'tɑ̃], a. constant, faithful, unshaken; persevering.

constatation [kɔ̃stata'sjɔ̃], n.f. authentication; statement; findings.

constater [kɔ̃sta'te], v.t. to prove, to verify; to ascertain; to state, to declare.

constellation [kɔ̃stɛla'sjɔ̃], n.f. constellation.

constellé [kɔ̃stɛ'le], a. constellated; studded.

consteller [kɔ̃stɛ'le], v.t. to constellate, to stud.

consternation [kɔ̃stɛrna'sjɔ̃], n.f. consternation, dismay.

consterné [kɔ̃stɛr'ne], a. dismayed, overwhelmed.

consterner [kɔ̃stɛr'ne], v.t. to dismay, to dishearten; to astound, to amaze.

constipation [kɔ̃stipa'sjɔ̃], n.f. constipation, costiveness.

constipé [kɔ̃sti'pe], a. costive, constipated.

constiper [kɔ̃sti'pe], v.t. to constipate, to bind.

constituant [kɔ̃sti'tɥɑ̃], a. constituent.

constituer [kɔ̃sti'tɥe], v.t. to constitute; to establish; to appoint; to settle, to assign. **se constituer**, v.r. to constitute oneself.

constitution [kɔ̃stity'sjɔ̃], n.f. constitution; establishment; settlement (of an annuity etc.); temperament.

constitutionnel [kɔ̃stitysjɔ'nɛl], a. (fem. -elle) constitutional.

constitutionnellement [kɔ̃stitysjɔnɛl'mɑ̃], adv. constitutionally.

constriction [kɔ̃strik'sjɔ̃], n.f. constriction.

constringent [kɔ̃strɛ̃'ʒɑ̃], a. constringent.

constructeur [kɔ̃stryk'tœ:r], n.m. constructor, builder; shipbuilder, shipwright.

construction [kɔ̃stryk'sjɔ̃], n.f. building, construction; erection, structure.

constructivité [kɔ̃stryktivi'te], n.f. constructiveness.

construire [kɔ̃s'trɥi:r], v.t. irr. (conjug. like CONDUIRE) to construct, to build, to erect.

consul [kɔ̃'syl], n.m. consul.

consulaire [kɔ̃sy'lɛ:r], a. consular.

consulat [kɔ̃sy'la], n.m. consulate, consulship.

consultant [kɔ̃syl'tɑ̃], a. consulting.—n.m. (fem. -e) consultant, consulting physician.

consultatif [kɔ̃sylta'tif], a. (fem. -tive) consultative, deliberative.

consultation [kɔ̃sylta'sjɔ̃], n.f. consultation; opinion, advice; *cabinet de consultation*, surgery.

consulter [kɔ̃syl'te], v.t. to consult; to refer to.—v.i. to deliberate, to take counsel (together). **se consulter**, v.r. to consider, to reflect, to deliberate.

consumable [kɔ̃sy'mabl], a. consumable.

consumant [kɔ̃sy'mɑ̃], a. consuming, devouring, burning.

consumer [kɔ̃sy'me], v.t. to consume; to destroy, to wear out, to wear away, to squander, to waste. **se consumer**, v.r. to decay, to waste away, to wear out; to undermine one's health.

contact [kɔ̃'takt], n.m. contact; touch; connection; (Motor.) *clé de contact*, ignition key; (Opt.) *verres de contact*, contact lenses.

contagieux [kɔ̃ta'ʒjø], a. (fem. -euse) contagious, infectious.

contagion [kɔ̃ta'ʒjɔ̃], n.f. contagion, infection.

contamination [kɔ̃tamina'sjɔ̃], n.f. contamination, pollution.

contaminé [kɔ̃tami'ne], a. polluted, contaminated.

contaminer [kɔ̃tami'ne], v.t. to contaminate.

conte [kɔ̃:t], n.m. story, tale; (fig.) fib, fairytale.

contemplateur [kɔ̃tãpla'tœːr], _n.m._ (_fem._ **-trice**) contemplator.

contemplatif [kɔ̃tãpla'tif], _a._ (_fem._ **-tive**) contemplative.

contemplation [kɔ̃tãpla'sjɔ̃], _n.f._ contemplation, meditation.

contempler [kɔ̃tã'ple], _v.t._ to contemplate, to survey, to gaze on.—_v.i._ to contemplate, to meditate, to reflect.

contemporain [kɔ̃tãpo'rɛ̃], _a._ and _n.m._ (_fem._ **-e**) contemporary.

contempteur [kɔ̃tãp'tœːr], _a._ (_fem._ **-trice**) contemptuous, scornful, insolent, disdainful.—_n.m._ contemner, despiser, scorner.

contenance [kɔ̃t'nãːs], _n.f._ capacity; volume; (_fig._) countenance, air, bearing.

contenant [kɔ̃t'nã], _a._ holding, containing.—_n.m._ holder, container.

contenir [kɔ̃t'niːr], _v.t._ irr. (_conjug. like_ TENIR) to contain, to comprise, to hold, to include; to restrain. **se contenir**, _v.r._ to keep within bounds, to be moderate, to control oneself.

content [kɔ̃'tã], _a._ content, satisfied; pleased, glad, gratified.

contentement [kɔ̃tãt'mã], _n.m._ contentment, satisfaction; comfort, pleasure.

contenter [kɔ̃tã'te], _v.t._ to content, to satisfy; to please, to gratify. **se contenter**, _v.r._ to be satisfied, to be content.

contentieusement [kɔ̃tãsjøz'mã], _adv._ contentiously, litigiously.

contentieux [kɔ̃tã'sjø], _a._ (_fem._ **-euse**) contentious, disputable; litigious; in dispute; quarrelsome. — _n.m._ debatable matter; _bureau du contentieux_, legal department.

contention [kɔ̃tã'sjɔ̃], _n.f._ application, vehemence; contention, contest, debate, strife.

contenu [kɔ̃t'ny], _a._ contained; (_fig._) kept in control.—_n.m._ contents; enclosure; terms (_of a letter etc._).

conter [kɔ̃'te], _v.t._ to tell, to relate; _en conter_, to tell fibs.

contestable [kɔ̃tɛs'tabl], _a._ disputable, debatable.

contestant [kɔ̃tɛs'tã], _a._ contending (_at law_). —_n.m._ (_fem._ **-e**) contesting party, litigant.

contestation [kɔ̃tɛsta'sjɔ̃], _n.f._ contestation, contest; dispute, debate; litigation.

contester [kɔ̃tɛs'te], _v.t._ to dispute, to contest; to contend, to debate.—_v.i._ to quarrel; to be contentious.

conteur [kɔ̃'tœːr], _a._ (_fem._ **-euse**) who tells stories.—_n.m._ (_fem._ **-euse**) story teller; (_fig._) fibber.

contexte [kɔ̃'tɛkst], _n.m._ context; text (_of a deed_).

contexture [kɔ̃tɛks'tyːr], _n.f._ contexture (_of the muscles etc._); texture (_of materials_).

contigu [kɔ̃ti'gy], _a._ (_fem._ **-ë**) contiguous, adjoining.

contiguïté [kɔ̃tigɥi'te], _n.f._ contiguity.

continence [kɔ̃ti'nãːs], _n.f._ continency, chastity.

continent (1) [kɔ̃ti'nã], _a._ chaste, continent.

continent (2) [kɔ̃ti'nã], _n.m._ continent, mainland.

continental [kɔ̃tinã'tal], _a._ (_m. pl._ **-aux**) continental.

contingence [kɔ̃tɛ̃'ʒãːs], _n.f._ contingency, casualty.

contingent [kɔ̃tɛ̃'ʒã], _a._ contingent, accidental, casual.—_n.m._ quota; contingent.

continu [kɔ̃ti'ny], _a._ continuous, continual, uninterrupted; incessant.

continuation [kɔ̃tinɥa'sjɔ̃], _n.f._ continuation.

continuel [kɔ̃ti'nɥɛl], _a._ (_fem._ **-elle**) continual, perpetual.

continuellement [kɔ̃tinɥɛl'mã], _adv._ continually, perpetually.

continuer [kɔ̃ti'nɥe], _v.t._ to continue, to proceed with; to lengthen.—_v.i._ to continue, to keep on. **se continuer**, _v.r._ to be continued, to last.

continuité [kɔ̃tinɥi'te], _n.f._ continuity; continuance.

continûment [kɔ̃tiny'mã], _adv._ unremittingly, continuously, without cessation.

contorsion [kɔ̃tor'sjɔ̃], _n.f._ contortion; grimace.

contorsionniste [kɔ̃torsjo'nist], _n._ contortionist.

contour [kɔ̃'tuːr], _n.m._ circuit, circumference; contour, outline.

contourné [kɔ̃tur'ne], _a._ distorted, bizarre.

contournement [kɔ̃turne'mã], _n.m._ outlining, tracing; winding, convolution; _route de contournement_, by-pass (_road_).

contourner [kɔ̃tur'ne], _v.t._ to outline; to distort, to twist; to twist, turn, go _or_ wind round. **se contourner**, _v.r._ to grow crooked, to become bent.

contractant [kɔ̃trak'tã], _a._ _partie contractante_, contracting party.—_n.m._ (_fem._ **-e**) stipulator.

contracté [kɔ̃trak'te], _a._ contracted, shortened.

contracter [kɔ̃trak'te], _v.t._ to contract; to covenant, to stipulate, to bargain; to make a contract; to acquire. **se contracter**, _v.r._ to contract, to shrink; to shorten; to be settled by contract.

contraction [kɔ̃trak'sjɔ̃], _n.f._ contraction.

contractuel [kɔ̃trak'tɥɛl], _a._ (_fem._ **-elle**) stipulated, done by contract.

contractuellement [kɔ̃trak.ɥɛl'mã], _adv._ by contract.

contradicteur [kɔ̃tradik'tœːr], _n.m._ contradictor; (_Law_) adversary.

contradiction [kɔ̃tradik'sjɔ̃], _n.f._ contradiction, denial; opposition; discrepancy.

contradictoire [kɔ̃tradik'twaːr], _a._ contradictory, inconsistent, conflicting; _examen contradictoire_, cross-examination.

contraindre [kɔ̃'trɛ̃ːdr], _v.t._ irr. (_conjug. like_ CRAINDRE) to constrain, to compel, to coerce; to restrain; to squeeze. **se contraindre**, _v.r._ to restrain oneself, to refrain.

contraint [kɔ̃'trɛ̃], _a._ constrained, forced.

contrainte [kɔ̃'trɛ̃ːt], _n.f._ constraint, compulsion, coercion; restraint; uneasiness.

contraire [kɔ̃'trɛːr], _a._ contrary, opposite, inconsistent; adverse; prejudicial.—_n.m._ contrary, opposite, reverse.

contrairement [kɔ̃trɛr'mã], _adv._ contrarily, in opposition.

contralte [kɔ̃'tralt], **contralto** [kɔ̃tral'to], _n.m._ contralto, counter-tenor.

contrariant [kɔ̃tra'rjã], _a._ thwarting, annoying.

contrarier [kɔ̃tra'rje], _v.t._ to thwart, to counteract, to baffle; to annoy; to disappoint.

contrariété [kɔ̃trarje'te], n.f. contrariety, contradiction; annoyance; hindrance, disappointment; *quelle contrariété !* how annoying!

contrastant [kɔ̃tras'tɑ̃], a. contrasting.

contraste [kɔ̃'trast], n.m. contrast, opposition.

contraster [kɔ̃tras'te], v.t., v.i. to contrast.

contrat [kɔ̃'tra], n.m. contract, deed; agreement, bargain.

contravention [kɔ̃travɑ̃'sjɔ̃], n.f. contravention.

contre [kɔ̃:tr], prep. against, versus, contrary to; close up against, near; in exchange for; *ci-contre*, opposite, in the margin; *par contre*, on the other hand; *pour et contre*, pro and con.—adv. against.—n.m. the opposite side of the question; *le pour et le contre*, the pros and cons.

contre-allée [kɔ̃tra'le], n.f. side lane, side alley.

contre-amiral [kɔ̃trami'ral], n.m. (*pl.* contre-amiraux) rear-admiral.

contre-attaque [kɔ̃tra'tak], n.f. (*Mil.*) counter-attack.

contre-avions [kɔ̃tra'vjɔ̃], a. anti-aircraft.

contrebalancer [kɔ̃trəbalɑ̃'se], v.t. (*conjug. like* COMMENCER) to counterbalance, to counterpoise.

contrebande [kɔ̃trə'bɑ̃:d], n.f. contraband, smuggling; smuggled goods.

contrebandier [kɔ̃trəbɑ̃'dje], n.m. smuggler, gunrunner; smuggling vessel.

contre-bas (en) [ɑ̃kɔ̃trə'bɑ], adv. downwards.

contrebasse [kɔ̃trə'bɑ:s], n.f. double bass.

contre-bord (à) [akɔ̃trə'bɔ:r], adv. (*Naut.*) on the opposite tack.

contre-boutant [kɔ̃trəbu'tɑ̃], contreboutement [kɔ̃trəbut'mɑ̃], n.m. abutment, buttress.

contre-bouter [kɔ̃trəbu'te], v.t. to buttress; to shore up.

contrecarrer [kɔ̃trəka're], v.t. to thwart, to oppose.

contre-cœur [kɔ̃trə'kœ:r], n.m. chimneyback; *à contre-cœur*, reluctantly.

contre-coup [kɔ̃trə'ku], n.m. rebound, repercussion; (*fig.*) consequence, result; *par contre-coup*, as a consequence.

contredanse [kɔ̃trə'dɑ̃:s], n.f. quadrille.

contredire [kɔ̃trə'di:r], v.t. irr. (*conjug. like* MÉDIRE) to contradict, to gainsay; (*Law*) to disprove. se contredire, v.r. to contradict oneself; to be contradictory.

contredisant [kɔ̃trədi'zɑ̃], a. contradicting.

contredit [kɔ̃trə'di], n.m. contradiction; answer, reply; *sans contredit*, incontestably.

contrée [kɔ̃'tre], n.f. country, region, district.

contre-échange [kɔ̃tre'ʃɑ̃:ʒ], n.m. mutual exchange.

contre-écrou [kɔ̃tre'kru], n.m. lock nut.

contre-épreuve [kɔ̃tre'prœ:v], n.f. (*Engraving*) counter-proof; (*fig.*) feeble imitation.

contre-espionnage [kɔ̃trespjɔ'na:ʒ], n.m. counter-espionage.

contrefaçon [kɔ̃trəfa'sɔ̃], n.f. counterfeiting, forgery.

contrefacteur [kɔ̃trəfak'tœ:r], n.m. counterfeiter (*of coins etc.*); forger (*of bills etc.*); infringer (*of patents etc.*).

contrefaire [kɔ̃trə'fɛ:r], v.t. irr. (*conjug. like* FAIRE) to counterfeit, to imitate; to copy; to forge; to mimic; to disguise. se contrefaire, v.r. to dissemble, to sham.

contrefaiseur [kɔ̃trəfə'zœ:r], n.m. (*fem.* -euse) counterfeiter, mimic, imitator.

contrefait [kɔ̃trə'fɛ], a. counterfeit; deformed.

contre-fiche [kɔ̃trə'fiʃ], n.f. (*Carp.*) prop, strut.

contre-haut (en) [ɑ̃kɔ̃trə'o], adv. upwards.

contre-jour [kɔ̃trə'ʒu:r], n.m. (*Phot.*) low light; *à contre-jour*, against the light.

contremaître [kɔ̃trə'mɛ:tr], n.m. overseer, foreman.

contremander [kɔ̃trəmɑ̃'de], v.t. to countermand.

contremarche [kɔ̃trə'marʃ], n.f. countermarch.

contremarcher [kɔ̃trəmar'ʃe], v.i. to countermarch.

contremarque [kɔ̃trə'mark], n.f. countermark; (*Theat.*) pass-out check.

contre-mesure [kɔ̃trəmə'zy:r], n.f. countermeasure.

contre-offensive [kɔ̃trɔfɑ̃'si:v], n.f. counterattack.

contre-partie [kɔ̃trəpar'ti], n.f. counterpart; (*fig.*) opposite, contrary; return match.

contre-pédaler [kɔ̃trəpeda'le], v.i. to backpedal.

contre-pied [kɔ̃trə'pje], n.m. (*Hunt.*) backscent; (*fig.*) reverse way, contrary.

contre-plaqué [kɔ̃trəpla'ke], a. laminated. —n.m. two- (*or* three-) ply wood.

contrepoids [kɔ̃trə'pwa], n.m. inv. counterpoise, counter-balance; (*fig.*) equilibrium.

contre-poil [kɔ̃trə'pwal], n.m. wrong way of the hair *or* of the nap; *à contre-poil*, against the grain.

contrepoint [kɔ̃trə'pwɛ̃], n.m. counterpoint.

contrepoison [kɔ̃trəpwa'zɔ̃], n.m. antidote, counter-poison.

contre-poser [kɔ̃trəpo'ze], v.t. to misplace; (*Comm.*) to set down wrong.

contrer [kɔ̃'tre], v.t. (*Bridge*) to double.

contre-ressort [kɔ̃trərə'sɔ:r], n.m. shock absorber.

contre-révolution [kɔ̃trərevɔly'sjɔ̃], n.f. counter-revolution.

contre-saison (à) [akɔ̃trəsɛ'zɔ̃], adv. phr. (*flower*) produced out of season; ill-timed.

contresens [kɔ̃trə'sɑ̃:s], n.m. contrary sense, wrong construction *or* meaning; mistranslation; wrong side (*of material*).

contresigner [kɔ̃trəsi'ɲe], v.t. to countersign.

contretemps [kɔ̃trə'tɑ̃], n.m. inv. untoward accident, disappointment, mishap; (*Mus.*) syncopation; *à contretemps*, at the wrong time.

contre-torpilleur [kɔ̃trətɔrpi'jœ:r] n.m. torpedo-boat destroyer.

contrevenant [kɔ̃trəv'nɑ̃], n.m. (*fem.* -e) contravener, infringer, offender, transgressor.

contrevenir [kɔ̃trəv'ni:r], v.i. irr. (*conjug. like* TENIR) to contravene, infringe.

contrevent [kɔ̃trə'vɑ̃], n.m. outside windowshutter.

contribuable [kɔ̃tri'bɥabl], a. taxable. —n. tax-payer.

contribuer [kɔ̃tri'bɥe], v.i. to contribute, to pay; (*fig.*) to conduce, to be an accessory (à).

contributaire [kɔ̃triby'tɛːr], *a.* contributory.

contribution [kɔ̃triby'sjɔ̃], *n.f.* contribution; tax; share, portion; *contribution foncière*, land tax.

contrister [kɔ̃tris'te], *v.t.* to grieve, to vex, to sadden.

contrit [kɔ̃'tri], *a.* contrite, penitent; afflicted.

contrition [kɔ̃tri'sjɔ̃], *n.f.* contrition.

contrôlable [kɔ̃tro'labl], *a.* that may be checked, verified.

contrôle [kɔ̃'troːl], *n.m.* muster roll; roll, list; controller's office; stamp, hallmark; (*Theat.*) ticket-checking counter; (*fig.*) control, censure.

contrôler [kɔ̃tro'le], *v.t.* to register; to stamp; to check, to verify; to audit; to censure.

contrôleur [kɔ̃tro'lœːr], *n.m.* (*fem.* -euse) controller; (*Taxes, Theat., Rail.*) inspector; time-keeper; ticket collector; (*fig.*) critic.

controuver [kɔ̃tru've], *v.t.* to forge, to fabricate.

controversable [kɔ̃trover'sabl], *a.* controvertible, controversial.

controverse [kɔ̃tro'vɛrs], *n.f.* controversy, discussion, dispute.

controverser [kɔ̃trover'se], *v.t.* to dispute, to discuss.

contumace [kɔ̃ty'mas], *n.f.* contumacy, nonappearance or default, contempt of court; obstinacy.—*a.* contumacious.—*n.* defaulter.

contus [kɔ̃'ty], *a.* bruised, contused.

contusion [kɔ̃ty'zjɔ̃], *n.f.* contusion, bruise.

contusionner [kɔ̃tyzjɔ'ne], *v.t.* to contuse, to bruise.

convaincant [kɔ̃vɛ̃'kɑ̃], *a.* convincing.

convaincre [kɔ̃'vɛ̃ːkr], *v.t. irr.* (*conjug. like* VAINCRE) to convince; to persuade. **se convaincre,** *v.r.* to convince oneself.

convaincu [kɔ̃vɛ̃'ky], *a.* convinced; sincere; convicted.

convalescence [kɔ̃valɛ'sɑ̃ːs], *n.f.* convalescence.

convalescent [kɔ̃valɛ'sɑ̃], *a.* and *n.m.* (*fem.* -e) convalescent (person).

convection [kɔ̃vɛk'sjɔ̃], *n.f.* convection.

convenable [kɔ̃v'nabl], *a.* suitable, fit, proper; convenient; becoming.

convenablement [kɔ̃vnablə'mɑ̃], *adv.* suitably, becomingly, decently.

convenance [kɔ̃v'nɑ̃ːs], *n.f.* fitness, propriety; seasonableness (*of time*); decency, seemliness; (*pl.*) propriety, decorum; *mariage de convenance,* marriage of convenience.

convenir [kɔ̃v'niːr], *v.i. irr.* (*conjug. like* TENIR, *but with aux.* ÊTRE) to agree; to admit, to own, to acknowledge (*de*); (*with aux.* AVOIR) to suit, to fit, to match; (*impers.*) to be fitting. **se convenir,** *v.r.* to suit each other, to agree.

convention [kɔ̃vɑ̃'sjɔ̃], *n.f.* agreement, treaty; (*social and other*) convention; (*pl.*) conditions (*of an agreement*).

conventionnel [kɔ̃vɑ̃sjɔ'nɛl], *a.* (*fem.* -elle) conventional.

conventionnellement [kɔ̃vɑ̃sjɔnɛl'mɑ̃], *adv.* by agreement.

convenu [kɔ̃v'ny], *a.* agreed; conventional; banal.

convergent [kɔ̃vɛr'ʒɑ̃], *a.* convergent.

converger [kɔ̃vɛr'ʒe], *v.i.* (*conjug. like* MANGER) to converge.

conversation [kɔ̃vɛrsa'sjɔ̃], *n.f.* conversation, converse, talk.

converse [kɔ̃'vɛrs], *a.* and *n.f.* (*Log.*) converse; (*Math.*) inverted.

converser [kɔ̃vɛr'se], *v.i.* to converse, to discourse.

conversible [kɔ̃vɛr'sibl], [CONVERTIBLE].

conversion [kɔ̃vɛr'sjɔ̃], *n.f.* conversion; transformation; change.

converti [kɔ̃vɛr'ti], *n.m.* (*fem.* -e) convert.

convertible [kɔ̃vɛr'tibl], *a.* convertible.

convertir [kɔ̃vɛr'tiːr], *v.t.* to convert, to transform, to change, to turn. **se convertir,** *v.r.* to be converted, to turn.

convertissement [kɔ̃vɛrtis'mɑ̃], *n.m.* conversion.

convexe [kɔ̃'vɛks], *a.* convex.

convexité [kɔ̃vɛksi'te], *n.f.* convexity.

conviction [kɔ̃vik'sjɔ̃], *n.f.* conviction, convincing proof.

convié [kɔ̃'vje], *a.* invited.—*n.m.* (*fem.* -ée) guest.

convier [kɔ̃'vje], *v.t.* to invite, to bid; (*fig.*) to urge.

convive [kɔ̃'viv], *n.* guest; fellow diner.

convocation [kɔ̃voka'sjɔ̃], *n.f.* convocation; summons.

convoi [kɔ̃'vwa], *n.m.* (*Mil., Navy*) convoy; (*Rail. etc.*) train; *convoi funèbre,* funeral procession.

convoiter [kɔ̃vwa'te], *v.t.* to covet, to hanker after.

convoitise [kɔ̃vwa'tiːz], *n.f.* covetousness; lust.

convolution [kɔ̃voly'sjɔ̃], *n.f.* convolution.

convolvulus [kɔ̃volvy'lyːs], *n.m.* (*Bot.*) convolvulus.

convoquer [kɔ̃vo'ke], *v.t.* to convoke, to convene; to summon.

convoyer [kɔ̃vwa'je], *v.t.* (*conjug. like* EMPLOYER) to convoy, to escort.

convoyeur [kɔ̃vwa'jœːr], *n.m.* convoy (*ship*); (*Mech.*) conveyor.

convulser [kɔ̃vyl'se], *v.t.* to convulse. **se convulser,** *v.r.* to be or become convulsed.

convulsif [kɔ̃vyl'sif], *a.* (*fem.* -sive) convulsive.

convulsion [kɔ̃vyl'sjɔ̃], *n.f.* convulsion.

convulsionner [kɔ̃vylsjɔ'ne], *v.t.* (*Med.*) to convulse.

convulsivement [kɔ̃vylsiv'mɑ̃], *adv.* convulsively.

coolie or **coulis** [ku'li], *n.m.* coolie.

coopérateur [koopera'tœːr], *n.m.* (*fem.* -trice) co-operator, fellow workman.—*a.* (*fem.* -trice) co-operating.

coopératif [koopera'tif], *a.* (*fem.* -tive) co-operative.

coopération [koopera'sjɔ̃], *n.f.* co-operation.

coopérer [koope're], *v.i.* (*conjug. like* CÉDER) to co-operate.

coopter [koop'te], *v.t.* to co-opt.

coordination [koordina'sjɔ̃], *n.f.* co-ordination.

coordonné [koordo'ne], *a.* co-ordinate.—*n.f. pl.* (-ées) (*Gram., Geom.*) co-ordinates.

coordonner [koordo'ne], *v.t.* to co-ordinate.

copain [kɔ'pɛ̃], *n.m.* (*colloq.*) pal, mate.

copal [kɔ'pal], *n.m.* copal.

copeau [kɔ'po], *n.m.* (*pl.* -eaux) shaving, chip (*of wood*).

Copenhague [kɔpə'nag], *f.* Copenhagen.

85

cophte

cophte [COPTE].
copie [kɔ'pi], n.f. copy, transcript; reproduction; (Print.) 'copy'; candidate's paper.
copier [kɔ'pje], v.t. to copy; to imitate; to mimic.
copieusement [kɔpjøz'mã], adv. copiously, heartily (of drinking, eating).
copieux [kɔ'pjø], a. (fem. -euse) copious, plentiful.
co-pilote [kopi'lɔt], n.m. second pilot.
copiste [kɔ'pist], n. copier, transcriber, copyist.
copte or cophte [kɔpt], a. Coptic.—n. (Copte, Cophte) Copt.
coq [kɔk], n.m. cock, rooster; cock- (as opposed to hen); weathercock; au chant du coq, at cock-crow; coq de bruyère, grouse; coq d'Inde, turkey cock; poids coq, (Box.) bantam weight.
coq-à-l'âne [kɔka'la:n], n.m. inv. nonsense, cock-and-bull story.
coque [kɔk], n.f. shell (of eggs, walnuts, fruits, snails etc.); cocoon; cockle-shell (small boat); (Naut.) hull.
coquelicot [kɔkli'ko], n.m. corn-poppy.
coqueluche [kɔ'klyʃ], n.f. the rage, favorite; (Med.) whooping-cough.
coquerico [kɔkri'ko], n.m. cock-a-doodle-doo.
coqueriquer [kɔkri'ke], v.i. to crow.
coquet [kɔ'kɛ], a. (fem. -ette) coquettish; stylish, smart.—n.m. (fem. -ette) coquette, flirt; dandy.
coqueter [kɔk'te], v.i. (conjug. like APPELER) to coquet, to flirt.
coquetier [kɔk'tje], n.m. egg merchant, poulterer; egg cup.
coquetterie [kɔkɛ'tri], n.f. coquettishness, flirtation; affectation (in dress etc.).
coquillage [kɔki'ja:ʒ], n.m. shell-fish; shell.
coquille [kɔ'ki:j], n.f. shell (of shell-fish, egg, fruits etc.); (Cook.) Dutch oven; pat (of butter); (Print.) wrong letter; thumb (of a latch); (Ornament) conch.
coquin [kɔ'kɛ̃], a. roguish; rascally.—n.m. knave, rascal, rogue, scamp.—n.f. (-e) slut, hussy, jade.
coquinerie [kɔki'nri], n.f. knavery, rascality, roguery.
coquinet [kɔki'nɛ], n.m. little rascal.
cor (1) [kɔ:r], n.m. horn, hunting horn.
cor (2) [kɔ:r], n.m. corn (on the foot).
cor (3) [kɔ:r], n.m. tine (of antler).
corail [kɔ'ra:j], n.m. (pl. -aux) coral.
corailleur [kɔra'jœ:r], n.m. coral fisher; coral-fishing boat.
Coran [kɔ'rã], n.m. Koran.
corbeau [kɔr'bo], n.m. (pl. -eaux) crow; raven.
corbeille [kɔr'bɛ:j], n.f. flat, wide basket.
corbillard [kɔrbi'ja:r], n.m. hearse.
corbillon [kɔrbi'jõ], n.m. small basket; crambo (game).
corbin [kɔr'bɛ̃], n.m. crow.
corbine [kɔr'bin], n.f. carrion crow.
corbleu! [kɔr'blø], int. by Jove!
cordage [kɔr'da:ʒ], n.m. cord, rope, cordage, rigging.
corde [kɔrd], n.f. cord, rope; twine, twist; string (musical instrument, racquet); line; (Mus., Geom. etc.) chord; tone, note; corde à boyau, catgut.
cordé (1) [kɔr'de], a. twisted, corded.

cordé (2) [kɔr'de], a. cordate, heart-shaped.
cordeau [kɔr'do], n.m. (pl. -eaux) cord; line; fuse; tape.
cordée [kɔr'de], n.f. fishing line; line of roped mountaineers.
cordeler [kɔrdə'le], v.t. (conjug. like APPELER) to twist, to twine.
cordelette [kɔrdə'lɛt], n.f. small cord; string.
cordelier [kɔrdə'lje], n.m. Franciscan friar.
cordelière [kɔrdə'ljɛ:r], n.f. girdle (of dressing-gown etc.).
cordelle [kɔr'dɛl], n.f. towline, tow-rope.
corder [kɔr'de], v.t. to twist (into cord); to cord; to bind with a cord; to string (racquet). se corder, v.r. to be corded; to become stringy (of plants etc.).
corderie [kɔr'dri], n.f. rope walk.
cordial [kɔr'djal], a. (m. pl. -aux) cordial, hearty, sincere.—n.m. cordial.
cordialement [kɔrdjal'mã], adv. cordially, heartily, sincerely.
cordialité [kɔrdjali'te], n.f. cordiality, heartiness.
cordier [kɔr'dje], n.m. rope maker.
Cordillères [kɔrdi'jɛ:r], les, f.pl. the Cordilleras.
cordite [kɔr'dit], n.f. cordite.
cordon [kɔr'dõ], n.m. strand (of a rope); twist; string; cord; ribbon (of an order); border, edging; cordon bleu, blue ribbon, first-rate cook.
cordonner [kɔrdɔ'ne], v.t. to twist, to twine, to braid; to mill (coins).
cordonnerie [kɔrdɔn'ri], n.f. shoe-making; cobbler's shop.
cordonnet [kɔrdɔ'nɛ], n.m. twist; milled edge (of coins).
cordonnier [kɔrdɔ'nje], n.m. shoe-maker.
Corée [kɔ're], la, f. Korea.
coréen [kɔre'ɛ̃], a. (fem. -enne) Korean.—n.m. Korean (language); (Coréen, fem. -enne) Korean (person).
coriace [kɔ'rjas], a. tough, leathery; (fig.) close, niggardly; dogged.
coricide [kɔri'sid], n.m. corn cure.
corinthien [kɔrɛ̃'tjɛ̃], a. (fem. -enne) Corinthian.—n.m. (Corinthien, fem.-enne) Corinthian.
coris [CAURI].
corli [kɔr'li], courlis [kur'li], corlieu [kɔr'ljø], n.m. curlew.
cormoran [kɔrmɔ'rã], n.m. cormorant.
cornac [kɔr'nak], n.m. elephant driver, mahout; mentor.
corne [kɔrn], n.f. horn, hoof; shoe horn; dog's-ear (on books, leaves); chapeau à trois cornes, three-cornered hat.
corné [kɔr'ne], a. corneous, horny.
cornée [kɔr'ne], n.f. cornea.
corneille [kɔr'nɛ:j], n.f. crow, rook, jackdaw.
cornement [kɔrnə'mã], n.m. buzzing in the ears.
cornemuse [kɔrnə'my:z], n.f. bagpipes.
corner (1) [kɔr'ne], v.t. to blurt out, to trumpet; to dog's-ear (a leaf).—v.i. to blow, wind or sound a horn; to tingle (of the ears).
corner (2) [kɔr'nɛ], n.m. (Ftb.) corner (-kick).
cornet [kɔr'nɛ], n.m. horn, hooter; ink-horn; cone.
cornette [kɔr'nɛt], n.f. mob-cap; pennant of cavalry.
corniche [kɔr'niʃ], n.f. cornice; ledge.

cornichon [kɔrni'ʃɔ̃], n.m. gherkin; (fig.) greenhorn.
corniste [kɔr'nist], n. horn player.
Cornouaille [kɔr'nwa:j], la, f. Cornwall.
cornu [kɔr'ny], a. horned; angular, cornered; (fig.) absurd.
cornue [kɔr'ny], n.f. (Chem.) retort.
corollaire [kɔrɔ'lɛ:r], n.m. corollary.
corolle [kɔ'rɔl], n.f. corolla.
coronaire [kɔrɔ'nɛ:r], a. (Anat.) coronary.
coronal [kɔrɔ'nal], a. (m. pl. -aux) (Anat.) coronal.
corporation [kɔrpɔra'sjɔ̃], n.f. corporation, corporate body.
corporel [kɔrpɔ'rɛl], a. (fem. -elle) corporal, bodily.
corps [kɔ:r], n.m. body; matter, substance; thickness, consistence; chief part; corporation, company; society, college; corps; fellow creature; à corps perdu, desperately; à son corps défendant, (fig.) reluctantly; corps à corps, hand to hand, (Box.) in-fight(ing); corps morts, (Naut.) fixed moorings; garde du corps, life-guard; sombrer corps et biens, to founder with all hands.
corpulence [kɔrpy'lɑ̃:s], n.f. corpulence, stoutness.
corpulent [kɔrpy'lɑ̃], a. corpulent, stout.
corpuscule [kɔrpys'kyl], n.m. corpuscule, corpuscle.
correct [kɔ'rɛkt], a. correct, accurate.
correctement [kɔrɛkt'mɑ̃], adv. correctly, accurately.
correctif [kɔrɛk'tif], a. (fem. -tive) corrective.—n.m. corrective.
correction [kɔrɛk'sjɔ̃], n.f. correction; correctness, accuracy; (Print.) reading, alteration (of a proof etc.); (fig.) reprimand, reproof; punishment; thrashing.
correctionnel [kɔrɛksjɔ'nɛl], a. (fem. -elle) within the jurisdiction of the tribunal de police correctionnelle, court of petty sessions.
corrélation [kɔrela'sjɔ̃], n.f. correlation.
correspondance [kɔrɛspɔ̃'dɑ̃:s], n.f. correspondence; connection; intercourse; conformity; (Rail.) connection.
correspondant [kɔrɛspɔ̃'dɑ̃], a. correspondent, corresponding.—n.m. (fem. -e) correspondent, corresponding member.
correspondre [kɔrɛs'pɔ̃:dr], v.i. to correspond, to communicate, to be in correspondence; to agree.
corridor [kɔri'dɔ:r], n.m. corridor, gallery, passage.
corrigé [kɔri'ʒe], n.m. corrected (schoolboy's) exercise; key (book), crib.
corriger [kɔri'ʒe], v.t. (conjug. like MANGER) to correct, to rectify; to repair, to amend; to reprove, to chide, to chastise. se corriger, v.r. to correct oneself, to amend, to reform.
corroboration [kɔrɔbɔra'sjɔ̃], n.f. corroboration, strengthening.
corroborer [kɔrɔbɔ're], v.t. to strengthen; to corroborate.
corrodant [kɔrɔ'dɑ̃], a. corroding, corrosive.
corroder [kɔrɔ'de], v.t. to corrode.
corrompre [kɔ'rɔ̃:pr], v.t. (conjug. like ROMPRE) to corrupt, to infect; to spoil; to taint (meat); (fig.) to pervert; to bribe. se

corrompre, v.r. to grow corrupt; to become tainted.
corrompu [kɔrɔ̃'py], a. corrupted, unsound; bribed.
corrosif [kɔrɔ'zif], a. (fem. -sive) and n.m. corrosive.
corrosion [kɔrɔ'zjɔ̃], n.f. corrosion.
corroyer [kɔrwa'je], v.t. (conjug. like EMPLOYER) to curry (leather); to plane (wood).
corroyeur [kɔrwa'jœːr], n.m. currier.
corrupteur [kɔryp'tœːr], a. (fem. -trice) corrupting, perverting, infectious.—n.m. (fem. -trice) corrupter, seducer; briber.
corruptibilité [kɔryptibili'te], n.f. corruptibility.
corruptible [kɔryp'tibl], a. corruptible.
corruptif [kɔryp'tif], a. (fem. -tive) corruptive.
corruption [kɔryp'sjɔ̃], n.f. corruption; rottenness; (fig.) depravity; (Polit.) bribery.
corsage [kɔr'sa:ʒ], n.m. chest (of the body); corsage, bodice.
corsaire [kɔr'sɛːr], n.m. privateer, corsair; (fig.) shark.
Corse [kɔrs], la, f. Corsica.—n. Corsican (person).
corse [kɔrs], a. Corsican.
corsé [kɔr'se], a. rich, full-bodied; (colloq.) strong, thick; (of stories etc.) spicy.
corser [kɔr'se], v.t. to stiffen, to thicken; to complicate.
corset [kɔr'sɛ], n.m. corset, stays.
corsetier [kɔrsə'tje], n.m. (fem. -ière) corset maker.
cortège [kɔr'tɛ:ʒ], n.m. train, retinue, suite, procession.
corvée [kɔr've], n.f. (Feud.) forced or statute labor; fatigue party; (fig.) drudgery.
corvette [kɔr'vɛt], n.f. corvette, sloop of war.
Cosaque [kɔ'zak], n.m. Cossack.
cosinus [kɔsi'ny:s], n.m. cosine.
cosmétique [kɔsme'tik], a. and n.m. cosmetic.
cosmique [kɔs'mik], a. cosmic.
cosmographie [kɔsmɔgra'fi], n.f. cosmography.
cosmopolite [kɔsmɔpɔ'lit], n. cosmopolite.—a. cosmopolitan.
cosmos [kɔs'mos], n.m. cosmos.
cosse [kɔs], n.f. pod, shell, husk, rind.
cossu [kɔ'sy], a. substantial, wealthy.
costume [kɔs'tym], n.m. costume, dress; uniform.
costumer [kɔsty'me], v.t. to dress (in a certain style etc.). se costumer, v.r. to dress (oneself) up.
costumier [kɔsty'mje], n.m. (fem. -ière) costumier.
cote [kɔt], n.f. quota, share; letter, number, figure (to indicate order etc.); (St. Exch.) quotation; (Comm.) price list; odds.
côte [ko:t], n.f. rib (of the body, cloth, fruit etc.); slope, hill; shore, sea coast; à mi-côte, half-way up.
côté [ko'te], n.m. side; part, quarter, hand, way, direction; face, aspect; à côté de, by, near; d'à côté, adjoining, next.
coté [kɔ'te], a. marked; classed; backed; point coté, (on a map) trig-point; cheval bien coté, well-backed horse.
coteau [kɔ'to], n.m. (pl. -eaux) slope; little hill.

côtelette [ko'tlɛt], n.f. cutlet, chop.

coter [ko'te], v.t. to number; to price; (*St. Exch.*) to quote.

coterie [ko'tri], n.f. coterie, set, circle, clique.

cothurne [ko'tyrn], n.m. buskin.

côtier [ko'tje], a. (*fem.* **-ière**) coasting.—n.m. coaster (*ship*).

cotillon [koti'jɔ̃], n.m. under-petticoat; cotillion.

cotisation [kotiza'sjɔ̃], n.f. assessment, quota, share; subscription.

cotiser [koti'ze], v.t. to assess, to rate. **se cotiser**, v.r. to club together; to get up a subscription, to subscribe.

coton [ko'tɔ̃], n.m. cotton; fluff, down (*of fruit, and hair on the face*);absorbent cotton.

cotonnade [koto'nad], n.f. cotton cloth.

cotonné [koto'ne], a. covered with or full of cotton; downy; woolly (*of hair*); padded.

cotonner [koto'ne], v.t. to fill or to stuff with cotton; to pad. **se cotonner**, v.r. to be covered with down.

cotonneux [koto'nø], a. (*fem.* **-euse**) cottony, downy; spongy, mealy.

cotonnier [koto'nje], n.m. cotton bush.

côtoyer [kotwa'je], v.t. (*conjug. like* EMPLOYER) to go by the side of, to skirt; to coast; (*fig.*) to keep close to.

cotre [ko:tr], n.m. cutter (*vessel*).

cotret [ko'trɛ], n.m. faggot; stick.

cottage [ko'ta:ʒ], n.m. cottage.

cotte [kot], n.f. short petticoat; (*engineer's*) overalls.

cotuteur [koty'tœ:r], n.m. (*fem.* **-trice**) joint guardian.

cou [ku], n.m. neck.

couac [kwak], n.m. false note; squawk.

couard [kwa:r], a. coward, cowardly.—n.m. (*fem.* **-e**) coward.

couardise [kwar'di:z], n.f. cowardice.

couchage [ku'ʃa:ʒ], n.m. act of lying in bed; bed, night's lodging; bedding.

couchant [ku'ʃɑ̃], a. setting; lying; (*fig.*) fawning; *un chien couchant*, a setter.—n.m. west; (*fig.*) decline.

couche [kuʃ], n.f. bed, couch; confinement; diaper; layer, row; (*Min.*) seam; (*Gard.*) hotbed, bed; coat (*of varnish or color*); (*fig.*) social stratum.

couché [ku'ʃe], a. in bed, gone to bed, lying down, recumbent; (*Her.*) couchant.

couchée [ku'ʃe], n.f. act of lying down; sleeping place; night's lodging.

coucher [ku'ʃe], v.t. to put to bed; to lay down; to knock down; to lay on; to stake.—v.i. to sleep, to lie (down), to rest; *coucher à la belle étoile*, to sleep in the open air. **se coucher**, v.r. to go to bed; to lie down; to set, to go down (*of the sun etc.*).—n.m. going to bed; bed time; setting (*of the sun etc.*).

couchette [ku'ʃɛt], n.f. small bed, crib; berth; bunk (*on a ship*); *wagon à couchettes*, second-class sleeper.

coucou [ku'ku], n.m. cuckoo; cuckoo clock; (*Bot.*) cowslip.

coude [kud], n.m. elbow; bend, angle; turning.

coudé [ku'de], a. bent, elbowed, cranked.

coudée [ku'de], n.f. length of arm from elbow to tip of middle finger, cubit.

cou-de-pied [kud'pje], n.m. (*pl.* **cous-depied**) instep.

couder [ku'de], v.t. to bend, to make an elbow in. **se couder**, v.r. to elbow, to form an elbow.

coudoyer [kudwa'je], v.t. (*conjug. like* EMPLOYER) to elbow, to jostle. **se coudoyer**, v.r. to elbow or jostle each other.

coudraie [ku'drɛ], n.f. hazel copse; filbert orchard.

coudre [kudr], v.t. irr. to sew, to stitch; (*fig.*) to attach, to connect.

coudrier [ku'drje], n.m. hazel tree.

couenne [kwan], n.f. scraped pig-skin; crackling (*of pork*); rind; (*Med.*) birthmark.

couette [kwɛt], **coit(t)e** (2) [kwat], n.f. feather-bed; sea-gull; (*hare's*) scut.

couguar [ku'ga:r], n.m. cougar, puma.

coulage [ku'la:ʒ], n.m. flow (*of metal in fusion*); melting, casting; leakage, waste; pilferage.

coulant [ku'lɑ̃], a. flowing, smooth, natural (*of style etc.*); (*fig.*) easy; *nœud coulant*, slip knot.—n.m. sliding ring (*for a necktie, umbrella etc.*).

coulé [ku'le], n.m. (*Mus.*) slur; (*Billiards*) follow through; (*Swim.*) plunge.

coulée [ku'le], n.f. running hand (*of writing*); (*Metal.*) tapping; flow, rush (*of a torrent etc.*); (*Hunt.*) track, path.

couler [ku'le], v.t. to cast; to strain; to slip (*dans*); to sink, to run down; (*Mus.*) to slur.—v.i. to flow; to glide; to trickle; to leak; to slip away (*of time etc.*); to founder (*of a ship etc.*). **se couler**, v.r. to slip, to creep, to steal, to glide; to be cast (*of metals*).

couleur [ku'lœ:r], n.f. color; coloring-matter, paint; coloring; (*fig.*) appearance; pretence; suit (*at cards*).

couleuvre [ku'lœ:vr], n.f. (grass) snake.

coulis [ku'li], n.m. strained juice from meat etc. slowly stewed.

coulisse [ku'lis], n.f. groove, channel; running string; (*Theat.*) wing; (*fig.*) behind the scenes; *porte à coulisse*, sliding door; *faire les yeux en coulisse*, to make sheep's eyes.

coulissé [kuli'se], a. grooved.

coulissier [kuli'sje], n.m. stock jobber, outside broker.

couloir [ku'lwa:r], n.m. passage, corridor, lobby, gangway.

couloire [ku'lwa:r], n.f. colander, strainer.

coup [ku], n.m. blow, stroke, hit, thump, knock, stab, thrust; beat (*of a drum*); draft (*of liquids*); clap (*of thunder*); (*Artill.*) charge; gust (*of wind*); throw; shot; moment; bout; attempt; deed; event; *à coup sûr*, unquestionably; (*Ftb.*) *coup d'envoi*, kick-off; *coup d'œil*, glance; *coup de téléphone*, telephone call; *le coup de grâce*, the finishing stroke; *tout à coup*, all of a sudden; *tout d'un coup*, all at once.

coupable [ku'pabl], a. culpable, guilty.—n. guilty person, culprit.

coupage [ku'pa:ʒ], n.m. cutting; diluting (*of wine*); blending (*of spirits*).

coupant [ku'pɑ̃], a. cutting, sharp.—n.m. edge (*of a sword etc.*).

coupe (1) [kup], n.f. cutting, felling (*of wood*); wood felled; the cut end; cut (*clothes etc.*); shape; (*Pros.*) cadence; (*Swim.*) overarm stroke.

coupe (2) [kup], *n.f.* cup, goblet, chalice; basin (*of a fountain etc.*).

coupé (1) [ku'pe], *a.* intersected; diluted; (*fig.*) laconic.

coupé (2) [ku'pe], *n.m.* coupé (*kind of brougham*); a dance step.

[In the following compounds *coupe* is *inv.*]

coupe-circuit [kupsir'kɥi], *n.m. inv.* cut-out, circuit breaker; fuse.

coupée [ku'pe], *n.f.* (*Naut.*) gangway; *échelle de coupée*, accommodation ladder.

coupe-file [kup'fil], *n.m. inv.* police pass.

coupe-gorge [kup'gɔrʒ], *n.m. inv.* cut-throat place, den.

coupe-jarret [kupʒa'rɛ], *n.m.* cut-throat, assassin, ruffian.

coupe-papier [kuppa'pje], *n.m. inv.* paper knife.

couper [ku'pe], *v.t.* to cut; to dock; to strike off; to clip; to pare; to geld; (*Mil.*) to intercept; to dilute (*milk, wine, with water*); to intersect; to interrupt.—*v.i.* to make an incision; to cut, to trump (*at cards*). **se couper**, *v.r.* to cut oneself; to intersect.

couperet [ku'prɛ], *n.m.* (*butcher's*) chopper; knife (*of guillotine*).

couperose [ku'pro:z], *n.f.* copperas.

couperosé [kupro'ze], *a.* blotched.

coupeur [ku'pœ:r], *n.m.* (*fem.* **-euse**) cutter. —*n.f.* (**-euse**) cutting machine.

(C) **coupe-vent** [kup'vã], *n.m.* wind breaker.

couplage [ku'pla:ʒ], *n.m.* coupling.

couple [kupl], *n.f.* brace, couple.—*n.m.* married couple; pair (*of animals, male and female*); (*Naut.*) frame.

coupler [ku'ple], *v.t.* to couple, to link.

couplet [ku'plɛ], *n.m.* couplet; verse of song; (*fig.*) tirade; (*Tech.*) hinge.

coupleur [ku'plœ:r], *n.m.* (*Elec.*) make-and-break, cut-out.

coupoir [ku'pwa:r], *n.m.* cutter (*instrument*).

coupole [ku'pɔl], *n.f.* cupola; (*Naut.*) revolving gun turret.

coupon [ku'pɔ̃], *n.m.* remnant; coupon; dividend check, check; (*Theat.*) ticket.

coupure [ku'py:r], *n.f.* cut, incision, slit; cutting; suppression; drain; (*Banking*) small note.

cour [ku:r], *n.f.* court (*of a prince, of justice etc.*); yard, courtyard; (*fig.*) courtship, suit.

courage [ku'ra:ʒ], *n.m.* courage, daring; spirit, mettle; fortitude, greatness of soul.

courageusement [kuraʒøz'mã], *adv.* courageously, bravely, resolutely.

courageux [kura'ʒø], *a.* (*fem.* **-euse**) courageous, daring, fearless, plucky.

couramment [kura'mã], *adv.* fluently, readily.

courant [ku'rã], *a.* running; current, present; usual; fair, middling (*of goods*); lineal (*of measures*).—*n.m.* stream, current, tide; course (*of time etc.*); routine; present price; present (*time*).

courbage [kur'ba:ʒ], *n.m.* bending, curving.

courbatu [kurba'ty], *a.* foundered (*of horses*); stiff in the joints; (*Med.*) affected with lumbago.

courbature [kurba'ty:r], *n.f.* foundering, lameness; (*Path.*) stiffness in the limbs, lumbago.

courbaturer [kurbaty're], *v.t.* to make (*someone*) feel stiff all over.

courbe [kurb], *a.* curved, bent, crooked.—*n.f.* curve; (*Naut., Carp.*) knee; (*Vet.*) curb; (*Math.*) graph.

courber [kur'be], *v.t.* to curve, to bend, to warp, to make crooked.—*v.i.* to bend, to sag. **se courber**, *v.r.* to bend, to stoop; to bow down.

courbette [kur'bɛt], *n.f.* curvet; (*pl.*) bowing and scraping, cringing.

courbetter [kurbe'te], *v.i.* to curvet.

courbure [kur'by:r], *n.f.* curvature, curve; bend; sagging.

coureur [ku'rœ:r], *a.* (*fem.* **-euse**) swift.— *n.m.* runner, racer; hunter (*horse*); light porter; rover; rake, libertine; (*Mil.*) scout.

courge [kurʒ], *n.f.* gourd; *courge à la moelle*, vegetable marrow, squash.

courir [ku'ri:r], *v.t. irr.* to pursue; to travel over; to hunt, to frequent; to expose oneself to.—*v.i.* to run; to hasten; to ramble, to rove; to flow; to stretch; to circulate.

courlis [kur'li], **courlieu** [kur'ljø], *n.m.* curlew.

couronne [ku'rɔn], *n.f.* crown; coronet; wreath; crown (*a coin*).

couronnement [kurɔn'mã], *n.m.* crowning, coronation; completion.

couronner [kurɔ'ne], *v.t.* to crown; to award a prize, to honor (*avec*); to consummate; to wreathe.

courre [ku:r], *v.t.* only used in *chasse à courre*, hunting.

courrier [ku'rje], *n.m.* messenger, courier; mail, post; letters, correspondence.

courriériste [kurje'rist], *n.m.* columnist.

courroie [ku'rwa], *n.f.* strap, thong; driving belt or band.

courroucer [kuru'se], *v.t.* (*conjug. like* COMMENCER) to provoke, to anger, to incense, to irritate. **se courroucer**, *v.r.* to become angry, to rage.

courroux [ku'ru], *n.m.* wrath, anger, rage.

cours [ku:r], *n.m.* course, stream, current, flow; lapse; path, orbit; vent, scope; public drive or walk; vogue; currency; series of lectures; (*pl.*) classes; (*St. Exch.*) market price, rate.

course [kurs], *n.f.* running, run; course; drive, walk, excursion; career; race; errand; privateering; cruise; length of the stroke (*of a piece of machinery*).

coursier [kur'sje], *n.m.* charger; (*poet.*) steed; (*Naut.*) bow gun.

coursive [kur'si:v], *n.f.* (*Naut.*) gangway.

court (1) [ku:r], *a.* short; brief; concise, curt; limited, scanty; fleeting.—*adv.* short, abruptly; *demeurer court*, to stop short; *être à court d'argent*, to be short of money.

court (2) [kort, ku:r], *n.m.* tennis court.

courtage [kur'ta:ʒ], *n.m.* brokerage, commission.

courtaud [kur'to], *a.* thick-set, dumpy; docked, crop-eared.—*n.m.* (*fem.* **-e**) short, thick-set person; docked or crop-eared horse.

courtauder [kurto'de], *v.t.* to dock, to crop (*horses etc.*).

court-circuit [kursir'kɥi], *n.m.* (*pl.* **courts-circuits**) short circuit.

court-circuiter [kursirkɥi'te], *v.t.* to short-circuit.

courtement [kurtə'mã], *adv.* shortly, briefly.

courtepointe [kurtə'pwɛ:t], *n.f.* counterpane, quilt.

courtier [kur'tje], *n.m.* (*fem.* **-ière**) broker, agent.

courtil [kur'til], *n.m.* *small garden; garth.

courtisan [kurti'zã], *n.m.* courtier; fawner.

courtisane [kurti'zan], *n.f.* courtesan.

courtisanerie [kurtizan'ri], *n.f.* court flattery, toadyism.

courtisanesque [kurtiza'nɛsk], *a.* courtier-like.

courtiser [kurti'ze], *v.t.* to court; to woo; to flatter.

courtois [kur'twa] *a.* courteous, polite.

courtoisement [kurtwaz'mã], *adv.* courteously.

courtoisie [kurtwa'zi], *n.f.* courtesy; kindness, good turn.

couseur [ku'zœ:r], *n.m.* (*fem.* **-euse**) sewer, stitcher (*of books*).

cousin [ku'zɛ̃], *n.m.* (*fem.* **-e**) cousin; (*fig.*) friend, crony.

cousinage [kuzi'na:ʒ], *n.m.* cousinhood; cousins; relationship.

cousiner [kuzi'ne], *v.t.* to call cousin; to hob-nob with.—*v.i.* to live on others; to be friends *or* cronies.

coussin [ku'sɛ̃], *n.m.* cushion, hassock; pad.

coussiner [kusi'ne], *v.t.* to pad, to cushion.

coussinet [kusi'ne], *n.m.* small cushion, pad; iron wedge; pillion.

cousu [ku'zy], *a.* sewn, stitched.

coût [ku], *n.m.* costs, charge; *le coût de la vie*, the cost of living.

coûtant [ku'tã], *a.* costing; *à prix coûtant*, at cost price.

couteau [ku'to], *n.m.* (*pl.* **-eaux**) knife.

coutelas [kut'la], *n.m.* cutlass.

coutelier [kutə'lje], *n.m.* cutler.

coutelière [kutə'ljɛ:r], *n.f.* knife case; cutler's wife.

coutellerie [kutɛl'ri], *n.f.* cutler's shop *or* business; cutlery.

coûter [ku'te], *v.t.* to cost, to cause, to occasion.—*v.i.* to cost (*cher etc.*); to be expensive; (*fig.*) to be painful, troublesome.

coûteusement [kutøz'mã], *adv.* expensively.

coûteux [ku'tø], *a.* (*fem.* **-euse**) expensive, costly.

coutil [ku'ti], *n.m.* tick, ticking; (*Tex.*) drill.

coutre [kutr], *n.m.* plough-share, coulter, axe.

coutume [ku'tym], *n.f.* custom, habit, practice.

coutumier [kuty'mje], *a.* (*fem.* **-ière**) customary, common, ordinary; habitual.

couture [ku'ty:r], *n.f.* sewing, needlework; seam, suture; scar.

couturer [kuty're], *v.t.* to seam.

couturier [kuty'rje], *n.m.* ladies' tailor.—*a.* sartorial.

couturière [kuty'rjɛ:r], *n.f.* dressmaker, seamstress.

couvage [ku'va:ʒ], **couvaison** [kuve'zõ], *n.f.* brooding-time, sitting, incubation.

couvée [ku've], *n.f.* sitting (*of eggs*); brood, covey.

couvent [ku'vã], *n.m.* convent, monastery, nunnery; convent school.

couver [ku've], *v.t.* to sit on, to incubate, to hatch; to brood, to prepare in secret (*a plot etc.*); to brood over.—*v.i.* to lie hidden, to lurk; to smoulder.

couvercle [ku'vɛrkl], *n.m.* cover, lid, cap, shutter.

couvert [ku'vɛ:r], *a.* covered; clad, clothed; cloudy, overcast; obscure, ambiguous (*of words*).—*n.m.* cover (*plate, spoon, knife, fork*); shelter; cover, wrapper; covert, thicket; *le vivre et le couvert*, board and lodging.

couverte [ku'vɛrt], *n.f.* glaze, glazing.

couverture [kuver'ty:r], *n.f.* covering, wrapper; blanket, rug, counterpane, quilt; cover (*of a book*); (*Comm.*) guaranty, security; *couverture chauffante*, electric blanket.

couveuse [ku'vø:z], *n.f.* broody hen; *couveuse artificielle*, incubator.

couvi [ku'vi], *a.* addled, rotten (*egg*).

couvoir [ku'vwa:r], *n.m.* incubator.

[In the following compounds *couvre* is *inv.*]

couvre-chef [kuvrə'ʃɛf], *n.m.* headgear.

couvre-feu [kuvrə'fø], *n.m. inv.* curfew; curfew-bell; fire cover, fire plate; black-out.

couvre-plat [kuvrə'pla], *n.m.* dish cover.

couvre-théière [kuvrəte'jɛ:r], *n.m.* tea cosy.

couvreur [ku'vrœ:r], *n.m.* roofer.

couvrir [ku'vri:r], *v.t. irr.* (*conjug. like* OUVRIR) to cover; to wrap up; to roof; to overwhelm; to clothe; to defend, to protect; to overrun, to overflow; to excuse; to disguise; to defray (*expenses etc.*). **se couvrir,** *v.r.* to cover oneself, to put on (*one's hat*); to get under cover; to be overcast (*of the weather*); (*Comm.*) to reimburse oneself.

coyote [kɔ'jɔt], *n.m.* prairie wolf.

crabe [kra:b], *n.m.* crab.

crac! [krak], *int.* crack! pop!

crachat [kra'ʃa], *n.m.* spittle, expectoration.

crachement [kraʃ'mã], *n.m.* spitting.

cracher [kra'ʃe], *v.t.* to spit; (*fig.*) to spit out, to come out with.—*v.i.* to spit, to splutter; (*Mach. etc.*) to spark, to backfire.

crachoir [kra'ʃwa:r], *n.m.* spittoon.

crachoter [kraʃɔ'te], *v.i.* to spit often.

Cracovie [krakɔ'vi], *f.* Cracow.

craie [krɛ], *n.f.* chalk.

craillement [krɑj'mã], *n.m.* cawing (*of crows*).

crailler [krɑ'je], *v.i.* to caw.

craindre [krɛ̃:dr], *v.t. irr.* to fear; to dread; to dislike.

crainte [krɛ̃:t], *n.f.* fear, apprehension; dread, awe.

craintif [krɛ̃'tif], *a.* (*fem.* **-tive**) fearful, apprehensive, timid.

craintivement [krɛ̃tiv'mã], *adv.* fearfully, timorously.

cramoisi [kramwa'zi], *a.* and *n.m.* crimson.

crampe [krɑ̃:p], *n.f.* cramp; crampon.

crampon [krɑ̃'põ], *n.m.* crampon, cramp-iron, grappling iron.

cramponner [krɑ̃pɔ'ne], *v.t.* to cramp, to fasten with a cramp-iron. **se cramponner,** *v.r.* to hold fast, to cling like grim death.

cramponnet [krɑ̃pɔ'nɛ], *n.m.* small cramp, tack; staple (*of a lock*).

cran (1) [krɑ̃], *n.m.* notch; cog; (*Print.*) nick; (*fam.*) pluck.

cran (2) [krɑ̃], *n.m.* horse-radish.

crâne [krɑːn], *a.* bold, plucky.—*n.m.* skull, cranium.

crânement [krɑn'mɑ̃], *adv.* pluckily; in style, famously.

craner [kra'ne], *v.t.* to notch, to indent (*a clock wheel*).

crâner [krɑ'ne], *v.i.* to swagger.

cranologie [kranɔlɔ'ʒi], **craniologie** [kranjɔlɔ'ʒi], *n.f.* craniology.

crapaud [kra'po], *n.m.* toad; jumping cracker; (*fig.*) urchin, brat.

crapaudière [krapo'djɛːr], *n.f.* nest of toads; (*fig.*) low, swampy place.

crapaudine [krapo'din], *n.f.* toadstone; grating (*of an escape-pipe*); *à la crapaudine*, cut open and broiled.

crapouillot [krapu'jo], *n.m.* trench-mortar.

crapule [kra'pyl], *n.f.* low vulgar debauchery, gluttony, drunkenness; blackguards.

crapuleusement [krapyløz'mɑ̃], *adv.* dissolutely.

crapuleux [krapy'lø], *a.* (*fem.* **-euse**) low, debauched, vicious, dissolute.

craque [krak], *n.f.* fib, humbug.

craqueler [kra'kle], *v.t.* (*conjug. like* APPELER) to crackle (*china*).

craquelot [kra'klo], *n.m.* bloater.

craquelure [kra'klyːr], *n.f.* crack (*in china*).

craquement [krak'mɑ̃], *n.m.* cracking noise, creaking, snapping (*boughs*).

craquer [kra'ke], *v.i.* to crack, to crackle, to snap, to creak, to crunch.

craquètement [krakɛt'mɑ̃], *n.m.* crackling; chattering (*of the teeth*); gabbling (*of a stork and other birds*).

craqueter [krak'te], *v.i.* (*conjug. like* APPELER) to crackle, to crepitate; to gabble (*birds*).

crasse (1) [kras], *a.* gross, thick, coarse, crass.

crasse (2) [kras], *n.f.* dirt, filth, squalor; stinginess; dross.

crasser [kra'se], *v.t.* to foul, to dirty (*fire-arms etc.*). **se crasser**, *v.r.* to become foul (*of fire-arms etc.*).

crasseux [kra'sø], *a.* (*fem.* **-euse**) dirty, filthy, nasty, squalid, sordid; stingy, mean.—*n.m.* (*fem.* **-euse**) sloven, slut; skinflint.

crassier [kra'sje], *n.m.* slag heap; rubbish dump.

cratère [kra'tɛːr], *n.m.* crater (*mouth of volcano*); (*Gr. or Rom.*) bowl or cup.

cravache [kra'vaʃ], *n.f.* riding whip.

cravacher [krava'ʃe], *v.t.* to horse whip.

cravate [kra'vat], *n.f.* cravat, (neck-)tie.

cravater (se) [səkrava'te], *v.r.* to put on one's (neck-)tie.

cravatier [krava'tje], *n.m.* maker or vendor of neckties.

crawl [krol], *n.m.* (*Swim.*) crawl.

crawleur [kro'lœːr], *n.m.* crawl swimmer.

crayer [krɛ'je], *v.t.* (*conjug. like* PAYER) to chalk, to mark up etc. with chalk.

crayère [krɛ'jɛːr], *n.f.* chalk pit.

crayeux [krɛ'jø], *a.* (*fem.* **-euse**) chalky.

crayon [krɛ'jɔ̃], *n.m.* pencil; drawing or portrait in crayon; (*fig.*) style; sketch; *crayon à bille*, ball-point pen.

crayonnage [krɛjɔ'naːʒ], *n.m.* pencil drawing.

crayonner [krɛjɔ'ne], *v.t.* to draw with a pencil; to mark with a pencil; (*fig.*) to sketch.

crayonneux [krɛjɔ'nø], *a.* (*fem.* **-euse**) chalky.

créance [kre'ɑ̃ːs], *n.f.* credence, trust, belief; credit; money owing; (*Hunt.*) command.

créancier [kreɑ̃'sje], *n.m.* (*fem.* **-ière**) creditor.

créateur [krea'tœːr], *a.* (*fem.* **-trice**) creative, inventive.—*n.m.* (*fem.* **-trice**) creator, maker, author.

création [krea'sjɔ̃], *n.f.* creation; universe; establishment; (*Dress.*) design.

créature [krea'tyːr], *n.f.* creature; man, as opposed to God.

crécelle [kre'sɛl], *n.f.* child's or hand rattle.

crécerelle [kres'rɛl], *n.f.* (*Orn.*) kestrel.

crèche [krɛːʃ], *n.f.* manger; crib; crèche.

crédence [kre'dɑ̃ːs], *n.f.* credence table; side-board.

crédibilité [kredibili'te], *n.f.* credibility.

crédit [kre'di], *n.m.* credit; trust; authority, influence; esteem; vogue; parliamentary grant.

créditer [kredi'te], *v.t.* to credit.

créditeur [kredi'tœːr], *a.* credit.—*n.m.* (*fem.* **-trice**) creditor.

credo [kre'do], *n.m.* (*no pl.*) creed, belief.

crédule [kre'dyl], *a.* credulous.

crédulement [kredyl'mɑ̃], *adv.* credulously.

crédulité [kredyli'te], *n.f.* credulity.

créer [kre'e], *v.t.* to create; to produce; to invent, to imagine; to establish.

crémaillère [kremɑ'jɛːr], *n.f.* pot-hook.

crémation [krema'sjɔ̃], *n.f.* cremation.

crématorium [kremato'rjɔm], *n.m.* (*pl.* **-ia**) crematorium.

crème [krɛm], *n.f.* cream; custard; sweet liqueur; the best part of a thing.

crémer (1) [kre'me], *v.t.* (*conjug. like* CÉDER) to dye cream color. —*v.i.* to cream.

crémer (2) [kre'me], *v.i.* (*conjug. like* CÉDER) to cremate.

crémerie [krem'ri], *n.f.* creamery, dairy.

crémeux [kre'mø], *a.* (*fem.* **-euse**) creamy.

crémier [kre'mje], *n.m.* (*fem.* **-ière**) milkman, dairyman or -woman.—*n.f.* (*-ière*) cream pitcher.

créneau [kre'no], *n.m.* (*pl.* **-eaux**) battlement.

crénelage [kren'laːʒ], *n.m.* milling, milled edge (*on coins*), crenation.

créneler [kren'le], *v.t.* (*conjug. like* APPELER) to embattle; to indent, to notch.

crénelure [kren'lyːr], *n.f.* crenellation; notching.

créole [kre'ɔl], *a.* Creole.—*n.* (**Créole**) Creole.

créosote [kreɔ'zɔt], *n.f.* creosote.

créosoter [kreɔzɔ'te], *v.t.* to creosote.

crêpe (1) [krɛːp], *n.m.* crape; (*fig.*) veil; crêpe rubber.

crêpe (2) [krɛːp], *n.f.* pancake.

crépelu [krep'ly], *a.* frizzy (*hair*).

crêper [krɛ'pe], *v.t.* to crisp, to frizz.

crépi [kre'pi], *n.m.* rough-cast, parget.

crépir [kre'piːr], *v.t.* to rough-cast, to plaster.

crépissage [krepi'saːʒ], **crépissement** [krepis'mɑ̃], *n.m.* plastering, pargeting, rough-casting.

crépissure [krepi'syːr], *n.m.* parget; rough-casting.

crépitant

crépitant [krepi'tɑ̃], *a.* crepitating; crackling.

crépitation [krepitɑ'sjɔ̃], *n.f.*, **crépitement** [krepit'mɑ̃], *n.m.* crepitation; crackling.

crépiter [krepi'te], *v.i.* to crackle; to crepitate.

crépu [kre'py], *a.* crisped, frizzy; woolly.

crêpure [kre'py:r], *n.f.* crisping; craping.

crépusculaire [krepysky'lɛ:r], *a.* crepuscular, twilight.

crépuscule [krepys'kyl], *n.m.* twilight; dawn.

créquier [kre'kje], *n.m.* sloe tree.

cresson [krɛ'sɔ̃], *n.m.* cress.

cressonnière [krɛsɔ'njɛ:r], *n.f.* water-cress bed.

Crésus [kre'zy:s], *m.* Croesus.

crésus [kre'zy:s], *n.m. inv.* very rich man.

crétacé [kreta'se], *a.* cretaceous, chalky.

Crète [krɛ:t], **la**, *f.* Crete.

crête [krɛ:t], *n.f.* crest, comb (*of a cock or hen*); tuft; ridge; coping.

crêté [kre'te], *a.* crested, tufted.

crêteler [krɛ'tle], *v.i.* (*conjug. like* APPELER) to cackle (*of hens*).

crétin [kre'tɛ̃], *a.* cretinous; idiotic.—*n.m.* (*fem.* -e) cretin; idiot, dunce.

crétinerie [kretin'ri], *n.f.* idiotic behavior; foolishness.

crétiniser [kretini'ze], *v.t.* to make cretinous, to brutalize, to make an idiot of.

crétinisme [kreti'nism], *n.m.* cretinism.

crétois [kre'twa], *a.* Cretan.—*n.m.* (**Crétois**, *fem.* -oise) Cretan (*person*).

cretonne [krə'tɔn], *n.f.* cretonne.

creusage [krø'za:ʒ], **creusement** [krøz'mɑ̃], *n.m.* deepening, hollowing; excavation.

creuser [krø'ze], *v.t.* to dig, to hollow, to excavate, to scoop out; to sink, to drive (*a well, shaft etc.*); to make hollow *or* empty. **se creuser**, *v.r.* to become hollow.

creuset [krø'ze], *n.m.* crucible, melting pot; (*fig.*) test, trial.

creux [krø], *a.* (*fem.* **creuse**) hollow; cavernous; deep; empty; (*fig.*) airy, extravagant. —*n.m.* hollow, cavity; pit, hole, chasm; mold, mortar, trough.—*adv.* hollow; **sonner creux**, to sound hollow.

crevaison [krəvɛ'zɔ̃], *n.f.* puncture (*of a tire*).

crevant [krə'vɑ̃], *a.* (*vulg.*) tiresome; killing (*toil etc.*); killing (*funny*).

crevasse [krə'vas], *n.f.* crevice, rift, crack, chink, crevasse; gap, cranny; chap (*in the hands etc.*).

crevasser [krəva'se], *v.t.* to split; to crack; to chap. **se crevasser**, *v.r.* to crack, to become chapped.

crevé [krə've], *n.m.* (*Dress.*) opening, slash (*in sleeves*).

crève-cœur [krɛv'kœ:r], *n.m. inv.* heart-break; heart-breaking thing.

crever [krə've], *v.t.* (*conjug. like* AMENER) to burst, to split, to break open, to rend; to stave in; to puncture.—*v.i.* to burst; to die (*animals*); (*vulg.*) to die (*human beings*). **se crever**, *v.r.* to burst; to kill oneself.

crevette [krə'vɛt], *n.f.* shrimp, prawn.

cri [kri], *n.m.* cry; scream, roar, yell, shriek, screech, wail, outcry, clamor.

criaillement [kriaj'mɑ̃], *n.m.* shouting, wrangling, brawling; scolding.

criailler [kria'je], *v.i.* to bawl, to cry, to clamor; to scold; to brawl; to gabble (*of geese*).

criaillerie [kriaj'ri], *n.f.* brawling, clamoring, wrangling.

criailleur [kria'jœ:r], *n.m.* (*fem.* -euse) brawler, wrangler; shrew, scold.

criant [kri'ɑ̃], *a.* crying; (*fig.*) glaring, shocking.

criard [kri'a:r], *a.* crying, noisy, clamorous; scolding; (*fig.*) shrill, discordant, crude.— *n.m.* (*fem.* -e) bawler, clamorer; scold, shrew.

criblage [kri'bla:ʒ], *n.m.* sifting, screening (*of coals etc.*).

crible [kribl], *n.m.* sieve, riddle.

cribler [kri'ble], *v.t.* to sift, to riddle; to pierce all over, to riddle (*with wounds etc.*); (*fig.*) to overwhelm.

eric [krij], *n.m.* jack, screw-jack, hand-screw.

cri-cri [kri'kri], *n.m. inv.* (*fam.*) cricket (*insect*); chirping.

criée [kri'e], *n.f.* (*public*) auction.

crier [kri'e], *v.t.* to cry, to proclaim, to put up for sale; to publish, to announce.—*v.i.* to cry out; to shout, to scream, to shriek; to call out; to whine; to complain loudly, to exclaim; to chirp; to creak.

crieur [kri'jœ:r], *n.m.* (*fem.* -euse) bawler; crier; (*Theat.*) call-boy; auctioneer; hawker; **crieur public**, town crier; **crieur de journaux**, newsboy.

crime [krim], *n.m.* crime, offence.

Crimée [kri'me], **la**, *f.* the Crimea.

criminel [krimi'nɛl], *a.* (*fem.* -elle) criminal, felonious, guilty.—*n.m.* (*fem.* -elle) criminal, felon, culprit, offender.

criminellement [kriminɛl'mɑ̃], *adv.* criminally, culpably, guiltily.

crin [krɛ̃], *n.m.* horse-hair, bristles, fibres, mane.

crinière [kri'njɛ:r], *n.f.* mane (*of animal*).

crinoline [krino'lin], *n.f.* crinoline.

crique [krik], *n.f.* creek, cove; flaw, crack.

criquet [kri'kɛ], *n.m.* locust; (*fig.*) bad horse.

criqueter [krik'te], *v.i.* (*conjug. like* APPELER) to rasp, to grate.

crise [kri:z], *n.f.* crisis; fit, convulsion; slump.

crispation [krispɑ'sjɔ̃], *n.f.* shrivelling, crispation; fidgets.

crisper [kris'pe], *v.t.* to shrivel; to irritate (*the nerves*); to give (*someone*) the fidgets. **se crisper**, *v.r.* to shrivel, to contract.

crissement [kris'mɑ̃], *n.m.* grating (*of teeth, of brakes etc.*).

crisser [kris'e], *v.i.* to grate, to squeak.

cristal [kris'tal], *n.m.* (*pl.* -aux) crystal, cut glass; (*fig.*) limpidity; **cristal de mine**, quartz; **cristal de roche**, rock crystal.

cristallerie [kristal'ri], *n.f.* crystal-cutting; crystal manufactory, glass works.

cristallier [krista'lje], *n.m.* glass-cutter; glass cupboard.

cristallière [krista'ljɛ:r], *n.f.* rock-crystal mine; machine for glass-cutting.

cristallin [krista'lɛ̃], *a.* crystalline; pellucid. —*n.m.* (*Anat.*) crystalline lens (*of the eye*); (*Astron.*) crystalline heaven.

cristallisant [kristali'zɑ̃], *a.* crystallizing.

cristallisation [kristaliza'sjɔ̃], *n.f.* crystallization.

cristalliser [kristali'ze], *v.t.*, *v.i.* to crystallize. **se cristalliser**, *v.r.* to crystallize; to candy.

critère [kri'tɛ:r], **critérium** [krite'rjɔm], *n.m.* criterion, standard, test.

critiquable [kriti'kabl], *a.* open to criticism, censurable, exceptionable.

critique [kri'tik], *a.* critical; censorious, carping; ticklish, momentous; critical (*in the literary sense*).—*n.m.* critic; censor, carper.—*n.f.* criticism, science of criticism; review.

critiquer [kriti'ke], *v.t.* to criticize unfavorably; to censure, to find fault with.

critiqueur [kriti'kœ:r], *n.m.* (*fem.* **-euse**) criticizer, fault-finder, carper.

croassement [kroas'mã], *n.m.* croak, croaking, cawing (*of rooks*).

croasser [kroa'se], *v.i.* to croak, to caw (*of crows, rooks etc.*).

croate [krɔ'at], *a.* Croatian.—*n.m.* Croatian (*language*).—*n.* (**Croate**) Croat.

Croatie [krɔa'si], la, *f.* Croatia.

croc [kro], *n.m.* hook; fang (*of dog*), tusk (*of walrus*).

croc-en-jambe [krɔkã'ʒã:b], *n.m.* (*pl.* **crocs-en-jambe**) trip up; dirty trick.

croche [krɔʃ], *a.* crooked, bent.—*n.f.* (*Mus.*) quaver; (*pl.*) smith's tongs; **double croche**, semi-quaver; **triple croche**, demi-quaver.

crocher [krɔ'ʃe], *v.t.* to hook; to bend like a hook.

crochet [krɔ'ʃɛ], *n.m.* small hook; knitting needle, crochet hook; (*Print.*) square bracket; teeth of certain animals.

crochetable [krɔʃ'tabl], *a.* pickable (*of locks*).

crochetage [krɔʃ'ta:ʒ], *n.m.* lock picking.

crocheter [krɔʃ'te], *v.t.* (*conjug. like* AMENER) to pick (*a lock*); to crochet.

crochetier [krɔʃ'tje], *n.m.* hook maker, clasp maker.

crochu [krɔ'ʃy], *a.* crooked, hooked.

crocodile [krɔkɔ'dil], *n.m.* crocodile; (*Rail.*) automatic stop.

crocus [krɔ'ky:s], *n.m.* (*Bot.*) crocus.

croire [krwa:r], *v.t.* *irr.* to believe; to have faith in; to think, to deem.—*v.i.* to believe, to have faith (*à*), to be a believer. **se croire**, *v.r.* to believe *or* think oneself. to consider oneself; to be believed, to be credible.

croisade [krwa'zad], *n.f.* crusade.

croisé [krwa'ze], *a.* crossed; twilled, double-milled (*of cloth*); cross (*of breeds of animals*); **mots croisés**, a crossword.—*n.m.* crusader; twill; crossing (*a step in dancing*).

croisée [krwa'ze], *n.f.* crossing point; casement window (*opening inside*).

croisement [krwaz'mã], *n.m.* crossing (*of two roads etc.*); meeting; cross-breeding (*of animals*).

croiser [krwa'ze], *v.t.* to cross; to lay across; to cross (*breeds of animals*); to pass (*a person*); to thwart.—*v.i.* to overlap; to cruise. **se croiser**, *v.r.* to cross *or* pass each other; to be crossed; to thwart one another.

croiseur [krwa'zœ:r], *n.m.* cruiser.

croisière [krwa'zjɛ:r], *n.f.* cruise, cruising; (*Rail.*) crossing.

croissance [krwa'sã:s], *n.f.* growth, increase.

croissant [krwa'sã], *a.* growing, increasing.—*n.m.* the moon in her increase; crescent; pruning hook, hedging bill; crescent roll.

croît [krwa], *n.m.* increase (*from breeding*).

croître [krwa:tr], *v.i.* *irr.* to grow; to increase; to wax (*moon*); to spring up, to sprout; to lengthen; to swell.

croix [krwa], *n.f.* cross; the Holy Rood; (*fig.*) affliction; (*Coin.*) obverse.

cromlech [krom'lɛk], *n.m.* (*Archaeol.*) stone circle.

crône [kro:n], *n.m.* crane (*on a wharf*).

croquade [krɔ'kad], *n.f.* rough sketch.

croquant [krɔ'kã], *a.* crisp, crackling, short.—*n.m.* poor wretch; clodhopper.—*n.f.* crisp almond cake.

croque-au-sel (à la) [krɔko'sɛl], *adv. phr.* with salt only.

croque-mitaine [krɔkmi'tɛn], *n.m.* (*pl.* **croque-mitaines**) bogy man.

croquer [krɔ'ke], *v.t.* to crunch; to devour; to draft, to sketch.—*v.i.* to crackle between the teeth, to make a scrunching noise.

croquet [krɔ'kɛ], *n.m.* crisp biscuit; croquet (*game*).

croquette [krɔ'kɛt], *n.f.* croquette.

croquignole [krɔki'nɔl], *n.f.* cracknel; fillip; (*C*) doughnut.

croquis [krɔ'ki], *n.m.* first sketch, rough draft, outline.

cross [krɔs], *n.m.* (*Box.*) cross-counter; cross-country running.

crosse [krɔs], *n.f.* crooked stick, crosier (*of bishops*); butt (*of rifle*); stock; hockey stick, golf club etc.; (*C*) **jeu de crosse**, lacrosse.

crossé [krɔ'se], *a.* crosiered, mitred.

crosser [krɔ'se], *v.t.* to strike (*a ball etc.*).

crosseur [krɔ'sœ:r], *n.m.* hockey player, lacrosse player.

crotale [krɔ'tal], *n.m.* rattlesnake.

crotte [krɔt], *n.f.* dung; dirt, mud, mire.

crotté [krɔ'te], *a.* dirty, muddy; (*fig.*) squalid.

crotter [krɔ'te], *v.t.* to dirty; to draggle, to bespatter. **se crotter**, *v.r.* to get dirty.

crottin [krɔ'tɛ̃], *n.m.* dung.

croulant [kru'lã], *a.* sinking, crumbling; tottering, tumbledown.

croulement [krul'mã], *n.m.* sinking, falling in, collapse.

crouler [kru'le], *v.i.* to give way, to fall in, to collapse.

croup [krup], *n.m.* (*Path.*) croup, diphtheria.

croupal [kru'pal], *a.* (*m. pl.* **-aux**) pertaining to the croup; laryngitic.

croupe [krup], *n.f.* croup, crupper, buttocks (*of a horse*), rump; top *or* brow (*of a hill*); **monter en croupe**, to ride pillion.

croupé [kru'pe], *a.* with a rump *or* crupper.

croupi [kru'pi], *a.* stagnant, putrid; **de l'eau croupie**, ditch water.

croupier [kru'pje], *n.m.* croupier (*at a gaming table*); partner (*of a financier etc.*).

croupière [kru'pjɛ:r], *n.f.* saddle tie, crupper.

croupion [kru'pjɔ̃], *n.m.* rump; **le croupion** (*d'une volaille*), the parson's nose.

croupir [kru'pi:r], *v.i.* to stagnate; to wallow.

croupissant [krupi'sã], *a.* stagnant, putrescent.

croupon [kru'pɔ̃], *n.m.* butt (*leather*).

croustillant [krusti'jã], *a.* crisp, crusty.

croustille [krus'ti:j], *n.f.* little crust; (*fig.*) snack.

croustiller [krusti'je], *v.i.* to bite, eat, crunch a crust, to munch.

croûte [krut], *n.f.* crust; pie crust; scab; *casser la croûte,* to have a snack; (*C*) crust (*of the snow*); (*fig.*) bad painting, daub.

croûton [kru'tɔ̃], *n.m.* bit of crust, crusty end; sippet.

croyable [krwa'jabl], *a.* credible, likely.

croyance [krwa'jɑ̃:s], *n.f.* belief; creed, faith.

croyant [krwa'jɑ̃], *a.* believing.—*n.m.* (*fem. -e*) believer.

cru (1) [kry], *n.m.* growth; production (*esp. of wine*).

cru (2) [kry], *a.* raw, uncooked; unwrought; (*fig.*) crude, coarse, indecent; *à cru,* on the bare skin.

cruauté [kryo'te], *n.f.* cruelty, inhumanity.

cruche [kryʃ], *n.f.* pitcher, jar, jug; (*colloq.*) blockhead.

cruchée [kry'ʃe], *n.f.* pitcherful, jugful, jarful.

cruchon [kry'ʃɔ̃], *n.m.* little pitcher; (*stone*) hot-water bottle.

crucial [kry'sjal], *a.* (*m. pl. -aux*) cross-shaped, crucial; (*fig.*) decisive.

crucifiement [krysifi'mɑ̃], *n.m.* crucifixion.

crucifier [krysi'fje], *v.t.* to crucify.

crucifix [krysi'fi], *n.m.* crucifix.

crucifixion [krysifik'sjɔ̃], *n.f.* crucifixion.

cruciforme [krysi'fɔrm], *a.* cruciform, cross-shaped.

crudité [krydi'te], *n.f.* crudity, rawness; coarse expression; (*pl.*) raw vegetables *or* fruit.

crue [kry], *n.f.* growth, increase; rise, swelling (*of river etc.*); flood.

cruel [kry'ɛl], *a.* (*fem. -elle*) cruel, merciless; bloodthirsty; hard; grievous, sad.

cruellement [kryɛl'mɑ̃], *adv.* cruelly; unmercifully; severely.

crûment [kry'mɑ̃], *adv.* roughly, coarsely; crudely.

crustacé [krysta'se], *a.* crustaceous.—*n.m.* crustacean; shell-fish.

crypte [kript], *n.f.* crypt.

cryptogramme [kripto'gram], *n.m.* cryptogram, cipher.

cryptographe [kripto'graf], *n.* cryptographer.

cryptographie [kriptɔgra'fi], *n.f.* cryptography.

cryptographique [kriptɔgra'fik], *a.* cryptographic.

cubage [ky'ba:ʒ], *n.m.* cubage, cubature; cubic content.

cubain [ky'bɛ̃], *a.* Cuban.—*n.m.* (**Cubain,** *fem. -aine*) Cuban (*person*).

cubature [kyba'ty:r], *n.f.* cubature.

cube [kyb], *a.* cubic.—*n.m.* cube (*shape and measure*).

cuber [ky'be], *v.t.* to cube.

cubique [ky'bik], *a.* cubic; cubical.

cubisme [ky'bism], *n.m.* (*Art*) cubism.

cubiste [ky'bist], *a.* and *n.* cubist.

cueillage [kœ'ja:ʒ], *n.m.,* **cueillaison** [kœjɛ'zɔ̃], **cueille** [kœ:j], *n.f.* gathering time, gathering.

cueillette [kœ'jɛt], *n.f.* gathering of a crop; harvesting time.

cueilleur [kœ'jœ:r], *n.m.* (*fem. -euse*) gatherer, picker.

cueillir [kœ'ji:r], *v.t. irr.* to gather, to cull, to pick, to pluck; to acquire.

cueilloir [kœj'wa:r], *n.m.* fruit basket; implement for picking fruit.

cuiller [kɥi'je], **cuillère** [kɥi'jɛ:r], *n.f.* spoon; scoop.

cuillerée [kɥij're], *n.f.* spoonful.

cuilleron [kɥij'rɔ̃], *n.m.* bowl of a spoon.

cuir [kɥi:r], *n.m.* hide; leather; strop.

cuirasse [kɥi'ras], *n.f.* cuirass, breast-plate.

cuirassé [kɥira'se], *a.* armed with a cuirass; armour-plated; hardened; secret.—*n.m.* (*Naut.*) battleship.

cuirassement [kɥiras'mɑ̃], *n.m.* armor-plating.

cuirasser [kɥira'se], *v.t.* to arm with a cuirass; to armor-plate; (*fig.*) to steel, to harden. **se cuirasser,** *v.r.* to put on a cuirass; to harden *or* fortify oneself.

cuirassier [kɥira'sje], *n.m.* cuirassier.

cuire [kɥi:r], *v.t. irr.* (*conjug. like* CONDUIRE) to cook; to burn (*of the sun*); to ripen.—*v.i.* to cook, to be cooked, to be done; to bake, boil etc.; to smart.

cuisage [kɥi'za:ʒ], *n.m.* burning (*of charcoal*), charring.

cuisant [kɥi'zɑ̃], *a.* sharp, smarting; piercing.

cuiseur [kɥi'zœ:r], *n.m.* pressure cooker.

cuisine [kɥi'zin], *n.f.* kitchen; cookery; cooks; fare, living; (*Naut.*) galley.

cuisiner [kɥizi'ne], *v.t., v.i.* to cook.

cuisinier [kɥizi'nje], *n.m.* (*fem. -ière*) cook.—*n.f.* (*-ière*) Dutch oven.

cuisse [kɥis], *n.f.* thigh; quarter (*of venison*); leg (*of poultry*).

cuisseau [kɥi'so], *n.m.* (*pl. -eaux*) leg (*of veal*).

cuisson [kɥi'sɔ̃], *n.f.* cooking (*baking, boiling, roasting etc.*); smart (*pain*).

cuissot [kɥi'so], *n.m.* haunch (*of venison*).

cuit [kɥi], *a.* cooked, done (*roasted, boiled, baked etc.*); (*fig.*) done for, dished.

cuite [kɥit], *n.f.* baking; burning (*of bricks etc.*); ovenful, kilnful; (*slang*) intoxication.

cuivrage [kɥi'vra:ʒ], *n.m.* coppering; copper-plating.

cuivre [kɥi:vr], *n.m.* copper; copper money; copper-plate; *cuivre battu,* wrought copper; *cuivre jaune,* brass; *cuivre rouge,* copper.

cuivré [kɥi'vre], *a.* copper-colored; (*fig.*) bronzed (*complexion*); ringing, clear.

cuivrer [kɥi'vre], *v.t.* to cover with copper.

cuivrerie [kɥivrə'ri], *n.f.* copper-works; copper wares.

cuivreux [kɥi'vrø], *a.* (*fem. -euse*) coppery.

cul [ky], *n.m.* (*indec.*) backside, posterior; bottom (*of bottle or bag*); stern (*of ship*).

culasse [ky'las], *n.f.* breech (*of a cannon etc.*); cylinder head (*of car engine*).

culbute [kyl'byt], *n.f.* somersault; fall, tumble; (*fig.*) ruin, bankruptcy.

culbuter [kylby'te], *v.t.* to throw over, to upset violently; to overthrow.—*v.i.* to fall head over heels.

culbutis [kylby'ti], *n.m.* confused heap, jumble.

cul de bouteille [kydbu'tɛ:j], *a.* bottle-green. —*n.m.* bottom of bottle.

cul-de-jatte [kyd'ʒat], *n.m.* (*pl. culs-de-jatte*) legless cripple.

cul-de-lampe [kyd'lɑ̃p], *n.m.* (*Print.*) tail-piece.

cul-de-sac [kyd'sak], *n.m.* (*pl. culs-de-sac*) blind alley, cul-de-sac; (*fig.*) deadlock.

culée [ky'le], *n.f.* abutment (*of bridges*); (*Naut.*) stern-way.

culer [ky'le], *v.i.* to go backwards; to fall astern.

culière [ky'ljɛːr], *n.f.* hind girth, crupper (*of harness*); gutter stone.

culinaire [kyli'nɛːr], *a.* culinary.

culminance [kylmi'nãːs], *n.f.* culmination, highest point.

culminant [kylmi'nã], *a.* culminating; prominent.

culmination [kylmina'sjõ], *n.f.* culmination.

culminer [kylmi'ne], *v.i.* to culminate.

culot [ky'lo], *n.m.* bottom (*of lamps, crucibles etc.*); residuum, (*fam.*) dottle (*in a pipe*).

culottage [kylɔ'taːʒ], *n.m.* coloring, seasoning (*of pipes*).

culotte [ky'lɔt], *n.f.* breeches; (*pl.*) shorts; tights; (*Cook.*) rump (*of an ox*).

culotter [kylɔ'te], *v.t.* to breech; to put in breeches; to color (*pipes*). **se culotter**, *v.r.* to put on one's breeches; to become colored (*of pipes*).

culottier [kylɔ'tje], *n.m.* (*fem.* **-ière**) breeches maker.

culpabilité [kylpabili'te], *n.f.* culpability, guilt.

culte [kylt], *n.m.* worship, adoration; (*fig.*) cult, religion, creed; veneration, love.

cultivable [kylti'vabl], *a.* cultivable, arable.

cultivateur [kyltiva'tœːr], *a.* agricultural.—*n.m.* (*fem.* **-trice**) cultivator, farmer, agriculturist; cultivator (*implement*).

cultivé [kylti've], *a.* cultivated; (*of the mind*) cultured.

cultiver [kylti've], *v.t.* to cultivate; to till; to improve (*the mind*); to study, to practise; to cultivate the acquaintance of.

cultural [kylty'ral], *a.* (*m. pl.* **-aux**) cultural (*in relation to agriculture*).

culture [kyl'tyːr], *n.f.* culture, cultivation, tillage, husbandry; education, improvement.

culturel [kylty'rɛl], *a.* (*fem.* **-elle**) cultural (*in relation to intellectual culture*).

cumulatif [kymyla'tif], *a.* (*fem.* **-tive**) cumulative.

cumulativement [kymylativ'mã], *adv.* by accumulation.

cumuler [kymy'le], *v.t.* to accumulate; to hold several (*offices, salaries etc.*).

cumulus [kymy'lyːs], *n.m.* cumulus.

cupide [ky'pid], *a.* covetous, greedy, grasping.

cupidement [kypid'mã], *adv.* greedily, covetously.

cupidité [kypidi'te], *n.f.* cupidity, covetousness, greed.

Cupidon [kypi'dõ], *n.m.* (*Myth.*) Cupid, Love.

curable [ky'rabl], *a.* curable.

curaçao [kyra'so], *n.m.* curaçao (*liqueur*).

curage [ky'raːʒ], **curement** [kyr'mã], *n.m.* cleansing.

curatelle [kyra'tɛl], *n.f.* guardianship, trusteeship.

curateur [kyra'tœːr], *n.m.* (*fem.* **-trice**) guardian, trustee.

curatif [kyra'tif], *a.* (*fem.* **-tive**) curative.—*n.m.* curative agent.

cure [kyːr], *n.f.* medical treatment, cure, healing; living, rectorship; vicarage, rectory.

curé [ky're], *n.m.* parish priest; parson, rector, vicar.

cure-dent [kyr'dã], *n.m.* (*pl.* **cure-dents**) tooth-pick.

curée [ky're], *n.f.* (*Hunt.*) quarry, chase; (*fig.*) prey, booty.

curement [CURAGE].

cure-môle [kyr'moːl], *n.m.* (*pl.* **cure-môles**) dredging machine.

cure-ongles [kyr'rõgl], *n.m. inv.* nail file.

curer [ky're], *v.t.* to cleanse, to clean out (*harbors, sewers etc.*); to pick (*teeth, ears etc.*).

curial (1) [ky'rjal], *a.* (*m. pl.* **-aux**) vicarial, rectorial.

curial (2) or **curiale** [ky'rjal], *a.* (*Rom. Ant.*) curial.

curie [ky'ri], *n.f.* (*Rom. Ant.*) curia.

curieusement [kyrjøz'mã], *adv.* curiously; inquisitively; carefully; quaintly.

curieux [ky'rjø], *a.* (*fem.* **-euse**) curious, inquisitive, prying; inquiring; careful; dainty; particular; strange.—*n.m.* (*fem.* **-euse**) interested person; inquisitive person; sightseer, looker-on.—*n.m.* curious fact.

curiosité [kyrjozi'te], *n.f.* curiosity; inquisitiveness; curio, rarity; quaintness.

cursif [kyr'sif], *a.* (*fem.* **-sive**) cursive, running; cursory.

cursivement [kyrsiv'mã], *adv.* cursively; cursorily.

curure [ky'ryːr], *n.f.* dirt, sewage.

cussonné [kyso'ne], *a.* worm-eaten (*of wood*).

custode [kys'tod], *n.m.* warden (*among monks*); custodian, inspector.

cutané [kyta'ne], *a.* cutaneous.

cuticule [kyti'kyl], *n.f.* cuticle.

cuvage [ky'vaːʒ], *n.m.*, **cuvaison** [kyvɛ'zõ], *n.f.* fermenting (*of wine*).

cuve [ky:v], *n.f.* tub, vat.

cuvée [ky've], *n.f.* tubful; vatful.

cuvelage [ky'vlaːʒ], **cuvellement** [kyvɛl'mã], *n.m.* lining, casing (*of mine shafts*).

cuveler [ky'vle], *v.t.* (*conjug. like* APPELER) to line, to case (*mine shafts etc.*).

cuver [ky've], *v.t.* to ferment; (*fam.*) to sleep off the effects of (*wine*).—*v.i.* to work, to ferment, to settle.

cuvette [ky'vɛt], *n.f.* shallow basin; wash basin; lavatory bowl.

cuvier [ky'vje], *n.m.* wash tub.

cyanure [sja'nyːr], *n.m.* (*Chem.*) cyanide.

cybernétique [siberne'tik], *n.f.* cybernetics.

cyclamen [sikla'mɛn], *n.m.* cyclamen, sow-bread.

cycle [sikl], *n.m.* cycle (*of events*); **cycle à 4 temps** (*d'un moteur*), 4-stroke cycle (*of an engine*).

cyclique [si'klik], *a.* cyclical.

cyclisme [si'klism], *n.m.* cycling.

cycliste [si'klist], *n.* cyclist.

cyclomoteur [siklomo'tœːr], *n.m.* motorbike.

cyclonal [siklo'nal], *a.* (*m. pl.* **-aux**) cyclonic.

cyclone [si'kloːn], *n.m.* cyclone.

cyclonique [siklo'nik], *a.* cyclonic.

Cyclope [si'klop], *n.m.* Cyclops.

cygne [siɲ], *n.m.* swan.

cylindrage [silɛ̃'draːʒ], *n.m.* mangling (*of linen etc.*); rolling (*of roads*).

cylindre [si'lɛːdr], *n.m.* cylinder; roller; garden roller; mangle, calender.

cylindrée [silɛ̃'dre], n.f. cubic capacity of an engine.

cylindrer [silɛ̃'dre], v.t. to calender; to roll.

cylindrique [silɛ̃'drik], a. cylindrical.

cymaise [CIMAISE].

cymbale [sɛ̃'bal], n.f. (Mus.) cymbal.

cymbalier [sɛ̃ba'lje], n.m. cymbal player.

cynancie [sinɑ̃'si], [ESQUINANCIE].

cynégétique [sineze'tik], a. relating to hunting and dogs.—n.f. the art of hunting with dogs, cynegetics.

cynique [si'nik], a. cynical; snarling, snappish; impudent.—n. cynic.

cyniquement [sinik'mɑ̃], adv. cynically.

cynisme [si'nism], n.m. cynicism; impudence.

cynodrome [sino'dro:m], n.m. greyhound racing track.

cynosure [sino'sy:r], n.f. (Astron.) Cynosure, Little Bear.

cyprès [si'prɛ], n.m. cypress, cypress tree.

cyprière [si'prjɛ:r], n.f. cypress grove.

cypriote [si'prjɔt], a. Cypriot.—n. (Cypriote) Cypriot (person).

cytise [si'ti:z], n.m. cytisus, laburnum.

czar [tsa:r], [TZAR].

D

D, d [de], n.m. the fourth letter of the alphabet.

d', abbr. [DE].

da [da], particle (used after oui, non) truly, indeed; oui-da, yes indeed.

d'abord [da'bo:r], [ABORD].

dactylo [dakti'lo], n.f. abbr. of [DACTYLOGRAPHE].

dactylographe [daktilo'graf], n.m. typist.

dactylographie [daktilɔgra'fi], n.f. typewriting.

dactylographier [daktilɔgra'fje], v.t. to type(write).

dactylographique [daktilɔgra'fik], a. typewritten (report); typewriting (material).

dactyloptère [daktilɔp'tɛ:r], n.m. flying fish.

dada [da'da], n.m. (childish) horse, cockhorse; gee-gee.

dadais [da'dɛ], n.m. booby, clown, ninny.

dague [dag], n.f. dagger, dirk.

daguerréotype [dagɛreo'tip], n.m. daguerreotype.

dahlia [da'lja], n.m. dahlia.

daigner [dɛ'ɲe], v.i. to deign, to condescend.

d'ailleurs [da'jœ:r], [AILLEURS].

daim [dɛ̃], n.m. deer, fallow deer; buck.

daine [dɛn], n.f. doe.

dais [dɛ], n.m. canopy.

dallage [da'la:ʒ], n.m. paving with flagstones.

dalle [dal], n.f. flag, flagstone; slab.

daller [da'le], v.t. to pave with flagstones, to flag.

dalleur [da'lœ:r], n.m. pavior.

dalmate [dal'mat], a. Dalmatian.—n. (Dalmate) Dalmatian (person).

dalmatique [dalma'tik], n.f. dalmatic.

daltonisme [dalto'nism], n.m. color blindness.

96

damas [da'ma], n.m. damask; damson; Damascus blade.

damasquiner [damaski'ne], v.t. to damascene.

damassé [dama'se], n.m. damask linen, damask cloth.

damasser [dama'se], v.t. to damask.

damassin [dama'sɛ̃], n.m. figured linen cloth.

damassure [dama'sy:r], n.f. damasking (of linen); damask work.

dame (1) [dam], n.f. (married) lady, dame; rowlock; beetle, rammer; (Cards, and Chess) queen.

dame (2) [dam], int. dame oui! why, yes!

dame-jeanne [dam'ʒɑ:n], n.f. (pl. dames-jeannes) demijohn, carboy.

damer [da'me], v.t. (Draughts) to crown (a man); (Chess) to queen; to ram (earth etc.).

damier [da'mje], n.m. draught board.

damnable [da'nabl], a. damnable.

damnablement [danablə'mɑ̃], adv. damnably.

damnation [dana'sjɔ̃], n.f. damnation.

damné [da'ne], a. and n.m. (fem. -ée) damned (person).

damner [da'ne], v.t. to damn. se damner, v.r. to damn oneself.

dancing [dɑ̃'siŋ], n.m. dance hall, palais de danse.

dandin [dɑ̃'dɛ̃], n.m. ninny.

dandinement [dɑ̃din'mɑ̃], n.m. swinging (of the body); rolling gait.

dandiner [dɑ̃di'ne], v.i. to swing (of the body) to dandle (of a baby). se dandiner, v.r. to waddle.

dandy [dɑ̃'di], n.m. dandy.

dandysme [dɑ̃'dism], n.m. dandyism.

Danemark [dan'mark], le, m. Denmark.

danger [dɑ̃'ʒe], n.m. danger, peril, risk, hazard.

dangereusement [dɑ̃ʒrøz'mɑ̃], adv. dangerously.

dangereux [dɑ̃'ʒrø], a. (fem. -euse) dangerous.

danois [da'nwa], a. Danish.—n.m. Danish (language); Great Dane (dog); (Danois, fem. -oise) Dane (person).

dans [dɑ̃], prep. in, within; into; with, according to; during; out of.

danse [dɑ̃:s], n.f. dance; dancing; (fig.) beating, hiding; danse de Saint-Guy, St. Vitus's dance.

danser [dɑ̃'se], v.t., v.i. to dance.

danseur [dɑ̃'sœ:r], n.m. (fem. -euse) dancer, ballet girl.

dard [da:r], n.m. dart; sting; forked tongue (of a snake); pistil.

darder [dar'de], v.t. to hurl; to spear; to shoot forth, to beam, to dart.

dardillon [dardi'jɔ̃], n.m. small dart; barb (of a fish-hook).

dare-dare [dar'da:r], adv. (fam.) in great haste, in double-quick time.

darne [darn], n.f. slice (of fish).

dartre [dartr], n.f. slight and dry eruption (of the skin); scurf.

dartreux [dar'trø], a. (fem. -euse) herpetic, scurfy.

date [dat], n.f. date.

dater [da'te], v.t. to date (a letter etc.).—v.i. to date (de); to reckon.

datif [da'tif], n.m. (Gram.) dative, dative case.

datte [dat], *n.f.* date.

dattier [da'tje], *n.m.* date palm.

datura [daty'ra], *n.m.* datura, thorn apple.

daube [do:b], *n.f.* stew.

dauber [do'be], *v.t.* to cuff, to drub; *(fig.)* to banter, to jeer at; *(Cook.)* to stew.

daubeur [do'bœ:r], *n.m. (fem. -euse)* jeerer, banterer, sneerer.

daubière [do'bjɛ:r], *n.f.* stew pan.

dauphin [do'fɛ̃], *n.m.* dolphin; dauphin *(eldest son of the king of France).*

dauphine [do'fin], *n.f.* wife of the dauphin.

dauphinelle [dofi'nɛl], *n.f. (Bot.)* larkspur, delphinium.

daurade [do'rad], *n.f.* gilt-head *(fish).*

davantage [davã'ta:3], *adv.* more, any more; any longer, any further.

davier [da'vje], *n.m.* dentist's forceps; cramp; *(Naut.)* davit.

de [də], *prep.* of; out of, made of, composed of, from, by, with, at, for; concerning, about.

dé (1) [de], *n.m.* die *(for playing)*; *(fig.)* throw, hazard.

dé (2) [de], *n.m.* thimble.

débâcher [deba'ʃe], *v.t.* to uncover, to untilt.

débâcle [de'bɑ:kl], *n.f.* breaking up *(of ice)*; *(fig.)* downfall, collapse.

débâcler [deba'kle], *v.i.* to break up *(of ice).*

débâcleur [deba'klœ:r], *n.m.* water or port bailiff.

déballage [deba'la:3], *n.m.* unpacking.

déballer [deba'le], *v.t.* to unpack.

débandade [debã'dad], *n.f.* rout, stampede; *à la débandade,* in confusion.

débander [debã'de], *v.t.* to unbind; to loosen; to remove a bandage from. **se débander,** *v.r.* to slacken, to relax; to disband.

débaptiser [debati'ze], *v.t.* to change the name of.

débarbouillage [debarbu'ja:3], *n.m.* washing, cleansing.

débarbouiller [debarbu'je], *v.t.* to wash, to cleanse. **se débarbouiller,** *v.r.* to wash one's face etc.; *(fig.)* to extricate oneself.

débarcadère [debarka'dɛ:r], *n.m.* landing place, wharf; *(Rail.)* station; arrival platform.

débardage [debar'da:3], *n.m.* unloading *(of wood etc.).*

débarder [debar'de], *v.t.* to unload *(wood etc.)*; to clear *(a wood etc.)* of felled trees.

débardeur [debar'dœ:r], *n.m.* stevedore, lighterman, docker.

débarquement [debarkə'mã], *n.m.* landing, disembarkation *(of persons)*; unloading *(of goods).*

débarquer [debar'ke], *v.t., v.i.* to disembark, to land.

débarras [deba'rɑ], *n.m.* riddance, disencumbrance; *chambre de débarras,* lumber-room, box room.

débarrasser [debara'se], *v.t.* to disencumber, to rid; to disentangle, to extricate; to clear *(the table).* **se débarrasser,** *v.r.* to extricate oneself, to rid oneself of, to shake off; to get clear.

débarrer [deba're], *v.t.* to unbar.

débat [de'ba], *n.m.* dispute, contest; debate, discussion; *(pl.)* parliamentary debates.

débateler [debatə'le], *v.t. (conjug. like APPELER)* to unlade *(boats etc.).*

débâter [debɑ'te], *v.t.* to unsaddle; to take a packsaddle off.

débâtir [debɑ'ti:r], *v.t.* to pull down, to demolish; to unbaste, to untack *(garments).*

débattre [de'batr], *v.t. irr. (conjug. like BATTRE)* to debate, to discuss, to argue. **se débattre,** *v.r.* to struggle, to strive; to flounder, to flutter.

débauche [de'bo:ʃ], *n.f.* debauchery; dissoluteness.

débauché [debo'ʃe], *n.m.* debauchee, rake.

débaucher [debo'ʃe], *v.t.* to debauch; to corrupt; to lead astray. **se débaucher,** *v.r.* to become debauched.

débet [de'be], *n.m.* debit.

débile [de'bil], *a.* weak, feeble.

débilement [debil'mã], *adv.* feebly, weakly.

débilité [debili'te], *n.f.* debility, weakness.

débiliter [debili'te], *v.t.* to debilitate, to enfeeble.

débit [de'bi], *n.m.* sale; market; retail; retail shop; *(fig.)* delivery, utterance; *(Bookkeeping)* debit.

débitage [debi'ta:3], *n.m.* cutting up *(of stones, timber etc.).*

débitant [debi'tã], *n.m. (fem. -e)* retailer, dealer.

débiter [debi'te], *v.t.* to sell; to retail; to supply; to debit; to cut up *(wood, stone etc.)*; *(fig.)* to spread, to report, to utter.

débiteur (1) [debi'tœ:r], *n.m. (fem. -trice)* debtor.

débiteur (2) [debi'tœ:r], *n.m. (fem. -euse)* prattler, gossipmonger.

déblai [de'blɛ], *n.m.* clearing; excavation; *(pl.)* earth, stones etc. cleared away.

déblaiement or **déblayement** [deblɛ'mã], *n.m.* clearance; cutting, excavation, digging.

déblatérer [deblate're], *v.i. (conjug. like CÉDER)* to utter violent abuse, to rail *(contre).*

déblayement [DÉBLAIEMENT].

déblayer [deblɛ'je], *v.t. (conjug. like PAYER)* to clear away; to clear; *(fig.)* to sweep away *(obstacles etc.).*

déblocage [deblɔ'ka:3], *n.m. (Print.)* turning letters.

débloquer [deblɔ'ke], *v.t.* to raise the blockade from; *(Print.)* to turn letters; to unlock; to release.

débobiner [debɔbi'ne], *v.t.* to unwind.

déboire [de'bwa:r], *n.m.* after-taste; *(fig.)* disappointment, vexation.

déboisement [debwaz'mã], *n.m.* clearing of trees, deforestation.

déboiser [debwa'ze], *v.t.* to clear of trees.

déboîtement [debwat'mã], *n.m.* dislocation.

déboîter [debwa'te], *v.t.* to put out of joint, to dislocate; *(Elec.)* to disconnect. **se déboîter,** *v.r.* to be dislocated.

débonder [debõ'de], *v.t.* to unplug, to unstopper; to loosen, to unbind.—*v.i.* or **se débonder,** *v.r.* to gush, to break out, to burst forth; to be relaxed *(of a person).*

débonnaire [debɔ'nɛ:r], *a.* good-natured, easy-tempered.

débonnairement [debɔnɛr'mã], *adv.* compliantly, easily.

débonnaireté [debɔnɛr'te], *n.f.* compliance, good nature.

débordé [debɔr'de], *a.* overflowing *(river)*; overwhelmed *(man)*; outflanked *(troops).*

débordement

débordement [debɔrdə'mã], *n.m.* overflowing, flood; outburst; (*fig.*) dissoluteness.

déborder [debɔr'de], *v.t.* to take off the border from; to go beyond; to outrun.—*v.i.* to overflow, to run over; to project, to jut out. **se déborder**, *v.r.* to overflow; to run over, to burst forth.

débordoir [debɔr'dwa:r], *n.m.* edging tool; spoke shave.

débosseler [debos'le], *v.t.* (*conjug. like* APPELER) to take the dents out of.

débotté *or* **débotter** (1) [debo'te], *n.m.* the moment of taking boots off; (*fig.*) **au débotté**, at once.

débotter (2) [debo'te], *v.t.* to pull off (*someone's*) boots. **se débotter**, *v.r.* to take off one's boots.

débouché [debu'ʃe], *n.m.* outlet, issue; waterway; (*Comm.*) market, sale.

débouchage [debu'ʃa:3], **débouchement** [debuʃ'mã], *n.m.* uncorking; outlet; market, sale.

déboucher [debu'ʃe], *v.t.* to open, to clear; to uncork; to unplug.—*v.i.* to emerge; to empty itself (*of rivers*); (*Mil.*) to debouch.

déboucler [debu'kle], *v.t.* to unbuckle; to uncurl.

débouler [debu'le], *v.i.* to roll down (*like a ball*); to start off suddenly (*like a hare*).

déboulonner [debulɔ'ne], *v.t.* to unrivet, to unbolt.

débourrer [debu're], *v.t.* to draw the wad *or* wadding out of (*fire arms*); to empty the tobacco out of (*a pipe*); (*fig.*) to polish (*a person's manners*).

débours [de'bu:r], **déboursé** [debur'se], *n.m.* disbursement, outlay.

déboursement [deburs'mã], *n.m.* outlay, expenditure.

débourser [debur'se], *v.t.* to disburse, to expend, to lay out.

debout [də'bu], *adv.* upright, on end, standing up; out of bed, up; in existence; (*Naut.*) ahead (*of the wind*).

déboutonner [debutɔ'ne], *v.t.* to unbutton. **se déboutonner**, *v.r.* to unbutton oneself; (*colloq.*) to unbosom oneself.

débraillé [debra'je], *a.* loosely dressed, in disorder.—*n.m.* disorder, untidiness; (*fig.*) license.

débrailler (se) [sədebra'je], *v.r.* to uncover one's breast, to be untidy *or* disordered.

débrancher [debrã'ʃe], *v.t.* (*Elec.*) to disconnect.

débrayage [debre'ja:3], **désembrayage** [dezãbre'ja:3], *n.m.* disengaging gear (*of motors etc.*); declutching.

débrayer [debre'je], *v.t.* (*conjug. like* PAYER) to throw out of gear, to disengage, to declutch.

débridement [debrid'mã], *n.m.* unbridling; (*fig.*) dispatch, hurry.

débrider [debri'de], *v.t. v.i.* to unbridle (*horse*); to halt.

débris [de'bri], *n.m.* (*usu. in pl.*) remains, debris; rubbish.

débrouillard [debru'ja:r], *a.* and *n.m.* (*fem.* -e) (*colloq.*) resourceful (person).

débrouiller [debru'je], *v.t.* to disentangle, to unravel; (*fig.*) to explain. **se débrouiller**, *v.r.* to be cleared up; to get out of difficulties, to manage.

débusquement [debyskə'mã], *n.m.* driving out, dislodging.

débusquer [debys'ke], *v.t.* to turn out, to oust, to expel; (*Hunt.*) to start.

début [de'by], *n.m.* lead; outset; début.

débutant [deby'tã], *n.m.* (*fem.* -e) actor *or* actress appearing for the first time; beginner.

débuter [deby'te], *v.i.* to lead, to play first; to open; to start; to make one's début.

deçà [də'sa], *prep.* on this side of; short of, well within.—*adv.* here, on this side; *deçà (et) delà*, here and there.

décachetage [dekaʃ'ta:3], *n.m.* unsealing, opening.

décacheter [dekaʃ'te], *v.t.* (*conjug. like* APPELER) to unseal, to open.

décadaire [deka'dɛ:r], *a.* decadal.

décade [de'kad], *n.f.* decade, group of ten.

décadenasser [dekadna'se], *v.t.* to unpadlock.

décadence [deka'dã:s], *n.f.* decadence, decline, wane.

décadent [deka'dã], *a.* and *n.m.* (*fem.* -e) decadent (person).

décaèdre [deka'ɛdr], *a.* decahedral.—*n.m.* decahedron.

décagonal [dekago'nal], *a.* (*pl.* -aux) decagonal (*ten-sided*).

décagone [deka'gɔn], *n.m.* decagon.

décagramme [deka'gram], *n.m.* decagramme, ten grammes.

décaissement [dekes'mã], **décaissage** [deke'sa:3], *n.m.* uncasing, unpacking.

décaisser [deke'se], *v.t.* to unpack; to pay out.

décaler [deka'le], *v.t.* to unwedge.

décalaminage [dekalami'na:3], *n.m.* (*Motor.*) decarbonizing.

décalaminer [dekalami'ne], *v.t.* to decarbonize.

décalitre [deka'litr], *n.m.* decalitre (2·2 *gallons*).

décalquer [dekal'ke], *v.t.* to transfer (*a tracing*), to countertrace.

décamètre [deka'mɛtr], *n.m.* decametre.

décamper [dekã'pe], *v.i.* to decamp; (*fig.*) to bolt.

décanter [dekã'te], *v.t.* to decant, to pour off gently.

décapitation [dekapita'sjɔ̃], *n.f.* decapitation, beheading.

décapiter [dekapi'te], *v.t.* to behead, to decapitate.

décapotable [dekapo'tabl], *a.* (*Motor.*) convertible.

décarboniser [dekarbɔni'ze], *v.t.* to decarbonize.

décarburation [dekarbyra'sjɔ̃], *n.f.* decarbonization.

décarburer [dekarby're], *v.t.* to decarburize, to decarbonize.

décastère [deka'stɛ:r], *n.m.* measure of 10 steres *or* cubic metres (13.1 cubic yards).

décathlon [dekat'lɔ̃], *n.m.* (*spt.*) decathlon.

décauville [dəko'vil], *n.m.* narrow gauge railway.

décaver [deka've], *v.t.* to win the whole of the stakes from, (*fam.*) to clean out; (*fig.*) to ruin, to beggar.

décédé [dese'de], *n.m.* (*fem.* -ée) deceased (*person*).

décéder [dese'de], *v.i.* (*conjug. like* CÉDER) to die, to decease.

décèlement [desɛl'mɑ̃], *n.m.* disclosure, exposure, discovery.

déceler [des'le], *v.t.* (*conjug. like* AMENER) to disclose, to reveal, to betray. **se déceler**, *v.r.* to betray oneself.

déceleur [des'lœːr], *n.m.* (*fem.* **-euse**) betrayer, revealer.

décembre [de'sɑ̃:br], *n.m.* December.

décemment [desa'mɑ̃], *adv.* decently.

décence [de'sɑ̃:s], *n.f.* decency, propriety.

décent [de'sɑ̃], *a.* decent, becoming; modest.

décentralisation [desɑ̃traliza'sjɔ̃], *n.f.* decentralization.

décentraliser [desɑ̃trali'ze], *v.t.* to decentralize.

déception [desɛp'sjɔ̃], *n.f.* disappointment; deception, deceit.

décernement [desɛrnə'mɑ̃], *n.m.* awarding.

décerner [desɛr'ne], *v.t.* to decree, to enact, to award, to confer (*an honor*); to issue (*a summons etc.*).

décès [de'sɛ], *n.m.* decease, demise, death.

décevant [des'vɑ̃], *a.* deceptive; disappointing.

décevoir [desə'vwaːr], *v.t. irr.* (*conjug. like* RECEVOIR) to deceive; to disappoint.

déchaînement [deʃɛn'mɑ̃], *n.m.* unbridling, bursting (*of storm*); outburst (*of passion*); fury, rage; invective.

déchaîner [deʃɛ'ne], *v.t.* to unchain, to let loose; to give vent to (*passion*). **se déchaîner**, *v.r.* to break loose; to burst out; to run wild (*of passions etc.*).

déchaler [deʃa'le], *v.i.* to ebb; to lie dry.

déchanter [deʃɑ̃'te], *v.i.* to lower one's key (*in singing*); (*fig.*) to lower one's pretensions, to sing another tune.

déchaperonner [deʃaprɔ'ne], *v.t.* to unhood (*a hawk etc.*); to uncope (*a wall*).

décharge [de'ʃarʒ], *n.f.* unloading; rebate (*on a tax*); outlet, discharge (*of water etc.*); (*Law*) discharge, acquittal; (*Mil.*) volley.

déchargement [deʃarʒə'mɑ̃], *n.m.* unloading, unlading.

décharger [deʃar'ʒe], *v.t.* (*conjug. like* MANGER) to unload; to empty; to disburden; to discharge; to fire (*fire-arms*); to acquit (*de*). **se décharger**, *v.r.* to be unloaded, to discharge; to give vent (*to*); to unburden oneself.

déchargeur [deʃar'ʒœːr], *n.m.* unloader, wharf porter, heaver, lumper.

décharné [deʃar'ne], *a.* fleshless; lean, emaciated.

décharnement [deʃarnə'mɑ̃], *n.m.* emaciation.

décharner [deʃar'ne], *v.t.* to strip the flesh off; to emaciate.

déchaumage [deʃo'maːʒ], *n.m.* (*Agric.*) ploughing up fallow ground.

déchaumer [deʃo'me], *v.t.* to plough up the stubble on; to break up (*fallow land*).

déchaussé [deʃo'se], *a.* barefooted.

déchausser [deʃo'se], *v.t.* to pull off (*someone's* shoes and stockings; to lay bare the root or base (*of trees, buildings, teeth etc.*). **se déchausser**, *v.r.* to take off one's shoes and stockings.

déchéance [deʃe'ɑ̃:s], *n.f.* forfeiture; disgrace; deposition.

déchet [de'ʃɛ], *n.m.* loss, waste, offal.

décheveler [deʃə'vle], *v.t.* (*conjug. like* APPELER) to dishevel [ÉCHEVELER].

déchevêtrer [deʃəvɛ'tre], *v.t.* to unhalter (*a beast of burden*).

décheviller [deʃəvi'je], *v.t.* to unpeg, to unpin.

déchiffrable [deʃi'frabl], *a.* legible.

déchiffrement [deʃifrə'mɑ̃], *n.m.* deciphering; reading *or* playing at sight.

déchiffrer [deʃi'fre], *v.t.* to decipher, to unravel; to read *or* play at sight. **se déchiffrer**, *v.r.* to be deciphered.

déchiffreur [deʃi'frœːr], *n.m.* (*fem.* **-euse**) decipherer; sight reader; **déchiffreur de radar**, radar scanner.

déchiqueté [deʃik'te], *a.* jagged, indented.

déchiqueter [deʃik'te], *v.t.* (*conjug. like* APPELER) to cut, to slash, to hack; to cut into long pieces.

déchiqueture [deʃik'tyːr], *n.f.* tear, slash.

déchirage [deʃi'raːʒ], *n.m.* ripping up, breaking up (*of a ship etc.*).

déchirant [deʃi'rɑ̃], *a.* heart-rending, piercing; excruciating.

déchirement [deʃir'mɑ̃], *n.m.* rending, tearing, laceration; (*fig.*) heart-break.

déchirer [deʃi're], *v.t.* to tear to pieces, to rend; (*fig.*) to torture; to revile. **se déchirer**, *v.r.* to tear, to be torn; to defame each other.

déchirure [deʃi'ryːr], *n.f.* rent, tear; fissure.

déchoir [de'ʃwaːr], *v.i. irr.* to decay, to fall off, to decline; to sink.

déchouer [deʃu'e], *v.t.* to get off, to set afloat.

déchu [de'ʃy], *a.* fallen, decayed; sunken; **ange déchu**, fallen angel.

décidé [desi'de], *a.* decided, determined, resolved.

décidément [deside'mɑ̃], *adv.* decidedly, positively; firmly; definitely.

décider [desi'de], *v.t.* to decide, to determine, to settle; to induce, to persuade.—*v.i.* to decide. **se décider**, *v.r.* to decide, to determine, to make up one's mind.

décigramme [desi'gram], *n.m.* decigram (*one-tenth of a gramme*, 1.54 *grains*).

décilitre [desi'litr], *n.m.* decilitre (*one-tenth of a litre*).

décimal [desi'mal], *a.* (*m.pl.* **-aux**) decimal.—*n.f.* (**-e**) a decimal.

décimalisation [desimaliza'sjɔ̃], *n.f.* decimalization.

décimaliser [desimali'ze], *v.t.* to decimalize.

décimateur [desima'tœːr], *n.m.* tithe owner.

décime [de'sim], *n.f.* tithe.

décimer [desi'me], *v.t.* to decimate, to destroy, to annihilate.

décimètre [desi'mɛtr], *n.m.* decimetre (3.937 *inches*).

décimo [desi'mo], *adv.* tenthly.

décintrer [desɛ̃'tre], *v.t.* to remove the centerings from (*arches*).

décisif [desi'zif], *a.* (*fem.* **-sive**) decisive, conclusive.

décision [desi'zjɔ̃], *n.f.* decision, determination; resolution.

décisivement [desiziv'mɑ̃], *adv.* decisively; peremptorily, positively.

décistère [desi'stɛːr], *n.m.* tenth of a stere (3.53 *cubic feet*).

déciviliser [desivili'ze], *v.t.* to decivilize.

déclamateur [deklama'tœ:r], *n.m.* (*fem.* **-trice**) declaimer; (*fig.*) tub-thumper.—*a.* (*fem.* **-trice**) declamatory, bombastic.

déclamation [deklama'sjõ], *n.f.* declamation, elocution.

déclamatoire [deklama'twa:r], *a.* declamatory.

déclamer [dekla'me], *v.t., v.i.* to declaim; to spout, to mouth.

déclarant [dekla'rã], *n.m.* (*Law*) informant.

déclaration [deklara'sjõ], *n.f.* declaration, proclamation; disclosure; notification; *déclaration sous serment,* affidavit.

déclaratoire [deklara'twa:r], *a.* declaratory.

déclarer [dekla're], *v.t.* to declare, to make known; to proclaim; to certify. **se déclarer,** *v.r.* to speak one's mind; to declare oneself *or* itself; to show oneself *or* itself.

déclassé [dekla'se], *a.* come down in the world.—*n.m.* (*fem.* **-ée**) one who has come down in the world; one rejected by his own class *or* sphere.

déclassement [deklas'mã], *n.m.* loss of social position.

déclasser [dekla'se], *v.t.* to alter the classing of; to transfer from one class to another (*on trains, boats etc.*); to strike off the rolls, to dismiss from the service.

déclencher [deklã'ʃe], *v.t.* to unlatch (*a door*); to unhook, to detach; to release; (*Mil.*) to launch (*an attack*).

déclic [de'klik], *n.m.* pawl, catch.

déclin [de'klɛ̃], *n.m.* decline; decay; wane (*of the moon*); ebb; close (*of day etc.*).

déclinaison [deklinɛ'zõ], *n.f.* (*Gram.*) declension.

déclinant [dekli'nã], *a.* declining.

décliner [dekli'ne], *v.t.* to refuse; (*Gram.*) to decline; to state.—*v.i.* to decline, to be on the wane, to fall off.

déclive [de'kli:v], *a.* declivous, sloping.

déclivité [deklivi'te], *n.f.* declivity, slope.

décloîtrer (se) [sədeklwa'tre], *v.r.* to leave the cloister, to return to the world.

déclore [de'klɔ:r], *v.t. irr.* (*conjug. like* CLORE) to unclose, to throw open.

décochement [dekɔʃ'mã], *n.m.* discharge, shooting (*of arrows, shafts etc.*).

décocher [dekɔ'ʃe], *v.t.* to discharge, to dart (*arrows etc.*); to let fly (*insults etc.*).

décoiffer [dekwa'fe], *v.t.* to remove *or* undo the coiffure of, to undress the hair of. **se décoiffer,** *v.r.* to undo one's head-dress; to take off one's hat.

décoincer (se) [sədekwɛ̃'se], *v.r.* (*conjug. like* COMMENCER) to work loose.

décollage [dekɔ'la:ʒ], *n.m.* (*Av.*) taking off.

décollement [dekɔl'mã], *n.m.* ungluing, unpasting; coming off; detachment (*of retina*).

décoller [dekɔ'le], *v.t.* to unglue.—*v.i.* (*Av.*) to take off. **se décoller,** *v.r.* to become unglued,to come off.

décolletage [dekɔl'ta:ʒ], *n.m.* lowness in the neck (*of dresses*); baring the neck and shoulders.

décolleté [dekɔl'te], *a.* (*Dress.*) low-necked.

décolleter [dekɔl'te], *v.t.* (*conjug. like* APPELER) to uncover the neck, shoulders etc., of; to cut (*a dress*) low. **se décolleter,** *v.r.* to bare one's shoulders; to wear a low dress.

décoloration [dekɔlɔra'sjõ], *n.f.* discoloration.

décoloré [dekɔlɔ're], *a.* discolored, faded.

décolorer [dekɔlɔ're], *v.t.* to discolor. **se décolorer,** *v.r.* to become discolored, to fade.

décombres [de'kõ:br], *n.m.* (*used only in pl.*) rubbish, debris, ruins.

décommander [dekɔmã'de], *v.t.* to countermand; to cancel.

décomposé [dekõpo'ze], *a.* decomposed.

décomposer [dekõpo'ze], *v.t.* to decompose; to break up; to distort. **se décomposer,** *v.r.* to decompose, to rot; (*fig.*) to be distorted (*of the face etc.*).

décomposition [dekõpozi'sjõ], *n.f.* decomposition, analysis.

décompresseur [dekõprɛ'sœ:r], *n.m.* (*Motor.*) exhaust valve.

décompte [de'kõ:t], *n.m.* deduction, discount, allowance; deficit; balance due; (*fig.*) drawback; disappointment.

décompter [dekõ'te], *v.t.* to deduct.—*v.i.* (*fig.*) to be disappointed.

déconcertant [dekõsɛr'tã], *a.* disconcerting.

déconcerter [dekõsɛr'te], *v.t.* to disconcert; to baffle. **se déconcerter,** *v.r.* to be disconcerted *or* put out.

déconfiture [dekõfi'ty:r], *n.f.* discomfiture; break-down; insolvency.

décongeler [dekõ'ʒle], *v.t.* (*conjug. like* AMENER) to thaw (*chilled meat*).

déconseiller [dekõsɛ'je], *v.t.* to dissuade.

déconsidération [dekõsidera'sjõ], *n.f.* disrepute, discredit.

déconsidérer [dekõside're], *v.t.* (*conjug. like* CÉDER) to bring into disrepute, to discredit. **se déconsidérer,** *v.r.* to fall into disrepute.

décontenancement [dekõtnãs'mã], *n.m.* mortification, embarrassment.

décontenancer [dekõtnã'se], *v.t.* (*conjug. like* COMMENCER) to abash, to put out of countenance. **se décontenancer,** *v.r.* to be put out of countenance, to be abashed.

déconvenue [dekõv'ny], *n.f.* discomfiture; disappointment, set-back.

décor [de'kɔ:r], *n.m.* decoration; (*Theat., pl.*) scenery.

décorateur [dekɔra'tœ:r], *n.m.* (*fem.* **-trice**) ornamental painter, decorator; scene painter.

décoratif [dekɔra'tif], *a.* (*fem.* **-tive**) decorative, ornamental.

décoration [dekɔra'sjõ], *n.f.* decoration, embellishment; medal, insignia (*of an order*).

décorder [dekɔr'de], *v.t.* to untwist, to untwine (*a cord etc.*); to untie the rope (*of a box*).

décoré [dekɔ're], *a.* decorated; wearing the insignia of some order *or* its ribbon in one's buttonhole.

décorer [dekɔ're], *v.t.* to decorate; to set off; to confer the Legion of Honor etc. upon.

décorner [dekɔr'ne], *v.t.* to dishorn.

décortiquer [dekɔrti'ke], *v.t.* to decorticate, to bark, to husk, to shell, to peel.

décorum [dekɔ'rɔm], *n.m.* decorum, propriety.

découcher [deku'ʃe], *v.i.* to sleep away from home; to stay out all night.

découdre [de'kudr] *v.t. irr. (conjug. like* COUDRE*)* to unsew, to unstitch; to rip up. **se découdre,** *v.r.* to come unstitched.

découler [deku'le], *v.i.* to trickle, to flow; to spring, to proceed *(from).*

découpage [deku'pa:ʒ], *n.m.* cutting out, carving out.

découpé [deku'pe], *a.* (Bot.) cut, denticulated.

découper [deku'pe], *v.t.* to cut up; to pink, to cut out; to punch. **se découper,** *v.r.* to stand out, to show up *(against).*

découpeur [deku'pœ:r], *n.m.* (fem. **-euse**) carver; pinker, cutter.

découplé [deku'ple], *a.* strapping.

découpler [deku'ple], *v.t.* to uncouple, to unleash, to let loose *(in pursuit).*

découpoir [deku'pwa:r], *n.m.* punch, stamping machine, stamping press.

découpure [deku'py:r], *n.f.* cutting out, pinking, work cut out; cut paper-work; indentation.

décourageant [dekura'ʒã], *a.* discouraging, disheartening.

découragement [dekuraʒ'mã], *n.m.* discouragement.

décourager [dekura'ʒe], *v.t. (conjug. like* MANGER*)* to discourage, to dishearten. **se décourager,** *v.r.* to be disheartened.

décours [de'ku:r], *n.m.* decrease; wane *(of the moon).*

décousu [deku'zy], *a.* unsewn, unstitched; *(fig.)* desultory *(of style etc.).*

décousure [deku'zy:r], *n.f.* unpicked stitching.

découvert [deku've:r], *a.* uncovered; discovered; open, unguarded; bare, bareheaded.—*n.m.* (Comm.) overdraft, deficit.

découverte [deku'vert], *n.f.* discovery, detection; (Mil.) reconnoitring; (Naut.) look out.

découvreur [deku'vrœ:r], *n.m.* (fem. **-euse**) discoverer.

découvrir [deku'vri:r], *v.t. (conjug. like* OUVRIR*)* to uncover, to expose; to discover, to disclose, to detect. **se découvrir,** *v.r.* to uncover oneself, to take off one's hat; to unbosom oneself; to expose oneself; to lie open *or* bare; to clear up *(of the sky).*

décramponner (se) [sədekrãpɔ'ne], *v.r.* to let go one's hold.

décrasser [dekra'se], *v.t.* to take the dirt off, to scour; *(fig.)* to make presentable. **se décrasser,** *v.r.* to wash, to clean oneself; to become polished.

décrassoir [dekra'swa:r], *n.m.* fine-tooth comb.

décréditement [dekredit'mã], *n.m.* discrediting.

décrépi [dekre'pi], *a.* unplastered.

décrépir (se) [sədekre'pi:r], *v.r.* to lose its plaster *(of a wall etc.).*

décrépit [dekre'pi], *a.* decrepit, broken-down.

décrépitude [dekrepi'tyd], *n.f.* decrepitude.

décret [de'krɛ], *n.m.* decree, order, enactment; (Law) writ, warrant.

décret-loi [dekrɛ'lwa], *n.m.* Order in Council.

décréter [dekre'te], *v.t. (conjug. like* CÉDER*)* to decree, to order, to enact.

décri [de'kri], *n.m.* official crying down *or* depreciation *(of coinage);* (fig.) discredit.

décrier [dekri'e], *v.t.* to decry, to run down;

(fig.) to discredit. **se décrier,** *v.r.* to bring oneself into disrepute; to decry one another.

décrire [de'kri:r], *v.t. (conjug. like* ÉCRIRE*)* to describe, to depict.

décrocher [dekrɔ'ʃe], *v.t.* to unhook, to take down, to disconnect.

décroiser [dekrwa'ze], *v.t.* to uncross *(the legs etc.).*

décroissant [dekrwa'sã], *a.* decreasing, diminishing; subsiding.

décroissement [dekrwas'mã], *n.m.*, **décroissance** [dekrwa'sã:s], *n.f.* decrease, diminution, wane.

décroît [de'krwa], *n.m.* wane *(of the moon).*

décroître [de'krwa:tr], *v.i. irr. (conjug. like* CROÎTRE *but p.p.* décru, *without circumflex)* to decrease, to diminish, to wane.

décrottage [dekrɔ'ta:ʒ], *n.m.* cleaning *(of boots, trousers etc.).*

décrotter [dekrɔ'te], *v.t.* to rub the dirt off; *(fig.)* to improve the manners of. **se décrotter,** *v.r.* to clean oneself; to clean one's shoes etc.

décrotteur [dekrɔ'tœ:r], *n.m.* (fem. **-euse**) bootblack.

décrottoir [dekrɔ'twa:r], *n.m.* scraper *(for shoes).*

décrottoire [dekrɔ'twa:r], *n.f.* shoe brush.

décrue [de'kry], *n.f.* decrease; fall *(of water).*

décrypter [dekrip'te], *v.t.* to decipher.

déculotter [dekylɔ'te], *v.t.* to take off *(s.o.'s)* breeches, *(a child's)* pants.

décuple [de'kypl], *a.* and *n.m.* tenfold.

décupler [deky'ple], *v.t.* to increase tenfold.

décuvage [deky'va:ʒ], *n.m.*, **décuvaison** [dekyvɛ'zõ], *n.f.* tunning *(of wine).*

décuver [deky've], *v.t.* to tun.

dédaigner [dede'ɲe], *v.t.* to disdain, to scorn, to despise.

dédaigneusement [dedɛɲøz'mã], *adv.* disdainfully, scornfully.

dédaigneux [dedɛ'ɲø], *a.* (fem. **-euse**) disdainful, scornful.

dédain [de'dɛ̃], *n.m.* disdain, scorn, disregard.

dédale [de'dal], *n.m.* labyrinth, maze.

dedans [də'dã], *adv.* within, in, inside; at home.—*n.m.* inside, interior.

dédicace [dedi'kas], *n.f.* dedication, consecration *(of a church etc.).*

dédication [dedika'sjõ], *n.f.* (Law) dedication *(of a temple etc.).*

dédier [de'dje], *v.t.* to dedicate, to consecrate; to devote; to inscribe *(a book etc.).*

dédire [de'di:r], *v.t. irr. (conjug. like* MÉDIRE*)* to disown; gainsay, to contradict. **se dédire,** *v.r.* to recant, to retract, to go back on one's word.

dédit [de'di], *n.m.* retraction; forfeit.

dédommagement [dedɔmaʒ'mã], *n.m.* indemnification; compensation, damages.

dédommager [dedɔma'ʒe], *v.t. (conjug. like* MANGER*)* to make amends for; to compensate, to make up for. **se dédommager,** *v.r.* to indemnify oneself.

dédorer [dedɔ're], *v.t.* to ungild. **se dédorer,** *v.r.* to lose its gilt *(of metal etc.).*

dédouanement [dedwan'mã], *n.m.* (customs) clearance.

dédouaner [dedwa'ne], *v.t.* to clear *(goods)* from the custom house.

dédoublement [dedublə'mã], **dédoublage** [dedu'bla:ʒ], *n.m.* dividing into two; unlining (*of a garment*); diluting.

dédoubler [dedu'ble], *v.t.* to take out the lining of; to divide into two; *dédoubler un autocar* (*un train*), to run a relief coach (train). **se dédoubler**, *v.r.* to be divided into two.

déductif [dedyk'tif], *a.* (*fem.* **-tive**) deductive.

déduction [dedyk'sjõ], *n.f.* deduction, allowance; inference.

déduire [de'dɥi:r], *v.t. irr.* (*conjug. like* CONDUIRE) to deduct, to subtract; to deduce, to infer.

déesse [de'ɛs], *n.f.* goddess, female deity.

défâcher [defa'ʃe], *v.t.* to pacify. **se défâcher**, *v.r.* to be pacified, to cool down.

défaillance [defa'jã:s], *n.f.* fainting fit, swoon, faintness; exhaustion; extinction (*of a family etc.*).

défaillant [defa'jã], *a.* failing, falling off; decaying; without heirs; weak, feeble.— *n.m.* (*fem.* **-e**) (*Law*) defaulter.

défaillir [defa'ji:r], *v.i. irr.* (*conjug. like* ASSAILLIR) to fail, to default; to decay; to swoon, to faint away.

défaire [de'fɛ:r], *v.t. irr.* (*conjug. like.* FAIRE) to undo, to unmake; to defeat; to emaciate; to embarrass; to rid. **se défaire**, *v.r.* to come undone; *se défaire de*, to get rid of, to give up.

défait [de'fɛ], *a.* undone, defeated; meager, wasted; worn out.

défaite [de'fɛt], *n.f.* defeat, overthrow; evasion, pretence, excuse.

défaitisme [defɛ'tism], *n.m.* defeatism.

défaitiste [defɛ'tist], *a.* and *n.* defeatist.

défalcation [defalka'sjõ], *n.f.* deduction.

défalquer [defal'ke], *v.t.* to take off, to deduct.

défausser [defo'se], *v.t.* to straighten.

défaut [de'fo], *n.m.* absence, lack, default; defect, fault, flaw; (*Law*) non-appearance; *à défaut de*, instead of, for want of; *faire défaut*, to be wanting, to be missing.

défaveur [defa'vœ:r], *n.f.* disfavor, discredit.

défavorable [defavɔ'rabl], *a.* unfavorable.

défavorablement [defavɔrablə'mã], *adv.* unfavorably.

défectif [defɛk'tif], *a.* (*fem.* **-tive**) (*Gram.*) defective.

défection [defɛk'sjõ], *n.f.* defection, falling off, disloyalty.

défectueux [defɛk'tɥø], *a.* (*fem.* **-euse**) defective, imperfect.

défectuosité [defɛktɥozi'te], *n.f.* defect, imperfection, flaw.

défendable [defã'dabl], *a.* defensible, tenable.

défendeur [defã'dœ:r], *n.m.* (*fem.* **-eresse**) defendant; respondent.

défendre [de'fã:dr], *v.t.* to defend, to protect; to shield; to support; to forbid. **se défendre**, *v.r.* to defend oneself; to clear oneself; to deny.

défense [de'fã:s], *n.f.* defense, protection; prohibition; apology, plea; (*Law*) the defense; (*Fort., pl.*) outworks; tusk, fang (*of animals*); (*Naut.*) fender; *défense de fumer*, no smoking.

défenseur [defã'sœ:r], *n.m.* defender, supporter; advocate, counsel.

défensif [defã'sif], *a.* (*fem.* **-sive**) defensive.—*n.f.* (**-sive**) defensive.

déféquer [defe'ke], *v.t.* (*conjug. like* CÉDER) to purify.—*v.i.* to defecate.

déférence [defe'rã:s], *n.f.* deference, regard, respect.

déférent [defe'rã], *a.* deferential, compliant.

déférer [defe're], *v.t.* (*conjug. like* CÉDER) * to confer, to bestow; to tender; to accuse, to inform against.—*v.i.* to defer, to yield, to comply.

déferler [defɛr'le], *v.t.* (*Naut.*) to unfurl.—*v.i.* to break into foam (*of the sea*).

déferrer [defe're], *v.t.* to unshoe (*a horse*). **se déferrer**, *v.r.* to come unshod, to lose a shoe.

défeuiller [defœ'je], *v.t.* to take the leaves off. **se défeuiller**, *v.r.* to shed its leaves.

défi [de'fi], *n.m.* defiance, challenge.

défiance [de'fjã:s], *n.f.* distrust, mistrust; caution.

défiant [de'fjã], *a.* distrustful, suspicious.

déficeler [defis'le], *v.t.* (*conjug. like* APPELER) to untie; to undo.

déficient [defi'sjõ], *a.* deficient.

déficit [defi'sit], *n.m.* deficit, deficiency.

défier [de'fje], *v.t.* to defy, to challenge; to brave, to face; to set at defiance. **se défier**, *v.r.* to defy *or* to challenge each other; to distrust, to beware (*de*).

défiger [defi'ʒe], *v.t.* (*conjug. like* MANGER) to liquefy.

défiguration [defigyra'sjõ], *n.f.*, **défigurement** [defigyr'mã], *n.m.* disfigurement, defacement.

défigurer [defigy're], *v.t.* to disfigure, to mar; to distort. **se défigurer**, *v.r.* to disfigure oneself; to become deformed.

défilade [defi'lad], *n.f.* filing off *or* past, marching past; succession.

défilé [defi'le], *n.m.* defile, narrow pass, gorge; (*fig.*) strait, difficulty; (*Mil.*) filing past; *un défilé de mannequins*, a mannequin parade.

défiler [defi'le], *v.t.* to unstring, to unthread; to untwist.—*v.i.* to file off, to march past. **se défiler**, *v.r.* to come unthreaded *or* unstrung; (*Mil.*) to take cover; to slip away.

défini [defi'ni], *a.* definite, determined, defined.

définir [defi'ni:r], *v.t.* to define; to determine; to describe.

définissable [defini'sabl], *a.* definable.

définitif [defini'tif], *a.* (*fem.* **-tive**) definitive, final; ultimate, eventual.

définition [defini'sjõ], *n.f.* definition.

définitivement [definitiv'mã], *adv.* definitively, positively, decidedly; eventually.

déflation [defla'sjõ], *n.f.* deflation.

défléchir [defle'ʃi:r], *v.t.*, *v.i.* to turn from *or* aside, to deflect.

déflecteur [deflɛk'tœ:r], *n.m.* (*Motor.*) ventilating window; deflector.

défleuraison [DÉFLORAISON].

défleurir [deflœ'ri:r], *v.t.* to nip *or* strip off blossoms.—*v.i.* to lose its flowers.

déflexion [deflɛk'sjõ], *n.f.* deviation; (*Gram.*) deflection.

défloraison [deflɔrɛ'zõ], **défleuraison** [deflœrɛ'zõ], *n.f.* fall *or* withering of the blossom.

déflorer [deflɔ're], *v.t.* to deflower, to seduce.

défonçage [defɔ̃'sa:ʒ], **défoncement** [defɔ̃s'mã], *n.m.* staving in (*of the head of casks*), breaking *or* smashing in; (*Agric.*) deep trenching.

défoncer [defɔ̃'se], *v.t.* (*conjug. like* COMMENCER) to stave in, to bilge (*a cask*); to dig deeply, to trench (*ground*). **se défoncer,** *v.r.* to give way; to break up (*of roads*); to get battered.

défonceuse [defɔ̃'søːz], *n.f.* trenching plough.

déforestation [deforesta'sjɔ̃], *n.f.* deforestation.

déformant [defɔr'mã], *a.* a distorting (*mirror etc.*).

déformation [deforma'sjɔ̃], *n.f.* distortion, buckling.

déformer [defɔr'me], *v.t.* to deform, to distort. **se déformer,** *v.r.* to lose its shape.

défortifier [deforti'fje], *v.t.* to dismantle the fortifications of.

défourner [defur'ne], *v.t.* to draw out of an oven *or* kiln.

défourrer [defu're], *v.t.* to unwrap, to take out of its cover; to thresh (*grain*).

défraîchir [defrɛ'ʃiːr], *v.t.* to tarnish, to take away the brilliancy, gloss *or* freshness of. **se défraîchir,** *v.r.* to lose its brilliancy, freshness etc., to tarnish.

défrayer [defrɛ'je], *v.t.* (*conjug. like* PAYER) to defray, to bear the cost of; to amuse.

défriche [de'friʃ], *n.f.,* **défriché** [defri'ʃe], *n.m.* piece of cleared land.

défrichement [defriʃ'mã], **défrichage** [defri'ʃa:ʒ], *n.m.* clearing, breaking up (*of land for tillage*).

défricher [defri'ʃe], *v.t.* to clear, to break up (*ground*) for tillage; to reclaim.

défricheur [defri'ʃœːr], *n.m.* clearer; settler.

défriper [defri'pe], *v.t.* to smooth out.

défrisement [defriz'mã], *n.m.* uncurling.

défriser [defri'ze], *v.t.* to uncurl; (*fam.*) to disappoint, to ruffle.

défroque [de'frɔk], *n.f.* the effects left by a dying monk; *hence,* old things, effects, cast-off clothes, etc.

défroqué [defrɔ'ke], *a.* and *n.m.* unfrocked (*priest*).

défroquer [defrɔ'ke], *v.t.* to unfrock. **se défroquer,** *v.r.* to renounce one's order (*of monks*).

défunt [de'fœ̃], *a.* defunct, deceased, late.—*n.m.* (*fem.* -e) the deceased.

dégagé [dega'ʒe], *a.* free, easy, unconstrained; flippant; bold; slender, graceful.

dégagement [degaʒ'mã], *n.m.* disengagement, redemption; clearance; discharge (*of gas etc.*); (*fig.*) unconcern.

dégager [dega'ʒe], *v.t.* (*conjug. like* MANGER) to disengage, to extricate; to clear; to deliver, to rescue; to release, to emit (*fumes etc.*); to redeem, to take out of pawn. **se dégager,** *v.r.* to be liberated (*de*); to extricate, disengage *or* disentangle oneself; to get away; (*Chem.*) to be emitted.

dégaine [de'gɛːn], *n.f.* (*colloq.*) awkward gait.

dégainer [degɛ'ne], *v.t.* to unsheathe (*one's sword etc.*).

déganter [degã'te], *v.t.* to unglove. **se déganter,** *v.r.* to take off one's gloves.

dégarnir [degar'niːr], *v.t.* to strip; to dismantle; to thin (*trees, woods etc.*). **se dégarnir,** *v.r.* to strip oneself (*de*); to become empty; to grow thin; to lose branches etc.

dégât [de'ga], *n.m.* havoc, damage, ravage.

dégauchir [dego'ʃiːr], *v.t.* to smooth, to plane, to level, to straighten; (*fig.*) to polish.

dégauchissement [degoʃis'mã], **dégauchissage** [degoʃi'sa:ʒ], *n.m.* planing, straightening, levelling, smoothing.

dégazonner [degazɔ'ne], *v.t.* to remove the turf from.

dégel [de'ʒɛl], *n.m.* thaw.

dégeler [de'ʒle], *v.t., v.i.* (*conjug. like* AMENER) to thaw. **se dégeler,** *v.r.* to thaw (*of persons*).

dégénération [deʒenera'sjɔ̃], *n.f.* degeneration, degeneracy.

dégénéré [deʒene're], *a.* and *n.m.* (*fem.* -ée) degenerate (person).

dégénérer [deʒene're], *v.i. irr.* (*conjug. like* CÉDER) to decline, to degenerate.

dégénérescence [deʒenere'sã:s], *n.f.* degeneracy, degeneration.

dégénérescent [deʒenere'sã], *a.* degenerating.

dégingandé [deʒɛ̃gã'de], *a.* ungainly, gawky, awkward in one's gait; clumsy, disjointed, irregular.

dégivrer [deʒi'vre], *v.t.* to de-ice.

dégivreur [deʒi'vrœːr], *n.m.* (*Motor., Av.*) de-icer.

déglutir [degly'tiːr], *v.t.* to swallow.

déglutition [deglyti'sjɔ̃], *n.f.* deglutition, swallowing.

dégommer [degɔ'me], *v.t.* to wash the gum out of; (*slang*) to sack.

dégonflement [degɔ̃flə'mã], *n.m.* deflating (*of tire, balloon*); collapse; reduction.

dégonfler [degɔ̃'fle], *v.t.* to cause to collapse; to deflate; to reduce (*a swelling*). **se dégonfler,** *v.r.* to go down, to be reduced; to subside; (*pop.*) to sing small.

dégorgement [degɔrʒ'mã], *n.m.* breaking out, overflow; unstopping.

dégorger [degɔr'ʒe], *v.t.* (*conjug. like* MANGER) to disgorge; to unstop, to clear; to cleanse.—*v.i.* to discharge, to overflow. **se dégorger,** *v.r.* to discharge *or* empty itself *or* oneself, to be unstopped, to be cleared.

dégourdi [degur'di], *a.* quick, sharp, acute, smart; tepid (*of water*).—*n.m.* (*fem.* -e) a shrewd *or* forward person.

dégourdir [degur'diːr], *v.t.* to revive, to quicken; to take the chill off; (*fig.*) to sharpen, to render shrewd; to polish. **se dégourdir,** *v.r.* to lose numbness, to feel warmer; to brighten up.

dégourdissement [degurdis'mã], *n.m.* return of circulation; quickening, reviving.

dégoût [de'gu], *n.m.* dislike, distaste; disgust, aversion; mortification.

dégoûtant [degu'tã], *a.* disgusting, distasteful, nauseous; loathsome; unpleasant.

dégoûté [degu'te], *a.* disgusted; fastidious.—*n.m.* (*fem.* -ée) fastidious person.

dégoûter [degu'te], *v.t.* to disgust. **se dégoûter,** *v.r.* to take a dislike to.

dégouttant [degu'tã], *a.* dripping.

dégouttement [degut'mã], *n.m.* dripping, falling in drops.

dégoutter [degu'te], *v.i.* to drip, to fall in drops, to trickle.

dégradant [degra'dã], *a.* degrading, debasing.

103

dégradation

dégradation [degradɑ'sjɔ̃], *n.f.* degradation; debasement; (*Paint.*) gradation of light and shade; (*Law*) **dégradation nationale** or **civile**, loss of civil rights; **dégradation militaire**, cashiering.

dégrader [degra'de], *v.t.* to degrade, to debase; to deface; (*Mil.*) to reduce to the ranks; to cashier; (*Paint.*) to graduate the light and shade. **se dégrader**, *v.r.* to degrade, debase or disgrace oneself; to become damaged or defaced.

dégrafer [degra'fe], *v.t.* to unclasp, to un-hook. **se dégrafer**, *v.r.* to come unfastened (*of garments etc.*); to unfasten one's clothes.

dégraissage [degrɛ'sa:ʒ], **dégraissement** [degrɛs'mɑ̃], *n.m.* dry-cleaning (*garments*); scouring (*wool*).

dégraisser [degrɛ'se], *v.t.* to remove greasy stains from.

dégraisseur [degrɛ'sœ:r], *n.m.* (*fem.* **-euse**) scourer (*of wool*); dry-cleaner (*of clothes etc.*).

dégraissoir [degrɛ'swa:r], *n.m.* scraper.

degré [də'gre], *n.m.* step, stair; stage, grade, degree; point, extent, height, pitch.

dégréer [degre'e], *v.t.* to unrig; to strip a mast.

dégrèvement [degrɛv'mɑ̃], *n.m.* reduction; tax allowance, relief.

dégrever [degrə've], *v.t.* (*conjug. like* AMENER) to diminish, to reduce (*a tax etc.*); to relieve (*someone of a tax*); to disencumber (*an estate etc.*); to pay off (*a mortgage*).

dégringolade [degrɛ̃gɔ'lad], *n.f.* (*fam.*) fall, tumble.

dégringoler [degrɛ̃gɔ'le], *v.i.* to tumble down, to topple over.

dégrisement [degriz'mɑ̃], *n.m.* (*colloq.*) sobering, getting sober; (*fig.*) cooling down.

dégriser [degri'ze], *v.t.* to sober; (*fig.*) to cool down, to bring to one's senses. **se dégriser**, *v.r.* to sober up; (*fig.*) to come to one's senses; to lose one's illusions.

dégrossir [degro'si:r], *v.t.* to rough-hew; (*fig.*) to make a rough sketch of.

dégrossissage [degrosi'sa:ʒ], **dégrossissement** [degrosis'mɑ̃], *n.m.* rough-hewing; (*Carp.*) dressing, trimming.

déguenillé [degəni'je], *a.* tattered, ragged.—*n.m.* (*fem.* **-ée**) ragamuffin.

déguerpir [deger'pi:r], *v.i.* to move off; to be gone.

déguerpissement [degɛrpis'mɑ̃], *n.m.* quitting, giving up, abandonment.

dégueuler [degœ'le], *v.t.* (*vulg.*) to spew.

déguignonner [degiɲɔ'ne], *v.t.* to lift a curse from, to bring better luck to.

déguisable [degi'zabl], *a.* disguisable.

déguisement [degiz'mɑ̃], *n.m.* disguise, concealment; **parlez sans déguisement**, speak openly.

déguiser [degi'ze], *v.t.* to disguise, to cloak; to misrepresent. **se déguiser**, *v.r.* to disguise oneself, to put on fancy dress.

dégustateur [degysta'tœ:r], *n.m.* (*fem.* **-trice**) taster (*of wines etc.*).

dégustation [degysta'sjɔ̃], *n.f.* tasting (*of wines etc.*).

déguster [degys'te], *v.t.* to taste; to sip, to savor.

déhaler [dea'le], *v.t.* (*Naut.*) to tow out; to haul off.

déhâler [dea'le], *v.t.* to take away sun-burn, freckles, tan etc. from. **se déhâler**, *v.r.* to clear one's complexion.

déhanché [deɑ̃'ʃe], *a.* having the hip dislocated; (*fig.*) ungainly.

déhanchement [deɑ̃ʃ'mɑ̃], *n.m.* waddling gait, waddle.

déhancher (se) [sədeɑ̃'ʃe], *v.r.* to sway one's hips; to have a waddling, loose gait.

déharnachement [dearnaʃ'mɑ̃], *n.m.* un-harnessing.

déharnacher [dearna'ʃe], *v.t.* to unharness.

dehors [də'ɔ:r], *adv.* *without, outside; out of doors; abroad; externally; (*Naut.*) at sea; **au dedans et au dehors**, at home and abroad; **au dehors**, outwardly; **de dehors**, from without; **en dehors**, outside, *without; **mettre quelqu'un dehors**, to turn someone out.—*n.m. inv.* outside, exterior; (*pl.*) appearances; (*Fort.*) outworks; dependencies, approaches, grounds (*of a house*); **sauver les dehors**, to save appearances.

déification [deifika'sjɔ̃], *n.f.* deification.

déifier [dei'fje], *v.t.* to deify.

déisme [de'ism], *n.m.* deism.

déiste [de'ist], *a.* deistic.—*n.* deist.

déité [dei'te], *n.f.* deity (*god, goddess*), divinity.

déjà [de'ʒa], *adv.* already, before, previously.

déjection [deʒɛk'sjɔ̃], *n.f.* (*Med.*) dejection, ejection, evacuation.

déjeté [deʒ'te], *a.* awry, lopsided, off the straight.

déjeter [deʒ'te], *v.t.* (*conjug. like* APPELER) to warp. **se déjeter**, *v.r.* to warp (*of wood etc.*); (*Path.*) to deviate.

déjettement [deʒɛt'mɑ̃], *n.m.* warping, deviation.

déjeuner [deʒœ'ne], *n.m.* lunch; **petit déjeuner**, breakfast; **un déjeuner de porcelaine**, a china breakfast-set.—*v.i.* to breakfast, to lunch.

déjouer [de'ʒwe], *v.t.* to baffle, to frustrate, to foil; (*Mil.*) to outmaneuver.

déjucher [deʒy'ʃe], *v.t.* to dislodge.—*v.i.* to come down from the roost or from one's perch.

déjuger (se) [sədeʒy'ʒe], *v.r.* (*conjug. like* MANGER) to reverse one's opinion or decision.

delà [də'la], *prep.* on the other side of; beyond; **au delà, de delà, par delà**, or **en delà**, beyond; **deçà et delà**, both here and there, both this and that; **l'au-delà**, the hereafter.

délabré [dela'bre], *a.* tattered, shabby (*garments*); tumbledown, ramshackle (*building*).

délabrement [delabrə'mɑ̃], *n.m.* decay, dilapidation; shabbiness.

délabrer [dela'bre], *v.t.* to shatter, to ruin, to tear to tatters. **se délabrer**, *v.r.* to fall to pieces, to go to ruin.

délacer [dela'se], *v.t.* (*conjug. like* COMMENCER) to unlace (*shoes etc.*). **se délacer**, *v.r.* to unlace oneself; to come undone (*of shoes, strings etc.*).

délai [de'le], *n.m.* delay; respite.

délaissé [delɛ'se], *a.* abandoned, friendless.

délaissement [delɛs'mã], *n.m.* desertion; destitution, helplessness.

délaisser [delɛ'se], *v.t.* to forsake, to abandon; to neglect.

délassant [dela'sã], *a.* refreshing, diverting.

délassement [delas'mã], *n.m.* relaxation; repose.

délasser [dela'se], *v.t.* to refresh, to relax, to divert. **se délasser**, *v.r.* to refresh oneself, to rest.

délateur [dela'tœːr], *n.m.* (*fem.* **-trice**) informer, accuser.

délation [dela'sjɔ̃], *n.f.* informing.

délavage [dela'vaːʒ], *n.m.* diluting of color; soaking.

délaver [dela've], *v.t.* to dilute *or* wash (*color*); to soak into. **se délaver**, *v.r.* to become soaked; to lose color.

délayable [dele'jabl], *a.* dilutable.

délayage [dele'jaːʒ], *n.m.* diluting, dilution.

délayé [dele'je], *a.* watery.

délayer [dele'je], *v.t.* (*conjug. like* PAYER) to dilute; (*fig.*) to spin out.

délectable [delɛk'tabl], *a.* delectable, delightful.

délecter (se) [sədelɛk'te], *v.r.* to take delight.

délégation [delega'sjɔ̃], *n.f.* delegation, assignment.

délégatoire [delega'twaːr], *a.* delegatory.

délégué [dele'ge], *n.m.* (*fem.* **-ée**) delegate, deputy; proxy.

déléguer [dele'ge], *v.t.* (*conjug. like* CÉDER) to delegate; to assign. **se déléguer**, *v.r.* to be delegated.

délester [delɛs'te], *v.t.* to unballast.

délétère [dele'tɛːr], *a.* deleterious.

délibérant [delibe'rã], *a.* deliberative.

délibératif [delibera'tif], *a.* (*fem.* **-tive**) deliberative.

délibération [delibera'sjɔ̃], *n.f.* deliberation; resolution.

délibéré [delibe're], *a.* deliberate, determined, resolute.

délibérément [delibere'mã], *adv.* deliberately, resolutely.

délibérer [delibe're], *v.i.* (*conjug. like* CÉDER) to deliberate; to resolve.

délicat [deli'ka], *a.* delicate, dainty; nice, fastidious; frail.—*n.m.* (*fem.* **-e**) fastidious person.

délicatement [delikat'mã], *adv.* delicately, daintily, tenderly.

délicatesse [delika'tɛs], *n.f.* delicacy, fragility; tenderness; daintiness, fastidiousness; refinement, squeamishness; nicety (*of language etc.*); considerateness; (*pl.*) dainties.

délice [de'lis], *n.m. in sing.* (*used chiefly in f.pl.*) delight, pleasure.

délicieusement [delisjøz'mã], *adv.* deliciously, delightfully.

délicieux [deli'sjø], *a.* (*fem.* **-euse**) delicious, delightful.

délié [de'lje], *a.* slender, fine; sharp, shrewd; glib, flowing (*of style etc.*); untied, loose.

délier [de'lje], *v.t.* to unbind, to untie; to liberate; to release; to absolve. **se délier**, *v.r.* to come untied; to get loose.

délimitation [delimita'sjɔ̃], *n.f.* delimitation, fixing of boundaries.

délimiter [delimi'te], *v.t.* to delimit, to settle the boundaries of.

délinéation [delinea'sjɔ̃], *n.f.* delineation.

délinéer [deline'e], *v.t.* to delineate.

délinquance [delɛ̃'kãːs], *n.f.* delinquency.

délinquant [delɛ̃'kã], *n;a.* (*fem.* **-e**) delinquent, offender.— **enfance délinquante**, juvenile delinquents.

délirant [deli'rã], *a.* delirious, frenzied, frantic; rapturous, ecstatic.—*n.m.* (*fem.* **-e**) a delirious *or* ecstatic person.

délire [de'liːr], *n.m.* delirium, frenzy, folly.

délirer [deli're], *v.i.* to be delirious, to rave, to wander.

délit [de'li], *n.m.* misdemeanor, offence; **en flagrant délit**, in the very act, redhanded.

délivrance [deli'vrãːs], *n.f.* rescue, deliverance; issue (*of tickets*); delivery (*of certificates etc.*); accouchement.

délivre [de'livr], *n.m.* (*Anat.*) after-birth, placenta.

délivrer [deli'vre], *v.t.* to deliver, to release, to set free; to hand over; to issue; to deliver (*a woman of a baby*).

délogement [deloʒ'mã], *n.m.* removal, change of quarters, decamping.

déloger [delo'ʒe], *v.t.* (*conjug. like* MANGER) to turn out (*of house etc.*), to oust; to drive away; (*Mil.*) to dislodge.—*v.i.* to remove, to go (*from one's house etc.*), to go away, to march off.

déloyal [delwa'jal], *a.* (*m.pl.* **-aux**) disloyal, false, treacherous, unfair; foul.

déloyalement [delwajal'mã], *adv.* disloyally, unfairly.

déloyauté [delwajo'te], *n.f.* disloyalty, treachery.

delta [del'ta], *n.m.* delta.

déluge [de'lyːʒ], *n.m.* deluge, flood.

déluré [dely're], *a.* wide-awake, sharp.

délustrer [delys'tre], *v.t.* to take the luster *or* gloss from.

démagnétiser [demaɲeti'ze], *v.t.* to demagnetize.

démagogue [dema'gɔg], *n.* demagogue.

démailler [dema'je], *v.t.* to undo the meshes of (*. net etc.*).

demain [də'mɛ̃] *adv.* and *n.m.* tomorrow; **à demain!** see you tomorrow!

démancher [demã'ʃe], *v.t.* to take off the handle of; (*fig.*) to dislocate. **se démancher**, *v.r.* to lose its handle; to go wrong.

demande [də'mãːd], *n.f.* question; request, application, petition; claim; (*Comm.*) demand; order.

demander [dəmã'de], *v.t.* to ask, to beg, to request; to desire, to wish; to require, to call for; to need, to want; to inquire about; to ask to see; to seek in marriage; (*Comm.*) to order. **se demander**, *v.r.* to ask oneself, to wonder.

demandeur [dəmã'dœːr], *a.* (*fem.* **-euse**) always asking.—*n.m.* (*fem.* **-eresse**) asker, applicant; (*Law*) plaintiff.

démangeaison [demãʒɛ'zɔ̃], *n.f.* itching; longing.

démanger [demã'ʒe], *v.i.* (*conjug. like* MANGER) to itch; to long.

démantibuler [demãtiby'le], *v.t.* to break, to dislocate.

démaquiller [demaki'je], *v.t.* to take off someone's make-up. **se démaquiller**, *v.r.* to take off one's make-up.

démarcation

démarcation [demarkɑ'sjɔ̃], *n.f.* demarcation; *ligne de démarcation*, line of demarcation.

démarche [de'marʃ], *n.f.* gait, walk, bearing; proceeding, measure, step, course.

démarcheur [demar'ʃœːr], *n.m.* canvasser.

démarier [dema'rje], *v.t.* (*fam.*) to annul the marriage of; (*Hort.*) to thin out. **se démarier,** *v.r.* to be divorced.

démarrer [dema're], *v.t.* to cast off; to unfasten.—*v.i.* to leave, to slip her moorings (*of a ship*); to move, to get away, to start.

démarreur [dema'rœːr], *n.m.* (*Motor.*) self-starter.

démasquer [demas'ke], *v.t.* to unmask; to show up.

démâter [demɑ'te], *v.t.* to dismast.—*v.i.* to lose her masts (*of a ship*).

démêlage [deme'laːʒ], *n.m.* combing (*of wool*).

démêlé [deme'le], *n.m.* strife, contest, quarrel.

démêler [deme'le], *v.t.* to unravel, to disentangle, to separate; to clear up; to distinguish, to discern; to comb out (*hair*), to tease (*wool*). **se démêler,** *v.r.* to be disentangled; to extricate oneself; to stand out (*clearly*); to comb out one's hair.

démembrement [demɑ̃brə'mɑ̃], *n.m.* dismemberment; breaking up.

démembrer [demɑ̃'bre], *v.t.* to tear limb from limb, to dismember; to break up.

déménagement [demenaʒ'mɑ̃], *n.m.* (*household*) removal.

déménager [demena'ʒe], *v.t.* (*conjug. like* MANGER) to remove (*one's furniture*).—*v.i.* to (re)move.

déménageur [demena'ʒœːr], *n.m.* furniture mover.

démence [de'mɑ̃:s], *n.f.* insanity, madness.

démener (se) [sadem'ne], *v.r.* (*conjug. like* AMENER) to stir, to struggle, to make a great fuss, to strive hard.

démenti [demɑ̃'ti], *n.m.* denial, flat contradiction; lie.

démentir [demɑ̃'tiːr], *v.t.* (*conjug. like* SENTIR) to give the lie to, to contradict; to deny; to belie, to refute. **se démentir,** *v.r.* to contradict oneself; to fall off, to flag.

démérite [deme'rit], *n.m.* demerit.

démériter [demeri'te], *v.i.* to lose esteem *or* favor.

démesuré [demǝzy're], *a.* inordinate, excessive, enormous.

démesurément [demǝzyre'mɑ̃], *adv.* inordinately, excessively.

démettre [de'mɛtr], *v.t.* irr. (*conjug. like* METTRE) to put out of joint, to dislocate; to dismiss; (*Law*) to overrule. **se démettre,** *v.r.* to be put out of joint; to resign.

démeubler [demœ'ble], *v.t.* to strip of furniture.

demeurant [demœ'rɑ̃], *a.* dwelling, living.—*n.m.* remainder; *au demeurant,* after all, nevertheless.

demeure [dǝ'mœːr], *n.f.* abode, home, dwelling; stay; (*Law*) delay.

demeurer [demœ're], *v.i.* to live, to lodge, to reside; to stop, to stand; to continue, to stay.

demi [dǝ'mi], *a.* and *adv.* half.—*n.m.* (*Arith.*) half; (*Ftb. etc.*) half-back; glass of beer.—*n.f.* (-e) (the) half-hour.

[In the following compounds *demi* is *inv.* The noun has its regular plural, unless otherwise indicated.]

demi-bain [dǝmi'bɛ̃], *n.m.* hip bath.

demi-bas [dǝmi'bɑ], *n.m. inv.* knee-length stocking.

demi-botte [dǝmi'bot], *n.f.* Wellington boot.

demi-cercle [dǝmi'sɛrkl], *n.m.* semicircle.

demi-finale [dǝmifi'nal], *n.f.* (*Spt.*) semifinal.

demi-fond [dǝmi'fɔ̃], *n.m. inv.* middle distance (*race*).

demi-heure [dǝmi'œːr], *n.f.* half-hour; *une demi-heure,* half an hour.

demi-jour [dǝmi'ʒuːr], *n.m.* twilight.

demi-mot [dǝmi'mo], *adv. phr. comprendre à demi-mot,* to take the hint.

déminage [demi'naːʒ], *n.m.* mine clearing.

déminer [demi'ne], *v.t.* to clear of mines.

demi-pension [dǝmipɑ̃'sjɔ̃], *n.f.* half-board.

demi-pensionnaire [dǝmipɑ̃sjɔ'nɛːr], *n.* dayboarder.

demi-place [dǝmi'plas], *n.f.* half-fare.

demi-saison [dǝmi'sɛzɔ̃], *n.f.* autumn *or* spring.

demi-sang [dǝmi'sɑ̃], *n.m. inv.* half-bred horse.

demi-sel [dǝmi'sɛl], *n.m.* slightly salted cream cheese.

demi-solde [dǝmi'sold], *n.f.* half-pay.

démission [demi'sjɔ̃], *n.f.* resignation.

démissionnaire [demisjɔ'nɛːr], *a.* who has resigned *or* vacated his seat, outgoing.

démissionner [demisjɔ'ne], *v.i.* to resign.

demi-tour [dǝmi'tuːr], *n.m.* half-turn; (*Mil.*) about turn; *faire demi-tour,* to turn back.

démobilisation [demɔbiliza'sjɔ̃], *n.f.* demobilization.

démobiliser [demɔbili'ze], *v.t.* to demobilize.

démocrate [demɔ'krat], *a.* democratic.—*n.* democrat.

démocratie [demɔkra'si], *n.f.* democracy.

démocratique [demɔkra'tik], *a.* democratic.

démocratiquement [demɔkratik'mɑ̃], *adv.* democratically.

démocratiser [demɔkrati'ze], *v.t.* to democratize.

démodé [demɔ'de], *a.* old-fashioned, antiquated.

demoiselle [demwa'zɛl], *n.f.* young lady; unmarried woman, spinster; young girl; dragon-fly; *demoiselle d'honneur,* bridesmaid.

démolir [demɔ'liːr], *v.t.* to demolish, to pull down.

démolisseur [demɔli'sœːr], *n.m.* (*fem.* **-euse**) demolisher.

démolition [demɔli'sjɔ̃], *n.f.* demolition; (*pl.*) old building materials.

démon [de'mɔ̃], *n.m.* demon; (*good* or *evil*) genius; devil, fiend.

démonétisation [demɔnetiza'sjɔ̃], *n.f.* withdrawal from circulation (*of money*).

démonétiser [demɔneti'ze], *v.t.* to withdraw from circulation, to call in (*money*).

démoniaque [demɔ'njak], *a.* demoniac(al).—*n.* demoniac, demon, devil.

démonstrateur [demɔ̃stra'tœːr], *n.m.* (*fem.* **-euse**) demonstrator, lecturer.

démonstratif [demɔ̃stra'tif], *a.* (*fem.* **-tive**) demonstrative.

démonstration [demõstra'sjõ], *n.f.* demonstration, proof; exhibition.

démontable [demõ'tabl], *a.* that can be taken to pieces; collapsible (*canoe*).

démontage [demõ'ta:ʒ], *n.m.* taking to pieces, dismantling.

démonte-pneu [demõt'pnø], *n.m.* tire lever.

démonter [demõ'te], *v.t.* to unhorse, to dismount; to take to pieces, to dismantle; (*fig.*) to nonplus, to baffle; *mer démontée*, very rough sea. **se démonter**, *v.r.* to take or come to pieces (*of machinery*); to lose countenance; to be nonplussed; to be getting out of order (*of machinery etc.*).

démontrer [demõ'tre], *v.t.* to demonstrate, to prove.

démoralisant [demɔrali'zã], *a.* demoralizing.

démoralisateur [demɔraliza'tœ:r], *a.* (*fem.* **-trice**) corrupting, demoralizing.

démoralisation [demɔraliza'sjõ], *n.f.* demoralization.

démoraliser [demɔrali'ze], *v.t.* to demoralize; to corrupt.

démordre [de'mɔrdr], *v.i.* to let go one's hold; to desist, to yield, to give in.

démoucheter [demuʃ'te], *v.t.* (*conjug. like* APPELER) to take off the button from (*a foil*), to uncap.

démoulage [demu'la:ʒ], *n.m.* taking from the mold.

démouler [demu'le], *v.t.* to take from the mold.

démunir [demy'ni:r], *v.t.* to strip (*of ammunition*), to leave unprovided. **se démunir**, *v.r.* to deprive oneself, to leave oneself unprovided for.

démuseler [demyz'le], *v.t.* (*conjug. like* APPELER) to unmuzzle; (*fig.*) to let loose.

dénatalité [denatali'te], *n.f.* fall in the birthrate.

dénationalisation [denasjɔnaliza'sjõ], *n.f.* denationalization.

dénationaliser [denasjɔnali'ze], *v.t.* to denationalize.

dénatter [dena'te], *v.t.* to unplait (*hair etc.*).

dénaturé [denaty're], *a.* unnatural, barbarous, cruel.

dénaturer [denaty're], *v.t.* to alter the nature of; to misrepresent, to distort; to disfigure; to methylate (*alcohol*).

dénégation [denega'sjõ], *n.f.* denial, denegation.

déni [de'ni], *n.m.* denial, refusal.

déniaiser [denjɛ'ze], *v.t.* to sharpen the wits of; to initiate; to seduce. **se déniaiser**, *v.r.* to learn to be sharp, to grow cunning; (*fam.*) to lose one's innocence.

dénicher [deni'ʃe], *v.t.* to take out of the nest; to hunt out, to find out.—*v.i.* to forsake its nest (*of a bird*); to make off, to run away.

dénicheur [deni'ʃœ:r], *n.m.* nest robber.

denier [də'nje], *n.m.* (*Rom. Ant.*) denarius; (*Fr. Ant.*) denier; penny; farthing, mite; (*pl.*) state revenues.

dénier [de'nje], *v.t.* to deny, to refuse.

dénigrant [deni'grã], *a.* disparaging.

dénigrement [denigrə'mã], *n.m.* disparagement.

dénigrer [deni'gre], *v.t.* to disparage; to vilify.

dénivellation [denivella'sjõ], *n.f.*, **dénivellement** [denivɛl'mã], *n.m.* difference of level; unevenness.

dénombrement [denõbrə'mã], *n.m.* enumeration; census.

dénombrer [denõ'bre], *v.t.* to number, to enumerate.

dénominateur [denɔmina'tœ:r], *n.m.* (*Arith.*) denominator.

dénomination [denɔmina'sjõ], *n.f.* denomination, name.

dénommer [denɔ'me], *v.t.* to designate.

dénoncer [denõ'se], *v.t.* (*conjug. like* COMMENCER) to denounce, to inform against; to give notice of, to declare (*war etc.*). **se dénoncer**, *v.r.* to own up; to give oneself up.

dénonciateur [denõsja'tœ:r], *n.m.* (*fem.* **-trice**) informer, accuser.

dénonciation [denõsja'sjõ], *n.f.* denunciation, declaration.

dénoter [denɔ'te], *v.t.* to denote, to betoken.

dénouement or **dénoûment** [denu'mã], *n.m.* dénouement, unravelling (*esp. of a play etc.*).

dénouer [denu'e], *v.t.* to untie, to loosen; to solve (*difficulties etc.*); to unravel (*plots*). **se dénouer**, *v.r.* to come untied, to be unravelled; to be solved.

denrée [dã're], *n.f.* commodity, produce provisions.

dense [dã:s], *a.* dense, close, thick.

densité [dãsi'te], *n.f.* density, thickness.

dent [dã], *n.f.* tooth; fang; notch; cog; prong; *faire ses dents*, to cut one's teeth.

dentaire [dã'tɛ:r], *a.* dental.

dental [dã'tal], *a.* (*m.pl.* **-aux**) (*Phon.*) dental.

dent-de-lion [dãdə'ljõ], *n.m.* (*pl.* **dents-de-lion**) dandelion.

denté [dã'te], *a.* toothed; (*Bot.*) dentate; *roue dentée*, cogged wheel.

dentelé [dã'tle], *a.* notched, denticulated, indented, jagged.

denteler [dã'tle], *v.t.* (*conjug. like* APPELER) to indent, to notch.

dentelle [dã'tɛl], *n.f.* lace, lace work.

dentellier [dãtɛ'lje], *n.m.* (*fem.* **-ière**) lace maker.

dentelure [dã'tly:r], *n.f.* denticulation, indenting; scallop.

denticule [dãti'kyl], *n.m.* denticle.

dentier [dã'tje], *n.m.* set of teeth (*esp. artificial*), denture.

dentifrice [dãti'fris], *n.m.* toothpaste.

dentiste [dã'tist], *n.m.* dentist.

denture [dã'ty:r], *n.f.* set of teeth; (*Horol.*) teeth of a wheel.

dénudation [denyda'sjõ], *n.f.* denudation.

dénuder [deny'de], *v.t.* to denude; to lay bare.

dénuement or **dénûment** [deny'mã], *n.m.* destitution, penury, want.

dénuer [de'nɥe], *v.t.* to strip, to leave destitute. **se dénuer**, *v.r.* to strip oneself; to leave oneself destitute.

dépannage [depa'na:ʒ], *n.m.* (*Mach., Elec.*) repairing; *service de dépannage*, breakdown or repair service.

dépanner [depa'ne], *v.t.* (*Mach., Elec.*) to repair (*a breakdown*).

dépanneuse [depa'nø:z], *n.f.* breakdown vehicle, repair car, wrecker.

dépaqueter [depak'te], *v.t.* (*conjug. like* APPELER) to unpack.

dépareillé [depare'je], *a.* unmatched, odd.
déparer [depa're], *v.t.* to strip (*of ornaments*); (*fig.*) to mar, to disfigure.
déparier [depa'rje], *v.t.* to take away one (*of a pair*); to separate (*a pair of animals*).
départ [de'pa:r], *n.m.* departure, start, setting out.
départager [departa'ʒe], *v.t.* (*conjug. like* MANGER) to settle by a vote.
département [departə'mã], *n.m.* department; line, business.
départemental [departəmã'tal], *a.* (*m. pl.* -**aux**) departmental.
départir [depar'ti:r], *v.t. irr.* (*conjug. like* SENTIR) to separate; to distribute, to divide, to endow; to bestow. **se départir**, *v.r.* to desist; to deviate (*from*).
dépassement [depas'mã], *n.m.* overstepping (*of credit etc.*); (*Motor.*) passing.
dépasser [depa'se], *v.t.* to go beyond, to pass, to overtake; to exceed, to surpass; to be taller etc. than; to show; *son jupon dépasse*, her slip is showing.
dépaver [depa've], *v.t.* to unpave, to take up the pavement of.
dépaysé [depei'ze], *a.* away from home, out of one's element.
dépayser [depei'ze], *v.t.* to send away from home; to remove from his natural sphere etc.; (*fig.*) to bewilder. **se dépayser**, *v.r.* to leave one's home; to go abroad; to get out of one's element.
dépècement [depes'mã], **dépeçage** [depə-sa:ʒ], *n.m.* cutting up, carving, dismemberment.
dépecer [dep'se], *v.t.* (*see Verb Tables*) to cut up (*a carcass*), to carve.
dépêche [de'pe:ʃ], *n.f.* dispatch (*letter on affairs of State*); communication (*esp. a telegram*).
dépêcher [depe'ʃe], *v.t.* to dispatch, to do quickly; to send quickly, to send by messenger; to kill. **se dépêcher**, *v.r.* to hurry, to make haste; *dépêchez-vous*, hurry up.
dépeigner [depe'ɲe], *v.t.* to ruffle (*hair*).
dépeindre [de'pɛ̃:dr], *v.t. irr.* (*conjug. like* CRAINDRE) to depict, to describe; to portray, to paint.
dépelotonner [deplɔtɔ'ne], *v.t.* to unwind. **se dépelotonner**, *v.r.* to come unwound; to uncurl (*of cat*).
dépenaillé [depna'je], *a.* tattered, ragged.
dépendance [depã'dã:s], *n.f.* subordination; dependence; appendage, annex, outhouse, (*pl.*) out-buildings.
dépendant [depã'dã], *a.* dependent.
dépendre (1) [de'pã:dr], *v.t.* to take down; to unhang.
dépendre (2) [de'pã:dr], *v.i.* to depend, to be dependent (*de*).
dépens [de'pã], *n.m.* (*used only in pl.*) expense, cost.
dépense [de'pã:s], *n.f.* expense; expenditure, outlay; waste, flow.
dépenser [depã'se], *v.t.* to spend, to consume; to waste.
dépensier [depã'sje], *a.* (*fem.* -**ière**) extravagant.—*n.m.* (*fem.* -**ière**) extravagant person, spend-thrift; bursar.
déperdition [deperdi'sjõ], *n.f.* loss, waste.
dépérir [depe'ri:r], *v.i.* to decline, to pine away, to wither, to dwindle, to waste away.

dépérissement [deperis'mã], *n.m.* decay, withering, wasting away.
dépêtrer [depe'tre], *v.t.* to disentangle, to extricate. **se dépêtrer**, *v.r.* to get clear of.
dépeuplement [depœplə'mã], *n.m.* depopulation; thinning (*of forests etc.*).
dépeupler [depœ'ple], *v.t.* to depopulate; to thin. **se dépeupler**, *v.r.* to become depopulated, to be unstocked (*of river*).
dépilage [depi'la:ʒ], *n.m.* removal of hairs, bristles, etc. (*from hides etc.*).
dépilation [depila'sjõ], *n.f.* depilation.
dépiquage [depi'ka:ʒ], *n.m.* threshing *or* treading out (*grain*).
dépiquer (1) [depi'ke], *v.t.* to unquilt, to unstitch.
dépiquer (2) [depi'ke], *v.t.* to tread out (*grain*).
dépister [depis'te], *v.t.* to track down; to hunt out; (*fig.*) to throw off the scent.
dépit [de'pi], *n.m.* spite; vexation.
dépiter [depi'te], *v.t.* to vex, to spite. **se dépiter**, *v.r.* to be vexed, to fret.
déplacé [depla'se], *a.* displaced, misplaced, ill-timed, unbecoming.
déplacement [deplas'mã], *n.m.* removal; displacement; *frais de déplacement*, travelling expenses.
déplacer [depla'se], *v.t.* (*conjug. like* COMMENCER) to displace; to remove, to change; to misplace. **se déplacer**, *v.r.* to move, to change one's place, to leave one's residence; to be displaced (*of things*).
déplaire [de'plɛ:r], *v.i. irr.* (*conjug. like* PLAIRE) to displease, to offend; to be disagreable, to give offence. **se déplaire**, *v.r.* to be displeased *or* dissatisfied (*with*).
déplaisant [deplɛ'zã], *a.* unpleasant, disagreable.
déplaisir [deplɛ'zi:r], *n.m.* displeasure, annoyance; grief.
déplanter [deplã'te], *v.t.* to dig *or* take up (*a plant*).
déplantoir [deplã'twa:r], *n.m.* garden trowel.
dépliant [depli'ã], *n.m.* folding page; folder, prospectus, leaflet.
déplier [depli'e], *v.t.* to unfold, to open out; to lay out.
déplisser [depli'se], *v.t.* to unpleat. **se déplisser**, *v.r.* to come unpleated; to lose its pleats (*of a skirt etc.*).
déploiement *or* **déploîment** [deplwa'mã], *n.m.* unfolding; display, show; (*Mil.*) deployment.
déplombage [deplõ'ba:ʒ], *n.m.* unsealing; unstopping.
déplomber [deplõ'be], *v.t.* to take the customhouse seal off (*goods*); to unstop (*a tooth*).
déplorable [deplɔ'rabl], *a.* deplorable, lamentable.
déplorablement [deplɔrablə'mã], *adv.* deplorably, wretchedly.
déplorer [deplɔ're], *v.t.* to deplore, to bewail, to lament, to mourn.
déployer [deplwa'je], *v.t.* (*conjug. like* EMPLOYER) to unfold, to unroll, to unfurl, to spread out; to display, to show; (*Mil.*) to deploy; *à gorge déployée*, at the top of one's voice. **se déployer**, *v.r.* to unroll; to display oneself; (*Mil.*) to deploy.
déplumer [deply'me], *v.t.* to pluck; (*fig.*) to despoil; to tear the hair from. **se déplumer**, *v.r.* to molt, to shed feathers.

dépolariser [depolari'ze], *v.t.* to depolarize.
dépolir [depo'li:r], *v.t.* to make the surface (*of metal etc.*) dull, to frost (*glass*).
dépopulation [depopyla'sjɔ̃], *n.m.* depopulation.
déportation [deporta'sjɔ̃], *n.f.* deportation.
déporté [depor'te], *n.m.* (*fem.* -ée) deported person.
déportements [deporta'mɑ̃], *n.m. pl.* misconduct, evil-doings.
déporter [depor'te], *v.t.* to deport, to transport for life; to swerve; to carry away, to drift. **se déporter**, *v.r.* (*Law*) to desist (*from*).
déposant [depo'zɑ̃], *a.* giving evidence; depositing.—*n.m.* (*fem.* -e) witness; depositor.
déposer [depo'ze], *v.t.* to lay down *or* aside; to divest oneself of, to depose; to deposit; to lodge (*a complaint etc.*); **marque déposée**, registered trademark.—*v.i.* to give evidence; to settle, to leave a sediment.
dépositaire [depozi'tɛ:r], *n.m.* depositary, trustee; agent.
déposition [depozi'sjɔ̃], *n.f.* deposition, evidence.
dépositoire [depozi'twa:r], *n.m.* depository, mortuary.
déposséder [depose'de], *v.t.* (*conjug. like* CÉDER) to dispossess, to oust.
dépossession [depose'sjɔ̃], *n.f.* dispossession, deprivation.
dépôt [de'po], *n.m.* depositing; deposit; sediment; depository, warehouse; (*Mil.*) depot; (*Med.*) tumor, abscess; **dépôt d'essence**, gas station; **en dépôt**, as a deposit in trust, (*Comm.*) on sale; **mandat de dépôt**, writ of imprisonment.
dépotage [depo'ta:ʒ], **dépotement** [depot'mɑ̃], *n.m.* unpotting; decanting.
dépoter [depo'te], *v.t.* to take out of a pot; to decant.
dépouille [de'pu:j], *n.f.* slough, cast-off skin *or* hide; spoil; remains, wardrobe (*of persons deceased*); (*pl.*) spoils, booty; **dépouille mortelle**, mortal remains.
dépouillement [depuj'mɑ̃], *n.m.* spoliation, despoiling; scrutiny (*of a ballot box*); abstract (*of an account*).
dépouiller [depu'je], *v.t.* to strip, to skin; to unclothe; to despoil; to throw off; to cast (*of insects*); to reap (*crops*); to inspect, to count up (*a ballot-box*); to present an abstract (*of accounts*). **se dépouiller**, *v.r.* to shed its skin (*of insects and animals*), to molt; **se dépouiller de**, to divest oneself of, to strip oneself of, to renounce (*possessions etc.*).
dépourvoir [depur'vwa:r], *v.t. irr.* (*conjug. like* POURVOIR) to leave unprovided (*with*) *or* destitute (*of*). **se dépourvoir**, *v.r.* to leave oneself unequipped.
dépourvu [depur'vy], *a.* destitute, unprovided; **au dépourvu**, unawares, unexpectedly.
dépravation [deprava'sjɔ̃], *n.f.* vitiation, depravity.
dépravé [depra've], *a.* vitiated, depraved, corrupt.
dépraver [depra've], *v.t.* to deprave, to corrupt, to pervert. **se dépraver**, *v.r.* to become depraved *or* corrupted.

dépréciation [depresja'sjɔ̃], *n.f.* depreciation.
déprécier [depre'sje], *v.t.* to depreciate, to undervalue, to underrate; to disparage. **se déprécier**, *v.r.* to underrate oneself; to fall in value (*of things*).
déprédateur [depreda'tœ:r], *n.m.* (*fem.* -trice) depredator, plunderer.
déprédation [depreda'sjɔ̃], *n.f.* plundering, depredation.
déprendre [de'prɑ̃:dr], *v.t. irr.* (*conjug. like* PRENDRE) to loosen, to detach. **se déprendre**, *v.r.* to get loose; to detach oneself (*de*).
dépression [depre'sjɔ̃], *n.f.* depression, hollow; (*fig.*) recession, slump (*of business*); **dépression nerveuse**, nervous breakdown.
déprimer [depri'me], *v.t.* to press down, to depress; (*fig.*) to discourage.
depuis [da'pɥi], *prep.* since, for; from, after; **depuis longtemps**, for a long time; **depuis peu**, lately; **depuis quand?** since when?—*adv.* since (then), afterwards, since that time.—*conj. phr.* **depuis que**, since.
députation [depyta'sjɔ̃], *n.f.* deputation; deputyship.
député [depy'te], *n.m.* deputy, delegate; Member of Parliament.
députer [depy'te], *v.t.* to send as representative, to depute.
déracinement [derasin'mɑ̃], *n.m.* uprooting, eradication.
déraciner [derasi'ne], *v.t.* to uproot; to eradicate, to extirpate.
déraidir [dere'di:r], *v.t.* to unstiffen; to make pliant. **se déraidir**, *v.r.* to grow soft *or* supple; to unbend.
déraillement [deraj'mɑ̃], *n.m.* derailment.
dérailler [dera'je], *v.i.* to run off the rails.
déraison [dere'zɔ̃], *n.f.* unreasonableness, folly.
déraisonnable [derezo'nabl], *a.* unreasonable, senseless.
déraisonnablement [derezonablə'mɑ̃], *adv.* unreasonably, irrationally.
déraisonner [derezo'ne], *v.i.* to reason falsely, to talk nonsense; to rave.
dérangement [derɑ̃ʒ'mɑ̃], *n.m.* derangement; trouble; disorder, disturbance.
déranger [derɑ̃'ʒe], *v.t.* (*conjug. like* MANGER) to derange, to put out of place *or* order; to discompose, to disconcert; to disturb, to upset; to unsettle. **se déranger**, *v.r.* to move; to be deranged, to get out of order; to trouble *or* disturb oneself, to put oneself out.
déraper [dera'pe], *v.i.* to skid, to side-slip (*bicycle, car etc.*).
dératé [dera'te], *n.m. only used in* **courir comme un dératé**, to run like a greyhound.
derechef [dər'ʃef], *adv.* over again, afresh, anew.
déréglé [dere'gle], *a.* out of order; irregular; intemperate, (*fig.*) unruly, dissolute.
déréglement [dereglə'mɑ̃], *n.m.* irregularity, disorder; dissoluteness, licentiousness.
dérégler [dere'gle], *v.t.* (*conjug. like* CÉDER) to put out of order, to derange; **se dérégler**, *v.r.* to get out of order, to be deranged; to lead a disorderly life.

dérider [deri'de], *v.t.* to unwrinkle, to smooth; to brighten, to cheer up. **se dérider,** *v.r.* to smooth one's brow; to cheer up.

dérision [deri'zjɔ̃], *n.f.* derision, mockery, ridicule.

dérisoire [deri'zwa:r], *a.* derisive, mocking.

dérivatif [deriva'tif], *a.* (*fem.* **-tive**) derivative.—*n.m.* (*Med.*) derivative, counter-irritant.

dérivation [deriva'sjɔ̃], *n.f.* derivation; diversion (*of water etc.*); (*Elec.*) branching, shunting; (*Naut.*) drift, leeway; (*Av.*) windage; (*Elec.*) **circuit en dérivation**, branch circuit.

dérive [de'ri:v], *n.f.* (*Naut.*) drift, leeway; (*Av.*) fin.

dérivé [deri've], *a.* drifted.—*n.m.* (*Gram.*) derivative.

dériver [deri've], *v.t.* to divert; to derive.—*v.i.* to be turned from its proper course; (*Naut.*) to drift (*from the shore*), to go adrift.

dermatite [dɛrma'tit], *n.f.* dermatitis.

dernier [dɛr'nje], *a.* (*fem.* **-ière**) last, latest; vilest, meanest; extreme (*highest, greatest etc.*); the one just past; youngest (*of a family of children*).—*n.m.* (*fem.* **-ière**) the last; the highest, lowest etc.

dernièrement [dɛrnjɛr'mɑ̃], *adv.* lately, recently.

dérobé [derɔ'be], *a.* stolen, hidden, secret; **à la dérobée,** stealthily.

dérober [derɔ'be], *v.t.* to steal; to remove; to conceal; to protect, to screen. **se dérober,** *v.r.* to steal away, to escape, to disappear.

dérogation [derɔga'sjɔ̃], *n.f.* derogation.

dérogatoire [derɔga'twa:r], *a.* derogatory.

déroger [derɔ'ʒe], *v.i.* (*conjug. like* MANGER) to derogate; to detract; to condescend, to stoop.

dérouillement [deruj'mɑ̃], *n.m.* removal of rust.

dérouiller [deru'je], *v.t.* to remove the rust from; (*fig.*) to polish. **se dérouiller,** *v.r.* to lose its *or* one's rust; to brighten up; to read a subject up again.

déroulement [derul'mɑ̃], *n.m.* unrolling, unfolding.

dérouler [deru'le], *v.t.* to unroll; to spread out, to display. **se dérouler,** *v.r.* to unroll; to open to the view; to roll in (*of the waves*); to take place (*of events*).

déroutant [deru'tɑ̃], *a.* baffling, confusing.

déroute [de'rut], *n.f.* rout, overthrow; ruin; disorder, confusion.

dérouter [deru'te], *v.t.* to lead astray; to embarrass, to disconcert; to baffle; to divert (*ship, train etc.*).

derrière [dɛ'rjɛ:r], *prep.* behind, on the other side of.—*adv.* behind, after.—*n.m.* back, hinder part; posterior; behind; *pattes de derrière,* hind legs; *porte de derrière,* back door.

derviche [dɛr'viʃ], **dervis** [dɛr'vi], *n.m.* dervish.

des [de], [*contr. of* DE LES].

dès [dɛ], *prep.* from, since, as early as.—*conj. phr.* **dès que,** when, as soon as, since.

désabonnement [dezabɔn'mɑ̃], *n.m.* withdrawal of subscription.

désabonner (se) [sədezabɔ'ne], *v.r.* to withdraw one's subscription (*to a magazine etc.*).

désabuser [dezaby'ze], *v.t.* to disabuse, to undeceive. **se désabuser,** *v.r.* to be undeceived, to face the facts.

désaccord [deza'kɔ:r], *n.m.* disagreement, discord.

désaccorder [dezakɔr'de], *v.t.* to untune; (*fig.*) to set at variance. **se désaccorder,** *v.r.* to get out of tune.

désaccouplement [dezakuplə'mɑ̃], *n.m.* uncoupling.

désaccoupler [dezaku'ple], *v.t.* to uncouple. **se désaccoupler,** *v.r.* to become uncoupled; to come asunder.

désaccoutumer [dezakuty'me], *v.t.* to disaccustom. **se désaccoutumer,** *v.r.* to break oneself of, to lose the habit of.

désaffecter [dezafɛk'te], *v.t.* to secularize (*a church*); (*Mil.*) to transfer; to put a building to another use.

désaffection [dezafɛk'sjɔ̃], *n.f.* loss of affection.

désaffectionner [dezafɛksjɔ'ne], *v.t.* to cause (*someone*) to lose his *or* her affection, to disaffect. **se désaffectionner,** *v.r.* to lose affection.

désagencement [dezaʒɑ̃s'mɑ̃], *n.m.* throwing out of gear.

désagencer [dezaʒɑ̃'se], *v.t.* (*conjug. like* COMMENCER) to throw out of gear, to disarrange.

désagréable [dezagre'abl], *a.* disagreeable, unpleasant.

désagréablement [dezagreablə'mɑ̃], *adv.* disagreeably, unpleasantly.

désagréger [dezagre'ʒe], *v.t.* (*conjug. like* ASSIÉGER) to disaggregate, to break up, to separate.

désagrément [dezagre'mɑ̃], *n.m.* disagreeableness, unpleasantness; annoyance, discomfort.

désaimanter [dezemɑ̃'te], *v.t.* to demagnetize.

désajustement [dezaʒystə'mɑ̃], *n.m.* disarrangement, disorder.

désajuster [dezaʒys'te], *v.t.* to disarrange, to disturb, to put out of order. **se désajuster,** *v.r.* to become disarranged, to get out of order.

désaltérant [dezalte'rɑ̃], *a.* thirst-quenching.

désaltérer [dezalte're], *v.t.* (*conjug. like* CÉDER) to quench the thirst of, to refresh. **se désaltérer,** *v.r.* to quench one's thirst.

désamorcer [dezamɔr'se], *v.t.* (*conjug. like* COMMENCER) to unprime, to uncap (*fire-arms etc.*). **se désamorcer,** *v.r.* to run down (*dynamo*); to run dry (*pump*).

désappointement [dezapwɛ̃t'mɑ̃], *n.m.* disappointment.

désappointer [dezapwɛ̃'te], *v.t.* to disappoint.

désapprendre [deza'prɑ̃:dr], *v.t. irr.* (*conjug. like* PRENDRE) to unlearn, to forget.

désapprobateur [dezaprɔba'tœ:r], *a.* (*fem.* **-trice**) disapproving, censuring, carping.—*n.m.* (*fem.* **-trice**) censurer, fault-finder.

désapprobation [dezaprɔba'sjɔ̃], *n.f.* disapprobation, disapproval.

désappropriation [dezaprɔpria'sjɔ̃], *n.f.* renunciation (*of property*).

désapprouver [dezapru've], *v.t.* to disapprove of, to blame.

désarçonner [dezarsɔ'ne], v.t. to unhorse; (fig.) to baffle, to floor.

désarmement [dezarmə'mã], n.m. disarming, disarmament; (Naut.) laying up.

désarmer [dezar'me], v.t. to disarm, to unarm; (fig.) to appease, to calm; to uncock (a gun); (Naut.) to lay up (a vessel).—v.i. to disarm; to give up maintaining troops.

désarroi [deza'rwa], n.m. disorder, disarray, confusion.

désarticulation [dezartikyla'sjõ], n.f. disarticulation.

désarticuler [dezartiky'le], v.t. to disarticulate, to disjoint.

désassemblage [dezasã'bla:ʒ], **désassemblement** [dezasãblə'mã], n.m. dismantling.

désassembler [dezasã'ble], v.t. to take to pieces, to separate, to dismantle.

désassocier [dezasɔ'sje], v.t. to disassociate, to dissociate.

désassortiment [dezasɔrti'mã], n.m. unmatching, ill-assortment; unstocking.

désastre [de'zastr], n.m. disaster.

désastreusement [dezastrøz'mã], adv. disastrously.

désastreux [dezas'trø], a. (fem. -euse) disastrous, unfortunate, very sad.

désavantage [dezavã'ta:ʒ], n.m. disadvantage; detriment, prejudice; drawback, handicap.

désavantager [dezavãta'ʒe], v.t. (conjug. like MANGER) to disadvantage, to handicap.

désavantageusement [dezavãtaʒøz'mã], adv. disadvantageously; disparagingly.

désavantageux [dezavãta'ʒø], a. (fem. -euse) disadvantageous; detrimental, prejudicial, unfavorable.

désaveu [deza'vø], n.m. (pl. -eux) disavowal; denial; retractation.

désavouer [deza'vwe], v.t. to disown, to disclaim, to disavow; to retract.

désaxé [deza'kse], a. offset, out of true (of a wheel, etc.); (fig.) out of joint.

descellement [desel'mã], n.m. loosening, unsealing.

desceller [desɛ'le], v.t. to unseal; to loosen (masonry etc.). **se desceller,** v.r. to become loose or unsealed.

descendance [desã'dã:s], n.f. descent, lineage.

descendant [desã'dã], a. descending, going down; (Mil.) coming off duty.—n.m. (fem. -e) descendant, offspring, issue.

descendre [de'sã:dr], v.t. (with aux. AVOIR) to take down, bring or let down; to go or come down (a staircase etc.); to drop off (of a cab etc.); to land.—v.i. (with aux. ÊTRE) to descend, to go down; to go downstairs; to alight, to land; to slope, to incline; to fall, to subside.

descente [de'sã:t], n.f. descent; taking down; subsidence (of waters etc.); dismounting; disembarkation; declivity; raid; (pop.) rupture; **descente de lit,** bedside rug; **descente de bain,** bath mat.

descriptif [deskrip'tif], a. (fem. -tive) descriptive.

description [deskrip'sjõ], n.f. description; inventory.

désemballage [dezãba'la:ʒ], n.m. unpacking.

désemballer [dezãba'le], v.t. to unpack.

désembarquement [dezãbarkə'mã], n.m. disembarkation, landing.

désembarquer [dezãbar'ke], v.t. to disembark, to land; to unship, to unload.

désemboîter [dezãbwa'te], v.t. to dislocate. **se désemboîter,** v.r. to become disjointed.

désembourber [dezãbur'be], v.t. to draw out of the mire.

désemparé [dezãpa're], a. in distress, helpless.

désemparer [dezãpa're], v.t. (Naut.) to disable.—v.i. to quit, to go away; **sans désemparer,** on the spot, at once.

désempeser [dezãpə'ze], v.t. (conjug. like AMENER) to unstarch. **se désempeser,** v.r. to become limp.

désemplir [dezã'pli:r], v.t. to make less full, to empty in part.—v.i. to become less full (used only in negative). **se désemplir,** v.r. to become less full.

désenchaîner [dezãʃɛ'ne], v.t. to unchain.

désenchantement [dezãʃãt'mã], n.m. disenchantment, disillusion.

désenchanter [dezãʃã'te], v.t. to disenchant, to disillusion.

désenchanteur [dezãʃã'tœ:r], a. (fem. -eresse) disenchanting.

désencombrement [dezãkõbrə'mã], n.m. disencumbrance; dispersal.

désencombrer [dezãkõ'bre], v.t. to disencumber, to clear (a road etc.).

désenfiler [dezãfi'le], v.t. to unthread, to unstring. **se désenfiler,** v.r. to come unthreaded or unstrung.

désenfler [dezã'fle], v.t. to reduce the swelling of.—v.i. and **se désenfler,** v.r. to become less swollen.

désenflure [dezã'fly:r], n.f., **désenflement** [dezãflə'mã], n.m. diminution or disappearance of a swelling.

désengager [dezãga'ʒe], v.t. (conjug. like MANGER) to disengage, to release from an engagement.

désengrener [dezãgrə'ne], v.t. (conjug. like AMENER) to throw out of gear.

désenivrer [dezãni'vre], v.t., to make sober again.—v.i. to sober. **se désenivrer,** v.r. to become sober (again), to sober up.

désenlaidir [dezãlɛ'di:r], v.t. to render less ugly.—v.i. to become less ugly.

désennuyer [dezãnɥi'je], v.t. (conjug. like EMPLOYER) to enliven, to cheer. **se désennuyer,** v.r. to find amusement, to kill time.

désenrayer [dezãrɛ'je], v.t. (conjug. like PAYER) to unlock or unskid (a wheel etc.).

désenrhumer [dezãry'me], v.t. to cure (someone) of a cold. **se désenrhumer,** v.r. to get rid of a cold.

désenrôlement [dezãrol'mã], n.m. (Mil.) discharge.

désenrôler [dezãro'le], v.t. to discharge.

désensevelir [dezãsə'vli:r], v.t. to unshroud; to exhume.

désensevelissement [dezãsəvlis'mã], n.m. unshrouding, exhumation, disinterment.

désentortiller [dezãtɔrti'je], v.t. to untwist, to unravel.

désentraver [dezãtra've], v.t. to untrammel, to unhobble (a horse etc.).

déséquilibre [dezeki'libr], n.m. lack of balance, unbalance; imbalance.

111

déséquilibré

déséquilibré [dezekili'bre], *a.* and *n.m.* (*fem.* -**ée**) unbalanced (person).
déséquilibrer [dezekili'bre], *v.t.* to unbalance.
désert [de'zɛːr], *a.* uninhabited, solitary; wild, waste, deserted.—*n.m.* desert, wilderness; solitary place; (C) clearing in a forest.
déserter [dezɛrte], *v.t.* to desert, to abandon, to forsake; to quit, to leave; (C) to clear land, to break up (*ground*) for tillage.—*v.i.* to desert, to go over to the enemy.
déserteur [dezɛr'tœːr], *n.m.* deserter.
désertion [dezɛr'sjɔ̃], *n.f.* desertion.
désespérance [dezɛspe'rãːs], *n.f.* despair.
désespérant [dezɛspe'rã], *a.* desperate, hopeless; disheartening, distressing.
désespéré [dezɛspe're], *a.* hopeless, desperate; disconsolate.—*n.m.* (*fem.* -**ée**) person in despair; madman, madwoman.
désespérément [dezɛspere'mã], *adv.* desperately, despairingly.
désespérer [dezɛspe're], *v.t.* (*conjug. like* CÉDER) to drive to despair; to dishearten; to distress.—*v.i.* to despair. **se désespérer**, *v.r.* to be in despair.
désespoir [dezɛs'pwaːr], *n.m.* despair, hopelessness, despondency, grief; **en désespoir de cause,** as a last resource.
déshabiliter [dezabili'te], *v.t.* to disqualify.
déshabillé [dezabi'je], *n.m.* deshabille, undress; **en déshabillé,** partly *or* scantily dressed.
déshabiller [dezabi'je], *v.t.* to undress, to strip. **se déshabiller,** *v.r.* to undress oneself.
déshabituer [dezabi'tɥe], *v.t.* to disaccustom, to break off. **se déshabituer,** *v.r.* to lose the habit of; to break oneself of.
déshérence [deze'rãːs], *n.f.* (*Law*) escheat.
déshériter [dezeri'te], *v.t.* to disinherit.
déshonnête [dezɔ'nɛːt], *a.* immodest, indecent, unseemly.
déshonnêtement [dezɔnɛt'mã], *adv.* indecently, immodestly.
déshonnêteté [dezɔnɛt'te], *n.f.* indecency, unseemliness.
déshonneur [dezɔ'nœːr], *n.m.* dishonor, disgrace, shame.
déshonorable [dezɔnɔ'rabl], *a.* dishonorable.
déshonorablement [dezɔnɔrablə'mã], *adv.* dishonorably.
déshonorant [dezɔnɔ'rã], *a.* dishonorable, disgraceful.
déshonorer [dezɔnɔ're], *v.t.* to dishonor, to disgrace. **se déshonorer,** *v.r.* to dishonor *or* disgrace oneself.
déshydrater [dezidra'te], *v.t.* to dehydrate.
désignatif [dezina'tif], *a.* (*fem.* -**tive**) indicative.
désignation [dezina'sjɔ̃], *n.f.* designation, indication.
désigner [dezi'ne], *v.t.* to designate, to denote; to appoint, to nominate, to point out; (*Mil.*) to detail.
désillusion [dezily'zjɔ̃], *n.f.*, **désillusionnement** [dezilyzjɔn'mã], *n.m.* disillusion.
désillusionner [dezilyzjɔ'ne], *v.t.* to disillusion, to disappoint.
désinfectant [dezɛ̃fɛk'tã], *a.* disinfecting.—*n.m.* disinfectant.

désinfecter [dezɛ̃fɛk'te], *v.t.* to disinfect, to decontaminate.
désinfection [dezɛ̃fɛk'sjɔ̃], *n.f.* disinfection.
désintégration [dezɛ̃tegra'sjɔ̃], *n.f.* disintegration; fission.
désintégrer [dezɛ̃te'gre], *v.t.* (*conjug. like* CÉDER) to disintegrate; to split (*atom*).
désintéressé [dezɛ̃tere'se], *a.* disinterested, unselfish, unbiased.
désintéressement [dezɛ̃teres'mã], *n.m.* disinterestedness.
désintéresser [dezɛ̃tere'se], *v.t.* to indemnify.
désinvestir [dezɛ̃vɛs'tiːr], *v.t.* (*Mil.*) to raise the siege of.
désinvolte [dezɛ̃'vɔlt], *a.* free, easy; offhand.
désinvolture [dezɛ̃vɔl'tyːr], *n.f.* casual, easy bearing *or* gait; offhandedness.
désir [de'ziːr], *n.m.* desire, wish, longing.
désirable [dezi'rabl], *a.* desirable.
désirer [dezi're], *v.t.* to desire, to wish for, to long for, to want.
désireux [dezi'rø], *a.* (*fem.* -**euse**) desirous, anxious, eager (*to*).
désistement [dezistə'mã], *n.m.* desistance, withdrawal.
désister (se) [sədezis'te], *v.r.* to desist from, to renounce, to withdraw.
désobéir [dezɔbe'iːr], *v.i.* to disobey.
désobéissance [dezɔbei'sãːs], *n.f.* disobedience.
désobéissant [dezɔbei'sã], *a.* disobedient.
désobligeamment [dezɔbliʒa'mã], *adv.* disobligingly; unkindly.
désobligeance [dezɔbli'ʒãːs], *n.f.* lack of complaisance; unkindness.
désobligeant [dezɔbli'ʒã], *a.* disobliging; uncivil.
désobliger [dezɔbli'ʒe], *v.t.* (*conjug. like* MANGER) to disoblige, to displease.
désodorisant [dezɔdɔri'zã], *a.* and *n.m.* deodorant.
désœuvré [dezœ'vre], *a.* unoccupied, idle.
désœuvrement [dezœvrə'mã], *n.m.* want of occupation, idleness.
désolant [dezɔ'lã], *a.* grievous, distressing.
désolation [dezɔla'sjɔ̃], *n.f.* desolation, ruin; deep affliction, grief.
désolé [dezɔ'le], *a.* afflicted, broken-hearted; very sorry, grieved; dreary, desolate (*place*).
désoler [dezɔ'le], *v.t.* to devastate, to desolate, to lay waste; to afflict, to grieve; to annoy, to torment. **se désoler,** *v.r.* to grieve, to be disconsolate.
désolidariser [desɔlidari'ze], *v.t.* to break the ties which keep together (*a party, friends etc.*).
désopilant [dezɔpi'lã], *a.* very funny, side-splitting.
désopiler [dezɔpi'le], *v.t.* to clear of obstruction; (*fig.*) to cheer up, to enliven.
désordonné [dezɔrdɔ'ne], *a.* disorderly; (*fig.*) dissolute, unruly; inordinate.
désordonner [dezɔrdɔ'ne], *v.t.* to disturb; to throw into confusion.
désordre [de'zɔrdr], *n.m.* disorder, confusion; disorderly life; perturbation; (*pl.*) disturbances, riots.
désorganisation [dezɔrganiza'sjɔ̃], *n.f.* disorganization.
désorganiser [dezɔrgani'ze], *v.t.* to disorganize. **se désorganiser,** *v.r.* to become disorganized.

désorienter [dezɔrjɑ̃'te], v.t. to lead astray, to mislead, to bewilder; to put out, to disconcert.

désormais [dezɔr'mɛ], adv. henceforth, hereafter.

désossé [dezo'se], a. boneless, flabby.

désosser [dezo'se], v.t. to bone. **se désosser**, v.r. to become disjointed, limp, flabby etc.

despote [dɛs'pɔt], n.m. despot.

despotique [dɛspo'tik], a. despotic.

despotiquement [dɛspotik'mɑ̃], adv. despotically.

despotisme [dɛspo'tism], n.m. despotism.

desquels [de'kɛl], m.pl. (fem. -elles) [DUQUEL].

dessaisir [desɛ'ziːr], v.t. to let go; to dispossess. **se dessaisir**, v.r. to give up, to part with.

dessaisissement [desɛzis'mɑ̃], n.m. parting with, abandonment.

dessalé [desa'le], a. unsalted, free from salt; (fam.) sharp.—n.m. (fem. -ée) sharp person.

dessaler [desa'le], v.t. to remove salt from (meat etc.); (fig.) to make sharp, cunning etc.

dessangler [desɑ̃'gle], v.t. to loosen the girth of (a horse etc.).

desséchant [dese'ʃɑ̃], a. drying, parching.

dessèchement [desɛʃ'mɑ̃], n.m. drying up; dryness.

dessécher [dese'ʃe], v.t. to dry up; to parch; (fig.) to wither (the heart etc.); to emaciate. **se dessécher**, v.r. to become dry, to dry up; (fig.) to wither, to waste away.

dessein [de'sɛ̃], n.m. design, plan, scheme; intention, resolution.

desseller [desɛ'le], v.t. to unsaddle.

desserrer [desɛ're], v.t. to loosen, to relax; to ease. **se desserrer**, v.r. to become loose, to relax.

dessert [de'sɛːr], n.m. dessert.

desserte [de'sɛrt], n.f. leavings, remains (of a meal); small sideboard; parochial duty; railway service.

desservant [desɛr'vɑ̃], n.m. officiating minister (of a parish etc.).

desservir [desɛr'viːr], v.t. irr. (conjug. like SENTIR) to clear (a table); to officiate (of clergymen); to ply between (of boats etc.); (fig.) to do someone a disservice.

dessiller or **déciller** [desi'je], v.t. to open (someone's eyes); to undeceive.

dessin [de'sɛ̃], n.m. drawing; sketch; pattern, design; **dessin animé**, (Cine.) cartoon.

dessinateur [desina'tœːr], n.m. (fem. -trice) draftsman; designer.

dessiner [desi'ne], v.t. to draw, to sketch; to set off, to indicate; to lay out. **se dessiner**, v.r. to be delineated, to be visible, to stand out.

dessous [də'su], adv. under, underneath, below.—n.m. lower part; under, hidden or wrong side; worst; lee (of the wind); (pl.) underclothing (of women).—prep. phr. **au-dessous de**, beneath.

dessus [də'sy], adv. on, upon, over, above; **là-dessus**, thereupon; **par-dessus**, over, besides; **sens dessus dessous**, upside down.—n.m. top, upper part; right side; upper hand, advantage.—prep. phr. **au-dessus de**, above.

destin [dɛs'tɛ̃], n.m. destiny, fate; career.

destinataire [dɛstina'tɛːr], n. addressee; recipient; (Comm.) consignee; payee.

destination [dɛstina'sjɔ̃], n.f. destination; object, end.

destinée [dɛsti'ne], n.f. fate, destiny, doom.

destiner [dɛsti'ne], v.t. to destine, to purpose; to reserve (for a particular fate etc.). **se destiner**, v.r. to be destined.

destituer [dɛsti'tɥe], v.t. to dismiss, to discharge.

destitution [dɛstity'sjɔ̃], n.f. dismissal, removal (from office).

destroyer [dɛstrwa'jœːr], n.m. (Navy) destroyer.

destructeur [dɛstryk'tœːr], a. (fem. -trice) destructive, deadly, ruinous.—n.m. (fem. -trice) ravager, spoiler.

destructif [dɛstryk'tif], a. (fem. -tive) destructive, destroying.

destruction [dɛstryk'sjɔ̃], n.f. destruction.

désuet [desɥ'ɛ], a. (fem. -ète) obsolete, out-of-date.

désuétude [desɥe'tyd], n.f. disuse, desuetude.

désunion [dezy'njɔ̃], n.f. disunion; disjunction.

désunir [dezy'niːr], v.t. to disunite, to disjoin, to part. **se désunir**, v.r. to disunite, to come asunder.

détachage [deta'ʃaːʒ], n.m. cleaning, scouring.

détachant [deta'ʃɑ̃], n.m. cleaner, stain-remover.

détachement [detaʃ'mɑ̃], n.m. indifference, unconcern; (Mil.) detachment, draft.

détacher (1) [deta'ʃe], v.t. to remove stains, spots etc.

détacher (2) [deta'ʃe], v.t. to detach, to untie, to unfasten, to undo; to cut off; (Mil.) to detail. **se détacher**, v.r. to come unfastened, to come undone; to disengage oneself; to break away; to stand out clearly.

détail [de'taːj], n.m. detail, small matter, trifle; retail.

détaillant [deta'jɑ̃], n.m. (fem. -e) retailer, small dealer.

détailler [deta'je], v.t. to cut in pieces; to retail; to relate minutely.

détaxation [detaksa'sjɔ̃], n.f. decontrol (of prices).

détaxer [detak'se], v.t. to reduce or take off a tax; to decontrol.

détecter [detɛk'te], v.t. to detect.

détecteur [detɛk'tœːr], n.m. detector.

détection [detɛk'sjɔ̃], n.f. detection.

détective [detɛk'tiːv], n.m. detective.

déteindre [de'tɛ̃ːdr], v.t. irr. (conjug. like CRAINDRE) to take the dye or color out of.—v.i. to lose color, to run, to fade.

dételage [de'tla:ʒ], n.m. unharnessing.

dételer [de'tle], v.t. (conjug. like APPELER) to unharness, to unyoke.

détendre [de'tɑ̃ːdr], v.t. to slacken, to relax; to reduce the pressure of; to take down. **se détendre**, v.r. to slacken, to unbend, to become easier, to relax.

détenir [det'niːr], v.t. irr. (conjug. like TENIR) to detain, to withhold; to confine.

détente [de'tɑ̃ːt], n.f. trigger (of a gun etc.); cut-off (of an engine); relaxation, easing.

détenteur [detɑ̃'tœːr], n.m. (fem. -trice) holder, detainer.

détention [detɑ̃'sjɔ̃], *n.f.* detention; imprisonment.

détenu [det'ny], *a.* detained, imprisoned.—*n.m.* (*fem.* **-e**) prisoner.

détergent [deter'ʒɑ̃], *a.* (*Med.*) detergent.—*n.m.* detergent.

déterger [deter'ʒe], *v.t.* (*conjug. like* MANGER) to cleanse, to purify.

détérioration [deterjɔra'sjɔ̃], *n.f.* deterioration; wear and tear.

détériorer [deterjɔ're], *v.t.* to impair, to make worse. **se détériorer**, *v.r.* to deteriorate.

déterminable [determi'nabl], *a.* determinable.

déterminant [determi'nɑ̃], *a.* determinative, decisive.—*n.m.* (*Math.*) determinant.

détermination [determina'sjɔ̃], *n.f.* determination, resolution.

déterminé [determi'ne], *a.* determined, decided, fixed; resolute, firm.

déterminer [determi'ne], *v.t.* to determine, to settle; to ascertain; to decide; to cause to take a resolution. **se déterminer**, *v.r.* to resolve, to determine.

déterré [dete're], *n.m.* exhumed body.

déterrer [dete're], *v.t.* to dig up, to disinter; to unearth, to bring to light.

détestable [detes'tabl], *a.* detestable, hateful, odious; wretched.

détestablement [detestablə'mɑ̃], *adv.* detestably, abominably.

détestation [detesta'sjɔ̃], *n.f.* detestation, abhorrence.

détester [detes'te], *v.t.* to detest, to hate.

détirer [deti're], *v.t.* to draw out, to stretch.

détisser [deti'se], *v.t.* to unweave.

détonateur [detɔna'tœːr], *n.m.* detonator.

détonation [detɔna'sjɔ̃], *n.f.* detonation, report.

détoner [detɔ'ne], *v.t., v.i.* to detonate.

détonneler [detɔn'le], *v.t.* (*conjug. like* APPELER) to draw from a cask.

détonner [detɔ'ne], *v.i.* to be out of tune; to jar.

détordre [de'tɔrdr], *v.t.* to untwist; to unravel. **se détordre**, *v.r.* to come untwisted.

détors [de'tɔːr], *a.* untwisted.

détortiller [detɔrti'je], *v.t.* to untwist; to unravel. **se détortiller**, *v.r.* to become untwisted; to be unravelled.

détour [de'tuːr], *n.m.* turning, change of direction; roundabout way; (*fig.*) shift, evasion, trick.

détourné [detur'ne], *a.* out of the way, unfrequented; indirect.

détournement [deturnə'mɑ̃], *n.m.* turning aside; embezzlement; *détournement de mineur*, (*Law*) abduction of a minor.

détourner [detur'ne], *v.t.* to turn away; to lead astray; to divert; to ward off; to embezzle; to deter.—*v.i.* to turn, to turn off. **se détourner**, *v.r.* to turn aside; to abandon (*de*).

détracteur [detrak'tœːr], *a.* (*fem.* **-trice**) detractive, detracting.—*n.m.* (*fem.* **-trice**) detractor, disparager.

détraqué [detra'ke], *a.* out of order; deranged. (*colloq.*) crazy.—*n.m.* (*fem.* **-ée**) person shattered in mind or body.

détraquement [detrak'mɑ̃], *n.m.* breakdown (*of mechanism, mind, health*).

détraquer [detra'ke], *v.t.* to spoil (*a horse's*) paces; (*fig.*) to put out of order. **se détraquer**, *v.r.* to lose its paces (*of a horse*); (*fig.*) to be disordered.

détrempe [de'trɑ̃ːp], *n.f.* calcimine (*paint*).

détremper [detrɑ̃'pe], *v.t.* to dilute, to dissolve.

détresse [de'trɛs], *n.f.* distress, grief, trouble.

détresser [detrɛ'se], *v.t.* to unravel; to unplait.

détriment [detri'mɑ̃], *n.m.* detriment, injury, prejudice.

détritus [detri'tys], *n.m.* residue, refuse; offal.

détroit [de'trwa], *n.m.* strait, channel, sound, narrow firth.

détromper [detrɔ'pe], *v.t.* to undeceive. **se détromper**, *v.r.* to be undeceived.

détrônement [detron'mɑ̃], *n.m.* dethronement.

détrôner [detro'ne], *v.t.* to dethrone.

détrousser [detru'se], *v.t.* to untruss, to let down; (*fig.*) to rob.

détrousseur [detru'sœːr], *n.m.* (*fem.* **-euse**) highwayman, robber.

détruire [de'trɥiːr], *v.t. irr.* (*conjug. like* CONDUIRE) to destroy, to demolish, to ruin; to exterminate, to do away with, to efface, to suppress. **se détruire**, *v.r.* to fall into ruin or decay; to destroy each other.

dette [dɛt], *n.f.* debt; obligation.

deuil [dœːj], *n.m.* mourning; grief, sorrow; gloom; period of mourning; bereavement; mourning clothes; funeral cortège.

Deutéronome [døtero'nɔm], *n.m.* Deuteronomy.

deux [dø], *a.* two, both; second.—*n.m.* two; second (*of the month*); (*Cards, Dice etc.*) deuce.

deuxième [dø'zjɛm], *a.* second.—*n.m.* second; second floor.

deuxièmement [døzjɛm'mɑ̃], *adv.* secondly.

deux-pièces [dø'pjɛs], *n.m. inv.* (*women's*) two-piece (*suit*).

deux-points [dø'pwɛ̃], *n.m. inv.* (*Print.*) colon.

dévaler [deva'le], *v.t.* to descend; to lower.—*v.i.* to descend, to slope; to go *or* rush down (*of streams etc.*).

dévaliser [devali'ze], *v.t.* to rifle, to strip, to rob.

dévaliseur [devali'zœːr], *n.m.* (*fem.* **-euse**) thief, burglar.

dévaluation [devalɥa'sjɔ̃], *n.f.* devaluation.

dévaluer [deva'lɥe], *v.t.* to devalue.

devancer [devɑ̃'se], *v.t.* (*conjug. like* COMMENCER) to precede; to outstrip; to forestall, to anticipate; to surpass.

devancier [devɑ̃'sje], *n.m.* (*fem.* **-ière**) predecessor; (*pl.*) ancestors, forefathers.

devant [də'vɑ̃], *prep.* before; in front of, over against.—*adv.* in front, ahead.—*n.m.* front, forepart.

devanture [dəvɑ̃'tyːr], *n.f.* front(age) (*of a building*); shop front.

dévaser [deva'ze], *v.t.* to dredge.

dévastateur [devasta'tœːr], *a.* (*fem.* **-trice**) devastating, destructive.—*n.m.* (*fem.* **-trice**) devastator.

dévastation [devasta'sjɔ̃], *n.f.* devastation, ravage, havoc.

dévaster [devas'te], *v.t.* to devastate, to lay waste.

développement [devlɔp'mɑ̃], *n.m.* unfolding, opening; development, progress; (*Mil.*) deployment.

développer [devlɔ'pe], *v.t.* to open, to unwrap; to expand, to explain; to develop. **se développer**, *v.r.* to expand, to unfold; to be unravelled; to extend; to develop.

devenir [dəv'ni:r], *v.i. irr.* (*conjug. like* TENIR) to become, to grow, to get, to turn into.— *n.m.* gradual development (*of beings or of things*).

dévergondage [devergɔ̃'da:ʒ], *n.m.* shamelessness; profligacy, dissoluteness.

dévergonder (se) [sədevergɔ̃'de], *v.r.* to become dissolute.

déverrouillement [deveruj'mɑ̃], *n.m.* unbolting.

déverrouiller [deveru'je], *v.t.* to unbolt; (*fig.*) to set free.

devers [də'vɛ:r], *prep.* towards; **par devers**, in the presence of.

dévers [de'vɛ:r], *a.* inclined; out of alignment. —*n.m.* inclination; warping.

déverser [dever'se], *v.t.* to bend; to dump; to pour out (*water etc.*).—*v.i.* to lean, to jut out; to warp. **se déverser**, *v.r.* to empty (*of rivers, canals etc.*).

déversoir [dever'swa:r], *n.m.* overflow (*of a canal etc.*); outfall.

dévêtir [deve'ti:r], *v.t. irr.* (*conjug. like* VÊTIR) to undress, to strip of clothes; (*Law*) to divest. **se dévêtir**, *v.r.* to take off one's clothes, to undress.

déviation [devja'sjɔ̃], *n.f.* deviation, curvature; detour (*of a road*).

déviationnisme [devjasjɔ'nism], *n.m.* (*Polit.*) deviationism.

déviationniste [devjasjɔ'nist], *n.* deviationist.

dévidage [devi'da:ʒ], *n.m.* winding *or* reeling off.

dévider [devi'de], *v.t.* to wind off (*into skeins etc.*); (*fig.*) to explain.

dévideur [devi'dœ:r], *n.m.* (*fem.* -**euse**) winder, reeler.

dévidoir [devi'dwa:r], *n.m.* reel, skein winder, spool.

dévier [de'vje], *v.i.* and **se dévier**, *v.r.* to deviate; to swerve.

devin [də'vɛ̃], *n.m.* (*fem.* **devin\resse**) diviner, augur; fortune-teller.

deviner [dəvi'ne], *v.t.* to divine, to predict; to guess. **se deviner**, *v.r.* to understand each other.

devinette [dəvi'nɛt], *n.f.* poser, riddle, conundrum.

devineur [dəvi'nœ:r], *n.m.* (*fem.* -**euse**) guesser.

devis [də'vi], *n.m.* estimate; specification.

dévisager [deviza'ʒe], *v.t.* (*conjug. like* MANGER) to disfigure; to stare at.

devise [də'vi:z], *n.f.* device, emblem; motto, slogan; (*Fin.*) currency; **des devises étrangères**, foreign currency.

deviser [dəvi'ze], *v.i.* to talk casually, to chat.

dévissage [devi'sa:ʒ], **dévissement** [devis'mɑ̃], *n.m.* unscrewing.

dévisser [devi'se], *v.t.* to unscrew. **se dévisser**, *v.r.* to come unscrewed.

dévitaliser [devitali'ze], *v.t.* to kill the nerve (*of a tooth etc.*).

dévoiement [devwa'mɑ̃], *n.m.* looseness (*of the bowels*); (*Arch.*) inclination, slope; (*fig.*) departure from the normal path.

dévoilement [devwal'mɑ̃], *n.m.* unveiling, disclosure.

dévoiler [devwa'le], *v.t.* to unveil, to reveal, to disclose. **se dévoiler**, *v.r.* to be revealed.

dévoiment [DÉVOIEMENT].

devoir [də'vwa:r], *v.t. irr.* to owe (*money, gratitude*); to be obliged to, to be bound to, to have to, must. **se devoir**, *v.r.* to owe oneself; to owe it to oneself.—*n.m.* duty; (*Sch.*) work set, homework; (*pl.*) respects, compliments.

dévoltage [devɔl'ta:ʒ], *n.m.* (*Elec.*) reduction of voltage.

dévolter [devɔl'te], *v.t.* to reduce the voltage, to step down (*current*).

dévolteur [devɔl'tœ:r], *n.m.* reducing transformer.

dévolu [devɔ'ly], *a.* (*Law*) devolved, vested.— *n.m.* choice, preference.

dévolution [devɔly'sjɔ̃], *n.f.* devolution; escheat.

dévorant [devɔ'rɑ̃], *a.* devouring, ravenous; (*fig.*) wasting.

dévorateur [devɔra'tœ:r], *a.* (*fem.* -**trice**) devouring.—*n.m.* (*fem.* -**trice**) devourer, destroyer.

dévorer [devɔ're], *v.t.* to devour; to destroy; to squander; to gaze at eagerly.

dévot [de'vo], *a.* devout, pious; sanctimonious; holy (*of books etc.*).—*n.m.* (*fem.* -**e**) devout person, devotee; bigot.

dévotement [devɔt'mɑ̃], *adv.* devoutly, piously.

dévotion [devɔ'sjɔ̃], *n.f.* devotion, piety; disposal; devoutness.

dévouement *or* **dévoûment** [devu'mɑ̃], *n.m.* self-sacrifice; devotion, devotedness; zeal.

dévouer [de'vwe], *v.t.* to devote, to dedicate. **se dévouer**, *v.r.* to devote oneself; to dedicate oneself.

dévoyé [devwa'je], *a.* stray, gone astray.—*n.m.* (*fem.* -**ée**) (*fig.*) black sheep.

dévoyer [devwa'je], *v.t.* (*conjug. like* EMPLOYER) to corrupt; to lead astray. **se dévoyer**, *v.r.* to become corrupted.

dextérité [dɛksteri'te], *n.f.* dexterity, skill.

dextrine [dɛks'trin], *n.f.* dextrin.

dextrose [dɛks'tro:z], *n.f.* dextrose, glucose.

diabète [dja'bɛt], *n.m.* diabetes.

diabétique [djabe'tik], *a.* and *n.* diabetic.

diable [dja:bl], *n.m.* devil; wayward child; jack-in-the-box; luggage-truck; drag; *un bon diable*, a good-natured fellow; *un pauvre diable*, a poor wretch.—*int.* the devil! the deuce! confound it! hang it!

diablement [djablə'mɑ̃], *adv.* devilishly.

diablerie [djablə'ri], *n.f.* deviltry, witchcraft; mischief.

diablesse [dja'blɛs], *n.f.* she-devil; shrew, vixen.

diablotin [djablɔ'tɛ̃], *n.m.* imp; (Christmas) cracker.

diabolique [djabɔ'lik], *a.* diabolical, devilish.

diaboliquement [djabɔlik'mɑ̃], *adv.* diabolically, devilishly.

diaconal [djakɔ'nal], *a.* (*m. pl.* -**aux**) diaconal.

diaconat [djakɔ'na], *n.m.* diaconate, deaconry.

diaconesse [djakɔ'nɛs], *n.f.* deaconess.
diacre [djakr], *n.m.* deacon.
diadème [dja'dɛ:m], *n.m.* diadem; coronet.
diagnose [djag'no:z], *n.f.* (*art of*) diagnosis.
diagnostic [djagnɔs'tik], *n.m.* diagnosis.
diagnostique [djagnɔs'tik], *a.* diagnostic.
diagnostiquer [djagnosti'ke], *v.t.* to diagnose.
diagonal [djagɔ'nal], *a.* (*m. pl.* **-aux**) diagonal.—*n.f.* (**-e**) diagonal.
diagonalement [djagɔnal'mɑ̃], *adv.* diagonally.
diagramme [dja'gram], *n.m.* diagram.
dialecte [dja'lɛkt], *n.m.* dialect.
dialecticien [djalɛkti'sjɛ̃], *n.m.* dialectician.
dialectique [djalɛk'tik], *a.* dialectical.—*n.f.* dialectics, logic.
dialogue [dja'lɔg], *n.m.* dialogue, colloquy.
dialoguer [djalɔ'ge], *v.t.* to write in dialogue form.—*v.i.* to converse, to chat.
dialoguiste [djalɔ'gist], *n.m.* (*Cine.*) script writer.
diamant [dja'mɑ̃], *n.m.* diamond.
diamantaire [djamɑ̃'tɛ:r], *a.* of diamond brilliancy.—*n.m.* diamond cutter *or* seller.
diamanter [djamɑ̃'te], *v.t.* to set with diamonds; to tinsel, to frost.
diamétral [djame'tral], *a.* (*m. pl.* **-aux**) diametrical.
diamétralement [djametral'mɑ̃], *adv.* diametrically.
diamètre [dja'mɛtr], *n.m.* diameter.
diane [djan], *n.f.* reveille.
diantre [djɑ̃:tr], *int.* the deuce! dash! blast!
diapason [djapa'zɔ̃], *n.m.* diapason, pitch; tuning fork.
diaphane [dja'fan], *a.* diaphanous, transparent.
diaphragme [dja'fragm], *n.m.* diaphragm, midriff.
diapositive [djapozi'ti:v], *n.f.* transparency, slide.
diapré [dja'pre], *a.* dappled, variegated.
diaprer [dja'pre], *v.t.* to dapple, to variegate, to mottle.
diarrhée [dja're], *n.f.* diarrhoea.
diatribe [dja'trib], *n.f.* diatribe, bitter criticism *or* dissertation.
dictamen [dikta'mɛn], *n.m.* dictate (*of one's conscience*).
dictateur [dikta'tœ:r], *n.m.* dictator.
dictatorial [diktatɔ'rjal], *a.* (*m. pl.* **-aux**) dictatorial.
dictature [dikta'ty:r], *n.f.* dictatorship.
dictée [dik'te], *n.f.* act of dictating, dictation.
dicter [dik'te], *v.t.* to dictate; (*fig.*) to suggest, to inspire.
diction [dik'sjɔ̃], *n.f.* diction; delivery.
dictionnaire [diksjɔ'nɛ:r], *n.m.* dictionary.
dicton [dik'tɔ̃], *n.m.* common saying, saw, proverb.
didactique [didak'tik], *a.* didactic.—*n.f.* didactic art.
didactiquement [didaktik'mɑ̃], *adv.* didactically.
dièse [dje:z], *n.m.* (*Mus.*) sharp.
diesel [dje'zɛl], *n.m.* diesel (*engine*).
diète (1) [djɛt], *n.f.* diet (*regimen*).
diète (2) [djɛt], *n.f.* (*Hist.*) diet.
diététicien [djeteti'sjɛ̃], *n.m.* (*fem.* **-enne**) dietician, dietist.

diététique [djete'tik], *a.* dietetical.—*n.f.* dietetics.
Dieu [djø], *n.m.* God.
dieu [djø], *n.m.* (*pl.* **dieux**) god.
diffamant [difa'mɑ̃], *a.* defamatory, libellous, slanderous.
diffamateur [difama'tœ:r], *n.m.* (*fem.* **-trice**) defamer, slanderer.
diffamation [difama'sjɔ̃], *n.f.* defamation, aspersion, calumny.
diffamatoire [difama'twa:r], *a.* defamatory, libelous, slanderous.
diffamer [difa'me], *v.t.* to defame, to slander, to libel.
différemment [difera'mɑ̃], *adv.* differently.
différence [dife'rɑ̃:s], *n.f.* difference, diversity, contrast.
différenciation [diferɑ̃sja'sjɔ̃], *n.f.* differentiation.
différencier [diferɑ̃'sje], *v.t.* to make a difference, to distinguish; (*Math.*) to differentiate.
différend [dife'rɑ̃], *n.m.* difference, quarrel, dispute.
différent [dife'rɑ̃], *a.* different, dissimilar, unlike.
différentiel [diferɑ̃'sjɛl], *a.* (*fem.* **-elle**) differential.—*n.m.* (*Motor.*) differential.
différer [dife're], *v.t.* (*conjug. like* CÉDER) to defer, to postpone, to adjourn.—*v.i.* to defer, to put off; to differ, to disagree.
difficile [difi'sil], *a.* difficult; hard, trying; hard to please, particular.
difficilement [difisil'mɑ̃], *adv.* with difficulty.
difficulté [difikyl'te], *n.f.* difficulty; obstacle; rub; objection.
difficultueux [difikyl'tɥø], *a.* (*fem.* **-euse**) prone to raise difficulties; hard to please.
difforme [di'fɔrm], *a.* deformed, misshapen.
difformité [difɔrmi'te], *n.f.* deformity; hideousness.
diffus [di'fy], *a.* diffuse, prolix, verbose.
diffusément [difyze'mɑ̃], *adv.* diffusely, wordily.
diffuser [dify'ze], *v.t.* to diffuse; (*Rad. Tel.*) to broadcast.
diffuseur [dify'zœ:r], *n.m.* diffuser, spray cone; loudspeaker.
diffusion [dify'zjɔ̃], *n.f.* diffusion; diffusiveness, wordiness; propagation; broadcasting.
digérer [diʒe're], *v.t.* (*conjug. like* CÉDER) to digest; to ponder, to discuss; to put up with.
digestible [diʒɛs'tibl], *a.* digestible.
digestif [diʒɛs'tif], *a.* (*fem.* **-tive**) and *n.m.* digestive.
digestion [diʒɛs'tjɔ̃], *n.f.* digestion.
digital [diʒi'tall], *a.* (*m. pl.* **-aux**) digital; *empreinte digitale*, finger-print.
digitale [diʒi'tall], *n.f.* foxglove.
digitaline [diʒita'lin], *n.f.* (*Pharm.*) digitalis.
digne [diɲ], *a.* deserving, worthy; dignified.
dignement [diɲ'mɑ̃], *adv.* worthily, deservedly; with dignity.
dignitaire [diɲi'tɛ:r], *n.m.* dignitary.
dignité [diɲi'te], *n.f.* dignity, nobility, seriousness; self-respect.
digresser [digre'se], *v.i.* to digress, to depart from the main subject.
digressif [digre'sif], *a.* (*fem.* **-ive**) digressive.
digression [digre'sjɔ̃], *n.f.* digression.

digressivement [digresiv'mã], *adv.* digressively.

digue [dig], *n.f.* dike, dam, embankment; (*fig.*) limit; security.

diguer [di'ge], *v.t.* to dam, to embank.

dilacération [dilasero'sjõ], *n.f.* tearing, rending.

dilacérer [dilase're], *v.t.* (*conjug. like* CÉDER) to tear to pieces.

dilapidateur [dilapida'tœːr], *a.* (*fem.* -**trice**) wasteful, extravagant.—*n.m.* (*fem.* -**trice**) squanderer.

dilapidation [dilapida'sjõ], *n.f.* waste; embezzlement.

dilapider [dilapi'de], *v.t.* to waste, to squander (*a fortune*); to embezzle.

dilatation [dilata'sjõ], *n.f.* dilatation, expansion, distension.

dilater [dila'te], *v.t.* to dilate, to distend, to expand. **se dilater**, *v.r.* to dilate, to be dilated.

dilatoire [dila'twaːr], *a.* (*Law*) dilatory.

dilemme [di'lɛm], *n.m.* dilemma.

dilettante [dile'tãːt], *n.* dilettante.

dilettantisme [dilɛtã'tism], *n.m.* dilettantism, amateurism.

diligemment [dili3a'mã], *adv.* diligently, promptly.

diligence [dili'3ãːs], *n.f.* diligence; dispatch, application; stage-coach.

diligent [dili'3ã], *a.* diligent, assiduous, active.

diluer [di'lɥe], *v.t.* to dilute.

dilution [dily'sjõ], *n.f.* dilution.

diluvien [dily'vjɛ̃], *a.* (*fem.* -**enne**) diluvian.

dimanche [di'mãːʃ], *n.m.* Sunday, Sabbath.

dîme [dim], *n.f.* tithe; (*U.S.*) dime.

dimension [dimã'sjõ], *n.f.* dimension, size.

dimer [di'me], *v.t.* to tithe.—*v.i.* to levy a tithe.

diminuer [dimi'nɥe], *v.t.* to diminish, to lessen; to impair.—*v.i.* to diminish, to abate, to fall (*in price etc.*); to grow shorter (*of days*).

diminutif [diminy'tif], *a.* (*fem.* **ive**) and *n.m.* diminutive.

diminution [diminy'sjõ], *n.f.* diminution, reduction, abatement.

dinde [dɛ̃ːd], *n.f.* turkey hen; turkey.

dindon [dɛ̃'dõ], *n.m.* turkey cock.

dindonneau [dɛ̃dɔ'no], *n.m.* (*pl.* -**eaux**) young turkey.

dindonner [dɛ̃dɔ'ne], *v.t.* to dupe, to take in.

dindonnier [dɛ̃dɔ'nje], *n.m.* (*fem.* -**ière**) turkey keeper.

dîné [DÎNER].

dîner [di'ne], *v.i.* to dine, to have dinner.—*n.m.* or **dîné** [di'ne], dinner; dinner party.

dînette [di'nɛt], *n.f.* child's or doll's dinner.

dîneur [di'nœːr], *n.m.* (*fem.* -**euse**) diner; diner-out.

diocésain [djose'zɛ̃], *a.* diocesan.

diocèse [djo'sɛːz], *n.m.* diocese.

diphasé [difa'ze], *a.* (*Elec.*) two-phase, diphasic.

diphtérie [difte'ri], *n.f.* diphtheria.

diphtongue [dif'tõːg], *n.f.* diphthong.

diplomate [diplo'mat], *a.* diplomatic.—*n.* diplomatist, diplomat.

diplomatie [diploma'si], *n.f.* diplomacy; diplomatic service.

diplomatique [diploma'tik], *a.* diplomatic; tactful.

diplomatiquement [diplomatik'mã], *adv.* diplomatically.

diplôme [di'ploːm], *n.m.* diploma.

diplômé [diplo'me], *a.* (*fem.* -**ée**) qualified.—*n.m.* (*fem.* -**ée**) qualified person.

dipsomane [dipso'man], *n.m.* dipsomaniac.

dipsomanie [dipsoma'ni], *n.f.* dipsomania.

dire [diːr], *v.t. irr.* to say, to speak; to tell; to recite; to order; to express. **se dire**, *v.r.* to call oneself, to be called; to say to oneself; to be said.—*n.m.* what one says, statement; (*Law*) allegation.

direct [di'rɛkt], *a.* direct, straight, immediate. —*n.m.* (*Box.*) straight blow; **un direct du gauche**, a straight left.

directement [dirɛktə'mã], *adv.* directly, point-blank.

directeur [dirɛk'tœːr], *n.m.* (*fem.* -**trice**) director, manager, superintendent, head; principal, head master, head mistress; conductor (*of orchestra*).

direction [dirɛk'sjõ], *n.f.* directing, direction; management; directorship; (*Motor.*) steering.

directives [dirɛk'tiːv], *n.f. pl.* general rules, directives.

directoire [dirɛk'twaːr], *n.m.* (*Eccles.*) directory.

directorat [dirɛkto'ra], *n.m.* directorship, directorate.

dirigeable [diri'3abl], *n.m.* dirigible balloon or airship.

dirigeant [diri'3ã], *a.* directing, leading.—*n.* ruler, leader.

diriger [diri'3e], *v.t.* (*conjug. like* MANGER) to direct; to control; to steer, to manage, to govern; to send, to aim. **se diriger**, *v.r.* to make for, to go (*towards*); to govern oneself.

dirigisme [diri'3ism], *n.m.* (*Polit.*) state planning or controls.

discernement [disɛrnə'mã], *n.m.* discernment; discrimination; judgment.

discerner [disɛr'ne], *v.t.* to discern; to distinguish, to discriminate.

disciple [di'sipl], *n.m.* disciple, follower.

disciplinaire [disipli'nɛːr], *a.* disciplinary.

discipline [disi'plin], *n.f.* discipline; education, training; (*sch.*) subject.

discipliner [disipli'ne], *v.t.* to discipline. **se discipliner**, *v.r.* to be disciplined.

discontinu [diskõti'ny], *a.* discontinuous.

discontinuation [diskõtinɥa'sjõ], *n.f.* discontinuance, discontinuation.

discontinuer [diskõti'nɥe], *v.t.* to discontinue, to interrupt, to suspend.—*v.i.* to cease, to leave off.

discontinuité [diskõtinɥi'te], *n.f.* discontinuity, discontinuance, interruption.

disconvenance [diskõv'nãːs], *n.f.* incongruity, unsuitability; dissimilarity.

disconvenir [diskõv'niːr], *v.i. irr.* (*conjug. like* TENIR) to deny, to disown; to disagree.

discord [dis'kɔːr], *a.* (*Mus.*) out of tune, discordant.

discordance [diskɔr'dãːs], *n.f.* discordancy, dissonance.

discordant [diskɔr'dã], *a.* discordant, dissonant, out of tune; inharmonious, incongruous.

discorde [dis'kɔrd], *n.f.* discord, disagreement, strife.

discorder [diskɔr'de], *v.i.* (*Mus.*) to be out of tune; to be in a state of dissension.

discothèque [diskɔ'tɛk], *n.f.* record library; discothèque.

discoureur [disku'rœːr], *n.m.* (*fem.* **-euse**) talker, chatterer.

discourir [disku'riːr], *v.i.* irr. (*conjug. like* COURIR) to discourse; to descant (*sur*); to babble.

discours [dis'kuːr], *n.m.* discourse; speech; address; diction; treatise.

discourtois [diskur'twa], *a.* discourteous.

discourtoisement [diskurtwaz'mã], *adv.* discourteously.

discourtoisie [diskurtwa'zi], *n.f.* discourtesy, incivility.

discrédit [diskre'di], *n.m.* discredit, disrepute.

discréditer [diskredi'te], *v.t.* to discredit.

discret [dis'krɛ], *a.* (*fem.* **-ète**) discreet; cautious, shy; secret, close.

discrètement [diskrɛt'mã], *adv.* discreetly, warily.

discrétion [diskre'sjõ], *n.f.* circumspection, prudence; discretion; reserve; *pain à discrétion*, bread ad lib.

discrétionnaire [diskresjɔ'nɛːr], *a.* discretionary.

discrimination [diskrimina'sjõ], *n.f.* discrimination.

discriminer [diskrimi'ne], *v.t.* to discriminate.

disculper [diskyl'pe], *v.t.* to exculpate, to vindicate, to exonerate.

discursif [diskyr'sif], *a.* (*fem.* **-sive**) discursive.

discussion [disky'sjõ], *n.f.* discussion, debate; altercation, dispute.

discutable [disky'tabl], *a.* debatable, disputable, contestable.

discuter [disky'te], *v.t.* to discuss, to debate, to argue; to examine, to inquire into, to sift.

discuteur [disky'tœːr] *n.m.* (*fem.* **-euse**) disputant.

disert [di'zɛːr], *a.* copious, fluent, eloquent.

disertement [dizɛrtə'mã], *adv.* copiously, fluently.

disette [di'zɛt], *n.f.* scarcity, dearth, famine; poverty, penury.

diseur [di'zœːr], *n.m.* (*fem.* **-euse**) sayer, teller; diseuse.

disgrâce [diz'grɑːs], *n.f.* disfavor; disgrace, misfortune; plainness (*of features*).

disgracié [dizgra'sje], *a.* out of favor; (*fig.*) ill-favored, deformed.

disgracier [dizgra'sje], *v.t.* to disgrace, to put out of favor.

disgracieusement [dizgrasjøz'mã], *adv.* awkwardly, ungracefully.

disgracieux [dizgra'sjø], *a.* (*fem.* **-euse**) awkward, uncouth, disagreeable.

disjoindre [diz'ʒwɛ̃ːdr], *v.t.* irr. (*conjug. like* CRAINDRE) to disjoin, to disunite. **se disjoindre**, *v.r.* to come apart, to disunite.

disjoncteur [dizʒɔ̃k'tœːr], *n.m.* (*Elec.*) circuit breaker.

disjonction [dizʒɔ̃k'sjõ], *n.f.* disjunction, separation.

dislocation [dislɔka'sjõ], *n.f.* dislocation, dismemberment.

disloquement [dislɔk'mã], *n.m.* dislocation.

disloquer [dislɔ'ke], *v.t.* to dislocate, to dismember; to take to pieces (*machines etc.*); (*Mil.*) to break up (*an army*). **se disloquer**, *v.r.* to dislocate one's arm etc.; to be taken to pieces; to come apart.

dispache [dis'paʃ], *n.f.* (*Maritime Insurance*) assessment; average adjustment.

dispacheur [dispa'ʃœːr], **dispatcheur** [dispa'tʃœːr], *n.m.* assessor, average adjuster.

disparaître [dispa'rɛːtr], *v.i.* irr. (*conjug. like* CONNAÎTRE) to vanish, to disappear; to abscond; to die.

disparate [dispa'rat], *a.* dissimilar, incongruous, unlike, ill-matched.—*n.f.* incongruity, dissimilarity.

disparité [dispari'te], *n.f.* disparity, dissimilarity.

disparition [dispari'sjõ], *n.f.* disappearance.

dispendieusement [dispãdjøz'mã], *adv.* expensively.

dispendieux [dispã'djø], *a.* (*fem.* **-euse**) expensively, costly.

dispensaire [dispã'sɛːr], *n.m.* dispensary; out-patients' department.

dispensateur [dispãsa'tœːr], *n.m.* (*fem.* **-trice**) dispenser; bestower, giver.

dispensation [dispãsa'sjõ], *n.f.* dispensation; distribution; dispensing.

dispense [dis'pãːs], *n.f.* dispensation (*from fasting*); exemption (*from military service*).

dispenser [dispã'se], *v.t.* to dispense, to bestow; to exempt; to dispense (*with*). **se dispenser**, *v.r.* to dispense with; to exempt or excuse oneself (*from*); to spare oneself.

disperser [dispɛr'se], *v.t.* to disperse, to scatter. **se disperser**, *v.r.* to be dispersed, to break up, to be scattered.

dispersion [dispɛr'sjõ], *n.f.* dispersion, breaking up.

disponibilité [dispɔnibili'te], *n.f.* (*Law*) state of being disposable, disposal (*of property*); (*Mil.*) state of being unattached.

disponible [dispɔ'nibl], *a.* disposable, available; disengaged.—*n.m.* realizable assets.

dispos [dis'po], *a.* fit and well, in good fettle, nimble; cheerful.

disposer [dispo'ze], *v.t.* to dispose, to arrange, to prepare; to incline, to prevail upon.—*v.i.* to dispose (*de*); to prescribe, to ordain. **se disposer**, *v.r.* to dispose oneself, to be disposed; to get ready.

disposition [dispozi'sjõ], *n.f.* disposition, arrangement; inclination, frame of mind; mind, intention.

disproportion [disprɔpɔr'sjõ], *n.f.* disproportion.

disproportionné [disprɔpɔrsjɔ'ne], *a.* disproportionate, inadequate.

disproportionnel [disprɔpɔrsjɔ'nɛl], *a.* (*fem.* **-elle**) disproportional.

disputable [dispy'tabl], *a.* disputable, debatable, doubtful.

dispute [dis'pyt], *n.f.* dispute, debate, controversy, wrangle; quarrel.

disputer [dispy'te], *v.t.* to contend for; to dispute, to call in question.—*v.i.* to discuss, to argue, to dispute; to contend, to wrangle. **se disputer**, *v.r.* to dispute; to contend, to quarrel.

disputeur [dispy'tœːr], *a.* (*fem.* **-euse**) contentious, quarrelsome.—*n.m.* (*fem.* **-euse**) wrangler.

disqualification [diskalifika'sjɔ̃], *n.f.* disqualification.

disqualifier [diskali'fje], *v.t.* to disqualify.

disquaire [dis'kɛːr], *n.* phonograph record seller.

disque [disk], *n.m.* discus, queit; disk; (*Rail.*) signal disk; phonograph record; *disque longue durée* or *microsillon*, long-playing record.

disruptif [disryp'tif], *a.* (*fem.* **-tive**) disruptive.

disrupteur [disryp'tœːr], *n.m.* (*Elec.*) interrupter.

dissecteur [disɛk'tœːr], *n.m.* dissector.

dissection [disɛk'sjɔ̃], *n.f.* dissection.

dissemblable [disɑ̃'blabl], *a.* dissimilar, unlike.

dissemblablement [disɑ̃blablə'mɑ̃], *adv.* dissimilarly.

dissemblance [disɑ̃'blɑ̃ːs], *n.f.* dissimilarity, difference.

dissemblant [disɑ̃'blɑ̃], *a.* dissimilar, different.

dissémination [disemina'sjɔ̃], *n.f.* dissemination, scattering (*of seeds etc.*).

disséminer [disemi'ne], *v.t.* to disseminate, to scatter.

dissension [disɑ̃'sjɔ̃], *n.f.* dissension, discord, strife.

dissentiment [disɑ̃ti'mɑ̃], *n.m.* dissent, disagreement.

disséquer [dise'ke], *v.t.* (*conjug. like* CÉDER) to dissect; to analyse.

disséqueur [dise'kœːr], [DISSECTEUR].

dissertation [disɛrta'sjɔ̃], *n.f.* dissertation, treatise; essay (*in schools*).

disserter [disɛr'te], *v.i.* to dissert.

dissidence [disi'dɑ̃ːs], *n.f.* dissidence, difference of opinion, dissent.

dissident [disi'dɑ̃], *a.* dissident.—*n.m.* (*fem.* **-e**) dissenter, rebel.

dissimilaire [disimi'lɛːr], *a.* dissimilar, different, unlike.

dissimilarité [disimilari'te], *n.f.* dissimilarity.

dissimilitude [disimili'tyd], *n.f.* dissimilitude, difference.

dissimulateur [disimyla'tœːr], *n.m.* (*fem.* **-trice**) dissembler; hypocrite.

dissimulation [disimyla'sjɔ̃], *n.f.* dissimulation; double-dealing.

dissimulé [disimy'le], *a.* two-faced, artful.—*n.m.* (*fem.* **-ée**) dissembler; hypocrite.

dissimuler [disimy'le], *v.t.* to dissemble, to conceal. **se dissimuler**, *v.r.* to hide oneself, to pass unnoticed.

dissipateur [disipa'tœːr], *a.* (*fem.* **-trice**) lavish, extravagant.—*n.m.* (*fem.* **-trice**) squanderer, spendthrift.

dissipation [disipa'sjɔ̃], *n.f.* dissipation, waste; idleness.

dissipé [disi'pe], *a.* dissipated, profligate; inattentive.

dissiper [disi'pe], *v.t.* to dissipate, to dispel; to scatter, to squander. **se dissiper**, *v.r.* to be dispersed; to vanish; to be squandered; to be inattentive (*in class-room*).

dissolu [diso'ly], *a.* dissolute, profligate, licentious.

dissolubilité [disɔlybili'te], *n.f.* dissolubility.

dissoluble [diso'lybl], *a.* dissoluble, dissolvable.

dissolution [disɔly'sjɔ̃], *n.f.* dissolution; solution; dissoluteness.

dissolvant [disɔl'vɑ̃], *a.* and *n.m.* dissolvent, solutive, solvent.

dissonance [disɔ'nɑ̃ːs], *n.f.* dissonance, discord.

dissonant [disɔ'nɑ̃], *a.* dissonant, discordant.

dissoudre [di'sudr], *v.t. irr.* (*conjug. like* ABSOUDRE) to dissolve; to break up; to annul. **se dissoudre**, *v.r.* to dissolve, to be dissolved; to break up.

dissous [di'su], *a.* (*fem.* **-oute**) dissolved; broken up.

dissuader [disɥa'de], *v.t.* to dissuade.

dissuasif [disɥa'zif], *a.* (*fem.* **-sive**) dissuasive.

dissymétrique [disime'trik], *a.* assymetric(al).

distance [dis'tɑ̃ːs], *n.f.* distance; interval (*of place or time*).

distancer [distɑ̃'se], *v.t.* (*conjug. like* COMMENCER) to out-distance, to outrun; (*fig.*) to surpass, to outdo.

distant [dis'tɑ̃], *a.* distant, remote; aloof, stand-offish.

distendre [dis'tɑ̃ːdr], *v.t.* to distend.

distension [dis'tɑ̃ːsjɔ̃], *n.f.* distension, strain.

distillable [disti'labl], *a.* distillable.

distillateur [distila'tœːr], *n.m.* distiller.

distillation [distila'sjɔ̃], *n.f.* distillation.

distiller [disti'le], *v.t.* to distil; to discharge; to vent.—*v.i.* to drop, to distil, to trickle.

distillerie [distil'ri], *n.f.* distillery; distilling.

distinct [dis'tɛ̃], *a.* distinct, different, separate.

distinctement [distɛ̃ktə'mɑ̃], *adv.* distinctly, clearly, plainly.

distinctif [distɛ̃k'tif], *a.* (*fem.* **-tive**) distinctive, characteristic.

distinction [distɛ̃k'sjɔ̃], *n.f.* distinction; division, difference; eminence; refinement.

distinctivement [distɛ̃ktiv'mɑ̃], *adv.* distinctively.

distingué [distɛ̃'ge], *a.* distinguished, eminent, noted; elegant, well-bred.

distinguer [distɛ̃'ge], *v.t.* to distinguish, to discern; to discriminate; to honor. **se distinguer**, *v.r.* to be conspicuous; to gain distinction.

distique [dis'tik], *n.m.* distich; couplet.

distordre [dis'tɔrdr], *v.t.* to distort; to sprain. **se distordre**, *v.r.* to become distorted.

distorsion [distɔr'sjɔ̃], *n.f.* distortion; sprain.

distraction [distrak'sjɔ̃], *n.f.* separation; absence of mind, inattention; diversion, hobby.

distraire [dis'trɛːr], *v.t. irr.* (*conjug. like* TRAIRE) to separate; to distract, to disturb; to entertain. **se distraire**, *v.r.* to be disturbed; to be diverted (*de*); to amuse oneself.

distrait [dis'trɛ], *a.* absent-minded, heedless; vacant (*person*).—*n.m.* (*fem.* **-e**) absent-minded person.

distraitement [distrɛt'mɑ̃], *adv.* absent-mindedly.

distrayant [distrɛ'jɑ̃], *a.* diverting, pleasing.

distribuable [distri'bɥabl], *a.* distributable.

distribuer [distri'bɥe], *v.t.* to distribute, to divide; to dispose; to arrange.

distributaire [distriby'tɛːr], *n.* recipient, receiver; sharer.

distributeur [distriby'tœːr], *a.* (*fem.* **-trice**) distributing.—*n.m.* (*fem.* **-trice**) distributer, bestower, dispenser; **distributeur automatique,** vending machine.

distributif [distriby'tif], *a.* (*fem.* **-tive**) distributive.

distribution [distriby'sjɔ̃], *n.f.* distribution; division; disposition; delivery (*of mail*).

district [dis'trikt], *n.m.* (administrative) district; region.

dit [di], *a.* said, spoken; surnamed, called; *aussitôt dit, aussitôt fait,* no sooner said than done; *autrement dit,* in other words. —*n.m.* maxim; saying.

dito [di'to], *adv.* (Comm.) ditto, (*abbr.*) do.

diurnal [diyr'nal], *a.* (*m. pl.* **-aux**) diurnal.—*n.m.* diurnal, daily-prayer book.

diurne [djyrn], *a.* diurnal, daily.—*n.m.* diurnal insect.

divagant [diva'gɑ̃], *a.* wandering, rambling.

divagateur [divaga'tœːr], *a.* (*fem.* **-trice**) desultory, rambling.—*n.m.* (*fem.* **-trice**) rambling speaker.

divagation [divaga'sjɔ̃], *n.f.* divagation, wandering.

divaguer [diva'ge], *v.i.* to ramble, to wander from the question; to be incoherent (*in writing* or *speaking*).

divan [di'vɑ̃], *n.m.* divan; couch.

divergence [diver'ʒɑ̃ːs], *n.f.* divergence.

divergent [diver'ʒɑ̃], *a.* divergent; different.

diverger [diver'ʒe], *v.i.* (*conjug. like* MANGER) to diverge, to branch off.

divers [di'veːr], *a.* diverse, miscellaneous; changing; (*pl.*) various, divers, sundry.

diversement [diverse'mɑ̃], *adv.* diversely, variously.

diversifier [diversi'fje], *v.t.* to diversify; to variegate. **se diversifier,** *v.r.* to be varied *or* diversified.

diversion [diver'sjɔ̃], *n.f.* diversion; change.

diversité [diversi'te], *n.f.* diversity, variety, difference.

divertir [diver'tiːr], *v.t.* to amuse, to delight; to divert; to embezzle. **se divertir,** *v.r.* to amuse oneself.

divertissant [diverti'sɑ̃], *a.* diverting, entertaining.

divertissement [divertis'mɑ̃], *n.m.* diversion, amusement, entertainment; (*Law*) embezzlement.

divette [di'vet], *n.f.* musical comedy actress.

dividende [divi'dɑ̃ːd], *n.m.* dividend.

divin [di'vɛ̃], *a.* divine, heavenly; (*fig.*) admirable, exquisite.

divinateur [divina'tœːr], *a.* (*fem.* **-trice**) prophetic.—*n.m.* (*fem.* **-trice**) diviner, seer.

divination [divina'sjɔ̃], *n.f.* divination.

divinatoire [divina'twaːr], *a.* divinatory, divining.

divinement [divin'mɑ̃], *adv.* divinely; (*fig.*) admirably, exquisitely.

diviniser [divini'ze], *v.t.* to deify; to laud to the skies.

divinité [divini'te], *n.f.* divinity, godhead, deity.

diviser [divi'ze], *v.t.* to divide, to portion out; to disunite. **se diviser,** *v.r.* to be divided; to fall (*into*), to break up (*into*).

diviseur [divi'zœːr], *a.* divisive, dividing.— *n.m.* (Arith.) divisor; divider.

divisibilité [divizibili'te], *n.f.* divisibility.

divisible [divi'zibl], *a.* divisible.

division [divi'zjɔ̃], *n.f.* division, partition, dividing; (Mil.) division.

divisionnaire [divizjo'nɛːr], *a.* divisional, divisionary.

divorce [di'vors], *n.m.* divorce; (*fig.*) variance.

divorcer [divor'se], *v.i.* (*conjug. like* COMMENCER) to divorce oneself (*de*); to break with; to divorce *or* get a divorce from someone (*d'avec quelqu'un*).

divulgation [divylga'sjɔ̃], *n.f.* divulgence; revelation.

divulguer [divyl'ge], *v.t.* to divulge, to reveal, to make public. **se divulguer,** *v.r.* to leak out (*secret*).

dix [dis], *when other words follow* [di] *or* [diz], *a.* ten; tenth.—*n.m.* ten.

dix-huit [di'zɥit], *a.* and *n.m.* eighteen.

dix-huitième [dizɥi'tjem],*a.* and *n.*eighteenth.

dixième [di'zjem], *a.* and *n.* tenth.

dixièmement [dizjem'mɑ̃], *adv.* tenthly, ninteenth.

dix-neuf [diz'nœf], *a.* and *n.m.* nineteen.

dix-neuvième [diznœ'vjem], *a.* and *n.* nineteenth.

dix-sept [dis'set], *a.* and *n.m.* seventeen; seventeenth.

dix-septième [disse'tjem], *a.* and *n.* seventeenth.

dizaine [di'zen], *n.f.* half a score; about ten.

djinn [dʒin], *n.m.* jinn(ee).

do [do], *n.m.* (Mus.) do *or* ut; (the note) C.

docile [do'sil], *a.* docile, tractable, submissive.

docilement [dosil'mɑ̃], *adv.* with docility.

docilité [dosili'te], *n.f.* docility, tractability.

dock [dok], *n.m.* dock; warehouse.

docker [dɔ'kɛːr], *n.m.* docker.

docte [dokt], *a.* erudite, learned.

doctement [dɔkta'mɑ̃], *adv.* learnedly; pedantically.

docteur [dɔk'tœːr], *n.* doctor.

doctoral [dɔkto'ral], *a.* (*m. pl.* **-aux**) doctoral.

doctorat [dɔkto'ra], *n.m.* doctorate, doctor's degree.

doctrinaire [dɔktri'nɛːr], *a.* stiff, formal, pedantic.—*n.m.* doctrinaire.

doctrinairement [dɔktrinɛr'mɑ̃], *adv.* stiffly, formally, pedantically.

doctrine [dɔk'trin], *n.f.* doctrine.

document [dɔky'mɑ̃], *n.m.* document; (*pl.*) records.

documentaire [dɔkymɑ̃'tɛːr], *a.* documentary.—*n.m.* (Cine.) documentary film.

documentation [dɔkymɑ̃ta'sjɔ̃], *n.f.* documentation.

documenter [dɔkymɑ̃'te], *v.t.* to give information. **se documenter,** *v.r.* to gather evidence.

dodelinement [dɔdlin'mɑ̃], *n.m.* wagging, nodding (*of head*); dandling.

dodeliner [dɔdli'ne], *v.t.* to dandle, to rock (*a child*).—*v.i.* to wag, nod (*head*).

dodiner [dɔdi'ne], *v.t.* to rock, to dandle.— *v.i.* to oscillate. **se dodiner,** *v.r.* to rock one's body; to nurse *or* coddle oneself.

dodo [do'do], *n.m.* (Infantile) bye-bye; (*fig.*) sleep, bed.

dodu [dɔ'dy], *a.* plump.

dogaresse [dɔga'res], *n.f.* dogaressa, wife of a doge.

doge [dɔːʒ], *n.m.* doge.

dogmatique [dɔgma'tik], *a.* dogmatic.
dogmatiquement [dɔgmatik'mã], *adv.* dogmatically.
dogmatiser [dɔgmati'ze], *v.t.* to state dogmatically.—*v.i.* to dogmatize.
dogmatisme [dɔgma'tism], *n.m.* dogmatism.
dogmatiste [dɔgma'tist], *n.* dogmatist.
dogme [dɔgm], *n.m.* dogma, tenet.
dogue [dɔg], *n.m.* mastiff; (*fig.*) bull-dog (*of a man*).
doguin [dɔ'gɛ̃], *n.m.* pug.
doigt [dwa], *n.m.* finger, digit; toe.
doigté [dwa'te], *n.m.* (*Mus.*) fingering, touch; (*fig.*) tact, adroitness.
doigtier [dwa'tje], *n.m.* finger-stall.
dol [dɔl], *n.m.* deceit, fraud.
dolage [dɔ'la:ʒ], *n.m.* planing.
doléances [dɔle'ã:s], *n.f. pl.* complaints; grievances.
dolemment [dɔla'mã], *adv.* dolefully.
dolent [dɔ'lã], *a.* doleful, piteous, plaintive.
doler [dɔ'le], *v.t.* to smooth with the adze; to plane.
dolmen [dɔl'mɛn], *n.m.* dolmen.
doloir [dɔ'lwa:r], *n.m.* paring knife, parer.
doloire [dɔ'lwa:r], *n.f.* cooper's adze; mason's axe.
dolosif [dɔlo'zif], *a.* (*fem.* **-sive**) fraudulent.
domaine [dɔ'mɛːn], *n.m.* domain, estate, property; province, sphere.
dôme [do:m], *n.m.* dome; canopy, vault.
domestication [dɔmɛstika'sjɔ̃], *n.f.* domestication.
domesticité [dɔmɛstisi'te], *n.f.* domesticity; (*collect.*) domestic servants.
domestique [dɔmɛs'tik], *a.* domestic; tame, domesticated.—*n.* servant, domestic.—*n.m.* household.
domestiquer [dɔmɛsti'ke], *v.t.* to domesticate, to tame.
domicile [dɔmi'sil], *n.m.* domicile, residence.
domiciliaire [dɔmisi'ljɛːr], *a.* domiciliary.
domicilié [dɔmisi'lje], *a.* resident, domiciled.
domicilier (se) [sədɔmisi'lje], *v.r.* to settle down in a place.
dominance [dɔmi'nã:s], *n.f.* dominance.
dominant [dɔmi'nã], *a.* dominant, predominant, prevalent.
dominateur [dɔmina'tœːr], *a.* (*fem.* **-trice**) ruling, domineering, arrogant.—*n.m.* (*fem.* **-trice**) dominator, ruler, tyrant.
domination [dɔmina'sjɔ̃], *n.f.* domination, dominion, rule, sway.
dominer [dɔmi'ne], *v.t.* to dominate; to rule; to prevail over; to overlook, to tower over.—*v.i.* to rule, to control; to dominate, to prevail; to lord it; to tower. **se dominer** *v.r.* to control oneself.
dominicain [dɔmini'kɛ̃], *a.* (*Relig.*, *Polit.*) Dominican.—*n.m.* (**Dominicain**, *fem.* **-aine**) (*Polit.*) Dominican (*person*), Dominican friar *or* nun; **la République Dominicaine**, the Dominican Republic.
dominical [dɔmini'kal], *a.* (*m. pl.* **-aux**) dominical.
dominicale [dɔmini'kal], *n.f.* Sunday sermon.
dominion [dɔmi'njɔ̃], *n.m.* dominion.
domino [dɔmi'no], *n.m.* domino.
dommage [dɔ'ma:ʒ], *n.m.* damage, injury, loss; *c'est dommage*, it is a pity.

dommageable [dɔma'ʒabl], *a.* hurtful, prejudicial, injurious; damageable (*goods*).
domptable [dɔ̃'tabl], *a.* tamable, manageable.
dompter [dɔ̃'te], *v.t.* to subdue, to subjugate, to tame. **se dompter**, *v.r.* to quell *or* overcome one's passions.
dompteur [dɔ̃'tœːr], *n.m.* (*fem.* **-euse**) subduer; tamer; breaker-in.
don [dɔ̃], *n.m.* gift, donation; (*fig.*) aptitude, talent.
donataire [dɔna'tɛːr], *n.* donee, recipient.
donateur [dɔna'tœːr], *n.m.* (*fem.* **-trice**) donor, giver.
donation [dɔna'sjɔ̃], *n.f.* donation, free gift.
donc [dɔ̃ːk, dɔ̃], *conj.* then, therefore, accordingly, hence; consequently; of course, to be sure.
donjon [dɔ̃'ʒɔ̃], *n.m.* keep, castle keep; turret.
donnant [dɔ'nã], *a.* open-handed, generous; *donnant donnant*, give and take.
donne [dɔn], *n.f.* deal (*at cards*).
donnée [dɔ'ne], *n.f.* given fact, datum; notion; (*Math.*) known quantity; (*pl.*) data.
donner [dɔ'ne], *v.t.* to give, to bestow; to grant; to present (*a play etc.*); to deal (*at cards*).—*v.i.* to give way; to hit, to stumble (*dans*); to be addicted to (*dans*); to attack (*of troops etc.*); to yield; to overlook. **se donner**, *v.r.* to procure; to take place (*of battles etc.*); to give oneself out (*pour*).
donneur [dɔ'nœːr], *n.m.* (*fem.* **-euse**) giver, donor; dealer (*of cards*); *donneur de sang*, blood donor.
don Quichotte [dɔ̃ki'ʃɔt], *n.m.* Don Quixote, quixotic person.
dont [dɔ̃], *pron.* whose, of which, of whom, from whom etc.
doper [dɔ'pe], *v.t.* (*Spt.*) to dope (*a horse etc.*).
doping [dɔ'piŋ], *n.m.* dope; doping.
dorade [dɔ'rad], *n.f.* (*Ichth.*) sea bream.
doré [dɔ're], *a.* gilt, gilded, golden.
dorénavant [dɔrena'vã], *adv.* henceforth, hereafter.
dorer [dɔ're], *v.t.* to gild; to glaze (*pastry*). **se dorer**, *v.r.* to gild; to become yellow.
doreur [dɔ'rœːr], *n.m.* (*fem.* **-euse**) gilder.
dorien [dɔ'rjɛ̃], *a.* and *n.m.* (*fem.* **-enne**) Dorian; Doric.
dorique [dɔ'rik], *a.* and *n.m.* Doric.
dorloter [dɔrlɔ'te], *v.t.* to fondle, to pamper, to coddle, to pet. **se dorloter**, *v.r.* to coddle oneself; to indulge oneself.
dormant [dɔr'mã], *a.* sleeping, asleep; dormant, stagnant.—*n.m.* fixed frame (*of window etc.*).
dormeur [dɔr'mœːr], *a.* (*fem.* **-euse**) sleepy, drowsy, sluggish.—*n.m.* (*fem.* **-euse**) sleeper; sluggard.—*n.f.* (**-euse** (1)) sort of chaise longue.
dormeuse (2) [dɔr'møːz], *n.f.* stud ear-ring.
dormir [dɔr'mi:r], *v.i. irr.* (*conjug. like* SENTIR) to sleep, to be asleep; to lie still; to lie dormant (*of money*); to be stagnant (*of water*).
dormitif [dɔrmi'tif], *a.* (*fem.* **-tive**) soporific, dormitive.
Dorothée [dɔro'te], *f.* Dorothy.
dorsal [dɔr'sal], *a.* dorsal.
dortoir [dɔr'twa:r], *n.m.* dormitory.
dorure [dɔ'ry:r], *n.f.* gilding; glazing (*of pastry*).

doryphore [dɔri'fɔːr], *n.m.* Colorado beetle.
dos [do], *n.m. inv.* back; rear; top, ridge.
dosable [do'zabl], *a.* measurable.
dosage [do'zaːʒ], *n.m.* dosage; titration.
dose [doːz], *n.f.* dose; quantity; portion.
doser [do'ze], *v.t.* to dose; to proportion.
dossier [do'sje], *n.m.* back (*of chair etc.*); brief (*of a lawyer*); record, file, dossier.
dossière [do'sjɛːr], *n.f.* back band, ridge band (*of harness*); back plate (*of a cuirass*).
dot [dɔt], *n.f.* marriage portion, dowry.
dotal [do'tal], *a.* (*m. pl.* **-aux**) of or concerning dowry.
dotation [dɔta'sjɔ̃], *n.f.* endowment.
doter [do'te], *v.t.* to endow; to make a grant.
douaire [dwɛːr], *n.m.* (*widow's*) dower; jointure, marriage settlement.
douairière [dwɛ'rjɛːr], *n.f.* dowager.
douane [dwan], *n.f.* customs; custom house; custom duty.
douanier [dwa'nje], *a.* relating to the custom house, of customs.—*n.m.* customs officer.
doublage [du'blaːʒ], *n.m.* lining, plating; (*Cine.*) dubbing.
double [dubl], *a.* twofold, double, duplicate; (*fig.*) deceitful, downright.—*n.m.* double; carbon copy, duplicate, replica; (*Ten.*) doubles.—*adv.* double; *voir double*, to see double.
doublé [du'ble], *n.m.* gold- or silver-plated ware; (*Billiards*) carom off the cushion.
doubleau [du'blo], *n.m.* (*pl.* **-eaux**) ceiling beam.
doublement [dublə'mɑ̃], *n.m.* doubling.—*adv.* doubly.
doubler [du'ble], *v.t.* to double; to line (*clothes etc.*); to overtake, to pass; (*Theat.*) to understudy; (*Cine.*) to dub.
doublet [du'blɛ], *n.m.* doublet.
doubleur [du'blœːr], *n.m.* (*fem.* **-euse**) doubler, twister.
doublure [du'blyːr], *n.f.* lining; (*Theat.*) understudy.
douce-amère [dusa'mɛːr], *n.f.* (*pl.* **douces-amères**) woody nightshade, bitter-sweet.
douceâtre [du'saːtr], *a.* sweetish, sickly.
doucement [dus'mɑ̃], *adv.* gently, tenderly; slowly, quietly; mildly, calmly; so-so.
doucereux [dus'rø], *a.* (*fem.* **-euse**) sweetish; mawkish, mealy-mouthed.
doucet [du'sɛ], *a.* and *n.m.* (*fem.* **-ette** (1)) demure, mild, affected (person).
doucette (2) [du'sɛt], *n.f.* corn salad.
doucette (3) [du'sɛt], *n.f.* Venus's-looking-glass.
douceur [du'sœːr], *n.f.* sweetness, softness; fragrance; kindness; peacefulness; gentleness; (*pl.*) sweets; gallantries.
douche [duʃ], *n.f.* shower-bath.
doucher [du'ʃe], *v.t.* to give someone a shower-bath; to cool down (*excitement etc.*). **se doucher**, *v.r.* to take a shower.
doucir [du'siːr], *v.t.* to polish (*looking-glasses etc.*).
doucissage [dusi'saːʒ], *n.m.* polishing.
doucisseur [dusi'sœːr], *n.m.* polisher.
doué [dwe], *a.* gifted.
douer [dwe], *v.t.* to endow, to bestow upon.
douille [duːj], *n.f.* socket; case or shell (*of cartridges*); *douille d'embrayage*, clutch casing; *douille de lampe*, lamp socket, lamp holder.

douillet [du'jɛ], *a.* effeminate, delicate; sensitive; soft.
douillettement [dujɛt'mɑ̃], *adv.* softly; delicately; cosily.
douleur [du'lœːr], *n.f.* pain, suffering, ache; anguish, grief, sorrow.
douloureusement [dulurøz'mɑ̃], *adv.* painfully; grievously.
douloureux [dulu'rø], *a.* (*fem.* **-euse**) painful, smarting, sore; grievous, afflicting, sad.
doute [dut], *n.m.* doubt, irresolution; suspicion; scepticism; fear; *sans doute*, no doubt.
douter [du'te], *v.i.* (**de**) to doubt, to question; to hesitate; to distrust; to fear. **se douter**, *v.r.* (**de, que**) to suspect, to conjecture.
douteur [du'tœːr], *a.* (*fem.* **-euse** (1)) doubting.—*n.m.* (*fem.* **-euse**) doubter.
douteusement [dutøz'mɑ̃], *adv.* doubtfully.
douteux [du'tø], *a.* (*fem.* **-euse** (2)) doubtful, questionable.
douve [duːv], *n.f.* stave (*for casks*); trench, moat.
Douvres [duːvr], *m.* Dover.
doux [du], *a.* (*fem.* **douce**) sweet; fragrant; kindly, charming; easy; gentle; calm; fresh (*of water*).—*adv.* gently; submissively.
douzaine [du'zɛn], *n.f.* dozen.
douze [duːz], *a.* twelve, twelfth.—*n.m.* twelve.
douzième [du'zjɛm], *a.* and *n.* twelfth.
douzièmement [duzjɛm'mɑ̃], *adv.* twelfthly.
doyen [dwa'jɛ̃], *n.m.* (*fem.* **-enne**) senior, oldest member; dean.
doyenné [dwajɛ'ne], *n.m.* deanship, deanery.
drachme [drakm], *n.f.* drachma; (*Pharm.*) dram.
draconien [drakɔ'njɛ̃], *a.* (*fem.* **-enne**) draconian, harsh, severe.
dragage [dra'gaːʒ], *n.m.* dredging, dragging (*of a river etc.*).
dragée [dra'ʒe], *n.f.* sugar-almond, sugar-plum; small shot.
drageoir [dra'ʒwaːr], *n.m.* comfit dish.
drageon [dra'ʒɔ̃], *n.m.* sucker.
drageonner [draʒɔ'ne], *v.i.* to put forth suckers.
dragon [dra'gɔ̃], *a.* dragonish.—*n.m.* dragon; (*fig.*) vixen; dragoon.
dragonne [dra'gɔn], *n.f.* sword-knot.
drague [drag], *n.f.* dredger; dredge net; grappling iron.
draguer [dra'ge], *v.t.* to drag, to dredge.
dragueur [dra'gœːr], *n.m.* dredger; *dragueur de mines*, minesweeper.
drain [drɛ̃], *n.m.* drain, drain-pipe.
drainage [drɛ'naːʒ], *n.m.* drainage.
drainer [drɛ'ne], *v.t.* to drain.
dramatique [drama'tik], *a.* dramatic.
dramatiser [dramati'ze], *v.t.* to dramatize.
dramaturge [drama'tyrʒ], *n.m.* dramatist, playwright.
drame [dram], *n.m.* drama.
drap [dra], *n.m.* cloth; (*bed*) sheet; pall.
drapeau [dra'po], *n.m.* (*pl.* **-eaux**) flag, standard, ensign, streamer, colors.
draper [dra'pe], *v.t.* to cover with cloth; to drape. **se draper**, *v.r.* to wrap oneself up; to make a show, to parade.
draperie [dra'pri], *n.f.* drapery; cloth trade, cloth making.
drapier [dra'pje], *n.m.* draper, clothier.

drastique [dras'tik], *a.* and *n.m.* (*Med.*) drastic.

(C) **drave** [drav], *n.f.* drive, log-running.

(C) **draver** [dra've], *v.t.* to drive, to drift.

(C) **draveur** [dra'vœːr], *n.m.* wood-floater, rafter.

drayage [drɛ'jaːʒ], *n.m.* fleshing (*of hides*).

drayer [drɛ'je], *v.t.* (*conjug. like* PAYER) to flesh (*hides*).

dressage [drɛ'saːʒ], *n.m.* erection; training (*of animals*); pitching (*of a tent*).

dresser [drɛ'se], *v.t.* to erect, to set up, to raise; to straighten; to lay out; to lay (*a snare*); to pitch (*a tent*); to draw up (*a report*); to prick up (*the ears*); to train (*animals*). **se dresser**, *v.r.* to stand on end (*of hair*); to stand erect; to rear.

dresseur [drɛ'sœːr], *n.m.* (*fem.* **-euse**) trainer (*of dogs etc.*).

dressoir [drɛ'swaːr], *n.m.* dresser, sideboard.

drille [driːj], *n.f.* hand-drill, borer.

driller [dri'je], *v.t.* to drill, to bore.

drive [driv], *n.m.* (*Ten.*) drive.

drogue [drɔg], *n.f.* drug; rubbish; dope.

droguer [drɔ'ge], *v.t.* to drug, to physic. **se droguer**, *v.r.* to physic *or* doctor oneself, to dope oneself.

droguerie [drɔ'gri], *n.f.* drug-store; drug-trade, drysaltery.

droguiste [drɔ'gist], *n.* retailer in drugs and chemicals.

droguet [drɔ'gɛ], *n.m.* (*Tex.*) drugget.

droit [drwa], *a.* straight, right, direct; vertical, upright; just, sincere; right (*opposed to left*).—*adv.* straight, straight on.—*n.m.* right, equity; law; right (*to*), claim, title; fee; due (*tax*), duty, customs duty.

droite [drwat], *n.f.* right hand, right.

droitement [drwat'mã], *adv.* rightly; sincerely, straighforwardly.

droitier [drwa'tje], *a.* and *n.m.* (*fem.* **-ière**) right-handed (person).

droiture [drwa'tyːr], *n.f.* equity, justice; uprightness, integrity.

drolatique [drola'tik], *a.* amusing, laughable, facetious.

drôle [droːl], *a.* funny, droll, ludicrous; strange, curious.—*n.* rogue, rascal, scoundrel.

drôlement [drol'mã], *adv.* comically, facetiously, jocosely.

drôlerie [drol'ri], *n.f.* drollery; buffoonery.

drôlesse [dro'lɛs], *n.f.* jade, hussy.

dromadaire [drɔma'dɛːr], *n.m.* dromedary.

dru [dry], *a.* sturdy; dense (*of rain*); brisk, lively; close-planted; fledged (*of birds*).—*adv.* thick, fast, hard.

druide [drɥid], *n.m.* druid.

druidesse [drɥi'dɛs], *n.f.* druidess.

druidique [drɥi'dik], *a.* druidical.

druidisme [drɥi'dism], *n.m.* druidism.

dryade [dri'ad], *n.f.* dryad; (*Bot.*) dryas.

du [dy], (*contraction of* DE LE) of the, from the, by the; some, any.

dû [dy], *n.m.* due, what is owed, what is owing.

dualisme [dɥa'lism], *n.m.* dualism.

dualiste [dɥa'list], *a.* and *n.* dualist.

dualité [dɥali'te], *n.f.* duality; dualism.

duc [dyk], *n.m.* duke; horned owl.

ducal [dy'kal], *a.* (*m. pl.* **-aux**) ducal.

ducat [dy'ka], *n.m.* ducat.

duché [dy'ʃe], *n.m.* dukedom, duchy.

duchesse [dy'ʃɛs], *n.f.* duchess.

ductile [dyk'til], *a.* ductile, malleable.

ductilité [dyktili'te], *n.f.* ductility.

duègne [dɥɛɲ], *n.f.* duenna, chaperon.

duel [dɥɛl], *n.m.* duel; struggle.

duelliste [dɥe'list], *n.* duellist.

dulcifier [dylsi'fje], *v.t.* to dulcify.

dulcinée [dylsi'ne], *n.f.* sweetheart.

dûment [dy'mã], *adv.* duly, properly.

dumping [dʌm'piŋ], *n.m.* dumping, unfair competition.

dune [dyn], *n.f.* dune, sand-hill.

dunette [dy'nɛt], *n.f.* poop-deck.

duo [dɥo], *n.m.* duet.

duodécimal [dɥodesi'mal], *a.* (*m. pl.* **-aux**) duodecimal.

duodénal [dɥode'nal], *a.* (*m. pl.* **-aux**) duodenal.

duodénum [dɥode'nɔm], *n.m.* duodenum.

dupe [dyp], *n.f.* dupe.

duper [dy'pe], *v.t.* to dupe, to gull, to take in.

duperie [dy'pri], *n.f.* dupery, trickery.

dupeur [dy'pœːr], *n.m.* (*fem.* **-euse**) cheat, trickster.

duplicata [dyplika'ta], *n.m.* duplicate.

duplicateur [dyplika'tœːr], *n.m.* (*Elec.*) duplicator; duplicating machine.

duplicité [dyplisi'te], *n.f.* duplicity, double-dealing, deceit.

duquel [dy'kɛl], (*contraction of* DE LEQUEL) of whom, of which.

dur [dyːr], *a.* hard; tough; (*fig.*) unyielding, harsh, unkind; difficult.—*adv.* hard; firmly; *travailler dur*, to work hard.

durabilité [dyrabili'te], *n.f.* durability.

durable [dy'rabl], *a.* durable, lasting, solid.

durablement [dyrablə'mã], *adv.* durably, lastingly.

duralumin [dyraly'mɛ̃], *n.m.* duralumin.

durant [dy'rã], *prep.* during.

durcir [dyr'siːr], *v.t.* to harden.—*v.i.* to harden, to stiffen. **se durcir**, *v.r.* to harden.

durcissement [dyrsis'mã], *n.m.* hardening, stiffening, induration.

dure [dyːr], *n.f.* hard ground *or* floor *in coucher sur la dure*.

durée [dy're], *n.f.* duration; continuance.

durement [dyr'mã], *adv.* hard; harshly, roughly.

durer [dy're], *v.i.* to last, to remain; to endure.

dureté [dyr'te], *n.f.* hardness; harshness, austerity, unkindness; (*pl.*) harsh *or* offensive words.

durillon [dyri'jõ], *n.m.* callosity, corn.

duvet [dy've], *n.m.* down; wool, nap; fluff.

duveté [dyv'te], *a.* downy (*of birds etc.*); like down.

duveteux [dyv'tø], *a.* (*fem.* **-euse**) downy, fluffy.

dynamique [dina'mik], *a.* dynamic.—*n.f.* dynamics.

dynamisme [dina'mism], *n.m.* dynamism.

dynamiste [dina'mist], *n.* dynamist.

dynamitage [dinami'taːʒ], *n.m.* blasting, blowing up.

dynamite [dina'mit], *n.f.* dynamite.

dynamiter [dinami'te], *v.t.* to dynamite, to blow up.

dynamo [dina'mo], *n.f.* dynamo.

dynastie [dinas'ti], *n.f.* dynasty.

123

dynastique [dinas'tik], a. dynastic.
dysenterie [disā'tri], n.f. dysentery.
dyspepsie [dispɛp'si], n.f. dyspepsia.
dyspepsique [dispɛp'sik], dyspeptique [dispɛp'tik], a. dyspeptic.

E

E, e [ə], n.m. the fifth letter of the alphabet.
eau [o], n.f. water; rain, flood; (pl.) mineral or thermal waters; watering place; stream; track; gloss; à fleur d'eau, on a level with the water; (Chem.) eau lourde, heavy water.
eau-de-vie [o'dvi], n.f. (pl. eaux-de-vie) brandy.
ébahi [eba'i], a. astonished, dumbfounded.
ébahir (s') [seba'i:r], v.r. to wonder (at), to be amazed.
ébahissement [ebais'mã], n.m. amazement, astonishment.
ébats [e'ba], n.m. pl. pastime, sport, gambol, frolic.
ébattre (s') [se'batr], v.r. (conjug. like BATTRE) to sport, to gambol, to frolic.
ébauchage [ebo'ʃa:ʒ], n.m. sketching.
ébauche [e'bo:ʃ], n.f. rough draft, outline.
ébaucher [ebo'ʃe], v.t. to make the first draft of, to draw an outline of, to sketch.
ébauchoir [ebo'ʃwa:r], n.m. (Sculp.) roughing chisel; (Carp.) mortise chisel.
ébène [e'bɛ:n], n.f. ebony, ebony work.
ébéner [ebe'ne], v.t. (conjug. like CÉDER) to ebonize.
ébénier [ebe'nje], n.m. ebony tree.
ébéniste [ebe'nist], n. cabinet-maker.
ébénisterie [ebenis'tri], n.f. cabinet-work.
ébiseler [ebi'zle], v.t. (conjug. like APPELER) to chamfer, to bevel.
éblouir [eblu'i:r], v.t. to dazzle; (fig.) to fascinate, to amaze. s'éblouir, v.r. to be dazzled or fascinated.
éblouissant [eblui'sã], a. dazzling, resplendent.
éblouissement [ebluis'mã], n.m. dazzle, daze; (fig.) bewilderment.
ébonite [ebo'nit], n.f. ebonite; vulcanite.
ébouage [ebu'a:ʒ], n.m. scavenging.
ébouer [ebu'e], v.t. to scavenge.
éboueur [ebu'œ:r], n.m. (fem. -euse) road-sweeper, scavenger.—n.f. (-euse) road-sweeping machine.
ébouillanter [ebujã'te], v.t. to dip in hot water, to scald.
éboulement [ebul'mã], n.m. falling in, fall; caving in, collapse; landslide, landslip.
ébouler [ebu'le], v.i. to fall in, to fall down, to sink. s'ébouler, v.r. to fall in, to cave in.
éboulis [ebu'li], n.m. inv. debris, fallen rocks.
ébourgeonner [eburʒɔ'ne], v.t. to disbud.
ébouriffé [eburi'fe], a. disordered, ruffled, in disorder; (fig.) in a flutter.
ébouriffer [eburi'fe], v.t. to ruffle, to disorder; (fig.) to startle, to amaze.
ébouter [ebu'te], v.t. to cut off (the end).

ébranchage [ebrã'ʃa:ʒ], ébranchement [ebrãʃ'mã], n.m. (Hort.) pruning, lopping, trimming.
ébrancher [ebrã'ʃe], v.t. to prune, to lop, to trim.
ébranlement [ebrãl'mã], n.m. shock, shaking; (fig.) perturbation, disturbance.
ébranler [ebrã'le], v.t. to shake; to disturb, to unsettle. s'ébranler, v.r. to get under way, to move off.
ébrécher [ebre'ʃe], v.t. (conjug. like CÉDER) to notch, to indent; to crack, to chip; (fig.) to impair.
ébriété [ebrie'te], n.f. drunkenness, inebriety.
ébrouement [ebru'mã], n.m. snorting.
ébrouer (s') [sebru'e], v.r. to snort from fear (of horses).
ébruiter [ebrɥi'te], v.t. to make known, to spread about. s'ébruiter, v.r. to spread, to be noised abroad.
ébullition [ebyli'sjɔ̃], n.f. boiling, ebullition.
écaille [eka'j], n.f. scale; shell.
écaillé [eka'je], a. scaly.
écailler (1) [eka'je], v.t. to scale. s'écailler v.r. to peel off, to scale.
écailler (2) [eka'je], n.m. (fem. -ère) oyster-man, oyster-woman.
écailleux [eka'jø], a. (fem. -euse) scaly, squamous.
écale [e'kal], n.f. shell, pod (of peas etc.); hull, husk (of walnut).
écaler [eka'le], v.t. to shell (beans, peas etc.); to hull, to husk (almonds, nuts etc.). s'écaler, v.r. to come out of the shell.
écarlate [ekar'lat], a. and n.f. scarlet; hectic red.
écarquillement [ekarkij'mã], n.m. spreading out, opening wide (of one's eyes, legs etc.).
écarquiller [ekarki'je], v.t. to spread out, to open wide.
écart [e'ka:r], n.m. stepping aside, swerving; fault; deviation; à l'écart, aside; faire un écart, to step aside.
écarté (1) [ekar'te], n.m. écarté (game of cards).
écarté (2) [ekar'te], a. remote, lonely, secluded.
écartelé [ekartə'le], a. (of mind, heart, etc.) divided, torn asunder; (Her.) quartered.
écartèlement [ekartɛl'mã], n.m. tearing to pieces, quartering.
écarteler [ekartə'le], v.t. (conjug. like AMENER) to tear to pieces; (Her.) to quarter.
écartement [ekartə'mã], n.m. putting aside, removal; spacing; spread.
écarter [ekar'te], v.t. to open, to throw wide apart; to set aside; to avert; to dispel, to deviate; to spread. s'écarter, v.r. to turn aside, to swerve; to stray; to make way.
ecchymose [ɛki'mo:z], n.f. (Med.) ecchymosis.
ecclésiastique [eklezjas'tik], a. ecclesiastic, clerical.—n.m. clergyman, ecclesiastic.
écervelé [esɛrvə'le], a. hare-brained, rash, giddy.—n.m. (fem. -ée) madcap; scatter-brain.
échafaud [eʃa'fo], n.m. scaffold.
échafaudage [eʃafo'da:ʒ], n.m. scaffolding; (fig.) structure.
échafauder [eʃafo'de], v.t. to pile up; (fig.) to lay out (a plan).—v.i. to erect scaffolding.

échalas [eʃɑ'la], *n.m.* vine prop; hop pole.
échalassage [eʃala'sa:ʒ], **échalassement** [eʃalas'mɑ̃], *n.m.* propping.
échalasser [eʃala'se], *v.t.* to prop (*vines etc.*).
échalier [eʃa'lje], **échalis** [eʃa'li], *n.m.* stile; wooden fence.
échalote [eʃa'lɔt], *n.f.* (*Bot.*) shallot.
échancrer [eʃɑ̃'kre], *v.t.* to make a crescent-shaped cut; to indent.
échancrure [eʃɑ̃'kry:r], *n.f.* notch, cut, indentation; opening.
échandole [eʃɑ̃'dɔl], *n.f.* shingle (*for roofing*).
échange [e'ʃɑ̃:ʒ], *n.m.* exchange, barter; *libre échange*, free trade.
échangeable [eʃɑ̃'ʒabl], *a.* exchangeable.
échanger [eʃɑ̃'ʒe], *v.t.* (*conjug. like* MANGER) to exchange, to barter; to interchange.
échanson [eʃɑ̃'sɔ̃], *n.m.* cup bearer; butler.
échantillon [eʃɑ̃ti'jɔ̃], *n.m.* sample, pattern, specimen; (*fig.*) model.
échantillonner [eʃɑ̃tijɔ'ne], *v.t.* to sample.
échappatoire [eʃapa'twa:r], *n.f.* shift, subterfuge, loop-hole, evasion.
échappé [eʃa'pe], *a.* runaway.—*n.m.* (*fem.* -ée (1)) one who has escaped, runaway.
échappée (2) [eʃa'pe], *n.f.* escapade, prank; short space of time.
échappement [eʃap'mɑ̃], *n.m.* escape; leakage; (*Horol.*) escapement; exhaust.
échapper [eʃa'pe], *v.t.* to escape, to avoid; *l'échapper belle*, to have a narrow escape.—*v.i.* to escape, to make good one's escape; to be overlooked. **s'échapper**, *v.r.* to escape; to vanish.
écharde [e'ʃard], *n.f.* prickle (*of a thistle etc.*); splinter.
écharner [eʃar'ne], *v.t.* to flesh *or* scrape (*hides*).
écharnoir [eʃar'nwa:r], *n.m.* fleshing-knife.
écharpe [e'ʃarp], *n.f.* scarf, sash; arm-sling.
écharper [eʃar'pe], *v.t.* to slash, to cut.
échasse [e'ʃa:s], *n.f.* stilt; long-legged plover.
échassier [eʃa'sje], *n.m.* (*fem.* -ière) stilt-walker; (*colloq.*) long-legged person.—*n.m.* (*Orn.*) wader.
échauboulure [eʃobu'ly:r], *n.f.* pimple, blotch.
échaudage [eʃo'da:ʒ], *n.m.* whitewash; white-washing; scalding.
échaudé (1) [eʃo'de], *n.m.* simnel, cracknel.
échaudé (2) [eʃo'de], *a.* scalded.
échauder [eʃo'de], *v.t.* to scald. **s'échauder**, *v.r.* to burn oneself.
échaudoir [eʃo'dwa:r], *n.m.* scalding-house; scalding-tub.
échaudure [eʃo'dy:r], *n.f.* scald.
échauffant [eʃo'fɑ̃], *a.* heating; binding (*food*).
échauffement [eʃof'mɑ̃], *n.m.* heating; over-excitement.
échauffer [eʃo'fe], *v.t.* to warm, to heat, to over-heat; to excite, to irritate. **s'échauffer**, *v.r.* to grow warm, to overheat oneself; to grow angry, to chafe.
échauffourée [eʃofu're], *n.f.* rash *or* blundering enterprise; brush, scuffle.
échauffure [eʃo'fy:r], *n.f.* red rash.
échauguette [eʃo'gɛt], *n.f.* (*Mil.*) watch-tower.
échéable [eʃe'abl], *a.* due, payable.
échéance [eʃe'ɑ̃:s], *n.f.* falling due (*of bill*); date (*of payment, of maturity*); expiration (*of tenancy*).

échéant [eʃe'ɑ̃], *a.* falling due; *le cas échéant*, in that case, if need be.
échec [e'ʃɛk], *n.m.* check, defeat, blow, loss.
échecs [e'ʃɛk], *n.m. pl.* chess; chess-men.
échelle [e'ʃɛl], *n.f.* ladder; scale; gradation.
échelon [eʃ'lɔ̃], *n.m.* round, rung, step (*of a ladder*); degree; (*Mil.*) echelon.
échelonner [eʃlɔ'ne], *v.t.* to draw up in echelon; to arrange according to gradation; to spread (*over a period of time*); to place (*at regular intervals*); *vacances échelonnées*, staggered holidays. **s'échelonner**, *v.r.* to be graduated; to slope gradually; to be arranged in echelon.
écheniller [eʃni'je], *v.t.* to rid (*plants, trees etc.*) of caterpillars.
écheveau [eʃ'vo], *n.m.* (*pl.* -eaux) hank, skein.
échevelé [eʃə'vle], *a.* dishevelled; (*fig.*) wild, extravagant.
écheveler [eʃə'vle], *v.t.* (*conjug. like* APPELER) to dishevel.
***échevin** [eʃ'vɛ̃], *n.m.* sheriff; alderman; (*C*) municipal magistrate.
échine [e'ʃin], *n.f.* spine, backbone, chine.
échiner [eʃi'ne], *v.t.* to beat unmercifully; to tire out. **s'échiner**, *v.r.* (*pop.*) to work oneself to death.
échiqueté [eʃik'te], *a.* chequered.
échiquier [eʃi'kje], *n.m.* chess-board; exchequer; square net.
écho [e'ko], *n.m.* echo.
échoir [e'ʃwa:r], *v.i. irr.* (*aux.* ÊTRE) to expire, to fall due, to lapse; to happen, to befall.
échoppe [e'ʃɔp], *n.f.* booth, covered stall.
échopper [eʃɔ'pe], *v.t.* to gouge.
échotier [eko'tje], *n.m.* (*fem.* -ière) gossip writer, columnist.
échouage [e'ʃwa:ʒ], **échouement** [eʃu'mɑ̃], *n.m.* (*Naut.*) beaching, running aground.
échouer [e'ʃwe], *v.t.* to run (*a vessel*) aground. —*v.i.* to run aground, to be stranded; (*fig.*) to miscarry, to fail.
écimer [esi'me], *v.t.* to top (*plants etc.*), to pollard (*trees*).
éclaboussement [eklabus'mɑ̃], *n.m.* splashing, bespattering.
éclabousser [eklabu'se], *v.t.* to splash, to bespatter.
éclaboussure [eklabu'sy:r], *n.f.* splash.
éclair [e'klɛ:r], *n.m.* lightning, flash of lightning; variety of chocolate cake.
éclairage [eklɛ'ra:ʒ], *n.m.* lighting, illumination, light.
éclaircie [eklɛr'si], *n.f.* opening, rift (*in clouds etc.*); glade, clearing; (*fig.*) favorable change of affairs.
éclaircir [eklɛr'si:r], *v.t.* to make clear *or* clearer, to brighten; to clarify; to make thin *or* thinner; to elucidate, to explain. **s'éclaircir**, *v.r.* to become clear, bright *or* fine; to grow light; to be explained.
éclaircissement [eklɛrsis'mɑ̃], *n.m.* clearing up, explanation, solution; hint, light.
éclaire [e'klɛ:r], *n.f.* celandine.
éclairé [ekle're], *a.* lighted; well-lighted; (*fig.*) well-informed, intelligent; enlightened.
éclairer [ekle're], *v.t.* to light, to give light to, to illuminate; to enlighten; to observe; (*Mil.*) to reconnoitre.—*v.i.* to sparkle, to shine, to glitter. **s'éclairer**, *v.r.* to become enlightened; to instruct *or* enlighten one another; to light up.

éclaireur [eklɛ'rœːr], *n.m.* (*Mil.*) scout; boy scout.

éclanche [e'klãːʃ], *n.f.* shoulder of mutton.

éclat [e'kla], *n.m.* burst; crash, peal; splinter (*of wood, stone, brick etc.*); brightness, glare, glitter; luster, pomp; renown; gaudiness (*of colors*); rumor, scandal; *un éclat de voix*, a burst of laughter; *un grand éclat de rire*, a loud shout; *voler en éclats*, to fly into a thousand pieces.

éclatant [ekla'tã], *a.* bright, sparkling, brilliant; striking; piercing, shrill.

éclatement [eklat'mã], *n.m.* bursting, explosion.

éclater [ekla'te], *v.i.* to split, to burst, to explode; to cry out; to shine, to sparkle, to flash; to break out (*war etc.*); *éclater de rire*, to burst out laughing.

éclectique [eklɛk'tik], *a.* and *n.f.* eclectic; dilettante.

éclectisme [eklɛk'tism], *n.m.* eclecticism.

éclipse [e'klips], *n.f.* eclipse; (*fig.*) disappearance.

éclipser [eklip'se], *v.t.* to eclipse, (*fig.*) to surpass. **s'éclipser**, *v.r.* (*fig.*) to disappear, to vanish.

écliptique [eklip'tik], *a.* and *n.f.* ecliptic.

éclisse [e'klis], *n.f.* (*Surg.*) splint.

éclisser [ekli'se], *v.t.* (*Surg.*) to splint.

éclopé [eklo'pe], *a.* a crippled, footsore, lame.—*n.m.* (*fem.* -ée) cripple.

écloper [eklo'pe], *v.t.* to lame, to disable.

éclore [e'klɔːr], *v.i. irr.* (*conjug. like* CLORE, *but with aux.* ÊTRE) to hatch; to open, to bloom (*of flowers*); (*fig.*) to show itself.

éclosion [eklo'zjɔ̃], *n.f.* hatching; (*fig.*) opening, blooming; appearance.

écluse [e'klyːz], *n.f.* lock (*on canals etc.*); dam, weir; *porte d'écluse*, sluice, floodgate.

écluser [ekly'ze], *v.t.* to furnish with locks; to take (*a boat etc.*) through a lock.

éclusier [ekly'zje], *n.m.* (*fem.* -ière) lock keeper.

écœurant [ekœ'rã], *a.* disgusting, nauseating.

écœurement [ekœr'mã], *n.m.* disgust; nausea.

écœurer [ekœ're], *v.t.* to disgust, to sicken; (*fig.*) to shock, to dishearten.

école [e'kɔl], *n.f.* school, college; scholastic philosophy; sect; (*Mil.*) training; (*fig.*) manner, practice.

écolier [eko'lje], *n.m.* (*fem.* -ière) schoolboy, schoolgirl, pupil, student.

éconduire [ekɔ̃'dɥiːr], *v.t. irr.* (*conjug. like* CONDUIRE) to show out, to dismiss; to refuse.

économat [ekɔnɔ'ma], *n.m.* stewardship, bursarship.

économe [eko'nɔm], *a.* economical, saving, thrifty.—*n.* steward, housekeeper, bursar, treasurer (*of colleges, hospitals etc.*).

économie [ekɔnɔ'mi], *n.f.* economy; thrift, saving.

économique [ekɔnɔ'mik], *a.* (*applied to things only*) economic, economical, cheap.—*n.f.* economics.

économiquement [ekɔnɔmik'mã], *adv.* economically.

économiser [ekɔnɔmi'ze], *v.t, v.i.* to economize, to save (up).

économiste [ekɔnɔ'mist], *n.* economist.

écope [e'kɔp], *n.f.* scoop, ladle; (*Naut.*) bailer.

écorce [e'kɔrs], *n.f.* bark, rind, peel; shell; (*Geol.*) crust (*of the earth*).

écorcement [ekɔrs'mã], **écorçage** [ekɔr'saː3], *n.m.* barking or stripping (*of trees etc.*); peeling.

écorcer [ekɔr'se], *v.t.* (*conjug. like* COMMENCER) to bark, to strip (*trees etc.*), to peel.

écorchement [ekɔrʃə'mã], *n.m.* excoriation, flaying, skinning.

écorcher [ekɔr'ʃe], *v.t.* to flay, to skin; to graze (*skin*); to peel, to bark; (*fig.*) to strip, to fleece. **s'écorcher**, *v.r.* to graze oneself.

écorcheur [ekɔr'ʃœːr], *n.m.* (*fem.* -euse) knacker, flayer; (*fig.*) fleecer.

écorchure [ekɔr'ʃyːr], *n.f.* scratch, graze.

écorner [ekɔr'ne], *v.t.* to break the horns of; to break the corners of, to dog-ear; to curtail, to impair.

écornifler [ekɔrni'fle], *v.t.* to sponge upon.

écornure [ekɔr'nyːr], *n.f.* broken-off corner, chip.

écossais [eko'sɛ], *a.* Scottish.—*n.m.* Scots (*language*); plaid, tartan cloth; (**Écossais**, *fem.* -aise) Scot, Scotsman, Scotswoman.

Écosse [e'kɔs], l', *f.* Scotland; *La Nouvelle Écosse*, *f.* Nova Scotia.

écosser [eko'se], *v.t.* to shell, to husk (*peas or beans*).

écosseur [eko'sœːr], *n.m.* (*fem.* -euse) sheller.

écot (1) [e'ko], *n.m.* share (*of a reckoning*); bill, reckoning, score (*usually in the expression payer son écot*, to pay one's share).

écot (2) [e'ko], *n.m.* stump of a tree.

écoulement [ekul'mã], *n.m.* flowing, flow, running; outlet; (*Comm.*) sale, disposal; export.

écouler [eku'le], *v.t.* to dispose of, to sell. **s'écouler**, *v.r.* to run or flow away, to pass, to slip away; (*Comm.*) to be disposed of.

écourter [ekur'te], *v.t.* to shorten, to dock, to crop.

écoutant [eku'tã], *a.* listening; *avocat écoutant*, briefless attorney.

écoute (1) [e'kut], *n.f.* hiding place for listening; *être aux écoutes*, to be on the watch.

écoute (2) [e'kut], *n.f.* (*Naut.*) sheet (*of sail*).

écouter [eku'te], *v.t.* to listen to, to hearken to; to pay attention to. **s'écouter**, *v.r.* to like the sound of one's own voice; to indulge oneself.

écouteur [eku'tœːr], *n.m.* (*fem.* -euse) listener, listener-in; (*Teleph.*) receiver; (*Teleg.*) ear-phone.

écoutille [eku'tiːj], *n.f.* (*Naut.*) hatchway.

écran [e'krã], *n.m.* screen; *vedette de l'écran*, film star.

écrasant [ekra'zã], *a.* crushing; (*fig.*) humiliating, excessive; overwhelming.

écrasé [ekra'ze], *a.* crushed, ruined.

écrasement [ekraz'mã], *n.m.* crushing, bruising; (*fig.*) overwhelming.

écraser [ekra'ze], *v.t.* to crush; to bruise; to overwhelm, to ruin; to run over.

écraseur [ekra'zœːr], *n.m.* crusher; (*Motor.*) road hog; steam-roller.

écrémer [ekre'me], *v.t.* (*conjug. like* CÉDER) to take the cream off, to skim.

écrémeuse [ekre'møːz]. *n.f.* separator.

écrevisse [ekrə'vis], *n.f.* crayfish; (*Am.*) crawfish; (*Astron.*) Cancer.

écrier (s') [sekri'je], *v.r.* to cry out, to exclaim.

écrin [e'krɛ̃], *n.m.* casket, jewel box *or* case.

écrire [e'kri:r], *v.t. irr.* to write; to spell. **s'écrire**, *v.r.* to be written; to be spelled; to write to each other.

écrit [e'kri], *n.m.* writing; pamphlet.

écriteau [ekri'to], *n.m.* (*pl.* **-eaux**) bill (*poster*); board.

écritoire [ekri'twa:r], *n.f.* writing desk; inkstand.

écriture [ekri'ty:r], *n.f.* writing, handwriting; scripture; (*pl.*) accounts, documents.

écrivain [ekri'vɛ̃], *n.m.* writer, author; **femme écrivain**, authoress, woman writer.

écrivassier [ekriva'sje], *n.m.* (*fem.* **-ière**) (*colloq.*) scribbler.

écrou [e'kru], *n.m.* screw nut; **écrou à oreilles**, wing nut.

écrouelles [ekru'el], *n.f. pl.* king's evil, scrofula.

écrouelleux [ekrue'lø], *a.* (*fem.* **-euse**) scrofulous.

écrouer [ekru'e], *v.t.* to imprison, to lock up.

écroulement [ekrul'mã], *n.m.* falling in, collapse; wreck, ruin.

écrouler (s') [sekru'le], *v.r.* to fall in, to fall to pieces, to collapse.

écru [e'kry], *a.* raw, unbleached; **toile écrue**, (brown) holland.

ectoplasme [ɛkto'plasm], *n.m.* ectoplasm.

écu [e'ky], *n.m.* shield; crown (*coin*); (*fig.*) money, cash.

écueil [e'kœ:j], *n.m.* reef, rock; (*fig.*) danger, stumbling-block.

écuelle [e'kɥel], *n.f.* porringer, bowl, basin.

écuellée [ekɥe'le], *n.f.* bowlful.

éculer [eky'le], *v.t.* to tread down at heel; **des souliers éculés**, down-at-heel shoes.

écumage [eky'ma:ʒ], *n.m.* skimming.

écumant [eky'mã], *a.* foaming, frothing, seething.

écume [e'kym], *n.f.* foam, froth; lather; (*fig.*) scum, dregs.

écumer [eky'me], *v.t.* to skim; to scour; **écumer la marmite**, to be a sponger.—*v.i.* to foam, to froth.

écumeur [eky'mœ:r], *n.m.* (*fem.* **écumeuse** (1)) skimmer; hanger-on, parasite.

écumeux [eky'mø], *a.* (*fem.* **écumeuse** (2)) frothy, foaming.

écumoire [eky'mwa:r], *n.f.* skimmer.

écurage [eky'ra:ʒ], *n.m.* scouring, cleaning.

écurer [eky're], *v.t.* to scour, to cleanse.

écureuil [eky'rœ:j], *n.m.* squirrel.

écurie [eky'ri], *n.f.* stable, mews; stud.

écusson [eky'sõ], *n.m.* escutcheon; shield.

écuyer [ekɥi'je], *n.m.* squire; equerry; ridingmaster; rider; wall hand-rail (*of a staircase*).

écuyère [ekɥi'jɛ:r], *n.f.* horsewoman; female equestrian performer; **bottes à l'écuyère**, top boots, riding boots.

eczéma [ɛgze'ma], *n.m.* eczema.

édenté [edã'te], *a.* toothless.

édenter [edã'te], *v.t.* to break the teeth of (*combs, saws etc.*).

édicter [edik'te], *v.t.* to enact, to decree.

édicule [edi'kyl], *n.m.* small building (*pavilion, kiosk etc.*).

édifiant [edi'fjã], *a.* edifying.

édification [edifika'sjõ], *n.f.* building, erection; (*fig.*) edification.

édifice [edi'fis], *n.m.* edifice, building, pile.

édifier [edi'fje], *v.t.* to build, to erect, to construct; (*fig.*) to edify, to improve; to instruct, to enlighten; to satisfy.

édile [e'dil], *n.m.* ædile; town councillor.

Édimbourg [edɛ̃'bu:r], *m. or f.* Edinburgh.

édit [e'di], *n.m.* edict.

éditer [edi'te], *v.t.* to publish; to edit.

éditeur [edi'tœ:r], *n.m.* (*fem.* **-trice**) publisher.

édition [edi'sjõ], *n.f.* edition.

éditorial [edito'rjal], *n.m.* (*pl.* **-aux**) leading article, leader, editorial.

éditorialiste [editorja'list], *n.* leader writer.

Édouard [e'dwa:r], *m.* Edward.

édredon [edrə'dõ], *n.m.* eider-down; eider-down quilt.

éducateur [edyka'tœ:r], *a.* (*fem.* **-trice**) educative, instructing.—*n.m.* (*fem.* **-trice**) educator; breeder.

éducatif [edyka'tif], *a.* (*fem.* **-tive**) educational.

éducation [edyka'sjõ], *n.f.* education; training; rearing (*of animals*); breeding, manners.

éduquer [edy'ke], *v.t.* to bring up, to educate (*children*).

effacement [efas'mã], *n.m.* effacement, obliteration; disappearance; humility, self-effacement.

effacer [efa'se], *v.t.* (*conjug. like* COMMENCER) to efface, to erase, to rub out, to blot out, to obliterate. **s'effacer**, *v.r.* to become obliterated; to wear away; to draw aside, to give way.

effaçure [efa'sy:r], *n.f.* erasure, blotting out, obliteration.

effaré [efa're], *a.* wild, scared, bewildered; astounded.

effarement [efar'mã], *n.m.* bewilderment, terror, affright.

effarer [efa're], *v.t.* to frighten, to scare. **s'effarer**, *v.r.* to be scared, to take fright.

effarouchant [efaru'ʃã], *a.* startling, disquieting; shocking; annoying.

effaroucher [efaru'ʃe], *v.t.* to startle, to frighten away. **s'effaroucher**, *v.r.* to be scared, to be startled.

effectif [efɛk'tif], *a.* (*fem.* **-tive**) actual, real, positive.—*n.m.* effective force (*of troops etc.*); size (*of a class*).

effectivement [efɛktiv'mã], *adv.* in effect, actually, indeed, in fact; (*in answer*) that is so.

effectuer [efɛk'tɥe], *v.t.* to effect, to accomplish, to carry out. **s'effectuer**, *v.r.* to be accomplished, to take place.

efféminer [efemina'sjõ], *n.f.* effeminacy.

efféminé [efemi'ne], *a.* effeminate, womanish.

effervescence [efɛrvɛ'sã:s], *n.f.* effervescence; (*fig.*) agitation, ferment.

effervescent [efɛrvɛ'sã], *a.* effervescent; (*fig.*) excitable, irascible.

effet [e'fɛ], *n.m.* effect, result; performance; impression; power (*transmitted by machinery etc.*); (*Comm.*) bill of exchange; (*pl.*) belongings; **en effet**, indeed, in fact.

effeuillaison [efœje'zõ], *n.f.*, **effeuillement** [efœj'mã], *n.m.* fall of the leaves.

effeuiller [efœ'je], *v.t.* to strip off leaves, to pick (*a flower*) to pieces. **s'effeuiller**, *v.r.* to lose *or* shed its leaves.

efficace [efi'kas], *a.* efficacious, effective.

efficacité [efikasi'te], *n.f.* efficacy, effectiveness; efficiency.

effigie [efi'ʒi], *n.f.* effigy.

effilé [efi'le], *a.* slender, slim; sharp, keen, trenchant.—*n.m.* fringe.

effiler [efi'le], *v.t.* to unweave, to unravel; to taper. **s'effiler**, *v.r.* to unravel; to taper, to become sharp; to fray.

effiloche [efi'lɔʃ], **effiloque** [efi'lɔk], *n.f.* floss silk, light refuse silk.

effilocher [efilɔ'ʃe], **effiloquer** [efilɔ'ke], *v.t.* to unravel, to undo.

efflanqué [eflɑ̃'ke], *a.* lean, thin, lank.

efflanquer [eflɑ̃'ke], *v.t.* to make lean, to emaciate.

effleurer [eflœ're], *v.t.* to graze, to skim the surface of, to touch lightly; (*fig.*) to touch upon.

efflorescence [eflɔrɛ'sɑ̃:s], *n.f.* efflorescence.

efflorescent [eflɔrɛ'sɑ̃], *a.* efflorescent.

effluent [efly'ɑ̃], *a.* effluent.

effluve [e'fly:v], *n.m.* effluvium.

effondrement [efɔ̃drə'mɑ̃], *n.m.* (*Agric.*) trenching; falling in, sinking; collapse.

effondrer [efɔ̃'dre], *v.t.* to dig deeply; to break in; to overwhelm. **s'effondrer**, *v.r.* to fall in, to collapse.

efforcer (s') [sefɔr'se], *v.r.* (*conjug. like* COMMENCER) to exert oneself, to strain, to strive.

effort [e'fɔ:r], *n.m.* effort, exertion, endeavor; stress; (*Med.*) strain, rupture.

effraction [efrak'sjɔ̃], *n.f.* breaking into, house-breaking; *vol avec effraction*, burglary.

effraie [e'frɛ], *n.f.* barn owl, screech owl.

effrayant [efrɛ'jɑ̃], *a.* frightful, dreadful.

effrayer [efrɛ'je], *v.t.* (*conjug. like* PAYER) to frighten, to alarm, to terrify. **s'effrayer**, *v.r.* to be frightened, to be startled.

effréné [efre'ne], *a.* unrestrained; lawless; wild.

effritement [efrit'mɑ̃], *n.m.* crumbling into dust.

effriter (s') [sefri'te], *v.r.* to crumble.

effroi [e'frwa], *n.m.* fright, terror, dread.

effronté [efrɔ̃'te], *a.* and *n.m.* (*fem.* -ée) shameless, brazen, impudent (person).

effrontément [efrɔ̃te'mɑ̃], *adv.* impudently, shamelessly.

effronterie [efrɔ̃'tri], *n.f.* effrontery, impudence.

effroyable [efrwa'jabl], *a.* frightful, dreadful, hideous.

effroyablement [efrwajablə'mɑ̃], *adv.* frightfully, horribly, dreadfully.

effusion [efy'zjɔ̃], *n.f.* effusion; overflowing.

égal [e'gal], *a.* (*m. pl.* -aux) equal, alike; even, level, smooth; all the same.—*n.m.* (*fem.* -e) equal.

également [egal'mɑ̃], *adv.* equally, alike.

égaler [ega'le], *v.t.* to equal; to make equal; to compare. **s'égaler**, *v.r.* to equal; to compare oneself (*à*).

égalisation [egaliza'sjɔ̃], *n.f.* equalization.

égaliser [egali'ze], *v.t.* to equalize; to level.

égalitaire [egali'tɛ:r], *a.* and *n.* egalitarian.

égalité [egali'te], *n.f.* equality, parity; uniformity.

égard [e'ga:r], *n.m.* regard, consideration, respect.

égaré [ega're], *a.* wandering, strayed; misled; mislaid; distracted.

égarement [egar'mɑ̃], *n.m.* straying, losing one's way; mistake; ill-conduct.

égarer [ega're], *v.t.* to mislead; to lose; to lead astray; to bewilder; to impair (*intellect*). **s'égarer**, *v.r.* to lose one's way, to stray; to err.

égayer [ege'je], *v.t.* (*conjug. like* PAYER) to enliven, to cheer up; (*Hort.*) to prune (*trees*). **s'égayer**, *v.r.* to brighten up; to make merry.

églantier [eglɑ̃'tje], *n.m.* eglantine, briar, dog-rose (*bush*).

églantine [eglɑ̃'tin], *n.f.* eglantine, dog-rose (*flower*).

église [e'gli:z], *n.f.* church.

églogue [e'glɔg], *n.f.* eclogue.

égocentrique [egosɑ̃'trik], *a.* egocentric, self-centered.

égoïsme [ego'ism], *n.m.* egoism, selfishness.

égoïste [ego'ist], *a.* egoistic, selfish.—*n.* egoist, selfish person.

égorger [egɔr'ʒe], *v.t.* (*conjug. like* MANGER) to cut the throat of, to slaughter.

égorgeur [egɔr'ʒœ:r], *n.m.* (*fem.* -euse) slaughterer, murderer.

égosiller (s') [segozi'je], *v.r.* to make oneself hoarse; to bawl.

égotisme [ego'tism], *n.m.* egotism.

égotiste [ego'tist], *a.* egotistic(al).—*n.* egotist.

égout [e'gu], *n.m.* running *or* falling of water; sink, drain, sewer.

égouttage [egu'ta:ʒ], **égouttement** [egut'mɑ̃], *n.m.* drainage, draining; dripping.

égoutter [egu'te], *v.t., v.i.* to drain, to drip. **s'égoutter**, *v.r.* to drip, to drain.

égouttoir [egu'twa:r], *n.m.* drainer (*plate-rack etc.*).

égrapper [egra'pe], *v.t.* to pick (*grapes, currants etc.*) from the bunch.

égratigner [egrati'ɲe], *v.t.* to scratch.

égratignure [egrati'ɲy:r], *n.f.* scratch; slight wound.

égrenage [egra'na:ʒ], *n.m.* picking off (*of grapes etc.*).

égrener [egra'ne], *v.t.* (*conjug. like* AMENER) to tell (*beads*); to unstring (*beads etc.*); to pick off (*grapes etc.*) from the bunch. **s'égrener**, *v.r.* to fall from the stalk, to drop one by one.

égrillard [egri'ja:r], *a.* lewd, broad, naughty; *propos égrillards*, spicy talk.

égrilloir [egri'jwa:r], *n.m.* weir; grate (*to confine fish in a pond*).

égrisé [egri'ze], *n.m. or* **égrisée** [egri'ze], *n.f.* diamond dust.

égriser [egri'ze], *v.t.* to grind, to polish (*diamonds etc.*).

égrugeoir [egry'ʒwa:r], *n.m.* mortar.

égruger [egry'ʒe], *v.t.* (*conjug. like* MANGER) to pound, to grind in a mortar.

égueuler [egœ'le], *v.t.* to break off the mouth *or* neck (*of glass and other vessels*).

Égypte [e'ʒipt], **l'**, *f.* Egypt.

égyptien [eʒip'sjɛ̃], *a.* (*fem.* -enne) Egyptian.—*n.m.* (**Égyptien**, *fem.* -enne) Egyptian (*person*).

eh! [e], *int.* ah! well! hey! *eh bien !* well!

éhonté [eɔ̃'te], *a.* shameless.

éjaculation [eʒakylɑ'sjɔ̃], *n.f.* throwing out with force, discharge; ejaculation.

éjaculer [eʒaky'le], *v.t.* to discharge, to ejaculate.

éjecter [eʒɛk'te], *v.t.* to eject.

éjecteur [eʒɛk'tœːr], *a.* (*fem.* **-trice**) ejecting; (*Av.*) *siège éjecteur*, ejector seat.—*n.m.* ejector (*of firearm*).

élaboration [elabɔra'sjɔ̃], *n.f.* elaboration.

élaboré [elabɔ're], *a.* wrought; elaborate.

élaborer [elabɔ're], *v.t.* to elaborate, to work out.

élaguer [ela'ge], *v.t.* to lop, to prune; (*fig.*) to curtail, to cut down.

élagueur [ela'gœːr], *n.m.* (*Hort.*) pruner.

élan (1) [e'lɑ̃], *n.m.* start, spring, bound; flight; burst; dash.

élan (2) [e'lɑ̃], *n.m.* elk; moose, wapiti (*Canada*), eland (*S. Africa*).

élancé [elɑ̃'se], *a.* slender, slim.

élancement [elɑ̃s'mɑ̃], *n.m.* darting forward; shooting pain, twinge; (*pl.*) transports.

élancer [elɑ̃'se], *v.t.* (*conjug. like* COMMENCER) to dart, to hurl.—*v.i.* to shoot, to twitch (*of pain*). **s'élancer**, *v.r.* to bound, to shoot *or* dart forth, to rush, to dash; to soar up.

élargir [elar'ʒiːr], *v.t.* to widen, to enlarge; to release. **s'élargir**, *v.r.* to widen; to stretch; to enlarge one's estate.

élargissement [elarʒis'mɑ̃], *n.m.* widening, enlarging; discharge (*from prison etc.*).

élasticité [elastisi'te], *n.f.* elasticity, springiness.

élastique [elas'tik], *a.* elastic, springy.—*n.m.* India rubber; elastic band.

électeur [elɛk'tœːr], *n.m.* (*fem.* **-trice**) (*Hist.*) elector, electress; (*Polit.*) voter.

élection [elɛk'sjɔ̃], *n.f.* election, polling; choice; appointment.

électoral [elɛktɔ'ral], *a.* (*m. pl.* **-aux**) electoral.

électorat [elɛktɔ'ra], *n.m.* electorate.

électricien [elɛktri'sjɛ̃], *n.m.* electrician.

électricité [elɛktrisi'te], *n.f.* electricity.

électrification [elɛktrifika'sjɔ̃], *n.f.* electrification.

électrifier [elɛktri'fje], *v.t.* to provide with current, to electrify.

électrique [elɛk'trik], *a.* electric; *secousse électrique*, electric shock.

électriquement [elɛktrik'mɑ̃], *adv.* electrically.

électriser [elɛktri'ze], *v.t.* to electrify.

électro-aimant [elɛktroɛ'mɑ̃], *n.m.* (*pl.* **électro-aimants**) electro-magnet.

électrocuter [elɛktrɔky'te], *v.t.* to electrocute.

électrocution [elɛktrɔky'sjɔ̃], *n.f.* electrocution.

électron [elɛk'trɔ̃], *n.m.* electron.

électronique [elɛktrɔ'nik], *a.* electronic.

élégamment [elega'mɑ̃], *adv.* elegantly, stylishly.

élégance [ele'gɑ̃ːs], *n.f.* elegance, style.

élégant [ele'gɑ̃], *a.* elegant, smart, fashionable, stylish.—*n.m.* (*fem.* **-ée**) gentleman *or* lady of fashion.

élégiaque [ele'ʒjak], *a.* elegiac.—*n.* elegist.

élégie [ele'ʒi], *n.f.* elegy.

élément [ele'mɑ̃], *n.m.* element, component part.

élémentaire [elemɑ̃'tɛːr], *a.* elementary, elemental.

éléphant [ele'fɑ̃], *n.m.* elephant.

éléphantin [elefɑ̃'tɛ̃], *a.* elephantine.

élevage [el'vaːʒ], *n.m.* breeding, rearing (*of cattle*); stud.

élévateur [eleva'tœːr], *a.* (*fem.* **-trice**) raising, lifting.—*n.m.* elevator, lift, hoist.

élévation [eleva'sjɔ̃], *n.f.* elevation, raising; eminence, height; promotion; greatness (*of soul*); rise (*in prices etc.*).

élève [e'lɛːv], *n.* pupil; student, disciple; apprentice.

élevé [el've], *a.* raised, grand; reared; heroic, eminent; high (*of prices etc.*); exalted; *bien élevé*, well-bred; *mal élevé*, ill-bred.

élever [el've], *v.t.* (*conjug. like* AMENER) to raise, to lift up; to erect; to exalt; to run up (*accounts etc.*); to bring up, to rear; to educate; to foster. **s'élever**, *v.r.* to rise, to ascend, to go up; to be constructed; to increase; to break out.

éleveur [el'vœːr], *n.m.* (*fem.* **-euse**) raiser; cattle breeder.—*n.f.* (**-euse**) incubator.

elfe [ɛlf], *n.m.* elf, brownie.

élider [eli'de], *v.t.* (*Gram.*) to cut off, to elide. **s'élider**, *v.r.* to be elided.

éligibilité [eliʒibili'te], *n.f.* eligibility.

éligible [eli'ʒibl], *a.* eligible.

élimer [eli'me], *v.t.* to wear out. **s'élimer**, *v.r.* to wear threadbare (*of clothes etc.*).

élimination [elimina'sjɔ̃], *n.f.* elimination.

éliminatoire [elimina'twaːr], *a.* and *n.f.* (*Spt.*) eliminating (heat); disqualifying.

éliminer [elimi'ne], *v.t.* to eliminate; to expel; to remove.

élire [e'liːr], *v.t.* irr. (*conjug. like* LIRE) to elect, to choose; to return, to appoint.

élision [eli'zjɔ̃], *n.f.* elision.

élite [e'lit], *n.f.* choice, pick, select few, élite.

élixir [elik'siːr], *n.m.* elixir.

elle [ɛl], *pron.* (*pl.* **elles**) she, her, it; (*pl.*) they.

ellébore [ele'boːr], *n.m.* hellebore.

ellipse [e'lips], *n.f.* ellipse; (*Gram.*) ellipsis.

elliptique [elip'tik], *a.* elliptical.

élocution [elɔky'sjɔ̃], *n.f.* elocution.

éloge [e'lɔːʒ], *n.m.* eulogy, praise; panegyric.

élogieux [elɔ'ʒjø], *a.* (*fem.* **-euse**) laudatory, eulogistic, flattering.

éloigné [elwa'ɲe], *a.* removed, distant, remote; absent.

éloignement [elwaɲ'mɑ̃], *n.m.* removal; remoteness; dislike; unwillingness.

éloigner [elwa'ɲe], *v.t.* to remove; to dismiss; to set aside, to repudiate; to waive; to banish; to put off; to alienate. **s'éloigner**, *v.r.* to go away, to withdraw; to digress; to deviate; to be alienated.

éloquemment [elɔka'mɑ̃], *adv.* eloquently.

éloquence [elɔ'kɑ̃ːs], *n.f.* eloquence, oratory.

éloquent [elɔ'kɑ̃], *a.* eloquent.

élu [e'ly], *a.* elected, chosen, elect; appointed. —*n.m.* (*fem.* **-e**) elected *or* chosen person.

élucidation [elysida'sjɔ̃], *n.f.* elucidation.

élucider [elysi'de], *v.t.* to elucidate, to clear up.

éluder [ely'de], *v.t.* to elude, to evade.

Élysée [eli'ze], *n.m.* Elysium; *l'Élysée*, the residence (*in Paris*) of the President of the Republic.

émaciation [emasja'sjɔ̃], *n.f.* emaciation.

émacié [ema'sje], *a.* emaciated.

émail

émail [e'ma:j], *n.m.* (*pl.* **émaux**) enamel.
émaillage [ema'ja:3], *n.m.* enamelling.
émailler [ema'je], *v.t.* to enamel; (*fig.*) to adorn.
émailleur [ema'jœr], *n.m.* enameller.
émaillure [ema'jy:r], *n.f.* enamelling.
émanation [emana'sjɔ̃], *n.f.* emanation.
émancipation [emɑ̃sipa'sjɔ̃], *n.f.* emancipation.
émanciper [emɑ̃si'pe], *v.t.* to emancipate. **s'émanciper**, *v.r.* to gain one's liberty; to overstep the mark, to forget oneself.
émaner [ema'ne], *v.i.* to emanate.
émargement [emarʒə'mɑ̃], *n.m.* writing in the margin, marginal note; signature in the margin.
émarger [emar'ʒe], *v.t.* (*conjug. like* MANGER) to write or sign in the margin, *esp. on receipt*; *hence*, to draw one's salary.
embâcle [ɑ̃'bɑ:kl], *n.m.* ice-pack (*in a river etc.*).
emballage [ɑ̃ba'la:3], *n.m.* packing up, packing; package; (*Spt.*) spurt.
emballement [ɑ̃bal'mɑ̃], *n.m.* excitement; flying into a temper; burst of enthusiasm.
emballer [ɑ̃ba'le], *v.t.* to pack up, to wrap up; (*colloq.*) to pack off; to arrest; to tell (*someone*) off. **s'emballer**, *v.r.* to bolt (*of a horse etc.*); to wrap oneself up; to be carried away (*by rage, enthusiasm etc.*), to race (*of an engine*).
emballeur [ɑ̃ba'lœr], *n.m.* packer.
embarbouiller [ɑ̃barbu'je], *v.t.* to besmear. **s'embarbouiller**, *v.r.* to get muddled.
embarcadère [ɑ̃barka'dɛ:r], *n.m.* wharf, pier, landing-stage.
embarcation [ɑ̃barka'sjɔ̃], *n.f.* small boat, craft.
embardée [ɑ̃bar'de], *n.f.* lurch (*of a boat, a car etc.*); **faire une embardée**, to lurch (*of boat*); to swerve, to skid (*of car*).
embargo [ɑ̃bar'go], *n.m.* embargo.
embarquement [ɑ̃barkə'mɑ̃], *n.m.* embarkation, embarking; shipment.
embarquer [ɑ̃bar'ke], *v.t.* to embark, to take on board; to ship (*water etc.*). **s'embarquer**, *v.r.* to embark, to go on board; **s'embarquer dans**, (*fig.*) to embark upon.
embarras [ɑ̃ba'ra], *n.m.* encumbrance, hindrance; difficulty; fuss; (*pl.*) embarrassing circumstances; trouble, nervousness.
embarrassant [ɑ̃bara'sɑ̃], *a.* embarrassing, puzzling, awkward; troublesome.
embarrassé [ɑ̃bara'se], *a.* embarrassed, perplexed.
embarrasser [ɑ̃bara'se], *v.t.* to embarrass, to obstruct; to trouble, to confound; to puzzle. **s'embarrasser**, *v.r.* to entangle oneself; to be embarrassed; to concern oneself (*with*).
embâter [ɑ̃ba'te], *v.t.* to put a pack-saddle on, to saddle.
embauchage [ɑ̃bo'ʃa:3], *n.m.*, **embauche** [ɑ̃'boʃ], *n.f.* hiring, engaging (*of workmen*); enlisting, recruiting (*soldiers*).
embaucher [ɑ̃bo'ʃe], *v.t.* to hire, to engage, to sign on (*workmen*); to enlist (*soldiers*).
embaucheur [ɑ̃bo'ʃœr], *n.m.* (*fem.* -euse) hirer, recruiting officer.
embauchoir [ɑ̃bo'ʃwa:r], *n.m.* boot tree, boot last.

embaumement [ɑ̃bom'mɑ̃], *n.m.* embalming.
embaumer [ɑ̃bo'me], *v.t.* to embalm; to perfume.—*v.i.* to smell sweet.
embaumeur [ɑ̃bo'mœr], *n.m.* embalmer.
embecquer [ɑ̃bɛ'ke], *v.t.* to feed (*a bird*); to bait (*a hook*).
embéguiner [ɑ̃begi'ne], *v.t.* to muffle up. **s'embéguiner**, *v.r.* to wrap oneself up; (*fig.*) to be infatuated with.
embellir [ɑ̃bɛ'li:r], *v.t.* to embellish, to beautify.—*v.i.* to grow more beautiful. **s'embellir**, *v.r.* to grow more beautiful; to enhance one's looks.
embellissement [ɑ̃bɛlis'mɑ̃], *n.m.* embellishment; improvement.
embêtant [ɑ̃bɛ'tɑ̃], *a.* (*colloq.*) boring, annoying.
embêtement [ɑ̃bɛt'mɑ̃], *n.m.* (*colloq.*) annoyance; nuisance, bore.
embêter [ɑ̃bɛ'te], *v.t.* to bore; to annoy, to rile; to worry. **s'embêter**, *v.r.* to feel dull or bored.
emblée (d') [dɑ̃'ble], *adv.* at the first, at the first attempt, immediately.
emblématique [ɑ̃blema'tik], *a.* emblematical.
emblème [ɑ̃'blɛ:m], *n.m.* emblem.
emboîtage [ɑ̃bwa'ta:3], *n.m.* boards, cover (*book*).
emboîtement [ɑ̃bwat'mɑ̃], *n.m.* fitting in, jointing, clamping.
emboîter [ɑ̃bwa'te], *v.t.* to fit in, to put (*a book*) into its boards; to clamp. **s'emboîter**, *v.r.* to fit, to fit in; (*fig.*) to model oneself upon.
emboîture [ɑ̃bwa'ty:r], *n.f.* socket, clamp.
embolie [ɑ̃bɔ'li], *n.f.* (*Path.*) embolism.
embonpoint [ɑ̃bɔ̃'pwɛ̃], *n.m.* plumpness, stoutness, obesity.
emboucher [ɑ̃bu'ʃe], *v.t.* to put to one's mouth, to sound (*wind instruments*); to bit (*a horse*).
embouchure [ɑ̃bu'ʃy:r], *n.f.* mouth (*of a river, harbor etc.*); mouth-piece (*of wind instruments*); opening (*of a receptacle*).
embourber [ɑ̃bur'be], *v.t.* to put in the mire; (*fig.*) to implicate in a dirty affair. **s'embourber**, *v.r.* to stick in the mire, to get bogged down; (*fig.*) to be involved (*in some trouble*); to put one's foot in it.
embourser [ɑ̃bur'se], *v.t.* to receive, to swallow (*affronts etc.*).
embout [ɑ̃'bu], *n.m.* ferrule.
embouteillage [ɑ̃bute'ja:3], *n.m.* bottling; traffic jam.
embouteiller [ɑ̃bute'je], *v.t.* to bottle; to bottle up; to block up.
emboutir [ɑ̃bu'ti:r], *v.t.* to beat out (*coppersmith's work etc.*); to scoop out, to stamp; (*fam.*) to bump into. **s'emboutir**, *v.r.* to crash into, to collide with.
embranchement [ɑ̃brɑ̃ʃ'mɑ̃], *n.m.* branching off; branch road, branch line etc.; junction.
embrancher [ɑ̃brɑ̃'ʃe], *v.t.* to put together, to join up (*roads, railways, pipes etc.*). **s'embrancher**, *v.r.* to join (*of a minor road or line joining a major one*).
embrasement [ɑ̃braz'mɑ̃], *n.m.* conflagration; illumination.

embraser [ăbra'ze], *v.t.* to fire, to set on fire; (*fig.*) to inflame; to illuminate. **s'embraser,** *v.r.* to kindle, to catch fire; to glow.

embrassade [ăbra'sad], *n.f.* embrace, hug; kissing, kiss.

embrasse [ă'bras], *n.f.* curtain loop.

embrassement [ăbras'mã], *n.m.* embrace, embracing.

embrasser [ăbra'se], *v.t.* to embrace, to clasp; to kiss; (*fig.*) to encircle; to comprise. **s'embrasser,** *v.r.* to embrace *or* kiss one another; to be included.

embrassure [ăbra'sy:r], *n.f.* band of iron.

embrasure [ăbra'zy:r], *n.f.* embrasure, recess.

embrayage [ăbrɛ'ja:ʒ], *n.m.* (*Motor.*) coupling gear, clutch.

embrayer [ăbrɛ'je], *v.t.* (*conjug. like* PAYER) to connect up, to throw into gear.—*v.i.* to let in the clutch.

embrèvement [ăbrɛv'mã], *n.m.* (*Carp.*) mortise.

embrocation [ăbroka'sjɔ̃], *n.f.* embrocation.

embrocher [ăbrɔ'ʃe], *v.t.* to put on the spit.

embrouillement [ăbruj'mã], *n.m.* embroilment, entanglement, perplexity.

embrouiller [ăbru'je], *v.t.* to embroil, to confuse; to perplex; to obscure. **s'embrouiller,** *v.r.* to become intricate *or* entangled; to get confused *or* muddled.

embrouilleur [ăbruj'œ:r], *n.m.* (*fem.* -euse) muddler, blunderer.

embrumer (s') [să'bry'me], *v.r.* to be covered with fog etc; to become misty *or* hazy; (*fig.*) to grow somber *or* gloomy.

embrun [ă'brœ̃], *n.m.* (*usu. pl.*) spray, spindrift.

embrunir [ăbry'ni:r], *v.t.* to brown.

embryon [ăbri'jɔ̃], *n.m.* embryo; germ; (*fig.*) dwarf, shrimp.

embryonnaire [ăbrijɔ'nɛ:r], *a.* embryonic, in embryo.

embûche [ă'byʃ], *n.f.* ambush, snare.

embuscade [ăbys'kad], *n.f.* ambuscade, ambush.

embusqué [ăbys'ke], *n.m.* (*Mil. slang*) shirker.

embusquer [ăbys'ke], *v.t.* to place in ambuscade, to post. **s'embusquer,** *v.r.* to lie in wait.

émender [ămã'de], *v.t.* (*Law*) to amend, to correct.

émeraude [em'ro:d], *n.f.* emerald.

émergence [emɛr'ʒã:s], *n.f.* emergence; emersion.

émergent [emɛr'ʒã], *a.* emergent.

émerger [emɛr'ʒe], *v.i.* (*conjug. like* MANGER) to emerge, to rise out.

émeri [em'ri], *n.m.* emery.

émerillon [emri'jɔ̃], *n.m.* (*Orn.*) merlin.

émeriser [emri'ze], *v.t.* to cover with emery; *papier émerisé,* emery paper.

émérite [eme'rit], *a.* emeritus; practised, perfect; eminent.

émersion [emɛr'sjɔ̃], *n.f.* emersion.

émerveillement [emɛrvɛj'mã], *n.m.* wonder, astonishment.

émerveiller [emɛrvɛ'je], *v.t.* to astonish, to amaze. **s'émerveiller,** *v.r.* to marvel, to be astonished.

émétique [eme'tik], *a.* and *n.m.* emetic.

émetteur [eme'tœ:r] *a.* (*fem.* -trice)

(*Rad., Tel.*) *poste émetteur or station émettrice,* broadcasting station.—*n.m.* transmitter; *émetteur-récepteur,* transmitter-receiver, (*fam.*) walkie-talkie.

émettre [e'mɛtr], *v.t. irr.* (*conjug. like* METTRE) to emit, to give out; to utter, to express; (*Rad., Tel.*) to broadcast.

émeu [e'mø], *n.m.* (*Orn.*) emu.

émeute [e'mø:t], *n.f.* riot, disturbance, tumult, rising; *chef d'émeute,* ringleader.

émeuter [emø'te], *v.t.* to rouse, to stir up, to excite.

émeutier [emø'tje], *n.m.* (*fem.* -ière) rioter.

émiettement [emjɛt'mã], *n.m.* crumbling.

émietter [emjɛ'te], *v.t.* to crumble. **s'émietter,** *v.r.* to crumble.

émigrant [emi'grã], *a.* emigrating.—*n.m.* (*fem.* -e) emigrant.

émigration [emigra'sjɔ̃], *n.f.* emigration, migration.

émigré [emi'gre], *n.m.* (*fem.* -ée) emigrant; refugee.

émigrer [emi'gre], *v.i.* to emigrate; to migrate.

émincé [emɛ̃'se], *n.m.* (*Cook.*) thin slices (*of meat*).

émincer [emɛ̃'se], *v.t.* (*conjug. like* COMMENCER) to slice (*meat*).

éminemment [emina'mã], *adv.* eminently.

éminence [emi'nã:s], *n.f.* eminence, elevation, rising ground, height.

éminent [emi'nã], *a.* eminent, high, lofty.

émissaire [emi'sɛ:r], *n.m.* emissary, messenger; *bouc émissaire,* scapegoat.

émission [emi'sjɔ̃], *n.f.* emission; issue, uttering; broadcasting.

emmagasinage [ămagazi'na:ʒ], *n.m.* storage, warehousing.

emmagasiner [ămagazi'ne], *v.t.* to warehouse, to store.

emmaillotement [ămajot'mã], *n.m.* swaddling, swathing.

emmailloter [ămajo'te], *v.t.* to swaddle, to swathe.

emmanchement [ămãʃ'mã], *n.m.* hafting, helving (*putting a handle on*); (*fig.*) joining.

emmancher [ămã'ʃe], *v.t.* to put a handle to, to haft, to helve. **s'emmancher,** *v.r.* to fit on a handle; (*fig.*) to start (*of an affair*).

emmanchure [ămã'ʃy:r], *n.f.* armhole.

emmarchement [ămarʃə'mã], *n.m.* tread (*of stair*).

emmêlement [ămɛl'mã], *n.m.* tangle, muddle.

emmêler [ămɛ'le], *v.t.* to entangle. **s'emmêler,** *v.r.* to get entangled.

emménagement [ămenaʒ'mã], *n.m.* moving into (*a new house*), installation.

emménager [ămena'ʒe], *v.t.* (*conjug. like* MANGER) to move in; to fit out (*a ship etc.*). —*v.i. and* **s'emménager,** *v.r.* to move in.

emmener [ăm'ne], *v.t.* (*conjug. like* AMENER) to take away, to lead away, to fetch away; to convey away.

emmenotter [ămnɔ'te], *v.t.* to handcuff.

emmeuler [ămø'le], *v.t.* to stack (*hay etc.*).

emmiellé [ămjɛ'le], *a.* honeyed, sweet.

emmieller [ămjɛ'le], *v.t.* to honey, to sweeten with *or* as with honey.

emmitoufler [ămitu'fle], *v.t.* to wrap up warmly.

émoi [e'mwa], *n.m.* emotion, anxiety, flutter.

émollient [emɔ'ljã], *a.* emollient, softening. —*n.m.* emollient.

émolument [emɔly'mã], *n.m.* emolument, fee; (*pl.*) salary.

émondage [emɔ̃'da:ʒ], *n.m.* pruning, lopping, trimming.

émonder [emɔ̃'de], *v.t.* to prune, to lop.

émondeur [emɔ̃'dœ:r], *n.m.* (*fem.* -euse) pruner, trimmer.

émotion [emo'sjɔ̃], *n.f.* emotion; stir, commotion.

émotter [emɔ'te], *v.t.* to break up (*soil, a field etc.*).

émoucher [emu'ʃe], *v.t.* to drive flies away from. **s'émoucher,** *v.r.* to whisk away the flies.

émouchet [emu'ʃɛ], *n.m.* sparrow hawk.

émouchette [emu'ʃɛt], *n.f.* fly net (*for horses etc.*).

émouchoir [emu'ʃwa:r], *n.m.* fly whisk.

émoudre [e'mudr], *v.t. irr.* (*conjug. like* MOUDRE) to grind, to sharpen.

émouleur [emu'lœ:r], *n.m.* knifegrinder.

émoulu [emu'ly], *a.* sharpened, sharp.

émousser [emu'se], *v.t.* to blunt, to take the edge off; (*fig.*) to dull; to deaden. **s'émousser,** *v.r.* to get blunt; to become dull.

émoustiller [emusti'je], *v.t.* (*colloq.*) to exhilarate, to put into good spirits; (*fam.*) to ginger up. **s'émoustiller,** *v.r.* to bestir oneself.

émouvant [emu'vã], *a.* touching, moving, stirring.

émouvoir [emu'vwa:r], *v.t. irr.* (*conjug. like* MOUVOIR) to move, to affect; to excite, to rouse. **s'émouvoir,** *v.r.* to be roused *or* moved; to be agitated.

empaillage [ãpa'ja:ʒ], **empaillement** [ãpaj'mã], *n.m.* bottoming (*with straw*); stuffing (*of animals*).

empaillé [ãpa'je], *a.* stuffed; (*fam.*) *avoir l'air empaillé,* to be slow *or* dull-witted.

empailler [ãpa'je], *v.t.* to pack in straw; to straw-bottom; to stuff (*birds etc.*).

empailleur [ãpa'jœ:r], *n.m.* (*fem.* -euse) chair mender; bird *or* animal stuffer, taxidermist.

empaler [ãpa'le], *v.t.* to impale.

empanacher [ãpana'ʃe], *v.t.* to adorn with a plume; (*colloq.*) to touch up.

empaquetage [ãpakta:ʒ], *n.m.* wheel-base.

empaqueter [ãpak'te], *v.t.* (*conjug. like* APPELER) to pack up, to make up into a bundle, to do up. **s'empaqueter,** *v.r.* to wrap oneself up.

emparer (s') [ãpa're], *v.r.* to possess oneself (*of*), to get hold (*of*); to seize, to secure.

empâtement [ãpat'mã], *n.m.* stickiness, clamminess.

empâter [ãpa'te], *v.t.* to make clammy *or* sticky; to cram (*fowls*).

empattement [ãpat'mã], *n.m.* footing, foundation, base; (*Motor. etc.*) wheel-base.

empaumer [ãpo'me], *v.t.* to catch *or* strike (*a ball etc.*) in *or* with the palm of the hand; (*fig.*) to get hold of, to grasp, to take possession of.

empêchement [ãpɛʃ'mã], *n.m.* hindrance, obstacle, impediment, objection.

empêcher [ãpɛ'ʃe], *v.t.* to oppose, to prevent; to hinder. **s'empêcher,** *v.r.* (*always in the*

negative) to forbear, to refrain from; *je ne peux m'empêcher de rire,* I cannot help laughing.

empeigne [ã'pɛɲ], *n.f.* upper (leather) (*of shoe*).

empenner [ãpɛ'ne], *v.t.* to feather (*arrows*); to fit on (*fins*).

empereur [ã'prœ:r], *n.m.* emperor.

empesage [ãpə'za:ʒ], *n.m.* starching.

empesé [ãpə'ze], *a.* starched; stiff (*of style etc.*), formal.

empeser [ãpə'ze], *v.t.* (*conjug. like* AMENER) to starch.

empester [ãpɛs'te], *v.t.* to infect, to taint; to cause to stink horribly; (*fig.*) to corrupt.

empêtrer [ãpɛ'tre], *v.t.* to entangle; to embarrass. **s'empêtrer,** *v.r.* to become entangled.

emphase [ã'fa:z], *n.f.* grandiloquence; emphasis, stress.

emphatique [ãfa'tik], *a.* bombastic, affected; emphatic.

empiècement [ãpjɛs'mã], *n.m.* yoke (*of blouse*).

empierrement [ãpjɛr'mã], *n.m.* stoning, metalling, surfacing (*a road etc.*).

empierrer [ãpjɛ're], *v.t.* to stone, to metal, to surface (*roads etc.*).

empiétement [ãpjet'mã], *n.m.* encroaching, infringement.

empiéter [ãpje'te], *v.t.* (*conjug. like* CÉDER) to encroach upon, to invade, to trespass upon.—*v.i.* to encroach (*sur*).

empilement [ãpil'mã], *n.m.* piling, stacking.

empiler [ãpi'le], *v.t.* to pile up, to stack.

empire [ã'pi:r], *n.m.* empire, sovereignty, control, authority, dominion; (*fig.*) prestige, sway, mastery.

empirer [ãpi're], *v.t.* to make worse.—*v.i* to grow worse.

empirique [ãpi'rik], *a.* empiric(al).

empirisme [ãpi'rism], *n.m.* empiricism.

emplacement [ãplas'mã], *n.m.* site, place, piece of ground.

emplâtre [ã'pla:tr], *n.m.* plaster, ointment; (*fig.*) palliative; (*colloq.*) helpless creature.

emplette [ã'plɛt], *n.f.* purchase; *faire des emplettes,* to go shopping.

emplir [ã'pli:r], *v.t.* to fill. **s'emplir,** *v.r.* to fill; to be filled.

emploi [ã'plwa], *n.m.* employ, employment; use, function; situation, post.

employé [ãplwa'je], *a.* employed.—*n.m.* (*fem.* -ée) employee, assistant, clerk.

employer [ãplwa'je], *v.t.* (*see Verb Tables*) to employ, to use; to give employment to; to spend, to invest. **s'employer,** *v.r.* to employ oneself, to exert *or* busy oneself; to use one's interest; to be used.

employeur [ãplwa'jœ:r], *n.m.* (*fem.* -euse) employer.

emplumer (s') [ãply'me], *v.r.* to become fledged.

empocher [ãpɔ'ʃe], *v.t.* to pocket.

empoignade [ãpɔ'nad, ãpwa'nad], *n.f.* (*colloq.*) dispute, row, set-to.

empoignant [ãpɔ'nã, ãpwa'nã], *a.* thrilling, poignant.

empoigner [ãpɔ'ne, ãpwa'ne], *v.t.* to grasp, to seize. **s'empoigner,** *v.r.* to lay hold of each other, to grapple.

empois [ã'pwa], *n.m.* starch.

empoisonné [ãpwazɔ'ne], *a.* poisoned; (*fig.*) poisonous.

empoisonner [ãpwazɔ'ne], *v.t.* to poison; (*fig.*) to infect; to corrupt; to embitter; (*slang*) to bore to death. **s'empoisonner**, *v.r.* to poison oneself.

empoisonneur [ãpwazɔ'nœːr], *a.* (*fem.* **-euse**) poisonous; (*fig.*) corrupting.—*n.m.* (*fem.* **-euse**) poisoner; (*fig.*) corrupter.

empoissonner [ãpwasɔ'ne], *v.t.* to stock with fish.

emporté [ãpɔr'te], *a.* fiery, passionate, hot-headed; runaway, unmanageable.

emportement [ãpɔrt'mã], *n.m.* transport, fit of passion, outburst (*of anger, rage etc.*).

emporte-pièce [ãpɔrtə'pjɛs], *n.m.* punch (*instrument*), cutting-out machine; *c'est une réponse à l'emporte-pièce*, it is a very cutting answer.

emporter [ãpɔr'te], *v.t.* to carry away, to take away; to remove (*stains etc.*); to transport (*of emotion etc.*); to entail, to involve; to gain, to obtain. **s'emporter**, *v.r.* to fly into a passion, to flare up; to declaim (*contre*); to bolt (*of horses*).

empotage [ãpɔ'taːʒ], *n.m.* potting (*of plants*).

empoter [ãpɔ'te], *v.t.* to pot (*plants*).

empourpré [ãpur'pre], *a.* crimson.

empourprer [ãpur'pre], *v.t.* to color red *or* purple. **s'empourprer**, *v.r.* to turn red *or* purple; to flush, to blush.

empreindre [ã'prɛ̃ːdr], *v.t. irr.* (*conjug. like* CRAINDRE) to imprint, to stamp, to impress. **s'empreindre**, *v.r.* to become tinged.

empreinte [ã'prɛ̃ːt], *n.f.* stamp, print, impression; mark; *empreintes digitales*, fingerprints.

empressé [ãpre'se], *a.* eager, earnest; assiduous.

empressement [ãprɛs'mã], *n.m.* alacrity, cagerness; haste, hurry.

empresser (s') [sãpre'se], *v.r.* to be eager (*to*); to crowd, to press.

emprisonnement [ãprizɔn'mã], *n.m.* imprisonment.

emprisonner [ãprizɔ'ne], *v.t.* to imprison, to confine.

emprunt [ã'prœ̃], *n.m.* borrowing; loan.

emprunter [ãprœ̃'te], *v.t.* to borrow; to assume.

emprunteur [ãprœ̃'tœːr], *a.* (*fem.* **-euse**) borrowing.—*n.m.* (*fem.* **-euse**) borrower.

empuantir [ãpɥã'tiːr], *v.t.* to give an ill smell to, to infect.

ému [e'my], *a.* moved, affected.

émulation [emyla'sjɔ̃], *n.f.* emulation, rivalry.

émule [e'myl], *n.* rival, competitor.

émulgent [emyl'ʒã], *a.* (*Physiol.*) emulgent.

émulsif [emyl'sif], *a.* (*fem.* **-sive**) emulsive.

émulsion [emyl'sjɔ̃], *n.f.* emulsion.

en (1) [ã], *prep.* in; to; within; into; at; like, in the form of, as; out of, by, through, from; for, on.

en (2) [ã], *pron. inv.* of him, of her, of it, its, of them, their; from him, by him, about him etc.; thence, from thence; some of it, any.

enamourer (s') [sãnamu're], *v.r.* to fall in love; to be enamored (*de*).

encadrement [ãkadrə'mã], *n.m.* framing, frame; border; (*fig.*) environment.

encadrer [ãka'dre], *v.t.* to frame; to surround, to insert; (*Mil.*) to bracket (*target*); to officer (*troops*). **s'encadrer**, *v.r.* to be inserted *or* enclosed.

encadreur [ãka'drœːr], *n.m.* (*fem.* **-euse**) picture-frame maker.

encager [ãka'ʒe], *v.t.* (*conjug. like* MANGER) to cage, to put in a cage.

encaissage [ãkɛ'saːʒ], *n.m.* encasing.

encaisse [ã'kɛs], *n.f.* cash in hand, cash balance.

encaissé [ãkɛ'se], *a.* encased; sunk, hollow; steeply *or* deeply embanked.

encaissement [ãkɛs'mã], *n.m.* packing, putting in boxes etc.; embankment; paying in (*of money*).

encaisser [ãkɛ'se], *v.t.* to encase, to pack; to bank, pay in; to collect, to receive (*money*).

encaisseur [ãkɛ'sœːr], *n.m.* (*fem.* **-euse**) cashier.

encan [ã'kã], *n.m.* public auction.

encapuchonner (s') [sãkapyʃɔ'ne], *v.r.* to put on a cowl; to wrap one's head up; to arch the neck (*of horses*).

encarter [ãkar'te], *v.t.* to card-index.

en-cas [ã'ka], *n.m. inv.* anything kept for use in emergency; small umbrella; light meal prepared in case of need.

encastrement [ãkastrə'mã], *n.m.* fitting, fitting in.

encastrer [ãkas'tre], *v.t.* to fit in, to imbed.

encaustiquage [ãkosti'ka:ʒ], *n.m.* wax-polishing.

encavement [ãkav'mã], *n.m.* storing (*in cellar*), cellaring.

encaver [ãka've], *v.t.* to put *or* store in a cellar.

enceindre [ã'sɛ̃ːdr], *v.t. irr.* (*conjug. like* CRAINDRE) to surround, to enclose.

enceinte [ã'sɛ̃ːt], *n.f.* circuit, enclosure; (*Fort.*) enceinte. *a.* pregnant

encens [ã'sã], *n.m.* incense; (*fig.*) fragrance; flattery.

encensement [ãsãs'mã], *n.m.* incensing; (*fig.*) flattery.

encenser [ãsã'se], *v.t.* to incense; (*fig.*) to flatter.

encenseur [ãsã'sœːr], *n.m.* (*fem.* **-euse**) burner of incense; (*fig.*) flatterer.

encensoir [ãsã'swaːr], *n.m.* censer; (*fig.*) flattery.

encerclement [ãsɛrklə'mã], *n.m.* encircling; (*Polit.*) encirclement.

encercler [ãsɛr'kle], *v.t.* to encircle.

enchaînement [ãʃɛn'mã], *n.m.* chaining, linking; series, connection.

enchaîner [ãʃɛ'ne], *v.t.* to chain up, to bind in chains; (*Cine.*) to fade in; (*fig.*) to restrain; to captivate; to link. **s'enchaîner**, *v.r.* to be connected *or* linked together.

enchanté [ãʃã'te], *a.* enchanted; (*fig.*) charmed, delighted.

enchantement [ãʃãt'mã], *n.m.* enchantment, magic; (*fig.*) charm, delight.

enchanter [ãʃã'te], *v.t.* to enchant; (*fig.*) to fascinate, to charm.

enchanteur [ãʃã'tœːr], *a.* (*fem.* **-eresse**) enchanting, entrancing, captivating.—*n.m.* (*fem.* **-eresse**) enchanter, enchantress, charmer.

enchâsser [ãʃã'se], *v.t.* to enchase; to enshrine; to insert.

enchâssure [ãʃã'syːr], *n.f.* setting, mount; insertion.

enchère [ɑ̃'ʃɛːr], n.f. bid (at an auction); auction.

enchérir [ɑ̃ʃe'riːr], v.t. to bid for, to outbid; to raise (prices etc.).—v.i. to rise (in price); (fig.) to surpass, to outdo; to bid, to outbid (sur).

enchérissement [ɑ̃ʃeris'mɑ̃], n.m. rise, increase.

enchérisseur [ɑ̃ʃeri'sœːr], n.m. bidder (at an auction).

enchevêtrement [ɑ̃ʃvetrə'mɑ̃], n.m. entanglement.

enchevêtrer [ɑ̃ʃve'tre], v.t. to halter (a horse etc.); to entangle. s'enchevêtrer, v.r. to get entangled, confused or embarrassed.

enclave [ɑ̃'klaːv], n.f. enclave, piece of enclosed land.

enclaver [ɑ̃kla've], v.t. to enclose, to hem in.

enclenchement [ɑ̃klɑ̃ʃ'mɑ̃], n.m. throwing into gear; automatic clutch.

enclin [ɑ̃'klɛ̃], a. inclined; prone, addicted, apt, given to.

enclore [ɑ̃'kloːr], v.t. irr. (conjug. like CLORE) to enclose, to fence in, to take in, to shut in.

enclos [ɑ̃'klo], n.m. enclosure, yard; paddock; fencing, wall.

enclume [ɑ̃'klym], n.f. anvil.

encoche [ɑ̃'kɔʃ], n.f. notch.

encoffrer [ɑ̃'kɔfre], v.t. to shut in a coffer; (fig.) to cage.

encoignure [ɑ̃kɔ'nyːr], n.f. corner, angle (of a street); corner piece; corner cupboard.

encollage [ɑ̃kɔ'laːʒ], n.m. sizing, gluing; glue, size.

encoller [ɑ̃kɔ'le], v.t. to size, to glue.

encolure [ɑ̃kɔ'lyːr], n.f. neck and shoulders (of a horse); neck-line (of a garment); size (of collars); (fig.) appearance (of a person).

encombrant [ɑ̃kɔ̃'brɑ̃], a. cumbersome.

encombre [ɑ̃'kɔ̃ːbr], n.m. (now only used after sans) impediment, hindrance.

encombrement [ɑ̃kɔ̃brə'mɑ̃], n.m. obstruction; crowding, congestion (of traffic).

encombrer [ɑ̃kɔ̃'bre], v.t. to obstruct; to crowd, to throng.

encontre (à l'... de) [alɑ̃'kɔ̃ːtrdə], prep. phr. against, counter to.

encore [ɑ̃'kɔːr], adv. yet, still, as yet; anew, again, once more; further, moreover, besides; even, but, only.

encorner [ɑ̃kɔr'ne], v.t. to gore, to toss.

encourageant [ɑ̃kura'ʒɑ̃], a. encouraging, cheering.

encouragement [ɑ̃kuraʒ'mɑ̃], n.m. encouragement.

encourager [ɑ̃kura'ʒe], v.t. (conjug. like MANGER) to encourage, to stimulate. s'encourager, v.r. to encourage each other, to take courage.

encourir [ɑ̃ku'riːr], v.t. irr. (conjug. like COURIR) to incur (disgrace, reproach, obligation etc.).

encrasser [ɑ̃kra'se], v.t. to make dirty, to foul. s'encrasser, v.r. to become dirty.

encre [ɑ̃ːkr], n.f. ink.

encrier [ɑ̃kri'e], n.m. ink-stand, ink-pot.

encroûté [ɑ̃kru'te], a. covered with a crust; (fig.) full of prejudices.—n.m. (fem. -ée) old fogy.

encroûter (s') [sɑ̃kru'te], v.r. to crust, to get hard; to become dull, stupid or hide-bound.

encuvage [ɑ̃ky'va:ʒ], encuvement [ɑ̃kyv'mɑ̃], n.m. tubbing.

encuver [ɑ̃ky've], v.t. to put into a vat, to tub.

encyclopédie [ɑ̃siklɔpe'di], n.f. encyclopaedia.

endémique [ɑ̃de'mik], a. endemic.

endenté [ɑ̃dɑ̃'te], a. indented.

endenter [ɑ̃dɑ̃'te], v.t. to cog, to tooth.

endetter [ɑ̃de'te], v.t. to get (a person) into debt. s'endetter, v.r. to run into debt.

endeuiller [ɑ̃dœ'je], v.t. to put into mourning; to sadden.

endiablé [ɑ̃dja'ble], a. possessed; (fig.) devilish.

endiabler [ɑ̃dja'ble], v.i. to be furious; faire endiabler, to torment.

endiguement [ɑ̃dig'mɑ̃], n.m. damming up.

endiguer [ɑ̃di'ge], v.t. to dam up, to embank.

endimancher (s') [sɑ̃dimɑ̃'ʃe], v.r. to put on one's Sunday best.

endive [ɑ̃'diːv], n.f. (broad-leaved) chicory.

endoctrinement [ɑ̃dɔktrin'mɑ̃], n.m. indoctrination.

endoctriner [ɑ̃dɔktri'ne], v.t. to indoctrinate.

endolorir [ɑ̃dɔlɔ'riːr], v.t. to make sore; to make (the heart etc.) ache. s'endolorir, v.r. to become sore.

endolorissement [ɑ̃dɔlɔris'mɑ̃], n.m. pain, soreness.

endommagement [ɑ̃dɔmaʒ'mɑ̃], n.m. loss, injury, damage.

endommager [ɑ̃dɔma'ʒe], v.t. (conjug. like MANGER) to damage, to injure.

endormeur [ɑ̃dɔr'mœːr], n.m. (fem. -euse) cajoler, flatterer; bore.

endormi [ɑ̃dɔr'mi], a. asleep; sleepy; benumbed.—n.m. (fem. -e) sleepy-head.

endormir [ɑ̃dɔr'miːr], v.t. irr. (conjug. like SENTIR) to send to sleep, to rock to sleep; to anesthetize; to wheedle, to deceive; to benumb; to bore. s'endormir, v.r. to fall asleep.

endos [ɑ̃'do], endossement [ɑ̃dɔs'mɑ̃], n.m. endorsement.

endosser [ɑ̃do'se], v.t. to put on one's back, to put on; to saddle oneself with (an obligation etc.); to endorse.

endroit [ɑ̃'drwa], n.m. place, spot; point; right side (of a material); part, passage (of a book etc.).

enduire [ɑ̃'dɥiːr], v.t. irr. (conjug. like CONDUIRE) to do over, to coat, to smear.

enduit [ɑ̃'dɥi], n.m. coating, layer, plaster, glaze, varnish, polish.

endurance [ɑ̃dy'rɑ̃ːs], n.f. endurance, fortitude; épreuve d'endurance, endurance or reliability test.

endurant [ɑ̃dy'rɑ̃], a. patient, tolerant.

endurci [ɑ̃dyr'si], a. hardened; inured, callous.

endurcir [ɑ̃dyr'siːr], v.t. to harden, to toughen, to inure; to render callous. s'endurcir, v.r. to harden, to grow hard; to become callous.

endurcissement [ɑ̃dyrsis'mɑ̃], n.m. hardening, obduracy; callousness.

endurer [ɑ̃dy're], v.t. to endure, to bear; to put up with.

énergie [ener'ʒi], n.f. energy, strength, vigor, power.

énergique [ener'ʒik], a. energetic, vigorous.

énergiquement [enɛrʒik'mɑ̃], *adv.* energetically, vigorously.
énervant [enɛr'vɑ̃], *a.* enervating; debilitat-
ing, nerve-racking.
énervé [enɛr've], *a.* nerveless; on edge, fidgety.
énervement [enɛrv'mɑ̃], *n.m.* nervous tension.
énerver [enɛr've], *v.t.* to enervate, to debilitate; to weaken; to unnerve; (*fam.*) to get
on the nerves. **s'énerver,** *v.r.* to become
enervated, unnerved, irritable *or* fidgety.
enfance [ɑ̃'fɑ̃:s], *n.f.* infancy, childhood;
childishness.
enfant [ɑ̃'fɑ̃], *n.* child; infant, baby; descendant; citizen, native.
enfantement [ɑ̃fɑ̃t'mɑ̃], *n.m.* childbirth.
enfanter [ɑ̃fɑ̃'te], *v.t.* to bring forth, to bear;
(*fig.*) to beget, to give birth to.
enfantillage [ɑ̃fɑ̃ti'ja:ʒ], *n.m.* child's-play,
childishness.
enfantin [ɑ̃fɑ̃'tɛ̃], *a.* infantile, childish.
enfariner [ɑ̃fari'ne], *v.t.* to flour, to sprinkle
with flour.
enfer [ɑ̃'fɛ:r], *n.m.* hell; (*fig.*) torment,
misery.
enfermer [ɑ̃fɛr'me], *v.t.* to shut in *or* up; to
lock up; to enclose; to conceal; to comprise.
s'enfermer, *v.r.* to lock oneself in.
enficeler [ɑ̃fis'le], *v.t.* (*conjug. like* APPELER)
to tie with string etc.
enfièvrement [ɑ̃fjɛvra'mɑ̃], *n.m.* feverishness.
enfilade [ɑ̃fi'lad], *n.f.* suite (*of chambers etc.*);
string (*of phrases etc.*); (*Mil.*) enfilade.
enfiler [ɑ̃fi'le], *v.t.* to thread (*a needle*); to
string (*beads*); to pierce; to pass through;
(*Mil.*) to enfilade; to slip on (*clothes*).
s'enfiler, *v.r.* to be threaded; to be pierced;
to get involved in.
enfin [ɑ̃'fɛ̃], *adv.* at last, finally, at length,
after all, lastly; in short, in a word.
enflammé [ɑ̃flɑ̃'me], *a.* on fire, in flames,
ignited.
enflammer [ɑ̃flɑ̃'me], *v.t.* to set on fire, to
kindle; (*fig.*) to incense, to provoke. **s'enflammer,** *v.r.* to catch fire, to blaze; (*fig.*)
to be incensed.
enflé [ɑ̃'fle], *a.* swollen, puffed up; (*fig.*) bombastic, high-flown (*style etc.*).
enfler [ɑ̃'fle], *v.t.* to swell out, to puff up, to
distend; (*fig.*) to excite; to exaggerate.
s'enfler, *v.r.* to swell; (*fig.*) to be puffed up.
enflure [ɑ̃'fly:r], *n.f.* bloatedness, swelling;
bombast.
enfoncé [ɑ̃fɔ̃'se], *a.* broken open; sunken;
(*pop.*) done for.
enfoncement [ɑ̃fɔ̃s'mɑ̃], *n.m.* breaking in;
sinking; recess; (*Paint.*) background.
enfoncer [ɑ̃fɔ̃'se], *v.t.* (*conjug. like* COM-
MENCER) to push *or* drive in, down etc.; to
sink; to break in; to get the better of.—
v.i. to sink, to founder. **s'enfoncer,** *v.r.*
to sink; to bury oneself; to plunge; (*fig.*)
to fail.
enfonçure [ɑ̃fɔ̃'sy:r], *n.f.* cavity, hole, hollow.
enforcir [ɑ̃fɔr'si:r], *v.t.* to strengthen.—*v.i.*
and **s'enforcir,** *v.r.* to gather strength; to
grow stronger.
enfouir [ɑ̃'fwi:r], *v.t.* to put *or* bury in the
ground; (*fig.*) to hide. **s'enfouir,** *v.r.* to
bury oneself (*in an out-of-the-way place etc.*).
enfourcher [ɑ̃fur'ʃe], *v.t.* to bestride, to
straddle; to pierce with a pitch-fork etc.

enfourchure [ɑ̃fur'ʃy:r], *n.f.* fork; crotch.
enfourner [ɑ̃fur'ne], *v.t.* to put in the oven.
s'enfourner, *v.r.* to get into a blind alley, a
scrape etc.
enfreindre [ɑ̃'frɛ̃:dr], *v.t. irr.* (*conjug. like*
CRAINDRE) to infringe, to break, to violate.
enfuir (s') [sɑ̃'fɥi:r], *v.r. irr.* (*conjug. like*
FUIR) to run away, to escape.
enfumer [ɑ̃fy'me], *v.t.* to smoke, to fill with
smoke, to smoke (*vermin etc.*) out.
enfûtage [ɑ̃fy'ta:ʒ], *n.m.* casking.
enfutailler [ɑ̃fyta'je], **enfûter** [ɑ̃fy'te], *v.t.*
to cask, to barrel, to tun (*wine etc.*).
engagé [ɑ̃ga'ʒe], *a.* pledged; engaged, en-
listed; in action; (*Naut.*) water-logged.
engageant [ɑ̃ga'ʒɑ̃], *a.* engaging, winning.
engagement [ɑ̃gaʒ'mɑ̃], *n.m.* engagement,
commitment; pledging; mortgage; appointment; (*Mil.*) enlisting; action; entry (*for a
sporting event*); (*pl.*) liabilities.
engager [ɑ̃ga'ʒe], *v.t.* (*conjug. like* MANGER)
to pledge, to pawn; to engage; to begin; to
invite, to induce, to urge; to involve.
s'engager, *v.r.* to engage oneself, to undertake, to promise; to stand security; to
begin; to enter; to enlist; to get involved.
engeance [ɑ̃'ʒɑ̃:s], *n.f.* breed; brood (*esp. of
poultry*).
engelure [ɑ̃ʒ'ly:r], *n.f.* chilblain.
engendrer [ɑ̃ʒɑ̃'dre], *v.t.* to beget, to engender; (*fig.*) to produce.
engin [ɑ̃'ʒɛ̃], *n.m.* machine, engine; snare;
tool; *engin téléguidé,* guided missile.
englober [ɑ̃glɔ'be], *v.t.* to unite, to put
together; (*fig.*) to include, to embrace.
engloutir [ɑ̃glu'ti:r], *v.t.* to swallow, to
devour. **s'engloutir,** *v.r.* to be swallowed
up.
engloutissement [ɑ̃glutis'mɑ̃], *n.m.* engul-
fing, swallowing up.
engoncé [ɑ̃gɔ̃'se], *a. avoir l'air engoncé,* to
look awkward and stiff.
engorgement [ɑ̃gɔrʒə'mɑ̃], *n.m.* obstruction,
stopping up (*of a pipe etc.*); (*Med.*) congestion; (*Econ.*) glut.
engorger [ɑ̃gɔr'ʒe], *v.t.* (*conjug. like* MANGER)
to obstruct, to block. **s'engorger,** *v.r.* to be
obstructed *or* choked up.
engouement *or* **engoûment** [ɑ̃gu'mɑ̃], *n.m.*
(*Med.*) choking, obstruction; (*fig.*) infatuation.
engouer [ɑ̃'gwe], *v.t.* to obstruct (*the throat
etc.*); (*fig.*) to infatuate. **s'engouer,** *v.r.* to
half choke oneself; (*fig.*) to be infatuated.
engouffrer [ɑ̃gu'fre], *v.t.* to engulf; (*fig.*) to
swallow up. **s'engouffrer,** *v.r.* to be engulfed; to be swallowed up; to blow hard (*of
the wind*).
engourdi [ɑ̃gur'di], *a.* torpid; benumbed.
engourdir [ɑ̃gur'di:r], *v.t.* to benumb; to dull,
to enervate. **s'engourdir,** *v.r.* to get benumbed; to become sluggish.
engourdissement [ɑ̃gurdis'mɑ̃], *n.m.* numbness; torpor, enervation.
engrais [ɑ̃'grɛ], *n.m.* manure, fertilizer;
fattening (*cattle*).
engraissant [ɑ̃grɛ'sɑ̃], *a.* fattening.
engraissement [ɑ̃grɛs'mɑ̃], *n.m.* fattening.
engraisser [ɑ̃grɛ'se], *v.t.* to fatten; to
manure; (*fig.*) to enrich.—*v.i.* to grow fat;
(*fig.*) to thrive. **s'engraisser,** *v.r.* to grow
fat *or* stout.

engrenage [ãgrə'na:ȝ], *n.m.* gear, gearing etc.; action of these; (*fig.*) correlation (*of circumstances etc.*).

engrener (1) [ãgrə'ne], *v.t.* (*conjug. like* AMENER) to put corn into (*the mill-hopper*); to feed with corn.

engrener (2) [ãgrə'ne], *v.t.* (*conjug. like* AMENER) (*Mach.*) to throw into gear. **s'engrener**, *v.r.* to work into each other (*of toothed wheels*); to be put in gear.

engrenure [ãgrə'ny:r], *n.f.* engagement of teeth, cogs etc.

engrumeler (s') [sãgrym'le], *v.r.* (*conjug. like* APPELER) to clot, to coagulate.

enhardir [ãar'di:r], *v.t.* to embolden, to encourage. **s'enhardir**, *v.r.* to grow bold.

enherber [ãnɛr'be], *v.t.* to put land under grass.

énigmatique [enigma'tik], *a.* enigmatical.

énigmatiquement [enigmatik'mã], *adv.* enigmatically.

énigme [e'nigm], *n.f.* enigma, riddle.

enivrant [ãni'vrã], *a.* intoxicating.

enivrement [ãnivrə'mã], *n.m.* intoxication; (*fig.*) elation.

enivrer [ãni'vre], *v.t.* to intoxicate, to inebriate; (*fig.*) to elate. **s'enivrer**, *v.r.* to get intoxicated; (*fig.*) to be elated.

enjambée [ãȝã'be], *n.f.* stride.

enjambement [ãȝãb'mã], *n.m.* (*Pros.*) run-on line, enjambment.

enjamber [ãȝã'be], *v.t.* to skip *or* leap over; to stride; (*fig.*) to encroach upon; (*Pros.*) to make enjambment.

enjeu [ã'ȝø], *n.m.* (*pl.* **-eux**) stake (*gaming and fig.*).

enjoindre [ã'ȝwɛ̃:dr], *v.t.* irr. (*conjug. like* CRAINDRE) to enjoin, to charge, to direct, to prescribe.

enjôlement [ãȝol'mã], *n.m.* wheedling, coaxing, cajoling.

enjôler [ãȝo'le], *v.t.* to coax, to wheedle.

enjôleur [ãȝo'lœ:r], *n.m.* (*fem.* **-euse**) wheedler, coaxer.

enjolivement [ãȝoliv'mã], *n.m.* embellishment, decoration, ornament.

enjoliver [ãȝoli've], *v.t.* to embellish, to set off.

enjoliveur [ãȝoli'vœ:r], *n.m.* (*fem.* **-euse**) embellisher.

enjolivure [ãȝoli'vy:r], *n.f.* (small) embellishment.

enjoué [ã'ȝwe], *a.* playful, sprightly, lively, jovial, sportive.

enjouement *or* **enjoûment** [ãȝu'mã], *n.m.* playfulness, sportiveness, sprightliness.

enlacement [ãlas'mã], *n.m.* lacing, interlacing, entwining.

enlacer [ãla'se], *v.t.* (*conjug. like* COMMENCER) to lace; to entwine; to clasp. **s'enlacer**, *v.r.* to entwine, to be interlaced.

enlaidir [ãlɛ'di:r], *v.t.* to make ugly; to disfigure.—*v.i.* to grow ugly, to be disfigured.

enlaidissement [ãledis'mã], *n.m.* disfigurement.

enlèvement [ãlev'mã], *n.m.* carrying off; removal; wiping off; kidnapping.

enlever [ãlə've], *v.t.* (*conjug. like* AMENER) to remove, to take off; to carry off; to kidnap; to wipe off; to charm. **s'enlever**, *v.r.* to rise, to be lifted; to come off, to peel off; to come

out; to be snapped up (*of goods on sale*); to get into a passion.

enlève-taches [ãlɛv'taʃ], *n.m. inv.* stain remover.

enliasser [ãlja'se], *v.t.* to tie up in a bundle.

enlignement [ãliɲ'mã], *n.m.* alignment.

enligner [ãli'ɲe], *v.t.* to put in line.

enlisement [ãliz'mã], *n.m.* sinking, swallowing up (*in quicksand*).

enliser [ãli'ze], *v.t.* to engulf. **s'enliser**, *v.r.* to be engulfed *or* swallowed up.

enluminer [ãlymi'ne], *v.t.* to color; to illuminate. **s'enluminer**, *v.r.* to rouge, to paint; to flush.

enlumineur [ãlymi'nœ:r], *n.m.* (*fem.* **-euse**) colorer of maps, prints etc.

enluminure [ãlymi'ny:r], *n.f.* coloring; colored print; tinsel (*of style*).

enneigé [ãnɛ'ȝe], *a.* snow-covered.

ennemi [ɛn'mi], *a.* hostile; injurious.—*n.m.* (*fem.* **-e**) enemy, foe.

ennoblir [ãno'bli:r], *v.t.* to dignify, to exalt. **s'ennoblir**, *v.r.* to be ennobled *or* exalted.

ennoblissement [ãnoblis'mã], *n.m.* ennoblement, exaltation.

ennui [ã'nɥi], *n.m.* trouble, worry; nuisance; boredom.

ennuyer [ãnɥi'je], *v.t.* (*conjug. like* EMPLOYER) to bore, to weary; to pester; (*fig.*) to annoy. **s'ennuyer**, *v.r.* to be bored, to feel dull; to miss.

ennuyeusement [ãnɥijøz'mã], *adv.* tediously, irksomely.

ennuyeux [ãnɥi'jø], *a.* (*fem.* **-euse**) boring, tedious, dull, tiresome; annoying.—*n.m.* (*fem.* **-euse**) tiresome person, bore.

énoncé [enõ'se], *n.m.* statement.

énoncer [enõ'se], *v.t.* (*conjug. like* COMMENCER) to state, to express, to enunciate. **s'énoncer**, *v.r.* to be worded *or* expressed.

énonciatif [enõsja'tif], *a.* (*fem.* **-tive**) enunciative.

énonciation [enõsja'sjõ], *n.f.* enunciation, delivery; statement; wording.

enorgueillir [ãnorgœ'ji:r], *v.t.* to make proud, to elate. **s'enorgueillir**, *v.r.* to be *or* grow proud of; to be elated, to glory in (*de*).

énorme [e'norm], *a.* enormous, huge.

énormément [enorme'mã], *adv.* enormously, beyond measure.

énormité [enormi'te], *n.f.* hugeness, vastness; enormity.

enquérir (s') [sãke'ri:r], *v.r. irr.* (*conjug. like* ACQUÉRIR) to inquire, to make inquiries.

enquête [ã'kɛ:t], *n.f.* inquiry, investigation; inquest.

enquêter [ãkɛ'te], *v.i.* to inquire into a matter (*sur*), to conduct an inquiry.

enquêteur [ãkɛ'tœ:r], *n.m.* (*fem.* **-euse**) investigator.

enraciner [ãrasi'ne], *v.t.* to root; (*fig.*) to implant. **s'enraciner**, *v.r.* to take root.

enragé [ãra'ȝe], *a.* mad, rabid; (*fig.*) enthusiastic.—*n.m.* (*fem.* **-ée**) madman, mad woman; desperate person.

enrageant [ãra'ȝã], *a.* maddening, vexing.

enrager [ãra'ȝe], *v.i.* (*conjug. like* MANGER) to be mad, to go mad; to be enraged, to fume.

enrayage [ãrɛ'ja:ȝ], *n.m.* (*Mil.*) jam (*in rifle*).

136

enrayement or **enraiement** [ɑ̃rɛj'mɑ̃], n.m. skidding, locking.

enrayer (1) [ɑ̃rɛ'je], v.t. (conjug. like PAYER) to put spokes to (a wheel); to skid (a wheel), to apply brakes to; (fig.) to check, to slow up (an attack); to stem (an epidemic); to jam (a machine-gun).

enrayer (2) [ɑ̃rɛ'je], v.t. (conjug. like PAYER) (Agric.) to plough the first furrow in.

enrayure (1) [ɑ̃rɛ'jy:r], n.f. drag, skid, lock-chain.

enrayure (2) [ɑ̃rɛ'jy:r], n.m. (Agric.) first furrow.

enrégimenter [ɑ̃reʒimɑ̃'te], v.t. to form into regiments; (fig.) to enroll.

enregistrement [ɑ̃rəʒistrə'mɑ̃], n.m. registration, recording; checking (of luggage).

enregistrer [ɑ̃rəʒis'tre], v.t. to register, to record; to check (luggage).

enregistreur [ɑ̃rəʒis'trœ:r], n.m. registrar, recording machine.

enrêner [ɑ̃rɛ'ne], v.t. to rein in; to tie up by the reins.

enrhumer [ɑ̃ry'me], v.t. to give a cold to (someone). **s'enrhumer**, v.r. to catch a cold.

enrichi [ɑ̃ri'ʃi], n.m. (fem. -e) upstart, parvenu, new rich.

enrichir [ɑ̃ri'ʃi:r], v.t. to enrich; (fig.) to embellish. **s'enrichir**, v.r. to enrich oneself, to thrive.

enrichissement [ɑ̃riʃis'mɑ̃], n.m. enrichment; (fig.) embellishment.

enrôlement [ɑ̃rol'mɑ̃], n.m. enrolment; (Mil.) enlistment.

enrôler [ɑ̃ro'le], v.t. to enlist; to enroll. **s'enrôler**, v.r. to enroll oneself, to enlist.

enroué [ɑ̃'rwe], a. hoarse, husky.

enrouement [ɑ̃ru'mɑ̃], n.m. hoarseness, huskiness.

enrouer [ɑ̃'rwe], v.t. to make hoarse. **s'enrouer**, v.r. to become hoarse or husky.

enroulement [ɑ̃rul'mɑ̃], n.m. rolling up; (Arch.) scroll.

enrouler [ɑ̃ru'le], v.t. to roll up, to coil. **s'enrouler**, v.r. to roll oneself up; to twine (of plants etc.).

enrubanner [ɑ̃ryba'ne], v.t. to deck out with ribbons. **s'enrubanner**, v.r. to beribbon oneself.

ensablement [ɑ̃sabla'mɑ̃], n.m. sand-bank; ballasting; stranding (of a ship).

ensabler [ɑ̃sa'ble], v.t. to ballast; to run aground, to strand. **s'ensabler**, v.r. to run aground; to sink in sand; to silt up.

ensacher [ɑ̃sa'ʃe], v.t. to put in bags or sacks.

ensanglanter [ɑ̃sɑ̃glɑ̃'te], v.t. to make bloody, to stain with blood.

enseignant [ɑ̃sɛ'ɲɑ̃], a. teaching.—n.m. (pl.) teachers.

enseigne [ɑ̃'sɛɲ], n.f. sign, signboard; mark, token; ensign, flag.—n.m. (Navy) sub-lieutenant; (U.S.) ensign.

enseignement [ɑ̃sɛɲ'mɑ̃], n.m. teaching, education; teaching profession.

enseigner [ɑ̃sɛ'ɲe], v.t. to teach, to instruct, to inform, to direct.

ensemble [ɑ̃'sɑ̃:bl], adv. together, at the same time.—n.m. whole, general effect, mass; two- or three-piece (clothing); suite (furniture); (Math.) set.

ensemencement [ɑ̃smɑ̃s'mɑ̃], n.m. sowing.

ensemencer [ɑ̃smɑ̃'se], v.t. (conjug. like COMMENCER) to sow.

enserrer [ɑ̃sɛ're], v.t. to enclose; to lock up; to hem in.

ensevelir [ɑ̃sə'vli:r], v.t. to shroud; (fig.) to bury; to swallow up, to entomb; to absorb. **s'ensevelir**, v.r. to bury oneself.

ensevelissement [ɑ̃səvlis'mɑ̃], n.m. putting in a shroud; burial.

ensoleillé [ɑ̃sɔlɛ'je], a. sunny.

ensoleiller [ɑ̃sɔlɛ'je], v.t. to light up with sunshine; (fig.) to brighten.

ensommeillé [ɑ̃sɔmɛ'je], a. heavy with sleep; (fig.) torpid.

ensorceler [ɑ̃sɔrsə'le], v.t. (conjug. like APPELER) to bewitch.

ensorceleur [ɑ̃sɔrsə'lœ:r], a. (fem. -euse) bewitching.—n.m. (fem. -euse) enchanter, enchantress.

ensorcellement [ɑ̃sɔrsɛl'mɑ̃], n.m. bewitchment.

ensuite [ɑ̃'sɥit], adv. after, afterwards, then, in the next place; what then? what next? well!

ensuivre (s') [sɑ̃'sɥi:vr], v.r. irr. (conjug. like SUIVRE) to follow, to result, to ensue.

entacher [ɑ̃ta'ʃe], v.t. to sully; to taint, to cast a slur on.

entaille [ɑ̃'ta:j], n.f. notch; cut; gash; groove.

entailler [ɑ̃ta'je], v.t. to notch, to cut.

entamer [ɑ̃ta'me], v.t. to make the first cut in; to make an incision in; to broach; to break into.

entartrer (s') [sɑ̃tar'tre], v.r. to scale, to become furred.

entassement [ɑ̃tas'mɑ̃], n.m. accumulation; heap, pile; crowding together.

entasser [ɑ̃ta'se], v.t. to heap or pile up, to accumulate; to hoard up; to pack together. **s'entasser**, v.r. to heap up; to crowd together.

entendement [ɑ̃tɑ̃d'mɑ̃], n.m. understanding; judgment, sense.

entendre [ɑ̃'tɑ̃:dr], v.t. to hear; to understand; to know; to intend; to mean. **s'entendre**, v.r. to hear each other; to hear one's own voice; to be heard; to be understood; to understand one another; to act in concert; to come to terms (avec); to agree with; to be skilful in.

entendu [ɑ̃'tɑ̃dy], a. heard; understood; agreed; skilful.

enténébrer [ɑ̃tene'bre], v.t. (conjug. like CÉDER) to plunge or wrap in darkness.

entente [ɑ̃'tɑ̃:t], n.f. meaning; skill, judgment; understanding, agreement.

enter [ɑ̃'te], v.t. to graft upon, to engraft; to join.

entériner [ɑ̃teri'ne], v.t. to ratify, to confirm.

entérique [ɑ̃te'rik], a. enteric.

entérite [ɑ̃te'rit], n.f. enteritis.

enterrement [ɑ̃tɛr'mɑ̃], n.m. burial, interment, funeral.

enterrer [ɑ̃tɛ're], v.t. to bury, to inter; (fig.) to survive, to outlive; to end. **s'enterrer**, v.r. to bury oneself.

en-tête [ɑ̃'tɛ:t], n.m. (pl. -têtes) heading, headline.

entêté [ɑ̃tɛ'te], a. stubborn, obstinate.—n.m. (fem. -ée) stubborn person.

entêtement

entêtement [ãtɛt'mã], *n.m.* stubbornness, obstinacy; infatuation.

entêter [ãtɛ'te], *v.t.* to give a headache to; to make giddy, to intoxicate. **s'entêter**, *v.r.* to be stubborn, to persist (*in*); to be infatuated (*de*).

enthousiasme [ãtu'zjasm], *n.m.* enthusiasm, rapture, ecstasy.

enthousiasmer [ãtuzjas'me], *v.t.* to render enthusiastic, to enrapture. **s'enthousiasmer**, *v.r.* to be enthusiastic, to be in raptures (*de*).

enthousiaste [ãtu'zjast], *a.* enthusiastic.—*n.* enthusiast.

entiché [ãti'ʃe], *a.* infatuated, keen on.

entichement [ãtiʃ'mã], *n.m.* infatuation, addiction.

enticher [ãti'ʃe], *v.t.* to infatuate. **s'enticher**, *v.r.* to be infatuated with (*de*).

entier [ã'tje], *a.* (*fem.* **-ière**) entire, whole; total; positive.—*n.m.* entirety, totality; (*Arith.*) integral.

entièrement [ãtjɛr'mã], *adv.* entirely, wholly.

entité [ãti'te], *n.f.* entity.

entonner (1) [ãtɔ'ne], *v.t.* to tun, to put into casks.

entonner (2) [ãtɔ'ne], *v.t.* to begin to sing, to strike up.

entonnoir [ãtɔ'nwa:r], *n.m.* funnel; shell hole.

entorse [ã'tɔrs], *n.f.* sprain; strain, twist.

entortillage [ãtɔrti'ja:ʒ], **entortillement** [ãtɔrtij'mã], *n.m.* entanglement; winding, coiling; abstruseness; subterfuge; equivocation.

entortiller [ãtɔrti'je], *v.t.* to wrap, to roll round; to distort; to entangle. **s'entortiller**, *v.r.* to twist oneself round; to twine; to be obscure.

entour [ã'tu:r], *n.m.* (*used only in pl. except in the adverbial expression* **à l'entour**, around) environs, adjacent parts.

entourage [ãtu'ra:ʒ], *n.m.* frame; entourage, friends, relations, circle, attendants.

entourer [ãtu're], *v.t.* to surround; to gather round.

entournure [ãtur'ny:r], *n.f.* arm-hole.

entracte [ã'trakt], *n.m.* intermission (*Theat.*); interlude.

entraide [ã'trɛd], *n.f.* (*no pl.*) mutual aid.

entraider (**s'**) or **entr'aider** (**s'**) [sãtrɛ'de], *v.r.* to help one another.

entrailles [ã'tra:j], *n.f. pl.* intestines, entrails, bowels; (*fig.*) feelings, tenderness, pity.

entrain [ã'trɛ̃], *n.m.* warmth, heartiness; spirit, animation, life, go.

entraînant [ãtrɛ'nã], *a.* captivating, seductive.

entraînement [ãtrɛn'mã], *n.m.* enthusiasm, rapture; impulse, temptation; (*Spt.*) coaching, training.

entraîner [ãtrɛ'ne], *v.t.* to drag along; to carry away; to win over; to involve; to train.

entraîneur [ãtrɛ'nœ:r], *n.m.* (*fem.* **-euse**) trainer (*esp. of horses*); pace-maker; coach (*of teams*).

entrant [ã'trã], *a.* ingoing, incoming.—*n.m.* (*fem.* **-e**) person going or coming in.

entr'apercevoir [ãtrapɛrsə'vwa:r], *v.t. irr.* (*conjug. like* RECEVOIR) to catch a quick glimpse of.

entr'appeler (**s'**) [sãtra'ple], *v.r.* (*conjug. like* APPELER) to call one another.

138

entrave [ã'tra:v], *n.f.* clog, fetter, hobble; (*fig.*) hindrance, impediment.

entraver [ãtra've], *v.t.* to shackle; to hinder, to thwart.

entre [ã:tr], *prep.* between, betwixt; among, amongst; into.

entrebâillé [ãtrəba'je], *a.* ajar, half-open.

entrebâillement [ãtrəbaj'mã], *n.m.* small opening, gap, chink.

entrebâiller [ãtrəba'je], *v.t.* to half-open.

entrechat [ãtrə'ʃa], *n.m.* caper in dancing, entrechat.

entrechoquement [ãtrəʃɔk'mã], *n.m.* clash, collision, conflict.

entrechoquer (**s'**) [sãtrəʃɔ'ke], *v.r.* to knock, to run or dash against each other.

entre-clos [ãtrə'klo], *a.* half-closed; half-drawn.

entr'éclos [ãtre'klo], *a.* half-opened (*flower*).

entrecôte [ãtrə'ko:t], *n.f.* steak cut from between the ribs.

entrecoupé [ãtrəku'pe], *a.* broken (*of words, speech etc.*).

entrecouper [ãtrəku'pe], *v.t.* to intersect; to interrupt; to intersperse.

entrecroisement [ãtrəkrwaz'mã], *n.m.* intersection, crossing.

entrecroiser [ãtrəkrwa'ze], *v.t.* to intersect. **s'entrecroiser**, *v.r.* to cross one other, to intersect.

entre-deux [ãtrə'dø], *n.m. inv.* partition; insertion (*of lace etc.*).

entrée [ã'tre], *n.f.* entry, entrance; mouth; reception; beginning; first course.

entrefaites [ãtrə'fɛt], *n.f. pl.* interval, meantime; *sur ces entrefaites*, meanwhile.

entrefilet [ãtrəfi'le], *n.m.* (short) paragraph, note (*in a newspaper*).

entregent [ãtrə'ʒã], *n.m.* tact, cleverness (*in dealing with people*).

entrelacement [ãtrəlas'mã], *n.m.* interlacing, interweaving, intertwining.

entrelacer [ãtrəla'se], *v.t.* (*conjug. like* COMMENCER) to interlace, to intertwine. **s'entrelacer**, *v.r.* to entwine, to twist round each other.

entrelardé [ãtrəlar'de], *a.* interlarded; streaky.

entrelarder [ãtrəlar'de], *v.t.* to lard.

entremêlement [ãtrəmɛl'mã], *n.m.* intermixing, intermingling.

entremêler [ãtrəmɛ'le], *v.t.* to intermingle, to intermix. **s'entremêler**, *v.r.* to intermingle, to meddle.

entremets [ãtrə'me], *n.m. inv.* side dish, sweet.

entremetteur [ãtrəmɛ'tœ:r], *n.m.* (*fem.* **-euse**) go-between, mediator.

entremettre (**s'**) [sãtrə'mɛtr], *v.r. irr.* (*conjug. like* METTRE) to interpose; to interfere, to meddle.

entremise [ãtrə'mi:z], *n.f.* intervention, mediation.

entrepont [ãtrə'pɔ̃], *n.m.* (*Naut.*) between decks; *passagers d'entrepont*, steerage passengers.

entreposer [ãtrəpo'ze], *v.t.* to store, to warehouse; to put in bond.

entrepositaire [ãtrəpozi'tɛ:r], *n.* bonder; depositor (*of goods*).

entrepôt [ãtrə'po], *n.m.* bonded warehouse, store; mart, emporium, depot.

entreprenant [ãtrəprə'nã], *a.* enterprising, adventurous; daring, bold.

entreprendre [ãtrə'prã:dr], *v.t. irr.* (*conjug. like* PRENDRE) to undertake, to attempt; to contract for *or* to; to venture.—*v.i.* to encroach, to infringe (*sur*).

entrepreneur [ãtrəprə'nœ:r], *n.m.* (*fem.* -**euse**) contractor; master builder; *entrepreneur de pompes funèbres*, undertaker.

entreprise [ãtrə'pri:z], *n.f.* enterprise, undertaking; concern, company.

entrer [ã'tre], *v.i.* (*with aux.* ÊTRE) to enter, to come *or* go in; to run into.

entre-rail [ãtrə'ra:j], *n.m.* (*pl.* -**rails**) (*Rail.*) gauge.

entresol [ãtrə'sɔl], *n.m.* mezzanine, entresol (*rooms between the ground floor and the first floor*).

entre-temps [ãtrə'tã], *n.m. inv.* interval; *dans l'entre-temps*, meanwhile.—*adv.* meanwhile.

entretenir [ãtrət'ni:r], *v.t. irr.* (*conjug. like* TENIR) to hold together, to keep up, to keep in good order; to maintain, to support; to entertain. **s'entretenir**, *v.r.* to be kept up, to be maintained; to subsist; to converse.

entretien [ãtrə'tjɛ̃], *n.m.* maintenance, servicing (*of car etc.*); preservation; living, livelihood; conversation, interview, conference.

entrevoir [ãtrə'vwa:r], *v.t. irr.* (*conjug. like* VOIR) to catch a glimpse of; to foresee confusedly.

entrevue [ãtrə'vy], *n.f.* interview.

entr'ouvert [ãtru've:r], *a.* partly open, ajar; gaping.

entr'ouvrir [ãtru'vri:r], *v.t. irr.* (*conjug. like* OUVRIR) to open a little, to half-open. **s'entr'ouvrir**, *v.r.* to be ajar; to open up.

énumérateur [enymera'tœ:r], *n.m.* (*fem.* -**trice**) enumerator.

énumératif [enymera'tif], *a.* (*fem.* -**tive**) enumerative.

énumération [enymera'sjɔ̃], *n.f.* enumeration.

énumérer [enyme're] *v.t.* (*conjug. like* CÉDER) to enumerate, to count, to reckon.

envahir [ãva'i:r], *v.t.* to invade, to overrun; to encroach upon.

envahissant [ãvai'sã], *a.* invading, encroaching.

envahissement [ãvais'mã], *n.m.* invasion, overrunning; encroachment.

envahisseur [ãvai'sœ:r], *a.* (*fem.* -**euse**) invading, encroaching.—*n.m.* (*fem.* -**euse**) invader.

envaser [ãva'ze], *v.t.* to fill up *or* choke with silt. **s'envaser**, *v.r.* to stick fast in the mud; to silt up.

enveloppe [ã'vlɔp], *n.f.* wrapper, cover; envelope; exterior; tire casing.

enveloppement [ãvlɔp'mã], *n.m.* enveloping, wrapping up.

envelopper [ãvlɔ'pe], *v.t.* to envelop, to wrap up, to cover; to surround; to disguise. **s'envelopper**, *v.r.* to cover *or* wrap oneself up.

envenimement [ãvnima'mã], *n.m.* poisoning; aggravation (*of a quarrel*).

envenimer [ãvni'me], *v.t.* to poison; to inflame, to exasperate. **s'envenimer**, *v.r.* to be envenomed; to fester, to rankle.

envergure [ãvɛr'gy:r], *n.f.* spread (*of sail*); spread, span (*of a bird's wings, of an airplane*).

envers [ã've:r], *prep.* towards, to (*in respect of*).—*n.m.* wrong side, reverse side, back; *à l'envers*, on the wrong side, inside out.

envi (**à l'**) [alã'vi], *adv. phr.* emulously, vying with each other.

enviable [ã'vjabl], *a.* enviable, to be envied.

envie [ã'vi], *n.f.* envy; desire, longing; birthmark; *avoir envie de*, to have a mind to, to long for, to feel like.

envier [ã'vje], *v.t.* to envy; to long for; to grudge.

envieux [ã'vjø], *a.* and *n.m.* (*fem.* -**euse**) envious, jealous (person).

environ [ãvi'rɔ̃], *adv.* about, nearly, thereabouts.—*n.m.* (*pl.*) environs, vicinity, neighborhood.

environnant [ãvirɔ'nã], *a.* surrounding.

environner [ãvirɔ'ne], *v.t.* to surround, to stand round, to encircle, to enclose.

envisager [ãviza'ʒe], *v.t.* (*conjug. like* MANGER) to look, to stare in the face, to face; to consider, to envisage.

envoi [ã'vwa], *n.m.* sending (*of thing sent*); packet, parcel, consignment, shipment; (*Pros.*) envoy.

envol [ã'vɔl], *n.m.* taking wing (*of birds*), taking off (*of airplanes*), start; *piste d'envol*, runway.

envolée [ãvɔ'le], *n.f.* flight; (*fig.*) élan.

envoler (**s'**) [sãvɔ'le], *v.r.* to fly away; to take off; (*fig.*) to be carried off (*by the wind etc.*); (*fig.*) to disappear.

envoûtement [ãvut'mã], *n.m.* spell, magical charm.

envoûter [ãvu'te], *v.t.* to cast a spell on (*someone*).

envoyé [ãvwa'je], *n.m.* (*fem.* -**ée**) envoy, delegate, messenger; *envoyé spécial* (*of a paper*), special correspondent.

envoyer [ãvwa'je], *v.t. irr.* to send, to forward, to dispatch.

envoyeur [ãvwa'jœ:r], *n.m.* (*fem.* -**euse**) sender.

enzyme [ã'ʒim], *n.f.* enzyme.

éon [e'ɔ̃], *n.m.* eon.

épagneul [epa'nœl], *n.m.* spaniel.

épais [e'pɛ], *a.* thick, dense; thickset; (*fig.*) dull, gross.—*adv.* thick, thickly.

épaisseur [epɛ'sœ:r], *n.f.* thickness, density; stoutness; dullness.

épaissir [epɛ'si:r], *v.t.* to thicken.—*v.i.* and **s'épaissir**, *v.r.* to become thick, to grow big; to become heavy.

épaississement [epɛsis'mã], *n.m.* thickening.

épanchement [epãʃ'mã], *n.m.* pouring out, discharge; (*fig.*) outpouring (*emotion etc.*).

épancher [epã'ʃe], *v.t.* to pour out, to shed; to discharge. **s'épancher**, *v.r.* to be discharged, to overflow; to open one's heart.

épanchoir [epã'ʃwa:r], *n.m.* outlet, overflow.

épandre [e'pã:dr], *v.t.* to scatter, to strew; to shed (*light etc.*). **s'épandre**, *v.r.* to spread; (*fig.*) to stretch (*of a sheet of water etc.*).

épanoui [epa'nwi], *a.* in full bloom; (*fig.*) beaming.

épanouir [epa'nwi:r], *v.t.* to cause to open *or* expand; (*fig.*) to gladden. **s'épanouir**, *v.r.* to blossom, to open (*of flowers*); to brighten up (*of the face etc.*).

épanouissement [epanwis'mã], *n.m.* blossoming, opening (*of flowers*); (*fig.*) brightness, glow.

épargnant [epar'nã], *a.* sparing, saving; parsimonious.—*n.m.* (*fem.* **-e**) small investor.

épargne [e'parn], *n.f.* saving, thrift; parsimony; *caisse d'épargne*, savings bank.

épargner [epar'ne], *v.t.* to save; to spare; to economize.

éparpillement [eparpij'mã], *n.m.* scattering, dispersion.

éparpiller [eparpi'je], *v.t.* to scatter, to spread, to disperse; to squander.

épars [e'pa:r], *a.* scattered, dispersed, sparse; dishevelled (*of hair*).

épaté [epa'te], *a.* flat (*of noses*); (*fam.*) amazed.

épaule [e'po:l], *n.f.* shoulder.

épaulement [epol'mã], *n.m.* shoulder; (*Naut.*) bows; (*Fort.*) breast-work.

épauler [epo'le], *v.t.* to splay the shoulder (*a horse etc.*); to bring (*a rifle*) to the shoulder.

épaulette [epo'let], *n.f.* shoulder strap; epaulet.

épave [e'pa:v], *n.f.* wreck; flotsam, jetsam; waif.

épée [e'pe], *n.f.* sword; (*fig.*) brand, steel.

épeler [e'ple], *v.t.* (*conjug. like* APPELER) to spell.

épellation [epela'sjɔ̃], *n.f.* spelling.

éperdu [eper'dy], *a.* distracted, bewildered.

éperdument [eperdy'mã], *adv.* madly, distractedly.

éperon [e'prɔ̃], *n.m.* spur; (*Arch.*) buttress, starling (*of a bridge etc.*); (*Naut.*) prow.

éperonné [epro'ne], *a.* spurred.

éperonner [epro'ne], *v.t.* to spur; to urge forward.

éperonnière [epro'njɛ:r], *n.f.* (*Bot.*) larkspur.

épervier [eper'vje], *n.m.* sparrow hawk; casting net.

épeuré [epœ're], *a.* scared.

éphélide [efe'lid], *n.f.* sunburn; freckle.

éphémère [efe'mɛ:r], *a.* ephemeral, short-lived.—*n.m.* ephemera, May fly.

épi [e'pi], *n.m.* ear of corn; (*Rail.*) system of marshalling tracks, spur tracks.

épice [e'pis], *n.f.* spice.

épicé [epi'se], *a.* spiced; seasoned.

épicer [epi'se], *v.t.* (*conjug. like* COMMENCER) to spice.

épicerie [epi'sri], *n.f.* spices; grocery.

épicier [epi'sje], *n.m.* (*fem.* **-ière**) grocer.

épicurien [epiky'rjɛ̃], *a.* (*fem.* **-enne**) epicurean, voluptuous.—*n.m.* (*fem.* **-enne**) epicure.

épicurisme [epiky'rism], *n.m.* epicureanism, epicurism.

épidémie [epide'mi], *n.f.* epidemic.

épidémique [epide'mik], *a.* epidemic.

épiderme [epi'derm], *n.m.* epidermis, cuticle.

épidermique [epider'mik], *a.* epidermic, epidermal.

épier (1) [e'pje], *v.i.* to ear (*of grain*).

épier (2) [e'pje], *v.t.* to watch; to spy upon; to lie in wait for.

épieu [e'pjø], *n.m.* (*pl.* **-eux**) boar spear, hunting pole.

épigrammatique [epigrama'tik], *a.* epigrammatical.

épigrammatiste [epigrama'tist], *n.* epigrammatist.

épigramme [epi'gram], *n.f.* epigram.

épigraphe [epi'graf], *n.f.* epigraph.

épilation [epila'sjɔ̃], *n.f.* depilation.

épilatoire [epila'twa:r], *a.* depilatory.

épilepsie [epilɛp'si], *n.f.* epilepsy.

épileptique [epilɛp'tik], *a.* and *n.* epileptic.

épiler [epi'le], *v.t.* to depilate. **s'épiler**, *v.r.* to pluck out one's hairs.

épileur [epi'lœ:r], *n.m.* (*fem.* **-euse**) depilator (*person*).

épilogue [epi'lɔg], *n.m.* epilogue.

épiloguer [epilo'ge], *v.t.* to censure, to criticize.—*v.i.* to carp, to find fault.

épilogueur [epilo'gœ:r], *a.* (*fem.* **-euse**) fault-finding.—*n.m.* (*fem.* **-euse**) critic, fault-finder, carper.

épiloir [epi'lwa:r], *n.m.* tweezers.

épinaie [epi'nɛ], *n.f.* brake, thorny thicket.

épinard [epi'na:r], *n.m.* spinach.

épine [e'pin], *n.f.* thorn, prickle; (*fig.*) obstacle, difficulty; (*Anat.*) spine.

épinette [epi'nɛt], *n.f.* *spinet; (*Bot.*) spruce.

épineux [epi'nø], *a.* (*fem.* **-euse**) thorny, prickly; (*fig.*) irritable; ticklish, intricate.

épingle [e'pɛ̃gl], *n.f.* pin; scarf pin, breast pin.

épinglé [epɛ̃'gle], *a.* pinned; corded, terry.—*n.m.* terry velvet.

épingler [epɛ̃'gle], *v.t.* to pin.

épinglier [epɛ̃'glje], *n.m.* pin tray; (*fem.* **-ière**) pin maker.

épinière [epi'njɛ:r], *a.* (*Anat.*) spinal.

Épiphanie [epifa'ni], *n.f.* Epiphany.

épique [e'pik], *a.* epic(al).

épiscopal [episko'pal], *a.* (*m.pl.* **-aux**) episcopal.

épiscopalien [episkopa'ljɛ̃], *a.* and *n.m.* (*fem.* **-enne**) episcopalian.

épiscopat [episko'pa], *n.m.* episcopate, episcopacy.

épisode [epi'zod], *n.m.* episode.

épistolaire [episto'lɛ:r], *a.* epistolary.

épitaphe [epi'taf], *n.f.* epitaph.

épithète [epi'tɛt], *n.f.* epithet.

épitomé [epito'me], *n.m.* epitome, abridgment.

épître [e'pi:tr], *n.f.* epistle, letter, missive.

éploré [eplo're], *a.* in tears, distressed.

épluchage [eply'ʃa:3], *n.m.* cleaning; picking; peeling.

épluchement [eplyʃ'mã], *n.m.* cleaning; picking; peeling.

éplucher [eply'ʃe], *v.t.* to pick; to clean; to peel; (*fig.*) to sift.

éplucheur [eply'ʃœ:r], *n.m.* (*fem.* **-euse**) picker; fault-finder, hair-splitter.

épluchures [eply'ʃy:r], *n.f. pl.* parings, peelings.

épointé [epwɛ̃'te], *a.* blunt (*pencil, needle*).

épointement [epwɛ̃t'mã], *n.m.* bluntness.

épointer [epwɛ̃'te], *v.t.* to break the point off, to blunt. **s'épointer**, *v.r.* to have its point broken off.

éponge [e'pɔ̃:3], *n.f.* sponge.

épongeage [epɔ̃'3a:3], *n.m.* sponging.

éponger [epɔ̃'3e], *v.t.* (*conjug. like* MANGER) to sponge.

épopée [epo'pe], *n.f.* epic.

époque [e'pok], *n.f.* epoch, period, era; time.

époumoner [epumo'ne], *v.t.* to tire the lungs of, to exhaust. **s'époumoner**, *v.r.* to tire one's lungs; (*fig.*) to shout oneself hoarse.

épouse [e'pu:z], *n.f.* spouse, bride, wife.

épouser [epu'ze], *v.t.* to marry, to wed; (*fig.*) to take up. **s'épouser**, *v.r.* to marry (*each other*).

époussetage [epus'ta:ʒ], *n.m.* dusting.
épousseter [epus'te], *v.t.* (*conjug. like* AP-PELER) to dust.
époussette [epu'sɛt], *n.f.* dusting brush, duster.
épouvantable [epuvɑ̃'tabl], *a.* frightful, dreadful, horrible, appalling.
épouvantablement [epuvɑ̃tablə'mɑ̃], *adv.* frightfully; dreadfully.
épouvantail [epuvɑ̃'ta:j], *n.m.* scarecrow; (*fig.*) bugbear.
épouvante [epu'vɑ̃:t], *n.f.* terror, fright; dismay.
épouvanter [epuvɑ̃'te], *v.t.* to terrify, to frighten. **s'épouvanter**, *v.r.* to be frightened *or* terrified.
époux [e'pu], *n.m.* husband, bridegroom; (*pl.*) married couple.
éprendre (s') [se'prɑ̃:dr], *v.r. irr.* (*conjug. like* PRENDRE) to fall in love (*de*).
épreuve [e'prœ:v], *n.f.* proof, test; ordeal; examination; (*Print.*) proof sheet; (*Phot.*) print.
épris [e'pri], *a.* in love, taken with.
éprouvé [epru've], *a.* tried, tested; stricken with misfortune.
éprouver [epru've], *v.t.* to try, to test; to put to the proof; (*fig.*) to feel, to experience.
éprouvette [epru'vɛt], *n.f.* gauge; test tube; eprouvette (*for testing gunpowder*); (*Surg.*) probe.
épuisable [epʮi'zabl], *a.* exhaustible.
épuisement [epʮiz'mɑ̃], *n.m.* exhaustion, draining; enervation.
épuiser [epʮi'ze], *v.t.* to exhaust, to drain; to use up; to tire out, to wear out. **s'épuiser**, *v.r.* to be exhausted; to use up one's strength.
épulsette [epʮi'zɛt], *n.f.* landing-net; scoop.
épurateur [epyra'tœ:r], *a.* (*fem.* -trice) purifying.—*n.m.* purifier.
épuratif [epyra'tif], *a.* (*fem.* -tive) purifying, refining.
épuration [epyra'sjɔ̃], *n.f.* purification; refining; (*Polit.*) purge.
épuratoire [epyra'twa:r], *a.* purifying.
épurement [epyr'mɑ̃], *n.m.* purifying.
épurer [epy're], *v.t.* to purify; to clarify; to refine; to purge. **s'épurer**, *v.r.* to be purified, to become pure.
équanime [ekwa'nim], *a.* even-tempered.
équanimité [ekwanimi'te], *n.f.* equanimity.
équarrir [eka'ri:r], *v.t.* to square; to cut up (*a carcass*).
équarrissage [ekari'sa:ʒ], **équarrissement** [ekaris'mɑ̃], *n.m.* squaring; squareness; flaying and cutting up (*of horses etc.*).
équarrisseur [ekari'sœ:r], *n.m.* knacker.
Équateur [ekwa'tœ:r], **l'**, *m.* Ecuador.
équateur [ekwa'tœ:r], *n.m.* equator.
équation [ekwa'sjɔ̃], *n.f.* equation.
équatorial [ekwatɔ'rjal], *a.* (*m. pl.* -aux) equatorial.
équatorien [ekwatɔ'rjɛ̃], *a.* (*fem.* -enne) Ecuadorean.—*n.m.* (**Équatorien**, *fem.* -enne) Ecuadorean (*person*).
équerre [e'kɛ:r], *n.f.* square, set-square.
équerrer [eke're], *v.t.* to square, to bevel.
équestre [e'kɛstr], *a.* equestrian.

équilibre [eki'libr], *n.m.* equilibrium, poise, balance; (*Hist.*) balance of power.
équilibrer [ekili'bre], *v.t.* to equilibrate, to balance.
équilibriste [ekili'brist], *n.* tight-rope walker, acrobat.
équin [e'kɛ̃], *a.* equine; *pied équin*, club foot.
équinoxe [eki'nɔks], *n.m.* equinox.
équinoxial [ekinɔk'sjal], *a.* (*m. pl.* -aux) equinoctial.
équipage [eki'pa:ʒ], *n.m.* equipage; carriage; dress; gear, tackle; personnel, crew.
équipe [e'kip], *n.f.* train of boats; gang (*of workmen etc.*); team (*of sportmen*).
équipement [ekip'mɑ̃], *n.m.* outfit, fitting out; equipment.
équiper [eki'pe], *v.t.* to equip, to fit out; to furnish; to man. **s'équiper**, *v.r.* to fit oneself out; to rig oneself out.
équitable [eki'tabl], *a.* equitable, just, fair.
équitablement [ekitablə'mɑ̃], *adv.* equitably, justly, fairly.
équitation [ekita'sjɔ̃], *n.f.* horsemanship, riding.
équité [eki'te], *n.f.* equity, fairness.
équivalence [ekiva'lɑ̃:s], *n.f.* equivalence.
équivalent [ekiva'lɑ̃], *a.* equivalent; tantamount (to).—*n.m.* equivalent.
équivaloir [ekiva'lwa:r], *v.i. irr.* (*conjug. like* VALOIR) to be equivalent, to be tantamount (*à*).
équivoque [eki'vɔk], *a.* equivocal, ambiguous; doubtful.—*n.f.* equivocation, ambiguity; evasion.
équivoquer [ekivɔ'ke], *v.t.* to equivocate, to speak ambiguously, to quibble.
érable [e'rabl], *n.m.* maple, maple tree.
éradication [eradika'sjɔ̃], *n.f.* eradication.
érafler [era'fle], *v.t.* to scratch slightly, to graze.
éraflure [era'fly:r], *n.f.* slight scratch, graze.
éraillé [era'je], *a.* frayed; wrinkled; bloodshot (*of the eyes*); raucous, hoarse (*of the voice*).
éraillement [eraj'mɑ̃], *n.m.* eversion of the eyelids; fraying; huskiness.
érailler [era'je], *v.t.* to unravel; to fray. **s'érailler**, *v.r.* to fray; to become bloodshot (*of the eyes*); to become husky (*of the voice*).
éraillure [era'jy:r], *n.f.* fret, fraying; scratch.
ère [ɛ:r], *n.f.* era, epoch.
érection [erɛk'sjɔ̃], *n.f.* erection, erecting.
éreinter [erɛ̃'te], *v.t.* to break the back (*of*); to tire out; to beat unmercifully; (*fig.*) to slate, to lash (*satire etc.*). **s'éreinter**, *v.r.* to break one's back, to tire oneself out, to drudge.
érésipèle [ERYSIPÈLE].
ergot [ɛr'go], *n.m.* spur (*of certain birds etc.*); catch, stop (*of machine*).
ergotage [ɛrgɔ'ta:ʒ], **ergotement** [ɛrgɔt'mɑ̃] *n.m.*, **ergoterie** [ɛrgɔ'tri], *n.f.* cavilling, quibbling.
ergoter [ɛrgɔ'te], *v.i.* (*colloq.*) to cavil; to wrangle.
ergoteur [ɛrgɔ'tœ:r], *a.* (*fem.* -euse) cavilling.—*n.m.* (*fem.* -euse) caviller, quibbler.
ériger [eri'ʒe], *v.t.* (*conjug. like* MANGER) to erect, to raise, to rear; to set up; to exalt. **s'ériger**, *v.r.* to set up for, to pose (*en*); to be erected.
ermitage [ɛrmi'ta:ʒ], *n.m.* hermitage.

ermite

ermite [ɛr'mit], *n.* hermit, recluse.
éroder [ero'de], *v.t.* to erode.
érosif [ero'zif], *a.* (*fem.* **-sive**) erosive.
érosion [ero'zjõ], *n.f.* erosion.
érotique [ero'tik], *a.* erotic.
errant [ɛ'rã], *a.* wandering, roving, errant; erring; *chevalier errant*, knight errant.
erratique [ɛra'tik], *a.* erratic.
erre [ɛːr], *n.f.* course, way; (*pl.*) track (*of a stag etc.*).
errements [ɛr'mã], *n.m.* (*used only in pl.*) manner, way; vagaries, follies.
errer [ɛ're], *v.i.* to wander, to stray; to range; to rove; to err, to go astray.
erreur [ɛ'rœːr], *n.f.* error, mistake.
erroné [ero'ne], *a.* erroneous, mistaken, false.
erronément [erone'mã], *adv.* erroneously.
érudit [ery'di], *a.* erudite, learned.—*n.m.* (*fem.* **-e**) scholar, learned person.
érudition [erydi'sjõ], *n.f.* erudition, scholarship.
éruptif [eryp'tif], *a.* (*fem.* **-tive**) eruptive.
éruption [eryp'sjõ], *n.f.* eruption; cutting (*of teeth*); breaking out (*of a rash*).
érysipèle [erizi'pɛl], **érésipèle** [erezi'pɛl], *n.m.* erysipelas.
ès [ɛs], *contraction of* EN (I) LES (*survives only in a few set expressions*) in, of; *licencié ès lettres*, bachelor of arts.
escabeau [ɛska'bo], *n.m.* (*pl.* **-eaux**) stool; step ladder.
escabelle [ɛska'bɛl], *n.f.* three-legged stool.
escadre [ɛs'ka:dr], *n.f.* (*Naut.*) squadron; (*Av.*) wing.
escadrille [ɛska'dri:j], *n.f.* small squadron, flotilla.
escadron [ɛska'drõ], *n.m.* squadron (*of horse*).
escalade [ɛska'lad], *n.f.* scaling (*a wall*); rock-climbing; escalation (*of a war etc.*).
escalader [ɛskala'de], *v.t.* to scale, to climb over.
escale [ɛs'kal], *n.f.* port of call, stopping place.
escalier [ɛska'lje], *n.m.* staircase, stairs, steps; *escalier roulant*, escalator.
escalope [ɛska'lɔp], *n.f.* escalope, collop (*of veal*); steak (*of fish*).
escamotable [ɛskamɔ'tabl], *a.* which can be tucked away; (*Av.*) *train escamotable*, retractable landing-gear.
escamotage [ɛskamɔ'ta:3], *n.m.* juggling, sleight of hand; (*fig.*) filching.
escamoter [ɛskamɔ'te], *v.t.* to conjure away; to pilfer, to make away with; (*Av.*) to retract (*the undercarriage*).
escamoteur [ɛskamɔ'tœːr], *n.m.* (*fem.* **-euse**) juggler, conjurer; pilferer, pickpocket.
escapade [ɛska'pad], *n.f.* escapade, prank.
escarbille [ɛskar'bi:j], *n.f.* cinder (*of coal*).
escarboucle [ɛskar'bukl], *n.f.* carbuncle (*precious stone*).
escargot [ɛskar'go], *n.m.* snail (*edible*).
escarmouche [ɛskar'muʃ], *n.f.* skirmish; brush; (*fig.*) bickering.
escarmoucher [ɛskarmu'ʃe], *v.i.* to skirmish; (*fig.*) to bicker.
escarpé [ɛskar'pe], *a.* scarped, steep, precipitous; (*fig.*) difficult.
escarpement [ɛskarpə'mã], *n.m.* escarpment; steep face or slope.
escarpin [ɛskar'pɛ̃], *n.m.* pump, dancing shoe.

escarpolette [ɛskarpɔ'lɛt], *n.f.* (*child's*) swing.
escarre or **eschare** [ɛs'ka:r], *n.f.* scab.
escient [ɛ'sjã], *n.m.* used only in *à bon escient*, wittingly, knowingly.
esclaffer (s') [sɛskla'fe], *v.r.* to laugh noisily, to guffaw.
esclandre [ɛs'klã:dr]. *n.m.* scandal, exposure, scene.
esclavage [ɛskla'va:3], *n.m.* slavery; bondage.
esclave [ɛs'kla:v], *a.* slavish.—*n.* slave, bondsman; drudge.
escogriffe [ɛskɔ'grif], *n.m.* (*colloq.*) tall, lanky, ungainly fellow.
escompte [ɛs'kõ:t], *n.m.* discount, rebate.
escompter [ɛskõ'te], *v.t.* to discount; (*fig.*) to anticipate; *escompter un billet*, to cash a bill.
escorte [ɛs'kort], *n.f.* escort; (*Navy*) convoy; (*fig.*) retinue, attendants.
escorter [ɛskɔr'te], *v.t.* to escort, to accompany, to attend.
escorteur [ɛskɔr'tœːr], *n.m.* escort vessel.
escouade [ɛs'kwad], *n.f.* squad, small party (*of soldiers*); gang (*of workmen*).
escrime [ɛs'krim], *n.f.* fencing.
escrimer [ɛskri'me], *v.i.* to fence; (*fig.*) to have a trial of skill etc. **s'escrimer**, *v.r.* (*colloq.*) to strive; to try hard.
escrimeur [ɛskri'mœːr], *n.m.* (*fem.* **-euse**) fencer.
escroc [ɛs'kro], *n.m.* sharper, swindler.
escroquer [ɛskrɔ'ke], *v.t.* to swindle out of; to cheat.
escroquerie [ɛskrɔ'kri], *n.f.* swindling.
espace [ɛs'pa:s], *n.m.* space, room; duration.—*n.f.* (*Print.*) space.
espacement [ɛspas'mã], *n.m.* interval; (*Print.*) spacing.
espacer [ɛspa'se], *v.t.* (*conjug. like* COMMENCER) to leave a space between; to separate. **s'espacer**, *v.r.* to become less frequent *or* numerous.
espadrille [ɛspa'dri:j], *n.f.* canvas shoe with cord soles.
Espagne [ɛs'paɲ], **l'**, *f.* Spain.
espagnol [ɛspa'ɲɔl], *a.* Spanish.—*n.m.* Spanish (*language*); (**Espagnol**, *fem.* **-ole**) Spaniard.
espagnolette [ɛspaɲɔ'lɛt], *n.f.* bolt of French window.
espalier [ɛspa'lje], *n.m.* espalier (*tree or wall*).
espèce [ɛs'pɛs], *n.f.* species; sort, nature; (*pl.*) ready money, hard cash.
espérance [ɛspe'rã:s], *n.f.* hope, trust, expectation.
espéranto [ɛspe'rã'to], *n.m.* Esperanto.
espérer [ɛspe're], *v.t.* (*conjug. like* CÉDER) to hope for; to expect; to trust.—*v.i.* to hope; to put one's trust in.
espiègle [ɛs'pjɛgl], *a.* and *n.* mischievous, roguish (*person*).
espièglerie [ɛspjɛgla'ri], *n.f.* frolic, roguish trick, prank.
espion [ɛs'pjõ], *n.m.* (*fem.* **-onne**) spy.
espionnage [ɛspjɔ'na:3], *n.m.* espionage.
espionner [ɛspjɔ'ne], *v.t.* to spy, to pry into.
esplanade [ɛspla'nad], *n.f.* esplanade, parade.
espoir [ɛs'pwaːr], *n.m.* hope.
esprit [ɛs'pri], *n.m.* spirit, ghost; soul; mind, sense, intellect; wit; humor, character.
esquif [ɛs'kif], *n.m.* small boat.
esquille [ɛs'ki:j], *n.f.* splinter (*of a bone*).

142

esquimau [ɛski'mo], a. (pl. -aux) and n. (Esquimau or Eskimo) Eskimo.

esquinancie [ɛskinã'si], **cynancie** [sinã'si], n.f. quinsy.

esquisse [ɛs'kis], n.f. sketch, outline, rough draft or plan.

esquisser [ɛski'se], v.t. to sketch, to outline.

esquiver [ɛski've], v.t. to avoid, to elude; to duck; to dodge. **s'esquiver**, v.r. to escape; to give the slip.

essai [ɛ'sɛ], n.m. trial; attempt; experiment, testing; (Rugby) try; (Lit.) essay.

essaim [ɛ'sɛ̃], n.m. swarm; (fig.) crowd, host.

essaimer [ɛsɛ'me], v.i. to swarm; to hive off.

essarter [ɛsar'te], v.t. to clear, to grub (land).

essayage [ɛsɛ'ja:3], n.m. trying, testing; trying-on (of clothes).

essayer [ɛsɛ'je], v.t. (conjug. like PAYER) to try; to try on; to attempt; to assay.—v.i. to try, to make an attempt. **s'essayer**, v.r. to try one's strength or skill.

essayeur [ɛsɛ'jœ:r], n.m. (fem. -euse) assayer; (cloth) fitter.

essayiste [ɛsɛ'jist], n. essayist.

essence [ɛ'sã:s], n.f. essence; gasoline; attar (of roses).

essentiel [ɛsã'sjɛl], a. (fem. -elle) essential, material.—n.m. essential, main point.

essentiellement [ɛsãsjɛl'mã], adv. essentially, absolutely, above all.

essieu [ɛ'sjø], n.m. (pl. -eux) axle-tree; spindle; pin (of a block); écartement des essieux, wheel base (motor); essieu moteur, driving-shaft.

essor [ɛ'sɔ:r], n.m. flight, soaring; (fig.) impulse, vigor.

essorer [ɛsɔ're], v.t. to hang in the air to dry, to wring out (washing).

essoreuse [ɛsɔ'rø:z], n.f. wringer, mangle.

essoriller [ɛsɔri'je], v.t. to cut the ears (of a dog etc.); to crop.

essoufflement [ɛsuflə'mã], n.m. panting, breathlessness.

essouffler [ɛsu'fle], v.t. to wind (horses etc.). **s'essouffler**, v.r. to be out of breath; to be winded.

essuie-glaces [ɛsɥi'glas], n.m. pl. windshield wipers.

essuie-main(s) [ɛsɥi'mɛ̃], n.m. inv. hand towel.

essuie-pieds [ɛsɥi'pje], n.m. inv. doormat.

essuyage [ɛsɥi'ja:3], n.m. wiping, drying.

essuyer [ɛsɥi'je], v.t. (conjug. like EMPLOYER) to wipe; to dry; to sustain, to endure, to undergo. **s'essuyer**, v.r. to dry oneself; **s'essuyer les mains, la figure etc.**, to dry one's hands, one's face etc.

est [ɛst], n.m. east.

estacade [ɛsta'kad], n.f. breakwater; pier or boom made of timbers.

estafette [ɛsta'fɛt], n.f. courier, express messenger; dispatch rider.

estafilade [ɛstafi'lad], n.f. cut, gash; slash, rent.

estaminet [ɛstami'nɛ], n.m. coffee house or room; tavern.

estampage [ɛstã'pa:3], n.m. stamping (of metal etc.).

estampe [ɛs'tã:p], n.f. print, engraving.

estamper [ɛstã'pe], v.t. to stamp, to punch.

estampeur [ɛstã'pœ:r], a. (fem. -euse) stamp-

ing.—n.m. (fem. -euse) stamper.—n.f. (-euse) stamping machine.

estampillage [ɛstãpi'ja:3], n.m. stamping, marking.

estampille [ɛstã'pi:j], n.f. stamp, mark, trade mark.

estampiller [ɛstãpi'je], v.t. to stamp, to mark.

esthétique [ɛste'tik], a. esthetic.—n.f. esthetics.

Esthonie [ɛstɔ'ni], l', f. Estonia.

esthonien [ɛstɔ'njɛ̃], a. (fem. -enne) Estonian.—n.m. Estonian (language); (Esthonien, fem. -enne) Estonian (person).

estimable [ɛsti'mabl], a. estimable.

estimateur [ɛstima'tœ:r], n.m. (fem. -trice) appraiser, valuer.

estimation [ɛstima'sjɔ̃], n.f. estimation, appraising, valuation, estimate.

estime [ɛs'tim], n.f. esteem, regard, estimation; (Naut.) reckoning.

estimer [ɛsti'me], v.t. to estimate, to value, to assess; to esteem; to deem. **s'estimer**, v.r. to esteem oneself; to deem oneself.

estival [ɛsti'val], a. (m. pl. -aux) estival, summer (plant, resort etc.).

estivant [ɛsti'vã], n.m. (fem. -e) summer visitor.

estomac [ɛstɔ'ma], n.m. stomach; (fig.) pluck.

estompage [ɛstɔ̃'pa:3], n.m. (Drawing) stumping.

estompe [ɛs'tɔ̃:p], n.f. (Drawing) stump.

estomper [ɛstɔ̃'pe], v.t. (Drawing) to stump; to shade off, to blur. **s'estomper**, v.r. to become blurred.

Estonie [ESTHONIE].

estonien [ESTHONIEN].

estrade [ɛs'trad], n.f. platform, stand, stage.

estragon [ɛstra'gɔ̃], n.m. (Bot.) tarragon.

estropié [ɛstrɔ'pje], a. crippled, lame, disabled.—n.m. (fem. -ée) cripple.

estropier [ɛstrɔ'pje], v.t. to cripple, to maim, to disable; (fig.) to distort, to mangle.

estuaire [ɛs'tɥɛ:r], n.m. estuary.

esturgeon [ɛstyr'3ɔ̃], n.m. sturgeon.

et [e], conj. and.

étable [e'tabl], n.f. shed (for oxen, sheep, goats etc.); stall; pigsty, sty.

établi [eta'bli], n.m. bench (tailor's etc.).

établir [eta'bli:r], v.t. to fix, to erect, to set up; to establish, to found; to assert. **s'établir**, v.r. to establish oneself; to take up one's residence; to settle down; to set up in business.

établissement [etablis'mã], n.m. establishment, setting up; placing, erecting; proving; imposition (of taxes).

étage [e'ta:3], n.m. storey, floor, flight (of stairs); (fig.) stage; tier; (Geol., Mining) layer, stratum.

étager [eta'3e], v.t. (conjug. like MANGER) to dispose in tiers. **s'étager**, v.r. to rise tier upon tier.

étagère [eta'3ɛ:r], n.f. whatnot, set of shelves, shelf.

étai [e'tɛ], n.m. stay, shore, prop, strut.

étaiement [ÉTAYAGE].

étain [e'tɛ̃], n.m. tin; pewter.

étal [e'tal], n.m. (pl. -aux or -als) butcher's stall, butcher's shop.

étalage [eta'la:3], n.m. laying out of goods for sale; goods exposed for sale; shop window, frontage; (fig.) showing off.

143

étalager [etala'ʒe], *v.t.* (*conjug. like* MANGER) to display (*goods*) for sale.

étalagiste [etala'ʒist], *n.* stall keeper; window dresser.

étale [e'tal], *a.* slack (*of water or wind*).

étalement [etal'mã], *n.m.* display, parade; staggering (*of holidays*).

étaler [eta'le], *v.t.* to expose for sale; to spread out; to display; (*Naut.*) to stem (*current*); to weather (*gale*). **s'étaler**, *v.r.* to stretch oneself out, to sprawl; to show off.

étalon (1) [eta'lɔ̃], *n.m.* stallion.

étalon (2) [eta'lɔ̃], *n.m.* standard (*of weights and measures*).

étalonnage [etalɔ'naːʒ], **étalonnement** [etalɔn'mã], *n.m.* standardization; stamping (*of weights etc.*); gauging.

étalonner [etalɔ'ne], *v.t.* to standardize; to gauge.

étalonneur [etalɔ'nœːr], *n.m.* inspector of weights and measures.

étamage [eta'maːʒ], *n.m.* tinning; quicksilvering (*of glass*).

étamer [eta'me], *v.t.* to tin; to quicksilver.

étameur [eta'mœːr], *n.m.* tinner; silverer (*of mirrors*).

étamine (1) [eta'min], *n.f.* sieve, strainer; (*Naut.*) bunting.

étamine (2) [eta'min], *n.f.* (*Bot.*) stamen.

étampe [e'tãːp], *n.f.* die; punch.

étamper [etã'pe], *v.t.* to punch (*horse-shoes etc.*); to stamp (*sheet metal etc.*).

étanche [e'tãːʃ], *a.* water-tight, air-tight etc.

étanchement [etãʃ'mã], *n.m.* stanching, stopping; slaking; quenching.

étancher [etã'ʃe], *v.t.* to stanch, to stop; to render water-tight; (*fig.*) to quench.

étang [e'tã], *n.m.* pond, mere, pool.

étape [e'tap], *n.f.* halting-place, stage, station; day's march.

état [e'ta], *n.m.* state, case, condition; circumstance, predicament; statement; list, estimate; profession.

étatique [eta'tik], *a.* nationalized.

étatiser [etati'ze], *v.t.* to nationalize.

étatisme [eta'tism], *n.m.* State socialism, State control, nationalization.

état-major [etama'ʒɔːr], *n.m.* (*pl.* **états-majors**) (*Mil.*) staff, general staff.

étau [e'to], *n.m.* (*pl.* **-aux**) (*Tech.*) vise.

étayage [etɛ'jaːʒ], **étayement** [etɛj'mã], **étaiement** [etɛ'mã], *n.m.* staying, shoring, supporting.

étayer [etɛ'je], *v.t.* (*conjug. like* PAYER) to stay, to shore; to support (*a theory etc.*).

été [e'te], *n.m.* summer; (C) *Été des Sauvages*, Indian summer.

éteignoir [etɛ'nwaːr], *n.m.* extinguisher (*for candles*).

éteindre [e'tɛ̃ːdr], *v.t. irr.* (*conjug. like* CRAINDRE) to put out, to extinguish; to appease; to destroy. **s'éteindre**, *v.r.* to be extinguished, to be put out; to die out; to become extinct.

éteint [e'tɛ̃], *a.* extinguished; extinct; (*fig.*) dull.

étendard [etã'daːr], *n.m.* standard, banner, flag.

étendre [e'tãːdr], *v.t.* to extend, to spread out; to stretch; to dilute; to prolong; to lay (down) (*a person*). **s'étendre**, *v.r.* to stretch oneself out; to reach, to extend; to dwell on.

étendu [etã'dy], *a.* outstretched, outspread; extensive; diluted.

étendue [etã'dy], *n.f.* extent; scope, length.

éternel [etɛr'nɛl], *a.* (*fem.* **-elle**) eternal, everlasting.—*n.m.* (**l'Éternel**) God, the Eternal.

éternellement [etɛrnɛl'mã], *adv.* eternally.

éterniser [etɛrni'ze], *v.t.* to perpetuate. **s'éterniser**, *v.r.* to be perpetuated, to last forever.

éternité [etɛrni'te], *n.f.* eternity.

éternuement or **éternûment** [etɛrny'mã], *n.m.* sneezing, sneeze.

éternuer [etɛr'nɥe], *v.i.* to sneeze.

éternueur [etɛr'nɥœːr], *n.m.* (*fem.* **-euse**) sneezer.

éteule [e'tøːl], *n.f.* stubble.

éther [e'teːr], *n.m.* ether.

éthéré [ete're], *a.* ethereal.

éthériser [eteri'ze], *v.t.* to etherize.

Éthiopie [etjɔ'pi], **l'**, *f.* Ethiopia.

Éthiopien [etjɔ'pjɛ̃], *a.* (*fem.* **-enne**) Ethiopian.—*n.m.* (**Éthiopien**, *fem.* **-enne**) Ethiopian (*person*).

éthique [e'tik], *a.* ethic(al).—*n.f.* ethics, morals.

ethnique [et'nik], *a.* ethnic(al).

ethnographe [etnɔ'graf], *n.* ethnographer.

ethnographie [etnɔgra'fi], *n.f.* ethnography.

ethnographique [etnɔgra'fik], *a.* ethnographic.

ethnologie [etnɔlɔ'ʒi], *n.f.* ethnology.

ethnologique [etnɔlɔ'ʒik], *a.* ethnological.

ethnologue [etnɔ'lɔg], **ethnologiste** [etnɔlɔ'ʒist], *n.* ethnologist.

éthologie [etɔlɔ'ʒi], *n.f.* ethology.

éthyle [e'tiːl], *n.m.* ethyl.

étiage [e'tjaːʒ], *n.m.* low-water mark; (*fig.*) level.

Étienne [e'tjɛn], *m.* Stephen.

étincelant [etɛ̃s'lã], *a.* sparkling, glittering, glistening.

étinceler [etɛ̃s'le], *v.i.* (*conjug. like* APPELER) to sparkle, to flash; to gleam, to glitter.

étincelle [etɛ̃'sɛl], *n.f.* spark, flash; brilliance.

étincellement [etɛ̃sɛl'mã], *n.m.* sparkling, twinkling, scintillation.

étiolement [etjɔl'mã], *n.m.* etiolation, sickliness (*of plants etc.*); paleness, emaciation.

étioler [etjɔ'le], *v.t.* to etiolate (*plants*); (*fig.*) to enervate. **s'étioler**, *v.r.* to become etiolated (*of plants*); (*fig.*) to waste away.

étique [e'tik], *a.* consumptive; emaciated.

étiqueter [etik'te], *v.t.* (*conjug. like* APPELER) to label, to ticket.

étiquette [eti'kɛt], *n.f.* ticket, label, tag; etiquette.

étirage [eti'raːʒ], *n.m.* stretching.

étirer [eti're], *v.t.* to stretch; to lengthen. **s'étirer**, *v.r.* to stretch one's limbs.

étisie [eti'zi], *n.f.* consumption.

étoffe [e'tɔf], *n.f.* material; stuff, cloth; quality, worth; (C) *étoffe du pays*, homespun.

étoffé [etɔ'fe], *a.* stuffed full; upholstered; stout, substantial.

étoffer [etɔ'fe], *v.t.* to stuff; to upholster.

étoile [e'twal], *n.f.* star; (*fig.*) fate, destiny; blaze (*on horse's head*); star (*crack in glass*).

étoilé [etwa'le], *a.* starry; star-shaped.

étoiler [etwa'le], *v.t.* to star, to stud with stars; to crack (*of glass*). **s'étoiler**, *v.r.* to star, to crack (*of glass*).

étole [e'tɔl], *n.f.* stole.

étonnamment [etɔna'mɑ̃], *adv.* astonishingly, wonderfully, amazingly.

étonnant [etɔ'nɑ̃], *a.* astonishing, wonderful, marvellous.

étonnement [etɔn'mɑ̃], *n.m.* astonishment, amazement; wonder; crack, fissure.

étonner [etɔ'ne], *v.t.* to astonish, to amaze, to astound; to shock; to cause to crack. **s'étonner**, *v.r.* to be astonished, to wonder; to become cracked.

étouffant [etu'fɑ̃], *a.* suffocating, sultry, close.

étouffement [etuf'mɑ̃], *n.m.* suffocation.

étouffer [etu'fe], *v.t.* to suffocate, to choke, to smother; (*fig.*) to stifle, to hush up; to deaden (*sound etc.*).—*v.i.* to choke, to suffocate. **s'étouffer**, *v.r.* to be choking, to be suffocated; to swelter.

étoupe [e'tup], *n.f.* tow, oakum.

étouper [etu'pe], *v.t.* to stop (*with tow or oakum*); to caulk.

étoupiller [etupi'je], *v.t.* to prime (*a friction tube*).

étourderie [eturdə'ri], *n.f.* heedlessness, thoughtlessness; blunder.

étourdi [etur'di], *a.* giddy, thoughtless, heedless.—*n.m.* (*fem.* -e) madcap.

étourdiment [eturdi'mɑ̃], *adv.* heedlessly, thoughtlessly.

étourdir [etur'di:r], *v.t.* to stun, to deafen, to make giddy; to din; to astound. **s'étourdir**, *v.r.* to divert one's thoughts; to try to forget something.

étourdissant [eturdi'sɑ̃], *a.* deafening; stunning, astounding.

étourdissement [eturdis'mɑ̃], *n.m.* dizziness, giddiness; stupefaction; shock.

étourneau [etur'no], *n.m.* (*pl.* -eaux) starling; (*fig.*) giddy fellow.

étrange [e'trɑ̃:ʒ], *a.* strange, odd, queer.

étrangement [etrɑ̃ʒ'mɑ̃], *adv.* strangely, queerly, extraordinarily.

étranger [etrɑ̃'ʒe], *a.* (*fem.* -ère) foreign; strange; unknown; irrelevant.—*n.m.* (*fem.* -ère) foreigner, alien; stranger; *à l'étranger*, abroad.

étrangeté [etrɑ̃ʒ'te], *n.f.* strangeness, oddness.

étranglé [etrɑ̃'gle], *a.* strangled; restricted, scanty, too narrow.

étranglement [etrɑ̃glə'mɑ̃], *n.m.* strangling; garotting; constriction.

étrangler [etrɑ̃'gle], *v.t.* to strangle, to choke, to stifle; to constrict, to confine; (*fig.*) to smother, to suppress.—*v.i.* to be choked, to be short of breath. **s'étrangler**, *v.r.* to strangle oneself; to choke.

étrangleur [etrɑ̃'glœ:r], *n.m.* (*fem.* -euse) strangler; garotter.

être [ɛ:tr], *v.i. irr.* to be, to exist; to belong (*à*); to stand; to take part (*à*); to be a member (*de*).—*n.m.* being, existence; creature.

étreindre [e'trɛ̃:dr], *v.t. irr.* (*conjug. like* CRAINDRE) to embrace, to clasp, to grip.

étreinte [e'trɛ̃:t], *n.f.* embrace, hug; grip.

étrenne [e'trɛn], *n.f.* New Year's gift (*usually in pl.*); gift, present.

étrenner [etre'ne], *v.t.* to give a New Year's gift; to handsel; to try *or* put on for the first time; to buy the first lot from.

étrier [etri'e], *n.m.* stirrup; (*Surg.*) caliper.

étrille [e'tri:j], *n.f.* curry-comb.

étriller [etri'je], *v.t.* to curry, to comb (*a horse*); (*fig.*) to fleece; to drub.

étriper [etri'pe], *v.t.* to gut (*an animal*).

étriqué [etri'ke], *a.* scanty, narrow, curtailed.

étriquer [etri'ke], *v.t.* to shorten, to curtail, to make too small.

étrivière [etri'vjɛ:r], *n.f.* stirrup leather.

étroit [e'trwa], *a.* narrow, tight, strait; limited; (*fig.*) strict, rigorous.

étroitement [etrwat'mɑ̃], *adv.* narrowly, tightly; intimately, closely.

étroitesse [etrwa'tes], *n.f.* narrowness, straitness; tightness, closeness.

Étrurie [etry'ri], l', *f.* Etruria.

étrusque [e'trysk], *a.* Etruscan.—*n.m.* Etruscan (*language*).—*n.* (**Étrusque**) Etruscan (*person*).

étude [e'tyd], *n.f.* study; room for study; time of preparation; office, practice (*of attorneys*); essay, article.

étudiant [ety'djɑ̃], *n.m.* (*fem.* -e) student; undergraduate.

étudié [ety'dje], *a.* studied; affected.

étudier [ety'dje], *v.t.* to study, to learn; to practice (*music*); to rehearse (*a play*); to observe.—*v.i.* to study, to learn; to practice (*music*). **s'étudier**, *v.r.* to make (*it*) one's study, to school oneself.

étui [e'tɥi], *n.m.* case, box, sheath.

étuve [e'ty:v], *n.f.* sweating room; stove; drying room; incubator.

étuvée [ety've], *n.f.* stew.

étuver [ety've], *v.t.* to stew; (*Med.*) to bathe, to foment.

étymologie [etimɔlɔ'ʒi], *n.f.* etymology.

étymologique [etimɔlɔ'ʒik], *a.* etymological.

étymologiste [etimɔlɔ'ʒist], *n.* etymologist.

eucharistie [økaris'ti], *n.f.* eucharist.

eucharistique [økaris'tik], *a.* eucharistic.

eugénique [øʒe'nik], *n.f.*, **eugénisme** [øʒe'nism], *n.m.* eugenics.

euh [ø], *int.* aha! oh! hum!

eunuque [ø'nyk], *n.m.* eunuch.

euphémique [øfe'mik], *a.* euphemistic.

euphémisme [øfe'mism], *n.m.* euphemism.

euphonie [øfɔ'ni], *n.f.* euphony.

euphonique [øfɔ'nik], *a.* euphonious.

Euphrate [ø'frat], l', *m.* the Euphrates.

euphuisme [øfy'ism], *n.m.* euphuism.

eurasien [øra'zjɛ̃], *a.* (*fem.* -enne) Eurasian. —*n.m.* (**Eurasien**, *fem.* -enne) Eurasian (*person*).

Euripide [øri'pid], *m.* Euripides.

Europe [ø'rɔp], *f.* (*Myth.*) Europa; *l'Europe*, (*Geog.*) Europe.

européaniser [øropeani'ze], *v.t.* to Europeanize.

européen [øropeɛ̃], *a.* (*fem.* -éenne) European.—*n.m.* (**Européen**, *fem.* -éenne) European (*person*).

euthanasie [øtana'zi], *n.f.* euthanasia.

eux [ø], *pron. pers. m. pl.* (*fem.* -elles) they; them.

évacuant [eva'kɥɑ̃], **évacuatif** [evakɥa'tif] (*fem.* -tive), *a.* and *n.m.* evacuant.

évacuation [evakɥa'sjɔ̃], *n.f.* evacuation; ejection.

évacué [eva'kɥe], *n.m.* (*fem.* -ée) evacuee.

évacuer [eva'kɥe], *v.t.* to evacuate; to throw off, to eject, to clear. **s'évacuer**, *v.r.* to discharge (*into*).

145

évadé [eva'de], *a.* and *n.m.* (*fem.* **-ée**) escaped (*person*); escapee.

évader (s') [seva'de], *v.r.* to escape; to get away or out of (*de*).

évaluable [eva'lyabl], *a.* appraisable.

évaluateur [evalya'tœ:r], *n.m.* (*fem.* **-trice**) valuer, appraiser.

évaluation [evalya'sjɔ̃], *n.f.* valuation, estimate.

évaluer [eva'lɥe], *v.t.* to value, to estimate, to appreciate.

évangélique [evãʒe'lik], *a.* evangelical.

évangéliser [evãʒeli'ze], *v.t.* to evangelize, to preach the Gospel to.

évangélisme [evãʒe'lism], *n.m.* evangelism.

évangéliste [evãʒe'list], *n.m.* evangelist.

évangile [evã'ʒil], *n.m.* Gospel.

évanouir (s') [seva'nwi:r], *v.r.* to faint, to swoon, to lose consciousness; (*fig.*) to vanish, to disappear.

évanouissement [evanwis'mã], *n.m.* swoon, fainting fit; disappearance; (*Math.*) cancelling out.

évaporatif [evapɔra'tif], *a.* (*fem.* **-tive**) evaporative.

évaporation [evapɔra'sjɔ̃], *n.f.* evaporation.

évaporé [evapɔ're], *a.* and *n.m.* (*fem.* **-ée**) frivolous, thoughtless (person).

évaporer [evapɔ're], *v.t.* to evaporate; (*fig.*) to exhale, to give vent to; *évaporer son chagrin*, to give vent to one's grief. **s'évaporer**, *v.r.* to evaporate; (*fig.*) to get giddy.

évasé [eva'ze], *a.* wide, bell-shaped; flared (*skirt*).

évasement [evaz'mã], *n.m.* width, widening (*at the mouth of a vase etc.*); flare (*of a skirt*).

évaser [eva'ze], *v.t.* to widen (*an opening*); to flare (*a skirt*). **s'évaser**, *v.r.* to be widened; to extend, to spread.

évasif [eva'zif], *a.* (*fem.* **-sive**) evasive.

évasion [eva'zjɔ̃], *n.f.* escape, flight; evasion; escapism.

évasivement [evaziv'mã], *adv.* evasively.

évêché [eve'ʃe], *n.m.* bishopric, episcopate, see; bishop's palace.

éveil [e've:j], *n.m.* awakening; warning, hint, alarm.

éveillé [eve'je], *a.* wide-awake; lively, sprightly; sharp, intelligent.

éveiller [eve'je], *v.t.* to awaken, to rouse; to excite, to enliven. **s'éveiller**, *v.r.* to wake up; to become animated.

événement [even'mã], *n.m.* event, occurrence; result; climax; emergency.

évent [e'vã], *n.m.* open air; vent hole, air hole; (*fig.*) flatness, vapidness.

éventail [evã'ta:j], *n.m.* (*pl.* **éventails**) fan; fan-light.

éventaire [evã'tɛ:r], *n.m.* flat tray (*carried by hawkers*).

éventé [evã'te], *a.* fanned, aired; flat, stale (*beer etc.*); (*fig.*) giddy, thoughtless.

éventer [evã'te], *v.t.* to fan; to winnow(*grain*); to air; to let (*wine etc.*) get flat; to get wind of; to divulge. **s'éventer**, *v.r.* to fan oneself; to evaporate; to become flat; to be divulged.

éventrer [evã'tre], *v.t.* to disembowel, to gut (*fish etc.*); to rip up, to break open. **s'éventrer**, *v.r.* to rip one's bowels open; to commit hara-kiri.

éventualité [evãtɥali'te], *n.f.* contingency, eventuality.

éventuel [evã'tɥɛl], *a.* (*fem.* **-elle**) contingent, possible.

éventuellement [evãtɥɛl'mã], *adv.* possibly; on occasion.

évêque [e'vɛ:k], *n.m.* bishop.

évertuer (s') [sever'tɥe], *v.r.* to strive, to exert *or* bestir oneself.

éviction [evik'sjɔ̃], *n.f.* eviction, ejectment.

évidemment [evida'mã], *adv.* evidently.

évidence [evi'dã:s], *n.f.* obviousness, clearness; conspicuousness.

évident [evi'dã], *a.* evident, plain, clear, obvious.

évider [evi'de], *v.t.* to hollow, to groove, to scoop out.

évier [e'vje], *n.m.* sink.

évincer [evɛ̃'se], *v.t.* (*conjug. like* COMMENCER) to evict, to eject, to oust.

éviscérer [evise're], *v.t.* (*conjug. like* CÉDER) to disembowel.

évitable [evi'tabl], *a.* avoidable.

évitement [evit'mã], *n.m.* (*Rail.*) siding, shunting; by-pass.

éviter [evi'te], *v.t.* to shun, to avoid, to evade; to abstain from.

évocateur [evɔka'tœ:r], *a.* (*fem.* **-trice**) evocative.

évocation [evɔka'sjɔ̃], *n.f.* evocation; recollection.

évolué [evɔ'lɥe], *a.* highly civilized.

évoluer [evɔ'lɥe], *v.i.* to evolve; to develop.

évolution [evɔly'sjɔ̃], *n.f.* evolution.

évoquer [evɔ'ke], *v.t.* to evoke; to allude to.

exacerbation [egzasɛrba'sjɔ̃], *n.f.* exacerbation.

exacerber [egzasɛr'be], *v.t.* to exacerbate.

exact [eg'zakt], *a.* exact, correct; punctual.

exactement [egzakta'mã], *adv.* exactly, accurately; punctually.

exaction [egzak'sjɔ̃], *n.f.* exaction, impost, extortion.

exactitude [egzakti'tyd], *n.f.* exactness, accuracy; punctuality.

exagération [egzaʒera'sjɔ̃], *n.f.* exaggeration; overrating.

exagérer [egzaʒe're], *v.t.* (*conjug. like* CÉDER) to exaggerate, to magnify.

exaltation [egzalta'sjɔ̃], *n.f.* exaltation; extolling.

exalté [egzal'te], *a.* exalted, feverish.—*n.m.* (*fem.* **-ée**) enthusiast, fanatic.

exalter [egzal'te], *v.t.* to exalt, to magnify; to excite, to inflame. **s'exalter**, *v.r.* to become excited, to be elated.

examen [egza'mɛ̃], *n.m.* examination; inspection; research.

examinateur [egzamina'tœ:r], *n.m.* (*fem.* **-trice**) examiner.

examiner [egzami'ne], *v.t.* to examine, to inspect, to survey; to discuss, to investigate. **s'examiner**, *v.r.* to examine *or* search oneself; to observe each other attentively.

exaspération [egzaspera'sjɔ̃], *n.f.* exasperation, aggravation.

exaspérer [egzaspe're], *v.t.* (*conjug. like* CÉDER) to exasperate, to incense, to inflame; to aggravate (*pain etc.*). **s'exaspérer**, *v.r.* to become exasperated *or* incensed; to become aggravated (*pain etc.*).

exaucer [ɛgzo'se], *v.t. (conjug. like* COM-
MENCER) to hearken to, to grant.

excavateur [ɛkskava'tœːr], *n.m.* excavator,
digging machine.

excavation [ɛkskava'sjɔ̃], *n.f.* excavation.

excaver [ɛkska've], *v.t.* to excavate, to hollow
out.

excédant [ɛkse'dɑ̃], *a.* exceeding, excessive;
unbearable.

excédent [ɛkse'dɑ̃], *n.m.* surplus, excess.

excéder [ɛkse'de], *v.t. (conjug. like* CÉDER)
to exceed, to surpass, to rise above (*in level,
price etc.*); (*fig.*) to wear out, to tire out.

excellemment [ɛksɛla'mɑ̃], *adv.* excellently,
surpassingly.

Excellence [ɛksɛ'lɑ̃ːs], *f.* (*title*) Excellency.

excellence [ɛksɛ'lɑ̃ːs], *n.f.* excellence; *par
excellence, pre eminently, above all.*

excellent [ɛksɛ'lɑ̃], *a.* excellent; delightful.

excellentissime [ɛksɛlɑ̃ti'sim], *a.* most
excellent.

exceller [ɛksɛ'le], *v.i.* to excel, to be eminent;
to surpass.

excentricité [ɛksɑ̃trisi'te], *n.f.* eccentricity.

excentrique [ɛksɑ̃'trik], *a.* eccentric, odd.

excepté [ɛksɛp'te], *prep.* except, excepting, but.

excepter [ɛksɛp'te], *v.t.* to except.

exception [ɛksɛp'sjɔ̃], *n.f.* exception.

exceptionnel [ɛksɛpsjɔ'nɛl], *a.* (*fem.* **-elle**)
exceptional; rare, infrequent.

excès [ɛk'sɛ], *n.m. inv.* excess; (*pl.*) riot, out-
rages, violence.

excessif [ɛksɛ'sif], *a.* (*fem.* **-ive**) excessive,
exorbitant; intemperate.

excessivement [ɛksɛsiv'mɑ̃], *adv.* excessively, to excess.

excise [ɛk'siːz], *n.f.* excise; excise office.

excitabilité [ɛksitabili'te], *n.f.* excitability.

excitable [ɛksi'tabl], *a.* excitable.

excitant [ɛksi'tɑ̃], *a.* exciting.—*n.m.* (*Med.*)
excitant.

excitateur [ɛksita'tœːr], *a.* (*fem.* **-trice**)
provocative.—*n.m.* (*fem.* **-trice**) instigator.

excitation [ɛksita'sjɔ̃], *n.f.* exciting, excitation; excitement.

exciter [ɛksi'te], *v.t.* to excite, to stir up, to
rouse; to stimulate, to animate; to instigate,
to prompt; to irritate. **s'exciter**, *v.r.* to
excite oneself, to work oneself up; to
encourage each other; to be excited.

exclamation [ɛksklama'sjɔ̃], *n.f.* exclamation;
point d'exclamation, exclamation mark.

exclamer (s') [sɛkskla'me], *v.r.* to exclaim, to
cry out; to protest.

exclure [ɛks'klyːr], *v.t. irr. (conjug. like*
CONCLURE) to exclude, to debar, to shut out;
to bar; to be incompatible with.

exclusif [ɛkskly'zif], *a.* (*fem.* **-sive**) exclusive,
intolerant.

exclusion [ɛkskly'zjɔ̃], *n.f.* exclusion.

exclusivement [ɛkskluziv'mɑ̃], *adv.* exclu-
sively.

excommunication [ɛkskɔmynika'sjɔ̃], *n.f.*
excommunication.

excommunié [ɛkskɔmy'nje], *a.* excom-
municated.—*n.m.* (*fem.* **-ée**) excommuni-
cated person.

excommunier [ɛkskɔmy'nje], *v.t.* to excommunicate.

excrément [ɛkskre'mɑ̃], *n.m.* excrement.

excréter [ɛkskre'te], *v.t. (conjug. like* CÉDER)
to excrete.

excrétion [ɛkskre'sjɔ̃], *n.f.* excretion.

excroissance [ɛkskrwa'sɑ̃ːs], *n.f.* excrescence
(*tumor etc.*).

excursion [ɛkskyr'sjɔ̃], *n.f.* excursion, ramble,
tour, trip; raid; (*fig.*) digression.

excursionniste [ɛkskyrsjɔ'nist], *n.* tripper.

excusable [ɛksky'zabl], *a.* excusable, pardonable.

excuse [ɛks'kyːz], *n.f.* excuse, (*pl.*) apology.

excuser [ɛksky'ze], *v.t.* to excuse, to pardon;
to bear with; to apologize for. **s'excuser**,
v.r. to excuse or exculpate oneself; to
apologize; to decline; *qui s'excuse,
s'accuse*, excuses indicate a guilty conscience.

exécrable [ɛgze'krabl], *a.* execrable; abominable.

exécrablement [ɛgzekrablə'mɑ̃], *adv.* exe-
crably.

exécration [ɛgzekra'sjɔ̃], *n.f.* execration.

exécrer [ɛgze'kre], *v.t. (conjug. like* CÉDER)
to execrate, to abhor.

exécutable [ɛgzeky'tabl], *a.* feasible, practicable.

exécutant [ɛgzeky'tɑ̃], *n.m.* (*fem.* **-e**) performer, player (*esp. of music*).

exécuter [ɛgzeky'te], *v.t.* to execute, to perform, to accomplish; to carry out, to fulfil.
s'exécuter, *v.r.* to be performed, to be
done, to take place; to yield, to comply, to
submit; *allons, exécutez-vous*, come, do
the needful.

exécuteur [ɛgzeky'tœːr], *n.m.* (*fem.* **-trice**)
executor, executrix; *exécuteur (des
hautes œuvres)*, executioner.

exécutif [ɛgzeky'tif], *a.* (*fem.* **-tive**) executive.—*n.m.* the executive.

exécution [ɛgzeky'sjɔ̃], *n.f.* execution, accomplishment, performance, fulfilment; (*St.
Exch.*) suspension. (*of defaulter*).

exemplaire [ɛgzɑ̃'plɛːr], *a.* exemplary.—
n.m. model, pattern; copy (*of printed books,
engravings etc.*); specimen.

exemplairement [ɛgzɑ̃plɛr'mɑ̃], *adv.* in an
exemplary manner.

exemple [ɛg'zɑ̃ːpl], *n.m.* example, pattern,
model; precedent, parallel, instance; *à
l'exemple de*, in imitation of; *par
exemple*, for instance; upon my word!
sans exemple, unparalleled.

exempt [ɛg'zɑ̃], *a.* exempt, free (*from*).

exempté [ɛgzɑ̃'te], *a.* and *n.m.* (*fem.* **-ée**)
exempt(ed) (person).

exempter [ɛgzɑ̃'te], *v.t.* to exempt, to free;
to dispense, to exonerate.

exemption [ɛgzɑ̃'sjɔ̃], *n.f.* exemption, immunity; dispensation.

exercer [ɛgzɛr'se], *v.t. (conjug. like* COM-
MENCER) to exercise, to train; to fulfil (*an
office etc.*); to follow, to practice (*a trade or
profession*); (*fig.*) to try (*one's patience etc.*).
s'exercer, *v.r.* to exercise, to practice; to
exert oneself.

exercice [ɛgzɛr'sis], *n.m.* exercise, practice,
use; (*Customs*) inspection; (*Administration*)
financial year; (*Mil.*) drill.

exerciseur [ɛgzɛrsi'zœːr], *n.m.* (*Gym.*) chest
expander.

exhalaison [ɛgzalɛ'zɔ̃], *n.f.* exhalation,
effluvium.

exhalation [ɛgzala'sjɔ̃], *n.f.* exhalation.

exhaler [egza'le], *v.t.* to send forth, to exhale; to give vent to, to emit. **s'exhaler**, *v.r.* to be emitted, to be exhaled; to give vent to.

exhausser [egzo'se], *v.t.* to raise, to make higher.

exhaustif [egzos'tif], *a.* (*fem.* **-tive**) exhaustive.

exhaustion [egzos'tjɔ̃], *n.f.* exhaustion.

exhiber [egzi'be], *v.t.* to exhibit (*in a law court*); to produce, to show. **s'exhiber**, *v.r.* (*pej.*) to show off.

exhibition [egzibi'sjɔ̃], *n.f.* producing, show, exhibiting, exhibition.

exhilarant [egzila'rɑ̃], *a.* exhilarating.

exhortation [egzɔrta'sjɔ̃], *n.f.* exhortation.

exhorter [egzɔr'te], *v.t.* to exhort, to encourage.

exhumation [egzyma'sjɔ̃], *n.f.* exhumation, disinterment.

exhumer [egzy'me], *v.t.* to exhume, to disinter; (*fig.*) to rake up.

exigeant [egzi'ʒɑ̃], *a.* exacting, hard to please.

exigence [egzi'ʒɑ̃:s], *n.f.* unreasonableness; exigency; demand, requirement.

exiger [egzi'ʒe], *v.t.* (*conjug. like* MANGER) to exact, to require, to demand.

exigu [egzi'gy], *a.* (*fem.* **-uë**) very small; scanty, slender, slight.

exiguïté [egzigui'te], *n.f.* scantiness, slenderness, slightness.

exil [eg'zil], *n.m.* exile, banishment.

exilé [egzi'le], *a.* exiled.—*n.m.* (*fem.* **-ée**) exile.

exiler [egzi'le], *v.t.* to exile, to banish. **s'exiler**, *v.r.* to go into exile.

existant [egzis'tɑ̃], *a.* existing, in being, existent; extant.

existence [egzis'tɑ̃:s], *n.f.* existence; subsistence, living; (*pl.*) (*Comm.*) stock on hand.

existentialisme [egzistɑ̃sja'lism], *n.m.* existentialism.

exister [egzis'te], *v.i.* to exist, to live; to be extant.

exocet [egzɔ'sɛ], *n.m.* flying fish.

exode [eg'zɔd], *n.m.* exodus.

exonération [egzɔnera'sjɔ̃], *n.f.* exoneration.

exonérer [egzɔne're], *v.t.* (*conjug. like* CÉDER) to exonerate, to discharge.

exorable [egzɔ'rabl], *a.* lenient, merciful.

exorbitant [egzɔrbi'tɑ̃], *a.* exorbitant.

exorciser [egzɔrsi'ze], *v.t.* to exorcize.

exorde [ɛg'zɔrd], *n.m.* exordium, beginning (*of a speech etc.*).

exotique [egzɔ'tik], *a.* exotic; foreign, outlandish.

expansif [ɛkspɑ̃'sif], *a.* (*fem.* **-sive**) expansive; (*fig.*) unreserved, open-hearted.

expansion [ɛkspɑ̃'sjɔ̃], *n.f.* expansion; (*fig.*) unreservedness.

expatriation [ɛkspatria'sjɔ̃], *n.f.* expatriation; self-banishment.

expatrier [ɛkspatri'e], *v.t.* to expatriate, to exile. **s'expatrier**, *v.r.* to leave one's country.

expectant [ɛkspɛk'tɑ̃], *a.* expectant.

expectative [ɛkspɛkta'ti:v], *n.f.* expectation, hope, expectancy.

expectoration [ɛkspɛktɔra'sjɔ̃], *n.f.* expectoration; sputum.

expectorer [ɛkspɛktɔ're], *v.t.* to expectorate, to spit.

expédient [ɛkspe'djɑ̃], *a.* expedient, fit, meet.—*n.m.* expedient, device; shift.

expédier [ɛkspe'dje], *v.t.* to dispatch, to send off, to forward; to do quickly; to clear (*at the customs*); to draw up (*a deed etc.*).

expéditeur [ɛkspedi'tœ:r], *n.m.* (*fem.* **-trice**) sender (*by post*); shipper, consigner.

expéditif [ɛkspedi'tif], *a.* (*fem.* **-tive**) expeditious, quick.

expédition [ɛkspedi'sjɔ̃], *n.f.* expedition, dispatch; shipment; thing sent; performance; (*Law*) copy (*of a deed etc.*).

expéditionnaire [ɛkspedisjɔ'nɛ:r], *a.* expeditionary.—*n.* sender, shipper; commission-agent; copying clerk.

expérience [ɛkspe'rjɑ̃:s], *n.f.* experience; experiment, test.

expérimental [ɛksperimɑ̃'tal], *a.* (*m.pl.* **-aux**) experimental.

expérimenté [ɛksperimɑ̃'te], *a.* experienced.

expérimenter [ɛksperimɑ̃'te], *v.t.* to try out, to test; to experience.

expert [ɛks'pɛ:r], *a.* expert, skillful.—*n.m.* connoisseur; valuer, surveyor; expert; **expert comptable**, C. P. A., accountant.

expertement [ɛkspɛrt'mɑ̃], *adv.* expertly skilfully.

expertise [ɛkspɛr'ti:z], *n.f.* survey, valuation; appraisal.

expertiser [ɛkspɛrti'ze], *v.t.* to make a survey of; to appraise, to value, to assess.

expiation [ɛkspja'sjɔ̃], *n.f.* expiation, atonement.

expiatoire [ɛkspja'twa:r], *a.* expiatory.

expier [ɛks'pje], *v.t.* to expiate, to atone for.

expirant [ɛkspi'rɑ̃], *a.* expiring, dying.

expiration [ɛkspira'sjɔ̃], *n.f.* expiration.

expirer [ɛkspi're], *v.t.* to breathe out; exhale. —*v.i.* to expire, to die; to come to an end.

explicable [ɛkspli'kabl], *a.* explicable.

explicatif [ɛksplika'tif], *a.* (*fem.* **-tive**) explicative, explanatory.

explication [ɛksplika'sjɔ̃], *n.f.* explanation; interpretation; meaning.

explicite [ɛkspli'sit], *a.* explicit, clear, express.

explicitement [ɛksplisit'mɑ̃], *adv.* explicitly, clearly.

expliquer [ɛkspli'ke], *v.t.* to explain, to expound; to interpret; to make known. **s'expliquer**, *v.r.* to explain oneself; to be explained.

exploit [ɛks'plwa], *n.m.* exploit, achievement, feat; (*Law*) writ, process.

exploitable [ɛksplwa'tabl], *a.* workable; (*Law*) distrainable.

exploitant [ɛksplwa'tɑ̃], *n.m.* operator (*of mines etc.*); farmer, grower.

exploitation [ɛksplwato'sjɔ̃], *n.f.* working, improving (*of lands etc.*); employing, using; taking advantage of, exploitation.

exploiter [ɛksplwa'te], *v.t.* to work, to improve, to cultivate; to use; to exploit, to take (*unfair*) advantage of.

exploiteur [ɛksplwa'tœ:r], *n.m.* (*fem.* **-euse**) exploiter, person who takes advantage (*of others*).

explorateur [ɛksplɔra'tœ:r], *a.* (*fem.* **-trice**) exploratory.—*n.m.* (*fem.* **-trice**) explorer.

exploration [ɛksplɔrɑ'sjɔ̃], *n.f.* exploration.
explorer [ɛksplɔ're], *v.t.* to explore.
exploser [ɛksplo'ze], *v.i.* to explode, to blow up.
explosible [ɛksplo'zibl], *a.* explosive.
explosif [ɛksplo'zif], *a.* (*fem.* **-sive**) and *n.m.* explosive.
explosion [ɛksplo'zjɔ̃], *n.f.* explosion; (*fig.*) outbreak.
exportateur [ɛkspɔrtɑ'tœːr], *a.* (*fem.* **-trice**) exporting.—*n.m.* (*fem.* **-trice**) exporter.
exportation [ɛkspɔrtɑ'sjɔ̃], *n.f.* exportation, export.
exporter [ɛkspɔr'te], *v.t.* to export.
exposant [ɛkspo'zɑ̃], *n.m.* (*fem.* **-e**) exhibitor; (*Law*) petitioner.—*n.m.* (*Math.*) exponent.
exposé [ɛkspo'ze], *a.* exposed, on view; dangerous (*position*).—*n.m.* statement, explanation; account, report.
exposer [ɛkspo'ze], *v.t.* to expose, to show, to exhibit; to lay bare; to state, to explain; to endanger.—*v.i.* to explain; to exhibit. **s'exposer**, *v.r.* to expose oneself; to be liable.
exposition [ɛkspozi'sjɔ̃], *n.f.* exhibition; exposure; situation, aspect; explanation, account.
exprès [ɛks'prɛs], *a.* (*fem.* **-presse**) express, formal, positive.—[ɛks'prɛ], *adv.* expressly, on purpose.—*n.m.* express (*messenger*).
express [ɛks'prɛs], *a.* (*Rail.*) express.—*n.m.* express train.
expressément [ɛksprɛsɛ'mɑ̃], *adv.* expressly, positively.
expressif [ɛksprɛ'sif], *a.* (*fem.* **-ive**) expressive.
expression [ɛksprɛ'sjɔ̃], *n.f.* expression; expressiveness.
exprimer [ɛkspri'me], *v.t.* to express; to press *or* squeeze out; to utter; to betoken. **s'exprimer**, *v.r.* to express oneself.
expropriation [ɛksprɔpriɑ'sjɔ̃], *n.f.* expropriation, dispossession, compulsory purchase.
exproprier [ɛksprɔpri'e], *v.t.* to expropriate, to dispossess; to requisition (*buildings*).
expulser [ɛkspyl'se], *v.t.* to expel, to turn out; to evict.
expulsion [ɛkspyl'sjɔ̃], *n.f.* expulsion; (*Law*) ejection.
expurger [ɛkspyr'ʒe], *v.t.* (*conjug. like* MANGER) to expurgate, to bowdlerize (*a book*).
exquis [ɛks'ki], *a.* exquisite, nice, refined.
exquisement [ɛkskiz'mɑ̃], *adv.* exquisitely.
exsangue [ɛk'sɑ̃ːg], *a.* bloodless, anaemic.
extase [ɛks'taːz], *n.f.* ecstasy, rapture.
extasier (s') [sɛksta'zje], *v.r.* to be enraptured, to go into raptures.
extatique [ɛksta'tik], *a.* ecstatic, rapturous.
extenseur [ɛkstɑ̃'sœːr], *a.* extensor.—*n.m.* (*Anat.*) extensor; chest-expander.
extension [ɛkstɑ̃'sjɔ̃], *n.f.* extension, stretching; extent; increase.
exténuant [ɛkste'nɥɑ̃], *a.* extenuating.
exténuation [ɛkstenɥɑ'sjɔ̃], *n.f.* extenuation, debility.
exténuer [ɛkste'nɥe], *v.t.* to extenuate, to enfeeble.

extérieur [ɛkste'rjœːr], *a.* exterior, external, outward; foreign.—*n.m.* exterior; outward appearance; abroad.
extérieurement [ɛksterjœr'mɑ̃], *adv.* externally, outwardly.
exterminateur [ɛkstɛrminɑ'tœːr], *a.* (*fem.* **-trice**) exterminating, destroying.—*n.m.* (*fem.* **-trice**) destroyer, exterminator.
extermination [ɛkstɛrminɑ'sjɔ̃], *n.f.* extermination.
exterminer [ɛkstɛrmi'ne], *v.t.* to exterminate, to destroy.
externat [ɛkstɛr'na], *n.m.* day school.
externe [ɛks'tɛrn], *a.* external, exterior, outer.—*n.* day scholar.
extincteur [ɛkstɛ̃k'tœːr], *a.* (*fem.* **-trice**) extinguishing (*fire*).—*n.m.* fire extinguisher.
extinction [ɛkstɛ̃k'sjɔ̃], *n.f.* extinction, destruction; liquidation; quelling; quenching (*of thirst*); slaking (*of lime*).
extinguible [ɛkstɛ̃'gibl], *a.* extinguishable.
extirpateur [ɛkstirpɑ'tœːr], *n.m.* extirpator, destroyer; (*Agric.*) scarifier, weeder.
extirpation [ɛkstirpɑ'sjɔ̃], *n.f.* extirpation.
extirper [ɛkstir'pe], *v.t.* to extirpate.
extorquer [ɛkstɔr'ke], *v.t.* to extort, to wrest.
extorsion [ɛkstɔr'sjɔ̃], *n.f.* extortion.
extra [ɛks'tra], *n.m. inv.* extra.
extra-conjugal [ɛkstrakɔ̃ʒy'gal], *a.* (*m.pl.* **-aux**) extra-marital.
extracteur [ɛkstrak'tœːr], *n.m.* extractor.
extraction [ɛkstrak'sjɔ̃], *n.f.* extraction; origin, descent.
extrader [ɛkstra'de], *v.t.* to extradite.
extradition [ɛkstradi'sjɔ̃], *n.f.* extradition.
extraire [ɛks'trɛːr], *v.t. irr.* (*conjug. like* TRAIRE) to extract, to take out; to make extracts from.
extrait [ɛks'trɛ], *n.m.* extract; selection; abstract; certificate.
extraordinaire [ɛkstraɔrdi'nɛːr], *a.* extraordinary, unusual.—*n.m.* extraordinary thing.
extraordinairement [ɛkstraɔrdinɛr'mɑ̃], *adv.* extraordinarily, unusually; oddly.
extrapolation [ɛkstrapɔlɑ'sjɔ̃], *n.f.* (*Math.*) extrapolation.
extra-scolaire [ɛkstraskɔ'lɛːr], *a.* out-of-school (*activities*).
extravagamment [ɛkstravaga'mɑ̃], *adv.* extravagantly, unreasonably.
extravagance [ɛkstrava'gɑ̃ːs], *n.f.* extravagance, folly.
extravagant [ɛkstrava'gɑ̃], *a.* and *n.m.* (*fem.* **-e**) extravagant (person).
extravaguer [ɛkstrava'ge], *v.i.* to talk wildly.
extrême [ɛks'trɛːm], *a.* extreme, utmost; excessive.—*n.m.* extreme *or* utmost point.
extrêmement [ɛkstrɛm'mɑ̃], *adv.* extremely.
Extrême-Orient [ɛkstrɛmo'rjɑ̃], l', *m.* Far East.
extrémiste [ɛkstre'mist], *n.* extremist, diehard.
extrémité [ɛkstremi'te], *n.f.* extremity, end; last moment; (*fig.*) border, brink.
exubérance [ɛgzybe'rɑ̃ːs], *n.f.* exuberance.
exubérant [ɛgzybe'rɑ̃], *a.* exuberant, luxuriant.
exultation [ɛgzyltɑ'sjɔ̃], *n.f.* exultation, rapture.

F, f

F, f (1) [ɛf], *n.m.* the sixth letter of the alphabet.
f. (2) or **fr.**, (*abbr.*) franc.
fa [fa], *n.m.* (*Mus.*) fa; F.
fable [fɑːbl], *n.f.* fable; story, tale; (*fig.*) untruth; byword.
fablier [fabli'e], *n.m.* book of fables; fabulist.
fabricant [fabri'kɑ̃], *n.m.* (*fem.* -e) manufacturer, maker.
fabricateur [fabrika'tœːr], *n.m.* (*fem.* -trice) fabricator; counterfeiter; forger.
fabrication [fabrika'sjɔ̃], *n.f.* fabrication, manufacture.
fabrique [fa'brik], *n.f.* building and maintenance (*esp. of churches*); factory; fabrication.
fabriquer [fabri'ke], *v.t.* to manufacture, to make; to fabricate.
fabuleusement [fabyløz'mɑ̃], *adv.* fabulously; (*fig.*) incredibly.
fabuleux [faby'lø], *a.* (*fem.* -euse) fabulous, fictitious; (*fig.*) incredible.
fabuliste [faby'list], *n.* fabulist.
façade [fa'sad], *n.f.* façade, front (*of an edifice*); (*fig.*) appearance.
face [fas], *n.f.* face; front; side (*of a record*); (*fig.*) state, appearance; turn (*of affairs*); **en face de**, opposite.
facétie [fase'si], *n.f.* facetiousness; jest, joke.
facétieusement [fasesjøz'mɑ̃], *adv.* facetiously.
facétieux [fase'sjø], *a.* (*fem.* -euse) facetious, humorous.
facette [fa'sɛt], *n.f.* facet, face.
fâcher [fa'ʃe], *v.t.* to anger, to offend, to displease; **être fâché avec**, to be on bad terms with; **fâché (contre)**, angry (*with*); **fâché (de)**, sorry. **se fâcher**, *v.r.* to get angry, to be offended.
fâcherie [fa'ʃri], *n.f.* angry feeling; quarrel.
fâcheusement [faʃøz'mɑ̃], *adv.* unfortunately, unpleasantly; inopportunely, disagreeably; awkwardly.
fâcheux [fa'ʃø], *a.* (*fem.* -euse) troublesome, vexatious; unfortunate; cross.—*n.m.* (*fem.* -euse) troublesome or disagreeable person or thing, pesterer, bore.
facial [fa'sjal], *a.* (*m. pl.* -aux) (*Anat.*) facial.
facile [fa'sil], *a.* easy; facile; fluent; ready, quick; weak.
facilement [fasil'mɑ̃], *adv.* easily, readily.
facilité [fasili'te], *n.f.* facility, ease; readiness; (*pl.*) easy terms (*for payment*).
faciliter [fasili'te], *v.t.* to facilitate, to make easy.
façon [fa'sɔ̃], *n.f.* make, shape, fashion; making, workmanship; (*fig.*) manner; appearance; sort; affectation; fuss; (*pl.*) ceremony.
faconde [fa'kɔ̃ːd], *n.f.* talkativeness, loquacity.
façonné [fasɔ'ne], *a.* figured (*of materials*); wrought.
façonnement [fasɔn'mɑ̃], **façonnage** [fasɔ'naːʒ], *n.m.* fashioning, making.
façonner [fasɔ'ne], *v.t.* to make, to fashion, to form; to work, to mold; to accustom, to use (*to discipline etc.*).
façonnier [fasɔ'nje], *a.* (*fem.* -ière) ceremonious, affected.—*n.m.* custom tailor.
fac-similé [faksimi'le], *n.m.* facsimile.

factage [fak'taːʒ], *n.m.* porterage, carriage.
facteur [fak'tœːr], *n.m.* (*fem.* -trice) maker (*of musical instruments*); agent; postman; railway porter; (*Math., Biol.*) factor.
factice [fak'tis], *a.* factitious, artificial; unnatural.
factieux [fak'sjø], *a.* (*fem.* -euse) factious, mutinous.—*n.m.* (*fem.* -euse) rebel.
faction [fak'sjɔ̃], *n.f.* watch, sentry duty; faction.
factionnaire [faksjɔ'nɛːr], *n.m.* sentry.
factorerie [faktɔrə'ri], *n.f.* trading depot, factory (*in a colony etc.*).
facture [fak'tyːr], *n.f.* composition, workmanship (*of music, verse etc.*); (*Comm.*) bill (*of sale*), invoice.
facturer [fakty're], *v.t.* to invoice.
facultatif [fakylta'tif], *a.* (*fem.* -tive) optional; **arrêt facultatif**, request stop.
faculté [fakyl'te], *n.f.* faculty, ability, power; quality; option; right; (*pl.*) mental faculties.
fadaise [fa'dɛːz], *n.f.* trifle, stuff, nonsense, twaddle.
fade [fad], *a.* insipid, tasteless, dull; (*fig.*) flat, stale.
fadement [fad'mɑ̃], *adv.* insipidly, tastelessly; mawkishly.
fadeur [fa'dœːr], *n.f.* insipidity, tastelessness; (*fig.*) pointlessness.
fagot [fa'go], *n.m.* faggot, bundle of sticks etc.
fagoter [fago'te], *v.t.* to tie into faggots; (*fig.*) to jumble together; to dress in a slovenly manner; **comme le voilà fagoté**, what a sight he looks. **se fagoter**, *v.r.* to dress in a slovenly manner.
faible [fɛːbl], *a.* and *n.* weak, feeble (*person*).—*n.m.* weak part; defect, failing; partiality, weakness (*for*).
faiblement [fɛblə'mɑ̃], *adv.* weakly, feebly.
faiblesse [fɛ'blɛs], *n.f.* weakness, feebleness; faintness; deficiency; backwardness; defect; partiality.
faiblir [fɛ'bliːr], *v.i.* to become weak, to flag, to yield, to abate, to relax.
faïence [fa'jɑ̃ːs], *n.f.* crockery, earthenware.
faïencier [fajɑ̃'sje], *n.m.* (*fem.* -ière) dealer in or maker of crockery.
faille [faːj], *n.f.* (*Geol.*) fault.
failli [fa'ji], *a.* and *n.m.* (*fem.* -e) bankrupt, insolvent (*person*).
faillibilité [fajibili'te], *n.f.* fallibility.
faillible [fa'jibl], *a.* fallible.
faillir [fa'jiːr], *v.i. irr.* to err, to transgress; to yield; to fail; to be on the point of; **j'ai failli tomber**, I nearly fell.
faillite [fa'jit], *n.f.* bankruptcy, insolvency; **faire faillite**, to become bankrupt.
faim [fɛ̃], *n.f.* hunger, appetite; (*fig.*) longing; **avoir faim**, to be hungry.
faîne [fɛːn], *n.f.* beechnut; beechmast.
fainéant [fene'ɑ̃], *a.* idle, lazy.—*n.m.* (*fem.* -e) idler.
fainéanter [feneɑ̃'te], *v.i.* (*colloq.*) to be idle, to loaf.
fainéantise [feneɑ̃'tiːz], *n.f.* idleness, laziness, sloth.
faire (1) [fɛːr], *v. irr.* (*The most frequently used verb in the language; faire not only translates to do or to make, but, followed by a noun or an infinitive, it may take the place of practically any verb; followed by an adjective*

or an adverb it forms many current idioms.)

I. *v.t.* to do; to make; to form; to be; *cela fait mon affaire*, this is exactly what I want; *cela fait beaucoup*, that makes a great difference; *cela ne fait rien*, that makes no difference; *faire accueil à*, to welcome; *faire attention*, to pay attention; *faire bâtir*, to have built; *faire cas de*, to have a high opinion of; (*Motor.*) *faire du 50 à l'heure*, to do 50 kilometres an hour; *faire le mort*, to sham dead; *faire part de*, to inform, to announce; *faire peu de cas de*, to set little store by; *faire ses dents*, to cut one's teeth; *faire une promenade*, to take a walk; *faire venir*, to send for; *faire voir*, to show; *faites-le entrer*, show him in; *il ne fait que d'arriver*, he has only just arrived; *je n'ai que faire de lui*, I am in no way interested in him; *qu'est-ce que cela vous fait?* what is that to you? *que faire?* what is to be done? *se laisser faire*, to offer no resistance.

II. *v.i.* to do; to mean, to signify, to look; to fit, to suit; to deal (*at cards*); to arrange, to manage; *avoir à faire*, to have work to do; *c'en est fait de*, it is all up with.

III. *v. impers.* to be; *il fait beau*, it is fine; *quel temps fait-il?* what sort of weather is it?

IV. *se faire*, *v.r.* to be done, to be made; to happen, to become; to pretend to be; to have, make *or* get oneself; to be used (*à*), to accustom oneself (*à*); to improve; *cela ne se fait pas*, that is not done.

faire (2) [fɛːr], *n.m.* doing, making; (*Paint. etc.*) execution, style.

faire-part [fɛr'paːr], *n.m. inv.* *un faire-part* *or* *une lettre de faire-part de décès* *or* *de mariage*, notification of death, wedding-card.

faisable [fə'zabl], *a.* practicable, feasible.

faisan [fə'zɑ̃], *n.m.* pheasant.

faisandé [fəzɑ̃'de], *a.* gamy, high.

faisandeau [fəzɑ̃'do], *n.m.* (*pl.* -eaux) young pheasant.

faisceau [fɛ'so], *n.m.* (*pl.* -eaux) bundle; sheaf (*of arrows etc.*); pile (*of arms etc.*); (*fig.*) union; (*Elec.*) beam; (*Antiq.*, *pl.*) fasces.

faiseur [fə'zœːr], *n.m.* (*fem.* -euse) maker; doer; charlatan, quack.

fait [fɛ, fɛt], *a.* made; done; fit, qualified; dressed, got up; full grown; mature.—*n.m.* act, deed; fact, actual event; case, matter point in business; *tout à fait*, quite.

faîte [fɛːt], *n.m.* top, pinnacle; ridge, coping (*of a building*); (*fig.*) zenith, height.

faits divers [fedi'vɛr], *n.m. pl.* news items, news in brief.

faix [fɛ], *n.m. inv.* weight, burden, load.

falaise [fa'lɛːz], *n.f.* cliff.

fallacieusement [falasjøz'mɑ̃], *adv.* fallaciously, falsely.

fallacieux [fala'sjø], *a.* (*fem.* -euse) fallacious, deceptive.

falloir [fa'lwaːr], *v. impers. irr.* to be necessary, to be obligatory, proper *or* expedient (*should*, *must*); to be needful, to be wanting *or* lacking; *comme il faut*, properly, well-bred (*of people*); *peu s'en*

faut, very nearly; *tant s'en faut*, far from it.

falot [fa'lo], *n.m.* large hand-lantern.

falsification [falsifika'sjɔ̃], *n.f.* falsification; adulteration, debasement.

falsifier [falsi'fje], *v.t.* to falsify; to alter (*texts etc.*); to adulterate (*milk*, *metals*); to tamper with.

faluche [fa'lyʃ], *n.f.* student's beret.

famé [fa'me], *a.* used only in *bien* or *mal famé*, of good *or* evil repute.

famélique [fame'lik], *a.* starving.—*n.* starveling.

fameux [fa'mø], *a.* (*fem.* -euse) famous, celebrated; first-rate; (*iron. adj. before noun*) perfect.

familial [fami'ljal], *a.* (*m. pl.* -aux) pertaining to family.

familiariser [familjari'se], *v.t.* to accustom to, to familiarize. **se familiariser**, *v.r.* to familiarize oneself (*avec*), to become accustomed; to grow familiar.

familiarité [familjari'te], *n.f.* familiarity, familiar terms, intimacy; (*pl.*) liberties.

familier [fami'lje], *a.* (*fem.* -ère) familiar, intimate; free; homely.—*n.m.* familiar.

familièrement [familjɛr'mɑ̃], *adv.* familiarly.

famille [fa'miːj], *n.f.* family, kindred, kin; race, tribe; (*fig.*) host.

famine [fa'min], *n.f.* famine, dearth.

fanal [fa'nal], *n.m.* (*pl.* -aux) signal light; ship's lantern.

fanatique [fana'tik], *a.* fanatical.—*n.* fanatic, enthusiast.

fanatiquement [fanatik'mɑ̃], *adv.* fanatically.

fanatisme [fana'tism], *n.m.* fanaticism.

faner [fa'ne], *v.t.* to toss *or* ted (*hay*); to cause to fade; to tarnish. **se faner**, *v.r.* to fade, to droop, to wither; to tarnish.

faneur [fa'nœːr], *n.m.* (*fem.* -euse) haymaker.—*n.f.* (-euse) haymaking machine.

fanfare [fɑ̃'faːr], *n.f.* flourish (*of trumpets*), fanfare; brass band.

fanfaron [fɑ̃fa'rɔ̃], *a.* (*fem.* -onne) blustering, swaggering, boasting.—*n.m.* (*fem.* -onne) blusterer, swaggerer; braggart.

fanfreluche [fɑ̃frə'lyʃ], *n.f.* bauble, gewgaw.

fange [fɑ̃ːʒ], *n.f.* mire, mud, dirt; vileness.

fangeux [fɑ̃'ʒø], *a.* (*fem.* -euse) miry, muddy, dirty.

fanon [fa'nɔ̃], *n.m.* dewlap (*oxen*); fetlock (*horse*); horny strip (*in whales*); (*Mil.*) pennon (*of lance*).

fantaisie [fɑ̃tɛ'zi], *n.f.* imagination; fancy; whim, caprice; (*Mus.*) fantasia.

fantaisiste [fɑ̃tɛ'zist], *a.* whimsical, fantastic.—*n.* whimsical painter, writer *or* other artist.

fantasmagorie [fɑ̃tasmago'ri], *n.f.* phantasmagoria.

fantasque [fɑ̃'task], *a.* fantastic, whimsical; strange, odd.

fantassin [fɑ̃ta'sɛ̃], *n.m.* foot soldier, infantryman.

fantastique [fɑ̃tas'tik], *a.* fantastic, fanciful.—*n.m.* uncanny.

fantastiquement [fɑ̃tastik'mɑ̃], *adv.* fantastically.

fantoche [fɑ̃'tɔʃ], *n.m.* marionette, puppet.

fantôme [fɑ̃'toːm], *n.m.* phantom, specter, ghost.

faon

faon [fɑ̃], *n.m.* fawn, calf of deer.
faquin [fa'kɛ̃], *n.m.* cad, rascal.
farandole [farɑ̃'dɔl], *n.f.* farandole (*Provençal dance*).
farce [fars], *n.f.* stuffing, force-meat; farce; buffoonery; practical joke; prank.
farceur [far'sœːr], *a.* (*fem.* **-euse**) waggish, facetious.—*n.m.* (*fem.* **-euse**) practical joker; humbug.
farcir [far'siːr], *v.t.* to stuff with force-meat etc.; to cram.
fard [faːr], *n.m.* paint (*for the complexion*), rouge, make-up; (*fig.*) varnish, disguise; *sans fard*, plainly, frankly.
fardeau [far'do], *n.m.* (*pl.* **-eaux**) burden, load; mash (*for brewing*); (*Mining*) mass.
farder [far'de], *v.t.* to paint (*the face*), to make up; (*fig.*) to varnish, to gloss over. **se farder**, *v.r.* to paint one's face, to make up. (C) **fardoches** [far'dɔʃ], *n.f. pl.* brushwood.
farfadet [farfa'dɛ], *n.m.* goblin, elf.
farfouiller [farfu'je], *v.i.* (*fam.*) to rummage.
faribole [fari'bɔl], *n.f.* idle story; trifle.
farine [fa'rin], *n.f.* flour; meal.
farineux [fari'nø], *a.* (*fem.* **-euse**) mealy, farinaceous; white with flour.
farouche [fa'ruʃ], *a.* wild; fierce; sullen; shy.
fascicule [fasi'kyl], *n.m.* fascicle.
fascinateur [fasina'tœːr], *a.* (*fem.* **-trice**) fascinating.
fascination [fasina'sjɔ̃], *n.f.* fascination.
fasciner [fasi'ne], *v.t.* to fascinate.
fascisme [fa'ʃism], *n.m.* fascism.
fasciste [fa'ʃist], *a.* and *n.* fascist.
faste [fast], *a.* favourable, lucky.—*n.m.* (*used only in sing.*) pomp, ostentation.
fastidieusement [fastidjøz'mɑ̃], *adv.* tediously.
fastidieux [fasti'djø], *a.* (*fem.* **-euse**) irksome, tedious.
fastueusement [fastɥøz'mɑ̃], *adv.* ostentatiously, pompously; splendidly.
fastueux [fas'tɥø], *a.* (*fem.* **-euse**) ostentatious, pompous, showy; stately.
fat [fat], *a.* conceited, vain, foppish.—*n.m.* fop, coxcomb.
fatal [fa'tal], *a.* fatal; inevitable; *une femme fatale*, a vamp.
fatalement [fatal'mɑ̃], *adv.* fatally; inevitably.
fatalisme [fata'lism], *n.m.* fatalism.
fataliste [fata'list], *n.* fatalist.
fatalité [fatali'te], *n.f.* fatality.
fatigant [fati'gɑ̃], *a.* fatiguing, tiring, wearisome.
fatigue [fa'tig], *n.f.* fatigue, weariness; toil, hardship; *habits de fatigue*, working clothes.
fatigué [fati'ge], *a.* fatigued, tired; (*fig.*) worn out.
fatiguer [fati'ge], *v.t.* to fatigue; to tire.—*v.i.* to tire; to be fatiguing. **se fatiguer**, *v.r.* to tire oneself out, to get tired, to be jaded.
fatras [fa'trɑ], *n.m.* jumble; rubbish, trash.
fatuité [fatɥi'te], *n.f.* fatuity, self-conceit.
faubourg [fo'buːr], *n.m.* outskirts, suburb.
faubourien [fobu'rjɛ̃], *a.* (*fem.* **-enne**) suburban, working-class; common.—*n.m.* (*fem.* **-enne**) person living in the suburbs; (*pej.*) common person.
fauchage [fo'jaːʒ], *n.m.* mowing.
fauchaison [foʃe'zɔ̃], *n.f.* mowing time.
fauché [fo'ʃe], *a.* mown; (*slang*) broke.

faucher [fo'ʃe], *v.t.* to mow, to reap.
faucheur [fo'ʃœːr], *n.m.* (*fem.* **-euse**) mower, reaper.—*n.f.* (**-euse**) (*mechanical*) mower.
faucille [fo'siːj], *n.f.* sickle, reaping-hook.
faucon [fo'kɔ̃], *n.m.* falcon, hawk.
fauconnerie [fokon'ri], *n.f.* falconry.
fauconnier [foko'nje], *n.m.* falconer.
faufiler [fofi'le], *v.t.* to tack, to baste (*needlework*). **se faufiler**, *v.r.* to insinuate oneself, to sneak in; to find a way in.
faune (1) [foːn], *n.m.* faun.
faune (2) [foːn], *n.f.* (*Zool.*) fauna.
faussaire [fo'sɛːr], *n.* forger.
fausse [fos], [FAUX].
faussement [fos'mɑ̃], *adv.* falsely, wrongfully.
fausser [fo'se], *v.t.* to bend; to falsify, to pervert; (*narrow*) to break, to force or strain (*a lock*).
fausset [fo'sɛ], *n.m.* (*Mus.*) falsetto.
fausseté [fos'te], *n.f.* falsity, falsehood; duplicity.
faute [foːt], *n.f.* want; defect; fault, mistake, error; *faute de*, for want of.
fauteuil [fo'tœːj], *n.m.* arm-chair; chair (*speaker's, president's seat*).
fauteur [fo'tœːr], *n.m.* abettor, favorer.
fautif [fo'tif], *a.* (*fem.* **-tive**) faulty, at fault, defective.
fauve [foːv], *a.* fawn-colored, tawny.—*n.m.* wild animal; *Les Fauves*, group of French painters at the beginning of this century.
fauvette [fo'vɛt], *n.f.* warbler.
faux (1) [fo], *n.f. inv.* scythe.
faux (2) [fo], *a.* (*fem.* **fausse**) false, untrue, wrong; base, counterfeit, forged (*coinage*); sham; insincere; (*Mus.*) out of tune; *faire un faux pas*, to stumble; (*fig.*) to make a slip.—*n.m.* falsehood; error; forgery.—*adv.* falsely, erroneously; (*Mus.*) out of tune.
faux-filet [fofi'lɛ], *n.m.* sirloin.
faux-fuyant [fofɥi'jɑ̃], *n.m.* subterfuge, evasion.
faux-monnayeur [fomone'jœːr], *n.m.* counterfeiter.
faveur [fa'vœːr], *n.f.* favor, boon; grace; vogue; (*narrow*) silk ribbon; *à la faveur de*, by means of; *en faveur de*, on behalf of.
favorable [favo'rabl], *a.* favorable, propitious.
favorablement [favorablə'mɑ̃], *adv.* favorably.
favori [favo'ri], *a.* and *n.m.* (*fem.* **-Ite**) favorite.—*n.m.* (*pl.*) side whiskers.
favoriser [favori'ze], *v.t.* to favor, to befriend; to assist, to protect.
favoritisme [favori'tism], *n.m.* favoritism.
fébrile [fe'bril], *a.* febrile, feverish.
fécond [fe'kɔ̃], *a.* fruitful, prolific; copious, abundant, fertile.
fécondation [fekɔ̃da'sjɔ̃], *n.f.* impregnation; fertilization.
féconder [fekɔ̃'de], *v.t.* to make fruitful, to fertilize.
fécondité [fekɔ̃di'te], *n.f.* fecundity, fruitfulness, fertility.
fécule [fe'kyl], *n.f.* faecula, starch.
féculent [feky'lɑ̃], *a.* feculent.—*n.m.* starchy food.
fédéral [fede'ral], *a.* (*m. pl.* **-aux**) federal.
fédéralisme [federa'lism], *n.m.* federalism.
fédéraliste [federa'list], *a.* and *n.* federalist.

fédération [federɑ'sjɔ̃], *n.f.* federation, alliance.

fédéré [fede're], *a.* federate, confederate; amalgamated.

fédérer (se) [səfede're], *v.r.* (*conjug. like* CÉDER) to federate, to band together.

fée [fe], *n.f.* fairy, fay.

féerie [fea'ri], *n.f.* enchantment; fairy scene; fairy-land.

féerique [fea'rik], *a.* fairy-like; wonderful.

feindre [fɛ̃:dr], *v.t. irr* (*conjug. like* CRAINDRE) to feign, to simulate, to sham, to pretend.—*v.i.* to feign, to sham.

feint [fɛ̃], *a.* feigned, pretended, sham.

feinte [fɛ̃:t], *n.f.* feint; pretence, dissimulation.

feld-maréchal [fɛldmare'ʃal], *n.m.* (*pl.* -**aux**) field marshal.

feldspath [fɛls'pat], *n.m.* feldspar.

fêlé [fɛ'le], *a.* cracked (*of glass*); (*fig.*) crack-brained.

fêler [fɛ'le], *v.t.* and **se fêler**, *v.r.* to crack (*of glass etc.*).

félicitation [felisita'sjɔ̃], *n.f.* felicitation, congratulation.

félicité [felisi'te], *n.f.* felicity, bliss.

féliciter [felisi'te], *v.t.* to congratulate, to felicitate. **se féliciter**, *v.r.* to congratulate oneself.

félin [fe'lɛ̃], *a.* and *n.m.* (*fem.* -**e**) feline.

félon [fe'lɔ̃], *a.* (*fem.* -**onne**) disloyal, traitorous.—*n.m.* (*fem.* -**onne**) traitor, caitiff.

félonie [felɔ'ni], *n.f.* (*Feud.*) felony, treason.

fêlure [fɛ'ly:r], *n.f.* crack, fissure.

femelle [fə'mɛl], *a.* female, feminine, she-.—*n.f.* female, (*pej.*) woman.

féminin [femi'nɛ̃], *a.* feminine, female, womanish, womanly, effeminate.—*n.m.* (*Gram.*) feminine.

femme [fam], *n.f.* woman; married woman; wife; female attendant; lady.

femme-agent [fama'ʒɑ̃], *n.f.* police-woman.

femmelette [fam'lɛt], *n.f.* silly, weak woman; effeminate man.

femme-soldat [famsɔl'da], *n.f.* service-woman.

fémur [fe'my:r], *n.m.* femur, thigh-bone.

fenaison [fənɛ'zɔ̃], *n.f.* hay time, hay-making.

fendiller (se) [səfɑ̃di'je], *v.r.* to be covered with small cracks, to crack, to split.

fendre [fɑ̃:dr], *v.t.* to cleave, to split, to crack, to cut open; to plough (*the sea*). **se fendre**, *v.r.* to burst asunder, to split, to be ready to burst.

fendu [fɑ̃'dy], *a.* cleft, split, cloven.

fenêtre [fə'nɛ:tr], *n.f.* window, casement.

fenil [fə'ni], *n.m.* hayloft.

fenouil [fə'nu:j], *n.m.* fennel.

fente [fɑ̃:t], *n.f.* slit, chink, cleft; gap, crevice.

féodal [feɔ'dal], *a.* (*m. pl.* -**aux**) feudal.

féodalisme [feɔda'lism], *n.m.* feudalism.

fer [fɛ:r], *n.m.* iron; iron tool; horseshoe; head, point, etc.; (*fig.*) sword, brand; (*Golf*) club; (*pl.*) irons, chains, fetters; *fer battu* or *forgé*, wrought iron; *fil de fer*, wire.

fer-blanc [fɛr'blɑ̃], *n.m.* (*pl.* **fers-blancs**) tin, tin plate.

férié [fe'rje], *a.* holiday; *jour férié*, holiday, general holiday, bank holiday.

férir [fe'rir], *v.t.* used only in *sans coup férir*, without striking a blow.

ferler [fɛr'le], *v.t.* to furl (*sails*).

fermage [fɛr'ma:ʒ], *n.m.* rent (*of a farm*).

fermail [fɛr'ma:j], *n.m.* clasp, buckle.

ferme (1) [fɛrm], *a.* firm; fixed, stable; strong, stout, stiff, steady; resolute.—*adv.* firmly, fast, hard.

ferme (2) [fɛrm], *n.f.* farm, farmhouse, farmstead; farming (*of taxes*); letting out on lease.

ferme (3) [fɛrm], *n.f.* framework of beams.

fermement [fɛrmə'mɑ̃], *adv.* firmly, steadily, resolutely.

ferment [fɛr'mɑ̃], *n.m.* ferment, leaven.

fermentation [fɛrmɑ̃tɑ'sjɔ̃], *n.f.* fermentation, working; (*fig.*) ferment.

fermenter [fɛrmɑ̃'te], *v.i.* to ferment, to rise, to work.

fermer [fɛr'me], *v.t.* to shut, to close; to fasten; to turn off (*water, gas etc.*); to put an end to (*a discussion etc.*); to enclose.—*v.i.* to shut, to be shut. **se fermer**, *v.r.* to shut, to close, to be closed; to lock.

fermeté [fɛrmə'te], *n.f.* firmness; steadiness; resolution.

fermeture [fɛrmə'ty:r], *n.f.* closing, shutting; *fermeture à glissière*, zip fastener.

fermier [fɛr'mje], *n.m.* (tenant) farmer.

fermière [fɛr'mjɛ:r], *n.f.* farmer's wife.

fermoir [fɛr'mwa:r], *n.m.* clasp, fastener.

féroce [fe'rɔs], *a.* ferocious, fierce, savage.

férocement [ferɔs'mɑ̃], *adv.* ferociously.

férocité [ferɔsi'te], *n.f.* ferocity, fierceness.

ferraille [fɛ'rɑ:j], *n.f.* old iron, scrap iron.

ferrailler [fɛrɑ'je], *v.i.* (*Spt.*) to fence clumsily; (*fig.*) to squabble.

ferrailleur [fɛrɑ'jœ:r], *n.m.* dealer in old iron, scrap merchant; (*Spt.*) clumsy fencer.

ferrant [fɛ'rɑ̃], *a.* **maréchal ferrant**, farrier, shoeing-smith.

ferré [fɛ're], *a.* bound, shod etc., with iron; metalled; (*colloq.*) skilled; *voie ferrée*, railway.

ferrer [fɛ're], *v.t.* to bind, hoop, etc., with iron; to shoe (*a horse etc.*).

ferret [fɛ're], *n.m.* tag (*of a lace*).

ferronnerie [fɛrɔn'ri], *n.f.* iron foundry; ironmongery; wrought iron.

ferronnier [fɛrɔ'nje], *n.m.* (*fem.* -**ière**) ironmonger, iron worker.

ferroviaire [fɛrɔ'vjɛ:r], *a.* pertaining to railways.

ferrure [fɛ'ry:r], *n.f.* iron work; shoeing (*of a horse etc.*).

fertile [fɛr'til], *a.* fertile, fruitful.

fertilement [fɛrtil'mɑ̃], *adv.* fertilely, abundantly.

fertilisant [fɛrtili'zɑ̃], *a.* fertilizing.

fertiliser [fɛrtili'ze], *v.t.* to fertilize, to manure.

fertilité [fɛrtili'te], *n.f.* fertility, fruitfulness.

féru [fe'ry], *a.* smitten; keen on (*something or someone*).

férule [fe'ryl], *n.f.* (*Sch.*) cane, ferule, rod; stroke, cut.

fervent [fɛr'vɑ̃], *a.* fervent.—*n.m.* (*fem.* -**e**) enthusiast, devotee, fan.

ferveur [fɛr'vœ:r], *n.f.* fervor, ardor.

fesse [fɛs], *n.f.* buttock, rump; (*pl.*) bottom.

fessée [fɛ'se], *n.f.* spanking.

fesse-mathieu [fɛsma'tjø], *n.m.* (*pl.* **fesse-mathieux**) miser, skinflint.

fesser [fɛ'se], *v.t.* to spank, to smack.

153

fessier [fɛ'sje], *n.m.* buttocks, bottom.
festin [fɛs'tɛ̃], *n.m.* feast, banquet.
*__festiner__ [fɛsti'ne], *v.i.* to banquet, to carouse.
festival [fɛsti'val], *n.m.* festival.
festivité [fɛstivi'te], *n.f.* festivity.
feston [fɛs'tɔ̃], *n.m.* festoon; scallop.
festonner [fɛstɔ'ne], *v.t.* to festoon; to cut in festoons, to scallop.
festoyer [fɛstwa'je], *v.t.* (*conjug. like* EMPLOYER) to entertain, to feast.
fête [fɛːt], *n.f.* holiday, festival; saint's day; feast; birthday; festivity, merry-making.
fête-Dieu [fɛːt'djø], *n.f.* Corpus Christi day.
fêter [fɛ'te], *v.t.* to keep (as a holiday); to entertain, to feast.
fétiche [fe'tiʃ], *n.m.* fetish.
fétide [fe'tid], *a.* fetid, rank, offensive.
fétidité [fetidi'te], *n.f.* fetidity, offensive smell.
fétu [fe'ty], *n.m.* straw; (*fig.*) pin, rap.
feu (1) [fø], *n.m.* (*pl.* **feux**) fire; burning; heat; discharge of fire-arms; fire-place; (*fig.*) light; brilliancy; passion; vivacity; *crier 'au feu'*, to cry 'fire!'; *faire feu*, to fire; *feu d'artifice*, fireworks; *feu de joie*, bonfire; *feux de position*, (*Motor.*) parking lights; *le coin du feu*, the fireside; *prendre feu*, to catch fire.
feu (2) [fø], *a.* late, deceased.
feuillage [fœ'jaːʒ], *n.m.* foliage, leaves.
feuille [fœːj], *n.f.* leaf; sheet (*of paper, metal etc.*); newspaper; list; foil (*of mirrors*).
feuillet [fœ'jɛ], *n.m.* leaf (*of a book*).
feuilleter [fœj'te], *v.t.* (*conjug. like* APPELER) to turn over; to peruse rapidly; *gâteau feuilleté*, flaky puff.
feuillu [fœ'jy], *a.* leafy.
feutrage [fø'traːʒ], *n.m.* felting.
feutre [fø:tr], *n.m.* felt; felt hat.
feutrer [fø'tre], *v.t.* to felt; to pad, to pack.
feutrier [føtri'e], *n.m.* (*fem.* **-ière**) felt maker.
fève [fɛːv], *n.f.* bean, broad bean.
février [fevri'e], *n.m.* February.
fez [fɛːz], *n.m. inv.* fez (Turkish cap).
fi! [fi], *int.* fie!
fiacre [fjakr], *n.m.* hackney-coach, cab.
fiançailles [fjɑ̃'saːj], *n.f.* (*used only in pl.*) betrothal, engagement.
fiancé [fjɑ̃'se], *n.m.* (*fem.* **-ée**) betrothed, fiancé, fiancée.
fiancer [fjɑ̃'se], *v.t.* (*conjug. like* COMMENCER) to betroth, to affiance. **se fiancer**, *v.r.* to become engaged to each other.
fiasco [fjas'ko], *n.m. inv.* fiasco, failure.
fibre [fibr], *n.f.* fiber, filament; (*fig.*) feeling.
fibreux [fi'brø], *a.* (*fem.* **-euse**) fibrous, stringy.
ficeler [fis'le], *v.t.* (*conjug. like* APPELER) to bind *or* tie up with string; to do up; to dress up.
ficeleur [fis'lœːr], *n.m.* (*fem.* **-euse**) packer.
ficelle [fi'sɛl], *n.f.* string, packthread, twine; (*fig.*) dodge.
fiche [fiʃ], *n.f.* peg, pin (*for a hinge etc.*); (*Teleph.*) plug; small card; (*Whist*) booby prize; (*colloq.*) slip of paper, memo.
ficher [fi'ʃe], *v.t.* to drive in, to fasten in. **se ficher**, *v.r.* (*colloq.*) to laugh at (*de*).
fichier [fi'ʃje], *n.m.* card index (*cabinet*).
fichoir [fi'ʃwaːr], *n.m.* clothespin.
fichtre! [fiʃtr], *int.* (*colloq.*) dash it! hang it!
fichu (1) [fi'ʃy], *n.m.* neckerchief.

fichu (2) [fi'ʃy], *a.* sorry, pitiful; got up (*dressed*); (*slang*) done for.
fictif [fik'tif], *a.* (*fem.* **-tive**) supposed, fictitious.
fiction [fik'sjɔ̃], *n.f.* fiction; fable.
fictivement [fiktiv'mɑ̃], *adv.* fictitiously.
fidèle [fi'dɛl], *a.* faithful, loyal, true.—*n.* faithful friend etc.; (*pl.*) worshippers, faithful.
fidèlement [fidɛl'mɑ̃], *adv.* faithfully, truly.
fidélité [fideli'te], *n.f.* fidelity, faithfulness, loyalty; accuracy.
fief [fjɛf], *n.m.* fief, fee.
fieffé [fje'fe], *a.* (*colloq.*) arrant, downright.
fiel [fjɛl], *n.m.* gall; (*fig.*) hatred, bitterness, rancour.
fier [fje], *v.t.* to trust, to entrust. **se fier**, *v.r.* to trust to *or* in, to depend upon (*à*).
fier [fjɛːr], *a.* (*fem.* **fière**) proud, haughty; bold; (*colloq.*) fine, capital.
fièrement [fjɛr'mɑ̃], *adv.* proudly, arrogantly, haughtily; boldly.
fierté [fjɛr'te], *n.f.* pride, arrogance; dignity.
fièvre [fjɛːvr], *n.f.* fever, feverishness; (*fig.*) restlessness, excitement.
fiévreux [fje'vrø], *a.* (*fem.* **-euse**) feverish; (*fig.*) restless.—*n.m.* (*fem.* **-euse**) fever-patient.
fifre [fifr], *n.m.* fife; fifer.
figé [fi'ʒe], *a.* stiff, cold, set (*features, smile etc.*).
figement [fiʒ'mɑ̃], *n.m.* congealment, coagulation, curdling.
figer [fi'ʒe], *v.t.* and **se figer**, *v.r.* (*conjug. like* MANGER) to congeal, to coagulate, to curdle.
figue [fig], *n.f.* fig.
figuier [fi'gje], *n.m.* fig tree.
figurant [figy'rɑ̃], *n.m.* (*fem.* **-e**) (*Theat., Cine.*) figurant; extra.
figuratif [figyra'tif], *a.* (*fem.* **-tive**) figurative.
figurativement [figyrativ'mɑ̃], *adv.* figuratively.
figure [fi'gyːr], *n.f.* figure, shape; face, appearance; symbol, type.
figuré [figy're], *a.* figured; figurative.
figurer [figy're], *v.t.* to figure, to represent.—*v.i.* to figure, to appear. **se figurer**, *v.r.* to imagine, fancy *or* picture to oneself.
figurine [figy'rin], *n.f.* figurine, statuette.
fil [fil], *n.m.* thread; wire; yarn; (cutting) edge; grain, vein (*in stones etc.*); course (*of a stream etc.*); chain, series; *de fil en aiguille*, one thing leading to another; *donner un coup de fil*, to give a ring; *être au bout du fil*, to be speaking (*on the phone*); *fil à coudre*, sewing thread; *fil de la Vierge*, gossamer; *laine deux fils*, two-ply wool.
filage [fi'laːʒ], *n.m.* spinning.
filament [fila'mɑ̃], *n.m.* filament, thread.
filamenteux [filamɑ̃'tø], *a.* (*fem.* **-euse**) thready, stringy.
filandière [filɑ̃'djɛːr], *n.f.* spinner.
filandreux [filɑ̃'drø], *a.* (*fem.* **-euse**) fibrous, stringy, thready.
filant [fi'lɑ̃], *a.* flowing; ropy; shooting (*of stars*).
filasse [fi'las], *n.f.* harl, tow (*of flax, hemp etc.*); oakum.
filateur [fila'tœːr], *n.m.* spinning-mill owner; spinner.

filature [fila'ty:r], *n.f.* spinning-mill; spinning; shadowing (*by a detective*).

file [fil], *n.f.* file; *à la file*, one after another; *prendre la file*, to take one's place in the line.

filé [fi'le], *a.* drawn out, sustained.—*n.m.* gold or silver thread.

filer [fi'le], *v.t.* to spin; (*fig.*) to carry on; to spin out (*a story etc.*); (*Naut.*) to pay out (*a rope*); to trail, to shadow.—*v.i.* to become ropy; to go, to travel; to shoot (*of stars*); to flare (*of a lamp etc.*); to take oneself off; *filer à l'anglaise*, to take French leave; *filer doux*, to sing small.

filet [fi'le], *n.m.* slender thread, string; net; (*Rail.*) rack; filament, fiber; (*Bot., Arch. etc.*) fillet; drop (*of water etc.*); (*fig.*) streak; trickle, streamlet; snaffle-bridle; (*fig.*) snare.

fileur [fi'lœ:r], *n.m.* (*fem.* **-euse**) spinner; wire-drawer.

filial [fi'ljal], *a.* (*m. pl.* **-aux**) filial.

filiale [fi'ljal], *n.f.* subsidiary company, branch.

filiation [filja'sjɔ̃], *n.f.* filiation; (*fig.*) connection, relationship.

filière [fi'ljɛ:r], *n.f.* draw-plate; screw-plate; (*Carp.*) purlin; (*fig.*) channel, series.

filigrane [fili'gran], *n.m.* filigree, filigree work; water-mark (*in paper*); embossing.

filigraner [filigra'ne], *v.t.* to work in filigree; to emboss.

fille [fi:j], *n.f.* daughter; girl, young unmarried woman; maiden; servant-maid; *arrière-petite-fille*, great-granddaughter; *belle-fille*, daughter-in-law, stepdaughter; *jeune fille*, girl; *petite-fille*, granddaughter; *vieille fille*, old maid.

fillette [fi'jet], *n.f.* little girl; lass.

filleul [fi'jœ:l], *n.m.* godson.

filleule [fi'jœ:l], *n.f.* goddaughter.

film [film], *n.m.* film; *film fixe*, film strip.

filmer [fil'me], *v.t.* to film.

filon [fi'lɔ̃], *n.m.* metallic vein; (*fig.*) good job; tip.

filou [fi'lu], *n.m.* pickpocket, thief; swindler.

filouter [filu'te], *v.t.* to steal; to cheat, to swindle.

filouterie [filu'tri], *n.f.* picking pockets; swindling, cheating.

fils [fis], *n.m. inv.* son, male child; offspring; *arrière-petit-fils*, great-grandson; *beau-fils*, stepson, son-in-law; *petit-fils*, grandson.

filtrage [fil'tra:3], *n.m.* filtering, straining.

filtrant [fil'trɑ̃], *a.* filtering, straining; *bout filtrant*, filter-tip.

filtration [filtra'sjɔ̃], *n.f.* filtration, straining; percolation.

filtre (1) [filtr], *n.m.* filter; cup of filtered coffee; *filtre à café*, percolator.

filtre (2) [PHILTRE].

filtrer [fil'tre], *v.t.* to filter, to strain.—*v.i.* and se filtrer, *v.r.* to filter; to percolate.

filure [fi'ly:r], *n.f.* texture of a spun fabric.

fin (1) [fɛ̃], *n.f.* end, conclusion, close; death; destination; aim, design.

fin (2) [fɛ̃], *a.* fine, thin, slender; delicate; refined, polite; acute; cunning.—*n.m.* sharp fellow; main point.—*n.f.* (**-e**) type of liqueur brandy.

final [fi'nal], *a.* final, last, ultimate.

finale [fi'nal], *n.m.* (*Mus.*) finale.—*n.f.* (*Spt.*) final.

finalement [final'mɑ̃], *adv.* finally, lastly.

finalité [finali'te], *n.f.* finality.

finance [fi'nɑ̃:s], *n.f.* ready money; (*pl.*) (*public*) finances, exchequer, treasury.

financer [finɑ̃'se], *v.t.* (*conjug. like* COMMENCER) to finance.—*v.i.* to lay out money.

financier [finɑ̃'sje], *a.* (*fem.* **-ière**) financial. —*n.m.* financier.

financièrement [finɑ̃sjɛr'mɑ̃], *adv.* financially.

finaud [fi'no], *a.* sly, artful, cunning.—*n.m.* (*fem.* **-e**) sly, artful person.

fine [fin], [FIN (2)].

finement [fin'mɑ̃], *adv.* finely, delicately; ingeniously; artfully.

finesse [fi'nɛs], *n.f.* fineness; delicacy; ingenuity; finesse, artifice, slyness.

finette [fi'net], *n.f.* thin material of wool or cotton, flannelette.

fini [fi'ni], *a.* finished, ended.—*n.m.* finish, high finish, perfection.

finir [fi'ni:r], *v.t.* to finish, to complete; to end, to terminate.—*v.i.* to end, to conclude, to be over; to expire.

finissage [fini'sa:3], *n.m.* finishing touches.

finissant [fini'sɑ̃], *a.* declining, dying.

finlandais [fɛ̃lɑ̃'dɛ], *a.* Finnish.—*n.m.* Finnish (*language*); (Finlandais, *fem.* **-aise**) Finn.

Finlande [fɛ̃'lɑ̃:d], **la**, *f.* Finland.

finnois [fi'nwa], *a.* Finnish.—*n.m.* Finnish (*language*); (Finnois, *fem.* **-oise**) Finn.

fiole [fjɔl], *n.f.* phial.

firmament [firma'mɑ̃], *n.m.* firmament, sky.

fisc [fisk], *n.m.* public treasury, fisc.

fiscal [fis'kal], *a.* (*m. pl.* **-aux**) fiscal, financial.

fissible [fi'sibl], *a.* fissile (*of radio-active materials*).

fission [fi'sjɔ̃], *n.f.* fission, splitting (*of atom*); *fission de l'atome*, nuclear fission.

fissure [fi'sy:r], *n.f.* fissure, crack, rent.

fissurer (se) [səfisy're], *v.r.* to become fissured.

five-o'clock [faivɔ'klɔk], *n.m.* afternoon tea.

fixation [fiksa'sjɔ̃], *n.f.* fixation, fixing; settlement; rating, assessment.

fixe [fiks], *a.* fixed; settled; appointed, regular. —*n.m.* fixed salary.—*int.* (*Mil.*) eyes front! steady!

fixement [fiksə'mɑ̃], *adv.* fixedly, steadily.

fixer [fik'se], *v.t.* to fix, to fasten; to settle; to establish; to stare at; to attract. se fixer, *v.r.* to be fixed; to settle down.

fixité [fiksi'te], *n.f.* fixity, stability.

flac [flak], *int.* slap! bang! plop!—*n.m.* anti-aircraft gunfire, flak.

flaccidité [flaksidi'te], *n.f.* flaccidity.

flacon [fla'kɔ̃], *n.m.* bottle; decanter; phial.

flagellant [flaʒe'lɑ̃], *n.m.* flagellant.

flagellation [flaʒela'sjɔ̃], *n.f.* flagellation, flogging.

flageller [flaʒe'le], *v.t.* to flagellate, to scourge, to flog; (*fig.*) to lash with words.

flageoler [flaʒɔ'le], *v.i.* to tremble, to shake (*of legs*).

flageolet [flaʒɔ'le], *n.m.* flageolet (*music*); (*small*) green kidney bean.

flagorner [flagor'ne], *v.t.* to flatter servilely, to toady to.

flagornerie [flagɔrnəˈri], *n.f.* sycophancy, base flattery.

flagorneur [flagɔrˈnœːr], *n.m.* (*fem.* **-euse**) sycophant, toady.

flagrant [flaˈgrɑ̃], *a.* flagrant, gross; *en flagrant délit*, red-handed.

flair [flɛːr], *n.m.* (*Hunt.*) nose; (*fig.*) perspicacity.

flairer [flɛˈre], *v.t.* to smell, to scent; (*colloq.*) to smell of; to find out.

flamand [flaˈmɑ̃], *a.* Flemish.—*n.m.* Flemmish (*language*); (**Flamand**, *fem.* **-ande**) Fleming.

flamant (rose) [flaˈmɑ̃(roːz)], *n.m.* flamingo.

flambant [flɑ̃ˈbɑ̃], *a.* blazing, flaming; (*pop.*) smart, flashy; *flambant neuf*, brand new.

flambeau [flɑ̃ˈbo], *n.m.* (*pl.* **-eaux**) torch, link; candle, candlestick.

flambée [flɑ̃ˈbe], *n.f.* blaze.

flamber [flɑ̃ˈbe], *v.t.* to singe; to fumigate, to disinfect.—*v.i.* to blaze, to flame, to flare.

flamboiement [flɑ̃bwaˈmɑ̃], *n.m.* flaming, blaze.

flamboyant [flɑ̃bwaˈjɑ̃], *a.* flaming, blazing; flashing.

flamboyer [flɑ̃bwaˈje], *v.i.* (*conjug. like* EMPLOYER) to flame, to blaze, to flare.

flamme [flaːm], *n.f.* flame; (*fig.*) fire; glow; ardor, passion.

flammèche [flaˈmɛʃ], *n.f.* flake of fire, spark.

flammer [flaˈme], *v.t.* to singe (*material*).

flan [flɑ̃], *n.m.* (*baked*) custard tart; flan.

flanc [flɑ̃], *n.m.* flank, side; (*fig.*) womb, bowels.

flancher [flɑ̃ˈʃe], *v.i.* (*fam.*) to give in, to rat, to scab; (*Motor.*) to stop, to break down.

flandrin [flɑ̃ˈdrɛ̃], *n.m.* (*colloq.*) *un grand flandrin*, a long, lanky fellow.

flanelle [flaˈnɛl], *n.f.* flannel.

flâner [flɑˈne], *v.i.* to lounge, to stroll, to loaf.

flânerie [flɑˈnri], *n.f.* lounging; stroll; loafing.

flâneur [flɑˈnœːr], *n.m.* (*fem.* **-euse**) stroller; lounger, loafer.

flanquer [flɑ̃ˈke], *v.t.* to flank; (*Mil.*) to defend, to guard; (*colloq.*) to deal (*a blow*); to fling. **se flanquer**, *v.r. se flanquer par terre*, to throw oneself down.

flaque [flak], *n.f.* small pool, puddle.

flash [flaʃ], *n.m.* (*Phot.*) flash-light; (*Cine.*) flash.

flasque (1) [flask], *a.* limp, slack, flabby, flaccid.

flasque (2) [flask], *n.f.* powder horn.

flatter [flaˈte], *v.t.* to stroke, to caress; to flatter; to soothe; to cajole. **se flatter**, *v.r.* to flatter oneself; to pride oneself; to hope, to expect.

flatterie [flaˈtri], *n.f.* flattery, adulation.

flatteur [flaˈtœːr], *a.* (*fem.* **-euse**) flattering, complimentary.—*n.m.* (*fem.* **-euse**) flatterer.

flatteusement [flatœzˈmɑ̃], *adv.* flatteringly.

flatulence [flatyˈlɑ̃ːs], *n.f.* flatulence, wind.

flatulent [flatyˈlɑ̃], *a.* flatulent, windy.

fléau [fleˈo], *n.m.* (*pl.* **fléaux**) flail; (*fig.*) scourge, plague; beam (*of a balance*).

flèche [flɛʃ], *n.f.* arrow, dart; shaft; (*Arch.*) slender spire; *faire flèche de tout bois*, to leave no stone unturned.

fléchette [fleˈʃɛt], *n.f.* dart (*game*).

fléchir [fleˈʃiːr], *v.t.* to bend, to bow; (*fig.*) to move, to persuade.—*v.i.* to bend, to bow, to yield; to stagger.

fléchissement [fleʃisˈmɑ̃], *n.m.* bending, giving way.

flegmatique [flɛgmaˈtik], *a.* (*Med.*) phlegmatic; (*fig.*) stolid, sluggish.

flegme [flɛgm], *n.m.* phlegm; (*fig.*) coolness, impassivity.

flet [flɛ], **flétan** [fleˈtɑ̃], *n.m. grand flétan*, halibut; *petit flétan* or *flet*, flounder.

flétrir [fleˈtriːr], *v.t.* to wither; (*fig.*) to blight, to tarnish, to blemish. **se flétrir**, *v.r.* to fade, to wither.

flétrissant [fletriˈsɑ̃], *a.* dishonoring, blighting.

flétrissure [fletriˈsyːr], *n.f.* fading, withering; stigma, disgrace.

fleur [flœːr], *n.f.* flower, blossom; bloom; (*fig.*) best, pick; surface; *à fleur d'eau*, at water level; *à fleur de peau*, superficially; *yeux à fleur de tête*, prominent *or* goggle eyes.

fleurer [flœˈre], *v.i.* to smell, to exhale.

fleuret [flœˈre], *n.m.* (*Fenc.*) foil; miner's drill.

fleurette [flœˈrɛt], *n.f.* little flower, floweret; amorous discourse, gallant speech.

fleuri [flœˈri], *a.* flowery; florid.

fleurir [flœˈriːr], *v.t.* to decorate with flowers.—*v.i.* to flower, to blossom; to flourish. **se fleurir**, *v.r.* to adorn oneself with flowers.

fleurissant [flœriˈsɑ̃], *a.* blossoming, blooming.

fleuriste [flœˈrist], *a.* and *n.* florist; artificial flower maker *or* seller.

fleuron [flœˈrɔ̃], *n.m.* carved *or* painted flower; (*fig.*) flower work; jewel.

fleuve [flœːv], *n.m.* river (*flowing into the sea*), large stream.

flexibilité [flɛksibiliˈte], *n.f.* flexibility, pliancy.

flexible [flɛkˈsibl], *a.* flexible, pliable, supple.

flexion [flɛkˈsjɔ̃], *n.f.* flexion, bending.

flibuster [flibysˈte], *v.i.* to buccaneer, to filibuster, to freeboot.

flibusterie [flibysˈtri], *n.f.* filibustering; robbery, theft.

flibustier [flibysˈtje], *n.m.* buccaneer, pirate; filibuster.

flirt [flœrt], *n.m.* flirtation, flirting.

flirter [flœrˈte], *v.i.* to flirt.

floc [flɔk], *n.m.* tuft, tassel.—*int.* flop!

floche [flɔʃ], *a.* flossy, shaggy.

flocon [flɔˈkɔ̃], *n.m.* flock, tuft; flake (*of snow*).

floconneux [flɔkɔˈnø], *a.* (*fem.* **-euse**) flaky.

floraison [flɔrɛˈzɔ̃], *n.f.* efflorescence, flowering.

floral [flɔˈral], *a.* (*m. pl.* **-aux**) floral.

flore [flɔːr], *n.f.* flora.

florentin [flɔrɑ̃ˈtɛ̃], *a.* Florentine.

florin [flɔˈrɛ̃], *n.m.* florin.

florir [flɔˈriːr], [FLEURIR].

florissant [flɔriˈsɑ̃], *a.* prosperous, flourishing.

floriste [flɔˈrist], *n.* florist.

flot [flo], *n.m.* wave, billow; (*fig.*) tide, flood; crowd; (*pl.*) sea, stream, torrent.

flottage [flɔˈtaːʒ], *n.m.* floating of wood, rafting.

flottaison [flɔtɛˈzɔ̃], *n.f.* floating.

flottant [flɔˈtɑ̃], *a.* floating, waving; (*fig.*) irresolute.

flotte [flɔt], *n.f.* fleet; navy.

flottement [flɔtˈmɑ̃], *n.m.* floating; (*fig.*) wavering, irresolution.

flotter [flɔ'te], *v.i.* to float; to flutter (*of flag*); to be irresolute.

flotteur [flɔ'tœːr], *n.m.* raftsman; fishing-float; cable-buoy.

flottille [flɔ'tiːj], *n.f.* flotilla.

flou [flu], *a.* hazy, soft, blurred, out of focus. —*n.m.* softness, haziness (*of outlines*); (*Dress.*) looseness.

fluctuation [flyktɥa'sjɔ̃], *n.f.* fluctuation.

fluctuer [flyk'tɥe], *v.i.* to fluctuate.

fluctueux [flyk'tɥø], *a.* (*fem.* -**euse**) fluctuating, agitated, boisterous.

fluet [flɥ'ɛ], *a.* (*fem.* -**ette**) slender, thin, slim.

fluide [flɥ'id], *a.* fluid (*liquid*).—*n.m.* fluid.

fluidité [flɥidi'te], *n.f.* fluidity.

fluorescence [flyɔrɛ'sãːs], *n.f.* fluorescence.

fluorescent [flyɔrɛ'sã], *a.* fluorescent.

fluorure [flyɔ'yr], *n.m.* fluoride.

flûte [flyt], *n.f.* flute; long French roll; tall glass (*for champagne*).

flûté [fly'te], *a.* soft, fluted, fluty (*of a voice*).

flûtiste [fly'tist], *n.* flautist, flute player.

fluvial [fly'vjal], *a.* (*m. pl.* -**aux**) fluvial.

flux [fly], *n.m.* flux, flow, flood, rising.

fluxion [flyk'sjɔ̃], *n.f.* inflammation, swelling.

foc [fɔk], *n.m.* (*Naut.*) jib.

focal [fɔ'kal], *a.* (*m. pl.* -**aux**) focal.

foi [fwa], *n.f.* faith, belief; trust; fidelity, honor; proof, testimony.

foie [fwa], *n.m.* liver.

foin [fwɛ̃], *n.m.* hay.

foire [fwaːr], *n.f.* fair (*market*); fairing.

fois [fwa], *n.f. inv.* time (*turn, occasion*); *une fois*, once; *trois fois*, three times.

foison [fwa'zɔ̃], *n.f.* plenty, abundance.

foisonner [fwazɔ'ne], *v.i.* to abound, to increase, to multiply.

fol [fɔl], [FOU].

folâtre [fɔ'laːtr], *a.* playful, gay, frolicsome.

folâtrer [fɔla'tre], *v.i.* to play, to sport, to frolic.

folâtrerie [fɔlatrə'ri], *n.f.* frolic, prank, gambol.

foliacé [fɔlja'se], *a.* (*Bot.*) foliaceous.

foliation [fɔlja'sjɔ̃], *n.f.* foliation.

folichon [fɔli'ʃɔ̃], *a.* (*fam.*) frolicsome, waggish, wanton.

folie [fɔ'li], *n.f.* madness, distraction, folly; foolery, jest; mania; hobby.

folio [fɔ'ljo], *n.m.* folio.

folle [fɔl], [FOU].

follement [fɔl'mã], *adv.* madly, foolishly.

follet [fɔ'lɛ], *a.* (*fem.* -**ette**) wanton, playful, frolicsome; *feu follet*, will o' the wisp.

fomentation [fɔmãta'sjɔ̃], *n.f.* fomentation.

fomenter [fɔmã'te], *v.t.* to foment; (*fig.*) to feed, to excite.

foncé [fɔ̃'se], *a.* dark, deep (*of color*).

foncer [fɔ̃'se], *v.t.* (*conjug. like* COMMENCER) to fit a bottom to (*a cask etc.*); to sink (*wells etc.*); to deepen (*colors*). —*v.i.* to dash, to swoop (*sur*).

foncier [fɔ̃'sje], *a.* (*fem.* -**ière**) landed; based on *or* derived from land; (*fig.*) thorough.—*n.m.* land tax.

foncièrement [fɔ̃sjɛr'mã], *adv.* thoroughly, completely, fundamentally.

fonction [fɔ̃k'sjɔ̃], *n.f.* function, office; occupation.

fonctionnaire [fɔ̃ksjɔ'nɛːr], *n.m.* civil servant, officer, official.

fonctionnel [fɔ̃ksjɔ'nɛl], *a.* (*fem.* -**elle**) functional.

fonctionnement [fɔ̃ksjɔn'mã], *n.m.* operation, working, action.

fonctionner [fɔ̃ksjɔ'ne], *v.i.* to work, to act, to operate.

fond [fɔ̃], *n.m.* bottom; bed, ground; farther end; foundation; (*fig.*) essence; basis; subject matter; (*Paint.*) background; (*Theat.*) back-cloth.

fondage [fɔ̃'daːʒ], *n.m.* casting, smelting.

fondamental [fɔ̃damã'tal], *a.* (*m. pl.* -**aux**) fundamental, essential.

fondamentalement [fɔ̃damãtal'mã], *adv.* fundamentally, essentially, radically.

fondant [fɔ̃'dã], *a.* melting, dissolving; luscious.—*n.m.* fondant (*sweetmeat*); flux (*for metals*).

fondateur [fɔ̃da'tœːr], *n.m.* (*fem.* -**trice**) founder; promoter.

fondation [fɔ̃da'sjɔ̃], *n.f.* foundation; groundwork; founding; endowment.

fondé [fɔ̃'de], *a.* founded, well-founded; (*Fin.*) consolidated.—*n.m.* proxy.

fondement [fɔ̃d'mã], *n.m.* foundation; basis, ground, cause.

fonder [fɔ̃'de], *v.t.* to lay the foundation of, to establish; to institute; to base; to endow. **se fonder**, *v.r.* to rely *or* rest (*upon*), to be founded (*sur*).

fonderie [fɔ̃'dri], *n.f.* foundry; smelting-house; casting.

fondeur [fɔ̃'dœːr], *n.m.* founder, caster, smelter.

fondre [fɔ̃:dr], *v.t.* to melt; to dissolve; to smelt; to cast.—*v.i.* to melt; to pounce (*sur*); to vanish; to blow (*of a fuse*); *fondre en larmes*, to burst into tears. **se fondre**, *v.r.* to melt; to dissolve; to be cast; to blend; to diminish, to melt away.

fondrière [fɔ̃dri'ɛːr], *n.f.* bog, quagmire; rut, pothole; slough.

fonds [fɔ̃], *n.m.* land, soil; landed property; funds, capital; business assets; (*pl.*) funds, stocks etc.

fondue [fɔ̃'dy], *n.f.* dish of melted cheese and eggs.

fongicide [fɔ̃ʒi'sid], *a.* fungicide.

fongoïde [fɔ̃gɔ'id], *a.* fungoid.

fongueux [fɔ̃'gø], *a.* (*fem.* -**euse**) fungous.

fongus [fɔ̃'gys], *n.m.* (*Med.*) fungus.

fontaine [fɔ̃'tɛːn], *n.f.* fountain, spring; cistern.

fonte [fɔ̃:t], *n.f.* melting, smelting; cast-iron; casting; holster (*of saddles*).

fonts [fɔ̃], *n.m. pl.* (*no sing.*) font.

football [fut'bɔl], *n.m.* Association Football.

footballeur [futbɔ'lœːr], *n.m.* football player.

footing [fu'tiŋ], *n.m.* walking (*for training or exercise*).

forage [fɔ'raːʒ], *n.m.* boring, drilling; sinking (*of well*).

forain [fɔ'rɛ̃], *a.* non-resident, travelling, itinerant; *marchand forain*, hawker, pedlar.

forban [fɔr'bã], *n.m.* pirate, corsair, freebooter.

forçat [fɔr'sa], *n.m.* convict.

force [fɔrs], *n.f.* strength, might, power; authority; violence, constraint; vigor; resolution; skill; (*pl.*) troops, forces.— *†adv.* a great deal, a great many.

forcé [fɔr'se], a. forced, compulsory; un-natural, strained, far-fetched.

forcément [fɔrse'mã], adv. forcibly; neces-sarily, inevitably.

forcené [fɔrsa'ne], a. mad, furious; passion-ate, infuriated.—n.m. (fem. **-ée**) mad person.

forceps [fɔr'seps], n.m. inv. forceps.

forcer [fɔr'se], v.t. (conjug. like COMMENCER) to force; to compel; to impel; to strain; to break open; to storm; to outrage. **se forcer**, v.r. to strain oneself; to do violence to one's feelings.

forer [fɔ're], v.t. to bore, to drill, to perforate.

forestier [fɔres'tje], a. (fem. **-ière**) pertaining to forests.—n.m. ranger, keeper, forester.

foret [fɔ're], n.m. borer, drill.

forêt [fɔ're], n.f. forest; woodland.

forfaire [fɔr'fɛːr], v.t. irr. to forfeit (a fief).—v.i. (used only in inf., p.p. (**forfait** (1) and compound tenses) to fail (in one's duty); to trespass, to be false to.

forfait (2) [fɔr'fɛ], n.m. crime, heinous offence.

forfait (3) [fɔr'fɛ], n.m. contract.

forfaiture [fɔrfɛ'tyːr], n.f. forfeiture; breach of duty.

forfanterie [fɔrfɑ'tri], n.f. romancing, bragging, boasting.

forge [fɔrʒ], n.f. forge, smithy; iron-works.

forger [fɔr'ʒe], v.t. (conjug. like MANGER) to forge, to hammer; (fig.) to invent, to fabri-cate. **se forger**, v.r. to imagine, to conjure up, to fancy.

forgeron [fɔrʒə'rɔ̃], n.m. smith, blacksmith.

formaliser (**se**) [səfɔrmali'ze], v.r. to take exception or offence (de).

formalisme [fɔrma'lism], n.m. formalism.

formaliste [fɔrma'list], a. formal, precise.—n. formalist; quibbler.

formalité [fɔrmali'te], n.f. formality; form, ceremony.

format [fɔr'ma], n.m. format (size, shape etc., of a book).

formateur [fɔrma'tœːr], a. (fem. **-trice**) for-mative, creative.

formation [fɔrma'sjɔ̃], n.f. formation; educa-tion; (Geol.) structure.

forme [fɔrm], n.f. form, shape, figure; etiquette; crown (of a hat).

formé [fɔr'me], a. formed, mature.

formel [fɔr'mɛl], a. (fem. **-elle**) formal; express, precise.

formellement [fɔrmɛl'mã], adv. formally; expressly, precisely, strictly.

former [fɔr'me], v.t. to form, to frame; to make up; to bring up; to train; to mold. **se former**, v.r. to be formed; to take shape.

formidable [fɔrmi'dabl], a. formidable, fear-ful; (fam.) terrific.

Formose [fɔr'moːz], **la**, f. Formosa, Taiwan.

formule [fɔr'myl], n.f. formula, form; model; recipe.

formuler [fɔrmy'le], v.t. to formulate; to detail; (Med.) to write (a prescription).

fort [fɔːr], a. strong, sturdy; powerful; clever; plentiful; shocking; painful; high (wind); heavy (ground, rain).—n.m. strong part; stronghold, fort; strength; depth, heat, height; centre.—adv. very, very much, extremely; hard.

fortement [fɔrtə'mã], adv. strongly, vigor-ously; much, exceedingly.

forteresse [fɔrtə'rɛs], n.f. fortress, strong-hold.

fortifiant [fɔrti'fjã], a. strengthening, brac-ing.—n.m. (Med.) tonic.

fortification [fɔrtifika'sjɔ̃], n.f. fortification; fort, redoubt.

fortifier [fɔrti'fje], v.t. to strengthen, to invigorate; to fortify; to confirm. **se fortifier**, v.r. to fortify oneself, to grow strong.

fortuit [fɔr'tɥi], a. fortuitous, casual.

fortuitement [fɔrtɥit'mã], adv. fortuitously, casually, by chance.

fortune [fɔr'tyn], n.f. fortune, chance, hazard, risk; success, luck; wealth.

fortuné [fɔrty'ne], a. fortunate, lucky; happy; well-to-do.

fosse [foːs], n.f. hole, pit; grave; (Hort.) trench.

fossé [fo'se], n.m. ditch, drain, trench; moat.

fossette [fo'sɛt], n.f. dimple.

fossile [fɔ'sil], a. fossilized.—n.m. fossil.

fossiliser [fɔsili'ze], v.t. to fossilize. **se fossiliser**, v.r. to become fossilized.

fossoyage [fɔswa'jaːʒ], n.m. ditching; grave-digging.

fossoyer [fɔswa'je], v.t. (conjug. like EM-PLOYER) to ditch, to dig a trench round.

fossoyeur [fɔswa'jœːr], n.m. grave digger; sexton beetle.

fou [fu], a. (before vowels **fol**, fem. **folle**) mad, demented; wild, foolish; tremendous.—n.m. (fem. **folle**) madman, madwoman.—n.m. jester, fool; (Chess) bishop.

foudre (1) [fudr], n.f. lightning; thunder, thunderbolt; (fig.) sudden calamity; coup de foudre, clap of thunder.—n.m. (fig.) un foudre de guerre a great captain; un foudre d'éloquence, a mighty speaker.

foudre (2) [fudr], n.m. large cask, tun.

foudroiement [fudrwa'mã], n.m. striking, blasting (by thunder or lightning); (fig.) destruction.

foudroyant [fudrwa'jã], a. thundering; terrible, crushing (news).

foudroyer [fudrwa'je], v.t. (conjug. like EMPLOYER) to strike (thunder or lightning); to riddle with shot; (fig.) to blast, to crush.—v.i. to thunder; (fig.) to fulminate.

fouet [fwe], n.m. whip; lash; whipping, slating (criticism).

fouetter [fwɛ'te], v.t. to whip, to flog; to beat (eggs etc.); to flick; (fig.) to excite.—v.i. to beat, to patter (of hail, rain).

fougeraie [fuʒ're], n.f. fern patch, fernery.

fougère [fu'ʒɛːr], n.f. fern.

fougue [fug], n.f. ardor, impetuosity; fire, spirit, mettle; (Naut.) mizzen-top.

fougueux [fu'gø], a. (fem. **-euse**) fiery, impetuous, ardent, passionate, high-mettled.

fouille [fuːj], n.f. excavation, digging; search.

fouiller [fu'je], v.t. to excavate; (fig.) to pry into, to rummage, to ransack; to search; to think out (problems etc.).—v.i. to dig, to search; (fig.) to rummage.

fouillis [fu'ji], n.m. medley, jumble; confused mass (of foliage etc.).

fouine (1) [fwin], n.f. marten.

fouine (2) [fwin], *n.f.* pitchfork; fish spear.
fouiner [fwi'ne], *v.i.* (*colloq.*) to nose about, to ferret; to slink off.
fouir [fwi:r], *v.t.* to dig; to burrow.
fouissement [fwis'mã], *n.m.* digging; burrowing.
fouisseur [fwi'sœ:r], *a.* (*fem.* **-euse**) burrowing (*animal*).
foulage [fu'la:ʒ], *n.m.* fulling; treading, pressing (*of grapes*).
foulant [fu'lã], *a.* pressing; forcing; **pompe foulante**, force pump.
foulard [fu'la:r], *n.m.* silk neckerchief; scarf.
foule [ful], *n.f.* crowd, throng, multitude; mob.
foulée [fu'le], *n.f.* tread (*of steps*); stride (*of a horse or runner*).
fouler [fu'le], *v.t.* to tread; to trample down; to press; to oppress; to sprain (*ankle*).—*v.i.* (*Print.*) to press. **se fouler**, *v.r.* **se fouler le pied**, to sprain one's foot.
fouleur [fu'lœ:r], *n.m.* (*fem.* **-euse**) fuller; wine presser.
foulure [fu'ly:r], *n.f.* sprain, wrench, strain.
four [fu:r], *n.m.* oven; bakehouse; furnace; kiln; **des petits fours**, fancy biscuits, small cakes.
fourbe [furb], *a.* cheating, deceitful.—*n.* cheat, swindler, impostor.
fourberie [furbə'ri], *n.f.* cheating, knavery, imposture, deceit.
fourbir [fur'bi:r], *v.t.* to furbish, to polish.
fourbisseur [furbi'sœ:r], *n.m.* furbisher; sword-cutler.
fourbissure [furbi'sy:r], *n.f.* furbishing, polishing.
fourbu [fur'by], *a.* foundered, run down (*of horses*); dead tired (*of persons*).
fourbure [fur'by:r], *n.f.* foundering, inflammation of the feet.
fourche [furʃ], *n.f.* pitchfork, (garden) fork, fork (*of roads*).
fourchée [fur'ʃe], *n.f.* pitchforkful.
fourcher [fur'ʃe], *v.i.* to fork; to divide. **se fourcher**, *v.r.* to fork, to branch off.
fourchette [fur'ʃet], *n.f.* table-forkful.
fourchette [fur'ʃet], *n.f.* table fork; breast bone (*of birds*).
fourchu [fur'ʃy], *a.* forked; cloven; furcate.
fourgon (1) [fur'gõ], *n.m.* van, truck, freight *or* baggage car.
fourgon (2) [fur'gõ], *n.m.* poker, fire-iron (*for ovens etc.*).
fourgonner [furgɔ'ne], *v.i.* to poke the fire (*of an oven*); (*colloq.*) to poke, to rummage.
fourmi [fur'mi], *n.f.* ant.
fourmilière [furmi'ljɛ:r], *n.f.* ant hill, ants' nest; (*fig.*) swarm; crowd.
fourmillement [furmij'mã], *n.m.* tingling, pins and needles; swarming.
fourmiller [furmi'je], *v.i.* to swarm, to be full (*de*); to have pins and needles (*in one's limbs etc.*).
fournaise [fur'ne:z], *n.f.* (*Lit.*) furnace; (*fig.*) oven.
fourneau [fur'no], *n.m.* (*pl.* **-eaux**) stove, cooker, cooking range; furnace.
fournée [fur'ne], *n.f.* batch, baking; kilnful (*of bricks*).
fournil [fur'ni], *n.m.* bakehouse.
fourniment [furni'mã], *n.m.* (*Mil.*) equipment.

fournir [fur'ni:r], *v.t.* to furnish, to supply, to stock, to provide; to make up (*a sum of money*).—*v.i.* to contribute (*à*); to suffice.
fournisseur [furni'sœ:r], *n.m.* army contractor; purveyor; tradesman.
fourniture [furni'ty:r], *n.f.* furnishing; supply, provision; equipment.
fourrage [fu'ra:ʒ], *n.m.* fodder; forage; foraging party.
fourrager [fura'ʒe], *v.t.* (*conjug. like* MANGER) to ravage; to upset.—*v.i.* to forage; to plunder, to ravage; (*fig.*) to rummage.
fourrageur [fura'ʒœ:r], *n.m.* forager; (*fig.*) marauder; rummager.
fourré [fu're], *a.* thick, furry; wooded; (*fig.*) underhand (*of a blow etc.*).—*n.m.* thicket, brake.
fourreau [fu'ro], *n.m.* (*pl.* **-eaux**) sheath, case; scabbard; cover; tight-fitting *or* sheath dress.
fourrer [fu're], *v.t.* to line with fur; to poke; to cram, to stuff. **se fourrer**, *v.r.* to thrust oneself in, to intrude; to wrap oneself up warmly.
fourreur [fu'rœ:r], *n.m.* furrier.
fourrier [fu'rje], *n.m.* quartermaster-sergeant; (*fig.*) harbinger.
fourrière [fu'rjɛ:r], *n.f.* pound (*for vehicles, strayed animals*).
fourrure [fu'ry:r], *n.f.* fur, furred gown.
fourvoyer [furvwa'je], *v.t.* (*conjug. like* EMPLOYER) to lead astray, to mislead; (*fig.*) to baffle. **se fourvoyer**, *v.r.* to go astray, to lose one's way; (*fig.*) to blunder badly.
fox (1) [foks], *n.m.* fox terrier.
fox (2) [foks], *n.m.* foxtrot.
foyer [fwa'je], *n.m.* hearth; fire; fire box (*of an engine*); (*fig.*) home, family; (*Theat.*) foyer; focus, source.
frac [frak], *n.m.* frock coat.
fracas [fra'ka], *n.m.* noise, din; disturbance; fuss.
fracasser [fraka'se], *v.t.* to break into pieces, to shatter. **se fracasser**, *v.r.* to crash to pieces.
fraction [frak'sjõ], *n.f.* breaking; fraction, portion.
fractionnaire [fraksjɔ'nɛ:r], *a.* fractional.
fracture [frak'ty:r], *n.f.* breaking (*with violence*), rupture; (*Surg.*) fracture.
fracturer [frakty're], *v.t.* to break, to smash; (*Surg.*) to fracture. **se fracturer**, *v.r.* to fracture oneself; to be fractured.
fragile [fra'ʒil], *a.* fragile, brittle; frail.
fragilité [fraʒili'te], *n.f.* fragility, brittleness; frailty.
fragment [frag'mã], *n.m.* fragment, piece, remnant.
fragmentaire [fragmã'tɛ:r], *a.* fragmentary.
fragmentation [fragmãta'sjõ], *n.f.* fragmenting, fragmentation.
fragmenter [fragmã'te], *v.t.* to reduce to fragments.
fragrance [fra'grã:s], *n.f.* fragrance.
fragrant [fra'grã], *a.* fragrant.
frai [fre], *n.m.* fraying; spawning (*of fish*).
fraîche [freʃ], [FRAIS (1)].
fraîchement [freʃ'mã], *adv.* coolly, freshly; newly, recently.
fraîcheur [fre'ʃœ:r], *n.f.* coolness, freshness, coldness; ruddiness; brilliancy.
fraîchir [fre'ʃi:r], *v.i.* to freshen; to get cool.

159

frais

frais (1) [frɛ], *a.* (*fem.* **fraîche**) cool; fresh; new; youthful; ruddy; new-laid (*of eggs*).—*n.m.* coolness, freshness; cool spot.—*adv.* freshly, newly, recently, just.

frais (2) [frɛ], *n.m.* (*used only in pl.*) expense, expenses; charge, charges, cost, outlay; *menus frais*, petty expenses; *sans frais*, free of charge.

fraise (1) [frɛːz], *n.f.* strawberry; strawberry mark, birthmark; ruff.

fraise (2) [frɛːz], *n.f.* fraise (*tool for enlarging a drill hole etc.*); (dentist's) drill.

fraiser [frɛ'ze], *v.t.* to plait, to ruffle; to countersink.

fraisier [frɛ'zje], *n.m.* strawberry plant; strawberry grower.

framboise [frɑ̃'bwaːz], *n.f.* raspberry.

framboiser [frɑ̃bwa'ze], *v.t.* to give a raspberry flavor to.

framboisier [frɑ̃bwa'zje], *n.m.* raspberry-bush.

franc (1) [frɑ̃], *n.m.* franc (*French coin*); new franc (*of 1960*).

franc (2) [frɑ̃], *a.* (*fem.* **franche**) free; exempt; frank, candid, sincere; clear.—*adv.* frankly, openly, sincerely; clean; quite, completely.

franc (3) [frɑ̃], *a.* (*fem.* **franque**) Frankish.—*n.m.* Frankish (*language*); (**Franc**, *fem.* **Franque**) Frank.

français [frɑ̃'sɛ], *a.* French.—*n.m.* French (*language*); (**Français**, *fem.* **-aise**) Frenchman, Frenchwoman.

France [frɑ̃ːs], **la**, *f.* France.

franche [frɑ̃ʃ], [FRANC (2)].

franchement [frɑ̃ʃ'mɑ̃], *adv.* frankly, sincerely; plainly; boldly.

franchir [frɑ̃'ʃiːr], *v.t.* to leap, to jump over; to clear; to pass over; to surmount.

franchise [frɑ̃'ʃiːz], *n.f.* exemption, immunity; freedom (*of a city*); (*fig.*) frankness, sincerity.

franchissable [frɑ̃ʃi'sabl], *a.* passable, capable of being crossed.

franchissement [frɑ̃ʃis'mɑ̃], *n.m.* leaping over, crossing.

francisation [frɑ̃siza'sjɔ̃], *n.f.* Gallicizing of foreign word; registration as a French ship.

franciscain [frɑ̃sis'kɛ̃], *a.* and *n.m.* (*fem.* **-e**) Franciscan, grey friar, Franciscan nun.

franciser [frɑ̃si'ze], *v.t.* to Gallicize; to Frenchify. **se franciser**, *v.r.* to become French *or* Frenchified.

franc-maçon [frɑ̃ma'sɔ̃], *n.m.* (*pl.* **francs-maçons**) freemason.

franc-maçonnerie [frɑ̃masɔn'ri], *n.f.* freemasonry.

franco [frɑ̃'ko], *adv.* free of charge; prepaid.

François [frɑ̃'swa], *m.* Francis.

Françoise [frɑ̃'swaːz], *f.* Frances.

francophile [frɑ̃ko'fil], *a.* and *n.* Francophile.

francophobe [frɑ̃ko'fɔb], *a.* and *n.* Francophobe.

franc-parler [frɑ̃par'le], *n.m.* frankness *or* freedom of speech.

franc-tireur [frɑ̃ti'rœːr], *n.m.* franc-tireur; sniper.

frange [frɑ̃ːʒ], *n.f.* fringe.

franger [frɑ̃'ʒe], *v.t.* (*conjug. like* MANGER) to fringe.

franque [frɑ̃k], [FRANC (3)].

frappant [fra'pɑ̃], *a.* striking, impressive.

frappé [fra'pe], *a.* struck, astounded; iced (*of liquids etc.*); (*fig.*) powerful.

frappement [frap'mɑ̃], *n.m.* striking, stamping; clapping (*of hands*).

frapper [fra'pe], *v.t.* to strike, to slap, to hit; to make an impression on, to affect; to surprise, to frighten; to ice (*liquids*).—*v.i.* to knock, to rap. **se frapper**, *v.r.* to strike oneself; to strike each other; to be impressed.

frappeur [fra'pœːr], *a.* (*fem.* **-euse**) striking, rapping.—*n.m.* (*fem.* **-euse**) beater, striker.

frasque [frask], *n.f.* prank, escapade.

fraternel [fratɛr'nɛl], *a.* (*fem.* **-elle**) fraternal, brotherly.

fraternellement [fratɛrnɛl'mɑ̃], *adv.* fraternally.

fraternisation [fratɛrniza'sjɔ̃], *n.f.* fraternization.

fraterniser [fratɛrni'ze], *v.t.* to fraternize.

fraternité [fratɛrni'te], *n.f.* fraternity, brotherhood.

fratricide [fratri'sid], *a.* fratricidal.—*n.m.* fratricide.

fraude [froːd], *n.f.* fraud, deceit.

frauder [fro'de], *v.t.* to defraud.—*v.i.* to smuggle.

fraudeur [fro'dœːr], *n.m.* (*fem.* **-euse**) defrauder; smuggler.

frauduleusement [frodyløz'mɑ̃], *adv.* fraudulently.

frauduleux [frody'lø], *a.* (*fem.* **-euse**) fraudulent.

frayer [frɛ'je], *v.t.* to trace out, to open out; to make (*a way etc.*); to rub against, to graze.—*v.i.* to wear away; to spawn (*of fish*); (*fig.*) to frequent, to be on good terms (*avec*). **se frayer**, *v.r.* to open for oneself; to prepare *or* carve out (*a way*) for oneself.

frayeur [frɛ'jœːr], *n.f.* fright, terror, fear.

fredaine [frə'dɛn], *n.f.* (*colloq.*) frolic, prank; freak.

Frédéric [frede'rik], *m.* Frederick.

Frédérique [frede'rik], *f.* Frederica.

fredon [frə'dɔ̃], *n.m.* song, refrain.

fredonnement [frədɔn'mɑ̃], *n.m.* humming.

fredonner [frədɔ'ne], *v.t.*, *v.i.* to hum.

frégate [fre'gat], *n.f.* frigate; frigate bird; (*Navy*) *capitaine de frégate*, commander.

frein [frɛ̃], *n.m.* bit, bridle; curb, check; brake.

freinage [frɛ'naːʒ], *n.m.* braking.

freiner [frɛ'ne], *v.t.* to brake; to curb.

frelatage [frəla'taːʒ], **frelatement** [frəlat'mɑ̃], *n.m.*, **frelaterie** [frəla'tri], **frelatation** [frəlata'sjɔ̃], *n.f.* adulteration.

frelater [frəla'te], *v.t.* to adulterate.

frêle [frɛːl], *a.* frail, fragile, weak.

frelon [frə'lɔ̃], *n.m.* hornet.

freluquet [frəly'kɛ], *n.m.* conceited young man, puppy.

frémir [fre'miːr], *v.i.* to quiver, to shudder, to tremble; to vibrate; to rustle.

frémissant [fremi'sɑ̃], *a.* quivering, trembling.

frémissement [fremis'mɑ̃], *n.m.* quivering, trembling, shuddering; thrill, vibration; rustling.

frênaie [frɛ'nɛ], *n.f.* ash grove.

frêne [frɛːn], *n.m.* ash, ash tree.

frénésie [frene'zi], *n.f.* frenzy, madness.

frénétique [frene'tik], a. frantic, frenzied.—
n. raving, frantic person.
frénétiquement [frenetik'mɑ̃], adv. frantically.
fréquemment [freka'mɑ̃], adv. frequently.
fréquence [fre'kɑ̃:s], n.f. frequency.
fréquent [fre'kɑ̃], a. frequent.
fréquentation [frekɑ̃ta'sjɔ̃], n.f. frequenta-
tion, company.
fréquenter [frekɑ̃'te], v.t. to frequent, to
keep company with; to haunt.—v.i. to
associate (chez); to be a frequent caller
(at).
frère [frɛːr], n.m. brother; fellow member;
monk.
fresque [frɛsk], n.f. fresco.
fret [frɛ], n.m. freight, cargo.
fréter [fre'te], v.t. (conjug. like CÉDER) to
charter; to freight; to hire (a car).
fréteur [fre'tœːr], n.m. freighter, charterer.
frétillant [freti'jɑ̃], a. wriggling, lively;
frisky.
frétillement [fretij'mɑ̃], n.m. wriggling;
frisking.
frétiller [freti'je], v.i. to wriggle, to jump
about; to frisk.
fretin [frə'tɛ̃], n.m. fry, young fish; (fig.)
trash.
freudien [frø'djɛ̃], a. (fem. -enne) Freudian.
freux [frø], n.m. inv. (Orn.) rook.
friable [fri'abl], a. friable; crisp, short.
friand [fri'ɑ̃], a. dainty, nice; partial to;
appetizing.
friandise [friɑ̃'diːz], n.f. daintiness; dainty,
titbit.
fricassée [frika'se], n.f. fricassee.
fricasser [frika'se], v.t. to fricassee.
friche [friʃ], n.f. waste or fallow land.
fricot [fri'ko], n.m. (colloq.) ragout, stew.
fricoter [friko'te], v.t. to squander.—v.i. to
cook.
fricoteur [friko'tœːr], n.m. (fem. -euse)
feaster; fast liver.
friction [frik'sjɔ̃], n.f. friction, rubbing.
frictionner [friksjo'ne], v.t. to rub.
frigide [fri'ʒid], a. frigid.
frigidité [friʒidi'te], n.f. frigidity.
frigorifier [frigori'fje], v.t. to chill, to freeze
(meat etc.).
frileux [fri'lø], a. (fem. -euse) chilly; susceptible to cold.—n.m. redbreast, robin.
frimas [fri'mɑ], n.m. *rime, hoar-frost.
frime [frim], n.f. (pop.) show, pretence, sham.
fringant [frɛ̃'gɑ̃], a. brisk, frisky; smart.
fringuer [frɛ̃'ge], v.i. to skip; to prance (of a
horse).
fripe [frip], n.f. rag, scrap (of cloth etc.).
friper [fri'pe], v.t. to crumple, to rumple. se
friper, v.r. to become rumpled or shabby.
friperie [fri'pri], n.f. frippery, old clothes;
junk shop.
fripier [fri'pje], n.m. (fem. -ière) dealer in
old clothes, furniture etc.
fripon [fri'pɔ̃], a. (fem. -onne) cheating,
rascally.—n.m. (fem. -onne) rogue, cheat.
friponnerie [fripɔn'ri], n.f. cheating, roguery,
knavery.
friquet [fri'kɛ], n.m. tree sparrow.
frire [friːr], v.t., v.i. irr. to fry.
frisage [fri'zaːʒ], n.m. curling, frizzing (of
hair etc.).
frise [friːz], n.f. (Arch. etc.) frieze.

friser [fri'ze], v.t. to curl, to frizz (hair); to
graze; to border upon.—v.i. to curl. se
friser, v.r. to curl; to curl one's hair.
frisson [fri'sɔ̃], n.m. shiver, shudder; thrill.
frissonnant [frisɔ'nɑ̃], a. shuddering, shivering.
frissonnement [frisɔn'mɑ̃], n.m. shivering,
shudder; thrill.
frissonner [frisɔ'ne], v.i. to shiver, to
shudder; to feel a thrill; to tremble.
frisure [fri'zyːr], n.f. crisping; curling.
frit [fri], a. fried.—n.f. pl. des frites, chips,
French fried potatoes.
friture [fri'tyːr], n.f. frying; fried fish etc.;
grease (for frying).
frivole [fri'vɔl], a. frivolous, trifling, futile.
frivolité [frivɔli'te], n.f. frivolity; trifle.
froc [frɔk], n.m. cowl, monk's gown.
froid [frwa], a. cold; (fig.) indifferent, lifeless;
reserved.—n.m. cold, coldness; chilliness;
(fig.) unconcern, dullness; reserve.
froidement [frwad'mɑ̃], adv. coldly, frigidly;
dispassionately.
froideur [frwa'dœːr], n.f. coldness; chilliness; (fig.) indifference, coolness.
froidure [frwa'dyːr], n.f. coldness (of the
weather); cold; (fig.) winter.
froissement [frwas'mɑ̃], n.m. rumpling;
bruising; (fig.) clash; slight, affront, annoyance.
froisser [frwa'se], v.t. to rumple; to crease;
to bruise slightly; (fig.) to offend, to wound.
se **froisser**, v.r. to become bruised (of a
muscle); to take offence.
froissure [frwa'syːr], n.f. crease; bruise.
frôlement [frol'mɑ̃], n.m. grazing; rustle.
frôler [fro'le], v.t. to graze, to touch slightly in
passing; to brush past.
fromage [fro'maːʒ], n.m. cheese; (fig.) un
(bon) fromage, a nice soft job.
fromagerie [fromaʒ'ri], n.f. cheese farm or
dairy; cheese trade.
fromageux [froma'ʒø], a. (fem. -euse)
cheesy.
froment [fro'mɑ̃], n.m. wheat.
fronce [frɔ̃:s], n.f. gather, pucker (in needlework etc.); crease (in paper).
froncement [frɔ̃s'mɑ̃], n.m. contraction,
knitting (of the brows etc.); (fig.) frown.
froncer [frɔ̃'se], v.t. (conjug. like COMMENCER)
to contract; to wrinkle; to purse (the
lips); to gather (needlework); froncer les
sourcils, to frown. se froncer, v.r. to contract, to pucker; to wrinkle.
frondaison [frɔ̃dɛ'zɔ̃], n.f. foliation; foliage.
fronde [frɔ̃:d], n.f. sling; frond; (Surg.)
bandage.
fronder [frɔ̃'de], v.t. to sling, to fling with a
sling; to banter; to jeer at.
frondeur [frɔ̃'dœːr], n.m. (fem. -euse) slinger;
censurer, fault-finder; rioter.
front [frɔ̃], n.m. forehead, brow; face; (fig.)
boldness, impudence; (Polit.) Front populaire, Popular Front.
frontal [frɔ̃'tal], a. (m. pl. -aux) (Anat.)
frontal.—n.m. headband.
frontière [frɔ̃'tjɛːr], n.f. frontier, border.
frontispice [frɔ̃tis'pis], n.m. frontispiece;
title page.
fronton [frɔ̃'tɔ̃], n.m. (Arch.) fronton, pediment.
frottage [frɔ'taːʒ], n.m. rubbing; polishing.

frottée [fro'te], *n.f.* (*colloq.*) drubbing.

frottement [frot'mɑ̃], *n.m.* rubbing, friction; (*fig.*) interaction.

frotter [fro'te], *v.t.* to rub; to polish; (*fig.*) to pommel, to warm (*the ears of*).—*v.i.* to rub. **se frotter**, *v.r.* to rub oneself; to provoke, to meddle (*à*).

frotteur [fro'tœːr], *n.m.* (*fem.* **-euse**) rubber; scrubber; floor polisher.

frottoir [fro'twaːr], *n.m.* (*pl.* **-frous**) rustling (*of silk etc.*).

frou-frou [fru'fru], *n.m.* (*pl.* **-frous**) rustling (*of silk etc.*).

fructification [fryktifika'sjɔ̃], *n.f.* fructification.

fructifier [frykti'fje], *v.i.* to fructify, to bear fruit; (*fig.*) to thrive.

fructueusement [fryktɥøz'mɑ̃], *adv.* fruitfully, profitably.

fructueux [fryk'tɥø], *a.* (*fem.* **-euse**) fruitful, profitable.

frugal [fry'gal], *a.* (*m. pl.* **-aux**) frugal.

frugalement [frygal'mɑ̃], *adv.* frugally.

frugalité [frygali'te], *n.f.* frugality.

fruit [frɥi], *n.m.* fruit; (*fig.*) offspring; advantage, utility; (*pl.*) fruits; result.

fruiterie [frɥi'tri], *n.f.* fruit loft; fruit trade.

fruitier [frɥi'tje], *a.* (*fem.* **-ière**) fruit-bearing.—*n.m.* (*fem.* **-ière**) fruiterer, greengrocer.

fruste [fryst], *a.* worn, defaced; unpolished (*person*).

frustration [frystra'sjɔ̃], *n.f.* frustration.

frustrer [frys'tre], *v.t.* to defraud; to frustrate, to disappoint; to baffle.

fuchsia [fyk'sja], *n.m.* fuchsia.

fugace [fy'gas], *a.* fugitive, fleeting, transient.

fugitif [fyʒi'tif], *a.* (*fem.* **-tive**) fugitive, fleeting.—*n.m.* (*fem.* **-tive**) fugitive, runaway.

fugue [fyg], *n.f.* fugue; (*colloq.*) flight, escapade.

fuir [fɥiːr], *v.t. irr.* to fly, to avoid; to shun.—*v.i.* to fly, to flee, to run away; to elude; to leak. **se fuir**, *v.r.* to fly from oneself; to shun *or* avoid each other.

fuite [fɥit], *n.f.* flight, escaping; avoiding; evasion, shift; leakage.

fulgurant [fylgy'rɑ̃], *a.* flashing, vivid, sharp.

fulguration [fylgyra'sjɔ̃], *n.f.* (*Chem.*) fulguration; lightning.

fuligineux [fyliʒi'nø], *a.* (*fem.* **-euse**) fuliginous.

fulminant [fylmi'nɑ̃], *a.* fulminant, fulminating.

fulminer [fylmi'ne], *v.t.* to fulminate, to send forth (*maledictions or religious decrees*).—*v.i.* to explode; (*fig.*) to storm, to thunder, to inveigh (*against*).

fumage [fy'maːʒ], *n.m.*, **fumaison** [fymɛ'zɔ̃], *n.f.* manuring, spreading of dung on land.

fumant [fy'mɑ̃], *a.* smoking, reeking, fuming.

fumé [fy'me], *a.* smoked; manured.

fumée [fy'me], *n.f.* smoke; steam; fume, reek; phantom, dream.

fumer [fy'me], *v.t.* to smoke (*a cigarette etc.*); to smoke-dry; to manure.—*v.i.* to smoke; to reek, to steam; (*fig.*) to fret, to fume.

fumerolle [fym'rol], *n.f.* fumarole.

fumet [fy'me], *n.m.* flavor (*of meat*); bouquet (*of wines*); (*fig.*) raciness; (*Hunt.*) scent.

fumeur [fy'mœːr], *n.m.* (*fem.* **-euse** (1)) smoker.

fumeux [fy'mø], *a.* (*fem.* **-euse** (2)) smoky, fumy; hazy (*of brain, ideas etc.*).

fumier [fy'mje], *n.m.* manure, dung, dunghill; (*fig.*) trash.

fumigateur [fymiga'tœːr], *n.m.* fumigator.

fumigation [fymiga'sjɔ̃], *n.f.* fumigation.

fumiger [fymi'ʒe], *v.t.* (*conjug. like* MANGER) to fumigate.

fumiste [fy'mist], *n.m.* stove *or* chimney repairer; (*fig.*) practical joker; humbug, trickster.

fumisterie [fymis'tri], *n.f.* (*fig.*) practical joke.

fumoir [fy'mwaːr], *n.m.* smoking shed (*for curing fish etc.*); smoking room.

fumure [FUMAGE].

funèbre [fy'nebr], *a.* funeral; funereal, mournful; dismal.

funérailles [fyne'rɑːj], *n.f. pl.* funeral ceremonies, obsequies.

funéraire [fyne'rɛːr], *a.* funeral, funereal.

funeste [fy'nest], *a.* fatal, deadly; (*fig.*) disastrous; distressing.

funestement [fynest'mɑ̃], *adv.* fatally, disastrously.

funiculaire [fyniky'lɛːr], *a.* funicular.—*n.m.* funicular railway.

fur [fyːr], *n.m.*, used only in the expression *au fur et à mesure* (*que*), gradually (as), in proportion (as).

furet [fy'rɛ], *n.m.* ferret; inquisitive, prying person.

fureter [fyr'te], *v.i.* (*conjug. like* AMENER) to ferret, to hunt with a ferret; (*fig.*) to rummage.

fureteur [fyr'tœːr], *n.m.* (*fem.* **-euse**) ferreter; (*fig.*) Nosey Parker.

fureur [fy'rœːr], *n.f.* rage, fury; passion, frenzy.

furibond [fyri'bɔ̃], *a.* furious, raging, wild.—*n.m.* (*fem.* **-e**) furious person.

furie [fy'ri], *n.f.* fury, rage; ardour, intensity.

furieusement [fyrjøz'mɑ̃], *adv.* furiously.

furieux [fy'rjø], *a.* (*fem.* **-euse**) furious; mad, fierce, impetuous; (*colloq.*) monstrous.—*n.m.* (*fem.* **-euse**) mad person.

furoncle [fy'rɔ̃kl], *n.m.* (*Med.*) furuncle, boil.

furtif [fyr'tif], *a.* (*fem.* **-tive**) furtive, stealthy, secret.

furtivement [fyrtiv'mɑ̃], *adv.* furtively.

fusain [fy'zɛ̃], *n.m.* spindle-tree; charcoal (*for drawing*).

fuseau [fy'zo], *n.m.* (*pl.* **-eaux**) spindle; distaff.

fusée [fy'ze], *n.f.* spindleful; spindle (*of axle*); (*Motor.*) stub axle; (*Mil. etc.*) fuse; rocket; (*Vet.*) splint.

fuselage [fyz'laːʒ], *n.m.* framework, fuselage (*of an aeroplane*).

fuselé [fyz'le], *a.* slender, tapering (*fingers*); streamlined.

fuser [fy'ze], *v.i.* to spirt; to liquefy, to dissolve, to fuse.

fusibilité [fyzibili'te], *n.f.* fusibility.

fusible [fy'zibl], *a.* fusible.—*n.m.* (*Elec.*) fuse.

fusil [fy'zi], *n.m.* gun, rifle; steel (*for sharpening knives*).

fusilier [fyzi'lje], *n.m.* fusilier; *fusilier marin*, marine.

fusillade [fyzi'jad], *n.f.* discharge of musketry, fusillade; execution by shooting.

fusiller [fyzi'je], *v.t.* to shoot (down); to execute by shooting.
fusil-mitrailleur [fyzimitra'jœːr], *n.m.* submachine gun.
fusion [fy'zjɔ̃], *n.f.* fusion, melting; (*fig.*) blending, merger.
fusionner [fyzjɔ'ne], *v.t., v.i.* to amalgamate, to unite, to merge; to blend.
fustigation [fystiga'sjɔ̃], *n.f.* fustigation, whipping, flogging.
fustiger [fysti'ʒe], *v.t.* (*conjug. like* MANGER) to flog, to whip.
fût [fy], *n.m.* stock (*of a gun or pistol*); shaft (*of a column*); cask; barrel (*of a drum*).
futaie [fy'te], *n.f.* forest of high trees; high forest tree.
futaille [fy'tɑːj], *n.f.* cask, barrel.
futaine [fy'tɛːn], *n.f.* fustian.
futé [fy'te], *a.* (*colloq.*) sharp, cunning, sly.
futile [fy'til], *a.* futile, frivolous, trifling.
futilité [fytili'te], *n.f.* futility; trifle.
futur [fy'tyːr], *a.* future.—*n.m.* (*Gram.*) future. —*n.m.* (*fem.* -e) intended husband *or* wife.
futurisme [fyty'rism], *n.m.* futurism.
futuriste [fyty'rist], *a.* futuristic.—*n.* futurist.
fuyant [fɥi'jɑ̃], *a.* flying, fleeing, retreating; receding (*of the forehead etc.*); fleeting.— *n.m.* perspective.
fuyard [fɥi'jaːr], *a.* and *n.m.* (*fem.* -e) fugitive, runaway.

G

G, g [ʒe], *n.m.* the seventh letter of the alphabet.
gabardine [gabar'din], *n.f.* gabardine.
gabare [ga'baːr], *n.f.* lighter, flat-bottomed barge; store ship.
gabarier [gaba'rje], *n.m.* lighterman.
gabelle [ga'bɛl], *n.f.* gabelle, salt tax.
gâche (1) [gɑːʃ], *n.f.* staple, wall hook.
gâche (2) [gɑːʃ], *n.f.* trowel; (baker's) spatula.
gâcher [gɑ'ʃe], *v.t.* to mix (*mortar*); (*fig.*) to bungle, to botch.
gâchette [gɑ'ʃet], *n.f.* tumbler, sear (*of a gun-lock*); follower, catch (*of a lock*); (*fam.*) trigger.
gâcheur [gɑ'ʃœːr], *n.m.* mason's helper; (*fig.*) bungler.
gâchis [gɑ'ʃi], *n.m.* wet mortar; sludge; (*fig.*) mess.
gaélique [gae'lik], *a.* Gaelic.—*n.m.* Gaelic (*language*).
gaffe [gaf], *n.f.* boat-hook, gaff; (*fam.*) gross blunder, howler.
gaffer [ga'fe], *v.t.* to hook with a gaff.—*n.i.* (*fam.*) to blunder; (*Row.*) to catch a crab.
gage [gaːʒ], *n.m.* pawn, pledge; security, deposit; stake, token; (*pl.*) wages.
gager [ga'ʒe], *v.t.* (*conjug. like* MANGER) to wager, to bet, to stake; to pay wages to; to engage.
gageur [ga'ʒœːr], *n.m.* (*fem.* -euse) bettor, one who wagers, punter.

gageure [ga'ʒyːr], *n.f.* wager, stake.
gagnant [ga'nɑ̃], *a.* winning.—*n.m.* (*fem.* -e) winner.
gagne-pain [gan'pɛ̃], *n.m. inv.* livelihood, daily bread; bread-winner.
gagner [ga'ne], *v.t.* to gain, to earn; to win; to deserve; to prevail upon, to gain over; to allure; to seize; to overtake.—*v.i.* to spread; to gain (*à*); to improve. **se gagner**, *v.r.* to be gained; to be contagious.
gai [ge], *a.* gay, merry; exhilarating; vivid (*of colors*).
gaiement or **gaîment** [ge'mɑ̃], *adv.* gaily, merrily, cheerfully; briskly, willingly.
gaieté or **gaîté** [ge'te], *n.f.* gaiety, cheerfulness, good humor.
gaillard (1) [ga'jaːr], *n.m.* (*Naut.*) castle; **gaillard d'arrière**, quarter-deck; **gaillard d'avant**, forecastle.
gaillard (2) [ga'jaːr], *a.* strong; jolly, lively; wanton; gallant.—*n.m.* (*fem.* -e) lively, merry, strapping fellow *or* girl.
gaillardement [gajardə'mɑ̃], *adv.* joyously, merrily; boldly.
gaillardise [gajar'diːz], *n.f.* sprightliness, liveliness, jollity; broad language, risky story.
gaîment [GAIEMENT].
gain [gɛ̃], *n.m.* gain, profit; earnings; winnings.
gaine [gɛːn], *n.f.* sheath; foundation garment; case (*of a clock etc.*).
gaîté [GAIETÉ].
gala [ga'la], *n.m.* gala.
galamment [gala'mɑ̃], *adv.* gallantly, courteously; gracefully, handsomely.
galant [ga'lɑ̃], *a.* attentive to ladies; elegant, correct, courteous; complimentary, flattering; *c'est un galant homme*, he is a man of honor; *femme galante*, courtesan.— *n.m.* gallant; sweetheart, suitor; *faire le galant*, to court the ladies.
galanterie [galɑ̃'tri], *n.f.* politeness; gallantry (*towards the ladies*); intrigue, love affair.
galantin [galɑ̃'tɛ̃], *n.m.* fop, coxcomb.
galbe [galb], *n.m.* graceful curve *or* contour.
gale [gal], *n.f.* scabies; itch; scab; mange.
galène [ga'lɛːn], *n.f.* galena; *poste à galène*, crystal set.
galère [ga'lɛːr], *n.f.* galley; (*pl.*) galleys, imprisonment with hard labor.
galerie [gal'ri], *n.f.* gallery; corridor; picture gallery; (*Theat.*) upper circle, gallery; (*fig.*) spectators; (*Mining*) drift.
galérien [gale'rjɛ̃], *n.m.* galley slave, convict.
galet [ga'le], *n.m.* pebble, shingle; friction roller.
galetas [gal'tɑ], *n.m. inv.* garret, attic; (*fig.*) hole, hovel.
galette [ga'let], *n.f.* broad thin cake; sea biscuit.
galeux [ga'lø], *a.* (*fem.* -euse) itchy; scabby; mangy; *brebis galeuse*, (*fig.*) black sheep.
Galilée [gali'le], *m.* Galileo.
Galilée [gali'le], *a.* Galilee.
galimatias [galima'tjɑ], *n.m.* balderdash; rigmarole.
galion [ga'ljɔ̃], *n.m.* galleon.
galiote [ga'ljɔt], *n.f.* galliot, half galley.
galle [gal], *n.f.* gall.
Galles, le Pays de [ləpeidə'gall], *m.* Wales.

163

gallican [gali'kɑ̃], *a.* gallican.

gallicisme [gali'sism], *n.m.*Gallicism, French idiom.

gallois [ga'lwa], *a.* Welsh.—*n.m.* Welsh (*language*); (**Gallois**, *fem.* **-oise**) Welshman, Welshwoman.

galoche [ga'lɔʃ], *n.f.* clog.

galon [ga'lɔ̃], *n.m.* braid; lace; (*pl.*) (*Mil.*) bands *or* stripes (*officers and N.C.O.s*).

galonner [galɔ'ne], *v.t.* to lace, to adorn with gold *or* silver lace.

galonnier [galɔ'nje], *n.m.* gold *or* silver lace maker.

galop [ga'lo], *n.m.* gallop, galloping.

galopade [galɔ'pad], *n.f.* galloping, gallop.

galoper [galɔ'pe], *v.t.* to gallop (*a horse etc.*); to run after.—*v.i.* to gallop; (*fig.*) to run on.

galopin [galɔ'pɛ̃], *n.m.* errand boy; (*fig.*) urchin, rogue, imp.

galvanique [galva'nik], *a.* galvanic.

galvaniser [galvani'ze], *v.t.* to galvanize; (*fig.*) to stimulate.

galvanisme [galva'nism], *n.m.* galvanism.

galvanomètre [galvanɔ'mɛ:tr], *n.m.* galvanometer.

galvanoplastie [galvanɔplas'ti], *n.f.* electroplating.

galvauder [galvo'de], *v.t.* to muddle; to lower, to dishonor.

gambade [gɑ̃'bad], *n.f.* skip, gambol.

gambader [gɑ̃ba'de], *v.i.* to skip, to gambol, to romp, to frisk about.

Gambie [gɑ̃'bi], **la**, *f.* Gambia.

gambit [gɑ̃'bi], *n.m.* gambit.

gamelle [ga'mɛl], *n.f.* (*Mil.*, *Naut.*) mess tin *or* pot; (*fig.*) company-mess.

gamète [ga'mɛt], *n.m.* (*Biol.*) gamete.

gamin [ga'mɛ̃], *n.m.* boy, youngster, urchin.

gamine [ga'min], *n.f.* hoyden, chit of a girl.

gamme [gam], *n.f.* gamut, scale.

gammée [ga'me], *a. used in* **'croix gammée',** swastika.

ganache [ga'naʃ], *n.f.* lower jaw (*of a horse*); (*colloq.*) booby, blockhead.

gandin [gɑ̃'dɛ̃], *n.m.* dandy, swell.

gang [gɑ̃g], *n.m.* gang (*of thieves*).

Gange [gɑ̃:ʒ], **le**, *m.* Ganges.

gangrène [gɑ̃'grɛ:n], *n.f.* gangrene; (*fig.*) corruption.

gangrené [gɑ̃grə'ne], *a.* gangrened; (*fig.*) cankered, corrupt.

gangrener [gɑ̃grə'ne], *v.t.* (*conjug. like* AMENER) to gangrene, to mortify; (*fig.*) to corrupt.

gangreneux [gɑ̃grə'nø], *a.* (*fem.* **-euse**) gangrenous, cankered.

gangster [gɑ̃gs'tɛ:r], *n.m.* gangster.

ganse [gɑ̃:s], *n.f.* braid; cord, twist; edging; string.

gant [gɑ̃], *n.m.* glove, gauntlet.

gantelet [gɑ̃'tlɛ], *n.m.* gauntlet; handleather; (*Surg.*) glove bandage.

ganter [gɑ̃'te], *v.t.* to glove, to put gloves on; (*fig.*) to fit, to suit. **se ganter**, *v.r.* to put on one's gloves.

ganterie [gɑ̃'tri], *n.f.* glove-making; glove trade; glove shop.

gantier [gɑ̃'tje], *n.m.* (*fem.* **-ière**) glover.

garage [ga'ra:ʒ], *n.m.* parking, storing away; (*Rail.*) shunting; siding; (*on rivers, canals etc.*) putting into wet dock; (*Motor. etc.*) garage; (*Row.*) boat-house.

garagiste [gara'ʒist], *n.m.* garage keeper; garage mechanic *or* owner.

garance [ga'rɑ̃:s], *a.* madder-colored. —*n.f.* madder; madder root.

garant [ga'rɑ̃], *n.m.* (*fem.* **-e**) guarantor, surety.—*n.m.* guaranty, voucher, proof.

garanti [garɑ̃'ti], *a.* guaranteed, warranted.

garantie [garɑ̃'ti], *n.f.* guarantee, guaranty; indemnity; security; voucher, pledge.

garantir [garɑ̃'ti:r], *v.t.* to guarantee, to vouch for; to ensure; to indemnify; to protect, to shield. **se garantir**, *v.r.* to secure oneself, to preserve oneself.

garantisseur [garɑ̃ti'sœ:r], *n.m.* warranter.

garçon [gar'sɔ̃], *n.m.* boy, lad; bachelor; workman; porter; waiter; stable boy; steward (*on ship*).

garçonnet [garsɔ'nɛ], *n.m.* little boy.

garçonnière [garsɔ'njɛ:r], *n.f.* bachelor's flat.

garde [gard], *n.f.* keeping; defense, guard; custody, watch; heed; nurse; hilt (*of sword*).—*n.m.* guard, guardsman, keeper, warder; watchman.

garde-à-vous [garda'vu], *n.m. inv.* (*Mil.*) position at attention.

garde-barrière [gardba'rjɛ:r], *n.m.* (*pl. unchanged or* **gardes-barrières**) (*Rail.*) signalman at level crossing.

garde-boue [gard'bu], *n.m. inv.* mudguard.

garde-cendre(s) [gard'sɑ̃:dr], *n.m. inv.* fender, fire guard.

garde-chasse [gard'ʃas], *n.m.* (*pl. unchanged or* **gardes-chasses**) game-keeper.

garde-chiourme [gard'ʃjurm], *n.m.* (*pl. unchanged or* **gardes-chiourme**) overseer of convict gangs; warder.

garde-corps [gard'kɔ:r], *n.m. inv.* rail, handrail; (*Naut.*) life-line.

garde-côte(s) [gard'kot], *n.m.* (*pl.* **garde-côtes** *or* **gardes-côtes**) guard ship, coast guard.

garde-crotte [gard'krɔt], *n.m. inv.* mudguard.

garde-feu [gard'fø], *n.m.* (*pl. unchanged or* **garde-feux**) fire-guard; fender.

garde-fou [gard'fu], *n.m.* (*pl.* **-fous**) parapet; railings.

garde-frein [gard'frɛ̃], *n.m.* (*pl.* **garde-freins** *or* **gardes-freins**) brakeman.

garde-magasin [gardmaga'zɛ̃], *n.m.* (*pl. unchanged or* **gardes-magasins**) warehouse keeper, storekeeper.

garde-malade [gardma'lad], *n.* (*pl. unchanged or* **gardes-malades**) sick-nurse, attendant.

garde-manger [gardmɑ̃'ʒe], *n.m. inv.* larder, pantry, meat safe.

garde-meuble(s) [gard'mœbl], *n.m. inv.* furniture repository.

garde-pêche [gard'pɛ:ʃ], *n.m.* (*pl.* **gardes-pêche**) river keeper, water bailiff.

garde-port [gard'pɔ:r], *n.m.* (*pl.* **gardes-port** *or* **gardes-ports**) harbor-master.

garder [gar'de], *v.t.* to keep, to preserve; to retain; to watch over, to take care of, to nurse; to guard, to defend; to observe (*silence etc.*); to keep up. **se garder**, *v.r.* to keep, to last; to beware, to take care not to; to refrain (*de*); to guard.

garderie [gardə'ri], *n.f.* day nursery.

garde-robe (1) [gard'rɔb], n.m. (pl. **-robes**) apron; overall].

garde-robe (2) [gard'rɔb], n.f. (pl. **-robes**) wardrobe (*cupboard for clothes*).

gardeur [gar'dœ:r], n.m. (*fem.* **-euse**) herd-boy *or* -girl, keeper.

gardien [gar'djɛ̃], a. (*fem.* **-enne**) tutelary, guardian.—n.m. (*fem.* **-enne**) guardian, keeper, door-keeper; trustee; *gardien de but*, goalkeeper.

gardon [gar'dɔ̃], n.m. roach.

gare! (1) [ga:r], int. beware! take care! look out!

gare (2) [ga:r], n.f. railway station, terminus; (*wet*) dock; *gare routière*, coach station.

garenne [ga'rɛn], n.f. warren.

garer [ga're], v.t. to side-track (*a train*); to garage, to park. **se garer**, v.r. to keep *or* get out of the way; to take cover; to park.

Gargantua [gargɑ̃'tɥa], n.m. Gargantua; glutton.

gargantuesque [gargɑ̃'tɥɛsk], a. gluttonous.

gargariser (se) [səgargari'ze], v.r. to gargle.

gargarisme [garga'rism], n.m. gargle, gargling.

gargote [gar'gɔt], n.f. cheap eating-house, cook-shop.

gargotier [gargɔ'tje], n.m. (*fem.* **-ière**) keeper of a cook-shop; bad cook.

gargouille [gar'gu:j], n.f. gargoyle, water-spout.

gargouillement [garguj'mɑ̃], n.m. rumbling (*in the stomach*); gurgling, bubbling (*of water*).

gargouiller [gargu'je], v.i. to rumble, to gurgle.

gargouillis [gargu'ji], n.m. gurgling (*of water*).

gargousse [gar'gus], n.f. cannon cartridge; *papier à gargousse*, cartridge paper.

garnement [garnə'mɑ̃], n.m. scapegrace, scamp, (*young*) rogue.

garni [gar'ni], a. furnished; trimmed, garnished.—n.m. furnished lodgings *or* house.

garnir [gar'ni:r], v.t. to furnish, to stock; to trim, to garnish, to adorn; to fill. **se garnir**, v.r. to furnish *or* provide oneself (*with*).

garnison [garni'zɔ̃], n.f. garrison, station.

garnissage [garni'sa:ʒ], **garnissement** [garnis'mɑ̃], n.m. trimming (*of clothes etc.*).

garnisseur [garni'sœ:r], n.m. (*fem.* **-euse**) trimmer.

garniture [garni'ty:r], n.f. furniture, trimmings; ornaments.

garrot (1) [ga'ro], n.m. withers (*of a horse etc.*).

garrot (2) [ga'ro], n.m. tightener, garrot; (*Surg.*) tourniquet.

garrotte [ga'rɔt], n.f. garrotting, strangulation.

garrotter [garo'te], v.t. to tie down, to pinion; to strangle.

gars [ga], n.m. lad, stripling, young fellow.

Gascogne [gas'kɔɲ], la, f. Gascony; *le Golfe de Gascogne*, the Bay of Biscay.

gascon [gas'kɔ̃], a. (*fem.* **-onne**) Gascon.—n.m. Gascon (*dialect*); (**Gascon**, *fem.* **-onne**) Gascon (*person*); (*fig.*) boaster, braggart.

gasconnade [gaskɔ'nad], n.f. gasconade, boast, brag.

gasconner [gaskɔ'ne], v.i. to speak with a Gascon accent; to brag.

gaspillage [gaspi'ja:ʒ], n.m. waste, squandering.

gaspiller [gaspi'je], v.t. to waste, to squander.

gaspilleur [gaspi'jœ:r], a. (*fem.* **-euse**) wasting, squandering.—n.m. (*fem.* **-euse**) waster, squanderer, spendthrift.

gastrique [gas'trik], a. gastric.

gastrite [gas'trit], n.f. gastritis.

gastro-entérite [gastroɑ̃te'rit], n.f. gastro-enteritis.

gâté [ga'te], a. marred, damaged, tainted; (*fig.*) spoiled.

gâteau [ga'to], n.m. (pl. **-eaux**) cake.

gâte-métier [gatme'tje], n.m. (pl. *unchanged* or **gâte-métiers**) underseller.

gâte-papier [gatpa'pje], n. *inv.* scribbler, poor writer.

gâter [ga'te], v.t. to spoil, to damage, to injure, to mar; to corrupt. **se gâter**, v.r. to taint, to spoil, to get spoiled; to break up (*of weather*).

gâterie [ga'tri], n.f. spoiling (*of children*), foolish indulgence.

gâte-sauce [gat'so:s], n.m. (pl. *unchanged* or **gâte-sauces**) scullion; (*colloq.*) bad cook.

gâteux [ga'tø], a. and n.m. (*fem.* **-euse**) idiot.

gauche [go:ʃ], a. left; (*fig.*) crooked, ugly; clumsy.—n.f. left hand, left side; (*Mil.*) left wing, left flank.

gauchement [goʃ'mɑ̃], adv. awkwardly, clumsily.

gaucher [go'ʃe], a. and n.m. (*fem.* **-ère**) left-handed (*person*).

gaucherie [go'ʃri], n.f. awkwardness, clumsiness.

gauchir [go'ʃi:r], v.t. to warp.—v.i. to turn aside; to flinch; to become warped; (*fig.*) to dodge.

gaudriole [godri'ɔl], n.f. broad joke, coarse jest.

gaufrage [go'fra:ʒ], n.m. goffering.

gaufre [go:fr], n.f. wafer, waffle (*thin cake*); honeycomb.

gaufrer [go'fre], v.t. to goffer.

gaufrette [go'frɛt], n.f. small wafer.

gaufreur [go'frœ:r], n.m. (*fem.* **-euse**) gofferer.

gaufrier [gofri'e], n.m. waffle iron.

gaufrure [go'fry:r], n.f. goffering.

Gaule [go:l], la, f. Gaul.

gaule [go:l], n.f. pole, switch, long stick.

gauler [go'le], v.t. to beat (*trees*) with a long pole; to knock down (*fruit*).

gaullisme [go'lism], n.m. policy *or* partisanship of General de Gaulle.

gaulliste [go'list], a. and n. follower of General de Gaulle.

gaulois [go'lwa], a. Gaulish, Gallic; (*fig.*) free.—n.m. Gallic (*language*); (**Gaulois**, *fem.* **-oise**) Gaul (*person*).

gausser (se) [səgo'se], v.r. (*colloq.*) to banter, to chaff.

Gauthier [go'tje], m. Walter.

gave (1) [ga:v], n.m. torrent, mountain stream (*in the Pyrenees*).

gave (2) [ga:v], n.f. crop (*of birds*).

gaver [ga've], v.t. (*colloq.*) to cram, to gorge.

gavotte [ga'vɔt], n.f. gavotte (*dance*).

gavroche [ga'vrɔʃ], n.m. Parisian urchin.

gaz [ga:z], n.m. gas; *bec de gaz*, gas burner.

gaze

gaze [gɑːz], *n.f.* gauze.
gazé [gɑ'ze], *a.* covered with gauze, veiled; softened, toned down; (*Mil.*) gassed (*soldier*).
gazelle [gɑ'zɛl], *n.f.* gazelle.
gazer (1) [gɑ'ze], *v.t.* to cover with gauze; (*fig.*) to veil, to tone down.
gazer (2) [gɑ'ze], *v.t.* (*Mil.*) to gas (*men*).
gazette [gɑ'zɛt], *n.f.* gazette, newspaper; (*fig.*) gossipmonger.
gazeux [gɑ'zø], *a.* (*fem.* **-euse**) gaseous; aerated.
gazier (1) [gɑ'zje], *n.m.* gas-fitter.
gazier (2) [gɑ'zje], *n.m.* (*fem.* **-ière**) gauze maker.
gazolène [gɑzɔ'lɛn], **gazoléine** [gɑzɔle'in], **gazoline** [gɑzɔ'lin], *n.f.* gasoline.
gazomètre [gɑzɔ'mɛtr], *n.m.* gasometer.
gazon [gɑ'zɔ̃], *n.m.* grass; sod, turf; lawn.
gazonnant [gɑzɔ'nɑ̃], *a.* producing grass; grassy.
gazonner [gɑzɔ'ne], *v.t.* to cover with turf, to turf.
gazonneux [gɑzɔ'nø], *a.* (*fem.* **-euse**) turfy, swarded.
gazouillement [gɑzuj'mɑ̃], *n.m.* chirping, warbling (*of birds*); babbling (*of a brook etc.*); prattle.
gazouiller [gɑzu'je], *v.i.* to chirp, to warble; to twitter; to prattle, to babble.
gazouillis [gɑzu'ji], *n.m.* warbling, twittering.
geai [ʒɛ], *n.m.* jay.
géant [ʒe'ɑ̃], *a.* gigantic.—*n.m.* (*fem.* **-e**) giant.
geignard [ʒɛ'naːr], *a.* always whining, querulous.
geignement [ʒɛɲ'mɑ̃], *n.m.* moan, whine.
geindre [ʒɛ̃ːdr], *v.i. irr.* (*conjug. like* CRAINDRE) to moan, to whine, to fret, to complain.
gel [ʒɛl], *n.m.* frost, freezing.
gélatine [ʒela'tin], *n.f.* gelatine.
gélatiner [ʒelati'ne], *v.t.* to gelatinize.
gélatineux [ʒelati'nø], *a.* (*fem.* **-euse**) gelatinous.
gelé [ʒə'le], *a.* frozen, cold.
gelée [ʒə'le], *n.f.* frost; jelly; aspic.
geler [ʒə'le], *v.t., v.i.* (*conjug. like* AMENER) and *se geler*, *v.r.* to freeze.
gélignite [ʒeli'nit], *n.f.* gelignite.
gelinotte [ʒəli'nɔt], *n.f.* grouse (*bird*).
gémir [ʒe'miːr], *v.i.* to groan, to moan; to lament; (*fig.*) to suffer.
gémissant [ʒemi'sɑ̃], *a.* groaning, moaning, lamenting.
gémissement [ʒemis'mɑ̃], *n.m.* groan, moan; (*fig.*) lament, cooing.
gemme [ʒɛm], *n.f.* gem; resin; (*Bot.*) bud.
gemmer [ʒɛ'me], *v.i.* to bud.
gênant [ʒɛ'nɑ̃], *a.* troublesome, inconvenient, embarrassing.
gencive [ʒɑ̃'siːv], *n.f.* gum (*of the teeth*).
gendarme [ʒɑ̃'darm], *n.m.* gendarme (*armed policeman*); constable; virago (*woman*).
gendarmerie [ʒɑ̃darm'ri], *n.f.* gendarmery (*armed police*); constabulary; barracks (*of gendarmes*).
gendre [ʒɑ̃ːdr], *n.m.* son-in-law.
gêne [ʒɛn], *n.f.* constraint, uneasiness, annoyance; difficulty; financial difficulties, penury.
gêné [ʒɛ'ne], *a.* constrained, ill at ease; hard up.

généalogie [ʒenealɔ'ʒi], *n.f.* genealogy; pedigree.
généalogique [ʒenealɔ'ʒik], *a.* genealogical.
généalogiste [ʒenealɔ'ʒist], *n.m.* genealogist.
gêner [ʒɛ'ne], *v.t.* to constrain, to constrict; to impede; to obstruct; to thwart, to restrain; to inconvenience, to embarrass; to annoy. *se gêner*, *v.r.* to constrain oneself, to put oneself out.
général [ʒene'ral], *a.* (*m. pl.* **-aux**) general, universal; vague.—*adv. phr. en général*, in general.—*n.m.* (*Mil.*) general.
générale [ʒene'ral], *n.f.* general's wife; drumbeat (*to give alarm of fire etc.*).
généralement [ʒeneral'mɑ̃], *adv.* generally, in general.
généralisation [ʒeneraliza'sjɔ̃], *n.f.* generalization.
généraliser [ʒenerali'ze], *v.t.* to generalize.
généralissime [ʒenerali'sim], *n.m.* generalissimo, commander-in-chief of allied armies.
généralité [ʒenerali'te], *n.f.* generality.
générateur [ʒenera'tœːr], *a.* (*fem.* **-trice**) generating, generative.—*n.m.* generator.
génératif [ʒenera'tif], *a.* (*fem.* **-tive**) generative.
génération [ʒenera'sjɔ̃], *n.f.* generation; procreation.
générer [ʒene're], *v.t.* (*conjug. like* CÉDER) to generate.
généreusement [ʒenerøz'mɑ̃], *adv.* generously, bountifully; nobly, bravely.
généreux [ʒene'rø], *a.* (*fem.* **-euse**) generous, liberal, bountiful; noble; courageous.
générique [ʒene'rik], *a.* generic.—*n.m.* (*Cine.*) credits.
générosité [ʒenerozi'te], *n.f.* generosity, liberality; magnanimity.
Gênes [ʒɛn], *f.* Genoa.
genèse [ʒə'nɛːz], *n.f.* genesis.
genêt [ʒə'nɛ], *n.m.* (*Bot.*) broom.
genette [ʒə'nɛt], *n.f.* genet, civet cat.
gêneur [ʒɛ'nœːr], *n.m.* (*fem.* **-euse**) intruder; spoil-sport.
Genève [ʒə'nɛv], *f.* Geneva.
genevois [ʒən'vwa], *a.* Genevese.
genévrier [ʒənevri'e], *n.m.* juniper tree.
génie [ʒe'ni], *n.m.* genius; spirit, nature, bent, talent; (*Mil.*) corps of engineers.
genièvre [ʒə'njɛːvr], *n.m.* juniper berry; juniper tree; gin.
génisse [ʒe'nis], *n.f.* heifer.
génital [ʒeni'tal], *a.* (*m. pl.* **-aux**) genital.
génitif [ʒeni'tif], *n.m.* (*Gram.*) genitive.
génocide [ʒeno'sid], *n.m.* genocide.
génois [ʒe'nwa], *a.* Genoese.
genou [ʒə'nu], *n.m.* (*pl.* **-oux**) knee; (*Mech.*) ball and socket; (*pl.*) lap.
genouillère [ʒənu'jɛːr], *n.f.* knee piece (*of armor*); top (*of a high boot*); knee-cap; ball-and-socket joint.
genre [ʒɑ̃ːr], *n.m.* genus; species, kind, sort; fashion, style; (*Gram.*) gender.
gens [ʒɑ̃], *n.m. pl.* (*but adjectives directly preceding the word take the feminine form*) people, persons, folk; men, hands; servants.
gent [ʒɑ̃], *n.f.* brood, race, tribe.
gentiane [ʒɑ̃'sjan], *n.f.* (*Bot.*) gentian.
gentil (1) [ʒɑ̃'ti], *n.m.* Gentile.
gentil (2) [ʒɑ̃'ti], *a.* (*fem.* **-ille**) noble, gentle; pretty, nice, graceful; amiable, pleasing.

gentilhomme [ʒɑ̃ti'jɔm], n.m. (pl. gentils-
hommes) nobleman, gentleman.
gentillesse [ʒɑ̃ti'jɛs], n.f. kindness, sweetness
(of temperament); prettiness, gracefulness,
pretty thing, thought etc.
gentiment [ʒɑ̃ti'mɑ̃], adv. prettily, gracefully, like a good boy or girl.
génuflexion [ʒenyflɛk'sjɔ̃], n.f. genuflexion.
géocentrique [ʒeosɑ̃'trik], a. geocentric.
Geoffroy [ʒɔ'frwa], m. Geoffrey, Jeffrey.
géographe [ʒeo'graf], n.m. geographer.
géographie [ʒeogra'fi], n.f. geography.
géographique [ʒeogra'fik], a. geographical.
geôle [ʒo:l], n.f. jail, prison.
geôlier [ʒo'lje], n.m. jailer.
géologie [ʒeolɔ'ʒi], n.f. geology.
géologique [ʒeolɔ'ʒik], a. geological.
géologue [ʒeo'lɔg], n.m. geologist.
géométral [ʒeome'tral], a. (m. pl. -aux)
geometrical.
géomètre [ʒeo'metr], n.m. geometrician; geo-
meter.
géométrie [ʒeome'tri], n.f. geometry.
géométrique [ʒeome'trik], a. geometrical.
Georges [ʒɔrʒ], m. George.
gérance [ʒe'rɑ̃:s], n.f. management, manager-
ship; editorship.
géranium [ʒera'njɔm], n.m. geranium.
gérant [ʒe'rɑ̃], n.m. (fem. -e) manager; editor;
rédacteur gérant, managing editor.
gerbe [ʒɛrb], n.f. sheaf, bundle; bunch of
flowers.
gerber [ʒɛr'be], v.t. to make up or bind into
sheaves.
gerbier [ʒɛr'bje], n.m. cornstack.
gerce [ʒɛrs], n.f. chap, crack.
gercé [ʒɛr'se], a. chapped (hands).
gercer [ʒɛr'se], v.t., v.i. (conjug. like
COMMENCER) and se gercer, v.r. to chap, to
crack.
gerçure [ʒɛr'sy:r], n.f. chap, crack; chink,
cleft.
gérer [ʒe're], v.t. (conjug. like CÉDER) to
manage, to administer.
gerfaut [ʒɛr'fo], n.m. gerfalcon.
germain [ʒɛr'mɛ̃], a. german, first (of
cousins etc.); (Law) full (brother etc.).
germanique [ʒɛrma'nik], a. Germanic.
germe [ʒɛrm], n.m. germ, embryo; seed; bud,
sprout, shoot; (fig.) origin.
germer [ʒɛr'me], v.i. to shoot, to sprout, to
germinate.
germination [ʒɛrmina'sjɔ̃], n.f. germination.
gésier [ʒe'zje], n.m. gizzard.
*gésir [ʒe'zi:r], v.i. irr. to lie; ci-gît, here lies.
gestation [ʒɛsta'sjɔ̃], n.f. gestation.
gestatoire [ʒɛsta'twa:r], a. gestatory.
geste [ʒɛst], n.m. gesture, action; sign.
gesticulateur [ʒɛstikyla'tœ:r], n.m. (fem.
-trice) gesticulator.
gesticulation [ʒɛstikyla'sjɔ̃], n.f. gesticulation.
gesticuler [ʒɛstiky'le], v.i. to gesticulate.
gestion [ʒɛs'tjɔ̃], n.f. management, administration.
geyser [ge'zɛ:r], n.m. geyser.
Ghana [ga'na], le, m. Ghana.
ghetto [ge'to], n.m. Jewish quarter, ghetto.
gibbeux [ʒi'bø], a. (fem. -euse) gibbous,
hump-backed.
gibbon [ʒi'bɔ̃], n.m. gibbon (ape).
gibbosité [ʒibozi'te], n.f. gibbosity; hump.

gibecière [ʒib'sjɛ:r], n.f. game bag, satchel;
juggler's pocket.
gibelet [ʒi'blɛ], n.m. gimlet.
giberne [ʒi'bɛrn], n.f. cartridge box or pouch.
gibet [ʒi'bɛ], n.m. gibbet, gallows.
gibier [ʒi'bje], n.m. (Hunt.) game.
giboulée [ʒibu'le], n.f. sudden shower, hail
storm
gibus [ʒi'by:s], n.m. inv. gibus (crush-hat,
opera hat).
giclage [ʒi'kla:ʒ], n.m. spraying; carburateur à giclage, jet carburetor.
giclée [ʒi'kle], n.f. squirt, spirt.
gicleur [ʒi'klœ:r], n.m. spray nozzle, jet.
gicler [ʒi'kle], v.i. to spout, to squirt.
gifle [ʒifl], n.f. slap in the face, box on the
ear.
gifler [ʒi'fle], v.t. to slap in the face, to box the
ears of.
gigantesque [ʒigɑ̃'tɛsk], a. gigantic, colossal.
gigot [ʒi'go], n.m. leg of mutton.
gigue [ʒig], n.f. shank, leg, haunch (of
venison); jig (dance).
gilet [ʒi'le], n.m. waistcoat; vest.
Gilles [ʒil], m. Giles.
gingembre [ʒɛ̃'ʒɑ̃:br], n.m. ginger.
gingivite [ʒɛ̃ʒi'vit], n.f. gingivitis.
ginguet [ʒɛ̃'gɛ], a. (fem. -ette) (colloq.) weak,
worthless, scanty.—n.m. thin wine.
girandole [ʒirɑ̃'dɔl], n.f. girandole, epergne.
giration [ʒira'sjɔ̃], n.f. gyration.
giratoire [ʒira'twa:r], a. gyratory.
girofle [ʒi'rɔfl], n.m. clove.
giroflée [ʒiro'fle], n.f. gillyflower; stock;
giroflée jaune, wallflower.
giron [ʒi'rɔ̃], n.m. lap; (fig.) bosom.
girouette [ʒi'rwɛt], n.f. weathercock, vane.
gisant [ʒi'zɑ̃], a. lying (ill, dead etc.); out-
stretched [GÉSIR].
gisement [ʒiz'mɑ̃], n.m. (Geol. etc.) lie (of
strata); layer, bed; (Naut.) bearing (of coast
etc.).
gitan [ʒi'tɑ̃], n.m. (fem. -e) gipsy.
gîte [ʒit], n.m. home, lodging; refuge; lair (of
deer); (Min.) seam, layer.—n.f. (Naut.) list.
gîter [ʒi'te], v.t. to lodge, to house, to put
up, to shelter.—v.i. to lie, to lodge; (Naut.)
to list; to run aground. se gîter, v.r. to
lodge, to sleep.
givrage [ʒi'vra:ʒ], n.m. (Av.) frosting, icing.
givre [ʒi'vr], n.m. hoar-frost, *rime.
givré [ʒi'vre], a. rimed, rimy.
glabre [gla:br], a. (Bot.) glabrous, smooth,
without down; hairless.
glaçage [gla'sa:ʒ], n.m. frosting, glazing.
glaçant [gla'sɑ̃], a. freezing; icy, chilling.
glace [glas], n.f. ice; ice cream; glass, plate
glass; mirror; carriage window; flaw (in a
diamond etc.); icing (on cakes etc.).
glacé [gla'se], a. frozen, freezing; icy-cold;
iced; glazed; glossy (paper); candied.
glacer [gla'se], v.t. (conjug. like COMMENCER)
to freeze; to ice; (fig.) to paralyze; to glaze.
—v.i. and se glacer, v.r. to freeze.
glaciaire [gla'sjɛ:r], a. of glaciers, glacial.
glacial [gla'sjal], a. frozen, glacial, icy.
glaciale [gla'sjal], n.f. (Bot.) ice-plant.
glacier [gla'sje], n.m. glacier, field of ice; ice-
cream vendor.
glaçon [gla'sɔ̃], n.m. block of ice; floe; ice
cube; petit glaçon, icicle.
gladiateur [gladja'tœ:r], n.m. gladiator.

167

glaïeul

glaïeul [gla'jœl], *n.m.* gladiolus; iris.
glaire [glɛːr], *n.f.* glair, white of egg; phlegm, mucus.
glaise [glɛːz], *a.* clayey.—*n.f.* clay, loam; potter's earth.
glaiseux [glɛ'zø], *a.* (*fem.* **-euse**) clayey, loamy.
glaisière [glɛ'zjɛːr], *n.f.* clay pit.
glaive [glɛːv], *n.m.* sword, blade, steel.
gland [glɑ̃], *n.m.* acorn; tassel.
glande [glɑ̃ːd], *n.f.* (*Anat.*) gland; (*pop.*) tumor; kernel.
glanduleux [glɑ̃dy'lø], *a.* (*fem.* **-euse**) glandulous, glandular.
glaner [gla'ne], *v.t., v.i.* to glean.
glaneur [gla'nœːr], *n.m.* (*fem.* **-euse**) gleaner.
glapir [gla'piːr], *v.i.* to yelp (*of puppies etc.*); to screech, to scream (*of persons*).
glapissant [glapi'sɑ̃], *a.* yelping; screeching, shrill.
glapissement [glapis'mɑ̃], *n.m.* yelping; screeching.
glas [glɑ], *n.m.* knell.
glauque [gloːk], *a.* glaucous, sea-green.
glèbe [glɛb], *n.f.* glebe; land, soil.
glissade [gli'sad], *n.f.* sliding, slide; slipping.
glissant [gli'sɑ̃], *a.* slippery; (*fig.*) ticklish, delicate.
glissement [glis'mɑ̃], *n.m.* slipping, sliding, gliding; (*Polit.*) landslide.
glisser [gli'se], *v.t.* to slip, to slide; to insinuate.—*v.i.* to slip, to slide; to glide. **se glisser**, *v.r.* to slip, to slide, to creep, to steal, to insinuate oneself (*dans*).
glissière [gli'sjɛːr], *n.f.* slide; *porte à glissière*, sliding door.
glissoire [gli'swaːr], *n.f.* slide on ice.
global [glɔ'bal], *a.* (*m. pl.* **-aux**) in a mass, entire; *somme globale*, lump sum.
globe [glɔb], *n.m.* globe, sphere, orb; glass shade.
globulaire [glɔby'lɛːr], *a.* globular.
globule [glɔ'byl], *n.m.* globule.
gloire [glwaːr], *n.f.* glory, fame.
gloriette [glɔ'rjɛt], *n.f.* arbor, summer-house.
glorieusement [glɔrjøz'mɑ̃], *adv.* gloriously.
glorieux [glɔ'rjø], *a.* (*fem.* **-euse**) glorious; vainglorious.—*n.m.* braggart, boaster.
glorification [glɔrifika'sjɔ̃], *n.f.* glorification.
glorifier [glɔri'fje], *v.t.* to glorify, to honor. **se glorifier**, *v.r.* to glory in, to boast (*de*).
gloriole [glɔ'rjɔl], *n.f.* vainglory, petty vanity.
glose [glo'z], *n.f.* gloss; criticism; comment; parody.
gloser [glo'ze], *v.t.* to gloss; to criticize.—*v.i.* to carp, to find fault.
gloseur [glo'zœːr], *n.m.* (*fem.* **-euse**) carper, fault-finder.
glossaire [glɔ'sɛːr], *n.m.* glossary, vocabulary.
glouglou [glu'glu], *n.m.* gurgling, gurgle.
glouglouter [gluglu'te], *v.i.* to gurgle.
gloussement [glus'mɑ̃], *n.m.* clucking.
glousser [glu'se], *v.i.* to cluck (*of hens*).
glouton [glu'tɔ̃], *a.* (*fem.* **-onne**) gluttonous, greedy.—*n.m.* (*fem.* **-onne**) glutton.
gloutonnement [glutɔn'mɑ̃], *adv.* gluttonously, greedily.
gloutonnerie [glutɔn'ri], *n.f.* gluttony, greediness.
glu [gly], *n.f.* bird-lime, glue.
gluant [gly'ɑ̃], *a.* glutinous, sticky; slimy.

glucose [gly'koːz], *n.m.* glucose.
glutineux [glyti'nø], *a.* (*fem.* **-euse**) glutinous, viscous.
glycérine [glise'rin], *n.f.* glycerine.
glycine [gli'sin], *n.f.* wistaria.
gnome [gno:m], *n.m.* (*fem.* **gnomide**) gnome.
gnou [gnu], *n.m.* gnu.
gobelet [gɔ'blɛ], *n.m.* goblet, mug; dice box; *tour de gobelet*, juggler's trick.
gobelin [gɔ'blɛ̃], *n.m.* goblin, imp.
gobe-mouches [gɔb'muʃ], *n.m. inv.* fly-catcher (*bird*); fly-trap (*plant*); (*fig.*) simpleton.
gober [gɔ'be], *v.t.* to gulp down, to swallow; (*colloq.*) to believe easily; to have a liking for (*a person*).
(C) godendard [gɔdɑ̃'daːr], *n.m.* cross-cut saw, whip-saw, two-handle saw.
goder [gɔ'de], *v.i.* to crease, to bag (*of clothes*), to pucker (*of needlework etc.*).
godiche [gɔ'diʃ], *a.* clumsy, boobyish, simple.
godille [gɔ'diːj], *n.f.* stern oar; scull.
goéland [gɔe'lɑ̃], *n.m.* gull, sea-gull.
goélette [gɔe'lɛt], *n.f.* schooner.
goémon [gɔe'mɔ̃], *n.m.* seaweed.
gogo [gɔ'go] (*in adv. phr.*) *à gogo*, galore.
goguenard [gɔg'naːr], *a.* bantering, jeering, mocking, scoffing.—*n.m.* (*fem.* **-e**) banterer, jeerer, chaffer.
goguenarder [gɔgnar'de], *v.i.* to jeer, to banter, to chaff.
goguette [gɔ'gɛt], *n.f.* *être en goguette*, to be in a merry mood, to be on the spree.
goinfre [gwɛ̃:fr], *n.m.* (*fam.*) guzzler, gormandizer.
goinfrer [gwɛ̃'fre], *v.i.* to gorge, to gormandize.
goinfrerie [gwɛ̃frə'ri], *n.f.* gluttony.
goitre [gwaːtr], *n.m.* goitre; wen.
goitreux [gwa'trø], *a.* (*fem.* **-euse**) goitrous.—*n.m.* (*fem.* **-euse**) goitrous person, (*colloq.*) imbecile, idiot.
golfe [golf], *n.m.* gulf, bay.
gommage [gɔ'maːʒ], *n.m.* gumming.
gomme [gɔm], *n.f.* gum; rubber, eraser.
gommer [gɔ'me], *v.t.* to gum; to rub out.
gommeux [gɔ'mø], *a.* (*fem.* **-euse**) gummy.
gommier [gɔ'mje], *n.m.* gum tree.
gond [gɔ̃], *n.m.* hinge; *hors des gonds*, unhinged, (*fig.*) enraged, beside oneself.
gondole [gɔ'dɔl], *n.f.* gondola; car *or* gondola (*of a balloon etc.*); eye-bath.
gondoler [gɔdɔ'le], *v.i.* to bulge; to warp (*of wood*); to buckle.
gondolier [gɔdɔ'lje], *n.m.* gondolier.
gonflement [gɔ̃flə'mɑ̃], *n.m.* swelling, inflation.
gonfler [gɔ̃'fle], *v.t.* to swell, to inflate; to pump up (*a tire*); to puff up.—*v.i.* to swell, to be swollen. **se gonfler**, *v.r.* to swell, to be swollen, to be puffed up; (*fam.*) to swank.
gonfleur [gɔ̃'flœːr], *n.m.* air-pump, inflator.
gong [gɔ̃:g], *n.m.* gong.
gorge [gɔrʒ], *n.f.* throat, gullet; bosom, neck; defile, strait; (*Bot.*) mouth; (*Arch., Fort.*) gorge; *avoir mal à la gorge*, to have a sore throat; *avoir la gorge serrée*, to have a lump in one's throat; *rendre gorge*, to refund, to pay up; *faire des gorges chaudes*, to gloat over.
gorge-de-pigeon [gɔrʒdəpi'ʒɔ̃], *a. inv.* iridescent, shot (*of colors*).

168

gorgée [gɔrˈʒe], *n.f.* draft; gulp; *petite gorgée*, sip.

gorger [gɔrˈʒe], *v.t.* (*conjug. like* MANGER) to gorge, to cram. **se gorger**, *v.r.* to gorge oneself.

gorille [gɔˈriːj], *n.m.* gorilla.

gosier [goˈzje], *n.m.* throat, gullet; (*fig.*) voice.

gosse [gɔs], *n.* (*fam.*) brat, urchin, kid.

gothique [gɔˈtik], *a.* Gothic.—*n.f.* (*Print.*) Old English.

gouache [gwaʃ], *n.f.* gouache; painting in this.

goudron [guˈdrɔ̃], *n.m.* tar.

goudronnage [gudrɔˈnaːʒ], *n.m.* tarring.

goudronner [gudrɔˈne], *v.t.* to tar.

goudronneux [gudrɔˈnø], *a.* (*fem.* **-euse**) tarry.

gouffre [gufr], *n.m.* gulf, abyss, pit.

gouge [guːʒ], *n.f.* gouge.

goujat [guˈʒa], *n.m.* (*fig.*) cad, vulgar fellow.

goujon [guˈʒɔ̃], *n.m.* gudgeon (*pin or fish*).

goule [gul], *n.f.* ghoul.

goulet [guˈlɛ], *n.m.* narrow entrance (*to a harbour etc.*); inlet; mouth, neck (*of a bottle etc.*); gully, gorge (*between mountains etc.*).

goulot [guˈlo], *n.m.* neck (*of a bottle etc.*).

goulu [guˈly], *a.* gluttonous, greedy.—*n.m.* (*fem.* **-e**) glutton, greedy person.

goulûment [gulyˈmɑ̃], *adv.* greedily.

goupille [guˈpiːj], *n.f.* (cotter) pin, peg, bolt.

goupiller [gupiˈje], *v.t.* to pin, to bolt.

gourd [guːr], *a.* benumbed, numb.

gourde [gurd], *n.f.* gourd; flask, wineskin.

gourdin [gurˈdɛ̃], *n.m.* cudgel, club, thick stick.

gourmade [gurˈmad], *n.f.* smack in the face.

gourmand [gurˈmɑ̃], *a.* greedy.—*n.m.* (*fem.* **-e**) glutton.

gourmander [gurmɑ̃ˈde], *v.t.* to chide, to reprimand; to prune (*trees*).

gourmandise [gurmɑ̃ˈdiːz], *n.f.* gluttony, greediness; (*pl.*) sweetmeats.

gourmé [gurˈme], *a.* stiff, stuck-up, formal, solemn.

gourmer [gurˈme], *v.t.* to box, to thump; to curb (*a horse*). **se gourmer**, *v.r.* to thump, to pummel each other.

gourmet [gurˈmɛ], *n.m.* connoisseur in wines etc.; epicure.

gourmette [gurˈmɛt], *n.f.* bit, curb chain.

gousse [gus], *n.f.* shell, pod, husk; *gousse d'ail*, clove of garlic.

gousset [guˈsɛ], *n.m.* armpit; fob, (waistcoat-) pocket; gusset (*of a shirt etc.*); bracket.

goût [gu], *n.m.* taste, flavor, relish; savor; inclination, liking; style, manner; *chacun à son goût*, every man to his taste; *chacun son goût*, tastes differ; *viande de haut goût*, highly seasoned meat.

goûter [guˈte], *v.t.* to taste, to try; to like; to enjoy; to feel.—*v.i.* to taste; to try; to have a snack.—*n.m.* a snack taken between lunch and dinner (*the equivalent of English tea*).

goutte (1) [gut], *n.f.* drop, small quantity; sip, dram; (*Arch., Pharm.*) drop.—*adv. phr. ne . . . goutte*; *n'entendre goutte*, not to hear *or* understand in the least; *n'y voir goutte*, not to make it out at all.

goutte (2) [gut], *n.f.* gout.

gouttelette [guˈtlɛt], *n.f.* small drop, drip.

goutter [guˈte], *v.i.* to drip.

goutteux [guˈtø], *a.* and *n.m.* (*fem.* **-euse**) gouty (person).

gouttière [guˈtjɛːr], *n.f.* gutter of a roof; shoot, spout (*for rain water*); cradle splint.

gouvernable [guverˈnabl], *a.* governable, manageable.

gouvernail [guverˈnaj], *n.m.* rudder, helm.

gouvernant [guverˈnɑ̃], *a.* governing, ruling.—*n.m.* governor, ruler.—*n.f.* (**-e**) governor's wife; governess; housekeeper (*of bachelor*).

gouvernement [guvernəˈmɑ̃], *n.m.* government, rule, sway; management; governorship.

gouvernemental [guvernəmɑ̃ˈtal], *a.* (*m. pl.* **-aux**) governmental.

gouverner [guverˈne], *v.t.* to govern, to control, to govern, to direct, to steer; to rule, to command, to manage, to regulate.—*v.i.* to steer, to answer the helm.

gouverneur [guverˈnœːr], *n.m.* governor; manager; tutor.

grabat [graˈba], *n.m.* pallet, litter (*of straw etc.*), trundle bed.

grabuge [graˈbyːʒ], *n.m.* (*fam.*) wrangling, squabble, brawl.

grâce [graːs], *n.f.* grace, favor, mercy, forgiveness; gracefulness, elegance; (*pl.*) thanks; (*Myth.*) *les Grâces*, the Graces.

graciable [graˈsjabl], *a.* pardonable.

gracier [graˈsje], *v.t.* to pardon, to reprieve.

gracieusement [grasjøzˈmɑ̃], *adv.* graciously, kindly, gracefully.

gracieuseté [grasjøzˈte], *n.f.* graciousness, kindness; act of courtesy; gratuity.

gracieux [graˈsjø], *a.* (*fem.* **-euse**) graceful, gracious, obliging.

gracilité [grasiliˈte], *n.f.* slimness, slenderness.

gradation [gradaˈsjɔ̃], *n.f.* gradation; climax.

grade [grad], *n.m.* grade, rank; degree; *monter en grade*, to be promoted.

gradé [graˈde], *n.m.* (*Mil.*) non-commissioned officer.

gradin [graˈdɛ̃], *n.m.* step; tier.

graduation [graduaˈsjɔ̃], *n.f.* graduation; scale.

gradué [graˈdɥe], *a.* graduated; progressive (*exercises*).—*n.m.* (*fem.* **-ée**) graduate (*of a university*).

graduel [graˈdɥɛl], *a.* (*fem.* **-elle**) gradual.

graduellement [gradɥɛlˈmɑ̃], *adv.* gradually.

graduer [graˈdɥe], *v.t.* to graduate, to proportion.

graillon [graˈjɔ̃], *n.m.* smell of burnt meat *or* fat; (*pl.*) scraps (*of meat etc.*) from a meal.

grain (1) [grɛ̃], *n.m.* grain, berry; bead; jot, bit; *avoir un grain*, to have a bee in one's bonnet; *grain de beauté*, mole, beauty-spot; *grain de café*, coffee bean; *grain de poivre*, peppercorn; *grain de raisin*, grape.

grain (2) [grɛ̃], *n.m.* (*Naut.*) squall.

graine [grɛːn], *n.f.* seed; breed; *c'est une mauvaise graine*, he is a bad lot.

grainetier [grɛnˈtje], **grainier** [grɛˈnje], *n.m.* (*fem.* **-ière**) seedsman, seedswoman; grain and seed dealer.

graissage [grɛˈsaːʒ], *n.m.* greasing, oiling, lubrication.

graisse [grɛ:s], *n.f.* fat, grease.
graisser [grɛ'se], *v.t.* to grease; to make greasy; to lubricate, to oil.
graisseur [grɛ'sœ:r], *n.m.* greaser, oiler.
graisseux [grɛ'sø], *a.* (*fem.* **-euse**) greasy; oily; fatty.
grammaire [gra'mɛ:r], *n.f.* grammar.
grammairien [grame'rjɛ̃], *n.m.* (*fem.* **-enne**) grammarian.
grammatical [gramati'kal], *a.* (*m. pl.* **-aux**) grammatical.
grammaticalement [gramatikal'mɑ̃], *adv.* grammatically.
gramme [gram], *n.m.* gramme *or* gram.
grand [grɑ̃], *a.* great; large, big; high, tall; wide, spacious; grown-up; capital (*of letters*); broad (*of daylight*); grand, noble.—*adv.* **voir grand**, to have big ideas; *en grand*, on a large scale; (*of portraits*) full length.—*n.m.* the grand, the sublime.—*n.m.* (*fem.* **-e**) great person; grown-up person; *grand d'Espagne*, Spanish grandee; (*pl.*) the great, grand people; (*sch.*) the big (*or* senior) boys *or* girls.
(C) **grand-bois** [grɑ̃'bwa], *n.m.* virgin forest.
grand-duc [grɑ̃'dyk], *n.m.* (*pl.* **grands-ducs**) grand duke; eagle-owl.
grand-duché [grɑ̃dy'ʃe], *n.m.* (*pl.* **grands-duchés**) grand duchy.
grande-duchesse [grɑ̃ddy'ʃes], *n.f.* (*pl.* **grandes-duchesses**) grand duchess.
grandement [grɑ̃d'mɑ̃], *adv.* greatly, extremely, very much; grandly, nobly, handsomely.
grandeur [grɑ̃'dœ:r], *n.f.* extent, size; height; length; breadth; bulk; greatness, magnitude; tallness; grandeur, magnificence; grace, highness (*titles*).
grandiose [grɑ̃'djo:z], *a.* grandiose.
grandir [grɑ̃'di:r], *v.t.* to increase; to magnify.—*v.i.* to grow; to grow (tall, big, up etc.). **se grandir**, *v.r.* to make oneself appear taller; to grow taller; to raise oneself, to rise.
grandissement [grɑ̃dis'mɑ̃], *n.m.* growth, increase; rise; (*Opt.*) magnification.
grand-maman [grɑ̃ma'mɑ̃], *n.f.* (*pl.* **-mamans**) granny.
grand-mère [grɑ̃'mɛ:r], *n.f.* (*pl.* **-mères**) grandmother.
grand-père [grɑ̃'pɛ:r], *n.m.* (*pl.* **grands-pères**) grandfather.
grand-route [grɑ̃'rut], *n.f.* (*pl.* **-routes**) high-road, main road.
grand-rue [grɑ̃'ry], *n.f.* (*pl.* **-rues**) high street, main street.
grange [grɑ̃:ʒ], *n.f.* barn.
granit [gra'nit, gra'ni], **granite** [gra'nit], *n.m.* granite.
granulaire [grany'lɛ:r], *a.* granular.
granule [gra'nyl], *n.m.* granule.
granulé [grany'le], *a.* granulated, granular.
graphique [gra'fik], *a.* graphic.—*n.m.* diagram; graph.
graphiquement [grafik'mɑ̃], *adv.* graphically.
graphite [gra'fit], *n.m.* graphite; plumbago.
grappe [grap], *n.f.* bunch (*of grapes, currants etc.*); cluster (*of fruit etc.*); (*Artill.*) grapeshot.
grappillage [grapi'ja:ʒ], *n.m.* vine gleaning *or* pickings.

grappiller [grapi'je], *v.t.* to glean.—*v.i.* to glean; to get pickings, to make a little profit.
grappilleur [grapi'jœ:r], *n.m.* (*fem.* **-euse**) gleaner; petty thief, profiteer.
grappin [gra'pɛ̃], *n.m.* grapnel, grappling iron; grab.
gras [grɑ], *a.* (*fem.* **grasse**) fat; fleshy, corpulent; greasy, oily, unctuous; rich; broad, indecent; *eaux grasses*, dishwater; *faire la grasse matinée*, to get up late; *mardi gras*, Shrove Tuesday; *matières grasses*, fats.—*n.m.* fat, fat part (*of meat etc.*); meat, flesh; meat diet.
gras-double [grɑ'dubl], *n.m.* tripe.
grassement [grɑs'mɑ̃], *adv.* plentifully, liberally; in affluence.
grasseyement [grasɛj'mɑ̃], *n.m.* exaggerated rolling of uvular r.
grasseyer [grasɛ'je], *v.i.* to roll one's r's.
grassouillet [grasu'jɛ], *a.* (*fem.* **-ette**) (*fam.*) plump, chubby.
gratification [gratifika'sjɔ̃], *n.f.* gratuity, extra pay, reward.
gratifier [grati'fje], *v.t.* to confer (*a favor*) on; to ascribe.
gratin [gra'tɛ̃], *n.m.* burnt part; *au gratin*, (*Cook.*) dressed with crust of bread-crumbs.
gratis [gra'tis], *adv.* gratis, for nothing.
gratitude [grati'tyd], *n.f.* gratitude.
gratte-ciel [grat'sjɛl], *n.m. inv.* skyscraper.
grattelle [gra'tɛl], *n.f.* rash, itching.
gratte-papier [gratpa'pje], *n.m. inv.* scribbler, pen pusher.
gratter [gra'te], *v.t.* to scratch; to scrape. **se gratter**, *v.r.* to scratch oneself.
grattoir [gra'twa:r], *n.m.* scraper; eraser, paint scraper.
gratuit [gra'tɥi], *a.* free (of charge); gratuitous.
gratuité [gratɥi'te], *n.f.* gratuitousness.
gratuitement [gratɥit'mɑ̃], *adv.* for nothing; gratuitously.
gravats [gra'va], *n.m. pl.* rubbish, debris (*of a building*).
grave [gra:v], *a.* heavy, grave, serious; weighty; dangerous; low, deep (*of voice*); (*Mus.*) low-pitched.
gravé [gra've], *a.* pitted; engraved.
graveleux [gra'vlø], *a.* (*fem.* **-euse**) gravelly, sandy, gritty; (*fig.*) smutty.
gravelle [gra'vɛl], *n.f.* (*Path.*) gravel.
gravement [grav'mɑ̃], *adv.* gravely, seriously.
graver [gra've], *v.t.* to engrave; to impress, to imprint. **se graver**, *v.r.* to be engraved, to be impressed *or* imprinted.
graveur [gra'vœ:r], *n.m.* engraver.
gravier [gra'vje], *n.m.* gravel, grit; (*Path.*) gravel.
gravir [gra'vi:r], *v.t.* to clamber up, to climb, to ascend.
gravitation [gravita'sjɔ̃], *n.f.* gravitation.
gravité [gravi'te], *n.f.* gravity; seriousness, solemnity; weight, importance.
graviter [gravi'te], *v.i.* to gravitate.
gravure [gra'vy:r], *n.f.* engraving, print; illustration (*in book*).
gré [gre], *n.m.* will, wish; liking, pleasure; mind, taste; accord, consent *bon gré mal gré* or *de gré ou de force*, willy nilly; *de bon gré*, willingly; *de mauvais gré*, unwillingly; *savoir (bon) gré*, to be thankful; *vendre de gré à gré*, to sell by private contract.

grèbe [grɛb], n.m. (Orn.) grebe.
grec [grɛk], a. (fem. **grecque**) Greek; Grecian.—n.m. Greek (language); (**Grec**, fem. **Grecque**) Greek (person).
Grèce [grɛs], la, f. Greece.
gredin [grə'dɛ̃], n.m. rascal, scoundrel.
gréer [gre'e], v.t. to rig.
greffe (1) [grɛf], n.m. (Law) registry, record office.
greffe (2) [grɛf], n.f. graft; grafting.
greffer [grɛ'fe], v.t. to graft.
greffier [grɛ'fje], n.m. registrar, recorder, clerk of the court.
greffoir [grɛ'fwaːr], n.m. grafting knife.
greffon [grɛ'fɔ̃], n.m. graft, scion, slip.
grégaire [gre'gɛːr], **grégarien** [grega'rjɛ̃] (fem. **-enne**), a. gregarious.
grêle (1) [grɛːl], a. slender, slim; shrill.
grêle (2) [grɛːl], n.f. hail; hailstorm.
grêlé [grɛ'le], a. ravaged by hail; pock-marked.
grêler [grɛ'le], v. impers. to hail.—v.t. to ravage, ruin or spoil by hail.
grêlon [grɛ'lɔ̃], n.m. hailstone.
grelot [grə'lo], n.m. small (round) bell.
grelotter [grələ'te], v.i. to tremble, to shake, to shiver (with cold, fear); to tinkle.
grenade [grə'nad], n.f. pomegranate; (Mil.) grenade.
grenadier [grəna'dje], n.m. pomegranate tree; (Mil.) grenadier.
grenadine [grəna'din], n.f. grenadine (silk or syrup).
grenat [grə'na], n.m. garnet.—a. garnet-red.
grener [grə'ne], v.t. (conjug. like AMENER) to granulate; to grain (leather etc.); (Engr.) to stipple.—v.i. to seed, to run to seed.
grènetis [grɛn'ti], n.m. milling, milled edge.
grenier [grə'nje], n.m. loft; attic; corn loft, granary.
grenouille [grə'nuːj], n.f. frog.
grenu [grə'ny], a. full of grains, rough-grained.
grès [grɛ], n.m. sandstone, stoneware.
grésil [gre'zi], n.m. sleet.
grésillement [grezij'mɑ̃], n.m. pattering (like sleet); shrivelling, crackling; chirping.
grésiller [grezi'je], v. impers. to sleet, to patter.—v.t. to shrivel up.—v.i. to crackle.
grève [grɛːv], n.f. strand, beach of sand or shingle; strike of workmen; **grève du zèle**, slowdown (strike).
grever [grə've], v.t. (conjug. like AMENER) to wrong, to injure; to burden; to encumber (with debt etc.).
gréviste [gre'vist], n. striker.
gribouillage [gribu'jaːʒ], **gribouillis** [gribu'ji], n.m. (Paint.) daub; scrawl.
gribouiller [gribu'je], v.t., v.i. to daub; to scrawl, to scribble.
gribouilleur [gribu'jœːr], n.m. (fem. **-euse**) dauber; scrawler, scribbler.
grief [gri'ɛf], n.m. wrong, injury, grievance.
grièvement [griɛv'mɑ̃], adv. grievously, gravely.
grièveté [griɛv'te], n.f. gravity, seriousness.
griffade [gri'fad], n.f. clawing, scratch.
griffe [grif], n.f. claw, talon; (pl.) clutches; paper-clip, clamp; **griffe d'asperge**, root of asparagus.
griffer [gri'fe], v.t. to claw, to scratch (of cats etc.); to stamp (with signature etc.).

griffon [gri'fɔ̃], n.m. griffin; griffon.
griffonnage [grifɔ'naːʒ], n.m. scrawl, scribble.
griffonner [grifɔ'ne], v.t. to scrawl, to scribble.
griffonneur [grifɔ'nœːr], n.m. (fem. **-euse**) scrawler, scribbler.
grignoter [griɲɔ'te], v.t. to nibble; (fig.) to get pickings out of.
gril [gri], n.m. gridiron, grill.
grillade [gri'jad], n.f. grilling, broiling; grill, grilled steak.
grillage [gri'jaːʒ], n.m. grilling, broiling, toasting; wire guard or mesh; light iron railing.
grille [griːj], n.f. railing, grating; grill; iron gate or bars; (Elec.) grid.
grille-pain [grij'pɛ̃], n.m. inv. toaster.
griller (1) [gri'je], v.t. to broil, to grill (meat); to roast (coffee); to toast (bread).—v.i. to broil, to be burned up or scorched; to burn out (electric bulbs); (fig.) to be itching (to do something). **se griller**, v.r. to be scorched, to be parched.
griller (2) [gri'je], v.t. to enclose with iron rails.
grillon [gri'jɔ̃], n.m. cricket.
grimaçant [grima'sɑ̃], a. grimacing, grinning; (fig.) gaping, ill-fitting.
grimace [gri'mas], n.f. grimace, wry face; (fig.) affectations, airs and graces.
grimacer [grima'se], v.i. (conjug. like COMMENCER) to make faces, to grimace, to grin; to simper; to pucker.
grimer (se) [səgri'me], v.r. to make up.
grimpant [grɛ̃'pɑ̃], a. climbing, creeping (of plants).
grimper [grɛ̃'pe], v.i. to climb, to clamber up; to creep up (of plants).
grimpeur [grɛ̃'pœːr], a. (fem. **-euse**) climbing, twining.—n.m. (fem. **-euse**) (Orn.) climber.
grincement [grɛs'mɔ̃], n.m. gnashing, grinding (of the teeth etc.); grating.
grincer [grɛ̃'se], v.i. (conjug. like COMMENCER) to grind, to gnash, to grate.
grincheux [grɛ̃'ʃø], a. (fem. **-euse**) ill-tempered, peevish, crabbed, surly.—n.m. (fem. **-euse**) grumbler.
gringalet [grɛ̃ga'lɛ], n.m. weak, puny man.
griotte [gri'ɔt], n.f. morello cherry.
grippage [gri'paːʒ], **grippement** [grip'mɔ̃], n.m. friction (of two surfaces); seizing, jamming (of bearing).
grippe [grip], n.f. influenza, flu; (colloq.) dislike.
grippé [gri'pe], a. shrunk, contracted (of the face); ill with influenza; run hot, seized up (of motors).
gripper [gri'pe], v.t. to pounce upon, to clutch, to seize.—v.i. to run hot, to seize up, to jam. **se gripper**, v.r. to shrivel, to shrink.
grippe-sou [grip'su], n.m. (pl. unchanged or **grippe-sous**) miser, money-grubber.
gris [gri], a. grey; grey-haired; dull (of the weather); (fig.) tipsy; **papier gris**, brown paper.—n.m. grey.
grisaille [gri'zaːj], n.f. sketch or painting in tones of grey; greyness (of weather).
grisâtre [gri'zɑːtr], a. greyish.
griser [gri'ze], v.t. to give a gray tint to; to intoxicate. **se griser**, v.r. to get tipsy.
grisette [gri'zɛt], n.f. gray gown; (Orn.) whitethroat.

171

grison

grison [gri'zɔ̃], *a.* (*fem.* **-onne**) gray, gray-haired.—*n.m.* (*colloq.*) gray-beard (*old man*); donkey.

grisonnant [grizo'nɑ̃], *a.* turning gray.

grisonner [grizo'ne], *v.i.* to grow gray (*of hair etc.*).

grisou [gri'zu], *n.m.* fire-damp.

grive [gri:v], *n.f.* thrush.

grivelé [gri'vle], *a.* speckled.

grivois [gri'vwa], *a.* loose, broad, obscene.

grivoiserie [grivwaz'ri], *n.f.* smutty story.

Groenland [grɔen'lɑ̃d], **le**, *m.* Greenland.

groenlandais [grɔenlɑ̃de], *a.* of Greenland.—*n.m.* (**Groenlandais**, *fem.* **-aise**) Greenlander.

grognard [grɔ'naːr], *a.* grumbling, growling.—*n.* grumbler, grouser; veteran of Napoleon's Old Guard.

grognement [grɔɲ'mɑ̃], *n.m.* grunt, grunting; growling, grumbling.

grogner [grɔ'ɲe], *v.i.* to grunt; to growl, to grumble, to grouse.

grognon [grɔ'ɲɔ̃], *a.* (*fem.* **-onne**, *but usu. unchanged*) grumbling, querulous.—*n.m.* (*fem.* **-onne**) grumbler, growler.

groin [grwɛ̃], *n.m.* snout (*of a hog*).

grommeler [grɔm'le], *v.t.*, *v.i.* (*conjug. like* APPELER) to mutter, to grumble.

grondant [grɔ̃'dɑ̃], *a.* scolding; roaring, rumbling.

grondement [grɔ̃d'mɑ̃], *n.m.* rumbling, growling, snarling; roar.

gronder [grɔ̃'de], *v.t.* to chide, to scold.—*v.i.* to growl, to mutter; to snarl, to rumble, to roar.

gronderie [grɔ̃'dri], *n.f.* scolding, chiding.

grondeur [grɔ̃'dœːr], *a.* (*fem.* **-euse**) grumbling, scolding.—*n.m.* (*fem.* **-euse**) scold; grumbler.

grondin [grɔ̃'dɛ̃], *n.m.* (*Ichth.*) gurnard, gurnet.

groom [grum], *n.m.* page, (*U.S.*) bell-boy; stable lad.

gros [gro], *a.* (*fem.* **grosse** (1)) big, large, bulky; stout; coarse; pregnant; loud (*of laughter*); gruff (*of the voice*); substantial, foul (*of the weather*); high (*of the sea etc.*); dark, deep (*in color*); (*Cine.*) **gros plan**, close-up.—*n.m.* large or main part; bulk, mass; main body (*of an army*); **en gros et en détail**, wholesale and retail.—*adv.* much.

groseille [gro'zɛːj], *n.f.* currant; **groseille à maquereau**, gooseberry.

groseillier [grozɛ'je], *n.m.* currant bush.

grosse (1) [gros], *a.* [GROS].

grosse (2) [gros], *n.f.* gross (*twelve dozen*).

grossement [gros'mɑ̃], *adv.* grossly, coarsely.

grossesse [gro'sɛs], *n.f.* pregnancy.

grosseur [gro'sœːr], *n.f.* size, bulk; bigness; swelling, tumor.

grossier [gro'sje], *a.* (*fem.* **-ière**) gross, coarse, thick; plain, common; rough, rude, unpolished, unmannerly, boorish.

grossièrement [grosjɛr'mɑ̃], *adv.* coarsely, rudely, roughly, uncouthly.

grossièreté [grosjɛr'te], *n.f.* coarseness, grossness; rudeness; coarse language.

grossir [gro'siːr], *v.t.* to make bigger or greater.—*v.i.* to grow bigger; to put on weight.

grossissant [grosi'sɑ̃], *a.* magnifying.

grossissement [grosis'mɑ̃], *n.m.* magnifying, magnifying power; increase; exaggeration.

grosso-modo [grɔsomo'do], *adv.* summarily.

grotesque [grɔ'tɛsk], *a.* and *n.m.* grotesque.

grotte [grɔt], *n.f.* grotto, cave.

grouillant [gru'jɑ̃], *a.* stirring, swarming, crawling.

grouillement [gruj'mɑ̃], *n.m.* stirring, swarming; rumbling (*of the intestines*).

grouiller [gru'je], *v.i.* to stir, to move; to swarm; to rumble (*of the intestines*).

groupe [grup], *n.m.* group, party (*of people*); cluster (*of stars*); clump (*of trees etc.*).

groupement [grup'mɑ̃], *n.m.* grouping.

grouper [gru'pe], *v.t.* to group. **se grouper**, *v.r.* to form groups, to gather.

gruau [gry'o], *n.m.* flour of wheat; **gruau d'avoine**, groats; oatmeal; **tisane de gruau**, gruel.

grue [gry], *n.f.* (*Orn.*, *Eng.*) crane.

gruger [gry'ʒe], *v.t.* (*conjug. like* MANGER) to crunch; to eat, to devour.

grume [grym], *n.f.* bark (*of tree*); **bois de** or **en grume**, wood with the bark on.

grumeau [gry'mo], *n.m.* (*pl.* **-eaux**) clot, small lump.

grumeler (**se**) [səgry'mle], *v.r.* (*conjug. like* APPELER) to clot.

grumeleux [grym'lø], *a.* (*fem.* **-euse**) clotted, rough.

gruyère [gry'jɛːr], *n.m.* Gruyère cheese.

guano [gwa'no], *n.m.* guano.

Guatémala [gwatema'la], **le**, *m.* Guatemala.

guatémaltèque [gwatemal'tɛk], *a.* Guatemalan.—*n.* (**Guatémaltèque**) Guatemalan (*person*).

gué [ge], *n.m.* ford.

guéable [ge'abl], *a.* fordable.

guéer [ge'e], *v.t.* to ford.

guenille [gə'niːj], *n.f.* rag, tatter; (*pl.*) tattered clothes.

guenilleux [gəni'jø], *a.* (*fem.* **-euse**) tattered, ragged.

guenon [gə'nɔ̃], *n.f.* monkey, ape; she-monkey; (*fig.*) fright, ugly woman.

guépard [ge'paːr], *n.m.* cheetah.

guêpe [gɛ:p], *n.f.* wasp.

guêpier [gɛ:'pje], *n.m.* wasps' nest; bee-eater (*bird*); scrape, difficulty.

guère [gɛːr], *adv.* but little, not much, not very; not long; hardly, scarcely.

guères (*poet.*) [GUÈRE].

guéret [ge're], *n.m.* ploughed but unsown land; fallow land; (*pl.*, *poet.*) fields.

guéridon [geri'dɔ̃], *n.m.* (small) round table.

guérilla [geri'ja], *n.f.* guerrilla war or troops.

guérir [ge'riːr], *v.t.* to heal, to cure.—*v.i.* to heal, to heal up; to recover, to be cured.

guérison [geri'zɔ̃], *n.f.* recovery, healing, cure.

guérissable [geri'sabl], *a.* curable.

guérisseur [geri'sœːr], *n.m.* (*fem.* **-euse**) healer, faith healer; quack.

guérite [ge'rit], *n.f.* sentry box; look-out turret.

Guernesey [gɛrnə'ze], *f.* Guernsey.

guerre [gɛːr], *n.f.* war; warfare, hostilities; strife.

guerrier [ge'rje], *a.* (*fem.* **-ière**) warlike, martial.—*n.m.* (*fem.* **-ière**) warrior, fighting man or woman.

guerroyant [gɛrwa'jã], a. bellicose, pugnacious.

guerroyer [gɛrwa'je], v.i. (conjug. like EMPLOYER) to make war, to wage war.

guet [gɛ], n.m. watch; watching; *au guet*, on the look-out.

guet-apens [gɛta'pã], n.m. (pl. guets-apens) ambush; trap.

guêtre [gɛːtr], n.f. gaiter; *grandes guêtres*, leggings; *petites guêtres*, spats.

guetter [gɛ'te], v.t. to lie in wait for, to watch for, to waylay.

guetteur [gɛ'tœːr], n.m. signalman, look-out man.

gueulard [gœ'laːr], a. (pop.) bawling, mouthing; gluttonous; hard-mouthed (of horses). —n.m. (fem. -e) bawler; glutton.—n.m. mouth of a furnace.

gueule [gœl], n.f. mouth (of animals); (vulg.) mouth, face, mug (of human).

gueule-de-lion [gœldə'ljõ], n.f. (pl. gueules-de-lion) antirrhinum.

gueule-de-loup [gœldə'lu], n.f. (pl. gueules-de-loup) snapdragon; chimney cowl.

gueuler [gœ'le], v.i. (pop.) to bawl.

gueuse (1) [gøːz], n.f. pig iron.

gueuser [gø'ze], v.t., v.i. to beg.

gueuserie [gø'zri], n.f. beggary; destitution; (fig.) trash.

gueux [gø], a. (fem. -euse) poor, destitute; wretched.—n.m. beggar, tramp; knave, rascal.—n.f. (-euse (2)) wench, bitch.

gui [gi], n.m. mistletoe.

guichet [gi'ʃɛ], n.m. wicket gate (of prison); spyhole (of door); position at counter (banks, post office), pay desk; ticket office (railways).

guichetier [giʃ'tje], n.m. turnkey.

guide [gid], n.m. guide; guide-book.—n.f. girl scout; rein.

guider [gi'de], v.t. to guide, to lead; to direct.

guidon [gi'dõ], n.m. (Mil.) guidon; (Navy) burgee; (fore)sight, bead (of fire-arms); reference mark (in a book); handle-bar (of bicycle).

guigner [gi'ne], v.t. to peer or peep at; to ogle; to covet.—v.i. to peep, to peer.

guignol [gi'nɔl], n.m. Punch; puppet show, Punch and Judy show.

guignolet [gino'lɛ], n.m. cherry brandy.

guignon [gi'nõ], n.m. bad luck, ill-luck.

Guillaume [gi'joːm], m. William.

guillemet [gij'mɛ], n.m. quotation mark, inverted comma.

guillemot [gij'mo], n.m. (Orn.) guillemot.

guilleret [gij'rɛ], a. (fem. -ette) brisk, lively.

guilleri [gij'ri], n.m. chirping (of sparrows).

guillotine [gijo'tin], n.f. guillotine; *fenêtre à guillotine*, sash-window.

guillotiner [gijoti'ne], v.t. to guillotine.

guimauve [gi'moːv], n.f. marsh-mallow.

guimbarde [gɛ'bard], n.f. Jew's harp; (colloq.) rickety old vehicle, boneshaker.

guimpe [gɛːp], n.f. stomacher; wimple (for nuns etc.).

guindé [gɛ'de], a. stiff, forced, unnatural; formal (of style).

guindeau [gɛ'do], n.m. (pl. -eaux) windlass.

guinder [gɛ'de], v.t. to hoist; to strain, to force. se guinder, v.r. to hoist oneself up; to be strained, to be forced.

Guinée [gi'ne], la, f. Guinea.

guinéen [gine'ɛ̃], a. (fem. -éenne) Guinean. —n.m. (Guinéen, fem. -éenne) Guinean (person).

guingan [gɛ'gã], n.m. gingham.

guingois [gɛ'gwa], n.m. crookedness; *de guingois*, awry, askew.

guinguette [gɛ'gɛt], n.f. small suburban tavern (usually with pleasure garden).

guirlande [gir'lãd], n.f. garland, wreath.

guise [giːz], n.f. manner, way, guise; fancy; *en guise de*, by way of.

guitare [gi'taːr], n.f. guitar.

guitariste [gita'rist], n. guitarist, guitar player.

gustatif [gysta'tif], a. (fem. -tive) gustatory.

gustation [gysta'sjõ], n.f. tasting, gustation.

guttural [gyty'ral], a. (m. pl. -aux) guttural.

guyanais [guija'nɛ], a. (fem. -aise) Guyanese. —n.m. (Guyanais, fem. -aise) Guyanese (person).

Guyane [gui'jan], la, f. Guyana.

gymnase [ʒim'naːz], n.m. gymnasium.

gymnaste [ʒim'nast], n. gymnast.

gymnastique [ʒimnas'tik], a. gymnastic.— n.f. gymnastics.

gynécologie [ʒinekɔlɔ'ʒi], n.f. gynecology.

gynécologiste [ʒinekɔlɔ'ʒist], gynécologue [ʒinekɔ'lɔg], n. gynecologist.

gypse [ʒips], n.m. gypsum; plaster of Paris.

gyroscope [ʒirɔs'kɔp], n.m. gyroscope.

H

[In words marked thus † the *h* is 'aspirated'.]

H, h [aʃ], n.m. or f. the eighth letter of the alphabet. *H* is mute or aspirated. The so-called aspirated *h* is a graphic symbol which indicates that there is neither elision nor liaison; *e.g. la halle* [la'al], *les halles* [le'al]; *l'heure H*, (Mil.) zero hour.

habile [a'bil], a. able, clever; capable; skilful; sharp, cunning.

habilement [abil'mã], adv. cleverly, skilfully.

habileté [abil'te], n.f. ability, skill, cleverness.

habilité [abili'te], a. entitled, qualified.—n.f. (Law) competency, qualification.

habiliter [abili'te], v.t. to qualify, to enable, to entitle.

habillage [abi'jaːʒ], n.m. dressing; trussing (poultry).

habillant [abi'jã], a. dressy or suiting well (of clothes etc.).

habillé [abi'je], a. dressed, clad, decked out.

habillement [abij'mã] n.m. clothes, dress, attire.

habiller [abi'je], v.t. to dress; to make clothes for; to become, to fit; to wrap up; (Cook.) to truss (fowls, fish etc.); (fig.) to adorn. s'habiller, v.r. to dress; to have one's clothes made.

habilleur [abi'jœːr], n.m. (fem. -euse) (Theat.) dresser.

habit

habit [a'bi], n.m. clothes; dress coat; *habit complet*, suit of clothes.

habitable [abi'tabl], a. habitable.

habitant [abi'tā], n.m. (*fem.* -e) inhabitant, resident; occupier; denizen; (C) farmer.

habitation [abita'sjɔ̃], n.f. habitation, residence, abode.

habiter [abi'te], v.t. to inhabit, to dwell in, to live in; to frequent; *habiter un lieu*, to live in a place.—v.i. to inhabit, to dwell, to reside; *habiter avec*, (Law) to cohabit.

habitude [abi'tyd], n.f. habit, custom, practice; *d'habitude*, usually.

habitué [abi'tчe], n.m. (*fem.* -ée) frequenter, customer.

habituel [abi'tчɛl], a. (*fem.* -elle) habitual, usual.

habituellement [abitчɛl'mã], adv. habitually, usually.

habituer [abi'tчe], v.t. to accustom. s'habituer, v.r. to accustom oneself; to get used (à).

†hâbler [a'ble], v.i. to brag, to boast.

†hâblerie [abla'ri], n.f. bragging, boasting.

†hâbleur [a'blœ:r], n.m. (*fem.* -euse) braggart, boaster.

†hache [aʃ], n.f. axe, hatchet.

†haché [a'ʃe], a. chopped up, mixed; (*fig.*) abrupt.

†hacher [a'ʃe], v.t. to chop, to cut to pieces; to hash, to mince; to hack; to cross-hatch.

†hachis [a'ʃi], n.m. minced meat, hash.

†hachoir [a'ʃwa:r], n.m. chopping board; chopping knife; mincer.

†hachure [a'ʃy:r], n.f. (Engr.) hatching, hachure.

†hagard [a'ga:r], a. wild-looking, haggard.

†haie [ɛ], n.f. hedge, hedgerow; hurdle; row, line.

†haillon [a'jɔ̃], n.m. rag, tatter.

†haine [ɛ:n], n.f. hate, hatred; dislike; spite.

†haineusement [ɛnøz'mã], adv. hatefully, spitefully.

†haineux [ɛ'nø], a. (*fem.* -euse) hating, spiteful.

†haïr [a'i:r], v.t. irr. to hate, to detest, to loathe.

†haire [ɛ:r], n.f. hair shirt.

†haïssable [ai'sabl], a. hateful, odious.

Haïti [ai'ti], m. or f. Haiti.

†haïtien [ai'sjɛ̃], a. (*fem.* -enne) Haitian.— n.m. (Haïtien, *fem.* -enne) Haitian (*person*).

†halage [a'la:ʒ], n.m. towage, hauling.

†hale [a:l], n.m. tow-line, tow-rope.

†hâle [a:l], n.m. heat of the sun; sunburn.

†hâlé [a'le], a. sunburnt; tanned; swarthy.

haleine [a'lɛn], n.f. breath, wind.

†haler [a'le], v.t. (Naut.) to haul, to tow.

†hâler [a'le], v.t. to tan, to burn (*of the sun*). se hâler, v.r. to become sunburnt or tanned.

†haletant [al'tã], a. out of breath, panting.

†haleter [al'te], v.i. (*conjug. like* AMENER) to pant, to gasp for breath.

†hall [ɔl], n.m. large entrance hall (*of hotel, station*).

†halle [al], n.f. market; market hall, market-place.

†hallebarde [al'bard], n.f. halberd; *pleuvoir des hallebardes*, to rain cats and dogs.

†hallebardier [albar'dje], n.m. halberdier.

†hallier [a'lje], n.m. thicket, coppice.

hallucination [alysina'sjɔ̃], n.f. hallucination, delusion.

halluciné [alysi'ne], a. hallucinated; (*fig.*) deluded.—n.m. (*fem.* -ée) person suffering from delusions.

halluciner [alysi'ne], v.t. to hallucinate; (*fig.*) to delude.

halo [a'lo], n.m. halo; (Phot.) halation.

halot [a'lo], n.m. rabbit-burrow.

halte [alt], n.f. halt; stand, stop; halting-place.—int. halt! stop!

haltère [al'tɛ:r], n.m. dumb-bell.

†hamac [a'mak], n.m. hammock.

†hameau [a'mo], n.m. (*pl.* -eaux) hamlet.

hameçon [am'sɔ̃], n.m. hook, fish-hook; bait.

†hampe [ã:p], n.f. staff (*of a lance, flag etc.*); stem, flower stalk.

†hamster [ams'tɛ:r], n.m. hamster.

†hanche [ã:ʃ], n.f. hip; haunch (*of horse*).

†handicap [ãdi'kap], n.m. handicap.

†hangar [ã'ga:r], n.m. outhouse, shed, cart shed; hangar (*for airplanes*).

†hanneton [an'tɔ̃], n.m. May-bug, cockchafer; (*fig.*) thoughtless person.

†hanter [ã'te], v.t. to haunt; to frequent.

†hantise [ã'ti:z], n.f. obsession.

†happer [a'pe], v.t. to snap up, to snatch; to seize.

†happeur [a'pœ:r], n.m. paper-clip.

†haquenée [ak'ne], n.f. hack, quiet horse; (*fig.*) ungainly woman.

†haquet [a'kɛ], n.m. dray.

harangue [a'rã:g], n.f. harangue, speech; (*boring*) address.

haranguer [arã'ge], v.t., v.i. to harangue.

harangueur [arã'gœ:r], n.m. (*fem.* -euse) haranguer, orator, speechifier.

haras [a'rɑ], n.m. stud, breeding-stud.

harasser [ara'se], v.t. to harass, to tire out, to weary.

harceler [arsə'le], v.t. (*conjug. like* APPELER) to worry, to pester, to torment, to harass.

†harde [ard], n.f. herd (*of deer etc.*); leash (*for hounds*).

†hardes [ard], n.f. (*used only in pl.*) wearing apparel, attire; worn clothes.

†hardi [ar'di], a. bold, daring, fearless; rash; impudent.

†hardiesse [ar'djɛs], n.f. boldness, daring; rashness; assurance, impudence.

†hardiment [ardi'mã], adv. boldly, daringly; impudently.

†harem [a'rɛm], n.m. harem.

†hareng [a'rã], n.m. herring.

†harengère [arã'ʒɛ:r], n.f. fish-wife.

†harenguet [arã'ge], n.m. sprat.

†hargneux [ar'nø], a. (*fem.* -euse) cross, cross-grained, peevish, surly.

†haricot [ari'ko], n.m. kidney bean; *haricot de mouton*, Irish stew; *haricots d'Espagne*, scarlet runners; *haricots verts*, French beans.

†haridelle [ari'dɛl], n.f. jade, hack; (*fig.*) gawky woman.

†harle [arl], n.m. (Orn.) merganser.

harmonica [armɔni'ka], n.m. harmonica; mouth-organ.

harmonie [armɔ'ni], n.f. harmony; concord; (Mus.) harmonics.

harmonieusement [armɔnjøz'mã], adv. harmoniously.

174

harmonieux [armɔ'njø], *a.* (*fem.* **-euse**) harmonious; musical, melodious; in keeping; blending (*of colors*).

harmonique [armɔ'nik], *a.* harmonic.—*n.f.* harmonics.

harmoniser [armɔni'ze], *v.t.* and **s'harmoniser**, *v.r.* to harmonize.

harmonium [armɔ'njɔm], *n.m.* harmonium.

†**harnachement** [arnaʃ'mɑ̃], *n.m.* harness, trappings.

†**harnacher** [arna'ʃe], *v.t.* to harness; to rig out.

†**harnais** [ar'nɛ], *n.m.* harness; horse-trappings; armor; equipment, tackle.

†**haro** [a'ro], *n.m.* hue and cry.

†**harpagon** [arpa'gɔ̃], *n.m.* miser, skinflint.

†**harpe** [arp], *n.f.* harp.

†**harper** [ar'pe], *v.t.* to grasp, to clutch.

†**harpie** [ar'pi], *n.f.* harpy, vixen, shrew.

†**harpiste** [ar'pist], *n.* harpist.

†**harpon** [ar'pɔ̃], *n.m.* harpoon.

†**harponner** [arpɔ'ne], *v.t.* to harpoon.

†**hasard** [a'za:r], *n.m.* chance; hazard; risk, danger; *à tout hasard*, on the off chance; *au hasard*, at random; *par hasard*, by chance.

†**hasardé** [azar'de], *a.* hazarded, ventured; hazardous, bold.

†**hasarder** [azar'de], *v.t.* to hazard, to risk; to venture. **se hasarder**, *v.r.* to hazard, to venture, to take the risk.

†**hasardeusement** [azardøz'mɑ̃], *adv.* hazardously.

†**hasardeux** [azar'dø], *a.* (*fem.* **-euse**) venturesome, daring; hazardous, unsafe.

†**hâte** [ɑ:t], *n.f.* hurry, haste; *à la hâte*, in a hurry.

†**hâter** [ɑ'te], *v.t.* to hasten, to forward, to hurry, to urge on; to expedite; to force (*fruit*). **se hâter**, *v.r.* to make haste, to hurry.

†**hâtif** [ɑ'tif], *a.* (*fem.* **-tive**) forward; precocious, premature; (*Hort.*) early.

†**hâtivement** [ɑtiv'mɑ̃], *adv.* early, prematurely; hastily.

†**hauban** [o'bɑ̃], *n.m.* (*Naut.*) shroud, guy, stay.

†**hausse** [o:s], *n.f.* lift, block (*for raising anything*); (*Comm.*) rise, advance; (back) sight (*of a rifle*).

†**haussement** [os'mɑ̃], *n.m.* raising, lifting; *haussement d'épaules*, shrugging of the shoulders.

†**hausser** [o'se], *v.t.* to raise, to lift up; to increase; to shrug; (*Comm.*) to advance.— *v.i.* to rise; to get higher; to increase. **se hausser**, *v.r.* to be raised, to rise; to raise oneself; to clear up (*of the weather*); to increase.

†**haussier** [o'sje], *n.m.* (*St. Exch.*) bull.

†**haussière** [o'sjɛ:r], *n.f.* hawser.

†**haut** [o], *a.* high, tall, lofty; elevated; upper; principal; eminent; haughty; loud (*of sound*); *lire à haute voix*, to read aloud; *pousser les hauts cris*, to complain loudly.—*n.m.* height; top, summit; upper part; *d'en haut*, from above.—*n.f.* (*colloq.*) *la haute*, the wealthy, the upper crust.— *adv.* high; loud, aloud, loudly; haughtily; *ainsi qu'il a été dit plus haut*, as has already been said; *parlez plus haut*, speak louder.—*adv. phr.* **en haut**, upstairs.

†**hautain** [o'tɛ̃], *a.* haughty, proud.

†**hautainement** [otɛn'mɑ̃], *adv.* haughtily, superciliously, proudly.

†**hautbois** [o'bwa], *n.m.* hautboy, oboe; oboe player.

†**haut-de-forme** [od'fɔrm], *n.m.* (*pl.* **hauts-de-forme**) top hat.

†**hautement** [ot'mɑ̃], *adv.* boldly, resolutely, proudly; aloud.

†**hauteur** [o'tœ:r], *n.f.* height, elevation, altitude; depth; rising ground; haughtiness, arrogance; pitch (*of the voice etc.*); (*Naut.*) bearing; *être à la hauteur de quelqu'un*, to be a match for someone; *être à la hauteur d'une tâche*, to be equal to a task.

†**haut-fond** [o'fɔ̃], *n.m.* (*pl.* **hauts-fonds**) shoal, shallow.

|**haut-le-corps** [ol'kɔ:r] *n.m. inv.* spring, bound; start.

†**haut-le-pied** [ol'pje], *a. inv. cheval haut-le-pied*, spare horse; *locomotive haut-le-pied*, engine running light.

†**haut-parleur** [opar'lœ:r], *n.m.* (*pl.* **-parleurs**) loud-speaker; amplifier.

†**Havane** [a'van], **la**, *f.* Havana.

†**havane** [a'van], *a.* brown, tan.—*n.m.* Havana cigar.

†**hâve** [ɑ:v], *a.* pale, wan, emaciated.

†**havre** [ɑ:vr], *n.m.* haven, harbor, port.

†**havresac** [ɑvrə'sak], *n.m.* knapsack, pack.

†**Haye** [ɛ], **La**, *f.* The Hague.

†**hé!** [e], *int.* hoy! (*for calling, warning etc.*); why! well! I say! (*emphat.*).

†**heaume** [o:m], *n.m.* helmet.

hebdomadaire [ɛbdɔma'dɛ:r], *a.* weekly.— *n.m.* weekly newspaper.

hébergement [ebɛrʒə'mɑ̃], *n.m.* lodging.

héberger [ebɛr'ʒe], *v.t.* (*conjug. like* MANGER) to lodge.

hébété [ebe'te], *a.* dazed, stupid, bewildered.

hébéter [ebe'te], *v.t.* (*conjug. like* CÉDER) to make stupid, to besot.

hébraïque [ebra'ik], *a.* Hebrew, Hebraic.

hébreu [e'brø], *a.* (*fem.* **hébraïque**) Hebrew.— *n.m.* Hebrew (*language*); (**Hébreu**, *fem.* **Juive**, *pl.* **Hébreux**) Hebrew (*person*).

hécatombe [eka'tɔ̃b], *n.f.* hecatomb.

hectare [ɛk'ta:r], *n.m.* hectare (*2 acres, 1 rood, 35 perches or 2.4711 acres*).

hectogramme [ɛktɔ'gram], **hecto** [ɛk'to], *n.m.* hectogramme (*3.527 oz. avoirdupois*).

hectolitre [ɛktɔ'litr], *n.m.* hectolitre (*22.009668 imperial gallons*).

hectomètre [ɛktɔ'mɛtr], *n.m.* hectometre (*109.936 yds.*).

hégire [e'ʒi:r], *n.f.* Hegira (*Mohammedan era*).

†**hein!** [ɛ̃], *int.* (*before a sentence*) hey! what! (*after a sentence* = *n'est-ce pas*) isn't it etc.?

hélas! [e'lɑːs], *int.* alas!

Hélène [e'lɛn], *f.* Helen.

héler [e'le], *v.t.* (*conjug. like* CÉDER) to hail, to call (*a taxi, a boat etc.*).

hélice [e'lis], *n.f.* screw; propeller.

hélicoptère [elikɔp'tɛ:r], *n.m.* helicopter.

héliport [eli'pɔ:r], *n.m.* heliport, helicopter landing-ground.

hélium [e'ljɔm], *n.m.* helium.

helvétique [ɛlve'tik], *a.* Helvetic, Helvetian, Swiss.

hémisphère [emis'fɛ:r], *n.m.* hemisphere.

hémisphérique [emisfe'rik], *a.* hemispheric.
hémistiche [emis'tiʃ], *n.m.* hemistich.
hémoglobine [emoglɔ'bin], *n.f.* hemoglobin.
hémophylie [emofi'li], *n.f.* hemophilia.
hémorragie [emora'ʒi], *n.f.* hemorrhage.
hémorroïdes [emɔro'id], *n.f. pl.* hemorrhoids, piles.
†**henné** [ɛ'ne], *n.m.* (*Bot.*) henna.
†**hennir** [ɛ'niːr], *v.i.* to neigh, to whinny.
†**hennissement** [enis'mã], *n.m.* neighing.
Henri [ã'ri], *m.* Henry.
hépatique [epa'tik], *a.* hepatic.—*n.f.* (*Bot.*) liverwort.
hépatite [epa'tit], *n.f.* hepatitis (*inflammation of the liver*); (*Min.*) hepatite (*liver stone*).
heptagone [ɛpta'gɔn], *a.* heptagonal.—*n.m.* heptagon.
héraldique [ɛral'dik], *a.* heraldic.—*n.f.* heraldry.
†**héraut** [e'ro], *n.m.* herald.
herbacé [ɛrba'se], *a.* (*Bot.*) herbaceous.
herbage [ɛr'baːʒ], *n.m.* herbage, grass-land; pasture.
herbager [ɛrba'ʒe] *v.t.* (*conjug. like* MANGER) to graze (*cattle*).
herbe [ɛrb], *n.f.* herb, grass, wort; *blé en herbe,* grain in the blade; *brin d'herbe,* blade of grass; *fines herbes,* herbs for seasoning; *mauvaise herbe,* weed; (*fig.*) scamp.
herbette [ɛr'bɛt], *n.f.* (*Poet.*) short grass, green-sward.
herbeux [ɛr'bø], *a.* (*fem.* **-euse**) grassy, herbous.
herbicide [ɛrbi'sid], *a.* weed-killing.—*n.m.* weed-killer.
herbivore [ɛrbi'vɔːr], *a.* herbivorous.—*n.m.* herbivore.
herboriste [ɛrbɔ'rist], *n.* herbalist, dealer in medicinal herbs.
herbu [ɛr'by], *a.* grassy, covered with grass.
Hercule [ɛr'kyl], *m.* Hercules.
hercule [ɛr'kyl], *n.m.* man of herculean strength; strong-arm man.
herculéen [ɛrkyle'ɛ], *a.* (*fem.* **-éenne**) herculean.
†**hère** [ɛːr], *n.m.* **un pauvre hère,** a sorry fellow, a poor devil.
héréditaire [eredi'tɛːr], *a.* hereditary.
hérédité [eredi'te], *n.f.* hereditary transmission, inheritance *or* succession, hereditary right; heredity.
hérésie [ere'zi], *n.f.* heresy.
hérétique [ere'tik], *a.* heretical.—*n.* heretic.
†**hérissé** [eri'se], *a.* bristling, on end; rough, shaggy; (*Bot.*) hairy, prickly.
†**hérissement** [eris'mã], *n.m.* bristling, shagginess.
†**hérisser** [eri'se], *v.t.* to bristle, to erect. **se hérisser,** *v.r.* to stand on end; to bristle up; to be bristling with.
†**hérisson** [eri'sɔ̃], *n.m.* hedgehog; (*fig.*) cross-grained person; *hérisson de mer,* sea-urchin.
héritage [eri'taːʒ], *n.m.* heritage, inheritance, legacy.
hériter [eri'te], *v.t.* to inherit.—*v.i.* to inherit, to be heir (*de*); to succeed.
héritier [eri'tje], *n.m.* (*fem.* **-ière**) heir, heiress.
hermétique [ɛrme'tik], *a.* hermetic, air-tight, water-tight.

hermétiquement [ɛrmetik'mã], *adv.* hermetically.
hermine [ɛr'min], *n.f.* ermine.
hermitage [ɛrmi'taːʒ], [ERMITAGE].
†**herniaire** [ɛr'njɛːr], *a.* hernial; *bandage herniaire,* truss.
†**hernie** [ɛr'ni], *n.f.* hernia, rupture.
héroïne [erɔ'in], *n.f.* heroine; (*Chem.*) heroin.
héroïque [erɔ'ik], *a.* heroic.
héroïquement [erɔik'mã], *adv.* heroically.
héroïsme [erɔ'ism], *n.m.* heroism.
†**héron** [e'rɔ̃], *n.m.* heron.
†**héros** [e'ro], *n.m.* hero.
†**hersage** [ɛr'saːʒ], *n.m.* harrowing.
†**herse** [ɛrs], *n.f.* harrow; portcullis,**°herse;** (*pl.*) (*Theat.*) battens, lights (*above stage*).
†**hersé** [ɛr'se], *a.* harrowed; (*Her.*) represented with a herse.
†**herser** [ɛr'se], *v.t.* to harrow.
hésitant [ezi'tã], *a.* hesitating, wavering.
hésitation [ezito'sjɔ̃], *n.f.* hesitation.
hésiter [ezi'te], *v.i.* to hesitate, to falter, to pause, to waver.
†**hessois** [e'swa], *a.* Hessian.—*n.m.* (**Hessois,** *fem.* **-oise**) Hessian (*person*).
hétéroclite [eterɔ'klit], *a.* heteroclite, anomalous; irregular.
hétérodoxe [eterɔ'dɔks], *a.* heterodox.
hétérodyne [eterɔ'din], *a.* and *n.f.* (*Rad.*) heterodyne.
hétérogène [eterɔ'ʒɛ:n], *a.* heterogeneous; incongruous.
†**hêtre** [ɛ:tr], *n.m.* beech, beech tree.
heure [œ:r], *n.f.* hour; o'clock; time of day; moment; (*pl.*) primer (*prayer-book*); *heures d'affluence* or *de pointe,* rush hours, peak periods; (*nouvelles de la*) *dernière heure,* latest news; *quelle heure est-il?* what time is it? *tout à l'heure,* in a few minutes, just now; *de bonne heure,* early.
heureusement [œrøz'mã], *adv.* happily, luckily, fortunately; successfully.
heureux [œ'rø], *a.* (*fem.* **-euse**) happy, blissful; blessed, lucky; successful; pleasing; delighted.
†**heurt** [œ:r], *n.m.* blow; knock, shock, collision; bruise.
†**heurté** [œr'te], *a.* abrupt, harsh, jerky (*of style*).
†**heurtement** [œrtə'mã], *n.m.* clash, collision; hiatus.
†**heurter** [œr'te], *v.t.* to knock against, to strike against; to jostle; to shock, to offend; to jar with.—*v.i.* to strike, to knock, to hit. **se heurter,** *v.r.* to strike *or* hit oneself; to strike against each other; to jostle each other, to clash.
hiatus [ja'ty:s], *n.m.* hiatus; gap.
hibernal [iber'nal], *a.* (*m. pl.* **-aux**) hibernal.
hibernant [iber'nã], *a.* hibernating.
hibernation [iberna'sjɔ̃], *n.f.* hibernation.
hiberner [iber'ne], *v.i.* to hibernate.
†**hibou** [i'bu], *n.m.* (*pl.* **-oux**) owl; (*fig.*) moper.
†**hic** [ik], *n.m.* knot, difficulty, rub.
†**hideur** [i'dœ:r], *n.f.* hideousness.
†**hideusement** [idøz'mã], *adv.* hideously.
†**hideux** [i'dø], *a.* (*fem.* **-euse**) hideous, frightful, shocking.
hier [jɛ:r], *adv.* yesterday; *avant-hier,* the day before yesterday; *hier matin,* yesterday morning; *hier (au) soir,* last night.

†**hiérarchie** [jerar'ʃi], *n.f.* hierarchy.
†**hiérarchique** [jerar'ʃik], *a.* hierarchical.
hiératique [jera'tik], *a.* hieratic.
hiéroglyphe [jerɔ'glif], *n.m.* hieroglyph.
hiéroglyphique [jerɔgli'fik], *a.* hieroglyphical.
Hilaire [i'lɛːr], *m.* Hilary.
hilarant [ila'rɑ̃], *a.* screamingly funny, rollicking; *gaz hilarant*, laughing-gas.
hilare [i'laːr], *a.* hilarious.
hilarité [ilari'te], *n.f.* hilarity, mirth, laughter.
hindou [ɛ̃'du], *a.* Hindu; Indian (*of India*).—*n.m.* (**Hindou**, *fem.* **-oue**) Hindu; Indian (*of India*).
hindouisme [ɛ̃du'ism], *n.m.* Hinduism.
hindoustani [ɛ̃dusta'ni], *n.m.* Hindustani, Urdu (*language*).
hippique [i'pik], *a.* hippic; *concours hippique*, horse show.
hippodrome [ipɔ'drom], *n.m.* hippodrome, circus; race-course.
hippopotame [ipɔpɔ'tam], *n.m.* hippopotamus.
hirondelle [irɔ̃'dɛl], *n.f.* swallow.
hirsute [ir'syt], *a.* hirsute, hairy; shaggy, dishevelled; (*fig.*) boorish.
†**hisser** [i'se], *v.t.* to hoist, to lift, to run up, to raise. **se hisser**, *v.r.* to raise, hoist *or* lift oneself up.
histoire [is'twaːr], *n.f.* history; tale, story; idle story, untruth, falsehood; trifle; (*pl.*) fuss.
historien [istɔ'rjɛ̃], *n.m.* historian.
historier [istɔ'rje], *v.t.* to illustrate, to embellish, to adorn.
historiette [istɔ'rjɛt], *n.f.* little story, short tale.
historiographe [istɔrjɔ'graf], *n.* historiographer.
historique [istɔ'rik], *a.* historic(al).—*n.m.* historical account.
historiquement [istɔrik'mɑ̃], *adv.* historically.
histrion [istri'jɔ̃], *n.m.* histrion, actor; mountebank.
histrionique [istriɔ'nik], *a.* histrionic.
hitlérien [itle'rjɛ̃], *a.* (*fem.* **-enne**) Hitlerite.
hitlérisme [itle'rism], *n.m.* Hitlerism.
hiver [i'vɛːr], *n.m.* winter.
hivernage [ivɛr'naːʒ], *n.m.* winter season, winter-time; wintering place.
hivernal [ivɛr'nal], *a.* (*m. pl.* **-aux**) wintry.
hiverner [ivɛr'ne], *v.t.* (*Agric.*) to winter-fallow.—*v.i.* to winter.
†**hobereau** [ɔ'bro], *n.m.* (*pl.* **-eaux**) hobby (*bird*); country squire, squireen.
†**hochement** [ɔʃ'mɑ̃], *n.m.* shaking, tossing, wagging (*of the head*).
†**hochequeue** [ɔʃ'kø], *n.m.* (*Orn.*) wagtail.
†**hocher** [ɔ'ʃe], *v.t.* to shake, to toss; to wag (*the tail etc.*).
†**hochet** [ɔ'ʃɛ], *n.m.* rattle (*for children*); (*fig.*) toy, bauble, plaything.
†**hockey** [ɔ'kɛ], *n.m.* hockey; (*C*) hockey, hockey stick; *hockey sur glace*, ice hockey.
†**holà!** [ɔ'la], *int.* stop! hold on! hallo, there!—*n.m.* stop, end; *mettre le holà*, to put a stop to (*a quarrel*).
†**hollandais** [ɔlɑ̃'dɛ], *a.* Dutch.—*n.m.* Dutch (*language*). (**Hollandais**, *fem.* **-aise**) Dutchman, Dutchwoman.

†**Hollande** [ɔ'lɑ̃ːd], **la**, *f.* Holland, the Netherlands.
holocauste [ɔlɔ'koːst], *n.m.* holocaust, burnt offering; sacrifice.
†**homard** [ɔ'maːr], *n.m.* lobster.
homélie [ɔme'li], *n.f.* homily, familiar sermon.
homéopathe [ɔmeɔ'pat], *a.* homeopathic.—*n.* homœopath.
homéopathie [ɔmeɔpa'ti], *n.f.* homeopathy.
homéopathique [ɔmeɔpa'tik], *a.* homeopathic.
Homère [ɔ'mɛːr], *m.* Homer.
homérique [ɔme'rik], *a.* Homeric.
homicide [ɔmi'sid], *a.* murderous.—*n.m.* homicide, manslaughter.—*n.* murderer.
hommage [ɔ'maʒ], *n.m.* homage; respect; service; acknowledgment; token, gift; (*pl.*) respects.
homme [ɔm], *n.m.* man; (*colloq.*) husband, old man.
homme-grenouille [ɔmgrə'nuːj], *n.m.* (*pl.* **hommes-grenouilles**) frogman.
homme-sandwich [ɔmsɑ̃'dwitʃ], *n.m.* (*pl.* **hommes-sandwich(e)s**) sandwich man.
homogène [ɔmɔ'ʒɛːn], *a.* homogeneous.
homogénéité [ɔmɔʒenei'te], *n.f.* homogeneity.
homonyme [ɔmɔ'nim], *a.* homonymous.—*n.m.* homonym; namesake.
†**Honduras** [ɔ̃dy'ras], **le**, *m.* Honduras.
†**hondurien** [ɔ̃dy'rjɛ̃], *a.* (*fem.* **-enne**) Honduran.—*n.m.* (**Hondurien**, *fem.* **-enne**) Honduran (*person*).
†**hongre** [ɔ̃ːgr], *a.* gelded.—*n.m.* gelding.
†**hongrer** [ɔ̃'gre], *v.t.* to geld (*a horse*).
†**Hongrie** [ɔ̃'gri], **la**, *f.* Hungary.
†**hongrois** [ɔ̃'grwa], *a.* Hungarian.—*n.m.* Hungarian (*language*); (**Hongrois**, *fem.* **-oise**) Hungarian (*person*).
honnête [ɔ'nɛːt], *a.* honest, upright; modest (*of women*); respectable; decorous; proper; handsome; reasonable.—*n.m.* honesty, probity.
honnêtement [ɔnɛt'mɑ̃], *adv.* honestly, honorably; virtuously; becomingly; handsomely; suitably; reasonably.
honnêteté [ɔnɛt'te], *n.f.* honesty, integrity; modesty, chastity, virtue; propriety; respectability.
honneur [ɔ'nœːr], *n.m.* honor; virtue; integrity; repute; credit; distinction; respect; (*Cards*) honor.
†**honnir** [ɔ'niːr], *v.t.* to dishonor, to disgrace, to cover with shame.
honorabilité [ɔnɔrabili'te], *n.f.* honor, respectability.
honorable [ɔnɔ'rabl], *a.* honorable; respectable, creditable; suitable.
honorablement [ɔnɔrablə'mɑ̃], *adv.* honorably, respectably, creditably; nobly.
honoraire [ɔnɔ'rɛːr], *a.* honorary, titular.—*n.m.* (*pl.*) honorarium, fee.
honorer [ɔnɔ're], *v.t.* to honor; to do credit to, to be an honor to; *honorer une traite*, to meet a bill. **s'honorer**, *v.r.* to do oneself honor; to acquire honor; to deem it an honor; to pride oneself.
honorifique [ɔnɔri'fik], *a.* honorary, titular, gratuitous.

honte

†**honte** [ɔ̃:t], *n.f.* shame; disgrace, infamy; reproach; scandal; *avoir honte de*, to be ashamed of; *mauvaise honte* or *fausse honte*, self-consciousness, bashfulness.

†**honteusement** [ɔ̃tøz'mɑ̃], *adv.* shamefully, disgracefully; infamously.

†**honteux** [ɔ̃'tø], *a.* (*fem.* **-euse**) ashamed; bashful, shy; shameful, disgraceful.

hôpital [ɔpi'tal], *n.m.* (*pl.* **-aux**) hospital.

†**hoquet** [ɔ'kɛ], *n.m.* hiccup.

hoqueter [ɔk'te], *v.i.* (*conjug. like* APPELER) to hiccup.

horaire [ɔ'rɛːr], *a.* hourly; horary, horal.— *n.m.* time-table, schedule.

†**horde** [ɔrd], *n.f.* horde; pack; rabble.

horizon [ɔri'zɔ̃], *n.m.* horizon, sky-line.

horizontal [ɔrizɔ̃'tal], *a.* (*m. pl.* **-aux**) horizontal.

horizontalement [ɔrizɔ̃tal'mɑ̃], *adv.* horizontally.

horloge [ɔr'lɔːʒ], *n.f.* clock; time-keeper.

horloger [ɔrlɔ'ʒe], *a.* (*fem.* **-ère**) pertaining to clock-making.—*n.m.* (*fem.* **-ère**) clockmaker, watch-maker.

horlogerie [ɔrlɔ'ʒri], *n.f.* watch- and clock-making; clocks and watches.

hormis [ɔr'mi], *prep.* except, excepting, but.

hormone [ɔr'mɔn], *n.f.* hormone.

horoscope [ɔrɔs'kɔp], *n.m.* horoscope.

horreur [ɔ'rœːr], *n.f.* horror, dread; detestation; enormity.

horrible [ɔ'ribl], *a.* horrible, dreadful; hideous, frightful, shocking.

horriblement [ɔribla'mɑ̃], *adv.* horribly, awfully.

horrifier [ɔri'fje], *v.t.* to horrify.

horrifique [ɔri'fik], *a.* hair-raising.

horripilant [ɔripi'lɑ̃], *a.* exasperating.

horripiler [ɔripi'le], *v.t.* to horripilate; to exasperate.

†**hors** [ɔːr], *prep.* out of, outside of; beyond, past; but, except, save; *hors d'affaire*, out of danger; *hors de combat*, disabled; *hors de doute*, beyond doubt; *hors d'ici!* away with you! out of my sight! *hors de prix*, exorbitant; *hors de service*, unserviceable, out of order; *hors la loi*, outlawed.

†**hors-bord** [ɔr'bɔr], *n.m. inv.* outboard; speed-boat.

†**hors-caste** [ɔr'kast], *a.* and *n. inv.* outcaste, untouchable.

†**hors-d'œuvre** [ɔr'dœːvr], *n.m. inv.* (*Arch.*) outwork, outbuilding; (*Lit.*) digression, episode; (*Cook.*) dish served at the beginning of a meal.

†**hors-jeu** [ɔr'ʒø], *n.m. inv.* (*Ftb.*) off-side.

†**hors-la-loi** [ɔrla'lwa], *n.m. inv.* outlaw.

hortensia [ɔrtɑ̃'sja], *n.m.* hydrangea.

horticulteur [ɔrtikyl'tœːr], *n.m.* horticulturist.

horticultural [ɔrtikylty'ral], *a.* (*m. pl.* **-aux**) horticultural.

horticulture [ɔrtikyl'tyr], *n.f.* horticulture.

hospice [ɔs'pis], *n.m.* refuge; asylum; almshouse.

hospitalier [ɔspita'lje], *a.* (*fem.* **-ière**) hospitable.—*n.m.* (*fem.* **-ière**) hospitaller.

hospitalièrement [ɔspitaljɛr'mɑ̃], *adv.* hospitably.

hospitalité [ɔspitali'te], *n.f.* hospitality.

hostellerie [ɔstɛl'ri], *n.f.* inn.

hostie [ɔs'ti], *n.f.* (*Jewish Ant.*) offering, victim, sacrifice; (*R.-C. Ch.*) host.

hostile [ɔs'til], *a.* hostile, adverse.

hostilement [ɔstil'mɑ̃], *adv.* hostilely, adversely.

hostilité [ɔstili'te], *n.f.* hostility, enmity.

hôte [oːt], *n.m.* (*fem.* **-esse**) host, hostess; landlord, innkeeper; guest; lodger; occupier, inmate.

hôtel [o'tɛl], *n.m.* town mansion, large house; hotel, inn; *hôtel de ville*, town hall; *hôtel des ventes*, auction mart; *hôtel meublé*, furnished lodgings, lodging-house.

hôtelier [otə'lje], *n.m.* (*fem.* **-ière**) innkeeper, host, hostess.

hôtellerie [otɛl'ri], *n.f.* inn, hotel; hotel trade.

hôtesse [o'tɛs], (**HÔTE**).

†**hotte** [ɔt], *n.f.* basket (*carried on the back*); dosser, hod.

†**hottée** [ɔ'te], *n.f.* basketful.

†**hottentot** [ɔtɑ̃'to], *a.* Hottentot.—*n.m.* (Hottentot, *fem.* **-e**) Hottentot (*person*).

†**houage** [wa:ʒ], *n.m.* hoeing.

houblon [u'blɔ̃], *n.m.* (*Bot.*) hop.

houblonnière [ublɔ'njɛːr], *n.f.* hop field.

houe [u], *n.f.* hoe.

houer [u'e], *v.t.* to hoe.

houille [u:j], *n.f.* coal.

houiller [u'je], *a.* (*fem.* **-ère**) coal-bearing. —*n.f.* (**-ère**) coal mine, colliery.

†**houilleur** [u'jœːr], *n.m.* collier, coal miner.

†**houilleux** [u'jø], *a.* (*fem.* **-euse**) containing coal.

†**houle** [ul], *n.f.* swell, surge.

†**houlette** [u'lɛt], *n.f.* (shepherd's) crook; crosier.

†**houleux** [u'lø], *a.* (*fem.* **-euse**) swelling, rough (*of sea*).

†**houppe** [up], *n.f.* tuft; top-knot; tassel.

†**houppé** [u'pe], *a.* tufted, crested.

†**houppelande** [u'plɑ̃:d], *n.f.* overcoat, cloak.

†**houpper** [u'pe], *v.t.* to tuft; to comb (*wool*).

†**houppette** [u'pɛt], *n.f.* powder puff.

†**hourdage** [ur'da:ʒ], †**hourdis** [ur'di], *n.m.* rough-walling; pugging.

†**hourder** [ur'de], *v.t.* to rough-wall; to pug.

†**hourdis** [HOURDAGE].

†**hourra** [u'ra], *n.m.* hurrah.

†**houspiller** [uspi'je], *v.t.* to manhandle, to rough-house; to abuse.

†**housse** [us], *n.f.* housing, horse-cloth; dust-sheet, loose cover.

†**housser** [u'se], *v.t.* to cover up.

†**houssine** [u'sin], *n.f.* switch; riding-whip.

†**houssiner** [usi'ne], *v.t.* to switch; to beat.

†**houx** [u], *n.m.* holly, holly tree.

†**hoyau** [wa'jo], *n.m.* (*pl.* **-aux**) mattock, grubbing-hoe.

†**huard** [ɥa:r], *n.m.* osprey; sea-eagle.

†**hublot** [y'blo], *n.m.* (*Naut.*) side-light, port-hole.

†**huche** [yʃ], *n.f.* kneading trough; bread pan.

†**hue!** [y], *int.* gee! get up!

†**huée** [ɥe], *n.f.* whoop, shouting; hooting, booing.

†**huer** [ɥe], *v.t.* to shout after; to hoot at, to boo.—*v.i.* to boo.

†**huguenot** [yg'no], a. Huguenot.—n.m. (**Huguenot**, fem. -e) Huguenot (*person*).
huilage [ɥi'la:ʒ], n.m. oiling.
huile [ɥil], n.f. oil.
huiler [ɥi'le], v.t. to oil; to anoint with oil; to lubricate.—v.i. (*Bot.*) to exude oil.
huilerie [ɥil'ri], n.f. oil works.
huileux [ɥi'lø], a. (*fem.* -euse) oily, greasy.
huilier [ɥi'lje], n.m. cruet-stand; oil merchant.
†**huis** [ɥi], n.m. door; **à huis clos**, behind closed doors, in camera.
huisserie [ɥis'ri], n.f. door frame.
huissier [ɥi'sje], n.m. usher; gentleman-usher; door-keeper; sheriff's officer, bailiff.
†**huit** [ɥit], a. and n.m. eight; eighth.
†**huitaine** [ɥi'tɛn], n.f. eight days, week.
†**huitième** [ɥi'tjɛm], a. eighth.—n.m. eighth, eighth part.
†**huitièmement** [ɥitjɛm'mã], adv. eighthly.
huître [ɥitr], n.f. oyster; (*fig.*) blockhead, dunce.
huîtrier [ɥit'rje], n.m. (*Orn.*) oyster-catcher.
huîtrière [ɥitri'ɛ:r], n.f. oyster bed.
hululer [ULULER].
humain [y'mɛ̃], a. human; humane, benevolent.—n.m. humanity, mankind.
humainement [ymɛn'mã], adv. humanly, humanely.
humaniser [ymani'ze], v.t. to humanize, to civilize. **s'humaniser**, v.r. to become humanized.
humanisme [yma'nism], n.m. humanism.
humaniste [yma'nist], a. and n. humanist; classical scholar.
humanitaire [ymani'tɛ:r], a. and n. humanitarian.
humanité [ymani'te], n.f. humanity; human nature; mankind.
humble [œ̃:bl], a. humble, meek, modest.
humblement [œ̃blə'mã], adv. humbly, meekly.
humectant [ymɛk'tã], a. refreshing, moistening.—n.m. humectant.
humectation [ymɛkta'sjɔ̃], n.f. moistening.
humecter [ymɛk'te], v.t. to damp, to moisten, to refresh. **s'humecter**, v.r. to be moistened; to refresh oneself.
†**humer** [y'me], v.t. to inhale.
humeur [y'mœ:r], n.f. humor; temperament, disposition; mood, fancy; ill-humor.
humide [y'mid], a. damp, wet, moist, humid.
humidité [ymidi'te], n.f. humidity, moisture, dampness.
humiliant [ymi'ljã], a. humiliating, degrading.
humiliation [ymilja'sjɔ̃], n.f. humiliation, abasement.
humilier [ymi'lje], v.t. to humble, to humiliate. **s'humilier**, v.r. to humble or abase oneself.
humilité [ymili'te], n.f. humility, meekness, lowliness.
humoriste [ymɔ'rist], a. humorous.—n. humorist.
humoristique [ymɔris'tik] a. humorous (*writer etc.*).
humour [y'mur], n.m. humor.
humus [y'mys], n.m. humus, mold.
†**hune** [yn], n.f. (*Naut.*) top.
†**hunier** [y'nje], n.m. topsail.
†**huppe** [yp], n.f. hoopoe; tuft, crest.

†**huppé** [y'pe], a. tufted, crested (*of birds*); (*colloq.*) well off, smartly dressed.
†**hurlement** [yrlə'mã], n.m. howling; howl, roar, yell.
†**hurler** [yr'le], v.i. to howl, to yell; to roar; **hurler avec les loups**, to do as others do.
†**hurleur** [yr'lœ:r], a. (*fem.* -euse) howling.—n.m. (*fem.* -euse) howler.
hurluberlu [yrlyber'ly], n. hare-brained person, harum-scarum.
†**hussard** [y'sa:r], n.m. hussar.
†**hutte** [yt], n.f. hut, cabin, shanty.
hyacinthe [ja'sɛ̃:t], n.f. jacinth; hyacinth.
hybride [i'brid], a. and n.m. hybrid, mongrel.
hydrangée [idrã'ʒe], n.f. (*Bot.*) hydrangea.
hydrater [idra'te], v.t. to hydrate.
hydraulique [idro'lik], a. hydraulic.—n.f. hydraulics.
hydravion [idra'vjɔ̃], n.m. flying boat, seaplane.
hydre [idr], n.f. hydra.
hydro-électrique [idroelɛk'trik], a. hydroelectric.
hydrogène [idro'ʒɛ:n], n.m. hydrogen.
hydrophobe [idro'fɔb], a. and n. hydrophobic (person).
hydrophobie [idrofɔ'bi], n.f. hydrophobia, rabies.
hydropique [idro'pik], a. and n. dropsical (person).
hydropisie [idropi'zi], n.f. dropsy.
hydroplane [idro'plan], n.m. hydroplane.
hydroscope [idros'kɔp], n.m. water diviner.
hyène [je:n], n.f. hyena.
hygiène [i'ʒjɛ:n], n.f. hygiene.
hygiénique [iʒje'nik], a. hygienic; sanitary.
hymen [i'mɛn], **hyménée** [ime'ne], n.m. hymen, marriage, wedlock.
hymnaire [im'nɛ:r], n.m. hymn book, hymnal.
hymne [imn], n.m. (*patriotic*) song, anthem.—n.f. hymn.
hyperbole [iper'bɔl], n.f. hyperbole, exaggeration; (*Math.*) hyperbola.
hyperbolique [iperbɔ'lik], a. hyperbolic.
hypermétrope [iperme'trɔp], a. long-sighted.
hypersensible [ipersã'sibl], a. over-sensitive.
hypertension [ipertã'sjɔ̃], n.f. high blood pressure.
hypnose [ip'no:z], n.f. hypnosis.
hypnotique [ipnɔ'tik], a. and n.m. hypnotic.
hypnotiser [ipnɔti'ze], v.t. to hypnotize; to fascinate.
hypnotiseur [ipnɔti'zœ:r], n.m. (*fem.* -euse) hypnotist.
hypnotisme [ipnɔ'tism], n.m. hypnotism.
hypocondriaque [ipokɔ̃'driak], a. and n. hypochondriac.
hypocondrie [ipokɔ̃'dri], n.f. hypochondria.
hypocrisie [ipɔkri'zi], n.f. hypocrisy.
hypocrite [ipɔ'krit], a. hypocritical.—n. hypocrite.
hypodermique [ipɔder'mik], a. hypodermic, under the skin.
hypotension [ipotã'sjɔ̃], n.f. low blood pressure.
hypothécaire [ipote'kɛ:r], a. on mortgage.
hypothèque [ipo'tɛk], n.f. mortgage.
hypothéquer [ipote'ke], v.t. (*conjug. like* CÉDER) to mortgage.
hypothèse [ipo'tɛ:z], n.f. hypothesis, supposition.

179

hypothétique [ipote′tik], a. hypothetical.
hystérie [iste′ri], n.f. hysteria.
hystérique [iste′rik], a. hysteric, hysterical.

I

I, i [i], n.m. the ninth letter of the alphabet.
iceberg [is′bɛrg], n.m. iceberg.
ici [i′si], adv. here, in this place; hither; now, this time.
iconoclaste [ikono′klast], a. iconoclastic.— n. iconoclast.
iconolâtre [ikono′lɑːtr], n.m. image-worshipper.
iconolâtrie [ikonola′tri], n.f. image-worship.
idéal [ide′al], a. (m. pl. -aux) ideal; unreal, imaginary.—n.m. (pl. -als or -aux) ideal.
idéalement [ideal′mɑ̃], adv. ideally.
idéaliser [ideali′ze], v.t. to idealize.
idéalisme [idea′lism], n.m. idealism.
idéaliste [idea′list], a. idealistic.—n. idealist.
idée [i′de], n.f. idea; notion; conception; opinion; plan; fancy; sketch, suggestion.
idem [i′dɛm], adv. idem, ditto.
identification [idɑ̃tifika′sjɔ̃], n.f. identification.
identifier [idɑ̃ti′fje], v.t. to identify. **s'identifier**, v.r. to identify oneself.
identique [idɑ̃′tik], a. identical, the same.
identiquement [idɑ̃tik′mɑ̃], adv. identically.
identité [idɑ̃ti′te], n.f. identity.
idéologie [ideolo′ʒi], n.f. ideology.
idéologique [ideolo′ʒik], a. ideological.
idéologue [ideo′log], n.m. ideologist.
ides [id], n.f. pl. Ides (15 March etc.).
idiomatique [idjoma′tik], a. idiomatic.
idiome [i′djoːm], n.m. idiom, dialect.
idiosyncrasie [idjosɛ̃kra′zi], n.f. idiosyncrasy.
idiot [i′djo], a. idiotic, absurd.—n.m. (fem. -e) idiot, imbecile, fool.
idiotie [idjo′si], n.f. idiocy, imbecility.
idiotisme [idjo′tism], n.m. (Gram.) idiom; (Path.) idiocy.
idolâtre [ido′lɑːtr], a. idolatrous.—n. idolater.
idolâtrer [idola′tre], v.t. to idolize, to dote upon.
idolâtrie [idola′tri], n.f. idolatry.
idole [i′dɔl], n.f. idol.
idylle [i′dil], n.f. idyll.
idyllique [idi′lik], a. idyllic.
if [if], n.m. yew, yew tree.
igloo or **iglou** [i′glu], n.m. igloo.
ignare [i′naːr], a. illiterate, ignorant.—n. dunce, ignoramus.
igné [ig′ne], a. igneous.
ignifuge [igni′fyːʒ], a. fire-resisting, fire-proof; **grenade ignifuge**, fire extinguisher.
ignifuger [ignify′ʒe], v.t. (conjug. like MANGER) to fireproof.
ignition [igni′sjɔ̃], n.f. ignition.
ignoble [i′nɔbl], a. ignoble; vile, base; beastly, filthy.
ignoblement [inɔblə′mɑ̃], adv. ignobly, vilely, basely.

ignominie [inɔmi′ni], n.f. ignominy, shame, dishonor.
ignominieusement [inɔminjøz′mɑ̃], adv. ignominiously.
ignominieux [inɔmi′njø], a. (fem. -euse) ignominious.
ignorance [ino′rɑ̃ːs], n.f. ignorance; error, mistake, blunder.
ignorant [ino′rɑ̃], a. ignorant, illiterate, unlearned.—n.m. (fem. -e) ignoramus.
ignorer [ino′re], v.t. to be ignorant of, not to know, not to be aware of. **s'ignorer**, v.r. not to know oneself; to be ignorant of one's own capabilities.
iguane [i′gwan], n.m. iguana.
il [il], pron. m. (pl. **ils**) he; it; there; (pl.) they.
île [il], n.f. island, isle.
illégal [ille′gal], a. (m. pl. -aux) illegal, unlawful.
illégalement [illegal′mɑ̃], adv. illegally.
illégalité [illegali′te], n.f. illegality.
illégitime [illeʒi′tim], a. illegitimate; unlawful, unjust.
illégitimement [illeʒitim′mɑ̃], adv. illegitimately, unlawfully.
illégitimité [illeʒitimi′te], n.f. illegitimacy; unlawfulness; spuriousness.
illettré [ille′tre], a. and n.m. (fem. -ée) illiterate, unlettered (person).
illicite [illi′sit], a. illicit, unlawful.
illicitement [illisit′mɑ̃], adv. illicitly, unlawfully.
illimitable [illimi′tabl], a. illimitable.
illimité [illimi′te], a. unlimited, unbounded, boundless.
illisibilité [illizibili′te], n.f. illegibility.
illisible [illi′zibl], a. illegible.
illisiblement [illizibləˈmɑ̃], adv. illegibly.
illogique [illo′ʒik], a. illogical.
illogiquement [illoʒik′mɑ̃], adv. illogically.
illuminant [illymi′nɑ̃], a. illuminating.— n.m. illuminant.
illuminateur [illymina′tœːr], n.m. illuminator, enlightener.
illumination [illymina′sjɔ̃], n.f. illumination.
illuminé [illymi′ne], a. illuminated, enlightened.—n.m. (fem. -ée) visionary, fanatic.
illuminer [illymi′ne], v.t. to illuminate, to illumine, to light up; to enlighten (the mind etc.). **s'illuminer**, v.r. to light or brighten up.
illusion [illy′zjɔ̃], n.f. illusion, self-deception, delusion; fallacy, chimera.
illusionner [illyzjo′ne], v.t. to delude, to deceive.
illusionniste [illyzjo′nist], n.m. conjurer.
illusoire [illy′zwaːr], a. illusive, illusory, delusive.
illusoirement [illyzwar′mɑ̃], adv. illusively.
illustration [illystra′sjɔ̃], n.f. illustriousness, renown; explanation; illustration.
illustre [il′lystr], a. illustrious, famous.
illustrer [illys′tre], v.t. to do honor to; to illustrate, to make clear. **s'illustrer**, v.r. to win fame.
illustrissime [illystri′sim], a. most illustrious.
îlot [i′lo], n.m. islet (in sea); holm (in river); block (of houses).
ilote [i′lɔt], n.m. helot.
ils [il], pl. pron. [IL].
image [i′maːʒ], n.f. image; likeness; picture; statue.

imaginable [imaʒi'nabl], *a.* imaginable.
imaginaire [imaʒi'nɛːr], *a.* imaginary, visionary, unreal, fantastic.
imaginatif [imaʒina'tif], *a.* (*fem.* **-tive**) imaginative.
imagination [imaʒina'sjɔ̃], *n.f.* imagination; conception, thought; fancy.
imaginer [imaʒi'ne], *v.t.* to imagine, to conceive; to fancy, to suppose; to devise. **s'imaginer**, *v.r.* to imagine oneself; to imagine, to fancy, to surmise.
imbécile [ɛ̃be'sil], *a.* imbecile; foolish, idiotic.—*n.* imbecile, idiot; fool.
imbécilement [ɛ̃besil'mã], *adv.* foolishly.
imbécillité [ɛ̃besili'te], *n.f.* imbecility, idiocy; stupidity.
imberbe [ɛ̃'bɛrb], *a.* beardless; (*fig.*) green.
imbiber [ɛ̃bi'be], *v.t.* to imbibe; to imbue; to steep. **s'imbiber**, *v.r.* to imbibe, to drink in.
imbroglio [ɛ̃brɔ'ljo], *n.m.* imbroglio, intricacy.
imbu [ɛ̃'by], *a.* imbued, saturated.
imbuvable [ɛ̃by'vabl], *a.* undrinkable.
imitable [imi'tabl], *a.* imitable.
imitateur [imita'tœːr], *a.* (*fem.* **-trice**) imitative.—*n.m.* (*fem.* **-trice**) imitator.
imitatif [imita'tif], *a.* (*fem.* **-tive**) imitative.
imitation [imita'sjɔ̃], *n.f.* imitation.
imiter [imi'te], *v.t.* to imitate, to copy; to mimic; to resemble.
immaculé [immaky'le], *a.* immaculate, spotless.
immanent [imma'nã], *a.* immanent.
immangeable [ɛ̃mã'ʒabl, imã'ʒabl], *a.* uneatable.
immanquable [ɛ̃mã'kabl], *a.* infallible, certain, sure.
immanquablement [ɛ̃mãkablə'mã], *adv.* infallibly, certainly, without fail.
immatériel [immate'rjɛl], *a.* (*fem.* **-elle**) immaterial, incorporeal.
immatriculation [immatrikyla'sjɔ̃], *n.f.* matriculation; registering; enrolment; (*Motor.*) **plaque d'immatriculation**, license plate.
immatriculé [immatriky'le], *a.* registered; matriculated.
immatriculer [immatriky'le], *v.t.* to matriculate; to register.
immaturité [immatyri'te], *n.f.* unripeness, immaturity.
immédiat [imme'dja], *a.* immediate.
immédiatement [immedjat'mã] *adv.* immediately.
immémorial [immemɔ'rjal], *a.* (*m. pl.* **-aux** immemorial.
immense [im'mãːs], *a.* immense, immeasurable; boundless, huge.
immensément [immãse'mã], *adv.* immensely.
immensité [immãsi'te], *n.f.* immensity.
immerger [immɛr'ʒe], *v.t.* (*conjug. like* MANGER) to immerse, to plunge.
immersion [immɛr'sjɔ̃], *n.f.* immersion; submergence; committal to the deep.
immesurable [immazy'rabl], *a.* unmeasurable, immeasurable.
immeuble [im'mœbl], *a.* fixed, real (*of estate*).—*n.m.* real estate; property; premises.

immigrant [immi'grã], *a.* and *n.m.* (*fem.* **-e**) immigrant.
immigration [immigra'sjɔ̃], *n.f.* immigration.
immigrer [immi'gre], *v.i.* to immigrate.
imminence [immi'nãːs], *n.f.* imminence.
imminent [immi'nã], *a.* imminent, impending.
immiscer (s') [simmi'se], *v.r.* (*conjug. like* COMMENCER) to interfere.
immobile [immɔ'bil], *a.* motionless, still; (*fig.*) firm, immovable, unshaken.
immobilier [immɔbi'lje], *a.* (*fem.* **-lère**) real, landed (*of estate*); **agent immobilier**, real estate agent; **société immobilière**, building society.
immobilisation [immɔbiliza'sjɔ̃], *n.f.* immobilization; (*Law*) conversion of movable property into real estate.
immobiliser [immɔbili'ze], *v.t.* to immobilize; to convert into real estate, to tie up (*capital*).
immobilité [immɔbili'te], *n.f.* immobility, immovability.
immodération [immɔdera'sjɔ̃], *n.f.* immoderation.
immodéré [immɔde're], *a.* immoderate, excessive, violent.
immodérément [immɔdere'mã], *adv.* immoderately, intemperately; excessively.
immodeste [immɔ'dɛst], *a.* immodest, indecent.
immodestement [immɔdɛste'mã], *adv.* immodestly.
immodestie [immɔdɛs'ti], *n.f.* immodesty.
immolation [immɔla'sjɔ̃], *n.f.* immolation; (*fig.*) sacrifice.
immoler [immɔ'le], *v.t.* to immolate, to sacrifice; to slay. **s'immoler**, *v.r.* to immolate *or* sacrifice oneself.
immonde [im'mɔ̃ːd], *a.* unclean, impure.
immondice [immɔ̃'dis], *n.f.* (*usu. in pl.*) filth, dirt; rubbish.
immoral [immɔ'ral], *a.* (*m. pl.* **-aux**) immoral.
immoralité [immɔrali'te], *n.f.* immorality.
immortaliser [immɔrtali'ze], *v.t.* to immortalize. **s'immortaliser**, *v.r.* to immortalize oneself.
immortalité [immɔrtali'te], *n.f.* immortality.
immortel [immɔr'tel], *a.* (*fem.* **-elle**) immortal, everlasting.
immuable [im'myabl], *a.* immutable, unalterable, unchangeable.
immuablement [immyablə'mã], *adv.* immutably, unalterably, unchangeably.
immunisation [immyniza'sjɔ̃], *n.f.* (*Med.*) immunization.
immuniser [immyni'ze], *v.t.* to immunize.
immunité [immyni'te], *n.f.* immunity; privilege; exemption.
immutabilité [immytabili'te], *n.f.* immutability, unchangeableness, fixity.
impact [ɛ̃'pakt], *n.m.* impact; hit.
impaction [ɛ̃pak'sjɔ̃], *n.f.* (*Surg.*) impaction.
impair [ɛ̃'pɛːr], *a.* odd, uneven.—*n.m.* blunder, bloomer.
impalpabilité [ɛ̃palpabili'te], *n.f.* impalpability.
impalpable [ɛ̃pal'pabl], *a.* impalpable.
impardonnable [ɛ̃pardɔ'nabl], *a.* unpardonable, unforgivable.

imparfait [ɛpar'fɛ], *a.* imperfect, incomplete, defective.—*n.m.* (*Gram.*) imperfect (tense).

imparfaitement [ɛparfɛt'mã], *adv.* imperfectly.

imparité [ɛpari'te], *n.f.* imparity, inequality; oddness.

impartageable [ɛparta'ʒabl], *a.* indivisible.

impartial [ɛpar'sjal], *a.* (*m. pl.* **-aux**) impartial.

impartialement [ɛparsjal'mã], *adv.* impartially, even-handedly.

impartialité [ɛparsjali'te], *n.f.* impartiality.

impasse [ɛ'pɑːs], *n.f.* blind alley, cul-de-sac; deadlock, dilemma.

impassibilité [ɛpɑsibili'te], *n.f.* impassibility, insensibility.

impassible [ɛpɑ'sibl], *a.* impassive, unmoved.

impassiblement [ɛpɑsiblə'mã], *adv.* impassively, impassibly.

impatiemment [ɛpasja'mã], *adv.* impatiently, eagerly.

impatience [ɛpa'sjɑːs], *n.f.* impatience; restlessness; eagerness, longing.

impatient [ɛpa'sjã], *a.* impatient; anxious, restless, eager.

impatientant [ɛpasjã'tã], *a.* provoking, vexing, tiresome.

impatienter [ɛpasjã'te], *v.t.* to make impatient, to put out of patience; to provoke. **s'impatienter**, *v.r.* to lose one's patience; to fret, to worry.

impayable [ɛpe'jabl], *a.* invaluable, priceless; inimitable, extraordinarily funny.

impayé [ɛpe'je], *a.* unpaid.

impeccabilité [ɛpekabili'te], *n.f.* impeccability.

impeccable [ɛpe'kabl], *a.* impeccable, faultless.

impécunieux [ɛpeky'njø], *a.* (*fem.* **-euse**) impecunious.

impénétrabilité [ɛpenetrabili'te], *n.f.* impenetrability, imperviousness.

impénétrable [ɛpene'trabl], *a.* impenetrable, impervious; inscrutable.

impénitence [ɛpeni'tɑːs], *n.f.* impenitence, obduracy.

impénitent [ɛpeni'tã], *a.* and *n.m.* (*fem.* **-e**) impenitent, obdurate (person).

impératif [ɛpera'tif], *a.* (*fem.* **-tive**) imperative, peremptory.—*n.m.* (*Gram.*) imperative.

impérativement [ɛperativ'mã], *adv.* imperatively.

impératrice [ɛpera'tris], *n.f.* empress.

imperceptible [ɛpersɛp'tibl], *a.* imperceptible, unperceivable.

imperceptiblement [ɛpersɛptiblə'mã], *adv.* imperceptibly.

imperfectible [ɛpɛrfɛk'tibl], *a.* imperfectible.

imperfection [ɛpɛrfɛk'sjɔ̃], *n.f.* imperfection, defect, flaw.

impérial [ɛpe'rjal], *a.* (*m. pl.* **-aux**) imperial.

impériale [ɛpe'rjal], *n.f.* top, outside (*of a coach*); imperial (*small beard under the lip*).

impérieusement [ɛperjøz'mã], *adv.* imperiously.

impérieux [ɛpe'rjø], *a.* (*fem.* **-euse**) imperious, supercilious, haughty, lordly.

impérissable [ɛperi'sabl], *a.* imperishable.

impérissablement [ɛperisablə'mã], *adv.* imperishably.

impéritie [ɛperi'si], *n.f.* incapacity, incompetence.

imperméabilité [ɛpermeabili'te], *n.f.* impermeability.

imperméable [ɛperme'abl], *a.* impermeable, impervious.—*n.m.* raincoat, mackintosh.

impersonnalité [ɛpersɔnali'te], *n.f.* impersonality.

impersonnel [ɛpersɔ'nɛl], *a.* (*fem.* **-elle**) impersonal.—*n.m.* (*Gram.*) impersonal verb.

impersonnellement [ɛpersɔnɛl'mã], *adv.* impersonally.

impertinemment [ɛpertina mã], *adv.* impertinently.

impertinence [ɛperti'nɑːs], *n.f.* impertinence, insolence; silliness.

impertinent [ɛperti'nã], *a.* impertinent, insolent, pert.—*n.m.* (*fem.* **-e**) impertinent, saucy person.

imperturbabilité [ɛpertyrbabili'te], *n.f.* imperturbability.

imperturbable [ɛpertyr'babl], *a.* imperturbable.

imperturbablement [ɛpertyrbablə'mã], *adv.* imperturbably.

impétigo [ɛpeti'go], *n.m.* (*Med.*) impetigo.

impétueusement [ɛpetɥøz'mã], *adv.* impetuously.

impétueux [ɛpe'tɥø], *a.* (*fem.* **-euse**) impetuous, vehement, violent.

impétuosité [ɛpetɥozi'te], *n.f.* impetuosity, vehemence; impetus.

impie [ɛ'pi], *a.* impious, godless; irreligious.—*n.* impious, ungodly *or* irreligious person.

impiété [ɛpje'te], *n.f.* impiety, godlessness.

impitoyable [ɛpitwa'jabl], *a.* pitiless, merciless, ruthless; unrelenting.

impitoyablement [ɛpitwajablə'mã], *adv.* pitilessly.

implacabilité [ɛplakabili'te], *n.f.* implacability.

implacable [ɛpla'kabl], *a.* implacable.

implacablement [ɛplakablə'mã], *adv.* implacably.

implantation [ɛplɑ̃ta'sjɔ̃], *n.f.* implantation.

implanter [ɛplɑ̃'te], *v.t.* to implant; to plant. **s'implanter**, *v.r.* to be implanted, fixed, rooted *or* lodged.

implication [ɛplika'sjɔ̃], *n.f.* implication, involving; discrepancy.

implicite [ɛpli'sit], *a.* implicit.

implicitement [ɛplisit'mã], *adv.* implicitly.

impliquer [ɛpli'ke], *v.t.* to implicate, to involve, to entangle; to imply.

implorateur [ɛplɔra'tœːr], *n.m.* (*fem.* **-trice**) implorer, supplicant.

imploration [ɛplɔra'sjɔ̃], *n.f.* supplication, imploration.

implorer [ɛplɔ're], *v.t.* to implore, to entreat, to beseech; to crave.

imployable [ɛplwa'jabl], *a.* unbending.

impoli [ɛpɔ'li], *a.* impolite, discourteous, uncivil, rude.

impoliment [ɛpɔli'mã], *adv.* impolitely, discourteously.

impolitesse [ɛpɔli'tɛs], *n.f.* impoliteness, incivility; rudeness.

impolitique [ɛpɔli'tik], *a.* impolitic, ill-advised.

impolitiquement [ɛpɔlitik'mɑ̃], *adv.* unwisely.

impopulaire [ɛpɔpy'lɛːr], *a.* unpopular.

impopularité [ɛpɔpylari'te], *n.f.* unpopularity.

importable [ɛpɔr'tabl], *a.* importable.

importance [ɛpɔr'tɑ̃ːs], *n.f.* importance, consequence; authority, credit; self-conceit.

important [ɛpɔr'tɑ̃], *a.* important, of consequence, weighty.—*n.m.* the essential, the main point; (*fem.* -**e**) person of importance.

importateur [ɛpɔrta'tœːr], *a.* (*fem.* -**trice**) importing.—*n.m.* (*fem.* -**trice**) importer.

importation [ɛpɔrta'sjɔ̃], *n.f.* importation; (*pl.*) imports.

importer [ɛpɔr'te], *v.t.* to import; (*fig.*) to introduce.—*v.i.* to import, to be of moment, to matter; *n'importe*, no matter, never mind; *n'importe où*, anywhere; *n'importe qui*, anyone; *n'importe quoi*, anything; *peu importe*, it does not much matter; *venez n'importe quand*, come when you like.

importun [ɛpɔr'tœ̃], *a.* importunate, tiresome, obtrusive, irksome.—*n.m.* (*fem.* -**e**) tiresome person; intruder, bore.

importuner [ɛpɔrty'ne], *v.t.* to importune, to pester; to inconvenience; to tease.

importunité [ɛpɔrtyni'te], *n.f.* importunity.

imposable [ɛpo'zabl], *a.* taxable.

imposant [ɛpo'zɑ̃], *a.* imposing, impressive, striking.

imposer [ɛpo'ze], *v.t.* to lay on (*hands*); to impose, to tax; to force (*à*).—*v.i.* or **en imposer**, to awe, to overawe. **s'imposer**, *v.r.* to assert oneself; to thrust oneself (*upon somebody*); to be indispensable.

imposition [ɛpozi'sjɔ̃], *n.f.* imposition, laying on (*of hands*); tax, assessment.

impossibilité [ɛpɔsibili'te], *n.f.* impossibility.

impossible [ɛpo'sibl], *a.* impossible.—*n.m.* one's utmost, a great deal.

imposte [ɛ'pɔst], *n.f.* (*Arch.*) impost, fanlight.

imposteur [ɛpos'tœːr], *n.m.* impostor, cheat.

imposture [ɛpos'tyːr], *n.f.* imposture, deception.

impôt [ɛ'po], *n.m.* tax, duty, impost; *percevoir les impôts*, to collect the taxes.

impotence [ɛpo'tɑ̃ːs], *n.f.* helplessness, infirmity.

impotent [ɛpo'tɑ̃], *a.* infirm, crippled.—*n.m.* (*fem.* -**e**) cripple, helpless invalid.

impraticabilité [ɛpratikabili'te], *n.f.* impracticability.

impraticable [ɛprati'kabl], *a.* impracticable; impassable; unmanageable.

imprécation [ɛpreka'sjɔ̃], *n.f.* imprecation, curse.

imprécatoire [ɛpreka'twaːr], *a.* imprecatory.

imprécis [ɛpre'si], *a.* unprecise, indefinite (*words*); (*Mil.*) inaccurate (*fire*).

imprécision [ɛpresi'zjɔ̃], *n.f.* lack of precision, vagueness (*of statement*); looseness (*of terms*); (*Mil.*) inaccuracy (*in firing*).

imprégnation [ɛpreɲa'sjɔ̃], *n.f.* impregnation.

imprégner [ɛpre'ne], *v.t.* (*conjug. like* CÉDER) to impregnate; (*fig.*) to imbue. **s'imprégner**, *v.r.* to become impregnated; to be imbued.

imprenable [ɛprə'nabl], *a.* impregnable.

impressif [ɛpre'sif], *a.* (*fem.* -**ive**) impressive, striking.

impression [ɛpre'sjɔ̃], *n.f.* impression; mark, stamp; print; edition; *faute d'impression*, misprint.

impressionnable [ɛpresjɔ'nabl], *a.* impressionable, sensitive.

impressionnant [ɛpresjɔ'nɑ̃], *a.* impressive.

impressionner [ɛpresjɔ'ne], *v.t.* to move, to affect, to impress.

impressionnisme [ɛpresjɔ'nism], *n.m.* impressionism.

impressionniste [ɛpresjɔ'nist], *a.* and *n.* impressionist.

imprévisible [ɛprevi'zibl], *a.* unforeseeable.

imprévoyance [ɛprevwa'jɑ̃ːs], *n.f.* want of foresight, improvidence.

imprévoyant [ɛprevwa'jɑ̃], *a.* improvident.

imprévu [ɛpre'vy], *a.* unforeseen, unexpected.

imprimable [ɛpri'mabl], *a.* fit to be printed.

imprimé [ɛpri'me], *n.m.* printed book, paper, document etc.; *service des imprimés*, book post.

imprimer [ɛpri'me], *v.t.* to imprint, to impress, to stamp; to print; to instil; to impart. **s'imprimer**, *v.r.* to be printed.

imprimerie [ɛprim'ri], *n.f.* printing; printing office, printing establishment.

imprimeur [ɛpri'mœːr], *n.m.* printer; (*Print.*) press-man.

improbabilité [ɛprobabili'te], *n.f.* improbability, unlikelihood.

improbable [ɛprɔ'babl], *a.* improbable, unlikely.

improbablement [ɛprobablə'mɑ̃], *adv.* improbably.

improbité [ɛprobi'te], *n.f.* improbity, dishonesty.

improductible [ɛprodyk'tibl], *a.* unproducible.

improductif [ɛprodyk'tif], *a.* (*fem.* -**ive**) unproductive, idle.

impromptu [ɛprɔp'ty], *a. inv.* impromptu, extemporary.—*n.m.* impromptu.—*adv.* offhand, extempore.

imprononçable [ɛpronɔ̃'sabl], *a.* unpronounceable (*word*).

impropre [ɛ'prɔpr], *a.* improper, wrong; unfit.

improprement [ɛproprə'mɑ̃], *adv.* improperly.

impropriété [ɛproprie'te], *n.f.* impropriety; unfitness.

improvisateur [ɛproviza'tœːr], *n.m.* (*fem.* -**trice**) improviser, extemporary speaker.

improvisation [ɛproviza'sjɔ̃], *n.f.* improvisation; (*Mus.*) voluntary.

improviser [ɛprovi'ze], *v.t.* to improvise, to extemporize.

improviste (à l') [alɛpro'vist], *adv. phr.* all of a sudden, unawares, unexpectedly.

imprudemment [ɛpryda'mɑ̃], *adv.* imprudently, indiscreetly.

imprudence [ɛpry'dɑ̃ːs], *n.f.* imprudence, rashness; indiscretion.

imprudent [ɛpry'dɑ̃], *a.* imprudent, foolhardy, unwise, incautious.

impudemment [ɛpyda'mɑ̃], *adv.* impudently, shamelessly.

impudence [ɛpy'dɑ̃ːs], *n.f.* impudence, shamelessness.

impudent [ɛpy'dã], *a.* impudent, shameless, saucy.—*n.m.* (*fem.* **-e**) impudent person.

impudeur [ɛpy'dœːr], *n.f.* immodesty, indecency; effrontery.

impudicité [ɛpydisi'te], *n.f.* impudicity, immodesty, lewdness.

impudique [ɛpy'dik], *a.* unchaste, lewd, immodest.

impudiquement [ɛpydik'mã], *adv.* immodestly, unchastely, lewdly.

impuissance [ɛpɥi'sãːs], *n.f.* impotence, incapacity, powerlessness.

impuissant [ɛpɥi'sã], *a.* impotent, powerless, unable.

impulsif [ɛpɥl'sif], *a.* (*fem.* **-sive**) impulsive.

impulsion [ɛpɥl'sjɔ̃], *n.f.* impulsion, impulse; impetus; motive.

impunément [ɛpyne'mã], *adv.* with impunity.

impuni [ɛpy'ni], *a.* unpunished.

impunité [ɛpyni'te], *n.f.* impunity.

impur [ɛ'pyːr], *a.* impure, foul; unchaste, immodest; unclean.

impurement [ɛpyr'mã], *adv.* impurely, immodestly.

impureté [ɛpyr'te], *n.f.* impurity, foulness; immodesty; obscenity.

imputabilité [ɛpytabili'te], *n.f.* imputability.

imputable [ɛpy'tabl], *a.* imputable, chargeable; to be deducted.

imputation [ɛpyta'sjɔ̃], *n.f.* imputation, charge; deduction.

imputer [ɛpy'te], *v.t.* to impute, to attribute; to deduct.

imputrescible [ɛpytre'sibl], *a.* not liable to putrefaction; rot-proof.

inabordable [inabor'dabl], *a.* inaccessible, unapproachable.

inabrité [inabri'te], *a.* unsheltered, open.

inabrogé [inabrɔ'ʒe], *a.* unrepealed.

inacceptable [inaksɛp'tabl], *a.* unacceptable.

inaccessibilité [inaksɛsibili'te], *n.f.* inaccessibility.

inaccessible [inaksɛ'sibl], *a.* inaccessible.

inaccordable [inakɔr'dabl], *a.* irreconcilable; unallowable, inadmissible.

inaccoutumé [inakuty'me], *a.* unaccustomed, unusual.

inachevé [inaʃ've], *a.* unfinished.

inactif [inak'tif], *a.* (*fem.* **-tive**) inactive; inert, indolent.

inaction [inak'sjɔ̃], *n.f.* inaction; indolence, inertness.

inactivement [inaktiv'mã], *adv.* inactively.

inactivité [inaktivi'te], *n.f.* inactivity.

inadaptation [inadapta'sjɔ̃], *n.f.* maladjustment.

inadapté [inadap'te], *a.* maladjusted.—*n.m.* (*fem.* **-ée**) social misfit.

inadmissible [inadmi'sibl], *a.* inadmissible.

inadmission [inadmi'sjɔ̃], *n.f.* non-admission.

inadvertance [inadvɛr'tãːs], *n.f.* inadvertence, oversight.

inaliénable [inalje'nabl], *a.* inalienable.

inaliéné [inalje'ne], *a.* unalienated.

inalliable [ina'ljabl], *a.* that cannot be alloyed; incompatible.

inaltérable [inalte'rabl], *a.* unalterable, invariable.

inamical [inami'kal], *a.* (*m. pl.* **-aux**) unfriendly.

inamovibilité [inamɔvibili'te], *n.f.* irremovability, fixity of tenure.

inamovible [inamɔ'vibl], *a.* irremovable, permanent; built in.

inanimé [inani'me], *a.* inanimate, lifeless.

inanité [ɪnani'te], *n.f.* inanity, emptiness.

inanition [inani'sjɔ̃], *n.f.* inanition, starvation.

inapaisé [inape'ze], *a.* unappeased; unquenched.

inaperçu [inapɛr'sy], *a.* unperceived, unobserved, unnoticed.

inapparent [inapa'rã], *a.* unapparent; inconspicuous.

inapplicable [inapli'kabl], *a.* inapplicable.

inappliqué [inapli'ke], *a.* inattentive, heedless.

inappréciable [inapre'sjabl], *a.* inappreciable; invaluable.

inappréciablement [inapresjablə'mã], *adv.* inappreciably.

inapprécié [inapre'sje], *a.* unappreciated.

inapprêté [inapre'te], *a.* unprepared, undressed, uncooked.

inapprochable [inaprɔ'ʃabl], *a.* unapproachable.

inapte [i'napt], *a.* inapt, unfit, unqualified.

inaptitude [inapti'tyd], *n.f.* inaptitude, unfitness; disqualification.

inarticulé [inartiky'le], *a.* inarticulate.

inassouvi [inasu'vi], *a.* unsatiated.

inassouvissable [inasuvi'sabl], *a.* insatiable.

inattaquable [inata'kabl], *a.* unassailable; (*fig.*) unimpeachable, irreproachable.

inattendu [inatɑ̃'dy], *a.* unexpected, unforeseen; unhoped for.

inattentif [inatɑ̃'tif], *a.* (*fem.* **-tive**) inattentive, unmindful.

inattention [inatɑ̃'sjɔ̃], *n.f.* inattention, carelessness; *faute d'inattention*, slip.

inaudible [ino'dibl], *a.* inaudible.

inaugural [inogy'ral], *a.* (*m. pl.* **-aux**) inaugural.

inauguration [inogyra'sjɔ̃], *n.f.* inauguration.

inaugurer [inogy're], *v.t.* to inaugurate, to open; to usher in.

inavouable [ina'vwabl], *a.* unavowable; shameful.

incalculable [ɛ̃kalky'labl], *a.* incalculable, numberless.

incandescence [ɛ̃kɑ̃de'sãːs], *n.f.* incandescence.

incandescent [ɛ̃kɑ̃de'sã], *a.* incandescent.

incapable [ɛ̃ka'pabl], *a.* incapable, unable (*de*); unfit, incompetent.

incapacité [ɛ̃kapasi'te], *n.f.* incapacity, incapability; inability, unfitness; incompetence, disability; disqualification, (*Mil.*) disablement; *frapper d'incapacité*, to incapacitate.

incarcération [ɛ̃karsera'sjɔ̃], *n.f.* incarceration.

incarcérer [ɛ̃karse're], *v.t.* (*conjug. like* CÉDER) to incarcerate, to imprison.

incarnat [ɛ̃kar'na], *a.* flesh-colored, rosy.—*n.m.* carnation, flesh-color.

incarnation [ɛ̃karnɑ'sjɔ̃], *n.f.* incarnation.

incarné [ɛ̃kar'ne], *a.* incarnate; ingrowing (*nail*).

incarner [ɛkar'ne], v.t. to incarnate, to embody. **s'incarner**, v.r. to become incarnate; to grow in (of nails).

incartade [ɛkar'tad], n.f. thoughtless insult; prank, folly.

incassable [ɛka'sabl], a. unbreakable.

incendiaire [ɛsɑ̃'djɛːr], a. and n. incendiary.

incendie [ɛsɑ̃'di], n.m. fire, conflagration.

incendié [ɛsɑ̃'dje], a. burnt-out, gutted.— n.m. (fem. -ée) sufferer by fire.

incendier [ɛsɑ̃'dje], v.t. to set fire to, to burn down.

incertain [ɛsɛr'tɛ̃], a. uncertain; unsettled, inconstant; vague.

incertitude [ɛsɛrti'tyd], n.f. uncertainty, doubt, suspense; instability, fickleness.

incessamment [ɛsɛsa'mɑ̃], adv. immediately, at once; incessantly.

incessant [ɛsɛ'sɑ̃], a. incessant, ceaseless, unremitting.

inceste [ɛ̃'sɛst], a. incestuous.—n.m. incest. —n. incestuous person.

incestueusement [ɛsɛstɥøz'mɑ̃], adv. incestuously.

incestueux [ɛsɛs'tɥø], a. (fem. -euse) incestuous.—n.m. (fem. -euse) incestuous person.

incidemment [ɛsida'mɑ̃], adv. incidentally.

incidence [ɛsi'dɑ̃ːs], n.f. incidence.

incident [ɛsi'dɑ̃], a. incidental; incident.— n.m. incident, occurrence.

incinération [ɛsinera'sjɔ̃], n.f. incineration; cremation.

incinérer [ɛsine're], v.t. (conjug. like CÉDER) to incinerate; to cremate.

inciser [ɛsi'ze], v.t. to make an incision in, to notch, to gash; to tap (a tree).

incisif [ɛsi'zif], a. (fem. -sive) sharp, cutting, incisive.—n.f. (-sive) incisive tooth, incisor.

incision [ɛsi'zjɔ̃], n.f. incision.

incitation [ɛsita'sjɔ̃], n.f. incitement, instigation; (Med.) stimulus.

inciter [ɛsi'te], v.t. to incite; to instigate, to induce.

incivil [ɛsi'vil], a. uncivil, unmannerly.

incivilement [ɛsivil'mɑ̃], adv. uncivilly.

incivilisé [ɛsivili'ze], a. uncivilized.

incivilité [ɛsivili'te], n.f. incivility; rude remark.

inclémence [ɛkle'mɑ̃ːs], n.f. inclemency.

inclément [ɛkle'mɑ̃], a. inclement.

inclinaison [ɛklinɛ'zɔ̃], n.f. inclination; incline, gradient; pitch, slant.

inclination [ɛklina'sjɔ̃], n.f. bow, bending; proneness, propensity; attachment, passion.

incliner [ɛkli'ne], v.t. to incline, to slope; to bow; to bend; (fig.) to dispose, to turn.— v.i. to incline, to lean; to be inclined (à or vers). **s'incliner**, v.r. to incline, to lean; to bow to bend, to yield.

inclure [ɛ'klyːr] v.t. irr. (conjug. like CONCLURE but p.p. **inclus**) to include, to enclose, to insert.

inclus [ɛ'kly], a. enclosed, included.

inclusif [ɛkly'zif], a. (fem. -sive) inclusive.

inclusion [ɛkly'zjɔ̃], n.f. enclosing; inclusion.

inclusivement [ɛklyziv'mɑ̃], adv. inclusively.

incognito [ɛkɔɲi'to], adv. incognito.

incohérence [ɛkɔe'rɑ̃ːs], n.f. incoherence.

incohérent [ɛkɔe'rɑ̃], a. incoherent.

incolore [ɛkɔ'lɔːr], a. colorless.

incomber [ɛkɔ̃'be], v.i. to be incumbent (on anyone).

incombustible [ɛkɔ̃bys'tibl], a. incombustible, fire-proof.

incomestible [ɛkɔmɛs'tibl], a. inedible.

incommode [ɛkɔ'mɔd], a. inconvenient, uncomfortable; annoying, disagreeable.

incommodé [ɛkɔmɔ'de], a. indisposed, unwell, poorly.

incommodément [ɛkɔmɔde'mɑ̃], adv. incommodiously, inconveniently.

incommoder [ɛkɔmɔ'de], v.t. to inconvenience, to trouble; to disturb, to annoy; to make unwell.

incommodité [ɛkɔmɔdi'te], n.f. inconvenience, incommodiousness; annoyance; indisposition.

incommunicable [ɛkɔmyni'kabl], a. incommunicable.

incomparable [ɛkɔpa'rabl], a. incomparable, unequalled, peerless.

incomparablement [ɛkɔparablə'mɑ̃], adv. incomparably.

incompatibilité [ɛkɔpatibili'te], n.f. incompatibility.

incompatible [ɛkɔpa'tibl], a. incompatible, inconsistent.

incompétence [ɛkɔpe'tɑ̃ːs], n.f. incompetence.

incompétent [ɛkɔpe'tɑ̃], a. incompetent.

incomplet [ɛkɔ̃'plɛ], a. (fem. -ète) incomplete.

incomplètement [ɛkɔ̃plɛt'mɑ̃], adv. incompletely.

incompréhensible [ɛkɔprea'sibl], a. incomprehensible, inscrutable.

incompréhension [ɛkɔprea'sjɔ̃], n.f. lack of understanding, obtuseness.

incompressible [ɛkɔpre'sibl], a. incompressible.

incompris [ɛkɔ̃'pri], a. and n.m. (fem. -e) misunderstood, unappreciated (person).

inconcevable [ɛkɔs'vabl], a. inconceivable, unthinkable.

inconcevablement [ɛkɔsvablə'mɑ̃], adv. inconceivably.

inconciliable [ɛkɔsi'ljabl], a. irreconcilable, incompatible.

inconduite [ɛkɔ̃'dɥit], n.f. misconduct.

inconfort [ɛkɔ̃'fɔːr], n.m. discomfort, lack of comfort.

inconfortable [ɛkɔfɔr'tabl], a. uncomfortable.

incongru [ɛkɔ̃'gry], a. incongruous, improper, unseemly.

incongruité [ɛkɔgryi'te], n.f. incongruity, impropriety.

incongrûment [ɛkɔgry'mɑ̃], adv. incongruously, improperly.

inconnu [ɛkɔ'ny], a. unknown.—n.m. the unknown.—n.m. (fem. -e) stranger. —n.f. (-e) (Math.) unknown quantity.

inconquis [ɛkɔ̃'ki], a. unconquered.

inconsciemment [ɛkɔsja'mɑ̃], adv. unconsciously, unawares.

inconscience [ɛkɔ̃'sjɑ̃ːs], n.f. unconsciousness; failure to realize.

inconscient [ɛkɔ̃'sjɑ̃], a. unconscious.—n.m. the unconscious.

inconséquemment [ɛkɔseka'mɑ̃], adv. inconsistently, inconsequentially.

inconséquence [ɛkɔse'kɑ̃ːs], n.f. inconsistency, inconsequence.

inconséquent [ɛkɔse'kɑ̃], a. inconsistent; inconsequential.

inconsidéré

inconsidéré [ɛ̃kɔ̃sideˈre], *a.* inconsiderate, thoughtless.

inconsistance [ɛ̃kɔ̃sisˈtãːs], *n.f.* inconsistency.

inconsistant [ɛ̃kɔ̃sisˈtã], *a.* inconsistent.

inconsolable [ɛ̃kɔ̃sɔˈlabl], *a.* disconsolate; inconsolable.

inconsolablement [ɛ̃kɔ̃sɔlabləˈmã], *adv.* disconsolately, inconsolably.

inconsolé [ɛ̃kɔ̃sɔˈle], *a.* unconsoled, uncomforted.

inconstamment [ɛ̃kɔ̃staˈmã], *adv.* inconstantly; unsteadily.

inconstance [ɛ̃kɔ̃sˈtãːs], *n.f.* inconstancy, fickleness; instability.

inconstant [ɛ̃kɔ̃sˈtã], *a.* inconstant, fickle; changeable; unsettled, unsteady.—*n.m.* (*fem.* -**e**) fickle person.

inconstitutionnel [ɛ̃kɔ̃stitysjɔˈnɛl], *a.* (*fem.* -**elle**) unconstitutional.

incontestable [ɛ̃kɔ̃tɛsˈtabl], *a.* incontestable, indisputable.

incontestablement [ɛ̃kɔ̃testabləˈmã], *adv.* incontestably.

incontesté [ɛ̃kɔ̃tɛsˈte], *a.* uncontested, unquestioned, undisputed.

incontinence [ɛ̃kɔ̃tiˈnãːs], *n.f.* incontinence.

incontinent (1) [ɛ̃kɔ̃tiˈnã], *a.* incontinent, unchaste.

incontinent (2) [ɛ̃kɔ̃tiˈnã], *adv.* at once, immediately, forthwith.

incontrôlable [ɛ̃kɔ̃troˈlabl], *a.* that cannot be checked *or* verified.

inconvenance [ɛ̃kɔ̃vˈnãːs], *n.f.* impropriety, unseemliness; indecorum; *quelle inconvenance !* how very improper!

inconvenant [ɛ̃kɔ̃vˈnã], *a.* improper, unbecoming, unseemly.

inconvénient [ɛ̃kɔ̃veˈnjã], *n.m.* inconvenience, harm; drawback, objection.

inconvertible [ɛ̃kɔ̃vɛrˈtibl], *a.* unconvertible.

incorporation [ɛ̃kɔrpɔraˈsjɔ̃], *n.f.* incorporation.

incorporer [ɛ̃kɔrpɔˈre], *v.t.* to incorporate, to embody; to fuse. **s'incorporer**, *v.r.* to be embodied; to unite, to be blended.

incorrect [ɛ̃kɔˈrɛkt], *a.* incorrect, inaccurate.

incorrectement [ɛ̃kɔrɛktəˈmã], *adv.* incorrectly, inaccurately.

incorrection [ɛ̃kɔrɛkˈsjɔ̃], *n.f.* incorrectness, inaccuracy.

incorrigible [ɛ̃kɔriˈʒibl], *a.* incorrigible.

incorrigiblement [ɛ̃kɔriʒibləˈmã], *adv.* incorrigibly.

incorruptible [ɛ̃kɔrypˈtibl], *a.* incorruptible, unbribable.

incrédibilité [ɛ̃kredibiliˈte], *n.f.* incredibility.

incrédule [ɛ̃kreˈdyl], *a.* incredulous, unbelieving.—*n.* unbeliever, infidel.

incrédulité [ɛ̃kredyliˈte], *n.f.* incredulity, unbelief.

incriminer [ɛ̃krimiˈne], *v.t.* to incriminate, to accuse.

incroyable [ɛ̃krwaˈjabl], *a.* incredible, past belief.

incroyablement [ɛ̃krwajabləˈmã], *adv.* incredibly.

incroyance [ɛ̃krwaˈjãːs], *n.f.* unbelief.

incroyant [ɛ̃krwaˈjã], *a.* unbelieving.—*n.m.* (*fem.* -**e**) unbeliever.

incruster [ɛ̃krysˈte], *v.t.* to encrust, to inlay. **s'incruster**, *v.r.* to become encrusted.

incubateur [ɛ̃kybaˈtœːr], *a.* (*fem.* -**trice**) incubating.—*n.m.* incubator.

incubation [ɛ̃kybaˈsjɔ̃], *n.f.* incubation, hatching.

incuber [ɛ̃kyˈbe], *v.t.* to incubate.

inculcation [ɛ̃kylkaˈsjɔ̃], *n.f.* inculcation.

inculpation [ɛ̃kylpaˈsjɔ̃], *n.f.* indictment, charge.

inculpé [ɛ̃kylˈpe], *n.m.* (*fem.* -**ée**) defendant, accused.

inculper [ɛ̃kylˈpe], *v.t.* to indict, to inculpate, to charge.

inculquer [ɛ̃kylˈke], *v.t.* to inculcate, to impress.

inculte [ɛ̃ˈkylt], *a.* uncultivated; untilled; unpolished; unkempt.

incultivable [ɛ̃kyltiˈvabl], *a.* untillable, uncultivable.

incultivé [ɛ̃kyltiˈve], *a.* uncultivated; (*fig.*) uncultured.

incurable [ɛ̃kyˈrabl], *a.* and *n.* incurable.

incurablement [ɛ̃kyrabləˈmã], *adv.* incurably.

incurie [ɛ̃kyˈri], *n.f.* carelessness, heedlessness; negligence.

incursion [ɛ̃kyrˈsjɔ̃], *n.f.* incursion, inroad, irruption; expedition.

incurver [ɛ̃kyrˈve], *v.t.* to curve (*something*) inwards.

Inde [ɛ̃ːd], l', *f.* India; ***les Indes**, the Indies; *les Indes occidentales*, the West Indies.

indécemment [ɛ̃desaˈmã], *adv.* indecently.

indécence [ɛ̃deˈsãːs], *n.f.* indecency, impropriety.

indécent [ɛ̃deˈsã], *a.* indecent; unseemly.

indéchiffrable [ɛ̃deʃiˈfrabl], *a.* undecipherable, illegible; obscure, incomprehensible.

indéchirable [ɛ̃deʃiˈrabl], *a.* untearable.

indécis [ɛ̃deˈsi], *a.* undecided, doubtful; irresolute.

indécision [ɛ̃desiˈzjɔ̃], *n.f.* indecision, irresolution.

indécrottable [ɛ̃dekrɔˈtabl], *a.* uncleanable; (*fig.*) incorrigible.

indéfendable [ɛ̃defãˈdabl], *a.* indefensible, untenable.

indéfini [ɛ̃defiˈni], *a.* indefinite, unlimited.

indéfiniment [ɛ̃definiˈmã], *adv.* indefinitely.

indéfinissable [ɛ̃definiˈsabl], *a.* undefinable; nondescript.

indéfrichable [ɛ̃defriˈʃabl], *a.* unclearable (*of land*).

indéfrisable [ɛ̃defriˈzabl], *n.f.* permanent wave.

indélébile [ɛ̃deleˈbil], *a.* indelible, ineffaceable.

indélicat [ɛ̃deliˈka], *a.* indelicate; unhandsome.

indélicatement [ɛ̃delikatˈmã], *adv.* indelicately; unhandsomely.

indélicatesse [ɛ̃delikaˈtɛs], *n.f.* tactlessness; unscrupulousness; objectionable action.

indémaillable [ɛ̃demaˈjabl], *a.* run-proof (*stocking*).

indemne [ɛ̃ˈdɛmn], *a.* uninjured.

indemnisation [ɛ̃dɛmnizaˈsjɔ̃], *n.f.* indemnification, compensation.

indemniser [ɛ̃dɛmniˈze], *v.t.* to indemnify; to make good.

indemnité [ɛdɛmni'te], *n.f.* indemnity; *indemnité de charges de famille,* family allowance; *indemnité de chômage,* unemployment benefit; *indemnité de vie chère,* cost of living bonus.
indéniable [ɛde'njabl], *a.* undeniable; self-evident.
indépendamment [ɛdepɑ̃da'mɑ̃], *adv.* independently.
indépendance [ɛdepɑ̃'dɑ̃:s], *n.f.* independence.
indépendant [ɛdepɑ̃'dɑ̃], *a.* independent.
indescriptible [ɛdɛskrip'tibl], *a.* indescribable.
indésirable [ɛdezi'rabl], *a.* and *n.* undesirable.
indestructible [ɛdɛstryk'tibl], *a.* indestructible.
indéterminable [ɛdetɛrmi'nabl], *a.* indeterminable.
indétermination [ɛdetɛrmina'sjɔ̃], *n.f.* indetermination, irresolution.
indéterminé [ɛdetɛrmi'ne], *a.* undetermined, irresolute.
index [ɛ'dɛks], *n.m. inv.* fore-finger; index.
indicateur [ɛdika'tœ:r], *a.* (*fem.* -trice) indicating, indicatory.—*n.m.* indicator, guide; time-table; (*fem.* -trice) (*fig.*) informer.
indicatif [ɛdika'tif], *a.* (*fem.* -tive) indicative.—*n.m.* (*Gram.*) indicative mood; call-sign; signature tune.
indication [ɛdika'sjɔ̃], *n.f.* indication, information; sign, mark.
indice [ɛ'dis], *n.m.* indication, sign, mark, clue.
indicible [ɛdi'sibl], *a.* inexpressible, unspeakable, indescribable.
indiciblement [ɛdisiblə'mɑ̃], *adv.* inexpressibly.
indien [ɛ'djɛ̃], *a.* (*fem.* -enne) Indian.—*n.m.* (**Indien**, *fem.* -enne) Indian (*person*).—*n.f.* (-enne) printed calico, printed cotton.
indifféremment [ɛdifera'mɑ̃], *adv.* indifferently; alike.
indifférence [ɛdife'rɑ̃:s], *n.f.* indifference, unconcern.
indifférent [ɛdife'rɑ̃], *a.* indifferent, immaterial; unconcerned, heedless.—*n.m.* (*fem.* -e) indifferent person.
indigence [ɛdi'ʒɑ̃:s], *n.f.* indigence, poverty, need.
indigène [ɛdi'ʒɛ:n], *a.* indigenous, native.—*n.* native.
indigent [ɛdi'ʒɑ̃], *a.* indigent, needy.—*n.m.* (*fem.* -e) pauper, destitute person.
indigéré [ɛdiʒe're], *a.* undigested, crude.
indigeste [ɛdi'ʒɛst], *a.* indigestible; undigested.
indigestion [ɛdiʒɛs'tjɔ̃], *n.f.* indigestion, surfeit.
indignation [ɛdina'sjɔ̃], *n.f.* indignation.
indigne [ɛ'din], *a.* unworthy; infamous, worthless.
indigné [ɛdi'ne], *a.* indignant; shocked.
indignement [ɛdinə'mɑ̃], *adv.* unworthily; scandalously.
indigner [ɛdi'ne], *v.t.* to render indignant; to shock. **s'indigner,** *v.r.* to be indignant; to be shocked.
indignité [ɛdini'te], *n.f.* unworthiness, worthlessness; indignity; infamy.

indigo [ɛdi'go], *a. inv.* and *n.m.* indigo.
indigotier [ɛdigo'tje], *n.m.* indigo plant *or* manufacturer.
indiquer [ɛdi'ke], *v.t.* to indicate, to point out; to mention; to denote; to appoint, to recommend; to outline.
indirect [ɛdi'rɛkt], *a.* indirect; circumstantial (*of evidence*); collateral (*of heirs*).
indirectement [ɛdirɛktə'mɑ̃], *a.* indirectly.
indiscipline [ɛdisi'plin], *n.f.* indiscipline, insubordination.
indiscipliné [ɛdisipli'ne], *a.* undisciplined.
indiscret [ɛdis'krɛ], *a.* (*fem.* -ète) indiscreet, inconsiderate; inquisitive; tell-tale.—*n.m.* (*fem.* -ète) babbler.
indiscrètement [ɛdiskrɛt'mɑ̃], *adv.* indiscreetly, inconsiderately.
indiscrétion [ɛdiskre'sjɔ̃], *n.f.* indiscretion; unwariness.
indiscutable [ɛdisky'tabl], *a.* incontestable, indisputable, obvious.
indispensable [ɛdispɑ̃'sabl], *a.* indispensable.
indispensablement [ɛdispɑ̃sablə'mɑ̃], *adv.* indispensably.
indisponible [ɛdispo'nibl], *a.* unavailable.
indisposé [ɛdispo'ze], *a.* unwell; unfriendly.
indisposer [ɛdispo'ze], *v.t.* to indispose, to make unwell; to disincline, to set against (*contre*).
indisposition [ɛdispozi'sjɔ̃], *n.f.* indisposition; disinclination.
indisputé [ɛdispy'te], *a.* unquestioned.
indissoluble [ɛdiso'lybl], *a.* indissoluble.
indissolublement [ɛdisolyblə'mɑ̃], *adv.* indissolubly.
indistinct [ɛdis'tɛ̃:kt], *a.* indistinct.
indistinctement [ɛdistɛ̃ktə'mɑ̃], *adv.* indistinctly.
individu [ɛdivi'dy], *n.m.* individual; (*colloq.*) fellow.
individualisme [ɛdividɥa'lism], *n.m.* individualism.
individualiste [ɛdividɥa'list], *a.* individualistic.—*n.* individualist.
individualité [ɛdividɥali'te], *n.f.* individuality.
individuel [ɛdivi'dɥɛl], *a.* (*fem.* -elle) individual.
individuellement [ɛdividɥɛl'mɑ̃], *adv.* individually.
indivis [ɛdivi'ze], *a.* undivided.
indivisément [ɛdivize'mɑ̃], *adv.* jointly.
indivisibilité [ɛdivizibili'te], *n.f.* indivisibility.
indivisible [ɛdivi'zibl], *a.* indivisible.
indivisiblement [ɛdiviziblə'mɑ̃], *adv.* indivisibly.
indivision [ɛdivi'zjɔ̃], *n.f.* joint possession.
Indochine [ɛdo'ʃin], **l',** *f.* Indo-China.
indochinois [ɛdoʃi'nwa], *a.* Indo-Chinese.—*n.m.* (**Indochinois,** *fem.* -oise) Indo-Chinese (*person*).
indocile [ɛdo'sil], *a.* indocile, unmanageable.
indocilité [ɛdosili'te], *n.f.* indocility, intractability.
indolemment [ɛdola'mɑ̃], *adv.* indolently.
indolence [ɛdo'lɑ̃:s], *n.f.* indolence, sloth.
indolent [ɛdo'lɑ̃], *a.* indolent, slothful.—*n.m.* (*fem.* -e) sluggard.
indolore [ɛdo'lɔ:r], *a.* painless.
indomptable [ɛdɔ̃'tabl], *a.* indomitable, untamable; unmanageable.

187

indompté [ɛ̃dɔ̃'te], *a.* untamed, wild; unsubdued.

Indonésie [ɛ̃dɔne'zi], l', *f.* Indonesia.

indonésien [ɛ̃dɔne'zjɛ̃], *a.* Indonesian.—*n.m.* Indonesian (*language*); (**Indonésien**, *fem.* **-enne**) Indonesian (*person*).

indou [HINDOU].

indu [ɛ̃'dy], *a.* undue, unseasonable, late.

indubitable [ɛ̃dybi'tabl], *a.* indubitable, certain.

indubitablement [ɛ̃dybitablə'mɑ̃], *adv.* undoubtedly.

inductif [ɛ̃dyk'tif], *a.* (*fem.* **-tive**) inductive.

induction [ɛ̃dyk'sjɔ̃], *n.f.* induction, inference.

induire [ɛ̃'dɥiːr], *v.t. irr.* (*conjug. like* CONDUIRE) to induce, to lead; to infer.

indulgence [ɛ̃dyl'ʒɑ̃ːs], *n.f.* indulgence, leniency.

indulgent [ɛ̃dyl'ʒɑ̃], *a.* indulgent, forbearing.

indûment [ɛ̃dy'mɑ̃] *adv.* unduly.

industrialiser [ɛ̃dystriali'ze], *v.t.* to industrialize.

industrialisme [ɛ̃dystria'lism], *n.m.* industrialism.

industrie [ɛ̃dys'tri], *n.f.* skill, ingenuity; business; manufacturing; industry, work; *chevalier d'industrie*, swindler, sharper; *industrie de base* or *industrie clef*, key industry.

industriel [ɛ̃dystri'ɛl], *a.* (*fem.* **-elle**) industrial, manufacturing.—*n.m.* manufacturer, mill owner.

industrieusement [ɛ̃dystriøz'mɑ̃], *adv.* ingeniously, skilfully; industriously.

industrieux [ɛ̃dystri'ø], *a.* (*fem.* **-euse**) ingenious, skilful; industrious.

inébranlable [inebrɑ̃'labl], *a.* immovable; firm, resolute.

inébranlablement [inebrɑ̃lablə'mɑ̃], *adv.* immovably, steadily; resolutely.

inédit [ine'di], *a.* unpublished; new.

ineffable [ine'fabl], *a.* ineffable, inexpressible, unutterable.

ineffaçable [inefa'sabl], *a.* indelible, ineffaceable.

inefficace [inefi'kas], *a.* ineffectual, ineffective.

inefficacité [inefikasi'te], *n.f.* inefficacy, ineffectiveness.

inégal [ine'gal], *a.* (*m. pl.* **-aux**) unequal; rough; (*fig.*) ill-matched; irregular.

inégalement [inegal'mɑ̃], *adv.* unequally, unevenly.

inégalité [inegali'te], *n.f.* inequality; unevenness; irregularity.

inélégance [inele'gɑ̃ːs], *n.f.* inelegance.

inélégant [inele'gɑ̃], *a.* inelegant.

inéligible [ineli'ʒibl], *a.* ineligible.

inéluctable [inelyk'tabl], *a.* unavoidable; unescapable.

inénarrable [inena'rabl], *a.* untellable; incredible.

inepte [i'nɛpt], *a.* foolish, silly, inept, absurd.

ineptie [inɛp'si], *n.f.* ineptitude, foolishness, absurdity.

inépuisable [inepɥi'zabl], *a.* inexhaustible.

inépuisablement [inepɥizablə'mɑ̃], *adv.* inexhaustibly.

inéquitable [ineki'tabl], *a.* unfair.

inerte [i'nɛrt], *a.* inert, sluggish, inactive.

inertie [inɛr'si], *n.f.* inertia; indolence.

inespéré [inɛspe're], *a.* unhoped for, unexpected.

inestimable [inɛsti'mabl], *a.* inestimable.

inévitable [inevi'tabl], *a.* inevitable, unavoidable.

inévitablement [inevitablə'mɑ̃], *adv.* inevitably, unavoidably.

inexact [inɛg'zakt], *a.* inexact, inaccurate, incorrect.

inexactement [inɛgzakta'mɑ̃], *adv.* inaccurately, incorrectly.

inexactitude [inɛgzakti'tyd], *n.f.* incorrectness; inaccuracy, slip.

inexcusable [inɛksky'zabl], *a.* inexcusable, unwarrantable.

inexécutable [inɛgzeky'tabl], *a.* impracticable.

inexercé [inɛgzɛr'se], *a.* untrained.

inexistant [inɛgzis'tɑ̃], *a.* non-existent.

inexorable [inɛgzɔ'rabl], *a.* inexorable, inflexible; pitiless.

inexorablement [inɛgzɔrablə'mɑ̃], *adv.* inexorably.

inexpérience [inɛkspe'rjɑ̃ːs], *n.f.* inexperience.

inexpérimenté [inɛksperimɑ̃'te], *a.* inexperienced; untried (*of things*).

inexplicable [inɛkspli'kabl], *a.* inexplicable, unaccountable.

inexpliqué [inɛkspli'ke], *a.* unexplained.

inexploitable [inɛksplwa'tabl], *a.* unworkable, useless.

inexploité [inɛksplwa'te], *a.* uncultivated (*of land*); unworked (*of mines etc.*); untapped (*resources*).

inexploré [inɛksplɔ're], *a.* unexplored.

inexplosible [inɛksplɔ'zibl], *a.* unexplosive.

inexpressible [inɛkspre'sibl], *a.* inexpressible.

inexpressif [inɛkspre'sif], *a.* (*fem.* **-ive**) inexpressive, lacking expression.

inexprimable [inɛkspri'mabl], *a.* inexpressible, unspeakable.

inextinguible [inɛkstɛ̃'gibl], *a.* inextinguishable; unquenchable (*thirst, fire*); irrepressible (*laughter*).

inextricable [inɛkstri'kabl], *a.* inextricable.

inextricablement [inɛkstrikablə'mɑ̃], *adv.* inextricably.

infaillibilité [ɛ̃fajibili'te], *n.f.* infallibility.

infaillible [ɛ̃fa'jibl], *a.* infallible.

infailliblement [ɛ̃fajiblə'mɑ̃], *adv.* infallibly.

infaisable [ɛ̃fə'zabl], *a.* impracticable.

infamant [ɛ̃fa'mɑ̃], *a.* infamous, ignominious.

infâme [ɛ̃'fɑːm], *a.* infamous; squalid, sordid.—*n.* infamous person, wretch.

infamie [ɛ̃fa'mi], *n.f.* infamy, ignominy; baseness.

infant [ɛ̃'fɑ̃], *n.m.* (*fem.* **-e**) infante, infanta (*Spanish prince* or *princess*).

infanterie [ɛ̃fɑ̃'tri], *n.f.* infantry.

infanticide [ɛ̃fɑ̃ti'sid], *n.m.* infanticide.—*n.* child-murderer.

infantile [ɛ̃fɑ̃'til], *a.* infantile.

infatigable [ɛ̃fati'gabl], *a.* indefatigable, untiring.

infatuation [ɛ̃fatɥa'sjɔ̃], *n.f.* infatuation.

infatuer [ɛ̃fa'tɥe], *v.t.* to infatuate. **s'infatuer**, *v.r.* to become infatuated.

infécond [ɛ̃fe'kɔ̃], *a.* unfruitful, barren, sterile.

infécondité [ɛ̃fekɔ̃di'te], *n.f.* unfruitfulness, barrenness, sterility.

infect [ɛ̃'fɛkt], *a.* infected, foul, noisome, stinking.

infectant [ɛ̃fɛk'tã], *a.* infecting.

infecter [ɛ̃fɛk'te], *v.t.* to infect, to contaminate; to taint.—*v.i.* to stink.

infectieux [ɛ̃fɛk'sjø], *a.* (*fem.* -euse) infectious.

infection [ɛ̃fɛk'sjɔ̃], *n.f.* infection; infectious disease; stench; *foyer d'infection,* hotbed of disease.

inférence [ɛ̃fe'rã:s], *n.f.* conclusion, inference.

inférer [ɛ̃fe're], *v.t.* (*conjug. like* CÉDER) to infer, to conclude.

inférieur [ɛ̃fe'rjœ:r], *a.* inferior, lower.—*n.m.* (*fem.* -e) inferior; subordinate.

infériorité [ɛ̃terjɔri'te], *n.f.* inferiority.

infernal [ɛ̃fɛr'nal], *a.* (*m. pl.* -aux) infernal, hellish.

infernalement [ɛ̃fɛrnal'mã], *adv.* infernally.

infertile [ɛ̃fɛr'til], *a.* infertile, unfruitful; sterile, barren.

infertilité [ɛ̃fɛrtili'te], *n.f.* unfruitfulness.

infester [ɛ̃fɛs'te], *v.t.* to infest, to overrun; to haunt.

infidèle [ɛ̃fi'dɛl], *a.* unfaithful, disloyal; unbelieving.—*n.* unfaithful person; infidel.

infidèlement [ɛ̃fidɛl'mã], *adv.* unfaithfully; inaccurately.

infidélité [ɛ̃fideli'te], *n.f.* infidelity; unbelief; dishonesty.

infiltration [ɛ̃filtra'sjɔ̃], *n.f.* infiltration.

infiltrer (s') [sɛ̃fil'tre], *v.r.* to infiltrate, to percolate.

infime [ɛ̃'fim], *a.* lowest (*of ranks*); tiny.

infini [ɛ̃fi'ni], *a.* infinite, boundless.—*n.m.* infinite, infinity.

infiniment [ɛ̃fini'mã], *adv.* infinitely, without end; exceedingly, extremely.

infinité [ɛ̃fini'te], *n.f.* infinity, infiniteness; (*fig.*) crowd; no end.

infinitif [ɛ̃fini'tif], *a.* (*fem.* -tive) and *n.m.* infinitive (mood).

infirme [ɛ̃'firm], *a.* crippled, invalid; infirm; feeble.—*n.* invalid, cripple.

infirmerie [ɛ̃firm'ri], *n.f.* infirmary, sick ward; (*sch.*) sanatorium, sick-bay.

infirmier [ɛ̃fir'mje], *n.m.* (*fem.* -ière) hospital attendant; nurse.

infirmité [ɛ̃firmi'te], *n.f.* infirmity, weakness, failing.

inflammable [ɛ̃fla'mabl], *a.* inflammable.

inflammation [ɛ̃flama'sjɔ̃], *n.f.* inflammation.

inflammatoire [ɛ̃flama'twa:r], *a.* inflammatory.

inflation [ɛ̃fla'sjɔ̃], *n.f.* inflation, swelling.

inflexible [ɛ̃flɛk'sibl], *a.* inflexible; unyielding, unbending.

inflexiblement [ɛ̃flɛksiblə'mã], *adv.* inflexibly.

inflexion [ɛ̃flɛk'sjɔ̃], *n.f.* inflexion; modulation, variation.

infliction [ɛ̃flik'sjɔ̃], *n.f.* infliction.

infliger [ɛ̃fli'ʒe], *v.t.* (*conjug. like* MANGER) to inflict, to impose.

influence [ɛ̃fly'ã:s], *n.f.* influence; sway, power, authority.

influencer [ɛ̃flyã'se], *v.t.* (*conjug. like* COMMENCER) to influence, to sway, to bias.

influent [ɛ̃fly'ã], *a.* influential.

influenza [ɛ̃flyã'za], *n.f.* influenza.

influer [ɛ̃fly'e], *v.i.* to have an influence (*sur, on*).

informateur [ɛ̃forma'tœ:r], *n.m.* (*fem.* -trice) informant.

information [ɛ̃forma'sjɔ̃], *n.f.* inquiry; information; (*pl.*) news (bulletin).

informe [ɛ̃'form], *a.* shapeless; misshapen; crude, imperfect.

informer [ɛ̃for'me], *v.t.* to inform, to acquaint, to apprise. **s'informer,** *v.r.* to inquire, to make inquiries, to investigate.

infortune [ɛ̃for'tyn], *n.f.* misfortune, adversity.

infortuné [ɛ̃forty'ne], *a.* unfortunate, unhappy, ill-fated, wretched.—*n.m.* (*fem.* -ée) unfortunate, unhappy *or* wretched person.

infraction [ɛ̃frak'sjɔ̃], *n.f.* infringement, breach, violation.

infranchissable [ɛ̃frãʃi'sabl], *a.* insurmountable, insuperable.

infra-rouge [ɛ̃fra'ru:ʒ], *a.* infra-red.

infréquenté [ɛ̃frekã'te], *a.* unfrequented.

infructueusement [ɛ̃fryktɥøz'mã], *adv.* fruitlessly, to no purpose, in vain.

infructueux [ɛ̃fryk'tɥø], *a.* (*fem.* -euse) unfruitful, vain, unavailing.

infus [ɛ̃'fy], *a.* infused, innate, native (*of knowledge etc.*).

infuser [ɛ̃fy'ze], *v.t.* to infuse, to instill; to steep.

infusion [ɛ̃fy'zjɔ̃], *n.f.* infusion, decoction.

ingambe [ɛ̃'gã:b], *a.* nimble, brisk, active.

ingénier (s') [sɛ̃ʒe'nje], *v.r.* to tax one's ingenuity, to contrive.

ingénieur [ɛ̃ʒe'njœ:r], *n.m.* engineer.

ingénieusement [ɛ̃ʒenjøz'mã], *adv.* ingeniously.

ingénieux [ɛ̃ʒe'njø], *a.* (*fem.* -euse) ingenious, clever, witty.

ingéniosité [ɛ̃ʒenjozi'te], *n.f.* ingenuity; cleverness.

ingénu [ɛ̃ʒe'ny], *a.* ingenuous; guileless, unsophisticated; simple, artless.—*n.m.* (*fem.* -e) ingenuous person, artless *or* simpleminded person.

ingénuité [ɛ̃ʒenɥi'te], *n.f.* ingenuousness.

ingénument [ɛ̃ʒeny'mã], *adv.* ingenuously.

ingérence [ɛ̃ʒe'rã:s], *n.f.* interference, meddling.

ingérer (s') [sɛ̃ʒe're], *v.r.* (*conjug. like* CÉDER) to meddle with, to interfere, to obtrude.

inglorieux [ɛ̃glɔ'rjø], *a.* (*fem.* -euse) inglorious.

ingouvernable [ɛ̃guvɛr'nabl], *a.* ungovernable, uncontrollable.

ingrat [ɛ̃'gra], *a.* unthankful, ungrateful; thankless, unprofitable.

ingratitude [ɛ̃grati'tyd], *n.f.* ingratitude, thanklessness.

ingrédient [ɛ̃gre'djã], *n.m.* ingredient.

inguérissable [ɛ̃geri'sabl], *a.* incurable.

inhabile [ina'bil], *a.* unskillful, unskilled, inexpert.

inhabilement [inabil'mã], *adv.* unskillfully.

inhabileté [inabil'te], *n.f.* unskillfulness, incompetence, inability.

inhabitable [inabi'tabl], *a.* uninhabitable.

inhabité [inabi'te], *a.* uninhabited.

inhabitué [inabi'tɥe], *a.* unaccustomed, unused.

189

inhalation [inalɑ'sjɔ̃], *n.f.* inhalation.
inhaler [ina'le], *v.t.* to inhale.
inharmonieux [inarmɔ'njø], *a.* (*fem.* **-euse**) inharmonious, unmusical.
inhérent [ine'rɑ̃], *a.* inherent.
inhospitalier [inɔspitɑ'lje], *a.* (*fem.* **-ière**) inhospitable; (*fig.*) unfriendly, forbidding.
inhumain [iny'mɛ̃], *a.* inhuman, cruel.
inhumainement [inymɛn'mɑ̃], *adv.* inhumanly.
inhumanité [inymani'te], *n.f.* inhumanity, cruelty.
inhumation [inymɑ'sjɔ̃], *n.f.* inhumation, interment.
inhumer [iny'me], *v.t.* to bury, to inter.
inimaginable [inimaʒi'nabl], *a.* unimaginable, inconceivable.
inimitable [inimi'tabl], *a.* inimitable.
inimitié [inimi'tje], *n.f.* enmity, antipathy, aversion.
ininflammable [inɛ̃flɑ'mabl], *a.* non-inflammable, fire-proof.
inintelligemment [inɛ̃teliʒa'mɑ̃], *adv.* unintelligently.
inintelligence [inɛ̃teli'ʒɑ̃:s], *n.f.* lack of intelligence.
inintelligent [inɛ̃teli'ʒɑ̃], *a.* unintelligent.
inintelligible [inɛ̃teli'ʒibl], *a.* unintelligible.
inintéressant [inɛ̃tere'sɑ̃], *a.* uninteresting.
ininterrompu [inɛ̃terɔ̃'py], *a.* uninterrupted.
inique [i'nik], *a.* iniquitous; unrighteous.
iniquement [inik'mɑ̃], *adv.* iniquitously.
iniquité [iniki'te], *n.f.* iniquity, unrighteousness; injustice.
initial [ini'sjal], *a.* (*m. pl.* **-aux**) initial.
initiale [ini'sjal], *n.f.* initial.
initialement [inisjal'mɑ̃], *adv.* initially.
initiateur [inisja'tœ:r], *n.m.* (*fem.* **-trice**) initiator.
initiation [inisja'sjɔ̃], *n.f.* initiation.
initiative [inisja'ti:v], *n.f.* initiative.
initier [ini'sje], *v.t.* to initiate, to admit.
injecté [ɛ̃ʒɛk'te], *a.* injected; bloodshot; creosoted.
injecter [ɛ̃ʒɛk'te], *v.t.* to inject.
injection [ɛ̃ʒɛk'sjɔ̃], *n.f.* injection.
injonction [ɛ̃ʒɔ̃k'sjɔ̃], *n.f.* injunction, order.
injudicieux [ɛ̃ʒydi'sjø], *a.* (*fem.* **-euse**) injudicious.
injure [ɛ̃'ʒy:r], *n.f.* injury; insult; (*pl.*) abuse, abusive language; slander.
injurier [ɛ̃ʒy'rje], *v.t.* to abuse, to insult.
injurieux [ɛ̃ʒy'rjø], *a.* (*fem.* **-euse**) wrongful; abusive, insulting.
injuste [ɛ̃'ʒyst], *a.* unjust, unfair, wrong.
injustement [ɛ̃ʒystə'mɑ̃], *adv.* unjustly, wrongly.
injustice [ɛ̃ʒys'tis], *n.f.* injustice; wrong.
injustifiable [ɛ̃ʒysti'fjabl], *a.* unjustifiable.
injustifié [ɛ̃ʒysti'fje], *a.* unjustified, groundless.
inlassable [ɛ̃lɑ'sabl], *a.* untirable.
inné [in'ne], *a.* innate, inborn.
innocemment [inɔsa'mɑ̃], *adv.* innocently.
innocence [inɔ'sɑ̃:s], *n.f.* innocence; inoffensiveness; simplicity.
innocent [inɔ'sɑ̃], *a.* innocent; harmless, inoffensive; guileless, simple.—*n.m.* (*fem.* **-e**) simpleton; idiot.
innocenter [inɔsɑ̃'te], *v.t.* to acquit.
innombrable [innɔ̃'brabl], *a.* innumerable, numberless.

innombrablement [inɔ̃brablə'mɑ̃], *adv.* innumerably.
innovateur [innɔva'tœ:r], *n.m.* (*fem.* **-trice**) innovator.
innovation [innɔva'sjɔ̃], *n.f.* innovation.
innover [innɔ've], *v.i.* to make innovations.
inobservable [inɔpsɛr'vabl], *a.* inobservable.
inobservance [inɔpsɛr'vɑ̃:s], **inobservation** [inɔpsɛrva'sjɔ̃], *n.f.* non-observance.
inobservé [inɔpsɛr've], *a.* unobserved, unnoticed.
inoccupé [inɔky'pe], *a.* unoccupied; idle; vacant.
inoculateur [inɔkyla'tœ:r], *n.m.* (*fem.* **-trice**) inoculator.
inoculation [inɔkyla'sjɔ̃], *n.f.* inoculation.
inoculer [inɔky'le], *v.t.* to inoculate.
inodore [inɔ'dɔ:r], *a.* odorless.
inoffensif [inɔfɑ̃'sif], *a.* (*fem.* **-sive**) inoffensive; innocuous.
inoffensivement [inɔfɑ̃siv'mɑ̃], *adv.* inoffensively.
inofficiel [inɔfi'sjɛl], *a.* (*fem.* **-elle**) unofficial.
inofficiellement [inɔfisjɛl'mɑ̃], *adv.* unofficially.
inondation [inɔ̃dɑ'sjɔ̃], *n.f.* inundation, flood, deluge.
inonder [inɔ̃'de], *v.t.* to inundate, to overflow; (*fig.*) to overrun.
inopérant [inɔpe'rɑ̃], *a.* inoperative; inefficient.
inopiné [inɔpi'ne], *a.* unforeseen, unexpected, sudden.
inopinément [inɔpine'mɑ̃], *adv.* unawares, unexpectedly, suddenly.
inopportun [inɔpɔr'tœ̃], *a.* inopportune, untimely.
inorganique [inɔrga'nik], *a.* inorganic.
inoubliable [inu'bljabl], *a.* unforgettable.
inoublié [inu'blje], *a.* unforgotten, well-remembered.
inouï [i'nwi], *a.* unheard of, unprecedented.
inoxydable [inɔksi'dabl], *a.* rustless, stainless.
inqualifiable [ɛ̃kali'fjabl], *a.* unspeakable.
inquiet [ɛ̃'kjɛ], *a.* (*fem.* **-ète**) anxious; restless.
inquiétant [ɛ̃kje'tɑ̃], *a.* disquieting, alarming.
inquiéter [ɛ̃kje'te], *v.t.* (*conjug. like* CÉDER) to disquiet; to worry; to disturb. **s'inquiéter**, *v.r.* to be anxious, to be uneasy; to worry.
inquiétude [ɛ̃kje'tyd], *n.f.* anxiety, uneasiness, concern.
inquisiteur [ɛ̃kizi'tœ:r], *a.* inquisitorial; inquisitive.—*n.m.* inquisitor.
inquisitif [ɛ̃kizi'tif], *a.* (*fem.* **-tive**) inquisitive.
inquisition [ɛ̃kizi'sjɔ̃], *n.f.* inquisition.
insaisissable [ɛ̃sɛzi'sabl], *a.* unseizable, imperceptible.
insalubre [ɛ̃sa'lybr], *a.* insalubrious, unhealthy, unwholesome.
insalubrement [ɛ̃salybrə'mɑ̃], *adv.* insalubriously, unhealthily.
insalubrité [ɛ̃salybri'te], *n.f.* insalubrity, unhealthiness.
insanité [ɛ̃sa'nite], *n.f.* insanity.
insatiabilité [ɛ̃sasjabili'te], *n.f.* insatiability.
insatiable [ɛ̃sa'sjabl], *a.* insatiable.
insciemment [ɛ̃sja'mɑ̃], *adv.* unwittingly.
inscription [ɛ̃skrip'sjɔ̃], *n.f.* inscription; registration, enrolment; matriculation.

inscrire [ɛs'kri:r], *v.t. irr. (conjug. like* ÉCRIRE) to inscribe, to set down, to register. **s'inscrire**, *v.r.* to inscribe oneself; to enter one's name; to register, to enroll.

inscrutable [ɛskry'tabl], *a.* inscrutable, unfathomable.

insecte [ɛ'sɛkt], *n.m.* insect.

insecticide [ɛsɛkti'sid], *a.* insecticidal.—*n.m.* insecticide.

insectivore [ɛsɛkti'vɔ:r], *a.* insectivorous.

insécurité [ɛsekyri'te], *n.f.* insecurity.

insémination [ɛsemina'sjɔ̃], *n.f.* insemination (*cows, ewes etc.*).

inséminer [ɛsemi'ne], *v.t.* to inseminate.

insensé [ɛsɑ̃'se], *a.* insane, mad; foolish, senseless.—*n.m.* (*fem.* **-ée**) madman, mad woman, maniac.

insensibiliser [ɛsɑ̃sibili'ze], *v.t.* to anesthetize.

insensibilité [ɛsɑ̃sibili'te], *n.f.* insensibility; callousness.

insensible [ɛsɑ̃'sibl], *a.* insensible, unconscious; hard-hearted, unfeeling.

insensiblement [ɛsɑ̃siblə'mɑ̃], *adv.* insensibly; gradually, imperceptibly.

inséparable [ɛsepa'rabl], *a.* inseparable.—*n.m. (pl.)* (*Orn.*) love-birds.

inséparablement [ɛseparablə'mɑ̃], *adv.* inseparably.

insérer [ɛse're], *v.t. (conjug. like* CÉDER) to insert, to put in.

insertion [ɛsɛr'sjɔ̃], *n.f.* insertion.

insidieusement [ɛsidjøz'mɑ̃], *adv.* insidiously.

insidieux [ɛsi'djø], *a. (fem.* **-euse**) insidious.

insigne [ɛ'siɲ], *a.* distinguished; conspicuous; notorious.—*n.m.* badge, mark; (*pl.*) insignia.

insignifiance [ɛsiɲi'fjɑ̃:s], *n.f.* insignificance.

insignifiant [ɛsiɲi'fjɑ̃], *a.* insignificant, trivial.

insincère [ɛsɛ̃'sɛ:r], *a.* insincere.

insinuant [ɛsi'nɥɑ̃], *a.* insinuating; ingratiating.

insinuation [ɛsinɥa'sjɔ̃], *n.f.* insinuation, hint, innuendo.

insinuer [ɛsi'nɥe], *v.t.* to insinuate; to hint, to suggest. **s'insinuer**, *v.r.* to insinuate oneself (*dans*), to creep *or* worm one's way (*into*).

insipide [ɛsi'pid], *a.* insipid, tasteless; dull.

insipidité [ɛsipidi'te], *n.f.* insipidity.

insistance [ɛsis'tɑ̃:s], *n.f.* insistence, persistence.

insister [ɛsis'te], *v.i.* to insist, to lay stress (*sur*).

insociable [ɛsɔ'sjabl], *a.* unsociable; difficult to live with.

insolation [ɛsɔla'sjɔ̃], *n.f.* insolation, sunstroke.

insolemment [ɛsɔla'mɑ̃], *adv.* insolently.

insolence [ɛsɔ'lɑ̃:s], *n.f.* insolence, impertinence.

insolent [ɛsɔ'lɑ̃], *a.* insolent, impudent, rude.—*n.m. (fem.* **-e**) insolent person.

insolite [ɛsɔ'lit], *a.* unusual, unwonted.

insolubilité [ɛsɔlybili'te], *n.f.* insolubility.

insoluble [ɛsɔ'lybl], *a.* insoluble.

insolvabilité [ɛsɔlvabili'te], *n.f.* insolvency.

insolvable [ɛsɔl'vabl], *a.* insolvent.

insomnie [ɛsɔm'ni], *n.f.* insomnia.

insondable [ɛsɔ̃'dabl], *a.* unfathomable.

insonore [ɛsɔ'nɔ:r], *a.* sound-proof.

insouciance [ɛsu'sjɑ̃:s], *n.f.* carelessness, thoughtlessness.

insouciant [ɛsu'sjɑ̃], **insoucieux** [ɛsu'sjø] (*fem.* **-euse**), *a.* careless, thoughtless; unconcerned, easy-going.

insoumis [ɛsu'mi], *a.* unsubdued; refractory, unruly.—*n.m.* (*Mil.*) defaulter.

insoumission [ɛsumi'sjɔ̃], *n.f.* insubordination.

insoutenable [ɛsut'nabl], *a.* indefensible; unbearable.

inspecter [ɛspɛk'te], *v.t.* to inspect, to survey, to scan.

inspecteur [ɛspɛk'tœ:r], *n.m.* (*fem.* **-trice**) inspector, superintendent, surveyor.

inspection [ɛspɛk'sjɔ̃], *n.f.* inspection, survey; superintendence; **faire l'inspection de**, to inspect; **passer à l'inspection**, to undergo inspection.

inspirateur [ɛspira'tœ:r], *a. (fem.* **-trice**) inspiring; (*Anat.*) inspiratory.—*n.m. (fem.* **-trice**) inspirer.

inspiration [ɛspira'sjɔ̃], *n.f.* inspiration; suggestion; inhaling.

inspiré [ɛspi're], *a.* and *n.m. (fem.* **-ée**) inspired (person).

inspirer [ɛspi're], *v.t.* to inspire, to breathe in; (*fig.*) to suggest, to instill. **s'inspirer**, *v.r.* to draw one's inspiration (*de*).

instabilité [ɛstabili'te], *n.f.* instability, fickleness.

instable [ɛ'stabl], *a.* unstable; unsteady, wobbly.

installation [ɛstala'sjɔ̃], *n.f.* installation; equipment.

installer [ɛsta'le], *v.t.* to install; to inaugurate, to establish. **s'installer**, *v.r.* to install oneself; to settle.

instamment [ɛsta'mɑ̃], *adv.* earnestly, urgently.

instance [ɛs'tɑ̃:s], *n.f.* entreaty; urgency, earnestness; (*Law*) instance; (*pl.*) entreaties.

instant (1) [ɛs'tɑ̃], *n.m.* instant, moment; **à l'instant**, in an instant, immediately.

instant (2) [ɛs'tɑ̃], *a.* pressing, urgent; imminent.

instantané [ɛstɑ̃ta'ne], *a.* instantaneous.—*n.m.* snapshot.

instantanément [ɛstɑ̃tane'mɑ̃], *adv.* instantaneously.

instar (à l') [alɛs'ta:r], *prep. phr.* **à l'instar de**, like; in imitation of.

instigateur [ɛstiga'tœ:r], *n.m. (fem.* **-trice**) instigator.

instigation [ɛstiga'sjɔ̃], *n.f.* instigation.

instiller [ɛsti'le], *v.t.* to instil.

instinct [ɛs'tɛ̃], *n.m.* instinct.

instinctif [ɛstɛ̃k'tif], *a. (fem.* **-tive**) instinctive.

instinctivement [ɛstɛ̃ktiv'mɑ̃], *adv.* instinctively.

instituer [ɛsti'tɥe], *v.t.* to institute, to establish.

institut [ɛsti'ty], *n.m.* institution; institute; order (*of monks*).

instituteur [ɛstity'tœ:r], *n.m. (fem.* **-trice**) teacher, schoolmaster, schoolmistress (*in primary schools*); **institutrice (particulière)**, governess.

institution [ɛstity'sjɔ̃], *n.f.* institution; establishment; (*Law*) appointment.

191

instructeur [ɛ̃stryk'tœːr], *n.m.* instructor, drill-master.

instructif [ɛ̃stryk'tif], *a.* (*fem.* **-tive**) instructive.

instruction [ɛ̃stryk'sjɔ̃], *n.f.* instruction, tuition, education, learning; (*Law*) inquiry, examination; (*pl.*) directions.

instruire [ɛs'trɥiːr], *v.t. irr.* (*conjug. like* CONDUIRE) to instruct, to teach, to educate; to inform (*de*). **s'instruire**, *v.r.* to instruct, inform *or* improve oneself.

instruit [ɛ̃'strɥi], *a.* instructed, informed; aware; educated.

instrument [ɛ̃stry'mã], *n.m.* instrument, tool; document.

instrumental [ɛ̃strymã'tal], *a.* (*m. pl.* **-aux**) instrumental.

instrumentiste [ɛ̃strymã'tist], *n.* instrumentalist.

insu [ɛ̃'sy], *prep. phr.* **à l'insu de**, unknown to; **à mon insu**, unknown to me.

insubmersible [ɛ̃sybmɛr'sibl], *a.* unsinkable.

insubordination [ɛ̃sybɔrdinɑ'sjɔ̃], *n.f.* insubordination.

insubordonné [ɛ̃sybɔrdɔ'ne], *a.* insubordinate.

insuccès [ɛ̃syk'sɛ], *n.m. inv.* failure, lack of success.

insuffisamment [ɛ̃syfiza'mã], *adv.* insufficiently.

insuffisance [ɛ̃syfi'zãːs], *n.f.* insufficiency.

insuffisant [ɛ̃syfi'zã], *a.* insufficient, inadequate.

insulaire [ɛ̃sy'lɛːr], *a.* insular.—*n.* islander.

insularité [ɛ̃sylari'te], *n.f.* insularity.

insuline [ɛ̃sy'lin], *n.f.* insulin.

insultant [ɛ̃syl'tã], *a.* insulting.

insulte [ɛ̃'sylt], *n.f.* insult.

insulter [ɛ̃syl'te], *v.t.* to insult, to affront.

insupportable [ɛ̃sypɔr'tabl], *a.* intolerable, unbearable.

insupportablement [ɛ̃sypɔrtablə'mã], *adv.* intolerably, unbearably.

insurgé [ɛ̃syr'ʒe], *a.* and *n.m.* (*fem.* **-ée**) rebel, insurgent.

insurger (s') [sɛ̃syr'ʒe], *v.r.* (*conjug. like* MANGER) to revolt, to rebel.

insurmontable [ɛ̃syrmɔ̃'tabl], *a.* insurmountable, insuperable.

insurrection [ɛ̃syrɛk'sjɔ̃], *n.f.* insurrection, rising.

intact [ɛ̃'takt], *a.* intact, entire, whole.

intangible [ɛ̃tã'ʒibl], *a.* intangible.

intarissable [ɛ̃tari'sabl], *a.* inexhaustible.

intégral [ɛ̃te'gral], *a.* (*m. pl.* **-aux**) integral, whole, entire.

intégrale [ɛ̃te'gral], *n.f.* (*Math.*) integral.

intégralement [ɛ̃tegral'mã], *adv.* integrally, entirely, in full.

intègre [ɛ̃'tɛgr], *a.* honest, upright, just.

intègrement [ɛ̃tegrə'mã], *adv.* honestly, uprightly.

intégrer [ɛ̃te'gre], *v.t.* (*conjug. like* CÉDER) to integrate. **s'intégrer**, *v.r.* to combine into; to form an integral part of.

intégrité [ɛ̃tegri'te], *n.f.* integrity, uprightness, probity.

intellect [ɛ̃tɛ'lɛkt], *n.m.* intellect, understanding.

intellectuel [ɛ̃tɛlɛk'tɥɛl], *a.* (*fem.* **-elle**) and *n.m.* (*fem.* **-elle**) intellectual.

intellectuellement [ɛ̃tɛlɛktɥɛl'mã], *adv.* intellectually.

intelligemment [ɛ̃teliʒa'mã], *adv.* intelligently.

intelligence [ɛ̃teli'ʒãːs], *n.f.* intelligence, intellect; clear comprehension; cleverness, skill, ability; mutual understanding; **avec intelligence**, skillfully, cleverly; **en bonne intelligence avec**, on good terms with; **être d'intelligence avec**, to be in collusion with.

intelligent [ɛ̃teli'ʒã], *a.* intelligent; bright, clever, sharp.

intelligible [ɛ̃teli'ʒibl], *a.* intelligible; distinct, clear.

intelligiblement [ɛ̃teliʒiblə'mã], *adv.* intelligibly, clearly.

intempérance [ɛ̃tãpe'rãːs], *n.f.* intemperance, insobriety.

intempérant [ɛ̃tãpe'rã], *a.* intemperate.

intempérie [ɛ̃tãpe'ri], *n.f.* (*usu. in pl.*) inclemency (*of the weather*).

intempestif [ɛ̃tãpɛs'tif], *a.* (*fem.* **-tive**) unseasonable, untimely.

intenable [ɛ̃ta'nabl], *a.* untenable; insufferable.

intendance [ɛ̃tã'dãːs], *n.f.* stewardship (*of an estate*); (*Mil.*) commissariat; the Army Service Corps.

intendant [ɛ̃tã'dã], *n.m.* intendant, steward; major-domo; (*Mil.*) administrative officer (*having the rank of a general*).

intense [ɛ̃'tãːs], *a.* intense, violent; severe.

intensité [ɛ̃tãsi'te], *n.f.* intensity, violence, severity.

intensivement [ɛ̃tãsiv'mã], *adv.* intensively.

intenter [ɛ̃tã'te], *v.t.* (*Law*) **intenter une action** *or* **un procès à** *or* **contre quelqu'un**, to enter *or* bring an action against someone.

intention [ɛ̃tã'sjɔ̃], *n.f.* intention; (*Law*) intent; purpose; **à l'intention de**, for the sake of; **avec intention**, on purpose; **avoir l'intention de**, to intend to; **sans intention**, unintentionally.

intentionné [ɛ̃tãsjɔ'ne], *a.* intentioned, disposed, meaning.

intentionnel [ɛ̃tãsjɔ'nɛl], *a.* (*fem.* **-elle**) intentional.

inter [ɛ̃'tɛr], *n.m.* (*Ftb.*) inside-forward.

interaction [ɛ̃terak'sjɔ̃], *n.f.* interaction.

intercaler [ɛ̃terka'le], *v.t.* to intercalate; to interpolate; (*Elec.*) to switch in.

intercéder [ɛ̃terse'de], *v.i.* (*conjug. like* CÉDER) to intercede, to plead.

intercepter [ɛ̃tersɛp'te], *v.t.* to intercept.

intercession [ɛ̃tersɛ'sjɔ̃], *n.f.* intercession; mediation.

intercontinental [ɛ̃terkɔ̃tinã'tal], *a.* (*m. pl.* **-aux**) intercontinental.

interdépartemental [ɛ̃terdepartəmã'tal], *a.* (*m. pl.* **-aux**) interdepartmental.

interdiction [ɛ̃terdik'sjɔ̃], *n.f.* interdiction, prohibition.

interdire [ɛ̃ter'diːr], *v.t. irr.* (*conjug. like* MÉDIRE) to interdict, to prohibit, to forbid; to suspend; (*fig.*) to confound, to nonplus.

interdit [ɛ̃ter'di], *a.* forbidden, prohibited; (*fig.*) abashed, confused; **entrée interdite**, no admittance; **passage interdit**, no thoroughfare.—*n.m.* interdict.—*n.m.* (*fem.* **-e**) person interdicted.

intéressant [ɛ̃terɛ'sɑ̃], *a.* interesting; attractive (*price*).

intéressé [ɛ̃tere'se], *a.* interested; selfish.— *n.m.* (*fem.* **-ée**) interested party.

intéresser [ɛ̃tere'se], *v.t.* to interest; to concern, to affect. **s'intéresser**, *v.r.* to take an interest in, to be interested (*à*).

intérêt [ɛ̃te'rɛ], *n.m.* interest, concern; share.

interférence [ɛ̃terfe'rɑ̃:s], *n.f.* interference; (*pl.*) (*Rad., Tel.*) interference.

interférer [ɛ̃terfe're], *v.i.* (*conjug. like* CÉDER) to interfere.

intérieur [ɛ̃te'rjœ:r], *a.* inner, inward, internal, interior; inland.—*n.m.* interior; home, private life; *à l'intérieur*, inside; *Ministre de l'Intérieur*, Home Secretary.

interlocuteur [ɛ̃terlɔky'tœ:r], *n.m.* (*fem.* **-trice**) speaker (*in a conversation*).

interloquer [ɛ̃terlɔ'ke], *v.t.* to nonplus, to disconcert.

intermède [ɛ̃ter'mɛd], *n.m.* interlude.

intermédiaire [ɛ̃terme'djɛ:r], *a.* intermediate, intervening.—*n.m.* medium, agency; intermediary, middleman, agent.

interminable [ɛ̃termi'nabl], *a.* interminable, endless.

intermission [ɛ̃termi'sjɔ̃], *n.f.* intermission, pause.

intermittence [ɛ̃termi'tɑ̃:s], *n.f.* intermission, cessation.

intermittent [ɛ̃termi'tɑ̃], *a.* intermittent.

internat [ɛ̃ter'na], *n.m.* boarding school; house-surgeonship (*of hospitals*).

international [ɛ̃ternasjɔ'nal], *a.* (*m. pl.* **-aux**) international.

interne [ɛ̃'tɛrn], *a.* internal, inward, resident. —*n.* boarder (*in schools*).

interné [ɛ̃ter'ne], *a.* interned.—*n.m.* (*fem.* **-ée**) internee.

interner [ɛ̃ter'ne], *v.t.* to intern.

interpellation [ɛ̃terpɛla'sjɔ̃], *n.f.* interpellation.

interpeller [ɛ̃terpɛ'le], *v.t.* to hail, to call upon, to challenge; (*Polit.*) to interpellate.

interplanétaire [ɛ̃terplane'tɛ:r], *a.* interplanetary.

interpoler [ɛ̃terpɔ'le], *v.t.* to interpolate.

interposer [ɛ̃terpo'ze], *v.t.* to interpose. **s'interposer**, *v.r.* to interpose, to come between.

interprétation [ɛ̃terpreta'sjɔ̃], *n.f.* interpretation; rendering (*of a play*).

interprète [ɛ̃ter'prɛt], *n.* interpreter, expounder; artist, actor, actress.

interpréter [ɛ̃terpre'te], *v.t.* (*conjug. like* CÉDER) to interpret, to explain; to construe.

interrègne [ɛ̃ter'rɛɲ], *n.m.* interregnum.

interrogateur [ɛ̃terɔga'tœr], *n.m.* (*fem.* **-trice**) interrogator, questioner, examiner.

interrogatif [ɛ̃terɔga'tif], *a.* (*fem.* **-tive**) interrogative.

interrogation [ɛ̃terɔga'sjɔ̃], *n.f.* interrogation, question; *point d'interrogation*, question mark.

interrogatoire [ɛ̃terɔga'twa:r], *n.m.* examination.

interroger [ɛ̃terɔ'ʒe], *v.t.* (*conjug. like* MANGER) to interrogate, to question; to examine.

interrompre [ɛ̃te'rɔ̃:pr], *v.t.* (*conjug. like* RÔMPRE) to interrupt, to break off; to stop.

interrupteur [ɛ̃terryp'tœ:r], *a.* and *n.m.* (*fem.* **-trice**) interrupting; interrupter.—*n.m.* (*Elec.*) switch, cut-out.

interruption [ɛ̃terryp'sjɔ̃], *n.f.* interruption; (*Elec.*) disconnection.

interscolaire [ɛ̃tersko'lɛ:r], *a.* inter-school (*competition etc.*).

intersection [ɛ̃tersɛk'sjɔ̃], *n.f.* intersection.

interstice [ɛ̃ter'stis], *n.m.* interstice, chink, crack.

intervalle [ɛ̃ter'val], *n.m.* interval; distance, gap; *dans l'intervalle*, in the meantime.

intervenir [ɛ̃tervə'ni:r], *v.i. irr.* (*conjug. like* TENIR) to intervene, to interfere; to happen.

intervention [ɛ̃tervɑ̃'sjɔ̃], *n.f.* intervention, interference.

interversion [ɛ̃terver'sjɔ̃], *n.f.* inversion.

intervertir [ɛ̃terver'ti:r], *v.t.* to invert, to reverse.

intestin [ɛ̃tɛs'tɛ̃], *a.* intestine; internal, domestic, civil.—*n.m.* intestine.

intimation [ɛ̃tima'sjɔ̃], *n.f.* notification.

intime [ɛ̃'tim], *a.* intimate, inmost, secret; close.—*n.* intimate.

intimement [ɛ̃tim'mɑ̃], *adv.* intimately.

intimider [ɛ̃timi'de], *v.t.* to intimidate, to frighten.

intimité [ɛ̃timi'te], *n.f.* intimacy, closeness.

intitulé [ɛ̃tity'le], *a.* entitled.—*n.m.* title (*of deeds, books etc.*).

intituler [ɛ̃tity'le], *v.t.* to entitle, to call, to name. **s'intituler**, *v.r.* to entitle *or* call oneself.

intolérable [ɛ̃tɔle'rabl], *a.* intolerable, insufferable.

intolérablement [ɛ̃tɔlerablə'mɑ̃], *adv.* unbearably.

intolérance [ɛ̃tɔle'rɑ̃:s], *n.f.* intolerance.

intolérant [ɛ̃tɔle'rɑ̃], *a.* intolerant.

intonation [ɛ̃tɔna'sjɔ̃], *n.f.* intonation; pitch.

intoxicant [ɛ̃tɔksi'kɑ̃], *a.* poisonous.

intoxication [ɛ̃tɔksika'sjɔ̃], *n.f.* poisoning.

intoxiquer [ɛ̃tɔksi'ke], *v.t.* to poison.

intraduisible [ɛ̃tradɥi'zibl], *a.* untranslatable.

intraitable [ɛ̃trɛ'tabl], *a.* intractable, unmanageable.

intransigeant [ɛ̃trɑ̃zi'ʒɑ̃], *a.* intransigent, uncompromising.—*n.m.* (*fem.* **-e**) intransigent, diehard.

intransitif [ɛ̃trɑ̃zi'tif], *a.* (*fem.* **-tive**) (*Gram.*) intransitive.

intraversable [ɛ̃traver'sabl], *a.* impassable.

intrépide [ɛ̃tre'pid], *a.* intrepid, dauntless, fearless.

intrigant [ɛ̃tri'gɑ̃], *a.* intriguing.—*n.m.* (*fem.* **-e**) intriguer, schemer.

intrigue [ɛ̃'trig], *n.f.* intrigue; plot (*of a novel etc.*).

intrigueur [ɛ̃tri'gœ:r], *n.m.* (*fem.* **-euse**) intriguer, plotter.

intrinsèque [ɛ̃trɛ̃'sɛk], *a.* intrinsic.

introduction [ɛ̃trɔdyk'sjɔ̃], *n.f.* introduction; preamble.

introductoire [ɛ̃trɔdyk'twa:r], *a.* introductory, preliminary.

introduire [ɛ̃trɔ'dɥi:r], *v.t. irr.* (*conjug. like* CONDUIRE) to show *or* bring in, to introduce. **s'introduire**, *v.r.* to get in, to find one's way in; to intrude.

introniser [ɛ̃trɔni'ze], *v.t.* to install, to enthrone; (*fig.*) to establish (*a fashion*).

introspectif [ɛ̃trɔspɛk'tif], *a.* (*fem.* **-tive**) introspective.

introuvable [ɛtru'vabl], *a.* not to be found; matchless.
introverti [ɛtrɔvɛr'ti], *a.* introverted.—*n.m.* (*fem.* -e) introvert.
intrus [ɛ'try], *a.* intruding, intruded.—*n.m.* (*fem.* -e) intruder.
intrusion [ɛtry'zjɔ̃], *n.f.* intrusion.
intuitif [ɛtɥi'tif], *a.* (*fem.* -tive) intuitive.
intuition [ɛtɥi'sjɔ̃], *n.f.* intuition.
inusable [iny'zabl], *a.* durable, everlasting.
inusité [inyzi'te], *a.* unused; unusual; obsolete.
inutile [iny'til], *a.* useless, unnecessary.
inutilement [inytil'mã], *adv.* uselessly, to no purpose, needlessly.
inutilisable [inytili'zabl], *a.* that cannot be utilized, worthless.
inutilité [inytili'te], *n.f.* uselessness; useless thing.
invaincu [ɛvɛ̃'ky], *a.* unvanquished, unconquered.
invalidation [ɛvalida'sjɔ̃], *n.f.* invalidation.
invalide [ɛva'lid], *a.* disabled, crippled, infirm, invalid; (*Law*) not valid.—*n.* invalid, pensioner; *Hôtel des Invalides*, the veterans hospital of France.
invalider [ɛvali'de], *v.t.* to invalidate, to annul.
invariable [ɛva'rjabl], *a.* invariable, unchangeable.
invariablement [ɛvarjablə'mã], *adv.* invariably.
invasion [ɛva'zjɔ̃], *n.f.* invasion; inroad.
invective [ɛvɛk'ti:v], *n.f.* invective, (*pl.*) abuse.
invectiver [ɛvɛkti've] *v.t.* to abuse.—*v.i.* to inveigh against, to revile (*contre*).
inventaire [ɛvã'tɛ:r], *n.m.* inventory; stock-taking.
inventer [ɛvã'te], *v.t.* to invent, to devise; to find out; to imagine; to forge.
inventeur [ɛvã'tœ:r], *n.m.* (*fem.* -trice) inventor.
inventif [ɛvã'tif], *a.* (*fem.* -tive) inventive.
invention [ɛvã'sjɔ̃], *n.f.* invention; inventiveness; device, trick; falsehood; *brevet d'invention*, patent.
inventorier [ɛvãtɔ'rje], *v.t.* to draw up an inventory of; to schedule, to catalogue.
inversable [ɛvɛr'sabl], *a.* that cannot be upset.
inverse [ɛ'vɛrs], *a.* inverse, inverted.—*n.m.* reverse, contrary.
inversement [ɛvɛrs'mã], *adv.* inversely.
invertébré [ɛvɛrte'bre], *a.* and *n.m.* (*fem.* -ée) invertebrate.
inverti [ɛvɛr'ti], *a.* inverted, reversed.
investigateur [ɛvɛstiga'tœ:r], *a.* (*fem.* -trice) searching, inquiring.—*n.m.* (*fem.* -trice) investigator.
investigation [ɛvɛstiga'sjɔ̃], *n.f.* investigation, inquiry.
investir [ɛvɛs'ti:r], *v.t.* to invest; to surround, to lay siege to.
investiture [ɛvɛsti'ty:r], *n.f.* investiture.
invétéré [ɛvete're], *a.* inveterate.
invincibilité [ɛvɛ̃sibili'te], *n.f.* invincibility.
invincible [ɛvɛ̃'sibl], *a.* invincible, unconquerable.
inviolable [ɛvjɔ'labl], *a.* inviolable.
inviolé [ɛvjɔ'le], *a.* inviolate.
invisible [ɛvi'zibl], *a.* invisible.

invisiblement [ɛviziblə'mã], *adv.* invisibly.
invitation [ɛvita'sjɔ̃], *n.f.* invitation.
invité [ɛvi'te], *n.m.* (*fem.* -ée) guest.
inviter [ɛvi'te], *v.t.* to invite, to request; to incite, to tempt.
invocation [ɛvɔka'sjɔ̃], *n.f.* invocation.
involontaire [ɛvɔlɔ̃'tɛ:r], *a.* involuntary, unwilling.
involontairement [ɛvɔlɔ̃tɛr'mã], *adv.* involuntarily.
invoquer [ɛvɔ'ke], *v.t.* to invoke, to call upon; to appeal to.
invraisemblable [ɛvrɛsã'blabl], *a.* unlikely, improbable.
invraisemblablement [ɛvrɛsãblablə'mã], *adv.* improbably.
invraisemblance [ɛvrɛsã'blã:s], *n.f.* unlikelihood, improbability.
invulnérable [ɛvylne'rabl], *a.* invulnerable.
iode [jɔd], *n.m.* iodine.
ion [jɔ̃], *n.m.* (*Phys.*) ion.
ionisation [jɔniza'sjɔ̃], *n.f.* ionization.
ionosphère [jɔnɔs'fɛ:r], *n.f.* ionosphere.
iota [jo'ta], *n.m.* iota, jot, tittle.
Irak [i'rak], **l'**, *m.* Iraq.
irakien [ira'kjɛ̃], *a.* (*fem.* -enne) Iraqi.—*n.m.* (**Irakien**, *fem.* -enne) Iraqi (*person*).
Iran [i'rã], **l'**, *m.* Iran.
iranien [ira'njɛ̃], *a.* (*fem.* -enne) Iranian.—*n.m.* (**Iranien**, *fem.* -enne) Iranian (*person*).
irascibilité [irasibili'te], *n.f.* irascibility.
irascible [ira'sibl], *a.* irascible, irritable.
iridescence [iride'sã:s], *n.f.* iridescence.
iridescent [iride'sã], *a.* iridescent.
iris [i'ri:s], *n.m. inv.* iris; rainbow.
irisé [iri'ze], *a.* rainbow-colored, iridescent.
irlandais [irlã'dɛ], *a.* Irish.—*n.m.* Irish (*language*); (**Irlandais**, *fem.* -aise) Irishman, Irishwoman.
Irlande [ir'lãd], **l'**, *f.* Ireland.
ironie [irɔ'ni], *n.f.* irony, mockery, raillery.
ironique [irɔ'nik], *a.* ironical.
irradiation [irradja'sjɔ̃], *n.f.* irradiation.
irradier [irra'dje], *v.t.* to radiate through; (*C*) to broadcast.
irraisonnable [irrɛzɔ'nabl], *a.* irrational.
irraisonnablement [irrɛzɔnablə'mã], *adv.* irrationally.
irrationnel [irrasjɔ'nɛl], *a.* (*fem.* -elle) irrational.
irrationnellement [irrasjɔnɛl'mã], *adv.* irrationally.
irréalisable [irreali'zabl], *a.* impossible, impracticable.
irréconciliable [irrekɔ̃si'ljabl], *a.* irreconcilable.
irrécusable [irreky'zabl], *a.* unexceptionable, unimpeachable.
irréductible [irredyk'tibl], *a.* irreducible; (*fig.*) unyielding.
irréel [irre'ɛl], *a.* (*fem.* -éelle) unreal.—*n.m.* unreality.
irréfléchi [irrefle'ʃi], *a.* thoughtless, inconsiderate.
irréflexion [irreflɛk'sjɔ̃], *n.f.* thoughtlessness, heedlessness.
irréfutable [irrefy'tabl], *a.* irrefutable.
irrégularité [irregylari'te], *n.f.* irregularity.
irrégulier [irregy'lje], *a.* (*fem.* -ière) irregular.
irrégulièrement [irregyljɛr'mã], *adv.* irregularly.

irréligieux [irreli'ʒjø], a. (fem. -euse) irreligious.

irrémédiable [irreme'djabl], a. irremediable, irreparable, irretrievable.

irrémédiablement [irremedjablə'mɑ̃], adv. irremediably, irreparably.

irrémissible [irremi'sibl], a. irremissible, unpardonable.

irremplaçable [irrɑ̃plaˈsabl], a. irreplaceable.

irréparable [irrepa'rabl], a. irreparable.

irrépressible [irrepreˈsibl], a. irrepressible.

irréprochable [irreproˈʃabl], a. irreproachable.

irrésistible [irrezis'tibl], a. irresistible.

irrésistiblement [irrezistiblə'mɑ̃], adv. irresistibly.

irrésolu [irrezo'ly], a. irresolute, wavering.

irrésolument [irrezoly'mɑ̃], adv. irresolutely.

irrésolution [irrezoly'sjɔ̃], n.f. irresolution, indecision.

irrespectueusement [irrespɛktɥøz'mɑ̃], adv. disrespectfully.

irrespectueux [irrespɛk'tɥø], a. (fem. -euse) disrespectful.

irresponsabilité [irrespɔ̃sabili'te], n.f. irresponsibility.

irresponsable [irrespɔ̃'sabl], a. irresponsible.

irrétrécissable [irretresi'sabl], a. unshrinkable.

irrévérence [irreve'rɑ̃ːs], n.f. irreverence, disrespect.

irrévocable [irrevoˈkabl], a. irrevocable.

irrévocablement [irrevokablə'mɑ̃], adv. irrevocably.

irrigateur [irriga'tœːr], n.m. watering engine; garden hose.

irrigation [irriga'sjɔ̃], n.f. irrigation.

irriguer [irri'ge], v.t. to irrigate, to water.

irritabilité [irritabili'te], n.f. irritability.

irritable [irri'tabl], a. irritable.

irritant [irri'tɑ̃], a. irritating, provoking.

irritation [irrita'sjɔ̃], n.f. irritation, exasperation.

irriter [irri'te], v.t. to irritate, to incense, to anger; to provoke, to excite. **s'irriter**, v.r. to grow angry; to become irritated.

irruption [irryp'sjɔ̃], n.f. irruption, raid; overflow, flood; *faire irruption dans*, to invade.

Isaïe [iza'i], m. Isaiah.

Islam [is'lam], n.m. Islam.

islandais [islɑ̃'dɛ], a. Icelandic.—n.m. Icelandic (language); (**Islandais**, fem. -aise) Icelander.

Islande [is'lɑ̃d], l', f. Iceland.

isobare [izo'bar], n.f. isobar.

isocèle or **isoscèle** [izo'sɛl], a. (Geom.) isosceles.

isolant [izo'lɑ̃], a. insulating; *bouteille isolante*, vacuum flask.

isolateur [izola'tœːr], a. (fem. -trice) insulating.—n.m. insulator.

isolation [izola'sjɔ̃], n.f. insulation; isolation.

isolé [izo'le], a. isolated; lonely, solitary; detached; insulated; apart.

isolement [izol'mɑ̃], n.m. loneliness, isolation; insulation.

isolément [izole'mɑ̃], adv. separately.

isoler [izo'le], v.t. to isolate; to insulate; to detach; to separate.

isotope [izo'top], n.m. isotope.

Israël [isra'ɛl], l', m. Israel.

israélien [israe'ljɛ̃], a. (fem. -enne) Israeli(i). —n.m. (**Israélien**, fem. -enne) Israeli (person).

issu [i'sy], a. born, descended, sprung from.

issue [i'sy], n.f. issue, outlet; escape; (fig.) end, event.

isthme [ism], n.m. isthmus.

Italie [ita'li], l', f. Italy.

italien [ita'ljɛ̃], a. (fem. -enne) Italian.— n.m. Italian (language); (**Italien**, fem. -enne) Italian (person).

italique [ita'lik], a. and n.m. italic.

itinéraire [itine'rɛːr], a. pertaining to roads etc.—n.m. itinerary, route; guide-book.

itinérant [itine'rɑ̃], a. itinerant.

ivoire [i'vwaːr], n.m. ivory; (fig.) whiteness; *la Côte d'Ivoire*, Ivory Coast.

ivraie [i'vrɛ], n.f. darnel, tare.

ivre [iːvr], a. drunk; intoxicated; (fig.) transported; *ivre mort*, dead drunk.

ivresse [i'vrɛs], n.f. drunkenness, intoxication; (fig.) frenzy, rapture.

ivrogne [i'vrɔɲ], a. drunken.—n. drunkard.

ivrognerie [ivro'ɲri], n.f. habitual drunkenness.

J

J, j [ʒi], n.m. the tenth letter of the alphabet.

jabot [ʒa'bo], n.m. crop (of a bird); frill (of a shirt or blouse); jabot.

jaboter [ʒabo'te], v.i. (colloq.) to prattle, to chatter.

jacasser [ʒaka'se], v.i. to chatter (of the magpie); (fig.) to chatter, to jabber.

jachère [ʒa'ʃɛːr], n.f. fallow.

jacinthe [ʒa'sɛ̃ːt], n.f. jacinthe; hyacinth.

Jacques [ʒɑːk], m. James.

jade [ʒad], n.m. jade.

jadis [ʒɑ'dis], adv. of old, formerly.

jaguar [ʒa'gwaːr], n.m. jaguar.

jaillir [ʒa'jiːr], v.i. to spout, to gush; to shoot out or up.

jaillissant [ʒaji'sɑ̃], a. spouting, gushing.

jaillissement [ʒajis'mɑ̃], n.m. gushing, spouting, flashing.

jais [ʒɛ], n.m. jet.

jalon [ʒa'lɔ̃], n.m. levelling staff, surveying staff; (fig.) landmark, beacon.

jalonnement [ʒalon'mɑ̃], n.m. (Land surveying) staking out, marking out.

jalonner [ʒalo'ne], v.t. to mark or stake out.—v.i. to place land marks etc.

jalousement [ʒaluz'mɑ̃], adv. jealously.

jalouser [ʒalu'ze], v.t. to be jealous of, to envy.

jalousie [ʒalu'zi], n.f. jealousy, envy; Venetian blind; (Bot.) sweet william.

jaloux [ʒa'lu], a. (fem. -ouse) jealous; envious; desirous, anxious.—n.m. (fem. -ouse) jealous person.

195

jamaïquain [ʒamai'kɛ̃], *a.* Jamaican.—*n.m.* (**Jamaïquain,** *fem.* **-aine**) Jamaican (*person*).

Jamaïque [ʒama'ik], **la**, *f.* Jamaica.

jamais [ʒa'mɛ], *adv.* (*neg.*) never, (*affirm.*) ever; *à jamais,* for ever; *jamais de la vie,* not on your life!; *mieux vaut tard que jamais,* better late than never.

jambage [ʒɑ̃'ba:ʒ], *n.m.* jamb (*of a door etc.*); down-stroke, pot-hook (*in writing*).

jambe [ʒɑ̃:b], *n.f.* leg; shank; *courir à toutes jambes,* to run as fast as one can; *prendre ses jambes à son cou,* to take to one's heels.

jambière [ʒɑ̃'bjɛ:r], *n.f.* legging, leg guard.

jambon [ʒɑ̃'bɔ̃], *n.m.* ham.

jamboree [ʒãbɔ'ri], *n.m.* jamboree.

jante [ʒɑ̃:t], *n.f.* felloe, rim (*of a wheel*).

janvier [ʒɑ̃'vje], *n.m.* January.

Japon [ʒa'pɔ̃], **le**, *m.* Japan.

japonais [ʒapo'nɛ], *a.* Japanese.—*n.m.* Japanese (*language*); (**Japonais,** *fem.* **-aise**) Japanese (*person*).

japper [ʒa'pe], *v.i.* to yelp, to yap.

jaquette [ʒa'kɛt], *n.f.* morning coat, tail-coat; woman's jacket; dust cover (*of book*).

jardin [ʒar'dɛ̃], *n.m.* garden.

jardinage [ʒardi'na:ʒ], *n.m.* gardening; garden produce.

jardiner [ʒardi'ne], *v.i.* to garden.

jardinier [ʒardi'nje], *a.* (*fem.* **-ière**) (of the) garden.—*n.m.* (*fem.* **-ière**) gardener.—*n.f.* (**-ière**) flower-stand, jardinière.

jardiniste [ʒardi'nist], *n.* landscape-gardener.

jargon [ʒar'gɔ̃], *n.m.* jargon, gibberish; lingo.

jarre [ʒa:r], *n.f.* jar.

jarret [ʒa're], *n.m.* ham (*of man*); hough, hock (*of horse*).

jarretière [ʒar'tjɛr], *n.f.* (lady's) garter.

jars (1) [ʒa:r], *n.m.* gander.

jars (2) [ʒa:r], *n.m.* (*another form of jargon*) slang.

jaser [ʒa'ze], *v.i.* to chatter, to gossip.

jaserie [ʒaz'ri], *n.f.* chatter; gossip.

jaseur [ʒa'zœ:r], *a.* (*fem.* **-euse**) talkative.—*n.m.* (*fem.* **-euse**) chatterer, chatterbox.

jasmin [ʒas'mɛ̃], *n.m.* jasmine.

jaspe [ʒasp], *n.m.* jasper.

jasper [ʒas'pe], *v.t.* to marble, to vein, to variegate.

jaspure [ʒas'py:r], *n.f.* marbling, veining.

jatte [ʒat], *n.f.* bowl, platter; dog's bowl.

jauge [ʒo:ʒ], *n.f.* gauge; (*Naut.*) tonnage.

jaugeage [ʒo'ʒa:ʒ], *n.m.* gauging.

jauger [ʒo'ʒe], *v.t.* (*conjug. like* MANGER) to gauge, to measure the capacity of; (*Naut.*) to draw (*so many feet of water*).

jaunâtre [ʒo'nɑ:tr], *a.* yellowish.

jaune [ʒo:n], *a.* yellow; *rire jaune,* to give a sickly smile.—*n.m.* yellow; *jaune d'œuf,* egg yolk.

jaunir [ʒo'ni:r], *v.t.* to make yellow, to dye yellow.—*v.i.* to grow yellow, to turn yellow.

jaunissant [ʒoni'sɑ̃], *a.* turning yellow, yellowing; ripening.

jaunisse [ʒo'nis], *n.f.* jaundice.

javanais [ʒava'nɛ], *a.* Javanese.—*n.m.* (**Javanais,** *fem.* **-aise**) Javanese (*person*).

javeau [ʒa'vo], *n.m.* (*pl.* **-eaux**) sandbank.

javeline [ʒa'vlin], *n.f.* javelin.

javelle [ʒa'vɛl], *n.f.* swathe, loose sheaf.

javelot [ʒa'vlo], *n.m.* javelin.

jazz [(d)ʒɑ:z], *n.m.* jazz.

je [ʒə], (**j'**, *before a vowel sound*), *pron.* I.

Jean [ʒɑ̃], *m.* John [JEANNOT].

Jeanne [ʒɑ(:)n], *f.* Joan, Jane, Jean.

Jeannot [ʒa'no], *m.* Johnny, Jock.

jeep [(d)ʒip], *n.f.* jeep.

jésuite [ʒe'zɥit], *a.* Jesuit.—*n.m.* (**Jésuite**) Jesuit.

Jésus [ʒe'zy], *m.* Jesus.

jet [ʒɛ], *n.m.* casting, cast, throw; jet, gush, spurt (*of water*); sudden ray (*of light*); casting (*of metal*); shoot, sprout (*of plants*); spout (*of pump etc.*); new swarm (*of bees*); *arme de jet,* missile weapon.

jetée [ʒə'te], *n.f.* jetty, pier; breakwater.

jeter [ʒə'te], *v.t.* (*conjug. like* APPELER) to throw, to fling, to hurl; to throw up; to throw down, to knock down; to throw out; to mold; to shoot out; to send forth; to empty; to discharge. **se jeter,** *v.r.* to throw oneself, to fling oneself; to fall upon (*attack*); to flow (*of rivers etc.*).

jeton [ʒə'tɔ̃], *n.m.* token, counter; voucher.

jeu [ʒø], *n.m.* (*pl.* **jeux**) play, sport; game; fun; gambling; (*fig.*) stake; manner of playing; performance (*of players*); (*Mach.*) working; clearance; play.

jeudi [ʒø'di], *n.m.* Thursday.

jeun (à) [a'ʒœ̃], *adv.* fasting, sober, on an empty stomach.

jeune [ʒœn], *a.* young, youthful; junior; new; early, unripe, green.—*n.* young person *or* animal.

jeûne [ʒø:n], *n.m.* fasting; fast, abstinence.

jeûner [ʒø'ne], *v.i.* to fast.

jeunesse [ʒœ'nɛs], *n.f.* youth, young days; youthfulness; freshness, prime; young people.

jeunet [ʒœ'nɛ], *a.* (*fem.* **-ette**) (*colloq.*) very young.

jiu-jitsu [(d)ʒyʒi'tsy], *n.m.* ju-jitsu.

joaillerie [ʒwaj'ri], *n.f.* jeweller's trade *or* business; jewelry, jewels.

joaillier [ʒwa'je], *n.m.* (*fem.* **-ière**) jeweller.

jobard [ʒo'ba:r], *n.m.* (*colloq.*) sucker, mug, fool.

jockey [ʒo'kɛ], *n.m.* jockey.

jocrisse [ʒo'kris], *n.m.* dolt, simpleton.

joie [ʒwa], *n.f.* joy, happiness, joyfulness, gladness; glee, mirth.

joignant [ʒwa'ɲɑ̃], *a.* and *prep.* next to, adjoining.

joindre [ʒwɛ̃:dr], *v.t. irr.* (*conjug. like* CRAINDRE) to join, to put together, to unite, to combine; to add; to meet; to overtake.—*v.i.* to join, to meet. **se joindre,** *v.r.* to join, to be joined, to be united; to be adjoining, to be adjacent; to be added.

joint [ʒwɛ̃], *a.* joined, united; added.—*n.m.* joint; seam, junction.

jointé [ʒwɛ̃'te], *a.* jointed.

jointure [ʒwɛ̃'ty:r], *n.f.* joint, jointing, articulation.

joli [ʒo'li], *a.* pretty, pleasing, neat; fine; nice.—*n.m.* what is pretty; *le joli de la chose c'est que . . . ,* the best of the thing is that . . .

joliment [ʒoli'mɑ̃], *adv.* prettily; (*iron.*) nicely, finely; (*colloq.*) awfully, jolly, much, very.

jonc [ʒɔ̃], *n.m.* (*Bot.*) rush; cane, Malacca cane; keeper, guard (*ring*).

jupe

jonchée [ʒɔ̃'ʃe], *n.f.* strewing (*of flowers*).
joncher [ʒɔ̃'ʃe], *v.t.* to strew; to heap; to scatter.
jonction [ʒɔ̃k'sjɔ̃], *n.f.* junction, joining.
jongler [ʒɔ̃'gle], *v.i.* to juggle.
jonglerie [ʒɔ̃glə'ri], *n.f.* juggling.
jongleur [ʒɔ̃'glœːr], *n.m.* juggler; (*fig.*) trickster.
jonque [ʒɔ̃ːk], *n.f.* junk (*Chinese vessel*).
jonquille [ʒɔ̃'kiːj], *n.f.* jonquil.—*a. inv.* and *n.m.* pale yellow, jonquil (*color*).
Jordanie [ʒɔrda'ni], **la**, *f.* Jordan.
jordanien [ʒɔrda'njɛ̃], *a.* Jordanian.—*n.m.* (**Jordanien**, *fem.* -**enne**) Jordanian (*person*).
Joseph [ʒɔ'zef], *m.* Joseph.
jouable [ʒwabl], *a.* playable.
joue [ʒu], *n.f.* cheek; **coucher** or **mettre en joue**, to take aim at.
jouer [ʒwe], *v.t.* to play; to stake; to gamble away; to move (*a piece*); to perform, to act; to pretend to be; to imitate; to ridicule; to deceive.—*v.i.* to play, to amuse oneself; to gambol, to frolic; to gamble, to run the risk; to speculate (*on the funds*); to work, to work loose (*of machinery etc.*); to act, to perform. **se jouer**, *v.r.* to sport, to play; to make game (*of*); to make light of.
jouet [ʒwɛ], *n.m.* plaything, toy; laughing-stock, jest, sport.
joueur [ʒwœːr], *n.m.* (*fem.* -**euse**) player; gambler; speculator; performer (*on an instrument*).
joufflu [ʒu'fly], *a.* chubby, chubby-cheeked.
joug [ʒu(g)], *n.m.* yoke; bondage, slavery.
jouir [ʒwiːr], *v.i.* to enjoy, to revel; to be in possession (*de*).
jouissance [ʒwi'sãːs], *n.f.* enjoyment; possession, use; delight; interest payable.
jouissant [ʒwi'sã], *a.* enjoying, in possession (*de*).
joujou [ʒu'ʒu], *n.m.* (*pl.* -**oux**) plaything, toy.
jour [ʒuːr], *n.m.* day, daylight; light; daybreak; day time; opening, gap; **broderie à jours**, open-work embroidery; **donner le jour à**, to give birth to; **plat du jour**, today's special; **se faire jour**, to force one's way through; **un jour de fête**, a holiday.
Jourdain [ʒur'dɛ̃], **le**, *m.* Jordan (*river*).
journal [ʒur'nal], *n.m.* (*pl.* -**aux**) journal, diary; newspaper; (*Comm.*) day-book.
journalier [ʒurna'lje], *a.* (*fem.* -**ière**) daily, diurnal.—*n.m.* journeyman, day laborer.
journalisme [ʒurna'lism], *n.m.* journalism.
journaliste [ʒurna'list], *n.* journalist.
journée [ʒur'ne], *n.f.* day (time), day's work or wages; day's journey; battle; historic day; **toute la journée**, all day (long).
journellement [ʒurnɛl'mã], *adv.* daily, every day.
joute [ʒut], *n.f.* joust, tilting match; contest; (*C*) game.
jouter [ʒu'te], *v.i.* to joust, to tilt.
jouteur [ʒu'tœːr], *n.m.* tilter; (*fig.*) antagonist, adversary.
jovial [ʒɔ'vjal], *a.* (*m. pl.* -**aux**) jovial, jolly, merry.
jovialement [ʒɔvjal'mã], *adv.* jovially.
jovialité [ʒɔvjali'te], *n.f.* joviality, jollity.
joyau [ʒwa'jo], *n.m.* (*pl.* -**aux**) jewel.
joyeusement [ʒwajøz'mã], *adv.* cheerfully, joyfully.
joyeuseté [ʒwajøz'te], *n.f.* (*fam.*) joke, jest.

joyeux [ʒwa'jø], *a.* (*fem.* -**euse**) joyful, merry; cheerful.
jubilaire [ʒybi'lɛːr], *a.* jubilee; (*fig.*) of fifty years' standing (*of persons etc.*).
jubilant [ʒybi'lã], *a.* jubilant, delighted.
jubilation [ʒybila'sjɔ̃], *n.f.* jubilation, rejoicing.
jubilé [ʒybi'le], *n.m.* jubilee; (*fig.*) golden wedding.
jubiler [ʒybi'le], *v.i.* to jubilate, to exult.
jucher [ʒy'ʃe], *v.i.* to roost, to perch; to lodge (*at the top of a house etc.*). **se jucher**, *v.r.* to go to roost; to perch (*oneself*).
juchoir [ʒy'ʃwaːr], *n.m.* roosting-place, perch.
judaïque [ʒyda'ik], *a.* Judaical, Jewish.
judaïsme [ʒyda'ism], *n.m.* Judaism.
judas [ʒy'da], *n.m.* Judas, traitor; peep-hole (*in a door etc.*).
Judée [ʒy'de], **la**, *f.* Judaea.
judicature [ʒydika'tyːr], *n.f.* judicature, magistracy.
judiciaire [ʒydi'sjɛːr], *a.* judiciary, judicial; legal.
judiciairement [ʒydisjɛr'mã], *adv.* judicially, by authority of justice.
judicieusement [ʒydisjøz'mã], *adv.* judiciously, discreetly.
judicieux [ʒydi'sjø], *a.* (*fem.* -**euse**) judicious, wise, discreet.
juge [ʒyːʒ], *n.m.* judge; magistrate, justice; (*pl.*) bench.
jugé [ʒy'ʒe], *a.* judged.—*n.m.* **au jugé**, at a guess.
jugement [ʒyʒ'mã], *n.m.* judgment; opinion; trial; sentence; good sense; **jugement arbitral**, award; **jugement provisoire**, decree nisi; **jugement définitif**, decree absolute.
juger [ʒy'ʒe], *v.t.* (*conjug. like* MANGER) to judge; to try; to pass sentence on; to consider, to think.—*v.i.* to judge (*de*); to give judgment, to deem. **se juger**, *v.r.* to judge oneself; to deem oneself; to be judged.
jugulaire [ʒygy'lɛːr], *a.* (*Anat.*) jugular.—*n.f.* jugular vein; chin strap.
juguler [ʒygy'le], *v.t.* to strangle; (*fig.*) to torment; to fleece.
juif [ʒɥif], *a.* (*fem.* **juive**) Jewish.—*n.m.* (**Juif**, *fem.* **Juive**) Jew, Jewess.
juillet [ʒɥi'jɛ], *n.m.* July.
juin [ʒɥɛ̃], *n.m.* June.
juiverie [ʒɥi'vri], *n.f.* ghetto (*Jews' quarter*).
jujube [ʒy'ʒyb], *n.f.* jujube (*fruit*).—*n.m.* or **pâte de jujube**, jujube (*lozenge*).
julep [ʒy'lɛp], *n.m.* julep.
julienne [ʒy'ljɛn], *n.f.* julienne (*vegetable soup*).
jumeau [ʒy'mo], *a.* (*fem.* -**elle**, *m. pl.* -**eaux**) twin; double (*of fruit etc.*).—*n.m.* twin (brother).
jumelage [ʒym'la:ʒ], *n.m.* twinning (*of towns etc.*).
jumelé [ʒym'le], *a.* twin, in couples; **maison jumelée**, semi-detached house; (*horse racing*) **pari jumelé**, each-way bet.
jumelle [ʒy'mɛl], *n.f.* twin (sister); (*pl.*) binoculars; **jumelles de campagne**, field glasses; **jumelles de théâtre**, opera glasses; **jumelles de manchettes**, cuff links.
jument [ʒy'mã], *n.f.* mare.
jungle [ʒɔ̃:gl], *n.f.* jungle.
jupe [ʒyp], *n.f.* skirt.

197

Jupiter [ʒypi'tɛr], *m.* Jupiter, Jove.
jupon [ʒy'pɔ̃], *n.m.* petticoat.
juré [ʒy're], *a.* sworn.—*n.m.* juror, juryman.
jurement [ʒyr'mɑ̃], *n.m.* oath; swearing.
jurer [ʒy're], *v.t.* to swear by; to swear, to vow, to take an oath that; to blaspheme.—*v.i.* to swear, to take an oath; to blaspheme; (*fig.*) to contrast, to jar, to clash (*of colors etc.*).
juridiction [ʒyridik'sjɔ̃], *n.f.* jurisdiction; department, province.
juridique [ʒyri'dik], *a.* juridical, judicial, legal.
juridiquement [ʒyridik'mɑ̃], *adv.* juridically, judicially.
jurisprudence [ʒyrispry'dɑ̃:s], *n.f.* jurisprudence.
juriste [ʒy'rist], *n.m.* jurist.
juron [ʒy'rɔ̃], *n.m.* oath, curse, swear word.
jury [ʒy'ri], *n.m.* jury; board, committee.
jus [ʒy], *n.m.* juice; gravy.
jusque or *jusques [ʒysk], *prep.* even to, as far as; till, until; down to; up to.
juste [ʒyst], *a.* just, equitable; fair, legitimate, lawful; proper, fit; exact; well-fitting; tight; *au plus juste prix*, at the lowest price; *un homme juste*, a righteous man.—*n.m.* upright man, virtuous man; what is just.—*adv.* just, exactly, precisely; (*Mus.*) true.
justement [ʒystə'mɑ̃], *adv.* justly, precisely; justifiably.
justesse [ʒys'tɛs], *n.f.* justness, exactness, precision, accuracy; appropriateness.
justice [ʒys'tis], *n.f.* justice; righteousness, probity; fairness, impartiality; reason; courts of justice, judges; *palais de justice*, law court.
justifiable [ʒysti'fjabl], *a.* justifiable; warrantable.
justification [ʒystifika'sjɔ̃], *n.f.* justification, vindication, proof.
justifier [ʒysti'fje], *v.t.* to justify, to vindicate, to make good. se justifier, *v.r.* to justify, clear *or* vindicate oneself.
jute [ʒyt], *n.m.* jute.
juteux [ʒy'tø], *a.* (*fem.* -euse) juicy.
juvénile [ʒyve'nil], *a.* juvenile, youthful.
juvénilement [ʒyvenil'mɑ̃], *adv.* boyishly, in a juvenile manner.
juxtaposer [ʒykstapo'ze], *v.t.* to place side by side. se juxtaposer, *v.r.* to be in juxtaposition.
juxtaposition [ʒykstapozi'sjɔ̃], *n.f.* juxtaposition.

K

K, k [kɑ], *n.m.* the eleventh letter of the alphabet; *Échelle K* (*viz.* Kelvin), absolute scale (*of temperature*).
kakatoès [kakatɔ'ɛs], [CACATOIS].
kaki [ka'ki], *a. inv.* khaki (*color*).
kaléidoscope [kaleidɔs'kɔp], *n.m.* kaleidoscope.
kangourou [kɑ̃gu'ru], *n.m.* kangaroo.

kaolin [kaɔ'lɛ̃], *n.m.* kaolin, porcelain clay, china clay.
kapok or kapoc [ka'pɔk], *n.m.* kapok.
kascher or kacher [ka'ʃɛr], kachir [ka'ʃir], *a.* (*Jew. Relig.*) kosher.
kayac [ka'jak], *n.m.* kayak.
Kénia [ke'nja], le, *m.* Kenya.
képi [ke'pi], *n.m.* kepi, military cap; peak cap.
kermesse [kɛr'mɛs], *n.f.* kermis (*in the Netherlands*); kermesse; village fair.
kérosène [kerɔ'zɛ:n], *n.m.* kerosene, coal oil.
kidnapper [kidna'pe], *v.t.* to kidnap.
kilo [ki'lo], *n.m.* (*abbr.*) kilogramme.
kilocycle [kilɔ'sikl], *n.m.* kilocycle.
kilogramme [kilɔ'gram], *n.m.* kilogramme (*2.2 lb. avoirdupois*).
kilomètre [kilɔ'mɛtr], *n.m.* kilometre (*1093.6 yards*).
kilowatt [kilɔ'wat], *n.m.* kilowatt.
kimono [kimɔ'no], *n.m.* kimono.
kiosque [kjɔsk], *n.m.* kiosk; (*Naut.*) house; *kiosque à journaux*, newspaper stand; *kiosque à musique*, bandstand.
klakson or klaxon [klak'sɔ̃], *n.m.* klaxon, hooter, horn.
kleptomane [klɛptɔ'man], *a.* and *n.* kleptomaniac.
kleptomanie [klɛptɔma'ni], *n.f.* kleptomania.
kola or cola [kɔ'la], *n.m.* kola.
Kominform [kɔmɛ̃'fɔrm], *n.m.* Cominform.
Komintern [kɔmɛ̃'tɛrn], *n.m.* Comintern.
Koweit [kɔ'weit], le, *m.* Kuwait.
kyrielle [ki'rjɛl], *n.f.* litany; (*fig.*) long string (*of words etc.*), long tedious story.
kyste [kist], *n.m.* (*Path.*) cyst.

L

L, 1 [ɛl], *n.m.* or *f.* the twelfth letter of the alphabet.
l', *art.* and *pron.* (*by elision of* le *or* la) the; him, her, it.
la (1) [la], *art.* and *pron. f.* the; her, it.
la (2) [la], *n.m.* (*Mus.*) la; the note A.
là [la], *adv.* and *int.* there, thither; then (*of time*); *çà et là*, here and there; *là là*, now now! there! there now! *là où*, where; *par là*, that way.
là-bas [la'ba], *adv.* there, over there.
labbe [lab], *n.m.* (*Orn.*) skua.
label [la'bɛl], *n.m.* (*Ind.*) label; brand, mark.
labeur [la'bœ:r], *n.m.* labor, work, toil.
laboratoire [labɔra'twa:r], *n.m.* laboratory.
laborieusement [labɔrjøz'mɑ̃], *adv.* laboriously; painfully.
laborieux [labɔ'rjø], *a.* (*fem.* -euse) laborious, hard-working.
labour [la'bu:r], *n.m.* ploughing, tillage; arable land.
labourable [labu'rabl], *a.* arable.
labourage [labu'ra:ʒ], *n.m.* tillage, ploughing; dressing.
labourer [labu're], *v.t.* to plough, to till; to dig, to turn up; to dress; to toil through.

laboureur [labu'rœ:r], *n.m.* husbandman, plowman.

laboureuse [labu'rø:z], *n.f.* tractor plow.

laburne [la'byrn], *n.m.* laburnum.

labyrinthe [labi'rɛ̃:t], *n.m.* labyrinth, maze.

lac [lak], *n.m.* lake.

laçage [la'sa:ʒ], *n.m.* lacing.

lacer [la'se], *v.t.* (*conjug. like* COMMENCER) to lace.

lacération [lasera'sjɔ̃], *n.f.* laceration.

lacérer [lase're], *v.t.* (*conjug. like* CÉDER) to lacerate, to tear.

lacet [la'sɛ], *n.m.* lace, shoe-lace; noose; bow-string (*for strangling*); winding, hairpin bend (*of road etc.*); (*pl.*) toils.

lâche [lɑːʃ], *a.* loose, slack; faint-hearted, cowardly; base, mean, shameful; craven; dastard.—*adv.* loosely.

lâché [la'ʃe], *a.* loosely, slipshod.

lâchement [lɑʃ'mɑ̃], *adv.* in a dastardly *or* cowardly manner; loosely; shamefully.

lâcher [la'ʃe], *v.t.* to loosen, to slacken; to let go, to release; to unbind; to blurt out; to let fly, to discharge; to let down (*someone*).—*v.i.* to slacken, to become loose; to slip; (*Spt.*) to give up.

lâcheté [lɑʃ'te], *n.f.* cowardice; baseness, meanness.

lacis [la'si], *n.m.* network.

laconique [lakɔ'nik], *a.* laconic.

laconiquement [lakɔnik'mɑ̃], *adv.* laconically.

lacs [lɑ], *n.m. inv.* string; noose; trap; *lacs d'amour*, love-knot.

lacté [lak'te], *a.* lacteous, milky; *la voie lactée*, the Milky Way.

lacune [la'kyn], *n.f.* gap, break, hiatus, blank.

là-dedans [lada'dɑ̃], *adv.* in there.

là-dehors [lada'ɔ:r], *adv.* outside.

là-dessous [la'tsu], *adv.* under there.

là-dessus [la'tsy], *adv.* on that; thereupon.

ladite [la'dit], [LEDIT].

ladre [lɑ:dr], *a.* leprous; (*fig.*) mean, sordid, stingy; unfeeling.—*n.m.* (*fem.* -esse) leper; (*fig.*) sordid person.

ladrerie [ladrə'ri], *n.f.* sordid avarice, stinginess.

lagune [la'gyn], *n.f.* lagoon.

là-haut [la'o], *adv.* up there; upstairs.

lai [lɛ]. *n.m.* lay (*poem, song*).

laïc [LAÏQUE].

laid [lɛ], *a.* ugly, unsightly; unseemly, unbecoming.—*n.m.* ugliness; (*fem.* -e) ugly person, creature etc.; naughty boy *or* girl.

laidement [lɛd'mɑ̃], *adv.* in an ugly way.

laideron [lɛd'rɔ̃], *n.m.* (*fem.* -onne) ugly creature.

laideur [lɛ'dœ:r], *n.f.* ugliness, uncomeliness; unseemliness.

laie [lɛ], *n.f.* path (*in a forest*).

lainage [lɛ'na:ʒ], *n.m.* woollens, woollen goods.

laine [lɛn], *n.f.* wool; *laine filée*, yarn; *laine peignée*, worsted; *tapis de haute laine*, thick-pile carpet; *tout laine*, pure wool.

lainerie [lɛn'ri], *n.f.* woollen goods, woollens; wool trade, shop etc.

laineux [lɛ'nø], *a.* (*fem.* -euse) woolly, fleecy.

lainier [lɛ'nje], *a.* (*fem.* -ière) of wool, woollen.—*n.m.* (*fem.* -ière) wool merchant, wool worker.

laïque *or* **laïc** [la'ik], *a.* lay, secular.—*n.* layman, lay person.

laisse [lɛ:s], *n.f.* string, leash, lead.

laisser [lɛ'se], *v.t.* to leave, to quit; to leave behind, to part with; to bequeath; to permit, to let, to allow; to let alone; to leave off; to give up. **se laisser**, *v.r.* to allow oneself, to let oneself.

laisser-aller [lɛsea'le], *n.m.* unconstraint, negligence; slovenliness; indolence.

laisser-faire [lɛse'fɛ:r], *n.m.* non-interference.

laissez-passer [lɛsɛpa'se], *n.m. inv.* permit, leave, pass.

lait [lɛ], *n.m.* milk; *au lait*, with milk; *lait de chaux*, whitewash; *lait de poule*, egg-flip; *petit-lait* *or* *lait clair*, whey.

laitage [lɛ'ta:ʒ], *n.m.* milk puddings; milk products.

laiterie [lɛ'tri], *n.f.* dairy, dairy-farm.

laiteux [lɛ'tø], *a.* (*fem.* -euse) lacteous, milky.

laitier [lɛ'tje], *a.* (*fem.* -ière) pertaining to milk; having milk, milch (*of cows*).—*n.m.* (*fem.*-ière) milkman; milkmaid, dairy maid.—*n.f.* (*-ière*) milch cow; milk truck *or* cart.

laiton [lɛ'tɔ̃], *n.m.* brass, latten.

laitue [lɛ'ty], *n.f.* lettuce.

lama [la'ma], *n.m.* lama (*priest*); llama.

lambeau [lɑ̃'bo], *n.m.* (*pl.* -eaux) shred; rag; fragment, scrap.

lambin [lɑ̃'bɛ̃], *a.* slow, dawdling.—*n.m.* (*fem.* -e) dawdler, slowcoach.

lambiner [lɑ̃bi'ne], *v.i.* to dawdle, to dilly-dally.

lambrequin [lɑ̃brə'kɛ̃], *n.m.* valance, cut-out, pelmet.

lambris [lɑ̃'bri], *n.m.* panelling; wainscot; ceiling; (*fig.*) mansion, palace; canopy.

lambrissage [lɑ̃bri'sa:ʒ], *n.m.* wainscoting, panelling.

lambrisser [lɑ̃bri'se], *v.t.* to panel, to wainscot.

lame [lam], *n.f.* thin plate, leaf of metal; foil; knife (*of mower etc.*), blade; (*fig.*) sword; wave, billow.

lamé [la'me], *a.* spangled with gold or silver.

lamentable [lamɑ̃'tabl], *a.* lamentable, sad, distressing; pitiful.

lamentablement [lamɑ̃tablə'mɑ̃], *adv.* woefully.

lamentation [lamɑ̃ta'sjɔ̃], *n.f.* lamentation, wailing; lament; whining.

lamenter (se) [səlamɑ̃'te], *v.r.* to lament, to bewail.

laminage [lami'na:ʒ], *n.m.* laminating; rolling (*of gold etc.*).

laminer [lami'ne], *v.t.* to laminate, to roll.

laminoir [lami'nwa:r], *n.m.* flattening mill; rolling mill.

lampe [lɑ̃:p], *n.f.* lamp; (*Rad. Tel.*) tube; *lampe de bord*, (*Motor.*) dashboard light; *lampe de poche*, electric flashlight.

lampion [lɑ̃'pjɔ̃], *n.m.* illumination lamp, fairy-light; Chinese lantern; (*slang*) cocked hat.

lampiste [lɑ̃'pist], *n.m.* lamp maker; lamp lighter.

lampisterie [lɑ̃pis'tri], *n.f.* lamp room.

lamproie [lɑ̃'prwa], *n.f.* lamprey.

lance [lɑ̃:s], *n.f.* lance, spear; staff, flagstaff; nozzle (*of a fire-hose*).

lance-flammes [lãs'flam], *n.m. inv.* flame-thrower.
lancement [lãs'mã], *n.m.* throwing, darting; launching, launch.
lance-pierres [lãs'pjɛːr], *n.m. inv.* catapult.
lancer [lã'se], *v.t.* (*conjug. like* COMMENCER) to fling, to hurl, to throw; to launch; to shoot forth, to dart; to issue (*a warrant etc.*). **se lancer,** *v.r.* to dart, to spring; to rush, to fly; to launch out; (*fig.*) to make a start.
lancette [lã'sɛt], *n.f.* lancet.
lancier [lã'sje], *n.m.* lancer.
lancinant [lãsi'nã], *a.* shooting (*of pains*).
lande [lã:d], *n.f.* waste land, moor, heath.
langage [lã'ga:ʒ], *n.m.* language; speech, diction.
lange [lã:ʒ], *n.m.* diaper; swaddling-cloth; (*pl.*) swaddling clothes.
langoureusement [lãgurøz'mã], *adv.* languishingly, languidly.
langoureux [lãgu'rø], *a.* (*fem.* **-euse**) languishing, languid.
langouste [lã'gust], *n.f.* spiny lobster.
langoustine [lãgus'tin], *n.f.* large Brittany prawn; Dublin Bay prawn.
langue [lã:g], *n.f.* tongue; language; strip (*of land*); **avoir la langue bien pendue** or **bien affilée,** to have the gift of the gab; **avoir la langue liée,** to be tongue-tied.
languette [lã'gɛt], *n.f.* small tongue; tongue-like strip; partition; tongue (*of instruments*); index (*of a balance*); tongue (*of shoe*).
langueur [lã'gœːr], *n.f.* apathy, languor; weakness, weariness; debility.
languir [lã'giːr], *v.i.* to languish, to pine away; to droop; to linger; to flag.
languissant [lãgi'sã], *a.* languid, languishing, pining; (*Comm.*) dull, inactive.
lanière [la'njɛːr], *n.f.* thong, lash.
lanoline [lano'lin], *n.f.* lanoline.
lanterne [lã'tɛrn], *n.f.* lantern; street lamp; (*Arch.*) skylight; dawdler; **lanterne vénitienne,** Chinese lantern.
lanterner [lãtɛr'ne], *v.i.* to dawdle, to trifle away one's time.
Laos [laos], le, *m.* Laos.
laotien [lao'sjɛ̃], *a.* (*fem.* **-enne**) Laotian.— *n.m.* (**Laotien,** *fem.* **-enne**) Laotian (*person*).
lapement [lap'mã], *n.m.* lapping.
laper [la'pe], *v.i., v.t.* to lap (up).
lapidaire [lapi'dɛːr], *a.* and *n.m.* lapidary.
lapidation [lapida'sjõ], *n.f.* lapidation, stoning.
lapider [lapi'de], *v.t.* to lapidate, to stone to death; (*fig.*) to pelt, to abuse.
lapin [la'pɛ̃], *n.m.* rabbit.
lapis [la'piːs], **lapis lazuli** [lapislazy'li], *n.m. inv.* lapis lazuli.
lapon [la'põ], *a.* (*fem.* **-onne**) Lapp.—*n.m.* Lappish (*language*); (**Lapon,** *fem.* **-onne**) Laplander.
Laponie [lapo'ni], **la,** *f.* Lapland.
laps (1) [laps], *n.m.* lapse (*of time*).
laps (2) [laps], *a.* *lapsed, fallen into heresy.
lapsus [lap'sy:s], *n.m. inv.* slip, mistake.
laquais [la'kɛ], *n.m. inv.* lackey, footman.
laque [lak], *n.f.* lacquer, lac, lake (*paint*).— *n.m.* lacquer.
laquelle [la'kɛl], [LEQUEL].
laquer [la'ke], *v.t.* to lacquer, to japan.
larcin [lar'sɛ̃], *n.m.* larceny, pilfering; petty theft; **larcin littéraire,** plagiarism.

lard [laːr], *n.m.* fat (*esp. of pigs*); bacon; **flèche de lard,** flitch of bacon; **tranche de lard,** rasher of bacon.
larder [lar'de], *v.t.* to lard; to pink, to run through, to pierce.
lardon [lar'dõ], *n.m.* thin slice of bacon; (*fam.*) child, kid, brat.
large [larʒ], *a.* broad, wide; large, great, extensive; generous, liberal; lax, loose.— *n.m.* breadth, width; offing, open sea; **au large!** keep off! sheer off! **au large de Dieppe,** off Dieppe.
largement [larʒ'mã], *adv.* largely, abundantly; fully; liberally.
largesse [lar'ʒɛs], *n.f.* largess, bounty, munificence.
largeur [lar'ʒœːr], *n.f.* breadth, width; amplitude.
larme [larm], *n.f.* tear; drop; **fondre en larmes,** to burst into tears.
larmoiement [larmwa'mã], *n.m.* watering of the eyes.
larmoyant [larmwa'jã], *a.* weeping, in tears; tearful, whining.
larmoyer [larmwa'je], *v.i.* (*conjug. like* EMPLOYER) to shed tears; to whine, to snivel; to water (*of the eyes*).
larron [la'rõ], *n.m.* thief.
larve [larv], *n.f.* larva, grub.
laryngite [larɛ̃'ʒit], *n.f.* laryngitis.
larynx [la'rɛ̃:ks], *n.m. inv.* larynx.
las! (1) [lɑ], *int.* alas!
las (2) [lɑ], *a.* (*fem.* **lasse**) tired, weary, fatigued; bored; disgusted.
lascif [la'sif], *a.* (*fem.* **-cive**) lascivious, lewd, wanton.
lascivement [lasiv'mã], *adv.* lasciviously.
lassant [la'sã], *a.* tiresome, wearisome, tedious.
lasser [la'se], *v.t.* to tire, to weary, to fatigue, to wear out. **se lasser,** *v.r.* to tire, to grow tired, to be wearied.
lassitude [lasi'tyd], *n.f.* lassitude, weariness.
lasso [la'so], *n.m.* lasso.
latent [la'tã], *a.* latent, concealed, secret.
latéral [late'ral], *a.* (*m. pl.* **-aux**) lateral, side.
latéralement [lateral'mã], *adv.* laterally.
latin [la'tɛ̃], *a.* Latin.—*n.m.* Latin (*language*); **latin de cuisine,** dog Latin.—*n.m.* (**Latin,** (*fem.* **-ine**) Latin (*person*).
latitude [lati'tyd], *n.f.* latitude; room, space, margin.
latte [lat], *n.f.* lath.
latter [la'te], *v.t.* to lath.
lattis [la'ti], *n.m.* lathing, lath-work; laths.
laudanum [loda'nom], *n.m.* laudanum.
laudatif [loda'tif], *a.* (*fem.* **-tive**) laudatory.
lauréat [lore'a], *a.* laureate.—*n.m.* (*fem.* **-e**) prize-winner.
laurier [lo'rje], *n.m.* laurel, bay tree; (*fig.*) glory, honor.
lavable [la'vabl], *a.* washable.
lavabo [lava'bo], *n.m.* wash-basin; wash-stand; (*pl.*) conveniences.
lavage [la'vaʒ], *n.m.* washing; dilution.
lavande [la'vã:d], *n.f.* lavender.
lavandière [lavã'djɛːr], *n.f.* laundress, washerwoman; (*Orn.*) gray wagtail.
lavasse [la'vas], *n.f.* washy soup *or* wine.
lave [la:v], *n.f.* lava.
lavé [la've], *a.* washed out, faint.

lave-dos [lav'do], *n.m. inv.* back brush.
lavement [lav'mɑ̃], *n.m.* (*Med.*) enema.
laver [la've], *v.t.* to wash; to cleanse; to purify; to expiate; *laver à grande eau*, to swill; *laver la vaisselle*, to wash up; *machine à laver*, washing machine. **se laver**, *v.r.* to wash, to wash oneself; to clear oneself (*of an accusation*).
lavette [la'vɛt], *n.f.* dish mop.
laveur [la'vœːr], *n.m.* (*fem.* **-euse**) washer, scourer; *laveuse de vaisselle*, scullery maid.
lavoir [la'vwaːr], *n.m.* wash house.
laxatif [laksa'tif], *a.* (*fem.* **-tive**) laxative, opening.—*n.m.* laxative.
layette [lɛ'jɛt], *n.f.* box; baby's trousseau *or* outfit.
le [lə], *art.* and *pron. m.* the; him, it; so; *je le crois*, I think so.
lécher [le'ʃe], *v.t.* (*conjug. like* CÉDER) to lick; to lick up; (*fig.*) to labor, to polish, to elaborate, to overdo; *lécher les vitrines*, to go window-shopping.
leçon [lə'sɔ̃], *n.f.* lesson; reading (*of a text*).
lecteur [lɛk'tœːr], *n.m.* (*fem.* **-trice**) reader, lector.
lecture [lɛk'tyːr], *n.f.* reading; perusal.
ledit [lə'di], *a.* (*fem.* **ladite**, *pl.* **lesdit(e)s**) the (afore)said, the same.
légal [le'gal], *a.* (*m. pl.* **-aux**) legal, lawful, legitimate.
légalement [legal'mɑ̃], *adv.* legally, lawfully.
légaliser [legali'ze], *v.t.* to legalize.
légalité [legali'te], *n.f.* legality, lawfulness.
légataire [lega'tɛːr], *n.* legatee.
légation [lega'sjɔ̃], *n.f.* legateship; legation.
légendaire [leʒɑ̃'dɛːr], *a.* and *n.m.* legendary.
légende [le'ʒɑ̃ːd], *n.f.* legend; inscription; caption; key (*to map etc.*).
léger [le'ʒe], *a.* (*fem.* **-ère**) light; slight; buoyant; fleet, fast; nimble; fickle; faint; thoughtless.
légèrement [leʒɛr'mɑ̃], *adv.* lightly, slightly, swiftly; thoughtlessly.
légèreté [leʒɛr'te], *n.f.* lightness; swiftness; fickleness; frivolity; thoughtlessness.
légiférer [leʒife're], *v.i.* (*conjug. like* CÉDER) to legislate.
légion [le'ʒɔ̃], *n.f.* legion; great number, host.
légionnaire [leʒjɔ'nɛːr], *n.m.* legionary; member of the Legion of Honor; soldier of the Foreign Legion.
législateur [leʒisla'tœːr], *a.* (*fem.* **-trice**) legislative, lawgiving.—*n.m.* (*fem.* **-trice**) legislator.
législatif [leʒisla'tif], *a.* (*fem.* **-tive**) legislative.
législation [leʒisla'sjɔ̃], *n.f.* legislation.
législature [leʒisla'tyːr], *n.f.* legislature.
légitime [leʒi'tim], *a.* lawful, legitimate, rightful; justifiable.
légitimement [leʒitim'mɑ̃], *adv.* legitimately, lawfully; justifiably.
légitimer [leʒiti'me], *v.t.* to legitimate; to justify; to recognize.
légitimité [leʒitimi'te], *n.f.* legitimacy, lawfulness.
legs [lɛ], *n.m.* legacy, bequest.
léguer [le'ge], *v.t.* (*conjug. like* CÉDER) to leave by will, to bequeath.
légume [le'gym], *n.m.* vegetable.—*n.f. pl.* (*fam.*) *les grosses légumes*, the bigwigs.

légumier [legy'mje], *a.* (*fem.* **-ière**) of vegetables.—*n.m.* vegetable dish.
lendemain [lɑ̃d'mɛ̃], *n.m.* morrow, next day, day after.
lent [lɑ̃], *a.* slow, tardy; backward; sluggish, slack.
lentement [lɑ̃t'mɑ̃], *adv.* slowly, tardily; sluggishly.
lenteur [lɑ̃'tœːr], *n.f.* slowness; tardiness.
lenticulaire [lɑ̃tiky'lɛːr], **lenticulé** [lɑ̃tiky'le], *a.* lenticular.
lentille [lɑ̃'tiːj], *n.f.* lentil; lens; (*pl.*) freckles; *lentille d'eau*, duckweed.
léonin [leɔ'nɛ̃], *a.* leonine.
léopard [leɔ'paːr], *n.m.* leopard.
lèpre [lɛpr], *n.f.* leprosy.
lépreux [le'prø], *a.* (*fem.* **-euse**) leprous.—*n.m.* (*fem.* **-euse**) leper.
léproserie [lepro'ri], *n.f.* leper hospital.
lequel [lə'kɛl], *pron. m.* (*fem.* **laquelle**, *m. pl.* **lesquels**, *f. pl.* **lesquelles**) who, whom, that, which; (*inter.*) which one, which?
les [le], *art.* and *pron. pl.* the; them.
lèse-majesté [lɛzmaʒɛs'te], *n.f.* high treason, lese-majesty.
léser [le'ze], *v.t.* (*conjug. like* CÉDER) to wrong; to injure, to hurt.
lésine [le'zin], *n.f.* niggardliness, stinginess.
lésiner [lezi'ne], *v.i.* to be stingy *or* mean; to haggle.
lésinerie [lezin'ri], *n.f.* stinginess, meanness.
lésion [le'zjɔ̃], *n.f.* (*Law*) wrong, injury; (*Surg.*) lesion.
lessive [le'siːv], *n.f.* wash, linen washed *or* to be washed, washing.
leste [lɛst], *a.* brisk, nimble, active; light; smart; sharp; improper, free.
lestement [lɛst'mɑ̃], *adv.* briskly; cleverly; flippantly; freely.
lester [lɛs'te], *v.t.* to ballast. **se lester**, *v.r.* (*fam.*) to take in ballast; to line one's stomach.
léthargie [letar'ʒi], *n.f.* lethargy.
léthargique [letar'ʒik], *a.* lethargic.
lette [lɛt], **letton** [le'tɔ̃] (*fem.* **-onne**), *a.* Latvian.—*n.m.* Latvian (*language*); (**Lette, Letton**, *fem.* **-onne**) Latvian (*person*).
Lettonie [letɔ'ni], **la**, *f.* Latvia.
lettre [lɛtr], *n.f.* letter, note; (*Print.*) character, type; (*pl.*) literature, letters; *les belles-lettres*, humanities; *lettre de change*, bill of exchange; *lettre d'envoi*, covering letter; *lettre de voiture*, way-bill.
lettré [le'tre], *a.* cultured, literate, well-read; literary.—*n.m.* (*fem.* **-ée**) scholar.
leur [lœːr], *a. poss. their.—poss. pron. le leur, la leur* or *les leurs*, theirs.—*pers. pron.* to them, them.
leurre [lœːr], *n.m.* lure, decoy; bait; snare, trap.
leurrer [lœ're], *v.t.* to lure, to entice, to decoy; to ensnare. **se leurrer**, *v.r.* to delude oneself.
levage [lə'vaːʒ], *n.m.* raising, lifting.
levain [lə'vɛ̃], *n.m.* leaven; (*fig.*) germ.
levant [lə'vɑ̃], *a.* rising.—*n.m.* east; rising sun; Levant.
levantin [ləvɑ̃'tɛ̃], *a.* Levantine.—*n.m.* (**Levantin**, *fem.* **-ine**) Levantine (*person*).
levé [lə've], *a.* lifted up, raised; up, out of bed.

levée [lə've], *n.f.* raising, lifting; levying; gathering (*crop, fruit etc.*); collection (*post-office*); embankment; swell (*of the sea*); (*Cards*) trick.

lever [lə've], *v.t.* (*conjug. like* AMENER) to lift, to lift up, to raise; to heave; to pull up; to weigh (*anchor*); to take away; to take out; to collect; to levy.—*v.i.* to come up; to spring up, to rise. **se lever,** *v.r.* to rise, to get up; to stand up; to heave (*of the sea*); to clear up (*of the weather*).

lever [lə've], *n.m.* rising, getting up; levee (*of king*).

levier [lə'vje], *n.m.* lever; crowbar, hand-spike.

levraut [lə'vro], *n.m.* leveret, young hare.

lèvre [lɛ:vr], *n.f.* lip; rim.

lévrier [levri'e], *n.m.* greyhound.

levure [lə'vy:r], *n.f.* yeast.

lexique [lɛk'sik], *n.m.* lexicon; abridged dictionary.

lézard [le'za:r], *n.m.* lizard.

lézarde [le'zard], *n.f.* crevice, crack, chink.

lézardé [lezar'de], *a.* cracked (*of walls etc.*).

lézarder [lezar'de], *v.t.* to crack (*walls etc.*). **se lézarder,** *v.r.* to crack, to become cracked.

liais [lje], *n.m.* lias; blue limestone.

liaison [ljɛ'zõ], *n.f.* joining; connection, acquaintance; intimacy; (*Mil.*) liaison.

liane [ljan], *n.f.* liana, tropical creeper.

liant [ljã], *a.* supple, flexible; affable, sociable. —*n.m.* suppleness; sociability; gentleness.

liard [lja:r], *n.m.* liard (*half-farthing*).

liasse [ljas], *n.f.* bundle, file (*of papers*); wad (*of banknotes*).

Liban [li'bã], **le,** *m.* Lebanon.

libanais [liba'nɛ], *a.* Lebanese.—*n.m.* (**Libanais,** *fem.* **-aise**) Lebanese (*person*).

libation [liba'sjõ], *n.f.* libation; (*fig.*) potation.

libelle [li'bɛl], *n.m.* libel, lampoon.

libellé [libɛl'le], *a.* drawn up, specified.—*n.m.* wording, contents.

libellule [libɛl'lyl], *n.f.* dragon-fly.

libéral [libe'ral], *a.* (*m. pl.* **-aux**) liberal, generous, bountiful; (*Polit.*) liberal.

libéralement [liberal'mã], *adv.* liberally, bountifully, generously.

libéralisme [libera'lism], *n.m.* liberalism.

libéralité [liberali'te], *n.f.* generosity, open-handedness.

libérateur [libera'tœ:r], *n.m.* (*fem.* **-trice**) deliverer, liberator, rescuer.

libération [libera'sjõ], *n.f.* liberation, deliverance; rescue, discharge.

libéré [libe're], *a.* liberated, discharged.

libérer [libe're], *v.t.* (*conjug. like* CÉDER) to liberate, to free; to discharge. **se libérer,** *v.r.* to free oneself, to clear oneself (*de*) to pay off one's debts.

Libéria [libe'rja], **le,** *m.* Liberia.

libérien [libe'rjɛ̃], *a.* (*fem.* **-enne**) Liberian. —*n.m.* (**Libérien,** *fem.* **-enne**) Liberian (*person*).

liberté [liber'te], *n.f.* liberty, freedom, ease.

libertin [liber'tɛ̃], *a.* libertine, licentious; dissolute.—*n.m.* (*fem.* **-e**) libertine, rake.

libertinage [libɛrti'na:ʒ], *n.m.* libertinism, debauchery.

libraire [li'brɛ:r], *n.* bookseller; **libraire-éditeur,** publisher and bookseller.

librairie [librɛ'ri], *n.f.* book trade; bookseller's shop.

libre [libr], *a.* free; at liberty; independent; undisciplined, unconfined; bold, broad; exempt; irregular (*of verse*).

libre-échange [librɛ'ʃãːʒ], *n.m.* free trade.

libre-échangiste [librɛʃã'ʒist], *n.m.* (*pl.* **libre-échangistes**) free-trader.

librement [librə'mã], *adv.* freely, without restraint; boldly.

librettiste [librɛ'tist], *n.m.* librettist.

Libye [li'bi], **la,** *f.* Libya.

libyen [li'bjɛ̃], *a.* (*fem.* **-enne**) Libyan.—*n.m.* (**Libyen,** *fem.* **-enne**) Libyan (*person*).

lice [lis], *n.f.* lists, tilt yard.

licence [li'sãːs], *n.f.* license, leave, permission; licentiousness; licentiate's degree.

licencié [lisã'sje], *a.* licentiate; (*C*) **épicier licencié,** licensed grocer.—*n.m.* (*fem.* **-ée**) licenciate.

licenciement [lisãsi'mã], *n.m.* disbanding.

licencier [lisã'sje], *v.t.* to disband (*troops*); to declare redundant, to lay off; to dismiss.

licencieusement [lisãsjøz'mã], *adv.* licentiously, dissolutely.

licencieux [lisã'sjø], *a.* (*fem.* **-euse**) licentious, dissolute.

licite [li'sit], *a.* licit, lawful, allowable.

licitement [lisit'mã], *adv.* lawfully, licitly.

licol [LICOU].

licorne [li'kɔrn], *n.f.* unicorn.

licou [li'ku], **licol** [li'kɔl], *n.m.* halter.

licteur [lik'tœ:r], *n.m.* (*Rom. Ant.*) lictor.

lie [li], *n.f.* lees, dregs; (*fig.*) scum, refuse.

liège [ljɛ:ʒ], *n.m.* cork; cork tree.

lien [ljɛ̃], *n.m.* bond, tie, link; (*pl.*) bonds, shackles.

lier [lje], *v.t.* to fasten, to tie; to bind, to tie up; to join, to connect (*avec*); to engage in; (*Mus.*) to slur; to thicken (*a sauce etc.*). **se lier,** *v.r.* to become acquainted; to thicken (*of sauce etc.*).

lierre [ljɛ:r], *n.m.* ivy.

lieu [ljø], *n.m.* (*pl.* **lieux**) place, spot; position; cause; (*pl.*) premises, apartments; **au lieu de,** instead of; **avoir lieu,** to take place; **lieu commun,** commonplace.

lieue [ljø], *n.f.* league (4 *kilometres,* 2½ *miles*).

lieur [ljœ:r], *n.m.* (*fem.* **-euse**) (*Agric.*) binder (*person*).—*n.f.* (**-euse**) binder (*machine*).

lieutenance [ljøt'nãːs], *n.f.* lieutenancy.

lieutenant [ljøt'nã], *n.m.* lieutenant; right-hand man.

lièvre [ljɛ:vr], *n.m.* hare.

liftier [lif'tje], *n.m.* (*fem.* **-ière**) elevator operator.

ligament [liga'mã], *n.m.* ligament.

ligature [liga'ty:r], *n.f.* ligature.

ligaturer [ligaty're], *v.t.* to ligature, to splice.

lignage [li'na:ʒ], *n.m.* lineage.

ligne [liɲ], *n.f.* line; row; path, way; cord; fishing line; order.

lignée [li'ɲe], *n.f.* issue, progeny, offspring.

ligoter [ligo'te], *v.t.* to bind, to tie up.

ligue [lig], *n.f.* league, confederacy.

liguer [li'ge], *v.t.* to unite in a league. **se liguer,** *v.r.* to league, to combine.

ligueur [li'gœ:r], *n.m.* (*fem.* **-euse**) leaguer; plotter.

lilas [li'la], *a. inv.* lilac-colored. —*n.m.* lilac.

lilliputien [lilipy'sjɛ̃], *a.* (*fem.* **-enne**) Lilliputian.

limace [li'mas], *n.f.* slug; Archimedean screw.

limaçon [lima'sɔ̃], *n.m.* snail.

limbe [lɛ̃:b], *n.m.* (*Math.*, *Bot. etc.*) limb; (*Astron.*) border, halo; (*pl.*) limbo.

lime (1) [lim], *n.f.* file.

lime (2) [lim], *n.f.* lime, citron.

limer [li'me], *v.t.* to file, to smooth.

limeur [li'mœːr], *n.m.* (*fem.* -euse) filer.—*n.f.* (-euse) finishing tool *or* machine.

limier [li'mje], *n.m.* bloodhound; (*fig.*) police spy, detective.

liminaire [limi'nɛːr], *a.* prefatory.

limitatif [limita'tif], *a.* (*fem.* -tive) limiting, restrictive.

limitation [limita'sjɔ̃], *n.f.* limitation.

limite [li'mit], *n.f.* limit, boundary; border; landmark.

limiter [limi'te], *v.t.* to limit, to bound; to confine.

limitrophe [limi'trɔf], *a.* neighboring, bordering.

limon [li'mɔ̃], *n.m.* silt, ooze, mud; shaft (*of a carriage*); sour lime (*fruit*).

limonade [limɔ'nad], *n.f.* lemonade.

limonadier [limɔna'dje], *n.m.* (*fem.* -ière) seller of lemonade.

limoneux [limɔ'nø], *a.* (*fem.* -euse) muddy, turbid, slimy; alluvial.

limonier [limɔ'nje], *n.m.* carriage horse; lime tree.

limonière [limɔ'njɛːr], *n.f.* pair of shafts (*of wagon etc.*); wagon with two shafts.

limousin [limu'zɛ̃], *n.m.* stonemason.

limousine [limu'zin], *n.f.* limousine (*car*); coarse woollen cloak.

limpide [lɛ̃'pid], *a.* limpid, clear.

limpidité [lɛ̃pidi'te], *n.f.* limpidity.

lin [lɛ̃], *n.m.* flax; *graine de lin*, linseed; *huile de lin*, linseed oil; *toile de lin*, linen cloth.

linceul [lɛ̃'sœl], *n.m.* winding-sheet, shroud.

linéaire [line'ɛːr], *a.* linear.

linéal [line'al], *a.* (*m. pl.* -aux) lineal, in a direct line.

linéament [linea'mɑ̃], *n.m.* lineament, feature; (*fig.*) trace, vestige.

linge [lɛ̃:ʒ], *n.m.* linen; piece, rag.

linger [lɛ̃'ʒe], *n.m.* (*fem.* -ère) linen dealer; maker of linen goods; seamstress (*of same*). —*n.f.* (-ère) wardrobe woman.

lingerie [lɛ̃'ʒri], *n.f.* linen trade; linen room; linen goods.

lingot [lɛ̃'go], *n.m.* ingot; bullion.

lingue [lɛ̃:g], *n.f.* (*Ichth.*) ling.

linguiste [lɛ̃'gɥist], *n.* linguist.

linguistique [lɛ̃gɥis'tik], *a.* linguistic.—*n.f.* linguistics.

linier [li'nje], *a.* (*fem.* -ière) of flax *or* linen.— *n.f.* (-ière) flax field.

linoléum [linɔle'ɔm], *n.m.* linoleum.

linon [li'nɔ̃], *n.m.* lawn (*fine linen*).

linot [li'no], *n.m.*, linotte [li'nɔt], *n.f.* linnet.

linotype [linɔ'tip], *n.f.* linotype.

linotypiste [linɔti'pist], *n.* linotype operator.

linteau [lɛ̃'to], *n.m.* (*pl.* -eaux) lintel.

lion [ljɔ̃], *n.m.* (*fem.* lionne) lion, lioness; (*fig.*) a bold, brave fellow.

lionceau [ljɔ̃'so], *n.m.* (*pl.* -eaux) young lion, lion's cub.

lippe [lip], *n.f.* thick lower lip; pouting lip.

lippu [li'py], *a.* thick-lipped.

liquéfaction [likefak'sjɔ̃], *n.f.* liquefaction.

liquéfiable [like'fjabl], *a.* liquefiable.

liquéfier [like'fje], *v.t.* and se liquéfier, *v.r.* to liquefy.

liqueur [li'kœːr], *n.f.* liquid; liqueur, cordial; (*Chem.*) spirit.

liquidateur [likida'tœːr], *n.m.* liquidator.

liquidation [likida'sjɔ̃], *n.f.* liquidation; settlement (*of debts etc.*); winding up (*of a business*); clearance sale.

liquide [li'kid], *a.* liquid; clear, net (*of money*).—*n.m.* liquid, fluid; drink.

liquider [liki'de], *v.t.* to liquidate, to settle; to wind up; to sell off; (*fam.*) to get rid of.

liquidité [likidi'te], *n.f.* liquidity, fluidity.

liquoreux [likɔ'rø], *a.* (*fem.* -euse) luscious, sweet.

liquoriste [likɔ'rist], *n.m.* wine and spirit merchant.

lire [liːr], *v.t. irr.* to read, to peruse, to study.

lis [lis], *n.m.* lily.

liseré [lizə're], *n.m.* piping; border, edge.

lisérer [lize're], *v.t.* (*conjug. like* CÉDER) to trim (*a dress etc.*) with piping.

liseron [liz'rɔ̃], liset [li'zɛ], *n.m.* (*Bot.*) convolvulus.

liseur [li'zœːr], *n.m.* (*fem.* -euse) reader.

lisibilité [lizibili'te], *n.f.* legibility, readableness.

lisible [li'zibl], *a.* legible, readable.

lisiblement [liziblə'mɑ̃], *adv.* legibly.

lisière [li'zjɛːr], *n.f.* selvedge, edge (*of cloth etc.*); border, verge, outskirts.

lissage [li'saːʒ], *n.m.* smoothing, glossing.

lisse (1) [lis], *a.* smooth; sleek; glossy.—*n.m.* smoothness, gloss.

lisse (2) [lis], *n.f.* rail, railing (*of ship*).

lisser [li'se], *v.t.* to smooth, to polish.

lisseur [li'sœːr], *n.m.* (*fem.* -euse) polisher.

liste [list], *n.f.* list, roll; catalogue; schedule.

lit [li], *n.m.* bed; layer (*of clay, mortar*); direction, set (*of tide, current*); (*fig.*) marriage.

litanie [lita'ni], *n.f.* (*fig.*) rigmarole; (*pl.*) litany.

litée [li'te], *n.f.* litter (*of animals*).

literie [li'tri], *n.f.* bedding.

lithographe [litɔ'graf], *n.m.* lithographer.

lithographie [litɔgra'fi], *n.f.* lithography; lithograph.

lithographier [litɔgra'fje], *v.t.* to lithograph.

lithographique [litɔgra'fik], *a.* lithographic.

Lithuanie [LITUANIE].

lithuanien [LITUANIEN].

litière [li'tjɛːr], *n.f.* stable litter; litter (*for carrying sick persons etc.*).

litigant [liti'gɑ̃], *a.* litigant.

litige [li'tiːʒ], *n.m.* litigation, legal dispute; (*fig.*) strife.

litigieux [liti'ʒjø], *a.* (*fem.* -euse) litigious, given to lawsuits.

litre [litr], *n.m.* litre (1.76 pints).

littéraire [lite'rɛːr], *a.* literary; *propriété littéraire*, copyright.

littérairement [literɛr'mɑ̃], *adv.* in a literary manner *or* way.

littéral [lite'ral], *a.* (*m. pl.* -aux) literal.

littéralement [literal'mɑ̃], *adv.* literally, word for word.

littérateur [litera'tœːr], *n.m.* literary man, author, man of letters.

littérature [litera'tyːr], *n.f.* literature.

littoral [litɔ′ral], *a.* (*m. pl.* -**aux**) littoral, coastal.—*n.m.* littoral, seaboard.

Lituanie [litɥa′ni], la, *f.* Lithuania.

lituanien [litɥa′njɛ̃], *a.* Lithuanian.—*n.m.* Lithuanian (*language*); (**Lituanien**, *fem.* -**enne**) Lithuanian (*person*).

liturgie [lityr′ʒi], *n.f.* liturgy.

liturgique [lityr′ʒik], *a.* liturgic, liturgical.

liturgiste [lityr′ʒist], *n.* liturgist.

livide [li′vid], *a.* livid, ghastly.

lividité [lividi′te], *n.f.* lividness.

livrable [li′vrabl], *a.* deliverable.

livraison [livrɛ′zɔ̃], *n.f.* delivery (*of goods*); part, number, issue (*of a magazine etc.*).

livre (1) [li′vr], *n.m.* book; register, account book.

livre (2) [li:vr], *n.f.* pound (*1.1 lb. avoirdupois*); *livre sterling*, pound sterling.

livrée [li′vre], *n.f.* livery; livery servants.

livrer [li′vre], *v.t.* to deliver; to give up, to hand over; to betray (*a secret*). **se livrer**, *v.r.* to give oneself up (*à*); to surrender; to devote oneself; to entrust oneself to; to indulge in (*a vice*).

livret [li′vrɛ], *n.m.* little book; memorandum book; libretto.

livreur [li′vrœ:r], *n.m.* (*fem.* -**euse**) deliverer (*of goods*); delivery man, van man.—*n.f.* (-**euse**) delivery van.

lobe [lɔb], *n.m.* lobe (*of ear, liver etc.*).

lobélie [lɔbe′li], *n.f.* (*Bot.*) lobelia.

local [lɔ′kal], *a.* (*m. pl.* -**aux**) local.—*n.m.* place, premises; quarters.

localement [lɔkal′mɑ̃], *adv.* locally.

localisation [lɔkaliza′sjɔ̃], *n.f.* localization.

localiser [lɔkali′ze], *v.t.* to localize. **se localiser**, *v.r.* to become localized.

localité [lɔkali′te], *n.f.* locality.

locataire [lɔka′tɛ:r], *n.* tenant, lodger, occupier.

location [lɔka′sjɔ̃], *n.f.* letting out; hiring, renting; (*Theat.*) booking of seat.

lock-out [lɔ′kaut], *n.m. inv.* lock-out.

lock-outer [lɔkau′te], *v.t.* to lock-out.

locomoteur [lɔkɔmɔ′tœ:r], *a.* (*fem.* -**trice**) locomotor.

locomotif [lɔkɔmɔ′tif], *a.* (*fem.* -**tive**) locomotive.—*n.f.* (-**tive**) locomotive, engine.

locomotion [lɔkɔmɔ′sjɔ̃], *n.f.* locomotion.

locomotive [LOCOMOTIF].

locuste [lɔ′kyst], *n.f.* locust.

locution [lɔky′sjɔ̃], *n.f.* locution, expression, form of speech; term, phrase.

logarithme [lɔga′ritm], *n.m.* logarithm.

loge [lɔ:ʒ], *n.f.* hut; lodge; (*Theat.*) box, dressing room; stand, stall; kennel; booth.

logeable [lɔ′ʒabl], *a.* tenantable, fit to live in.

logement [lɔʒ′mɑ̃], *n.m.* lodgings; dwelling; house-room, accommodation; quarters.

loger [lɔ′ʒe], *v.t.* (*conjug. like* MANGER) to lodge; to put up, to accommodate, to house; to quarter; to stable.—*v.i.* to lodge, to live; to put up. **se loger**, *v.r.* to lodge, to take up one's abode; to lodge itself.

logette [lɔ′ʒɛt], *n.f.* small lodge.

logeur [lɔ′ʒœ:r], *n.m.* (*fem.* -**euse**) lodging-house keeper.

logicien [lɔʒi′sjɛ̃], *n.m.* (*fem.* -**enne**) logician.

logique [lɔ′ʒik], *a.* logical.—*n.f.* logic.

logiquement [lɔʒik′mɑ̃], *adv.* logically.

logis [lɔ′ʒi], *n.m.* (*rare*) house, dwelling.

loi [lwa], *n.f.* law, statute, act; rule.

loin [lwɛ̃], *adv.* far, at a distance; remote, distant; *au loin*, far away, far and wide; *de loin*, from afar, from a distance; *de loin en loin*, at long intervals.

lointain [lwɛ̃′tɛ̃], *a.* remote, far off, distant.—*n.m.* distance, distant prospect.

loir [lwa:r], *n.m.* dormouse.

loisible [lwa′zibl], *a.* optional, lawful, allowable.

loisir [lwa′zi:r], *n.m.* leisure, spare time.

lombes [lɔ̃:b], *n.m. pl.* (*Anat.*) lumbar region, loins.

londonien [lɔ̃dɔ′njɛ̃], *a.* (*fem.* -**enne**) of *or* pertaining to London.—*n.m.* (**Londonien**, *fem.* -**enne**) Londoner.

Londres [′lɔ̃drə], *f.* London.

long [lɔ̃], *a.* (*fem.* **longue**) long; slow, tedious; diffuse, drawn out.—*n.m.* length; extent; (*tout*) *au long*, in full; *de long en large*, up and down, to and fro.—*n.f. à la longue*, in the long run.—*adv.* much, great deal.

longanimité [lɔ̃ganimi′te], *n.f.* longanimity, forbearance, long-suffering.

long-courrier [lɔ̃ku′rje], *n.m.* (*pl.* -**courriers**) ocean-going ship.

longe (1) [lɔ̃:ʒ], *n.f.* tether, leading-rein; thong.

longe (2) [lɔ̃:ʒ], *n.f. longe de veau*, loin of veal.

longer [lɔ̃′ʒe], *v.t.* (*conjug. like* MANGER) to go, to run along; to skirt; to extend along.

longévité [lɔ̃ʒevi′te], *n.f.* longevity.

longitude [lɔ̃ʒi′tyd], *n.f.* longitude.

longitudinal [lɔ̃ʒitydi′nal], *a.* (*m. pl.* -**aux**) longitudinal.

longitudinalement [lɔ̃ʒitydinal′mɑ̃], *adv.* lengthwise.

longtemps [lɔ̃′tɑ̃], *adv.* long, a long while.

longuement [lɔ̃g′mɑ̃], *adv.* long, a long time, for a great while.

longueur [lɔ̃′gœ:r], *n.f.* length, extent in time; slowness; prolixity.

longue-vue [lɔ̃g′vy], *n.f.* (*pl.* **longues-vues**) telescope, spy-glass.

lopin [lɔ′pɛ̃], *n.m.* small piece *or* share; *lopin de terre*, plot of ground.

loquace [lɔ′kwas], *a.* loquacious, talkative.

loquacement [lɔkwas′mɑ̃], *adv.* talkatively, loquaciously.

loquacité [lɔkwasi′te], *n.f.* loquacity, talkativeness.

loque [lɔk], *n.f.* rag, tatter.

loquet [lɔkɛ], *n.m.* latch; *fermé au loquet*, on the latch.

loqueteau [lɔk′to], *n.m.* (*pl.* -**eaux**) small latch.

loqueteux [lɔk′tø], *a.* (*fem.* -**euse**) in rags.—*n.m.* (*fem.* -**euse**) ragged person.

lorgner [lɔr′ɲe], *v.t.* to leer at, to ogle.

lorgnette [lɔr′ɲɛt], *n.f.* field *or* opera glasses.

lorgnon [lɔr′ɲɔ̃], *n.m.* (*sometimes pl.*) eye-glasses; lorgnette.

lorry [lɔ′ri], *n.m.* (*Rail.*) trolley, repair *or* construction car.

lors [lɔ:r], *adv.* then; *depuis lors* or *dès lors*, from that time, since then; *lors de*, at the time of; *lors même que*, even though; *pour lors*, then, at the time; so, therefore.

lorsque [lɔrsk, ′lɔrskə], *conj.* when; at the time *or* moment of.

losange [lɔ'zɑ̃:ʒ], n.m. diamond-shape, lozenge.

losangé [lɔzɑ̃'ʒe], a. in lozenges.

lot [lo], n.m. lot; portion, share; prize (in a lottery); (fig.) fate.

loterie [lo'tri], n.f. lottery, raffle.

lotion [lo'sjɔ̃], n.f. lotion; ablution.

lotir [lo'ti:r], v.t. to divide into lots, to portion off.

lotissement [lotis'mɑ̃], n.m. dividing into lots; building plot.

loto [lo'to], n.m. lotto (game of chance); bingo.

lotus [lo'ty:s], n.m. inv. lotus.

louable [lwabl], a. laudable, praiseworthy, commendable.

louablement [lwablə'mɑ̃], adv. commendably.

louage [lwa:ʒ], n.m. letting out, hiring, renting; hire.

louange [lwɑ̃:ʒ], n.f. praise, commendation, eulogy.

louanger [lwɑ̃'ʒe], v.t. (conjug. like MANGER) to praise, to flatter, to extol.

louangeur [lwɑ̃'ʒœ:r], a. (fem. -euse) laudatory, eulogistic.—n.m. (fem. -euse) praiser, flatterer.

louche (1) [luʃ], n.f. (soup) ladle; scoop; countersink bit.

louche (2) [luʃ], a. squint-eyed; dubious, ambiguous; suspicious, shady.

loucher [lu'ʃe], v.i. to squint.

loucheur [lu'ʃœ:r], a. (fem. -euse) squinting.—n.m. (fem. -euse) squinter.

louer (1) [lwe], v.t. to let or hire out; to lease, to rent, to hire; to book. **se louer** (1), v.r. to hire oneself out; to be let or rented.

louer (2) [lwe], v.t. to praise, to commend, to extol. **se louer** (2), v.r. to praise oneself; to rejoice.

loueur [lwœ:r], n.m. (fem. -euse) hirer, letter out.

lougre [lugr], n.m. lugger.

Louis [lwi], m. Lewis, Louis.

louis [lwi], n.m. inv. louis (a French coin worth 20 gold francs).

loup [lu], n.m. wolf; black velvet mask.

loup-cervier [lusɛr'vje], n.m. (pl. **loups-cerviers**) lynx; (fig.) profiteer.

loupe (1) [lup], n.f. magnifying glass.

loupe (2) [lup], n.f. wen; gnarl (on trees).

louper [lu'pe], v.t. (pop.) to botch (a piece of work); (Exam.) to fail; to miss (train).

loupeux [lu'pø], a. (fem. -euse) wenny, knobby.

loup-garou [luga'ru], n.m. (pl. **loups-garous**) wer(e)wolf; bugbear.

lourd [lu:r], a. heavy, clumsy; stupid; sultry.

lourdaud [lur'do], a. loutish.—n.m. (fem. -e) blockhead.

lourdement [lurdə'mɑ̃], adv. heavily, clumsily.

lourdeur [lur'dœ:r], n.f. heaviness; clumsiness; stupidity; sultriness.

loutre [lutr], n.f. otter; otter fur.

louve [lu:v], n.f. she-wolf.

louveteau [luv'to], n.m. (pl. **-eaux**) wolf cub.

louveterie [luv'tri], n.f. wolf-hunting equipage; wolf hunting.

louvetier [luv'tje], n.m. wolf hunter.

louvoyer [luvwa'je], v.i. (conjug. like EM-PLOYER) to tack, to tack about; (fig.) to maneuver, to dodge.

lover [lo've], v.t. to coil (rope etc.). **se lover**, v.r. to coil up (of snakes).

loyal [lwa'jal], a. (m. pl. **-aux**) fair, honest, upright; loyal; (Comm.) unadulterated.

loyalement [lwajal'mɑ̃], adv. fairly, honestly; loyally.

loyauté [lwajo'te], n.f. honesty, fairness; loyalty, faithfulness.

loyer [lwa'je], n.m. hire, rent.

lubie [ly'bi] n.f. crotchet, whim, fad.

lubrifiant [lybri'fjɑ̃], a. lubricating.—n.m. lubricant.

lubrification [lybrifika'sjɔ̃], n.f. lubrication.

lubrifier [lybri'fje], v.t. to lubricate.

Luc [lyk], m. Luke.

lucarne [ly'karn], n.f. dormer window, skylight.

lucide [ly'sid], a. lucid, clear.

lucidement [lysid'mɑ̃], adv. lucidly.

lucidité [lysidi'te], n.f. lucidity, clearness.

luciole [ly'sjɔl], n.f. (Ent.) fire-fly; winged glow-worm.

lucratif [lykra'tif], a. (fem. -tive) lucrative.

lucre [lykr], n.m. lucre, gain.

lueur [lɥœ:r], n.f. glimmer, gleam; flash.

luffa [ly'fa], n.m. or f. loofah.

lugubre [ly'gybr], a. lugubrious, doleful, dismal.

lugubrement [lygybrə'mɑ̃], adv. ominously; dismally.

lui [lɥi], pers. pron. he, it; to him, to her, to it.

luire [lɥi:r], v.i. irr. to shine; to glitter, to gleam, to glisten; to dawn.

luisant [lɥi'zɑ̃], a. glistening, glittering, bright; glossy.—n.m. gloss, shine.

lumbago [lɛ̃ba'go], n.m. lumbago.

lumière [ly'mjɛ:r], n.f. light; daylight, day; (fig.) enlightenment; knowledge, wisdom.

luminaire [lymi'nɛ:r], n.m. luminary, light.

lumineux [lymi'nø], a. (fem. -euse) luminous; bright.

lunaire [ly'nɛ:r], a. lunar.

lunatique [lyna'tik], a. fantastical, whimsical.—n. incalculable or whimsical person.

lundi [lɛ̃'di], n.m. Monday.

lune [lyn], n.f. moon.

lunetier [lyn'tje], n.m. (fem. -ière) spectacle maker; optician.

lunette [ly'nɛt], n.f. telescope, field glass; (pl.) spectacles.

lupin [ly'pɛ̃], n.m. (Bot.) lupin(e).

lupus [ly'py:s], n.m. lupus.

luron [ly'rɔ̃], n.m. (fem. -onne) jolly fellow, gay dog; carefree type of girl.

lustrage [lys'tra:ʒ], n.m. glossing.

lustral [lys'tral], a. (m. pl. **-aux**) lustral.

lustration [lystra'sjɔ̃], n.f. lustration.

lustre (1) [lystr], n.m. luster, brilliancy, brightness; (fig.) distinction; chandelier.

lustre (2) [lystr], n.m. (Rom. Ant.) lustrum, space of five years.

lustré [lys'tre], a. glossy, shiny.

lustrer [lys'tre], v.t. to give a luster or gloss to, to glaze.

lustrine [lys'trin], n.f. lustering, cotton luster.

luth [lyt], n.m. lute.

luthérien [lyte'rjɛ̃], a. Lutheran.—n.m. (**Luthérien**, fem. **-enne**) Lutheran (person).

lutin

lutin [ly'tɛ̃], *a.* roguish, sprightly.—*n.m.* goblin, sprite, elf, imp.

lutiner [lyti'ne], *v.t.* to plague, to tease, to pester.—*v.i.* to be mischievous, to play the imp.

lutrin [ly'trɛ̃], *n.m.* music lectern *or* desk; choir.

lutte [lyt], *n.f.* wrestling; struggle, contest, strife; *de bonne lutte*, by fair play; *de haute lutte*, by force.

lutter [ly'te], *v.i.* to wrestle; to struggle, to contend.

lutteur [ly'tœ:r], *n.m.* (*fem.* **-euse**) wrestler.

luxation [lyksɑ'sjɔ̃], *n.f.* luxation, dislocation.

luxe [lyks], *n.m.* luxury; profusion; extravagance, excess.

Luxembourg [lyksɑ̃'bu:r], **le**, *m.* Luxembourg.

luxembourgeois [lyksɑ̃bur'ʒwa], *a.* (of) Luxembourg.—*n.m.* (**Luxembourgeois**, *fem.* **-oise**) citizen of Luxembourg.

luxer [lyk'se], *v.t.* to luxate, to dislocate.

luxueusement [lyksɥøz'mɑ̃], *a.* luxuriously, sumptuously, richly.

luxueux [lyk'sɥø], *a.* (*fem.* **-euse**) luxurious; magnificent, rich, sumptuous.

luxure [lyk'sy:r], *n.f.* lust.

luxuriance [lyksy'rjɑ̃:s], *n.f.* luxuriance.

luxuriant [lyksy'rjɑ̃], *a.* luxuriant.

luxurieux [lyksy'rjø], *a.* (*fem.* **-euse**) lustful, lecherous.

lycée [li'se], *n.m.* French grammar *or* high school.

lycéen [lise'ɛ̃], *n.m.* (*fem.* **-éenne**) grammar-school pupil.

lymphatique [lɛ̃fa'tik], *a.* lymphatic.

lymphe [lɛ̃:f], *n.f.* lymph; (*Bot.*) sap.

lynchage [lɛ̃'ʃa:ʒ], *n.m.* lynching.

lyncher [lɛ̃'ʃe], *v.t.* to lynch.

lynx [lɛ̃:ks], *n.m. inv.* lynx.

Lyon [ljɔ̃], *m.* Lyons.

lyre [li:r], *n.f.* lyre; (*fig.*) poetry.

lyrique [li'rik], *a.* lyric, lyrical.

lyrisme [li'rism], *n.m.* lyric poetry; poetic fire.

M

M m [ɛm], *n.m. or f.* the thirteenth letter of the alphabet; *M*, 1000; *M. MM.*, abbr. of *Monsieur, Messieurs.*

m' [ME].

ma [ma], *a. poss. f.* [MON].

macabre [ma'kɑ:br], *a.* gruesome, macabre, deathly, ghastly; *la danse macabre*, the dance of death.

macadam [maka'dam], *n.m.* macadam.

macadamiser [makadami'ze], *v.t.* to macadamize.

macaque [ma'kak], *n.m.* macaco (*monkey*).

macaron [maka'rɔ̃], *n.m.* macaroon.

macaroni [makaro'ni], *n.m.* macaroni.

Macédoine [mase'dwan], **la**, *f.* Macedonia.

macédoine [mase'dwan], *n.f.* vegetable hotchpotch; fruit salad; (*fig.*) medley, hotchpotch.

macédonien [masedɔ'njɛ̃], *a.* Macedonian.—*n.m.* (**Macédonien**, *fem.* **-enne**) Macedonian (*person*).

macération [masera'sjɔ̃], *n.f.* maceration.

macérer [mase're], *v.t.* (*conjug. like* CÉDER) to macerate; (*fig.*) to mortify.—*v.i.* to soak. **se macérer**, *v.r.* to macerate one's body; (*fig.*) to mortify oneself.

mâcher [mɑ'ʃe], *v.t.* to chew, to masticate; *ne pas mâcher ses mots*, not to mince matters.

machiavélique [makjave'lik], *a.* Machiavellian.

machiavélisme [makjave'lism], *n.m.* Machiavellism.

machiavéliste [makjave'list], *n.* Machiavellian.

machinal [maʃi'nal], *a.* (*m. pl.* **-aux**) mechanical, automatic, instinctive.

machinalement [maʃinal'mɑ̃], *adv.* mechanically, automatically, instinctively.

machinateur [maʃina'tœ:r], *n.m.* (*fem.* **-trice**) plotter, schemer.

machination [maʃinɑ'sjɔ̃], *n.f.* machination, plot, scheme.

machine [ma'ʃin], *n.f.* machine, engine, piece of machinery; apparatus; scheme, plot; *machine à coudre*, sewing machine; *machine à écrire*, typewriter; *machine à laver*, washing machine; *machine pneumatique*, air pump.

machine-outil [maʃinu'ti], *n.f.* (*pl.* **machines-outils**) machine tool.

machiner [maʃi'ne], *v.t.* to contrive, to plot.

machiniste [maʃi'nist], *n.m.* machinist, engine man; (*Theat.*) scene shifter.

mâchoire [mɑ'ʃwa:r], *n.f.* jaw; jawbone.

mâchonner [mɑʃo'ne], *v.t.* to chew with difficulty; to munch; to mumble; to champ (*the bit*).

mâchurer [mɑʃy're], *v.t.* to daub, to smudge; to bruise.

maçon [ma'sɔ̃], *n.m.* mason, bricklayer; freemason.

maçonnage [maso'na:ʒ], *n.m.* mason's work, stonework.

maçonner [maso'ne], *v.t.* to build; to wall up.

maçonnerie [maso'ri], *n.f.* masonry, mason's work, stone work; freemasonry.

maçonnique [maso'nik], *a.* masonic.

macule [ma'kyl], *n.f.* stain, spot.

maculer [maky'le], *v.t.* to blot, to spot.

Madagascar [madagas'ka:r], **le**, *n.m.* Malagasy Republic.

madame [ma'dam], *n.f.* (*pl.* **mesdames**) madam, ma'am; Mrs.; your ladyship.

madécasse [made'kas], *a.* Madagascan.—*n.* (**Madécasse**) Madagascan (*person*).

madeleine [ma'dlɛn], *n.f.* shell-shaped sponge-cake; early pear.

Madelon [ma'dlɔ̃], *f.* Maud.

mademoiselle [madmwa'zɛl], *n.f.* (*pl.* **mesdemoiselles**) Miss; young lady.

Madère [ma'dɛ:r], **la**, *f.* Madeira.

madère [ma'dɛ:r], *n.m.* Madeira wine.

madone [ma'dɔn], *n.f.* Madonna.

madré [mɑ'dre], *a.* veined, mottled; (*fig.*) cunning, sly, sharp.—*n.m.* (*fem.* **-ée**) cunning, sharp *or* sly person.

madrier [madri'e], *n.m.* thick plank.

maestria [maes'trija], *n.f.* masterliness; *avec maestria*, in a masterly manner.

magasin [maga′zɛ̃], *n.m.* warehouse, storehouse; shop, store; magazine (*of fire-arm, camera etc.*).

(C) **magasiner** [magazi′ne], *v.i.* to shop.

magasinier [magazi′nje], *n.m.* warehouse keeper, storeman.

magazine [maga′zin], *n.m.* magazine (*usu. illustrated*).

mage [ma:ʒ], *n.m.* mage, magus; seer; *les rois mages*, the three wise men.

magicien [maʒi′sjɛ̃], *n.m.* (*fem.* **-enne**) magician, wizard, sorcerer, sorceress.

magie [ma′ʒi], *n.f.* magic.

magique [ma′ʒik], *a.* magic(al).

magister [maʒis′tɛ:r], *n.m.* village schoolmaster; pedant.

magistral [maʒis′tral], *a.* (*m. pl.* **-aux**) magisterial; masterly, authoritative, sovereign.

magistralement [maʒistral′mɑ̃], *adv.* magisterially; in a masterly fashion.

magistrat [maʒis′tra], *n.m.* magistrate, justice; civic officer.

magistrature [maʒistra′ty:r], *n.f.* magistracy; bench.

magnanime [mana′nim], *a.* magnanimous, high-minded.

magnanimement [mananim′mɑ̃], *adv.* magnanimously.

magnanimité [mananimi′te], *n.f.* magnanimity.

magnat [mag′na], *n.m.* magnate.

magnésie [mane′zi], *n.f.* magnesia.

magnétique [mane′tik], *a.* magnetic.

magnétiser [maneti′ze], *v.t.* to magnetize.

magnetiseur [maneti′zœ:r], *n.m.* magnetizer.

magnétisme [mane′tism], *n.m.* magnetism; (*fig.*) attraction.

magnétophone [maneto′fɔn], *n.m.* (*Reg. trade mark*) tape recorder.

magnificence [manifi′sɑ̃:s], *n.f.* magnificence, splendor.

magnifier [mani′fje], *v.t.* to magnify, to glorify.

magnifique [mani′fik], *a.* magnificent, splendid; gorgeous.

magnifiquement [manifik′mɑ̃], *adv.* magnificently.

magot [ma′go], *n.m.* magot, ape; grotesque figure (*of china*); (*fig.*) ugly person; (*fam.*) hoard, hidden savings.

Mahomet [maɔ′mɛ], *m.* Mohammed.

mahométan [maɔme′tɑ̃], *a.* Mohammedan. —*n.m.* (**Mahométan**, *fem.* **-ane**) Mohammedan (*person*).

mahométisme [maɔme′tism], *n.m.* Mohammedanism.

mai [mɛ], *n.m.* May; maypole.

maigre [mɛ:gr], *a.* meager, lean, thin; poor, scanty; barren; fasting; *repas maigre*, meatless meal; *maigre repas*, slender meal.

maigrement [mɛgrə′mɑ̃], *adv.* meagerly; poorly; sparingly.

maigreur [mɛ′grœ:r], *n.f.* leanness, meagerness; thinness, poorness, barrenness.

maigrir [mɛ′gri:r], *v.i.* to grow thin, to lose weight.

mail [ma:j], *n.m.* mall (*game, promenade, avenue of trees*).

maille [mɑ:j], *n.f.* mesh; ring of cable; link of mail; stitch.

maillé [mu′je], *a.* stitched; mailed.

mailler [mɑ′je], *v.t.* to make with meshes, to lattice; to mail.

maillet [mɑ′jɛ], *n.m.* mallet.

maillon [mɑ′jɔ̃], *n.m.* link (*of chain*).

maillot [mɑ′jo], *n.m.* swaddling-band; swaddling clothes; pair of tights (*for theatre*); bathing suit, (*Spt.*) jersey, vest; *enfant au maillot*, baby in arms.

main [mɛ̃], *n.f.* hand; handwriting; lead, deal (*at cards*); handle; quire (*of paper*); *à la main*, in his *or* her hand, by hand; *à la portée de la main*, within reach; *à main armée*, by force of arms, armed; *à pleines mains*, by handfuls, liberally; *vol à main armée*, armed robbery.

main-d'œuvre [mɛ′dœ:vr], *n.f.* (*pl.* **mains-d'œuvre**) man-power, labor; workmanship.

main-forte [mɛ′fɔrt], *n.f.* assistance, help.

maint [mɛ̃], *a.* many; *maintes fois*, many a time.

maintenant [mɛt′nɑ̃], *adv.* now, at this moment, at present, nowadays.

maintenir [mɛt′ni:r], *v.t. irr.* (*conjug. like* TENIR) to uphold, to sustain; to maintain; to enforce. **se maintenir**, *v.r.* to keep up; to subsist; to hold out, to stand one's ground; to remain in force.

maintien [mɛ′tjɛ̃], *n.m.* maintenance, keeping up; deportment; attitude.

maire [mɛ:r], *n.m.* mayor.

mairesse [mɛ′rɛs], *n.f.* mayoress.

mairie [mɛ′ri], *n.f.* mayoralty; town hall.

mais [mɛ], *conj.* but; why.

maïs [ma′is], *n.m.* maize, Indian corn.

maison [mɛ′zɔ̃], *n.f.* house; home; housekeeping; family; (*Comm.*) firm; *à la maison*, at home.

maisonnée [mɛzɔ′ne], *n.f.* (*fam.*) whole house *or* family, household.

maisonnette [mɛzɔ′nɛt], *n.f.* small house, cottage, lodge.

maître [mɛ:tr], *n.m.* master; ruler, lord; proprietor, landlord; teacher, tutor; (*Naut.*) chief petty officer; *coup de maître*, masterly stroke; *maître chanteur*, blackmailer.

maître-autel [mɛtro′tɛl], *n.m.* (*pl.* **maîtres-autels**) high altar.

maîtresse [mɛ′trɛs], *a.* chief, leading, main.—*n.f.* mistress; ruler, lady; proprietress; teacher; sweetheart.

maîtrise [mɛ′tri:z], *n.f.* mastery; control; music school (*in a cathedral*).

maîtriser [mɛtri′ze], *v.t.* to master, to control; to lord (it) over.

majesté [maʒɛs′te], *n.f.* majesty; stateliness.

majestueusement [maʒɛstɥœz′mɑ̃], *adv.* majestically.

majestueux [maʒɛs′tɥø], *a.* (*fem.* **-euse**) majestic.

majeur [ma′ʒœ:r], *a.* major, greater; superior, main, chief, most important; of full age.—*n.m.* (*fem.* **-e**) a male *or* female of full age, major.—*n.m.* middle finger.

majolique [maʒɔ′llk], *n.f.* majolica.

major [ma′ʒɔ:r], *n.m.* major; medical officer.

majordome [maʒɔr′dɔm], *n.m.* major-domo.

majorer [maʒɔ′re], *v.t.* to raise (*the price*).

majorité [maʒɔri′te], *n.f.* majority.

majuscule [maʒys′kyl], *a.* capital, large.—*n.f.* capital letter.

mal

mal [mal], *n.m.* (*pl.* **maux**) evil, ill; harm; pain, ache, sickness; hardship, misfortune; trouble; repugnance.—*adv.* wrong, badly; *mal à propos*, improperly.

malade [ma'lad], *a.* sick, ill; unhealthy.—*n.* sick person, invalid; patient.

maladie [mala'di], *n.f.* illness, sickness, malady.

maladif [mala'dif], *a.* (*fem.* **-dive**) sickly, puny, ailing, unhealthy.

maladivement [maladiv'mã], *adv.* morbidly.

maladresse [mala'drɛs], *n.f.* awkwardness, clumsiness; blunder.

maladroit [mala'drwa], *a.* and *n.m.* (*fem.* **-e**) awkward, clumsy, stupid (person).

maladroitement [maladrwat'mã], *adv.* clumsily.

malais [ma'lɛ], *a.* Malay, Malayan, Malaysian.—*n.m.* Malay (*language*); (**Malais**, *fem.* **-aise**) Malay, Malayan, Malaysian (*person*).

malaise [ma'lɛ:z], *n.m.* uneasiness, discomfort; indisposition.

malaisé [malɛ'ze], *a.* hard, difficult, rough, arduous.

malaisément [malɛze'mã], *adv.* with difficulty, painfully.

Malaisie [malɛ'zi], **la**, *f.* Malaysia.

malappris [mala'pri], *a.* unmannerly, ill-bred.—*n.m.* (*fem.* **-e**) ill-bred person, lout.

malard [ma'la:r], *n.m.* mallard, wild drake.

malaria [mala'rja], *n.f.* malaria.

malart [MALARD].

malavisé [malavi'ze], *a.* ill-advised, imprudent, unwise, indiscreet.

malaxer [malak'ze], *v.t.* to mix, knead *or* work up; to massage.

malbâti [malbɑ'ti], *a.* ill-shaped, gawky.—*n.m.* (*fem.* **-e**) ill-favored person.

malchance [mal'ʃã:s], *n.f.* ill-luck, mishap, mischance.

malchanceux [malʃã'sø], *a.* (*fem.* **-euse**) unlucky.

mâle [mɑ:l], *a.* male; manly, virile; masculine.—*n.m.* male; cock.

malédiction [maledik'sjɔ̃], *n.f.* malediction, curse.

maléfice [male'fis], *n.m.* evil spell, sorcery.

maléfique [male'fik], *a.* harmful, malefic, baleful.

malencontre [malã'kɔ̃:tr], *n.f.* mishap, mischance.

malencontreusement [malãkɔ̃trøz'mã], *adv.* unluckily, untowardly.

malencontreux [malãkɔ̃'trø], *a.* (*fem.* **-euse**) unlucky, untoward.

mal-en-point [malã'pwɛ̃], *adv.* badly off; in a sorry plight.

malentendu [malãtã'dy], *n.m.* misunderstanding, misapprehension, mistake.

malfaçon [malfa'sɔ̃], *n.f.* bad work; malpractice, illicit profit.

malfaire [mal'fɛ:r], *v.i.* (*used only in the inf.*) to do evil.

malfaisant [malfə'zã], *a.* mischievous; spiteful, malevolent.

malfaiteur [malfɛ'tœ:r], *n.m.* (*fem.* **-trice**) malefactor, evil-doer; offender; thief.

malfamé [malfa'me], *a.* ill-famed, of bad repute.

malformation [malfɔrma'sjɔ̃], *n.f.* malformation.

malgache [mal'gaʃ], *a.* Madagascan.—*n.* (**Malgache**) Malagasy, Madagascan.

malgracieusement [malgrasjøz'mã], *adv.* ungraciously, rudely, uncivilly.

malgracieux [malgra'sjø], *a.* (*fem.* **-euse**) rude, ungracious, uncivil.

malgré [mal'gre], *prep.* in spite of, notwithstanding.

malhabile [mala'bil], *a.* unskilled, awkward.

malhabilement [malabil'mã], *adv.* unskilfully, awkwardly.

malhabileté [malabil'te], *n.f.* unskilfulness, awkwardness, clumsiness.

malheur [ma'lœ:r], *n.m.* unhappiness, misfortune, bad luck; mischance; calamity, disaster; woe, adversity; poverty.

malheureusement [malœrøz'mã], *adv.* unfortunately.

malheureux [malœ'rø], *a.* (*fem.* **-euse**) unfortunate, unlucky; unsuccessful; unpleasant; unhappy, miserable, wretched.—*n.m.* (*fem.* **-euse**) unhappy person.

malhonnête [malɔ'nɛ:t], *a.* dishonest, uncivil, rude.—*n.* rude person.

malhonnêtement [malɔnɛt'mã], *adv.* dishonestly; rudely.

malhonnêteté [malɔnɛt'te], *n.f.* rudeness, incivility; dishonesty.

malice [ma'lis], *n.f.* malice, spite; mischievousness; prank, trick.

malicieusement [malisjøz'mã], *adv.* maliciously; mischievously; slyly.

malicieux [mali'sjø], *a.* (*fem.* **-euse**) malicious, spiteful; mischievous; roguish.

malignement [maliɲ'mã], *adv.* malignantly; maliciously.

malignité [maliɲi'te], *n.f.* malignity, spite.

malin [ma'lɛ̃], *a.* (*fem.* **maligne**) malicious, mischievous; malignant; waggish, roguish; cunning, clever.—*n.m.* (*fem.* **maligne**) malignant *or* malicious person.—*n.m.* devil, evil spirit, fiend.

maline [ma'lin], *n.f.* spring tide.

malingre [ma'lɛ̃:gr], *a.* sickly, weakly, puny.

malintentionné [malɛ̃tãsjo'ne], *a.* evil-minded, ill-disposed.

malle [mal], *n.f.* trunk, box; mail car, mail boat.

malléabilité [maleabili'te], *n.f.* malleability; pliability.

malléable [male'abl], *a.* malleable.

malle-poste [mal'pɔst], *n.f.* (*pl.* **malles-poste(s)**) mail car.

mallette [ma'lɛt], *n.f.* small case, suitcase, attaché-case.

malmener [malmə'ne], *v.t.* (*conjug. like* AMENER) to ill-treat, to handle roughly; to abuse.

malodorant [malɔdɔ'rã], *a.* malodorous, ill-smelling.

malotru [malɔ'try], *a.* coarse, uncouth, vulgar.—*n.m.* (*fem.* **-e**) ill-bred person; lout.

Malouines [ma'lwin], **les îles**, *f. pl.* the Falkland Islands.

malpeigné [malpɛ'ɲe], *a.* unkempt.—*n.m.* (*fem.* **-ée**) unkempt *or* dirty person.

malplaisant [malplɛ'zã], *a.* unpleasant, disagreeable.

malpropre [mal'prɔpr], *a.* slovenly, dirty; dishonest; unfit (*à*).

malproprement [malprɔprə'mã], *adv.* in a slovenly way, dirtily; improperly.

208

malpropreté [malprɔprə'te], n.f. dirtiness.
malsain [mal'sɛ̃], a. unhealthy; unwholesome, injurious.
malséant [malse'ã], a. unbecoming, unseemly, improper.
malsonnant [malsɔ'nã], a. ill-sounding; offensive.
malt [malt], n.m. malt.
maltais [mal'te], a. Maltese.—n.m. Maltese (*language*); (**Maltais**, *fem.* **-aise**) Maltese (*person*).
Malte [malt], **la**, f. Malta.
maltraiter [maltrɛ'te], v.t. to ill-use, to maltreat, to abuse.
malveillamment [malvɛja'mã], adv. malevolently.
malveillance [malvɛ'jã:s], n.f. malevolence, ill-will, malice.
malveillant [malvɛ'jã], a. malevolent, malignant, ill-disposed, spiteful.—n.m. (*fem.* **-e**) evil-minded person.
malversation [malvɛrsa'sjɔ̃], n.f. malversation, peculation, embezzlement.
maman [ma'mã], n.f. mamma, mummy.
mamelle [ma'mɛl], n.f. breast; udder.
mamelon [mam'lɔ̃], n.m. nipple, teat; dug (*of animals*); pap, hillock, knoll.
mameluk [mam'luk], n.m. Mameluke.
mammouth [ma'mut], n.m. mammoth.
manant [ma'nã], n.m. peasant, clodhopper.
manche (1) [mã:ʃ], n.m. handle; neck (*of violin etc.*).
manche (2) [mã:ʃ], n.f. sleeve; hose; channel; (*Spt.*) rubber, game, heat.
Manche [mã:ʃ], **la**, f. The (English) Channel. *Les Îles de la Manche*, the Channel Islands.
manchette [mã'ʃɛt], n.f. cuff; ruffle; wristband.
manchon [mã'ʃɔ̃], n.m. muff.
manchot [mã'ʃo], a. one-handed, one-armed.—n.m. penguin; (*fem.* **-e**) one-handed, one-armed person.
mandarin [mãda'rɛ̃], a. and n.m. (*fem.* **-ine** (1)) mandarin.
mandarine [mãda'rin], n.f. tangerine.
mandat [mã'da], n.m. mandate, authority; warrant, writ; money order, order.
mandataire [mãda'tɛːr], n.m. mandatory; proxy, attorney, agent.
mandchou [mãt'ʃu], a. Manchu(rian).—n.m. Manchu(rian) (*language*); (**Mandchou**, *fem.* **-oue**) Manchu(rian) (*person*).
Mandchourie [mãtʃu'ri], **la**, f. Manchuria.
mandement [mãd'mã], n.m. mandate; bishop's letter.
mander [mã'de], v.t. to write, to send word, to inform; to send for.
mandoline [mãdɔ'lin], n.f. mandolin.
mandoliniste [mãdɔli'nist], n. mandolin player.
manège [ma'nɛ:ʒ], n.m. horsemanship; riding school; merry-go-round; (*fig.*) trick, intrigue.
mânes [mɑ:n], n.m. pl. manes, shades.
manette [ma'nɛt], n.f. hand lever, grip; (*Hort.*) trowel.
mangeable [mã'ʒabl], a. eatable, edible.
mangeoire [mã'ʒwa:r], n.f. manger, crib.
manger [mã'ʒe], v.t. (*see Verb Tables*) to eat; (*fig.*) to squander, to run through.—v.i. to eat; to feed.—n.m. eating; victuals, food.

se manger, v.r. to eat each other; to hurt each other; to be edible.
mangeur [mã'ʒœːr], n.m. (*fem.* **-euse**) eater; spendthrift.
mangouste [mã'gust], n.f. mongoose.
maniable [ma'njabl], a. easy to handle; tractable, supple, pliable.
maniaque [ma'njak], a. eccentric, having a mania.—n. crank, faddist.
manicure [mani'ky:r], [MANUCURE].
manie [ma'ni], n.f. mania; fad, hobby; inveterate habit, craze.
maniement [mani'mã], n.m. handling; management, use.
manier [ma'nje], v.t. to handle; to touch; to use, to wield; to manage, to govern.
manière [ma'njɛːr], n.f. manner, way, style; sort; affectation; (*pl.*) manners; *de manière à*, so as to; *de quelle manière*, how; *manière d'être*, bearing, attitude.
maniéré [manje're], a. affected, unnatural, forced.
maniérisme [manje'rism], n.m. mannerism.
manifestation [manifesta'sjɔ̃], n.f. manifestation; (*Polit.*) demonstration.
manifeste [mani'fɛst], a. manifest, obvious.—n.m. manifesto.
manifestement [manifɛstə'mã], adv. manifestly.
manifester [manifɛs'te], v.t. to manifest, to display, to show.—v.i. to attend a (*political*) demonstration. **se manifester**, v.r. to manifest oneself, to make oneself known.
manigance [mani'gã:s], n.f. (*fam.*) maneuver, intrigue.
manigancer [manigã'se], v.t. (*conjug. like* COMMENCER) to contrive, to plot.
Manille [ma'ni:j], **la**, f. Manila.
manipulateur [manipyla'tœ:r], n.m. (*fem.* **-trice**) manipulator.
manipulation [manipyla'sjɔ̃], n.f. manipulation.
manipuler [manipy'le], v.t. to manipulate; (*Teleg.*) to operate.
manivelle [mani'vɛl], n.f. crank; handle.
manne (1) [ma:n], n.f. manna.
manne (2) [ma:n], n.f. hamper, flat basket.
mannequin (1) [man'kɛ̃], n.m. small hamper.
mannequin (2) [man'kɛ̃], n.m. lay figure; tailor's dummy; model girl; mannequin.
manœuvre [ma'nœ:vr], n.f. working; drilling (*of soldiers*); maneuver; scheme; move; (*Rail.*) marshalling.—n.m. unskilled workman, laborer.
manœuvrer [manœ'vre], v.t. to maneuver; to work (*a machine*); to shunt (*trains*).
manœuvrier [manœvri'e], a. (*fem.* **-ière**) highly trained.—n.m. expert seaman; tactician.
manoir [ma'nwa:r], n.m. manor; country house.
manouvrier [manuvri'e], n.m. (*fem.* **-ière**) day laborer.
manquant [mã'kã], a. missing, absent, wanting.—n.m. (*fem.* **-e**) absentee, defaulter.—n.m. (*pl.*) shortages, deficiencies.
manque [mã:k], n.m. want, lack; defect; deficiency.
manqué [mã'ke], a. missed; defective; unsuccessful, abortive.
manquement [mãkə'mã], n.m. omission, oversight; failure; breach.

209

manquer [mã'ke], v.t. to miss, to lose; to spoil.—v.i. to miss, to fail; to be wanting; to be deficient; to slip; to misfire; to go bankrupt; to miscarry.

mansarde [mã'sard], n.f. roof window, dormer; garret.

mansardé [mãsar'de], a. with attics.

mansuétude [mãsɥe'tyd], n.f. mildness, gentleness, forbearance.

mante (1) [mã:t], n.f. mantle (woman's).

mante (2) [mã:t], n.f. mantis; *mante religieuse*, praying mantis.

manteau [mã'to], n.m. (pl. **-eaux**) cloak, mantle; overcoat; (fig.) pretence.

mantille [mã'ti:j], n.f. mantilla.

manucure [many'ky:r], **manicure** [mani'ky:r], n. manicure (person), manicurist.

manuel [ma'nɥɛl], a. (fem. **-elle**) manual, portable.—n.m. manual, textbook.

manuellement [manɥɛl'mã], adv. by hand, manually.

manufacture [manyfak'ty:r], n.f. manufacture, making; factory, mill, works.

manufacturer [manyfakty're], v.t. to manufacture.

manufacturier [manyfakty'rje], a. (fem. **-ière**) manufacturing.—n.m. manufacturer.

manuscrit [manys'kri], a. handwritten.—n.m. manuscript.

manutention [manytã'sjɔ̃], n.f. management, administration; manipulation; handling (of goods etc.); army bakery.

mappemonde [map'mɔ̃:d], n.f. map of the world, planisphere.

maquereau [ma'kro], n.m. (pl. **-eaux**) mackerel.

maquette [ma'kɛt], n.f. (Sculp.) small rough model (in clay, wax etc.); (Paint.) rough sketch; lay figure; (Theat., Cine.) model.

maquignon [maki'ɲɔ̃], n.m. (fem. **-onne**) horse dealer, jobber.

maquignonnage [makiɲɔ'na:ʒ], n.m. horse-dealing; underhand work, jobbery.

maquignonner [makiɲɔ'ne], v.t. to jockey, to bishop (a horse for sale); to job.

maquillage [maki'ja:ʒ], n.m. make-up.

maquiller [maki'je], v.t. to make up; to fake up. **se maquiller**, v.r. to make up or paint oneself.

maquilleur [maki'jœ:r], n.m. (fem. **-euse**) (Theat.) maker-up; faker (of paintings etc.).

maquis [ma'ki], n.m. inv. scrub (in Corsica); (1941-44) underground forces.

maquisard [maki'za:r], n.m. free fighter in the maquis.

maraîcher [mare'ʃe], a. (fem. **-ère**) of market gardening.—n.m. market gardener.

marais [ma'rɛ], n.m. marsh, fen, bog, swamp.

marasme [ma'rasm], n.m. emaciation; (fig.) depression; stagnation, slump.

marâtre [ma'ra:tr], n.f. stepmother; (fig.) harsh mother.

maraudage [maro'da:ʒ], n.m. marauding.

maraude [ma'ro:d], n.f. pilfering.

marauder [maro'de], v.i. to pilfer, to go scrounging.

maraudeur [maro'dœ:r], n.m. (fem. **-euse**) marauder; plunderer.

marbre [marbr], n.m. marble.

marbré [mar'bre], a. marbled.

marbrer [mar'bre], v.t. to marble, to vein.

marbrerie [marbrə'ri], n.f. marble-cutting; marble works.

marbrier [marbri'e], a. (fem. **-ière**) of marble.—n.m. marble cutter, marble polisher; dealer in marble.—n.f. (**-ière**) marble quarry.

marbrure [mar'bry:r], n.f. marbling; mottling (on the skin).

marc [ma:r], n.m. residuum (of fruit etc. squeezed, boiled or strained); dregs, grounds.

Marc [mark], m. Mark.

marchand [mar'ʃɑ̃], a. saleable, trading.—n.m. (fem. **-e**) dealer, tradesman, shopkeeper; merchant; *marchand des quatre saisons*, hawker of fruits etc.; *marchand au détail*, retail merchant; *marchand en gros*, wholesale dealer.

marchandage [marʃɑ̃'da:ʒ], n.m. bargaining, haggling; piece-work.

marchander [marʃɑ̃'de], v.t. to bargain for; to haggle over; (fig.) to spare; to grudge.—v.i. to haggle; to hesitate.

marchandeur [marʃɑ̃'dœ:r], n.m. (fem. **-euse**) bargainer, haggler; contractor on small scale.

marchandise [marʃɑ̃'di:z], n.f. merchandise; goods, wares, commodities.

marche (1) [marʃ], n.f. walk; gait; march, journey; procession; movement; conduct; *marche arrière*, reversing (of a car); *mettre en marche*, to set going.

marche (2) [marʃ], n.f. step, stair; treadle.

marché [mar'ʃe], n.m. market; market-place; bargain, purchase; price, rate; contract; *à bon marché*, cheaply; *bon marché*, cheap, cheapness.

marchepied [marʃə'pje], n.m. step (of a coach, altar etc.); step-ladder; running-board.

marcher [mar'ʃe], v.i. to walk; to progress; to step, to tread; to march; to run, to ply; to work (of a machine).

marcheur [mar'ʃœ:r], n.m. (fem. **-euse**) walker.

mardi [mar'di], n.m. Tuesday; *mardi gras*, Shrove Tuesday.

mare [ma:r], n.f. pool, pond.

marécage [mare'ka:ʒ], n.m. marsh, bog, fen, swamp.

marécageux [mareka'ʒø], a. (fem. **-euse**) marshy, swampy, boggy.

maréchal [mare'ʃal], n.m. (pl. **-aux**) marshal, field marshal.

maréchalerie [mareʃal'ri], n.f. farriery, smithy.

maréchal-ferrant [mareʃalfe'rɑ̃], n.m. (pl. **maréchaux-ferrants**) farrier, shoeing smith.

marée [ma're], n.f. tide, flood; fresh sea-fish.

marelle [ma'rɛl], n.f. hopscotch.

mareyeur [mare'jœ:r] n.m. fish dealer, fish-salesman.

margarine [marga'rin], n.f. margarine.

marge [marʒ], n.f. margin, border, edge; (fig.) freedom, latitude, scope; means.

margelle [mar'ʒɛl], n.f. curb, edge (of a well etc.).

Marguerite [margə'rit], f. Margaret.

marguerite [margə'rit], n.f. daisy.

marguillier [margi'je], n.m. churchwarden.

mari [ma'ri], n.m. husband.

mariable [ma'rjabl], a. marriageable.

mariage [ma'rja:ʒ], *n.m.* marriage; matrimony; wedding; union, blending.

Marie [ma'ri], *f.* Mary, Maria.

marié [ma'rje], *a.* married.—*n.m.* (*fem.* **-ée**) married man; bridegroom; married woman; bride.

marier [ma'rje], *v.t.* to give in marriage, to marry off; to match. **se marier**, *v.r.* to marry, to get married (*avec*).

marieur [ma'rjœ:r], *n.m.* (*fem.* **-euse**) matchmaker.

marin [ma'rɛ̃], *a.* marine; sea-going.—*n.m.* sailor.

marinade [mari'nad], *n.f.* pickle, souse.

marine [ma'rin], *n.f.* sea service; Admiralty; navy.

mariner [mari'ne], *v.t.* to pickle, to souse.

marinier [mari'nje], *a.* (*fem.* **-ière** (1)) *officiers mariniers*, petty officers.—*n.m.* bargeman, lighter-man.—*n.f.* (**-ière**) (*Swim.*) side stroke.

marinière (2) [mari'nje:r], *n.f.* (*Cook.*) onion sauce.

marionnette [marjo'nɛt], *n.f.* puppet, marionette; (*pl.*) puppet show.

marital [mari'tal], *a.* (*m. pl.* **-aux**) marital.

maritalement [marital'mã], *adv.* maritally, as man and wife.

maritime [mari'tim], *a.* maritime, naval.

marmaille [mar'ma:j], *n.f.* (*colloq.*) brats.

marmelade [marmə'lad], *n.f.* compote; (*fig.*) jelly, soup.

marmite [mar'mit], *n.f.* cooking pot.

marmiteux [marmi'tø], *a.* (*fem.* **-euse**) pitiful, wretched, miserable.—*n.m.* (*fem.* **-euse**) poor devil.

marmiton [marmi'tɔ̃], *n.m.* scullion.

marmonner [marmɔ'ne], *v.t.* to mutter.

marmoréen [marmɔre'ɛ̃], *a.* (*fem.* **-éenne**) marmorean.

marmot [mar'mo], *n.m.* kid, brat, urchin.

marmotte [mar'mɔt], *n.f.* marmot.

marmotter [marmɔ'te], *v.t., v.i.* to mutter, to mumble.

marmouset [marmu'zɛ], *n.m.* grotesque figure; young monkey (*little boy*); fire-dog.

marne [marn], *n.f.* marl, chalk, clay.

marner [mar'ne], *v.t.* to marl.

marneux [mar'nø], *a.* (*fem.* **-euse**) marly.

marnière [mar'nje:r], *n.f.* marlpit.

Maroc [ma'rɔk], le, *m.* Morocco.

marocain [marɔ'kɛ̃], *a.* Moroccan.—*n.m.* (**Marocain**, *fem.* **-aine**) Moroccan (*person*).

maroquin [marɔ'kɛ̃], *n.m.* morocco leather.

maroquiner [marɔki'ne], *v.t.* to morocco.

maroquinerie [marɔkin'ri], *n.f.* morocco leather manufacture or factory.

maroquinier [marɔki'nje], *n.m.* morocco leather tanner.

marotte [ma'rɔt], *n.f.* cap and bells; hairdresser's dummy head; (*fig.*) fancy, hobby.

marquant [mar'kã], *a.* conspicuous, striking.

marque [mark], *n.f.* mark, imprint, stamp; cipher, trade mark, make; badge, sign, token; proof; distinction.

marqué [mar'ke], *a.* marked, conspicuous, obvious; determined.

marquer [mar'ke], *v.t.* to mark; to stamp; to brand; to indicate; to denote; to testify; to score.—*v.i.* to mark, to be remarkable; to show off.

marqueter [markə'te], *v.t.* (*conjug. like* APPELER) to speckle, to spot; to inlay.

marqueterie [markə'tri], *n.f.* marquetry, inlaid work, inlaying.

marqueur [mar'kœ:r], *n.m.* (*fem.* **-euse**) marker; scorer.

marquis [mar'ki], *n.m.* marquess, marquis.

marquise [mar'ki:z], *n.f.* marchioness; marquee, glass porch or roof.

marraine [ma'rɛn], *n.f.* godmother; sponsor.

marron (1) [ma'rɔ̃], *a. inv.* maroon, chestnut-color.—*n.m.* chestnut; cracker (*fireworks*); *marron d'Inde*, horse chestnut.

marron (2) [ma'rɔ̃] *a.* (*fem.* **-onne**) fugitive, runaway (*of slaves*); (*Comm.*) unlicensed; unqualified (*doctor etc.*).

marronnier [marɔ'nje], *n.m.* chestnut tree; *marronnier d'Inde*, horse chestnut tree.

mars [mars], *n.m.* March.

Marseillaise [marsɛ'jɛ:z], *n.f.* Marseillaise (*French national anthem*).

marsouin [mar'swɛ̃], *n.m.* porpoise.

marte [MARTRE].

marteau [mar'to], *n.m.* (*pl.* **-eaux**) hammer; *marteau de porte*, knocker; *marteau pneumatique*, pneumatic drill.

marteau-pilon [martopi'lɔ̃], *n.m.* (*pl.* **marteaux-pilons**) steam hammer.

martelage [martə'la:ʒ], *n.m.* hammering; marking (*of trees*).

martelé [martə'le], *a.* hammered; (*Mus.*) brilliant and distinct.

marteler [martə'le], *v.t.* (*conjug. like* AMENER) to hammer; to mark (*trees*).

Marthe [mart], *f.* Martha.

martial [mar'sjal], *a.* (*m. pl.* **-aux**) martial, warlike, soldierly.

martinet (1) [marti'nɛ], *n.m.* (*Orn.*) swift, martlet.

martinet (2) [marti'nɛ], *n.m.* tilt hammer; cat-o'-nine-tails.

martingale [martɛ̃'gal], *n.f.* martingale; *jouer la martingale*, to play double or quits.

martin-pêcheur [martɛ̃pɛ'ʃœ:r], *n.m.* (*pl.* **martins-pêcheurs**) kingfisher; *martin-pêcheur d'Australie*, laughing jackass.

martre [martr], **marte** [mart], *n.f.* marten.

martyr [mar'ti:r], *n.m.* (*fem.* **martyre** (1)) martyr.

martyre (2) [mar'ti:r], *n.m.* martyrdom.

martyriser [martiri'ze], *v.t.* to martyrize; to torment, to torture.

marxisme [mark'sism], *n.m.* Marxism.

marxiste [mark'sist], *a.* and *n.* Marxist.

mascarade [maska'rad], *n.f.* masquerade.

mascotte [mas'kɔt], *n.f.* mascot, charm.

masculin [masky'lɛ̃], *a.* masculine, male.—*n.m.* (*Gram.*) masculine.

masculiniser [maskylini'ze], *v.t.* to make masculine.

masculinité [maskylini'te], *n.f.* masculinity.

masque [mask], *n.m.* mask; (*fig.*) blind, cloak, pretence; masquerader, mummer; (*Fenc.*) face guard.

masqué [mas'ke], *a.* masked; disguised; concealed; *virage masqué*, blind corner.

masquer [mas'ke], *v.t.* to mask; to cloak, to disguise; to conceal.

massacrant [masa'krã], *a.* used chiefly in *être d'une humeur massacrante*, to be in an awful temper.

massacre [ma'sakr], *n.m.* massacre, butchery, slaughter; (*fig.*) havoc, waste.

massacrer [masa'kre], *v.t.* to massacre, to butcher, to murder, to slaughter; (*fig.*) to bungle.

massacreur [masa'krœːr], *n.m.* (*fem.* -**euse**) slaughterer, slayer; (*fig.*) bungler.

massage [ma'saːʒ], *n.m.* massage.

masse (1) [mas], *n.f.* mass, heap, lump; mob; stock; (*Elec.*) ground.

masse (2) [mas], *n.f.* sledge-hammer.

massepain [mas'pɛ̃], *n.m.* marzipan.

masser [ma'se], *v.t.* to mass (*troops etc.*); to massage.

masseur [ma'sœːr], *n.m.* (*fem.* -**euse**) masseur, masseuse.

massier [ma'sje], *n.m.* mace bearer.

massif [ma'sif], *a.* (*fem.* -**ive**) massive, bulky, massy, solid; lumpish, heavy.—*n.m.* clump (*of trees, flowers etc.*); solid mass *or* block (*of masonry*); (*Geog.*) massif.

massivement [masiv'mɑ̃], *adv.* massively, heavily, solidly.

massiveté [masiv'te], *n.f.* massiveness.

massue [ma'sy], *n.f.* club (*weapon*).

mastic [mas'tik], *n.m.* mastic; cement; putty; filling (*for teeth*); plastic wood.

masticage [masti'kaːʒ], *n.m.* cementing; puttying; filling.

mastication [mastika'sjɔ̃], *n.f.* mastication, chewing.

mastiquer (1) [masti'ke], *v.t.* to masticate.

mastiquer (2) [masti'ke], *v.t.* to putty, to cement.

mastodonte [masto'dɔ̃ːt], *n.m.* mastodon.

mastoïde [masto'id], *a.* mastoid.

masure [ma'zyːr], *n.f.* hovel, tumbledown cottage.

mat (1) [mat], *n.m.* (*Chess*) mate.

mat (2) [mat], *a.* mat, dull, unpolished; dull-sounding; heavy, sodden.

mât [mɑ], *n.m.* mast; pole.

matador [mata'dɔːr], *n.m.* matador.

matamore [mata'mɔːr], *n.m.* blusterer, braggart.

match [matʃ], *n.m.* (*pl.* **matches**) (*Spt.*) match; *match nul*, draw.

matelas [ma'tlɑ], *n.m.* mattress; pad, cushion; *toile à matelas*, ticking.

matelasser [matla'se], *v.t.* to stuff, to pad.

matelot [ma'tlo], *n.m.* sailor, seaman.

matelote [ma'tlɔt], *n.f.* sailor's wife; fish stew.

mater (1) [ma'te], *v.t.* to checkmate; to bring down, to subdue.

mater (2) [ma'te], *v.t.* to make mat *or* dull, to deaden.

matérialiser [materjali'ze], *v.t.* to materialize.

matérialisme [materja'lism], *n.m.* materialism.

matérialiste [materja'list], *a.* materialistic.—*n.* materialist.

matériaux [mate'rjo], *n.m. pl.* materials.

matériel [mate'rjɛl], *a.* (*fem.* -**elle**) material; gross, rough; heavy, dull.—*n.m.* material, working stock, implements, plant.

matériellement [materjɛl'mɑ̃], *adv.* materially; positively; sensually.

maternel [mater'nɛl], *a.* (*fem.* -**elle**) maternal, motherly; *école maternelle*, nursery school.

maternité [materni'te], *n.f.* maternity.

mathématicien [matemati'sjɛ̃], *n.m.* (*fem.* -**enne**) mathematician.

mathématique [matema'tik], *a.* mathematical.—*n.f.* (*usu. in pl.*) mathematics.

mathématiquement [matematik'mɑ̃], *adv.* mathematically.

matière [ma'tjɛːr], *n.f.* matter; material; subject matter; cause, motive; contents; *matière première*, raw material.

matin [ma'tɛ̃], *n.m.* morning, forenoon; prime, dawn.—*adv.* early, early in the morning.

mâtin [mɑ'tɛ̃], *n.m.* mastiff; big mongrel dog.

matinal [mati'nal], *a.* (*m. pl.* -**aux**) morning, early; early-rising.

matinée [mati'ne], *n.f.* morning, forenoon; afternoon performance, matinée.

matines [ma'tin], *n.f. pl.* matins.

matineux [mati'nø], *a.* (*fem.* -**euse**) rising early.

matois [ma'twa], *a.* cunning, artful, sly.—*n.m.* (*fem.* -**e**) cunning person, sly dog.

matoisement [matwaz'mɑ̃], *adv.* cunningly, slyly.

matoiserie [matwaz'ri], *n.f.* cunning; wile.

matou [ma'tu], *n.m.* tom-cat; (*fam.*) curmudgeon.

matraque [ma'trak], *n.f.* bludgeon; truncheon.

matriarcal [matriar'kal], *a.* (*m. pl.* -**aux**) matriarchal.

matriarcat [matriar'ka], *n.m.* matriarchy.

matrice [ma'tris], *n.f.* womb, matrix.

matricide [matri'sid], *a.* matricidal.—*n.* matricide (*person*).—*n.m.* matricide (*crime*).

matricule [matri'kyl], *n.f.* register, roll; matriculation.—*n.m.* regimental number (*of a soldier*); number (*of a rifle etc.*).

matrimonial [matrimo'njal], *a.* (*m. pl.* -**aux**) matrimonial.

Matthieu [ma'tjø], *m.* Matthew.

maturation [matyra'sjɔ̃], *n.f.* maturation.

mâture [mɑ'tyːr], *n.f.* masting, masts and spars.

maturité [matyri'te], *n.f.* maturity, ripeness.

maudire [mo'diːr], *v.t. irr.* to curse; to detest.

maudissable [modi'sabl], *a.* execrable, detestable.

maudit [mo'di], *a.* cursed, accursed; wretched.

maugréer [mogre'e], *v.i.* to fret and fume, to curse and swear.

maure [MORE].

Maurice [mɔ'ris], *m.* Maurice; *l'île Maurice*, Mauritius.

Mauritanie [mɔrita'ni], **la,** *f.* Mauritania.

mauritanien [mɔrita'njɛ̃], *a.* (*fem.* -**enne**) Mauritanian.—*n.m.* (**Mauritanien,** *fem.* -**enne**) Mauritanian (*person*).

mausolée [mozo'le], *n.m.* mausoleum.

maussade [mo'sad], *a.* sulky, sullen, cross; disagreeable, dull.

maussadement [mosad'mɑ̃], *adv.* disagreeably, sullenly, peevishly.

maussaderie [mosa'dri], *n.f.* sullenness, sulkiness.

mauvais [mo'vɛ], *a.* bad, ill, evil; naughty; mischievous; hurtful; wrong; unpleasant; wretched; nasty.—*n.m.* bad.—*adv.* bad, badly, wrong.

mauve [moːv] *a.* mauve.—*n.f.* (*Bot.*) mallow.

maxillaire [maksi'lɛ:r], a. maxillary.—n.m. jaw-bone.
maxime [mak'sim], n.f. maxim.
maximum [maksi'nɔm], a. (fem. **maxima**) maximum.—n.m. (pl. **maxima** or **maximums**) maximum; acme.
mayonnaise [majɔ'nɛ:z], n.f. mayonnaise.
mazout [ma'ʒut], n.m. fuel oil.
me [mə], pron. pers. me; to me.
méandre [me'ɑ̃:dr], n.m. meander, winding.
mécanicien [mekani'sjɛ̃], n.m. mechanic; engine driver, (Am.) engineer; **ingénieur mécanicien**, mechanical engineer.
mécanique [meka'nik], a. mechanical.—n.f. mechanics; mechanism, machinery; machine.
mécaniquement [mekanik'mɑ̃], adv. mechanically.
mécanisation [mekaniza'sjɔ̃], n.f. mechanization.
mécaniser [mekani'ze], v.t. to mechanize.
mécanisme [meka'nism], n.m. mechanism, machinery.
méchamment [meʃa'mɑ̃], adv. wickedly; maliciously.
méchanceté [meʃɑ̃s'te], n.f. wickedness; spitefulness; naughtiness.
méchant [me'ʃɑ̃], a. wicked, evil, bad; spiteful, malicious; naughty; paltry; vicious (of an animal); nasty.—n.m. (fem. -e) wicked person, evil-doer; naughty child.
mèche [mɛːʃ], n.f. wick (of candle); fuse; bit, drill; worm (of screws); lock (of hair).
mécompte [me'kɔ̃:t], n.m. miscalculation; mistake; disappointment.
méconnaissable [mekɔnɛ'sabl], a. unrecognizable.
méconnaissance [mekɔnɛ'sɑ̃:s], n.f. misappreciation, misreading; ingratitude.
méconnaître [mekɔ'nɛ:tr], v.t. irr. (conjug. like CONNAÎTRE) not to recognize; to disown, to disregard, to ignore; to misjudge. **se méconnaître**, v.r. to forget oneself.
méconnu [mekɔ'ny], a. unrecognized, unacknowledged; ignored, disowned.
mécontent [mekɔ̃'tɑ̃], a. displeased, dissatisfied.—n.m. (fem. -e) malcontent.
mécontentement [mekɔ̃tɑ̃t'mɑ̃], n.m. dissatisfaction, discontent.
mécontenter [mekɔ̃tɑ̃'te], v.t. to displease.
Mecque [mɛk], **la**, f. Mecca.
mécréant [mekre'ɑ̃], n.m. (fem. -e) unbeliever, infidel.
médaille [me'da:j], n.f. medal; (Arch.) medallion.
médaillé [meda'je], a. with a medal as a reward; having a badge (of hawker, porter etc.).—n.m. (fem. -ée) holder of a medal.
médaillon [meda'jɔ̃], n.m. medallion; locket.
médecin [med'sɛ̃], n.m. physician, doctor; **faire venir le médecin**, to send for the doctor.
médecine [med'sin], n.f. medicine.
médiateur [medja'tœ:r], a. (fem. -trice) mediatory.—n.m. (fem. -trice) mediator.
médiation [medja'sjɔ̃], n.f. mediation.
médical [medi'kal], a. (m. pl. -aux) medical.
médicament [medika'mɑ̃], n.m. medicine, drug.
médicamenter [medikamɑ̃'te], v.t. to physic, to doctor.
médication [medikɑ'sjɔ̃], n.f. medication.

médicinal [medisi'nal], a. (m. pl. -aux) medicinal.
médiéval [medje'val], a. (m. pl. -aux) medi(a)eval.
médiocre [me'djɔkr], a. mediocre, middling; moderate.—n.m. mediocrity.
médiocrement [medjɔkrə'mɑ̃], adv. middlingly, indifferently; poorly; barely.
médiocrité [medjɔkri'te], n.f. mediocrity.
médire [me'di:r], v.i. irr. to slander, to speak ill of, to traduce.
médisance [medi'zɑ̃:s], n.f. slander, scandal.
médisant [medi'zɑ̃], a. slanderous, scandalous.—n.m. (fem. -e) slanderer, scandalmonger.
méditatif [medita'tif], a. (fem. -tive) meditative, pensive.
méditation [medita'sjɔ̃], n.f. meditation.
méditer [medi'te], v.t. to meditate, to think over; to plan.—v.i. to meditate, to muse.
méditerrané [mediteʁa'ne], a. inland; **la (Mer) Méditerranée**, the Mediterranean (Sea).
méditerranéen [mediteʁane'ɛ̃], a. (fem. -enne) Mediterranean.
médium [me'djɔm], n.m. medium.
médoc [me'dɔk], n.m. or **vin de Médoc**, Médoc (claret).
meeting [mi'tiŋ], n.m. (Polit., Spt.) meeting.
méfait [me'fɛ], n.m. misdeed, crime.
méfiance [me'fjɑ̃:s], n.f. mistrust, distrust, suspicion.
méfiant [me'fjɑ̃], a. distrustful, suspicious.
méfier (se) [səme'fje], v.r. to mistrust, to distrust, to be suspicious of (de).
mégaphone [mega'fɔn], n.m. megaphone.
mégarde [me'gard], n.f. inadvertence; **par mégarde**, inadvertently.
mégère [me'ʒɛ:r], n.f. shrew, vixen.
mégot [me'go], n.m. (pop.) cigar stump, cigarette end.
meilleur [me'jœ:r], a. better; preferable; **le meilleur**, the best; **meilleur marché**, cheaper; **de meilleure heure**, earlier.—n.m. best.
mélancolie [melɑ̃kɔ'li], n.f. melancholy, sadness, gloom, dejection.
mélancolique [melɑ̃kɔ'lik], a. melancholy; dismal, gloomy.
mélancoliquement [melɑ̃kɔlik'mɑ̃], adv. gloomily.
mélange [me'lɑ̃:ʒ], n.m. mixture, mingling; blending (of tea); medley; mash (for brewing).
mélanger [melɑ̃'ʒe], v.t. and **se mélanger**, v.r. (conjug. like MANGER) to mix, to mingle, to blend.
mélasse [me'las], n.f. molasses treacle.
mêlé [mɛ'le], a. mixed; miscellaneous.
mêlée [mɛ'le], n.f. conflict, fray; scramble, scuffle, free fight.
mêler [mɛ'le], v.t. to mingle, to mix; to blend; to jumble; to entangle, to involve; to shuffle (cards). **se mêler**, v.r. to mingle to blend, to intermingle; to trouble oneself (de); to interfere (de); to have a hand in; to get entangled, to be mixed up (dans); **mêlez-vous de vos affaires**, mind your own business.
mélèze [me'lɛ:z], n.m. larch.
mélodie [melɔ'di], n.f. melody; melodiousness.

213

mélodieusement [melɔdjøz'mã], *adv.* tunefully.

mélodieux [melɔ'djø], *a.* (*fem.* **-euse**) melodious, musical, tuneful.

mélodramatique [melɔdrama'tik], *a.* melodramatic.

mélodrame [melɔ'dram], *n.m.* melodrama.

melon [mə'lɔ̃], *n.m.* melon; derby (hat).

membrane [mã'bran], *n.f.* membrane; web (*of duck's foot etc.*).

membraneux [mãbra'nø], *a.* (*fem.* **-euse**) membranous.

membre [mã:br], *n.m.* limb; member.

membrure [mã'bry:r], *n.f.* limbs, frame (*of a person etc.*); ribs, timbers (*of a ship*).

même [mɛ:m], *a.* same; self, self-same, very same; **moi-même**, myself.—*adv.* even, also; **à même de**, in a position to, able to; **de même**, likewise; **quand même**, even though; **tout de même**, all the same.

mémoire (1) [me'mwa:r], *n.f.* memory; remembrance; commemoration; fame; **de mémoire** from memory; **de mémoire d'homme**, within living memory.

mémoire (2) [me'mwa:r], *n.m.* memorandum, bill, statement of account; (*Sci., Lit.*) treatise; memorial; (*pl.*) memoirs.

mémorable [memɔ'rabl], *a.* memorable.

mémorandum [memɔrã'dɔm], *n.m.* memorandum; notebook.

mémorial [memɔ'rjal], *n.m.* (*pl.* **-aux**) memorial; memoirs; (*Comm.*) daybook.

menaçant [məna'sã], *a.* menacing, threatening.

menace [mə'nas], *n.f.* menace, threat.

menacer [məna'se], *v.t.* (*conjug. like* COMMENCER) to threaten, to menace; to forebode; to impend.

ménage [me'na:ʒ], *n.m.* housekeeping; household, family, married couple; household equipment; economy; **faire bon ménage**, to live happily together; **faire des ménages**, to do housework by the day; **femme de ménage**, housemaid.

ménagement [menaʒ'mã], *n.m.* regard, circumspection, caution, discretion.

ménager [mena'ʒe], *v.t.* (*conjug. like* MANGER) to be sparing of, to save; to be careful of, to treat with caution, to humor; to procure; to contrive. **se ménager**, *v.r.* to take care of oneself; to spare oneself.—*a.* (*fem.* **-ère**) thrifty, sparing, frugal; household.—*n.f.* (**-ère**) housewife, housekeeper; cruet stand; tableware.

ménagerie [menaʒ'ri], *n.f.* menagerie.

mendiant [mã'djɔ̃], *n.m.* (*fem.* **-e**) beggar, mendicant.

mendicité [mãdisi'te], *n.f.* begging, mendicity.

mendier [mã'dje], *v.t.* to beg for.—*v.i.* to beg.

mener [mə'ne], *v.t.* (*conjug. like* AMENER) to guide, to conduct, to lead; to drive (*a carriage*); to steer (*a boat etc.*); to bring, to take; to manage.—*v.i.* to lead, to conduct, to go.

ménestrel [menɛs'trɛl], *n.m.* minstrel.

meneur [mə'nœ:r], *n.m.* (*fem.* **-euse**) driver, leader; agitator, ringleader.

méningite [menɛ̃'ʒit], *n.f.* meningitis.

menotte [mə'nɔt], *n.f.* (*colloq.*) little hand (*of a child*); (*pl.*) handcuffs.

menotter [mənɔ'te], *v.t.* to handcuff.

mensonge [mã's3:3], *n.m.* lie, falsehood, untruth.

mensonger [mãsɔ̃'ʒe], *a.* (*fem.* **-ère**) lying, untrue, false.

menstruation [mãstryɑ'sjɔ̃], *n.f.* menstruation.

menstrues [mã'stry], *n.f. pl.* menses, periods.

mensualité [mãsɥali'te], *n.f.* monthly payment.

mensuel [mã'sɥɛl], *a.* (*fem.* **-elle**) monthly.

mensuellement [mãsɥɛl'mã], *adv.* · onthly.

mensuration [mãsyrɑ'sjɔ̃], *n.f.* measurement.

mental [mã'tal], *a.* (*m. pl.* **-aux**) mental.

mentalement [mãtal'mã], *adv.* mentally.

mentalité [mãtali'te], *n.f.* mentality.

menteur [mã'tœ:r], *a.* (*fem.* **-euse**) lying, false, deceitful.—*n.m.* (*fem.* **-euse**) liar, story-teller.

menthe [mã:t], *n.f.* mint.

mention [mã'sjɔ̃], *n.f.* mention; (*sch.*) **reçu avec mention**, passed with distinction.

mentionner [mãsjɔ'ne], *v.t.* to mention, to name.

mentir [mã'ti:r], *v.i. irr.* (*conjug. like* SENTIR) to lie, to tell a lie or untruth.

menton [mã'tɔ̃], *n.m.* chin.

mentor [mã'tɔ:r], *n.m.* mentor, guide, tutor.

menu [mə'ny], *a.* slender, spare, thin, small; petty.—*n.m.* minute detail, particulars; menu, bill of fare; **par le menu**, in detail.—*adv.* small, fine, minutely, in small pieces; **hacher menu**, to mince.

menuet [mə'nɥɛ], *n.m.* minuet.

menuiser [mənɥi'ze], *v.t.* to saw, cut etc. (*wood*).—*v.i.* to do carpenter's work.

menuiserie [mənɥiz'ri], *n.f.* woodwork, joinery, carpentry.

menuisier [mənɥi'zje], *n.m.* joiner, carpenter.

méprendre (**se**) [səme'prã:dr], *v.r. irr.* (*conjug. like* PRENDRE) to mistake, to be mistaken.

mépris [me'pri], *n.m.* contempt, scorn.

méprisable [mepri'zabl], *a.* contemptible, despicable.

méprisant [mepri'zã], *a.* contemptuous, scornful.

méprise [me'pri:z], *n.f.* mistake, misunderstanding.

mépriser [mepri'ze], *v.t.* to despise, to scorn.

mer [mɛ:r], *n.f.* sea; **aller au bord de la mer**, to go to the seaside; **en pleine mer**, on the open sea; **mal de mer**, seasickness.

mercantile [mɛrkã'til], *a.* mercantile, commercial; (*fig.*) mercenary.

mercenaire [mɛrsə'nɛ:r], *a.* mercenary, venal.—*n.m.* mercenary, hireling.

mercerie [mɛrsə'ri], *n.f.* notions (store).

merci [mɛr'si], *n.f.* (*no pl.*) mercy, discretion, will.—*n.m.* thanks.—*int.* thank you, thanks.

mercier [mɛr'sje], *n.m.* (*fem.* **-ière**) dealer in notions.

mercredi [mɛrkrə'di], *n.m.* Wednesday; **mercredi des Cendres**, Ash Wednesday.

mercure [mɛr'ky:r], *n.m.* mercury, quicksilver.

mercuriel [mɛrky'rjɛl], *a.* (*fem.* **-elle**) mercurial.

mère [mɛ:r], *n.f.* mother; dam (*of animals*); (*fig.*) cause, reason.

méridien [meri'djɛ̃], *a.* (*fem.* **-enne**) and *n.m.* meridian.—*n.f.* (**-enne**) siesta.

méridional [meridjɔ'nal], *a.* (*m. pl.* **-aux**) meridional, southern.—*n.m.* (*fem.* **-e**) person of the Midi, southerner.

meringue [mə'rɛ̃:g], *n.f.* meringue (*confection*).

mérinos [meri'nɔːs], *n.m.* merino sheep; merino wool; merino (*material*).

merise [mə'riːz], *n.f.* wild cherry.

merisier [mari'zje], *n.m.* wild-cherry tree.

méritant [meri'tɑ̃], *a.* meritorious, worthy.

mérite [me'rit], *n.m.* merit, worth; desert.

mériter [meri'te], *v.t.* to deserve, to merit; to earn.—*v.i.* to be deserving (*de*).

méritoire [meri'twaːr], *a.* meritorious.

méritoirement [meritwar'mɑ̃], *adv.* meritoriously, deservingly.

merlan [mɛr'lɑ̃], *n.m.* whiting.

merle [mɛrl], *n.m.* blackbird.

merluche [mɛr'lyʃ], *n.f.* hake; dried cod.

merveille [mɛr'vɛːj], *n.f.* wonder, marvel, prodigy; *à merveille*, wonderfully well.

merveilleusement [mɛrvɛjøz'mɑ̃], *adv.* wonderfully, admirably.

merveilleux [mɛrvɛ'jø], *a.* (*fem.* **-euse**) wonderful, marvellous.—*n.m.* the wonderful, the marvellous part.

mes [me], *pl.* [MON].

mésalliance [meza'ljɑ̃:s], *n.f.* misalliance, bad match.

mésallier [meza'lje], *v.t.* to marry off (*somebody*) badly; (*fig.*) to disparage. **se mésallier**, *v.r.* to marry beneath one.

mésange [me'zɑ̃:ʒ], *n.f.* (*Orn.*) tit.

mésangette [mezɑ̃'ʒɛt], *n.f.* bird trap.

mésaventure [mezavɑ̃'tyːr], *n.f.* mischance, misadventure, misfortune.

mésentente [mezɑ̃'tɑ̃:t], *n.f.* misunderstanding; disagreement.

mésestime [mezes'tim], *n.f.* low esteem.

mésestimer [mezesti'me], *v.t.* to underestimate, to underrate.

mésintelligence [mezɛ̃teli'ʒɑ̃:s], *n.f.* misunderstanding, variance, disagreement.

mesmérisme [mɛsme'rism], *n.m.* mesmerism.

mesquin [mɛs'kɛ̃], *a.* shabby; paltry; mean.

mesquinement [mɛskin'mɑ̃], *adv.* shabbily, meanly.

mesquinerie [mɛskin'ri], *n.f.* meanness, shabbiness.

mess [mɛs], *n.m. inv.* (*Mil.*) mess.

message [me'saːʒ], *n.m.* message.

messager [mesa'ʒe], *n.m.* (*fem.* **-ère**) messenger; carrier; (*fig.*) forerunner.

messagerie [mesa'ʒri], *n.f.* shipping office; carriage of goods; goods department; parcels office; *messageries maritimes*, shipping service.

messe [mɛs], *n.f.* (*R.-C. Ch.*) mass.

messéance [mese'ɑ̃:s], *n.f.* unseemliness, impropriety.

messéant [mese'ɑ̃], *a.* unseemly, unbecoming, improper.

messeigneurs [mesɛ'nœːr], *pl.* [MONSEIGNEUR].

Messie [me'si], *m.* Messiah.

messieurs [me'sjø], *pl.* [MONSIEUR].

mesurable [mazy'rabl], *a.* measurable.

mesurage [mazy'raːʒ], *n.m.* measurement, measuring.

mesure [mə'zyːr], *n.f.* measure; gauge, standard; measurement, extent, limit; (*fig.*)

moderation; dimension; (*Mus.*) bar; (*Pros.*) metre; *à mesure que*, in proportion as, as; *outre mesure*, excessively; *se mettre en mesure de*, to prepare to, to get ready to.

mesuré [mazy're], *a.* measured, regular; cautious.

mesurer [mazy're], *v.t.* to measure; to proportion; to calculate; to compare, to consider. **se mesurer**, *v.r.* to try one's strength; (*fig.*) to vie, to contend, to cope.

mesureur [mazy'rœːr], *n.m.* measurer; meter.

mésusage [mezy'zaːʒ], *n.m.* misuse, abuse.

mésuser [mezy'ze], *v.i.* to misuse, to abuse (*de*).

métabolisme [metabɔ'lism], *n.m.* metabolism.

métairie [mete'ri], *n.f.* land, small farm.

métal [me'tal], *n.m.* (*pl.* **-aux**) metal.

métallique [meta'lik], *a.* metallic.

métallurgie [metalyr'ʒi], *n.f.* metallurgy.

métallurgiste [metalyr'ʒist], *n.m.* metallurgist.

métamorphose [metamɔr'foːz], *n.f.* metamorphosis, transformation.

métaphore [meta'foːr], *n.f.* metaphor.

métaphorique [metafɔ'rik], *a.* metaphorical.

métaphoriquement [metafɔrik'mɑ̃], *adv.* metaphorically.

métaphysique [metafi'zik], *a.* metaphysical. —*n.f.* metaphysics.

métatarse [meta'tars], *n.m.* (*Anat.*) metatarsus.

métayage [metɛ'jaːʒ], *n.m.* metayage.

métayer [metɛ'je], *n.m.* (*fem.* **-ère**) small farmer.

météo [mete'o], *n.f.* (*fam.*) meteorology; weather report; meteorological office.

météore [mete'oːr], *n.m.* meteor.

météorique [mete'rik], *a.* meteoric.

météorite [mete'rit], *n.m.* or *f.* meteorite.

météorologie [meteorolɔ'ʒi], *n.f.* meteorology.

météorologique [meteorolɔ'ʒik], *a.* meteorological.

météorologiste [meteorolɔ'ʒist], **météorologue** [meteoro'lɔg], *n.* meteorologist.

méthane [me'tan], *n.m.* marsh gas, methane.

méthode [me'tɔd], *n.f.* method, system; way.

méthodique [metɔ'dik], *a.* methodical, systematic.

méthodiquement [metɔdik'mɑ̃], *adv.* methodically.

méthodisme [metɔ'dism], *n.m.* Methodism.

méthodiste [metɔ'dist], *a.* and *n.* Methodist.

méticuleusement [metikyløz'mɑ̃], *adv.* meticulously.

méticuleux [metiky'lø], *a.* (*fem.* **-euse**) meticulous, fastidious.

méticulosité [metikylozi'te], *n.f.* meticulousness.

métier [me'tje], *n.m.* trade, business, calling, craft, profession; loom, frame; *arts et métiers*, arts and crafts; *corps de métier*, corporation, guild; *gens de métier*, professionals; *homme de métier*, craftsman; *métier manuel*, handicraft.

métis [me'tiːs], *a.* (*fem.* **-isse**) half-caste, cross-bred; hybrid (*plant*); mongrel (*dog*).— *n.m.* (*fem.* **-isse**) half-caste; mongrel (*dog*).

métissage [meti'saːʒ], *n.m.* cross-breeding.

métisser [meti'se], *v.t.* to cross-breed.

métrage

métrage [me'traːʒ], *n.m.* measurement (*in metres*); (*Cine.*) *court métrage*, short film.

mètre [mɛtr], *n.m.* metre (*1.09 yards*); rule, measure (*of 1 metre*); (*Pros.*) metre.

métrer [me'tre], *v.t.* (*conjug. like* CÉDER) to measure (*by the metre*).

métreur [me'trœːr], *n.m.* quantity surveyor.

métrique [me'trik], *a.* metric (*system etc.*); (*Pros.*) metrical.—*n.f.* scansion.

métro [me'tro], *n.m.* (*colloq. abbr. of chemin de fer métropolitain*) the underground (railway), the tube (*in Paris*), (*Am.*) the subway.

métropole [metrɔ'pɔl], *n.f.* mother country; metropolis.

métropolitain [metrɔpoli'tɛ̃], *a.* metropolitan.—*n.m.* metropolitan, archbishop; underground railway, subway.

mets [mɛ], *n.m.* dish, food, viands.

mettable [mɛ'tabl], *a.* fit to be worn, wearable.

metteur [mɛ'tœːr], *n.m. metteur en scène*, (*Theat.*) producer, (*Cine.*) director.

mettre [mɛtr], *v.t. irr.* to put, to set, to place; to put on, to wear; to employ; to contribute, to expend; to suppose, to imagine; *mettre en marche* or *en mouvement*, to start up, to set going; *mettre quelqu'un en état de*, to enable someone to; *mettre un habit*, to put on a coat. **se mettre**, *v.r.* to put or place oneself; to dress; to begin (*à*); to take to; *se mettre à parler*, to begin to speak; *se mettre à table*, to sit down to table; *se mettre bien*, to dress well; *se mettre en route*, to start.

meuble [mœbl], *a.* movable; *biens meubles*, (*Law*) personal property.—*n.m.* piece of furniture; (*pl.*) furniture.

meublé [mœ'ble], *a.* furnished.—*n.m.* a furnished room or flat.

meubler [mœ'ble], *v.t.* to furnish; to stock, to store. **se meubler**, *v.r.* to furnish one's home.

meule [møːl], *n.f.* millstone, grindstone; (*Agric.*) stack, rick (*of grain, hay etc.*); (*Hort.*) hotbed.

meunerie [møn'ri], *n.f.* miller's trade; (*collect.*) millers.

meunier [mø'nje], *n.m.* miller; chub (*fish*).

meunière [mø'njɛːr], *n.f.* miller's wife.

meurtre [mœrtr], *n.m.* murder.

meurtrier [mœrtri'e], *a.* (*fem.* -**ière**) murdering, murderous, deadly; killing.—*n.m.* (*fem.* -**ière** (1)) murderer, murderess.

meurtrière (2) [mœrtri'ɛːr], *n.f.* (*Fort.*) loophole.

meurtrir [mœr'triːr], *v.t.* to bruise, to make black and blue.

meurtrissure [mœrtri'syːr], *n.f.* bruise.

mévendre [me'vãːdr], *v.t.* to sell at a loss.

mévente [me'vãːt], *n.f.* selling at a loss; slump.

mexicain [mɛksi'kɛ̃], *a.* Mexican.—*n.m.* (**Mexicain** *fem.* -**aine**) Mexican (*person*).

Mexico [mɛksi'ko], *m.* Mexico City.

Mexique [mɛk'sik], *le, m.* Mexico.

mi [mi], *n.m.* (*Mus.*) mi; the note E.

mi- [mi], *comb. form.* half, demi-, semi-; mid, middle; *à mi-chemin*, half-way; *à mi-corps*, up to the waist; *à mi-côte*, half-way up the hill; *à mi-jambe*, half-way up the leg; *la mi-août*, the middle of August.

miaou [mjau], *n.m. inv.* (*fam.*) mew, miaow; cat.

miaulement [mjol'mã], *n.m.* mewing.

miauler [mjo'le], *v.i.* to mew; to caterwaul.

mica [mi'ka], *n.m.* mica.

miche [miʃ], *n.f.* round loaf.

Michel [mi'ʃɛl], *m.* Michael; *la Saint-Michel*, Michaelmas.

Michel-Ange [mikɛl'ãːʒ], *m.* Michelangelo.

Micheline [miʃ'lin], *n.f.* rail-car, autorail.

micro [mi'kro], *n.m.* (*fam. abbr. of* **microphone**) mike.

microbe [mi'krɔb], *n.m.* microbe.

microcosme [mikrɔ'kɔsm], *n.m.* microcosm.

microfilm [mikrɔ'film], *n.m.* microfilm.

micromètre [mikrɔ'mɛtr], *n.m.* micrometer.

micro-organisme [mikroorga'nism], *n.m.* micro-organism.

microphone [mikrɔ'fɔn], *n.m.* microphone.

microscope [mikrɔs'kɔp], *n.m.* microscope.

microscopique [mikrɔskɔ'pik], *a.* microscopic.

midi [mi'di], *n.m.* noon, midday, twelve o'clock (*in the day*); meridian; south; *le Midi (de la France)*, the South of France.

midinette [midi'nɛt], *n.f.* (*fam.*) young dressmaker or milliner in Paris.

mie [mi], *n.f.* crumb; soft part of loaf.

miel [mjɛl], *n.m.* honey; *lune de miel*, honeymoon.

miellé [mjɛ'le], *a.* honeyed; like honey; (*fig.*) sweet, bland.

miellée [mjɛ'le], **miellure** [mjɛ'lyːr], *n.f.* honeydew.

mielleusement [mjɛløz'mã], *adv.* sweetly, blandly, honey-like.

mielleux [mjɛ'lø], *a.* (*fem.* -**euse**) honeyed; sweet, bland.

mien [mjɛ̃], *a. poss. and pron. poss.* (*fem.* **mienne**) mine; *le mien, la mienne, les miens, les miennes*, mine, my own.

miette [mjɛt], *n.f.* crumb, bit, morsel.

mieux [mjø], *adv.* better; correctly; more agreeably, more comfortably etc.; rather, more; *faute de mieux*, for want of better; *mieux vaut tard que jamais*, better late than never; *tant mieux*, so much the better; *valoir mieux*, to be better, to be worth more.—*n.m.* best thing; improvement.

mièvre [mjɛːvr], *a.* finical, affected; delicate (*child*), fragile.

mièvrerie [mjɛvrə'ri], **mièvreté** [mjɛvrə'te], *n.f.* affectation.

mignard [mi'naːr], *a.* delicate, pretty, dainty; mincing, affected.

mignardement [miɲardə'mã], *adv.* delicately, daintily; mincingly.

mignarder [miɲar'de], *v.t.* to fondle, to pet; to indulge.

mignardise [miɲar'diːz], *n.f.* delicacy, prettiness, daintiness; affectation, mincing ways.

mignon [mi'nɔ̃], *a.* (*fem.* -**onne**) delicate, pretty, dainty; sweet; neat, tiny.—*n.m.* (*fem.* -**onne**) darling, pet, favorite.

mignonnement [miɲɔn'mã], *adv.* daintily, prettily.

migraine [mi'grɛn], *n.f.* sick headache; migraine.

216

migrateur [migra'tœːr], *a.* (*fem.* **-trice**) migratory.

migration [migra'sjɔ̃], *n.f.* migration.

migratoire [migra'twaːr], *a.* migratory.

mijoter [miʒɔ'te], *v.t., v.i.* to cook slowly, to stew; to simmer; (*fig.*) to plot, to brew.

mil (1) [MILLE (2)].

mil (2) [mil], *n.m.* millet.

milan [mi'lɑ̃], *n.m.* kite (*bird*).

milice [mi'lis], *n.f.* militia; (*fig.*) troops, soldiery.

milicien [mili'sjɛ̃], *n.m.* militiaman.

milieu [mi'ljø], *n.m.* (*pl.* **-eux**) middle, midst; heart, center; mean; environment, surroundings; *au beau milieu*, in the very middle.

militaire [mili'tɛːr], *a.* military.—*n.m.* soldier.

militairement [militɛr'mɑ̃], *adv.* in a soldier-like manner.

militant [mili'tɑ̃], *a.* militant.

militer [mili'te], *v.i.* to militate (*pour* or *contre*).

(C) **millage** [mi'la:ʒ], *n.m.* mileage.

mille (1) [mil], *n.m.* mile (*English*, *American mile, 1609.35 metres*).

mille (2) [mil], *a. inv.* and *n.m. inv.* (**mil** *in dates of the Christian era*) thousand, a thousand, one thousand.

millénaire [mille'nɛːr], *a.* millenary.—*n.m.* millennium.

mille-pattes [mil'pat], *n.m. inv.* centipede.

millésime [mile'zim], *n.m.* date (*on a coin, monument etc.*).

millet [mi'je], *n.m.* millet, millet grass.

milliard [mi'ljaːr], *n.m.* one thousand millions, (*Am.*) one billion.

milliardaire [miljar'dɛːr], *a.* and *n.* multi-millionaire(ss).

millibar [milli'bar], *n.m.* (*Meteor.*) millibar.

millième [mi'ljɛm], *a.* and *n.m.* thousandth.

millier [mi'lje], *n.m.* thousand.

milligramme [milli'gram], *n.m.* milligramme (*.0154 grain*).

millimètre [milli'mɛtr], *n.m.* millimetre (*.03937 in.*).

million [mi'ljɔ̃], *n.m.* million.

millionième [miljɔ'njɛːm], *a.* and *n.m.* millionth.

millionnaire [miljɔ'nɛːr], *a.* and *n.* millionaire(ss).

mime [mim], *n.m.* mime; mimic.

mimer [mi'me], *v.t., v.i.* to mimic, to mime.

mimi [mi'mi], *n.m.* (*Childish*) cat, pussy, darling, ducky.

mimique [mi'mik], *a.* mimic, mimetic.—*n.f.* art of mimicry.

mimosa [mimo'za], *n.m.* mimosa.

minable [mi'nabl], *a.* (*colloq.*) seedy, shabby.

minaret [mina'rɛ], *n.m.* minaret.

minauder [mino'de], *v.i.* to smirk, to simper.

minauderie [mino'dri], *n.f.* affected or mincing manners, simpering, smirking.

minaudier [mino'dje], *a.* (*fem.* **-ière**) affected, lackadaisical.—*n.m.* (*fem.* **-ière**) affected person.

mince [mɛ̃s], *a.* thin, slender, slim; puny, slight, trivial; scanty, small.—*int.* (*pop.*) *ah ! mince !* or *mince alors !* my word! well, I never!

minceur [mɛ̃'sœːr], *n.f.* slenderness, slimness.

mine (1) [min], *n.f.* look, bearing; face, expression; appearance, aspect; (*pl.*) airs.

mine (2) [min], *n.f.* (*Min.*) mine; (*fig.*) source, store.

mine (3) [min], *n.f.* (*Mil.*, *Pyro.*) mine.

miner [mi'ne], *v.t.* to mine, to undermine, to sap; to wear away.

minerai [min'rɛ], *n.m.* ore.

minéral [mine'ral], *a.* (*m. pl.* **-aux**) mineral. —*n.m.* (*pl.* **-aux**) mineral; ore.

minéralogie [mineralɔ'ʒi], *n.f.* mineralogy.

minéralogique [mineralɔ'ʒik], *a.* mineralogical.

minéralogiste [mineralɔ'ʒist], *n.* mineralogist.

Minerve [mi'nɛrv], *f.* Minerva.

minet [mi'nɛ], *n.m.* (*fem.* **-ette**) (*colloq.*) puss, kitten.

mineur (1) [mi'nœːr], *n.m.* miner; pitman; (*Mil.*) sapper.

mineur (2) [mi'nœːr], *a.* lesser, minor; under age.—*n.m.* (*fem.* **-e**) minor; (*Law*) infant.

miniature [minja'tyːr], *n.f.* miniature.

miniaturiste [minjaty'rist], *a.* of miniatures. —*n.* miniature painter.

minier [mi'nje], *a.* (*fem.* **-ière**) pertaining to mines, mining.—*n.f.* (**-ière**) open mine.

minime [mi'nim], *a.* very small, trifling.

minimum [mini'mɔm], *a.* (*usu. inv.*) minimum.—*n.m.* (*pl.* **minimums** or **minima**) minimum.

ministère [minis'tɛːr], *n.m.* ministry; department; minister's office; offices, services; administration.

ministériel [ministe'rjɛl], *a.* (*fem.* **-elle**) ministerial.

ministre [mi'nistr], *n.m.* (*Polit.*, *Ch.*) minister; clergyman.

minois [mi'nwa], *n.m. inv.* pretty face; looks, appearance.

minoritaire [minɔri'tɛːr], *a.* minority.

minorité [minɔri'te], *n.f.* minority; (*Law*) infancy.

Minorque [mi'nɔrk], *f.* Minorca.

minoterie [minɔ'tri], *n.f.* flour mill; flour trade.

minotier [minɔ'tje], *n.m.* flour dealer, grain dealer.

minuit [mi'nɥi], *n.m.* midnight.

minuscule [minys'kyl], *a.* small (*of letters*), minute, tiny.—*n.f.* small letter.

minute [mi'nyt], *n.f.* minute (*of time*), moment, instant; rough draft; minute, record; *minute !* (*fam.*) just a moment!

minuter [miny'te], *v.t.* to record; to time.

minuterie [minyt'ri], *n.f.* time switch.

minutie [miny'si], *n.f.* trifle, (*pl.*) minutiae.

minutieusement [minysjøz'mɑ̃], *adv.* minutely.

minutieux [miny'sjø], *a.* (*fem.* **-euse**) minute; meticulous.

mioche [mjɔʃ], *n.* (*colloq.*) brat, urchin.

mi-parti [mipar'ti], *a.* bipartite, half and half.

mirabelle [mira'bɛl], *n.f.* yellow variety of plum.

miracle [mi'raːkl], *n.m.* miracle; (*fig.*) wonder; *à miracle*, wonderfully well.

miraculeusement [mirakyløz'mɑ̃], *adv.* miraculously; wonderfully.

miraculeux [miraky'lø], *a.* (*fem.* **-euse**) miraculous; wonderful, marvellous.

mirage [mi'ra:ʒ], *n.m.* mirage; (*Naut.*) looming; (*fig.*) shadow.

mire [mi:r], *n.f.* land-surveyor's pole; (*Artill.*) aim; sight (*of fire-arms*).

mirer [mi're], *v.t.* to aim at; to have in view, to look at; to covet. **se mirer**, *v.r.* to look at oneself; to admire oneself; to be reflected.

mirliton [mirli'tɔ̃], *n.m.* reed pipe.

mirobolant [mirɔbɔ'lɑ̃], *a.* (*colloq.*) wonderful, prodigious.

miroir [mi'rwa:r], *n.m.* mirror, looking-glass.

miroitant [mirwa'tɑ̃], *a.* reflecting (*like a mirror*), glistening.

miroité [mirwa'te], *a.* shot, shiny; dappled (*of horses*).

miroitement [mirwat'mɑ̃], *n.m.* reflection of the light by polished surfaces; sheen, brilliancy.

miroiter [mirwa'te], *v.i.* to reflect light, to shine, to glisten, to shimmer.

mis [mi], *p.p.* [METTRE] **bien** or **mal mis**, well or badly dressed.

misaine [mi'zɛːn], *n.f.* **mât de misaine,** foremast; *voile de misaine,* foresail.

misanthrope [mizɑ̃'trɔp], *n.* misanthrope.

misanthropie [mizɑ̃trɔ'pi], *n.f.* misanthropy.

misanthropique [mizɑ̃trɔ'pik], *a.* misanthropic.

miscellanées [misɛla'ne], *n.f. pl.* miscellanea, miscellany.

mise [mi:z], *n.f.* placing; stake; investment; bidding (*at auctions*); capital; dress; *mise en marche,* starting; starting-handle; *mise en marche automatique,* self-starter; *mise en scène,* (*Theat.*) production, (*Cine.*) direction.

misérable [mize'rabl], *a.* miserable, pitiable; worthless; despicable.—*n.* wretch, miserable person; miscreant.

misérablement [mizerablə'mɑ̃], *adv.* miserably.

misère [mi'zɛːr], *n.f.* misery, wretchedness, distress; poverty; trouble; trifling thing.

miséreux [mize'rø], *a.* and *n.m.* (*fem.* **-euse**) poor, destitute; seedy looking (*person*).

miséricorde [mizeri'kɔrd], *n.f.* mercy, pardon, grace.

miséricordieux [mizerikor'djø], *a.* (*fem.* **-euse**) merciful, compassionate.

missel [mi'sɛl], *n.m.* missal, mass book.

mission [mi'sjɔ̃], *n.f.* mission.

missionnaire [misjɔ'nɛːr], *n.* missionary.

missive [mi'siːv], *a.f.* and *n.f.* missive.

mistral [mis'tral], *n.m.* mistral (*cold north wind in southern France*).

mitaine [mi'tɛn], *n.f.* mitten.

mite [mit], *n.f.* mite; moth; *mangé des mites,* moth-eaten.

mité [mi'te], *a.* moth-eaten, maggoty.

mi-temps [mi'tɑ̃], *n.f.* (*Ftb.*) half-time.

miteux [mi'tø], *a.* (*fem.* **-euse**) full of mites; (*fig.*) shabby, poverty-stricken.

mitigation [mitiga'sjɔ̃], *n.f.* mitigation.

mitiger [miti'ʒe], *v.t.* (*conjug. like* MANGER) to mitigate, to alleviate, to modify.

mitonner [mitɔ'ne], *v.t.* to coddle, to fondle; to nurse.—*v.i.* to let slices of bread simmer in the broth, to simmer.

mitoyen [mitwa'jɛ̃], *a.* (*fem.* **-enne**) middle; intermediate; party, joint; *mur mitoyen,* party wall.

mitraille [mi'trɑ:j], *n.f.* grape-shot.

mitrailler [mitra'je], *v.t., v.i.* to machine-gun.

mitraillette [mitra'jɛt], *n.f.* Tommy gun.

mitrailleuse [mitra'jøːz], *n.f.* machine gun.

mitre [mitr], *n.f.* miter.

mitré [mi'tre], *a.* mitered.

mitron [mi'trɔ̃], *n.m.* journeyman baker; pastry-cook's boy.

mixte [mikst], *a.* mixed.

mixture [miks'ty:r], *n.f.* mixture.

mobile [mɔ'bil], *a.* mobile, movable; unsteady, variable.—*n.m.* body in motion; mover, motive power.

mobilier [mɔbi'lje], *a.* (*fem.* **-ière**) movable; personal (*of property*).—*n.m.* furniture.

mobilisation [mɔbiliza'sjɔ̃], *n.f.* mobilization; liquidation (*of capital*).

mobiliser [mɔbili'ze], *v.t.* (*Law*) to liquidate; (*Mil.*) to mobilize.

mobilité [mɔbili'te], *n.f.* mobility; variability; instability.

mode (1) [mɔd], *n.f.* fashion; manner, way, custom; (*pl.*) millinery.

mode (2) [mɔd], *n.m.* (*Mus. etc.*) mode; (*Gram.*) mood; method; *mode d'emploi,* directions for use.

modelage [mɔ'dla:ʒ], *n.m.* modelling.

modèle [mɔ'dɛl], *a.* exemplary.—*n.m.* model; pattern, design.

modelé [mɔ'dle], *n.m.* (*Sculp., Paint.*) relief; reproduction.

modeler [mɔ'dle], *v.t.* (*conjug. like* AMENER) to model; to shape; to mould (*clay*). **se modeler,** *v.r.* to model oneself (*sur*).

modeleur [mɔ'dlœːr], *n.m.* modeller.

modérateur [mɔdera'tœːr], *a.* (*fem.* **-trice**) moderating.—*n.m.* (*fem.* **-trice**) moderator.—*n.m.* (*Mech.*) regulator.

modération [mɔdera'sjɔ̃], *n.f.* moderation; abatement.

modéré [mode're], *a.* moderate, reasonable. —*n.m.* (*fem.* **-e**) (*Polit.*) moderate.

modérément [mɔdere'mɑ̃], *adv.* moderately, in moderation.

modérer [mɔde're], *v.t.* (*conjug. like* CÉDER) to moderate, to mitigate; to restrain. **se modérer,** *v.r.* to keep one's temper; to restrain oneself.

moderne [mɔ'dɛrn], *a.* modern, up-to-date. —*n.m.* modern style.

modernisation [mɔderniza'sjɔ̃], *n.f.* modernization.

moderniser [mɔderni'ze], *v.t.* to modernize.

modeste [mɔ'dɛst], *a.* modest, unassuming; quiet; simple.

modestement [mɔdɛstə'mɑ̃], *adv.* modestly, quietly, simply.

modestie [mɔdɛs'ti], *n.f.* modesty, simplicity.

modicité [mɔdisi'te], *n.f.* smallness; modicum.

modification [mɔdifika'sjɔ̃], *n.f.* modification.

modifier [mɔdi'fje], *v.t.* to modify, to change, to alter. **se modifier,** *v.r.* to become modified.

modique [mɔ'dik], *a.* moderate; small.

modiquement [mɔdik'mɑ̃], *adv.* moderately.

modiste [mɔ'dist], *n.* modiste, milliner.

modulation [mɔdyla'sjɔ̃], *n.f.* modulation; (*Rad.*) *modulation de fréquence,* very high frequency, V.H.F.

moduler [mɔdy'le], v.t. to modulate.
moelle [mwal], n.f. marrow (of bone); (Bot.) pith.
moelleusement [mwaløz'mã], adv. softly; (Paint.) with mellowness.
moelleux [mwa'lø], a. (fem. -euse) full of marrow; pithy; soft; mellow.—n.m. softness; mellowness.
moellon [mwa'lɔ̃], n.m. rubble; building stone.
mœurs [mœrs], n.f. pl. morals; manners, habits, ways, customs; *certificat de bonne vie et mœurs*, certificate of good character.
Mogol [mɔ'gɔl], m. Mogul.
moi [mwa], pron. pers. I; me, to me; *moi-même*, myself.—n.m. self, ego.
moignon [mwa'ɲɔ̃], n.m. stump (of limbs, trees etc.).
moindre [mwɛ̃:dr], a. lesser; least.
moine [mwan], n.m. monk, friar; bed-warmer.
moineau [mwa'no], n.m. (pl. -eaux) sparrow.
moins [mwɛ̃], adv. less; fewer (de or que); not so; *à moins de* (or que), unless; *du moins*, at least, at any rate; *les moins de seize ans*, the under sixteens.—prep. less, minus.—n.m. (Math.) minus sign; (Print.) dash.
moire [mwar], n.f. watering; moire, watered silk.
moiré [mwa're], a. watered, moiré.—n.m. watered effect.
moirer [mwa're], v.t. to moiré, to give a watered appearance to.
mois [mwa], n.m. month; monthly allowance, month's pay.
Moïse [mɔ'i:z], m. Moses.
moisi [mwa'zi], a. moldy, musty.—n.m. moldiness, mustiness.
moisir [mwa'zi:r], v.t. to make moldy or musty.—v.i. and **se moisir**, v.r. to grow moldy or musty.
moisissure [mwazi'sy:r], n.f. moldiness, mustiness, mildew.
moisson [mwa'sɔ̃], n.f. harvest, harvest time.
moissonner [mwasɔ'ne], v.t. to reap, to gather in, to mow.
moissonneur [mwasɔ'nœ:r], n.m. (fem. -euse) reaper, harvester.—n.f. (-euse) reaping machine.
moissonneuse-batteuse [mwasɔ'nøzba'tø:z] n.f. (pl. moissonneuses-batteuses) combine harvester.
moite [mwat], a. moist, damp; clammy.
moiteur [mwa'tœ:r], n.f. moistness, damp-ness.
moitié [mwa'tje], n.f. half; (colloq.) better half, wife.—adv. half; *à moitié fait*, half done; *trop cher de moitié*, too dear by half.
moka [mɔ'ka], n.m. mocha (coffee or cake).
mol [mɔl], [MOU].
molaire [mɔ'lɛ:r], a. molar.—n.f. molar (tooth).
môle [mo:l], n.m. mole, pier.
moléculaire [mɔleky'lɛ:r], a. molecular.
molécule [mɔle'kyl], n.f. molecule.
molestation [mɔlɛsta'sjɔ̃], n.f. molestation, annoyance.
molester [mɔlɛs'te], v.t. to molest, to trouble.

mollasse [mɔ'las], a. flabby; spineless.
molle [mɔl], [MOU].
mollement [mɔl'mã], adv. softly; feebly; indolently.
mollesse [mɔ'lɛs], n.f. softness; flabbiness; slackness; indolence.
mollet [mɔ'lɛ], a. (fem. -ette) soft; light (of bread).—n.m. calf (of the leg).
molletière [mɔl'tjɛ:r], n.f. legging, puttee.
molleton [mɔl'tɔ̃], n.m. thick flannel, duffel.
mollir [mɔ'li:r], v.i. to soften; to mellow (of fruit); to slacken, to give way.
mollusque [mɔ'lysk], n.m. mollusc.
molosse [mɔ'lɔs], n.m. mastiff, watch-dog.
môme [mo:m], n. (pop.) brat, urchin.
moment [mɔ'mã], n.m. moment, instant; favorable occasion; *au moment de*, just as; *du moment que*, since.
momentané [mɔmãta'ne], a. momentary
momentanément [mɔmãtane'mã], adv. momentarily.
momie [mɔ'mi], n.f. mummy; (fig.) old fogy.
momifier [mɔmi'fje], v.t. to mummify.
mon [mɔ̃], a.poss.m. (fem. **ma**, pl. **mes**) my.
monarchie [mɔnar'ʃi], n.f. monarchy.
monarchique [mɔnar'ʃik], a. monarchical.
monarchiste [mɔnar'ʃist], a. and n. monar-chist.
monarque [mɔ'nark], n.m. monarch.
monastère [mɔnas'tɛ:r], n.m. monastery, convent.
monastique [mɔnas'tik], a. monastic.
monceau [mɔ̃'so], n.m. (pl. -eaux) heap, pile.
mondain [mɔ̃'dɛ̃], a. worldly, mundane.—n.m. (fem. -e) worldly person.
mondanité [mɔ̃dani'te], n.f. worldliness, (pl.) social events.
monde [mɔ̃:d], n.m. world; universe; man-kind; people; society; company, set; men; customers; *tout le monde*, everybody.
monder [mɔ̃'de], v.t. to cleanse; to hull (barley), to blanch (almonds).
mondial [mɔ̃'djal], a. (m. pl. -aux) world, world-wide.
monétaire [mɔne'tɛ:r], a. monetary.
mongol [mɔ̃'gɔl], a. Mongolian.—n.m. Mon-golian (language); (**Mongol**, fem. -ole) Mongol(ian) (person).
Mongolie [mɔ̃gɔ'li], **la**, f. Mongolia.
Monique [mɔ'nik], f. Monica.
moniteur [mɔni'tœ:r], n.m. (fem. -trice) (sch.) prefect, monitor; instructor.
monnaie [mɔ'nɛ], n.f. coin, money; change; mint; *monnaie forte*, hard currency; *monnaie légale*, legal tender.
monnayage [mɔnɛ'ja:ʒ], n.m. coining, mint-ing.
monnayer [mɔnɛ'je], v.t. (conjug. like PAYER) to coin into money, to mint; (fig.) to make money out of, to sell.
monnayeur [mɔnɛ'jœ:r], n.m. coiner, minter; *faux monnayeur*, counterfeiter, forger.
monochrome [mɔnɔ'krom], a. monochrome.
monocle [mɔ'nɔkl], n.m. monocle, eyeglass.
monogramme [mɔnɔ'gram], n.m. mono-gram.
monologue [mɔnɔ'lɔg], n.m. monologue, soliloquy.
monopole [mɔnɔ'pɔl], n.m. monopoly.
monopoliser [mɔnɔpɔli'ze], v.t. to mono-polize.
monorail [mɔnɔ'ra:j], a. and n.m. monorail.

monosyllabe [mɔnɔsil'lab], *a.* monosyllabic.
—*n.f.* monosyllable.
monosyllabique [mɔnɔsilla'bik], *a.* monosyllabic.
monotone [mɔnɔ'tɔn], *a.* monotonous.
monotonie [mɔnɔtɔ'ni], *n.f.* monotony. ·
monseigneur [mɔ̃sɛ'ɲœːr], *n.m.* (*pl.* **messeigneurs** or **nosseigneurs**) my lord;
your Grace; your Royal *or* Imperial Highness.
monsieur [mə'sjø, msjø], *n.m.* (*pl.* **messieurs**) sir; gentleman; Mr.
monstre [mɔ̃ːstr], *a.* (*fam.*) huge.—*n.m.*
monster.
monstrueusement [mɔ̃strɥøz'mɑ̃], *adv.*
monstrously, prodigiously.
monstrueux [mɔ̃s'trɥø], *a.* (*fem.* **-euse**)
monstrous, prodigious.
monstruosité [mɔ̃strɥozi'te], *n.f.* monstrosity.
mont [mɔ̃], *n.m.* hill, mount, mountain.
montage [mɔ̃'taːʒ], *n.m.* carrying up;
mounting, setting; assembling; (*Cine.*)
editing (*of film*); (*Ind.*) **chaîne de montage**, assembly line.
montagnard [mɔ̃ta'naːr], *a.* mountain, highland.—*n.m.* (*fem.* **-e**) mountaineer, highlander.
montagne [mɔ̃'taɲ], *n.f.* mountain; hill.
montagneux [mɔ̃ta'ɲø], *a.* (*fem.* **-euse**)
mountainous, hilly.
montant (1) [mɔ̃'tɑ̃], *n.m.* upright (*of a
ladder etc.*); post (*of door etc.*); (*Naut.*)
stanchion; amount, sum total; rising tide;
high flavor, pungency; (*Ftb.*) goal post.
montant (2) [mɔ̃'tɑ̃], *a.* rising; ascending;
flowing, coming in; high-necked (*of dresses*).
monte [mɔ̃ːt], *n.f.* mounting, mount (*of a
jockey*); serving (*of animals*), covering
season.
monte-charge [mɔ̃t'ʃarʒ], *n.m. inv.* hoist,
goods lift; (*Am.*) freight elevator.
montée [mɔ̃'te], *n.f.* gradient, slope; ascent;
(*Arch. etc.*) height.
monter [mɔ̃'te], *v.t.* to mount, to ascend, to
go up: to walk, ride, row etc. up; to get up
on, to ride; to raise; to wind up; to equip;
to make up; to rouse.—*v.i.* (*with aux.* AVOIR
or ÊTRE *according as action or condition is
meant*) to go (*or* come) up, to mount; to
climb; to rise; to increase; to amount.
se monter, *v.r.* to amount, to rise; to get
excited; to supply oneself with (*en*).
monteur [mɔ̃'tœːr], *n.m.* (*fem.* **-euse**) setter,
mounter (*of jewels, machinery etc.*); (*Cine.*)
(film-)editor.
monticule [mɔ̃ti'kyl], *n.m.* hillock, knoll.
montoir [mɔ̃'twaːr], *n.m.* horse-block; **côté
du montoir**, near side; **côté hors montoir**, off side.
montre (1) [mɔ̃ːtr], *n.f.* show-case, shop-
window; show, display, exhibition.
montre (2) [mɔ̃ːtr], *n.f.* watch.
montre-bracelet [mɔ̃trabras'lɛ], *n.f.* (*pl.*
montres-bracelets) wrist watch.
montrer [mɔ̃'tre], *v.t.* to show, to display;
to demonstrate; to teach; to indicate. **se
montrer**, *v.r.* to show oneself; to appear; to
prove oneself to be, to turn out.
montreur [mɔ̃'trœːr], *n.m.* (*fem.* **-euse**)
showman, exhibitor.
montueux [mɔ̃'tɥø], *a.* (*fem.* **-euse**) hilly.

monture [mɔ̃'tyːr], *n.f.* animal for riding,
mount; setting (*of gems etc.*); frame.
monument [mɔny'mɑ̃], *n.m.* monument;
memorial.
monumental [mɔnymɑ̃'tal], *a.* (*m. pl.* **-aux**)
monumental.
moquer (se) [sǝmɔ'ke], *v.r.* (*de*) to mock, to
jeer, to laugh at; to make fun of.
moquerie [mɔk'ri], *n.f.* mockery, derision;
jest.
moquette [mɔ'kɛt], *n.f.* carpet; fitted carpet;
velvet pile.
moqueur [mɔ'kœːr], *a.* (*fem.* **-euse**) mocking,
jeering, derisive.—*n.m.* (*fem.* **-euse**) mocker,
scoffer; wag.
moral [mɔ'ral], *a.* (*m. pl.* **-aux**) moral;
mental.—*n.m.* mind, mental faculties,
spirit, morale.
morale [mɔ'ral], *n.f.* ethics, moral philosophy; morals, morality; rebuke, lecture;
moral (*of a story etc.*).
moralement [mɔral'mɑ̃], *adv.* morally.
moraliste [mɔra'list], *a.* and *n.* moralist.
moralité [mɔrali'te], *n.f.* morality; morals.
morbide [mɔr'bid], *a.* morbid.
morbleu! [mɔr'blø], *int.* the devil! hang it!
morceau [mɔr'so], *n.m.* (*pl.* **-eaux**) bit, piece,
morsel, fragment.
morceler [mɔrsə'le], *v.t.* (*conjug. like* APPELER)
to parcel out, to cut up.
mordant [mɔr'dɑ̃], *a.* biting; cutting, sarcastic.—*n.m.* mordant; pungency, keenness.
mordiller [mɔrdi'je], *v.t.* to nibble, to bite
at.
mordoré [mɔrdɔ're], *a.* and *n.m.* reddish
brown.
mordre [mɔrdr], *v.t.* to bite; to gnaw; to eat
into.—*v.i.* to bite, to nibble; to take hold;
to succeed; to criticize. **se mordre**, *v.r.* to
bite oneself; **s'en mordre les doigts**, to
repent of a thing.
more [mɔːr], **moresque** [mɔ'rɛsk], *a.*
Moorish.—*n.* (**More**) Moor; Negro.
morfondre [mɔr'fɔ̃ːdr], *v.t.* to chill. **se
morfondre**, *v.r.* to be chilled, to shiver; to
kick one's heels; (*fig.*) to mope.
morfondu [mɔrfɔ̃'dy], *a.* chilled, shivering,
benumbed.
morganatique [mɔrgana'tik], *a.* morganatic.
morgue (1) [mɔrg], *n.f.* haughtiness, arrogance.
morgue (2) [mɔrg], *n.f.* morgue, mortuary.
moribond [mɔri'bɔ̃], *a.* moribund, dying.—
n.m. (*fem.* **-e**) person in a dying state.
moricaud [mɔri'ko], *a.* dark, darkish.—*n.m.*
(*fem.* **-e**) (*pej.*) blackamoor, (*pej.*) Negro.
morigéner [mɔriʒe'ne], *v.t.* (*conjug. like*
CÉDER) to scold, to reprimand.
mormon [mɔr'mɔ̃], *a.* Mormon.—*n.m.*
(**Mormon**, *fem.* **-e**) Mormon (*person*).
morne [mɔrn], *a.* gloomy, dejected, dreary.
morose [mɔ'roːz], *a.* morose, sullen, surly.
morosité [mɔrozi'te], *n.f.* moroseness, sullenness, surliness.
Morphée [mɔr'fe], *m.* Morpheus.
morphine [mɔr'fin], *n.f.* morphia.
morphologie [mɔrfɔlɔ'ʒi], *n.f.* morphology.
mors [mɔːr], *n.m. inv.* bit (*of a bridle*); (*fig.*)
curb, check.
morse (1) [mɔrs], *n.m.* morse, walrus.
morse (2) [mɔrs], *n.m.* Morse (code).
morsure [mɔr'syːr], *n.f.* bite, biting.

mort [mɔːr], *a.* dead; lifeless, inanimate; dormant; stagnant; out (*of a candle etc.*); *nature morte,* still life; *au point mort,* at a standstill, in neutral (gear) (*of a car*).—*n.m.* (*fem.* **-e**) dead person, corpse.—*n.m.* dummy (*at cards*).—*n.f.* death; *à mort,* mortally, to the death.

mortalité [mɔrtali'te], *n.f.* mortality.

mort-bois [mɔr'bwa], *n.m.* (*no pl.*) brushwood, undergrowth.

morte-eau [mɔr'to], *n.f.* (*pl.* **mortes-eaux**) neap tide.

mortel [mɔr'tɛl], *a.* (*fem.* **-elle**) mortal, deadly; grievous.—*n.m.* (*fem.* **-elle**) mortal.

mortellement [mɔrtɛl'mã], *adv.* fatally, deadly.

morte-saison [mɔrtsɛ'zɔ̃], *n.f.* (*pl.* **mortes-saisons**) slack time, off season.

mortier [mɔr'tje], *n.m.* mortar (*cement, artillery, vessel*).

mortifiant [mɔrti'fjã], *a.* mortifying, humiliating.

mortification [mɔrtifika'sjɔ̃], *n.f.* mortification, humiliation.

mortifier [mɔrti'fje], *v.t.* to mortify; to humiliate. **se mortifier,** *v.r.* to mortify oneself.

mort-né [mɔr'ne], *a.* and *n.m.* (*fem.* **mort-née,** *pl.* **mort-nés, mort-nées**) stillborn (child).

mortuaire [mɔr'tɥɛːr], *a.* mortuary; *drap mortuaire,* pall.

morue [mɔ'ry], *n.f.* cod, codfish; *huile de foie de morue,* cod-liver oil.

morveux [mɔr'vø], *a.* (*fem.* **-euse**) snotty; *qui se sent morveux se mouche,* if the cap fits, wear it.

mosaïque [mɔza'ik], *a.* and *n.f.* mosaic.

Moscou [mɔs'ku], **le,** *m.* Moscow.

mosquée [mɔs'ke], *n.f.* mosque.

mot [mo], *n.m.* word; remark, saying, sentence; motto; note; (*Mil.*) parole, watchword; *au bas mot,* at the least; *bon mot,* witticism; *mots croisés,* crossword.

motel [mɔ'tɛl], *n.m.* motel.

moteur [mɔ'tœːr], *a.* (*fem.* **-trice**) motive, driving.—*n.m.* mover; motor, engine; motive power.

motif [mɔ'tif], *a.* (*fem.* **-tive**) moving, inciting.—*n.m.* motive, incentive; cause; (*Mus. etc.*) motif, design.

motion [mɔ'sjɔ̃], *n.f.* (*Polit.*) motion.

motiver [mɔti've], *v.t.* to justify; to allege as a motive; to be the cause of, to bring about.

moto [mɔ'to], *n.f.* (*fam.*) motor bike.

motocyclette [mɔtosi'klɛt], *n.f.* motor-cycle.

motte [mɔt], *n.f.* clod; *motte de beurre,* pat of butter.

motus! [mɔ'tyːs], *int.* (*colloq.*) mum's the word!

mou [mu], *a.* (**mol** before vowel or *h* mute, *fem.* **molle**) soft; limp; flabby; weak; slack, sluggish, indolent.—*n.m.* soft part of thing; slack (*of a rope*); lights (*of animals*).

mouchard [mu'ʃaːr], *n.m.* sneak, *esp.* police spy, nark, informer.

moucharder [muʃar'de], *v.t., v.i.* to inform (*on*), to spy (*on*); to sneak.

mouche [muʃ], *n.f.* fly; patch (*on the face*), beauty spot; bull's-eye (*of a target*); river passenger-steamer.

(C) **mouche à feu** [muʃa'fø], *n.f.* firefly.

moucher [mu'ʃe], *v.t.* to wipe the nose of; to snuff. **se moucher,** *v.r.* to blow one's nose.

moucheron [muʃ'rɔ̃], *n.m.* gnat, very small fly.

moucheté [muʃ'te], *a.* spotted, speckled, flecked; capped (*of foils*).

moucheter [muʃ'te], *v.t.* (*conjug. like* APPELER) to spot, to speckle, to fleck; to cap (*foils*).

mouchoir [mu'ʃwaːr], *n.m.* handkerchief.

moudre [mudr], *v.t. irr.* to grind, to crush.

moue [mu], *n.f.* pout; *faire la moue,* to pout.

mouette [mwɛt], *n.f.* gull, sea-mew.

moufle [mufl], *n.f.* mitten; tackle-block.

mouillage [mu'ja:ʒ], *n.m.* soaking, wetting; anchorage.

mouillé [mu'je], *a.* wet, watery; liquid (*of the letter l*); at anchor.

mouiller [mu'je], *v.t.* to wet, to moisten.—*v.i.* to drop anchor; to moor.

moulage [mu'la:ʒ], *n.m.* molding, casting; mold, cast; grinding, milling.

moule (1) [mul], *n.m.* mold, matrix; pattern.

moule (2) [mul], *n.f.* mussel.

moulé [mu'le], *a.* molded; cast; well-formed; *lettre moulée,* block letter.

mouler [mu'le], *v.t.* to cast, to mold; to shape. **se mouler,** *v.r.* to model oneself (*sur*).

mouleur [mu'lœːr], *n.m.* molder.

moulin [mu'lɛ̃], *n.m.* mill; grinder; (*Geol.*) pothole; *jeter son bonnet par-dessus les moulins,* to throw off all restraint.

moulinet [muli'nɛ], *n.m.* small mill; winch; turnstile; fishing reel.

moulu [mu'ly], *a.* ground; bruised.

moulure [mu'lyːr], *n.f.* (*Arch.*) molding.

mourant [mu'rã], *a.* dying, expiring; fading.—*n.m.* (*fem.* **-e**) dying person.

mourir [mu'riːr], *v.i. irr.* (*with aux.* ÊTRE) to die, to expire; to perish; to stop; to go out (*of fire*); to be out (*at play*). **se mourir,** *v.r.* (*Poet., only used in pres. and imp. indic.*) to be dying.

mouron [mu'rɔ̃], *n.m.* (*Bot.*) *mouron rouge,* scarlet pimpernel; *mouron des oiseaux,* chickweed.

mousquet [mus'kɛ], *n.m.* musket; *mousquet à pierre,* flintlock.

mousquetaire [muskə'tɛːr], *n.m.* musketeer.

mousse (1) [mus], *a.* blunt (*of tools*).

mousse (2) [mus], *n.f.* moss; froth, foam; lather; whipped cream.

mousse (3) [mus], *n.m.* ship's boy.

mousseline [mus'lin], *n.f.* muslin.

mousser [mu'se], *v.i.* to froth, to foam; to sparkle (*of wine*).

mousseux [mu'sø], *a.* (*fem.* **-euse**) foaming, frothy; sparkling (*of wine etc.*).

mousson [mu'sɔ̃], *n.f.* monsoon.

moussu [mu'sy], *a.* mossy.

moustache [mus'taʃ], *n.f.* moustache; whiskers (*of animals*).

moustiquaire [musti'kɛːr], *n.f.* mosquito net.

moustique [mus'tik], *n.m.* mosquito.

moût [mu], *n.m.* must (*wine not fermented*); wort (*of beer*).

moutarde [mu'tard], *n.f.* mustard.

moutardier [mutar'dje], *n.m.* mustard pot; mustard maker.

mouton [mu'tɔ̃], *n.m.* sheep; mutton; sheep-skin (*leather*); ram; (*fig.*) ninny; (*slang*) decoy, prison spy; (*pl.*) white-crested waves; *revenons à nos moutons*, let us return to the subject.

moutonné [muto'ne], *a.* fleecy, curled; white with foam (*of the sea*).

moutonner [muto'ne], *v.t.* to make woolly *or* fleecy; to curl, to frizzle.—*v.i.* to be ruffled, to foam.

moutonneux [muto'nø], *a.* (*fem.* -euse) fleecy; foaming (*of waves*).

moutonnier [muto'nje], *a.* (*fem.* -ière) sheep-like.

mouvant [mu'vɑ̃], *a.* moving, shifting; unstable.

mouvement [muv'mɑ̃], *n.m.* movement, motion; march; animation, bustle; emotion, commotion; spirit, impulse; (*Mus.*) time; (*Mil.*) maneuver.

mouvementé [muvmɑ̃'te], *a.* animated, lively; undulating (*ground*).

mouvoir [mu'vwa:r], *v.t. irr.* to move, to stir; to prompt. **se mouvoir**, *v.r.* to move, to stir.

moyen [mwa'jɛ̃], *a.* (*fem.* -enne) mean, middle, medium; average.—*n.m.* means; way, manner, medium; (*pl.*) resources; talents.

moyennant [mwajɛ'nɑ̃], *prep.* by means of; in consideration of.—*conj. phr. moyennant que*, on condition that.

moyenne [mwa'jɛn], *n.f.* average; (*sch.*) passing mark.

moyeu [mwa'jø], *n.m.* (*pl.* -eux) nave (*of cartwheel*); hub (*of bicycle*).

muable [mɥabl], *a.* mutable, changeable.

mucosité [mykozi'te], *n.f.* mucus.

mucus [my'ky:s], *n.m.* mucus.

mue [my], *n.f.* molting; skin, slough; mew, coop (*cage*).

muer [mɥe], *v.i.* to molt, to cast *or* slough horns etc.; to break (*of the voice*).

muet [mɥɛ], *a.* (*fem.* **muette**) dumb, mute; silent (*of letters*); blank (*of maps*).—*n.m.* (*fem.* **muette** (1)) dumb man *or* woman.

muette (2) [mɥɛt], *n.f.* mews; hunting lodge.

mufle [myfl], *n.m.* snout, muzzle (*of animals*); (*pop.*) beast, cad.

muflier [myfli'e], *n.m.* (*Bot.*) antirrhinum.

mugir [my'ʒi:r], *v.i.* to bellow, to low; (*fig.*) to roar; to sough (*of the wind*).

mugissement [myʒis'mɑ̃], *n.m.* bellowing, lowing, roaring; soughing (*of the wind*).

muguet [my'gɛ], *n.m.* lily of the valley.

mulâtre [my'lɑ:tr], *a* and *n.m.* (*fem. inv.* or **-esse**) mulatto, half-caste.

mule [myl], *n.f.* mule, slipper; she-mule.

mulet [my'lɛ], *n.m.* he-mule; mullet.

muletier [myl'tje], *a.* (*fem.* -ière) pertaining to mules.—*n.m.* muleteer.

mulot [my'lo], *n.m.* field-mouse.

multicolore [myltiko'lɔ:r], *a.* many-colored; motley; variegated.

multiforme [mylti'fɔrm], *a.* multiform.

multilatéral [myltilate'ral], *a.* (*m. pl.* -aux) multilateral.

multiple [myl'tipl], *a.* multiple; multifarious. —*n.m.* multiple.

multiplicateur [myltiplika'tœ:r], *a.* (*fem.* -trice) multiplying.—*n.m.* (*Arith.*) multiplier, multiplicator.

multiplication [myltiplika'sjɔ̃], *n.f.* multiplication; gearing (-ratio).

multiplicité [myltiplisi'te], *n.f.* multiplicity.

multiplié [myltipli'e], *a.* multiplied; manifold; frequent.

multiplier [myltipli'e], *v.t., v.i.* to multiply; to gear up to. **se multiplier**, *v.r.* to multiply; to be repeated.

multitude [mylti'tyd], *n.f.* multitude; crowd.

muni [my'ni], *a.* supplied, provided (*de*); fortified.

municipal [mynisi'pal], *a.* (*m. pl.* -aux) municipal.—*n.m.* soldier of the municipal guard.

municipalité [mynisipali'te], *n.f.* municipality; town council and staff.

munificence [mynifi'sɑ̃:s], *n.f.* bounty, munificence.

munificent [mynifi'sɑ̃], *a.* bountiful.

munir [my'ni:r], *v.t.* to provide, to supply; to arm, to secure. **se munir**, *v.r.* to provide oneself, to be provided (*de*).

munitions [myni'sjɔ̃], *n.f. pl.* ammunition, munitions; military stores.

muqueux [my'kø], *a.* (*fem.* -euse (1)) mucous.

muqueuse (2) [my'kø:z], *n.f.* mucous membrane.

mur [my:r], *n.m.* wall; *le mur du son*, the sound barrier.

mûr [my:r], *a.* ripe, mature, matured.

murage [my'ra:ʒ], *n.m.* walling.

muraille [my'ra:j], *n.f.* thick, high wall; (*pl.*) ramparts.

mural [my'ral], *a.* (*m. pl.* -aux) mural; *peinture murale*, mural.

mûre [my:r], *n.f.* mulberry.

mûrement [myr'mɑ̃], *adv.* maturely.

murer [my're], *v.t.* to wall in, to brick up; (*fig.*) to screen.

mûrier [my'rje], *n.m.* mulberry tree, bramble bush.

mûrir [my'ri:r], *v.t.* to ripen, to mature.—*v.i.* to ripen, to grow ripe, to mature.

murmurant [myrmy'rɑ̃], *a.* murmuring; babbling; grumbling.

murmure [myr'my:r], *n.m.* murmur; grumbling; whispering, babbling; soughing (*of the wind*).

murmurer [myrmy're], *v.t.* to mutter, to whisper.—*v.i.* to murmur, to whisper; to grumble; to gurgle, to prattle, to babble; to sough.

musard [my'za:r], *a.* loitering, dawdling.—*n.m.* (*fem.* -e) (*colloq.*) loiterer, dawdler.

musarder [myzar'de], *v.i.* to dawdle.

musarderie [myzar'dri], **musardise** [myzar'di:z], *n.f.* loitering, dawdling, trifling.

musc [mysk], *n.m.* musk deer, musk.

muscade [mys'kad], *n.f.* nutmeg; juggler's ball.

muscadier [myska'dje], *n.m.* nutmeg tree.

muscat [mys'ka], *a.* and *n.m.* muscat (grape), muscadine; dried muscatel wine; variety of pear.

muscle [myskl], *n.m.* muscle.

musculaire [mysky'lɛ:r], *a.* muscular.

musculeux [mysky'lø], *a.* (*fem.* -euse) muscular, brawny.

muse [my:z], *n.f.* muse.

museau [my'zo], *n.m.* (*pl.* **-eaux**) muzzle, snout, nose.

musée [my'ze], *n.m.* museum, art gallery.

museler [myz'le], *v.t.* (*conjug. like* APPELER) to muzzle; (*fig.*) to gag, to silence.

muselière [myz'ljɛːr], *n.f.* muzzle.

musellement [myzɛl'mɑ̃], *n.m.* muzzling; (*fig.*) gagging, silencing.

muser [my'ze], *v.i.* to loiter, to moon, to dawdle.

musette [my'zɛt], *n.f.* bagpipe; (*Mil.*) haversack; nosebag (*for horses*).

muséum [myze'ɔm], *n.m.* natural history museum.

musical [myzi'kal], *a.* (*m. pl.* **-aux**) musical.

musicalement [myzikal'mɑ̃], *adv.* musically.

musicien [myzi'sjɛ̃], *n.m.* (*fem.* **-enne**) musician

musique [my'zik], *n.f.* music; band, musicians.

musoir [my'zwaːr], *n.m.* pier head, jetty head.

musqué [mys'ke], *a.* musked, perfumed; (*fig.*) affected (*language etc.*).

musquer [mys'ke], *v.t.* to perfume with musk.

musulman [myzyl'mɑ̃], *a.* Moslem.—*n.m.* (**Musulman**, *fem.* **-ane**) Moslem (*person*).

mutabilité [mytabili'te], *n.f.* mutability, changeableness.

mutation [mytɑ'sjɔ̃], *n.f.* change; (*Biol.*) mutation.

muter [my'te], *v.t.* (*Mil., Adm.*) to transfer.

mutilateur [mytila'tœːr], *n.m.* (*fem.* **-trice**) mutilator, maimer, defacer.

mutilation [mytila'sjɔ̃], *n.f.* mutilation, maiming.

mutiler [myti'le], *v.t.* to mutilate, to maim; (*fig.*) to disfigure.

mutin [my'tɛ̃], *a.* obstinate; fractious; pert.—*n.m.* (*fem.* **-e**) mutineer, rebel.

mutiné [myti'ne], *a.* mutinous, riotous.

mutiner (se) [səmyti'ne], *v.r.* to mutiny.

mutinerie [mytin'ri], *n.f.* unruliness; mutiny, riot; pertness.

mutisme [my'tism], *n.m.* dumbness; speechlessness.

mutualité [mytuali'te], *n.f.* mutuality.

mutuel [my'tuɛl], *a.* (*fem.* **-elle**) mutual, reciprocal; *société de secours mutuels*, mutual benefit society.

mutuellement [mytuɛl'mɑ̃], *adv.* mutually.

myope [mjɔp], *a.* myopic, short-sighted.—*n.* short-sighted person.

myopie [mjɔ'pi], *n.f.* myopia, short-sightedness.

myosotis [mjɔzɔ'ti:], *n.m.* myosotis, forget-me-not.

myriade [mi'rjad], *n.f.* myriad.

myrrhe [miːr], *n.f.* myrrh.

myrte [mirt], *n.m.* myrtle.

myrtille [mir'ti:j], *n.f.* bilberry.

mystère [mis'tɛːr], *n.m.* mystery; secret; (*fig.*) fuss.

mystérieusement [misterjøz'mɑ̃], *adv.* mysteriously.

mystérieux [miste'rjø], *a.* (*fem.* **-euse**) mysterious.

mysticisme [misti'sism], *n.m.* mysticism.

mystificateur [mistifika'tœːr], *a.* (*fem.*

-trice) mystifying, hoaxing.—*n.m.* (*fem.* **-trice**) mystifier, hoaxer.

mystification [mistifika'sjɔ̃], *n.f.* hoax.

mystifier [misti'fje], *v.t.* to mystify; to hoax.

mystique [mis'tik], *a.* mystical, mystic.—*n.* mystic.

mythe [mit], *n.m.* myth; fable, fiction.

mythique [mi'tik], *a.* mythical.

mythologie [mitɔlɔ'ʒi], *n.f.* mythology.

mythologique [mitɔlɔ'ʒik], *a.* mythological.

mythologiste [mitɔlɔ'ʒist], **mythologue** [mitɔ'lɔg], *n.* mythologist.

myxomatose [miksɔma'to:z], *n.f.* myxomatosis.

N

N, n [ɛn], *n.m.* the fourteenth letter of the alphabet.

nabab [na'bab], *n.m.* nabob.

nacelle [na'sɛl], *n.f.* wherry, skiff; gondola (*of airship etc.*).

nacre [nakr], *n.f.* mother-of-pearl.

nacré [na'kre], *a.* nacreous, pearly.

nage [na:ʒ], *n.f.* swimming; rowing, sculling; (*fam.*) *être en nage*, to be bathed in perspiration.

nageoire [na'ʒwaːr], *n.f.* fin (*of a fish*).

nager [na'ʒe], *v.i.* (*conjug. like* MANGER) to swim; to float; to row.

nageur [na'ʒœːr], *a.* (*fem.* **-euse**) swimming.—*n.m.* (*fem.* **-euse**) swimmer; rower, oarsman.

naguère [na'gɛːr], *adv.* lately, not long ago.

naïade [na'jad], *n.f.* naiad, water nymph.

naïf [na'if], *a.* (*fem.* **naïve**) naïve, artless, ingenuous, unaffected; simple.

nain [nɛ̃], *a.* dwarfish.—*n.m.* (*fem.* **-e**) dwarf.

naissance [nɛ'sɑ̃:s], *n.f.* birth; descent; (*fig.*) beginning, dawn, rise.

naissant [nɛ'sɑ̃], *a.* new-born, in its infancy; beginning, rising.

naître [nɛ:tr], *v.i. irr.* (*with aux.* ÊTRE) to be born, (*fig.*) to originate; to dawn.

naïvement [naiv'mɑ̃], *adv.* naïvely, ingenuously, artlessly.

naïveté [naiv'te], *n.f.* artlessness, simplicity, naïvety.

nantir [nɑ̃'ti:r], *v.t.* to give as a pledge, to secure; (*fig.*) to furnish. **se nantir**, *v.r.* to provide oneself (*de*); to take possession (*de*).

nantissement [nɑ̃tis'mɑ̃], *n.m.* security, pledge.

naphte [naft], *n.m.* naphtha.

napolitain [napoli'tɛ̃], *a.* Neapolitan.—*n.m.* (**Napolitain**, *fem.* **-aine**) Neapolitan (*person*).

nappe [nap], *n.f.* table-cloth, cover; sheet (*of water etc.*).

napperon [na'prɔ̃], *n.m.* tray cloth; doily.

narcisse [nar'sis], *n.m.* (*Bot.*) narcissus.

narcotique [narkɔ'tik], *a. and n.m.* narcotic.

narcotisme [narkɔ'tism], *n.m.* narcotism.

narguer [nar'ge], *v.t.* to defy, to flout.

narine [na'rin], *n.f.* nostril.
narquois [nar'kwa], *a.* cunning, sly; chaffing.
narquoisement [narkwaz'mɑ̃], *adv.* slyly, quizzingly.
narrateur [nara'tœːr], *n.m.* (*fem.* **-trice**) narrator, relater.
narratif [nara'tif], *a.* (*fem.* **-tive**) narrative.
narration [narɑ'sjɔ̃], *n.f.* narration, narrative.
narrer [na're], *v.t.* to narrate, to tell.
nasal [na'zal], *a.* (*m. pl.* **-aux**) nasal.
nasalement [nazal'mɑ̃], *adv.* nasally, with a nasal sound.
naseau [na'zo], *n.m.* (*pl.* **-eaux**) nostril (*of animals*).
nasillard [nazi'jɑ], *a.* speaking through the nose.
nasillard [nazi'jaːr], *a.* snuffling, nasal.
nasillement [nazij'mɑ̃], *n.m.* speaking through the nose, snuffling; twang.
nasiller [nazi'je], *v.i.* to speak through the nose, to snuffle.
nasse [nɑːs], *n.f.* bow net, weir, eel pot.
natal [na'tal], *a.* (*m. pl.* **-als** (*rare*)) natal, native.
natalité [natali'te], *n.f.* birth-rate.
natation [natɑ'sjɔ̃], *n.f.* swimming.
natif [na'tif], *a.* (*fem.* **-tive**) native; natural. —*n.m.* native.
nation [nɑ'sjɔ̃], *n.f.* nation.
national [nasjɔ'nal], *a.* (*m. pl.* **-aux**) national.
nationalement [nasjɔnal'mɑ̃], *adv.* nationally.
nationalisation [nasjɔnaliza'sjɔ̃], *n.f.* nationalization.
nationaliser [nasjɔnali'ze], *v.t.* to nationalize.
nationaliste [nasjɔna'list], *n.* nationalist.
nationalité [nasjɔnali'te], *n.f.* nationality.
nativité [nativi'te], *n.f.* nativity, birth.
natte [nat], *n.f.* mat, matting (*of straw*); plait.
natter [na'te], *v.t.* to mat; to plait, to twist.
naturalisation [natyraliza'sjɔ̃], *n.f.* naturalization; taxidermy.
naturaliser [natyrali'ze], *v.t.* to naturalize; to stuff (*animal*).
naturalisme [natyra'lism], *n.m.* naturalism; naturalism.
naturaliste [natyra'list], *a.* naturalistic.—*n.* naturalist; taxidermist.
nature [na'tyːr], *n.f.* nature; kind, sort; temperament; life, life-size; *de nature à*, likely to; *dessiner d'après nature*, to draw from life; *nature morte*, still life; *payer en nature*, to pay in kind.
naturel [naty'rɛl], *a.* (*fem.* **-elle**) natural; native, innate; artless, plain; *enfant naturel*, illegitimate child.—*n.m.* (*fem.* **-elle**) native (*of a country*).—*n.m.* disposition, nature; genuineness, simplicity.
naturellement [natyrɛl'mɑ̃], *adv.* naturally. —*int.* of course!
naturiste [naty'rist], *a.* naturistic.—*n.* naturist.
naufrage [no'fraːʒ], *n.m.* shipwreck.
naufragé [nofra'ʒe], *a.* shipwrecked, wrecked. —*n.m.* (*fem.* **-ée**) shipwrecked person, castaway.
nauséabond [nozea'bɔ̃], *a.* nauseating, loathsome, disgusting.
nausée [no'ze], *n.f.* nausea, sickness; (*fig.*) loathing, disgust.
nauséeux [noze'ø], *a.* (*fem.* **-éeuse**) nauseating.

nautique [no'tik], *a.* nautical.
naval [na'val] *a.* (*m. pl.* **-als**) naval, nautical.
navet [na'vɛ], *n.m.* turnip.
navette [na'vɛt], *n.f.* incense box; weaver's shuttle; (*Bot.*) rape; *faire la navette*, to run a shuttle service.
navigabilité [navigabili'te], *n.f.* airworthiness, seaworthiness.
navigable [navi'gabl], *a.* navigable; seaworthy, airworthy.
navigateur [naviga'tœːr], *n.m.* navigator.—*a.m.* seafaring; swimming (*birds etc.*).
navigation [navigɑ'sjɔ̃], *n.f.* navigation; voyage, sailing.
naviguer [navi'ge], *v.i.* to navigate; to row, to sail etc.
navire [na'viːr], *n.m.* vessel, ship.
navrant [na'vrɑ̃], *a.* heartrending, harrowing, distressing.
navrer [na'vre], *v.t.* to distress, to rend (*the heart*).
nazaréen [nazare'ɛ̃], *a.* (*fem.* **-éenne**) of Nazareth.—*n.m.* (**Nazaréen**, *fem.* **-éenne**) Nazarene; Nazarite.
nazi [na'zi], *a.* Nazi.—*n.* (**Nazi**) Nazi.
nazisme [na'zism], *n.m.* Nazism.
ne [nə], *adv.* no, not.
né [ne], *a.* born.
néanmoins [neɑ̃'mwɛ̃], *adv.* nevertheless, however, for all that.
néant [ne'ɑ̃], *n.m.* naught, nothingness; nil.
nébuleux [neby'lø], *a.* (*fem.* **-euse**) cloudy, misty; nebulous; (*fig.*) obscure.—*n.f.* (**-euse**) nebula.
nébulosité [nebylozi'te], *n.f.* patch of haze.
nécessaire [nese'sɛːr], *a.* necessary; inevitable.—*n.m.* the needful; necessities (*of life etc.*); dressing-case, work-box.
nécessairement [nesesɛr'mɑ̃], *adv.* necessarily; inevitably, of course.
nécessité [nesesi'te], *n.f.* necessity; need, want.
nécessiter [nesesi'te], *v.t.* to necessitate, to compel, to oblige.
nécessiteux [nesesi'tø], *a.* (*fem.* **-euse**) necessitous, needy.—*n.m.* (*fem.* **-euse**) pauper.
nécrologe [nekrɔ'lɔːʒ], *n.m.* obituary list; death roll.
nécrologie [nekrɔlɔ'ʒi], *n.f.* necrology, obituary.
nécrologique [nekrɔlɔ'ʒik], *a.* necrological.
nécromancie [nekrɔmɑ̃'si], *n.f.* necromancy.
nécromancien [nekrɔmɑ̃'sjɛ̃], *n.m.* (*fem.* **-enne**) necromancer.
nécropole [nekrɔ'pɔl], *n.f.* necropolis.
nectar [nɛk'taːr], *n.m.* nectar.
néerlandais [neɛrlɑ̃'dɛ], *a.* Dutch.—*n.m.* Dutch (*language*); (**Néerlandais**, *fem.* **-aise**) Dutchman, Dutchwoman.
nef [nɛf], *n.f.* nave (*of a church*).
néfaste [ne'fast], *a.* inauspicious; disastrous.
nèfle [nɛfl], *n.f.* medlar.
néflier [ne'flje], *n.m.* medlar tree.
négatif [nega'tif], *a.* (*fem.* **-tive**) negative.—*n.m.* (*Phot.*) negative.—*n.f.* (**-tive**) negative, refusal.
négation [negɑ'sjɔ̃], *n.f.* negation; (*Gram.*) negative.
négativement [negativ'mɑ̃], *adv.* negatively.

négligé [negli'ʒe], a. neglected, unnoticed; careless; slovenly.—*n.m.* undress, negligee.

négligeable [negli'ʒabl], a. negligible; trifling, unimportant.

négligemment [negliʒa'mɑ̃], adv. nonchalantly; negligently.

négligence [negli'ʒɑ̃:s], *n.f.* negligence, neglect, oversight.

négligent [negli'ʒɑ̃], a. negligent, careless.—*n.m.* (*fem.* **-e**) negligent person.

négliger [negli'ʒe], *v.t.* (*conjug. like* MANGER) to neglect; to omit. **se négliger**, *v.r.* to neglect oneself; to be careless.

négoce [ne'gɔs], *n.m.* trade, business; trafficking.

négociabilité [negɔsjabili'te], *n.f.* negotiability.

négociable [negɔ'sjabl], a. negotiable, transferrable.

négociant [negɔ'sjɑ̃], *n.m.* (*fem.* **-e**) merchant (*wholesale*).

négociateur [negɔsja'tœ:r], *n.m.* (*fem.* **-trice**) negotiator, transactor.

négociation [negɔsja'sjɔ̃], *n.f.* negotiation, transaction.

négocier [negɔ'sje], *v.t.* to negotiate.—*v.i.* to trade.

nègre [nɛ:gr], a. and *n.m.* (*fem.* **négresse**) (*pej.*) Negro; (*pl.*) (*pej.*) blacks.

négrier [negri'e], *n.m.* slave ship; slaver; slave dealer.

négrillon [negri'jɔ̃], *n.m.* (*fem.* **-onne**) (*pej.*) little Negro, Negro boy *or* girl.

neige [nɛ:ʒ], *n.f.* snow; **boule de neige**, snowball.

neiger [nɛ'ʒe], *v. impers.* (*conjug. like* MANGER) to snow.

neigeux [nɛ'ʒø], a. (*fem.* **-euse**) snowy, snow-covered.

nénuphar [neny'fa:r], *n.m.* water lily.

néon [ne'ɔ̃], *n.m.* neon.

néo-zélandais [neozelɑ̃'dɛ], a. New Zealand (*butter, cheese etc.*).—*n.m.* (**Néo-Zélandais**, *fem.* **-aise**) New Zealander.

Népal [ne'pa:l], **le**, *m.* Nepal.

népalais [nepa'lɛ], a. Nepalese.—*n.m.* (**Népalais**, *fem.* **-aise**) Nepalese (*person*).

népotisme [nepo'tism], *n.m.* nepotism.

nerf [nɛ:r], *n.m.* nerve; sinew; fortitude, strength.

nerveusement [nɛrvøz'mɑ̃], adv. impatiently; nervously.

nerveux [nɛr'vø], a. (*fem.* **-euse**) nervous; excitable; muscular.

nervosité [nɛrvozi'te], *n.f.* nervousness.

nervure [nɛr'vy:r], *n.f.* (*Bot. etc.*) nervure, nerve; (*Arch.*) : molding; (*Carp.*) rib, fillet; (*Bookb.*) tapes, cording; (*Needlework*) piping.

net [nɛt], a. (*fem.* **nette**) clean; pure; clear, distinct; flat, frank, pointblank; net (*of prices*).—*n.m.* fair copy; **mettre au net**, to make a fair copy.—*adv.* clean off, at once; flatly, point-blank.

nettement [nɛt'mɑ̃], adv. cleanly; clearly, plainly, flatly.

netteté [nɛt'te], *n.f.* cleanness; clearness, distinctness.

nettoiement [nɛtwa'mɑ̃], **nettoyage** [nɛtwa'ja:ʒ], *n.m.* cleaning; clearing; wiping.

nettoyer [nɛtwa'je], *v.t.* (*conjug. like* EMPLOYER) to clean; to wipe; to rid (*de*).

neuf (1) [nœf], a. and *n.m.* nine, ninth.

neuf (2) [nœf], a. (*fem.* **neuve**) new, brand-new; young, raw.—*n.m.* something new.

neurologie [nørɔlɔ'ʒi], *n.f.* neurology.

neutralisation [nøtraliza'sjɔ̃], *n.f.* neutralization.

neutraliser [nøtrali'ze], *v.t.* to neutralize. **se neutraliser**, *v.r.* to neutralize each other.

neutralité [nøtrali'te], *n.f.* neutrality.

neutre [nø:tr], a. and *n.m.* neuter; neutral.

neutron [nø'trɔ̃], *n.m.* neutron.

neuvième [nœ'vjɛm], a. and *n.* ninth.

neveu [nə'vø], *n.m.* (*pl.* **-eux**) nephew; (*pl. poet.*) descendants.

névralgie [nevral'ʒi], *n.f.* neuralgia.

névralgique [nevral'ʒik], a. neuralgic.

névrite [ne'vrit], *n.f.* neuritis.

névritique [nevri'tik], a. neuritic.

névrose [ne'vro:z], *n.f.* neurosis, nervous disorder.

névrosé [nevro'ze], a. and *n.m.* (*fem.* **-ée**) neurotic.

nez [ne], *n.m. inv.* nose; face; scent (*of dogs etc.*).

ni [ni], *conj.* nor, neither . . . nor; (*after sans, sans que, etc.*) either . . . or.

niable [njabl], a. deniable.

niais [njɛ], a. silly, foolish.—*n.m.* (*fem.* **-e**) ninny, simpleton.

niaisement [njɛz'mɑ̃], adv. foolishly.

niaiser [njɛ'ze], *v.i.* to play the fool.

niaiserie [njɛz'ri], *n.f.* foolishness; nonsense.

Nicaragua [nikara'gwa], **le**, *m.* Nicaragua.

nicaraguayen [nikaragwa'jɛ̃], a. (*fem.* **-enne**) Nicaraguan.—*n.m.* (**Nicaraguayen**, *fem.* **-enne**) Nicaraguan (*person*).

niche [niʃ], *n.f.* niche, nook; recess; kennel; (*fam.*) prank.

nichée [ni'ʃe], *n.f.* nestful (*of young birds*); brood (*of animals, children etc.*).

nicher [ni'ʃe], *v.t.* to lodge, to put.—*v.i.* to build a nest; to nestle. **se nicher**, *v.r.* to nest, to nestle; to hide oneself.

nickel [ni'kɛl], *n.m.* nickel.

nickelage [ni'kla:ʒ], *n.m.* nickel-plating.

nickeler [ni'kle], *v.t.* (*conjug. like* APPELER) to nickel-plate.

Nicolas [niko'lɑ], *m.* Nicholas.

nicotine [niko'tin], *n.f.* nicotine.

nid [ni], *n.m.* nest; berth, post.

nièce [njɛs], *n.f.* niece.

nier [nje], *v.t.* to deny; to repudiate, to disown.

nigaud [ni'go], a. (*colloq.*) silly, simple.—*n.m.* (*fem.* **-e**) booby, simpleton.

Nigéria [niʒe'rja], **le**, *m.* Nigeria.

nigérien [niʒe'rjɛ̃], a. (*fem.* **-enne**) Nigerian.—*n.m.* (**Nigérien**, *fem.* **-enne**) Nigerian (*person*).

nihilisme [nii'lism], *n.m.* nihilism.

nihiliste [nii'list], a. nihilistic.—*n.* nihilist.

Nil [nil], **le**, *m.* the Nile.

nimbe [nɛ̃:b], *n.m.* nimbus, halo.

nippe [nip], *n.f. usu. pl.* (*colloq.*) old clothes, togs.

nipper [ni'pe], *v.t.* (*colloq.*) to fit out, to rig out. **se nipper**, *v.r.* to rig oneself out.

nippon [ni'pɔ̃], a. Japanese.—*n.m.* (**Nippon**, *fem.* **-one**) Japanese (*person*).

nitrate [ni'trat], *n.m.* nitrate.

nitre [nitr], *n.m.* nitre, saltpeter.

nitrique [ni'trik], a. nitric.

225

nitrogène [nitro'ʒɛn], *n.m.* nitrogen.
niveau [ni'vo], *n.m.* (*pl.* **-eaux**) level; standard; *passage à niveau*, level crossing.
niveler [ni'vle], *v.t.* (*conjug. like* APPELER) to level, to flatten (out).
niveleur [ni'vlœ:r], *a.* (*fem.* **-euse**) levelling.
—*n.m.* (*fem.* **-euse**) leveller.
nivellement [nivɛl'mɑ̃], *n.m.* levelling.
nobiliaire [nɔbi'ljɛ:r], *a.* of the nobility, nobiliary.
noble [nɔbl], *a.* noble; great, high, exalted.—*n.* noble, nobleman, noblewoman.
noblement [nɔblə'mɑ̃], *adv.* nobly; honorably.
noblesse [no'blɛs], *n.f.* nobility; nobleness, loftiness.
noce [nɔs], *n.f.* wedding; wedding party; (*colloq.*) jollification.
noceur [nɔ'sœ:r], *n.m.* (*fem.* **-euse**) gay dog, gay woman, rake.
nocif [nɔ'sif], *a.* (*fem.* **-cive**) injurious, noxious.
noctambule [nɔktɑ̃'byl], *a.* noctambulant, noctambulous.—*n.* sleep-walker.
noctambulisme [nɔktɑ̃by'lism], *n.m.* noctambulism, sleep-walking.
nocturne [nɔk'tyrn], *a.* nocturnal, nightly.—*n.m.* (*Mus.*) nocturne.
Noël [nɔ'ɛl], *n.m.* Christmas, Yule-tide; (**noël**) Christmas carol.
nœud [nø], *n.m.* knot; bow; difficulty, intricacy; (*fig.*) tie; bond.
noir [nwa:r], *a.* black; swarthy; gloomy, dismal; foul; *bête noire*, pet aversion.—*n.m.* black (*color*); (*fem.* **-e**) Negro.
noirâtre [nwa'sɑ:tr], *a.* blackish.
noiraud [nwa'ro], *a.* dark, swarthy-looking.
noirceur [nwar'sœ:r], *n.f.* blackness; baseness; foul deed.
noircir [nwar'si:r], *v.t.* to blacken; to sully; to defame; to darken.—*v.i.* and **se noircir**, *v.r.* to blacken, to darken, to grow black or dark.
noircissure [nwarsi'sy:r], *n.f.* black spot, smudge.
noire (2) [nwa:r], *n.f.* (*Mus.*) crotchet.
noisetier [nwaz'tje], *n.m.* hazel (*tree or bush*).
noisette [nwa'zɛt], *n.f.* hazel-nut.
noix [nwa], *n.f. inv.* walnut; nut.
nom [nɔ̃], *n.m.* name; fame, celebrity; noun.
nomade [nɔ'mad], *a.* nomad, nomadic, wandering.—*n.* nomad.
nombre [nɔ̃:br], *n.m.* number; quantity; numbers.
nombrer [nɔ̃'bre], *v.t.* to number, to reckon.
nombreux [nɔ̃'brø], *a.* (*fem.* **-euse**) numerous; harmonious (*prose, style*).
nombril [nɔ̃'bri], *n.m.* navel.
nomenclature [nɔmɑ̃kla'ty:r], *n.f.* nomenclature; list, catalogue.
nominal [nɔmi'nal], *a.* (*m. pl.* **-aux**) nominal.
nominalement [nɔminal'mɑ̃], *adv.* nominally.
nominatif [nɔmina'tif], *a.* (*fem.* **-tive**) and *n.m.* nominative.
nomination [nɔmina'sjɔ̃], *n.f.* nomination; appointment.
nominativement [nɔminativ'mɑ̃], *adv.* by name.
nommé [nɔ'me], *a.* named, called; appointed.
nommément [nɔme'mɑ̃], *adv.* namely; particularly, especially.

nommer [nɔ'me], *v.t.* to name, to call; to mention; to nominate, to appoint. **se nommer**, *v.r.* to state one's name; to be called.
non [nɔ̃], *adv.* no, not.
non-activité [nɔ̃naktivi'te], *n.f.* state of being unattached *or* unemployed.
nonagénaire [nɔnaʒe'nɛ:r], *a.* ninety years of age.—*n.* nonagenarian.
non-agression [nɔ̃nagrɛ'sjɔ̃], *n.f.* non-aggression.
nonce [nɔ̃:s], *n.m.* nuncio.
nonchalamment [nɔ̃ʃala'mɑ̃], *adv.* nonchalantly, carelessly, heedlessly.
nonchalance [nɔ̃ʃa'lɑ̃:s], *n.f.* carelessness, heedlessness, nonchalance.
nonchalant [nɔ̃ʃa'lɑ̃], *a.* nonchalant, careless; listless.—*n.m.* (*fem.* **-e**) such a person.
non-lieu [nɔ̃'ljø], *n.m.* (*Law*) no true bill.
nonne [nɔn], *n.f.* nun.
nonobstant [nɔnɔps'tɑ̃], *prep.* notwithstanding, in spite of.—*adv.* nevertheless.
nonpareil [nɔ̃pa'rɛ:j], *a.* (*fem.* **-eille**) nonpareil, matchless.
non-sens [nɔ̃'sɑ̃:s], *n.m.* meaningless sentence, translation, *or* action.
nord [nɔ:r], *a. inv.* north, *Pôle nord*, North Pole.—*n.m.* north; north-wind; *nord-est*, north-east; *nord-ouest*, north-west.
nordique [nɔr'dik], *a.* Nordic, Scandinavian.—*n.* (**Nordique**) Nordic, Scandinavian (*person*).
normal [nɔr'mal], *a.* (*m. pl.* **-aux**) normal; (*Geom.*) perpendicular.
normalement [nɔrmal'mɑ̃], *adv.* normally.
normalien [nɔrma'ljɛ̃], *n.m.* (*fem.* **-enne**) training-college student *or* ex-student.
normalité [nɔrmali'te], *n.f.* normality.
normand [nɔr'mɑ̃], *a.* Norman.—*n.m.* (**Normand**, *fem.* **-ande**) Norman (*person*).
Normandie [nɔrmɑ̃'di], **la**, *f.* Normandy.
norme [nɔrm], *n.f.* norm, average.
Norvège [nɔr've:ʒ], **la**, *f.* Norway.
norvégien [nɔrve'ʒjɛ̃], *a.* (*fem.* **-enne**) Norwegian.—*n.m.* Norwegian (*language*); (**Norvégien**, *fem.* **-enne**) Norwegian (*person*).
nos [no], *pl.* [NOTRE].
nostalgie [nɔstal'ʒi], *n.f.* nostalgia, homesickness.
nostalgique [nɔstal'ʒik], *a.* nostalgic; sad.
notabilité [nɔtabili'te], *n.f.* respectability; person of note.
notable [nɔ'tabl], *a.* notable, of influence.—*n.* notable, person of note.
notablement [nɔtablə'mɑ̃], *adv.* notably.
notaire [nɔ'tɛ:r], *n.m.* notary; solicitor.
notamment [nɔta'mɑ̃], *adv.* specially; more particularly.
notariat [nɔta'rja], *n.m.* profession, business *or* function of notary.
notation [nɔta'sjɔ̃], *n.f.* notation.
note [nɔt], *n.f.* note, memorandum; mark; statement; bill.
noter [nɔ'te], *v.t.* to note; to mark; to note down; to observe, to notice.
notice [nɔ'tis], *n.f.* notice, account; review (*of a book*); notification.
notification [nɔtifika'sjɔ̃], *n.f.* notification, notice, intimation.
notifier [nɔti'fje], *v.t.* to notify; to intimate.
notion [no'sjɔ̃], *n.f.* notion, idea; (*pl.*) elements, rudiments.

notoire [nɔ'twaːr], a. notorious; well-known.

notoirement [nɔtwar'mɑ̃], adv. notoriously.

notoriété [nɔtɔrjɛ'te], n.f. notoriety (of fact); repute (of person).

notre [nɔtr], a. poss. (pl. nos) our.

nôtre [noːtr], pron. poss. (pl. nôtres) ours; our own; our things, friends, relatives etc.

noué [nwe], a. knotty, tied; rickety.

nouer [nwe], v.t. to tie, to knot; (fig.) to devise; to establish. **se nouer**, v.r. to be twisted or tied; to fasten oneself.

noueux [nu'ø], a. (fem. **-euse**) knotty, gnarled.

nougat [nu'ga], n.m. nougat; almond cake.

nouilles [nuːj], n.f. pl. noodles, spaghetti.

nourri [nu'ri], a. nourished, fed; full, rich, copious; brisk (fire).

nourrice [nu'ris], n.f. nurse; wet-nurse; (Motor., Av.) feed-tank.

nourricier [nuri'sje], a. (fem. **-ière**) lifegiving, nourishing; producing food.—n.m. (fem. **-ière**) foster parent.

nourrir [nu'riːr], v.t. to nourish, to feed; to keep, to maintain; to nurse; to foster; to rear; to cherish. **se nourrir**, v.r. to feed, to live upon.

nourrissage [nuri'saːʒ], n.m. rearing, feeding (of cattle).

nourrissant [nuri'sɑ̃], a. nutritious; nourishing; sustaining.

nourrisseur [nuri'sœːr], n.m. cow keeper; stock raiser.

nourrisson [nuri'sɔ̃], n.m. (fem. **-onne**) infant; foster child; nursling.

nourriture [nuri'tyːr], n.f. nourishment, food; livelihood.

nous [nu], pers. pron. we; us; to us; ourselves; each other.

nouveau [nu'vo], (before a vowel or unaspirated h, **nouvel**), a. (fem. **-elle** (1)) new; recent, novel; additional; inexperienced.—n.m. (pl. **-eaux**) new, something new; à nouveau, afresh; de nouveau, again.

nouveau-né [nuvo'ne], n.m. (fem. **nouveau-née**, pl. **nouveau-né(e)s**) new-born child.

nouveauté [nuvo'te], n.f. novelty; change, innovation; (pl.) fancy articles; (fig.) new book, new play.

nouvelle (2) [nu'vɛl], n.f. (often in pl.) news, tidings; short story, short novel.

nouvellement [nuvɛl'mɑ̃], adv. newly, lately, recently.

Nouvelle-Zélande [nuvɛlze'lɑ̃ːd], la, f. New Zealand.

nouvelliste [nuve'list], n. newswriter; short story writer.

novateur [nova'tœːr], a. (fem. **-trice**) innovating.—n.m. (fem. **-trice**) innovator.

novembre [nɔ'vɑ̃ːbr], n.m. November.

novice [nɔ'vis], a. novice, inexperienced.—n. novice, probationer.

noviciat [nɔvi'sja], n.m. noviciate.

noyade [nwa'jad], n.f. drowning.

noyau [nwa'jo], n.m. (pl. **-aux**) stone (of fruit), nucleus; core (of statues, casts etc.).

noyé [nwa'je], a. drowned.—n.m. (fem. **-ée**) drowned person.

noyer (1) [nwa'je], n.m. walnut tree; walnut (wood).

noyer (2) [nwa'je], v.t. (conjug. like EMPLOYER) to drown; to swamp; to deluge. **se noyer**, v.r. to be drowned; to be plunged (dans).

nu [ny], a. naked, nude, bare; uncovered; unadorned; destitute.—n.m. the nude, nudity.

nuage [nɥaːʒ], n.m. cloud; mist; (fig.) gloom, dejection.

nuageux [nɥa'ʒø], a. (fem. **-euse**) cloudy, overcast.

nuance [nɥɑ̃ːs], n.f. shade, hue; gradation; tinge.

nuancer [nɥɑ̃'se], v.t. (conjug. like COMMENCER) to shade; to vary slightly.

nubile [ny'bil], a. nubile, marriageable.

nubilité [nybili'te], n.f. nubility, marriageable age.

nucléaire [nykle'ɛːr], a. nuclear.

nudité [nydi'te], n.f. nudity, nakedness.

nuée [nɥe], n.f. cloud; (fig.) swarm, host, multitude, flock.

nues [ny], n.f. pl. (Poet.) skies.

nuire [nɥiːr], v.i. irr. to be hurtful, to jeopardize, to harm (à).

nuisible [nɥi'zibl], harmful, noxious, prejudicial.

nuit [nɥi], n.f. night, night-time; darkness; il fait nuit, it is dark; nuit blanche, sleepless night.

nuitamment [nɥita'mɑ̃], adv. by night, in the night.

nul [nyl], a. (fem. **nulle**) no, not any; void, null.—pron. no one, nobody, not one.

nullement [nyl'mɑ̃], adv. not at all, by no means.

nullifier [nyli'fje], v.t. to nullify.

nullité [nyli'te], n.f. nullity; nonentity; (fig.) incapacity.

numéraire [nyme'rɛːr], a. legal (of coin).—n.m. metallic currency, cash.

numéral [nyme'ral], a. (m. pl. **-aux**) numeral.

numérateur [nymera'tœːr], n.m. (Arith.) numerator.

numération [nymera'sjɔ̃], n.f. numeration, notation.

numérique [nyme'rik], a. numerical.

numériquement [nymerik'mɑ̃], adv. numerically.

numéro [nyme'ro], n.m. number.

numérotage [nymero'taːʒ], n.m., **numérotation** [nymero'sjɔ̃], n.f. numbering.

numéroter [nymero'te], v.t. to number.

numismate [nymis'mat], **numismatiste** [nymisma'tist], n. numismatist.

numismatique [nymisma'tik], a. numismatic.—n.f. numismatics.

nuptial [nyp'sjal], a. (m. pl. **-aux**) nuptial, bridal.

nuque [nyk], n.f. nape (of the neck).

nutritif [nytri'tif], a. (fem. **-tive**) nutritious, nourishing.

nutrition [nytri'sjɔ̃], n.f. nutrition.

nylon [ni'lɔ̃], n.m. nylon; des bas nylon, nylon stockings.

nymphe [nɛ̃ːf], n.f. nymph.

O

O, o [o], n.m. the fifteenth letter of the alphabet.

ô! [o] int. oh!

oasis

oasis [oa'zi:s], *n.f. inv.* oasis.

obéir [obe'i:r], *v.i.* to obey; to comply, to yield, to submit (à).

obéissance [obei'sã:s], *n.f.* obedience; allegiance.

obéissant [obei'sã], *a.* obedient; docile.

obélisque [obe'lɪsk], *n.m.* obelisk, needle.

obérer [obe're], *v.t. (conjug. like* CÉDER) to encumber *or* involve in debt.

obèse [o'bɛ:z], *a.* obese, stout.

obésité [obezi'te], *n.f.* obesity, stoutness.

obituaire [obity'ɛ:r], *a.* and *n.m.* obituary, register of deaths; mortuary.

objecter [obʒɛk'te], *v.t.* to object; to allege.

objecteur [obʒɛk'tœ:r], *n.m.* objector.

objectif [obʒɛk'tif], *a. (fem.* -tive) objective.—*n.m.* objective, aim; lens; *(Mil.)* target.

objection [obʒɛk'sjõ], *n.f.* objection.

objectivement [obʒɛktiv'mã], *adv.* objectively.

objectivité [obʒɛktivi'te], *n.f.* objectivity.

objet [ob'ʒɛ], *n.m.* object; subject, matter; aim; *(pl.)* articles, goods.

obligation [obliga'twa:r], *n.f.* obligation; *(Law)* bond; *(Comm.)* debenture.

obligatoire [obliga'twa:r], *a.* compulsory, obligatory, incumbent.

obligatoirement [obligatwar'mã], *adv.* compulsorily.

obligeamment [obliʒa'mã], *adv.* obligingly.

obligeance [obli'ʒã:s], *n.f.* obligingness; kindness.

obligeant [obli'ʒã] *a.* obliging, kind, helpful.

obliger [obli'ʒe], *v.t. (conjug. like* MANGER) to oblige, to bind; to compel; to gratify. **s'obliger,** *v.r.* to put oneself under an obligation.

oblique [o'blik], *a.* oblique, slanting; *(fig.)* indirect, underhand.

obliquement [oblik'mã], *adv.* obliquely, indirectly; unfairly.

obliquer [obli'ke], *v.i.* to slant, to swerve.

obliquité [obliki'te], *n.f.* obliquity.

oblitération [oblitera'sjõ], *n.f.* obliteration.

oblitérer [oblite're], *v.t. (conjug. like* CÉDER) to obliterate; to cancel *(stamps).*

oblong [o'blõ], *a. (fem.* -ue) oblong.

obole [o'bɔl] *n.f.* obolus; *(fig.)* farthing, mite.

obscène [op'sɛn], *a.* obscene.

obscénité [opseni'te], *n.f.* obscenity, lewdness.

obscur [ops'ky:r], *a.* obscure; dark, gloomy; *(fig.)* humble; mean.

obscurcir [opskyr'si:r], *v.t.* to obscure, to darken, to dim; to tarnish. **s'obscurcir,** *v.r.* to grow dim.

obscurcissement [opskyrsis'mã], *n.m.* darkening; *(Mil.)* black-out.

obscurément [opskyre'mã], *adv.* obscurely, dimly.

obscurité [opskyri'te], *n.f.* obscurity, darkness.

obséder [opse'de], *v.t. (conjug. like* CÉDER) to beset; to haunt; to importune, to obsess.

obsèques [op'sɛk], *n.f. pl.* obsequies, funeral.

obséquieusement [opsekjøz'mã], *adv.* obsequiously.

obséquieux [opse'kjø], *a. (fem.* -euse) obsequious, fawning.

observable [opser'vabl], *a.* observable.

observance [opsɛr'vã:s], *n.f.* observance.

observateur [opserva'tœ:r], *a. (fem.* -trice) observant.—*n.m. (fem.* -trice) observer, onlooker.

observation [opserva'sjõ], *n.f.* observation; observance; remark.

observatoire [opsɛrva'twa:r], *n.m.* observatory; look-out.

observer [opser've], *v.t.* to observe, to notice; to watch; to remark; to perform. **s'observer,** *v.r.* to be circumspect, to be on one's guard; to observe each other.

obsession [opsɛ'sjõ], *n.f.* obsession.

obstacle [ops'takl], *n.m.* obstacle, bar, hindrance.

obstination [opstina'sjõ], *n.f.* obstinacy, stubbornness, wilfulness.

obstiné [opsti'ne], *a.* obstinate, self-willed, stubborn; persistent.

obstinément [opstine'mã], *adv.* obstinately, stubbornly.

obstiner (s') [sopsti'ne], *v.r.* to be obstinately resolved (à), to insist, to persist.

obstructif [opstryk'tif], *a. (fem.* -tive) obstructive.

obstruction [opstryk'sjõ], *n.f.* obstruction; stoppage.

obstruer [opstry'e], *v.t.* to obstruct, to block.

obtempérer [optãpe're], *v.i. (conjug. like* CÉDER) to obey, to comply (à).

obtenir [optə'ni:r], *v.t. trr. (conjug. like* TENIR) to obtain, to procure, to get. **s'obtenir,** *v.r.* to be obtained; to be obtainable.

obtention [optã'sjõ], *n.f.* obtaining, getting.

obturer [opty're], *v.t.* to seal, to obturate; to fill *(gap),* to fill *(a tooth etc.).*

obtus [op'ty], *a.* obtuse; dull, blunt.

obus [o'by], *n.m. (Artill.)* shell.

obusier [aby'zje], *n.m.* howitzer.

obvier [ob'vje], *v.i.* to obviate, to prevent (à).

occasion [oka'zjõ], *n.f.* opportunity, occasion; cause; bargain, job lot; *livres d'occasion,* second-hand books.

occasionnel [okazjo'nɛl], *a. (fem.* -elle) occasional.

occasionnellement [okazjonɛl'mã], *adv.* occasionally.

occasionner [okazjo'ne], *v.t.* to occasion, to cause.

occident [oksi'dã], *n.m.* west.

occidental [oksidã'tal], *a. (m. pl.* -aux) occidental, western.

Occidentaux [oksidã'to], *n.m. pl.* natives *or* inhabitants of the western countries, members of the western bloc.

occulte [o'kylt], *a.* occult.

occupant [oky'pã], *a.* occupying.—*n.m. (fem.* -e) occupant, occupier.

occupation [okypa'sjõ], *n.f.* occupation; occupancy; capture.

occupé [oky'pe], *a.* occupied, busy, engaged; seized.

occuper [oky'pe], *v.t.* to occupy; to employ; to inhabit. **s'occuper,** *v.r.* to occupy oneself; to be busy; to look after; to see to (de).

occurrence [oky'rã:s], *n.f.* occurrence; event; *en l'occurrence,* under the circumstances.

océan [ose'ã], *n.m.* ocean, high sea.

océanique [osea'nik], *a.* oceanic.

ocre [okr], *n.f.* ochre.

octane [ok'tan], *n.m.* octane.

octave [ok'ta:v], *n.f.* octave.

228

octavo [ɔkta'vo], *adv.* eighthly.—*n.m.* octavo.
octobre [ɔk'tɔbr], *n.m.* October.
octogénaire [ɔktɔʒe'nɛːr], *a.* and *n.* octogenarian.
octogone [ɔktɔ'gɔn], *a.* octagonal, eight-sided.—*n.m.* octagon.
octroi [ɔk'trwa], *n.m.* grant, concession; town dues, toll; toll house *or* office.
octroyer [ɔktrwa'je], *v.t. (conjug. like* EMPLOYER) to grant, to concede.
oculaire [ɔky'lɛːr], *a.* ocular; *témoin oculaire,* eyewitness.—*n.m.* eye-piece.
oculiste [ɔky'list], *n.m.* oculist.
odalisque [ɔda'lisk], *n.f.* odalisque.
ode [ɔd], *n.f.* ode.
odeur [ɔ'dœːr], *n.f.* odor, smell; scent.
odieusement [ɔdjøz'mɑ̃], *adv.* odiously, hatefully.
odieux [ɔ'djø], *a. (fem.* **-euse)** odious, hateful, loathsome.—*n.m.* odiousness, hatefulness.
odorant [ɔdɔ'rɑ̃], *a.* fragrant, sweet-smelling.
odorat [ɔdɔ'ra], *n.m.* smell, sense of smell.
odoriférant [ɔdɔrife'rɑ̃], *a.* sweet-smelling.
Odyssée [ɔdi'se], *n.f.* Odyssey.
œil [œːj], *n.m. (pl.* **yeux)** eye; look; luster; bud; dint, hole *(in bread, cheese); des yeux à fleur de tête,* prominent eyes; *d'un coup d'œil,* at a glance; *en un clin d'œil,* in the twinkling of an eye.
œil-de-bœuf [œjdə'bœf], *n.m. (pl.* **œils-de-bœuf)** round *or* oval window.
œillade [œ'jad], *n.f.* glance; ogle, leer; wink.
œillère [œ'jɛːr], *n.f.* blinker; canine tooth; eye bath.
œillet [œ'je], *n.m.* eyelet; *(Bot.)* dianthus, pink; *œillet des fleuristes,* carnation; *œillet de poète,* sweet william; *petit œillet d'Inde,* French marigold.
œuf [œf], *n.m. (pl.* **œufs)** egg; ovum; spawn, roe *(of fish).*
œuvre [œːvr], *n.f.* work; performance; production; *(pl.)* works *(of an author).*—*n.m. (no pl.)* work *(of an author, painter, musician etc.)*
œuvrer [œ'vre], [OUVRER].
offensant [ɔfɑ̃'sɑ̃], *a.* offensive, insulting.
offense [ɔ'fɑ̃ːs], *n.f.* offense; injury, wrong, trespass.
offensé [ɔfɑ̃'se], *n.m. (fem.* **-ée)** offended party.
offenser [ɔfɑ̃'se], *v.t.* to offend; to sin against; to hurt, to injure *(feelings);* to shock. **s'offenser,** *v.r.* to be offended, to take offense.
offenseur [ɔfɑ̃'sœːr], *n.m.* offender.
offensif [ɔfɑ̃'sif], *a. (fem.* **-sive)** offensive.—*n.f.* **(-sive)** offensive *(attack).*
offensivement [ɔfɑ̃siv'mɑ̃], *adv.* offensively.
office [ɔ'fis], *n.m.* office; duty; employment; service; Divine worship.—*n.f.* servants' hall, pantry, larder.
officiant [ɔfi'sjɑ̃], *a.* officiating.—*n.m.* officiating priest.
officiel [ɔfi'sjɛl], *a. (fem.* **-elle)** official, formal.
officiellement [ɔfisjɛl'mɑ̃], *adv.* officially.
officier (1) [ɔfi'sje], *v.n.* to officiate *(at divine service).*
officier (2) [ɔfi'sje], *n.m.* officer.
officieusement [ɔfisjøz'mɑ̃], *adv.* officiously.
officieux [ɔfi'sjø], *a. (fem.* **-euse)** officious; semi-official; obliging.—*n.m. (fem.* **-euse)** busybody.

offrande [ɔ'frɑ̃ːd], *n.f.* offertory; offering.
offre [ɔfr], *n.f.* offer, tender.
offrir [ɔ'friːr], *v.t. (conjug. like* OUVRIR) to offer, to tender; to present, to give. **s'offrir,** *v.r.* to offer oneself; to present itself.
offusquer [ɔfys'ke], *v.t.* to obscure; to dazzle; to offend. **s'offusquer,** *v.r. (rare)* to become darkened; *(fig.)* to take offense.
ogival [ɔʒi'val], *a. (m. pl.* **-aux)** *(Arch.)* pointed; gothic.
ogive [ɔ'ʒiːv], *n.f.* ogive, pointed arch; nose *(of missile, rocket).*
ogre [ɔgr], *n.m. (fem.* **-esse)** ogre, ogress.
oh! [o], *int.* O! ho!
ohm [om], *n.m.* ohm.
oie [wa], *n.f.* goose; *(fig.)* simpleton.
oignon [ɔ'nɔ̃], *n.m.* onion; bulb; bunion.
oindre [wɛ̃dr], *v.t. irr.* to anoint.
oiseau [wa'zo], *n.m. (pl.* **-eaux)** bird; *(colloq.)* fellow, chap; *à vol d'oiseau,* as the crow flies.
oiseau-mouche [wazo'muʃ], *n.m. (pl.* **oiseaux-mouches)** humming-bird.
oiselet [wa'zlɛ], *n.m.* small bird.
oiseleur [wa'zlœːr], *n.m.* bird-catcher, fowler.
oiselier [waz'lje], *n.m.* bird seller; bird fancier.
oiseux [wa'zø], *a. (fem.* **-euse)** idle, useless, trifling.
oisif [wa'zif], *a. (fem.* **-ive)** idle, unoccupied; lying dead *(money).*—*n.m. (fem.* **-ive)** idler.
oisillon [wazi'jɔ̃], *n.m.* young bird, fledg(e)ling.
oisivement [waziv'mɑ̃], *adv.* idly.
oisiveté [waziv'te], *n.f.* idleness; hours of ease.
oison [wa'zɔ̃], *n.m.* gosling; *(fig.)* simpleton.
oléagineux [ɔlea'ʒinø], *a. (fem.* **-euse)** oleaginous, oily.
oléoduc [ɔleɔ'dyk], *n.m.* pipeline.
oligarchie [ɔligar'ʃi], *n.f.* oligarchy.
oligarchique [ɔligar'ʃik], *a.* oligarchical.
oligarque [ɔli'gark], *n.* oligarch.
olivâtre [ɔli'vɑːtr], *a.* olivaceous, olive-hued; sallow.
olive [ɔ'liːv], *a. inv.* olive-colored.—*n.f.* olive.
Olivier [ɔli'vje], *m.* Oliver.
olivier [ɔli'vje], *n.m.* olive tree; olive wood.
olographe [ɔlɔ'graf], *a.* holograph(ic) *(will).*
Olympe [ɔ'lɛ̃ːp], *n.m.* Olympus; *(fig.)* heaven.
olympien [ɔlɛ̃'pjɛ̃], *a. (fem.* **-enne)** Olympian.—*n.m.* **(Olympien,** *fem.* **-enne)** Olympian.
olympique [ɔlɛ̃'pik], *a.* Olympic.
ombrage [ɔ̃'braːʒ], *n.m.* shade; umbrage, suspicion.
ombrager [ɔ̃bra'ʒe], *v.t. (conjug. like* MANGER) to shade; *(fig.)* to protect.
ombrageux [ɔ̃bra'ʒø], *a. (fem.* **-euse)** skittish *(of horses);* suspicious, touchy.
ombre [ɔ̃ːbr], *n.f.* shadow; shade; darkness; ghost; *à l'ombre,* in the shade.
ombré [ɔ̃'bre], *a.* tinted, shaded.
ombrelle [ɔ̃'brɛl], *n.f.* parasol, sunshade.
ombrer [ɔ̃'bre], *v.t.* to shade; to darken.
ombreux [ɔ̃'brø], *a. (fem.* **-euse)** shady.
omelette [ɔm'lɛt], *n.f.* omelet(te).
omettre [ɔ'mɛtr], *v.t. irr. (conjug. like* METTRE) to omit.
omission [ɔmi'sjɔ̃], *n.f.* omission.
omnibus [ɔmni'byːs], *a.* suitable for all; *train omnibus,* slow train, local train.—*n.m. inv.* omnibus, bus.

omnipotence [ɔmnipo'tã:s], *n.f.* omnipotence.

omnipotent [ɔmnipo'tã], *a.* omnipotent.

omnivore [ɔmni'vɔːr], *a.* omnivorous.—*n.m.* omnivore.

omoplate [ɔmɔ'plat], *n.f.* shoulder-blade; scapula.

on [ɔ̃], *indef. pron.* one, they, we, you, people, men, somebody.

once (1) [ɔ̃:s], *n.f.* ounce (*weight*).

once (2) [ɔ̃:s], *n.f.* ounce, snow leopard.

oncle [ɔ̃:kl], *n.m.* uncle.

onction [ɔ̃k'sjɔ̃], *n.f.* unction, anointing; (*fig.*) unctuousness.

onctueusement [ɔ̃ktɥøz'mã], *adv.* unctuously.

onctueux [ɔ̃k'tɥø], *a.* (*fem.* **-euse**) unctuous, oily.

onctuosité [ɔ̃ktɥozi'te], *n.f.* unctuousness, smoothness.

onde [ɔ̃:d], *n.f.* wave, billow; (*fig.*) sea.

ondé [ɔ̃'de], *a.* undulating, wavy; watered (*of silk etc.*).

ondée [ɔ̃'de], *n.f.* shower (*of rain*).

ondoyant [ɔ̃dwa'jã], *a.* undulating; (*fig.*) changeable.

ondoyer [ɔ̃dwa'je], *v.t.* (*conjug. like* EMPLOYER) to baptize privately.—*v.i.* to undulate; to ripple (*water*).

ondulant [ɔ̃dy'lã], *a.* undulating; waving, flowing.

ondulation [ɔ̃dyla'sjɔ̃], *n.f.* undulation; wave (*of hair*).

ondulé [ɔ̃dy'le], *a.* rolling, undulating; waved (*hair*); corrugated (*iron*).

onduler [ɔ̃dy'le], *v.t.* to wave (*hair*).—*v.i.* to undulate; to ripple.

onduleux [ɔ̃dy'lø], *a.* (*fem.* **-euse**) sinuous, wavy.

onéreux [one'rø], *a.* (*fem.* **-euse**) burdensome, onerous; expensive.

ongle [ɔ̃:gl], *n.m.* nail (*of fingers, claws etc.*); claw, talon; hoof.

onglée [ɔ̃'gle], *n.f.* numbness of the fingers (*from cold*).

onglet [ɔ̃'glɛ], *n.m.* miter, miter-joint.

onglier [ɔ̃'glje], *n.m.* manicure case; (*pl.*) (*curved*) nail scissors.

onguent [ɔ̃'gã], *n.m.* ointment, salve.

ongulé [ɔ̃gy'le], *a.* hoofed, ungulate.

onyx [ɔ'niks], *a.* and *n.m. inv.* onyx.

onze [ɔ̃:z], *a.* and *n.m.* eleven, eleventh.

onzième [ɔ̃'zjɛm], *a.* and *n.m.* eleventh.

onzièmement [ɔ̃zjɛm'mã], *adv.* eleventhly, in the eleventh place.

opacité [opasi'te], *n.f.* opacity; (*fig.*) darkness.

opale [ɔ'pal], *n.f.* opal.

opalescence [opalɛ'sã:s], *n.f.* opalescence.

opalescent [opalɛ'sã], *a.* opalescent.

opaque [ɔ'pak], *a.* opaque.

opéra [ope'ra], *n.m.* opera; opera house.

opéra-bouffe [opera'buf], *n.m.* comic opera; musical comedy.

opérateur [opera'tœːr], *n.m.* (*fem.* **-trice**) operator; operative.

opératif [opera'tif], *a.* (*fem.* **-tive**) operative.

opération [opera'sjɔ̃], *n.f.* operation, working, performance; (*Comm.*) transaction.

opératoire [opera'twaːr], *a.* operative, surgical.

opérer [ope're], *v.t.* (*conjug. like* CÉDER) to operate, to bring about, to perform; to operate upon.—*v.i.* to work, to operate. **s'opérer**, *v.r.* to take place, to be brought about.

opérette [ope'rɛt], *n.f.* operetta, light opera.

ophtalmie [ɔftal'mi], *n.f.* ophthalmia.

ophtalmique [ɔftal'mik], *a.* ophthalmic.

opiner [ɔpi'ne], *v.i.* to opine, to give *or* be of opinion; to speak.

opiniâtre [ɔpi'njɑːtr], *a.* stubborn, obstinate.—*n.* stubborn person.

opiniâtrement [ɔpinjɑtrə'mã], *adv.* doggedly.

opiniâtrer (s') [sɔpinja'tre], *v.r.* to be obstinate, to insist.

opiniâtreté [ɔpinjɑtrə'te], *n.f.* obstinacy.

opinion [ɔpi'njɔ̃], *n.f.* opinion; judgment, view; (*pl.*) votes.

opium [ɔ'pjɔm], *n.m.* opium.

opossum [ɔpɔ'sɔm], *n.m.* opossum.

opportun [ɔpɔr'tœ̃], *a.* opportune, timely; expedient.

opportunément [ɔpɔrtyne'mã], *adv.* seasonably.

opportunisme [ɔpɔrty'nism], *n.m.* opportunism.

opportuniste [ɔpɔrty'nist], *a.* and *n.* opportunist.

opportunité [ɔpɔrtyni'te], *n.f.* opportuneness, expediency.

opposant [opo'zã], *a.* opposing, adverse.—*n.m.* (*fem.* **-e**) opponent, adversary.

opposé [opo'ze], *a.* opposite, contrary.—*n.m.* the opposite, the reverse, the contrary.

opposer [opo'ze], *v.t.* to oppose; to object; to urge. **s'opposer**, *v.r.* to be opposed *or* contrary (*à*), to set oneself against, to resist.

opposition [opozi'sjɔ̃], *n.f.* opposition, resistance; contrast.

oppresser [ɔprɛ'se], *v.t.* (*fig.*) to depress; *†*to oppress.

oppresseur [ɔprɛ'sœːr], *a.m.* oppressive.—*n.m.* oppressor.

oppressif [ɔprɛ'sif], *a.* (*fem.* **-ive**) oppressive.

oppression [ɔprɛ'sjɔ̃], *n.f.* oppression.

oppressivement [ɔprɛsiv'mã], *adv.* tyrannically, oppressively (*person*).

opprimant [ɔpri'mã], *a.* oppressing.

opprimé [ɔpri'me], *a.* oppressed.—*n.m.* (*fem.* **-ée**) the oppressed.

opprimer [ɔpri'me], *v.t.* to oppress, to crush.

opprobre [ɔ'prɔbr], *n.m.* opprobrium, shame, disgrace.

opter [ɔp'te], *v.i.* to choose, to decide.

opticien [ɔpti'sjɛ̃], *n.m.* optician.

optimisme [ɔpti'mism], *n.m.* optimism.

optimiste [ɔpti'mist], *a.* optimistic.—*n.* optimist.

option [ɔp'sjɔ̃], *n.f.* option, choice.

optique [ɔp'tik], *a.* optic, optical.—*n.f.* optics; perspective.

opulence [ɔpy'lã:s], *n.f.* opulence, wealth.

opulent [ɔpy'lã], *a.* opulent, wealthy.

or (1) [ɔːr], *n.m.* gold; (*Her.*) or.

or (2) [ɔːr], *conj.* but, now; well.

oracle [ɔ'raːkl], *n.m.* oracle.

orage [ɔ'raːʒ], *n.m.* storm; thunder-storm; (*fig.*) tumult, disorder.

orageusement [ɔraʒøz'mã], *adv.* tempestuously; boisterously.

orageux [ɔra'ʒø], *a.* (*fem.* **-euse**) stormy, tempestuous; restless.

oraison [orɛ'zɔ̃], *n.f.* speech, oration; prayer.

oral [o'ral], *a.* (*m. pl.* -**aux**) oral, by word of mouth.

oralement [oral'mã], *adv.* orally, by word of mouth.

orange [o'rãːʒ], *n.f.* orange (*fruit*).—*a. inv.* and *n.m.* orange (*color*).

orangé [orã'ʒe], *a.* orange(-colored).

orangeade [orã'ʒad], *n.f.* orangeade, orange squash.

oranger [orã'ʒe], *n.m.* orange tree.

orangerie [orã'ʒri], *n.f.* orange house; orange grove, orangery.

orang-outan(g) [orãu'tã], *n.m.* (*pl.* **orangs-outans**) orang-utan.

orateur [ora'tœːr], *n.m.* (*fem.* -**trice**) orator, speaker.

oratoire [ora'twaːr], *a.* oratorical; oratorial.—*n.m.* oratory; private chapel.

orbe [orb], *n.m.* orb, orbit; globe; sphere; coil (*snake*).

orbite [or'bit], *n.f.* orbit; (*Anat.*) socket; (*fig.*) sphere (*of action*).

Orcades [or'kad], **les**, *f. pl.* the Orkneys.

orchestral [orkɛs'tral], *a.* (*m. pl.* -**aux**) orchestral.

orchestration [orkɛstra'sjɔ̃], *n.f.* scoring, orchestration.

orchestre [or'kɛstr], *n.m.* orchestra; band.

orchestrer [orkɛs'tre], *v.t.* to score, to orchestrate.

orchidée [orki'de], *n.f.* orchid; (*pl.*) Orchidaceae.

ordinaire [ordi'nɛːr], *a.* ordinary, common, usual.—*n.m.* ordinary practice; usual fare.

ordinairement [ordinɛr'mã], *adv.* usually.

ordinal [ordi'nal], *a.* (*m. pl.* -**aux**) ordinal.

ordination [ordina'sjɔ̃], *n.f.* ordination.

ordonnance [ordo'nãːs], *n.f.* order, ordinance, regulation; disposition, arrangement; (*Med.*) prescription.—*n.* (*usu. fem.*) (*Mil.*) orderly.

ordonnateur [ordona'tœːr], *a.* (*fem.* -**trice**) ordaining, ordering.—*n.m.* (*fem.* -**trice**) organizer, manager; master of ceremonies.

ordonné [ordo'ne], *a.* ordered; tidy; ordained (*priest*).

ordonner [ordo'ne], *v.t.* to order, to regulate; to direct, to command; to ordain; (*Med.*) to prescribe.

ordre [ordr], *n.m.* order, command; class, tribe; (*pl.*) holy orders.

ordure [or'dyːr], *n.f.* filth, dirt; (*pl.*) sweepings, refuse, garbage.

ordurier [ordy'rje], *a.* (*fem.* -**ière**) filthy, ribald, lewd.

oreille [o'rɛːj], *n.f.* ear; hearing; flange; handle (*of a vase etc.*); *avoir l'oreille basse*, to be crestfallen; *avoir mal aux oreilles*, to have ear-ache; *faire la sourde oreille*, to turn a deaf ear; *prêter l'oreille à*, to listen to.

oreiller [orɛ'je], *n.m.* pillow.

oreillons [orɛ'jɔ̃], *n.m. pl.* mumps.

orfèvre [or'fɛːvr], *n.m.* goldsmith, silversmith.

orfraie [or'frɛ], *n.f.* osprey.

organdi [orgã'di], *n.m.* organdie.

organe [or'gan], *n.m.* organ; voice; agent, agency; spokesman.

organique [orga'nik], *a.* organic.

organisateur [organiza'tœːr], *a.* (*fem.* -**trice**) organizing.—*n.m.* (*fem.* -**trice**) organizer.

organisation [organiza'sjɔ̃], *n.f.* organization; (*fig.*) set-up; constitution.

organisé [organi'ze], *a.* organized.

organiser [organi'ze], *v.t.* to organize; to get up, to arrange. **s'organiser**, *v.r.* to become organized.

organisme [orga'nism], *n.m.* organism.

organiste [orga'nist], *n.* organist.

orge [orʒ], *n.f.* barley; (*masc. in orge mondé*, hulled barley, *and orge perlé*, pearl barley).

orgelet [orʒ'lɛ], *n.m.* sty (*in the eye*).

orgie [or'ʒi], *n.f.* orgy; (*fig.*) profusion.

orgue [org], *n.m.* (*fem. in pl.*) (*Mus.*) organ.

orgueil [or'gœːj], *n.m.* pride; arrogance.

orgueilleusement [orgœjøz'mã], *adv.* proudly, haughtily.

orgueilleux [orgœ'jø], *a.* proud, haughty, arrogant.—*n.m.* (*fem.* -**euse**) proud and haughty person.

orient [o'rjã], *n.m.* East, Orient; rise; water (*of pearls*).

oriental [orjã'tal], *a.* (*m. pl.* -**aux**) oriental, eastern.—*n.m.* (*fem.* -**e**) oriental (*person*).

orientation [orjãta'sjɔ̃], *n.f.* orientation.

orienter [orjã'te], *v.t.* to orientate; to set (*a map*) by the compass; (*fig.*) to guide; (*Naut.*) to trim (*sails*). **s'orienter**, *v.r.* to take one's bearings, to ascertain one's position; (*fig.*) to see what one is about.

orifice [ori'fis], *n.m.* orifice, aperture, hole.

originaire [oriʒi'nɛːr], *a.* originally (*coming*) from; native (*de*); primitive.

originairement [oriʒinɛr'mã], *adv.* originally, primitively.

original [oriʒi'nal], *a.* (*m. pl.* -**aux**) original; singular, odd, peculiar, quaint.—*n.m.* original manuscript, drawing etc. (*not a copy*).—*n.m.* (*fem.* -**e**) queer person, character, oddity.

originalement [oriʒinal'mã], *adv.* originally; singularly, oddly.

originalité [oriʒinali'te], *n.f.* originality; eccentricity.

origine [ori'ʒin], *n.f.* origin, source; descent, derivation, extraction; *d'origine*, authentic; vintage (*wine*).

originel [oriʒi'nɛl], *a.* (*fem.* -**elle**) original, primitive.

originellement [oriʒinɛl'mã], *adv.* originally.

orignal [ori'nal], *n.m.* elk (*of Canada*), moose.

Orion [o'rjɔ̃], *n.m.* (*Astron.*) Orion.

oripeau [ori'po], *n.m.* (*pl.* -**eaux**) tinsel; foil; (*pl.*) tawdry finery; (*more usually*) rags.

orme [orm], *n.m.* elm.

ormeau [or'mo], *n.m.* (*pl.* -**eaux**) young elm.

orné [or'ne], *a.* ornate.

ornement [orna'mã], *n.m.* ornament, embellishment.

ornemental [ornamã'tal], *a.* (*m. pl.* -**aux**) ornamental.

ornementation [ornamãta'sjɔ̃], *n.f.* ornamentation.

orner [or'ne], *v.t.* to adorn, to decorate, to deck, to embellish. **s'orner**, *v.r.* to adorn oneself; to be adorned.

ornière [or'njɛːr], *n.f.* rut.

ornithologie [ornitolo'ʒi], *n.f.* ornithology.

ornithologiste [ornitolo'ʒist], **ornithologue** [ornito'log], *n.m.* ornithologist.

231

Orphée [ɔr'fe], m. Orpheus.

orphelin [ɔrfə'lɛ̃], a. and n.m. (fem. -e) orphan.

orphelinat [ɔrfəli'na], n.m. orphanage.

orphéon [ɔrfe'ɔ̃], n.m. male-voice choir.

ort [ɔːr], a. inv. and adv. (Comm.) gross, gross weight.

orteil [ɔr'tɛːj], n.m. toe, esp. the big toe.

orthodoxe [ɔrtɔ'dɔks], a. orthodox.

orthodoxie [ɔrtɔdɔk'si], n.f. orthodoxy.

orthographe [ɔrtɔ'graf], n.f. orthography, spelling.

orthopédie [ɔrtɔpe'di], n.f. orthopedics.

ortie [ɔr'ti], n.f. nettle.

orvet [ɔr'vɛ], n.m. slow-worm.

os [ɔs; pl. o], n.m. inv. bone.

oscillant [ɔsi'lɑ̃], a. oscillating.

oscillation [ɔsila'sjɔ̃], n.f. oscillation, vibration.

oscillatoire [ɔsila'twaːr], a. oscillatory.

osciller [ɔsi'le], v.i. to oscillate, to swing, to vibrate; (fig.) to fluctuate.

oscillographe [ɔsilɔ'graf], n.m. (Elec.) oscillograph.

osé [o'ze], a. bold, daring.

oseille [o'zɛːj], n.f. sorrel.

oser [o'ze], v.t., v.i. to dare, to venture.

oseraie [oz'rɛ], n.f. osier bed.

osier [o'zje], n.m. osier, withy, wicker.

osselet [ɔs'lɛ], n.m. knuckle bone (of sheep); ossicle (of ear).

ossements [ɔs'mɑ̃], n.m. pl. bones (of the dead).

osseux [ɔ'sø], a. (fem. -euse) bony, osseous.

ossification [ɔsifika'sjɔ̃], n.f. ossification.

ossifier [ɔsi'fje], v.t. to ossify. **s'ossifier**, v.r. to become ossified.

ossuaire [ɔ'sɥɛːr], n.m. ossuary, charnel-house.

ostensible [ɔstɑ̃'sibl], a. open; above-board.

ostensiblement [ɔstɑ̃siblə'mɑ̃], adv. openly, publicly.

ostensoir [ɔstɑ̃'swaːr], n.m. monstrance.

ostentateur [ɔstɑ̃ta'tœːr], a. (fem. -trice) ostentatious.

ostentation [ɔstɑ̃ta'sjɔ̃], n.f. ostentation, show.

ostraciser [ɔstrasi'ze], v.t. to ostracize.

ostracisme [ɔstra'sism], n.m. ostracism.

ostréiculture [ɔstreikyl'tyːr], n.f. oyster culture.

otage [o'taːʒ], n.m. hostage; pledge.

ôter [o'te], v.t. to take away; to remove; to take off; to deprive of; to deduct; to rid of. **s'ôter**, v.r. to remove oneself, to get away; to rid oneself; ôtez-vous de mon chemin, stand aside.

ou [u], conj. or, either, else; ou bien, or else; ou . . . ou, either . . . or.

où [u], adv. where; whither; at which, in which, to which, through which; when, that; par où? which way?

ouais! [wɛ], int. well now! my word!

ouate [wat], n.f. l'ouate or la ouate, wadding, padding; cotton-wool.

ouater [wa'te], v.t. to wad, to pad; to coddle.

oubli [u'bli], n.m. forgetfulness; oblivion; oversight, slip; pardon.

oubliable [u'bljabl], a. liable or deserving to be forgotten.

oublier [u'blje], v.t. to forget, to omit, to neglect; to pardon. **s'oublier**, v.r. to forget oneself; to be forgotten.

oubliettes [u'bljɛt], n.f. pl. oubliette, trap-dungeon.

oublieux [u'bljø], a. (fem. -euse) forgetful, unmindful.

ouest [wɛst], a. inv. westerly, western.—n.m. west.

ouf! [uf], int. oh! (of relief).

Ouganda [ugɑ̃'da], l', m. Uganda.

oui [wi], adv. yes.—n.m. yes.

ouï [wi], p.p. [OUÏR].

ouï-dire [wi'diːr], n.m. inv. hearsay.

ouïe [wi], n.f. *hearing; hole (of a violin etc.); (pl.) gills (of fish).

ouïr [wiːr], v.t. irr. (rarely used except in the infinitive and compound tenses) to hear; j'ai ouï dire, I have heard say.

ouragan [ura'gɑ̃], n.m. hurricane; (fig.) storm.

ourdir [ur'diːr], v.t. to warp (cloth); (fig.) to weave, to plot, to concoct.

ourdissage [urdi'saːʒ], n.m. warping.

ourdou [ur'du], n.m. Urdu (language), Hindustani.

ourler [ur'le], v.t. to hem; ourler à jour, to hemstitch.

ourlet [ur'lɛ], n.m. hem.

ours [urs], n.m. bear.

ourse [urs], n.f. she-bear.

oursin [ur'sɛ̃], n.m. sea-urchin.

ourson [ur'sɔ̃], n.m. bear cub.

outil [u'ti], n.m. tool, implement.

outillage [uti'jaːʒ], n.m. stock of tools; equipment.

outillé [uti'je], a. furnished with tools.

outiller [uti'je], v.t. to furnish with tools; to equip.

outrage [u'traːʒ], n.m. outrage, gross insult; injury, wrong.

outrageant [utra'ʒɑ̃], a. outrageous; insulting, abusive.

outrager [utra'ʒe], v.t. (conjug. like MANGER) to outrage; to insult, to offend.

outrageusement [utraʒøz'mɑ̃], adv. insultingly.

outrageux [utra'ʒø], a. (fem. -euse) outrageous.

outrance [u'trɑ̃s], n.f. extreme; excess; à outrance, to the death.

outre (1) [utr], n.f. goatskin or leather bottle.

outre (2) [utr], adv. further, beyond; en outre, besides; passer outre, to go on, to take no notice of a thing.—prep. beyond; besides, in addition to; outre que, besides.

outré [u'tre], a. exaggerated, strained, excessive; incensed.

outrecuidance [utrəkɥi'dɑ̃s], n.f. presumption.

outrecuidant [utrəkɥi'dɑ̃], a. presumptuous, bumptious.

outre-Manche [utrə'mɑ̃ːʃ], adv. across the Channel.

outremer [utrə'mɛːr], n.m. ultramarine (color).

outre-mer [utrə'mɛːr], adv. overseas.

outrepasser [utrəpa'se], v.t. to go beyond, to transgress.

outrer [u'tre], v.t. to overdo; to exaggerate.

ouvert [u'vɛːr], a. open; unfortified (of towns); (fig.) frank.

ouvertement [uvɛrtə'mᾶ], *adv.* openly, frankly.

ouverture [uvɛr'ty:r], *n.f.* opening; aperture, gap, hole; (*Mus.*) overture; (*Arch.*) span, width (*of a doorway etc.*); (*Av.*) (parachute) drop.

ouvrable [u'vrabl], *a.* working, workable; *jour ouvrable*, working day.

ouvrage [u'vra:ʒ], *n.m.* work, piece of work; performance, workmanship.

ouvragé [uvra'ʒe], *a.* wrought, figured.

ouvrager [uvra'ʒe], *v.t.* (*conjug. like* MANGER) to work, to figure.

ouvrant [u'vrᾶ], *a.* opening.

ouvré [u'vre], *a.* wrought; diapered, figured.

ouvre-boîte [uvrə'bwa:t], *n.m.* (*pl.* -**boîtes**) can opener.

ouvrer [u'vre], *v.t.* to work (*material*); to diaper (*linen*).—*v.i.* to work.

ouvrier [uvri'e], *a.* (*fem.* -**ière**) operative, working.—*n.m.* (*fem.* -**ière**) workman, (female) worker, hand, operative; laborer.

ouvrir [u'vri:r], *v.t. irr.* to open, to unlock; to sharpen (*the appetite*); to broach (*opinions etc.*).—*v.i.* to open; to expand. **s'ouvrir**, *v.r.* to open; to open for oneself; to open one's mind.

ouvroir [u'vrwa:r], *n.m.* charity workshop; workroom.

ovaire [ɔ'vɛ:r], *n.m.* ovary.

ovalaire [ova'lɛ:r], *a.* (*Anat.*) oval.

ovale [ɔ'val], *a.* and *n.m.* oval.

ovation [ova'sjɔ̃], *n.f.* ovation.

ovoïde [ɔvɔ'id], *a.* ovoid, egg-shaped.

ovule [ɔ'vyl], *n.m.* ovule.

oxalique [ɔksa'lik], *a.* oxalic.

oxyacétylénique [ɔksiasetile'nik], *a.* oxyacetylene (*welding etc.*).

oxyde [ɔk'sid], *n.m.* oxide.

oxyder [ɔksi'de], *v.t.* to oxidize.

oxygène [ɔksi'ʒɛ:n], *n.m.* oxygen.

oxygéné [ɔksiʒe'ne], *a.* *eau oxygénée*, hydrogen peroxide.

ozone [ɔ'zɔn], *n.m.* ozone.

P

F, p [pe], *n.m.* the sixteenth letter of the alphabet.

pacage [pa'ka:ʒ], *n.m.* pasture land; *droit de pacage*, grazing rights.

pacificateur [pasifika'tœ:r], *a.* (*fem.* -**trice**) pacifying, peace-making.—*n.m.* (*fem.* -**trice**) peacemaker.

pacification [pasifika'sjɔ̃], *n.f.* pacification.

pacifier [pasi'fje], *v.t.* to pacify, to appease

pacifique [pasi'fik], *a.* pacific, peaceful.

pacifiquement [pasifik'mᾶ], *adv.* peaceably, quietly.

pacifisme [pasi'fism], *n.m.* pacifism.

pacifiste [pasi'fist], *a.* and *n.* pacifist.

pacotille [pako'ti:j], *n.f.* goods carried free of charge by passengers or seamen; shoddy goods; pack, bale.

pacte [pakt], *n.m.* compact, contract, pact, agreement; *pacte de préférence*, preference clause.

pactiser [pakti'ze], *v.i.* to covenant, to make a compact (*avec*).

paf! [paf], *int.* slap! bang!

pagaie [pa'gɛ], *n.f.* paddle (*for canoe etc.*).

pagaie or **pagaille** [pa'gaj], *n.f.* hurry; disorder; *en pagaïe*, (*pop.*) higgledy-piggledy.

paganisme [paga'nism], *n.m.* paganism.

pagayer [page'je], *v.t., v.i.* (*conjug. like* PAYER) to paddle.

page (1) [pa:ʒ], *n.m.* page (boy).

page (2) [pa:ʒ], *n.f.* page (*of a book*).

pagode [pa'gɔd], *n.f.* pagoda.

paiement [PAYEMENT].

païen [pa'jɛ̃], *a.* and *n.m.* (*fem.* -**enne**) pagan, heathen.

paillard [pa'ja:r], *a.* lecherous, lewd. *n.m.* (*fem.* -**e**) wanton, sensual person, bawd.

paillasse (1) [pa'jas], *n.f.* straw mattress.

paillasse (2) [pa'jas], *n.m.* clown, buffoon.

paillasson [puja'sɔ̃], *n.m.* straw mat; doormat.

paille [pa:j], *a.* straw-colored.—*n.f.* straw; flaw (*in gems, metals etc.*); *botte de paille*, bale of straw.

paillé [pa'je], *a.* straw-colored; faulty (*of metals etc.*).

pailler (1) [pa'je], *n.m.* farm yard; heap *or* stack of straw.

pailler (2) [pa'je], *v.t.* to mulch (*plants*).

pailleter [paj'te], *v.t.* (*conjug. like* APPELER) to spangle.

paillette [pa'jɛt], *n.f.* spangle; flaw (*in a gem*); *savon en paillettes*, soap flakes.

paillis [pa'ji], *n.m.* mulch.

paillon [pa'jɔ̃], *n.m.* large spangle, tinsel; wisp of straw; straw wrapper (*for bottle*).

pain [pɛ̃], *n.m.* bread; loaf; cake (*of soap etc.*); (*pop.*) blow, punch; *pain grillé*, toast; *un pain*, a loaf; *un petit pain*, a roll.

pair [pɛ:r], *a.* equal, even (*of numbers*).—*n.m.* peer; equal; mate (*of birds*); par, equality; *au pair*, at par, even (*with*), 'au pair'; *de pair*, on a par; *hors* (*de*) *pair*, beyond comparison.

paire [pɛ:r], *n.f.* pair, brace, couple.

pairesse [pɛ'rɛs], *n.f.* peeress.

pairie [pɛ'ri], *n.f.* peerage.

paisible [pɛ'zibl], *a.* peaceful, quiet, calm.

paisiblement [pɛzibl'mᾶ], *adv.* peacefully.

paître [pɛ:tr], *v.t., v.i. irr.* to graze, to feed.

paix [pɛ], *n.f.* peace; quiet; stillness; rest.—*int.* be quiet!

Pakistan [pakis'tᾶ], le, *m.* Pakistan.

pakistanais [pakista'nɛ], *a.* Pakistani.—*n.* (**Pakistanais**, *fem.* -**aise**) Pakistani (*person*).

paladin [pala'dɛ̃], *n.m.* paladin, champion.

palais (1) [pa'lɛ], *n.m.* palace; (*fig.*) the bar, the law; *palais de justice*, law-courts.

palais (2) [pa'lɛ], *n.m.* palate, roof (*of the mouth*).

palan [pa'lᾶ], *n.m.* tackle, pulley block.

pale [pal], *n.f.* blade (*of oar, propeller etc.*); sluice, flood-gate.

pâle [pɑ:l], *a.* pale, wan, pallid, ghastly.

palefrenier [palfrə'nje], *n.m.* groom, ostler.

palefroi [pal'frwa], *n.m.* palfrey.

Palestine [palɛs'tin], la, *f.* Palestine.

palestinien [palɛsti'njɛ̃], *a.* (*fem.* -**enne**) Palestinian.

palet [pa'lɛ], *n.m.* quoit.
palette [pa'lɛt], *n.f.* paddle (*of paddle-wheel*); bat (*ping-pong*); palette (*of painter*).
pâleur [pɑ'lœːr], *n.f.* pallor, wanness.
pâli [pɑ'li], *a.* grown pale.
palier [pa'lje], *n.m.* landing (*on a staircase*), floor; stage, degree; level stretch; *vitesse en palier*, speed on the flat.
pâlir [pɑ'liːr], *v.t.* to make pale, to bleach.— *v.i.* to (grow, turn *or* become) pale; to grow dim.
palis [pa'li], *n.m.* stake, pale; paling, enclosure.
palissade [pali'sad], *n.f.* palisade, paling; wooden fence; hedgerow; stockade.
palissader [palisa'de], *v.t.* to palisade; to stockade; to fence in.
pâlissant [pɑli'sɑ̃], *a.* turning pale, fading.
pallier [pa'lje], *v.t.* to palliate, to excuse.
palmarès [palma'rɛːs], *n.m. inv.* prize list, list of honors.
palme [palm], *n.f.* palm, palm branch; palm tree; (*fig.*) victory, triumph.
palmé [pal'me], *a.* palmate; web-footed.
palmier [pal'mje], *n.m.* palm tree, palm.
palombe [pa'lɔ̃ːb], *n.f.* wood pigeon, ringdove.
palonnier [palɔ'nje], *n.m.* pole (*of a coach*); (*Motor.*) compensator (*of brake*); (*Av.*) rudder bar.
pâlot [pɑ'lo], *a.* (*fem.* **-otte**) palish, rather pale.
palourde [pa'lurd], *n.f.* clam.
palpable [pal'pabl], *a.* palpable.
palpablement [palpablə'mɑ̃], *adv.* palpably.
palper [pal'pe], *v.t.* to feel, to touch; (*colloq.*) to pocket.
palpitant [palpi'tɑ̃], *a.* palpitating; thrilling.
palpitation [palpita'sjɔ̃], *n.f.* palpitation; throbbing; thrill, flutter.
palpiter [palpi'te], *v.i.* to palpitate, to throb; to quiver, to flutter.
paludéen [palyde'ɛ̃], *a.* (*fem.* **-éenne**) paludal, marshy.
pâmer [pɑ'me], *v.i.* and **se pâmer**, *v.r.* to swoon.
pâmoison [pamwa'zɔ̃], *n.f.* swoon, fainting fit.
pamphlet [pɑ'flɛ], *n.m.* satirical booklet, lampoon.
pamphlétaire [pɑfle'tɛːr], *n.* pamphleteer.
pamplemousse [pɑplə'mus], *n.m. or f.* grapefruit.
pampre [pɑ̃ːpr], *n.m.* vine branch.
pan (1) [pɑ̃], *n.m.* flap, coat tails, panel (*of dress*); side, section (*of a wall etc.*); *pan de ciel*, stretch *or* patch of sky; *pan de mur*, bare wall, piece of wall.
pan! (2) [pɑ̃], *int.* slap! bang! smack!
panacée [pana'se], *n.f.* panacea.
panache [pa'naʃ], *n.m.* plume, bunch of feathers etc.; (*fig.*) show, swagger.
panaché [pana'ʃe], *a.* plumed, tufted; striped; (*colloq.*) variegated, motley; *glace panachée*, mixed ice-cream.
panacher [pana'ʃe], *v.t.* to plume; to streak, to variegate, to mix.
panais [pa'nɛ], *n.m.* parsnip.
Panama [pana'ma], **le**, *m.* Panama.
panama [pana'ma], *n.m.* panama hat.
panamien [pana'mjɛ̃], *a.* (*fem.* **-enne**) Panama(nian).—*n.m.* (**Panamien**, *fem.* **-enne**) Panamanian (*person*).

panaris [pana'ri], *n.m.* whitlow.
pancarte [pɑ̃'kart], *n.f.* large placard *or* bill.
pancréas [pɑ̃kre'ɑːs], *n.m. inv.* pancreas; sweetbread.
panda [pɑ̃'da], *n.m.* panda.
pandémonium [pɑ̃demɔ'njɔm], *n.m.* pandemonium.
pandit [pɑ̃'di], *n.m.* pundit.
Pandore [pɑ̃'dɔːr], *f.* Pandora.
pané [pa'ne], *a.* covered *or* fried, in breadcrumbs.
panégyrique [paneʒi'rik], *n.m.* panegyric.
paner [pa'ne], *v.t.* to cover with breadcrumbs.
panier [pa'nje], *n.m.* basket, hamper, pannier; hoop-petticoat; *le dessus du panier*, the pick of the basket; *panier à salade*, (*wire*) salad washer; (*slang*) black Maria; *panier percé*, spendthrift.
panique [pa'nik], *a.* and *n.f.* panic.
panne [pan], *n.f.* plush; fat, lard; purlin; breakdown, mishap; *panne d'allumage*, (*Motor.*) ignition trouble; *rester en panne* (*Motor.*) to have a breakdown.
panneau [pa'no], *n.m.* (*pl.* **-eaux**) panel; snare, trap; (*Naut.*) hatch; (*Hort.*) glass frame.
panoplie [panɔ'pli], *n.f.* panoply; trophy (*of arms*).
panorama [panɔra'ma], *n.m.* panorama.
panoramique [panɔra'mik], *a.* panoramic.
pansage [pɑ̃'saːʒ], *n.m.* grooming (*of horses etc.*).
panse [pɑ̃ːs], *n.f.* belly, paunch.
pansement [pɑ̃s'mɑ̃], *n.m.* dressing (*of wounds*); *pansement sommaire*, first aid; dressing.
panser [pɑ̃'se], *v.t.* to dress (*wounds*); to groom (*a horse*).
pansu [pɑ̃'sy], *a.* and *n.m.* (*fem.* **-e**) pot-bellied (*person*); bulging.
pantalon [pɑ̃ta'lɔ̃], *n.m.* (pair of) trousers; *pantalon de femme*, women's drawers, panties.
pantelant [pɑ̃'tlɑ̃], *a.* panting, gasping.
panteler [pɑ̃'tle], *v.i.* (*conjug. like* APPELER) to gasp, to pant.
panthère [pɑ̃'tɛːr], *n.f.* panther.
pantin [pɑ̃'tɛ̃], *n.m.* nonentity, puppet; (*fig.*) jumping-jack.
pantois [pɑ̃'twa], *a.* (*fig.*) astonished, flabbergasted.
pantomime [pɑ̃tɔ'mim], *a.* pantomimic.— *n f* dumb show, pantomime.—*n.m.* pantomime (*actor*).
pantoufle [pɑ̃'tufl], *n.f.* slipper; *en pantoufles*, slipshod.
paon [pɑ̃], *n.m.* peacock; emperor moth; (*fig.*) vain person.
paonne [pan], *n.f.* peahen.
papa [pa'pa], *n.m.* papa, daddy.
papal [pa'pal], *a.* (*m. pl.* **-aux**) papal.
papauté [papo'te], *n.f.* papacy.
pape [pap], *n.m.* pope.
paperasse [pa'pras], *n.f.* useless papers, documents; red tape; paper work.
paperasser [papra'se], *v.i.* to rummage among old papers; to scribble.
paperasserie [papras'ri], *n.f.* red tape.
paperassier [papra'sje], *a.* (*fem.* **-ière**) red-tape; formal.—*n.m.* (*fem.* **-ière**) everlasting scribbler; rummager through old papers.

papeterie [pap'tri], *n.f.* paper mill, paper trade; stationery; stationer's shop; stationery case.

papetier [papǝ'tje], *a.* (*fem.* **-ière**) paper (*industry etc.*).—*n.m.* (*fem.* **-ière**) paper maker; stationer.

papier [pa'pje], *n.m.* paper; *papier buvard*, blotting paper; *papier d'emballage*, brown paper; *papier de verre*, glass-paper, sand-paper; *papier hygiénique*, toilet paper.

papillon [papi'jɔ̃], *n.m.* butterfly.

papillonner [papijɔ'ne], *v.i.* to flutter about, to hover; (*fig.*) to trifle, to flirt.

papillotage [papijɔ'ta:ʒ], *n.m.* blinking (*of the eyes*); dazzle, glitter, tinsel (*of style*).

papillote [papi'jɔt], *n.f.* curl paper; bonbon; *fer à papillotes*, curling irons; *papillotes à pétard*, Christmas crackers.

papilloter [papijɔ'te], *v.t.* to put (*hair etc.*) in paper.—*v.i.* to blink; to dazzle, to be gaudy.

papisme [pa'pism], *n.m.* papism, popery.

papiste [pa'pist], *a.* popish.—*n.* papist.

papou [pa'pu], *a.* Papuan.—*n.m.* (**Papou**, *fem.* **-oue**) Papuan (*person*).

Papouasie [papwa'zi], **la**, *f.* Papua.

papyrus [papi'ry:s], *n.m.* papyrus.

pâque [pɑ:k], *n.f.* Passover (*among Jews*).

paquebot [pak'bo], *n.m.* packet boat, steamer, liner.

pâquerette [pɑ'krɛt], *n.f.* daisy.

Pâques [pɑ:k], *n.m.* Easter.

paquet [pa'kɛ], *n.m.* package, bundle, parcel; packet; (*fig.*) clumsy lout.

paqueter [pak'te], *v.t.* (*conjug. like* APPELER) to make into a packet, parcel etc.

par [pa:r], *prep.* by, through, out of, from; about, in, into; for, for the sake of.

parabole [para'bɔl], *n.f.* parabola; parable.

parabolique [parabɔ'lik], *a.* parabolic.

parachutage [paraʃy'ta:ʒ], *n.m.* parachuting; parachute landing.

parachute [para'ʃyt], *n.m.* parachute; *sauter en parachute*, to bale out.

parachuter [paraʃy'te], *v.t., v.i.* to parachute, to drop (by parachute).

parachutiste [paraʃy'tist], *n.* parachutist, paratrooper.

parade [pa'rad], *n.f.* parade, show, display; pageantry; (*Fenc.*) parry.

parader [para'de], *v.i.* to show off.

paradis [para'di], *n.m.* paradise; (*Theat.*) upper gallery, the gods.

paradoxal [paradɔk'sal], *a.* (*m. pl.* **-aux**) paradoxical.

paradoxe [para'dɔks], *n.m.* paradox.

parafe or **paraphe** [pa'raf], *n.m.* paraph; flourish (*after one's signature*); initials and flourish.

parafer or **parapher** [para'fe], *v.t.* to paraph, to put one's flourish, dash or initials to.

paraffine [para'fin], *n.f.* paraffin, paraffin wax; *huile de paraffine*, liquid paraffin.

parage [pa'ra:ʒ], *n.m.* extraction, descent, lineage; (*usually in pl.*) localities, latitudes, waters; *dans ces parages*, in these parts.

paragraphe [para'graf], *n.m.* paragraph.

Paraguay [para'gwɛ], **le**, *m.* Paraguay.

paraguayen [paragwɛ'jɛ̃], *a.* (*fem.* **-enne**) Paraguayan.—*n.m.* (**Paraguayen**, *fem.* **-enne**) Paraguayan (*person*).

paraître [pa'rɛ:tr], *v.i. irr.* (*conjug. like* CONNAÎTRE) to appear, to come into sight; to make a show, to seem, to look like; to come out, to be published; *à ce qu'il paraît*, as it would seem.

parallèle [para'lɛl], *a.* parallel.—*n.f.* parallel line.—*n.m.* parallel, comparison; (*Geog.*) parallel of latitude.

parallèlement [paralɛl'mɑ̃], *adv.* in a parallel way or direction.

parallélogramme [paralelɔ'gram], *n.m.* parallelogram.

paralysateur [paraliza'tœ:r] (*fem.* **-trice**), **paralysant** [parali'zɑ̃], *a.* paralysing.

paralyser [parali'ze], *v.t.* to paralyse.

paralysie [parali'zi], *n.f.* paralysis, palsy.

paralytique [parali'tik], *a.* and *n.* paralytic.

parangon [parɑ̃'gɔ̃], *n.m.* model, paragon; comparison; flawless precious stone.

paranoïa [paranɔ'ja], *n.f.* (*Med.*) paranoia.

parapet [para'pɛ], *n.m.* parapet.

paraphrase [para'frɑ:z], *n.f.* paraphrase, amplification.

paraphraser [parafrɑ'ze], *v.t.* to paraphrase; to amplify.

parapluie [para'plɥi], *n.m.* umbrella.

parasite [para'zit], *a.* parasitic; superfluous; extraneous.—*n.m.* parasite; (*fig.*) hanger-on; (*pl.*) (*Rad.*) atmospherics.

parasol [para'sɔl], *n.m.* sunshade.

paratonnerre [paratɔ'nɛ:r], *n.m.* lightning-conductor.

paratyphoïde [paratifɔ'id], *a.* and *n.f.* (*Med.*) paratyphoid (fever).

paravent [para'vɑ̃], *n.m.* folding screen; (*fig.*) screen.

parbleu! [par'blø], *int.* by Jove! why, of course!

parc [park], *n.m.* park; pen; *parc à huîtres*, oyster-bed; *parc d'attractions*, carnival.

parcage [par'ka:ʒ], *n.m.* folding (*of sheep*); penning (*of cattle*); parking (*of cars*).

parcellaire [parsɛ'lɛ:r], *a.* by small portions, by lots, in detail.

parcelle [par'sɛl], *n.f.* portion; particle; piece (*of land*).

parceller [parsɛ'le], *v.t.* to portion or parcel out.

parce que [parsǝ'kǝ, pars'kǝ], *conj.* because, as.—*n.m. inv. les pourquoi et les parce que*, the whys and the wherefores.

parchemin [parʃǝ'mɛ̃], *n.m.* parchment; (*fam.*) diploma; (*pl.*) titles of nobility.

parcimonie [parsimɔ'ni], *n.f.* parsimony.

parcimonieusement [parsimɔnjøz'mɑ̃], *adv.* parsimoniously.

parcimonieux [parsimɔ'njø], *a.* (*fem.* **-euse**) parsimonious, stingy.

(C) parcomètre [parkɔ'mɛtr], *n.m.* parking meter.

parcourir [parku'ri:r], *v.t. irr.* (*conjug. like* COURIR) to travel through; to run over or through; to scour; to look over; to peruse, to glance through (*a book*).

parcours [par'ku:r], *n.m.* line, course, road, way; route (*of bus*); distance; course (*golf*).

par-dessous [pardǝ'su], *prep.* and *adv.* under, beneath, underneath.

par-dessus [pardǝ'sy], *prep.* and *adv.* over, above.

pardessus [pardəˈsy], *n.m.* overcoat.

pardon [parˈdɔ̃], *n.m.* pardon, forgiveness; pilgrimage (*in Brittany*); **pardon !** excuse me!

pardonnable [pardoˈnabl] *a.* pardonable, excusable.

pardonner [pardoˈne], *v.t.* to pardon, to forgive; to overlook; to excuse.

paré [paˈre], *a.* adorned, got up; dressed.

pare-boue [parˈbu], *n.m. inv.* fender.

pare-brise [parˈbriːz], *n.m. inv.* windshield (*of motor-car*).

pare-chocs [parˈʃɔk], *n.m. inv.* bumper (*of car*).

pare-étincelles [paretɛˈsɛl], *n.m. inv.* fire-screen, fire-guard.

pareil [paˈrɛːj], *a.* (*fem.* **-eille**) like, equal, similar; such, like that; same, identical.— *n.m.* (*fem.* **-eille**) similar *or* equal person. —*n.m.* equal, fellow.—*n.f.* (**-eille**) the like, tit for tat.

pareillement [parɛjˈmɑ̃], *adv.* in like manner; likewise, also.

parement [parˈmɑ̃], *n.m.* ornament; facing (*of dress*); cuff (*of sleeves*); (*Build.*) curbstone.

parent [paˈrɑ̃], *n.m.* (*fem.* **-e**) relative, kinsman, kinswoman; (*pl.*) parents, relations, relatives; **être parent**, to be related; **parents par alliance**, related by marriage.

parenté [parɑ̃ˈte], *n.f.* relationship, kinship; relatives, kith and kin.

parenthèse [parɑ̃ˈtɛːz], *n.f.* parenthesis, digression; (*Print.*) bracket.

parer [paˈre], *v.t.* to adorn, to set off, to embellish; to attire, to trim; (*Box.*) to parry; to shelter, to guard.—*v.i.* to fend, to guard (*against*). **se parer**, *v.r.* to adorn oneself; to deck oneself out; to screen *or* guard oneself, to ward off.

pare-soleil [parsoˈlɛːj], *n.m. inv.* (*Motor.*) sun visor.

paresse [paˈrɛs], *n.f.* idleness, sloth, laziness, indolence.

paresser [parɛˈse], *v.i.* to idle, to fritter away one's time.

paresseusement [parɛsøzˈmɑ̃], *adv.* lazily, idly.

paresseux [parɛˈsø], *a.* (*fem.* **-euse**) lazy, idle, slothful.—*n.m.* (*fem.* **-euse**) sluggard, lazy person.—*n.m.* (*Zool.*) sloth.

parfaire [parˈfɛːr], *v.t. irr.* (*conjug. like* FAIRE) to complete, to perfect.

parfait [parˈfɛ], *a.* perfect, faultless; complete, full.—*n.m.* perfection; (*Gram.*) perfect; **un parfait au café**, a coffee ice-cream.

parfaitement [parfɛtˈmɑ̃], *adv.* perfectly, completely; exactly, just so, decidedly.

parfilage [parfiˈlaːʒ], *n.m.* unravelling.

parfois [parˈfwa], *adv.* sometimes, occasionally.

parfum [parˈfœ̃], *n.m.* perfume, odor, scent.

parfumer [parfyˈme], *v.t.* to perfume, to sweeten; to scent; to fumigate. **se parfumer** *v.r.* to use perfume, to scent oneself.

parfumerie [parfymˈri], *n.f.* perfumery.

pari [paˈri], *n.m.* bet, wager, stake; **pari mutuel**, totalizator; (*fam.*) tote.

paria [paˈrja], *n.m.* pariah, outcast.

parier [paˈrje], *v.t.* to bet, to stake.

parieur [paˈrjœːr], *n.m.* (*fem.* **-euse**) bettor; backer.

parisien [pariˈzjɛ̃], *a.* (*fem.* **-enne**) Parisian.— *n.m.* (**Parisien**, *fem.* **-enne**) Parisian (*person*).

parité [pariˈte], *n.f.* parity, likeness, equality; (*Fin.*) par.

parjure [parˈʒyːr], *a.* perjured.—*n.m.* perjury, false oath.—*n.* perjurer.

parjurer (se) [səparʒyˈre], *v.r.* to perjure oneself.

parking [parˈkiŋ], *n.m.* parking place, parking lot.

parlant [parˈlɑ̃], *a.* speaking; (*colloq.*) talkative.

parlement [parləˈmɑ̃], *n.m.* parliament.

parlementaire [parləmɑ̃ˈtɛːr], *a.* parliamentary.—*n.m.* bearer of a flag of truce; parliamentarian.

parlementer [parləmɑ̃ˈte], *v.i.* to parley, to come to terms.

parler [parˈle], *v.t.* to speak, to talk.—*v.i.* to speak, to talk; to discourse, to converse, to treat (*de*); (*pop.*) **tu parles !** you're telling me! **se parler**, *v.r.* to be spoken; to talk to oneself; to talk to each other.—*n.m.* speech.

parleur [parˈlœːr], *n.m.* (*fem.* **-euse**) glib talker.

parloir [parˈlwaːr], *n.m.* parlor (*of convent, school, prison*).

parmentier [parmɑ̃ˈtje], *a.* and *n.m.* **potage parmentier**, thick potato soup.

parmesan [parməˈzɑ̃], *n.m.* Parmesan (*cheese*).

parmi [parˈmi], *prep.* among, amongst, amid, amidst.

parodie [paroˈdi], *n.f.* parody.

parodier [paroˈdje], *v.t.* to parody, to burlesque.

paroi [paˈrwa], *n.f.* wall; partition; inner surface; lining; (*Theat.*) flat.

paroisse [paˈrwas], *n.f.* parish; (*collect.*) parishioners.

paroissial [parwaˈsjal], *a.* (*m. pl.* **-aux**) parochial, parish.

paroissien [parwaˈsjɛ̃], *n.m.* (*fem.* **-enne**) parishioner.—*n.m.* prayer book.

parole [paˈrɔl], *n.f.* (spoken) word; speech, utterance, voice; eloquence; promise; parole; **engager sa parole**, to pledge one's word; **manquer à sa parole**, to break one's word; **tenir parole**, to keep one's word.

paroxysme [parɔkˈsism], *n.m.* paroxysm; culminating point.

parpaing [parˈpɛ̃], *n.m.* (*Build.*) through stone, bondstone.

parquer [parˈke], *v.t.* to fold, to pen; to enclose; (*Motor.*) to park.—*v.i.* to be penned up (*of cattle etc.*). **se parquer**, *v.r.* to be placed in an enclosure.

parquet [parˈke], *n.m.* well (*of a court of justice*); prosecuting magistrates; (inlaid) floor.

parquetage [parkəˈtaːʒ], *n.m.* making a floor; flooring.

parqueter [parkəˈte], *v.t.* (*conjug. like* APPELER) to floor, to lay a floor.

parqueterie [parkəˈtri], *n.f.* floor-making; inlaid flooring.

parrain [pa'rɛ̃], *n.m.* godfather, sponsor; proposer.
parricide [pari'sid], *a.* parricidal.—*n.* parricide (*person*).—*n.m.* parricide (*crime*).
parsemer [parsə'me], *v.t.* (*conjug. like* AMENER) to strew, to sprinkle; to be strewn on, to stud, to spangle.
parsi [par'si], *a.* Parsee.—*n.m.* (**Parsi**, *fem.* -ie) Parsee (*person*).
part [pa:r], *n.f.* share, part; concern, interest; place (*where*); *à part*, aside; apart from; *de part en part*, through and through; *de toutes parts*, on all sides; *dites-lui de ma part*, tell him from me; *nulle part*, nowhere; *quelque part*, somewhere (or other).
partage [par'ta:ʒ], *n.m.* sharing, share; partition.
partageable [parta'ʒabl], *a.* divisible into shares.
partageant [parta'ʒɑ̃], *n.m.* (*fem.* -e) (*Law*) sharer.
partager [parta'ʒe], *v.t.* (*conjug. like* MANGER) to divide, to share out; to participate in; to endow.—*v.i.* to share, to receive a share. **se partager**, *v.r.* to divide, to be divided.
partance [par'tɑ̃:s], *n.f.* (*Naut.*) sailing, departure; *en partance pour*, bound for.
partant [par'tɑ̃], *adv.* consequently, hence, therefore.—*n.m.* (*Turf*) starter.
partenaire [partə'nɛ:r], *n.* (*Spt. etc.*) partner.
parterre [par'tɛ:r], *n.m.* flower bed; (*Theat.*) pit.
parti [par'ti], *n.m.* (*Polit.*) party; part, cause; resolution, course; profit, advantage; match (*marriage*); (*Mil.*) detachment; *parti pris*, set purpose; rank prejudice; *le parti conservateur*, the Conservative party; *le parti travailliste*, the Labour party.
partial [par'sjal], *a.* (*m. pl.* -aux) partial, biased.
partialement [parsjal'mɑ̃], *adv.* partially, with partiality.
partialité [parsjali'te], *n.f.* partiality, bias.
participant [partisi'pɑ̃], *a.* participating.—*n.m.* (*fem.* -e) participant, sharer.
participation [partisipa'sjɔ̃], *n.f.* participation, share.
participe [parti'sip], *n.m.* (*Gram.*) participle.
participer [partisi'pe], *v.i.* to participate in, to share in; to be a party to (à); to partake of (de).
particularité [partikylari'te], *n.f.* peculiarity, particular circumstance.
particule [parti'kyl], *n.f.* particle.
particulier [partiky'lje], *a.* (*fem.* -ière) particular, peculiar; private; special; singular; personal.—*n.m.* (*fem.* -ière) private person, individual; (*colloq.*) fellow.
particulièrement [partikyljɛr'mɑ̃], *adv.* particularly, especially.
partie [par'ti] *n.f.* part (*of a whole*); line of business; party, amusement; game, match; client; opponent; (*Law*) party; (*Comm.*) parcel; *partie nulle*, drawn game.
partiel [par'sjɛl], *a.* (*fem.* -elle) partial.
partiellement [parsjɛl'mɑ̃], *adv.* partially, in part.
partir [par'ti:r], *v.i. irr.* (*with aux.* ÊTRE) to set out, to start, to depart, to leave; to rise (*of birds*); to proceed, to emanate (*from*); to go

off (*of firearms*); *à partir d'aujourd'hui*, from this day forward.
partisan [parti'zɑ̃], *n.m.* (*fem.* -e) partisan.
partition [parti'sjɔ̃], *n.f.* (*Her.*) partition; (*Mus.*) score.
partout [par'tu], *adv.* everywhere, on all sides.
parure [pa'ry:r]. *n.f.* attire, dress, finery, ornament.
parvenir [parvə'ni:r], *v.i. irr.* (*conjug. like* TENIR *but with aux.* ÊTRE) to attain, to reach; to succeed; to get; to arrive; to rise in the world.
parvenu [parvə'ny], *n.m.* (*fem.* -e) upstart, self-made person.
parvis [par'vi], *n.m.* parvis, open space (*in front of a church*); (*Poet.*) hall, temple.
pas (1) [pɑ], *n.m. inv.* step, pace; footprint; gait; dance; precedence; threshold; step of stair; strait, pass; thread (*of screw*); *aller à pas mesurés*, to proceed with circumspection; *au pas*, at a walking pace; in step; *faire un faux pas*, to stumble, (*fig.*) to blunder; *le pas de Calais*, the Straits of Dover; *pas à pas*, slowly, little by little.
pas (2) [pɑ], *adv.* no; not; *pas du tout*, not at all.
pascal [pas'kal], *a.* (*m. pl.* -aux) paschal.
passable [pɑ'sabl], *a.* passable, tolerable; (*fig.*) middling, so-so.
passablement [pɑsablə'mɑ̃], *adv.* fairly, passably.
passade [pɑ'sad], *n.f.* short stay; (*fig.*) passing fancy.
passage [pɑ'sa:ʒ], *n.m.* passage, transit; thoroughfare; arcade; crossing (*on railway etc.*); *passage clouté*, pedestrian crossing.
passager [pɑsa'ʒe], *a.* (*fem.* -ère) passing, transitory, short-lived; migratory.—*n.m.* (*fem.* -ère) passenger (*by sea or air*); passer-by.
passagèrement [pɑsaʒɛr'mɑ̃], *adv.* transiently.
passant [pɑ'sɑ̃], *a.* much-frequented.—*n.m.* (*fem.* -e) passer-by, wayfarer.
passavant [pɑsa'vɑ̃], *n.m.* pass, permit; (*Naut.*) gangway.
passe [pɑs], *n.f.* passing, passage; permit, pass; situation, state; (*Fenc.*) thrust; channel, narrow passage (*of harbors, rivers etc.*); stake (*at play*); (*Ftb.*) pass; *être dans une mauvaise passe*, to be in a fix; *en passe de*, in a fair way to.
passé [pɑ'se], *a.* past, bygone; faded, worn, withered.—*n.m.* past, past life, time past.—*prep.* after, beyond.
passée [pɑ'se], *n.f.* (*Hunt.*) flight, passage (*of woodcock etc.*).
passefiler [pasfi'le], *v.t.* to darn.
passement [pas'mɑ̃], *n.m.* lace (*of gold, silk etc.*).
passe-partout [paspar'tu], *n.m. inv.* master key; latch-key; passe-partout (*frame*); cross-cut saw.
passeport [pas'po:r], *n.m.* passport.
passer [pɑ'se], *v.t.* (*takes the auxiliary* AVOIR *or* ÊTRE *according as action or condition is implied*) to pass; to cross; to go over; to transport; to strain (*liquids*); to sift (*flour*); to put on (*wearing apparel*); to omit; to waive; to allow; to spend (*time*); to take (*an examination*).—*v.i.* to pass to pass on;

to pass away; to die; to pass for; to fade. **se passer**, *v.r.* to pass, to pass away; to fade; to happen; to do without (*de*).

passereau [pas'ro], *n.m.* (*pl.* **-eaux**) sparrow.

passerelle [pas'rɛl], *n.f.* foot bridge; (*Naut.*) bridge, gangway.

passe-temps [pas'tɑ̃], *n.m. inv.* pastime, hobby.

passeur [pa'sœːr], *n.m.* (*fem.* **-euse**) ferryman, ferrywoman.

passibilité [pasibili'te], *n.f.* liability.

passible [pa'sibl], *a.* passible; liable (*to*).

passif [pa'sif], *a.* (*fem.* **-ive**) passive; (*Comm.*) on debit side.—*n.m.* (*Gram.*) passive; (*Comm.*) liabilities.

passion [pa'sjɔ̃], *n.f.* suffering, agony; passion, *esp.* love; (*fig.*) fondness.

passionnant [pasjo'nɑ̃], *a.* exciting, thrilling.

passionné [pasjo'ne], *a.* passionate, impassioned, very fond of (*de*).

passionnel [pasjo'nɛl], *a.* (*fem.* **-elle**) *crime passionnel*, crime due to jealous love.

passionnément [pasjone'mɑ̃], *adv.* passionately, fondly.

passionner [pasjo'ne], *v.t.* to impassion, to interest deeply. **se passionner**, *v.r.* to be passionately fond of; to become enamored of.

passivement [pasiv'mɑ̃], *adv.* passively.

passiveté [pasiv'te], **passivité** [pasivi'te], *n.f.* passivity.

passoire [pa'swaːr], *n.f.* strainer.

pastel [pas'tɛl], *n.m.* pastel, crayon.

pastèque [pas'tɛk], *n.f.* water-melon.

pasteur [pas'tœːr], *n.m.* pastor, (*Protestant*) minister; clergyman.

pasteurisation [pastœriza'sjɔ̃], *n.f.* pasteurization.

pasteuriser [pastœri'ze], *v.t.* to pasteurize.

pastiche [pas'tiʃ], *n.m.* pastiche; (*Mus.*) medley.

pastille [pas'tiːj], *n.f.* pastille; lozenge; rubber patch (*for tubes of tire*).

pastoral [pasto'ral] *a.* (*m. pl.* **-aux**) pastoral.—*n.f.* (**-e**) pastoral (*play or poem*).

patapouf [pata'puf], *int. faire patapouf*, to fall flat.—*n.m. gros patapouf*, fat fellow, fatty.

patate [pa'tat], *n.f.* sweet potato.

patati [pata'ti], *only used in the phrase, et patati et patata*, and so on and so forth.

patatras! [pata'tra], *int.* crack! slap! bang!

pataud [pa'to], *a.* awkward, clumsy.—*n.m.* (*fem.* **-e**) pup with large paws; (*fig.*) lout, clumsy person.

patauger [pato'ʒe], *v.i.* (*conjug. like* MANGER) to splash, to flounder.

pâte [paːt], *n.f.* paste; dough, batter; (*fig.*) kind sort; (*Print.*) pie.

pâté [pa'te], *n.m.* pie, pasty, patty; blot (*of ink*); block (*of buildings*); (*Print.*) pie.

pâtée [pa'te], *n.f.* mash (*to fatten poultry*); mess (*for dogs or cats*).

patelin [pa'tlɛ̃], *a.* smooth-tongued, wheedling.—*n.m.* (*fem.* **-e**) wheedler.—*n.m.* (*fam.*) village.

patent [pa'tɑ̃], *a.* patent; obvious, manifest.

patenté [patɑ̃'te], *a.* licensed.—*n.m.* (*fem.* **-ée**) licensed dealer.

patenter [patɑ̃'te], *v.t.* to license.

patère [pa'tɛːr], *n.f.* coat hook; curtain hook.

paternel [patɛr'nɛl], *a.* (*fem.* **-elle**) paternal, fatherly.

paternité [patɛrni'te], *n.f.* paternity, fatherhood.

pâteux [pa'tø], *a.* (*fem.* **-euse**) pasty, clammy, sticky.

pathétique [pate'tik], *a.* pathetic, moving.—*n.m.* pathos.

pathétiquement [patetik'mɑ̃], *adv.* pathetically.

pathologie [patɔlɔ'ʒi], *n.f.* pathology.

pathologiste [patɔlɔ'ʒist], *n.m.* pathologist.

pathos [pa'toːs], *n.m.* bathos; (*fig.*) bombast.

patiemment [pasja'mɑ̃], *adv.* patiently.

patience [pa'sjɑ̃ːs], *n.f.* patience, endurance.

patient [pa'sjɑ̃], *a.* patient, enduring, forbearing.—*n.m.* (*fem.* **-e**) sufferer; (*Med.*) patient.

patienter [pasjɑ̃'te], *v.i.* to be patient.

patin [pa'tɛ̃], *n.m.* skate; flange (*of rail*); skid (*of airplane*); shoe (*of brake*); *patins à roulettes*, roller skates.

patinage [pati'naːʒ], *n.m.* skating; skidding (*of locomotive, car etc.*).

patine [pa'tin], *n.f.* patina (*of bronze*).

patiner [pati'ne], *v.i.* to skate; to skid (*of wheels*).

patinette [pati'nɛt], *n.f.* scooter.

patineur [pati'nœːr], *n.m.* (*fem.* **-euse**) skater.

patinoire [pati'nwaːr], *n.f.* skating rink.

pâtir [pa'tiːr], *v.i.* to suffer; to be in distress.

pâtisser [pati'se], *v.t.*, to knead (*flour*).—*v.i.* to knead, to make pastry.

pâtisserie [patis'ri], *n.f.* pastry, fancy cake; pastry-cook's shop *or* business.

pâtissier [pati'sje], *n.m.* (*fem.* **-ière**) pastrycook.—*a.f.* (**-ière**) *crème pâtissière*, custard.

patois [pa'twa], *n.m. inv.* patois, provincial dialect; brogue; jargon.

patouiller [patu'je], [PATAUGER.]

patraque [pa'trak], *a.* seedy, broken-down.—*n.f.* broken-down person *or* machine.

pâtre [paːtr], *n.m.* herdsman, shepherd.

patriarcal [patriar'kal], *a.* (*m. pl.* **-aux**) patriarchal.

patriarche [patri'arʃ], *n.m.* patriarch.

Patrice [pa'tris], *m.* Patrick.

patrice [pa'tris], *n.m.* patrician.

patricien [patri'sjɛ̃], *a.* and *n.m.* (*fem.* **-enne**) patrician.

patrie [pa'tri], *n.f.* native land, fatherland.

patrimoine [patri'mwan], *n.m.* patrimony, inheritance.

patriote [patri'ɔt], *a.* patriotic (*person*).—*n.* patriot.

patriotique [patriɔ'tik], *a.* patriotic (*song, speech etc.*).

patriotisme [patriɔ'tism], *n.m.* patriotism.

patron (1) [pa'trɔ̃], *n.m.* pattern, model.

patron (2) [pa'trɔ̃], *n.m.* (*fem.* **-onne**) patron; master, mistress, employer; proprietor; (*colloq.*) boss; (*Naut.*) skipper, coxswain.

patronage [patro'naːʒ], *n.m.* patronage.

patronat [patro'na], *n.m.* management.

patronner [patro'ne], *v.t.* to patronize; to support.

patrouille [pa'truːj], *n.f.* patrol.

patrouiller [patru'je], *v.i.* to patrol.

patrouilleur [patru'jœːr], *n.m.* (*Naut.*) patrol boat.

patte [pat], *n.f.* paw (*of quadruped*); foot (*of bird*); leg (*of insect*); bracket, cramp; flap (*of pocket etc.*); tab, strap (*of clothes*); (*fig.*) claws, clutches.

pâturage [pɑty'ra:ʒ], *n.m.* pasture.

pâture [pɑ'ty:r], *n.f.* food (*for animals*); pasture; fodder.

pâturer [pɑty're], *v.t.* to graze on.—*v.i.* to pasture, to graze, to feed.

pâturon or paturon [pɑty'rɔ̃], *n.m.* pastern.

paume [po:m], *n.f.* palm (*of the hand*); *jeu de paume*, (*court*) tennis, 'real' tennis.

paupérisme [pope'rism], *n.m.* pauperism.

paupière [po'pjɛ:r], *n.f.* eyelid; (*fig.*) eye(s).

pause [po:z], *n.f.* pause, stop; (*Mus.*) rest.

pauser [po'ze], *v.i.* to pause.

pauvre [po:vr], *a.* poor, needy; wretched, paltry, mean.—*n.m.* poor person pauper; beggar.

pauvrement [povrə'mã], *adv.* poorly, wretchedly.

pauvresse [po'vrɛs], *n.f.* poor woman, beggar-woman.

pauvret [po'vrɛ], *n.m.* (*fem.* -ette) poor creature, poor little thing.

pauvreté [povrə'te], *n.f.* poverty; wretchedness; sorry thing.

pavage [pa'va:ʒ], *n.m.* paving; pavement.

pavane [pa'van], *n.f.* pavan (*dance*).

pavaner (se) [səpava'ne], *v.r.* to strut, to stalk proudly.

pavé [pa've], *a.* paved.—*n.m.* paving stone; paved part of road; (*fig.*) road, street(s).

pavement [pav'mã], *n.m.* paving; flooring.

paver [pa've], *v.t.* to pave.

paveur [pa'vœ:r], *n.m.* pavior.

pavillon [pavi'jɔ̃], *n.m.* pavilion, tent; summerhouse; detached house; wing (*of a house*), outhouse, lodge; (*Naut.*) flag.

pavoiser [pavwa'ze], *v.t.* to deck with flags, to dress (*ship*).

pavot [pa'vo], *n.m.* poppy.

payable [pɛ'jabl], *a.* payable.

payant [pɛ'jã], *a.* paying; to be paid for.— *n.m.* (*fem.* -e) payer.

paye [pɛ:], **paie** [pɛ], *n.f.* pay, wages.

payement or **paiement** [pɛ'mã], *n.m.* payment.

payer [pɛ'je], *v.t.* (*see Verb Tables*) to pay (for); to reward; to expiate, to atone for. se payer, *v.r.* to be paid *or* satisfied; to treat oneself to.

payeur [pɛ'jœ:r], *n.m.* (*fem.* -euse) payer; pay-clerk; (*Mil.*) pay-master.

pays [pe'i], *n.m. inv.* country, land; region, district; fatherland, home; *avoir le mal du pays*, to be home-sick; *pays perdu*, out-of-the-way place.

paysage [pei'za:ʒ], *n.m.* landscape, scenery.

paysagiste [peiza'ʒist], *a.* and *n.m.* landscape (painter).

paysan [pei'zã], *a.* (*fem.* -anne) rustic.—*n.m.* (*fem.* -anne) peasant, country man, country woman; farmer.

paysannerie [peizan'ri], *n.f.* rusticity; peasantry.

Pays-Bas [pei'bɑ], les, *m.pl.* the Netherlands.

péage [pe'a:ʒ], *n.m.* toll; toll house.

péan or **pæan** [pe'ã], *n.m.* pæan, song of triumph or joy.

peau [po] *n.f.* (*pl.* peaux) skin; hide; peel, rind.

Peau-Rouge [po'ru:ʒ], *n.* (*pl.* Peaux-Rouges) Redskin, Red Indian.

peccadille [pɛka'di:j], *n.f.* peccadillo.

pêche (1) [pɛ:ʃ], *n.f.* peach.

pêche (2) [pɛ:ʃ], *n.f.* fishing, angling.

péché [pe'ʃe], *n.m.* sin, transgression.

pécher [pe'ʃe], *v.i.* (*conjug. like* CÉDER) to sin, to transgress; to offend; to be deficient.

pêcher (1) [pe'ʃe], *n.m.* peach tree.

pêcher (2) [pe'ʃe], *v.t.* to fish for; to drag out; (*fig.*) to get hold of.—*v.i.* to fish, to angle.

pécheresse [peʃ'rɛs], [PÉCHEUR].

pêcherie [pɛʃ'ri], *n.f.* fishing ground, fishery.

pécheur [pe'ʃœ:r], *n.m.* (*fem.* -eresse) sinner.

pêcheur [pe'ʃœ:r], *n.m.* (*fem.* -euse) fisher, fisherman, fisherwoman.

pécore [pe'ko:r], *n.f.* stupid creature, blockhead; *esp.* silly girl.

pécule [pe'kyl], *n.m.* savings; earnings (*of a prisoner*).

pécuniaire [peky'njɛ:r], *a.* pecuniary.

pédagogie [pedagɔ'ʒi], *n.f.* pedagogy.

pédagogue [peda'gɔg], *n.* pedagogue.

pédale [pe'dal], *n.f.* pedal; treadle.

pédaler [peda'le], *v.i.* to pedal; (*colloq.*) to cycle.

pédant [pe'dã], *a.* pedantic.—*n.m.* (*fem.* -e) pedant.

pédanterie [pedã'tri], *n.f.* pedantry.

pédantesque [pedã'tɛsk], *a.* pedantic.

pédantisme [pedã'tism], *n.m.* pedantry.

pédestre [pe'dɛstr], *a.* pedestrian, on foot.

pédestrement [pedɛstrə'mã], *adv.* on foot.

pédicure [pedi'ky:r], *n.* chiropodist.

Pégase [pe'ga:z], *m.* Pegasus.

peignage [pɛ'na:ʒ], *n.m.* combing, wool-combing.

peigne [pɛɲ], *n.m.* comb.

peigné [pɛ'ɲe], *a.* combed; (*fig.*) arranged.— *n.m.* worsted.

peigner [pɛ'ɲe], *v.t.* to comb; to card; (*fig.*) to polish (*style*). se peigner, *v.r.* to comb one's hair.

peignoir [pɛ'ɲwa:r], *n.m.* dressing-gown; (*Am.*) bath-robe.

peindre [pɛ̃:dr], *v.t. irr.* (*conjug. like* CRAINDRE) to paint, to portray; to represent, to express; *se faire peindre*, to sit for one's portrait. se peindre, *v.r.* to paint oneself; to be represented.

peine [pɛn], *n.f.* punishment, penalty; pain, grief, sorrow; anxiety; trouble; difficulty; reluctance; *à peine*, hardly, scarcely; *un homme de peine*, an unskilled laborer.

peiné [pɛ'ne], *a.* a pained, grieved; labored; elaborate.

peiner [pɛ'ne], *v.t.* to pain, to trouble, to grieve; (*fig.*) to elaborate.—*v.i.* to labor, to toil; to be reluctant.

peintre [pɛ̃:tr], *n.m.* painter.

peinture [pɛ̃'ty:r], *n.f.* painting; picture; description, appearance; paint, color.

péjoratif [peʒɔra'tif], *a.* (*fem.* -tive) pejorative.

Pékin [pe'kɛ̃], *m.* Peking.

pékinois [peki'nwa], *a.* Pekinese.—*n.m.* Pekinese (*dog*); (**Pékinois**, *fem.* -oise) Pekinese (*person*).

pelage [pə'la:ʒ], *n.m.* hair, fur, coat (*of animal*).

pelé [pə'le], *a.* bald; which has lost its hair (*animals*).—*n.m.* (*fem.* -ée) bald-headed person.

pêle-mêle [pɛl'mɛll], *adv.* pell-mell, higgledy-piggledy.—*n.m. inv.* disorder, jumble.

peler

peler [pə'le], *v.t.* (*conjug. like* AMENER) to skin, to peel.—*v.i.* to peel off (*of the skin etc.*). **se peler**, *v.r.* to come off, to peel.

pèlerin [pɛl'rɛ̃], *n.m.* (*fem.* -ine (1)) pilgrim; peregrine falcon; basking shark.

pèlerinage [pɛlri'na:ʒ], *n.m.* pilgrimage.

pèlerine (2) [pɛl'rin], *n.f.* tippet, cape (*with hood*).

pélican [peli'kɑ̃], *n.m.* pelican.

pelisse [pə'lis], *n.f.* pelisse; fur-lined coat.

pelle [pɛl], *n.f.* shovel, scoop, blade (*of an oar*); (*fam.*) spill, cropper.

pelletée [pɛl'te], *n.f.* shovelful.

pelleter [pɛl'te], *v.t.* (*conjug. like* APPELER) to shovel.

pelletier [pɛl'tje], *n.m.* (*fem.* -ière) furrier.

pellicule [peli'kyl], *n.f.* pellicle; (*Phot.*) film; (*pl.*) scurf (*of scalp*), dandruff.

pelotage [pələ'ta:ʒ], *n.m.* winding skeins into balls; (*Billiards, Ten.*) warmup.

pelote [pə'lɔt], *n.f.* ball; ball of thread; pellet; pin-cushion; (*Spt.*) *pelote basque*, pelota.

peloter [pələ'te], *v.t.* to make *or* wind into a ball.—*v.i.* (*Spt.*) to warm up.

peloton [pələ'tɔ̃], *n.m.* ball; cluster (*of bees*); (*Mil.*) squad; (*Racing*) bunch (*of runners*).

pelotonner [pələtɔ'ne], *v.t.* to wind into balls. **se pelotonner**, *v.r.* to roll oneself up; to curl up.

pelouse [pə'lu:z], *n.f.* lawn, greensward.

peluche [pə'lyʃ], *n.f.* plush.

peluché [pəly'ʃe], *a.* shaggy.

pelucher [pəly'ʃe], *v.i.* to become shaggy, to wear rough.

pelucheux [pəly'ʃø], *a.* (*fem.* -euse) shaggy; fluffy.

pelure [pə'ly:r], *n.f.* paring; peel, skin; rind.

pénal [pe'nal], *a.* (*m. pl.* -aux) penal.

pénaliser [penali'ze], *v.t.* to penalize.

pénalité [penali'te], *n.f.* penal law; penalty.

pénates [pe'nat], *n.m. pl.* penates, household gods; (*fig.*) home.

penaud [pə'no], *a.* abashed, sheepish, crest-fallen.

penchant [pɑ̃'ʃɑ̃], *a.* inclined, sloping, leaning.—*n.m.* declivity, slope; inclination, bent.

pencher [pɑ̃'ʃe], *v.t.* to incline, to bend.—*v.i.* to lean; to tilt, to slope. **se pencher**, *v.r.* to bend, to stoop; to slope, to be inclined.

pendable [pɑ̃'dabl], *a.* deserving hanging, abominable.

pendaison [pɑ̃dɛ'zɔ̃], *n.f.* hanging (*on the gallows*), death by hanging.

pendant [pɑ̃'dɑ̃], *a.* pendent, hanging; pending; depending.—*n.m.* thing hanging, pendant; counterpart.—*prep.* during; for; *pendant que*, while.

pendard [pɑ̃'da:r], *n.m.* (*fem.* -e) (*colloq.*) rascal, rogue, jade.

pendeloque [pɑ̃'dlɔk], *n.f.* ear-drop; pendant.

pendiller [pɑ̃di'je], *v.i.* to hang loose, to dangle.

pendre [pɑ̃:dr], *v.t.* to hang, to hang up, to suspend.—*v.i.* to hang; to dangle, to droop. **se pendre**, *v.r.* to hang oneself.

pendu [pɑ̃'dy], *a.* hanging; hanged; hung.—*n.m.* (*fem.* -e) one that has been hanged.

pendule [pɑ̃'dyl], *n.f.* clock, time-piece.—*n.m.* pendulum.

pêne [pɛ:n], *n.m.* bolt (*of a lock*).

---

pénétrabilité [penetrabili'te], *n.f.* penetrability.

pénétrable [pene'trabl], *a.* penetrable.

pénétrant [pene'trɑ̃], *a.* penetrating; piercing, keen; acute; impressive.

pénétration [penetra'sjɔ̃], *n.f.* penetration; acuteness, shrewdness.

pénétré [pene'tre], *a.* penetrated; moved, impressed.

pénétrer [pene'tre], *v.t.* (*conjug. like* CÉDER) to penetrate, to go through; to pierce; to pervade; to fathom; to impress, to affect.—*v.i.* to penetrate (*dans*); to reach (*à*). **se pénétrer**, *v.r.* to penetrate each other; to be impressed.

pénible [pe'nibl], *a.* painful, laborious; troublesome.

péniblement [peniblə'mɑ̃]. *adv.* laboriously.

pénicilline [penisi'lin], *n.f.* penicillin.

péninsulaire [penɛ̃sy'lɛ:r], *a.* peninsular.

péninsule [penɛ̃'syl], *n.f.* peninsula.

pénitence [peni'tɑ̃:s], *n.f.* penitence, repentance; penance; punishment.

pénitencier [penitɑ̃'sje], *a.* penitentiary.—*n.m.* penitentiary, reformatory.

pénitent [peni'tɑ̃], *a.* penitent, repentant.—*n.m.* (*fem.* -e) penitent.

pénitentiaire [penitɑ̃'sje:r], *a.* penitentiary.

penne [pɛn], *n.f.* tail feather, wing feather.

penniforme [peni'fɔrm], *a.* penniform.

pennon [pe'nɔ̃], *n.m.* pennon.

pénombre [pe'nɔ̃:br], *n.f.* penumbra; semidarkness, half-light.

pensée [pɑ̃'se], *n.f.* thought; opinion; idea, conception; meaning; (*Bot.*) pansy.

penser [pɑ̃'se], *v.t.* to think, to think of (*à or de*).—*v.i.* to think, to reflect, to consider; to expect; to take heed, to take care.—*n.m.* (*poet.*) inward reasoning, thought.

penseur [pɑ̃'sœ:r], *a.* (*fem.* -euse) thinking, thoughtful.—*n.m.* (*fem.* -euse) thinker.

pensif [pɑ̃'sif], *a.* (*fem.* -sive) pensive, thoughtful.

pension [pɑ̃'sjɔ̃], *n.f.* board and lodging; boarding house; boarding school; pension, allowance, annuity.

pensionnaire [pɑ̃sjɔ'nɛ:r], *n.* boarder; schoolboy *or* -girl; pensioner, resident.

pensionnat [pɑ̃sjɔ'na], *n.m.* private boarding school.

pensionné [pɑ̃sjɔ'ne], *a.* pensioned.—*n.m.* (*fem.* -ée) pensioner.

pensionner [pɑ̃sjɔ'ne], *v.t.* to pension, to grant a pension to.

pensum [pɛ̃'sɔm], *n.m.* imposition, extra task (*at school*).

pente [pɑ̃:t], *n.f.* declivity, slope; acclivity, ascent; gradient; pitch (*of roofs*); (*fig.*) propensity, bent.

Pentecôte [pɑ̃t'ko:t], *n.f.* Pentecost, Whitsuntide.

pénultième [penyl'tjɛm], *a.* last but one, penultimate.

pénurie [peny'ri], *n.f.* scarcity, dearth; penury, want.

pépier [pe'pje], *v.i.* to chirp, to cheep.

pépin [pe'pɛ̃], *n.m.* pip (*of apple etc.*); stone (*of grape*).

pépinière [pepi'njɛ:r], *n.f.* nursery (*of trees*).

pépiniériste [pepinje'rist], *n.m.* nurseryman.

pépite [pe'pit], *n.f.* nugget (*of gold*).

pepsine [pɛp'sin], *n.f.* pepsine.

peptique [pɛp'tik], *a.* peptic.

percale [pɛr'kal], *n.f.* cotton cambric, percale.

percaline [pɛrka'lin], *n.f.* glazed calico *or* lining, percaline.

perçant [pɛr'sã], *a.* piercing; sharp; shrill, acute.

perce [pɛrs], *n.f.* piercer, borer.

percé [pɛr'se], *a.* pierced, bored, in holes.

percée [pɛr'se], *n.f.* opening, cutting (*in a wood*), vista, glade; (*fig.*) break-through.

percement [pɛrsə'mã], *n.m.* piercing, boring, perforation.

perce-neige [pɛrs'nɛ:ʒ], *n.f. inv.* snowdrop.

perce-oreille [pɛrsɔ'rɛ:j], *n.m.* (*pl.* **-oreilles**) earwig.

percepteur [pɛrsɛp'tœ:r], *n.m.* collector of taxes.

perceptible [pɛrsɛp'tibl], *a.* collectible; perceptible.

perceptiblement [pɛrsɛptiblə'mã], *adv.* perceptibly.

perceptif [pɛrsɛp'tif], *a.* (*fem.* **-tive**) perceptive.

perception [pɛrsɛp'sjã], *n.f.* perception; collecting, receipt; collectorship, collector's office.

percer [pɛr'se], *v.t.* (*conjug. like* COMMENCER) to pierce, to bore, to drill; to make an opening; to tunnel; to wet through (*of rain etc.*).—*v.i.* to pierce through, to come through; to transpire; to manifest itself. **se percer**, *v.r.* to pierce oneself, to be pierced.

perceur [pɛr'sœ:r], *n.m.* (*fem.* **-euse**) borer.— *n.f.* (**-euse**) boring machine, drill.

percevoir [pɛrsə'vwa:r], *v.t. irr.* (*conjug. like* RECEVOIR) to collect (*taxes etc.*); (*Phil.*) to perceive.

perche [pɛrʃ], *n.f.* perch, pole; (*Ichth.*) perch.

perché [pɛr'ʃe], *a.* perched, perched up, roosting.

percher [pɛr'ʃe], *v.i.* and **se percher**, *v.r.* to perch, to roost.

percheur [pɛr'ʃœ:r], *a.* (*fem.* **-euse**) perching, roosting (*of birds*).

perchoir [pɛr'ʃwa:r], *n.m.* roost.

perclus [pɛr'kly], *a.* crippled, impotent.

percolateur [pɛrkɔla'tœ:r], *n.m.* percolator.

percussion [pɛrky'sjã], *n.f.* percussion.

percutant [pɛrky'tã], *a.* producing percussion; (*colloq.*) fabulous.

percuter [pɛrky'te], *v.t.* to strike; to percuss. —*v.i.* to crash.

perdable [pɛr'dabl], *a.* losable.

perdant [pɛr'dã], *a.* losing.—*n.m.* (*fem.* **-e**) loser.

perdition [pɛrdi'sjã], *n.f.* perdition.

perdre [pɛrdr], *v.t.* to lose, to be deprived of; to waste, to ruin, to corrupt, to lead astray. —*v.i.* to lose, to be a loser; to leak. **se perdre**, *v.r.* to be lost; to lose one's way, to be bewildered; to disappear.

perdreau [pɛr'dro], *n.m.* (*pl.* **-eaux**) young partridge.

perdrix [pɛr'dri], *n.f. inv.* partridge.

perdu [pɛr'dy], *a.* lost; ruined; spoilt; stray; obsolete; out of the way; bewildered; **salle des pas perdus**, waiting hall (*in courts of law*).

père [pɛ:r], *n.m.* father; sire.

pérégrination [peregrina'sjã], *n.f.* peregrination.

péremptoire [perãp'twa:r], *a.* peremptory.

péremptoirement [perãptwar'mã], *adv.* peremptorily.

pérennité [pereni'te], *n.f.* perpetuity.

perfectibilité [pɛrfɛktibili'te], *n.f.* perfectibility.

perfectible [pɛrfɛk'tibl], *a.* perfectible.

perfection [pɛrfɛk'sjã], *n.f.* perfection; faultlessness; completeness.

perfectionnement [pɛrfɛksjɔn'mã], *n.m.* improvement, perfecting.

perfectionner [pɛrfɛksjɔ'ne], *v.t.* to perfect; to improve. **se perfectionner**, *v.r.* to perfect oneself; to improve.

perfide [pɛr'fid], *a.* perfidious, treacherous, false.—*n.* perfidious *or* treacherous person.

perfidement [pɛrfid'mã], *adv.* perfidiously, falsely, treacherously.

perfidie [pɛrfi'di], *n.f.* perfidy, treachery.

perforage [pɛrfɔ'ra:ʒ], *n.m.* boring, perforation.

perforant [pɛrfɔ'rã], *a.* perforating, penetrating.

perforateur [pɛrfɔra'tœ:r], *a.* (*fem.* **-trice** (1)) perforative.—*n.m.* perforator.

perforation [pɛrfɔra'sjã], *n.f.* perforation.

perforatrice (2) [pɛrfɔra'tris], *n.f.* drilling machine.

perforer [pɛrfɔ're], *v.t.* to perforate, to bore, to drill.

péricliter [perikli'te], *v.i.* to be in jeopardy.

péril [pe'ril], *n.m.* peril, danger, hazard, risk.

périlleusement [perijøz'mã], *adv.* perilously.

périlleux [peri'jø], *a.* (*fem.* **-euse**) perilous, dangerous.

périmé [peri'me], *a.* out-of-date, no longer valid.

période [pe'rjɔd], *n.f.* period of time, era; (*Gram.*) period, sentence; (*Mus.*) phrase.— *n.m.* pitch, summit, degree, acme.

périodicité [perjodisi'te], *n.f.* periodicity.

périodique [perjo'dik], *a.* periodic, periodical.—*n.m.* periodical.

périodiquement [perjodik'mã], *adv.* periodically.

péripétie [peripe'si], *n.f.* sudden turn of fortune; (*pl.*) vicissitudes.

périr [pe'ri:r], *v.i.* to perish, to die; to be wrecked; to decay.

périscope [peris'kɔp], *n.m.* periscope.

périssable [peri'sabl], *a.* perishable.

péristyle [peris'til], *a.* and *n.m.* peristyle.

péritoine [peri'twan], *n.m.* peritoneum.

péritonite [perito'nit], *n.f.* peritonitis.

perle [pɛrl], *n.f.* pearl; bead, bugle (*for bracelets, necklaces etc.*); (*fig.*) gem, jewel, the best.

perlé [pɛr'le], *a.* pearled, set with pearls; pearly.

perler [pɛr'le], *v.t.* to bead, to form into beads; to pearl.—*v.i.* to form beads (*of sweat etc.*).

perlier [pɛr'lje], *a.* (*fem.* **-ière**) of pearl.

permanence [pɛrma'nã:s], *n.f.* permanence; headquarters (*of a political party*).

permanent [pɛrma'nã], *a.* permanent, lasting.

permanente [pɛrma'nã:t], *n.f.* (*Hairdressing*) permanent wave.

241

perméabilité [pɛrmeabili'te], n.f. permeability.

perméable [pɛrme'abl], a. permeable, pervious (to).

permettre [pɛr'mɛtr], v.t. irr. (conjug. like METTRE) to permit, to allow; to enable, to afford room for. **se permettre**, v.r. to permit oneself; to indulge, to venture, to take the liberty (de).

permis [pɛr'mi], a. allowed, permitted, lawful.—n.m. permission, leave; permit, license, pass.

permission [pɛrmi'sjɔ̃], n.f. permission, leave, permit.

permutant [pɛrmy'tɑ̃], n.m. permuter, exchanger.

permutation [pɛrmyta'sjɔ̃], n.f. permutation, exchange; (Mil.) transfer.

permuter [pɛrmy'te], v.t. to exchange, to permute, to transpose.

pernicieusement [pɛrnisjøz'mɑ̃], adv. perniciously, mischievously, injuriously.

pernicieux [pɛrni'sjø], a. (fem. -euse) pernicious, mischievous, hurtful.

péronnelle [pero'nɛl], n.f. pert hussy, saucy baggage.

péroraison [perore'zɔ̃], n.f. peroration.

pérorer [pero're], v.i. to hold forth, to speechify.

péroreur [pero'rœ:r], n.m. (fem. -euse) speechifier, spouter.

Pérou [pe'ru], le, m. Peru.

perpendiculaire [pɛrpɑ̃diky'lɛ:r], a. and n.f. perpendicular.

perpendiculairement [pɛrpɑ̃dikylɛr'mɑ̃], adv. perpendicularly.

perpétration [pɛrpetra'sjɔ̃], n.f. perpetration.

perpétrer [pɛrpe'tre], v.t. (conjug. like CÉDER) to perpetrate, to commit.

perpétuation [pɛrpetɥa'sjɔ̃], n.f. perpetuation.

perpétuel [pɛrpe'tɥɛl], a. (fem. -elle) perpetual, permanent; for life.

perpétuellement [pɛrpetɥɛl'mɑ̃], adv. perpetually; everlastingly.

perpétuer [pɛrpe'tɥe], v.t. to perpetuate. **se perpétuer**, v.r. to be perpetuated, to continue.

perpétuité [pɛrpetɥi'te], n.f. perpetuity; à perpétuité, for ever, for life.

perplexe [pɛr'plɛks], a. perplexed, embarrassed, irresolute; perplexing.

perplexité [pɛrplɛksi'te], n.f. perplexity.

perquisition [pɛrkizi'sjɔ̃], n.f. perquisition, search; investigation.

perquisitionner [pɛrkizisjo'ne], v.i. to make a search.

perron [pɛ'rɔ̃], n.m. steps (before a house).

perroquet [pero'kɛ], n.m. parrot.

perruche [pe'ryʃ], n.f. parakeet, budgerigar; (pop.) hen-parrot.

perruque [pe'ryk], n.f. wig, periwig.

perruquier [pery'kje], n.m. wig-maker; (obs.) hair-dresser, barber.

persan [pɛr'sɑ̃], a. Persian.—n.m. Persian (language); (**Persan**, fem. -ane) Persian (person).

Perse [pɛrs], la, f. Persia.

perse [pɛrs], n.f. chintz.

persécuter [pɛrseky'te], v.t. to persecute; (fig.) to bore, to dun.

persécuteur [pɛrseky'tœ:r], a. (fem. -trice) persecuting; troublesome.—n.m. (fem. -trice) persecutor; troublesome person.

persécution [pɛrseky'sjɔ̃], n.f. persecution; annoyance, importunity.

persévérance [pɛrseve'rɑ̃:s], n.f. perseverance; firmness, steadiness.

persévérant [pɛrseve'rɑ̃], a. persevering; steady, resolute.

persévérer [pɛrseve're], v.i. (conjug. like CÉDER) to persevere; to be steadfast; to persist.

persienne [pɛr'sjɛn], n.f. Venetian shutter.

persiflage [pɛrsi'fla:ʒ], n.m. banter, chaff, persiflage.

persifler [pɛrsi'fle], v.t., v.i. to rally, to banter, to chaff.

persifleur [pɛrsi'flœ:r], a. (fem. -euse) bantering, chaffing.—n.m. (fem. -euse) banterer, tease.

persil [pɛr'si], n.m. parsley.

persillé [pɛrsi'je], a. spotted; blue-molded (cheese).

persique [pɛr'sik], a. ancient Persian; le Golfe Persique, Persian Gulf.

persistance [pɛrsis'tɑ̃:s], n.f. persistence.

persistant [pɛrsis'tɑ̃], a. persistent.

persister [pɛrsis'te], v.i. to persist.

personnage [pɛrso'na:ʒ], n.m. personage, person; (Theat.) character, part.

personnalité [pɛrsonali'te], n.f. personality, personal character; person; selfishness.

personne [pɛr'son], n.f. person; own self; appearance.—pron. indef. anyone, no one, nobody.

personnel [pɛrso'nɛl], a. (fem. -elle) personal; selfish.—n.m. personnel, staff.

personnellement [pɛrsonɛl'mɑ̃], adv. personally.

personnification [pɛrsonifika'sjɔ̃], n.f. personification.

personnifier [pɛrsoni'fje], v.t. to personify; to embody.

perspectif [pɛrspɛk'tif], a. (fem. -tive) perspective.—n.f. (-tive) perspective; view, prospect, distance, vista.

perspicace [pɛrspi'kas], a. perspicacious, shrewd.

perspicacité [pɛrspikasi'te], n.f. perspicacity, insight.

persuader [pɛrsɥa'de], v.t. to persuade; to convince, to satisfy. **se persuader**, v.r. to persuade or convince oneself; to be persuaded.

persuasible [pɛrsɥa'zibl], a. persuadable.

persuasif [pɛrsɥa'zif], a. (fem. -sive) persuasive; convincing.

persuasion [pɛrsɥa'zjɔ̃], n.f. persuasion; conviction, belief, opinion.

persuasivement [pɛrsɥaziv'mɑ̃], adv. persuasively.

perte [pɛrt], n.f. loss; waste; ruin, fall, doom; à perte, at a loss; en pure perte, in vain.

pertinemment [pɛrtina'mɑ̃], adv. pertinently.

pertinence [pɛrti'nɑ̃:s], n.f. pertinence.

pertinent [pɛrti'nɑ̃], a. pertinent, relevant.

pertuis [pɛr'tɥi], n.m. opening, sluice; straits.

perturbateur [pɛrtyrba'tœ:r], a. (fem. -trice) disturbing.—n.m. (fem. -trice) disturber.

perturbation [pɛrtyrba'sjɔ̃], n.f. perturbation, disturbance.

perturber [pɛrtyr'be], *v.t.* to perturb, to disturb.

péruvien [pery'vjɛ̃], *a.* (*fem.* -enne) Peruvian.—*n.m.* (**Péruvien**, *fem.* -enne) Peruvian (*person*).

pervenche [pɛr'vɑ̃:ʃ], *n.f.* (*Bot.*) periwinkle.

pervers [pɛr'vɛ:r], *a.* perverse, wicked, depraved.—*n.m.* (*fem.* -e) perverse person; wrongdoer.

perversion [pɛrvɛr'sjɔ̃], *n.f.* perversion.

perversité [pɛrvɛrsi'te], *n.f.* perverseness.

pervertir [pɛrvɛr'ti:r], *v.t.* to pervert.

pervertissement [pɛrvɛrtis'mɑ̃], *n.m.* perversion.

pervertisseur [pɛrvɛrti'sœ:r], *a.* (*fem.* -euse) perverting.—*n.m.* (*fem.* -euse) perverter, corrupter.

pesage [pə'za:ʒ], *n.m.* weighing; (*Turf.*) weighing-in room; paddock (*on race-course*), the enclosure.

pesamment [pɔza'mɑ̃], *adv.* heavily, ponderously; clumsily.

pesant [pə'zɑ̃], *a.* heavy, ponderous, unwieldy; sluggish.—*n.m.* weight.—*adv.* in weight.

pesanteur [pɔzɑ̃'tœ:r], *n.f.* weight; heaviness; unwieldiness; dullness, ponderousness; (*Phys.*) gravity.

pesée [pə'ze], *n.f.* weighing.

pèse-lettre [pɛz'lɛtr], *n.m.* (*pl.* -lettres) letter-scales.

peser [pə'ze], *v.t.* (*conjug. like* AMENER) to weigh; (*fig.*) to ponder, to estimate.—*v.i.* to weigh; to be heavy; to be of importance; to lie heavy; to dwell (*sur*).

peseur [pə'zœ:r], *n.m.* (*fem.* -euse) weigher.

pessimisme [pɛsi'mism], *n.m.* pessimism.

pessimiste [pɛsi'mist], *a.* pessimistic.—*n.* pessimist.

peste [pɛst], *n.f.* plague, pestilence; (*fig.*) pest, bore, nuisance.—*int.* the deuce! hang it!

pester [pɛs'te], *v.i.* to inveigh, to storm, to rave.

pestiféré [pɛstife're], *a.* and *n.m.* (*fem.* -ée) plague-stricken (person).

pestilence [pɛsti'lɑ̃:s], *n.f.* pestilence.

pestilent [pɛsti'lɑ̃], *a.* pestilent.

pestilentiel [pɛstilɑ̃'sjɛl], *a.* (*fem.* -elle) pestilential.

pétale [pe'tal], *n.m.* petal.

pétarade [peta'rad], *n.f.* cracking (*noise*); back-fire (*of car*).

pétard [pe'ta:r], *n.m.* petard; cracker (*firework*); (*Rail.*) detonator, fog signal.

pétaudière [peto'djɛ:r], *n.f.* noisy *or* disorderly assembly.

pétillant [peti'jɑ̃], *a.* crackling; sparkling.

pétillement [petij'mɑ̃], *n.m.* crackling; sparkling.

pétiller [peti'je], *v.i.* to crackle (*of burning wood*); to sparkle.

petlot [pə'tjo], *a.* (*fam.*) tiny, wee.—*n.m.* (*fem.* -e) little one; darling.

petit [pə'ti], *a.* little, small; short; very young; petty, slight; shabby; humble.—*n.m.* (*fem.* -e) little child, little one; young one; whelp, pup, kitten, cub.

petite-fille [pɔtit'fij], *n.f.* (*pl.* **petites-filles**) granddaughter.

petitement [pɔtit'mɑ̃], *adv.* in small quantity; not much, poorly, meanly.

petitesse [pɔti'tɛs], *n.f.* smallness, littleness; insignificance; meanness; narrowness.

petit-fils [pɔti'fis], *n.m.* (*pl.* **petits-fils**) grandson.

pétition [peti'sjɔ̃], *n.f.* petition, request.

pétitionnaire [petisjɔ'nɛ:r], *n.* petitioner.

pétitionnement [petisjɔn'mɑ̃], *n.m.* petitioning.

pétitionner [petisjɔ'ne], *v.i.* to make a request, to petition.

petit-lait [pɔti'lɛ], *n.m.* whey.

petits-enfants [pɔtizɑ̃'fɑ̃], *n.m. pl.* grandchildren.

pétrel [pe'trɛl], *n.m.* petrel.

pétri [pe'tri], *a.* kneaded.

pétrifiant [petri'fjɑ̃], *a.* petrifying.

pétrification [petrifika'sjɔ̃], *n.f.* petrifaction.

pétrifier [petri'fje], *v.t.* to petrify. **se pétrifier**, *v.r.* to turn into stone.

pétrin [pe'trɛ̃], *n.m.* kneading trough; (*fig.*) scrape.

pétrir [pe'tri:r], *v.t.* to knead; (*fig.*) to mold, to form.

pétrissable [petri'sabl], *a.* that can be kneaded; (*fig.*) yielding, pliant.

pétrissage [petri'sa:ʒ], **pétrissement** [petris'mɑ̃], *n.m.* kneading; (*fig.*) forming.

pétrisseur [petri'sœ:r], *n.m.* (*fem.* -euse) kneader.—*n.f.* (-euse) kneading-machine.

pétrole [pe'trɔl], *n.m.* petroleum, (mineral) oil; kerosene.

pétrolier [petro'lje], *a.* (*fem.* -lère) pertaining to oil.—*n.m.* oil tanker.

pétulance [pety'lɑ̃:s], *n.f.* liveliness, ebulliency; friskiness.

pétulant [pety'lɑ̃], *a.* lively, ebullient, frisky.

pétunia [pety'nja], *n.m.* petunia.

peu [pø], *adv.* little, not much; few, not many; not very.—*n.m.* little; bit.

peuplade [pœ'plad], *n.f.* clan, tribe, horde.

peuple [pœpl], *a.* plebeian, common, vulgar.—*n.m.* people, nation; the people, the multitude, the lower classes.

peuplé [pœ'ple], *a.* heavily populated, populous.

peuplement [pœplə'mɑ̃], *n.m.* peopling; stocking of a poultry yard, pond etc.

peupler [pœ'ple], *v.t.* to people; to stock with animals etc.; to populate; to throng.—*v.i.* to multiply, to breed. **se peupler**, *v.r.* to become peopled; to be populated.

peuplier [pœ'plje], *n.m.* poplar.

peur [pœ:r], *n.f.* fear, dread, terror; apprehension; **avoir peur**, to be afraid; **de peur de**, for fear of.

peureusement [pœrøz'mɑ̃], *adv.* timorously.

peureux [pœ'rø], *a.* (*fem.* -euse) fearful, timid, timorous.—*n.m.* (*fem.* -euse) timid person.

peut-être [pø'tɛ:tr], *adv.* perhaps, maybe.

phalange [fa'lɑ̃:ʒ], *n.f.* phalanx; (*poet.*) army, host.

phalène [fa'lɛ:n], *n.f.* moth.

pharaon [fara'ɔ̃], *n.m.* Pharaoh.

phare [fa:r], *n.m.* lighthouse; beacon; (*Motor.*) head-light.

pharisien [fari'zjɛ̃], *n.m.* Pharisee; (*fig.*) hypocrite; self-righteous person.

pharmaceutique [farmasø'tik], *a.* pharmaceutical.—*n.f.* pharmaceutics.

243

pharmacie [farma'si], *n.f.* pharmacy, druggist's shop, dispensary; medicine chest.

pharmacien [farma'sjɛ̃], *n.m.* (*fem.* **-enne**) pharmacist.

phase [fɑ:z], *n.f.* phasis (*of planet*); phase; aspect, period.

phénicien [feni'sjɛ̃], *a.* (*fem.* **-enne**) Phoenician.—*n.m.* (**Phénicien**, *fem.* **-enne**) Phoenician (*person*).

phénix [fe'niks], *n.m.* phoenix; paragon.

phénoménal [fenɔme'nal], *a.* (*m. pl.* **-aux**) phenomenal; (*colloq.*) extraordinary.

phénomène [fenɔ'mɛːn], *n.m.* phenomenon; (*colloq.*) remarkable person *or* thing; freak.

philanthrope [filɑ̃'trɔp], *n.* philanthropist.

philanthropie [filɑ̃trɔ'pi], *n.f.* philanthropy.

philanthropique [filɑ̃trɔ'pik], *a.* philanthropic.

philatélie [filate'li], *n.f.* philately, stamp collecting.

philatéliste [filate'list], *n.* stamp collector.

Philippe [fi'lip], *m.* Philip.

philippine [fili'pin], *a.* Philippine, Filipino.—*n.* (**Philippine**) Filipino (*person*).

Philippines [fili'pin], **les**, *f. pl.* Philippines, Philippine Islands.

Philistin [filis'tɛ̃], *n.m.* (*fem.* **-e**) Philistine, person of vulgar taste.

philosophale [filozɔ'fal], *a.* **la pierre philosophale**, the philosopher's stone.

philosophe [filɔ'zɔf], *a.* philosophical.—*n.* philosopher.

philosopher [filozɔ'fe], *v.i.* to philosophize.

philosophie [filozɔ'fi], *n.f.* philosophy; class in French school roughly equivalent to English sixth.

philosophique [filozɔ'fik], *a.* philosophical.

philosophiquement [filozɔfik'mɑ̃], *adv.* philosophically.

philtre *or* **filtre** [filtr], *n.m.* philtre.

phlébite [fle'bit], *n.f.* phlebitis.

phlegmatique [FLEGMATIQUE].

phobie [fɔ'bi], *n.f.* phobia, morbid dread.

phonétique [fɔne'tik], *a.* phonetic.—*n.f.* phonetics.

phonique [fɔ'nik], *a.* a phonic.

phonographe [fɔnɔ'graf], *n.m.* phonograph, gramophone.

phonographie [fɔnɔgra'fi], *n.f.* phonography, sound recording.

phonographique [fɔnɔgra'fik], *a.* phonographic.

phoque [fɔk], *n.m.* (*Zool.*) seal.

phosphate [fɔs'fat], *n.m.* phosphate.

phosphore [fɔs'fɔːr], *n.m.* phosphorus.

phosphorescence [fɔsfɔrɛ'sɑ̃ːs], *n.f.* phosphorescence.

phosphorescent [fɔsfɔrɛ'sɑ̃], *a.* phosphorescent.

phosphoreux [fɔsfɔ'rø], *a.m.* phosphorous.

phosphorique [fɔsfɔ'rik], *a.* phosphoric.

photo [fɔ'to], *n.f. abbr.* [PHOTOGRAPHIE].

photocopie [fɔtɔkɔ'pi], *n.f.* photocopy, photostat.

photogénique [fɔtɔʒe'nik], *a.* photogenic.

photographe [fɔtɔ'graf], *n.* photographer.

photographie [fɔtɔgra'fi], *n.f.* photography; photograph.

photographier [fɔtɔgra'fje], *v.t.* to photograph.

photographique [fɔtɔgra'fik], *a.* photographic; **appareil photographique**, camera.

photogravure [fɔtɔgra'vyːr], *n.f.* photogravure.

phrase [frɑ:z], *n.f.* sentence; (*Mus.*) phrase; **phrase toute faite**, commonplace, stock phrase.

phraséologie [frazeɔlɔ'zi], *n.f.* phraseology.

phraser [frɑ'ze], *v.t.* to express in phrases; (*Mus.*) to phrase.—*v.i.* to phrase.

phraseur [frɑ'zœːr], *n.m.* (*fem.* **-euse**) (*fam.*) verbose writer *or* talker.

phtisie [fti'zi], *n.f.* phthisis, consumption.

phtisique [fti'zik], *a.* consumptive.—*n.* consumptive person.

physicien [fizi'sjɛ̃], *n.m.* (*fem.* **-enne**) physicist.

physionomie [fizjɔnɔ'mi], *n.f.* physiognomy, countenance, aspect, look.

physionomiste [fizjɔnɔ'mist], *n.* physiognomist.

physiothérapie [fizjɔtera'pi], *n.f.* (*Med.*) physiotherapy.

physiothérapiste [fizjɔtera'pist], *n.* physiotherapist.

physique [fi'zik], *a.* physical, material, bodily.—*n.f.* physics.—*n.m.* physique, natural constitution; outward appearance.

physiquement [fizik'mɑ̃], *adv.* physically.

piaffer [pja'fe], *v.i.* to paw the ground, to prance (*of horses*).

piaffeur [pja'fœːr], *a.* (*fem.* **-euse**) pawing, prancing.—*n.m.* (*fem.* **-euse**) pawer, prancer.

piailler [pja'je], *v.i.* to cheep (*of small birds*); (*fig.*) to squall; to rant.

piaillerie [pjaj'ri], *n.f.* cheeping; squealing.

piailleur [pja'jœːr], *n.m.* (*fem.* **-euse**) cheeper; squaller.

pianiste [pja'nist], *n.* pianist.

piano [pja'no], *n.m.* piano, pianoforte; **piano à queue**, grand piano.

piaulement [pjol'mɑ̃], *n.m.* whining, puling; cheeping (*of chickens*).

piauler [pjo'le], *v.i.* to cheep (*of chickens etc.*); (*fig.*) to pule, to whine.

pic [pik], *n.m.* pick, pickaxe; gaff; peak (*of a mountain*); woodpecker.

pick-up [pi'kœp], *n.m. inv.* record player.

picoté [pikɔ'te], *a.* pricked, marked.

picotement [pikɔt'mɑ̃], *n.m.* pricking, tingling.

picoter [pikɔ'te], *v.t.* to cause to tingle; to prick; to peck (*of birds*).

picvert *or* **pivert** [pi'vɛːr], *n.m.* green woodpecker.

pie [pi], *a. inv.* and *n.* piebald (*horse*).—*n.f.* magpie.

pièce [pjɛs], *n.f.* piece; patch; cask (*of wine etc.*); head (*of cattle, poultry etc.*); apartment, room; piece of ordnance, cannon; (*Theat.*) play; coin; joint (*of meat*).

pied [pje], *n.m.* foot; footing; footprint, track; leg (*of furniture*); stand, rest; stalk (*of plants*).

pied-à-terre [pjeta'tɛːr], *n.m. inv.* occasional lodging.

pied-de-biche [pjed'biʃ], *n.m.* (*pl.* **pieds-de-biche**) bell-pull; (*Surg.*) forceps; nail-clench.

piédestal [pjedɛs'tal], *n.m.* (*pl.* **-aux**) pedestal.

piège [pjɛːʒ], *n.m.* trap, snare.

piéger [pje'ʒe], *v.t.* (*conjug. like* CÉDER) to trap (*animals*); (*Mil.*) to set a booby trap.

pie-grièche [pigri'ɛʃ], *n.f.* (*pl.* **pies-grièches**) (*Orn.*) shrike; (*fig.*) shrew.

pierraille [pjɛ'raːj], *n.f.* rubble, ballast.

Pierre [pjɛːr], *m.* Peter.

pierre [pjɛːr], *n.f.* stone; (*Path.*) calculus.

pierreries [pjɛr'ri], *n.f. pl.* precious stones, gems.

pierreux [pjɛ'rø], *a.* (*fem.* **-euse**) stony, flinty, gritty, gravelly; calculous.

pierrot [pjɛ'ro], *n.m.* pierrot, merry-andrew; house sparrow.

piété [pje'te], *n.f.* piety, godliness; affection.

piétinement [pjetin'mã], *n.m.* stamping, trampling.

piétiner [pjeti'ne], *v.t.* to tread *or* trample under foot.—*v.i.* to stamp; to paw the ground (*of horses*).

piéton [pje'tõ], *n.m.* (*fem.* **-onne**) pedestrian.

piètre [pjɛtr], *a.* poor, paltry, pitiful.

piètrement [pjetrə'mã], *adv.* pitifully, wretchedly.

pieu [pjø], *n.m.* (*pl.* **pieux** (1)) stake, pile, post.

pieusement [pjøz'mã], *adv.* piously, devoutly; obediently; reverently.

pieuvre [pjœːvr], *n.f.* octopus, poulpe.

pieux (2) [pjø], *a.* (*fem.* **pieuse**) pious, godly.

pigeon [pi'ʒõ], *n.m.* pigeon, dove; (*slang*) dupe, gull.

pigeonneau [piʒɔ'no], *n.m.* (*pl.* **-eaux**) young pigeon, squab.

pigeonnier [piʒɔ'nje], *n.m.* pigeon house, dove-cot.

pigment [pig'mã], *n.m.* (*Anat.*) pigment.

pignon [pi'ɲõ], *n.m.* gable end; pinion; kernel (*of fir cone*).

pilaire [pi'lɛːr], *a.* pilous, pilose.

pilastre [pi'lastr], *n.m.* (*Arch.*) pilaster.

pilchard [pil'ʃaːr], *n.m.* pilchard.

pile [pil], *n.f.* pile, heap; pier (*of a bridge etc.*); mole (*masonry*); (*Elec.*) battery; reverse (*of coins*); **pile atomique**, atomic pile.

piler [pi'le], *v.t.* to pound, to crush, to powder.

pileur [pi'lœːr], *n.m.* (*fem.* **-euse** (1)) pounder, beater.

pileux [pi'lø], *a.* (*fem.* **-euse** (2)) pilous, hairy.

pilier [pi'lje], *n.m.* pillar, column, post; (*fig.*) supporter, prop.

pillage [pi'jaːʒ], *n.m.* pillage, plunder; (*fig.*) pilfering.

pillard [pi'jaːr], *a.* plundering; predatory.—*n.m.* (*fem.* **-e**) pillager, plunderer.

piller [pi'je], *v.t.* to pillage, to plunder; to ransack; to pilfer.

pillerie [pij'ri], *n.f.* pillage, plunder; extortion.

pilleur [pi'jœːr], *n.m.* (*fem.* **-euse**) pillager, plunderer, pilferer.

pilon [pi'lõ], *n.m.* pestle; rammer, stamper; wooden leg.

pilonnage [pilɔ'naːʒ], *n.m.* ramming, pounding, stamping, milling.

pilonner [pilɔ'ne], *v.t.* to ram, to pound, to mill; to stamp (*ore*).

pilori [pilɔ'ri], *n.m.* pillory.

pilorier [pilɔ'rje], *v.t.* to pillory.

pilotage [pilɔ'taːʒ], *n.m.* (*Civ. Eng.*) pile-driving; (*Naut.*) piloting.

pilote [pi'lɔt], *n.m.* pilot; guide; pilot fish.

piloter [pilɔ'te], *v.t.* to pile, to drive piles into; (*Naut.*, *Av.*) to pilot; (*fig.*) to guide.

pilotis [pilɔ'ti], *n.m.* pilework.

pilule [pi'lyl], *n.f.* pill.

pimbêche [pɛ̃'bɛʃ], *n.f.* uppish and impertinent woman.

piment [pi'mã], *n.m.* pimento, allspice.

pimenter [pimã'te], *v.t.* to flavor with pimento.

pimpant [pɛ̃'pã], *a.* natty, spruce, smart.

pin [pɛ̃], *n.m.* pine tree; **pomme de pin**, fir cone.

pinacle [pi'nakl], *n.m.* pinnacle.

pince [pɛ̃ːs], *n.f.* pinching, nipping; hold, grip; pincers, pliers, forceps; tongs, clip; crowbar (*lever*); toe (*of a horse's foot*); claw (*of a lobster etc.*).

pincé [pɛ̃'se], *a.* affected, stiff, prim.

pinceau [pɛ̃'so], *n.m.* (*pl.* **-eaux**) paint-brush.

pincée [pɛ̃'se], *n.f.* pinch (*of snuff, salt etc.*).

pince-nez [pɛ̃s'ne], *n.m. inv.* pince-nez, (*folding*) eye glasses.

pince-notes [pɛ̃s'nɔt], *n.m. inv.* paper clip.

pincer [pɛ̃'se], *v.t.* (*conjug. like* COMMENCER) to pinch, to nip; to grip; to bite (*of cold etc.*); to pluck (*a musical instrument*); (*Naut.*) to hug (*the wind*).

pince-sans-rire [pɛ̃ssã'riːr], *n.m. inv.* sly *or* malicious person, dry joker.

pincette(s) [pɛ̃'sɛt], *n.f.* (*pl.*) tongs; tweezers, nippers.

pinçure [pɛ̃'syːr], *n.f.* pinching; crease in cloth.

pingouin [pɛ̃'gwɛ̃], *n.m.* auk.

pingre [pɛ̃ːgr], *a.* avaricious, stingy.—*n.* miser, skinflint.

pinson [pɛ̃'sõ], *n.m.* finch, chaffinch.

pintade [pɛ̃'tad], *n.f.* guinea fowl.

piochage [pjɔ'ʃaːʒ], *n.m.* digging; (*fig.*) working, fagging.

pioche [pjɔʃ], *n.f.* pickaxe.

piocher [pjɔ'ʃe], *v.t.* to dig.—*v.i.* to dig; (*fig.*) to fag, to work hard, to grind.

piocheur [pjɔ'ʃœːr], *n.m.* (*fem.* **-euse**) digger; (*slang*) hard-working student, grind. —*n.f.* (**-euse**) (*Civ. Eng.*) excavator.

piolet [pjɔ'lɛ], *n.m.* piolet, ice axe.

pion [pjõ], *n.m.* pawn (*at chess*); piece (*at checkers*); (*Sch. slang*) assistant teacher.

pionnier [pjɔ'nje], *n.m.* pioneer.

pipe [pip], *n.f.* pipe; tobacco-pipe; pipe (*cask*).

pipeau [pi'po], *n.m.* (*pl.* **-eaux**) pipe, reed-pipe; bird-call; limed twig, snare.

pipée [pi'pe], *n.f.* bird-catching (*with a bird-call*); (*fig.*) deceit, trickery.

piper [pi'pe], *v.t.* to catch (*birds*) with a bird-call etc.; (*fig.*) to trick, to decoy.

pipeur [pi'pœːr], *a.* (*fem.* **-euse**) cheating, deceitful.—*n.m.* (*fem.* **-euse**) one who decoys birds; cheat, trickster (*at play*).

piquant [pi'kã], *a.* prickling, stinging; pungent; biting, cutting, keen; piquant, pointed; smart.—*n.m.* prickle; quill (*of porcupine*); pungency, point, piquancy.

pique [pik], *n.f.* pike (*weapon*); pique, spite, quarrel.—*n.m.* (*Cards*) spade(s).

piqué [pi'ke], *a.* quilted, pinked; worm-eaten; sour (*wine*).—*n.m.* quilting; piqué; nose-dive; **bombardement en piqué**, dive-bombing.

pique-nique

pique-nique [pik'nik], *n.m.* (*pl.* **-niques**) picnic.

piquer [pi'ke], *v.t.* to prick; to sting; to goad, to spur; to puncture; to bite (*of insects*); to quilt; to lard; to prick off; to excite, to stimulate; to nettle, to rouse; (*Med.*) to inject.—*v.i.* to turn sour (*of wine etc.*). **se piquer,** *v.r.* to prick oneself; to be offended, to be piqued; to pride oneself; to turn sour.

piquet [pi'ke], *n.m.* peg, stake; (*Mil.*) picket; piquet (*card game*).

piqueter [pik'te], *v.t.* (*conjug. like* APPELER) to mark out with stakes *or* pegs; to mark with little points.

piquette [pi'ket], *n.f.*, **piqueton** [pik'tɔ̃], *n.m.* thin wine.

piqueur (1) [pi'kœːr], *n.m.* outrider; overseer (*of workmen*); stud groom; huntsman.

piqueur (2) [pi'kœːr], *n.m.* (*fem.* **-euse**) stitcher.

piqûre [pi'kyːr], *n.f.* prick; sting; bite; puncture; (*Needlework*) quilting, stitching; (*Med.*) injection, shot.

pirate [pi'rat], *n.m.* pirate; (*fig.*) extortioner, plagiarist.

pirater [pira'te], *v.i.* to commit piracy.

piraterie [pira'tri], *n.f.* piracy; act of piracy *or* plagiarism.

pire [piːr], *a. and n.m.* worse; the worst.

pirogue [pi'rɔg], *n.f.* pirogue, dug-out, canoe.

pirouette [pi'rwɛt], *n.f.* pirouette, whirligig.

pirouetter [pirwe'te], *v.i.* to pirouette, to whirl about.

pis (1) [pi], *n.m.* udder, dug (*of cow*).

pis (2) [pi], *adv. and n.m.* worse.—*n.m. inv.* **pis-aller,** the worst, last resource, make-shift.

pisciculture [pisikyl'tyːr], *n.f.* fish culture.

piscine [pi'sin], *n.f.* piscina; swimming pool.

pissenlit [pisɑ̃'li], *n.m.* dandelion.

pistache [pis'taʃ], *n.f.* pistachio, pistachio nut.

pistachier [pista'ʃje], *n.m.* pistachio tree.

piste [pist], *n.f.* track, footprint, trail, scent; course, race-course.

pistolet [pistɔ'lɛ], *n.m.* pistol; spray gun.

piston [pis'tɔ̃], *n.m.* piston; sucker (*of a pump*); press button; (*Mus.*) cornet.

pitance [pi'tɑ̃ːs], *n.f.* pittance; allowance (*of food*), dole.

piteusement [pitøz'mɑ̃], *adv.* piteously, woefully, sadly.

piteux [pi'tø], *a.* (*fem.* **-euse**) piteous, pitiable, woeful.

pitié [pi'tje], *n.f.* pity, compassion; object of pity.

piton [pi'tɔ̃], *n.m.* eye-bolt, screw-ring, ring-bolt; peak (*of mountain*).

pitoyable [pitwa'jabl], *a.* pitiful, piteous; paltry.

pitoyablement [pitwajablə'mɑ̃], *adv.* pitifully.

pittoresque [pitɔ'rɛsk], *a.* picturesque; graphic.—*n.m.* the picturesque, picturesqueness.

pittoresquement [pitɔrɛsk'mɑ̃], *adv.* picturesquely.

pivert [PICVERT].

pivoine [pi'vwan], *n.m.* bullfinch.—*n.f.* peony.

pivot [pi'vo], *n.m.* pivot, pin, spindle, hinge.

pivoter [pivɔ'te], *v.i.* to pivot, to turn on a pivot, to revolve, to turn.

placage [pla'kaːʒ], *n.m.* plating (*metal-work*); veneering (*of wood*); (*Lit.*) patchwork.

placard [pla'kaːr], *n.m.* placard, poster, bill; (*Print.*) slip; cupboard (*in a wall*).

placarder [plakar'de], *v.t.* to placard, to post up.

place [plas], *n.f.* place; room; seat; stead; post, job, situation; town; public square; **faire place,** to make room; **retenir des places,** to book seats; **sur place,** on the spot.

placement [plas'mɑ̃], *n.m.* placing; sale; employment; investment.

placer [pla'se], *v.t.* (*conjug. like* COMMENCER) to place, to put; to find a place *or* situation for; to invest; to deposit; to sell. **se placer** *v.r.* to place oneself; to find a job.

placet [pla'sɛ], *n.m.* petition, address.

placide [pla'sid], *a.* placid, calm.

placidement [plasid'mɑ̃], *adv.* placidly, calmly.

placidité [plasidi'te], *n.f.* placidity.

plafond [pla'fɔ̃], *n.m.* ceiling.

plafonnage [plafɔ'naːʒ], *n.m.* ceiling (*action, work*); (*Av.*) visibility.

plafonner [plafɔ'ne], *v.t.* to ceil, to put a ceiling to.—*v.i.* to reach the highest point (*of prices etc.*); (*Av.*) to fly at the ceiling; (*Motor.*) to travel at maximum speed.

plafonneur [plafɔ'nœːr], *n.m.* plasterer.

plafonnier [plafɔ'nje], *n.m.* ceiling light.

plage [plaːʒ], *n.f.* beach, shore; sea-side resort.

plagiaire [pla'ʒjɛːr], *a. and n.* plagiarist.

plagiat [pla'ʒja], *n.m.* plagiarism.

plagier [pla'ʒje], *v.t.* to plagiarize.

plaid [plɛd], *n.m.* plaid, travelling rug.

plaidant [plɛ'dɑ̃], *a.* pleading, litigant.

plaider [plɛ'de], *v.t.* to defend; to allege.—*v.i.* to go to law, to litigate; to plead, to argue.

plaideur [plɛ'dœːr], *n.m.* (*fem.* **-euse**) litigant, suitor.

plaidoirie [plɛdwa'ri], *n.f.* pleading; counsel's speech.

plaidoyer [plɛdwa'je], *n.m.* speech for the defence, counsel's address.

plaie [plɛ], *n.f.* wound; sore; (*fig.*) plague; evil.

plaignant [plɛ'ɲɑ̃], *a.* complaining; **la partie plaignante,** the plaintiff.—*n.m.* (*fem.* **-e**) plaintiff, prosecutor.

plain [plɛ̃], *a.* plain, even, flat, level.

plaindre [plɛ̃ːdr], *v.t. irr.* (*conjug. like* CRAINDRE) to pity, to be sorry for. **se plaindre,** *v.r.* to complain; to grumble.

plaine [plɛn], *n.f.* plain; flat country.

plain-pied (de) [daplɛ̃'pje], *adv. phr.* on a level; (*fig.*) without difficulty.

plainte [plɛ̃ːt], *n.f.* complaint, plaint; lamentation, wail; plaint at law.

plaintif [plɛ̃'tif], *a.* (*fem.* **-tive**) plaintive, complaining; querulous.

plaintivement [plɛtiv'mɑ̃], *adv.* dolefully; querulously.

plaire [plɛːr], *v.i. irr.* to please; to be pleasant *or* agreeable (à); **s'il vous plaît,** please. **se plaire,** *v.r.* to delight, to take pleasure; to like.

plaisamment [plɛza'mɑ̃], *adv.* humorously, amusingly; ludicrously.

plaisance [plɛ'zɑ̃:s], *n.f.* pleasure.

plaisant [plɛ'zɑ̃], *a.* humorous, amusing, funny; (*iron.*) odd, strange.—*n.m.* jester, wag; the funny side; *un mauvais plaisant*, a practical joker.

plaisanter [plɛzɑ̃'te], *v.t.* to chaff, to banter. —*v.i.* to jest, to joke.

plaisanterie [plɛzɑ̃'tri], *n.f.* jest, joke, witticism; mockery, trifle.

plaisir [plɛ'zi:r], *n.m.* pleasure; delight; diversion, entertainment; favor.

plan [plɑ̃], *a.* even, level, flat.—*n.m.* plane, plan; drawing; scheme, project; (*Paint.*) ground.

planche [plɑ̃:ʃ], *n.f.* board, plank; shelf; (*Engr.*) plate; (*Gard.*) bed, border.

planchéiage [plɑ̃ʃe'ja:ʒ], *n.m.* boarding, planking; flooring.

planchéier [plɑ̃ʃe'je], *v.t.* to board over, to floor.

plancher [plɑ̃'ʃe], *n.m.* floor, deck planking.

planchette [plɑ̃'ʃɛt], *n.f.* small board; (*Math.*) plane table.

plancton [plɑ̃k'tɔ̃], *n.m.* plankton.

plane [plan], *n.f.* drawing-knife; planisher.

plané [pla'ne], *a.* soaring, gliding; *un vol plané*, gliding descent.

planer [pla'ne], *v.t.* to make smooth, to plane. —*v.i.* to hover, to soar; to look down (*on*) (*sur*); (*Av.*) to glide.

planétaire [plane'tɛ:r], *a.* planetary.

planète [pla'nɛ:t], *n.f.* planet.

planeur [pla'nœ:r], *n.m.* planisher; glider (*airplane*).

planeuse [pla'nø:z], *n.f.* planing machine.

planification [planifika'sjɔ̃], *n.f.* (*Polit. Econ.*) planning.

planifier [plani'fje], *v.t.* to plan.

plant [plɑ̃], *n.m.* young plant, seedling; slip; sapling; plantation.

plantation [plɑ̃ta'sjɔ̃], *n.f.* planting; plantation.

plante [plɑ̃:t], *n.f.* plant; *la plante du pied*, (*Anat.*) the sole of the foot.

planter [plɑ̃'te], *v.t.* to plant; to set, to drive in; to set up, to erect. **se planter**, *v.r.* to station oneself.

planteur [plɑ̃'tœ:r], *n.m.* planter.

planteuse [plɑ̃'tø:z], *n.f.* potato-planting machine.

plantoir [plɑ̃'twa:r], *n.m.* dibble.

planton [plɑ̃'tɔ̃], *n.m.* (*Mil.*) orderly.

plantureusement [plɑ̃tyrøz'mɑ̃], *adv.* copiously, abundantly, luxuriantly.

plantureux [plɑ̃ty'rø], *a.* (*fem.* **-euse**) plentiful, copious; fertile.

plaquage [pla'ka:ʒ], *n.m.* (*Ftb.*) rugby tackle.

plaque [plak], *n.f.* plate, slab; plaque; badge, star; *plaque tournante*, (*Rail.*) turn-table.

plaqué [pla'ke], *a.* plated, covered with.

plaquer [pla'ke], *v.t.* to plate (*metal*); to veneer (*wood*); (*Ftb.*) to tackle.

plaquette [pla'kɛt], *n.f.* small thin book; small plate; thin slab.

plasticité [plastisi'te], *n.f.* plasticity.

plastique [plas'tik], *a.* plastic.—*n.m.* plastics. —*n.f.* plastic art; figure.

plastron [plas'trɔ̃], *n.m.* breast-plate; fencing pad; shirt front.

plastronner [plastro'ne], *v.i.* to strut, to swagger.

plat (1) [pla], *a.* flat; level; regular, (*fig.*) dull, insipid.—*n.m.* flat part, side; flat racing.

plat (2) [pla], *n.m.* dish (*the vessel and the food*), (*Naut.*) mess; course (*of a meal*).

platane [pla'tan], *n.m.* plane-tree, platan.

plateau [pla'to], *n.m.* (*pl.* **-eaux**) scale (*of a balance*); tray; table-land, plateau; turntable (*of gramophone*).

plate-bande [plat'bɑ̃:d], *n.f.* (*pl.* **plates-bandes**) border, flower bed.

plate-forme [plat'fɔrm], *n.f.* (*pl.* **plates-formes**) platform (*of a bus etc.*).

platement [plat'mɑ̃], *adv.* flatly, dully.

platine [pla'tin], *n.f.* lock (*of fire-arms*); plate (*of lock, watch, machine*); platen (*of typewriter*).—*n.m.* platinum.

platiné [plati'ne], *a.* platinum-plated; platinum-colored (*of hair*).

platitude [plati'tyd], *n.f.* platitude; flatness, dullness.

Platon [pla'tɔ̃], *m.* Plato.

platonique [plato'nik], *a.* Platonic.

platonisme [plato'nism], *n.m.* Platonism.

plâtrage [plɑ'tra:ʒ], *n.m.* plaster work, plastering.

plâtras [plɑ'tra], *n.m.* debris of plaster work; rubbish.

plâtre [plɑ:tr], *n.m.* plaster.

plâtré [plɑ'tre], *a.* plastered.

plâtrer [plɑ'tre], *v.t.* to plaster; (*fig.*) to patch up, to disguise.

plâtreux [plɑ'trø], *a.* (*fem.* **-euse**) chalky.

plâtrier [plɑtri'e], *n.m.* plasterer.

plâtrière [plɑtri'jɛ:r], *n.f.* chalk pit; plaster kiln.

plâtroir [plɑ'trwa:r], *n.m.* plasterer's trowel.

plausibilité [plozibili'te], *n.f.* plausibility.

plausible [plo'zibl], *a.* plausible (*never of person*).

plausiblement [plozibl'mɑ̃], *adv.* plausibly.

plèbe [plɛb], *n.f.* common people.

plébéien [plebe'jɛ̃], *a.* and *n.m.* (*fem.* **-enne**) plebeian.

plébiscite [plebi'sit], *n.m.* plebiscite.

plein [plɛ̃], *a.* full; fraught (*de*); filled, replete; entire, whole; thorough; copious; solid; *en plein air*, in the open air; *en plein hiver*, in the heart of winter.—*n.m.* full part; plenum.—*adv.* full.

pleinement [plɛn'mɑ̃], *adv.* fully, entirely, thoroughly.

plénier [ple'nje], *a.* (*fem.* **-ière**) plenary; full, complete.

plénipotentiaire [plenipotɑ̃'sjɛ:r], *a.* and *n.m.* plenipotentiary.

plénitude [pleni'tyd], *n.f.* plenitude, fullness.

pleur [plœ:r], *n.m.* (*poet.*) tear; lament.

pleurard [plœ'ra:r], *a.* whimpering, tearful.—*n.m.* (*fem.* **-e**) whimperer, blubberer.

pleurer [plœ're], *v.t.* to weep, to bewail, to mourn, to deplore the loss of.—*v.i.* to weep, to cry, to shed tears; to mourn; to run (*of the eyes*); to drip (*of a tap*).

pleurésie [plœre'zi], *n.f.* pleurisy.

pleureur [plœ'rœ:r], *a.* (*fem.* **-euse**) whimpering, tearful; *saule pleureur*, weeping willow.—*n.m.* (*fem.* **-euse**) whimperer, weeper.—*n.f.* (**-euse**) paid mourner.

247

pleurnichement [plœrniʃˈmã], *n.m.* whimpering, snivelling.

pleurnicher [plœrniˈʃe], *v.i.* to whimper, to whine, to snivel.

pleurnicheur [plœrniˈʃœːr], *a.* (*fem.* -euse) whimpering, snivelling.—*n.m.* (*fem.* -euse) whimperer, sniveller.

pleutre [pløːtr], *n.m.* contemptible fellow.

pleuvoir [plœˈvwaːr], *v. impers. irr.* to rain; *il pleut à verse* or *à seaux*, it is pouring in buckets; *pleuvoir des hallebardes*, to rain cats and dogs.

pli [pli], *n.m.* fold; wrinkle; coil; bend; undulation, depression; cover, envelope; habit; (*Cards*) trick; *mise en pli*, setting (*the hair*); *sous pli recommandé*, in a registered envelope; *un faux pli*, a crease.

pliable [pliˈjabl], *a.* pliable, flexible, supple.

pliage [pliˈjaːʒ], **pliement** [pliˈmã], *n.m.* folding.

pliant [pliˈjã], *a.* pliant, docile; folding, collapsible.—*n.m.* folding chair, deck chair.

plie [pli], *n.f.* plaice.

plier [pliˈje], *v.t.* to fold, to fold up; to bend.—*v.i.* to bend, to bow; to give way. **se plier**, *v.r.* to bow, to bend, to yield.

plieur [pliˈjœːr], *n.m.* (*fem.* -euse) folder.—*n.f.* (-euse) folding-machine.

plinthe [plɛ̃ːt], *n.f.* plinth; skirting-board.

plissage [pliˈsaːʒ], *n.m.* pleating, kilting.

plissé [pliˈse], *a.* kilted, pleated.—*n.m.* kilting, pleats.

plissement [plisˈmã], *n.m.* folding, doubling over; crumpling.

plisser [pliˈse], *v.t.* to fold; to crumple, to wrinkle; to pleat.—*v.i.* and **se plisser**, *v.r.* to be wrinkled, to pucker.

plissure [pliˈsyːr], *n.f.* pleating; pleats.

ploiement [plwaˈmã], *n.m.* folding, bending.

plomb [plɔ̃], *n.m.* lead; bullet, shot; plumbline; sinker; custom-house seal; fuse; *à plomb*, vertically.

plombage [plɔ̃ˈbaːʒ], *n.m.* leading, plumbing; filling (*of teeth*).

plombagine [plɔ̃baˈʒin], *n.f.* plumbago, blacklead, graphite.

plomber [plɔ̃ˈbe], *v.t.* to cover with lead, to seal; to fill (*a tooth*); to plumb.

plomberie [plɔ̃ˈbri], *n.f.* plumber's shop; plumbing; lead-making; lead works.

plombier [plɔ̃ˈbje], *n.m.* lead worker; plumber.

plongée [plɔ̃ˈʒe], *n.f.* slope; dive.

plongeoir [plɔ̃ˈʒwaːr], *n.m.* diving-board.

plongeon [plɔ̃ˈʒɔ̃], *n.m.* plunge, dive; (*Orn.*) diver.

plonger [plɔ̃ˈʒe], *v.t.* (*conjug. like* MANGER) to plunge, to dip, to immerse; to throw, to involve.—*v.i.* to dive, to plunge; to submerge (*of submarine*); to pitch (*of ships*). **se plonger**, *v.r.* to be plunged; to immerse oneself (*in*).

plongeur [plɔ̃ˈʒœːr], *a.* (*fem.* -euse) plunging, diving (*bird*).—*n.m.* (*fem.* -euse) diver; dish washer (*in hotels etc.*).

ploutocrate [plutoˈkrat], *n.m.* plutocrat.

ploutocratie [plutokraˈsi], *n.f.* plutocracy.

ploutocratique [plutokraˈtik], *a.* plutocratic.

ployable [plwaˈjabl], *a.* pliable, flexible.

ployer [plwaˈje], *v.t.* (*conjug. like* EMPLOYER) to bend; to fold up.—*v.i.* and **se ployer**,

v.r. to bend, to be folded; to yield, to give way.

pluie [plɥi], *n.f.* rain; (*fig.*) shower.

plumage [plyˈmaːʒ], *n.m.* plumage, feathers.

plumassier [plymaˈsje], *n.m.* (*fem.* -ière) feather merchant or dresser.

plume [plym], *n.f.* feather; plume; quill, pen; nib.

plumeau [plyˈmo], *n.m.* (*pl.* -eaux) feather broom; feather duster.

plumée [plyˈme], *n.f.* penful (*of ink*); plucking (*of poultry*).

plumer [plyˈme], *v.t.* to pluck, to plume; (*fig.*) to fleece.

plumet [plyˈme], *n.m.* plume.

plumetis [plymˈti], *n.m.* feather-stitch.

plumier [plyˈmje], *n.m.* pen box, pen tray.

plupart [plyˈpaːr], *n.f. la plupart*, most, most part, the majority (*de*), most people.

pluralité [plyraliˈte], *n.f.* plurality; pluralism.

pluriel [plyˈrjɛl], *a.* (*fem.* -elle) plural.—*n.m.* plural.

plus [ply], *adv.* more, -er (*que*, than); -est, the most; also, moreover, further, besides; (*with ne*) no more, no longer, never again; *de plus*, besides, moreover.—*n.m.* the most, the maximum; the more.

plusieurs [plyˈzjœːr], *a. pl.* and *pron. indef.* several, some.

plus-que-parfait [plyskaparˈfe], *n.m.* pluperfect.

plutonium [plytoˈnjɔm], *n.m.* plutonium.

plutôt [plyˈto], *adv.* rather, sooner (*que*).

pluvial [plyˈvjal], *a.* (*m. pl.* -aux) pluvial, of rain, rainy.

pluvier [plyˈvje], *n.m.* plover.

pluvieux [plyˈvjø], *a.* (*fem.* -euse) rainy, wet, pluvious.

pluviomètre [plyvjoˈmɛtr], *n.m.* rain gauge.

pluviosité [plyvjoziˈte], *n.f.* rainfall.

pneu [pnø], *n.m.* (*pl.* pneus) *fam. abbr.* [PNEUMATIQUE].

pneumatique [pnømaˈtik], *a.* pneumatic.—*n.m.* tire; express letter (*in Paris*).—*n.f.* pneumatics.

pneumonie [pnømoˈni], *n.f.* pneumonia.

pochade [poˈʃad], *n.f.* rough sketch; (*fig.*) hurried piece of writing etc.

poche [poʃ], *n.f.* pocket; pouch; sack, bag; wrinkle (*in clothes*); crop (*of a bird*).

pocher [poˈʃe], *v.t.* to poach (*eggs*); to give a black eye to; to stencil; to make a rough sketch of.—*v.i.* to become baggy, to bag.

pochet [poˈʃe], *n.m.* nosebag (*of horse*).

pochette [poˈʃɛt], *n.f.* small pocket; small net; folder, jacket (*containers*); fancy handkerchief.

pochoir [poˈʃwaːr], *n.m.* stencil.

podagre [poˈdagr], *a.* gouty.—*n.f.* gout.—*n.* gouty person.

podomètre [podoˈmɛtr], *n.m.* pedometer.

poêle [pwaːl], *n.f.* frying pan.—*n.m.* stove; pall (*at a funeral*).

poêlée [pwaˈle], *n.f.* panful.

poêlon [pwaˈlɔ̃], *n.m.* small saucepan.

poème [poˈɛːm], *n.m.* poem.

poésie [poeˈzi], *n.f.* poetry, verse; poem.

poète [poˈɛːt], *n.m.* poet.

poétesse [poeˈtɛs], *n.f.* poetess.

poétique [poeˈtik], *a.* poetical.—*n.f.* poetics.

poétiquement [poetikˈmã], *adv.* poetically.

poétiser [poeti'ze], *v.t.* to make poetical, to idealize, to poeticize.

pogrom [pɔ'grɔm], *n.m.* pogrom.

poids [pwɑ], *n.m. inv.* weight; heaviness; gravity; load; (*fig.*) importance, consequence; **les poids lourds,** heavy vehicles.

poignant [pwa'nɑ̃], *a.* poignant; sharp, acute, keen.

poignard [pwa'naːr], *n.m.* dagger.

poignarder [pwanar'de], *v.t.* to stab; to knife; (*fig.*) to grieve to the heart.

poigne [pwaɲ], *n.f.* (*colloq.*) grasp, grip; (*fig.*) strength.

poignée [pwa'ɲe], *n.f.* handful; handle, hilt; shake (*of the hand*).

poignet [pwa'nɛ], *n.m.* wrist; wristband, cuff.

poil [pwal], *n.m.* hair (*of animals*); hair (*of persons, other than that of the head*); (*fig.*) beard; nap (*of cloth, of hats etc.*); **à contre-poil,** against the grain.

poilu [pwa'ly], *a.* hairy, shaggy.

poinçon [pwɛ̃'sɔ̃], *n.m.* punch; point, stiletto; awl, stamp, die.

poinçonnage [pwɛ̃sɔ'naːʒ], **poinçonnement** [pwɛ̃sɔn'mɑ̃], *n.m.* stamping, punching.

poinçonner [pwɛ̃sɔ'ne], *v.t.* to punch, to stamp.

poinçonneuse [pwɛ̃sɔ'nøːz], *n.f.* stamping *or* punching machine.

poindre [pwɛ̃ːdr], *v.i. irr.* to dawn, to break; (*fig.*) to appear.

poing [pwɛ̃], *n.m.* fist, hand; (*fig.*) force, brute strength; (*fig.*) **dormir à poings fermés,** to sleep like a log.

point [pwɛ̃], *adv.* (*used with negative*) no, not at all; none (*more emphatic than* **pas**).—*n.m.* point; speck; dot, mark; (*Sch.*) mark; full stop; hole (*of a strap etc.*); (*Needlework*) stitch; matter, question; particular; state, case; degree; place; **à point,** in the nick of time; well done (*of meat*); **en tout point,** in every respect; **sur ce** *or* **en ce point,** on that score.

pointage [pwɛ̃'taːʒ], **pointement** [pwɛ̃t'mɑ̃], *n.m.* pointing, levelling (*of guns*); checking; scrutiny (*of votes*), tally.

pointe [pwɛ̃ːt], *n.f.* point (*sharp end*); tip, head (*of an arrow etc.*); nose (*of a bullet*); cape; peak; etching needle; nail, tack; (*Print.*) bodkin; (*fig.*) dash, flavor; pungency, sharpness; witticism.

pointement [POINTAGE].

pointer [pwɛ̃'te], *v.t.* to point, to aim (*a gun etc.*); to pierce, to stab, to prick; to mark; to tally, to scrutinize (*votes*); to pick up (*ears etc.*); to sharpen.—*v.i.* to point; to spring, to soar; to rear; to sprout.

pointeur [pwɛ̃'tœːr], *n.m.* (*fem.* **-euse**) pointer, marker, checker; (*Artill.*) gun layer.

pointillage [pwɛ̃ti'jaːʒ], **pointillement** [pwɛ̃tij'mɑ̃], *n.m.* dotting, stippling; dotted line.

pointillé [pwɛ̃ti'je], *n.m.* stipple drawing *or* engraving; dotted line.

pointiller [pwɛ̃ti'je], *v.t.* to dot, to stipple; (*fig.*) to tease.—*v.i.* to bicker, to cavil.

pointilleux [pwɛ̃ti'jø], *a.* (*fem.* **-euse**) cavilling, captious; fastidious.

pointu [pwɛ̃'ty], *a.* pointed, sharp; (*fig.*) subtle, captious.

pointure [pwɛ̃'tyːr], *n.f.* (*Print.*) point; size, number (*of shoes, gloves etc.*).

poire [pwaːr], *n.f.* pear; bulb (*rubber*).

poiré [pwa're], *n.m.* perry.

poireau [pwa'ro], **porreau** [pɔ'ro], *n.m.* (*pl.* **-eaux**) leek; wart.

poirée [pwa're], *n.f.* white beet.

poirier [pwa'rje], *n.m.* pear tree.

pois [pwɑ], *n.m. inv.* pea, peas.

poison [pwa'zɔ̃], *n.m.* poison.

poissard [pwa'saːr], *a.* vulgar, low.

poisser [pwa'se], *v.t.* to pitch; to make sticky.

poisseux [pwa'sø], *a.* (*fem.* **-euse**) pitchy, gluey, sticky.

poisson [pwa'sɔ̃], *n.m.* fish; **poisson d'avril,** April fool.

poissonnerie [pwasɔn'ri], *n.f.* fishmarket; fish shop.

poissonneux [pwasɔ'nø], *a.* (*fem.* **-euse**) abounding in fish.

poissonnier [pwasɔ'nje], *n.m.* (*fem.* **-ière**) fishmonger, fishwife.—*n.f.* (**-ière**) fishkettle.

poitrail [pwa'traːj], *n.m.* breast (*of a horse*); breast piece (*of harness*).

poitrinaire [pwatri'nɛːr], *a.* and *n.* consumptive.

poitrine [pwa'trin], *n.f.* chest, breast; breasts; lungs; brisket.

poivrade [pwa'vrad], *n.f.* pepper sauce.

poivre [pwa'vr], *n.m.* pepper.

poivrer [pwa'vre], *v.t.* to pepper.

poivrier [pwavri'je], *n.m.* pepper plant; pepper box.

poivrière [pwavri'jɛːr], *n.f.* pepper plantation; (*Fort.*) corner turret; pepper box.

poix [pwɑ], *n.f.* pitch; shoemakers' wax.

polaire [pɔ'lɛːr], *a.* polar.

polariser [pɔlari'ze], *v.t.* to polarize.

pôle [poːl], *n.m.* (*Astron., Geog.*) pole.

polémique [pɔle'mik], *a.* polemical.—*n.f.* polemics, controversy.

poli [pɔ'li], *a.* polished, glossy, sleek; polite, civil; refined.—*n.m.* polish, finish, gloss.

police [pɔ'lis], *n.f.* police; police regulations; insurance policy; **agent de police,** police constable.

policer [pɔli'se], *v.t.* (*conjug. like* COMMENCER) to establish law and order in; to civilize, to polish, to refine.

polichinelle [pɔliʃi'nɛl], *n.m.* Punch; buffoon; Punch and Judy show.

policier [pɔli'sje], *a.* (*fem.* **-ière**) pertaining to the police; **roman policier,** detective story.—*n.m.* policeman; detective.

policlinique [pɔlikli'nik], *n.f.* out-patients' department.

poliment [pɔli'mɑ̃], *adv.* politely.

poliomyélite [pɔljɔmje'lit], *n.f.* poliomyelitis.

polir [pɔ'liːr], *v.t.* to polish, to burnish; (*fig.*) to civilize, to refine. **se polir,** *v.r.* to become polished; to become refined.

polissage [pɔli'saːʒ], **polissement** [pɔlis'mɑ̃], *n.m.* polishing, finishing.

polisseur [pɔli'sœːr], *n.m.* (*fem.* **-euse**) polisher.

polissoir [pɔli'swaːr], *n.m.* polisher (*tool*).

polisson [pɔli'sɔ̃], *a.* (*fem.* **-onne**) loose, naughty, licentious, smutty.—*n.m.* (*fem.* **-onne**) mischievous child, scamp; loose person.

249

polissonner [pɔliso'ne], *v.i.* to run about the streets (*of children*).

polissonnerie [pɔlisɔn'ri], *n.f.* smutty joke, lewd act.

polissure [pɔli'sy:r], *n.f.* polishing.

politesse [pɔli'tɛs], *n.f.* politeness, civility, polite attention; compliment.

politicien [pɔliti'sjɛ̃], *n.m.* (*fem.* **-enne**) (*usu. pej.*) politician.

politique [pɔli'tik], *a.* political; (*fig.*) politic, prudent, wise.—*n.f.* politics; policy, discretion.—*n.m.* politician, statesman.

politiquement [pɔlitik'mɑ̃], *adv.* politically; (*fig.*) shrewdly.

polka [pɔl'ka], *n.f.* polka.

pollen [pɔl'lɛn], *n.m.* pollen.

pollinisation [pɔlliniza'sjɔ̃], *n.f.* pollinization.

polluer [pɔl'lɥe], *v.t.* to pollute; to defile; to profane.

pollution [pɔly'sjɔ̃], *n.f.* pollution; profanation.

polo [pɔ'lo], *n.m.* polo.

Pologne [pɔ'lɔɲ], la, *f.* Poland.

polonais [pɔlo'nɛ], *a.* Polish.—*n.m.* Polish (*language*); (**Polonais,** *fem.* **-aise**) Pole.—*n.f.* (**-aise**) Polonaise (*dress, dance, tune*).

poltron [pɔl'trɔ̃], *a.* (*fem.* **-onne**) cowardly, chicken-hearted. —*n.m.* (*fem.* **-onne**) coward, poltroon.

poltronnerie [pɔltrɔn'ri], *n.f.* cowardice, poltroonery.

polycopier [pɔlikɔ'pje], *v.t.* to cyclostyle.

polygamie [pɔliga'mi], *n.f.* polygamy.

polyglotte [pɔli'glɔt], *a.* and *n.* polyglot.

polytechnique [pɔlitɛk'nik], *a.* polytechnic.

pommade [pɔ'mad], *n.f.* pomade; ointment.

pomme [pɔm], *n.f.* apple; ball, knob; head (*of a cabbage, lettuce, walking-stick etc.*); (*pop.*) head, nut; *pomme de pin,* fir cone; *pomme de terre,* potato.

pommé [pɔ'me], *a.* grown to a round head; (*colloq.*) complete, downright.

pommeau [pɔ'mo], *n.m.* (*pl.* **-eaux**) pommel (*of a saddle, sword etc.*); head, knob.

pommelé [pɔm'le], *a.* dappled, mottled.

pommeler (se) [səpɔm'le], *v.r.* (*conjug. like* APPELER) to become dappled.

pommer [pɔ'me], *v.i.* and **se pommer,** *v.r.* to grow to a firm round head (*of cabbage, lettuce etc.*).

pommette [pɔ'mɛt], *n.f.* apple-like ball or knob; cheek bone; (*C*) crab apple.

pommier [pɔ'mje], *n.m.* apple tree.

pompe [pɔ̃:p], *n.f.* pomp, ceremony; display; pump, inflator; *pompe à incendie,* fire-engine.

pomper [pɔ̃'pe], *v.t.* to pump; (*fig.*) to suck up.—*v.i.* to pump.

pompeusement [pɔ̃pøz'mɑ̃], *adv.* solemnly, with pomp.

pompeux [pɔ̃'pø], *a.* (*fem.* **-euse**) stately, solemn; pompous.

pompier [pɔ̃'pje], *a. inv.* conventional (*art, style*).—*n.m.* fireman.

pompiste [pɔ̃'pist], *n.* pump attendant (*at gas pump etc.*).

pompon [pɔ̃'pɔ̃], *n.m.* pompon, top-knot.

pomponner [pɔ̃pɔ'ne], *v.t.* to ornament with pompons, to deck out. **se pomponner,** *v.r.* to dress oneself up.

ponce [pɔ̃:s], *n.f.* pumice; (*Drawing*) pounce.

ponceau (1) [pɔ̃'so], *n.m.* (*pl.* **-eaux**) small bridge, culvert.

ponceau (2) [pɔ̃'so], *a.* poppy-red.—*n.m.* (*pl.* **-eaux**) corn poppy.

Ponce Pilate [pɔ̃spi'lat], *m.* Pontius Pilate.

poncer [pɔ̃'se], *v.t.* (*conjug. like* COMMENCER) to pumice; (*Drawing*) to pounce.

poncif [pɔ̃'sif], *n.m.* pounced drawing; (*fig.*) commonplace piece of work.

ponctualité [pɔ̃ktɥali'te], *n.f.* punctuality.

ponctuation [pɔ̃ktɥa'sjɔ̃], *n.f.* punctuation.

ponctué [pɔ̃k'tɥe], *a.* punctuated; dotted; *ligne ponctuée,* dotted line.

ponctuel [pɔ̃k'tɥɛl], *a.* (*fem.* **-elle**) punctual, exact.

ponctuellement [pɔ̃ktɥɛl'mɑ̃], *adv.* punctually.

ponctuer [pɔ̃k'tɥe], *v.t.* to punctuate; to point.

pondéré [pɔ̃de're], *a.* poised, calm, self-controlled.

pondérer [pɔ̃de're], *v.t.* (*conjug. like* CÉDER) to poise, to balance.

pondeur [pɔ̃'dœ:r], *a.* (*fem.* **-euse**) good laying (*of poultry etc.*); (*colloq.*) productive.—*n.f.* (**-euse**) good layer.

pondre [pɔ̃:dr], *v.t.* to lay (*eggs*).

poney [pɔ'ne], *n.m.* pony.

pont [pɔ̃], *n.m.* bridge; deck; *Ponts et Chaussées,* (*France*) Department of Bridges and Highways.

ponte (1) [pɔ̃:t], *n.f.* laying of eggs.

ponte (2) [pɔ̃:t], *n.m.* better; (*fam.*) V.I.P.

ponté [pɔ̃'te], *a.* decked (*of ship*); *non ponté,* open (*boat*).

ponter [pɔ̃'te], *v.i.* to punt, to gamble.

pontet [pɔ̃'te], *n.m.* trigger guard; saddle-tree.

pontife [pɔ̃'tif], *n.m.* pontiff.

pontifier [pɔ̃ti'fje], *v.i.* (*fam.*) to act or speak solemnly or pompously; to pontificate, to lay down the law.

pont-levis [pɔ̃l'vi], *n.m.* (*pl.* **ponts-levis**) drawbridge.

ponton [pɔ̃'tɔ̃], *n.m.* bridge of boats; pontoon.

popeline [pɔ'plin], *n.f.* poplin.

populace [pɔpy'las], *n.f.* populace, mob, rabble.

populacier [pɔpyla'sje], *a.* (*fem.* **-ière**) low, vulgar.

populaire [pɔpy'lɛ:r], *a.* popular; common. —*n.m.* populace, rabble.

populairement [pɔpylɛr'mɑ̃], *adv.* popularly.

populariser [pɔpylari'ze], *v.t.* to popularize.

popularité [pɔpylari'te], *n.f.* popularity.

population [pɔpyla'sjɔ̃], *n.f.* population.

populeux [pɔpy'lø], *a.* (*fem.* **-euse**) populous.

porc [pɔ:r], *n.m.* pig; swine; pork.

porcelaine [pɔrsa'lɛn], *n.f.* porcelain, china, chinaware.

porcelet [pɔrsa'lɛ], *n.m.* young pig, piglet.

porc-épic [pɔrke'pik], *n.m.* (*pl.* **porcs-épics**) porcupine; (*Am.*) hedgehog.

porche [pɔrʃ], *n.m.* porch.

porcher [pɔr'ʃe], *n.m.* (*fem.* **-ère**) swineherd.

porcherie [pɔrʃ'ri], *n.f.* pigsty, piggery.

porcin [pɔr'sɛ̃], *a.* porcine.—*n.m.* (*pl.*) pigs.

pore [pɔ:r], *n.m.* pore.

poreux [pɔ're], *a.* (*fem.* **-euse**) porous.

pornographie [pɔrnɔgra'fi], *n.f.* pornography.

pornographique [pɔrnɔgra'fik], *a.* pornographic.

porphyre [pɔr'fi:r], n.m. porphyry.
porphyriser [pɔrfiri'ze], v.t. to porphyrize; to pulverize.
porreau [POIREAU].
port (1) [pɔ:r], n.m. haven, harbor, port; seaport town; *arriver à bon port*, to arrive safely; (*fig.*) to end happily; *port d'escale*, port of call.
port (2) [pɔ:r], n.m. carrying, carriage; postage; bearing, gait; (*Naut.*) tonnage.
portable [pɔr'tabl], a. portable; wearable.
portage [pɔr'ta:ʒ], n.m. carriage, transport.
portail [pɔr'ta:j], n.m. (pl. **-s**) portal, front gate (of a church etc.).
portant [pɔr'tɑ̃], a. bearing, carrying; *être bien portant*, to be in good health.
portatif [pɔrta'tif], a. (fem. **-tive**) portable.
porte [pɔrt], n.f. doorway, gateway; door; gate; entrance; eye (of hooks etc.); defile.
porté [pɔr'te], a. carried; inclined, prone, disposed (à); projected (of shadows).
porte-à-faux [pɔrta'fo], n.m. inv. overhang; *en porte-à-faux*, overhanging; unsteady.
porte-affiches [pɔrta'fiʃ], n.m. inv. advertising board.
porte-avions [pɔrta'vjɔ̃], n.m. inv. aircraft carrier.
porte-bagages [pɔrtba'ga:ʒ], n.m. inv. luggage rack.
porte-billets [pɔrtbi'jɛ], n.m. inv. note case; (Am.) bill-fold.
porte-bonheur [pɔrtbɔ'nœ:r], n.m. inv. good-luck charm; mascot.
porte-bouteilles [pɔrtbu'tɛ:j], n.m. inv. bottle rack, wine bin.
porte-chapeaux [pɔrtʃa'po], n.m. inv. hat-stand.
porte-cigarettes [pɔrtsiga'rɛt], n.m. inv. cigarette case.
porte-clefs [pɔrta'kle], n.m. inv. key ring.
porte-couteau [pɔrtku'to], n.m. inv. knife rest.
porte-crayon [pɔrtkrɛ'jɔ̃], n.m. inv. pencil case.
porte-documents [pɔrtdɔky'mɑ̃], n.m. inv. dispatch case.
porte-drapeau [pɔrtdra'po], n.m. inv. ensign, color bearer.
portée [pɔr'te], n.f. brood, litter; reach (of the hand, arm etc.); hearing; range, shot; scope; capacity; import, significance; bearing; resting-point; (Mus.) stave.
porte-étendard [pɔrtetɑ̃'da:r], n.m. inv. standard bearer.
porte-fenêtre [pɔrtfə'nɛ:tr], n.f. (pl. **portes-fenêtres**) French window.
portefeuille [pɔrtə'fœ:j], n.m. wallet; (fig.) portfolio; office.
porte-flambeau [pɔrtflɑ̃'bo], n.m. inv. torch bearer, linkman.
porte-jupe [pɔrtə'ʒyp], n.m. inv. skirt-hanger.
porte-livres [pɔrtə'li:vr], n.m. inv. book rest.
porte-malheur [pɔrtma'lœ:r], n.m. inv. bird of ill omen, bearer of ill luck.
portemanteau [pɔrtmɑ̃'to], n.m. (pl. **-eaux**) coat stand, coat rail; peg.
porte-masse [pɔrtə'mas], n.m. inv. mace bearer.
porte-mine(s) [pɔrtə'min], n.m. inv. mechanical pencil.

porte-monnaie [pɔrtmɔ'nɛ], n.m. inv. purse.
porte-musique [pɔrtmy'zik], n.m. inv. music case.
porte-parapluies [pɔrtpara'plɥi], n.m. inv. umbrella stand.
porte-parole [pɔrtpa'rɔl], n.m. inv. mouthpiece, spokesman.
porte-plume [pɔrtə'plym], n.m. inv. pen holder.
porte-queue [pɔrtə'kø], n.m. inv. train bearer; swallowtail butterfly.
porter [pɔr'te], v.t. to carry, to bear, to support; to endure; to bring, to take; to wear; to deal (blows etc.); to turn (the eyes etc.); to declare, to show.—v.i. to bear; to rest, to lie; to take effect; to hit; to reach; to carry (of a gun etc.); (Naut.) to stand, to bear off; to be with young (of animals). **se porter**, v.r. to go, to repair, to move; to resort, to flock; to be inclined or disposed, to tend; to be, to do (of health); to be worn; to present oneself, to stand forth; to turn, to be directed.
porte-rame [pɔrt'ram], n.m. inv. oarlock.
porte-serviette(s) [pɔrtsɛr'vjɛt], n.m. inv. towel rail.
porteur [pɔr'tœ:r], n.m. (fem. **-euse**) porter, carrier, bearer; holder; sleeper (on railway track).
porte-voix [pɔrt'vwa], n.m. inv. megaphone.
portier [pɔr'tje], n.m. (fem. **-ière** (1)) porter, door-keeper.
portière (2) [pɔr'tjɛ:r], n.f. door-curtain, door (of vehicle).
portion [pɔr'sjɔ̃], n.f. portion, part, share, allowance.
portionner [pɔrsjɔ'ne], v.t. to share out.
portique [pɔr'tik], n.m. portico; porch.
porto [pɔr'to], n.m. port (wine).
portrait [pɔr'trɛ], n.m. portrait, likeness, picture.
portraitiste [pɔrtrɛ'tist], n. portrait painter.
portugais [pɔrty'gɛ], a. Portuguese.—n.m. Portuguese (language); (**Portugais**, fem. **-aise**) Portuguese (person).
Portugal [pɔrty'gal], le, m. Portugal.
pose [po:z], n.f. laying, setting; pose, posture, attitude; posing, affectation; sitting (for one's portrait etc.); hanging (of bells); (Mil.) posting (of sentries); (Phot.) time exposure.
posé [po'ze], a. laid, set, poised; bearing, resting; sedate, staid, sober; *cela posé*, this being granted.
posément [poze'mɑ̃], adv. calmly; sedately.
poser [po'ze], v.t. to put, to put in (a lock, a window pane); to place, to lay down; to hang; to suppose, to grant; to post (sentries etc.); to lay down, to state; (Mus.) to pitch; to sit (for portrait); *poser une question*, to ask a question.—v.i. to lie, to rest (sur); to stand, to pose, to sit (for one's portrait); to show off. **se poser**, v.r. to perch (of birds etc.); to come down, to land (plane); to set up (en), to play the part (en).
poseur [po'zœ:r], n.m. (Rail.) track layer.—n.m. (fem. **-euse**) (colloq.) poseur, snob, prig.
positif [pozi'tif], a. (fem. **-tive**) positive, certain; practical, actual, matter-of-fact.—n.m. positive reality; certainty, fact; (Phot., Ciné., Gram.) positive.

251

position

position [pɔzi′sjɔ̃], *n.f.* position, situation; status, standing; case, state, circumstances.
positivement [pozitiv′mã], *adv.* positively, exactly.
possédé [pose′de], *a.* possessed.—*n.m.* (*fem.* **-ée**) person possessed, madman, maniac.
posséder [pɔse′de], *v.t.* (*conjug. like* CÉDER) to possess, to be possessed of, to own; to be master of; to be conversant with; to dominate (*a person*); (*pop.*) to deceive. **se posséder**, *v.r.* to master one's passions, to contain oneself.
possesseur [pɔse′sœːr], *n.m.* possessor, owner, occupier.
possessif [pɔse′sif], *a.* (*fem.* **-lve**) possessive.—*n.m.* (*Gram.*) possessive adjective or pronoun.
possession [pɔse′sjɔ̃], *n.f.* possession; property.
possibilité [pɔsibili′te], *n.f.* possibility; (*pl.*) facilities.
possible [pɔ′sibl], *a.* possible.—*n.m.* possibility; *au possible*, extremely; *je ferai tout mon possible*, I'll do the best I can.
postal [pɔs′tal], *a.* (*m. pl.* **-aux**) postal, of the post.
poste (1) [pɔst], *n.m.* post, station; guardhouse; place, employment, post; (*Naut.*) berth; (*Teleph.*) extension; entry (*in books*); *poste de radio*, radio set; *poste d'incendie*, fire station.
poste (2) [pɔst], *n.f.* post (*relay*); post stage; postal service; post office, mail; *bureau de poste*, post office.
poster [pɔs′te], *v.t.* to station, to post (*sentry or letter*).
postérieur [pɔste′rjœːr], *a.* posterior, later; behind.—*n.m.* (*colloq.*) posterior.
postérieurement [pɔsterjœr′mã], *adv.* subsequently.
postérité [pɔsteri′te], *n.f.* posterity.
posthume [pɔs′tym], *a.* posthumous.
postiche [pɔs′tiʃ], *a.* superadded; false, artificial.—*n.m.* wig.
postier [pɔs′tje], *n.m.* (*fem.* **-lère**) postoffice employee.
postillon [pɔsti′jɔ̃], *n.m.* postilion; post boy.
postscolaire [pɔstskɔ′leːr], *a.* continuation (*class*); *enseignement postscolaire*, adult education.
post-scriptum [pɔstskrip′tɔm] (*abbr.* **P.S.**), *n.m. inv.* postscript.
postulant [pɔsty′lã], *n.m.* (*fem.* **-e**) candidate, applicant; postulant.
postuler [pɔsty′le], *v.t.* to solicit, to apply for.—*v.i.* (*Law*) to act on behalf of a client.
posture [pɔs′tyːr], *n.f.* posture, attitude; situation.
pot [po], *n.m.* pot; jug, tankard, flagon, can, jar; (*C*) half a gallon.
potable [pɔ′tabl], *a.* drinkable (*water*).
potage [pɔ′taːʒ], *n.m.* soup.
potager (1) [pɔta′ʒe], *n.m.* kitchen garden; kitchen stove.
potager (2) [pɔta′ʒe], *a.* (*fem.* **-ère**) culinary; *jardin potager*, kitchen garden.
potasse [pɔ′tas], *n.f.* potash.
potassium [pɔta′sjɔm], *n.m.* potassium.
pot-au-feu [pɔto′fø], *n.m. inv.* beef boiled with carrots etc.; broth of this.
pot-de-vin [pod′vɛ̃], *n.m.* (*pl.* **pots-de-vin**) gratuity; bribe; hush money.

poteau [pɔ′to], *n.m.* (*pl.* **-eaux**) post, stake.
potée [pɔ′te], *n.f.* potful; (*colloq.*) swarm (*of children etc.*); putty; (*Metal.*) molding.
potelé [pɔ′tle], *a.* plump, chubby.
potence [pɔ′tãːs], *n.f.* gallows, gibbet; bracket; crutch; *gibier de potence*, jailbird.
potentat [pɔtã′ta], *n.m.* potentate.
potentiel [pɔtã′sjɛ], *a.* (*fem.* **-elle**) potential, —*n.m.* potentialities.
potentiellement [pɔtãsjɛl′mã], *adv.* potentially.
poterie [pɔ′tri], *n.f.* pottery, earthenware.
poterne [pɔ′tɛrn], *n.f.* postern.
potiche [pɔ′tiʃ], *n.f.* China *or* Japan porcelain vase.
potier [pɔ′tje], *n.m.* potter.
potin [pɔ′tɛ̃], *n.m.* pinchbeck; (*pl.*) gossip.
potion [po′sjɔ̃], *n.f.* potion, draft.
potiron [pɔti′rɔ̃], *n.m.* pumpkin.
pou [pu], *n.m.* (*pl.* **poux**) louse.
pouah! [pwa], *int.* ugh! disgusting!
poubelle [pu′bɛl], *n.f.* dustbin; (*Am.*) ashcan.
pouce [pus], *n.m.* thumb; big toe; inch; *un morceau sur le pouce*, a snack; (*C*) *faire du pouce*, to hitch-hike.
poucet [pu′sɛ], *n.m.* *le petit Poucet*, Tom Thumb.
pouding [pu′diŋ], *n.m.* plum pudding.
poudre [pudr], *n.f.* powder; gunpowder; dust; *sucre en poudre*, powdered sugar.
poudrer [pu′dre], *v.t.* to powder, to sprinkle with powder.
poudrerie [pudrə′ri], *n.f.* gunpowderfactory; (*C*) blizzard.
poudreux [pu′drø], *a.* (*fem.* **-euse**) dusty, powdery.
poudrier [pudri′e], *n.m.* (powder) compact.
poudrière [pudri′ɛːr], *n.f.* powder mill, magazine; sand box.
poudroyer [pudrwa′je], *v.i.* (*conjug. like* EMPLOYER) to rise in dust; to be dusty (*of roads etc.*).
pouf! (1) [puf], *int.* plop! flop! phew!
pouf (2) [puf], *n.m.* ottoman (*seat*), pouf; blurb(*advertisement*).
pouffer [pu′fe], *v.i.* *pouffer de rire*, to burst out laughing, to guffaw.
pouilleux [pu′jø], *a.* and *n.m.* (*fem.* **-euse**) lousy; wretched, mean (person).
poulailler [pula′je], *n.m.* hen house; (*of persons*) poulterer; (*Theat.*) gods, gallery.
poulain [pu′lɛ̃], *n.m.* foal, colt.
poularde [pu′lard], *n.f.* fat pullet.
poulbot [pul′bo], *n.m.* Paris street urchin.
poule [pul], *n.f.* hen; fowl; pool (*at games*); eliminating round (*in a competition*).
poulet [pu′lɛ], *n.m.* chicken; love letter.
poulette [pu′lɛt], *n.f.* pullet.
pouliche [pu′liʃ], *n.f.* filly.
poulie [pu′li], *n.f.* pulley; (*Naut.*) block.
pouliner [puli′ne], *v.i.* to foal (*of mares*).
poulinière [puli′njeːr], *a.f.* and *n.f.* (*jument poulinière*, brood mare.
poulpe [pulp], *n.m.* octopus, devil-fish.
pouls [pu], *n.m.* pulse; *se tâter le pouls*, to feel one's pulse.
poumon [pu′mɔ̃], *n.m.* lung; *poumon d'acier*, iron lung.

poupard [pu'pa:r], *a.* chubby.—*n.m.* baby; doll.

poupe [pup], *n.f.* stern, poop.

poupée [pu'pe], *n.f.* doll; puppet; tailor's dummy.

poupin [pu'pɛ̃], *a.* fresh-colored; rosy.

poupon [pu'pɔ̃], *n.m.* (*fem.* **-onne**) baby; plump, chubby-cheeked boy *or* girl.

pouponnière [pupɔ'njɛ:r], *n.f.* (*public*) day nursery.

pour [pu:r], *prep.* for; on account of; on behalf of; as regards, as for; in order; although.—*n.m.* for, pro.

pourboire [pur'bwa:r], *n.m.* tip, gratuity.

pourceau [pur'so], *n.m.* (*pl.* **-eaux**) hog, pig, swine.

pour-cent [pur'sɑ̃], **pourcentage** [pursɑ̃'ta:ʒ], *n.m.* percentage.

pourchasser [purʃa'se], *v.t.* to pursue, to chase, to badger.

pourfendre [pur'fɑ̃:dr], *v.t.* to cleave asunder.

pourlécher [purle'ʃe], *v.t.* (*conjug. like* CÉDER) to lick all over. **se pourlécher**, *v.r.* to lick one's lips.

pourparler [purpar'le], *n.m.* (*usu. in pl.*) parley, negotiations; talks.

pourpoint [pur'pwɛ̃], *n.m.* doublet.

pourpre [purpr], *a.* purple, dark red.—*n.f.* purple (*stuff*); (*fig.*) sovereign dignity; cardinalate.—*n.m.* purple, crimson (*color*).

pourpré [pur'pre], *a.* purple.

pourquoi [pur'kwa], *adv.* and *conj.* why, wherefore; *pourquoi pas?* why not?—*n.m. inv.* the reason why.

pourri [pu'ri], *a.* rotten; *temps pourri*, muggy weather.—*n.m.* the rotten part, rottenness.

pourrir [pu'ri:r], *v.t.* to make rotten, to corrupt.—*v.i.* to rot; (*fig.*) to perish. **se pourrir**, *v.r.* to become rotten, to go bad.

pourrissable [puri'sabl], *a.* perishable.

pourrissant [puri'sɑ̃], *a.* rotting, causing rot.

pourriture [puri'ty:r], *n.f.* rot, rottenness, putrefaction; (*fig.*) corruption.

poursuite [pur'sɥit], *n.f.* pursuit, chase; prosecution; (*Law*) suit, proceedings.

poursuivable [pursɥi'vabl], *a.* actionable.

poursuivant [pursɥi'vɑ̃], *a.* suing, prosecuting.—*n.m.* suitor.—*n.m.* (*fem.* **-e**) prosecutor, plaintiff.

poursuivre [pur'sɥi:vr], *v.t. irr.* (*conjug. like* SUIVRE) to pursue; to seek; to persecute; to haunt; to go on with; to follow up; (*Law*) to sue, to prosecute.—*v.i.* to pursue, to go on, to continue. **se poursuivre**, *v.r.* to continue, to follow its course.

pourtant [pur'tɑ̃], *adv.* however, yet, still, nevertheless.

pourtour [pur'tu:r], *n.m.* periphery, circumference; aisle (*in a theatre etc.*); precincts (*of cathedral*).

pourvoi [pur'vwa], *n.m.* (*Law*) appeal.

pourvoir [pur'vwa:r], *v.t. irr.* to invest with, to appoint; to provide, to supply, to endow. —*v.i.* (*followed by* à) to see to, to attend to, to provide for; to make an appointment to. **se pourvoir**, *v.r.* to provide oneself; to appeal.

pourvoyeur [purvwa'jœ:r], *n.m.* (*fem.* **-euse**) purveyor, provider, caterer.

pourvu que [pur'vykə], *conj. phr.* provided that, provided.

pousse [pus], *n.f.* shoot, sprout.

pousse-café [puska'fe], *n.m. inv.* (*fam.*) liqueur (*after coffee*).

poussée [pu'se], *n.f.* pushing; shove; thrust (*of arches etc.*); pressure (*of business etc.*).

pousse-pousse [pus'pus], *n.m. inv.* rickshaw (*carriage or man*).

pousser [pu'se], *v.t.* to push, to thrust, to shove; to drive on; to carry on, to extend; to grow, to send forth (*of plants etc.*); to urge, to provoke; to assist, to help on; to utter, to heave (*a sigh etc.*); to deal (*a blow etc.*).—*v.i.* to sprout, to shoot (*of plants*); to grow (*of the hair, nails etc.*); to push on, to go on; to bulge; to be broken-winded (*of horses*). **se pousser**, *v.r.* to push forward, to push oneself forward; to push each other, to jostle.

poussette [pu'sɛt], *n.f.* go-cart; movement in dancing.

poussier [pu'sje], *n.m.* coal dust, screenings.

poussière [pu'sjɛ:r], *n.f.* dust; spray (*of water*).

poussiéreux [pusje'rø], *a.* (*fem.* **-euse**) dusty.

poussif [pu'sif], *a.* (*fem.* **-ive**) shortwinded.

poussin [pu'sɛ̃], *n.m.* chick, chicken just hatched.

poussinière [pusi'njɛ:r], *n.f.* chicken coop; incubator.

poutre [putr], *n.f.* beam; girder.

poutrelle [pu'trɛl], *n.f.* small beam.

pouvoir [pu'vwa:r], *v.t. irr.* to be able to do.— *v.i.* to be able (*can etc.*); to have power; to be allowed (*may etc.*); (*impers.*) to be possible; *il peut arriver que*, it may happen that; *il se peut que*, it is possible that; *on ne peut plus*, (*followed by adj.*) exceedingly; *sauve qui peut*, every man for himself.—*n.m.* power; might; authority; command, government.

prairie [prɛ'ri], *n.f.* meadow, grass-land, grass field; (*U.S.*) prairie.

praline [pra'lin], *n.f.* burnt almond.

praliner [prali'ne], *v.t.* to brown in sugar (*like burnt almonds*).

praticabilité [pratikabili'te], *n.f.* practicability, feasibility.

praticable [prati'kabl], *a.* practicable, feasible; passable (*of roads*); accessible; (*Theat.*) real, usable.

praticien [prati'sjɛ̃], *a.* (*fem.* **-enne**) practicing.—*n.m.* (*fem.* **-enne**) practitioner.

pratiquant [prati'kɑ̃], *a.* church-going.— *n.m.* (*fem.* **-e**) church-goer.

pratique [pra'tik], *a.* practical; experienced. —*n.f.* practice; execution; method; experience; usage; custom (*of tradesman*), practice (*of attorneys, physicians etc.*); customer; (*pl.*) dealings.

pratiquement [pratik'mɑ̃], *adv.* in actual fact, practically; in a practical way.

pratiquer [prati'ke], *v.t.* to practice, to exercise; to frequent; to tamper with, to bribe; to obtain; (*Arch.*) to contrive. **se pratiquer**, *v.r.* to be in use, to be practiced.

pré [pre], *n.m.* meadow.

préalable [prea'labl], *a.* preliminary; previous.—*n.m. au préalable*, previously, first of all.

préalablement [prealablə'mɑ̃], *adv.* previously, first, to begin with.

préambule [preã'byl], *n.m.* preamble, preface.

préau [pre'o], *n.m.* (*pl.* **-aux**) courtyard (*of a convent* or *prison*); (*sch.*) covered playground.

préavis [prea'vi], *n.m. inv.* (previous) notice.

précaire [pre'kɛːr], *a.* precarious; uncertain.

précairement [prekɛr'mã], *adv.* precariously.

précaution [preko'sjɔ̃], *n.f.* precaution; caution, care.

précautionner [prekosjo'ne], *v.t.* to warn, to caution. **se précautionner**, *v.r.* to take precautions.

précédemment [preseda'mã], *adv.* before, previously.

précédent [prese'dã], *a.* preceding, former.—*n.m.* precedent.

précéder [prese'de], *v.t.* (*conjug. like* CÉDER) to precede, to go before; to take precedence (*of*).

précepte [pre'sɛpt], *n.m.* precept, rule.

précepteur [presɛp'tœːr], *n.m.* (*fem.* **-trice**) tutor, teacher.

prêche [prɛːʃ], *n.m.* sermon (*Protestant*); Protestant church.

prêcher [prɛ'ʃe], *v.t.* to preach; to exhort; to extol, to praise.—*v.i.* to preach.

prêcheur [prɛ'ʃœːr], *n.m.* (*fem.* **-euse**) preacher.

précieusement [presjøz'mã], *adv.* preciously; carefully; affectedly.

précieux [pre'sjø], *a.* (*fem.* **-euse**) precious, valuable; affected.—*n.m.* affectation.—*n.m.* (*fem.* **-euse**) affected person.

préciosité [presjozi'te], *n.f.* affectation.

précipice [presi'pis], *n.m.* precipice.

précipitamment [presipita'mã], *adv.* precipitately, hurriedly, rashly.

précipitation [presipita'sjɔ̃], *n.f.* haste, hurry; (*Chem.*) precipitation.

précipité [presipi'te], *a.* precipitated, hurled; precipitate, hasty, sudden.—*n.m.* (*Chem.*) precipitate.

précipiter [presipi'te], *v.t.* to precipitate, to hurl; to hasten, to accelerate; (*Chem.*) to precipitate. **se précipiter**, *v.r.* to precipitate, throw or hurl oneself; to rush forward, to spring forth, to dart.

précis [pre'si], *a.* fixed, precise, exact; formal, terse, concise.—*n.m.* summary, abstract.

précisément [presize'mã], *adv.* precisely, exactly; quite; just so.

préciser [presi'ze], *v.t.* to state precisely, to specify.

précision [presi'zjɔ̃], *n.f.* precision, preciseness.

précité [presi'te], *a.* afore-mentioned.

précoce [pre'kɔs], *a.* precocious, early, forward.

précocité [prekosi'te], *n.f.* precocity.

préconçu [prekɔ̃'sy], *a.* preconceived.

préconiser [prekɔni'ze], *v.t.* to advocate, to recommend.

préconnaissance [prekɔnɛ'sãːs], *n.f.* foreknowledge.

précurseur [prekyr'sœːr], *n.m.* forerunner, precursor, harbinger.

prédateur [preda'tœːr], *a.* (*fem.* **-trice**) (*Ent.*) predatory.

prédécéder [predese'de], *v.i.* (*conjug. like* CÉDER) to predecease (*someone*).

prédestination [predɛstinɑ'sjɔ̃], *n.f.* predestination.

prédestiné [predɛsti'ne], *a.* predestined; predetermined.—*n.m.* (*fem.* **-ée**) one of the elect.

prédicateur [predika'tœːr], *n.m.* (*fem.* **-trice**) preacher.

prédiction [predik'sjɔ̃], *n.f.* prediction, forecast.

prédilection [predilɛk'sjɔ̃], *n.f.* predilection, preference.

prédire [pre'diːr], *v.t. irr.* (*conjug. like* MÉDIRE) to predict, to foretell.

prédisposer [predispo'ze], *v.t.* to predispose.

prédisposition [predispozi'sjɔ̃], *n.f.* predisposition.

prédominance [predomi'nãːs], *n.f.* predominance, ascendancy.

prédominant [predomi'nã], *a.* predominant.

prédominer [predomi'ne], *v.t.* to prevail over.—*v.i.* to predominate.

prééminence [preemi'nãːs], *n.f.* pre-eminence.

prééminent [preemi'nã], *a.* pre-eminent.

préemption [preãp'sjɔ̃], *n.f.* pre-emption.

préfabriqué [prefabri'ke], *a.* prefabricated.

préface [pre'fas], *n.f.* preface; foreword.

préfecture [prefɛk'tyːr], *n.f.* prefecture; **préfecture de police**, Paris police headquarters.

préférable [prefe'rabl], *a.* preferable.

préférablement [preferabla'mã], *adv.* preferably.

préféré [prefe're], *a.* favorite.

préférence [prefe'rãːs], *n.f.* preference.

préférer [prefe're], *v.t.* (*conjug. like* CÉDER) to prefer.

préfet [pre'fɛ], *n.m.* prefect; chief administrator of a department in France; **préfet de police**, chief commissioner of Parisian police.

préhensile [preã'sil], *a.* prehensile.

préhistorique [preisto'rik], *a.* prehistoric.

préjudice [preʒy'dis], *n.m.* detriment, injury, damage, prejudice.

préjudiciable [preʒydi'sjabl], *a.* prejudicial, detrimental.

préjudicier [preʒydi'sje], *v.i.* to be prejudicial or detrimental.

préjugé [preʒy'ʒe], *n.m.* presumption, prejudice; (*Law*) precedent.

préjuger [preʒy'ʒe], *v.t.* (*conjug. like* MANGER) to prejudge.

prélasser (se) [saprela'se], *v.r.* to strut, to stalk along.

prélat [pre'la], *n.m.* prelate.

prélèvement [prelɛv'mã], *n.m.* deduction; sample; (*Med.*) swab.

prélever [prela've], *v.t.* (*conjug. like* AMENER) to deduct; to appropriate.

préliminaire [prelimi'nɛːr], *a.* and *n.m.* preliminary.

prélude [pre'lyd], *n.m.* prelude.

prématuré [prematy're], *a.* premature, untimely.

prématurément [prematyre'mã], *adv.* prematurely.

préméditation [premedita'sjɔ̃], *n.f.* premeditation.

préméditer [premedi'te], *v.t.* to premeditate.

prémices [pre'mis], *n.f. pl.* first-fruits; *(fig.)* beginning.

premier [prə'mje], *a.* *(fem.* **-ière)** first; foremost, best, chief; former *(of two)*; early, pristine, primeval; *(Arith.)* prime; *au premier abord*, at first sight; *le premier rang*, the front rank; *matières premières*, raw materials.—*n.m.* *(fem.* **-ière)** chief, head, leader.—*n.m.* first floor; first of the month etc.—*n.f.* **(-ière)** *(Theat.)* first night.

premièrement [prəmjɛr'mã], *adv.* firstly, in the first place.

prémonition [premoni'sjɔ̃], *n.f.* premonition.

prémunir [premy'ni:r], *v.t.* to forewarn, to caution, to secure beforehand. **se prémunir**, *v.r.* to provide *(contre)*.

prenant [prə'nã], *a.* taking, prehensile; *(fig.)* fascinating; *partie prenante*, payee.

prendre [prã:dr], *v.t.* *irr.* to take; to take up; to snatch; to seize; to capture; to contract, to catch *(a cold etc.)*; to choose; to fetch; to assume; to collect *(votes etc.)*; to help oneself to; to conduct *(an affair etc.)*; to entertain *(a feeling etc.)*; *en prendre à son aise*, to take it easy; *prendre pour dit*, to take for granted; *que je t'y prenne un peu!* just let me catch you at it!—*v.i.* to take; to take root; to congeal, to freeze; to curdle *(of milk etc.)*; to succeed; to begin to burn. **se prendre**, *v.r.* to be taken, to be caught; to catch; to freeze, to congeal *(of liquids)*; to begin.

preneur [prə'nœ:r], *n.m.* *(fem.* **-euse)** taker; lessee; purchaser; catcher *(of animals)*.

prénom [pre'nɔ̃], *n.m.* Christian name.

prénommé [prenɔ'me], *a.* and *n.m.* *(fem.* **-ée)** (the) above-named, aforesaid; named.

préoccupation [preɔkypa'sjɔ̃], *n.f.* preoccupation; anxiety, concern.

préoccupé [preɔky'pe], *a.* preoccupied, absorbed; worried.

préoccuper [preɔky'pe], *v.t.* to engross, to preoccupy; to worry. **se préoccuper**, *v.r.* to see to, to be engaged in *(de)*, to be anxious about.

préparateur [prepara'tœ:r], *n.m.* *(fem.* **-trice)** preparer, assistant *(in laboratory or in a dispensing druggist's)*.

préparatif(s) [prepara'tif], *n.m. sing.* or *pl.* preparation.

préparation [prepara'sjɔ̃], *n.f.* preparation; *sans préparation*, extempore.

préparatoire [prepara'twa:r], *a.* preparatory.

préparer [prepa're], *v.t.* to prepare, to make ready; to fit; to make up, to manufacture. **se préparer**, *v.r.* to prepare, to prepare oneself, to get ready.

prépondérance [prepɔ̃de'rã:s], *n.f.* preponderance.

prépondérant [prepɔ̃de'rã], *a.* preponderant; *voix prépondérante*, casting-vote.

préposé [prepo'ze], *n.m.* *(fem.* **-ée)** officer in charge, superintendent, agent.

préposer [prepo'ze], *v.t.* to set over, to appoint to, to put in charge of.

préposition [prepozi'sjɔ̃], *n.f.* preposition.

prérogative [prerɔga'ti:v], *n.f.* prerogative.

près [prɛ], *adv.* by, near, hard by; nearly, almost, about; on the point of; *à beaucoup près*, by a great deal; *à cela près*, with

that exception; *à peu près*, pretty near, nearly so; *de près*, close, near; *tout près*, very near.—*prep.* *(usu. près de)* near, close to.

présage [pre'za:ʒ], *n.m.* presage, omen, foreboding.

présager [preza'ʒe], *v.t.* *(conjug. like* MANGER*)* to presage, to portend.

pré-salé [presa'le], *n.m.* *(pl.* **prés-salés)** salt-marsh sheep *or* mutton.

presbyte [prɛz'bit], *a.* long-sighted.—*n.* long-sighted person.

presbytère [prɛzbi'tɛ:r], *n.m.* parsonage, vicarage, rectory; presbytery *(R.-C. Ch.)*.

presbytérien [prɛzbite'rjɛ̃], *a.* and *n.m.* *(fem.* **-enne)** Presbyterian.

presbytie [prɛzbi'si], *n.f.* far- *or* long-sightedness.

prescience [pre'sjã:s], *n.f.* prescience, fore-knowledge.

prescription [preskrip'sjɔ̃], *n.f.* prescription; regulation.

prescrire [prɛs'kri:r], *v.t.* *irr.* *(conjug. like* ÉCRIRE*)* to prescribe, to stipulate; *(Law)* to bar.

préséance [prese'ã:s], *n.f.* precedence.

présence [pre'zã:s], *n.f.* presence, attendance, appearance; *mettre en présence*, to bring face to face.

présent [pre'zã], *a.* present; *présent!* here!—*n.m.* present, present time; gift; *dès à présent*, from now on.

présentable [preza'tabl], *a.* presentable, fit to be seen.

présentation [prezãta'sjɔ̃], *n.f.* presentation, introduction.

présentement [prezãt'mã], *adv.* now, at present.

présenter [prezã'te], *v.t.* to present, to offer; to show; to introduce. **se présenter**, *v.r.* to present oneself, to appear.

préservateur [prezɛrva'tœ:r], *a.* *(fem.* **-trice)** preservative.

préservatif [prezɛrva'tif], *a.* *(fem.* **-tive)** preservative.

préservation [prezɛrva'sjɔ̃], *n.f.* preservation.

préserver [prezɛr've], *v.t.* to preserve; to defend, to keep safe; *le ciel m'en préserve!* heaven forbid! **se préserver**, *v.r.* to preserve oneself, to guard against.

présidence [prezi'dã:s], *n.f.* presidency, chairmanship.

président [prezi'dã], *n.m.* president *(of tribunal)*, presiding judge; speaker *(of the House of Commons)*, chairman.

présidente [prezi'dã:t], *n.f.* lady president; president's wife.

présider [prezi'de], *v.t.* to preside over, to be president *or* chairman of.—*v.i.* to preside, to be president, to be in the chair.

présomptif [prezɔ̃p'tif], *a.* *(fem.* **-tive)** presumptive, apparent, presumed *(of heirs)*.

présomption [prezɔ̃p'sjɔ̃], *n.f.* presumption, self-conceit.

présomptueusement [prezɔ̃ptɥøz'mã], *adv.* presumptuously.

présomptueux [prezɔ̃p'tɥø], *a.* *(fem.* **-euse)** presumptuous.

presque [prɛsk], *adv.* almost, nearly, all but; hardly, scarcely; *presque jamais*, hardly ever; *presque plus (de)*, scarcely any left; *presque rien*, hardly anything.

presqu'île [prɛs'kil], *n.f.* peninsula.
pressage [prɛ'saːʒ], *n.m.* pressing.
pressant [prɛ'sɑ̃], *a.* pressing, urgent, earnest.
presse [prɛs], *n.f.* throng, crowd; hurry; urgency; (*Navy*) press-gang; press (*newspapers*); printing-press.
pressé [prɛ'se], *a.* pressed; crowded; close, thick; in haste, hurried; urgent; eager; very busy; (*fig.*) condensed, concise.
presse-citron [prɛssi'trɔ̃], *n.m.* (*pl. unchanged or* **-citrons**) lemon-squeezer.
pressée [prɛ'se], *n.f.* pressing, pressure; pressful (*of print etc.*).
pressentiment [prɛsɑ̃ti'mɑ̃], *n.m.* presentiment; foreboding.
pressentir [prɛsɑ̃'tiːr], *v.t. irr.* (*conjug. like* SENTIR) to have a presentiment of; to sound.
presse-papiers [prɛspa'pje], *n.m. inv.* paperweight.
presse-purée [prɛspy're], *n.m. inv.* potato masher.
presser [prɛ'se], *v.t.* to press, to squeeze; to tread down; to crowd; to hasten; to entreat, to urge.—*v.i.* to be urgent. **se presser**, *v.r.* to press, to squeeze, to crowd; to make haste, to hurry.
pression [prɛ'sjɔ̃], *n.f.* pressure.
pressoir [prɛ'swaːr], *n.m.* press (*wine etc.*).
pressurer [prɛsy're], *v.t.* to press (*grapes, apples etc.*); (*fig.*) to squeeze money etc. out of; to oppress.
pressureur [prɛsy'rœːr], *n.m.* (*fem.* **-euse**) presser (*of fruit etc.*); (*fig.*) squeezer, sponger; oppressor.
prestance [prɛs'tɑ̃ːs], *n.f.* commanding appearance, fine presence.
prestation [prɛsta'sjɔ̃], *n.f.* taking (*of an oath*); prestation (*payment of toll etc.*).
preste [prɛst], *a.* agile, nimble; smart.
prestement [prɛstə'mɑ̃], *adv.* nimbly, quickly.
prestesse [prɛs'tɛs], *n.f.* agility, quickness.
prestidigitateur [prɛstidiʒita'tœːr], *n.m.* conjurer, juggler.
prestidigitation [prɛstidiʒita'sjɔ̃], *n.f.* conjuring, sleight of hand.
prestige [prɛs'tiːʒ], *n.m.* marvel; illusion, magic spell; prestige.
prestigieux [prɛsti'ʒjø], *a.* (*fem.* **-euse**) marvellous, amazing.
(C) **presto** [prɛs'to], *n.m.* pressure cooker.
présumer [prezy'me], *v.t.* to presume, to suppose.
présure [pre'zyːr], *n.f.* rennet.
prêt (1) [prɛ], *a.* ready, prepared.
prêt (2) [prɛ], *n.m.* loan; (*Mil.*) pay.
prétantaine [pretɑ̃'tɛn], *n.f.* **courir la prétantaine**, to gad about.
prêté [prɛ'te], *a.* lent.
prétendant [pretɑ̃'dɑ̃], *n.m.* (*fem.* **-e**) claimant.—*n.m.* suitor; pretender (*to the throne*).
prétendre [pre'tɑ̃ːdr], *v.t.* to claim, to lay claim to; to mean; affirm.—*v.i.* to lay claim (*to*); to aspire (*à*).
prétendu [pretɑ̃'dy], *a.* pretended, supposed, sham, so-called, would-be.—*n.m.* (*fem.* **-e**) future husband *or* wife.
prétentieux [pretɑ̃'sjø], *a.* (*fem.* **-euse**) pretentious, assuming.
prétention [pretɑ̃'sjɔ̃], *n.f.* pretension, claim; intention, wish; expectation.

prêter [prɛ'te], *v.t.* to lend; to impart; to attribute; to bestow.—*v.i.* to give, to stretch; to invite, to give rise to. **se prêter**, *v.r.* to give way; to lend oneself *or* itself; to countenance, to favor.
prêteur [prɛ'tœːr], *n.m.* (*fem.* **-euse**) lender.
prétexte [pre'tɛkst], *n.m.* pretext, pretence; plea.
prétexter [pretɛks'te], *v.t.* to allege (*as pretext*), to pretend, to feign.
prétoire [pre'twaːr], *n.m.* (*Rom. Ant.*) praetorium.
prétorien [preto'rjɛ̃], *a.* (*fem.* **-enne**) praetorian.
prêtre [prɛːtr], *n.m.* priest.
prêtresse [prɛ'trɛs], *n.f.* priestess.
prêtrise [prɛ'triːz], *n.f.* priesthood.
preuve [prœːv], *n.f.* proof; evidence, testimony.
preux [prø], *a. inv.* gallant, doughty, valiant.—*n.m.* valiant knight.
prévaloir [preva'lwaːr], *v.i. irr.* (*conjug. like* VALOIR) to prevail. **se prévaloir**, *v.r.* to take advantage, to avail oneself; to boast.
prévaricateur [prevarika'tœːr], *a.* (*fem.* **-trice**) dishonest, unjust.—*n.m.* (*fem.* **-trice**) betrayer of trust.
prévarication [prevarika'sjɔ̃], *n.f.* betrayal of trust, maladministration of justice.
prévariquer [prevari'ke], *v.i.* to betray one's trust.
prévenance [prev'nɑ̃ːs], *n.f.* (*pl.*) kind attentions.
prévenant [prev'nɑ̃], *a.* obliging, kind; prepossessing, engaging.
prévenir [prev'niːr], *v.t. irr.* (*conjug. like* TENIR) to precede; to forestall; to prevent; to prepossess, to predispose; to warn. **se prévenir**, *v.r.* to be prejudiced.
préventif [prevɑ̃'tif], *a.* (*fem.* **-tive**) preventive.
prévention [prevɑ̃'sjɔ̃], *n.f.* prepossession, prejudice; suspicion; accusation.
préventivement [prevɑ̃tiv'mɑ̃], *adv.* by way of prevention; while awaiting trial.
prévenu [prev'ny], *a.* forestalled, anticipated; prejudiced; accused.—*n.m.* (*fem.* **-e**) the accused.
prévisible [previ'zibl], *a.* foreseeable.
prévision [previ'zjɔ̃], *n.f.* forecast; estimate, expectation.
prévoir [pre'vwaːr], *v.t. irr.* to foresee, to anticipate.
prévôt [pre'vo], *n.m.* provost.
prévôté [prevo'te], *n.f.* provostship; military police.
prévoyance [prevwa'jɑ̃ːs], *n.f.* foresight, forethought, prudence.
prévoyant [prevwa'jɑ̃], *a.* a provident, prudent, careful.
prié [pri'je], *a.* invited (*to a feast etc.*).
prie-Dieu [pri'djø], *n.m. inv.* praying-stool.
prier [pri'je], *v.t.* to pray, to beseech; to request; to invite.
prière [pri'jɛːr], *n.f.* prayer; request, entreaty; invitation.
prieur [pri'jœːr], *n.m.* prior (*superior of a convent*).
prieure [pri'jœːr], *n.f.* prioress.
prieuré [prijœ're], *n.m.* priory.
primaire [pri'mɛːr], *a.* primary.

primat [pri'ma], *n.m.* primate, metropolitan.
primauté [primo'te], *n.f.* primacy, priority, pre-eminence; the lead (*at cards, dice etc.*).
prime [prim], *a.* first.—*n.f.* premium; subsidy; (*Mil.*) bounty; bonus, prize; (*Fenc.*) prime; (*Comm.*) free gift; *certificat de primes*, debenture; *faire prime*, to be at a premium.
primer [pri'me], *v.t.* to surpass, to excel.—*v.i.* to play first, to lead (*at games*); to excel.
primeur [pri'mœːr], *n.f.* early vegetables, fruit, flowers, etc.; early sentiment, love etc.; freshness, bloom.
primevère [prim'vɛːr], *n.f.* (*Bot.*) primula, primrose, cowslip.
primitif [primi'tif], *a.* (*fem.* -ive) first, early, primitive, aboriginal; pristine.—*n.m.* (*Gram., Paint.*) primitive.
primitivement [primitiv'mã], *adv.* primitively, originally.
primo [pri'mo], *adv.* first, in the first place.
primordial [primor'djal], *a.* (*m. pl.* -aux) primordial.
prince [prɛːs], *n.m.* prince.
princeps [prɛ̃'sɛps], *a. inv. édition princeps,* first edition.
princesse [prɛ̃'sɛs], *n.f.* princess.
princier [prɛ̃'sje], *a.* (*fem.* -ière) princely, like a prince.
principal [prɛ̃si'pal], *a.* (*m. pl.* -aux) principal, chief, most important.—*n.m.* chief thing, principal point; principal, capital (*money*); headmaster (*of a collège*); (*pl.*) chief personages (*of a town etc.*).
principalement [prɛ̃sipal'mã], *adv.* principally, chiefly.
principauté [prɛ̃sipo'te], *n.f.* principality, princedom.
principe [prɛ̃'sip], *n.m.* beginning, source, basis; principle; (*pl.*) principles, rudiments; *dès le principe*, from the very first; *en principe*, as a rule.
printanier [prɛ̃ta'nje], *a.* (*fem.* -ière) spring-like, vernal; (*fig.*) youthful, early.
printemps [prɛ̃'tã], *n.m.* spring, spring-time; (*fig.*) prime, bloom.
priorité [priori'te], *n.f.* priority.
pris [pri], *a.* taken, caught, seized; frozen.
prisable [pri'zabl], *a.* estimable, worthy of esteem.
prise [priːz], *n.f.* taking, capture; prize; hold, purchase; grip; quarrel; dose; pinch (*of snuff etc.*); (*pl.*) fighting.
priser (1) [pri'ze], *v.t., v.i.* to (take) snuff.
priser (2) [pri'ze], *v.t.* to appraise, to estimate; to esteem.
priseur [pri'zœːr], *n.m. commissaire priseur,* auctioneer, valuer.
prismatique [prisma'tik], *a.* prismatic.
prisme [prism], *n.m.* prism.
prison [pri'zɔ̃], *n.f.* prison, jail; imprisonment.
prisonnier [prizo'nje], *n.m.* (*fem.* -ière) prisoner.
privation [priva'sjɔ̃], *n.f.* privation; want, need.
privauté [privo'te], *n.f.* extreme familiarity *or* liberty.
privé [pri've], *a.* and *n.m.* (*fem.* -ée) private; familiar, intimate; tame (*of animals*).

priver [pri've], *v.t.* to deprive, to bereave; to tame (*animals etc.*). **se priver,** *v.r.* to deprive *or* stint oneself; to abstain (*de*).
privilège [privi'lɛːʒ], *n.m.* privilege; license; prerogative, grant.
privilégié [privile'ʒje], *a.* privileged; licensed; entitled to preference (*of creditors*); preference (*of shares*).—*n.m.* (*fem.* -ée) privileged person.
privilégier [privile'ʒje], *v.t.* to privilege; to license.
prix [pri], *n.m. inv.* price, cost, value; rate, return; reward, prize; stakes (*race for prize*); *à prix d'argent*, for money; *à vil prix*, dirt cheap; *prix coûtant*, cost price; *prix de gros*, wholesale price; *remporter le prix*, to carry off the prize.
probabilité [probabili'te], *n.f.* probability, likelihood.
probable [prɔ'babl], *a.* probable, likely, credible.
probablement [probablə'mã], *adv.* probably.
probant [prɔ'bã], *a.* convincing, conclusive.
probation [prɔba'sjɔ̃], *n.f.* (*Eccles.*) probation.
probe [prɔb], *a.* honest, upright.
probité [probi'te], *n.f.* probity, honesty, integrity.
problématique [problema'tik], *a.* problematical; questionable, doubtful.
problématiquement [problematik'mã], *adv.* problematically.
problème [prɔ'blɛm], *n.m.* problem.
procédé [prɔse'de], *n.m.* behavior, proceeding, conduct; process, operation; (*Billiards*) cue tip.
procéder [prɔse'de], *v.i.* (*conjug. like* CÉDER) to proceed, to arise, to originate (*de*); to behave.
procédure [prɔse'dyːr], *n.f.* procedure; proceedings.
procès [prɔ'sɛ], *n.m.* lawsuit, action, trial; (*Anat.*) process.
procession [prɔsɛ'sjɔ̃], *n.f.* procession.
processionnel [prɔsɛsjɔ'nɛl], *a.* (*fem.* -elle) processional.
procès-verbal [prɔsɛvɛr'bal], *n.m.* (*pl.* -verbaux) official report; minute of proceedings; police report.
prochain [prɔ'ʃɛ̃], *a.* near, nearest, next.—*n.m.* neighbor, fellow creature.
prochainement [prɔʃɛn'mã], *adv.* shortly, soon.
proche [prɔʃ], *a.* near, neighboring; nigh, approaching.—*prep.* and *adv.* near, nigh; *de proche en proche*, gradually.—*n.m.* (*usu. in pl.*) near relation, kin, kindred.
proclamation [prɔklama'sjɔ̃], *n.f.* proclamation.
proclamer [prɔkla'me], *v.t.* to proclaim, to announce; to publish; to disclose.
proclivité [prɔklivi'te], *n.f.* proclivity, slope.
procréateur [prɔkrea'tœːr], *a.* (*fem.* -trice) procreative.—*n.m.* (*fem.* -trice) procreator.
procréation [prɔkrea'sjɔ̃], *n.f.* procreation.
procréer [prɔkre'e], *v.t.* to procreate, to beget.
procurateur [prɔkyra'tœːr], *n.m.* (*Hist.*) procurator.
procuration [prɔkyra'sjɔ̃], *n.f.* procuration, power of attorney, proxy (*deed*).

procurer

procurer [prɔky're], *v.t.* to procure, to obtain. **se procurer,** *v.r.* to procure, to get for oneself.

procureur [prɔky'rœ:r], *n.m.* (*fem.* **procuratrice**) attorney, procurator, proxy.

prodigalement [prɔdigal'mɑ̃], *adv.* prodigally, extravagantly.

prodigalité [prɔdigali'te], *n.f.* prodigality, lavishness.

prodige [prɔ'di:ʒ], *n.m.* prodigy, marvel.

prodigieusement [prɔdiʒjøz'mɑ̃], *adv.* prodigiously.

prodigieux [prɔdi'ʒjø], *a.* (*fem.* **-euse**) prodigious, wonderful; stupendous.

prodigue [prɔ'dig], *a.* prodigal, lavish; wasteful.—*n.* prodigal, spendthrift.

prodiguer [prɔdi'ge], *v.t.* to be prodigal of; to waste, to squander. **se prodiguer,** *v.r.* to make oneself cheap; not to spare oneself.

prodrome [prɔ'drɔ:m], *n.m.* introduction, preface, preamble.

producteur [prɔdyk'tœ:r], *a.* (*fem.* **-trice**) productive.—*n.m.* (*fem.* **-trice**) producer.

productif [prɔdyk'tif], *a.* (*fem.* **-tive**) productive.

production [prɔdyk'sjɔ̃], *n.f.* production; produce, product (*of nature*); yield, output.

productivité [prɔdyktivi'te], *n.f.* productivity; productiveness.

produire [prɔ'dɥi:r], *v.t. irr.* (*conjug. like* CONDUIRE) to produce; to bear; to exhibit; to introduce. **se produire,** *v.r.* to put oneself forward; to occur, to happen.

produit [prɔ'dɥi], *n.m.* produce, product, production; proceeds.

proéminence [prɔemi'nɑ̃:s], *n.f.* prominence; protuberance.

proéminent [prɔemi'nɑ̃], *a.* prominent, protuberant.

profanateur [prɔfana'tœ:r], *n.m.* (*fem.* **-trice**) profaner.

profanation [prɔfana'sjɔ̃], *n.f.* profanation.

profane [prɔ'fan], *a.* profane; secular.—*n.* profane person; outsider; layman.

profaner [prɔfa'ne], *v.t.* to profane, to desecrate; to defile.

proférer [prɔfe're], *v.t.* (*conjug. like* CÉDER) to utter, to pronounce.

professer [prɔfe'se], *v.t.* to profess; to exercise, to practice; to teach, to lecture on.—*v.i.* to lecture, to teach.

professeur [prɔfe'sœ:r], *n.m.* (*fem.* **femme professeur**) professor, lecturer (*at university*); teacher in secondary schools.

profession [prɔfe'sjɔ̃], *n.f.* profession, declaration; calling, business.

professionnel [prɔfesjɔ'nɛl], *a.* and *n.m.* (*fem.* **-elle**) (*Spt. etc.*) professional.

professoral [prɔfesɔ'ral], *a.* (*m. pl.* **-aux**) professorial.

professorat [prɔfesɔ'ra], *n.m.* professorship, lectureship; mastership (*of* **lycée** or **collège**).

profil [prɔ'fil], *n.m.* profile, side view; outline; (*Drawing*) section.

profiler [prɔfi'le], *v.t.* to represent *or* show in profile. **se profiler,** *v.r.* to appear in profile, to be outlined.

profit [prɔ'fi], *n.m.* profit, gain; benefit, utility, use; (*pl.*) perquisites.

profitable [prɔfi'tabl], *a.* profitable, advantageous.

profiter [prɔfi'te], *v.i.* to profit, to gain, to benefit; to take advantage of (*de*).

profiteur [prɔfi'tœ:r], *n.m.* (*fem.* **-euse**) (*pej.*) profiteer.

profond [prɔ'fɔ̃], *a.* deep; profound; vast; sound (*of sleep etc.*); downright; dark (*of night etc.*).—*n.m.* depth, abyss.

profondément [prɔfɔ̃de'mɑ̃], *adv.* deeply, profoundly, greatly; soundly.

profondeur [prɔfɔ̃'dœ:r], *n.f.* depth; profundity; penetration; extent.

profus [prɔ'fy], *a.* profuse.

profusément [prɔfyze'mɑ̃], *adv.* profusely.

profusion [prɔfy'zjɔ̃], *n.f.* profusion.

progéniture [prɔʒeni'ty:r], *n.f.* progeny.

prognostique [prɔgnɔs'tik], *a.* (*Med.*) prognostic.

programmation [prɔgramɑ'sjɔ̃], *n.f.* programming.

programme [prɔ'gram], *n.m.* (*Theat. etc.*) program; (*sch.*) curriculum, syllabus.

progrès [prɔ'grɛ], *n.m.* progress; advancement, improvement, development.

progresser [prɔgrɛ'se], *v.i.* to progress, to get on.

progressif [prɔgrɛ'sif], *a.* (*fem.* **-ive**) progressive.

progression [prɔgrɛ'sjɔ̃], *n.f.* progression.

progressiste [prɔgrɛ'sist], *a.* progressive.—*n.* progressist, progressive.

progressivement [prɔgrɛsiv'mɑ̃], *adv.* progressively.

prohiber [prɔi'be], *v.t.* to forbid, to prohibit.

prohibitif [prɔibi'tif], *a.* (*fem.* **-tive**) prohibitive, exorbitant.

prohibition [prɔibi'sjɔ̃], *n.f.* prohibition.

proie [prwa], *n.f.* prey, prize, booty.

projecteur [prɔʒɛk'tœ:r], *n.m.* searchlight; projector; floodlight.

projectile [prɔʒɛk'til], *a.* and *n.m.* projectile, missile.

projection [prɔʒɛk'sjɔ̃], *n.f.* projection; (*Cine.*) **appareil de projection,** projector.

projectionniste [prɔʒɛksjɔ'nist], *n.* (*Cine.*) projectionist.

projet [prɔ'ʒɛ], *n.m.* project, plan, idea; rough draft; **homme à projets,** schemer.

projeter [prɔʒ'te], *v.t.* (*conjug. like* APPELER) to project, to throw; to delineate, to plan, to design; to contemplate, to intend.—*v.i.* to scheme, to form projects. **se projeter,** *v.r.* to project, to stand out.

prolétaire [prɔle'tɛ:r], *a.* and *n.m.* proletarian.

prolétariat [prɔleta'rja], *n.m.* proletariat.

prolifique [prɔli'fik], *a.* prolific.

prolixe [prɔ'liks], *a.* verbose.

prologue [prɔ'lɔg], *n.m.* prologue.

prolongation [prɔlɔ̃ga'sjɔ̃], *n.f.* prolongation; extension.

prolongement [prɔlɔ̃ʒ'mɑ̃], *n.m.* prolongation, extension.

prolonger [prɔlɔ̃'ʒe], *v.t.* (*conjug. like* MANGER) to prolong, to lengthen, to protract; to draw out. **se prolonger,** *v.r.* to be protracted; to extend; to continue.

promenade [prɔm'nad], *n.f.* walk, walking; promenade; drive, excursion, pleasure trip.

promener [prɔm'ne], *v.t.* to take out for a walk, for a drive, for a ride, for an airing; to cast (*one's eyes*) over; to run or pass (*one's hand, fingers*) over. **se promener,** *v.r.* to

258

walk, to go for a walk, ramble, drive, row, sail etc.; to stroll.

promeneur [prɔm'nœːr], *n.m.* (*fem.* **-euse**) walker; rider; person taking a drive.

promenoir [prɔm'nwaːr], *n.m.* covered walk; promenade (*in a concert hall etc.*).

promesse [prɔ'mɛs], *n.f.* promise; promissory note.

promettre [prɔ'mɛtr], *v.t. irr.* (*conjug. like* METTRE) to promise; to forebode.—*v.i.* to be promising. **se promettre**, *v.r.* to promise oneself; to purpose; to promise each other.

promis [prɔ'mi], *a.* promised; intended, engaged.—*n.m.* (*fem.* **-e**) fiancé *or* fiancée.

promiscuité [prɔmiskɥi'te], *n.f.* promiscuity.

promontoire [prɔmɔ̃'twaːr], *n.m.* promontory, headland.

promoteur [prɔmɔ'tœːr], *n.m.* (*fem.* **-trice**) promoter.

promotion [prɔmɔ'sjɔ̃], *n.f.* promotion, preferment.

promouvoir [prɔmu'vwaːr], *v.t. irr.* (*conjug. like* MOUVOIR) to promote, to advance.

prompt [prɔ̃], *a.* prompt, quick, active; sudden, swift; hasty.

promptement [prɔ̃t'mɑ̃], *adv.* promptly.

promptitude [prɔ̃ti'ty:d], *n.f.* promptitude, promptness; suddenness; hastiness.

promulgation [prɔmylga'sjɔ̃], *n.f.* promulgation.

promulguer [prɔmyl'ge], *v.t.* to promulgate.

prône [proːn], *n.m.* sermon (*at* Mass); (*fig.*) lecture, rebuke.

prôner [pro'ne], *v.t.* to lecture, to sermonize; to extol.—*v.i.* to sermonize.

prôneur [pro'nœːr], *n.m.* (*fem.* **-euse**) longwinded preacher.

pronom [prɔ'nɔ̃], *n.m.* (Gram.) pronoun.

prononçable [prɔnɔ̃'sabl], *a.* pronounceable.

prononcé [prɔnɔ̃'se], *a.* pronounced, decided, marked; (*Paint. etc.*) prominent; broad (*of speech*).—*n.m.* judgment delivered, sentence.

prononcer [prɔnɔ̃'se], *v.t.* (*conjug. like* COMMENCER) to pronounce, to utter, to say; to declare; to pass (*a verdict etc.*).—*v.i.* to declare one's sentiments, to decide with authority. **se prononcer**, *v.r.* to declare oneself, to express one's opinion, to give a verdict; to be pronounced.

prononciation [prɔnɔ̃sja'sjɔ̃], *n.f.* pronunciation; utterance.

pronostic [prɔnɔs'tik], *n.m.* prognostic; prognostication; (Med.) prognosis; weather forecast; (*racing*) tip.

propagande [prɔpa'gɑ̃:d], *n.f.* propaganda.

propagandiste [prɔpagɑ̃'dist], *n.* propagandist.

propagateur [prɔpaga'tœːr], *a.* (*fem.* **-trice**) propagating, spreading.—*n.m.* (*fem.* **-trice**) propagator.

propagation [prɔpaga'sjɔ̃], *n.f.* propagation, spreading, diffusion.

propager [prɔpa'ʒe], *v.t.* (*conjug. like* MANGER) to propagate, to spread abroad, to diffuse. **se propager**, *v.r.* to be propagated, to spread.

propension [prɔpɑ̃'sjɔ̃], *n.f.* propensity, tendency.

prophète [prɔ'fɛːt], *n.m.* prophet, seer.

prophétesse [prɔfe'tɛs], *n.f.* prophetess.

prophétie [prɔfe'si], *n.f.* prophecy, prophesying.

prophétique [prɔfe'tik], *a.* prophetic.

prophétiser [prɔfeti'ze], *v.t.* to prophesy, to foretell.

propice [prɔ'pis], *a.* propitious, favorable.

propitiation [prɔpisja'sjɔ̃], *n.f.* propitiation.

propitiatoire [prɔpisja'twaːr], *a.* propitiatory.

proportion [prɔpɔr'sjɔ̃], *n.f.* proportion, ratio.

proportionné [prɔpɔrsjɔ'ne], *a.* proportioned, suited.

proportionnel [prɔpɔrsjɔ'nɛl], *a.* (*fem.* **-elle**) proportional.

proportionner [prɔpɔrsjɔ'ne], *v.t.* to proportion, to adjust, to adapt.

propos [prɔ'po], *n.m.* talk, words; remark; purpose, resolution; (*pl.*) idle remarks, tittle-tattle; *à propos*, apt, to the purpose; by the way; *à propos de*, with respect to; *à quel propos?* what about? *de propos délibéré*, of set purpose; *mal à propos*, ill-timed; *propos de table*, table-talk; *venir fort à propos*, to come in the nick of time.

proposer [prɔpo'ze], *v.t.* to propose; to propound, to move; to designate, to set up.—*v.i.* to propose. **se proposer**, *v.r.* to propose oneself; to intend, to have in view.

proposeur [prɔpo'zœːr], *n.m.* (*fem.* **-euse**) proposer, propounder.

proposition [prɔpozi'sjɔ̃], *n.f.* proposal; proposition; motion; (Gram.) clause.

propre [prɔpr], *a.* own; very, same, selfsame; proper; appropriate, suitable; good, right, correct; clean, neat, tidy; *le mot propre*, the right word; *peu propre*, inappropriate; dirty—*n.m.* characteristic, property; proper sense; (Law) real property.

propre à rien [prɔpra'rjɛ̃], *n. inv.* good for nothing.

proprement [prɔprə'mɑ̃], *adv.* properly, correctly; cleanly, neatly.

propret [prɔ'prɛ], *a.* (*fem.* **-ette**) spruce, neat, tidy.

propreté [prɔprə'te], *n.f.* cleanliness; neatness.

propriétaire [prɔprie'tɛːr], *n.* owner, proprietor, proprietress; landlord, householder.

propriété [prɔprie'te], *n.f.* property; estate; characteristic; *propriété littéraire*, copyright.

propulser [prɔpyl'se], *v.t.* (Naut., Av.) to propel.

propulseur [prɔpyl'sœːr], *n.m.* propeller.

propulsif [prɔpyl'sif], *a.* (*fem.* **-sive**) propelling, propellent.

propulsion [prɔpyl'sjɔ̃], *n.f.* propulsion.

prorogation [prɔrɔga'sjɔ̃], *n.f.* adjournment, prorogation (*of Parliament etc.*); extension.

proroger [prɔrɔ'ʒe], *v.t.* (*conjug. like* MANGER) to prolong the time of; to prorogue (*Parliament etc.*).

prosaïque [prɔza'ik], *a.* prosaic; banal; prosy.

prosaïquement [prɔzaik'mɑ̃], *adv.* prosaically.

prosateur [prɔza'tœːr], *n.m.* prose writer.

proscription [prɔskrip'sjɔ̃], *n.f.* proscription.

proscrire [prɔs'kriːr], *v.t. irr.* (*conjug. like* ÉCRIRE) to proscribe, to outlaw; to banish.

259

proscrit [pros'kri], *a.* proscribed, forbidden. —*n.m.* (*fem.* **-e**) proscribed person, outlaw; exile.

prose [pro:z], *n.f.* prose.

prosodie [prozo'di], *n.f.* prosody.

prospecter [prospɛk'te], *v.t.* to prospect (*for oil, minerals*).

prospecteur [prospɛk'tœ:r], *n.m.* prospector.

prospectus [prospɛk'ty:s], *n.m. inv.* prospectus; handbill.

prospère [pros'pɛ:r], *a.* prosperous, thriving.

prospérer [prospe're], *v.i.* (*conjug. like* CÉDER) to prosper, to be prosperous, to thrive.

prospérité [prosperi'te], *n.f.* prosperity.

prostate [pros'tat], *n.f.* (*Anat.*) prostate.

prosternation [prosterna'sjɔ̃], *n.f.*, **prosternement** [prosterna'mɑ̃], *n.m.* prostration, obeisance.

prosterner [proster'ne], *v.t.* to prostrate. **se prosterner**, *v.r.* to prostrate oneself, to bow low.

prostituée [prosti'tɥe], *n.f.* prostitute.

prostituer [prosti'tɥe], *v.t.* to prostitute. **se prostituer**, *v.r.* to prostitute oneself.

prostitution [prostity'sjɔ̃], *n.f.* prostitution.

prostration [prostra'sjɔ̃], *n.f.* prostration.

protagoniste [protago'nist], *n.m.* protagonist.

protecteur [protɛk'tœ:r], *a.* (*fem.* **-trice**) protective; patronizing.—*n.m.* (*fem.* **-trice**) protector, protectress; patron, patroness.—*n.m.* (*Eng.*) guard (*for machine tool*).

protection [protɛk'sjɔ̃], *n.f.* protection, shelter; support, patronage.

protectorat [protɛkto'ra], *n.m.* protectorate.

protégé [prote'ʒe], *n.m.* (*fem.* **-ée**) favorite, dependant.

protéger [prote'ʒe], *v.t.* (*conjug. like* ASSIÉGER) to protect, to defend; to patronize, to favor.

protège-vue [protɛ'ʒvy], *n.m. inv.* eye-shade.

protéine [prote'in], *n.f.* protein.

protestant [protɛs'tɑ̃], *a.* and *n.m.* (*fem.* **-e**) Protestant.

protestantisme [protɛstɑ̃'tism], *n.m.* Protestantism.

protestation [protɛsta'sjɔ̃], *n.f.* protestation, protest.

protester [protɛs'te], *v.t.* to protest, to affirm.—*v.i.* to protest.

protocole [proto'kɔl], *n.m.* protocol.

proton [pro'tɔ̃], *n.m.* proton.

protoplasma [protoplas'ma], **protoplasme** [proto'plasm], *n.m.* protoplasm.

prototype [proto'tip], *n.m.* prototype.

protubérance [protybe'rɑ̃:s], *n.f.* protuberance.

protubérant [protybe'rɑ̃], *a.* protuberant.

proue [pru], *n.f.* prow, stem, bows (*of ship*).

prouesse [pru'ɛs], *n.f.* prowess, valor; feat.

prouver [pru've], *v.t.* to prove; to substantiate; to show.

provenance [prov'nɑ̃:s], *n.f.* origin, source; (*pl.*) produce, commodities.

provençal [provɑ̃'sal], *a.* (*m. pl.* **-aux**) Provençal.—*n.m.* Provençal (*language*); (**Provençal**, *fem.* **-ale**) Provençal (*person*).

provenir [prov'ni:r], *v.i. irr.* (*conjug. like* TENIR *but with aux.* ÊTRE) to issue, proceed, spring, originate *or* come from (*de*).

proverbe [pro'vɛrb], *n.m.* proverb, saying.

proverbial [provɛr'bjal], *a.* (*m. pl.* **-aux**) proverbial.

providence [provi'dɑ̃:s], *n.f.* providence.

providentiel [providɑ̃'sjɛl], *a.* (*fem.* **-elle**) providential.

provigner [provi'ɲe], *v.t.* to layer (*vines*).

provin [pro'vɛ̃], *n.m.* layer (*of a vine*).

province [pro'vɛ̃:s], *n.f.* province, shire; country; **en province**, in the country, in the provinces.

provincial [provɛ̃'sjal], *a.* (*m. pl.* **-aux**) provincial; countrified.—*n.m.* (*fem.* **-e**) provincial, country person.

proviseur [provi'zœ:r], *n.m.* headmaster (*of a lycée*).

provision [provi'zjɔ̃], *n.f.* provision, stock, store, supply; deposit; (*Comm.*) reserve funds.

provisionnel [provizjo'nɛl], *a.* (*fem.* **-elle**) provisional.

provisoire [provi'zwa:r], *a.* provisional, temporary.—*n.m.* provisional nature (*of something*).

provisoirement [provizwar'mɑ̃], *adv.* provisionally, temporarily.

provocant [provo'kɑ̃], *a.* provoking, provocative; exciting.

provocateur [provoka'tœ:r], *a.* (*fem.* **-trice**) provoking, provocative; **agent provocateur**, agent hired to instigate a riot etc.—*n.m.* (*fem.* **-trice**) provoker; aggressor.

provocation [provoka'sjɔ̃], *n.f.* provocation.

provoquer [provo'ke], *v.t.* to provoke, to incite, to call forth; to instigate.

proximité [proksimi'te], *n.f.* proximity, nearness.

prude [pryd], *a.* prudish.—*n.f.* prude.

prudemment [pryda'mɑ̃], *adv.* prudently, discreetly, cautiously.

prudence [pry'dɑ̃:s], *n.f.* carefulness, prudence.

prudent [pry'dɑ̃], *a.* prudent, discreet; advisable.

pruderie [pry'dri], *n.f.* prudery, prudishness.

prud'homme [pry'dɔm], *n.m.* upright, honest man; (*Ind.*) arbitrator.

pruine [prɥin], *n.f.* bloom (*on fruits*).

prune [pryn], *n.f.* plum.

pruneau [pry'no], *n.m.* (*pl.* **-eaux**) prune.

prunelle (1) [pry'nɛl], *n.f.* sloe; sloe gin.

prunelle (2) [pry'nɛl], *n.f.* pupil, apple (*of the eye*), eyeball.

prunellier [prynɛ'lje], *n.m.* sloe tree, blackthorn.

prunier [pry'nje], *n.m.* plum tree.

Prusse [prys], **la**, *f.* Prussia.

prussien [pry'sjɛ̃], *a.* (*fem.* **-enne**) Prussian. —*n.m.* (**Prussien**, *fem.* **-enne**) Prussian (*person*).

prussique [pry'sik], *a.* (*Chem.*) prussic.

psalmiste [psal'mist], *n.m.* psalmist.

psalmodie [psalmo'di], *n.f.* psalmody, intoning; (*fig.*) sing-song.

psalmodier [psalmo'dje], *v.t.*, *v.i.* to recite, to chant (*as the psalms*); to read *or* recite in a sing-song manner.

psaume [pso:m], *n.m.* psalm.

psautier [pso'tje], *n.m.* psalter, psalm book.

pseudonyme [psødo'nim], *a.* pseudonymous. —*n.m.* pseudonym, nom-de-plume.

psychanalyse [psikana'li:z], *n.f.* psychoanalysis.

psychanalyste [psikana'list], *n.m.* psycho-analyst.
psychiatre [psi'kja:tr], *n.m.* psychiatrist.
psychiatrie [psikja'tri], *n.f.* psychiatry.
psychologie [psikɔlɔ'ʒi], *n.f.* psychology.
psychologique [psikɔlɔ'ʒik], *a.* psychological.
psychologue [psikɔ'lɔg], *n.* psychologist.
puant [pɥã], *a.* stinking; foul.
puanteur [pɥã'tœ:r], *n.f.* stench, stink.
pubère [py'be:r], *a.* pubescent, puberal.
puberté [pyber'te], *n.f.* puberty.
public [py'blik], *a.* (*fem.* **-ique**) public; notorious; *la chose publique*, the common weal, the State.—*n.m.* public.
publication [pyblika'sjɔ̃], *n.f.* publication; publishing, proclamation.
publiciste [pybli'sist], *n.m.* publicist, journalist.
publicité [pyblisi'te], *n.f.* publicity; advertising.
publier [py'blje], *v.t.* to publish, to make public, to proclaim; to issue.
publiquement [pyblik'mã], *adv.* in public.
puce (1) [pys], *a. inv.* puce, puce-colored.
puce (2) [pys], *n.f.* flea.
puceron [pys'rɔ̃], *n.m.* plant louse, greenfly.
pudeur [py'dœ:r], *n.f.* modesty; bashfulness, shame, reserve.
pudibond [pydi'bɔ̃], *a.* bashful; prudish.
pudicité [pydisi'te], *n.f.* modesty, chastity.
pudique [py'dik], *a.* chaste, modest, bashful.
pudiquement [pydik'mã], *adv.* modestly.
puer [pɥe], *v.t.* (*fam.*) to smell of, to reek of.—*v.i.* to stink.
puéril [pɥe'ril], *a.* juvenile, childish, puerile.
puérilement [pɥeril'mã], *adv.* childishly.
puérilité [pɥerili'te], *n.f.* puerility, childishness.
pugilat [pyʒi'la], *n.m.* pugilism, boxing.
pugiliste [pyʒi'list], *n.m.* pugilist, boxer.
pugnace [pyg'nas], *a.* pugnacious.
pugnacité [pygnasi'te], *n.f.* pugnacity.
puîné [pɥi'ne], *a.* (*fem.* **-ée**) younger (*brother or sister*).
puis [pɥi], *adv.* then, afterwards, after that, next; besides.
puisage [pɥi'za:ʒ], **puisement** [pɥiz'mã], *n.m.* drawing up; drawing water.
puisard [pɥi'za:r], *n.m.* cesspool; sump, water-sump.
puisatier [pɥiza'tje], *n.m.* well-sinker; shaft-sinker (*in mining*).
puisement [PUISAGE].
puiser [pɥi'ze], *v.t.* to draw, to fetch up (*a liquid*); (*fig.*) to imbibe.
puisque [pɥisk], *conj.* since, as, seeing that.
puissamment [pɥisa'mã], *adv.* powerfully; extremely, very.
puissance [pɥi'sã:s], *n.f.* power; force; dominion, sway; influence.
puissant [pɥi'sã], *a.* powerful, mighty; lusty, stout; strong.
puits [pɥi], *n.m. inv.* well; pit, shaft.
pullulation [pylyla'sjɔ̃], *n.f.*, **pullulement** [pylyl'mã], *n.m.* pullulation, swarming.
pulluler [pyly'le], *v.i.* to multiply, to pullulate, to swarm.
pulmonaire [pylmɔ'nɛ:r], *a.* pulmonary; *phthisie pulmonaire*, consumption.
pulmonique [pylmɔ'nik], *a.* and *n.* consumptive.
pulpe [pylp], *n.f.* pulp.

pulper [pyl'pe], *v.t.* to pulp.
pulpeux [pyl'pø], *a.* (*fem.* **-euse**) pulpous, pulpy.
pulsatif [pylsa'tif], *a.* (*fem.* **-tive**) pulsatory, throbbing.
pulsation [pylsa'sjɔ̃], *n.f.* beating of the pulse, pulsation, throbbing.
pulvérin [pylve'rɛ̃], *n.m.* spray (*from water-falls*).
pulvérisateur [pylveriza'tœ:r], *n.m.* pulverizator, vaporizer; spray, atomiser.
pulvérisation [pylveriza'sjɔ̃], *n.f.* pulverization.
pulvériser [pylveri'ze], *v.t.* to reduce to powder *or* dust, to pulverize; to atomize; (*fig.*) to annihilate.
pulvérulent [pylvery'lã], *a.* pulverulent, powdery.
puma [py'ma], *n.m.* puma, cougar.
pumicin [pymi'sɛ̃], *n.m.* palm oil.
punaise [py'nɛ:z], *n.f.* bug; thumbtack.
punch [pɔ̃:ʃ], *n.m.* (*Box.*) punch; punch (*beverage*).
punique [py'nik], *a.* Punic.
punir [py'ni:r], *v.t.* to punish, to chastise.
punissable [pyni'sabl], *a.* punishable.
punisseur [pyni'sœ:r], *a.* (*fem.* **-euse**) punishing, avenging.—*n.m.* (*fem.* **-euse**) punisher; avenger.
punitif [pyni'tif], *a.* (*fem.* **-tive**) punitive.
punition [pyni'sjɔ̃], *n.f.* punishment.
pupille [py'pil], *n.* ward, minor in charge of guardian.—*n.f.* pupil (*of the eye*).
pupitre [py'pitr], *n.m.* desk; music stand.
pur [py:r], *a.* pure, unalloyed; unadulterated; unblemished; innocent, chaste; mere, sheer; neat (*of liquor*); *en pure perte*, to no purpose.
purée [py're], *n.f.* mash, purée, thick soup.
purement [pyr'mã], *adv.* purely; merely.
pureté [pyr'te], *n.f.* purity, guilelessness, innocence; chastity.
purgatif [pyrga'tif], *a.* (*fem.* **-tive**) purgative, purging.—*n.m.* (*Med.*) purgative.
purgation [pyrga'sjɔ̃], *n.f.* purgation, purge.
purgatoire [pyrga'twa:r], *n.m.* purgatory.
purge [pyrʒ], *n.f.* purge; cleansing; disinfection.
purger [pyr'ʒe], *v.t.* (*conjug. like* MANGER) to purge; to cleanse, to purify. **se purger**, *v.r.* to purge oneself; to clear oneself (*of*).
purificateur [pyrifika'tœ:r], *a.* (*fem.* **-trice**) purifying.—*n.m.* (*fem.* **-trice**) purifier.
purification [pyrifika'sjɔ̃], *n.f.* purification.
purifier [pyri'fje], *v.t.* to purify, to cleanse; to refine (*metals etc.*). **se purifier**, *v.r.* to purify oneself, to become refined.
puritain [pyri'tɛ̃], *a.* and *n.m.* (*fem.* **-e**) Puritan, puritan.
puritanisme [pyrita'nism], *n.m.* puritanism.
purpurin [pyrpy'rɛ̃], *a.* purplish.
pur-sang [pyr'sã], *n.m. inv.* thoroughbred.
pus [py], *n.m.* pus, matter.
pusillanime [pyzila'nim], *a.* pusillanimous, faint-hearted.
pusillanimité [pyzllanimi'te], *n.f.* pusillanimity.
pustule [pys'tyl], *n.f.* pustule, pimple, blotch.
putatif [pyta'tif], *a.* (*fem.* **-tive**) putative, reputed, supposed.
putativement [pytativ'mã], *adv.* reputedly.
putois [py'twa], *n.m.* polecat, skunk.

putréfaction [pytrefak'sjõ], *n.f.* putrefaction; putrescence.
putréfier [pytre'fje], *v.t.* to putrefy; to rot. **se putréfier**, *v.r.* to putrefy; to rot; to decompose.
putride [py'trid], *a.* putrid.
pygmée [pig'me], *n.m.* pygmy.
pyjama [piʒa'ma], *n.m.* pajamas.
pylône [pi'lo:n], *n.m.* pylon; mast.
pyorrhée [pio're], *n.f.* pyorrhœa.
pyramidal [pirami'dal], *a.* (*m. pl.* **-aux**) pyramidal.
pyramide [pira'mid], *n.f.* pyramid.
python [pi'tõ], *n.m.* python (*snake*).

Q

Q, q [ky] *n.m.* the seventeenth letter of the alphabet.
qu' [k], *elision* [QUE].
quadragénaire [kwadraʒe'nɛːr], *a.* forty years of age.—*n.* person forty years old.
quadrangle [kwa'drɑ̃:gl], *n.m.* quadrangle.
quadrangulaire [kwadrɑ̃gy'lɛːr], *a.* quadrangular, four-cornered.
quadrillage [kadri'jaːʒ], *n.m.* checker-work, pattern in squares; map grid.
quadrille [ka'driːj], *n.m.* quadrille (*card game*); quadrille (*dance*); check (*in tapestry*).
quadrillé [kadri'je], *a.* checkered (*of cloth*); ruled in squares (*of paper*).
quadriréacteur [kwadrireak'tœːr], *n.m.* four-engined jet plane.
quadrupède [kwadry'pɛd], *a.* and *n.m.* quadruped.
quadruple [kwa'drypl], *a.* quadruple, four-fold.
quadruplé [kwadry'ple], *n.m.* (*fem.* **-ée**) quadruplet, (*fam.*) quad.
quadrupler [kwadry'ple], *v.t., v.i.* to quadruple, to increase fourfold.
quai [ke], *n.m.* quay, wharf, pier; embankment (*along river*); platform (*railway*).
qualifiable [kali'fjabl], *a.* qualifiable, characterized (*as*).
qualification [kalifika'sjõ], *n.f.* title; designation, qualification.
qualifié [kali'fje], *a.* qualified; named.
qualifier [kali'fje], *v.t.* to qualify; to style. **se qualifier**, *v.r.* to style oneself; to qualify (*for*).
qualité [kali'te], *n.f.* quality; property; excellence; talent; qualification; title; *en qualité de*, in the capacity of.
quand [kɑ̃], *adv.* when, whenever, what time; while.—*conj.* though; *quand même*, even though; all the same.
quant [kɑ̃], *adv.* (*followed by à*) as for, with regard to.
quant-à-soi [kɑ̃ta'swa], *n.m.* reserve, dignity.
quantième [kɑ̃'tjɛm], *n.m.* which (*day of the month etc.*).
quantité [kɑ̃ti'te], *n.f.* quantity; abundance, plenty; variety.

quarantaine [karɑ̃'tɛn], *n.f.* about forty; age of forty; quarantine.
quarante [ka'rɑ̃t], *a.* and *n.m.* forty.
quarantième [karɑ̃'tjɛm], *a.* and *n.* fortieth.
quart [kaːr], *a.* fourth.—*n.m.* quarter, fourth part; point (*of the compass*); quart (*measure*); (*Mil.*) tin cup; (*Naut.*) watch.
quarte [kart], *n.f.* (*Mus.*) fourth; (*Fenc., Piquet*) carte.
quartier [kar'tje], *n.m.* quarter, fourth part; piece, part; ward, district; gammon; (*Mil.*) quarters, barracks.
quartier-maître [kartje'mɛːtr], *n.m.* (*pl.* **quartiers-maîtres**) (*Naut.*) leading seaman.
quarto [kwar'to], *adv.* fourthly, in the fourth place.
quartz [kwaːrts], *n.m.* quartz.
quasi [ka'zi], *adv.* almost, as if, quasi.
quasiment [kazi'mɑ̃], *adv.* (*dial.*) almost, nearly, as you might say.
quaternaire [kwatɛr'nɛːr], *a.* quaternary.
quatorze [ka'tɔrz], *a.* and *n.m.* fourteen; fourteenth.
quatorzième [katɔr'zjɛm], *a.* and *n.* fourteenth.
quatrain [ka'trɛ̃], *n.m.* quatrain.
quatre ['katrə, katr], *a.* and *n.m. inv.* four, fourth.
quatre-temps [katrə'tɑ̃], *n.m. pl.* Ember days.
quatre-vingtième [katrəvɛ̃'tjɛm], *a.* and *n.m.* eightieth.
quatre-vingt(s) [katrə'vɛ̃], *a.* and *n.m.* eighty.
quatrième [kat'rjɛm], *a.* and *n.* fourth.—*n.m.* fourth floor, fourth storey. —*n.f.* (*Piquet*) quart.
quatrièmement [katrjɛm'mɑ̃], *adv.* fourthly.
quatuor [kwaty'ɔr], *n.m.* (*Mus.*) quartet.
que (1) [kə, k], *pron. rel.* whom, that; which; what? on which; *qu'est-ce que c'est?* what is it?
que (2) [kə, k], *conj.* that; than; than that; as, if, whether; when; without; yet; lest; in order that; oh that, may; let; before; so; only, but; *afin que*, in order that; *attendez qu'il vienne*, wait till he comes; *de sorte que*, so that.—*adv.* how, how much, how many; why, wherefore?
quel [kɛl], *a.* (*fem.* **quelle**) what, which, what sort of.
quelconque [kɛl'kõːk], *a. indef.* any; any whatsoever; mediocre.
quelque ['kɛlkə, kɛlk], *adj.* some, any; a few; whatever, whatsoever.—*adv.* however, howsoever; some, about.
quelquefois [kɛlkə'fwa], *adv.* sometimes.
quelqu'un [kɛl'kœ̃], *pron. indef. m.* someone, somebody; anyone, anybody.—*n.m.* (*fem.* **quel-qu'une**, *pl.* **quelques-uns, quelques-unes**, one (or other), some.
quémander [kemɑ̃'de], *v.t.. v.i.* to beg, to solicit.
quémandeur [kemɑ̃'dœːr], *n.m.* (*fem.* **-euse**) importunate beggar.
qu'en-dira-t-on [kɑ̃dira'tõ], *n.m. inv.* public talk, tittle-tattle.
quenelle [kə'nɛl], *n.f.* forcemeat *or* fish ball.
quenotte [kə'nɔt], *n.f.* (*colloq.*) tooth (*of young children*).
quenouille [kə'nuːj], *n.f.* distaff; bed-post.

querelle [kə'rɛl], *n.f.* quarrel; row, brawl; feud; cause of dispute; *chercher querelle à,* to pick a quarrel with.

quereller [kərɛ'le], *v.t.* to quarrel with; to scold. **se quereller,** *v.r.* to quarrel, to wrangle, to have words.

querelleur [kərɛ'lœːr], *a.* (*fem.* **-euse**) quarrelsome.—*n.m.* (*fem.* **-euse**) quarreller, wrangler.

quérir [ke'riːr], *v.t.* to fetch (*employed only in the infinitive with* aller, envoyer, venir).

questeur [kɥɛs'tœːr], *n.m.* quaestor.

question [kɛs'tjɔ̃], *n.f.* question, interrogation; query, point, issue; rack, torture.

questionnaire [kɛstjɔ'nɛːr], *n.m.* questionnaire; book of questions.

questionner [kɛstjɔ'ne], *v.t.* to question, to interrogate.

questionneur [kɛstjɔ'nœːr], *a.* (*fem.* **-euse**) inquisitive.—*n.m.* (*fem.* **-euse**) questioner.

questure [kɥɛs'tyːr], *n.f.* quaestorship; quaestors' office.

quête [kɛːt], *n.f.* quest, search; collection, offertory; (*Hunt.*) beating about.

quêter [kɛ'te], *v.t.* to look for, to seek, to go in quest of, to gather.—*v.i.* to beg.

quêteur [kɛ'tœːr], *n.m.* (*fem.* **-euse**) collector; mendicant (friar).

queue [kø], *n.f.* tail; stalk; stem; end; rear; billiard cue; handle; train (*of robes etc.*); queue, line.

queue-d'aronde [køda'rɔ̃ːd], *n.f.* (*pl.* **queues-d'aronde**) dovetail.

qui [ki], *pron. rel. and inter.* who, that, whom, which; whoever, whomsoever, whatever; what; some.

quiconque [ki'kɔ̃ːk], *pron. indef.* whoever, whosoever; whomsoever, whichever.

quiétude [kɥie'tyd], *n.f.* quietude.

quignon [ki'nɔ̃], *n.m.* hunch, chunk, hunk (*of bread*).

quille [kiːj], *n.f.* keel; skittle, ninepin.

quiller [ki'je], *v.i.* to throw for partners *or* for first play (*at skittles*).

quillier [ki'je], *n.m.* skittle alley.

quincaillerie [kɛ̃kaj'ri], *n.f.* ironmongery, hardware.

quincailllier [kɛ̃ka'je], *n.m.* hardware dealer.

quinconce [kɛ̃'kɔ̃ːs], *n.m.* quincunx.

quine [kin], *n.m.* two fives (*at trictrac*); five winning numbers (*in a lottery*).

quinine [ki'nin], *n.f.* quinine.

quinquagénaire [kɥɛ̃kwaʒe'nɛːr], *a.* fifty years old.—*n.* person of fifty.

quinquennal [kɥɛ̃kɥɛ'nal], *a.* (*m. pl.* **-aux**) quinquennial.

quinquet [kɛ̃'kɛ], *n.m.* Argand lamp.

quinquina [kɛ̃ki'na], *n.m.* Peruvian bark.

quintal [kɛ̃'tal], *n.m.* (*pl.* **-aux**) quintal, hundredweight; 100 kilogr.

quinte [kɛ̃ːt], *n.f.* (*Mus.*) fifth; (*Piquet*) quint; (*fig.*) freak, whim; (*Fenc.*) quinte, *quinte de toux,* fit of coughing.

quintessence [kɛ̃te'sɑ̃ːs], *n.f.* quintessence; (*fig.*) pith, essential part.

quintette [kɛ̃'tɛt], *n.m.* quintette.

quinteux [kɛ̃'tø], *a.* (*fem.* **-euse**) whimsical, crotchety; jibbing (*of a horse*).

quintuple [kɛ̃'typl], *a. and n.m.* quintuple.

quintuplé [kɛ̃ty'ple], *n.m.* quintuplet.

quintupler [kɛ̃ty'ple], *v.t.* to quintuple.

quinzaine [kɛ̃'zɛn], *n.f.* about fifteen; fortnight.

quinze [kɛ̃ːʒ], *a. and n.m.* fifteen; fifteenth.

quinzième [kɛ̃'zjɛm], *a. and n.* fifteenth.

quinzièmement [kɛ̃zjɛm'mɑ̃], *adv.* fifteenthly, in the fifteenth place.

quiproquo [kipro'ko], *n.m.* mistake; substitution.

quittance [ki'tɑ̃ːs], *n.f.* receipt, discharge.

quittancer [kitɑ̃'se], *v.t.* (*conjug. like* COMMENCER) to receipt.

quitte [kit], *a.* discharged (*from debt*); clear, free.

quitter [ki'te], *v.t.* to leave; to discharge; to give up; to leave off, to lay aside; to depart (*life*); *ne quittez pas!* (*Teleph.*) hold the line! **se quitter,** *v.r.* to part company, to separate.

qui va là? [kiva'la], *inter. phr.* who goes there?

qui-vive [ki'viːv], *n.m.* who goes there? (*challenge of a sentry*); *être sur le qui-vive,* to be on the alert.

quoi [kwa], *pron. rel. and inter.* which; what; *il n'y a pas de quoi,* don't mention it! *le je ne sais quoi,* the indefinable something; *quoi que,* whatever.—*int.* what!

quoique ['kwakə], *conj.* although, though.

quolibet [kɔli'bɛ], *n.m.* gibe, jeer.

quote-part [kɔt'paːr], *n.f.* (*pl.* **quotes-parts**) quota, portion, share.

quotidien [kɔti'djɛ̃], *a.* (*fem.* **-enne**) daily, quotidian.—*n.m.* daily (newspaper).

quotidiennement [kɔtidjɛn'mɑ̃], *adv.* daily.

quotient [kɔ'sjɑ̃], *n.m.* quotient.

quotité [kɔti'te], *n.f.* (*Fin.*) quota, share; proportion.

R

R, r [ɛːr], *n.m.* the eighteenth letter of the alphabet.

rabâchage [rabɑ'ʃaːʒ], *n.m.* tiresome repetition; drivel.

rabâcher [rabɑ'ʃe], *v.t., v.i.* to repeat (*the same thing*) over and over again.

rabâcheur [rabɑ'ʃœːr], *n.m.* (*fem.* **-euse**) eternal repeater, twaddler.

rabais [ra'bɛ], *n.m. inv.* abatement, reduction; discount.

rabaissement [rabɛs'mɑ̃], *n.m.* lowering, depreciation; (*fig.*) humiliation.

rabaisser [rabɛ'se], *v.t.* to lower; to abate, to lessen; to depreciate; to humble, to disparage.

rabat [ra'ba], *n.m.* clerical *or* academic band, Geneva bands; beating (*for game*).

rabat-joie [raba'ʒwa], *n.m. inv.* damper, wet blanket, spoil-sport.

rabattre [ra'batr], *v.t.* (*conjug. like* BATTRE) to beat down, to bring *or* cut down; to smooth down; to humble, (*Hunt.*) to beat up; to abate.—*v.i.* to reduce one's pretensions. **se**

rabattre, *v.r.* to turn off, to change one's road; to come down; to fall back on.

rabbin [ra'bɛ̃], *n.m.* rabbi.

rabbinique [rabi'nik], *a.* rabbinical.

rabique [ra'bik], *a.* rabid, rabic.

râble [rɑːbl], *n.m.* back (*of hare, rabbit etc.*); fire rake.

râblé [rɑː'ble], *a.* broad-backed; (*fig.*) vigorous, strapping.

rabonnir [rabɔ'niːr], *v.t., v.i.* to improve (*wine*).

rabot [ra'bo], *n.m.* plane.

rabotage [rabɔ'taːʒ], **rabotement** [rabɔt'mɑ̃], *n.m.* planing.

raboter [rabɔ'te], *v.t.* to plane; (*fig.*) to polish; (*slang*) to pilfer, to filch.

raboteur [rabɔ'tœːr], *n.m.* planer.

raboteuse (1) [rabɔ'tøːz], *n.f.* planing machine.

raboteux [rabɔ'tø], *a.* (*fem.* -euse (2)) knotty; rough, rugged, uneven; (*fig.*) harsh (*of style*).

rabougri [rabu'gri], *a.* stunted, dwarfed.

rabougrir [rabu'griːr], *v.t.* to stunt.

raboutir [rabu'tiːr], **rabouter** [rabu'te], *v.t.* to join end to end, to join on.

rabrouer [rabru'e], *v.t.* to snub, to rebuke sharply.

rabroueur [rabru'œːr], *n.m.* (*fem.* -euse) snappish person, scold.

racaille [ra'kɑːj], *n.f.* rabble, riffraff; rubbish, trash.

raccommodage [rakɔmɔ'daːʒ], *n.m.* mending, repairing; darning.

raccommodement [rakɔmɔd'mɑ̃], *n.m.* reconciliation.

raccommoder [rakɔmɔ'de], *v.t.* to mend, to repair; to darn; to patch; to set right, to correct; to reconcile. **se raccommoder**, *v.r.* to be reconciled.

raccommodeur [rakɔmɔ'dœːr], *n.m.* (*fem.* -euse) mender.

raccompagner [rakɔ̃pa'ne], *v.t.* to accompany back.

raccord [ra'kɔːr], *n.m.* joining, fitting; joint, connection.

raccordement [rakɔrdə'mɑ̃], *n.m.* joining, union, junction; levelling; *voie de raccordement*, loop *or* junction line.

raccorder [rakɔr'de], *v.t.* to join, to unite, to connect. **se raccorder**, *v.r.* to fit together, to blend.

raccourci [rakur'si], *a.* shortened, abridged. —*n.m.* abridgment, epitome; short cut.

raccourcir [rakur'siːr], *v.t.* to shorten, to curtail, to abridge.—*v.i.* to become shorter; to take a short cut. **se raccourcir**, *v.r.* to grow shorter, to contract, to shrink.

raccourcissement [rakursis'mɑ̃], *n.m.* shortening, abridgment, shrinking.

raccoutrage [raku'traːʒ], **raccoutrement** [rakutrə'mɑ̃], *n.m.* mending (*of clothes etc.*).

raccoutrer [raku'tre], *v.t.* to mend, to repair (*garment*).

raccoutumer (se) [sərakuty'me], *v.r.* to reaccustom oneself, to get used to again.

raccroc [ra'kro], *n.m.* chance, lucky stroke (*esp. at billiards*), fluke.

raccrocher [rakrɔ'ʃe], *v.t.* to hook up again, to hang up again; (*colloq.*) to recover.—*v.i.* to make flukes (*at play*); (*Teleph.*) to ring off. **se raccrocher**, *v.r.* to cling; to retrieve one's losses; to grasp *or* snatch at.

race [ras], *n.f.* race; stock, breed; family, ancestry; generation; *un cheval de race*, a thoroughbred horse.

rachat [ra'ʃa], *n.m.* repurchase, redemption.

rachetable [raʃ'tabl], *a.* redeemable.

racheter [raʃ'te], *v.t.* (*conjug. like* AMENER) to buy back, to repurchase; to redeem; to ransom; to compensate; to atone for. **se racheter**, *v.r.* to redeem oneself; to be made up for.

rachitique [raʃi'tik], *a.* rachitic, rickety.—*n.* rickety person.

rachitis [raʃi'tis], **rachitisme** [raʃi'tism], *n.m.* rachitis, rickets; (*Bot.*) blight.

racial [ra'sjal], *a.* (*m. pl.* -aux) racial.

racine [ra'sin], *n.f.* root; (*fig.*) principle, origin.

racisme [ra'sism], *n.m.* racialism, racism.

raciste [ra'sist], *a.* racial.—*n.* racialist, racist.

raclage [ra'klaːʒ], *n.m.* scraping, raking.

racle [rɑːkl], *n.f.* scraper.

raclée [rɑ'kle], *n.f.* (*fam.*) thrashing, hiding.

racler [rɑ'kle], *v.t.* to scrape, to rake; to rasp.

racleur [rɑ'klœːr], *n.m.* (*fem.* -euse) scraper; (*fam.*) bad violinist.

racloir [rɑ'klwaːr], *n.m.* scraper, road scraper.

raclure [rɑ'klyːr], *n.f.* scrapings.

racolage [rakɔ'laːʒ], *n.m.* impressing; recruiting.

racoler [rakɔ'le], *v.t.* to enlist.

racoleur [rakɔ'lœːr], *n.m.* tout.

racontable [rakɔ̃'tabl], *a.* relatable.

racontar [rakɔ̃'taːr], *n.m.* gossip, tittle-tattle.

raconter [rakɔ̃'te], *v.t.* to relate, to tell, to narrate.

raconteur [rakɔ̃'tœːr], *n.m.* (*fem.* -euse) story-teller, narrator, raconteur.

racornir [rakɔr'niːr], *v.t.* to harden; to dry up, to shrivel up. **se racornir**, *v.r.* to grow hard; to shrivel up; to grow callous.

racornissement [rakɔrnis'mɑ̃], *n.m.* hardening.

racquit [ra'ki], *n.m.* winning back.

racquitter [raki'te], *v.t.* to indemnify, to recoup. **se racquitter**, *v.r.* to retrieve one's losses.

radar [ra'dar], *n.m.* radar.

radariste [rada'rist], *n.* radar operator.

rade [rad], *n.f.* (*Naut.*) roads, roadstead.

radeau [ra'do], *n.m.* (*pl.* -eaux) raft.

radiance [ra'djɑ̃ːs], *n.f.* radiance, luster.

radiant [ra'djɑ̃], *a.* radiant.

radiateur [radja'tœːr], *a.* (*fem.* -trice) radiating.—*n.m.* radiator.

radiation [radja'sjɔ̃], *n.f.* radiation, irradiation; obliteration.

radical [radi'kal], *a.* (*m. pl.* -aux) radical; complete.—*n.m.* radical; root.

radicalement [radikal'mɑ̃], *adv.* radically.

radicalisme [radika'lism], *n.m.* radicalism.

radier (1) [ra'dje], *n.m.* floor *or* apron (*of docks, locks, basins etc.*); invert (*of tunnel*).

radier (2) [ra'dje], *v.t.* to strike out, to erase.—*v.i.* to radiate, to beam (*with satisfaction*).

radieux [ra'djø], *a.* (*fem.* -euse) radiant, beaming, shining.

radio [ra'djo], *n.f.* broadcasting, radio; radio set; radiography.—*n.m.* radio message; radio operator.

radio-actif [radjoak'tif], *a.* (*fem.* -tive) radio-active.

radio-activité [radjoaktivi'te], *n.f.* radio-activity.

radiodiffuser [radjodify'ze], *v.t.* to broadcast.

radiodiffusion [radjodify'zjɔ̃], *n.f.* broadcasting.

radiographie [radjɔgra'fi], *n.f.* radiography.

radio-reporter [radjɔrɔpɔr'tɛːr], *n.m.* commentator.

radio-thérapie [radjotera'pi], *n.f.* X-ray treatment, radio-therapy.

radis [ra'di], *n.m.* radish.

radium [ra'djɔm], *n.m.* radium.

radotage [rado'ta:ʒ], *n.m.* nonsense, drivel; dotage.

radoter [rado'te], *v.i.* to talk idly, to talk drivel; to dote.

radoteur [rado'tœːr], *n.m.* (*fem.* **-euse**) driveller; dotard.

radoucir [radu'siːr], *v.t.* to soften; to appease, to pacify. **se radoucir**, *v.r.* to grow milder; to soften, to be appeased, to relent, to relax.

radoucissement [radusis'mɑ̃], *n.m.* softening; getting milder (*of the weather*); mitigation, appeasement.

rafale [ra'fal], *n.f.* squall; gust of wind; (*Mil.*) burst of fire.

raffermir [rafɛr'miːr], *v.t.* to make firm, to secure, to strengthen; to confirm. **se raffermir**, *v.r.* to grow stronger; to be established; to improve in strength *or* health.

raffermissement [rafɛrmis'mɑ̃], *n.m.* hardening; securing; strengthening; confirmation.

raffinage [rafi'na:ʒ], *n.m.* refining.

raffiné [rafi'ne], *a.* refined, delicate; subtle, clever; polished.—*n.m.* (*fem.* **-ée**) exquisite; sophisticated person.

raffinement [rafin'mɑ̃], *n.m.* refinement, affectation.

raffiner [rafi'ne], *v.t.* to refine.—*v.i.* to split hairs. **se raffiner**, *v.r.* to become refined.

raffinerie [rafin'ri], *n.f.* refinery.

raffineur [rafi'nœːr], *n.m.* (*fem.* **-euse**) refiner.

raffoler [rafɔ'le], *v.i.* to dote, to be passionately fond (*de*).

rafistolage [rafisto'la:ʒ], *n.m.* (*colloq.*) patching up, mending.

rafistoler [rafisto'le], *v.t.* to mend, to patch up.

rafle [ra:fl], *n.f.* clean sweep (*by thieves*); raid, round-up in the streets by police.

rafler [ra'fle], *v.t.* to sweep off, to carry off; to round up (*of police*).

rafraîchir [rafrɛ'ʃiːr], *v.t.* to cool; to refresh, to restore, to renew; to rub up; to trim.—*v.i.* to cool; to freshen. **se rafraîchir**, *v.r.* to cool, to take refreshment; to be refreshed, to rest.

rafraîchissant [rafrɛʃi'sɑ̃], *a.* cooling, refreshing; laxative.

rafraîchissement [rafrɛʃis'mɑ̃], *n.m.* cooling; (*pl.*) cool drinks.

ragaillardir [ragaiar'diːr], *v.t.* to enliven, to cheer up, to buck up.

rage [ra:ʒ], *n.f.* rabies; hydrophobia; violent pain; rage, fury; passion; mania.

rager [ra'ʒe], *v.i.* (*conjug. like* MANGER) (*colloq.*) to be in a passion; to be angry, to fume.

rageur [ra'ʒœːr], *a.* and *n.m.* (*fem.* **-euse**) ill-tempered (person).

ragot [ra'go], *a.* thick-set.—*n.m.* tittle-tattle.

ragoût [ra'gu], *n.m.* ragout; stew; (*fig.*) relish.

ragoûtant [ragu'tɑ̃], *a.* relishing, savory, (*fig.*) inviting, tempting.

ragoûter [ragu'te], *v.t.* to restore the appetite of; to stimulate, to stir up.

ragrafer [ragra'fe], *v.t.* to reclasp, to hook again.

ragréer [ragre'e], *v.t.* to give the finishing touch to (*wall, building*); to renovate (*building*).

ragrément *or* **ragréement** [ragre'mɑ̃], *n.m.* finishing; restoration, renovation.

rai [RAIS].

raid [rɛd], *n.m.* long-distance run *or* flight; raid; *un raid aérien*, an air-raid.

raide [rɛd], *a.* stiff, rigid; taut; steep; firm; rapid.—*adv.* quickly, swiftly, suddenly.

raideur [rɛ'dœːr], *n.f.* stiffness; inflexibility; steepness; harshness.

raidillon [rɛdi'jɔ̃], *n.m.* stiff ascent.

raidir [rɛ'diːr], *v.t.* to stiffen; to tighten; to make inflexible.—*v.i.* and **se raidir**, *v.r.* to stiffen; to be inflexible; (*fig.*) to harden oneself (*contre*).

raidissement [rɛdis'mɑ̃], *n.m.* stiffening, tautening.

raie [rɛ], *n.f.* line, stroke; stripe; parting (*of hair*); (*Ichth.*) ray, skate.

raifort [rɛ'fɔːr], *n.m.* horse-radish.

rail [ra:j, ra:j], *n.m.* (*Rail.*) rail.

railler [ra'je], *v.t.* to chaff; to scoff at.—*v.i.* to banter, to jest. **se railler**, *v.r.* to jest, to mock, to make game (*de*).

raillerie [roj'ri], *n.f.* raillery, bantering; jesting.

railleur [ra'jœːr], *a.* (*fem.* **-euse**) bantering, joking; jeering, scoffing.—*n.m.* (*fem.* **-euse**) banterer, joker; scoffer.

rainette [rɛ'nɛt], *n.f.* (*Zool.*) tree toad.

rainure [rɛ'nyːr], *n.f.* groove, rabbet, slot.

rais *or* **rai** [rɛ], *n.m.* spoke (*of a wheel*); ray (*of light*).

raisin [rɛ'zɛ̃], *n.m.* grapes; *des raisins secs*, raisins.

raisiné [rɛzi'ne], *n.m.* grape jam.

raison [rɛ'zɔ̃], *n.f.* reason; sense, judgment; satisfaction; justice, right; proof, ground; motive; *avoir raison*, to be right.

raisonnable [rɛzɔ'nabl], *a.* rational, reasonable, sensible; just, right; adequate, moderate, fair.

raisonnablement [rɛzɔnablə'mɑ̃], *adv.* reasonably, sensibly; fairly, justly, moderately; tolerably.

raisonné [rɛzɔ'ne], *a.* rational, intelligent; systematic; classified, analytical.

raisonnement [rɛzɔn'mɑ̃], *n.m.* reasoning, argument.

raisonner [rɛzɔ'ne], *v.t.* to study; to talk *or* discourse upon.—*v.i.* to reason; to argue; to answer, to murmur. **se raisonner**, *v.r.* to reason with oneself.

raisonneur [rɛzɔ'nœːr], *a.* (*fem.* **-euse**) reasoning; argumentative.—*n.m.* (*fem.* **-euse**) reasoner, logician; argufier, pertinacious answerer.

rajeunir [raʒœ'niːr], *v.t.* to rejuvenate; to make look young *or* younger; to renew; to modernize.—*v.i.* to grow young again. **se**

rajeunir, *v.r.* to make oneself look young again.

rajeunissant [raʒœni'sɑ̃], *a.* that makes one look younger, rejuvenating.

rajeunissement [raʒœnis'mɑ̃], *n.m.* rejuvenation; renewal, renovation.

rajouter [raʒu'te], *v.t.* to add again; to add more of.

rajustement [raʒysta'mɑ̃], *n.m.* readjustment, setting in order; (*fig.*) reconciliation.

rajuster [raʒys'te], *v.t.* to readjust; (*fig.*) to settle, to reconcile. **se rajuster**, *v.r.* to readjust *or* straighten one's dress; to be reconciled.

râle (1) [rɑːl], **râlement** [rɑːl'mɑ̃], *n.m.* rattling in the throat; death rattle.

râle (2) [rɑːl], *n.m.* (*Orn.*) rail.

ralenti [ralɑ̃'ti], *a.* slower.—*n.m.* (*Cine.*) slow motion; *tourner au ralenti*, (*Motor.*) to idle.

ralentir [ralɑ̃'tiːr], *v.t.*, *v.i.* to slow down, to ease up; to lessen, to moderate. **se ralentir**, *v.r.* to slacken, to slow up; to abate, to relax.

ralentissement [ralɑ̃tis'mɑ̃], *n.m.* slackening; decrease; cooling (*of zeal*).

râler [rɑ'le], *v.i.* to be at one's last gasp.

ralliement [rali'mɑ̃], *n.m.* rallying, rally; winning over; *mot de ralliement*, (*Mil.*) password.

rallier [ra'lje], *v.t.* to rally; to rejoin; to win over. **se rallier**, *v.r.* to rally; to join.

rallonge [ra'lɔ̃ːʒ], *n.f.* lengthening-piece, leaf; *table à rallonges*, draw-table.

rallongement [ralɔ̃ʒ'mɑ̃], *n.m.* lengthening, extension.

rallonger [ralɔ̃'ʒe], *v.t.* (*conjug. like* MANGER) to lengthen; to let out (*skirt*).

rallumer [raly'me], *v.t.* to relight; to rekindle; to revive. **se rallumer**, *v.r.* to light again; (*fig.*) to rekindle.

rallye [ra'li], *n.m.* (*Motor.*) race meeting, rally.

ramage [ra'maːʒ], *n.m.* floral pattern (*on materials*); chirping, warbling (*of birds*); (*fig.*) prattle (*of children*).

ramaigrir [ramɛ'griːr], *v.t.* to make lean *or* thin again.—*v.i.* to grow thin again.

ramaigrissement [ramɛgris'mɑ̃], *n.m.* emaciation, leanness.

ramas [ra'mɑ], *n.m. inv.* heap, disorderly collection; set, troop, lot, rabble.

ramassé [rama'se], *a.* thick-set, stocky; compact.

ramasser [rama'se], *v.t.* to collect, to gather; to pick up, to take up. **se ramasser**, *v.r.* to assemble, to gather together; to roll itself up (*of an animal*); to crouch; to pick oneself up (*after a spill*).

ramasseur [rama'sœːr], *n.m.* (*fem.* **-euse**) gatherer, collector.

ramassis [rama'si], [RAMAS].

rame [ram], *n.f.* scull, oar; (*Hort.*) stick, prop; (*Manuf.*) tenter frame; ream (*of paper*); made-up train *or* portion of train; *une rame de Métro*, an Underground train, a subway train.

ramé [ra'me], *a.* supported with sticks (*of peas*), staked (*of plants*).

rameau [ra'mo], *n.m.* (*pl.* **-eaux**) bough, small branch (*of a tree*); subdivision.

ramée [ra'me], *n.f.* green boughs, green arbor.

ramener [ram'ne], *v.t.* (*conjug. like* AMENER) to bring back; to take home; to restore; to reclaim; to recall.

ramer (1) [ra'me], *v.t.* to stick (*peas*), to stake (*plants*).

ramer (2) [ra'me], *v.i.* to row, to scull.

rameur [ra'mœːr], *n.m.* (*fem.* **-euse**) rower.

ramier [ra'mje], *n.m.* wood pigeon, ring dove.

ramification [ramifika'sjɔ̃], *n.f.* ramification.

ramifier [rami'fje], *v.t.* to ramify. **se ramifier**, *v.r.* to ramify, to divide.

ramille [ra'miːj], *n.f.*, **ramillon** [rami'jɔ̃], *n.m.* twig.

ramollir [ramɔ'liːr], *v.t.* to soften, (*fig.*) to enervate, to unman. **se ramollir**, *v.r.* to soften; (*fig.*) to relent.

ramollissant [ramɔli'sɑ̃], *a.* softening, emollient.

ramollissement [ramɔlis'mɑ̃], *n.m.* softening.

ramonage [ramɔ'naːʒ], *n.m.* chimney sweeping.

ramoner [ramɔ'ne], *v.t.* to sweep (*a chimney*).

ramoneur [ramɔ'nœːr], *n.m.* chimney sweeper, sweep.

rampant [rɑ̃'pɑ̃], *a.* creeping, crawling; (*fig.*) cringing, servile.

rampe [rɑ̃ːp], *n.f.* banister; flight of stairs; slope, ramp, incline, gradient; (*Theat.*) footlights.

rampement [rɑ̃p'mɑ̃], *n.m.* creeping, crawling.

ramper [rɑ̃'pe], *v.i.* to creep, to crawl; (*fig.*) to crouch, to grovel.

ramure [ra'myːr], *n.f.* branches, boughs; antlers (*of a stag*).

rancart [rɑ̃'kaːr], *n.m. mettre au rancart*, to throw aside, to cast off; to put on the shelf.

rance [rɑ̃ːs], *a.* rancid, rank.—*n.m.* rancidness.

ranci [rɑ̃'si], *a.* rancid.

rancidité [rɑ̃sidi'te], **rancissure** [rɑ̃si'syːr], *n.f.*, **rancissement** [rɑ̃sis'mɑ̃], *n.m.* rancidity.

rancir [rɑ̃'siːr], *v.i.* to grow rancid.

rancœur [rɑ̃'kœːr], *n.f.* rancor, bitterness.

rançon [rɑ̃'sɔ̃], *n.f.* ransom.

rançonnement [rɑ̃sɔn'mɑ̃], *n.m.* ransoming; (*fig.*) extortion.

rançonner [rɑ̃sɔ'ne], *v.t.* to ransom; (*fig.*) to fleece.

rancune [rɑ̃'kyn], *n.f.* rancor, spite, grudge, malice.

rancunier [rɑ̃ky'nje], *a.* and *n.m.* (*fem.* **-ière**) rancorous, spiteful (person).

randonnée [rɑ̃dɔ'ne], *n.f.* outing, run, ramble, tour.

rang [rɑ̃], *n.m.* row, line; order, class; rank.

rangé [rɑ̃'ʒe], *a.* tidy; steady; *en bataille rangée*, in a pitched battle.

rangée [rɑ̃'ʒe], *n.f.* row, range, line, tier, set.

rangement [rɑ̃ʒ'mɑ̃], *n.m.* arranging, putting in order.

ranger [rɑ̃'ʒe], *v.t.* (*conjug. like* MANGER) to put in order, to set to rights; to draw up; to arrange; to range; to rank; to reduce, to subdue. **se ranger**, *v.r.* to make room, to make way (*for*); to draw up (*of carriages,* *troops etc.*), to pull up (*at curb*); to fall in (*of soldiers*).

ranimer [rani'me], *v.t.* to restore to life, to revive; to rouse, to enliven; to cheer up. **se ranimer**, *v.r.* to revive, to brighten up, to be enlivened; to cheer up.

Raoul [ra'ul], *m.* Ralph.

rapace [ra'pas], *a.* rapacious; grasping (*of person*).—*n.m.* rapacious bird, bird of prey.

rapacement [rapas'mã], *adv.* rapaciously.

rapacité [rapasi'te], *n.f.* rapacity; cupidity.

râpage [rɑ'pa:ʒ], *n.m.* rasping; grating.

rapatriement [rapatri'mã], *n.m.* repatriation.

rapatrier [rapatri'je], *v.t.* to repatriate; (*dial.*) to reconcile.

râpe [rɑ:p], *n.f.* grater; rasp; stalk (*of grapes*).

râpé [rɑ'pe], *a.* grated; rasped; threadbare (*of clothes*).

râper [rɑ'pe], *v.t.* to grate (*cheese*), to rasp; to make threadbare.

rapetassage [rapta'sa:ʒ], *n.m.* patching up, mending, cobbling.

rapetasser [rapta'se], *v.t.* to patch, to mend, to cobble.

rapetasseur [rapta'sœ:r], *n.m.* (*fem.* **-euse**) piecer, patcher; cobbler; (*fig.*) compiler, adapter.

rapetissement [raptis'mã], *n.m.* shortening, shrinking; (*fig.*) belittling.

rapetisser [rapti'se], *v.t.* to shorten, to make smaller; (*fig.*) to belittle.—*v.i.* to grow less, to shorten, to shrink.

raphia [ra'fja], *n.m.* raffia.

rapide [ra'pid], *a.* rapid, quick, fast; sudden; steep.—*n.m.* rapid; fast train.

rapidement [rapid'mã], *adv.* rapidly, swiftly, steeply.

rapidité [rapidi'te], *n.f.* rapidity; speed; steepness.

rapiéçage [rapje'sa:ʒ], **rapiècement** [rapjes'mã], *n.m.* piecing, patching.

rapiécer [rapje'se], (*see Verb Tables*), **rapiéceter** [rapjes'te] (*conjug. like* AMENER), *v.t.* to piece, to patch.

rapière [ra'pje:r], *n.f.* rapier.

rapin [ra'pɛ̃], *n.m.* art student; (*fig.*) dauber.

rapine [ra'pin], *n.f.* rapine, robbery; plunder; graft.

rapiner [rapi'ne], *v.t., v.i.* to pillage, to plunder.

rapineur [rapi'nœ:r], *n.m.* (*fem.* **-euse**) plunderer, pillager, pilferer.

rappareiller [rapare'je], **rapparier** [rapa'rje], *v.t.* to match, to complete.

rappel [ra'pel], *n.m.* recall, reminder, call (*to order*); tattoo, assembly; revocation; back pay; (*Theat.*) curtain call.

rappeler [ra'ple], *v.t.* (*conjug. like* APPELER) to call back, to recall; to restore (*to life etc.*); to muster; to retract; to recall to mind; to remind. **se rappeler**, *v.r.* to recollect, to remember.

rapport [ra'pɔ:r], *n.m.* revenue, profit; produce; productiveness; report, account, information, tale; return, statement; resemblance, conformity; agreement; connection; communication; proportion; reimbursement; **faire un rapport**, to draw up a report; **maison de rapport**, tenement house; **sous tous les rapports**, in every respect.

rapporter [rapɔr'te], *v.t.* to bring back; to bring home; to yield; to retrieve (*of dog*); to refund; to recall; to give an account of; to attribute.—*v.i.* to retrieve (*of dog*); (*sch.*) to tell tales; to be profitable. **se rapporter**, *v.r.* to agree, to correspond, to tally; to be related.

rapporteur [rapɔr'tœ:r], *n.m.* (*fem.* **-euse**) tale-bearer; reporter.—*n.m.* (*Geom.*) protractor.

rapprendre [ra'prã:dr], *v.t. irr.* (*conjug. like* PRENDRE) to learn anew; to teach again.

rapprochement [raprɔʃ'mã], *n.m.* drawing closer, bringing together; reconciliation; junction; comparison.

rapprocher [raprɔ'ʃe], *v.t.* to bring near again; to bring together; to reconcile; to compare. **se rapprocher**, *v.r.* to come near again; to draw nearer; to be brought together; to become reconciled; to approximate (*de*).

rapsodie [rapso'di], *n.f.* rhapsody.

rapt [rapt], *n.m.* abduction; kidnapping.

raquette [ra'ket], *n.f.* racket, battledore; snow-shoe.

rare [ra:r], *a.* rare, uncommon; scarce; thin, scanty.

raréfaction [rarefak'sjõ], *n.f.* rarefaction.

raréfiant [rare'fjã], *a.* rarefying. **se raréfier**, *v.r.* to become rare; to become rarefied.

raréfier [rare'fje], *v.t.* to rarefy. **se raréfier**, *v.r.* to become rare; to become rarefied.

rarement [rar'mã], *adv.* rarely, seldom.

rareté [rar'te], *n.f.* rarity; scarcity.

rarissime [rari'sim], *a.* very rare, most rare.

ras [rɑ], *a.* close-shaven, shorn; bare, smooth, open, flat, low; **faire table rase**, to sweep away all preconceptions; **rase campagne**, open country.—*n.m.* short-nap cloth; level; raft; race (*of a mill*) [RAZ].

rasade [rɑ'zad], *n.f.* brimful glass (*of wine*).

rasant [rɑ'zã], *a.* shaving, grazing; sweeping; (*fam.*) boring.

raser [rɑ'ze], *v.t.* to shave; to demolish; to graze, to skim over; (*fam.*) to bore. **se raser**, *v.r.* to shave, to be shaved.

rasoir [rɑ'zwa:r], *n.m.* razor; (*fam.*) bore.

rassasiant [rasa'zjã], *a.* satiating, filling (*food*).

rassasiement [rasazi'mã], *n.m.* satiety.

rassasier [rasa'zje], *v.t.* to satisfy, to fill; to satiate; to surfeit. **se rassasier**, *v.r.* to be cloyed; to take one's fill.

rassemblement [rasãblə'mã], *n.m.* assembly, muster, crowd, mob; political group.

rassembler [rasã'ble], *v.t.* to gather together, to collect; to put together; to assemble. **se rassembler**, *v.r.* to assemble, to congregate, to muster.

rasseoir [ra'swa:r], *v.t. irr.* (*conjug. like* ASSEOIR) to seat again, to reseat; to replace; to calm, to compose. **se rasseoir**, *v.r.* to sit down again; to settle (*of liquids*); to become composed again.

rasséréner [rasere'ne], *v.t.* (*conjug. like* CÉDER) to clear up; to restore serenity to. **se rasséréner**, *v.r.* to clear up; to recover one's serenity.

rassis [ra'si], *a.* settled; calm, staid, sedate; stale.

rassortiment [rasɔrti'mã], **réassortiment** [reasɔrti'mã], *n.m.* rematching (*of colors, materials etc.*), resorting; restocking.

rassortir [rasɔr'tiːr], **réassortir** [reasɔr'tiːr], *v.t.* to sort *or* match again; to stock (*a shop etc.*).

rassurant [rasy'rɑ̃], *a.* tranquillizing; encouraging, reassuring.

rassurer [rasy're], *v.t.* to make firm; to strengthen; to tranquillize, to reassure. **se rassurer**, *v.r.* to be reassured; to reassure oneself; to clear up (*of the weather*); *rassurez-vous*, set your mind at rest.

rat [ra], *n.m.* rat; *rat des champs*, field mouse; *rat d'hôtel*, hotel thief.

ratafia [rata'fja], *n.m.* ratafia.

ratatiné [ratati'ne], *a.* shrivelled, shrunken.

ratatiner (se) [səratati'ne], *v.r.* to shrink, to shrivel up.

rate (1) [rat], *n.f.* spleen.

rate (2) [rat], *n.f.* female rat.

râteau [rɑ'to], *n.m.* (*pl.* **-eaux**) rake.

râtelage [rɑt'laːʒ], *n.m.* raking.

râtelée [rɑt'le], *n.f.* rakeful, raking.

râteler [rɑt'le], *v.t.* (*conjug. like* APPELER) to rake.

râteleur [rɑt'lœːr], *n.m.* (*fem.* **-euse**) raker.

râtelier [rɑtə'lje], *n.m.* rack; set of teeth, denture.

rater [ra'te], *v.t.* to miss; (*fig.*) to fail to obtain.—*v.i.* to misfire, to miss (*one's shot*); (*fig.*) to miscarry.

ratière [ra'tjeːr], *n.f.* rat trap.

ratification [ratifika'sjɔ̃], *n.f.* ratification.

ratifier [rati'fje], *v.t.* to ratify.

ratine [ra'tin], *n.f.* ratteen, petersham (*cloth*).

ration [ra'sjɔ̃], *n.f.* ration, allowance.

rationaliser [rasjonali'ze], *v.t.* to rationalize.

rationalisme [rasjona'lism], *n.m.* rationalism.

rationaliste [rasjona'list], *a.* and *n.* rationalist.

rationalité [rasjonali'te], *n.f.* rationality.

rationnel [rasjo'nɛl], *a.* (*fem.* **-elle**) rational.

rationnement [rasjon'mɑ̃], *n.m.* rationing.

rationner [rasjo'ne], *v.t.* to ration.

ratissage [rati'saːʒ], *n.m.* scraping; raking.

ratisser [rati'se], *v.t.* to rake; to scrape.

ratissoire [rati'swaːr], *n.f.* scraper, light rake, hoe.

ratissure [rati'syːr], *n.f.* scrapings.

raton [ra'tɔ̃], *n.m.* little rat; (*fig.*) little pet, darling.

rattacher [rata'ʃe], *v.t.* to refasten; to attach; (*fig.*) to link. **se rattacher**, *v.r.* to be attached *or* connected; to be linked up (*with*).

ratteindre [ra'tɛ̃ːdr], *v.t. irr.* (*conjug. like* CRAINDRE) to retake, to catch again; to overtake.

rattendrir [ratɑ̃'driːr], *v.t.* to soften again.

rattraper [ratra'pe], *v.t.* to catch again, to retake; to overtake; to recover. **se rattraper**, *v.r.* to catch hold (à); to be caught again; to make up for one's losses.

rature [ra'tyːr], *n.f.* erasure.

raturer [raty're], *v.t.* to erase.

raucité [rosi'te], *n.f.* raucity, hoarseness.

rauque [roːk], *a.* hoarse, raucous, rough.

ravage [ra'vaːʒ], *n.m.* ravage, havoc.

ravager [rava'ʒe], *v.t.* (*conjug. like* MANGER) to ravage, to lay waste; to spoil, to ruin.

ravageur [rava'ʒœːr], *n.m.* (*fem.* **-euse**) ravager, spoiler.

ravalement [raval'mɑ̃], *n.m.* scraping and pointing (*of a wall*); rough-casting; repainting.

ravaler [rava'le], *v.t.* to swallow again; (*fig.*) to disparage; to point (*stonework*); to rough-cast (*wall*). **se ravaler**, *v.r.* to debase oneself, to lower oneself.

ravaudage [ravo'daːʒ], *n.m.* mending (*of old clothes etc.*).

ravauder [ravo'de], *v.t.* to mend, to darn; (*dial.*) to scold.

ravaudeur [ravo'dœːr], *n.m.* (*fem.* **-euse**) mender (*of stockings, old clothes etc.*).

rave [raːv], *n.f.* (*Bot.*) **grosse rave**, French turnip; *petite rave*, radish.

ravenelle [rav'nɛl], *n.f.* wallflower.

ravi [ra'vi], *a.* carried away, enraptured, delighted.

ravier [ra'vje], *n.m.* radish dish.

ravière [ra'vjɛːr], *n.f.* radish bed.

ravigote [ravi'got], *n.f.* ravigote sauce.

ravigoter [ravigo'te], *v.t.* to revive, to refresh, to buck up. **se ravigoter**, *v.r.* to recover one's spirits, to perk up.

ravilir [ravi'liːr], *v.t.* to degrade, to lower.

ravin [ra'vɛ̃], *n.m.* ravine; gully.

ravine [ra'viːn], *n.f.* mountain torrent; small gully.

ravinement [ravin'mɑ̃], *n.m.* hollowing out *or* furrowing (*by waters*).

raviner [ravi'ne], *v.t.* to channel, to furrow.

ravir [ra'viːr], *v.t.* to carry off, to ravish; (*fig.*) to charm, to enrapture.

raviser (se) [səravi'ze], *v.r.* to change one's mind; to think better of it.

ravissant [ravi'sɑ̃], *a.* ravishing, delightful, charming.

ravissement [ravis'mɑ̃], *n.m.* carrying off; *rape; rapture, delight.

ravisseur [ravi'sœːr], *n.m.* (*fem.* **-euse**) ravisher; kidnapper.

ravitaillement [ravitaj'mɑ̃], *n.m.* revictualling; supplying; supplies; food.

ravitailler [ravita'je], *v.t.* to provision; to supply.

raviver [ravi've], *v.t.* to revive, to cheer; to freshen up (*colors*).

ravoir [ra'vwaːr], *v.t.* (*usu. in infin.*) to get back again, to recover.

rayé [rɛ'je], *a.* striped (*garment*); rifled (*gun*); scratched (*glass*); struck off (*a list*).

rayer [rɛ'je], *v.t.* (*conjug. like* PAYER) to scratch (*dishes etc.*); to streak, to stripe; to erase; (*Artill.*) to rifle.

rayon [rɛ'jɔ̃], *n.m.* ray; beam, gleam; radius; spoke (*of a wheel*); shelf; department (*of a shop*); *rayon de miel*, honeycomb.

rayonnant [rɛjo'nɑ̃], *a.* radiant, beaming.

rayonne [rɛ'jɔn], *n.f.* rayon.

rayonnement [rɛjon'mɑ̃], *n.m.* radiance; radiation.

rayonner [rɛjo'ne], *v.i.* to radiate; to shine; to beam; to sparkle.

rayure [rɛ'jyːr], *n.f.* stripe; streak, scratch; rifling (*of fire-arms*); erasure.

raz *or* **ras** [rɑ], *n.m. inv.* race (*a violent current*); *ras de marée*, tidal wave.

razzia [ra'zja], *n.f.* (*Algerian*) razzia, raid, inroad, foray.

ré [re], *n.m.* (*Mus.*) re, D.

réabonnement [reabon'mɑ̃], *n.m.* renewed subscription.

réabonner (se) [səreabɔ'ne], *v.r.* to renew one's subscription.
réacteur [reak'tœ:r], *n.m.* reactor; (*Av.*) jet engine.
réaction [reak'sjɔ̃], *n.f.* reaction; *les avions à réaction*, jet aircraft.
réactionnaire [reaksjɔ'nɛ:r], *a.* and *n.* reactionary.
réactionner [reaksjɔ'ne], *v.t.* to sue again.—*v.i.* (*St. Exch.*) to react against a rise.
réadmettre [read'mɛtr], *v.t. irr.* (*conjug. like* METTRE) to admit again, to readmit.
réadmission [readmi'sjɔ̃], *n.f.* readmission.
réagir [rea'ʒi:r], *v.i.* to react.
réajourner [reaʒur'ne], *v.t.* to readjourn.
réalisable [reali'zabl], *a.* realizable; feasible.
réalisateur [realiza'tœ:r], *n.m.* (*Cine.*) film director.
réalisation [realiza'sjɔ̃], *n.f.* realization; achievement; conversion into money; clearance sale.
réaliser [reali'ze], *v.t.* to realize; to achieve; to convert into money. **se réaliser**, *v.r.* to be realized, to come true.
réalisme [rea'lism], *n.m.* realism.
réaliste [rea'list], *a.* realistic.—*n.* realist.
réalité [reali'te], *n.f.* reality.
réapparaître [reapa'rɛ:tr], *v.i. irr.* (*conjug. like* CONNAÎTRE) to reappear.
réapparition [reapari'sjɔ̃], *n.f.* reappearance.
réarmement [rearmə'mɑ̃], *n.m.* rearmament.
réarmer [rear'me], *v.t.* to rearm; (*Navy*) to refit.
réassortiment [RASSORTIMENT].
rebaisser [rəbɛ'se], *v.t.* to lower again.
rébarbatif [rebarba'tif], *a.* (*fem.* **-tive**) stern, surly, forbidding.
rebâtir [rəba'ti:r], *v.t.* to rebuild.
rebattre [rə'batr], *v.t.* (*conjug. like* BATTRE) to beat again; to repeat; to shuffle (*cards*) again.
rebattu [rəba'ty], *a.* hackneyed, trite.
rebelle [rə'bɛl], *a.* rebellious; disobedient; unyielding; refractory.—*n.* rebel.
rebeller (se) [sərəbɛ'le], *v.r.* to rebel, to revolt.
rébellion [rebɛ'ljɔ̃], *n.f.* rebellion; resistance.
rebiffer (se) [sərəbi'fe], *v.r.* (*fam.*) to bridle up, to kick over the traces.
reblanchir [rəblɑ̃'ʃi:r], *v.t.* to bleach again; to whitewash again.
reboire [rə'bwa:r], *v.t. irr.* (*conjug. like* BOIRE) to drink again.
reboisement [rəbwaz'mɑ̃], *n.m.* retimbering, reforestation.
reboiser [rəbwa'ze], *v.t.* to retimber, to reforest.
rebond [rə'bɔ̃], *n.m.* rebound; bounce (*of ball*).
rebondi [rəbɔ̃'di], *a.* plump, chubby.
rebondir [rəbɔ̃'di:r], *v.i.* to rebound; to bounce.
rebondissement [rəbɔ̃dis'mɑ̃], *n.m.* rebounding; bounce.
rebord [rə'bɔ:r], *n.m.* edge, brink; sill (*of window*); border, hem.
reborder [rəbɔr'de], *v.t.* to border again, to re-hem.
rebouillir [rəbu'ji:r], *v.i. irr.* (*conjug. like* BOUILLIR) to boil again.
rebours [rə'bu:r], *a.* cross-grained (*wood*); intractable (*horse*).—*n.m.* wrong side (*of

material etc.*); wrong way (*of the grain*); contrary, reverse; *à rebours* or *au rebours*, the wrong way, against the grain, backwards.
reboutage [rəbu'ta:ʒ], *n.m.* bone-setting.
rebouter [rəbu'te], *v.t.* to set (*bones*).
rebouteur [rəbu'tœ:r], **rebouteux** [rəbu'tø], *n.m.* (*fem.* **-euse**) bone setter.
reboutonner [rəbuto'ne], *v.t.* to rebutton. **se reboutonner**, *v.r.* to button up one's clothes again.
rebroussement [rəbrus'mɑ̃], *n.m.* turning back, turning up.
rebrousse-poil (à) [arəbrus'pwal], *adv. phr.* against the grain; the wrong way.
rebrousser [rəbru'se], *v.t.* to turn up (*the hair*); *rebrousser chemin*, to turn back.
rebuffade [rəby'fad], *n.f.* rebuff, repulse; snub.
rébus [re'by:s], *n.m.* rebus; riddle.
rebut [rə'by], *n.m.* repulse, rebuff; refuse, rubbish; scum.
rebutant [rəby'tɑ̃], *a.* repulsive, disgusting, forbidding.
rebuter [rəby'te], *v.t.* to repulse, to rebuff, to reject, to snub; to disgust. **se rebuter**, *v.r.* to become discouraged.
récalcitrant [rekalsi'trɑ̃], *a.* refractory, recalcitrant; rebellious.
récalcitrer [rekalsi'tre], *v.i.* to kick (*of horses*); (*fig.*) to be refractory.
recaler [rəka'le], *v.t.* to wedge up again, to refix; (*Sch.*) to fail (*s. o. in an examination*).
récapitulation [rekapityla'sjɔ̃], *n.f.* recapitulation, summing up; summary.
récapituler [rekapity'le], *v.t.* to recapitulate, to sum up; (*colloq.*) to recap.
recel [rə'sɛl], **recèlement** [rəsɛl'mɑ̃], *n.m.* receiving of stolen goods.
receler [rəs'le] (*conjug. like* AMENER), **recéler** [rəse'le] (*conjug. like* CÉDER), *v.t.* to receive (*stolen goods*); to embezzle; to conceal from justice; to contain.
receleur [rəs'lœ:r], *n.m.* (*fem.* **-euse**) receiver of stolen goods, fence.
récemment [resa'mɑ̃], *adv.* recently, newly.
recensement [rəsɑ̃s'mɑ̃], *n.m.* census; return, inventory; verification.
recenser [rəsɑ̃'se], *v.t.* to take the census of; to record; to verify.
recenseur [rəsɑ̃'sœ:r], *n.m.* (*fem.* **-euse**) census taker; enumerator.
recension [rəsɑ̃'sjɔ̃], *n.f.* recension; collation (*of books etc.*).
récent [re'sɑ̃], *a.* recent, new, fresh, late.
receper [rəsə'pe] (*conjug. like* AMENER), **recéper** [rəse'pe] (*conjug. like* CÉDER), *v.t.* to cut back; to clear (*a wood*).
récépissé [resepi'se], *n.m.* receipt, acknowledgment (*for documents, papers etc.*).
réceptacle [resɛp'takl], *n.m.* receptacle; repository.
récepteur [resɛp'tœ:r], *a.* (*fem.* **-trice**) receiving; *poste récepteur*, receiving set.—*n.m.* receiver; reservoir (*in a machine, etc.*); receiving instrument (*of telegraphs*).
réception [resɛp'sjɔ̃], *n.f.* receiving, receipt; admission; (*hotel*) reception desk; reception, party.
réceptionnaire [resɛpsjɔ'nɛ:r], *a.* receiving.—*n.* receiver, receiving clerk; consignee.
réceptionniste [resɛpsjɔ'nist], *n.* receptionist.

269

recette [rə'sɛt], *n.f.* receipts, returns; takings; (*Cook.*) recipe; receiver's office; **faire recette**, to be a hit (*of a play*).

recevable [rəsə'vabl], *a.* receivable, admissible.

receveur [rəsə'vœ:r], *n.m.* (*fem.* **-euse**) receiver, collector (*of taxes etc.*); (*bus*) conductor.

recevoir [rəsə'vwa:r], *v.t. irr.* to receive, to accept, to take, to let in, to admit; to welcome; to entertain.—*v.i.* to receive, to be at home to visitors.

rechange [rə'ʃɑ̃:ʒ], *n.m.* change (*of anything*), replacement; spare things; (*Comm.*) re-exchange; **roue de rechange**, spare wheel.

rechanter [rəʃɑ̃'te], *v.t.* to sing again; to retell.

rechaper [rəʃa'pe], *v.t.* to retread (*a tire*).

réchapper [reʃa'pe], *v.i.* to escape; **réchapper d'une maladie**, to recover from an illness.

recharge [rə'ʃarʒ], *n.f.* fresh *or* second charge.

rechargement [rəʃarʒə'mɑ̃], *n.m.* reloading, relading; reballasting.

recharger [rəʃar'ʒe], *v.t.* (*conjug. like* MANGER) to load again; to recharge.

réchaud [re'ʃo], *n.m.* small portable stove; chafing dish; dish warmer.

réchauffage [reʃo'fa:ʒ], *n.m.* warming up again, reheating.

réchauffé [reʃo'fe], *n.m.* dish *or* food warmed up again; rehash, stale stuff *or* news.

réchauffer [reʃo'fe], *v.t.* to warm up, to reheat; to reanimate, to stir up. **se réchauffer**, *v.r.* to warm oneself, to get warm.

réchauffoir [reʃo'fwa:r], *n.m.* plate warmer, hot plate.

rechausser [rəʃo'se], *v.t.* to put shoes *or* stockings on (*a person*) again; (*Build.*) to u.iderpin.

rêche [rɛ:ʃ], *a.* rough (*to the taste, touch etc.*); (*fig.*) sour, crabbed (*of persons*).

recherche [rə'ʃɛrʃ], *n.f.* search, pursuit; inquiry, investigation; research; (*fig.*) studied elegance *or* refinement, affectation.

recherché [rəʃɛr'ʃe], *a.* choice, exquisite; affected; far-fetched; in great demand.

rechercher [rəʃɛr'ʃe], *v.t.* to seek again; to seek, to search for; to investigate, to pry into; to desire; to court, to woo.

rechigné [rəʃi'ɲe], *a.* sour-faced, surly, crabbed.

rechignement [rəʃiɲə'mɑ̃], *n.m.* sulking, sullenness.

rechigner [rəʃi'ɲe], *v.i.* to look sulky, sullen, grim etc; to balk (*at something*).

rechute [rə'ʃyt], *n.f.* relapse, set-back.

rechuter [rəʃy'te], *v.i.* to have a relapse; to backslide.

récidive [resi'di:v], *n.f.* recidivism; second offence.

récidiver [residi've], *v.i.* to repeat the offence; to relapse; to recur (*of disease*).

récidiviste [residi'vist], *n.* recidivist, old lag.

récif [re'sif], *n.m.* reef (*of rocks*).

récipé [resi'pe], *n.m.* recipe, prescription.

récipient [resi'pjɑ̃], *n.m.* container, receptacle; reservoir.

réciprocité [resiprəsi'te], *n.f.* reciprocity, reciprocation.

réciproque [resi'prɔk], *a.* reciprocal, mutual.

réciproquement [resiprɔk'mɑ̃], *adv.* reciprocally, mutually; vice versa.

récit [re'si], *n.m.* recital, account, story narrative, report.

récital [resi'tal], *n.m.* (*pl.* **-als**) musical recital.

récitant [resi'tɑ̃], *a.* (*Mus.*) solo (*instrument, voice*).—*n.m.* (*fem.* **-e**) soloist; narrator.

récitateur [resita'tœ:r], *n.m.* (*fem.* **-trice**) reciter, repeater.

récitatif [resita'tif], *n.m.* (*Mus.*) recitative.

récitation [resita'sjɔ̃], *n.f.* recitation, reciting; repetition.

réciter [resi'te], *v.t.* to recite, to rehearse; to repeat, to say; to tell, to relate, to recount.

réclamant [rekla'mɑ̃], *a.* claiming.—*n.m.* (*fem.* **-e**) claimant.

réclamation [reklama'sjɔ̃], *n.f.* claim, request, demand; complaint.

réclame [re'kla:m], *n.f.* advertisement; publicity; (*Print.*) catch-word; blurb.

réclamer [rekla'me], *v.t.* to crave, to entreat; to beseech; to claim.—*v.i.* to object, to complain; to protest (*contre*). **se réclamer**, *v.r.* to refer to.

reclus [rə'kly], *a.* shut up, secluded.—*n.m.* (*fem.* **-e**) recluse; monk, nun.

reclusion [rəkly'zjɔ̃], **réclusion** [rekly'zjɔ̃], *n.f.* reclusion, confinement; (*Law*) solitary confinement (*with hard labor*).

recoin [rə'kwɛ̃], *n.m.* corner, nook; **coins et recoins**, nooks and crannies.

récolte [re'kɔlt], *n.f.* harvest, crop, vintage.

récolter [rekɔl'te], *v.t.* to reap, to gather in; to get in.

recommandable [rəkəmɑ̃'dabl], *a.* respectable; commendable.

recommandation [rəkəmɑ̃da'sjɔ̃], *n.f.* recommendation; reference; (*fig.*) esteem; (*Post*) registration.

recommander [rəkəmɑ̃'de], *v.t.* to recommend; to enjoin; to request; to commend; (*Post*) to register. **se recommander**, *v.r.* to recommend oneself; to refer to.

recommencement [rəkəmɑ̃s'mɑ̃], *n.m.* re-commencement, fresh start.

recommencer [rəkəmɑ̃'se], *v.t., v.i.* (*conjug. like* COMMENCER) to recommence, to begin again; to do (*it*) again.

récompense [rekɔ̃'pɑ̃:s], *n.f.* reward, recompense; prize; compensation; **en récompense de**, in return for.

récompenser [rekɔ̃pɑ̃'se], *v.t.* to reward; to compensate; to repay.

recomposer [rəkɔ̃po'ze], *v.t.* to recompose.

recomposition [rəkɔ̃pozi'sjɔ̃], *n.f.* recomposition.

réconciliable [rekɔ̃si'ljabl], *a.* reconcilable.

réconciliateur [rekɔ̃silja'tœ:r], *n.m.* (*fem.* **-trice**) reconciler.

réconciliation [rekɔ̃silja'sjɔ̃], *n.f.* reconciliation.

réconcilier [rekɔ̃si'lje], *v.t.* to reconcile. **se réconcilier**, *v.r.* to be(come) reconciled; (*colloq.*) to make it up.

reconduire [rəkɔ̃'dɥi:r], *v.t. irr.* (*conjug. like* CONDUIRE) to lead back, to see home; to show out.

reconduite [rəkɔ̃'dɥit], *n.f.* showing out, seeing out, seeing home.

réconfort [rekɔ̃'fɔ:r], *n.m.* comfort, relief.

réconforter [rekɔ̃fɔr'te], *v.t.* to comfort, to cheer up; to fortify.

reconnaissable [rəkɔnɛ'sabl], *a.* recognizable.

reconnaissance [rəkɔnɛ'sɑ̃:s], *n.f.* recognition; discovery; gratitude, thankfulness; survey; acknowledgment, confession; reward; recognizance; pawn ticket; (*Mil.*) reconnaissance.

reconnaissant [rəkɔnɛ'sɑ̃], *a.* grateful, thankful.

reconnaître [rəkɔ'nɛ:tr], *v.t. irr.* (*conjug. like* CONNAÎTRE) to recognize, to identify; to discover; to acknowledge, to admit; to be grateful for; to reconnoitre. **se reconnaître,** *v.r.* to recognize oneself; to be recognizable; to make out where one is.

reconquérir [rəkɔ̃ke'ri:r], *v.t. irr.* (*conjug. like* ACQUÉRIR) to reconquer; to regain.

reconstituer [rəkɔ̃sti'tɥe], *v.t.* to reconstitute, to restore.

reconstitution [rəkɔ̃stity'sjɔ̃], *n.f.* reconstitution, reorganization; reconstruction (*of a murder*).

reconstruction [rəkɔ̃stryk'sjɔ̃], *n.f.* reconstruction, rebuilding.

reconstruire [rəkɔ̃s'trɥi:r], *v.t. irr.* (*conjug. like* CONDUIRE) to rebuild, to reconstruct; to rehabilitate.

recopier [rəkɔ'pje], *v.t.* to make a copy of.

recoquillement [rəkɔkij'mɑ̃], *n.m.* curling up, dog('s)-earing (*of pages of book*).

recoquiller [rəkɔki'je], *v.t.* to turn up *or* back. **se recoquiller,** *v.r.* to curl up, to shrivel.

record [rə'kɔ:r], *n.m.* record (*in sports etc.*).

recorder [rəkɔr'de], *v.t.* to learn by heart; to tie up again.

recors [rə'kɔ:r], *n.m.* local magistrate's helper.

recoucher [rəku'ʃe], *v.t.* to put to bed again; to lay down again. **se recoucher,** *v.r.* to go to bed again, to lie down again.

recoudre [rə'kudr], *v.t. irr.* (*conjug. like* COUDRE) to sew again, to sew up.

recoupement [rəkup'mɑ̃], *n.m.* (*Build.*) offset; cross-checking.

recouper [rəku'pe], *v.t.* to cut again; to cross-check.

recourbé [rəkur'be], *a.* curved, bent (back).

recourber [rəkur'be], *v.t.* to bend back, to bend round. **se recourber,** *v.r.* to be curved, to bend.

recourir [rəku'ri:r], *v.i. irr.* (*conjug. like* COURIR) to run again; to resort (*à*); (*Law*) to appeal.

recours [rə'kur], *n.m.* recourse; (*fig.*) resource, remedy; (*Law*) appeal.

recousu [rəku'zy], *a.* sewn *or* stitched again.

recouvrement [rəkuvrə'mɑ̃], *n.m.* recovery, regaining; recovering (*of debts etc.*); covering up, overlapping; cap (*of a watch*).

recouvrer [rəku'vre], *v.t.* to recover, to retrieve, to collect.

recouvrir [rəku'vri:r], *v.t. irr.* (*conjug. like* OUVRIR) to cover up, to cover over; to overlay; to hide. **se recouvrir,** *v.r.* to cover oneself again; to cloud over.

recracher [rəkra'ʃe], *v.t.* to spit out again; to disgorge.—*v.i.* to spit again.

récréatif [rekrea'tif], *a.* (*fem.* -**tive**) recreative, entertaining.

récréation [rekrea'sjɔ̃], *n.f.* recreation, amusement; (*Sch.*) playtime, break.

recréer [rəkre'e], *v.t.* to re-create, to create again.

récréer [rekre'e], *v.t.* to entertain; to amuse. **se récréer,** *v.r.* to amuse oneself, to take recreation.

recrépir [rəkre'pi:r], *v.t.* to give a fresh coat of plaster to; to repoint (*a wall*); (*fig.* and *fam.*) to paint (*one's face*); to recast.

recrépissement [rəkrepis'mɑ̃], **recrépissage** [rəkrepi'sa:ʒ], *n.m.* replastering; repatching.

récrier (se) [sərekri'je], *v.r.* to exclaim, to cry out; to protest (*contre*); to be amazed.

récrimination [rekrimina'sjɔ̃], *n.f.* recrimination.

récriminatoire [rekrimina'twa:r], *a.* recriminatory.

récriminer [rekrimi'ne], *v.i.* to recriminate.

récrire [re'kri:r], *v.t. irr.* (*conjug. like* ÉCRIRE) to rewrite; to write back.

recroqueviller (se) [sərəkrəkvi'je], *v.r.* to curl up, to shrivel.

recru [rə'kry], *a.* tired out, worn out.

recrudescence [rəkrydɛ'sɑ̃:s], *n.f.* recrudescence.

recrudescent [rəkrydɛ'sɑ̃], *a.* recrudescent.

recrue [rə'kry], *n.f.* recruiting; recruit.

recrutement [rəkryt'mɑ̃], *n.m.* recruiting, recruitment.

recruter [rəkry'te], *v.t.* to recruit; to enroll. **se recruter,** *v.r.* to be recruited.

recruteur [rəkry'tœ:r], *n.m.* recruiter; recruiting officer.

rectangle [rɛk'tɑ̃:gl], *n.m.* rectangle.

rectangulaire [rɛktɑ̃gy'lɛ:r], *a.* rectangular, right-angled.

recteur [rɛk'tœ:r], *n.m.* rector, vice-chancellor (*of a University*); parish priest (*in Brittany*).

rectifiable [rɛkti'fjabl], *a.* rectifiable.

rectification [rɛktifika'sjɔ̃], *n.f.* rectification; adjustment.

rectifier [rɛkti'fje], *v.t.* to rectify; to adjust; to reform.

rectiligne [rɛkti'liɲ], *a.* rectilinear.

rectitude [rɛkti'tyd], *n.f.* rectitude, uprightness.

recto [rɛk'to], *n.m.* first page of a leaf, right-hand page, recto.

rectorat [rɛktɔ'ra], *n.m.* rectorship.

reçu [rə'sy], *a.* received; admitted, recognized; *être reçu (à un examen)*, to pass (an examination).—*n.m.* receipt.

recueil [rə'kœ:j], *n.m.* collection, selection; anthology.

recueillement [rəkœj'mɑ̃], *n.m.* meditation; peaceful contemplation.

recueilli [rəkœ'ji], *a.* meditative, calm, rapt.

recueillir [rəkœ'ji:r], *v.t. irr.* (*conjug. like* CUEILLIR) to gather; to collect; to reap; to receive; to shelter. **se recueillir,** *v.r.* to collect one's thoughts; to be plunged in meditation.

recuire [rə'kɥi:r], *v.t. irr.* (*conjug. like* CONDUIRE) to cook again.

recuit [rə'kɥi], *a.* cooked, baked *or* roasted again.

recul [rə'kyl], *n.m.* recoil (*of cannon*), kick (*of rifle*); backing (*of horse, car*).

reculade [rəky'lad], *n.f.* falling back, retreat.

reculé [rəky'le], *a.* distant, remote.

reculement [rəkyl'mã], *n.m.* drawing back, backing (*of carriages etc.*); breech (*of saddles*).

reculer [rəky'le], *v.t.* to draw back, to move back, to back; (*fig.*) to put off, to defer.—*v.i.* to go back, to draw back, to retreat; to recoil; to give way. **se reculer**, *v.r.* to draw back, to become more remote.

reculons (à) [arəky'lõ], *adv. phr.* backwards.

récupérage [rekype'ra:ʒ], *n.m.*, **récupération** [rekypera'sjõ], *n.f.* recovery, recuperation.

récupérer [rekype're], *v.t.* (*conjug. like* CÉDER) to recover, to retrieve, to recuperate.

récurer [reky're], *v.t.* to scour, to clean.

récusable [reky'zabl], *a.* (*Law*) exceptionable, doubtful (*of witnesses etc.*).

récusation [rekyza'sjõ], *n.f.* (*Law*) challenge; exception.

récuser [reky'ze], *v.t.* to challenge, to object to (*witnesses, jurors etc.*); to reject. **se récuser**, *v.r.* to excuse oneself, to decline; to decline, to give a decision (*of judges, jurors etc.*).

rédacteur [redak'tœ:r], *n.m.* (*fem.* **-trice**) writer, inditer (*of deed*); clerk (*in public office*); **rédacteur en chef**, editor.

rédaction [redak'sjõ], *n.f.* drawing up (*deeds etc.*); wording; editing (*periodicals*); essay.

reddition [redi'sjõ], *n.f.* surrender; rendering (*of accounts*).

rédempteur [redãp'tœ:r], *a.* (*fem.* **-trice**) redeeming, redemptory.—*n.m.* redeemer, savior.

rédemption [redãp'sjõ], *n.f.* redemption; redeeming.

redescendre [rədɛ'sã:dr], *v.t.* (*with aux.* AVOIR) to carry or take down again.—*v.i.* (*with aux.* ÊTRE) to come, go or step down again.

redevable [rəd'vabl], *a.* indebted, owing.

redevance [rəd'vã:s], *n.f.* rent, due, tax.

redevenir [rədəv'ni:r], *v.i. irr.* (*conjug. like* TENIR, *but with aux.* ÊTRE) to become again.

redevoir [rəd(ə)'vwa:r], *v.t. irr.* (*conjug. like* DEVOIR) to owe still.

rédiger [redi'ʒe], *v.t.* (*conjug. like* MANGER) to draw up, to draft; to edit.

redingote [rədɛ̃'got], *n.f.* frock coat.

redire [rə'di:r], *v.t. irr.* (*conjug. like* DIRE) to repeat, to reveal.—*v.i.* to criticize; *trouver à redire à*, to find fault with.

redondance [rədõ'dã:s], *n.f.* superfluity of words, redundancy.

redondant [rədõ'dã], *a.* redundant.

redonner [rədɔ'ne], *v.t.* to give back again, to restore.—*v.i.* to fall again; to begin again; to charge again.

redoublé [radu'ble], *a.* redoubled, increased.

redoublement [rədublə'mã], *n.m.* redoubling, increase; (*Med.*) paroxysm.

redoubler [radu'ble], *v.t.* to redouble, to reiterate; to increase; to reline (*dress*).—*v.i.* to increase, to redouble.

redoutable [radu'tabl], *a.* formidable, redoubtable.

redoute [rə'dut], *n.f.* redoubt.

redouter [radu'te], *v.t.* to dread, to fear.

redressement [rədrɛs'mã], *n.m.* straightening; rectification, redress.

redresser [radrɛ'se], *v.t.* to make straight; to set up again; to put right; (*colloq.*) to rebuke. **se redresser**, *v.r.* to become

straight again; to right itself (*of a ship etc.*); to be redressed; *redressez-vous*, sit up.

redû [rə'dy], *n.m.* balance due.

réducteur [redyk'tœ:r], *a.* (*fem.* **-trice**) reducing.—*n.m.* (*Chem.*) reducer.

réductible [redyk'tibl], *a.* reducible.

réduction [redyk'sjõ], *n.f.* reduction; subjugation; allowance.

réduire [re'dɥi:r], *v.t. irr.* (*conjug. like* CONDUIRE) to reduce, to diminish; to subdue; to compel, to oblige. **se réduire**, *v.r.* to be reduced, to diminish, to abate, to vanish; to be subdued; to amount to.

réduit [re'dɥi], *a.* reduced; dimmed (*of light*).—*n.m.* retreat, nook; hovel; (*Fort.*) keep.

réédification [reedifika'sjõ], *n.f.* rebuilding.

réédifier [reedi'fje], *v.t.* to rebuild.

rééducatif [reedyka'tif], *a.* (*fem.* **-tive**) **thérapie rééducative**, occupational therapy.

réel [re'ɛl], *a.* (*fem.* **-elle**) real, actual; genuine.—*n.m.* reality.

réélection [reelɛk'sjõ], *n.f.* re-election.

réélire [ree'li:r], *v.t. irr.* (*conjug. like* LIRE) to re-elect.

réellement [reɛl'mã], *adv.* really, in reality.

réembobiner [reãbɔbi'ne], *v.t.* to rewind.

réemploi [reã'plwa], *n.m.* re-employment.

réexpédier [reɛkspe'dje], *v.t.* to send on, to (re)forward; to send back.

refaçonner [rəfasɔ'ne], *v.t.* to make again, to refashion.

réfaction [refak'sjõ], *n.f.* rebate, allowance.

refaire [rə'fɛ:r], *v.t. irr.* (*conjug. like* FAIRE) to do again, to remake; to recommence; to do up; to deal again (*at cards*); to revive; (*slang*) to cheat. **se refaire**, *v.r.* to recover one's strength; to recoup oneself.

refait [rə'fɛ], *a.* set up, done again; (*slang*) *j'ai été refait(e)*, I have been had.—*n.m.* drawn game.

réfection [refɛk'sjõ], *n.f.* repairs (*to buildings etc.*).

réfectoire [refɛk'twa:r], *n.m.* refectory, dining room or hall (*in college, convent etc.*).

refend [rə'fã], *n.m.* splitting, sawing, dividing; *mur de refend*, partition wall.

refendre [rə'fã:dr], *v.t.* to cleave or split again; to quarter (*timber*); to saw (*stone*) into slabs.

référence [refe'rã:s], *n.f.* reference.

referendum [referã'dom], **référendum** [referã'dom], *n.m.* referendum.

référer [refe're], *v.t.* (*conjug. like* CÉDER) to refer; to ascribe.—*v.i.* to refer; *en référer à*, to refer to. **se référer**, *v.r.* to refer, to have reference; to leave it (*à*); to trust (*à*).

refermer [rəfɛr'me], *v.t.* to shut again; to close up. **se refermer**, *v.r.* to shut itself; to close up; to heal up (*of wound*).

réfléchi [refle'ʃi], *a.* reflected; deliberate; reflective, thoughtful; wary; (*Gram.*) reflexive.

réfléchir [refle'ʃi:r], *v.t.* to reflect, to throw back; to reverberate.—*v.i.* to reflect, to consider, to ponder. **se réfléchir**, *v.r.* to be reflected.

réfléchissant [refleʃi'sã], *a.* reflecting.

réflecteur [reflɛk'tœ:r], *a.* reflecting.—*n.m.* reflector.

reflet [rə'flɛ], *n.m.* reflection, reflex; reflected light.

refléter [rəfle'te], *v.t.* (*conjug. like* CÉDER) to reflect (*light etc.*).—*v.i.* and **se refléter**, *v.r.* to be reflected.

refleurir [rəflœ'riːr], *v.i.* to blossom again.

réflexe [re'flɛks], *a.* and *n.m.* reflex.

réflexion [reflɛk'sjɔ̃], *n.f.* reflection; thought, consideration.

refluer [rə'flɥe], *v.i.* to reflow, to ebb; (*fig.*) to swing back.

reflux [rə'fly], *n.m.* reflux, ebb; flowing back.

refondre [rə'fɔ̃:dr], *v.t.* to refound (*metal*), to melt down again, to cast again; (*fig.*) to remodel.

refonte [rə'fɔ̃t], *n.f.* refounding, recasting; recoining; remodelling.

réformateur [reforma'tœ:r], *a.* (*fem.* -**trice**) reforming.—*n.m.* (*fem.* -**trice**) reformer.

réformation [reforma'sjɔ̃], *n.f.* reformation.

réforme [re'form], *n.f.* reform, reformation, amendment; (*Mil.*) reduction, discharge.

réformé [refor'me], *a.* reformed; (*Mil.*) invalided out of the service.

réformer [refor'me], *v.t.* to reform, to improve; (*Mil.*) to invalid. **se réformer**, *v.r.* to reform, to mend one's ways.

reformer [rəfor'me], *v.t.* to form again. **se reformer**, *v.r.* to form anew, to re-form (*of troops etc.*).

réformiste [refor'mist], *a.* and *n.* reformist.

refoulement [rəful'mɑ̃], *n.m.* driving back; (*Psych.*) inhibition, repression.

refouler [rəfu'le], *v.t.* to drive back; to compress; to suppress; to expel (*aliens*); to stem (*the tide*).—*v.i.* to ebb, to flow back; **la marée refoule**, the tide is ebbing.

réfractaire [refrak'tɛːr], *a.* refractory, obstinate, rebellious; **terre réfractaire**, fireproof clay.—*n.m.* defaulter.

réfracter [refrak'te], *v.t.* to refract. **se réfracter**, *v.r.* to be refracted.

réfraction [refrak'sjɔ̃], *n.f.* refraction.

refrain [rə'frɛ̃], *n.m.* refrain, chorus; (*fig.*) constant theme.

refréner [rəfre'ne], *v.t.* (*conjug. like* CÉDER) to curb, to control (*passions*); to bridle, to restrain.

réfrigérant [refriʒe'rɑ̃], *a.* refrigerant, cooling.—*n.m.* refrigerator.

réfrigérateur [refriʒera'tœ:r], *n.m.* refrigerating chamber; refrigerator, (*colloq.*) fridge; (*Am.*) icebox.

réfrigération [refriʒera'sjɔ̃], *n.f.* refrigeration.

réfrigérer [refriʒe're], *v.t.* (*conjug. like* CÉDER) to chill, to freeze (*food etc.*).

refroidir [rəfrwa'di:r], *v.t.* to cool, to chill.—*v.i.* to cool, to become cold. **se refroidir**, *v.r.* to cool, to grow cold; to catch cold; to slacken, to relax.

refroidissement [rəfrwadis'mɑ̃], *n.m.* cooling, refrigeration; coldness; chill, cold.

refuge [rə'fy:ʒ], *n.m.* refuge, shelter; (*street-*) island; lay-by.

réfugié [refy'ʒje], *n.m.* (*fem.* -**ée**) refugee.

réfugier (se) [sərefy'ʒje], *v.r.* to take refuge; (*fig.*) to have recourse (*to*) (*dans*).

refus [rə'fy], *n.m. inv.* refusal, denial.

refuser [rəfy'ze], *v.t.* to refuse, to deny, to decline, to reject.—*v.i.* to refuse; to decline.

se refuser, *v.r.* to deny oneself; to shun; to resist.

réfuter [refy'te], *v.t.* to refute, to disprove.

regagner [rəga'ne], *v.t.* to regain, to recover, to retrieve; to rejoin, to reach.

regain [rə'gɛ̃], *n.m.* aftermath; second crop; (*fig.*) revival, new lease (*of life*).

régal [re'gal], *n.m.* feast, entertainment, treat.

régalade [rega'lad], *n.f.* giving a treat, regaling; blazing fire.

régalant [rega'lɑ̃], *a.* pleasant, entertaining.

régaler [rega'le], *v.t.* to regale, to treat, to entertain. **se régaler**, *v.r.* to regale oneself; to enjoy oneself; to entertain *or* treat each other.

regard [rə'ga:r], *n.m.* look; glance; gaze, notice, attention; inspection hole; (*pl.*) eyes; **au regard de**, in comparison with; **d'un seul regard**, at one glance; **en regard**, opposite; **un regard de côté**, a sidelong glance.

regardant [rəgar'dɑ̃], *a.* particular, meticulous; stingy, niggardly.

regarder [rəgar'de], *v.t.* to look at, to behold; to look into, to consider; to face, to be opposite; to concern; **cela vous regarde**, that concerns you.—*v.i.* to look; to mind, to pay heed. **se regarder**, *v.r.* to look at oneself; to look at each other; to look upon oneself (*comme*); to consider one another (*comme*); to face each other.

regarnir [rəgar'ni:r], *v.t.* to furnish again; to retrim (*dress*); to re-cover (*furniture*) etc.

régate [re'gat], *n.f.* regatta, boat race.

régence [re'ʒɑ̃:s], *n.f.* regency.

régénérateur [reʒenera'tœ:r], *a.* (*fem.* -**trice**) regenerating.—*n.m.* regenerator.

régénération [reʒenera'sjɔ̃], *n.f.* regeneration; reclamation (*of land*).

régénérer [reʒene're], *v.t.* (*conjug. like* CÉDER) to regenerate.

régent [re'ʒɑ̃], *a.* and *n.m.* (*fem.* -**e**) regent.

régenter [reʒɑ̃'te], *v.t.* to domineer, to lord it over.

régie [re'ʒi], *n.f.* administration; (*public*) corporation; excise.

regimbement [rəʒɛ̃bə'mɑ̃], *n.m.* kicking (*of horses*); resistance, recalcitrance.

regimber [rəʒɛ̃'be], *v.i.* to kick (*of horses*); (*fig.*) to resist, to jib.

régime [re'ʒim], *n.m.* regimen; diet; form of government; rules, regulations; régime, system; speed (*of motor etc.*); bunch (*of bananas etc.*).

régiment [reʒi'mɑ̃], *n.m.* regiment.

régimentaire [reʒimɑ̃'tɛ:r], *a.* regimental.

région [re'ʒjɔ̃], *n.f.* region; district.

régional [reʒjɔ'nal], *a.* (*m. pl.* -**aux**) local.

régir [re'ʒi:r], *v.t.* to govern, to rule; to administer.

régisseur [reʒi'sœ:r], *n.m.* manager, steward; (*Theat.*) stage manager.

registre [re'ʒistr], *n.m.* register; account book; damper (*in chimneys*).

réglable [re'glabl], *a.* adjustable.

réglage [re'gla:ʒ], *n.m.* ruling (*of paper*); regulating, adjusting, tuning.

règle [rɛgl], *n.f.* ruler, rule; order, regularity; model.

réglé [re'gle], *a.* regular, steady; ruled; paid.

règlement [rɛglə'mã], *n.m.* regulation; settlement (*of accounts*).

réglementaire [rɛgləmã'tɛːr], *a.* according to regulations, lawful; usual.

réglementer [rɛgləmã'te], *v.t.* to regulate.— *v.i.* to make regulations.

régler [re'gle], *v.t.* (*conjug. like* CÉDER) to rule (*paper etc.*); to regulate, to order, to adjust, to time (*a watch etc.*); to settle (*an account*). **se régler**, *v.r.* to regulate oneself, to be regulated; to be guided (*sur*).

régleur [re'glœːr], *n.m.* (*fem.* -**euse**) regulator (*of clocks etc.*).

réglisse [re'glis], *n.f.* liquorice.

réglure [re'glyːr], *n.f.* ruling (*of paper*).

régnant [re'nã], *a.* reigning; (*fig.*) prevailing, predominant.

règne [rɛɲ], *n.m.* reign; prevalence, vogue; (*Nat. Hist.*) kingdom.

régner [re'ne], *v.i.* (*conjug. like* CÉDER) to reign, to rule; to prevail, to be in fashion.

regonfler [rəgɔ̃'fle], *v.t.* to swell again; to pump up (*tire*).—*v.i.* to swell again.

regorgeant [rəgɔr'ʒã], *a.* overflowing; abounding.

regorger [rəgɔr'ʒe], *v.t.* (*conjug. like* MANGER) to regurgitate, to disgorge.—*v.i.* to overflow, to run over; to be crammed (*with*); to be plentiful, to abound.

régressif [regrɛ'sif], *a.* (*fem.* -**ive**) regressive, retrogressive.

régression [regrɛ'sjɔ̃], *n.f.* regression, recession; retrogression; (*fig.*) decline.

regret [rə'grɛ], *n.m.* regret; *à regret*, with reluctance.

regrettable [rəgrɛ'tabl], *a.* regrettable, deplorable.

regrettablement [rəgrɛtablə'mã], *adv.* regrettably.

regretter [rəgrɛ'te], *v.t.* to regret; to grieve; to be sorry for, to repent; to miss.

régularisation [regylariza'sjɔ̃], *n.f.* putting in order, regularization.

régulariser [regylari'ze], *v.t.* to put in order, to regularize.

régularité [regylari'te], *n.f.* regularity.

régulateur [regyla'tœːr], *a.* (*fem.* -**trice**) regulating.—*n.m.* regulator; (*Eng. etc.*) governor.

régulier [regy'lje], *a.* (*fem.* -**ière**) regular; steady, exact.—*n.m.* regular (*monk, soldier etc.*).

régulièrement [regyljer'mã], *adv.* regularly.

régurgitation [regyrʒita'sjɔ̃], *n.f.* regurgitation.

régurgiter [regyrʒi'te], *v.t.* to regurgitate.

réhabilitation [reabilita'sjɔ̃], *n.f.* rehabilitation.

réhabiliter [reabili'te], *v.t.* to rehabilitate; to reinstate. **se réhabiliter**, *v.r.* to rehabilitate oneself, to recover one's good name.

rehaussement [rəos'mã], *n.m.* raising; heightening, enhancing; increase of value (*of coin*).

rehausser [rəo'se], *v.t.* to raise; to heighten, to enhance; to raise the value of; to enrich; to set off.

réimposer [reɛ̃po'ze], *v.t.* to reassess (*tax*); (*Print.*) to reimpose.

réimpression [reɛ̃prɛ'sjɔ̃], *n.f.* reprinting; reprint.

réimprimer [reɛ̃pri'me], *v.t.* to print again, to reprint.

rein [rɛ̃], *n.m.* kidney; (*pl.*) loins, back.

réincarnation [reɛ̃karna'sjɔ̃], *n.f.* reincarnation.

reine [rɛn], *n.f.* queen.

reine-claude [rɛːn'kloːd], *n.f.* (*pl.* **reines-claude**) greengage.

reine-des-prés [rɛːnde'pre], *n.f.* (*pl.* **reines-des-prés**) meadowsweet.

réinstallation [reɛ̃stala'sjɔ̃], *n.f.* reinstallment, re-establishment.

réinstaller [reɛ̃sta'le], *v.t.* to reinstall.

réintégration [reɛ̃tegra'sjɔ̃], *n.f.* reinstatement.

réintégrer [reɛ̃te'gre], *v.t.* (*conjug. like* CÉDER) to reinstate.

réitératif [reitera'tif], *a.* (*fem.* -**tive**) reiterative.

réitération [reitera'sjɔ̃], *n.f.* reiteration, repetition.

réitérer [reite're], *v.t.* (*conjug. like* CÉDER) to reiterate, to repeat.

rejaillir [rəʒa'jiːr], *v.i.* to gush, to spurt out; to spring, to spout; (*fig.*) to flash; to reflect; to rebound.

rejaillissement [rəʒajis'mã], *n.m.* gushing out; spouting, springing; reflection, flashing; rebound.

réjection [reʒɛk'sjɔ̃], *n.f.* rejection.

rejet [rə'ʒɛ], *n.m.* rejection; throwing out; young shoot, sprout.

rejeter [rəʒ'te], *v.t.* (*conjug. like* APPELER) to throw again; to throw back; to tilt back (*one's hat*); to repel; to throw away; to throw up (*of plants*); to reject; to deny.— *v.i.* to shoot (*of plants*). **se rejeter**, *v.r.* to have recourse to; to fall back (*upon*).

rejeton [rəʒ'tɔ̃], *n.m.* shoot, sprout; (*fig.*) scion.

rejoindre [rə'ʒwɛ̃ːdr], *v.t. irr.* (*conjug. like* CRAINDRE) to rejoin, to join; to reunite; to overtake, to catch up. **se rejoindre**, *v.r.* to reunite; to meet; to catch each other up again.

rejouer [rə'ʒwe], *v.t.*, *v.i.* to play again, to replay.

réjoui [re'ʒwi], *a.* and *n.m.* (*fem.* -**e**) jovial, joyous, merry (*person*).

réjouir [re'ʒwiːr], *v.t.* to rejoice, to delight, to cheer. **se réjouir**, *v.r.* to be or to make merry; to rejoice, to be delighted (*de*).

réjouissance [reʒwi'sãːs], *n.f.* rejoicing; (*pl.*) merry-making.

réjouissant [reʒwi'sã], *a.* cheering; diverting, amusing.

relâchant [rəla'ʃã], *a.* relaxing; laxative, loosening.—*n.m.* (*Med.*) laxative.

relâche (1) [rə'laːʃ], *n.m.* intermission, discontinuance, respite; relaxation; (*Theat.*) suspension of performance; *relâche ce soir*, no performance this evening.

relâche (2) [rə'laːʃ], *n.f.* (*Naut.*) putting into a port; port of call.

relâché [rəla'ʃe], *a.* lax, relaxed; loose, remiss.

relâchement [rəlaʃ'mã], *n.m.* slackening; slackness; laxity (*of morals*); looseness (*of bowels*).

relâcher [rəla'ʃe], *v.t.* to slacken, to loosen, to relax; to release, to unbend (*the mind etc.*); to yield, to abate.—*v.i.* (*Naut.*) to put into port. **se relâcher**, *v.r.* to grow slack *or* loose; to abate; to relax, to unbend.

relais [rə'lɛ], *n.m.* relay (*fresh horses*); stage; shift (*of workmen*).

relancer [rəlɑ̃'se], *v.t.* (*conjug. like COMMENCER*) to throw back; (*Ten.*) to return (*the ball*); (*Cards*) to raise (*a bid*); (*fig.*) to harry (*someone*).

relaps [rə'laps], *a.* relapsed, relapsed into heresy.—*n.m.* (*fem.* -e) relapsed heretic.

rélargir [relar'ʒiːr], *v.t.* to widen, to let out (*clothes etc.*).

relater [rəla'te], *v.t.* to state, to tell.

relatif [rəla'tif], *a.* (*fem.* -tive) relative; relating (*à*).

relation [rəla'sjɔ̃], *n.f.* relation, account; statement; respect; connection; communication, correspondence; (*pl.*) connections.

relativement [rəlativ'mɑ̃], *adv.* relatively.

relativité [rəlativi'te], *n.f.* relativity.

relaxation [rəlaksa'sjɔ̃], *n.f.* release; relaxation (*of muscles*).

relaxer [rəlak'se], *v.t.* to release (*a prisoner*); to relax (*muscles*).

relayer [rəlɛ'je], *v.t.* (*conjug. like PAYER*) to take the place of, to relieve; (*Elec. Eng., Rad., Teleg. etc.*) to relay.—*v.i.* to change horses. **se relayer**, *v.r.* to relieve each other; to work in shifts.

relégation [rəlega'sjɔ̃], *n.f.* relegation; deportation (*of convict*).

reléguer [rəle'ge], *v.t.* (*conjug. like CÉDER*) to deport (*for life*); to shut up; to relegate, to consign (*à*). **se reléguer**, *v.r.* to shut oneself up.

relent [rə'lɑ̃], *a.* moldy, musty.—*n.m.* mustiness, moldiness.

relève [rə'lɛːv], *n.f.* (*Mil.*) relief.

relevé [rəl've], *a.* raised, erect; exalted, lofty; refined; highly seasoned.—*n.m.* abstract; statement, return; survey.

relèvement [rəlɛv'mɑ̃], *n.m.* raising again; recovery (*of business*); relieving (*of sentry*); raise, increase (*of salary*); (*Naut.*) bearing.

relever [rəl've], *v.t.* (*conjug. like AMENER*) to raise again, to lift up again; to turn up; to restore; to relieve (*troops*), to change (*sentry*); to raise (*prices, salary*); to set off, to enhance; to extol; to remark; to note, take down (*name, address etc.*); to release (*from vows, oath*); to survey; (*Naut.*) to take the bearings of.—*v.i.* to recover; to turn up; to depend. **se relever**, *v.r.* to rise again; to get up, to pick oneself up; to recover; to be raised; to relieve each other.

relief [rə'ljɛf], *n.m.* relief, embossment; enhancement; (*pl.*) scraps (*from the table*).

relier [rə'lje], *v.t.* to connect; to hoop (*casks*); to bind (*books*).

relieur [rə'ljœːr], *n.m.* (*fem.* -euse) binder, book-binder.

religieusement [rəliʒjøz'mɑ̃], *adv.* religiously; scrupulously.

religieux [rəli'ʒjø], *a.* (*fem.* -euse) religious, strict.—*n.m.* (*fem.* -euse) monk, nun.

religion [rəli'ʒjɔ̃], *n.f.* religion.

reliquaire [rəli'kɛːr], *n.m.* reliquary, shrine.

reliquat [rəli'ka], *n.m.* balance, remainder (*of an account*); after-effects (*of a disease etc.*).

relique [rə'lik], *n.f.* relic (*of a saint*).

relire [rə'liːr], *v.t. irr.* (*conjug. like LIRE*) to re-read.

reliure [rə'ljyːr], *n.f.* binding (*of books*).

relouer [rəlu'e], *v.t.* to relet, to sub-let.

reluire [rəlɥiːr], *v.i. irr.* (*conjug. like LUIRE*) to shine, to glitter.

reluisant [rəlɥi'zɑ̃], *a.* gleaming, shining, glittering.

reluquer [rəly'ke], *v.t.* (*colloq.*) to ogle, to leer at; (*fig.*) to have an eye on.

remâcher [rəmɑ'ʃe], *v.t.* to chew again; (*fig.*) to turn over in one's mind.

remailler [rəma'je], *v.t.* to repair the meshes (*of fishing nets etc.*); to mend a run (*in stocking*).

remaniement *or* **remaniment** [rəmani'mɑ̃], *n.m.* (*Polit.*) shakeup; handling again, touching up; repairing; changing.

remanier [rəma'nje], *v.t.* to handle again; to remodel; to adapt, to revise.

remariage [rəma'rjaːʒ], *n.m.* re-marriage.

remarier [rəma'rje], *v.t.* to remarry. **se remarier**, *v.r.* to marry again, to remarry.

remarquable [rəmar'kabl], *a.* remarkable, notable.

remarquablement [rəmarkablə'mɑ̃], *adv.* remarkably.

remarque [rə'mark], *n.f.* remark; notice.

remarquer [rəmar'ke], *v.t.* to mark again; to notice; to distinguish; *faire remarquer*, to point out. **se remarquer**, *v.r.* to be remarked.

remballer [rɑ̃ba'le], *v.t.* to pack up again.

rembarquement [rɑ̃barkə'mɑ̃], *n.m.* re-embarkation.

rembarquer [rɑ̃bar'ke], *v.t.* to re-embark, to ship again. **se rembarquer**, *v.r.* to go on board again.

rembarrer [rɑ̃ba're], *v.t.* to repulse; to snub; (*fam.*) to tell someone off.

remblai [rɑ̃'blɛ], *n.m.* filling up; embankment.

remblayer [rɑ̃blɛ'je], *v.t.* (*conjug. like PAYER*) to embank, to fill up (*with earth*).

remboîter [rɑ̃bwa'te], *v.t.* to fit in again; to reassemble; to reset (*a bone*).

rembourrage [rɑ̃bu'raːʒ], **rembourrement** [rɑ̃bur'mɑ̃], *n.m.* stuffing, padding.

rembourrer [rɑ̃bu're], *v.t.* to stuff, to pad; to upholster.

remboursable [rɑ̃bur'sabl], *a.* repayable; redeemable.

remboursement [rɑ̃bursə'mɑ̃], *n.m.* reimbursement, repayment.

rembourser [rɑ̃bur'se], *v.t.* to repay; to reimburse; to redeem (*an annuity etc.*).

rembruni [rɑ̃bry'ni], *a.* dark, gloomy.

rembrunir [rɑ̃bry'niːr], *v.t.* to darken; to cloud over; (*fig.*) to sadden. **se rembrunir**, *v.r.* to grow darker; to become cloudy *or* gloomy.

remède [rə'mɛd], *n.m.* remedy, medicine.

remédiable [rəme'djabl], *a.* remediable.

remédier [rəme'dje], *v.i.* to remedy, to cure (*à*).

remêler [rəmɛ'le], *v.t.* to mix again, to reshuffle.

remembrement [rəmɑ̃brə'mɑ̃], *n.m.* consolidation (*of land*).

remémoratif [rəmemɔra'tif], *a.* (*fem.* -tive) commemorative.

remémorer [rəmemɔ're], *v.t.* to bring (*a thing*) to someone's mind. **se remémorer**, *v.r.* to recollect.

remerciement or **remercîment** [rəmεrsi
'mɑ̃], *n.m.* thanking; (*pl.*) thanks; *faire
des remerciements*, to thank.

remercier [rəmεr'sje], *v.t.* to thank; to
dismiss; *non, je vous remercie*, no, thank
you.

remettre [rə'mεtr], *v.t. irr.* (*conjug. like*
METTRE) to put back; to put on again; to lay
down again; to make well again; to deliver;
to postpone; to entrust; to forgive; to
remember; (*Ten.*) (*balle*) *à remettre*, let
(ball); *je vous remets*, I remember your
face; *remettre dans l'esprit*, to remind.
se remettre, *v.r.* to recover (*oneself*); to
resume, to start again; to recollect; to refer;
to improve (*of weather*).

réminiscence [remini'sɑ̃:s], *n.f.* reminiscence.

remis [rə'mi], *a.* put back, put off, postponed.

remisage [rəmi'za:ʒ], *n.m.* housing, putting
away (*vehicle*).

remise [rə'mi:z], *n.f.* delivery; remittance;
discount; commission; delay; coach house,
mews, shed.

remiser [rəmi'ze], *v.t.* to put up, to put away
(*vehicle*); to house; (*colloq.*) to put by.

rémissible [remi'si:bl], *a.* remissible, pardonable.

rémission [remi'sjɔ̃], *n.f.* remission, forgiveness.

remmener [rɑ̃m'ne], *v.t.* (*conjug. like*
AMENER) to take back, to lead back.

remodeler [rəmɔ'dle], *v.t.* (*conjug. like*
AMENER) to remodel.

remontage [rəmɔ̃'ta:ʒ], *n.m.* going up; winding up (*of clock etc.*); assembling; refitting
(*of parts of machinery*); restocking (*of shop*).

remonte [rə'mɔ̃:t], *n.f.* remounting, going
upstream; run (*of fish*); (*Mil.*) remount.

remonter [rəmɔ̃'te], *v.t.* (*with aux.* AVOIR *or*
ÊTRE *according as action or condition is meant*)
to go up again; to take up again; to raise;
to stock; to wind up (*clock etc.*); to re-string
(*instruments*).—*v.i.* to go up again; to go back;
to rise *or* increase (*in value etc.*); to date
back; to remount (*cavalry*). **se remonter**,
v.r. to take in a fresh supply (*de*); to be
wound up (*of watches etc.*); to recover one's
strength *or* spirits.

remontoir [rəmɔ̃'twa:r], *n.m.* winder, key (*of
clock, watch*).

remontrance [rəmɔ̃'trɑ̃:s], *n.f.* remonstrance.

remontrer [rəmɔ̃'tre], *v.t.* to show again; to
point out; to represent.—*v.i. en remontrer*,
(*fig.*) to give advice.

remordre [rə'mɔrdr], *v.t.* to bite again.—
v.i. to try again.

remords [rə'mɔ:r], *n.m.* remorse.

remorquage [rəmɔr'ka:ʒ], *n.m.* towing,
hauling.

remorque [rə'mɔrk], *n.f.* towing; tow; tow-
line; trailer (*car*).

remorquer [rəmɔr'ke], *v.t.* to tow, to haul.

remorqueur [rəmɔr'kœ:r], *a.* (*fem.* **-euse**)
towing, hauling.—*n.m.* tug-boat, tug.

rémoulade [remu'lad], *n.f.* sharp sauce.

rémouleur [remu'lœ:r], *n.m.* knife-grinder.

remous [rə'mu], *n.m.* eddy; back-wash (*of
ship*); slip-stream.

rempailler [rɑ̃pa'je], *v.t.* to re-seat (*a straw-
bottomed chair*); to re-stuff with straw.

rempailleur [rɑ̃pa'jœ:r], *n.m.* (*fem.* **-euse**)
chair mender.

rempaqueter [rɑ̃pak'te], *v.t.* (*conjug. like*
APPELER) to pack up again.

rempart [rɑ̃'pa:r], *n.m.* rampart; (*fig.*) bulwark.

remplaçable [rɑ̃pla'sabl], *a.* replaceable.

remplaçant [rɑ̃pla'sɑ̃], *n.m.* (*fem.* **-e**) substitute; locum.

remplacement [rɑ̃plas'mɑ̃], *n.m.* replacing,
replacement.

remplacer [rɑ̃pla'se], *v.t.* (*conjug. like* COM-
MENCER) to take the place of, to replace; to
reinvest. **se remplacer**, *v.r.* to be replaced.

rempli [rɑ̃'pli], *a.* filled, full.—*n.m.* tuck,
take-up.

remplier [rɑ̃pli'je], *v.t.* to make a tuck in; to
turn in.

remplir [rɑ̃'pli:r], *v.t.* to refill, to replenish;
to fill, to fill up; to fill in (*form*); to cram; to
supply; to occupy (*time etc.*); to fulfil. **se
remplir**, *v.r.* to fill oneself; to become full.

remplissage [rɑ̃pli'sa:ʒ], *n.m.* filling, filling
up (*of casks etc.*); (*fig.*) rubbish, padding.

remploi [rɑ̃'plwa], *n.m.* reinvestment.

remployer [rɑ̃plwa'je], *v.t.* (*conjug. like*
EMPLOYER) to use again; to reinvest.

remplumer [rɑ̃ply'me], *v.t.* to feather again.
se remplumer, *v.r.* to get new feathers;
(*fig.*) to retrieve one's losses; to get plump
again.

rempocher [rɑ̃pɔ'ʃe], *v.t.* to put (*something*)
back in one's pocket.

remporter [rɑ̃pɔr'te], *v.t.* to carry *or* take
back; to carry off, to take away with one; to
get; to win.

rempoter [rɑ̃pɔ'te], *v.t.* to repot.

remuant [rə'mɥɑ̃], *a.* restless; bustling;
(*fam.*) on the go.

remue-ménage [rəmyme'na:ʒ], *n.m. inv.*
stir, disturbance, bustle.

remuement or **remûment** [rəmy'mɑ̃], *n.m.*
stir, stirring; removal; disturbance.

remuer [rə'mɥe], *v.t.* to move, to stir; to
rouse; to turn up; to shake.—*v.i.* and **se
remuer**, *v.r.* to stir, to move; to fidget.

rémunérateur [remynera'tœ:r], *a.* (*fem.*
-trice) remunerative, profitable.—*n.m.*
(*fem.* **-trice**) rewarder.

rémunération [remynera'sjɔ̃], *n.f.* remuneration, reward.

rémunératoire [remynera'twa:r], *a.* remunerative.

rémunérer [remyne're], *v.t.* (*conjug. like*
CÉDER) to remunerate; to reward.

renâcler [rəna'kle], *v.i.* to snort; (*fam.*) to
turn up one's nose; to balk (*at something*).

renaissance [rənε'sɑ̃:s], *n.f.* rebirth; renaissance.

renaissant [rənε'sɑ̃], *a.* springing up again,
reviving.

renaître [rə'nε:tr], *v.i. irr.* (*conjug. like*
NAÎTRE, *but no p.p.*) to be born again; to grow
again; to appear again; to revive.

rénal [re'nal], *a.* (*m. pl.* **-aux**) (*Anat.*) renal.

renard [rə'na:r], *n.m.* fox; (*fig.*) sly fellow;
(*pop.*) strikebreaker.

renarde [rə'nard], *n.f.* vixen.

renardeau [rənar'do], *n.m.* (*pl.* **-eaux**) fox
cub.

Renaud [rə'no], *m.* Reginald.

renchéri [rãʃeˈri], a. particular, over-nice (of a person).—n.m. (fem. -e) fastidious person; faire le renchéri, to put on airs.

renchérir [rãʃeˈriːr], v.t. to raise the price of. —v.i. to get dearer, to rise in price; renchérir sur, to improve upon.

renchérissement [rãʃerisˈmã], n.m. rise in price.

rencogner (se) [sərãkoˈɲe], v.r. to retreat, to crouch in a corner.

rencontre [rãˈkõːtr], n.f. meeting, encounter; duel; accidental meeting, discovery etc.; collision; chance, coincidence.

rencontrer, [rãˈkõːtre], v.t. to meet, to meet with; to light upon, to encounter. se rencontrer, v.r. to meet, to meet each other; to be met with; to agree, to coincide.

rendement [rãdˈmã], n.m. produce, yield, output; efficiency (of a machine etc.); (Spt.) handicap; (Comm.) return, profit.

rendez-vous [rãdeˈvu], n.m. inv. rendezvous, appointment; engagement; place of meeting.

rendormir [rãdorˈmiːr], v.t. irr. (conjug. like SENTIR) to put to sleep again. se rendormir, v.r. to fall asleep again.

rendre [rãːdr], v.t. to return, to restore, to give back; to repay; to deliver; to give up; to pay; to produce; to reward; to carry; to eject, to emit; to express; to translate; rendre visite, to pay a visit.—v.i. to lead (of roads); to be lucrative; to function, to work. se rendre, v.r. to go; to resort; to make oneself, to render oneself; to become; to surrender, to give up; to be worn out.

rendu [rãˈdy], a. rendered, delivered; exhausted, tired out; arrived.—n.m. return, tit for tat.

rendurcir [rãdyrˈsiːr], v.t. to make harder. se rendurcir, v.r. to become harder.

rêne [rɛːn], n.f. rein.

renégat [reneˈga], a. and n.m. (fem. -e) renegade, turncoat.

rêner [reˈne], v.t. to bridle (a horse).

renfermé [rãferˈme], a. personne renfermée, close, uncommunicative person.—n.m. odeur de renfermé, fustiness; musty smell; sentir le renfermé, to smell close, fusty or stuffy.

renfermer [rãferˈme], v.t. to shut up; to contain; to include, to comprise; to conceal. se renfermer, v.r. to shut oneself up; to confine oneself.

renfiler [rãfiˈle], v.t. to thread, to string again.

renflammer [rãflaˈme], v.t. to rekindle. se renflammer, v.r. to flare up again.

renflé [rãˈfle], a. swollen, swelling; (Bot.) inflated.

renflement [rãflaˈmã], n.m. swelling, bulge.

renfler [rãˈfle], v.t., v.i. to swell.

renflouage [rãfluˈaːʒ], renflouement [rãfluˈmã], n.m. refloating (of a ship).

renflouer [rãfluˈe], v.t. to refloat, to raise (a ship); (fig.) to salvage (firm, company etc.).

renfoncement [rãfõsˈmã], n.m. cavity, hollow, recess.

renfoncer [rãfõˈse], v.t. (conjug. like COMMENCER) to drive deeper; to pull (a hat etc.) further on.

renforçage [rãforˈsaːʒ], n.m. strengthening.

renforcé [rãforˈse], a. downright, regular; reinforced.

renforcement [rãforsˈmã], n.m. strengthening; reinforcement.

renforcer [rãforˈse], v.t. (conjug. like COMMENCER) to strengthen, to reinforce; to increase. se renforcer, v.r. to gather strength, to grow stronger; (Mil.) to be reinforced.

renfort [rãˈfoːr], n.m. reinforcement; (fig.) help, aid, relief; strengthening-piece.

renfrogné [rãfroˈɲe], a. frowning, scowling, surly.

renfrognement [rãfroɲəˈmã], n.m. frown, scowl.

renfrogner (se) [sərãfroˈɲe], v.r. to frown.

rengagement [rãgaʒˈmã], n.m. re-engagement; (Mil.) re-enlistment.

rengager [rãgaˈʒe], v.t. (conjug. like MANGER) to re-engage.—v.i. (Mil.) to re-enlist. se rengager, v.r. to re-engage; to begin afresh; to re-enlist.

rengaine [rãˈgɛːn], n.f. catch phrase; (fam.) hackneyed story; popular tune.

rengainer [rãgeˈne], v.t. to sheathe, to put up (one's sword); to withdraw, to put away.

rengorgement [rãgorʒəˈmã], n.m. swaggering, puffing out the neck (of peacock).

rengorger (se) [sərãgorˈʒe], v.r. to carry one's head high; (fig.) to give oneself airs.

reniable [rəˈnjabl], a. deniable.

reniement or **reniment** [rəniˈmã], n.m. denying, disowning.

renier [rəˈnje], v.t. to disown (son, friend etc.); to deny (God, doctrine).

reniflement [rəniflaˈmã], n.m. sniffing, snuffling, snivelling.

renifler [rəniˈfle], v.i. to sniff, to snivel; (fig.) to turn up one's nose (sur); to hang back.

renne [rɛn], n.m. reindeer.

renom [rəˈnõ], n.m. renown, fame, reputation.

renommé [rənoˈme], a. renowned, famed.

renommée [rənoˈme], n.f. renown, fame reputation; rumor.

renommer [rənoˈme], v.t. to name again, to re-elect; to make famous, to praise.

renoncement [rənõsˈmã], n.m. renouncement; renunciation.

renoncer [rənõˈse], v.t. (conjug. like COMMENCER) to renounce, to disclaim, to disown.—v.i. to give up, to renounce (à).

renonciation [rənõsjaˈsjõ], n.f. renunciation, self-denial.

renoncule [rənõˈkyl], n.f. (Bot.) ranunculus, buttercup, crowfoot.

renouer [rənuˈe], v.t. to tie again, to knot again; to put together; to resume.—v.i. to resume relations (avec).

renouveau [rənuˈvo], n.m. (pl. -eaux) (poet.) spring.

renouvelable [rənuˈvlabl], a. renewable.

renouveler [rənuˈvle], v.t. (conjug. like APPELER) to renew, to renovate; to revive; to recommence, to repeat. se renouveler, v.r. to be renewed, to be revived, to occur again.

renouvellement [rənuvelˈmã], n.m. renewal, revival, renovation; increase.

rénovateur [renovaˈtœːr], a. (fem. -trice) renovating.—n.m. (fem. -trice) renovator, restorer.

rénovation [renɔva'sjɔ̃], *n.f.* rénovation, renewal.

renseignement [rɑ̃sɛɲ'mɑ̃], *n.m.* (piece of) information, (piece of) intelligence, account; (*pl.*) information; references; *bureau de renseignements*, information bureau, inquiry office.

renseigner [rɑ̃sɛ'ɲe], *v.t.* to give information to; to direct. **se renseigner**, *v.r.* to seek information, to make inquiries.

rente [rɑ̃:t], *n.f.* yearly income; revenue; stock, funds.

renté [rɑ̃'te], *a.* of independent means; endowed (*of hospital etc.*).

renter [rɑ̃'te], *v.t.* to allow a yearly income to, to endow (*public services etc.*).

rentier [rɑ̃'tje], *n.m.* (*fem.* -**ière**) stockholder; person of independent means.

rentrant [rɑ̃'trɑ̃], *a.* re-entering, returning; (*Av.*) retractable.—*n.m.* recess (*in a wall*); (*fem.* -**e**) new player.

rentré [rɑ̃'tre], *a.* returned; suppressed; depressed.

rentrée [rɑ̃'tre], *n.f.* re-entrance; return, home-coming; reopening (*of schools etc.*); reappearance; ingathering (*of crops etc.*); receipt, collection.

rentrer [rɑ̃'tre], *v.t.* to take in, to bring in; to suppress.—*v.i.* (*aux.* ÊTRE) to re-enter, to go in again; to return home; to join again; to reopen (*of schools etc.*).

renversable [rɑ̃vɛr'sabl], *a.* liable to be upset; reversible.

renversant [rɑ̃vɛr'sɑ̃], *a.* (*colloq.*) amazing, stunning.

renverse [rɑ̃'vɛrs], *n.f. à la renverse*, backwards.

renversé [rɑ̃vɛr'se], *a.* thrown down, thrown back; upside-down.

renversement [rɑ̃vɛrsə'mɑ̃], *n.m.* reversing; overturning; overthrow; turning upside down; confusion; subversion.

renverser [rɑ̃vɛr'se], *v.t.* to turn upside down, to upset; to reverse; to knock over; to spill (*a liquid*); to destroy; to confuse; to turn (*the brain*); (*fam.*) to astound; to rout; (*Arith., Mus.*) to invert. **se renverser**, *v.r.* to fall back; to fall down; to capsize; to be spilt.

renvoi [rɑ̃'vwa], *n.m.* sending back, return; dismissal; referring (*to a committee etc.*).

renvoyer [rɑ̃vwa'je], *v.t. irr.* (*conjug. like* ENVOYER) to send again; to send back, to return; to dismiss; to refer; to postpone; to throw back; to reflect (*light, heat etc.*); to reverberate (*sound*). **se renvoyer**, *v.r.* to be sent back *or* returned; to send from one to the other.

réoccupation [reɔkypa'sjɔ̃], *n.f.* reoccupation.

réoccuper [reɔky'pe], *v.t.* to reoccupy.

réorganisation [reɔrganiza'sjɔ̃], *n.f.* reorganization.

réorganiser [reɔrgani'ze], *v.t.* to reorganize.

réouverture [reuvɛr'ty:r], *n.f.* reopening (*of a theatre*).

repaire (1) [rə'pɛ:r], *n.m.* haunt (*of criminals*); den, lair (*of animals*).

repaire (2) [REPÈRE].

repaître [rə'pɛ:tr], *v.t. irr.* (*conjug. like* PAÎTRE) to feed, to nourish. **se repaître**, *v.r.*

to feed on, to feast on; to delight in, to indulge in.

répandre [re'pɑ̃:dr], *v.t.* to pour out, to shed; to spill; to scatter; to distribute; to exhale; to spread abroad. **se répandre**, *v.r.* to be poured out, to be shed, to be spilt; to be spread; to be exhaled; to be spread abroad; to be current; to go into society.

répandu [repɑ̃'dy], *a.* spilt, shed; widespread.

réparable [repa'rabl], *a.* reparable; rectifiable.

reparaître [rəpa're:tr], *v.i. irr.* (*conjug. like* CONNAÎTRE) to reappear.

réparateur [repara'tœ:r], *a.* (*fem.* -**trice**) restorative, refreshing.—*n.m.* (*fem.* -**trice**) repairer, restorer.

réparation [repara'sjɔ̃], *n.f.* repairing, mending; amends; compensation; *en réparation*, under repair.

réparer [repa're], *v.t.* to repair, to mend; to make amends for, to make up for.

répareur [repa'rœ:r], *n.m.* (*fem.* -**euse**) repairer.

reparler [rəpar'le], *v.i.* to speak again.

repartie [rəpar'ti], *n.f.* repartee, retort.

repartir (1) [rəpar'ti:r], *v.t., v.i.* (*conjug. like* SENTIR) to answer, to retort.

repartir (2) [rəpar'ti:r], *v.i. irr.* (*conjug. like* SENTIR, *but with aux.* ÊTRE) to set out again, to go away again.

répartir [repar'ti:r], *v.t.* to divide, to distribute; to assess.

répartissable [reparti'sabl], *a.* divisible, assessable.

répartiteur [reparti'tœ:r], *n.m.* (*fem.* -**trice**) distributor; assessor (*of taxes etc.*).

répartition [reparti'sjɔ̃], *n.f.* distribution; assessment.

repas [rə'pɑ], *n.m. inv.* meal, repast.

repassage [rəpa'sa:ʒ], *n.m.* repassing; grinding, sharpening (*of cutlery*); ironing (*of linen etc.*).

repasser [rəpa'se], *v.t.* (*aux.* AVOIR) to pass again; to cross again; to think over; to sharpen, to grind (*tools*); to iron; to repeat; to look over again.—*v.i.* (*aux.* ÊTRE) to pass again; to go, come, call etc., again.

repasseur [rəpa'sœ:r], *n.m.* (*fem.* -**euse**) (*Ind.*) examiner; grinder.—*n.f.* (-**euse**) ironer (*person or machine*).

repavage [rəpa'va:ʒ], **repavement** [rəpav'mɑ̃], *n.m.* repaving.

repaver [rəpa've], *v.t.* to repave.

repêchage [rəpɛ'ʃa:ʒ], *n.m.* rescuing; (*Spt.*) *épreuve de repêchage*, supplementary heat; (*Sch.*) second chance (*for candidate who has failed an examination*).

repêcher [rəpɛ'ʃe], *v.t.* to fish up *or* out again; (*fig.*) to recover, to retrieve.

repeindre [rə'pɛ̃:dr], *v.t. irr.* (*conjug. like* CRAINDRE) to repaint.

repenser [rəpɑ̃'se], *v.t., v.i.* to think over; to think again (of).

repentance [rəpɑ̃'tɑ̃:s], *n.f.* repentance, contrition.

repentant [rəpɑ̃'tɑ̃], *a.* repentant.

repenti [rəpɑ̃'ti], *a.* penitent.

repentir [rəpɑ̃'ti:r], *n.m.* repentance, contrition, regret.

repentir (se) [sərəpɑ̃'ti:r], *v.r. irr.* (*conjug. like* SENTIR) to repent; to rue (*de*).

repérage [rəpe'ra:ʒ], *n.m.* locating; (*Cine.*) synchronization; (*Mil.*) spotting.

répercussion [reperky'sjɔ̃], *n.f.* repercussion, reverberation.

répercuter [reperky'te], *v.t.* to reverberate, to echo; to reflect. **se répercuter**, *v.r.* to be reflected (*light*); to reverberate (*sound*); (*fig.*) to have repercussions.

repère or **repaire** [rə'pɛ:r], *n.m.* mark; benchmark; (*fig.*) landmark.

repérer [rəpe're], *v.t.* (*conjug. like* CÉDER) to locate, to spot; to make a guiding mark upon. **se repérer**, *v.r.* to find one's bearings.

répertoire [reper'twa:r], *n.m.* table, list, catalogue; repertory.

répéter [repe'te], *v.t.* (*conjug. like* CÉDER) to repeat, to tell again; to rehearse; to reflect; (*Law*) to demand back. **se répéter**, *v.r.* to be repeated; to repeat oneself.

répétiteur [repeti'tœ:r], *n.m.* (*fem.* **-trice**) private teacher, tutor.

répétition [repeti'sjɔ̃], *n.f.* repetition; recurrence; private lesson; (*Theat.*) rehearsal.

repétrir [rəpe'tri:r], *v.t.* to remold; to re-fashion.

repeupler [rəpœ'ple], *v.t.* to repeople; to restock. **se repeupler**, *v.r.* to be repeopled; to be restocked.

repiquage [rəpi'ka:ʒ], *n.m.* transplanting, pricking or planting out (again); repairing (*of road*).

repiquer [rəpi'ke], *v.t.* to prick again; to prick out, to transplant; to repair (*road*).

répit [re'pi], *n.m.* respite; (*fig.*) rest, breathing space.

replacement [rəplas'mɑ̃], *n.m.* replacing, putting or setting again; reinvestment (*of funds*).

replacer [rəpla'se], *v.t.* (*conjug. like* COMMENCER) to replace, to put in place again; to bring back; to reinvest (*funds*). **se replacer**, *v.r.* to find oneself a new situation.

replanir [rəpla'ni:r], *v.t.* to plane down (*wood*).

replanter [rəpla'te], *v.t.* to replant.

replâtrer [rəpla'tre], *v.t.* to replaster; to patch up (*temporarily*).

replet [rə'ple], *a.* (*fem.* **-ète**) obese, stout; (*fam.*) pudgy.

réplétion [reple'sjɔ̃], *n.f.* stoutness, repletion, surfeit.

repli [rə'pli], *n.m.* fold, crease; (*fig.*) winding, coil, meander (*of river*); (*Mil.*) withdrawal.

repliable [rəpli'jabl], *a.* folding, collapsible.

replier [rəpli'je], *v.t.* to fold again, to fold up; to bend back; to coil (*a rope etc.*). **se replier**, *v.r.* to twist oneself, to writhe, to wind, to coil; (*Mil.*) to retreat.

réplique [re'plik], *n.f.* reply, answer, retort; (*Mus.*) repeat; (*Theat.*) cue.

répliquer [repli'ke], *v.t.*, *v.i.* to reply, to retort.

replonger [rəplɔ̃'ʒe], *v.t.* (*conjug. like* MANGER) to plunge again, to dip again.—*v.i.* and **se replonger**, *v.r.* to plunge again; to dive again.

répondant [repɔ̃'dɑ̃], *n.m.* candidate (*at an examination*); bail, surety.

répondre [re'pɔ̃:dr], *v.t.* to answer, to reply.—*v.i.* to answer, to reply; to write back; to come up (*à*); to correspond; to re-echo; to be answerable (*de*); to pledge oneself (*pour*); *je vous en réponds*, take my word for it.

répons [re'pɔ̃], *n.m.* response (*in church*).

réponse [re'pɔ̃:s], *n.f.* answer, reply, response.

report [rə'pɔ:r], *n.m.* (*Book-keeping*) carrying forward, bringing forward; amount brought forward.

reportage [rəpɔr'ta:ʒ], *n.m.* (*Journ.*) reporting; feature article.

reporter (1) [rəpɔr'tɛ:r], *n.m.* (*Journ.*) reporter.

reporter (2) [rəpɔr'te], *v.t.* to carry back; to take back; (*Book-keeping*) to carry forward. **se reporter**, *v.r.* to go back; to refer; *se reporter à*, please refer to.

repos [rə'po], *n.m.* rest, repose; sleep; quiet; resting place; *en repos*, at rest; (*Mil.*) *repos!* stand at ease!

reposant [rəpo'zɑ̃], *a.* restful, refreshing.

reposé [rəpo'ze], *a.* rested, refreshed; quiet, calm, cool.

reposer [rəpo'ze], *v.t.* to place again, to lay again, to replace; to rest (*on anything*); to refresh.—*v.i.* to rest, to lie down; to sleep; to be at rest. **se reposer**, *v.r.* to rest, to lie down; to settle down; to alight again (*of birds*); *se reposer sur*, to rely on.

reposoir [rəpo'zwa:r], *n.m.* resting place; pause.

repoussant [rəpu'sɑ̃], *a.* repulsive, loathsome.

repoussé [rəpu'se], *a.* chased (*silver*), embossed.

repousser [rəpu'se], *v.t.* to push back, to repel; to spurn, to reject; to rebuff; to shoot out (*branches etc.*) again; *repousser du cuir*, to emboss leather; *repousser du cuivre*, to chase copper.—*v.i.* to recoil; to spring up again (*of plants etc.*); to grow again (*of hair*); to be repulsive.

repoussoir [rəpu'swa:r], *n.m.* (*Paint.*) foil.

répréhensible [repreɑ̃'sibl], *a.* reprehensible.

répréhension [repreɑ̃'sjɔ̃], *n.f.* reprehension, reproof.

reprendre [rə'prɑ̃:dr], *v.t. irr.* (*conjug. like* PRENDRE) to recover, to recapture; to take up again; to reprove; to repair.—*v.i.* to take root again; to freeze again; to close up again (*of wounds etc.*); to begin again, to return to; to improve; to reply; to resume. **se reprendre**, *v.r.* to correct oneself; to be caught again; to begin again.

représaille [rəpre'za:j], *n.f.* (*usu. pl.*) reprisal; *user de représailles*, to retaliate.

représentant [rəprezɑ̃'tɑ̃], *n.m.* (*fem.* **-e**) representative.

représentatif [rəprezɑ̃ta'tif], *a.* (*fem.* **-tive**) representative.

représentation [rəprezɑ̃ta'sjɔ̃], *n.f.* representation; performance; show; remonstrance; agency.

représenter [rəprezɑ̃'te], *v.t.* to present again; to show; to produce; to represent; to resemble; to act (*a play*); to be the representative of.—*v.i.* to have an imposing appearance; to make a good show. **se représenter**, *v.r.* to present oneself again; to picture to oneself; to occur.

répressible [repre'sibl], *a.* repressible.

répressif [repre'sif], *a.* (*fem.* **-ive**) repressive.

répression [repre'sjɔ̃], *n.f.* repression.

réprimande [repri'mɑ̃:d], *n.f.* reprimand, rebuke.

réprimander [reprimɑ̃'de], *v.t.* to reprimand, to reprove.

réprimant [repri'mɑ̃], *a.* repressive.

réprimer [repri'me], *v.t.* to repress, to restrain.

repris [rə'pri], *a.* retaken, taken up again; reset (*of a bone*).—*n.m.* **repris de justice**, old offender, (*fam.*) old lag.

reprisage [rəpri'za:ʒ], *n.m.* darn; darning.

reprise [rə'pri:z], *n.f.* resumption; recapture, recovery; revival; darn; (*Mus.*) repetition; refrain (*of a song*); (*Ftb. etc.*) second half; (*Fenc.*) bout; (*Box.*) round; **à plusieurs reprises**, several times, repeatedly.

repriser [rəpri'ze], *v.t.* to darn.

réprobateur [reprɔba'tœ:r], *a.* (*fem.* **-trice**) reproving.

réprobation [reprɔba'sjɔ̃], *n.f.* reprobation.

reprochable [rəprɔ'ʃabl], *a.* reproachable.

reproche [rə'prɔʃ], *n.m.* reproach.

reprocher [rəprɔ'ʃe], *v.t.* to reproach, to upbraid; to taunt. **se reprocher**, *v.r.* to reproach oneself; to blame oneself.

reproducteur [rəprɔdyk'tœ:r], *a.* (*fem.* **-trice**) reproductive.

reproductif [rəprɔdyk'tif], *a.* (*fem.* **-tive**) reproductive.

reproduction [rəprɔdyk'sjɔ̃], *n.f.* reproduction; copy.

reproduire [rəprɔ'dɥi:r], *v.t. irr.* (*conjug. like* CONDUIRE) to reproduce; to reprint. **se reproduire**, *v.r.* to reproduce; to breed; to recur.

réprouvable [repru'vabl], *a.* censurable, reprehensible.

réprouvé [repru've], *a.* and *n.m.* (*fem.* **-ée**) reprobate.

réprouver [repru've], *v.t.* to disapprove of; (*Theol.*) to condemn.

reps [rɛps], *n.m.* rep (*silk or woollen fabric*).

reptile [rɛp'til], *a.* creeping, crawling.—*n.m.* reptile.

repu [rə'py], *a.* and *p.p.* of **repaître**, full, satiated.

républicain [repybli'kɛ̃], *a.* and *n.m.* (*fem.* **-e**) republican.

republier [rəpybli'je], *v.t.* to republish.

république [repy'blik], *n.f.* republic; commonwealth.

répudiation [repydja'sjɔ̃], *n.f.* repudiation.

répudier [repy'dje], *v.t.* to repudiate.

répugnance [repy'nɑ̃:s], *n.f.* repugnance; reluctance.

répugnant [repy'nɑ̃], *a.* repugnant.

répugner [repy'ne], *v.i.* to be repugnant; to feel repugnance; to clash with.

répulsif [repyl'sif], *a.* (*fem.* **-sive**) repulsive, repellent; (*fig.*) disgusting.

répulsion [repyl'sjɔ̃], *n.f.* repulsion; (*fig.*) aversion, disgust.

réputation [repyta'sjɔ̃], *n.f.* reputation; character; fame.

réputé [repy'te], *a.* well-known.

réputer [repy'te], *v.t.* to repute, to consider, to deem.

requérant [rəke'rɑ̃], *n.m.* (*fem.* **-e**) plaintiff, petitioner.

requérir [rəke'ri:r], *v.t. irr.* (*conjug. like* ACQUÉRIR) to request; to require; to claim; to requisition.

requête [rə'kɛ:t], *n.f.* request, petition, demand.

requiem [rekɥi'ɛm], *n.m.* requiem.

requin [rə'kɛ̃], *n.m.* shark.

requis [rə'ki], *a.* required, requisite, necessary.

réquisition [rekizi'sjɔ̃], *n.f.* requisition; summons; levy.

réquisitionner [rekizisjɔ'ne], *v.t.* to requisition, to commandeer.

rescapé [rɛska'pe], *a.* and *n.m.* (*fem.* **-ée**) survivor of a disaster.

rescousse [rɛs'kus], *n.f.* **venir** (**aller**) **à la rescousse**, to come (to go) to the rescue.

réseau [re'zo], *n.m.* (*pl.* **-eaux**) net; network; (*fig.*) web, tangle; (*Rail., Elec. etc.*) network, system.

réséda [reze'da], *n.m.* reseda; mignonette.

réservation [rezɛrva'sjɔ̃], *n.f.* reservation, reserving; booking (*of seats*).

réserve [re'zɛrv], *n.f.* reserve; reservation, caution; modesty; stock, store; preserve (*for game*).

réservé [rezɛr've], *a.* reserved; cautious.

réserver [rezɛr've], *v.t.* to reserve; to keep (*pour*). **se réserver**, *v.r.* to reserve for oneself; to reserve oneself, to wait.

réserviste [rezɛr'vist], *n.m.* (*Mil.*) reservist.

réservoir [rezɛr'vwa:r], *n.m.* reservoir; tank, cistern, well.

résidant [rezi'dɑ̃], *a.* resident.

résidence [rezi'dɑ̃:s], *n.f.* residence, dwelling.

résident [rezi'dɑ̃], *n.m.* (*fem.* **-e**) resident.

résidentiel [rezidɑ̃'sjɛl], *a.* (*fem.* **-elle**) residential.

résider [rezi'de], *v.i.* to reside, to dwell.

résidu [rezi'dy], *n.m.* residue; remainder.

résiduaire [rezi'dɥɛ:r], *a.* waste.

résignation [rezina'sjɔ̃], *n.f.* resignation.

résigné [rezi'ne], *a.* resigned, submissive.

résigner [rezi'ne], *v.t.* to resign, to give up. **se résigner**, *v.r.* to resign oneself, to submit.

résiliation [rezilja'sjɔ̃], *n.f.*, **résiliement** or **résiliment** [rezili'mɑ̃], *n.m.* cancelling, annulment.

résilience [rezi'ljɑ̃:s], *n.f.* resilience (*in metals*).

résilier [rezi'lje], *v.t.* to cancel, to annul.

résille [re'zi:j], *n.f.* hair net.

résine [re'zin], *n.f.* resin, rosin.

résineux [rezi'nø], *a.* (*fem.* **-euse**) resinous.

résistance [rezis'tɑ̃:s], *n.f.* resistance, opposition; **la Résistance**, the Resistance Movement (1940–45).

résistant [rezis'tɑ̃], *a.* unyielding; resistant, tough.—*n.m.* (*fem.* **-e**) member of the Resistance Movement.

résister [rezis'te], *v.i.* to resist, to withstand (**à**).

résistible [rezis'tibl], *a.* resistible.

résistivité [rezistivi'te], *n.f.* (*Elec.*) resistivity.

résolu [rezɔ'ly], *a.* resolved, resolute, determined; solved.

résoluble [rezɔ'lybl], *a.* soluble.

résolument [rezɔly'mɑ̃], *adv.* resolutely, boldly.

résolution [rezɔly'sjɔ̃], *n.f.* resolution, solution; decision, determination; resolve.

résonance [rezɔ'nɑ̃:s], *n.f.* resonance.

résonnant [rezɔ'nɑ̃], *a.* resonant, resounding, sonorous.

résonnement [rezɔn'mɑ̃], *n.m.* resounding, re-echoing.

résonner [rezɔ'ne], *v.i.* to resound, to reverberate, to re-echo.

résoudre [re'zu:dr], *v.t. irr.* to resolve; to dissolve; to solve; to decide upon; to cancel; to persuade. **se résoudre**, *v.r.* to resolve, to determine; to be resolved, to be solved; to dissolve.

respect [rɛs'pɛ], *n.m.* respect, regard, reverence.

respectabilité [rɛspɛktabili'te], *n.f.* respectability.

respectable [rɛspɛk'tabl], *a.* respectable.

respectablement [rɛspɛktablə'mɑ̃], *adv.* respectably.

respecter [rɛspɛk'te], *v.t.* to respect, to revere; to spare.

respectif [rɛspɛk'tif], *a.* (*fem.* **-tive**) respective.

respectivement [rɛspɛktiv'mɑ̃], *adv.* respectively.

respectueusement [rɛspɛktɥøz'mɑ̃], *adv.* respectfully, deferentially.

respectueux [rɛspɛk'tɥø], *a.* (*fem.* **-euse**) respectful, deferential.

respirable [rɛspi'rabl], *a.* respirable, breathable.

respirateur [rɛspira'tœ:r], *a.m.* respiratory. —*n.m.* respirator.

respiration [rɛspira'sjɔ̃], *n.f.* respiration, breathing.

respiratoire [rɛspira'twa:r], *a.* respiratory, breathing.

respirer [rɛspi're], *v.t.* to breathe; (*fig.*) to express; to long for.—*v.i.* to breathe; to catch one's breath, to rest.

resplendir [rɛsplɑ̃'di:r], *v.i.* to shine brightly; to glitter.

resplendissant [rɛsplɑ̃di'sɑ̃], *a.* resplendent, glittering.

resplendissement [rɛsplɑ̃dis'mɑ̃], *n.m.* splendor, refulgence.

responsabilité [rɛspɔ̃sabili'te], *n.f.* responsibility, liability.

responsable [rɛspɔ̃'sabl], *a.* responsible, accountable.

resquillage [rɛski'ja:ʒ], *n.m.*, **resquille** [rɛs'ki:j], *n.f.* (*slang*) gate-crashing; **entrer à la resquille**, to gate-crash.

resquiller [rɛski'je], *v.i.* to gate-crash; to wangle.

ressac [rə'sak], *n.m.* surf.

ressaisir [rəse'zi:r], *v.t.* to seize again. **se ressaisir**, *v.r.* to regain one's self-control.

ressasser [rəsa'se], *v.t.* (*fig.*) to scrutinize; (*fig.*) to repeat tediously, to harp on.

ressaut [rə'so], *n.m.* projection; abrupt fall, dip.

ressauter [rəso'te], *v.t.* to leap over again.— *v.i.* to leap again; (*Arch.*) to project.

ressemblance [rəsɑ̃'blɑ̃:s], *n.f.* resemblance, likeness.

ressemblant [rəsɑ̃'blɑ̃], *a.* like, similar.

ressembler [rəsɑ̃'ble], *v.i.* to look like, to resemble (à). **se ressembler**, *v.r.* to be like each other; to look alike.

ressemelage [rəsəm'la:ʒ], *n.m.* resoling (of shoes).

ressemeler [rəsə'mle], *v.t.* (*conjug. like* APPELER) to re-sole (*shoes etc.*).

ressenti [rəsɑ̃'ti], *a.* felt; (*Paint.*) strongly expressed.

ressentiment [rəsɑ̃ti'mɑ̃], *n.m.* resentment.

ressentir [rəsɑ̃'ti:r], *v.t. irr.* (*conjug. like* SENTIR) to feel, to experience; to manifest; to resent. **se ressentir**, *v.r.* to feel the effects (*de*); to be felt.

resserrement [rəsɛr'mɑ̃], *n.m.* contraction, tightening; restriction.

resserrer [rəsɛ're], *v.t.* to tighten; to pen in; to restrain; to abridge; to close up; to lock up again. **se resserrer**, *v.r.* to contract, to be contracted; to confine oneself; to curtail one's expenses.

ressort (1) [rə'sɔ:r], *n.m.* spring; elasticity; energy, activity, strength; means.

ressort (2) [rə'sɔ:r], *n.m.* extent of jurisdiction; (*fig.*) department, line.

ressortir (1) [rəsɔr'ti:r], *v.i. irr.* (*conjug. like* SENTIR, *but with aux.* ÊTRE) to go *or* come out again; (*fig.*) to stand out; to result (*de*); **faire ressortir**, to throw into relief.

ressortir (2) [rəsɔr'ti:r], *v.i.* to be under the jurisdiction of, to be dependent on.

ressortissant [rəsɔrti'sɑ̃], *n.m.* (*fem.* **-e**) national.

ressource [rə'surs], *n.f.* resource, resort, expedient, shift; (*pl.*) resources; **il n'y a point de ressource**, there's no help for it; **ressources personnelles**, private means.

ressouvenir [rəsuv'ni:r], *n.m.* remembrance, recollection, reminiscence.

ressouvenir (se) [sərəsuv'ni:r], *v.r. irr.* (*conjug. like* TENIR, *but with aux.* ÊTRE) to recollect, to remember.

ressuscitation [resysita'sjɔ̃], *n.f.* resuscitation, revival.

ressusciter [resysi'te], *v.t.* to resuscitate; to revive (*a custom etc.*).—*v.i.* to come to life again.

restant [rɛs'tɑ̃], *a.* remaining, left.—*n.m.* remainder, rest.

restaurant [rɛsto'rɑ̃], *n.m.* restaurant; restorative.

restaurateur [rɛstora'tœ:r], *n.m.* (*fem.* **-trice**) restorer; restaurant keeper.

restauration [rɛstora'sjɔ̃], *n.f.* restoration, repair.

restaurer [rɛsto're], *v.t.* to restore; to refresh. **se restaurer**, *v.r.* to take refreshment; to build up one's strength (*after illness*).

reste [rɛst], *n.m.* rest, remainder; trace, vestige; (*pl.*) remnants, relics; remains; **au reste** *or* **du reste**, besides, moreover; **de reste**, over and above; **et le reste**, and so on, and so forth; **être en reste**, to be in arrears; **les restes**, remnants (*of meal*); mortal remains.

rester [rɛs'te], *v.i.* (*aux.* ÊTRE) to remain; to stay; to last; to pause; **rester court**, to stop short.

restituable [rɛsti'tɥabl], *a.* repayable, returnable.

restituer [rɛsti'tɥe], *v.t.* to restore; to return, to refund.

restitution [rɛstity'sjɔ̃], *n.f.* restitution, restoration.

restreindre [rɛs'trɛ̃:dr], *v.t. irr.* (*conjug. like* CRAINDRE) to restrict; to limit; to restrain. **se restreindre**, *v.r.* to restrain oneself; to curtail one's expenses.

restreint [rɛs'trɛ̃], *a.* restricted, limited.

restrictif [rɛstrik'tif], *a.* (*fem.* **-tive**) restrictive.

restriction [rɛstrik'sjɔ̃], *n.f.* restriction, restraint; **restriction mentale**, mental reservation.

restringent [rɛstrɛ̃'ʒɑ̃], *a.* and *n.m.* (*Med.*) astringent.

résultant [rezyl'tɑ̃], *a.* resulting.

résultat [rezyl'ta], *n.m.* result.

résulter [rezyl'te], *v.i.* to result.

résumé [rezy'me], *n.m.* recapitulation, summary; **en résumé**, to sum up.

résumer [rezy'me], *v.t.* to summarize. **se résumer**, *v.r.* to recapitulate, to sum up.

résurrection [rezyrɛk'sjɔ̃], *n.f.* resurrection; revival.

rétablir [reta'bliːr], *v.t.* to re-establish, to restore; to repair; to recover; to retrieve. **se rétablir**, *v.r.* to recover one's health; to be restored.

rétablissement [retablis'mɑ̃], *n.m.* re-establishment, restoration; repair; recovery.

retailler [rəta'je], *v.t.* to cut again, to prune again.

rétamer [reta'me], *v.t.* to tin over again; to resilver.

rétameur [reta'mœːr], *n.m.* tinker.

retaper [rəta'pe], *v.t.* (*colloq.*) to do up (*a hat etc.*), to straighten (*bedclothes*). **se retaper**, *v.r.* (*fam.*) to buck up.

retard [rə'taːr], *n.m.* delay; slowness (*of a clock etc.*); to be late. **être en retard**, to be late.

retardataire [rətarda'tɛːr], *a.* in arrears, late; backward.—*n.* late-comer; defaulter.

retardement [rətardə'mɑ̃], *n.m.* , delay, retardment.

retarder [ratar'de], *v.t.* to retard, to delay; to defer (*payment*); to set back (*clocks and watches*).—*v.i.* to lose time; to be slow (*of clocks and watches*); to be behind the times.

retenir [rət'niːr] *v.t. irr.* (*conjug. like* TENIR) to hold back; to retain; to detain; to remember; to reserve; to hold in, to restrain; to engage; to prevent; to get hold of again; (*Arith.*) to carry. **se retenir**, *v.r.* to control oneself; to refrain; to catch hold.

retenteur [rətɑ̃'tœːr], *a.* (*fem.* **-trice**) retaining.

rétentif [retɑ̃'tif], *a.* (*fem.* **-tive**) retentive.

rétention [retɑ̃'sjɔ̃], *n.f.* reservation.

retentir [rətɑ̃'tiːr], *v.i.* to resound, to re-echo, to ring.

retentissant [rətɑ̃ti'sɑ̃], *a.* resounding, echoing; ringing, loud; (*fig.*) famous.

retentissement [rətɑ̃tis'mɑ̃], *n.m.* resounding, echo; ringing; (*fig.*) fame, celebrity.

retenu [rət'ny], *a.* reserved, cautious, wary.

retenue [rət'ny], *n.f.* discretion, circumspection, caution; detention; (*Comm.*) deduction; guy rope.

réticence [reti'sɑ̃ːs], *n.f.* reserve, silence; concealment (*of some particular*).

rétif [re'tif], *a.* (*fem.* **-tive**) restive; stubborn.

rétine [re'tin], *n.f.* retina (*of the eye*).

retirable [rəti'rabl], *a.* withdrawable.

retiré [rəti're], *a.* retired, secluded; in retirement.

retirement [rətir'mɑ̃], *n.m.* contraction; shrinking.

retirer [rəti're], *v.t.* to draw again; to pull back, to withdraw; to take away; to retract; to derive. **se retirer**, *v.r.* to retire, to withdraw; to subside (*of waters*); to contract.

retombée [rətɔ̃'be], *n.f.* fall, fall-out;

retombée de particules radioactives, radio-active fall-out.

retomber [rətɔ̃'be], *v.i.* (*aux.* ÊTRE) to fall again; to have a relapse; to subside.

retordre [rə'tɔrdr], *v.t.* to twist again; to twist (*silk, thread etc.*).

rétorquer [retɔr'ke], *v.t.* to retort.

retors [rə'tɔːr], *a.* twisted; artful, cunning, crafty.—*n.m.* twisted thread; crafty person.

retouche [rə'tuʃ], *n.f.* retouching, touching up.

retoucher [rətu'ʃe], *v.t.* to retouch; to touch up.

retour [rə'tuːr], *n.m.* return; repetition, recurrence; sending back; (*fig.*) change; reverse; turning, winding; (*Law*) reversion; **billet d'aller et retour**, return ticket.

retourne [rə'turn], *n.f.* trump card.

retourner [rətur'ne], *v.t.* (*aux.* AVOIR) to turn, to turn up, to turn over, round, about etc.; to send back.—*v.i.* (*aux.* ÊTRE) to return, to go again, to go back (*again*); to recoil upon; to turn up (*cards*). **se retourner**, *v.r.* to turn, to turn round, to look round.

retracer [rətra'se], *v.t.* (*conjug. like* COMMENCER) to trace again, to retrace; to relate. **se retracer**, *v.r.* to recall to mind; to recur, to be retraced (*in mind*).

rétracter [retrak'te], *v.t.* and **se rétracter** *v.r.* to retract; to recant.

retrait [rə'trɛ], *a.* shrunk (*of grain, wood etc.*).—*n.m.* shrinkage; recess (*in wall*), closet; withdrawal.

retraite [rə'trɛt], *n.f.* retreat, retiring; privacy; refuge; haunt; retirement (*from office*); superannuation; retiring pension; **battre en retraite**, to beat a retreat.

retraité [rətrɛ'te], *a.* superannuated, retired, pensioned off.

retraiter [rətrɛ'te], *v.t.* to retire, to pension off.

retranchement [rətrɑ̃ʃ'mɑ̃], *n.m.* retrenchment, curtailment; (*Mil.*) entrenchment.

retrancher [rətrɑ̃'ʃe], *v.t.* to retrench, to curtail, to cut short; to cut out; to abridge; (*Arith.*) to subtract; (*Mil.*) to entrench. **se retrancher**, *v.r.* to restrain oneself; to curtail one's expenses; (*Mil.*) to entrench oneself; (*fig.*) to fall back upon.

rétrécir [retre'siːr], *v.t.* to take in, to contract; to narrow, to limit.—*v.i.* and **se rétrécir**, *v.r.* to grow narrower; to shrink, to contract.

rétrécissement [retresis'mɑ̃], *n.m.* narrowing; shrinking.

retremper [rətrɑ̃'pe], *v.t.* to soak again; to temper again; (*fig.*) to strengthen. **se retremper**, *v.r.* to be strengthened *or* invigorated.

rétribuer [retri'bɥe], *v.t.* to remunerate.

rétribution [retriby'sjɔ̃], *n.f.* payment, reward.

rétroactif [retroak'tif], *a.* (*fem.* **-tive**) retro-active.

rétroaction [retroak'sjɔ̃], *n.f.* retroaction; (*Rad. Teleg.*) feed-back.

rétrograde [retro'grad], *a.* retrograde; backward.

rétrograder [retrogra'de], *v.i.* to retrograde; to go back, (*Mil.*) to fall back.

rétrogressif [retrogre'sif], *a.* (*fem.* **-ive**) retrogressive.

rétrogression [retrɔgrɛ'sjɔ̃], *n.f.* retrogression.

rétrospectif [retrɔspɛk'tif], *a.* (*fem.* -**tive**) retrospective.

retroussé [rətru'se], *a.* turned up; tucked up; *nez retroussé,* turned-up nose, snub nose.

retrousser [rətru'se], *v.t.* to turn up, to roll up (*trousers*); to tuck up; to cock (*one's hat*). **se retrousser,** *v.r.* to tuck up one's skirt *or* other garment.

retroussis [rətru'si], *n.m.* cock (*of a hat*); top (*of a shoe*); facing (*of a uniform*).

retrouver [rətru've], *v.t.* to find again, to regain, to recover. **se retrouver,** *v.r.* to find each other again; to be oneself again.

rétroviseur [retrɔvi'zœːr], *n.m.* (*Motor.*) rearview mirror.

rets [rɛ], *n.m. inv.* net; (*fig.*) snare, toils.

réunion [rey'njɔ̃], *n.f.* reunion; reconciliation; junction; meeting, assembly, gathering; reception.

réunir [rey'niːr], *v.t.* to reunite, to join again, to bring together again, to reconcile; to connect; to collect. **se réunir,** *v.r.* to assemble again, to reunite; to meet; to amalgamate.

réussi [rey'si], *a.* successful, brilliant.

réussir [rey'siːr], *v.t.* to carry out well, to accomplish, to perform successfully.—*v.i.* to succeed, to be successful, to prosper, to thrive; to pass (*Exam*).

réussite [rey'sit], *n.f.* success; (*happy*) issue *or* result; (*Cards*) solitaire.

revaloir [rəva'lwaːr], *v.t. irr.* (*conjug. like* VALOIR) to return like for like, to be even with.

revanche [rə'vãːʃ], *n.f.* revenge; return match.

rêvasser [rɛva'se], *v.i.* to day-dream, to muse.

rêvasserie [rɛvas'ri], *n.f.* day-dreams; idle musing.

rêvasseur [rɛva'sœːr], *n.m.* (*fem.* -**euse**) (*colloq.*) dreamer, muser.

rêve [rɛːv], *n.m.* dream; day-dream, illusion.

revêche [rə'vɛːʃ], *a.* rough; cross, ill-natured, cantankerous.

réveil [re've:j], *n.m.* waking, awaking; alarm clock; (*Mil.*) reveille.

réveille-matin [revejma'tɛ̃], *n.m. inv.* alarm clock.

réveiller [reve'je], *v.t.* to awake, to arouse; to recall. **se réveiller,** *v.r.* to awake, to wake up; to be roused; to revive.

réveillon [reve'jɔ̃], *n.m.* midnight repast, *esp.* Christmas Eve revel.

réveillonner [revejɔ'ne], *v.i.* to take part in a *réveillon.*

révélateur [revela'tœːr], *a.* (*fem.* -**trice**) revealing, tell-tale.—*n.m.* (*fem.* -**trice**) revealer, informer.—*n.m.* (*Phot.*) developer.

révélation [revela'sjɔ̃], *n.f.* revelation, disclosure.

révéler [reve'le], *v.t.* (*conjug. like* CÉDER) to reveal, to disclose; to betray; (*Phot.*) to develop. **se révéler,** *v.r.* to reveal oneself; to prove (to be).

revenant [rəv'nã], *a.* pleasing, prepossessing.—*n.m.* ghost.

revendeur [rəvã'dœːr], *n.m.* (*fem.* -**euse**) retail dealer, dealer in old clothes etc.

revendicable [rəvãdi'kabl], *a.* claimable.

revendicateur [rəvãdika'tœːr], *n.m.* (*fem.* -**trice**) claimant.

revendication [rəvãdika'sjɔ̃], *n.f.* claim, demand.

revendiquer [rəvãdi'ke], *v.t.* to claim.

revendre [rə'vãːdr], *v.t.* to sell again, to resell.

revenir [rəv'niːr], *v.i. irr.* (*conjug. like* TENIR but with aux. ÊTRE) to come again, to come back, to return; to reappear, to haunt; to walk (*of ghosts*); to recur; to recover; to amount, to cost; to retract; to please.

revente [rə'vãːt], *n.f.* resale.

revenu [rəv'ny], *n.m.* revenue, income.

revenue [rəv'ny], *n.f.* young wood, aftergrowth.

rêver [rɛ've], *v.t.* to dream, to dream of.—*v.i.* to dream; to have day dreams; to muse.

réverbérant [reverbe'rã], *a.* reverberating.

réverbération [reverbera'sjɔ̃], *n.f.* reverberation; reflection (*of light, heat*).

réverbère [rever'bɛːr], *n.m.* reflector; street lamp.

réverbérer [reverbe're], *v.t., v.i.* (*conjug. like* CÉDER) to reverberate; to reflect (*light, heat*).

reverdir [rəver'diːr], *v.t.* to make green again, to revive.—*v.i.* to become green again; (*fig.*) to grow young again.

reverdissement [rəverdis'mã], *n.m.* growing green again.

révéremment [revera'mã], *adv.* reverently.

révérence [reve'rãːs], *n.f.* reverence; bow, curtsy.

révérenciel [reverã'sjɛl], *a.* (*fem.* -**elle**) reverential.

révérencieusement [reverãsjøz'mã], *adv.* reverentially.

révérencieux [reverã'sjø], *a.* (*fem.* -**euse**) ceremonious, obsequious.

révérend [reve'rã], *a.* reverend.

révérendissime [reverãdi'sim], *a.* most reverend, right reverend.

révérer [reve're], *v.t.* (*conjug. like* CÉDER) to revere.

rêverie [rɛ'vri], *n.f.* reverie, musing, dreaming.

revers [rə'vɛːr], *n.m.* back, reverse; facing (*of clothes*); lapel (*of a coat*); turn-up (*of trousers*); top (*of shoes*); (*Ten.*) back-hand stroke; misfortune, set back.

reverser [rəver'se], *v.t.* to pour out again; to pour back; to transfer; to pay back.

réversible [rever'sibl], *a.* reversible; revertible.

réversion [rever'sjɔ̃], *n.f.* reversion.

reversoir [rəver'swaːr], *n.m.* weir.

revêtement [rəvɛt'mã], *n.m.* facing (*of masonry etc.*); surface (*of road*).

revêtir [rəvɛ'tiːr], *v.t. irr.* (*conjug. like* VÊTIR) to give clothes to, to dress; to put on; to assume; to cover; (*fig.*) to invest *or* endow with. **se revêtir,** *v.r.* to clothe oneself, to array oneself; to put on, to assume.

rêveur [rɛ'vœːr], *a.* (*fem.* -**euse**) dreaming; (*fig.*) pensive, dreamy.—*n.m.* (*fem.* -**euse**) dreamer; muser.

revient [rə'vjɛ̃], *n.m. prix de revient,* net cost.

revirement [ravir'mã], *n.m.* tacking about; (*fig.*) sudden change.

revirer [ləvi're], *v.i.* to tack, to put about; (*fig.*) to change sides.

revisable [rəvi'zabl], **révisable** [revi'zabl], *a.* revisable.

reviser [rəvi'ze], **réviser** [revi'ze], *v.t.* to revise, to review, to examine; to overhaul (*engine*).

reviseur [rəvi'zœ:r], **réviseur** [revi'zœ:r], *n.m.* reviser, examiner; auditor; proofreader.

revision [rəvi'zjɔ̃], **révision** [revi'zjɔ̃], *n.f.* revision, review; overhaul (*of engine*).

revivifier [rəvivi'fje], *v.t.* to revivify, to regenerate, to revive.

revivre [rə'vi:vr], *v.t. irr.* (*conjug. like* VIVRE) to relive.—*v.i.* to come to life again, to live again.

révocable [revɔ'kabl], *a.* revocable; removable (*of an official*).

révocation [revɔka'sjɔ̃], *n.f.* revocation (*of will*), repeal; dismissal (*of an official*).

revoici [rəvwa'si], **revoilà** [rəvwa'la], *adv.* (*colloq.*) *me revoici*, here I am again; *le revoilà*, there he is again.

revoir [rə'vwa:r], *v.t. irr.* (*conjug. like* VOIR) to see again; to meet again; to revise, to review. **se revoir**, *v.r.* to see *or* meet each other again.—*n.m. inv. au revoir*, good-bye (*for the present*).

revoler (1) [rəvɔ'le], *v.t.* to steal again.

revoler (2) [rəvɔ'le], *v.i.* to fly again; to fly back.

révoltant [revɔl'tɑ̃], *a.* revolting, shocking.

révolte [re'vɔlt], *n.f.* revolt, rebellion.

révolté [revɔl'te], *n.m.* (*fem.* **-ée**) rebel; mutineer.

révolter [revɔl'te], *v.t.* to stir up, to rouse; to shock, to disgust. **se révolter**, *v.r.* to revolt, to rebel; to be indignant, to be shocked.

révolu [revɔ'ly], *a.* accomplished, completed; elapsed.

révolution [revɔly'sjɔ̃], *n.f.* revolution.

révolutionnaire [revɔlysjɔ'nɛ:r], *a.* revolutionary.—*n.* revolutionary; revolutionist.

révolutionner [revɔlysjɔ'ne], *v.t.* to revolutionize.

revolver [revɔl'vɛ:r], *n.m.* revolver.

révoquer [revɔ'ke], *v.t.* to dismiss (*an official etc.*); to recall (*an ambassador etc.*); to repeal, to cancel.

revue [rə'vy], *n.f.* review, survey; revision; magazine; review (*critical article*); (*Mil.*) review; (*Theat.*) revue.

révulsion [revyl'sjɔ̃], *n.f.* revulsion.

rez [re], *prep.* on a level with, even with.

rez-de-chaussée [redʒo'se], *n.m. inv.* ground-level; ground floor.

rhabillage [rabi'ja:ʒ], *n.m.* mending, overhaul.

rhabiller [rabi'je], *v.t.* to dress again; to mend.

rhétoricien [retɔri'sjɛ̃], *n.m.* rhetorician.

rhétorique [retɔ'rik], *n.f.* rhetoric.

Rhin [rɛ̃], **le**, *m.* the Rhine.

rhinocéros [rinɔse'rɔs], *n.m. inv.* rhinoceros.

rhododendron [rɔdɔdɛ̃'drɔ̃], *n.m.* rhododendron.

rhombe [rɔ̃:b], *a.* rhombic.—*n.m.* rhomb; rhombus.

rhubarbe [ry'barb], *n.f.* rhubarb.

rhum [rɔm], *n.m.* rum.

rhumatisant [rymati'zɑ̃], *a.* suffering from rheumatism, rheumatic.—*n.m.* (*fem.* **-e**) sufferer from rheumatism.

rhumatismal [rymatis'mal], *a.* (*m. pl.* **-aux**) rheumatic.

rhumatisme [ryma'tism], *n.m.* rheumatism.

rhume [rym], *n.m.* cold (*illness*).

riant [ri'jɑ̃], *a.* smiling, cheerful, pleasant, pleasing.

ribambelle [ribɑ̃'bɛl], *n.f.* (*colloq.*) swarm, string, lot.

ribaud [ri'bo], *a.* and *n.m.* (*fem.* **-e**) ribald.

ribauderie [ribod'ri], *n.f.* ribaldry.

ricanement [rikan'mɑ̃], *n.m.* sneering, sneer; mocking laughter.

ricaner [rika'ne], *v.i.* to sneer, to snigger.

ricaneur [rika'nœ:r], *a.* (*fem.* **-euse**) sneering, derisive.—*n.m.* (*fem.* **-euse**) sneerer.

Richard [ri'ʃa:r], *m.* Richard.

richard [ri'ʃa:r], *n.m.* (*fam.* and *pej.*) moneyed person, capitalist.

riche [riʃ], *a.* rich, wealthy; copious; valuable.—*n.* rich person.

richement [riʃ'mɑ̃], *adv.* richly; splendidly.

richesse [ri'ʃɛs], *n.f.* riches, wealth; copiousness; richness.

richissime [riʃi'sim], *a.* (*colloq.*) rolling in money.

ricin [ri'sɛ̃], *n.m.* castor-oil plant.

ricocher [rikɔ'ʃe], *v.i.* to rebound; to ricochet.

ricochet [rikɔ'ʃɛ], *n.m.* rebound (*on the water*); (*Artill.*) ricochet; (*fig.*) chain (*of events*).

rictus [rik'ty:s], *n.m. inv.* grin; rictus.

ride [rid], *n.f.* wrinkle; ripple.

ridé [ri'de], *a.* wrinkled; rippling; corrugated.

rideau [ri'do], *n.m.* (*pl.* **-eaux**) curtain; screen (*of trees etc.*).

rider [ri'de], *v.t.* to wrinkle; to corrugate; to shrivel; to ruffle (*water*). **se rider**, *v.r.* to be wrinkled; to shrivel up; to ripple (*of water*).

ridicule [ridi'kyl], *a.* ridiculous.—*n.m.* ridicule; ridiculousness.

ridiculement [ridikyl'mɑ̃], *adv.* ridiculously.

ridiculiser [ridikyli'ze], *v.t.* to ridicule, to make fun of.

rien [rjɛ̃], *n.m.* trifle, mere nothing.—*indef. pron.* nothing, nought, not anything; anything.

rieur [ri'jœ:r], *a.* (*fem.* **rieuse**) laughing, joking.

rigide [ri'ʒid], *a.* rigid, stiff; strict, severe.

rigidement [riʒid'mɑ̃], *adv.* rigidly, strictly.

rigidité [riʒidi'te], *n.f.* rigidity, stiffness, strictness, severity.

rigole [ri'gɔl], *n.f.* trench, small ditch *or* channel; gutter.

rigoler [rigɔ'le], *v.i.* (*pop.*) to laugh; to have fun; to joke.

rigorisme [rigɔ'rism], *n.m.* rigorism, austerity.

rigoriste [rigɔ'rist], *a.* over-severe.—*n.* rigorist, stickler.

rigoureusement [rigurøz'mɑ̃], *adv.* rigorously, severely, strictly.

rigoureux [rigu'rø], *a.* (*fem.* **-euse**) rigorous, harsh; strict; stern; inclement.

rigueur [ri'gœ:r], *n.f.* rigor, strictness; precision; severity; inclemency; *à la rigueur*, at a pinch; if necessary; *de rigueur*, indispensable, compulsory.

rimailler [rima'je], *v.i.* to write doggerel.

rimailleur [rimɑ'jœ:r], *n.m.* (*fem.* **-euse**) sorry rhymer, rhymester.

rime [rim], *n.f.* rhyme; (*fig.*) verse.

rimer [ri'me], *v.i.* to rhyme; to write verses.

rimeur [ri'mœ:r], *n.m.* rhymer, versifier.

rinçage [rɛ̃'sa:ʒ], *n.m.* rinsing, washing.

rincer [rɛ̃'se], *v.t.* (*conjug. like* COMMENCER) to rinse, to wash. **se rincer,** *v.r.* to rinse.

ripaille [ri'pɑ:j], *n.f.* feasting, junketing.

riposte [ri'pɔst], *n.f.* (*Fenc.*) ripost, return; (*fig.*) retort, repartee.

riposter [ripɔs'te], *v.i.* (*Fenc.*) to ripost, to parry and thrust; (*fig.*) to make a smart reply.

rire [ri:r], *v.i.* irr. to laugh; to smile; to be favorable; to joke; to mock. **se rire,** *v.r.* to make sport, to scoff (*de*).—*n.m.* laughter, laughing.

ris [ri], *n.m. inv.* laugh, smile, laughter; (*Naut.*) reef (*of sails*); sweetbread.

risée [ri'ze], *n.f.* laugh, laughter; mockery; laughing-stock.

risette [ri'zɛt], *n.f.* pleasant little laugh.

risible [ri'zibl], *a.* comical, laughable; ridiculous.

risiblement [riziblə'mɑ̃], *adv.* laughably, ludicrously.

risque [risk], *n.m.* risk, hazard.

risqué [ris'ke], *a.* risky; *une plaisanterie risquée,* a doubtful joke.

risquer [ris'ke], *v.t.* to risk, to venture; (*fam.*) to chance. **se risquer,** *v.r.* to risk, to venture.

risque-tout [riskə'tu], *n.m. inv.* (*colloq.*) dare-devil.

rissole [ri'sɔl], *n.f.* rissole.

rissoler [risɔ'le], *v.t.* (*Cook.*) to brown.

ristourne [ris'turn], *n.f.* refund; rebate.

rit or **rite** [rit], *n.m.* rite.

ritournelle [ritur'nɛl], *n.f.* (*Mus.*) ritornello, flourish.

rituel [ri'tɥɛl], *a.* (*fem.* **-elle**) ritual.—*n.m.* ritual (*prayer book*).

rivage [ri'va:ʒ], *n.m.* shore, strand, beach; bank, waterside.

rival [ri'val], *a.* (*m. pl.* **-aux**) rival, competitive.—*n.m.* (*fem.* **-e,** *m. pl.* **-aux**) rival.

rivaliser [rivali'ze], *v.i.* to rival, to vie, to compete.

rivalité [rivali'te], *n.f.* rivalry, emulation.

rive [ri:v], *n.f.* bank, shore (*of rivers, lakes etc.*); (*fig.*) seashore; border.

rivement [riv'mɑ̃], *n.m.* riveting.

river [ri've], *v.t.* to clinch, to rivet.

riverain [ri'vrɛ̃], *a.* riparian; bordering (*on rivers or woods*).—*n.m.* (*fem.* **-e**) riverside resident; borderer.

rivet [ri'vɛ], *n.m.* rivet; clinch.

rivetage [riv'ta:ʒ], *n.m.* riveting.

riveter [riv'te], *v.t.* (*conjug. like* APPELER) to rivet.

riveteur [riv'tœ:r], **riveur** [ri'vœ:r], *n.m.* riveter.

rivière [ri'vjɛ:r], *n.f.* river, stream.

rivoir [ri'vwa:r], or **rivoire** [ri'vwa:r], *n.f.* riveting hammer *or* machine.

rivure [ri'vy:r], *n.f.* clinching, riveting.

rixe [riks], *n.f.* fight, scuffle; brawl, affray.

riz [ri], *n.m.* rice.

rizière [ri'zjɛ:r], *n.f.* rice field, paddy field, rice plantation; rice swamp.

robe [rɔb], *n.f.* gown, dress, frock; robe; long robe (*lawyers*), the cloth (*clergy*); coat (*of certain animals*); skin, husk, peel (*of certain fruits etc.*).

robinet [rɔbi'nɛ], *n.m.* tap; cock; *ouvrir* (*fermer*) *le robinet,* to turn on (off) the tap.

robot [rɔ'bo], *a. inv. avion robot,* pilotless plane; *fusée, satellite robot,* unmanned rocket, satellite.—*n.m.* automaton, robot.

robuste [rɔ'byst], *a.* robust, sturdy; hardy, strong.

robustement [rɔbystə'mɑ̃], *adv.* robustly, athletically.

robustesse [rɔbys'tɛs], *n.f.* robustness, strength, vigor.

roc [rɔk], *n.m.* rock.

rocaille [rɔ'kɑ:j], *n.f.* rock work, grotto work.

rocailleux [rɔkɑ'jø], *a.* (*fem.* **-euse**) pebbly, stony; rugged, rough.

roche [rɔʃ], *n.f.* rock; boulder; stony mass.

rocher [rɔ'ʃe], *n.m.* rock, crag.

rochet [rɔ'ʃɛ], *n.m.* rochet (*surplice*); ratchet.

rocheux [rɔ'ʃø], *a.* (*fem.* **-euse**) rocky, stony.

rococo [rɔkɔ'ko], *a. inv.* rococo; antiquated.—*n.m.* rococo, antiquated style.

rodage [rɔ'da:ʒ], *n.m.* grinding in; polishing; *en rodage,* breaking in (*engine*).

roder [rɔ'de], *v.t.* to break in (*car*); to grind, to polish.

rôder [ro'de], *v.i.* to prowl.

rôdeur [ro'dœ:r], *a.* (*fem.* **-euse**) prowling.—*n.m.* (*fem.* **-euse**) prowler; vagrant.

rodomontade [rɔdɔmɔ̃'tad], *n.f.* bluster, swagger.

Rodrigue [rɔ'drig], *m.* Roderick.

rogaton [rɔga'tɔ̃], *n.m.* (*pl.*) scraps, odds and ends.

Roger [rɔ'ʒe], *m.* Roger; *c'est un vrai Roger Bontemps,* he is a happy-go-lucky sort of chap.

rogner [rɔ'ɲe], *v.t.* to cut, to pare, to crop; to clip, to prune.

rogneux [rɔ'ɲø], *a.* (*fem.* **-euse**) mangy, scabby.

rognon [rɔ'ɲɔ̃], *n.m.* kidney (*as food*).

rognure [rɔ'ɲy:r], *n.f.* a paring, a clipping; (*pl.*) scraps, refuse, leavings.

rogue [rɔg], *a.* arrogant, haughty.

roi [rwa], *n.m.* king.

roitelet [rwa'tlɛ], *n.m.* petty king; wren.

rôle [ro:l], *n.m.* roll; list, roster, catalogue; (*Theat.*) part, character.

romain [rɔ'mɛ̃], *a.* Roman.—*n.m.* (**Romain,** *fem.* **-aine**) Roman (*person*).

roman (1) [rɔ'mɑ̃], *a.* Romance, Romanic.

roman (2) [rɔ'mɑ̃], *n.m.* novel, romance, fiction.

romance [rɔ'mɑ̃:s], *n.f.* (*Mus.*) ballad, sentimental song.

romancier [rɔmɑ̃'sje], *n.m.* (*fem.* **-ière**) novelist.

romanesque [rɔma'nɛsk], *a.* romantic.—*n.m.* the romantic.

roman-feuilleton [rɔmɑ̃fœj'tɔ̃], *n.m.* (*pl.* **romans-feuilletons**) newspaper serial (story).

romantique [rɔmɑ̃'tik], *a.* romantic.—*n.* romanticist.

romantiquement [rɔmɑ̃tik'mɑ̃], *adv.* romantically.

romantisme [rɔmɑ̃'tism], *n.m.* (*Lit. Hist.*) romanticism.

285

romarin

romarin [rɔma'rɛ̃], *n.m.* rosemary.
rompre [rɔ̃:pr], *v.t.* (*see Verb Tables*) to break; to snap; to break off; to rout; to dissolve; to break in; to divert; to interrupt. —*v.i.* to break; to fall out. **se rompre**, *v.r.* to break off, to snap.
rompu [rɔ̃'py], *a.* broken, snapped; broken in.
romsteck [rɔm'stɛk], *n.m.* rump steak.
ronce [rɔ̃:s], *n.f.* bramble, blackberry bush.
ronceraie [rɔ̃s'rɛ], *n.f.* brake, brambly ground.
ronchonner [rɔ̃ʃɔ'ne], *v.i.* (*fam.*) to grumble.
rond [rɔ̃], *a.* round; plump, rotund; frank; even (*of money or accounts*).—*adv.* normally, true (*of motor*).—*n.m.* round, ring, orb, circle, disk.
ronde [rɔ̃:d], *n.f.* round; patrol; beat; (*Mus.*) whole note; roundelay; round-hand (*writing*).
rondeau [rɔ̃'do], *n.m.* (*pl.* **-eaux**) rondeau (*French poem*); (*Mus.*) rondo; roller.
rondelet [rɔ̃'dlɛ], *a.* (*fem.* **-ette**) roundish, plump, pudgy.
rondelle [rɔ̃'dɛl], *n.f.* rondelle, washer; rundle, ring.
rondement [rɔ̃d'mɑ̃], *adv.* roundly; briskly; frankly, bluntly.
rondeur [rɔ̃'dœ:r], *n.f.* roundness, rotundity; fullness; plain dealing.
rondin [rɔ̃'dɛ̃], *n.m.* round log; cudgel.
rond-point [rɔ̃'pwɛ̃], *n.m.* (*pl.* **ronds-points**) (*Arch.*) apsis; circle (*place where several roads etc. meet*); traffic circle.
ronflant [rɔ̃'flɑ̃], *a.* snoring; humming, whirring; sonorous.
ronflement [rɔ̃flǝ'mɑ̃], *n.m.* snoring; roaring, rumbling; boom; snorting (*of horses*).
ronfler [rɔ̃'fle], *v.i.* to snore; to snort (*of horses*); to roar (*cannon, thunder etc.*); to boom; to peal (*organs*); to hum (*spinning-tops*).
ronfleur [rɔ̃'flœ:r], *n.m.* (*fem.* **-euse**) snorer.
rongeant [rɔ̃'ʒɑ̃], *a.* gnawing, corroding; (*fig.*) tormenting.
ronger [rɔ̃'ʒe], *v.t.* (*conjug. like* MANGER) to gnaw, to nibble; to consume, to corrode; to prey upon (*the mind etc.*); **ronger son frein**, to champ the bit. **se ronger**, *v.r.* to fret.
rongeur [rɔ̃'ʒœ:r], *a.* (*fem.* **-euse**) gnawing, biting; corroding; consuming.—*n.m.* (*Zool.*) rodent.
ronron [rɔ̃'rɔ̃], *n.m.* purr, purring.
ronronner [rɔ̃rɔ'ne], *v.i.* to purr, to hum.
roquet [rɔ'kɛ], *n.m.* pug dog; cur, mongrel.
rosace [ro'zas], *n.f.* (*Arch.*) rose; rose window.
rosage [ro'za:ʒ], *n.m.* rhododendron; azalea.
rosaire [ro'zɛ:r], *n.m.* (*R.-C. Ch.*) rosary.
rosâtre [ro'zɑ:tr], *a.* pinkish.
rosbif [rɔs'bif], *n.m.* roast beef.
rose [ro:z], *a.* rosy; pink, rose-colored. —*n.f.* rose; rose window; **rose trémière**, hollyhock.—*n.m.* rose-color, pink.
rosé [ro'ze], *a.* rosy, roseate; **vin rosé**, light-red wine.
roseau [ro'zo], *n.m.* (*pl.* **-eaux**) reed.
rosée [ro'ze], *n.f.* dew.
roselière [rozǝ'ljɛ:r], *n.f.* reed bed.
roséole [roze'ɔl], *n.f.* scarlet rash; German measles.
roser [ro'ze], *v.t.* to make pink.

roseraie [roz're], *n.f.* rosery, rose garden.
rosette [ro'zɛt], *n.f.* small rose; rosette.
rosier [ro'zje], *n.m.* rose tree, rose-bush.
rosière [ro'zjɛ:r], *n.f.* rose queen; queen of the May.
rosiériste [rozje'rist], *n.* rose grower.
rosse [rɔs], *a.* bad, malicious.—*n.f.* old horse; (*fig.* and *fam.*) worthless or nasty person.
rossée [rɔ'se], *n.f.* shower of blows, thrashing.
rosser [rɔ'se], *v.t.* (*colloq.*) to thrash, to beat up.
rossignol [rɔsi'nɔl], *n.m.* nightingale; picklock, skeleton key; (*Carp.*) wedge; (*fig.*) unsaleable article (*in a shop*).
rot [ro], *n.m.* (*pop.*) belch, eructation.
rôt [ro], *n.m.* roast, roast meat.
rotarien [rɔta'rjɛ̃], *n.m.* member of a Rotary Club.
rotateur [rɔta'tœ:r], *a.* (*fem.* **-trice**) (*Anat.*) rotatory.—*n.m.* (*Anat.*) rotator.
rotatif [rɔta'tif], *a.* (*fem.* **-tive**) rotary.
rotation [rɔta'sjɔ̃], *n.f.* rotation.
rotatoire [rɔta'twa:r], *a.* rotatory.
roter [rɔ'te], *v.i.* to belch.
rôti [ro'ti], *n.m.* roast, roast meat.
rôtie [ro'ti], *n.f.* slice of toast.
rôtir [ro'ti:r], *v.t., v.i.* to roast; to broil; to toast (*bread etc.*); (*fig.*) to parch.
rôtissage [roti'sa:ʒ], *n.m.* roasting.
rôtisserie [rotis'ri], *n.f.* cook-shop.
rôtisseur [roti'sœ:r], *n.m.* (*fem.* **-euse**) cook-shop keeper.
rôtissoire [roti'swa:r], *n.f.* roaster, Dutch oven.
rotonde [rɔ'tɔ̃:d], *n.f.* rotunda; long sleeveless cloak.
rotondité [rɔtɔ̃di'te], *n.f.* rotundity; plumpness.
rotor [rɔ'tɔ:r], *n.m.* rotor.
roturier [rɔty'rje], *a.* (*fem.* **-ière**) plebeian; vulgar, mean.—*n.m.* (*fem.* **-ière**) commoner.
rouage [rwa:ʒ], *n.m.* wheelwork, cog-wheel; machinery; (*Horol.*) movement.
rouan [rwɑ̃], *a.* (*fem.* **rouanne**) roan (*of horses, cattle etc.*).—*n.m.* roan horse.
roublard [ru'bla:r], *a.* and *n.m.* (*fem.* **-e**) (*fam.*) wily, crafty (person).
rouble [rubl], *n.m.* rouble (*Russian coin*).
roucoulement [rukul'mɑ̃], *n.m.* cooing; gurgling (*of babies*).
roucouler [ruku'le], *v.t., v.i.* to coo.
roue [ru], *n.f.* wheel; paddle-wheel; **faire la roue**, to spread (out) its tail (*of peacocks etc.*); to show off; **mettre or jeter des bâtons dans les roues**, to put spokes into the wheel (*of*); to interfere.
roué [rwe], *a.* cunning, sharp, artful; exhausted.—*n.m.* rake, profligate; (*fem.* **-ée**) cunning or unscrupulous person.
rouelle [rwɛl], *n.f.* round slice (*meat*).
rouer [rwe], *v.t.* to break upon the wheel; **rouer de coups**, to beat unmercifully.
rouerie [ru'ri], *n.f.* piece of knavery, trick, sharp practice.
rouet [rwɛ], *n.m.* spinning-wheel.
rouge [ru:ʒ], *a.* red; red-hot; bloodshot.—*n.m.* rouge; redness.—*n.* (*fam.*) left-winger, communist.
rougeâtre [ru'ʒa:tr], *a.* reddish.
rougeaud [ru'ʒo], *a.* (*colloq.*) red-faced, ruddy.—*n.m.* (*fem.* **-e**) red-faced person.

rouge-gorge [ruʒˈgɔrʒ], *n.m.* (*pl.* **rouges-gorges**) red-breast, robin redbreast.

rougeole [ruˈʒɔl], *n.f.* measles.

rougeoyer [ruʒwaˈje], *v.i.* (*conjug. like* EM-PLOYER) to turn red; to glow.

rouget [ruˈʒɛ], *a.* (*fem.* **-ette**) reddish.—*n.m.* (*Ichth.*) red mullet.

rougeur [ruˈʒœːr], *n.f.* redness; flush, glow, blush.

rougir [ruˈʒiːr], *v.t.* to redden, to tinge with red.—*v.i.* to redden, to grow red, to color, to blush.

rouille [ruːj], *n.f.* rust, rustiness; (*Agric.*) mildew, blight.

rouillé [ruˈje], *a.* rusty; blighted (*of grain*).

rouiller [ruˈje], *v.t.*, *v.i.* to rust; to blight; to impair. **se rouiller**, *v.r.* to rust; to grow rusty; to be impaired.

rouilleux [ruˈjø], *a.* (*fem.* **-euse**) rust-colored.

rouillure [ruˈjyːr], *n.f.* rustiness; (*Agric.*) rust.

rouir [rwiːr], *v.t.* to steep, to soak, to ret.

rouissage [rwiˈsaːʒ], *n.m.* steeping, retting.

roulade [ruˈlad], *n.f.* roll, rolling down; (*Mus.*) trill.

roulage [ruˈlaːʒ], *n.m.* rolling; haulage, carriage (*in wagons etc.*); road traffic.

roulant [ruˈlɑ̃], *a.* rolling; travelling (*crane*); easy (*of roads*); (*Print.*) at work.

rouleau [ruˈlo], *n.m.* (*pl.* **-eaux**) roll; roller; rolling-pin; coil (*rope*).

roulement [rulˈmɑ̃], *n.m.* rolling, roll; rumbling, rattle; rotation; *par roulement*, in rotation; *roulement à billes*, ball-bearing.

rouler [ruˈle], *v.t.* to roll up; to roll up; to wind up; to revolve; (*colloq.*) to cheat; (*Golf*) *coup roulé*, putt.—*v.i.* to roll, to roll along; to revolve; to ride (*en*); to ramble; to keep going. **se rouler**, *v.r.* to roll, to tumble, to wallow.

roulette [ruˈlɛt], *n.f.* small wheel; roller; castor, truckle; roulette (*game*).

roulier [ruˈlje], *a.* carrying (*trade*).—*n.m.* wagoner, carter, carrier.

roulis [ruˈli], *n.m.* rolling, roll (*waves or ships*), lurch.

roulotte [ruˈlɔt], *n.f.* gipsy van; (*Motor.*) trailer.

roumain [ruˈmɛ̃], *a.* Rumanian.—*n.m.* Rumanian (*language*); (**Roumain**, *fem.* **-aine**) Rumanian (*person*).

Roumanie [rumaˈni], la, *f.* Rumania.

roupie [ruˈpi], *n.f.* rupee.

roupiller [rupiˈje], *v.i.* (*colloq.*) to doze, to snooze.

rouquin [ruˈkɛ̃], *a.* (*pop.*) ginger-haired, carroty-haired.

roussâtre [ruˈsɑːtr], *a.* reddish, russet.

rousseur [ruˈsœːr], *n.f.* redness.

roussi [ruˈsi], *a.* browned, scorched.—*n.m.* burnt smell; burning.

roussir [ruˈsiːr], *v.t.*, *v.i.* to redden; to singe, to scorch; *faire roussir*, to brown (*meat etc.*).

roussissage [rusiˈsaːʒ], **roussissement** [rusisˈmɑ̃], *n.m.* reddening; browning; scorching.

routage [ruˈtaːʒ], *n.m.* sorting (*of mail*).

route [rut], *n.f.* road, way; route, path, course; track (*of a ship etc.*); highway.

router [ruˈte], *v.t.* to sort (*mail*).

routier [ruˈtje], *a.* (*fem.* **-ière**) of roads; *carte routière*, road map.—*n.m.* truck driver; (*fig.*) old hand; road racer (*cyclist*).

routine [ruˈtin], *n.f.* routine, habit, practice.

routinier [rutiˈnje], *a.* (*fem.* **-ière**) routine, following a routine.—*n.m.* (*fem.* **-ière**) person following a routine; stick-in-the-mud.

rouvrir [ruˈvriːr], *v.t.*, *v.i. irr.* (*conjug. like* OUVRIR) to reopen.

roux [ru], *a.* (*fem.* **rousse**) reddish; red-haired, sandy.—*n.m.* (*fem.* **rousse**) red-haired *or* sandy person.—*n.m.* reddish color.

royal [rwaˈjal], *a.* (*m. pl.* **-aux**) royal; regal, kingly.

royalement [rwajalˈmɑ̃], *adv.* royally; regally.

royalisme [rwajaˈlism], *n.m.* royalism.

royaliste [rwajaˈlist], *a.* and *n.* royalist.

royaume [rwaˈjuːm], *n.m.* kingdom, realm; *le Royaume-Uni*, the United Kingdom.

royauté [rwajoˈte], *n.f.* royalty, kingship, monarchy.

ruade [rɥad], *n.f.* kick (*by horse etc.*); lashing out.

Ruanda [RWANDA].

ruban [ryˈbɑ̃], *n.m.* ribbon; (*fig.*) strip; tape.

rubané [rybaˈne], *a.* covered with ribbons.

rubaner [rybaˈne], *v.t.* to trim with ribbons; to cut into ribbons.

rubanerie [rybanˈri], *n.f.* ribbon-weaving; ribbon trade.

rubéole [rybeˈɔl], *n.f.* rubeola, German measles.

rubescent [rybɛˈsɑ̃], *a.* reddish; growing red.

rubicond [rybiˈkɔ̃], *a.* rubicund.

rubis [ryˈbi], *n.m. inv.* ruby.

rubrique [ryˈbrik], *n.f.* red chalk; (*pl.*) rubric; (*fig.*) heading (*of article*).

ruche [ryʃ], *n.f.* hive; (*Needlework*) frilling, ruche.

ruchée [ryˈʃe], *n.f.* hiveful.

rucher (1) [ryˈʃe], *n.m.* stand *or* shed for bee-hives; apiary.

rucher (2) [ryˈʃe], *v.t.* (*Needlework*) to ruche, to frill.

rude [ryd], *a.* harsh, rough, rugged; violent; severe; uncouth; churlish; arduous, difficult.

rudement [rydˈmɑ̃], *adv.* roughly, harshly, severely, violently; (*pop.*) awfully, very.

rudesse [ryˈdɛs], *n.f.* roughness, coarseness; ruggedness, uncouthness; harshness; unkindness.

rudiment [rydiˈmɑ̃], *n.m.* rudiment; primer.

rudimentaire [rydimɑ̃ˈtɛːr], *a.* rudimentary.

rudoiement [rydwaˈmɑ̃], *n.m.* bullying, brow-beating.

rudoyer [rydwaˈje], *v.t.* (*conjug. like* EM-PLOYER) to treat roughly; to bully, to ill-treat.

rue [ry], *n.f.* street; rue (*plant*).

ruée [rɥe], *n.f.* rush; onslaught.

ruelle [rɥɛl], *n.f.* lane, alley.

ruer [rɥe], *v.t.* to kick (*of horses etc.*). **se ruer**, *v.r.* to throw oneself, to rush (*sur*).

rugby [rygˈbi], *n.m.* rugby football, rugger.

rugir [ryˈʒiːr], *v.i.* to roar, to bellow.

rugissant [ryʒiˈsɑ̃], *a.* roaring.

rugissement [ryʒisˈmɑ̃], *n.m.* roaring, roar.

rugosité [rygoziˈte], *n.f.* rugosity, roughness.

rugueux [ryˈgø], *a.* (*fem.* **-euse**) rugose, rough.

ruine [rɥin], *n.f.* ruin; decay, destruction.
ruiner [rɥi'ne], *v.t.* to ruin, to lay waste; to destroy; to spoil. **se ruiner**, *v.r.* to ruin oneself; to fall into decay.
ruineux [rɥi'nø], *a.* (*fem.* **-euse**) ruinous.
ruisseau [rɥi'so], *n.m.* (*pl.* **-eaux**) brook, stream; gutter.
ruisselant [rɥi'slɑ̃], *a.* streaming, dripping.
ruisseler [rɥi'sle], *v.i.* (*conjug. like* APPELER) to run, to be very wet, to stream (with) (*de*).
rumeur [ry'mœ:r], *n.f.* clamor, uproar; (*fig.*) report, rumor.
ruminant [rymi'nɑ̃], *a.* ruminant, ruminating.—*n.m.* ruminant.
rumination [rymina'sjɔ̃], *n.f.* rumination (*chewing the cud*).
ruminer [rymi'ne], *v.t.* to ruminate on; (*fig.*) to think over.—*v.i.* to ruminate, to chew the cud; (*fig.*) to ponder, to muse.
rupture [ryp'ty:r], *n.f.* breaking, rupture; annulment; hernia.
rural [ry'ral], *a.* (*m. pl.* **-aux**) rural, rustic.
ruse [ry:z], *n.f.* guile, cunning; trick, wile, ruse.
rusé [ry'ze], *a.* artful, crafty, sly.—*n.m.* (*fem.* **-ée**) artful, crafty *or* sly person.
ruser [ry'ze], *v.i.* to use deceit, craft *or* guile.
russe [rys], *a.* Russian.—*n.m.* Russian (*language*).—*n.* (Russe) Russian (*person*).
Russie [ry'si], la, *f.* Russia.
rustaud [rys'to], *a.* rustic, boorish, uncouth.—*n.m.* (*fem.* **-e**) rustic, clodhopper.
rusticité [rystisi'te], *n.f.* rusticity, simplicity.
rustique [rys'tik], *a.* rustic, rural; homely, simple.
rustiquement [rystik'mɑ̃], *adv.* rustically; boorishly, uncouthly.
rustre [rystr], *a.* boorish, rude.—*n.m.* boor, lout.
rutabaga [rytaba'ga], *n.m.* rutabaga, Swedish turnip.
rutilant [ryti'lɑ̃], *a.* glowing, gleaming, rutilant.
rutiler [ryti'le], *v.i.* to glow, to gleam (*red*).
Rwanda, Ruanda [rwɑ̃'da], le, *m.* Rwanda.
rythme [ritm], *n.m.* rhythm.
rythmique [rit'mik], *a.* rhythmical.

S

S, s [ɛs], *n.m.* the nineteenth letter of the alphabet.
s' [s], *elision*, [SE].
sa [sa], [SON (1)].
sabbat [sa'ba], *n.m.* Sabbath.
sable [sa:bl], *n.m.* sand; gravel; (*Zool., Her.*) sable.
sablé [sa'ble], *a.* covered with sand *or* gravel.
sabler [sa'ble], *v.t.* to sand, to gravel; (*fig.*) to drink off.
sableux [sa'blø], *a.* (*fem.* **-euse**) sandy.
sablier [sabli'je], *n.m.* sand-glass, hour-glass, egg-timer.
sablière [sabli'jɛ:r], *n.f.* sand pit; gravel pit.

sablon [sa'blɔ̃], *n.m.* fine sand, scouring sand.
sablonner [sablɔ'ne], *v.t.* to scour with sand.
sablonneux [sablɔ'nø], *a.* (*fem.* **-euse**) sandy, gritty.
sablonnière [sablɔ'njɛ:r], *n.f.* sand pit.
sabord [sa'bo:r], *n.m.* (*Naut.*) port-hole.
saborder [sabɔr'de], *v.t.* to scuttle.
sabot [sa'bo], *n.m.* sabot, clog; hoof (*of horse etc.*); trig (*of carriages*); **dormir comme un sabot**, to sleep like a top.
sabotage [sabɔ'ta:ʒ], *n.m.* sabotage.
saboter [sabɔ'te], *v.t.* (*colloq.*) to bungle; to damage wilfully, to sabotage.
saboteur [sabɔ'tœ:r], *n.m.* (*fem.* **-euse**) bungler; saboteur.
sabotier [sabɔ'tje], *n.m.* (*fem.* **-lère**) sabot maker.
sabre [sa:br], *n.m.* saber; broadsword.
sabrer [sa'bre], *v.t.* to strike *or* cut with a saber, to saber; (*colloq.*) to hurry over, to botch.
sabreur [sa'brœ:r], *n.m.* swashbuckler; (*colloq.*) botcher.
sac (1) [sak], *n.m.* sack, bag; pouch (*of certain animals*).
sac (2) [sak], *n.m.* sack (*plunder*), pillage.
saccade [sa'kad], *n.f.* jerk, jolt.
saccadé [saka'de], *a.* jerky, broken, abrupt, irregular.
saccader [saka'de], *v.t.* to jerk.
saccage [sa'ka:ʒ], *n.m.* upset, confusion; pillage.
saccager [saka'ʒe], *v.t.* (*conjug. like* MANGER) to sack, to plunder; (*fig.*) to play havoc with.
saccharine [saka'rin], *n.f.* saccharine.
sacerdoce [saɛr'dɔs], *n.m.* priesthood.
sacerdotal [saɛrdɔ'tal], *a.* (*m. pl.* **-aux**) sacerdotal.
sachée [sa'ʃe], *n.f.* sackful, bagful.
sachet [sa'ʃɛ], *n.m.* small bag, sachet.
sacoche [sa'kɔʃ], *n.f.* (*Mil.*) saddle-bag; money-bag; tool-bag.
sacramental [sakramɑ̃'tal], (*m. pl.* **-aux**), **sacramentel** [sakramɑ̃'tɛl] (*fem.* **-elle**), *a.* sacramental.
sacre [sakr], *n.m.* anointing and coronation of a king; consecration of a bishop.
sacré [sa'kre], *a.* holy, consecrated; sacred, inviolable.
sacrebleu! [sakrə'blø], *int.* confound it! curse it!
sacrement [sakrə'mɑ̃], *n.m.* sacrament, *esp.* matrimony.
sacrer [sa'kre], *v.t.* to anoint, to crown; to consecrate.—*v.i.* to curse and swear.
sacrificateur [sakrifika'tœ:r], *n.m.* (*fem.* **-trice**) sacrificer.
sacrificatoire [sakrifika'twa:r], *a.* sacrificial.
sacrifice [sakri'fis], *n.m.* sacrifice; renunciation.
sacrifier [sakri'fje], *v.t.* to sacrifice; to devote; to give up.—*v.i.* to sacrifice.
sacrilège [sakri'lɛ:ʒ], *a.* sacrilegious.—*n.m.* sacrilege.
sacrilègement [sakrilɛʒ'mɑ̃], *adv.* sacrilegiously.
sacripant [sakri'pɑ̃], *n.m.* rascal, scoundrel.
sacristain [sakris'tɛ̃], *n.m.* sacristan, sexton.
sacristie [sakris'ti], *n.f.* sacristy, vestry; church plate.
sacristine [sakris'tin], *n.f.* vestry nun, sacristine.

sacro-saint [sakro'sɛ̃], *a.* sacrosanct.
sadique [sa'dik], *a.* sadistic.—*n.* sadist.
sadisme [sa'dism], *n.m.* sadism.
saducéen [sadyse'ɛ̃], *a.* (*fem.* **-éenne**) Sadducean.—*n.m.* (*fem.* **-éenne**) Sadducee.
safran [sa'frɑ̃], *n.m.* saffron; crocus.
safrané [safra'ne], *a.* saffron-colored.
saga [sa'ga], *n.f.* saga.
sagace [sa'gas], *a.* sagacious, shrewd.
sagacité [sagasi'te], *n.f.* sagacity.
sage [sa:ʒ], *a.* wise; sage, sensible, prudent; sober, well-behaved, good; virtuous, modest; gentle (*of animals*).—*n.m.* wise man, sage.
sage-femme [saʒ'fam], *n.f.* (*pl.* **sages-femmes**) midwife.
sagement [saʒ'mɑ̃], *adv.* wisely; prudently; soberly, steadily.
sagesse [sa'ʒɛs], *n.f.* wisdom; prudence; steadiness; chastity; good behavior (*of children*); gentleness (*of animals*).
sagittaire [saʒi'tɛ:r], *n.m.* (*Rom. Ant.*) archer; (*Astron.*) Sagittarius.
sagou [sa'gu], *n.m.* sago.
sagouier [sagu'je] or (*preferably*) **sagoutier** [sagu'tje], *n.m.* sago tree.
sagouin [sa'gwɛ̃], *n.m.* squirrel-monkey; (*fem.* **-e**) (*fig.*) slovenly fellow *or* woman.
Sahara [saa'ra], **le**, *m.* the Sahara.
saignant [sɛ'nɑ̃], *a.* bleeding, bloody; underdone (*of meat*).
saignée [sɛ'ne], *n.f.* blood-letting, phlebotomy; small of the arm; (*fig.*) drain on the purse.
saignement [sɛɲə'mɑ̃], *n.m.* bleeding.
saigner [sɛ'ne], *v.t.* to bleed; to stick (*an animal*); (*fig.*) to drain.—*v.i.* to bleed. **se saigner**, *v.r.* to bleed oneself; to drain oneself *or* one's purse.
saigneux [sɛ'nø], *a.* (*fem.* **-euse**) bloody.
saillant [sa'jɑ̃], *a.* jutting out, projecting; (*fig.*) striking, remarkable.—*n.m.* (*Fort.*) salient.
saillie [sa'ji], *n.f.* start, sudden spurt; sally; (*fig.*) witticism; projection.
saillir [sa'ji:r], *v.i.* to gush (*of liquids*); to ripple (*of muscles*).
sain [sɛ̃], *a.* hale, healthy; sound; sane; **sain et sauf**, safe and sound.
saindoux [sɛ̃'du], *n.m. inv.* lard.
sainement [sɛn'mɑ̃], *adv.* wholesomely; healthily, soundly; judiciously.
sainfoin [sɛ̃'fwɛ̃], *n.m.* sainfoin.
saint [sɛ̃], *a.* holy, sacred; godly, saintly; sanctified, consecrated.—*n.m.* (*fem.* **-e**) saint; patron saint.
saintement [sɛ̃t'mɑ̃], *adv.* sacredly; piously, religiously.
sainteté [sɛ̃tə'te], *n.f.* holiness, sanctity, sacredness, saintliness; **Sa Sainteté le Pape**, His Holiness the Pope.
saisi [sɛ'zi], *a.* seized, possessed, struck (*de*).
saisie [sɛ'zi], *n.f.* (*Law*) seizure; distraint, execution.
saisir [sɛ'zi:r], *v.t.* to seize, to take hold of; to understand; (*fig.*) to impress, to shock, to startle; to distrain. **se saisir**, *v.r.* to seize, to catch hold (*de*); to take possession (*de*); to arrest.
saisissable [sɛzi'sabl], *a.* distrainable, seizable.
saisissant [sɛzi'sɑ̃], *a.* keen, sharp, piercing (*of cold*); striking, impressive.

saisissement [sɛzis'mɑ̃], *n.m.* shock, violent impression, seizure.
saison [sɛ'zɔ̃], *n.f.* season; **marchand des quatre saisons**, street vendor (*of produce*).
saisonnier [sɛzɔ'nje], *a.* (*fem.* **-ière**) seasonal.
salade [sa'lad], *n.f.* salad, herb grown for salad; (*fig.*) medley, confusion.
saladier [sala'dje], *n.m.* salad bowl.
salage [sa'la:ʒ], *n.m.* salting.
salaire [sa'lɛ:r], *n.m.* wages, pay, hire; reward.
salaison [salɛ'zɔ̃], *n.f.* salting; salt provisions; curing (*of bacon etc.*).
salamalec [salama'lek], *n.m.* (*used chiefly in pl.*) salaam; (*fig.*) exaggerated politeness.
salamandre [sala'mɑ̃:dr], *n.f.* salamander; slow-combustion stove.
salant [sa'lɑ̃], *a.m.* **marais salant**, salt-marsh.
salarié [sala'rje], *a.* paid, wage-earning.—*n.m.* (*fem.* **-ée**) wage-earner.
salarier [sala'rje], *v.t.* to pay, to give wages to.
salaud [sa'lo], *n.m.* (*fem.* **-e**) (*pop.* and *rude*) sloven, dirty person, slut; **quel salaud!** dirty beast! dirty dog!
sale [sal], *a.* dirty; nasty, foul; coarse, obscene; squalid.
salé [sa'le], *a.* salted, salt; briny; (*fig.*) keen, biting; coarse; spicy.—*n.m.* salt pork; **du petit salé**, pickled pork.
salement [sal'mɑ̃], *adv.* dirtily; nastily.
saler [sa'le], *v.t.* to salt; (*fig.*) to overcharge for; to fleece (*customers*).
saleté [sal'te], *n.f.* dirtiness, filthiness; filth, dirt; dirty trick; obscenity.
saleur [sa'lœ:r], *n.m.* (*fem.* **-euse**) salter, curer.
salière [sa'ljɛ:r], *n.f.* salt-cellar; salt box; eye-pit (*in horses*).
salin [sa'lɛ̃], *a.* salt, saline, briny.—*n.m.* salt works; salt marsh.
saline [sa'lin], *n.f.* salt marsh, salt mine, salt pit.
salinier [sali'nje], *n.m.* owner of salt works; salt worker *or* vendor.
salique [sa'lik], *a.* **loi salique**, Salic law.
salir [sa'li:r], *v.t.* to dirty, to soil; to taint, to sully. **se salir**, *v.r.* to get dirty; to sully one's reputation.
salissant [sali'sɑ̃], *a.* that soils *or* gets dirty easily; dirty (*of job, work etc.*).
salive [sa'li:v], *n.f.* saliva, spittle.
saliver [sali've], *v.i.* to salivate.
salle [sal], *n.f.* hall; large room; gallery (*of museum*); ward (*in hospitals*); (*Theat.*) house; **salle à manger**, dining room; **salle d'attente**, waiting room; **salle de bain(s)**, bathroom; **salle de spectacle**, playhouse.
saloir [sa'lwa:r], *n.m.* salt box; salting-tub.
salon [sa'lɔ̃], *n.m.* drawing-room, parlor; lounge; saloon; exhibition (*art*); (*pl.*) world of fashion.
salopette [salo'pɛt], *n.f.* overall, dungarees.
salpêtrage [salpe'tra:ʒ], *n.m.* saltpeter-making; nitrification.
salpêtre [sal'pɛ:tr], *n.m.* saltpeter.
salpêtrer [salpe'tre], *v.t.* to cover with saltpeter.
salpêtrerie [salpetrə'ri], *n.f.* saltpeter-works.

salpêtreux [salpɛ'trø], *a.* (*fem.* **-euse**) saltpetrous.
salpêtrière [salpetri'jɛːr], *n.f.* saltpeter works.
salsepareille [salspa'rɛːj], *n.f.* sarsaparilla.
saltimbanque [saltɛ̃'bãːk], *n.m.* mountebank, buffoon; (*fig.*) humbug.
salubre [sa'lybr], *a.* salubrious, healthy (*climate*).
salubrité [salybri'te], *n.f.* salubrity, healthfulness, wholesomeness.
saluer [sa'lɥe], *v.t.* to salute, to bow to; to greet; to cheer; to proclaim. **se saluer,** *v.r.* to bow to *or* salute each other.
salure [sa'lyːr], *n.f.* saltness, salinity.
salut [sa'ly], *n.m.* safety; salvation; welfare; escape; salutation, greeting; hail, cheers.
salutaire [saly'tɛːr], *a.* salutary, advantageous, beneficial.
salutairement [salytɛr'mã], *adv.* beneficially.
salutation [salyta'sjõ], *n.f.* salutation, greeting; (*pl.*) compliments.
Salvador [salva'dɔr], **le,** *m.* El Salvador.
salvadorègne [salvadɔ'rɛɲ], *a.* Salvadorean. —*n.* (**Salvadorègne**) Salvadorean (*person*).
salve [salv], *n.f.* salvo, volley; salute (*of artillery*).
samedi [sam'di], *n.m.* Saturday.
sanatorium [sanatɔ'rjɔm], *n.m.* sanatorium.
sanctifiant [sãkti'fjã], *a.* sanctifying.
sanctificateur [sãktifika'tœːr], *a.* (*fem.* **-trice**) sanctifying.—*n.m.* sanctifier.
sanctification [sãktifika'sjõ], *n.f.* sanctification.
sanctifier [sãkti'fje], *v.t.* to sanctify, to hallow.
sanction [sãk'sjõ], *n.f.* sanction; approbation; penalty.
sanctionner [sãksjɔ'ne], *v.t.* to sanction, to approve; to penalize.
sanctuaire [sãk'tɥɛːr], *n.m.* sanctuary (*of the temple etc.*), shrine; chancel (*of church*).
sandale [sã'dal], *n.f.* sandal; fencing shoe.
sandalier [sãda'lje], *n.m.* sandal-maker.
sandow [sã'dof], *n.m.* chest-expander; rubber shock-absorber.
sandwich [sã'dwitʃ], *n.m.* (*pl.* **sandwichs** or **sandwiches**) sandwich.
sang [sã], *n.m.* blood; race; kindred; *pur sang,* thoroughbred.
sang-froid [sã'frwa], *n.m.* coolness, composure, sang-froid.
sanglade [sã'glad], *n.f.* lash, cut (*with a whip*).
sanglant [sã'glã], *a.* bloody, bleeding; (*fig.*) biting, outrageous.
sangle [sã'gl], *n.f.* strap, belt; saddle-girth; *lit de sangle,* camp bed.
sangler [sã'gle], *v.t.* to girth, to strap; to lace too tightly; to deal (*a slashing blow*). **se sangler,** *v.r.* to lace oneself tightly.
sanglier [sã'glje], *n.m.* wild boar.
sanglot [sã'glo], *n.m.* sob.
sangloter [sãglo'te], *v.i.* to sob.
sang-mêlé [sãme'le], *n.m. inv.* half-caste.
sangsue [sã'sy], *n.f.* leech; (*fig.*) extortioner.
sanguin [sã'gɛ̃], *a.* of blood; full-blooded; blood-red.
sanguinaire [sãgi'nɛːr], *a.* sanguinary, bloody, blood-thirsty.
sanitaire [sani'tɛːr], *a.* sanitary.

sans [sã], *prep.* without; free from; but for; had it not been for, were it not for; *cela va sans dire,* of course; *sans abri, sans gîte, sans logis,* homeless; *sans cela,* otherwise; *sans quoi,* otherwise.
sans-atout [sãza'tu], *n.m.* no trumps.
sans-cœur [sã'kœːr], *n. inv.* heartless, unfeeling person.
sanscrit [sãs'kri], *n.m.* Sanskrit.
sans-façon [sãfa'sõ], *n.m.* bluntness; offhandedness.
sans-gêne [sã'ʒɛːn], *n.m.* unceremoniousness, coolness; (*fam.*) cheek.
sansonnet [sãsɔ'nɛ], *n.m.* (*Orn.*) starling.
sans-patrie [sãpa'tri], *n. inv.* stateless person.
sans-souci [sãsu'si], *a.* carefree, happy-go-lucky.—*n. inv.* (*colloq.*) carefree, easy-going person.—*n.m. inv.* free-and-easy manners.
sans-travail [sãtra'vaj], *n.m. inv.* **les sans-travail,** the unemployed.
santal [sã'tal], *n.m.* (*pl.* **-als**) sandalwood, santal.
santé [sã'te], *n.f.* health, healthiness; state of health.
saoul [soul].
sape [sap], *n.f.* sapping, undermining; mine; trench.
saper [sa'pe], *v.t.* to sap, to undermine.
sapeur [sa'pœːr], *n.m.* sapper.
sapeur-pompier [sapœrpõ'pje], *n.m.* (*pl.* **sapeurs-pompiers**) fireman.
sapeur-télégraphiste [sapœrtelegra'fist], *n.m.* (*pl.* **sapeurs-télégraphistes**) soldier of the signal corps; (*pl.*) (*fam.*) signals.
saphir [sa'fiːr], *n.m.* sapphire.
sapin [sa'pɛ̃], *n.m.* fir, fir tree; (*bois de*) *sapin,* deal.
sapinette [sapi'nɛt], *n.f.* spruce.
sapinière [sapi'njɛːr], *n.f.* fir wood, fir plantation.
sarabande [sara'bãːd], *n.f.* saraband (*dance*); (*fam.*) song-and-dance.
sarcasme [sar'kasm], *n.m.* sarcasm, sarcastic remark.
sarcastique [sarkas'tik], *a.* sarcastic.
sarcelle [sar'sɛl], *n.f.* (*Orn.*) teal.
sarclage [sar'klaːʒ], *n.m.* weeding.
sarcler [sar'kle], *v.t.* to weed; to hoe; (*fig.*) to extirpate.
sarcleur [sar'klœːr], *n.m.* (*fem.* **-euse**) weeder.
sarcloir [sar'klwaːr], *n.m.* hoe.
sarcophage (1) [sarkɔ'faːʒ], *n.m.* sarcophagus.
sarcophage (2) [sarkɔ'faːʒ], *n.f.* (*Ent.*) blow-fly.
Sardaigne [sar'dɛɲ], *n.f.* Sardinia.
sarde [sard], *a.* Sardinian.—*n.* (**Sarde**) Sardinian (*person*).
sardine [sar'din], *n.f.* sardine.
sardinerie [sardin'ri], *n.f.* sardine packing and curing factory.
sardinier [sardi'nje], *n.m.* (*fem.* **-ière**) sardine fisher; sardine packer *or* curer. —*n.m.* sardine net; sardine boat.
sardoine [sar'dwan], *n.f.* sardonyx.
sardonique [sardɔ'nik], *a.* sardonic.
sarigue [sa'rig], *n.* sarigue (*opossum*).
sarment [sar'mã], *n.m.* vine shoot, vine branch.
sarmenteux [sarmã'tø], *a.* (*fem.* **-euse**) branchy, climbing; rambling (*of roses*).
sarrasin [sara'zɛ̃], *n.m.* buckwheat.

sarrau [sa'ro], *n.m.* (*pl.* **-aux**) smock frock; child's blouse.

sas [sɑ], *n.m. inv.* sieve, screen; (*Naut.*) floating chamber (*of submarine*).

Satan [sa'tɑ̃], *m.* Satan.

satané [sata'ne], *a.* (*colloq.*) devilish, confounded.

satanique [sata'nik], *a.* satanic, diabolical.

sataniquement [satanik'mɑ̃], *adv.* fiendishly, diabolically.

satellite [satɛl'lit], *a.* satellite.—*n.m.* satellite.

satiété [sasje'te], *n.f.* satiety, repletion.

satin [sa'tɛ̃], *n.m.* satin.

satiné [sati'ne], *a.* satin-like, satiny; glazed (*of paper etc.*).

satiner [sati'ne], *v.t.* to satin; to glaze (*paper etc.*).—*v.i.* to look like satin.

satire [sa'tiːr], *n.f.* satire; lampoon.

satirique [sati'rik], *a.* satirical.—*n.m.* satirist.

satiriquement [satirik'mɑ̃], *adv.* satirically.

satiriser [satiri'ze], *v.t.* to satirize.

satisfaction [satisfak'sjɔ̃], *n.f.* satisfaction; gratification; atonement.

satisfaire [satis'fɛːr], *v.t. irr.* (*conjug. like* FAIRE) to satisfy; to gratify; to answer; to give satisfaction to, to make amends to.—*v.i.* to be satisfactory (**à**); to fulfil (**à**). **se satisfaire**, *v.r.* to satisfy oneself, to indulge oneself.

satisfaisant [satisfə'zɑ̃], *a.* satisfactory.

satisfait [satis'fɛ], *a.* satisfied, contented, pleased.

saturant [saty'rɑ̃], *a.* saturating.

saturation [satyra'sjɔ̃], *n.f.* saturation.

saturer [saty're], *v.t.* to saturate; (*fig.*) to surfeit.

saturnales [satyr'nal], *n.f. pl.* saturnalia.

Saturne [sa'tyrn], *m.* Saturn.

satyre [sa'tiːr], *n.m.* satyr.

sauce [soːs], *n.f.* sauce; *sauce hollandaise*, egg yolks and melted butter.

saucé [so'se], *a.* soused, wet through.

saucer [so'se], *v.t.* (*conjug. like* COMMENCER) to dip in sauce; to sop, to souse.

saucière [so'sjɛːr], *n.f.* sauce dish.

saucisse [so'sis], *n.f.* (*fresh*) sausage.

saucisson [sosi'sɔ̃], *n.m.* large dry sausage; salami.

sauf (1) [sof], *a.* (*fem.* **sauve**) safe; unhurt, unscathed; *sain et sauf*, safe and sound.

sauf (2) [sof], *prep.* save, except; unless.

sauf-conduit [sofkɔ̃'dɥi], *n.m.* (*pl.* **-conduits**) safe-conduct.

sauge [soːʒ], *n.f.* sage (*herb*).

saugrenu [sogrə'ny], *a.* absurd, ridiculous, preposterous.

saulaie [so'lɛ], *n.f.* willow grove.

saule [soːl], *n.m.* willow.

saumâtre [so'mɑːtr], *a.* brackish, briny.

saumon [so'mɔ̃], *n.m.* salmon.

saumoné [somo'ne], *a.* salmon-colored; *truite saumonée*, salmon trout.

saumurage [somy'raːʒ], *n.m.* pickling (*in brine*), brining.

saumure [so'myːr], *n.f.* brine, pickle.

saumuré [somy're], *a.* pickled, brined.

saunage [so'naːʒ], *n.m.*, **saunaison** [sonɛ'zɔ̃], *n.f.* salt-making; salt trade.

sauner [so'ne], *v.i.* to make salt.

saunerie [son'ri], *n.f.* saltworks.

saunier [so'nje], *n.m.* salt-maker; **salt merchant.**

saunière [so'njɛːr], *n.f.* salt bin.

saupoudrage [sopu'draːʒ], *n.m.* salting; sprinkling, powdering.

saupoudrer [sopu'dre], *v.t.* to sprinkle with salt, pepper etc.; to powder, to sprinkle.

saur or **sor** [soːr], *a.m.* smoked and salted; red (*of herrings*).

saure [soːr], *a.* yellowish-brown; sorrel (*of horses*); red, smoked (*of herrings*).

saurer [so're], *v.t.* to smoke (*herrings*).

saurin [so'rɛ̃], *n.m.* freshly smoked herring, bloater.

saurisserie [soris'ri], *n.f.* kippering factory.

saut [so], *n.m.* leap, jump, hop, bound; *de plein saut*, at once, suddenly; *saut périlleux*, somersault.

sautage [so'taːʒ], *n.m.* exploding (*mines*).

saut-de-mouton [sodmu'tɔ̃], *n.m.* (*pl.* **sauts-de-mouton**) overpass.

saute [sot], *n.f.* (*Naut.*) sudden shift or change (*of wind*).

sauté [so'te], *a.* fried, tossed in the pan.

saute-mouton [sotmu'tɔ̃], *n.m.* leap-frog (*game*).

sauter [so'te], *v.t.* to leap over; to leave out, to skip; to toss in the pan.—*v.i.* to leap, to jump; to explode; to spring; to blow out (*of fuse*).

sauterelle [so'trɛl], *n.f.* grasshopper, locust.

sauterie [sot'ri], *n.f.* (*fam.*) informal dance, hop.

saute-ruisseau [sotrɥi'so], *n.m. inv.* messenger boy (*in offices*).

sauteur [so'tœːr], *a.* (*fem.* **-euse**) jumping, leaping.—*n.m.* (*fem.* **-euse**) leaper, jumper; vaulter.

sautillant [soti'jɑ̃], *a.* hopping, skipping.

sautiller [soti'je], *v.i.* to hop, to skip, to jump about.

sautoir [so'twaːr], *n.m.* Saint Andrew's cross.

sauvage [so'vaːʒ], *a.* savage, wild; uncivilized; brutal; shy; unsociable.—*n.* savage; unsociable person.

sauvagement [sovaʒ'mɑ̃], *adv.* wildly, savagely; barbarously, fiercely.

sauvageon [sova'ʒɔ̃], *n.m.* (*Agric.*) wild stock (*for grafting*); briar (*of roses*).

sauvagerie [sovaʒ'ri], *n.f.* unsociableness, shyness; wildness.

sauvagesse [sova'ʒɛs], *n.f.* uncivilized woman; hoyden.

sauvagin [sova'ʒɛ̃], *a.* fishy (*in taste, smell, etc.*).—*n.m.* fishy taste or smell.—*n.f.* (**-e**) wild waterfowl.

sauvegarde [sov'gard], *n.f.* safe-keeping, safeguard; safe-conduct; (*Naut.*) life-line.

sauvegarder [sovgar'de], *v.t.* to watch over, to protect, to safeguard.

sauve-qui-peut [sovki'pø], *n.m. inv.* headlong flight, stampede; every man for himself.

sauver [so've], *v.t.* to save, to rescue; to preserve; to exempt; to conceal. **se sauver**, *v.r.* to escape, to make off; (*fam.*) to abscond; to take refuge.

sauvetage [sov'taːʒ], *n.m.* salvage; lifesaving, rescue; *appareil de sauvetage*, rescue apparatus; fire escape; *bouée de*

sauvetage, life buoy; *canot de sauvetage*, life-boat; *ceinture de sauvetage*, life-belt.

sauveteur [sov'tœːr], *n.m.* rescuer, lifeboat man.

sauveur [so'vœːr], *a.* saving, redeeming.—*n.m.* saver, deliverer; Saviour.

savamment [sava'mã], *adv.* learnedly; knowingly.

savane [sa'van], *n.f.* savanna; (C) swamp.

savant [sa'vã], *a.* learned, expert (*en*); scholarly; clever.—*n.m.* (*fem.* -e) scholar, scientist.

savarin [sava'rɛ̃], *n.m.* round, hollow cake.

savate [sa'vat], *n.f.* old shoe; clumsy person.

savetier [sav'tje], *n.m.* cobbler; (*fig.*) bungler.

saveur [sa'vœːr], *n.f.* savor, flavor, relish.

savoir [sa'vwaːr], *v.t. irr.* to know, to be aware of; to understand; to know how (*can*), to be able. **se savoir**, *v.r.* to get known.—*n.m.* knowledge, learning, scholarship.

savoir-faire [savwar'fɛːr], *n.m.* tact; savoir-faire; cleverness.

savoir-vivre [savwar'viːvr], *n.m.* good manners, good breeding.

savon [sa'võ], *n.m.* soap; (*colloq.*) scolding.

savonnage [savo'naːʒ], *n.m.* soaping, washing with soap.

savonner [savo'ne], *v.t.* to soap; to lather; (*colloq.*) to scold. **se savonner**, *v.r.* to be washable, to wash (*of fabrics*); to lather (*oneself*).

savonnerie [savon'ri], *n.f.* soap manufacture; soap trade; soap works.

savonnette [savo'nɛt], *n.f.* cake of toilet soap.

savonneux [savo'nø], *a.* (*fem.* -euse) soapy.

savourer [savu're], *v.t.* to savor, to relish; (*fig.*) to enjoy.

savoureusement [savurøz'mã], *adv.* with relish.

savoureux [savu'rø], *a.* (*fem.* -euse) savory, tasty (*dish*); racy (*story*).

savoyard [savwa'jaːr], *a.* of Savoy.—*n.m.* (Savoyard, *fem.* -arde) Savoyard (*person*); *petit Savoyard*, little chimney-sweep.

saxifrage [saksi'fraːʒ], *a.* saxifragous.—*n.f.* saxifrage.

saxon [sak'sõ], *a.* (*fem.* -onne) Saxon.—*n.m.* (Saxon, *fem.* -onne) Saxon (*person*).

saxophone [sakso'fon], *n.m.* saxophone.

saynète [se'nɛt], *n.f.* playlet, sketch.

scabieux [ska'bjø], *a.* (*fem.* -euse) scabious, scabby.—*n.f.* (-euse) scabious (*plant*).

scabreux [ska'brø], *a.* (*fem.* -euse) scabrous, rugged, rough; (*fig.*) dangerous, difficult, ticklish; improper.

scalp [skalp], *n.m.* scalp (*of an enemy*).

scalpel [skal'pɛl], *n.m.* scalpel.

scalper [skal'pe], *v.t.* to scalp.

scandale [skã'dal], *n.m.* scandal; shame, dismay, disgust.

scandaleusement [skãdaløz'mã], *adv.* scandalously.

scandaleux [skãda'lø], *a.* (*fem.* -euse) scandalous.

scandaliser [skãdali'ze], *v.t.* to scandalize, to shock. **se scandaliser**, *v.r.* to be shocked.

scander [skã'de], *v.t.* to scan; to stress (*a phrase*).

scandinave [skãdi'naːv], *a.* Scandinavian.—*n.* (Scandinave) Scandinavian (*person*).

Scandinavie [skãdina'vi], **la**, *f.* Scandinavia.

scansion [skã'sjõ], *n.f.* scansion.

scaphandre [ska'fãːdr], *n.m.* diving suit.

scaphandrier [skafãdri'je], *n.m.* diver.

scapulaire [skapy'lɛːr], *a.* and *n.m.* scapular.

scarabée [skara'be], *n.m.* scarabaeus (*beetle*); scarab.

scarlatine [skarla'tin], *a.* and *n.f.* (*fièvre*) *scarlatine*, scarlet fever.

sceau [so], *n.m.* (*pl.* sceaux) seal; (*fig.*) sanction; *mettre le sceau à*, to seal, (*fig.*) to complete.

scélérat [sele'ra], *a.* wicked, villainous, criminal, vile.—*n.m.* (*fem.* -e) scoundrel, villain, miscreant, jade.

scélératesse [selera'tɛs], *n.f.* villainy.

scellé [sɛ'le], *n.m.* seal.

scellement [sɛl'mã], *n.m.* sealing; fastening.

sceller [sɛ'le], *v.t.* to put an official seal on, to seal; (*Build.*) to fasten; (*fig.*) to ratify.

scénario [sena'rjo], *n.m.* (*pl.* **scénarios** or **scénarii**) scenario (*of ballet etc.*); film script.

scénariste [sena'rist], *n.* script writer, scenario writer.

scène [sɛːn], *n.f.* stage; scenery; (*colloq.*) scene, quarrel.

scénique [se'nik], *a.* scenic, theatrical; *indications scéniques*, stage directions.

scepticisme [sɛpti'sism], *n.m.* scepticism.

sceptique [sɛp'tik], *a.* sceptical.—*n.* sceptic.

sceptre [sɛptr], *n.m.* scepter; (*fig.*) sway, dominion.

schah [ʃa], *n.m.* shah (*of Persia*).

scheik or **cheik** [ʃɛk], *n.m.* sheik.

schéma [ʃe'ma], **schème** [ʃɛm], *n.m.* diagram; rough sketch.

schématique [ʃema'tik], *a.* diagrammatic; *dessin schématique*, draft, diagram.

schibboleth [ʃibo'lɛt], *n.m.* catchword, shibboleth.

schisme [ʃism], *n.m.* schism.

schiste [ʃist], *n.m.* schist, slaty rock, shale.

schizophrène [skizo'frɛn], *a.* and *n.* schizophrenic.

schizophrénie [skizofre'ni], *n.f.* schizophrenia.

schnorkel [ʃnɔr'kɛl], *n.m.* snorkel; submarine's air-tube.

schooner [ʃku'nɔːr], *n.m.* schooner.

sciage [sja:ʒ], *n.m.* sawing.

sciatique [sja'tik], *a.* sciatic.—*n.m.* sciatic nerve.—*n.f.* sciatica.

scie [si], *n.f.* saw; (*pop.*) bore, nuisance.

sciemment [sja'mã], *adv.* wittingly, knowingly.

science [sjã:s], *n.f.* science, knowledge, learning; skill.

scientifique [sjãti'fik], *a.* scientific.

scientifiquement [sjãtifik'mã], *adv.* scientifically.

scier [sje], *v.t.* to saw; to cut down.—*v.i.* (*Row.*) to back water.

scierie [si'ri], *n.f.* sawmill.

scieur [sjœːr], *n.m.* sawyer.

scinder [sɛ̃'de], *v.t.* to divide, to split up.

scintillant [sɛ̃ti'jã], *a.* scintillating; twinkling.

scintillation [sɛ̃tija'sjõ], *n.f.*, **scintillement** [sɛ̃tij'mã], *n.m.* scintillation, sparkling; twinkling.

scintiller [sɛ̃ti'je], *v.i.* to scintillate, to sparkle; to twinkle (*of star*); to flicker.

scion [sjø], *n.m.* scion, shoot.

scission [si'sjõ], *n.f.* scission; split, secession.

scissure [si'sy:r], *n.f.* fissure, crack, cleft.

sciure [sjy:r], *n.f. sciure de bois*, sawdust.

sclérose [skle'ro:z], *n.f.* sclerosis.

scolaire [skɔ'lɛ:r], *a.* of schools; *année scolaire*, school year.

scolarité [skɔlari'te], *n.f.* course of study; school attendance.

scolastique [skɔlas'tik], *a.* scholastic.—*n.m.* scholastic; schoolman.—*n.f.* scholasticism.

scolastiquement [skɔlastik'mã], *adv.* scholastically.

scooter [sku'tɛ:r], *n.m.* motor-scooter; *autos scooters*, 3-wheeled delivery vehicles.

scorbut [skɔr'byt], *n.m.* scurvy.

scorbutique [skɔrby'tik], *a.* and *n.* scorbutic.

scorie [skɔ'ri], *n.f.* scoria, slag, dross.

scorifier [skɔri'fje], *v.t.* to scorify.

scorpion [skɔr'pjõ], *n.m.* scorpion.

scout [skut], *a.* of scouting.—*n.m.* (boy) scout.

scoutisme [sku'tism], *n.m.* scouting, boy-scout movement.

scratch [skratʃ], *n.m.* (*Spt.*) *être* or *partir scratch*, to start at scratch.

scratcher [skrat'ʃe], *v.t.* (*Spt.*) to scratch (*horse, competitor etc.*).

scribe [skrib], *n.m.* scribe; copyist.

script [skript], *n.m.* script (*film* or *play*).

scriptural [skripty'ral], *a.* (*m. pl.* -aux) scriptural.

scrofule [skrɔ'fyl], *n.f.* scrofula, king's evil.

scrofuleux [skrɔfy'lø], *a.* and *n.m.* (*fem. -euse*) scrofulous (person).

scrupule [skry'pyl], *n.m.* scruple, qualm, doubt; scrupulousness.

scrupulcusement [skrypyløz'mã], *adv.* scrupulously.

scrupuleux [skrypy'lø], *a.* (*fem. -euse*) scrupulous, strict, punctilious.

scrutateur [skryta'tœ:r], *a.* (*fem. -trice*) searching, scrutinizing.—*n.m.* (*fem. -trice*) investigator, scrutinizer; scrutineer; teller (*of a ballot etc.*).

scruter [skry'te], *v.t.* to scrutinize, to investigate.

scrutin [skry'tɛ̃], *n.m.* ballot, balloting, poll.

sculpter [skyl'te], *v.t.* to sculpture, to carve.

sculpteur [skyl'tœ:r], *n.m.* sculptor, carver.

sculptural [skylty'ral], *a.* (*m. pl.* -aux) sculptural.

sculpture [skyl'ty:r], *n.f.* sculpture, carving.

se [sə], **s'** [s], *pron. inv.* oneself, himself, herself, itself, themselves; to oneself etc.; one another, each other; *cela se peut*, that may be.

séance [se'ãːs], *n.f.* seat (*right to sit*); session, duration, meeting; sitting (*for one's portrait etc.*); seance; *être en séance*, to be in session; *lever la séance*, to close the meeting; *séance tenante*, there and then, forthwith.

séant [se'ã], *a.* sitting; fitting, seemly, becoming.—*n.m.* sitting posture; seat.

seau [so], *n.m.* (*pl.* seaux) pail, bucket.

sébile [se'bil], *n.f.* small wooden bowl (*used by beggars*); pan (*in gold mining*).

sec [sɛk], *a.* (*fem. sèche*) dry, arid; withered; lean; plain; unfeeling, sharp; *à pied sec*, dry-shod; *coup sec*, sharp stroke; *perte*

sèche, dead loss.—*n.m.* dryness.—*adv.* dryly, sharply.

sécateur [seka'tœ:r], *n.m.* (*Gard.*) pruning-shears; secateurs.

seccotine [sekɔ'tin], *n.f.* (*reg. trade mark*) Seccotine.

sécession [sesɛ'sjõ], *n.f.* secession.

séchage [se'ʃaːʒ], *n.m.* drying.

sèchement [sɛʃ'mã], *adv.* dryly; curtly.

sécher [se'ʃe], *v.t.* (*conjug. like* CÉDER) to dry; to dry up; to cure.—*v.i.* to dry; to wither; to pine away. **se sécher**, *v.r.* to dry oneself; to dry (*of a thing*).

sécheresse [se'ʃrɛs], *n.f.* dryness; drought; (*fig.*) sharpness.

séchoir [se'ʃwaːr], *n.m.* drying room; clothes-horse, clothes airer; hair dryer.

second [sə'gõ, zgõ], *a.* second.—*n.m.* (*fem. -e*) second, assistant.—*n.m.* second floor.—*n.f.* (-e) second class; (*Sch.*) fifth grade; second (*of time*).

secondaire [səgõ'dɛːr], *a.* secondary; accessory.

secondairement [səgõdɛr'mã], *adv.* secondarily.

secondement [səgõd'mã], *adv.* secondly.

seconder [səgõ'de], *v.t.* to second, to assist; to back (up), to support; to promote.

secouement [səku'mã], **secouage** [sə'kwa:ʒ], *n.m.* shaking, jogging, jolting.

secouer [sə'kwe], *v.t.* to shake, to jolt; to shake off; to shock; to rouse. **se secouer**, *v.r.* to shake oneself; to bestir oneself.

secourable [səku'rabl], *a.* helpful, helping; relievable.

secourir [səku'riːr], *v.t. irr.* (*conjug. like* COURIR) to succor, to assist, to help, to relieve.

secourisme [səku'rism], *n.m.* first aid.

secouriste [səku'rist], *n.* qualified first-aider.

secours [sə'kuːr], *n.m.* help, assistance, aid; rescue; *appeler police secours*, to call police emergency; *au secours !* help!

secousse [sə'kus], *n.f.* shake, shock; blow, concussion; jerk, jolt.

secret [sə'krɛ], *a.* (*fem. -ète*) secret, private, hidden; reserved.—*n.m.* secret; secrecy, privacy, mystery.

secrétaire [səkre'tɛːr], *n.* secretary.—*n.m.* writing desk.

secrétariat [səkreta'rja], *n.m.* secretaryship; secretary's office; secretariat.

secrètement [səkrɛt'mã], *adv.* secretly, in secret, inwardly.

sécréter [sekre'te], *v.t.* (*conjug. like* CÉDER) to secrete (*of glands etc.*).

sécréteur [sekre'tœːr], *a.* (*fem. -euse* or *-trice*) secretory.

sécrétion [sekre'sjõ], *n.f.* secretion.

sectaire [sɛk'tɛːr], *a.* sectarian.—*n.* sectary.

sectateur [sɛkta'tœːr], *n.m.* (*fem. -trice*) follower, votary.

secte [sɛkt], *n.f.* sect.

secteur [sɛk'tœːr], *n.m.* sector, section, district.

section [sɛk'sjõ], *n.f.* section; division.

sectionnement [sɛksjɔn'mã], *n.m.* division into parts.

sectionner [sɛksjɔ'ne], *v.t.* to divide into sections; to cut off.

séculaire [seky'lɛːr], *a.* secular, coming once in a century; ancient; time-honored.

séculier [seky'lje], *a.* (*fem.* **-ière**) secular, lay; temporal, worldly.—*n.m.* layman.

secundo [sǝgɔ̃'do], *adv.* secondly.

sécurité [sekyri'te], *n.f.* security, safety.

sédatif [seda'tif], *a.* (*fem.* **-tive**) and *n.m.* sedative.

sédentaire [sedɑ̃'tɛːr], *a.* sedentary; settled, stationary.

sédiment [sedi'mɑ̃], *n.m.* sediment.

sédimentaire [sedimɑ̃'tɛːr], *a.* sedimentary.

séditieusement [sedisjøz'mɑ̃], *adv.* seditiously.

séditieux [sedi'sjø], *a.* (*fem.* **-euse**) seditious; mutinous.—*n.m.* rebel, mutineer.

sédition [sedi'sjɔ̃], *n.f.* sedition, mutiny, riot.

séducteur [sedyk'tœːr], *a.* (*fem.* **-trice**) seductive; enticing, alluring.—*n.m.* (*fem.* **-trice**) seducer, enticer.

séduction [sedyk'sjɔ̃], *n.f.* seduction; allurement; bribing.

séduire [se'dɥiːr], *v.t. irr.* (*conjug. like* CONDUIRE) to seduce; to beguile; to charm; to fascinate; to bribe.

séduisant [sedɥi'zɑ̃], *a.* seductive, alluring, fascinating; tempting.

segment [sɛg'mɑ̃], *n.m.* segment.

ségrégation [segregɑ'sjɔ̃], *n.f.* segregation.

seigle [sɛgl], *n.m.* rye.

seigneur [sɛ'nœːr], *n.m.* lord; lord of the manor, squire; nobleman; *le Seigneur,* the Lord.

seigneurial [sɛɲœ'rjal], *a.* (*m. pl.* **-aux**) manorial; lordly.

seigneurie [sɛɲœ'ri], *n.f.* lordship; manor.

sein [sɛ̃], *n.m.* breast, bosom; (*fig.*) heart, midst; womb.

seine [sɛːn], *n.f.* seine, (fishing-) net.

séisme [se'ism], *n.m.* earthquake.

seize [sɛːz], *a.* and *n.m.* sixteen, sixteenth.

seizième [sɛ'zjɛm], *a.* and *n.* sixteenth.

séjour [se'ʒuːr], *n.m.* stay, abode, sojourn; place where one sojourns.

séjourner [seʒur'ne], *v.i.* to stay, to sojourn.

sel [sɛl], *n.m.* salt; (*fig.*) wit, pungency; (*pl.*) smelling salts.

sélecteur [selɛk'tœːr], *a.* (*fem.* **-trice**) selecting; selective.

sélection [selɛk'sjɔ̃], *n.f.* selection.

sélectivité [selɛktivi'te], *n.f.* selectivity.

sellage [sɛ'laːʒ], *n.m.* saddling.

selle [sɛl], *n.f.* saddle; bowel movement.

seller [sɛ'le], *v.t.* to saddle.

sellerie [sɛl'ri], *n.f.* saddlery; harness room.

sellette [sɛ'lɛt], *n.f.* stool of repentance; shoeblack's box; (*Naut.*) slung cradle.

sellier [sɛ'lje], *n.m.* saddler.

selon [sǝ'lɔ̃], *prep.* according to; *c'est selon,* that depends; *selon moi,* in my opinion; *selon que,* according as.

semailles [sǝ'maːj], *n.f. pl.* seeds; sowing; sowing time.

semaine [sǝ'mɛn], *n.f.* week; week's work; week's money.

semainier [sǝmɛ'nje], *n.m.* (*fem.* **-ière**) person on duty for the week.—*n.m.* (*Ind.*) time-sheet; weekly output.

sémaphore [sema'fɔːr], *n.m.* semaphore, signal post.

semblable [sɑ̃'blabl], *a.* like, similar, alike.—*n.* like; fellow, match, equal.—*n.m.* fellow creature.

semblablement [sɑ̃blablǝ'mɑ̃], *adv.* likewise, also.

semblant [sɑ̃'blɑ̃], *n.m.* appearance, semblance, look; pretence; *faire semblant,* to pretend.

sembler [sɑ̃'ble], *v.i.* to seem, to appear.

semé [sǝ'me], *a.* sowed, sown; strewn (*de*).

semelle [sǝ'mɛl], *n.f.* sole (*of boots, shoes etc.*); foot (*of stockings*); length of a foot.

semence [sǝ'mɑ̃ːs], *n.f.* seed; semen; (*fig.*) cause.

semer [sǝ'me], *v.t.* (*conjug. like* AMENER) to sow; to scatter, to strew, to sprinkle.

semestre [sǝ'mɛstr], *n.m.* half-year, six months.

semestriel [sǝmɛstri'ɛl], *a.* (*fem.* **-elle**) half-yearly.

semeur [sǝ'mœːr], *n.m.* (*fem.* **-euse**) sower; (*fig.*) disseminator.

semi-circulaire [sǝmisirky'lɛːr], *a.* semi-circular.

sémillance [semi'jɑ̃ːs], *n.f.* sprightliness, liveliness.

sémillant [semi'jɑ̃], *a.* brisk, lively, sprightly.

semi-mensuel [sǝmimɑ̃'sɥɛl], *a.* (*fem.* **-elle**) fortnightly.

séminaire [semi'nɛːr], *n.m.* seminary, theological college; specialized course.

semis [sǝ'mi], *n.m.* sowing; seed bed; seedlings.

sémitique [semi'tik], *a.* Semitic.

sémitisme [semi'tism], *n.m.* Semitism.

semi-ton [sǝmi'tɔ̃], *n.m.* (*pl.* **-tons**) semitone.

semoir [sǝ'mwaːr], *n.m.* seed bag; seed drill.

semonce [sǝ'mɔ̃ːs], *n.f.* rebuke, reprimand, lecture.

semoncer [sǝmɔ̃'se], *v.t.* (*conjug. like* COMMENCER) to reprimand, to lecture.

semoule [sǝ'mul], *n.f.* semolina.

sempiternel [sɛpitɛr'nɛl], *a.* (*fem.* **-elle**) sempiternal, everlasting.

sénat [se'na], *n.m.* senate; senate building.

sénateur [sena'tœːr], *n.m.* senator.

sénatorial [senatɔ'rjal], *a.* (*m. pl.* **-aux**) senatorial.

séné [se'ne], *n.m.* senna.

seneçon [sǝn'sɔ̃], *n.m.* groundsel.

Sénégal [sene'gal], **le**, *m.* Senegal.

sénégalais [senega'lɛ], *a.* Senegalese.—*n.m.* (**Sénégalais**, *fem.* **-aise**) Senegalese (*person*).

Sénèque [se'nɛk], *m.* Seneca.

*****senestre** [se'nɛstr], **senestre** [sǝ'nɛstr], *a.* left, (*Her.*) sinister.

sénile [se'nil], *a.* senile.

sénilité [senili'te], *n.f.* senility, old age.

senne [sɛn], *n.f.* [SEINE].

sens [sɑ̃ːs], *n.m. inv.* sense; senses, feelings; intelligence; consciousness; meaning; opinion; way, direction; *à contre-sens,* in a wrong sense; *à double sens,* with double meaning; *sens dessus dessous,* upside down; *sens interdit,* no entry.

sensation [sɑ̃sa'sjɔ̃], *n.f.* sensation, feeling.

sensationnel [sɑ̃sasjɔ'nɛl], *a.* (*fem.* **-elle**) sensational.

sensé [sɑ̃'se], *a.* sensible, intelligent.

sensément [sɑ̃se'mɑ̃], *adv.* sensibly, judiciously.

sensibilité [sɑ̃sibili'te], *n.f.* sensibility, sensitiveness, feeling; compassion.

sensible [sã'sibl], *a.* sensitive, susceptible, sympathetic; tender; sore (*skin etc.*); perceptible, noticeable, tangible.

sensiblement [sãsiblə'mã], *adv.* appreciably; feelingly, deeply; obviously; considerably.

sensiblerie [sãsiblə'ri], *n.f.* sentimentality; (*fam.*) sob stuff.

sensitif [sãsi'tif], *a.* (*fem.* **-tive**) sensitive; sensory.—*n.f.* (**-tive**) sensitive plant.

sensitivité [sãsitivi'te], *n.f.* sensitivity.

sensualiste [sãsɥa'list], *a.* sensual.—*n.* sensualist.

sensualité [sãsɥali'te], *n.f.* sensuality.

sensuel [sã'sɥɛl], *a.* (*fem.* **-elle**) sensual.—*n.m.* (*fem.* **-elle**) sensualist.

sensuellement [sãsɥɛl'mã], *adv.* sensually.

sentence [sã'tã:s], *n.f.* maxim; sentence, judgment, verdict.

sentencieusement [sãtãsjøz'mã], *adv.* sententiously.

sentencieux [sãtã'sjø], *a.* (*fem.* **-euse**) sententious.

senteur [sã'tœ:r], *n.f.* smell; scent, perfume; *pois de senteur*, sweet pea.

senti [sã'ti], *a.* felt, experienced.

sentier [sã'tje], *n.m.* path, footpath; *sentier battu*, beaten track.

sentiment [sãti'mã], *n.m.* feeling; sensation; sentiment; affection, *esp.* love; perception, sense; opinion.

sentimental [sãtimã'tal], *a.* (*m. pl.* **-aux**) sentimental.

sentimentalement [sãtimãtal'mã], *adv.* sentimentally.

sentimentaliste [sãtimãta'list], *n.* sentimentalist.

sentimentalité [sãtimãtali'te], *n.f.* sentimentality.

sentinelle [sãti'nɛl], *n.f.* sentinel, sentry.

sentir [sã'ti:r], *v.t. irr.* to feel; to guess; to perceive; to smell; to savor of; to seem.—*v.i.* to smell. **se sentir**, *v.r.* to feel oneself, to feel; to be conscious; to feel the effects (*de*); to be perceived, felt etc.

seoir (1) [swa:r], *v.i. irr.* (*only used in pres. p.* **séant** *and p.p.* **sis**) to sit, to be sitting.

seoir (2) [swa:r], *v.i. irr.* (*pres. p.* **seyant**, *no p.p.*) to suit, to become.

Séoudite [seu'dit], [ARABIE].

séparable [sepa'rabl], *a.* separable.

séparation [separa'sjõ], *n.f.* separation, parting.

séparé [sepa're], *a.* separate; distinct.

séparément [separe'mã], *adv.* separately; apart.

séparer [sepa're], *v.t.* to separate, to part; to sever. **se séparer**, *v.r.* to separate, to part; to divide.

sépia [se'pja], *n.f.* sepia.

sept [sɛt], *a.* and *n.m. inv.* seven; seventh.

septembre [sɛp'tã:br], *n.m.* September.

septénaire [sɛpte'nɛ:r], *a.* and *n.m.* septenary.

septennal [sɛptɛ'nal], *a.* (*m. pl.* **-aux**) septennial.

septentrion [sɛptãtri'õ], *n.m.* north.

septentrional [sɛptãtrio'nal], *a.* (*m. pl.* **-aux**) north, northern.

septicémie [sɛptise'mi], *n.f.* (*Méd.*) septicemia, blood poisoning.

septième [se'tjɛm], *a.* and *n.* seventh.

septique [sɛp'tik], *a.* septic.

septuagénaire [sɛptɥaʒe'nɛ:r], *a.* and *n.* septuagenarian.

sépulcral [sepyl'kral], *a.* (*m. pl.* **-aux**) sepulchral.

sépulcre [se'pylkr], *n.m.* sepulcher.

sépulture [sepyl'ty:r], *n.f.* burial, interment; burial place, tomb.

séquelle [se'kɛl], *n.f.* (*pl.*) after-effects (*of illness*).

séquence [se'kã:s], *n.f.* sequence.

séquestration [sekɛstra'sjõ], *n.f.* sequestration.

séquestre [se'kɛstr], *n.m.* sequestration; sequestrator; depository.

séquestrer [sekɛs'tre], *v.t.* to sequester, to sequestrate; to shut up illegally. **se séquestrer**, *v.r.* to sequester oneself.

sequin [sə'kɛ̃], *n.m.* sequin (gold coin).

sérail [se'ra:j], *n.m.* seraglio.

séraphin [sera'fɛ̃], *n.m.* seraph.

séraphique [sera'fik], *a.* seraphic.

serbe [sɛrb], *a.* Serbian.—*n.* (**Serbe**) Serb. **Serbie** [sɛr'bi], **la**, *f.* Serbia.

serein [sə'rɛ̃], *a.* serene, placid, calm.—*n.m.* (*poet.*) night dew.

sérénade [sere'nad], *n.f.* serenade.

sérénité [sereni'te], *n.f.* serenity, calmness; equanimity.

séreux [se'rø], *a.* (*fem.* **-euse**) serous, watery.

serf [sɛrf], *a.* (*fem.* **serve**) in bondage, servile.—*n.m.* (*fem.* **serve**) serf, bondsman, bondswoman.

serge [sɛrʒ], *n.f.* serge.

sergent [sɛr'ʒã], *n.m.* sergeant; *sergent de ville*, police constable.

séricicole [serisi'kɔl], *a.* silk-producing.

sériciculteur [serisikyl'tœːr], *n.m.* silk grower.

sériciculture [serisikyl'ty:r], *n.f.* silk culture.

série [se'ri], *n.f.* series; succession; run; (*Spt.*) heat; *fabrication en série*, mass production.

sérieusement [serjøz'mã], *adv.* seriously, gravely.

sérieux [se'rjø], *a.* (*fem.* **-euse**) serious, grave; earnest; real, true.—*n.m.* seriousness, importance, gravity.

serin [sə'rɛ̃], *n.m.* canary; (*fig.*) duffer, fool.

seriner [səri'ne], *v.t.* to din (*something*) into someone.

seringue [sə'rɛ̃:g], *n.f.* syringe, squirt.

seringuer [sərɛ̃'ge], *v.t.* to syringe, to squirt; to inject.

serment [sɛr'mã], *n.m.* oath, promise, solemn declaration; (*pl.*) swearing.

sermon [sɛr'mõ], *n.m.* sermon; lecture.

sermonner [sɛrmɔ'ne], *v.t., v.i.* to sermonize, to lecture, to reprimand.

sermonneur [sɛrmɔ'nœːr], *n.m.* (*fem.* **-euse**) sermonizer, preacher, fault-finder.

sérosité [serozi'te], *n.f.* serosity, wateriness.

serpe [sɛrp], *n.f.* bill-hook.

serpent [sɛr'pã], *n.m.* serpent, snake; *serpent à sonnettes*, rattlesnake.

serpenter [sɛrpã'te], *v.i.* to meander, to wind.

serpentin [sɛrpã'tɛ̃], *a.* serpentine.—*n.m.* paper streamer.

serpette [sɛr'pɛt], *n.f.* pruning knife.

serpolet [sɛrpɔ'le], *n.m.* wild thyme.

serrage [se'ra:ʒ], *n.m.* tightening, pressing.

serre [sɛːr], n.f. squeeze, pressure; talon, claw (of birds); clip; hot-house, greenhouse, conservatory.

serré [sɛˈre], a. close; compact; tight; clenched; (fam.) close-fisted.

serre-frein(s) [sɛrˈfrɛ̃], n.m. inv. (Rail.) brakeman.

serre-livres [sɛːrˈlivr], n.m. inv. book ends.

serrement [sɛrˈmɑ̃], n.m. pressing, squeezing; **serrement de cœur**, pang (of grief); **serrement de main**, handshake.

serre-papiers [sɛrpaˈpje], n.m. inv. paper clip; file (for papers); set of pigeon-holes (for papers).

serrer [sɛˈre], v.t. to press, to squeeze; to fasten, to lock; to grip; to condense, to put close together; to press; to close (the ranks); to clench (one's fist, teeth etc.). **se serrer**, v.r. to press each other close; to sit, lie or stand close together; to stint oneself.

serre-tête [sɛrˈtɛːt], n.m. inv. headband; crash helmet.

serrure [sɛˈryːr], n.f. lock.

serrurier [sɛryˈrje], n.m. locksmith.

sérum [seˈrɔm], n.m. serum.

servage [sɛrˈvaːʒ], n.m. servitude, bondage.

servant [sɛrˈvɑ̃], a.m. serving; in waiting.—n.m. (Artill.) gunner.

servante [sɛrˈvɑ̃ːt], n.f. maid-servant; servant-girl; dinner wagon.

serveur [sɛrˈvœːr], n.m. (fem. -euse) (Ten.) server; waiter, barman; (Cards) dealer.

serviable [sɛrˈvjabl], a. willing, obliging.

service [sɛrˈvis], n.m. service; attendance; duty; function; divine service.

serviette [sɛrˈvjɛt], n.f. napkin, serviette; towel; briefcase.

servile [sɛrˈvil], a. servile, menial; slavish.

servilement [sɛrvilˈmɑ̃], adv. servilely, slavishly.

servir [sɛrˈviːr], v.t. irr. (conjug. like SENTIR) to serve, to attend; to serve up; to be of service to; to assist.—v.i. to serve, to be of use; to serve up a meal. **se servir**, v.r. to serve oneself; to be served up (of dishes); **servez-vous**, help yourself.

serviteur [sɛrviˈtœːr], n.m. servant, man-servant.

servitude [sɛrviˈtyd], n.f. servitude, slavery.

ses [se], [SON].

session [sɛˈsjɔ̃], n.f. session, sitting; term (of law courts etc.).

seuil [sœːj], n.m. threshold; door-step; shelf (of ocean bed).

seul [sœl], a. alone; single, only, sole; mere, bare.—n.m. one only, the only one.

seulement [sœlˈmɑ̃], adv. only; but; solely, merely.

sève [sɛːv], n.f. sap; (fig.) pith, vigor, strength.

sévère [seˈvɛːr], a. severe, stern, austere, strict.

sévèrement [severˈmɑ̃], adv. severely, sternly; strictly.

sévérité [severiˈte], n.f. severity; strictness; purity.

séveux [seˈvø], a. (fem. -euse) (Bot.) sappy; (fig.) vigorous.

sévices [seˈvis], n.m. pl. (Law) cruelty, ill-treatment.

sévir [seˈviːr], v.i. to deal severely (contre); to rage (of war etc.).

sevrage [səˈvraːʒ], n.m. weaning.

sevrer [səˈvre], v.t. (conjug. like AMENER) to wean; (fig.) to deprive (de).

sexagénaire [sɛkzaʒeˈnɛːr], a. and n. sexagenarian.

sexe [sɛks], n.m. sex.

sextant [sɛksˈtɑ̃], n.m. sextant.

sextuple [sɛksˈtypl], a. and n.m. sextuple, sixfold.

sexualité [sɛksɥaliˈte], n.f. sexuality.

sexuel [sɛkˈsɥɛl], a. (fem. -elle) sexual.

shampooing [ʃɑ̃ˈpwɛ], n.m. shampoo, hairwash.

shérif [ʃeˈrif], n.m. sheriff.

short [ʃort], n.m. (Cost.) shorts.

shunt [ʃœ̃t], n.m. (Elec.) shunt.

shunter [ʃœ̃ˈte], v.t. to shunt.

si (1) [si], conj. if; whether; supposing, what if.

si (2) [si], adv. so, so much, however much; yes.

si (3) [si], n.m. inv. (Mus.) si; the note B.

Siam [sjam], le, m. Thailand, Siam.

siamois [sjaˈmwa], a. Siamese.—n.m. Siamese (language); (**Siamois**, fem. **-oise**) Siamese (person).

Sibérie [sibeˈri], la, f. Siberia.

sibérien [sibeˈrjɛ̃], a. (fem. -enne) Siberian.—n.m. (**Sibérien**, fem. **-enne**) Siberian (person).

sibilant [sibiˈlɑ̃], a. sibilant, hissing.

siccatif [sikaˈtif], a. (fem. -tive) siccative, drying.

Sicile [siˈsil], la, f. Sicily.

sicilien [sisiˈljɛ̃], a. (fem. -enne) Sicilian.—n.m. (**Sicilien**, fem. **-enne**) Sicilian (person).

sidérurgie [sideryrˈʒi], n.f. iron and steel industry.

siècle [sjɛkl], n.m. century; age, period.

siège [sjɛːʒ], n.m. seat; bench (of a court of justice); headquarters (of society etc.); (Eccles.) see; siege.

siéger [sjeˈʒe], v.i. (conjug. like ASSIÉGER) to sit (of assemblies, courts etc.); to hold one's see (of bishops); to be seated; (fig.) to lie (of a thing); to have one's headquarters (of business, society).

sien [sjɛ̃], pron. poss. 3rd pers. sing. (fem. **sienne**) his, hers, its, one's.—n.m. one's own (property, work etc.).

Sienne [sjɛn], f. Sienna.

Sierra-Leone [sjɛraleˈon], le, m. Sierra Leone.

sieste [sjɛst], n.f. siesta.

sifflant [siˈflɑ̃], a. hissing; whistling; wheezing.

sifflement [sifləˈmɑ̃], n.m. hissing, hiss; whistling, whistle; whizzing; wheezing.

siffler [siˈfle], v.t. to whistle; to hiss.—v.i. to hiss; to whistle; to whizz; to wheeze.

sifflet [siˈflɛ], n.m. whistle (instrument and sound); catcall; hiss; (colloq.) windpipe.

siffleur [siˈflœːr], a. (fem. -euse) whistling, piping (of birds); wheezing (of horses).—n.m. (fem. -euse) whistler; hisser.

sigle [sigl], n.m. initial letter; group of initial letters used as abbreviation of phrase (U.N. etc.).

signal [siˈnal], n.m. (pl. -aux) signal.

signalé [siɲaˈle], a. signal, remarkable, conspicuous.

signalement [siɲalˈmɑ̃], n.m. description (of a man etc.), particulars.

signaler [siɲaˈle], *v.t.* to signal; to give the description of; to point out, to mark out; to signalize. **se signaler,** *v.r.* to signalize *or* distinguish oneself.

signaleur [siɲaˈlœːr], *n.m.* signalman; (*Mil.*) signaller.

signalisateur [siɲalizaˈtœːr], *n.m.*(*Motor.*) directional signal.

signataire [siɲaˈtɛːr], *n.* signer, subscriber, signatory.

signature [siɲaˈtyːr], *n.f.* signature; signing.

signe [siɲ], *n.m.* sign; mark, indication; badge; omen; **faire signe de la main,** to beckon; **signe de la tête,** nod.

signer [siˈɲe], *v.t., v.i.* to sign, to subscribe. **se signer,** *v.r.* to cross oneself.

signet [siˈɲɛ], *n.m.* signet; book mark; signet ring.

significatif [siɲifikaˈtif], *a.* (*fem.* **-tive**) significant.

signification [siɲifikaˈsjɔ̃], *n.f.* signification, meaning; (*Law*) legal notice.

significativement [siɲifikativˈmɑ̃], *adv.* significantly.

signifier [siɲiˈfje], *v.t.* to signify, to mean; to notify, to intimate; (*Law*) to serve.

silence [siˈlɑ̃ːs], *n.m.* silence; stillness; secrecy; (*Mus.*) rest.

silencieusement [silɑ̃sjøzˈmɑ̃], *adv.* silently.

silencieux [silɑ̃ˈsjø], *a.* (*fem.* **-euse**) silent; still.—*n.m.* (*Motor.*) muffler.

silex [siˈlɛks], *n.m.* silex, flint.

silhouette [siˈlwɛt], *n.f.* silhouette; outline, profile.

silice [siˈlis], *n.f.* (*Chem.*) silica, flint.

sillage [siˈjaːʒ], *n.m.* wake, wash; ship-stream.

sillon [siˈjɔ̃], *n.m.* furrow made by plow; seed drill; (*fig.*) track, wake (*of a ship etc.*); wrinkle.

sillonner [sijɔˈne], *v.t.* to furrow; to streak.

silo [siˈlo], *n.m.* silo (*pit or tower for preserving fodder*).

silotage [siloˈtaːʒ], *n.m.* silage.

simagrée [simaˈgre], *n.f.* pretence, affectation; (*pl.*) fuss.

simiesque [siˈmjɛsk], *a.* ape-like, apish (*face*).

similaire [simiˈlɛːr], *a.* similar.

similarité [similariˈte], *n.f.* similarity, likeness.

similitude [similiˈtyd], *n.f.* similitude, resemblance; simile.

simoun [siˈmuːn], *n.m.* simoom, simoon.

simple [sɛ̃ːpl], *a.* simple, single; easy; only, mere; common, plain; private (*soldier*); simple-minded, silly; natural.—*n.m.* that which is simple; (*Ten.*) singles; **simple dames,** women's singles.

simplement [sɛ̃plɔˈmɑ̃], *adv.* simply.

simplet [sɛ̃ˈplɛ], *a.* (*fem.* **-ette**) naïve, simple; (*fam.*) a bit off; (*Am.*) green.—*n.m.* (*fem.* **-ette**) simpleton, silly.

simplicité [sɛ̃plisiˈte], *n.f.* simplicity; artlessness; silliness.

simplification [sɛ̃plifikaˈsjɔ̃], *n.f.* simplification.

simplifier [sɛ̃pliˈfje], *v.t.* to simplify.

simulacre [simyˈlakr], *n.m.* image; phantom; semblance, sham.

simulé [simyˈle], *a.* feigned, sham.

simuler [simyˈle], *v.t.* to feign, to sham.

simultané [simyltaˈne], *a.* simultaneous.

simultanément [simyltaneˈmɑ̃], *adv.* simultaneously.

sincère [sɛ̃ˈsɛːr], *a.* sincere, frank; honest.

sincèrement [sɛ̃sɛrˈmɑ̃], *adv.* sincerely, honestly.

sincérité [sɛ̃seriˈte], *n.f.* sincerity.

sinécure [sineˈkyːr], *n.f.* sinecure.

Singapour [sɛ̃gaˈpuːr], *m.* Singapore.

singe [sɛ̃ːʒ], *n.m.* ape, monkey; hoist; (*Mil. slang*) bully beef.

singer [sɛ̃ˈʒe], *v.t.* (*conjug. like* MANGER) to ape, to mimic.

singerie [sɛ̃ˈʒri], *n.f.* monkey house; grimace; antic; mimicry.

singeur [sɛ̃ˈʒœːr], *a.* (*fem.* **-euse**) aping, mimicking.—*n.m.* (*fem.* **-euse**) ape, mimic.

singulariser [sɛ̃gylariˈze], *v.t.* to singularize; to make conspicuous. **se singulariser,** *v.r.* to make oneself conspicuous.

singularité [sɛ̃gylariˈte], *n.f.* singularity, peculiarity.

singulier [sɛ̃gyˈlje], *a.* (*fem.* **-ière**) singular; peculiar; odd.—*n.m.* (*Gram.*) singular.

singulièrement [sɛ̃gyljerˈmɑ̃], *adv.* singularly, oddly.

sinistre [siˈnistr], *a.* sinister; dismal; evil.—*n.m.* disaster, calamity.

sinistré [sinisˈtre], *a.* affected by disaster (*shipwreck, fire etc.*).—*n.m.* (*fem.* **-ée**) victim of disaster; casualty.

sinon [siˈnɔ̃], *conj.* otherwise, if not, else; except, unless; **sinon que,** except that.

sinueux [siˈnɥø], *a.* (*fem.* **-euse**) sinuous, winding.

sinuosité [sinɥoziˈte], *n.f.* sinuosity, winding.

sinus [siˈnyːs], *n.m. inv.* sine; (*Anat.*) sinus.

sinusite [sinyˈzit], *n.f.* sinusitis.

siphon [siˈfɔ̃], *n.m.* siphon; (*Naut.*) water-spout.

sire [siːr], *n.m.* sire (*title of kings and emperors*).

sirène [siˈrɛn], *n.f.* siren, mermaid; horn, fog-horn.

sirocco [siroˈko], *n.m.* sirocco.

sirop [siˈro], *n.m.* syrup.

siroter [siroˈte], *v.t.* to sip; (*pop.*) to tipple.

sirupeux [siryˈpø], *a.* (*fem.* **-euse**) syrupy.

sis [si], *a.* seated, situated [SEOIR (1)].

Sisyphe [siˈzif], *m.* Sisyphus.

site [sit], *n.m.* site (*situation with regard to scenery etc.*); **un beau site,** a beauty spot.

sitôt [siˈto], *adv.* so soon, as soon; **sitôt dit, sitôt fait,** no sooner said than done; **sitôt que,** as soon as.

situation [sitɥaˈsjɔ̃], *n.f.* situation, site, position; state of affairs, predicament.

situé [siˈtɥe], *a.* situated, lying.

situer [siˈtɥe], *v.t.* to place.

six [si *before a consonant,* siz *before a vowel,* sis *at the end of a sentence*], *a.* six; sixth.—[sis], *n.m.* six; sixth; sixth day.

sixième [siˈzjɛm], *a.* and *n.* sixth.—*n.m.* sixth (part); sixth floor.—*n.f.* (*in France*) sixth class, (*in England*) first form (*of upper school*).

ski [ski], *n.m.* ski; **faire du ski,** to go in for skiing; **ski nautique,** water-skiing.

slave [slav], *a.* Slav, Slavonic.—*n.* (**Slave**) Slav (*person*).

slip [slip], *n.m.* (*Cost.*) trunks, briefs; **slip de bain,** (swimming) trunks.

297

slovène [slɔ'vɛn], a. Slovenian.—n. (Slovène)
Slovene.

smoking [smɔ'kiŋ], n.m. dinner jacket.

snob [snɔb], a. (fam.) swanky.—n.m. person
who tries to be always in the swim.

snobisme [snɔ'bism], n.m. affected up-to-
dateness.

sobre [sɔbr], a. (of persons) abstemious, temperate, moderate; (of colors, style etc.)
sober, quiet, unadorned.

sobrement [sɔbrə'mɑ̃], adv. soberly, moderately.

sobriété [sɔbrie'te], n.f. sobriety; abstemiousness (in food and drink).

sobriquet [sɔbri'kɛ], n.m. nickname.

soc [sɔk], n.m. ploughshare.

sociabilité [sɔsjabili'te], n.f. sociability, good
fellowship.

sociable [sɔ'sjabl], a. sociable, companion-
able.

sociablement [sɔsjablə'mɑ̃], adv. sociably.

social [sɔ'sjal], a. (m. pl. -aux) social; siège
social, registered office; head office.

socialement [sɔsjal'mɑ̃], adv. socially.

socialisme [sɔsja'lism], n.m. socialism.

socialiste [sɔsja'list], a. and n. socialist.

sociétaire [sɔsje'tɛːr], n. associate, member;
partner; shareholder.

société [sɔsje'te], n.f. society, association;
community; firm; partnership; société
anonyme, incorporated company.

sociologie [sɔsjɔlɔ'ʒi], n.f. sociology.

sociologiste [sɔsjɔlɔ'ʒist], sociologue [sɔsjɔ-
'lɔg], n. sociologist.

socle [sɔkl], n.m. socle, pedestal, stand, base.

socque [sɔk], n.m. clog, patten.

Socrate [sɔ'krat], m. Socrates.

sœur [sœːr], n.f. sister; nun.

sœurette [sœ'rɛt], n.f. (colloq.) little sister,
sis(s).

sofa [sɔ'fa], n.m. sofa, settee.

soi [swa], soi-même [swa'mɛm], impers.
pron. 3rd pers. sing. oneself, itself; self.

soi-disant [swadi'zɑ̃], a. inv. self-styled,
would-be, so-called.

soie [swa], n.f. silk; silken hair; bristle (of
hogs); papier de soie, tissue paper.

soierie [swa'ri], n.f. silks, silk goods; silk-
trade; silk-factory.

soif [swaf], n.f. thirst; avoir soif, to be
thirsty.

soigné [swa'ne], a. carefully done; neat,
smart; (colloq.) first-rate.

soigner [swa'ne], v.t. to take care of, to look
after; to nurse. se soigner, v.r. to take
care of oneself.

soigneusement [swaɲøz'mɑ̃], adv. carefully.

soigneux [swa'ɲø], a. (fem. -euse) careful;
solicitous.

soi-même [swa'mɛm].

soin [swɛ̃], n.m. care; attendance; (pl.) attentions, pains, trouble.

soir [swaːr], n.m. evening; night.

soirée [swa're], n.f. evening (duration);
evening party.

soit [swa, swa], adv. be it so, well and good,
granted; (swat, swa], let us say.—conj. either, or;
whether.

soixantaine [swasɑ̃'tɛn], n.f. about sixty.

soixante [swa'sɑ̃ːt], a. and n.m. sixty.

soixantième [swasɑ̃'tjɛːm], a. and n.
sixtieth.

sol [sɔl], n.m. ground; soil; earth.

solaire [sɔ'lɛːr], a. solar.

soldat [sɔl'da], n.m. soldier; simple soldat,
private; les simples soldats, the rank and
file.

soldatesque [sɔlda'tɛsk], n.f. (usu. pej.)
soldiery.

solde (1) [sɔld], n.f. (Mil.) pay.

solde (2) [sɔld], n.m. balance (between debit
and credit); clearance sale; (pl.) sale bargains, reductions.

solder (1) [sɔl'de], v.t. to pay (soldiers); to
have in one's pay.

solder (2) [sɔl'de], v.t. to settle (an account);
to sell off, to clear.

sole [sɔl], n.f. sole (of animal's foot); sole
(fish).

solécisme [sɔle'sism], n.m. solecism.

soleil [sɔ'lɛːj], n.m. sun; sunshine; (fig.) star;
catherine wheel (firework); sunflower.

solennel [sɔla'nɛl], a. (fem. -elle) solemn.

solennellement [sɔlanɛl'mɑ̃], adv. solemnly.

solenniser [sɔlani'ze], v.t. to solemnize.

solennité [sɔlani'te], n.f. solemnity.

solénoïde [sɔleno'id], n.m. solenoid.

solidaire [sɔli'dɛːr], a. jointly and separately
liable.

solidairement [sɔlidɛr'mɑ̃], adv. jointly and
severally.

solidariser [sɔlidari'ze], v.t. to render jointly
liable.

solidarité [sɔlidari'te], n.f. joint and separate
liability; solidarity, fellowship.

solide [sɔ'lid], a. solid; strong; substantial,
sound; reliable.—n.m. solid, solid body.

solidement [sɔlid'mɑ̃], adv. solidly; firmly;
soundly.

solidification [sɔlidifika'sjɔ̃], n.f. solidification.

solidifier [sɔlidi'fje], v.t. and se solidifier,
v.r. to solidify.

solidité [sɔlidi'te], n.f. solidity; strength;
stability; soundness.

soliloque [sɔli'lɔk], n.m. soliloquy.

soliste [sɔ'list], a. solo.—n. soloist.

solitaire [sɔli'tɛːr], a. solitary, single, alone;
lonely, desert.—n.m. lonely person, recluse;
solitaire (diamond or game).

solitairement [sɔlitɛr'mɑ̃], adv. solitarily,
alone.

solitude [sɔli'tyd], n.f. solitude, loneliness;
desert.

solive [sɔ'liːv], n.f. joist.

soliveau [sɔli'vo], n.m. (pl. -eaux) small joist.

sollicitation [sɔlisita'sjɔ̃], n.f. solicitation;
pull (of magnet).

solliciter [sɔlisi'te], v.t. to incite; to solicit, to
entreat; to call into action; to attract (of
magnet).

sollicitude [sɔlisi'tyd], n.f. solicitude, care;
concern.

solo [sɔ'lo], a. inv. solo.—n.m. (pl. solos or
soli) solo.

solstice [sɔls'tis], n.m. solstice.

solubilité [sɔlybili'te], n.f. solubility.

soluble [sɔ'lybl], a. soluble.

solution [sɔly'sjɔ̃], n.f. solution; resolution;
(Law) discharge; solution de continuité,
interruption, break, fault.

solvabilité [sɔlvabili'te], n.f. solvency.

solvable [sɔl'vabl], a. solvent.

solvant [sɔl'vɑ̃], n.m. solvent.

somali [sɔmɑ'li], *a.* Somali.—*n.m.* Somali (*language*).—*n.* (**Somali**) Somali (*person*); *Côte Française des Somalis*, French Somaliland.

Somalie [sɔmɑ'li], **la**, *f.* Somalia, Somaliland.

sombre [sɔ̃:br], *a.* dark, somber, gloomy; dim; overcast; melancholy.

sombrer [sɔ̃'bre], *v.i.* (*Naut.*) to founder.

sombrero [sɔ̃bre'ro], *n.m.* sombrero.

sommaire [sɔ'mɛ:r], *a.* summary, concise; scanty.—*n.m.* summary, abstract.

sommairement [sɔmɛr'mɑ̃], *adv.* summarily; hastily.

sommation [sɔmɑ'sjɔ̃], *n.f.* summons, demand; (*Mil.*) challenge.

somme [sɔm], *n.f.* sum, total; amount; summary; burden.—*n.m.* nap, *faire un somme*, to have forty winks.

sommeil [sɔ'mɛ:j], *n.m.* sleep; *avoir sommeil*, to be sleepy.

sommeiller [sɔmɛ'je], *v.i.* to slumber; to doze.

sommelier [sɔmə'lje], *n.m.* butler, cellarman, wine waiter.

sommellerie [sɔmɛl'ri], *n.f.* butler's pantry.

sommer [sɔ'me], *v.t.* to summon, to call upon; to sum up.

sommet [sɔ'me], *n.m.* top, summit; acme; crown (*of the head etc.*).

sommier (1) [sɔ'mje], *n.m.* pack horse; box mattress; wind chest (*of organ*); (*Arch.*) cross-beam.

sommier (2) [sɔ'mje], *n.m.* cash book, register.

sommité [sɔmi'te], *n.f.* summit, top; head, principal; chief point; prominent person.

somnambule [sɔmnɑ̃'byl], *a.* somnambulistic.—*n.* sleepwalker.

somnambulisme [sɔmnɑ̃by'lism], *n.m.* somnambulism, sleep-walking.

somnolence [sɔmnɔ'lɑ̃:s], *n.f.* somnolence.

somnolent [sɔmnɔ'lɑ̃], *a.* somnolent, sleepy.

somptuaire [sɔ̃p'tɥɛ:r], *a.* sumptuary.

somptueusement [sɔ̃ptɥøz'mɑ̃], *adv.* sumptuously.

somptueux [sɔ̃p'tɥø], *a.* (*fem.* -euse) sumptuous; magnificent.

somptuosité [sɔ̃ptɥozi'te], *n.f.* sumptuousness.

son (1) [sɔ̃], *a.* (*fem.* **sa**, *pl.* **ses**) his, her, its; one's.

son (2) [sɔ̃], *n.m.* sound.

son (3) [sɔ̃], *n.m.* bran; *tache de son*, freckle.

sonate [sɔ'nat], *n.f.* sonata.

sondage [sɔ̃'da:ʒ], *n.m.* sounding; (*Mining*) boring.

sonde [sɔ̃:d], *n.f.* sounding-line, lead; (*Surg. etc.*) probe; (*Mining*) drill, boring machine.

sonder [sɔ̃'de], *v.t.* to sound; to taste; to search, to fathom, to investigate.

sondeur [sɔ̃'dœ:r], *n.m.* (*Naut.*) leadsman; (*Mining*) driller, borer.

songe [sɔ̃:ʒ], *n.m.* dream; dreaming.

songe-creux [sɔ̃ʒ'krø], *n.m. inv.* dreamer, visionary.

songer [sɔ̃'ʒe], *v.t.* (*conjug. like* MANGER) to dream; (*fig.*) to imagine; to think of.—*v.i.* to dream; (*fig.*) to day-dream; to think; to mean, to intend, to propose.

songerie [sɔ̃'ʒri], *n.f.* dreaming; musing; day-dreaming.

songeur [sɔ̃'ʒœ:r], *a.* (*fem.* -euse) thoughtful, dreamy.—*n.m.* (*fem.* -euse) dreamer.

sonique [sɔ'nik], *a.* sonic.

sonnant [sɔ'nɑ̃], *a.* sounding; sonorous.

sonner [sɔ'ne], *v.t., v.i.* to sound; to ring, to toll, to strike (*of clocks etc.*).

sonnerie [sɔn'ri], *n.f.* ring, ringing (*of bells*); bells, chimes; striking part (*of a clock etc.*); (*Mil.*) bugle call.

sonnet [sɔ'ne], *n.m.* sonnet.

sonnette [sɔ'net], *n.f.* small bell; hand bell.

sonneur [sɔ'nœ:r], *n.m.* bell ringer.

sonore [sɔ'nɔ:r], *a.* resonant; clear; *ondes sonores*, sound waves.

sonorité [sɔnɔri'te], *n.f.* resonance.

sophisme [sɔ'fism], *n.m.* sophism, fallacy.

sophiste [sɔ'fist], *a.* sophistical.—*n.* sophist.

sophistiqué [sɔfisti'ke], *a.* sophisticated; affected.

soporifique [sɔpɔri'fik], *a.* soporific; (*fig.*) tedious.—*n.m.* soporific.

soprano [sɔpra'no], *n.* (*pl.* **soprani** or **sopranos**) soprano, treble.

sorbet [sɔr'be], *n.m.* sherbet.

sorbier [sɔr'bje], *n.m.* mountain ash, rowan tree.

sorcellerie [sɔrsɛl'ri], *n.f.* sorcery, witchcraft.

sorcier [sɔr'sje], *n.m.* (*fem.* -ière) sorcerer, wizard, sorceress, witch.

sordide [sɔr'did], *a.* sordid, filthy; mean, vile.

sordidement [sɔrdid'mɑ̃], *adv.* sordidly.

Sorlingues [sɔr'lɛ̃:g], **les**, *f. pl.* the Scilly Isles.

sornette [sɔr'net], *n.f.* (*usu. in pl.*) idle talk, small talk.

sort [sɔ:r], *n.m.* fate, destiny; lot; condition; fortune; chance; spell, charm; *au sort*, by lot; *le sort en est jeté*, the die is cast; *tirer au sort*, to draw lots; to toss.

sortable [sɔr'tabl], *a.* suitable.

sortablement [sɔrtablə'mɑ̃], *adv.* suitably.

sortant [sɔr'tɑ̃], *a.* outgoing, retiring, leaving (*office etc.*); drawn (*of numbers in lotteries*).—*n.m.* person going out; person leaving office etc.; *les entrants et les sortants*, the incomers and outgoers.

sorte [sɔrt], *n.f.* sort, kind, species; manner, way; *de la sorte*, thus, in that way; *de sorte que* or *en sorte que*, so that.

sortie [sɔr'ti], *n.f.* going or coming out; exit, way out; outing, trip; exportation; sortie; (*collog.*) outburst, attack; *droit de sortie*, export duty; *jour de sortie*, day off, holiday.

sortilège [sɔrti'lɛ:ʒ], *n.m.* sorcery, magic; spell, charm.

sortir [sɔr'ti:r], *v.t. irr.* (*conjug. like* SENTIR *with aux.* AVOIR) to bring out, to take out; to pull out, to extricate.—*v.i.* (*with aux.* ÊTRE) to go out, to come out, to come forth, to emerge; to make one's exit; to leave, to depart; to swerve; to wander (*from a subject*); to proceed, to result; to spring, to come up; to sally forth; to burst forth; to escape; (*Paint. etc.*) to stand out; to be in relief.—*n.m.* going out, leaving; rising.

sosie [sɔ'zi], *n.m.* double, counterpart.

sot [so], *a.* (*fem.* **sotte**) stupid, silly, foolish; (*fig.*) embarrassed, sheepish.—*n.m.* (*fem.* **sotte**) fool, ass, idiot.

sottement [sɔt'mɑ̃], *adv.* stupidly; foolishly.

299

sottise [sɔ'ti:z], *n.f.* silliness, folly; foolish trick, nonsense; insult; (*pl.*) abusive language.

sou [su], *n.m.* sou (*copper coin worth 5 centimes*); copper, penny.

soubresaut [subrə'so], *n.m.* sudden leap *or* bound; plunge (*of a horse*); start; jolt.

soubresauter [subrə'sote], *v.i.* to start, to jump, to plunge.

soubrette [su'brɛt], *n.f.* lady's maid, waiting-woman.

souche [suʃ], *n.f.* stump, stock, stub, stem; (*fig.*) blockhead; founder (*of a family etc.*); origin; chimney-stack; counterfoil; tally; *faire souche,* to found a family.

souci (1) [su'si], *n.m.* care, anxiety.

souci (2) [su'si], *n.m.* (*Bot.*) marigold.

soucier (**se**) [səsu'sje], *v.r.* to care, to mind, to be concerned, to be anxious (*de*).

soucieux [su'sjø], *a.* (*fem.* **-euse**) anxious, full of care; pensive, thoughtful.

soucoupe [su'kup], *n.f.* saucer.

soudage [su'da:ʒ], *n.m.* soldering, welding; (*fig.*) reconciliation.

soudain [su'dɛ̃], *a.* sudden, unexpected.—*adv.* suddenly.

soudainement [sudɛn'mã], *adv.* suddenly, all of a sudden.

soudaineté [sudɛn'te], *n.f.* suddenness.

Soudan [su'dã], **le**, *n.m.* the Sudan.

soudanais [suda'nɛ], *a.* Sudanese.—*n.m.* (**Soudanais**, *fem.* **-aise**) Sudanese (*person*).

soude [sud], *n.f.* soda.

souder [su'de], *v.t.* to solder, to braze, to weld; (*fig.*) to unite. **se souder**, *v.r.* to be soldered *or* welded; to knit (*of bones*).

soudeur [su'dœ:r], *n.m.* welder.

soudoyer [sudwa'je], *v.t.* (*conjug. like* EMPLOYER) to keep in one's pay; to hire; to bribe.

soudure [su'dy:r], *n.f.* solder; soldering, welding; *soudure autogène,* oxyacetylene welding.

soue [su], *n.f.* pigsty.

soufflage [su'fla:ʒ], *n.m.* glass-blowing.

soufflant [su'flã], *a.* blowing.

souffle [sufl], *n.m.* breath, breathing; puff (*of wind etc.*); (*fig.*) inspiration, influence.

soufflé [su'fle], *a.* soufflé (*of pastry etc.*); exaggerated (*reputation*).—*n.m.* soufflé (*light dish*).

soufflement [suflə'mã], *n.m.* blowing.

souffler [su'fle], *v.t.* to blow, to blow out; to inflate; to whisper; (*Theat.*) to prompt; to huff (*at checkers*); (*Naut.*) to sheathe.—*v.i.* to blow, to breathe; to pant, to puff; (*fig.*) to breathe a word etc.; *souffler aux oreilles de quelqu'un,* to whisper in someone's ear.

soufflerie [suflə'ri], *n.f.* bellows (*of an organ*); wind-tunnel.

soufflet [su'flɛ], *n.m.* pair of bellows; box on the ear, slap in the face; affront.

souffleter [suflə'te], *v.t.* (*conjug. like* APPELER) to slap in the face, to box the ears of; (*fig.*) to insult.

souffleur [su'flœ:r], *a.* (*fem.* **-euse**) blowing, puffing.—*n.m.* (*fem.* **-euse**) blower; (*Theat.*) prompter.—(C) *n.f.* (**-euse**) snow blower.

souffrance [su'frã:s], *n.f.* suffering, pain; suspense; (*Law*) sufferance; *en souffrance,* awaiting delivery; in abeyance.

souffrant [su'frã], *a.* suffering; unwell; long-suffering.

souffre-douleur [sufrədu'lœ:r], *n.m. inv.* drudge; butt, laughing-stock.

souffreteux [sufrə'tø], *a.* (*fem.* **-euse**) needy; poorly, sickly, weakly.

souffrir [su'fri:r], *v.t. irr.* (*conjug. like* OUVRIR) to suffer; to bear, to endure, to undergo, to sustain; to stand, to tolerate; to admit of; *faire souffrir,* to cause pain, to grieve.—*v.i.* to suffer, to be in pain; to be pained; to be injured.

soufre [sufr], *n.m.* sulphur, brimstone.

souhait [swɛ], *n.m.* wish, desire; *à souhait,* to one's heart's content, as one would have it.

souhaitable [swɛ'tabl], *a.* desirable.

souhaiter [swɛ'te], *v.t.* to desire, to wish for.

souiller [su'je], *v.t.* to soil, to dirty; to stain, to blemish, to sully; to defile. **se souiller**, *v.r.* to soil oneself, to get dirty; to tarnish one's good name.

souillon [su'jɔ̃], *n.* sloven, slut; scullion.

souillure [su'jy:r], *n.f.* spot, stain; blot, blemish; contamination.

soûl or **saoul** [su], *a.* glutted, surfeited (*de*); drunk; satiated, heartily sick (*de*).—*n.m.* fill, bellyful; *tout son soûl,* to one's heart's content.

soulagement [sulaʒ'mã], *n.m.* relief, alleviation; solace, help.

soulager [sula'ʒe], *v.t.* (*conjug. like* MANGER) to relieve, to ease; to alleviate, to allay; to soothe, to comfort. **se soulager**, *v.r.* to relieve oneself; to help each other.

soûlard [su'la:r], *a.* drunken.—*n.m.* (*fem.* **-e**) drunkard, sot.

soûler [su'le], *v.t.* to fill, to glut; to make drunk. **se soûler**, *v.r.* to gorge; to get drunk.

soûlerie [sul'ri], *n.f.* drinking bout, 'binge'.

soulèvement [sulɛv'mã], *n.m.* heaving; swelling (*of sea waves etc.*); rising (*of the stomach*); (*fig.*) insurrection, revolt.

soulever [sul've], *v.t.* (*conjug. like* AMENER) to raise, to lift up; to heave; to take up; (*fig.*) to excite, to stir up; to sicken; to rouse the indignation of. **se soulever**, *v.r.* to raise oneself, to rise; to heave, to swell; to rise in insurrection.

soulier [su'lje], *n.m.* shoe; *être dans ses petits souliers,* to be ill at ease; *souliers ferrés,* hobnailed boots.

soulignement [sulɲ'mã], *n.m.* underlining.

souligner [suli'ɲe], *v.t.* to underline; (*fig.*) to emphasize.

soumettre [su'mɛtr], *v.t. irr.* (*conjug. like* METTRE) to subdue, to subject; to submit, to refer; to subordinate. **se soumettre**, *v.r.* to submit, to yield; to comply, to assent (*à*).

soumis [su'mi], *a.* submissive.

soumission [sumi'sjɔ̃], *n.f.* submission, compliance, obedience; subjection; mark of respect; bid for a contract etc.

soumissionner [sumisjɔ'ne], *v.t.* to bid for.

soupape [su'pap], *n.f.* valve; *soupape de sûreté,* safety-valve.

soupçon [sup'sɔ̃], *n.m.* suspicion; surmise, conjecture; (*fig.*) slight taste, dash, touch.

soupçonner [supsɔ'ne], *v.t.* to suspect; to surmise.

soupçonneux [supsɔ'nø], *a.* (*fem.* **-euse**) suspicious.

soupe [sup], *n.f.* soup; sop; *c'est une soupe au lait*, he has a quick temper; *trempé comme une soupe*, drenched to the skin.

soupente [su'pɑ̃:t], *n.f.* straps (*of a horse*); loft, garret.

souper [su'pe], *v.i.* to sup, to have supper. —*n.m.* supper.

soupeser [supə'ze], *v.t.* (*conjug. like* AMENER) to weigh in one's hand, to try the weight of.

soupière [su'pjɛ:r], *n.f.* soup tureen.

soupir [su'pi:r], *n.m.* sigh; breath, gasp; (*Mus.*) quarter rest.

soupirail [supi'ra:j], *n.m.* (*pl.* **-aux**) air-hole, ventilator.

soupirant [supi'rɑ̃], *a.* sighing.—*n.m.* wooer, lover.

soupirer [supi're], *v.t.* to breathe forth, to sigh out.—*v.i.* to sigh; to gasp; to long.

souple [supl], *a.* supple, pliant, flexible, yielding; docile.

souplesse [su'plɛs], *n.f.* suppleness, flexibility; compliance, pliancy; versatility; toughness.

souquenille [suk'ni:j], *n.f.* smock frock; (shabby) old garment.

source [surs], *n.f.* spring, source, fountain.

sourcier [sur'sje], *n.m.* (*fem.* **-ière**) water diviner.

sourcil [sur'si], *n.m.* eyebrow, brow; *froncer le sourcil*, to frown.

sourciller [sursi'je], *v.i.* to knit one's brows, to frown; to wince.

sourcilleux [sursi'jø], *a.* (*fem.* **-euse**) haughty, proud, supercilious; frowning; uneasy.

sourd [su:r], *a.* deaf; (*fig.*) dull; insensible; hollow, muffled (*of sound*); underhand.—*n.m.* (*fem.* **-e**) deaf person.

sourdement [surdə'mɑ̃], *adv.* indistinctly; with a hollow voice; in an underhand manner.

sourdine [sur'din], *n.f.* mute (*of a musical instrument*); damper (*of a piano etc.*); *en sourdine*, secretly, on the sly.

sourd-muet [sur'mɥɛ], *a.* and *n.m.* (*fem.* **sourde-muette**) deaf-and-dumb (person), deaf-mute.

sourdre [surdr], *v.i.* to spring, to gush, to well; (*fig.*) to result.

souriant [su'rjɑ̃], *a.* smiling.

souricière [suri'sjɛ:r], *n.f.* mouse-trap.

sourire [su'ri:r], *v.i. irr.* (*conjug. like* RIRE) to smile; to be agreeable, to delight, to please; to be propitious.—*n.m.* smile; *large sourire*, grin; *sourire affecté*, smirk.

souris [su'ri], *a. inv.* mouse-colored.—*n.f.* mouse; mouse-color; knuckle (*of a leg of mutton*).

sournois [sur'nwa], *a.* artful, cunning, sly.—*n.m.* (*fem.* **-e**) sneak.

sournoisement [surnwaz'mɑ̃], *adv.* cunningly, slyly.

sournoiserie [surnwaz'ri], *n.f.* slyness, cunning; underhand trick.

sous [su], *prep.* under, beneath, below; on, upon; with; in; by; *affirmer sous serment*, to swear under oath; *sous dix jours*, within ten days; *sous peu*, in a short time.

sous-alimentation [suzalimɑ̃ta'sjɔ̃], *n.f.* malnutrition.

sous-alimenté [suzalimɑ̃'te], *a.* underfed.

sous-chef [su'ʃɛf], *n.m.* deputy head-clerk; assistant manager.

souscripteur [suskrip'tœ:r], *n.m.* subscriber; (*Comm.*) underwriter.

souscription [suskrip'sjɔ̃], *n.f.* subscription; signature.

souscrire [sus'kri:r], *v.t. irr.* (*conjug. like* ÉCRIRE) to subscribe, to sign.—*v.i.* to consent, to agree (*à*).

sous-développé [sudevlɔ'pe], *a.* underdeveloped (*country*).

sous-dit [su'di], *a.* undermentioned.

sous-entendre [suzɑ̃'tɑ̃:dr], *v.t.* not to express fully, to hint, to imply.

sous-entendu [suzɑ̃tɑ̃'dy], *n.m.* thing understood, implication.

sous-entente [suzɑ̃'tɑ̃:t], *n.f.* mental reservation.

sous-lieutenant [suljøt'nɑ̃], *n.m.* second-lieutenant; *sous-lieutenant aviateur*, pilot officer.

sous-louer [su'lwe], *v.t.* to sub-let.

sous-main [su'mɛ̃], *n.m. inv.* writing pad; *en sous-main*, behind the scenes.

sous-marin [suma'rɛ̃], *a.* and *n.m.* submarine.

sous-off [su'zɔf], *abbr. fam.* of **sous-officier** [suzɔfi'sje], *n.m.* non-commissioned officer, N.C.O.

sous-ordre [su'zɔrdr], *n.m. inv.* subordinate.

sous-préfet [supre'fɛ], *n.m.* subprefect, under-sheriff.

sous-produit [supro'dɥi], *n.m.* by-product.

sous-secrétaire [susəkre'tɛ:r], *n.* under-secretary.

soussigné [susi'ɲe], *a.* undersigned; *nous soussignés certifions*, we, the undersigned, certify.

sous-sol [su'sɔl], *n.m.* subsoil; basement.

sous-titre [su'titr], *n.m.* sub-title.

soustraction [sustrak'sjɔ̃], *n.f.* taking away, subtraction.

soustraire [sus'trɛ:r], *v.t. irr.* (*conjug. like* TRAIRE) to take away, to withdraw, to screen; (*Arith.*) to subtract. **se soustraire**, *v.r.* to escape, to flee, to avoid; to withdraw oneself; to be subtracted.

sous-traitant [sutrɛ'tɑ̃], *n.m.* subcontractor.

soutache [su'taʃ], *n.f.* braid.

soutane [su'tan], *n.f.* cassock; (*fig.*) the cloth.

soute [sut], *n.f.* (*Naut.*) store-room; (*Av.*) luggage bay, bomb bay.

soutenable [sut'nabl], *a.* sustainable; tenable.

soutènement [sutɛn'mɑ̃], *n.m.* (*Arch.*) support.

soutenir [sut'ni:r], *v.t.* (*conjug. like* TENIR) to hold up, to support, to sustain, to keep up, to prop up; (*fig.*) to maintain, to uphold; to countenance; to afford (*an expense*); to endure. **se soutenir**, *v.r.* to support oneself; to hold oneself up; to bear up, to hold out; to stand firm; to succeed; to continue; to sustain one another.

soutenu [sut'ny], *a.* sustained; unremitting, unceasing, constant; lofty, elevated.

souterrain [sutɛ'rɛ̃], *a.* underground; (*fig.*) underhand.—*n.m.* underground vault, cavern; (*Rail.*) tunnel; underground passage.

soutien [su'tjɛ̃], *n.m.* support, prop, stay, staff.

soutien-gorge [sutjɛ̃'gɔrʒ], *n.m. inv.* brassiere.

soutirer [suti're], *v.t.* to draw off, to rack (*liquors*); (*fig.*) to worm out (*à*), to extract (*money, information*).

souvenir [suv'niːr], *n.m.* recollection; reminder, souvenir, keepsake.—*v. impers. irr.* (*conjug. like* TENIR *but with aux.* ÊTRE) to occur to the mind; *il m'en souvient*, I remember it. **se souvenir**, *v.r.* to remember, to call to mind, to recollect.

souvent [su'vã], *adv.* often, frequently.

souverain [suv'rɛ̃], *a.* sovereign, supreme; highest, extreme; infallible.—*n.m.* (*fem.* -e) sovereign (*monarch*).—*n.m.* sovereign (*coin*).

souverainement [suvrɛn'mã], *adv.* in the extreme; supremely.

souveraineté [suvrɛn'te], *n.f.* sovereignty, dominion.

soviet [sɔ'vjɛt], *n.m.* soviet.

soviétique [sɔvje'tik], *a.* *l'Union des Républiques socialistes soviétiques* (*U.R.S.S.*), the Union of Soviet Socialist Republics (*U.S.S.R.*).—*n.* (**Soviétique**) Soviet citizen.

soyeux [swa'jø], *a.* (*fem.* -euse) silky, silken.

spacieusement [spasjøz'mã], *adv.* spaciously.

spacieux [spa'sjø], *a.* (*fem.* -euse) spacious, wide, roomy.

spahi [spa'i], *n.m.* spahi (*Algerian native trooper*).

sparadrap [spara'dra], *n.m.* sticking plaster.

Sparte [spart], **la**, *f.* Sparta.

spartiate [spar'sjat], *a.* Spartan.—*n.* (**Spartiate**) Spartan (*person*).

spasme [spasm], *n.m.* spasm.

spasmodique [spasmɔ'dik], *a.* spasmodic.

spasmodiquement [spasmɔdik'mã], *adv.* spasmodically.

spatule [spa'tyl], *n.f.* spatula.

speaker [spi'kœːr], *n.m.* (*fem.* **speakerine**) (*Rad.*) announcer.

spécial [spe'sjal], *a.* (*m. pl.* -aux) special, especial, particular; professional.

spécialement [spesjal'mã], *adv.* especially, particularly.

spécialisation [spesjaliza'sjɔ̃], *n.f.* specialization.

spécialiser [spesjali'ze], *v.t.* to specialize.

spécialiste [spesja'list], *n.* specialist, expert.

spécialité [spesjali'te], *n.f.* peculiarity, specialty; patent medicine.

spécieux [spe'sjø], *a.* (*fem.* -euse) specious, plausible.

spécification [spesifika'sjɔ̃], *n.f.* specification.

spécifier [spesi'fje], *v.t.* to specify.

spécifique [spesi'fik], *a.* and *n.m.* specific.

spécifiquement [spesifik'mã], *adv.* specifically.

spécimen [spesi'mɛn], *n.m.* specimen.

spectacle [spɛk'takl], *n.m.* spectacle, scene, sight; theatre; play, performance; show; *se donner en spectacle*, to make an exhibition of oneself.

spectaculaire [spɛktaky'lɛːr], *a.* spectacular.

spectateur [spɛkta'tœːr], *n.m.* (*fem.* -trice) spectator, looker-on.

spectral [spɛk'tral], *a.* (*m. pl.* -aux) spectral.

spectre [spɛktr], *n.m.* specter, ghost; spectrum.

spéculateur [spekyla'tœːr], *n.m.* (*fem.* -trice) speculator.

spéculatif [spekyla'tif], *a.* (*fem.* -tive) speculative.

spéculation [spekylɑ'sjɔ̃], *n.f.* speculation.

spéculativement [spekylativ'mã], *adv.* in a speculative manner.

spéculer [speky'le], *v.i.* to speculate.

sperme [spɛrm], *n.m.* sperm, seed.

sphaigne [sfɛːɲ], *n.f.* sphagnum moss.

sphère [sfɛːr], *n.f.* sphere, orb, globe; (*fig.*) circle.

sphérique [sfe'rik], *a.* spherical.

sphinx [sfɛːks], *n.m.* sphinx.

spinal [spi'nal], *a.* (*m. pl.* -aux) spinal.

spiral [spi'ral], *a.* (*m. pl.* -aux) spiral.—*n.m.* hair-spring (*of watch*).

spirale [spi'ral], *n.f.* spiral.

spirite [spi'rit], *a.* spiritualistic.—*n.* spiritualist.

spiritisme [spiri'tism], *n.m.* spiritualism.

spiritualisme [spiritɥa'lism], *n.m.* spiritualism.

spiritualiste [spiritɥa'list], *a.* and *n.* spiritualist.

spirituel [spiri'tɥɛl], *a.* (*fem.* -elle) spiritual; intellectual; witty, shrewd, lively, intelligent.

spirituellement [spiritɥɛl'mã], *adv.* spiritually; wittily, cleverly.

spiritueux [spiri'tɥø], *a.* (*fem.* -euse) spirituous.—*n.m.* spirit, spirituous liquor.

spleen [splin], *n.m.* spleen; (*fam.*) *avoir le spleen*, to be in the dumps.

splendeur [splã'dœːr], *n.f.* splendor, brilliance; magnificence.

splendide [splã'did], *a.* sumptuous, magnificent.

splendidement [splãdid'mã], *adv.* splendidly.

spoliateur [spolja'tœːr], *a.* (*fem.* -trice) despoiling.—*n.m.* (*fem.* -trice) spoiler, despoiler.

spoliation [spolja'sjɔ̃], *n.f.* spoliation.

spolier [spɔ'lje], *v.t.* to despoil, to plunder.

spongieux [spɔ̃'ʒjø], *a.* (*fem.* -euse) spongy.

spontané [spɔ̃ta'ne], *a.* spontaneous.

spontanéité [spɔ̃tanei'te], *n.f.* spontaneity.

spontanément [spɔ̃tane'mã], *adv.* spontaneously.

sporadique [spora'dik], *a.* sporadic.

spore [spɔːr], *n.f.* spore.

sport [spɔːr], *n.m.* games, outdoor games; *faire du sport*, to play games.

sportif [spɔr'tif], *a.* (*fem.* -tive) sporting; *réunion sportive*, athletics meeting.—*n.m.* (*fem.* -tive) athlete; devotee of out-door games; sportsman, sportswoman.

spumeux [spy'mø], *a.* (*fem.* -euse) spumy.

square [skwaːr], *n.m.* residential square with enclosed garden.

squelette [skə'lɛt], *n.m.* skeleton; carcass, frame (*of a ship*).

squelettique [skəlɛ'tik], *a.* lanky.

stabilisateur [stabiliza'tœːr], *a.* (*fem.* -trice) stabilizing.—*n.m.* (*Av., Naut.*) stabilizer.

stabiliser [stabili'ze], *v.t.* to stabilize.

stabilité [stabili'te], *n.f.* stability, durability.

stable [sta:bl], *a.* stable, firm; durable, lasting, permanent.

stade [stad], *n.m.* sports ground, stadium; (*fig.*) stage, period.

stage [staːʒ], *n.m.* term of probation, study, residence etc.; training course; (*fig.*) probation.

stagiaire [staˈʒjɛːr], *n.* probationer, trainee.

stagnant [stagˈnã], *a.* stagnant, at a standstill.

stagnation [stagnaˈsjõ], *n.f.* stagnation.

stagner [stagˈne], *v.i.* to stagnate.

stalactite [stalakˈtit], *n.f.* stalactite.

stalagmite [stalagˈmit], *n.f.* stalagmite.

stalle [stal], *n.f.* stall; box (*for horses*) (*Theat.*) stall, seat.

stance [stãːs], *n.f.* stanza.

stand [stãːd], *n.m.* rifle range; shooting gallery; stall, stand (*at exhibitions etc.*).

standard [stãˈdaːr], *n.m.* (*in house* or *office*) switchboard; standard (*of living*).

standardiser [stãdardiˈze], *v.t.* to standardize.

standardiste [stãdarˈdist], *n.* switchboard operator.

star [staːr], *n.f.* (*Cine.*) star.

starlette [starˈlɛt], *n.f.* starlet.

starter [starˈtɛːr], *n.m.* (*Motor.*) choke; (*Racing*) starter.

station [staˈsjõ], *n.f.* station, standing; stop (*of bus etc.*); taxi stand; resort.

stationnaire [stasjoˈnɛːr], *a.* stationary.

stationnement [stasjonˈmã], *n.m.* stationing, standing; parking; *stationnement interdit*, no parking, no standing.

stationner [stasjoˈne], *v.i.* to stop, to stand, to park (*of cars*).

statique [staˈtik], *a.* static.—*n.f.* statics.

statisticien [statistiˈsjɛ̃], *n.m.* statistician.

statistique [statisˈtik], *a.* statistical.—*n.f.* statistics.

statuaire [staˈtɥɛːr], *a.* statuary.—*n.* sculptor.—*n.f.* statuary (*art*).

statue [staˈty], *n.f.* statue.

statuer [staˈtɥe], *v.t.* to decree, to resolve, to ordain.—*v.i.* to give a ruling.

statuette [staˈtɥɛt], *n.f.* statuette.

stature [staˈtyːr], *n.f.* stature, height.

statut [staˈty], *n.m.* statute, ordinance, by-law; status.

statutaire [statyˈtɛːr], *a.* statutory.

stellaire [stɛlˈlɛːr], *a.* stellar, starry.

stencil [stɛnˈsil], *n.m.* stencil.

sténo [steˈno], *abbr.* of **sténographe** or **sténographie**.

sténo-dactylo(graphe) [stenodaktiˈlo(ˈgraf)], *n.* shorthand typist.

sténographe [stenoˈgraf], *n.* stenographer, shorthand writer.

sténographie [stenograˈfi], *n.f.* stenography, shorthand.

sténographier [stenograˈfje], *v.t.* to take down in shorthand.

stentor [stãˈtoːr], *n.m.* stentor; *d'une voix de stentor*, in a stentorian voice.

steppe [stɛp], *n.f.* steppe.

stéréoscope [stereosˈkɔp], *n.m.* stereoscope.

stéréotypé [stereotiˈpe], *a.* stereotyped, hackneyed.

stérile [steˈril], *a.* sterile, barren; (*fig.*) fruitless, vain.

stérilisant [steriliˈzã], *a.* sterilizing.—*n.m.* sterilizing agent.

stérilisation [steriliza·sjõ], *n.f.* sterilization.

stériliser [steriliˈze], *v.t.* to sterilize.

stérilité [steriliˈte], *n.f.* sterility, barrenness.

sterling [stɛrˈliŋ], *a. inv.* and *n.m.* sterling.

stéthoscope [stetosˈkɔp], *n.m.* stethoscope.

stigmate [stigˈmat], *n.m.* scar, stigma, stain; brand.

stigmatiser [stigmatiˈze], *v.t.* to stigmatize, to brand.

stimulant [stimyˈlã], *a.* stimulating.—*n.m.* stimulant; stimulus; incentive.

stimulation [stimylaˈsjõ], *n.f.* stimulation.

stimuler [stimyˈle], *v.t.* to stimulate; to excite, to rouse.

stipendiaire [stipãˈdjɛːr], *a.* and *n.m.* stipendiary, mercenary.

stipendié [stipãˈdje], *a.* hired.—*n.m.* stipendiary, hireling.

stipendier [stipãˈdje], *v.t.* to hire, to keep on the payroll.

stipulation [stipylaˈsjõ], *n.f.* stipulation.

stipuler [stipyˈle], *v.t.* to stipulate; to contract.

stock [stɔk], *n.m.* (*Comm.*) stock.

stocker [stɔˈke], *v.t.* to stock; to stockpile.

stockiste [stɔˈkist], *n.m.* warehouseman; dealer; agent (*for a certain make of car*); service station (*with spare parts*).

stoïcien [stɔiˈsjɛ̃], *a.* stoic, stoical.—*n.m.* (*fem.* -enne) stoic.

stoïcisme [stɔiˈsism], *n.m.* stoicism.

stoïque [stɔˈik], *a.* stoic, stoical.—*n.* stoic.

stoïquement [stɔikˈmã], *adv.* stoically.

stop [stɔp], *int.* stop!—*n.m.* (*Motor.*) stop-light.

stoppage [stɔˈpaːʒ], *n.m.* invisible mending; stoppage (*of motion, current*).

stopper [stɔˈpe], *v.t.* to mend invisibly; to stop.—*v.i.* to stop (*of a train, steamboat etc.*).

store [stɔːr], *n.m.* (*spring-roller*) blind.

strabisme [straˈbism], *n.m.* squinting.

strangulation [strãgylaˈsjõ], *n.f.* strangulation.

strapontin [strapõˈtɛ̃], *n.m.* folding seat, tip-up seat.

strass or **stras** [stras], *n.m.* strass, paste jewels.

stratagème [strataˈʒɛm], *n.m.* stratagem.

strate [strat], *n.f.* stratum.

stratégie [strateˈʒi], *n.f.* strategy.

stratégique [strateˈʒik], *a.* strategic.

stratégiquement [strateʒikˈmã], *adv.* strategically.

stratégiste [strateˈʒist], *n.m.* strategist.

stratosphère [stratosˈfɛːr], *n.f.* stratosphere.

strict [strikt], *a.* strict, precise; severe.

strictement [striktəˈmã], *adv.* strictly; severely.

strident [striˈdã], *a.* strident, jarring.

strié [striˈe], *a.* striate, streaked; corrugated; scored.

strontium [strõˈsjɔm], *n.m.* strontium.

strophe [strɔf], *n.f.* strophe; stanza.

structural [stryktyˈral], *a.* (*m. pl.* -aux) structural.

structure [strykˈtyːr], *n.f.* structure; form, make.

strychnine [strikˈnin], *n.f.* strychnin(e).

stuc [styk], *n.m.* stucco.

stucage [styˈkaːʒ], *n.m.* stucco-work.

studieusement [stydjøzˈmã], *adv.* studiously.

studieux [styˈdjø], *a.* (*fem.* -euse) studious.

studio [styˈdjo], *n.m.* (*Cine.*) film studio; (*Rad., Tel.*) broadcasting studio; one-room flat.

stupéfaction

stupéfaction [stypefak'sjɔ̃], *n.f.* stupefaction, amazement.
stupéfait [stype'fɛ], *a.* amazed, dumbfounded.
stupéfiant [stype'fjɑ̃], *a.* stupefactive; amazing, astounding.—*n.m.* narcotic.
stupéfier [stype'fje], *v.t.* to stupefy, to astound, to dumbfound.
stupeur [sty'pœːr], *n.f.* stupor; amazement.
stupide [sty'pid], *a.* stunned; stupid, foolish, dull.
stupidement [stypid'mɑ̃], *adv.* stupidly.
stupidité [stypidi'te], *n.f.* stupidity.
style (1) [stil], *n.m.* style.
style (2) [stil], *n.m.* stylus.
stylé [sti'le], *a.* stylate; (*colloq.*) trained, taught, clever.
styler [sti'le], *v.t.* to train, to form, to school.
stylet [sti'lɛ], *n.m.* stiletto; (*Surg.*) probe.
stylo [sti'lo], *abbr. of* **stylographe** [stilo'graf], *n.m.* fountain pen; *stylo à bille*, ballpoint pen.
stylomine [stilo'min], *n.m.* mechanical pencil.
styptique [stip'tik], *a.* and *n.m.* styptic.
su (1) [sy], *n.m.* knowledge; *au vu et au su de tout le monde*, as everybody knows.
su (2) [sy], *p.p.* [SAVOIR].
suaire [sɥɛːr], *n.m.* winding sheet, shroud.
suant [sɥɑ̃], *a.* sweating, in a sweat.
suave [sɥaːv], *a.* sweet, agreeable; suave, bland; soft.
suavement [sɥav'mɑ̃], *adv.* suavely; sweetly.
suavité [sɥavi'te], *n.f.* suavity; sweetness.
subalterne [sybal'tɛrn], *a.* and *n.* subaltern; subordinate; inferior.
subdiviser [sybdivi'ze], *v.t.* to subdivide. **se subdiviser**, *v.r.* to be subdivided.
subdivision [sybdivi'zjɔ̃], *n.f.* subdivision.
subir [sy'biːr], *v.t.* to support; to go through, to undergo, to suffer; to submit to.
subit [sy'bit], *a.* sudden, unexpected.
subitement [sybit'mɑ̃], *adv.* suddenly, all of a sudden.
subjectif [sybʒɛk'tif], *a.* (*fem.* **-tive**) subjective.
subjection [sybʒɛk'sjɔ̃], *n.f.* subjection.
subjectivement [sybʒɛktiv'mɑ̃], *adv.* subjectively.
subjonctif [sybʒɔ̃k'tif], *a.* (*fem.* **-tive**) and *n.m.* subjunctive.
subjugation [sybʒyga'sjɔ̃], *n.f.* subjugation.
subjuguer [sybʒy'ge], *v.t.* to subjugate, to subdue.
sublimation [syblima'sjɔ̃], *n.f.* sublimation.
sublime [sy'blim], *a.* lofty, sublime, splendid.—*n.m.* the sublime.
sublimement [syblim'mɑ̃], *adv.* sublimely.
submerger [sybmɛr'ʒe], *v.t.* (*conjug. like* MANGER) to submerge, to swamp, to flood; (*fig.*) to overwhelm.
submersible [sybmɛr'sibl], *a.* submersible.—*n.m.* submarine (*boat*).
submersion [sybmɛr'sjɔ̃], *n.f.* submersion.
subordination [sybordina'sjɔ̃], *n.f.* subordination.
subordonné [sybordo'ne], *a.* and *n.m.* (*fem.* **-ée**) subordinate, dependent.
subordonner [sybordo'ne], *v.t.* to subordinate.
suborner [sybor'ne], *v.t.* to suborn, to bribe.
suborneur [sybor'nœːr], *a.* (*fem.* **-euse**)

suborning, bribing.—*n.m.* (*fem.* **-euse** suborner, briber.
subreptice [sybrɛp'tis], *a.* surreptitious.
subrepticement [sybrɛptis'mɑ̃], *adv.* surreptitiously.
subséquemment [sybseka'mɑ̃], *adv.* subsequently.
subséquent [sybse'kɑ̃], *a.* subsequent.
subside [syb'sid], *n.m.* subsidy; (*colloq.*) aid.
subsidiaire [sybsi'djɛːr], *a.* subsidiary, auxiliary.
subsidiairement [sybsidjɛr'mɑ̃], *adv.* further, also, additionally.
subsistance [sybzis'tɑ̃ːs], *n.f.* subsistence, sustenance, maintenance; (*pl.*) provisions.
subsistant [sybzis'tɑ̃], *a.* subsisting, existing
subsister [sybzis'te], *v.i.* to subsist, to stand; to hold good; to exist, to live.
substance [sybs'tɑ̃ːs], *n.f.* substance.
substantiel [sybstɑ̃'sjɛl], *a.* (*fem.* **-elle**) substantial.
substantiellement [sybstɑ̃sjɛl'mɑ̃], *adv.* substantially.
substantif [sybstɑ̃'tif], *a.* (*fem.* **-tive**) substantive.—*n.m.* (*Gram.*) noun.
substituer [sybsti'tɥe], *v.t.* to substitute; (*Law*) to entail.
substitut [sybsti'ty], *n.m.* substitute, deputy (*to someone*).
substitution [sybstity'sjɔ̃], *n.f.* substitution; (*Law*) entail.
subterfuge [sybtɛr'fy:ʒ], *n.m.* subterfuge, evasion, shift.
subtil [syb'til], *a.* subtile, tenuous; penetrating; acute, keen, sharp; cunning; fine-spun, subtle.
subtilement [sybtil'mɑ̃], *adv.* subtly, craftily.
subtiliser [sybtili'ze], *v.t.* to subtilize, to refine; (*colloq.*) to sneak, to steal.
subtilité [sybtili'te], *n.f.* subtlety, fineness; acuteness; shrewdness.
suburbain [sybyr'bɛ̃], *a.* suburban.
subvenir [sybvə'niːr], *v.i. irr.* (*conjug. like* TENIR) to be helpful; to supply, to provide.
subvention [sybvɑ̃'sjɔ̃], *n.f.* subsidy, aid.
subventionner [sybvɑ̃sjɔ'ne], *v.t.* to subsidize, to make a grant to.
subversif [sybvɛr'sif], *a.* (*fem.* **-sive**) subversive.
subversion [sybvɛr'sjɔ̃], *n.f.* subversion, overthrow.
suc [syk], *n.m.* juice; (*fig.*) essence, quintessence.
succéder [sykse'de], *v.i.* (*conjug. like* CÉDER) to succeed, to follow after (*à*). **se succéder**, *v.r.* to succeed each other.
succès [syk'sɛ], *n.m.* success.
successeur [sykse'sœːr], *n.m.* successor.
successif [sykse'sif], *a.* (*fem.* **-ive**) successive, in succession.
succession [sykse'sjɔ̃], *n.f.* succession; inheritance; heritage, estate.
successivement [syksesiv'mɑ̃], *adv.* successively, in succession.
succinct [syk'sɛ̃], *a.* succinct, concise.
succinctement [syksɛt'mɑ̃], *adv.* succinctly, briefly.
succion [syk'sjɔ̃], *n.f.* suction.
succomber [sykɔ̃'be], *v.i.* to sink, to faint; to yield, to succumb; to fail; to die.
succulence [syky'lɑ̃ːs], *n.f.* succulence.
succulent [syky'lɑ̃], *a.* succulent, juicy; rich.

succursale [sykyr'sal], *n.f.* branch (*of a bank etc.*).

sucement [sys'mã], *n.m.* sucking, suck.

sucer [sy'se], *v.t.* (*conjug. like* COMMENCER) to suck, to suck in; to imbibe.

sucette [sy'sɛt], *n.f.* lollipop; pacifier (*for baby*).

suceur [sy'sœːr], *a.* (*fem.* **-euse**) sucking.— *n.m.* sucker; nozzle (*of a vacuum cleaner*).

suçoir [sy'swaːr], *n.m.* sucker.

sucre [sykr], *n.m.* sugar; *sucre cristallisé*, granulated sugar; *sucre d'orge*, barley-sugar; *sucre en poudre*, powdered sugar.

sucré [sy'kre], *a.* sugared, sweet, sugary; (*fig.*) demure, prim.

sucrer [sy'kre], *v.t.* to sugar, to sweeten.

sucrerie [sykrə'ri], *n.f.* sugar refinery; (*pl.*) sweets.

sucrier [sykri'e], *n.m.* sugar bowl; sugar maker.

sud [syd], *a. inv.* south, southerly (*of the wind*).—*n.m.* south; south wind.

sud-est [sy'dɛst], *a. inv.* and *n.m.* south-east.

Sudètes [sy'dɛt], **les**, *m. pl.* Sudetenland.

sud-ouest [sy'dwɛst], *a. inv.* and *n.m.* south-west.

Suède [sųɛd], **la**, *f.* Sweden.

suède [sųɛd], *n.m.* suede (*glove leather*).

suédois [sųe'dwa], *a.* Swedish.—*n.m.* Swedish (*language*); (**Suédois**, *fem.* **-oise**) Swede.

suée [sųe], *n.f.* sweating.

suer [sųe], *v.t.* to sweat.—*v.i.* to sweat, to perspire; (*fig.*) to toil, to drudge; to ooze (*of walls*).

sueur [sųœːr], *n.f.* sweat, perspiration; (*pl.*) labor, toil.

suffire [sy'fiːr], *v.i. irr.* to suffice, to be sufficient; to be adequate; *cela suffit*, that's enough. **se suffire**, *v.r.* to provide for oneself.

suffisamment [syfiza'mã], *adv.* sufficiently.

suffisance [syfi'zãːs], *n.f.* sufficiency, adequacy; conceit, self-sufficiency.

suffisant [syfi'zã], *a.* sufficient; conceited.— *n.m.* (*fem.* **-e**) conceited person.

suffixe [sy'fiks], *n.m.* suffix.

suffocant [syfɔ'kã], *a.* suffocating, choking.

suffocation [syfɔka'sjõ], *n.f.* suffocation.

suffoquer [syfɔ'ke], *v.t.* to suffocate, to choke.—*v.i.* to choke.

suffrage [sy'fraː3], *n.m.* suffrage, vote; approbation, commendation.

suggérer [syg3e're], *v.t.* (*conjug. like* CÉDER) to suggest.

suggestif [syg3ɛs'tif], *a.* (*fem.* **-tive**) suggestive; erotic.

suggestion [syg3ɛs'tjõ], *n.f.* suggestion, hint, instigation.

suicide [sųi'sid], *n.m.* suicide.

suicidé [sųisi'de], *n.m.* (*fem.* **-ée**) suicide.

suicider (**se**) [səsųisi'de], *v.r.* to commit suicide.

suie [sųi], *n.f.* soot.

suif [sųif], *n.m.* tallow.

suintement [sųɛ̃t'mã], *n.m.* oozing, sweating.

suinter [sųɛ̃'te], *v.i.* to ooze, to sweat (*of walls etc.*); to leak, to run (*of vessels*).

Suisse [sųis], **la**, *f.* Switzerland.

suisse [sųis], *a.* Swiss.—*n.m.* porter (*of a mansion*); church officer; (**Suisse**, *fem.* **Suissesse**) Swiss (*person*).

suite [sųit], *n.f.* the rest; retinue, attendants; sequel, continuation; series; set; connection; result; *à la suite*, after, behind; *de suite*, consecutively; *et ainsi de suite*, and so on; *tout de suite*, immediately.

suivant [sųi'vã], *prep.* according to; in the direction of; *suivant que*, as, according as. —*a.* next, following, subsequent.—*n.m.* (*fem.* **-e**) follower, attendant.—*n.f.* (**-e**) lady's maid.

suivi [sųi'vi], *a.* followed; connected; consistent; popular.

suivre [sųiːvr], *v.t. irr.* to follow; to be next to; to attend; to observe; to pursue; to practise (*a profession etc.*).—*v.i.* to follow; to come after; to result, to ensue; *à faire suivre*, to be forwarded; *à suivre*, to be continued. **se suivre**, *v.r.* to follow each other, to be continuous.

sujet [sy'3ɛ], *a.* (*fem.* **-ette**) subject, subjected, liable, exposed; apt, addicted, inclined (*à*).—*n.m.* subject; topic; cause.

sujétion [sy3e'sjõ], *n.f.* subjection, servitude, constraint.

sulfate [syl'fat], *n.m.* sulphate.

sulfureux [sylfy'rø], *a.* (*fem.* **-euse**) sulphurous, sulphureous.

sulfurique [sylfy'rik], *a.* sulphuric (*acid*).

sultan [syl'tã], *n.m.* sultan.

sultane [syl'tan], *n.f.* sultana, sultaness.

sumac [sy'mak], *n.m.* sumac.

superbe [sy'pɛrb], *a.* proud, arrogant; superb; stately; lofty; vainglorious.—*n.* proud person.—*n.f.* arrogance; vainglory.

superbement [sypɛrbə'mã], *adv.* haughtily, superbly.

supercarburant [sypɛrkarby'rã], *n.m.* high-octane gasoline.

supercherie [sypɛrʃə'ri], *n.f.* deceit, fraud.

superficie [sypɛrfi'si], *n.f.* area, surface; (*fig.*) superficiality.

superficiel [sypɛrfi'sjɛl], *a.* (*fem.* **-elle**) superficial; shallow.

superficiellement [sypɛrfisjɛl'mã], *adv.* superficially.

superfin [sypɛr'fɛ̃], *a.* superfine, of superior quality.

superflu [sypɛr'fly], *a.* superfluous; unnecessary.—*n.m.* superfluity, excess.

superfluité [sypɛrflųi'te], *n.f.* superfluity.

supérieur [sype'rjœːr], *a.* superior; upper, higher.—*n.m.* (*fem.* **-e**) superior.

supérieurement [syperjœr'mã], *adv.* in a superior manner; superlatively.

supériorité [syperjori'te], *n.f.* superiority.

superlatif [sypɛrla'tif], *a.* (*fem.* **-tive**) superlative.—*n.m.* (*Gram.*) superlative.

superlativement [sypɛrlativ'mã], *adv.* superlatively.

superposer [sypɛrpo'ze], *v.t.* to superpose; to superimpose.

superposition [sypɛrpozi'sjõ], *n.f.* superposition; superimposition.

supersonique [sypɛrsɔ'nik], *a.* supersonic.

superstitieusement [sypɛrstisjøz'mã], *adv.* superstitiously.

superstitieux [sypɛrsti'sjø], *a.* (*fem.* **-euse**) superstitious.

superstition [sypɛrsti'sjõ], *n.f.* superstition.

superstructure [sypɛrstryk'tyːr], *n.f.* superstructure; right of way (*of railway*).

supin [sy'pɛ̃], *n.m.* (*Gram.*) supine.

305

supplantation [syplāta′sjɔ̃], *n.f.* supplantation; supersession.

supplanter [syplā′te], *v.t.* to supplant, to oust, to supersede.

suppléance [syple′ā:s], *n.f.* substitution, deputyship.

suppléant [syple′ā], *a.* and *n.m.* (*fem.* -e) substitute, assistant, deputy, understudy.

suppléer [syple′e], *v.t.* to supply, to fill up; to take the place of.—*v.i.* to make up the deficiency, to compensate for (*à*).

supplément [syple′mā], *n.m.* supplement; additional price, excess fare.

supplémentaire [syplemā′tɛ:r], *a.* supplementary, supplemental, additional, extra.

suppliant [sypli′ā], *a.* suppliant, beseeching. —*n.m.* (*fem.* -e) suppliant, supplicant, petitioner.

supplication [syplika′sjɔ̃], *n.f.* supplication, entreaty.

supplice [sy′plis], *n.m.* corporal punishment; torture; (*fig.*) torment, ordeal; *être au supplice*, to be upon the rack.

supplicié [sypli′sje], *n.m.* (*fem.* -ée) executed criminal.

supplicier [sypli′sje], *v.t.* to put to death, to execute.

supplier [sypli′e], *v.t.* to beseech, to entreat, to beg.

supplique [sy′plik], *n.f.* petition, entreaty.

support [sy′pɔ:r], *n.m.* support, prop; rest, stand, bracket.

supportable [sypor′tabl], *a.* supportable, bearable, tolerable.

supportablement [syportabla′mā], *adv.* tolerably.

supporter (1) [sypor′tœ:r], *n.m.* (*Spt.*) supporter, partisan.

supporter (2) [sypor′te], *v.t.* to support, to uphold; to endure, to suffer; to stand. **se supporter**, *v.r.* to be borne; to bear with each other.

supposable [sypo′zabl], *a.* supposable.

supposé [sypo′ze], *a.* pretended, forged, assumed; reputed.

supposer [sypo′ze], *v.t.* to suppose; to admit, to imply; to conjecture; to forge (*a will*).

supposition [sypozi′sjɔ̃], *n.f.* supposition; substitution; forgery.

suppôt [sy′po], *n.m.* agent, tool, abettor.

suppressif [sypre′sif], *a.* (*fem.* -ive) suppressive.

suppression [sypre′sjɔ̃], *n.f.* suppression; cancelling (*of passage*); concealment.

supprimer [sypri′me], *v.t.* to suppress; to omit; to abolish, to cancel.

suppuration [sypyra′sjɔ̃], *n.f.* suppuration.

suppurer [sypy′re], *v.i.* to suppurate, to run.

supputation [sypyta′sjɔ̃], *n.f.* computation, calculation.

supputer [sypy′te], *v.t.* to calculate, to compute, to reckon.

suprématie [syprema′si], *n.f.* supremacy.

suprême [sy′prɛ:m], *a.* supreme, highest; last.

suprêmement [syprɛma′mā], *adv.* supremely.

sur (1) [syr], *prep.* on, upon; over; in; towards; about; concerning; out of.

sur (2) [sy:r], *a.* sour, tart.

sûr [sy:r], *a.* sure, certain; safe, secure; firm, steady; trustworthy; *à coup sûr*, for certain; *en lieu sûr*, in a place of safety; *je suis sûr de vous*, I can depend on you; *sûr et certain*, positive.

surabondamment [syrabɔ̃da′mā], *adv.* superabundantly.

surabondance [syrabɔ̃′dā:s], *n.f.* superabundance; glut.

surabondant [syrabɔ̃′dā], *a.* superabundant.

surabonder [syrabɔ̃′de], *v.i.* to superabound; to be glutted (*de*).

suraigu [syre′gy], *a.* (*fem.* -ë) overshrill; very acute (*inflammation*).

suralimenté [syralimā′te], *a.* overfed.

suralimenter [syralimā′te], *v.t.* to overfeed, to feed up; (*Motor.*) to supercharge.

suranné [syra′ne], *a.* expired; superannuated, antiquated.

surcharge [syr′ʃarʒ], *n.f.* overloading; (*stamp*) surcharge; excess.

surcharger [syrʃar′ʒe], *v.t.* (*conjug. like* MANGER) to overload, to overtax; (*fig.*) to overwhelm; to oppress; *surcharger d'impôts*, to overtax.

surchauffer [syrʃo′fe], *v.t.* to overheat.

surclasser [syrkla′se], *v.t.* to outclass.

surcompresseur [syrkɔ̃prɛ′sœ:r], *n.m.* supercharger.

surcompression [syrkɔ̃prɛ′sjɔ̃], *n.f.* supercharging.

surcomprimé [syrkɔ̃pri′me], *a.* supercharged.

surcroît [syr′krwa], *n.m.* addition, increase; surplus, excess.

surcuit [syr′kɥi], *a.* overdone.

surdité [syrdi′te], *n.f.* deafness.

sureau [sy′ro], *n.m.* (*pl.* -eaux) elder (tree).

surélever [syrel′ve], *v.t.* (*conjug. like* AMENER) to raise higher; (*Golf*) to tee.

sûrement [syr′mā], *adv.* surely, certainly, to be sure; safely.

surenchère [syrā′ʃɛ:r], *n.f.* higher bid, outbidding.

surenchérir [syrāʃe′ri:r], *v.i.* to overbid; to bid higher.

surestimation [syrɛstima′sjɔ̃], *n.f.* overestimate, overvaluation.

surestimer [syrɛsti′me], *v.t.* to overestimate; to overrate.

sûreté [syr′te], *n.f.* safety, security; warranty; *la Sûreté*, Criminal Investigation Department.

surexcitation [syrɛksita′sjɔ̃], *n.f.* excitement, overexcitement.

surexciter [syrɛksi′te], *v.t.* to overexcite.

surexposer [syrɛkspo′ze], *v.t.* (*Phot.*) to overexpose.

surexposition [syrɛkspozi′sjɔ̃], *n.f.* (*Phot.*) overexposure.

surface [syr′fas], *n.f.* surface; outside.

surfaire [syr′fɛ:r], *v.t. irr.* (*conjug. like* FAIRE) to ask too much for; to overrate, to overpraise.

surfin [syr′fɛ̃], *a.* (*Comm.*) superfine.

surgir [syr′ʒi:r], *v.i.* to rise, to surge; to loom up.

surgissement [syrʒis′mā], *n.m.* upheaval.

surhomme [sy′rom], *n.m.* superman.

surhumain [syry′mɛ̃], *a.* superhuman.

surintendant [syrɛ̃tā′dā], *n.m.* superintendent, overseer; steward (*of large estate*).

surintendante [syrɛ̃tā′dā:t], *n.f.* woman superintendent; superintendent's wife.

surir [sy′ri:r], *v.i.* to turn sour.

sur-le-champ [syrla′ʃā], *adv.* at once.

sympathique

surlendemain [syrlãd'mɛ̃], n.m. two days after.
surmenage [syrmə'na:ʒ], n.m. excess fatigue; overworking.
surmener [syrmə'ne], v.t. (conjug. like AMENER) to overwork, to overtire. **se surmener**, v.r. to overwork.
surmontable [syrmɔ̃'tabl], a. surmountable, superable.
surmonter [syrmɔ̃'te], v.t. to surmount; to overcome, to surpass.
surmultiplication [syrmyltiplika'sjɔ̃], n.f. (Motor.) overdrive.
surnager [syrna'ʒe], v.i. (conjug. like MANGER) to float on the surface; (fig.) to survive.
surnaturel [syrnaty'rɛl], a. (fem. -elle) supernatural.—n.m. supernatural.
surnaturellement [syrnatyrɛl mã], adv. supernaturally.
surnom [syr'nɔ̃], n.m. nickname.
surnommer [syrnɔ'me], v.t. to nickname.
surnuméraire [syrnyme'rɛ:r], a. and n.m. supernumerary.
surpasser [syrpɑ'se], v.t. to surpass, to excel, to outdo; to exceed.
surpeuplé [syrpœ'ple], a. overpopulated.
surpeuplement [syrpœplə'mã], n.m. overpopulation, overcrowding.
surplis [syr'pli], n.m. inv. surplice.
surplomb [syr'plɔ̃], n.m. overhang (of buildings); **en surplomb**, overhanging.
surplomber [syrplɔ̃'be], v.t., v.i. to overhang.
surplus [syr'ply], n.m. inv. surplus, remainder, excess.
surpoids [syr'pwa], n.m. overweight, excess weight.
surprenant [syrprə'nã], a. surprising, astonishing.
surprendre [syr'prã:dr], v.t. irr. (conjug. like PRENDRE) to surprise, to catch, to overhear; to entrap; to intercept. **se surprendre**, v.r. to surprise oneself; to catch oneself (napping etc.).
surprise [syr'pri:z], n.f. surprise; amazement.
surproduction [syrprɔdyk'sjɔ̃], n.f. overproduction.
surréalisme [syrrea'lism], n.m. surrealism.
surréaliste [syrrea'list], a. and n. surrealist.
sursaut [syr'so], n.m. start, jump.
sursauter [syrso'te], v.i. to start up; **faire sursauter (quelqu'un)**, to startle (someone).
surseoir [syr'swa:r], v.t., v.i. irr. to suspend, to delay, to postpone.
sursis [syr'si], n.m. delay, respite, reprieve.
surtaxe [syr'taks], n.f. surtax; surcharge.
surtaxer [syrtak'se], v.t. to overtax.
surtout [syr'tu], adv. above all, chiefly.—n.m. overcoat; centrepiece (for table).
surveillance [syrvɛ'jã:s], n.f. supervision; surveillance.
surveillant [syrvɛ'jã], n.m. (fem. -e) inspector, superintendent; supervisor.
surveiller [syrvɛ'je], v.t. to superintend, to inspect; to watch, to supervise.
survenir [syrvə'ni:r], v.i. irr. (conjug. like TENIR, but with aux. ÊTRE) to arrive or happen unexpectedly; to drop in.
survêtement [syrvɛt'mã], n.m. (Spt.) track suit.

survivant [syrvi'vã], a. surviving.—n.m. (fem. -e) survivor.
survivre [syr'vi:vr], v.i. irr. (conjug. like VIVRE) to survive, to outlive someone (à). **se survivre**, v.r. to live or exist again.
survoler [syrvɔ'le], v.t. to fly over (of aircraft).
sus [sys], prep. upon; **en sus**, over and above. —int. courage! come on!
susceptibilité [syseptibili'te], n.f. susceptibility; irritability.
susceptible [sysɛp'tibl], a. susceptible, capable; likely to; touchy; irascible.
susciter [sysi'te], v.t. to raise up, to set up; to create; to arouse, to instigate.
suscription [syskrip'sjɔ̃], n.f. superscription, address.
susdit [sys'di], a. and n.m. (fem. -e) aforesaid.
suspect [sys'pɛkt, sys'pɛ], a. suspected, suspicious, suspect, doubtful.—n.m. suspect.
suspecter [syspɛk'te], v.t. to suspect.
suspendre [sys'pã:dr], v.t. to suspend, to hang up; to delay, to defer.
suspendu [syspã'dy], a. suspended, hung up; in suspense.
suspens [sys'pã], adv. phr. **en suspens**, in suspense; (person) in doubt; (thing) in abeyance.
suspension [syspã'sjɔ̃], n.f. suspension, interruption; hanging lamp.
suspicion [syspi'sjɔ̃], n.f. suspicion.
susurration [sysyra'sjɔ̃], n.f., **susurrement** [sysyr'mã], n.m. susurration, whispering, murmur; rustling.
suttée [sy'te], **suttie** [sy'ti], n.f. suttee.
suture [sy'ty:r], n.f. suture; joint; stitching.
Suzanne [sy'zan], f. Susan.
suzerain [syz're], a. paramount, suzerain.—n.m. (fem. -e) suzerain, lord or lady paramount.
suzeraineté [syzrɛn'te], n.f. suzerainty.
svastika [zvasti'ka], n.m. swastika.
svelte [zvɛlt], a. slender, slim.
sveltesse [zvɛl'tɛs], n.f. slenderness, slimness.
sybarite [siba'rit], a. sybaritic.—n. sybarite, voluptuary.
sycomore [sikɔ'mɔ:r], n.m. sycamore.
sycophante [sikɔ'fã:t], a. sycophantic.—n.m. informer; hypocrite, impostor; sycophant, (fam.) toady.
syllabe [sil'lab], n.f. syllable.
syllabique [silla'bik], a. syllabic.
syllogisme [sillɔ'ʒism], n.m. syllogism.
sylphe [silf], n.m., **sylphide** [sil'fid], n.f. sylph.
sylvain [sil've], n.m. sylvan.
sylvestre [sil'vɛstr], a. sylvan, growing in woods.
Sylvie [sil'vi], f. Sylvia.
symbole [sɛ̃'bɔl], n.m. symbol, sign, emblem; creed.
symbolique [sɛ̃bɔ'lik], a. symbolic, symbolical.
symboliser [sɛ̃bɔli'ze], v.t. to symbolize.
symbolisme [sɛ̃bɔ'lism], n.m. symbolism.
symétrie [sime'tri], n.f. symmetry.
symétrique [sime'trik], a. symmetrical.
symétriquement [simetrik'mã], adv. symmetrically.
sympathie [sɛ̃pa'ti], n.f. liking, fellow feeling.
sympathique [sɛ̃pa'tik], a. congenial, likeable.

307

sympathisant [sɛpati'zɑ̃], *a.* sympathizing.—*n.m.* (*Pol.*) fellow traveller.

sympathiser [sɛpati'ze], *v.i.* to get on well together.

symphonie [sɛfo'ni], *n.f.* symphony.

symptomatique [sɛ̃ptoma'tik], *a.* symptomatic.

symptôme [sɛ̃p'to:m], *n.m.* symptom; indication, sign; token.

synagogue [sina'gɔg], *n.f.* synagogue.

synchronisation [sɛ̃kroniza'sjɔ̃], *n.f.* synchronization.

synchroniser [sɛ̃kroni'ze], *v.t.* to synchronize.

syncope [sɛ̃'kɔp], *n.f.* syncope, swoon, fainting fit; (*Mus.*) syncopation.

syndic [sɛ̃'dik], *n.m.* syndic, trustee; assignee (*in bankruptcy*).

syndicalisme [sɛ̃dika'lism], *n.m.* **syndicalisme ouvrier**, trade-unionism.

syndicaliste [sɛ̃dika'list], *a.* and *n.* trade-unionist.

syndicat [sɛ̃di'ka], *n.m.* syndicate, trusteeship; **syndicat d'initiative**, tourists' information bureau; **syndicat ouvrier**, trade union.

synonyme [sino'nim], *a.* synonymous.—*n.m.* synonym.

syntaxe [sɛ̃'taks], *n.f.* syntax.

synthétique [sɛ̃te'tik], *a.* synthetic.

syriaque [si'rjak], *a.* Syriac.—*n.m.* Syriac (*language*).

Syrie [si'ri], **la**, *f.* Syria.

syrien [si'rjɛ̃], *a.* Syrian.—*n.m.* Syrian (*language*); (**Syrien**, *fem.* **-enne**) Syrian (*person*).

systématique [sistema'tik], *a.* systematic(al).

systématiquement [sistematik'mɑ̃], *adv.* systematically.

système [sis'tɛm], *n.m.* system, scheme, plan; device.

T

T, t [te], *n.m.* the twentieth letter of the alphabet.

t' [t], *elision* [TE].

ta [ta], [TON (1)].

tabac [ta'ba], *n.m.* tobacco; snuff.

tabatière [taba'tjɛːr], *n.f.* snuff box.

tabernacle [tabɛr'nakl], *n.m.* tent; tabernacle.

table [tabl], *n.f.* table; board (*food, fare*); mess (*of officers etc.*); slab; face (*of anvil etc.*); table of contents etc.; **faire table rase**, to make a clean sweep; **mettre** or **dresser la table**, to lay the table.

tableau [ta'blo], *n.m.* (*pl.* **-eaux**) picture, painting, tableau; scene; description; list; blackboard.

tablée [ta'ble], *n.f.* company at table.

tablette [ta'blɛt], *n.f.* shelf; tablet; slab, bar (*of chocolate*); (*Pharm.*) lozenge; note-book.

tablier [ta'blje], *n.m.* apron (*in all senses*); chess or checker board.

tabou [ta'bu], *a.* and *n.m.* taboo.

tabouret [tabu'rɛ], *n.m.* stool, foot-stool.

tabourin [tabu'rɛ̃], *n.m.* chimney cowl.

tabulateur [tabyla'tœːr], *n.m.* tabulator; (*Teleph.*) dial.

tachant [ta'ʃɑ̃], *a.* easily soiled.

tache [taʃ], *n.f.* spot, stain; (*fig.*) blot.

tâche [tɑːʃ], *n.f.* task, job.

tacher [ta'ʃe], *v.t.* to stain, to spot; (*fig.*) to taint.

tâcher [tɑ'ʃe], *v.i.* to try, to endeavor, to strive.

tacheter [taʃ'te], *v.t.* (*conjug. like* APPELER) to fleck, to speckle, to mottle.

tacite [ta'sit], *a.* tacit, implied.

tacitement [tasit'mɑ̃], *adv.* tacitly.

taciturne [tasi'tyrn], *a.* taciturn.

taciturnité [tasityrni'te], *n.f.* taciturnity.

tact [takt], *n.m.* feeling, touch; tact.

tacticien [takti'sjɛ̃], *n.m.* tactician.

tactile [tak'til], *a.* tactile.

tactilité [taktili'te], *n.f.* tactility.

tactique [tak'tik], *a.* tactical.—*n.f.* tactics; (*fig.*) stratagem, move.

taffetas [taf'ta], *n.m.* taffeta.

taie (1) [tɛ], *n.f.* **taie d'oreiller**, pillow-case.

taie (2) [tɛ], *n.f.* film, speck (*in the eye*).

taillade [ta'jad], *n.f.* slash, gash, cut.

taillader [taja'de], *v.t.* to slash, to cut, to gash.

taillant [ta'jɑ̃], *n.m.* edge (*of a knife etc.*).

taille [tɑːj], *n.f.* cutting, cut, fashion; edge (*of a sword*); height, stature; waist, figure; (*Hort.*) pruning; **de taille à**, quite capable of.

taillé [ta'je], *a.* cut, carved; well-built (*person*).

taille-crayon [tajkrɛ'jɔ̃], *n.m.* (*pl.* **-crayons**) pencil sharpener.

taille-ongles [taj'ɔ̃:gl], *n.m. inv.* nail clippers.

tailler [ta'je], *v.t.* to cut, to cut out; to carve; to hew; to prune; to sharpen; to shape; to deal (*cards*).

tailleur [ta'jœːr], *n.m.* tailor; cutter; hewer; (*woman's two-piece*) suit.

tailleuse [ta'jøːz], *n.f.* tailoress.

taillis [ta'ji], *n.m. inv.* copse; brushwood.

tain [tɛ̃], *n.m.* foil; silvering (*for mirrors*).

taire [tɛːr], *v.t. irr.* to say nothing of, to pass over in silence, to suppress, to keep dark. **se taire**, *v.r.* to be silent; to remain unsaid.

talc [talk], *n.m.* talc, talcum powder.

talent [ta'lɑ̃], *n.m.* talent; (*fig.*) ability.

talion [ta'ljɔ̃], *n.m.* talion, retaliation.

talisman [talis'mɑ̃], *n.m.* talisman.

taloche [ta'lɔʃ], *n.f.* cuff, thump, buffet.

talocher [talo'ʃe], *v.t.* to cuff, to box (*someone's*) ears.

talon [ta'lɔ̃], *n.m.* heel; counterfoil, stub.

talonner [talo'ne], *v.t.* to be close on the heels of; to press hard, to spur.—*v.i.* (*Naut.*) to ground; (*Ftb.*) to heel out (*of the scrum*).

talonneur [talo'nœːr], *n.m.* (*Ftb.*) hooker.

talus [ta'ly], *n.m.* slope, ramp; embankment.

taluter [taly'ta:3], *n.m.* sloping, embanking.

tamarin [tama'rɛ̃], *n.m.* tamarind.

tamaris [tama'ris], **tamarisc** [tama'risk], *n.m.* tamarisk.

tambour [tɑ̃'buːr], *n.m.* drum; drummer; embroidery frame; (*Anat.*) tympanum; **tambour de ville**, town crier.

tambourin [tɑ̃bu'rɛ̃], *n.m.* Provençal tabor.

tambourinage [tɑ̃buri'naːʒ], *n.m.* drumming.

tambouriner [tɑ̃buri'ne], *v.t.* to advertise.—*v.i.* to drum, to tattoo.

tambour-major [tăburma'ʒɔːr], *n.m.* (*pl.* **tambours-majors**) drum major.

tamis [ta'mi], *n.m. inv.* sieve, sifter, strainer.

tamisage [tami'za:ʒ], *n.m.* sifting, straining.

Tamise [ta'mi:z], **la**, *f.* the Thames.

tamiser [tami'ze], *v.t.* to sift, to strain; to filter.

tamiseur [tami'zœːr], *n.m.* (*fem.* **-euse**) sifter.

tampon [tã'põ], *n.m.* stopper; plug; bung; buffer; pad (*used in engraving etc.*).

tamponnement [tãpɔn'mã], *n.m.* plugging, stopping; (*Rail.*) head-on collision.

tamponner [tãpɔ'ne], *v.t.* to plug, to stop up; to run into (*another train etc.*). **se tamponner**, *v.r.* to collide.

tan [tã], *a. inv.* tan(-colored). —*n.m.* tan, tanner's bark.

tancer [tã'se], *v.t.* (*conjug. like* COMMENCER) to rate, to lecture, to scold.

tanche [tã:ʃ], *n.f.* tench.

tandem [tã'dɛm], *n.m.* tandem.

tandis [tã'di] que, *conj. phr.* while; whereas.

tangage [tã'ga:ʒ], *n.m.* pitching (*of ship, airplane*).

tangent [tã'ʒã], *a.* tangential. —*n.f.* (**-e**) tangent.

tangible [tã'ʒibl], *a.* tangible.

tangiblement [tãʒiblə'mã], *adv.* tangibly.

tangue [tã:g], *n.f.* slimy sand (*used as manure*).

tanguer [tã'ge], *v.i.* (*Naut.*) to pitch.

tanière [ta'njɛːr], *n.f.* den, hole, lair (*of beasts*).

tank [tãk], *n.m.* (*Mil.*) tank.

tannage [ta'na:ʒ], *n.m.* tanning.

tannant [ta'nã], *a.* tanning; (*pop.*) tiresome, annoying.

tanné [ta'ne], *a.* tanned, sunburnt (*skin*); tawny. —*n.m.* tan (*color*).

tanner [ta'ne], *v.t.* to tan; (*pop.*) to tease; to beat.

tannerie [tan'ri], *n.f.* tan-yard, tannery.

tanneur [ta'nœːr], *n.m.* tanner.

tant [tã], *adv.* so much, such; so many; as much, as many; to such a degree, so; so far; so long, as long: *tant bien que mal*, somehow or other, after a fashion; *tant pis*, too bad, never mind.

tantaliser [tãtali'ze], *v.t.* to tantalize.

tante [tã:t], *n.f.* aunt; (*pop.*) pawnbroker, 'uncle'.

tantôt [tã'to], *adv.* presently, by and by, anon; soon; a little while ago, just now; sometimes.

Tanzanie [tãza'ni], **la**, *f.* Tanzania.

taon [tã], *n.m.* botfly, gadfly, cleg.

tapage [ta'pa:ʒ], *n.m.* noise, uproar, row; (*colloq.*) show.

tapageur [tapa'ʒœːr], *a.* (*fem.* **-euse**) rackety, boisterous, noisy; flashy. —*n.m.* (*fem.* **-euse**) noisy person, blusterer.

tape [tap], *n.f.* rap, slap, tap, thump.

taper [ta'pe], *v.t.* to hit, to slap; to smack, to tap. —*v.i.* to hit, to stamp; to strum; to beat down (*of sun*).

tapinois [tapi'nwa], *only in en tapinois, adv. phr.* stealthily, slyly.

tapioca [tapjɔ'ka], *n.m.* tapioca.

tapir [ta'pi:r], *n.m.* tapir (*animal*).

tapir (se) [sɔta'piːr], *v.r.* to squat, to crouch, to cower, to lurk.

tapis [ta'pi], *n.m.* carpet, rug; cover cloth (*for tables etc.*).

tapis-brosse [tapi'brɔs], *n.m.* (*pl.* **-brosses**) door-mat.

tapisser [tapi'se], *v.t.* to hang with tapestry; to cover; to deck, to adorn; to paper; to carpet.

tapisserie [tapis'ri], *n.f.* tapestry, hangings; wallpaper; upholstery.

tapissier [tapi'sje], *n.m.* (*fem.* **-ière**) upholsterer; tapestry worker.

tapoter [tapo'te], *v.t.* to pat, to tap; to strum.

taquin [ta'kɛ̃], *a.* teasing. —*n.m.* (*fem.* **-e**) tease, teasing person.

taquiner [taki'ne], *v.t.* to tease, to plague.

taquinerie [takin'ri], *n.f.* teasing; teasing disposition.

tard [ta:r], *adv.* late. —*n.m.* late hour.

tarder [tar'de], *v.i.* to delay; to tarry, to loiter; to be long; (*impers.*) to long (*de*).

tardif [tar'dif], *a.* (*fem.* **-dive**) tardy, late; slow, belated; backward.

tardivement [tardiv'mã], *adv.* tardily, slowly, belatedly.

tare [ta:r], *n.f.* tare; (*Comm.*) waste, damage; (*fig.*) blemish, defect.

taré [ta're], *a.* damaged, spoiled; disreputable.

tarentule [tarã'tyl], *n.f.* tarantula.

tarer [ta're], *v.t.* to injure, to damage, to spoil; (*Comm.*) to tare. **se tarer**, *v.r.* to spoil, to deteriorate.

targuer (se) [sɔtar'ge], *v.r.* to boast, to brag.

tarif [ta'rif], *n.m.* tariff, rate, scale of prices.

tarifer [tari'fe], *v.t.* to tariff, to price, to rate.

tarir [ta'ri:r], *v.t.* to dry up; to exhaust. —*v.i.* to dry up; to be exhausted; to cease. **se tarir**, *v.r.* to dry up.

tarissable [tari'sabl], *a.* exhaustible.

tarissement [taris'mã], *n.m.* exhausting, drying up.

tartan [tar'tã], *n.m.* tartan, plaid.

tarte [tart], *n.f.* tart; flan.

tartelette [tar'tlet], *n.f.* tartlet.

tartine [tar'tin], *n.f.* slice of bread (*with butter, jam etc.*).

tartufe [tar'tyf], *n.m.* hypocrite.

tas [tã], *n.m. inv.* heap, pile; (*fig.*) lot, set (*of persons etc.*).

Tasmanie [tasma'ni], **la**, *f.* Tasmania.

tasmanien [tasma'njɛ̃], *a.* Tasmanian. —*n.m.* (**Tasmanien**, *fem.* **-enne**) Tasmanian (*person*).

tasse [tɔ:s], *n.f.* cup.

tassement [tɔs'mã], *n.m.* settling, sinking, subsidence.

tasser [ta'se], *v.t.* to heap or pile up; to compress, to squeeze, to cram. —*v.i.* to grow thick. **se tasser**, *v.r.* to sink, to settle, to subside; to huddle together (*of persons*).

tâter [ta'te], *v.t.* to feel; to try, to taste; to sound, to test. —*v.i.* to taste, to try (*de or à*). **se tâter**, *v.r.* to examine oneself.

tatillon [tati'jõ], *a.* (*fem.* **-onne**) niggling, finical.

tâtonnement [taton'mã], *n.m.* groping.

tâtonner [tato'ne], *v.i.* to feel one's way, to grope.

tâtons (à) [atɔ'tõ], *adv. phr.* gropingly.

tatouage [ta'twa:ʒ], *n.m.* tattooing.

tatouer [ta'twe], *v.t.* to tattoo.

taudis [to'di], *n.m.* hovel, slum, hole.

taupe [to:p], *n.f.* mole; moleskin.

taupier [to'pje], *n.m.* mole catcher.
taupière [to'pjɛːr], *n.f.* mole trap.
taupinière [topi'njɛːr], **taupinée** [topi'ne], *n.f.* mole-hill; hillock, knoll.
taure [toːr], *n.f.* heifer.
taureau [to'ro], *n.m.* (*pl.* **-eaux**) bull; (*Astron.*) Taurus.
taux [to], *n.m. inv.* price, rate; rate of interest.
taverne [ta'vɛrn], *n.f.* tavern, café, restaurant.
tavernier [tavɛr'nje], *n.m.* (*fem.* **-ière**) innkeeper.
taxation [taksɑ'sjɔ̃], *n.f.* taxation; fixing of prices.
taxe [taks], *n.f.* tax; duty, rate; fixing of prices; controlled price.
taxer [tak'se], *v.t.* to tax; to rate, to fix the price of; to accuse (*de*).
taxi [tak'si], *n.m.* taxi (-cab).
taxiphone [taksi'fɔn], *n.m.* public telephone booth.
Tchécoslovaquie [tʃekɔslɔva'ki], **la**, *f.* Czechoslovakia.
tchèque [tʃɛk], *a.* Czech.—*n.m.* Czech (*language*).—*n.* (**Tchèque**) Czech (*person*).
te [tə, t], *pron. obj.* *thee, you.
technicien [tɛkni'sjɛ̃], *n.m.* (*fem.* **-enne**) technician.
technique [tɛk'nik], *a.* technical.—*n.f.* technique.
techniquement [tɛknik'mɑ̃], *adv.* technically.
technologie [tɛknɔlɔ'ʒi], *n.f.* technology.
technologique [tɛknɔlɔ'ʒik], *a.* technological.
technologue [tɛknɔ'lɔg], *n.* technologist.
teck or **tek** [tɛk], *n.m.* teak, teak-wood.
teigne [tɛɲ], *n.f.* tinea (*moth*); tinea (*skin disease, such as ringworm*).
teigneux [tɛ'ɲø], *a.* (*fem.* **-euse**) scurvy.—*n.m.* (*fem.* **-euse**) scurfy person.
teindre [tɛ̃ːdr], *v.t. irr.* (*conjug. like* CRAINDRE) to dye, to stain.
teint [tɛ̃], *n.m.* dye, color; complexion; hue.
teinte [tɛ̃ːt], *n.f.* tint, color, shade, hue; (*fig.*) smack, touch.
teinter [tɛ̃'te], *v.t.* to tint; to give a color to.
teinture [tɛ̃'tyːr], *n.f.* dye; dyeing; color, hue; (*Pharm.*) tincture.
teinturerie [tɛ̃ty'ri], *n.f.* dyeing; dye works; dry cleaning.
teinturier [tɛ̃ty'rje], *n.m.* (*fem.* **-ière**) dyer; dry cleaner.
tek [TECK].
tel [tɛl], *a.* (*fem.* **telle**) such; like, similar.—*pron. indef.* such a one; *M.* **un tel**, Mr. So-and-so.
télécommande [telekɔ'mɑ̃ːd], *n.f.* remote control.
télécommunications [telekɔmynika'sjɔ̃], *n.f. pl.* telecommunications.
télégramme [tele'gram], *n.m.* telegram.
télégraphe [tele'graf], *n.m.* telegraph.
télégraphie [telegra'fi], *n.f.* telegraphy; *télégraphie sans fil*, wireless telegraphy.
télégraphier [telegra'fje], *v.t., v.i.* to telegraph; to wire, to cable.
télégraphique [telegra'fik], *a.* telegraphic.
télégraphiste [telegra'fist], *n.* telegraphist.
téléguidé [telegi'de], *a.* guided; *engin téléguidé*, guided missile.
téléimprimeur [teleɛ̃pri'mœːr], **téléscripteur** [teleskrip'tœr], *n.m.* teleprinter.
télémètre [tele'mɛtr], *n.m.* rangefinder.

télépathie [telepa'ti], *n.f.* telepathy.
télépathique [telepa'tik], *a.* telepathic.
téléphérique [telefe'rik], *a.* and *n.m.* teleferic.
téléphone [tele'fɔn], *n.m.* telephone; *un coup de téléphone*, a telephone call.
téléphoner [telefɔ'ne], *v.t., v.i.* to telephone, to ring up.
téléphonique [telefɔ'nik], *a.* *cabine téléphonique*, telephone booth.
téléphoniste [telefɔ'nist], *n.* telephone operator.
télescope [teles'kɔp], *n.m.* telescope.
télescopique [teleskɔ'pik], *a.* telescopic.
téléscripteur [teleskrip'tœːr], [TÉLÉIMPRIMEUR].
télespectateur [telespekta'tœːr], *n.m.* (*fem.* **-trice**) televiewer.
téléviser [televi'ze], *v.t.* to televise.
téléviseur [televi'zœːr], *n.m.* television (receiving-)set.
télévision [televi'zjɔ̃], *n.f.* television.
tellement [tɛl'mɑ̃], *adv.* so, in such a manner; so much, so far.
téméraire [teme'rɛːr], *a.* rash, reckless.—*n.* reckless person, daredevil.
témérairement [temerɛr'mɑ̃], *adv.* rashly, recklessly.
témérité [temeri'te], *n.f.* temerity.
témoignage [temwa'ɲaːʒ], *n.m.* testimony, evidence, witness; testimonial; (*fig.*) token, mark, proof.
témoigner [temwa'ɲe], *v.t.* to testify; to show, to prove, to be the sign of.—*v.i.* to testify, to give evidence (*de*).
témoin [te'mwɛ̃], *n.m.* witness, evidence, proof, mark; second (*in duels*).
tempe [tɑ̃ːp], *n.f.* (*Anat.*) temple.
tempérament [tɑ̃pera'mɑ̃], *n.m.* constitution, temperament; temper; (*fig.*) moderation, compromise; *à tempérament*, by instalments.
tempérance [tɑ̃pe'rɑ̃ːs], *n.f.* temperance.
température [tɑ̃pera'tyːr], *n.f.* temperature.
tempéré [tɑ̃pe're], *a.* temperate (*of climate*); limited, constitutional (*of governments*); restrained, sober (*of style*).
tempérer [tɑ̃pe're], *v.t.* (*conjug. like* CÉDER) to temper, to moderate, to allay, to assuage, to check. **se tempérer**, *v.r.* to become mild (*of the weather*).
tempête [tɑ̃'pɛːt], *n.f.* storm, tempest.
tempêter [tɑ̃pe'te], *v.i.* to storm, to bluster, to fume.
tempétueusement [tɑ̃petɥœz'mɑ̃], *adv.* tempestuously, violently.
tempétueux [tɑ̃pe'tɥø], *a.* (*fem.* **-euse**) tempestuous, boisterous, stormy.
temple [tɑ̃ːpl], *n.m.* temple; French Protestant church.
templier [tɑ̃pli'e], *n.m.* Knight Templar.
temporaire [tɑ̃pɔ'rɛːr], *a.* temporary.
temporairement [tɑ̃pɔrɛr'mɑ̃], *adv.* temporarily, provisionally.
temporel [tɑ̃pɔ'rɛl], *a.* (*fem.* **-elle**) temporal.
temporisateur [tɑ̃pɔriza'tœːr], *a.* (*fem.* **-trice**) procrastinating, temporizing.—*n.m.* (*fem.* **-trice**) temporizer, procrastinator.
temporisation [tɑ̃pɔriza'sjɔ̃], *n.f.* temporizing, procrastination.
temporiser [tɑ̃pɔri'ze], *v.i.* to temporize, to delay.

temps [tã], *n.m. inv.* time, while, period, term; occasion; season; weather; (*Gram.*) tense; *à temps*, in time; *avec le temps*, in course of time; *dans le temps*, formerly; *en temps et lieu*, in proper time and place.

tenable [tə'nabl], *a.* tenable; bearable.

tenace [tə'nas], *a.* tenacious, adhesive, sticky.

ténacité [tenasi'te], *n.f.* tenacity, toughness; retentiveness (*of memory*).

tenaille [tə'na:j], *n.f.* (*usu. in pl.*) pincers, nippers, pliers.

tenailler [tənɑ'je], *v.t.* to torture with red-hot pincers; (*fig.*) to torture.

tenant [tə'nã], *a séance tenante*, during the sitting; forthwith, then and there.— *n.m.* titlist (*at a tournament*); (*fig.*) champion, defender.

tendance [tã'dã:s], *n.f.* tendency; leaning, bent, inclination.

tendancieux [tãdã'sjø], *a.* (*fem.* **-euse**) tendentious; insinuating, suggestive.

tendeur [tã'dœ:r], *n.m.* (*fem.* **-euse**) spreader, layer, setter (*of snares*); wire-stretcher.

tendoir [tã'dwa:r], *n.m.* clothes-line.

tendon [tã'dõ], *n.m.* tendon, sinew.

tendre (1) [tã:dr], *a.* tender, soft; delicate, sensitive; affectionate; moving; early, young, new.

tendre (2) [tã:dr], *v.t.* to stretch, to strain; to bend (*a bow etc.*); to spread, to lay, to set; to hold out; to pitch (*tents*); to hang (*tapestry etc.*).—*v.i.* to lead; to tend, to conduce.

tendrement [tãdrə'mã], *adv.* tenderly, affectionately.

tendresse [tã'drɛs], *n.f.* tenderness, fondness; (*pl.*) endearments.

tendron [tã'drõ], *n.m.* shoot (*of plants*).

tendu [tã'dy], *a.* stretched, held out; tight, tense; strained.

ténèbres [te'nɛːbr], *n.f.* (*used only in pl.*) darkness, night, gloom.

ténébreusement [tenebrøz'mã], *adv.* darkly, gloomily; secretly.

ténébreux [tene'brø], *a.* (*fem.* **-euse**) dark, gloomy, overcast; obscure, mysterious.

teneur (1) [tə'nœ:r], *n.f.* tenor, terms, text; purport.

teneur (2) [tə'nœ:r], *n.m.* (*fem.* **-euse**) holder; *teneur de livres*, book-keeper.

ténia [te'nja], *n.m.* tapeworm.

tenir [tə'ni:r], *v.t. irr.* to hold, to have hold of; to have, to possess; to seize; to occupy; to keep, to follow; to retain; to perform; to consider.—*v.i.* to hold; to adhere, to stick; to hold together; to cling; to prize (*à*); to be attached *or* related (*à*); to be contiguous; to depend, to result (*de*); to be held (*of fairs, markets, assemblies etc.*); to take after; to savor; to persist; to resist; to be anxious (*à*). **se tenir**, *v.r.* to hold fast, to remain; to adhere; to consider oneself; to contain oneself; to refrain.

tennis [te'nis], *n.m.* lawn tennis.

tenon [tə'nõ], *n.m.* tenon; bolt (*of fire-arms*).

ténor [te'nɔ:r], *n.m.* (*Mus.*) tenor.

tension [tã'sjõ], *n.f.* tension, strain; tense-ness; (*Elec.*) voltage.

tentacule [tãta'kyl], *n.m.* tentacle, feeler.

tentant [tã'tã], *a.* tempting.

tentateur [tãta'tœ:r], *a.* (*fem.* **-trice**) tempting.—*n.m.* (*fem.* **-trice**) tempter, temptress.

tentation [tãta'sjõ], *n.f.* temptation.

tentative [tãta'ti:v], *n.f.* attempt, trial, endeavor.

tente [tã:t], *n.f.* tent, pavilion; (*Naut.*) awning.

tenter [tã'te], *v.t.* to attempt, to try; to tempt.

tenture [tã'ty:r], *n.f.* hangings, tapestry; wall-paper; paper-hanging.

ténu [te'ny], *a.* tenuous, thin, slender.

tenue [tə'ny], *n.f.* holding (*of assemblies etc.*); session; attitude (*of a person*); behavior, bearing; dress; keeping (*of books*); *grande tenue*, (*Mil.*) full dress; *petite tenue*, undress.

ténuité [tenɥi'te], *n.f.* tenuity, thinness; (*fig.*) insignificance.

tenure [tə'ny:r], *n.f.* tenure.

ter [tɛ:r], *adv.* thrice; for the third time.

térébenthine [terebã'tin], *n.f.* turpentine.

térébinthe [tere'bɛ̃:t], *n.m.* turpentine tree, terebinth.

tergiversation [tɛrʒivɛrsa'sjõ], *n.f.* tergiver-sation, evasion.

tergiverser [tɛrʒivɛr'se], *v.i.* to waver, to beat about the bush.

terme [tɛrm], *n.m.* term; termination, end; limit, boundary; time; three months; quarter's rent; expression; (*pl.*) state, con-ditions, terms; *avant terme*, prematurely.

terminaison [tɛrmine'zõ], *n.f.* termination, ending.

terminer [tɛrmi'ne], *v.t.* to bound, to limit; to terminate, to conclude. **se terminer**, *v.r.* to terminate; to be bounded.

terminus [tɛrmi'nys], *n.m.* terminus (*of rail-way*).

terne [tɛrn], *a.* dull, dim; wan; spiritless.

ternir [tɛr'ni:r], *v.t.* to dull, to deaden; to tarnish. **se ternir**, *v.r.* to tarnish, to grow dull; to fade (*of colors*).

ternissure [tɛrni'sy:r], *n.f.* tarnishing, fading, stain.

terrain [tɛ'rɛ̃], *n.m.* piece of ground; soil, earth; site; field, course.

terrassant [tɛra'sã], *a.* crushing (*news etc.*).

terrasse [tɛ'ras], *n.f.* terrace; flat roof, balcony.

terrassement [tɛras'mã], *n.m.* earthwork, embankment; ballasting.

terrasser [tɛra'se], *v.t.* to embank; to throw to the ground; to beat; to confound, to dismay.

terrassier [tɛra'sje], *n.m.* digger, excavator, laborer; earthwork contractor.

terre [tɛ:r], *n.f.* earth; land; ground, soil; dominion, territory; grounds, estate, prop-erty; (*C*) farm.

terreau [tɛ'ro], *n.m.* (*pl.* **-eaux**) compost.

Terre-Neuve [tɛr'nœ:v], *f.* Newfoundland.

terre-neuve [tɛr'nœ:v], *n.m. inv.* New-foundland (*dog*).

terrer [tɛ're], *v.t.* to earth up (*a tree etc.*). *v.i.* to burrow. **se terrer**, *v.r.* to dig oneself in.

terrestre [tɛ'rɛstr], *a.* terrestrial, earthly.

terreur [tɛ'rœ:r], *n.f.* terror; awe, dread.

terreux [tɛ'rø], *a.* (*fem.* **-euse**) terreous, earthy; dirty; dull (*of colors*); ashen (*of the face*).

terrible [tɛ'ribl], *a.* terrible, dreadful; un-manageable (*of children*).

311

terriblement [tɛriblə'mɑ̃], *adv.* terribly; (*colloq.*) with a vengeance.

terrier [tɛ'rje], *n.m.* burrow, hole; earth (*of fox*); terrier (*dog*).

terrifier [tɛri'fje], *v.t.* to terrify, to dismay.

terrine [tɛ'rin], *n.f.* earthen pan, dish; potted meat.

territoire [tɛri'twa:r], *n.m.* territory, district

territorial [tɛrito'rjal], *a.* (*m. pl.* **-aux**) territorial.

terroir [tɛ'rwa:r], *n.m.* soil, ground; *goût de terroir*, raciness (*of style*); native tang (*of wine*).

terroriser [tɛrɔri'ze], *v.t.* to terrorize.

terrorisme [tɛrɔ'rism], *n.m.* terrorism.

terroriste [tɛrɔ'rist], *n.m.* terrorist.

tertiaire [tɛr'sjɛ:r], *a.* tertiary.

tertre [tɛrtr], *n.m.*, knoll, hillock.

tes [te], [TON (1).]

tesson [tɛ'sɔ̃], *n.m.* potsherd, fragment of broken glass etc.

test [tɛst], *n.m.* shell; trial, test.

testacé [tɛsta'se], *a.* testaceous.—*n.m.* testacean.

testament [tɛsta'mɑ̃], *n.m.* will.

tester [tɛs'te], *v.t.* to test.—*v.i.* to make one's will.

testimonial [tɛstimɔ'njal], *a.* (*m. pl.* **-aux**) testifying, testimonial.

tétanos [teta'nɔs], *n.m.* tetanus, lock-jaw.

têtard [tɛ'ta:r], *n.m.* tadpole.

tête [tɛ:t], *n.f.* head; head-piece; face; beginning; top; van, vanguard; (*fig.*) brains, sense, judgment; presence of mind; *en tête*, in one's head; in front, ahead; *mal de tête*, headache; *tête de mort*, skull.

tête-à-tête [tɛta'tɛ:t], *n.m. inv.* tête-à-tête, private interview or conversation; settee (*for two*)

téter [te'te], *v.t.* (*conjug. like* CÉDER) to suck.

têtière [tɛ'tjɛ:r], *n.f.* infant's cap; head-stall (*of a bridle*); antimacassar.

tétin [te'tɛ̃], *n.m.* nipple, teat; breast.

téton [te'tɔ̃], *n.m.* teat; (*fam.*) breast.

tétrarque [te'trark], *n.m.* tetrarch.

tétras [te'tra], *n.m. inv.* (*Orn.*) grouse.

têtu [tɛ'ty], *a.* headstrong, stubborn, obstinate.

teutonique [tøtɔ'nik], *a.* teutonic.

texte [tɛkst], *n.m.* text; theme, matter, subject; passage (*of Scripture*)

textile [tɛks'til], *a.* and *n.m.* textile.

textuel [tɛks'tɥɛl], *a* (*fem.* **-elle**) textual, word for word.

textuellement [tɛkstɥɛl'mɑ̃], *adv.* textually.

texture [tɛks'ty:r], *n.f.* texture; disposition.

thaïlandais [tailɑ̃'dɛ], *a.* Thai.—*n.m.* Thai (*language*); (**Thaïlandais**, *fem.* **-aise**) Thai (*person*).

Thaïlande [tai'lɑ̃:d], **la**, *f.* Thailand, Siam.

thé [te], *n.m.* tea; tea party.

théâtral [tea'tral], *a.* (*m. pl.* **-aux**) theatrical.

théâtre [te'a:tr], *n.m.* theatre, playhouse; stage; plays (*collection*), scene; *coup de théâtre*, striking event.

théerie [te'ri], *n.f.* tea plantation.

théière [te'jɛ:r], *n.f.* teapot.

théisme [te'ism], *n.m.* theism.

thème [tɛ:m], *n.m.* topic, subject, theme; (*sch.*) prose, composition.

théodolite [teɔdɔ'lit], *n.m.* theodolite.

théologie [teɔlɔ'ʒi], *n.f.* theology; divinity.

théologien [teɔlɔ'ʒjɛ̃], *n.m.* theologian.

théorème [teɔ'rɛm], *n.m.* theorem.

théorie [teɔ'ri], *n.f.* theory, speculation.

théorique [teɔ'rik], *a.* theoretical.

théoriquement [teɔrik'mɑ̃], *adv.* theoretically.

théoriser [teɔri'ze], *v.t.*, *v.i.* to theorize.

théoriste [teɔ'rist], *n.* theorist.

thérapie [tera'pi], *n.f.* therapy.

Thérèse [te'rɛ:z], *f.* Theresa.

thermal [tɛr'mal], *a.* (*m. pl.* **-aux**) thermal; *eaux thermales*, hot springs.

thermomètre [tɛrmɔ'mɛtr], *n.m.* thermometer.

thermos [tɛr'mɔs], *n.m.* thermos (flask).

thermostat [tɛrmɔ'sta], *n.m.* thermostat.

thésauriser [tezɔri'ze], *v.t.* to treasure.—*v.i.* to hoard treasure.

thèse [tɛ:z], *n.f.* thesis, proposition.

thibaude [ti'bo:d], *n.f.* hair-cloth, coarse drugget.

Thomas [tɔ'ma], *m.* Thomas.

thon [tɔ̃], *n.m.* tunny-fish.

thoracique [tɔra'sik], *a.* thoracic.

thorax [tɔ'raks], *n.m.* thorax, chest.

thrombose [trɔ̃'bo:z], *n.f.* thrombosis.

thym [tɛ̃], *n.m.* thyme.

thyroïde [tirɔ'id], *a.* thyroid.

tiare [tja:r], *n.f.* tiara.

Tibet [ti'be], **le** *m.* Tibet.

tibétain [tibe'tɛ̃], *a.* Tibetan.—*n.m.* Tibetan (*language*); (**Tibétain**, *fem.* **-aine**) Tibetan (*person*).

tibia [ti'bja], *n.m.* (*Anat.*) tibia, shin-bone.

tic [tik], *n.m.* tic, twitching; bad habit.

ticket [ti'kɛ], *n.m.* ticket (*for bus, underground etc., but not railways*).

tiède [tjɛd], *a.* lukewarm, tepid, mild; (*fig.*) indifferent.

tièdement [tjɛd'mɑ̃], *adv.* with indifference.

tiédeur [tje'dœ:r], *n.f.* lukewarmness; (*fig.*) indifference.

tiédir [tje'di:r], *v.t.* to take the chill off, to tepefy.—*v.i.* to cool, to grow lukewarm.

tien [tjɛ̃], *pron. poss. m.* (*fem.* **tienne**) *thine, yours.—n.* (*pl.*) *les tiens*, your relations and friends.

tiens! [tjɛ̃], *2nd sing. imper.* [TENIR], *int.* well! hello! look here! here! really? you don't say so!

tierce (1) [tjɛrs], *n.f.* a third (*of time*); tierce (*at cards etc.*).

tiers [tjɛ:r], *a.* (*fem.* **tierce** (2)) third.—*n.m.* third person, third party; (*fig.*) stranger; third part.

tige [ti:ʒ], *n.f.* stem, stalk; trunk (*of tree*); straw (*of grain*); shank (*of a key, anchor etc.*); stock (*of a family*).

tignasse [ti'nas], *n.f.* old wig; (*pop.*) mop, shock (*of hair*).

tigre [tigr], *n.m.* (*fem.* **-esse**) tiger, tigress.

tigrer [ti'gre], *v.t.* to stripe, to spot, to speckle.

tillac [ti'jak], *n.m.* deck.

tilleul [ti'jœl], *n.m.* lime tree, linden tree.

timbale [tɛ̃'bal], *n.f.* kettledrum, timbal; metal cup or mug; kitchen mould.

timbre [tɛ̃:br], *n.m.* bell, clock chime; sound, tone; stamp; stamp duty; postmark.

timbré [tɛ̃'bre], *a.* stamped; (*fam.*) cracked.

timbre-poste [tɛ̃brə'pɔst], *n.m.* (*pl.* **timbres-poste**) postage stamp.

timbrer [tɛ̃'bre], *v.t.* to stamp; to stick a stamp on (*a letter*).

timide [ti'mid], *a.* shy, bashful, self-conscious; timid.

timidement [timid'mɑ̃], *adv.* shyly; timidly.

timidité [timidi'te], *n.f.* shyness, bashfulness; timidity.

timon [ti'mɔ̃], *n.m.* pole (*of a carriage, cart etc.*); shaft; beam (*of a plough*); (*Naut.*) helm, tiller; (*fig.*) direction, government.

timonerie [timon'ri], *n.f.* steerage, steering.

timonier [timo'nje], *n.m.* steersman, helmsman; wheel horse.

timoré [timo're], *a.* timorous, fearful.

Timothée [timo'te], *m.* Timothy.

tine [tin], *n.f.* tub, water cask.

tintamarre [tɛ̃ta'maːr], *n.m.* hubbub, uproar, hurly-burly, din.

tintement [tɛ̃t'mɑ̃], *n.m.* ringing sound, tinkling; tolling; singing or buzzing (*in the ears etc.*).

tinter [tɛ̃'te], *v.t.* to ring, to toll; to sound (*a knell etc.*); (*Naut.*) to prop, to support.—*v.i.* to ring, to toll; to tinkle, to jingle; to tingle.

tintouin [tɛ̃'twɛ̃], *n.m.* (*fam.*) anxiety, trouble.

tique [tik], *n.f.* cattle tick, dog tick.

tiquer [ti'ke], *v.i.* to have a tic, to twitch.

tiqueté [tik'te], *a.* speckled, spotted.

tiqueture [tik'tyːr], *n.f.* mottling, speckles.

tir [tiːr], *n.m.* shooting; firing, fire; shooting gallery, rifle range.

tirade [ti'rad], *n.f.* passage (*of prose or verse*); tirade.

tirage [ti'raːʒ], *n.m.* drawing, hauling, towing; tow-path; (*fig.*) difficulties; working off; printing, circulation (*of newspaper*); drawing (*of a lottery*); focal length (*of camera*).

tiraillement [tiraj'mɑ̃], *n.m.* pulling, hauling about; twinge, pain; (*fig.*) jarring, wrangling, vexation.

tirailler [tira'je], *v.t.* to pull about; to tease, to pester.—*v.i.* to shoot wildly; to skirmish. **se tirailler,** *v.r.* to pull each other about.

tirailleur [tiraj'œːr], *n.m.* sharpshooter; skirmisher.

tirant [ti'rɑ̃], *n.m.* purse-string; boot-strap; (*Carp. etc.*) tie-beam; brace (*of a drum*); *tirant d'eau,* ship's draft.

tire [tiːr], *n.f.* pull.

tiré [ti're], *a.* drawn; fatigued.—*n.m.* (*Comm.*) drawee (*of a bill*).

tire-bouchon [tirbu'ʃɔ̃], *n.m.* (*pl.* -bouchons) corkscrew; ringlet (*of hair*).

tire-bouton [tirbu'tɔ̃], *n.m.* (*pl.* -boutons) button-hook.

tire-d'aile (à) [atir'dɛl], *adv. phr.* at full speed (*of a bird flying*).

tire-larigot (à) [atirlari'go], *adv. phr.* (*fam.*) to one's heart's content.

tirelire [tir'liːr], *n.f.* money box.

tirer [ti're], *v.t.* to draw, to pull; to take out, to extract; to tap (*liquors*); to stretch, to tighten; to receive, to reap; to infer; to put on; to get; to shoot, to fire; (*Print.*) to print.—*v.i.* to draw, to pull; to fire; to tend, to border, to verge (*sur*). **se tirer,** *v.r.* to extricate oneself; to get out; to recover (*from illness*).

tiret [ti're], *n.m.* hyphen, dash.

tiretaine [tir'tɛːn], *n.f.* linsey-woolsey.

tireur [ti'rœːr], *n.m.* (*fem.* -euse) one who draws; marksman, sharpshooter.

tiroir [ti'rwaːr], *n.m.* drawer (*in a table etc.*); slide, slide-valve (*steam engine*).

tisane [ti'zan], *n.f.* infusion of herbs etc.

tison [ti'zɔ̃], *n.m.* brand, fire-brand; (*fig.*) embers.

tisonner [tizo'ne], *v.t.*, *v.i.* to poke (*the fire*).

tisonnier [tizo'nje], *n.m.* poker, fire iron.

tissage [ti'saːʒ], *n.m.* weaving; cloth mill.

tisser [ti'se], *v.t.* to weave; *métier à tisser* weaving-loom.

tisserand [tis'rɑ̃], *n.m.* (*fem.* -e) weaver.

tissu [ti'sy], *a.* woven.—*n.m.* material, fabric; tissue.

tissure [ti'syːr], *n.f.* tissue, texture.

titan [ti'tɑ̃], *n.m.* Titan, titan.

titanesque [tita'nɛsk], **titanique** [tita'nik], *a.* titanic, Titanic.

titillant [titil'lɑ̃], *a.* titillating, tickling.

titillation [titilla'sjɔ̃], *n.f.* titillation, tickling.

titiller [titil'le], *v.t.*, *v.i.* to titillate, to tickle.

titre [titr], *n.m.* title, style, denomination; title page; head, heading; right, claim, reason; voucher; title deed; *titre de circulation,* (railway) ticket *or* pass; *à bon titre or à juste titre,* deservedly, justly.

titrer [ti'tre], *v.t.* to give a title to.

titubant [tity'bɑ̃], *a.* staggering.

titubation [tityba'sjɔ̃], *n.f.* reeling, staggering.

tituber [tity'be], *v.i.* to stagger, to reel.

titulaire [tity'lɛːr], *a.* titular.—*n.* titular incumbent, holder, chief.

toast [tost], *n.m.* toast, health; toast(ed bread); *porter un toast* (*à quelqu'un*), to toast (*someone*).

toboggan [tobo'gɑ̃], *n.m.* toboggan.

toc [tok], *int.* tap, rap.—*n.m.* rap, knock (*at a door etc.*).

tocsin [tok'sɛ̃], *n.m.* tocsin, alarm bell.

toge [toːʒ], *n.f.* toga; (*fig.*) robe, gown (*of a judge etc.*).

Togo [to'go], **le,** *m.* Togo.

togolais [togo'lɛ], *a. of* Togo.—*n.m.* (**Togolais** *fem.* -aise) native of Togo.

tohu-bohu [toybo'y], *n.m.* chaos; (*fig.*) confusion; jumble, hubbub.

toi [twa], *pron. pers.* *thou, *thee, you.

toile [twal], *n.f.* linen, cloth; canvas; sail; painting, picture; web; *toile cirée,* oilcloth; *toile d'araignée,* cobweb, spider's web.

toilette [twa'lɛt], *n.f.* doily; toilet set; dressing table, wash-stand; dress, attire; *cabinet de toilette,* dressing room; *grande toilette,* full dress; *les toilettes,* toilets.

toise [twaːz], *n.f.* fathom; fathom measure; (*fig.*) measure, standard.

toiser [twa'ze], *v.t.* to measure; to survey; (*fig.*) to eye from head to foot.

toiseur [twa'zœːr], *n.m.* measurer; quantity surveyor.

toison [twa'zɔ̃], *n.f.* fleece; (*fig.*) mop, thick head of hair.

toit [twa], *n.m.* roof, house-top; top, roof (*of a mine*); (*fig.*) house, home; *toit à cochons* pigsty.

toiture [twa'tyːr], *n.f.* roofing, roof.

tôle [toːl], *n.f.* sheet iron; plate of steel; *tôle ondulée,* corrugated iron.

313

tolérable [tole'rabl], *a.* tolerable, bearable; middling.

tolérablement [tolerablə'mã], *adv.* tolerably.

tolérance [tole'rã:s], *n.f.* tolerance, toleration; endurance, forbearance; indulgence; tolerance (*in coins*).

tolérant [tole'rã], *a.* tolerant.

tolérer [tole're], *v.t.* (*conjug. like* CÉDER) to tolerate, to allow; to endure, to bear; to wink at.

tomate [to'mat], *n.f.* tomato.

tombal [tɔ̃'bal], *a.* (*m. pl.* **-aux**) pertaining to a tomb; *pierre tombale*, tombstone.

tombe [tɔ̃:b], *n.f.* tomb, grave; tombstone.

tombeau [tɔ̃'bo], *n.m.* (*pl.* **-eaux**) tomb, grave; (*fig.*) sepulcher, death.

tombée [tɔ̃'be], *n.f.* fall (*of night etc.*).

tomber [tɔ̃'be], *v.i.* (*with aux.* ÊTRE) to fall, to fall down; to sink; to decay, to droop; to abate; to sag; to fall into; to meet, to light (upon) (*sur*); *laisser tomber*, to drop; *tomber amoureux* (*de*), to fall in love (with); *tomber bien* or *mal*, to come at the right or wrong moment; *tomber d'accord*, to agree; *tomber malade*, to fall ill.

tombereau [tɔ̃'bro], *n.m.* (*pl.* **-eaux**) tip-cart.

tombola [tɔ̃bɔ'la], *n.f.* tombola; raffle.

tome [to:m], *n.m.* volume, tome.

ton (1) [tɔ̃], *a. poss. m.* (*fem.* **ta**, *pl.* **tes**) *thy, your.

ton (2) [tɔ̃], *n.m.* tone; intonation, accent; tint; (*fig.*) manner, style; breeding; (*Mus.*) pitch, key.

tondaison [TONTE].

tondeur [tɔ̃'dœ:r], *n.m.* (*fem.* **-euse**) shearer, clipper.—*n.f.* (**-euse**) shearing machine, clipper; *tondeuse* (*de gazon*), lawn-mower.

tondre [tɔ̃:dr], *v.t.* to shear, to clip, to crop; to cut, to mow, to trim.

tondu [tɔ̃'dy], *a.* shorn.

tonique [tɔ'nik], *a.* tonic; stressed.—*n.m.* (*Med.*) tonic.—*n.f.* (*Mus.*) keynote.

tonnage [tɔ'na:ʒ], *n.m.* tonnage; displacement.

tonne [tɔn], *n.f.* tun (*wooden vessel*); ton (*20 cwt., approx. 1000 kil.*).

tonneau [tɔ'no], *n.m.* (*pl.* **-eaux**) tun (*cask*); tun (*measure*); ton [TONNE]; (*collog.*) drunkard; *mettre un tonneau en perce*, to broach a cask; *tonneau percé*, (*fig.*) spendthrift.

tonnelier [tɔnə'lje], *n.m.* cooper.

tonnelle [tɔ'nɛl], *n.f.* arbor, bower.

tonnellerie [tɔnɛl'ri], *n.f.* cooperage.

tonner [tɔ'ne], *v.i.* to thunder; (*fig.*) to inveigh.

tonnerre [tɔ'nɛ:r], *n.m.* thunder, thunderbolt; *coup* or *éclat de tonnerre*, clap of thunder.

tonsure [tɔ̃'sy:r], *n.f.* tonsure.

tonsuré [tɔ̃sy're], *a.m.* tonsured, shaven.—*n.m.* cleric, priest.

tonte [tɔ̃:t], **tondaison** [tɔ̃dɛ'zɔ̃], *n.f.* sheepshearing, clipping.

tonture [tɔ̃'ty:r], *n.f.* shearings, clippings; flock (*of cloth*); (*Naut.*) sheer.

top [tɔp], *n.m.* time signal; *les tops*, the pips.

topaze [tɔ'pɑ:z], *n.f.* topaz.

toper [tɔ'pe], *v.i.* to agree; *tope là !* done! agreed!

topinambour [tɔpinã'bu:r], *n.m.* Jerusalem artichoke.

topographe [tɔpɔ'graf], *n.m.* topographer.

topographie [tɔpɔgra'fi], *n.f.* topography.

topographique [tɔpɔgra'fik], *a.* topographical.

toquade or **tocade** [tɔ'kad], *n.f.* (*collog.*) infatuation, whim, fad, craze.

toque [tɔk], *n.f.* toque; jockey's cap; magistrate's cap.

toqué [tɔ'ke], *a.* (*fam.*) cracked, touched; infatuated.

torche [tɔrʃ], *n.f.* torch; twist (*of straw etc.*); pad (*on head*).

torcher [tɔr'ʃe], *v.t.* to wipe, to clean; (*fig.*) to polish off. **se torcher**, *v.r.* to wipe oneself.

torchère [tɔr'ʃɛ:r], *n.f.* torch-holder, tall candelabrum, hall lamp.

torchis [tɔr'ʃi], *n.m.* loam; *mur de torchis*, mud wall.

torchon [tɔr'ʃɔ̃], *n.m.* duster, house-cloth, dish-cloth.

tordage [tɔr'da:ʒ], *n.m.* twisting, twist.

tordeur [tɔr'dœ:r], *n.m.* (*fem.* **-euse**) twister (*of wool etc.*); throwster (*of silk*).

tordoir [tɔr'dwa:r], *n.m.* mangle, wringer.

tordre [tɔrdr], *v.t.* to twist, to wring; to contort, to disfigure. **se tordre**, *v.r.* to twist; to writhe.

tordu [tɔr'dy], *a.* twisted, distorted.

toréador [tɔrea'dɔ:r], *n.m.* toreador, bullfighter.

tornade [tɔr'nad], *n.f.* tornado.

torpeur [tɔr'pœ:r], *n.f.* torpor.

torpide [tɔr'pid], *a.* torpid.

torpille [tɔr'pi:j], *n.f.* torpedo (*numb-fish*); (*Navy, Av.*) torpedo.

torpiller [tɔrpi'je], *v.t.* to torpedo.

torpilleur [tɔrpi'jœ:r], *n.m.* torpedo boat.

torréfier [tɔre'fje], *v.t.* to torrefy, to roast (*coffee*).

torrent [tɔ'rã], *n.m.* torrent, stream; flood (*of tears etc.*); flow (*of words etc.*).

torrentiel [tɔrã'sjɛl], **torrentueux** [tɔrã'tɥø], *a.* (*fem.* **-elle, -euse**) torrential; impetuous.

torride [tɔ'rid], *a.* torrid.

tors [tɔr], *a.* (*fem.* **torse** (1) or **torte**) twisted, wreathed, contorted; wry, crooked.—*n.m.* twisting (*of ropes etc.*); torsion.

torsade [tɔr'sad], *n.f.* twisted fringe or cord; bullion (*on epaulets etc.*).

torse (2) [tɔrs], *n.m.* torso, trunk, bust.

torsion [tɔr'sjɔ̃], *n.f.* torsion, twisting.

tort [tɔ:r], *n.m.* wrong, injustice; harm, injury, mischief, offence; prejudice, detriment; *à tort ou à raison*, rightly or wrongly; *avoir tort*, to be wrong.

torticolis [tɔrtikɔ'li], *n.m.* wryneck, stiff neck; crick (*in the neck*).

tortiller [tɔrti'je], *v.t.* to twist.—*v.i.* to wriggle, to shuffle; to prevaricate. **se tortiller**, *v.r.* to wriggle, to writhe.

tortionnaire [tɔrsjɔ'nɛ:r], *n.m.* executioner, torturer.

tortu [tɔr'ty], *a.* crooked, tortuous; *jambes tortues*, bandy legs.

tortue [tɔr'ty], *n.f.* tortoise; *tortue de mer*, turtle.

tortueux [tɔr'tɥø], a. (fem. -euse) tortuous, winding, crooked; (fig.) artful, crafty.

torture [tɔr'ty:r], n.f. torture; the rack.

torturer [tɔrty're], v.t. to torture, to put on the rack.

tôt [to], adv. soon, quickly; early; au plus tôt or le plus tôt possible, as soon as possible; tôt ou tard, sooner or later.

total [tɔ'tal], a. (m. pl. -aux) total, whole, entire; utter.—n.m. whole, total, sum total.

totalement [tɔtal'mɑ̃], adv. totally, wholly, utterly, completely.

totalisateur [tɔtaliza'tœ:r], n.m. calculating-machine; totalisator.

totaliser [tɔtali'ze], v.t. to tot up, to total up.

totalitaire [tɔtali'tɛ:r], a. totalitarian.

totalitarisme [tɔtalita'rism], n.m. totalitarianism.

totalité [tɔtali'te], n.f. totality, whole.

touage [twa:ʒ], n.m. towage, towing, warping.

toucan [tu'kɑ̃], n.m. toucan.

touchant [tu'ʃɑ̃], a. touching, moving, affecting.—n.m. the moving, affecting or impressive part.—prep. concerning, with regard to.

touche [tuʃ], n.f. touch; assay, trial; (Paint. etc.) manner, style; key (of piano, typewriter etc.); stop (of organ); (Fishing) nibble, bite; (Fenc. etc.) hit; drove of cattle; pierre de touche, touchstone.

touche-à-tout [tuʃa'tu], a. inv. meddling.—n. inv. meddler; jack-of-all-trades.

toucher [tu'ʃe], v.t. to touch; to handle, to feel, to finger; to assay, to try (precious metals etc.); to receive (money); to hit; to offend; to move, to affect; to whip, to drive (animals); to play on (a musical instrument); to express, to describe; to allude to; to concern, to regard; toucher un chèque, to cash a check.—v.i. to touch, to meddle (à); to reach; to play (on a musical instrument); to draw near; to be related, to be like; to concern; (Naut.) to go aground. se toucher, v.r. to touch, to touch each other; to be adjoining.—n.m. touch, feeling.

toue [tu], n.f. barge.

touée [tu'e], n.f. towing, warping; towline.

touer [tu'e], v.t. to tow, to warp.

toueur [tu'œ:r], n.m. towboat, tug.

touffe [tuf], n.f. tuft, clump, bunch, wisp.

touffer [tu'fe], v.t. to arrange in tufts.—v.i. to grow in a tuft or tufts.

touffu [tu'fy], a. tufted, bushy; leafy; full, thick; labored (of style).

toujours [tu'ʒu:r], adv. always, ever, for ever; still; all the same, nevertheless, at least; toujours est-il que . . ., still, the fact remains that . . . .

toupet [tu'pɛ], n.m. tuft of hair; forelock; front, foretop (on a horse); (colloq.) effrontery, cheek, impudence.

toupie [tu'pi], n.f. top, spinning-top.

toupiller [tupi'je], v.i. to spin, to whirl round and round.

tour (1) [tu:r], n.f. tower; (Chess) rook, castle.

tour (2) [tu:r], n.m. turn, winding; revolution; circumference, circuit; twist, strain; tour, trip; trick; feat; à tour de rôle, in turn; tour de force, feat of strength; tour de reins, sprain in the back.

tour (3) [tu:r], n.m. lathe.

tourangeau [turɑ̃'ʒo], a. (fem. -elle, m. pl. -eaux) of Touraine.—n.m. (Tourangeau, fem. -elle) native of Touraine.

tourbe [turb], n.f. mob, rabble; peat, turf.

tourbeux [tur'bø], a. (fem. -euse) peaty.

tourbillon [turbi'jɔ̃], n.m. whirlwind; whirlpool, eddy; (fig.) hurly-burly, bustle.

tourbillonner [turbijɔ'ne], v.i. to whirl, to eddy; to swirl.

tourelle [tu'rɛl], n.f. turret; gun turret; tourelle de veille, conning tower.

touret [tu'rɛ], n.m. wheel (of a lathe etc.); angler's reel.

tourie [tu'ri], n.f. carboy.

tourillon [turi'jɔ̃], n.m. axle; axle-tree, arbor; spindle, pivot.

tourisme [tu'rism], n.m. touring, tourism.

touriste [tu'rist], n. tourist.

tourment [tur'mɑ̃], n.m. torment, torture; anguish, pain; agony of mind.

tourmente [tur'mɑ̃:t], n.f. tempest, storm; (fig.) disturbance, turmoil.

tourmenter [turmɑ̃'te], v.t. to torment, to torture, to rack; to distress, to harass; to worry; to jolt; to toss. se tourmenter, v.r. to be uneasy, to fret; to warp (of wood); to labor hard (of a ship).

tourmenteur [turmɑ̃'tœ:r], a. (fem. -euse) torturing, tormenting.—n.m. (fem. -euse) torturer, tormentor.

tournailler [turna'je], v.i. (colloq.) to prowl round.

tournant [tur'nɑ̃], a. turning, winding; plaque tournante, turn-table; pont tournant, swing-bridge.—n.m. turn, turning, bend; street corner; (fig.) indirect means; turning-point.

tourné [tur'ne], a. turned, shaped; expressed; sour, spoilt; avoir l'esprit mal tourné, to be cross-grained.

tournebroche [turnə'brɔʃ], n.m. roasting-jack; turnspit.

tourne-disques [turnə'disk], n.m. inv. record player.

tournedos [turnə'do], n.m. inv. filet mignon.

tournée [tur'ne], n.f. round, turn, visit, journey; circuit.

tournemain (en un) [ɑ̃nœ̃turnə'mɛ̃], adv. phr. in a trice.

tourner [tur'ne], v.t. to turn; to turn round, to revolve, to twirl; to wind; (Cine.) to shoot (a film); to convert; to interpret; to shape.—v.i. to turn, to turn round, to revolve; to turn out; to change; to ripen; to spoil, to curdle (of liquids). se tourner, v.r. to turn round; to turn; to change.

tournesol [turnə'sɔl], n.m. turnsole, sunflower; (Chem.) litmus.

tourneur [tur'nœ:r], n.m. turner.

tournevent [turnə'vɑ̃], n.m. cowl (for chimney).

tournevis [turnə'vis], n.m. screwdriver.

tourniole [tur'njɔl], n.f. whitlow.

tourniquet [turni'kɛ], n.m. turnstile; swivel; (Surg.) tourniquet.

tournoi [tur'nwa], n.m. tournament.

tournoiement [turnwa'mɑ̃], n.m. turning round, whirling, swirling; dizziness.

tournoyer [turnwa'je], v.i. (conjug. like EMPLOYER) to turn round and round, to wind; to eddy; (fig.) to beat about the bush, to shilly-shally.

tournure [tur'ny:r], *n.f.* turn, direction, course; figure, shape; (*fig.*) cast (*of mind, style etc.*); phrase, construction (*of language*); *les choses commencent à prendre une mauvaise tournure,* things are beginning to look bad.

tourte [turt], *n.f.* covered pie; round loaf.

tourtereau [turtə'ro], *n.m.* (*pl.* **-eaux**) young turtle-dove; (*pl.*) (*fam.*) lovers.

tourterelle [turtə'rɛl], *n.f.* turtle-dove.

Toussaint [tu'sɛ̃], **la,** *f.* All Saints' Day.

tousser [tu'se], *v.i.* to cough.

tout [tu; *liaison-form,* tut], *a.* (*m.* (*pl.* **tous**) all; whole, the whole of; every; each; any; *tous les jours,* every day; *toutes les fois que,* as often as, every time that; *tout le monde,* all the world, everybody.—*pron. indef.* (*m. pl. pronounced* tu:s) all, everything; (*pl.*) all men; *à tout prendre,* on the whole; *comme tout,* exceedingly, extremely; *du tout,* not at all; *en tout,* in all, on the whole.—*n.m.* whole, the whole; the chief point, only thing.—*adv.* wholly, entirely, quite, thoroughly; all, altogether; although, however, for all; *parler tout haut,* to speak aloud; presently; *tout à coup,* suddenly; *tout à fait,* quite, entirely; *tout à l'heure,* just now; presently; *tout à vous,* sincerely yours; *tout beau* or *tout doux,* softly, gently, not so fast; *tout de bon,* in earnest; *tout de suite,* immediately; *tout nu,* stark naked.

toutefois [tut'fwa], *adv.* yet, nevertheless, however, still.

toute-puissance [tutpɥi'sã:s], *n.f.* omnipotence, almighty power.

tout-puissant [tupɥi'sã], *a.* (*fem.* **toute-puissante**) almighty. — *n.m.* (**Tout-Puissant**) the Almighty.

toux [tu], *n.f. inv.* cough.

toxémie [tɔkse'mi], *n.f.* (*Med.*) toxemia, blood poisoning.

toxique [tɔk'sik], *a.* toxic, poisonous.—*n.m.* poison.

tracas [tra'ka], *n.m.* bustle, turmoil, disturbance; worry, annoyance.

tracassement [trakas'mã], *n.m.* worrying.

tracasser [traka'se], *v.t.* to worry, to pester. **se tracasser,** *v.r.* to worry.

tracasserie [trakas'ri], *n.f.* worry, pestering, annoyance, vexation; (*pl.*) bickering.

tracassier [traka'sje], *a.* (*fem.* **-ière**) pestering, worrying, annoying; fussy; mischief-making.—*n.m.* (*fem.* **-ière**) pesterer, busybody; troublesome person, mischief-maker.

trace [tras], *n.f.* trace, track, footprint; spoor, trail; mark, impression, vestige; outline, sketch.

tracé [tra'se], *n.m.* outline, sketch (*of figure*); marking out; laying out (*of grounds etc.*); direction.

tracement [tras'mã], *n.m.* tracing, laying out (*of grounds, roads etc.*).

tracer [tra'se], *v.t.* (*conjug. like* COMMENCER) to trace, to draw, to trace out; to sketch; to portray; to lay out (*grounds, roads etc.*); (*fig.*) to set forth, to mark out.—*v.i.* to spread roots (*of trees*); to burrow (*of moles*).

trachée [tra'ʃe], *n.f.* trachea, air vessel.

trachée-artère [traʃear'tɛ:r], *n.f.* (*pl.* **trachées-artères**) trachea, windpipe.

tract [trakt], *n.m.* tract, leaflet (*for propaganda*).

tracteur [trak'tœ:r], *n.m.* tractor, traction engine.

traction [trak'sjɔ̃], *n.f.* traction; pulling; draft. t; *traction avant,* front-wheel drive.

tradition [tradi'sjɔ̃], *n.f.* tradition; (*Law*) delivery.

traditionnel [tradisjɔ'nɛl], *a.* (*fem.* **-elle**) traditional.

traducteur [tradyk'tœ:r], *n.m.* (*fem.* **-trice**) translator.

traduction [tradyk'sjɔ̃], *n.f.* translation, (*sch.*) crib, pony.

traduire [tra'dɥi:r], *v.t. irr.* (*conjug. like* CONDUIRE) to translate; to interpret, to construe; to convey, to express; to indicate, to denote.

traduisible [tradɥi'zibl], *a.* translatable.

trafic [tra'fik], *n.m.* traffic; trading, trade; dealings.

trafiquant [trafi'kã], *n.m.* (*fem.* **-e**) trafficker.

trafiquer [trafi'ke], *v.i.* to traffic, to trade, to deal (*de*).

tragédie [traʒe'di], *n.f.* tragedy.

tragédien [traʒe'djɛ̃], *n.m.* (*fem.* **-enne**) tragedian.

tragique [tra'ʒik], *a.* tragic, tragical.—*n.m.* tragedy, tragic art; tragic writer.

trahir [tra'i:r], *v.t.* to betray; to deceive; to divulge, to reveal. **se trahir,** *v.r.* to betray oneself; to betray each other.

trahison [trai'zɔ̃], *n.f.* treachery, treason, perfidy; breach of faith.

train [trɛ̃], *n.m.* pace, rate; train, suite, attendants; way, manner; noise, clatter, dust; carriage; quarters (*of a horse etc.*); (*Rail.*) train; *à fond de train,* at full speed; *être en train de faire quelque chose,* to be (in the act of) doing something; *train de maison,* style of living; *train de marchandises,* freight train; *train omnibus,* slow or local train.

traînage [trɛ'na:ʒ], *n.m.* dragging, drawing; sledging, sleighing.

traînant [trɛ'nã], *a.* dragging, trailing (*dress*); drawling (*voice*); shuffling (*gait*).

traînard [trɛ'na:r], *n.m.* straggler, laggard, slow-coach.

traîne [trɛ:n], *n.f.* dragging, being dragged or drawn; train (*of a dress etc.*).

traîneau [trɛ'no], *n.m.* (*pl.* **-eaux**) sledge, sleigh; drag-net.

traînée [trɛ'ne], *n.f.* train (*of gunpowder etc.*); trail, track.

traîner [trɛ'ne], *v.t.* to drag, to draw; to track; to spin out, to drag out, to protract; to drawl; to put off.—*v.i.* to trail, to draggle, to lag; to droop; to languish, to flag; to lie about; to loiter, to linger, to be protracted. **se traîner,** *v.r.* to crawl along, to creep; to lag, to drag oneself along.

train-train [trɛ̃'trɛ̃], *n.m.* (*colloq.*) routine, regular course.

traire [trɛ:r], *v.t. irr.* to milk; to draw (*milk*).

trait [trɛ], *n.m.* arrow, dart, bolt, shaft; thunderbolt; stroke, hit; trace (*of harness*); leash (*for dogs*); turn (*of the scale*); draft, gulp; dash (*of the pen etc.*); flash (*of light*); stroke, touch, trait, feature, lineament; act, deed; prime move (*at chess, draughts etc.*); *avoir trait à*, to have reference to; *boire à longs traits*, to drink long draughts of; *d'un seul trait*, at one gulp; *trait de génie*, stroke of genius, (*fam.*) brain-wave; *trait d'union*, hyphen.

traite [trɛt], *n.f.* stage, journey, stretch; milking; (*Comm.*) draft, bill; *traite des noirs*, slave trade.

traité [trɛ'te], *n.m.* treatise, tract, dissertation; treaty; agreement.

traitement [trɛt'mã], *n.m.* treatment; (*Ind.*) processing; reception; salary, pay.

traiter [trɛ'te], *v.t.* to treat; (*Ind.*) to process; to entertain; to use, to behave to; to discuss, to handle; to call, to style; to negotiate; to execute, to do.—*v.i.* to treat, to negotiate.

traiteur [trɛ'tœːr], *n.m.* restaurant keeper; caterer.

traître-[trɛːtr], *a.* (*fem.* **-esse**) treacherous, perfidious.—*n.m.* (*fem.* **-esse**) treacherous person, traitor, traitress.

traîtreusement [trɛtrœz'mã], *adv.* treacherously.

traîtrise [trɛ'triːz], *n.f.* treachery.

trajectoire [traʒɛk'twaːr], *a.* and *n.f.* trajectory.

trajet [tra'ʒɛ], *n.m.* passage, journey, crossing, voyage; (*Med.*) course.

trame [tram], *n.f.* weft, woof; plot, conspiracy; course, progress, thread.

tramer [tra'me], *v.t.* to weave; (*fig.*) to plot, to contrive, to hatch.

tramontane [tramõ'tan], *n.f.* tramontane, north wind; North; North Star.

tramway [tra'mwɛ], *n.m.* trolley car.

tranchant [trã'ʃã], *a.* sharp, cutting; (*fig.*) trenchant, decisive; salient, prominent.—*n.m.* edge.

tranche [trãːʃ], *n.f.* slice, chop; slab; edge (*of a book*); *doré sur tranche*, gilt-edged (*of a book*); *tranche de lard*, rasher of bacon.

tranchée [trã'ʃe], *n.f.* trench, cutting; (*pl.*) colic.

trancher [trã'ʃe], *v.t.* to cut; to cut off; to slice; to decide, to determine, to settle.—*v.i.* to cut; to decide; to set up for; to affect; to be glaring (*of colors*).

tranchoir [trã'ʃwaːr], *n.m.* trencher, cutting-board.

tranquille [trã'kil], *a.* quiet, calm, tranquil, placid, peaceful; undisturbed (*in mind etc.*); *soyez tranquille*, set your mind at ease.

tranquillement [trãkil'mã], *adv.* peacefully, quietly.

tranquillisant [trãkili'zã], *a.* tranquillizing.—*n.m.* tranquillizer.

tranquilliser [trãkili'ze], *v.t.* to tranquillize, to make easy, to soothe. **se tranquilliser**, *v.r.* to become tranquil, to calm down.

tranquillité [trãkili'te], *n.f.* tranquillity, quiet, peace.

transaction [trãzak'sjõ], *n.f.* transaction, arrangement.

transalpin [trãzal'pɛ̃], *a.* transalpine.

transatlantique [trãzatlã'tik], *a.* transatlantic.—*n.m.* liner; deck-chair.

transborder [trãsbɔr'de], *v.t.* to tranship.

transbordeur [trãsbɔr'dœːr], *n.m.* transporter; *pont transbordeur*, transporter bridge.

transcendant [trãsã'dã], *a.* transcendent.

transcription [trãskrip'sjõ], *n.f.* transcription, transcript, copy.

transcrire [trã'skriːr], *v.t. irr.* (*conjug. like* ÉCRIRE) to transcribe, to copy out.

transe [trãːs], *n.f.* fright, apprehension; trance.

transférable [trãsfe'rabl], *a.* transferable.

transférer [trãsfe're], *v.t.* (*conjug. like* CÉDER) to transfer, to transport, to convey, to move.

transfert [trãs'fɛːr], *n.m.* transfer.

transfiguration [trãsfigyra'sjõ], *n.f.* transfiguration.

transfigurer [trãsfigy're], *v.t.* to transfigure. **se transfigurer**, *v.r.* to be transfigured.

transformateur [trãsfɔrma'tœːr], *n.m.* (*Elec.*) transformer.

transformation [trãsfɔrma'sjõ], *n.f.* transformation.

transformer [trãsfɔr'me], *v.t.* to transform; to change, to convert. **se transformer**, *v.r.* to be transformed.

transfuge [trãs'fyːʒ], *n.m.* deserter; fugitive; turncoat.

transgresser [trãsgrɛ'se], *v.t.* to transgress, to infringe, to contravene.

transgression [trãsgrɛ'sjõ], *n.f.* transgression.

transhumance [trãzy'mãːs], *n.f.* transhumance.

transi [trã'zi], *a.* chilled, benumbed.

transiger [trãzi'ʒe], *v.i.* (*conjug. like* MANGER) to compound, to compromise, to come to terms (*avec*).

transir [trã'ziːr], *v.t.* to chill, to benumb; to paralyse.—*v.i.* to be chilled; to be paralyzed (*with fear etc.*).

transissement [trãzis'mã], *n.m.* chill, numbness; shivering (*with terror etc.*).

transistor [trãzis'tɔr], *n.m.* transistor.

transit [trã'zit], *n.m.* transit.

transitaire [trãzi'tɛːr], *a.* pertaining to the transit of goods.

transitif [trãzi'tif], *a.* (*fem.* **-tive**) transitive.

transition [trãzi'sjõ], *n.f.* transition.

transitoire [trãzi'twaːr], *a.* transitory.

translation [trãslɑ'sjõ], *n.f.* transfer(ring), relaying.

translucide [trãsly'sid], *a.* translucent.

translucidité [trãslysidi'te], *n.f.* translucence.

transmarin [trãsma'rɛ̃], *a.* transmarine, oversea.

transmetteur [trãsmɛ'tœːr], *n.m.* (*Rad.*) transmitter.

transmettre [trãs'mɛtr], *v.t. irr.* (*conjug. like* METTRE) to transmit, to convey, to send on; to transfer.

transmigration [trãsmigra'sjõ], *n.f.* transmigration.

transmigrer [trãsmi'gre], *v.i.* to transmigrate.

transparence [trãspa'rãːs], *n.f.* transparency.

transparent [trãspa'rã], *a.* transparent.—*n.m.* paper ruled with black lines; transparency.

transpercer [trãspɛr'se], *v.t.* (*conjug. like* COMMENCER) to pierce through; to run through (*with a sword etc.*), to transfix.

transpiration [trãspira'sjõ], *n.f.* perspiration, perspiring.

transpirer [trãspi're], *v.i.* to perspire; to ooze out; to transpire.

transplanter [trăsplă'te], *v.t.* to transplant.
transport [trăs'pɔːr], *n.m.* carriage, conveyance; transport, removal; transfer, assignment; (*fig.*) rapture, ecstasy; transport ship; *transport au cerveau,* stroke, fit of delirium.
transportation [trăsporta'sjɔ̃], *n.f.* transportation.
transporté [trăspor'te], *n.m.* (*fem.* **-ée**) deported person, convict.
transporter [trăspor'te], *v.t.* to convey, to transport; to transfer; to banish; to enrapture. **se transporter,** *v.r.* to transport oneself, to go.
transporteur [trăspor'tœːr], *n.m.* carrier, conveyor.
transposer [trăspo'ze], *v.t.* to transpose.
transposition [trăspozi'sjɔ̃], *n.f.* transposition.
transrhénan [trăsre'nɑ̃], *a.* from beyond the Rhine.
transsubstantiation [trăssybstɑ̃sja'sjɔ̃], *n.f.* transubstantiation.
transvaser [trăsva'ze], *v.t.* to decant.
transversal [trăzver'sal], *a.* (*m.pl.* **-aux**) transversal, transverse.
trapèze [tra'pɛːz], *n.m.* trapezium; trapeze.
trappe [trap], *n.f.* trap door; trap, pitfall; curtain, register (*of chimney*).
trappeur [tra'pœːr], *n.m.* trapper.
trappiste [tra'pist], *a.* and *n.m.* Trappist.
trapu [tra'py], *a.* squat, dumpy, thick-set, stocky.
traquer [tra'ke], *v.t.* (*Hunt.*) to beat for game; to enclose, to encircle; to track down.
travail [tra'vaːj], *n.m.* (*pl.* **-aux**) labor, work; toil; travail; piece of work; workmanship; occupation; study; *cabinet de travail,* study (*room*); *travaux forcés,* hard labor.
travaillé [trava'je], *a.* worked, wrought; labored, elaborate; laboring (*under*).
travailler [trava'je], *v.t.* to work, to work at; to do with care; to fashion; to till (*the ground*).—*v.i.* to labor, to work; to study; to strive; to ferment (*of wines*); to warp (*of wood*). **se travailler,** *v.r.* to torment oneself; to be overwrought.
travailleur [trava'jœːr], *a.* (*fem.* **-euse**) industrious, hard-working; painstaking.—*n.m.* (*fem.* **-euse**) workman, laborer; hard-working person.
travailliste [trava'jist], *a.* Labour, Socialist.—*n.* member of the Labour Party.
travée [tra've], *n.f.* (*Arch.*) bay; truss (*of bridges*); (*Av.*) rib (*of wing*).
travers [tra'vɛːr], *n.m.* breadth; fault, failing; oddity; (*Naut.*) side, broadside; *à travers,* across; *au travers de,* through; *de travers,* obliquely, awry, askew; *en travers,* across, crosswise; *à tort et à travers,* at random.
traverse [tra'vɛrs], *n.f.* cross-bar, cross-piece; cross-road, short cut; (*Rail.*) tie; (*pl.*) (*fig.*) setbacks.
traversée [traver'se], *n.f.* passage, crossing.
traverser [traver'se], *v.t.* to cross, to go over or through, to traverse, to get through or across; to run through (*with a sword etc.*); to lie across, to span; to intersect; to penetrate; to thwart.

traversier [traver'sje], *a.* (*fem.* **-ière**) cross-; that plies across.
traversin [traver'sɛ̃], *n.m.* bolster; (*Carp. etc.*) cross-beam; (*Naut.*) stretcher (*in boats*).
travesti [traves'ti], *a.* disguised; travestied, parodied.
travestir [traves'tiːr], *v.t.* to disguise, to travesty; (*fig.*) to misrepresent.
travestissement [travestis'mɑ̃], *n.m.* disguise; travesty.
trébuchant [treby'ʃɑ̃], *a.* of full weight (*of coins*); stumbling.
trébucher [treby'ʃe], *v.i.* to stumble, to slip; to err; (*fig.*) to turn the scale.
trébuchet [treby'ʃɛ], *n.m.* bird trap; assay-balance.
tréfiler [trefi'le], *v.t.* to wire-draw.
trèfle [trɛfl], *n.m.* trefoil, clover; (*Cards*) clubs; *trèfle blanc,* shamrock.
tréfonds [tre'ʃɔ̃], *n.m.* subsoil; (*fig.*) bottom, heart.
treillage [trɛ'jaːʒ], *n.m.* trellis(-work), lattice-work.
treille [trɛːj], *n.f.* vine trellis; shrimp net.
treillis [trɛ'ji], *n.m.* trellis, lattice; coarse canvas etc., sackcloth.
treizaine [trɛ'zɛn], *n.f.* baker's dozen.
treize [trɛːz], *a.* and *n.m.* thirteen; thirteenth.
treizième [trɛ'zjɛm], *a.* and *n.* thirteenth (*part*).
tréma [tre'ma], *n.m.* dieresis.
tremblant [trɑ̃'blɑ̃], *a.* trembling, quivering; flickering (*of light etc.*).
tremble [trɑ̃:bl], *n.m.* aspen.
tremblé [trɑ̃'ble], *a.* wavy (*of lines*); shaky (*of writing*).
tremblement [trɑ̃blə'mɑ̃], *n.m.* trembling, shaking, quaking, trepidation, tremor; flickering (*of light*); (*Mus.*) tremolo; *tremblement de terre,* earthquake.
trembler [trɑ̃'ble], *v.i.* to tremble, to shake, to shiver; to quake, to fear; to flutter (*of wings*).
tremblotant [trɑ̃blɔ'tɑ̃], *a.* trembling, tremulous (*of sound etc.*); shivering, quivering, fluttering.
tremblotement [trɑ̃blɔt'mɑ̃], *n.m.* trembling, shivering.
trembloter [trɑ̃blɔ'te], *v.i.* to tremble (*of sound*); to quiver, to shiver; to flutter (*of wings*); to flicker (*of light*).
trémousser [tremu'se], *v.t.* to bestir, to move about, to flutter.—*v.i.* to shake, to stir. **se trémousser,** *v.r.* to flutter or frisk about; to bestir oneself.
trempage [trɑ̃'paːʒ], *n.m.* steeping, soaking; (*Print.*) wetting.
trempe [trɑ̃:p], *n.f.* temper (*of steel etc.*); (*fig.*) character, stamp, quality.
tremper [trɑ̃'pe], *v.t.* to soak, to steep, to wet, to drench; to temper (*iron, steel etc.*); to dilute (*wine etc.*).—*v.i.* to soak, to be steeped; to be implicated (*in a crime*).
tremplin [trɑ̃'plɛ̃], *n.m.* spring-board, diving board; trampoline.
trentaine [trɑ̃'tɛn], *n.f.* about thirty; age of thirty.
trente [trɑ̃:t], *a.* and *n.m.* thirty; thirtieth.
trentième [trɑ̃'tjɛm], *a.* and *n.* thirtieth (*part*).

trépan [tre'pɑ̃], *n.m.* trepan (*instrument*); trepanning.

trépaner [trepa'ne], *v.t.* to trepan.

trépas [tre'pɑ], *n.m. inv.* (*poet.*) decease, death.

trépassé [trepa'se], *n.m.* (*fem.* **-ée**) dead person.

trépasser [trepa'se], *v.i.* to depart this life, to pass away.

trépidant [trepi'dɑ̃], *a.* vibrating; (*fig.*) agitated, hectic.

trépidation [trepida'sjɔ̃], *n.f.* trepidation, trembling; agitation.

trépied [tre'pje], *n.m.* trivet; tripod.

trépignement [trepiɲ'mɑ̃], *n.m.* stamping (*of feet*).

trépigner [trepi'ɲe], *v.i.* to stamp, to stamp one's foot.

très [trɛ], *adv.* very; most; very much.

trésor [tre'zɔːr], *n.m.* treasure; treasury; exchequer; thesaurus.

trésorerie [trezɔr'ri], *n.f.* treasury; treasurership.

trésorier [trezɔ'rje], *n.m.* treasurer; (*Mil.*) paymaster.

tressage [trɛ'saːʒ], *n.m.* plaiting, braiding.

tressaillement [trɛsaj'mɑ̃], *n.m.* start, bound, thrill, shudder; flutter.

tressaillir [trɛsa'jiːr], *v.i. irr.* (*conjug. like* ASSAILLIR) to start, to thrill; to quake, to tremble, to shudder.

tresse [trɛs], *n.f.* tress, plait (*of hair*); braid.

tresser [trɛ'se], *v.t.* to weave, to plait, to braid; to wreathe.

tréteau [tre'to], *n.m.* (*pl.* **-eaux**) trestle; (*pl.*) stage.

treuil [trœːj], *n.m.* windlass; winch.

trêve [trɛːv], *n.f.* truce.

tri [tri], *n.m.* sorting (*of letters etc.*).

triage [tri'aːʒ], *n.m.* picking, sorting; choice, selection.

triangle [tri'ɑ̃ːgl], *n.m.* triangle.

triangulaire [trijɑ̃gy'lɛːr], *a.* triangular.

tribord [tri'bɔːr], *n.m.* (*Naut.*) starboard.

tribu [tri'by], *n.f.* tribe.

tribulation [tribyla'sjɔ̃], *n.f.* tribulation.

tribun [tri'bœ̃], *n.m.* tribune; (*fig.*) democratic leader.

tribunal [triby'nal], *n.m.* (*pl.* **-aux**) tribunal, bench; court of justice.

tribune [tri'byn], *n.f.* tribune (*rostrum*); hustings; gallery.

tribut [tri'by], *n.m.* tribute; grant, contribution; *duty; (fig.)* debt.

tributaire [triby'tɛːr], *a.* dependent (*upon*).—*n.m.* tributary.

tricher [tri'ʃe], *v.t., v.i.* to cheat, to trick.

tricherie [triʃ'ri], *n.f.* cheating, trick, trickery.

tricheur [tri'ʃœːr], *n.m.* (*fem.* **-euse**) cheat, trickster.

tricolore [trikɔ'lɔːr], *a.* tricolored.

tricorne [tri'kɔrn], *a.* three-cornered.—*n.m.* three-cornered hat.

tricot [tri'ko], *n.m.* knitting; jersey, jumper, (*fam.*) woolly; *tricot de corps*, vest.

tricotage [trikɔ'taːʒ], *n.m.* knitting.

tricoter [trikɔ'te], *v.t., v.i.* to knit.

trictrac [trik'trak], *n.m.* tric-trac (*form of backgammon*).

tricycle [tri'sikl], *n.m.* three-wheeled vehicle; tricycle.

trident [tri'dɑ̃], *n.m.* trident.

triennal [triɛ'nal], *a.* (*m. pl.* **-aux**) triennial.

trier [tri'je], *v.t.* to pick, to choose, to sort, to select; to route (*freight cars*).

trieur [tri'jœːr], *n.m.* (*fem.* **-euse**) sorter, picker.

trigonométrie [trigɔnɔme'tri], *n.f.* trigonometry.

trille [triːj], *n.m.* quaver, trill.

triller [tri'je], *v.t.* to trill, to quaver.

trillion [tri'ljɔ̃], *n.m.* (*since* 1948 = 1 *followed by* 18 *ciphers*) trillion, one million billion(s); (*Am.*) quintillion.

trilogie [trilɔ'ʒi], *n.f.* trilogy.

trimbaler [trɛ̃ba'le], *v.t.* (*fam.*) to drag *or* lug about (*parcels*); to trail (*children*) about. **se trimbaler**, *v.r.* (*pop.*) to traipse round.

trimer [tri'me], *v.i.* (*pop.*) to drudge, to wear oneself out.

trimestre [tri'mɛstr], *n.m.* quarter (*three months*); quarter's pay; (*Sch.*) term.

trimestriel [trimɛstri'ɛl], *a.* (*fem.* **-elle**) quarterly.

tringle [trɛ̃ːgl], *n.f.* rod.

Trinité [trini'te], *n.f.* Trinity; *la Trinité*, Trinity Sunday; (*l'Île de*) *la Trinité*, Trinidad.

trinquer [trɛ̃'ke], *v.i.* to clink glasses (*before drinking*); to drink to one another's health; (*pop.*) to suffer, to be hurt.

trio [tri'o], *n.m.* trio.

triomphal [triɔ̃'fal], *a.* (*m. pl.* **-aux**) triumphal.

triomphalement [triɔ̃fal'mɑ̃], *adv.* triumphantly.

triomphant [triɔ̃'fɑ̃], *a.* triumphant.

triomphe [tri'ɔ̃ːf], *n.m.* triumph.

triompher [triɔ̃'fe], *v.i.* to triumph; to overcome; to exult; to excel.

triparti [tripar'ti], **tripartite** [tripar'tit], *a.* tripartite.

tripe [trip], *n.f.* tripe; imitation velvet, velveteen (*also called tripe de velours*).

triperie [trip'ri], *n.f.* tripe shop.

triple [tripl], *a.* and *n.m.* treble, triple, threefold.

tripler [tri'ple], *v.t., v.i.* to treble, to triple.

triplicata [triplika'ta], *n.m. inv.* triplicate.

tripode [tri'pɔd], *a.* and *n.m.* tripod.

tripot [tri'po], *n.m.* gambling den; house of ill fame.

tripotage [tripɔ'taːʒ], *n.m.* mess; underhand dealing; chore.

tripoter [tripɔ'te], *v.t.* to meddle with; to speculate in.—*v.i.* to make mischief, to mess about; to act in an underhand way.

tripoteur [tripɔ'tœːr], *n.m.* (*fem.* **-euse**) mischief-maker, shady speculator.

trique [trik], *n.f.* (*fam.*) cudgel, stick, bludgeon.

trisaïeul [triza'jœl], *n.m.* (*pl.* **-aïeuls**) great-great-grandfather.

trisaïeule [triza'jœl], *n.f.* great-great-grandmother.

triste [trist], *a.* sorrowful, mournful, sad, melancholy, dejected; dull, dreary, dismal; poor, sorry (*of persons*); mean, paltry.

tristement [trista'mɑ̃], *adv.* sadly.

tristesse [tris'tɛs], *n.f.* sadness; melancholy; dreariness.

triton [tri'tɔ̃], *n.m.* triton, newt.

trivial [tri'vjal], *a.* (*m. pl.* **-aux**) vulgar, trifling; trite, hackneyed.—*n.m.* vulgarity.

trivialité

trivialité [trivjali'te], *n.f.* vulgarity; triteness.
troc [trok], *n.m.* trade, barter, swap.
troène [trɔ'ɛn], *n.m.* privet.
troglodyte [trɔglo'dit], *n.m.* troglodyte.
trogne [trɔɲ], *n.f.* reddish *or* bloated face.
trognon [trɔ'ɲɔ̃], *n.m.* core (*of a pear or apple*); stump (*of a cabbage*).
Troie [trwa], *f.* Troy.
trois [trwa], *a.* and *n.m. inv.* three; third.
troisième [trwa'zjɛm], *a.* third.—*n.* third.—*n.m.* third floor.
troisièmement [trwazjɛm'mɑ̃], *adv.* thirdly.
trombe [trɔ̃ːb], *n.f.* waterspout.
tromblon [trɔ̃'blɔ̃], *n.m.* blunderbuss.
trombone [trɔ̃'bon], *n.m.* trombone; paper clip (*of wire*).
trompe [trɔ̃ːp], *n.f.* *trump, horn; proboscis, trunk (*of elephants*).
tromper [trɔ̃'pe], *v.t.* to deceive, to impose upon; to delude; to cheat, to take in; to betray, to be unfaithful to (*wife, husband*). **se tromper,** *v.r.* to be mistaken, to make a mistake, to deceive oneself.
tromperie [trɔ̃'pri], *n.f.* cheat, fraud; illusion, delusion.
trompeter [trɔ̃pə'te], *v.t.* (*conjug. like* APPELER) to trumpet abroad.
trompette [trɔ̃'pɛt], *n.f.* trumpet.—*n.m.* trumpeter.
trompeur [trɔ̃'pœːr], *a.* (*fem.* **-euse**) deceitful; false, misleading.—*n.m.* (*fem.* **-euse**) deceiver, cheat, impostor; betrayer.
trompeusement [trɔ̃pøz'mɑ̃], *adv.* deceitfully, deceptively.
tronc [trɔ̃], *n.m.* trunk, bole (*of tree*); stock; poor box.
tronçon [trɔ̃'sɔ̃], *n.m.* broken piece, fragment, stump.
tronçonner [trɔ̃sɔ'ne], *v.t.* to cut into pieces.
trône [troːn], *n.m.* throne.
trôner [tro'ne], *v.i.* to sit on a throne; (*fig.*) to lord it.
tronquer [trɔ̃'ke], *v.t.* to mutilate, to truncate; (*fig.*) to garble, to mangle.
trop [tro], *adv.* too much, too, over, too many; *de trop,* too much, too many; *être de trop,* to be in the way, not to be wanted; *par trop,* excessively.—*n.m.* excess, superfluity.
trophée [tro'fe], *n.m.* trophy.
tropical [trɔpi'kal], *a.* (*m. pl.* **-aux**) tropical.
tropique [trɔ'pik], *n.m.* tropic.
trop-plein [tro'plɛ̃], *n.m.* (*pl.* **-pleins**) overflow, waste; surplus, excess.
troquer [trɔ'ke], *v.t.* to trade, to barter, to exchange.
trot [tro], *n.m.* trot.
trotte-menu [trotmə'ny] *a. inv.* running with little steps, pitter-pattering.
trotter [trɔ'te], *v.i.* to trot; to run about, to toddle (*children*).
trotteur [trɔ'tœːr], *n.m.* (*fem.* **-euse**) trotter.—*n.f.* (**-euse**) second hand (*of watch*).
trottin [trɔ'tɛ̃], *n.m.* errand girl.
trottiner [trɔti'ne], *v.i.* to go at a jog-trot; to toddle along.
trottinette [trɔti'nɛt], *n.f.* (*child's*) scooter.
trottoir [trɔ'twaːr], *n.m.* foot-path, pavement, (*Am.*) sidewalk; *le bord du trottoir,* the curb.
trou [tru], *n.m.* hole; gap; orifice, mouth; *boucher un trou,* to stop a gap, to pay a

debt; *trou d'air,* air pocket; *trou de la serrure,* keyhole; *trou du souffleur,* (*Theat.*) prompter's box.
troubadour [truba'duːr], *n.m.* troubadour.
troublant [tru'blɑ̃], *a.* disturbing, troubling.
trouble [trubl], *a.* thick, muddy, turbid, cloudy; dull.—*adv.* dimly, confusedly.—*n.m.* confusion, disorder, disturbance; perplexity, uneasiness; dispute, quarrel; (*pl.*) disturbances, dissensions.
trouble-fête [trublə'fɛːt], *n.m. inv.* kill-joy.
troubler [tru'ble], *v.t.* to disturb, to make thick, to make muddy; to muddle, to turn; to confuse, to agitate; to perplex, to disconcert; to trouble; to interrupt; to ruffle, to annoy; to dim, to dull. **se troubler,** *v.r.* to grow thick, to become muddy; to be confused, to be disconcerted; to become cloudy; to become confused.
trouée [tru'e], *n.f.* opening, gap, breach; pass.
trouer [tru'e], *v.t.* to bore, to make a hole in. **se trouer,** *v.r.* to get holes in it.
trouille [truːj], *n.f.* (*vulg.*) fear.
troupe [truːp], *n.f.* troop, band; crew, gang, set; company (*of actors*); flock, crowd; (*pl.*) troops, forces.
troupeau [tru'po], *n.m.* (*pl.* **-eaux**) flock, herd, drove.
troupier [tru'pje], *n.m.* soldier.
trousse [truːs], *n.f.* bundle, truss; (*Surg.*) case of instruments; case for razors, toilet articles etc; *je suis à ses trousses,* I am after him.
troussé [tru'se], *a.* tucked up; *bien troussé,* well set up, neat, dapper.
trousseau [tru'so], *n.m.* (*pl.* **-eaux**) bunch (*of keys*); trousseau; outfit, kit.
trousser [tru'se], *v.t.* to tuck up, to turn up, to pin up; to truss; to dispatch (*business etc.*). **se trousser,** *v.r.* to tuck up one's clothes.
trouvaille [tru'vaːj], *n.f.* godsend, windfall; find.
trouvé [tru've], *a.* found; *bien trouvé,* felicitous; *enfant trouvé,* foundling.
trouver [tru've], *v.t.* to find, to discover, to meet with, to hit upon; to detect; to find out; to deem, to judge; *trouver à dire* or *à redire à,* to find fault with; *trouver bon,* to think fit; *trouver mauvais,* to blame, to be displeased with; *vous trouvez?* you think so, do you? **se trouver,** *v.r.* to find oneself; to be, to exist; to feel; to prove, to turn out; *se trouver mal,* to faint.
truand [try'ɑ̃], *a.* vagrant.—*n.m.* (*fem.* **-e**) vagrant, beggar, tramp; crook.
truc (1) [tryk], *n.m.* knack, dodge, trick; (*Theat.*) machinery; (*pop.*) thing, thingumajig, gadget.
truc (2) **or truck** [tryk], *n.m.* (*Rail.*) flatcar.
trucheman or truchement [tryʃ'mɑ̃], *n.m.* interpreter; go-between.
truculent [tryky'lɑ̃], *a.* truculent.
truelle [try'ɛl], *n.f.* trowel; *truelle à poisson,* slice of fish.
truffe [tryf], *n.f.* truffle.
truie [truji], *n.f.* sow.
truite [truit], *n.f.* trout.
truité [truji'te], *a.* spotted, speckled.
trumeau [try'mo], *n.m.* (*pl.* **-eaux**) pier; pier glass; leg of beef.

tsar [tsa:r], *n.m.* Tsar.

tsigane [TZIGANE].

tu [ty], *pron.* *thou, you.

tuant [tyˈɑ̃], *a.* killing, tiresome, laborious.

tube [tyb], *n.m.* tube, pipe; (*Anat.*) duct.

tuberculeux [tybɛrkyˈlø], *a.* (*fem.* **-euse**) tuberculous.

tuberculose [tybɛrkyˈloːz], *n.f.* tuberculosis.

tubulaire [tybyˈlɛːr], *a.* tubular.

tuer [tɥe], *v.t.* to kill, to slay; to slaughter, to butcher; to tire to death; to while away. **se tuer**, *v.r.* to kill oneself, to be killed; (*fig.*) to wear oneself out.

tuerie [tyˈri], *n.f.* slaughter, butchery; slaughter-house.

tue-tête (à) [atyˈtɛːt], *adv. phr.* at the top of one's voice.

tueur [tɥœːr], *n.m.* (*fem.* **-euse**) killer, thug.

tuile [tɥil], *n.f.* tile.

tuilerie [tɥilˈri], *n.f.* tile-works; **les Tuileries**, the Tuileries (*before 1871 a Royal palace, now a garden in Paris*).

tulipe [tyˈlip], *n.f.* tulip.

tulle [tyl], *n.m.* tulle, net.

tumeur [tyˈmœːr], *n.f.* tumor, swelling.

tumulte [tyˈmylt], *n.m.* tumult, uproar; hubbub.

tumultueux [tymylˈtɥø], *a.* (*fem.* **-euse**) tumultuous, riotous.

tunique [tyˈnik], *n.f.* tunic; envelope, film.

Tunisie [tyniˈzi], **la**, *f.* Tunisia.

tunisien [tyniˈzjɛ̃], *a.* Tunisian.—*n.m.* (**Tunisien**, *fem.* **-enne**) Tunisian (*person*).

tunnel [tyˈnɛl], *n.m.* tunnel.

turban [tyrˈbɑ̃], *n.m.* turban.

turbine [tyrˈbin], *n.f.* turbine.

turbopropulseur [tyrbopropylˈsœːr], *n.m.* turbo-prop.

turboréacteur [tyrboreakˈtœːr], *n.m.* jet engine; turbo-jet.

turbot [tyrˈbo], *n.m.* turbot.

turbulence [tyrbyˈlɑ̃ːs], *n.f.* turbulence.

turbulent [tyrbyˈlɑ̃], *a.* turbulent, boisterous; rowdy.

turc [tyrk], *a.* (*fem.* **turque**) Turkish.—*n.m.* Turkish (*language*); (**Turc**, *fem.* **Turque**) Turk.

turelure [tyrˈlyːr], *n.f.* fol-de-rol (*burden of a song*).

turf [tyrf], *n.m.* the turf, horse racing.

turpitude [tyrpiˈtyd], *n.f.* turpitude, baseness, ignominy.

turque [TURC].

Turquie [tɥiˈki], **la**, *f.* Turkey.

turquoise [tyrˈkwaːz], *a.* and *n.f.* turquoise.

tussor [tyˈsoːr], *n.m.* tussore (*silk*).

tutelle [tyˈtɛl], *n.f.* tutelage, guardianship; (*Polit.*) trusteeship.

tuteur [tyˈtœːr], *n.m.* (*fem.* **tutrice**) guardian, trustee, protector.—*n.m.* (*Hort.*) stake.

tutoiement or **tutoîment** [tytwaˈmɑ̃], *n.m.* addressing a person as 'tu', 'theeing and thouing'.

tutoyer [tytwaˈje], *v.t.* (*conjug. like* EMPLOYER) to be on intimate terms with. **se tutoyer**, *v.r.* to be on familiar terms.

tutrice [tyˈtris], [TUTEUR].

tuyau [tɥiˈjo], *n.m.* (*pl.* **-aux**) pipe; tube; (chimney-)flue; shaft, funnel; stalk (*of grain*); nozzle (*of bellows etc.*); stem (*of a tobacco pipe*); **tuyau d'arrosage**, garden

hose; **tuyau d'incendie**, fire hose; **tuyau de poêle**, stove-pipe.

tuyautage [tɥijoˈtaːʒ], *n.m.* frilling, fluting; tubing.

tuyauter [tɥijoˈte], *v.t.* to goffer, to frill.

tuyauterie [tɥijoˈtri], *n.f.* system of pipes; plumbing; pipe trade.

tympan [tɛ̃ˈpɑ̃], *n.m.* ear-drum, tympanum; tympan; spandrel.

type [tip], *n.m.* type; model, pattern; symbol, emblem; standard; (*Astron.*) plan, drawing; (*colloq.*) guy, chap, fellow.

typhoïde [tifoˈid], *a.* typhoid.

typhon [tiˈfɔ̃], *n.m.* typhoon.

typhus [tiˈfyːs], *n.m.* typhus.

typique [tiˈpik], *a.* typical; characteristic.

typographe [tipoˈgraf], *n.m.* typographer.

typographie [tipograˈfi], *n.f.* typography.

tyran [tiˈrɑ̃], *n.m.* tyrant.

tyrannie [tiraˈni], *n.f.* tyranny.

tyrannique [tiraˈnik], *a.* tyrannical.

tyranniser [tiraniˈze], *v.t.* to tyrannize, to oppress.

tzar [TSAR].

tzigane or **tsigane** [tsiˈgan], *a.* and *n.* gipsy.

U

U, u [y], *n.m.* the twenty-first letter of the alphabet.

ubiquité [ybikɥiˈte], *n.f.* ubiquity.

Ukraine [yˈkrɛn], **l'**, *f.* the Ukraine.

ukrainien [ykrɛˈnjɛ̃], *a.* Ukrainian.—*n.m.* (**Ukrainien**, *fem.* **-enne**) Ukrainian (*person*).

ulcère [ylˈsɛːr], *n.m.* ulcer.

ulcéré [ylseˈre], *a.* ulcerated; (*fig.*) embittered.

ulcérer [ylseˈre], *v.t.* (*conjug. like* CÉDER) to ulcerate; (*fig.*) to embitter, to incense.

ultérieur [ylteˈrjœːr], *a.* ulterior, further, later, subsequent.

ultérieurement [ylterjœrˈmɑ̃], *adv.* later on.

ultimatum [ultimaˈtɔm], *n.m.* ultimatum.

ultime [ylˈtim], *a.* last, final, ultimate.

ultra-sonore [yltrasoˈnoːr], *a.* supersonic.

ultra-violet [yltravioˈlɛ], *a.* (*fem.* **-ette**) ultra-violet.

ululer [ylyˈle], *v.i.* to ululate, to hoot.

Ulysse [yˈlis], *m.* Ulysses.

umbre [ɔ̃ːbr], **omble** [ɔ̃ːbl], **ombre** [ɔ̃ːbr], *n.m.* grayling (*fish*).

un [œ̃], *a.* and *art. indef.* (*fem.* **une**) one, the first; single; a, an; any, a certain.—*pron. indef.* one thing; one; *c'est tout un*, it is all one; *les uns disent oui, les autres disent non*, some say yes, others say no; *les uns et les autres*, all, all together; *l'un et l'autre*, both; *l'un ou l'autre*, the one or the other; *l'un vaut l'autre*, one is as good as the other; *un à un*, one by one.—*n.m.* one.

unanime [ynaˈnim], *a.* unanimous.

unanimement [ynanimˈmɑ̃], *adv.* unanimously.

unanimité [ynanimiˈte], *n.f.* unanimity.

uni [y'ni], *a.* united; smooth, even, level; uniform; plain, unaffected.

unicorne [yni'kɔrn], *n.m.* unicorn.

unième [y'njɛm], *a.* (*in compounds only*) first; *vingt et unième*, 21st.

unification [ynifika'sjɔ̃], *n.f.* unification.

unifier [yni'fje], *v.t.* to unify, to unite; to amalgamate.

uniforme [yni'fɔrm], *a.* uniform.—*n.m.* uniform, regimentals.

uniformément [ynifɔrme'mɑ̃], *adv.* uniformly.

uniformité [ynifɔrmi'te], *n.f.* uniformity.

unilatéral [ynilate'ral], *a.* (*m. pl.* **-aux**) unilateral.

uniment [yni'mɑ̃], *adv.* evenly, smoothly; plainly.

union [y'njɔ̃], *n.f.* union; concord, agreement; mixture; marriage.

unique [y'nik], *a.* only, sole; single, unique, unparalleled; odd, singular; *fils unique*, only son; *sens unique*, one way (*street*).

uniquement [ynik'mɑ̃], *adv.* solely.

unir [y'ni:r], *v.t.* to unite, to join; to smooth, to level; to pair. **s'unir**, *v.r.* to unite, to join together.

unisson [yni'sɔ̃], *n.m.* unison; (*fig.*) harmony, concert.

unité [yni'te], *n.f.* unity; unit; (*fig.*) concord, agreement.

univers [yni've:r], *n.m. inv.* universe.

universalité [yniversali'te], *n.f.* universality; sum total, whole.

universel [yniver'sɛl], *a.* (*fem.* **-elle**) universal; residuary (*of legacies*).

universellement [yniversɛl'mɑ̃], *adv.* universally.

universitaire [yniversi'tɛ:r], *a.* of the university, academic.—*n.* teacher, professor.

université [yniversi'te], *n.f.* university.

uranium [yra'njɔm], *n.m.* uranium.

urbain [yr'bɛ̃], *a.* urban.

urbanisme [yrba'nism], *n.m.* town-planning.

urbaniste [yrba'nist], *n.m.* town-planner.

urbanité [yrbani'te], *n.f.* urbanity.

urgence [yr'ʒɑ̃:s], *n.f.* urgency; emergency; *d'urgence*, urgently, immediately.

urgent [yr'ʒɑ̃], *a.* urgent, pressing.

urinaire [yri'nɛ:r], *a.* urinary.

urine [y'rin], *n.f.* urine.

uriner [yri'ne], *v.i.* to urinate, to make water.

urinoir [yri'nwa:r], *n.m.* (public) urinal.

urne [yrn], *n.f.* urn; *urne électorale*, ballot box.

Ursule [yr'syl], *f.* Ursula.

urticaire [yrti'kɛ:r], *n.f.* nettle rash; urticaria.

Uruguay [yry'gɛ], l', *m.* Uruguay.

uruguayen [yrygɛ'jɛ̃], *a.* Uruguayan.—*n.m.* (**Uruguayen**, *fem.* **-enne**) Uruguayan (*person*).

us [ys, yz], *n.m. pl. les us et coutumes*, the ways and customs.

usage [y'za:ʒ], *n.m.* custom, practice, usage; use; wear (*of clothes etc.*); *avoir de l'usage*, to have breeding; *hors d'usage*, out of use; *faire de l'usage* or *faire un bon usage*, to last or wear a long time.

usagé [yza'ʒe], *a.* used, worn, second-hand.

usager [yza'ʒe], *n.m.* user; *les usagers de la route*, road-users.

usé [y'ze], *a.* worn-out, threadbare; stale, trite, hackneyed.

user [y'ze], *v.t.* to use up, to consume; to wear out; to spend, to waste.—*v.i.* to make use of. **s'user**, *v.r.* to wear oneself out; to wear away.

usine [y'zin], *n.f.* works, mills, factory.

usinier [yzi'nje], *n.m.* manufacturer, mill owner.

usité [yzi'te], *a.* used, usual, in common use.

ustensile [ystɑ̃'sil], *n.m.* utensil; tool, implement.

usuel [y'zɥɛl], *a.* (*fem.* **-elle**) usual, customary, ordinary.

usuellement [ysɥɛl'mɑ̃], *adv.* habitually, ordinarily.

usure [y'zy:r], *n.f.* usury, excessive interest; wear and tear.

usurier [yzy'rje], *a.* (*fem.* **-ière**) usurious.—*n.m.* (*fem.* **-ière**) usurer.

usurpateur [yzyrpa'tœ:r], *a.* (*fem.* **-trice**) usurping.—*n.m.* (*fem.* **-trice**) usurper.

usurpation [yzyrpa'sjɔ̃], *n.f.* usurpation; encroachment.

usurper [yzyr'pe], *v.t.* to usurp; to encroach upon.

ut [yt], *n.m.* (*Mus.*) ut, do, the note C.

utérus [yte'rys], *n.m.* uterus, womb.

utile [y'til], *a.* useful, serviceable; advantageous, expedient, beneficial; *en temps utile*, in due or good time.—*n.m.* utility, usefulness.

utilement [ytil'mɑ̃], *adv.* usefully.

utilisation [ytiliza'sjɔ̃], *n.f.* use, utilization.

utiliser [ytili'ze], *v.t.* to use, to find use for, to employ.

utilité [ytili'te], *n.f.* utility, usefulness; benefit, profit, service, avail.

utopie [ytɔ'pi], *n.f.* utopia.

utopique [ytɔ'pik], *a.* utopian.

V

V, v [ve], *n.m.* the twenty-second letter of the alphabet.

vacance [va'kɑ̃:s], *n.f.* vacancy; (*pl.*) vacation, holiday; recess (*of parliament etc.*).

vacant [va'kɑ̃], *a.* vacant; unoccupied, empty.

vacarme [va'karm], *n.m.* hubbub, uproar, fuss.

vacation [vaka'sjɔ̃], *n.f.* attendance, sitting (*of public officers etc.*); day's sale (*at auctions*); vacation (*of courts*).

vaccin [vak'sɛ̃], *n.m.* vaccine.

vaccination [vaksina'sjɔ̃], *n.f.* inoculation, vaccination.

vacciner [vaksi'ne], *v.t.* to inoculate, to vaccinate; to immunize.

vache [vaʃ], *n.f.* cow; cow-hide.

vacher [va'ʃe], *n.m.* (*fem.* **-ère**) cow-herd.

vacherie [va'ʃri], *n.f.* cow-house, byre.

vacillant [vasi'jɑ̃], *a.* vacillating, wavering, flickering; shaky, uncertain, unsteady.

vacillation [vasija'sjɔ̃], *n.f.* wobbling, flickering.

vaciller [vasi'je], *v.i.* to vacillate; to waver, to stagger; to flicker (*of light etc.*).

vacuité [vakɥi'te], *n.f.* vacuity, emptiness.

vacuum [va'kɥɔm], *n.m.* vacuum.

va-et-vient [vae'vjɛ̃], *n.m. inv.* reciprocating motion, swing, see-saw motion, oscillation; (*fig.*) coming and going.

vagabond [vaga'bɔ̃], *a.* and *n.m.* (*fem. -e*) vagabond, vagrant.

vagabondage [vagabɔ̃'da:ʒ], *n.m.* vagrancy.

vagabonder [vagabɔ̃'de], *v.i.* to be a vagabond; to roam; (*fig.*) to flit from one thing to another.

vagin [va'ʒɛ̃], *n.m.* (*Anat.*) vagina.

vagir [va'ʒi:r], *v.i.* to wail, to pule (*of infants*).

vague (1) [vag], *n.f.* wave, billow.

vague (2) [vag], *a.* vague, indeterminate, uncertain; faint, indistinct, hazy; empty, vacant; *terres vagues*, waste-land; *terrain vague*, vacant site, piece of waste ground. —*n.m.* vagueness, looseness, uncertainty; empty space.

vaguement [vag'mɑ̃], *adv.* vaguely, dimly.

vaguer [va'ge], *v.i.* to ramble, to wander, to stray.

vaillamment [vaja'mɑ̃], *adv.* valiantly.

vaillance [va'jɑ̃:s], *n.f.* valor, bravery.

vaillant [va'jɑ̃], *a.* valiant, brave, gallant; stout (*heart*); *n'avoir pas un sou vaillant*, to be penniless.

vain [vɛ̃], *a.* vain, fruitless, ineffectual; empty, hollow; trifling; vainglorious; conceited; *en vain*, vainly, in vain.

vaincre [vɛ̃:kr], *v.t. irr.* to vanquish, to conquer, to overcome; to defeat; to outdo, to surpass; *se laisser vaincre*, to give way to, to yield.

vaincu [vɛ̃'ky], *a.* conquered, vanquished. —*n.m.* (*fem. -e*) conquered person, loser.

vainement [vɛn'mɑ̃], *adv.* vainly, in vain.

vainqueur [vɛ̃'kœ:r], *a.* conquering, victorious. —*n.m.* vanquisher, conqueror, victor; prize winner.

vairon [vɛ'rɔ̃], *n.m.* minnow.

vaisseau [vɛ'so], *n.m.* (*pl. -eaux*) vessel, receptacle; ship; large covered space (*of a building*); (*Anat., Bot.*) vessel, tube, duct; (*pl.*) shipping.

vaisselle [vɛ'sɛl], *n.f.* plates and dishes; plate (*of gold or silver*); *faire la vaisselle*, to wash up.

val [val], *n.m.* (*pl.* **vals** or **vaux**) narrow valley, vale, dale.

valable [va'labl], *a.* valid, good.

valet [va'lɛ], *n.m.* footman, valet, man-servant; jack (*at cards*); door weight; holdfast; *valet de chambre*, valet; *valet de chiens*, whipper-in; *valet de ferme*, farm worker.

valeter [val'te], *v.i.* (*conjug. like* APPELER) to cringe, to dance attendance.

valétudinaire [valetydi'nɛ:r], *a.* valetudinary. —*n.* valetudinarian, invalid.

valeur [va'lœ:r], *n.f.* value, worth, price; consideration; import, meaning; valor, bravery; (*pl.*) bills, paper, stocks, shares, securities.

valeureusement [valœrøz'mɑ̃], *adv.* bravely, courageously.

valeureux [valœ'rø], *a.* (*fem. -euse*) brave, courageous, gallant.

valide [va'lid], *a.* valid, good; healthy, able-bodied. —*n.* person in good health.

valider [vali'de], *v.t.* to make valid; to ratify, to validate.

validité [validi'te], *n.f.* validity; availability (*of a ticket*).

valise [va'li:z], *n.f.* suit-case; valise, portmanteau.

vallée [va'le], *n.f.* valley.

vallon [va'lɔ̃], *n.m.* small valley, vale, dale.

valoir [va'lwa:r], *v.t. irr.* to yield, to bring in; to procure, to furnish. —*v.i.* to be worth, to be as good as, to be equal to; to deserve, to merit; *autant vaut*, to all intents and purposes; *à valoir*, on account; *faire valoir son droit*, to assert one's right; *se faire valoir*, to boast; *vaille que vaille*, for better or worse; *valoir mieux*, to be better.

valse [vals], *n.f.* waltz.

valser [val'se], *v.i.* to waltz.

valve [valv], *n.f.* valve; electron tube.

vampire [vɑ̃'pi:r], *n.m.* vampire.

van [vɑ̃], *n.m.* (*Agric.*) winnowing basket.

vandale [vɑ̃'dal], *n.* vandal.

vandalisme [vɑ̃da'lism], *n.m.* vandalism.

vanille [va'ni:j], *n.f.* vanilla.

vanité [vani'te], *n.f.* vanity, conceit.

vaniteux [vani'tø], *a.* (*fem. -euse*) vainglorious, vain.

vannage [va'na:ʒ], *n.m.* winnowing.

vanne [van], *n.f.* sluice, sluice gate.

vanneau [va'no], *n.m.* (*pl. -eaux*) lapwing, peewit.

vanner [va'ne], *v.t.* to winnow, to fan, to sift; (*pop.*) to tire out.

vannerie [van'ri], *n.f.* basket-making, basket trade.

vanneur [va'nœ:r], *a.* (*fem. -euse*) winnowing. —*n.m.* (*fem. -euse*) winnower. —*n.f.* (*-euse*) winnowing machine.

vannier [va'nje], *n.m.* (*fem. -ière*) basket-maker.

vannure [va'ny:r], *n.f.* chaff.

vantard [vɑ̃'ta:r], *a.* boasting, boastful, bragging. —*n.m.* (*fem. -e*) boaster, braggart.

vantardise [vɑ̃tar'di:z], *n.f.* boasting, bragging.

vanter [vɑ̃'te], *v.t.* to praise, to commend, to extol. **se vanter**, *v.r.* to boast, to pride oneself on (*de*).

vanterie [vɑ̃'tri], *n.f.* boasting, bragging.

va-nu-pieds [vany'pje], *n. inv.* ragamuffin.

vapeur [va'pœ:r], *n.f.* vapor; steam; haze, mist; *à la vapeur* or *à toute vapeur*, at full speed. —*n.m.* steamer, steamship.

vaporeux [vapo'rø], *a.* (*fem. -euse*) vaporous; steamy, hazy.

vaquer [va'ke], *v.i.* to be vacant; to attend, to devote oneself (*à*).

varech or **varec** [va'rɛk], *n.m* sea-wrack, sea-weed.

variabilité [varjabili'te], *n.f.* variability, changeableness.

variable [va'rjabl], *a.* variable, fickle, unsettled. —*n.f.* (*Math.*) variable.

variant [va'rjɑ̃], *a.* variable, fickle. —*n.f.* (*-e*) variant (*reading or interpretation*).

variation [varja'sjɔ̃], *n.f.* variation.

varice [va'ris], *n.f.* varix, varicose vein.

varier [va'rje], *v.t.* to vary, to change; to variegate. —*v.i.* to vary, to be changeable; to disagree.

323

variété [varje'te], *n.f.* variety, diversity, change; (*pl.*) miscellanea.

variole [va'rjɔl], *n.f.* smallpox.

Varsovie [varsɔ'vi], *f.* Warsaw.

vase (1) [va:z], *n.m.* vase, vessel.

vase (2) [va:z], *n.f.* slime, mud, mire, ooze.

vaseline [vaz'lin], *n.f.* petroleum jelly, Vaseline (*reg. trade mark*).

vaseux [va'zø], *a.* (*fem.* -euse) slimy, muddy, miry.

vasistas [vazis'ta:s], *n.m. inv.* transom, fan-light (*over a door or a window*).

vassal [va'sal], *n.m.* (*fem.* -e, *m. pl.* -aux) vassal.

vaste [vast], *a.* vast, wide, spacious.

vastement [vastə'mɑ̃], *adv.* vastly, widely.

Vatican [vati'kɑ̃], le, *m.* the Vatican.

va-tout [va'tu], *n.m. inv.* one's all (*at cards*); jouer son va-tout, to stake one's all.

vaudeville [vod'vil], *n.m.* vaudeville; light form of comedy.

vau-l'eau (à) [avo'lo], *adv. phr.* with the current, down-stream; to rack and ruin.

vaurien [vo'rjɛ̃], *n.m.* (*fem.* -enne) good-for-nothing, scamp; rogue.

vautour [vo'tu:r], *n.m.* vulture.

vautre [vo:tr], *n.m.* boar-hound.

vautrer (se) [səvo'tre], *v.r.* to wallow; to sprawl.

veau [vo], *n.m.* (*pl.* veaux) calf; (*Cook.*) veal; calf-skin, calf leather; (*fig.*) slow-witted fellow; *veau marin*, seal, seal-skin.

vedette [və'dɛt], *n.f.* vedette, mounted sentinel; scout; observation post, watch-tower; (*Theat.*) star.

végétal [veʒe'tal], *a.* (*m. pl.* -aux) vegetable. —*n.m.* (*pl.* -aux) vegetable, plant.

végétarien [veʒeta'rjɛ̃], *a.* and *n.m.* (*fem.* -enne) vegetarian.

végétation [veʒeta'sjɔ̃], *n.f.* vegetation; (*pl.*) adenoids.

végéter [veʒe'te], *v.i.* (*conjug. like* CÉDER) to vegetate.

véhémence [vee'mɑ̃:s], *n.f.* vehemence.

véhément [vee'mɑ̃], *a.* vehement, impetuous, hot, passionate.

véhiculaire [veiky'lɛ:r], *a.* vehicular.

véhicule [vei'kyl], *n.m.* vehicle; medium.

veille [vɛ:j], *n.f.* sleeplessness, watching; being awake; vigil; eve, day before; point, verge; (*pl.*) midnight work; *être à la veille de*, to be on the point of; *la veille de Noël*, Christmas Eve.

veillée [vɛ'je], *n.f.* time from supper to bed-time, evening (*in company*); sitting up to work etc. in company; night attendance (*upon a sick person*).

veiller [vɛ'je], *v.t.* to watch by, to nurse, to look after, to sit up with.—*v.i.* to sit up, to watch; to attend, to take care, to have an eye (*à*).

veilleur [vɛ'jœ:r], *n.m.* (*fem.* -euse) watcher; *veilleur de nuit*, night watchman.—*n.f.* (-euse) night-light.

veinard [vɛ'na:r], *a.* and *n.m.* (*fem.* -e) (*pop.*) lucky (person), lucky dog.

veine [vɛ:n], *n.f.* vein; (*Geol. etc.*) seam; (*pop.*) good luck; *avoir de la veine*, to be in luck; *en veine de*, in the mood for; *un coup de veine*, a fluke.

veiné [vɛ'ne], *a.* veined, veiny.

veineux [vɛ'nø], *a.* (*fem.* -euse) veined, veiny; venous (*system, blood*).

vélin [ve'lɛ̃], *n.m.* vellum.

velléité [vɛlei'te], *n.f.* passing fancy, wish, whim.

vélo [ve'lo], *n.m.* (*fam.*) bike.

vélocité [velɔsi'te], *n.f.* velocity.

vélodrome [velɔ'drɔm], *n.m.* cycle-racing track.

vélomoteur [velɔmɔ'tœ:r], *n.m.* motorbike.

velours [və'lu:r], *n.m.* velvet; *velours à côtes*, corduroy; *velours de coton*, velveteen.

velouté [vəlu'te], *a.* velvet, velvety, velvet-like; soft and smooth to the palate (*of wines*).—*n.m.* velvet pile; softness; bloom (*of fruit*); smooth rich soup *or* sauce; *velouté de laine*, velours.

velu [və'ly], *a.* hairy, shaggy, rough.—*n.m.* shagginess.

vélum [ve'lɔm], *n.m.* awning.

venaison [vənɛ'zɔ̃], *n.f.* venison.

vénal [ve'nal], *a.* (*m. pl.* -aux) venal, mercenary.

vénalité [venali'te], *n.f.* venality.

venant [və'nɑ̃], *a.* coming, thriving.—*n.m.* comer; *tout-venant*, unsorted (*of produce*).

vendable [vɑ̃'dabl], *a.* saleable, marketable.

vendange [vɑ̃'dɑ̃:ʒ], *n.f.* vintage, grape gathering.

vendanger [vɑ̃dɑ̃'ʒe], *v.t.* (*conjug. like* MANGER) to gather in the grapes from; (*fig.*) to ravage, to spoil.—*v.i.* to pick (*the grapes*); (*fig.*) to make illicit profits.

vendangeur [vɑ̃dɑ̃'ʒœ:r], *n.m.* (*fem.* -euse) vintager, grape gatherer.

vendéen [vɑ̃de'ɛ̃], *a.* (*fem.* -éenne) Vendean.

vendetta [vɑ̃dɛ'ta], *n.f.* vendetta.

vendeur [vɑ̃'dœ:r], *n.m.* (*fem.* -euse) vendor, seller, dealer; salesman, shop assistant.

vendre [vɑ̃:dr], *v.t.* to sell; (*fig.*) to betray; *à vendre*, for sale. se vendre, *v.r.* to sell one-self; to be sold; to go off (*well etc.*).

vendredi [vɑ̃drə'di], *n.m.* Friday; *le Vendredi saint*, Good Friday.

vené [və'ne], *a.* high (*of meat*).

vénéneux [vene'nø], *a.* (*fem.* -euse) poison-ous (*when eaten*).

vénérable [vene'rabl], *a.* venerable.

vénération [venera'sjɔ̃], *n.f.* veneration.

vénérer [vene're], *v.t.* (*conjug. like* CÉDER) to venerate, to hold in reverence.

vénerie [ven'ri], *n.f.* venery, hunting.

veneur [və'nœ:r], *n.m.* huntsman.

Vénézuéla [venezɥe'la], le, *m.* Venezuela.

vénézuélien [venezɥe'ljɛ̃], *a.* (*fem.* -enne) Venezuelan.—*n.m.* (Vénézuélien, *fem.* -enne) Venezuelan (*person*).

vengeance [vɑ̃'ʒɑ̃:s], *n.f.* vengeance, revenge.

venger [vɑ̃'ʒe], *v.t.* (*conjug. like* MANGER) to revenge, to avenge. se venger, *v.r. se venger de quelqu'un*, to revenge oneself on someone.

vengeur [vɑ̃'ʒœ:r], *a.* (*fem.* -eresse) revenge-ful, avenging.—*n.m.* (*fem.* -eresse) avenger, revenger.

véniel [ve'njɛl], *a.* (*fem.* -elle) venial.

venimeux [vəni'mø], *a.* (*fem.* -euse) com-municating poison (*from outside*), venomous (*snake etc.*); (*fig.*) malignant, harmful.

venin [vəˈnɛ̃], *n.m.* venom, poison; (*fig.*) spite, malice.

venir [vəˈniːr], *v.i. irr.* (*conjug. like* TENIR, *but with aux.* ÊTRE) to come, to be coming; to arrive; to reach; to occur, to happen; to grow, to grow up; to thrive; to issue, to arise; to be descended; *d'où vient cela?* what is the cause of that? *en venir aux mains,* to come to blows; *faire venir le médecin,* to send for the doctor; *il va et vient,* he goes in and out; *je ne ferai qu'aller et venir,* I will not stay, I shall come straight back; *le voilà qui vient,* here he comes; *où voulez-vous en venir?* what are you getting at? *s'en venir,* to come away; *si ma lettre venait à se perdre,* if my letter should happen to go astray; *venir à bout de,* to master; *venir de,* to come from, (*followed by an infinitive*) to have just—*je viens de le voir,* I have just seen him; *je venais de le quitter,* I had just left him).

Venise [vəˈniːz], *f.* Venice.

vent [vɑ̃], *n.m.* wind; breeze; breath, breathing; (*Med.*) (*pl.*) flatulence; (*Hunt.*) scent; (*fig.*) vanity, emptiness; *autant en emporte le vent,* all that is idle talk; *avoir vent de,* to get wind of; *coup de vent,* gust of wind; (*colloq.*) *dans le vent,* 'with it'; *en plein vent,* in the open air; *il fait du vent,* it is windy.

vente [vɑ̃ːt], *n.f.* sale; selling; auction; felling *or* cutting (*of timber*); *en vente,* for sale, on sale; *vente aux enchères,* sale at auction.

venter [vɑ̃ˈte], *v.i.* (*usu. impers.*) to blow, to be windy.

venteux [vɑ̃ˈtə], *a.* (*fem.* -**euse**) windy, gusty.

ventilateur [vɑ̃tilaˈtœːr], *n.m.* ventilator, fan, blower.

ventilation [vɑ̃tilaˈsjɔ̃], *n.f.* ventilation, airing.

ventiler [vɑ̃tiˈle], *v.t.* to ventilate, to air; (*fig.*) to discuss.

ventosité [vɑ̃toziˈte], *n.f.* flatulence.

ventouse [vɑ̃ˈtuːz], *n.f.* cupping-glass; vent, air-hole; sucker (*of leech*); nozzle (*of vacuum cleaner*).

ventre [vɑ̃ːtr], *n.m.* belly, abdomen; stomach; womb; bowels, one's inside; bulge; *à plat ventre,* flat on one's face; *ventre à terre,* at full speed; *j'ai mal au ventre,* I have a stomach ache.

ventrière [vɑ̃triˈɛːr], *n.f.* abdominal belt; sling, brace; girth (*of horse*).

ventriloque [vɑ̃triˈlɔk], *n.m.* ventriloquist.

ventriloquie [vɑ̃triloˈki], *n.f.* ventriloquy.

ventru [vɑ̃ˈtry], *a.* big-bellied, corpulent; bulging.—*n.m.* (*fem.* -**e**) pot-bellied person.

venu [vəˈny], *a.* come; done; come up, grown; *bien venu* [BIENVENU]; *enfant bien venu,* well-grown child; *mal venu,* unwelcome; open to censure.—*n.m.* (*fem.* -**e**) *le dernier venu,* the last arrival; *le premier venu* or *la première venue,* the first comer, anyone.—*n.f.* (-**e**) coming, arrival, advent; growth.

Vénus [veˈnys], *f.* Venus.

vêpres [vɛːpr], *n.f. pl.* vespers.

ver [vɛːr], *n.m.* worm; maggot, mite; moth; *mangé* or *rongé des vers,* worm-eaten; *nu comme un ver,* stark naked; *ver blanc,* grub; *ver à soie,* silkworm; *ver luisant,* glow-worm; *ver solitaire,* tapeworm.

véracité [verasiˈte], *n.f.* veracity.

véranda [verɑ̃ˈda], *n.f.* veranda.

verbal [vɛrˈbal], *a.* (*m. pl.* -**aux**) verbal.

verbalement [vɛrbalˈmɑ̃], *adv.* verbally; (*colloq.*) by word of mouth.

verbaliser [vɛrbaliˈze], *v.i.* to draw up a written statement.

verbe [vɛrb], *n.m.* verb; (*Theol.*) *le Verbe,* the Word.

verbeux [vɛrˈbə], *a.* (*fem.* -**euse**) verbose.

verbiage [vɛrˈbjaːʒ], *n.m.* verbiage.

verbosité [vɛrboziˈte], *n.f.* verbosity.

verdâtre [vɛrˈdɑːtr], *a.* greenish.

verdelet [vɛrdˈlɛ], *a.* (*fem.* -**ette**) greenish; tart (*of wine*); hale (*of old people*).

verdeur [vɛrˈdœːr], *n.f.* greenness, sap (*of wood*); tartness, harshness (*of wine*); vigor, spryness (*of old people*); (*fig.*) crudeness (*of language*).

verdict [vɛrˈdikt], *n.m.* verdict, finding.

verdier [vɛrˈdje], *n.m.* greenfinch; verderer, ranger.

verdir [vɛrˈdiːr], *v.t.* to make *or* paint green.—*v.i.* to turn green.

verdoyant [vɛrdwaˈjɑ̃], *a.* verdant, green.

verdoyer [vɛrdwaˈje], *v.i.* (*conjug. like* EMPLOYER) to become green.

verdure [vɛrˈdyːr], *n.f.* verdure; greenery; pot-herbs.

verdurier [vɛrdyˈrje], *n.m.* (*fem.* -**ière**) greengrocer, fruit and vegetable grocer.

véreux [veˈrə], *a.* (*fem.* -**euse**) worm-eaten, maggoty; rotten; (*fig.*) suspect; insecure (*of bills etc.*).

verge [vɛːrʒ], *n.f.* rod, wand; shaft, pin; shank (*of an anchor etc.*); (C) yard (*measure*).

verger [vɛrˈʒe], *n.m.* orchard.

vergeté [vɛrʒəˈte], *a.* streaky.

vergette [vɛrˈʒet], *n.f.* clothes brush; bundle of rods, switch.

verglacé [vɛrglaˈse], *a.* covered with glazed frost; icy.

verglas [vɛrˈgla], *n.m.* thin coating of ice, frost after a thaw *or* rain; glazed frost.

vergne [vɛrɲ], **verne** [vɛrn], *n.m.* alder (*tree*).

vergogne [vɛrˈgɔɲ], *n.f.* shame; *sans vergogne,* shameless(ly).

vergue [vɛrg], *n.f.* yard (*for sail*).

véridicité [veridisiˈte], *n.f.* veracity, truthfulness.

véridique [veriˈdik], *a.* veracious, truthful.

vérificateur [verifikaˈtœːr], *n.m.* verifier, examiner, inspector; (*Eng.*) calipers; gauge; *vérificateur des comptes,* auditor.

vérification [verifikaˈsjɔ̃], *n.f.* verification, auditing, probate.

vérifier [veriˈfje], *v.t.* to verify, to inspect, to examine, to audit; to prove.

vérin [veˈrɛ̃], *n.m.* (*Eng.*) jack.

véritable [veriˈtabl], *a.* true, genuine, real; staunch, downright, thorough.

véritablement [veritabləˈmɑ̃], *adv.* truly, in reality, indeed.

vérité [veriˈte], *n.f.* truth, verity, truthfulness; *à la vérité,* indeed, it is true, I admit; *dire la vérité,* to speak the truth; *en vérité,* indeed, truly.

verjus [vɛrˈʒy], *n.m.* verjuice; sour grapes.

verjuté [vɛrʒyˈte], *a.* sharp, tart, acid.

vermeil [vɛr'mɛːj], a. (fem. **-eille**) vermilion, ruddy, rosy.—n.m. vermeil, silver-gilt.
vermicelle [vɛrmi'sɛl], n.m. vermicelli.
vermiculaire [vɛrmiky'lɛːr], a. vermicular, worm-shaped.
vermillon [vɛrmi'jɔ̃], a. inv. and n.m. vermilion.
vermine [vɛr'min], n.f. vermin (only insects such as fleas, lice etc.); (fig.) rabble.
vermoulu [vɛrmu'ly], a. worm-eaten.
vermoulure [vɛrmu'lyːr], n.f. worm hole, rottenness caused by worms (in wood).
vermout(h) [vɛr'mut], n.m. vermouth.
vernaculaire [vɛrnaky'lɛːr], a. and n.m. vernacular.
vernal [vɛr'nal], a. (m. pl. **-aux**) vernal, spring-like.
vernier [vɛr'nje], n.m. vernier, sliding scale.
vernir [vɛr'niːr], v.t. to varnish; to glaze, to polish.
vernis [vɛr'ni], n.m. varnish, polish, glaze.
vernissage [vɛrni'saːʒ], n.m. varnishing; private view (of art exhibition).
vernisser [vɛrni'se], v.t. to glaze (pottery etc.).
vérole [ve'rɔl], n.f. petite vérole, smallpox; petite vérole volante, chicken pox.
véronal [vero'nal], n.m. (Chem.) veronal, barbitone.
Véronique [vero'nik], f. Veronica.
véronique [vero'nik], n.f. veronica, speedwell.
verrat [vɛ'ra], n.m. boar.
verre [vɛːr], n.m. glass; verre à eau or verre gobelet, tumbler; verre à vin, wine glass; verre de vin, glass of wine.
verrerie [vɛr'ri], n.f. glass-works; glass-ware.
verrier [vɛ'rje], n.m. glass-maker.
verrière [vɛ'rjɛːr], n.f. stained-glass window.
verroterie [vero'tri], n.f. small glass-ware, glass beads.
verrou [vɛ'ru], n.m. bolt, bar.
verrouiller [vɛru'je], v.t. to bolt. **se verrouiller**, v.r. to bolt oneself in.
verrue [vɛ'ry], n.f. wart; verrues plantaire, verruca.
vers (1) [vɛːr], n.m. inv. verse, line (of poetry).
vers (2) [vɛːr], prep. towards, to; about; vers (les) quatre heures, about four o'clock.
versable [vɛr'sabl], a. apt to overturn, liable to upset.
versage [vɛr'saːʒ], n.m. emptying, tipping; (Agric.) first ploughing (of fallow land).
versant (1) [vɛr'sã], a. liable to be overturned.
versant (2) [vɛr'sã], n.m. declivity, side, slope; watershed.
versatile [vɛrsa'til], a. inconstant, changeable.
versatilité [vɛrsatili'te], n.f. inconstancy.
verse (à) [a'vɛrs], adv. abundantly; il pleut à verse, it is pouring down rain.
versé [vɛr'se], a. spilt; well versed, conversant.
versement [vɛrsə'mã], n.m. payment; deposit.
verser [vɛr'se], v.t. to pour, to pour out; to discharge, to empty; to shed, to spill; to pay in, to deposit; to overturn, to upset; to lay (grain).—v.i. to overturn, to upset (of vehicles); to be laid flat (of standing grain).
verset [vɛr'sɛ], n.m. (Bibl. etc.) verse.

versificateur [vɛrsifika'tœːr], n.m. (fem. **-trice**) versifier.
versification [vɛrsifika'sjɔ̃], n.f. versification.
versifier [vɛrsi'fje], v.t., v.i. to versify.
version [vɛr'sjɔ̃], n.f. version; (Sch.) translation.
verso [vɛr'so], n.m. verso, back, left-hand page.
vert [vɛːr], a. green; sharp, harsh (of things); tart (of wine); raw; sour; (fig.) vigorous, robust; spicy (of stories).—n.m. green, green color; green food; sharpness (of wine etc.); (Golf) (putting-)green.
vert-de-gris [vɛrdə'gri], n.m. verdigris.
vertèbre [vɛr'tɛːbr], n.f. vertebra.
vertébré [vɛrte'bre], a. and n.m. vertebrate.
vertement [vɛrtə'mã], adv. sharply; harshly, severely.
vertical [vɛrti'kal], a. (m. pl. **-aux**) vertical.
verticalement [vɛrtikal'mã], adv. vertically.
vertige [vɛr'tiːʒ], n.m. dizziness, giddiness, vertigo; (fig.) breath-taking.
vertigineux [vɛrtiʒi'nø], a. (fem. **-euse**) dizzy, giddy; (fig.) breath-taking.
vertigo [vɛrti'go], n.m. staggers; (fig.) whim.
vertu [vɛr'ty], n.f. virtue, chastity; property, faculty, quality; efficacy, force.
vertueusement [vɛrtɥøz'mã], adv. virtuously.
vertueux [vɛr'tɥø], a. (fem. **-euse**) virtuous, chaste.
verve [vɛrv], n.f. warmth, animation, verve, spirit, zest.
verveine [vɛr'vɛːn], n.f. vervain, verbena.
vésicule [vezi'kyl], n.f. vesicle, bladder; vésicule biliaire, gall bladder.
vespasienne [vɛspa'zjɛn], n.f. public urinal; public convenience.
vessie [vɛ'si], n.f. bladder.
veste [vɛst], n.f. jacket.
vestiaire [vɛs'tjɛːr], n.m. cloakroom; changing room; robing room (for judges); hat-and-coat rack.
vestibule [vɛsti'byːl], n.m. vestibule, lobby, hall.
vestige [vɛs'tiːʒ], n.m. footprint, vestige, sign, mark; trace, remains.
veston [vɛs'tɔ̃], n.m. jacket, coat; complet veston, business suit.
Vésuve [ve'zyːv], le, m. Vesuvius.
vêtement [vɛt'mã], n.m. garment; (pl.) dress, clothes; (poet.) raiment; vêtements de dessous, underwear.
vétéran [vete'rã], n.m. veteran; (Sch.) boy who stays in a grade a second year.
vétérinaire [veteri'nɛːr], a. veterinary.—n.m. veterinary surgeon.
vétille [ve'tiːj], n.f. trifle, bagatelle.
vétiller [veti'je], v.i. to trifle; to split hairs.
vétilleux [veti'jø], a. (fem. **-euse**) particular, finicky.
vêtir [vɛ'tiːr], v.t. irr. to clothe; to array, to dress; to put on. **se vêtir**, v.r. to dress oneself.
véto [ve'to], n.m. veto.
vêtu [vɛ'ty], a. dressed, clothed, arrayed.
vétuste [ve'tyst], a. old, antiquated; dilapidated, worn out.
vétusté [vetys'te], n.f. antiquity, old age, decay.

veuf [vœf], *a.* (*fem.* **veuve**) widowed.—*n.m.* widower.—*n.f.* (**veuve**) widow.

veule [vœːl], *a.* feckless, weak, feeble.

veuvage [vœˈvaːʒ], *n.m.* widowhood, widowerhood.

vexant [vɛkˈsɑ̃], *a.* vexing, provoking.

vexer [vɛkˈse], *v.t.* to vex, to plague, to annoy.

viable [vjabl], *a.* likely to live, viable; fit for traffic.

viaduc [vjaˈdyk], *n.m.* viaduct.

viager [vjaˈʒe], *a.* (*fem.* **-ère**) for life, during life; *rente viagère*, life annuity.

viande [vjɑ̃ːd], *n.f.* meat; *menue viande*, fowl and game; *grosse viande*, butcher's meat.

vibrant [vlˈbrɑ̃], *a.* vibrating; vibrant, resonant.

vibration [vibraˈsjɔ̃], *n.f.* vibration.

vibrer [viˈbre], *v.i.* to vibrate.

vicaire [viˈkɛːr], *n.m.* curate (*of a parish*).

vicariat [vikaˈrja], *n.m.*, **vicairie** [vikɛˈri], *n.f.* curacy; vicariate.

vice [vis], *n.m.* fault, defect, flaw, blemish; vice, viciousness.

vice-amiral [visamiˈral], *n.m.* (*pl.* **-aux**) vice admiral; second ship of a fleet.

vice-roi [visˈrwa], *n.m.* (*pl.* **vice-rois**) viceroy.

vicié [viˈsje], *a.* vitiated, depraved, corrupted; foul (*of air etc.*).

vicier [viˈsje], *v.t.* to vitiate, to taint, to corrupt.

vicieusement [visjøzˈmɑ̃], *adv.* viciously.

vicieux [viˈsjø], *a.* (*fem.* **-euse**) vicious, faulty, defective.

vicinal [visiˈnal], *a.* (*m. pl.* **-aux**) local, connecting (*of roads*); *chemin vicinal*, by-road.

vicissitude [visisiˈtyd], *n.f.* vicissitude, change.

vicomte [viˈkɔ̃ːt], *n.m.* viscount.

vicomtesse [vikɔ̃ˈtɛs], *n.f.* viscountess.

victime [vikˈtim], *n.f.* victim; sufferer; casualty.

Victoire [vikˈtwaːr], **Victoria** [viktɔˈrja], *f.* Victoria.

victoire [vikˈtwaːr], *n.f.* victory.

victorieux [viktɔˈrjø], *a.* (*fem.* **-euse**) victorious.

victuaille [vikˈtɥaj], *n.f.* (*colloq.*) provisions.

vidange [viˈdɑ̃ːʒ], *n.f.* emptying; draining off; night soil; *tonneau en vidange*, broached cask.

vidanger [vidɑ̃ˈʒe], *v.t.* (*conjug. like* MANGER) to empty, to clean out, to drain, to blow off.

vidangeur [vidɑ̃ˈʒœːr], *n.m.* scavenger.

vide [vid], *a.* empty; void, vacant, blank; destitute.—*n.m.* empty space, blank; vacuum; gap, hole; emptiness.—*adv. phr.* *à vide*, empty.

vidé [viˈde], *a.* emptied, exhausted.

vider [viˈde], *v.t.* to empty; to drain; to hollow out; to draw (*poultry*); to gut (*fish*); to vacate; to decide, to settle.

vie [vi], *n.f.* life; lifetime; existence, days; vitality; livelihood, living; food, subsistence; spirit, animation; noise; *être en vie*, to be alive; *le coût de la vie*, the cost of living; *niveau de vie*, standard of living.

vieil [vjɛj], [VIEUX].

vieillard [vjɛˈjaːr], *n.m.* old man.

vieille [vjɛj], [VIEUX].

vieillerie [vjɛjˈri], *n.f.* (*usu. pl.*) old things, old clothes, old lumber, rubbish; obsolete ideas.

vieillesse [vjɛˈjɛs], *n.f.* old age; oldness.

vieillir [vjɛˈjiːr], *v.t.* to make old; to make look old.—*v.i.* to grow old; to become obsolete.

vieillissant [vjɛjiˈsɑ̃], *a.* growing old.

vieillot [vjɛˈjo], *a.* (*fem.* **-otte**) oldish.

vielle [vjɛl], *n.f.* *hurdy-gurdy.

Vienne [vjɛn], *f.* Vienna.

viennois [vjɛˈnwa], *a.* Viennese.—*n.m.* (**Viennois**, *fem.* **-oise**) Viennese (*person*).

vierge [vjɛrʒ], *a.* virgin, virginal, maiden; pure, untrodden; unwrought; free (*from*).—*n.f.* virgin, maid; (*Astron.*) Virgo.

Viet-Nam [vjɛtˈnam], **le**, *m.* Vietnam.

vietnamien [vjɛtnaˈmjɛ̃], *a.* (*fem.* **-enne**) Vietnamese.—*n.m.* Vietnamese (*language*); (**Vietnamien**, *fem.* **-enne**) Vietnamese (*person*).

vieux [vjø], *a.* (*before a vowel or h mute*, **vieil**, *fem.* **vieille**) old, aged, advanced in years; ancient, venerable; *vieux jeu*, old-fashioned.—*n.m.* (*fem.* **vieille**) old man, old woman; *la retraite des vieux*, old-age pension; *mon vieux*, (*a term of endearment*) old friend, old chap.

vif [vif], *a.* (*fem.* **vive**) alive, live, living; quick; lively, brisk, sprightly, animated, fiery, mettlesome, ardent, eager; hasty; keen; sharp, violent (*of pain etc.*); bracing (*of air etc.*); vivid, bright (*of colors*). —*n.m.* the quick (*live flesh*); living person; *être pris sur le vif*, to be very lifelike; *piquer au vif*, to sting to the quick.

vif-argent [vifarˈʒɑ̃], *n.m.* quicksilver.

vigie [viˈʒi], *n.f.* look-out man; look-out (*station or ship*); (*Rail.*) seat on the top of trainmen's car.

vigilance [viʒiˈlɑ̃ːs], *n.f.* vigilance.

vigilant [viʒiˈlɑ̃], *a.* vigilant, watchful.

vigile [viˈʒil], *n.f.* vigil, eve.

vigne [viɲ], *n.f.* vine; vineyard; *vigne vierge*, wild grape; Virginia creeper.

vigneron [viɲəˈrɔ̃], *n.m.* (*fem.* **-onne**) vine dresser, wine grower.

vignette [viˈɲɛt], *n.f.* vignette; (*pop.*) meadow-sweet.

vignoble [viˈɲɔbl], *n.m.* vineyard.

vigoureusement [viɡurøzˈmɑ̃], *adv.* vigorously, energetically.

vigoureux [viɡuˈrø], *a.* (*fem.* **-euse**) vigorous, energetic; stout, stalwart.

vigueur [viˈɡœːr], *n.f.* vigor, strength; force, power, energy; *entrer en vigueur*, to come into force (*of laws etc.*).

vil [vil], *a.* vile, base, mean; abject, low; worthless; *à vil prix*, dirt cheap.

vilain [viˈlɛ̃], *a.* ugly; unsightly; pitiful; nasty; sordid, wretched; naughty (*of a child*); *un vilain tour*, a dirty trick; *vilain temps*, vile weather.—*n.m.* (*fem.* **-e**) *villein (*bondman*); nasty fellow; (*childish*) naughty boy or girl.

vilainement [vilɛnˈmɑ̃], *adv.* uglily; basely, shamefully, deplorably.

vilebrequin [vilbrəˈkɛ̃], *n.m.* brace, wimble; (*Mech.*) crankshaft.

vilement [vilˈmɑ̃], *adv.* vilely, basely.

vilenie [vil'ni], *n.f.* nastiness, foulness; vile action; stinginess, meanness; (*pl.*) offensive words.

vileté [vil'te], *n.f.* cheapness, low price; vileness; mean action.

vilipender [vilipã'de], *v.t.* to vilify; to disparage.

villa [vil'la], *n.f.* villa.

village [vi'la:ʒ], *n.m.* village.

villageois [vila'ʒwa], *a.* rustic.—*n.m.* (*fem.* **-e**) villager.

ville [vil], *n.f.* town, city; *être en ville*, to be out (*not at home*); *hôtel de ville*, town hall; *ville d'eaux*, spa.

villégiature [vileʒja'ty:r], *n.f.* sojourn in the country; *en villégiature*, staying in the country.

vin [vɛ̃], *n.m.* wine; *à bon vin point d'enseigne*, good wine needs no bush; *vin de Bordeaux rouge*, claret; *vin de marque*, vintage wine; *vin mousseux*, sparkling wine; *vin ordinaire*, dinner wine.

vinaigre [vi'nɛ:gr], *n.m.* vinegar.

vinaigrer [vine'gre], *v.t.* to season with vinegar.

vindicatif [vɛ̃dika'tif], *a.* (*fem.* **-tive**) vindictive, revengeful.

vingt [vɛ̃], *a.* and *n.m. inv.* twenty, score; twentieth.

vingtaine [vɛ̃'tɛ:n], *n.f.* a score, about twenty.

vingt-et-un [vɛ̃te'œ̃], *n.m.* twenty-one (*card game*).

vingtième [vɛ̃'tjɛ:m], *a.* and *n.* twentieth.

vinicole [vini'kɔl], *a.* wine-growing, wine-producing.

viol [vjɔl], *n.m.* rape (*Law*).

violateur [vjɔla'tœ:r], *a.* (*fem.* **-trice**) violating, transgressing, infringing.—*n.m.* (*fem.* **-trice**) violator, infringer, breaker.

violation [vjɔla'sjɔ̃], *n.f.* violation, breach, infringement.

violâtre [vjɔ'lɑ:tr], *a.* purplish.

viole [vjɔl], *n.f.* viol.

violemment [vjɔla'mã], *adv.* violently.

violence [vjɔ'lã:s], *n.f.* violence; (*Law*) duress; (*fig.*) stress, fury.

violent [vjɔ'lã], *a.* violent; strong (*of suspicion etc.*); (*colloq.*) excessive; *c'est par trop violent*, it really is too bad.

violenter [vjɔlã'te], *v.t.* to offer *or* do violence to, to force; to constrain; to violate.

violer [vjɔ'le], *v.t.* to violate; to outrage, to transgress.

violet [vjɔ'lɛ], *a.* (*fem.* **-ette**) violet-colored, purple.—*n.m.* violet(color). —*n.f.* (**-ette**) (*Bot.*) violet.

violier [vjɔ'lje], *n.m.* wallflower, gillyflower.

violon [vjɔ'lɔ̃], *n.m.* violin, fiddle; violinist, fiddler; (*pop.*) lock-up, cells (*prison*).

violoncelle [vjɔlɔ̃'sɛl], *n.m.* violoncello, cello.

violoncelliste [vjɔlɔ̃sɛ'list], *n.* violoncellist, cellist.

violoniste [vjɔlɔ'nist], *n.* violinist.

viorne [vjɔrn], *n.f.* viburnum.

vipère [vi'pɛ:r], *n.f.* viper, adder.

virage [vi'ra:ʒ], *n.m.* turning, cornering; turn, bend, corner; (*Naut.*) tacking; *virage incliné*, bank; *virage en épingle à cheveux*, hair-pin bend.

virago [vira'go], *n.f.* virago, termagant.

virée [vi're], *n.f.* turning; winding.

virement [vir'mã], *n.m.* turning; (*Naut.*) veering about, tacking; (*Book-keeping*) clearing, transfer; *banque de virement*, clearing-bank.

virer [vi're], *v.t.* to transfer, to clear (*a sum o money*).—*v.i.* to turn, to turn about; (*Naut.*) to tack, to veer about.

vireux [vi'rø], *a.* (*fem.* **-euse**) poisonous, noxious, nauseous.

virginal [virʒi'nal], *a.* (*m. pl.* **-aux**) virginal, maidenly.

Virginie [virʒi'ni], *f.* Virginia; (*Geog.*) *La Virginie*, Virginia.

virginité [virʒini'te], *n.f.* virginity, maidenhood.

virgule [vir'gyl], *n.f.* comma; *point et virgule*, semi-colon.

viril [vi'ril], *a.* virile, male; manly.

virilement [viril'mã], *adv.* like a man; in a manly way.

virilité [virili'te], *n.f.* virility; manhood.

virole [vi'rɔl], *n.f.* ferrule.

virtuel [vir'tɥɛl], *a.* (*fem.* **-elle**) virtual.

virtuellement [virtɥɛl'mã], *adv.* virtually; potentially.

virtuose [vir'tɥo:z], *n.* virtuoso.

virtuosité [virtɥozi'te], *n.f.* virtuosity.

virulence [viry'lã:s], *n.f.* virulence.

virulent [viry'lã], *a.* virulent.

virus [vi'ry:s], *n.m.* virus.

vis [vis], *n.f. inv.* screw; *escalier à vis*, spiral staircase.

visa [vi'za], *n.m.* visa, signature, endorsement (*on passports etc.*).

visage [vi'za:ʒ], *n.m.* face, visage, countenance; aspect, look, air; *à deux visages*, double-faced; *à visage découvert*, openly, barefacedly; *avoir bon visage*, to look well.

vis-à-vis [viza'vi], *prep. phr.* opposite, over against; towards, in relation to; *vis-à-vis de l'église*, opposite the church.—*adv. phr.* opposite.—*n.m. inv.* vis-à-vis (*in dancing etc.*); person opposite (*at table etc.*).

viscère [vi'sɛ:r], *n.m.* any of the viscera *or* vital organs.

viscosité [viskozi'te], *n.f.* viscosity, viscidity stickiness.

visée [vi'ze], *n.f.* aim, end; design, plan.

viser [vi'ze], *v.t.* to aim at; to allude to; to pursue; to endorse.—*v.i.* to aim, to take aim; to aspire (*à*).

viseur [vi'zœ:r], *n.m.* (*Phot.*) view finder.

visibilité [vizibili'te], *n.f.* visibility.

visible [vi'zibl], *a.* visible; evident, manifest, obvious.

visiblement [vizibla'mã], *adv.* visibly, obviously.

visière [vi'zjɛ:r], *n.f.* visor (*of a helmet*); peak (*of caps etc.*), eye shade; sight (*on fire-arms*).

vision [vi'zjɔ̃], *n.f.* vision, sight; dream, phantom, fancy.

visionnaire [vizjɔ'nɛ:r], *a.* visionary, fanciful. —*n.* seer; dreamer, visionary.

visite [vi'zit], *n.f.* visit; call; visitation (*of a bishop etc.*); examination, inspection; search; *droit de visite*, right of search; *faire la visite des bagages*, to examine luggage; *faire une visite* or *rendre visite*, to pay a visit.

visiter [vizi'te], *v.t.* to visit (*patients, clients etc.*); to visit (*cathedral etc.*); to search, to examine, to inspect.

visiteur [vizi'tœːr], *n.m.* (*fem.* **-euse**) visitor, caller; inspector, searcher.

vison [vi'zɔ̃], *n.m.* mink (*animal*).

visqueux [vis'kø], *a.* (*fem.* **-euse**) viscous, sticky; slimy; clammy.

visser [vi'se], *v.t.* to screw, to screw on, up *or* down. **se visser**, *v.r.* to fix *or* attach oneself firmly.

visserie [vi'sri], *n.f.* screws, nuts and bolts.

Vistule [vis'tyl], **la.** *f.* the Vistula.

visuel [vi'zɥɛl], *a.* (*fem.* **-elle**) visual.

vital [vi'tal], *a.* (*m.* *pl.* **-aux**) vital; (*fig.*) essential.

vitalement [vital'mɑ̃], *adv.* vitally.

vitalité [vitali'te], *n.f.* vitality.

vitamine [vita'min], *n.f.* vitamin.

vite [vit], *a.* swift, quick, speedy, rapid.— *adv.* quick, quickly, fast, rapidly, expeditiously; *vite!* quick! look sharp!

vitesse [vi'tɛs], *n.f.* quickness, rapidity, celerity, swiftness, speed; (*Motor.*) gear; *à grande* *or* *à toute vitesse*, at full speed; *boîte de vitesse*, gear box; *changement de vitesse*, change of gear; *gagner (quelqu'un) de vitesse*, to outrun (someone).

Viti [vi'ti], **les Îles**, *f.pl.* the Fiji Islands.

viticole [viti'kɔl], *a.* pertaining to vine culture, vinicultural.

viticulture [vitikyl'tyːr], *n.f.* vine-growing.

vitrage [vi'traːʒ], *n.m.* glazing; glass windows.

vitrail [vi'traːj], *n.m.* (*pl.* **-aux**) stained-glass window.

vitre [vitr], *n.f.* pane of glass; window.

vitré [vi'tre], *a.* glazed, of glass; (*Anat. etc.*) vitreous; *porte vitrée*, glass door.

vitrer [vi'tre], *v.t.* to furnish with glass windows, to glaze.

vitreux [vi'trø], *a.* (*fem.* **-euse**) vitreous, glassy.

vitrier [vitri'e], *n.m.* glass-maker; glazier.

vitrine [vi'trin], *n.f.* shop window; showcase.

vitriol [vitri'ɔl], *n.m.* vitriol.

vitupération [vitypera'sjɔ̃], *n.f.* vituperation.

vitupérer [vitype're], *v.t.* (*conjug. like* CÉDER) to vituperate, to reprimand.

vivace [vi'vas], *a.* long-lived, perennial (*of plants*); inveterate, deep-rooted.

vivacité [vivasi'te], *n.f.* vivacity, liveliness, sprightliness; spirit, life, ardor.

vivant [vi'vɑ̃], *a.* living, alive; lively, animated; *langue vivante*, modern language; *portrait vivant*, lifelike portrait.—*n.m.* life, lifetime; *de son vivant*, in his lifetime. —*n.m.* (*fem.* **-e**) living person.

vivat! [vi'vat], *int.* and *n.m.* hurrah! huzza!

vivement [viv'mɑ̃], *adv.* quickly, briskly, sharply, vigorously; eagerly, keenly, acutely; smartly, angrily, spiritedly.

viveur [vi'vœːr], *n.m.* (*fem.* **-euse**) rake, gay dog, person who leads a fast life.

vivier [vi'vje], *n.m.* fish pond.

vivifiant [vivi'fjɑ̃], *a.* vivifying, quickening; refreshing, invigorating.

vivifier [vivi'fje], *v.t.* to vivify, to quicken, to give life to; to enliven, to revive.

vivisection [vivisɛk'sjɔ̃], *n.f.* vivisection.

(C) **vivoir** [vi'vwaːr], *n.m.* living room.

vivoter [vivo'te], *v.i.* to live poorly, to scrape along.

vivre [viːvr], *v.i.* irr. to live, to be alive; to subsist, to live on, to be maintained; to board, to take one's meals; to behave; to last; *vive la France!* long live France! *qui vive?* who goes there? *il ne sait pas vivre*, he has no manners.—*n.m.* living, board, food; (*pl.*) provisions, victuals, rations.

vocable [vɔ'kabl], *n.m.* vocable, word, name.

vocabulaire [vɔkaby'lɛːr], *n.m.* vocabulary.

vocal [vɔ'kal], *a.* (*m. pl.* **-aux**) vocal.

vocation [vɔka'sjɔ̃], *n.f.* vocation, calling, call; inclination; bent, talent.

vociférant [vosife'rɑ̃], *a.* vociferous.

vociférer [vosife're], *v.t.* (*conjug. like* CÉDER) to vociferate, to bawl.

vœu [vø], *n.m.* (*pl.* **vœux**) vow; prayer, wish, desire; vote, suffrage.

vogue [vɔg], *n.f.* vogue, fashion; credit, craze; *avoir de la vogue*, to be in fashion.

voguer [vo'ge], *v.i.* to move forward by rowing (*of a galley etc.*); to sail, to float, to move along.

voici [vwa'si], *prep.* see here, behold; here is, here are, this is, these are; ago, past; *le voilà, me voici*, there he is, here I am; *monsieur que voici*, this gentleman; *voici trois mois que je suis à l'hôpital*, I have been in hospital for the past three months.

voie [vwa], *n.f.* way, road; line, path, track, (*fig.*) organ, medium, channel, course; conveyance; gauge; breadth (*between the wheels of carriages*); load; (*Chem.*) process; *être en voie de*, to be in a fair way to; *voie d'eau*, (*Naut.*) leak; *voie ferrée*, railway track; *voie libre*, line clear.

voilà [vwa'la], *prep.* there, behold, there now, there is, there are, that is; *ah! vous voilà*, oh! there you are! *voilà une heure qu'il parle*, he has been speaking for an hour.

voile (1) [vwal], *n.m.* veil; (*fig.*) cover, mask, disguise, show, pretence.

voile (2) [vwal], *n.f.* sail; canvas; (*fig.*) ship; *faire voile*, to sail, to set sail.

voilé [vwa'le], *a.* rigged; veiled; clouded, dull, dim; (*wheel*) buckled, out of true.

voiler [vwa'le], *v.t.* to veil; to cover, to cloak, to blind, to disguise, to conceal; to buckle (*wheel*).—*v.i.* and **se voiler**, *v.r.* to wear a veil; to cloud over (*of the sky*); to buckle (*of a wheel*).

voilier [vwa'lje], *n.m.* sail maker; sailing ship.

voir [vwaːr], *v.t.* irr. to see; to behold; to witness; to look at, to observe, to view; to inspect, to superintend; to overlook; to visit; to frequent; *faire voir*, to show, to let see; *voyons!* let us see! now then!—*v.i.* to see, to look, to watch; to have one's sight; *voir à* *or* *voir à ce que*, to see to it that. **se voir**, *v.r.* to see oneself; to see each other; to visit each other; to be obvious.

voire [vwaːr], *adv.* and even, and indeed.

voirie [vwa'ri], *n.f.* roads, system of roads; commission of public streets and highways; refuse dump.

voisin [vwa'zɛ̃], *a.* bordering, adjacent, next; next door, neighboring. —*n.m.* (*fem.* **-e**) neighbor.

329

voisinage [vwazi'na:ʒ], *n.m.* neighborhood; vicinity, proximity, nearness; neighbors.

voiturage [vwaty'ra:ʒ], *n.m.* carriage, cartage (*of goods etc.*).

voiture [vwa'ty:r], *n.f.* vehicle, conveyance; carriage; coach; cart, car; cart-load; *descendre de voiture*, to alight from a carriage; *en voiture !* all aboard! *se promener en voiture* or *aller en voiture*, to drive; *voiture d'enfant*, perambulator, baby carriage, (*fam.*) pram.

voiturer [vwaty're], *v.t.* to carry, to convey, to cart.

voiturier [vwaty'rje], *n.m.* carrier, carter.

voix [vwa], *n.f. inv.* voice; tone, sound; vote, suffrage; opinion, judgment; singer; *à demi-voix*, in a low voice; *à haute voix*, aloud; loudly; *de vive voix*, by word of mouth.

vol (1) [vɔl], *n.m.* flying, soaring; flight; flock (*of birds*); spread (*of wings*); *au vol*, on the wing; *à vol d'oiseau*, as the crow flies.

vol (2) [vɔl], *n.m.* theft, robbery, stealing, larceny; stolen goods; *vol à l'étalage*, shoplifting; *vol avec effraction*, burglary.

volage [vɔ'la:ʒ], *a.* fickle, inconstant, flighty.

volaille [vɔ'la:j], *n.f.* poultry, fowls; *marchand de volaille*, poultry dealer.

volant [vɔ'lɑ̃], *a.* flying; loose, floating; movable, portable.—*n.m.* shuttlecock; flounce (*of a dress*); flywheel (*of machinery*); steering wheel (*of a car*); sail (*of a windmill*).

volatil [vɔla'til], *a.* (*Chem.*) volatile; (*fig.*) volatile (*of temperament*).

volatile [vɔla'til], *a.* winged.—*n.m.* winged creature, bird.

vol-au-vent [vɔlo'vɑ̃], *n.m. inv.* vol-au-vent, puff-pie.

volcan [vɔl'kɑ̃], *n.m.* volcano.

volcanique [vɔlka'nik], *a.* volcanic, fiery.

volée [vɔ'le], *n.f.* flight (*of birds etc.*); flock, covey; brood; bevy; volley (*of guns*); shower (*of blows*); thrashing; peal (*of bells*); *à la volée*, flying, as it flies, in the air; (*fig.*) rashly, at random; *sonner à toute volée*, to ring a full peal; *volée d'escalier*, flight of stairs.

voler (1) [vɔ'le], *v.i.* to fly; to take wing, to soar; *entendre voler une mouche*, to hear a pin drop.

voler (2) [vɔ'le], *v.t.* to steal, to rob; to fleece, to plunder; (*fig.*) to embezzle, to usurp.—*v.i.* to steal.

volerie [vɔl'ri], *n.f.* robbery; pilfering.

volet [vɔ'le], *n.m.* (window-)shutter; dovecot; (*Av.*) flap.

voleter [vɔl'te], *v.i.* (*conjug. like* APPELER) to flutter.

voleur [vɔ'lœ:r], *n.m.* (*fem.* -**euse**) thief, robber; plunderer, extortioner; stealer; *au voleur !* stop thief!

volière [vɔ'ljɛ:r], *n.f.* aviary, large bird cage.

volontaire [vɔlɔ̃'tɛ:r], *a.* voluntary, willing; intended, intentional; spontaneous; obstinate, wilful.—*n.* volunteer.

volontairement [vɔlɔ̃tɛr'mɑ̃], *adv.* voluntarily; wilfully.

volonté [vɔlɔ̃'te], *n.f.* will; (*pl.*) whims, caprices; *avoir de la bonne volonté*, to be willing; *à volonté*, at pleasure, at will; *dernières volontés*, last will and testament; *faire ses quatre volontés*, (*colloq.*)

to do as one pleases; *mauvaise volonté*, illwill; unwillingness.

volontiers [vɔlɔ̃'tje], *adv.* willingly, gladly, with pleasure.

volt [vɔlt], *n.m.* (*Elec.*) volt.

voltage [vɔl'ta:ʒ], *n.m.* voltage.

volte-face [vɔlt'fas], *n.f. inv.* turning round; *faire volte-face*, to face about; (*fig.*) to reverse one's opinions completely.

voltige [vɔl'ti:ʒ], *n.f.* slack-rope gymnastics, flying-trapeze exercises.

voltigeant [vɔlti'ʒɑ̃], *a.* fluttering, hovering.

voltigement [vɔltiʒ'mɑ̃], *n.m.* tumbling; fluttering.

voltiger [vɔlti'ʒe], *v.i.* (*conjug. like* MANGER) to flutter, to fly about; to hover.

voltigeur [vɔlti'ʒœ:r], *n.m.* vaulter; light-infantry soldier, rifleman.

voltmètre [vɔlt'mɛtr], *n.m.* voltmeter.

volubilis [vɔlybi'lis], *n.m.* convolvulus.

volubilité [vɔlybili'te], *n.f.* volubility, fluency, glibness.

volume [vɔ'lym], *n.m.* volume; bulk, size, mass.

volumineux [vɔlymi'nø], *a.* (*fem.* -**euse**) voluminous, bulky.

volupté [vɔlyp'te], *n.f.* voluptuousness, sensual pleasure.

voluptueux [vɔlyp'tɥø], *a.* (*fem.* -**euse**) voluptuous, sensual.—*n.m.* (*fem.* -**euse**) voluptuary.

volute [vɔ'ly:t], *n.f.* volute; scroll.

vomir [vɔ'mi:r], *v.t.* to vomit, to throw up, (*fig.*) to belch forth.—*v.i.* to vomit, to be sick.

vomissement [vɔmis'mɑ̃], *n.m.* vomit(ing).

vorace [vɔ'ras], *a.* voracious, ravenous.

voracité [vɔrasi'te], *n.f.* voracity.

vos [vo], [VOTRE].

votant [vɔ'tɑ̃], *n.m.* (*fem.* -**e**) voter.

vote [vɔt], *n.m.* vote; division, voting, poll.

voter [vɔ'te], *v.t., v.i.* to vote; to pass (*a bill*).

votif [vɔ'tif], *a.* (*fem.* -**tive**) votive.

votre [vɔtr], *a. poss.* (*pl.* **vos**) your.

vôtre [vo:tr], *pron.poss.* (*m. sing.* **le vôtre**, *fem. sing.* **la vôtre**, *pl.* **les vôtres**) yours.—*n.* your own, your own property; (*pl.*) your relations, friends etc.; your pranks, tricks.

vouer [vwe], *v.t.* to devote, to dedicate; to vow, to swear. **se vouer**, *v.r.* to devote oneself.

vouloir [vu'lwa:r], *v.t. irr.* to want; to desire, to wish, to require; to consent; to please; to choose; to determine; to try, to attempt; to admit, to grant; to mean; *en vouloir à quelqu'un*, to bear someone a grudge; *oui, je (le) veux bien*, yes, I am willing; *que veut dire cela?* what does that mean? *que voulez-vous?* what do you want? what can I do for you? what can you expect? *veuillez me dire*, please tell me.—*n.m.* will; *bon vouloir*, goodwill, *mauvais vouloir*, illwill.

voulu [vu'ly], *a.* wished, desired, required, requisite; due, received; deliberate, studied.

vous [vu], *pron. pers.* you; to you.

voûte [vut], *n.f.* arch, vault. (*fig.*) roof, canopy; *clef de voûte*, keystone.

voûté [vu'te], *a.* vaulted, curved.

voûter [vu'te], *v.t.* to vault, to arch over; to bend. **se voûter**, *v.r.* to arch, to vault; to be bent, to stoop.

vouvoyer [vuvwa'je], v.t. (conjug. like EM-PLOYER) to say vous instead of tu when addressing somebody.

voyage [vwa'ja:ʒ], n.m. travel; journey, voyage, trip; visit; (pl.) travels; bon voyage! pleasant journey to you! être en voyage, to be travelling.

voyager [vwaja'ʒe], v.i. (conjug. like MANGER) to travel, to journey.

voyageur [vwaja'ʒœ:r], a. (fem. -euse) travelling; migrating; commis voyageur, commercial traveller; oiseau voyageur, migratory bird; pigeon voyageur, carrier pigeon.—n.m. (fem. -euse) traveller; passenger.

voyant [vwa'jɑ̃], a. gaudy, showy (of colors).—n.m. (fem. -e) seer, clairvoyant.

voyelle [vwa'jɛl], n.f. vowel.

voyou [vwa'ju], n.m. (fam.) guttersnipe, hooligan; loafer.

vrac (en) [ɑ̃'vrak], adv. phr. in bulk, loose, pell-mell.

vrai [vrɛ], a. true, real, genuine; right, proper, fit; downright, arrant.—int. truly, really, in truth!—n.m. truth; à vrai dire, to tell the truth, as a matter of fact.

vraiment [vrɛ'mɑ̃], adv. truly, in truth; indeed, really!

vraisemblable [vrɛsɑ̃'blabl], a. likely, probable.—n.m. probability, likelihood.

vraisemblance [vrɛsɑ̃'blɑ̃:s], n.f. probability, likelihood, verisimilitude.

vrille [vri:j], n.f. gimlet, borer, piercer; (Bot.) tendril; (Av.) tail-spin.

vriller [vri'je], v.t. to bore.—v.i. to ascend spirally.

vrillette [vri'jɛt], n.f. death-watch beetle.

vrombir [vrɔ̃'bi:r], v.i. to buzz, to hum, to whirr, to purr, to throb.

vu [vy], a. considered, regarded; seen, observed.—prep. considering, in view of.—n.m. sight, examination, inspection; (Law) preamble.—conj. phr. vu que, seeing that, whereas.

vue [vy], n.f. sight, eyesight; eyes; view, survey, inspection; prospect; appearance; light, window; design; à perte de vue, as far as the eye can reach, out of sight; à vue d'œil, visibly.

Vulcain [vyl'kɛ̃], m. Vulcan.

vulcaniser [vylkani'ze], v.t. to vulcanize.

vulgaire [vyl'gɛ:r], a. vulgar, common.—n.m. the common herd.

vulgairement [vylgɛr'mɑ̃], adv. vulgarly, commonly.

vulgariser [vylgari'ze], v.t. to popularize.

vulgarité [vylgari'te], n.f. vulgarity.

vulnérabilité [vylnerabili'te], n.f. vulnerability.

vulnérable [vylne'rabl], a. vulnerable.

W

W, w [dublə've], n.m. this twenty-third letter of the alphabet is used only in borrowed words.

wagon [va'gɔ̃], n.m. (Rail.) coach, (Am.) car; truck, van, (Am.) freight car.

wagon-lit [vagɔ̃'li], n.m. (pl. wagons-lits) sleeping-car, sleeper.

wagonnet [vagɔ'nɛ], n.m. tip-truck.

wallon [wa'lɔ̃], a. (fem. -onne) Walloon.—n.m. Walloon (language); (Wallon, fem. -onne) Walloon (person).

warrant [va'rɑ̃], n.m. warrant.

warranter [varɑ̃'te], v.t. to warrant, to guarantee, to certify.

water [wa'tɛr], les W.C. [ɛvɛ'se], n.m. pl. water closet, lavatory, toilet.

watt [wat], n.m. (Elec.) watt.

wattman [wat'man], n.m. (pl.-men) motorman.

week-end [wik'ɛnd], n.m. (pl. week-ends) week-end.

whisky [wis'ki], n.m. whisky.

whist [wist], n.m. whist.

wigwam [wig'wam], n.m. wigwam.

wolfram [vɔl'fram], n.m. wolfram (tungsten ore).

X

X, x [iks], n.m. the twenty-fourth letter of the alphabet; rayons X, X-rays.

xénophobe [ksenɔ'fɔb], a. and n. xenophobe.

xérès [kse'rɛs], n.m. sherry (wine).

xylophone [ksilɔ'fɔn], n.m. (Mus.) xylophone.

Y

Y, y [i grɛk], n.m. the twenty-fifth letter of the alphabet.

y [i], adv. there; thither; within, at home; ça y est! that's it! il y a, there is, there are; je l'y ai vu, I saw him there; j'y suis, I follow you, I get you; y compris, included.—pron. by, for, in, at or to him, her, it or them.

yacht [jɔt, jak], n.m. yacht.

Yémen [je'mɛn], le, m. Yemen.

yéménite [jema'nit], a. Yemeni.—n. (Yéménite) Yemeni (person).

yeuse [jø:z], n.f. ilex, holm oak.

yeux [jø:], [ŒIL].

yodler [jo'dle], v.i. (Mus.) to yodel.

yogi or **yogui** [jo'gi], n.m. yogi.

yole [jɔl], n.f. yawl, gig.

yougoslave [jugos'lav], a. Yugoslav.—n.m. Yugoslav (language).—n. (Yougoslave) Yugoslav (person).

Yougoslavie [jugɔsla'vi], la, f. Yugoslavia.

youyou [ju'ju], n.m. dinghy.

Z

Z, z [zed], *n.m.* the twenty-sixth letter of the alphabet.

Zambie [zā'bi], **la**, *f.* Zambia.

zèbre [zɛbr], *n.m.* zebra.

zébré [ze'bre], *a.* striped like the zebra.

zèle [zɛːl], *n.m.* zeal, warmth, ardor, enthusiasm.

zélé [ze'le], *a.* zealous.

zélote [ze'lɔt], *n.m.* zealot.

zénith [ze'nit], *n.m.* zenith.

zéphire, zéphyr or **zéphyre** [ze'fiːr], *n.m.* zephyr, gentle breeze.

zéro [ze'ro], *n.m.* nought; zero (*of the thermometer*); (*fig.*) a mere cipher, nonentity.

zeste [zɛst], *n.m.* woody skin dividing sections of a walnut; peel (*of orange, lemon etc.*), rind; (*fig.*) straw, fig, nothing.

zézaiement or **zézayement** [zezɛ(j)'mā] *n.m.* ·lisping, lisp (*incorrect pronunciation of* [z] *instead of* [ʒ]).

zézayer [zeze'je], *v.i.* (*conjug. like* PAYER) to lisp.

zibeline [zi'blin], *n.f.* sable.

zigzag [zig'zag], *n.m.* zigzag; *éclair en zigzag*, forked lightning.

zinc [zɛ̃ːg], *n.m.* zinc; (*slang*) bar or counter of a bistro.

zingaro [zɛ̃ga'ro], *n.m.* (*pl.* **zingari**) gipsy.

zinguer [zɛ̃'ge], *v.t.* to cover with zinc; to zinc.

zizanie [ziza'ni], *n.f.* tare, *darnel; (*fig.*) discord, bickering.

zodiaque [zɔ'djak], *n.m.* zodiac.

zone [zoːn], *n.f.* zone, belt, area.

zoo [zo'o], *n.m.* (*fam.*) zoo.

zoologie [zɔɔlɔ'ʒi], *n.f.* zoology.

zoologique [zɔɔlɔ'ʒik], *a.* zoological.

zoologiste [zɔɔlɔ'ʒist], *n.* zoologist.

zouave [zwa:v], *n.m.* Zouave (*soldier*).

zut! [zyt], *int.* (*fam.*) (to convey anger, scorn, disappointment, flat refusal); *zut! zut alors! non, zut!* be blowed! no go! never! bother!

A

A, a (1) [ei]. première lettre de l'alphabet; (*Mus.*) la, *m.*; *a.m.*, du matin.

a (2) [ei, ə], **an** [æn, ən] (*before vowel*), *indef. art.* un, *m.*, une, *f.*; *a shilling a pound*, un shilling la livre; *three a day*, trois par jour.

aback [ə'bæk], *adv.* en arrière; (*fig.*) à l'improviste, au dépourvu.

abacus ['æbəkəs], *n.* (*pl.* **abaci** ['æbəkai]) (*Arch., Math.*) abaque, *m.*

abaft [ə'bɑːft], *adv.* sur l'arrière, en arrière.—*prep.* en arrière de, à l'arrière de.

abandon [ə'bændən], *v.t.* abandonner; délaisser, quitter; renoncer à, se désister de. —*n.* abandon, *m.*; désinvolture, *f.*

abandoned [ə'bændənd], *a.* abandonné; dépravé.

abandonment [ə'bændənmənt], *n.* abandonnement; délaissement; abandon, *m.*

abase [ə'beis], *v.t.* abaisser; ravaler.

abasement [ə'beismənt], *n.* abaissement; ravalement, *m.*; humiliation, *f.*

abash [ə'bæʃ], *v.t.* déconcerter, décontenancer; interdire, confondre.

abate [ə'beit], *v.t.* diminuer; rabattre; affaiblir, atténuer; amortir; calmer, apaiser. —*v.i.* diminuer; s'affaiblir; se calmer, s'apaiser (*temps etc.*); tomber, baisser, s'abattre (*vent etc.*).

abatement [ə'beitmənt], *n.* diminution, réduction, *f.*, rabais; affaiblissement, adoucissement; apaisement, *m.*

abbacy ['æbəsi], *n.* dignité d'abbé, *f.*

abbess ['æbes], *n.* abbesse, *f.*

abbey ['æbi], *n.* abbaye, *f.*

abbot ['æbət], *n.* abbé, supérieur (*d'abbaye*), *m.*

abbreviate [ə'briːvieit], *v.t.* abréger; raccourcir.

abbreviation [əbriːvi'eiʃən], *n.* abréviation, *f.*

abdicate ['æbdikeit], *v.t.*, *v.i.* abdiquer.

abdication [æbdi'keiʃən], *n.* abdication, *f.*

abdomen [æb'doumən, 'æbdəmən], *n.* abdomen, bas-ventre, *m.*

abdominal [æb'dɔminəl], *a.* abdominal.

abduct [æb'dʌkt], *v.t.* détourner, enlever (*clandestinement* ou *par force*).

abduction [æb'dʌkʃən], *n.* abduction, *f.*, enlèvement (*de mineur etc.*), détournement, *m.*

abductor [æb'dʌktə], *n.* (*Anat.*) abducteur; (*Law*) ravisseur, *m.*

abed [ə'bed], *adv.* au lit, couché.

aberration [æbə'reiʃən], *n.* aberration, *f.*; éloignement, écart, égarement, *m.*; erreur (*de jugement*), *f.*

abet [ə'bet], *v.t.* soutenir, encourager (*à un crime*); *to aid and abet*, être le complice.

abetment [ə'betmənt], *n.* encouragement (*à un crime*), *m.*

abetting [ə'betiŋ], *n.*

abettor [ə'betə], *n.* instigateur (*d'un crime*), *m.*; complice, *m.*, *f.*

abeyance [ə'beiəns], *n.* vacance; suspension, *f.*; *in abeyance*, en suspens; *to fall into abeyance*, tomber en désuétude.

abhor [əb'hɔː], *v.t.* abhorrer, détester.

abhorrence [əb'hɔrəns], *n.* horreur, *f.*

abhorrent [əb'hɔrənt], *a.* odieux, répugnant (*à*).

abide [ə'baid], *v.t. irr.* attendre; supporter; subir, souffrir.—*v.i.* demeurer, rester; séjourner; durer; *to abide by* (*a decision etc.*), rester fidèle à; *to abide by* (*the laws etc.*), se conformer à.

abiding [ə'baidiŋ], *a.* constant, immuable.

ability [ə'biliti], *n.* capacité, *f.*; pouvoir; talent, *m.*; habileté, *f.*

abject ['æbdʒekt], *a.* abject, bas, vil.

abjection [æb'dʒekʃən], **abjectness** ['æbdʒektnis], *n.* abjection, misère, *f.*

abjectly ['æbdʒektli], *adv.* d'une manière abjecte.

abjure [æb'dʒuə], *v.t.* abjurer; renoncer à, renier.

ablative ['æblətiv], *a.* and *n.* (*Gram.*) ablatif, *m.*

ablaze [ə'bleiz], *a.* en feu, en flammes; (*fig.*) enflammé.

able [eibl], *a.* capable (*de*), à même (*de*); habile; *to be able to*, pouvoir.

able-bodied ['eiblbɔdid], *a.* fort, robuste, vigoureux.

ablution [ə'bluːʃən], *n.* ablution, *f.*

ably ['eibli], *adv.* habilement, avec talent.

abnegation [æbni'geiʃən], *n.* abnégation, renonciation, *f.*; désaveu, *m.*

abnormal [æb'nɔːməl], *a.* anormal.

abnormality [æbnɔː'mæliti], *n.* anomalie; difformité, *f.*

abnormally [æb'nɔːməli], *adv.* anormalement.

aboard [ə'bɔːd], *adv.* à bord (*de*).

abode (1) [ə'boud], *n.* demeure, habitation, *f.*; séjour, *m.*

abode (2) [ə'boud], *past* and *p.p.* [ABIDE].

abolish [ə'bɔliʃ], *v.t.* abolir; supprimer.

abolishment [ə'bɔliʃmənt], **abolition** [æbə'liʃən], *n.* abolition, suppression, *f.*; abolissement, *m.*

abominable [ə'bɔminəbl], *a.* abominable, infâme, détestable.

abominably [ə'bɔminəbli], *adv.* abominablement.

abominate [ə'bɔmineit], *v.t.* abominer, détester.

abomination [əbɔmi'neiʃən], *n.* abomination, horreur, *f.*

aboriginal [æbə'ridʒinəl], *a.* aborigène, primitif.—*n.* aborigène, *m.*, *f.*

aborigine [æbə'ridʒini], *n.* aborigène, *m.*, *f.*

abortion [ə'bɔːʃən], *n.* avortement (*acte*); avorton (*embryon*), *m.*

abortive [ə'bɔːtiv], *a.* abortif, manqué; avorté.

abortively [ə'bɔːtivli], *adv.* avant terme; (*fig.*) sans résultat, sans succès.

abortiveness [ə'bɔːtivnis], *n.* (*fig.*) insuccès, *m.*

abound [ə'baund], *v.i.* abonder (*de* ou *en*), regorger (*de*).

333

abounding [ə'baundiŋ], a. abondant.
about [ə'baut], prep. autour de; auprès de;
sur; vers; environ; touchant, au sujet de, à
l'égard de; à peu près; sur le point de; dans,
par; *about that*, là-dessus, à ce sujet;
about two o'clock, vers (les) deux heures;
what is it all about? de quoi s'agit-il ?—
adv. tout autour, à l'entour, à la ronde; çà
et là; *to be about to*, être sur le point de.
above [ə'bʌv], prep. au-dessus de, par-dessus;
en amont de; plus de; au delà de; *above
all*, surtout, par-dessus tout; *above board*,
ouvertement, franchement.—adv. en haut;
là-haut; au-dessus; ci-dessus.
abrasion [ə'breiʒən], n. abrasion, écorchure, f.
abrasive [ə'breisiv], a. and n. abrasif, m.
abreast [ə'brest], adv. de front, à côté l'un de
l'autre; (fig.) de pair avec.
abridge [ə'bridʒ], v.t. abréger, raccourcir;
restreindre, priver; *abridged edition (of
book)*, édition réduite, f.
abridgment [ə'bridʒmənt], n. abrégé, précis,
m.; réduction, diminution, f.
abroad [ə'brɔːd], adv. à l'étranger; au loin, de
tous côtés; *to get abroad*, se répandre
(nouvelles).
abrogate ['æbrogeit], v.t. abroger.
abrogation [æbro'geiʃən], n. abrogation, f.
abrupt [ə'brʌpt], a. brusque; brisé, saccadé;
précipité, soudain; abrupt, escarpé, à pic.
abruptly [ə'brʌptli], adv. brusquement, tout
à coup.
abruptness [ə'brʌptnis], n. précipitation; (fig.)
brusquerie, rudesse, f.; escarpement, m.
abscess ['æbses], n. abcès, dépôt, m.
abscond [əb'skɔnd], v.i. se soustraire (furtivement) aux poursuites de la justice; disparaître; (fam.) décamper.
absconder [əb'skɔndə], n. fugitif, m.; (Law)
contumace, m., f.
absence ['æbsəns], n. absence, f.; éloignement, m.; absence d'esprit, distraction, f.;
manque, m.
absent ['æbsənt], a. absent.—[æb'sent], v.t.
to absent oneself, s'absenter.
absentee [æbsən'tiː], n. absent, manquant, m.
absenteeism [æbsən'tiːizm], n. absentéisme,
m.
absent-minded ['æbsənt'maindid], a. distrait.
absinthe ['æbsinθ], n. absinthe, f.
absolute ['æbsəluːt], a. absolu, illimité;
irrévocable (décret); véritable.
absolutely ['æbsə'luːtli], adv. absolument.
absolution [æbsə'luːʃən], n. absolution, f.;
(R.-C. Ch.) absoute, f.
absolve [əb'zɔlv], v.t. absoudre (de); délier,
décharger, dégager, affranchir.
absorb [əb'sɔːb], v.t. absorber; amortir (un
choc).
absorbent [əb'sɔːbənt], a. and n. absorbant,
m.
absorption [əb'sɔːpʃən], n. absorption, f.;
absorbement, amortissement, m.
abstain [əb'stein], v.i. s'abstenir (de).
abstainer [əb'steinə], n. buveur d'eau, m.,
abstème, m., f.; *total abstainer*, personne
qui ne boit jamais d'alcool, f.
abstemious [əb'stiːmiəs], a. tempérant,
sobre.
abstemiously [əb'stiːmiəsli], adv. sobrement, avec modération.

abstemiousness [əb'stiːmiəsnis], n. abstinence; modération, sobriété, f.
abstention [əb'stenʃən], n. abstention, f.
abstinence ['æbstinəns], n. abstinence, f.
abstinent ['æbstinənt], a. abstinent, sobre.
abstract (1) [æb'strækt], v.t. soustraire
dérober, détourner; faire abstraction de;
résumer, abréger.
abstract (2) ['æbstrækt], a. abstrait.—n.
abrégé, résumé, précis, m.; analyse, f.;
(Comm.) relevé, m.
abstracted [æb'stræktid], a. séparé; distrait,
rêveur, pensif; soustrait, dérobé.
abstractedness [æb'stræktidnis], n. caractère abstrait, m.; préoccupation, f.
abstraction [æb'strækʃən], n. soustraction,
distraction; abstraction; préoccupation, f.
abstractly ['æbstræktli], adv. abstractive-
ment, d'une manière abstraite.
abstruse [æb'struːs], a. caché; abstrus,
obscur.
absurd [əb'səːd], a. absurde.
absurdity [əb'səːditi], n. absurdité, f.
absurdly [əb'səːdli], adv. absurdement.
abundance [ə'bʌndəns], n. abondance,
grande quantité, f.; grand nombre, m.; (fig.)
prospérité, f.
abundant [ə'bʌndənt], a. abondant.
abundantly [ə'bʌndəntli], adv. abondamment, en abondance, à foison.
abuse (1) [ə'bjuːz], v.t. abuser de; maltraiter;
médire de; injurier, dire des injures à;
séduire.
abuse (2) [ə'bjuːs], n. abus, m.; insultes,
injures, f. pl.
abuser [ə'bjuːzə], n. détracteur; séducteur;
trompeur, m.
abusive [ə'bjuːsiv], a. abusif; injurieux.
abusively [ə'bjuːsivli], adv. abusivement;
injurieusement.
abusiveness [ə'bjuːsivnis], n. langage injurieux ou grossier, m.
abut [ə'bʌt], v.i. aboutir (à); (Build.) s'appuyer
(contre).
abysmal [ə'bizməl], a. sans fond; (ignorance)
profonde.
abyss [ə'bis], n. abîme, gouffre, m.
Abyssinia [æbi'sinjə], l'Abyssinie, l'Éthiopie,
f.
Abyssinian [æbi'sinjən], a. abyssinien.—n.
Abyssinien (personne), m.
acacia [ə'keiʃə], n. acacia, m.
academic [ækə'demik], **academical** [ækə-
'demikəl], a. académique, universitaire,
classique, scolaire.
academician [əkædə'miʃən], n. académicien, m.
academy [ə'kædəmi], n. académie (société
savante); école libre, f., pensionnat, m.,
institution, f.
acanthus [ə'kænθəs], n. acanthe, f.
accede [æk'siːd], v.i. accéder, consentir (à);
monter (sur le trône).
accelerate [æk'seləreit], v.t. accélérer; hâter.
—v.i. s'accélérer.
acceleration [ækselə'reiʃən], n. accélération, f.
accelerator [æk'seləreitə], n. accélérateur,
m.
accent (1) [æk'sent], v.t. accentuer.
accent (2) ['æksənt], n. accent, m.
accentuate [æk'sentjueit], v.t. accentuer.

accept [ək'sept], v.t. accepter, agréer, admettre.

acceptability [əkseptə'biliti], acceptableness [ək'septəblnis], n. acceptabilité, f.; droit au bon accueil, m.

acceptable [ək'septəbl], a. acceptable; agréable.

acceptance [ək'septəns], n. acceptation, f.; accueil favorable, m.

acceptation [æksep'teiʃən], n. acception, f., sens (d'un mot), m.

access ['ækses], n. accès, abord, m.; entrée, admission, f.

accessible [æk'sesibl], a. accessible, abordable.

accession [æk'seʃən], n. acquisition; augmentation, addition, f.; accroissement; avènement (au trône etc.), m.

accessory [æk'sesəri], a. accessoire.—n. accessoire (chose), m.; complice (personne), m., f.

accidence ['æksidəns], n. morphologie, f.; rudiments (de grammaire), m. pl.

accident ['æksidənt], n. accident, m., avarie, f., hasard; incident; malheur, m.

accidental [æksi'dentəl], a. accidentel, fortuit.

accidentally [æksi'dentəli], adv. accidentellement; par hasard.

acclaim [ə'kleim], v.t. acclamer, applaudir à; proclamer.—n. acclamation, f.

acclamation [æklə'meiʃən], n. acclamation, f.

acclimatation [əklaimə'teiʃən], acclimation [æklai'meiʃən], n. acclimatement, m.; acclimatation, f.

acclimatization [əklaimətai'zeiʃən], n. acclimatation, f.

acclimatize [ə'klaimətaiz], v.t. acclimater; to become acclimatized, s'acclimater; s'accoutumer.

acclivity [ə'kliviti], n. montée, côte, rampe, f.

accolade [ækə'leid], n. accolade, f.

accommodate [ə'kɒmədeit], v.t. accommoder, ajuster; loger, recevoir; fournir, obliger (par), servir (de).

accommodating [ə'kɒmədeitiŋ], a. accommodant, obligeant; complaisant.

accommodation [əkɒmə'deiʃən], n. ajustement, accommodement, m.; complaisance, convenance, f.; logement, m.; facilités, f.pl.

accompaniment [ə'kʌmpnimənt], n. accompagnement, m.

accompanist [ə'kʌmpənist], n. (Mus.) accompagnateur, m., accompagnatrice, f.

accompany [ə'kʌmpəni], v.t. accompagner; reconduire (à sa voiture etc.).

accomplice [ə'kʌmplis], n. complice, m., f., compère, m.

accomplish [ə'kʌmpliʃ], v.t. accomplir, achever; effectuer; réaliser (une prédiction etc.).

accomplished [ə'kʌmpliʃt], a. accompli, achevé; parfait.

accomplishment [ə'kʌmpliʃmənt], n. accomplissement, m.; exécution, f.; (usu. pl.) arts d'agrément, talents, m.pl.

accord [ə'kɔːd], v.t. accorder, concéder.—v.i. s'accorder, être d'accord.—n. accord, consentement, m.; of one's own accord, de son propre gré, spontanément; with one accord, d'un commun accord.

accordance [ə'kɔːdəns], n. accord, rapport, m.; conformité, f.

according [ə'kɔːdiŋ], a. conforme (à); according as, selon que, suivant que; according to, selon, suivant, conformément à, d'après.

accordingly [ə'kɔːdiŋli], adv. en conséquence; donc, aussi.

accordion [ə'kɔːdiən], n. accordéon, m.

accost [ə'kɒst], v.t. accoster, aborder.

account [ə'kaunt], n. compte; mémoire, rapport, exposé, compte rendu, m.; relation, f., récit, m.; raison; cause; (fig.) considération, valeur, f.; cas, poids, m.; by all accounts, au dire de tout le monde; current account, compte courant; on account of, à cause de; to keep accounts, tenir les livres.—v.t. compter, estimer (de), regarder (comme), tenir (pour).—v.i. to account for, rendre compte de, expliquer; répondre de, rendre raison de.

accountable [ə'kauntəbl], a. responsable; comptable.

accountancy [ə'kauntənsi], n. comptabilité, f.

accountant [ə'kauntənt], n. comptable, agent comptable, m.; chartered accountant, expert comptable, m.

account book [ə'kauntbuk], n. livre de comptes, m.

accouter [ə'kuːtə], v.t. habiller, équiper; accoutrer (un chevalier etc.).

accouterment [ə'kuːtəmənt], n. harnachement; équipement (du soldat), m.

accredit [ə'kredit], v.t. accréditer.

accretion [ə'kriːʃən], n. accroissement, m.

accrue [ə'kruː], v.i. provenir, résulter (de); s'accumuler.

accumulate [ə'kjuːmjuleit], v.t. accumuler, entasser; amonceler.—v.i. s'accumuler, s'amonceler.

accumulation [əkjuːmju'leiʃən], n. accumulation, f.; amoncellement, amas, entassement, m.

accumulative [ə'kjuːmjulətiv], a. (chose) qui s'accumule; (personne) qui accumule, thésauriseur.

accumulator [ə'kjuːmjuleitə], n. accumulateur, m.

accuracy ['ækjurisi], accurateness ['ækjuritnis], n. exactitude, justesse; précision, f.; soin, m.

accurate ['ækjurit], a. exact, juste, correct, précis.

accurately ['ækjuritli], adv. exactement, avec justesse.

accurateness [ACCURACY].

accursed [ə'kɔːsid], a. maudit; détestable, exécrable.

accusation [ækju'zeiʃən], n. accusation, f.

accusative [ə'kjuːzətiv], a. and n. (Gram.), accusatif, m.

accusatory [ə'kjuːzətri], a. accusatoire.

accuse [ə'kjuːz], v.t. accuser.

accuser [ə'kjuːzə], n. accusateur, m.

accustom [ə'kʌstəm], v.t. accoutumer, habituer.

ace [eis], n. as; (fig.) point, iota, m.; within an ace of, à deux doigts de.

acerb [ə'sɔːb], a. acerbe, aigre.

acerbity [ə'sɔːbiti], n. acerbité, aigreur; (fig.) âpreté, sévérité, f.

acetic [ə'siːtik, ə'setik], a. acétique.

acetylene [ə'setili:n], *n.* acétylène, *m.*
ache [eik], *n.* mal, *m.*; douleur, *f.*; *headache,*
mal de tête; *toothache,* mal de dents.—
v.i. faire mal; (*fig.*) souffrir (*de*); *my head
aches,* j'ai mal à la tête.
achieve [ə'tʃi:v], *v.t.* exécuter, accomplir;
remporter (*une victoire*); atteindre (*à*).
achievement [ə'tʃi:vmənt], *n.* exploit, fait
d'armes; accomplissement, succès, *m.*;
réalisation, *f.*
aching ['eikiŋ], *a.* endolori, douloureux; *an
aching heart,* un cœur dolent.
acid ['æsid], *a.* and *n.* acide, *m.*; *acid
drops,* bonbons acidulés, *m.pl.*
acidity [ə'siditi], *n.* acidité, *f.*
acknowledge [ək'nɔlidʒ], *v.t.* reconnaître;
avouer, confesser; accuser réception de
(*lettre*); répondre à.
acknowledgment [ək'nɔlidʒmənt], *n.* reconnaissance, *f.*; aveu; accusé de réception, *m.*;
remerciements, *m.pl.*
acme ['ækmi], *n.* comble, faîte; apogée, *m.*
acolyte ['ækolait], *n.* acolyte, *m.*
aconite ['ækonait], *n.* (*Bot.*) aconit, *m.*
acorn ['eikɔːn], *n.* gland, *m.*
acoustic [ə'ku:stik], *a.* acoustique.—*n.* (*pl.*)
acoustique, *f.*
acquaint [ə'kweint], *v.t.* informer (*de*); faire
savoir à, faire part à; *to be acquainted
with,* connaître, savoir.
acquaintance [ə'kweintəns], *n.* connaissance (*de*); personne de ma (sa *etc.*) connaissance, *f.*
acquainted [ə'kweintid], *a.* connu; instruit
(*de*), familier (*avec*).
acquiesce [ækwi'es], *v.i.* acquiescer (*à*);
accéder (*à*).
acquiescence [ækwi'esəns], *n.* acquiescement; consentement, *m.*
acquiescent [ækwi'esənt], *a.* résigné, soumis,
consentant.
acquire [ə'kwaiə], *v.t.* acquérir, obtenir,
gagner.
acquirement [ə'kwaiəmənt], *n.* acquisition;
connaissance, *f.*
acquisition [ækwi'ziʃən], *n.* acquisition, *f.*
acquisitive [ə'kwizitiv], *a.* âpre au gain.
acquit [ə'kwit], *v.t.* régler (*une dette*);
absoudre, acquitter (*un accusé*); s'acquitter
(*d'un devoir*); *to acquit oneself well,* faire
son devoir.
acquittal [ə'kwitəl], *n.* acquittement, *m.*
acre ['eikə], *n.* arpent, *m.*, acre, *f.*
acreage ['eikəridʒ], *n.* superficie, *f.*
acrid ['ækrid], *a.* âcre; (*fig.*) acerbe.
acridity [æ'kriditi], *n.* âcreté, *f.*
acrimonious [ækri'mouniəs], *a.* acrimonieux.
acrimoniously [ækri'mouniəsli], *adv.* avec
aigreur, avec acrimonie.
acrimony ['ækrimən i], *n.* acrimonie, aigreur,
f.
acrobat ['ækrobæt], *n.* acrobate, *m.*, *f.*
acrobatic [ækro'bætik], *a.* acrobatique.—
n. (*pl.*) acrobatie, *f.*
acropolis [ə'krɔpolis], *n.* acropole, *f.*
across [ə'krɔs, ə'krɔːs], *prep.* à travers, sur; *to
come across,* rencontrer.—*adv.* à travers,
en travers; de l'autre côté; *across the
street,* de l'autre côté de la rue.
acrostic [ə'krɔstik], *n.* acrostiche, *m.*
act [ækt], *n.* acte, *m.*, loi; action, *f.*; *in the
act,* sur le fait; *in the act of doing it,* en

train de le faire; *in the very act,* en
flagrant délit.—*v.t.* jouer, représenter;
feindre, contrefaire.—*v.i.* agir (*en, sur etc.*);
se conduire; se comporter; opérer.
acting ['æktiŋ], *a.* qui agit; suppléant;
(*Comm.*) gérant; *acting manager,* directeur gérant, *m.*—*n.* (*Theat.*) jeu, *m.*; (*fig.*)
feinte, *f.*
action ['ækʃən], *n.* action, *f.*, fait; (*Law*)
procès, *m.*; bataille, *f.*
actionable ['ækʃənəbl], *a.* actionnable,
sujet à procès.
activate ['æktiveit], *v.t.* activer; rendre
radioactif.
active ['æktiv], *a.* actif, agile, alerte.
actively ['æktivli], *adv.* activement.
activity [æk'tiviti], *n.* activité, *f.*
actor ['æktə], *n.* acteur, comédien, *m.*
actress ['æktris], *n.* actrice, comédienne, *f.*
actual ['æktjuəl], *a.* réel, véritable, effectif.
actuality [æktju'æliti], *n.* réalité, *f.*
actually ['æktjuəli], *adv.* réellement, en
effet, positivement, véritablement; à vrai
dire.
actuarial [æktju'εəriəl], *a.* actuariel.
actuary ['æktjuari], *n.* actuaire, *m.*
actuate ['æktjueit], *v.t.* mettre en action;
pousser, animer.
acuity [ə'kjuiti], *n.* acuité, *f.*
acumen [ə'kju:mən], *n.* finesse, pénétration, *f.*
acute [ə'kju:t], *a.* aigu, pointu, fin; (*fig.*)
violent, poignant; perçant, pénétrant.
acutely [ə'kju:tli], *adv.* vivement; avec finesse.
acuteness [ə'kju:tnis], *n.* acuité; intensité;
finesse, pénétration, *f.*
adage ['ædidʒ], *n.* adage, proverbe, *m.*
adamant ['ædəmənt], *a.* inflexible, intransigeant.—*n.* diamant, *m.*
adamantine [ædə'mæntain], *a.* adamantin,
inflexible.
adapt [ə'dæpt], *v.t.* adapter, approprier,
ajuster (*à*).
adaptability [ədæptə'biliti], *n.* faculté
d'adaptation, souplesse, *f.*
adaptable [ə'dæptəbl], *a.* adaptable, qui peut
s'adapter.
adapter [ə'dæptə], *n.* (*Elec.*) raccord, *m.*
add [æd], *v.t.* ajouter, joindre; additionner.
adder ['ædə], *n.* vipère, *f.*
addict ['ædikt], *n.* personne adonnée à (*stupé-
fiants etc.*), *f.*—[ə'dikt], *v.i.* s'adonner, se
livrer (*à*).
addictedness [ə'diktidnis], *addiction* [ə'dik
ʃən], *n.* attachement, goût (*pour*), penchant
(*à*), *m.*
addition [ə'diʃən], *n.* addition, *f.*; surcroît,
supplément, accroissement, *m.*
additional [ə'diʃənəl], *a.* additionnel, supplémentaire, de plus.
additionally [ə'diʃənəli], *adv.* par addition,
en sus, de plus, en outre.
addle [ædl], *v.t.* rendre couvi, corrompre; (*fig.*)
brouiller (*le cerveau*).—*a.* or *addled* [ædld],
couvi (*œuf*); pourri; (*fig.*) stérile.
addle-headed ['ædl'hedid], *a.* à cerveau vide,
écervelé, à l'esprit brouillon.
address [ə'dres], *n.* adresse; habileté, dextérité; allocution, *f.*, discours; (*fig.*) abord,
m.—*v.t.* adresser (*une lettre*); adresser la
parole à, aborder (*quelqu'un*); (*Golf*) *to
address the ball,* viser la balle.
addressee [ædre'si:], *n.* destinataire, *m.*, *f.*

adduce [ə'dju:s], *v.t.* alléguer; apporter, avancer, produire.
Adela ['ædilə]. Adèle, *f.*
Adelaide ['ædəleid]. Adélaïde, *f.*
adenoid ['ædinɔid], *a.* adénoïde.—*n.* (*pl.*) adénite, *f.*; végétations, *f. pl.*
adept [æ'dept], *a.* adepte, habile, versé (*dans*).—*n.* adepte, *m.*, *f.*
adequacy ['ædikwəsi], **adequateness** ['ædikwitnis], *n.* juste proportion, suffisance, *f.*
adequate ['ædikwit], *a.* proportionné, suffisant (*à*), compétent.
adequately ['ædikwitli], *adv.* en juste proportion, suffisamment, convenablement.
adequateness [ADEQUACY].
adhere [əd'hiə], *v.i.* adhérer, s'attacher, s'en tenir (*à*).
adherence [əd'hiərəns], *n.* adhérence, *f.*, attachement, *m.*
adherent [əd'hiərənt], *n.* adhérent, *m.*
adhesion [əd'hi:ʒən], *n.* adhésion, *f.*
adhesive [əd'hi:siv], *a.* adhésif, tenace; gommé, agglutinant.
adieu [ə'dju:], *adv. and n.* adieu, *m.*; *to bid someone adieu*, faire ses adieux à quelqu'un.
adipose ['ædipous], *a.* adipeux.
adjacency [ə'dʒeisənsi], *n.* contiguïté, *f.*, voisinage, *m.*
adjacent [ə'dʒeisənt], *a.* adjacent, contigu (*à*), avoisinant.
adjectival [ædʒək'taivəl], *a.* comme adjectif.
adjectivally [ædʒək'taivali], *adv.* adjectivement.
adjective ['ædʒəktiv], *a. and n.* adjectif, *m.*
adjoin [ə'dʒɔin], *v.t.* adjoindre, joindre; toucher, se joindre à.—*v.i.* se toucher, être contigu.
adjoining [ə'dʒɔiniŋ],.*a.* adjacent, avoisinant, contigu (*à*).
adjourn [ə'dʒə:n], *v.t.* ajourner, différer, remettre.—*v.i.* s'ajourner, lever la séance.
adjournment [ə'dʒə:nmənt], *n.* ajournement, *m.*; remise, *f.*
adjudge [ə'dʒʌdʒ], *v.t.* adjuger; juger, condamner; (*fig.*) estimer.
adjudicate [ə'dʒu:dikeit], *v.t.* adjuger; prononcer.
adjudication [ədʒu:di'keiʃən], *n.* jugement, *m.*; décision, *f.*, arrêt, *m.*
adjudicator [ə'dʒu:dikeitə], *n.* juge, arbitre, *m.*, *f.*
adjunct ['ædʒʌŋkt], *a.* adjoint, accessoire.—*n.* accessoire; adjoint, *m.*
adjure [ə'dʒuə], *v.t.* adjurer.
adjust [ə'dʒʌst], *v.t.* ajuster, régler, arranger.
adjustable [ə'dʒʌstəbl], *a.* réglable.
adjustment [ə'dʒʌstmənt], *n.* ajustement, arrangement, accord, *m.*; mise au point, *f.*, réglage, *m.*
adjutant ['ædʒutənt], *n.* capitaine adjudant major; major de la garnison, *m.*
administer [əd'ministə], *v.t.* administrer, gérer, régir; faire prêter (*un serment*).
administrate [əd'ministreit], *v.t.* administrer; régir.
administration [ədminis'treiʃən], *n.* administration, *f.*, gouvernement, *m.*
administrative [əd'ministrativ], *a.* administratif.
administrator [əd'ministreitə], *n.* administrateur; (*Law*) curateur, *m.*

admirable ['ædmərəbl], *a.* admirable.
admirably ['ædmərəbli], *adv.* admirablement, à ravir, à merveille.
admiral ['ædmərəl], *n.* amiral, *m.*; *rear admiral*, contre-amiral, *m.*; *vice admiral*, vice-amiral, *m.*
admiralty ['ædmərəlti], *n.* amirauté, *f.*; Ministère de la Marine (*en France*), *m.*; *Board of Admiralty*, conseil d'amirauté, *m.*; *First Lord of the Admiralty*, ministre de la marine, *m.*
admiration [ædmə'reiʃən], *n.* admiration, *f.*; étonnement, *m.*
admire [əd'maiə], *v.t.* admirer; aimer; s'étonner de.—*v.i.* s'étonner.
admirer [əd'maiərə], *n.* admirateur, *m.*, admiratrice, *f.*
admissible [əd'misibl], *a.* admissible.
admission [əd'miʃən], *n.* admission, entrée, *f.*; accès; aveu, *m.*, concession, *f.*
admit [əd'mit], *v.t.* admettre, laisser entrer; avouer, reconnaître; tolérer.—*v.i. to admit of*, comporter, permettre; souffrir.
admittance [əd'mitəns], *n.* accès, *m.*; admission, entrée, *f.*; *no admittance*, défense d'entrer.
admittedly [əd'mitidli], *adv.* de l'aveu général; il est vrai que.
admixture [əd'mikstʃə], *n.* mélange, *m.*
admonish [əd'məniʃ], *v.t.* avertir, exhorter; reprendre, réprimander.
admonishment [əd'məniʃmənt], **admonition** [ædmə'niʃən], *n.* admonition, *f.*, avertissement, *m.*; remontrance, réprimande, *f.*
ado [ə'du:], *n.* bruit, fracas, *m.*, façons, cérémonies, *f.pl.*, embarras, *m.*, peine, difficulté, *f.*; *much ado about nothing*, beaucoup de bruit pour rien; *without any more ado*, sans plus de façons.
adolescence [ædo'lesəns], *n.* adolescence, *f.*
adolescent [ædo'lesənt], *a. and n.* adolescent, *m.*
Adolphus [ə'dɔlfəs]. Adolphe, *m.*
adopt [ə'dɔpt], *v.t.* adopter.
adopted [ə'dɔptid], **adoptive** [ə'dɔptiv], *a.* adoptif, adopté, d'adoption.
adoption [ə'dɔpʃən], *n.* adoption, *f.*
adoptive [ADOPTED].
adorable [ə'dɔ:rəbl], *a.* adorable.
adorably [ə'dɔ:rəbli], *adv.* d'une manière adorable, adorablement.
adoration [ædo'reiʃən], *n.* adoration, *f.*
adore [ə'dɔ:], *v.t.* adorer.
adorer [ə'dɔ:rə], *n.* adorateur, *m.*
adoringly [ə'dɔ:riŋli], *adv.* avec adoration.
adorn [ə'dɔ:n], *v.t.* orner; parer, embellir; (*fig.*) faire l'ornement de.
adornment [ə'dɔ:nmənt], *n.* ornement, *m.*, parure; ornementation, *f.*
Adrian ['eidriən]. Adrien, *m.*
Adriatic Sea [eidri'ætik'si:]. la mer Adriatique, l'Adriatique, *f.*
adrift [ə'drift], *adv.* en ou à la dérive; à l'abandon.
adroit [ə'drɔit], *a.* adroit, habile.
adroitly [ə'drɔitli], *adv.* adroitement.
adroitness [ə'drɔitnis], *n.* adresse, dextérité, *f.*
adulate ['ædjuleit], *v.t.* aduler.
adulation [ædju'leiʃən], *n.* adulation, *f.*
adulatory ['ædjuleitəri], *a.* adulateur.
adult [ə'dʌlt, 'ædʌlt], *a. and n.* adulte, *m.*, *f.*

adulterate

adulterate [ə'dʌltəreit], v.t. adultérer, frelater, falsifier, sophistiquer; (fig.) corrompre.

adulteration [ədʌltə'reiʃən], n. falsification, sophistication, f., frelatage, m.

adulterator [ə'dʌltəreitə], n. frelateur, falsificateur, m.

adulterer [ə'dʌltərə], n. adultère, m.

adulteress [ə'dʌltəris], n. (femme) adultère, f.

adulterous [ə'dʌltərəs], a. adultère; (fig.) altéré, faux.

adultery [ə'dʌltəri], n. adultère, m.

advance [əd'vɑːns], v.t. avancer, faire avancer; élever, hausser, augmenter.—v.i. avancer, s'avancer, se porter en avant.—n. mouvement en avant, m.; avance (de fonds), f.; avancement, progrès, m.; in advance, d'avance.

advance guard [əd'vɑːnsgɑːd], n. avant-garde, f.

advancement [əd'vɑːnsmənt], n. avancement, progrès, m.; (Comm.) avance, f.

advantage [əd'vɑːntidʒ], n. avantage; profit, intérêt, m.; to have the advantage, avoir le dessus; to take advantage of, profiter de; to take advantage of someone's kindness, abuser de la bonté de quelqu'un.

advantageous [ædvən'teidʒəs], a. avantageux (à ou de).

advantageously [ædvən'teidʒəsli], adv. avantageusement.

Advent ['ædvənt]. (Eccles.) l'Avent, m.

advent ['ædvənt], n. venue, f.

adventitious [ædvən'tiʃəs], a. adventice, fortuit.

adventure [əd'ventʃə], n. aventure, entreprise hasardeuse, f.—v.t. aventurer, hasarder.—v.i. s'aventurer, se hasarder.

adventurer [əd'ventʃərə], n. aventurier, m.

adventuress [əd'ventʃəris], n. aventurière, f.

adventurous [əd'ventʃərəs], a. aventureux, hardi.

adventurously [əd'ventʃərəsli], adv. aventureusement.

adverb ['ædvəːb], n. adverbe, m.

adverbial [əd'vəːbjəl], a. adverbial.

adverbially [əd'vəːbjəli], adv. adverbialement.

adversary ['ædvəsəri], n. adversaire, m., f.

adverse ['ædvəːs], a. adverse, contraire (à); défavorable.

adversely ['ædvəːsli], adv. d'une manière hostile, malheureusement.

adversity [əd'vəːsiti], n. adversité, f.

advert [əd'vəːt], v.i. faire allusion (à); parler (de).

advertise ['ædvətaiz], v.t. annoncer, faire annoncer, afficher, faire de la publicité pour.

advertisement [əd'vəːtizmənt], n. annonce (journal), publicité, réclame, f.; avis, m.; classified advertisements, petites annonces, f.pl.

advertiser ['ædvətaizə], n. personne qui fait des annonces, f.; journal d'annonces, m.

advertising ['ædvətaiziŋ], n. publicité, réclame, f.; advertising agency, agence de publicité, f.

advice [əd'vais], n. avis, conseil, m.; if you take my advice, si vous m'en croyez; to take advice, prendre conseil (de), consulter (un médecin etc.).

advisable [əd'vaizəbl], a. judicieux, convenable (pour ou de); opportun.

advisability [ədvaizə'biliti], n. convenance, utilité, opportunité, f.

advise [əd'vaiz], v.t. conseiller; donner avis (de); prévenir (de); annoncer.—v.i. délibérer, prendre conseil, consulter.

advisedly [əd'vaizidli], adv. avec réflexion, de propos délibéré.

adviser [əd'vaizə], n. conseiller, m.

advisory [əd'vaizəri], a. consultatif.

advocacy ['ædvəkəsi], n. profession d'avocat; défense, f., plaidoyer, m.

advocate ['ædvəkət], n. avocat, défenseur; intercesseur, m.—['ædvəkeit], v.t. défendre, plaider; soutenir, appuyer, préconiser.

adze [ædz], n. herminette, doloire; aissette, f.—v.t. entailler à l'herminette, doler.

Aegean Sea [iː'dʒiːənsiː]. la mer Égée, f.

aegis ['iːdʒis], n. égide, f.

Aeneas [iː'niːəs]. Énée, m.

Aeneid [iː'niːid]. l'Énéide, f.

aeon ['iːən], n. éternité, f., éon, m.

aerate ['εəreit], v.t. aérer; gazéifier.

aeration [εə'reiʃən], n. aération, f.

aerial ['εəriəl], a. aérien.—n. antenne, f.

aerie, aery, eyrie, eyry ['εəri, 'iəri], n. aire, f.

aerobatics [εərο'bætiks], n.pl. acrobaties aériennes, f.pl.

aerodrome ['εərodroum], n. aérodrome, m.

aerodynamic [εərodai'næmik], a. aérodynamique.— (n. pl.) aérodynamique, f.

aerolite ['εərolait], aerolith ['εəroliθ], n. aérolithe, bolide, m.

aeronaut ['εəronɔːt], n. aéronaute, m., f.

aeronautic [εəro'nɔːtik], a. aéronautique.

aeroplane ['εəroplein], n. aéroplane, avion, m.

aerostat ['εərostæt], n. aérostat, m.

Aeschylus ['iːskiləs]. Eschyle, m.

Aesop ['iːsɔp]. Ésope, m.

aesthete ['iːsθiːt], n. esthète, m., f.

aesthetic [iːs'θetik], aesthetical [iːs'θetikəl], a. esthétique.

aesthetically [iːs'θetikəli], adv. esthétiquement.

aestival [iːs'taivəl], a. estival.

aether [ETHER].

afar [ə'fɑː], adv. loin, de loin, au loin.

affability [æfə'biliti], affableness ['æfəblnis], n. affabilité, f.

affable ['æfəbl], a. affable, doux, gracieux.

affably ['æfəbli], adv. affablement, avec affabilité.

affair [ə'fεə], n. affaire, f.

affect [ə'fekt], v.t. affecter; intéresser, toucher, émouvoir.

affectation [æfek'teiʃən], affectedness [ə'fektidnis], n. affectation, f.

affected [ə'fektid], a. disposé (pour etc.); affecté, précieux; maniéré, prétentieux (style).

affecting [ə'fektiŋ], a. touchant, émouvant, attendrissant.

affection [ə'fekʃən], n. affection, f., amour; goût, attachement, penchant, m.; maladie, f.

affectionate [ə'fekʃənit], a. affectueux, affectionné.

affectionately [ə'fekʃənitli], adv. affectueusement.

affiance [ə'faiəns], v.t. fiancer.—n. fiançailles, f.pl.

affianced [ə'faiənst], *a.* fiancé.

affidavit [æfi'deivit], *n.* déclaration par écrit sous serment, attestation, *f.*

affiliate [ə'filieit], *v.t.* affilier; attribuer, rattacher (*à*).

affiliation [əfili'eiʃən], *n.* affiliation, *f.*

affinity [ə'finiti], *n.* affinité, *f.*

affirm [ə'fə:m], *v.t.* affirmer.

affirmation [æfə'meiʃən], *n.* affirmation, *f.*

affirmative [ə'fə:mətiv], *a.* affirmatif.—*n.* affirmative, *f.*

affirmatively [ə'fə:mətivli], *adv.* affirmativement.

affix [ə'fiks], *v.t.* apposer, attacher (*à*).

afflatus [ə'fleitəs], *n.* souffle, *m.*, inspiration, *f.*

afflict [ə'flikt], *v.t.* affliger (*de*); tourmenter.

afflicting [ə'fliktiŋ], *a.* affligeant.

affliction [ə'flikʃən], *n.* affliction; calamité, *f.*, malheur, *m.*

affluence ['æfluəns], *n.* opulence, affluence; abondance, *f.*, concours (*de personnes*), *m.*

affluent ['æfluənt], *a.* opulent, riche; affluent.

afford [ə'fɔ:d], *v.t.* donner, fournir, accorder; avoir les moyens de, pouvoir.

afforestation [əfɔris'teiʃən], *n.* boisement; reboisement, *m.*

affranchise [ə'fræntʃaiz], *v.t.* affranchir.

affray [ə'frei], *n.* bagarre, échauffourée, *f.*

affright [ə'frait], *v.t.* effrayer.

affront [ə'frʌnt], *n.* affront, *m.*, insulte, injure, *f.*, outrage, *m.—v.t.* affronter, offenser, insulter.

afield [ə'fi:ld], *adv.* aux champs, à la campagne; *to go far afield*, aller très loin.

afire [ə'faiə], *adv.* en feu.

aflame [ə'fleim], *adv.* en flammes.

afloat [ə'flout], *adv.* à flot; (*fig.*) en circulation.

afoot [ə'fut], *adv.* à pied; en marche, en route; (*fig.*) sur pied; en train.

afore [ə'fɔ:], *adv.* précédemment, auparavant; par devant.

aforementioned [ə'fɔ:menʃənd], *a.* mentionné plus haut, susdit, précité.

aforesaid [ə'fɔ:sed], *a.* susdit, ledit, susnommé.

aforethought [ə'fɔ:θɔ:t], *a.* *with malice aforethought*, avec intention criminelle.

afraid [ə'freid], *a.* effrayé, pris de peur; *I am afraid not*, je crains que non; *I am afraid she's gone*, je crains bien qu'elle ne soit partie; *to be afraid of*, avoir peur de.

afresh [ə'freʃ], *adv.* de nouveau, de plus belle.

Africa ['æfrikə]. l'Afrique, *f.*

African ['æfrikən], *a.* africain.—*n.* Africain (*personne*), *m.*

aft [ɑ:ft], *a.* arrière, de l'arrière.—*adv.* (*Naut.*) à l'arrière.

after ['ɑ:ftə], *a.* subséquent, ultérieur, futur; arrière.—*prep.* après; sur, à la suite de; selon, d'après.—*adv.* après, d'après, ensuite. —*conj.* après que.

aftercrop ['ɑ:ftəkrɔp], *n.* seconde récolte, *f.*; regain, *m.*

aftereffects ['ɑ:ftərifekts], *n. pl.* suites, *f. pl.*, répercussion, *f.*

afterlife ['ɑ:ftəlaif], *n.* suite de la vie, *f.*; au-delà, *m.*

aftermath ['ɑ:ftəmæθ], *n.* regain, *m.*; (*fig.*) suites, *f.pl.*

afternoon [ɑ:ftə'nu:n], *n.* après-midi, *m.* ou *f.*

afterthought ['ɑ:ftəθɔ:t], *n.* réflexion après coup, *f.*

afterward ['ɑ:ftəwəd], **afterwards** ['ɑ:ftəwədz], *adv.* après, ensuite, plus tard.

again [ə'gein], *adv.* encore; encore une fois, de nouveau; *again and again*, à plusieurs reprises; *as much again*, encore autant; *never again*, jamais plus.

against [ə'geinst], *prep.* contre; vis-à-vis; vers; pour.

agape [ə'geip], *adv.* bouche bée.

agate ['ægeit], *n.* agate, *f.*

Agatha ['ægəθə]. Agathe, *f.*

age [eidʒ], *n.* âge, *m.*; époque, *f.*; *of age*, majeur; *under age*, mineur; *Middle Ages*, moyen âge.—*v.t.*, *v.i.* vieillir.

aged ['eidʒid, (*after prefix*) eidʒd], *a.* vieux, âgé; *middle-aged*, entre deux âges.

ageless ['eidʒlis], *a.* toujours jeune.

agency ['eidʒənsi], *n.* action, entremise; (*Comm.*) agence, *f.*

agenda [ə'dʒendə], *n.* ordre du jour; programme, *m.*

agent ['eidʒənt], *n.* représentant, agent, mandataire, *m.*

agglomerate [ə'gloməreit], *v.t.* agglomérer.—*v.i.* s'agglomérer.—*a.* aggloméré.

agglomeration [əglomə'reiʃən], *n.* agglomération, *f.*

aggrandize [ə'grændaiz], *v.t.* agrandir.

aggrandizement [ə'grændizmənt], *n.* agrandissement, *m.*

aggravate ['ægrəveit], *v.t.* aggraver; exagérer; (*colloq.*) agacer, pousser à bout, exaspérer.

aggravation [ægrə'veiʃən], *n.* aggravation; circonstance aggravante, *f.*, agacement, *m.*

aggregate ['ægrigit], *a.* collectif, global, réuni. —*n.* masse, *f.*; ensemble, *m.*, somme totale, *f.*—['ægrigeit], *v.t.* rassembler.

aggregation [ægri'geiʃən], *n.* agrégation, *f.*, assemblage, *m.*

aggression [ə'greʃən], *n.* agression, *f.*

aggressive [ə'gresiv], *a.* agressif.

aggressiveness [ə'gresivnis], *n.* caractère agressif, *m.*

aggressor [ə'gresə], *n.* agresseur, *m.*

aggrieve [ə'gri:v], *v.t.* chagriner, affliger; blesser, léser.

aghast [ə'gɑ:st], *a.* consterné, ébahi, médusé, tout pantois.

agile ['ædʒail], *a.* agile, leste.

agility [ə'dʒiliti], *n.* agilité, *f.*

agio ['ædʒiou], *n.* prix du change, agio, *m.*

agiotage ['ædʒiɔtidʒ], *n.* agiotage, *m.*

agitate ['ædʒiteit], *v.t.* agiter, exciter; remuer, troubler.

agitation [ædʒi'teiʃən], *n.* agitation; discussion, *f.*, examen, *m.*

agitator ['ædʒiteitə], *n.* agitateur; meneur, *m.*

aglow [ə'glou], *a.* enflammé, resplendissant.

agnostic [æg'nɔstik], *a.* and *n.* agnosticiste, agnostique, *m.*, *f.*

agnosticism [æg'nɔstisizm], *n.* agnosticisme, *m.*

ago [ə'gou], *adv.* passé, il y a; *two days ago*, il y a deux jours.

agog [ə'gɔg], *adv.* excité, impatient, empressé; en train, en l'air; *to be all agog*, avoir la tête montée.

agonize ['ægənaiz], *v.t.* torturer, mettre au supplice.—*v.i.* souffrir l'agonie, être au supplice.

agonizing ['ægənaiziŋ], a. atroce, déchirant.

agony ['ægəni], n. douleur, angoisse, f., paroxysme, m.

agrarian [ə'grɛəriən], a. agraire.

agree [ə'gri:], v.i. s'accorder (à ou avec); être d'accord; consentir (à); convenir (de); être conforme (à).

agreeable [ə'gri:əbl], a. agréable, aimable; conforme (à); consentant.

agreeably [ə'gri:əbli], adv. agréablement; conformément (à).

agreed [ə'gri:d], a. convenu, d'accord; *it's agreed*, c'est entendu.

agreement [ə'gri:mənt], n. accord, m.; convention, f., contrat, pacte, marché, m.; conformité, f.

agricultural [ægri'kʌltʃərəl], a. agricole, d'agriculture.

agriculture ['ægrikʌltʃə], n. agriculture, f.

agriculturist [ægri'kʌltʃərist], n. agriculteur, agronome, m.

aground [ə'graund], adv. échoué; à terre.

ague [eigju:], n. fièvre intermittente, f.

ahead [ə'hed], adv. en avant; (fig.) en tête; *go ahead!* en avant! vas-y! *straight ahead*, tout droit; *ahead of time*, en avance.

aid [eid], v.t. aider, assister; secourir; *to aid each other*, s'entr'aider.—n. aide, assistance, f.; secours, concours, subside, m.; *with the aid of*, à l'aide de.

aide-de-camp [eiddə'kã], n. aide de camp, m.

aigrette ['eigret], n. aigrette, f.

ail [eil], v.t. faire mal à; chagriner; *what ails him?* qu'est-ce qu'il a ?—v.i. être souffrant.

aileron ['eilərɔn], n. aileron, m.

ailing ['eiliŋ], a. souffrant, indisposé, mal portant.

ailment ['eilmənt], n. mal, malaise, m., indisposition, f.

aim [eim], v.t. viser; diriger, lancer (un coup etc.).—v.i. viser (à); aspirer (à); avoir pour but (de).—n. point de mire, but, objet, dessein, m.; visée, f.; *to take aim at*, viser, coucher en joue.

aimless ['eimlis], a. sans but, sans objet.

air [ɛə], n. air; vent, m., brise; (fig.) mine, expression, f.; *in the air*, en l'air; *in the open air*, en plein air.—v.t. aérer, donner de l'air à, mettre à l'air; sécher.

air- [ɛə], see also **aero-**.

airborne ['ɛəbɔ:n], a. (Av.) aéroporté.

air-conditioned ['ɛəkəndiʃənd], a. climatisé.

air conditioning ['ɛəkəndiʃəniŋ], n. climatisation, f.

air cooling ['ɛəku:liŋ], n. refroidissement par air, m.

aircraft ['ɛəkra:ft], n. avion, m.; les avions, m.pl.

aircrew ['ɛəkru:], n. équipage (d'avion), m.

airfield ['ɛəfi:ld], n. terrain d'aviation, m.

air hostess ['ɛəhoustis], n. hôtesse de l'air, f.

airily ['ɛərili], adv. allègrement, légèrement.

airiness ['ɛərinis], n. situation aérée; (fig.) légèreté, vivacité, désinvolture, f.

airing ['ɛəriŋ], n. aérage, m., exposition à l'air, f., éventage, m.; promenade, f.

airlift ['ɛəlift], n. pont aérien, m.

airline ['ɛəlain], n. ligne aérienne, f.

airliner ['ɛəlainə], n. avion de ligne, m.

air mail ['ɛəmeil], n. poste aérienne, f.

airman ['ɛəmən], n. aviateur, m.

air mattress ['ɛəmætris], n. matelas à air, m.

air pocket ['ɛəpɔkit], n. (Av.) trou d'air, m.

airport ['ɛəpɔ:t], n. aéroport, m.

airship ['ɛəʃip], n. dirigeable, m.

airsickness ['ɛəsiknis], n. mal de l'air, m.

airstrip ['ɛəstrip], n. piste d'atterrissage, f.

airtight ['ɛətait], a. imperméable à l'air, hermétique.

airworthy ['ɛəwə:ði], a. navigable.

airy ['ɛəri], a. ouvert à l'air; aérien, aéré; (fig.) léger, dégagé, gai, enjoué, insouciant; *airy words*, paroles en l'air, f.pl.

aisle [ail], n. bas-côté, passage, m.

ajar [ə'dʒa:], a. entr'ouvert, entrebâillé.

akimbo [ə'kimbou], adv. appuyé sur la hanche; *with one's arms akimbo*, les poings sur les hanches.

akin [ə'kin], a. allié (à); parent (de); (fig.) qui a rapport (avec).

alabaster ['æləba:stə], a. d'albâtre.—n. albâtre, m.

alacrity [ə'lækriti], n. alacrité, f., empressement, m., promptitude, f.

Alan, Allan, Allen ['ælən], Alain, m.

alarm [ə'la:m], n. alarme, alerte, f.; réveil (réveille-matin), m.—v.t. alarmer; effrayer, faire peur à.

alarm bell [ə'la:mbel], n. cloche d'alarme, f., tocsin, m.

alarm clock [ə'la:mklɔk], n. réveille-matin, m.

alarming [ə'la:miŋ], a. alarmant.

alarmingly [ə'la:miŋli], adv. d'une manière alarmante.

alarmist [ə'la:mist], n. alarmiste, m., f.

alas! [ə'læs], int. hélas!

Albania [æl'beinjə], l'Albanie, f.

Albanian [æl'beinjən], a. albanais.—n. Albanais (personne), m.

albatross ['ælbətrɔs], n. albatros, m.

albeit [ɔ:l'bi:it], conj. quoique, bien que (with subj.).

albino [æl'bi:nou], a. and n. albinos, m., f.

album ['ælbəm], n. album, m.

albumen [æl'bju:min], n. albumen; blanc d'œuf, m.; albumine, f.

albuminous [æl'bju:minəs], a. albumineux.

alburnum [æl'bə:nəm], n. aubier, m.

alchemic [æl'kemik], **alchemical** [æl'kemikəl], a. alchimique.

alchemist ['ælkimist], n. alchimiste, m.

alchemistic [ælki'mistik], **alchemistical** [ælki'mistikəl], a. d'alchimiste, alchimique.

alchemy ['ælkimi], n. alchimie, f.

alcohol ['ælkəhɔl], n. alcool, m. [see **spirit**]

alcoholic [ælkə'hɔlik], a. and n. alcoolique, m., f.

alcoholism ['ælkəhɔlizm], n. alcoolisme, m.

Alcoran [ælkə'ra:n], le Coran, le Koran.

alcove ['ælkouv], n. alcôve; niche, f., enfoncement, m.

alder ['ɔ:ldə], n. aune, vergne, m.

alder grove ['ɔ:ldəgrouv], n. aunaie, f.

alderman ['ɔ:ldəmən], n. (pl. -men [men]) conseiller municipal, alderman, échevin, m.

ale [eil], n. ale, bière, f.

alehouse ['eilhaus], n. taverne, f.

alembic [ə'lembik], n. alambic, m.

alert [ə'lə:t], a. alerte, vigilant, éveillé.—n. alerte, f.; *on the alert*, sur le qui-vive.

alertness [ə'lə:tnis], n. vigilance, promptitude, prestesse, f.

Alexander [ælig'zɑ:ndə]. Alexandre, m.

alexandrine [ælig'zɑ:ndrin], n. (Pros.) alexandrin, m.

alfresco [æl'freskou], adv. en plein air.

algebra [æld3əbrə], n. algèbre, f.

algebraic [æld3ə'breiik], **algebraical** [æld3ə'breiikəl], a. algébrique.

Algeria [æl'd3iəriə]. l'Algérie, f.

Algerian [æl'd3iəriən], a. algérien.—n. Algérien (personne), m.

Algiers [æl'd3iəz]. Alger, m.

alias ['eiliəs], n. nom d'emprunt ou de rechange, m.—adv. dit, autrement nommé, alias.

alibi ['ælibai], n. alibi, m.

alien ['eiljən], a. étranger (à); éloigné (de).—n. étranger, m.

alienate ['eiljəneit], v.t. aliéner (de).

alienation [eiljə'neiʃən], n. aliénation, f.

alienist ['eiljənist], n. aliéniste, m., f.

alight [ə'lait], a. allumé, embrasé.—v.i. descendre; mettre pied à terre; s'abattre (oiseau etc.); atterrir (aviateur), amerrir (sur l'eau).

align [ALINE].

alike [ə'laik], adv. également; de même, de la même manière; à la fois.—a. semblable, pareil; to be alike, se ressembler.

aliment ['ælimənt], n. aliment, m.

alimentary [æli'mentəri], a. alimentaire.

alimony ['æliməni], n. pension alimentaire, f.

aline, align [ə'lain], v.t. aligner; dresser.—v.i. s'aligner.

alinement, alignment [ə'lainmənt], n. alignement, m.

alive [ə'laiv], a. en vie, vivant; vif, éveillé; au monde; animé, sensible (à); dead or alive, mort ou vif; to be alive with, grouiller de, fourmiller de; alive to, sensible à; while alive, de son vivant.

alkali ['ælkəlai], n. alcali, m.

Alkoran [ALCORAN].

all [ɔ:l], a. tout, tous; all of you, vous tous; for all that, malgré cela; it is all the same to me, cela m'est égal; with all speed, au plus vite, à toute vitesse.—adv. tout, entièrement; all at once, tout à coup, tout d'un coup; all the better, tant mieux; not at all, point du tout.—n. and pron. tout, m.; above all, surtout; all but, presque; all aboard! en voiture!

allay [ə'lei], v.t. apaiser, adoucir, calmer.

allegation [ælə'geiʃən], n. allégation, f.

allege [ə'led3], v.t. alléguer, prétendre (that, que).

allegiance [ə'li:d3əns], n. fidélité; obéissance, f.

allegorical [ælə'gɔrikəl], a. allégorique.

allegorically [ælə'gɔrikəli], adv. allégoriquement.

allegory ['æləgəri], n. allégorie, f.

allelujah [æli'lu:jə], n. and int. alléluia, m.

allergic [ə'lə:d3ik], a. (Med.) allergique.

allergy ['æləd3i], n. allergie, f.

alleviate [ə'li:vieit], v.t. alléger, soulager, adoucir.

alleviation [əli:vi'eiʃən], n. allégement, adoucissement, soulagement, m.

alley ['æli], n. ruelle (d'une ville); allée (jardin),

f.; blind alley, impasse, f., cul de sac; m.

All Fools' Day [ɔ:l'fu:lzdei]. le 1er avril.

alliance [ə'laiəns], n. alliance, f.

allied ['ælaid, ə'laid], a. allié; parent, voisin (de).

alligator ['æligeitə], n. alligator, caïman, m.

alliteration [əlitə'reiʃən], n. allitération, f.

alliterative [ə'litərətiv], a. allitératif.

allocate ['æləkeit], v.t. allouer, assigner.

allocation [ælo'keiʃən], n. allocation, f.

allot [ə'lɔt], v.t. assigner, donner en partage; répartir.

allotment [ə'lɔtmənt], n. partage, lot, lotissement, m., portion; distribution, f.; lopin de terre, jardin ouvrier, m.

allow [ə'lau], v.t. permettre, autoriser; accorder, allouer; admettre, reconnaître; to allow someone to do something, permettre à quelqu'un de faire quelque chose.

allowable [ə'lauəbl], a. permis, admissible, légitime.

allowance [ə'lauəns], n. pension, rente; allocation; ration; remise, réduction; indulgence, indemnité, f.; to make allowance for, tenir compte de; to put on short allowance, rationner.

alloy [ə'lɔi], n. alliage, mélange, m.—v.t. allier; (fig.) altérer, diminuer, corrompre.

All Saints' Day [ɔ:l'seintsdei]. la Toussaint, f.

All Souls' Day [ɔ:l'soulzdei]. Jour des Morts, m.

allude [ə'lju:d], v.i. faire allusion (à).

allure [ə'ljuə], v.t. amorcer, attirer, séduire, inviter (à).

allurement [ə'ljuəmənt], n. amorce, f., appât, charme, attrait, m.

alluring [ə'ljuəriŋ], a. attrayant, séduisant.

alluringly [ə'ljuəriŋli], adv. d'une manière séduisante.

allusion [ə'lju:3ən], n. allusion, f.

allusive [ə'lju:siv], a. allusif, plein d'allusions.

allusively [ə'lju:sivli], adv. par allusion.

alluvia [ə'lju:viə], n.pl. terres d'alluvion, f.pl., alluvion, f.

alluvial [ə'lju:viəl], a. alluvial, d'alluvion.

alluvium [ə'lju:viəm], n. alluvion, f.

ally [ə'lai], v.t. allier.—v.i. s'allier (à ou avec).—['ælai, ə'lai], n. allié, confédéré, m.

almanac ['ɔ:lmənæk], n. almanach, m.

almighty [ɔ:l'maiti], a. tout-puissant; the Almighty, le Tout-Puissant.

almond ['ɑ:mənd], n. amande, f.; burnt almond, praline, f.

almond-tree ['ɑ:məndtri:], n. amandier, m.

almost ['ɔ:lmoust], adv. presque, à peu près; I almost fell, j'ai failli tomber.

alms [ɑ:mz], n. aumône, f.; to give alms, faire l'aumône.

almshouse ['ɑ:mzhaus], n. maison de retraite, f., asile, m.

aloe ['ælou], n. aloès, m.; bitter aloes, amer d'aloès, m.

aloft [ə'lɔft], adv. en haut, en l'air; (Naut.) dans la mâture.

alone [ə'loun], a. seul, solitaire; leave me alone, laissez-moi tranquille.

along [ə'lɔŋ], adv. and prep. le long de; all along (time), tout le temps; (place) tout le long du chemin; along with, avec; come along, venez donc; get along with you, allez-vous en, allez-vous promener.

alongside

alongside [ə'lɒŋsaid], *adv.* bord à bord; bord à quai.—*prep.* à côté de.

aloof [ə'lu:f], *a.* distant.—*adv.* au loin, (*Naut.*) au large; éloigné, à l'écart; *to keep aloof,* se tenir à l'écart.

aloofness [ə'lu:fnis], *n.* attitude distante, *f.*

aloud [ə'laud], *adv.* à haute voix, haut.

alpaca [æl'pækə], *n.* alpaga (*tissu*); alpaca (*animal*), *m.*

alphabet ['ælfəbet], *n.* alphabet; abécédaire (*livre d'enfant*), *m.*

alphabetic [ælfə'betik], **alphabetical** [ælfə'betikəl], *a.* alphabétique.

alphabetically [ælfə'betikəli], *adv.* alphabétiquement.

alpine ['ælpain], *a.* alpin; des Alpes, alpestre.

alpinist ['ælpinist], *n.* alpiniste, *m., f.*

Alps [ælps]. les Alpes, *f. pl.*

already [ɔ:l'redi], *adv.* déjà.

Alsatian [æl'seiʃən], *a.* alsacien.—*n.* (*chien*) chien-loup; (*personne*) Alsacien, *m.*

also [ɔ:lsou], *adv.* aussi, également.

altar ['ɔ:ltə], *n.* autel, *m.*; *high altar,* maître-autel, *m.*

altar cloth ['ɔ:ltəklɔθ], *n.* nappe d'autel, *f.*

altar screen ['ɔ:ltəskri:n], *n.* rétable, *m.*

alter ['ɔ:ltə], *v.t.* changer, modifier; retoucher, corriger.—*v.i.* changer, se changer.

alteration [ɔ:ltə'reiʃən], *n.* changement, *m.,* modification, *f.*

altercation [ɔ:ltə'keiʃən], *n.* altercation, dispute, *f.*

alternate ['ɔ:ltəneit], *v.t.* alterner, faire alternativement.—*v.i.* alterner; se succéder; *alternating current,* courant alternatif, *m.*— ['ɔ:ltənit], *a.* alternatif; alternant; *alternate rhymes,* rimes croisées, *f.pl.*

alternately [ɔ:l'tə:nitli], *adv.* alternativement, tour à tour.

alternative [ɔ:l'tə:nətiv], *a.* alternatif.—*n.* alternative; autre solution, *f.*

alternatively [ɔ:l'tə:nətivli], *adv.* alternativement, tour à tour.

alternator [ɔ:l'tə:neitə], *n.* (*Elec.*) alternateur, *m.*

although [ɔ:l'ðou], *conj.* quoique, bien que (*with subj.*).

altimeter [ælti'mi:tə], *n.* altimètre, *m.*

altitude ['æltitju:d], *n.* altitude, élévation, hauteur, *f.*

alto ['æltou], *n.* alto, *m.*

altogether [ɔ:ltə'geðə], *adv.* tout à fait, entièrement.

altruistic [æltru'istik], *a.* altruiste.

alum ['æləm], *n.* alun, *m.*

aluminum [æ'lu:minəm], *n.* aluminium, *m.*

always ['ɔ:lweiz], *adv.* toujours.

*amain [ə'mein], *adv.* avec force, de toutes ses forces.

amalgam [ə'mælgəm], *n.* amalgame, *m.*

amalgamate [ə'mælgəmeit], *v.t.* amalgamer; (*Comm.*) fusionner.—*v.i.* s'amalgamer; (*Comm.*) fusionner.

amalgamation [əmælgə'meiʃən], *n.* amalgamation, *f.*; (*fig.*) amalgame, fusionnement, *m.*

amanuensis [əmænju'ensis], *n.* (*pl.* **amanuenses** [əmænju'ensi:z]) secrétaire, *m., f.*

amaranth ['æmərænθ], *n.* amarante, *f.*

amass [ə'mæs], *v.t.* amasser.

amateur ['æmətə:, 'æmətjuə], *n.* amateur, *m.*

amateurish [æmə'tə:riʃ, 'æmətjuəriʃ], *a.* d'amateur.

amateurism ['æmətə:rizm, 'æmətjuərizm], *n.* (*Spt.*) amateurisme, *m.*

amatory ['æmətəri], *a.* d'amour, amoureux.

amaze [ə'meiz], *v.t.* étonner, confondre, stupéfier; *to be amazed,* s'étonner.

amazement [ə'meizmənt], **amazedness** [ə'meizidnis], *n.* étonnement, *m.,* stupeur, stupéfaction, *f.*

amazing [ə'meizin], *a.* étonnant.

Amazon ['æməzən], **the.** l'Amazone, *m.*

amazon ['æməzən], *n.* amazone, *f.*

ambassador [æm'bæsədə], *n.* ambassadeur, *m.*

ambassadress [æm'bæsədris], *n.* ambassadrice, *f.*

amber ['æmbə], *a.* d'ambre; *amber light* (*traffic*), feu orange, *m.*—*n.* ambre, *m.*

amber-colored ['æmbəkʌləd], *a.* ambré.

ambergris ['æmbəgris], *n.* ambre gris, *m.*

ambidexter [æmbi'dekstə], *a.* and *n.* ambidextre, *m., f.*

ambidextrous [æmbi'dekstrəs], *a.* ambidextre.

ambient ['æmbiənt], *a.* ambiant.

ambiguity [æmbi'gju:iti], **ambiguousness** [æm'bigjuəsnis], *n.* ambiguïté; équivoque, *f.*

ambiguous [æm'bigjuəs], *a.* ambigu; équivoque; douteux.

ambiguously [æm'bigjuəsli], *adv.* ambigument, d'une manière équivoque.

ambit ['æmbit], *n.* tour, circuit, *m.*; (*fig.*) étendue, portée, *f.*

ambition [æm'biʃən], *n.* ambition, *f.*

ambitious [æm'biʃəs], *a.* ambitieux.

ambitiously [æm'biʃəsli], *adv.* ambitieusement.

amble [æmbl], *v.i.* aller (à) l'amble (*cheval*); (*fig.*) trottiner, aller son chemin, déambuler. —*n.* amble, *m.*

Ambrose ['æmbrouz]. Ambroise, *m.*

ambrosia [æm'brouziə], *n.* ambroisie, *f.*

ambulance ['æmbjuləns], *n.* ambulance, *f.*; hôpital militaire, *m.*

ambulant ['æmbjulənt], *a.* ambulant.

ambulatory ['æmbjulətri], *a.* ambulatoire.

ambuscade [æmbəs'keid], *n.* embuscade, *f.*; *to lay an ambuscade for,* dresser une embuscade à.—*v.t.* embusquer; mettre en embuscade.

ambush ['æmbuʃ], *n.* embuscade, *f.,* guet-apens, *m.*—*v.t.* embusquer.

Amelia [ə'mi:liə]. Amélie, *f.*

ameliorate [ə'mi:ljəreit], *v.t.* améliorer.—*v.i.* s'améliorer.

amelioration [əmi:ljə'reiʃən], *n.* amélioration, *f.*

amen [ɑ:'men], *int.* amen, ainsi soit-il.

amenable [ə'mi:nəbl], *a.* responsable, comptable; docile, soumis, sujet (*à*).

amend [ə'mend], *v.t.* amender, corriger; réformer.—*v.i.* s'amender, se corriger.

amendment [ə'mendmənt], *n.* modification, *f.,* amendement, *m.,* amélioration, *f.*

amends [ə'mendz], *n.pl.* dédommagement, *m.,* compensation, réparation, *f.*; *to make amends for,* dédommager de, faire réparation de.

amenity [ə'mi:niti, ə'meniti], *n.* aménité, *f.,* agrément, *m.*

America [ə'merikə]. l'Amérique, *f.*

American [ə'merikən], *a.* américain.—*n.* Américain (*personne*), *m.*
amethyst [æməθist], *n.* améthyste, *f.*
amiability [eimjə'biliti], **amiableness** ['eimjəblnis], *n.* amabilité, *f.*
amiable ['eimjəbl], *a.* aimable.
amiably ['eimjəbli], *adv.* aimablement, avec amabilité.
amicable ['æmikəbl], *a.* amical; *amicable settlement*, arrangement à l'amiable, *m.*
amicably ['æmikəbli], *adv.* amicalement; à l'amiable.
amid [ə'mid], *prep.* au milieu de; parmi.
amidships [ə'midʃips], *adv.* (*Naut.*) par le travers.
amidst [ə'midst], [AMID].
amiss [ə'mis], *adv.* mal, **en mauvaise** part; (*unseasonably*) mal à propos.
amity ['æmiti], *n.* amitié, *f.*
ammeter ['æmitə], *n.* ampèremètre, *m.*
ammonia [ə'mouniə], *n.* ammoniaque, *f.*
ammunition [æmju'niʃən], *n.* munitions de guerre; cartouches, *f.pl.*
amnesia [æm'ni:ziə], *n.* amnésie, *f.*
amnesty ['æmnəsti], *n.* amnistie, *f.*—*v.t.* amnistier.
amoeba [ə'mi:bə], *n.* (*pl.* **amoebae** [ə'mi:bai], **amoebas** [ə'mi:bəz]) amibe, *f.*
amok [AMUCK].
among [ə'mʌŋ], **amongst** [ə'mʌŋst], *prep.* entre; parmi; au milieu de, chez, avec; *among other things*, entre autres choses; *from among*, d'entre.
amorous ['æmərəs], *a.* amoureux; porté à l'amour.
amorously ['æmərəsli], *adv.* amoureusement.
amorousness ['æmərəsnis], *n.* tempérament amoureux, *m.*, tendance à l'amour, *f.*
amorphous [ə'mɔ:fəs], *a.* amorphe.
amount [ə'maunt], *n.* montant, total, *m.*, somme; quantité; (*fig.*) valeur, *f.*, résultat, *m.*; *to the amount of*, jusqu'à concurrence de.—*v.i.* s'élever, se monter (à); revenir (à), se réduire (à); *that amounts to the same thing*, cela revient au même.
amour [ə'muə], *n.* intrigue amoureuse, *f.*
ampere [æmpɛə], *n.* (*Elec.*) ampère, *m.*
amphibian [æm'fibiən], *n.* amphibie, *m.*
amphibious [æm'fibiəs], *a.* amphibie.
amphitheater [æmfi'θiətə], *n.* amphithéâtre, *m.*
amphitheatrical [æmfiθi'ætrikəl], *a.* amphithéâtral, d'amphithéâtre.
amphora ['æmfərə], *n.* amphore, *f.*
ample [æmpl], *a.* ample, large, abondant, copieux; très suffisant.
ampleness ['æmplnis], *n.* ampleur; grandeur, *f.*
amplification [æmplifi'keiʃən], *n.* amplification, *f.*
amplifier ['æmplifaiə], *n.* (*Rad., Tel.*) amplificateur, *m.*
amplify ['æmplifai], *v.t.* amplifier; exagérer.
amplitude ['æmplitju:d], *n.* amplitude, étendue, largeur, *f.*
amply ['æmpli], *adv.* amplement.
amputate ['æmpjuteit], *v.t.* amputer.
amputation [æmpju'teiʃən], *n.* amputation, *f.*
amuck [ə'mʌk], **amock**, **amok** [ə'mɔk], *adv. to run amuck*, devenir fou furieux.
amulet ['æmjulit], *n.* amulette, *f.*

amuse [ə'mju:z], *v.t.* amuser, divertir; *to be amused at*, s'amuser *ou* se divertir de.
amusement [ə'mju:zmənt], *n.* amusement, divertissement, *m.*
amusing [ə'mju:ziŋ], *a.* amusant, divertissant.
amusingly [ə'mju:ziŋli], *adv.* d'une manière amusante.
Amy ['eimi]. Aimée, *f.*
an [ʌ (2)].
anachronism [ə'nækrənizm], *n.* anachronisme, *m.*
anachronistic [ənækrə'nistik], *a.* anachronique.
anaconda [ænə'kɔndə], *n.* anaconda, eunecte, *m.*
anaemia [ə'ni:miə], *n.* anémie, *f.*
anaemic [ə'ni:mik], *a.* anémique.
anaesthesia [ænəs'θi:ziə], *n.* anesthésie, *f.*
anaesthetic [ænəs'θetik], *a.* and *n.* anesthésique, *m.*
anaesthetist [ə'ni:sθətist], *n.* anesthésiste, *m., f.*
anaesthetize [ə'ni:sθətaiz], *v.t.* anesthésier.
anagram ['ænəgræm], *n.* anagramme, *f.*
analgesia [ænæl'dʒi:ziə], *n.* analgésie, analgie, *f.*
analogical [ænə'lɔdʒikəl], *a.* analogique.
analogism [ə'nælədʒizm], *n.* (*Phil.*) analogisme, *m.*
analogous [ə'næləgəs], *a.* analogue.
analogy [ə'nælədʒi], *n.* analogie, *f.*
analysis [ə'nælisis], *n.* analyse, *f.*
analyst ['ænəlist], *n.* analyste, *m., f.*
analytic [ænə'litik], **analytical** [ænə'litikəl], *a.* analytique.
analytically [ænə'litikəli], *adv.* analytiquement.
analyze ['ænəlaiz], *v.t.* analyser, faire l'analyse de.
anarchism ['ænəkizm], *n.* anarchisme, *m.*
anarchist ['ænəkist], *a.* and *n.* anarchiste, *m., f.*
anarchy ['ænəki], *n.* anarchie, *f.*
anathema [ə'næθimə], *n.* anathème, *m.*
anathematize [ə'næθimataiz], *v.t.* anathématiser, frapper d'anathème; maudire.
anatomical [ænə'tɔmikəl], *a.* anatomique.
anatomically [ænə'tɔmikəli], *adv.* anatomiquement.
anatomist [ə'nætəmist], *n.* anatomiste, *m., f.*
anatomize [ə'nætəmaiz], *v.t.* anatomiser.
anatomy [ə'nætəmi], *n.* anatomie, *f.*
ancestor ['ænsəstə], *n.* aïeul, *m.*
ancestors ['ænsəstəz], *n.pl.* ancêtres, pères, aïeux, *m.pl.*
ancestral [æn'sestrəl], *a.* ancestral, d'ancêtres, de ses ancêtres; héréditaire.
ancestry ['ænsəstri], *n.* ancêtres, *m.pl.*; race, origine, naissance, *f.*, lignage, *m.*
anchor ['æŋkə], *n.* ancre, *f.*; *sheet anchor*, maîtresse ancre, (*fig.*) ancre de miséricorde; *to ride at anchor*, être à l'ancre; *to weigh anchor*, lever l'ancre.—*v.t.* mouiller, ancrer.—*v.i.* ancrer, s'ancrer, jeter l'ancre, mouiller; (*fig.*) se fixer.
anchorage ['æŋkəridʒ], *n.* mouillage, ancrage, *m.*; retraite (*d'anachorète*).
anchoret ['æŋkərɛt], **anchorite** ['æŋkərait], *n.* anachorète, ermite, *m., f.*
anchovy [æn'tʃouvi, 'æntʃəvi], *n.* anchois, *m.*

ancient ['einʃənt], a. ancien; antique.—n. ancien, m.; the Ancient of Days, l'Éternel, m.

anciently ['einʃəntli], adv. anciennement.

ancillary [æn'siləri], a. ancillaire, subordonné, auxiliaire.

and [ænd], conj. et; and so on, et ainsi de suite; better and better, de mieux en mieux; carriage and pair, voiture à deux chevaux, f.; go and see, allez voir.

Andes ['ændi:z], the. les Andes, f.pl.

andiron ['ændaiən], n. landier; chenet, m.

Andrew ['ændru:]. André, m.

anecdote ['ænikdout], n. anecdote, f.

anecdotal [ænik'doutl], a. anecdotique.

anemone [ə'neməni], n. anémone, f.

***anent** [ə'nent], prep. touchant.

aneroid ['ænərɔid], a. and n. anéroïde, m.

anes— see **anaes—**

aneurism ['ænjurizm], n. anévrisme, m.

anew [ə'nju:], adv. de nouveau.

angel ['eindʒəl], n. ange, m.

Angela ['ændʒələ]. Angèle, f.

angelic [æn'dʒelik], **angelical** [æn'dʒelikəl], a. angélique.

angelica [æn'dʒelikə], n. angélique, f.

angelus ['ændʒələs], n. angélus, m.

anger ['æŋgə], n. colère, f.; emportement; courroux, m.—v.t. fâcher, irriter, mettre en colère.

angina [æn'dʒainə], n. (Path.) angine, f.

angle (1) [æŋgl], n. angle; coin, m.

angle (2) [æŋgl], v.i. pêcher à la ligne.

angled [æŋgld], a. à angles; right-angled, rectangulaire.

angler ['æŋglə], n. pêcheur à la ligne, m.; (Ichth.) baudroie, f.; crapaud de mer, m.

Anglican ['æŋglikən], a. anglican.—n. Anglican, m.

Anglicism ['æŋglisizm], n. anglicisme, m.

Anglicize ['æŋglisaiz], v.t. angliciser.

angling ['æŋgliŋ], n. pêche à la ligne, f.

Anglophil(e) ['æŋgloufail], n. anglophile, m.,f.

Anglo-Saxon ['æŋglo'sæksən], a. anglo-saxon.—n. Anglo-Saxon, m.

angrily ['æŋgrili], adv. en colère, avec colère.

angry ['æŋgri], a. en colère, fâché, irrité (contre ou de), courroucé; to be angry with, être en colère contre, en vouloir à.

anguish ['æŋgwiʃ], n. angoisse, douleur, f.—v.t. angoisser, navrer de douleur.

angular ['æŋgjulə], a. angulaire, angulé; anguleux; maigre, décharné.

angularity [æŋgju'læriti], n. angularité, f.

angularly ['æŋgjuləli], adv. angulairement.

anile ['einail], a. de vieille femme, débile.

aniline ['ænilain], n. (Chem.) aniline, f.

anility [ə'niliti], n. seconde enfance, f., radotage, m.

animadversion [ænimæd'və:ʃən], n. animadversion, censure, critique, f.

animadvert [ænimæd'və:t], v.i. to animadvert upon, critiquer, censurer.

animal ['æniməl], a. and n. animal, m.

animalism ['æniməlizm], **animality** [æni'mæliti], n. animalité, f.

animalize ['æniməlaiz], v.t. animaliser.

animate ['ænimeit], v.t. animer (de).—['ænimit], a. animé.

animated ['ænimeitid], a. animé, vif.

animatedly ['ænimeitidli], adv. vivement.

animating ['ænimeitiŋ], a. qui anime, qui ranime.

animation [æni'meiʃən], n. animation, vivacité, vie, f.

animator ['ænimeitə], n. animateur, m.

animosity [æni'mɔsiti], n. animosité, f.

animus ['æniməs], n. animosité, hostilité, f.; esprit (de), m.

anise ['ænis], n. anis, m.

aniseed ['ænisi:d], n. graine d'anis, f.

ankle [æŋkl], n. cheville du pied, f.

ankle bone ['æŋklboun], n. astragale, m.

ankle deep ['æŋkldi:p], adv. jusqu'aux chevilles.

Anna ['ænə]. Anne, f.

annalist ['ænəlist], n. annaliste, m., f.

annals ['ænəlz], n.pl. annales, f.pl.

Ann(e) [æn]. Anne, f.

anneal [ə'ni:l], v.t. détremper; adoucir (acier etc.), recuire (verre).

annealing [ə'ni:liŋ], n. recuite, f.

annex [ə'neks], v.t. annexer, joindre (à).—['æneks], n. annexe, f.

annexation [ænek'seiʃən], n. annexation, f.

annexed [ə'nekst], a. ci-joint, annexé.

annihilate [ə'naiileit], v.t. anéantir, annihiler.

annihilation [ənaii'leiʃən], n. anéantissement, m., annihilation, f.

annihilator [ə'naiileitə], n. annihilateur, m.

anniversary [æni'və:səri], a. and n. anniversaire, m.

Anno Domini ['ænou'dɔminai], (abbr. **A.D.** [ei'di:]). l'an du Seigneur; l'an de grâce; ap. J.-C.

annotate ['ænoteit], v.t. annoter.

annotation [æno'teiʃən], n. annotation, f.

annotator ['ænoteitə], n. annotateur, m.

announce [ə'nauns], v.t. annoncer, proclamer.

announcement [ə'naunsmənt], n. annonce, f., avis, m.; lettre de faire-part, f.

announcer [ə'naunsə], n. annonciateur; (Theat.) compère, m., commère, f.; (Rad., Tel.) speaker, m., speakerine, f.

annoy [ə'nɔi], v.t. gêner; incommoder, ennuyer, importuner; contrarier, tracasser.

annoyance [ə'nɔiəns], n. ennui, désagrément, chagrin, m.; contrariété, f.

annoying [ə'nɔiiŋ], a. ennuyeux, contrariant, vexant.

annoyingly [ə'nɔiiŋli], adv. ennuyeusement.

annual ['ænjuəl], a. annuel.—n. annuaire, m.

annually ['ænjuəli], adv. annuellement, tous les ans.

annuitant [ə'nju:itənt], n. bénéficiaire d'une pension ou d'une rente viagère, m., f.

annuity [ə'nju:iti], n. annuité, rente annuelle, pension, f.; life annuity, rente viagère, f.

annul [ə'nʌl], v.t. annuler.

annular ['ænjulə], a. annulaire.

annulet ['ænjulit], n. annelet, filet, m.

annulment [ə'nʌlmənt], n. annulation, f.; decree of annulment, décret abolitif, m.

Annunciation [ənʌnsi'eiʃən], the. (Eccles.) l'Annonciation, f.

annunciation [ənʌnsi'eiʃən], n. annonce, proclamation, f., avis, m.

anode ['ænoud], n. (Elec.) anode, f.

anodyne ['ænədain], a. anodin, calmant.—n. anodin (remède), m.

anoint [ə'nɔint], v.t. oindre.

anointed [ə'nɔintid], *a.* oint; *the Lord's Anointed*, l'Oint du Seigneur, *m.*

anomalous [ə'nɔmələs], *a.* anomal, irrégulier.

anomaly [ə'nɔməli], *n.* anomalie, *f.*

anon [ə'nɔn], *adv.* tout à l'heure, bientôt; à l'instant.

anonymity [æno'nimiti], *n.* anonymat, *m.*

anonymous [ə'nɔniməs], *a.* anonyme.

anonymously [ə'nɔniməsli], *adv.* anonymement.

another [ə'nʌðə], *a.* and *pron.* autre, un autre; encore un; *one another*, l'un l'autre, les uns les autres.

answer [a:nsə], *v.t.* répondre; répondre à; satisfaire, suffire à. *v.i.* faire réponse; répondre (*de* ou *pour*); raisonner; réussir.—*n.* réponse; solution (*d'un problème*), *f.*

answerable ['a:nsərəbl], *a.* susceptible de réponse; responsable (*for*, *de*).

ant [ænt], *n.* fourmi, *f.*

antagonism [æn'tægənizm], *n.* antagonisme, *m.*, opposition, *f.*

antagonist [æn'tægənist], *n.* antagoniste, *m.*,*f.*

antagonistic [æntægə'nistik], *a.* opposé (*à*); antagonique.

antagonize [æn'tægənaiz], *v.t.* eveiller l'antagonisme (*de*).

Antarctic [ænt'a:ktik], *a.* antarctique.—*n.* Antarctique, *m.*

ant-eater ['ænti:tə], *n.* fourmilier, *m.*

antecedence [ænti'si:dəns], *n.* antériorité, *f.*

antecedent [ænti'si:dənt], *a.* and *n.* antécédent, *m.*

ante-chamber ['æntitʃeimbə], *n.* antichambre, *f.*

antediluvian [æntidi'lu:viən], *a.* and *n.* antédiluvien, *m.*

antelope ['æntiloup], *n.* antilope, *f.*

ante-meridiem [æntimə'ridiəm], (*abbr.* **a.m.** [ei'em]), *adv.* avant midi; *at* II *a.m.*, à onze heures du matin.

ante-natal ['ænti'neitəl], *a.* prénatal.

antenna [æn'tenə], *n.* (*pl.* **antennae** [æn'teni:]) antenne, *f.*

antepenult [æntipi'nʌlt], **antepenultimate** [æntipi'nʌltimit], *a.* and *n.* antépénultième, *f.*

anterior [æn'tiəriə], *a.* antérieur.

anteroom ['æntiru:m], *n.* antichambre, *f.*

anthem ['ænθəm], *n.* hymne (national), *m.*; antienne, *f.*

ant-hill ['ænthil], *n.* fourmilière, *f.*

anthology [æn'θɔlədʒi], *n.* anthologie, chrestomathie, *f.*

Anthony ['æntəni], Antoine, *m.*

anthracite ['ænθrəsait], *n.* anthracite, *m.*

anthrax ['ænθræks], *n.* (*Med.*) anthrax, *m.*

anthropoid ['ænθrəpoid], *a.* and *n.* anthropoïde, *m.*

anthropological [ænθrəpə'lɔdʒikəl], *a.* anthropologique.

anthropologist [ænθrə'pɔlədʒist], *n.* anthropologiste, anthropologue, *m.*,*f.*

anthropology [ænθrə'pɔlədʒi], *n.* anthropologie, *f.*

anti-aircraft [ænti'ɛəkra:ft], *a.* contre-avion, antiaérien.

antibiotic ['æntibai'ɔtik], *a.* and *n.* antibiotique, *m.*

antic ['æntik], *n.* bouffonnerie, farce, *f.*

Antichrist ['æntikraist], *n.* antéchrist, *m.*

antichristian ['ænti'kristjən], *a.* and *n.* antichrétien, *m.*

anticipate [æn'tisipeit], *v.t.* anticiper; prévenir, devancer; s'attendre à, prévoir, envisager; jouir d'avance de; se promettre.

anticipation [æntisi'peiʃən], *n.* anticipation, *f.*; avant-goût, *m.*; attente, *f.*

anticipatory [æn'tisipətri], *a.* par anticipation.

anticlerical [ænti'klerikəl], *a.* and *n.* anticlérical, *m.*

anticlericalism [ænti'klerikəlizm], *n.* anticléricalisme, *m.*

anti-climax [ænti'klaimæks], *n.* anticlimax, *m.*

anti-clockwise [COUNTER-CLOCKWISE].

anticyclone [ænti'saikloun], *n.* anticyclone, *m.*

anti-dazzle ['ænti'dæzl], *a.* anti-aveuglant; (*Motor*) *anti-dazzle head lights*, phares-code, *m.pl.*

antidote ['æntidout], *n.* antidote, contre-poison, *m.*

anti-freeze ['æntifri:z], *n.* anti-gel, *m.*

Antilles [æn'tili:z], *the.* les Antilles, *f.pl.*

antimacassar [æntimə'kæsə], *n.* têtière, *f.*

antimony ['æntiməni], *n.* antimoine, *m.*

antinomy [æn'tinəmi], *n.* antinomie, *f.*

antipathetic [æntipə'θetik], **antipathetical** [æntipə'θetikəl], *a.* antipathique.

antipathy [æn'tipəθi], *n.* antipathie, aversion, *f.*

antiphony [æn'tifəni], *n.* contre-chant, *m.*

antiphrasis [æn'tifrəsis], *n.* antiphrase, *f.*

antipodal [æn'tipədl], *a.* antipodal.

antipodes [æn'tipədi:z], *n. pl.* antipodes, *m.pl.*

anti-pope ['æntipoup], *n.* antipape *m.*

antiquarian [ænti'kwɛəriən], *a.* d'antiquaire; archéologique.—*n.* antiquaire, *m.*

antiquary ['æntikwəri], *n.* archéologue; antiquaire, *m.*

antiquated ['æntikweitid], *a.* vieilli, vétuste; suranné, démodé.

antique [æn'ti:k], *a.* antique, ancien.—*n. the antique*, l'antique, *m.*; *an antique*, un objet antique, une antiquité.

antiquity [æn'tikwiti], *n.* antiquité; ancienneté, *f.*

antirrhinum [ænti'rainəm], *n.* antirrhine, *f.*

anti-Semitism [ænti'semitizm], *n.* antisémitisme, *m.*

antiseptic [ænti'septik], *a.* and *n.* antiseptique, *m.*

anti-tank [ænti'tæŋk], *a.* anti-chars.

antithesis [æn'tiθisis], *n.* antithèse, *f.*

antithetic [ænti'θetik], **antithetical** [ænti'θetikəl], *a.* antithétique.

antler ['æntlə], *n.* andouiller, bois (*de cerf*), *m.*

Antony ['æntəni], Antoine, *m.*

Antwerp ['æntwə:p], Anvers, *m.*

anvil ['ænvil], *n.* enclume, *f.*; (*fig.*) *on the anvil*, sur le métier, en préparation.

anxiety [æŋ'zaiəti], *n.* anxiété, inquiétude, sollicitude, *f.*; désir, *m.*

anxious ['æŋkʃəs], *a.* inquiet, soucieux, plein de sollicitude (*pour*); désireux (*de*); *to be anxious to*, désirer vivement (*de*); tenir à.

anxiously ['æŋkʃəsli], *adv.* anxieusement, avec anxiété, avec inquiétude.

any ['eni], *a.* and *pron.* du, de la, etc.; en; aucun; quelque; n'importe lequel; *any man*, tout homme; *any others*, d'autres; *at any rate*, en tout cas; *I haven't any*, je n'en ai pas; *scarcely any*, presque pas.

anybody ['enibɔdi], **anyone** ['eniwʌn], *pron.* quelqu'un, chacun, qui que ce soit, n'importe qui, tout le monde; *I didn't see anybody*, je n'ai vu personne.

anyhow ['enihau], **anyway** ['eniwei], *adv.* de toute façon, de quelque manière que ce soit, en tout cas, quand même.

anyone [ANYBODY].

anything ['eniθiŋ], *pron.* quelque chose, *m.*, quoi que ce soit, n'importe quoi; *not to say anything*, ne rien dire.

anyway [ANYHOW].

anywhere ['eniwɛə], *adv.* quelque part, dans quelque endroit que ce soit, n'importe où; *not anywhere*, nulle part.

apace [ə'peis], *adv.* vite, à grands pas.

apanage, **appanage** [æ'pənidʒ], *n.* apanage, *m.*

apart [ə'pɑːt], *adv.* à part; de côté, séparément.

apartheid [ə'pɑːtheit], *n.* (*en Afrique du Sud*) ségrégation, *f.*

apartment [ə'pɑːtmənt], *n.* chambre; pièce (*d'un appartement*), *f.*; logement; (*Am.*) appartement; (*pl.*) appartement, *m.*

apathetic [æpə'θetik], *a.* apathique.

apathy ['æpəθi], *n.* apathie, *f.*

ape [eip], *n.* singe, *m.*, guenon, *f.*—*v.t.* singer.

aperient [ə'piəriənt], **aperitive** [ə'peritiv], *a.* and *n.* laxatif, *m.*

aperture ['æpətjuə], *n.* ouverture, *f.*; orifice, *m.*

apex ['eipeks], *n.* (*pl.* **apices** ['eipisiːz], **apexes** ['eipeksiz]) sommet, *m.*, pointe, *f.*

aphorism ['æfərizm], *n.* aphorisme, *m.*

apiary ['eipiəri], *n.* rucher, *m.*

apiece [ə'piːs], *adv.* la pièce; par tête, par personne, chacun.

apish ['eipiʃ], *a.* de singe, simiesque; *apish trick*, singerie, *f.*

apocalypse [ə'pɔkəlips], *n.* apocalypse, *f.*

apocalyptic [əpɔkə'liptik], **apocalyptical** [əpɔkə'liptikəl], *a.* apocalyptique.

Apocrypha [ə'pɔkrifə], *n.pl.* les Apocryphes, *m.pl.*

apocryphal [ə'pɔkrifəl], *a.* apocryphe.

apogee ['æpədʒiː], *n.* apogée, *m.*

apologetic [əpɔlə'dʒetik], **apologetical** [əpɔlə'dʒetikəl], *a.* qui s'excuse, qui regrette; *he was quite apologetic about it*, il s'en excusa vivement.

apologetically [əpɔlə'dʒetikəli], *adv.* pour s'excuser, en s'excusant.

apologia [æpə'loudʒiə], *n.* apologie; justification, *f.*

apologist [ə'pɔlədʒist], *n.* apologiste, *m.*, *f.*

apologize [ə'pɔlədʒaiz], *v.i.* s'excuser, faire des excuses (*de* ou *auprès de*).

apologue ['æpəlɔg], *n.* apologue, *m.*

apology [ə'pɔlədʒi], *n.* excuses, *f.pl.*, apologie, *f.*

apoplectic [æpə'plektik], *a.* apoplectique; *apoplectic stroke*, coup de sang, *m.*

apoplexy ['æpəpleksi], *n.* apoplexie, *f.*; *a fit of apoplexy*, congestion cérébrale, *f.*

apostasy [ə'pɔstəsi], *n.* apostasie, *f.*

apostate [ə'pɔsteit], *a.* and *n.* apostat, *m.*

apostle [ə'pɔsl], *n.* apôtre, *m.*; *the Acts of the Apostles*, les Actes des Apôtres, *m.pl.*

apostolic [æpəs'tɔlik], **apostolical** [æpəs'tɔlikəl], *a.* apostolique.

apostrophe [ə'pɔstrəfi], *n.* apostrophe, *f.*

apostrophize [ə'pɔstrəfaiz], *v.t.* apostropher.

apothecary [ə'pɔθikəri], *n.* apothicaire; pharmacien, *m.*

apotheosis [əpɔθi'ousis], *n.* apothéose, *f.*

appal [ə'pɔːl], *v.t.* épouvanter, consterner.

appalling [ə'pɔːliŋ], *a.* épouvantable, effrayant.

appallingly [ə'pɔːliŋli], *adv.* épouvantablement.

appanage [APANAGE].

apparatus [æpə'reitəs], *n.* appareil, dispositif, *m.*

apparel [ə'pærəl], *v.t.* vêtir; parer.—*n.* habillement, vêtement, *m.*

apparent [ə'pærənt], *a.* évident, manifeste, apparent; *heir apparent*, héritier présomptif, *m.*

apparently [ə'pærəntli], *adv.* en apparence, apparemment.

apparition [æpə'riʃən], *n.* apparition, *f.*

appeal [ə'piːl], *v.i.* appeler, en appeler (*de*), faire appel (*à*); (*Law*) se pourvoir en cassation, réclamer (*contre* ou *à*); (*fig.*) attirer, séduire.—*n.* appel, attrait, *m.*; *Court of Appeal*, cour de cassation, *f.*

appealing [ə'piːliŋ], *a.* suppliant, attrayant, séduisant.

appear [ə'piə], *v.i.* paraître, apparaître; se montrer, se présenter (à).

appearance [ə'piərəns], *n.* apparition; apparence, figure, mine, *f.*, air, aspect, *m.*; (*Law*) comparution, *f.*; *at first appearance*, au premier abord, au premier coup d'œil.

appeasable [ə'piːzəbl], *a.* qu'on peut apaiser.

appease [ə'piːz], *v.t.* apaiser, pacifier.

appeasement [ə'piːzmənt], *n.* apaisement, adoucissement, *m.*; conciliation, *f.*

appellant [ə'pelənt], *a.* and *n.* (*Law*) appellant, *m.*

appellation [æpə'leiʃən], *n.* nom, *m.*, appellation, dénomination, *f.*

append [ə'pend], *v.t.* apposer, attacher (à).

appendage [ə'pendidʒ], *n.* accessoire, apanage, *m.*

appendant [ə'pendənt], *a.* accessoire, attaché, annexé (à).

appendicitis [əpendi'saitis], *n.* appendicite, *f.*

appendix [ə'pendiks], *n.* (*pl.* **appendixes** [ə'pendiksiz], **appendices** [ə'pendisiːz]) appendice, *m.*

appertain [æpə'tein], *v.i.* appartenir (à).

appetite ['æpitait], *n.* appétit; (*fig.*) désir, *m.*, soif, *f.*

appetize ['æpitaiz], *v.t.* mettre en appétit.

appetizer ['æpitaizə], *n.* apéritif, *m.*

appetizing ['æpitaiziŋ], *a.* appétissant.

applaud [ə'plɔːd], *v.t.*, *v.i.* applaudir (à).

applause [ə'plɔːz], *n.* applaudissements, *m.pl.*

apple [æpl], *n.* pomme, *f.*; *apple of the eye*, prunelle, *f.*

apple pie [æpl'pai], *n.* tourte aux pommes, *f.*

apple-sauce ['æpl'sɔːs], *n.* compote de pommes, *f.*

apple tart [æpl'tɑːt], *n.* tarte aux pommes, *f.*

apple tree ['æpltriː], *n.* pommier, *m.*

appliance [ə'plaiəns], *n.* instrument, appareil, dispositif, *m.*
applicability [æplikə'biliti], **applicableness** ['æplikəblnis], *n.* applicabilité, *f.*
applicable ['æplikəbl], *a.* applicable.
applicant ['æplikənt], *n.* postulant, candidat; (*Law*) demandeur, *m.*
application [æpli'keiʃən], *n.* application; sollicitation, demande, *f.*; usage, *m.*; *for external application*, usage externe; *on application*, sur demande; *to make application to*, s'adresser à, faire une demande à.
apply [ə'plai], *v.t.* appliquer (*à*); *to apply the brake*, freiner; serrer le frein.—*v.i.* s'adresser (*à*); s'appliquer, être applicable; *to apply for* (*a job*), faire une demande (d'emploi); *to apply to*, s'adresser à *ou* chez.
appoint [ə'point], *v.t.* arrêter, désigner, fixer; nommer; installer; équiper; *at the appointed hour*, à l'heure convenue; *a well-appointed house*, une maison bien installée.
appointment [ə'pointmənt], *n.* nomination, *f.*; décret, arrêt; établissement; emploi; rendez-vous, *m.*; convocation, *f.*
apportion [ə'pɔ:ʃən], *v.t.* partager, répartir, assigner.
apportionment [ə'pɔ:ʃənmənt], *n.* répartition, *f.*, partage, *m.*
apposite ['æpəzait], *a.* juste; à propos; approprié, convenable (*à*).
appositely ['æpəzaitli], *adv.* convenablement, justement, à propos.
appositeness ['æpəzaitnis], *n.* à-propos, *m.*, opportunité, *f.*
appraisal [APPRAISMENT].
appraise [ə'preiz], *v.t.* priser, évaluer, estimer.
appraisement [ə'preizmənt], **appraisal** [ə'preizəl], *n.* évaluation, estimation; expertise, *f.*
appraiser [ə'preizə], *n.* commissaire-priseur, expert, *m.*
appreciable [ə'pri:ʃəbl], *a.* appréciable, sensible.
appreciably [ə'pri:ʃəbli], *adv.* sensiblement.
appreciate [ə'pri:ʃieit], *v.t.* apprécier, estimer.—*v.i.* (*Comm. etc.*) augmenter de valeur.
appreciation [əpri:ʃi'eiʃən], *n.* appréciation; hausse de valeur, *f.*
appreciative [ə'pri:ʃiətiv], *a.* appréciateur.
apprehend [æpri'hend], *v.t.* comprendre; prendre, saisir, arrêter, appréhender; craindre.
apprehension [æpri'henʃən], *n.* appréhension; arrestation, prise de corps; crainte, inquiétude, *f.*
apprehensive [æpri'hensiv], *a.* intelligent, prompt à saisir; appréhensif, inquiet.
apprentice [ə'prentis], *n.* apprenti, *m.*—*v.t.* mettre en apprentissage.
apprenticeship [ə'prentisʃip], *n.* apprentissage, *m.*
apprise [ə'praiz], *v.t.* prévenir, informer, instruire.
approach [ə'proutʃ], *n.* approche, *f.*; abord, accès; rapprochement, *m.*; (*Math.*) approximation, *f.*—*v.t.* approcher de, s'approcher de, aborder; (*fig.*) pressentir, tâter (*quelqu'un*). —*v.i.* approcher, s'approcher.

approachable [ə'proutʃəbl], *a.* abordable, accessible.
approbation [æpro'beiʃən], *n.* approbation, *f.*; *on approbation*, à condition, à l'essai.
appropriate [ə'prouprieit], *v.t.* s'approprier, affecter (*à*); s'approprier; s'emparer de.—[ə'proupriət], *a.* approprié; propre, convenable (*à*).
appropriately [ə'proupriətli], *adv.* à juste titre; convenablement.
appropriateness [ə'proupriətnis], *n.* convenance, *f.*, à-propos, *m.*, justesse, *f.*
appropriation [əproupri'eiʃən], *n.* application, destination, appropriation, *f.*; crédit (*budgétaire*), *m.*
approval [ə'pru:vəl], *n.* approbation, *f.*; *on approval*, à condition.
approve [ə'pru:v], *v.t.* approuver; trouver bon. (*que, with subj.*).
approver [ə'pru:və], *n.* approbateur, *m.*
approving [ə'pru:viŋ], *a.* approbateur, approbatif.
approvingly [ə'pru:viŋli], *adv.* avec approbation, d'un air approbateur.
approximate [ə'proksimeit], *v.t.* rapprocher.—*v.i.* se rapprocher (*de*).—[ə'proksimit], *a.* approximatif.
approximately [ə'proksimitli], *adv.* approximativement, à peu près.
approximation [əproksi'meiʃən], *n.* approximation, *f.*; rapprochement, *m.*
appulse [ə'pʌls], *n.* choc, *m.*
appurtenance [ə'pə:tinəns], *n.* appartenance, dépendance, *f.*; (*pl.*) accessoires, *m.pl.*
appurtenant [ə'pə:tinənt], *a.* appartenant (*à*), dépendant (*de*).
apricot ['eiprikɔt], *n.* abricot, *m.*
apricot tree ['eiprikɔttri:], *n.* abricotier, *m.*
April ['eipril], avril, *m.*; *to make an April fool of*, donner un poisson d'avril à.
apron ['eiprən], *n.* tablier, *m.*; (*Av.*) aire de manœuvre *ou* d'atterrissage, *f.*
apron-stage ['eiprənsteidʒ], *n.* avant-scène, *f.*
apse [æps], **apsis** ['æpsis], *n.* (*pl.* **apses** ['æpsi:z], **apsides** [æp'saidi:z]) abside; (*Astron.*) apside, *f.*
apt [æpt], *a.* sujet, enclin, porté (*à*); propre, convenable (*à*); capable; juste (*mot*).
aptitude ['æptitju:d], **aptness** ['æptnis], *n.* aptitude, disposition, *f.*
aptly ['æptli], *adv.* à propos; convenablement.
aqua fortis [ækwə'fɔ:tis], *n.* eau-forte, *f.*
aquamarine [ækwəmə'ri:n], *n.* aigue-marine, *f.*
aqua regia [ækwə'ri:dʒiə], *n.* eau régale, *f.*
aquarium [ə'kwɛəriəm], *n.* aquarium, *m.*
aquatic [ə'kwɔtik, ə'kwætik], *a.* aquatique.
aquatics [ə'kwætiks], **aquatic sports** [ə'kwætikspɔːts], *n.pl.* sports nautiques, *m.pl.*
aqua vitae [ækwə'vaiti:], *n.* eau de vie, *f.*
aqueduct ['ækwidʌkt], *n.* aqueduc, *m.*
aqueous ['eikwiəs], *a.* aqueux.
aquiline ['ækwilain], *a.* aquilin, d'aigle.
Arab ['ærəb], *a.* arabe.—*n.* Arabe, *m.*
arabesque [ærə'besk], *a.* and *n.* arabesque, *f.*
Arabia [ə'reibjə], l'Arabie, *f.*; *Saudi Arabia*, l'Arabie Séoudite.
Arabian [ə'reibiən], *a.* arabe.

Arabic ['ærəbik], *a.* arabe, arabique; *Arabic figures*, chiffres arabes, *m.pl.*—*n.* arabe (*langue*), *m.*

arable ['ærəbl], *a.* arable, labourable.

arbalest ['a:bələst], *n.* arbalète, *f.*

arbiter ['a:bitə], *n.* arbitre, *m., f.*

arbitrament [a:'bitrəmənt], *n.* arbitrage, *m.*, arbitration, *f.*; jugement, *m.*

arbitrarily [a:'bitrərəli], *adv.* arbitrairement.

arbitrary ['a:bitrəri], *a.* arbitraire.

arbitrate ['a:bitreit], *v.t., v.i.* arbitrer, décider.

arbitration [a:bi'treiʃən], *n.* arbitrage, *m.*

arbitrator ['a:bitreitə], *n.* arbitre, *m., f.*

arbor ['a:bə], *n.* berceau, *m.*, tonnelle, *f.*

arbutus [a:'bju:təs], *n.* arbousier, *f.*

arc [a:k], *n.* arc, *m.*

arcade [a:'keid], *n.* arcade, *f.*; passage, *m.*

arch [a:tʃ], *a.* moqueur, malin, espiègle; grand, maître, archi-, insigne, fieffé.—*n.* arche, *f.*; arc, cintre, *m.*, voûte, *f.*; *pointed arch*, ogive, *f.*; *triumphal arch*, arc de triomphe.—*v.t.* voûter, cintrer, arquer.

archaeological [a:kiə'lɔdʒikəl], *a.* archéologique.

archaeologist [a:ki'ɔlədʒist], *n.* archéologue, *m., f.*

archaeology [a:ki'ɔlədʒi], *n.* archéologie, *f.*

archaic [a:'keiik], *a.* archaïque.

archaism ['a:keiizm], *n.* archaïsme, *m.*

archangel ['a:keindʒəl], *n.* archange, *m.*

archbishop [a:tʃ'biʃəp], *n.* archevêque, *m.*

archbishopric [a:tʃ'biʃəprik], *n.* archevêché, *m.*

archdeacon [a:tʃ'di:kən], *n.* archidiacre, *m.*

archduchess [a:tʃ'dʌtʃis], *n.* archiduchesse, *f.*

archduchy [a:tʃ'dʌtʃi], *n.* archiduché, *m.*

archduke [a:tʃ'dju:k], *n.* archiduc, *m.*

archer ['a:tʃə], *n.* archer, *m.*; (*Astron.*) *the Archer*, Sagittaire, *m.*

archery ['a:tʃəri], *n.* tir à l'arc, *m.*

archetype ['a:kitaip], *n.* archétype; étalon (*mesure*), *m.*

archiepiscopal [a:kiə'piskəpəl], *a.* archiépiscopal.

archipelago [a:ki'peləgou], *n.* archipel, *m.*

architect ['a:kitekt], *n.* architecte; (*fig.*) artisan, *m.*

architectural [a:ki'tektʃərəl], *a.* architectural.

architecture ['a:kitektʃə], *n.* architecture, *f.*

archives ['a:kaivz], *n. pl.* archives, *f.pl.*

archivist ['a:kivist], *n.* archiviste, *m., f.*

archly ['a:tʃli], *adv.* avec espièglerie, d'un air malin.

archness ['a:tʃnis], *n.* malice, espièglerie, *f.*

arc light ['a:k'klæmp], *n.* lampe à arc, *f.*

Arctic ['a:ktik], *a.* arctique.

ardent ['a:dənt], *a.* ardent; *ardent spirits*, spiritueux, *m.pl.*

ardently ['a:dəntli], *adv.* ardemment, avec ardeur.

ardor ['a:də], *n.* ardeur, *f.*

arduous ['a:djuəs], *a.* ardu, rude, pénible, difficile.

arduously ['a:djuəsli], *adv.* difficilement, péniblement.

arduousness ['a:djuəsnis], *n.* difficulté, *f.*

area ['ɛəriə], *n.* étendue; aire, surface, superficie; région, zone; courette d'entrée (*devant la maison*), *f.*; *area steps*, escalier de service, *m.*; *postal area*, zone postale, *f.*

arena [ə'ri:nə], *n.* arène, *f.*

argent ['a:dʒənt], *a.* argenté.—*n.* (*Her.*) argent, *m.*

Argentina [a:dʒən'ti:nə], l'Argentine, la République Argentine, *f.*

Argentine ['a:dʒəntain], *a.* argentin.—*n.* Argentin, *m.*; *the Argentine* [ARGENTINA].

Argentinian [a:dʒən'tinjən], *a.* argentin.—*n.* Argentin (*personne*), *m.*

argil ['a:dʒil], *n.* argile, *f.*

argonaut ['a:gənɔ:t], *n.* argonaute, *m.*

argosy ['a:gəsi], *n.* caraque, *f.*

argue ['a:gju:], *v.t.* discuter; soutenir; (*fig.*) dénoter, indiquer, accuser.—*v.i.* argumenter (*contre*), raisonner (*sur*), discuter (*avec*); (*Law*) plaider.

argument ['a:gjumənt], *n.* argument, raisonnement, *m.*; discussion, dispute; thèse, *f.*; *for argument's sake*, à titre d'exemple.

argumentative [a:gju'mentətiv], *a.* raisonneur; disposé à argumenter.

aria ['a:riə], *n.* aria, *f.*

arid ['ærid], *a.* aride.

aridity [ə'riditi], **aridness** ['æridnis], *n.* aridité, *f.*

aright [ə'rait], *adv.* correctement; bien.

arise [ə'raiz], *v.i. irr.* (*conjug. like* RISE) se lever; s'élever; survenir, se présenter; provenir, résulter (*de*); *if the question arises*, le cas échéant.

aristocracy [æris'tɔkrəsi], *n.* aristocratie, *f.*

aristocrat ['æristəkræt], *n.* aristocrate, *m., f.*

aristocratic [æristə'krætik], *a.* aristocratique.

arithmetic [ə'riθmətik], *n.* arithmétique, *f.*, calcul, *m.*

arithmetical [æriθ'metikəl], *a.* arithmétique.

arithmetically [æriθ'metikəli], *adv.* arithmétiquement.

arithmetician [æriθmə'tiʃən], *n.* arithméticien, *m.*

ark [a:k], *n.* arche, *f.*; *Noah's ark*, l'arche de Noé.

arm [a:m], *n.* bras, *m.*; arme (*à feu*), *f.*; (*pl.*) (*Her.*) armes, armoiries, *f.pl.*; *arm in arm*, bras dessus bras dessous; *with arms folded*, les bras croisés; *with open arms*, à bras ouverts.—*v.t.* armer; donner des armes à.—*v.i.* armer; s'armer (*de*); prendre les armes.

armada [a:'ma:də], *n.* armada, *f.*

armadillo [a:mə'dilou], *n.* tatou, *m.*

armament ['a:məmənt], *n.* armement, *m.*, armée, flotte, *f.*; *armaments race*, course aux armements, *f.*

armature ['a:mətjuə], *n.* armature, *f.*, induit, *m.*

arm band [a:'mbænd], *n.* brassard, *m.*

arm-chair ['a:mtʃɛə], *n.* fauteuil, *m.*

Armenia [a:'mi:niə], l'Arménie, *f.*

Armenian [a:'mi:niən], *a.* arménien.—*n.* arménien (*langue*); Arménien (*personne*), *m.*

armful ['a:mful], *n.* brassée, *f.*

arm-hole ['a:mhoul], *n.* emmanchure, entournure, *f.*

armistice ['a:mistis], *n.* armistice, *m.*

armless ['a:mlis], *a.* sans bras.

armlet ['a:mlit], *n.* brassard; bracelet; petit bras (*de mer*), *m.*

armor ['a:mə], *n.* armure, *f.*; blindés, *m.pl.*—*v.t.* cuirasser, blinder.

armored ['a:məd], *a.* cuirassé, blindé.

armorer ['a:mərə], *n.* armurier, *m.*

armorial [ɑːˈmɔːriəl], a. armorial; *armorial bearings*, armoiries, f.pl.

armor plate [ˈɑːməˈpleit], n. plaque de blindage, f.

armor-plated [ˈɑːməˈpleitid], a. cuirassé, blindé.

armory [ˈɑːməri], n. arsenal, m.; salle d'armes; armurerie, f.

armpit [ˈɑːmpit], n. aisselle, f.

army [ˈɑːmi], n. armée; (*fig.*) foule, multitude, f.; *the Salvation Army*, l'Armée du Salut.

Arnold [ˈɑːnəld]. Arnaud, m.

aroma [əˈroumə], n. arome *ou* arôme; bouquet (*de vin*), m.

aromatic [æroˈmætik], a. aromatique.

around [əˈraund], *prep.* autour de; (*colloq.*) environ, vers, à peu près.—*adv.* autour, à l'entour, aux alentours.

arouse [əˈrauz], v.t. réveiller, éveiller; exciter, provoquer.

arraign [əˈrein], v.t. accuser, poursuivre en justice, attaquer.

arraignment [əˈreinmənt], n. mise en accusation, f.

arrange [əˈreindʒ], v.t. arranger, régler, disposer, distribuer; organiser.

arrangement [əˈreindʒmənt], n. arrangement, m., disposition, organisation, f., dispositif, m.

arrant [ˈærənt], a. insigne, achevé, fieffé.

arrantly [ˈærəntli], adv. notoirement, impudemment.

array [əˈrei], v.t. ranger, déployer; revêtir, parer.—n. ordre, rang; étalage; appareil, m.

arrear [əˈriə], n. arriéré, m.; (*pl.*) arrérages, m.pl.; *to be in arrears*, être en retard, avoir de l'arriéré.

arrest [əˈrest], v.t. arrêter; fixer; suspendre.—n. arrestation, prise de corps, f.; arrêt, m., suspension, f.

arresting [əˈrestiŋ], a. frappant, qui arrête l'attention.

arrival [əˈraivəl], n. arrivée, f.; arrivage (*de marchandises etc.*), m.; *arrival platform*, quai d'arrivée, débarcadère, m.

arrive [əˈraiv], v.i. arriver (à); parvenir (à).

arrogance [ˈærəgəns], n. arrogance, f.

arrogant [ˈærəgənt], a. arrogant.

arrogantly [ˈærəgəntli], adv. arrogamment.

arrogate [ˈærəgeit], v.t. attribuer injustement; *to arrogate to oneself*, s'arroger.

arrogation [ærəˈgeiʃən], n. prétention, usurpation, f.

arrow [ˈærou], n. flèche, f.; (*fig.*) trait, m.—v.t. indiquer par des flèches.

arrow-root [ˈærourut], n. arrow-root, m.

arsenal [ˈɑːsənəl], n. arsenal, m.

arsenic [ˈɑːsenik], a. arsénique.—[ˈɑːsenik], n. arsenic, m.

arson [ˈɑːsən], n. incendie volontaire, m.

art [ɑːt], n. art, m.; adresse, habileté, f.; *faculty of arts*, faculté des lettres, f.; *fine arts*, beaux-arts, m.pl.; *school of art*, école de dessin, académie, f.

arterial [ɑːˈtiəriəl], a. artériel; *arterial road*, route à grande circulation, f.

artery [ˈɑːtəri], n. artère, f.

artesian [ɑːˈtiːʒən], a. artésien.

artful [ˈɑːtful], a. rusé, fin, artificieux.

artfully [ˈɑːtfuli], adv. avec artifice, artificieusement, adroitement.

artfulness [ˈɑːtfulnis], n. ruse, finesse, f., artifice, m.

arthritic [ɑːˈθritik], a. arthritique.

arthritis [ɑːˈθraitis], n. arthrite, f.

artichoke [ˈɑːtitʃouk], n. *Chinese artichoke*, crosne (du Japon), m.; *globe artichoke*, artichaut, m.; *Jerusalem artichoke*, topinambour, m.

article [ˈɑːtikl], n. article; objet; statut, m.—v.t. engager par contrat; placer (*chez un avoué*) comme clerc; *articled clerk*, clerc d'avoué, m.

articulate [ɑːˈtikjuleit], v.t., v.i. articuler; énoncer, parler distinctement.—[ɑːˈtikjulit], a. articulé.

artifice [ˈɑːtifis], n. artifice, m., ruse, finesse, f.

artificer [ɑːˈtifisə], n. artisan, ouvrier; mécanicien, m.

artificial [ɑːtiˈfiʃəl], a. artificiel; factice.

artificiality [ɑːtifiʃiˈæliti], n. nature artificielle, f.

artificially [ɑːtiˈfiʃəli], adv. artificiellement.

artillery [ɑːˈtiləri], n. artillerie, f.

artilleryman [ɑːˈtilərimən], n. (*pl.* -men [men]) artilleur, m.

artisan [ɑːtiˈzæn], n. artisan, ouvrier, m.

artist [ˈɑːtist], n. artiste, m., f.

artistic [ɑːˈtistik], a. artistique.

artistically [ɑːˈtistikli], adv. artistement, avec art.

artless [ˈɑːtlis], a. ingénu, naïf; sans art, naturel.

artlessly [ˈɑːtlisli], adv. ingénument, naïvement; sans art.

artlessness [ˈɑːtlisnis], n. naïveté; simplicité, f.

as [æz], *conj.* comme; tel que; à titre de; aussi ... que; à mesure que; en, pour; parce que; *as big as*, aussi gros que; *as cold as charity*, froid comme le marbre; *as for*, quant à, pour; *as he advanced*, à mesure qu'il avançait; *as he was walking*, comme il marchait; *as if*, comme si; *as it were*, pour ainsi dire; *as much as*, autant que, tant que; *as yet*, jusqu'à présent, encore; *as you were*, (*Mil.*) au temps! be that as it may, quoi qu'il en soit; *do as you wish*, faites comme vous voudrez; *rich as she is*, toute riche qu'elle est; *she was dressed as a page*, elle était habillée en page; *that's as may be*, c'est selon; *to act as*, agir en.

asbestos [æzˈbestos], n. asbeste, amiante, m.

ascend [əˈsend], v.t. monter; gravir, faire l'ascension de; remonter (*un fleuve*).—v.i. monter (à ou *sur*); remonter; s'élever (*montagne etc.*).

ascendancy [əˈsendənsi], n. ascendant, m.; supériorité, influence, f.

ascendant [əˈsendənt], a. ascendant; supérieur.—n. ascendant, m.; supériorité, f., dessus, m.

Ascension [əˈsenʃən], n. (*Eccles.*) Ascension, f.; *Ascension Day*, jour de l'Ascension, m.

ascent [əˈsent], n. ascension; élévation, montée, pente, f.

ascertain [æsəˈtein], v.t. s'assurer, s'informer de, constater, vérifier.

ascetic [əˈsetik], a. ascétique.—n. ascète, ascétique, m., f.

asceticism [əˈsetisizm], n. ascétisme, m.

ascribable [ə'skraibəbl], a. attribuable, imputable.

ascribe [ə'skraib], v.t. attribuer, imputer (à).

aseptic [æ'septik], a. and n. aseptique, m.

asexual [æ'seksjuəl], a. asexué, asexuel.

ash (1) [æʃ], a. de frêne.—n. frêne (arbre); bâton, m.; **mountain ash**, sorbier, m.

ash (2) [æʃ], n. cendre, f.; cendres, f.pl.

ashamed [ə'ʃeimd], a. honteux, confus; **to be ashamed of**, avoir honte de.

ash bin, **pit** [æʃbin, -pit], n. cendrier, m.

ashcan [æʃkæn], n. (Am.) boîte à ordures, f.

ashen (1) [æʃn], a. de frêne.

ashen (2) [æʃn], a. cendré; gris pâle.

ashore [ə'ʃɔ:], adv. à terre; échoué (navire); **to go ashore**, débarquer.

ash pit [ASH BIN].

ashtray [æʃtrei], n. cendrier, m.

Ash Wednesday [æʃ'wenzdi]. mercredi des Cendres, m.

ashy [æʃi], a. cendré; gris pâle.

Asia ['eiʃə]. l'Asie, f.

Asia Minor ['eiʃə'mainə]. l'Asie-Mineure, f.

Asiatic [eiʃi'ætik], **Asian** ['eiʃən], a. asiatique.—n. Asiatique (personne), m., f.

aside [ə'said], adv. de côté, à; (Theat.) à part; à l'écart.—n. (Theat.) aparté, m.

asinine ['æsinain], a. d'âne; sot.

ask [ɑ:sk], v.t., v.i. demander, prier (de); inviter (à); s'informer, se renseigner; poser (une question); **to ask in**, prier d'entrer; **to ask someone to do something**, demander à quelqu'un de faire quelque chose; **to ask to see**, demander à voir.

askance [ə'skɑ:ns], adv. de travers, obliquement.

askew [ə'skju:], adv. de côté, de biais.

aslant [ə'slɑ:nt], adv. obliquement, de biais, de côté, en travers.

asleep [ə'sli:p], a. endormi; **to be asleep**, dormir; **to fall asleep**, s'endormir.

asp (1) [æsp], **aspic** ['æspik], n. aspic, m.

asp (2) [æsp], **aspen** ['æspən], n. tremble, m.

asparagus [əs'pærəgəs], n. asperges, f.pl.

aspect ['æspekt], n. aspect, m.; exposition, f.; **to have a southern aspect**, être exposé au midi.

aspen ['æspən], a. de tremble.—n. [ASP (2)].

asperity [æs'periti], n. aspérité, âpreté, rudesse, f.

aspersion [æs'pə:ʃən], n. calomnie, f.; **to cast aspersions on**, répandre des calomnies sur.

asphalt ['æsfælt], a. d'asphalte.—n. asphalte, m.

asphyxia [æs'fiksiə], n. asphyxie, f.

asphyxiate [æs'fiksieit], v.t. asphyxier.

aspic [ASP (1)].

aspirant [ə'spaiərənt], n. aspirant, candidat, m.

aspirate ['æspireit], v.t. aspirer.—['æspirit], a. aspiré.

aspiration [æspi'reiʃən], n. aspiration, f.

aspire [ə'spaiə], v.i. aspirer (à), ambitionner.

aspirin ['æspirin], n. aspirine, f.

asquint [ə'skwint], adv. de travers, en louchant.

ass [æs], n. âne, m.; **he is a silly ass**, il est bête à manger du foin; **she-ass**, ânesse, f.; **to make an ass of oneself**, agir sottement; **young ass**, ânon, m.

assail [ə'seil], v.t. assaillir, attaquer.

assailant [ə'seilənt], n. assaillant, m.

assassin [ə'sæsin], n. assassin (politique), m.

assassinate [ə'sæsineit], v.t. assassiner.

assassination [əsæsi'neiʃən], n. assassinat, m.

assault [ə'sɔ:lt], n. assaut, m., attaque brusquée; (Law) tentative de voie de fait, f.; **assault and battery**, voies de fait, f.pl.; **indecent assault**, outrage aux mœurs, m.—v.t. assaillir, attaquer.

assay [ə'sei], n. épreuve, vérification, f.; essai, m.—v.t. essayer.

assemble [ə'sembl], v.t. assembler, réunir.—v.i. s'assembler, se réunir.

assembly [ə'sembli], n. assemblée, réunion, f.; assemblage (d'une machine), m.; **assembly line**, chaîne de montage, f.

assent [ə'sent], v.i. donner son assentiment (à), admettre.—n. assentiment, consentement, m.

assert [ə'sə:t], v.t. affirmer, prétendre, soutenir; revendiquer, faire valoir (ses droits etc.).

assertion [ə'sə:ʃən], n. assertion, revendication, f.

assertive [ə'sə:tiv], a. assertif.

assertively [ə'sə:tivli], adv. d'un ton péremptoire.

assess [ə'ses], v.t. répartir, fixer; imposer; évaluer.

assessment [ə'sesmənt], n. imposition, répartition, assiette; évaluation, f.

assessor [ə'sesə], n. assesseur; répartiteur, m.

asset [æset], n. avoir; avantage, m.

assets ['æsets], n.pl. actif, m; **assets and liabilities**, actif et passif, m.; **personal assets**, biens meubles, m.pl.; **real assets**, biens immobiliers, m.pl.

asseverate [ə'sevəreit], v.t. affirmer solennellement.

assiduity [æsi'dju:iti], n. assiduité, f.

assiduous [ə'sidjuəs], a. assidu.

assiduously [ə'sidjuəsli], adv. assidûment.

assign [ə'sain], v.t. assigner, attribuer; transférer (à).—n. (Law) ayant droit, m.

assignation [æsig'neiʃən], n. attribution, assignation, cession, f.; rendez-vous, m.

assignee [æsi'ni:], n. cessionnaire, m., f.; syndic (de faillite), m.

assimilate [ə'simileit], v.t. assimiler.—v.i. s'assimiler.

assimilation [əsimi'leiʃən], n. assimilation, f.

assist [ə'sist], v.t. aider; **to assist each other**, s'entr'aider.

assistance [ə'sistəns], n. assistance, aide, f.; secours, concours, m.

assistant [ə'sistənt], a. qui aide, auxiliaire.—n. aide; adjoint; commis (dans une boutique), m.; **assistant examiner**, examinateur adjoint, m.; **assistant manager**, sous-directeur, m.

assizes [ə'saiziz], n. pl. assises, f.pl.

associate [ə'souʃieit], v.t. associer (avec ou à).—v.i. s'associer (avec ou à); **to associate with**, fréquenter.—[ə'souʃiit], a. associé.—n. associé, m.; complice, m., f.

association [əsousi'eiʃən], n. association, f.; souvenir, m.

assort [ə'sɔ:t], v.t. assortir.

assorted [ə'sɔ:tid], a. assorti.

assortment [ə'sɔ:tmənt], n. assortiment, m.; classification, f.

assuage [ə'sweidʒ], *v.t.* adoucir, apaiser, calmer, soulager.—*v.i.* s'apaiser, se calmer.

assume [ə'sju:m], *v.t.* prendre sur soi, s'arroger, s'attribuer; assumer (*une responsabilité*); supposer, présumer; se donner; affecter.

assuming [ə'sju:miŋ], *a.* arrogant, présomptueux, prétentieux; *assuming that*, en supposant que.

assumption [ə'sʌmpʃən], *n.* supposition; prétention, *f.*; (*Eccles.*) *the Assumption*, l'Assomption (*de la Sainte Vierge*), *f.*

assurance [ə'ʃuərəns], *n.* assurance, *f.*

assure [ə'ʃuə], *v.t.* assurer.

assuredly [ə'ʃuəridli], *adv.* assurément, à coup sûr.

Assyria [ə'siriə], l'Assyrie, *f.*

Assyrian [ə'siriən], *a.* assyrien.—*n.* assyrien (*langue*); Assyrien (*personne*), *m.*

aster ['æstə], *n.* (*Bot., Biol.*) aster, *m.*

asterisk ['æstərisk], *n.* astérisque, *m.*

astern [ə'stə:n], *adv.* (*Naut.*) à l'arrière, sur l'arrière; *to go astern*, culer.

asteroid ['æstərɔid], *n.* astéroïde, *m.*

asthma ['æsθmə], *n.* asthme, *m.*

asthmatic [æsθ'mætik], *a.* asthmatique.

astigmatism [ə'stigmətizm], *n.* astigmatisme, *m.*

astir [ə'stə:], *a.* en mouvement, agité, en émoi; debout.

astonish [ə'stɔniʃ], *v.t.* étonner.

astonishing [ə'stɔniʃiŋ], *a.* étonnant.

astonishment [ə'stɔniʃmənt], *n.* étonnement, *m.*

astound [ə'staund], *v.t.* étonner, ébahir, étourdir.

astounding [ə'staundiŋ], *a.* renversant, abasourdissant.

astray [ə'strei], *adv.* égaré, (*fig.*) dévoyé; *to go astray*, s'égarer.

astride [ə'straid], *adv.* à califourchon; *astride upon*, à cheval sur.

astringent [ə'strindʒənt], *a.* and *n.* astringent, *m.*

astrologer [ə'strɔlədʒə], *n.* astrologue, *m.,f.*

astrology [ə'strɔlədʒi], *n.* astrologie, *f.*

astronaut ['æstrənɔ:t], *n.* astronaute, *m.,f.*

astronomer [ə'strɔnəmə], *n.* astronome, *m.,f.*

astronomic [æstrə'nɔmik], **astronomical** [æstrə'nɔmikəl], *a.* astronomique.

astronomy [ə'strɔnəmi], *n.* astronomie, *f.*

astute [ə'stju:t], *a.* fin, avisé; rusé, astucieux.

astuteness [ə'stju:tnis], *n.* astuce, sagacité, *f.*

asunder [ə'sʌndə], *adv.* en deux.

asylum [ə'sailəm], *n.* asile, refuge; hospice, *m.*

at [æt], *prep.* à, en, dans; après; *at first*, d'abord; *at hand*, sous la main; *at home*, chez soi; *at last*, enfin; *at least*, (*quantity*) au moins; (*fig.*) du moins; *at once*, tout de suite; à la fois; *at school*, à l'école; *at the same time*, en même temps; *at work*, à l'ouvrage.

atheism ['eiθiizm], *n.* athéisme, *m.*

atheist ['eiθiist], *n.* athée, *m., f.*

atheistic [eiθi'istik], *a.* athée, athéistique.

Athens ['æθənz]. Athènes, *f.*

athirst [ə'θə:st], *a.* altéré, assoiffé.

athlete ['æθli:t], *n.* athlète, *m., f.*

athletic [æθ'letik], *a.* athlétique.

athletics [æθ'letiks], *n. pl.* l'athlétisme, *m.*

Atlantic [ət'læntik], *a.* atlantique.—*n.* l'(Océan) Atlantique, *m.*

atlas ['ætləs], *n.* atlas, *m.*

atmosphere ['ætməsfiə], *n.* atmosphère, *f.*

atmospheric [ætməs'ferik], **atmospherical** [ætməs'ferikəl], *a.* atmosphérique.

atmospherics [ætməs'feriks], *n.pl.* (*Rad.*) parasites, *m.pl.*

atoll ['ætɔl], *n.* atoll, attoll, *m.*

atom ['ætəm], *n.* atome, *m.*; *atom bomb*, bombe atomique, *f.*

atomic [ə'tɔmik], *a.* atomique.

atomize ['ætəmaiz], *v.t.* pulvériser, vaporiser.

atomizer ['ætəmaizə], *n.* pulvérisateur, *m.*

atone [ə'toun], *v.t., v.i.* expier; racheter.

atonement [ə'tounmənt], *n.* expiation, *f.*

atop [ə'tɔp], *adv.* au sommet, en haut.

atrocious [ə'trouʃəs], *a.* atroce.

atrociously [ə'trouʃəsli], *adv.* atrocement.

atrocity [ə'trɔsiti], *n.* atrocité, *f.*

atrophy ['ætrəfi], *n.* atrophie, *f.*—*v.t.* atrophier.—*v.i.* s'atrophier.

attach [ə'tætʃ], *v.t.* attacher, lier (à).

attachable [ə'tætʃəbl], *a.* qu'on peut attacher.

attaché case [ə'tæʃikeis], *n.* mallette, *f.*

attachment [ə'tætʃmənt], *n.* attachement, *m.*

attack [ə'tæk], *v.t.* attaquer.—*n.* attaque, *m.*, accès, assaut, *m.*

attacker [ə'tækə], *n.* agresseur, *m.*

attain [ə'tein], *v.t.* atteindre, parvenir à.

attainable [ə'teinəbl], *a.* qu'on peut atteindre.

attainment [ə'teinmənt], *n.* acquisition, *f.*; talent, *m.*; (*pl.*) connaissances, *f.pl.*

attaint [ə'teint], *v.t.* accuser; condamner; flétrir, dégrader.

attempt [ə'tempt], *v.t.* tenter, essayer tâcher (*de*).—*n.* tentative, *f.*, essai, effort; attentat, *m.*

attend [ə'tend], *v.t.* s'occuper de; soigner (*un malade*); servir; assister (à).—*v.i.* faire attention, écouter; assister (à); servir; s'appliquer (à).

attendance [ə'tendəns], *n.* service, *m.*; assistance (à *une réunion*); présence; fréquentation (*scolaire*), *f.*; soins (*pour un malade*), *m.pl.*

attendant [ə'tendənt], *a.* qui suit.—*n.* assistant, aide; serviteur, *m.*

attention [ə'tenʃən], *n.* attention, *f.*; (*pl.*) soins, *m.pl.*

attentive [ə'tentiv], *a.* attentif (à), assidu (*auprès de*).

attentively [ə'tentivli], *adv.* attentivement.

attest [ə'test], *v.t.* attester.

attic ['ætik], *n.* mansarde, *f.*, grenier, *m.*

attire [ə'taiə], *v.t.* vêtir, parer.—*n.* vêtements *m.pl.*, costume, *m.*; parure, *f.*, atours, *m.pl.*

attitude ['ætitju:d], *n.* attitude, pose, *f.*

attorney [ə'tə:ni], *n.* (*Am.*) avoué; mandataire, *m.*; *power of attorney*, procuration, *f.*; [*see* prosecutor]

attorney general [ə'tə:ni'dʒenərəl], *n.* procureur-général, *m.*

attract [ə'trækt], *v.t.* attirer.

attraction [ə'trækʃən], *n.* attraction, *f.*; (*pl.*) attraits, appas, *m.pl.*

attractive [ə'træktiv], *a.* attrayant, séduisant; attractif (*de l'aimant etc.*).

attractiveness [ə'træktivnis], *n.* attrait, charme, *m.*

attributable [ə'tribjutəbl], *a.* attribuable.

attribute [ə'tribju:t], *v.t.* attribuer, imputer (à).—['ætribju:t], *n.* attribut, *m.*, qualité, *f.*

351

attrition [əˈtriʃən], *n.* attrition, *f.*; *war of attrition*, guerre d'usure, *f.*

attune [əˈtjuːn], *v.t.* accorder.

auburn [ˈɔːbən], *a.* châtain roux.

auction [ˈɔːkʃən], *n.* enchère, *f.*—*v.t.* vendre aux enchères.

auctioneer [ɔːkʃəˈniə], *n.* commissaire-priseur.

auction-room [ˈɔːkʃənruːm], *n.* salle des ventes, *f.*

audacious [ɔːˈdeiʃəs], *a.* audacieux.

audaciously [ɔːˈdeiʃəsli], *adv.* audacieusement.

audacity [ɔːˈdæsiti], *n.* audace, *f.*

audible [ˈɔːdibl], *a.* qu'on peut entendre, audible; distinct, intelligible.

audibly [ˈɔːdibli], *adv.* de manière à être entendu.

audience [ˈɔːdjəns], *n.* auditoire, *m.*, assistance, audience, *f.*

audio-visual [ˈɔːdjoˈvizjuəl], *a.* audio-visuel.

audit [ˈɔːdit], *v.t.* apurer, vérifier (*des comptes*).—*n.* apurement, *m.*, vérification de comptes, *f.*; *audit office*, cour des comptes, *f.*

audition [ɔːˈdiʃən], *n.* audition, *f.*—*v.t.* (*fam.*) auditionner.

auditor [ˈɔːditə], *n.* vérificateur; expert comptable, *m.*

auger [ˈɔːgə], *n.* tarière, *f.*

aught [ɔːt], *n.* quelque chose; quoi que ce soit, *m.*; *for aught I know*, pour autant que je sache.

augment [ɔːgˈment], *v.t.* augmenter, accroître.

augur [ˈɔːgə], *v.t.*, *v.i.* augurer, présager.—*n.* augure, *m.*

augury [ˈɔːgjuri], *n.* augure, *m.*

August [ˈɔːgəst], août, *m.*; *in August*, en août.

august [ɔːˈgast], *a.* auguste, imposant.

auk [ɔːk], *n.* (Orn.) pingouin, *m.*

aunt [ɑːnt], *n.* tante, *f.*

auntie [ˈɑːnti], *n.* (*colloq.*) tata, *f.*

aura [ˈɔːrə], *n.* exhalaison, *f.*; effluve, *m.*

aural [ˈɔːrəl], *a.* de l'oreille.

Aurora [ɔːˈrɔːrə], *n.* aurore, *f.*; *Aurora Borealis*, aurore boréale.

auspice [ˈɔːspis], *n.* (*usu. in pl.*) auspice, *m.*

auspicious [ɔːˈspiʃəs], *a.* de bon augure, propice.

auspiciously [ɔːˈspiʃəsli], *adv.* sous d'heureux auspices.

austere [ɔːsˈtiə], *a.* austère; âpre.

austerity [ɔːsˈteriti], *n.* austérité, *f.*

Australasia [ɔːstrəˈleiʃiə], l'Australasie, *f.*

Australia [ɔːsˈtreiliə], l'Australie, *f.*

Australian [ɔːsˈtreiliən], *a.* australien.—*n.* Australien (*personne*).

Austria [ˈɔːstriə], l'Autriche, *f.*

Austrian [ˈɔːstriən], *a.* autrichien.—*n.* Autrichien (*personne*), *m.*

authentic [ɔːˈθentik], *a.* authentique.

authentically [ɔːˈθentikli], *adv.* authentiquement.

authenticate [ɔːˈθentikeit], *v.t.* authentiquer, constater.

authenticated [ɔːˈθentikeitid], *a.* authentique, avéré.

authenticity [ɔːθenˈtisiti], *n.* authenticité, *f.*

author [ˈɔːθə], *n.* auteur, *m.*

authoress [ˈɔːθəris], *n.* femme auteur, femme écrivain, *f.*

authoritative [ɔːˈθɔritətiv], *a.* d'autorité; autorisé; autoritaire, impérieux.

authority [ɔːˈθɔriti], *n.* autorité; autorisation, *f.*, mandat, *m.*

authorization [ɔːθəraiˈzeiʃən], *n.* autorisation, *f.*

authorize [ˈɔːθəraiz], *v.t.* autoriser.

authorship [ˈɔːθəʃip], *n.* qualité d'auteur; (*colloq.*) paternité, *f.*

autobiographer [ɔːtəbaiˈɔgrəfə], *n.* autobiographe, *m.*, *f.*

autobiography [ɔːtəbaiˈɔgrəfi], *n.* autobiographie, *f.*

autocracy [ɔːˈtɔkrəsi], *n.* autocratie, *f.*

autocrat [ˈɔːtəkræt], *n.* autocrate, *m.*, *f.*

auto-cycle [ˈɔːtosaikl], *n.* cyclomoteur, *m.*

autograph [ˈɔːtəgrɑːf], *n.* autographe, *m.*—*v.t.* signer, autographier.

autogyro [ɔːtoˈdʒairou], *n.* autogyre, *m.*

automatic [ɔːtəˈmætik], *a.* automatique.

automatically [ɔːtəˈmætikli], *adv.* automatiquement; machinalement.

automation [ɔːtəˈmeiʃən], *n.* automation, *f.*

automaton [ɔːˈtɔmətən], *n.* (*pl.* **automata** [ɔːˈtɔmətə]) automate, *m.*

automobile [ˈɔːtəməbiːl], *n.* (*Am.*) automobile, auto, voiture, *f.*

autonomous [ɔːˈtɔnəməs], *a.* autonome.

autonomy [ɔːˈtɔnəmi], *n.* autonomie, *f.*

autopsy [ˈɔːtɔpsi, ɔːˈtɔpsi], *n.* autopsie, *f.*

autumn [ˈɔːtəm], *n.* automne, *m.* ou *f.*

autumnal [ɔːˈtamnəl], *a.* automnal, d'automne.

auxiliary [ɔːgˈziljəri], *a.* and *n.* auxiliaire, *m.*

avail [əˈveil], *v.t.*, *v.i.* profiter, servir; *to avail oneself of*, se servir de.—*n.* service, avantage, *m.*, utilité, *f.*; *of what avail is it?* à quoi bon?

available [əˈveiləbl], *a.* disponible; valable.

avalanche [ˈævəlɑːnʃ], *n.* avalanche, *f.*

avarice [ˈævəris], *n.* avarice, *f.*

avaricious [ævəˈriʃəs], *a.* avare, avaricieux.

avenge [əˈvendʒ], *v.t.* venger; *to avenge oneself*, se venger (*de* ou *sur*).

avenger [əˈvendʒə], *n.* vengeur, *m.*

avenging [əˈvendʒiŋ], *a.* vengeur.—*n.* vengeance, *f.*

avenue [ˈævənjuː], *n.* avenue, *f.*

aver [əˈvəː], *v.t.* affirmer.

average [ˈævəridʒ], *a.* commun, moyen.—*n.* moyenne, *f.*, prix moyen, terme moyen, *m.*; (*Naut.*) avarie, *f.*; *on an average*, en moyenne.—*v.t.* établir la moyenne de; atteindre une moyenne de.

averse [əˈvəːs], *a.* opposé (*à*), ennemi (*de*).

aversely [əˈvəːsli], *adv.* à contre-cœur.

aversion [əˈvəːʃən], *n.* répugnance, aversion, *f.*; *it is his pet aversion*, c'est sa bête noire.

avert [əˈvəːt], *v.t.* détourner, écarter.

aviary [ˈeiviəri], *n.* volière, *f.*

aviation [eiviˈeiʃən], *n.* aviation, *f.*

aviator [ˈeivieitə], *n.* aviateur, *m.*

avid [ˈævid], *a.* avide.

avidly [ˈævidli], *adv.* avec avidité, avidement.

avoid [əˈvoid], *v.t.* éviter.

avoidable [əˈvoidəbl], *a.* évitable.

avoidance [əˈvoidəns], *n.* action d'éviter, *f.*

avoirdupois [ævədəˈpoiz], *n.* poids du commerce, *m.*

avow [əˈvau], *v.t.* avouer, confesser, déclarer.

avowal [ə'vauəl], *n.* aveu, *m.*

avowedly [ə'vauidli], *adv.* de son propre aveu.

await [ə'weit], *v.t.* attendre.

awake [ə'weik], *v.t. irr.* éveiller, réveiller.—*v.i.* s'éveiller, se réveiller.—*a.* éveillé; attentif.

awaken [ə'weikən], *v.t.* éveiller, réveiller.

awakening [ə'weikniŋ], *n.* réveil, *m.*

award [ə'wɔːd], *v.t.* décerner, adjuger.—*n.* décision, *f.*; jugement, *m.*, sentence; (*Sch.*) récompense, *f.*

aware [ə'wɛə], *a.* qui sait; instruit; *to be aware of*, savoir, avoir connaissance de; *not to be aware of*, ignorer.

awareness [ə'wɛənis], *n.* conscience, *f.*

away [ə'wei], *adv.* absent; loin, au loin; *away with you!* allez-vous en! *far away*, au loin; *right away*, immédiatement.

awe [ɔː], *n.* crainte, terreur, *f.*, respect, *m.*

awe-inspiring [ɔː'inspaiəriŋ], *a.* terrifiant.

awestruck ['ɔːstrʌk], *a.* frappé de terreur.

awful ['ɔːful], *a.* terrible, redoutable, effroyable; solennel; *what awful weather!* quel temps affreux!

awfully ['ɔːfuli], *adv.* horriblement, terriblement; (*fam.*) diablement.

awhile [ə'wail], *adv.* un instant, un peu.

awkward ['ɔːkwəd], *a.* gauche, maladroit; embarrassant.

awkwardly ['ɔːkwədli], *adv.* gauchement, maladroitement.

awkwardness ['ɔːkwədnis], *n.* gaucherie, maladresse, *f.*

awl [ɔːl], *n.* alène, *f.*; poinçon, *m.*

awning ['ɔːniŋ], *n.* tente, banne, bâche, *f.*

awry [ə'rai], *a.* and *adv.* de travers.

axe [æks], *n.* hache, cognée, *f.*

axiom ['æksiəm], *n.* axiome, *m.*

axiomatic [æksiə'mætik], *a.* axiomatique.

axis ['æksis], *n.* (*pl.* **axes** ['æksiːz]) axe, *m.*

axle [æksl], *n.* arbre, essieu, *m.*; (*Motor.*) *rear axle*, pont arrière, *m.*

ay, aye [ai], *adv.* oui, c'est vrai; *aye, aye!* (*Naut.*) bon quart!—*n.* **ayes and noes**, voix pour et contre, *f.pl.*

azalea [ə'zeiliə], *n.* (*Bot.*) azalée, *f.*

Azores [ə'zɔːz], the. les Açores, *f.pl.*

azote [ə'zout], *n.* (*Chem.*) azote, *m.*

azure ['æʒuə, 'eiʒə], *a.* d'azur.—*n.* azur, *m.*

B

B, b [biː]. deuxième lettre de l'alphabet; (*Mus.*) si, *m.*

baa [baː], *v.i.* bêler.—*n.* bêlement, *m.*

babble [bæbl], *v.i.* babiller; gazouiller, jaser; (*fig.*) murmurer (*ruisseau*).—*n.* babil, caquet; (*fig.*) murmure, *m.*, jaserie, *f.*

babbler ['bæblə], *n.* babillard, *m.*

babbling ['bæbliŋ], *a.* babillard, bavard.

babe [beib], *n.* enfant nouveau-né, petit enfant, *m.*

Babel ['beibəl]. Babel, *f.*

baboon [bə'buːn], *n.* babouin, *m.*

baby ['beibi], *n.* bébé, *m.*; *baby grand (piano)*, piano à demi-queue, *m.*; *baby linen*, layette, *f.* [**carriage, see pram**]

babyhood ['beibihud], *n.* première enfance, *f.*

babyish ['beibiiʃ], *a.* enfantin.

bacchanalia [bækə'neiliə], *n.pl.* bacchanales, *f.pl.*

bacchanalian [bækə'neiliən], *a.* bachique.—*n.* ivrogne, *m.*

bachelor ['bætʃələ], *n.* célibataire, vieux garçon; bachelier (*ès lettres*), *m.*

back [bæk], *n.* arrière, de derrière; *a back street*, une petite rue.—*n.* dos, *m.*, reins, *m.pl.*; envers (*d'un tissu*); verso (*d'une page etc.*); fond (*d'une salle etc.*); (*Ftb.*) arrière; revers (*d'une colline etc.*); derrière (*d'une maison etc.*); dossier (*d'une chaise*), *m.*; *at the back of*, derrière; *back to back*, dos à dos; *on the back of (a letter etc.)*, au verso.—*adv.* en arrière; de retour, rentré; *a few years back*, il y a quelques années; *to be back*, être de retour; *to call back*, rappeler; *to come back*, revenir.—*v.t.* soutenir; (*Betting*) jouer (*un cheval*); faire reculer.—*v.i.* reculer.

backbite ['bækbait], *v.t.* médire de, calomnier.

backbiting ['bækbaitiŋ], *n.* médisance, *f.*

backbone ['bækboun], *n.* épine dorsale, *f.*

back door ['bæk'dɔː], *n.* porte de derrière, *f.*

backer ['bækə], *n.* partisan, second; parieur pour, *m.*

back-fire [bæk'faiə], *v.i.* (*Motor.*) pétarader.

backgammon [bæk'gæmən], *n.* trictrac, *m.*

back garden ['bæk'gɑːdn], *n.* jardin de derrière, *m.*

background ['bækgraund], *n.* arrière-plan, fond, *m.*

back room ['bæk'ruːm], *n.* chambre de derrière, *f.*

backside ['bæk'said], *n.* (*pop.*) derrière, *m.*

backslide ['bæk'slaid], *v.i.* retomber dans le vice ou le péché.

backstage ['bæk'steidʒ], *adv.* derrière la scène; dans les coulisses.

backstairs ['bæk'stɛəz], *n.* escalier de service, *m.*

backward ['bækwəd], *a.* arriéré; en retard; en arrière; lent, tardif.

backward(s) ['bækwəd(z)], *adv.* à reculons; en arrière; à la renverse.

backwoodsman ['bækwudzmən], *n.* (*pl.* **-men** [men]) défricheur de forêts, *m.*

back-yard ['bæk'jɑːd], *n.* cour de derrière, *f.*

bacon ['beikən], *n.* lard, *m.*

bacterium [bæk'tiəriəm], *n.* (*pl.* **bacteria** [bæk'tiəriə]) bactérie, *f.*

bad [bæd], *a.* mauvais; méchant (*enfant etc.*); gâté (*aliment etc.*); malade; *that is too bad*, c'est trop fort.

badge [bædʒ], *n.* insigne, *m.*; plaque, *f.*; (*Mil.*) écusson; brassard, *m.*

badger ['bædʒə], *n.* blaireau, *m.*—*v.t.* harceler.

badly ['bædli], *adv.* mal; grièvement, fort, beaucoup.

badness ['bædnis], *n.* méchanceté, *f.*; mauvais état, *m.*

baffle [bæfl], *v.t.* déjouer; confondre.

353

bag

bag [bæg], *n.* sac; cornet (*papier*), *m.*; **game bag**, gibecière, *f.*; **with bag and baggage**, avec armes et bagages.—*v.t.* mettre en sac; abattre (*du gibier*); (*colloq.*) s'emparer de; (*slang*) chiper.—*v.i.* bouffer (*pantalon*).

baggage ['bægidʒ], *n.* (*chiefly Am.*) bagages, *m.pl.*

bagpipes ['bægpaips], *n. pl.* cornemuse, *f.*

bail (1) [beil], *n.* caution, *f.*; **on bail**, sous caution.

bail (2) [beil], *v.t.* vider l'eau d' (*un bateau*), écoper.—*v.i.* **to bail out**, (*Av.*) sauter en parachute.

bailiff ['beilif], *n.* huissier, *m.*; **farm bailiff**, régisseur, *m.*

bait [beit], *v.t.* amorcer (*un hameçon*); (*fig.*) harceler, tourmenter.—*n.* amorce, *f.*; appât, leurre, *m.*

baize [beiz], *n.* serge, *f.*; **green baize**, tapis vert, *m.*

bake [beik], *v.t., v.i.* cuire au four.

bakehouse ['beikhaus], *n.* fournil, *m.*, boulangerie, *f.*

Bakelite ['beikəlait], *n.* bakélite (*reg. trade mark*), *f.*

baker ['beikə], *n.* boulanger, *m.*

bakery ['beikəri], *n.* boulangerie, *f.*

baking ['beikiŋ], *n.* cuisson; fournée, *f.*

balance ['bæləns], *n.* balance, *f.*; équilibre; balancier (*d'une pendule*), *m.*—*v.t.* équilibrer, balancer; **to balance up**, arrêter.

balance-sheet ['bælənsʃi:t], *n.* bilan, *m.*

balance-weight ['bælənsweit], *n.* contre-poids, *m.*

balcony ['bælkəni], *n.* balcon, *m.*

bald [bɔ:ld], *a.* chauve; (*fig.*) plat, sec (*style*).

baldly ['bɔ:ldli], *adv.* pauvrement, platement, sèchement.

baldness ['bɔ:ldnis], *n.* calvitie; (*fig.*) platitude, *f.*

bale (2) [beil], *n.* balle, *f.*, ballot, *m.*—*v.t.* emballer.

baleful ['beilful], *a.* sinistre, funeste.

balefully ['beilfuli], *adv.* d'une manière funeste.

balk, baulk [bɔ:k], *n.* poutre, bille; (*Billiards*) ligne de départ, *f.*—*v.t.* frustrer, contrarier, déjouer.

Balkan ['bɔ:lkən], *a.* balkanique.

Balkans ['bɔ:lkənz], **the.** les Balkans, les États Balkaniques, *m.pl.*

ball (1) [bɔ:l], *n.* balle; boule (*de neige*); pelote, *f.*, peloton (*de laine, de ficelle*); boulet (*de canon*), *m.*; (*Billiards*) bille (*Cook.*) boulette, *f.*; ballon (*plein d'air*), *m.*; prunelle (*d'œil*), *f.*; **ball-point pen**, stylo à bille, *m.*

ball (2) [bɔ:l], *n.* bal, *m.*; **fancy-dress ball**, bal masqué.

ballad ['bæləd], *n.* (*Mus.*) romance; ballade, *f.*

ballast ['bæləst], *n.* lest, (*Rail.*) ballast, *m.*; **in ballast**, sur lest.—*v.t.* lester; (*Rail.*) ensabler.

ballerina [bælə'ri:nə], *n.* ballerine, *f.*

ballet ['bælei], *n.* ballet, *m.*

balloon [bə'lu:n], *n.* ballon, aérostat, *m.*—*v.i.* se ballonner.

ballot ['bælət], *n.* boule, *f.*; bulletin, scrutin, *m.*; **by ballot**, au scrutin.—*v.i.* voter au scrutin.

ballot box ['bælətbɒks], *n.* urne électorale, *f.*

ballot (paper) ['bælətpeipə], *n.* bulletin de vote, *m.*

balm [ba:m], *n.* baume, *m.*; mélisse, *f.*—*v.t.* parfumer.

balmy ['ba:mi], *a.* embaumé, parfumé.

balsam ['bɔ:lsəm], *n.* baume, *m.*

Baltic ['bɔ:ltik], **the.** la Baltique, *f.*

balustrade [bæləs'treid], *n.* balustrade, *f.*

bamboo [bæm'bu:], *n.* bambou, *m.*

bamboozle [bæm'bu:zl], *v.t.* (*colloq.*) tromper, duper, enjôler.

ban [bæn], *n.* ban, *m.*; interdiction, *f.*; (*Eccles.*) interdit, *m.*—*v.t.* interdire, proscrire.

banal [bə'næl, 'beinəl], *a.* banal.

banality [bə'næliti], *n.* banalité, *f.*

banana [bə'nɑ:nə], *n.* banane, *f.*

banana tree [bə'nɑ:nətri:], *n.* bananier, *m.*

band (1) [bænd], *n.* bande, *f.*, lien; ruban, *m.*; raie, *f.*—*v.t.* bander.

band (2) [bænd], *n.* bande, troupe; (*Mil.*) musique, *f.*; orchestre, *m.*; **brass band**, fanfare, *f.*—*v.t.* liguer, réunir en troupe.—*v.i.* se liguer.

bandage ['bændidʒ], *n.* bandeau; (*Surg.*) bandage, pansement, *m.*

bandbox ['bændbɒks], *n.* carton (*de modiste*), *m.*

bandit ['bændit], *n.* bandit, *m.*

bandmaster ['bændma:stə], *n.* chef de musique, *m.*

bandoleer, bandolier [bændə'liə], *n.* bandoulière, *f.*

bandsman ['bændzmən], *n.* (*pl.* **-men** [men]) musicien, *m.*

bandstand ['bændstænd], *n.* kiosque à musique, *m.*

bandy ['bændi], *v.t.* renvoyer; échanger; se renvoyer; **to bandy words**, se renvoyer des paroles.—*v.i.* se disputer.

bandy-legged ['bændilegd], *a.* bancal.

bane [bein], *n.* poison; (*fig.*) fléau, *m.*

baneful ['beinful], *a.* pernicieux, funeste, nuisible.

bang [bæŋ], *n.* coup, grand bruit, *m.*, détonation, *f.*—*v.t.* frapper violemment, taper; **to bang a door**, claquer une porte.—*int.* pan! paf! boum!

bangle ['bæŋgl], *n.* porte-bonheur, bracelet, *m.*

banish ['bæniʃ], *v.t.* bannir, exiler.

banishment ['bæniʃmənt], *n.* bannissement, exil, *m.*

bank (1) [bæŋk], *n.* rivage, bord, *m.*; berge, rive, terrasse, *f.*, remblai, talus; banc (*de sable, de gazon etc.*), *m.*; digue, *f.*; carreau (*de mine*), *m.*—*v.t.* terrasser, remblayer.

bank (2) [bæŋk], *n.* (*Comm.*) banque, *f.*; **savings bank**, caisse d'épargne, *f.*—*v.t.* encaisser (*de l'argent*).

banker ['bæŋkə], *n.* banquier, *m.*

banking ['bæŋkiŋ], *n.* banque, *f.*

bank note ['bæŋknout], *n.* billet de banque, *m.*

bankrupt ['bæŋkrʌpt], *a.* failli, en faillite; (*fig.*) ruiné.—*v.t.* mettre en faillite, ruiner.—*n.* banqueroutier, failli, *m.*; **to go bankrupt**, faire faillite.

bankruptcy ['bæŋkrʌptsi], *n.* banqueroute, faillite, *f.*

banner ['bænə], *n.* bannière, *f.*

bannock ['bænək], *n.* (*grosse*) galette d'avoine, *f.*

banns [bænz], *n.pl.* **banns of marriage**, bans de mariage, *m.pl.*

banquet ['bæŋkwit], *n.* banquet; *festin, *m.*

banter ['bæntə], *v.t.* railler, badiner.—*n.* badinage, *m.*, raillerie, *f.*

baptism ['bæptizm], *n.* baptême, *m.*

baptismal [bæp'tizməl], *a.* baptismal.

baptist ['bæptist], *n.* baptiste, *m.*, *f.*

baptize [bæp'taiz], *v.t.* baptiser.

bar (1) [ba:], *n.* barre, *f.*; (*Law etc.*) barreau, parquet, *m.*; (*fig.*) barrière; buvette, *f.*, comptoir, bar (*de café, hôtel etc.*); (*Law*) banc des accusés, *m.*; (*Mus.*) mesure; tablette (*de chocolat*), *f.*; *to be admitted to the bar,* être reçu avocat.—*v.t.* barrer, empêcher; exclure.

bar (2) [BARRING].

barb [ba:b], *n.* barbillon, dardillon (*hameçon*), *m.*; pointe (*flèche*); barbe, arête (*blé*), *f.*

Barbados [ba:'beidos]. la Barbade, *f.*

barbarian [ba:'bɛəriən], *a.* and *n.* barbare, *m.*, *f.*

barbaric [ba:'bærik], *a.* barbare.

barbarism ['ba:bərizm], *n.* barbarie, *f.*; (*Gram.*) barbarisme, *m.*

barbarity [ba:'bæriti], *n.* barbarie, cruauté, *f.*

barbarous ['ba:bərəs], *a.* barbare.

barbecue ['ba:bəkju:], *n.* grand gril; grand pique-nique (en plein air), *m.*—*v.t.* rôtir à la broche.

barbed [ba:bd], *a.* barbelé; (*fig.*) acéré; *barbed wire,* fil de fer barbelé, *m.*

barbel ['ba:bəl], *n.* (*Ichth.*) barbeau, *m.*

barber ['ba:bə], *n.* coiffeur, *m.*

Barcelona [ba:sə'lounə]. Barcelone, *f.*

bard [ba:d], *n.* barde, trouvère, *m.*

bare [bɛə], *a.* nu, découvert; (*fig.*) seul, simple; pauvre.—*v.t.* découvrir, dépouiller; mettre à nu.

bareback ['bɛəbæk], *adv.* à dos nu.

barefaced ['bɛəfeist], *a.* à visage découvert; éhonté, sans déguisement.

barefoot ['bɛəfut], *a.* nu-pieds, les pieds nus.

bareheaded ['bɛə'hedid], *a.* nu-tête, la tête nue.

barely ['bɛəli], *adv.* à peine; tout juste, simplement, seulement; pauvrement.

bareness ['bɛənis], *n.* nudité; misère, *f.*

bargain ['ba:gin], *n.* marché, *m.*, affaire; occasion, *f.*; *into the bargain,* par-dessus le marché; *it is a bargain,* c'est convenu; *to strike a bargain,* conclure un marché. —*v.i.* marchander, faire marché.

barge [ba:dʒ], *n.* chaland, *m.*; péniche, *f.*— *v.i. to barge into,* se heurter contre, bousculer.

bargee [ba:'dʒi:], **bargeman** ['ba:dʒmən] (*pl.* -**men** [men]), *n.* batelier, *m.*

baritone ['bæritoun], *a.* de baryton.—*n.* baryton, *m.*

bark (1) [ba:k], *n.* écorce, *f.*; tan, *m.*

bark (2) [ba:k], *n.* aboiement, *m.*—*v.i.* aboyer.

bark (3), **barque** [ba:k], *n.* trois-mâts, *m.*

barking ['ba:kiŋ], *n.* aboiement, *m.*

barley ['ba:li], *n.* orge, *f.*

barmaid ['ba:meid], *n.* barmaid, *f.*

barman ['ba:mən], *n.* (*pl.* -**men** [men]) barman, *m.*

barmy ['ba:mi], *a.* (*colloq.*) fou, toqué.

barn [ba:n], *n.* grange; (*Am.*) étable, *f.*

barnacle ['ba:nəkl], *n.* barnache (*oie*), *f.*; balane, anatife (*crustacé*), *m.*

barometer [bə'rɔmitə], *n.* baromètre, *m.*

barometric [bærə'metrik], *a.* barométrique.

baron ['bærən], *n.* baron, *m.*; *baron of beef,* double aloyau, *m.*

baroness ['bærənis], *n.* baronne, *f.*

baronet ['bærənet], *n.* baronnet, *m.*

baronial [bə'rouniəl], *a.* baronnial, seigneurial.

barony ['bærəni], *n.* baronnie, *f.*

barouche [bə'ru:ʃ], *n.* calèche, *f.*

barque [BARK (3)].

barrack ['bærək], *n.* (*usu. in pl.*) caserne, *f.*; quartier (*pour la cavalerie*), *m.*

barrage ['bærid3, 'bæra:3], *n.* barrage, *m.*

barrel ['bærəl], *n.* baril, *m.*; gonne, caque (*de poissons etc.*), *f.*; corps (*de pompe*); cylindre, tambour (*de machine*); canon (*de fusil*), *m.* —*v.t.* embariller, entonner, mettre en baril, encaquer.

barrel organ ['bærələ:gən], *n.* orgue de Barbarie, *m.*

barren ['bærən], *a.* stérile; infertile (*terre*).

barrenness ['bærənnis], *n.* stérilité, *f.*

barricade [bæri'keid], *n.* barricade, *f.*—*v.t.* barricader.

barrier ['bæriə], *n.* barrière, *f.*

barring ['ba:riŋ], **bar** (2) [ba:], *prep.* excepté, hormis, sauf.

barrister ['bæristə], *n.* avocat, *m.*

barrow ['bærou], *n.* brouette, *f.*

barrow-boy ['bæroubɔi], *n.* (*fam.*) marchand des quatre saisons, *m.*

barter ['ba:tə], *n.* échange, troc; trafic, *m.*— *v.t.* troquer, échanger.—*v.i.* échanger, faire échange.

basalt [bə'sɔ:lt], *n.* basalte, *m.*

base (1) [beis], *a.* bas, vil, indigne, méprisable; illégitime (*enfant*); de mauvais aloi; non précieux, faux (*monnaie*).

base (2) [beis], *n.* base, *f.*, fondement; fond, *m.*—*v.t.* fonder (*sur*); asseoir (*l'impôt*).

baseball ['beisbɔ:l], *n.* (*Spt.*) base-ball, *m.*

baseless ['beislis], *a.* sans fondement.

basely ['beisli], *adv.* bassement, lâchement.

basement ['beismənt], *n.* sous-sol, *m.*

baseness ['beisnis], *n.* bassesse, lâcheté, *f.*

bashful ['bæʃful], *a.* timide, intimidé.

bashfully ['bæʃfuli], *adv.* timidement, en rougissant.

bashfulness ['bæʃfulnis], *n.* timidité, fausse honte, *f.*

basic ['beisik], *a.* (*Chem.*) basique; de base.

basilica [bə'zilikə], *n.* basilique, *f.*

basilisk ['bæzilisk], *n.* basilic, *m.*

basin ['beisən], *n.* bassin; bol, *m.*; cuvette, *f.*

basis ['beisis], *n.* (*pl.* **bases** ['beisi:z]) base, *f.*, fondement, *m.*

bask [ba:sk], *v.i.* se chauffer.

basket ['ba:skit], *n.* panier, *m.*, corbeille, *f.*

basketball ['ba:skitbɔ:l], *n.* (*Spt.*) basket-ball, (*fam.*) basket, *m.*

Basle [ba:l]. Bâle, *f.*

bas-relief [ba:rə'li:f], *n.* bas-relief, *m.*

bass (1) [beis], *n.* (*Mus.*) basse; basse-taille, *f.*; *double bass,* contre-basse, *f.*

bass (2) [bæs], *n.* (*Ichth.*) bar, *m.*; perche, *f.*

bassinet [bæsi'net], *n.* bercelonnette, *f.*, moïse, *m.*

bassoon [bə'su:n], *n.* basson, *m.*

bastard ['bæstəd], *a.* bâtard; (*fig.*) faux.—*n.* bâtard, *m.*, bâtarde, *f.*; (*pop.*) salaud, *m.*

baste [beist], *v.t.* arroser (*viande*); (*fig.*) bâtonner; (*Needlework*) bâtir.

355

bastion ['bæstiən], *n.* bastion, *m.*
bat (1) [bæt], *n.* (*Cricket*) batte, *f.*; *off his own bat*, de sa propre initiative.—*v.i.* être au guichet.
bat (2) [bæt], *n.* (*Zool.*) chauve-souris, *f.*
Batavian [bə'teiviən], *a.* batave.—*n.* Batave (*personne*), *m.*, *f.*
batch [bætʃ], *n.* fournée (*pain*); (*fig.*) troupe, bande, *f.*; tas; lot, *m.*
bate [beit], *v.t.* rabattre, rabaisser.
bath [bɑːθ], *n.* bain, *m.*; baignoire, *f.*; *shower bath*, douche, *f.*—*v.t.* donner un bain à, baigner.—*v.i.* prendre un bain.
bathe [beið], *v.t.* baigner; tremper, mouiller.—*v.i.* se baigner.—*n.* baignade, *f.*
bather ['beiðə], *n.* baigneur, *m.*, baigneuse, *f.*
bathing ['beiðiŋ], *n.* baignade, *f.*; bains, *m.pl.*
bathing suit ['beiðiŋsjuːt], *n.* costume de bain, maillot, *m.*
bathos ['beiθɔs], *n.* pathos, *m.*, enflure, *f.*
bathroom ['bɑːθrum], *n.* salle de bain(s), *f.*
batman ['bætmən], *n.* (*pl.* **-men** [men]) ordonnance, brosseur, *m.*
baton ['bætən], *n.* bâton, *m.*; baguette, *f.*
batsman ['bætsmən], *n.* (*Cricket*) batteur, *m.*
battalion [bə'tæliən], *n.* bataillon, *m.*
batten ['bætən], *n.* volige, latte, *f.*—*v.t.* fermer; (*Carp.*) voliger.—*v.i.* s'engraisser.
batter ['bætə], *v.t.* battre en brèche; battre; délabrer, ébranler, démolir.—*n.* pâte, *f.*
battered ['bætəd], *a.* délabré.
battering-ram ['bætəriŋræm], *n.* bélier, *m.*
battery ['bætəri], *n.* batterie (*Elec.*) pile, batterie, *f.*, accumulateur, *m.*; action de battre en brèche, *f.*; (*Law*) voies de fait, *f.pl.*
battle [bætl], *n.* bataille, *f.*, combat, *m.*; *pitched battle*, bataille rangée; *to give battle*, livrer bataille.—*v.i.* lutter, combattre; (*colloq.*) batailler.
battle-axe ['bætlæks], *n.* hache d'armes, *f.*
battledore ['bætldɔː], *n.* raquette, *f.*
battle dress ['bætldres], *n.* tenue de campagne, *f.*
battle-field ['bætlfiːld], *n.* champ de bataille, *m.*
battlement ['bætlmənt], *n.* créneau, *m.*
battleship ['bætlʃip], *n.* cuirassé, *m.*
bauble [bɔːbl], *n.* babiole, fanfreluche, *f.*; *fool's bauble*, marotte, *f.*
baulk [BALK].
bauxite ['bɔːksait, 'bouzait], *n.* bauxite, *f.*
Bavaria [bə'veəriə], la Bavière, *f.*
Bavarian [bə'veəriən], *a.* bavarois.—*n.* Bavarois (*personne*).
bawdy ['bɔːdi], *a.* obscène, paillard.
bawl [bɔːl], *v.i.* crier, brailler.
bay (1) [bei], *a.* bai (*cheval*).
bay (2) [bei], *n.* baie, *f.*, golfe *m.*; (*Arch.*) baie, *f.*
bay (3) [bei], *n.* (*Bot.*) baie, *f.*; laurier, *m.*
bay (4) [bei], *n.* abois, *m.pl.*; *at bay*, aux abois.—*v.i.* aboyer.
bayonet ['beiənit], *n.* baïonnette, *f.*—*v.t.* tuer *ou* percer à coups de baïonnette.
bay window ['beiwindou], *n.* fenêtre en saillie *ou* à baie, *f.*
bazaar [bə'zɑː], *n.* bazar, *m.*; vente de charité, *f.*
bazooka [bə'zuːkə], *n.* bazooka, *m.*
be [biː], *v.i.* irr. être; exister; subsister; y

avoir, se trouver; avoir; faire; devoir, falloir; *be it so*, soit; *be that as it may*, quoi qu'il en soit; *how is it that . . .?* comment se fait-il que . . .? *I was to*, je devais; *to be better*, valoir mieux; se porter mieux; *to be mistaken*, se tromper; *to be right*, avoir raison.
beach [biːtʃ], *n.* plage, grève, *f.*, rivage, *m.*—*v.t.* échouer.
beacon ['biːkən], *n.* phare, fanal, *m.*; balise, *f.*—*v.t.* baliser, éclairer.
bead [biːd], *n.* grain (*de chapelet, de bracelet, de collier*), globule, *m.*; (*pl.*) chapelet, collier, chapelet, *m.*; *to tell one's beads*, égrener son chapelet.
beadle [biːdl], *n.* bedeau; appariteur, *m.*
beagle [biːgl], *n.* chien briquet, bigle, *m.*
beak [biːk], *n.* bec, *m.*; bigorne (*enclume*), *f.*; (*Naut.*) éperon, *m.*
beaker ['biːkə], *n.* gobelet, *m.*, coupe, *f.*
beakful ['biːkful], *n.* becquée, *f.*
beam [biːm], *n.* poutre, *f.*; timon (*charrue, voiture etc.*); rayon (*lumière*); large sourire (*de joie etc.*), *m.*—*v.t.* lancer, darder (*des rayons*).—*v.i.* rayonner.
beaming ['biːmiŋ], *a.* rayonnant, radieux.—*n.* rayonnement, *m.*
bean [biːn], *n.* fève, *f.*; haricot; grain (*de café*), *m.*; *French beans*, haricots verts; *kidney beans*, haricots, soissons.
bear (1) [beə], *n.* ours; (*St. Exch.*) joueur à la baisse, baissier, *m.*; *polar bear*, ours blanc.
bear (2) [beə], *v.t. irr.* porter, soutenir; endurer, supporter, souffrir, subir; avoir, produire (*fruits etc.*); enfanter; donner naissance à; y tenir; remporter.—*v.i.* endurer, souffrir; porter, peser; avoir rapport (à); appuyer; porter (*sur*); rapporter.
bearable ['beərəbl], *a.* supportable.
beard [biəd], *n.* barbe, *f.*—*v.t.* braver, défier.
bearded ['biədid], *a.* barbu.
beardless ['biədlis], *a.* imberbe.
bearer ['beərə], *n.* porteur; (*Arch.*) support, *m.*
bearing ['beəriŋ], *n.* rapport; maintien, port, *m.*, conduite, relation, *f.*, aspect, *m.*, portée; face, *f.*; (*Arch.*) support; (*Mech.*) coussinet, *m.*; *ball bearings*, roulement à billes, *m.*; *to take one's bearings*, s'orienter.
bearskin ['beəskin], *n.* (*Mil.*) bonnet d'oursin, *m.*
beast [biːst], *n.* bête, *f.*; (*fig.*) animal, cochon, *m.*
beastliness ['biːstlinis], *n.* saleté, saloperie, *f.*
beastly ['biːstli], *a.* bestial; sale, malpropre, dégoûtant.
beat [biːt], *v.t. irr.* battre; frapper; piler, broyer; l'emporter sur; fouetter (*pluie, neige etc.*); se frapper (*la poitrine etc.*); *beat it!* fiche-moi le camp! *that beats all*, cela dépasse tout; *to beat a retreat*, battre en retraite.—*v.i.* battre; être agité.—*n.* coup, battement; son; itinéraire, *m.*; ronde (*d'un agent de police*), *f.*, parcours (*facteurs etc.*), *m.*; (*Hunt.*) battue; (*Mus.*) mesure, *f.*, temps, *m.*; *beat of the drum*, batterie de tambour, *f.* [see **whisk**]
beaten [biːtn], *a.* battu.
beater ['biːtə], *n.* batteur; (*Spt.*) rabatteur, *m.*; batte (*instrument*), *f.* [see **whisk**]
beating ['biːtiŋ], *n.* battement, *m.*; rossée, *f.*; coups, *m.pl.*; batterie, *f.*; roulement (*tambour etc.*), *m.*

beau [bou], *n.* (*pl.* **beaux** [bouz]) petit-maître; prétendant (*amant*), *m.*
beauteous ['bju:tiəs], *a.* (*Poet.*) beau.
beauteously ['bju:tiəsli], *adv.* avec beauté.
beautiful ['bju:tiful], *a.* très beau; (*colloq.*) magnifique.
beautifully ['bju:tifuli], *adv.* admirablement.
beautify ['bju:tifai], *v.t.* embellir, orner.—*v.i.* s'embellir.
beauty ['bju:ti], *n.* beauté (*personne et qualité*), *f.*
beauty spot ['bju:tispɔt], *n.* mouche, *f.*, grain de beauté; site pittoresque, *m.*
beaver ['bi:və], *n.* castor; chapeau de castor, *m.*
becalm [bi'kɑ:m], *v.t.* apaiser, calmer; abriter (*navire*).
because [bi'kɔz], *conj.* parce que; *because of*, à cause de.
beck (1) [bek], *n.* signe (*du doigt etc.*), *m.*—*v.i.* faire signe (*du doigt etc.*).
beck (2) [bek], *n.* ruisseau, *m.*
beckon ['bekən], *v.t.* faire signe à, appeler.—*v.i.* faire signe (à).
become [bi'kʌm], *v.t. irr.* (*conjug. like* COME) aller bien à, convenir à, être propre à.—*v.i.* devenir, commencer à être.
becoming [bi'kʌmiŋ], *a.* bienséant, convenable, qui va bien, attrayant.
becomingly [bi'kʌmiŋli], *adv.* avec bienséance.
bed [bed], *n.* lit, *m.*; couche; (*Geol.*) assise, *f.*; encaissement (*rue*); parterre, *m.*, plate-bande (*fleurs*), *f.*; carré, *m.*—*v.t.* coucher, mettre au lit; loger, fixer, enfoncer; parquer (*huîtres*).—*v.i.* coucher, se coucher.
bedaub [bi'dɔ:b], *v.t.* barbouiller.
bedazzle [bi'dæzl], *v.t.* éblouir.
***bed-chamber** [BEDROOM].
bedclothes ['bedklouðz], *n.pl.* les draps et les couvertures, *m.pl.*
bedding ['bediŋ], *n.* literie; litière (*pour animaux*), *f.*
bedeck [bi'dek], *v.t.* parer (*de*).
bedfellow ['bedfelou], *n.* camarade de lit, *m.*
***bedizen** [bi'daizn], *v.t.* attifer, parer.
bedraggle [bi'drægl], *v.t.* crotter, traîner dans la boue.
bedridden ['bedridn], *a.* alité.
bedroom ['bedrum], *n.*, ***bed-chamber** [bed tʃeimbə], *n.* chambre (à coucher), *f.*
bedside ['bedsaid], *n.* ruelle, *f.*, chevet, bord du lit, *m.*
bed-spread ['bedspred], *n.* couvrelit, dessus de lit, *m.*
bedstead ['bedsted], *n.* lit, bois de lit, *m.*; couchette, *f.*
bee [bi:], *n.* abeille, *f.*; *to have a bee in one's bonnet*, avoir une araignée dans le plafond.
beech [bi:tʃ], *n.* hêtre, *m.*
beef [bi:f], *n.* bœuf (*viande*); (*pl.* **beeves** [bi:vz]) bœuf (*animal*), *m.*
beef-steak ['bi:f steik], *n.* bifteck, *m.*
beehive ['bi:haiv], *n.* ruche, *f.*
bee-line [bi:lain], *n.* ligne droite, *f.*; *in a bee-line*, à vol d'oiseau; *to make a bee-line for*, se diriger tout droit vers.
Beelzebub [bi'elzəbəb], Belzébuth, *m.*
beer [biə], *n.* bière, *f.*; *glass of beer*, bock, *m.*
beet [bi:t], *n.* betterave, *f.*
beetle (1) [bi:tl], *n.* coléoptère, scarabée, escarbot, *m.*

beetle (2) [bi:tl], *n.* maillet, *m.*, mailloche, batte, *f.*, battoir (*de laveuse*), *m.*; hie, demoiselle (*d'un paveur*), *f.*; mouton (à enfoncer les pieux), *m.*
beetle (3) [bi:tl], *v.i.* surplomber.—*a.* en surplomb.
beets ['bi:tz], *n.* betterave rouge, *f.*
beet-sugar ['bi:tʃugə], *n.* sucre de betterave, *m.*
befall [bi'fɔ:l], *v.t., v.i. irr.* (*conjug. like* FALL) arriver, survenir (à).
befit [bi'fit], *v.t.* convenir à.
befitting [bi'fitiŋ], *a.* convenable à.
before [bi'fɔ:], *adv.* avant (*temps, ordre etc.*); auparavant, en avant; plus haut; jusqu'alors, naguère, jusqu'ici.—*prep.* devant (*endroit*); avant (*temps etc.*), *before going there*, avant d'y aller.—*conj.* avant que (*with subj.*).
beforehand [bi'fɔ:hænd], *adv.* à l'avance, d'avance.
befriend [bi'frend], *v.t.* seconder, aider, secourir; devenir l'ami de (*quelqu'un*).
beg [beg], *v.t.* mendier (*demander l'aumône*); demander, prier (*de*).—*v.i.* mendier.
beget [bi'get], *v.t. irr.* engendrer; (*fig.*) produire, causer.
beggar ['begə], *n.* mendiant, *m.*, mendiante, *f.*; gueux, *m.*, gueuse, *f.*—*v.t.* appauvrir, ruiner; (*fig.*) épuiser.
beggarly ['begəli], *a.* chétif, pauvre, misérable.
beggary ['begəri], *n.* mendicité, misère, *f.*
begging ['begiŋ], *n.* mendicité, *f.*
begin [bi'gin], *v.t. irr.* commencer; entamer, débuter; se mettre à.—*v.i.* commencer (*by, with, par*); begin afresh, recommencer.
beginner [bi'ginə], *n.* commençant; débutant, *m.*
beginning [bi'giniŋ], *n.* commencement, début, *m.*, origine, *f.*
begone! [bi'gɔn], *int.* va-t'en! allez-vous-en!
begonia [bi'gounjə], *n.* (*Bot.*) bégonia, *m.*
begrudge [bi'grʌdʒ], *v.t.* envier; refuser (à).
begrudgingly [bi'grʌdʒiŋli], *adv.* à contre-cœur.
beguile [bi'gail], *v.t.* tromper, séduire; (*fig.*) passer (*le temps*).
behalf [bi'hɑ:f], *n.* faveur, part, *f.*; *on behalf of*, au nom de.
behave [bi'heiv], *v.i.* se comporter, se conduire; *well-behaved*, sage.
behavior [bi'heivjə], *n.* conduite, tenue, *f.*; comportement, *m.*; manières, *f.pl.*
behead [bi'hed], *v.t.* décapiter.
behest [bi'hest], *n.* commandement, ordre, *m.*
behind [bi'haind], *adv.* derrière, par derrière, en arrière.—*prep.* derrière, en arrière de; après, en retard de.—*n.* (*colloq.*) derrière, *m.*
behindhand [bi'haindhænd], *a. and adv.* en arrière, en retard.
behold [bi'hould], *v.t. irr.* (*conjug. like* HOLD) voir, regarder.—*int.* voyez! voici! voilà!
beholden [bi'houldən], *a.* redevable (à).
behoove [bi'houv], *v.i.impers.* incomber à; *it behooves*, il faut, il convient.
beige [beiʒ], *a. and n.* beige, *m.*
being [bi:iŋ], *n.* être, *m.*; existence, *f.*; *in being*, existant, vivant.—*pres.p.* [BE] étant; *for the time being*, pour le moment.
Beirut [bei'ru:t], Beyrouth, *m.*
belated [bi'leitid], *a.* attardé; tardif.

357

belch [beltʃ], v.t., v.i. roter, éructer; *to belch forth*, vomir; *to belch out flames*, vomir des flammes.—n. rot, m., éructation, f.
beleaguer [bi'li:gə], v.t. assiéger, investir.
belfry ['belfri], n. clocher, beffroi, m.
Belgian ['beldʒən], a. belge.—n. Belge (*personne*), m., f.
Belgium ['beldʒəm]. la Belgique, f.
belie [bi'lai], v.t. démentir.
belief [bi'li:f], n. croyance, f.; credo, m.
believable [bi'li:vəbl], a. croyable.
believe [bi'li:v], v.t. croire.—v.i. croire (*en ou à*); *I believe not*, je crois que non, je ne le crois pas; *I believe so*, je crois que oui, je le crois.
believer [bi'li:və], n. croyant, m.
bell [bel], n. cloche, clochette, f.; grelot (*de chevaux etc.*), m.; sonnette (*de maison*), f.; timbre (*horloge, bicyclette*); (*Arch.*) vase, m.
belle [bel], n. belle, beauté, f.
bellicose ['belikous], a. belliqueux.
belligerent [bi'lidʒərənt], a. and n. belligérant, m.
bellow ['belou], v.i. beugler; mugir (*mer*); gronder (*tonnerre*).—n. beuglement, m.
bellows ['belouz], n.pl. soufflet, m.
bell ringer ['belriŋə], n. sonneur, m.
bell rope ['belroup], n. corde de cloche, f.
bell tower ['beltauə], n. campanile, clocher, m.
belly ['beli], n. ventre, m.—v.i. bomber, s'enfler, se gonfler.
belong [bi'lɔŋ], v.i. appartenir, être (à).
belongings [bi'lɔŋiŋz], n.pl. effets, m.pl., affaires, f.pl.
beloved [bi'lʌvd, bi'lʌvid], a. cher, chéri, bien-aimé.
below [bi'lou], prep. sous, au-dessous de; en aval de.—adv. au-dessous, dessous, en bas; *here below*, ici-bas.
belt [belt], n. ceinture, f.; ceinturon; baudrier, m. (*Mach.*) courroie, f.; *green belt*, zone verte, f.—v.t. ceindre, entourer.
bemoan [bi'moun], v.t. pleurer, déplorer.—v.i. gémir (*sur*).
bemuse [bi'mju:z], v.t. stupéfier.
bench [bentʃ], n. banc; gradin, m.; banquette, f.; établi (*de menuisier*); siège, tribunal, m.
bend [bend], v.t. irr. plier; courber, faire plier; incliner, tendre (*un arc*); fléchir (*le genou*); (*fig.*) appliquer.—v.i. plier, ployer; se courber, se pencher, s'incliner; s'appliquer (à); tourner; fléchir.—n. courbure, f.; coude (*Motor.*) tournant, virage, m.
beneath [bi'ni:θ], prep. sous, au-dessous de.—adv. au-dessous, en bas.
Benedict ['benidikt]. Benoît, m.
benediction [beni'dikʃən], n. bénédiction, f.
benefaction [beni'fækʃən], n. bienfait, m.
benefactor ['benifæktə], n. bienfaiteur, m.
benefactress ['benifæktris], n. bienfaitrice, f.
benefice ['benifis], n. bénéfice, m.
beneficence [bə'nefisəns], n. bienfaisance, f.
beneficial [beni'fiʃəl], a. salutaire, avantageux.
beneficiary [beni'fiʃəri], a. and n. bénéficiaire, m., f.
benefit ['benifit], n. bienfait, profit; bénéfice, m.; indemnité (*de chômage etc.*), f.—v.t. faire du bien à.—v.i. profiter.
Benelux ['beniləks]. Bénélux, m.
benevolence [bə'nevələns], n. bienveillance, f.

benevolent [bə'nevələnt], a. bienveillant, bienfaisant.
benighted [bi'naitid], a. anuité, surpris par la nuit; (*fig.*) ignorant.
benign [bi'nain], a. bénin, bénigne (*maladie, médecine etc.*), f.; bienfaisant (*personne*); doux, affable.
benignant [bi'nignənt], a. bon, bienveillant.
bent (1) [bent], *past and p.p.* [BEND].
bent (2) [bent], a. courbé, plié; *bent on*, résolu à.—n. penchant, m., disposition, tendance, f.
benumb [bi'nʌm], v.t. engourdir.
benzene, ['benzi:n], n. benzène, benzol, m.
benzine ['benzi:n], n. benzine, f.
bequeath [bi'kwi:ð], v.t. léguer.
bequest [bi'kwest], n. legs, m.
bereave [bi'ri:v], v.t. irr. priver (*de*).
bereavement [bi'ri:vmənt], n. privation, perte, f.; deuil, m.
beret ['berei], n. béret, m.
Bermuda(s) [bə:'mju:də(z)], (the). les (Îles) Bermudes, f.pl.
berry ['beri], n. baie, f.; grain, m.
berth [bə:θ], n. mouillage; lit, m., couchette, f.; poste, m., place, f., emploi, m.—v.t. amarrer à quai.—v.i. mouiller.
Bertha ['bə:θə]. Berthe, f.
beseech [bi'si:tʃ], v.t. irr. supplier, implorer.
beset [bi'set], v.t. irr. (*conjug. like* SET) obséder, entourer, assaillir.
besetting [bi'setiŋ], a. habituel, obsesseur.
beside [bi'said], prep. à côté de, auprès de; hors, hormis, excepté.
besides [bi'saidz], prep. outre, hors, hormis, excepté.—adv. d'ailleurs, du reste, en outre, de plus.
besiege [bi'si:dʒ], v.t. assiéger.
besmear [bi'smiə], v.t. barbouiller; souiller.
besmirch [bi'smə:tʃ], v.t. tacher, salir.
besom ['bi:zəm], n. balai, m.
bespatter [bi'spætə], v.t. éclabousser, couvrir de boue.
bespeak [bi'spi:k], v.t. irr. (*conjug. like* SPEAK) commander; retenir; annoncer, dénoter, accuser.
best [best], a. and n. le meilleur, la meilleure, le mieux; *at best*, au mieux, tout au plus; *best man* (*at weddings*), garçon d'honneur, m.; *to do one's best*, faire de son mieux; *to have the best of it*, avoir le dessus; *to make the best of it*, tirer le meilleur parti; *to the best of my belief*, autant que je sache.—adv. le mieux.
bestial ['bestjəl], a. bestial, de bête.
bestir [bi'stə:], v.t. remuer, mettre en mouvement.
bestow [bi'stou], v.t. donner, accorder.
bestrew [bi'stru:], v.t. irr. (*conjug. like* STREW) joncher (*de*), parsemer (*de*).
bestride [bi'straid], v.t. irr. (*conjug. like* STRIDE) enjamber, enfourcher (*un cheval*); être à cheval sur.
bet [bet], n. pari, m., gageure, f.—v.t., v.i. parier.
betake [bi'teik], v.r. irr. (*conjug. like* TAKE) *to betake oneself to*, se mettre à, s'en aller à, avoir recours à.
bethink [bi'θiŋk], v.t. irr. (*conjug. like* THINK) s'aviser (*de*); *to bethink oneself of*, se rappeler.

Bethlehem ['beθlihem, 'beθliəm]. Bethléem, *m.*

betide [bi'taid], *v.t.* **woe betide you**, malheur à vous.—*v.i.* arriver, advenir.

betimes [bi'taimz], *adv.* de bonne heure.

betoken [bi'toukn], *v.t.* annoncer, présager.

betray [bi'trei], *v.t.* trahir; tromper; révéler; faire tomber, entraîner.

betrayal [bi'treiəl], *n.* trahison, perfidie, *f.*

betrayer [bi'treiə], *n.* traître, *m.*

betroth [bi'trouð], *v.t.* fiancer.

betrothal [bi'trouðəl], *n.* fiançailles, *f.pl.*

betrothed [bi'trouðd], *a.* and *n.* fiancé, *m.* fiancée, *f.*

better ['betə], *a.* meilleur; **to get the better of,** l'emporter sur.—*adv.* mieux; **better late than never,** mieux vaut tard que jamais; **better and better,** de mieux en mieux; **for better for worse,** vaille que vaille; **I had better,** je ferais mieux; **so much the better!** tant mieux!—*n.* meilleur; supérieur, *m.*—*v.t.* améliorer, avancer.

betterment ['betəmənt], *n.* amélioration, *f.*

betting ['betiŋ], *n.* paris, *m.pl.*

Betty ['beti]. Babette, *f.*

between [bi'twi:n], *prep.* entre.

*****betwixt** [bi'twikst], *prep.* entre; **betwixt and between,** entre les deux.

bevel ['bevəl], *a.* de biais, en biseau.—*n.* fausse équerre (*outil*), *f.*—*v.t.* tailler en biseau.—*v.i.* biaiser.

beverage ['bevəridʒ], *n.* boisson, *f.*; *****breuvage, *m.*

bevy ['bevi], *n.* volée; troupe, compagnie, *f.*

bewail [bi'weil], *v.t.* pleurer, lamenter.

bewailing [bi'weiliŋ], *n.* lamentation, *f.*

beware [bi'wɛə], *v.i.* se garder (*de*), prendre garde (*à*); se méfier (*de*).

bewilder [bi'wildə], *v.t.* égarer, embarrasser.

bewildering [bi'wildəriŋ], *a.* déroutant, ahurissant.

bewilderment [bi'wildəmənt], *n.* égarement, *m.*

bewitch [bi'witʃ], *v.t.* ensorceler.

bewitching [bi'witʃiŋ], *a.* enchanteur, séduisant.

beyond [bi'jɔnd], *prep.* par delà, au delà de; au-dessus de; outre, hors de.—*adv.* là-bas.—*n.* au-delà, *m.*

bias ['baiəs], *a.* and *adv.* de biais, de travers.—*n.* biais, *m.*, pente, *f.*; penchant, parti pris, préjugé, *m.*—*v.t.* décentrer (*boule*); faire pencher; prévenir; influencer.

biased ['baiəst], *a.* décentré; partial, prédisposé.

bib (1) [bib], *n.* bavette, *f.*

bib (2) [bib], *n.* tacaud (*poisson*), *m.*

Bible [baibl], *n.* Bible, *f.*

biblical ['biblikəl], *a.* biblique.

biceps ['baiseps], *n.* (*Anat.*) biceps, *m.*

bicker ['bikə], *v.i.* se quereller, se chamailler.

bickering ['bikəriŋ], *n.* bisbille, *f.*, querelles, *f.pl.*

bicycle ['baisikl], *n.* bicyclette, *f.*; (*pop.*) vélo, *m.*, bécane, *f.*

bid [bid], *v.t. irr.* ordonner, dire, commander (*de*); inviter (*à*); offrir, enchérir; **to bid good-bye to,** dire adieu à.—*n.* enchère, *f.*

bidder ['bidə], *n.* enchérisseur, acheteur, *m.*

bidding ['bidiŋ], *n.* commandement, ordre, *m.*; invitation, prière, *f.*; enchères, *f.pl.*

bide [baid], *v.t. irr. archaic except in* **to bide one's time,** attendre le bon moment.

biennial [bai'eniəl], *a.* biennal; (*Bot.*) bisannuel.

biennially [bai'eniəli], *adv.* tous les deux ans.

bier [biə], *n.* civière, *f.*, corbillard, *m.*

big [big], *a.* gros; grand, vaste; enceinte, grosse (*d'enfant*), pleine (*bête*); (*fig.*) fier, hautain.

bigamist ['bigəmist], *n.* bigame, *m., f.*

bigamy ['bigəmi], *n.* bigamie, *f.*

bigness ['bignis], *n.* grosseur, grandeur, *f.*

bigot ['bigət], *n.* bigot, cagot, *m.*, fanatique, *m., f.*

bigoted ['bigətid], *a.* bigot.

bigotry ['bigətri], *n.* bigoterie, *f.*, sectarisme, fanatisme, *m.*

bigwig ['bigwig], *n.* (*fam*) gros bonnet, *m.*

bike [baik], *n.* (*colloq.*) vélo, *m.*, bécane, *f.*

bikini [bi'ki:ni], *n.* (*Cost.*) bikini, *m.*

bile [bail], *n.* bile, *f.*

bilge [bildʒ], *n.* (*Naut.*) sentine, *f.*; (*colloq.*) bêtises, *f.pl.*

bilge water ['bildʒwɔ:tə], *n.* eau de la cale, *f.*

bilingual [bai'liŋgwəl], *a.* bilingue.

bilious ['biljəs], *a.* bilieux.

bill (1) [bil], *n.* bec (*d'oiseau*), *m.*

bill (2) [bil], *n.* hallebarde, *f.*

bill (3) [bil], *n.* mémoire, compte, *m.*; facture (*invoice*), note (*hôtels etc.*), addition (*restaurants*); (*Comm.*) note, *f.*, billet, effet, *m.*; (*Banking*) lettre de change, *f.*; (*Parl.*) projet de loi, *m.*; affiche, placard, *m.*; **bill of fare,** menu, *m.*, carte, *f.*; **bill of health,** patente de santé, *f.*; **post no bills!** défense d'afficher!

billet ['bilit], *n.* bûche, *f.*; (*Mil.*) billet de logement, *m.*—*v.t., v.i.* loger chez l'habitant.

bill-hook ['bilhuk], *n.* serpe, *f.*, vouge, *m.*

billiard ['biljəd], *a.* de billard.

billiard ball ['biljədbɔ:l], *n.* bille, *f.*

billiards ['biljədz], *n.pl.* billard, *m.*; **to play a game of billiards,** faire une partie de billard.

billiard table ['biljədteibl], *n.* billard, *m.*

billion ['biljən], *n.* (*since 1948*) billion; (*Am.*) milliard, *m.*

billow ['bilou], *n.* grande vague, lame, *f.*—*v.i.* s'élever en vagues, rouler.

billowy ['biloui], *a.* houleux.

bill-sticker ['bilstikə], *n.* afficheur, colleur d'affiches, *m.*

billy goat ['biligout], *n.* bouc, *m.*

bin [bin], *n.* huche, *f.*, bac; coffre, *m.*

binary ['bainəri], *a.* binaire.

bind [baind], *v.t. irr.* lier; obliger; resserrer; border (*chaussures etc.*); garrotter, serrer; rendre constipé; relier (*livres*); **to be bound to,** être tenu de.—*n.* (*pop.*) **that's a bind,** quelle scie!

binder ['baində], *n.* lieur; relieur, *m.*; bande, attache, *f.*

binding ['baindiŋ], *a.* obligatoire; (*Med.*) astringent.—*n.* reliure, *f.*; bandeau, galon, *m.*, bordure, *f.*

bindweed ['baindwi:d], *n.* liseron, *m.*

binge [bindʒ], *n.* (*pop.*) bombe, *f.*; **to be on a binge,** faire la bombe.

binoculars [bi'nɔkjulaz], *n.pl.* jumelles, *f.pl.*

binomial [bai'noumiəl], *a.* (*Alg.*) binôme.

biochemist [baio'kemist], *n.* biochimiste, *m.*

biochemistry [baio'kemistri], *n.* biochimie, *f.*

biographer

biographer [bai'ɔgrəfə], n. biographe, m.
biography [bai'ɔgrəfi], n. biographie, f.
biologist [bai'ɔlədʒist], n. biologiste, biologue, m.
biology [bai'ɔlədʒi], n. biologie, f.
biped ['baiped], n. bipède, m.
birch [bə:tʃ], n. bouleau, m.; verges, f.pl.; *silver birch*, bouleau blanc.—*v.t.* fouetter.
bird [bə:d], n. oiseau; (*pop.*) type, m.; *little bird*, oiselet, m.
bird cage [bə:dkeidʒ], n. cage d'oiseau, f.
bird-lime ['bə:dlaim], n. glu, f.
bird's-eye view ['bə:dzai'vju:], n. vue à vol d'oiseau, f.
bird's nest ['bə:dznest], n. nid d'oiseau, m.
birth [bə:θ], n. naissance, f.; enfantement, m.; (*fig.*) origine, source, f.
birth control ['bə:θkəntroul], n. limitation des naissances, f.
birthday ['bə:θdei], n. anniversaire, m.
birthplace ['bə:θpleis], n. lieu de naissance, pays natal, m.
birth rate ['bə:θreit], n. natalité, f.
birthright ['bə:θrait], n. droit d'aînesse, m.
Biscay ['biskei], f.; *the Bay of Biscay*, le Golfe de Gascogne, m.
biscuit ['biskit], n. biscuit, m.
bisect [bai'sekt], v.t. couper en deux.
bishop ['biʃəp], n. évêque; (*Chess*) fou, m.
bishopric ['biʃəprik], n. évêché, m.
bit (1) [bit], n. morceau, m.; pièce (*de monnaie*), f.; (*colloq.*) brin, bout, peu, m.; mèche (*outil*); (*Naut.*) bitte, f.; mors (*de bride*), m.
bit (2) [bit], *past* [BITE].
bitch [bitʃ], n. chienne; femelle (*in compounds*), f.
bite [bait], n. morsure; piqûre, f.; coup de dent, m., bouchée; (*Fishing*) touche, f.—*v.t. irr.* mordre; piquer; ronger; (*fig.*) attraper, pincer, couper (*vent*).—*v.i.* mordre.
biting ['baitiŋ], a. mordant, piquant; coupant (*vent*).
bitter ['bitə], a. amer, acerbe; (*fig.*) acharné, mordant, aigre.—n. amer, m.
bitterly ['bitəli], adv. avec amertume; amèrement.
bittern ['bitə:n], n. butor, m.
bitterness ['bitənis], n. amertume, aigreur, âpreté, f.
bitumen [bi'tju:mən], n. bitume, m.
bivouac ['bivuæk], n. bivouac, m.—*v.i.* bivouaquer.
blab [blæb], v.i. jaser, bavarder.—n. bavard, m.
black [blæk], a. noir; (*fig.*) obscur, sombre, triste.—*v.t.* noircir; cirer (*chaussures*).—n. noir, m.
black-ball ['blækbɔ:l], n. boule noire, f.—*v.t.* rejeter au scrutin.
black beetle ['blæk'bi:tl], n. cafard, m., blatte, f.
blackberry ['blækbəri], n. mûre (sauvage), f.
blackbird ['blækbə:d], n. merle, m.
blackboard ['blækbɔ:d], n. tableau noir, m.
black currant ['blæk'kʌrənt], n. cassis, m.
blacken ['blækən], v.t., v.i. noircir.
blackguard ['blægɑ:d], n. polisson, gredin, vaurien, m.
blacking ['blækiŋ], n. cirage (*chaussures*); noircissement, m.
blackish ['blækiʃ], a. noirâtre.
black lead [blæk'led], n. mine de plomb, f.

blackleg ['blækleg], n. (*Gambling*) escroc; (*Strikes*) renard, jaune, m.
blackmail ['blækmeil], n. chantage, m.—*v.t.* faire chanter.
blackmailer ['blækmeilə], n. maître-chanteur, m.
black market [blæk'mɑ:kit], n. marché noir, m.
blackness ['blæknis], n. noirceur, f.
black-out ['blækaut], n. extinction des lumières, f.; black-out, m.
blacksmith ['blæksmiθ], n. forgeron, m.
bladder ['blædə], n. vessie; (*Bot.*) vésicule, f.
blade [bleid], n. lame (*de couteau etc.*), f.; brin (*d'herbe*), m.; pelle (*d'un aviron*); pale (*d'hélice*), f.; (*fig.*) gaillard (*personne*), m.
blain [blein], n. pustule, f.
blame [bleim], n. blâme, m.; faute, f.—*v.t.* blâmer, s'en prendre à; censurer, reprocher.
blameless ['bleimlis], a. innocent, sans tache.
blanch [blɑ:ntʃ], v.t. blanchir; pâlir; faire pâlir; monder (*amandes*).—*v.i.* blanchir; pâlir.
blancmange [blə'mɔnʒ], n. blanc-manger, m.
bland [blænd], a. doux, aimable, affable.
blandish ['blændiʃ], v.t. caresser, flatter, cajoler.
blandishment ['blændiʃmənt], n. flatterie, f.
blank [blæŋk], a. blanc, en blanc; (*fig.*) vide, confus, déconcerté.—n. blanc; (*Lotteries*) billet blanc; (*fig.*) vide, m., lacune, f.
blanket ['blæŋkit], n. couverture, f.
blare [bleə], v.t. faire retentir.—v.i. sonner (*comme une trompette*), cuivrer.—v. sonnerie, f.
blaspheme [blæs'fi:m], v.t., v.i. blasphémer.
blasphemer [blæs'fi:mə], n.blasphémateur, m.
blasphemous ['blæsfəməs], a. blasphématoire.
blasphemy ['blæsfəmi], n. blasphème, m.
blast [blɑ:st], n. vent, coup de vent; son (*d'un instrument à vent*), m.; explosion, f.—*v.t.* flétrir, brûler; détruire, ruiner; faire sauter.—*int.* sacrebleu!
blast furnace ['blɑ:stfə:nis], n. haut fourneau, m.
blasting ['blɑ:stiŋ], a. destructeur, m. coup de mine, m., explosion, f.
blatant ['bleitənt], a. bruyant, criard.
blatantly ['bleitəntli], adv. avec une vulgarité criarde.
blaze (1) [bleiz], n. flamme; flambée, f.; feu; (*fig.*) éclat, m.; étoile (*de cheval*), f.—*v.t. to blaze a trail*, se frayer un chemin.—v.i. être en flammes; flamber, brûler.
blaze (2) [bleiz], blazon (1) ['bleizən], v t. proclamer; *to blaze abroad*, répandre, crier par-dessus les toits.
blazing ['bleiziŋ], a. flambant; enflammé, embrasé; (*fig.*) brillant.
blazon (2) ['bleizən], n. blason, m.—*v.t.* blasonner.
bleach [bli:tʃ], v.t., v.i. blanchir; (*Hairdressing*) oxygéner.—n. agent de blanchiment, m., eau de javel; (*Hairdressing*) oxygénée, f.
bleak [bli:k], a. ouvert, sans abri; froid; désert; triste, morne.
bleakness ['bli:knis], n. exposition découverte, f.; froid, m.; tristesse, f.; aspect morne, m.
blear [bliə], bleary ['bliəri], a. larmoyant.
bleat [bli:t], v.i. bêler.—n. bêlement, m.

bleed [bli:d], *v.t.* irr. saigner; *(colloq.)* débourser.—*v.i.* saigner; pleurer *(vignes etc.)*.

bleeding ['bli:diŋ], *a.* saignant.—*n.* saignement, *m.*; *(Surg.)* saignée, *f.*

blemish ['blemiʃ], *v.t.* tacher, flétrir.—*n.* tache, flétrissure, *f.*, défaut, *m.*

blend [blend], *v.t.* mêler, mélanger; fondre.—*v.i.* se fondre, se marier *(à ou avec)*.—*n.* mélange, *m.*

bless [bles], *v.t.* bénir; rendre heureux, réjouir.

blessed [blest, 'blesid], *a.* béni, saint; bienheureux.

blessedness ['blesidnis], *n.* béatitude, félicité, *f.*, bonheur, *m.*

blessing ['blesiŋ], *n.* bénédiction, *f.*; bonheur, bien, *m.*

blight [blait], *v.t.* flétrir *(vent)*; brouir *(soleil)*; *(fig.)* frustrer, détruire.—*n.* brouissure *(des fleurs et des fruits)*; rouille *(du blé etc.)*; *(fig.)* flétrissure, *f.*

blind [blaind], *a.* aveugle; obscur; *blind alley*, impasse, *f.*; *blind in one eye*, borgne; *blind side*, côté faible, *m.*—*n.* store *(fenêtre)*; abat-jour, *m.*; banne *(de boutique)*; persienne *(à l'extérieur)*, *f.*; *(fig.)* voile, *m.*; *Venetian blind*, jalousie, *f.*—*v.t.* aveugler; *(fig.)* éblouir.

blindfold ['blaindfould], *v.t.* bander les yeux à.—*a.* les yeux bandés.

blindly ['blaindli], *adv.* aveuglément.

blind-man's buff ['blaindmænz'bʌf], *n.* colin-maillard, *m.*

blindness ['blaindnis], *n.* cécité, *f.*; aveuglement, *m.*

blink [bliŋk], *v.i.* clignoter, cligner des yeux; vaciller *(lumière)*.—*n.* clignotement, *m.*

blinker ['bliŋkə], *n.* œillère *(de cheval)*, *f.*

bliss [blis], *n.* félicité, béatitude, *f.*

blissful ['blisful], *a.* bienheureux.

blister ['blistə], *n.* ampoule, bulle; cloque *(peinture)*, *f.*—*v.t.* faire venir des ampoules à.—*v.i.* se couvrir d'ampoules; se cloquer *(peinture)*.

blithe [blaið], **blithesome** ['blaiðsəm], *a.* gai, joyeux.

blitz [blits], *n.* bombardement aérien *(2me guerre mondiale)*.

blizzard ['blizəd], *n.* tempête de neige, *f.*

bloat [blout], *v.t.* gonfler, bouffir, enfler.

bloater ['bloutə], *n.* hareng saur, *m.*

blob [blɔb], *n.* goutte *(d'eau)*, *f.*; pâté *(d'encre)*, *m.*

block [blɔk], *n.* bloc, *m.*, bille, *f.*; billot; *(fig.)* obstacle, *m.*; *block of houses*, pâté de maisons, *m.*; *block of flats*, immeuble, *m.*—*v.t.* bloquer; *to block up*, fermer, boucher.

blockade [blɔ'keid], *n.* blocus, *m.*—*v.t.* bloquer.

blockhead ['blɔkhed], *n.* imbécile, sot, *m.*

bloke [blouk], *n.* *(pop.)* type, *m.*

blond(e) [blɔnd], *a.* and *n.* blond, *m.*

blood [blʌd], *n.* sang, *m.*; *(fig.)* parenté, *f.*; tempérament, *m.*; race *(de cheval)*, *f.*

blood group ['blʌdgru:p], *n.* groupe sanguin, *m.*

bloodhound ['blʌdhaund], *n.* limier, *m.*

bloodless ['blʌdlis], *a.* exsangue; pâle.

bloodshed ['blʌdʃed], *n.* effusion de sang, *f.*

bloodshot ['blʌdʃɔt], *a.* injecté de sang.

bloodthirsty ['blʌdθə:sti], *a.* sanguinaire.

bloody ['blʌdi], *a.* sanglant, ensanglanté, sanguinaire.

bloom [blu:m], *n.* fleur, *f.*; duvet, velouté *(de fruit)*, *m.*; *(Metal.)* loupe, *f.*—*v.i.* fleurir; *(fig.)* être éclatant.

blooming ['blu:miŋ], *a.* fleurissant; *(pop.)* sacré, satané.—*n.* floraison, *f.*

blossom ['blɔsəm], *n.* fleur, *f.*—*v.i.* fleurir; être en fleur; *to blossom out*, s'épanouir.

blossoming ['blɔsəmiŋ], *n.* floraison, *f.*

blot [blɔt], *n.* tache, *f.*; pâté *(d'encre)*, *m.*—*v.t.* tacher, salir; faire sauter *(avec papier buvard)*; *to blot out*, rayer, effacer.—*v.i.* boire *(papier)*.

blotch [blɔtʃ], *n.* pustule, tache, *f.*

blotchy ['blɔtʃi], *a.* tacheté.

blotting paper ['blɔtiŋpeipə], *n.* papier buvard, *m.*

blouse [blauz], *n.* blouse; chemisette, *f.*; corsage, chemisier, *m.*

blow (1) [blou], *n.* coup, *m.*; *to come to blows*, en venir aux mains.

blow (2) [blou], *v.t.* irr. souffler; sonner *(un instrument à vent)*; faire sauter *(plomb)*; *to blow away*, chasser; *to blow out*, éteindre *(une lumière)*; faire sauter *(la cervelle)*; *to blow up*, faire sauter; gonfler *(un pneu)*.—*v.i.* souffler; faire du vent; sauter *(plomb)*; claquer *(ampoule électrique)*; *to blow up*, sauter, éclater.

blow (3) [blou], *v.i.* s'épanouir *(fleurs)*.

blower [blouə], *n.* souffleur; rideau de cheminée, *m.*

blow-lamp ['bloulæmp], *n.* lampe à souder, *f.*

blubber ['blʌbə], *n.* graisse de baleine, *f.*

bludgeon ['blʌdʒən], *n.* gourdin, *m.*; trique, *f.*

blue [blu:], *a.* bleu.—*n.* bleu; azur, *m.*—*v.t.* bleuir.

blue-bell ['blu:bel], *n.* jacinthe des prés, *f.*

blueness ['blu:nis], *n.* couleur bleue, *f.*

blue-print ['blu:print], *n.* dessin négatif; *(fam.)* bleu, projet, *m.*

bluestocking ['blu:stɔkiŋ], *n.* bas bleu, *m.*

bluff (1) [blʌf], *a.* escarpé, accore; brusque *(personne)*.—*n.* à-pic, *m.*, falaise, *f.*, escarpement, *m.*

bluff (2) [blʌf], *n.* bluff *(feinte)*, *m.*—*v.t.* bluffer.

bluffness ['blʌfnis], *n.* rudesse, brusquerie, *f.*

bluish ['blu:iʃ], *a.* bleuâtre.

blunder ['blʌndə], *n.* bévue, étourderie, balourdise, *f.*—*v.i.* embrouiller.—*v.i.* faire une bévue.

blunderbuss ['blʌndəbʌs], *n.* tromblon, *m.*

blunderer ['blʌndərə], *n.* maladroit, étourdi, *m.*

blundering ['blʌndəriŋ], *a.* maladroit.

blunt [blʌnt], *a.* émoussé; *(fig.)* brusque, bourru.—*v.t.* émousser; épointer; *(fig.)* amortir.

bluntly ['blʌntli], *adv.* brusquement, carrément.

bluntness ['blʌntnis], *n.* état émoussé, *m.*; brusquerie, *f.*

blur [blə:], *v.t.* tacher, barbouiller; *(fig.)* brouiller.

blurt [blə:t], *v.t.* *to blurt out*, laisser échapper.

blush [blʌʃ], *v.i.* rougir.—*n.* rougeur, *f.*; *at the first blush*, au premier abord.

blushing ['blʌʃiŋ], *a.* rougissant.

bluster

bluster ['blʌstə], *v.i.* tempêter, crier (*contre*), fanfaronner.—*n.* fracas, tapage, *m.*, fanfaronnade, fureur (*d'une tempête*), *f.*

blusterer ['blʌstərə], *n.* fanfaron, *m.*, bravache, *m.*, *f.*

blustering ['blʌstəriŋ], *a.* orageux; bruyant; bravache.

boa ['bouə], *n.* boa, *m.*

boar [bɔ:], *n.* verrat, *m.*; *wild boar*, sanglier, *m.*

board [bɔ:d], *n.* planche, *f.*; écriteau, *m.*; table, pension, *f.*; conseil, *m.*, administration, *f.*; (*Bookb.*) carton; (*Tailors*) établi; (*Naut.*) bord; (*Chess*) échiquier, *m.*; *Board of Trade*, ministère du commerce, *m.*; *on board*, à bord.—*v.t.* planchéier; nourrir; (*Naut.*) aborder; *to board out*, mettre en pension.—*v.i.* se mettre en pension.

boarder ['bɔ:də], *n.* pensionnaire; interne, *m.*, *f.*

boarding ['bɔ:diŋ], *n.* planchéiage, plancher, *m.*; table, pension, *f.*; (*Naut.*) abordage, *m.*

boarding house ['bɔ:diŋhaus], *n.* pension de famille, *f.*

boarding school ['bɔ:diŋsku:l], *n.* pensionnat, internat, *m.*

boast [boust], *v.i.* se vanter, se glorifier.—*n.* vanterie, *f.*

boaster ['boustə], *n.* vantard, *m.*

boastful ['boustful], *a.* vantard.

boat [bout], *n.* bateau, canot, *m.*, barque, *f.*

boating ['boutiŋ], *n.* canotage, *m.*

boatman ['boutmən], *n.* batelier, *m.*

boatswain, bosun [bousn], *n.* maître d'équipage, *m.*

bob [bɔb], *n.* (*Hairdressing*) perruque ronde; lentille (*d'un pendule*); secousse, *f.*; coup, *m.*, tape; petite révérence, *f.*—*v.t.* écourter (*la queue*); secouer, ballotter, balancer.—*v.i.* pendiller, osciller, s'agiter; *to bob up*, revenir à la surface.

bobbin ['bɔbin], *n.* bobine, *f.*

bode [boud], *v.t.*, *v.i.* présager; *to bode well* (*ill*), être de bon (mauvais) augure.

bodice ['bɔdis], *n.* corsage, *m.*

bodiless ['bɔdilis], *a.* sans corps.

bodily ['bɔdili], *a.* corporel, matériel.—*adv.* corporellement; entièrement, en masse.

boding ['boudiŋ], *n.* présage, pressentiment, *m.*

bodkin ['bɔdkin], *n.* poinçon; passe-lacet, *m.*

body ['bɔdi], *n.* corps; fond; cœur, centre; gros (*d'une armée*), *m.*; bande, troupe; nef (*d'une église*); personne; sève (*de vin*), carrosserie (*d'un véhicule*), *f.*; corsage (*d'une robe*), *m.*

body-guard ['bɔdiga:d], *n.* garde du corps, *m.*

body-work ['bɔdiwə:k], *n.* carrosserie, *f.*

boffin ['bɔfin], *n.* (*fam.*) savant, inventeur, *m.*

bog [bɔg], *n.* marécage, *m.*, fondrière, *f.*; *to get bogged down*, s'embourber.

boggle [bɔgl], *v.i.* hésiter (à); reculer (*devant*).

boggy ['bɔgi], *a.* marécageux.

bogie ['bougi], *n.* (*Rail.*) bogie, *m.*

bogus ['bougəs], *a.* faux, simulé.

boil (1) [bɔil], *v.t.* faire bouillir; faire cuire à l'eau.—*v.i.* bouillir; bouillonner; *to boil over*, déborder.

boil (2) [bɔil], *n.* (*Med.*) furoncle, clou, *m.*

boiled [bɔild], *a.* bouilli, cuit à l'eau; *a boiled egg*, un œuf à la coque.

boiler ['bɔilə], *n.* chaudière, *f.*; réservoir à eau chaude, *m.*

boiler house ['bɔiləhaus], *n.* salle des chaudières, *f.*

boiler maker ['bɔiləmeikə], *n.* chaudronnier, *m.*

boiler suit ['bɔiləsju:t], *n.* bleus, *m.pl.*

boiling ['bɔiliŋ], *a.* en ébullition.—*n.* bouillonnement, *m.*

boisterous ['bɔistərəs], *a.* orageux, violent; bruyant, turbulent.

boisterously ['bɔistərəsli], *adv.* impétueusement; violemment; bruyamment.

boisterousness ['bɔistərəsnis], *n.* impétuosité, turbulence; violence, *f.*

bold [bould], *a.* hardi; audacieux, téméraire; impudent, effronté; saillant, net.

bold-faced ['bouldfeist], *a.* impudent, effronté.

boldly ['bouldli], *adv.* hardiment, intrépidement; impudemment.

boldness ['bouldnis], *n.* hardiesse, audace; assurance, effronterie, *f.*

bole [boul], *n.* tronc, fût (*d'un arbre*), *m.*

Bolivia [bə'liviə]. la Bolivie, *f.*

Bolivian [bə'liviən], *a.* bolivien.—*n.* Bolivien (*personne*), *m.*

bollard ['bɔləd], *n.* (*Naut.*) pieu d'amarrage, *m.*

Bolshevik ['bɔlʃivik], *a.* bolchevik.—*n.* Bolchevik, *m.*

Bolshevism ['bɔlʃivizm], *n.* bolchevisme, *m.*

bolster ['boulstə], *n.* traversin; coussin, *m.*—*v.t.* mettre un traversin sous; (*fig.*) appuyer, soutenir.

bolt [boult], *n.* verrou; pêne; (*Tech.*) boulon, *m.*, cheville, *f.*; (*fig.*) trait, *m.*, flèche; fuite, *f.*; *thunder-bolt*, éclair, *m.*—*v.t.* verrouiller; fermer au verrou; gober, avaler (*to swallow*).—*v.i.* décamper, filer; s'emporter, s'emballer (*cheval*).

bomb [bɔm], *n.* bombe, *f.*—*v.t.* bombarder.

bombard [bɔm'ba:d], *v.t.* bombarder.

bombardier [bɔmbə'diə], *n.* bombardier, *m.*

bombardment [bɔm'ba:dmənt], *n.* bombardement, *m.*

bombast ['bɔmbæst], *n.* emphase, enflure, *f.*, boursouflage, *m.*

bombastic [bɔm'bæstik], *a.* enflé, ampoulé.

bomber ['bɔmə], *n.* avion de bombardement, *m.*

bombing ['bɔmiŋ], *n.* bombardement, *m.*

bona fide [bounə'faidi], *a.* sérieux, de bonne foi.

bond [bɔnd], *n.* lien, *m.*; liaison, *f.*; engagement, *m.*; obligation, *f.*; (*Fin.*) bon, *m.*; *in bonds*, dans les fers.—*v.t.* entreposer; *bonded goods*, marchandises entreposées, *f.pl.*

bondage ['bɔndidʒ], *n.* esclavage, *m.*, servitude, *f.*

bond-holder ['bɔndhouldə], *n.* obligataire, *m.*, *f.*, porteur d'obligation, *m.*

bondman ['bɔndmən], **bondsman** ['bɔndzmən], *n.* (*pl.* -men [men]) serf, esclave, *m.*

bondwoman ['bɔndwumən], **bondswoman** ['bɔndzwumən], *n.* (*pl.* -women [wimin]) esclave, *f.*

bone [boun], *n.* os, *m.*; arête (*de poisson*); baleine (*whale bone*); ivoire (*des dents*), *f.*; (*pl.*) ossements, *m.pl.*; *bone of contention*, pomme de discorde, *f.*—*v.t.* désosser.

362

bonfire ['bɔnfaiə], *n.* feu de joie *ou* de jardin, *m.*

bonnet ['bɔnit], *n.* chapeau (*de femme*); bonnet (*d'un Ecossais*).

bonny ['bɔni], *a.* gentil, joli, joyeux, gai.

bonus ['bounəs], *n.* boni, *m.*; prime, *f.*

bony ['bouni], *a.* osseux; plein d'arêtes (*poisson*).

boo [bu:], *v.t., v.i.* huer.—*n.* huée, *f.*—*int.* hou!

booby ['bu:bi], *n.* nigaud, benêt, *m.*

booby trap ['bu:bitræp], *n.* attrape-nigaud, *m.*; (*Mil.*) mine-piège, *f.*

book [buk], *n.* livre, livret; registre; bouquin (*vieux livre*), *m.*; **exercise book**, cahier, *m.*—*v.t.* retenir, réserver; enregistrer, inscrire.

bookbinder ['bukbaində], *n.* relieur, *m.*

bookbinding ['bukbaindiŋ], *n.* reliure, *f.*

book-case ['bukkeis], *n.* bibliothèque, *f.*

booking office ['bukiŋɔfis], *n.* bureau d'enregistrement; guichet (*de gare etc.*), *m.*

bookish ['bukiʃ], *a.* studieux; livresque (*style*).

book-keeper ['bukki:pə], *n.* teneur de livres, *m.*

book-keeping ['bukki:piŋ], *n.* comptabilité, *f.*

book lover ['buklʌvə], *n.* bibliophile, *m., f.*

bookseller ['buksela], *n.* libraire, *m., f.*

bookshelf ['bukʃelf], *n.* rayon (*de bibliothèque*), *m.*

book-shop ['bukʃɔp], (*Am.*) **bookstore** ['buksto:], *n.* librairie, *f.*

book-stall ['buksto:l], *n.* (*Rail.*) bibliothèque, *f.*, étalage de livres, *m.*

boom [bu:m], *n.* (*Naut.*) bout-dehors, *m.*; chaîne (*des ports etc.*); (*Cine.*) perche, *f.*; grondement, retentissement, *m.*; (*fig., Comm.*) grande (*et rapide*) hausse, *f.*—*v.i.* gronder, retentir; (*Comm.*) être en hausse, prospérer.

boomerang ['bu:məræŋ], *n.* boumerang, *m.*

boon (1) [bu:n], *n.* bienfait, *m.*, faveur, *f.*; bien, avantage, *m.*

boon (2) [bu:n], *a.* gai, joyeux.

boor [buə], *n.* rustre, *m.*

boorish ['buəriʃ], *a.* rustre, grossier.

boost [bu:st], *v.t.* (*Am.*) pousser (*par derrière*); lancer; (*Elec.*) survolter.

boot (1) [bu:t], *n.* chaussure, bottine, botte, *f.*

boot (2) [bu:t], *n.* (used only in) **to boot**, en sus, par-dessus le marché.

booth [bu:ð], *n.* baraque, tente; cabine, *f.*

booty ['bu:ti], *n.* butin, *m.*

borax ['bo:ræks], *n.* borax, *m.*

border ['bo:də], *n.* bord, *m.*; bordure (*de vêtement etc.*); frontière (*d'un pays*), *f.*; (*Gard.*) parterre, *m.*, platebande, *f.*—*v.t.* border.—*v.i.* aboutir, toucher (à); avoisiner.

bordering ['bo:dəriŋ], *a.* contigu, voisin.

border-line ['bo:dəlain], *a.* indéterminé.—*n.* ligne de démarcation, *f.*

bore (1) [bo:], *v.t.* percer, forer; sonder, creuser; (*fig.*) ennuyer, embêter.—*v.i.* percer.—*n.* trou; calibre; (*fig.*) fâcheux (*personne*); ennui (*chose*); mascaret (*d'un fleuve*), *m.*

bore (2) [bo:], *past* [BEAR].

boredom ['bo:dəm], *n.* ennui, *m.*

born [bo:n], *a.* né; **to be born**, naître.

borough ['bʌrə], *n.* bourg, *m.*, ville, *f.*

borrow ['bɔrou], *v.t.* emprunter (à).

borrower ['bɔrouə], *n.* emprunteur, *m.*

bosh [bɔʃ], *n.* blague, farce, *f.*; bêtises, *f.pl.* galimatias, *m.*

bosom ['buzəm], *n.* sein; (*fig.*) cœur, *m.*

boss (1) [bɔs], *n.* bosse, *f.*; moyeu (*d'une roue*), *m.*

boss (2) [bɔs], *n.* patron, chef, contremaître, *m.*—*v.t.* diriger, contrôler; régenter.

bosun [BOATSWAIN].

botanic [bə'tænik], **botanical** [bə'tænikəl] *a.* botanique.

botanist ['bɔtənist], *n.* botaniste, *m., f.*

botany ['bɔtəni], *n.* botanique, *f.*

botch [bɔtʃ], *n.* pustule, *f.*; (*fig.*) ravaudage, replâtrage, travail mal fait, *m.*—*v.t.* ravauder, replâtrer, saboter.

both [bouθ], *a. and pron.* tous les deux, tous deux, l'un et l'autre.—*conj.* tant, à la fois.

bother ['bɔðə], *v.t.* ennuyer, tracasser; (*colloq.*) embêter.—*n.* ennui, tracas, embêtement, *m.*

bottle ['bɔtl], *n.* bouteille, *f.*; flacon; biberon (*d'enfant*), *m.*; botte (*de foin*), *f.*; **hot water bottle**, bouillotte, *f.*—*v.t.* mettre en bouteille.

bottle-neck ['bɔtlnek], *n.* goulot; embouteillage (*de circulation routière*), *m.*

bottling ['bɔtliŋ], *n.* mise en bouteilles, *f.*

bottom ['bɔtəm], *n.* fond; bas; dessous, pied; derrière, *m.*; base; (*Naut.*) carène, *f.*

bottomless ['bɔtəmlis], *a.* sans fond.

boudoir ['bu:dwa:], *n.* boudoir, *m.*

bough [bau], *n.* branche, *f.*, rameau, *m.*

boulder ['bouldə], *n.* grosse pierre, *f.*, bloc, *m.*

bounce [bauns], *v.i.* sauter, (re)bondir.—*n.* saut, (re)bond, *m.*

bouncer ['baunsə], *n.* (*pop.*) expulseur, videur, *m.*

bound (1) [baund], *n.* bond, saut, *m.*—*v.i.* bondir, sauter.

bound (2) [baund], *n.* borne, limite, *f.*—*v.t.* borner, limiter.

bound (3) [baund], *a.* (*Naut.*) allant (à), en partance (*pour*).

bound (4) [baund], *past and p.p.* [BIND].

boundary ['baundri], *n.* limite, borne, frontière, *f.*

bounden ['baundən], *a.* obligatoire, impérieux.

boundless ['baundlis], *a.* sans bornes; illimité.

bounteous ['bauntiəs], **bountiful** ['bauntiful], *a.* libéral, généreux; abondant.

bounty ['baunti], *n.* bonté, générosité, libéralité, *f.*; don, *m.*

bouquet [bu'kei], *n.pl.* bouquet, *m.*

bourne, bourn [bo:n], *n.* borne, frontière, limite, *f.*; terme, but, *m.*

bout [baut], *n.* tour, *m.*, partie, *f.*; accès, *m.*, crise, *f.*

bovine ['bouvain], *a.* bovin.

bow (1) [bau], *v.t.* courber, plier, fléchir, incliner.—*v.i.* se courber, s'incliner; saluer; se soumettre (à).—*n.* salut, *m.*, révérence, *f.*

bow (2) [bau], *n.* (*Naut.*) avant, bossoir, *m.*

bow (3) [bou], *n.* arc; archet (*de violon*); nœud (*rubans*), *m.*

bowels ['bauəlz], *n.pl.* entrailles, *f.pl.*, intestins, boyaux, *m.pl.*; (*fig.*); compassion, *f.*

bower ['bauə], *n.* berceau de verdure, *m.*, tonnelle, *f.*

bowl [boul], *n.* bol, vase, *m.*; coupe; jatte, *f.*; fourneau (*d'une pipe*), *m.*; boule (*sphère*), *f.*; (*pl.*) boules, *f.pl.*; *to play (at) bowls*, jouer aux boules.—*v.t.* rouler, faire rouler; (*Cricket*) lancer, bôler.

bow-legged ['bouleg(i)d], *a.* à jambes arquées, bancal.

bowler(-hat) ['boulǝ(hæt)], *n.* chapeau melon, *m.*

bowsprit ['bousprit], *n.* (*Naut.*) beaupré, *m.*

bow tie ['bou'tai], *n.* nœud carré, *m.*

bow window ['bou'windou], *n.* fenêtre en saillie, *f.*

box (1) [bɔks], *n.* boîte, *f.*; coffret (*petit*); coffre (*grand*), *m.*, caisse; malle; (*Theat.*) loge, *f.*; buis (*arbre*), *m.*—*v.t.* enfermer dans une boîte, emboîter, encaisser.

box (2) [bɔks], *v.t.* souffleter, gifler.—*v.i.* boxer.—*n.* soufflet, *m.*, gifle, *f.*

boxer ['bɔksǝ], *n.* boxeur, pugiliste, *m.*

boxing ['bɔksiŋ], *n.* la boxe, *f.*

box office ['bɔksɔfis], *n.* (*Theat.*) bureau de location, *m.*

boy [bɔi], *n.* garçon, petit garçon; fils, *m.*

boycott ['bɔikɔt], *v.t.* boycotter.

boycotting ['bɔikɔtiŋ], *n.* boycottage, *m.*

boyhood ['bɔihud], *n.* enfance, adolescence, *f.*

boyish ['bɔiiʃ], *a.* puéril; d'enfant, enfantin.

boy scout ['bɔi'skaut], *n.* (jeune) éclaireur, scout, *m.*

bra [brɑ:], (*pop.*) [BRASSIÈRE].

brace [breis], *n.* couple (*gibier*); paire (*pistolets*), *f.*; vilebrequin (*outil*), *m.*; (*pl.*) bretelles, *f.pl.*—*v.t.* lier, serrer, attacher; (*fig.*) fortifier.

bracelet ['breislit], *n.* bracelet, *m.*

bracing ['breisiŋ], *a.* fortifiant, tonifiant.

bracken ['brækǝn], *n.* fougère, *f.*

bracket ['brækit], *n.* console, applique, *f.*, tasseau, *m.*; accolade, *f.*; bras (*pour une lampe etc.*), *m.*; (*Print.*) parenthèse, *f.*

brackish ['brækiʃ], *a.* saumâtre.

bradawl ['brædɔːl], *n.* poinçon, *m.*

brag [bræg], *v.i.* se vanter.—*n.* fanfaronnade, vanterie, *f.*

braggart ['brægǝt], *n.* fanfaron, *m.*

braid [breid], *n.* tresse; soutache, ganse, *f.*; lacet; galon, *m.*—*v.t.* tresser, natter, soutacher.

braille [breil], *n.* braille, *m.*

brain [brein], *n.* cerveau (*organe*), *m.*; cervelle (*substance*), *f.*; (*fig.*) jugement, esprit, *m.*; tête, *f.*

brainless ['breinlis], *a.* sans cervelle; stupide.

brainy ['breini], *a.* intelligent.

braise [breiz], *v.t.* braiser.

brake (1) [breik], *n.* fourré, hallier, *m.*, fougère (*thicket*), *f.*

brake (2) [breik], *n.* frein; *m.*; *to put on the brake*, serrer le frein.—*v.t.*, *v.i.* freiner.

braking ['breikiŋ], *n.* freinage, *m.*

bramble ['bræmbl], *n.* ronce, *f.*

bran [bræn], *n.* son, *m.*

branch [brɑ:ntʃ], *n.* branche, *f.*, rameau, *m.*; succursale (*d'une banque etc.*), *f.*—*v.i.* *to branch off*, s'embrancher, bifurquer; *to branch out*, se ramifier.

brand [brænd], *n.* brandon, tison; fer chaud, stigmate, *m.*; flétrissure (*d'infamie*); (*Comm.*) marque, *f.*—*v.t.* marquer au fer chaud; flétrir; (*fig.*) stigmatiser (*de*).

brandish ['brændiʃ], *v.t.* brandir.

brand-new ['brænd'nju:], *a.* tout (flambant) neuf.

brandy ['brændi], *n.* eau-de-vie, *f.*, cognac, *m.*

brash [bræʃ], *a.* effronté, présomptueux.

brass [brɑ:s], *n.* cuivre jaune, laiton; (*fig.*) toupet, *m.*, effronterie, *f.*

brassière ['bræsjeǝ], *n.* soutien-gorge, *m.*

brat [bræt], *n.* marmot, bambin, *m.*

bravado [brǝ'vɑ:dou], *n.* bravade, *f.*

brave [breiv], *a.* courageux, brave, vaillant; (*fig.*) fameux, excellent.—*v.t.* braver, défier.

bravely ['breivli], *adv.* courageusement, bravement.

bravery ['breivǝri], *n.* bravoure, *f.*, courage, *m.*

brawl [brɔ:l], *n.* dispute, rixe, querelle, *f.*; bruit, tapage, *m.*—*v.i.* brailler, disputer.

brawler ['brɔ:lǝ], *n.* tapageur; braillard, querelleur, *m.*

brawn [brɔ:n], *n.* pâté de cochon, fromage de tête, *m.*; (*fig.*) muscles, *m.pl.*

brawny ['brɔ:ni], *a.* charnu, musculeux.

bray (1) [brei], *v.t.* broyer, piler.

bray (2) [brei], *v.i.* braire (*ânes etc.*); (*fig.*) résonner.—*n.* braiment, *m.*

brazen ['breizǝn], *a.* d'airain; (*fig.*) effronté, impudent.—*v.t.* *to brazen it out*, payer d'effronterie.

brazen-faced ['breizǝnfeist], *a.* à front d'airain, effronté.

brazier ['breiziǝ], *n.* chaudronnier, *m.*

Brazil [brǝ'zil], le Brésil, *m.*

Brazilian [brǝ'ziljǝn], *a.* brésilien.—*n.* Brésilien (*personne*), *m.*

Brazil nut [brǝ'zilnʌt], *n.* noix du Brésil, *f.*

breach [bri:tʃ], *n.* brèche, rupture; (*fig.*) violation, infraction, *f.*—*v.t.* battre en brèche.

bread [bred], *n.* pain, *m.*; *brown bread*, pain bis; *stale bread*, pain rassis.

breadcrumb ['bredkrʌm], *n.* miette, *f.*; (*pl.*) (*Cook.*) chapelure, *f.*, gratin, *m.*

breadth [bredθ], *n.* largeur, *f.*

bread-winner ['bredwinǝ], *n.* soutien de famille, *m.*

break [breik], *v.t. irr.* casser; briser; rompre; violer, enfreindre; ruiner; défricher (*terrain inculte*); (*fig.*) faire part de, communiquer (*une nouvelle*); amortir (*un choc*); *to break through the sound barrier*, franchir le mur du son.—*v.i.* se casser, se briser, se rompre, casser, rompre; éclater (*tempête etc.*); (*Comm.*) faire faillite; poindre (*jour*); changer (*temps*); *to break away*, se détacher; (*Mil.*) rompre les rangs; (*Box.*) cesser le corps-à-corps; *to break down*, s'abattre, se délabrer, s'effondrer, s'écrouler; (*Motor.*) tomber en panne; défaillir, s'altérer (*santé*); fondre en larmes; *to break in*, pénétrer dans; (*Motor.*) roder; *to break into*, entamer; éclater en; *to break loose*, s'échapper, s'évader, (*fig.*) s'émanciper; *to break off*, rompre, s'arrêter; *to break out*, éclater, se déclarer (*maladie*); jaillir, paraître, s'échapper; *to break up*, se disperser, entrer en vacances; *to break with*, rompre avec.—*n.* rupture, brisure, fracture; trouée, fente; (*fig.*) interruption, *f.*; changement (*de temps*); arrêt (*dans un voyage*), *m.*; (*Sch.*) récréation, *f.*; *break of day*, point du jour, *m.*

breakage ['breikidʒ], *n.* rupture, cassure; (*Comm.*) casse, *f.*

breakdown ['breikdaun], *n.* (*Motor., Mech.*) panne; (*fig.*) débâcle, *f.*; **nervous breakdown**, dépression nerveuse, *f.*

breaker ['breikə], *n.* infracteur, briseur; violateur; brisant (*mer*), *m.*

breakfast ['brekfəst], *n.* petit déjeuner, *m.*—*v.i.* prendre le petit déjeuner.

breakwater ['breikwɔːtə], *n.* brise-lames, *m.*, digue, jetée, *f.*

bream [briːm], *n.* (*Ichth.*) brème, *f.*

breast [brest], *n.* sein, *m.*; poitrine, *f.*; (*fig.*) cœur, *m.*, âme, conscience, *f.*; poitrail (*d'un cheval*), *m.*

breastplate ['brestpleit], *n.* cuirasse, *f.*

breath [breθ], *n.* haleine, respiration, *f.* souffle, *m.*; (*fig.*) vie, existence, *f.*; **to be out of breath**, être hors d'haleine *ou* tout essoufflé.

breathe [briːð], *v.t.* respirer, souffler; **to breathe in**, aspirer; **to breathe one's last**, rendre le dernier soupir; **to breathe out**, exhaler.—*v.i.* respirer; souffler, reprendre haleine.

breathing-space ['briːðiŋ'speis], *n.* temps de respirer, relâche, répit, *m.*

breathless ['breθlis], *a.* hors d'haleine, essoufflé, haletant.

breech [briːtʃ], *n.* culasse (*fusil*), *f.*—*v.t.* culotter.

breeches ['britʃiz], *n.pl.* culotte, *f.*

breed [briːd], *v.t. irr.* élever; faire naître.—*v.i.* multiplier, se reproduire.—*n.* race, *f.*

breeder ['briːdə], *n.* éleveur, *m.*

breeding ['briːdiŋ], *n.* élevage (*de bestiaux etc.*), *m.*; reproduction; éducation, *f.*; **good breeding**, politesse, *f.*, savoir-vivre, *m.*

breeze [briːz], *n.* (*forte*) brise, *f.*, vent assez fort, *m.*

breezy ['briːzi], *a.* frais; jovial.

brevity ['breviti], *n.* brièveté, concision, *f.*

brew [bruː], *v.t.* brasser; faire une infusion; (*fig.*) tramer, machiner.—*v.i.* faire de la bière; (*fig.*) se préparer, se tramer, couver.

brewer ['bruːə], *n.* brasseur, *m.*

brewery ['bruːəri], *n.* brasserie, *f.*

bribe [braib], *n.* présent (*dans le but de corrompre*); pot-de-vin, *m.*—*v.t.* gagner, corrompre, acheter.

bribery ['braibəri], *n.* corruption, *f.*

brick [brik], *a.* de briques, en briques.—*n.* brique, *f.*; (*fig.*) brave garçon, bon enfant, *m.*

brickbat ['brikbæt], *n.* briqueton, *m.*

brick kiln ['brikkiln], *n.* four à briques, *m.*

bricklayer ['brikleiə], *n.* maçon, *m.*

bridal ['braidl], *a.* nuptial, de noces.—*n.* fête nuptiale, noce, *f.*

bride [braid], *n.* nouvelle mariée, mariée, *f.*

bridegroom ['braidgruːm], *n.* nouveau marié, *m.*

bridesmaid ['braidzmeid], *n.* demoiselle d'honneur, *f.*

bridge [bridʒ], *n.* pont, *m.*; passerelle (*de navire etc.*), *f.*; chevalet (*d'instrument à cordes*); dos (*du nez*); (*Cards*) bridge, *m.*—*v.t.* jeter un pont sur; (*fig.*) combler (*une lacune*).

bridge-head ['bridʒhed], *n.* tête de pont, *f.*, point d'appui, *m.*

Bridget ['bridʒit]. Brigitte, *f.*

bridle [braidl], *n.* bride, *f.*; (*fig.*) frein, *m.*—*v.t.* brider; (*fig.*) mettre un frein à.—*v.i.* redresser la tête, se rebiffer.

brief [briːf], *a.* bref, court; (*fig.*) concis.—*n.* abrégé; dossier, *m.*—*v.t.* confier une cause à; donner des instructions à.

brief-case ['briːfkeis], *n.* serviette, *f.*

briefly ['briːfli], *adv.* brièvement, en peu de mots.

brier ['braiə], *n.* bruyère, *f.*; églantier, *m.*; (*pl.*) ronces, *f.pl.*

brig [brig], *n.* (*Naut.*) brick, *m.*

brigade [bri'geid], *n.* brigade, *f.*

brigadier [brigə'diə], *n.* général de brigade, *m.*

brigand ['brigənd], *n.* brigand, *m.*

brigantine ['brigənti:n], *n.* brigantin, *m.*

bright [brait], *a.* brillant, poli, clair, lumineux; éclatant, vif; (*fig.*) joyeux, intelligent.

brighten [braitn], *v.t.* faire briller; éclaircir, égayer; polir; (*fig.*) illustrer, embellir; dégourdir.—*v.i.* s'éclaircir; briller, étinceler.

brightly ['braitli], *adv.* brillamment, avec éclat.

brightness ['braitnis], *n.* brillant, *m.*; clarté, *f.*; éclat, *m.*; (*fig.*) joie, vivacité; intelligence, *f.*

brill [bril], *n.* (*Ichth.*) barbue, *f.*

brilliance ['briljəns], **brilliancy** ['briljənsi], *n.* lustre, éclat, *m.*

brilliant ['briljənt], *a.* brillant, éclatant.—*n.* brillant (*diamant*), *m.*

brilliantly ['briljəntli], *adv.* brillamment, avec éclat.

brim [brim], *n.* bord, *m.*—*v.i.* être plein jusqu'au bord; **brimming over**, débordant.

brimful ['brimful], *a.* rempli jusqu'au bord, tout plein.

brimstone ['brimstən], *n.* soufre, *m.*

brindle(d) [brindl(d)], *a.* tacheté, bringé.

brine [brain], *n.* saumure, *f.*

bring [briŋ], *v.t. irr.* apporter (*choses*); amener (*personnes et animaux*); conduire; porter (*to carry*); transporter; réduire (*to reduce*); (*fig.*) mettre; **to bring about**, amener, causer, opérer, provoquer; **to bring down**, descendre, abattre; **to bring forth**, produire, mettre au monde, mettre bas; **to bring forward**, amener, avancer; **to bring in**, faire entrer, rapporter; **to bring into play**, mettre en œuvre; **to bring off**, tirer d'affaire, sauver; conduire à bien, réussir; **to bring on**, amener, occasionner; **to bring to again**, faire reprendre connaissance à; **to bring together**, réunir, assembler, réconcilier; **to bring up**, nourrir, élever.

brink [briŋk], *n.* bord, *m.*

briny ['braini], *a.* saumâtre, salé; (*fig.*) amer.

brisk [brisk], *a.* vif; (*fig.*) animé, actif, gai, frais, dispos.

briskly ['briskli], *adv.* vivement.

briskness ['brisknis], *n.* vivacité; activité, *f.*

bristle [brisl], *n.* soie, *f.*; poil raide, *m.*—*v.i.* se hérisser (*de*); se raidir (*contre*).

bristling ['brisliŋ], **bristly** ['brisli], *a.* hérissé (*de*); (*Bot.*) poilu.

Britain ['britən]. la Grande-Bretagne, *f.*

Britannic [bri'tænik], *a.* (*rare*) britannique.

British ['britiʃ], *a.* britannique; **the British**, les Anglais, les Britanniques, *m.pl.*

Brittany ['britəni]. la Bretagne, *f.*
brittle [britl], *a.* fragile, cassant.
brittleness ['britlnis], *n.* fragilité, *f.*
broach [brəutʃ], *n.* broche, *f.*—*v.t.* embrocher; mettre (*un tonneau*) en perce; introduire, entamer (*un sujet*).
broad [brɔːd], *a.* large, grand, gros, vaste; (*fig.*) libre, grossier, hardi; peu voilé (*allusion*); prononcé (*accent*).
broadcast ['brɔːdkɑːst], *a.* à la volée; radiodiffusé.—*v.t. irr.* semer (*du grain*) à la volée; répandre (*une nouvelle*); radiodiffuser.—*n.* émission, *f.*
broadcaster ['brɔːdkɑːstə], *n.* speaker, *m.*
broadcasting ['brɔːdkɑːstiŋ], *n.* radiodiffusion, *f.*; **broadcasting station**, poste émetteur, *m.*
broaden [brɔːdn], *v.t.* élargir.—*v.i.* s'élargir, s'étendre.
broadly ['brɔːdli], *adv.* largement.
broad-minded ['brɔːd'maindid], *a.* tolérant, à l'esprit large.
broadness ['brɔːdnis], *n.* largeur, *f.*; (*fig.*) grossièreté, *f.*
broadside ['brɔːdsaid], *n.* (*Naut.*) côté, flanc, *m.*; bordée, *f.*
brocade [bro'keid], *n.* brocart, *m.*
brogue (1) [broug], *n.* accent irlandais, *m.*
brogue (2) [broug], *n.* brogue (*chaussure*), *f.*
broil (1) [brɔil], *n.* querelle, *f.*, tumulte, *m.*
broil (2) [brɔil], *v.t.* griller.—*v.i.* se griller.
broken ['broukan], *a.* cassé, brisé, rompu; (*fig.*) navré; entrecoupé, décousu (*discours etc.*); accidenté (*terrain*); interrompu (*sommeil*); délabré (*santé*).
broker ['broukə], *n.* courtier; brocanteur (*articles d'occasion*), *m.*; **ship broker**, courtier maritime; **stockbroker**, agent de change, *m.*
brokerage ['broukəridʒ], *n.* courtage, *m.*
bromide ['broumaid], *n.* bromure, *f.*
bromine ['broumi:n, 'broumain], *n.* brome, *m.*
bronchia ['brɔŋkiə], *n.pl.* bronches, *f.pl.*
bronchial ['brɔŋkiəl], *a.* bronchial.
bronchitis [brɔŋ'kaitis], *n.* bronchite, *f.*
bronze [brɔnz], *n.* bronze, *m.*
bronzed [brɔnzd], *a.* bronzé, basané.
brooch [broutʃ], *n.* broche, *f.*
brood [bruːd], *v.i.* couver; **to brood over**, rêver à, ruminer.—*n.* couvée, *f.*
broody ['bruːdi], *a.* couveuse (*poule*); distrait (*personne*).
brook (1) [bruk], *n.* ruisseau, *m.*
brook (2) [bruk], *v.t.* (*always neg.*) souffrir; avaler, digérer.
broom [bruːm], *n.* balai; genêt (*plante*), *m.*
broth [brɔθ], *n.* bouillon, potage, *m.*
brother ['brʌðə], *n.* (*pl.* **brothers** ['brʌðəz], *rhet.* **brethren** ['breðrin]) frère, *m.*; **brother in arms**, frère d'armes; **foster brother**, frère de lait.
brotherhood ['brʌðəhud], *n.* fraternité; confrérie, confraternité, *f.*
brother-in-law ['brʌðərinlɔː], *n.* beau-frère, *m.*
brotherly ['brʌðəli], *a.* fraternel.
brow [brau], *n.* front; sourcil; (*fig.*) sommet, *m.*
browbeat ['braubiːt], *v.t. irr.* (*conjug. like* BEAT) intimider, rudoyer.
brown [braun], *a.* brun; sombre, rembruni; châtain (*chevelure*); (*Cook.*) rissolé; **brown bread**, pain bis, *m.*; **brown study**, rêverie, *f.*; **brown sugar**, sucre brut, *m.*—

n. brun, *m.*—*v.t.* brunir; (*Cook.*) rissoler, faire dorer.
brownie ['brauni], *n.* jeannette, *f.*
brownish ['brauniʃ], *a.* brunâtre.
browse [brauz], *v.i.* brouter.
bruise [bruːz], *v.t.* meurtrir, contusionner; écraser, froisser.—*n.* meurtrissure, contusion, *f.*
brunette [bruː'net], *a.* and *n.* brune, *f.*
brunt [brʌnt], *n.* choc, *m.*, violence, fureur, *f.*; **to bear the brunt of**, faire tous les frais de.
brush [brʌʃ], *n.* brosse, *f.*; balai; pinceau, *m.*; (*fig.*) escarmouche; queue (*d'un renard*), *f.*—*v.t.* brosser; balayer; (*fig.*) effleurer, raser.
brush-maker ['brʌʃmeikə], *n.* brossier, *m.*
brushwood ['brʌʃwud], *n.* broussailles, *f.pl.*, fourré, *m.*
brusque [brusk], *a.* brusque.
Brussels ['brʌslz]. Bruxelles, *f*; **Brussels sprouts**, choux de Bruxelles, *m.pl.*
brutal [bruːtl], *a.* brutal, cruel, inhumain.
brutality [bruː'tæliti], *n.* brutalité, cruauté, *f.*
brutally ['bruːtəli], *adv.* brutalement.
brute [bruːt], *a.* brut, insensible; sauvage; brutal (*animaux*).—*n.* animal, *m.*, brute, bête, *f.*, brutal, *m.*
bubble [bʌbl], *n.* bulle; (*fig.*) chimère, illusion; duperie, *f.*—*v.i.* bouillonner; pétiller (*vin*).
bubonic [bjuː'bɔnik], *a.* bubonique.
buccaneer [bʌkə'niə], *n.* boucanier, flibustier, *m.*
buck [bʌk], *n.* daim; chevreuil; mâle (*lièvre ou lapin*); (*fig.*) gaillard, beau, élégant, *m.*
bucket ['bʌkit], *n.* seau; baquet, *m.*
buckle [bʌkl], *n.* boucle, agrafe, *f.*—*v.t.* boucler, agrafer.—*v.i.* se boucler; se courber.
buckler ['bʌklə], *n.* bouclier, *m.*
buckram ['bʌkrəm], *n.* bougran, *m.*
buckwheat ['bʌkwiːt], *n.* sarrasin, blé noir, *m.*
bucolic [bjuː'kɔlik], *a.* bucolique.—*n.* poème bucolique, *m.*
bud [bʌd], *n.* bourgeon, bouton; (*fig.*) germe, *m.*—*v.t.* écussonner.—*v.i.* bourgeonner.
Buddha ['budə]. Bouddha, *m.*
Buddhism ['budizm], *n.* bouddhisme, *m.*
Buddhist ['budist], *n.* bouddhiste, *m.*, *f.*
budge [bʌdʒ], *v.t.* bouger.—*v.i.* bouger, se remuer.
budgerigar [bʌdʒəri'gɑː], *n.* (*Orn.*) perruche inséparable, *f.*
budget ['bʌdʒit], *n.* sac; (*Fin.*) budget, *m.*
buff [bʌf], *a.* de couleur chamois.—*n.* buffle, *m.*, peau de buffle; couleur chamois, *f.*—*v.t.* polir au buffle.
buffalo ['bʌfəlou], *n.* buffle, *m.*
buffer ['bʌfə], *n.* tampon, amortisseur, *m.*
buffet (1) [bu'fei], *n.* buffet (*sideboard*); buffet (*meal*), *m.*
buffet (2) ['bʌfit], *v.t.* frapper à coups de poing, souffleter.—*v.i.* se battre à coups de poing.—*n.* soufflet, coup de poing, *m.*
buffoon [bʌ'fuːn], *n.* bouffon, *m.*
buffoonery [bʌ'fuːnəri], *n.* bouffonnerie, *f.*
bug [bʌg], *n.* punaise, *f.*, insecte, *m.*
bugle [bjuːgl], *n.* cor de chasse; (*Mil.*) clairon, *m.*
bugler ['bjuːglə], *n.* clairon, *m.*
build [bild], *v.t. irr.* bâtir, faire bâtir, construire; (*fig.*) édifier, fonder, baser.—*n.* construction; forme, carrure, taille, *f.*

builder ['bɪldə], n. constructeur, entrepreneur de maçonnerie, m.

building ['bɪldɪŋ], n. construction, f.; édifice, bâtiment, m.; *building and loan association*, société immobilière, f.

bulb [bʌlb], n. bulbe, oignon, m.; cuvette (*de thermomètre*); poire (*en caoutchouc*); (*Elec.*) ampoule, lampe, f.

bulbous ['bʌlbəs], a. bulbeux.

Bulgaria [bʌl'gɛəriə]. la Bulgarie, f.

Bulgarian [bʌl'gɛəriən], a. bulgare.—n. bulgare (*langue*), m.; Bulgare (*personne*), m., f.

bulge [bʌldʒ], n. bombement, m., bosse, f.—v.t., v.i. faire saillie, bomber.

bulging ['bʌldʒɪŋ], a. bombé.

bulk [bʌlk], n. volume, m., grosseur, masse, f., gros, m.; (*Naut.*) charge, f.; *in bulk*, en bloc, en gros.

bulkhead ['bʌlkhed], n. cloison étanche, f.

bulky ['bʌlkɪ], a. gros, encombrant.

bull (1) [bul], n. taureau, m.; (*St. Exch.*) haussier, m.

bull (2) [bul], n. bulle (*du Pape*), f.

bulldog ['buldɒg], n. bouledogue, m.

bulldozer ['buldouzə], n. bulldozer, m.

bullet ['bulit], n. balle, f.

bulletin ['bulitin], n. bulletin, communiqué, m. [**bulletin board**, see notice-board]

bullet-proof ['bulitpruːf], a. à l'épreuve des balles.

bullfinch ['bulfintʃ], n. (*Orn.*) bouvreuil, m.

bullion ['buljən], n. or ou argent en lingots, m.

bullock ['bulək], n. bœuf, bouvillon, m.

bull's-eye ['bulzaɪ], n. centre, noir (*d'une cible*); œil-de-bœuf (*fenêtre*), m.

bully ['bulɪ], n. matamore, bravache, m.; brute, f.—v.t. malmener, intimider.—v.i. faire le matamore.

bulrush ['bulrʌʃ], n. (*Bot.*) jonc, m.

bulwark ['bulwək], n. rempart; (*Naut.*) pavois, m.

bumble-bee ['bʌmblbiː], n. bourdon, m.

bump [bʌmp], n. bosse, f.; heurt, cahot, coup, choc, m.—v.t. frapper, cogner.—v.i. se cogner, se heurter.

bumper ['bʌmpə], n. rasade, f., rouge-bord; (*Motor.*) pare-choc, m.

bumpkin ['bʌmpkin], n. rustre, lourdaud, m.

bumpy ['bʌmpɪ], a. cahoteux (*route*).

bun [bʌn], n. petit pain rond (au lait); chignon (*coiffure*), m.

bunch [bʌntʃ], n. botte, f.; bouquet, m., gerbe (*de fleurs*); grappe (*de raisins*), f.; régime (*de bananes*); trousseau (*de clefs*), m.

bundle [bʌndl], n. paquet; ballot; faisceau; fagot (*de bois etc.*), m.; liasse (*de papiers*), f.—v.t. empaqueter.

bung [bʌŋ], n. bondon, tampon, m.—v.t. boucher.

bungalow ['bʌŋgəlou], n. maison sans étage, f.

bung-hole ['bʌŋhoul], n. bonde, f.

bungle [bʌŋgl], v.t. bousiller, gâcher, rater.—v.i. s'y prendre gauchement, faire de la mauvaise besogne.—n. bousillage, gâchis, m.

bungler ['bʌŋglə], n. maladroit, savetier, bousilleur, m.

bungling ['bʌŋglɪŋ], a. maladroit, gauche.

bunion ['bʌnjən], n. oignon (*de pied*), m.

bunk [bʌŋk], n. (*Naut.*) couchette, f.

bunker ['bʌŋkə], n. soute (*à charbon*); (*Golf*) banquette, f.

bunting ['bʌntɪŋ], n. étamine, f.; (*Orn.*) bruant, m.; (*fig.*) drapeaux, pavillons, m.pl.

buoy [bɔi], n. bouée, f.; life *buoy*, bouée de sauvetage; *mooring buoy*, coffre d'amarrage, m.—v.t. to *buoy up*, soutenir sur l'eau; (*fig.*) encourager.

buoyancy ['bɔiənsi], n. légèreté, f.; élan, m.; vivacité, animation, f.

buoyant ['bɔiənt], a. léger, flottant; animé, vif.

burble [bə:bl], v.i. murmurer, bafouiller.—n. murmure, m.

burden [bə:dn], n. fardeau, m.; charge, f.; poids; refrain (*d'une chanson*), m.—v.t. charger.

burdensome ['bə:dnsəm], a. pesant, lourd; ennuyeux.

bureau [bjuə'rou], n. bureau, m.

bureaucracy [bjuə'rokrəsi], n. bureaucratie, f.

bureaucrat ['bjuərokræt], n. bureaucrate, m., f.

bureaucratic [bjuəro'krætik], a. bureaucratique.

burgess ['bə:dʒis], n. bourgeois, citoyen, électeur, m.

burgh ['bʌrə], n. (*Sc.*) bourg, m.

burglar ['bə:glə], n. cambrioleur, m.

burglary ['bə:gləri], n. vol avec effraction; cambriolage, m.

burgle [bə:gl], v.t., v.i. cambrioler.

burgomaster ['bə:goma:stə], n. bourgmestre, m.

burial ['beriəl], n. enterrement, m., obsèques, f.pl.; inhumation, f.

burlesque [bə:'lesk], a. and n. burlesque, m.—v.t. parodier, travestir.

burliness ['bə:linis], n. grosseur, corpulence, f.

burly ['bə:li], a. de forte carrure.

Burma(h) ['bə:mə]. la Birmanie, f.

Burmese [bə:'mi:z], a. birman.—n. birman (*langue*); Birman (*personne*), m.

burn [bə:n], v.t. irr. brûler; cuire (*briques etc.*); incendier.—v.i. brûler; (*fig.*) brûler, être impatient de.—n. brûlure, f.

burner ['bə:nə], n. brûleur; bec (*de gaz etc.*), m.

burning ['bə:niŋ], a. en feu; brûlant, ardent.—n. brûlure, f.; incendie, m.

burnish ['bə:niʃ], v.t. brunir, polir.

burrow ['bʌrou], n. terrier, trou, m.—v.t. creuser.—v.i. se terrer; (*fig.*) se cacher.

bursar ['bə:sə], n. économe, intendant; trésorier; boursier, m.

bursary ['bə:səri], n. bourse (*d'études*), f.

burst [bə:st], v.t. irr. crever; faire éclater; fendre; rompre.—v.i. cæver, éclater; sauter; jaillir; s'élancer; éclore (*bourgeon*); to *burst into tears*, fondre en larmes; to *burst out laughing*, éclater de rire.—n. éclat, éclatement, m., explosion; rupture, hernie, f.

bury ['beri], v.t. enterrer, ensevelir; (*fig.*) enfoncer; cacher.

bus [bʌs], n. autobus, m.

bus conductor ['bʌskəndʌktə], n. receveur (d'autobus), m.

bush [buʃ], n. buisson; fourré, m.

bushel [buʃl], n. boisseau, m.

bushy ['buʃi], a. buissonneux; touffu.

367

busily ['bizili], *adv.* activement; avec empressement.

business ['biznis], *n.* affaire, occupation, *f.*, devoir; état, métier, *m.*; affaires, *f.pl.*, commerce, *m.*; *what business is that of yours?* est-ce que cela vous regarde? *you have no business here*, vous n'avez que faire ici; *business suit*, complet veston, *m.*

businesslike ['biznislaik], *a.* pratique, régulier, méthodique; franc, droit, sérieux.

buskin ['bʌskin], *n.* brodequin; (*fig.*) cothurne, *m.*

bust [bʌst], *n.* (*Sculp.*) buste, *m.*; gorge (*de femme*); (*Art*) bosse, *f.*

bustard ['bʌstəd], *n.* (*Orn.*) outarde, *f.*

bustle [bʌsl], *n.* mouvement; bruit, *m.*, confusion, activité, agitation, *f.*—*v.i.* se remuer, s'empresser.

bustling ['bʌsliŋ], *a.* empressé, affairé, remuant; bruyant.

busy ['bizi], *a.* affairé, occupé, empressé, diligent.—*v.r.* *to busy oneself*, s'occuper.

busybody ['bizibɔdi], *n.* officieux, *m.*

but [bʌt], *conj.* mais, que; sauf que; qui ne; *but that*, sans que.—*adv.* ne . . . que; seulement; *all but*, presque.—*prep.* sans, excepté, à part.

butcher ['butʃə], *n.* boucher, *m.*; *butcher's shop*, boucherie, *f.*—*v.t.* égorger, massacrer.

butchery ['butʃəri], *n.* boucherie; tuerie, *f.*, massacre, carnage, *m.*

butler ['bʌtlə], *n.* maître d'hôtel, *m.*

butt (1) [bʌt], *n.* bout, *m.*; crosse (*d'un fusil*); masse (*d'une queue de billard*), *f.*

butt (2) [bʌt], *n.* cible, *f.*; (*fig.*) point de mire; plastron (*personne*), *m.*

butt (3) [bʌt], *n.* coup de tête, *m.*—*v.t.* cosser, frapper de le tête (*animal*).

butt (4) [bʌt], *n.* barrique, *f.*

butter ['bʌtə], *n.* beurre, *m.*—*v.t.* beurrer.

buttercup ['bʌtəkʌp], *n.* bouton d'or, *m.*

butter dish ['bʌtədiʃ], *n.* beurrier, *m.*

butterfly ['bʌtəflai], *n.* papillon, *m.*

buttermilk ['bʌtəmilk], *n.* petit-lait, *m.*

buttery ['bʌtəri], *a.* de beurre, graisseux.—*n.* dépense, *f.*

buttock ['bʌtək], *n.* fesse (*de cheval*); culotte (*de bœuf*), *f.*

button [bʌtn], *n.* bouton, *m.*—*v.t.* boutonner. —*v.i.* se boutonner.

buttonhole ['bʌtnhoul], *n.* boutonnière, *f.*— *v.t.* accrocher (*quelqu'un*).

button-hook ['bʌtnhuk], *n.* tire-bouton, *m.*

buttress ['bʌtris], *n.* contrefort, éperon, *m.*; *flying buttress*, arc-boutant, *m.*—*v.t.* arcbouter.

buxom ['bʌksəm], *a.* plein de santé et d'entrain; rondelette et fraîche (*femme*).

buy [bai], *v.t. irr.* acheter; prendre (*billet*); corrompre, acheter (*quelqu'un*); *to buy up*, accaparer.

buyer ['baiə], *n.* acheteur, acquéreur, *m.*

buying ['baiiŋ], *n.* achat, *m.*

buzz [bʌz], *v.i.* bourdonner.—*n.* bourdonnement; brouhaha (*de conversation*), *m.*

buzzard ['bʌzəd], *n.* (*Orn.*) buse, *f.*

buzzer ['bʌzə], *n.* trompe, *f.*; vibreur, appel vibré, *m.*

by [bai], *prep.* par; de; à; sur; près de, auprès de, à côté de; en (*with participles*); *by far*, de beaucoup; *by no means*, nullement; *by sight*, de vue.—*adv.* près; passé.

by-election ['baiilekʃən], *n.* élection partielle, *f.*

bygone ['baigɔn], *a.* passé, d'autrefois.

by-pass ['baipɑːs], *n.* route d'évitement, déviation, *f.*—*v.t.* contourner, éviter (*une ville*).

by-play ['baiplei], *n.* jeu de scène, jeu muet, *m.*

by-product ['baiprɔdʌkt], *n.* sous-produit, *m.*

byre ['baiə], *n.* étable à vaches, *f.*

bystander ['baistændə], *n.* spectateur, assistant, *m.*

byword ['baiwəːd], *n.* dicton, proverbe, *m.*; (*fig.*) risée, *f.*

C

C, c [siː], troisième lettre de l'alphabet; (*Mus.*) ut, do, *m.*

cab [kæb], *n.* fiacre, taxi, *m.*

cabal [kə'bæl], *n.* cabale, *f.*—*v.i.* cabaler.

cabbage ['kæbidʒ], *n.* chou, *m.*

cabin ['kæbin], *n.* cabine, chambre (*pour officiers etc.*); (*Av.*) carlingue; cabane, case, hutte, *f.*

cabin boy ['kæbinbɔi], *n.* mousse, *m.*

cabinet ['kæbinit], *n.* meuble à tiroirs; classeur; cabinet; ministère, *m.*

cabinet-maker ['kæbiniˈtmeikə], *n.* ébéniste, *m.*, *f.*

cable [keibl], *n.* câble; câblogramme, *m.*— *v.t.* câbler, télégraphier.

cablegram ['keiblgræm], *n.* câblogramme, *m.*

caboose [kə'buːs], *n.* (*Naut.*) cuisine, cambuse, *f.*

cackle [kækl], *n.* caquet, *m.*—*v.i.* caqueter; (*fig.*) ricaner, glousser; cacarder (*oie*).

cackling ['kækliŋ], *n.* caquetage, *m.*

cactus ['kæktəs], *n.* cactus, *m.*

cad [kæd], *n.* goujat, *m.*; canaille, *f.*

cadaverous [kə'dævərəs], *a.* cadavéreux.

caddie ['kædi], *n.* (*Golf*) cadet, *m.*—*v.i.* servir de cadet.

caddy ['kædi], *n.* boîte à thé, *f.*

cadet [kə'det], *n.* cadet; élève-officier (*d'une école militaire ou d'une école navale*), *m.*

cadge [kædʒ], *v.t.*, *v.i.* colporter; quémander; écornifler.

cage [keidʒ], *n.* cage, *f.*—*v.t.* mettre en cage.

Cairo ['kaiərou], le Caire, *m.*

cajole [kə'dʒoul], *v.t.* cajoler, enjôler.

cake [keik], *n.* gâteau, *m.*; masse, croûte (*matière solidifiée*), *f.*; *cake of soap*, savonnette, *f.*—*v.i.* se cailler, se prendre, se coller.

calamitous [kə'læmitəs], *a.* calamiteux, désastreux, funeste.

calamity [kə'læmiti], *n.* calamité, *f.*, désastre, malheur, *m.*

calculate ['kælkjuleit], *v.t.* calculer; compter; évaluer.

calculation [kælkju'leiʃən], *n.* calcul, compte, *m.*

calculus ['kælkjuləs], *n.* (*Med.*) calcul; (*Math.*) calcul infinitésimal, *m.*
Caledonia [kæli'dəuniə]. la Calédonie, *f.*
calendar ['kæləndə], *n.* calendrier, *m.*; (*Law*) liste, *f.*
calender ['kæləndə], *n.* calandre, *f.pl.*
calends ['kæləndz], *n.pl.* calendes, *f.pl.*
calf [kɑːf], *n.* (*pl.* **calves** [kɑːvz]) veau, *m.*; mollet (*de la jambe*), *m.*
calibre ['kælibə], *n.* calibre, *m.*; (*Tech.*) compas, *m.*
calibrate ['kælibreit], *v.t.* calibrer, graduer.
calico ['kælikou], *n.* indienne, *f.*
California [kæli'fɔːniə]. la Californie, *f.*
caliph ['keilif], *n.* calife, *m.*
calk [kɔːk], *v.t.* ferrer à glace (*cheval etc.*).
call [kɔːl], *n.* appel, cri, *m.*; voix, *f.*; (*Naut.*) sifflet, *m.*; (*fig.*) obligation, *f.*, devoir, *m.*; demande, invitation; visite, *f.*; coup de téléphone, *m.*; *within call*, à portée de voix.—*v.t.* appeler; nommer, qualifier (*de*); convoquer; rappeler; *to be called Peter*, s'appeler Pierre; *to call for*, demander, exiger; aller chercher; *to call in*, faire rentrer; *to call in a doctor*, faire venir un médecin; *to call off*, rappeler, rompre, décommander; *to call out*, appeler, crier; *to call to mind*, se rappeler; *to call up*, faire monter; réveiller; appeler sous les drapeaux, mobiliser.—*v.i.* appeler, crier; venir *ou* aller (*chez*), rendre visite (*à*); (*Naut.*) toucher (*à*); *to call at*, passer par, s'arrêter à; *to call on*, inviter, prier; rendre visite à; *to call upon*, faire appel (*à quelqu'un*).
call-box ['kɔːlbɔks], *n.* cabine téléphonique, *f.*
call-boy ['kɔːlbɔi], *n.* (*Theat.*) avertisseur, *m.*
caller ['kɔːlə], *n.* visiteur, *m.*; (*Teleph.*) celui *ou* celle qui appelle, *m.*, *f.*
calling ['kɔːliŋ], *n.* appel, *m.*; profession, vocation, *f.*, métier, état, *m.*
callipers ['kælipəz], *n.* compas de calibre, *m.*
callous ['kæləs], *a.* calleux, endurci; insensible.
callously ['kæləsli], *adv.* durement, impitoyablement.
callousness ['kæləsnis], *n.* insensibilité, *f.*, endurcissement, *m.*
callow ['kælou], *a.* sans plume; (*fig.*) jeune, novice.
call-up ['kɔːlʌp], *n.* (*Mil.*) appel sous les drapeaux, *m.*
calm [kɑːm], *a.* and *n.* calme, *m.*—*v.t.* calmer, apaiser.
calmly ['kɑːmli], *adv.* avec calme, tranquillement.
calorie ['kæləri], *n.* calorie, *f.*
calumniate [kə'lʌmnieit], *v.t.* calomnier.
calumnious [kə'lʌmniəs], *a.* calomnieux.
calumny ['kæləmni], *n.* calomnie, *f.*
calvary ['kælvəri], *n.* calvaire; chemin de la croix, *m.*
calve [kɑːv], *v.i.* vêler.
calves [CALF.]
calyx ['keiliks, 'kæliks], *n.* calice, *m.*
cam [kæm], *n.* (*Mech.*) came, *f.*
camber ['kæmbə], *n.* cambrure, *f.*
Cambodia [kæm'boudiə]. le Cambodge, *m.*
Cambodian [kæm'boudiən], *a.* cambodgien. —*n.* cambodgien (*langue*); Cambodgien (*personne*), *m.*
cambric ['keimbrik], *n.* batiste, *f.*

camel ['kæməl], *n.* chameau, *m.*
camellia [kə'miːliə], *n.* camélia, *m.*
camel hair ['kæməlhɛə], *n.* poil de chameau, *m.*
cameo ['kæmiou], *n.* camée, *m.*
camera ['kæmərə], *n.* appareil (photographique), *m.*; *movie camera*, (ciné)caméra, *f.*
cameraman ['kæmərəmæn], *n.* (*pl.* **cameramen** ['kæmərəmen]) photographe (*de presse*); (*Cine., Tel.*) opérateur, cameraman, *m.*
camouflage ['kæmuflɑːʒ], *n.* camouflage, *m.* —*v.t.* camoufler.
camp [kæmp], *n.* camp, *m.*; *to break up a camp*, lever un camp; *to pitch a camp*, établir un camp.—*v.i.* camper.
campaign [kæm'pein], *n.* campagne, *f.*—*v.i.* faire campagne.
campaigner [kæm'peinə], *n.* vieux soldat, *m.*
campanile [kæmpə'niːli], *n.* campanile, *m.*
campanula [kæm'pænjulə], *n.* (*Bot.*) campanule, *f.*
camp bed ['kæmpbed], *n.* lit de camp, *m.*
camper ['kæmpə], *n.* campeur, *m.*
camphor ['kæmfə], *n.* camphre, *m.*
camping ['kæmpiŋ], *n.* (*Mil.*) campement; camping, *m.*; *to go camping*, faire du camping.
can (1) [kæn], *n.* pot, broc, bidon, *m.*; boîte en fer blanc, *f.*—*v.t.* mettre en boîte.
can (2) [kæn], *v. aux. irr.* (*inf.* to be able) pouvoir (*to be able*); savoir (*to know how to*); *he can read*, il sait lire; *I can do it*, je peux *ou* je sais le faire.
Canada ['kænədə]. le Canada, *m.*
Canadian [kə'neidiən], *a.* canadien.—*n.* Canadien (*personne*), *m.*
canal [kə'næl], *n.* canal, *m.*
canary [kə'nɛəri], *n.* (*Orn.*) serin, *m.*
cancel ['kænsəl], *v.t.* annuler; effacer, biffer, rayer; oblitérer (*un timbre*); décommander; (*Comm.*) résilier.
cancellation [kænsə'leiʃən], *n.* annulation; résiliation, oblitération, *f.*
cancer ['kænsə], *n.* cancer, *m.*
cancerous ['kænsərəs], *a.* cancéreux.
candelabrum [kændi'lɑːbrəm], **candelabra** [kændi'lɑːbrə], *n.* candélabre, *m.*
candid ['kændid], *a.* sincère, franc.
candidate ['kændidit], *n.* aspirant, candidat, *m.*
candidature ['kændiditʃə], *n.* candidature, *f.*
candidly ['kændidli], *adv.* franchement, de bonne foi.
candle ['kændl], *n.* chandelle; bougie; (*fig.*) lumière, *f.*; (*Ch.*) cierge, *m.*
Candlemas ['kændlməs]. la Chandeleur, *f.*
candlestick ['kændlstik], *n.* chandelier; bougeoir, *m.*
candle wax ['kændlwæks], *n.* suif, *m.*
candor ['kændə], *n.* franchise, sincérité, bonne foi, *f.*
candy ['kændi], *n.* candi, *m.*; (*Am.*) bonbons, *m.pl.*
cane [kein], *n.* canne, *f.*
canine ['kænain, 'keinain], *a.* canin, de chien.
caning ['keiniŋ], *n.* coups de canne, *m.pl.*, râclée, *f.*

canister ['kænistə], *n.* boîte en fer blanc; boîte à thé, *f.*

canker ['kæŋkə], *n.* chancre; (*fig.*) ver rongeur; fléau, *m.*—*v.t.* ronger; (*fig.*) corrompre, empoisonner.—*v.i.* se ronger; (*fig.*) se gangrener, se corrompre.

canned [kænd], *a.* (*Am.*) conservé en boîtes (*fruits etc.*); (*fam.*) enregistré (*musique*).

cannibal ['kænibəl], *n.* cannibale, anthropophage, *m., f.*

cannibalism ['kænibəlizm], *n.* cannibalisme, *m.*

cannon ['kænən], *n.* canon; (*Billiards*) carambolage, *m.*—*v.i.* caramboler.

cannonade [kænə'neid], *n.* cannonade, *f.*

cannon ball ['kænənbɔ:l], *n.* boulet de canon, *m.*

canoe [kə'nu:], *n.* canoë, *m.*; périssoire; pirogue, *f.*

canoeist [kə'nu:ist], *n.* canoëiste, *m., f.*

canon ['kænən], *n.* chanoine; canon (*règle*), *m.*

canonical [kə'nɔnikl], *a.* canonique.

canonization [kænənai'zeiʃən], *n.* canonisation, *f.*

canonize ['kænənaiz], *v.t.* canoniser.

can opener ['kænoupənə], *n.* (*Am.*) ouvre-boîte, *m.*

canopy ['kænəpi], *n.* dais; (*Arch.*) baldaquin, *m.*; voûte (*du ciel*), *f.*

cant (1) [kænt], *n.* cant, langage hypocrite, *m.*; afféterie; hypocrisie, *f.*—*v.i.* parler avec afféterie *ou* avec affectation.

cant (2) [kænt], *n.* (*Arch.*) pan coupé, *m.*—*v.t.* pousser, jeter de côté, incliner.

cantankerous [kæn'tæŋkərəs], *a.* acariâtre, revêche, bourru.

cantankerousness [kæn'tæŋkərəsnis], *n.* humeur acariâtre, *f.*

cantata [kæn'ta:tə], *n.* cantate, *f.*

canteen [kæn'ti:n], *n.* cantine, *f.*, restaurant; bidon (*boîte*), *m.*; *canteen of cutlery*, ménagère, *f.*

canter ['kæntə], *n.* petit galop, *m.*—*v.i.* aller au petit galop.

canticle ['kæntikl], *n.* cantique, *m.*

cantilever ['kæntili:və], *n.* (*Arch.*) encorbellement, modillon, *m.*

canto ['kæntou], *n.* chant, *m.*

canton ['kæntən], *n.* canton, *m.*

cantonment [kæn'tu:nmənt], *n.* cantonnement, *m.*

canvas ['kænvəs], *n.* toile, *f.*; tableau, *m.*, peinture; voile, toile à voiles, *f.*; *under canvas*, sous la tente.

canvass ['kænvəs], *n.* débat, *m.*, discussion; sollicitation de suffrages, *f.*—*v.t.* agiter, discuter; solliciter.—*v.i.* solliciter des suffrages; faire la place.

canvasser ['kænvəsə], *n.* agent électoral, (*Comm.*) représentant, *m.*

canvassing ['kænvəsiŋ], *n.* propagande électorale; (*Comm.*) prospection, *f.*

canyon ['kænjən], *n.* gorge, *f.*, défilé, *m.*

cap [kæp], *n.* bonnet (*de femme*), *m.*; casquette (*d'homme*); barrette (*d'un cardinal*); capsule, amorce (*d'armes à feu*), *f.*; (*Phot.*) chapeau (*d'un objectif etc.*); capuchon (*d'un stylo*), *m.*—*v.t.* coiffer, couvrir; (*fig.*) couronner, surpasser.

capability [keipə'biliti], *n.* capacité, *f.*

capable ['keipəbl], *a.* capable; susceptible (*de*); compétent.

capacious [kə'peiʃəs], *a.* ample, vaste, spacieux.

capaciousness [kə'peiʃəsnis], *n.* capacité, étendue, *f.*

capacitate [kə'pæsiteit], *v.t.* rendre capable de.

capacity [kə'pæsiti], *n.* capacité, *f.*; *in the capacity of*, en qualité de.

cap-à-pie [kæpə'pi:], *adv.* de pied en cap.

caparison [kə'pærizn], *n.* caparaçon, *m.*—*v.t.* caparaçonner.

cape (1) [keip], *n.* cap, promontoire, *m.*

cape (2) [keip], *n.* pèlerine, cape (*manteau*), *f.*

caper (1) ['keipə], *n.* bond, entrechat, *m.*—*v.i.* cabrioler; bondir, sauter.

caper (2) ['keipə], *n.* (*Bot.*) câpre, *f.*

capillary [kə'piləri], *a.* capillaire.

capital ['kæpitl], *a.* capital; (*colloq.*) excellent; (*Print.*) majuscule.—*n.* capital, *m.*, capitaux, *m.pl.*; capitale (*ville*), *f.*; (*Comm.*) fonds; (*Arch.*) chapiteau, *m.*; (*Print.*) majuscule, *f.*

capitalism ['kæpitəlizm], *n.* capitalisme, *m.*

capitalist ['kæpitəlist], *n.* capitaliste, *m., f.*

capitalize ['kæpitəlaiz], *v.t.* capitaliser.

capitally ['kæpitəli], *adv.* principalement; admirablement, à merveille.

capitulate [kə'pitjuleit], *v.i.* capituler.

capitulation [kəpitju'leiʃən], *n.* capitulation, *f.*

capon ['keipən], *n.* chapon, *m.*

caprice [kə'pri:s], *n.* caprice, *m.*

capricious [kə'priʃəs], *a.* capricieux.

capriciously [kə'priʃəsli], *adv.* capricieusement.

capsize [kæp'saiz], *v.t.* faire chavirer.—*v.i.* chavirer (*bateau*).

capstan ['kæpstən], *n.* cabestan, *m.*

capsule ['kæpsju:l], *n.* capsule, *f.*

captain ['kæptin], *n.* capitaine, *m.*

caption ['kæpʃən], *n.* arrestation; saisie (*choses*), *f.*; en-tête (*d'un chapitre etc.*), *m.*, légende (*d'une photographie etc.*), *f.*; (*Cine.*) sous-titre, *m.*

captious ['kæpʃəs], *a.* insidieux, chicaneur.

captiousness ['kæpʃəsnis], *n.* esprit de chicane; sophisme, *m.*

captivate ['kæptiveit], *v.t.* captiver; charmer, séduire.

captivating ['kæptiveitiŋ], *a.* enchanteur, séduisant.

captive ['kæptiv], *a.* captif.—*n.* captif, prisonnier, *m.*

captivity [kæp'tiviti], *n.* captivité, *f.*

capture ['kæptʃə], *n.* capture; prise, arrestation, *f.*—*v.t.* capturer, prendre, arrêter.

car [ka:], *n.* (*Motor.*) auto, voiture, *f.*; (*Rail.*) wagon; (*Lit.*) char, chariot, *m.*; nacelle (*d'un ballon*), *f.*; *dining car*, wagon-restaurant, *m.*; *sleeping car*, wagon-lit, *m.* [freight car, see van]

caramel ['kærəmel], *n.* caramel, *m.*

carat ['kærət], *n.* carat, *m.*

caravan [kærə'væn, 'kærəvæn], *n.* caravane; roulotte, *f.*

caravanseral [kærə'vænsərai], *n.* caravansérail, *m.*

caraway ['kærəwei], *n.* (*Bot.*) carvi, cumin des prés, *m.*

carbide ['ka:baid], *n.* carbure, *m.*

carbine ['ka:bain], *n.* carabine, *f.*

carbohydrate [ka:bou'haidreit], *n.* hydrate de carbone, *m.*

carbolic [ka:'bolik], *a.* phénique.
carbon ['ka:bən], *n.* (*Chem.*) carbone; (*Elec.*) charbon, *m.*
carbonic [ka:'bonik], *a.* carbonique.
carboniferous [ka:bə'nifərəs], *a.* carbonifère.
carboy ['ka:boi], *n.* tourie, bonbonne, *f.*
carbuncle ['ka:baŋkl], *n.* escarboucle, *f.*; (*Med.*) charbon, furoncle, *m.*
carburation [ka:bju'reiʃən], *n.* carburation, *f.*
carburetor [ka:bju'retə], *n.* carburateur, *m.*
carcase, carcass ['ka:kəs], *n.* carcasse, *f.*; cadavre, *m.*
card [ka:d], *n.* carte à jouer; fiche, carte; (*Manuf.*) carde, *f.*—*v.t.* carder.
cardboard ['ka:dbɔ:d], *n.* carton, *m.*
cardiac ['ka:diæk], *a.* cardiaque.
cardigan ['ka:digən], *n.* gilet de tricot, *m.*
cardinal ['ka:dinl], *a.* cardinal, fondamental. —*n.* cardinal, *m.*
card index ['ka:dindeks], *n.* fichier, *m.*—*v.t.* encarter.
cardiograph ['ka:diogræf, -gra:f], *n.* cardiographe, *m.*
card-sharper ['ka:dʃa:pə], *n.* grec, fileur de cartes, *m.*
card table ['ka:dteibl], *n.* table de jeu, *f.*
care [keə], *n.* soin; souci, *m.*, sollicitude; précaution, attention, *f.*; *care of* (*abbr. c/o*) aux bons soins de, chez; *to take care of*, avoir soin de, s'occuper de,—*v.i.* se soucier, s'inquiéter (*de*); *I dont care!* cela m'est égal! je m'en moque!
career [kə'riə], *n.* carrière, course, *f.*—*v.i.* courir rapidement.
carefree ['keəfri:], *a.* libre de soucis; insouciant.
careful ['keəful], *a.* soigneux, attentif; prudent, économe; soucieux.
carefully ['keəfuli], *adv.* soigneusement, avec soin.
carefulness ['keəfulnis], *n.* attention, *f.*; soin, *m.*
careless ['keəlis], *a.* insouciant, nonchalant; négligent (*de*).
carelessly ['keəlisli], *adv.* nonchalamment, négligemment.
carelessness ['keəlisnis], *n.* insouciance, nonchalance; négligence, *f.*
caress [kə'res], *n.* caresse, *f.*—*v.t.* caresser.
caretaker ['keəteikə], *n.* gardien, *m.*, concierge, *m.,f.*
cargo ['ka:gou], *n.* cargaison, *f.*, chargement, *m.*
cargo boat ['ka:goubout], *n.* cargo, *m.*
Caribbean [kæri'bi:ən], *a.* antillais; *Caribbean Sea*, la mer des Antilles, *f.*—*n. the Caribbean*, les Antilles, *f.pl.*
caribou [kæri'bu:], *n.* caribou, *m.*
caricature [kærikə'tjuə], *n.* caricature, charge, *f.*—*v.t.* caricaturer, faire la charge de.
carking ['ka:kiŋ], *a.* cuisant (*souci*); rongeur.
carmine ['ka:main], *a.* and *n.* carmin, *m.*
carnage ['ka:nidʒ], *n.* carnage, *m.*
carnal [ka:nl], *a.* charnel.
carnally ['ka:nəli], *adv.* charnellement.
carnation [ka:'neiʃən], *n.* (*Bot.*) œillet; incarnat, *m.*, carnation (*couleur*), *f.*
carnival ['ka:nivl], *n.* carnaval, *m.*

carnivorous [ka:'nivərəs], *a.* carnivore, carnassier.
carol ['kærəl], *n.* chanson, *f.*, chant, *m.*; *Christmas carol*, noël, *m.*—*v.i.* chanter.
carousal [kə'rauzəl], *n.* orgie, débauche, ripaille, *f.*; festin, *m.*
carouse [kə'rauz], *v.i.* boire, faire la fête.
carp (1) [ka:p], *n.* (*Ichth.*) carpe, *f.*
carp (2) [ka:p], *v.i.* critiquer, chicaner (*sur*).
car-park ['ka:pa:k], *n.* parc de stationnement, *m.*
carpenter ['ka:pintə], *n.* menuisier, charpentier, *m.*
carpentry ['ka:pintri], *n.* grosse menuiserie, charpenterie, *f.*
carpet ['ka:pit], *n.* tapis. *m.*; *fitted carpet*, moquette, *f.*—*v.t.* garnir de tapis, tapisser.
carpet sweeper ['ka:pitswi:pə], *n.* balai mécanique, *m.*
carping ['ka:piŋ], *a.* chicanier, pointilleux.
carpingly ['ka:piŋli], *adv.* en glosant; malignement.
carriage ['kæridʒ], *n.* voiture, *f.*; équipage; (*Rail.*) wagon, *m.*, voiture, *f.*; port, factage (*de paquets etc.*); affût (*de canon*), *m.*; (*Comm.*) frais de transport, *m.pl.*; (*fig.*) maintien, *m.*, tenue, démarche, *f.*
carriageway ['kæridʒwei], *n.* **dual carriageway**, route à double circulation, *f.*
carrier ['kæriə], *n.* camionneur; porteur, messager; (*Cycl.*) porte-bagages, *m.*; *aircraft carrier*, porte-avions, *m.inv.*; *carrier pigeon*, pigeon voyageur, *m.*
carrion ['kæriən], *n.* charogne, *f.*
carrion crow ['kæriən'krou], *n.* corbeau, *m.*, corbine, *f.*
carrot ['kærət], *n.* carotte, *f.*
carry ['kæri], *v.t.* porter; emporter; rapporter (*chien*); mener, conduire, entraîner (*jeter*, *voter*, *adopter*, (*Arith.*) retenir; *to carry away*, emporter, enlever, emmener; *to carry off*, emporter, enlever, remporter; *to carry on*, poursuivre, continuer; *to carry out*, porter dehors; mettre à exécution; *to carry through*, mener à bonne fin. —*v.i.* porter (*sons*).
cart [ka:t], *n.* charrette, *f.*; (*Mil.*) fourgon, *m.*; carriole (*de paysan*), *f.*—*v.t.* charrier, transporter, voiturer.
cartage ['ka:tidʒ], *n.* charriage, transport, *m.*
carte [ka:t], *n.* carte, *f.*; menu, *m.*
carter ['ka:tə], *n.* charretier, roulier, voiturier, *m.*
cart horse ['ka:thɔ:s], *n.* cheval de trait, *m.*
cartilage ['ka:tilidʒ], *n.* cartilage, *m.*
cart-load ['ka:tloud], *n.* charretée, *f.*
carton ['ka:tən], *n.* carton, *m.*; petite boîte en carton, *f.*
cartoon [ka:'tu:n], *n.* carton, *m.*; (*Polit.*) caricature, *f.*; dessin humoristique; (*Cine.*) dessin animé, *m.*
cartoonist [ka:'tu:nist], *n.* caricaturiste, *m.,f.*
cartridge ['ka:tridʒ], *n.* cartouche, *f.*
cartridge paper ['ka:tridʒpeipə], *n.* (*Ind.*) papier à cartouche, *m.*
cartridge pouch ['ka:tridʒpautʃ], *n.* cartouchière, giberne, *f.*
cart shed ['ka:tʃed], *n.* hangar, *m.*
cartwright ['ka:trait], *n.* charron, *m.*
carve [ka:v], *v.t.* sculpter, tailler; graver, ciseler; découper (*viande etc.*).

carver ['kɑːvə], n. découpeur; (Art.) sculpteur, graveur, ciseleur, m.

carving ['kɑːviŋ], n. découpage (de viande), m.; (Art.) sculpture, gravure, ciselure, f.

cascade [kæs'keid], n. cascade, f.—v.i. tomber en cascade, cascader.

case (1) [keis], n. cas, état, m.; question; (Law) cause, affaire, f.; (Med.) malade, blessé, m.; *in any case*, en tout cas; *in case*, dans le cas où.

case (2) [keis], n. étui, fourreau, m.; caisse (d'emballage), f.; écrin (à bijoux), m.—v.t. enfermer; emballer; encaisser.

casemate ['keismeit], n. casemate, f.—v.t. casemater.

easement ['keismənt], n. châssis de fenêtre, m.

cash [kæʃ], n. argent, numéraire, m.; espèces (argent), f.pl.; *cash down*, argent comptant; *cash on delivery*, contre remboursement; *to pay cash*, payer en espèces; *to sell for cash*, vendre au comptant.—v.t. toucher, encaisser (chèque, mandat-poste); changer (billet); *to cash in on*, tirer profit de, tirer parti de.

cash-book ['kæʃbuk], n. livre de caisse, m.

cash box ['kæʃbɔks], n. caisse, f.

cash-desk ['kæʃdesk], n. caisse, f.

cashier (1) [kæ'ʃiə], n. caissier, m.

cashier (2) [kæ'ʃiə], v.t. (Mil.) casser, dégrader.

cashmere ['kæʃmiə], n. cachemire, m.

cash register ['kæʃredʒistə], n. caisse enregistreuse, f.

cask [kɑːsk], n. fût, baril, m., barrique, f., tonneau, m.

casket ['kɑːskit], n. écrin, m., cassette, f.

Caspian (Sea) ['kæspiən(siː)], the. la mer Caspienne, f.

cassock ['kæsək], n. soutane, f.

cast [kɑːst], v.t. irr. jeter; se dépouiller de (arbre, animal); (Metal.) couler, fondre; (Theat.) distribuer les rôles; *to cast a glance at*, jeter un regard sur; *to cast aside*, mettre de côté, rejeter; *to cast down*, jeter par terre, abattre, décourager; *to cast its slough*, faire peau neuve; *to cast off*, rejeter, repousser, abandonner.—v.i. se jeter; se déjeter (arbre).—a. fondu.—n. coup, jet; moule, m.; (Metal.) fonte; (Theat.) distribution des rôles, f.; rôles, acteurs, m.pl.; (fig.) nuance, tournure, f., air, caractère, m.; (Sculp.) statuette, figure, f., plâtre, m.

castanet [kæstə'net], n. castagnette, f.

castaway ['kɑːstəwei], a. rejeté.—n. naufragé, m.

caste [kɑːst], n. caste, f.

castigate ['kæstigeit], v.t. châtier, punir; critiquer sévèrement.

castigation [kæsti'geiʃən], n. châtiment, m., correction, discipline, f.

casting ['kɑːstiŋ], n. (Metal.) coulée, fonte, f., moulage, m.; (Theat.) distribution des rôles, f.

cast-iron ['kɑːst'aiən], a. en fonte; (fig.) de fer, rigide.—n. fonte, f.

castle [kɑːsl], n. château, château fort, m.; (Chess) tour, f.; *castles in the air*, châteaux en Espagne.

castor ['kɑːstə], n. roulette (de meuble); poivrière, f.; (pair of) castors, huilier, m.

castor oil ['kɑːstər'ɔil], n. huile de ricin, f.

castrate [kæs'treit], v.t. châtrer.

casual ['kæʒjuəl], a. fortuit, accidentel, casuel, de passage; insouciant.

casually ['kæʒjuəli], adv. fortuitement, par hasard; négligemment.

casualty ['kæʒjuəlti], n. accident; accidenté (personne), m.; (pl.) (Mil.) pertes, f.pl.

cat [kæt], n. chat; (Mil., Navy) fouet, martinet (à neuf queues), m.; *tom-cat*, matou, m.

catacombs ['kætəkuːmz], n.pl. catacombes, f.pl.

catalepsy ['kætəlepsi], n. catalepsie, f.

catalogue ['kætəlɔg], n. catalogue, m., liste, f.

catamaran [kætəmə'ræn], n. catamaran, m.

catapult ['kætəpʌlt], n. catapulte, f.; lance-pierre (jouet), m.

cataract ['kætərækt], n. cataracte, f.

catarrh [kə'tɑː], n. catarrhe, m.

catastrophe [kə'tæstrəfi], n. catastrophe, f.; désastre, m.

catch [kætʃ], v.t. irr. attraper, prendre, saisir; (colloq.) pincer; frapper (l'œil etc.); *to catch a cold*, s'enrhumer; *to catch on*, avoir du succès, réussir; *to catch up*, atteindre, rattraper.—v.i. s'accrocher (à), se prendre (à).—n. prise; attrape; (fig.) aubaine, belle affaire, f.; cliquet (d'une roue); crampon (d'une porte); mentonnet (d'un loquet), m.

catching ['kætʃiŋ], a. contagieux; communicatif (rire); facile à retenir (air).—n. prise, capture, f.

catechism ['kætəkizm], n. catéchisme, m.

categorical [kætə'gɔrikəl], a. catégorique.

categorically [kætə'gɔrikəli], adv. catégoriquement.

category ['kætəgəri], n. catégorie, f.

cater ['keitə], v.i. pourvoir (à).

caterer ['keitərə], n. pourvoyeur, fournisseur, m.

caterpillar ['kætəpilə], n. chenille, f.; *caterpillar tractor*, tracteur à chenilles, m.

cathedral [kə'θiːdrəl], n. cathédrale, f.

catholic ['kæθəlik], a. universel; éclectique; catholique.

catkin ['kætkin], n. (Bot.) chaton, m.

cattiness ['kætinis], cattishness ['kætiʃnis], n. méchanceté, sournoiserie, f.

cattish ['kætiʃ], catty ['kæti], a. méchant, sournois, rosse.

cattle [kætl], n. bétail, m., bestiaux, m.pl.

Caucasus ['kɔːkəsəs], the. le Caucase, m.

cauldron ['kɔːldrən], n. chaudron, m., chaudière, f.

cauliflower ['kɔliflauə], n. chou-fleur, m.

caulk [kɔːk], v.t. calfater (navire).

cause [kɔːz], n. raison, cause, f., motif, sujet, m.—v.t. causer, être cause de; occasionner, provoquer (un accident).

causeway ['kɔːzwei], n. chaussée, f.

caustic ['kɔːstik], a. caustique, corrosif; (fig.) mordant.

cauterize ['kɔːtəraiz], v.t. cautériser.

cautery ['kɔːtəri], n. cautère, m.

caution ['kɔːʃən], n. avis (avertissement), m.; précaution, prévoyance, prudence; caution, garantie, f.—v.t. avertir, aviser (de); réprimander.

cautious ['kɔːʃəs], a. circonspect, prudent, en garde.

cautiously ['kɔːʃəsli], *adv.* avec précaution, prudemment.

cavalcade [kævəl'keid], *n.* cavalcade, *f.*

cavalier [kævə'liə], *a.* cavalier, désinvolte.—*n.* cavalier, *m.*

cavalry ['kævəlri], *n.* cavalerie, *f.*

cave [keiv], *n.* caverne, *f.*, antre, souterrain, *m.* —*v.t.* creuser.—*v.i.* **to cave in**, céder, s'affaisser, s'effondrer (*édifice*).

cavern ['kævən], *n.* caverne, *f.*

cavernous ['kævənəs], *a.* caverneux.

caviare [kævi'ɑː], *n.* caviar, *m.*

cavil ['kævil], *v.i.* chicaner (*sur*).

cavilling ['kæviliŋ], *a.* chicaneur.—*n.* chicanerie, *f.*

cavity ['kæviti], *n.* cavité, *f.*

cavort [kə'vɔːt], *v.i.* cabrioler.

caw [kɔː], *v.i.* croasser.

cawing ['kɔːiŋ], *n.* croassement, *m.*

cease [siːs], *v.t.* cesser; faire cesser.—*v.i.* cesser, discontinuer.

ceaseless ['siːslis], *a.* incessant, continuel.

ceaselessly ['siːslisli], *adv.* sans cesse.

Cecilia [sə'siliə], Cécile, *f.*

cedar ['siːdə], *n.* cèdre, *m.*

cede [siːd], *v.t.*, *v.i.* (*Law*) céder.

cedilla [sə'dilə], *n.* (*Gram.*) cédille, *f.*

ceiling ['siːliŋ], *n.* plafond, *m.*

celebrate ['selibreit], *v.t.* célébrer, fêter.

celebrated ['selibreitid], *a.* célèbre, fameux.

celebration [seli'breiʃən], *n.* célébration, *f.*

celebrity [sə'lebriti], *n.* célébrité, *f.*

celerity [sə'leriti], *n.* célérité, vitesse, *f.*

celery ['seləri], *n.* céleri, *m.*

celestial [sə'lestjəl], *a.* céleste.

celibacy ['selibəsi], *n.* célibat, *m.*

celibate ['selibit], *a.* and *n.* célibataire, *m.*, *f.*

cell [sel], *n.* cellule, case; alvéole (*d'abeilles*), *f.*; compartiment; cachot; (*Elec.*) élément, *m.*, pile, *f.*

cellar ['selə], *n.* cave, *f.*; cellier, caveau, *m.*

cello ['tʃelou], *n.* (*abbr.* of **violoncello**) violoncelle, *m.*

cellophane ['seləfein], *n.* cellophane, *f.*

celluloid ['seljuloid], *n.* celluloïd, celluloïde, *m.*

Celt [kelt, selt], *n.* Celte, *m.*, *f.*

Celtic ['keltik, 'seltik], *a.* celtique.

cement [si'ment], *n.* ciment, *m.*—*v.t.* cimenter; (*fig.*) consolider, fortifier.

cement mixer [si'mentmiksə], *n.* bétonnière, *f.*

cemetery ['semətri], *n.* cimetière, *m.*

cenotaph ['senotæf, -tɑːf], *n.* cénotaphe, *m.*

censer ['sensə], *n.* encensoir, *m.*

censor ['sensə], *n.* censeur, *m.*—*v.t.* soumettre à des coupures; censurer.

censorious [sen'sɔːriəs], *a.* critique, hargneux.

censorship ['sensəʃip], *n.* censure, *f.*; fonctions de censeur, *f.pl.*

censure ['senʃə], *n.* censure, critique, *f.*, blâme, *m.*—*v.t.* censurer, critiquer, blâmer.

census ['sensəs], *n.* recensement, *m.*

cent [sent], *n.* cent; sou (*pièce de monnaie*), *m.*; **ten per cent**, dix pour cent.

centaur ['sentɔː], *n.* centaure, *m.*

centenarian [senti'nɛəriən], *n.* centenaire, *m.*, *f.*

centenary [sen'tiːnəri], *a.* and *n.* centenaire, *m.*

centennial [sen'teniəl], *a.* de cent ans, séculaire.

center ['sentə], *n.* centre; milieu; (*fig.*) foyer, *m.*—*v.t.* placer au centre; concentrer.—*v.i.* se concentrer.

centesimal [sen'tesiməl], *a.* centésimal.—*n.* centième, *m.*

centigrade ['sentigreid], *a.* centigrade.

centipede ['sentipiːd], *n.* scolopendre, *f.*, mille-pattes, *m.*

central ['sentrəl], *a.* central; **central heating**, chauffage central, *m.*

centralization [sentrəlai'zeiʃən], *n.* centralisation, *f.*

centralize ['sentrəlaiz], *v.t.* centraliser.

centrifugal [sen'trifjugəl], *a.* centrifuge.

centripetal [sen'tripitl], *a.* centripète.

centuple ['sentjupl], *a.* and *n.* centuple, *m.*—*v.t.* centupler.

centurion [sen'tjuəriən], *n.* centurion, (*Bibl.*) centenier, *m.*

century ['sentʃuri], *n.* siècle, *m.*

ceramic [sə'ræmik], *a.* céramique.

ceramics [sə'ræmiks], *n.pl.* céramique, *f.*

cereal ['siəriəl], *a.* and *n.* céréale, *f.*

cerebral ['serəbrəl], *a.* cérébral.

ceremonial [seri'mouniəl], *a.* de cérémonie.—*n.* cérémonie, étiquette, *f.*, cérémonial, *m.*

ceremonially [seri'mouniəli], *adv.* rituellement.

ceremonious [seri'mouniəs], *a.* cérémonieux.

ceremoniously [seri'mouniəsli], *adv.* cérémonieusement.

ceremony ['seriməni], *n.* cérémonie, solennité, *f.*; **without ceremony**, sans façon.

cerise [sə'riːz], *a.* and *n.* cerise (*couleur*), *m.*

certain ['səːtin], *a.* certain, sûr; **he is certain to do it**, il le fera certainement; **to make certain of something**, s'assurer de quelque chose.

certainly ['səːtinli], *adv.* certainement.

certainty ['səːtinti], *n.* certitude; chose certaine, *f.*

certificate [sə'tifikit], *n.* certificat; diplôme, brevet; concordat (*de faillite*); acte (*de naissance, de mariage* ou *de mort*), *m.*

certify ['səːtifai], *v.t.* certifier; notifier, donner avis à.

certitude ['səːtitjuːd], *n.* certitude, *f.*

cessation [se'seiʃən], *n.* cessation, suspension, *f.*

cession ['seʃən], *n.* cession, *f.*

cesspit ['sespit], **cesspool** ['sespuːl], *n.* puisard, *m.*, fosse d'aisances; (*fig.*) sentine, *f.*

Ceylon [si'lɔn], le Ceylan, *m.*

Ceylonese [silə'niːz], *a.* cingalais.—*n.* Cingalais (*personne*), *m.*

chafe [tʃeif], *v.t.* échauffer, irriter; érailler (*un câble*).—*v.i.* frotter; s'user, s'érailler (*un câble*); s'irriter; s'enflammer.

chafer (1) ['tʃeifə], *n.* hanneton (*insecte*), *m.*

chafer (2) [tʃeifə], *n.* réchaud (*plat*), *m.*

chafing dish ['tʃeifiŋdiʃ], *n.* réchaud (*de table*), *m.*

chaff [tʃɑːf], *n.* menue paille; (*colloq.*) plaisanterie, raillerie, blague, *f.*—*v.t.* blaguer, taquiner, se moquer de.

chaffinch ['tʃæfintʃ], *n.* (*Orn.*) pinson, *m.*

chagrin ['ʃægrin], *n.* chagrin, *m.*; dépit, *m.*—*v.t.* chagriner, vexer.

chain [tʃein], *n.* chaîne; chaînée, *f.*—*v.t.* enchaîner. [**chain store**, see **multiple**]

chair [tʃɛə], *n.* chaise, *f.*; siège, *m.*; chaire (*à l'université*), *f.*; fauteuil (*d'un président*), *m.*; *arm-chair*, fauteuil, *m.*—*v.t.* blanchir avec de la craie; marquer *ou* écrire à la craie.

chairman ['tʃɛəmən], *n.* président, *m.*

chalice ['tʃælis], *n.* calice, *m.*, coupe, *f.*

chalk [tʃɔːk], *n.* craie, *f.*, calcaire; crayon (*pour dessiner*), *m.*—*v.t.* blanchir avec de la craie; marquer *ou* écrire à la craie.

chalk pit ['tʃɔːkpit], *n.* carrière de craie, *f.*

chalky ['tʃɔːki], *a.* crayeux, crétacé, calcaire.

challenge ['tʃælindʒ], *n.* défi, cartel, *m.*; (*fig.*) provocation, demande; (*Law*) récusation, *f.*; (*Mil.*) qui-vive; (*Spt.*) challenge, *m.*—*v.t.* défier; contester; (*Law*) récuser.

challenger ['tʃælindʒə], *n.* auteur d'un cartel; provocateur, agresseur, champion; (*Spt.*) challenger, *m.*

chamber ['tʃeimbə], *n.* chambre; salle, pièce, *f.*, cabinet, *m.*; (*Artill.*) âme, *f.*; (*pl.*) bureaux, *m.pl.*, étude, *f.*

chamberlain ['tʃeimbəlin], *n.* chambellan; camérier (*du Pape*), *m.*

chamber-maid ['tʃeimbəmeid], *n.* femme de chambre, *f.*

chamber music ['tʃeimbəmjuːzik], *n.* musique de chambre, *f.*

chameleon [kə'miːljən], *n.* caméléon, *m.*

chamfer ['tʃæmfə], *n.* chanfrein, *m.*—*v.t.* chanfreiner, biseauter.

chamois ['ʃæmwɑ], *n.* chamois, *m.*

chamois leather ['ʃæmi'leðə], *n.* chamois, *m.*, peau de chamois, *f.*

champ [tʃæmp], *v.t.* ronger, mâcher.—*v.i.* ronger son frein.

champagne [ʃæm'pein], *n.* champagne, vin de Champagne, *m.*

champion ['tʃæmpiən], *n.* champion, *m.*—*v.t.* soutenir, défendre.

championship ['tʃæmpiənʃip], *n.* championnat, *m.*

chance [tʃɑːns], *a.* accidentel, de hasard.—*n.* chance, *f.*, hasard, sort, *m.*; *by chance*, par hasard; *to stand a chance of*, avoir des chances de.—*v.t.* risquer.—*v.i.* arriver par hasard, venir à.

chancel ['tʃɑːnsəl], *n.* sanctuaire, chœur, *m.*

chancellery ['tʃɑːnsələri], *n.* chancellerie, *f.*

chancellor ['tʃɑːnsələ], *n.* chancelier, *m.*

chancery ['tʃɑːnsəri], *n.* cour de la chancellerie, *f.*

chandelier [ʃændi'liə], *n.* lustre, *m.*

chandler ['tʃɑːndlə], *n.* marchand *ou* fabricant de chandelles, *m.*; *corn-chandler*, marchand de blé; *ship chandler*, approvisionneur de navires, *m.*

change [tʃeindʒ], *n.* changement, *m.*; phase (*de la lune*); monnaie (*espèces*), *f.*; *change of life*, retour d'âge, *m.*; *changes of life*, vicissitudes, *f.pl.*; *for a change*, pour changer.—*v.t.* changer; modifier; donner la monnaie de.—*v.i.* changer (*de*); se renouveler (*la lune*); *to change for the better*, s'améliorer.

changeable ['tʃeindʒəbl], *a.* changeant, variable, inconstant.

changer ['tʃeindʒə], *n.* changeur, *m.*

channel [tʃænl], *n.* canal; lit (*de rivière*), *m.*; passe (*de port*), *f.*; (*Naut.*) détroit, *m.*;

(*fig.*) voie, *f.*, moyen, *m.*, entremise, *f.*; *the Channel Islands*, les îles Anglo-normandes, *f.pl.*; *the English Channel*, la Manche, *f.*—*v.t.* creuser.

chant [tʃɑːnt], *n.* chant, plain-chant, *m.*—*v.t.*, *v.i.* chanter.

chaos ['keiɔs], *n.* chaos, *m.*

chaotic [kei'ɔtik], *a.* chaotique.

chap (1) [tʃæp], *v.t.* gercer.—*v.i.* gercer, se gercer.—*n.* gerçure, crevasse (*dans la peau etc.*), *f.*

chap (2) [tʃæp], *n.* garçon, gaillard, type, *m.*; *old chap*, (*colloq.*) mon vieux.

chap (3) [tʃæp], **chop** (1) [tʃɔp], *n.* mâchoire, bouche; bajoue (*de cochon*), *f.*

chapel [tʃæpl], *n.* chapelle, *f.*

chaperon ['ʃæpəroun], *n.* chaperon, *m.*—*v.t.* chaperonner.

chap-fallen ['tʃæpfɔːlən], *a.* (*fam.*) penaud, abattu, consterné.

chaplain ['tʃæplin], *n.* aumônier, *m.*

chaplet ['tʃæplit], *n.* chapelet, *m.*, guirlande, *f.*

chapter ['tʃæptə], *n.* chapitre, *m.*

chapter house ['tʃæptəhaus], *n.* chapitre, *m.*

char (1) [tʃɑː], *v.t.* carboniser.—*v.i.* se carboniser.

char (2) [tʃɑː], *v.i.* faire des ménages.—*n.* (*pop. abbr. of* CHARWOMAN) femme de ménage, *f.*

character ['kæriktə], *n.* caractère, *m.*; (*Theat.*) rôle, personnage; genre, *m.*, nature, qualité, réputation, *f.*; certificat (*de mœurs*); (*fig.*) personnage, type, *m.*; *a bad character*, un mauvais sujet; *he is quite a character*, c'est un vrai original; *out of character*, déplacé.

characteristic [kæriktə'ristik], *a.* caractéristique.—*n.* trait caractéristique, *m.*

charade [ʃə'rɑːd], *n.* charade, *f.*

charcoal ['tʃɑːkoul], *n.* charbon de bois, *m.*

charge [tʃɑːdʒ], *v.t.* charger, accuser (*de*); faire payer; (*fig.*) adjurer; ordonner à.—*v.i.* (*Mil.*) charger.—*n.* charge, *f.*; prix, *m.*; garde, *f.*; soin; ordre, commandement; (*Law*) acte d'accusation, *m.*, accusation, *f.*; mandement (*d'un évêque*); résumé (*d'un juge*), *m.*; (*pl.*) frais, dépens, *m.pl.*; *free of charge*, gratis; *the officer in charge*, l'officier commandant, *m.*; *to take charge of*, se charger de.

chargeable ['tʃɑːdʒəbl], *a.* à charge (*à*); accusable (*de*).

charger ['tʃɑːdʒə], *n.* grand plat; cheval de bataille; (*Elec.*) chargeur, *m.*

charily ['tʃɛərili], *adv.* avec précaution; frugalement.

chariot ['tʃæriət], *n.* char, chariot, *m.*

charioteer [tʃæriə'tiə], *n.* conducteur de chariot, *m.*

charitable ['tʃæritəbl], *a.* de charité; charitable.

charitably ['tʃæritəbli], *adv.* charitablement.

charity ['tʃæriti], *n.* charité, bienveillance; aumône, *f.*

charlatan ['ʃɑːlətən], *n.* charlatan, *m.*

charm [tʃɑːm], *n.* charme, *m.*; breloque (*trinket*), *f.*, porte-bonheur, *m. inv.*; (*pl.*) attraits, *m.pl.*—*v.t.* charmer, enchanter.

charmer ['tʃɑːmə], *n.* enchanteur, charmeur, *m.*

charming ['tʃɑːmiŋ], *a.* enchanteur, charmant; ravissant.

charnel ['tʃɑːnəl], a. de charnier.
charnel house ['tʃɑːnəlhaus], n. charnier, ossuaire, m.
chart [tʃɑːt], n. carte marine, f.—v.t. porter sur une carte.
charter ['tʃɑːtə], n. charte, f., acte, m.; **on charter**, loué, affrété.—v.t. établir par un acte; (Comm.) fréter, affréter; **chartered accountant**, expert comptable, m.; **chartered plane**, avion-taxi, m.
charwoman ['tʃɑːwumən], n. (pl. -women [wimin]) femme de journée, femme de ménage, f.
chary ['tʃɛəri], a. prudent, économe.
chase (1) [tʃeis], n. chasse; poursuite, f.—v.t. chasser, poursuivre; **to chase away**, chasser.
chase (2) [tʃeis], v.t. (Metal.) ciseler.
chasm [kæzm], n. abîme; chasme; vide énorme, m., brèche, fissure, f.
chassis ['tʃæsi], n. (Motor.) châssis, m.
chaste [tʃeist], a. chaste, pudique; pur (langage); de bon goût.
chasten [tʃeisn], v.t. châtier; purifier.
chastise [tʃæs'taiz], v.t. châtier.
chastisement ['tʃæstizmənt], n. châtiment, m.
chastity ['tʃæstiti], n. chasteté, pureté, f.
chasuble ['tʃæzjubl], n. chasuble, f.
chat [tʃæt], n. causerie; (colloq.) causette, f., entretien, m.—v.i. causer, bavarder; (colloq.) faire la causette.
chattel [tʃætl], n. bien meuble, m.; **goods and chattels**, biens et effets, m.pl.
chatter ['tʃætə], v.i. jaser, bavarder; jacasser (singes etc.); babiller; claquer (dents).—n. caquetage, m., jaserie, f.
chatterbox ['tʃætəbɔks], n. moulin à paroles, jaseur, babillard, m.
chattering ['tʃætəriŋ], n. jaserie, f.; claquement (des dents), m.
chatty ['tʃæti], a. causeur, bavard.
chauffeur ['ʃoufə, ʃou'fəː], n. chauffeur, m.
cheap [tʃiːp], a. (à) bon marché; peu coûteux; de peu de valeur; **dirt cheap**, pour rien, à vil prix.
cheapen ['tʃiːpən], v.t. faire baisser le prix de; **to cheapen oneself**, se déprécier.
cheaper ['tʃiːpə], a. (à) meilleur marché.
cheaply ['tʃiːpli], adv. à bon marché, à bon compte.
cheapness ['tʃiːpnis], n. bon marché, bas prix, m.
cheat [tʃiːt], n. fourberie, tromperie, f.; trompeur; (Cards etc.) tricheur, m.—v.t. tromper; (Cards etc.) tricher.
cheating ['tʃiːtiŋ], n. tromperie; (Cards etc.) tricherie, f.
check [tʃek], v.t. réprimer; arrêter; contenir; (Comm.) vérifier; enregistrer (bagages etc.); contrôler (comptes); (Chess) faire échec à.—n. échec, obstacle; (Comm.) bon; (Am.) [CHEQUE] carreau, damier (dessin); (Chess) échec, m. [**checkroom**, see **luggage**]
checking ['tʃekiŋ], n. répression, f. contrôle, m.
checkmate ['tʃekmeit], n. échec et mat, m.—v.t. mettre échec et mat, mater.
cheek [tʃiːk], n. joue; bajoue (cochon); (fig.) impudence, f., front, toupet, m.; **cheek by jowl**, côte à côte.—v.t. narguer.
cheek-bone ['tʃiːkboun], n. pommette, f.
cheeky ['tʃiːki], a. impudent, effronté.

cheep [tʃiːp], n. piaulement, m.—v.i. piauler.
cheer [tʃiə], n. chère (aliment etc.); gaieté, f., courage, m.; acclamation, f., applaudissement, hourra, vivat, m.—v.t. égayer, réjouir; animer; applaudir, acclamer.—v.i. se réjouir; applaudir.
cheerful ['tʃiəful], a. joyeux, gai; riant (paysage etc.).
cheerfully ['tʃiəfuli], adv. gaiement, joyeusement.
cheerfulness ['tʃiəfulnis], n. gaieté, allégresse, bonne humeur, f.
cheerily ['tʃiərili], adv. gaiement.
cheering ['tʃiəriŋ], a. consolant, encourageant.—n. applaudissements, m.pl.
cheerio! ['tʃiəriou], int. (fam.) (good-bye) à bientôt! (when drinking) à votre santé!
cheerless ['tʃiəlis], a. triste, morne.
cheery ['tʃiəri], a. gai, joyeux, réjoui.
cheese [tʃiːz], n. fromage, m.
cheese-paring ['tʃiːzpɛəriŋ], n. (fig.) économie de bouts de chandelle, f.
cheetah, cheetah ['tʃiːtə], n. guépard, m.
chef [ʃef], n. chef (cuisinier), m.
chemical ['kemikəl], a. chimique.
chemically ['kemikli], adv. chimiquement.
chemicals ['kemikəlz], n.pl. produits chimiques, m.pl.
chemise [ʃi'miːz], n. chemise de femme, f.
chemist ['kemist], n. (scientist) chimiste, m., f.; (druggist) pharmacien, m.; **chemist's shop**, pharmacie, f.
chemistry ['kemistri], n. chimie, f.
cheque [tʃek], n. chèque, m.; **traveller's cheque**, chèque de voyage, m.
cheque-book ['tʃekbuk], n. carnet de chèques, m.
cherish ['tʃeriʃ], v.t. chérir; soigner; nourrir; entretenir (de l'espoir etc.).
cherry ['tʃeri], n. cerise, f.
cherry tree ['tʃeritriː], n. cerisier, m.
cherub ['tʃerəb], n. (pl. **cherubs** ['tʃerəbz], **cherubim** ['tʃerəbim]) chérubin, m.
cherubic [tʃə'ruːbik], a. de chérubin, angélique.
chess [tʃes], n. échecs, m.pl.
chess-board ['tʃesbɔːd], n. échiquier, m.
chessman ['tʃesmən], n. (pl. **chessmen** ['tʃesmen]) pièce, f.; **a set of chessmen**, un jeu d'échecs.
chest [tʃest], n. coffre, m., caisse, f.; (Anat.) poitrine, f.; poitrail (de cheval), m.; **chest of drawers**, commode, f.
chestnut ['tʃesnʌt], a. châtain, marron (couleur); alezan (cheval).—n. marron, m.; châtaigne, f.
chestnut tree ['tʃesnʌttriː], n. châtaignier (Spanish chestnut); marronnier (d'Inde) (horse chestnut), m.
chevalier [ʃevə'liə], n. chevalier, m.
chevron ['ʃevrən], n. chevron, m.
chew [tʃuː], v.t. mâcher; (fig.) **to chew over**, ruminer.
chick [tʃik], n. poussin (fig.) poulet, m.
chicken ['tʃikin], n. poussin; poulet, m.
chicken-hearted ['tʃikin'hɑːtid], a. peureux, poltron.
chicken pox ['tʃikinpɔks], n. varicelle, f.
chickweed ['tʃikwiːd], n. mouron des oiseaux, m.

chicory ['tʃikəri], n. chicorée (assaisonnement ou pour remplacer le café); endive (légume), f.
chide [tʃaid], v.t. gronder, blâmer.
chief [tʃi:f], a. principal.—n. chef, m.; partie principale, f.; (fam.) the chief, le patron, m.
chiefly ['tʃi:fli], adv. surtout, principalement.
chieftain ['tʃi:ftən], n. chef de clan, m.
chiffon ['ʃifɔn], n. chiffon, m.
chiffonier [ʃifə'niə], n. chiffonnier, m.
chilblain ['tʃilblein], n. engelure, f.
child [tʃaild], n. (pl. children ['tʃildrən]) enfant, m.,f.; with child, enceinte.
child-bed ['tʃaildbed], n. couches, f.pl.
child-birth ['tʃaildbə:θ], n. enfantement, m.
childhood ['tʃaildhud], n. enfance, f.
childish ['tʃaildiʃ], a. enfantin; puéril.
childishness ['tʃaildiʃnis], n. puérilité, f.; enfantillage, m.
Chile ['tʃili]. le Chili, m.
Chilean ['tʃilian], a. chilien.—n. Chilien (personne), m.
chill [tʃil], a. froid; glacé.—n. froid; refroidissement, frisson, m.; to catch a chill, prendre froid.—v.t. refroidir; (fig.) glacer; décourager.
chilli ['tʃili], n. piment, m.
chilliness ['tʃilinis], n. froid, frisson, m.; froideur, f.
chilly ['tʃili], a. un peu froid (chose); frileux (personne ou temps).
chime [tʃaim], n. carillon, m.—v.t., v.i. carillonner.
chimera [kai'miərə], n. chimère, f.
chimney ['tʃimni], n. cheminée, f.
chimney corner ['tʃimni'kɔ:nə], n. coin du feu, m.
chimney piece ['tʃimnipi:s], n. chambranle ou manteau de cheminée, m.; (colloq.) cheminée, f.
chimney pot ['tʃimnipɔt], n. tuyau de cheminée, m.
chimney sweep ['tʃimniswi:p], n. ramoneur, m.
chimpanzee [tʃimpæn'zi:], n. chimpanzé, m.
chin [tʃin], n. menton, m.
China ['tʃainə]. la Chine, f.
china ['tʃainə], n. porcelaine, f.
Chinese [tʃai'ni:z], a. chinois, de Chine.—n. chinois (langue); Chinois (personne), m.
chink [tʃiŋk], n. crevasse, fente, lézarde, f.; son, tintement, (slang) argent, m.—v.t. crevasser; faire sonner.—v.i. se fendiller; sonner.
chintz [tʃints], n. (Tex.) indienne, f.
chip [tʃip], n. copeau, fragment, éclat (de bois); (Cards) jeton, m.; (pl., Cook.) (pommes de terre) frites, f.pl.—v.t. tailler; railler.—v.i. s'écorner; s'écailler (porcelaine etc.).
chiropodist [ki'rɔpədist], n. pédicure, m.,f.
chirp [tʃə:p], v.i. pépier, gazouiller; crier (insectes).—n. gazouillement, pépiement; cri (insectes), m.
chirpy ['tʃə:pi], a. (colloq.) gai, réjoui.
chirrup ['tʃirəp], [CHIRP].
chisel ['tʃizl], n. ciseau, m.—v.t. ciseler.
chit [tʃit], n. marmot, bambin; billet (lettre), m.
chitchat ['tʃittʃæt], n. caquet, babillage, m.
chivalrous ['ʃivəlrəs], a. chevaleresque.
chivalry ['ʃivəlri], n. chevalerie, f.
chives [tʃaivz], n.pl. ciboulette, f.
chlorate ['klɔ:reit], n. (Chem.) chlorate, m.

chlorinate ['klɔ:rineit], v.t. verduniser (eau potable).
chlorine ['klɔ:ri:n], n. chlore, m.
chloroform ['klɔrəfɔ:m], n. chloroforme, m.—v.t. chloroformer.
chlorophyll ['klɔrəfil], n. chlorophylle, f.
choc-ice ['tʃɔkais], n. chocolat glacé, m.
chock-full [tʃɔk'ful], (fam.) chock-a-block ['tʃɔkə'blɔk], a. plein comme un œuf, comble.
chocolate ['tʃɔkəlit], n. chocolat, m.
choice [tʃɔis], a. choisi; de choix; recherché; fin (vin).—n. choix, m.; élite, f.; assortiment, m.
choir ['kwaiə], n. chœur, m.
choke [tʃouk], v.t. étouffer, suffoquer; engorger.—v.i. s'engorger.—n. étranglement (de voix); (Motor.) starter, m.
choking ['tʃoukiŋ], a. étouffant.—n. étouffement, m., suffocation, f.
choky ['tʃouki], a. étouffant, suffoquant.
choler ['kɔlə], n. colère, bile, f.
cholera ['kɔlərə], n. choléra, m.
choleric ['kɔlərik], a. colérique, irascible.
choose [tʃu:z], v.t. irr. choisir; élire; préférer; vouloir.
chop (1) [CHAP].
chop (2) [tʃɔp], v.t. couper en morceaux, hacher; trafiquer, troquer; to chop down, abattre.—v.i. trafiquer, troquer; (Naut.) tourner (vent); clapoter (mer); chopping block, hachoir, billot, m.—n. tranche; côtelette (de mouton); (colloq., pl.) gueule, f.
chopper ['tʃɔpə], n. couperet, m.
chopping ['tʃɔpiŋ], n. coupe, action de couper, f.
choppy ['tʃɔpi], a. crevassé, haché; clapoteux (mer).
choral ['kɔ:rəl], a. choral, en ou de chœur.
chord [kɔ:d], n. corde, f.; (Mus.) accord, m.
chores [tʃɔ:z], n.pl. corvées domestiques, f.pl.
chorister ['kɔristə], n. choriste, m.; enfant de chœur, m.,f.
chorus ['kɔ:rəs], n. chœur; refrain, m.
Christ [kraist]. le Christ, m.
christen [krisn], v.t. baptiser.
Christendom ['krisndəm], n. chrétienté, f.
christening ['krisniŋ], n. baptême, m.
Christian ['kristjən], a. and n. chrétien, m.; Christian name, prénom, m.
Christianity [kristi'æniti], n. christianisme, m.
Christmas ['krisməs]. Noël, m., la fête de Noël, f.; Christmas carol, chant de Noël, m.; Christmas Eve, la veille de Noël, f.
Christmas box ['krisməsbɔks], n. étrennes, f.pl.
Christopher ['kristəfə]. Christophe, m.
chrome [kroum], n. bichromate de potasse, m.; chrome leather, cuir chromé, m.
chromium ['kroumiəm], n. chrome, m.
chronic ['krɔnik], a. chronique.
chronicle ['krɔnikl], n. chronique, f.
chronicler ['krɔniklə], n. chroniqueur, m.
chronological [krɔnə'lɔdʒikəl], a. chronologique.
chrysalis ['krisəlis], n. chrysalide, f.
chrysanthemum [kri'sænθəmʌm], n. chrysanthème, m.
chub [tʃʌb], n. (Ichth.) chabot, chevesne, m.
chubby ['tʃʌbi], a. joufflu; potelé (mains).

chuck (1) [tʃʌk], *n.* gloussement, *m.—v.i.* glousser.

chuck (2) [tʃʌk], *n.* petite tape sous le menton, *f.*

chuckle [tʃʌkl], *v.i.* rire tout bas, rire sous cape (*de*).—*n.* rire étouffé, gloussement, *m.*

chum [tʃʌm], *n.* copain, *m.*

chummy ['tʃʌmi], *a.* intime.

chump [tʃʌmp], *n.* tronçon (*de bois*); (*colloq.*) idiot, *m.*; *chump chop*, côtelette de gigot, *f.*

chunk [tʃʌŋk], *n.* gros morceau, *m.*

church [tʃəːtʃ], *n.* église, *f.*; (*Protestant*) temple, *m.*

churchwarden ['tʃəːtʃwɔːdn], *n.* marguillier, *m.*

churchyard ['tʃəːtʃjɑːd], *n.* cimetière, *m.*

churl [tʃəːl], *n.* rustre, manant, ladre, *m.*

churlish ['tʃəːliʃ], *a.* grossier, rude, ladre.

churlishly ['tʃəːliʃli], *adv.* grossièrement.

churlishness ['tʃəːliʃnis], *n.* grossièreté, *f.*

churn [tʃəːn], *n.* baratte, *f.*; *milk churn*, bidon à lait, *m.—v.i.* baratter.

chute [ʃuːt], *n.* chute (*d'eau*); glissière, piste (*de luges*), *f.*

Cicero ['sisərou]. Cicéron, *m.*

cider ['saidə], *n.* cidre, *m.*

cigar [si'gɑː], *n.* cigare, *m.*

cigarette [sigə'ret], *n.* cigarette, *f.*

cinder ['sində], *n.* cendre, *f.*; (*pl.*) escarbilles (*de charbon*), *f.pl.*

Cinderella [sində'relə]. Cendrillon, *f.*

cine-camera ['sinikæmərə], *n.* (ciné)caméra, *f.*

cinema ['sinimə], *n.* cinéma, *m.*

cinnamon ['sinəmən], *n.* cannelle, *f.*

cipher ['saifə], *n.* zéro; chiffre, *m.—v.t.*, *v.i.* chiffrer; calculer.

circle ['səːkl], *n.* cercle, *m.*; (*fig.*) coterie, *f.—v.t.* entourer (*de*).—*v.i.* tournoyer.

circlet ['səːklit], *n.* petit cercle, anneau, *m.*

circuit ['səːkit], *n.* rotation, révolution, *f.*, tour; circuit, *m.*, circonférence; tournée (*de juge etc.*), *f.*

circuitous [səː'kjuːitəs], *a.* détourné, sinueux.

circular ['səːkjulə], *a.* circulaire.—*n.* circulaire, *f.*, bulletin, *m.*

circulate ['səːkjuleit], *v.t.* mettre en circulation, faire circuler, répandre.—*v.i.* circuler.

circulating ['səːkjuleitiŋ], *a.* circulant.

circulation [səːkju'leiʃən], *n.* circulation, *f.*; tirage (*d'un journal etc.*), *m.*

circumference [səː'kʌmfərəns], *n.* circonférence, périphérie, *f.*

circumflex ['səːkəmfleks], *a.* (*Gram.*) circonflexe.

circumlocution [səːkəmlə'kjuːʃən], *n.* circonlocution, *f.*

circumscribe ['səːkəmskraib], *v.t.* circonscrire.

circumspect ['səːkəmspekt], *a.* circonspect.

circumstance ['səːkəmstæns], *n.* circonstance, *f.*; état, *m.*; (*pl.*) moyens, *m.pl.*; *in straitened circumstances*, dans la gêne; *in easy circumstances*, dans l'aisance; *under no circumstances*, en aucun cas.

circumstantial [səːkəm'stænʃəl], *a.* circonstancié, minutieux; indirect (*témoignage*).

circumvent [səːkəm'vent], *v.t.* circonvenir.

circumvention [səːkəm'venʃən], *n.* circonvention, *f.*

circus ['səːkəs], *n.* cirque; rond-point (*de rues*), *m.*

cistern ['sistən], *n.* citerne, *f.*, réservoir, *m.*

citadel ['sitədl], *n.* citadelle, *f.*

citation [sai'teiʃən], *n.* citation, *f.*

cite [sait], *v.t.* citer; sommer (*de*).

citizen ['sitizn], *n.* citoyen, bourgeois; habitant, *m.*

citron ['sitrən], *n.* cédrat, *m.*

city ['siti], *n.* ville; cité, *f.* [see town etc.]

civet ['sivit], *n.* civette, *f.*

civic ['sivik], *a.* civique.

civil ['sivl], *a.* civil; municipal; honnête, poli; *civil servant*, fonctionnaire, *m.*; *in the Civil Service*, dans l'administration.

civilian [si'viljən], *n.* bourgeois, civil, *m.*

civility [si'viliti], *n.* civilité, politesse, *f.*

civilization [sivilai'zeiʃən], *n.* civilisation, *f.*

civilize ['sivilaiz], *v.t.* civiliser.

claim [kleim], *v.t.* demander, prétendre (*à*), réclamer, revendiquer.—*n.* demande, *f.*; titre, droit, *m.*

claimant ['kleimənt], *n.* réclamateur, prétendant, *m.*

clam [klæm], *n.* peigne (*bivalve*), *m.*, palourde, *f.*

clamber ['klæmbə], *v.i.* grimper (*sur* ou *à*).

clammy ['klæmi], *a.* visqueux, pâteux; moite (*mains*).

clamor ['klæmə], *n.* clameur, *f.*, bruit, *m.—v.i.* crier, vociférer.

clamorous ['klæmərəs], *a.* bruyant; criard.

clamp [klæmp], *n.* crampon; (*Carp.*) serre-joints, *m.—v.t.* cramponner; serrer; entasser.

clan [klæn], *n.* clan, *m.*; clique, coterie, *f.*

clandestine [klæn'destin], *a.* clandestin.

clang [klæŋ], clank [klæŋk], *n.* cliquetis, son métallique, *m.—v.t.* faire résonner.—*v.i.* résonner.

clap [klæp], *n.* coup, *m.*; claque, *f.*; battement de mains; coup (*de tonnerre*), *m.—v.t.* claquer, frapper, battre (*mains, ailes etc.*); applaudir.—*v.i.* claquer ou battre des mains; applaudir.

clapper ['klæpə], *n.* applaudisseur; battant (*d'une cloche*); claquet (*d'un moulin*), *m.*

clapping ['klæpiŋ], *n.* battement des mains, *m.*, applaudissements, *m.pl.*

Clara ['klɛərə], Clare [klɛə]. Claire, *f.*

claret ['klærət], *n.* vin de Bordeaux rouge, *m.*

clarify ['klærifai], *v.t.* clarifier.—*v.i.* se clarifier.

clarinet [klæri'net], *n.* clarinette, *f.*

clarion ['klæriən], *n.* clairon, *f.*

clarity ['klæriti], *n.* clarté, *f.*

clash [klæʃ], *v.t.* faire résonner (*en frappant*); choquer, heurter.—*v.i.* résonner, se heurter; (*fig.*) être aux prises (*avec*), s'opposer.—*n.* fracas, choc, conflit; cliquetis (*d'armes etc.*), *m.*

clasp [klɑːsp], *n.* fermoir, *m.*; agrafe, *f.*; (*fig.*) embrassement, *m.*, étreinte, *f.—v.t.* agrafer; serrer, presser.

clasp knife [klɑːspnaif], *n.* couteau de poche, *m.*

class [klɑːs], *n.* classe, *f.*; (*Sch.*) cours; genre, *m.*, catégorie, *f.—v.t.* classer.

classic ['klæsik], *a.* and *n.* classique, *m*; *to study classics*, faire ses humanités *f.pl.*

classical ['klæsikəl], *a.* classique.

classification [klæsifi'keiʃən], *n.* classification, *f.*

classify

classify ['klæsifai], *v.t.* classifier.
classroom ['klɑːsruːm], *n.* salle de classe, classe, *f.*
clatter ['klætə], *n.* bruit, tapage, fracas (*de ferraille etc.*), tintamarre, *m.*—*v.i.* faire du bruit, claquer.
clause [klɔːz], *n.* clause; proposition, *f.*
clavicle ['klævikl], *n.* (*Anat.*) clavicule, *f.*
claw [klɔː], *n.* griffe; (*Zool.*) serre; pince (*de crabes*), *f.*—*v.t.* griffer; déchirer; égratigner; (*fig.*) railler, gronder.
clay [klei], *n.* argile, terre glaise, glaise, *f.*—*v.t.* (*Agric.*) glaiser; terrer (*sucre*).
clayey ['kleii], *a.* argileux.
clean [kliːn], *a.* propre; blanc (*linge*); ciré (*chaussures*); (*fig.*) net, droit.—*adv.* entièrement, tout à fait, droit, raide.—*v.t.* nettoyer; décrotter, cirer (*chaussures*); écurer (*égouts, canaux etc.*)
cleaner ['kliːnə], *n.* nettoyeur (*personne*), *m.*
cleaning ['kliːniŋ], *n.* nettoyage, nettoiement, *m.*; *dry cleaning*, nettoyage à sec.
cleanliness ['klenlinis], **cleanness** ['kliːnnis], *n.* propreté; netteté, *f.*
cleanly [klenli], *a.* propre; (*fig.*) pur.— ['kliːnli], *adv.* proprement, nettement.
cleanness [CLEANLINESS].
cleanse [klenz], *v.t.* nettoyer; curer (*égouts etc.*); (*fig.*) purifier.
cleansing ['klenziŋ], *n.* nettoiement, nettoyage, *m.*; (*fig.*) purification, *f.*
clear [kliə], *a.* clair; net, évident; sûr; innocent, sans tache.—*adv.* clair.—*v.t.* éclaircir; clarifier (*liquides*); faire évacuer (*salle etc.*); déblayer (*débris etc.*); gagner (*profit etc.*); (*Agric.*) défricher; (*fig.*) acquitter; (*Customs*) passer.—*v.i.* s'éclaircir; *to clear off*, s'en aller, filer; *to clear out*, se retirer; *to clear up*, élucider (*problème, mystère*); s'éclaircir, se rasséréner (*temps*).
clearance ['kliərəns], *n.* dégagement; déblaiement (*débris*), *m.*; levée (*du courrier*), *f.*; (*Naut.*) congé; (*Customs*) dédouanement, *m.*; *clearance sale*, solde, *m.*; liquidation, *f.*
clear-cut ['kliəkʌt], *a.* net, d'une grande netteté.
clear-headed ['kliə'hedid], *a.* à l'esprit clair.
clearing ['kliəriŋ], *n.* éclaircissement; débrouillement; acquittement; (*Customs*) dédouanement; défrichement (*de terrain*), *m.*; éclaircie (*de forêt*), *f.*; déblaiement (*débris*), *m.*
clearing-house ['kliəriŋhaus], *n.* (*Rail.*) bureau de liquidation, *m.*; (*Banking*) banque de virement, *f.*
clearly ['kliəli], *adv.* nettement, clairement, évidemment.
clearness ['kliənis], *n.* clarté, netteté, pureté, *f.*
cleavage ['kliːvidʒ], *n.* clivage, *m.*; fissure, scission, *f.*
cleave [kliːv], *v.t. irr.* fendre, se fendre; *in a cleft stick*, (*fig.*) dans une impasse.
clef [klef], *n.* (*Mus.*) clef, *f.*
cleft [kleft], *n.* fente, fissure, crevasse, *f.*
clemency ['klemənsi], *n.* clémence; douceur (*du temps*), *f.*
clement ['klemənt], *a.* doux, clément.
clench [klentʃ], *v.t.* river (*clous etc.*); serrer (*poing*).
Cleopatra [kliə'pætrə]. Cléopâtre, *f.*
clergy ['kləːdʒi], *n.* clergé, *m.*

clergyman ['kləːdʒimən], *n.* (*pl.* **-men** [men]) ecclésiastique; (*R.-C. Ch.*) prêtre, abbé, curé; (*Protestant*) ministre, pasteur, *m.*
cleric ['klerik], *n.* ecclésiastique, prêtre, *m.*
clerical ['klerikəl], *a.* clérical; *clerical error*, faute de copiste, *f.*
clerk [klɑːk], *n.* (*Law*) clerc; (*Eccles.*) ecclésiastique; (*Comm.*) commis; (*Civil Service*) employé, *m.* [see **shop-assistant**]
clerkship ['klɑːkʃip], *n.* place de clerc, place de commis, *f.*
clever ['klevə], *a.* adroit, habile, (*colloq.*) malin; intelligent; bien fait; *to be clever at*, être fort en.
cleverly ['klevəli], *adv.* habilement, adroitement, avec adresse.
cleverness ['klevənis], *n.* habileté, dextérité, adresse; intelligence, *f.*
click [klik], *v.i.* faire tic-tac, cliqueter.—*n.* bruit sec, clic; cliquetis; déclic, *m.*
client ['klaiənt], *n.* client, *m.*
clientele [kliːõ'tel], *n.* clientèle, *f.*
cliff [klif], *n.* falaise, *f.*; rocher escarpé, *m.*
climate ['klaimit], *n.* climat, *m.*
climatic [klai'mætik], *a.* climatique.
climax ['klaimæks], *n.* gradation, *f.*; (*fig.*) comble, apogée, *m.*
climb [klaim], *v.t.* escalader, gravir, monter. —*v.i.* grimper; monter (*sur*); (*fig.*) s'élever. —*n.* ascension, montée, *f.*
climber ['klaimə], *n.* grimpeur, *m.*; alpiniste, *m., f.*; *social climber*, arriviste, *m., f.*
clime [klaim], *n.* (*poet.*) climat; pays, *m.*
clinch [klintʃ], *v.t.* river (*clous*); *to clinch an argument*, confirmer un argument.—*n.* (*Box.*) corps à corps, *m.*
cling [kliŋ], *v.i. irr.* se cramponner, s'attacher, s'accrocher (*à*); coller (*à*) (*robe*).
clinic ['klinik], *a.* and *n.* clinique, *f.*
clinical ['klinikəl], *a.* clinique.
clink [kliŋk], *n.* tintement, cliquetis, *m.*—*v.t.* faire tinter.—*v.i.* tinter.
clinker ['kliŋkə], *n.* mâchefer, *m.*
clip [klip], *v.t.* couper (*à ciseaux*); tondre (*chiens, chevaux*); écorcher, estropier (*paroles*); contrôler (*billets*).—*n.* tonte, *f.*; pince-notes, *m.*
clipper ['klipə], *n.* rogneur; (*Naut.*) fin voilier, *m.*
clippers ['klipəz], *n.pl.* tondeuse, *f.*
clique [kliːk], *n.* coterie, *f.*
cloak [klouk], *n.* manteau, *m.*; (*fig.*) voile, masque, prétexte, *m.*—*v.t.* couvrir d'un manteau, (*fig.*) masquer, voiler, cacher.
cloak-room ['kloukruːm], *n.* (*Rail.*) consigne, *f.*, (*Theat.*) vestiaire, *m.*
clock [klɔk], *n.* horloge (*grand*); pendule (*petit*), *f.*; *alarm clock*, réveille-matin, *m.* —*v.i.* (*Ind.*) *to clock in* or *out*, pointer à l'arrivée *ou* au départ.
clock-maker ['klɔkmeikə], *n.* horloger, *m.*
clockwise ['klɔkwaiz], *adv.* dans le sens des aiguilles d'une montre.
clockwork ['klɔkwəːk], *a.* mécanique.—*n.* mouvement, mécanisme d'horlogerie; (*fig.*) travail régulier, *m.*
clod [klɔd], *n.* motte de terre, *f.*
clodhopper ['klɔdhɔpə], *n.* rustre; manant, *m.*
clog [klɔg], *n.* sabot, *m.*—*v.t.* obstruer.—*v.i.* se boucher, s'obstruer.

cloister ['klɔistə], n. cloître, m.
close (1) [klouz], v.t. fermer; clore, terminer.
—v.i. se fermer; clore, se terminer, conclure, finir.—n. fin, conclusion, clôture, f.
close (2) [klous], a. clos, bien fermé; serré; lourd (temps); (fig.) mystérieux.—adv. près; de près; **close by**, tout près; **close to**, près de.
close-fisted ['klous'fistid], a. avare.
closely ['klousli], adv. de près; étroitement; secrètement.
closeness ['klousnis], n. proximité; exactitude; lourdeur (temps); intimité, f.
closet ['klɔzit], n. cabinet; boudoir, m.; garde-robe, armoire, f. v.t. **to be closeted with**, être en tête-à-tête avec.
close-up ['klousʌp], n. (Cine.) gros plan, m.
closing ['klouziŋ], a. dernier, final.—n. clôture, fermeture (de magasin); fin, conclusion, f.
closure ['klouʒə], n. clôture, fermeture, f.
clot [klɔt], n. grumeau, caillot, m.—v.i. se cailler, se figer.
cloth [klɔːθ], n. drap (de laine ou tissu d'or ou d'argent), m.; toile (de lin), f.; **table-cloth**, nappe, f.; tapis (de laine), m.
clothe [klouð], v.t. habiller, (re)vêtir.
clothes [klouðz], n.pl. habits, vêtements, m.pl., hardes, f.pl.; **bed-clothes**, draps et couvertures, m.pl.
clothing ['klouðiŋ], n. vêtement, habillement, m.; vêtements, m.pl.
cloud [klaud], n. nuage, m.; (poet.) nue; (fig.) nuée, f.; **every cloud has a silver lining**, après la pluie le beau temps; **to be under a cloud**, être mal vu du monde.—v.t. couvrir de nuages; obscurcir; (fig.) assombrir.—v.i. se couvrir (de nuages).
cloudburst ['klaudbəːst], n. trombe, rafale de pluie, f.
cloudless ['klaudlis], a. sans nuage.
cloudy ['klaudi], a. nuageux, couvert; trouble (liquides); (fig.) ténébreux.
clout [klaut], n. torchon, linge, m.; gifle, tape, f.—v.t. rapetasser; taper, souffleter.
clove [klouv], n. clou de girofle, m.; **clove of garlic**, gousse d'ail, f.
cloven [klouvn], a. fendu; fourchu; **to show the cloven foot**, laisser voir le bout de l'oreille.
clover ['klouvə], n. trèfle, m.
clown [klaun], n. rustre, manant, m.; (Theat.) bouffon, clown, m.
cloy [klɔi], v.t. écœurer, rassasier.
club [klʌb], n. massue, f.; (Golf) club (instrument), m.; crosse, f.; cercle, club, m., association, f.; (Cards) trèfle, m.—v.t. frapper avec une massue.—v.i. se cotiser, s'associer.
club-foot ['klʌbfut], n. pied bot, m.
club-house ['klʌbhaus], n. cercle; pavillon (de golf etc.), m.
cluck [klʌk], v.i. glousser.
clucking ['klʌkiŋ], n. gloussement, m.
clue [kluː], n. fil, indice, signe, m.; idée, f.
clueless ['kluːlis], a. (fam.) **to be clueless**, ne savoir rien de rien.
clump [klʌmp], n. masse, f., gros bloc; (fig.) groupe, m.; **clump of trees**, bouquet d'arbres, m.
clumsily ['klʌmzili], adv. gauchement, maladroitement.

clumsiness ['klʌmzinis], n. gaucherie, maladresse, f.
clumsy ['klʌmzi], a. gauche, maladroit; mal fait (chose).
cluster ['klʌstə], n. grappe (de raisin), f.; bouquet (de fleurs); régime (de bananes); nœud (de diamants), m.—v.i. se former en grappes; se grouper.
clutch [klʌtʃ], v.t. saisir, empoigner.—n. griffe, serre, étreinte, f.; (Motor.) embrayage, m.; couvée (d'œufs), f.
clutter ['klʌtə], n. fracas, vacarme; encombrement, désordre, m.—v.t. **to clutter up**, encombrer.
coach [koutʃ], n. voiture, f., carrosse, m.; (Rail.) voiture, f., wagon; autocar, car; (Sch.) répétiteur; (Spt.) entraîneur, m.—v.t. entraîner; préparer aux examens.
coaching ['koutʃiŋ], n. (Spt.) entraînement (d'équipe), m.; (Sch.) répétitions, f.pl.
coachman ['koutʃmən], n. (pl. -men [men]) cocher, m.
coachwork ['koutʃwəːk], n. carrosserie, f.
coagulate [kou'ægjuleit], v.t. coaguler.—v.i. se coaguler.
coal [koul], n. charbon, m.; houille, f.; **live coal**, charbon ardent.—v.t. charbonner.—v.i. s'approvisionner de charbon (navire).
coal cellar ['koulselə], n. cave à charbon, f.
coalesce [kouə'les], v.i. s'unir, se fondre, fusionner.
coal-field ['koulfiːld], n. bassin houiller, m.
coalition [kouə'liʃən], n. coalition, f.
coal mine ['koulmain], n. mine de charbon, houillère, f.
coal miner ['koulmainə], n. mineur, m.
coal scuttle ['koulskʌtl], n. seau à charbon, m.
coarse [kɔːs], a. gros, grossier.
coarseness ['kɔːsnis], n. grossièreté, f.
coast [koust], n. côte, plage, f., rivage, littoral, m.—v.t. côtoyer.—v.i. côtoyer, suivre la côte; caboter; planer (oiseau); (Motor.) rouler au débrayé.
coastal ['koustəl], a. côtier.
coaster ['koustə], n. caboteur, m.
coast guard ['koustgaːd], n. garde-côte, m.
coast-line ['koustlain], n. littoral, m.
coat [kout], n. habit; enduit (de goudron etc.), m.; robe (de certains animaux); (Mil.) tunique; (Paint.) couche, f.; **coat of mail**, cotte de mailles, f.; **double breasted coat**, veston croisé, m.—v.t. revêtir; enduire (de).
coat hanger ['kouthæŋə], n. cintre, m.; porte-vêtements, m. inv.
coax [kouks], v.t. amadouer, cajoler, flatter.
co-axial [kou'æksiəl], a. coaxial.
coaxing ['kouksiŋ], n. cajolerie, f., enjôlement, m.
cob [kɔb], n. bidet, goussant (cheval); épi (de mais), m.
cobalt ['koubɔːlt], n. cobalt, m.
cobble [kɔbl], v.t. saveter, raccommoder; paver en cailloutis.—n. galet rond, pavé, m.
cobbler ['kɔblə], n. cordonnier, m.
cobnut ['kɔbnʌt], n. aveline, f.
cobra ['koubrə], n. cobra, m.
cobweb ['kɔbweb], n. toile d'araignée, f.
cocaine [ko'kein], n. cocaïne, f.
cochineal ['kɔtʃiniːl], n. cochenille, f.

cock [kɔk], *n.* coq; mâle (*de petits oiseaux*); robinet (*tap*); chien (*de fusil*); tas, meulon (*de foin*), *m.*; *black-cock*, coq de bruyère; *cock-and-bull story*, coq-à-l'âne, *m.*—*v.t.* relever; retrousser; armer (*fusil*); *cocked hat*, chapeau à cornes, *m.*

cockade [kɔ'keid], *n.* cocarde, *f.*

cock-a-doodle-doo ['kɔkədu:dl'du:], *n.* coquerico, cocorico, *m.*

cockatoo [kɔkə'tu:], *n.* kakatoès, cacatois, *m.*

cockatrice ['kɔkətri:s], *n.* basilic, *m.*

cockchafer ['kɔktʃeifə], *n.* hanneton, *m.*

cock-crow ['kɔkkrou], *n.* chant du coq; (*fig.*) point du jour, *m.*

cockerel ['kɔkərəl], *n.* jeune coq, *m.*

cock-eyed ['kɔkaid], *a.* de biais, de travers.

cockle [kɔkl], *n.* bucarde, *f.*

cock-pit ['kɔkpit], *n.* arène des combats de coqs; (*Av.*) carlingue, *f.*

cockroach ['kɔkroutʃ], *n.* blatte, *f.*

cockscomb ['kɔkskoum], *n.* crête de coq, *f.*; [COXCOMB].

cocksure ['kɔkʃuə], *a.* sûr et certain, outrecuidant.

cocktail ['kɔkteil], *n.* cocktail, *m.*; *cocktail party*, cocktail.

cocky ['kɔki], *a.* effronté, suffisant.

coco ['koukou], *n.* coco, *m.*

cocoa ['koukou], *n.* cacao, *m.*

coconut, cocoa-nut ['koukənʌt], *n.* coco, *m.*, noix de coco, *f.*

cocoon [kə'ku:n], *n.* cocon, *m.*

cod [kɔd], *n.* morue, *f.*; cabillaud (*morue fraîche*), *m.*

coddle [kɔdl], *v.t.* mitonner; dorloter, choyer.

code [koud], *n.* code, *m.*—*v.t.* coder; chiffrer.

codicil ['kɔdisil], *n.* codicille, *m.*

codify ['koudifai], *v.t.* codifier.

cod-liver oil ['kɔdlivər'ɔil], *n.* huile de foie de morue, *f.*

co-education ['kouedju'keiʃən], *n.* enseignement mixte, *m.*

co-educational ['kouedju'keiʃənəl], *a.* (*Sch.*) mixte.

coefficient [koui'fiʃənt], *n.* coefficient, *m.*

coerce [kou'ə:s], *v.t.* forcer, contraindre.

coercion [kou'ə:ʃən], *n.* coercition, contrainte, *f.*

coexist [kouig'zist], *v.i.* coexister.

coexistence [kouig'zistəns], *n.* coexistence, *f.*

coffee ['kɔfi], *n.* café, *m.*; *white coffee*, café au lait.

coffee bean ['kɔfibi:n], *n.* grain de café, *m.*

coffee house ['kɔfihaus], *n.* café, *m.*

coffee mill ['kɔfimil], **coffee grinder** ['kɔfi graində], *n.* moulin à café, *m.*

coffee-pot ['kɔfipɔt], *n.* cafetière, *f.*

coffer ['kɔfə], *n.* coffre; caisson; sas, *m.*

coffin ['kɔfin], *n.* cercueil, *m.*, bière, *f.*

cog [kɔg], *n.* dent, *f.*

cogency ['koudʒənsi], *n.* force, puissance, *f.*

cogent ['koudʒənt], *a.* puissant, fort.

cogged [kɔgd], *a.* denté, à dents.

cogitate ['kɔdʒiteit], *v.t.* penser (à.)—*v.i.* méditer, penser.

cogitation [kɔdʒi'teiʃən], *n.* réflexion, pensée, méditation, *f.*

cognate ['kɔgneit], *a.* de la même famille; analogue.

cognizance ['kɔgnizəns], *n.* connaissance, *f.*; (*Her.*) insigne, *m.*

cognomen [kɔg'noumən], *n.* surnom; nom de guerre, sobriquet, *m.*

cog-wheel ['kɔgwi:l], *n.* roue d'engrenage, *f.*

cohabit [kou'hæbit], *v.i.* cohabiter.

cohabitation [kouhæbi'teiʃən], *n.* cohabitation, *f.*

coherence [kou'hiərəns], *n.* cohésion, cohérence, *f.*

coherent [kou'hiərənt], *a.* cohérent; conséquent.

coherently [kou'hiərəntli], *adv.* d'une manière cohérente.

cohesion [kou'hi:ʒən], *n.* cohésion, *f.*

cohesive [kou'hi:siv], *a.* cohésif.

cohort ['kouhɔ:t], *n.* cohorte, *f.*

coil [kɔil], *n.* rouleau (*de cheveux etc.*); repli (*de serpents*), *m.*; (*Elec.*) bobine, *f.*—*v.t.* replier, enrouler.—*v.i.* se replier, s'enrouler.

coin [kɔin], *n.* pièce de monnaie, *f.*—*v.t.* monnayer; forger, fabriquer, inventer.

coinage ['kɔinidʒ], *n.* monnayage, *m.*, monnaie; (*fig.*) fabrication, *f.*

coincide [kouin'said], *v.i.* s'accorder, coïncider (*avec*).

coincidence [kou'insidəns], *n.* coïncidence, *f.*

coincidental [kouinsi'dentl], *a.* de coïncidence.

coiner ['kɔinə], *n.* monnayeur; faux monnayeur, *m.*

coition [kou'iʃən], *n.* coït, *m.*

coke [kouk], *n.* coke, *m.*

colander ['kʌləndə], *n.* passoire, *f.*

cold [kould], *a.* froid; *it is cold*, il fait froid; *to be cold* (*of people*), avoir froid.—*n.* froid; rhume (*maladie*), refroidissement; frisson (*sensation*), *m.*; *to catch cold*, s'enrhumer.

coldly ['kouldli], *adv.* froidement.

cole [koul], *n.* chou marin, *m.*

colic ['kɔlik], *n.* colique, *f.*

collaborate [kə'læbəreit], *v.i.* collaborer.

collaboration [kəlæbə'reiʃən], *n.* collaboration, *f.*

collaborator [kə'læbəreitə] *n.* collaborateur, *m.*

collapse [kə'læps], *v.i.* s'affaisser, s'écrouler, s'effondrer.—*n.* affaissement, *m.*, débâcle, *f.*

collapsible [kə'læpsibl], *a.* pliant, démontable.

collar ['kɔlə], *n.* collier (*de chien, de cheval, de décoration*); col (*de chemise*); collet (*de pardessus*); collerette (*de dames*), *f.*—*v.t.* colleter, prendre au collet.

collar-bone ['kɔləboun], *n.* clavicule, *f.*

collar stud ['kɔləstʌd], *n.* bouton de col, *m.*

collate [kə'leit], *v.t.* collationner, comparer.

collateral [kə'lætərəl], *a.* collatéral.

collation [kə'leiʃən], *n.* collation, *f.*; don, présent; repas froid, *m.*

colleague ['kɔli:g], *n.* collègue, confrère, *m.*

collect (1) [kə'lekt], *v.t.* recueillir; ramasser; collectionner; percevoir, encaisser (*impôts*); recouvrer (*dettes*); quêter; faire la levée (*du courrier*).—*v.i.* s'amasser.

collect (2) ['kɔlikt], *n.* collecte; (*courte*) prière, *f.*

collected [kə'lektid], *a.* rassemblé; (*fig.*) recueilli, calme, tranquille.

collection [kə'lekʃən], *n.* collection, *f.*; assemblage, rassemblement, *m.*; collecte, quête; levée (*du courrier*), *f.*

collective [kə'lektiv], *a.* collectif.

collector [kə'lektə], *n.* collecteur; collectionneur; percepteur (*impôts*); quêteur (*aumône*); receveur (*douane*), *m.*

college ['kɔlidʒ], *n.* collège (d'Université), *m.*; école, *f.*

collide [kə'laid], *v.i.* se heurter.

collier ['kɔliə], *n.* mineur; (*Naut.*) (bateau) charbonnier, *m.*

colliery ['kɔljəri], *n.* houillère, mine de charbon, *f.*

collision [kə'liʒən], *n.* collision, *f.*, choc, *m.*

colloquial [kə'loukwiəl], *a.* de la conversation, familier; *colloquial French*, français parlé, *m.*

colloquialism [kə'loukwiəlizm], *n.* expression familière, *f.*

colloquy ['kɔləkwi], *n.* colloque, entretien, *m.*

collusion [kə'lu:ʒən], *n.* collusion, connivence, *f.*

Colombia [kə'lʌmbiə]. la Colombie, *f.*

colon (1) ['koulən], *n.* (*Anat.*) côlon, *m.*

colon (2) ['koulən], *n.* (*Gram.*) deux points, *m.pl.*

colonel [kə:nl], *n.* colonel, *m.*

colonial [kə'lounjəl], *a.* colonial.

colonist ['kɔlənist], *n.* colon, *m.*

colonization [kɔlənai'zeiʃən], *n.* colonisation, *f.*

colonize ['kɔlənaiz], *v.t.* coloniser.

colony ['kɔləni], *n.* colonie, *f.*

color ['kʌlə], *n.* couleur, *f.*; (*fig.*) prétexte, *m.*, apparence, *f.*; (*pl.*) (*Mil.*) drapeau; (*Navy*) pavillon, *m.*; *to be off color*, être pâle, n'être pas bien en train; *with the colors*, sous les drapeaux.—*v.t.* colorer; colorier, enluminer (*gravure etc.*).—*v.i.* rougir (*personne*); se colorer (*chose*).

Colorado-beetle ['kɔlərɑ:dou'bi:tl], *n.* doryphore, *m.*

color-blind ['kʌləblaind], *a.* daltonien.

color-blindness ['kʌləblaindnis], *n.* daltonisme, *m.*

colored ['kʌləd], *a.* coloré; colorié; de couleur.

colorful ['kʌləful], *a.* coloré, pittoresque.

coloring ['kʌləriŋ], *n.* coloris, couleur, *f.*

colorless ['kʌləlis], *a.* sans couleur.

colossal [kə'lɔsl], *a.* colossal.

Colosseum [kɔlə'si:əm]. Colisée, *m.*

colossus [kə'lɔsəs], *n.* (*pl.* colossi [kə'lɔsai], colossuses [kə'lɔsəsiz]) colosse, *m.*

colt [koult], *n.* poulain; (*fig.*) novice, *m.*

Columbus [kə'lʌmbəs]. Colomb, *m.*

column ['kɔləm], *n.* colonne, *f.*

coma ['koumə], *n.* coma; assoupissement, *m.*

comb [koum], *n.* peigne, *m.*; étrille (*chevaux*); crête (*coq*), *f.*; rayon (*miel*) *m.*—*v.t.* peigner; étriller (*cheval*).

combat ['kɔmbæt], *n.* combat, *m.*—*v.t.*, *v.i.* combattre.

combatant ['kɔmbətənt], *n.* combattant, *m.*

combination [kɔmbi'neiʃən], *n.* combinaison; association, coalition, *f.*; concours (*de circonstances*), *m.*

combine [kəm'bain], *v.t.* combiner; réunir, allier.—*v.i.* se combiner; se coaliser (*avec*); s'unir (*à*); se syndiquer.—['kɔmbain], *n.* (*Comm.*) cartel, *m.*

combine-harvester ['kɔmbain'hɑ:vistə], *n.* moissonneuse-batteuse, *f.*

combustion [kəm'bʌstʃən], *n.* combustion, *f.*

come [kʌm], *v.i. irr.* venir; arriver, parvenir; se présenter, advenir, se faire; devenir; *come in!* entrez! *come on!* allons! *to come back*, revenir; *to come down*, descendre; *to come for*, venir chercher; *to come forward*, s'avancer; *to come home*, rentrer; *to come in*, entrer; *to come off*, se détacher; *to come out*, sortir; *to come up*, monter.

comedian [kə'mi:diən], *n.* comédien, *m.*

comedy ['kɔmidi], *n.* comédie, *f.*

comeliness ['kʌmlinis], *n.* aspect gracieux, *m.*; agréments, *m.pl.*

comely ['kʌmli], *a.* avenant.

comer ['kʌmə], *n.* venant; venu, *m.*; *first comer*, premier venu; *newcomer*, nouveau venu.

comet ['kɔmit], *n.* comète, *f.*

comfort ['kʌmfət], *n.* réconfort; bien-être, agrément, confort, *m.*; aise(s); aisance, *f.*; *to take comfort*, se consoler.—*v.t.* réconforter, soulager; consoler.

comfortable ['kʌmfətəbl], *a.* à son aise, agréable, confortable.

comfortably ['kʌmfətəbli], *adv.* à son aise, confortablement.

comforter ['kʌmfətə], *n.* consolateur (*le Saint Esprit*); cache-nez (*foulard*), *m.*; couvre-pieds (*inv.*) piqué, *m.*

comfortless ['kʌmfətlis], *a.* sans consolation; désolé, triste.

comic ['kɔmik], **comical** ['kɔmikəl], *a.* comique, drôle.

comically ['kɔmikli], *adv.* comiquement.

coming ['kʌmiŋ], *n.* venue; arrivée; approche, *f.*

comma ['kɔmə], *n.* virgule, *f.*; *inverted commas*, guillemets, *m.pl.*

command [kə'mɑ:nd], *n.* ordre, commandement; pouvoir, *m.*; autorité, *f.*—*v.t.* commander; posséder; inspirer (*respect*).

commandant ['kɔməndænt], *n.* commandant, *m.*

commandeer [kɔmən'diə], *v.t.* réquisitionner.

commander [kə'mɑ:ndə], *n.* commandant; commandeur (*décoration*); (*Navy*) capitaine (*de frégate etc.*), *m.*

commander-in-chief [kəmə'ndərin'tʃi:f], *n.* généralissime, commandant en chef, *m.*

commanding [kə'mɑ:ndiŋ], *a.* commandant; imposant (*important*); qui domine (*surplombant*); impérieux (*de commandement*).

commandment [kə'mɑ:ndmənt], *n.* commandement (*de Dieu*), *m.*

commando [kə'mɑ:ndou], *n.* (*Mil.*) corps franc, commando, *m.*

commemorate [kə'meməreit], *v.t.* célébrer, solenniser; commémorer.

commemoration [kəmemə'reiʃən], *n.* célébration, commémoration, *f.*; souvenir, *m.*

commence [kə'mens], *v.t.*, *v.i.* commencer.

commencement [kə'mensmənt], *n.* commencement, début, *m.*

commend [kə'mend], *v.t.* confier (*à*); recommander; louer.

commendable [kə'mendəbl], *a.* louable.

commendation [kɔmen'deiʃən], *n.* éloge, *m.*, louange, *f.*

comment ['kɔment], *n.* commentaire, *m.*—*v.i.* commenter.

commentary ['kɔməntəri], *n.* commentaire, *m.*; ***running commentary***, radio-reportage (*d'un match*), *m.*

commerce ['kɔmə:s], *n.* commerce, *m.*

commercial [kə'mə:ʃəl], *a.* commercial, de commerce; commerçant (*ville etc.*); ***commercial traveller***, commis voyageur, *m.*— *n.* (*Tel.*) film publicitaire, *m.*

commingle [kɔ'miŋgl], *v.t.* mêler ensemble, mêler.—*v.i.* se mêler ensemble *ou* avec; se fondre (*dans ou en*).

commissariat [kɔmi'sɛəriət], *n.* commissariat, *m.*, intendance, *f.*

commission [kə'miʃən], *n.* commission, *f.*; (*Mil.*) brevet; (*Law*) mandat, *m.*—*v.t.* charger, commissionner.

commissionaire [kəmiʃə'nɛə], *n.* portier (*de magasin*); chasseur (*d'hôtel*); commissionnaire, *m.*

commissioner [kə'miʃənə], *n.* commissaire, *m.*

commit [kə'mit], *v.t.* commettre; confier, livrer, consigner; engager.

committee [kə'miti], *n.* comité, *m.*; (*Parl.*) commission, *f.*

commode [kə'moud], *n.* commode, *f.*

commodious [kə'moudjəs], *a.* spacieux.

commodity [kə'mɔditi], *n.* marchandise, denrée, *f.*, produit, *m.*

commodore ['kɔmədɔ:], *n.* (*Navy*) chef de division, *m.*; ***air-commodore***, général de brigade, *m.*

common [kɔmən], *a.* commun; ordinaire; vulgaire; (*fig.*) trivial; (*Mil.*) simple.—*n.* commune, *f.*; communal, *m.*; bruyère, lande, *f.*; ***House of Commons***, Chambre des Communes, *f.*

commoner ['kɔmənə], *n.* bourgeois, roturier, *m.*

commonly ['kɔmənli], *adv.* ordinairement.

commonplace ['kɔmənpleis], *a.* banal, commun, trivial.—*n.* lieu commun, *m.*, banalité, *f.*

commonweal ['kɔmən'wi:l], *n.* le bien public, *m.*

commonwealth ['kɔmənwelθ], *n.* la chose publique, *f.*, l'État, *m.*; ***the (British) Commonwealth***, le Commonwealth (britannique).

commotion [kə'mouʃən], *n.* secousse, agitation, *f.*, tumulte, *m.*

communal ['kɔmjunəl], *a.* communal.

commune (1) [kə'mju:n], *v.i.* parler, converser, s'entretenir (*avec*).

commune (2) ['kɔmju:n], *n.* commune, *f.*

communicate [kə'mju:nikeit], *v.t.* communiquer.—*v.i.* se communiquer.

communication [kəmju:ni'keiʃən], *n.* communication, *f.*

communion [kə'mju:njən], *n.* (*Eccles.*) communion, *f.*; commerce, *m.*

communiqué [kə'mju:nikei], *n.* communiqué, *m.*

Communism ['kɔmjunizm], *n.* communisme, *m.*

Communist ['kɔmjunist], *a.* and *n.* communiste, *m.*, *f.*

community [kə'mju:niti], *n.* communauté, société, *f.*

commutator ['kɔmjuteitə], *n.* commutateur, *m.*

compact (1) ['kɔmpækt], *n.* pacte, contrat; poudrier (*de dame*), *m.*

compact (2) [kəm'pækt], *a.* compact, serré, bien lié; concis.—*v.t.* rendre compact, unir.

companion [kəm'pænjən], *n.* compagnon, *m.*, compagne; dame *ou* demoiselle de compagnie (*to a lady*), *f.*; pendant (*mobilier*), *m.*

companionship [kəm'pænjənʃip], *n.* camaraderie; compagnie, *f.*

company ['kʌmpəni], *n.* compagnie; société, corporation; troupe (*acteurs*), *f.*; (*Naut.*) équipage, *m.*; ***we have company today***, nous avons du monde aujourd'hui.

comparable ['kɔmpərəbl], *a.* comparable.

comparative [kəm'pærətiv], *a.* comparatif.

comparatively [kəm'pærətivli], *adv.* relativement, comparativement.

compare [kəm'pɛə], *v.t.* comparer.—*v.i.* être comparable à, rivaliser.

comparison [kəm'pærisən], *n.* comparaison, *f.*

compartment [kəm'pɑ:tmənt], *n.* compartiment, *m.*

compass ['kʌmpəs], *n.* compas; circuit, cercle, *m.*; boussole; portée (*atteinte*); étendue (*de la voix*), *f.*; ***a pair of compasses***, un compas.—*v.t.* faire le tour de, entourer; accomplir; ***to compass about***, environner.

compassion [kəm'pæʃən], *n.* compassion, pitié, *f.*

compassionate [kəm'pæʃənit], *a.* compatissant.

compatible [kəm'pætəbl], *a.* compatible (*avec*).

compatriot [kəm'pætriət], *n.* compatriote, *m.*, *f.*

compel [kəm'pel], *v.t.* contraindre, forcer (*de*), obliger (*à ou de*).

compelling [kəm'peliŋ], *a.* compulsif, irrésistible.

compensate ['kɔmpənseit], *v.t.* dédommager (*de*); compenser.—*v.i.* ***to compensate for***, remplacer, racheter.

compensation [kɔmpən'seiʃən], *n.* dédommagement, *m.*; compensation, *f.*

compete [kəm'pi:t], *v.i.* concourir (*pour*), faire concurrence (*à*); disputer, rivaliser.

competence ['kɔmpitəns], *n.* capacité, aptitude; (*fig.*) aisance (*fortune*), *f.*

competent ['kɔmpitənt], *a.* compétent (*pour*), capable (*de*).

competently ['kɔmpitəntli], *adv.* avec compétence; suffisamment.

competition [kɔmpi'tiʃən], *n.* (*Comm.*) concurrence, *f.*; concours, *m.*

competitive [kəm'petitiv], *a.* compétitif, de concurrence; ***competitive examination***, concours, *m.*

competitor [kəm'petitə], *n.* compétiteur, *m.* (*Comm.*) concurrent, *m.*

compile [kəm'pail], *v.t.* compiler, composer.

complacent [kəm'pleisənt], *a.* suffisant, de suffisance.

complacently [kəm'pleisəntli], *adv.* avec un air *ou* ton suffisant.

complain [kəm'plein], *v.i.* se plaindre (*de*).

complaint [kəm'pleint], *n.* plainte; maladie, *f.*, mal (*illness*), *m.*; réclamation, *f.*; ***to lodge a complaint***, porter plainte.

complaisance [kəm'pleisəns], *n.* complaisance, *f.*

complement ['kɔmplimənt], *n.* complément, *m.*

complementary [kɔmpli'mentəri], _a._ complémentaire.

complete [kəm'pli:t], _a._ complet, entier; achevé.—_v.t._ compléter, achever; (_fig._) accomplir; remplir (_une fiche_).

completely [kəm'pli:tli], _adv._ complètement.

completion [kəm'pli:ʃən], _n._ achèvement, accomplissement, _m._, perfection, _f._

complex ['kɔmpleks], _a._ and _n._ complexe, _m._

complexion [kəm'plekʃən], _n._ teint, _m._, couleur, _f._; caractère, _m._; _to put a different complexion on_, présenter sous un autre jour.

complexity [kəm'pleksiti], _n._ complexité, _f._

compliance [kəm'plaiəns], _n._ acquiescement, _m._; obéissance, _f._; _in compliance with_, conformément à.

complicate ['kɔmplikeit], _v.t._ compliquer; embrouiller.

complicated ['kɔmplikeitid], _a._ compliqué.

complication [kɔmpli'keiʃən], _n._ complication, _f._

compliment ['kɔmplimənt], _n._ compliment, _m._; (_pl._) salutations, _f.pl._; hommages (_à une dame_), _m.pl._—[kɔmpli'ment], _v.t._ complimenter, féliciter.

complimentary [kɔmpli'mentəri], _a._ flatteur; en hommage; _complimentary ticket_, billet de faveur, _m._

comply [kəm'plai], _v.i._ se soumettre, se conformer; accéder (à).

component [kəm'pounənt], _a._ constituant, composant.—_n._ (_Mech._) composant, _m._

compose [kəm'pouz], _v.t._ composer; écrire, rédiger, arranger; calmer.

composed [kəm'pouzd], _a._ composé; calme.

composer [kəm'pouzə], _n._ auteur; (_Mus._) compositeur, _m._

composite ['kɔmpəzit], _a._ composé; (_Arch._) composite.

composition [kɔmpə'ziʃən], _n._ composition; (_Sch._) rédaction, _f._; _French composition_, thème français, _m._

compositor [kəm'pɔzitə], _n._ (_Print._) compositeur, _m._

compost ['kɔmpɔst], _n._ compost, terreau, _m._

composure [kəm'pouʒə], _n._ calme, _m._

compound ['kɔmpaund], _a._ and _n._ composé, _m._; _compound interest_, intérêts composés, _m.pl._—[kəm'paund], _v.t._ composer; mêler, combiner; (_Comm._) atermoyer.—_v.i._ s'arranger.

comprehend [kɔmpri'hend], _v.t._ comprendre.

comprehensible [kɔmpri'hensibl], _a._ compréhensible.

comprehension [kɔmpri'henʃən], _n._ compréhension, _f._

comprehensive [kɔmpri'hensiv], _a._ étendu, compréhensif; _comprehensive study_, étude d'ensemble, _f._

compress [kɔm'pres], _n._ compresse, _f._—[kɔm'pres], _v.t._ comprimer; (_fig._) resserrer.

comprise [kəm'praiz], _v.t._ contenir, renfermer, comporter.

compromise ['kɔmprəmaiz], _n._ compromis, arrangement, _m._—_v.t._ compromettre.—_v.i._ transiger.

compromising ['kɔmprəmaiziŋ], _a._ compromettant.

compulsion [kəm'pʌlʃən], _n._ contrainte, _f._

compulsorily [kəm'pʌlsərili], _adv._ par force, forcément.

compulsory [kəm'pʌlsəri], _a._ forcé, obligatoire.

compute [kəm'pju:t], _v.t._ calculer, supputer.

computer [kəm'pju:tə], _n._ machine à calculer, _f._; ordinateur, _m._

comrade ['kɔmrid], _n._ camarade, compagnon, _m._

comradeship ['kɔmridʃip], _n._ camaraderie, _f._

concave ['kɔnkeiv], _a._ concave, creux.

conceal [kən'si:l], _v.t._ cacher; (_fig._) dissimuler; celer _ou_ céler (à).

concealment [kən'si:lmənt], _n._ dissimulation, _f._; secret, mystère, _m._; retraite, cachette, _f._

concede [kən'si:d], _v.t._ concéder, accorder, admettre.—_v.i._ faire des concessions.

conceit [kən'si:t], _n._ suffisance, vanité, _f._

conceited [kən'si:tid], _a._ suffisant, vaniteux.

conceivable [kən'si:vəbl], _a._ concevable, imaginable.

conceive [kən'si:v], _v.t._ concevoir; imaginer.—_v.i._ concevoir, devenir enceinte (_femme_).

concentrate ['kɔnsəntreit], _v.t._ concentrer.—_v.i._ se concentrer.

concentration [kɔnsən'treiʃən], _n._ concentration, _f._

conception [kən'sepʃən], _n._ conception, idée, _f._

concern [kən'sə:n], _n._ intérêt; soin, souci, _m._, anxiété; (_Comm._) entreprise; (_fig._) affaire, _f._—_v.t._ concerner, regarder; intéresser; inquiéter.

concerning [kən'sə:niŋ], _prep._ touchant, concernant, en ce qui concerne, à l'égard de.

concert [kən'sə:t], _v.t._ concerter.—_v.i._ se concerter.—['kɔnsət], _n._ concert; accord, _m._

concerto [kən'tʃə:tou], _n._ (_Mus._) concerto, _m._

concession [kən'seʃən], _n._ concession, _f._

concessionary [kən'seʃənəri], _a._ concessionnaire.

conch [kɔŋk], _n._ conque, _f._

conciliate [kən'silieit], _v.t._ concilier.

conciliation [kənsili'eiʃən], _n._ conciliation, _f._

conciliator [kən'silieitə], _n._ conciliateur, _m._

conciliatory [kən'siljətri], _a._ conciliant, conciliatoire.

concise [kən'sais], _a._ concis.

concisely [kən'saisli], _adv._ succinctement.

conclude [kən'klu:d], _v.t._ conclure; terminer, achever; estimer.

concluding [kən'klu:diŋ], _a._ final, dernier.

conclusion [kən'klu:ʒən], _n._ conclusion, fin; décision, _f._

conclusive [kən'klu:siv], _a._ concluant; conclusif.

concoct [kən'kɔkt], _v.t._ confectionner; inventer, préparer; machiner (_un plan_), tramer.

concoction [kən'kɔkʃən], _n._ confection (_d'un plat_); potion; (_fig._) machination (_complot_), _f._

concord ['kɔnkɔ:d], _n._ concorde, harmonie, _f._; (_Mus._) accord, _m._

concourse ['kɔŋkɔ:s], _n._ concours, _m._, affluence, foule; réunion, _f._

concrete [kən'kri:t], _a._ concret.—_n._ béton; bétonnage, _m._; _reinforced concrete_, béton armé.—_v.t._ bétonner.

concubine ['kɔŋkjubain], _n._ concubine, _f._

concur [kən'kə:], _v.i._ s'accorder, être d'accord (_avec_).

concurrence [kən'kʌrəns], _n._ assentiment; concours, _m._

383

concurrent [kən'kʌrənt], *a.* qui concourt, qui s'accorde, concourant.

concurrently [kən'kʌrəntli], *adv.* concurremment.

concussion [kən'kʌʃən], *n.* secousse, *f.*; choc, *m.*; (*Med.*) commotion, *f.*

condemn [kən'dem], *v.t.* condamner (à); déclarer coupable; blâmer.

condemnation [kəndem'neiʃən], *n.* condamnation, censure, *f.*, blâme, *m.*

condensation [kənden'seiʃən], *n.* condensation, *f.*

condense [kən'dens], *v.t.* condenser; (*fig.*) resserrer, abréger.

condenser [kən'densə], *n.* condenseur, *f.*; (*Phys.*) condensateur, *m.*

condescend [kəndə'send], *v.i.* condescendre, daigner (à).

condescension [kəndə'senʃən], *n.* condescendance, *f.*; acte de condescendance, *m.*

condiment ['kəndimənt], *n.* assaisonnement, condiment, *m.*

condition [kən'diʃən], *n.* condition, *f.*, état, *m.*—*v.t.* conditionner.

conditional [kən'diʃənəl], *a.* conditionnel.

conditionally [kən'diʃənəli], *adv.* conditionnellement.

condole [kən'doul], *v.i.* prendre part à la douleur (*de*), exprimer ses condoléances.

condolence [kən'douləns], *n.* condoléance, *f.*

condone [kən'doun], *v.t.* excuser, pardonner.

condor ['kəndə], *n.* condor, *m.*

conduce [kən'dju:s], *v.i.* contribuer (à).

conducive [kən'dju:siv], *a.* qui contribue (à).

conduct ['kəndʌkt], *n.* conduite; direction, *f.*; *safeconduct*, sauf-conduit, *m.*—[kən'dʌkt], *v.t.* conduire (à); diriger, mener.

conductor [kən'dʌktə], *n.* receveur (d'autobus); (*Am.*)(*Rail.*) chef de train; (*Mus.*) chef d'orchestre; (*Phys.*) conducteur, *m.*; *lightning-conductor*, paratonnerre, *m.*

conductress [kən'dʌktris], *n.* receveuse (d'autobus), *f.*

conduit ['kʌndit, 'kəndit], *n.* conduit; tuyau, *m.*

cone [koun], *n.* cône; (*Bot.*) strobile, *m.*, pomme de pin, *f.*; *ice-cream cone*, cornet de glace, *m.*

confection [kən'fekʃən], *n.* bonbon, *m.*, friandise, *f.*

confectioner [kən'fekʃənə], *n.* confiseur, *m.*

confectionery [kən'fekʃənəri], *n.* confiserie, *f.*, bonbons, *m.pl.*

confederacy [kən'fedərəsi], *n.* confédération (*d'États*); ligue (*de conspirateurs*), *f.*

confederate [kən'fedərit], *a.* confédéré.—*n.* confédéré, *m.*, complice, *m.*, *f.*

confederation [kənfedə'reiʃən], *n.* confédération, *f.*

confer [kən'fə:], *v.t.* conférer, accorder.—*v.i.* conférer (à).

conference ['kənfərəns], *n.* conférence, *f.*, congrès, *m.*

confess [kən'fes], *v.t.* confesser, avouer.—*v.i.* se confesser.

confessed [kən'fest], *a.* reconnu, confessé, avoué.

confessedly [kən'fesidli], *adv.* de son propre aveu.

confession [kən'feʃən], *n.* confession, *f.*, aveu, *m.*

confessor [kən'fesə], *n.* confesseur, *m.*

confidant ['kənfidænt], *n.* confident, *m.*

confide [kən'faid], *v.t.* confier (à).—*v.i.* se confier, se fier (à).

confidence ['kənfidəns], *n.* confiance; hardiesse; assurance; confidence (*secret*), *f.*

confident ['kənfidənt], *a.* confiant, certain, sûr; assuré.

confidential [kənfi'denʃəl], *a.* de confiance (*personne*); confidentiel (*chose*).

confidentially [kənfi'denʃəli], *adv.* de confiance; confidentiellement.

confidently ['kənfidəntli], *adv.* avec confiance.

confine [kən'fain], *v.t.* confiner, enfermer; retenir; limiter; *to be confined* (*of woman*), faire ses couches, accoucher.—['kənfain], *n.* (*usu. in pl.*) confins, *m.pl.*; (*fig.*) limite, borne, *f.*

confinement [kən'fainmənt], *n.* emprisonnement, *m.*; (*Mil.*) arrêts, *m.pl.*; accouchement, *m.*, couches (*de femme*), *f.pl.*

confirm [kən'fə:m], *v.t.* confirmer; affermir.

confirmation [kənfə'meiʃən], *n.* confirmation, *f.*, affermissement, *m.*

confirmed [kən'fə:md], *a.* invétéré, fieffé, incorrigible.

confiscate ['kənfiskeit], *v.t.* confisquer.

confiscation [kənfis'keiʃən], *n.* confiscation, *f.*

conflagration [kənflə'greiʃən], *n.* conflagration, *f.*, incendie, *m.*

conflict ['kənflikt], *n.* conflit, *m.*; (*fig.*) lutte, contradiction, *f.*—[kən'flikt], *v.i.* s'entrechoquer, lutter (*contre*); être en conflit (*avec*).

conflicting [kən'fliktiŋ], *a.* en conflit, contradictoire.

confluence ['kənfluəns], *n.* confluent; concours, *m.*; (*Path.*) confluence, *f.*

conform [kən'fə:m], *v.t.* conformer.—*v.i.* se conformer.

conformity [kən'fə:miti], *n.* conformité, *f.*; *in conformity with*, conformément (à).

confound [kən'faund], *v.t.* confondre; (*fig.*) bouleverser; embarrasser; *confound it!* zut!

confounded [kən'faundid], *a.* maudit, sacré.

confoundedly [kən'faundidli], *adv.* terriblement, furieusement, diablement.

confront [kən'frʌnt], *v.t.* confronter; affronter, faire face à.

confuse [kən'fju:z], *v.t.* rendre confus, embrouiller; (*fig.*) déconcerter.

confused [kən'fju:zd], *a.* confus; embrouillé.

confusedly [kən'fju:zidli], *adv.* confusément.

confusion [kən'fju:ʒən], *n.* confusion, *f.*, désordre; (*fig.*) embarras, *m.*

confute [kən'fju:t], *v.t.* réfuter.

congeal [kən'dʒi:l], *v.t.* congeler, glacer, geler, figer.—*v.i.* se congeler, se geler, se figer.

congenial [kən'dʒi:niəl], *a.* de la même nature; sympathique (à ou *avec*); qui convient (à); *a congenial task*, une tâche agréable.

conger ['kəngə], *n.* (*Ichth.*) congre, *m.*, anguille de mer, *f.*

congest [kən'dʒest], *v.t.* entasser; engorger; *to become congested*, se congestionner; s'emboîteuiller (*rues*).

congestion [kən'dʒestʃən], *n.* amoncellement, *m.*; (*Path.*) congestion, *f.*; encombrement (*des rues*), *m.*

conglomerate [kən'glɔməreit], *v.t.* conglomérer.—*v.i.* se conglomérer.—[kən'glɔ
mərit], *n.* (*Geol.*) conglomérat, *m.*
conglomeration [kənglɔmə'reiʃən], *n.* conglomération, *f.*
Congo ['kɔŋgou]. le Congo, *m.*
Congolese [kɔŋgo'li:z], *a.* congolais.—*n.*
Congolais (*personne*).
congratulate [kən'grætjuleit], *v.t.* féliciter.
congratulation [kəngrætju'leiʃən], *n.* félicitation, *f.*
congregate ['kɔŋgrigeit], *v.t.* rassembler.—
v.i. se rassembler.
congregation [kɔŋgri'geiʃən], *n.* (*Eccles.*) congrégation, *f.*, fidèles, *m.pl.*; assemblée, *f.*,
auditoire, *m.*, assistance, *f.*
congress ['kɔŋgres], *n.* congrès, *m.*
congressional [kən'greʃənl], *a.* congres-
sionnel.
congressman ['kɔŋgresmən], *n.* (*pl.* **-men**
[men]) (*U.S.*) membre du Congrès, *m.*
conic ['kɔnik], **conical** ['kɔnikəl], *a.* conique.
conifer ['kounifə], *n.* conifère, *m.*
coniferous [ko'nifərəs], *a.* conifère.
conjecture [kən'dʒektʃə], *v.t., v.i.* conjecturer.—*n.* conjecture, *f.*
conjugal ['kɔndʒugəl], *a.* conjugal.
conjugate ['kɔndʒugeit], *v.t.* conjuguer.
conjugation [kɔndʒu'geiʃən], *n.* conjugaison,
f.
conjunction [kən'dʒʌŋkʃən], *n.* conjonction,
f.
conjure ['kʌndʒə], *v.t.* ensorceler; escamoter;
to conjure up, évoquer.
conjurer, conjuror ['kʌndʒərə], *n.* escamoteur, prestidigitateur, illusionniste, *m.*
conjuring ['kʌndʒəriŋ], *n.* prestidigitation, *f.*,
escamotage, *m.*
connect [kə'nekt], *v.t.* lier, joindre, rattacher,
unir (à); accoupler.—*v.i.* se lier; faire correspondance (*trains*).
connected [kə'nektid], *a.* joint, uni, lié;
cohérent; en relations.
connection (**connexion**) [kə'nekʃən], *n.* connexion, liaison, suite, *f.*; rapport, *m.*; (*Rail.*)
correspondance, *f.*; (*Elec.*) contact, *m.*;
(*Comm.*) clientèle, *f.*; (*pl.*) parents, *m.pl.*; *in
connection with*, à propos de.
connivance [kə'naivəns], *n.* connivence, *f.*
connive [kə'naiv], *v.i. to connive at*, fermer
les yeux sur, être de connivence dans.
connoisseur [kɔnə'sə:], *n.* connaisseur, *m.*
connubial [kə'nju:biəl], *a.* conjugal.
conquer ['kɔŋkə], *v.t.* vaincre, dompter;
conquérir.—*v.i.* vaincre, remporter la victoire.
conqueror ['kɔŋkərə], *n.* vainqueur, conquérant, *m.*
conquest ['kɔŋkwest], *n.* conquête, *f.*
conscience ['kɔnʃəns], *n.* conscience, *f.*;
conscience money, restitution anonyme,
f.
conscientious [kɔnʃi'enʃəs], *a.* consciencieux; de conscience; *conscientious
objector*, objecteur de conscience, *m.*
conscientiously [kɔnʃi'enʃəsli], *adv.* consciencieusement.
conscious ['kɔnʃəs], *a.* conscient; *to be conscious*, avoir sa connaissance; *to be conscious of*, avoir conscience de.
consciously ['kɔnʃəsli], *adv.* sciemment, en
connaissance de cause.

consciousness ['kɔnʃəsnis], *n.* conscience;
connaissance, *f.*
conscript ['kɔnskript], *a. and n.* conscrit, *m.*
—[kən'skript], *v.t.* enrôler (par la conscription).
conscription [kən'skripʃən], *n.* conscription,
f.
consecrate ['kɔnsikreit], *v.t.* consacrer (*une
église*); bénir (*pain*); sacrer (*évêque, roi*);
consecrated ground, terre sainte, *f.*
consecration [kɔnsi'kreiʃən], *n.* consécration; canonisation, *f.*; sacre (*d'évêque, de roi
etc.*), *m.*
consecutive [kən'sekjutiv], *a.* consécutif.
consent [kən'sent], *v.i.* consentir (à).—*n.*
consentement; accord, *m.*
consequence ['kɔnsikwəns], *n.* conséquence,
suite, *f.*, effet, *m.*; importance, *f.*
consequent ['kɔnsikwənt], *a.* résultant; (*Log.*)
conséquent.—*n.* conséquent, *m.*
consequential [kɔnsi'kwenʃəl], *a.* conséquent, logique; (*fig.*) suffisant, important.
consequently ['kɔnsikwəntli], *adv. and conj.*
par conséquent.
conservative [kən'sə:vətiv], *a. and n.* conservateur, *m.*
conservatory [kən'sə:vətri], *n.* conservatoire
(*théâtre, musique*), *m.*; (*Hort.*) serre, *f.*
consider [kən'sidə], *v.t.* considérer, examiner;
estimer.—*v.i.* considérer, réfléchir (à).
considerable [kən'sidərəbl], *a.* considérable,
grand, important.
considerably [kən'sidərəbli], *adv.* considérablement.
considerate [kən'sidərit], *a.* modéré, indulgent; attentif, plein d'égards; prévenant.
consideration [kənsidə'reiʃən], *n.* considération, *f.*, examen, *m.*; égards, *m.pl.*; récompense, *f.*, dédommagement, *m.*; *to take
into consideration*, tenir compte de.
considering [kən'sidəriŋ], *prep.* eu égard à,
étant donné, vu.—*conj.* vu que, attendu que,
étant donné que.
consign [kən'sain], *v.t.* consigner, livrer,
confier (à); (*Comm.*) expédier.
consignment [kən'sainmənt], *n.* expédition,
f., envoi, *m.*
consist [kən'sist], *v.i.* consister (*en*); *to consist of*, se composer (*de*).
consistency [kən'sistənsi], *n.* consistance,
suite, *f.*, esprit de suite; accord, *m.*, harmonie; stabilité, *f.*
consistent [kən'sistənt], *a.* consistant; compatible (*avec*), conséquent.
consistently [kən'sistəntli], *adv.* d'une
manière conséquente, conséquemment.
consolation [kɔnsə'leiʃən], *n.* consolation, *f.*
console [kən'soul], *v.t.* consoler (*de*).
consolidate [kən'sɔlideit], *v.t.* consolider.—
v.i. se consolider; *consolidated annuities*,
(*abbr.*) *consols*, consolidés, *m.pl.*
consolidation [kənsɔli'deiʃən], *n.* consolidation, *f.*
consoling [kən'souliŋ], *a.* consolant, consolateur.
consonant ['kɔnsənənt], *a.* consonant, conforme (à).—*n.* (*Phon.*) consonne, *f.*
consort ['kɔnsɔ:t], *n.* compagnon, *m.*, compagne, *f.*; époux, *m.*, épouse, *f.*—[kən'sɔ:t],
v.i. s'associer (à); *to consort with*, fréquenter.

385

conspicuous [kən'spikjuəs], *a.* bien visible, en évidence; remarquable, éminent.

conspicuously [kən'spikjuəsli], *adv.* visiblement, manifestement, éminemment.

conspiracy [kən'spirəsi], *n.* conspiration, conjuration, *f.*

conspirator [kən'spirətə], *n.* conspirateur; conjuré, *m.*

conspire [kən'spaiə], *v.i.* conspirer, comploter (*contre*); (*fig.*) se réunir (*pour*).

constable ['kʌnstəbl], *n.* gouverneur (*de château*); agent de police, *m.*; *chief constable*, commissaire de police, *m.*

constabulary [kən'stæbjulari], *n.* police; gendarmerie, *f.*

constancy ['kɒnstənsi], *n.* constance, fermeté, fidélité; régularité, *f.*

constant ['kɒnstənt], *a.* stable, constant, fidèle; continu.

constantly ['kɒnstəntli], *adv.* constamment, invariablement.

constellation [kɒnstə'leiʃən], *n.* constellation, *f.*

consternation [kɒnstə'neiʃən], *n.* consternation, *f.*, atterrement, *m.*

constipation [kɒnsti'peiʃən], *n.* constipation, *f.*

constituency [kən'stitjuənsi], *n.* circonscription électorale, *f.*, électeurs, *m.pl.*

constituent [kən'stitjuənt], *a.* constituant.— *n.* constituant; (*Polit.*) commettant, électeur, *m.*

constitute ['kɒnstitju:t], *v.t.* constituer, faire.

constitution [kɒnsti'tju:ʃən], *n.* constitution, *f.*, tempérament, *m.*

constitutional [kɒnsti'tju:ʃənəl], *a.* constitutionnel.—*n.* promenade de santé, *f.*

constrain [kən'strein], *v.t.* contraindre, forcer; retenir; gêner.

constraint [kən'streint], *n.* contrainte, gêne, *f.*

constrict [kən'strikt], *v.t.* resserrer, étrangler; brider.

construct [kən'strʌkt], *v.t.* construire, bâtir.

construction [kən'strʌkʃən], *n.* construction, *f.*; bâtiment, *m.*; (*fig.*) interprétation, *f.*, sens, *m.*

constructive [kən'strʌktiv], *a.* constructif; implicite.

construe [kən'stru:], *v.t.* traduire mot-à-mot; (*fig.*) expliquer, interpréter.

consul ['kɒnsəl], *n.* consul, *m.*

consular ['kɒnsjulə], *a.* consulaire.

consulate ['kɒnsjulit], **consulship** ['kɒnsəl ʃip], *n.* consulat, *m.*

consult [kən'sʌlt], *v.t.* consulter.—*v.i.* délibérer.

consultation [kɒnsəl'teiʃən], *n.* consultation, délibération, *f.*

consume [kən'sju:m], *v.t.* consumer, dissiper, dévorer; gaspiller; consommer (*to use*).

consumer [kən'sju:mə], *n.* consommateur; abonné (*de gaz etc.*), *m.*; *consumer goods*, biens de consommation, *m.pl.*

consummate ['kɒnsəmeit], *v.t.* consommer, achever, accomplir.—[kən'sʌmit], *a.* consommé, complet, achevé, fieffé.

consummation [kɒnsə'meiʃən], *n.* consommation, fin, *f.*; (*fig.*) comble, *m.*

consumption [kən'sʌmpʃən], *n.* consommation; phtisie, consomption (*maladie*), *f.*

consumptive [kən'sʌmptiv], *a.* poitrinaire, phtisique, tuberculeux.

contact ['kɒntækt], *n.* contact, rapport, *m.*— *v.t.* contacter, se mettre en relation avec, entrer en contact avec.

contagion [kən'teidʒən], *n.* contagion, *f.*

contagious [kən'teidʒəs], *a.* contagieux.

contain [kən'tein], *v.t.* contenir; retenir, renfermer.

container [kən'teinə], *n.* récipient, réservoir, *m.*; (*Comm.*) boîte, *f.*

contaminate [kən'tæmineit], *v.t.* souiller, contaminer.

contamination [kəntæmi'neiʃən], *n.* souillure, contamination, *f.*

contemplate ['kɒntəmpleit], *v.t.* contempler; méditer, projeter.—*v.i.* songer, méditer.

contemplation [kɒntəm'pleiʃən], *n.* contemplation; méditation, *f.*; projet, *m.*

contemplative [kən'templətiv], *a.* contemplatif; pensif.

contemporaneous [kəntempə'reinjəs], *a.* contemporain.

contemporary [kən'tempərəri], *a. and n.* contemporain, *m.*

contempt [kən'tempt], *n.* mépris, dédain, *m.*

contemptible [kən'temptəbl], *a.* méprisable, à dédaigner.

contemptuous [kən'temptjuəs], *a.* méprisant, dédaigneux.

contend [kən'tend], *v.i.* lutter, combattre; contester; prétendre (*que*).

contender [kən'tendə], *n.* compétiteur, concurrent, *m.*

content (1) [kən'tent], *a.* content, satisfait; *to be content with*, se contenter de.—*n.* contentement, *m.*—*v.t.* contenter, satisfaire.

content (2) ['kɒntent], *n.* contenu, *m.*; *table of contents*, table des matières, *f.*

contented [kən'tentid], *a.* satisfait, content (*de*).

contentedly [kən'tentidli], *adv.* avec contentement.

contention [kən'tenʃən], *n.* dispute, lutte, *f.*, débat, *m.*; prétention, *f.*; *bone of contention*, pomme de discorde, *f.*

contentious [kən'tenʃəs], *a.* contentieux, litigieux, querelleur.

contentiousness [kən'tenʃəsnis], *n.* humeur querelleuse, *f.*

contentment [kən'tentmənt], *n.* contentement, *m.*

conterminous [kən'tə:minəs], *a.* limitrophe, voisin (*de*); attenant (*à*).

contest ['kɒntest], *n.* lutte, *f.*, combat; concours, *m.*—[kən'test], *v.t.*, *v.i.* contester, disputer.

contestant [kən'testənt], *n.* contestant, concurrent, *m.*

context ['kɒntekst], *n.* contexte, *m.*; *in this context*, à ce sujet.

contiguity [kɒnti'gju:iti], *n.* contiguïté, *f.*

contiguous [kən'tigjuəs], *a.* contigu, attenant (*à*).

continence ['kɒntinəns], *n.* continence, chasteté; (*fig.*) retenue, *f.*

continent (1) ['kɒntinənt], *a.* continent, chaste; (*fig.*) modéré, retenu.

continent (2) ['kɒntinənt], *n.* continent, *m.*

continental [kɒnti'nentl], *a. and n.* continental, *m.*

contingence [kən'tindʒəns], **contingency** [kən'tindʒənsi], *n.* éventualité, *f.*, cas imprévu, *m.*

contingent [kən'tindʒənt], *a.* contingent, fortuit, imprévu.—*n.* (*Mil.*) contingent, *m.*

contingently [kən'tindʒəntli], *adv.* éventuellement, fortuitement.

continual [kən'tinjuəl], *a.* continuel.

continually [kən'tinjuəli], *adv.* continuellement.

continuance [kən'tinjuəns], *n.* continuation; durée, *f.*

continuation [kəntinju'eiʃən], *n.* continuation, durée, *f.*

continue [kən'tinju:], *v.t.* continuer; prolonger; reprendre; perpétuer.—*v.i.* continuer; demeurer; durer.

continued [kən'tinju:d], *a.* continu; suivi; à suivre (*feuilleton*); **to be continued,** à suivre.

continuity [kɔnti'nju:iti], *n.* continuité, *f.*

continuous [kən'tinjuəs], *a.* continu.

continuously [kən'tinjuəsli], *adv.* continûment, sans interruption.

contort [kən'tɔ:t], *v.t.* tordre, contourner, défigurer.

contorted [kən'tɔ:tid], *a.* tordu, contourné, défiguré.

contortion [kən'tɔ:ʃən], *n.* contorsion; (*Anat.*) luxation, *f.*

contortionist [kən'tɔ:ʃənist], *n.* contorsioniste, *m., f.*

contour [kən'tuə], *n.* contour, tracé (*de niveau*), *m.*

contra [kən'trə], *prep.* contre; (*Comm.*) d'autre part.

contraband [kən'trəbænd], *a.* de contrebande.—*n.* contrebande, *f.*

contraception [kɔntrə'sepʃən], *n.* procédés anticonceptionnels, *m.pl.*

contraceptive [kɔntrə'septiv], *a.* anticonceptionnel.—*n.* procédé *ou* appareil anticonceptionnel, *m.*

contract [kən'trækt], *v.t.* contracter (*dans tous les sens*); abréger; (*fig.*) resserrer; rider, froncer (*les sourcils etc.*); prendre (*habitude*).—*v.i.* se contracter, se resserrer, se rétrécir; (*Comm.*) traiter (*pour*), contracter, entreprendre, soumissionner; **to contract out of something,** renoncer à *ou* se dégager de quelquechose par contrat.—[′kɔntrækt], *n.* contrat; pacte, *m.,* convention; adjudication, *f.*

contractible [kən'træktəbl], *a.* contractile.

contraction [kən'trækʃən], *n.* contraction, *f.,* rétrécissement; raccourcissement; retrait (*métaux*), *m.;* (*Math.*) abréviation, *f.*

contractor [kən'træktə], *n.* contractant; entrepreneur (*constructeur*); fournisseur (*aux forces armées*); adjudicataire (*concesseur*), *m.*

contradict [kɔntrə'dikt], *v.t.* contredire; démentir.

contradiction [kɔntrə'dikʃən], *n.* contradiction, incompatibilité, *f.,* démenti (*négation*), *m.*

contradictory [kɔntrə'diktəri], *a.* contradictoire.

contralto [kən'træltou], *n.* (*Mus.*) contralto, contralte, *m.*

contrariety [kɔntrə'raiəti], *n.* contrariété, opposition, *f.*

contrarily [′kɔntrərili], *adv.* contrairement, en sens contraire.

contrary [′kɔntrəri], *a.* contraire, opposé; (*fam.*) [kən'treəri], contrariant (*personne*).—*n.* contraire, *m.;* **on the contrary,** au contraire.—*adv.* contrairement (*à*); à l'encontre (*de*).

contrast [′kɔntrɑ:st], *n.* contraste, *m.*—[kən'trɑ:st], *v.t.* faire contraster; mettre en contraste.—*v.i.* contraster, faire contraste.

contravene [kɔntrə'vi:n], *v.t.* contrevenir à, enfreindre.

contravention [kɔntrə'venʃən], *n.* contravention, infraction, *f.*

contribute [kən'tribju:t], *v.t.* contribuer, payer.—*v.i.* contribuer (*à*).

contribution [kɔntri'bju:ʃən], *n.* contribution, *f.*

contributor [kən'tribjutə], *n.* contribuant, (*Journ.*) collaborateur, *m.*

contributory [kən'tribjutəri], *a.* contribuant.

contrite [′kɔntrait], *a.* contrit, pénitent.

contritely [′kɔntraitli], *adv.* avec contrition.

contriteness [′kɔntraitnis], **contrition** [kən'triʃən], *n.* contrition, pénitence, *f.*

contrivance [kən'traivəns], *n.* invention; combinaison, idée, *f.;* artifice, *m.*

contrive [kən'traiv], *v.t.* inventer, imaginer; pratiquer, ménager.—*v.i.* s'arranger (*pour*), trouver moyen (*de*); parvenir (*à*).

contriver [kən'traivə], *n.* inventeur, *m.,* inventrice, *f.*

contriving [kən'traiviŋ], *a.* ingénieux.

control [kən'troul], *n.* autorité (*supérieure*); surveillance; (*Tech.*) commande, *f.;* **out of control,** désemparé; **remote control,** télécommande, *f.*—*v.t.* diriger, régler; gouverner, commander; **to control oneself,** se dominer, se retenir.

controller [kən'troulə], *n.* contrôleur, *m.*

controversial [kɔntrə'və:ʃəl], *a.* sujet à controverse, polémique.

controversy [′kɔntrəvə:si], *n.* controverse, polémique, *f.;* différend, *m.*

controvert [′kɔntrəvə:t], *v.t.* controverser, disputer.

contumacious [kɔntju'meiʃəs], *a.* obstiné, récalcitrant, opiniâtre; (*Law*) contumace.

contumaciousness [kɔntju'meiʃəsnis], **contumacy** [′kɔntjuməsi], *n.* obstination, opiniâtreté; (*Law*) contumace, *f.*

contumelious [kɔntju'mi:liəs], *a.* injurieux, outrageant.

contumely [′kɔntjuməli], *n.* injure, *f.,* outrage, *m.,* honte, *f.*

contuse [kən'tju:z], *v.t.* contusionner.

contusion [kən'tju:ʃən], *n.* contusion, meurtrissure, *f.*

conundrum [kə'nʌndrəm], *n.* énigme, devinette, *f.*

convalesce [kɔnvə'les], *v.i.* être en convalescence.

convalescence [kɔnvə'lesəns], *n.* convalescence, *f.*

convalescent [kɔnvə'lesənt], *a.* and *n.* convalescent, *m.,* convalescente, *f.*

convection [kən'vekʃən], *n.* convection, *f.*

convene [kən'vi:n], *v.t.* convoquer, réunir, assembler.—*v.i.* s'assembler, se réunir.

convenience [kən'vi:niəns], *n.* commodité, convenance, *f.*

convenient [kən'vi:niənt], *a.* commode, convenable.

conveniently [kən'vi:niəntli], *adv.* commodément, convenablement, sans inconvénient.

convent ['kɔnvənt], *n.* couvent, *m.*

conventicle [kən'ventikl], *n.* conventicule, *m.*

convention [kən'venʃən], *n.* convention; assemblée, *f.*; (*pl.*) convenances *f.pl.*

conventional [kən'venʃənəl], *a.* conventionnel, de convention.

conventual [kən'ventjuəl], *a.* conventuel.—*n.* conventuel, religieux, *m.*; religieuse, *f.*

converge [kən'və:dʒ], *v.i.* converger.

conversant [kən'və:sənt], *a.* versé (*dans*); familier (*avec*), au courant de.

conversation [kɔnvə'seiʃən], *n.* conversation, *f.*, entretien, *m.*

conversational [kɔnvə'seiʃənəl], *a.* de conversation.

conversationalist [kɔnvə'seiʃənəlist], *n.* causeur, *m.*

converse [kən'və:s], *v.i.* causer, converser, s'entretenir.—['kɔnvə:s], *n.* entretien, *m.*, conversation; (*Math.*) réciproque, *f.*

conversely ['kɔnvə:sli], *adv.* réciproquement.

conversion [kən'və:ʃən], *n.* conversion, *f.*

convert [kən'və:t], *v.t.* convertir, transformer; faire servir.—['kɔnvə:t], *n.* converti, *m.*, convertie, *f.*

converter [kən'və:tə], *n.* convertisseur, *m.*

convertible [kən'və:tibl], *a.* convertible (*chose*); convertissable (*personne*); (*Motor.*) décapotable.

convex ['kɔnveks], *a.* convexe.

convey [kən'vei], *v.t.* transporter (*marchandises etc.*); porter, conduire, amener; transmettre (*son etc.*); présenter (*remerciements etc.*); donner (*idée etc.*); communiquer (*nouvelle etc.*); céder (*propriété etc.*).

conveyable [kən'veiəbl], *a.* transportable; exprimable.

conveyance [kən'veiəns], *n.* transport, *m.*; transmission, *f.*; véhicule, *m.*; (*Law*) cession, *f.*

conveyor [kən'veiə], *n.* porteur, voiturier; (appareil) transporteur; conducteur (électrique), *m.*; **conveyor belt,** chaîne de montage, *f.*

convict [kən'vikt], *v.t.* condamner, déclarer coupable; convaincre (*quelqu'un de son erreur etc.*).—['kɔnvikt], *n.* forçat, *m.*

conviction [kən'vikʃən], *n.* conviction, persuasion; (*Law*) condamnation, *f.*

convince [kən'vins], *v.t.* convaincre, persuader.

convincing [kən'vinsiŋ], *a.* convaincant; persuasif.

convincingly [kən'vinsiŋli], *adv.* d'une manière convaincante.

convivial [kən'viviəl], *a.* joyeux, jovial.

conviviality [kənvivi'æliti], *n.* franche gaieté, *f.*; (*pl.*) joyeux repas, *m.pl.*

convocation [kɔnvə'keiʃən], *n.* convocation; (*Eccles.*) assemblée, *f.*, synode, *m.*

convoke [kən'vouk], *v.t.* convoquer, assembler.

convolvulus [kən'vɔlvjuləs], *n.* (*pl.* **convolvuli** [kən'vɔlvjulai]) volubilis, liseron, *m.*, belle-de-jour, *f.*

convoy ['kɔnvɔi], *n.* convoi, *m.*, escorte, *f.*

convulse [kən'vʌls], *v.t.* convulser; (*fig.*) ébranler, bouleverser.

convulsion [kən'vʌlʃən], *n.* convulsion; (*fig.*) commotion, *f.*

convulsive [kən'vʌlsiv], *a.* convulsif.

cony, coney ['kouni], *n.* lapin, *m.*

coo [ku:], *v.i.* roucouler.

cooing ['ku:iŋ], *n.* roucoulement, *m.*

cook [kuk], *n.* cuisinier, *m.*, cuisinière, *f.*; (*Naut.*) coq, *m.*; **head cook,** chef, *m.*—*v.t.* cuire, faire cuire.—*v.i.* cuire; faire la cuisine, cuisiner.

cooker ['kukə], *n.* cuisinière (*appareil*), *f.*; fruit à cuire, *m.*; **pressure cooker,** cocotte-minute, *f.*

cookery ['kukəri], *n.* cuisine (*art*), *f.*

cooking ['kukiŋ], *n.* cuisine; cuisson, *f.*

cool [ku:l], *a.* frais, (*fig.*) calme, tranquille; peu gêné.—*n.* frais, *m.*, fraicheur, *f.*—*v.t.* rafraîchir; refroidir; (*fig.*) calmer.—*v.i.* se refroidir; refroidir; **to cool down,** se calmer, s'apaiser.

cooling ['ku:liŋ], *a.* rafraîchissant, calmant; **cooler,** refroidisseur, *m.*

coolly ['ku:lli], *adv.* fraîchement; (*fig.*) de sangfroid, tranquillement.

coolness ['ku:lnis], *n.* fraîcheur, *f.*, frais, *m.*; (*fig.*) froideur (*indifférence*), *f.*; sang-froid; sans-gêne (*insolence*), *m.*

coop [ku:p], *n.* cage à poules, mue, *f.*—*v.t.* mettre en mue; **to coop up,** enfermer étroitement, claquemurer.

cooper ['ku:pə], *n.* tonnelier, *m.*

co-operate [kou'ɔpəreit], *v.i.* coopérer, concourir (à).

co-operation [kouɔpə'reiʃən], *n.* coopération, *f.*; concours, *m.*

co-operative [kou'ɔpərətiv], *a.* coopérant, coopératif.

co-opt [kou'ɔpt], *v.t.* coopter.

co-ordinate [kou'ɔ:dineit], *v.t.* coordonner.—[kou'ɔ:dinit], *a.* du même rang, égal; (*Math.*) coordonné.

coot [ku:t], *n.* (*Orn.*) foulque, *f.*

cop [kɔp], *n.* cime, *f.*, sommet, *m.*; huppe, aigrette (*d'oiseau*), *f.*; (*slang*) flic (*agent de police*), *m.*

copartner [kou'pɑ:tnə], *n.* associé, *m.*

copartnership [kou'pɑ:tnəʃip], *n.* société en nom collectif, *f.*

cope (1) [koup], *n.* chaperon, *m.*, chape (*vêtement sacerdotal*), *f.*—*v.t.* couvrir, chaperonner.

cope (2) [koup], *v.i.* se débrouiller; **to cope with,** tenir tête à; venir à bout de.

Copenhagen [koupən'heigən], Copenhague, *f.*

copier ['kɔpiə], **copyist** ['kɔpiist], *n.* copiste, *m.*, *f.*; (*fig.*) imitateur, *m.*

coping ['koupiŋ], *n.* faîte (*d'un édifice*); couronnement (*d'un mur*), *m.*

copious ['koupiəs], *a.* abondant, copieux.

copiously ['koupiəsli], *adv.* copieusement, abondamment.

copiousness ['koupiəsnis], *n.* abondance, *f.*

copper ['kɔpə], *a.* de cuivre, en cuivre.—*n.* cuivre (*rouge*), *m.*; chaudière (*boiler*), *f.*; (*slang*) flic (*agent de police*), *m.*; (*pl.*) petite monnaie, *f.*—*v.t.* cuivrer; (*Naut.*) doubler en cuivre.

copper-beech ['kɔpə'bi:tʃ], *n.* hêtre rouge, *m.*

copper-smith ['kɔpəsmiθ], *n.* chaudronnier, *m.*

coppice ['kɔpis], **copse** [kɔps], *n.* taillis, *m.*

copy ['kɔpi], *n.* copie, *f.*; exemple (*d'écriture*); exemplaire (*livre*); numéro (*journal*); modèle (*de dessin*), *m.*; *rough copy*, brouillon, *m.*—*v.t.* copier; imiter. [copy editor, see **sub-editor**]

copy-book ['kɔpibuk], *n.* cahier d'écriture, *m.*

copyist [COPIER].

copyright ['kɔpirait], *n.* droits d'auteur, *m.pl.*; propriété littéraire, *f.*

coquet [kɔ'ket], *v.i.* faire des coquetteries (*à*); faire la coquette (*avec*).

coquette [kɔ'ket], *n.* coquette, *f.*

coquetry ['koukətri], *n.* coquetterie, *f.*

coquettish [kɔ'ketiʃ], *a.* coquet, en coquette; provocant (*sourire*).

coquettishly [kɔ'ketiʃli], *adv.* d'un air provocant.

coral ['kɔrəl], *a.* de corail.—*n.* corail, *m.*

cord [kɔːd], *n.* corde, *f.*, cordon; cordage, *m.*, ganse, *f.*; (*fig.*) lien, *m.*—*v.t.* corder.

cordial ['kɔːdiəl], *a.* cordial.—*n.* cordial, *m.*, liqueur, *f.*

cordiality [kɔːdi'æliti], *n.* cordialité, *f.*

cordially ['kɔːdiəli], *adv.* cordialement.

cordon ['kɔːdən], *n.* cordon, *m.*—*v.t.* *to cordon off*, isoler par un cordon (*de police*).

corduroy ['kɔːdjurɔi], *n.* velours à côtes, *m.*

core [kɔː], *n.* cœur; noyau (*d'un moule*); (*fig.*) milieu, centre, *m.*; (*Naut.*) âme (*de corde*), *f.*; trognon (*de pomme*), *m.*—*v.t.* vider (*une pomme*); creuser, évider (*un moule*).

co-respondent [kouris'pɔndənt], *n.* complice, *m.*, *f.*, co-défendeur (*en adultère*), *m.*

corgi, corgy ['kɔːgi], *n.* basset gallois, *m.*

cork [kɔːk], *n.* liège; bouchon (*à bouteille etc.*), *m.*—*v.t.* boucher.

corkscrew ['kɔːkskru], *n.* tire-bouchon, *m.*; *corkscrew staircase*, escalier en colimaçon, *m.*

cork-tipped ['kɔːk'tipt], *a.* à bouts de liège (*cigarettes*).

corm [kɔːm], *n.* (*Bot.*) bulbe, *m.*

cormorant ['kɔːmərənt], *n.* cormoran, *m.*; (*fig.*) rapace, affameur, *m.*

corn (1) [kɔːn], *n.* grain, *m.*; céréales, *f.pl.*; blé, *m.*; (*Am.*) corn, maïs, *m.*—*v.t.* saler (*bœuf*).

corn (2) [kɔːn], *n.* cor (au pied), *m.*

corn-chandler ['kɔːntʃɑːndlə], *n.* blatier, marchand de blé, *m.*

corn-crake ['kɔːnkreik], *n.* râle de genêt, *m.*

cornea ['kɔːniə], *n.* (*Anat.*) cornée, *f.*

corned beef ['kɔːnd'biːf], *n.* bœuf salé, bœuf de conserve, *m.*

corner ['kɔːnə], *n.* coin, angle, *m.*; encoignure, *f.*; (*fig.*) monopole, accaparement, *m.*; *blind corner*, tournant (*ou* virage) masqué, *m.*—*v.t.* (*Comm.*) accaparer; (*fig.*) pousser dans un coin, acculer.—*v.i.* prendre un virage, virer.

corner-stone ['kɔːnəstoun], *n.* pierre angulaire, *f.*

cornet ['kɔːnit], *n.* cornet (*à pistons*), *m.*

cornfield ['kɔːnfiːld], *n.* champ de maïs, *m.*

cornflakes ['kɔːnfleiks], *n.pl.* paillettes de maïs, *f.pl.*

corn-flower ['kɔːnflauə], *n.* bluet, *m.*

cornice ['kɔːnis], *n.* corniche, *f.*

corn-poppy ['kɔːnpɔpi], *n.* coquelicot, *m.*

cornstarch ['kɔːnstɑːtʃ], *n.* farine de maïs, *f.*

corollary [kə'rɔləri], *n.* corollaire, *m.*

coronation [kɔrə'neiʃən], *n.* couronnement, sacre, *m.*

coroner ['kɔrənə], *n.* coroner, *m.*

coronet ['kɔrənit], *n.* (petite) couronne, *f.*

corporal ['kɔːpərəl], *a.* corporel.—*n.* caporal (*infanterie*); brigadier (*cavalerie*), *m.*

corporate ['kɔːpərit], *a.* érigé en corporation; de corporation.

corporately ['kɔːpəritli], *adv.* collectivement.

corporation [kɔːpə'reiʃən], *n.* corporation, *f.*; conseil municipal, *m.*, municipalité (*d'une ville*), *f.*

corporeal [kɔː'pɔːriəl], *a.* corporel, matériel.

corps [kɔː], *n.inv.* corps, *m.*, formation, *f.*

corpse [kɔːps], *n.* cadavre, *m.*

corpulence ['kɔːpjuləns], **corpulency** ['kɔːpjulənsi], *n.* corpulence, *f.*, embonpoint, *m.*

corpulent ['kɔːpjulənt], *a.* corpulent, gros, gras.

corpuscle ['kɔːpʌsl], *n.* corpuscule, globule, *m.*

correct [kə'rekt], *a.* correct, exact, juste; (*fig.*) convenable, en règle; pur, bon (*style*); bien élevé (*personne*); comme il faut.—*v.t.* corriger, rectifier, reprendre; punir.

correction [kə'rekʃən], *n.* correction; punition, *f.*

correctly [kə'rektli], *adv.* correctement, exactement, justement.

correctness [kə'rektnis], *n.* exactitude, justesse; pureté (*de style*), *f.*

correlate ['kɔrileit], *v.t.* mettre en corrélation.—*v.i.* correspondre.

correlation [kɔri'leiʃən], *n.* corrélation, *f.*

correspond [kɔris'pɔnd], *v.i.* correspondre (*à ou avec*); répondre (*à*); s'accorder (*avec*); être conforme (*à*).

correspondence [kɔris'pɔndəns], *n.* correspondance, *f.*, rapport, *m.*

correspondent [kɔris'pɔndənt], *a.* conforme, qui se rapporte (*à*).—*n.* correspondant, *m.*

corridor ['kɔridɔː], *n.* corridor; couloir, *m.*

corroborate [kə'rɔbəreit], *v.t.* corroborer, confirmer.

corroboration [kərɔbə'reiʃən], *n.* corroboration, confirmation, *f.*; *in corroboration of*, à l'appui de.

corrode [kə'roud], *v.t.* corroder, ronger; (*fig.*) détruire.—*v.i.* se corroder.

corrosion [kə'rouʒən], *n.* corrosion; (*fig.*) destruction, *f.*

corrosive [kə'rouziv], *a.* corrosif; (*fig.*) rongeur.—*n.* corrosif, *m.*

corrugate ['kɔrugeit], *v.t.* rider, plisser, froncer; onduler; *corrugated iron*, tôle ondulée, *f.*—*v.i.* se plisser, se froncer.

corrupt [kə'rʌpt], *v.t.* corrompre.—*v.i.* se corrompre.—*a.* corrompu, dépravé, vicié.

corruption [kə'rʌpʃən], *n.* corruption; (*fig.*) altération (*d'un texte etc.*), *f.*

corruptive [kə'rʌptiv], *a.* corruptif.

corruptly [kə'rʌptli], *adv.* par corruption.

corsair ['kɔːsɛə], *n.* corsaire, *m.*

corset ['kɔːsit], *n.* corset, *m.*

corset-maker ['kɔːsitmeikə], *n.* corsetier, *m.* corsetière, *f.*

Corsica ['kɔːsikə], la Corse, *f.*

Corsican ['kɔːsikən], *a.* corse.—*n.* Corse (*personne*), *m.*, *f.*

corslet ['kɔ:slit], n. corselet. m.

cortège [kɔ:'teiʒ], n. cortège (funèbre), m., procession; suite, f.

cortisone ['kɔ:tizoun], n. cortisone, f.

coruscate ['kɔrəskeit], v.i. scintiller, briller.

corvette [kɔ:'vet], n. (Naut.) corvette, f.

cosh [kɔʃ], n. matraque, f.—v.t. matraquer.

cosily ['kouzili], adv. à l'aise, bien au chaud, douillettement.

cosmetic [kɔz'metik], a. and n. cosmétique, m.

cosmic ['kɔzmik], cosmical ['kɔzmikəl], a. cosmique.

cosmopolitan [kɔzmo'pɔlitən], a. and n. cosmopolite, m., f.

cosmos ['kɔzmɔs], n. cosmos, m.

cosset ['kɔsit], v.t. dorloter, choyer.

cost [kɔst], n. prix; frais, m., dépense, f.; (Comm.) cout, m.; (Law, pl.) dépens, m.pl.; at any cost, at all costs, à tout prix; cost of living, coût de la vie.—v.i. irr. coûter; cost what it may, coûte que coûte.

coster ['kɔstə], costermonger ['kɔstəmʌŋgə], n. marchand des quatre saisons, m.

costive ['kɔstiv], a. constipé.

costliness ['kɔstlinis], n. haut prix, prix élevé, m.

costly ['kɔstli], a. coûteux, de prix; somptueux.

costume ['kɔstju:m], n. costume, m.

cosy ['kouzi], a. chaud, confortable, douillet; commode et petit (appartement).—n. (tea) cosy, couvre-théière, m.

cot [kɔt], n. cabane, chaumière, f.; bercail, parc (à moutons); petit lit, lit d'enfant, m.

coterie ['koutəri], n. coterie, clique, f.

cottage ['kɔtidʒ], n. chaumière; villa, f.

cotter pin, see split pin.

cotton [kɔtn], n. coton, m.

cotton mill ['kɔtnmil], n. filature de coton, f.

cotton plant ['kɔtnplɑ:nt], cotton bush ['kɔtnbuʃ], n. cotonnier, m.

cotton-spinning ['kɔtnspiniŋ], n. filage du coton, m.

cotton-wool ['kɔtn'wul], n. ouate, f.

couch [kautʃ], n. canapé, divan, m.—v.t. coucher; (fig.) rédiger, exprimer.—v.i. se coucher; se tapir.

cougar ['ku:gə], n. couguar, puma, m.

cough [kɔf], n. toux, f.; whooping cough, coqueluche, f.—v.i. tousser.

coughing ['kɔfiŋ], n. toux, f.; fit of coughing, quinte de toux, f.

council ['kaunsil], n. conseil; (Eccles.) concile, m.

councilor ['kaunsilə], n. conseiller, m.

counsel ['kaunsəl], n. conseil, avis; dessein; avocat, m.—v.t. conseiller.

counsellor ['kaunsələ], n. conseiller; avocat, m.

count (1) [kaunt], n. comte (titre), m.

count (2) [kaunt], n. calcul, compte, total, m. —v.t. compter; (fig.) regarder, considérer; to count on or upon, compter sur.

countenance ['kauntinəns], n. figure, mine, f., air, m.; (fig.) approbation, f., appui, m.; to give countenance to, favoriser, encourager; to keep one's countenance, garder son sérieux; to put out of countenance, décontenancer.—v.t. appuyer, encourager, favoriser; être en faveur de.

counter ['kauntə], n. calculateur; compteur (instrument); (Cards etc.) jeton; comptoir (de magasin), m.—adv. contre, contrairement (à), à l'encontre (de).—v.t., v.i. parer; contrer.

counteract [kauntə'rækt], v.t. contrecarrer, contre-balancer, neutraliser.

counteraction [kauntə'rækʃən], n. action contraire, opposition, résistance, f.

counter-clockwise ['kauntə'klɔkwaiz], anticlockwise ['ænti'klɔkwaiz], adv. dans le sens contraire des aiguilles d'une montre.

counter-espionage ['kauntər'espiənɑ:ʒ], n. contre-espionnage, m.

counterfeit ['kauntəfi:t], a. contrefait, imité; faux.—n. contrefaçon; fausse pièce, fausse monnaie; imitation, f.—v.t. contrefaire, imiter; feindre.—v.i. feindre.

counterfoil ['kauntəfɔil], n. talon (de registre), m., souche, f.

countermand [kauntə'mɑ:nd], v.t. contremander.—n. contremandement, m.

counterpane ['kauntəpein], n. couvre-pied, couvre-lit, m.

counterpart ['kauntəpɑ:t], n. contre-partie, f.; pendant, m.

countess ['kauntis], n. comtesse, f.

counting ['kauntiŋ], n. compte; dépouillement (élections), m.

counting house ['kauntiŋhaus], n. bureau, comptoir, m., caisse, f.

countless ['kauntlis], a. innombrable, sans nombre.

countrified ['kʌntrifaid], a. (devenu) campagnard ou provincial.

country ['kʌntri], n. pays, m.; contrée; région; campagne (opposée à la ville); province (opposée à la capitale); patrie (fatherland), f.; across country, à travers champs; in open country, en rase campagne; in the country, à la campagne.

countryman ['kʌntrimən], n. (pl. -men [men]) paysan, campagnard, m.; fellow countryman, compatriote, m.

countryside ['kʌntrisaid], n. campagne, f.; paysage, m.

country-woman ['kʌntriwumən], n. (pl. -women [wimin]) paysanne, f.

county ['kaunti], n. comté, m.; county council, conseil général, m.; county seat, chef-lieu m.

couple [kʌpl], n. couple, f.; couple (mâle et femelle), m.—v.t. coupler, accoupler; atteler; joindre.—v.i. s'accoupler.

couplet ['kʌplit], n. couplet, distique, m.

coupling ['kʌpliŋ], n. accouplement, m.

coupon ['ku:pɔn], n. coupon; bon, m.

courage ['kʌridʒ], n. courage, m.

courageous [kə'reidʒəs], a. courageux.

courageously [kə'reidʒəsli], adv. courageusement.

courier ['kuriə], n. courrier, m.

course [kɔ:s], n. cours, m.; carrière, voie, suite, f.; lit (d'une rivière); genre (de vie); service (de repas); courant (durée); (Racing) terrain de course; hippodrome, m.; (Naut.) route, f.; (Med., pl.) règles, f.pl.; in due course, en temps voulu; of course, naturellement, bien entendu.—v.t. courir; faire courir; chasser (le lièvre).—v.i. courir; circuler (sang).

courser ['kɔ:sə], n. coureur, coursier, m.

court [kɔːt], *n.* cour, *f.*; tribunal, *m.*; impasse, *f.*, passage (*petite rue*); (*Ten.*) court, *m.*—*v.t.* faire sa cour à, courtiser; rechercher; briguer.

courteous ['kɔːtiəs], *a.* courtois, poli.

courteously ['kɔːtiəsli], *adv.* courtoisement, poliment.

courtesan [kɔːti'zæn], *n.* courtisane, *f.*

courtesy ['kɔːtəsi], *n.* courtoisie, politesse, *f.*

court-house ['kɔːthaus], *n.* palais de justice, *m.*

courtier ['kɔːtiə], *n.* courtisan, homme de cour, *m.*

courtliness ['kɔːtlinis] *n.* élégance, politesse, *f.*

courtly ['kɔːtli], *a.* poli, élégant, courtois.

court-martial ['kɔːt'mɑːʃəl], *n.* conseil de guerre, *m.*—*v.t.* faire passer en conseil de guerre.

courtship ['kɔːtʃip], *n.* cour, *f.*

courtyard ['kɔːtjɑːd], *n.* cour (*de maison*), *f.*

cousin [kazn], *n.* cousin, *m.*

cove [kouv], *n.* anse, crique, *f.*

covenant ['kavənənt], *n.* convention, *f.*, pacte, contrat, *m.*—*v.t.* stipuler par contrat.—*v.i.* convenir (*de*), s'engager (à).

Coventry ['kovəntri, 'kavəntri]. (*colloq.*) **to send to Coventry**, mettre en quarantaine.

cover ['kavə], *v.t.* couvrir; voiler, déguiser; cacher.—*n.* couverture; cloche (*d'un plat etc.*); enveloppe (*d'une lettre etc.*); housse (*d'une chaise*), *f.*; couvercle (*d'une casserole etc.*); couvert (*gibier*); (*fig.*) voile, abri, *m.*; **under cover of**, sous la protection de, à la faveur de.

covering ['kavəriŋ], *n.* couverture; enveloppe; housse (*de chaise*), *f.*; habits (*vêtements*), *m.pl.*; **covering letter**, lettre d'envoi, *f.*

coverlet ['kavəlit], *n.* couvre-pied, couvre-lit, *m.*

covert ['kavəːt], *a.* couvert, caché, secret.—*n.* couvert, abri; gîte, *m.*, tanière, *f.*

covertly ['kavəːtli], *adv.* secrètement, en cachette.

covet ['kavit], *v.t.* convoiter, désirer ardemment.

covetous ['kavitəs], *a.* avide, avaricieux, cupide.

covetously ['kavitəsli], *adv.* avec convoitise, avidement.

covetousness ['kavitəsnis], *n.* convoitise, cupidité, *f.*

covey ['kavi], *n.* compagnie (*de perdrix*), *f.*

cow (I) [kau], *n.* vache, *f.*

cow (2) [kau], *v.t.* intimider, dompter.

coward ['kauəd], *n.* lâche, poltron, *m.*, poltronne, *f.*

cowardice ['kauədis], *n.* couardise, *f.*

cowardliness ['kauədlinis], *n.* couardise, poltronnerie, lâcheté, *f.*

cowardly ['kauədli], *a.* couard, lâche, poltron.—*adv.* lâchement.

cowboy ['kauboi], *n.* jeune vacher; (*Am.*) cowboy, *m.*

cower ['kauə], *v.i.* s'accroupir; se blottir, se tapir.

cowherd ['kauhəːd], *n.* vacher, *m.*

cowhide ['kauhaid], *n.* peau de vache, *f.*

cowl [kaul], *n.* capuchon; (*Naut., Av.*) capot; tabourin (*de cheminée*), *m.*

cow-shed ['kauʃed], *n.* vacherie, étable à vaches, *f.*

cowslip ['kauslip], *n.* primevère, *f.*, coucou, *m.*

coxcomb, cockscomb ['kɔkskoum], *n.* petit-maître, freluquet, fat, *m.*

coxswain [koksn], *n.* patron de chaloupe; (*Row.*) barreur, *m.*

coy [koi], *a.* timide, réservé.

coyly ['koili], *adv.* timidement, avec réserve.

coyness ['koinis], *n.* timidité, réserve, *f.*

coyote [koi'jouti], *n.* loup de prairie, coyote, *m.*

cozen [kazn], *v.t.* duper, tromper.

crab [kræb], *n.* crabe, cancre; (*Astron.*) cancer, *m.*

crab apple ['kræbæpl], *n.* pomme sauvage, *f.*

crabbed [kræbd], *a.* acariâtre, revêche, bourru.

crab tree ['kræbtriː], *n.* pommier sauvage, *m.*

crabwise ['kræbwaiz], *adv.* comme un crabe, de biais.

crack [kræk], *v.t.* fendre; fêler (*porcelaine etc.*); gercer (*la peau etc.*); casser (*noix etc.*); faire claquer (*fouet*); faire sauter (*bouteille de vin*); faire, lâcher (*plaisanterie*); (*fig.*) rompre, briser.—*v.i.* se fendre, se lézarder; se gercer (*la peau etc.*); claquer (*fouet*); se fêler (*verre etc.*); muer (*la voix*).—*a.* fameux, d'élite; **to be a crack shot**, être un fin tireur.—*n.* fente, crevasse, fissure; détonation (*de fusil*); lézarde, fêlure (*verre*), *f.*; craquement (*bruit*); claquement (*d'un fouet*), *m.*; mue (*de la voix*); hâblerie (*boast*), *f.*

crack-brained ['krækbreind], *a.* (*fam.*) timbré, fou.

cracked [krækd], *a.* fendu, fêlé; (*fig.*) timbré.

cracker ['krækə], *n.* vantard; pétard (*feu d'artifice*); (*Am.*) biscuit, *m.*; **nut-crackers**, casse-noix, *m.inv.*

crackle [krækl], *v.i.* pétiller, craqueter, crépiter.

crackling ['krækliŋ], *n.* pétillement, crépitement; (*fig.*) rissolé (*de rôti de porc*), *m.*

cracknel ['kræknəl], *n.* craquelin, *m.*, croquignole, *f.*

cradle [kreidl], *n.* berceau; (*Naut.*) ber, *m.*—*v.t.* bercer; endormir (*en berçant*).

cradle-song ['kreidlsɔŋ], *n.* berceuse, *f.*

craft [krɑːft], *n.* métier (*trade*), *m.*; ruse, astuce (*cunning*), *f.*; (*Naut.*) embarcation, *f.*, bâtiment, *m.*

craftily ['krɑːftili], *adv.* sournoisement, avec ruse.

craftiness ['krɑːftinis], *n.* artifice, *m.*, ruse, astuce, *f.*

craftsman ['krɑːftsmən], *n.* (*pl.* **-men** [men]) artisan; artiste dans son métier, *m.*

craftsmanship ['krɑːftsmənʃip], *n.* habileté technique, exécution, *f.*

crafty ['krɑːfti], *a.* rusé, astucieux.

crag [kræg], *n.* rocher escarpé, rocher à pic, *m.*

craggy ['krægi], *a.* rocailleux, escarpé, abrupt.

crake [kreik], *n.* (*Orn.*) râle, *m.*

cram [kræm], *v.t.* fourrer, remplir, bourrer; préparer, chauffer (*étudiants*).—*v.i.* se bourrer, s'empiffrer; (*fig.*) piocher, bûcher.

crammer ['kræmə], *n.* préparateur; (*colloq.*) colleur, *m.*

cramp [kræmp], *n.* crampe, *f.*; (*Tech.*) crampon, *m.*; (*fig.*) gêne, entrave, *f.*—*v.t.* cramponner; resserrer; (*fig.*) gêner, entraver, restreindre.

cramped [kræmpt], *a.* gêné; **to be cramped** (*for space*), être très à l'étroit.

cranberry ['krænbəri], *n.* (*Bot.*) canneberge, *f.*

crane [krein], *n.* (*Orn., Tech.*) grue, *f.*—*v.t.* allonger, tendre (*le cou*).

cranial ['kreiniəl], *a.* crânien.

cranium ['kreiniəm], *n.* crâne, *m.*

crank [kræŋk], *n.* manivelle, *f.*; coude, *m.*; (*fig.*) maniaque, excentrique, *m., f.*, original (*personne*).

crankshaft ['kræŋʃɑːft], *n.* arbre de manivelle; (*Motor.*) vilebrequin, *m.*

cranky ['kræŋki], *a.* capricieux, fantasque; impatient.

crannied ['krænid], *a.* crevassé, lézardé.

cranny ['kræni], *n.* crevasse, fente, lézarde, fissure, *f.*

crape [kreip], *n.* crêpe, *m.*

crash [kræʃ], *v.t.* fracasser, briser.—*v.i.* éclater, retentir; se tamponner (*deux autos etc.*).—*n.* fracas, grand bruit, *m.*; (*Motor.*) collision; (*fig.*) débâcle, ruine; faillite, *f.*

crash helmet ['kræʃhelmit], *n.* casque, *m.*

crash landing ['kræʃ'lændiŋ], *n.* (*Av.*) atterrissage brutal; crash, *m.*

crass [kræs], *a.* crasse, grossier, stupide.

crate [kreit], *n.* caisse à claire-voie, *f.*—*v.t.* emballer.

crater ['kreitə], *n.* cratère, *m.*

cravat [krə'væt], *n.* cravate, *f.*

crave [kreiv], *v.t.* implorer, solliciter; (*fig.*) soupirer après.

craven ['kreivn], *a.* and *n.* lâche, poltron, *m.*

craving ['kreiviŋ], *n.* désir ardent.

crawfish [CRAYFISH].

crawl [krɔːl], *v.i.* ramper, se traîner; *to crawl with*, grouiller de.—*n.* mouvement traînant; (*Swim.*) crawl, *m.*

crawling ['krɔːliŋ], *a.* rampant; grouillant, fourmillant (*de*).

crayfish ['kreifiʃ], **crawfish** ['krɔːfiʃ], *n.* écrevisse (*d'eau douce*), *f.*; *sea crayfish*, langouste, *f.*

crayon ['kreiən], *n.* crayon, pastel, fusain, *m.*—*v.t.* crayonner, dessiner au pastel.

craze [kreiz], *v.t.* craqueler (*porcelaine*); frapper de folie, rendre fou.—*n.* folie; (*fig.*) passion folle; toquade, *f.*

crazed [kreizd], *a.* craquelé (*porcelaine*); fou, dément.

crazily ['kreizili], *adv.* follement.

craziness ['kreizinis], *n.* délabrement, *m.*; démence, folie, *f.*

crazy ['kreizi], *a.* délabré; (*fam.*) fou, toqué.

creak [kriːk], *v.i.* crier, craquer, grincer.—*n.* cri, grincement, *m.*

creaking ['kriːkiŋ], *a.* qui crie, qui craque.—*n.* cri, grincement, *m.*

cream [kriːm], *n.* crème, *f.*—*v.i.* crémer, mousser.

cream-color(ed) ['kriːmkʌlə(d)], *a.* crème.

creamery ['kriːməri], *n.* crémerie, *f.*

cream pitcher ['kriːmpitʃə], *n.* pot à crème. *m.*

creamy ['kriːmi], *a.* crémeux; de crème.

crease [kriːs], *n.* pli, faux pli, *m.*—*v.t.* faire des plis à, plisser, chiffonner, friper.—*v.i.* se plisser; se friper.

create [kriː'eit], *v.t.* créer, faire naître; produire, engendrer, occasionner; faire.

creation [kriː'eiʃən], *n.* création; nature, *f.*, univers, *m.*; dernière mode, *f.*

creative [kriː'eitiv], *a.* créateur.

creator [kriː'eitə], *n.* créateur, *m.*

creature ['kriːtʃə], *n.* créature, personne, *f.*, être; animal, *m.*

crèche [kreiʃ], *n.* crèche, *f.*

credence ['kriːdəns], *n.* créance, croyance, foi, *f.*; *to give credence to*, ajouter foi à.

credentials [kri'denʃəlz], *n.pl.* lettres de créance, *f.pl.*

credibility [kredi'biliti], *n.* crédibilité, *f.*

credible ['kredibl], *a.* croyable, digne de foi.

credibly ['kredibli], *adv.* d'une manière digne de foi; *to be credibly informed*, tenir de bonne source.

credit ['kredit], *n.* croyance, foi; (*fig.*) influence; réputation, *f.*; mérite, honneur; (*Comm.*) crédit, *m.*; *on credit*, à crédit; *to do credit to*, faire honneur à; *to give credit to*, croire à; faire honneur à; (*Comm.*) faire crédit à.

creditable ['kreditəbl], *a.* honorable, estimable.

creditably ['kreditəbli], *adv.* honorablement.

creditor ['kreditə], *n.* créancier; (*Book-keeping*) créditeur, avoir, *m.*

credulity [kre'djuːliti], **credulousness** ['kredjuləsnis], *n.* crédulité, *f.*

credulous ['kredjuləs], *a.* crédule.

creed [kriːd], *n.* credo, *m.*; (*fig.*) profession de foi; croyance, foi, *f.*

creek [kriːk], *n.* ruisseau, *m.*

creel [kriːl], *n.* panier de pêche, *m.*

creep [kriːp], *v.i. irr.* se traîner, ramper, se glisser.

creeper ['kriːpə], *n.* reptile, *m.*; plante grimpante, *f.*; *tree creeper*, (*Orn.*) grimpereau, *m.*

creeping ['kriːpiŋ], *a.* rampant, grimpant; qui fait frissonner.—*n.* fourmillement (*sensation*), *m.*

creepy ['kriːpi], *a.* horrifique, qui donne la chair de poule; rampant.

cremate [kri'meit], *v.t.* incinérer.

cremation [kri'meiʃən], *n.* crémation, incinération, *f.*

crematorium [kremə'tɔːriəm], *n.* crématorium, *m.*

Creole ['kriːoul], *a.* créole.—*n.* Créole, *m., f.*

creosote ['kriːəsout], *n.* créosote, *f.*

crêpe [kreip], *n.* crêpe blanc (*ou* clair), *m.*

crescent ['kresənt], *a.* croissant.—*n.* croissant, *m.*, demi-lune; rue en demi-cercle, *f.*

cress [kres], *n.* cresson, *m.*

crest [krest], *n.* cimier, *m.*; crête (*d'un coq ou d'une montagne*), huppe (*d'un oiseau*); aigrette (*de paon*), *f.*; (*Her.*) écusson, *m.*; armoiries, *f.pl.*

crestfallen ['krestfɔːlən], *a.* abattu, découragé, l'oreille basse.

Cretan ['kriːtən], *a.* crétois.—*n.* Crétois, *m.*

Crete [kriːt], *n.* la Crète, la Candie, *f.*

crevasse [krə'væs], *n.* crevasse (*d'un glacier*), *f.*—*v.t.* se crevasser.

crevice ['krevis], *n.* crevasse, lézarde, fente (*mur*); fissure (*rocher*), *f.*—*v.t.* crevasser, lézarder, fissurer.

crew (1) [kruː], *n.* bande, troupe, *f.*; (*Naut.*) équipage, *m.*

crew (2) [kruː], *past* [CROW (2)].

crib [krib], *n.* lit d'enfant, *m.*; crèche, mangeoire, *f.*; (*colloq.*) livre de corrigés, *m.*—*v.t.* chiper; copier (*sur*).

crick [krik], *n.* crampe, *f.*, effort, torticolis, *m.* —*v.t.* **to crick one's neck**, se donner le torticolis.

cricket (1) ['krikit], *n.* (*Ent.*) grillon, *m.*

cricket (2) ['krikit], *n.* cricket (*jeu*), *m.*; (*colloq.*) **that's not cricket**, ça ne se fait pas, ce n'est pas loyal.

crier ['kraiə], *n.* crieur; huissier (*d'une cour*), *m.*

crime [kraim], *n.* crime, *m.*

Crimea [krai'mi:ə]. la Crimée, *f.*

criminal ['kriminl], *a.* and *n.* criminel, *m.*

criminologist [krimi'nɔlədʒist], *n.* criminaliste, *m.*, *f.*

criminology [krimi'nɔlədʒi], *n.* criminologie, *f.*

crimp [krimp], *v.t.* gaufrer; friser, boucler (*les cheveux*).

crimson [krimzn], *a.* and *n.* cramoisi; pourpre, *m.*—*v.t.* teindre en cramoisi.—*v.i.* devenir cramoisi.

cringe [krindʒ], *v.i.* faire des courbettes; s'humilier, ramper.

cringing ['krindʒiŋ], *a.* craintif; obséquieux. —*n.* basse servilité, *f.*

crinkle ['kriŋkl], *v.t.* froisser; former en zigzag.—*v.i.* serpenter, aller en zigzag.—*n.* sinuosité, *f.*; pli, *m.*; fronce, *f.*

crinkly ['kriŋkli], *a.* ratatiné.

cripple [kripl], *n.* boiteux; estropié, *m.*—*v.t.* estropier; (*fig.*) paralyser.

crisis ['kraisis], *n.* (*pl.* **crises** ['kraisi:z]) crise, *f.*; dénouement, *m.*

crisp [krisp], *a.* croquant, croustillant (*pâtisserie etc.*); crépu, frisé (*cheveux*).—*v.t.* friser (*cheveux etc.*); crêper (*tissu*).—*v.i.* se crêper.

crispness ['krispnis], *n.* qualité de ce qui est croquant *ou* cassant; frisure; netteté (*stylo etc.*), *f.*

criss-cross ['kriskrɔs], *a.* entrecroisé, croisé, en croix.—*n.* entrecroisement, *m.*—*v.t.* entrecroiser.—*v.i.* s'entrecroiser.

criterion [krai'tiəriən], *n.* critérium, *m.*

critic ['kritik], *n.* critique; censeur, *m.*; **dramatic critic**, critique de théâtre.

critical ['kritikl], *a.* critique, (*fig.*) difficile, délicat.

critically ['kritikli], *adv.* d'une manière critique; avec soin; **critically ill**, dangereusement malade.

criticism ['kritisizm], *n.* critique, appréciation, censure, *f.*

criticize ['kritisaiz], *v.t.* critiquer, faire la critique de, censurer.—*v.i.* faire de la critique.

croak [krouk], *v.i.* coasser (*grenouille*); croasser (*freux*); (*fig.*) gronder, grogner.—*n.* coassement (*grenouille*); croassement (*freux*); (*fig.*) grognement, *m.*

croaker ['kroukə], *n.* grognon, *m.*; (*fig.*) pessimiste, *m.*, *f.*

croaky ['krouki], *a.* enroué, rauque.

crochet ['krouʃei], *n.* ouvrage au crochet, *m.*—*v.t.*, *v.i.* broder au crochet.

crock [krɔk], *n.* cruche, *f.*; pot de terre, *m.*; (*fam.*) **old crock**, vieux clou, tacot (*bicyclette, auto etc.*); vieux débris, croulant (*personne*).

crockery ['krɔkəri], *n.* faïence, vaisselle, *f.*

crocodile ['krɔkədail], *n.* crocodile, *m.*; (*fig.*) procession, *f.*

crocus ['kroukəs], *n.* safran, crocus, *m.*

croft [krɔft], *n.* petit clos, *m.*, petite ferme, *f.*

crofter ['krɔftə], *n.* petit cultivateur, *m.*

crone [kroun], *n.* vieille femme, vieille, *f.*

crony ['krouni], *n.* vieux camarade; copain, compère, *m.*

crook [kruk], *n.* courbure; houlette (*de berger*); crosse (*d'évêque*), *f.*; (*fig.*) escroc (*personne*), *m.*; **by hook or by crook**, coûte que coûte, par un moyen ou par un autre.—*v.t.* courber; (*fig.*) pervertir.—*v.i.* se courber.

crook-backed ['krukbækt], *a.* bossu, voûté.

crooked ['krukid], *a.* courbé, crochu, tortueux; tortu; (*fig.*) malhonnête.

crookedly ['krukidli], *adv.* tortueusement, de travers.

crookedness ['krukidnis], *n.* nature tortueuse; difformité, *f.*; (*fig.*) travers, *m.*, perversité, *f.*

croon [kru:n], *v.i.* chantonner, fredonner.

crooner ['kru:nə], *n.* fredonneur, chanteur de charme, *m.*

crop [krɔp], *n.* récolte, moisson; cueillette (*de fruits*), *f.*; jabot (*d'un oiseau*), *m.*; coupe (*cheveux*), *f.*; **hunting crop**, fouet (*de chasse*), *m.*; **second crop**, regain, *m.*—*v.t.* tondre; couper; écourter (*chevaux*); brouter (*l'herbe*).

crosier, crozier ['krouziə], *n.* crosse (*d'évêque*), *f.*

cross [krɔs], *a.* en travers, de travers; fâcheux, contraire; maussade, de mauvaise humeur, fâché.—*n.* croix, *f.*; (*fig.*) malheur, *m.*, traverse, *f.*; croisement (*dans la reproduction*), *m.*; **criss-cross**, croisé, en croix.—*v.t.* croiser; marquer d'une croix, barrer (*un chèque*); (*fig.*) franchir; contrarier; **to cross off** *or* **out**, effacer, rayer, biffer; **to cross oneself**, faire le signe de la croix.—*v.i.* être mis en travers; faire la traversée; se croiser (*lettres*).

crossbow ['krɔsbou], *n.* arbalète, *f.*

cross-breed ['krɔsbri:d], *n.* race croisée, *f.*; métis, *m.*—*v.t.* croiser.

cross-country ['krɔs'kʌntri], *a.* à travers champs, *f.*; (*Racing*) **cross-country running**, cross, *m.*

cross-examination ['krɔsigzæmi'neiʃən], *n.* contre-interrogatoire, *m.*

cross-examine ['krɔsig'zæmin], *v.t.* interroger; (*Law*) contre-interroger.

crossing ['krɔsiŋ], *n.* traversée (*de la mer*), *f.*; passage; carrefour, croisement (*de routes*); croisement (*animaux*), *m.*; **pedestrian crossing**, passage clouté.

crossly ['krɔsli], *adv.* de travers; avec mauvaise humeur.

crossness ['krɔsnis], *n.* mauvaise humeur, méchanceté, *f.*

cross-roads ['krɔsroudz], *n.pl.* carrefour, *m.*

crossword ['krɔswɔ:d], *n.* **crossword** (**puzzle**), mots croisés, *m.pl.*

crotchet ['krɔtʃit], *n.* lubie, *f.*, caprice, *m.*, marotte, *f.*; (*Mus.*) noire, *f.*

crotchety ['krɔtʃiti], *a.* capricieux, d'humeur difficile.

crouch [krautʃ], *v.i.* se tapir, se blottir.

crouching ['krautʃiŋ], *a.* accroupi, tapi.

croup [kru:p], *n.* croupe (*animaux*), *f.*; croupion (*oiseaux*); (*Path.*) croup, *m.*

crow (1) [krou], *n.* corneille, *f.*; *as the crow
flies*, à vol d'oiseau; *crow's nest*, (*Naut.*)
hune, *f.*

crow (2) [krou], *v.i. irr.* chanter (*coq*).—*n.*
chant du coq, *m.*

crow-bar ['krouba:], *n.* pince, *f.*; levier, *m.*

crowd [kraud], *n.* foule, cohue, *f.*—*v.t.*
serrer, encombrer; presser.—*v.i.* se presser
en foule, se serrer.

crown [kraun], *n.* couronne; crête, *f.*, sommet; écu (*pièce de monnaie*); fond (*d'un
chapeau*), *m.*—*v.t.* couronner; combler.

crozier [CROSIER].

crucial ['kru:ʃəl], *a.* crucial; (*fig.*) définitif,
décisif.

crucible ['kru:sibl], *n.* creuset, *m.*

crucifix ['kru:sifiks], *n.* crucifix, *m.*

crucifixion [kru:si'fikʃən], *n.* crucifiement,
m., crucifixion, *f.*

crucify ['kru:sifai], *v.t.* crucifier.

crude [kru:d], *a.* cru; (*fig.*) informe, indigeste; grossier; brut.

crudely ['kru:dli], *adv.* crûment.

crudeness ['kru:dnis], **crudity** ['kru:diti], *n.*
crudité, nature informe, *f.*

cruel ['kru:əl], *a.* cruel.

cruelly ['kru:əli], *adv.* cruellement.

cruelty ['kru:əlti], *n.* cruauté, inhumanité, *f.*

cruet ['kru:it], *n.* burette, *f.*

cruet stand ['kru:itstænd], *n.* huilier, *m.*

cruise ['kru:z], *n.* croisière, course, *f.*—*v.i.*
croiser, faire la course; marauder (*taxi*).

cruiser ['kru:zə], *n.* croiseur, *m.*

crumb [krʌm], *n.* mie; miette, *f.*—*v.t.*
émietter.

crumble [krʌmbl], *v.t.* émietter; (*fig.*) pulvériser, broyer.—*v.i.* s'émietter; tomber en
poussière; *to crumble down*, tomber en
ruine, s'écrouler.

crump [krʌmp], *n.* coup violent, *m.*; chute, *f.*

crumpet ['krʌmpit], *n.* sorte de petite crêpe,
crêpe bretonne (*pour le thé*), *f.*

crumple [krʌmpl], *v.t.* chiffonner, froisser.—
v.i. se rider, se chiffonner.

crunch [krʌntʃ], *v.t.* croquer; broyer, écraser.
—*v.i.* crisser, s'écraser.—*n.* coup de dent;
grincement; crissement, *m.*

crupper ['krʌpə], *n.* croupe; croupière, *f.*

crusade [kru:'seid], *n.* croisade, *f.*

crusader [kru:'seidə], *n.* croisé, *m.*

crush [krʌʃ], *n.* écrasement, choc, *m.*; foule,
cohue, *f.*—*v.t.* écraser, broyer; froisser
(*une robe*); (*fig.*) accabler, anéantir.—*v.i.*
s'écraser.

crushing ['krʌʃiŋ], *a.* écrasant; (*fig.*) foudroyant.—*n.* broiement, écrasement, *m.*

crust [krʌst], *n.* croûte, *f.*, croûton, *m.*—*v.i.*
s'encroûter.

crustily ['krʌstili], *adv.* d'une manière
morose.

crusty ['krʌsti], *a.* couvert d'une croûte; (*fig.*)
bourru, hargneux.

crutch [krʌtʃ], *n.* béquille, *f.*

crux [krʌks], *n.* nœud (*d'une question*), *m.*;
crise, *f.*

cry [krai], *n.* cri, *m.*—*v.t.* crier.—*v.i.* pleurer;
crier; s'écrier.

crying ['kraiiŋ], *n.* larmes, *f.pl.*, pleurs, *m.pl.*;
cri, *m.*, cris, *m.pl.*

crypt [kript], *n.* crypte, *f.*

cryptic ['kriptik], *a.* secret; énigmatique.

crystal [kristl], *a.* de cristal.—*n.* cristal, *m.*

crystallize ['kristəlaiz], *v.t.* cristalliser.—*v.i.*
se cristalliser; *crystallized fruits*, fruits
glacés, *m.pl.*

cub [kʌb], *n.* petit (*d'une bête sauvage*); ourson
(*ours*); lionceau (*lion*); louveteau (*loup*);
renardeau (*renard*), *m.*

Cuba ['kju:bə]. le Cuba, *m.*

Cuban ['kju:bən], *a.* cubain.—*n.* Cubain, *m.*

cubby-hole ['kʌbihoul], *n.* retraite, *f.*; placard, *m.*; niche, *f.*

cube [kju:b], *n.* cube, *m.*

cubicle ['kju:bikl], *n.* compartiment, *m.*
cabine, *f.*

cubit ['kju:bit], *n.* coudée, *f.*

cuckoo ['kuku:], *n.* coucou, *m.*

cucumber ['kju:kʌmbə], *n.* concombre, *m.*

cud [kʌd], *n.* bol alimentaire, *m.*; *to chew the
cud*, ruminer.

cuddle [kʌdl], *v.t.* serrer (tendrement) dans
ses bras; étreindre.—*v.i.* s'étreindre (amoureusement); se blottir; se peloter.

cudgel ['kʌdʒəl], *n.* bâton, gourdin, *m.*—*v.t.*
bâtonner.

cue [kju:], *n.* queue de billard; (*Theat.*)
réplique, *f.*; (*fig.*) avis, mot, indice, *m.*

cuff (1) [kʌf], *v.t.* souffleter, calotter, battre.—
n. calotte, taloche, *f.*

cuff (2) [kʌf], *n.* manchette (*d'une manche*), *f.*;
parement (*d'un pardessus*); poignet (*d'une
robe*), *m.*

cuff link ['kʌfliŋk], *n.* bouton de manchette,
m.

cuirass [kwi'ræs], *n.* cuirasse, *f.*

cuirassier [kwi'ræsiə], *n.* cuirassier, *m.*

culinary ['kʌlinəri], *a.* de cuisine, culinaire.

cull [kʌl], *v.t.* recueillir, cueillir; (*fig.*) choisir.

culminate ['kʌlmineit], *v.i.* se terminer (*en*),
finir (*par*); (*Astron.*) culminer.

culmination [kʌlmi'neiʃən], *n.* point culminant, apogée, *m.*; (*Astron.*) culmination, *f.*

culpable ['kʌlpəbl], *a.* coupable.

culprit ['kʌlprit], *n.* accusé; inculpé, *m.*;
coupable, *m.*, *f.*

cult [kʌlt], *n.* culte, *m.*

cultivate ['kʌltiveit], *v.t.* cultiver.

cultivation [kʌlti'veiʃən], *n.* culture, *f.*

cultivator ['kʌltiveitə], *n.* cultivateur, *m.*

cultural ['kʌltʃərəl], *a.* agricole, cultural;
culturel.

culture ['kʌltʃə], *n.* culture; (*fig.*) instruction
éducation, *f.*

cultured ['kʌltʃəd], *a.* cultivé.

culvert ['kʌlvə:t], *n.* ponceau, petit aqueduc,
m.

cumber ['kʌmbə], *v.t.* embarrasser, encombrer (*de*).—*n.* embarras, obstacle, *m.*

cumbersome ['kʌmbəsəm], **cumbrous**
['kʌmbrəs], *a.* embarrassant, gênant.

cumulate ['kju:mjuleit], *v.t.* accumuler,
cumuler.

cunning ['kʌniŋ], *a.* fin, rusé, adroit, astucieux.—*n.* finesse, ruse, astuce, *f.*

cunningly ['kʌniŋli], *adv.* avec finesse, adroitement; par ruse.

cup [kʌp], *n.* tasse, coupe, *f.*; gobelet; (*Bot.
etc.*) calice, *m.*; (*Med.*) ventouse, *f.*—*v.t.*
(*Med.*) appliquer des ventouses à.

cupbearer ['kʌpbeərə], *n.* échanson, *m.*

cupboard ['kʌbəd], *n.* armoire (*pour vêtements etc.*), *f.*; placard (*dans un mur*), *m.*

cupidity [kju:'piditi], *n.* cupidité, *f.*

cupola ['kju:pələ], *n.* coupole, *f.*

cur [kə:], n. chien bâtard; roquet; (fig.) malotru, m., vilaine bête, f.

curable ['kjuərəbl], a. guérissable.

curate ['kjuərit], n. vicaire, desservant, m.

curator [kjuə'reitə], n. administrateur; conservateur (de musée), m.

curb [kə:b], n. gourmette, f.; (fig.) frein, m.; [KERB].—v.t. gourmer; (fig.) réprimer, contenir, brider; freiner.

curd [kə:d], n. caillé, lait caillé, m.—v.t. cailler, figer.

curdle [kə:dl], v.t. cailler, figer.—v.i. se cailler, se figer.

cure [kjuə], n. guérison, f.; remède, m.; (Eccles.) cure, f.—v.t. guérir; sécher (foin etc.); mariner (poisson etc.); saler (viande etc.); (fig.) corriger.

curfew ['kə:fju:], n. couvre-feu, m.

curio ['kjuəriou], n. curiosité, f.; bibelot, m.

curiosity [kjuəri'ositi], n. curiosité, f.

curious ['kjuəriəs], a. curieux; (fig.) remarquable, singulier.

curiously ['kjuəriəsli], adv. curieusement.

curl [kə:l], n. boucle (de cheveux); moue (de lèvres); spirale (de fumée); ondulation, f.—v.t. boucler, friser, (fig.) faire onduler.—v.i. friser; se replier (serpent etc.); s'entrelacer (vignes etc.); tourbillonner (fumée); onduler (vagues); to curl up, s'enrouler, se pelotonner (chat).

curled [kə:ld], a. frisé.

curlew ['kə:lju:], n. (Orn.) courlis, m.

curly ['kə:li], a. frisé, frisé bouclé.

curmudgeon [kə:'mʌdʒən], n. ladre, pingre, bourru, m.

currant ['kʌrənt], n. groseille (à grappes), f.; black currant, cassis, m.; (dried) currants, raisins de Corinthe, m.pl.

currant bush ['kʌrəntbuʃ], n. groseillier, m.

currency ['kʌrənsi], n. circulation (d'argent etc.); monnaie, f.; cours; crédit, m.; vogue, f.

current ['kʌrənt], a. courant; actuel; admis, reçu; current events, actualités, f.pl.—n. courant; cours d'eau, m.

currently ['kʌrəntli], adv. couramment; généralement.

curriculum [kə'rikjuləm], n. (Sch.) programme, plan d'études, m.

currier ['kʌriə], n. corroyeur, m.

curry (1) ['kʌri], v.t. corroyer (cuir); étriller (un cheval); (fig.) rosser.

curry (2) ['kʌri], v.t. (Cook.) apprêter au cari. —n. cari, m.

curry-comb ['kʌrikoum], n. étrille, f.

curse [kə:s], n. malédiction, f.; (fig.) fléau, malheur, m.—v.t. maudire; (fig.) affliger.—v.i. jurer; (colloq.) sacrer.

cursed ['kə:sid], a. maudit, exécrable.

cursorily ['kə:sərili], adv. rapidement, superficiellement.

cursory ['kə:səri], a. rapide, superficiel; général.

curt [kə:t], a. brusque, bref, sec.

curtail [kə:'teil], v.t. retrancher, raccourcir, abréger.

curtailment [kə:'teilmənt], n. raccourcissement, m., réduction, f.

curtain ['kə:tin], n. rideau, m.; toile, f.—v.t. garnir de rideaux; (fig.) voiler.

curtly ['kə:tli], adv. brusquement, sèchement.

curtsy, or curtsey ['kə:tsi], n. révérence, f.—v.i. faire la révérence.

curve [kə:v], n. courbe, f.—v.t. courber; cintrer.—v.i. se courber.

curvet [kə:'vet], v.i. faire des courbettes; sauter, gambader.—n. courbette, f.

cushion ['kuʃən], n. coussin, m.; (Billiards) bande, f.—v.t. garnir de coussins; amortir.

custard ['kʌstəd], n. crème (au lait), f.; flan, m.

custodian [kʌs'toudiən], n. gardien; conservateur, m.

custody ['kʌstədi], n. garde; prison, détention, f.

custom ['kʌstəm], n. coutume, habitude, f.; usage, m.; pratique (d'une boutique), f.; achalandage (d'un magasin), m., (pl.) douane, f.; droits (taxes), m.pl.

customarily ['kʌstəmərili], adv. ordinairement, d'habitude.

customary ['kʌstəməri], a. ordinaire, d'usage.

customer ['kʌstəmə], n. chaland, client, m.; pratique, f.; (colloq.) individu, m.

customs officer ['kʌstəmzɔfisə], n. douanier, m.

cut [kʌt], n. coup, m.; coupure (place cut open); coupe (de vêtements, cheveux, cartes à jouer); taille (forme), façon, tournure (silhouette); (Engr.) gravure, planche, f.; chemin de traverse (raccourci); (Ten. etc.) coup tranchant, m.—v.t. irr. couper, trancher; fendre; rogner; se rogner (les ongles); piquer, percer; faire (une dent); to cut down, abattre; réduire; to cut out, tailler, découper; to cut short, abréger; interrompre, couper la parole à; to be cut up, être blessé; avoir de la peine.—v.i. couper; se couper; percer (dent).

cute [kju:t], a. rusé, fin; (Am.) attirant (enfant, fille); amusant (chose, truc).

cuticle ['kju:tikl], n. cuticule, f.

cutler ['kʌtlə], n. coutelier, m.

cutlery ['kʌtləri], n. coutellerie, f.

cutlet ['kʌtlit], n. côtelette, escalope, f.

cut-price ['kʌtprais], n. prix réduit, m.

cutter ['kʌtə], n. coupeur; coupoir (outil), (Naut.) cutter, cotre, m.

cutting ['kʌtiŋ], a. incisif; (fig.) piquant, tranchant, mordant.—n. incision; rognure (morceau); coupe (bois, cartes, cheveux etc.), (Hort.) bouture, f.

cyanide ['saiənaid], n. cyanure, m.

cycle [saikl], n. cycle, m.; bicyclette, f., vélo, m.—v.i. aller à bicyclette.

cyclone ['saikloun], n. cyclone, m.

cygnet ['signit], n. jeune cygne, m.

cylinder ['silində], n. cylindre, m.

cymbal ['simbəl], n. cymbale, f.

cynic ['sinik], n. cynique; sceptique, m., f.

cynical ['sinikl], a. cynique.

cynically ['sinikli], adv. cyniquement.

cynicism ['sinisizm], n. cynisme, m.

cynosure ['sainəʃuə], n. (fig.) point de mire, m.

cypress ['saiprəs], n. cyprès, m.

Cyprian ['sipriən], a. cypriote.—n. Cypriote, m., f.

Cypriot ['sipriət], a. Cypriote, m., f.

Cyprus ['saiprəs], la Chypre, f.

cyst [sist], n. (Anat. etc.) kyste, m.

czar [TSAR].

Czech [tʃek], *a.* tchèque.—*n.* tchèque (*langue*), *m.*; Tchèque (*personne*), *m.*, *f.*
Czechoslovak [tʃeko'slouvæk], *a.* tchécoslovaque.—*n.* tchécoslovaque (*langue*), *m.*; Tchécoslovaque (*personne*), *m.*, *f.*
Czechoslovakia [tʃekoslo'vækiə]. la Tchécoslovaquie, *f.*

D

D, d [di:]. quatrième lettre de l'alphabet; (*Mus.*) ré, *m.*
dab [dæb], *n.* coup léger, *m.*, tape; éclaboussure, tache, *f.*; (*slang*) adepte, *m.*; (*Ichth.*) limande, *f.*—*v.t.* toucher légèrement; éponger à petits coups.
dabble [dæbl], *v.t.* humecter; éclabousser.—*v.i.* barboter, patauger; *to dabble in*, se mêler de.
dace [deis], *n.* (*Ichth.*) vandoise, *f.*, dard, *m.*
dachshund [dækshund], *n.* basset allemand, *m.*
dad [dæd], **daddy** [dædi], *n.* papa, *m.*
dado [deidou], *n.* lambris (*de mur*), *m.*
daffodil [dæfədil], *n.* jonquille, *f.*, narcisse des prés, *m.*
daft [dɑ:ft], *a.* niais, sot, à moitié fou.
dagger [dægə], *n.* poignard, *m.*, dague, *f.*
dahlia [deiljə], *n.* (*Bot.*) dahlia, *m.*
daily [deili], *a.* journalier, quotidien.—*n.* (*journal*) quotidien, *m.*; femme de ménage, *f.*—*adv.* journellement, tous les jours.
daintily [deintili], *adv.* délicatement; avec délicatesse.
daintiness [deintinis], *n.* délicatesse, *f.*, goût difficile, *m.*
dainty [deinti], *a.* friand; délicat, difficile.—*n.* friandise, *f.*
dairy [dɛəri], *n.* laiterie, *f.*
dairy farm [dɛərifɑːm], *n.* ferme laitière, *f.*
dairy-man [dɛərimən], *n.* (*pl.* **-men** [men]) nourrisseur; crémier, *m.*
dais [deis, 'deiis], *n.* estrade, *f.*
daisy [deizi], *n.* marguerite, pâquerette, *f.*
dale [deil], *n.* vallon, *m.*, vallée, *f.*
dalliance [dæliəns], *n.* folâtrerie, *f.*; badinage, *m.*; caresses, *f.pl.*
dally [dæli], *v.i.* folâtrer, perdre son temps; tarder; (*fig.*) badiner (*avec*).
dam (1) [dæm], *n.* mère (*animaux*), *f.*
dam (2) [dæm], *n.* digue (*d'un canal*), *f.*; barrage (*d'une rivière*), *m.*—*v.t.* diguer, barrer.
damage [dæmidʒ], *n.* dommage; tort, dégât; (*fig.*) préjudice, détriment, *m.*; (*pl.*) (*Law*) dommages-intérêts, *m.pl.*—*v.t.* endommager; avarier (*en transportant*); (*fig.*) faire tort à, nuire à.—*v.i.* s'endommager.
damask [dæməsk], *n.* damas; damassé, *m.*
dame [deim], *n.* (*poet.*) dame, *f.*
damn [dæm], *v.t.* damner; (*fig.*) condamner, désapprouver.
damnation [dæm'neiʃən], *n.* damnation, *f.*
damnatory [dæmnətəri], *a.* condamnatoire.
damned [dæmd], *a.* damné, maudit, exécrable.

damning [dæmiŋ], *a.* écrasant (*témoignage*).
damp [dæmp], *a.* humide; moite; (*fig.*) triste, abattu.—*n.* or **dampness** [dæmpnis], humidité; (*fig.*) tristesse, *f.*—*v.t.* rendre humide; (*fig.*) décourager.
damper [dæmpə], *n.* éteignoir; (*Piano*) étouffoir; (*fig.*) rabat-joie, *m.*
*****damsel** [dæmzəl], *n.* jeune fille, demoiselle, *f.*
damson [dæmzən], *n.* prune de Damas, *f.*
dance [dɑ:ns], *n.* danse, *f.*; bal, *m.*—*v.t.* danser; faire danser.—*v.i.* danser.
dancer [dɑ:nsə], *n.* danseur, *m.*, danseuse, *f.*
dandelion [dændilaiən], *n.* (*Bot.*) pissenlit, *m.*
dandle [dændl], *v.t.* dorloter, bercer.
dandruff [dændrʌf], *n.* pellicules, *f.pl.*
dandy [dændi], *n.* dandy, élégant, petit-maître, *m.*
Dane [dein], *n.* Danois (*personne*), *m.*
danger [deindʒə], *n.* danger, péril, *m.*
dangerous [deindʒərəs], *a.* dangereux.
dangerously [deindʒərəsli], *adv.* dangereusement.
dangle [dæŋgl], *v.t.* laisser pendre, balancer.—*v.i.* pendiller, baller.
Danish [deiniʃ], *a.* danois.—*n.* danois (*langue*), *m.*
dank [dæŋk], *a.* humide et froid.
Danube [dænjuːb], **the.** le Danube, *m.*
dapper [dæpə], *a.* petit et vif, pimpant; soigné (*homme*).
dapple [dæpl], *v.t.* tacheter, pommeler.—*v.i.* se pommeler, se tacheter.—*a.* or **dappled** [dæpld], pommelé, truité, miroité.
dare [dɛə], *v.t.* défier, braver; provoquer.—*v.i.* oser; *I dare say!* sans doute; je le crois bien.
dare-devil [dɛədevəl], *a.* and *n.* cassecou, *m.*
daring [dɛəriŋ], *a.* audacieux, hardi, cassecou.—*n.* hardiesse, audace, *f.*
dark [dɑ:k], *a.* obscur, sombre, noir; foncé (*couleur*); brun, basané (*teint*); (*fig.*) secret, mystérieux.—*n.* ténèbres, *f.pl.*, obscurité, *f.*; *after dark*, à la nuit close.
darken [dɑ:kən], *v.t.* obscurcir; brunir (*teint*); (*Paint.*) assombrir (*couleurs*).—*v.i.* s'obscurcir; s'assombrir.
darkening [dɑ:kniŋ], *n.* obscurcissement, assombrissement, *m.*
darkness [dɑ:knis], *n.* obscurité, *f.*, ténèbres, *f.pl.*, teint brun (*du visage*), *m.*
darling [dɑ:liŋ], *a.* and *n.* chéri, mignon, bien-aimé, *m.*; *my darling*, (*colloq.*) mon ange, mon chou, *m.*, ma chérie, *f.*
darn [dɑ:n], *n.* reprise, *f.*—*v.t.* repriser.
darning [dɑ:niŋ], *n.* reprise, *f.*
dart [dɑ:t], *n.* dard, trait, *m.*; fléchette, *f.*; élan soudain, *m.*—*v.t.* darder, lancer (*contre*).—*v.i.* se lancer, s'élancer (*sur*)
dash [dæʃ], *n.* choc, coup, *m.*; impétuosité, *f.*, entrain, cran; élan soudain; tiret; trait (*de plume*); (*fig.*) soupçon (*petite quantité*), *m.*—*v.t.* jeter; heurter, briser; abattre.—*v.i.* se briser; se précipiter.—*int.* zut!
dash-board [dæʃbo:d], *n.* (*Motor.*) tableau de bord, *m.*
dashing [dæʃiŋ], *a.* fougueux, brillant; pimpant, élégant.
dastard [dæstəd], *n.* lâche ignoble, *m.*
dastardly [dæstədli] *a.* lâche.

date (1) [deit], *n.* date, échéance, *f.*, millésime (*de pièce de monnaie*); (*Am. pop.*) rendez-vous, *m.*; *up to date*, à la page, à jour.—*v.t.* dater.—*v.i.* dater (*de*).

date (2) [deit], *n.* datte (*fruit*), *f.*

date palm ['deitpɑːm], *n.* dattier, *m.*

dative ['deitiv], *a.* and *n.* datif, *m.*

datum ['deitəm], *n.* (*pl.* **data** ['deitə]) donnée, *f.*

daub [dɔːb], *v.t.* barbouiller, enduire; (*fig.*) déguiser (*de*).—*n.* barbouillage, *m.*; (*Paint.*) croûte, *f.*

daughter ['dɔːtə], *n.* fille, *f.*

daughter-in-law ['dɔːtərinlɔː], *n.* belle-fille, bru, *f.*

daunt [dɔːnt], *v.t.* effrayer, intimider, décourager.

dauntless ['dɔːntlis], *a.* intrépide.

dauphin ['dɔːfin], *n.* dauphin, *m.*

David ['deivid]. David, *m.*

davit ['dævit], *n.* (*Naut.*) bossoir, *m.*

dawdle ['dɔːdl], *v.i.* flâner, muser.

dawdler ['dɔːdlə], *n.* flâneur, musard, *m.*

dawn [dɔːn], *v.i.* poindre, paraître; (*fig.*) naître, percer.—*n.* aube, *f.*, point du jour, *m.*; aurore, *f.*

day [dei], *n.* jour, *m.*; journée (*de travail etc.*); (*fig.*) bataille, victoire, *f.*; *at the present day*, de nos jours; *every day*, tous les jours; *the day after*, le lendemain; *the day before*, la veille; *today*, aujourd'hui.

day boarder ['deibɔːdə], *n.* demi-pensionnaire, *m.*, *f.*

day-book ['deibuk], *n.* journal, *m.*

day boy ['deibɔi], **day girl** ['deigəːl], *n.* externe, *m.*, *f.*

day-break ['deibreik], *n.* [DAWN].

daylight ['deilait], *n.* lumière du jour, *f.*

daze [deiz], *v.t.* éblouir; hébéter.—*n.* stupéfaction, *f.*; *in a daze*, hébété.

dazzle ['dæzl], *v.t.* éblouir, aveugler.

dazzling ['dæzliŋ], *a.* éblouissant.

deacon ['diːkən], *n.* diacre, *m.*

dead [ded], *a.* mort; inanimé, inerte, insensible; éventé (*boisson alcoolique*); mat (*couleur*); au rebut (*lettres*); *dead drunk*, ivre-mort; *dead loss*, perte sèche, *f.*; (*fig.*) crétin (*personne*), *m.*; *dead march*, marche funèbre, *f.*; *dead stop*, halte subite, *f.*; *dead weight*, poids mort, *m.*; *for a dead certainty*, à coup sûr.—*n.* cœur (*de l'hiver*), fort, *m.*; *at dead of night*, au plus profond de la nuit.

dead-beat ['ded'biːt], *a.* éreinté, épuisé.

deaden [dedn], *v.t.* amortir; émousser (*les sens*); éventer (*boisson alcoolique*); assourdir (*son*).

dead-end ['ded'end], *n.* cul-de-sac, *m.*; impasse, *f.*

deadlock ['dedlɔk], *n.* situation sans issue; impasse, *f.*

deadly ['dedli], *a.* mortel, à mort; meurtrier.—*adv.* mortellement.

deadness ['dednis], *n.* mort, *f.*; (*fig.*) engourdissement, *m.*, froideur, *f.*

deaf [def], *a.* sourd; (*fig.*) insensible.

deafen [defn], *v.t.* rendre sourd, assourdir.

deafening ['defniŋ], *a.* assourdissant.

deaf-mute ['def'mjuːt], *n.* sourd-muet, *m.*

deafness ['defnis], *n.* surdité, *f.*

deal (1) [diːl], *n.* quantité, *f.*; *a great* or *good*

deal, beaucoup (*de*); *by a good deal*, à beaucoup près.—*v.t. irr.* distribuer; répartir; (*Cards*) donner; porter, asséner (*coups*).—*v.i.* agir, traiter, en user (*avec*).

deal (2) [diːl], *n.* bois blanc, bois (*de sapin*), *m.*

dealer ['diːlə], *n.* marchand; (*Cards*) donneur, *m.*

dealing ['diːliŋ], *n.* conduite, *f.*; procédé, *m.*, affaire, *f.*; (*pl.*) relations, *f.pl.*, rapports, *m.pl.*

dean [diːn], *n.* doyen, *m.*

dear [diə], *a.* cher; précieux; (*fig.*) joli, gentil, charmant.—*adv.* cher; chèrement, beaucoup.—*n.* cher; cher ami, *m.*—*int.* **oh dear!** mon Dieu!

dearth [dəːθ], *n.* disette, *f.*

death [deθ], *n.* mort, *f.*; (*poet.*) trépas; (*Law*) décès, *m.*

death duties ['deθdjuːtiz], *n.pl.* droits de succession, *m.pl.*

death rate ['deθreit], *n.* taux de mortalité, *m.*

death rattle ['deθrætl], *n.* râle, *m.*

death throes ['deθθrouz], *n.* agonie, *f.*

debar [di'bɑː], *v.t.* exclure, priver (*de*).

debase [di'beis], *v.t.* avilir, abaisser; abâtardir; (*Chem.*) adultérer; (*Coin.*) altérer.

debasement [di'beismənt], *n.* abaissement, avilissement, *m.*; (*Coin.*) altération, dépréciation, *f.*

debasing [di'beisiŋ], *a.* avilissant.

debatable [di'beitəbl], *a.* contestable.

debate [di'beit], *n.* débat, *m.*; discussion, *f.*—*v.t.* débattre, discuter, disputer.—*v.i.* délibérer (*sur*); contester (*avec*).

debauch [di'bɔːtʃ], *n.* débauche, *f.*—*v.t.* débaucher, corrompre, pervertir.

debauchery [di'bɔːtʃəri], *n.* débauche, *f.*

debenture [di'bentʃə], *n.* obligation, *f.*

debilitate [di'biliteit], *v.t.* débiliter, affaiblir, anémier.

debilitation [dibili'teiʃən], *n.* débilitation, *f.*, affaiblissement, *m.*

debility [di'biliti], *n.* débilité, faiblesse, *f.*

debit ['debit], *n.* débit, *m.*—*v.t.* débiter (*de*).

debonair [debə'nɛə], *a.* jovial; de caractère enjoué; élégant.

debouch [di'buːʃ], *v.i.* déboucher.

débris, debris ['debriː], *n.* débris, *m.pl.*

debt [det], *n.* dette, *f.*; dettes, *f.pl.*; créance, *f.*

debtor ['detə], *n.* débiteur, *m.*

debutante ['deibjutɑːt], *n.* débutante (*à la cour*), *f.*

decade ['dekeid], *n.* décade; décennie, *f.*

decadence ['dekədəns], *n.* décadence, *f.*

decadent ['dekədənt], *a.* décadent.

decamp [di'kæmp], *v.i.* décamper; lever le camp.

decant [di'kænt], *v.t.* décanter, verser.

decanter [di'kæntə], *n.* carafe, *f.*

decapitate [di'kæpiteit], *v.t.* décapiter.

decapitation [dikæpi'teiʃən], *n.* décapitation, *f.*

decay [di'kei], *n.* décadence; pourriture; ruine; carie (*de dent*), *f.*—*v.i.* tomber en décadence; dépérir (*plante*); se carier (*dent*).

decease [di'siːs], *n.* (*Law*) décès, *m.*—*v.i.* décéder.

deceased [di'siːst], *a.* décédé, feu.—*n.* défunt, *m.*

deceit [di'siːt], *n.* supercherie, fourberie, tromperie, ruse, *f.*

deceitful [di'si:tful], *a.* trompeur; décevant (*choses*).

deceive [di'si:v], *v.t.* tromper, abuser.

deceiver [di'si:və], *n.* imposteur, trompeur, *m.*

decelerate [di:'seləreit], *v.t., v.i.* ralentir.

December [di'sembə], décembre, *m.*

decency ['di:sənsi], *n.* bienséance, *f.,* convenances, *f.pl.*; décence (*modestie*), *f.*

decennial [di'senjəl], *a.* décennal.

decent ['di:sənt], *a.* bienséant, décent; propre, convenable; gentil.

decently ['di:səntli], *adv.* décemment; convenablement.

decentralization ['di:sentrəlai'zei∫ən], *n.* décentralisation, *f.,* régionalisme, *m.*

decentralize [di:'sentrəlaiz], *v.t.* décentraliser.

deception [di'sep∫ən], *n.* tromperie, fraude, duperie, *f.*

deceptive [di'septiv], *a.* trompeur.

decibel ['desibel], *n.* décibel, *m.*

decide [di'said], *v.t.* décider; décider de.—*v.i.* se décider.

decided [di'saidid], *a.* décidé, prononcé; positif; résolu.

decidedly [di'saididli], *adv.* décidément; positivement.

decimal ['desiməl], *a.* décimal; *decimal point*, virgule, *f.*—*n.* (*fraction*) décimale, *f.*

decimate ['desimeit], *v.t.* décimer.

decipher [di'saifə], *v.t.* déchiffrer.

decision [di'siʒən], *n.* décision; (*fig.*) résolution, fermeté, *f.*

decisive [di'saisiv], *a.* décisif; concluant.

decisively [di'saisivli], *adv.* décisivement.

deck [dek], *n.* (*Naut.*) pont; tillac (*navire marchand*); plan (*avion*), *m.*—*v.t.* parer (*de*); orner.

deck chair ['dek't∫ɛə], *n.* transat(lantique), *m.*

declaim [di'kleim], *v.t., v.i.* déclamer (*contre*).

declamatory [di'klæmətəri], *a.* déclamatoire.

declaration [deklə'rei∫ən], *n.* déclaration; proclamation, *f.*

declare [di'klɛə], *v.t.* déclarer; (*fig.*) annoncer, affirmer.—*v.i.* se déclarer, se prononcer (*pour*).

decline [di'klain], *v.t.* pencher, incliner; refuser.—*v.i.* pencher; décliner; baisser (*prix*).—*n.* déclin, *m.,* décadence; (*Path.*) maladie de langueur, *f.*

declutch [di:'klʌt∫], *v.i.* débrayer.

decode [di:'koud], *v.t.* déchiffrer.

decompose [di:kəm'pouz], *v.t.* décomposer.—*v.i.* se décomposer.

decompression [di:kəm'pre∫ən], *n.* décompression, *f.*

decontaminate [di:kən'tæmineit], *v.t.* désinfecter.

decontrol [di:kən'troul], *v.t.* rendre libre de nouveau, libérer (*prix, loyers etc.*).—*n.* libération (*prix, loyers etc.*), *f.*

decorate ['dekəreit], *v.t.* décorer, orner.

decoration [dekə'rei∫ən], *n.* décoration, *f.*; ornement, *m.*

decorator ['dekəreitə], *n.* décorateur, *m.*

decorous ['dekərəs, di'kɔːrəs], *a.* bienséant, convenable.

decorously ['dekərəsli, di'kɔːrəsli], *adv.* convenablement.

decorum [di'kɔːrəm], *n.* bienséance, *f.,* décorum, *m.*

decoy [di'kɔi], *v.t.* leurrer, amorcer.—*n.* leurre; piège, *m.*

decrease ['di:kri:s], *n.* décroissement, *m.*; diminution; décrue (*eau*), *f.*—[di'kri:s], *v.t.* faire décroître.—*v.i.* diminuer; décroître.

decree [di'kri:], *n.* décret; (*Law*) arrêt, *m.*—*v.t.* arrêter, décréter.

decrepit [di'krepit], *a.* décrépit, caduc.

decry [di'krai], *v.t.* décrier, dénigrer.

dedicate ['dedikeit], *v.t.* dédier (*à*); consacrer (*à*).

dedication [dedi'kei∫ən], *n.* dédicace, *f.*

deduce [di'dju:s], *v.t.* déduire, inférer (*de*).

deduct [di'dʌkt], *v.t.* déduire, rabattre.

deduction [di'dʌk∫ən], *n.* déduction, *f.*

deed [di:d], *n.* action, *f.*; fait, exploit; (*Law*) titre, *m.*

deem [di:m], *v.t.* juger; penser, estimer.

deep [di:p], *a.* profond, extrême; foncé (*couleur*); grave (*son*); (*fig.*) rusé.—*n.* (*poet.*) océan, *m.*

deepen ['di:pən], *v.t.* approfondir; assombrir.—*v.i.* devenir plus profond *ou* plus foncé.

deep-freeze ['di:p'fri:z], *n.* réfrigérateur à basse température, *m.*

deeply ['di:pli], *adv.* profondément; extrêmement.

deep-rooted ['di:p'ru:tid], **deep-seated** ['di:p'si:tid], *a.* profond, enraciné.

deer [diə], *n.* cervidé, *m.*; *fallow deer*, daim, *m.,* daine, *f.*; *red deer*, cerf, *m.*

deface [di'feis], *v.t.* défigurer; mutiler.

defamation [defə'mei∫ən], *n.* diffamation, *f.*

defame [di'feim], *v.t.* diffamer.

default [di'fɔ:lt], *n.* défaut, manque, *m.*; (*Law*) contumace, *f.*

defaulter [di'fɔ:ltə], *n.* délinquant; (*Mil.*) réfractaire; (*Law*) défaillant, *m.*

defeat [di'fi:t], *n.* défaite, déroute, *f.*—*v.t.* battre, vaincre; (*fig.*) annuler, déjouer.

defeatism [di'fi:tizm], *n.* défaitisme, *m.*

defeatist [di'fi:tist], *a.* and *n.* défaitiste, *m.,f.*

defect [di'fekt], *n.* défaut, *m.*; imperfection, *f.*

defective [di'fektiv], *a.* défectueux, imparfait.

defend [di'fend], *v.t.* défendre (*de*), protéger (*contre*).

defender [di'fendə], *n.* défenseur, *m.*

defense [di'fens], *n.*défense, *f.*[see **war-office**]

defensible [di'fensəbl], *a.* défendable; (*fig.*) soutenable.

defensive [di'fensiv], *a.* défensif.—*n.* défensive, *f.*

defer [di'fə:], *v.t.* différer, remettre.—*v.i.* différer; déférer (*à*).

deference ['defərəns], *n.* déférence, *f.*

deferential [defə'ren∫əl], *a.* de déférence, respectueux.

deferment [di'fə:mənt], *n.* (*Mil.*) sursis, *m.*

defiance [di'faiəns], *n.* défi, *m.*

defiant [di'faiənt], *a.* défiant.

deficiency [di'fi∫ənsi], *n.* défaut, *m.*; insuffisance, *f.*

deficient [di'fi∫ənt], *a.* défectueux; insuffisant.

deficit ['defisit], *n.* déficit, *m.*

defile (1) [di:'fail], *n.* défilé, *m.*

defile (2) [di'fail], *v.t.* souiller; déshonorer.

define [di'fain], *v.t.* définir; déterminer.

definite ['definit], *a.* déterminé; (*Gram.*) défini.

definitely ['definitli], *adv.* absolument, nette- ment, d'une manière déterminée.

definition [defi'niʃən], *n.* définition, *f.*

deflate [di'fleit], *v.t.* dégonfler.

deflation [di'fleiʃən], *n.* dégonflement, *m.*; déflation monétaire, *f.*

deflect [di'flekt], *v.t.* faire dévier, détourner. —*v.i.* dévier.

deforestation [di:fɔris'teiʃən], *n.* déboise- ment, *m.*

deform [di'fɔ:m], *v.t.* déformer, défigurer.

deformation [di:fɔ:'meiʃən], *n.* déformation, *f.*

deformed [di'fɔ:md], *a.* difforme.

deformity [di'fɔ:miti], *n.* difformité; laideur, *f.*

defraud [di'frɔ:d], *v.t.* frauder.

defray [di'frei], *v.t.* défrayer; payer.

deft [deft], *a.* adroit, habile.

deftly ['deftli], *adv.* adroitement, lestement.

defunct [di'fʌŋkt], *a.* défunt, trépassé, décédé.—*n.* défunt, *m.*

defy [di'fai], *v.t.* défier, braver.

degeneracy [di'dʒenərəsi], **degeneration** [didʒenə'reiʃən], *n.* dégénérescence, *f.*

degenerate [di'dʒenərit], *a.* and *n.* dégénéré, *m.*—[di'dʒenəreit], *v.i.* dégénérer, s'abâ- tardir (*dans* ou *en*).

degradation [degrə'deiʃən], *n.* dégradation, *f.*; (*fig.*) avilissement, *m.*

degrade [di'greid], *v.t.* dégrader; (*fig.*) avilir.

degrading [di'greidiŋ], *a.* dégradant, avilis- sant.

degree [di'gri:], *n.* degré; rang, ordre, *m.*; qualité, *f.*; *university degree*, grade universitaire, *m.*

de-ice [di:'ais], *v.t.*, *v.i.* dégivrer.

deify ['di:ifai], *n.t.* déifier.

deign [dein], *v.t.*, *v.i.* daigner.

deity ['di:iti], *n.* divinité; (*Myth.*) déité, *f.*

dejected [di'dʒektid], *a.* abattu, triste.

dejection [di'dʒekʃən], *n.* abattement, *m.*

delay [di'lei], *n.* délai, retard, *m.*—*v.t.* différer; remettre.—*v.i.* tarder.

delegacy ['deligəsi], *n.* délégation, *f.*

delegate [di'ligit], *n.* délégué, *m.*—['deligeit], *v.t.* déléguer.

delegation [deli'geiʃən], *n.* délégation, *f.*

delete [di'li:t], *v.t.* effacer, rayer, biffer.

deletion [di'li:ʃən], *n.* rature, *f.*; grattage, *m.*

deliberate [di'libərit], *a.* délibéré, pré- médité; réfléchi.—[di'libəreit], *v.i.* dé- libérer.

deliberately [di'libəritli], *adv.* à dessein, lentement.

deliberation [dilibə'reiʃən], *n.* délibération, *f.*

delicacy ['delikəsi], *n.* délicatesse; friandise (*a titbit*), *f.*

delicate ['delikit], *a.* délicat.

delicious [di'liʃəs], *a.* délicieux.

deliciously [di'liʃəsli], *adv.* délicieusement.

delight [di'lait], *n.* délices, *f.pl.*, plaisir, *m.*— *v.t.* plaire à, réjouir, enchanter; *to be delighted to*, être enchanté de.—*v.i.* se plaire à.

delightful [di'laitful], *a.* délicieux; charmant (*personne*).

delineate [di'linieit], *v.t.* esquisser, dessiner; (*fig.*) décrire.

delinquency [di'liŋkwənsi], *n.* délit, *m.*; *juve- nile delinquency*, délinquance juvénile, *f.*

delinquent [di'liŋkwənt], *n.* délinquant, *m.*; *juvenile delinquent*, jeune délinquant.

delirious [di'liriəs], *a.* en délire; délirant.

delirium [di'liriəm], *n.* délire; (*fig.*) transport de joie, *m.*

deliver [di'livə], *v.t.* délivrer, sauver; dis- tribuer (*lettres etc.*); remettre (*lettre, paquet etc.*); livrer (*marchandises*), prononcer (*un discours*); (faire) accoucher (*femme*).

deliverance [di'livərəns], *n.* délivrance, *f.*

deliverer [di'livərə], *n.* libérateur, sauveur, *m.*

delivery [di'livəri], *n.* délivrance, remise, *f.*; débit, *m.*, diction (*d'un discours*); livraison (*de marchandises*); distribution (*du courrier*), *f.*; (*Med.*) accouchement, *m.*; *payment on delivery*, livraison contre remboursement.

delivery van [də'livərivæn], *n.* camion de livraison, *m.*; camionnette, *f.*

dell [del], *n.* vallon, *m.*

delta ['deltə], *n.* delta, *m.*

delude [di'lju:d], *v.t.* tromper, abuser.

deluge ['delju:dʒ], *n.* déluge, *m.*—*v.t.* inonder.

delusion [di'lju:ʒən], *n.* illusion, erreur, *f.*

delve [delv], *v.t.*, *v.i.* bêcher, creuser; (*fig.*) sonder.

demagnetize [di:'mægnitaiz], *v.t.* déma- gnétiser.

demagogue ['deməgɔg], *n.* démagogue, *m.*, *f.*

demand [di'mɑ:nd], *n.* exigence; réclama- tion; demande, requête, *f.*; *in great demand*, très demandé, très recherché; *on demand*, sur demande; *supply and demand*, l'offre et la demande, *f.*—*v.t.* exiger; réclamer; demander.

demarcation [di:mɑ:'keiʃən], *n.* démarca- tion, *f.*; *line of demarcation*, ligne de démarcation, *f.*

demean [di'mi:n], *v.i.* se comporter, se con- duire; (*colloq.*) s'abaisser, se dégrader.

demeanor [di'mi:nə], *n.* conduite, *f.*, main- tien, *m.*; tenue, *f.*

demented [di'mentid], *a.* fou, dément.

demi ['demi], *prep.* demi, à demi.

demigod ['demigɔd], *n.* demi-dieu, *m.*

demise [di'maiz], *n.* décès, *m.*, mort, *f.*—*v.t.* léguer; céder à bail.

demi-semiquaver ['demi'semikweivə], *n.* (*Mus.*) triple croche, *f.*

demister [di:'mistə], *n.* (*Motor.*) appareil antibuée, *m.*

demobilization [di:moubilai'zeiʃən], *n.* dé- mobilisation, *f.*

demobilize [di:'moubilaiz], *v.t.* démobiliser.

democracy [di'mɔkrəsi], *n.* démocratie, *f.*

democrat ['deməkræt], *n.* démocrate, *m.*, *f.*

democratic [demə'krætik], *a.* démocratique.

democratically [demə'krætikəli], *adv.* démo- cratiquement.

demolish [di'mɔliʃ], *v.t.* démolir.

demolition [demə'liʃən], *n.* démolition, *f.*

demon [di:mən], *n.* démon, diable, *m.*

demonstrate ['demənstreit], *v.t.* démontrer. —*v.i.* (*Polit.*) manifester.

demonstration [demən'streiʃən], *n.* démons- tration; (*Polit.*) manifestation, *f.*

demonstrative [di'mɔnstrətiv], *a.* démons- tratif.

demoralize [di:'mɔrəlaiz], *v.t.* démoraliser.

demote [di'mout], *v.t.* (*Mil.*) réduire à un grade inférieur, rétrograder.

demur [di'mə:], *n.* hésitation, objection, *f.*— *v.i.* hésiter, temporiser.

demure [di′mjuə], *a.* réservé, posé; d'une modestie affectée.

demurely [di′mjuəli], *adv.* d'un air posé; avec une modestie affectée.

den [den], *n.* antre; repaire (*de voleurs etc.*), *m.*; loge (*de ménagerie*), *f.*; (*fig.*) bouge, taudis; (*colloq.*) cabinet de travail, *m.*

denationalize [di:′næ∫nəlaiz], *v.t.* dénationaliser.

denial [di′naiəl], *n.* déni, *m.*, dénégation, *f.*

denier [′deniə], *n.* (*Hosiery*) denier, *m.*; *a* 15-denier stocking, un bas 15 deniers.

denigrate [′denigreit], *v.t.* noircir, dénigrer.

Denis [DENNIS].

denizen [′denizn], *n.* citoyen, habitant, *m.*

Denmark [′denma:k], le Danemark, *m.*

Dennis [′denis]. Denis, *m.*

denomination [dinɔmi′nei∫ən], *n.* dénomination, *f.*; culte, *m.*, secte, *f.*

denominational [dinɔmi′nei∫ənl], *a.* confessionnel (*école*).

denote [di′nout], *v.t.* dénoter, marquer, indiquer; signifier.

denounce [di′nauns], *v.t.* dénoncer.

dense [dens], *a.* dense, épais; compact; stupide.

densely [′densli], *adv.* en masse.

density [′densiti], *n.* densité, épaisseur, *f.*

dent [dent], *n.* renfoncement, *m.*, bosselure; coche, *f.*—*v.t.* bosseler, cabosser.

dental [dentl], *a.* dentaire; (*Phon.*) dental; *dental surgeon*, chirurgien dentiste, *m.*

dentifrice [′dentifris], *n.* dentifrice, *m.*

dentist [′dentist], *n.* dentiste, *m.*, *f.*

dentistry [′dentistri], *n.* dentisterie, *f.*

denture [′dent∫ə], *n.* dentier, (*fam.*) râtelier, *m.*

denude [di′nju:d], *v.t.* dénuder; (*fig.*) dénuer.

denunciation [dinʌnsi′ei∫ən], *n.* dénonciation, *f.*

deny [di′nai], *v.t.* nier, démentir; (*Law*) dénier, renier; refuser.

deodorant [di:′oudərənt], **deodorizer** [di:′oudəraizə], *n.* désinfectant, désinfecteur, désodorisant, *m.*

depart [di′pa:t], *v.i.* quitter.—*v.i.* partir, s'en aller, se retirer, s'éloigner; (*fig.*) mourir.

departed [di′pa:tid], *a.* mort, défunt; passé, évanoui.—*n.* *the departed*, le défunt, *m.*, les trépassés, *m.pl.*

department [di′pa:tmənt], *n.* département, service; (*Polit.*) bureau; comptoir, rayon (*de boutique*), *m.*; *department store*, grand magasin, *m.*

departmental [di:pa:t′mentl], *a.* départemental.

departure [di′pa:t∫ə], *n.* départ; éloignement, *m.*; déviation; (*fig.*) mort, *f.*

depend [di′pend], *v.i.* dépendre (*de*); compter (*sur*), se reposer (*sur*).

dependable [di′pendəbl], *a.* digne de confiance; sûr.

dependent [di′pendənt], *a.* dépendant; (*Law*) à la charge de; (*Gram.*) subordonné; *dependent relatives*, parents à charge, *m.pl.*

depict [di′pikt], *v.t.* peindre, dépeindre.

deplete [di′pli:t], *v.t.* amoindrir, épuiser.

deplorable [di′plɔ:rəbl], *a.* déplorable; pitoyable (*lamentable*).

deplore [di′plɔ:], *v.t.* déplorer.

deploy [di′plɔi], *v.t.* (*Mil.*) déployer.—*v.i.* se déployer.

depopulate [di:′pɔpjuleit], *v.t.* dépeupler.—*v.i.* se dépeupler.

deport [di′pɔ:t], *v.t.* déporter, expulser; *to deport oneself*, se comporter.

deportment [di′pɔ:tmənt], *n.* tenue, conduite, *f.*, manières, *f.pl.*

depose [di′pouz], *v.t.*, *v.i.* déposer (*de*).

deposit [di′pɔzit], *n.* dépôt, *m.*; (*Banking*) versement; gage, nantissement, *m.*, arrhes, *f.pl.*, caution, *f.*; (*Geol.*) gisement, gîte, *m.*; *deposit account*, compte de dépôt, *m.*—*v.t.* déposer; verser.

deposition [depə′zi∫ən, di:pə′zi∫ən], *n.* déposition, *f.*; dépôt, *m.*

depositor [di′pɔzitə], *n.* (*Comm.*) déposant, *m.*

depository [di′pɔzitri], *n.* dépôt; garde-meubles, *m.*

depot [′depou], *n.* dépôt, *m.*; (*Am.*) [′di:pou] gare, *f.*

deprave [di′preiv], *v.t.* dépraver, corrompre.

depraved [di′preivd], *a.* dépravé, corrompu.

depravity [di′præviti], *n.* dépravation, *f.*

deprecate [′deprikeit], *v.t.* désapprouver, désavouer, s'opposer à.

deprecatingly [′deprikeitiŋli], *adv.* avec désapprobation.

deprecative [′deprikeitiv], **deprecatory** [′deprikeitəri], *a.* de déprécation.

depreciate [di′pri:∫ieit], *v.t.* déprécier.—*v.i.* se déprécier.

depreciation [dipri:∫i′ei∫ən], *n.* dépréciation, *f.*

depress [di′pres], *v.t.* baisser, abaisser; abattre; accabler, décourager.

depressed [di′prest], *a.* abattu; bas.

depression [di′pre∫ən], *n.* abaissement, *m.*; dépression; (*Comm.*) crise, *f.*

deprivation [depri′vei∫ən], *n.* privation; perte, *f.*

deprive [di′praiv], *v.t.* priver (*de*); déposséder.

depth [depθ], *n.* profondeur, *f.*; enfoncement (*recoin*); fort (*des saisons*), *m.*; *in the depth of winter*, au cœur ou au plus fort de l'hiver, *m.*; *to get out of one's depth*, perdre pied.

depth charge [′depθt∫a:d3], *n.* grenade sous-marine, *f.*

deputation [depju′tei∫ən], *n.* députation, délégation, *f.*

depute [di′pju:t], *v.t.* députer, déléguer.

deputize [′depjutaiz], *v.i.* remplacer quelqu'un.

deputy [′depjuti], *n.* député, délégué; adjoint, *m.*

derail [di′reil], *v.t.* (*Rail.*) dérailler.

derailment [di:′reilmənt], *n.* déraillement, *m.*

derange [di′reind3], *v.t.* déranger.

derangement [di′reind3mənt], *n.* dérangement, *m.*

derelict [′derilikt], *a.* délaissé, abandonné.

deride [di′raid], *v.t.* tourner en dérision, se moquer de.

derision [di′ri3ən], *n.* dérision, moquerie, *f.*

derisive [di′raisiv], *a.* dérisoire.

derivation [deri′vei∫ən], *n.* dérivation; origine, *f.*

derivative [di′rivətiv], *n.* (*Gram.*) dérivé, *m.*

derive [di′raiv], *v.t.* dériver.—*v.i.* venir, dériver (*de*).

derogatory [di'rɔgətəri], *a.* péjoratif, dérogatoire, dérogeant (*à*).
derrick ['derik], *n.* grue, *f.*; derrick, *m.*
dervish ['dəːviʃ], *n.* derviche, *m.*
descend [di'send], *v.i.* descendre, tomber; s'abaisser; **to be descended from**, descendre de; **to descend upon**, tomber sur.
descendant [di'sendənt], *n.* descendant, *m.*
descendent [di'sendənt], *a.* descendant, qui descend, provenant (*de*).
descent [di'sent], *n.* descente; chute, pente; descendance, naissance, origine (*lignée*), *f.*
describe [dis'kraib], *v.t.* décrire, dépeindre, peindre.
description [dis'kripʃən], *n.* description; désignation (*d'une personne*), *f.*; (*l am*) signalement, *m.*; (*colloq.*) qualité, sorte, espèce, *f.*
descriptive [dis'kriptiv], *a.* descriptif.
descry [dis'krai], *v.t.* découvrir, apercevoir; aviser; reconnaître.
desecrate ['desəkreit], *v.t.* profaner.
desecration [desə'kreiʃən], *n.* profanation, *f.*
desert (1) [di'zəːt], *n.* mérite, *m.*; mérites, *m.pl.*
desert (2) ['dezət], *a.* désert; solitaire.—*n.* désert, *m.*; solitude, *f.*
desert (3) [di'zəːt], *v.t.* abandonner, déserter.
deserted [di'zəːtid], *a.* abandonné, désert.
deserter [di'zəːtə], *n.* déserteur, *m.*
desertion [di'zəːʃən], *n.* désertion, *f.*, abandon, *m.*
deserve [di'zəːv], *v.t.* mériter, être digne de.
deservedly [di'zəːvidli], *adv.* à bon droit, justement.
deserving [di'zəːviŋ], *a.* de mérite, méritoire.
desiccated ['desikeitid], *a.* desséché.
design [di'zain], *n.* dessein, projet; dessin (*drawing*); (*Manuf.*) modèle, *m.*; **by design**, à dessein.—*v.t.* projeter, se proposer de; dessiner.
designedly [di'zainidli], *adv.* à dessein.
designer [di'zainə], *n.* inventeur; auteur; architecte; dessinateur (*draftsman*), *m.*
designing [di'zainiŋ], *a.* artificieux, intrigant.
designate ['dezigneit], *v.t.* désigner, nommer.—['dezignit], *a.* désigné, nommé.
desirable [di'zaiərəbl], *a.* désirable, à souhaiter.
desire [di'zaiə], *n.* désir, *m.*; prière, demande, *f.*—*v.t.* désirer, souhaiter; prier.
desirous [di'zaiərəs], *a.* désireux (*de*), empressé (*à*); **to be desirous of**, avoir envie de.
desist [di'zist], *v.i.* se désister, cesser (*de*).
desk [desk], *n.* pupitre (*école*); bureau (*meuble*), *m.*; caisse (*boutique*); chaire (*de professeur*), *f.*
desolate ['desəlit], *a.* désolé, inhabité, solitaire, dévasté.
desolation [desə'leiʃən], *n.* désolation, *f.*
despair [dis'pɛə], *n.* désespoir, *m.*—*v.i.* désespérer (*de*).
despatch [DISPATCH].
desperado [despə'reidou, despə'raːdou], *n.* désespéré, *m.*
desperate ['despərit], *a.* désespéré; furieux, forcené; acharné, terrible.
desperately ['despəritli], *adv.* désespérément; (*fig.*) excessivement.

desperation [despə'reiʃən], *n.* désespoir, *m.*; fureur, *f.*, acharnement, *m.*
despicable ['dispikəbl], *a.* méprisable.
despise [dis'paiz], *v.t.* mépriser, dédaigner.
despite [dis'pait], *n.* (*Lit.*) dépit, *m.*—*prep.* en dépit de, malgré.
despoil [dis'pɔil], *v.t.* dépouiller.
despondency [dis'pɔndənsi], *n.* abattement, désespoir, *m.*
despondent [dis'pɔndənt], *a.* découragé, abattu.
despot ['despɔt], *n.* despote, *m.*, *f.*
despotic [des'pɔtik], *a.* despotique.
despotism ['despətizm], *n.* despotisme, *m.*
dessert [di'zəːt], *n.* dessert, *m.*
destination [desti'neiʃən], *n.* destination, *f.*
destine ['destin], *v.t.* destiner, désigner.
destiny ['destini], *n.* destin, *m.*, destinée, *f.*
destitute ['destitjuːt], *a.* dépourvu, destitué; indigent.
destitution [desti'tjuːʃən], *n.* dénuement, abandon, *m.*, indigence, *f.*
destroy [dis'trɔi], *v.t.* détruire, ruiner.
destroyer [dis'trɔiə], *n.* (*Naut.*) contre-torpilleur, *m.*
destroying [dis'trɔiiŋ], *a.* destructeur, destructif.
destruction [dis'trʌkʃən], *n.* destruction, *f.*, anéantissement, *m.*; ruine, *f.*
destructive [dis'trʌktiv], *a.* destructeur; funeste, fatal (*à*).
desultorily ['desəltərili], *adv.* à bâtons rompus, sans suite.
desultory ['desəltəri], *a.* à bâtons rompus, décousu, sans suite.
detach [di'tætʃ], *v.t.* détacher (*de*); isoler; **to become detached**, se détacher.
detachable [di'tætʃəbl], *a.* démontable, détachable.
detached [di'tætʃt], *a.* détaché, isolé.
detachment [di'tætʃmənt], *n.* détachement, *m.*
detail ['diːteil], *n.* détail, *m.*—[di'teil], *v.t.* détailler; (*Mil.*) désigner (*pour*).
detain [di'tein], *v.t.* retenir; détenir; (*Law*) empêcher.
detect [di'tekt], *v.t.* découvrir; détecter.
detection [di'tekʃən], *n.* découverte, *f.*
detective [di'tektiv], *n.* agent de la (police de) sûreté, policier, détective, *m.*; **a detective story**, un roman policier.
detention [di'tenʃən], *n.* action de retenir; (*Law*) détention; (*Sch.*) consigne, *f.*
deter [di'təː], *v.t.* détourner, empêcher (*de*); dissuader (*de*).
detergent [di'təːdʒənt], *a. and n.* détersif, détergent, *m.*
deteriorate [di'tiəriəreit], *v.i.* se détériorer.
deterioration [ditiəriə'reiʃən], *n.* détérioration, *f.*; dépérissement, *m.*
determination [ditəːmi'neiʃən], *n.* détermination, décision, *f.*
determine [di'təːmin], *v.t.* déterminer, décider.—*v.i.* se déterminer, se décider, résoudre.
determined [di'təːmind], *a.* résolu, obstiné.
deterrent [di'terənt], *a.* préventif.—*n.* arme préventive, *f.*
detest [di'test], *v.t.* détester.
detestable [di'testəbl], *a.* détestable; (*fig.*) odieux.
detestation [diːtes'teiʃən], *n.* détestation, *f.*

401

dethrone [di'θroun], *v.t.* détrôner.
detonation [detə'neiʃən], *n.* détonation, *f.*
detonator ['detəneitə], *n.* détonateur, *m.*
detour [di'tuə], *n.* déviation, *f.*
detract [di'trækt], *v.t.* enlever, ôter (à)
dénigrer.—*v.i.* déroger (à).
detriment ['detrimənt], *n.* détriment, préjudice, *m.*
detrimental [detri'mentl], *a.* préjudiciable,
nuisible (à).
deuce [dju:s], *n.* (*Cards*) deux; (*Ten.*) à deux;
à égalité; (*colloq.*) diable, diantre, *m.*
Deuteronomy [dju:tə'ronəmi]. Deutéronome,
m.
devaluation [di:vælju'eiʃən],*n.*dévaluation,*f.*
devalue [di:'vælju], **devaluate** [di:'væljueit],
v.t. dévaluer, déprécier.
devastate ['devəsteit], *v.t.* dévaster.
devastation [devəs'teiʃən], *n.* dévastation, *f.*
develop [di'veləp], *v.t.* développer.
developer [di'veləpə], *n.* (*Phot.*) révélateur,
m.
development [di'veləpmənt], *n.* développement, *m.*
deviate ['di:vieit], *v.i.* dévier, se dévier;
s'écarter (de).
deviation [di:vi'eiʃən], *n.* 'éviation, *f.*, écart,
m.
device [di'vais], *n.* dessein, moyen, stratagème; dispositif, mécanisme, *m.*; devise
(*motto*), *f.*
devil [devl], *n.* diable, démon, *m.*; **daredevil**, téméraire, *m.*, *f.*—*v.t.* griller et
poivrer; **devil-may-care**, étourdi, *m.*
devilish ['devliʃ], *a.* maudit, diabolique.
devilment ['devilmənt], **deviltry** ['devil
tri], *n.*diablerie, *f.*
devious [di:'viəs], *a.* détourné, écarté; (*fig.*)
errant.
devise [di'vaiz], *v.t.* imaginer, inventer;
tramer, machiner.
devitalize [di:'vaitəlaiz], *v.t.* dévitaliser.
devoid [di'void], *a.* exempt, dénué (de).
devote [di'vout], *v.t.* dévouer, consacrer (à).
devoted [di'voutid], *a.* dévoué, consacré.
devotee [devo'ti:], *n.* dévot; passionné, *n.*,
fanatique, *m.*, *f.*
devotion [di'vouʃən], *n.* dévotion, *f.*; dévouement, *m.*
devour [di'vauə], *v.t.* dévorer.
devout [di'vaut], *a.* dévot, pieux, fervent.
devoutly [di'vautli], *adv.* dévotement.
dew [dju:], *n.* rosée, *f.*
dewdrop ['dju:drop], *n.* goutte de rosée, *f.*
dewlap ['dju:læp], *n.* fanon, *m.*
dewy ['dju:i], *a.* (couvert) de rosée.
dexterity [deks'teriti], *n.* dextérité, adresse, *f.*
dexterous ['dekstrəs], *a.* adroit; habile.
diabetes [daiə'bi:ti:z], *n.* diabète, *m.*
diabetic [daiə'betik], *a.* and *n.* diabétique,
m., *f.*
diabolic [daiə'bolik], **diabolical** [daiə'bolikl],
a. diabolique.
diadem ['daiədem], *n.* diadème, *m.*
diæresis [dai'iərəsis], *n.* (*pl.* **diæreses**
[dai'iərəsi:z]) tréma, *m.*
diagnose [daiəg'nouz], *v.t.* diagnostiquer.
diagnosis [daiəg'nousis], *n.* diagnose, *f.*;
diagnostic, *m.*
diagonal [dai'ægənəl], *a.* diagonal.—*n.*
diagonale, *f.*

diagram ['daiəgræm], *n.* diagramme, schéma,
m., épure, *f.*
diagrammatic [daiəgrə'mætik], *a.* schématique.
dial ['daiəl], *n.* cadran, *m.*; **sun-dial**, cadran
solaire.—*v.t.* (*Teleph.*) composer (*un numéro*).
dialect ['daiəlekt], *n.* dialecte, patois; (*fig.*)
langage, *m.*
dialogue ['daiəlog], *n.* dialogue; entretien, *m.*
diameter [dai'æmitə], *n.* diamètre, *m.*
diamond ['daiəmənd], *n.* diamant; (*Cards*)
carreau, *m.*
diamond cutter ['daiəməndkʌtə], *n.* lapidaire, *m.*
diamond-shaped ['daiəmondʃeipt], *a.* en
losange.
Diana [dai'ænə]. (*Myth.*) Diane, *f.*
diaper ['daiəpə], *n.* linge ouvré, *m.*; (*Am.*)
serviette hygiénique, couche (*d'enfant*), *f.*
diarrhoea [daiə'ri:ə], *n.* diarrhée, *f.*
diary ['daiəri], *n.* journal (particulier); agenda,
m.
diatribe ['daiətraib], *n.* diatribe, *f.*
dice [dais], *n.pl.* dés, *m.pl.*—*v.i.* jouer aux dés.
dicky ['diki], *n.* faux plastron (de chemise)*m.*
dictate [dik'teit], *v.t.* dicter.—*v.i.* commander
(à).—['dikteit], *n.* précepte, ordre, *m.*
dictation [dik'teiʃən], *n.* dictée, *f.*
dictator [dik'teitə], *n.* dictateur, *m.*
dictatorial [diktə'to:riəl], *a.* dictatorial; impérieux.
dictatorship [dik'teitəʃip], *n.* dictature, *f.*
diction ['dikʃən], *n.* diction, *f.*; débit, *m.*
dictionary ['dikʃənri], *n.* dictionnaire, *m.*
dictum ['diktəm], *n.* (*pl.* **dicta** ['diktə])
dicton, *m.*
diddle [didl], *v.t.* (*colloq.*) duper, rouler.
die (1) [dai], *n.* (*pl.* **dies** [daiz]) coin (*pour
estamper*).
die (2) [dai], *n.* (*pl.* **dice** [dais]) dé (à jouer), *m.*;
(*fig.*) chance, *f.*
die (3) [dai], *v.i.* mourir; (*fig.*) s'éteindre;
to die down, s'apaiser, se calmer; **to die of**,
mourir de; **to die out**, s'éteindre, disparaître, s'oublier.
die-hard ['daiha:d], *n.* intransigeant, *m.*
diet ['daiət], *n.* diète, *f.*, régime, *m.*; diète
(*assemblée*), *f.*—*v.t.* mettre à la diète, mettre
au régime.—*v.i.* faire diète, être au régime.
dietetics [daiə'tetiks], *n.pl.* diététique, *f.*
differ ['difə], *v.i.* différer (de); se quereller
(avec).
difference ['difrəns], *n.* différence; dispute,
f.; différend (de valeur), *m.*; **to split the
difference**, partager le différend.
different ['difrənt], *a.* différent.
differentiate [difə'renʃieit], *v.t.* différencier,
distinguer.
differently ['difrəntli], *adv.* différemment,
autrement.
difficult ['difikəlt], *a.* difficile; malaisé.
difficulty ['difikəlti], *n.* difficulté; peine, *f.*,
embarras; (*pl.*) embarras pécuniaire, *m.*
diffidence ['difidəns], *n.* défiance (de soi),
modestie, timidité, *f.*
diffident ['difidənt], *a.* timide, hésitant.
diffidently ['difidəntli], *adv.* avec hésitation,
timidement.
diffuse [di'fju:s], *a.* répandu, étendu; diffus,
verbeux (*style*).—[di'fju:z], *v.t.* répandre.
diffusely [di'fju:sli], *adv.* diffusément.

dig [dig], *v.t. irr.* creuser; bêcher; piocher.—
v.i. bêcher, piocher; faire des fouilles.—*n.*
coup *(de coude)*; (*colloq.*) coup de patte, *m.*

digest [di'dʒest], *v.t.* digérer *(aliment etc.);*
résumer.—*v.i.* digérer.—['daidʒest], *n.* sommaire, abrégé, *m.*

digestion [di'dʒestʃən], *n.* digestion, *f.*

digestive [di'dʒestiv], *a. and n.* digestif, *m.*

digger ['digə], *n.* terrassier; mineur; fouil-
leur *(archéologue);* (*pop.*) Australien, *m.*

digging [digiŋ], *n.* fouille, *f.,* creusement, *m.*;
(*pl.*) (*pop.*) (*abbr.* **digs** [digz]) logement, *m.*

dignified ['dignifaid], *a.* plein de dignité,
digne; noble.

dignify ['dignifai], *v.t.* honorer, élever,
illustrer.

dignitary ['dignitri], *n.* dignitaire, *m., f.*

dignity ['digniti], *n.* dignité, *f.*

digress [dai'gres], *v.i.* faire une digression;
s'écarter *(de).*

digression [dai'greʃən], *n.* digression, *f.*

dike or **dyke** [daik], *n.* digue, *f.,* fossé, *m.*

dilapidated [di'læpideitid], *a.* délabré.

dilapidation [dilæpi'deiʃən], *n.* délabrement,
m.

dilate [dai'leit], *v.t.* dilater, élargir, étendre.—
v.i. se dilater.

dilatory ['dilətəri], *a.* négligent, lent.

dilemma [di'lemə, dai'lemə], *n.* dilemme, *f.*
(*fig.*) embarras, *m.*; **on the horns of a
dilemma**, enfermé dans un dilemme.

diligence ['dilidʒəns], *n.* diligence, assiduité,
f.

diligent ['dilidʒənt], *a.* diligent, appliqué.

dilute [dai'lju:t, di'lju:t], *v.t.* délayer; diluer;
couper *(vin)*; (*fig.*) affaiblir.—*a.* dilué,
mitigé.

dilution [dai'lju:ʃən, di'lju:ʃən], *n.* dilution
(liquides), *f.*; délayement *(fig.)* affaiblissement, *m.*

dim [dim], *a.* obscur, trouble; blafard; terne
(lumière); indécis.—*v.t.* obscurcir; ternir.

dimension [di'menʃən, dai'menʃən], *n.*
dimension, étendue, *f.*

dimensional [di'menʃənəl, dai'menʃənəl], *a.*
dimensionnel; (*Cine.*) **three-dimensional
(3-D) film,** film en relief, *m.*

diminish [di'miniʃ], *v.t.* diminuer; abaisser.
—*v.i.* diminuer.

diminutive [di'minjutiv], *a.* diminutif,
minuscule.

dimly ['dimli], *adv.* obscurément, indistinctement, faiblement, à peine; sans éclat.

dimness ['dimnis], *n.* obscurcissement, *m.*;
obscurité; faiblesse *(de vue),* *f.*

dimple [dimpl], *n.* fossette, *f.*—*v.i.* (*fig.*) se
rider *(eau etc.).*

din [din], *n.* vacarme, tapage, fracas; cliquetis
(d'armes etc.), *m.*

dine [dain], *v.i.* dîner *(de).*

diner ['dainə], *n.* dîneur, *m.*

dinghy [diŋgi], *n.* (*Naut.*) youyou, canot, *m.*

dinginess ['dindʒinis], *n.* couleur terne, *f.*;
aspect sale, *m.*

dingy ['dindʒi], *a.* terne; sale; défraîchi.

dining car ['daininka:], *n.* wagon-restaurant,
m.

dining room ['daininrum], *n.* salle à manger,
f.

dinner ['dinə], *n.* dîner, *m.*

dinner jacket ['dinədʒækit], *n.* smoking, *m*

dint (1) [dint], *n.* force, *f.,* pouvoir, *m.*; *by
dint of,* à force de.

dint (2) [dint], [DENT].

diocese ['daiəsis], *n.* diocèse, *m.*

dioxide [dai'oksaid], *n.* (*Chem.*) bioxyde, *m.*

dip [dip], *v.t.* plonger *(dans)*; tremper, mouiller; *(Motor.)* mettre en code *(phares).*—*v.i.*
plonger; *to dip into,* s'engager dans,
feuilleter *(un livre).*—*n.* plongeon, *m.,* baignade, *f.*

diphtheria [dif'θiəriə], *n.* diphtérie, *f.*

diphthong ['difθɔŋ], *n.* diphtongue, *f.*

diploma [di'ploumə], *n.* diplôme, *m.*

diplomacy [di'plouməsi], *n.* diplomatie, *f.*

diplomat ['diploumæt], **diplomatist** [di'plou
mətist], *n.* diplomate, *m., f.*

diplomatic [diplo'mætik], *a.* diplomatique.

dip-stick ['dipstik], *n.* (*Motor.*) réglette-
jauge, *f.*

dire ['daiə], *a.* terrible, affreux; cruel.

direct [di'rekt, dai'rekt], *a.* direct, droit;
exprès, clair.—*adv.* (*colloq.*) directement.—
v.t. diriger; ordonner, charger *(de);* indiquer, donner des renseignements à;
(Theat.) mettre en scène.

direction [di'rekʃən], *n.* direction, *f.*; ordre,
m., instruction, *f.*; sens, côté, *m.*; adresse
(d'une lettre), f.

directional signal [di'rekʃənəl 'signəl],
n. (*Motor.*) clignotant, *m.*

directly [di'rektli], *adv.* directement.

director [di'rektə], *n.* directeur, administrateur, gérant; (*Cine.*) réalisateur, *m.*

directory [di'rektəri], *n.* directoire; (*Postal,
Teleph.*) annuaire, *m.*

direful ['daiəful], *a.* terrible, affreux.

dirge [də:dʒ], *n.* chant funèbre, *m.*

dirt [də:t], *n.* saleté; crasse; boue, fange;
ordure, *f.*

dirtily ['də:tili], *adv.* salement; (*fig.*) vilainement.

dirtiness ['də:tinis], *n.* saleté; (*fig.*) bassesse, *f.*

dirty ['də:ti], *a.* sale, malpropre, crasseux;
(*fig.*) bas, vilain.—*v.t.* salir, crotter; (*fig.*)
souiller.

disability [disə'biliti], *n.* incapacité, *f.*

disable [dis'eibl], *v.t.* rendre incapable,
mettre hors d'état *(de).*

disabled [dis'eibld], *a.* hors de service; (*Mil.*)
hors de combat; *disabled ex-service
men,* mutilés de guerre, *m.pl.*

disadvantage [disəd'vɑ:ntidʒ], *n.* désavantage, inconvénient, *m.*; perte, *f.*

disagree [disə'gri:], *v.i.* différer, ne pas s'accorder; *my dinner disagreed with me,*
mon dîner m'a fait mal.

disagreeable [disə'gri:əbl], *a.* désagréable;
fâcheux.

disagreeableness [disə'gri:əblnis], *n.* désagrément, *m.,* nature désagréable, *f.*

disagreeably [disə'gri:əbli], *adv.* désagréablement.

disagreement [disə'gri:mənt], *n.* différence,
f., désaccord; différend, *m.*; brouille, *f.*

disallow [disə'lau], *v.t.* désapprouver; refuser,
défendre.

disappear [disə'piə], *v.i.* disparaître.

disappearance [disə'piərəns], *n.* disparition,
f.

disappoint [disə'point], *v.t.* désappointer,
décevoir.

disappointing [disə'pointiŋ], *a.* décevant.

disappointment [disə'pɔintmənt], *n.* désappointement, *m.*; déception, *f.*; contretemps, *m.*
disapprobation [disæprə'beiʃən], **disapproval** [disə'pru:vəl], *n.* désapprobation, *f.*
disapprove [disə'pru:v], *v.t.* désapprouver.—*v.i. to disapprove of,* désapprouver.
disarm [dis'ɑ:m], *v.t.* désarmer.
disarmament [dis'ɑ:məmənt], *n.* désarmement, *m.*
disarrange [disə'reindʒ], *v.t.* déranger.
disarray [disə'rei], *v.i.* mettre en désarroi *ou* en désordre.—*n.* désarroi, désordre, *m.*
disaster [di'zɑ:stə], *n.* désastre, malheur, *m.*
disastrous [di'zɑ:strəs], *a.* désastreux.
disavow [disə'vau], *v.t.* désavouer.
disband [dis'bænd], *v.t.* licencier, congédier; disperser.—*v.i.* se disperser.
disbelief [disbi'li:f], *n.* incrédulité, *f.*
disbelieve [disbi'li:v], *v.t.* ne pas croire, refuser de croire.
disbeliever [disbi'li:və], *n.* incrédule, *m.*, *f.*
disc [DISK].
discard [dis'kɑ:d], *v.t.* mettre de côté; congédier; écarter; éliminer; (*Cards*) faire son écart.—['diskɑ:d], *n.* (*Cards*) écart, *m.*
discern [di'sə:n, di'zə:n], *v.t.* discerner, distinguer.
discerning [di'sə:niŋ, di'zə:niŋ], *a.* judicieux, éclairé, attentif.
discernment [di'sə:nmənt, di'zə:nmənt], *n.* discernement, jugement, *m.*
discharge [dis'tʃɑ:dʒ], *n.* déchargement, *m.*; décharge (*arme à feu etc.*); mise en liberté (*d'un prisonnier*), *f.*; accomplissement (*d'un devoir*), *m.*; réhabilitation (*d'un failli*); quittance (*récépissé*), *f.*; congé (*d'employé*); (*Mil.*) congé définitif; (*Med.*) écoulement, *m.*—*v.t.* décharger; congédier (*employé*); libérer (*de prison*); acquitter (*dette*); décharger (*arme à feu*); remplir (*devoir*); (*Mil., Navy*) congédier; (*Law*) quitter.—*v.i.* suppurer (*blessure etc.*).
disciple [di'saipl], *n.* disciple, *m.*
disciplinarian [disipli'nɛəriən], *a.* disciplinaire.—*n.* personne rigide pour la discipline, *f.*
disciplinary ['disiplinəri], *a.* disciplinaire.
discipline ['disiplin], *n.* discipline, *f.*—*v.t.* discipliner.
disclaim [dis'kleim], *v.t.* désavouer, renier, nier.
disclose [dis'klouz], *v.t.* découvrir, révéler.
disclosure [dis'klouʒə], *n.* révélation, découverte, *f.*
discolor [dis'kʌlə], *v.t.* décolorer.
discomfort [dis'kʌmfət], *n.* incommodité, *f.*, inconfort, malaise, *m.*; gêne, *f.*
discompose [diskəm'pouz], *v.t.* déranger, troubler.
discomposure [diskəm'pouʒə], *n.* trouble, désordre, *m.*, agitation, *f.*
disconcert [diskən'sə:t], *v.t.* déconcerter.
disconnect [diskə'nekt], *v.t.* désunir, séparer; (*Elec.*) débrancher; (*Mach.*) désembrayer.
disconnected [diskə'nektid], *a.* débrayé; déconnecté; (*fig.*) décousu.
disconsolate [dis'kənsəlit], *a.* inconsolable, désolé.
discontent [diskən'tent], *n.* mécontentement, *m.*

discontented [diskən'tentid], *a.* mécontent (*de*).
discontinue [diskən'tinju:], *v.t., v.i.* discontinuer; cesser de.
discord ['diskɔ:d], *n.* discorde; (*Mus.*) dissonance, *f.*
discordant [dis'kɔ:dənt], *a.* discordant; (*fig.*) en désaccord.
discount ['diskaunt], *n.* escompte; rabais, *m. at a discount,* au rabais, en baisse.—[dis'kaunt], *v.t.* escompter; (*fig.*) décompter, rabattre.—*v.i.* faire l'escompte.
discourage [dis'kʌridʒ], *v.t.* décourager, détourner.
discouragement [dis'kʌridʒmənt], *n.* découragement, *m.*
discouraging [dis'kʌridʒiŋ], *a.* décourageant.
discourse (1) ['diskɔ:s], *n.* discours, entretien; (*fig.*) langage, propos, *m.*—[dis'kɔ:s], *v.i.* discourir, s'entretenir, traiter (*de*).
discourteous [dis'kə:tiəs], *a.* impoli.
discourtesy [dis'kə:tisi], *n.* impolitesse, *f.*
discover [dis'kʌvə], *v.t.* découvrir; révéler, montrer.
discovery [dis'kʌvəri], *n.* découverte, *f.*
discredit [dis'kredit], *n.* discrédit, *m.*; honte, *f.*—*v.t.* ne pas croire; déshonorer.
discreditable [dis'kreditəbl], *a.* peu honorable; honteux.
discreet [dis'kri:t], *a.* discret, prudent, circonspect, sage.
discreetly [dis'kri:tli], *adv.* discrètement, sagement, prudemment.
discrepancy [dis'krepənsi], *n.* désaccord, *m.*
discretion [dis'kreʃən], *n.* discrétion, prudence, sagesse, *f.*; jugement, discernement, *m.*
discriminate [dis'krimineit], *v.t.* discriminer, distinguer.—*v.i.* faire des distinctions.
discriminating [dis'krimineitiŋ], *a.* discriminatoire, distinctif.
discrimination [diskrimi'neiʃən], *n.* discrimination, *f.*, discernement, *m.*
discuss [dis'kʌs], *v.t.* discuter, débattre.
discussion [dis'kʌʃən], *n.* discussion, *f.*, débat, *m.*
disdain [dis'dein], *n.* dédain, mépris, *m.*—*v.t.* dédaigner, mépriser.
disdainful [dis'deinful], *a.* dédaigneux, méprisant.
disease [di'zi:z], *n.* maladie, *f.*, mal; (*fig.*) vice, *m.*
diseased [di'zi:zd], *a.* malade; (*fig.*) dérangé.
disembark [disim'bɑ:k], *v.t., v.i.* débarquer.
disembarkation [disembɑ:'keiʃən], *n.* débarquement, *m.*
disembodied [disim'bɔdid], *a.* désincarné.
disembowel [disim'bauəl], *v.t.* éventrer.
disengage [disin'geidʒ], *v.t.* dégager; (*Tech.*) débrayer.—*v.i.* se dégager.
disengaged [disin'geidʒd], *a.* dégagé; libre.
disentangle [disin'tæŋgl], *v.t.* démêler, débrouiller.
disentanglement [disin'tæŋglmənt], *n.* débrouillement, *m.*
disestablish [disis'tæbliʃ], *v.t.* séparer (*l'Église de l'État*).
disestablishment [disis'tæbliʃmənt], *n.* séparation de l'Église et de l'État, *f.*
disfavor [dis'feivə], *n.* défaveur, *f.*
disfigure [dis'figə], *v.t.* défigurer, enlaidir.

disfigurement [dis'figəmənt], n. action de défigurer; difformité, f.
disfranchisement [dis'fræntʃizinənt], n. privation ou perte de privilèges électoraux, f.
disgorge [dis'gɔ:dʒ], v.t. dégorger, rendre, vomir.—v.i. rendre gorge.
disgrace [dis'greis], n. disgrâce, honte, f., déshonneur, m.—v.t. disgracier; déshonorer.
disgraceful [dis'greisful], a. honteux; déshonorant, ignoble.
disgracefully [dis'greisfuli], adv. honteusement.
disgruntled [dis'grʌntld], a. mécontent; de mauvaise humeur.
disguise [dis'gaiz], n. déguisement, travestissement; (fig.) masque, voile, m.—v.t. déguiser; (fig.) cacher, voiler.
disguised [dis'gaizd], a. déguisé.
disgust [dis'gʌst], n. dégoût, m., aversion, f.; ennui, m.—v.t. dégoûter (de); écœurer.
disgusting [dis'gʌstiŋ], a. dégoûtant.
dish [diʃ], n. (pl. dishes ['diʃiz]) plat (vaisselle; mets (aliment), m.; (pl.) vaisselle, f.—v.t. dresser, servir, apprêter; (colloq.) enfoncer.
dish-cloth ['diʃklɔθ], n. torchon, m.
dishearten [dis'hɑ:tn], v.t. décourager.
disheartening [dis'hɑ:tniŋ], a. décourageant.
dishevel [di'ʃevəl], v.t. ébouriffer.
dishevelled [di'ʃevəld], a. dépeigné, ébouriffé.
dishonest [dis'ɔnist], a. malhonnête.
dishonestly [dis'ɔnistli], adv. malhonnêtement.
dishonesty [dis'ɔnisti], n. improbité, malhonnêteté, f.
dishonor [dis'ɔnə], n. déshonneur, m.—v.t. déshonorer; avilir; (Comm.) dishonored check, chèque impayé, m.
dishonorable [dis'ɔnərəbl], a. sans honneur; honteux (chose).
dishonorably [dis'ɔnərəbli], adv. malhonnêtement.
disillusion [disi'lju:ʒən], v.t. désillusionner.—n., also disillusionment [disi'lju:ʒənmənt], désillusionnement, m.
disinclination [disinkli'neiʃən], n. éloignement, m.; aversion, f.
disinclined [disin'klaind], a. peu disposé.
disinfect [disin'fekt], v.t.
disinfectant [disin'fektənt], n. désinfectant, m.
disingenuous [disin'dʒenjuəs], a. sans franchise, de mauvaise foi, dissimulé.
disingenuously [disin'dʒenjuəsli], adv. de mauvaise foi.
disingenuousness [disin'dʒenjuəsnis], n. dissimulation, mauvaise foi, fausseté, f.
disinherit [disin'herit], v.t. déshériter.
disinheritance [disin'heritəns], n. déshéritement, m.
disintegrate [dis'intigreit], v.t. désagréger; désintégrer.—v.i. se désagréger, se désintégrer.
disintegration [disinti'greiʃən], n. désagrégation; désintégration, f.
disinter [disin'tə:], v.t. déterrer, exhumer.
disinterested [dis'intrəstid], a. désintéressé.
disjointed [dis'dʒɔintid], a. désarticulé, disloqué; (fig.) décousu, sans suite (style etc.).

disjointedly [dis'dʒɔintidli], adv. d'une manière décousue ou incohérente.
disk [disk], n. disque, m.; (Med.) slipped disk, hernie discale, f.
dislike [dis'laik], v.t. ne pas aimer; avoir du dégoût pour.—n. aversion, f.; dégoût, m.
dislocate ['disloikeit], v.t. disloquer, démettre; déboîter (os etc.).
dislodge [dis'lɔdʒ], v.t. déloger; déplacer.
disloyal [dis'lɔiəl], a. perfide, déloyal.
disloyalty [dis'lɔiəlti], n. défection (de), déloyauté, perfidie, f.
dismal ['dizməl], a. sombre, morne, triste.
dismally ['dizməli], adv. lugubrement, tristement.
dismantle [dis'mæntl], v.t. dévêtir; démonter (machine).
dismay [dis'mei], n. effroi, m., terreur épouvante, f.—v.t. effarer, épouvanter, consterner.
dismiss [dis'mis], v.t. renvoyer (de); congédier; quitter (sujet etc.); rejeter (appel etc.); chasser (pensées etc.).
dismissal [dis'misəl], n. renvoi, congé; (Law) acquittement, m.
dismount [dis'maunt], v.t. démonter.—v.i. descendre de cheval.
disobedience [diso'bi:diəns], n. désobéissance, f.
disobedient [diso'bi:diənt], a. désobéissant.
disobey [diso'bei], v.t. désobéir à.
disobliging [diso'blaidʒiŋ], a. désobligeant.
disorder [dis'ɔ:də], n. désordre, dérèglement, m.; maladie (Med.), f.—v.t. déranger, troubler.
disordered [dis'ɔ:dəd], a. en désordre, dérangé; malade.
disorderly [dis'ɔ:dəli], a. en désordre, déréglé; vicieux; tumultueux.
disorganization [disɔ:gəni'zeiʃən], n. désorganisation, f.
disorganize [dis'ɔ:gənaiz], v.t. désorganiser.
disown [dis'oun], v.t. désavouer, nier.
disparage [dis'pæridʒ], v.t. déprécier, ravaler, dénigrer.
disparagement [dis'pæridʒmənt], n. dénigrement, déshonneur, reproche, m.; honte, f., tort, m.
disparaging [dis'pæridʒiŋ], a. dénigrant, injurieux.
disparagingly [dis'pæridʒiŋli], adv. avec mépris.
dispassionate [dis'pæʃənit], a. calme; impartial.
dispatch, despatch [dis'pætʃ], v.t. dépêcher, expédier; achever.—n. dépêche, f., envoi, m.; promptitude, f.; mentioned in dispatches, cité à l'ordre du jour.
dispel [dis'pel], v.t. dissiper, chasser.
dispensary [dis'pensəri], n. dispensaire, m.; pharmacie, f.
dispensation [dispən'seiʃən], n. dispensation, f.; (fig.) bienfait, don, m.
dispense [dis'pens], v.t. distribuer, dispenser, administrer; (Pharm.) préparer (médecine); to dispense with, se passer de.
dispenser [dis'pensə], n. dispensateur, pharmacien, m.
dispersal [dis'pə:səl], n. dispersion, f.
disperse [dis'pə:s], v.t. disperser; dissiper.—v.i. se disperser.
dispirited [dis'piritid], a. découragé, abattu.

displace

displace [dis'pleis], *v.t.* déplacer; destituer (*d'un emploi*).

displacement [dis'pleismənt], *n.* déplacement, *m.*

display [dis'plei], *n.* exposition, parade, *f.*; (*fig.*) étalage, *m.*—*v.t.* montrer, exposer, étaler.

displease [dis'pli:z], *v.t.* déplaire à; fâcher.

displeased [dis'pli:zd], *a.* mécontent, offensé (*de*).

displeasing [dis'pli:zin], *a.* désagréable.

displeasure [dis'pleʒə], *n.* déplaisir; courroux, *m.*

disport [dis'pɔ:t], *v.t.* **to disport oneself,** s'amuser, se divertir.

disposal [dis'pouzəl], *n.* disposition; vente, cession (*sale*), *f.*

dispose [dis'pouz], *v.t.* disposer; porter (*à croire*); **to dispose of,** céder, vendre, se défaire de, se débarrasser de.

disposition [dispə'ziʃən], *n.* disposition, *f.*; caractère, naturel, *m.*

dispossess [dispə'zes], *v.t.* déposséder (*de*).

disproportionate [disprə'pɔ:ʃənit], *a.* disproportionné.

disprove [dis'pru:v], *v.t.* réfuter.

dispute [dis'pju:t], *n.* différend; conflit, *m.*; **beyond dispute,** sans contredit.—*v.t.* disputer, discuter.

disqualification [diskwɔlifi'keiʃən], *n.* incapacité, *f.*

disqualify [dis'kwɔlifai], *v.t.* rendre incapable (*de*).

disquiet [dis'kwaiət], *n.* inquiétude, *f.*

disregard [disri'gɑ:d], *n.* insouciance, indifférence, *f.*—*v.t.* négliger, faire peu de cas de.

disrepair [disri'pɛə], *n.* délabrement, *m.*

disreputable [dis'repjutəbl], *a.* de mauvaise réputation; compromettant, déshonorant (*chose*).

disrepute [disri'pju:t], *n.* discrédit, déshonneur, *m.*; mauvaise réputation, *f.*

disrespect [disris'pekt], *n.* manque de respect, irrespect, *m.*

disrespectful [disris'pektful], *a.* irrespectueux.

disrobe [dis'roub], *v.t.* déshabiller, dévêtir.—*v.i.* se déshabiller.

disrupt [dis'rʌpt], *v.t.* rompre.

dissatisfaction [dissætis'fækʃən], *n.* mécontentement, *m.*

dissatisfied [dis'sætisfaid], *a.* mécontent (*de*).

dissect [di'sekt], *v.t.* disséquer.

dissection [di'sekʃən], *n.* dissection, *f.*

dissemble [di'sembl], *v.t.* dissimuler, déguiser, cacher.—*v.i.* dissimuler, feindre.

disseminate [di'semineit], *v.t.* disséminer, répandre, propager.

dissension [di'senʃən], *n.* dissension, *f.*; **to sow dissension,** semer la zizanie.

dissent [di'sent], *n.* dissentiment, *m.*; (*Relig.*) dissidence, *f.*—*v.i.* différer (*de*); différer de sentiment (*avec*).

dissenter [di'sentə], *n.* dissident, *m.*, nonconformiste, *m.,f.*

disservice [dis'sə:vis], *n.* mauvais service, *m.*

dissever [di'sevə], *v.t.* séparer (*de*).

dissimilar [di'similə], *a.* dissemblable (*à*); différent (*de*).

dissimulate [di'simjuleit], *v.t.* dissimuler.

dissipate ['disipeit], *v.t.* dissiper.—*v.i.* se dissiper.

dissociate [di'souʃieit], *v.t.* désassocier, dissocier.

dissolute ['disəlu:t], *a.* dissolu.

dissolve [di'zɔlv], *v.t.* dissoudre; désunir; supprimer; résoudre (*doute etc.*).—*v.i.* se dissoudre.

dissonance ['disənəns], *n.* dissonance; discordance, *f.*

dissuade [di'sweid], *v.t.* dissuader (*de*).

distaff ['distɑ:f], *n.* quenouille, *f.*; **the distaff side,** le côté maternel.

distance ['distəns], *n.* distance, *f.*; éloignement, lointain, *m.*; (*fig.*) réserve, *f.*

distant ['distənt], *a.* éloigné, lointain; (*fig.*) réservé, froid.

distaste [dis'teist], *n.* dégoût, *m.*, aversion (*pour*), *f.*

distasteful [dis'teistful], *a.* désagréable, offensant.

distemper [dis'tempə], *n.* maladie (*de chien*); (*Paint.*) détrempe, *f.*—*v.t.* peindre en détrempe.

distend [dis'tend], *v.t.* étendre; dilater, enfler.—*v.i.* se détendre.

distil [dis'til], *v.t., v.i.* distiller.

distillation [disti'leiʃən], *n.* distillation, *f.*

distiller [dis'tilə], *n.* distillateur, *m.*

distillery [dis'tiləri], *n.* distillerie, *f.*

distinct [dis'tiŋkt], *a.* distinct; exprès, clair, net.

distinction [dis'tiŋkʃən], *n.* distinction; (*Sch.*) mention, *f.*

distinctive [dis'tiŋktiv], *a.* distinctif.

distinctly [dis'tiŋktli], *adv.* distinctement, clairement; (*fig.*) indéniablement.

distinguish [dis'tiŋgwiʃ], *v.t.* distinguer (*de*).

distinguished [dis'tiŋgwiʃt], *a.* distingué; **a distinguished man,** un homme éminent.

distort [dis'tɔ:t], *v.t.* tordre, contourner; décomposer (*les traits*); (*fig.*) torturer, défigurer.

distorted [dis'tɔ:tid], *a.* tordu, décomposé; (*fig.*) torturé.

distortion [dis'tɔ:ʃən], *n.* contorsion, déformation, *f.*

distract [dis'trækt], *v.t.* distraire, détourner (*de*); tourmenter.

distracted [dis'træktid], *a.* bouleversé, fou, hors de soi.

distracting [dis'træktin], *a.* atroce, déchirant, affolant.

distraction [dis'trækʃən], *n.* distraction, *f.*, trouble, *m.*, confusion; démence, folie, *f.*; **to drive to distraction,** mettre hors de soi.

distraught [dis'trɔ:t], *a.* affolé, éperdu.

distress [dis'tres], *n.* détresse, affliction, peine, *f.*, chagrin, *m.*; misère (*pauvreté*), *f.*—*v.t.* affliger, désoler.

distressed [dis'trest], *a.* affligé, malheureux; dans la misère (*pauvre*).

distressing [dis'tresin], *a.* affligeant, désolant, pénible.

distribute [dis'tribju:t], *v.t.* distribuer.

distribution [distri'bju:ʃən], *n.* distribution, répartition, *f.*

district ['distrikt], *n.* contrée, région, *f.*, arrondissement, district; quartier (*de ville*); (*Postal*) secteur, *m.*

distrust [dis'trʌst], *n.* méfiance, *f.*—*v.t.* se méfier de.

distrustful [dis'trʌstful], *a.* défiant; méfiant, soupçonneux.

disturb [dis'tə:b], *v.t.* troubler; déranger.

disturbance [dis'tə:bəns], *n.* trouble, *m.*; confusion, émeute, *f.*; bruit, tapage; désordre, *m.*

disuse [dis'ju:s], *n.* désuétude, *f.*

disused [dis'ju:zd], *a.* hors d'usage.

ditch [ditʃ], *n.* fossé, *m.*—*v.t.* (*pop.*) abandonner.—*v.i.* creuser un fossé.

dither ['diðə], *n. to be all of a dither*, être tout agité.—*v.i.* trembler, trembloter, hésiter.

ditto ['ditou], *adv.* idem; (*Comm.*) dito.

ditty ['diti], *n.* chanson, chansonnette, *f.*

diurnal [dai'ə:nəl], *a.* journalier, du jour; (*Med.*) quotidien.

divan [di'væn], *n.* divan, *m.*

dive [daiv], *v.i.* plonger.—*n.* plongeon, *m.*; (*pop.*) boîte de nuit, *f.*

diver ['daivə], *n.* plongeur; plongeon (*oiseau*), *m.*

diverge [dai'və:dʒ], *v.i.* diverger (*de*).

divergent [dai'və:dʒənt], *a.* divergent.

diverse [dai'və:s], *a.* divers, varié.

diversify [dai'və:sifai], *v.t.* diversifier; varier (*couleurs*).

diversion [dai'və:ʃən], *n.* divertissement, amusement, *m.*; diversion, distraction, *f.*

diversity [dai'və:siti], *n.* diversité, variété, *f.*

divert [dai'və:t], *v.t.* divertir, réjouir; distraire; dévier, détourner (*de*).

diverting [dai'və:tiŋ], *a.* divertissant, amusant.

divest [di'vest, dai'vest], *v.t.* dépouiller (*de*).

divide [di'vaid], *v.t.* diviser; partager.—*v.i.* se diviser.

dividend ['dividend], *n.* dividende, *m.*

dividers [di'vaidəz], *n. pl.* compas à pointes sèches, *m.*

divine [di'vain], *a.* divin; (*fam.*) adorable.—*n.* théologien, ecclésiastique, *m.*—*v.t.* deviner, pressentir.

diving ['daiviŋ], *n.* plongement, plongeon, *m.*

diving board ['daivinbo:d], *n.* plongeoir, *m.*

divinity [di'viniti], *n.* divinité; théologie, *f.*

divisible [di'vizibl], *a.* divisible.

division [di'viʒən], *n.* division, *f.*, partage, *m.*; scission, *f.*; vote, *m.*

divorce [di'vɔ:s], *n.* divorce, *m.*; séparation, *f.*—*v.t.* séparer, divorcer avec.—*v.i.* se séparer (*de*).

divorcee [divɔ:'si:], *n.* divorcé, *m.*, divorcée, *f.*

divulge [dai'vʌldʒ, di'vʌldʒ], *v.t.* divulguer, publier.

dizziness ['dizinis], *n.* vertige, étourdissement, *m.*

dizzy ['dizi], *a.* étourdi; vertigineux (*élévation*).

do [du:], *v.t. irr.* faire; rendre (*service, justice etc.*); finir (*achever*); (*Cook.*) cuire; (*colloq.*) duper; *done!* c'est entendu! *done to a turn*, cuit à point; *he is done for*, c'en est fait de lui; *it can't be done*, pas moyen; *overdone*, trop cuit (*viande*); *to be doing well*, faire de bonnes affaires, réussir; *to do over*, enduire (*de*), couvrir (*de*); *to do up*, empaqueter, emballer, remettre en état, remettre à neuf; *underdone*, saignant (*viande*); *well done!* bravo! *what is to be done?* que faire?—*v.i.* se porter, se conduire; aller, convenir (*faire l'affaire*); suffire (*répondre à un besoin*); finir (*terminer*); *how do you do?* comment allez-vous? *to do away with*, supprimer, se défaire de, faire disparaître; *to do by*, agir envers; *to do without*, se passer de.—*n.* duperie; soirée, réception, *f.*

docile ['dousail], *a.* docile.

docility [dou'siliti], *n.* docilité, *f.*

dock [dɔk], *v.t.* écourter; rogner (*comptes etc.*); (*Naut.*) mettre dans le bassin.—*v.i.* entrer aux docks.—*n.* bassin, dock, *m.*; (*Bot.*) patience, *f.*; (*Law*) banc des accusés, *m.*

docker ['dɔkə], *n.* déchargeur, docker, *m.*

docket ['dɔkit], *n.* étiquette, fiche, *f.*—*v.t.* étiqueter; enregistrer.

doctor ['dɔktə], *n.* docteur, médecin, *m.*—*v.t.* soigner, droguer; (*fig.*) altérer; frelater (*vin*).

doctrinaire [dɔktri'nɛə], *a.* doctrinaire.

doctrinal [dɔk'trainəl], *a.* doctrinal.

doctrine ['dɔktrin], *n.* doctrine, *f.*

document ['dɔkjumənt], *n.* document, titre, *m.*—*v.t.* munir de documents.

documentary [dɔkju'mentəri], *a.* justificatif, authentique.—*n.* (*Cine.*) documentaire, *m.*

documentation [dɔkjumen'teiʃən], *n.* documentation, *f.*

dodge [dɔdʒ], *v.t.* éviter; esquiver.—*v.i.* s'esquiver; (*fig.*) ruser, faire des détours.—*n.* tour, détour, *m.*; (*fig.*) ruse, ficelle, *f.*

dodger ['dɔdʒə], *n.* rusé, malin, finaud, *m.*

doe [dou], *n.* daine, *f.*

doer ['du:ə], *n.* faiseur; auteur, *m.*

doff [dɔf], *v.t.* tirer, enlever, ôter.

dog [dɔg], *n.* chien; (*facet.*) coquin, gaillard, *m.*; *lucky dog!* quel veinard!—*v.t.* suivre à la piste; harceler, épier.

dog days ['dɔgdeiz], *n.pl.* canicule, *f.*

dogged ['dɔgid], *a.* obstiné; acharné.

doggedly ['dɔgidli], *adv.* avec acharnement.

doggedness ['dɔgidnis], *n.* obstination, *f.* acharnement, *m.*

doggerel ['dɔgərəl], *n.* vers burlesques, vers de mirliton, *m.pl.*

doggie ['dɔgi], *n.* (*Childish*) tou-tou, *m.*

doggo ['dɔgou], *adv. to lie doggo*, se tenir coi.

dogma ['dɔgmə], *n.* dogme, *m.*

dogmatic [dɔg'mætik], *a.* dogmatique.

dogmatism ['dɔgmətizm], *n.* dogmatisme, *m.*

doily ['dɔili], *n.* serviette de dessert, *f.*, napperon, *m.*

doing ['du:iŋ], *n.* (*usu. in pl.*) faits, *m.pl.*; actions, *f.pl.*, exploits, *m.pl.*

dole [doul], *n.* aumône, *f.*, partage, *m.*; allocation de chômage, *f.*—*v.t. to dole out*, distribuer, répartir avec parcimonie.

doleful ['doulful], *a.* plaintif, lugubre.

doll [dɔl], *n.* poupée, *f.*—*v.r. to doll oneself up*, se pomponner.

dollar ['dɔlə], *n.* dollar, *m.*

dolphin ['dɔlfin], *n.* dauphin, *m.*

dolt [doult], *n.* lourdaud, sot, butor, *m.*

domain [do'mein], *n.* domaine, *m.*

dome [doum], *n.* dôme, *m.*

domestic [də'mestik], *a.* de famille; domestique (*animaux*).—*n.* domestique, *m.*, *f.*, servante, *f.*

domesticate [də'mestikeit], *v.t.* domestiquer, apprivoiser; (*fig.*) rendre casanier.

domesticated [də'mestikeited], _a._ casanier (_personnes_); apprivoisé (_animaux_).
domicile ['dɔmisail, 'dɔmisil], _n._ domicile, _m._
dominance ['dɔminəns], _n._ dominance, _f._
dominant ['dɔminənt], _a._ dominant.
dominate ['dɔmineit], _v.t._ dominer sur.—_v.i._ dominer; prévaloir, prédominer.
domination [dɔmi'neiʃən], _n._ domination, _f._
domineer [dɔmi'niə], _v.i._ dominer (_sur_).
domineering [dɔmi'niəriŋ], _a._ impérieux, autoritaire.
Dominican [do'minikən], _a._ dominicain.—_n._ Dominicain (_personne_), _m._; _**Dominican nun**,_ Dominicaine, _f._
dominie ['dɔmini], _n._ (_Sc._) maître d'école, _m._
dominion [do'minjən], _n._ domination, autorité, _f._; empire, _m._; (_pl._) états, _m.pl._
domino ['dɔminou], _n._ domino (_capuchon, jeu_), _m._
don [dɔn], _n._ don (_titre_); (_fig._) grand seigneur; (_Univ._) professeur d'université, _m._—_v.t._ mettre, endosser.
donate [do'neit], _v.t._ faire un don de.
donation [do'neiʃən], _n._ donation, _f._, don, _m._
donkey ['dɔŋki], _n._ âne, baudet, _m._
donor ['douna], _n._ donateur, _m._
doodle [du:dl], _v.i._ griffonner.—_n._ griffonnage, _m._
doom [du:m], _v.t._ condamner (_à_); (_fig._) destiner (_à_).—_n._ jugement; destin funeste, _m._; perte, ruine, _f._
doomsday ['du:mzdei], _n._ jour du jugement dernier, _m._
door [dɔ:], _n._ porte; portière (_d'une voiture_), _f._; _folding doors,_ porte à deux battants; _next door,_ à côté; _indoors,_ à la maison; _out of doors,_ dehors; _behind closed doors,_ à huis clos.
door-bell ['dɔ:bel], _n._ sonnette, _f._
door-keeper ['dɔ:ki:pə], _n._ concierge, portier (_d'une maison_); gardien (_des monuments publics_), _m._
doorman ['dɔ:mən], _n._ portier, _m._
door mat ['dɔ:mæt], _n._ paillasson, _m._
door-step ['dɔ:step], _n._ seuil de la porte, pas de (la) porte, _m._
door-way ['dɔ:wei], _n._ entrée, porte, _f._
dope [doup], _n._ drogue, _f._, narcotique, _m._—_v.t._ droguer.
dormant ['dɔ:mənt], _a._ dormant; assoupi.
dormer window ['dɔ:məwindou], _n._ lucarne, _f._
dormitory ['dɔ:mitri], _n._ dortoir, _m._
dormouse ['dɔ:maus], _n._ (_pl._ **dormice** ['dɔ:mais]) loir, _m._
Dorothy ['dɔrəθi], Dorothée, _f._
dose [dous], _n._ dose, _f._—_v.t._ médicamenter; doser.
dossier ['dɔsjei], _n._ dossier, _m._
dot [dɔt], _n._ point, _m._—_v.t._ marquer d'un point, marquer avec des points; (_Paint._) pointiller.
dotage ['doutidʒ], _n._ seconde enfance, _f._, radotage, _m._
dote [dout], _v.i._ radoter; raffoler (_sur_).
double [dʌbl], _a._ double, en deux; _bent double,_ voûté.—_n._ double, pendant, sosie; (_Mil._) pas de course, _m._—_adv._ double; au double; _to fold double,_ plier en deux.—_v.t._ doubler; serrer (_poings_).—_v.i._ doubler;

user de ruse; _to double back,_ revenir sur ses pas.
double bed ['dʌbl'bed], _n._ lit à deux places, _m._
double-breasted ['dʌblbrestid], _a._ croisé.
double-cross ['dʌbl'krɔs], _v.t._ duper, tromper.
double-dealing ['dʌbl'di:liŋ], _n._ duplicité, _f._
double decker ['dʌbl'dekə], _n._ autobus à impériale, _m._
double-room ['dʌbl'ru:m], _n._ chambre pour deux personnes, _f._
doubt [daut], _n._ doute, _m._; hésitation, _f._; _beyond a doubt,_ sans aucun doute.—_v.t._ douter de.—_v.i._ douter; soupçonner.
doubtful ['dautful], _a._ douteux, incertain.
doubtless ['dautlis], _adv._ sans doute.
dough [dou], _n._ pâte, _f._
dough-nut ['dounʌt], _n._ pet-de-nonne, _m._
doughty ['dauti], _a._ vaillant, preux.
dour ['duə], _a._ (_Sc._) austère et froid.
douse [daus], _v.t._ plonger dans l'eau; éteindre.
dove [dʌv], _n._ colombe, _f._; pigeon, _m._
dove-cot(e) ['dʌvkɔt, 'dʌvkout], _n._ colombier, _m._
Dover ['douvə]. Douvres, _m._; _the Straits of Dover,_ le Pas-de-Calais, _m._
dowager ['dauədʒə], _n._ douairière, _f._
dowdy ['daudi], _a.f._ gauche et mal mise, mal fagotée.
dowel ['dauəl], _n._ (_Carp._) goujon, _m._
down (I) [daun], _n._ duvet (_poil follet_), _m._; dune (_colline_), _f._
down (2) [daun], _adv._ en bas; à bas; bas, à terre; tombé, apaisé (_vent_); couché (_soleil_); à plat (_pneu_); en baisse (_prix_); (_fig._) sur le déclin; _to go down,_ descendre.—_prep._ en bas de; vers le bas de.
downcast ['daunka:st], _a._ abattu.
downfall ['daunfɔ:l], _n._ chute, _f._; (_fig._) débâcle, _f._
downhill ['daunhil], _a._ incliné; en pente.—[daun'hil], _adv._ en descendant.
downpour ['daunpɔ:], _n._ averse, _f._
downright ['daunrait], _a._ direct; franc.—_adv._ net, tout à fait.
downstairs [daun'steəz], _adv._ en bas (de l'escalier).
downtrodden ['dauntrɔdn], _a._ opprimé.
downward ['daunwəd], _a._ de haut en bas, qui descend, descendant.—_adv._ (_also_ **downwards** ['daunwədz]) en bas, en descendant; en aval.
downy ['dauni] _a._ de duvet, duveteux.
dowry ['dauri], _n._ dot, _f._
doze [douz], _v.i._ s'assoupir, sommeiller, être assoupi.—_n._ petit somme, _m._
dozen [dʌzn], _n._ douzaine, _f._
drab [dræb], _a._ gris sale, brun terne; (_fig._) terne, décoloré.—_n._ (_fig._) traînée (_femme_), _f._
draft [dra:ft], _v.t._ dessiner, rédiger; (_Mil._) detacher.—_n._ dessin (_esquisse_); brouillon (_projet_), _m._; (_Comm._) traite, _f._; (_Mil._) détachement, _m._
draft [dra:ft], _n._ tirage; trait; courant d'air; coup (_boisson_); dessin (_esquisse_); coup de filet (_de pêcheur_); tirant (_d'un navire_), _m._; (_Med._) potion, _f._; (_pl._) jeu de dames, _m._
draft-board ['dra:ftbɔ:d], _n._ damier, _m._
draft-horse ['dra:fthɔ:s], _n._ cheval de trait, _m._
draftsman ['dra:ftsmən], _n._ (_pl._ **-men** [men]) dessinateur, _m._
drafty ['dra:fti], _a._ plein de courants

d'air.

drag [dræg], *v.t.* traîner, tirer; (*Naut.*) draguer; *to drag away from*, entraîner, arracher de; *to drag on*, entraîner; (*fig.*) traîner en longueur; *to drag out*, faire sortir de force.—*v.i.* se traîner; traîner; chasser (*ancre*).

draggle [drægl], *v.t.* traîner dans la boue.

drag-net ['drægnet], *n.* seine, *f.*, chalut, *m.*

dragoman ['drægoman], *n.* drogman, *m.*

dragon ['drægən], *n.* dragon, *m.*

dragon-fly ['drægənflai], *n.* demoiselle, libellule, *f.*, agrion, *m.*

dragoon [drə'gu:n], *n.* (*Mil.*) dragon, *m.*—*v.t.* (*fig.*) forcer par des mesures violentes.

drain [drein], *v.t.* faire écouler; dessécher; drainer; (*fig.*) épuiser; vider (*verre etc.*).—*v.i.* s'écouler.—*n.* tranchée, *f.*, égout, *m.*

drainage ['dreinidʒ], **draining** ['dreiniŋ] *n.* écoulement; (*Agric.*) drainage, *m.*

draining-board ['dreiniŋbo:d], *n.* égouttoir, *m.*

drake [dreik], *n.* canard, *m.*

dram [dræm], *n.* (*Pharm.*) drachme, *f.*

drama ['dra:mə], *n.* drame; (*fig.*) théâtre, *m.*

dramatic [drə'mætik], **dramatical** [drə'mætikəl], *a.* dramatique.

dramatist ['dra:mətist, 'dræmətist], *n.* auteur dramatique, *m.*, dramaturge, *m.*, *f.*

dramatize ['dra:mətaiz, 'dræmətaiz], *v.t.* dramatiser.

drape [dreip], *v.t.* draper, tendre (*de*).—*n.* (*Am.*) rideau, *m.*

draper ['dreipə], *n.* drapier; marchand de drap, *m.*

drapery ['dreipəri], *n.* draperie, *f.*

drastic ['dræstik], *a.* énergique, radical, brutal.

draw [dro:], *v.t. irr.* tirer; traîner; dessiner (*tableau etc.*); toucher (*rations, appointements etc.*); arracher (*dent*); puiser (*eau etc.*); (*fig.*) attirer (*à* ou *sur*); *to draw lots for*, tirer au sort.—*v.i.* tirer; dégainer; dessiner (*au crayon*); (*Spt.*) faire partie nulle *ou* match nul.—*n.* tirage (*au sort*), *m.*; attraction; (*Spt.*) partie nulle, *f.*

drawback ['dro:bæk], *n.* mécompte, désavantage, inconvénient, *m.*

drawbridge ['dro:bridʒ], *n.* pont-levis, *m.*

drawer ['dro:ə], *n.* tireur (*d'un chèque*); puiseur (*d'eau*); tiroir (*meuble*); (*pl.*) caleçon (*vêtement*), *m.*; *chest of drawers*, commode, *f.*

drawing ['dro:iŋ], *n.* tirage; dessin (*croquis*), *m.*

drawing board ['dro:iŋbo:d], *n.* planche à dessin, *f.*

drawing-pin ['dro:iŋpin], *n.* punaise (*pour le dessin*), *f.*

drawing room ['dro:iŋru:m], *n.* salon, *m.*; (*Court*) réception, *f.*

drawl [dro:l], *v.i.* parler d'une voix traînante. *n.* voix traînante *f.*

drawling ['dro:liŋ], *a.* traînant.

drawn [dro:n], *a.* indécis, égal (*bataille etc.*); tiré, nu (*épée*); *drawn game*, partie nulle, *f.*

dray [drei], *n.* camion, haquet, *m.*

dread [dred], *a.* redoutable, terrible; auguste.—*n.* terreur, crainte, *f.*—*v.t.* craindre, redouter.

dreadful ['dredful], *a.* affreux, terrible, épouvantable.

dreadfully ['dredfuli], *adv.* terriblement, affreusement.

dream [dri:m], *n.* songe, rêve, *m.*; *daydream*, rêverie, *f.*—*v.t.i. irr.* rêver.—*v.i.* rêver; (*fig.*) s'imaginer.

dreamer ['dri:mə], *n.* rêveur, *m.*; (*fig.*) visionnaire, *m.*, *f.*

dreamy ['dri:mi], *a.* rêveur; chimérique, visionnaire.

drear [driə], **dreary** ['driəri], *a.* triste, morne, lugubre.

drearily ['driərili], *adv.* tristement, lugubrement.

dreariness ['driərinis], *n.* tristesse, *f.*, aspect morne, *m.*

dredge (1) [dredʒ], *n.* drague, *f.*—*v.t.*, *v.i.* draguer.

dredge (2) [dredʒ], *v.t.* saupoudrer (*de farine etc.*).

dredger (1) ['dredʒə], *n.* dragueur (*bateau*), *m.*

dredger (2) ['dredʒə], *n.* saupoudreuse, *f.*

dregs [dregz], *n.pl.* lie, *f.*

drench [drentʃ], *v.t.* tremper, mouiller (*de*); noyer (*de*).

dress [dres], *v.t.* habiller, vêtir, parer, orner; panser (*blessure etc.*); apprêter (*aliments etc.*); (*Mil.*) aligner; (*Navy*) pavoiser.—*v.i.* s'habiller; faire sa toilette; (*Mil.*) s'aligner. —*n.* habillement, *m.*; robe (*de femme*); mise, toilette; (*Mil.*) tenue, *f.*; *dress rehearsal*, répétition générale, *f.*; *evening dress*, tenue de soirée, *f.*

dress circle ['dres'sə:kl], *n.* (*Theat.*) fauteuils de balcon, *m.pl.*

dresser ['dresə], *n.* habilleur (*personne*); dressoir (*de cuisine*), *m.*

dressing ['dresiŋ], *n.* toilette, *f.*, habillement; pansement (*de blessure etc.*); (*Cook.*) assaisonnement, *m.*; (*Agric.*) fumure, *f.*, engrais, *m.*

dressing case ['dresiŋkeis], *n.* mallette de toilette, *f.*

dressing gown ['dresiŋgaun], *n.* robe de chambre, *f.*, peignoir, *m.*

dressing room ['dresiŋru:m], *n.* cabinet de toilette, *m.*

dressing table ['dresiŋteibl], *n.* coiffeuse, table de toilette, *f.*

dressmaker ['dresmeikə], *n.* couturière, *f.*

dressmaking ['dresmeikiŋ], *n.* confections pour dames, *f.pl.*, couture, *f.*

dressy ['dresi], *a.* élégant, chic, coquet (*personne*); habillé (*robe*).

dribble [dribl], *v.t.* laisser dégoutter, laisser tomber goutte à goutte; (*Ftb.*) dribbler.—*v.i.* tomber goutte à goutte, dégoutter; baver; (*Ftb.*) dribbler.

drier ['draiə], *comp. a.* [DRY].—*n.* [DRYER].

drift [drift], *n.* monceau; tourbillon, *m.*, rafale, *f.*; objet flottant, *m.*; (*fig.*) tendance; (*Naut.*) dérive, *f.*—*v.t.* chasser, pousser; amonceler.—*v.i.* dériver, aller à la dérive, flotter; s'amonceler, s'amasser.

drifter ['driftə], *n.* (*Naut.*) chalutier, *m.*

drill [dril], *n.* foret, *m.*, mèche, *f.*; (*Agric.*) sillon, (*Mil.*) exercice, *m.*, manœuvre, *f.*—*v.t.* forer, percer; (*Mil.*) exercer.—*v.i.* (*Mil.*) faire l'exercice.

drilling ['drilin], n. forage; (Dent.) fraisage; (Mil.) exercice, m.

drink [drink], n. boisson; (fig.) ivresse (drunkenness), f.—v.t., v.i. irr. boire.

drinker ['drinkə], n. buveur; ivrogne, m.

drinking ['drinkin], a. potable; à boire.—n: boire, m.; ivrognerie, f.; alcoolisme, m.

drinking fountain ['drinkinfauntin], n. fontaine publique, f.

drip [drip], v.t. faire dégoutter.—v.i. dégoutter, tomber goutte à goutte.—n. goutte, f.; égout, m.

dripping ['dripin], n. graisse de rôti, f.; (pl.) gouttes, f.pl.

drive [draiv], v.t. irr. pousser; chasser; enfoncer (clou etc.); mener, conduire (voiture, cheval etc.); forcer, réduire (à); to drive away, chasser, éloigner; to drive back, repousser; to drive in, faire entrer, enfoncer; to drive out, faire sortir, chasser.—v.i. conduire; aller en voiture; to drive at, tendre à, vouloir en venir à; to drive up, arriver (en voiture).—n. promenade ou course en voiture; grande avenue ou allée, f.

drivel [drivl], n. bave, f.—v.i. baver; (fig.) radoter.

driver ['draivə], n. cocher (d'un carrosse); voiturier (d'une charrette); (Rail.) mécanicien; (Motor. etc.) chauffeur, conducteur, m.

driving ['draivin], n. action de conduire, f.; percement (d'un tunnel), m.

driving license ['draivinlaisəns], n. permis de conduire, m.

driving test ['draivintest], n. examen pour permis de conduire, m.

drizzle [drizl], v.i. bruiner.—n. bruine, pluie fine, f.

droll [droul], a. plaisant, drôle.

drollery ['drouləri], n. plaisanterie, drôlerie, farce, f.

dromedary ['drɒmədəri, 'drɒmədəri], n. dromadaire, m.

drone [droun], n. (Ent., Mus.) faux-bourdon; (fig.) frelon; fainéant (personne); bourdonnement (son), m.—v.i. bourdonner.

droning ['drounin], a. bourdonnant.—n. bourdonnement, m.

droop [dru:p], v.t. laisser tomber, laisser pendre.—v.i. languir, se pencher, tomber, pencher; (fig.) s'affaiblir.

drooping ['dru:pin], a. languissant, abattu, penché.—r. abattement, m., langueur, f.

drop [drɒp], n. goutte; chute (descente), f.; pendant (bijou), m.—v.t. laisser tomber; jeter (l'ancre); sauter (une maille); déposer (quelqu'un); abandonner (lâcher).—v.i. tomber goutte à goutte; dégoutter (de); échapper (glisser); to drop behind, se laisser dépasser, rester en arrière; to drop in, entrer en passant; to drop out, se retirer.

dropsy ['drɒpsi], n. hydropisie, f.

dross [drɒs], n. scorie, crasse, f.; (fig.) rebut, m.

drought [draut], n. sécheresse, f.

drove (1) [drouv], n. troupeau (en marche), m.; (fig.) foule (en marche), f.

drove (2) [drouv], past [DRIVE].

drover ['drouvə], n. conducteur de bestiaux, bouvier, m.

drown [draun], v.t. noyer; (fig.) submerger; étouffer (bruit).—v.i. se noyer.

drowsily ['drauzili], adv. comme endormi; (fig.) avec indolence.

drowsiness ['drauzinis], n. assoupissement, m.

drowsy ['drauzi], a. assoupi; somnolent; lourd, stupide.

drub [drʌb], v.t. rosser, battre.

drubbing ['drʌbin], n. volée (de coups), f.

drudge [drʌdʒ], n. homme (ou femme) de peine, souffre-douleur, m., f.—v.i. travailler sans relâche, peiner.

drudgery ['drʌdʒəri], n. travail pénible, m.; corvée, vile besogne, f.

drug [drʌg], n. drogue, f.—v.t. droguer; (fig.) empoisonner.

drug addict ['drʌgædikt], n. toxicomane, m., f.

druggist ['drʌgist], n. (Am.) pharmacien, m.

drug store ['drʌgstɔ:], n. (Am.) pharmacie, f.

druid ['dru:id], n. druide, m.

drum [drʌm], n. tambour, m.; caisse, f.; tympan (de l'oreille), m.—v.t. (Mil.) to drum out, dégrader.—v.i. battre du tambour (sur); (fig.) tinter.

drum major ['drʌmmeidʒə], n. tambour-major, m.

drummer ['drʌmə], n. tambour (homme), m.

drum-stick ['drʌmstik], n. baguette de tambour, f.

drunk [drʌnk], a. ivre, gris, soûl.

drunkard ['drʌnkəd], n. ivrogne, m.

drunkenness ['drʌnkənnis], n. ivresse; ivrognerie, f.

dry [drai], a. sec, desséché; aride; altéré; (fig.) caustique; ennuyeux.—v.t. sécher; dessécher.—v.i. sécher; to dry up, tarir; se taire.

dry-dock ['draidɒk], n. bassin de radoub, m., cale sèche, f.

dryer, drier ['draiə], n. (Ind. etc.) séchoir; (Paint.) siccatif, dessiccatif, m.

dryness ['drainis], n. sécheresse, aridité, f.

dry-shod ['draiʃɒd], a. and adv. à pied sec.

dual ['dju:əl], a. double; dual carriage-way, route à double circulation, f.—n. duel, m.

dub [dʌb], v.t. armer chevalier; (colloq.) qualifier, baptiser; (Cine.) doubler (film).

dubiety [dju'baiəti], n. dubiousness ['dju:biəsnis], n. doute, m., incertitude, f.

dubious ['dju:biəs], a. douteux, incertain.

dubiously ['dju:biəsli], adv. douteusement.

duchess ['dʌtʃis], n. duchesse, f.

duchy ['dʌtʃi], n. duché, m.

duck (1) [dʌk], n. cane, f.; canard; (colloq.) chou (mot tendre), m.

duck (2) [dʌk], n. (Box.) esquive, f.—v.t. plonger dans l'eau.—v.i. plonger; baisser la tête subitement; (Box.) esquiver.

duck (3) [dʌk], n. toile à voile, f.; (pl.) pantalon blanc, m.

ducking ['dʌkin], n. plongeon; (Naut.) baptême de la ligne, m.

duckling ['dʌklin], n. caneton, m.

duck-weed ['dʌkwi:d], n. lentille d'eau, f.

duct [dʌkt], n. conduit; (Anat.) canal, m.

dudgeon ['dʌdʒən], n. colère, f.; in high dudgeon, fort en colère.

due [dju:], *a.* dû; convenable, propre, juste; (*Comm.*) échu; (*fig.*) requis, voulu; *to fall due*, échoir.—*n.* dû; (*pl.*) droit, impôt, *m.*, redevance, *f.*—*adv.* droit, directement.
duel ['dju:əl], *n.* duel, *m.*, (*fig.*) lutte, *f.*
duellist ['dju:əlist], *n.* duelliste, *m.*
duenna [dju:'enə], *n.* duègne, *f.*
duet [dju:'et], *n.* duo, *m.*
duke [dju:k], *n.* duc, *m.*
dukedom ['dju:kdəm], *n.* duché, *m.*; dignité de duc, *f.*
dull [dʌl], *a.* lourd, hébété, stupide (*personne*); lourd, gris, sombre (*temps*); sourd (*son*); triste (*morne*); émoussé (*moins aigu*); terne (*couleur*); ennuyeux.—*v.t.* hébéter; émousser (*rendre moins aigu*); ternir (*ôter l'éclat de*); engourdir (*de froid*).—*v.i.* s'hébéter; s'engourdir; s'émousser.
dullard ['dʌləd], *n.* âne, lourdaud (*personne*), *m.*
dullness ['dʌlnis], *n.* lenteur, *f.*; assoupissement, ennui; manque d'éclat, *m.*, faiblesse (*de son*), *f.*
dully ['dʌli], *adv.* lourdement, tristement.
duly ['dju:li], *adv.* dûment, justement.
dumb [dʌm], *a.* muet, réduit au silence; (*Am.*) stupide.
dumb-bells ['dʌmbelz], *n.pl.* haltères, *m.pl.*
dumbfound [dʌm'faund], *v.t.* confondre, abasourdir, interdire.
dumbly ['dʌmli], *adv.* en silence.
dumbness ['dʌmnis], *n.* mutisme; (*fig.*) silence, *m.*
dumb show ['dʌmʃou], *n.* pantomime, *f.*, jeu muet, *m.*
dummy ['dʌmi], *n.* muet, *m.*, muette, *f.*; mannequin, objet imité; (*fig.*) homme de paille; (*Cards*) mort, *m.*
dump [dʌmp], *v.t.* déposer, décharger, déverser.—*n.* tas; dépotoir, *m.*
dumpling ['dʌmpliŋ], *n.* pâte cuite, *f.*
dumpy ['dʌmpi], *a.* trapu, gros et court.
dun (1) [dʌn], *a.* brun foncé; bai (*cheval*).
dun (2) [dʌn], *n.* créancier importun, *m.*—*v.t.* importuner.
dunce [dʌns], *n.* ignorant, âne, sot, *m.*
dune [dju:n], *n.* dune, *f.*
dung [dʌŋ], *n.* crotte, *f.*; crottin; (*Agric.*) fumier, *m.*
dung cart ['dʌŋkɑ:t], *n.* tombereau à fumier, *m.*
dungeon ['dʌndʒən], *n.* cachot, *m.*
dunghill ['dʌŋhil], *n.* fumier, *m.*
duodenal [dju:o'di:nl], *a.* (*Anat.*) duodénal; *duodenal ulcer*, ulcère au duodénum, *m.*
dupe [dju:p], *n.* dupe, *f.*—*v.t.* duper, tromper.
duplicate ['dju:plikit], *a.* double.—*n.* double, duplicata, *m.*—['dju:plikeit], *v.t.* doubler; copier.
duplicity [dju:'plisiti], *n.* duplicité, mauvaise foi, *f.*
durability [djuərə'biliti], **durableness** ['djuərəblnis], *n.* solidité, durabilité, *f.*
durable ['djuərəbl], *a.* durable.
duration [djuə'reiʃən], *n.* durée, *f.*
during ['djuəriŋ], *prep.* pendant, durant.
dusk [dʌsk], *n.* crépuscule, *m.*; obscurité, *f.*
duskiness ['dʌskinis], *n.* obscurité, teinte sombre, *f.*
dusky ['dʌski], *a.* foncé, sombre; noiraud, noirâtre.
dust [dʌst], *n.* poussière; poudre, *f.*; (*fig.*)

cendres (des morts), *f.pl.*; *sawdust*, sciure, *f.*—*v.t.* épousseter.
dust-bin ['dʌstbin], *n.* boîte à ordures, poubelle, *f.*
dust-cart ['dʌstkɑ:t], *n.* tombereau, *m.*
duster ['dʌstə], *n.* torchon, chiffon, *m.*
dustman ['dʌstmən], *n.* (*pl.* **-men** [men]) boueur, *m.*
dusty ['dʌsti], *a.* poussiéreux, couvert de poussière; poudreux.
Dutch [dʌtʃ], *a.* hollandais, de Hollande.—*n.* hollandais (*langue*), *m.*; *the Dutch*, les Hollandais, *m.pl.*
Dutchman ['dʌtʃmən], *n.* (*pl.* **-men** [men]) Hollandais, *m.*
Dutchwoman ['dʌtʃwumən], *n.* (*pl.* **-women** [wimin]) Hollandaise, *f.*
duteous ['dju:tiəs], **dutiful** ['dju:tiful], *a.* obéissant, soumis.
dutifully ['dju:tifuli], *adv.* avec soumission, respectueusement.
duty ['dju:ti], *n.* (*pl.* **duties** ['dju:tiz]) devoir; (*Customs*) droit; (*Mil. etc.*) service, *m.*; *on duty*, de service, de garde, en faction.
dwarf [dwɔ:f], *a.* and *n.* nain, *m.*, naine, *f.*—*v.t.* rapetisser; (*Hort.*) rabougrir.
dwell [dwel], *v.i. irr.* demeurer, habiter; rester; *to dwell on*, insister sur.
dweller ['dwelə], *n.* habitant, *m.*, habitante, *f.*
dwelling ['dweliŋ], *n.* habitation, demeure, *f.*
dwindle ['dwindl], *v.i.* diminuer, s'amoindrir; dépérir.
dye [dai], *v.t.* teindre.—*v.i.* teindre, se teindre.—*n.* teinture, teinte; couleur, nuance, *f.*; (*fig.*) caractère, *m.*
dyeing ['daiiŋ], *n.* teinture, *f.*
dyer ['daiə], *n.* teinturier, *m.*, teinturière, *f.*
dye-works ['daiwə:ks], *n.pl.* teinturerie, *f.*
dying ['daiiŋ], *a.* mourant, moribond; suprême, dernier.
dyke [DIKE].
dynamic [dai'næmik], **dynamical** [dai'næmikəl], *a.* dynamique.
dynamics [dai'næmiks], *n.pl.* dynamique, *f.*
dynamite ['dainəmait], *n.* dynamite, *f.*—*v.t.* dynamiter.
dynamo ['dainəmou], *n.* dynamo, *f.*
dynasty ['dinəsti], *n.* dynastie, *f.*
dysentery ['disəntri], *n.* dysenterie, *f.*
dyspepsia [dis'pepsiə], *n.* dyspepsie, *f.*
dyspeptic [dis'peptik], *a.* dyspepsique, dyspeptique.

E

E, e [i:]. cinquième lettre de l'alphabet; (*Mus.*) mi, *m.*
e-, see also **ae-**.
each [i:tʃ], *a.* chaque.—*pron.* chacun, *m.*, chacune, *f.*; *each other*, l'un l'autre, les uns les autres.
eager ['i:gə], *a.* vif, ardent (*à*); impatient (*de*); désireux; empressé (*à* ou *de*).
eagerly ['i:gəli], *adv.* ardemment; impatiemment.

411

eagerness ['i:gənis], *n.* ardeur, *f.*; empressement, *m.*

eagle [i:gl], *n.* aigle, *m.*, *f.*

eaglet ['i:glit], *n.* aiglon, *m.*

ear [iə], *n.* oreille, *f.*; épi (*de blé*), *m.*—*v.i.* monter en épi.

ear-ache ['iəreik], *n.* mal d'oreille, *m.*

ear-drum ['iədrʌm], *n.* tympan, tambour de l'oreille, *m.*

earl [ə:l], *n.* comte, *m.*

earldom ['ə:ldəm], *n.* comté, *m.*

earliness ['ə:linis], *n.* heure peu avancée; précocité (*de fruits*), *f.*

early ['ə:li], *a.* matinal; matineux (*personne*); ancien; précoce, hâtif (*fruit etc.*).—*adv.* de bonne heure, de bon matin, de grand matin; tôt.

ear-mark ['iəma:k], *v.t.* (*fig.*) réserver, mettre de côté.

earn [ə:n], *v.t.* gagner, acquérir; (*fig.*) mériter.

earnest (1) ['ə:nist], *a.* sérieux, empressé, sincère.

earnest (2) ['ə:nist], *n.* gage, *m.*, garantie, *f.*, arrhes, *f.pl.*

earnestly ['ə:nistli], *adv.* sérieusement, avec empressement.

earnestness ['ə:nistnis], *n.* ardeur, *f.*, empressement; sérieux, *m.*

earnings ['ə:niŋz], *n.pl.* gain, *m.*; gages, *m.pl.*

ear-phones ['iəfounz], *n.pl.* casque, *m.*

ear-ring ['iəriŋ], *n.* boucle d'oreille, *f.*

earth [ə:θ], *n.* terre, *f.*; terrier (*de renard etc.*), *m.*—*v.t.* enterrer, enfouir, couvrir de terre; (*Elec.*) joindre à la terre.

earthen ['ə:θən], *a.* de terre.

earthenware ['ə:θənwɛə], *n.* poterie, vaisselle de terre, faïence, *f.*

earthly ['ə:θli], *a.* terrestre.

earthquake ['ə:θkweik], *n.* tremblement de terre, *m.*

earthy ['ə:θi], *a.* de terre, terreux.

earwig ['iəwig], *n.* perce-oreille, *m.*

ease [i:z], *n.* aisance, aise; facilité; tranquillité, *f.*, repos; (*fig.*) abandon; soulagement (*de douleur*), *m.*—*v.t.* soulager, mettre à l'aise; (*fig.*) tranquilliser, calmer.

easel ['i:zl], *n.* chevalet, *m.*

easily ['i:zili], *adv.* facilement, sans peine; aisément.

east [i:st], *a.* d'est, d'orient; oriental.—*n.* est, orient; levant, *m.*

Easter ['i:stə], Pâques, *m.*

easterly ['i:stəli], *a.* d'est.—*adv.* vers l'orient, vers l'est.

eastern ['i:stən], *a.* d'est, d'orient, oriental.

eastward ['i:stwəd], *adv.* vers l'est, vers l'orient.

easy ['i:zi], *a.* facile; aisé; confortable; tranquille; naturel (*style*); à l'aise; *easy chair*, fauteuil, *m.*—*adv.* doucement.

easy-going ['i:zigouiŋ], *a.* accommodant, peu exigeant.

eat [i:t], *v.t.*, *v.i. irr.* manger; ronger (*corroder*); *to eat away*, consumer, ronger; *to eat up*, manger, achever de manger.

eatable ['i:təbl], *a.* mangeable, comestible.— *n.* comestible, *m.*; (*pl.*) vivres, *m.pl.*

eating ['i:tiŋ], *n.* action de manger, *f.*; manger, *m.*

eaves [i:vz], *n.* avance du toit, *f.*; gouttières, *f.pl.*

eavesdrop ['i:vzdrɔp], *v.i.* écouter aux portes.

eavesdropper ['i:vzdrɔpə], *n.* écouteur aux portes, *m.*

ebb [eb], *v.i.* baisser; décliner, refluer, se retirer.—*n.* reflux; (*fig.*) déclin, *m.*, décadence, *f.*

ebb tide ['ebtaid], *n.* jusant, *m.*

ebony ['ebəni], *a.* d'ébène.—*n.* ébène, *f.*, bois d'ébène, *m.*

ebony tree ['ebənitri:], *n.* ébénier, *m.*

ebullience [i'bʌliəns], **ebulliency** [i'bʌliənsi], *n.* ébullition, effervescence, *f.*

ebullient [i'bʌliənt], *a.* en ébullition, bouillonnant; (*fig.*) exubérant, pétulant.

ebullition [ebə'liʃən], *n.* ébullition; (*fig.*) effervescence, *f.*, transport, *m.*

eccentric [ek'sentrik], *a.* excentrique; désaxé; (*fig.*) singulier.

eccentricity [eksen'trisiti], *n.* excentricité, *f.*

ecclesiastic [ikli:zi'æstik], *a.* and *n.* ecclésiastique, *m.*

echo ['ekou], *n.* écho, *m.*—*v.t.* répercuter; (*fig.*) répéter.—*v.i.* faire écho; retentir, résonner (*de*).

eclipse [i'klips], *n.* éclipse, *f.*—*v.t.* éclipser; (*fig.*) surpasser.—*v.i.* s'éclipser.

economic [i:kə'nɔmik], **economical** [i:kə'nɔmikəl], *a.* économique (*chose*); économe, ménager (*personne*).

economically [i:kə'nɔmikəli], *adv.* économiquement.

economics [i:kə'nɔmiks], *n.pl.* économie politique, *f.*

economist [i'kɔnəmist], *n.* économiste, *m.*, *f.*

economize [i'kɔnəmaiz], *v.t.* économiser.— *v.i.* user d'économie.

economy [i'kɔnəmi], *n.* économie, *f.*; système, *m.*; *planned economy*, économie planifiée.

ecstasy ['ekstəsi], *n.* extase, *f.*, transport, *m.*

ecstatic [eks'tætik], **ecstatical** [eks'tætikəl], *a.* extatique, d'extase.

Ecuador [ekwə'dɔ:], (la République de) l'Équateur, *f.*

Ecuadorean [ekwə'dɔ:riən], *a.* équatorien.— *n.* Équatorien (*personne*), *m.*

eczema ['eksimə], *n.* eczéma, *m.*

eddy ['edi], *n.* remous (*eau*); tourbillon (*vent*), *m.*—*v.i.* tourbillonner.

Eden ['i:dən], Éden, *m.*

edge [edʒ], *n.* bord (*marge*); fil, tranchant (*de couteau etc.*), *m.*; lisière (*d'une forêt etc.*), *f.*; cordon (*d'une pièce de monnaie*), *m.*; tranche (*d'un livre*), *f.*—*v.t.* affiler, aiguiser; border (*entourer*).—*v.i. to edge away*, s'éloigner graduellement.

edged [edʒd], *a.* tranchant; bordé.

edgeways ['edʒweiz], **edgewise** ['edʒwaiz], *adv.* de côté, de champ.

edging ['edʒiŋ], *n.* bordure, *f.*

edible ['edibl], *a.* comestible, bon à manger.

edict ['i:dikt], *n.* édit, *m.*

edifice ['edifis], *n.* édifice, *m.*

edify ['edifai], *v.t.* édifier.

Edinburgh ['edinbrə], Édimbourg, *m.*

edit ['edit], *v.t.* éditer, rédiger.

edition [i'diʃən], *n.* édition, *f.*

editor ['editə], *n.* compilateur, annotateur, *m.*; (*Journ.*) rédacteur en chef, directeur, *m.*

editorial [edi'tɔ:riəl], *a.* de rédacteur.—*n.* article de fond, éditorial, *m.*

Edmund ['edmənd]. Edmond, *m.*
educate ['edjukeit], *v.t.* élever; instruire.
education [edju'keiʃən], *n.* éducation, *f.*;
  enseignement, *m.*; instruction, *f.*
Edward ['edwəd]. Édouard, *m.*
eel [i:l], *n.* ar.guille, *f.*
eerie ['iəri], *a.* étrange, mystérieux.
eeriness ['iərinis], *n.* étrangeté surnaturelle,
  f.
efface [i'feis], *v.t.* effacer.
effect [i'fekt], *n.* effet, *m.*; (*pl.*) effets, biens,
  m.pl.; *in effect*, en effet; *to carry into*
  effect, accomplir, exécuter, mettre à effet;
  to no effect, en vain, sans résultat; *to take*
  effect, faire son effet, opérer; (*Law*) entrer
  en vigueur.—*v.t.* effectuer, exécuter, accomplir.
effective [i'fektiv], *a.* effectif; efficace.
effectively [i'fektivli], *adv.* effectivement;
  efficacement.
effeminacy [i'feminəsi], *n.* mollesse, nature
  efféminée, *f.*
effeminate [i'feminit], *a.* efféminé.
effervesce [efə'ves], *v.i.* être en effervescence; mousser (*boisson*).
effervescence [efə'vesəns], *n.* effervescence,
  f.
effervescent [efə'vesənt], **effervescing** [efə
  'vesiŋ], *a.* effervescent; mousseux; gazeux
  (*eau minérale*).
effete [i'fi:t], *a.* usé; stérile, épuisé, caduc.
efficacious [efi'keiʃəs], *a.* efficace.
efficacy ['efikəsi], *n.* efficacité, *f.*
efficiency [i'fiʃənsi], *n.* efficacité; bonne condition, *f.*; (*Mach.*) rendement, *m.*
efficient [i'fiʃənt], *a.* efficace (*remède*);
  capable, compétent (*personne*).
efficiently [i'fiʃəntli], *adv.* efficacement.
effigy ['efidʒi], *n.* effigie, *f.*
effloresce [eflɔ'res], *v.i.* s'effleurir.
efflorescence [eflɔ'resəns], *n.* efflorescence;
  (*Bot.*) floraison, *f.*
efflorescent [eflɔ'resənt], *a.* efflorescent;
  (*Bot.*) fleurissant.
effluvium [i'flu:viəm], *n.* (*pl.* **effluvia** [i'flu:
  viə]) exhalaison, *f.*, effluve, *m.*
effort ['efət], *n.* effort, *m.*
effortless ['efətlis], *a.* sans effort.
effrontery [i'frʌntəri], *n.* effronterie, *f.*
effulgence [i'fʌldʒəns], *n.* splendeur, *f.*,
  éclat, *m.*
effulgent [i'fʌldʒənt], *a.* resplendissant,
  éclatant.
effusion [i'fju:ʒən], *n.* effusion, *f.*, épanchement, *m.*
effusive [i'fju:siv], *a.* expansif; (*fig.*) excessif,
  exubérant.
egg [eg], *n.* œuf, *m.*; *boiled egg*, œuf à la
  coque; *fried egg*, œuf sur le plat; *hard-*
  boiled egg, œuf dur; *new-laid egg*, œuf
  frais.—*v.t.* pousser (à).
egg cup ['egkʌp], *n.* coquetier, *m.*
egg-shell ['egʃel], *n.* coquille d'œuf, *f.*
eglantine ['eglantain], *n.* églantier, *m.*;
  églantine (*fleur*), *f.*
egoism ['egouizm], *n.* égoïsme, *m.*
egoist ['egouist], *n.* égoïste, *m.,f.*
egotism ['egətizm], *n.* égotisme, culte du
  moi, *m.*
egotist ['egətist], *n.* égotiste, *m.,f.*
egregious [i'gri:dʒəs], *a.* insigne, énorme;
  fameux.

egress ['i:gres], *n.* sortie, issue, *f.*
Egypt ['i:dʒipt]. l'Égypte, *f.*
Egyptian [i'dʒipʃən], *a.* égyptien.—*n.* Egyp-
  tien (*personne*), *m.*
eider ['aidə], **eider duck** ['aidədʌk], *n.*
  eider, *m.*
eiderdown ['aidədaun], *n.* édredon, *m.*
eight [eit], *a.* huit.
eighteen ['eiti:n], *a.* dix-huit.
eighteenth ['eiti:nθ], *a.* dix-huitième; dix-
  huit (*roi etc.*).—*n.* dix-huitième (*fraction*),
  m.
eighth [eitθ], *a.* huitième; huit (*roi etc.*).—*n.*
  huitième (*fraction*), *m.*; (*Mus.*) octave, *f.*
eightieth ['eitiiθ], *a.* quatre-vingtième.—*n.*
  quatre-vingtième (*fraction*), *m.*
eighty ['eiti], *a.* quatre-vingts.
Eire ['ɛərə]. l'Irlande, *f.*
either ['aiðə, 'i:ðə], *pron.* l'un ou l'autre, *m.*,
  l'une ou l'autre, *f.*; l'un d'eux, *m.*, l'une
  d'elles, *f.*; (*used negatively*) ni l'un ni l'autre,
  m., ni l'une ni l'autre, *f.*—*conj.* ou, soit.—
  adv. non plus.
ejaculate [i'dʒækjuleit], *v.t.* pousser (*un cri*).
  —*v.i.* s'écrier; éjaculer.
ejaculation [idʒækju'leiʃən], *n.* cri, *m.*
  exclamation, *f.*; éjaculation, *f.*
eject [i'dʒekt], *v.t.* rejeter; émettre (*flammes*);
  chasser, expulser.
ejection [i'dʒekʃən], **ejectment** [i'dʒekt
  mənt], *n.* expulsion, éjection; (*Law*) éviction,
  f.
eke [i:k], *v.t.* *to eke out*, allonger; suppléer à,
  augmenter; ménager; *to eke out a living*,
  se faire une maigre pitance.
elaborate [i'læbərit], *a.* élaboré, soigné;
  compliqué.—[i'læbəreit], *v.t.* élaborer.
elaboration [ilæbə'reiʃən], *n.* élaboration, *f.*
elapse [i'læps], *v.i.* s'écouler.
elastic [i'læstik], *a.* and *n.* élastique, *m.*
elasticity [elæs'tisiti], *n.* élasticité, *f.*
elate [i'leit], *v.t.* élever, exalter, transporter.
elation [i'leiʃən], *n.* transport de joie, *m.*,
  exaltation, ivresse, *f.*
elbow ['elbou], *n.* coude, *m.*—*v.t.* coudoyer,
  pousser du coude.
elder (1) ['eldə], *n.* sureau (*arbre*), *m.*
elder (2) ['eldə], *a.* aîné, plus âgé; plus
  ancien.—*n.* aîné; ancien, *m.*
elderly ['eldəli], *a.* d'un certain âge.
eldest ['eldist], *a.* le plus âgé, l'aîné.
Eleanor ['elinə]. Éléonore, *f.*
elect [i'lekt], *a.* élu, choisi, nommé.—*n.* élu,
  m.—*v.t.* élire, nommer, choisir; (*fig.*) se
  décider à.
election [i'lekʃən], *n.* élection, *f.*
electioneer [ilekʃə'niə], *v.i.* solliciter des
  votes, travailler les électeurs.
electioneering [ilekʃə'niəriŋ], *n.* manœuvres
  électorales, *f.pl.*
elective [i'lektiv], *a.* électif; électoral.
elector [i'lektə], *n.* électeur, votant, *m.*
electric [i'lektrik], **electrical** [i'lektrikəl], *a.*
  électrique; *electric shock*, secousse électrique, *f.*
electrician [elek'triʃən, ilek'triʃən], *n.* électricien, *m.*
electricity [elek'trisiti, ilek'trislti], *n.* électricité, *f.*
electrify [i'lektrifai], *v.t.* électriser; électrifier.
electrocute [i'lektrokju:t], *v.t.* électrocuter.
electron [i'lektrən], *n.* électron, *m.*

electronic [elek'trɔnik, ilek'trɔnik], *a.* électronique.

electronics [elek'trɔniks, ilek'trɔniks], *n.* électronique, *f.*

electro-plate [i'lektroupleit], *n.* argenture électrique, *f.—v.t.* plaquer, argenter.

elegance [e'eligəns], *n.* élégance, *f.*

elegant ['eligənt], *a.* élégant, chic.—*n.* élégant, beau, *m.*

elegantly ['eligəntli], *adv.* élégamment.

elegiac [eli'dʒaiæk], *a.* élégiaque.—*n.* vers élégiaque, *f.*

elegist ['elidʒist], *n.* poète élégiaque, *m.*

elegy ['elidʒi], *n.* élégie, *f.*

element ['elimənt], *n.* élément, *m.*; (*pl.*) rudiments, *m.pl.*

elemental [eli'mentl], **elementary** [eli'men tri], *a.* élémentaire.

elephant ['elifənt], *n.* éléphant, *m.*

elephantine [eli'fæntain], *a.* éléphantin.

elevate ['eliveit], *v.t.* élever; hausser, exalter, exciter.

elevation [eli'veiʃən], *n.* élévation; hauteur, altitude, *f.*

elevator [eli'veitə], *n.* (*Anat. etc.*) élévateur, (*Am.*) [LIFT].

eleven [i'levn], *a.* onze; *the eleven*, les apôtres, *m.pl.*; (*Spt.*) le onze, *m.*

eleventh [i'levnθ], *a.* onzième; onze (*roi etc.*). —*n.* onzième (*fraction*), *m.*

elf [elf], *n.* (*pl.* **elves** [elvz]) esprit follet, lutin, elfe, *m.*

elfin ['elfin], *a.* des lutins, des elfes.—*n.* gamin, bambin, *m.*

elicit [i'lisit], *v.t.* faire sortir, tirer (*de*); déduire, découvrir, faire avouer (*à*).

elide [i'laid], *v.t.* (*Gram.*) élider.—*v.i.* s'élider.

eligible ['elidʒibl], *a.* éligible; convenable (*pour*); acceptable.

eliminate [i'limineit], *v.t.* éliminer, supprimer.

eliminating [i'limineitiŋ], *a.* éliminateur, éliminatoire.

elimination [ilimi'neiʃən], *n.* élimination, *f.*

elision [i'liʒən], *n.* élision, *f.*

elixir [i'liksə], *n.* élixir, *m.*

Elizabeth [i'lizəbəθ]. Élisabeth, *f.*

elk [elk], *n.* (*Zool.*) élan, *m.*

ell [el], *n.* aune, *f.*

Ellen ['elin]. Hélène, *f.*

ellipse [i'lips], *n.* ellipse, *f.*

elliptic [i'liptik], **elliptical** [i'liptikəl], *a.* elliptique.

elm [elm], *n.* orme, *m.*

elocution [elo'kju:ʃən], *n.* élocution, diction, *f.*

elocutionist [elo'kju:ʃənist], *n.* déclamateur, *m.*

elongate ['i:lɔŋgeit], *v.t.* allonger, prolonger.

elongation [i:lɔŋ'geiʃən], *n.* allongement, prolongement, *m.*; (*Surg.*) élongation, *f.*

elope [i'loup], *v.i.* s'enfuir (*avec un amant*).

elopement [i'loupmənt], *n.* fuite, *f.*, enlèvement, *m.*

eloquence ['eləkwəns], *n.* éloquence, *f.*

eloquent ['eləkwənt], *a.* éloquent.

eloquently ['eləkwəntli], *adv.* éloquemment.

else [els], *adv.* autrement, ou bien, ailleurs.—*a.* autre; *anywhere else*, n'importe où ailleurs; *everything else*, tout le reste; *nobody else*, personne d'autre; *nothing else*, rien d'autre; *someone* (*somebody*) *else*, quelqu'un d'autre.

elsewhere ['elsweə], *adv.* ailleurs, autre part.

Elsie ['elsi]. Élise, *f.*

elucidate [i'lju:sideit], *v.t.* expliquer, éclaircir, élucider.

elucidation [ilju:si'deiʃən], *n.* éclaircissement, *m.*, élucidation, explication, *f.*

elude [i'lju:d], *v.t.* éluder, éviter, échapper à.

elusion [i'lju:ʒən], *n.* subterfuge, *m.*, réponse évasive, *f.*

elusive [i'lju:siv], *a.* artificieux (*réponse*); fuyant, insaisissable (*personne*).

elves [ELF].

emaciate [i'meiʃieit], *v.t.* amaigrir.—*v.i.* maigrir, s'amaigrir.

emaciated [i'meiʃieitid], *a.* amaigri, maigre, décharné.

emaciation [imeiʃi'eiʃən], *n.* amaigrissement, *m.*, maigreur, *f.*

emanate ['eməneit], *v.i.* émaner.

emancipate [i'mænsipeit], *v.t.* affranchir, émanciper (*de*).

emancipation [imænsi'peiʃən], *n.* affranchissement, *m.*, émancipation, *f.*

emasculate [i'mæskjuleit], *v.t.* châtrer; (*fig.*) affaiblir, efféminer.

embalm [im'bɑ:m], *v.t.* embaumer.

embalmer [im'bɑ:mə], *n.* embaumeur, *m.*

embalming [im'bɑ:miŋ], *n.* embaumement, *m.*

embank [im'bæŋk], *v.t.* endiguer, remblayer; encaisser (*canal etc.*).

embankment [im'bæŋkmənt], *n.* levée, *f.*; terrassement, talus, *m.*; (*Rail.*) remblai; quai (*rivière, canal*), *m.*

embarcation [EMBARKATION].

embargo [im'bɑ:gou], *n.* embargo, *m.—v.t.* mettre l'embargo sur; défendre, interdire.

embark [im'bɑ:k], *v.t.* embarquer.—*v.i.* s'embarquer (*sur*); (*fig.*) s'engager (*dans*).

embarkation or **embarcation** [embɑ:'kei ʃən], *n.* embarquement, *m.*

embarrass [im'bærəs], *v.t.* embarrasser; gêner.

embarrassment [im'bærəsmənt], *n.* embarras, *m.*; (*fig.*) perplexité; gêne (*manque d'argent*), *f.*

embassy ['embəsi], *n.* ambassade, *f.*

embellish [im'beliʃ], *v.t.* embellir, orner (*avec*).

embellishment [im'beliʃmənt], *n.* embellissement, ornement, *m.*

ember ['embə], *n.* braise, cendre ardente, *f.*

embezzle [im'bezl], *v.t.* détourner; s'approprier frauduleusement (*des fonds*).

embezzlement [im'bezlmənt], *n.* détournement, *m.*

embezzler [im'bezlə], *n.* détourneur (*de fonds*), *m.*

embitter [im'bitə], *v.t.* rendre amer; (*fig.*) empoisonner; aigrir.

emblazon [im'bleizn], *v.t.* blasonner (*de*); (*fig.*) publier, proclamer.

emblem ['embləm], *n.* emblème, *m.*; (*Her.*) devise, *f.*

embodiment [im'bɔdimənt], *n.* incarnation; personnification; (*Mil.*) incorporation, *f.*

embody [im'bɔdi], *v.t.* incarner; (*Mil. etc.*) incorporer (*dans*); (*fig.*) personnifier.

embolden [im'bouldn], *v.t.* enhardir.

emboss [im'bɔs], *v.t.* bosseler, relever en bosse; gaufrer (*papier*).

embossing [im'bosiŋ], *n.* bosselage; gaufrage, *m.*

embrace [im'breis], *n.* embrassement, *m.*, étreinte, *f.*—*v.t.* embrasser, étreindre; (*fig.*) accepter; comprendre.

embrocation [embrə'keiʃən], *n.* embrocation, *f.*

embroider [im'brɔidə], *v.t.* broder.

embroidery [im'brɔidəri], *n.* broderie, *f.*

embroil [im'brɔil], *v.t.* brouiller, embrouiller.

embryo ['embriou], *n.* embryon, germe, *m.*

emend [i'mend], *v.t.* corriger; (*Law*) émender.

emendation [i:men'deiʃən], *n.* correction, émendation, *f.*

emerald ['emərəld], *n.* émeraude, *f.*

emerge [i'mə:dʒ], *v.i.* surgir; sortir (*de*); ressortir.

emergency [i'mə:dʒənsi], *n.* circonstance critique; crise, *f.*, cas imprévu, *m.*; *in case of emergency*, en cas d'urgence; *emergency exit*, sortie de secours, *f.*

emery ['eməri], *n.* émeri, *m.*; *emery cloth*, toile d'émeri, *f.*

emetic [i'metik], *n.* émétique, *m.*

emigrant ['emigrənt], *n.* émigrant; (*Fr. Hist.*) émigré, *m.*

emigrate ['emigreit], *v.i.* émigrer.

emigration [emi'greiʃən], *n.* émigration, *f.*

Emily ['emili]. Émilie, *f.*

eminence ['eminəns], *n.* éminence, colline; (*fig.*) grandeur, distinction, *f.*

eminent ['eminənt], *a.* éminent; distingué, illustre.

eminently ['eminəntli], *adv.* éminemment, par excellence.

emissary ['emisəri], *n.* émissaire, messager, *m.*

emission [i'miʃən], *n.* émission, *f.*

emit [i'mit], *v.t.* jeter; exhaler, dégager; (*Fin.*) émettre.

emolument [i'mɔljumənt], *n.* (*usu. pl.*) émoluments, *m.pl.*, rémunération, *f.*; (*fig.*) profit, *m.*

emotion [i'mouʃən], *n.* émotion, *f.*

emotional [i'mouʃənəl], *a.* porté à l'émotion, émotif, *m.*

emperor ['empərə], *n.* empereur, *m.*

emphasis ['emfəsis], *n.* (*pl.* **emphases** ['emfəsi:z]) force, énergie, emphase, *f.*; accent, *m.*

emphasize ['emfəsaiz], *v.t.* appuyer sur; accentuer, souligner.

emphatic [im'fætik], *a.* fort, énergique; expressif; accentué, emphatique; (*fig.*) positif.

emphatically [im'fætikəli], *adv.* avec force, énergiquement; positivement.

empire ['empaiə], *n.* empire, *m.*

empiric [em'pirik], *n.* empirique; charlatan, *m.*—*a.* (*also* **empirical** [em'pirikəl]) empirique, guidé par l'expérience.

employ [im'plɔi], *v.t.* employer; se servir de.—*n.* emploi, *m.*; occupation, *f.*

employee [im'plɔii:], *n.* employé, *m.*

employer [im'plɔiə], *n.* patron; employeur, *m.*

employment [im'plɔimənt], *n.* emploi, *m.*, occupation, *f.*

emporium [em'pɔ:riəm], *n.* entrepôt; (*fam.*) grand magasin, *m.*

empower [em'pauə], *v.t.* autoriser (à), mettre à même (*de*).

empress ['empris], *n.* impératrice, *f.*

emptiness ['emptinis], *n.* vide, *m.*; (*fig.*) vanité, *f.*, néant, *m.*

empty ['empti], *a.* vide, à vide; désert (*rues etc.*); (*fig.*) vain, stérile.—*v.t.* vider, décharger.—*v.i.* se vider.

emu ['i:mju:], *n.* (*Orn.*) émeu, *m.*

emulate ['emjuleit], *v.t.* rivaliser avec; imiter.

emulation [emju'leiʃən], *n.* émulation, rivalité, *f.*

emulsion [i'mʌlʃən], *n.* émulsion, *f.*

enable [i'neibl], *v.t.* mettre à même (*de*); mettre en état (*de*); permettre (*de*).

enact [i'nækt], *v.t.* ordonner, arrêter; rendre (*loi*); jouer, faire (*un rôle*).

enactment [i'næktmənt], *n.* loi, ordonnance, *f.*, décret, *m.*

enamel [i'næml], *n.* émail, *m.*—*v.t.* émailler (*de*).—*v.i.* peindre en émail.

enamelling [i'næməliŋ], *n.* émaillure, *f.*; émaillage, *m.*

enamor [i'næmə], *v.t.* (*used now only in p.p.*) *to be enamored of*, être épris de.

encamp [in'kæmp], *v.t., v.i.* camper.

encase [in'keis], *v.t.* encaisser, enfermer.

enchain [in'tʃein], *v.t.* enchaîner.

enchant [in'tʃa:nt], *v.t.* enchanter; (*fig.*) charmer, ravir (*de*).

enchanter [in'tʃa:ntə], *n.* enchanteur, *m.*

enchanting [in'tʃa:ntiŋ], *a.* enchanteur, ravissant, charmant.

enchantment [in'tʃa:ntmənt], *n.* enchantement, charme, *m.*, fascination, *f.*

enchantress [in'tʃa:ntris], *n.* enchanteresse, *f.*

encircle [in'sə:kl], *v.t.* ceindre, entourer (*de*), encercler.

enclose [in'klouz], *v.t.* enclore; entourer, environner; renfermer; envoyer sous le même pli (*lettre etc.*).

enclosed [in'klouzd], *a.* entouré, environné; inclus, ci-inclus, sous ce pli (*paquet, lettre etc.*).

enclosure [in'klouʒə], *n.* clôture; enceinte (*espace clos*), *f.*; contenu (*objet renfermé*), *m.*

encomium [en'koumjəm], *n.* éloge, *m.*, louange, *f.*

encompass [in'kʌmpəs], *v.t.* entourer, environner; renfermer.

encore [ɔŋ'kɔ:], *n.* and *int.* bis.—*v.t.* bisser.

encounter [in'kauntə], *n.* rencontre, *f.*; combat, *m.*, lutte, *f.*—*v.t.* rencontrer, aborder; (*fig.*) éprouver, essuyer.

encourage [in'kʌridʒ], *v.t.* encourager.

encouragement [in'kʌridʒmənt], *n.* encouragement, *m.*

encroach [in'kroutʃ], *v.i.* empiéter (*sur*); abuser (*de*).

encroachment [in'kroutʃmənt], *n.* empiétement, *m.*, usurpation, *f.*

encumber [in'kʌmbə], *v.t.* encombrer, accabler, embarrasser (*de*); grever (*un héritage*).

encumbrance [in'kʌmbrəns], *n.* encombrement, embarras, *m.*; (*Law*) hypothèque, *f.*

encyclopaedia [insaiklə'pi:diə], *n.* encyclopédie, *f.*

encyclopaedic [insaiklə'pi:dik], *a.* encyclopédique.

415

end [end], *n.* fin; extrémité, *f.*, bout; but, objet; (*fig.*) dessein, *m.*, issue, *f.*; *at an end*, fini, terminé; *big end*, (*Motor.*) tête de bielle, *f.*; *from end to end*, d'un bout à l'autre; *in the end*, à la fin; *three days on end*, trois jours de suite; *to be at a loose end*, être désœuvré, se trouver sans avoir rien à faire; *to draw to an end*, tirer *ou* toucher à sa fin; *to make an end of*, en finir avec; *to make both ends meet*, joindre les deux bouts.—*v.t.* finir, terminer, achever.—*v.i.* finir, se terminer (*en*); cesser (*de*); aboutir (*à*).

endanger [in'deindʒə], *v.t.* mettre en danger, compromettre, risquer.

endear [in'diə], *v.t.* rendre cher (*à*).

endearing [in'diəriŋ], *a.* tendre, affectueux.

endearment [in'diəmənt], *n.* charme, *m.*; (*pl.*) caresses, *f.pl.*

endeavour [in'devə], *n.* effort, *m.*, tentative, *f.* —*v.i.* tâcher, essayer, tenter (*de*), chercher (*à*).

ending ['endiŋ], *n.* fin, conclusion; (*Gram.*) terminaison, *f.*

endive ['endiv], *n.* chicorée; escarole, *f.*

endless ['endlis], *a.* sans fin; éternel, perpétuel, interminable.

endlessly ['endlisli], *adv.* à l'infini, sans cesse.

endorse [in'dɔ:s], *v.t.* endosser; viser (*passeport*); (*fig.*) sanctionner, approuver.

endorsement [in'dɔ:smənt], *n.* suscription, *f.*; (*Comm.*) endossement (*signature au dos*); visa (*de passeport*), *m.*; (*fig.*) sanction, *f.*

endow [in'dau], *v.t.* doter (*de*); (*fig.*) douer (*de*).

endowment [in'daumənt], *n.* dotation, *f.*

endurable [in'djuərəbl], *a.* supportable, endurable.

endurance [in'djuərəns], *n.* endurance; souffrance, patience, *f.*

endure [in'djuə], *v.t.* supporter, souffrir, endurer.—*v.i.* durer; endurer, souffrir.

enduring [in'djuəriŋ], *a.* endurant, qui endure, patient; durable, qui dure (*permanent*).

endways ['endweiz], **endwise** ['endwaiz], *adv.* debout, de champ; bout à bout (*horizontalement*).

enema ['enimə, i'ni:mə], *n.* lavement, *m.*

enemy ['enəmi], *n.* ennemi, *m.*

energetic [enə'dʒetik], *a.* énergique.

energy ['enədʒi], *n.* énergie, *f.*

enervate ['enəveit], *v.t.* affaiblir, énerver.

enfeeble [in'fi:bl], *v.t.* affaiblir.

enfold [in'fould], *v.t.* envelopper.

enforce [in'fɔ:s], *v.t.* donner de la force à; faire respecter; faire exécuter; forcer.

enforcement [in'fɔ:smənt], *n.* mise en vigueur, exécution, *f.*

enfranchise [in'fræntʃaiz], *v.t.* affranchir (*un esclave*); donner le droit de vote à.

enfranchisement [in'fræntʃizmənt], *n.* affranchissement, *m.*; admission au suffrage, *f.*

engage [in'geidʒ], *v.t.* engager; retenir, prendre (*réserver*); louer (*prendre à louage*); arrêter (*un marché*); occuper (*attention etc.*); (*fig.*) en venir aux mains avec.—*v.i.* s'engager (*à*); livrer combat.

engaged [in'geidʒd], *a.* fiancé (*futur époux*);

occupé (*pris par le travail*); pas libre (*téléphone, cabinets*); aux prises (*combat*).

engagement [in'geidʒmənt], *n.* engagement, *m.*; occupation, *f.*; fiançailles, *f.pl.*; combat, *m.*

engaging [in'geidʒiŋ], *a.* engageant, attrayant.

engender [in'dʒendə], *v.t.* engendrer, faire naître, causer.

engine ['endʒin], *n.* machine, *f.*, moteur, *m.*; (*Rail.*) locomotive, *f.*; *fire engine*, pompe à incendie, *f.*; *steam engine*, machine à vapeur.

engine-driver ['endʒindraivə], *n.* (*Rail.*) mécanicien, *m.*

engineer [endʒi'niə], *n.* ingénieur (*Manuf.*) constructeur-mécanicien; (*Mil.*) soldat du génie; (*pl.*) le génie, *m.*

engineering [endʒi'niəriŋ], *n.* art de l'ingénieur, *m.*; *civil engineering*, génie civil, *m.*; *electrical engineering*, technique électrique, *f.*

England ['iŋglənd], l'Angleterre, *f.*

English ['iŋgliʃ], *a.* anglais; de l'Angleterre; *the English Channel*, la Manche, *f.*—*n.* anglais (*langue*), *m.*; *the English*, les Anglais, *m.pl.*

Englishman ['iŋgliʃmən], *n.* (*pl.* **-men** [men]) Anglais, *m.*

Englishwoman ['iŋgliʃwumən], *n.* (*pl.* **-women** [wimin]) Anglaise, *f.*

engrave [in'greiv], *v.t.* graver.

engraver [in'greivə], *n.* graveur, *m.*

engraving [in'greiviŋ], *n.* gravure; *copper-plate engraving*, taille-douce, *f.*

engross [in'grous], *v.t.* grossoyer (*copier*); accaparer (*monopoliser*); absorber, occuper (*l'esprit*).

engulf [in'gʌlf], *v.t.* engouffrer; (*fig.*) engloutir.

enhance [in'ha:ns], *v.t.* enchérir, renchérir; (*fig.*) rehausser.

enhancement [in'ha:nsmənt], *n.* hausse, *f.*; (*fig.*) rehaussement, *m.*

enigma [i'nigmə], *n.* énigme, *f.*

enigmatic [enig'mætik], **enigmatical** [enig'mætikal], *a.* énigmatique, obscur.

enjoin [in'dʒɔin], *v.t.* enjoindre; prescrire (*à*).

enjoy [in'dʒɔi], *v.t.* jouir de, posséder, goûter; *to enjoy oneself*, s'amuser.

enjoyable [in'dʒɔiəbl], *a.* agréable.

enjoyment [in'dʒɔimənt], *n.* jouissance (*de*) *f.*; plaisir, *m.*

enkindle [in'kindl], *v.t.* enflammer; (*fig.*) exciter.

enlace [in'leis], *v.t.* enlacer.

enlarge [in'la:dʒ], *v.t.* agrandir, étendre, dilater.—*v.i.* grandir, s'agrandir.

enlargement [in'la:dʒmənt], *n.* agrandissement (*also Phot.*), *m.*; augmentation, *f.*

enlighten [in'laitn], *v.t.* éclairer; (*fig.*) éclaircir.

enlightenment [in'laitnmənt], *n.* éclaircissement, *m.*; lumières, *f.pl.*

enlist [in'list], *v.t.* enrôler, engager.—*v.i.* s'engager.

enlistment [in'listmənt], *n.* engagement, enrôlement, *m.*

enliven [in'laivn], *v.t.* égayer, animer.

enmity ['enmiti], *n.* inimitié; animosité, haine, hostilité, *f.*

ennoble [i'noubl], *v.t.* anoblir; (*fig.*) ennoblir.

ennoblement [i'noublmənt], *n.* anoblissement; (*fig.*) ennoblissement, *m.*

enormity [i'nɔːmiti], **enormousness** [i'nɔːməsnis], *n.* énormité, *f.*

enormous [i'nɔːməs], *a.* énorme; (*fig.*) atroce, monstrueux.

enormously [i'nɔːməsli], *adv.* énormément.

enough [i'nʌf], *a.* and *adv.* assez; *large enough*, assez grand; *more than enough*, plus qu'il n'en faut.

enquire [INQUIRE].

enrage [in'reidʒ], *v.t.* faire enrager; exaspérer.

enrapture [in'ræptʃə], *v.t.* transporter, ravir.

enrich [in'ritʃ], *v.t.* enrichir.

enrichment [in'ritʃmənt], *n.* enrichissement, *m.*

enroll [in'roul], *v.t.* enrôler, enregistrer, inscrire.—*v.i.* s'enrôler, se faire inscrire.

enrollment [in'roulmənt], *n.* enrôlement, *m.*, inscription, *f.*

ensconce [in'skɔns], *v.t.* cacher; *to ensconce oneself*, se cacher (*dans*), se blottir.

enshrine [in'ʃrain], *v.t.* enchâsser (*dans*).

enshroud [in'ʃraud], *v.t.* mettre dans un linceul; (*fig.*) couvrir.

ensign ['ensain, (*R. Navy*) 'ensin], *n.* enseigne, *f.*, drapeau; (*Mil.*) porte-drapeau (*personne*), *m.*

enslave [in'sleiv], *v.t.* asservir; (*fig.*) captiver.

ensnare [in'snɛə], *v.t.* prendre au piège; (*fig.*) attraper séduire.

ensue [in'sjuː], *v.i.* s'ensuivre.

ensuing [in'sjuːiŋ], *a.* suivant; prochain.

ensure [in'ʃuə], *v.t.* assurer; garantir.

entail [en'teil], *v.t.* substituer (*à*); (*fig.*) entraîner; impliquer.

entangle [in'tæŋgl], *v.t.* emmêler; enchevêtrer; empêtrer (*les pieds*); (*fig.*) embrouiller.

entanglement [in'tæŋglmənt], *n.* embrouillement, embarras, *m.*

enter ['entə], *v.t.* entrer dans, pénétrer; inscrire (*nom etc.*); enregistrer (*paquet*).—*v.i.* entrer; s'engager (*dans*).

enteritis [entə'raitis], *n.* entérite, *f.*

enterprise ['entəpraiz], *n.* entreprise, hardiesse, *f.*; esprit d'entreprise, *m.*

entertain [entə'tein], *v.t.* recevoir (*des invités*); divertir, amuser (*distraire*); concevoir (*idée etc.*); accepter (*proposition*).—*v.i.* recevoir (*invités*).

entertainer [entə'teinə], *n.* (*Theat. etc.*) diseur, *m.*, diseuse, *f.*, comique, *m.*, *f.*; hôte, *m.*, hôtesse, *f.*

entertainment [entə'teinmənt], *n.* hospitalité, *f.*; accueil (*reception*); festin, *m.*, fête, *f.*; divertissement, spectacle (*amusement*), *m.*

enthrall [in'θrɔːl], *v.t.* asservir, assujettir; (*fig.*) ravir.

enthuse [in'θjuːz], *v.i.* s'enthousiasmer de ou pour.

enthusiasm [in'θjuːziæzm], *n.* enthousiasme, *m.*

enthusiast [in'θjuːziæst], *n.* enthousiaste, *m.*, *f.*

enthusiastic [inθjuːzi'æstik], *a.* enthousiaste.

entice [in'tais], *v.t.* attirer; entraîner (*dans*); séduire (*à*).

enticement [in'taismənt], *n.* appât, charme, *m.*; tentation, *f.*

enticer [in'taisə], *n.* tentateur, séducteur, *m.*

enticing [in'taisiŋ], *a.* séduisant, attrayant, tentant.

entire [in'taiə], *a.* entier, complet.

entirely [in'taiəli], *adv.* entièrement, complètement, tout entier.

entirety [in'taiəti], *n.* totalité; intégrité, *f.*

entitle [in'taitl], *v.t.* intituler, appeler; donner droit à.

entity [entiti], *n.* entité, *f.*, être de raison, *m.*

entomb [in'tuːm], *v.t.* ensevelir.

entrails ['entreilz], *n.pl.* entrailles, *f.pl.*

entrance (1) ['entrəns], *n.* entrée, *f.*; commencement, début (*de carrière*), *m.*; (*fig.*) initiation, *f.*

entrance (2) [in'traːns], *v.t.* extasier, ravir.

entrancing [in'traːnsiŋ], *a.* prenant; ravissant.

entrant ['entrənt], *n.* inscrit (*de concours*), *m.*; inscrite, *f.*; débutant (*dans une profession nouvelle*), *m.*, débutante, *f.*

entrap [in'træp], *v.t.* prendre au piège, attraper (*dans*).

entreat [in'triːt], *v.t.* supplier, prier instamment (*de*).

entreaty [in'triːti], *n.* prière; supplication; (*pl.*) sollicitation, *f.*, instances, *f.pl.*

entrust [in'trʌst], *v.t.* charger (*de*).

entry ['entri], *n.* entrée; inscription (*enregistrement*); (*Book-keeping*) écriture, *f.*, article, *m.*; (*Customs*) déclaration d'entrée, *f.*; *no entry*, sens interdit, passage interdit.

entwine [in'twain], *v.t.* enlacer, entortiller.—*v.i.* s'enlacer, s'entortiller.

enumerate [i'njuːməreit], *v.t.* énumérer, dénombrer.

enunciate [i'nʌnsieit], *v.t.* énoncer; prononcer.—*v.i.* articuler.

envelop [in'veləp], *v.t.* envelopper (*de ou dans*).

envelope ['enviloup, 'ɔnviloup], *n.* enveloppe, *f.*

envenom [in'venəm], *v.t.* envenimer; exaspérer (*aigrir*).

envious ['enviəs], *a.* envieux (*de*).

environ [in'vaiərən], *v.t.* environner (*de*).

environment [in'vaiərənmənt], *n.* milieu, entourage, environnement, *m.*

environs [in'vaiərənz], *n.pl.* environs, *m.pl.*

envisage [in'vizidʒ], *v.t.* envisager.

envoy ['envoi], *n.* envoyé, *m.*

envy ['envi], *n.* envie, *f.*—*v.t.* envier, porter envie à.

epaulet(te) ['epɔːlet], *n.* épaulette, *f.*

ephemeral [i'femərəl], *a.* éphémère.

epic ['epik], *a.* épique; (*fig.*) légendaire.—*n.* épopée, *f.*, poème épique, *m.*

epicure ['epikjuə], *n.* gourmet, *m.*, gastronome, *m.*, *f.*

epidemic [epi'demik], *a.* épidémique.—*n.* épidémie, *f.*

epigram ['epigræm], *n.* épigramme, *f.*

epilepsy ['epilepsi], *n.* épilepsie, *f.*

epileptic [epi'leptik], *a.* and *n.* épileptique, *m.*, *f.*

epilogue ['epilɔg], *n.* épilogue, *m.*

episcopacy [i'piskəpəsi], *n.* épiscopat, *m.*

episcopal [i'piskəpəl], *a.* épiscopal.

episode ['episoud], *n.* épisode, *m.*

epistle [i'pisl], *n.* épître, *f.*

epitaph ['epitaːf], *n.* épitaphe, *f.*

epithet ['epiθet], *n.* épithète, *f.*

epitome

epitome [i'pitəmi], *n.* épitomé, abrégé, précis, *m.*
epitomize [i'pitəmaiz], *v.t.* faire un abrégé de; être une image en petit de.
epoch ['i:pɔk], *n.* époque, *f.*
equable ['ekwəbl], *a.* uniforme, égal.
equal ['i:kwəl], *a.* égal; (*fig.*) impartial, juste; *equal to*, de force à, à la hauteur de.—*n.* égal, *m.*, égale, *f.*; (*pl.*) pareils, égaux, *m.pl.* —*v.t.* égaler, être égal à.
equality [i'kwɔliti], *n.* égalité, *f.*
equalize ['i:kwəlaiz], *v.t.* égaliser; compenser.
equally ['i:kwəli], *adv.* également, pareillement.
equanimity [i:kwə'nimiti], *n.* égalité d'âme, équanimité, *f.*
equation [i'kweiʃən], *n.* équation, *f.*
equator [i'kweitə], *n.* équateur, *m.*
equatorial [ekwə'tɔ:riəl], *a.* équatorial, de l'équateur.
equerry ['ekwəri], *n.* écuyer, *m.*
equestrian [i'kwestriən], *a.* équestre.—*n.* cavalier; (*Circus*) écuyer, *m.*
equilibrium [i:kwi'libriəm], *n.* équilibre, *m.*
equine ['i:kwain, 'ekwain], *a.* du cheval, équin.
equinox ['i:kwinɔks], *n.* équinoxe, *m.*
equip [i'kwip], *v.t.* équiper; (*Tech.*) outiller.
equipment [i'kwipmənt], *n.* équipement, matériel, outillage, *m.*
equitable ['ekwitəbl], *a.* équitable, juste.
equity ['ekwiti], *n.* équité, justice, *f.*
equivalent [i'kwivələnt], *a.* équivalent (à); *to be equivalent to*, être équivalent à, équivaloir à.—*n.* équivalent, *m.*
equivocal [i'kwivəkl], *a.* équivoque, ambigu.
equivocate [i'kwivəkeit], *v.i.* user d'équivoque, équivoquer.
era ['iərə], *n.* ère, *f.*
eradicate [i'rædikeit], *v.t.* déraciner; (*fig.*) exterminer.
erase [i'reiz], *v.t.* raturer, effacer, rayer.
eraser [i'reizə], *n.* grattoir, *m.*, gomme à effacer, *f.*
erasure [i'reiʒə], *n.* grattage, *m.*, rature, *f.*
***ere** [ɛə], *conj.* avant que; plutôt que.—*prep.* avant.
erect [i'rekt], *a.* debout, droit, élevé.—*v.t.* ériger, dresser; (*fig.*) établir.
erection [i'rekʃən], *n.* construction, érection, élévation; (*fig.*) fondation, *f.*
ermine ['ə:min], *a.* d'hermine.—*n.* hermine, *f.*
erode [i'roud], *v.t.* éroder, ronger.
erosion [i'rouʒən], *n.* érosion, *f.*
erotic [i'rɔtik], *a.* érotique.
err [ə:], *v.i.* s'écarter, s'égarer (*de*); (*fig.*) .se tromper.
errand ['erənd], *n.* message, *m.*, commission, course, *f.*
errand boy ['erəndbɔi], *n.* petit commissionnaire; saute-ruisseau (*de bureau*), chasseur (*dans un restaurant*), *m.*
erratic [i'rætik], *a.* erratique; errant, excentrique; irrégulier, inégal.
erroneous [i'rouniəs], *a.* erroné, faux.
erroneously [i'rouniəsli], *adv.* à faux, à tort.
error ['erə], *n.* erreur, faute, *f.*, écart, *m.*
erudite ['erudait], *a.* érudit, savant.
erudition [eru'diʃən], *n.* érudition, *f.*
erupt [i'rʌpt], *v.i.* faire éruption (*volcan*); percer (*dent*).

eruption [i'rʌpʃən], *n.* éruption, *f.*
erysipelas [eri'sipiləs], *n.* érysipèle, *m.*
escalade [eskə'leid], *n.* escalade, *f.*—*v.t.* escalader.
escalate [eskə'leit], *v.i.* escalader.
escalation [eskə'leiʃən], *n.* escalade, *f.*
escalator ['eskəleitə], *n.* escalier roulant, *m.*
escapade [eskə'peid], *n.* escapade, *f.*
escape [is'keip], *n.* évasion; fuite (*gaz*); (*fig.*) délivrance, *f.*; *fire escape*, échelle de sauvetage, *f.*; *to have a narrow escape*, l'échapper belle.—*v.t.* échapper à; éviter.—*v.i.* (s')échapper; s'évader (*de prison*).
escarpment [is'ka:pmənt], *n.* escarpement, talus, *m.*
eschew [is'tʃu:], *v.t.* éviter; renoncer à.
escort [is'kɔ:t], *v.t.* escorter.—['eskɔ:t], *n.* escorte, *f.*; cavalier, *m.*
escutcheon [is'kʌtʃən], *n.* écusson, *m.*
Eskimo ['eskimou], *a.* esquimau.—*n.* Esquimau (*personne*), *m.*
especial [is'peʃəl], *a.* spécial, particulier.
especially [is'peʃəli], *adv.* spécialement, surtout.
esplanade [esplə'neid], *n.* esplanade, promenade, *f.*
espouse [is'pauz], *v.t.* épouser; (*fig.*) adopter.
espy [is'pai], *v.t.* apercevoir, aviser, épier.
essay ['esei], *n.* essai; effort, *m.*; (*Sch.*) composition, dissertation, *f.*—[e'sei], *v.t.* essayer (*de*).
essence ['esəns], *n.* essence, *f.*
essential [i'senʃəl], *a.* essentiel.—*n.* (*also pl.*) essentiel, *m.*
essentially [i'senʃəli], *adv.* essentiellement.
establish [is'tæbliʃ], *v.t.* établir, fonder; (*fig.*) confirmer; prouver.
establishment [is'tæbliʃmənt], *n.* établissement, *m.*; maison; (*fig.*) confirmation, *f.*
estate [is'teit], *n.* état, rang (*condition*), *m.* propriété, *f.*, bien (*immeuble*), *m.*
estate agent [is'teiteidʒənt], *n.* agent immobilier, *m.*
estate duty [is'teitdju:ti], *n.* droits de succession, *m.pl.*
esteem [is'ti:m], *n.* estime, considération, *f.* —*v.t.* estimer, regarder comme.
estimate ['estimit], *n.* évaluation, *f.*, calcul, devis, *m.*; (*fig.*) appréciation, *f.*—['estimeit], *v.t.* estimer, apprécier; évaluer, calculer.
Estonia [es'tounia]. l'Esthonie, *f.*
Estonian [es'tounian], *a.* esthonien.—*n.* esthonien (*langue*); Esthonien (*personne*), *m.*
estrange [is'treindʒ], *v.t.* aliéner, éloigner (*de*).
estrangement [is'treindʒmənt], *n.* aliénation, *f.*, éloignement, *m.*, brouille, *f.*
estuary ['estjuari], *n.* estuaire, *m.*
etching ['etʃiŋ], *n.* gravure à l'eau-forte, *f.*
eternal [i'tə:nl], *a.* and *n.* éternel, *m.*
eternity [i'tə:niti], *n.* éternité, *f.*
ether ['i:θə], *n.* éther, *m.*
ethereal [i'θiəriəl], *a.* éthéré; céleste.
ethic ['eθik], **ethical** [i'θikəl], *a.* éthique; moral.
ethics ['eθiks], *n.pl.* morale, éthique, *f.*
Ethiopia [i:θi'oupiə]. l'Éthiopie, *f.*
Ethiopian [i:θi'oupiən], *a.* éthiopien.—*n.* Éthiopien (*personne*), *m.*
etiquette ['etiket], *n.* étiquette, *f.*, convenances, *f.pl.*
Etruria [i'truəriə]. l'Étrurie, *f.*

Etruscan [i'trʌskən], *a.* étrusque.—*n.* étrusque (*langue*); Étrusque (*personne*), *m.*, *f.*

etymology [eti'mɔlədʒi], *n.* étymologie, *f.*

eucharist ['ju:karist], *n.* eucharistie, *f.*

eulogium [ju:'loudʒiəm], **eulogy** ['ju:lədʒi], *n.* éloge, panégyrique, *m.*

eulogize ['ju:lədʒaiz], *v.t.* louer, faire l'éloge de.

eunuch ['ju:nək], *n.* eunuque, *m.*

euphemism ['ju:fimizm], *n.* euphémisme, *m.*

euphony ['ju:fəni], *n.* euphonie, *f.*

Eurasian [juə'reiʒən], *a.* eurasien.—*n.* Eurasien (*personne*), *m.*

Europe ['juərəp]. l'Europe, *f.*

European [juərə'pi:ən], *a.* européen.—*n.* Européen (*personne*), *m.*

euthanasia [ju:θə'neiziə], *n.* euthanasie, *f.*

evacuate [i'vækjueit], *v.t.* évacuer.

evacuation [ivækju'eiʃən], *n.* évacuation, *f.*

evade [i'veid], *v.t.* éluder, esquiver, éviter, se soustraire à; échapper à, déjouer (*la loi*).

evaluate [i'væljueit], *v.t.* évaluer.

evaporate [i'væpəreit], *v.t.* faire évaporer.—*v.i.* s'évaporer.

evaporation [ivæpə'reiʃən], *n.* évaporation, *f.*

evasion [i'veiʒən], *n.* subterfuge, *m.*; échappatoire, défaite, *f.*

eve [i:v], *n.* veille, *f.*; **on the eve of**, à la veille de.

even (1) [i:vn], *n.* (*Poet.*) soir, *m.*

even (2) [i:vn], *a.* égal; régulier (*respiration, pouls*); uni (*lisse*); de niveau (*avec*); pair (*numéro*).—*adv.* même, aussi bien; précisément.—*v.t.* égaler, égaliser; niveler.

evening ['i:vniŋ], *a.* du soir; **evening dress**, tenue de soirée, *f.*—*n.* soir, *m.*; soirée, *f.*; (*fig.*) déclin, *m.*

evenly ['i:vnli], *adv.* également; de niveau; (*fig.*) impartialement.

evenness ['i:vnnis], *n.* égalité, *f.*; régularité; sérénité, *f.*

evensong ['i:vnsɔŋ], *n.* chant du soir, *m.*, vêpres, *m.pl.*

event [i'vent], *n.* événement, *m.*; issue, *f.*; **at all events**, en tout cas, dans tous les cas; **in the event of**, au cas où.

even-tempered ['i:vntempəd], *a.* calme, placide, égal.

eventful [i'ventful], *a.* mouvementé.

eventual [i'ventjuəl], *a.* éventuel, aléatoire; final, définitif.

eventually [i'ventjuəli], *adv.* finalement, à la fin, par la suite.

ever ['evə], *adv.* toujours; jamais; **ever since**, depuis; **for ever**, à jamais.

evergreen ['evəgri:n], *a.* toujours vert.—*n.* arbre toujours vert, *m.*

everlasting [evə'la:stiŋ], *a.* éternel, perpétuel.—*n.* éternité, *f.*; éternel, *m.*

everlastingly [evə'la:stiŋli], *adv.* éternellement.

evermore ['evəmɔ:], *adv.* toujours; éternellement.

every ['evri], *a.* chaque, tout, tous les; **every one**, chacun, *m.*, chacune, *f.*, tous, *pl.*

everybody [EVERYONE].

everyday ['evridei], *a.* quotidien; ordinaire; de tous les jours.

everyone ['evriwʌn], **everybody** ['evribɔdi], *n.* tout le monde, *m.*

everything ['evriθiŋ], *n.* tout, *m.*

everywhere ['evriweə], *adv.* partout.

evict [i'vikt], *v.t.* évincer, expulser.

eviction [i'vikʃən], *n.* éviction, expulsion, *f.*

evidence ['evidəns], *n.* évidence; preuve, *f.*; témoignage; témoin (*personne*), *m.*—*v.t.* montrer, prouver, démontrer.

evident ['evidənt], *a.* évident, visible.

evidently ['evidəntli], *adv.* évidemment.

evil [i:vl], *a.* mauvais; malheureux, malfaisant, méchant (*esprit etc.*).—*n.* mal; malheur, *m.*, calamité, *f.*—*adv.* mal.

evil-doer ['i:vlduə], *n.* malfaiteur, méchant, *m.*

evil-speaking ['i:vl'spi:kiŋ], *n.* médisance, *f.*

evince [i'vins], *v.t.* montrer, manifester, démontrer.

evoke [i'vouk], *v.t.* évoquer; susciter.

evolution [i:və'lu:ʃən], *n.* évolution, *f.*

evolve [i'vɔlv], *v.t.* dérouler; développer.—*v.i.* se dérouler; se développer.

ewe [ju:], *n.* brebis, *f.*

ewer ['juə], *n.* aiguière, *f.*, broc, *m.*

exact [ig'zækt], *v.t.* exiger, extorquer.—*a.* exact, précis.

exaction [ig'zækʃən], *n.* exaction, *f.*

exactitude [ig'zæktitju:d], **exactness** [ig'zæktnis], *n.* exactitude, *f.*

exactly [ig'zæktli], *adv.* exactement, précisément, au juste; juste.

exaggerate [ig'zædʒəreit], *v.t.* exagérer.

exaggeration [igzædʒə'reiʃən], *n.* exagération, *f.*

exalt [ig'zɔ:lt], *v.t.* exalter, élever; (*fig.*) louer.

exaltation [egzɔ:l'teiʃən], *n.* exaltation, élévation, *f.*

examination [igzæmi'neiʃən], *n.* examen, *m.*; inspection, vérification, *f.*; (*Law*) interrogatoire (*de prisonniers*), *m.*; audition (*de témoins*), *f.*; **to pass an examination**, réussir à un examen; **to sit (for) an examination**, passer un examen.

examine [ig'zæmin], *v.t.* examiner; visiter; (*Law*) interroger.

examiner [ig'zæminə], *n.* examinateur; (*Law*) juge d'instruction, *m.*

example [ig'za:mpl], *n.* exemple, *m.*; **for example**, par exemple.

exasperate [ig'za:spəreit], *v.t.* exaspérer; irriter, aigrir.

exasperation [igza:spə'reiʃən], *n.* exaspération, irritation, *f.*

excavate ['ekskəveit], *v.t.* creuser, excaver.

excavation [ekskə'veiʃən], *n.* excavation, *f.*; fouilles, *f.pl.*

excavator ['ekskəveitə], *n.* piocheuse-défonceuse, *f.*

exceed [ik'si:d], *v.t.* excéder, dépasser; (*fig.*) surpasser.

exceeding [ik'si:diŋ], *a.* grand, extrême.

exceedingly [ik'si:diŋli], *adv.* très, fort, extrêmement.

excel [ik'sel], *v.t.* surpasser, l'emporter sur.—*v.i.* exceller, se distinguer (*à*).

excellence ['eksələns], *n.* excellence, supériorité, *f.*

excellent ['eksələnt], *a.* excellent.

excellently ['eksələntli], *adv.* excellemment, parfaitement.

except [ik'sept], *v.t.* excepter; exclure (*de*).—*prep.* à l'exception de, hors, sauf.—*conj.* à moins que, à moins de.

excepting [ik'septiŋ], *prep.* excepté, hormis.

exception [ik'sepʃən], *n.* exception; objection, *f.*; *to take exception to,* se formaliser de.

exceptionable [ik'sepʃənəbl], *a.* blâmable, à critiquer.

exceptional [ik'sepʃənl], *a.* exceptionnel.

exceptionally [ik'sepʃənəli], *adv.* exceptionnellement.

excerpt ['eksə:pt], *n.* extrait, *m.,* citation, *f.*

excess [ik'ses], *n.* excès; excédent (*poids*), *m.*

excessive [ik'sesiv], *a.* excessif, extrême; immodéré.

excessively [ik'sesivli], *adv.* excessivement, à l'excès.

exchange [iks'tʃeindʒ], *n.* échange; (*Comm.*) change, *m.;* Bourse (*édifice*), *f.; bill of exchange,* lettre de change, *f.; rate of exchange,* taux du change, *m.; telephone exchange,* central téléphonique, *m.—v.t.* échanger, changer (*contre* ou *pour*).

exchequer [iks'tʃekə], *n.* trésor; Ministère des Finances, *m.*

excisable [ek'saizəbl], *a.* imposable; sujet aux droits de l'accise.

excise ['eksaiz], *n.* (*England*) excise, *f.;* (*France*) contributions indirectes, *f.pl.,* régie, *f.*

excise-man ['eksaizman], *n.* (*pl.* **-men** [men]) préposé *ou* employé de la régie, *m.*

excitable [ik'saitəbl], *a.* excitable, impressionnable.

excite [ik'sait], *v.t.* exciter; irriter; émouvoir; (*fig.*) provoquer.

excitement [ik'saitmənt], *n.* émoi, *m.,* surexcitation; émotion, agitation, *f.*

exciting [ik'saitiŋ], *a.* émouvant, passionnant, palpitant.

exclaim [iks'kleim], *v.i.* s'écrier, se récrier, s'exclamer.

exclamation [eksklə'meiʃən], *n.* exclamation, *f.,* cri, *m.*

exclude [iks'klu:d], *v.t.* exclure (*de*); proscrire.

excluding [iks'klu:diŋ], *prep.* sans compter.

exclusion [iks'klu:ʒən], *n.* exclusion, *f.*

exclusive [iks'klu:siv], *a.* exclusif.

excommunicate [ekskə'mju:nikeit], *v.t.* excommunier.

excrement ['ekskrimənt], *n.* excrément, *m.*

excrescence [iks'kresəns], *n.* excroissance, *f.*

excruciate [iks'kru:ʃieit], *v.t.* tourmenter, torturer.

excruciating [iks'kru:ʃieitiŋ], *a.* atroce, affreux, horrible.

exculpate ['ekskʌlpeit], *v.t.* disculper, justifier.

excursion [iks'kə:ʃən], *n.* excursion, randonnée; (*fig.*) digression, *f.*

excusable [iks'kju:zəbl], *a.* excusable.

excuse [iks'kju:s], *n.* excuse, *f.;* prétexte, *m.; to find an excuse,* chercher des excuses; *to make excuses,* s'excuser.—[eks'kju:z], *v.t.* excuser, pardonner; *excuse me!* pardon! *to be excused from duty,* être exempt de service.

execrable ['eksikrəbl], *a.* exécrable.

execrate ['eksikreit], *v.t.* exécrer, maudire.

execute ['eksikju:t], *v.t.* exécuter, accomplir; remplir (*un ordre*); *to execute a deed,* signer un contrat.

execution [eksi'kju:ʃən], *n.* exécution, *f.;* accomplissement supplice, *m.*

executioner [eksi'kju:ʃənə], *n.* bourreau, *m.*

executive [ig'zekjutiv], *a.* exécutif.—*n.* pouvoir exécutif; (*Comm.*) directeur, *m.*

executor [ig'zekjutə], *n.* exécuteur testamentaire, *m.*

exemplar [ig'zemplə], *n.* modèle, exemplaire, *m.*

exemplary [ig'zempləri], *a.* exemplaire; modèle.

exemplify [ig'zemplifai], *v.t.* démontrer par des exemples, illustrer; donner un exemple de.

exempt [ig'zempt, eg'zemt], *v.t.* exempter (*de*).—*a.* exempt.

exemption [ig'zempʃən], *n.* exemption, *f.*

exercise ['eksəsaiz], *n.* exercice; (*Sch.*) thème, devoir, *m.—v.t.* exercer; promener (*un chien*).—*v.i.* s'exercer; (*Mil.*) faire l'exercice.

exercise book ['eksəsaizbuk], *n.* cahier (*de devoirs*), *m.*

exert [ig'zə:t], *v.t.* déployer; mettre en œuvre; exercer (*influence, pression etc.*); *to exert oneself,* faire des efforts (*pour*).

exertion [ig'zə:ʃən], *n.* effort, *m.*

exhale [eks'heil], *v.t.* exhaler, émettre.

exhaust [ig'zɔ:st], *v.t.* épuiser.—*n.* échappement, *m.*

exhausted [ig'zɔ:stid], *a.* épuisé.

exhaustion [ig'zɔ:stʃən], *n.* épuisement, *m.*

exhaustive [ig'zɔ:stiv], *a.* qui épuise; (*fig.*) complet.

exhaust pipe [ig'zɔ:stpaip], *n.* (*Motor.*) tuyau d'échappement, *m.*

exhibit [ig'zibit], *v.t.* montrer; exposer; (*fig.*) exhiber.—*n.* objet exposé, *m.*

exhibition [eksi'biʃən], *n.* exposition; représentation, *f.,* spectacle, *m.;* (*Univ.*) bourse, *f.*

exhibitioner [eksi'biʃənə], *n.* (*Univ.*) boursier, *m.*

exhibitor [ig'zibitə], *n.* exposant, *m.*

exhilarate [ig'ziləreit], *v.t.* réjouir, égayer.

exhilarating [ig'ziləreitiŋ], *a.* qui égaye, réjouissant.

exhilaration [igzilə'reiʃən], *n.* réjouissance, gaieté, joie de vivre, *f.*

exhort [ig'zɔ:t], *v.t.* exhorter (*à*).

exhortation [egzɔ:'teiʃən], *n.* exhortation, *f.*

exhume [eks'hju:m], *v.t.* exhumer, déterrer.

exile ['eksail], *n.* exil; exilé (*personne*), *m.—v.t.* exiler.

exist [ig'zist], *v.i.* exister.

existence [ig'zistəns], *n.* existence, *f.;* être, *m.*

exit ['eksit], *n.* sortie, *f.—v.i.* (*Theat.*) il (elle) sort.

exodus ['eksədəs], *n.* exode, *m.*

exonerate [ig'zɔnəreit], *v.t.* décharger, exempter, exonérer, justifier.

exorbitant [ig'zɔ:bitənt], *a.* exorbitant, excessif, exagéré.

exotic [eg'zotik], *a.* exotique.

expand [iks'pænd], *v.t.* étendre, faire épanouir; amplifier; dilater (*gaz*).—*v.i.* se dilater; s'épanouir; se développer.

expanse [iks'pæns], *n.* étendue, *f.*

expansion [iks'pænʃən], *n.* expansion, *f.*

expatiate [eks'peiʃieit], *v.i.* s'étendre (*sur*).

expatriate [eks'peitrieit], *v.t.* expatrier, bannir.

expect [iks'pekt], *v.t.* attendre; s'attendre à, compter sur (*choses*); espérer; *she is expecting,* elle attend un bébé; *to know what to expect,* savoir à quoi s'en tenir.

expectant [iks'pektənt], *a.* expectant.
expectation [ekspek'teiʃən], *n.* attente, espérance; expectative; probabilité, *f.*
expedience [iks'piːdiəns], **expediency** [iks'piːdiənsi], *n.* convenance, utilité, opportunité, *f.*
expedient [iks'piːdiənt], *a.* convenable, à propos, utile, opportun.—*n.* expédient, *m.*
expedite ['ekspədait], *v.t.* expédier, hâter, accélérer.
expedition [ekspə'diʃən], *n.* expédition; promptitude, *f.*
expeditious [ekspi'diʃəs], *a.* expéditif, prompt.
expel [iks'pel], *v.t.* expulser, chasser; (*Sch.*) renvoyer.
expend [iks'pend], *v.t.* dépenser; (*fig.*) employer.
expenditure [iks'penditʃə], *n.* dépense, *f.*, dépenses, *f.pl.*; (*fig.*) sacrifice, *m.*
expense [iks'pens], *n.* dépense, *f.*; dépens; frais, *m.pl.*; *at any expense*, à tout prix; *incidental expenses*, faux frais; *to clear one's expenses*, faire ses frais.
expensive [iks'pensiv], *a.* coûteux, cher (*chose*); dépensier (*personne*).
expensively [iks'pensivli], *adv.* à grands frais.
experience [iks'piəriəns], *n.* expérience, *f.*; sentiment, *m.*—*v.t.* éprouver, faire l'expérience de.
experienced [iks'piəriənst], *a.* éprouvé, expérimenté.
experiment [eks'perimənt], *n.* expérience, *f.* —*v.i.* expérimenter.
experimental [eksperi'mentl], *a.* expérimental.
expert ['ekspəːt], *a.* expert, habile.—*n.* expert, *m.*
expiate ['ekspieit], *v.t.* expier.
expiation [ekspi'eiʃən], *n.* expiation, *f.*
expiration [ekspi'reiʃən], **expiry** [iks'paiəri], *n.* expiration; fin, *f.*, terme, *m.*
expire [iks'paiə], *v.i.* expirer, mourir.
explain [iks'plein], *v.t.* expliquer.—*v.i.* s'expliquer.
explanation [eksplə'neiʃən], *n.* explication, *f.*
explanatory [iks'plænətri], *a.* explicatif.
explicit [iks'plisit], *a.* explicite, formel; franc.
explode [iks'ploud], *v.t.* faire éclater; faire sauter (*mine*); (*fig.*) discréditer; *exploded theory*, théorie abandonnée, *f.*—*v.i.* éclater, sauter, faire explosion.
exploit ['eksploit], *n.* exploit, haut fait, *m.* —[iks'ploit], *v.t.* exploiter.
exploitation [eksploi'teiʃən], *n.* exploitation, *f.*
exploration [eksplɔː'reiʃən], *n.* exploration, *f.*; (*fig.*) examen, *m.*
explore [iks'plɔː], *v.t.* explorer; (*fig.*) examiner.
explorer [iks'plɔːrə], *n.* explorateur, *m.*
explosion [iks'plouʒən], *n.* explosion, *f.*
explosive [iks'plousiv], *a.* and *n.* explosif, *m.*
exponent [eks'pounənt], *n.* (*Math.*) exposant; (*fig.*) représentant, *m.*
export ['ekspɔːt], *n.* exportation; marchandise exportée, *f.*—[eks'pɔːt], *v.t.* exporter, *f.*
expose [iks'pouz], *v.t.* exposer; (*fig.*) révéler, découvrir, démasquer.
expostulate [iks'pɔstjuleit], *v.i.* faire des remontrances (à).
exposure [iks'pouʒə], *n.* exposition (*aux*

intempéries, à un danger*), *f.*; étalage (*de marchandises*); esclandre, *m.*; (*Phot.*) pose, *f.*; *to die of exposure*, mourir de froid.
expound [iks'paund], *v.t.* expliquer, exposer.
express [iks'pres], *a.* exprès; formel, explicite; *by express delivery*, par exprès.—*n.* exprès (*messager*); train express, *m.*—*v.t.* exprimer.
expression [iks'preʃən], *n.* expression, *f.*
expressive [iks'presiv], *a.* expressif.
expressly [iks'presli], *adv.* expressément, formellement.
expropriate [eks'prouprieit], *v.t.* exproprier.
expulsion [iks'pʌlʃən], *n.* expulsion, *f.*
expurgate ['ekspəːgeit], *v.t.* corriger, expurger (*livre*).
exquisite ['ekskwizit], *a.* exquis; vif, extrême (*douleur*); raffiné, délicat.
exquisitely ['ekskwizitli], *adv.* d'une manière exquise; parfaitement.
ex-service man [eks'səːvismən], *n.* (*pl.* -men [men]) ancien combattant, *m.*
extant [ek'stænt], *a.* qui existe encore.
extempore [eks'tempəri], *a.* improvisé.—*adv.* impromptu, sans préparation.
extemporize [eks'tempəraiz], *v.t.* improviser.
extend [iks'tend], *v.t.* étendre; prolonger; tendre (*la main*); *to extend a welcome*, souhaiter la bienvenue.—*v.i.* s'étendre; se prolonger (*temps*).
extension [iks'tenʃən], *n.* extension; étendue, prolongation (*de temps*), *f.*; (*Teleph.*) poste, *m.*; (*Elec.*) [FLEX].
extensive [iks'tensiv], *a.* étendu, vaste; ample.
extensively [iks'tensivli], *adv.* d'une manière étendue; bien, très, au loin.
extent [iks'tent], *n.* étendue, *f.*; (*fig.*) degré, point, *m.*; *to a certain extent*, jusqu'à un certain point; *to the extent of*, jusqu'à.
extenuate [eks'tenjueit], *v.t.* atténuer, amoindrir.
extenuating [eks'tenjueitiŋ], *a.* (*Law*) atténuant.
exterior [eks'tiəriə], *a.* extérieur, en dehors.— *n.* extérieur, *m.*
exterminate [iks'təːmineit], *v.t.* exterminer; extirper.
extermination [ikstəːmi'neiʃən], *n.* extermination, *f.*
external [eks'təːnl], *a.* extérieur; externe (*étudiant* etc.).
extinct [iks'tiŋkt], *a.* éteint; qui n'existe plus (*espèce* etc.); aboli.
extinguish [iks'tiŋgwiʃ], *v.t.* éteindre; (*fig.*) éclipser.
extinguisher [iks'tiŋgwiʃə], *n.* extincteur (*appareil*), *m.*
extirpate ['ekstəpeit], *v.t.* extirper.
extol [iks'toul], *v.t.* exalter, vanter.
extort [iks'tɔːt], *v.t.* extorquer, arracher.
extortion [iks'tɔːʃən], *n.* extorsion, *f.*
extortionate [iks'tɔːʃənit], *a.* extorsionnaire, exorbitant.
extra ['ekstrə], *a.* en sus; supplémentaire. *extra charge*, prix en sus, supplément, *m.* —*n.* supplément; (*Cine.*) figurant, *m.*—*adv.* en sus, de plus; *extra strong*, extra-solide.
extract ['ekstrækt], *n.* extrait; concentré (*de viande* etc.), *m.*—[iks'trækt], *v.t.* extraire, tirer (*de*); arracher (*dent*) à.

extraction [iks'trækʃən], *n.* extraction; origine, *f.*

extraneous [eks'treinjəs], *a.* étranger (à); non-essentiel.

extraordinarily [iks'trɔːdnrili], *a.* extraordinairement.

extraordinary [iks'trɔːdnri], *a.* extraordinaire, rare.

extravagance [iks'trævəgəns], *n.* extravagance; prodigalité, *f.*, gaspillage, *m.*

extravagant [iks'trævəgənt], *a.* extravagant (*immodéré*); prodigue, dépensier; exorbitant (*prix*).

extravagantly [iks'trævəgəntli], *adv.* d'une manière extravagante.

extreme [iks'triːm], *a.* extrême.—*n.* extrémité, *f.*; extrême, *m.*

extremely [iks'triːmli], *adv.* extrêmement, au dernier degré.

extremist [iks'triːmist], *n.* extrémiste, *m.*, *f.*; ultra, *m.*

extremity [iks'tremiti], *n.* extrémité, *f.*, extrême; bout, comble, *m.*

extricate ['ekstrikeit], *v.t.* débarrasser, dégager; **to extricate oneself**, se tirer d'affaire.

extrovert ['ekstrəvəːt], *n.* extroverti, *m.*

exuberance [ig'zjuːbərəns], *n.* exubérance, surabondance, *f.*

exuberant [ig'zjuːbərənt], *a.* exubérant, surabondant.

exude [ek'sjuːd], *v.t.* faire exsuder.—*v.i.* exsuder.

exult [ig'zʌlt], *v.i.* se réjouir, exulter (*de*).

exultant [ig'zʌltənt], *a.* joyeux, triomphant.

exultation [egzʌl'teiʃən], *n.* triomphe, *m.*, exultation, *f.*

eye [ai], *n.* œil; trou (*d'une aiguille*); (*Bot.*) œil, bouton, *m.*; (*Needlework*) porte; (*fig.*) vue, *f.*; **black eye**, œil poché; **blind in one eye**, borgne; **in the twinkling of an eye**, en un clin d'œil; **to keep an eye on**, surveiller.—*v.t.* regarder; lorgner.

eyeball ['aibɔːl], *n.* bulbe de l'œil, *m.*

eyebrow ['aibrau], *n.* sourcil, *m.*

eyed [aid], *a.* **blue-eyed**, aux yeux bleus.

eyeglass ['aiglɑːs], *n.* monocle (*un seul verre*), lorgnon, pince-nez (*double*), *m.*

eye-hole ['aihoul], *n.* orbite; petit judas, *m.*

eyelash ['ailæʃ], *n.* cil, *m.*

eyelet ['ailit], *n.* œillet, *m.*

eyelid ['ailid], *n.* paupière, *f.*

eyesight ['aisait], *n.* vue, *f.*

eyesore ['aisɔː], *n.* chose qui blesse l'œil, *f.*, objet d'aversion, *m.*

eye-witness ['aiwitnis], *n.* témoin oculaire, *m.*

eyrie, eyry [ʌERIE].

F

F, f [ef]. sixième lettre de l'alphabet; (*Mus.*) fa, *m.*

fable [feibl], *n.* fable, *f.*, conte, *m.*

fabric ['fæbrik], *n.* construction, *f.*; édifice, ouvrage, *m.*; étoffe, *f.*; (*fig.*) système, *m.*

fabricate ['fæbrikeit], *v.t.* fabriquer, inventer, contrefaire.

fabrication [fæbri'keiʃən], *n.* fabrication, *f.*

fabulous ['fæbjuləs], *a.* fabuleux.

face [feis], *n.* figure, *f.*; visage, *m.*; face, surface (*des choses*); (*fig.*) apparence, *f.*, état, *m.*; mine, physionomie, *f.*; front (*insolence*), *m.*; façade, *f.*, devant (*front*), *m.*; facette (*d'un diamant*), *f.*; cadran (*de pendule*), *m.*; **face to face**, vis-à-vis; **to make faces at**, faire des grimaces à.—*v.t.* faire face à, affronter; mettre un revers à, parer (*vêtements*); revêtir (*mur etc.*); donner sur (*maison etc.*).—*v.i.* prendre un faux dehors; (*Mil.*) faire front; **face about!** volte-face!

facet ['fæsit], *n.* facette, *f.*—*v.t.* facetter.

facetious [fə'siːʃəs], *a.* facétieux.

facetiously [fə'siːʃəsli], *adv.* facétieusement.

facetiousness [fə'siːʃəsnis], *n.* plaisanterie, *f.*

facial ['feiʃəl], *a.* facial.

facile ['fæsail], *a.* facile; complaisant.

facility [fə'siliti], *n.* facilité, *f.*

facilitate [fə'siliteit], *v.t.* faciliter.

facing ['feisiŋ], *n.* parement (*de vêtements*); revers, *m.*

facsimile [fæk'simili], *n.* fac-similé, *m.*

fact [fækt], *n.* fait, *m.*; **as a matter of fact, in fact**, en réalité; **in point of fact**, au fait; **matter-of-fact man**, homme positif, *m.*

faction ['fækʃən], *n.* faction; (*fig.*) discorde, dissension, *f.*

factor ['fæktə], *n.* agent; facteur, *m.*

factory ['fæktri], *n.* usine, fabrique, *f.*; (*obs.*), comptoir (*d'outre-mer*) *m.*

faculty ['fækəlti], *n.* faculté, *f.*, pouvoir, talent, *m.*

fad [fæd], *n.* marotte, manie, *f.*

fade [feid], *v.t.* flétrir, faire flétrir.—*v.i.* se faner, se flétrir; disparaître, périr.

fag [fæg], *v.t.* forcer à piocher; fatiguer, éreinter; **fagged out**, éreinté.—*v.i.* travailler dur, piocher (à).—*n.* fatigue, peine, corvée, *f.*; (*pop.*) cigarette, *f.*

fag end ['fægend], *n.* (*pop.*) mégot (*de cigarette*), *m.*

faggot ['fægət], *n.* fagot, *m.*

fail [feil], *v.t.* manquer à, abandonner.—*v.i.* faillir; manquer (*to miss*); échouer (*ne pas réussir*); (*Comm.*) faire faillite.—*n.* manque, insuccès, *m.*

failing ['feiliŋ], *n.* défaut, *m.*, faute; (*Comm.*) faillite, *f.*—*prep.* à défaut de.

failure ['feiljə], *n.* manque, défaut (*want*); échec; insuccès, *m.*; affaire manquée, *f.*, fiasco, *m.*; chute (*d'une pièce etc.*); (*Comm.*) faillite, *f.*; **he is a failure**, c'est un raté.

***fain** [fein], *adv.* avec plaisir, volontiers.

faint [feint], *a.* faible; affaibli; languissant; découragé; timide.—*v.i.* s'évanouir, défaillir.—*n.* évanouissement, *m.*

faint-hearted ['feinthɑːtid], *a.* timide, sans courage, découragé.

fainting ['feintiŋ], *n.* évanouissement, *m.*, défaillance, *f.*

faintly ['feintli], *adv.* faiblement; mollement.

faintness ['feintnis], *n.* faiblesse, *f.*

fair [feə], *a.* beau; favorable (*vent*); clair (*teint*); blond (*cheveux etc.*); juste, équitable;

(*fig.*) assez bon, passable; *fair play*, franc jeu, *m.*; *fair price*, juste prix, *m.*; *that is not fair* (*at games*), cela n'est pas de jeu.—*adv.* bien; de bonne foi, honorablement.—*n.* foire (*marché*), *f.*

fairly ['feəli], *adv.* bien; loyalement; doucement; avec justesse; de bonne foi; passablement, assez.

fairness ['feənis], *n.* beauté; couleur blonde (*des cheveux*); blancheur (*du teint*); équité, impartialité, *f.*

fairy ['feəri], *a.* des fées, féerique.—*n.* fée, *f.*

fairy tale ['feəriteil], *n.* conte de fées, *m.*

faith [feiθ], *n.* foi, croyance; (*fig.*) fidélité, *f.*—*int.* ma [foi] en vérité!

faithful ['feiθful], *a.* fidèle.

faithfully ['feiθfuli], *adv.* fidèlement; *yours faithfully* (*lettre d'affaires*), veuillez agréer mes salutations distinguées.

faithfulness ['feiθfulnis], *n.* fidélité, *f.*

faithless ['feiθlis], *a.* sans foi, infidèle.

faithlessness ['feiθlisnis], *n.* infidélité; déloyauté, *f.*

fake [feik], *v.t.*, *v.i.* truquer, maquiller.

falcon ['fɔːlkən], *n.* faucon, *m.*

fall [fɔːl], *v.i. irr.* tomber; s'abaisser; baisser, diminuer; *to fall away from*, abandonner, quitter; *to fall back* tomber en arrière; (*Mil.*) reculer; *to fall down*, tomber par terre; *to fall for*, tomber amoureux de; *to fall for it*, s'y laisser prendre; *to fall in*, s'écrouler; (*Mil.*) se mettre en rangs, s'aligner; *to fall off*, tomber; diminuer; *to fall out*, tomber; se brouiller; (*Mil.*) *fall out!* rompez vos rangs! *to fall through*, échouer; *to fall to*, se mettre à; *to fall under*, être compris sous; tomber sous; *to fall upon*, tomber sur, attaquer; incomber à.—*n.* chute, *f.*; (*Am.*) automne, *m.* ou *f.*; tombée (*de la nuit*); baisse (*de prix*), *f.*; éboulement (*de terre*), *m.*; chute, cascade (*de rivières etc.*); décrue (*des eaux*); diminution (*de quantité*), *f.*

fallacy ['fæləsi], *n.* erreur, fausseté, illusion, *f.*

fallible ['fæləbl], *a.* faillible.

fall-out ['fɔːlaut], *n.* retombées radioactives, *f.pl.*

fallow ['fælou], *a.* en jachère; (*fig.*) inculte; fauve (*daim etc.*).—*n.* jachère, friche, *f.*

false [fɔːls], *a.* faux, perfide, déloyal; infidèle; prétendu; illégal (*détention*).

falsehood ['fɔːlshud], *n.* mensonge, *m.*

falsely ['fɔːlsli], *adv.* faussement.

falseness ['fɔːlsnis], *n.* fausseté; perfidie, *f.*

falsetto [fɔːl'setou], *n.* (*Mus.*) voix de fausset, *f.*

falsify ['fɔːlsifai], *v.t.* falsifier; fausser.

falter ['fɔːltə], *v.i.* hésiter; bégayer; chanceler.

faltering ['fɔːltəriŋ], *n.* hésitation, *f.*

fame [feim], *n.* gloire, renommée, *f.*

famed [feimd], *a.* renommé.

familiar [fə'miljə], *a.* familier, intime; de la famille; *to be familiar with*, être familier avec, connaître.—*n.* ami intime; esprit familier, *m.*

familiarity [fəmili'æriti], *n.* familiarité, *f.*

familiarly [fə'miljəli], *adv.* familièrement, sans cérémonie.

family ['fæmili], *a.* de famille, de la famille.—*n.* famille, *f.*

famine ['fæmin], *n.* famine, disette, *f.*

famished ['fæmiʃt], *a.* affamé.

famous ['feiməs], *a.* fameux, célèbre.

famously ['feiməsli], *adv.* fameusement; (*fig.*) prodigieusement.

fan [fæn], *n.* éventail; ventilateur; (*colloq.*) admirateur enthousiaste (*d'un artiste ou d'un sport*), *m.*—*v.t.* éventer; souffler (*feu*); (*Agric.*) vanner; (*fig.*) exciter, activer.

fanatic [fə'nætik], *a.* and *n.* fanatique, *m.*, *f.*

fanatical [fə'nætikəl], *a.* fanatique.

fanaticism [fə'nætisizm], *n.* fanatisme, *m.*

fancied ['fænsid], *a.* imaginaire, imaginé; (*Turf*) bien coté (*cheval*).

fancier ['fænsiə], *n.* amateur (*de*), *m.*

fanciful ['fænsiful], *a.* fantasque, capricieux.

fancy ['fænsi], *a.* de fantaisie.—*n.* fantaisie, imagination; idée, *f.*, caprice, goût (*pour*), *m.*, envie (*de*), *f.*—*v.t.* s'imaginer, se figurer; avoir du goût pour.—*v.i.* s'imaginer, se figurer; *just fancy!* figurez-vous!

fancy dress ['fænsidres], *n.* travesti, *m.*, *fancy-dress ball*, bal costumé, *m.*

fane [fein], *n.* temple, édifice sacré, *m.*

fanfare ['fænfeə], *n.* fanfare, *f.*

fang [fæŋ], *n.* croc (*de chien*), *m.*; racine (*d'une dent*); défense (*de sanglier*); (*fig.*) griffe, *f.*

fantastic [fæn'tæstik], *a.* fantastique; fantasque (*personne*).

fantasy ['fæntəsi], *n.* fantaisie, *f.*

far [fɑː], *a.* (*comp.* farther, further; *superl.* farthest, furthest) lointain, éloigné, reculé; *the Far East*, l'extrême Orient, *m.*—*adv.* loin, au loin; bien, fort, beaucoup; *as far as*, aussi loin que, jusqu'à; *by far*, de beaucoup; *far and wide*, de tous côtés; *how far?* jusqu'où?

far-away ['fɑːrəwei], *a.* rêveur (*regard*); lointain.

farce [fɑːs], *n.* farce, *f.*

farcical ['fɑːsikl], *a.* burlesque; (*fig.*) drôle.

fare [feə], *v.i.* aller, se porter; se nourrir, vivre.—*n.* prix de la course; prix de la place, *m.*, place, *f.*; voyageur (*personne*), *m.*; chère (*aliment*), *f.*; *bill of fare*, menu, *m.*, carte du jour, *f.*; *return fare*, aller et retour, *m.*; *single fare*, billet simple, *m.*

farewell [feə'wel], *a.* d'adieu.—*n.* adieu, *m.*

far-fetched [fɑː'fetʃt], *a.* recherché; tiré par les cheveux.

farm [fɑːm], *n.* ferme, *f.*—*v.t.* affermer, prendre à ferme; exploiter.

farmer ['fɑːmə], *n.* fermier, métayer; cultivateur, *m.*

farm-house ['fɑːmhaus], *n.* ferme, *f.*

farming ['fɑːmiŋ], *n.* agriculture, exploitation agricole, *f.*

farm-yard ['fɑːmjɑːd], *n.* basse-cour, *f.*

Faroe ['fɛərou] **Islands**, les îles Féroé, *f.pl.*

far-reaching ['fɑːriːtʃiŋ], *a.* d'une grande portée.

farrier ['færiə] *n.* maréchal ferrant, *m.*

farther [FURTHER].

farthest [FURTHERMOST].

fascinate ['fæsineit], *v.t.* fasciner; charmer, séduire.

fascinating ['fæsineitiŋ], *a.* fascinateur, enchanteur, séduisant.

fascination [fæsi'neiʃən], *n.* fascination, *f.*, charme, *m.*

fascism ['fæʃizm], *n.* fascisme, *m.*

fascist ['fæʃist], *a.* and *n.* fasciste, *m.*, *f.*

fashion ['fæʃən], n. façon, forme; mode, f.; le grand monde, m.; *after a fashion*, tant bien que mal; *in fashion*, à la mode; *to set the fashion*, donner le ton.—v.t. façonner, former.

fashionable ['fæʃnəbl], a. à la mode, élégant, de bon ton, (fam.) chic.

fashionably ['fæʃnəbli], adv. à la mode, élégamment.

fast (1) [fɑːst], n. jeûne, m.—v.i. jeûner.

fast (2) [fɑːst], a. ferme, fixe (solide); fidèle (constant); bon teint (couleur); serré (nœud); (Naut.) amarré (fixé); bien fermé (porte); vite, rapide; en avance (horloge etc.); (fig.) dissolu; *to make fast*, assujettir, fermer (porte, fenêtre); (Naut.) amarrer.—adv. ferme (stable); vite, rapidement (avec célérité); fort (pluie); *to hold fast*, tenir bon; *to stand fast*, ne pas broncher.

fasten [fɑːsn], v.t. attacher, fixer; lier; fermer (fenêtre, porte etc.).—v.i. s'attacher (à); se fermer.

fastener ['fɑːsnə], **fastening** ['fɑːsniŋ], n. attache; agrafe (de robe); fermeture, f.

fastidious [fæs'tidiəs], a. difficile; dédaigneux; délicat; exigeant.

fastness ['fɑːstnis], n. fermeté; vitesse; place forte (forteresse); légèreté de conduite, f.

fat [fæt], a. gras; gros (personne); (fig.) riche, fertile.—n. gras, m.; graisse; (fig.) substance, f.; (pl.) matières grasses, f.pl.

fatal [feitl], a. fatal, funeste; mortel.

fatality [fə'tæliti], n. fatalité, f.; accident mortel, m.

fatally ['feitəli], adv. fatalement, mortellement.

fate [feit], n. destin, sort, m.

fated ['feitid], a. destiné.

fateful ['feitful], a. fatal; décisif.

fat-head ['fæthed], n. (colloq.) nigaud, m.

father ['fɑːðə], n. père, m.; (pl.) pères, ancêtres, aïeux, m.pl.; *godfather*, parrain, m.; *grandfather*, grand-père, m.; *stepfather*, beau-père, m.

father-in-law ['fɑːðərinlɔː], n. beau-père, m.

fatherland ['fɑːðəlænd], n. pays natal, m., patrie, f.

fatherly ['fɑːðəli], a. paternel, de père.

fathom ['fæðəm], n. toise; (Naut.) brasse (= 6 pieds = 1 m. 829); (fig.) portée, profondeur, f.—v.t. sonder; (fig.) approfondir.

fatigue [fə'tiːg], n. fatigue; (Mil.) corvée, f.—v.t. fatiguer, lasser.

fatiguing [fə'tiːgiŋ], a. fatigant.—pres.p. fatiguant.

fatten [fætn], v.t. engraisser; (fig.) enrichir.

fattening ['fætniŋ], a. engraissant.—n. engraissement, m.

fatty ['fæti], a. graisseux.

fatuous ['fætjuəs], a. sot; béat.

fatuousness ['fætjuəsnis], n. fatuité, f.

fault [fɔːlt], n. faute, f.; défaut, vice, m.; (Geol.) faille, f.

faultless ['fɔːltlis], a. sans défaut, sans faute, impeccable.

faultlessly ['fɔːltlisli], adv. irréprochablement.

faultlessness ['fɔːltlisnis], n. perfection, f.

faulty ['fɔːlti], a. fautif, blâmable, défectueux.

favor ['feivə], n. faveur, f., bonnes grâces, f.pl.; bienfait, m.; grâce (permission), f.; couleurs, faveurs (rubans), f.pl.; (Comm.) honorée, f.—v.t. favoriser, honorer (de).

favorable ['feivərəbl], a. favorable.

favorably ['feivərəbli], adv. favorablement.

favorite ['feivərit], a. favori, préféré.—n. favori, m.

fawn [fɔːn], n. faon, m.—v.i. *to fawn upon*, caresser, flatter.

fawning ['fɔːniŋ], a. flatteur, servile.—n. caresse, flatterie, f.

fear [fiə], n. crainte, peur; inquiétude, f.; *for fear of*, de peur de.—v.t. craindre, redouter, avoir peur de.—v.i. craindre, avoir peur.

fearful ['fiəful], a. craintif, timide; terrible; affreux, effrayant.

fearless ['fiəlis], a. sans peur, intrépide.

fearlessly ['fiəlisli], adv. sans crainte, avec intrépidité.

feasible ['fiːzəbl], a. faisable, praticable.

feast [fiːst], n. festin, m.; fête, f.; régal, m.—v.t. fêter, régaler.—v.i. faire festin, se régaler.

feat [fiːt], n. exploit, fait, haut fait, m.

feather ['feðə], n. plume; penne (aile et queue d'oiseau), f.; (Mil.) plumet, m.—v.t. orner d'une plume; *to feather one's nest*, faire sa pelote.

feature ['fiːtʃə], n. trait, m.; (pl.) visage, m. figure; (fig.) spécialité, f.

February ['februəri], février, m.

feckless ['feklis], a. faible, veule.

fecundity [fə'kanditi], n. fécondité, f.

federal ['fedərəl], a. fédéral.

federate ['fedərit], a. fédéré.—['fedəreit], v.t. fédérer.—v.i. se fédérer.

federation [fedə'reiʃən], n. fédération, f.

fee [fiː], n. honoraires, m.pl.; cachet, salaire; (Eccles. etc.) droit, m.

feeble [fiːbl], a. faible; débile.

feebleness ['fiːblnis], n. faiblesse, f.

feebly ['fiːbli], adv. faiblement.

feed [fiːd], n. nourriture; pâture, f., pâturage (pour bestiaux), m.—v.t. irr. nourrir; donner à manger à; faire paître (bestiaux); (pop.) *to be fed up*, en avoir marre.—v.i. se nourrir; paître (animaux).

feed-back ['fiːdbæk], n. (Rad.) rétro-action, f.

feeding ['fiːdiŋ], n. nourriture; pâture (pour bestiaux), f.

feeding bottle ['fiːdiŋbɒtl], n. biberon, m.

feel [fiːl], n. tâter, toucher, sentir; éprouver; *to feel one's way*, avancer à tâtons.—v.i. sentir, se sentir; se trouver; *to feel cold*, avoir froid; *to feel like doing something*, avoir envie de faire quelque chose.—n. toucher; attouchement; tact, m.

feeler ['fiːlə], n. antenne (d'insecte), f.; (fig.) ballon d'essai, m.

feeling ['fiːliŋ], a. tendre, touchant.—n. toucher; sentiment, m., sensibilité, f., émotion, f.

feet [FOOT].

feign [fein], v.t. feindre, simuler.—v.i. feindre, faire semblant (de).

feigned [feind], a. feint, simulé.

feint [feint], n. feinte, f.—v.i. feinter.

felicitate [fi'lisiteit], v.t. féliciter.

felicitation [filisi'teiʃən], n. félicitation, f.

felicity [fi'lisiti], n. félicité, f., bonheur, m.

fell (1) [fel], v.t. abattre, assommer, terrasser.

fell (2) [fel], *past* [FALL].

fellow ['felou], *n.* compagnon, camarade, confrère; associé, membre; pendant, pareil (*choses*); (*colloq.*) garçon; individu, type, *m.*; *good fellow*, brave type.

fellow citizen ['felou'sitizn], *n.* concitoyen, *m.*

fellow countryman ['felou'kʌntrimən], *n.* (*pl.* -men [men]) compatriote, *m.*

fellow feeling (*animaux*), *n.* sympathie, *f.*

fellowship ['felouʃip], *n.* société, association; camaraderie, *f.*

fellow traveller ['felou'trævlə], *n.* compagnon de voyage; (*Polit.*) sympathisant communiste, communist, *m.*

felon ['felən], *a.* félon, traître.—*n.* criminel, *m.*

felony ['feləni], *n.* crime, *m.*

felt (1) [felt], *n.* feutre, chapeau de feutre, *m.*; *roofing felt*, carton bitumé, *m.*

felt (2) [felt], *past* [FEEL].

female ['fi:meil], *a.* féminin, de femme; femelle (*animaux*); *a female friend*, une amie.—*n.* femme; jeune personne; femelle (*animaux*), *f.*

feminine ['feminin], *a.* féminin.

fen [fen], *n.* marais, marécage, *m.*

fence [fens], *n.* clôture, enceinte; palissade, barrière; (*Turf*) haie; (*Spt.*) escrime (à l'épée); (*fig.*) défense, *f.*; (*slang*) receleur (*d'objets volés*), *m.*; *to sit on the fence*, (*fig.*) ne pas s'engager, ménager la chèvre et le chou.—*v.t.* enclore, mettre une clôture à, palissader; (*fig.*) protéger.—*v.i.* faire des armes.

fencing ['fensiŋ], *n.* (*Spt.*) escrime; enceinte, clôture, *f.*

fencing master ['fensiŋmɑ:stə], *n.* maître d'armes, *m.*

fend [fend], *v.t. to fend off*, parer.—*v.i. to fend for oneself*, se débrouiller, veiller à ses intérêts.

fender ['fendə], *n.* garde-feu, *m.*; (*Naut.*) défense, *f.*; (*Am. Motor.*) pare-boue, *m.*

ferment ['fə:mənt], *n.* ferment, *m.*; fermentation, *f.*—[fə:'ment], *v.t.* faire fermenter.—*v.i.* fermenter.

fermentation [fə:mən'teiʃən], *n.* fermentation, *f.*

fern [fə:n], *n.* fougère, *f.*

ferocious [fə'rouʃəs], *a.* féroce.

ferociously [fə'rouʃəsli], *adv.* avec férocité.

ferocity [fə'rɔsiti], *n.* férocité, *f.*

ferret ['ferit], *n.* furet, *m.*—*v.t.* fureter; *to ferret out*, dépister, dénicher.

ferrule ['feru:l], *n.* virole (*anneau*), *f.*

ferry ['feri], *v.t.* passer en bac.—*n.* bac, passage, *m.*; *air ferry*, avion transbordeur, *m.*

ferry-boat ['feribout], *n.* bac, bateau transbordeur de trains, *m.*

fertile ['fə:tail], *a.* fertile, fécond.

fertility [fə'tiliti], *n.* fertilité, fécondité, *f.*

fertilize ['fə:tilaiz], *v.t.* fertiliser.

fertilizer ['fə:tilaizə], *n.* fertilisant, engrais, *m.*

fervent ['fə:vənt], *a.* ardent, fervent, vif.

fervently ['fə:vəntli], *adv.* ardemment, avec ferveur.

fester ['festə], *v.i.* s'ulcérer; (*fig.*) se corrompre.—*n.* abcès, *m.*, pustule, *f.*

festival ['festivl], *a.* de fête, joyeux.—*n.* fête, *f.*; (*Mus., Theat.*) festival, *m.*

festive ['festiv], *a.* de fête, joyeux.

festivity [fes'tiviti], *n.* fête, *f.*; réjouissances, *f.pl.*

festoon [fes'tu:n], *n.* feston, *m.*—*v.t.* festonner (*de*).

fetch [fetʃ], *v.t.* chercher, aller chercher; apporter (*choses*); amener (*personnes etc.*); rapporter (*prix*).—*n.* ruse, *f.*; tour, *m.*

fête [feit], *n.* fête, *f.*—*v.t.* fêter.

fetlock ['fetlɔk], *n.* fanon (*de cheval*), *m.*

fetter ['fetə], *v.t.* entraver, enchaîner.

fetters ['fetəz], *n.pl.* (*fig.*) fers, *m.pl.*, chaînes, entraves (*de cheval*), *f.pl.*

fettle [fetl], *v.t.* arranger, préparer.—*n.* bon état, *m.*

feud [fju:d], *n.* querelle; vendetta, *f.*

feudal ['fju:dl], *a.* féodal.

feudalism ['fju:dlizm], *n.* féodalité, *f.*

fever ['fi:və], *n.* fièvre, *f.*

feverish ['fi:vəriʃ], *a.* fiévreux; (*fig.*) fébrile.

few [fju:], *a.* peu de; *a few*, quelques.—*n.* peu de gens, *m.pl.*; *a few*, quelques-uns, *m.pl.*, quelques-unes, *f.pl.*

fewer ['fju:ə], *a.* moins (*de*); moins nombreux.

fiasco [fi'æskou], *n.* fiasco, four, *m.*

fib [fib], *n.* petit mensonge, *m.*—*v.i.* mentir.

fibber ['fibə], *n.* menteur, *m.*

fibre ['faibə], *n.* fibre, *f.*

fibrositis [faibrə'saitis], *n.* (*Med.*) cellulite, *f.*

fibrous ['faibrəs], *a.* fibreux.

fickle [fikl], *a.* volage, inconstant.

fickleness ['fiklnis], *n.* inconstance, légèreté, *f.*

fiction ['fikʃən], *n.* fiction, *f.*; *works of fiction*, romans, *m.pl.*

fictitious [fik'tiʃəs], *a.* fictif, imaginaire; (*fig.*) faux, factice.

fiddle [fidl], *n.* violon; (*pej.*) crincrin, *m.*; (*pop.*) resquille, combine, *f.*—*v.t.* jouer du violon; (*fig.*) niaiser (*baguenauder*); (*pop.*) resquiller.

fiddler ['fidlə], *n.* joueur de violon; ménétrier, *m.*

fiddlesticks! ['fidlstiks], *int.* bah! quelle blague!

fidelity [fi'deliti], *n.* fidélité, *f.*

fidget ['fidʒit], *n.* agitation, *f.*; être remuant (*personne*).—*v.i.* se remuer, s'agiter.

fidgety ['fidʒiti], *a.* remuant, agité; ennuyeux (*gênant*).

field [fi:ld], *n.* champ; pré, *m.*, prairie; (*Mil.*) campagne, *f.*; champ de bataille, *m.*; (*Turf etc.*) courants, *m.pl.*; *in the scientific field*, dans le domaine des sciences.—*v.t.* (*Cricket*) arrêter (*une balle*); réunir (*équipe*).—*v.i.* (*Cricket*) tenir le champ.

field day ['fi:lddei], *n.* (*Mil.*) jour de manœuvres; (*fig.*) jour de grand succès, *m.*

field marshal ['fi:ldmɑ:ʃl], *n.* maréchal, *m.*

fiend [fi:nd], *n.* démon *m.*

fiendish ['fi:ndiʃ], *a.* diabolique, infernal.

fierce [fiəs], *a.* féroce, farouche, furieux.

fiercely ['fiəsli], *adv.* férocement, furieusement.

fierceness ['fiəsnis], *n.* violence, fureur, brutalité, *f.*; (*fig.*) acharnement, *m.*

fieriness ['faiərinis], *n.* fougue, ardeur, *f.*

fiery ['faiəri], *a.* de feu; (*fig.*) ardent, fougueux.

fife [faif], *n.* fifre, *m.*

fifteen [fif'ti:n], *a. and n.* quinze, *m.*

fifteenth [fif'ti:nθ], *a.* quinze (*jour du mois, roi etc.*).—*n.* quinzième (*fraction*), *m.*

fifth

fifth [fifθ], *a.* cinquième; cinq (*jour du mois, roi etc.*); **Charles the Fifth**, Charles-Quint.—*n.* cinquième (*fraction*), *m.*; (*Mus.*) quinte, *f.*

fiftieth [ˈfiftiəθ], *a.* cinquantième.—*n.* cinquantième (*fraction*), *m.*

fifty [ˈfifti], *a.* and *n.* cinquante, *m.*; **about fifty**, une cinquantaine.

fig [fig], *n.* figue, *f.*; figuier (*arbre*), *m.*

fight [fait], *v.t. irr.* se battre avec, combattre; livrer (*une bataille*).—*v.i.* se battre; combattre (*avec*).—*n.* combat, *m.*, bataille; (*fig.*) lutte, *f.*

fighter [ˈfaitə], *n.* combattant; (*pej.*) batailleur; (*Av.*) chasseur, *m.*

fighting [ˈfaitiŋ], *n.* combat, *m.*; lutte, *f.*

figment [ˈfigmənt], *n.* fiction, invention, *f.*

figurative [ˈfigjuərətiv], *a.* figuré; figuratif.

figuratively [ˈfigjuərətivli], *adv.* au figuré; figurativement.

figure [ˈfigə], *n.* figure; taille, tournure (*d'une personne*), *f.*; dessin (*sur un tissu*), *m.*; (*Arith.*) chiffre, *m.*; **figure of speech**, figure de rhétorique, métaphore; (*fam.*) façon de parler, *f.*; **to cut a figure**, faire figure. —*v.t.* figurer, former; façonner; (*fig.*) imaginer; **to figure out**, calculer.—*v.i.* figurer.

figure-head [ˈfigəhed], *n.* (*Naut.*) figure de proue, *f.*; (*fig.*) homme de paille; prête-nom, *m.*

Fiji [ˈfiːdʒiː], **the Fiji Islands**, les îles Fidji ou Viti, *f.pl.*

filament [ˈfiləmənt], *n.* filament, *m.*

filbert [ˈfilbət], *n.* aveline, grosse noisette, *f.*

filch [filtʃ], *v.t.* escamoter, filouter, chiper.

file [fail], *n.* lime (*outil*), liasse, *f.*, dossier, classeur (*de papiers*), *m.*; liste; collection (*de journaux*), *f.*; (*Mil.*) file; (*Theat. etc.*) queue, *f.*; **card-index file**, fichier, *m.*—*v.t.* limer, affiler; mettre en liasse; (*Law*) déposer (*une requête etc.*); **to file away**, classer.—*v.i.* (*Mil.*) marcher à la file; **to file off** or **past**, défiler.

filial [ˈfiliəl], *a.* filial.

filibuster [ˈfilibʌstə], *n.* flibustier, *m.*

filing [ˈfailiŋ], *n.* limage, *m.*; mise en liasse, *f.*, classement, *m.*; (*pl.*) limaille, *f.*

filing cabinet [ˈfailiŋkæbinit], *n.* cartonnier, classeur, *m.*

fill [fil], *v.t.* emplir, remplir; combler (*jusqu'au bord*); occuper; rassasier; **to fill a tooth**, plomber une dent.—*v.i.* se remplir, s'emplir. —*n.* suffisance, *f.*; (*colloq.*) **one's fill**, tout son soûl.

fillet [ˈfilit], *n.* bandeau; filet (*de poisson*), *m.*

filling [ˈfiliŋ], *a.* rassasiant.—*n.* plombage, *m.*

filling station [ˈfiliŋˈsteiʃən], *n.* poste d'essence, *m.*

filly [ˈfili], *n.* pouliche, *f.*

film [film], *n.* taie (*devant les yeux*), pellicule; (*Anat.*) tunique, *f.*; (*fig.*) nuage, voile, *m.*; (*Phot.*) pellicule, couche sensible, *f.*; (*Cine.*) film, *m.*; **film script**, scénario, script, *m.*; **film star**, vedette de cinéma, *f.*—*v.t.* couvrir d'une tunique, d'une pellicule etc.; filmer, mettre à l'écran.—*v.i.* tourner un film.

film-strip [ˈfilmstrip], *n.* film fixe, *m.*

filter [ˈfiltə], *n.* filtre, *m.*—*v.t.* filtrer.

filter tip [ˈfiltəˈtip], *n.* bout filtrant, *m.*

filth [filθ], *n.* ordure, saleté; (*fig.*) corruption, *f.*

filthy [ˈfilθi], *a.* sale, immonde; (*fig.*) obscène, infect.

fin [fin], *n.* nageoire, *f.*; aileron (*de requin*), *m.*; (*Naut., Av.*) dérive; (*Motor.*) ailette (*de radiateur*), *f.*

final [fainl], *a.* final, dernier; décisif.—*n.* (*Spt.*) finale, *f.*

finally [ˈfainəli], *adv.* enfin, finalement; définitivement.

finance [fiˈnæns, faiˈnæns], *n.* finance, *f.*

financial [fiˈnænʃəl], *a.* financier.

financier [fiˈnænsiə], *n.* financier, *m.*

finch [fintʃ], *n.* (*Orn.*) pinson, *m.*

find [faind], *v.t. irr.* trouver; estimer; (*Law*) déclarer (*coupable*); prononcer (*un verdict*); (*fig.*) pourvoir; **to find out**, trouver, découvrir, inventer, résoudre; démasquer; **to find out about**, se renseigner sur; **to find out the truth of**.—*v.n.* découverte, trouvaille, *f.*

finding [ˈfaindiŋ], *n.* (*Law*) verdict, *m.*

fine (1) [fain], *n.* amende, *f.*—*v.t.* mettre à l'amende.

fine (2) [fain], *a.* fin; raffiné; subtil; beau (*à voir*); (*fig.*) bon, accompli; (*colloq.*) fameux; **it is fine**, il fait beau (*temps*).

fine arts [fainˈɑːts], *n.pl.* beaux arts, *m.pl.*

finely [ˈfainli], *adv.* fin, délicatement; élégamment; (*colloq.*) bien; (*iron.*) joliment.

fineness [ˈfainnis], *n.* finesse, délicatesse, *f.*

finery [ˈfainəri], *n.* parure, *f.*, beaux habits, *m.pl.*

finesse [fiˈnes], *n.* finesse, *f.*

finger [ˈfiŋgə], *n.* doigt, *m.*; (*fig.*) main, *f.*—*v.t.* toucher, manier.—*v.i.* (*Mus.*) doigter.

fingering [ˈfiŋgəriŋ], *n.* maniement; (*Mus.*) doigté, *m.*

finger-nail [ˈfiŋgəneil], *n.* ongle de la main, *m.*

finger-print [ˈfiŋgəprint], *n.* empreinte digitale, *f.*

finger-stall [ˈfiŋgəstɔːl], *n.* doigtier, *m.*

finical [ˈfinikl], **finicking** [ˈfinikiŋ], (*colloq.*) **finicky** [ˈfiniki], *a.* précieux, méticuleux, vétilleux.

finish [ˈfiniʃ], *v.t.* finir, terminer; achever; (*Tech.*) usiner.—*v.i.* cesser, finir, prendre fin.—*n.* fini, *m.*; (*fig.*) fin; (*Spt.*) arrivée, *f.*

finished [ˈfiniʃt], *a.* fini; (*fig.*) parfait.

finishing [ˈfiniʃiŋ], *a.* dernier; (*Spt.*) **finishing line**, ligne d'arrivée, *f.*

finite [ˈfainait], *a.* fini; borné.

Finland [ˈfinlənd], la Finlande, *f.*

Finn [fin], *n.* Finlandais, Finnois, *m.*

Finnish [ˈfiniʃ], *a.* finlandais.—*n.* finnois (*langue*), *m.*

fir [fəː], *n.* sapin; bois de sapin, *m.*

fir cone [ˈfəːkoun], *n.* pomme de pin, *f.*

fire [faiə], *n.* feu; incendie (*accidentel*), *m.*; (*fig.*) ardeur, *f.*; **fire!** au feu! **to be on fire**, être en feu; **to catch fire**, prendre feu; **to hang fire**, faire long feu; **to miss fire**, rater; **to set on fire**, **to set fire to**, mettre le feu à.—*v.t.* mettre le feu à; embraser, incendier; tirer (*fusil*); (*pop.*) renvoyer.—*v.i.* prendre feu; tirer; (*Motor.*) donner; **fire!** (*Mil.*) feu!

fire alarm [ˈfaiərəlɑːm], *n.* avertisseur d'incendie, *m.*

fire-arms [ˈfaiərɑːmz], *n.pl.* armes à feu, *f.pl.*

426

fire brigade ['faiəbrigeid], *n.* (corps de) sapeurs pompiers, *m.*
fire engine ['faiərendʒin], *n.* pompe à incendie, *f.*
fire escape ['faiəriskeip], *n.* échelle de sauvetage, *f.*
fire extinguisher ['faiərikstiŋgwiʃə], *n.* extincteur, *m.*
fire-fly ['faiəflai], *n.* luciole, *f.*
fire-guard ['faiəgɑːd], *n.* garde-feu, *m.*
fireman ['faiəmən], *n.* (*pl.* **-men** [men]) pompier, *m.*
fireplace ['faiəpleis], *n.* cheminée, *f.*, foyer, âtre, *m.*
fireproof ['faiəpruːf], *a.* incombustible, ignifuge.
fireside ['faiəsaid], *n.* coin du feu; (*fig.*) foyer domestique, *m.*
fire station ['faiəsteiʃən], *n.* caserne de pompiers, *f.*
fireworks ['faiəwəːks], *n.pl.* feu d'artifice, *m.*
firing ['faiəriŋ], *n.* action d'incendier, *f.*; chauffage (*heating*), *m.*; cuisson (*de poterie etc.*), *f.*; combustible (*fuel*); (*Mil.*) feu, tir, *m.*, fusillade, *f.*
firm [fəːm], *a.* ferme, solide; constant.—*n.* maison de commerce, raison sociale, firme, *f.*
firmament ['fəːməmənt], *n.* firmament, *m.*
firmly ['fəːmli], *adv.* fermement, solidement.
firmness ['fəːmnis], *n.* fermeté, solidité, *f.*
first [fəːst], *a.* premier; (*in compounds*) unième; **twenty-first**, vingt et unième.—*n.* (le) premier, *m.*, (la) première, *f.*—*adv.* premièrement; **at first**, d'abord.
first aid ['fəːst'eid], *n.* premiers secours, *m.pl.*; **first-aid post**, poste de secours, *m.*
first-born ['fəːstbɔːn], *a.* premier-né, aîné.
first-class ['fəːst'klɑːs], **first-rate** ['fəːst'reit], *a.* de premier ordre; de premier choix; (*colloq.*) de première force; **first-class compartment**, compartiment de première classe, *m.*
firth [fəːθ], *n.* (*Sc.*) estuaire, *m.*
fiscal ['fiskəl], *a.* fiscal.
fiscally ['fiskəli], *adv.* fiscalement.
fish [fiʃ], *n.* poisson, *m.*; **a pretty kettle of fish**, un beau gâchis; **a queer fish**, un drôle de type.—*v.t.* pêcher.—*v.i.* pêcher; **to fish for**, pêcher; (*fig.*) rechercher, quêter.
fish bone ['fiʃboun], *n.* arête, *f.*
fisher ['fiʃə], **fisherman** ['fiʃəmən] (*pl.* **-men** [men]), *n.* pêcheur, *m.*
fishery ['fiʃəri], *n.* pêche; pêcherie, *f.*
fish-hook ['fiʃhuk], *n.* hameçon, *m.*
fishing ['fiʃiŋ], *n.* pêche, *f.*; **to go fishing**, aller à la pêche.
fishing boat ['fiʃiŋbout], *n.* bateau de pêche, *m.*
fishing rod ['fiʃiŋrɔd], *n.* canne à pêche, *f.*
fishmonger ['fiʃmʌŋgə], *n.* marchand de poisson, *m.*
fish-slice ['fiʃslais], *n.* truelle à poisson, *f.*
fishy ['fiʃi], *a.* de poisson, poissonneux; qui sent le poisson; (*slang*) louche, véreux.
fission ['fiʃən], *n.* (*Biol.*) fissiparité; (*Phys.*) fission, désintégration, *f.*; **nuclear fission**, fission nucléaire.
fissure ['fiʃə], *n.* fissure, fente, *f.*
fist [fist], *n.* poing, *m.*

fisted ['fistid], *a.* **close-fisted**, avare, dur à la détente.
fisticuffs ['fistikʌfs], *n.pl.* coups de poing, *m.pl.*
fit (1) [fit], *n.* accès (*de colère etc.*), *m.*; attaque (*de maladie*); convulsion, *f.*; **by fits and starts**, à bâtons rompus, par accès.
fit (2) [fit], *a.* propre, bon, convenable (à); juste, à propos; capable (*de*); en bonne santé, en forme; **to think fit**, juger convenable, juger bon.—*n.* ajustement (*de vêtements*), *m.*; (*fig.*) coupe, forme, *f.*—*v.t.* convenir à; aller à (*vêtements*); habiller; adapter, ajuster; **to fit out**, équiper, monter, armer (*un navire*).—*v.i.* convenir; s'adapter (à), aller bien (*vêtements*); **to fit in with**, s'accorder avec.
fitful ['fitful], *a.* agité; capricieux; irrégulier.
fitfully ['fitfuli], *adv.* par boutades; irrégulièrement.
fitly ['fitli], *adv.* à propos, convenablement.
fitness ['fitnis], *n.* convenance, *f.*; à-propos, *m.*; **physical fitness**, bonne forme, *f.*
fitter ['fitə], *n.* ajusteur; (*Dress.*) essayeur, *m.*
fitting ['fitiŋ], *a.* convenable, à propos, juste. —*n.* ajustement, essayage, *m.*, (*pl.*) garniture, *f.*
five [faiv], *a.* and *n.* cinq, *m.*
fix [fiks], *v.t.* fixer, attacher, arrêter, établir; (*colloq.*) réparer.—*v.i.* se fixer.—*n.* difficulté, impasse, *f.*, embarras, *m.*
fixation [fik'seiʃən], *n.* fixation, *f.*
fixed [fikst], *a.* fixe, fixé.
fixedly ['fiksidli], *adv.* fixement.
fixture ['fikstʃə], *n.* meuble à demeure, *m.*; agencements fixes, *m.pl.*; match, engagement (*prévu, annoncé*), *m.*
fizzy ['fizi], *a.* gazeux (*limonade etc.*), mousseux (*vin*).
flabby ['flæbi], *a.* flasque; mollasse (*personne*).
flag (1) [flæg], *v.i.* pendre mollement; se relâcher, faiblir; s'affaisser.
flag (2) [flæg], *n.* drapeau; (*Naut.*) pavillon; iris (*plante*); carreau, *m.*, dalle (*pierre*), *f.*—*v.t.* paver, daller; pavoiser.
flag day ['flægdei], *n.* jour de quête, *m.*
flag officer ['flægɔfisə], *n.* chef d'escadre, *m.*
flagon ['flægən], *n.* flacon, *m.*; burette (*d'église*), *f.*
flagrancy ['fleigrənsi], *n.* énormité, notoriété, *f.*
flagrant ['fleigrənt], *a.* flagrant, notoire, énorme.
flag-ship ['flægʃip], *n.* vaisseau amiral, *m.*
flagstaff ['flægstɑːf], *n.* mât de pavillon, *m.*
flagstone ['flægstoun], *n.* dalle, *f.*
flail [fleil], *n.* fléau, *m.*
flair [flɛə], *n.* perspicacité, *f.*, flair, *m.*; aptitude (à), *f.*
flake [fleik], *n.* flocon, *m.*; écaille; étincelle, *f.* —*v.t.* former en flocons, écailler.—*v.i.* s'écailler.
flaky ['fleiki], *a.* floconneux; écaillé; feuilleté (*pâtisserie*).
flame [fleim], *n.* flamme, *f.*; feu, *m.*—*v.i.* flamber.
flaming ['fleimiŋ], *a.* flamboyant, flambant; (*fig.*) violent, ardent; (*pop.*) sacré.
flamingo [flə'miŋgou], *n.* (*Orn.*) flamant, *m.*
flan [flæn], *n.* flan, *m.*
Flanders ['flɑːndəz], la Flandre, *f.*

flange [flændʒ], *n.* bride, *f.*, rebord (*d'un tube etc.*); (*Tech.*) boudin (*de roue*), *m.*; (*Motor.*) ailette, collerette, *f.*

flank [flæŋk], *n.* flanc; côté, *m.*—*v.t.* flanquer (*de*); (*Mil.*) prendre en flanc.—*v.i.* border.

flannel [flænl], *a.* de flanelle.—*n.* flanelle, *f.*; (*pl.*) pantalon de flanelle, *m.*

flap [flæp], *v.t.* frapper légèrement; battre, agiter.—*v.i.* battre légèrement; (*fig., pop.*) s'affoler.—*n.* battement (*d'aile*); claquement (*de voile*); petit coup (*de la main*), *m.*, tape, *f.*; battant (*d'une table etc.*), *m.*; patte (*d'une poche*), *f.*, pan (*d'un habit*); rabat (*d'une enveloppe*); (*fig., pop.*) affolement, *m.*

flare [fleə], *v.i.* flamboyer; s'évaser (*jupe*); **to flare up,** flamber; (*fig.*) se mettre en colère.—*n.* flamme, *f.*; (*Av.*) brûlot, *m.*

flash [flæʃ], *n.* éclair, éclat, jet de lumière; (*fig.*) trait; (*Mil.*) écusson, *m.*—*v.t.* faire jaillir, lancer.—*v.i.* luire, éclater, étinceler.

flashy [flæʃi], *a.* voyant, clinquant; superficiel.

flask [flɑːsk], *n.* flacon, *m.*, gourde, *f.*

flat [flæt], *a.* plat; étendu (*à terre*); éventé (*vin etc.*); (*Comm.*) languissant; (*Mus.*) bémol; grave (*son*); (*pl.*) (*pop.*) net, clair; fade, insipide (*goût*).—*n.* surface plane, *f.*; étage (*d'une maison*), appartement; (*Mus.*) bémol; (*Theat.*) châssis, *m.*

flat-iron [flætaiən], *n.* fer à repasser, *m.*

flatly [flætli], *adv.* à plat; (*fig.*) nettement, clairement.

flatten [flætn], *v.t.* aplatir, aplanir; éventer (*boisson alcoolique*); (*fig.*) abattre, attrister; (*Mus.*) rendre grave.—*v.i.* s'aplatir; s'éventer (*boisson alcoolique*).

flatter [flætə], *v.t.* flatter.

flatterer [flætərə], *n.* flatteur, *m.*

flattering [flætəriŋ], *a.* flatteur.

flattery [flætəri], *n.* flatterie, *f.*

flatulence [flætjuləns], *n.* flatuosité; flatulence, *f.*

flatulent [flætjulənt], *a.* flatueux.

flaunt [flɔːnt], *v.t.* faire parade de, étaler, déployer.—*v.i.* se pavaner, parader, flotter. —*n.* étalage, *m.*, parade, *f.*

flavor [fleivə], *n.* saveur, *f.*; goût, fumet (*de viande*); arome (*de thé, café etc.*); bouquet (*de vin*), *m.*—*v.t.* donner du goût, un arome etc. à, assaisonner (*de*).

flavoring [fleivəriŋ], *n.* assaisonnement, *m.*

flaw [flɔː], *n.* défaut, *m.*; fêlure; brèche. fente; paille (*de pierres précieuses*), *f.*

flawless [flɔːlis], *a.* parfait, sans défaut.

flax [flæks], *a.* de lin.—*n.* lin, *m.*

flaxen [flæksən], *a.* de lin; blond filasse (*cheveux*).

flay [flei], *v.t.* écorcher.

flaying [fleiiŋ], *n.* écorchement, *m.*

flea [fliː], *n.* puce, *f.*

fleck [flek], *n.* tache, moucheture, marque, *f.* —*v.t.* moucheter, tacheter (*de*).

fledg(e)ling [fledʒliŋ], *n.* oisillon, *m.*

flee [fliː], *v.t. irr.* fuir, éviter.—*v.i.* s'enfuir, se réfugier.

fleece [fliːs], *n.* toison, *f.*—*v.t.* tondre; (*fig.*) écorcher, plumer.

fleecy [fliːsi], *a.* laineux, (*fig.*) floconneux.

fleet (1) [fliːt], *n.* flotte, *f.*; **the Home Fleet,** la flotte métropolitaine.

fleet (2) [fliːt], *a.* vite, rapide, leste.

fleeting [fliːtiŋ], *a.* fugitif, passager.

Fleming [flemiŋ], *n.* Flamand, *m.*

Flemish [flemiʃ], *a.* flammand.—*n.* flamand (*langue*), *m.*

flesh [fleʃ], *n.* chair; viande (*meat*), *f.*; **in the flesh,** en chair et en os; **to put on flesh,** s'empâter, prendre de l'embonpoint.—*v.t.* (*Hunt.*) acharner; écharner (*peaux*).

fleshy [fleʃi], *a.* charnu.

flex (1) [fleks], *n.* fil électrique, *m.*

flex (2) [fleks], *v.t.* fléchir.

flexibility [fleksi'biliti], *n.* flexibilité, souplesse, *f.*

flexible [fleksibl], *a.* flexible, souple.

flick [flik], *n.* petit coup (*de fouet, de torchon*), *m.*; chiquenaude, *f.*; (*pl.*) (*pop.*) ciné, *m.*— *v.t.* effleurer; donner une chiquenaude à.

flicker [flikə], *v.i.* trembloter, vaciller (*lumière*); ciller (*paupières*).

flickering [flikəriŋ], *a.* vacillant, clignotant. —*n.* trémoussement; clignement, *m.*; vacillation, *f.*

flight [flait], *n.* vol, *m.*, volée (*d'oiseaux etc.*); fuite, *f.*; (*fig.*) élan, *m.*; (*Av.*) escadrille, *f.*; **flight of stairs,** escalier, *m.*; **flight of steps,** perron, *m.*; **in flight,** en déroute.

flightiness [flaitinis], *n.* légèreté, étourderie, *f.*

flighty [flaiti], *a.* étourdi, léger; volage.

flimsiness [flimzinis], *n.* légèrcté; (*fig.*) mesquinerie, *f.*

flimsy [flimzi], *a.* mollasse, léger, sans consistance.

flinch [flintʃ], *v.i.* reculer, céder.

fling [fliŋ], *v.t. irr.* jeter, lancer.—*n.* coup (*lancé*), *m.*; ruade (*de cheval*), *f.*; pas seul (*danse écossaise*); (*fig.*) essai; trait, coup de patte, *m.*, raillerie, *f.*

flint [flint], *n.* silex, *m.*, pierre à briquet; (*fig.*) roche, dureté, *f.*

flip [flip], *n.* petit coup, *m.*, chiquenaude, *f.*; flip (*boisson*), *m.*

flippancy [flipənsi], *n.* ton léger; bavardage, *m.*

flippant [flipənt], *a.* léger; désinvolte; cavalier (*manières, mine*).

flipper [flipə], *n.* nageoire, *f.*

flirt [fləːt], *v.i.* faire la coquette, flirter (*femme*); conter fleurette (*homme*).—*n.* coquette, *f.*

flirtation [fləː'teiʃən], *n.* coquetterie, *f.*; flirt, *m.*

flit [flit], *v.i.* fuir, voltiger; (*Sc.*) déménager.— *n.* **to do a moonlight flit,** déménager à la cloche de bois.

float [flout], *v.t.* faire flotter, (*fig.*) lancer.— *v.i.* flotter, surnager; **to float on one's back,** faire la planche.—*n.* train (*bois*); flotteur; char (*carnaval*), *m.*

floating [floutiŋ], *a.* flottant; **floating capital,** fonds de roulement, *m.*; **floating dock,** bassin à flot, *m.*

flock [flok], *n.* troupeau, *m.*; bande, troupe, *f.*; ouailles (*paroissiens*), *f.pl.*; flocon, *m.* bourre (*de laine etc.*), *f.*—*v.i.* s'attrouper, s'assembler.

floe [flou], *n.* nappe de glaçons flottants; banquise, *f.*

flog [flog], *v.t.* fouetter, flageller; (*pop.*) bazarder.

flogging [flogiŋ], *n.* fouet, *m.*; flagellation, *f.*

flood [flʌd], n. déluge, m.; inondation, crue, f.; (fig.) cours d'eau, torrent, m.; marée, f.— v.t. inonder, submerger, noyer.

flood-light ['flʌdlait], n. projecteur, m.—v.t. illuminer (un monument) avec des projecteurs.

flood tide ['flʌdtaid], n. marée montante, f.

floor [flɔ:], n. plancher; carreau, parquet (pavage); étage (storey), m.—v.t. planchéier, parqueter; (fig.) terrasser, réduire au silence.

flooring ['flɔ:riŋ], n. plancher, parquet, m.

floorwalker, see **shop-walker**.

flop [flɔp], int. plouf!—n. (Theat.) four, m.

floral ['flɔ:rəl, 'flɔ:rəl], a. floral; floral games, jeux floraux, m.pl.

Florence ['flɔrəns] Florence, f.

florid ['flɔrid], a. fleuri.

Florida ['flɔridə]. la Floride, f.

florist ['flɔrist], n. fleuriste, m., f.

floss [flɔs], n. bourre (de soie), f.; (Metal.) floss; (Bot.) duvet, m.

flotilla [flo'tilə], n. flottille, f.

flounder (1) ['flaundə], n. (Ichth.) flet, petit flétan, m.

flounder (2) ['flaundə], v.i. se débattre; patauger.

flour ['flauə] n. farine; fécule (des pommes de terre etc.), f.

flourish ['flʌriʃ], n. éclat, m.; fleur de rhétorique, f.; panache (manières, geste); moulinet, tour, m.; (Mus.) fioriture; fanfare (trompettes), f.—v.t. fleurir; parafer; brandir (épée etc.).—v.i. fleurir; venir bien (plantes); prospérer.

flourishing ['flʌriʃiŋ], a. florissant.

flout [flaut], v.t. railler; se moquer de.—n. moquerie, raillerie, f.

flow [flou], v.i. s'écouler, couler; monter (marée); (fig.) découler (de).—n. écoulement; flux; (fig.) épanchement, m.

flower ['flauə], n. fleur; (fig.) élite, f.—v.i. fleurir, être en fleur.

flower-bed ['flauəbed], n. plate-bande, f., parterre, m.

flowered ['flauəd], a. figuré: fleuri.

flower garden ['flauəga:dn], n. jardin d'agrément, m.

flower-pot ['flauəpɔt], n. pot à fleurs, m.

flowing ['flouiŋ], a. coulant; (fig.) naturel.—n. cours, écoulement, m.

flown [floun], a. envolé; high-flown, gonflé, outré (style).

flu [flu:], (colloq.) [INFLUENZA].

fluctuate ['flʌktjueit], v.i. balancer, flotter, varier.

fluctuating ['flʌktjueitiŋ], a. flottant; incertain; variable.

fluctuation [flʌktju'eiʃən], n. fluctuation, f.; (fig.) balancement, doute, m.

flue [flu:], n. tuyau de cheminée; carneau (d'un fourneau), m.

fluency ['flu:ənsi], n. facilité (de parole), f.

fluent ['flu:ənt], a. coulant, courant; facile.

fluently ['flu:əntli], adv. couramment, avec facilité.

fluff [flʌf], n. duvet, m., peluches, f.pl.

fluid ['flu:id], a. et n. fluide, liquide, m.

fluke [flu:k], n. patte (d'ancre), f.; carrelet (poisson); (fig.) coup de raccroc, m.

flunkey ['flʌŋki], n. laquais; (colloq.) sycophante, m.

flurry ['flʌri], n. agitation, f., désordre, émoi, m.—v.t. agiter, ahurir.

flush [flʌʃ], a. frais, plein de vigueur; à fleur, au ras (de niveau); flush with the ground, à ras de terre.—n. rougeur, f.; transport, m.; chasse d'eau, f.; (Cards) flush, m.—v.t. faire rougir; laver à grande eau; (Hunt.) lever; (fig.) animer.—v.i. rougir; partir tout à coup.

fluster ['flʌstə], v.t. déconcerter, agiter, ahurir.—n. agitation, f.

flute [flu:t], n. flûte, f.

fluted ['flu:tid], a. cannelé.

flutter ['flʌtə], n. trémoussement, émoi, m.; agitation, f.; battement d'ailes, m.—v.t. mettre en désordre, agiter, ahurir.—v.i. battre des ailes, s'agiter; palpiter.

flux [flʌks], n. flux, courant; (Metal.) fondant, f.

fly (1) [flai], n. (pl. flies [flaiz]) (Ent.) mouche, f.

fly (2) [flai], v.t. irr. faire voler; fuir, éviter.—v.i. voler, s'envoler, se sauver, prendre la fuite, fuir s'enfuir; to fly into a passion, s'emporter, se mettre en colère; to fly over, survoler.—a. (pop.) malin.

flyer ['flaiə], n. aviateur, m.

flying ['flaiiŋ], a. volant; flying squad, brigade mobile, f.

flying boat ['flaiiŋbout], n. hydravion, m.

flying buttress ['flaiiŋ'bʌtris], n. arc-boutant, m.

fly-over ['flaiouvə], n. enjambement, m.

fly-paper ['flaipeipə], n. papier tue-mouches, f.

fly-past ['flaipa:st], n. défilé aérien, m.

foal [foul], n. poulain, m., pouliche, f.—v.i. pouliner, mettre bas.

foam [foum], n. écume; bave; mousse, f.—v.i. écumer; moutonner (mer); baver (animaux).

foaming ['foumiŋ], a. écumant.

fob [fɔb], n. gousset (de pantalon), m.—v.t. (fam.) to fob someone off with something, refiler quelque chose à quelqu'un.

fo'c'sle [fouksl], [FORECASTLE].

focus ['foukəs], n. (pl. foci ['fousai], focuses ['foukəsiz]) foyer, m.—v.t. mettre au point.

fodder ['fɔdə], n. fourrage, m., pâture, f.; cannon fodder, chair à canon, f.

foe [fou], n. ennemi, adversaire, m.

fog [fɔg], n. brouillard, m.; (fig.) perplexité, f.; sea fog, brume, f.

fog-bound ['fɔgbaund], a. enveloppé de brouillard; arrêté par le brouillard.

foggy ['fɔgi], a. brumeux; (fig.) sombre; it is foggy, il fait du brouillard.

fogy, fogey ['fougi], n. ganache, vieille perruque, f.

foil [fɔil], n. feuille de métal, f.; tain (de miroir), m.; fleuret (check); contraste, repoussoir (set off); (Fenc.) fleuret, m.—v.t. déjouer, faire échouer; frustrer.

fold (1) [fould], v.t. plier, ployer; envelopper; serrer; to fold one's arms, croiser les bras.—n. pli, repli, m.; threefold, triple; twofold, double.

fold (2) [fould], n. parc (à moutons), m., bergerie, f.—v.t. to fold sheep, parquer des moutons.

folder ['fouldə], n. chemise (à documents), f.; dépliant, prospectus, m.

folding ['fouldiŋ], *a.* pliant; brisé, à deux battants (*porte*).
foliage ['fouliidʒ], *n.* feuillage, *m.*
folio ['fouliou], *n.* in-folio, *m.*; page, *f.*, folio, *m.*
folk(s) [fouk(s)], *n.* (*pl.*) gens, *m.pl.*, *f.pl.*, personnes, *f.pl.*
folklore ['fouklɔ:], *n.* folklore, *m.*, légendes, traditions populaires, *f.pl.*
folk song ['fouksɔŋ], *n.* chanson populaire, *f.*
follow ['folou], *v.t.* suivre; poursuivre; observer, imiter; exercer (*une profession*).—*v.i.* s'ensuivre, résulter; *as follows*, comme suit.
follower ['folouə], *n.* suivant; partisan; compagnon; (*colloq.*) amoureux, *m.*
following ['folouiŋ], *a.* suivant.—*n.* suite, *f.*, parti, *m.*
folly ['foli], *n.* folie, sottise, bêtise, *f.*
foment [fo'ment], *v.t.* fomenter.
fond [fond], *a.* passionné (*pour*); fou (*de*); indulgent (*pour*); doux, cher (*espoir*); vain, sot; *to be (passionately) fond of*, aimer (à la folie).
fondle [fondl], *v.t.* câliner, caresser.
fondly ['fondli], *adv.* tendrement.
fondness ['fondnis], *n.* tendresse; affection, *f.*; penchant, goût, *m.*
font [font], *n.* fonts baptismaux, *m.pl.*
food [fu:d], *n.* nourriture, *f.*, aliment, *m.*; vivres, *m.pl.*; denrées, *f.pl.*; pâture (*pour animaux*), *f.*
food-stuffs ['fu:dstʌfs], *n.pl.* comestibles, *m.pl.*
fool [fu:l], *n.* sot; insensé, imbécile, niais, *m.*; dupe, *f.*, fou (*bouffon*), *m.*; *to make a fool of*, se moquer de; *to make a fool of oneself*, se rendre ridicule, se faire moquer de soi.—*v.t.* duper; (*colloq.*) se moquer de.—*v.i.* faire la bête; *you are fooling*, vous plaisantez; vous blaguez.
foolery ['fu:ləri], *n.* folie, sottise; niaiserie, *f.*
foolhardy ['fu:lhɑ:di], *a.* téméraire.
foolish ['fu:liʃ], *a.* sot, insensé, bête, ridicule.
foolishly ['fu:liʃli], *adv.* follement, sottement.
foolishness ['fu:liʃnis], *n.* folie, sottise, *f.*
foolproof ['fu:lpru:f], *a.* inéréglable.
foot [fut], *n.* (*pl.* **feet** [fi:t]) pied, *m.*; patte (*d' insectes etc.*); base (*de colonne*), *f.*; bas (*d'une page*), *m.*; (*Mil.*) infanterie, *f.*; *on foot*, à pied.
football ['futbɔ:l], *n.* ballon; football (*jeu*), *m.*
foot-bridge ['futbridʒ], *n.* passerelle, *f.*
footfall ['futfɔ:l], *n.* pas, bruit de pas, *m.*
foothold ['futhould], *n.* prise pour le pied, *f.*; (*fig.*) point d'appui, *m.*
footing ['futiŋ], *n.* pied, point d'appui; établissement, *m.*; position, *f.*; *on an equal footing*, sur un pied d'égalité.
footlights ['futlaits], *n.pl.* (*Theat.*) rampe, *f.*
footman ['futmən], *n.* (*pl.* **-men** [men]) laquais, valet de pied, *m.*
footnote ['futnout], *n.* note au bas de la page, apostille, *f.*
foot-path ['futpɑ:θ], *n.* sentier; trottoir (*de rue*), *m.*
foot-print ['futprint], *n.* empreinte du pied, *f.*
foot soldier ['futsouldʒə], *n.* fantassin, *m.*
footstep ['futstep], *n.* pas, *m.*; trace, *f.*; vestige, *m.*
footstool ['futstu:l], *n.* tabouret, *m.*
footwear ['futweə], *n.* chaussures, *f.pl.*

fop [fɔp], *n.* fat, *m.*
foppery ['fɔpəri], *n.* affectation, fatuité, *f.*
foppish ['fɔpiʃ], *a.* affecté sot, fat.
for [fɔ:], *prep.* pour, par; de, à, vers, pendant; depuis; en place de, en lieu de; en faveur de; à cause de, pour le compte de; malgré; pour avoir; pour que (*with subj.*).—*conj.* car.
forage ['fɔridʒ], *n.* fourrage, *m.*—*v.i.* fourrager.
*forasmuch [fɔrəz'mʌtʃ], *conj.* **forasmuch as**, d'autant que, vu que.
foray ['fɔrei], *n.* incursion, razzia, *f.*, raid, *m.*
forbear (1) [FOREBEAR].
forbear (2) [fɔ:'bɛə], *v.t. irr.* cesser; épargner, supporter.—*v.i.* s'abstenir, se garder (*de*).
forbearance [fɔ:'bɛərəns], *n.* patience; indulgence, *f.*
forbid [fə'bid], *v.t. irr.* défendre, interdire (*de*); empêcher (*de*); *God forbid !* à Dieu ne plaise!
forbidding [fə'bidiŋ], *a.* rebutant, repoussant.
force [fɔ:s], *n.* force; violence; efficacité; valeur, *f.*; (*Mil.*, *pl.*) forces, *f.pl.*, armée, *f.*; *in force*, (*Law*) en vigueur.—*v.t.* forcer, contraindre (à ou *de*); violenter.
forced [fɔ:st], *a.* forcé, contraint; guindé (*style*).
forcedly ['fɔ:sidli], *adv.* de force.
forceps ['fɔ:seps], *n.pl.* (*Surg.*) pince, *f.*, forceps, *m.*
forcible ['fɔ:sibl], **forceful** ['fɔ:sful], *a.* fort; énergique.
forcibly ['fɔ:sibli], *adv.* par force; fortement.
ford [fɔ:d], *n.* gué, *m.*—*v.t.* passer à gué, guéer.
fore! (1) [fɔ:], *int.* (*Golf*) gare devant!
fore (2) [fɔ:], *a.* antérieur; de devant; (*Naut.*) de misaine; *fore and aft*, (*Naut.*) de l'avant à l'arrière.—*adv.* d'avant; (*Naut.*) de l'avant.
forearm (1) [fɔ:r'ɑ:m], *v.t.* prémunir.
forearm (2) [fɔ:r'ɑ:m], *n.* avant-bras, *m.*
forebear ['fɔ:bɛə], *n.* aïeul, ancêtre, *m.*
forebode [fɔ:'boud], *v.t.* présager, prédire, pressentir.
foreboding [fɔ:'boudiŋ], *n.* présage, pressentiment, *m.*
forecast [fɔ:'kɑ:st], *n.* prévoyance, prévision, *f.*; pronostic, *m.*; *weather forecast*, prévisions météorologiques, *f.pl.*—*v.t.* prévoir; pronostiquer.
forecastle ['fouksl, 'fɔ:kɑ:sl], *n.* gaillard d'avant, *m.*
fore-court [fɔ:'kɔ:t], *n.* avant-cour, *f.*
forefather ['fɔ:fɑ:ðə], *n.* aïeul, ancêtre, *m.*
forefinger ['fɔ:fiŋgə], *n.* index, *m.*
forego [fɔ:'gou], *v.t.* précéder, aller devant.
foregone [fɔ:'gɔ:n], *a.* prévu, résolu, décidé d'avance.
foreground ['fɔ:graund], *n.* premier plan, *m.*
forehead ['fɔrid], *n.* front, *m.*
foreign ['fɔrin], *a.* étranger; *Foreign Office*, Ministère des Affaires Étrangères, *m.*
foreigner ['fɔrinə], *n.* étranger, *m.*
foreland ['fɔ:lənd], *n.* promontoire, cap, *m.*
foreleg ['fɔ:leg], *n.* patte de devant, *f.*
forelock ['fɔ:lɔk], *n.* toupet, *m.*
foreman [fɔ:mən], *n.* (*pl.* **-men** [men]) chef (*d'un jury*); contremaître; chef d'atelier *ou* d'équipe; brigadier, *m.*
foremast ['fɔ:mɑ:st], *n.* mât de misaine, *m.*

foremost ['fɔːmoust], *a.* premier; en tête, au premier rang; **first and foremost**, tout d'abord.

forenoon ['fɔːnuːn], *n.* matin, *m.*, matinée, *f.*

forensic [fə'rensik], *a.* **forensic medicine**, médecine légale, *f.*

forerunner ['fɔːrʌnə], *n.* précurseur, *m.*

foresee [fɔː'siː], *v.t. irr. (conjug. like* SEE) prévoir.

foreseeable [fɔː'siːəbl], *a.* prévisible.

foreshore ['fɔːʃɔː], *n.* plage, *f.*

foreshorten [fɔː'ʃɔːtn], *v.t. (Paint.)* dessiner en raccourci.

foreshortening [fɔː'ʃɔːtniŋ], *n.* raccourci, *m.*

foresight ['fɔːsait], *n.* prévoyance, *f.*; guidon *(d'arme à feu)*, *m.*; **lack of foresight**, imprévoyance, *f.*

forest ['fɔrist], *a.* de forêt, forestier.—*n.* forêt, *f.*

forestall [fɔː'stɔːl], *v.t.* anticiper, devancer.

forester ['fɔristə], *n.* garde forestier; habitant d'une forêt, *m.*

forestry ['fɔristri], *n.* sylviculture, *f.*

foretaste ['fɔːteist], *n.* avant-goût, *m.*; anticipation, *f.*

foretell [fɔː'tel], *v.t. irr. (conjug. like* TELL) prédire.

forethought ['fɔːθɔːt], *n.* prévoyance, prescience, *f.*

forewarn [fɔː'wɔːn], *v.t.* prévenir, avertir.

foreword ['fɔːwəːd], *n.* préface, *f.*; avant-propos, *m.*

forfeit ['fɔːfit], *a.* confisqué; *(fig.)* perdu.—*n.* amende *(à payer)*; forfaiture, confiscation, *f.*; *(Games)* gage, *m.*—*v.t.* forfaire *(à)*; confisquer; perdre.

forfeiture ['fɔːfitʃə], *n.* forfaiture, confiscation; perte, déchéance, *f.*

forgather [fɔː'gæðə], *v.i.* s'assembler, se réunir.

forge [fɔːdʒ], *n.* forge, *f.*—*v.t.* forger; contrefaire *(monnaie etc.)*, fabriquer *(document etc.)*.—*v.t.* commettre un faux; **to forge ahead**, pousser de l'avant.

forger ['fɔːdʒə], *n.* faussaire; faux-monnayeur, *m.*

forgery ['fɔːdʒəri], *n.* falsification; contrefaçon, *f.*; faux, *m.*

forget [fə'get], *v.t., v.i. irr.* oublier.

forgetful [fə'getful], *a.* oublieux.

forgetfulness [fə'getfulnis], *n.* oubli, manque de mémoire, *m.*; négligence, *f.*

forget-me-not [fə'getminɔt], *n.* myosotis, *m.*

forgive [fə'giv], *v.t. irr. (conjug. like* GIVE) pardonner, faire grâce de; pardonner à.

forgiveness [fə'givnis], *n.* pardon, *m.*; clémence, grâce, *f.*

forgiving [fə'giviŋ], *a.* clément, miséricordieux.

forgo [fɔː'gou], *v.t. irr. (conjug. like* GO) renoncer à, s'abstenir de, se refuser à.

fork [fɔːk], *n.* fourchette; fourche; bifurcation *(de rues)*; pointe *(d'une flèche etc.)*, *f.*; zigzag *(d'éclair)*, *m.*—*v.t.* enlever avec une fourche.—*v.i.* fourcher; bifurquer.

forked [fɔːkt], *a.* fourchu; *(Bot.)* bifurqué.

forlorn [fə'lɔːn], *a.* abandonné, désespéré, délaissé.

forlornness [fə'lɔːnnis], *n.* délaissement, abandon; état désespéré, *m.*

form [fɔːm], *n.* forme, figure; formalité, *f.*; banc *(siège)*, *m.*; *(Sch.)* classe, *f.*; gîte *(de lièvre)*;

imprimé *(fiche)*, *m.*—*v.t.* former, faire; façonner.—*v.i.* se former; se giter *(lièvres)*.

formal ['fɔːməl], *a.* formel; pointilleux; affecté, cérémonieux. formaliste.

formality [fɔː'mæliti], *n.* formalité, cérémonie, *f.*

formally ['fɔːməli], *adv.* avec formalité, en forme, formellement.

formation [fɔː'meiʃən], *n.* formation, *f.*; ordre, *m.*

formative ['fɔːmətiv], *a.* formatif, formateur, plastique.

former ['fɔːmə], *a.* précédent, passé; ancien; premier *(de deux)*.—*pron.* celui-là, celle-là. —*n.* moule, *m.*

formerly ['fɔːməli], *adv.* autrefois, auparavant; jadis.

formidable ['fɔːmidəbl], *a.* formidable, redoutable.

formless ['fɔːmlis], *a.* informe, sans forme.

Formosa [fɔː'mouzə]. Formose, *f.*

formula ['fɔːmjulə], *n. (pl.* **formulæ** ['fɔːmjul(a)i]) formule, *f.*

forsake [fə'seik], *v.t. irr.* délaisser, abandonner.

forsaking [fə'seikiŋ], *n.* délaissement, abandon, *m.*

*****forsooth** [fə'suːθ], *adv.* en vérité ma foi.

forswear [fɔː'sweə], *v.t. irr. (conjug. like* SWEAR) abjurer, répudier.—*v.i.* se parjurer.

fort [fɔːt], *n.* fort, *m.*, forteresse, *f.*

forth [fɔːθ], *adv.* en avant; au dehors; **and so forth**, et ainsi de suite.

forthcoming [fɔːθ'kʌmiŋ], *a.* tout prêt, prêt à paraître; prochain, à venir.

forthright ['fɔːθrait], *a.* franc, carré, brutal.

forthwith [fɔːθ'wið], *adv.* incontinent, aussitôt, sur-le-champ, tout de suite.

fortieth ['fɔːtiəθ], *a.* quarantième.—*n.* quarantième *(fraction)*, *m.*

fortification [fɔːtifi'keiʃən], *n.* fortification, *f.*

fortify ['fɔːtifai], *v.t.* fortifier; munir *(de)*.

fortifying ['fɔːtifaiiŋ], *a. (fig.)* réconfortant, fortifiant.

fortitude ['fɔːtitjuːd], *n.* force d'âme, *f.* courage, *m.*

fortnight ['fɔːtnait], *n.* quinze jours, *m.pl.*, quinzaine, *f.*

fortnightly ['fɔːtnaitli], *a.* bimensuel.—*adv.* tous les quinze jours.

fortress ['fɔːtris], *n.* forteresse, place forte, *f.*

fortuitous [fɔː'tjuːitəs], *a.* fortuit.

fortuitously [fɔː'tjuːitəsli], *adv.* fortuitement, par hasard.

fortunate ['fɔːtʃənit, 'fɔːtʃunit], *a.* heureux.

fortunately ['fɔːtʃənitli], *adv.* heureusement.

fortune ['fɔːtʃən], *n.* fortune, *f.*, sort *(lot)*, destin, *m.*; **by good fortune**, par bonheur.

fortune hunter ['fɔːtʃənhʌntə], *n.* aventurier, coureur de dots, *m.*

fortune-teller ['fɔːtʃəntelə], *n.* diseur de bonne aventure, *m.*

forty ['fɔːti], *a.* quarante; précoce *(fruits etc.)*; **she must be nearly forty**, elle doit friser la quarantaine.

forward ['fɔːwəd], *a.* avancé; *(fig.)* empressé *(de)*, ardent *(à)*; précoce *(fruits etc.)*; présomptueux.—*n. (Ftb.)* avant, *m.*—*adv.* en avant; en évidence.—*v.t.* avancer, hâter; *(Comm.)* envoyer, expédier; faire suivre *(lettre)*.

forwardness ['fɔ:wədnis], *n.* empressement; progrès, *m.*; précocité (*fruits etc.*); hardiesse; effronterie, *f.*

fossil ['fosil], *a.* and *n.* fossile, *m.*

foster ['fostə], *v.t.* élever, nourrir; (*fig.*) encourager.

foster brother ['fostəbrʌðə], *n.* frère de lait, *m.*

foster child ['fostətʃaild], *n.* nourrisson, *m.*

foster father ['fostəfɑ:ðə], *n.* père nourricier, *m.*

foster mother ['fostəmʌðə], *n.* mère nourricière, *f.*

foster sister ['fostəsistə], *n.* sœur de lait, *f.*

foul [faul], *a.* sale, malpropre, immonde, trouble, bourbeux (*eau*); grossier (*langage*); **by fair means or foul**, de gré ou de force; **foul air**, air vicié, *m.*; **foul play**, trahison, *f.*—*n.* (*Spt.*) coup-bas, *m.*—*v.t.* salir, souiller, troubler; encrasser (*arme à feu*); (*Naut.*) aborder; s'engager (*cordes*).

foully ['fauli], *adv.* salement, honteusement.

foul-mouthed ['faulmauðd], *a.* grossier.

foulness ['faulnis], *n.* saleté, impureté; turpitude, noirceur, *f.*

found (1) [faund], *past* and *p.p.* [FIND].

found (2) [faund], *v.t.* fonder, établir; fondre (*to cast*).

foundation [faun'deiʃən], *n.* fondement, *m.*, fondation; (*fig.*) base, source, *f.*

founder (1) ['faundə], *n.* fondateur, auteur; (*Metal.*) fondeur, *m.*

founder (2) ['faundə], *v.t.* surmener (*un cheval*).—*v.i.* (*Naut.*) sombrer, couler bas; broncher (*un cheval*); (*fig.*) échouer.

foundered ['faundəd], *a.* courbatu (*cheval*); sombré (*navire*).

foundling ['faundliŋ], *n.* enfant trouvé, *m.*

foundry ['faundri], *n.* fonderie, *f.*

fount [faunt], *n.* fontaine, (*fig.*) cause, source, *f.*

fountain ['fauntin], *n.* fontaine, source, *f.*; jet d'eau, *m.*

fountain-head ['fauntinhed], *n.* source, origine, *f.*

fountain pen ['fauntinpen], *n.* stylo, *m.*

four [fɔ:], *a.* and *n.* quatre, *m.*; **carriage and four**, voiture à quatre chevaux, *f.*; **on all fours**, à quatre pattes.

four-engined ['fɔ:rendʒind], *a.* (*Av.*) quadrimoteur.

four-fold ['fɔ:fould], *a.* quatre fois, quatre fois autant, quadruple.

four-footed ['fɔ:futid], *a.* quadrupède, à quatre pieds.

fourteen ['fɔ:ti:n], *a.* and *n.* quatorze, *m.*

fourteenth ['fɔ:ti:nθ], *a.* quatorzième; quatorze (*date*; *rois etc.*).—*n.* quatorzième (*fraction*), *m.*

fourth [fɔ:θ], *a.* quatrième; quatre (*date*, *roi etc.*).—*n.* quart (*fraction*), *m.*; (*Mus.*) quarte, *f.*

fowl [faul], *n.* oiseau, *m.*, poule (*hen*); (*Cook.*) volaille, *f.*

fowler ['faulə], *n.* oiseleur, *m.*

fowl-house ['faulhaus], *n.* poulailler, *m.*

fowling piece ['faulinpi:s], *n.* fusil de chasse, *m.*

fox [foks], *n.* (*pl.* **foxes** ['foksiz]) renard, (*fig.*) rusé, *m.*

foxglove ['foksglʌv], *n.* digitale, *f.*

foxy ['foksi], *a.* de renard, rusé; roux (*red*).

fraction ['frækʃən], *n.* fraction, *f.*

fractious ['frækʃəs], *a.* revêche, maussade, hargneux, de mauvaise humeur.

fracture ['fræktʃə], *n.* fracture, cassure, *f.*—*v.t.* casser, rompre; (*Surg.*) fracturer.

fragile ['frædʒail], *a.* fragile.

fragility [frə'dʒiliti], *n.* fragilité, *f.*

fragment ['frægmənt], *n.* fragment, éclat, *m.*

fragrance ['freigrəns], *n.* odeur suave, *f.*, parfum, *m.*

fragrant ['freigrənt], *a.* odoriférant, parfumé.

frail [freil], *a.* frêle, fragile, faible.—*n.* cabas, panier d'emballage, *m.*

frailty ['freilti], *n.* faiblesse, fragilité, *f.*

frame [freim], *n.* charpente, *f.*; châssis (*de fenêtre etc.*), chambranle (*de porte*), *m.*; (*fig.*) forme, *f.*; cadre (*de tableau etc.*), *m.*; disposition (*d'esprit*), *f.*—*v.t.* former, construire; encadrer; inventer.

framer ['freimə], *n.* encadreur; (*fig.*) auteur (*d'un projet*), *m.*

France [frɑ:ns], la France, *f.*

Frances ['frɑ:nsis], Françoise, *f.*

franchise ['fræntʃaiz], *n.* franchise, *f.*, droit de vote, *m.*

Francis ['frɑ:nsis], François, Francis, *m.*

Franciscan [fræn'siskən], *a.* and *n.* Franciscain, *m.*

frank [fræŋk], *a.* franc, sincère, libéral; libre. —*v.t.* affranchir.

frankincense ['fræŋkinsens], *n.* encens, *m.*

frankly ['fræŋkli], *adv.* franchement.

frankness ['fræŋknis], *n.* franchise, sincérité, *f.*

frantic ['fræntik], *a.* frénétique, forcené, furieux.

frantically ['fræntikəli], *adv.* follement, avec frénésie.

fraternal [frə'tə:nəl], *a.* fraternel.

fraternity [frə'tə:niti], *n.* fraternité, confrérie, *f.*

fraud [frɔ:d], *n.* imposteur (*personne*), *m.*; (*also* **fraudulence** ['frɔ:djuləns]) fraude, supercherie, *f.*, dol, *m.*

fraudulent ['frɔ:djulənt], *a.* frauduleux, de mauvaise foi.

fraught [frɔ:t], *a.* rempli, plein (*de*); riche, fertile (*en*).

fray (1) [frei], *n.* échauffourée, mêlée, bagarre, *f.*

fray (2) [frei], *v.t.* érailler, effilocher.—*v.i.* s'érailler.

fraying ['freiiŋ], *n.* éraillure, *f.*

freak [fri:k], *n.* caprice, *m.*; bizarrerie, *f.*; monstre, *m.*; bigarrure, *f.*—*v.t.* bigarrer, tacheter (*de*).

freakish ['fri:kiʃ], *a.* bizarre, fantasque, capricieux.

freckle [frekl], *n.* tache de rousseur, tache de son, *f.*—*v.t.* tacheter.

Frederick ['fredrik], Frédéric, *m.*

free [fri:], *a.* libre; exempt; sincère, franc; gratuit; aisé, dégagé; **delivered free**, rendu franco à domicile; **free and easy**, sans façon.—*adv.* gratis.—*v.t.* délivrer, libérer.

freebooter ['fri:bu:tə], *n.* maraudeur; flibustier, *m.*

freedman ['fri:dmən], *n.* (*pl.* **-men** [men]) affranchi, *m.*

freedom ['fri:dəm], *n.* liberté; indépendance; aisance; bourgeoisie (*d'une ville*), *f.*

freehold ['fri:hould], *n.* propriété foncière libre, *f.*

free-holder ['fri:houldə], *n.* propriétaire foncier, *m.*

freely ['fri:li], *adv.* librement, sans contrainte, gratuitement; libéralement.

freeman ['fri:mən], *n.* (*pl.* **-men** [men]) citoyen, homme libre, *m.*

freemason ['fri:meisn], *n.* franc-maçon, *m.*

freemasonry ['fri:meisnri], *n.* franc-maçonnerie, *f.*

freestone ['fri:stoun], *n.* pierre de taille, *f.*

freestyle ['fri:stail], *n.* nage libre, *f.*

freethinker ['fri:θiŋkə], *n.* esprit fort, libre penseur, *m.*

free trade ['fri:'treid], *n.* libre échange, *m.*; *free-trade area*, zone de libre-échange, *f.*

free-trader ['fri:'treidə], *n.* libre-échangiste, *m.*, *f.*

freeze [fri:z], *v.t. irr.* geler; (*Fin.*) bloquer (*prix, salaires*).—*v.i.* se geler, se glacer.

freezing ['fri:ziŋ], *a.* glacial.—*n.* congélation, *f.*; (*Fin.*) blocage, *m.*

freight [freit], *n.* cargaison, *f.*, chargement; fret (*cost*), *m.*—*v.t.* fréter.

French [frentʃ], *a.* français; *French window*, porte-fenêtre, *f.*—*n.* français (*langue*), *m.*; *the French*, les Français, *m.pl.*

Frenchman ['frentʃmən], *n.* (*pl.* **-men** [men]) Français, *m.*

Frenchwoman ['frentʃwumən], *n.* (*pl.* **-women** [wimin]) Française, *f.*

frenzy ['frenzi], *n.* frénésie, *f.*; délire, *m.*

frequence ['fri:kwəns], **frequency** ['fri:kwənsi], *n.* fréquence; répétition fréquente, *f.*; *V.H.F.*, modulation de fréquence, *f.*

frequent ['fri:kwənt], *a.* fréquent, très répandu; rapide (*pouls*).—[fri'kwent], *v.t.* fréquenter; hanter.

frequently ['fri:kwəntli], *adv.* fréquemment, souvent.

fresco ['freskou], *n.* fresque, *f.*

fresh [freʃ], *a.* frais; récent, nouveau; (*fig.*) vigoureux, novice, vert; *fresh water*, eau douce, *f.*

freshen ['freʃən], *v.t.* rafraîchir.—*v.i.* se rafraîchir.

freshly ['freʃli], *adv.* fraîchement; récemment, depuis peu.

freshman ['freʃmən], *n.* (*pl.* **-men** [men]) étudiant de première année, bizuth, *m.*

freshness ['freʃnis], *n.* fraîcheur, *f.*; (*fig.*) nouveauté, *f.*

freshwater ['freʃwɔ:tə], *a.* d'eau douce *ou* de rivière.

fret [fret], *n.* fermentation; (*fig.*) agitation de l'âme, *f.*—*v.t.* frotter (*contre*); ronger, écorcher (*excorier*); chagriner, irriter; découper.—*v.i.* se chagriner, s'inquiéter; s'user, s'érailler.

fretful ['fretful], *a.* chagrin, maussade; agité, inquiet.

fretfulness ['fretfulnis], *n.* mauvaise humeur, irritation, *f.*

fretsaw ['fretsɔ:], *n.* scie à découper, *f.*

fretwork ['fretwə:k], *n.* ouvrage à claire-voie, découpage, *m.*

friable ['fraiəbl], *a.* friable.

friar ['fraiə], *n.* moine, *m.*

friction ['frikʃən], *n.* frottement, *m.*; (*Med.*) friction, *f.*

Friday ['fraid(e)i]. vendredi, *m.*; *Good Friday*, vendredi saint.

friend [frend], *n.* ami, *m.*, amie, *f.*

friendless ['frendlis], *a.* sans ami, délaissé.

friendliness ['frendlinis], *n.* bienveillance, *f.*

friendly ['frendli], *a.* d'ami, amical; bienveillant (*pour*).

friendship ['frendʃip], *n.* amitié, *f.*

frieze [fri:z], *a.* de frise.—*n.* frise, *f.*

frigate ['frigit], *n.* frégate, *f.*

fright [frait], *n.* effroi, *m.*, épouvante, frayeur, *f.*

frighten [fraitn], *v.t.* épouvanter, effrayer, faire peur à.

frightful ['fraitful], *a.* épouvantable, effroyable, affreux.

frightfulness ['fraitfulnis], *n.* horreur, frayeur, *f.*

frigid ['fridʒid], *a.* froid, glacial.

frigidity [fri'dʒiditi], **frigidness** ['fridʒidnis], *n.* frigidité, froideur, *f.*

frill [fril], *n.* volant, *m.*, ruche, *f.*, jabot (*de chemise*), *m.*; *without frills*, sans façons.—*v.t.* plisser, froncer; rucher.

fringe [frindʒ], *n.* frange; crépine, *f.*; bord, *m.*; bordure, *f.*; effilé, *m.*—*v.t.* franger, border.

frippery ['fripəri], *n.* parure sans valeur, *f.*; clinquant, *m.*

frisk [frisk], *n.* gambade, *f.*—*v.i.* sautiller, gambader, frétiller.

friskiness ['friskinis], *n.* folâtrerie, gaieté, vivacité, *f.*

frisky ['friski], *a.* vif, enjoué, folâtre; fringant (*cheval*).

fritter ['fritə], *n.* (*Cook.*) beignet, *m.*—*v.t.* couper en morceaux, morceler; *to fritter away* (*one's time* or *money*), gaspiller *ou* dissiper (*son temps ou son argent*).

frivolity [fri'voliti], *n.* frivolité, *f.*

frivolous ['frivaləs], *a.* frivole.

frivolousness ['frivaləsnis], *n.* frivolité, *f.*

frizz [friz], **frizzle** [frizl], *v.t.* friser, crêper.—*v.i.* frisotter (*cheveux*).—*n.* frisure, *f.*

frizzy ['frizi], *a.* frisottant, crêpé.

fro [frou], *adv.* en s'éloignant; *to go to and fro*, aller et venir.

frock [frok], *n.* robe d'enfant, robe, *f.*; froc (*de moine*), *m.*

frock coat ['frokkout], *n.* redingote, *f.*

frog [frog], *n.* grenouille, *f.*

frogman ['frogmən], *n.* (*pl.* **-men** [men]) homme-grenouille, *m.*

frolic ['frolik], *n.* espièglerie, *f.*, ébats, *m.pl.*, gambades, *f.pl.*—*v.i.* folâtrer, gambader.

frolicsome ['froliksəm], *a.* folâtre, espiègle.

from [from], *prep.* de; depuis, dès, à partir de; par (*à cause de*); d'après (*selon*); par suite de, en conséquence de (*en raison de*); de la part de (*comme représentant de*); *as from*, à partir de (*telle ou telle date*); *from above*, d'en haut; *from afar*, de loin; *from behind*, de derrière; *from hence*, d'ici; *from thence*, de là; *from* . . . *till*, depuis . . . jusqu'à; *from you*, de votre part.

front [frʌnt], *n.* devant, *m.*; face, façade (*d'un édifice*); audace, *f.*, front, *m.*—*v.t.* faire face à; s'opposer à; donner sur.

frontage ['frʌntidʒ], *n.* façade, devanture (*de magasin*), *f.*

front door ['frʌnt'dɔ:], *n.* porte d'entrée, *f.*

frontier ['frʌntiə], *a.* and *n.* frontière, *f.*
frontispiece ['frʌntispiːs], *n.* frontispice, *m.*
frost [frɒst], *n.* gelée, *f.*, gel, *m.*; **glazed frost**, verglas, *m.*; **ground frost**, gelée blanche; **hoar-frost**, givre, *m.*—*v.t.* glacer; damasquiner.
frost-bite ['frɒstbait], *n.* gelure, froidure, *f.*
frosted ['frɒstid], *a.* givré; dépoli (*verre*).
frosty ['frɒsti], *a.* de gelée; glacé; (*fig.*) froid.
froth [frɒθ], *n.* écume; mousse (*de boisson*), *f.*—*v.i.* écumer; mousser.
frothy ['frɒθi], *a.* écumeux; écumant; mousseux; (*fig.*) vain, frivole.
frown [fraun], *n.* froncement de sourcil, *m.*—*v.i.* froncer les sourcils; être contraire (à); (*fig.*) **to frown upon**, désapprouver.
frowning ['frauniŋ], *a.* rechigné, renfrogné; (*fig.*) menaçant.
frowzy ['frauzi], *a.* sale, malpropre.
frozen [frouzn], *a.* glacé, gelé; (*Fin.*) bloqué.
fructify ['frʌktifai], *v.t.* fertiliser, féconder.—*v.i.* fructifier.
frugal ['fruːgl], *a.* frugal, économe, ménager.
frugality [fruː'gæliti], *n.* économie, frugalité, *f.*
fruit [fruːt], *a.* à fruit, fruitier.—*n.* fruit, *m.*; fruits, *m.pl.*; (*fig.*) avantage, profit, *m.*; **first fruits**, prémices, *f.pl.*
fruiterer ['fruːtərə], *n.* fruitier, *m.*
fruitful ['fruːtful], *a.* fertile; (*fig.*) fécond.
fruitfully ['fruːtfuli], *adv.* fertilement, abondamment.
fruitfulness ['fruːtfulnis], *n.* fertilité, *f.*; (*fig.*) fécondité, *f.*
fruition [fruː'iʃən], *n.* jouissance, réalisation, *f.*
fruitless ['fruːtlis], *a.* stérile; (*fig.*) infructueux, inutile.
frump [frʌmp], *n.* femme désagréable et mal habillée, *f.*
frustrate [frʌs'treit], *v.t.* frustrer, rendre inutile, déjouer.
frustration [frʌs'treiʃən], *n.* frustration, *f.*, insuccès, *m.*
fry (1) [frai], *n.* fretin, frai (*petits poissons*), *m.*
fry (2) [frai], *n.* (*Cook.*) friture, *f.*—*v.t.* frire, faire frire, sauter; **fried eggs**, œufs au plat, *m.pl.*—*v.i.* frire.
frying pan ['fraiiŋpæn], *n.* poêle à frire, *f.*
fuchsia ['fjuːʃə], *n.* fuchsia, *m.*
fuddle [fʌdl], *v.t.* griser; hébéter.—*v.i.* se griser.
fudge [fʌdʒ], *int.* bah!—*n.* blague, faribole, *f.*; fondant américain (*bonbon*), *m.*
fuel ['fjuəl], *n.* combustible; (*fig.*) aliment, *m.*
fuel-oil ['fjuəlɔil], *n.* mazout, *m.*
fugitive ['fjuːdʒitiv], *a.* fugitif, fuyard, passager.—*n.* fugitif, transfuge, déserteur; (*Mil.*) fuyard, *m.*
fugue [fjuːg], *n.* (*Mus.*) fugue, *f.*
fulcrum ['fʌlkrəm], *n.* (*pl.* **fulcra** ['fʌlkrə]) point d'appui, *m.*
fulfil [ful'fil], *v.t.* accomplir, réaliser; satisfaire.
fulfilment [ful'filmənt], *n.* exécution, *f.*, accomplissement, *m.*
full [ful], *a.* plein, rempli; comble, replet, gras; entier, complet; ample; (*fig.*) repu; (*Gram.*) **full stop**, point, *m.*; **full up!** (*autobus etc.*) complet!—*adv.* tout à fait, entièrement; parfaitement.—*n.* plein; comble, *m.*, satiété, *f.*; soûl, *m.*

full-back ['fulbæk], *n.* (*Ftb.*) arrière, *m.*
full-blown ['fulbloun], *a.* épanoui; (*fig.*) dans tout son éclat.
full-bodied ['fulbɔdid], *a.* gros, replet; corsé (*vin*).
fuller ['fulə], *n.* foulon, *m.*
full-faced ['ful'feist], *a.* au visage plein.
full-length ['ful'leŋθ], *a.* en pied (*portrait*).
fullness ['fulnis], *n.* plénitude, abondance; ampleur, *f.*
fully ['fuli], *adv.* pleinement, entièrement; tout à fait; parfaitement.
fulmar ['fulmə], *n.* (*Orn.*) fulmar, *m.*
fulminate ['fʌlmineit], *v.t., v.i.* fulminer.
fulsome ['fulsəm], *a.* excessif, écœurant, servile; gonflé (*style*).
fumble [fʌmbl], *v.t.* manier maladroitement.—*v.i.* farfouiller; tâtonner.
fumbler ['fʌmblə], *n.* maladroit, *m.*
fume [fjuːm], *n.* fumée, vapeur; (*fig.*) colère, *f.*—*v.t.* fumer.—*v.i.* fumer, s'exhaler; (*fig.*) être en colère.
fumigate ['fjuːmigeit], *v.t.* fumiger; désinfecter.
fun [fʌn], *n.* amusement, *m.*, plaisanterie, drôlerie, *f.*
function ['fʌŋkʃən], *n.* fonction, *f.*, métier, *m.*; cérémonie, réception, *f.*—*v.i.* fonctionner, marcher.
fund [fʌnd], *n.* fonds, *m.*; caisse, *f.*
fundamental [fʌndə'mentl], *a.* fondamental.—*n.*(*pl.*) principe fondamental, *m.*
funeral ['fjuːnərəl], *a.* funèbre, funéraire.—*n.* enterrement, convoi funèbre, *m.*; funérailles, obsèques, *f.pl.*
funereal [fjuː'niəriəl], *a.* funèbre; lugubre.
fungus ['fʌŋgəs], *n.* (*pl.* **fungi** ['fʌndʒai]) champignon; (*Med.*) fongus, *m.*
funk [fʌŋk], *n.* peur, *f.*—*v.t.* éviter, avoir peur de.
funnel [fʌnl], *n.* entonnoir; tuyau, *m.*; cheminée (*de bateau à vapeur*), *f.*
funny ['fʌni], *a.* amusant, drôle, comique; bizarre.
fur [fəː], *n.* fourrure, *f.*; gibier à poil; (*fig.*) dépôt, *m.*, incrustation, *f.*—*v.t.* fourrer, garnir de fourrure.—*v.i.* s'incruster, s'encrasser (*la langue*).
furbish ['fəːbiʃ], *v.t.* fourbir.
furious ['fjuəriəs], *a.* furieux, acharné.
furiously ['fjuəriəsli], *adv.* avec fureur, avec acharnement.
furl [fəːl], *v.t.* (*Naut.*) ferler, serrer.
furlong ['fəːlɒŋ], *n.* furlong (*le huitième d'un mille anglais, 201 mètres*), *m.*
furlough ['fəːlou], *n.* (*Mil.*) congé, *m.*
furnace ['fəːnis], *n.* fournaise, *f.*; fourneau (*d'une forge*); foyer (*de locomotive*), *m.*; **blast furnace**, haut fourneau.
furnish ['fəːniʃ], *v.t.* fournir, garnir, pourvoir (*de*); meubler.
furnisher ['fəːniʃə], *n.* fournisseur, marchand de meubles, *m.*
furnishing ['fəːniʃiŋ], *n.* ameublement, *m.*, garniture, *f.*
furniture ['fəːnitʃəl], *n.* meubles, *m.pl.* mobilier, ameublement; équipage, *m.*; **a piece of furniture**, un meuble.
furrier ['fʌriə], *n.* fourreur, pelletier, *m.*
furrow ['fʌrou], *n.* sillon, *m.*; ride; rainure, *f.*—*v.t.* sillonner, rider (*la figure*).
furry ['fəːri], *a.* fourré.

further ['fəːðə], v.t. avancer; faciliter, favoriser, seconder.—a. (also **farther** ['faːðə]) plus éloigné, ultérieur; autre, nouveau; *further end*, extrémité, f.—adv. (also **farther** ['faːðə]) plus loin; de plus, en outre, davantage, encore; ultérieurement; au delà.
furtherance ['fəːðərəns], n. avancement; progrès, m.
furthermore ['fəːðəmɔː], adv. de plus, en outre, d'ailleurs.
furthermost ['fəːðəmoust], **furthest** ['fəːðist], **farthest** ['faːðist], a. le plus éloigné; le plus reculé.—adv. and n. le plus loin.
furtive ['fəːtiv], a. furtif.
furtively ['fəːtivli], adv. furtivement, à la dérobée.
fury ['fjuəri], n. furie, fureur, f.; acharnement, m.
furze [fəːz], n. ajonc, genêt épineux, m.
fuse [fjuːz], v.t. fondre, liquéfier.—v.i. se fondre.—n. mèche, fusée, f.; (Elec.) fusible, plomb, m.; *the fuse has gone*, le plomb a sauté.
fuselage ['fjuːzilaːʒ, 'fjuːziliːdʒ], n. fuselage, m.
fuse wire ['fjuːzwaiə], n. fil fusible, m.
fusible ['fjuːzibl], a. fusible.
fusilier [fjuːzi'liə], n. fusilier, m.
fusillade [fjuːzi'leid], n. fusillade, f.
fusion ['fjuːʒən], n. fusion, f.
fuss [fʌs], n. fracas, embarras, m., façons, f.pl.
fussily ['fʌsili], adv. avec embarras.
fussy ['fʌsi], a. qui fait des embarras; affairé.
fustian ['fʌstjən], n. futaine, f.; (fig.) galimatias, m.
fusty ['fʌsti], a. qui sent le renfermé ou le moisi.
futile ['fjuːtail], a. futile, vain, frivole.
futility [fjuː'tiliti], n. futilité, f.
future ['fjuːtʃə], a. futur, à venir.—n. avenir; (Gram.) futur, m.
fuzz [fʌz], n. bourre, f., duvet (de couverture); flou (de photographie), m.
fuzzy ['fʌzi], a. duveteux, floconneux; bouffant, moutonné (cheveux); flou (photographie).

G

G, g [dʒiː]. septième lettre de l'alphabet; (Mus.) sol, m.
gab [gæb], n. faconde, f., bagout, m.; *to have the gift of the gab*, (colloq.) avoir la langue bien pendue.
gabardine [GABERDINE].
gabble [gæbl], v.i. parler très vite, bredouiller; caqueter, jacasser.—n. bredouillement; caquet, m.
gaberdine, gabardine [gæbə'diːn], n. gabardine, f.
gable [geibl], n. pignon, gable, m.
gadfly ['gædflai], n. taon, m.
gadget ['gædʒit], n. instrument, accessoire; truc, machin, m.
gaff [gæf], n. gaffe, f.—v.t. gaffer (poisson).

gag [gæg], n. bâillon, m.; (Theat.) plaisanterie, f.; (Cine.) gag, m.—v.t. bâillonner.
gage [geidʒ], n. gage, m., assurance, f.
gaggle [gægl], n. troupeau d'oies, m.
gaiety ['geiəti], n. gaieté, f.; éclat, m.
gaily ['geili], adv. gaiement, joyeusement.
gain [gein], n. gain, profit, avantage, m.—v.t. gagner, acquérir; remporter (victoire); atteindre.—v.i. avancer (montre etc.).
gainings ['geiniŋz], n.pl. gains, profits, m.pl.
gainsay ['geinsei, gein'sei], v.t. contredire.
gait [geit], n. démarche, allure, f.
gaiter ['geitə], n. guêtre, f.
gala ['geilə, 'gaːlə], n. gala, m.; fête, f.
galaxy ['gæləksi], n. voie lactée, galaxie, f.; (fig.) assemblage brillant, m.
gale [geil], n. coup de vent, m., tempête, f.
Galilee ['gælili:]. la Galilée, f.
gall [gɔːl], n. fiel, m.; écorchure (plaie); noix de galle, galle (d'arbres etc.); (fig.) rancune, f., chagrin, m.—v.t. écorcher; (fig.) fâcher.
gallant ['gælənt], a. brave, intrépide; [gə'lænt] gallant.—n. brave; preux; [gə'lænt] galant; amant, m.
gallantry ['gæləntri], n. vaillance; galanterie, f.
gall bladder ['gɔːlblædə], n. vésicule bilaire, f.
galleon ['gæliən], n. galion, m.
gallery ['gæləri], n. galerie, f.; (Theat.) balcon, m.; (Parl.) tribune publique, f.
galley ['gæli], n. galère; (Naut.) cuisine, f.
galley slave ['gælisleiv], n. galérien, m.
Gallic ['gælik], a. gaulois.
galling ['gɔːliŋ], a. irritant, vexant.
gallon ['gælən], n. gallon (quatre litres et demi), m.
gallop ['gæləp], n. galop, m.—v.i. galoper, aller au galop.
gallows ['gælouz], n. potence, f.
galvanize ['gælvənaiz], v.t. galvaniser.
Gambia ['gæmbiə]. la Gambie, f.
gamble [gæmbl], v.i. jouer de l'argent.
gambler ['gæmblə], n. joueur, m.
gambling ['gæmbliŋ], n. jeu, m.
gambol [gæmbl], n. gambade, f.; ébats, m.pl.—v.i. gambader, folâtrer.
game (1) [geim], a. estropié (jambe, bras etc.).
game (2) [geim], a. courageux.—n. jeu, m., partie, f.; *drawn game*, partie nulle; *to make game of*, se moquer de.—v.i. jouer de l'argent.
game (3) [geim], n. gibier, m.
game bag ['geimbæg], n. carnassière, f.
game-keeper ['geimkiːpə], n. garde-chasse, m.
gamester ['geimstə], n. joueur, m.
gammon ['gæmən], n. quartier de lard fumé, m.—v.t. saler et fumer (jambon).
gamut ['gæmət], n. (Mus.) gamme, f.
gander ['gændə], n. jars, m.
gang [gæŋ], n. bande, troupe, brigade, équipe (d'ouvriers), f.
ganger ['gæŋə], n. chef d'équipe; cantonnier, m.
Ganges ['gændʒiːz]. le Gange, m.
gangrene ['gæŋgriːn], n. gangrène, f.
gangster ['gæŋstə], n. (Am.) bandit, gangster, m.
gangway ['gæŋwei], n. passage, m.; (Naut.) passerelle (pour débarquer), coupée, f.
gannet ['gænit], n. (Orn.) fou, m.

435

gaol

gaol [JAIL].

gap [gæp], *n.* brèche, ouverture, *f.*, trou, *m.*; *(fig.)* lacune; trouée *(dans une forêt), f.*

gape [geip], *v.i.* bâiller; s'entr'ouvrir *(porte etc.)*; *(fig.)* bayer; **to gape at,** regarder bouche bée.—*n.* bâillement, *m.*

gaping ['geipiŋ], *a.* béant.—*n.* bâillement, *m.*

garage ['gærɑːʒ], *n.* garage, *m.*—*v.t.* garer.

garb [gɑːb], *n.* costume, habit, habillement, *m.*

garbage ['gɑːbidʒ], *n.* entrailles, issues; *(Am.)* ordures, *f.pl.* [see also **dust-bin** etc.]

garble [gɑːbl], *v.t.* mutiler, tronquer *(citation etc.)*, altérer.

garden ['gɑːdn], *n.* jardin, *m.*—*v.i.* jardiner.

garden-city ['gɑːdn'siti], *n.* cité-jardin, *f.*

gardener ['gɑːdnə], *n.* jardinier, *m.*

gardenia [gɑːˈdiːnjə], *n.* gardenia, *m.*

gardening ['gɑːdniŋ], *n.* jardinage, *m.*

gargle [gɑːgl], *v.i.* se gargariser.—*n.* gargarisme, *m.*

gargoyle ['gɑːgoil], *n.* gargouille, *f.*

garish ['gɛəriʃ], *a.* éclatant, voyant.

garland ['gɑːlənd], *n.* guirlande, *f.*—*v.t.* enguirlander.

garlic ['gɑːlik], *n.* ail, *m.*

garment ['gɑːmənt], *n.* vêtement, *m.*

garner ['gɑːnə], *n.* grenier, *m.*—*v.t.* mettre en grenier, engranger; *(fig.)* amasser.

garnet ['gɑːnit], *n.* grenat, *m.*

garnish ['gɑːniʃ], *v.t.* garnir, orner de.—*n.* garniture, *f.*

garret ['gærət], *n.* galetas, *m.*, mansarde, soupente, *f.*

garrison ['gærisən], *n.* garnison, *f.*—*v.t.* mettre garnison dans; mettre en garnison.

garrotte [gəˈrɔt], *n.* garrotte, *f.*—*v.t.* garrotter.

garrulity [gəˈruːliti], *n.* garrulité, loquacité, *f.*

garrulous ['gærʊləs], *a.* babillard, loquace.

garter ['gɑːtə], *n.* jarretière, *f.*; *(Am.)* support-chaussette, *m.*

gas [gæs], *n.* (*pl.* **gases** ['gæsiz]) gaz, *m.*; *laughing gas,* gaz hilarant.—*v.t.* gazer; intoxiquer par un gaz. [see **petrol**]

gas cooker ['gæs'kukə], *n.* réchaud à gaz, four à gaz, *m.*

gaseous ['geisiəs], *a.* gazeux.

gash [gæʃ], *n.* balafre, estafilade, entaille, *f.*—*v.t.* balafrer, tailladar.

gas-holder ['gæshouldə], **gasometer** [gæ'sɔmitə], *n.* gazomètre, *m.*

gas mask ['gæsmɑːsk], *n.* masque à gaz, *m.*

gasometer [GAS-HOLDER].

gasp [gɑːsp], *v.i.* respirer avec peine.—*n.* respiration haletante, *f.*; sursaut *(de surprise),* soupir convulsif, *m.*

gasping ['gɑːspiŋ], *a.* haletant.—*n.* respiration haletante, *f.*

gas stove ['gæsstouv], *n.* fourneau à gaz, *m.*

gastric ['gæstrik], *a.* gastrique.

gastronomy [gæsˈtrɔnəmi], *n.* gastronomie, *f.*

gate [geit], *n.* porte; barrière *(de péage)*; grille *(en fer forgé), f.*

gate-keeper ['geitkiːpə], *n.* portier; *(Rail.)* garde-barrière, *m.*

gate-post ['geitpoust], *n.* montant de porte, *m.*

gateway ['geitwei], *n.* porte, porte cochère, *f.*; portail *(grand)*; guichet *(petit), m.*

gather ['gæðə], *v.t.* ramasser; assembler; recueillir *(réunir)*; cueillir *(fruits etc.)*; *(fig.)*

436

conclure; *(Dress.)* froncer.—*v.i.* se rassembler, se réunir, s'assembler; s'amasser. —*n.* pli, froncis, *m.*

gatherer ['gæðərə], *n.* cueilleur; percepteur *(des contributions directes)*; vendangeur *(de raisins), m.*

gathering ['gæðəriŋ], *n.* rassemblement, *m.*; assemblée, réunion; perception *(des contributions directes)*; récolte *(de fruits etc.), f.*: *(Dress.)* froncis; *(Med.)* abcès, *m.*

gaudiness ['gɔːdinis], *n.* faste, faux brillant, *m.*

gaudy ['gɔːdi], *a.* éclatant; criard, fastueux, de mauvais goût.

gauge [geidʒ], *v.t.* jauger, mesurer; *(fig.)* juger.—*n.* jauge, mesure, *f.*; calibre, *m.*; *(Rail.)* voie, *f.*

Gaul [gɔːl], la Gaule, *f.*

Gauls [gɔːlz], **the.** les Gaulois, *m.pl.*

gaunt [gɔːnt], *a.* maigre, décharné.

gauntlet ['gɔːntlit], *n.* gantelet, *m.*

gauze [gɔːz], *n.* gaze, *f.*

gawk [gɔːk], *n.* sot, maladroit, *m.*

gawky ['gɔːki], *a.* dégingandé.

gay [gei], *a.* gai, réjoui, joyeux; pimpant.

gayety [GAIETY].

gayly [GAILY].

gaze [geiz], *v.i.* regarder fixement.—*n.* regard fixe *ou* attentif, *m.*

gazelle [gəˈzel], *n.* gazelle, *f.*

gazette [gəˈzet], *n.* gazette, *f.*; bulletin officiel, *m.*—*v.t.* publier *ou* annoncer dans le journal officiel.

gazetteer [gæziˈtiə], *n.* dictionnaire géographique; gazetier, *m.*

gear [giə], *n.* appareil, attirail; harnais *(d'un cheval), m.*; *(colloq.)* vêtements; *(Naut.)* apparaux, *m.pl.*; *(Mach.)* engrenage, *m.*; *(Motor.)* vitesse, *f.*; *(Motor.)* **bottom, first** or **low gear,** première, *f.*; **neutral gear,** point mort, *m.*; **in top gear,** en prise.

gear-box ['giəbɔks], *n.* boîte de changement de vitesse, *f.*

geese [GOOSE].

gelatine ['dʒelətiːn], *n.* gélatine, *f.*

gelatinous [dʒeˈlætinəs], *a.* gélatineux.

gelding ['geldiŋ], *n.* cheval hongre, *m.*

gem [dʒem], *n.* pierre précieuse, *f.*, joyau, *m.*

gender ['dʒendə], *n.* genre, *m.*

genealogical [dʒiːniəˈlɔdʒikl], *a.* généalogique.

genealogist [dʒiːniˈælədʒist], *n.* généalogiste, *m.*, *f.*

genealogy [dʒiːniˈælədʒi], *n.* généalogie, *f.*

general ['dʒenərəl], *a.* général, commun.—*n.* général, *m.*

generalize ['dʒenrəlaiz], *v.t.* généraliser.

generally ['dʒenrəli], *adv.* en général, ordinairement, généralement.

generate ['dʒenəreit], *v.t.* produire, engendrer.

generation [dʒenəˈreiʃən], *n.* génération, famille; production, *f.*; âge, *m.*

generator ['dʒenəreitə], *n.* générateur, *m.*; *electricity generator,* génératrice, *f.*

generic [dʒəˈnerik], **generical** [dʒeˈnerikəl], *a.* générique.

generosity [dʒenəˈrɔsiti], *n.* générosité, magnanimité, libéralité, *f.*

generous ['dʒenərəs], *a.* généreux; *(fig.)* abondant, riche *(en)*.

generously ['dʒenərəsli], *adv.* généreusement.

genesis ['dʒenəsis], *n.* genèse, *f.*

genetics [dʒə'netiks], *n.* génétique, *f.*

Geneva [dʒə'niːvə]. Genève, *f.*

genial ['dʒiːniəl], *a.* bon; affable; cordial, joyeux.

geniality [dʒiːni'æliti], *n.* bonne humeur, nature sympathique, gaieté, *f.*, entrain, *m.*

genially ['dʒiːniəli], *adv.* avec bonté, d'un air affable.

genie ['dʒiːni], *n.* (*Myth.*) génie, djinn, *m.*

genitive ['dʒenitiv], *n.* (*Gram.*) génitif, *m.*

genius ['dʒiːniəs], *n.* génie, *m.*

Genoa ['dʒenouə]. Gênes, *f.*

genteel [dʒen'tiːl], *a.* (*now often iron.*) de bon ton, comme il faut, distingué.

gentility [dʒen'tiliti], *n.* bon ton, *m.*, distinction, *f.*

gentle [dʒentl], *a.* doux, aimable; paisible; modéré (*pente etc.*).

gentlefolk ['dʒentlfouk], *n.pl.* personnes de bon ton, *f.pl.*, gens comme il faut, *m.pl.*

gentleman ['dʒentlman], *n.* (*pl.* **gentlemen** [-men]) monsieur; homme comme il faut, galant homme, homme bien né, *m.*

gentlemanly ['dʒentlmanli], *a.* distingué, de bon ton, comme il faut.

gentleness ['dʒentlnis], *n.* douceur, bonté, *f.*

gentlewoman ['dʒentlwumən], *n.* (*pl.* **-women** [wimin]) dame *ou* jeune fille de bonne famille, *f.*

gently ['dʒentli], *adv.* doucement.

genuine ['dʒenjuin], *a.* pur, vrai, véritable, authentique, naturel; sincère.

genuinely ['dʒenjuinli], *adv.* purement, sincèrement, authentiquement.

genuineness ['dʒenjuinnis], *n.* authenticité, sincérité, *f.*

genus ['dʒiːnəs], *n.* (*pl.* **genera** ['dʒenərə]) genre, *m.*

Geoffrey ['dʒefri]. Geoffroi, *m.*

geographer [dʒi'ɔgrəfə], *n.* géographe, *m.*, *f.*

geographical [dʒiə'græfikl], *a.* géographique.

geography [dʒi'ɔgrəfi], *n.* géographie, *f.*

geology [dʒi'ɔlədʒi], *n.* géologie, *f.*

geometry [dʒi'ɔmitri], *n.* géométrie, *f.*

George [dʒɔːdʒ]. Georges, *m.*

geranium [dʒə'reiniəm], *n.* (*Bot.*) géranium, *m.*

germ [dʒəːm], *n.* germe, *m.*

German ['dʒəːmən], *a.* allemand.—*n.* allemand (*langue*); Allemand (*personne*), *m.*

Germany ['dʒəːməni]. l'Allemagne, *f.*

germinate ['dʒəːmineit], *v.t.* germer; pousser.

gesticulate [dʒes'tikjuleit], *v.i.* gesticuler.

gesticulation [dʒestikju'leiʃən], *n.* gesticulation, *f.*

gesture ['dʒestʃə], *n.* geste, *m.*, action, *f.*—*v.i.* gesticuler.

get [get], *v.t. irr.* (*se*) procurer, acquérir, obtenir; recevoir; remporter (*to gain*); gagner (*to earn*); avoir; acheter (*to buy*); arriver à, atteindre (*to reach*); aller chercher (*to fetch*); trouver (*to find*); faire, se faire (*to induce, make, cause etc.*); attraper, s'attirer (*to catch etc.*); **to get hold of,** s'emparer de, saisir, obtenir.—*v.i.* se mettre (*en*); devenir, se faire (*to become*); aller (*to go*); **to get about,** sortir, prendre de l'exercice; **to get at,** arriver à; attaquer; atteindre; **to get away,** s'en aller, se

sauver, échapper (*à*); **to get back,** revenir, regagner; recouvrer; **to get in,** entrer, faire entrer, rentrer; **to get off,** s'en tirer, s'échapper; descendre; ôter, enlever; **to get on,** avancer, réussir, faire des progrès; monter sur; **to get out,** sortir, s'en tirer, faire sortir; **to get over,** passer, surmonter, vaincre; se consoler de; **to get rid of,** se débarrasser de; **to get through,** passer par, parcourir; réussir (*à un examen*); **to get up,** se lever, monter, faire monter, lever; préparer.

gewgaw ['gjuːgɔː], *n.* babiole, bagatelle, *f.*, colifichet, *m.*

geyser ['giːzə], *n.* chauffe-bain; (*Geol.*) geyser, *m.*

Ghana ['gɑːnə]. le Ghana, *m.*

Ghanaian [gɑː'neiən], *a.* du Ghana.—*n.* citoyen(ne) du Ghana, *m.*, *f.*

ghastliness ['gɑːstlinis], *n.* pâleur, *f.*; aspect effrayant, *m.*

ghastly ['gɑːstli], *a.* pâle, pâle comme la mort; horrible, affreux.

gherkin ['gəːkin], *n.* cornichon, *m.*

ghetto ['getou], *n.* ghetto, *m.*

ghost [goust], *n.* revenant, fantôme, spectre, *m.*; ombre, *f.*; **the Holy Ghost,** le Saint-Esprit.

ghostly ['goustli], *a.* spirituel; de spectre.

ghoul [guːl], *n.* goule, *f.*

ghoulish ['guːliʃ], *a.* de goule.

ghyll [GILL (2)].

giant ['dʒaiənt], *a.* de géant.—*n.* géant, *m.*

gibber ['dʒibə], *v.i.* baragouiner.

gibberish ['dʒibəriʃ], *n.* baragouin, charabia, *m.*

gibbet ['dʒibit], *n.* potence, *f.*, gibet, *m.*

gibe [dʒaib], *v.t., v.i.* railler, se moquer (*de*).—*n.* sarcasme, *m.*; raillerie, moquerie, *f.*

giblets ['dʒiblits], *n.pl.* abatis, *m.pl.*

giddily ['gidili], *adv.* étourdiment, à l'étourdie.

giddiness ['gidinis], *n.* vertige, *m.*; (*fig.*) étourderie, *f.*

giddy ['gidi], *a.* étourdi; (*fig.*) volage; vertigineux; **I feel giddy,** la tête me tourne; **that makes me feel giddy,** cela me donne le vertige.

gift [gift], *n.* don, présent, cadeau; (*fig.*) talent, *m.*; **Christmas gifts,** étrennes, *f.pl.*—*v.t.* douer, doter (*de*).

gifted ['giftid], *a.* doué, de talent.

gigantic [dʒai'gæntik], *a.* gigantesque, de géant.

giggle [gigl], *v.i.* rire nerveusement, rire un peu bêtement.—*n.* ricanement, petit rire bête, *m.*

gild [gild], *v.t.* dorer; (*fig.*) embellir.

gilding ['gildin], *n.* dorure, *f.*

Giles [dʒailz]. Gilles, *m.*

gill (1) [gil], *n.* (*usu. pl.*) ouïe (*de poisson*), *f.*

gill (2), **ghyll** [gil], *n.* ravin boisé; ruisseau (*du ravin*), *m.*

gill (3) [dʒil], *n.* treize centilitres, *m.pl.*

gillyflower ['dʒiliflauə], *n.* giroflée, *f.*

gilt [gilt], *a.* doré.—*n.* dorure, *f.pl.*

gilt-edged ['gilted3d], *a.* **gilt-edged securities,** valeurs de tout repos, *f.pl.*

gimcrack ['dʒimkræk], *n.* pacotille, camelote, *f.*

gimlet ['gimlit], *n.* vrille, *f.*

gimmick ['gimik], *n.* machin; tour (*artifice*), *m.*

gin (1) [dʒin], *n.* trébuchet, piège, *m.*

gin (2) [dʒin], *n.* genièvre, gin (*liquor*), *m.*

ginger ['dʒindʒə], *n.* gingembre; (*fam.*) poil de carotte (*personne aux cheveux roux*), *m.*

gingerbread ['dʒindʒəbred], *n.* pain d'épice, *m.*

gingerly ['dʒindʒəli], *adv.* tout doucement, délicatement.

gipsy, gypsy ['dʒipsi], *n.* bohémien, tzigane, *m.*, bohémienne, *f.*

giraffe [dʒi'rɑːf], *n.* girafe, *f.*

gird [gəːd], *v.t. irr.* ceindre (*de*); entourer (*de*).

girder ['gəːdə], *n.* poutre, solive, traverse, *f.*

girdle [gəːdl], *n.* ceinture, *f.*; ceinturon, *m.*; gaine, *f.*—*v.t.* ceinturer.

girl [gəːl], *n.* fille, jeune fille; jeune personne, *f.*

girlish ['gəːliʃ], *a.* de jeune fille.

girl scout [gəːl'skaut], *n.* éclaireuse, *f.*

girth [gəːθ], *n.* sangle, *f.*; tour, *m.*, circonférence, *f.*

gist [dʒist], *n.* fond, fin mot; point principal, *m.*, substance (*d'un discours*), *f.*

give [giv], *v.t. irr.* donner; livrer, rendre, accorder; faire (*réponse, crédit, compliment, amitiés etc.*); remettre; porter (*un coup etc.*); pousser (*un gémissement etc.*); émettre (*un son*); **to give away**, donner; trahir; **to give up**, abandonner, renoncer à.—*v.i.* céder; plier (*se courber*); prêter (*s'allonger*); **give and take**, donnant donnant; **to give in**, céder; **to give oneself up**, se rendre; **to give way**, céder, se relâcher.

given [givn], *v.t.* adonné, porté (à); donné; **given these difficulties**, étant donné ces difficultés.

giver ['givə], *n.* donneur, *m.*

gizzard ['gizəd], *n.* gésier, *m.*

glacial ['gleiʃəl], *a.* glacial, glaciaire.

glacier ['glæsiə], *n.* glacier, *m.*

glad [glæd], *a.* content, aise, bien aise; heureux (*de*).

gladden [glædn], *v.t.* réjouir.

glade [gleid], *n.* clairière, percée, *f.*

gladiator ['glædieitə], *n.* gladiateur, *m.*

gladiolus [glædi'oulǝs], *n.* (*pl.* **gladioli** [glædi'oulai]) glaïeul, *m.*

gladly ['glædli], *adv.* volontiers, avec plaisir.

glamorous ['glæmərəs], *a.* charmeur, ensorceleur.

glamour ['glæmə], *n.* charme, prestige, éclat, *m.*

glance [glɑːns], *n.* ricochet, coup en biais; regard, coup d'œil, *m.*—*v.i.* jeter un coup d'œil (*sur*); étinceler; **to glance off**, ricocher.

gland [glænd], *n.* (*Anat.*) glande, *f.*

glare [glɛə], *n.* éclat, *m.*, lueur, *f.*; regard irrité *ou* farouche, *m.*—*v.i.* éblouir; luire; regarder d'un air furieux.

glaring ['glɛərin], *a.* voyant, éblouissant; choquant, manifeste.

glass [glɑːs], *a.* de verre.—*n.* (*pl.* **glasses** ['glɑːsiz]) verre, *m.*; vitre (*de fenêtre*), *f.*; (*pl.*) lunettes, *f. pl.*; **cut glass**, cristal taillé, *m.*; **field glasses**, jumelles, *f.pl.*; **looking glass**, miroir, *m.*; **magnifying glass**, loupe, *f.*; **stained glass**, vitraux, *m.pl.*; (**weather-**)**glass**, baromètre, *m.*

glass-maker ['glɑːsmeikə], *n.* verrier, *m.*

glass-ware ['glɑːswɛə], *n.* verrerie, *f.*

glassy ['glɑːsi], *a.* vitreux, transparent.

glaze [gleiz], *v.t.* vitrer; vernir.

glazier ['gleizjə], *n.* vitrier, *m.*

glazing ['gleizin], *n.* vitrage (*de fenêtres*); vernissage (*de peintures*), *m.*

gleam [gliːm], *n.* rayon, *m.*, lueur, *f.*—*v.i.* briller, luire (*de*).

gleaming ['gliːmin], *a.* miroitant, luisant.

glean [gliːn], *v.t.* glaner.

gleaner ['gliːnə], *n.* glaneur, *m.*

glebe [gliːb], *n.* glèbe, terre, *f.*, sol, *m.*

glee [gliː], *n.* joie, gaieté, *f.*

gleeful ['gliːful], *a.* joyeux, gai.

glen [glen], *n.* vallon, ravin, *m.*

glib [glib], *a.* coulant, délié, volubile.

glibly ['glibli], *adv.* avec volubilité; doucereusement.

glide [glaid], *v.i.* couler, glisser; se glisser (*dans*).—*n.* glissade, *f.*; (*Av.*) vol plané, *m.*

glider ['glaidə], *n.* (*Av.*) planeur, *m.*

glimmer ['glimə], *n.* lueur, *f.*, faible rayon, *m.*—*v.i.* entre-luire, luire faiblement; poindre (*l'aube*).

glimpse [glimps], *n.* coup d'œil, *m.*, vue rapide, *f.*; **to catch a glimpse of**, entrevoir.

glint [glint], *n.* trait de lumière, *m.*, lueur, *f.*—*v.i.* luire par moments.

glisten [glisn], **glister** ['glistə], **glitter** ['glitə], *v.i.* reluire, scintiller, chatoyer.—*n.* éclat, lustre, *m.*

gloaming ['gloumin], *n.* crépuscule, *m.*

gloat [glout], *v.i.* dévorer *ou* couver des yeux; (*fig.*) se régaler de.

global ['gloubl], *a.* global; **global war**, conflit mondial, *m.*

globe [gloub], *n.* globe, *m.*

globule ['glɔbjuːl], *n.* globule, *m.*

gloom [gluːm], **gloominess** ['gluːminis], *n.* obscurité, *f.*, ténèbres, *f.pl.*; (*fig.*) tristesse, *f.*

gloomily ['gluːmili], *adv.* obscurément; d'un air triste, lugubrement.

gloomy ['gluːmi], *a.* sombre, obscur; morne, triste.

glorify ['glɔːrifai], *v.t.* glorifier.

glorious ['glɔːriəs], *a.* glorieux; illustre, superbe.

glory ['glɔːri], *n.* gloire; (*Paint.*) auréole, *f.*—*v.i.* se glorifier (*de*).

gloss [glɔs], *n.* lustre, apprêt, *m.*; (*fig.*) glose, *f.*, commentaire, *m.*—*v.i.* gloser, interpréter; lustrer; **to gloss over**, glisser sur.

glossary ['glɔsəri], *n.* glossaire, *m.*

glossiness ['glɔsinis], *n.* lustre, brillant, glacé, *m.*

glossy ['glɔsi], *a.* lustré, brillant, luisant.

glove [glʌv], *n.* gant, *m.*

glover ['glʌvə], *n.* gantier, *m.*

glow [glou], *v.i.* brûler (*de*); briller; (*fig.*) s'échauffer.—*n.* lueur rouge, *f.*; (*fig.*) feu, éclat, *m.*, splendeur, *f.*

glowing ['glouin], *a.* embrasé; ardent, chaleureux.

glow-worm ['glouwəːm], *n.* ver luisant, *m.*

glue [gluː], *n.* colle-forte, *f.*—*v.t.* coller.

glum [glʌm], *a.* maussade, de mauvaise humeur, morne.

glut [glʌt], *v.t.* gorger, rassasier; engorger (*le marché*).—*n.* surabondance, *f.*, excès, *m.*

glutton [glʌtn], *n.* gourmand, goinfre, *m.*

gluttonous ['glʌtənəs], *a.* gourmand, glouton, vorace.

gluttony ['glʌtəni], *n.* gloutonnerie, *f.*

glycerine ['glisəri:n], *n.* glycérine, *f.*

gnarled [nɑ:ld], *a.* noueux.

gnash [næʃ], *v.t.* grincer.—*v.i.* grincer des dents.

gnashing ['næʃiŋ], *n.* grincement, *m.*

gnat [næt], *n.* cousin, moucheron, *m.*

gnaw [nɔ:], *v.t.* ronger.

gnawing ['nɔ:iŋ], *a.* rongeant, rongeur.—*n.* rongement, *m.*

gnome [noum], *n.* gnome, *m.*

gnu [nu:], *n.* gnou, *m.*

go [gou], *v.i. irr.* aller, se rendre; marcher, passer; s'en aller, partir (*to leave*); disparaître; devenir (*to become*); *to go astray*, s'égarer; *to go away*, s'en aller, partir; *to go back*, retourner, s'en retourner, reculer; *to go backward*, aller à reculons, reculer; *to go down*, descendre; se coucher (*soleil*); tomber; *to go off*, partir (*fusil*); s'en aller; *to go on*, aller, avancer, continuer; se passer; *to go through*, passer par, traverser; subir, souffrir; *to go to sleep*, s'endormir; *to go without*, se passer de; *to let go*, lâcher prise.—*n.* mode, vogue, *f.*; (*fig.*) entrain, coup, essai, *m.*

goad [goud], *n.* aiguillon, *m.*—*v.t.* aiguillonner; (*fig.*) stimuler.

goal [goul], *n.* but; terme, *m.*

goal-keeper ['goulki:pə], *n.* (*Ftb.*) gardien de but, *m.*

goat [gout], *n.* chèvre, *f.*; *he-goat*, bouc, *m.*

gobble [gɔbl], *v.t.* gober, avaler.—*v.i.* glouglouter (*dindon*).

goblet ['gɔblit], *n.* gobelet, *m.*

goblin ['gɔblin], *n.* lutin, *m.*

God [gɔd]. Dieu, *m.*

god [gɔd], *n.* dieu, *m.*

godchild ['gɔdtʃaild], *n.* filleul, *m.*, filleule, *f.*

goddaughter ['gɔddɔ:tə], *n.* filleule, *f.*

goddess ['gɔdis], *n.* déesse, *f.*

godfather ['gɔdfɑ:ðə], *n.* parrain, *m.*

Godfrey ['gɔdfri]. Godefroi, *m.*

godless ['gɔdlis], *a.* athée, impie.

godliness ['gɔdlinis], *n.* piété, *f.*

godly ['gɔdli], *a.* pieux, dévot.

godmother ['gɔdmʌðə], *n.* marraine, *f.*

godsend ['gɔdsend], *n.* aubaine, trouvaille, *f.*

godson ['gɔdsʌn], *n.* filleul, *m.*

godspeed ['gɔd'spi:d], *n.* succès, *m.*

goffer ['gɔfə], *v.t.* gaufrer.

goggle [gɔgl], *v.i.* rouler de gros yeux; *goggle eyes*, des yeux en boules de loto, *m.pl.*

goggles [gɔglz], *n.pl.* lunettes (protectrices), *f.pl.*

going ['gouiŋ], *n.* marche, démarche, allée, *f.*, départ, *m.*

goitre ['gɔitə], *n.* (*Med.*) goitre, *m.*

gold [gould], *a.* d'or, en or.—*n.* or, *m.*

golden [gouldn], *a.* d'or.

goldfinch ['gouldfintʃ], *n.* chardonneret, *m.*

goldfish ['gouldfiʃ], *n.* poisson rouge, *m.*

goldsmith ['gouldsmiθ], *n.* orfèvre, *m.*

golf [gɔlf, gɔf], *n.* golf, *m.*

golf club ['gɔlfklʌb], *n.* club de golf (*société ou instrument*), *m.*

golf course ['gɔlfkɔ:s], *n.* terrain de golf, *m.*

gondola ['gɔndələ], *n.* gondole; nacelle (*de ballon*), *f.*

gondolier [gɔndə'liə], *n.* gondolier, *m.*

gone [gɔ:n, gɔn], *a.* allé, parti; perdu, disparu; passé, écoulé; adjugé (*aux enchères*).

gong [gɔŋ], *n.* gong; timbre (*d'une horloge*), *m.*

good [gud], *a.* bon; de bien, honnête, convenable, avantageux; valide, solide; (*collog.*) sage; *good luck*, bonheur, *m.*, bonne chance, *f.*; *to make good*, exécuter; compenser, indemniser; assurer.—*n.* bien, bon, avantage, profit, *m.*; *for good (and all)*, pour (tout) de bon; *what's the good of?* à quoi bon? (*pl.*) effets, biens, *m.pl.*, marchandises, *f.pl.*—*adv.* bien.—*int.* bon! bien! c'est très bien!

good-bye! [gud'bai], *int.* adieu! good-bye! *for the present*, au revoir!

good-for-nothing [gudfə'nʌθiŋ], *n.* vaurien, *m.*

Good Friday [gud'fraid(e)i]. vendredi saint, *m.*

good-humored ['gud'hju:məd], *a.* de bonne humeur, enjoué, gai.

good-natured ['gud'neitʃəd], *a.* d'un bon naturel, bon, bienveillant.

goodness ['gudnis], *n.* bonté; probité, *f.*; *thank goodness!* Dieu merci!

goodwill [gud'wil], *n.* bienveillance, bonne volonté, bonté; (*Comm.*) clientèle, *f.*

goose [gu:s], *n.* (*pl.* **geese** [gi:s]) oie, *f.*; (*fig.*) imbécile, niqaud, *m.*

gooseberry ['guzbri], *n.* groseille à maquereau, *f.*

gooseberry bush ['guzbribuʃ], *n.* groseillier, *m.*

goose flesh ['gu:sfleʃ], *n.* chair de poule, *f.*

gore [gɔ:], *n.* sang, sang caillé, *m.*—*v.t.* donner un coup de corne à.

gorge [gɔ:dʒ], *n.* gorge, *f.*; gosier, *m.*—*v.t.* gorger, avaler, rassasier.—*v.i.* se gorger (*de*).

gorgeous [gɔ:dʒəs], *a.* magnifique, splendide, fastueux.

gorilla [gə'rilə], *n.* gorille, *m.*

gorse [gɔ:s], *n.* ajonc, *m.*

gory ['gɔ:ri], *a.* sanglant, couvert de sang.

gosling ['gɔzliŋ], *n.* oison, *m.*

gospel ['gɔspəl], *n.* évangile, *m.*

gossamer ['gɔsəmə], *n.* fil de la Vierge, *m.*

gossip ['gɔsip], *n.* commère, *f.*, causeur (*personne*), *m.*; causerie, *f.*, commérage, *m.*—*v.i.* bavarder, faire des commérages.

gossip writer ['gɔsipraitə], *n.* (*Journ.*) échotier, *m.*

Goth [gɔθ], *n.* Goth; (*fig.*) barbare, *m.*

Gothic ['gɔθik], *a.* gothique, ogival.

gouge [gaudʒ], *n.* gouge, *f.*—*v.t.* gouger; *to gouge out*, arracher (*l'œil etc.*).

gourd [guəd], *n.* gourde, calebasse, *f.*

gout [gaut], *n.* goutte, *f.*

gouty ['gauti], *a.* goutteux.

govern ['gʌvən], *v.t.* gouverner, régir, diriger.

governess ['gʌvənis], *n.* institutrice, gouvernante, *f.*

government ['gʌvənmənt], *n.* gouvernement, *m.*, administration, *f.*, régime, *m.*

governor ['gʌvənə], *n.* gouverneur, gouvernant; directeur (*d'une institution*); (*Mech.*) régulateur, *m.*

gown [gaun], *n.* robe, *f.*; *dressing gown*, peignoir, *m.*, robe de chambre, *f.*; *night-gown*, chemise de nuit, *f.*

grab [græb], *v.t.* empoigner, saisir (d'un geste brusque).

439

grace [greis], *n.* grâce; faveur, *f.*; pardon; (*Mus.*) agrément; bénédicité (*avant le repas*), *m.*; grâces (*après le repas*), *f.pl.*—*v.t.* orner, embellir; illustrer, honorer (*de*).

graceful ['greisful], *a.* gracieux, bien fait, élégant.

gracefully ['greisfuli], *adv.* gracieusement, élégamment.

gracefulness ['greisfulnis], *n.* grâce, *f.*

graceless ['greislis], *a.* sans grâce; dépravé.

gracious ['greiʃəs], *a.* gracieux, clément, bon, favorable, bénin.

graciously ['greiʃəsli], *adv.* avec bonté, favorablement.

graciousness ['greiʃəsnis], *n.* bonté, grâce, *f.*

grade [greid], *n.* grade; degré, rang, *m.*—*v.t.* classer; calibrer; graduer.

grading ['greidiŋ], *n.* classement; calibrage, *m.*; graduation, *f.*

gradient ['greidiənt], *n.* (*Rail.*) rampe, inclinaison, *f.*

gradual ['grædjuəl], *a.* graduel, par degrés, gradué.

gradually ['grædjuəli], *adv.* graduellement, par degrés, peu à peu.

graduate ['grædjueit], *v.t.* graduer.—*v.i.* être reçu à un examen d'enseignement supérieur.—['grædjuit], *n.* gradué, *m.*

graduation [grædju'eiʃən], *n.* graduation; (*Univ.*) remise d'un diplôme, *f.*

graft (1) [grɑːft], *v.t.* greffer, enter (*sur*).—*n.* greffe, *f.*

graft (2) [grɑːft], *n.* (*colloq.*) corruption, *f.*

grafting ['grɑːftiŋ], *n.* greffe, *f.*

grafting knife ['grɑːftiŋnaif], *n.* greffoir, *m.*

grain [grein], *n.* grain, *m.*; céréales; fibres (*de bois*), *f.pl.*; *against the grain*, contre le fil, (*fig.*) à contre-cœur, à rebrousse-poil.

gram, gramme [græm], *n.* gramme, *m.*

grammar ['græmə], *n.* grammaire, *f.*

grammar school ['græməskuːl], *n.* école primaire, *f.*

grammatical [grə'mætikəl], *a.* grammatical; de grammaire.

gramophone ['græməfoun], *n.* gramophone; phonographe, *m.*

grampus ['græmpəs], *n.* épaulard, *m.*

granary ['grænəri], *n.* grenier, *m.*

grand [grænd], *a.* grand, magnifique, sublime, grandiose; *grand* (*piano*), piano à queue, *m.*

grandchild ['græntʃaild], *n.* (*pl.* **grandchildren** ['græntʃildrən]) petit-fils, *m.*, petite-fille, *f.*

granddaughter ['grændɔːtə], *n.* petite-fille, *f.*

grandee [græn'diː], *n.* grand d'Espagne, *m.*

grandeur ['grændjə], *n.* grandeur, *f.*, éclat, *m.*

grandfather ['grænfɑːðə], *n.* grand-père, *m.*

grandiloquence [græn'diləkwəns], *n.* langage pompeux, *m.*; emphase, grandiloquence, *f.*

grandiloquent [græn'diləkwənt], *a.* pompeux, enflé, grandiloquent.

grandly ['grændli], *adv.* grandement, avec éclat.

grandmother ['grænmʌðə], *n.* grand-mère, *f.*

grandson ['qrænsʌn], *n.* petit-fils, *m.*

grandstand ['grændstænd], *n.* tribune, *f.*

grange [greindʒ], *n.* manoir (avec ferme), *m.*

granite ['grænit], *n.* granit, *m.*

grant [grɑːnt], *v.t.* accorder, concéder; convenir, avouer, admettre.—*n.* aide, bourse; concession, *f.*

granulate ['grænjuleit], *v.t.* grener, granuler.—*v.i.* se granuler.

granule ['grænjuːl], *n.* granule, *m.*

grape [greip], *n.* grain de raisin, *m.*; (*pl.*) raisins, *m.pl.*; *a bunch of grapes*, une grappe de raisin.

grape-fruit ['greipfruːt], *n.* pamplemousse, *f.*

grape-shot ['greipʃɔt], *n.* mitraille, *f.*

graph [grɑːf], *n.* (*Math.*) courbe, *f.*; graphique, *m.*—*v.t.* graphiquer.

graphic ['græfik], *a.* graphique, pittoresque.

graph paper ['grɑːfpeipə], *n.* papier quadrillé, *m.*

graphite ['græfait], *n.* graphite, *m.*

grapnel ['græpnəl], *n.* grappin, *f.*

grapple [græpl], *n.* grappin, *m.*; lutte, *f.*—*v.t.* accrocher; grappiner.—*v.i.* en venir aux prises; lutter (*contre*).

grasp [grɑːsp], *v.t.* empoigner, saisir, serrer; embrasser; vouloir se saisir de.—*n.* prise, étreinte, poignée; (*fig.*) portée; compréhension, *f.*; *within one's grasp*, à la portée de la main.

grasping ['grɑːspiŋ], *a.* avide, cupide, avare.

grass [grɑːs], *n.* herbe, *f.*; gazon, herbage, *m.*

grasshopper ['grɑːshɔpə], *n.* sauterelle, *f.*

grassy ['grɑːsi], *a.* herbeux, couvert de gazon, verdoyant.

grate [greit], *n.* grille, *f.*; foyer (*âtre*), *m.*—*v.t.* râper; frotter.—*v.i.* crisser (*sur* ou *contre*).

grateful ['greitful], *a.* reconnaissant; (*fig.*) agréable.

gratefully ['greitfuli], *adv.* avec reconnaissance; (*fig.*) agréablement.

grater ['greitə], *n.* râpe, *f.*

gratification [grætifi'keiʃən], *n.* satisfaction, *f.*; plaisir, *m.*; gratification, récompense, *f.*

gratify ['grætifai], *v.t.* satisfaire, faire plaisir à; récompenser.

gratifying ['grætifaiiŋ], *a.* agréable; (*fig.*) flatteur.

grating ['greitiŋ], *a.* grinçant, discordant, choquant, désagréable.—*n.* grille, *f.*, grillage; grincement (*bruit*), *m.*

gratis ['greitis], *adv.* gratuitement, gratis, pour rien.

gratitude ['grætitjuːd], *n.* gratitude, reconnaissance, *f.*

gratuitous [grə'tjuːitəs], *a.* gratuit; (*fig.*) volontaire; bénévole.

gratuitously [grə'tjuːitəsli], *adv.* gratuitement; (*fig.*) sans motif.

gratuity [grə'tjuːiti], *n.* don, présent, *m.* gratification, *f.*; pourboire, *m.*

grave (1) [greiv], *n.* tombe, fosse, *f.*; tombeau, *m.*

grave (2) [greiv], *a.* grave, sérieux.

grave (3) [greiv], *v.t.* graver, tailler, ciseler.

grave-digger ['greivdigə], *n.* fossoyeur, *m.*

gravel ['grævl], *n.* gravier, sable, *m.*—*v.t.* sabler.

gravely ['greivli], *adv.* gravement, sérieusement.

graven ['greivn], *a.* gravé, taillé, ciselé.

graver ['greivə], *n.* graveur, *m.*; burin (*instrument*), *m.*

gravity ['græviti], *n.* gravité, *f.*, air sérieux, *m.*; pesanteur, *f.*

gravy ['greivi], *n.* jus (*de viande*), *m.*; sauce, *f.*

gravy boat, see **sauce boat**.

gray (*Am.*) [GREY].

graze [greiz], *v.t.* effleurer, raser, frôler; érafler, écorcher (*la peau*).—*v.i.* paître, brouter.—*n.* écorchure, éraflure, *f.*

grease [gri:s], *n.* graisse, *f.*—*v.t.* graisser.

greasiness ['gri:sinis, 'gri:zinis], *n.* état graisseux, *m.*; (*fig.*) onctuosité, *f.*

greasy ['gri:si, 'gri:zi], *a.* gras, graisseux; (*fig.*) onctueux.

great [greit], *a.* grand; considérable; important, principal; gros (*de*); **a great deal** (*of*), **a great many** (*of*), beaucoup (de).

great-coat ['greitkout], *n.* pardessus, *m.*; (*Mil.*) capote, *f.*

great-grandparents ['greitgrændpɛərənts], *n.pl.* arrière-grands-parents, *m.pl.*

greatly ['greitli], *adv.* grandement, fort, beaucoup, de beaucoup.

greatness ['greitnis], *n.* grandeur; sublimité; force, *f.*

Grecian ['gri:ʃən], *a.* grec, de Grèce.—*n.* Helléniste, *m., f.*

Greece [gri:s], la Grèce, *f.*

greed [gri:d], **greediness** ['gri:dinis], *n.* cupidité, avidité; gourmandise, *f.*

greedily ['gri:dili], *adv.* avidement.

greedy ['gri:di], *a.* cupide, avide; glouton.

Greek [gri:k], *a.* grec, de Grèce.—*n.* grec (*langue*); Grec (*personne*), *m.*

green [gri:n], *a.* vert; (*fig.*) frais, nouveau; novice.—*n.* vert, *m.*; verdure, *f.*; gazon, *m.*; (*pl.*) légumes verts, *m.pl.*

greenfinch ['gri:nfintʃ], *n.* verdier, *m.*

greengage ['gri:ngeidʒ], *n.* reine-claude, *f.*

greengrocer ['gri:ngrousə], *n.* fruitier, marchand de légumes, *m.*

greenhorn ['gri:nhɔːn], *n.* blanc-bec, niais, *m.*

greenhouse ['gri:nhaus], *n.* serre, *f.*

greenish ['gri:niʃ], *a.* verdâtre.

Greenland ['gri:nlənd], le Groenland, *m.*

greet [gri:t], *v.t.* saluer, accueillir.

greeting ['gri:tiŋ], *n.* salutation, *f.*, salut, *m.*; (*pl.*) compliments, *m.pl.*

gregarious [gri'gɛəriəs], *a.* grégaire.

Gregory ['gregəri], Grégoire, *m.*

grenade [grə'neid], *n.* grenade, *f.*

grenadier [grenə'diə], *n.* grenadier, *m.*

grey [grei], *a.* gris.

greyhound ['greihaund], *n.* lévrier, *m.*

greyish ['greiiʃ], *a.* grisâtre.

grid [grid], **gridiron** ['gridaiən], *n.* gril, *m.*

grief [gri:f], *n.* douleur, tristesse, peine, *f.*; chagrin, *m.*

grievance ['gri:vəns], *n.* grief, *m.*; injustice, *f.*

grieve [gri:v], *v.t.* chagriner, attrister, faire de la peine à.—*v.i.* se chagriner, s'affliger.

grievous ['gri:vəs], *a.* lourd, douloureux, grave, affligeant; atroce.

grievously ['gri:vəsli], *adv.* grièvement, cruellement.

grill [gril], *v.t.* griller, faire griller.—*n.* gril, *m.*; grillade; viande grillée, *f.*

grim [grim], *a.* farouche, féroce; lugubre, effrayant; sinistre.

grimace [gri'meis], *n.* grimace; (*pl.*) grimacerie, *f.*—*v.i.* grimacer.

grime [graim], *n.* saleté, noirceur, *f.*

grimly ['grimli], *adv.* d'un air farouche *ou* sinistre.

grimness ['grimnis], *n.* air renfrogné, air farouche, *m.*

grimy ['graimi], *a.* sale, noirci, encrassé.

grin [grin], *n.* grimace, *f.*; ricanement, *m.*—*v.i.* ricaner, grimacer.

grind [graind], *v.t. irr.* moudre; broyer; aiguiser, repasser (*couteau etc.*); grincer (*dents*); (*fig.*) opprimer.

grinder ['graində], *n.* repasseur, émouleur; broyeur, *m.*; dent molaire, *f.*

grinding ['graindiŋ], *n.* broiement, grincement (*des dents etc.*); repassage (*de couteaux*), *m.*; (*fig.*) oppression, *f.*

grindstone ['graindstoun], *n.* meule, *f.*

grip [grip], *n.* prise, étreinte, *f.*, serrement, *m.*—*v.t.* empoigner, saisir, serrer.

gripe [graip], *v.t.* saisir; opprimer; donner la colique à.—*v.i.* avoir la colique.—*n.* saisine; (*pl.*) colique, *f.*

griping ['graipiŋ], *a.* (*fig.*) cuisant, affreux; avare (*pingre*).—*n.* colique, *f.*

grisly ['grizli], *a.* hideux, affreux, horrible.

grist [grist], *n.* blé à moudre, *m.*, mouture, *f.*; (*fig.*) gain, profit, *m.*

gristle [grisl], *n.* cartilage, *m.*

grit [grit], *n.* grès, sable; (*fig.*) courage, *m.*

gritty ['griti], *a.* graveleux.

grizzled [grizld], *a.* grison, grisâtre.

grizzly ['grizli], *a.* grisâtre; **grizzly bear**, ours gris d'Amérique, *m.*

groan [groun], *n.* gémissement, grognement, *m.*—*v.i.* gémir, grogner.

grocer ['grousə], *n.* épicier, *m.*

grocery ['grousəri], *n.* épicerie, *f.*

groggy ['grogi], *a.* gris, pochard; titubant; aux jambes faibles (*cheval*).

groin [groin], *n.* aine; (*Arch.*) arête, *f.*

groom [gru:m], *n.* palefrenier, valet d'écurie, *m.*—*v.t.* panser; **well-groomed**, bien soigné, *m.*

groove [gru:v], *n.* rainure, rayure, cannelure; (*fig.*) ornière (*rut*), *f.*—*v.t.* creuser, canneler.

grope [group], *v.i.* tâtonner.

gropingly ['groupiŋli], *adv.* à tâtons.

gross [grous], *a.* gros; grossier, rude; (*Comm.*) brut; (*fig.*) flagrant, énorme.—*n.* gros, *m.*, grosse; masse, *f.*

grossly ['grousli], *adv.* grossièrement; d'une manière flagrante.

grossness ['grousnis], *n.* grossièreté; énormité, *f.*

grotto ['grotou], *n.* grotte, *f.*

grotesque [gro'tesk], *a.* grotesque.

ground (1) [graund], *past* and *p.p.* [GRIND] and *a.* broyé, moulu; aiguisé (*affilé*).

ground (2) [graund], *n.* terre, *f.*; terrain (*plot*); sol (*soil*), *m.*; fond (*de tableau, de dessin textile etc.*); (*fig.*) fondement, sujet, motif, *m.*, cause, *f.*; (*pl.*) terrains, *m.pl.*, sédiment, marc de café, *m.*—*v.t.* fonder, baser, établir, appuyer (*sur*).—*v.i.* échouer.

grounded ['graundid], *a.* fondé, établi; **well-grounded**, bien fondé.

ground floor ['graund'flɔː], *n.* rez-de-chaussée, *m.*

groundless ['graundlis], *a.* sans fondement.

groundlessly ['graundlisli], *adv.* sans fondement.

group [gru:p], *n.* groupe, peloton, *m.*—*v.t.* grouper.

grouping ['gru:piŋ], *n.* groupement, *m.*

grouse (1) [graus], *n.* (*Orn.*) tétras; coq de bruyère, *m.*

grouse (2) [graus], *v.i.* grogner, grincher.

grove [grouv], n. bocage, bosquet, m.
grovel [grɔvl], v.i. ramper, se vautrer.
grovelling ['grɔvliŋ], a. rampant, abject, vil.
—n. bassesse, f.
grow [grou], v.i. irr. cultiver.—v.i. croître,
pousser; s'accroître; devenir, se faire (to
become); to grow up, croître, grandir,
arriver à maturité.
grower ['grouə], n. cultivateur, producteur, m.
growing ['grouiŋ], a. croissant.—n. croissance; culture, f.
growl [graul], v.i. grogner, gronder.—n.
grognement, grondement, m.
grown-up ['grounʌp], a. fait, grand.—n.
adulte, m., f.
growth [grouθ], n. croissance, f.; produit,
cru, m., récolte (produce), f.; (fig.) progrès,
m.
grub [grʌb], n. larve, f., ver blanc, m.—v.t.
défricher, fouiller.—v.i. bêcher, creuser.
grubby ['grʌbi], a. véreux; (fig.) sale.
grudge [grʌdʒ], n. rancune, animosité, f.; to
bear a grudge against, en vouloir à.—
v.t. donner à contre-cœur.
grudgingly ['grʌdʒiŋli], adv. à contre-cœur;
de mauvaise grâce.
gruel ['gru:əl], n. gruau, m.
gruesome ['gru:səm], a. macabre, horrible,
lugubre.
gruff [grʌf], a. bourru, rude, rébarbatif.
grumble [grʌmbl], v.i. se plaindre, grogner,
grommeler (contre ou de).
grumbler ['grʌmblə], n. grondeur, grogneur,
m.
grumbling ['grʌmbliŋ], n. grognement, m.
grunt [grʌnt], v.i. grogner.—n. grognement,
m.
guarantee [gærən'ti:], n. garant, m., caution,
garantie, f.—v.t. garantir.
guard [gɑ:d], n. garde; défense, protection, f.;
garde (personne), f.; (Rail.) conducteur, chef
de train, m.—v.t. garder, défendre, protéger, veiller sur.—v.i. se garder, se prémunir (contre).
guarded [gɑ:did], a. prudent, circonspect;
réservé.
guardedly ['gɑ:didli], adv. avec circonspection, avec réserve.
guardian ['gɑ:djən], a. gardien, tutélaire.—n.
gardien; tuteur (de jeunes), m.
guardianship ['gɑ:djənʃip], n. tutelle, protection, f.
guard-room ['gɑ:drum], n. corps de garde,
m., salle de police, f.
Guatemala [gwætə'mɑ:lə], le Guatemala, m.
gudgeon ['gʌdʒən], n. goujon, m.; (Mech.)
tourillon, m.; (fig.) dupe, f.
guess [ges], v.t., v.i. deviner, conjecturer.—
n. conjecture, f.
guest [gest], n. invité, m., convive, m., f.;
hôte, m.
guffaw [gə'fɔ:], n. gros rire, m.—v.i. pouffer
de rire.
guidance ['gaidəns], n. conduite, direction, f.
guide [gaid], n. guide, conducteur, m.;
Girl Guide, éclaireuse, f.—v.t. conduire,
guider; diriger; guided missile, (Mil.)
engin téléguidé, m.
guild [gild], n. corporation, guilde, f.
guildhall ['gildhɔ:l], n. hôtel de ville, m.
guile [gail], n. astuce, f., artifice, m.
guilt [gilt], n. culpabilité, f.

guiltily ['giltili], adv. criminellement.
guiltless ['giltlis], a. innocent.
guilty ['gilti], a. coupable; the guilty
party, le coupable, m.; to find guilty,
déclarer coupable; (Law) to plead guilty,
s'avouer coupable.
Guinea ['gini], la Guinée, f.
guinea ['gini], n. guinée, f.
guinea fowl ['ginifaul], n. pintade, f.
guinea pig ['ginipig], n. cochon d'Inde, m.
guise [gaiz], n. guise, façon, apparence, f.;
costume, m., dehors, m.pl.
guitar [gi'tɑ:], n. guitare, f.
gulf [gʌlf], n. golfe; (fig.) gouffre, m.
gull [gʌl], n. mouette, f., goéland; (fig.)
jobard, m.—v.t. duper, flouer.
gullet ['gʌlit], n. gosier, m.
gullible ['gʌlibl], a. crédule.
gully ['gʌli], n. ravin, m.
gulp [gʌlp], v.t. avaler, gober.—n. goulée,
gorgée, f., trait, m.; at a gulp, d'un trait.
gum [gʌm], n. gomme; (Anat.) gencive, f.
gumboil ['gʌmboil], n. abcès aux gencives, m.
gumption ['gʌmpʃən], n. (colloq.) sens
pratique, m., jugeotte, f.
gum tree ['gʌmtri:], n. gommier, m.; (fig.)
up a gum tree, dans le pétrin.
gun [gʌn], n. canon, m.; pièce d'artillerie,
bouche à feu, m.; fusil (non rayé); (Am.)
revolver, m.; machine gun, mitrailleuse
f.
gunboat ['gʌnbout], n. canonnière, f.
guncarriage ['gʌnkæridʒ], n. affût (de
canon), m.
gunnel [GUNWALE].
gunner ['gʌnə], n. canonnier, servant, artilleur, m.
gunnery ['gʌnəri], n. artillerie, f.; tir au
canon, m.
gunpowder ['gʌnpaudə], n. poudre à canon, f.
gunshot ['gʌnʃɔt], n. portée de fusil (distance),
f.; coup de canon (décharge); coup de feu
(blessure), m.
gunwale [gʌnl], n. (Naut.) plat-bord, m.
gurgle [gə:gl], v.i. faire glouglou; gargouiller.
gush [gʌʃ], n. jaillissement, m.; effusion, f.,
jet; débordement (de sentiments), m.—v.i.
jaillir; (fig.) être sentimental à l'excès.
gusher ['gʌʃə], n. (Min.) puits jaillissant, m.
gushing ['gʌʃiŋ], a. jaillissant; bouillonnant;
(fig.) expansif, empressé.
gusset ['gʌsit], n. gousset, m.
gust [gʌst], n. coup de vent, m., bouffée,
rafale, f.
gusty ['gʌsti], a. orageux, venteux.
gut [gʌt], n. boyau, intestin, m.; corde à
boyau (fabriqué), f.; (pl.) (fam.) intestins,
m.pl., ventre; courage, cran, m.—v.t.
éventrer, vider; (fig.) détruire.
gutter ['gʌtə], n. gouttière (d'une maison), f.;
ruisseau, caniveau (dans la rue), m.—v.i.
couler.
guttersnipe ['gʌtəsnaip], n. gamin, voyou, m.
guttural ['gʌtərəl], a. guttural.
guy [gai], n. épouvantail, m.; (Naut.) corde
soutien, f., guide; (Am.) type, individu, m.
Guyana [gi'ɑ:nə, gai'ɑ:nə], la Guyane, f.
guzzle [gʌzl], v.t., v.i. bouffer (aliment),
lamper (boisson).
gym [dʒim], [GYMNASIUM].
gymkhana [dʒim'kɑ:nə], n. gymkhana, m.
gymnasium [dʒim'neiziəm], n. gymnase, m.

gymnast ['dʒimnæst], n. gymnaste, m., f.
gymnastic [dʒim'næstik], a. gymnastique.—
n.(pl.) gymnastique, f.
gypsum ['dʒipsəm], n. gypse, m.
gypsy [GIPSY].
gyrate [dʒai'reit], v.i. tournoyer.
gyration [dʒai'reiʃən], n. mouvement giratoire, m.

H

H, h [eitʃ]. huitième lettre de l'alphabet, m.
ou f.; H-bomb, [HYDROGEN].
haberdasher ['hæbədæʃə], n. confectionneur
et chemisier, m.
haberdashery ['hæbədæʃəri], n. confection
pour hommes, f.
habit ['hæbit], n. habitude, coutume, f.; (pl.)
mœurs, f.pl.; riding habit, amazone, f.;
to be in the habit of, avoir coutume de.—
v.t. vêtir.
habitable ['hæbitəbl], a. habitable.
habitation [hæbi'teiʃən], n. habitation, demeure, f.
habitual [hə'bitjuəl], a. habituel.
habitually [hə'bitjuəli], adv. habituellement,
d'habitude.
habituate [hə'bitjueit], v.t. habituer, accoutumer.
hack (1) [hæk], v.t. hacher, couper; ébrécher;
(fig.) massacrer, écorcher.
hack (2) [hæk], n. cheval de louage, m.; rosse
(cheval sans force), f.; (fig.) écrivassier à
gages, m.
hackney ['hækni], n. hackney carriage,
fiacre, m.
hackneyed ['hæknid], a. banal, rebattu;
hackneyed phrase, cliché, m.
haddock ['hædək], n. (Ichth.) aiglefin, m.
Hades ['heidiːz]. les Enfers, m.pl.
haemoglobin [hiːmə'gloubin], n. hémoglobine, f.
haemorrhage ['hemərid3], n. hémorrhagie, f.
haft [hɑːft], n. manche, m., poignée, f.
hag [hæg], n. vieille sorcière; (pop.) vieille
fée, f.
haggard ['hægəd], a. hagard, farouche, égaré.
haggle [hægl], v.i. marchander.
Hague [heig], The. La Haye, f.
hail (1) [heil], n. grêle, f.—v.i. grêler.
hail (2) [heil], n. salut, appel, m.—int. salut!
—v.t. saluer; (Naut.) héler; to hail a
taxi, héler ou appeler un taxi; to hail
from, venir de.
hailstone ['heilstoun], n. grêlon, m.
hailstorm ['heilstɔːm], n. tempête de grêle, f.
hair [hɛə], n. cheveu (a single hair), m.;
cheveux, m.pl., chevelure (head of hair), f.;
poil (on the body, on animals etc.), crin
(horsehair), m.; soies (bristles), f.pl.; to do
one's hair, se coiffer; to split hairs,
chicaner sur les mots.
hair-brush ['hɛəbrʌʃ], n. brosse à cheveux, f.
hair-cut ['hɛəkʌt], n. coupe de cheveux, f.
hairdresser ['hɛədresə], n. coiffeur, m.
hairless ['hɛəlis], a. chauve, sans cheveux;
sans poil (animal).

hair net ['hɛənet], n. résille, f.
hairy ['hɛəri], a. velu, chevelu, poilu.
Haiti [hai'iːti]. Haïti, m. ou f.
Haitian [hai'iːʃən], a. haïtien.—n. Haïtien
(personne), m.
hake [heik], n. (Ichth.) merluche, f., (fam.)
colin, m.
halberd ['hælbəd], n. hallebarde, f.
hale [heil], a. robuste, sain, bien portant; to
be hale and hearty, avoir bon pied, bon
œil.
half [hɑːf], a. demi.—n. (pl. halves [hɑːvz])
moitié, f., demi, m., half an hour, une
demi-heure, f.; (pop.) not half! tu parles!
—adv. à demi, à moitié.
half-back ['hɑːfbæk], n. (Fib.) demi, m.
half brother ['hɑːf'brʌðə], n. demi-frère,
frère utérin, frère consanguin, m.
half-caste ['hɑːfkɑːst], n. métis, m.
half fare ['hɑːf'fɛə], n. demi-place, f., demi-
tarif, m.
half holiday ['hɑːf'hɔlidi], n. demi-congé, m.
half pay ['hɑːf'pei], n. demi-solde, f.
half time ['hɑːf'taim], n. (Spt.) la mi-temps, f.
half-way ['hɑːf'wei], adv. à mi-chemin; half-
way up the hill, à mi-côte.
half-witted ['hɑːf'witid], a. niais, sot, idiot.
half year ['hɑːf'jiə], n. semestre, m.
halibut ['hælibət], n. (Ichth.) flétan, m.
hall [hɔːl], n. salle, f.; vestibule (entrance-
hall); château, manoir (seat); réfectoire
(dining hall); hôtel de ville (town hall), m.;
hall porter, concierge, m.
hall-mark ['hɔːlmɑːk], n. poinçon de contrôle, m.—v.t. contrôler.
hallo! [hə'lou], int. holà! hé!
hallow ['hælou], v.t. sanctifier, consacrer.
hallucinate [hə'ljuːsineit], v.t. halluciner.
hallucination [həljuːsi'neiʃən], n. hallucination; (fig.) déception, illusion, f.
halo ['heilou], n. (Astron.) halo, m.; (Paint.
etc.) auréole, f.
halt (1) [hɔːlt], n. halte, f.; arrêt; clochement,
m.—v.i. faire halte.—int. halte-là!
***halt** (2) [hɔːlt], a. boiteux, estropié.
halter ['hɔːltə], n. licou, m., longe (à cheval);
corde (du gibet), f.
halve [hɑːv], v.t. diviser en deux.
ham [hæm], n. jambon; jarret (humain), m.
hamlet ['hæmlit], n. hameau, m.
hammer ['hæmə], n. marteau; chien (de
fusil), m.; to bring under the hammer,
mettre aux enchères.—v.t. marteler, forger.
—v.i. marteler.
hammock ['hæmək], n. hamac, m.
hamper (1) ['hæmpə], n. panier, m., manne, f.
hamper (2) ['hæmpə], v.t. empêtrer, embarrasser, gêner.
hamstring ['hæmstriŋ], n. tendon du jarret,
m.—v.t. irr. (conjug. like STRING) couper le
jarret à; (fig.) couper les moyens à.
hand [hænd], n. main; palme (mesure de 4
pouces); signature; écriture (calligraphie), f.;
(Cards) jeu, m.; aiguille (d'une montre etc.),
f.; ouvrier, employé, m.; at hand, sous la
main; off-hand, sur-le-champ; second-
hand, d'occasion.—v.t. passer, donner,
remettre; donner la main à; conduire,
guider; to hand about or round, faire
passer de main en main, faire circuler; to
hand down, transmettre; to hand over,
remettre, céder.

handbag ['hændbæg], *n.* sac à main, *m.*

hand bell ['hændbel], *n.* sonnette, clochette, *f.*

handbook ['hændbuk], *n.* manuel; guide, *m.*

handcuff ['hændkʌf], *n.* menotte, *f.—v.t.* mettres les menottes à.

handful ['hændful], *n.* poignée, *f.*; (*fig.*) petit nombre, peu, *m.*

handicap ['hændikæp], *n.* handicap, *m.—v.t.* handicaper.

handicraft ['hændikra:ft], *n.* métier, travail manuel, *m.*

handiwork ['hændiwə:k], *n.* ouvrage, travail manuel, *m.*

handkerchief ['hæŋkətʃif], *n.* mouchoir, *m.*

handle ['hændl], *n.* manche, *m.*; poignée (*d'une épée etc.*), *f.*; bouton (*d'une porte*), *m.*; anse (*d'une cruche*); queue (*d'une poêle*), *f.*; **starting handle**, (*Motor.*) manivelle (de mise en marche), *f.—v.t.* manier; toucher à, manipuler.

handle-bar ['hændlba:], *n.* guidon (*de bicyclette*), *m.*

handling ['hændliŋ], *n.* maniement, traitement, *m.*

handmaid ['hændmeid], *n.* servante, *f.*

handrail ['hændreil], *n.* garde-fou, *m.*, rampe, main courante, *f.*

handshake ['hændʃeik], *n.* poignée de main, *f.*, serrement de main, *m.*

handsome ['hænsəm], *a.* beau, élégant; (*fig.*) gracieux.

handsomely ['hænsəmli], *adv.* joliment, élégamment; généreusement.

handwriting ['hændraitiŋ], *n.* écriture, *f.*

handy ['hændi], *a.* adroit (*personne*); commode; à portée de la main.

hang [hæŋ], *v.t. irr.* pendre, suspendre; accrocher (*à*); tendre, tapisser (*de*); laisser pendre, pencher, baisser (*la tête etc.*); poser (*portes etc.*); **hang it!** fichtre! **go and be hanged,** va-t'en au diable! **to hang fire,** faire long feu; (*fig.*) vaciller.—*v.i.* pendre, être suspendu; s'accrocher, se pendre; baisser; se pencher (*à*); **to hang about,** rôder autour de; **to hang over,** être suspendu sur, surplomber.

hangar ['hæŋə], *n.* (*Av.*) hangar, *m.*

hang-dog ['hæŋdɔg], *n.* **hang-dog look,** mine patibulaire, *f.*

hanger-on ['hæŋə'rɔn], *n.* dépendant, parasite, *m.*

hanging ['hæŋiŋ], *a.* suspendu.—*n.* suspension, pendaison; pose (*papier de tenture*), *f.*; collage, *m.*; (*pl.*) tapisserie, tenture, *f.*

hangman ['hæŋmən], *n.* (*pl.* **-men** [men]) bourreau, *m.*

hank [hæŋk], *n.* poignée, *f.*, écheveau, *m.*

hanker ['hæŋkə], *v.i.* **to hanker after,** désirer ardemment.

hankering ['hæŋkəriŋ], *n.* grande envie, *f.*, vif désir, *m.*

haphazard [hæp'hæzəd], *a.* au petit bonheur, fortuit.—*n.* hasard, sort, *m.*

haply ['hæpli], *adv.* par hasard; peut-être.

happen ['hæpn], *v.i.* arriver, advenir, se passer; se trouver par hasard.

happily ['hæpili], *adv.* heureusement, par bonheur.

happiness ['hæpinis], *n.* bonheur, *m.*

happy ['hæpi], *a.* heureux, content.

harass ['hærəs], *v.t.* harasser, harceler.

harbinger ['ha:bindʒə], *n.* avant-coureur, précurseur, *m.*

harbor ['ha:bə], *n.* port, havre; (*fig.*) refuge, asile, gite, *m.—v.t.* héberger, recéler, donner asile à; (*fig.*) entretenir, nourrir.—*v.i.* se réfugier.

hard [ha:d], *a.* dur, ferme; (*fig.*) malaisé, difficile; pénible, rude, rigoureux; dur à la détente (*pingre*); **hard frost,** forte gelée, *f.*; **hard labor,** travaux forcés, *m.pl.*; **hard up,** à court (*d'argent*).—*adv.* dur, rudement, péniblement; fort, ferme.

harden [ha:dn], *v.t.* durcir; (*fig.*) endurcir (*à*).—*v.i.* s'endurcir, devenir dur.

hardening ['ha:dniŋ], *n.* durcissement; (*fig.*) endurcissement, *m.*; trempe (*d'acier*), *f.*

hardihood ['ha:dihud], *n.* hardiesse, audace, intrépidité, *f.*

hardily ['ha:dili], *adv.* durement, hardiment.

hardiness ['ha:dinis], *n.* tempérament robuste, *m.*; (*fig.*) effronterie, assurance, *f.*

hardly ['ha:dli], *adv.* durement, rudement, mal; à peine, guère (*presque pas*); **hardly ever,** presque jamais.

hardness ['ha:dnis], *n.* dureté, solidité; difficulté; crudité (*d'eau*), *f.*

hardship ['ha:dʃip], *n.* fatigue, peine, privation, *f.*; (*pl.*) épreuves, souffrances, *f.pl.*

hardware ['ha:dwɛə], *n.* quincaillerie, *f.*

hardy ['ha:di], *a.* hardi, courageux; fort; de pleine terre (*plantes*).

hare [hɛə], *n.* lièvre, *m.*

hare-brained ['hɛəbreind], *a.* écervelé, étourdi.

hare-lip ['hɛəlip], *n.* bec-de-lièvre, *m.*

hark [ha:k], *v.i.* écouter, prêter l'oreille.—*int.* écoutez!

harlequin ['ha:likwin], *n.* arlequin, *m.*

harm [ha:m], *n.* tort, dommage, mal, *m.—v.t.* nuire à, faire du mal à.

harmful ['ha:mful], *a.* nuisible, malfaisant, nocif.

harmless ['ha:mlis], *a.* innocent, inoffensif.

harmonic [ha:'mɔnik], *a.* harmonique; harmonieux.—*n.(pl.)* harmonique, *f.*

harmonious [ha:'mouniəs], *a.* harmonieux; mélodieux.

harmonize ['ha:mənaiz], *v.t.* rendre harmonieux, accorder, harmoniser.—*v.i.* s'harmoniser; (*fig.*) s'accorder.

harmony ['ha:məni], *n.* harmonie, *f.*; accord, *m.*

harness ['ha:nis], *n.* harnais, harnachement, *m.—v.t.* harnacher; atteler (*à une voiture*).

harp [ha:p], *n.* harpe, *f.*; **jew's harp,** guimbarde, *f.—v.i.* jouer de la harpe; **to harp on one string,** rabâcher toujours la même chose.

harpist ['ha:pist], *n.* harpiste, *m.*, *f.*

harpoon [ha:'pu:n], *n.* harpon, *m.—v.t.* harponner.

harpsichord ['ha:psikɔ:d], *n.* clavecin, *m.*

harridan ['hæridən], *n.* chipie, mégère, *f.*

harrow ['hærou], *n.* herse, *f.—v.t.* herser; (*fig.*) torturer.

harrowing ['hærouiŋ], *a.* navrant.—*n.* hersage; (*fig.*) déchirement, *m.*

Harry ['hæri], Henri, *m.*

harry ['hæri], *v.t.* harceler; piller.

harsh [ha:ʃ], *a.* âpre, rude, dur; discordant.

harshly ['ha:ʃli], *adv.* durement, sévèrement.

harshness ['hɑːʃnis], *n.* âpreté; discordance, *f.*
harum-scarum ['hɛərəm'skɛərəm], *a.* écervelé, étourdi.
harvest ['hɑːvist], *n.* moisson (*de blé*); récolte (*de fruits etc.*); vendange (*de raisins*), *f.*—*v.t.* moissonner; récolter; vendanger.
harvester. see **combine-harvester.**
hash [hæʃ], *n.* hachis, *m.*—*v.t.* hacher, hacher menu; (*fig.*) plagier.
hasp [hæsp, hɑːsp], *n.* loquet, *m.*
hassock ['hæsək], *n.* coussin (*pour les genoux ou les pieds*), *m.*
haste [heist], *n.* hâte, précipitation, *f.*, emportement, *m.*; diligence, *f.*; *in haste,* à la hâte; *to make haste,* se hâter, se dépêcher.—*v.i.* or **hasten** [heisn], se hâter, se dépêcher, s'empresser.
hasten [heisn], *v.t.* hâter, dépêcher.
hastily ['heistili], *adv.* à la hâte; brusquement.
hastiness ['heistinis], *n.* hâte, précipitation, *f.*; emportement, *m.*
hasty ['heisti], *a.* rapide, précipité; inconsidéré, emporté.
hat [hæt], *n.* chapeau, *m.*; *bowler-hat,* chapeau melon; *felt hat,* feutre, *m.*; *soft felt hat,* chapeau mou; *straw hat,* chapeau de paille; *top hat,* chapeau haut de forme.
hatch (1) [hætʃ], *n.* (*pl.* **hatches** ['hætʃiz]) couvée (*de poulets*); éclosion (*d'œufs*); porte coupée (*dans le mur*); (*Naut.*) écoutille, *f.*; (*pl.*) panneaux des écoutilles, *m.pl.*—*v.t.* couver (*incuber*); faire éclore; (*fig.*) tramer, produire.—*v.i.* éclore.
hatch (2) [hætʃ], *v.t.* hacher (*un dessin*).
hatchet ['hætʃit], *n.* cognée, hachette, hache, *f.*
hate [heit], *n.* haine, *f.*—*v.t.* haïr, détester.
hateful ['heitful], *a.* odieux, détestable.
hatred ['heitrid], *n.* haine, *f.*
hat stand ['hætstænd], *n.* porte-chapeaux, *m. inv.*
hatter ['hætə], *n.* chapelier, *m.*
haughtily ['hɔːtili], *adv.* hautainement, avec arrogance.
haughtiness ['hɔːtinis], *n.* arrogance, *f.*
haughty ['hɔːti], *a.* hautain, arrogant.
haul [hɔːl], *n.* tirage, remorquage; coup de filet, *m.*—*v.t.* tirer, remorquer, haler; charrier, transporter.
haulage ['hɔːlidʒ], *n.* camionnage, roulage; remorquage, *m.*
hauler ['hɔːlə], *n.* camionneur, *m.*
haunch [hɔːntʃ], *n.* hanche (*d'un animal*), *f.*, cuissot (*de venaison*), *m.*
haunt [hɔːnt], *n.* retraite, *f.*; repaire (*de voleurs etc.*), *m.*—*v.t.* hanter, fréquenter; (*fig.*) obséder.
Havana [hə'vænə]. la Havane, *f.*
have [hæv], *v.t.* and *aux. irr.* avoir; tenir, posséder; contenir; prendre; faire; *I had rather,* j'aimerais mieux; *I have it,* j'y suis; *to have to,* devoir, falloir, avoir à.
haven [heivn], *n.* havre, port; (*fig.*) asile, *m.*
haversack ['hævəsæk], *n.* (*Mil.*) musette, *f.*; havresac, *m.*
havoc ['hævək], *n.* dégât, ravage, *m.*
hawk [hɔːk], *n.* faucon, *m.*—*v.t.* chasser au faucon; colporter (*vendre*).
hawker ['hɔːkə], *n.* colporteur, *m.*
hawser ['hɔːzə], *n.* haussière, *f.*, grelin, *m.*

hawthorn ['hɔːθɔːn], *n.* aubépine, *f.*
hay [hei], *n.* foin, *m.*
hay fever ['hei'fiːvə], *n.* rhume des foins, *m.*
hay-making ['heimeikiŋ], *n.* fenaison, *f.*
hayrick ['heirik], **haystack** ['heistæk], *n.* meule de foin, *f.*
hazard ['hæzəd], *n.* hasard, danger, risque, *m.*—*v.t.* hasarder, risquer.—*v.i.* se hasarder, s'aventurer.
hazardous ['hæzədəs], *a.* hasardeux, risqué, dangereux.
haze [heiz], *n.* petite brume; (*fig.*) obscurité, *f.*
hazel [heizl], *a.* noisette.—*n.* noisetier, coudrier, *m.*
hazel-nut ['heizlnʌt], *n.* noisette, *f.*
hazily ['heizili], *adv.* indistinctement.
hazy ['heizi], *a.* brumeux; *to have hazy notions,* avoir des idées vagues.
he [hiː], *pron.* il, celui, lui; *he and I,* lui et moi; *he that* or *he who,* celui qui.
he- [hiː], *pref.* mâle.
head [hed], *a.* premier, principal, en chef.—*n.* tête, *f.*; chef, avant, *m.*; proue (*de navire*), *f.*; haut bout (*d'une table*); chevet (*d'un lit*), *m.*; chute (*d'eau*), *f.*; pièces (*de gibier*), *f.pl.*; source (*d'une rivière*), *f.*; (*fig.*) sujet, chapitre, *m.*—*v.t.* conduire, diriger.—*v.i. to head for,* (*Naut.*) mettre le cap sur; se diriger vers, s'avancer vers.
headache ['hedeik], *n.* mal de tête, *m.*, migraine, *f.*
head-dress ['heddres], *n.* coiffure, *f.*
heading ['hediŋ], *n.* titre, en-tête, *m.*
headland ['hedlənd], *n.* cap, promontoire, *m.*
head-light ['hedlait], *n.* (*Motor.*) phare, *m.*
headline ['hedlain], *n.* (*Journ.*) titre, soustitre, *m.*
headlong ['hedlɔŋ], *adv.* la tête la première; (*fig.*) tête baissée.—*a.* précipité, irréfléchi.
headmaster ['hed'mɑːstə], *n.* principal, directeur, proviseur, *m.*
head-mistress ['hed'mistris], *n.* directrice, *f.*
head-phone ['hedfoun], *n.* (*Teleph.*) écouteur, *m.*
head-quarters ['hed'kwɔːtəz], *n.pl.* quartier général, *m.*
headstone ['hedstoun], *n.* pierre tombale, *f.*
headstrong ['hedstrɔŋ], *a.* opiniâtre, obstiné, entêté.
headway ['hedwei], *n.* progrès, *m.*; *to make headway,* avancer, progresser.
heady ['hedi], *a.* capiteux (*boisson*).
heal [hiːl], *v.t.* guérir; (*fig.*) apaiser.—*v.i.* guérir, se guérir; se cicatriser.
healing ['hiːliŋ], *a.* curatif; (*fig.*) salutaire.—*n.* guérison, *f.*
health [helθ], *n.* santé, *f.*; toast, *m.*; *National Health Service,* sécurité sociale, *f.*; *bill of health,* patente de santé, *f.*
healthily ['helθili], *adv.* en santé; sainement.
healthy ['helθi], *a.* bien portant, en bonne santé; sain, salubre.
heap [hiːp], *n.* tas, monceau, amas, *m.*—*v.t.* entasser, amonceler.
hear [hiə], *v.t. irr.* entendre; entendre dire; écouter (*faire attention à*); (*fig.*) apprendre; *to hear it said,* entendre dire.—*v.i.* entendre; entendre parler; écouter; recevoir des nouvelles, avoir des nouvelles (*de*); *hear! hear!* très bien! bravo!

hearing ['hiəriŋ], *n.* ouïe (*sens auditif*); audition (*de témoins*), *f.*; *hard of hearing*, dur d'oreille; *within hearing*, à portée de la voix.

hearken [haːkn], *v.i.* écouter.

hearsay ['hiəsei], *n.* ouï-dire, *m.*

hearse [haːs], *n.* corbillard, *m.*

heart [haːt], *n.* cœur; (*fig.*) courage; centre, *m.*

heart attack ['haːtətæk], *n.* crise cardiaque, *f.*

heart-breaking ['haːtbreikiŋ], *a.* qui fend le cœur, navrant.

heart-broken ['haːtbroukən], *a.* qui a le cœur brisé.

heartburn ['haːtbəːn], *n.* brûlures d'estomac, aigreurs, *f.pl.*

hearten [haːtn], *v.t.* encourager, animer.

heart failure ['haːtfeiljə], *n.* arrêt du cœur, *m.*

heartfelt ['haːtfelt], *a.* qui vient du cœur.

hearth [haːθ], *n.* âtre, foyer, *m.*

heartily ['haːtili], *adv.* cordialement, de bon cœur; de bon appétit (*manger*).

heartiness ['haːtinis], *n.* cordialité; vigueur (*de l'appétit*), *f.*

heartless ['haːtlis], *a.* sans cœur, sans pitié.

hearty ['haːti], *a.* sincère, cordial; abondant, bon (*repas*).

heat [hiːt], *n.* chaleur; (*fig.*) ardeur; colère (*courroux*); (*Racing*) épreuve, *f.*—*v.t.* chauffer, échauffer.—*v.i.* s'échauffer.

heated ['hiːtid], *a.* chaud; échauffé; animé.

heath [hiːθ], *n.* bruyère, lande; brande (*plante*), *f.*

heathen ['hiːðn], *a. and n.* païen, *m.*

heather ['heðə], *n.* bruyère, brande, *f.*

heating ['hiːtiŋ], *n.* chauffage, *m.*

heave [hiːv], *n.* effort (*pour soulever*), *m.*, secousse, *f.*; soulèvement, *m.*—*v.t. irr.* lever; élever; soulever; pousser (*un soupir*).—*v.i.* se soulever; palpiter, battre (*sein, cœur etc.*).

heaven [hevn], *n.* ciel, *m.*, cieux, *m.pl.*

heavenly ['hevnli], *a.* céleste, divin.

heavily ['hevili], *adv.* pesamment, lourdement; fortement.

heaviness ['hevinis], *n.* pesanteur, lourdeur; (*fig.*) tristesse, *f.*

heavy ['hevi], *a.* lourd, pesant; (*fig.*) gros; triste.

Hebrew ['hiːbruː], *a.* hébreu, *m.*; hébraïque, *f.*—*n.* hebreu (*langue*); Hébreu, Juif (*personne*), *m.*

heckle [hekl], *v.t.* embarrasser de questions, harasser (*en public*).

hectic ['hektik], *a.* hectique; agité, fiévreux.

hedge [hedʒ], *n.* haie, *f.*—*v.t.* entourer d'une haie.—*v.i.* (*fig.*) éviter de se compromettre.

hedgehog ['hedʒhɔg], *n.* hérisson, *f.*

hedge sparrow ['hedʒspærou], *n.* mouchet, *m.*, fauvette d'hiver, *f.*

heed [hiːd], *n.* attention, *f.*, soin, *m.*—*v.t.* faire attention à, prendre garde à, écouter.

heedless ['hiːdlis], *a.* étourdi, inattentif, insouciant.

heedlessly ['hiːdlisli], *adv.* négligemment; étourdiment.

heel [hiːl], *n.* talon, *m.*; *to be down at heel*, traîner la savate; *to cool one's heels*, faire antichambre.—*v.i. to heel over*, (*Naut.*) donner de la bande.

hefty ['hefti], *a.* (*fam.*) solide, costaud.

heifer ['hefə], *n.* génisse, *f.*

height [hait], *n.* hauteur, élévation; taille, *f.*; (*fig.*) comble, faîte, *m.*; *the height of summer*, le cœur ou le fort de l'été.

heighten [haitn], *v.t.* rehausser, relever.

heinous ['heinəs], *a.* atroce.

heir [ɛə], *n.* héritier, *m.*

heiress ['ɛəris], *n.* héritière, *f.*

heirloom ['ɛəluːm], *n.* meuble *ou* bijou (de famille), *m.*

Helen ['helin]. (*Myth.*) Hélène, *f.*

helicopter ['helikɔptə], *n.* hélicoptère, *m.*

helium ['hiːliəm], *n.* (*Chem.*) hélium, *m.*

hell [hel], *n.* enfer, *m.*

hellish ['heliʃ], *a.* infernal, d'enfer.

hello! [he'lou], **hullo!** [hʌ'lou], *int.* holà! allô! (*au téléphone*); tiens! (*surprise*).

helm (1) [helm], *n.* (*Naut.*) gouvernail, timon, *m.*, barre, *f.*

helm (2) [helm], *n.* (*poet.*) heaume (*casque*), *m.*

helmet ['helmit], *n.* casque, *m.*

helmsman ['helmzmən], *n.* (*pl.* **-men** [men]) timonier, *m.*

help [help], *n.* secours, *m.*; aide, assistance, *f.*; remède (*recours*), *m.*; *help!* au secours!—*v.t.* aider, secourir, assister; servir (*à table*); empêcher (*prevent*); éviter (*avoid*); *help yourself* (*at table*), servez-vous; *how can I help it?* que voulez-vous que j'y fasse? *how can it be helped?* qu'y faire? *I can't help it*, je n'y puis rien; *I cannot help saying*, je ne puis m'empêcher de dire.—*v.i.* aider, servir, contribuer.

helper ['helpə], *n.* aide, *m.*, *f.*

helpful ['helpful], *a.* utile; secourable.

helpless ['helplis], *a.* faible, impuissant; sans appui.

helplessly ['helplisli], *adv.* faiblement; sans ressource.

helter-skelter ['heltə'skeltə], *adv.* pêle-mêle; en pagaille.

helve [helv], *n.* manche, *m.*

hem [hem], *n.* ourlet, bord, *m.*—*v.t.* ourler, border; *to hem in*, entourer.

hemisphere ['hemisfiə], *n.* hémisphère, *m.*

hemlock ['hemlɔk], *n.* ciguë, *f.*

hemorrhage [HAEMORRHAGE].

hemp [hemp], *n.* (*Bot.*) chanvre, *m.*; (*fig.*) corde, *f.*

hen [hen], *n.* poule; femelle (*d'oiseau*), *f.*

hence [hens], *adv.* d'ici; de là, ainsi (*pour cela*) désormais (*temps*).

henceforth ['hensfɔːθ], **henceforward** [hens'fɔːwəd], *adv.* désormais, dorénavant, à l'avenir.

henchman ['hentʃmən], *n.* (*pl.* **-men** [men]) écuyer, valet; (*fig.*) partisan, *m.*

hen house ['henhaus], *n.* poulailler, *m.*

hen-pecked ['henpekt], *a.* gouverné par sa femme.

Henry ['henri]. Henri, *m.*

her [həː], *pers. pron.* elle, la, lui.—*poss. a.* son, sa, ses.—*dem. pron.* celle, *f.*

herald ['herəld], *n.* héraut; (*fig.*) avant-coureur, précurseur, *m.*—*v.t.* annoncer.

heraldry ['herəldri], *n.* science héraldique, *f.*, blason, *m.*

herb [həːb], *n.* herbe, *f.*; *pot-herbs*, herbes potagères, *f.pl.*; *sweet herbs*, fines herbes, *f.pl.*

herbaceous [həː'beiʃəs], *a.* herbacé.

herbage ['həːbidʒ], *n.* herbage, *m.*

herbalist ['həːbəlist], *n.* herboriste, *m.*, *f.*
Hercules ['həːkjuːliːz]. Hercule, *m.*
herd [həːd], *n.* troupeau, *m.*, troupe, *f.*—*v.t.*
  garder.—*v.i.* vivre en troupeau.
herdsman ['həːdzmən], *n.* (*pl.* -men [men])
  bouvier, *m.*
here [hiə], *adv.* ici; voici, que voici; **here!**
  présent! **here and there**, çà et là; **here
  they are**, les voici; **I am here**, me voici;
  this one here, celui-ci.
hereafter [hiər'aːftə], *adv.* désormais; dans
  la vie à venir.—*n.* l'au-delà, *m.*
hereby [hiə'bai], *adv.* par ce moyen, par là.
hereditary [hi'reditəri], *a.* héréditaire.
heredity [hi'rediti], *n.* hérédité, *f.*
heresy ['herisi], *n.* hérésie, *f.*
heretic ['heritik], *n.* hérétique, *m.*, *f.*
heretical [hi'retikəl], *a.* hérétique.
heretofore [hiətuː'fɔː], *adv.* jadis, jusqu'ici.
hereupon [hiərə'pɔn], *adv.* là-dessus.
herewith [hiə'wið], *adv.* ci-joint.
heritage ['heritidʒ], *n.* héritage, *m.*
hermetic [həː'metik], *a.* hermétique.
hermetically [həː'metikli], *adv.* hermétiquement.
hermit ['həːmit], *n.* ermite, *m.*
hero ['hiərou], *n.* (*pl.* **heroes** ['hiərouz])
  héros, *m.*
heroic [hi'rouik], **heroical** [-əl], *a.* héroïque.
heroine ['herouin], *n.* héroïne, *f.*
heroism ['herouizm], *n.* héroïsme, *m.*
heron ['herən], *n.* héron, *m.*
herring ['heriŋ], *n.* hareng, *m.*; **red herring**,
  hareng saur; (*fig.*) diversion, *f.*
hers [həːz], *pron.* le sien, *m.*, la sienne, *f.*, les
  siens, *m.pl.*, les siennes, *f.pl.*; **a friend of
  hers**, une de ses amies, *f.*
herself [həː'self], *pron.* elle-même, elle,
  (*reflexive*) se; **by herself**, toute seule.
hesitant ['hezitənt], *a.* hésitant.
hesitate ['heziteit], *v.i.* hésiter.
hesitation [hezi'teiʃən], *n.* hésitation, *f.*
heterodox ['hetərədɔks], *a.* hétérodoxe.
heterogeneous [hetərə'dʒiːniəs], *a.* hétérogène.
hew [hjuː], *v.t.* *irr.* tailler, couper.
hewer ['hjuə], *n.* tailleur (*de pierre*); piqueur
  (*de charbon*); fendeur (*de bois*), *m.*
hexagon ['heksəgən], *n.* hexagone, *m.*
heyday ['heidei], *n.* beaux jours, *m.pl.*
hiatus [hai'eitəs], *n.* hiatus, *m.*; (*fig.*) lacune, *f.*
hibernate ['haibəneit], *v.i.* hiverner, hiberner.
hiccough, hiccup ['hikʌp], *n.* hoquet, *m.*—
  v.i. avoir le hoquet.
hidden [hidn], *a.* caché, secret; (*fig.*) occulte.
hide (1) [haid], *n.* peau, *f.*, cuir, *m.*
hide (2) [haid], *v.t.* *irr.* cacher; enfouir (*en
  terre*); **hide-and-seek**, cache-cache, *m.*—
  v.i. se cacher, se tenir caché.
hideous ['hidiəs], *a.* hideux, affreux.
hiding (1) ['haidiŋ], *n.* (*colloq.*) rossée, raclée,
  f.; **to give someone a good hiding**,
  tanner le cuir à quelqu'un.
hiding (2) ['haidiŋ], *n.* **in hiding**, caché;
  hiding place, cachette, *f.*
hie [hai], *v.i.* se hâter, se rendre (à).
hierarchy ['haiərɑːki], *n.* hiérarchie, *f.*
high [hai], *a.* haut, élevé; (*fig.*) grand; sublime; fier, altier; faisandé (*gibier*); avancé
  (*viande*); **from on high**, d'en haut; **high
  road**, grand-route, *f.*; **high street**, grand-

rue, *f.*; **it is high time**, il est grand temps.
  —*adv.* haut, hautement; grandement; fort;
  to run high, s'échauffer (*sentiments*).
highbrow ['haibrau], *a.* and *n.* (*fam.*) intellectuel, *m.*
higher ['haiə], *comp. a.* plus haut, plus élevé;
  supérieur.
highest ['haiist], *superl. a.* le plus haut, le plus
  élevé; **at the highest**, au comble.
high-flown ['haifloun], *a.* enflé; ampoulé
  (*style*).
high-handed ['hai'hændid], *a.* arbitraire.
Highland ['hailənd], *a.* de la Haute Écosse.
highland ['hailənd], *a.* des montagnes.
Highlander ['hailəndə], *n.* montagnard de
  l'Écosse, *m.*
Highlands ['hailəndz], **the**. les hautes terres
  d'Écosse, *f.pl.*; la haute Écosse, *f.*
highlands ['hailəndz], *n.pl.* pays montagneux,
  m.
highlight ['hailait], *n.* point culminant, (*fam.*)
  clou, *m.*
highly ['haili], *adv.* hautement; fortement.
Highness ['hainis], *n.* Altesse (*titre*), *f.*
highness ['hainis], *n.* hauteur, *f.*
high-pitched ['haipitʃt], *a.* aigu (*son*).
high-sounding ['haisaundiŋ], *a.* pompeux;
  ronflant (*style*).
high-spirited ['haispiritid], *a.* fougueux,
  plein de cœur.
highway ['haiwei], *n.* grand chemin, *m.*,
  grand-route, *f.*
highwayman ['haiweimən], *n.* (*pl.* -men
  [men]) voleur de grand chemin, *m.*
hijack ['haidʒæk], *v.t.* (*Av.*) détourner.
hijacking ['haidʒækiŋ], *n.* (*Av.*) détournement.
hike [haik], *n.* excursion à pied, *f.*—*v.i.* aller à
  pied, vagabonder, faire des excursions à
  pied.
hiker ['haikə], *n.* touriste à pied, *m.*, *f.*
hilarious [hi'lɛəriəs], *a.* gai, joyeux.
hilarity [hi'læriti], *n.* hilarité, *f.*
hill [hil], *n.* colline, montagne, *f.*, coteau, *m.*
hillock ['hilək], *n.* monticule, *m.*, butte, *f.*
hilly ['hili], *a.* montagneux, accidenté.
hilt [hilt], *n.* poignée, garde, *f.*
him [him], *pers. pron.* le, lui.—*dem. pron.* celui.
himself [him'self], *pron.* lui-même, lui;
  (*reflexive*) se; **by himself**, tout seul.
hind (1) [haind], *n.* (*Zool.*) biche, *f.*
hind (2) [haind], *a.* de derrière, postérieur,
  arrière.
hinder ['hində], *v.t.* empêcher; gêner, embarrasser, retarder.
hindrance ['hindrəns], *n.* empêchement, *m.*
Hindu [hin'duː], *a.* hindou.—*n.* Hindou, *m.*
hinge [hindʒ], *n.* gond, *m.*; paumelle, charnière (*butt hinge*), *f.*; (*fig.*) pivot, *m.*
hint [hint], *n.* insinuation, allusion, *f.*; (*fig.*)
  soupçon, *m.*; conseils, *m.pl.*; **broad hint**,
  allusion évidente; **to take the hint**, comprendre à demi-mot.—*v.i.* donner à entendre (à), insinuer, suggérer.
hip [hip], *n.* hanche, *f.*
hippopotamus [hipə'pɔtəməs], *n.* (*pl.* **hippo-
  potami** [hipə'pɔtəmai], **hippopotamuses**
  [hipə'pɔtəməsiz]) hippopotame, *m.*
hire ['haiə], *n.* louage, prix de louage; salaire,
  m., gages, *m.pl.*; **for hire**, à louer, libre
  (*taxi*).—*v.t.* louer; engager, employer.
hireling ['haiəliŋ], *a.* and *n.* mercenaire, *m.*

hire-purchase ['haiə'pəːtʃəs], *n.* vente à tempérament, location-vente, *f.*

hirsute ['həːsjuːt], *a.* velu, hirsute.

his [hiz], *a.* son, sa, ses.—*pron.* le sien, *m.*, la sienne, *f.*, les siens, *m.pl.*, les siennes, *f.pl.*; *a friend of his*, un de ses amis; *it is his*, c'est à lui.

hiss [his], *v.t.*, *v.i.* siffler.—*n.* sifflement, sifflet, *m.*

hissing ['hisiŋ], *a.* sifflant.—*n.* sifflement, *m.*

historian [his'tɔːriən], *n.* historien, *m.*

historic [his'tɔrik], **historical** [his'tɔrikəl], *a.* historique.

history ['histəri], *n.* histoire, *f.*

hit [hit], *v.t. irr.* frapper, heurter; atteindre (*le but*); donner (*un coup*); toucher.—*v.i.* frapper, heurter (*contre*).—*n.* coup, *m.*; chance, trouvaille; (*fig.*) invention, *f.*; (*Theat.*) succès, *m.*

hitch [hitʃ], *v.t.* accrocher, attacher; (*Naut.*) nouer, amarrer.—*n.* accroc, *m.pl.*, entrave, *f.*; empêchement; (*Naut.*) nœud, *m.*

hitch-hike ['hitʃhaik], *v.i.* faire de l'auto-stop.

hither ['hiðə], *adv.* ici; *hither and thither*, çà et là.

hitherto [hiðə'tuː], *adv.* jusqu'ici.

hive [haiv], *n.* ruche, *f.*; (*fig.*) essaim (*swarm*), *m.*

hoard [hɔːd], *n.* monceau, amas (*secret*); trésor, *m.*—*v.t.* amasser, accumuler.—*v.i.* thésauriser.

hoarding ['hɔːdiŋ], *n.* accumulation, *f.*; panneau-réclame, *m.*

hoar-frost ['hɔːfrɔst], *n.* gelée blanche, *f.*, givre, *m.*

hoarse [hɔːs], *a.* enroué, rauque.

hoary ['hɔːri], *a.* blanc; aux cheveux gris *ou* blancs.

hoax [houks], *n.* mystification, *f.*; mauvais tour (*brimade*); canard (*fausse nouvelle*), *m.* —*v.t.* mystifier; attraper.

hob [hɔb], *n.* plaque (*de l'âtre*), *f.*

hobble [hɔbl], *v.t.* entraver.—*v.i.* clocher, clopiner; aller clopin clopant.—*n.* clochement, *m.*, difficulté, *f.*, embarras, *m.*, entrave, *f.*

hobby ['hɔbi], *n.* marotte (*manie*), distraction, *f.*, passe-temps, *m.*

hobby-horse ['hɔbihɔːs], *n.* cheval de bois, dada, *m.*

hobgoblin [hɔb'gɔblin], *n.* lutin, *m*

hobnob ['hɔb'nɔb], *v.i.* trinquer ensemble.

hobo ['houbou], *n.* (*Am.*) chemineau, *m.*

hock [hɔk], *n.* jarret (*d'un cheval*); vin du Rhin, *m.*

hockey ['hɔki], *n.* hockey, *m.*

hockey stick ['hɔkistik], *n.* crosse de hockey, *f.*

hoe [hou], *n.* houe, binette, *f.*; *Dutch hoe*, sarcleur, *m.*—*v.t.*, *v.i.* houer; biner, sarcler.

hog [hɔg], *n.* cochon; goret; (*Comm.*) porc, pourceau; (*fam.*) glouton, *m.*

hogshead ['hɔgzhed], *n.* muid, *m.*; barrique de 240 litres (*tonneau*), *f.*

hoist [hoist], *v.t.* hisser; guinder (*avec un treuil*); lever; arborer (*un drapeau*).—*n.* grue, *f.*, palan, *m.*

hold [hould], *n.* prise, *f.*; soutien (*appui*), *m.*; garde (*custody*), *f.*; place forte (*forteresse*), *f.*; (*Naut.*) cale, *f.*; *to take hold of*, prendre, saisir; *to let go one's hold*, lâcher prise.— *v.t. irr.* tenir, retenir; arrêter; garder, maintenir; occuper, avoir; contenir (*to contain*);

regarder comme; célébrer; *to hold back*, retenir, cacher; *to hold fast*, tenir ferme, tenir bon; *to hold off*, tenir à distance; *to hold over*, remettre, ajourner; *to hold up*, lever, soulever, soutenir; arrêter, retarder. —*v.i.* tenir; se maintenir, durer; supporter; adhérer (*à*); rester; s'arrêter; être vrai; *hold on*, arrêtez! (*Teleph.*) ne quittez pas! *hold tight!* ne lâchez pas! *to hold back*, se tenir en arrière, hésiter; *to hold fast*, tenir ferme; *to hold forth*, haranguer, pérorer; *to hold on*, s'accrocher à; persévérer, poursuivre.

hold-all ['houldɔːl], *n.* enveloppe de voyage, *f.*

holder ['houldə], *n.* personne qui tient, *f.*; (*Spt.*) tenant, locataire, *m.*; poignée, anse, *f.*, manche, *m.*, (*in compound words*) porte-; (*Fin.*) titulaire, *m.*

holding ['houldiŋ], *n.* possession, tenure; ferme, *f.*

hold-up ['houldʌp], *n.* arrêt de la circulation; panne, *f.*; hold-up, *m.*

hole [houl], *n.* trou; antre, *m.*, caverne, *f.*; orifice, *m.*, ouverture, *f.*

holiday ['hɔlidei], *a.* de fête, de congé; de vacances.—*n.* fête, *f.*, jour de fête, jour férié, (*Sch. etc.*) congé, *m.*, (*pl.*) vacances, *f.pl.*; *bank holiday*, fête légale; *on holiday*, en vacances, *f.*

holiness ['houlinis], *n.* sainteté, *f.*

Holland ['hɔlənd], la Hollande, *f.*

hollow ['hɔlou], *a.* creux; vide; sourd (*son*).— *n.* creux, *m.*, cavité, *f.*; bas-fond, *m.*—*v.t.* creuser, évider.

holly ['hɔli], *n.* houx, *m.*

hollyhock ['hɔlihɔk], *n.* rose trémière, *f.*

holster ['houlstə], *n.* fonte (*de selle*), *f.*; étui (*de revolver*), *m.*

holy ['houli], *a.* saint, sacré; bénit; *Holy Ghost*, le Saint-Esprit; *Holy Land*, la Terre Sainte; *holy water*, eau bénite, *f.*; *Holy Week*, la semaine sainte, *f.*

homage ['hɔmidʒ], *n.* hommage, *m.*

home [houm], *a.* de la maison, domestique; (*fig.*) qui porte (*coup*).—*n.* foyer domestique, chez-soi; logis, *m.*, maison, *f.*, intérieur, *m.*; (*fig.*) demeure, *f.*; pays, *m.*, patrie (*pays natal*), *f.*; *at home*, chez soi, à la maison; *Home Office*, Ministère de l'Intérieur, *m.*; *to make oneself at home*, faire comme chez soi.—*adv.* chez soi, au logis, à la maison; dans son pays; (*fig.*) directement; *to bring home to*, faire admettre à; *homing pigeon*, pigeon voyageur, *m.*

home-coming ['houmkʌmiŋ], *n.* retour au foyer, *m.*

homeland ['houmlænd], *n.* patrie, *f.*; pays natal, *m.*

homeliness ['houmlinis], *n.* caractère domestique, *m.*; simplicité; rusticité, *f.*

homely ['houmli], *a.* de ménage; simple, sans façon; (*Am.*) laid.

Homer ['houmə]. Homère, *m.*

home-sick ['houmsik], *a.* qui a le mal du pays, nostalgique.

home-sickness ['houmsiknis], *n.* mal du pays, *m.*, nostalgie, *f.*

homestead ['houmsted], *n.* manoir, *m.*, ferme, *f.*

homeward(s) ['houmwəd(z)], *adv.* vers la maison; vers son pays.

homework ['houmwə:k], *n.* devoirs, *m.pl.*
homicide ['hɔmisaid], *n.* homicide, *m.*
homogeneous [hɔmə'dʒi:niəs], *a.* homogène.
homosexual [houmo'seksjuəl], *a.* and *n.* homosexuel, *m.*
Honduran [hɔn'djuərən], *a.* hondurien.—*n.* Hondurien (*personne*), *m.*
Honduras [hɔn'djuərəs]. l'Honduras, *m.*
hone [houn], *n.* pierre à aiguiser. *f.*—*v.t.* aiguiser.
honest ['ɔnist], *a.* honnête, loyal, probe, de bonne foi, sincère; *honest man*, homme de bien, honnête homme, *m.*
honestly ['ɔnistli], *adv.* honnêtement, sincèrement.
honesty ['ɔnisti], *n.* honnêteté, probité, bonne foi, sincérité, *f.*
honey ['hʌni], *n.* miel, *m.*; (*fig.*) (*Am.*) chérie, *f.*, ange, *m.*
honeycomb ['hʌnikoum], *n.* rayon de miel, *m.*
honeymoon ['hʌnimu:n], *n.* lune de miel, *f.*
honeysuckle ['hʌnisʌkl], *n.* chèvrefeuille, *m.*
honorary ['ɔnərəri], *a.* honoraire.
honor ['ɔnə], *n.* honneur, *m.*; (*fig.*) dignité, estime, *f.*—*v.t.* honorer (*de*); faire honneur à, faire bon accueil à (*une facture*).
honorable ['ɔnərəbl], *a.* honorable, d'honneur.
hood [hud], *n.* capuchon, *m.*; coiffe; capote (*de voiture*), *f.*; (*Am. Motor.*) [BONNET].
hoodwink ['hudwiŋk], *v.t.* bander les yeux à; (*fig.*) tromper.
hoof [hu:f, huf], *n.* (*pl.* hooves [hu:vz]) sabot, *m.*
hook [huk], *n.* crochet, croc; hameçon (*pour pêcher*), *m.*; faucille (*sickle*), *f.*; *hook and eye*, agrafe et porte, *f.*—*v.t.* accrocher; agrafer; attraper.
hooked [hukt], *a.* crochu, recourbé; aquilin (*nez*).
hooligan ['hu:ligən], *n.* voyou, *m.*
hooliganism ['hu:ligənizm], *n.* voyouterie, *f.*
hoop [hu:p], *n.* cercle; cerceau, *m.*; huppe (*d'oiseau*); jante (*de roue*), *f.*; panier (*de robe*); (*Croquet*) arceau, *m.*—*v.t.* cercler; (*fig.*) entourer.
hoot [hu:t], *v.t.*, *v.i.* hululer (*hibou*); huer; (*Motor.*) klaxonner.
hooter ['hu:tə], *n.* (*colloq.*) sirène d'usine, *f.* klaxon, *m.*
hop (1) [hɔp], *n.* saut, sautillement; bal populaire, *m.*—*v.i.* sauter, sautiller; (*pop.*) *to hop it*, ficher le camp.
hop (2) [hɔp], *n.* (*Bot.*) houblon, *m.*
hop-field ['hɔpfi:ld], *n.* houblonnière, *f.*
hopscotch ['hɔpskɔtʃ], *n.* marelle, *f.*
hope [houp], *n.* espérance, *f.*, espoir, *m.*, attente, *f.*—*v.t.* espérer, s'attendre à.—*v.i.* espérer.
hopeful ['houpful], *a.* plein d'espérance; qui promet beaucoup; encourageant.
hopefully ['houpfuli], *adv.* avec espoir, avec confiance; si tout va bien.
hopeless ['houplis], *a.* vain (*effort*); non valable (*excuse*); inextricable (*difficulté*); inconsolable (*douleur*); irrémédiable (*mal*); inutile (*négociation*); incorrigible (*personne*); désespéré (*situation*).
hopelessly ['houplisli], *adv.* sans espoir.
hopper ['hɔpə], *n.* trémie (*d'un moulin*), *f.*; (*Agric.*) semoir, *m.*

horizon [hə'raizən], *n.* horizon, *m.*
horizontal [hɔri'zɔntl], *a.* horizontal.
hormone ['hɔ:moun], *n.* hormone, *f.*
horn [hɔ:n], *a.* de corne.—*n.* corne, *f.*; bois (*de cerf*), *m.*; coupe (*à boire*); (*Ent.*) antenne *f.*; (*Mus.*) cor, cornet, *m.*;(*Motor.*)klaxon,*m.*
hornet ['hɔ:nit], *n.* frelon, *m.*
horrible ['hɔribl], *a.* horrible, affreux.
horribly ['hɔribli], *adv.* horriblement, affreusement.
horrid ['hɔrid], *a.* affreux, horrible.
horrific [hɔ'rifik], *a.* horrifique.
horrify ['hɔrifai], *v.t.* horrifier.
horror ['hɔrə], *n.* horreur, *f.*
horse [hɔ:s], *n.* cheval, *m.*, chevaux, *m.pl.*; (*Mil.*) cavalerie, *f.*; chevalet (*pour scier*), séchoir (*pour le linge*), *m.*
horseback ['hɔ:sbæk], *n.* dos de cheval, *m.*; *on horseback*, à cheval.
horseblock ['hɔ:sblɔk], *n.* montoir, *m.*
horse chestnut ['hɔ:s'tʃesnʌt], *n.* marron d'Inde; marronnier d'Inde (*arbre*), *m.*
horse dealer ['hɔ:sdi:lə], *n.* maquignon, *m.*
horse doctor ['hɔ:sdɔktə], *n.* vétérinaire, *m.*
horse-fly ['hɔ:sflai], *n.* taon, *m.*
horseman ['hɔ:smən], *n.* (*pl.* -men [men]) cavalier; écuyer, *m.*
horsemanship ['hɔ:smənʃip], *n.* équitation, *f.*; manège, *m.*
horse-play ['hɔ:splei], *n.* jeu de mains, *m.*
horse-power ['hɔ:spauə], *n.* cheval-vapeur, *m.*
horseshoe ['hɔ:sʃu:], *a.* en fer à cheval.—*n.* fer de cheval; fer à cheval, *m.*
horsewhip ['hɔ:swip], *n.* cravache, *f.*—*v.t.* cravacher.
horticulture ['hɔ:tikʌltʃə], *n.* horticulture, *f.*
hose [houz], *n.* bas, *m.pl.*; tuyau d'arrosage, boyau, *m.*
hosiery ['houʒəri], *n.* bonneterie, *f.*
hospitable ['hɔspitəbl], *a.* hospitalier.
hospital ['hɔspitl], *n.* hôpital, *m.*, infirmerie, *f.*; hospice, *m.*
hospitality [hɔspi'tæliti], *n.* hospitalité, *f.*
host [houst], *n.* hôte; hôtelier, aubergiste, *m.*; armée, foule; (*R.-C. Ch.*) hostie, *f.*
hostage ['hɔstidʒ], *n.* otage, *m.*
hostel ['hɔstəl], *n.* hôtel ou foyer pour les étudiants etc., *m.*; *youth hostel*, auberge de la jeunesse, *f.*
hostess ['houstis, 'houstes], *n.* hôtesse, *f.*
hostile ['hɔstail], *a.* hostile, ennemi; (*fig.*) opposé (*à*).
hostility [hɔs'tiliti], *n.* hostilité, *f.*
hot [hɔt], *a.* chaud, ardent; brûlant, piquant, épicé (*plat, sauce*); (*fig.*) vif, violent, échauffé; *boiling hot*, tout bouillant; *to be hot*, avoir chaud (*personne*), faire chaud (*temps*), être chaud (*chose*).
hotbed ['hɔtbed], *n.* couche, *f.*
hotel [ho'tel], *n.* hôtel, *m.*
hot-headed ['hɔt'hedid], *a.* violent, fougueux.
hot-house ['hɔthaus], *n.* serre, *f.*
hotly ['hɔtli], *adv.* avec chaleur, avec acharnement.
hotness ['hɔtnis], *n.* chaleur, *f.*; (*fig.*) passion, violence, *f.*
hot-water bottle [hɔt'wɔ:təbɔtl], *n.* bouillotte, *f.*
hough [hɔk], *n.* jarret (*d'animal*), *m.*
hound [haund], *n.* chien de chasse, *m.*—*v.t.* chasser; (*fig.*) traquer; exciter.

hour ['auə], n. heure, f.; an hour ago, il y a une heure; an hour and a half, une heure et demie; a quarter of an hour, un quart d'heure; half an hour, une demi-heure.

hourly ['auəli], a. continuel, d'heure en heure, à l'heure.—adv. d'heure en heure.

house [haus], n. maison, f., logis, m., demeure, habitation, f.; ménage (household), m.; famille; (Parl.) chambre; (Theat.) salle, f.; a country house, une maison de campagne; a nobleman's house, un hôtel; house full, (Theat.) salle comble; public house, café, m., brasserie, f.—[hauz], v.t. loger, héberger; garer (une voiture); rentrer (blé etc.); faire rentrer (bestiaux etc.).

house agent ['hauseidʒənt], n. agent de location, agent immobilier, m.

house-breaker ['hausbreikə], n. cambrioleur (voleur); démolisseur (ouvrier), m.

house-breaking ['hausbreikiŋ], n. vol avec effraction, m.

household ['haushould], a. de ménage, domestique.—n. maison, f., ménage, m., famille, f.

householder ['haushouldə], n. chef de famille, chef de maison, m.

housekeeper ['hauski:pə], n. femme de charge, ménagère, f.; concierge, m., f.

housekeeping ['hauski:piŋ], n. ménage, m.

housemaid ['hausmeid], n. bonne à tout faire, f.

house surgeon ['haussə:dʒən], n. interne (en chirurgie), m.

housewife ['hauswaif], n. ménagère, f.

housework ['hauswə:k], n. travaux ménagers, m.pl.; to do the housework, faire le ménage.

housing ['hauziŋ], n. logement, m.; rentrée, f., rentrage, m.; (Tech.) enchâssure, f.

hovel ['hɔvl], n. appentis, m., bicoque, f., taudis, m., masure, f.

hover ['hɔvə], v.i. planer; hésiter.

how [hau], adv. comment, de quelle façon; combien; comme, que; how are you? comment allez-vous? how far, jusqu'où; how many, how much, combien de; how old are you? quel âge avez-vous?

however [hau'evə], conj. cependant, pourtant, du reste, d'ailleurs, toutefois.—adv. de quelque manière que; quelque . . . que; however rich he may be, quelque riche qu'il soit, tout riche qu'il est; however that may be, quoi qu'il en soit.

howl [haul], n. hurlement, cri; mugissement, m.—v.i. hurler, crier; mugir.

howler ['haulə], n. faute grossière, bévue, f.

howling ['hauliŋ], a. hurlant; a howling success, un succès fou.—n. hurlement, m.

hoyden [hoidn], n. garçon manqué (se dit d'une jeune fille), m.

hub [hʌb], n. moyeu; (fig.) centre, m.

hubbub ['hʌbʌb], n. vacarme, brouhaha, tintamarre, m.

hub cap ['hʌbkæp], n. (Motor.) enjoliveur, m.

huddle [hʌdl], v.t. entasser pêle-mêle, (fig.) brouiller, confondre ensemble.—v.i. se mêler, se presser les uns contre les autres; (fig.) se confondre.—n. tas confus, fouillis, méli-mélo, ramassis, m.

hue [hju:], n. couleur, teinte, nuance; huée,

clameur, f.; to raise a hue and cry after, crier haro sur, élever un tollé contre.

huff [hʌf], n. emportement, accès de colère, m. —v.t. froisser; (checkers) souffler.—v.i. se gonfler, se mettre en colère.

hug [hʌg], v.t. embrasser, étreindre; étouffer (en serrant).—n. embrassement, m., étreinte, f.

huge [hju:dʒ], a. vaste, immense, énorme.

hulk [hʌlk], n. carcasse (d'un navire), f., ponton; (pl.) bagne, m.

hulking ['hʌlkiŋ], a. gros, lourd.

hull [hʌl], n. coque (d'un navire); cosse, gousse (de pois, fèves etc.); écale (de noix), f.—v.t. écaler (noix); écosser (fèves).

hullo [HELLO].

hum [hʌm], v.t., v.i. fredonner (personne); bourdonner (abeilles); to hum and ha(w), bredouiller.—n. bourdonnement; brouhaha (de conversation), m.

human ['hju:mən], a. humain.

humane [hju:'mein], a. humain, compatissant.

humanist ['hju:mənist], n. humaniste, m., f.

humanity [hju:'mæniti], n. humanité, f.

humanly ['hju:mənli], adv. humainement.

humble [hʌmbl], a. humble; modeste.—v.t. humilier, abaisser, mortifier.

humble-bee ['hʌmblbi:], n. bourdon, m.

humbly ['hʌmbli], adv. humblement, avec humilité; modestement.

humbug ['hʌmbʌg], n. blague, farce, f., charlatanisme; blagueur, farceur, charlatan, m.

humdrum ['hʌmdrʌm], a. monotone, assommant.

humid ['hju:mid], a. humide.

humidity [hju:'miditi], n. humidité, f.

humiliate [hju:'milieit], v.t. humilier, abaisser.

humiliating [hju:'milieitiŋ], a. humiliant.

humiliation [hju:mili'eiʃən], n. humiliation, f.

humility [hju:'militi], n. humilité, f.

humming ['hʌmiŋ], n. bourdonnement, fredonnement; (fig.) murmure, m.

humming-bird ['hʌmiŋbə:d], n. oiseau-mouche, colibri, m.

humor ['hju:mə], n. humeur, disposition, f.; humour, m.—v.t. complaire à, laisser faire.

humorist ['hju:mərist], n. humoriste, m., f., personne spirituelle, f.

humorous ['hju:mərəs], a. humoristique; plaisant, drôle, comique.

hump [hʌmp], n. bosse, f.; to have the hump, (slang) être maussade.

humpbacked ['hʌmpbækt], a. bossu.

hunch [hʌntʃ], n. gros morceau (de pain, de fromage), m.; bosse (du dos); (fig., fam.) idée, f., soupçon, m.; to have a hunch that, soupçonner que.

hunchback ['hʌntʃbæk], n. bossu, m.

hundred ['hʌndrəd], a. cent.—n. cent, m., centaine, f.; canton, district, m.

hundredth ['hʌndrətθ], a. centième.—n. centième (fraction), m.

hundredweight ['hʌndrədweit], n. quintal, m.

Hungarian [hʌŋ'gɛəriən], a. hongrois.—n. hongrois (langue); Hongrois (personne), m.

Hungary ['hʌŋgəri]. la Hongrie, f.

hunger ['hʌŋgə], n. faim, f.—v.i. avoir faim; être affamé (de).

hungrily ['hʌŋgrili], adv. avidement.

hungry ['hʌŋgri], *a.* affamé, qui a faim; maigre (*terre etc.*); *to be hungry*, avoir faim.
hunk [hʌŋk], *n.* gros morceau (*de gâteau, de fromage*), *m.*
hunt [hʌnt], *v.t.* chasser à courre; (*fig.*) poursuivre, chercher.—*v.i.* chasser, aller à la chasse.—*n.* chasse à courre, *f.*
hunter ['hʌntə], *n.* chasseur; cheval de chasse, *m.*
hunting ['hʌntiŋ], *n.* chasse; (*fig.*) recherche, *f.*
huntress ['hʌntris], *n.* chasseuse; (*poet.*) chasseresse, *f.*
huntsman ['hʌntsmən], *n.* (*pl.* -men [men]) veneur, piqueur, *m.*
hurdle [hə:dl], *n.* claie, *f.*; (*Spt.*) obstacle, *m.*, haie, *f.*; *hurdle race*, course de haies, *f.*
hurdy-gurdy ['hə:di'gə:di], *n.* vielle, *f.*
hurl [hə:l], *v.t.* lancer (avec force), précipiter, jeter.
hurly-burly ['hə:li'bə:li], *n.* tintamarre, brouhaha, tohu-bohu, *m.*
hurrah [hu'ra:], **hurray** [hu'rei], *n.* hourra, *m.*
hurricane ['hʌrikən], *n.* ouragan, *m.*
hurried ['hʌrid], *a.* précipité, pressé; fait à la hâte.
hurriedly ['hʌridli], *adv.* précipitamment, à la hâte.
hurry ['hʌri], *n.* hâte, précipitation, *f.*; (*fig.*) tumulte, *m.*, confusion, *f.*; *to be in a hurry*, être pressé.—*v.t.* hâter, presser, précipiter.—*v.i.* se hâter, se dépêcher, se presser.
hurt [hə:t], *n.* mal, *m.*, blessure, *f.*; (*fig.*) tort, *m.*—*v.t. irr.* faire mal à, (*fig.*) nuire à, offenser, blesser; *to hurt oneself*, se faire du mal.—*v.i.* faire du mal; faire mal.
hurtful ['hə:tful], *a.* nuisible (à).
hurtle [hə:tl], *v.t.* lancer.—*v.i.* se précipiter; se heurter.
husband ['hʌzbənd], *n.* mari, époux, *m.*—*v.t.* ménager, économiser.
husbandman ['hʌzbəndmən], *n.* (*pl.* -men [men]) laboureur, cultivateur, *m.*
husbandry ['hʌzbəndri], *n.* agriculture, industrie agricole; économie, *f.*
hush [hʌʃ], *n.* silence, calme, *m.*—*int.* chut! paix!—*v.t.* taire, faire taire; (*fig.*) calmer.—*v.i.* se taire, faire silence.
husk [hʌsk], *n.* cosse, gousse (*de pois etc.*), *f.*; brou, *m.*, écale (*de noix*); balle, pellicule (*de grain*), *f.*
huskiness ['hʌskinis], *n.* enrouement (*de la voix*), *m.*
husky ['hʌski], *a.* cossu; rauque, enroué (*voix*); (*colloq.*) costaud, fort.—*n.* chien esquimau, *m.*
hussar [hu'za:], *n.* hussard, *m.*
hussy ['hʌsi], *n.* friponne, coquine, *f.*
hustle [hʌsl], *v.t.* bousculer, presser, pousser.—*v.i.* se presser, se dépêcher.
hut [hʌt], *n.* hutte, cabane; (*Mil.*) baraque, *f.*
hutch [hʌtʃ], *n.* huche, *f.*; clapier (*de lapin*), *m.*
hyacinth ['haiəsinθ], *n.* (*Bot.*) jacinthe, *f.*
hybrid ['haibrid], *a.* and *n.* hybride, *m.*
hydrangea [hai'drændʒə, hai'dreindʒə], *n.* (*Bot.*) hortensia, *m.*
hydrant ['haidrənt], *n.* prise d'eau, *f.*; *fire hydrant*, bouche d'incendie, *f.*
hydraulic [hai'drɔ:lik], *a.* hydraulique.

hydrochloric [haidrə'klɔrik], *a.* (*acide*) chlorhydrique.
hydrogen ['haidridʒən], *n.* hydrogène, *m.*; *hydrogen bomb* or (*fam.*) *H-bomb*, bombe à hydrogène, bombe H, *f.*
hydrophobia [haidro'foubiə], *n.* hydrophobie, rage, *f.*
hyena [hai'i:nə], *n.* hyène, *f.*
hygiene ['haidʒi:n], *n.* hygiène, *f.*
hygienic [hai'dʒi:nik], *a.* hygiénique.
hymn [him], *n.* (*Eccles.*) hymne, *m.* ou *f.*, cantique, *m.*
hymn book ['himbuk], **hymnal** [himnl], *n.* hymnaire, *m.*
hyperbola [hai'pə:bələ], *n.* (*Geom.*) hyperbole, *f.*
hyperbole [hai'pə:bəli], *n.* (*Gram.*) hyperbole, *f.*
hyphen ['haifən], *n.* trait d'union, *m.*
hypnosis [hip'nousis], *n.* hypnose, *f.*
hypnotism ['hipnətizm], *n.* hypnotisme, *m.*
hypnotist ['hipnətist], *n.* hypnotiste, *m.*, *f.*
hypocrisy [hi'pɔkrisi], *n.* hypocrisie, *f.*
hypocrite ['hipəkrit], *n.* hypocrite, *m.*, *f.*
hypocritical [hipə'kritikl], *a.* hypocrite.
hypothesis [hai'pɔθisis], *n.* (*pl.* **hypotheses** [hai'pɔθisi:z]) hypothèse, *f.*
hysteria [his'tiəriə], *n.*, **hysterics** [his'teriks], *n.pl.* crise de nerfs, attaque de nerfs, *f.*
hysterical [his'terikəl], *a.* hystérique.

I

I (1), i [ai]. neuvième lettre de l'alphabet, *m.*
I (2) [ai], *pron.* je; moi.
ibex ['aibeks], *n.* bouquetin, *m.*
ibis ['aibis], *n.* (*Orn.*) ibis, *m.*
ice [ais], *n.* glace, *f.*—*v.t.* glacer (*gâteau*); frapper (*vin*).—*v.i.* (*Av.*) *to ice up*, givrer.
ice axe ['aisæks], *n.* piolet, *m.*
iceberg ['aisbə:g], *n.* iceberg, *m.*
ice-bound ['aisbaund], *a.* pris dans *ou* bloqué par les glaces.
ice-box ['aisbɔks], *n.* glacière, *f.*
ice-breaker ['aisbreikə], *n.* brise-glace, *m.*
ice cream ['ais'kri:m], *n.* glace, *f.*
iced [aist], *a.* glacé; frappé (*vin etc.*); *iced lollypop*, sucette, *f.*
ice-floe ['aisflou], *n.* banc de glace, *m.*
Iceland ['aislənd], l'Islande, *f.*
Icelander ['aisləndə], *n.* Islandais, *m.*
Icelandic [ais'lændik], *a.* islandais, d'Islande.
ice pack, see **pack-ice**.
icicle ['aisikl], *n.* petit glaçon, *m.*
icing ['aisiŋ], *n.* glacé; frappage (*de vin*), *m.*
icon ['aikɔn], *n.* icone, *f.*
icy ['aisi], *a.* glacé, glacial; *icy road*, route verglacée, *f.*
idea [ai'diə], *n.* idée, *f.*
ideal [ai'diəl], *a.* and *n.* idéal, *m.*
idealism [ai'diəlizm], *n.* idéalisme, *m.*
idealist [ai'diəlist], *n.* idéaliste, *m.*, *f.*
ideally [ai'diəli], *adv.* idéalement.
identical [ai'dentikl], *a.* identique.
identification [aidentifi'keiʃən], *n.* identification, *f.*

identify

identify [ai'dentifai], v.t. identifier (avec); reconnaître.

identity [ai'dentiti], n. identité, f.

idiocy ['idiəsi], n. idiotie, f.

idiom ['idiəm], n. idiome; idiotisme, m.

idiomatic [idiə'mætik], a. idiomatique.

idiot ['idiət], n. idiot, m.; imbécile, m., f.

idiotic [idi'ɔtik], a. idiot, d'imbécile.

idle [aidl], a. oisif, paresseux (*indolent*); désœuvré (*inactif*); en chômage (*personne sans travail*), en repos (*machine*); (*fig.*) inutile, frivole; *idle fellow*, fainéant, paresseux, m.; *idle talk*, balivernes, f.pl.— v.t. to idle away, perdre, gaspiller.— v.i. ne rien faire, faire le paresseux, fainéanter; (*Motor.*) tourner au ralenti.

idleness [aidlnis], n. paresse; oisiveté; (*fig.*) inutilité, f.; désœuvrement, m.

idler ['aidlə], n. oisif, fainéant, paresseux, m.

idly ['aidli], adv. dans l'oisiveté, en paresseux; inutilement.

idol [aidl], n. idole, f.

idolater [ai'dɔlətə], **idolatress** [ai'dɔlətris], n. idolâtre, m., f.

idolatry [ai'dɔlətri], n. idolâtrie, f.

idolize ['aidəlaiz], v.t. idolâtrer.

idyllic [ai'dilik, i'dilik], a. idyllique.

if [if], conj. si, quand, quand même; *even if*, même si, quand même; *if necessary*, s'il le faut, au besoin; *if not*, sinon, si ce n'est.

igloo ['iglu:], n. hutte de neige, f.; igloo (*des Esquimaux*), m.

ignite [ig'nait], v.t. allumer.—v.i. prendre feu.

ignition [ig'niʃən], n. ignition, f.; (*Motor.*) allumage, m.; *ignition key*, clé de contact, f.

ignoble [ig'noubl], a. roturier; ignoble.

ignominious [ignə'miniəs], a. ignominieux.

ignominy ['ignəmini], n. ignominie, f.

ignoramus [ignə'reiməs], n. ignorant, (*fam.*) âne bâté, m.

ignorance ['ignərəns], n. ignorance, f.

ignorant ['ignərənt], a. ignorant.

ignore [ig'nɔ:], v.t. feindre d'ignorer; ne tenir aucun compte de.

ill [il], a.; malade (*santé*); mauvais, méchant.— n. mal, m.—adv. mal; peu; *it ill becomes you*, il vous sied mal.

ill-bred ['il'bred], a. mal élevé.

illegal [i'li:gəl], a. illégal; illicite.

illegible [i'ledʒibl], a. illisible.

illegitimate [ilə'dʒitimit], a. illégitime; naturel (*enfant*).

ill-fated ['il'feitid], a. infortuné, malheureux.

ill-feeling ['il'fi:liŋ], n. ressentiment, m.

ill-gotten ['il'gɔtn], a. mal acquis.

ill-health ['il'helθ], n. mauvaise santé, f.

illicit [i'lisit], a. illicite.

ill-informed ['ilin'fɔ:md], a. mal renseigné.

illiteracy [i'litərəsi], n. analphabétisme, m.

illiterate [i'litərit], a. and n. illettré, m.

ill-mannered ['il'mænəd], a. malappris.

ill-natured ['il'neitʃəd], a. méchant, d'un mauvais naturel.

illness ['ilnis], n. maladie, indisposition, f.

illogical [i'lɔdʒikl], a. illogique, peu logique.

ill-tempered ['il'tempəd], a. maussade, de mauvaise humeur.

ill-treat ['il'tri:t], v.t. maltraiter.

illuminate [i'lju:mineit], v.t. illuminer, éclairer; enluminer (*un livre*).

illumination [ilju:mi'neiʃən], n. illumination; enluminure (*de livres etc.*), f.

illusion [i'lu:ʒən, i'lju:ʒən], n. illusion, f.

illustrate ['iləstreit], v.t. illustrer; (*fig.*) expliquer; orner, embellir.

illustration [iləs'treiʃən], n. illustration; explication, f.; éclaircissement, m.

illustrative [i'lʌstrətiv], a. explicatif.

illustrious [i'lʌstriəs], a. illustre, célèbre.

ill-will ['il'wil], n. mauvais vouloir, m.; rancune, f.

I'm [aim] (=**I am**) [BE].

image ['imidʒ], n. image, f.; (*fig.*) portrait, m.

imagery ['imidʒri], n. images, f.pl.; langage figuré, m.

imaginable [i'mædʒinəbl], a. imaginable.

imaginary [i'mædʒinri], a. imaginaire.

imagination [imædʒi'neiʃən], n. imagination; conception, idée, f.

imagine [i'mædʒin], v.t. imaginer; s'imaginer, se figurer.

imbecile ['imbisi:l], a. and n. faible d'esprit, m., f.

imbecility [imbi'siliti], n. faiblesse d'esprit, f.

imbibe [im'baib], v.t. imbiber, absorber; (*fig.*) puiser.

imbue [im'bju:], v.t. imprégner, teindre; (*fig.*) pénétrer, douer (*de*).

imbued [im'bju:d], a. imbu, pénétré (*de*).

imitate ['imiteit], v.t. imiter.

imitation [imi'teiʃən], n. imitation; (*Comm.*) contrefaçon, f.

imitative ['imitətiv], a. imitatif, imitateur.

immaculate [i'mækjulit], a. sans tache, immaculé.

immaterial [imə'tiəriəl], a. immatériel; peu important.

immature [imə'tjuə], a. pas mûr; prématuré.

immeasurable [i'meʒərəbl], a. infini; incommensurable.

immeasurably [i'meʒərəbli], adv. outre mesure, infiniment.

immediate [i'mi:djit], a. immédiat; urgent; très pressé (*sur enveloppe*).

immediately [i'mi:djitli], adv. immédiatement, tout de suite, sur-le-champ.—conj. aussitôt que, dès que.

immense [i'mens], a. immense.

immensely [i'mensli], adv. immensément.

immensity [i'mensiti], n. immensité, f.

immerse [i'mə:s], v.t. plonger, immerger.

immigrant ['imigrant], a. and n. immigrant, m.

immigrate ['imigreit], v.i. immigrer.

immigration [imi'greiʃən], n. immigration, f.

imminent ['iminənt], a. imminent.

immobilize [i'moubilaiz], v.t. immobiliser.

immodest [i'mɔdist], a. immodeste, peu modeste, impudique.

immoral [i'mɔrl], a. immoral; dissolu.

immorality [imɔ'ræliti], n. immoralité, f.

immortal [i'mɔ:tl], a. immortel.

immortality [imɔ:'tæliti], n. immortalité, f.

immortalize [i'mɔ:təlaiz], v.t. immortaliser, rendre immortel.

immovable [i'mu:vəbl], a. fixe, immuable, inébranlable.

immutable [i'mju:təbl], a. immuable.

imp [imp], n. diablotin, petit démon; petit diable (*gamin*), m.

impact ['impækt], n. choc, impact, m.— [im'pækt], v.t. serrer, encastrer.

impair [im'pɛə], v.t. altérer, affaiblir.

452

impale [im'peil], *v.t.* empaler.
impalpable [im'pælpəbl], *a.* impalpable; intangible.
impart [im'pa:t], *v.t.* accorder, donner; communiquer.
impartial [im'pa:ʃl], *a.* impartial, désintéressé.
impartially [im'pa:ʃəli], *adv.* impartialement.
impassable [im'pa:səbl], *a.* impraticable, infranchissable.
impassioned [im'pæʃənd], *a.* passionné.
impassive [im'pæsiv], *a.* impassible, insensible.
impatience [im'peiʃəns], *n.* impatience, *f.*
impatient [im'peiʃənt], *a.* impatient; (*fig.*) emporté.
impatiently [im'peiʃəntli], *adv.* impatiemment.
impeach [im'pi:tʃ], *v.t.* accuser; attaquer.
impeachment [im'pi:tʃmənt], *n.* mise en accusation; accusation, *f.*
impeccable [im'pekəbl], *a.* impeccable.
impecunious [impi'kju:niəs], *a.* besogneux.
impede [im'pi:d], *v.t.* empêcher; retarder, gêner.
impediment [im'pedimənt], *n.* empêchement, obstacle, *m.*; (*fig.*) difficulté, *f.*
impel [im'pel], *v.t.* pousser (à); forcer (de).
impelling [im'peliŋ], *a.* impulsif, moteur.
impend [im'pend], *v.i.* être suspendu sur, menacer; être imminent.
impending [im'pendiŋ], *a.* imminent, menaçant.
impenetrable [im'penitrəbl], *a.* impénétrable; (*fig.*) insensible.
impenitent [im'penitənt], *a.* impénitent.
imperative [im'perətiv], *a.* impératif, (*fig.*) obligatoire.—*n.* (*Gram.*) impératif, *m.*
imperceptible [impə'septibl], *a.* imperceptible, insensible.
imperceptibly [impə'septibli], *adv.* imperceptiblement.
imperfect [im'pə:fikt], *a.* imparfait; incomplet; (*Gram.*) imparfait.—*n.* (*Gram.*) imparfait, *m.*
imperfection [impə'fekʃən], *n.* imperfection, *f.*
imperfectly [im'pə:fiktli], *adv.* imparfaitement.
imperial [im'piəriəl], *a.* impérial; (*fig.*) princier.
imperil [im'peril], *v.t.* mettre en danger, hasarder.
imperious [im'piəriəs], *a.* impérieux.
imperishable [im'periʃəbl], *a.* impérissable.
impersonal [im'pə:sənəl], *a.* impersonnel.
impersonate [im'pə:səneit], *v.t.* personnifier; (*Theat.*) représenter, jouer le rôle de.
impertinence [im'pə:tinəns], *n.* impertinence, insolence, *f.*
impertinent [im'pə:tinənt], *a.* impertinent, insolent; hors de propos.
impertinently [im'pə:tinəntli], *adv.* d'un ton insolent; mal à propos.
imperturbable [impə'tə:bəbl], *a.* imperturbable.
impervious [im'pə:viəs], *a.* imperméable, impénétrable; (*fig.*) inaccessible.
impetuous [im'petjuəs], *a.* impétueux.
impetus ['impitəs], *n.* impulsion, *f.*; élan, essor, *m.*

impinge [im'pindʒ], *v.i.* se heurter (à ou *contre*); empiéter (*sur*).
impious ['impiəs], *a.* impie.
impiously ['impiəsli], *adv.* en impie, avec impiété.
impish ['impiʃ], *a.* espiègle, malicieux.
implacable [im'plækəbl], *a.* implacable, acharné.
implant [im'pla:nt], *v.t.* implanter; (*fig.*) imprimer, inculquer.
implement ['implimənt], *n.* outil; instrument; ustensile, *m.*—['impliment], *v.t.* exécuter; accomplir.
implicate ['implikeit], *v.t.* impliquer.
implication [impli'keiʃən], *n.* implication, *f.*; *by implication*, implicitement.
implicit [im'plisit], *a.* implicite; (*fig.*) aveugle.
implied [im'plaid], *a.* implicite, tacite.
implore [im'plɔ:], *v.t.* implorer, conjurer, supplier (*de*).
imply [im'plai], *v.t.* impliquer, signifier, vouloir dire; donner à entendre (*suggérer*).
impolite [impə'lait], *a.* impoli.
impoliteness [impə'laitnis], *n.* impolitesse, *f.*
import ['impɔ:t], *n.* portée, signification, *f.*, sens, *m.*; importance, *f.*; (*Comm.*) importation, *f.*—[im'pɔ:t], *v.t.* importer; introduire; signifier.
importance [im'pɔ:təns], *n.* importance, *f.*
important [im'pɔ:tənt], *a.* important.
importer [im'pɔ:tə], *n.* importateur, *m.*
importunate [im'pɔ:tjunit], *a.* importun; pressant.
importune [impɔ:'tju:n], *v.t.* importuner.
impose [im'pouz], *v.t.* imposer.—*v.i.* en imposer (à).
imposing [im'pouziŋ], *a.* imposant.
imposition [impə'ziʃən], *n.* impôt (*taxe*), *m.*; imposture (*tromperie*), *f.*; (*Sch.*) pensum, *m.*
impossibility [imposi'biliti], *n.* impossibilité, *f.*
impossible [im'pɔsibl], *a.* impossible.
impostor [im'pɔstə], *n.* imposteur, *m.*
imposture [im'pɔstʃə], *n.* imposture, tromperie, *f.*
impotence ['impətəns], **impotency** ['impətənsi], *n.* impuissance, *f.*
impotent ['impətənt], *a.* impuissant, faible.
impound [im'paund], *v.t.* mettre en fourrière; (*fig.*) enfermer, confisquer.
impoverish [im'pɔvəriʃ], *v.t.* appauvrir.
impracticable [im'præktikəbl], *a.* impossible, impraticable; intraitable (*personne*).
imprecation [imprə'keiʃən], *n.* imprécation, *f.*
impregnable [im'pregnəbl], *a.* imprenable; (*fig.*) inébranlable.
impregnate [im'pregneit], *v.t.* imprégner (*de*); féconder.
impress [im'pres], *v.t.* imprimer (à); faire bien comprendre (*quelque chose à quelqu'un*); pénétrer (*de*); impressionner.
impression [im'preʃən], *n.* impression, empreinte; (*fig.*) idée, *f.*
impressive [im'presiv], *a.* impressionnant, frappant, touchant, émouvant.
impressiveness [im'presivnis], *n.* force, puissance, grandeur, *f.*
imprint [im'print], *v.t.* imprimer, empreindre.—['imprint], *n.* empreinte, *f.*

imprison [im'prizn], *v.t.* emprisonner, enfermer.

imprisonment [im'priznmənt], *n.* emprisonnement, *m.*, détention, *f.*

improbability [imprɔbə'biliti], *n.* improbabilité; invraisemblance, *f.*

improbable [im'prɔbəbl], *a.* improbable, invraisemblable.

impromptu [im'prɔmptju:], *a.* impromptu, improvisé.—*adv.* par improvisation, impromptu.

improper [im'prɔpə], *a.* inconvenant; peu propre (*à*), impropre (*langage*).

improperly [im'prɔpəli], *adv.* d'une manière peu convenable; à tort, mal à propos.

impropriety [imprə'praiəti], *n.* inconvenance (*de conduite*); impropriété (*de langage*), *f.*

improve [im'pru:v], *v.t.* améliorer, perfectionner (*invention etc.*); faire avancer; utiliser; bonifier (*terre etc.*); embellir (*rendre plus beau*); exploiter (*cultiver*).—*v.i.* s'améliorer; se perfectionner; se bonifier (*vin etc.*); faire des progrès; (*Comm.*) hausser; augmenter de prix; *to improve upon*, améliorer, perfectionner, surpasser.

improvement [im'pru:vmənt], *n.* amélioration, *f.*; perfectionnement; progrès, avancement (*en connaissances*), *m.*

improvident [im'prɔvidənt], *a.* imprévoyant.

improvisation [imprɔvai'zeiʃən], *n.* improvisation, *f.*

improvise ['imprəvaiz], *v.t.* improviser.

imprudence [im'pru:dəns], *n.* imprudence, *f.*

imprudent [im'pru:dənt], *a.* imprudent.

imprudently [im'pru:dntli], *adv.* imprudemment.

impudence ['impjudəns], *n.* impudence, effronterie, *f.*

impudent ['impjudənt], *a.* impudent, effronté.

impudently ['impjudntli], *adv.* impudemment, effrontément.

impugn [im'pju:n], *v.t.* attaquer, contester; (*fig.*) mettre en doute.

impulse ['impʌls], **impulsion** [im'pʌlʃən], *n.* impulsion, *f.*, mouvement; (*fig.*) élan, *m.*; *sudden impulse*, coup de tête, *m.*

impulsive [im'pʌlsiv], *a.* impulsif, primesautier.

impulsively [im'pʌlsivli], *adv.* par impulsion, par un mouvement involontaire.

impunity [im'pju:niti], *n.* impunité, *f.*; *with impunity*, impunément.

impure [im'pjuə], *a.* impur; impudique.

impurity [im'pjuəriti], *n.* impureté; impudicité, *f.*

imputation [impju'teiʃən], *n.* imputation, accusation, *f.*

impute [im'pju:t], *v.t.* imputer, attribuer (*à*).

in [in], *prep.* en, dans; à; par; pour; sur, avec, chez, parmi (*en compagnie de*); *he will do it in one hour*, il fera cela en une heure; *he will start in one hour*, il partira dans une heure; *in bed*, au lit; *in England*, en Angleterre; *in Japan*, au Japon; *in Paris*, à Paris, *in spite of*, malgré; *in spring*, au printemps; *in summer* (*autumn, winter*), en été (automne, hiver); *in the morning*, le matin; *in the U.S.A.*, aux États-Unis; *in ten*, un sur dix; *to be clothed in*, être vêtu de.—*adv.* dedans, au dedans, rentré; chez soi, à la maison, y (*at home*); élu (*vainqueur aux élections*); au pouvoir (*parti politique*); *all in*, las, fatigué. —*n. to know all the ins and outs of a matter*, connaître les tenants et les aboutissants d'une affaire.

inability [inə'biliti], *n.* impuissance, incapacité, *f.*

inaccessible [inæk'sesibl], *a.* inaccessible; inabordable (*à*).

inaccuracy [in'ækjurəsi], *n.* inexactitude, *f.*

inaccurate [in'ækjurit], *a.* inexact.

inaction [in'ækʃən], *n.* inaction, inertie, *f.*

inactive [in'æktiv], *a.* inactif; inerte (*choses*).

inactivity [inæk'tiviti], *n.* inactivité, *f.*

inadequacy [in'ædikwəsi], *n.* insuffisance, imperfection, *f.*

inadequate [in'ædikwit], *a.* insuffisant; imparfait, défectueux, incomplet.

inadequately [in'ædikwitli], *adv.* insuffisamment.

inadmissible [inəd'misibl], *a.* inadmissible.

inadvertence [inəd'və:təns], **inadvertency** [inəd'və:tənsi], *n.* inadvertance, *f.*

inadvertent [inəd'və:tənt], *a.* négligent, inattentif.

inadvertently [inəd'və:təntli], *adv.* par inadvertance.

inalienable [in'eiliənəbl], *a.* inaliénable; inséparable.

inane [in'ein], *a.* vide; (*fig.*) inepte, absurde.

inanimate [in'ænimit], *a.* inanimé; mort.

inanition [inə'niʃən], *n.* inanition, *f.*

inanity [i'næniti], *n.* inanité, *f.*

inapplicable [in'æplikəbl], *a.* inapplicable.

inappreciable [inə'pri:ʃiəbl], *a.* inappréciable, insensible.

inappropriate [inə'proupriit], *a.* peu propre, qui ne convient pas.

inapt [in'æpt], *a.* inapte, impropre, peu propre (*à*).

inarticulate [ina:'tikjulit], *a.* inarticulé, qui s'exprime peu clairement.

inartistic [ina:'tistik], *a.* peu artistique.

inasmuch [inəz'mʌtʃ], *adv.* vu que, attendu que, d'autant que.

inattention [inə'tenʃən], *n.* inattention; distraction, *f.*

inattentive [inə'tentiv], *a.* inattentif, distrait; négligent.

inattentively [inə'tentivli], *adv.* sans attention, négligemment.

inaudible [in'ɔ:dibl], *a.* imperceptible, qu'on ne peut entendre.

inaudibly [in'ɔ:dibli], *adv.* à ne pouvoir être entendu.

inaugural [in'ɔ:gjurəl], *a.* inaugural.

inaugurate [in'ɔ:gjureit], *v.t.* inaugurer.

inauspicious [inɔ:'spiʃəs], *a.* malheureux, peu propice.

inauspiciously [inɔ:'spiʃəsli], *adv.* sous de mauvais auspices.

inborn ['inbɔ:n], **inbred** ['inbred], *a.* inné, naturel.

incalculable [in'kælkjuləbl], *a.* incalculable.

incapable [in'keipəbl], *a.* incapable (*de*).

incapacitate [inkə'pæsiteit], *v.t.* rendre incapable (*de*).

incarcerate [in'ka:səreit], *v.t.* incarcérer, mettre en prison.

incarnate [in'ka:nit], *a.* incarné.

incautious [in'kɔ:ʃəs], *a.* inconsidéré, imprudent.

incendiarism [in'sendjərizm], *n.* crime d'incendie, *m.*

incendiary [in'sendjəri], *a.* and *n.* incendiaire, *m.*, *f.*

incense ['insens], *n.* encens, *m.*—[in'sens], *v.t.* irriter, exaspérer (*contre*).

incentive [in'sentiv], *a.* excitant, stimulant.—*n.* motif, stimulant, encouragement, *m.*

inception [in'sepʃən], *n.* commencement, *m.*

incessant [in'sesənt], *a.* incessant; continuel.

incest ['insest], *n.* inceste, *m.*

inch [intʃ], *n.* pouce (2,539 *centimètres*), *m.*

incident ['insidənt], *a.* qui arrive; particulier.—*n.* incident, événement, *m.*

incidental [insi'dentl], *a.* fortuit, accidentel; accessoire; *incidental expenses*, faux frais, *m.pl.*

incidentally [insi'dentli], *adv.* fortuitement, par hasard; soit dit en passant.

incinerate [in'sinəreit], *v.t.* incinérer.

incipient [in'sipiənt], *a.* naissant, qui commence.

incise [in'saiz], *v.t.* inciser, graver.

incision [in'siʒən], *n.* incision, *f.*

incisive [in'saisiv], *a.* incisif.

incite [in'sait], *v.t.* inciter, stimuler; encourager (*à*).

incitement [in'saitmənt], *n.* encouragement, motif, stimulant, *m.*

incivility [insi'viliti], *n.* incivilité, impolitesse, *f.*

inclemency [in'klemənsi], *n.* inclémence, *f.*; intempéries, *f.pl.*, rigueur (*du temps etc.*), *f.*

inclement [in'klemənt], *a.* inclément; rigoureux.

inclination [inkli'neiʃən], *n.* inclinaison, pente; inclination (*de la tête* ou *du corps*), *f.*; penchant, goût (*disposition*), *m.*

incline ['inklain], *n.* pente, (*Rail.*) rampe, *f.*—[in'klain], *v.t.* incliner, (faire) pencher; (*fig.*) porter, disposer (*à*).—*v.i.* incliner, s'incliner, pencher; (*fig.*) être porté (*à*).

inclined [in'klaind], *a.* incliné, enclin (*à*); porté, disposé (*à*).

include [in'klu:d], *v.t.* comprendre, renfermer.

included [in'klu:did], *a.* compris, y compris.

including [in'klu:diŋ], *prep.* comprenant, y compris.

inclusion [in'klu:ʒən], *n.* inclusion, *f.*

inclusive [in'klu:siv], *a.* inclusif; qui renferme, qui comprend; *inclusive of*, y compris.

incoherence [inko'hiərəns], *n.* incohérence, *f.*

incoherent [inko'hierənt], *a.* incohérent.

incombustible [inkəm'bʌstibl], *a.* incombustible.

income ['inkəm], *n.* revenu, *m.*; *private income*, rente, *f.*, rentes, *f.pl.*

income tax ['inkəmtæks], *n.* impôt sur le revenu, *m.*

incommode [inkə'moud], *v.t.* incommoder, gêner, déranger.

incommodious [inkə'moudjəs], *a.* incommode.

incomparable [in'kɔmprəbl], *a.* incomparable.

incompatible [inkəm'pætibl], *a.* incompatible.

incompetence [in'kɔmpitəns], *n.* incompétence, insuffisance; incapacité, *f.*

incompetent [in'kɔmpitənt], *a.* incompétent, incapable.

incompetently [in'kɔmpitəntli], *adv.* avec incompétence.

incomplete [inkəm'pli:t], *a.* imparfait, inachevé, incomplet.

incompletely [inkəm'pli:tli], *adv.* incomplètement, imparfaitement.

incomprehensibility [inkɔmprihensi'biliti], *n.* incompréhensibilité, *f.*

incomprehensible [inkɔmpri'hensibl], *a.* incompréhensible.

inconceivable [inkən'si:vəbl], *a.* inconcevable.

inconclusive [inkən'klu:siv], *a.* qui n'est pas concluant.

incongruity [inkɔn'gru:iti], *n.* désaccord, *m.*, incongruité; inconvenance, *f.*

incongruous [in'kɔngruəs], *a.* incongru, inconvenant, (*fig.*) disparate.

inconsequence [in'kɔnsikwəns], *n.* inconséquence; fausse déduction, *f.*

inconsequent [in'kɔnsikwənt], *a.* inconséquent.

inconsiderable [inkən'sidərəbl], *a.* petit, insignifiant; de peu d'importance.

inconsiderate [inkən'sidərit], *a.* inconsidéré, irréfléchi; sans égards pour les autres.

inconsistency [inkən'sistənsi], *n.* inconséquence; contradiction, *f.*

inconsistent [inkən'sistənt], *a.* incompatible (*avec*), contradictoire (*à*); inconséquent.

inconsistently [inkən'sistəntli], *adv.* avec un manque de continuité.

inconspicuous [inkən'spikjuəs], *a.* peu apparent, peu remarquable; discret.

inconstancy [in'kɔnstənsi], *n.* inconstance, *f.*; caractère changeant, *m.*

inconstant [in'kɔnstənt], *a.* inconstant, volage, changeant.

incontestable [inkən'testəbl], *a.* incontestable, irrécusable.

incontrovertible [inkɔntrə'və:tibl], *a.* incontestable, indisputable.

inconvenience [inkən'vi:niəns], *n.* inconvénient; embarras, dérangement, *m.*—*v.t.* déranger, incommoder, gêner.

inconvenient [inkən'vi:niənt], *a.* incommode, gênant.

inconveniently [inkən'vi:niəntli], *adv.* incommodément, mal.

incorporate [in'kɔ:pareit], *v.t.* incorporer, former en société.—*v.i.* s'incorporer.

incorporated, see **joint-stock**.

incorrect [inkə'rekt], *a.* incorrect, inexact.

incorrectly [inkə'rektli], *adv.* incorrectement; inexactement.

incorrectness [inkə'rektnis], *n.* incorrection; inexactitude, *f.*

incorrigible [in'kɔridʒibl], *a.* incorrigible.

incorrupt [inkə'rʌpt], *a.* incorrompu, pur.

incorruptible [inkə'rʌptibl], *a.* incorruptible.

increase [in'kri:s], *v.t.* augmenter, agrandir, accroître.—*v.i.* croître, s'accroître; augmenter.—['inkri:s], *n.* augmentation (*de prix*), *f.*, accroissement (*de vitesse*); (*fig.*) produit, *m.*; crue (*de rivière*), *f.*

increasing [in'kri:siŋ], *a.* croissant.

increasingly [in'kri:siŋli], *adv.* de plus en plus.

incredible [in'kredibl], *a.* incroyable.

incredibly [in'kredibli], *adv.* incroyablement, d'une manière incroyable.
incredulity [inkrə'dju:liti], *n.* incrédulité, *f.*
incredulous [in'kredjuləs], *a.* incrédule.
increment ['inkrimənt], *n.* augmentation, *f.*; produit, *m.*
incriminate [in'krimineit], *v.t.* incriminer.
incubate ['inkjubeit], *v.t.* couver.
incubation [inkju'beiʃən], *n.* incubation, *f.*
incubator ['inkjubeitə], *n.* couveuse artificielle, *f.*
incubus ['inkjubəs], *n.* incube, cauchemar; (*fig.*) grand poids, *m.*
inculcate ['inkʌlkeit], *v.t.* inculquer (*à*).
incumbent [in'kʌmbənt], *a.* couché (*sur*); imposé, obligatoire; **to be incumbent on,** incomber à; **to feel it incumbent on one to do,** se faire un devoir de.—*n.* titulaire, bénéficier, *m.*
incur [in'kə:], *v.t.* encourir (*blâme*), s'attirer (*colère*); faire (*dettes*).
incurable [in'kjuərəbl], *a.* incurable, inguérissable.—*n.* incurable, *m.*, *f.*
incursion [in'kə:ʃən], *n.* incursion, irruption, *f.*
indebted [in'detid], *a.* endetté; redevable (*de*).
indebtedness [in'detidnis], *n.* dette, obligation, *f.*
indecency [in'di:sənsi], *n.* indécence, *f.*
indecent [in'di:sənt], *a.* indécent.
indecently [in'di:səntli], *adv.* indécemment.
indecision [indi'siʒən], *n.* irrésolution, *f.*
indecisive [indi'saisiv], *a.* peu décisif, indécis.
indecorous [in'dekərəs], *a.* inconvenant.
indecorousness [in'dekərəsnis], **indecorum** [indi'kɔ:rəm], *n.* manque de décorum, *m.*, inconvenance, *f.*
indeed [in'di:d], *adv.* en effet, en vérité; vraiment; à dire vrai, à la vérité.—*int.* vraiment! allons donc!
indefatigable [indi'fætigəbl], *a.* infatigable.
indefensible [indi'fensibl], *a.* indéfendable, inexcusable.
indefinable [indi'fainəbl], *a.* indéfinissable.
indefinite [in'definit], *a.* indéfini, vague.
indefinitely [in'definitli], *adv.* indéfiniment, vaguement.
indelible [in'delibl], *a.* indélébile, ineffaçable.
indelibly [in'delibli], *adv.* d'une manière indélébile, ineffaçablement.
indelicacy [in'delikəsi], *n.* indélicatesse, grossièreté, inconvenance, *f.*
indelicate [in'delikit], *a.* indélicat, grossier, inconvenant.
indemnify [in'demnifai], *v.t.* dédommager, indemniser (*de*).
indemnity [in'demniti], *n.* dédommagement, *m.*; indemnité, *f.*
indent [in'dent], *v.t.* denteler; ébrécher, échancrer.—*v.i.* **to indent for,** réquisitionner.—*n.* dentelure, bosselure, *f.*
indented [in'dentid], *a.* dentelé; échancré.
indenture [in'dentʃə], *n.* titre; (*esp. pl.*) contrat d'apprentissage, *m.*—*v.t.* mettre en apprentissage.
independence [indi'pendəns], **independency** [indi'pendənsi], *n.* indépendance, *f.*
independent [indi'pendənt], *a.* indépendant; libre.
independently [indi'pendəntli], *adv.* indépendamment; dans l'indépendance.
indescribable [indi'skraibəbl], *a.* indicible, indescriptible.

indestructible [indi'strʌktibl], *a.* indestructible.
index ['indeks], *n.* (*pl.* **indexes** ['indeksiz], **indices** ['indisi:z]) indice, signe, indicateur; index (*d'un livre*), *m.*; aiguille (*d'une montre etc.*), *f.*; (*Anat.*) index, doigt indicateur; (*Math.*) exposant, *m.*
India ['indjə], l'Inde, *f.*
Indian ['indjən], *a.* indien; des Indiens; de l'Inde, des Indes; *Indian corn,* maïs, *m.*—*n.* Indien (*personne*), *m.*; *Red Indian,* Peau-Rouge, *m.*, *f.*
India rubber ['indjə'rʌbə], *n.* caoutchouc, *m.*
indicate ['indikeit], *v.t.* indiquer.
indication [indi'keiʃən], *n.* indication, *f.*, signe, indice, *m.*
indicative [in'dikətiv], *a.* and *n.* indicatif, *m.*
indicator ['indikeitə], *n.* indicateur, *m.*
indict [in'dait], *v.t.* inculper, mettre en accusation.
indictment [in'daitmənt], *n.* accusation; mise en accusation, *f.*
Indies ['indiz], the. les Indes, *f.pl.*; *the West Indies,* les Antilles, *f.pl.*
indifference [in'difrəns], *n.* indifférence, apathie, *f.*
indifferent [in'difrənt], *a.* indifférent; impartial; passable, médiocre.
indifferently [in'difrəntli], *adv.* indifféremment; médiocrement.
indigence ['indidʒəns], *n.* indigence, *f.*
indigent ['indidʒənt], *a.* nécessiteux, indigent.
indigenous [in'didʒinəs], *a.* du pays, indigène.
indigestible [indi'dʒestibl], *a.* indigeste.
indigestion [indi'dʒestʃən], *n.* indigestion, dyspepsie, *f.*
indignant [in'dignənt], *a.* indigné (*de*); plein d'indignation.
indignantly [in'dignəntli], *adv.* avec indignation.
indignation [indig'neiʃən], *n.* indignation, *f.*
indignity [in'digniti], *n.* indignité, *f.*; outrage, affront, *m.*
indigo ['indigou], *n.* indigo, *m.*
indirect [indi'rekt], *a.* indirect; (*fig.*) oblique, insidieux.
indiscreet [indis'kri:t], *a.* indiscret, irréfléchi, imprudent.
indiscreetly [indis'kri:tli], *adv.* indiscrètement.
indiscretion [indis'kreʃən], *n.* indiscrétion, imprudence, *f.*
indiscriminate [indis'kriminit], *a.* confus, sans distinction; aveugle.
indiscriminately [indis'kriminitli], *adv.* sans distinction, à tort et à travers, aveuglément.
indispensable [indis'pensəbl], *a.* indispensable, nécessaire.
indispose [indis'pouz], *v.t.* indisposer (*contre*), déranger, détourner (*de*).
indisposed [indis'pouzd], *a.* souffrant.
indisposition [indispə'ziʃən], *n.* indisposition, *f.*; malaise, *m.*
indisputable [indis'pju:təbl], *a.* incontestable, indiscutable.
indisputably [indis'pju:təbli], *adv.* incontestablement.
indissoluble [indi'sɔljubl], *a.* indissoluble.
indistinct [indis'tiŋkt], *a.* indistinct, confus, imprécis, vague.

indistinctly [indis'tiŋktli], *adv.* indistinctement, confusément, vaguement.
indistinguishable [indis'tiŋgwiʃəbl], *a.* indistinct, imperceptible.
indite [in'dait], *v.t.* rédiger.
individual [indi'vidjuəl], *a.* individuel; seul, unique.—*n.* individu, particulier, *m.*
individuality [individju'æliti], *n.* individualité, personnalité, *f.*
individually [indi'vidjuəli], *adv.* individuellement.
indivisible [indi'vizibl], *a.* indivisible.
indoctrinate [in'dɔktrineit], *v.t.* instruire; endoctriner.
indolence ['indələns], *n.* indolence, paresse, *f.*
indolent ['indələnt], *a.* indolent, paresseux.
indolently ['indələntli], *adv.* indolemment, nonchalamment.
indomitable [in'dɔmitəbl], *a.* indomptable.
Indonesia [indo'ni:ziə], l'Indonésie, *f.*
Indonesian [indo'ni:ziən], *a.* indonésien.—*n.* indonésien (*langue*); Indonésien (*personne*), *m.*
indoors [in'dɔ:z], *adv.* à la maison, au dedans.
indubitable [in'dju:bitəbl], *a.* indubitable, incontestable.
induce [in'dju:s], *v.t.* porter, persuader, induire, pousser (à); amener, causer, produire.
inducement [in'dju:smənt], *n.* raison, tentation, *f.*, motif, mobile, *m.*
induction [in'dakʃən], *n.* installation; induction, *f.*
indulge [in'dʌldʒ], *v.t.* satisfaire; avoir trop d'indulgence pour; (*fig.*) flatter, caresser (*une espérance etc.*).—*v.i.* se laisser aller, se livrer à, s'abandonner (à).
indulgence [in'dʌldʒəns], *n.* faveur, *f.*, plaisir, agrément, *m.*; (*R.-C. Ch.*) indulgence, *f.*
indulgent [in'dʌldʒənt], *a.* indulgent, facile, complaisant.
industrial [in'dʌstriəl], *a.* industriel, de l'industrie.
industrialist [in'dʌstriəlist], *n.* industriel, *m.*
industrious [in'dʌstriəs], *a.* travailleur; diligent, laborieux.
industriously [in'dʌstriəsli], *adv.* assidûment, diligemment.
industry ['indəstri], *n.* travail, *m.*, diligence, assiduité, *f.*; (*fig.*) empressement, *m.*; industrie (*production*), *f.*
inebriate [i'ni:brieit], *v.t.* enivrer.—[i'ni:briit], *a.* enivré.—*n.* ivrogne, *m.*, *f.*
inebriation [ini:bri'eiʃən], **inebriety** [ini'braiəti], *n.* ivresse, ébriété, *f.*
inedible [in'edibl], *a.* immangeable; non comestible.
ineffable [in'efəbl], *a.* ineffable.
ineffaceable [ini'feisəbl], *a.* ineffaçable, indélébile.
ineffective [ini'fektiv], *a.* inefficace, sans effet.
ineffectual [ini'fektjuəl], *a.* inefficace, inutile, vain; incapable.
ineffectually [ini'fektjuəli], *adv.* inutilement, sans effet.
inefficacious [inefi'keiʃəs], *a.* inefficace.
inefficiency [ini'fiʃənsi], *n.* inefficacité, incapacité, incompétence, *f.*
inefficient [ini'fiʃənt], *a.* inefficace; incapable.

ineligible [in'elidʒibl], *a.* inéligible; peu propre (à).
inept [in'ept], *a.* inepte, sot, absurde, peu propre (à).
inequality [ini'kwɔliti], *n.* inégalité, disparité, *f.*
inert [i'nə:t], *a.* inerte.
inertia [i'nə:ʃə], *n.* inertie, inactivité, *f.*
inestimable [in'estiməbl], *a.* inestimable; incalculable.
inevitable [in'evitəbl], *a.* inévitable; fatal.
inevitably [in'evitəbli], *adv.* inévitablement.
inexact [inig'zækt], *a.* inexact.
inexcusable [iniks'kju:zəbl], *a.* inexcusable, sans excuse.
inexhaustible [inig'zɔ:stibl], *a.* inépuisable.
inexorable [in'eksərəbl], *a.* inexorable, inflexible.
inexpedient [iniks'pi:djənt], *a.* inopportun, mal à propos.
inexpensive [iniks'pensiv], *a.* peu coûteux, bon marché.
inexperience [iniks'piəriəns], *n.* inexpérience, *f.*
inexperienced [iniks'piəriənst], *a.* inexpérimenté, sans expérience.
inexplicable [in'eksplikəbl], *a.* inexplicable.
inexpressible [iniks'presibl], *a.* inexprimable, indicible.
inextricable [in'ekstrikəbl], *a.* inextricable.
infallible [in'fælibl], *a.* infaillible, immanquable.
infamous ['infaməs], *a.* infâme.
infamy ['infəmi], *n.* infamie, *f.*
infancy ['infənsi], *n.* première enfance, *f.*, bas âge, *m.*
infant ['infənt], *a.* en bas âge, dans l'enfance, petit; (*fig.*) naissant, qui commence.—*n.* enfant en bas âge, nourrisson, bébé; (*Law*) mineur, *m.*
infantile ['infəntail], *a.* enfantin, d'enfant.
infantry ['infəntri], *n.* infanterie, *f.*
infant-school ['infənt'sku:l], *n.* école maternelle, *f.*
infatuate [in'fætjueit], *v.t.* infatuer, entêter, affoler; **to become infatuated with**, s'engouer de, s'amouracher de.
infatuation [infætju'eiʃən], *n.* engouement, *m.*; infatuation; (*fam.*) toquade, *f.*
infect [in'fekt], *v.t.* infecter (de).
infection [in'fekʃən], *n.* infection, contagion, *f.*
infectious [in'fekʃəs], *a.* infect; contagieux, infectieux.
infectiousness [in'fekʃəsnis], *n.* nature contagieuse, contagion, *f.*
infer [in'fə:], *v.t.* inférer; (*fig.*) supposer.
inference ['infərəns], *n.* conséquence, conclusion, déduction, *f.*
inferior [in'fiəriə], *a.* inférieur; subordonné.—*n.* inférieur, *m.*
inferiority [infiəri'ɔriti], *n.* infériorité, *f.*
infernal [in'fə:nl], *a.* infernal, d'enfer; (*fig.*) diabolique.
inferno [in'fə:nou], *n.* enfer; brasier, *m.*
infest [in'fest], *v.t.* infester.
infidel ['infidəl], *a.* and *n.* infidèle; incrédule, *m.*, *f.*
infidelity [infi'deliti], *n.* infidélité; déloyauté (*d'un serviteur*), *f.*
infiltrate ['infiltreit], *v.i.* s'infiltrer (*dans*); pénétrer.

457

infinite ['infinit], *a.* and *n.* infini, *m.*
infinitely ['infinitli], *adv.* infiniment, à
l'infini; fort.
infinitive [in'finitiv], *a.* and *n.* infinitif, *m.*
infinity [in'finiti], *n.* infinité; immensité, *f.*
infirm [in'fə:m], *a.* infirme, faible; (*fig.*)
inconstant, irrésolu.
infirmary [in'fə:məri], *n.* hôpital, *m.*, infirmerie, *f.*
infirmity [in'fə:miti], *n.* infirmité, faiblesse,
f.
inflame [in'fleim], *v.t.* enflammer; (*fig.*)
exciter.—*v.i.* s'enflammer.
inflammable [in'flæməbl], *a.* inflammable.
inflammation [inflə'meiʃən], *n.* inflammation, fluxion, *f.*
inflammatory [in'flæmatri], *a.* inflammatoire; (*fig.*) incendiaire.
inflate [in'fleit], *v.t.* enfler, gonfler.
inflated [in'fleitid], *a.* enflé, gonflé; exagéré;
boursouflé (*style*).
inflation [in'fleiʃən], *n.* enflure, *f.*, gonflement, *m.*; inflation (monétaire), *f.*
inflect [in'flekt], *v.t.* fléchir; varier, moduler
(*la voix*).
inflection [in'flekʃən], *n.* inflexion, modulation, *f.*
inflexible [in'fleksibl], *a.* inflexible.
inflict [in'flikt], *v.t.* infliger, faire (*une peine*).
infliction [in'flikʃən], *n.* infliction; (*fig.*)
peine, *f.*
influence ['influəns], *n.* influence (*sur*), *f.*,
empire, *m.*—*v.t.* influencer; influer (*sur*).
influential [influ'enʃəl], *a.* influent, qui a de
l'influence.
influenza [influ'enzə], *n.* influenza, grippe, *f.*
influx ['inflʌks], *n.* affluence; invasion; embouchure, *f.*
inform [in'fɔ:m], *v.t.* informer, instruire,
renseigner, avertir; faire savoir à; *to inform
against*, dénoncer.
informal [in'fɔ:məl], *a.* sans cérémonie,
simple.
informality [infɔ:'mæliti], *n.* manque de
cérémonie, *m.*; simplicité, *f.*
informally [in'fɔ:məli], *adv.* sans cérémonie;
sans façon.
informant [in'fɔ:mənt], *n.* correspondant;
informateur, *m.*
information [infə'meiʃən], *n.* renseignements, *m.pl.*; *piece of information*,
renseignement, avis, *m.*, nouvelle, *f.*; savoir,
m.; (*Law*) dénonciation, *f.*
informative [in'fɔ:mətiv], *a.* instructif; éducatif.
informer [in'fɔ:mə], *n.* délateur, dénonciateur, *m.*
infraction [in'frækʃən], *n.* infraction, contravention, *f.*
infra-red [infrə'red], *a.* infra-rouge.
infrequent [in'fri:kwənt], *a.* rare.
infringe [in'frindʒ], *v.t.* enfreindre, violer,
transgresser.
infringement [in'frindʒmənt], *n.* infraction,
violation; contrefaçon (*d'un brevet*), *f.*
infuriate [in'fjuərieit], *v.t.* rendre furieux.
infuriated [in'fjuərieitid], *a.* furieux, en
fureur.
infuse [in'fju:z], *v.t.* infuser; faire infuser;
macérer; (*fig.*) inspirer (*à*).
infusion [in'fju:ʒən], *n.* infusion, *f.*
ingenious [in'dʒi:niəs], *a.* ingénieux, habile.

ingeniously [in'dʒi:niəsli], *adv.* ingénieusement; spirituellement.
ingeniousness [in'dʒi:niəsnis], **ingenuity**
[indʒi'nju:iti], *n.* ingéniosité, habileté, *f.*
ingenuous [in'dʒenjuəs], *a.* ingénu; naïf;
candide.
ingenuously [in'dʒenjuəsli], *adv.* ingénument, naivement.
ingenuousness [in'dʒenjuəsnis], *n.* ingénuité,
naiveté, *f.*
inglorious [in'glɔ:riəs], *a.* obscur; inconnu;
honteux.
ingloriously [in'glɔ:riəsli], *adv.* sans gloire;
honteusement.
ingoing ['ingouin], *a.* entrant, nouveau.—*n.*
entrée, *f.*
ingot ['ingət], *n.* lingot, *m.*
ingrained [in'greind], *a.* encrassé; (*fig.*)
enraciné, invétéré.
ingratiate [in'greiʃieit], *v.t.* insinuer (*dans*);
to ingratiate oneself with, s'insinuer
dans les bonnes grâces de.
ingratitude [in'grætitju:d], *n.* ingratitude, *f.*
ingredient [in'gri:diənt], *n.* ingrédient; élément, *m.*
ingrowing ['ingrouin], *a.* incarné (*ongle*).
inhabit [in'hæbit], *v.t.* habiter; habiter (*dans*).
inhabitable [in'hæbitəbl], *a.* habitable.
inhabitant [in'hæbitənt], *n.* habitant, *m.*
inhabited [in'hæbitid], *a.* habité.
inhalation [inhə'leiʃən], *n.* inhalation; inspiration, *f.*
inhale [in'heil], *v.t.* aspirer; respirer, humer.
inherent [in'hiərənt], *a.* inhérent, naturel (*à*).
inherit [in'herit], *v.t.* hériter (*de*).—*v.i.*
hériter.
inheritance [in'heritəns], *n.* héritage, patrimoine, *m.*
inheritance tax, see **death-duties**.
inhibit [in'hibit], *v.t.* arrêter, empêcher
interdire.
inhibition [inhi'biʃən], *n.* interdiction;
(*Psych.*) inhibition, *f.*
inhospitable [in'hɔspitəbl], *a.* inhospitalier.
inhuman [in'hju:mən], *a.* inhumain; dénaturé; cruel.
inhumanity [inhju'mæniti], *n.* inhumanité;
brutalité, *f.*
inhumation [inhju'meiʃən], *n.* inhumation,
f., enterrement, *m.*
inimical [i'nimikl], *a.* hostile, ennemi; contraire (*à*).
inimitable [i'nimitəbl], *a.* inimitable.
iniquitous [i'nikwitəs], *a.* inique, injuste.
iniquity [i'nikwiti], *n.* iniquité, *f.*
initial [i'niʃəl], *a.* initial; premier.—*n.*
initiale, *f.*—*v.t.* mettre ses initiales à.
initially [i'niʃəli], *adv.* au commencement.
initiate [i'niʃieit], *v.t.* initier (*à ou dans*);
amorcer, commencer.
initiation [iniʃi'eiʃən], *n.* initiation, *f.*
initiative [i'niʃiətiv], *n.* initiative, *f.*
inject [in'dʒekt], *v.t.* injecter; faire une
piqûre.
injection [in'dʒekʃən], *n.* injection; (*Med.*)
piqûre, *f.*
injudicious [indʒu'diʃəs], *a.* peu judicieux,
malavisé, imprudent.
injudiciously [indʒu'diʃəsli], *adv.* peu
judicieusement, imprudemment.
injunction [in'dʒʌŋkʃən], *n.* injonction;
recommandation, *f.*

injure ['indʒə], *v.t.* nuire à, faire tort à, léser; endommager (*to damage*); faire mal à, blesser.

injured ['indʒəd], *a.* offensé; blessé; *the injured*, les blessés, les accidentés, *m.pl.*

injurious [in'dʒuəriəs], *a.* nuisible, préjudiciable (*à*).

injuriously [in'dʒuəriəsli], *adv.* à tort.

injury ['indʒəri], *n.* tort, mal; dégât, dommage (*à des marchandises*), *m.*; (*Med.*) lésion, blessure, *f.*

injustice [in'dʒʌstis], *n.* injustice, *f.*

ink [iŋk], *n.* encre, *f.*; *India ink*, encre de Chine,—*v.t.* tacher *ou* barbouiller d'encre.

inkling ['iŋkliŋ], *n.* soupçon, vent (*d'une affaire*), *m.*

inkstand ['iŋkstænd], *n.* encrier de bureau, *m.*

ink-well ['iŋkwel], *n.* encrier, *m.*

inky ['iŋki], *a.* d'encre; taché d'encre.

inlaid [in'leid], *a.* incrusté, marqueté.

inland ['inlənd], *a.* intérieur, de l'intérieur.— *n.* intérieur (*d'un pays*), *m.*

inlay ['inlei], *n.* marqueterie, incrustation, *f.* —[in'lei], *v.t. irr.* (*conjug. like* LAY) marqueter, incruster.

inlet ['inlit], *n.* entrée, *f.*, passage, *m.*, voie, *f.*; petit bras de mer, *m.*

inmate ['inmeit], *n.* habitant, *m.*, locataire (*dans une maison*); interne, pensionnaire (*dans une maison de santé*), *m., f.*

inmost ['inmoust], *a.* le plus profond, le plus secret.

inn [in], *n.* auberge, *f.*; hôtel, *m.*; hôtellerie, *f.*; *to put up at an inn*, descendre à une auberge.

innate [i'neit], *a.* inné; foncier.

innavigable [i'nævigəbl], *a.* innavigable.

inner ['inə], *a.* intérieur, de l'intérieur; (*fig.*) interne, secret.

innermost ['inəmoust], *a.* le plus intérieur, le plus reculé.

innkeeper ['inki:pə], *n.* aubergiste, *m., f.*, hôtelier, *m.*

innocence ['inəsəns], *n.* innocence, *f.*

innocent ['inəsənt], *a.* innocent; permis, légitime.

innocently ['inəsəntli], *adv.* innocemment.

innocuous [i'nɔkjuəs], *a.* innocent, inoffensif.

innovate ['inəveit], *v.i.* innover.

innovation [inə'veiʃən], *n.* innovation, *f.*, changement, *m.*

innuendo [inju'endou], *n.* insinuation, allusion malveillante, *f.*

innumerable [i'nju:mərəbl], *a.* innombrable, sans nombre.

inoculate [i'nɔkjuleit], *v.t.* inoculer, vacciner.

inoculation [inɔkju'leiʃən], *n.* inoculation, *f.*, vaccin, *m.*

inodorous [in'oudərəs], *a.* inodore.

inoffensive [inə'fensiv], *a.* inoffensif.

inopportune [in'ɔpətju:n], *a.* inopportun, intempestif, mal à propos.

inopportunely [in'ɔpətju:nli], *adv.* inopportunément, mal à propos.

inordinate [i'nɔ:dinit], *a.* démesuré, immodéré.

inordinately [i'nɔ:dinitli], *adv.* démesurément, immodérément.

inorganic [inɔ:'gænik], *a.* inorganique.

inquest ['inkwest], *n.* enquête (*après une mort subite*), *f.*

inquire [in'kwaiə], *v.t.* demander.—*v.i.* s'enquérir, s'informer (*de*); s'adresser (*à ou chez*).

inquiring [in'kwaiəriŋ], *a.* investigateur, curieux.

inquiry [in'kwaiəri], *n.* demande, investigation, recherche, *f.*; (*pl.*) informations, *f.pl.* renseignements, *m.pl.*, (*Law*) enquête, *f.*

inquisition [inkwi'ziʃən], *n.* recherche, investigation; (*R.-C. Ch.*) inquisition, *f.*

inquisitive [in'kwizitiv], *a.* curieux.

inroad ['inroud], *n.* incursion, invasion, *f.*; (*fig.*) empiétement (*sur*), *m.*

insalubrious [insə'lju:briəs], *a.* insalubre.

insane [in'sein], *a.* fou, aliéné; dérangé; (*fig.*) insensé.

insanitary [in'sænitəri], *a.* insalubre, malsain.

insanity [in'sæniti], *n.* folie, démence, *f.*

insatiable [in'seiʃəbl], *a.* insatiable.

insatiate [in'seiʃiit], *a.* insatiable; inassouvi.

inscribe [in'skraib], *v.t.* inscrire; dédier (*à*).

inscription [in'skripʃən], *n.* inscription, *f.*; titre (*title*), *m.*; dédicace (*dedication*), *f.*

inscrutable [in'skru:təbl], *a.* inscrutable, impénétrable.

insect ['insekt], *n.* insecte, *m.*

insecticidal [in'sektisaidl], *a.* insecticide.

insecticide [in'sektisaid], *n.* insecticide, *m.*

insecure [insi'kjuə], *a.* en danger; chanceux, hasardeux; peu sûr, mal assuré.

insecurely [insi'kjuəli], *adv.* sans sûreté, en danger.

insecurity [insi'kjuəriti], *n.* manque de sûreté; danger, péril, *m.*; incertitude, *f.*

insensible [in'sensibl], *a.* imperceptible; insignifiant; inconscient (*unconscious*); sans connaissance.

insensibly [in'sensibli], *adv.* insensiblement, peu à peu.

insensitive [in'sensitiv], *a.* insensible.

inseparable [in'sepərəbl], *a.* inséparable.

insert [in'sə:t], *v.t.* insérer, faire insérer (*dans*).

insertion [in'sə:ʃən], *n.* insertion; interpolation, *f.*

inshore [in'ʃɔ:], *a.* and *adv.* près du rivage.

inside ['insaid], *a.* intérieur, d'intérieur.—*n.* dedans, intérieur, *m.*; *inside out*, à l'envers; [in'said] entrailles, *f.pl.*—[in'said] *adv.* à l'intérieur, en dedans—[in'said] *prep.* en, dans, à l'intérieur de, *m.*

insidious [in'sidiəs], *a.* insidieux, captieux, perfide.

insight ['insait], *n.* perspicacité, pénétration, *f.*

insignia [in'signiə], *n. pl.* insignes, *m.pl.*

insignificance [insig'nifikəns], *n.* insignifiance, *f.*, peu d'importance, *m.*

insignificant [insig'nifikənt], *a.* insignifiant.

insincere [insin'siə], *a.* peu sincère, faux, hypocrite.

insincerely [insin'siəli], *adv.* de mauvaise foi, hypocritement.

insincerity [insin'seriti], *n.* manque de sincérité, *m.*, fausseté, *f.*

insinuate [in'sinjueit], *v.t.* insinuer, glisser (*dans*); donner à entendre.—*v.i.* s'insinuer, se glisser (*dans*).

insinuation [insinju'eiʃən], *n.* insinuation, *f.*

insipid [in'sipid], *a.* insipide, fade.

insipidity [insi'piditi], *n.* insipidité, fadeur, *f.*

insist [in'sist], *v.i.* insister (*sur ou à*); persister; vouloir absolument.

insistence [in'sistəns], *n.* insistance, *f.*

insistent [in'sistənt], *a.* insistant.

insobriety [inso'braiəti], *n.* intempérance, *f.*

insolence ['insələns], *n.* insolence; effronterie, *f.*

insolent ['insələnt], *a.* insolent.

insolently ['insələntli], *adv.* insolemment.

insoluble [in'sɔljubl], *a.* insoluble.

insolvency [in'sɔlvənsi], *n.* insolvabilité, faillite, *f.*

insolvent [in'sɔlvənt], *a.* insolvable, en faillite.

insomnia [in'sɔmniə], *n.* insomnie, *f.*

insomuch [inso'mʌtʃ], *adv.* au point (*que*), à un tel point (*que*), tellement (*que*).

inspect [in'spekt], *v.t.* inspecter, examiner, visiter.

inspection [in'spekʃən], *n.* inspection, revue, *f.*, contrôle, examen, *m.*; surveillance, *f.*

inspector [in'spektə], *n.* inspecteur, *m.*

inspiration [inspi'reiʃən], *n.* inspiration, *f.*; encouragement, *m.*

inspire [in'spaiə], *v.t.* inspirer, souffler (*dans*); animer (*de*).—*v.i.* aspirer.

inspiring [in'spaiəriŋ], *a.* inspirateur; qui donne du courage; qui élève l'esprit.

instability [instə'biliti], *n.* instabilité, *f.*

install [in'stɔːl], *v.t.* installer; monter (*appareil, machine*).

installation [instə'leiʃən], *n.* installation, *f.*; montage (*de machine, équipement*), *m.*

installment [in'stɔːlmənt], *n.* installation, *f.*; (*Comm.*) accompte, versement (*partiel*); épisode (*de feuilleton*), *m.*

installment plan, see **hire-purchase**.

instance ['instəns], *n.* requête, demande, *f.*; exemple, *m.*, occasion, *f.*, cas, *m.*; *for instance*, par exemple; *in the first instance*, en premier lieu.—*v.t.* citer comme exemple.

instant ['instənt], *a.* instant, pressant, immédiat; courant (*mois*).—*n.* instant, moment, *m.*

instantaneous [instən'teiniəs], *a.* instantané.

instantaneously [instən'teiniəsli], *adv.* instantanément.

instantly ['instəntli], *adv.* à l'instant; tout de suite; sur-le-champ.

instead [in'sted], *adv.* à la place; *instead of*, au lieu de.

instep ['instep], *n.* cou-de-pied, *m.*

instigate ['instigeit], *v.t.* exciter, inciter, pousser (*à*).

instigation [insti'geiʃən], *n.* instigation, *f.*

instill [in'stil], *v.t.* instiller; (*fig.*) inspirer (*à*).

instillation [insti'leiʃən], *n.* instillation, (*fig.*) inspiration, *f.*

instinct ['instiŋkt], *n.* instinct, *m.*

instinctive [in'stiŋktiv], *a.* instinctif; (*fig.*) spontané.

instinctively [in'stiŋktivli], *adv.* d'instinct, instinctivement.

institute ['instituːt], *n.* institut, *m.*—*v.t.* instituer, établir; intenter (*un procès*).

institution [insti'tjuːʃən], *n.* institution, *f.*, établissement, *m.*

instruct [in'strʌkt], *v.t.* instruire, enseigner; charger (*de*).

instruction [in'strʌkʃən], *n.* instruction, *f.*, enseignement, *m.*

instructive [in'strʌktiv], *a.* instructif.

instructor [in'strʌktə], *n.* (*Mil.*) instructeur; précepteur, *m.*

instructress [in'strʌktris], *n.* préceptrice, monitrice, *f.*

instrument ['instrumənt], *n.* instrument; (*fig.*) agent, *m.*

instrumental [instru'mentl], *a.* instrumental; *to be instrumental in*, contribuer à.

insubordinate [insə'bɔːdinit], *a.* insubordonné; indocile.

insubordination [insəbɔːdi'neiʃən], *n.* insubordination; insoumission, *f.*

insufferable [in'sʌfərəbl], *a.* insupportable, intolérable.

insufficiency [insə'fiʃənsi], *n.* insuffisance, *f.*

insufficient [insə'fiʃənt], *a.* insuffisant.

insufficiently [insə'fiʃəntli], *adv.* insuffisamment.

insular ['insjulə], *a.* insulaire; (*fig.*) borné, rétréci.

insularity [insju'læriti], *n.* insularité, *f.*

insulate ['insjuleit], *v.t.* isoler; calorifuger.

insulation [insju'leiʃən], *n.* isolement, *m.*; (*Phys.*) isolation, *f.*

insulator ['insjuleitə], *n.* isolateur, isoloir, *m.*

insulin ['insjulin], *n.* insuline, *f.*

insult [in'sʌlt], *v.t.* insulter, faire insulte à, injurier.—['insʌlt], *n.* insulte, injure, *f.*, affront, *m.*

insulting [in'sʌltiŋ], *a.* insultant, outrageux, injurieux.

insultingly [in'sʌltiŋli], *adv.* insolemment, injurieusement.

insuperable [in'sjuːpərəbl], *a.* insurmontable, invincible.

insupportable [insə'pɔːtəbl], *a.* insupportable, intolérable.

insuppressible [insə'presibl], *a.* irrépressible, irrésistible, inextinguible (*rire*).

insurance [in'ʃuərəns], *n.* assurance, *f.*; *fire insurance*, assurance contre l'incendie; *life insurance*, assurance sur la vie.

insure [in'ʃuə], *v.t.* assurer, faire assurer; (*fig.*) garantir.

insurgent [in'səːdʒənt], *a. and n.* insurgé, *m.*

insurmountable [insə'mauntəbl], *a.* insurmontable, infranchissable.

insurrection [insə'rekʃən], *n.* insurrection, *f.* soulèvement, *m.*

intact [in'tækt], *a.* intact, indemne.

intangible [in'tændʒibl], *a.* intangible.

integer ['intədʒə], *n.* entier, nombre entier, *m.*

integral ['intəgrəl], *a.* intégral; *an integral part*, une partie intégrante.—*n.* totalité, *f.*, tout, *m.*

integrate ['intigreit], *v.t.* compléter, rendre entier.

integrity [in'tegriti], *n.* intégrité, probité, *f.*

intellect ['intilekt], *n.* intelligence, *f.*, esprit, *m.*

intellectual [inti'lektjuəl], *a.* intellectuel; intelligent.—*n.* intellectuel, *m.*

intellectually [inti'lektjuəli], *adv.* intellectuellement.

intelligence [in'telidʒəns], *n.* intelligence, *f.*, esprit; renseignement, avis, *m.*; nouvelle, *f.*

intelligent [in'telidʒənt], *a.* intelligent.

intelligently [in'telidʒəntli], *adv.* intelligemment, avec intelligence.

intelligibility [intelidʒi'biliti], *n.* intelligibilité, clarté, *f.*

intelligible [in'telidʒibl], *a.* intelligible.

intemperance [in'temperens], *n.* intempérance, *f.*
intemperate [in'temperit], *a.* démesuré, immodéré; intempérant; violent, emporté (*langage*).
intend [in'tend], *v.t.* se proposer de, avoir l'intention de, compter, vouloir; destiner (*à*); vouloir dire.
intended [in'tendid], *a.* projeté; intentionnel; *to be intended for*, être destiné à.
intense [in'tens], *a.* intense, véhément; (*fig.*) opiniâtre, très sérieux; vif, fort, aigu (*douleur etc.*).
intensely [in'tensli], *adv.* avec intensité, vivement, fortement.
intenseness [in'tensnis], **intensity** [in'tensiti], *n.* intensité; force, violence, *f.*
intensify [in'tensifai], *v.t.* rendre plus vif, intensifier.
intensive [in'tensiv], *a.* intensif.
intent [in'tent], *a.* attentif, absorbé (*par*); déterminé (*à*); fixe (*regard*).—*n.* dessein, but; sens, *m.*, intention, portée, *f.*; *to all intents and purposes*, à tous égards.
intention [in'tenʃən], *n.* intention, *f.*; dessein, but, *m.*
intentional [in'tenʃənəl], *a.* intentionnel, fait à dessein.
intentionally [in'tenʃənəli], *adv.* avec intention, à dessein, exprès.
intently [in'tentli], *adv.* attentivement.
intentness [in'tentnis], *n.* attention, force d'application, *f.*
inter [in'tə:], *v.t.* enterrer, inhumer, ensevelir.
intercede [intə'si:d], *v.t.* intercéder (*auprès de*).
intercept [intə'sept], *v.t.* intercepter; arrêter; (*fig.*) surprendre.
interchange [intə'tʃeindʒ], *v.t.* échanger.— ['intətʃeindʒ], *n.* échange, *m.*, succession; (*fig.*) variété, *f.*
intercourse ['intəkɔ:s], *n.* commerce, *m.*, relations, *f.pl.*, rapports, *m.pl.*
interdict [intə'dikt], *v.t.* interdire, interdire à, défendre à.—['intədikt], *n.* or **interdiction** [intə'dikʃən], interdit, *m.*, défense, interdiction, *f.*
interest ['intrəst], *v.t.* intéresser; *to be interested in*, s'intéresser à.—*n.* intérêt, *m.*; protection, *f.*, crédit, *m.*
interested ['intrəstid], *a.* intéressé.
interesting ['intrəstiŋ], *a.* intéressant.
interfere [intə'fiə], *v.i.* intervenir, se mêler (*de*); *to interfere with*, se mêler de, gêner, contrarier, déranger.
interference [intə'fiərəns], *n.* intervention, *f.*; (*Rad.*) brouillage, *m.*
interim ['intərim], *a.* provisoire.—*n.* intérim, intervalle, *m.*; *in the interim*, en attendant.
interior [in'tiəriə], *a. and n.* intérieur, *m.*; *interior angle*, angle interne, *m.*
interject [intə'dʒekt], *v.t.* interjecter; s'écrier (*en conversation*).
interjection [intə'dʒekʃən], *n.* interjection, *f.*
interlace [intə'leis], *v.t.* entrelacer.
interlacing [intə'leisiŋ], *n.* entrelacement, *m.*
interleave [intə'li:v], *v.t.* interfolier (*de*).
interloper ['intəloupə], *n.* intrus, *m.*
interlude ['intəlu:d], *n.* intermède, *m.*
intermediary [intə'mi:diəri], *a. and n.* intermédiaire, *m.*

intermediate [intə'mi:djit], *a.* intermédiaire, moyen.
interment [in'tə:mənt], *n.* enterrement, *m.*, inhumation, *f.*
interminable [in'tə:minəbl], *a.* interminable.
intermingle [intə'miŋgl], *v.t.* entremêler.— *v.i.* s'entremêler.
intermission [intə'miʃən], *n.* interruption momentanée, *f.*; relâche, intervalle; (*Theat.*) entr'acte, *m.*
intermittent [intə'mitənt], *a.* intermittent.
intermittently [intə'mitəntli], *adv.* par intervalles.
intern [in'tə:n], *v.t.* interner.
intern ['intə:n], *n.* (*Med.*) interne, *m.*, *f.*
internal [in'tə:nl], *a.* interne, intérieur.
international [intə'næʃənl], *a.* international. —*n.* (*joueur*) international, *m.*
internecine [intə'ni:sain], *a.* meurtrier.
internee [intə'ni:], *n.* interné, *m.*
internment [in'tə:nmənt], *n.* internement, *m.*; *internment camp*, camp de concentration, camp de prisonniers, *m.*
interplanetary [intə'plænətəri], *a.* interplanétaire.
interpolate [in'tə:poleit], *v.t.* interpoler; intercaler.
interpose [intə'pouz], *v.t.* interposer.—*v.i.* s'interposer, intervenir.
interpret [in'tə:prit], *v.t.* interpréter; expliquer.
interpretation [intə:pri'teiʃən], *n.* interprétation, *f.*
interpreter [in'tə:pritə], *n.* interprète, *m.*, *f.*
interracial [intə'reiʃəl], *a.* interracial.
interrogate [in'terəgeit], *v.t.* interroger, questionner.
interrogation [interə'geiʃən], *n.* interrogation, question, *f.*
interrogative [intə'rɔgətiv], *a.* interrogatif, interrogateur.
interrupt [intə'rʌpt], *v.t.* interrompre.
interruption [intə'rʌpʃən], *n.* interruption, *f.*; (*fig.*) obstacle, *m.*
intersect [intə'sekt], *v.t.* entrecouper; (*Geom.*) couper.—*v.i.* (*Geom.*) se couper, se croiser.
intersection [intə'sekʃən], *n.* intersection, *f.*
intersperse [intə'spə:s], *v.t.* entremêler (*de*); parsemer (*de*).
interstice [in'tə:stis], *n.* interstice; intervalle, *m.*
intertwine [intə'twain], *v.t.* entrelacer.—*v.i.* s'entrelacer.
interval ['intəvəl], *n.* intervalle, *m.*
intervene [intə'vi:n], *v.i.* intervenir, s'interposer; survenir; arriver (*événements*); s'écouler (*temps*).
intervening [intə'vi:niŋ], *a.* intervenant (*personnes*); intermédiaire (*espace, endroits, temps etc.*).
intervention [intə'venʃən], *n.* intervention, *f.*
interview ['intəvju:], *n.* entrevue; (*Journ.*) interview, *f.*—*v.t.* avoir une entrevue avec; (*Journ.*) interviewer.
interviewer ['intəvju:ə], *n.* interviewer, *m.*
interweave [intə'wi:v], *v.t. irr.* (*conjug. like* WEAVE) entrelacer; entremêler.
intestate [in'testit], *a.* intestat.
intestine [in'testin], *a. and n.* intestin, *m.*
intimacy ['intiməsi], *n.* intimité, *f.*
intimate ['intimit], *a.* intime, lié.—['intimeit], *v.t.* donner à entendre; intimer (*à*).

intimately ['intimitli], *adv.* intimement.
intimation [inti'meiʃən], *n.* avis, *m.*, indication, *f.*
intimidate [in'timideit], *v.t.* intimider.
intimidation [intimi'deiʃən], *n.* intimidation, *f.*
into ['intu], *prep.* dans, en, à, entre.
intolerable [in'tɔlərəbl], *a.* intolérable, insupportable.
intolerance [in'tɔlərəns], *n.* intolérance, *f.*
intolerant [in'tɔlərənt], *a.* intolérant.
intonation [intoʊ'neiʃən], *n.* intonation, *f.*
intone [in'toun], *v.t.*, *v.i.* psalmodier; entonner.
intoxicant [in'tɔksikənt], *n.* boisson alcoolique, *f.*
intoxicate [in'tɔksikeit], *v.t.* enivrer (*de*).
intoxicated [in'tɔksikeitid], *a.* ivre; (*fig.*) enivré (*de*).
intoxicating [in'tɔksikeitiŋ], *a.* enivrant.
intoxication [intɔksi'keiʃən], *n.* ivresse, *f.*; (*fig.*) enivrement, *m.*
intractability [intræktə'biliti], *n.* naturel intraitable, *m.*, indocilité, *f.*
intractable [in'træktəbl], *a.* intraitable, indocile.
intransigence [in'trænsidʒəns, in'trɑːnsidʒəns], *n.* intransigeance, *f.*
intransigent [in'trænsidʒənt, in'trɑːnsidʒənt], *a.* intransigeant.
intransitive [in'trænsitiv, in'trɑːnsitiv], *a.* intransitif.
intrepid [in'trepid], *a.* intrépide.
intricacy ['intrikəsi], *n.* embrouillement, *m.*; complication, *f.*, dédale, *m.*
intricate ['intrikit], *a.* embrouillé; embarrassé; obscur; compliqué.
intrigue [in'triːg], *n.* intrigue, *f.*—*v.t.* intriguer.—*v.i.* intriguer, s'intriguer.
intriguing [in'triːgiŋ], *a.* intrigant, qui excite la curiosité.
intrinsic [in'trinsik], **intrinsical** [in'trinsikəl], *a.* intrinsèque.
introduce [intrəˈdjuːs], *v.t.* introduire, faire entrer; présenter (*personnes*), faire connaître (*à*).
introduction [intrəˈdʌkʃən], *n.* introduction; présentation; recommandation (*par lettre*), *f.*; avant-propos (*de livre*), *m.*
introductory [intrəˈdʌktəri], *a.* introductoire, préliminaire.
introspection [introʊˈspekʃən], *n.* introspection, *f.*
introspective [introʊˈspektiv], *a.* introspectif; qui s'analyse.
introvert ['introvəːt], *n.* introverti, *m.*
intrude [in'truːd], *v.i.* s'introduire, se faufiler, se fourrer; *to intrude on*, importuner, déranger.
intruder [in'truːdə], *n.* intrus, *m.*
intrusion [in'truːʒən], *n.* intrusion, importunité; (*fig.*) usurpation, *f.*, empiètement, *m.*
intuition [intjuːˈiʃən], *n.* intuition, *f.*
intuitive [in'tjuːitiv], *a.* intuitif, d'intuition.
inundate ['inʌndeit], *v.t.* inonder (*de*).
inundation [inʌnˈdeiʃən], *n.* inondation, *f.*, débordement, *m.*
inure [i'njuə], *v.t.* habituer, endurcir, rompre.
invade [in'veid], *v.t.* envahir.
invader [in'veidə], *n.* envahisseur, *m.*
invading [in'veidiŋ], *a.* envahissant; d'invasion.

invalid ['invəliːd], *a.* malade, infirme; [in'vælid], (*Law*) invalide, de nul effet.—*n.* malade, *m.*, *f.*, personne malade, *f.*—*v.t. to invalid out* (*of the army*), réformer.
invalidate [in'vælideit], *v.t.* invalider, casser.
invaluable [in'væljuəbl], *a.* inestimable, sans prix.
invariable [in'veəriəbl], *a.* invariable, constant, uniforme.
invariably [in'veəriəbli], *adv.* invariablement; constamment.
invasion [in'veiʒən], *n.* invasion, *f.*, envahissement, *m.*; (*fig.*) violation, *f.*
invective [in'vektiv], *n.* invective, *f.*
inveigh [in'vei], *v.i.* invectiver (*contre*).
inveigle [in'viːgl, in'veigl], *v.t.* séduire, attirer, entraîner.
invent [in'vent], *v.t.* inventer.
invention [in'venʃən], *n.* invention, *f.*
inventive [in'ventiv], *a.* inventif.
inventor [in'ventə], *n.* inventeur, *m.*
inventory ['invəntri], *n.* inventaire, *m.*
inverse [in'vəːs], *a.* inverse.
inversely [in'vəːsli], *adv.* en sens inverse, inversement.
inversion [in'vəːʃən], *n.* inversion, *f.*
invert [in'vəːt], *v.t.* tourner sens dessus dessous, renverser.
invertebrate [in'vəːtibrit], *a.* and *n.* invertébré, *m.*
invest [in'vest], *v.t.* vêtir, revêtir (*de*); (*Mil.*) investir, bloquer; placer (*argent*).
investigate [in'vestigeit], *v.t.* rechercher, examiner; enquêter sur.
investigation [investi'geiʃən], *n.* investigation, recherche, enquête, *f.*
investigator [in'vestigeitə], *n.* investigateur, *m.*; *private investigator*, détective privé, *m.*
investment [in'vestmənt], *n.* placement (*d'argent*); (*Mil.*) investissement, *m.*
investor [in'vestə], *n.* actionnaire, *m.*, *f.*, personne qui place ses fonds, *f.*
inveterate [in'vetərit], *a.* invétéré, enraciné; acharné.
invidious [in'vidiəs], *a.* odieux; désagréable, ingrat (*tâche*).
invigorate [in'vigəreit], *v.t.* fortifier; donner de la vigueur à.
invigorating [in'vigəreitiŋ], *a.* fortifiant, vivifiant, tonifiant.
invincible [in'vinsibl], *a.* invincible.
inviolable [in'vaiələbl], *a.* inviolable.
inviolate [in'vaiəlit], *a.* inviolé, pur, intact.
invisible [in'vizibl], *a.* invisible.
invitation [invi'teiʃən], *n.* invitation, *f.*
invite [in'vait], *v.t.* inviter, engager (*à*); (*fig.*) appeler, provoquer.
inviting [in'vaitiŋ], *a.* attrayant, appétissant, tentant.
invoice ['invois], *n.* facture, *f.*—*v.t.* facturer.
invoke [in'vouk], *v.t.* invoquer.
involuntarily [in'vɔləntərili], *adv.* involontairement.
involuntary [in'vɔləntəri], *a.* involontaire.
involve [in'vɔlv], *v.t.* envelopper (*to envelop*); compromettre, impliquer, entraîner (*to entail*); comprendre, renfermer (*to comprise*); embarrasser, entortiller (*to entangle*).
involved [in'vɔlvd], *a.* embrouillé, entortillé, compliqué.
invulnerable [in'vʌlnərəbl], *a.* invulnérable.

inward ['inwəd], *a.* intérieur, interne.—*adv.* (*also* **inwards** ['inwədz]) en dedans, intérieurement.

inwardly ['inwədli], *adv.* intérieurement, intimement.

iodine ['aiədi:n, 'aiədain], *n.* iode, *m.*

ion ['aiən], *n.* ion, *m.*

ionosphere [ai'onəsfiə], *n.* ionosphère, *f.*

iota [ai'outə], *n.* iota; rien, *m.*

Iran [i'rɑ:n]. l'Iran, *m.*

Iranian [i'reiniən, ai'reiniən], *a.* iranien, *m.*—*n.* Iranien (*personne*), *m.*

Iraq, Irak [i'rɑ:k]. l'Irak, *m.*

Iraqi [i'rɑ:ki], *a.* irakien.—*n.* Irakien (*personne*), *m*

irascible [i'ræsibl], *a.* irascible.

irate [ai'reit], *a.* courroucé, irrité.

ire ['aiə], *n.* colère, *f.*, courroux, *m.*

Ireland ['aiələnd]. l'Irlande, *f.*

Irene [ai'ri:ni, ai'ri:n]. Irène, *f.*

iridescent [iri'desənt], *a.* iridescent, irisé; chatoyant.

iris ['aiəris], *n.* (*pl.* **irises** ['aiərisiz]) iris, *m.*

Irish ['aiəriʃ], *a.* irlandais.—*n.* irlandais (*langue*), *m.*; *the Irish*, les Irlandais, *m.pl.*

Irishman ['aiəriʃmən], *n.* (*pl.* **-men** [men]) Irlandais, *m.*

Irishwoman ['aiəriʃwumən], *n.* (*pl.* **-women** [wimin]) Irlandaise, *f.*

irk [ə:k], *v.t.* peiner, affliger; ennuyer.

irksome ['ə:ksəm], *a.* ingrat, ennuyeux.

iron ['aiən], *n.* fer à repasser, *m.*

iron ['aiən], *a.* de fer, en fer.—*n.* fer, *m.*; *cast iron*, fonte, *f.*; *corrugated iron*, tôle ondulée, *f.*; *sheet iron*, tôle, *f.*; *wrought iron*, fer forgé.—*v.t.* repasser (*linge etc.*).

ironic [ai'ronik], **ironical** [ai'ronikəl], *a.* ironique.

ironing ['aiəniŋ], *a.* à repasser.—*n.* repassage, *m.*

ironing board ['aiəniŋbɔ:d], *n.* planche à repasser, *f.*

ironmonger ['aiənmʌŋgə], *n.* quincaillier, *m.*

ironmongery ['aiənmʌŋgəri], *n.* quincaillerie, *f.*

iron ore ['aiən'ɔ:], *n.* minerai de fer, *m.*

iron-works ['aiənwə:ks], *n.pl.* forges, *f.pl.*; usine métallurgique, *f.*

irony ['aiərəni], *n.* ironie, *f.*

irradiate [i'reidieit], *v.t.* rayonner sur; éclairer.—*v.i.* rayonner.

irrational [i'ræʃənl], *a.* irraisonnable, déraisonnable; (*Math.*) irrationnel.

irreclaimable [iri'kleiməbl], *a.* incorrigible, invétéré.

irreconcilable [irekən'sailəbl], *a.* irréconciliable (*avec*); incompatible (*avec*); implacable.

irrecoverable [iri'kʌvərəbl], *a.* irrécouvrable; irréparable.

irredeemable [iri'di:məbl], *a.* irrachetable; irrémédiable.

irreducible [iri'dju:sibl], *a.* irréductible.

irreformable [iri'fɔ:məbl], *a.* inaltérable, irréformable.

irrefutable [i'refjutəbl], *a.* irréfutable.

irregular [i'regjulə], *a.* irrégulier, anormal; déréglé.

irregularity [iregju'læriti], *n.* irrégularité, *f.*, dérèglement, *m.*

irregularly [i'regjuləli], *adv.* irrégulièrement.

irrelevant [i'reləvənt], *a.* hors de propos, non pertinent; inapplicable (*à*).

irreligious [iri'lidʒəs], *a.* irréligieux.

irremediable [iri'mi:diəbl], *a.* irrémédiable, sans remède.

irremovable [iri'mu:vəbl], *a.* inébranlable, immuable; inamovible.

irreparable [i'repərəbl], *a.* irréparable.

irreplaceable [iri'pleisəbl], *a.* irremplaçable.

irrepressible [iri'presibl], *a.* irrépressible; inextinguible (*rire*).

irreproachable [iri'proutʃəbl], *a.* irréprochable, sans tache.

irresistible [iri'zistibl], *a.* irrésistible.

irresolute [i'rezolju:t], *a.* irrésolu, indécis.

irresolutely [i'rezolju:tli], *adv.* irrésolument, avec hésitation.

irresolution [irezo'lju:ʃən], **irresoluteness** [i'rezolju:tnis], *n.* irrésolution, indécision, *f.*

irrespective [iris'pektiv], *a.* indépendant (*de*), sans égard (*pour*); *irrespective of*, indépendamment de.

irrespectively [iris'pektivli], *adv.* indépendamment (*de*), sans égard (*pour*).

irresponsibility [irisponsi'biliti], *n.* irresponsabilité, étourderie, *f.*

irresponsible [iris'ponsibl], *a.* irresponsable; irréfléchi, étourdi.

irretrievable [iri'tri:vəbl], *a.* irréparable, irrémédiable.

irreverence [i'revərəns], *n.* irrévérence, *f.*, manque de respect, *m.*

irreverent [i'revərənt], *a.* irrévérencieux.

irrevocable [i'revəkəbl], *a.* irrévocable.

irrigate ['irigeit], *v.t.* arroser, irriguer.

irrigation [iri'geiʃən], *n.* arrosement, *m.* irrigation, *f.*

irritability [iritə'biliti], *n.* irritabilité, *f.*

irritable ['iritəbl], *a.* irritable.

irritate ['iriteit], *v.t.* irriter; agacer; *to be irritated*, s'irriter.

irritation [iri'teiʃən], *n.* irritation, *f.*

irruption [i'rʌpʃən], *n.* irruption, *f.*

Isabel ['izəbel], **Isabella** [izə'belə]. Isabelle, *f.*

island ['ailənd], *n.* île, *f.*; refuge (*au centre de la rue*), *m.*

islander ['ailəndə], *n.* insulaire, *m.*, *f.*

isle [ail], *n.* île, *f.*

islet ['ailit], *n.* îlot, *m.*

isobar ['aisobɑ:], *n.* isobare, *f.*

isolate ['aisəleit], *v.t.* isoler.

isolated ['aisəleitid], *a.* isolé, seul.

isolation [aisə'leiʃən], *n.* isolement, *m.*

isosceles [ai'sosəli:z], *a.* isocèle, isoscèle.

Israel ['izreil]. l'Israël, *m.*

Israeli [iz'reili], *a.* israélien.—*n.* Israélien (*personne*), *m.*

issue ['isju:, 'ifju:], *n.* issue, sortie (*egress*), *f.*; écoulement (*d'eau etc.*), *m.*; distribution (*envoi*); émission (*de billets de banque, timbres-poste*); publication (*de livres etc.*), *f.*; résultat (*conséquence*), *m.*; enfants, *m.pl.*; (*Law*) question, *f.*; *at issue*, en question.—*v.t.* publier; expédier, distribuer; émettre (*billets de banque*).—*v.i.* sortir, jaillir (*de*); (*fig.*) provenir.

isthmus ['isməs], *n.* isthme, *m.*

it [it], *pron.* il, *m.*, elle, *f.*; (*accusatif*) le, *m.*, la, *f.*; (*datif*) lui; (*impersonnel*) il, ce, cela.

Italian [i'tæliən], *a.* italien.—*n.* italien (*langue*); Italien (*personne*), *m.*

italic [i'tælik], *a.* italique.—*n.* (*pl.*) italiques, *m.pl.*

italicize [i'tælisaiz], *v.t.* mettre *ou* imprimer en italiques.

Italy ['itəli]. l'Italie, *f.*

itch [itʃ], *n.* démangeaison; gale (*maladie*), *f.*—*v.i.* démanger.

item ['aitəm], *n.* article; détail, *m.*, rubrique, *f.*; *item of news*, nouvelle, *f.*—*adv.* item, de plus.

itinerant [i'tinərənt], *a.* ambulant.

itinerary [i'tinərəri], *n.* itinéraire, *m.*

its [its], *poss. a.* son, *m.*, sa, *f.*; ses, *m.pl.*

itself [it'self], *pron.* lui, *m.*, elle, *f.*, soi, lui-même, *m.*, elle-même, *f.*, soi-même, *m.*; (*reflexive*) se.

ivory ['aivəri], *a.* d'ivoire.—*n.* ivoire, *m.*

ivy ['aivi], *n.* lierre, *m.*

J

J, j [dʒei]. dixième lettre de l'alphabet, *m.*

jabber ['dʒæbə], *v.i.* jaboter, baragouiner.—*n.* bavardage, baragouinage, *m.*

jack [dʒæk], *n.* chevalet (*de scieur*); cric (*pour auto*); (*Cards*) valet; (*Bowls*) cochonnet, *m.*—*v.t. to jack up*, soulever avec un cric.

jackal ['dʒækɔ:l], *n.* chacal, *m.*

jackanapes ['dʒækəneips], *n.* singe; fat, *m.*

jackass ['dʒækæs], *n.* âne, baudet, bourriquet; (*fig.*) idiot, *m.*

jackdaw ['dʒækdɔ:], *n.* choucas, *m.*

jacket ['dʒækit], *n.* veste, *f.*, veston, *m.*; (*Tech.*) chemise, enveloppe, jaquette, *f.*

jack-in-the-box ['dʒækinðəbɔks], *n.* boîte à surprise, *f.*

jack-tar ['dʒæk'tɑ:], *n.* marin, *m.*

jade (1) [dʒeid], *n.* rosse; haridelle; (*fig.*) coquine (*femme*), *f.*—*v.t.* surmener, harasser, éreinter.

jade (2) [dʒeid], *n.* (*Min.*) jade, *m.*

jaded ['dʒeidid], *a.* surmené, éreinté.

jagged ['dʒægid], **jaggy** ['dʒægi], *a.* dentelé, ébréché.

jaguar ['dʒægjuə], *n.* jaguar, *m.*

jail [dʒeil], *n.* prison, geôle, *f.*

jailer ['dʒeilə], *n.* geôlier, *m.*

jam [dʒæm], *n.* confitures, *f.pl.*; encombrement, embouteillage (*de circulation*), *m.*—*v.t.* serrer, presser, bloquer; (*Rad.*) brouiller.—*v.i.* se coincer.

jamming ['dʒæmiŋ], *n.* coincement; (*Rad.*) brouillage, *m.*

Jamaica [dʒə'meikə], la Jamaïque, *f.*

Jamaican [dʒə'meikən], *a.* jamaïquain.—*n.* Jamaïquain (*personne*), *m.*

James [dʒeimz]. Jacques, *m.*

Jane [dʒein]. Jeanne, *f.*

jangle ['dʒæŋgl], *v.t.* choquer avec bruit; (*fig.*) agacer (*nerfs*).—*v.i.* faire un bruit de ferraille.

janitor ['dʒænitə], *n.* portier, concierge, *m.*

January ['dʒænjuəri]. janvier, *m.*

Japan [dʒə'pæn]. le Japon, *m.*

japan [dʒə'pæn], *n.* laque, vernis, *m.*—*v.* laquer; vernir.

Japanese [dʒæpə'ni:z], *a.* japonais.—*n.* japonais (*langue*); Japonais (*personne*), *m.*

jar (1) [dʒɑ:], *v.t.* remuer, secouer; ébranler.—*v.i.* être discordant (*instrument de musique*); heurter, s'entrechoquer (*être en conflit*); jurer (*couleurs*); (*fig.*) se disputer.—*n.* son discordant, choc, *m.*; querelle, *f.*

jar (2) [dʒɑ:], *n.* jarre, cruche (*faience*), *f.*, bocal (*verre*), *m.*

jargon ['dʒɑ:gən], *n.* jargon, *m.*

jarring ['dʒɑ:riŋ], *a.* discordant; en conflit.—*n.* son discordant, *m.*; querelles, *f.pl.*

jasmine ['dʒæzmin], *n.* jasmin, *m.*

jasper ['dʒæspə], *n.* jaspe, *m.*

jaundice ['dʒɔ:ndis], *n.* jaunisse, *f.*

jaundiced ['dʒɔ:ndist], *a.* qui a la jaunisse; (*fig.*) prévenu (*contre*).

jaunt [dʒɔ:nt], *n.* petite promenade *ou* excursion, *f.*—*v.i.* faire une petite promenade *ou* excursion.

jauntily ['dʒɔ:ntili], *adv.* avec insouciance, légèrement.

jauntiness ['dʒɔ:ntinis], *n.* légèreté, *f.*, enjouement, *m.*

jaunty ['dʒɔ:nti], *a.* léger, enjoué, sémillant.

javelin ['dʒævəlin], *n.* javeline, *f.*, javelot, *m.*

jaw [dʒɔ:], *n.* mâchoire, *f.*; (*fig.*, *pl.*) portes, *f.pl.*; bras, *m.pl.*, étreintes, *f.pl.*

jawbone ['dʒɔ:boun], *n.* mâchoire, *f.*

jay [dʒei], *n.* geai, *m.*

jay-walker ['dʒeiwɔ:kə], *n.* piéton distrait, *m.*

jazz [dʒæz], *n.* jazz, *m.*

jealous ['dʒeləs], *a.* jaloux.

jealously ['dʒeləsli], *adv.* jalousement; par jalousie.

jealousy ['dʒeləsi], *n.* jalousie, *f.*

jean [dʒi:n], *n.* coutil, treillis; (*pl.*) pantalon (de coutil), *m.*

jeep [dʒi:p], *n.* jeep, *f.*

jeer [dʒiə], *n.* raillerie, moquerie, *f.*—*v.t.* railler, huer, se moquer de.—*v.i.* railler, se moquer, goguenarder.

jeering ['dʒiəriŋ], *a.* railleur, moqueur, goguenard.—*n.* raillerie, moquerie, *f.*

jeeringly ['dʒiəriŋli], *adv.* en raillant, d'un ton moqueur.

jelly ['dʒeli], *n.* gelée, *f.*

jelly-fish ['dʒelifiʃ], *n.* méduse, *f.*

jennet ['dʒenit], *n.* genet (*d'Espagne*), *m.*

jeopardize ['dʒepədaiz], *v.t.* hasarder, risquer, mettre en danger.

jeopardy ['dʒepədi], *n.* danger, hasard, *m.*

jerk [dʒə:k], *n.* saccade, secousse, *f.*—*v.t.* donner une poussée à; jeter.

jerkily ['dʒə:kili], *adv.* par saccades.

jerkin ['dʒə:kin], *n.* pourpoint; paletot (de cuir), *m.*

jerky ['dʒə:ki], *a.* saccadé; irrégulier.

jersey ['dʒə:zi], *n.* vareuse de laine, *f.*, maillot, tricot, *m.*

jest [dʒest], *n.* plaisanterie, facétie, *f.*, bon mot, *m.*; risée (*objet de rire*), *f.*—*v.i.* plaisanter (*de ou avec*), badiner (*sur*).

jester ['dʒestə], *n.* plaisant, railleur; bouffon, fou, *m.*

jesting ['dʒestiŋ], *a.* pour rire, badin.—*n.* raillerie, plaisanterie, *f.*, badinage, *m.*

jestingly ['dʒestiŋli], *adv.* en plaisantant, pour rire.

Jesuit ['dʒezjuit], *n.* Jésuite, *m.*

Jesus ['dʒiːzəs]. Jésus, *m.*

jet [dʒet], *n.* jet, jet d'eau; (*Min.*) jais, *m.*; **jet engine**, turbo-réacteur, *m.*; **jet plane**, avion à réaction, *m.*—*v.i.* s'élancer; gicler.

jet-black ['dʒet'blæk], *a.* noir comme du jais.

jetsam ['dʒetsəm], *n.* marchandise jetée à la mer, *f.*, épaves, *f.pl.*

jettison ['dʒetisən], *n.* jet à la mer, *m.*—*v.t.* jeter par-dessus bord.

jetty ['dʒeti], *n.* jetée, *f.*

Jew [dʒuː], *n.* Juif, *m.*

jewel ['dʒuːəl], *n.* joyau, bijou, *m.*, pierre précieuse, *f.*, (*pl.*) pierreries, *f.pl.*; rubis (*de montre*), *m.pl.*—*v.t.* orner de bijoux.

jeweler ['dʒuːələ], *n.* joaillier, bijoutier, *m.*

jewelry ['dʒuːəlri], *n.* joaillerie, bijouterie, *f.*

Jewess ['dʒuːis], *n.* Juive, *f.*

Jewish ['dʒuːiʃ], *a.* juif, des Juifs.

Jewry ['dʒuːri], *n.* Juiverie, *f.*

jib [dʒib], *n.* (*Naut.*) foc, *m.*—*v.i.* reculer; regimber.

jiffy ['dʒifi], *n.* **in a jiffy**, en un clin d'œil.

jig [dʒig], *n.* gigue (*danse*), *f.*, gabarit, *m.*—*v.i.* danser la gigue.

jilt [dʒilt], *n.* coquette, *f.*—*v.t.* planter là; abandonner, (*fam.*) plaquer (*un amoureux*).

jingle ['dʒiŋgl], *n.* tintement (*de cloches*); cliquetis (*de verres, métaux etc.*), *m.*—*v.t.* faire tinter, faire cliqueter.—*v.i.* tinter (*grelots etc.*); s'entrechoquer (*verres etc.*).

jingo ['dʒiŋgou], *n.* chauvin, *m.*; **by jingo!** par exemple!

jingoism ['dʒiŋgouizm], *n.* chauvinisme, *m.*

jinx [dʒiŋks], *n.* porte-guigne, *m.*

Joan [dʒoun]. Jeanne, *f.*; **Joan of Arc**, Jeanne d'Arc.

job [dʒɔb], *n.* travail, ouvrage, *m.*; tâche, pièce; besogne, affaire, *f.*; emploi, *m.*; **job lot**, solde, *m.*, occasion, *f.*; **that's just the job**, cela fait juste l'affaire.—*v.t.* louer; tripoter.—*v.i.* travailler à la tâche; (*Comm.*) agioter, spéculer.

jobber ['dʒɔbə], *n.* ouvrier à la tâche; (*Comm.*) agioteur, coulissier; exploiteur, *m.*

jobbing ['dʒɔbiŋ], *a.* **jobbing gardener**, jardinier à la journée, *m.*—*n.* ouvrage à la tâche; (*Comm.*) agiotage; tripotage, *m.*

jockey ['dʒɔki], *n.* jockey, *m.*

jocose [dʒo'kous], *a.* plaisant, jovial.

jocular ['dʒɔkjulə], *a.* plaisant, facétieux.

jocularly ['dʒɔkjuləli], *adv.* facétieusement.

jocund ['dʒɔkənd], *a.* joyeux, enjoué, gai.

jog [dʒɔg], *v.t.* pousser d'un coup de coude; secouer, cahoter; (*fig.*) rafraîchir (*la mémoire*).—*v.i.* se mouvoir; marcher lentement; **to jog along**, aller doucement.—*n.* secousse légère, *f.*, cahot; coup de coude, *m.*; **jog trot**, petit trot, *m.*

John [dʒɔn]. Jean, *m.*; **Johnnie**, (*colloq.*) Jeannot, *m.*

join [dʒɔin], *v.t.* joindre, unir; associer (à); rejoindre (*rattraper*); relier (*rues etc.*); **will you join us?** voulez-vous être des nôtres?—*v.i.* se joindre, s'unir; s'inscrire; s'associer; prendre part (à).

joiner ['dʒɔinə], *n.* menuisier, *m.*

joinery ['dʒɔinəri], *n.* menuiserie, *f.*

joint [dʒɔint], *a.* commun, ensemble, réuni.—*n.* jointure, *f.*, joint, *m.*; pièce, *f.*; rôti (*de viande*), *m.*; phalange (*du doigt*); charnière (*de porte*); soudure, (*Anat.*) articulation, *f.*; (*Bot.*) nœud, *m.*; (*slang*) boîte, *f.*; **out of**

joint, disloqué, (*fig.*) dérangé; **to put one's arm out of joint**, se démettre le bras.—*v.t.* couper aux jointures; joindre.

jointed ['dʒɔintid], *a.* articulé, jointé; séparé.

jointly ['dʒɔintli], *adv.* conjointement.

joint stock ['dʒɔintstɔk], *n.* capital, fonds commun, *m.*; **joint-stock bank**, banque par actions, *f.*; **joint-stock company**, société anonyme, *f.*

joist [dʒɔist], *n.* solive, poutre, poutrelle, *f.*

joke [dʒouk], *n.* bon mot, mot pour rire, *m.*, plaisanterie, (*fam.*) blague, *f.*; **a practical joke**, une farce, un mauvais tour; **to crack a joke**, dire un bon mot.—*v.t.* plaisanter sur, railler de.—*v.i.* plaisanter, badiner; rire de.

joker ['dʒoukə], *n.* plaisant, farceur; (*Cards*) joker, *m.*

joking ['dʒoukiŋ], *n.* plaisanterie, farce, *f.*

jokingly ['dʒoukinli], *adv.* en plaisantant, pour rire.

jollification [dʒɔlifi'keiʃən], *n.* partie de plaisir, *f.*

jollity ['dʒɔliti], *n.* joie, gaieté, *f.*

jolly ['dʒɔli], *a.* gai, joyeux, gaillard, réjoui.

jolt [dʒoult], *n.* cahot, choc, *m.*—*v.t.* cahoter.—*v.i.* faire des cahots.

Jonah ['dʒounə]. Jonas, *m.*—*n.* porte-malheur, *m.*

jonquil ['dʒɔŋkwil], *n.* (*Bot.*) jonquille, *f.*

Jordan ['dʒɔːdən]. le Jourdain (*rivière*), *m.*; la Jordanie (*pays*), *f.*

Jordanian [dʒɔː'deiniən], *a.* jordanien.—*n.* Jordanien (*personne*), *m.*

jostle [dʒɔsl], *v.t.* pousser, bousculer; (*Spt.*) gêner (*un concurrent*).—*v.i.* jouer des coudes.

jot [dʒɔt], *n.* iota, brin, *m.*—*v.t.* **to jot down**, noter, prendre note de.

journal ['dʒəːnəl], *n.* journal, *m.*; revue, *f.*

journalism ['dʒəːnəlizm], *n.* journalisme, *m.*

journalist ['dʒəːnəlist], *n.* journaliste, *m.*, *f.*

journey ['dʒəːni], *n.* voyage; trajet (*distance*), *m.*; **a pleasant journey to you!** bon voyage! **on the journey**, en route; **to go on a journey**, faire un voyage.—*v.i.* voyager.

journeyman ['dʒəːnimən], *n.* (*pl.* **-men** [men]) garçon, ouvrier, *m.*

joust [dʒaust], [dʒuːst], *n.* joute, *f.*—*v.t.* jouter.

Jove [dʒouv]. Jupiter, *m.*; **by Jove!** bigre! mâtin!

jovial ['dʒouviəl], *a.* joyeux, gai.

joviality [dʒouvi'æliti], *n.* humeur joviale, jovialité, *f.*

jowl [dʒaul], *n.* joue; hure (*de saumon*), *f.*; **cheek by jowl**, côte à côte.

joy [dʒɔi], *n.* joie, *f.*; **to wish someone joy**, féliciter quelqu'un.—*v.i.* se réjouir (*de* ou *avec*).

joyful ['dʒɔiful], *a.* joyeux.

joyfully ['dʒɔifuli], *adv.* joyeusement.

joyfulness ['dʒɔifulnis], *n.* allégresse, joie, *f.*

joyous ['dʒɔiəs], *a.* joyeux.

jubilant ['dʒuːbilənt], *a.* réjoui; jubilant.

jubilation [dʒuːbi'leiʃən], *n.* réjouissances de triomphe, *f.pl.*, jubilation, *f.*

jubilee ['dʒuːbiliː], *n.* jubilé, *m.*

Judaea [dʒuː'diə]. la Judée, *f.*

Judaism ['dʒuːdeiizm], *n.* judaïsme, *m.*

465

judge [dʒʌdʒ], n. juge; (fig.) connaisseur, m.; *to be a judge of*, se connaître à ou en.— v.t. juger; discerner, considérer.

judgment ['dʒʌdʒmənt], n. jugement; arrêt, m., sentence, f.; (fig.) avis, sens, m., opinion, f.

judicature ['dʒuːdikətʃə], n. judicature, justice; cour de justice, f.

judicial [dʒuː'diʃl], a. judiciaire, juridique.

judicious [dʒuː'diʃəs], a. judicieux, prudent.

judiciously [dʒuː'diʃəsli], adv. judicieusement.

judo ['dʒuːdou], n. jiu-jitsu, (fam.) judo, m.

jug [dʒʌg], n. broc, m.; cruche, f.; *water jug*, pot à eau, m.—v.t. faire un civet de (lièvre); *jugged hare*, civet de lièvre, m.

juggle [dʒʌgl], v.t. jouer, duper, escamoter.— v.i. faire des tours de passe-passe; (fig.) escamoter.—n. jonglerie, f.; escamotage, tour de passe-passe, m.

juggler ['dʒʌglə], n. jongleur; escamoteur; (fig.) charlatan, m.

juggling ['dʒʌgliŋ], n. jonglerie, f., escamotage, m.

jugular ['dʒʌgjulə], a. and n. jugulaire, f.

juice [dʒuːs], n. jus; suc, m.

juicy ['dʒuːsi], a. juteux; succulent.

ju-jitsu [dʒuː'dʒitsu], n. jiu-jitsu, m.

jukebox ['dʒuːkbɔks], n. phonographe à sous, jukebox, m.

Julian ['dʒuːliən]. Julien, m.

Juliet ['dʒuːliət]. Juliette, f.

July [dʒuː'lai]. juillet, m.

jumble [dʒʌmbl], v.t. jeter pêle-mêle, mêler ensemble, confondre.—n. pêle-mêle, méli-mélo, m., confusion, f.; *jumble sale*, vente de charité, f.

jump [dʒʌmp], n. saut, bond; sursaut; obstacle (à sauter), m.; *high jump*, saut en hauteur; *broad jump*, saut en longueur.— v.t sauter, franchir d'un bond; sauter de; faire sauter; (fam.) *to jump the queue*, resquiller (dans une queue).—v.i. sauter; se jeter, se précipiter (sur); *to jump at*, accepter avec empressement.

jumper (1) ['dʒʌmpə], n. sauteur, m.

jumper (2) ['dʒʌmpə], n. chandail, jersey, jumper, m.

jumpy ['dʒʌmpi], a. nerveux.

junction ['dʒʌŋkʃən], n. jonction, f.; (Rail.) embranchement, m.

juncture ['dʒʌŋktʃə], n. jointure, f.; moment critique, m.

June [dʒuːn]. juin, m.

jungle [dʒʌŋgl], n. jungle, f.; fourré, m.

junior ['dʒuːniə], a. jeune, cadet.—n. cadet, inférieur en âge, m.

juniper ['dʒuːnipə], n. genièvre, m.

junk (1) [dʒʌŋk], n. jonque (navire), f.

junk (2) [dʒʌŋk], n. objets de rebut, m.pl.

junket ['dʒʌŋkit], n. lait caillé, m.; jonchée (fromage), talmouse (gâteau), f.—v.t. régaler. —v.i. se régaler.

jurisdiction [dʒuəris'dikʃən], n. juridiction, f.

jurisprudence [dʒuəris'pruːdəns], n. jurisprudence, f.

jurist ['dʒuərist], n. juriste, m., f.

juror ['dʒuərə], n. juré, m.

jury ['dʒuəri], n. jury, m.

juryman ['dʒuərimən], n. (pl. -men [men]) juré, m.

just [dʒʌst], a. juste, équitable.—adv. juste, justement, précisément; tout, tout juste, seulement, un peu; *he has just gone out*, il vient de sortir; *just now*, à l'instant, tout à l'heure; *just so*, précisément.

justice ['dʒʌstis], n. justice, f.; juge (magistrat), m.; *Justice of the Peace*, juge de paix; *to do justice to*, (fig.) faire honneur à (un repas etc.).

justifiable [dʒʌsti'faiəbl], a. justifiable, légitime.

justification [dʒʌstifi'keiʃən], n. justification, f.

justify ['dʒʌstifai], v.t. justifier, autoriser, permettre; *to feel justified in*, se croire autorisé à, croire devoir.

justly ['dʒʌstli], adv. exactement, justement; à bon droit.

jut [dʒʌt], v.i. avancer, faire saillie.

jute [dʒuːt], n. jute, m.

jutting ['dʒʌtiŋ], a. en saillie, saillant.

juvenile ['dʒuːvənail], a. jeune; juvénile, de jeunesse; *juvenile delinquant*, jeune délinquant, m.—n. jeune, m., f.; adolescent, m.

juxtaposition [dʒʌkstəpə'ziʃən], n. juxtaposition, f.; *in juxtaposition*, juxtaposé.

K

K, k [kei]. onzième lettre de l'alphabet, m.

kale, kail [keil], n. (Sc.) chou, m.; *sea kale*, chou marin.

kaleidoscope [kə'laidəskoup], n. kaléidoscope, m.

kangaroo [kæŋgə'ruː], n. kangourou, m.

Katharine, Katherine ['kæθərin]. Catherine, f.

keel [kiːl], n. quille; carène, f.

keen [kiːn], a. affilé, aigu, aiguisé; (fig.) vif, ardent; amer, mordant (acerbe); pénétrant, perçant (brisant la surface de); dévorant (appétit).

keenly ['kiːnli], adv. vivement, ardemment, âprement.

keenness ['kiːnnis], n. finesse (de tranchant); (fig.) subtilité; vivacité, ardeur, f., empressement; mordant (de troupes), m., âpreté (du froid), f.

keep [kiːp], v.t. irr. tenir, retenir, garder; maintenir, conserver (ne pas perdre); avoir (volaille etc.); entretenir (subvenir aux besoins de); nourrir (avoir en pension); avoir à son service; (fig.) observer; célébrer, fêter; garantir, protéger; remplir; continuer; *keep it up!* continuez! *to keep away*, éloigner, tenir éloigné; *to keep back*, retenir, garder, tenir en réserve; retarder; *to keep from*, préserver de, empêcher de; *to keep in*, tenir enfermé, retenir; *to keep on*, continuer; *to keep out*, ne pas admettre, écarter, éloigner; *to keep to*, s'en tenir à; *to keep up*, tenir levé, soutenir; continuer; entretenir.—v.i. se tenir; rester, demeurer (ne pas cesser d'être); se garder, se conserver (*durer*); (*fig.*) se garder, s'abstenir; **to keep away**, se tenir éloigné; **to keep back**, se tenir en arrière; **to keep** (*doing, saying, telling* etc.), ne pas cesser de; **to keep silent**, se taire; **to keep up with**, aller de pair avec.—*n.* donjon, réduit (*forteresse*), *m.*; nourriture, *f.*, entretien (*substance*), *m.*

keeper ['ki:pə], *n.* garde; gardien; surveillant, *m.*

keeping ['ki:piŋ], *n.* garde, surveillance; conservation; (*fig.*) harmonie, *f.*

keepsake ['ki:pseik], *n.* souvenir, *m.*

keg [keg], *n.* caque (*de hareng*), *f.*, petit baril, *m.*

ken [ken], *n.* vue; portée, *f.*

kennel ['kenl], *n.* chenil, *m.*; niche, *f.*

Kenya ['kenjə]. le Kénya, *m.*

kept [kept], *a.* entretenu.—*p.p.* [KEEP].

kerb [kə:b], *n.* bordure (*de trottoir*), margelle (*de puits*), *f.* (*Am.* curb)

kerb-stone ['kə:bstoun], *n.* bordure (*de trottoir*), *f.*, parement, *m.*

*****kerchief** ['kə:tʃif], *n.* fichu, *m.*

kernel [kə:nl], *n.* graine, amande, *f.*, pignon (*de pomme de pin*); noyau (*de drupe*); (*fig.*) fond, essentiel, *m.*

kerosene ['kerosi:n], *n.* kérosène; pétrole lampant, *m.*

kestrel ['kestrəl], *n.* crécerelle, *f.*

ketch [ketʃ], *n.* (*Naut.*) quaiche, *f.*, ketch, *m.*

kettle [ketl], *n.* bouilloire, *f.*; chaudron (*bassine à confitures*), *m.*; **a pretty kettle of fish**, un beau gâchis.

kettledrum ['ketldram], *n.* timbale, *f.*

key [ki:], *n.* clef, clé, *f.*; (*Arith.* etc.) corrigé; (*Mus.*) ton, *m.*; touche (*sur le piano* etc.), *f.*; **under lock and key**, sous clef.

key-board ['ki:bɔ:d], *n.* clavier, *m.*

keyhole ['ki:houl], *n.* trou de la serrure, *m.*

key-note ['ki:nout], *n.* tonique; (*fig.*) idée maîtresse, *f.*

key-stone ['ki:stoun], *n.* clef de voûte, *f.*

khaki ['ka:ki], *n.* kaki, *m.*

khan [ka:n], *n.* kan, khan, *m.*

kick [kik], *n.* coup de pied, recul (*d'un fusil*), *m.*; ruade (*d'animal*), *f.*; (*Ftb.*) **free kick**, coup franc, *m.*—*v.t.* donner un coup de pied à; frapper ou pousser du pied; (*Ftb.*) botter; **to kick out**, chasser à coups de pied; **to kick up a row**, faire du tapage.—*v.i.* donner des coups de pied; ruer, regimber (*animal*); reculer (*fusil*).

kick-off ['kikɔf], *n.* (*Ftb.*) coup d'envoi, *m.*

kid [kid], *a.* de chevreau; **kid gloves**, gants de chevreau, *m.pl.*—*n.* chevreau; (*colloq.*) enfant, gosse, *m.*—*v.t.* (*fam.*) en conter à; **no kidding !** sans blague!

kidnap ['kidnæp], *v.t.* enlever.

kidney ['kidni], *n.* rein; rognon (*d'animal*), *m.*

kidney bean ['kidni'bi:n], *n.* haricot, *m.*

kill [kil], *v.t.* tuer; faire mourir; abattre (*assassiner*).

killer ['kilə], *n.* tueur, *m.*

killing ['kiliŋ], *a.* mortel; assommant (*travail*).—*n.* tuerie, boucherie, *f.*, massacre, *m.*

kiln [kiln], *n.* four, *m.*

kilogram ['kiləgræm], *n* kilogramme, *m.*

kilometer ['kiləmi:tə], *n.* kilomètre, *m.*

kilowatt ['kilowɔt], *n.* kilowatt, *m.*

kin [kin], *n.* parenté, *f.*; parent, allié, *m.*; **next of kin**, le plus proche parent.

kind [kaind], *a.* bon, bienveillant, bienfaisant; obligeant, complaisant (*accommodant*); **my kind regards to him**, faites-lui toutes mes amitiés; **will you be so kind as to**, voulez-vous avoir la bonté de.—*n.* genre, *m.*, sorte, espèce, *f.*; **in kind**, en nature.

kindergarten ['kindəga:tn], *n.* école maternelle, *f.*

kindhearted ['kaind'ha:tid], *a.* bon, bienveillant.

kindle [kindl], *v.t.* allumer, enflammer; (*fig.*) éveiller, exciter.—*v.i.* s'allumer, s'enflammer.

kindliness ['kaindlinis], *n.* bienveillance, bonté, *f.*

kindly ['kaindli], *a.* bon, bienveillant, favorable.—*adv.* avec bienveillance.

kindness ['kaindnis], *n.* bienveillance, bonté, *f.*; bienfait, *m.*

kindred ['kindrid], *a.* de même nature.—*n.* parenté, *f.*; parents, *m.pl.*

kinema ['kinimə], [CINEMA].

king [kiŋ], *n.* roi, *m.*; (*chockers*) dame, *f.*

kingdom ['kiŋdəm], *n.* royaume; (*fig.*) empire; (*Nat. Hist.*) règne, *m.*; **the United Kingdom**, le Royaume-Uni.

kingfisher ['kiŋfiʃə], *n.* (*Orn.*) martin-pêcheur, *m.*

kingly ['kiŋli], *a.* de roi, royal.

kink [kiŋk], *n.* nœud, *f.*; (*colloq.*) point faible, défaut, *m.*

kinsman ['kinzmən], *n.* (*pl.* **-men** [men]) parent, allié, *m.*

kiosk ['ki:ɔsk], *n.* kiosque, *m.*; **telephone kiosk**, cabine téléphonique, *f.*

kirk [kə:k], *n.* église d'Écosse, *f.*

kiss [kis], *n.* baiser, *m.*—*v.t.*, *v.i.* embrasser; **to kiss** (*zach other*), s'embrasser.

kit [kit], *n.* petit équipement, *m.*, effets, *m.pl.*; trousse, *f.*; outils (*d'un ouvrier*), *m.pl.*

kit bag ['kitbæg], *n.* sac, *m.*

kitchen ['kitʃin], *n.* cuisine, *f.*

kitchen garden ['kitʃinga:dn], *n.* jardin potager, *m.*

kitchen utensils ['kitʃinju:tenslz], *n.pl.* batterie de cuisine, *f.*

kite [kait], *n.* milan (*oiseau*); cerf-volant (*jouet*), *m.*

kith [kiθ], *n.* **kith and kin**, parents et amis, *m.pl.*

kitten [kitn], *n.* chaton, petit chat, *m.*

knack [næk], *n.* adresse, *f.*, tour de main, *m.*

knapsack ['næpsæk], *n.* havresac, *m.*

knave [neiv], *n.* fripon, coquin; (*Cards*) valet, *m.*

knavery ['neivəri], *n.* friponnerie, coquinerie, *f.*

knavish ['neiviʃ], *a.* fripon; malin.

knead [ni:d], *v.t.* pétrir.

knee [ni:], *n.* genou, *m.*

knee breeches ['ni:britʃiz], *n.pl.* culotte courte, *f.*

knee-cap ['ni:kæp], *n.* genouillère; (*Anat.*) rotule, *f.*

kneel [ni:l], *v.i. irr.* s'agenouiller.

knell [nel], *n.* glas, *m.*

knickers ['nikəz], *n.* culotte (*de femme*), *f.*

knick-knack ['niknæk], *n.* brimborion, *m.*, babiole, *f.*; colifichet, bibelot, *m.*

knife [naif], *n.* (*pl.* **knives** [naivz]) couteau; (*Tech.*) coupoir; (*Surg.*) scalpel, bistouri, *m.*; **carving knife**, couteau à découper; **pen-knife**, canif, *m.*—*v.t.* poignarder.

knife-grinder ['naifgraində], *n*. rémouleur, *m*.

knight [nait], *n*. chevalier; (*Chess*) cavalier, *m.—v.t.* créer chevalier.

knighthood ['naithud], *n*. chevalerie, *f*.

knightly ['naitli], *a*. chevaleresque, de chevalier.

knit [nit], *v.t.* tricoter; froncer (*les sourcils*); (*fig.*) joindre, attacher, lier.

knitting ['nitiŋ], *n*., tricot, *m*.

knitting needle ['nitiŋni:dl], *n*. aiguille à tricoter, *f*.

knives [KNIFE].

knob [nɔb], *n*. bosse, *f*.; bouton (*de porte*), *m*.

knock [nɔk], *v.t.* frapper, heurter, cogner; *to knock about*, bousculer, malmener; *to knock down*, renverser, assommer; adjuger (*aux enchères*).—*v.i.* to knock about, rouler sa bosse, aller de par le monde; *to knock off*, cesser le travail.—*n.* coup, choc; cognement, *m*.

knocker ['nɔkə], *n*. marteau (*de porte*), *m*.

knocking ['nɔkiŋ], *n*. coups, *m.pl.*

knoll [noul], *n*. monticule, tertre, *m*., butte, *f*.

knot [nɔt], *n*. nœud; groupe (*de personnes etc.*), *m*.; (*fig.*) difficulté, *f*., embarras, *m.—v.t.* nouer; lier; (*fig.*) embrouiller.—*v.i.* faire des nœuds; se nouer.

knotted ['nɔtid], *a*. noueux.

knotty ['nɔti], *a*. noueux; (*fig.*) dur (*difficile*); embrouillé, compliqué.

know [nou], *v.t.* irr. savoir, apprendre (*to learn*); connaître (*to be acquainted with*); reconnaître (*to recognize*); *to know by heart*, savoir par cœur; *to know by sight*, connaître de vue; *to know someone*, connaître quelqu'un; *to know something*, savoir quelque chose.—*n.* to be in the know, être dans le secret.

know-how ['nouhau], *n*. savoir-faire, *m*.

knowing ['nouiŋ], *a*. intelligent, instruit; fin, malin.

knowingly ['nouiŋli], *adv*. sciemment; avec ruse.

knowledge ['nɔlidʒ], *n*. connaissance, science, *f*.; savoir, *m*.; not to my knowledge, pas que je sache; *without my knowledge*, à mon insu.

knowledgeable ['nɔlidʒəbl], *a*. bien informé.

knuckle [nʌkl], *n*. jointure, articulation du doigt, *f*.; jarret (*de viande*), *m.—v.i.* to knuckle under, se soumettre, mettre les pouces.

knuckle-bone ['nʌklboun], *n*. osselet, *m*.

Korea [kə'ri:ə]. la Corée, *f*.

Korean [kə'ri:ən], *a*. coréen.—*n*. coréen (*langue*); Coréen (*personne*), *m*.

Kuwait [ku'weit]. le Koweit, *m*.

label [leibl], *n*. étiquette, *f*.; (*Ind.*) label, *m.— v.t.* étiqueter; (*fig.*) désigner sous le nom de.

labor ['leibə], *n*. travail, labeur, *m*., peine, *f*.; ouvrage (*piece of work*); travail d'enfant (*accouchement*), *m*.; *hard labor*, travaux forcés, *m.pl.*; *manual labor*, main-d'œuvre, *f*.; *the Labor Party*, le parti travailliste.—*v.t.* travailler; (*fig.*) élaborer.— *v.i.* travailler; souffrir, peiner; chercher (*à*), s'efforcer (*de*); *to labor under a delusion*, être dans l'erreur.

laboratory [lə'bɔrətəri, 'læbrətəri], *n*. laboratoire, *m*.

laborer ['leibərə], *n*. manœuvre, homme de peine, *m*.

labor-exchange ['leibəriks'tʃeindʒ], *n*. bureau de placement (*municipal ou d'état*), *m*.

laborious [lə'bɔːriəs], *a*. laborieux, pénible.

laboriously [lə'bɔːriəsli], *adv*. laborieusement, péniblement.

labor-saving ['leibəseiviŋ], *a*. *labor-saving device*, économiseur de travail, *m*.

Labrador ['læbrədɔ:]. le Labrador, *m*.

labrador ['læbrədɔ:], *n*. chien de Labrador, *m*.

laburnum [lə'bəːnəm], *n*. faux ébénier; cytise, *m*.

labyrinth ['læbirinθ], *n*. labyrinthe, *m*.

lace [leis], *n*. dentelle, *f*., point, galon; lacet (*cordon*); ruban (*bande*), *m*.; *shoelace*, lacet de bottine.—*v.t.* lacer (*ses souliers*); garnir de dentelle, galonner (*orner de dentelle*); (*fig.*) orner.

lacerate ['læsəreit], *v.t.* déchirer, lacérer.

laceration [læsə'reiʃən], *n*. déchirure, lacération, *f*.

lachrymose ['lækrimous], *a*. larmoyant.

lacing ['leisiŋ], *n*. lacement, *m*.

lack [læk], *n*. manque, besoin, défaut, *m*.; *for lack of*, faute de.—*v.t.* manquer de.— *v.i.* manquer.

lackey ['læki], *n*. laquais, *m*.

lacking ['lækiŋ], *a*. manquant (*de*), dépourvu (*de*).

laconic [lə'kɔnik], *a*. laconique.

lacquer ['lækə], *n*. laque, *m.*

lad [læd], *n*. garçon, jeune homme; gaillard, *m*.

ladder ['lædə], *n*. échelle, *f*.; démaillage (*d'un bas*) *m*.; *ladder-proof*, indémaillable (*bas*). —*v.t.* démailler (*un bas*).

lade [kid], *v.t.* (*Naut.*) charger.

laden ['leidn], *a*. chargé.

lading ['leidiŋ], *n*. chargement, *m*.; *bill of lading*, connaissement, *m*.

ladle ['leidl], *n*. louche, cuiller à pot, *f*.

lady ['leidi], *n*. (*pl.* ladies ['leidiz]) dame, *f*.; *young lady*, demoiselle, *f*.

lady-bird ['leidibə:d], *n*. coccinelle, bête à bon Dieu, *f*.

lady-killer ['leidikilə], *n*. bourreau des cœurs, *m*.

lady-like ['leidilaik], *a*. de dame, comme il faut, qui a l'air distingué.

lag [læg], *v.i.* se traîner; traîner (*choses*).—*n*. retard, *m*.

laggard ['lægəd], *n*. traînard, lambin, *m*.

lager ['lɑːgə], *n*. bière blonde (*allemande*), *f*.

lagoon [lə'guːn], *n*. lagune, *f*.

lair [lɛə], *n*. repaire, antre, *m*.

laird [lɛəd], *n*. (*Sc.*) propriétaire, châtelain, *m*.

laity ['leiiti], *n*. laïques, *m.pl.*

L

L, l [el]. douzième lettre de l'alphabet, *m*.

la [lɑ:], *n*. (*Mus.*) la, *m*.

lab [læb], *n*. (*fam.*) labo, *m*.

lake [leik], *n.* lac, *m.*; laque (*couleur*), *f.*

lamb [læm], *n.* agneau, *m.*—*v.i.* agneler.

lambkin ['læmkin], *n.* agnelet, petit agneau, *m.*

lame [leim], *a.* boiteux, estropié (*infirme*); (*fig.*) défectueux, imparfait; *a lame excuse*, une piètre excuse; *a lame man*, un boiteux.—*v.t.* estropier.

lamely ['leimli], *adv.* en boitant; (*fig.*) imparfaitement, mal.

lameness ['leimnis], *n.* claudication, *f.*; clochement, boitement, *m.*; (*fig.*) faiblesse (*d'une excuse*), *f.*

lament [lə'ment], *v.t.* se lamenter sur, pleurer, s'affliger de.—*v.i.* se lamenter, pleurer.—*n.* lamentation, complainte, plainte, *f.*

lamentable ['læməntəbl], *a.* lamentable, pitoyable.

lamentation [læmən'teiʃən], *n.* lamentation, plainte, jérémiade, *f.*

lamented [lə'mentid], *a.* regretté (*feu*).

lamp [læmp], *n.* lampe; lanterne (*carrosse etc.*); (*fig.*) lumière, *f.*; *street lamp*, réverbère, *m.*

lampoon [læm'pu:n], *n.* satire, *f.*, libelle, *m.*

lamp-post ['læmppoust], *n.* lampadaire, *m.*

lamp shade ['læmpʃeid], *n.* abat-jour, *m.*

lance [lɑ:ns], *n.* lance, *f.*—*v.t.* percer d'un coup de lance; (*Surg.*) donner un coup de lancette à, percer.

lance corporal ['lɑ:ns'kɔ:pərəl], *n.* soldat de première classe, *m.*

lancer ['lɑ:nsə], *n.* lancier, *m.*

lancet ['lɑ:nsit], *n.* lancette, *f.*; (*Arch.*) ogive, *f.*

land [lænd], *n.* terre, *f.*; pays (*territoire*); (*Law*) bien-fonds, *m.*; *Holy Land*, la Terre Sainte.—*v.t.* mettre à terre, prendre (*poisson*); débarquer.—*v.i.* débarquer (*à* ou *sur*), aborder; (*fig.*) arriver; (*Av.*) atterrir.

landed ['lændid], *a.* foncier; territorial.

landing ['lændiŋ], *n.* palier (*d'escalier*); (*Naut.*) débarquement; (*Av.*) atterrissage, *m.*

landing ground ['lændiŋgraund], *n.* terrain d'atterrissage, *m.*

landing stage ['lændiŋsteidʒ], *n.* débarcadère, *m.*

landing strip ['lændiŋstrip], *n.* piste d'atterrissage, *f.*

landlady ['lændleidi], *n.* propriétaire (*d'une maison*), logeuse (*d'un meuble*); aubergiste, hôtesse (*d'une auberge*), *f.*

landlord ['lændlɔ:d], *n.* propriétaire; hôte, hôtelier, aubergiste (*d'une auberge*), *m.*

landlubber ['lændlʌbə], *n.* marin d'eau douce, *m.*

landmark ['lændmɑ:k], *n.* borne, limite, *f.*; point de repère, *m.*

landowner ['lændounə], *n.* propriétaire foncier, *m.*

landscape ['lændskeip], *n.* paysage, *m.*; vue, *f.*

landscape garden ['lændskeip'gɑ:dən], *n.* jardin paysager, *m.*

land tax ['lændtæks], *n.* impôt foncier, *m.*

lane [lein], *n.* ruelle, *f.*, passage, *m.*; voie (*d'autoroute*), *f.*; chemin vicinal (*de campagne*), *m.*

language ['læŋgwidʒ], *n.* langage, *m.*, langue, expression, *f.*; *modern languages*, langues vivantes, *f.pl.*

languid ['læŋgwid], *a.* languissant.

languish ['læŋgwiʃ], *v.i.* languir.

languishing ['læŋgwiʃiŋ], *a.* languissant, langoureux.

languor ['læŋgə], *n.* langueur, *f.*

laniard [LANYARD].

lank [læŋk], *a.* efflanqué; maigre; décharné; fluet, grêle.

lanky ['læŋki], *a.* grand et maigre; *lanky fellow*, grand flandrin, *m.*

lantern ['læntən], *n.* lanterne, *f.*; (*Mil.*) falot; (*Naut.*) fanal, phare, *m.*; *Chinese lantern*, lanterne vénitienne; *dark lantern*, lanterne sourde; *lantern jaws*, joues creuses, *f.pl.*

lanyard ['lænjəd], *n.* (*Naut.*) ride, *f.*; (*Artill.*) (*cordon*) tire-feu, *m.*

Laos [laus], le Laos, *m.*

Laotian [lau'ʃən], *a.* laotien.—*n.* laotien (*langue*); Laotien (*personne*), *m.*

lap (1) [læp], *n.* pan (*de manteau etc.*); giron, *m.*; (*fig.*) genoux, *m.pl.*; sein; (*Racing*) tour de piste, *m.*; *in the lap of*, au sein de.—*v.i.* se replier.

lap (2) [læp], *v.t.* (*Racing*) prendre un tour (*à*).

lap (3) [læp], *v.t.* laper (*boire*).—*v.i.* laper; clapoter (*vagues*).

lap dog ['læpdɔg], *n.* bichon, petit chien, *m.*

lapel [lə'pel], *n.* revers (*d'habit*), *m.*

lapidary ['læpidəri], *a.* and *n.* lapidaire, *m.*—*v.t.* lapider.

lapidation [læpi'deiʃən], *n.* lapidation, *f.*

Lapland ['læplænd], la Laponie, *f.*

Laplander ['læpləndə], *n.* Lapon, *m.*

Lapp [læp], *a.* lapon.—*n.* lapon (*langue*); Lapon (*personne*), *m.*

lapse [læps], *n.* cours, laps (*temps*), *m.*; faute, erreur, *f.*; manquement, écart, manque (*divergence*), *m.*—*v.i.* s'écouler; tomber, faillir, manquer (*à*).

lapsed [læpst], *a.* périmé; caduc (*contrat, testament*).

lapwing ['læpwiŋ], *n.* vanneau, *m.*

larceny ['lɑ:səni], *n.* larcin, vol, *m.*

larch [lɑ:tʃ], *n.* (*Bot.*) mélèze, *m.*

lard [lɑ:d], *n.* saindoux, *m.*—*v.t.* larder (*de*).

larder ['lɑ:də], *n.* garde-manger, *m.*

large [lɑ:dʒ], *a.* grand, gros; étendu, considérable; fort; *as large as life*, grandeur nature; *at large*, en liberté, libre; en général.

largely ['lɑ:dʒli], *adv.* amplement, largement; au long, en grande partie.

largeness ['lɑ:dʒnis], *n.* grandeur, étendue, ampleur, *f.*

largess(e) ['lɑ:dʒes], *n.* largesse, libéralité, *f.*

lark [lɑ:k], *n.* alouette; (*fig.*) escapade, *f.*

larkspur ['lɑ:kspə:], *n.* pied-d'alouette, *m.*

larva ['lɑ:və], *n.* (*pl.* **larvae** ['lɑ:vi:]) larve, *f.*

laryngitis [lærin'dʒaitis], *n.* laryngite, *f.*

larynx ['læriŋks], *n.* (*pl.* **larynges** [læ'rindʒiz]) larynx, *m.*

lascar ['læskə], *n.* matelot indien, *m.*

lascivious [lə'siviəs], *a.* lascif.

lash [læʃ], *n.* coup de fouet; (*fig.*) coup, trait, *m.*; *eyelash* [EYE].—*v.t.* cingler, fouetter; châtier; lier, attacher (*to tie*).

lashing ['læʃiŋ], *a.* cinglant, fouettant.—*n.* coups de fouet, *m.pl.*; (*Naut.*) ligne d'amarrage, *f.*

lass [læs], *n.* (*Sc.*) jeune fille, *f.*

lassitude ['læsitju:d], *n.* lassitude, *f.*

last (1) [lɑːst], *a.* dernier, passé; *last but one*, avant-dernier; *last night*, hier soir; *last week*, la semaine dernière; *the last time*, la dernière fois; *this day last week*, il y a aujourd'hui huit jours.—*n.* bout, *m.*, fin, *f.*; *at last*, à la fin, enfin; *to the last*, jusqu'au bout, jusqu'à la fin.— *v.i.* durer.

last (2) [lɑːst], *n.* forme (*pour chaussures*), *f.*

lasting ['lɑːstiŋ], *a.* durable, permanent.

lastly ['lɑːstli], *adv.* en dernier lieu, enfin.

latch [lætʃ], *n.* loquet, *m.*—*v.t.* fermer au loquet.

latchkey ['lætʃkiː], *n.* passe-partout, *m.*, clef de la maison, *f.*

late [leit], *a.* tard; en retard; tardif (*fruits, légumes etc.*); avancé (*heure*); ancien, ex- (*autrefois*); feu (*décédé*); récent, dernier (*depuis peu*); *the late king*, feu le roi; *to be late*, être en retard.—*adv.* tard; sur la fin; récemment, depuis peu; *at latest*, au plus tard; *better late than never*, mieux vaut tard que jamais; *of late*, récemment, enfin; *to be getting late*, (*impers.*) se faire tard.

lately ['leitli], *adv.* dernièrement, récemment.

lateness ['leitnis], *n.* retard, *m.*; heure avancée, *f.*, temps avancé, *m.*; tardiveté, *f.*

latent ['leitənt], *a.* caché, secret, latent.

later ['leitə], *a.* postérieur, ultérieur.—*adv.* plus tard.

lateral ['lætərəl], *a.* de côté, latéral.

latest ['leitist], *a.* dernier; *at the latest*, au plus tard.

lath [lɑːθ], *n.* latte, *f.*

lathe [leið], *n.* tour, *m.*

lather ['læðə, lɑːðə], *n.* mousse, (*fig.*) écume, *f.*—*v.t.* savonner; (*colloq.*) rosser.

Latin ['lætin], *a.* latin.—*n.* latin (*langue*), *m.*

Latin-American ['lætinamerikən], *a.* latino-américain.—*n.* Latino-Américain (*personne*), *m.*

latish ['leitiʃ], *a.* un peu tard, un peu en retard.—*adv.* un peu tard.

latitude ['lætitjuːd], *n.* latitude; étendue (*breadth*), *f.*

latter ['lætə], *a.* dernier; moderne, récent; *the latter*, ce dernier, celui-ci, *m.*

lattice ['lætis], *n.* treillis, treillage, *m.*

Latvia ['lætviə]. la Lettonie, *f.*

Latvian ['lætviən], *a.* lette, letton.—*n.* lette, letton (*langue*), *m.*; Lette, *m.*, *f.*, Letton (*personne*), *m.*

laud [lɔːd], *v.t.* louer, célébrer.

laudable ['lɔːdəbl], *a.* louable, digne de louanges.

laugh [lɑːf], *n.* rire, *m.*, risée (*moquerie*), *f.*; *loud laugh*, gros rire, éclat de rire, *m.*— *v.i.* rire; *to burst out laughing*, éclater de rire; *to laugh at*, se moquer de.

laughable ['lɑːfəbl], *a.* risible.

laughing ['lɑːfiŋ], *a.* rieur, enjoué; *it is no laughing matter*, il n'y a pas de quoi rire.

laughing-stock ['lɑːfiŋstɔk], *n.* risée, *f.*

laughingly ['lɑːfiŋli], *adv.* en riant.

laughter ['lɑːftə], *n.* rire, *m.*, rires, *m.pl.*; risée, moquerie, *f.*; *burst of laughter*, éclat de rire, *m.*

launch [lɔːntʃ], *v.t.* lancer; mettre à la mer.— *v.i.* se lancer, se jeter.—*n.* lancement, *m.*; chaloupe (*bateau*), vedette, *f.*

launching ['lɔːntʃiŋ], *n.* (*Naut.*) mise à l'eau, *f.*, lancement, *m.*; *launching pad*, piste de lancement, *f.*

launder ['lɔːndə], *v.t.* blanchir; lessiver (*linge*).

launderette [lɔːndə'ret], *n.* laverie automatique, *f.*

laundress ['lɔːndris], *n.* blanchisseuse, *f.*

laundromat ['lɔːndrəmæt], (*Am.*) [LAUN-DERETTE]

laundry ['lɔːndri], *n.* buanderie; blanchisserie, *f.*; linge à blanchir, *m.*

laurel ['lɔrəl], *n.* laurier, *m.*

lava ['lɑːvə], *n.* lave, *f.*

lavatory ['lævət(ə)ri], *n.* water-closet, *m.*, les lavabos, les water, *m.pl.*

lavender ['lævində], *n.* lavande, *f.*

lavish ['læviʃ], *a.* prodigue.—*v.t.* prodiguer.

lavishly ['læviʃli], *adv.* prodigalement.

lavishness ['læviʃnis], *n.* prodigalité, *f.*

law [lɔː], *n.* loi, *f.*; droit, *m.*; *Law Courts*, Palais de Justice, *m.*

lawful ['lɔːful], *a.* légitime, licite, permis.

lawfully ['lɔːfuli], *adv.* légitimement.

lawless ['lɔːlis], *a.* sans loi; (*fig.*) sans frein, déréglé.

lawlessness ['lɔːlisnis], *n.* désordre, *m.* licence, *f.*

lawn (1) [lɔːn], *n.* pelouse, *f.*

lawn (2) [lɔːn], *n.* linon (*tissu*), *m.*

lawn mower ['lɔːnmouə], *n.* tondeuse de gazon, *f.*

lawsuit ['lɔːsjuːt], *n.* procès, *m.*

lawyer ['lɔːjə], *n.* homme de loi; avocat; avoué (*solicitor*); notaire (*notary*), *m.*

lax [læks], *a.* lâche, mou, flasque; (*fig.*) relâché, négligent.

laxative ['læksətiv], *a.* and *n.* laxatif, *m.*

laxity ['læksiti], **laxness** ['læksnis], *n.* relâchement, *m.*; flaccidité, *f.*; manque d'exactitude, *m.*

lay (1) [lei], *past* [LIE (2)].

lay (2) [lei], *v.t. irr.* placer, mettre, poser; coucher, étendre (*de tout son long*); faire; parier (*pari*); pondre (*œuf*); tendre, dresser (*piège*); abattre (*poussière*); calmer, apaiser (*rendre tranquille*); *to lay aside*, mettre de côté; *to lay claim to*, prétendre à; *to lay down*, mettre bas, poser (*principe*); *to lay down one's life for*, donner sa vie pour; *to lay hold of*, s'emparer de; *to lay in*, faire provision de; *to lay on*, appliquer, (*fam.*) arranger; *to lay out*, arranger; ensevelir (*cadavre*); disposer (*jardin etc.*); *to lay siege to*, assiéger; *to lay up*, mettre de côté, faire garder la chambre à; *to lay waste*, dévaster.—*v.i.* pondre (*œufs*).

lay (3) [lei], *n.* lai, *m.*, chanson, *f.*, chant, *m.*

lay (4) [lei], *a.* lai, laïque.

layer ['leiə], *n.* couche, *f.*, lit (*strate*), *m.*; (*Geol.*) assise; (*Hort.*) marcotte, *f.*; provin (*de vigne*), *m.*; pondeuse (*poule*), *f.*

laying ['leiiŋ], *n.* mise, pose; ponte (*d'œufs*), *f.*

layman ['leimən], *n.* (*pl.* -men [men]) laïque, profane, séculier, *m.*

lay-out ['leiaut], *n.* dessin, tracé, *m.*; disposition, *f.*

Lazarus ['læzərəs]. Lazare, *m.*

laze [leiz], *v.i. to laze about*, baguenauder.

lazily ['leizili], *adv.* lentement; en paresseux.

laziness ['leizinis], *n.* paresse, oisiveté, *f.*

lazy ['leizi], *a.* paresseux, indolent; *lazy fellow*, fainéant, *m.*

lea [li:], n. (*poet.*) prairie, f.
lead (1) [led], n. plomb (*métal*), m.; (*Naut.*) sonde; (*Print.*) interligne; mine de plomb (*pour des crayons*), f.;**black lead**, mine de plomb.
lead (2) [li:d], v.t. irr. mener, guider, conduire; porter, faire, induire (à); entraîner (à ou *dans*); **to lead astray**, égarer; **to lead back**, ramener, reconduire; **to lead in**, introduire; **to lead out**, emmener; **to lead someone to believe**, faire croire à quelqu'un; **to lead up to**, amener.—v.i. conduire, mener; (*Spt.*) jouer le premier. —n. conduite, direction, f., commandement, m.; laisse (*chien*), f.; battant (*Spt.*) début; (*Theat.*) premier rôle, m.; vedette, f.; (*Elec.*) conducteur, m.
leader ['li:də], n. conducteur, guide, chef, meneur; (*Journ.*) article de fond, éditorial; (*Polit.*) chef de parti, leader, m.
leadership ['li:dəʃip], n. conduite, direction, f.; qualités de chef, f.pl.
leading ['li:diŋ], a. premier, principal; **leading article**, article de fond, m.—n. conduite, direction, f.
leaf [li:f], n. (*pl.* **leaves** [li:vz]) feuille, f.; feuillet (*livre etc.*); battant (*porte*), m.; rallonge (*table*), f.; **to turn over a new leaf**, (*fig.*) changer de conduite; **to turn over the leaves of**, feuilleter.
leaflet ['li:flit], n. feuillet, imprimé, prospectus, m.
leafy ['li:fi], a. feuillu, couvert de feuilles.
league [li:g], n. ligue; lieue (*3 miles*), f.
leak [li:k], n. fuite, perte d'eau; (*Naut.*) voie d'eau, f.; **to spring a leak**, (*Naut.*) faire eau.—v.t. fuir, couler, faire eau; prendre l'eau (*chaussures*); **to leak out**, s'éventer.
leakage ['li:kidʒ], n. coulage, m.; fuite, f.
leaky ['li:ki], a. qui coule; (*Naut.*) qui fait eau.
lean (1) [li:n], a. and n. maigre, m.
lean (2) [li:n], v.t. irr. appuyer, faire pencher, incliner.—v.i. s'appuyer, s'incliner, se pencher; **to lean back against**, s'adosser à; **to lean out**, se pencher au dehors.
leaning ['li:niŋ], a. penché.—n. penchant, m.; (*fig.*) tendance, f.
lean-to ['li:ntu:], n. appentis, m.
leap [li:p], n. saut, bond, m.—v.t. irr. sauter, franchir.—v.i. sauter, bondir; s'élancer, se précipiter.
leap-frog ['li:pfrog], n. saute-mouton, m.
leap year ['li:pjiə], n. année bissextile, f.
learn [lə:n], v.t. irr. apprendre.—v.i. apprendre, s'instruire.
learned ['lə:nid], a. savant, instruit, érudit; **learned man**, savant, m.; **learned profession**, profession libérale, f.
learner ['lə:nə], n. élève, commençant, apprenti, m.; **learner driver**, élève chauffeur.
learning ['lə:niŋ], n. science, instruction, f., savoir, m., connaissances, f.pl.; érudition, f.
lease [li:s], n. bail, m.—v.t. louer, donner à bail; prendre à bail.
leasehold ['li:should], a. à bail.—n. tenure par bail, f.
leash [li:ʃ], n. laisse, f.—v.t. mener en laisse, attacher.
least [li:st], a. le moindre, le plus petit.—adv. le moins; **at least**, au moins, du moins; **not in the least**, point du tout, nullement.

leather ['leðə], a. de cuir.—n. cuir, m.; **upper leather**, empeigne, f.—v.t. (*colloq.*) étriller, rosser.
leave [li:v], n. permission, f., congé; adieu, m.; **on leave**, en congé (*un mois ou plus*), en permission (*moins d'un mois*); **with your leave**, avec votre permission.—v.t. irr. laisser; quitter, partir de (*s'en aller de*); cesser (*de*); **he left the house**, il quitta la maison, il partit de la maison; **he left the pen on the table**, il laissa le stylo sur la table; **to be left**, rester; **to leave about**, laisser trainer; **to leave alone**, laisser tranquille; **to leave off**, cesser (*de*); **to leave out**, supprimer, omettre, oublier. —v.i. partir, quitter; cesser.
leaven [levn], n. levain, m.—v.t. faire lever.
leaves [LEAF].
leave-taking ['li:vteikiŋ], n. adieux, m.pl.
leavings ['li:viŋz], n.pl. restes, m.pl.
Lebanese ['lebəni:z], a. libanais.—n. Libanais (*personne*), m.
Lebanon ['lebənən]. le Liban, m.
lecherous ['letʃərəs], a. lascif, libertin, lubrique.
lecherousness ['letʃərəsnis], **lechery** ['letʃəri], n. lasciveté, f.
lectern ['lektə:n], n. lutrin, m.
lecture ['lektʃə], n. conférence (*sur*), leçon (*de*), f.; (*fig.*) sermon, m., semonce, f.—v.t. faire un cours à; (*fig.*) sermonner, semoncer. —v.i. faire un cours (*de*), faire une conférence (*sur*).
lecturer ['lektʃərə], n. conférencier; maître de conférences, m.
lecture room ['lektʃəru:m], n. salle de conférences, f.
ledge [ledʒ], n. rebord, bord, m.; (*Arch.*) saillie, f.
ledger ['ledʒə], n. grand livre, m.
lee [li:], a. sous le vent.—n. (*Naut.*) côté sous le vent, m.
leech [li:tʃ], n. sangsue, f.
leek [li:k], n. poireau, m.
leer [liə], n. œillade, f.; regard de côté, m.—v.i. lorgner.
lees [li:z], n.pl. lie, f.
leeward ['lu:əd], a. and adv. (*Naut.*) sous le vent.
lee-way ['li:wei], n. dérive, f.; (*fig.*) marge, f.
left (1) [left], past and p.p. [LEAVE].
left (2) [left], a. and n. gauche, f.; **on the left**, à gauche.
left-handed ['left'hændid], a. gaucher; à gauche (*vis*); (*fig.*) gauche.
left-overs ['leftouvəz], n.pl. restes (*d'un repas*), m.pl.
leg [leg], n. jambe; patte (*d'oiseau, d'insecte etc.*); tige (*bottines*); cuisse (*volaille*), f.; pied (*meuble*); gigot (*mouton*), trumeau (*bœuf*), m.; branche (*compas*), f.; **to pull someone's leg**, se moquer de quelqu'un.
legacy ['legəsi], n. legs, m.
legal ['li:gl], a. légal, judiciaire, juridique.
legality [li'gæliti], n. légalité, f.
legalize ['li:gəlaiz], v.t. légaliser, (*fig.*) autoriser.
legally ['li:gəli], adv. légalement.
legation [li'geiʃən], n. légation, f.
legend ['ledʒənd], n. légende, f.
legendary ['ledʒəndri], a. légendaire, fabuleux.
legged [legd, 'legid], a. à jambes, à pieds;

four-legged, à quatre pattes; *two-legged*, à deux jambes, bipède.

leggings ['legiŋz], *n.pl.* jambières, guêtres, *f.pl.*

legibility [ledʒi'biliti], *n.* lisibilité, netteté d'écriture, *f.*

legible ['ledʒibl], *a.* lisible.

legion ['li:dʒən], *n.* légion, *f.*; *the Foreign Legion*, la Légion (étrangère).

legislate ['ledʒisleit], *v.t.* légiférer, faire des lois.

legislation [ledʒis'leiʃən], *n.* législation, *f.*

legislative ['ledʒislətiv], *a.* législatif.

legitimate [lə'dʒitimit], *a.* légitime; juste, correct.

leisure ['leʒə], *n.* loisir, *m.*; *at leisure*, de loisir; *at one's leisure*, à loisir; *you are at leisure to come or not*, il vous est loisible de venir ou non.

leisurely ['leʒəli], *a.* sans hâte, mesuré.—*adv.* à loisir.

lemon ['lemən], *n.* citron, limon, *m.*

lemonade [lemə'neid], *n.* citron pressé, *m.*

lemon squash ['lemən'skwɔʃ], *n.* citronnade, *f.*

lemon-squeezer ['lemən'skwi:zə], *n.* presse-citrons, *m.inv.*

lemon tree ['leməntri:], *n.* citronnier, *m.*

lend [lend], *v.t. irr.* prêter; (*fig.*) donner.

lender ['lendə], *n.* prêteur, *m.*

lending ['lendiŋ], *n.* prêt, *m.*; *lending library*, bibliothèque de prêt, *f.*

length [leŋθ], *n.* longueur; étendue, *f.*; degré, point (*extrémité*), *m.*; durée (*temps*), *f.*; *at full length*, tout au long (*non abrégé*); en toutes lettres (*mots*); de tout son long (*personnes*); *at great length*, longuement; *at length*, enfin; *full length*, de grandeur nature; *two feet in length*, deux pieds de longueur *ou* de long.

lengthen ['leŋθn], *v.t.* allonger, étendre; prolonger (*temps*).—*v.i.* s'allonger, s'étendre; se prolonger (*temps*); (*colloq.*) rallonger (*journées etc.*).

lengthening ['leŋθniŋ], *n.* allongement, *m.*; prolongation (*de temps*), *f.*; accroissement (*des journées*), *m.*

lengthways ['leŋθweiz], **lengthwise** ['leŋθwaiz], *adv.* en longueur, en long.

lengthy ['leŋθi], *a.* un peu long, ennuyeux.

leniency ['li:niənsi], *n.* douceur, clémence, indulgence (*pour*), *f.*

lenient ['li:niənt], *a.* doux, indulgent (*à, envers ou pour*).

leniently ['li:niəntli], *adv.* avec douceur, avec indulgence.

lens [lenz], *n.* (*pl.* **lenses** ['lenziz]) (*Opt.*) lentille, loupe, *f.*

Lent [lent], *n.* le carême, *m.*

lentil ['lentil], *n.* lentille, *f.*

leonine ['li:ənain], *a.* de lion, léonin.

leopard ['lepəd], *n.* léopard, *m.*

leper ['lepə], *n.* lépreux, *m.*

leprosy ['leprəsi], *n.* lèpre, *f.*

leprous ['leprəs], *a.* lépreux.

less [les], *a.* moindre, plus petit, inférieur; *to grow less*, diminuer.—*adv.* moins; *less and less*, de moins en moins; *no less*, rien moins, pas moins; *so much the less*, d'autant moins; *the less . . . the more . . .*, moins . . . plus . . .—*n.* moins; moindre, *m.*

lessee [le'si:], *n.* locataire à bail, *m., f.*

lessen [lesn], *v.t.* diminuer, amoindrir, rapetisser, rabaisser (*to lower*); ralentir (*la vitesse*).—*v.i.* diminuer, s'amoindrir.

lesser ['lesə], *a.* moindre, plus petit.

lesson [lesn], *n.* leçon, *f.*

lest [lest], *conj.* de peur que, de crainte que (*followed by ne with subj.*).

let (1) [let], *v.t. irr.* laisser, permettre à (*donner la permission à*); souffrir que (*with subjunctive*); faire (*causer*); louer (*maison*); *let him come*, qu'il vienne; *let me see*, voyons; *let us go*, allons; *to let alone*, laisser tranquille; *to let down*, descendre, faire descendre, baisser, rabattre; *to let fall*, laisser tomber; *to let go*, lâcher; *to let in*, faire entrer; *to let know*, faire savoir à; *to let off*, laisser échapper; tirer (*arme à feu*); *to let out*, faire sortir, laisser sortir; élargir (*vêtements*).

let (2) [let], *n.* empêchement; obstacle, délai, *m.*; (*Tennis*) (balle) à remettre.

lethal ['li:θl], *a.* mortel, fatal.

lethargic [lə'θɑ:dʒik], *a.* léthargique.

lethargy ['leθədʒi], *n.* léthargie, *f.*

letter ['letə], *n.* lettre, *f.*; (*pl., fig.*) belles-lettres, *f.pl.*; *registered letter*, lettre recommandée.

letter box ['letəbɔks], *n.* boîte aux lettres, *f.*

letter-card ['letəkɑ:d], *n.* carte-lettre, *f.*

lettered ['letəd], *a.* lettré, savant.

lettering ['letəriŋ], *n.* titre, *m.*

letting ['letiŋ], *n.* louage, *m.*; *letting out*, location, *f.*; agrandissement (*de vêtement*), *m.*

lettuce ['letis], *n.* laitue, *f.*

let-up ['letʌp], *n.* diminution, *f.*

Levant [lə'vænt], **the.** le Levant, *m.*

Levantine [li'væntain], *a.* du Levant, levantin.—*n.* Levantin (*personne*), *m.*; levantine (*soie*), *f.*

level [levl], *a.* de niveau (*avec*), au niveau (*de*); uni (*surface*); égal (*à*); *level crossing*, passage à niveau, *m.*—*n.* niveau, *m.*; surface unie, *f.*; *at ministerial level*, à l'échelon ministériel.—*v.t.* aplanir, niveler, mettre de niveau; braquer, pointer (*arme à feu*); porter (*coup*).—*v.i.* viser, mettre en joue, pointer.

level-headed ['levlhedid], *a.* équilibré, de sens rassis.

levelling ['levliŋ], *n.* nivellement; pointage (*de fusil*), *m.*

lever ['li:və], *n.* levier, *m.*; *hand lever* manette, *f.*

leveret ['levərit], *n.* levraut, *m.*

levity ['leviti], *n.* légèreté, *f.*; manque de sérieux, *m.*

levy ['levi], *n.* levée; perception (*d'impôts*), *f.*—*v.t.* lever; imposer (*amende etc.*).

lewd [lju:d], *a.* impudique, lascif.

lexicon ['leksikn], *n.* lexique, dictionnaire, *m.*

liability [laiə'biliti], *n.* responsabilité; tendance, *f.*; danger, *m.*; (*Comm.*) (*pl.*) engagements, *m.pl.*, passif, *m.*; *assets and liabilities*, actif et passif, *m.*

liable ['laiəbl], *a.* sujet à (*à*), exposé (*à*), responsable (*de*).

liar ['laiə], *n.* menteur, *m.*

libel [laibl], *n.* libelle, écrit diffamatoire, *m.*—*v.t.* diffamer.

libellous ['laibələs], *a.* diffamatoire.

liberal ['libərəl], *a.* libéral, généreux; prodigue, abondant, *m.* (*Polit.*) Libéral, *m.*

liberality [libə'ræliti], *n.* libéralité, *f.*

liberate ['libəreit], *v.t.* libérer, rendre libre; délivrer (*de*).

liberation [libə'reifən], *n.* mise en liberté, *f.*; élargissement (*de prisonniers*); affranchissement, *m.*; libération, délivrance, *f.*

liberator ['libəreitə], *n.* libérateur, *m.*

Liberia [lai'biəriə], le Libéria, *m.*

Liberian [lai'biəriən], *a.* libérien.—*n.* Libérien (*personne*), *m.*

liberty ['libəti], *n.* liberté, *f.*; privilèges, *m.pl.*, franchises, *f.pl.*

librarian [lai'breəriən], *n.* bibliothécaire, *m.,f.*

library ['laibrəri], *n.* bibliothèque, *f.*; *film library*, cinémathèque, *f.*; *record library*, disbothèque *f*

Libya ['libiə], la Lybie, *f.*

Libyan ['libiən], *a.* libyen.—*n.* Libyen (*personne*), *m.*

lice [LOUSE].

license ['laisəns], *n.* licence, liberté; permission, *f.*, permis; certificat; (*fig.*) dérèglement, *m.*; autorisation (*de prédicateur*), *f.*; brevet (*de libraire*), *m.*; (*Comm.*) patente, *f.*; *driving license*, permis de conduire; *gun license*, permis de port d'armes; permis de chasse; *marriage license*, dispense de bans, *f.* [see **number-plate**]

license ['laisəns], *v.t.* autoriser, accorder un permis à.

licensed ['laisənst], *a.* autorisé; breveté; (*Comm.*) patenté.

licentious [lai'senfəs], *a.* licencieux.

lichen ['laikən], *n.* lichen, *m.*

lick [lik], *v.t.* lécher; laper (*boire*); (*slang*) rosser (*battre*).—*n.* coup de langue, *m.*

licking ['likiŋ], *n.* (*slang*) coups, *m.pl.*, raclée, *f.*

licorice [LIQUORICE].

lid [lid], *n.* couvercle, *m.*; paupière (*d'œil*), *f.*

lie (1) [lai], *n.* mensonge; démenti, *m.*; *to give the lie to*, donner un démenti à; *white lie*, mensonge pieux.—*v.i.* mentir.

lie (2) [lai], *v.i. irr.* être couché, se coucher; reposer, être situé, se trouver; s'appuyer (*se soutenir*); rester (*to remain*); consister; *here lies*, ci-gît; *lie down!* (*à un chien*) couché! *to lie about* (*objets*), traîner çà et là; *to lie down*, se coucher, se reposer.—*n.* gisement, *f.*, position, situation, *f.*

lieutenant [lef'tenənt], *n.* lieutenant, *m.*

life [laif], *n.* (*pl.* **lives** [laivz]) vie, *f.*; homme vivant, *m.*; personne; (*fig.*) vie, âme, vivacité, *f.*, entrain; mouvement; (*Paint. etc.*) naturel, *m.*; *a double life*, une vie double; *for life*, à vie, à perpétuité; *from life*, d'après nature; *high life*, le grand monde, *m.*; *never in my life*, jamais de ma vie; *pension for life*, pension viagère, *f.*; *prime of life*, fleur de l'âge, *f.*; *single life*, célibat, *m.*; *to come to life*, s'animer.

life belt ['laifbelt], *n.* ceinture de sauvetage, *f.*

life boat ['laifbout], *n.* canot de sauvetage, *m.*

life buoy ['laifbɔi], *n.* bouée de sauvetage, *f.*

lifeguard ['laifga:d], *n.* garde du corps, *m.*; (*pl.*) les Gardes du corps, *m.pl.*; sauveteur, *m.*

life-insurance ['laifinʃuərəns], *n.* assurance sur la vie, *f.*

lifeless ['laiflis], *a.* sans vie, inanimé.

lifelike ['laiflaik], *a.* comme un être vivant, d'après nature, vivant.

lifelong ['laiflɔŋ], *a.* de toute la vie.

life-size ['laifsaiz], *a.* de grandeur nature.

lifetime ['laiftaim], *n.* vie, *f.*, vivant, *m.*; *in his* or *her lifetime*, de son vivant.

lift [lift], *n.* action de lever, élévation, *f.*, effort; coup de main (*aide*); monte-charge (*machine*); ascenseur, *m.*—*v.t.* lever, soulever, hausser, soupeser (*évaluer le poids de*); (*fig.*) élever, relever.

lift man ['liftmən], *n.* (*pl.* **men** [men]) liftier, *m.*

light (1) [lait], *n.* lumière, *f.*, jour (*du soleil*); clair (*de la lune etc.*), *m.*; clarté (*de l'œil etc.*); lueur, *f.*; (*fig.*) aspect, point de vue, *m.*; *electric light*, éclairage à l'électricité, *m.*; *it is light*, il fait jour; *light and shade*, clair-obscur, *m.*; *traffic lights*, feux de circulation, *m.pl.*; *will you give me a light?* voulez-vous me donner du feu?—*v.t. irr.* allumer; illuminer, éclairer (*fenêtres etc.*).—*v.i. to light up*, briller, s'enflammer.

light (2) [lait], *v.i. to light upon*, descendre *ou* tomber sur.

light (3) [lait], *a.* léger; (*fig.*) gai, frivole; clair (*couleur etc.*); blond (*teint*).

lighten (1) [laitn], *v.t.* éclairer, illuminer.—*v.i.* éclairer; faire des éclairs.

lighten (2) [laitn], *v.t.* soulager, alléger (*adoucir*).

lightening ['laitniŋ], *n.* éclaircissement; allègement; soulagement, *m.*

lighter ['laitə], *n.* allumeur; briquet (*pour cigarettes*), *m.*; (*Naut.*) allège, gabare, *f.*, chaland, *m.*

light-hearted [lait'ha:tid], *a.* gai, réjoui.

light-heartedness [lait'ha:tidnis], *n.* enjouement, *m.*, gaieté, *f.*

lighthouse ['laithaus], *n.* phare, *m.*

lighting ['laitiŋ], *n.* éclairage, *m.*; *lighting-up time*, heure d'éclairage, *f.*

lightly ['laitli], *adv.* légèrement, à la légère; lestement, facilement, aisément; gaiement.

lightness ['laitnis], *n.* légèreté, *f.*

lightning ['laitniŋ], *n.* éclair, *m.*, les éclairs, *m.pl.*; foudre, *f.*; *flash of lightning*, éclair.

lightning rod ['laitniŋrɔd], *n.* paratonnerre, *m.*

lights [laits], *n.pl.* mou (*d'animal*), *m.*

lightship ['laitʃip], *n.* bateau-feu, *m.*

like (1) [laik], *a.* semblable, tel, pareil; même, égal, *vraisemblable; as like as not*, probablement; *that is something like!* à la bonne heure! *to be like*, ressembler à; *to feel like doing something*, avoir envie de faire quelque chose; *what is he like?* comment est-il?—*prep.* comme, semblable à, pareil à.—*n.* chose pareille, *f.*, pareil, *m.*; même chose, *f.*; *the likes of you*, les gens de votre sorte, *m.pl.*, *f.pl.*

like (2) [laik], *v.t.* aimer, aimer bien, trouver bon, trouver bien; vouloir (bien), désirer, être bien aise (*de*); *as you like*, comme il vous plaira, comme vous voudrez.—*n.* goût, *m.*; préférence, *f.*; *everyone has his likes and dislikes*, chacun son goût.

likeable ['laikəbl], *a.* sympathique, aimable.

likelihood ['laiklihud], *n.* probabilité, vraisemblance, *f.*

likely ['laikli], *a.* probable, vraisemblable.—*adv.* probablement, vraisemblablement.

liken [laikn], *v.t.* comparer (*à* ou *avec*).
likeness ['laiknis], *n.* ressemblance, *f.*; portrait, *m.*
likewise ['laikwaiz], *adv.* également, pareillement, de même, aussi.
liking ['laikiŋ], *n.* gré, goût, penchant, *m.*, inclination; amitié, *f.*
lilac ['lailak], *n.* lilas, *m.*
lily ['lili], *n.* lis, *m.*; *lily of the valley,* muguet, *m.*
limb [lim], *n.* membre (*du corps*); (*colloq.*) enfant terrible, *m.*; grosse branche (*d'arbre*), *f.*
limber (1) ['limbə], *a.* souple, flexible; (*fig.*) agile.—*v.i. to limber up,* se chauffer les muscles.
limber (2) ['limbə], *n.* avant-train, *m.*
limbo ['limbou], *n.* limbes, *m.pl.*
lime (1) [laim], *n.* (*Bot.*) lime, limette, *f.*; *lime juice,* jus de limette, *m.*; *lime tree,* tilleul (*linden*); limettier, *m.*
lime (2) [laim], *n.* chaux; glu (*pour prendre des oiseaux*), *f.*
limelight ['laimlait], *n.* (*Theat.*) les feux de la lampe, *m.pl.*; *to be in the limelight,* être en évidence.
limestone ['laimstoun], *n.* pierre à chaux, *f.*; (*Geol.*) calcaire, *m.*
limit ['limit], *n.* limite, borne, *f.*; (*fam.*) *that's the limit!* ça c'est le comble!—*v.t.* limiter, borner, restreindre.
limitation [limi'teiʃən], *n.* limitation, restriction, *f.*
limited ['limitid], *a.* limité, borné; (*Comm.*) anonyme.
limitless ['limitlis], *a.* sans limite.
limp [limp], *a.* mou, flasque, sans consistance.—*v.i.* boiter.
limpet ['limpit], *n.* lépas, *m.*, patelle, *f.*
limpid ['limpid], *a.* limpide.
linden [lindn], *n.* (*Bot.*) tilleul, *m.*
line (1) [lain], *n.* ligne; corde, *f.*, cordeau (*ficelle*), *m.*; file, *f.*, alignement (*rang*); trait (*écrit*), *m.*; raie (*bande*), *f.*; contour (*profil*), *m.*; ride (*pli du visage*); (*Rail.*) voie; lignée, race (*descendance*), *f.*; (*fig.*) genre (*d'affaires etc.*); (*Pros.*) vers; mot, petit mot (*lettre brève*), *m.*; limite (*de territoire*), *f.*; air-line, ligne aérienne; (*Teleph.*) *hold the line!* ne quittez pas! *it is hard lines,* c'est dur; *not in my line,* pas de mon ressort.—*v.i.* ligner, régler; *to line up,* aligner. [queue]
line (2) [lain], *v.t.* doubler (*vêtement*); garnir (*de*); border (*de*).
lineage ['liniədʒ], *n.* lignée, race, famille, *f.*
lineal ['liniəl], *a.* linéaire.
lineally ['liniəli], *adv.* en ligne directe.
linear ['liniə], *a.* linéaire.
linen ['linin], *a.* de toile.—*n.* toile, toile de lin, *f.*, lin; linge (*habits*), *m.*
liner ['lainə], *n.* (*Naut.*) paquebot de ligne, transatlantique, *m.*
linesman ['lainzmən], *n.* (*pl.* **-men** [men]) (*Ftb.*) arbitre de touche, *m.*
linger ['liŋgə], *v.i.* traîner, tarder; hésiter.
lingering ['liŋgəriŋ], *a.* qui traîne, lent; languissant.—*n.* retard, *m.*, lenteur; hésitation, *f.*
lingo ['liŋgou], *n.* (*slang*) jargon, *m.*; langue, *f.*
linguist ['liŋgwist], *n.* linguiste, *m.*, *f.*
liniment ['linimənt], *n.* liniment, *m.*
lining ['lainiŋ], *n.* doublure; garniture (*de*

vêtement); coiffe (*de chapeau*), *f.*; (*Build.*) revêtement, *m.*
link [liŋk], *n.* chaînon, anneau; (*fig.*) lien; trait d'union, *m.*; *cuff links,* boutons de manchettes, *m.pl.*—*v.t.* lier, relier (*avec.*); enchaîner (*dans*); unir.—*v.i.* s'allier (*à*).
links [liŋks], *n.pl.* *golf links,* terrain de golf, *m.*
linnet ['linit], *n.* linotte, *f.*
linoleum [li'nouljəm], *n.* linoléum, *m.*
linotype ['lainotaip], *n.* linotype, *f.*
linseed ['linsi:d], *n.* graine de lin, *f.*; *linseed oil,* huile de lin, *f.*
lint [lint], *n.* charpie, *f.*
lintel [lintl], *n.* linteau, *m.*
lion ['laiən], *n.* lion, *m.*; (*fig.*) célébrité, *f.*; *lion's cub,* lionceau, *m.*
lioness ['laiənis], *n.* lionne, *f.*
lion tamer ['laiənteimə], *n.* dompteur de lions, *m.*
lip [lip], *n.* lèvre; babine (*de certains animaux*), *f.*; bord (*de choses*), *m.*; (*fig.*) impertinence, *f.*
lipstick ['lipstik], *n.* bâton de rouge, *m.*
liquefy ['likwifai], *v.t.* liquéfier.—*v.i.* se liquéfier.
liqueur [li'kjuə], *n.* liqueur, *f.*
liquid ['likwid], *a.* liquide; doux, coulant.—*n.* liquide, *m.*
liquidate ['likwideit], *v.t.* liquider.
liquidation [likwi'deiʃən], *n.* liquidation, *f.*, acquittement (*d'une dette*), *m.*
liquor ['likə], *n.* (*Chem.*) liqueur, solution; (*Am.*) boisson alcoolique, *f.*; (*Am.*) *hard liquor,* alcool, *m.*
liquorice ['likəris], *n.* réglisse, *f.*
Lisbon ['lizbən]. Lisbonne, *f.*
lisp [lisp], *v.t.*, *v.i.* dire (θ, ð) au lieu de (s, z); (*colloq.*) susurrer, zozoter.
lissom [lism], *a.* souple, leste.
list (1) [list], *n.* liste, *f.*, rôle, *m.*; *Army List,* annuaire de l'armée, *m.*—*v.t.* enrôler, enregistrer.
list (2) [list], *v.i.* (*Naut.*) donner de la bande.—*n.* (*Naut.*) bande, *f.*
listen [lisn], *v.i.* écouter.
listener ['lisnə], *n.* auditeur, *m.*
listless ['listlis], *a.* apathique.
listlessness ['listlisnis], *n.* apathie, *f.*
lists [lists], *n.pl.* lice, arène (*arena*), *f.*
litany ['litəni], *n.* litanie, *f.*
literal ['litərəl], *a.* littéral.
literally ['litərəli], *adv.* littéralement, à la lettre.
literary ['litərəri], *a.* littéraire; lettré (*personne*).
literature ['litəritʃə], *n.* littérature, *f.*
lithe [laið], *a.* pliant, flexible, souple.
lithograph ['liθogra:f], *n.* lithographie, *f.*
lithographer [li'θogrəfə], *n.* lithographe, *m.*, *f.*
Lithuania [liθju'einiə]. la Lituanie, la Lithuanie, *f.*
Lithuanian [liθju'einiən], *a.* lituanien, lithuanien.—*n.* lituanien, lithuanien (*langue*); Lituanien, Lithuanien (*personne*), *m.*
litigant ['litigənt], *n.* plaideur, *m.*
litigate ['litigeit], *v.t.* plaider, disputer.—*v.i.* être en procès.
litigation [liti'geiʃən], *n.* litige; procès, *m.*
litre ['li:tə], *n.* litre, *m.*
litter ['litə], *n.* litière, civière (*véhicule*), *f.*; ordures, *f.pl.*, détritus, *m.pl.*; (*fig.*) fouillis, désordre, *m.*; portée (*d'animal*), *f.*—*v.t.*

joncher; jeter çà et là; (*fig.*) mettre en désordre; mettre bas (*animal*); salir; *to litter down* (*of horse*), faire la litière à.

litter bin ['litəbin], *n.* boîte à ordures, *f.*

little [litl], *a.* petit; minime, exigu; mesquin; *little one,* enfant, *m.*, *f.*, petit, *m.*—*n.* peu, *m.*; *to think little of,* faire peu de cas de.—*adv.* peu, un peu, pas beaucoup, peu de chose, peu de; *a little,* un peu; *as little as possible,* le moins possible; *little by little,* petit à petit, peu à peu; *little or none,* peu ou point.

littleness ['litlnis], *n.* petitesse, *f.*

liturgy ['litədʒi], *n.* liturgie, *f.*

live (1) [liv], *v.t.* mener (une vie).—*v.i.* vivre; résider, demeurer, habiter; *long live the Queen!* vive la Reine! *to live by,* vivre de; *to live down a scandal,* faire oublier un scandale avec le temps; *to live on,* se nourrir de.

live (2) [laiv], *a.* en vie, vivant; ardent, vif (*charbons*); *live rail,* rail conducteur, *m.*; *livestock,* bétail, *m.*; *live wire,* fil sous tension, *m.*

lived [livd], *a.* de vie; *long-lived,* qui vit longtemps, de longue vie.

livelihood ['laivlihud], *n.* vie, subsistance, *f.*; gagne-pain, *m.*

liveliness ['laivlinis], *n.* vivacité, gaieté, *f.*

livelong ['livlɔŋ], *a.* durable, long, sans fin; *the livelong day,* toute la sainte journée.

lively ['laivli], *a.* vif, gai, enjoué, animé; vivant (*endroit*).

liven [laivn], *v.t.* *to liven up,* animer.

liver (1) ['livə], *n.* *fast liver,* viveur, noceur, *m.*

liver (2) ['livə], *n.* (*Anat.*) foie, *m.*

livery ['livəri], *n.* livrée; pension (*de chevaux*), *f.*

lives [LIFE].

livestock ['laivstɔk], [LIVE (2)].

livid ['livid], *a.* livide, blême.

living ['liviŋ], *a.* en vie, vivant; vif.—*n.* vie, subsistance, existence, *f.*; genre de vie, *m.*, chère, *f.*; (*Eccles.*) bénéfice, *m.*, cure, *f.*

living room ['liviŋrum], *n.* salle de séjour, *f.*

lizard ['lizəd], *n.* lézard, *m.*

llama ['lɑːmə], *n.* lama, *m.*

lo! [lou], *int.* voici! voilà! voyez! regardez!

load [loud], *n.* charge, *f.*, fardeau; (*fig.*) chargement, *m.*; charretée (*cartful*), *f.*—*v.t.* charger; (*fig.*) combler, accabler (*de*).

loaf [louf], *n.* (*pl.* **loaves** [louvz]) pain (*long*), *m.*; miche (*rond*), *f.*—*v.i.* flâner, fainéanter; *to loaf about town,* battre le pavé.

loafer ['loufə], *n.* fainéant, batteur de pavé, *m.*

loam [loum], *n.* terre grasse, *f.*

loamy ['loumi], *a.* glaiseux.

loan [loun], *n.* emprunt; prêt, *m.*; *to raise a loan,* faire un emprunt.—*v.t.* prêter.

loath [louθ], *a.* fâché, peiné; *to be loath to,* faire à contre-cœur.

loathe [louð], *v.t.* détester.

loathing ['louðiŋ], *n.* dégoût, *m.*, aversion, *f.*

loathsome ['louðsəm], *a.* dégoûtant, odieux.

loaves [LOAF].

lobby ['lɔbi], *n.* couloir, *m.*; salle d'attente (*vestibule*); (*Theat.*) entrée, *f.*—*v.t.*, *v.i.* (*Polit.*) faire les couloirs.

lobe [loub], *n.* lobe, *m.*

lobelia [lo'biːliə], *n.* lobélie, *f.*

lobster ['lɔbstə], *n.* homard, *m.*

local ['loukəl], *a.* local; topographique.

locality [lo'kæliti], *n.* localité, *f.*

localize ['loukəlaiz], *v.t.* localiser.

locally ['loukəli], *adv.* localement.

locate [lo'keit], *v.t.* placer, localiser; repérer.

location [lo'keiʃən], *n.* situation, *f.*, emplacement, *m.*; location, *f.*; (*Cine.*) extérieurs, *m.pl.*

loch [lɔx], *n.* (*Sc.*) lac, *m.*

lock [lɔk], *n.* serrure; écluse (*de canal*); platine (*de fusil*); mèche, boucle (*de cheveux*), *f.*; flocon (*de laine*), *m.*; (*pl.*) cheveux, *m.pl.*; *dead-lock,* impasse, *f.*; *padlock,* cadenas, *m.*—*v.t.* fermer à clef; accrocher (*roues etc.*); *to lock in,* enfermer; *to lock up,* serrer, enfermer, mettre en prison.—*v.i.* fermer à clef.

locker ['lɔkə], *n.* armoire, *f.*; coffre, *m.*

locket ['lɔkit], *n.* médaillon, *m.*

lock-jaw ['lɔkdʒɔː], *n.* trisme, tétanos, *m.*

locksmith ['lɔksmiθ], *n.* serrurier, *m.*

locomotion [loukə'mouʃən], *n.* locomotion, *f.*

locomotive ['loukəmoutiv], *a.* locomotif.—*n.* locomotive, *f.*

locust (1) ['loukəst], *n.* sauterelle d'Orient, *f.*, criquet, *m.*

locust (2) ['loukəst], *n.* caroubier (*plante*), *m.*; *locust tree,* robinier, *m.*

lodge [lɔdʒ], *n.* loge (*de concierge*), *f.*; pavillon, *m.*; maisonnette (*de garde*), *f.*—*v.t.* loger; abriter; enfoncer (*mettre dans*); déposer (*placer*); implanter (*dans le cœur*); interjeter (*appel*); *to lodge a complaint,* porter plainte.—*v.i.* loger, se loger; s'arrêter, se fixer.

lodger ['lɔdʒə], *n.* locataire; pensionnaire, *m.*, *f.*

lodging ['lɔdʒiŋ], *n.* logement; appartement, *m.*; *to live in furnished lodgings,* loger en garni *ou* en meublé.

lodging house ['lɔdʒiŋhaus], *n.* hôtel garni, hôtel meublé, *m.*

loft [lɔft], *n.* grenier, *m.*; tribune, *f.*; pigeonnier, *m.*

loftily ['lɔftili], *adv.* haut, avec hauteur, pompeusement.

loftiness ['lɔftinis], *n.* élévation; hauteur, fierté, pompe; sublimité, *f.*

lofty ['lɔfti], *a.* haut, élevé; altier; sublime (*style*).

log [lɔg], *n.* bûche, *f.*; (*Naut.*) loch, *m.*; *to sleep like a log,* dormir comme une souche.

loganberry ['lougənberi], *n.* ronce-framboise, *f.*

logarithm ['lɔgəriðm], *n.* logarithme, *m.*

log-book ['lɔgbuk], *n.* journal *ou* livre de bord; (*Motor.*) carnet de route, *m.*

loggerhead ['lɔgəhed], *n.* lourdaud, *m.*; *to be at loggerheads,* être aux prises *ou* à couteaux tirés.

logic ['lɔdʒik], *n.* logique, *f.*

logical ['lɔdʒikəl], *a.* logique, de la logique.

loin [lɔin], *n.* longe (*de veau*), *f.*; filet (*de mouton*), *m.*; (*pl.*) reins, lombes, *m.pl.*

loiter ['lɔitə], *v.t.* perdre, gaspiller.—*v.i.* flâner, traîner, s'amuser en chemin.

loiterer ['lɔitərə], *n.* musard, flâneur, *m.*

loitering ['lɔitəriŋ], *n.* flânerie, *f.*

loll [lɔl], *v.t.* laisser pendre (*la langue*).—*v.i.* s'étaler, se pencher; pendre (*la langue*).

lolling ['lɔliŋ], *a.* étendu, étalé..

lollipop ['lɔlipɔp], *n.* sucre d'orge, *m.*, sucette, *f.*

lolly ['lɔli], *n.* (*fam.*) sucette; (*slang*) galette (*argent*), *f.*

London ['lʌndən]. Londres, *m.* ou *f.*

Londoner ['lʌndənə], *n.* Londonien, *m.*

lone [loun], *a.* isolé, solitaire; délaissé.

loneliness ['lounlinis], *n.* solitude, *f.*; isolement, *m.*

lonely ['lounli], *a.* isolé; délaissé.

long (1) [lɔŋ], *v.i.* avoir bien envie, brûler (*de*); (*impers.*) tarder (*de*).

long (2) [lɔŋ], *a.* long; étendu, prolongé, allongé; *a long time*, longtemps, depuis longtemps, pendant longtemps; *in the long run*, à la longue; *to be three feet long*, avoir trois pieds de long, être long de trois pieds.—*n.* *the long and the short of*, le fort et le faible de.—*adv.* fort; longtemps, longuement; depuis longtemps; pendant longtemps; durant; *all night long*, tout le long de la nuit; *before long*, bientôt, avant peu, sous peu; *how long have you been here?* combien de temps y a-t-il que vous êtes ici? *long ago*, il y a longtemps, depuis longtemps; *not long after*, peu de temps après; *so long as*, tant que.

longer ['lɔŋgə], *a.* plus long.—*adv.* plus longtemps; de plus.

longing ['lɔŋiŋ], *n.* désir ardent, *m.*, envie, *f.*

longitude ['lɔndʒitjuːd], *n.* longitude, *f.*

long-sighted ['lɔŋsaitid], *a.* presbyte; (*fig.*) clairvoyant; *I am long-sighted*, j'ai la vue longue.

look [luk], *v.i.* regarder (*d'une fenêtre*); sembler, avoir l'air, paraître; donner sur (*maison etc.*); *look out!* attention! gare! *to look after*, soigner, s'occuper de; *to look away*, détourner ses regards; *to look back*, regarder en arrière; *to look down upon*, mépriser; *to look for*, chercher; *to look forward to*, attendre avec impatience; *to look in*, faire une petite visite, dire un petit bonjour à; *to look into*, examiner; *to look like*, ressembler à; *to look on*, regarder, considérer; *to look over*, jeter un coup d'œil sur, examiner.—*n.* regard, air, *m.*, apparence, mine, *f.*; coup d'œil, *m.*

looker-on ['lukərɔn], *n.* spectateur, *m.*

looking ['lukiŋ], *a.* à l'air . . .; à la mine . . .; *good-looking*, beau.

looking glass ['lukiŋglɑːs], *n.* miroir, *m.*, glace, *f.*

look-out ['lukaut], *n.* guet, *m.*, vigilance, vue, *f.*; (*Mil.*) guetteur, *m.*; (*Naut.*) vigie, *f.*; *to keep a look-out*, avoir l'œil au guet.

loom [luːm], *n.* métier à tisser, *m.*—*v.i.* apparaître indistinctement, surgir.

looming ['luːmiŋ], *a.* vague, estompé.

loop [luːp], *n.* boucle; bride (*pour bouton*), *f.*; (*Av.*) looping, *m.*

loop-hole ['luːphoul], *n.* meurtrière (*pour bouton*), *f.*; (*fig.*) échappatoire, *f.*, faux-fuyant, *m.*

loose [luːs], *a.* délié, défait; branlant; (*fig.*) relâché, lâche (*mœurs*); vague; licencieux; libre; *loose cash*, menue monnaie, *f.*; *on the loose*, dissolu, dissipé.—*v.t.* délier, lâcher, (*fig.*) déchaîner.

loosely ['luːsli], *adv.* librement, négligemment; licencieusement.

loosen ['luːsn], *v.t.* délier, détacher, défaire; desserrer; ébranler.—*v.i.* se délier; se défaire; se desserrer.

looseness ['luːsnis], *n.* état desserré, relâchement; caractère vague, *m.*

loot [luːt], *n.* butin; pillage, *m.*—*v.t.* piller.

looter ['luːtə], *n.* pillard, *m.*

lop [lɔp], *v.t.* élaguer, ébrancher.

lopsided ['lɔpsaidid], *a.* qui penche trop d'un côté, déjeté.

loquacious [lo'kweiʃəs], *a.* loquace.

lord [lɔːd], *n.* seigneur; (*fig.*) maître; lord (*titre anglais*); Monseigneur (*à un prince, noble, évêque etc.*); Seigneur; *the Lord's Prayer*, l'oraison dominicale, *f.*; *the year of our Lord*, l'an de grâce, *m.*—*v.t.* *to lord it over*, dominer, faire le maître.

lordliness ['lɔːdlinis], *n.* hauteur, *f.*, orgueil, *m.*

lordling ['lɔːdliŋ], *n.* petit seigneur; hobereau, *m.*

lordly ['lɔːdli], *a.* de seigneur, noble; hautain, fier.

lore [lɔː], *n.* savoir, *m.*; science, *f.*

lorry ['lɔri], *n.* camion, *m.*

lose [luːz], *v.t. irr.* perdre; égarer; *to lose one's temper*, s'emporter; *to lose one's way*, s'égarer; *to lose sight of*, perdre de vue.—*v.i.* perdre (*de valeur*); retarder (*horloge etc.*).

loss [lɔs], *n.* perte, *f.*; (*Hunt.*) défaut, *m.*; extinction (*de voix*), *f.*; *at a loss*, dans l'embarras; *dead loss*, perte sèche.

lost [lɔst], *a.* perdu; égaré (*fourvoyé*); abîmé (*endommagé*).

lot [lɔt], *n.* sort, destin, *m.*, part; quantité, *f.*; tas (*de personnes*); lot (*à une vente*), *m.*; *a lot of*, beaucoup de; *to draw* or *cast lots*, tirer au sort.   [see **plot**]

lotion ['louʃən], *n.* lotion, *f.*

lottery ['lɔtəri], *n.* loterie, *f.*

loud [laud], *a.* haut; fort, grand; bruyant, retentissant; tapageur (*tumultueux*); criard (*couleurs*).

loudly ['laudli], *adv.* haut, fort, à haute voix; avec grand bruit, à grands cris.

loudness ['laudnis], *n.* force, *f.*, grand bruit, éclat, *m.*

loud-speaker [laud'spiːkə], *n.* (*Rad.*) haut-parleur, *m.*

Louisa [luˈiːzə], **Louise** [luˈiːz]. Louise, *f.*

lounge [laundʒ], *v.i.* flâner; être couché *ou* étendu *ou* appuyé paresseusement (*sur*).—*n.* promenoir; sofa (*canapé*); petit salon; hall (*d'hôtel*), *m.*; *lounge jacket*, veston, *m.*; *lounge suit*, complet veston, *m.*

lounger ['laundʒə], *n.* flâneur, *m.*

lour, lower (1) ['lauə], *v.i.* froncer les sourcils; s'assombrir, s'obscurcir (*du temps*); *the sky lours*, le temps se couvre.

louring, lowering (1) ['lauəriŋ], *a.* couvert, sombre; (*fig.*) menaçant.

louse [laus], *n.* (*pl.* **lice** [lais]) pou, *m.*

lousy ['lauzi], *a.* pouilleux; (*fig.*) bas, vil, sale.

lout [laut], *n.* rustre, butor, *m.*

loutish ['lautiʃ], *a.* rustre.

lovable ['lʌvəbl], *a.* digne d'être aimé; aimable.

love [lʌv], *v.t.* aimer, adorer.—*n.* amour, *m.*, affection; amitié, *f.*; ami (*mot tendre*), *m.*; (*Ten.*) zéro, rien, *m.*; *my love to all*, mes amitiés à tous; *to be in love with*, être amoureux de.

love affair ['lʌvəfɛə], *n.* amourette, *f.*

love letter ['lʌvletə], *n.* billet doux, *m.*

loveliness ['lʌvlinis], *n.* amabilité; beauté, *f.*, charme, *m.*

lovely ['lʌvli], *a.* charmant, ravissant, séduisant, gracieux.

lover ['lʌvə], *n.* amant, amoureux; amateur (*de*), *m.*

lovesick ['lʌvsik], *a.* en mal d'amour.

loving ['lʌviŋ], *a.* aimant, affectueux, affectionné, tendre; d'amour (*choses*); *loving kindness*, bonté, miséricorde, *f.*

low (1) [lou], *a.* bas, petit; peu élevé, vulgaire; profond (*révérence*); (*fig.*) lent (*fièvre*); abattu (*humeur*); *at low water*, à marée basse; *in a low voice*, d'une voix basse. —*adv.* bas, en bas; à voix basse; profondément (*révérence*).

low (2) [lou], *v.i.* beugler.

low-brow ['loubrau], *a.* peu intellectuel.—*n.* philistin, *m.*

lower (1) [LOUR].

lower (2) ['louə], *a.* plus bas, inférieur; bas.— *v.t.* baisser, abaisser; descendre; rabaisser, humilier; diminuer, affaiblir.

lower class ['louəklɑ:s], *n.* peuple, *m.*

lowering (1) [LOURING].

lowering (2) ['louəriŋ], *n.* abaissement, *m.*, diminution, *f.*

lowest ['louist], *a.* le plus bas, le dernier.

lowing ['louiŋ], *n.* mugissement, beuglement, *m.*

lowliness ['loulinis], *n.* humilité, *f.*

lowly ['louli], *a.* humble.—*adv.* humblement.

lowness ['lounis], *n.* situation basse, petitesse; faiblesse (*santé*); dépression (*prix*), *f.*; abaissement (*température*); abattement (*humeur*), découragement, *m.*; vulgarité, *f.*

loyal ['lɔiəl], *a.* fidèle, loyal.

loyalty ['lɔiəlti], *n.* fidélité, *f.*

lozenge ['lɔzindʒ], *n.* pastille, *f.*; (*Geom.*, *Her. etc.*) losange, *m.*

lubber ['lʌbə], *n.* lourdaud, *m.*; *land-lubber*, marin d'eau douce, *m.*

lubricant ['lu:brikənt], *n.* lubrifiant, *m.*

lubricate ['lu:brikeit], *v.t.* lubrifier.

lubrication [lu:bri'keiʃən], *n.* lubrication, *f.*

lucid ['lu:sid], *a.* lucide; limpide, transparent.

lucidity [lu:'siditi], **lucidness** ['lu:sidnis], *n.* transparence, limpidité, lucidité, *f.*

luck [lʌk], *n.* chance, fortune, *f.*; bonheur, *m.*; *by good luck*, par bonheur; *by ill luck*, par malheur; *good luck*, bonne chance.

luckily ['lʌkili], *adv.* heureusement, par bonheur.

lucky ['lʌki], *a.* heureux; *to be lucky*, avoir de la chance; porter bonheur (*chose*).

lucrative ['lu:krətiv], *a.* lucratif.

lucre ['lu:kə], *n.* lucre, *m.*

Lucy ['lu:si]. Lucie, *f.*

ludicrous ['lu:dikrəs], *a.* risible, comique, ridicule.

luggage ['lʌgidʒ], *n.* bagage, *m.*, bagages, *m.pl.*; *left-luggage office*, consigne, *f.*

lugubrious [lu'gju:briəs], *a.* lugubre.

lukewarm ['lu:kwɔ:m], *a.* tiède; (*fig.*) peu zélé.

lull [lʌl], *v.t.* bercer, endormir; calmer.—*v.i.* se calmer, s'apaiser.—*n.* moment de calme, *m.*; (*Naut.*) accalmie, *f.*

lullaby ['lʌləbai], *n.* berceuse, *f.*

lumbago [lʌm'beigou], *n.* lumbago, *m.*

lumber ['lʌmbə], *n.* vieilleries, *f.pl.*; (*Am.*) bois de charpente, *m.*—*v.t.* entasser sans ordre; remplir de fatras.—*v.i.* se traîner lourdement.

lumbering ['lʌmbəriŋ], *a.* lourd, encombrant.

lumberjack ['lʌmbədʒæk], *n.* bûcheron, *m.*

luminous ['lju:minəs], *a.* lumineux.

lump [lʌmp], *n.* masse, *f.*; morceau, bloc (*piece*), *m.*—*v.t.* prendre en bloc; réunir ensemble.

lumpish ['lʌmpiʃ], *a.* gros, lourd, pesant.

lumpy ['lʌmpi], *a.* grumeleux.

lunacy ['lu:nəsi], *n.* aliénation mentale, *f.*

lunar ['lu:nə], *a.* lunaire.

lunatic ['lu:nətik], *a.* de fou, d'aliéné.—*n.* aliéné; fou, *m.*, folle, *f.*

lunatic asylum ['lu:nətikəsailəm], *n.* asile d'aliénés, *m.*

lunch [lʌntʃ], *n.* déjeuner (*vers midi*), *m.*— *v.i.* déjeuner.

lung [lʌŋ], *n.* (*usu. in pl.*) poumon; mou (*de veau*), *m.*; *iron lung*, poumon d'acier.

lunge [lʌndʒ], *n.* (*Fenc.*) botte, *f.*, coup droit, *m.*—*v.i.* porter une botte.

lupin ['lju:pin], *n.* (*Bot.*) lupin, *m.*

lurch [lə:tʃ], *n.* embardée, *f.*, cahot; (*fig.*) embarras, *m.*; *to leave in the lurch*, planter là.—*v.i.* faire une embardée (*navire*).

lure [ljuə], *n.* leurre, appât, piège; (*fig.*) attrait, *m.*—*v.t.* leurrer, attirer, séduire.

lurid ['ljuərid], *a.* sombre, blafard; sensationnel.

lurk [lə:k], *v.i.* être aux aguets; se tenir caché.

luscious ['lʌʃəs], *a.* délicieux, savoureux; liquoreux (*vin*).

lusciousness ['lʌʃəsnis], *n.* nature succulente, douceur extrême; volupté, *f.*

lush [lʌʃ], *a.* luxuriant.

lust [lʌst], *n.* luxure, *f.*; désir lascif, *m.*; (*fig.*) convoitise, *f.*—*v.i.* désirer immodérément; *to lust after*, convoiter.

luster ['lʌstə], *n.* brillant, lustre; (*fig.*) éclat, *m.*, splendeur, *f.*

lustily ['lʌstili], *adv.* vigoureusement.

lustrous ['lʌstrəs], *a.* brillant, lustré.

lusty ['lʌsti], *a.* vigoureux, robuste, fort.

lute [lju:t], *n.* luth, *m.*

Luxembourg ['lʌksəmbə:g]. le Luxembourg (*Duché*), *n.*

luxuriance [lʌg'zjuəriəns], *n.* exubérance, surabondance, luxuriance, *f.*

luxuriant [lʌg'zjuəriənt], *a.* exubérant, surabondant, luxuriant.

luxurious [lʌg'zjuəriəs], *a.* de luxe, somptueux, luxueux.

luxuriously [lʌg'zjuəriəsli], *adv.* avec luxe, somptueusement.

luxuriousness [lʌg'zjuəriəsnis], *n.* somptuosité, *f.*

luxury ['lʌkʃəri], *n.* luxe, *m.*, exubérance, *f.*; fin morceau; objet de luxe, *m.*

lying ['laiiŋ], *a.* menteur; mensonger (*choses*). —*n.* mensonge, *m.*

lymph [limf], *n.* lymphe, *f.*; vaccin, *m.*

lynch [lintʃ], *v.t.* lyncher (*exécuter sommairement*).

lynx [liŋks], *n.* lynx, *m.*

lyre ['laiǝ], n. lyre, f.
lyric ['lirik], a. lyrique.—n. poème lyrique, m.; (pl.) paroles (d'une chanson), f.pl.
lyrical ['lirikǝl], a. lyrique.

M

M, m [em]. treizième lettre de l'alphabet, m.
macadam [mǝ'kædǝm], n. macadam, m.
macaroni [mækǝ'rouni], n. macaroni, m.
macaroon [mækǝ'ru:n], n. macaron, m.
mace [mejs], n. masse (de cérémonie), f.
mace-bearer ['meisbɛǝrǝ], n. massier, m.
Macedonia [mæsǝ'douniǝ]. la Macédoine, f.
Macedonian [mæsǝ'douniǝn], a. macédonien.—n. Macédonien (personne), m.
macerate ['mæsǝreit], v.t. macérer.
machine [mǝ'ʃi:n], n. machine, f.; (fig.) instrument; appareil (avion), m.
machine gun [mǝ'ʃi:ngʌn], n. mitrailleuse, f.
machinery [mǝ'ʃi:nǝri], n. mécanique, f., mécanisme, m.; machines, f.pl.
machine tool [mǝ'ʃi:ntu:l], n. machine-outil, f.
mackerel ['mækǝrǝl], n. maquereau, m.
mackintosh ['mækintɔʃ], n. imperméable, m.
mad [mæd], a. fou, aliéné, insensé; affolé; furieux (déchaîné); enragé (animal).
Madagascan [mædǝ'gæskǝn], a. malgache.—n. Malgache (personne), m.
Madagascar [mædǝ'gæskǝ]. Madagascar, m.
madam ['mædǝm], n. madame, f.
madcap ['mædkæp], a. étourdi, fou.—n. fou, m.
madden [mædn], v.t. rendre fou; faire enrager.
maddening ['mædniŋ], a. à rendre fou, enrageant.
madder ['mædǝ], n. garance, f.
made [meid], a. fait, confectionné; self-made man, fils de ses œuvres, m.; made up, inventé (histoire); maquillé (visage).
Madeira [mǝ'diǝrǝ]. Madère, f.—n. madère (vin), m.
madly ['mædli], adv. follement, furieusement.
madman ['mædmǝn], n. (pl. -men [men]) aliéné, fou, m.
madness ['mædnis], n. démence, fureur, folie; rage (d'animal), f.
Madonna [mǝ'dɔnǝ]. la Madone, f.
maelstrom ['meilstroum, 'meilstrǝm], n. (Geog.) malstrom; (fig.) tourbillon, m.
magazine [mægǝ'zi:n], n. magasin (boutique; aussi chargeur d'arme à feu); magazine, m., revue (périodique), f.
magenta [mǝ'dʒentǝ], a. and n. magenta (couleur), m.
maggot ['mægǝt], n. larve, f., ver, asticot, m.
magic ['mædʒik], a. magique.—n. magie, f.
magical ['mædʒikǝl], a. magique.
magician [mǝ'dʒiʃǝn], n. magicien, m.
magisterial [mædʒis'tiǝriǝl], a. de maître; magistral.
magistrate ['mædʒistreit], n. magistrat, m.; examining magistrate, juge d'instruc-

tion, m.; police court magistrate, juge de paix, m.
magnanimity [mægnǝ'nimiti], n. magnanimité, f.
magnanimous [mæg'nænimǝs], a. magnanime.
magnate ['mægneit], n. magnat; grand; (colloq.) gros bonnet, m.
magnesia [mæg'ni:ʃǝ], n. magnésie, f.
magnesium [mæg'ni:ziǝm], n. magnésium, m.
magnet ['mægnit], n. aimant, m.
magnetic [mæg'netik], a. aimanté; magnétique; (fig.) attirant.
magnetism ['mægnitizm], n. magnétisme, m.; (Elec.) aimantation, f.
magnetize ['mægnitaiz], v.t. aimanter; (fig.) magnétiser.
magneto [mæg'ni:tou], n. magnéto, f.
magnificence [mæg'nifisǝns], n. magnificence, f.
magnificent [mæg'nifisǝnt], a. magnifique, superbe.
magnify ['mægnifai], v.t. magnifier, augmenter, grossir; (fig.) exalter.
magnifying ['mægnifaiŋ], a. qui grossit; magnifying glass, loupe, f.
magnitude ['mægnitju:d], n. grandeur; importance, f.
magnolia [mæg'nouliǝ], n. (Bot.) magnolia, magnolier, m.
magpie ['mægpai], n. pie, f.
mahogany [mǝ'hɔgǝni], n. acajou, bois d'acajou, m.
maid [meid], n. fille, jeune fille; vierge (virgin); bonne, servante, domestique, f.; chambermaid, fille de chambre; kitchen maid, fille de cuisine; maid of all work, bonne à tout faire; maid of honor, demoiselle d'honneur, f.
maiden [meidn], a. de fille, de jeune fille; virginal; (fig.) pur, neuf; maiden aunt, tante non mariée, f.; maiden name, nom de jeune fille, m.; maiden speech, premier discours (d'un nouveau membre du Parlement), m.; maiden voyage, premier voyage, m.—n. jeune fille, fille, f.
maidenly ['meidnli], a. de jeune fille; modeste, chaste.
mail (1) [meil], n. mailles (armure), f.pl.
mail (2) [meil], n. courrier, m., dépêches (lettres), f.pl.—v.t. (Am.) mettre à la poste.
mail-bag ['meilbæg], n. sac postal, m.
mail train ['meiltrein], n. train-postal, m.
maim [meim], v.t. mutiler, estropier.
main (1) [mein], a. principal, premier; grand; important, essentiel.—n. gros, m., plus grande partie, f.; principal océan, m.; in the main, pour la plupart, en général.
main (2) [mein], n. force, f.
main deck ['meindek], n. premier pont, m.
mainland ['meinlǝnd], n. continent, m.
mainly ['meinli], adv. principalement, surtout.
mainmast ['meinmɑ:st], n. grand mât, m.
mainstay ['meinstei], n. soutien, m.
maintain [mein'tein], v.t. maintenir; soutenir, alléguer; conserver; entretenir, nourrir (subvenir aux besoins de).
maintenance ['meintǝnǝns], n. maintien, soutien; entretien, m.
maize [meiz], n. maïs, m.

majestic [mə'dʒestik], a. majestueux.
majesty ['mædʒəsti], n. majesté, f.; *His* or *Her Majesty*, Sa Majesté.
major ['meidʒə], a. plus grand, majeur.—*n.* commandant, m.; (*Law*) personne majeure, f.; *drum major*, tambour-major, m.; *sergeant major*, adjudant, m.
Majorca [mə'jɔːkə]. Majorque, f.
majority [mə'dʒɔriti], n. majorité, f.
make [meik], v.t. irr. faire; créer, façonner, fabriquer, confectionner; rendre (*faire devenir*); forcer, contraindre (*obliger*); amasser, gagner (*argent*); *to make a mistake*, se tromper; *to make a noise*, faire du bruit, *to make believe*, faire accroire à; *to make fun of*, se moquer de; *to make good*, soutenir; réparer; dédommager de; *to make it up*, se raccommoder; *to make known*, faire connaître, faire savoir à; *to make out*, comprendre, déchiffrer, distinguer; *to make over to*, céder à; *to make sure of*, s'assurer de; *to make up*, compléter, inventer (*histoire*); arranger (*querelle*); régler (*comptes*); *to make up for*, suppléer à; rattraper (*temps*); *to make up one's mind*, se décider.—*v.i.* se diriger (*vers*); contribuer (*à*); faire (*comme si*); *to make believe*, faire semblant; *to make of*, comprendre; *to make off*, se sauver; *to make up*, se maquiller; *to make up for*, suppléer à; dédommager de, compenser.—*n.* façon, forme, tournure; fabrication, f.
make-believe ['meikbili:v], n. feinte, f., semblant, m.
maker ['meikə], n. créateur, auteur; faiseur; (*Comm.*) fabricant, m.
makeshift ['meikʃift], n. pis aller, expédient, m.
make-up ['meikʌp], n. contexture, f.; maquillage (*du visage*), m.
make-weight ['meikweit], n. supplément; (*fig.*) remplissage, m.
making ['meikiŋ], n. création; façon, fabrication, construction; confection (*de vêtements*), f.
maladjusted [mælə'dʒʌstid], a. inadapté.
maladjustment [mælə'dʒʌstmənt], n. inadaptation, f.
maladministration [mælədminis'treiʃən], n. mauvaise administration, f.
malady ['mælədi], n. maladie, f.
malaria [mə'lɛəriə], n. malaria, f., paludisme, m.
Malay [mə'lei], a. malais.—n. malais (*langue*); Malais (*personne*), m.
Malaysia [mə'leiziə]. la Malaisie, f.
Malaysian [mə'leiziən], a. malais.—n. Malais (*personne*), m.
malcontent ['mælkəntent], a. and n. mécontent, m.
male [meil], a. mâle; masculin.—n. mâle, m.
malediction [mæli'dikʃən], n. malédiction, f.
malefactor ['mælifæktə], n. malfaiteur, m.
malevolence [mə'levələns], n. malveillance, f.
malevolent [mə'levələnt], a. malveillant.
Mali ['maːli]. le Mali, m.
malice ['mælis], n. malice; malveillance, méchanceté; rancune, f.; *to bear malice*, vouloir du mal à, garder rancune à.
malicious [mə'liʃəs], a. malicieux, méchant.
maliciously [mə'liʃəsli], adv. méchamment.

maliciousness [mə'liʃəsnis], n. malice, malveillance, f.
malign [mə'lain], a. malin; méchant.—v.t. diffamer, noircir.
malignant [mə'lignənt], a. malin, méchant.
malignantly [mə'lignəntli], adv. malignement, méchamment.
malignity [mə'ligniti], n. malignité, malveillance, f.
malinger [mə'liŋgə], v.i. (*Mil.*) faire le malade; tirer au flanc.
mall (1) [mɔːl], n. gros maillet, m.
mall (2) [mæl], n. mail (*rue*), m.
mallard ['mæləd], n. (*Orn.*) canard sauvage, m.
malleability [mæliə'biliti], n. malléabilité, f.
malleable ['mæliəbl], a. malléable.
mallet ['mælit], n. maillet, m.; tapette, f.
mallow ['mælou], n. (*Bot.*) mauve, f.
malmsey ['maːmzi], n. malvoisie, f.
malnutrition [mælnju'triʃən], n. sous-alimentation, f.
malpractice [mæl'præktis], n. malversation, f., méfait, m.
malt [mɔːlt], n. malt, m.—v.t. malter.
Malta ['mɔːltə]. Malte, f.
Maltese [mɔːl'tiːz], a. maltais.—n. Maltais (*personne*), m.
maltreat [mæl'triːt], v.t. maltraiter.
maltreatment [mæl'triːtmənt], n. mauvais traitement, m.
mammal ['mæməl], n. mammifère, m.
mammoth ['mæməθ], n. mammouth, m.
man [mæn], n. (*pl.* men [men]) homme; domestique, valet (*servant*), m.; (*Chess*) pièce, f.; (*Draughts*) pion, m.; *the man in the street*, l'homme de la rue, le grand public.—v.t. garnir d'hommes; armer (*pompe, bateau*).
manacle ['mænəkl], v.t. mettre les menottes à.—n. (*pl.*) menottes, f.pl.
manage ['mænidʒ], v.t. diriger, mener, conduire; arranger (*choses*); gouverner, administrer, gérer; ménager (*habilement*); manier, dompter (*cheval*).—v.i. s'arranger (*pour*), parvenir à; venir à bout (*de*).
manageable ['mænidʒəbl], a. traitable, maniable.
management ['mænidʒmənt], n. conduite, administration, f.; (*Comm.*) gestion (*direction*), f.; artifice, savoir-faire (*manège*), m.
manager ['mænidʒə], n. directeur, administrateur; (*Comm.*) gérant; (*Theat.*) régisseur; (*Spt.*) manager, m.
manageress [mænidʒə'res], n. directrice, gérante, f.
Manchuria [mæn'tʃuəriə]. la Mandchourie, f.
Manchu(rian) [mæn'tʃu(əriən)], a. mandchou.—n. mandchou (*langue*); Mandchou (*personne*), m.
mandarin ['mændərin], n. mandarin, m.; mandarine (*orange*), f.
mandate ['mændeit], n. commandement, mandat; ordre, m.
mandatory ['mændətəri], a. and n. mandataire, m.
mandolin ['mændəlin], n. mandoline, f.
mane [mein], n. crinière, f.
maneuver, see **manœuvre**.
manfully ['mænfuli], adv. en homme, virilement, vaillamment.
manganese ['mæŋgəniːz], n. manganèse, m.

mange [meindʒ], *n.* gale (*d'animaux*), *f.*

manger ['meindʒə], *n.* mangeoire, crèche *f.*

mangle [mæŋgl], *v.t.* déchirer, mutiler; calandrer (*linge*).—*n.* calandre, *f.*

mango ['mæŋgou], *n.* (*Bot.*) mangue, *f.*; manguier (*arbre*), *m.*

mangrove ['mæŋgrouv], *n.* (*Bot.*) mangle, *f.*; manglier, manguier (*arbre*), *m.*

mangy [meindʒi], *a.* galeux.

man-handle ['mænhændl], *v.t.* manutentionner; (*fig.*) maltraiter.

man-hole ['mænhoul], *n.* bouche d'égout, *f.*

manhood ['mænhud], *n.* virilité, *f.*; âge viril, *m.*; nature humaine, *f.*

mania ['meiniə], *n.* folie, rage, manie, *f.*

maniac ['meiniæk], *a.* furieux, fou.—*n.* fou furieux, fou, *m.*; (*fig.*) maniaque, *m.*, *f.*

maniacal [mə'naiəkl], *a.* furieux, fou.

manicure ['mænikjuə], *n.* soin des ongles, *m.* —*v.t.* soigner les ongles.

manicurist ['mænikjuərist], *n.* manucure, *m.*, *f.*

manifest ['mænifest], *v.t.* manifester, témoigner, montrer; **to manifest a cargo**, déclarer une cargaison.—*a.* manifeste, évident.—*n.* manifeste, *m.*

manifestation [mænifes'teiʃən], *n.* manifestation, *f.*

manifesto [mæni'festou], *n.* manifeste, *m.*

manifold ['mænifould], *a.* divers, multiple; varié.

manikin ['mænikin], *n.* bout d'homme, mannequin, homuncule, *m.*

Manila [mə'nilə], Manille, *f.*

manipulate [mə'nipjuleit], *v.t.* manipuler.

mankind [mæn'kaind], *n.* genre humain, *m.*, l'humanité, *f.*

manlike ['mænlaik], *a.* d'homme, viril; mâle; hommasse (*femme*).

manliness ['mænlinis], *n.* caractère viril, *m.*

manly ['mænli], *a.* d'homme, viril, mâle.

manna ['mænə], *n.* manne, *f.*

mannequin ['mænikin], *n.* (*Dress.*) mannequin, *m.*; **mannequin parade**, défilé de mannequins, *m.*

manner ['mænə], *n.* manière, *f.*, air; genre, *m.*, sorte, façon, espèce; coutume, habitude, *f.*; (*pl.*) mœurs, *f.pl.*, politesse, *f.*; **after the manner of**, à la manière de, d'après; **all manner of things**, toutes sortes de choses, *f.pl.*; **in the same manner as**, de même que.

mannerism ['mænərizm], *n.* air maniéré, maniérisme; tic, *m.*

mannerly ['mænəli], *a.* poli.

manning ['mæniŋ], *n.* armement, équipement, *m.*

mannish ['mæniʃ], *a.* hommasse.

manœuvre [mə'nu:və], *n.* manœuvre, *f.*—*v.t.*, *v.i.* manœuvrer.

manor ['mænə], *n.* seigneurie, *f.*; manoir, château seigneurial, *m.*

manorial [mə'nɔ:riəl], *a.* seigneurial.

man-power ['mænpauə], *n.* main d'œuvre, *f.*

manse [mæns], *n.* presbytère, *m.*

mansion ['mænʃən], *n.* château (*à la campagne*); hôtel particulier (*en ville*), *m.*

manslaughter ['mænslɔ:tə], *n.* (*Law*) homicide involontaire, *m.*

mantel [mæntl], **mantelpiece** ['mæntlpi:s], *n.* manteau *ou* dessus de cheminée, *m.*, cheminée, *f.*

mantilla [mæn'tilə], *n.* mantille, *f.*

mantis ['mæntis], *n.* (*Ent.*) mante, *f.*; **praying mantis**, mante religieuse.

mantle [mæntl], *n.* manteau, *m.*—*v.t.* couvrir, voiler.

manual ['mænjuəl], *a.* manuel, de la main.—*n.* manuel (*livre*); (*Organ*) clavier, *m.*

manufacture [mænju'fæktʃə], *n.* manufacture, confection, fabrication, *f.*; (*pl.*) produits manufacturés, *m.pl.*—*v.t.* manufacturer, fabriquer.

manufacturer [mænju'fæktʃərə], *n.* fabricant, industriel, *m.*

manure [mə'njuə], *n.* engrais, fumier, *m.*—*v.t.* engraisser, fumer.

manuscript ['mænjuskript], *a.* and *n.* manuscrit, *m.*

Manx [mæŋks], *a.* de l'île de Man, mannois; **Manx cat**, chat sans queue, *m.*

many ['meni], *a.* beaucoup (*de*), bien (*des*); nombreux; plusieurs, maint; **as many as**, autant que, jusqu'à (*devant un numéro*); **how many?** combien? **many a time**, maintes fois; **so many**, tant, tant de; **too many**, trop, trop de.—*n.* **the many**, la multitude, la foule, *f.*

many-colored ['menikʌləd], *a.* multicolore.

many-sided ['menisaidid], *a.* polygone; (*fig.*) complexe.

map [mæp], *n.* carte, carte géographique, *f.*; **map of a town**, plan d'une ville, *m.*; **map of the world**, mappemonde, *f.*—*v.t.* faire une carte *ou* un plan de, tracer.

maple [meipl], *n.* érable, *m.*

mar [mɑ:], *v.t.* gâter, défigurer; (*fig.*) troubler.

marathon ['mærəθən], *n.* marathon, *m.*

marauder [mə'rɔ:də], *n.* maraudeur, malandrin, *m.*

marauding [mə'rɔ:diŋ], *n.* maraude, *f.*, maraudage, *f.*

marble [mɑ:bl], *a.* de marbre.—*n.* marbre, *m.*; bille (*jouet*), *f.*

marbled [mɑ:bld], *a.* marbré.

marbling ['mɑ:bliŋ], *n.* marbrure, *f.*

March [mɑ:tʃ]. mars (*mois*), *m.*

march (1) [mɑ:tʃ], *n.* (*Mil.*) marche, *f.*; (*fig.*) progrès, *m.*; **march past**, défilé, *m.*—*v.t.* mettre en marche; emmener.—*v.i.* marcher, se mettre en marche; (*fig.*) avancer; **to march past**, défiler devant.

march (2) [mɑ:tʃ], *n.* frontière, *f.*

marching ['mɑ:tʃiŋ], *a.* de marche.—*n.* marche, *f.*

marchioness [mɑ:ʃə'nes], *n.* marquise, *f.*

mare [mɛə], *n.* jument, *f.*

Margaret ['mɑ:gərit]. Marguerite, *f.*

margarine ['mɑ:gəri:n, mɑ:dʒəri:n], *n.* margarine, *f.*

margin ['mɑ:dʒin], *n.* marge (*de papier etc.*), *f.*; bord (*de rivière, de lac*), *m.*—*v.t.* border.

marginal ['mɑ:dʒinəl], *a.* en marge; marginal.

marigold ['mærigould], *n.* (*Bot.*) souci, *m.*

marine [mə'ri:n], *a.* marin, de mer; naval.—*n.* fusilier marin, *m.*; **tell that to the marines**, allez conter cela à d'autres.

mariner ['mærinə], *n.* marin, *m.*

maritime ['mæritaim], *a.* maritime.

Mark [mɑ:k]. Marc, *m.*

mark (1) [mɑ:k], *n.* marque, *f.*, signe, *m.*; empreinte; (*fig.*) distinction, importance, *f.*; témoignage (*d'estime*), *m.*; (*Sch.*) note, *f.*, point, *m.*; cible (*but*); croix (*signature*), *f.* —*v.t.* marquer, remarquer; (*Sch.*) noter; (*fig.*) observer, faire attention à.

mark (2) [mɑːk], *n.* marc (*pièce de monnaie*), *m.*

marked [mɑːkt], *a.* marqué, évident; prononcé (*accent*).

marker ['mɑːkə], *n.* marqueur; jeton (*au jeu*); signet (*de livre*), *m.*

market ['mɑːkit], *n.* marché, *m.*; halle, *f.*; débit (*vente*); cours (*prix*); (*Comm.*) débouché, *m.*—*v.t.* acheter au marché, vendre au marché.

market garden ['mɑːkit'gɑːdn], *n.* jardin maraîcher, *m.*

market gardener ['mɑːkit'gɑːdnə], *n.* maraîcher, *m.*

marking ['mɑːkiŋ], *n.* marquage, *m.*

marking ink ['mɑːkiŋiŋk], *n.* encre à marquer, *f.*

marksman ['mɑːksmən], *n.* (*pl.* -**men** [men]) bon tireur, *m.*

marksmanship ['mɑːksmənʃip], *n.* adresse au tir, *f.*

marl [mɑːl], *n.* marne, *f.*—*v.t.* marner.

marline-spike ['mɑːlinspaik], *n.* épissoir, *m.*

marmalade ['mɑːməleid], *n.* confiture d'oranges, *f.*

marmoset ['mɑːməzet], *n.* ouistiti, *m.*

marmot ['mɑːmət], *n.* marmotte, *f.*

maroon (1) [mə'ruːn], *n.* noir marron, *m.*—*v.t.* abandonner dans une île déserte.

maroon (2) [mə'ruːn], *a.* and *n.* marron pourpré (*couleur*), *m.*

marquee [mɑː'kiː], *n.* grande tente, *f.*

marquess, marquis ['mɑːkwis], *n.* marquis, *m.*

marquetry [mɑːkətri], *n.* marqueterie, *f.*

marquis [MARQUESS].

marriage ['mærid3], *n.* mariage, *m.*; noces (*fêtes*), *f.pl.*

marriageable ['mærid3əbl], *a.* mariable, nubile.

married ['mærid], *a.* marié; conjugal.

marrow ['mærou], *n.* moelle; (*fig.*) essence, *f.*; *vegetable marrow*, courgette, *f.*

marry ['mæri], *v.t.* marier (*donner ou unir en mariage*); se marier avec, épouser (*prendre pour époux*).—*v.i.* se marier.

Marseilles [mɑː'seilz]. Marseille, *f.*

marsh [mɑːʃ], *n.* marais, *m.*

marshal ['mɑːʃl], *n.* maréchal.—*v.t.* ranger; mettre en ordre; classer.

marsh-mallow ['mɑːʃ'mælou], *n.* (*Bot.*) guimauve, *f.*; bonbon à la guimauve, *m.*

marshy ['mɑːʃi], *a.* marécageux.

mart [mɑːt], *n.* marché, entrepôt, *m.*

marten [mɑːtn], *n.* martre, *f.*; *beech marten*, fouine, *f.*

Martha ['mɑːθə]. Marthe, *f.*

martial [mɑːʃl], *a.* martial; de guerre, de bataille; guerrier, belliqueux.

martin [mɑːtin], *n.* martin, martinet, *m.*

martinet [mɑːti'net], *n.* officier strict sur la discipline, *m.*

Martinmas ['mɑːtinmæs]. la Saint-Martin, *f.*

martyr ['mɑːtə], *n.* martyr, *m.*—*v.t.* martyriser.

martyrdom ['mɑːtədəm], *n.* martyre, *m.*

martyrize ['mɑːtəraiz], *v.t.* (*fam.*) faire souffrir, martyriser.

marvel [mɑːvl], *n.* merveille, *f.*—*v.i.* s'émerveiller, s'étonner.

marvellous ['mɑːv(i)ləs], *a.* merveilleux, étonnant.

marvellously ['mɑːv(i)ləsli], *adv.* à merveille.

Marxism ['mɑːksizm], *n.* Marxisme, *m.*

Marxist ['mɑːksist], *a.* marxiste.—*n.* Marxiste, *m.*, *f.*

Mary ['mɛəri]. Marie, *f.*

marzipan [mɑːzi'pæn], *n.* massepain, *m.*

mascot ['mæskət], *n.* mascotte, *f.*

masculine ['mæskjulin], *a.* mâle, d'homme; (*Gram.*) masculin; hommasse (*femme*).—*n.* masculin, *m.*

mash [mæʃ], *n.* mélange, *m.*, pâte, bouillie; mâche (*pour bestiaux*), *f.*; pâtée (*pour chien, volaille*), *f.*—*v.t.* broyer; mélanger; (*Brewing*) brasser; *mashed potatoes*, purée de pommes de terre, *f.*

mask [mɑːsk], *n.* masque; loup (*de soie, de velours*), *m.*—*v.t.* masquer; déguiser.—*v.i.* se masquer.

mason [meisn], *n.* maçon, *m.*; *freemason*, franc-maçon, *m.*

masonic [mə'sɔnik], *a.* maçonnique.

masonry ['meisənri], *n.* maçonnerie, *f.*; *freemasonry*, franc-maçonnerie, *f.*

masquerade [mæskə'reid], *n.* mascarade *f.* —*v.i.* se masquer; *to masquerade as*, se faire passer pour.

mass (1) [mæs], *n.* masse, *f.*; amas, gros, *m.*; multitude, foule (*de gens*), *f.*—*v.t.* se masser; s'amonceler (*nuages*).

mass (2) [mæs, mɑːs], *n.* (*R.-C. Ch.*) messe, *f.*

massacre ['mæsəkə], *n.* massacre, *m.*—*v.t.* massacrer.

massive ['mæsiv], *a.* massif.

mass meeting ['mæs'miːtiŋ], *n.* assemblée en masse, *f.*, grand meeting, *m.*

mast [mɑːst], *n.* mât, *m.*; (*pl.*) mâts, *m.pl.*, mâture, *f.*; *half-mast*, à mi-mât, en berne.

master ['mɑːstə], *n.* maître, directeur, chef; (*Naut.*) patron, maître (*d'un navire*); patron (*d'ouvriers*); (*Sch. etc.*) maître d'école, professeur; (*fig.*) possesseur, *m.*—*v.t.* maîtriser, surmonter, dompter, vaincre; se rendre maître de; l'emporter sur.

masterful ['mɑːstəful], *a.* de maître, impérieux, dominateur.

master key ['mɑːstəkiː], *n.* passe-partout, *m.*

masterly ['mɑːstəli], *a.* de maître; magistral.

master-mind ['mɑːstəmaind], *n.* esprit supérieur, *m.*

masterpiece ['mɑːstəpiːs], *n.* chef-d'œuvre, *m.*

master-stroke ['mɑːstəstrouk], **master-touch** ['mɑːstətʌtʃ], *n.* coup de maître, *m.*

mastery ['mɑːstəri], *n.* empire, pouvoir, *m.*; supériorité, maîtrise, *f.*

masticate ['mæstikeit], *v.t.* mâcher.

mastication [mæsti'keiʃən], *n.* mastication, *f.*

mastiff ['mæstif], *n.* mâtin, *m.*

mastitis [mæs'taitis], *n.* mastite, *f.*

mastodon ['mæstodon], *n.* mastodonte, *m.*

mastoid ['mæstoid], *a.* mastoïde.

mat [mæt], *n.* natte, *f.*; dessous de lampe, *m.*; *door mat*, paillasson, *m.*; *table mat*, dessous de plat, *m.*—*v.t.* natter, tresser.

match (1) [mætʃ], *n.* pareil, pendant, égal (*semblable*); mariage; parti (*futur époux*), *m.*; lutte (*concours*), *f.*; (*Spt.*) match, *m.*; partie; course, *f.*; **to be a bad match,** aller mal ensemble (*choses*); **to be more than a match for,** être trop fort pour; **to make a good match,** faire un bon mariage.—*v.t.* assortir, appareiller, égaler, apparier (*deux choses*); se mesurer avec (*opposer*).—*v.i.* s'assortir, être pareil.

match (2) [mætʃ], *n.* allumette, *f.*

match-box ['mætʃbɔks], *n.* boîte d'allumettes *ou* à allumettes, *f.*

matchless ['mætʃlis], *a.* incomparable, sans pareil.

match-maker (1) ['mætʃmeikə], *n.* marieur, *m.*

match-maker (2) ['mætʃmeikə], *n.* fabricant d'allumettes, *m.*

mate (1) [meit], *n.* camarade, compagnon, *m.*, compagne, *f.*; second (*de marine marchande*), *m.*—*v.t.* égaler, assortir, apparier; tenir compagnie avec; accoupler (*oiseaux*).—*v.i.* s'accoupler (*animaux*).

mate (2) [meit], *n.* (*Chess*) mat, *m.*—*v.t.* mater.

material [mə'tiəriəl], *a.* matériel; important. —*n.* matière; étoffe, *f.*, tissu (*textile*); matériel (*réserves*), *m.*; (*pl.*) matériaux, *m.pl.*; **raw material,** matière première.

materialism [mə'tiəriəlizm], *n.* matérialisme, *m.*

materialist [mə'tiəriəlist], *n.* matérialiste, *m.*, *f.*

materialistic [mətiəriə'listik], *a.* matérialiste.

materialize [mə'tiəriəlaiz], *v.t.* matérialiser. —*v.i.* se réaliser; se concrétiser.

materially [mə'tiəriəli], *adv.* matériellement; essentiellement.

maternal [mə'tə:nl], *a.* maternel.

maternity [mə'tə:niti], *n.* maternité, *f.*

mathematics [mæθə'mætiks], *n.pl.* mathématiques, *f.pl.*

Matilda [mə'tildə]. Mathilde, *f.*

matins ['mætinz], *n.pl.* matines, *f.pl.*

matriarch ['meitriɑːk], *n.* matriarche, *f.*

matricide ['mætrisaid], *n.* matricide (*crime*), *m.*; matricide (*criminel*), *m.*, *f.*

matrimonial [mætri'mouniəl], *a.* conjugal.

matrimony ['mætriməni], *n.* mariage, *m.*, vie conjugale, *f.*

matron ['meitrən], *n.* matrone, mère de famille; infirmière en chef, *f.*

matronly ['meitrənli], *a.* de matrone; d'un certain âge; respectable.

matt [mæt], *a.* mat.

matter ['mætə], *n.* matière; chose, affaire, *f.*; fond; sujet; (*Med.*) pus, *m.*; (*fig.*) importance, *f.*; **as a matter of fact,** le fait est que; **what is the matter? Nothing,** qu'y a-t-il? Il n'y a rien; **what is the matter with you? Nothing,** qu'avez-vous? Je n'ai rien.—*v.imp.* importer; **it doesn't matter,** n'importe; **it doesn't matter very much,** ce n'est pas grand'chose; **it matters little,** peu importe; **what matter?** qu'importe?

matter-of-fact ['mætərəvfækt], *a.* pratique, positif.

Matthew ['mæθju]. Mathieu, *m.*

mattock ['mætək], *n.* pioche, *f.*

mattress ['mætris], *n.* matelas, *m.*

mature [mə'tjuə], *a.* mûr, mûri.—*v.t.* mûrir, faire mûrir.—*v.i.* mûrir; (*Comm.*) échoir.

maturity [mə'tjuəriti], *n.* maturité; (*Comm.*) échéance, *f.*

matutinal [mætju'tainl], *a.* matutinal, du matin.

Maud [mɔːd]. Madelon, *f.*

maudlin ['mɔːdlin], *a.* pleurard, pleurnichard.

maul [mɔːl], *n.* maillet, *m.*—*v.t.* rosser, rouer de coups.

maul-stick ['mɔːlstik], *n.* (*Paint.*) appui-main, *m.*

Mauritania [mɔri'teiniə]. la Mauritanie, *f.*

Mauritanian [mɔri'teiniən], *a.* mauritanien. —*n.* Mauritanien (*personne*), *m.*

Mauritian [mə'riʃən], *a.* mauritien.—*n.* Mauritien (*personne*),.*m.*

Mauritius [mə'riʃəs]. l'Île Maurice, *f.*

mausoleum [mɔːsə'liːəm], *n.* mausolée, *m.*

mauve [mouv], *a.* mauve.

maw [mɔː], *n.* jabot (*d'oiseau*), *m.*; caillette (*de ruminant*), *f.*

mawkish ['mɔːkiʃ], *a.* fade, insipide; sottement sentimental.

maxim ['mæksim], *n.* maxime, *f.*

maximum ['mæksiməm], *n.* (*pl.* **maxima** ['mæksimə]) maximum, *m.*

May [mei]. mai (*mois*), *m.*

may [mei], *v.aux. irr.* pouvoir, être autorisé à; **he may go,** il peut sortir; **it may be that,** il se peut que (*with subj.*); **it might be,** cela se pourrait; **maybe,** peut-être; **may I? puis-je? one might as well,** autant vaudrait; **that may be,** cela se peut; **that might be,** cela pourrait être; **you might have gone there,** vous auriez pu y aller.

may-blossom ['meiblɔsəm], *n.* aubépine, *f.*

May Day ['meidei], *n.* premier mai, *m.*

mayor [mɛə], *n.* maire, *m.*

maze [meiz], *n.* labyrinthe, dédale; (*fig.*) embarras, *m.*

mazy ['meizi], *a.* sinueux; (*fig.*) compliqué.

mazurka [mə'zəːkə], *n.* mazurka, *f.*

me [miː], *pron.* me, moi.

mead [miːd], *n.* hydromel; (*poet.*) pré (*champ*), *m.*

meadow ['medou], *n.* pré, *m.*, prairie, *f.*

meager ['miːgə], *a.* maigre; pauvre.

meagerness ['miːgənis], *n.* maigreur; pauvreté, *f.*

meal (1) [miːl], *n.* repas, *m.*

meal (2) [miːl], *n.* farine, *f.*

mealy ['miːli], *a.* farineux, poudreux.

mealy-mouthed ['miːlimauðd], *a.* doucereux.

mean (1) [miːn], *a.* bas, méprisable, vil, abject; médiocre (*de peu de valeur*); mesquin; pauvre, humble; sordide; avare; **a mean trick,** un vilain tour.

mean (2) [miːn], *a.* moyen.—*n.* milieu, moyen terme, *m.*; (*Math.*) moyenne, *f.*; **golden mean,** le juste milieu.

mean (3) [miːn], *v.t. irr.* signifier, vouloir dire, entendre; se proposer de, avoir l'intention de, vouloir (*to intend*); destiner (*pour* ou *de*); **do you mean it?** êtes-vous sérieux? **what does that word mean?** que veut dire ce mot? **what do you mean?** que voulez-vous dire?—*v.i.* vouloir, entendre; **to mean well,** avoir de bonnes intentions.

meander [mi'ændə], *n.* détour, méandre, *m.*, sinuosité, *f.*—*v.i.* serpenter.

meandering [mi'ændəriŋ], *a.* onduleux, sinueux, tortueux.

meaning ['ni:niŋ], *a.* significatif; à intentions; **well-meaning**, bien intentionné.—*n.* signification, *f.*, sens, *m.*; intention, *f.*, dessein, *m.*; pensée (*idée*), *f.*; **double meaning**, double sens.

meaningless ['mi:niŋlis], *a.* qui n'a pas de sens, dénué de sens.

meanly ['mi:nli], *adv.* bassement; vilement; abjectement; pauvrement; médiocrement.

meanness ['mi:nnis], *n.* bassesse; pauvreté, mesquinerie; médiocrité, *f.*

means [mi:nz], *n.* moyen, *m.*, voie, *f.*; moyens, *m.pl.*, fortune, *f.*, ressources, *f.pl.*

meantime ['mi:ntaim], **meanwhile** ['mi:n wail], *n.* and *adv. in the meantime*, dans l'intervalle, en attendant, cependant, sur ces entrefaites.

measles [mi:zlz], *n.pl.* rougeole, *f.*; **German measles**, rubéole, *f.*

measurable ['meʒərəbl], *a.* mesurable.

measure ['meʒə], *n.* mesure; (*fig.*) capacité, portée, *f.*; (*Parl.*) projet de loi, *m.*; assise (*de charbon*), *f.*—*v.t.* mesurer; arpenter (*terre*); prendre mesure à (*une personne pour vêtements*); (*fig.*) considérer, toiser, métrer; **this measures ten feet**, ceci a dix pieds de longueur.

measured ['meʒəd], *a.* mesuré; égal, cadencé.

measurement ['meʒəmənt], *n.* mesurage; arpentage (*de terre*), *m.*; mesure, dimension, *f.*

meat [mi:t], *n.* viande; nourriture, *f.*, aliment (*manger*), *m.*

meat-safe ['mi:tseif], *n.* garde-manger, *m.*

meaty ['mi:ti], *a.* charnu; (*fig.*) bien rempli.

Mecca ['mekə], la Mecque, *f.*

mechanic [mi'kænik], *n.* artisan, ouvrier mécanicien, *m.*; **garage mechanic**, garagiste, *m.*

mechanical [mi'kænikəl], *a.* mécanique; d'ouvrier; machinal (*fait sans intelligence*).

mechanically [mi'kænikli], *adv.* mécaniquement; machinalement (*sans intelligence*).

mechanics [mi'kæniks], *n.pl.* mécanique, *f.*

mechanism ['mekənizm], *n.* mécanisme, *m.*

mechanization [mekənai'zeiʃən], *n.* mécanisation, *f.*

mechanize ['mekənaiz], *v.t.* mécaniser; **mechanized farming**, motoculture, *f.*; **mechanized army**, armée motorisée, *f.*

medal [medl], *n.* médaille, *f.*

medallion [mi'dæljən], *n.* médaillon, *m.*

medallist ['medlist], *n.* médaillé (*honoré*), *m.*

meddle [medl], *v.i.* se mêler (*de*), toucher (*à*), s'immiscer (*dans*).

meddler ['medlə], *n.* intrigant; officieux, *m.*

meddlesome ['medlsəm], **meddling** ['medliŋ], *a.* intrigant; officieux.

mediaeval [medi'i:vəl], *a.* du moyen âge.

medial ['mi:diəl], *a.* moyen; (*Gram.*) médial.

mediate ['mi:dieit], *v.i.* s'entremettre; s'interposer (*dans*).

mediation [mi:di'eiʃən], *n.* médiation, entremise, *f.*

mediator ['mi:dieitə], *n.* médiateur, *m.*

medical ['medikəl], *a.* médical; de médecine (*école*); en médecine (*étudiant*); **medical officer**, officier sanitaire, *m.*; **to take medical advice**, consulter un médecin.

medicament [me'dikəmənt], *n.* médicament, *m.*

medicinal [mə'disinl], *a.* médicinal.

medicine ['medsin], *n.* médecine, *f.*, médicament; (*fig.*) remède, *m.*

medicine chest ['medsintʃest], *n.* pharmacie, *f.*

medicine man ['medsinmæn], *n.* sorcier, *m.*

mediocre ['mi:dioukə], *a.* médiocre.

mediocrity [mi:di'ɔkriti], *n.* médiocrité, *f.*

meditate ['mediteit], *v.t.* se proposer de, projeter.—*v.i.* méditer (*sur.*).

meditation [medi'teiʃən], *n.* méditation, *f.*

Mediterranean [meditə'reinjən], *a.* méditerrané; méditerranéen.—*n.* la Méditerranée, *f.*

medium ['mi:djəm], *a.* moyen.—*n.* (*pl.* **media** ['mi:diə], **mediums** ['mi:djəmz]) milieu, moyen, *m.*; voie, entremise; (*Math.*) moyenne proportionnelle, *f.*; agent intermédiaire; (*Spiritualism*) médium, *m.*

medlar ['medlə], *n.* nèfle (*fruit*), *f.*; néflier (*arbre*), *m.*

medley ['medli], *a.* mêlé, hétéroclite.—*n.* mélange, *m.*; confusion, *f.*; (*Mus.*) pot pourri, *m.*

medulla [mi'dʌlə], *n.* médulle, moelle, *f.*

meed [mi:d], *n.* récompense; part (*portion*), *f.*

meek [mi:k], *a.* doux, humble, soumis.

meekly ['mi:kli], *adv.* avec douceur; humblement.

meekness ['mi:knis], *n.* douceur; humilité, *f.*

meet (1) [mi:t], *v.t. irr.* rencontrer, aller à la rencontre de; trouver, recevoir (*atteindre*); faire la connaissance de; faire face à, affronter (*braver*); se présenter devant (*paraître devant*); faire honneur à (*dette*); (*fig.*) satisfaire, remplir (*demande*). *v.i.* se rencontrer; se voir; se réunir, s'assembler; se joindre (*s'unir*); **to meet half-way**, se faire des concessions mutuelles.—*n.* rendez-vous de chasse, *m.*

meet (2) [mi:t], *a.* propre, convenable.

meeting ['mi:tiŋ], *n.* rencontre; entrevue; assemblée, réunion, *f.*; meeting, *m.*; séance (*session*), *f.*; confluent (*rivières*), *m.*; jonction (*routes*), *f.*

megaton ['megatɔn], *n.* mégatonne, *f.*

melancholy ['melənkəli], *a.* mélancolique, triste, affligeant.—*n.* mélancolie, tristesse, *f.*

mellifluous [mə'lifluəs], *a.* mielleux, doucereux.

mellow ['melou], *a.* mûr, fondant (*fruit*); moelleux, doux; gris (*à moitié ivre*); meuble (*terre*).—*v.t.* mûrir, faire mûrir; ameublir (*terre*); (*fig.*) adoucir.—*v.i.* mûrir; devenir meuble (*terre*); (*fig.*) s'adoucir.

mellowness ['melounis], *n.* maturité, *f.*; moelleux, *m.*; (*fig.*) douceur, *f.*

melodious [mə'loudiəs], *a.* mélodieux.

melodiously [mə'loudiəsli], *adv.* mélodieusement.

melodrama ['melədraːmə], *n.* mélodrame, *m.*

melodramatic [melədrə'mætik], *a.* mélodramatique.

melody ['melədi], *n.* mélodie, *f.*, air, *m.*

melon ['melən], *n.* melon, *m.*

melt [melt], *v.t.* fondre, faire fondre; (*fig.*) attendrir.—*v.i.* fondre, se fondre; (*fig.*) s'attendrir.

melting

melting ['meltiŋ], a. qui fond; fondant (glace); (fig.) attendrissant.—n. fusion, fonte, f.; attendrissement, m.
melting pot ['meltiŋpɔt], n. creuset, m.
member ['membə], n. membre; (Parl.) député, m.
membered ['membəd], a. membré; qui a des membres; large-membered, membru.
membership ['membəʃip], n. les membres d'une société etc., m.pl.
membrane ['membrein], n. membrane, f.
memento [mə'mentou], n. souvenir, mémento, m.
memoir ['memwɑː], n. mémoire, m.
memorable ['memərəbl], a. mémorable.
memorandum [memə'rændəm], n. (pl. memoranda [memə'rændə]) note, f., mémorandum, m.; (Comm.) bordereau, m.
memorial [mi'mɔːriəl], a. commémoratif.— n. souvenir, mémoire; monument commémoratif, m.; requête, pétition, f.
memorize ['meməraiz], v.t. apprendre par cœur.
memory ['meməri], n. mémoire, f.; (colloq.) souvenir, m.; in memory of, en souvenir de; to the best of my memory, autant qu'il m'en souvient.
men [MAN].
menace ['menəs], n. menace, f.—v.t. menacer.
menagerie [mə'nædʒəri], n. ménagerie, f.
mend [mend], v.t. raccommoder, réparer; corriger, améliorer; to mend one's ways, rentrer dans le bon chemin.—v.i. s'améliorer, se corriger; se rétablir (santé); se remettre au beau (temps).
mendacious [men'deiʃəs], a. mensonger.
mendacity [men'dæsiti], n. mensonge, m.; duplicité, f.
mendicant ['mendikənt], a. and n. mendiant, m.
mendicity [men'disiti], n. mendicité, f.
mending ['mendiŋ], n. raccommodage; reprisage (des bas), m.; réparation, f.
menial ['miːniəl], a. de domestique; (fig.) servile.—n. domestique, m., f.; (fig.) valet, laquais, m.
meningitis [menin'dʒaitis], n. méningite, f.
mental [mentl], a. mental; a mental case, un aliéné.
mentality [men'tæliti], n. mentalité, f.; esprit, m.
mention ['menʃən], n. mention, indication, f. —v.t. dire, faire mention de, mentionner, parler de; citer; don't mention it! il n'y a pas de quoi! not to mention, sans compter.
menu ['menju], n. menu, m., carte, f.
mercantile ['məːkəntail], a. marchand, de commerce, commerçant; mercantile marine, marine marchande, f.
mercenary ['məːsənri], a. mercenaire, vénal. —n. mercenaire, m.
merchandise ['məːtʃəndaiz], n. marchandise, f.
merchant ['məːtʃənt], a. marchand; commercial.—n. négociant, commerçant; marchand en gros, m.
merchantman ['məːtʃəntmən] (pl. -men [men]), merchant ship ['məːtʃəntʃip], n. navire marchand, m.
merchant marine ['məːtʃənt mə'riːn], n. marine marchande, f.

merciful ['məːsiful], a. miséricordieux.
merciless ['məːsilis], a. sans pitié, impitoyable.
mercurial [məː'kjuəriəl], a. de Mercure; de mercure; (fig.) mercuriel, vif.
mercury ['məːkjuəri], n. mercure, m.
mercy ['məːsi], n. miséricorde; pitié; grâce, indulgence (pardon), f.; for mercy's sake, par grâce; recommendation to mercy, recours en grâce, m.; sisters of mercy, sœurs de charité, f.pl.
mere (1) [miə], n. lac, étang, m.
mere (2) [miə], a. pur, simple, seul, rien que.
merely ['miəli], adv. simplement, seulement, rien que.
meretricious [meri'triʃəs], a. d'un éclat factice (style).
merge [məːdʒ], v.t. fondre, amalgamer, absorber.—v.i. se perdre (dans).
merger ['məːdʒə], n. fusion, f.
meridian [mə'ridiən], a. méridien; de midi. —n. méridien; (fig.) apogée, m.
merino [mə'riːnou], n. mérinos, m.
merit ['merit], n. mérite, m.—v.t. mériter.
meritorious [meri'tɔːriəs], a. méritoire (choses); méritant (personnes).
meritoriously [meri'tɔːriəsli], adv. d'une manière méritoire.
mermaid ['məːmeid], n. sirène, f.
merrily ['merili], adv. joyeusement, gaiement.
merriment ['merimənt], n. gaieté, réjouissance, f.
merry ['meri], a. joyeux, gai, plaisant; un peu gris; to make merry, se réjouir, se divertir.
merry-go-round ['merigouraund], n. chevaux de bois, m.pl.; manège, m.
merry-making ['merimeikiŋ], n. réjouissance, fête, f., divertissement, m.
mesh [meʃ], n. maille, f.; engrenage, m.
mesmerism ['mezmərizm], n. mesmérisme, magnétisme animal, m.
mesmerize ['mezməraiz], v.t. magnétiser; hypnotiser.
mess (1) [mes], n. gâchis, m.; saleté, f.; to be in a fine mess, être dans de beaux draps; what a mess! quel gâchis!—v.t. salir.— v.i. faire du gâchis.
mess (2) [mes], n. mets, plat; (Mil.) mess, m.; mess tin, gamelle (individuelle), f.—v.t. donner à manger à.—v.i. manger; manger ensemble.
message ['mesidʒ], n. message, m., commission, f.
messenger ['mesəndʒə], n. messager; commissionnaire; coursier (dans un bureau); (fig.) avant-coureur, m.
Messiah [mə'saiə], n. Messie, m.
messmate ['mesmeit], n. camarade de table, m.
messy ['mesi], a. sale; graisseux, salissant.
metabolism [mə'tæbolizm], n. métabolisme, m.
metal [metl], n. métal; cailloutis, empierrement (pour routes).
metalled [metld], a. empierré.
metallic [mə'tælik], a. métallique.
metallurgy [me'tælədʒi], n. métallurgie, f.
metamorphosis [metə'mɔːfəsis], n. métamorphose, f.
metaphor ['metəfə], n. métaphore, f.
metaphysical [metə'fizikl], a. métaphysique.

484

metaphysics [metə'fiziks], *n.pl.* métaphysique, *f.*

mete [mi:t], *v.t.* mesurer; *to mete out*, distribuer, décerner (*prix*); assigner (*punitions*).

meteor ['mi:tiə], *n.* météore, *m.*

meteoric [mi:ti'ɔrik], *a.* météorique.

meteorite ['mi:tiərait], *n.* météorite, *m.* ou *f.*

meteorological [mi:tiərə'lɔdʒikl], *a.* météorologique.

meteorologist [mi:tiə'rɔlədʒist], *n.* météorologiste, *m., f.*

meteorology [mi:tiə'rɔlədʒi], *n.* météorologie, *f.*

meter ['mi:tə], *n.* mesureur; compteur (*de gaz*), *m.*

method ['meθəd], *n.* méthode, *f.*; procédé, *m.*; modalité, (*fig.*) manière, *f.*, ordre, *m.*

methodical [mə'θɔdikəl], *a.* méthodique.

methylate ['meθileit], *v.t.* méthyler; *methylated spirit*, alcool à brûler, *m.*

meticulous [mə'tikjuləs], *a.* méticuleux.

meticulousness [mə'tikjuləsnis], *n.* méticulosité, *f.*

metre ['mi:tə], *n.* mètre, (*Pros.*) vers, *m.*, mesure, *f.*

metric ['metrik], *a.* métrique.

metrical ['metrikl], *a.* métrique; en vers.

metropolis [mə'trɔpəlis], *n.* capitale, métropole, *f.*

metropolitan [metrə'pɔlitən], *a.* de la capitale, métropolitain.

mettle [netl], *n.* courage, cœur, *m.*; fougue, ardeur, vivacité, *f.*; caractère, *m.*; *to put someone on his mettle*, piquer quelqu'un d'honneur.

mettled [metld], **mettlesome** ['metlsəm], *a.* fougueux, ardent, vif.

mew (1) [mju:], *n.* mue, cage, *f.*; (*pl.*) écuries, *f.pl.*; impasse, ruelle (*derrière les grandes maisons de ville*), *f.*—*v.t.* enfermer (*emprisonner*).

mew (2) [mju:], *v.i.* miauler (*chat*).

mew (3) [mju:], *n.* (*Orn.*) mouette, *f.*

mewing ['mju:in], *n.* miaulement (*de chat*), *m.*

Mexican ['meksikn], *a.* mexicain.—*n.* Mexicain (*personne*), *m.*

Mexico ['meksikou], le Mexique (*pays*), *Mexico City*, Mexico, *m.*

miasma [mi'æzmə], *n.* (*pl.* **miasmata** [mi'æzmətə]) miasme, *m.*

mica ['maikə], *n.* mica, *m.*

mice [MOUSE].

Michael [maikl], Michel, *m.*

Michaelmas ['miklməs], la Saint-Michel, *f.*

microbe ['maikroub], *n.* microbe, *m.*

microphone ['maikrəfoun], *n.* microphone, *m.*

microscope ['maikrəskoup], *n.* microscope, *m.*

microscopic [maikrə'skɔpik], *a.* microscopique.

mid [mid], *a.* du milieu, moyen.—*prep.* au milieu de.

mid-air [mid'eə], *n.* milieu de l'air, haut des airs, *m.*; *in mid-air*, entre ciel et terre.

midday ['middei], *a.* de midi.—*n.* midi, *m.*

middle [midl], *a.* du milieu, central; moyen; *Middle Ages*, Moyen Âge, *m.*; *middle class*, bourgeoisie, *f.*; *middle course*, moyen terme, *m.*—*n.* milieu, centre, *m.*; ceinture, *f.*

middle-aged ['midleidʒd], *a.* entre deux âges.

middle-man ['midlmæn], *n.* (*pl.* -**men** [men]) intermédiaire, tiers, *m.*

middling ['midlin], *a.* médiocre, passable, assez bien (*santé*); (*Comm.*) bon, ordinaire.

midget ['midʒit], *n.* nain, nabot, *m.*

midland ['midlənd], *a.* de l'intérieur, du centre.

Mid-Lent ['mid'lent], mi-carême, *f.*

midnight ['midnait], *a.* de minuit.—*n.* minuit, *m.*

midriff ['midrif], *n.* diaphragme, *m.*

midshipman ['midʃipmən], *n.* (*pl.* -**men** [men]) aspirant de marine, *m.*

midships ['midʃips], [AMIDSHIPS].

midst [midst], *n.* milieu; (*fig.*) fort, sein, cœur, *m.*—*prep.* au milieu de, parmi.

midstream ['midstri:m], *n.* milieu du courant; milieu du fleuve, *m.*

midsummer ['midsʌmə], *n.* milieu de l'été, cœur de l'été, *m.*; *Midsummer Day*, la Saint-Jean, *f.*

midway ['midwei], *a.* and *adv.* à mi-chemin, à mi-côte (*d'une colline*).

midwife ['midwaif], *n.* (*pl.* **midwives** ['midwaivz]) sage-femme, accoucheuse, *f.*

midwifery ['midwifri], *n.* obstétrique, *f.*

midwinter ['midwintə], *n.* fort de l'hiver, *m.*

mien [mi:n], *n.* mine, *f.*, air, *m.*

might (1) [mait], *past* [MAY].

might (2) [mait], *n.* force, puissance, *f.*

mightily ['maitili], *adv.* fortement, vigoureusement; extrêmement.

mighty ['maiti], *a.* fort, puissant; grand, important.—*adv.* fort, très, extrêmement.

mignonette [minjə'net], *n.* réséda, *m.*

migraine ['mi:grein], *n.* (*Med.*) migraine, *f.*

migrate [mai'greit], *v.i.* émigrer.

migration [mai'greiʃən], *n.* migration, *f.*

migratory ['maigrətəri], *a.* migratoire; migrateur.

milch [miltʃ], *a.* à lait, laitière.

mild [maild], *a.* doux; léger (*boisson, tabac etc.*); bénin.

mildew ['mildju:], *n.* rouille, moisissure, *f.*, taches d'humidité, *f.pl.*—*v.t.* gâter par l'humidité; souiller, tacher.

mildly ['maildli], *adv.* doucement, avec douceur; modérément.

mildness ['maildnis], *n.* douceur, *f.*

mile [mail], *n.* mille, *m.*

mileage ['mailidʒ], *n.* distance en milles, *f.*; prix par mille, *m.*

milestone ['mailstoun], *n.* borne milliaire, borne kilométrique, *f.*

militant ['militənt], *a.* militant.—*n.* activiste, *m., f.*

militarism ['militərizm], *n.* militarisme, *m.*

military ['militəri], *a.* militaire.—*n. the military*, les militaires, *m.pl.*, la troupe, *f.*

militate ['militeit], *v.i.* militer (*contre*).

militia [mi'liʃə], *n.* milice, *f.*

milk [milk], *n.* lait, *m.*; *milk and water*, lait coupé; (*fig.*) fade, insipide, sans caractère; *skim milk*, lait écrémé; *to come home with the milk*, rentrer à la première heure.—*v.t.* traire.

milk can ['milkkæn], *n.* pot au lait, *m.*

milkiness ['milkinis], *n.* nature laiteuse; (*fig.*) douceur, *f.*

milkmaid ['milkmeid], *n.* laitière, *f.*

milkman ['milkmən], n. (pl. -men [men]) laitier, m.
milk pail ['milkpeil], n. seau à lait, m.
milksop ['milksɔp], n. (colloq.) poule mouillée, f.
milky ['milki], a. laiteux; **Milky Way**, voie lactée, f.
mill [mil], n. moulin, m.; filature, fabrique (usine), f.—v.t. moudre; (Coin.) estamper.—v.i. fourmiller (foule).
millenary ['milənəri], a. millénaire.
millennium [mi'leniəm], n. millénaire, m., mille ans; les temps messianiques, m.pl.
miller ['milə], n. meunier, m.
millet ['milit], n. millet, mil, m.
millimetre ['milimi:tə], n. millimètre, m.
milliner ['milinə], n. marchande de modes, modiste, f.
millinery ['milinri], n. modes, f.pl.
million ['miljən], n. million, m.
millionaire [miljə'neə], n. millionnaire, m., f.
millstone ['milstoun], n. meule de moulin, f.
mime [maim], n. mime, m.—v.t. mimer (une scène).—v.i. jouer par gestes.
mimic ['mimik], a. imitateur, mimique; imitatif (animaux).—n. mime, imitateur, m.—v.t. contrefaire, imiter.
mimicry ['mimikri], n. mimique, imitation, f.
minatory ['minətəri], a. menaçant.
mince [mins], v.t. hacher menu.—v.i. marcher à petits pas; minauder (parler d'une façon affectée).—n. hachis, haché, m.
mincemeat ['minsmi:t], n. pâte d'épices, f., mincemeat, m.
mince pie ['mins'pai], n. tartelette au mincemeat, f.
mincing ['minsiŋ], a. affecté, minaudier.
mind [maind], n. esprit, m.; intelligence; envie, f., désir (inclination), m.; pensée, f., avis (opinion); souvenir (mémoire), m.—v.t. songer à, faire attention à; regarder à (s'occuper de); se défier de (se douter de); obéir à, écouter (se soumettre à); soigner, garder (veiller sur); surveiller, observer (étudier); **mind your own business**, mêlez-vous de ce qui vous regarde; **never mind**, peu importe, tant pis.
minded ['maindid], a. disposé, enclin.
mindful ['maindful], a. attentif (à), soigneux (de); qui se souvient (de).
mindfulness ['maindfulnis], n. attention, f.
mindless ['maindlis], a. inattentif (à); sans esprit.
mine (1) [main], pron.poss. le mien, m., la mienne, f.; les miens, m.pl., les miennes, f.pl.—a. à moi; **a friend of mine**, un de mes amis.
mine (2) [main], n. mine, f.—v.t. miner, saper.
mine-layer ['mainleiə], n. (Navy) mouilleur de mines, m.
miner ['mainə], n. mineur, m.
mineral ['minərəl], a. and n. minéral, m.
mineralogy [minə'rælədʒi], n. minéralogie, f.
mine-sweeper ['mainswi:pə], n. (Navy) dragueur de mines, m.
mingle [miŋgl], v.t. mélanger, mêler.—v.i. se mêler, se mélanger (avec, dans ou en).
mingling ['miŋgliŋ], n. mélange, m.
miniature ['mini(ə)tʃə], a. en miniature.—n. miniature, f.
minim ['minim], n. goutte, m.; (Mus.) blanche, f.

minimum ['miniməm], n. (pl. **minima** ['minimə]) minimum, m.
mining ['mainiŋ], a. des mines; de mineur, minier.—n. travail dans les mines, m.
minion ['minjən], n. favori, m., favorite, f.
minister ['ministə], n. ministre; (Eccles.) pasteur, m.—v.t. administrer; fournir.—v.i. servir (à); (Eccles.) officier à.
ministerial [minis'tiəriəl], a. de ministère, ministériel.
ministration [minis'treiʃən], n. ministère; service, m.
ministry ['ministri], n. ministère, département, m.
mink [miŋk], n. vison, m.
minnow ['minou], n. vairon, m.
minor ['mainə], a. moindre; secondaire; (Mus., Geog. etc.) mineur.—n. mineur, m.
Minorca [mi'nɔ:kə]. Minorque, f.
minority [mai'nɔriti], n. minorité, f.
minster ['minstə], n. cathédrale, église abbatiale, f.
minstrel ['minstrəl], n. ménestrel; (fam.) poète, musicien, chanteur, m.
mint (1) [mint], n. menthe, f.; **peppermint**, menthe poivrée.
mint (2) [mint], n. **The Mint**, la Monnaie, f.—v.t. monnayer, frapper; (fig.) forger.
mintage ['mintidʒ], n. objet monnayé, m.
minting ['mintiŋ], n. monnayage, m.
minuet [minju'et], n. menuet, m.
minus ['mainəs], prep. moins; sans (n'ayant pas de).—n. moins, m.
minute (1) [mai'nju:t], a. menu, minuscule, très petit; minutieux.
minute (2) ['minit], n. minute, f.; instant; moment, m.; note, f.; (pl.) procès-verbal, compte-rendu (d'une réunion), m.—v.t. minuter, prendre note de.
minute-book ['minitbuk], n. journal, m.
minute hand ['minithænd], n. grande aiguille, f.
minutely [mai'nju:tli], adv. minutieusement; exactement; en détail.
minuteness [mai'nju:tnis], n. petitesse; exactitude, f.; détails minutieux, m.pl.
minx [miŋks], n. coquine, friponne, f.
miracle ['mirəkl], n. miracle, m.
miraculous [mi'rækjuləs], a. miraculeux.
mirage [mi'rɑ:ʒ], n. mirage, m.
mire ['maiə], n. boue, bourbe, fange, vase, f.
miry ['maiəri], a. fangeux, bourbeux.
mirror ['mirə], n. miroir, m., glace, f.; **rearview mirror**, rétroviseur, m. —v.t. refléter.
mirth [mə:θ], n. gaieté, hilarité, f., rire, m.
mirthful ['mə:θful], a. gai, joyeux.
misadventure [misəd'ventʃə], n. mésaventure, f., contretemps, m.
misanthropist [mi'sænθrəpist], n. misanthrope, m., f.
misanthropy [mi'sænθrəpi], n. misanthropie, f.
misapplication [misæpli'keiʃən], n. mauvaise application, f.
misapply [misə'plai], v.t. mal appliquer, détourner (fonds etc.).
misapprehend [misæpri'hend], v.t. comprendre mal.
misapprehension [misæpri'henʃən], n. malentendu, m., méprise, f.

misappropriate [misə'prouprieit], *v.t.* détourner.

misappropriation [misəproupri'eiʃən], *n.* détournement, mauvais emploi, *m.*

misbehave [misbi'heiv], *v.i.* se conduire mal.

misbehavior [misbi'heivjə], *n.* mauvaise conduite, *f.*

miscalculate [mis'kælkjuleit], *v.t.* calculer mal.

miscalculation [miskælkju'leiʃən], *n.* calcul erroné; mécompte, *m.*

miscarriage [mis'kæridʒ], *n.* insuccès, coup manqué, *m.*; fausse couche (*de femme*), *f.*

miscarry [mis'kæri], *v.i.* manquer, échouer; faire une fausse couche (*femme*).

miscellaneous [misi'leinjəs], *a.* varié, divers; général; *miscellaneous news*, faits divers, *m.pl.*

miscellany [mi'seləni], *n.* (*pl.* **miscellanies** [mi'seləniz]) mélange, *m.*; mélanges (*livre*), *m.pl.*

mischance [mis'tʃɑːns], *n.* malheur, accident, *m.*, mésaventure, infortune, *f.*

mischief [mist'ʃif], *n.* mal, dommage, dégât, tort, *m.*

mischief-maker ['mistʃifmeikə], *n.* brouillon, *m.*

mischievous ['mistʃivəs], *a.* méchant, malicieux; malfaisant, mauvais, nuisible (*chose*); espiègle (*enfant*).

mischievously ['mistʃivəsli], *adv.* méchamment.

mischievousness ['mistʃivəsnis], *n.* méchanceté; espièglerie (*d'enfant*), *f.*

misconceive [miskən'siːv], *v.t.*, *v.i.* mal concevoir, juger mal.

misconception [miskən'sepʃən], *n.* malentendu, *m.*

misconduct [mis'kəndʌkt], *n.* mauvaise conduite, *f.*—[miskən'dʌkt], *v.t.* conduire mal; *to misconduct oneself*, se conduire mal.

misconstruction [miskən'strʌkʃən], *n.* fausse interprétation, *f.*, contresens, *m.*

misconstrue [miskən'struː], *v.t.* mal interpréter.

miscount [mis'kaunt], *v.t.* compter mal.—*v.i.* faire une erreur de compte.—*n.* mécompte, *m.*

miscreant ['miskriənt], *n.* mécréant, *m.*; (*fig.*) misérable, *m.*

misdeal [mis'diːl], *v.t.* maldonner.—*n.* maldonne, *f.*

misdeed [mis'diːd], *n.* méfait, *m.*

misdemean [misdə'miːn], *v.r.* *to misdemean oneself*, se comporter mal.

misdemeanor [misdə'miːnə], *n.* délit, crime, *m.*, offense, *f.*

misdirect [misdi'rekt], *v.t.* mal diriger, renseigner mal; mettre une fausse adresse à (*lettre*).

misdoing [mis'duːiŋ], *n.* méfait, *m.*

miser ['maizə], *n.* avare, *m.*, *f.*

miserable ['mizərəbl], *a.* misérable, pitoyable, malheureux; mesquin (*piètre*).

miserliness ['maizəlinis], *n.* avarice, *f.*

miserly ['maizəli], *a.* d'avare, avare, sordide.

misery ['mizəri], *n.* misère, *f.*; (*fig.*) tourment; supplice, *m.*; *to put out of misery*, mettre fin aux souffrances (*de*).

misfire [mis'faiə], *v.i.* rater; (*Motor.*) avoir des ratés.—*n.* raté d'allumage, *m.*

misfit ['misfit], *n.* vêtement manqué; inadapté (*personne*), *m.*

misfortune [mis'fɔːtʃən], *n.* malheur, *m.*, infortune, *f.*

misgiving [mis'giviŋ], *n.* pressentiment, soupçon, doute, *m.*; inquiétude, *f.*

misgovern [mis'gʌvən], *v.t.* gouverner mal.

misgovernment [mis'gʌvənmənt], *n.* mauvais gouvernement, *m.*

misguided [mis'gaidid], *a.* malencontreux; peu judicieux; dévoyé.

mishandle [mis'hændl], *v.t.* manier mal, malmener.

mishap [mis'hæp], *n.* contretemps, malheur, *m.*, mésaventure, *f.*

misinform [misin'fɔːm], *v.t.* mal renseigner.

misinterpret [misin'təːprit], *v.t.* interpréter mal.

misjudge [mis'dʒʌdʒ], *v.t.* juger mal, méjuger.

mislay [mis'lei], *v.t.* irr. (*conjug. like* LAY) égarer.

mislead [mis'liːd], *v.t.* irr. (*conjug. like* LEAD) égarer; induire en erreur, fourvoyer; tromper.

misleading [mis'liːdiŋ], *a.* trompeur.

mismanage [mis'mænidʒ], *v.t.* diriger mal.—*v.i.* s'y prendre mal, s'arranger mal (*pour*).

mismanagement [mis'mænidʒmənt], *n.* mauvaise administration, *f.*

misnomer [mis'noumə], *n.* faux nom, *m.*

misogynist [mi'sɔdʒinist], *n.* misogyne, *m.*

misogyny [mi'sɔdʒini], *n.* misogynie, *f.*

misplace [mis'pleis], *v.t.* mal placer; déplacer.

misprint ['misprint], *n.* faute d'impression, *f.* —[mis'print], *v.t.* imprimer incorrectement.

mispronounce [misprə'nauns], *v.t.* prononcer mal.

mispronunciation [misprənʌnsi'eiʃən], *n.* prononciation incorrecte, *f.*

misquote [mis'kwout], *v.t.* citer à faux.

misread [mis'riːd], *v.t.* irr. (*conjug. like* READ) mal lire, mal interpréter.

misrepresent [misrepri'zent], *v.t.* représenter mal, dénaturer.

misrepresentation [misreprizen'teiʃən], *n.* faux rapport, *m.*

misrule [mis'ruːl], *n.* désordre; mauvais gouvernement, *m.*

miss (1) [mis], *n.* mademoiselle, demoiselle, *f.*

miss (2) [mis], *n.* manque, *m.*; perte (*privation*); erreur (*méprise*), *f.*; coup manqué, *m.* —*v.t.* manquer; omettre; s'apercevoir de l'absence de, regretter vivement, ne plus trouver; *I miss my friend very much*, mon ami me manque beaucoup.—*v.i.* manquer; ne pas réussir, échouer, se tromper; *to be missing*, être absent, manquer.

missal [misl], *n.* missel, *m.*

misshapen [mis'ʃeipən], *a.* difforme.

missile ['misail], *a.* de jet, de trait.—*n.* projectile, *m.*; *guided missile*, engin téléguidé, *m.*

missing ['misiŋ], *a.* absent, perdu, disparu.

mission ['miʃən], *n.* mission, *f.*

missionary ['miʃənəri], *a.* des missions.—*n.* missionnaire, *m.*, *f.*

missive ['misiv], *a.* missive.—*n.* missive, lettre, *f.*

misspell [mis'spel], *v.t.* irr. (*conjug. like* SPELL) épeler mal.

misspelling [mis'spelin], *n.* faute d'ortho-graphe, *f.*
misspend [mis'spend], *v.t. irr. (conjug. like* SPEND) employer mal; gaspiller.
misstate [mis'steit], *v.t.* rapporter incorrecte-ment.
misstatement [mis'steitmənt], *n.* rapport erroné, *m.*
mist [mist], *n.* brume; buée (*sur une glace*), *f.*; *Scotch mist*, bruine, *f.*—*v.t.* couvrir (*une glace*) de buée.—*v.i.* se couvrir de buée.
mistake [mis'teik], *v.t. irr. (conjug. like* TAKE) se tromper de *ou* sur, se méprendre à *ou* sur; prendre (*pour*).—*v.i.* se tromper, se méprendre, s'abuser.—*n.* erreur, méprise, faute; bévue (*erreur grossière*), *f.*; *to make a mistake,* se tromper.
mistaken [mis'teikən] *a.* qui se trompe; faux, erroné (*chose*).
mistimed [mis'taimd], *a.* inopportun.
mistletoe [misltou], *n.* gui, *m.*
mistress [mistris], *n.* maîtresse; patronne; institutrice (*d'école primaire*), *f.*; head-mistress, *directrice, f.*
mistrust [mis'trʌst], *n.* méfiance, *f.*, soupçon, *m.*—*v.t.* se méfier de, soupçonner.
mistrustful [mis'trʌstful], *a.* méfiant.
misty [misti], *a.* brumeux; vaporeux (*lumière*); (*fig.*) confus.
misunderstand [misʌndə'stænd], *v.t. irr. (conjug. like* STAND) mal comprendre, entendre mal, se méprendre sur.
misunderstanding [misʌndə'stændiŋ], *n.* malentendu (*manque de compréhension*), *m.*; mésintelligence (*querelle*), *f.*
misuse [mis'ju:s], *n.* abus, *m.*—[mis'ju:z], *v.t.* mésuser de; maltraiter (*faire du mal à*).
mite (1) [mait], *n.* (*Zool.*) mite, *f.*
mite (2) [mait], *n.* denier (*argent*); (*fig.*) rien, *m.*, obole, *f.*; (*fam.*) petit gosse, *m.*
miter [maitə], *n.* mitre, *f.*
mitigate [mitigeit], *v.t.* mitiger, adoucir, modérer.
mitigating [mitigeitiŋ], *a.* adoucissant, atténuant.
mitigation [miti'geiʃən], *n.* mitigation, *f.*, adoucissement, *m.*
mitten [mitn], *n.* mitaine, *f.*
mix [miks], *v.t.* mêler, mélanger; couper (*boissons*); *to mix up,* mêler, embrouiller, confondre.—*v.i.* se mélanger, se mêler (*de*); s'associer (*à*).
mixed [mikst], *a.* mélangé, mêlé (*de*); mixte.
mixture [mikstʃə], *n.* mélange, *m.*; (*Pharm.*) potion, mixture, *f.*
mix-up [miksʌp], *n.* confusion, *f.*, embrouil-lement, *m.*; (*pop.*) pagaie, *f.*
mizzen [mizn], *n.* artimon, *m.*
mizzen-mast [miznmɑ:st], *n.* mât d'artimon, *m.*
moan [moun], *n.* gémissement, *m.*, plainte; (*fig.*) lamentation, *f.*—*v.t.* gémir de *ou* sur; se lamenter sur.—*v.i.* gémir, (*fig.*) se la-menter; (*pop.*) grognonner.
moat [mout], *n.* fossé, *m.*, douve, *f.*
mob [mob], *n.* foule; populace, canaille, *f.*—*v.t.* houspiller, malmener; assiéger.
mobile [moubail], *a.* mobile.
mobility [mou'biliti], *n.* mobilité; légèreté (*inconstance*), *f.*
mobilization [moubilai'zeiʃən], *n.* mobilisa-tion, *f.*

mobilize [moubilaiz], *v.t.* mobiliser.
mock [mɔk], *v.t.* se moquer de; narguer.—*v.i.* railler.—*a.* dérisoire; faux, simulé.
mocker [mɔkə], *n.* moqueur, *m.*
mockery [mɔkəri], *n.* moquerie, *f.*
mocking-bird [mɔkiŋbə:d], *n.* oiseau moqueur, *m.*
mode [moud], *n.* mode, façon, manière, *f.*
model [mɔdl], *n.* modèle; mannequin, *m.*—*v.t.* modeler; (*Cloth.*) présenter des vête-ments (*défilé de mannequins*).
moderate [mɔdərit], *a.* modéré; modique, ordinaire, passable, médiocre.—[mɔdəreit], *v.t.* modérer, adoucir, tempérer.—*v.i.* se modérer.
moderately [mɔdəritli], *adv.* modérément, passablement.
moderation [mɔdə'reiʃən], *n.* modération, *f.*
moderator [mɔdəreitə], *n.* modérateur, *m.*
modern [mɔdən], *a.* and *n.* moderne, *m.*, *f.*; *modern languages,* langues vivantes, *f.pl.*
modernize [mɔdənaiz], *v.t.* moderniser.
modest [mɔdist], *a.* modeste; pudique; modéré (*demandes etc.*).
modesty [mɔdisti], *n.* modestie, *f.*
modicum [mɔdikəm], *n.* petite portion, *f.*
modification [mɔdifi'keiʃən], *n.* modifica-tion, *f.*
modify [mɔdifai], *v.t.* modifier.
modulate [mɔdjuleit], *v.t.* moduler.
modulation [mɔdju'leiʃən], *n.* modulation, *f.*
mohair [mouhɛə], *n.* poil de chèvre angora, mohair, *m.*
Mohammed [mo'hæməd], Mahomet, *m.*
Mohammedan [mo'hæmədən], *a.* mahomé-tan.—*n.* Mahométan, *m.*
Mohammedanism [mo'hæmədənizm], *n.* mahométisme, *m.*
moist [mɔist], *a.* moite, humide.
moisten [mɔisn], *v.t.* humecter; mouiller.
moisture [mɔistʃə], **moistness** [mɔistnis], *n.* moiteur, humidité, *f.*
mol-, see **moul-.**
molasses [mo'læsiz], *n.pl.* mélasse, *f.*
mole (1) [moul], *n.* taupe (*animal*), *f.*
mole (2) [moul], *n.* tache, *f.*, grain de beauté (*sur la peau*), *m.*
mole (3) [moul], *n.* môle (*jetée*), *m.*
molecular [mo'lekjulə], *a.* moléculaire.
molecule [mɔlikju:l], *n.* molécule, *f.*
mole-hill [moulhil], *n.* taupinière, *f.*
moleskin [moulskin], *n.* peau de taupe, molesquine, *f.*, velours de coton, *m.*
molest [mo'lest], *v.t.* molester; vexer.
mollify [mɔlifai], *v.t.* amollir; adoucir.
molten [moultən], *a.* fondu.
moment [moumənt], *n.* moment, instant, *m.*; (*fig.*) importance, *f.*; *at the present moment,* actuellement; *at this moment,* en ce moment; *not for a moment,* pour rien au monde; *of no moment,* d'aucune importance; *the moment that,* dès que, aussitôt que.
momentarily [mouməntərili], *adv.* momen-tanément.
momentary [mouməntəri], *a.* momentané.
momentous [mo'mentəs], *a.* important, d'une importance capitale.
momentum [mo'mentəm], *n.* (*Phys.*) force vive; vitesse acquise, *f.*; élan, *m.*
monarch [mɔnək], *n.* monarque, *m.*

monarchy ['mɔnəki], n. monarchie, f.
monastery ['mɔnəstri], n. monastère, m.
monastic [mə'næstik], a. monastique.
monasticism [mə'næstisizm], n. monachisme, m.
Monday ['mʌndi], lundi, m.
monetary ['mʌnətəri], a. monétaire.
money ['mʌni], n. argent, m.; monnaie, f., espèces (pièces), f.pl.; made of money, cousu d'or; ready money, argent comptant; to make money, gagner de l'argent.
money box ['mʌnibɔks], n. tirelire, f.
money-changer ['mʌniʃeindʒə], n. changeur, m.
moneyed ['mʌnid], a. riche.
money grubber ['mʌnigrʌbə], n. grippe-sou, m.
money-lender ['mʌnilendə], n. prêteur d'argent, m.
money market ['mʌnimɑːkit], n. bourse, f.
money order ['mʌniɔːdə], n. mandat, m.
Mongol ['mɔŋgɔl], a. mongol.—n. Mongol (personne), m.
Mongolia [mɔŋ'gouliə], la Mongolie, f.
Mongolian [mɔŋ'gouliən], a. mongol.—n. mongol (langue); Mongol (personne), m.
mongrel ['mʌŋgrəl], a. métis.—n. métis, m., métisse, f.
monitor ['mɔnitə], n. moniteur, m.
monk [mʌŋk], n. moine, m.
monkey ['mʌŋki], n. singe, m.; guenon, f.
monkey wrench ['mʌŋkirentʃ], n. clé anglaise, f.
monocle ['mɔnəkl], n. monocle, m.
monogram ['mɔnəgræm], n. monogramme, m.
monologue ['mɔnəlɔg], n. monologue, m.
monoplane ['mɔnəplein], n. monoplan, m.
monopoly [mə'nɔpəli], n. monopole, accaparement, m.
monorail ['mɔnəreil], n. monorail, m.
monotonous [mə'nɔtənəs], a. monotone.
monotonously [mə'nɔtənəsli], adv. avec monotonie.
monotony [mə'nɔtəni], n. monotonie, f.
monsoon [mɔn'suːn], n. mousson, f.
monster ['mɔnstə], n. monstre, m.
monstrosity [mɔn'strɔsiti], n. monstruosité, f.
monstrous ['mɔnstrəs], a. monstrueux; prodigieux.
month [mʌnθ], n. mois, m.; calendar month, mois civil; the day of the month, le quantième du mois, m.
monthly ['mʌnθli], a. mensuel, de tous les mois.—n. (fam.) revue mensuelle, f.—adv. tous les mois, par mois.
monument ['mɔnjumənt], n. monument, m.
monumental [mɔnju'mentl], a. monumental.
moo [muː], v.i. meugler, beugler.—n. meuglement, m.
mood [muːd], n. humeur, f.; (Gram. etc.) mode, m.
moody ['muːdi], a. de mauvaise humeur, triste.
moon [muːn], n. lune, f.; by the light of the moon, au clair de la lune.—v.i. muser; to moon about, flâner.
moonbeam ['muːnbiːm], n. rayon de lune, m.
moonlight ['muːnlait], n. clair de lune, m.
moonlit ['muːnlit], a. éclairé par la lune.

moonshine ['muːnʃain], n. clair de lune, m.; (fig.) chimères, f.pl.
moonstrike ['muːnstraik], n. alunissage, m.
moonstruck ['muːnstrʌk], a. lunatique.
Moor [muə], n. Maure, m., f.
moor (1) [muə], n. lande, bruyère, f.; marais, m.
moor (2) [muə], v.t. amarrer.—v.i. s'amarrer.
moor hen ['muəhen], n. poule d'eau, f.
moorings ['muəriŋz], n. amarres, f.pl., mouillage, m.
moorland ['muələnd], n. lande, bruyère, f.; marais, m.
moose [muːs], n. élan du Canada, m.
moot [muːt], v.t. discuter, débattre, controverser.—a. moot point, question discutable, f.
mop [mɔp], n. balai à laver, m.—v.t. nettoyer avec un balai, éponger; to mop one's face, s'éponger la figure.
mope [moup], v.i. s'ennuyer; être hébété.
moping ['moupiŋ], a. triste, hébété.
moral ['mɔrəl], a. moral.—n. morale; moralité, f.; (pl.) mœurs, f.pl.
morale [mɔ'rɑːl], n. moral (de militaires etc.), m.
morality [mə'ræliti], n. morale; moralité, f.
moralize ['mɔrəlaiz], v.i. moraliser.
morally ['mɔrəli], adv. moralement.
morass [mə'ræs], n. marais, m., fondrière, f.
morbid ['mɔːbid], a. maladif, malsain, morbide.
morbidly ['mɔːbidli], adv. morbidement.
morbidity [mɔː'biditi], **morbidness** ['mɔːbidnis], n. état maladif, état morbide, m.
more [mɔː], a. and adv. plus; plus de; plus nombreux; encore; davantage; more and more, de plus en plus; more than, plus que, plus de (suivi d'un nombre); no more, pas davantage; no more of that! arrêtez cela! once more, encore une fois; some more, encore un peu, davantage.
moreover [mɔː'rouvə], adv. de plus, d'ailleurs, en outre.
moribund ['mɔribʌnd], a. moribond.
Mormon ['mɔːmən], a. mormon.—n. Mormon (personne), m.
morn [mɔːn], n. (poet.) matin, m., aurore, f.
morning ['mɔːniŋ], a. du matin.—n. matin, m., matinée, f.; good morning, bonjour; in the morning, le matin; the next morning, le lendemain matin.
Moroccan [mə'rɔkən], a. marocain.—n. Marocain (personne), m.
Morocco [mə'rɔkou], le Maroc, m.
morocco leather [mə'rɔkou'leðə], n. maroquin, m.
moron ['mɔːrɔn], n. crétin, idiot, m.
morose [mə'rous], a. morose.
morphia ['mɔːfiə], **morphine** ['mɔːfiːn], n. morphine, f.
morrow ['mɔrou], n. (poet.) demain, lendemain, m.; tomorrow, demain.
morsel ['mɔːsl], n. morceau, m.
mortal ['mɔːtl], a. mortel, funeste (fatal); des mortels, humain (terrestre); à outrance, à mort (combat); any mortal thing, n'importe quoi.—n. mortel, m.
mortality [mɔː'tæliti], n. mortalité; humanité, f.
mortally ['mɔːtəli], adv. mortellement, a mort.
mortar ['mɔːtə], n. mortier, m.

489

mortgage ['mɔːgidʒ], *n.* hypothèque, *f.*—*v.t.* hypothéquer.

mortician [mɔːˈtiʃən], *n.* (*Am.*) entrepreneur de pompes funèbres, *m.*

mortification [mɔːtifiˈkeiʃən], *n.* mortification; (*Path.*) gangrène, *f.*

mortify ['mɔːtifai], *v.t.* mortifier; (*Path.*) faire gangrener.—*v.i.* se gangrener.

mortise ['mɔːtis], *n.* mortaise, *f.*—*v.t.* mortaiser.

mortuary ['mɔːtjuəri], *a.* mortuaire.—*n.* morgue, *f.*, dépôt mortuaire, *m.*

mosaic [moˈzeiik], *a.* and *n.* mosaïque, *f.*

Moscow ['mɔskou], Moscou, *m.*

Moses ['mouziz]. Moïse, *m.*

Moslem ['mɔzlim, 'mɔzləm], *a.* musulman.—*n.* Musulman (*personne*), *m.*

mosque [mɔsk], *n.* mosquée, *f.*

mosquito [mɔsˈkiːtou], *n.* moustique, *m.*

mosquito net [mɔsˈkiːtounet], *n.* moustiquaire, *f.*

moss [mɔs], *n.* mousse, *f.*; marais, *m.*; tourbière (bog), *f.*

moss-grown ['mɔsgroun], *a.* couvert de mousse, moussu.

moss rose ['mɔsrouz], *n.* rose moussue, *f.*

most [moust], *a.* le plus; le plus grand; *most men,* la plupart des hommes; *the most part,* la plus grande partie.—*adv.* le plus, plus; très, fort; *a most valuable book,* un livre des plus précieux; *most likely,* très probablement.—*n.* la plupart, *f.*; le plus grand nombre, *m.*

mostly ['moustli], *adv.* pour la plupart; le plus souvent; principalement.

mote [mout], *n.* grain de poussière, *m.*; paille (*dans l'œil*), *f.*

motel [mouˈtel], *n.* motel, *m.*

motet [mouˈtet], *n.* (*Mus.*) motet, *m.*

moth [mɔθ], *n.* (*Ent.*) lépidoptère; papillon de nuit, *m.*; phalène; mite (*de vêtements*), *f.*

moth-eaten ['mɔθiːtn], *a.* mité.

mother ['mʌðə], *a.* mère; maternel; métropolitain (*église*); *mother tongue,* langue maternelle, *f.*—*n.* mère; bonne mère, bonne femme (*terme familier*), *f.*; *stepmother,* belle-mère, *f.*—*v.t.* servir de mère à; adopter; enfanter (*quelque chose*).

mother country ['mʌðəkʌntri], *n.* mère patrie, *f.*

mother-in-law ['mʌðərinlɔː], *n.* belle-mère, *f.*

motherly ['mʌðəli], *a.* maternel, de mère.—*adv.* maternellement, en mère.

mother-of-pearl [mʌðərəvˈpɔːl], *n.* nacre, *f.*

motion ['mouʃən], *n.* mouvement; signe (*signal*), *m.*; motion, proposition (*à une réunion*); (*Med.*) selle, *f.*—*v.t.* faire signe (*à*).

motionless ['mouʃənlis], *a.* immobile.

motivate ['moutiveit], *v.t.* motiver (*une action*).

motive ['moutiv], *a.* moteur, qui fait mouvoir; *motive power,* force motrice, *f.*—*n.* motif, mobile, *m.*

motley ['mɔtli], *a.* bigarré, mélangé.

motor ['moutə], *n.* moteur, *m.*—*v.i.* aller *ou* voyager en auto.

motor-boat ['moutəbout], *n.* canot automobile, *m.*

motor car ['moutəkaː], *n.* automobile, auto, voiture, *f.*

motor-cycle ['moutəsaikl], *n.* motocyclette, *f.*

motoring ['moutəriŋ], *n.* automobilisme, *m.*

motorist ['moutərist], *n.* automobiliste, *m.,f.*

motorway ['moutəwei], *n.* autoroute, *f.*

mottle [mɔtl], *v.t.* madrer; marbrer.

motto ['mɔtou], *n.* (*pl.* **mottoes** ['mɔtouz]) devise, *f.*

mould (1) [mould], *n.* moisi (*mousse*); terreau (*humus*), *m.*—*v.i.* se moisir.

mould (2) [mould], *n.* moule, *m.*, forme, *f.*—*v.t.* mouler; (*fig.*) petrir.

moulder ['mouldə], *v.i.* se réduire en poudre *ou* en poussière.

mouldiness ['mouldinis], *n.* moisissure, *f.*

moulding ['mouldiŋ], *n.* moulure, *f.*

mouldy ['mouldi], *a.* moisi.

moult [moult], *v.i.* muer.

moulting ['moultiŋ], *n.* mue, *f.*

mound [maund], *n.* butte, *f.*, tertre, *m.*; (*Fort.*) remparts, *m.pl.*

mount [maunt], *n.* mont, *m.*, montagne; monture (*cheval*); (*Turf*) monte, *f.*; (*Phot.*) carton, *m.*—*v.t.* monter, monter sur.—*v.i.* monter, s'élever; monter à cheval.

mountain ['mauntin], *a.* de montagne, des montagnes, montagnard, montagneux (*paysage*).—*n.* montagne, *f.*

mountaineer [maunti'niə], *n.* montagnard, *m.*; alpiniste, *m.,f.*

mountaineering [maunti'niəriŋ], *n.* alpinisme, *m.*

mountainous ['mauntinəs], *a.* montagneux, de montagnes; (*fig.*) énorme.

mountebank ['mauntibæŋk], *n.* charlatan, *m.*

mounted ['mauntid], *a.* monté, à cheval; (*Phot.*) collé.

mounting ['mauntiŋ], *n.* montage, *m.*, monture, *f.*; (*Phot.*) collage, *m.*

mourn [mɔːn], *v.t.* pleurer, déplorer.—*v.i.* pleurer, se lamenter.

mourner ['mɔːnə], *n.* personne affligée, *f.*; pleureur (*professionnel*), *m.*; personne qui suit le convoi, *f.*

mournful ['mɔːnful], *a.* triste, lugubre.

mourning ['mɔːniŋ], *a.* affligé, triste; de deuil.—*n.* affliction, lamentation, *f.*; deuil (*vêtements*), *m.*

mouse [maus], *n.* (*pl.* **mice** [mais]) souris, *f.*; *field mouse,* mulot, *m.*

mouse-trap ['maustræp], *n.* souricière, *f.*

moustache [mə'staːʃ], *n.* moustache, *f.*

mousy ['mausi], *a.* gris (*couleur*); timide.

mouth [mauθ], *n.* (*pl.* **mouths** [mauðz]) bouche; gueule (*de bête sauvage*); embouchure (*de rivière*); ouverture, entrée, *f.*; orifice (*donnant accès*); goulot (*d'une bouteille*), *m.*; *by word of mouth,* de vive voix.—[mauð], *v.t.*, *v.i.* crier.

mouthed [mauðd], *a.* **foul-mouthed,** mal embouché; **mealy-mouthed,** doucereux.

mouthful ['mauθful], *n.* bouchée; gorgée (*de vin*), *f.*

mouthpiece ['mauθpiːs], *n.* embouchure, *f.*; (*fig.*) interprète, porte-parole, *m.*

movable ['muːvəbl], *a.* mobile.—*n.* meuble, *m.*

move [muːv], *v.t.* remuer; déplacer; mouvoir, faire mouvoir, mettre en mouvement, faire marcher, faire aller; transporter (*marchandises etc.*); (*fig.*) émouvoir, toucher; exciter, pousser (*à*); proposer (*que*); (*Chess*) jouer; *to move forward,* avancer; *to move out,* déloger, sortir.—*v.i.* bouger, se remuer, se mouvoir, se déplacer; se mettre en mouvement, aller, partir, marcher, s'avancer; s'ébranler (*armée*); déménager (*changer de résidence*); (*Chess*) jouer; *move on!* circulez! *to move aside*, s'écarter; *to move away*, s'éloigner; *to move back*, reculer, se reculer; *to move in*, emménager; *to move off*, s'éloigner, s'en aller; *to move on*, avancer; *to move out*, sortir, déménager.—*n.* mouvement; coup; (*Chess*) trait, *m.*; *masterly move*, coup de maître; *to be on the move*, être en mouvement, se remuer; *to get a move on*, se presser.

movement ['mu:vmənt], *n.* mouvement, *m.*

mover ['mu:və], *n.* moteur; mobile, *m.*; force motrice, *f.*; déménageur, *m.*

movie ['mu:vi], *n.* (*Am.*) film, *m.*; *the movies*, le cinéma, *m.*

moving ['mu:viŋ], *a.* mouvant, mobile; (*fig.*) émouvant.—*n.* mouvement; déménagement (*de mobilier*); déplacement (*changement de place*), *m.*

movingly ['mu:viŋli], *adv.* d'une manière émouvante.

mow [mou], *v.t. irr.* faucher; tondre.

mower ['mouə], *n.* faucheur (*personne*), *m.*; faucheuse, tondeuse (*machine*), *f.*

Mr. ['mistə]. Monsieur (*abbr.* M.).

Mrs. ['misiz]. Madame (*abbr.* Mme.).

much [mʌtʃ], *adv.* beaucoup, bien, fort, très; *as much*, autant; *how much?* combien (*de*)? *much more*, bien plus; *nothing much*, pas grand'chose; *pretty much*, à peu près; *so much*, tant; *so much more*, d'autant plus; *so much the better*, tant mieux; *to make much of*, faire grand cas de; *too much*, trop (*de*).

muck [mʌk], *n.* fumier (*engrais*), *m.*; fange (*boue*); (*fig.*) saleté, *f.*—*v.t.* fumer; salir.

muckiness ['mʌkinis], *n.* saleté, ordure, *f.*

mucky ['mʌki], *a.* sale, malpropre.

mucous ['mju:kəs], *a.* muqueux; *mucous membrane*, muqueuse, *f.*

mucus ['mju:kəs], *n.* mucus, *m.*; mucosité, *f.*

mud [mʌd], *n.* boue, bourbe, vase, *f.*, limon, *m.*

mudguard ['mʌdgɑ:d], *n.* garde-boue, *m.*

muddle [mʌdl], *v.t.* brouiller; troubler; gâcher.—*v.i.* faire du gâchis.—*n.* confusion, *f.*, désordre, gâchis, *m.*

muddled ['mʌdld], *a.* troublé; hébété.

muddler ['mʌdlə], *n.* brouillon, *m.*

muddy ['mʌdi], *a.* boueux, bourbeux; crotté.

muff [mʌf], *n.* manchon, *m.*—*v.t.* gâcher.

muffle [mʌfl], *v.t.* emmitoufler, affubler; assourdir (*cloche*); voiler (*tambour*).—*n.* moufle, *f.*

muffler ['mʌflə], *n.* cache-nez, *m.*; (*Motor.*) pot d'échappement, *m.*

mug [mʌg], *n.* pot, *m.*, tasse; (*slang*) gueule, binette, *f.*; (*sl.*) imbécile, *m.*, *f.*

muggy ['mʌgi], *a.* humide, lourd.

mulberry ['mʌlbəri], *n.* mûre, *f.*; *mulberry bush*, mûrier, *m.*

mulch [mʌltʃ], *n.* paillis, *m.*—*v.t.* pailler, fumer.

mule [mju:l], *n.* mulet, *m.*, mule, *f.*

mulish ['mju:liʃ], *a.* de mulet; (*fig.*) têtu.

mull [mʌl], *v.t.* ruminer.—*v.t.* faire chauffer et épicer; *mulled wine*, vin chaud épicé.

multicolored ['mʌltikʌləd], *a.* multicolore.

multifarious [mʌlti'fɛəriəs], *a.* varié, divers, multiplié.

multi-millionaire ['mʌltimiljə'nɛə], *n.* milliardaire, *m.*, *f.*

multiple ['mʌltipl], *a.* and *n.* multiple, *m.*; *multiple store*, maison à succursales, *f.*

multiplication [mʌltipli'keiʃən], *n.* multiplication, *f.*

multiplicity [mʌlti'plisiti], *n.* multiplicité, *f.*

multiply ['mʌltiplai], *v.t.* multiplier.—*v.i.* multiplier, se multiplier.

multitude ['mʌltitju:d], *n.* multitude, *f.*

multitudinous [mʌlti'tju:dinəs], *a.* très nombreux, innombrable.

mum (1) [mʌm], *a.* muet.—*int.* bouche close! chut!

mum (2) [mʌm], *n.* (*fam.*) maman, *f.*

mumble [mʌmbl], *v.i.* marmotter.

mumbler ['mʌmblə], *n.* marmotteur, *m.*

mummer ['mʌmə], *n.* mime (*acteur*), *m.*

mummify ['mʌmifai], *v.t.* momifier.

mummy (1) ['mʌmi], *n.* momie, *f.*

mummy (2), **mummie** ['mʌmi], *n.* (*fam.*) maman, *f.*

mumps [mʌmps], *n.pl.* (*Med.*) oreillons, *m.pl.*

munch [mʌntʃ], *v.t.*, *v.i.* mâcher, croquer.

mundane ['mʌndein], *a.* mondain.

municipal [mju'nisipl], *a.* municipal.

municipality [mjunisi'pæliti], *n.* municipalité, *f.*

munificence [mju'nifisəns], *n.* munificence, *f.*

munificent [mju'nifisənt], *a.* libéral, généreux.

munition [mju'niʃən], *n.* munitions (*de guerre*), *f.pl.*—*v.t.* approvisionner.

mural ['mjuərəl], *a.* mural.—*n.* peinture murale, *f.*

murder ['mə:də], *n.* meurtre, homicide, *m.*; *wilful murder*, meurtre avec préméditation, assassinat, *m.*—*v.t.* assassiner, tuer; (*fig.*) écorcher (*une langue etc.*).

murderer ['mə:dərə], *n.* meurtrier, assassin, *m.*

murderess ['mə:dəris], *n.* meurtrière, *f.*

murdering ['mə:dəriŋ], **murderous** ['mə:dərəs], *a.* meurtrier, assassin.

murkiness ['mə:kinis], *n.* obscurité, *f.*

murky ['mə:ki], *a.* sombre, obscur, ténébreux.

murmur ['mə:mə], *n.* murmure, *m.*—*v.i.* murmurer.

murmuring ['mə:məriŋ], *a.* murmurant, murmurateur.—*n.* murmure, *m.*, murmures, *m.pl.*

muscle [mʌsl], *n.* muscle, *m.*

muscular ['mʌskjulə], *a.* musculaire (*force*); musculeux (*membres*).

Muse [mju:z], *n.* muse, *f.*

muse [mju:z], *v.i.* méditer (*sur*) rêver (*à*).—*n.* muse, rêverie, méditation, *f.*

museum [mju'zi:əm], *n.* musée, *m.*

mushroom ['mʌʃrum], *n.* champignon, *m.*

music ['mju:zik], *n.* musique, *f.*

musical ['mju:zikəl], *a.* musical; (*fig.*) harmonieux, mélodieux; qui aime la musique.

musician [mju'ziʃən], *n.* musicien, *m.*

music stand ['mju:zikstænd], *n.* pupitre à musique, *m.*

music stool ['mju:zikstu:l], *n.* tabouret de piano, *m.*

musing ['mju:ziŋ], *n.* méditation; (*pl.*) rêverie, *f.*

musk [mʌsk], *n.* musc, *m.*
musket ['mʌskit], *n.* fusil, mousquet, *m.*
musketeer [mʌski'tiə], *n.* mousquetaire, *m.*
musketry ['mʌskitri], *n.* mousqueterie, *f.*, tir, *m.*
musky ['mʌski], *a.* musqué, parfumé de musc.
Muslim ['mʌzlim], [MOSLEM].
muslin ['mʌzlin], *a.* de mousseline.—*n.* mousseline, *f.*
mussel [mʌsl], *n.* moule, *f.*
must (I) [mʌst], *v. aux.* falloir; devoir; *I must do it*, il faut que je le fasse; *you must know*, vous devez savoir.
must (2) [mʌst], *n.* moût (*de vin*), *m.*
mustard ['mʌstəd], *n.* moutarde, *f.*
muster ['mʌstə], *n.* appel, *m.*, revue, *f.*; rassemblement, *m.*; troupe, bande, *f.*; contrôles (*liste*), *m.pl.*—*v.t.* faire l'appel de; passer en revue; réunir, rassembler; se procurer; *to muster up courage*, prendre son courage à deux mains.—*v.i.* s'assembler, se réunir.
mustiness ['mʌstinis], *n.* moisi, *m.*
musty ['mʌsti], *a.* moisi; qui sent le renfermé.
mutability [mjuːtə'biliti], *n.* mutabilité, *f.*
mutation [mjuː'teiʃən], *n.* mutation, *f.*
mute [mjuːt], *a.* and *n.* muet, *m.*—*v.t.* amortir (*les cordes d'un violon etc.*).
mutely ['mjuːtli], *adv.* en silence.
mutilate ['mjuːtileit], *v.t.* mutiler, estropier.
mutilated ['mjuːtileitid], *a.* mutilé.
mutilation [mjuːti'leiʃən], *n.* mutilation, *f.*
mutineer [mjuːti'niə], *n.* révolté, rebelle, mutin, *m.*
mutinous ['mjuːtinəs], *a.* rebelle, mutiné, mutin.
mutinously ['mjuːtinəsli], *adv.* séditieusement.
mutiny ['mjuːtini], *n.* mutinerie, sédition, révolte, *f.*—*v.i.* se mutiner, s'insurger.
mutter ['mʌtə], *v.t.*, *v.i.* marmotter.—*n.* marmottement, *m.*
muttering ['mʌtəriŋ], *a.* marmotteur, murmurant.—*n.* murmure, marmottement, marmottage, *m.*
mutton [mʌtn], *n.* mouton (*viande*), *m.*; *leg of mutton*, gigot, *m.*
mutton chop ['mʌtn'tʃɔp], *n.* côtelette de mouton, *f.*
mutual ['mjuːtjuəl], *a.* mutuel, réciproque; *mutual friend*, ami commun, *m.*
mutually ['mjuːtjuəli], *adv.* mutuellement.
muzzle [mʌzl], *n.* museau (*d'animal*), *m.*; bouche, gueule (*de canon*), *f.*; bout (*de fusil etc.*), *m.*; muselière (*pour chien*), *f.*—*v.t.* museler.
muzzy ['mʌzi], *a.* brouillé, confus.
my [mai], *poss. a.* mon, *m.*, ma, *f.*, mes, *pl.*
myopic [mai'ɔpik], *a.* myope.
myriad ['miriəd], *a.* (*poet.*) innombrable.—*n.* myriade, *f.*
myrrh [məː], *n.* myrrhe, *f.*
myrtle [məːtl], *n.* myrte, *m.*
myself [mai'self], *pron.* me; moi-même; moi; *I consider myself*, je me crois.
mysterious [mis'tiəriəs], *a.* mystérieux.
mysteriously [mis'tiəriəsli], *adv.* mystérieusement.
mystery ['mistəri], *n.* mystère, *m.*
mystic ['mistik], *a.* and *n.* (*Theol.*) mystique, *m.*,*f.*

mysticism ['mistisizm], *n.* mysticisme, *m.*
mystify ['mistifai], *v.t.* envelopper de mystère, mystifier.
mystique [mis'tiːk], *n.* mystique, *f.*
myth [miθ], *n.* mythe, *m.*
mythical ['miθikl], *a.* mythique.
mythology [mi'θɔlədʒi], *n.* mythologie, *f.*

N

N, n [en]. quatorzième lettre de l'alphabet, *m.* ou *f.*
nab [næb], *v.t.* happer, saisir, pincer.
nag (I) [næg], *n.* bidet, petit cheval, *m.*
nag (2) [næg], *v.t.*, *v.i.* gronder, chamailler, criailler.
nagging ['nægiŋ], *a.* querelleur (*personne*); agaçant (*sensation*).
nail [neil], *n.* clou; ongle (*de griffes, de doigts*), *m.*—*v.t.* clouer; clouter.
nail brush ['neilbrʌʃ], *n.* brosse à ongles, *f.*
naïve [nai'iːv], *a.* naïf, ingénu.
naked ['neikid], *a.* nu, à nu; à découvert, ouvert (*sans protection*); dégarni (*sans meubles*); *stark naked*, tout nu.
nakedness ['neikidnis], *n.* nudité, *f.*
name [neim], *n.* nom; (*fig.*) renom, *m.*, renommée, réputation, *f.*; *Christian name*, nom de baptême, prénom, *m.*; *maiden name*, nom de jeune fille; *what is your name?* comment vous appelezvous?—*v.t.* nommer, appeler; désigner; *to be named*, s'appeler, se nommer.
named [neimd], *a.* nommé, désigné.
nameless ['neimlis], *a.* sans nom, anonyme; inconnu.
namely ['neimli], *adv.* à savoir, c'est-à-dire.
namesake ['neimseik], *n.* homonyme, *m.*
nanny ['næni], *n.* bonne d'enfant; (*childish*) nounou, *f.*
nap (I) [næp], *n.* somme (*sommeil*), *m.*; *afternoon nap*, sieste, *f.*; *to take a nap*, faire un somme; *to catch napping*, prendre au dépourvu.
nap (2) [næp], *n.* poil (*de tissu etc*), *m.*
nap (3) [næp], *n.* napoléon (*jeu*); tuyau certain (*courses de chevaux*), *m.*
nape [neip], *n.* nuque, *f.*
napkin ['næpkin], *n.* serviette; couche (*de bébé*), *f.*
Napoleon [nə'pouljən]. Napoléon, *m.*
narcissus [naː'sisəs], *n.* narcisse, *m.*
narcotic [naː'kɔtik], *a.* and *n.* narcotique, *m.*
narrate [nə'reit], *v.t.* raconter, narrer.
narration [nə'reiʃən], *n.* narration, *f.*, récit, *m.*
narrative ['nærətiv], *a.* narratif.—*n.* récit, narré, *m.*
narrator [nə'reitə], *n.* narrateur, *m.*
narrow ['nærou], *a.* étroit, resserré; à l'étroit, gêné; rétréci, limité, borné (*esprit*); *to have a narrow escape*, l'échapper belle.—*n.* (*pl.*) détroit, pas, *m.*—*v.t.* rétrécir, resserrer, limiter, borner.—*v.i.* se rétrécir, se resserrer.
narrowly ['nærouli], *adv.* étroitement, à l'étroit; de près.

narrow-minded ['nærou'maindid], *a.* à l'esprit étroit.
narrowness ['nærounis], *n.* étroitesse, *f.*
nasal [neizl], *a.* nasal, du nez.
nascent ['næsənt], *a.* naissant.
nastily ['nɑːstili], *adv.* salement, malproprement.
nastiness ['nɑːstinis], *n.* saleté; grossièreté, *f.*
nasturtium [nəs'təːʃəm], *n.* capucine, *f.*
nasty ['nɑːsti], *a.* sale, malpropre; (*fig.*) méchant, vilain; dégoûtant.
natal [neitl], *a.* natal, de naissance.
nation ['neiʃən], *n.* nation, *f.*
national ['næʃənl], *a.* national; ***national anthem***, hymne national, *m.*; ***national debt***, dette publique, *f.*; ***national insurance***, assurances sociales, *f.pl.*
nationalism ['næʃnəlizm], *n.* nationalisme, *m.*
nationality [næʃə'næliti], *n.* nationalité, *f.*
nationalization [næʃnəlai'zeiʃən], *n.* nationalisation (*d'une industrie*), *f.*; (*Am.*) naturalisation (*d'une personne*), *f.*
nationalize ['næʃnəlaiz], *v.t.* nationaliser.
native ['neitiv], *a.* natif, naturel; indigène (*personne ou plante*); maternel (*langue etc.*); ***native land***, patrie, *f.*—*n.* natif (*d'une ville*); habitant (*d'une île*); naturel (*de tribu sauvage*); indigène (*des pays d'outremer*), *m.*; ***a native of England***, Anglais de naissance, *m.*; ***a native of Paris***, natif de Paris.
nativity [nə'tiviti], *n.* nativité; naissance, *f.*
natty ['næti], *a.* pimpant, propret, coquet.
natural ['nætʃərəl], *a.* naturel; réel; naïf, simple; (*Mus.*) bécarre.
naturalist ['nætʃərəlist], *n.* naturaliste, *m.*, *f.*
naturalization [nætʃərəlai'zeiʃən], *n.* naturalisation, *f.*
naturally ['nætʃərəli], *adv.* naturellement.
nature ['neitʃə], *n.* nature, *f.*; naturel (*disposition*), *m.*
naught [nɔːt], *n.* néant, rien; (*Arith.*) zéro, *m.*; ***to come to naught***, échouer.
naughtily ['nɔːtili], *adv.* par méchanceté.
naughtiness ['nɔːtinis], *n.* méchanceté, *f.*
naughty ['nɔːti], *a.* méchant, vilain.
nausea ['nɔːziə], *n.* nausée, *f.*
nauseating ['nɔːzieitiŋ], *a.* nauséabond, dégoûtant, écœurant.
nautical ['nɔːtikl], *a.* nautique; marin (*milles etc.*).
naval [neivl], *a.* naval; maritime; de la marine (*de guerre*); ***naval officer***, officier de marine, *m.*
nave (1) [neiv], *n.* nef (*d'église*), *f.*
nave (2) [neiv], *n.* moyeu (*de roue*), *m.*
navel [neivl], *n.* nombril, *m.*
navigable ['nævigəbl], *a.* navigable.
navigate ['nævigeit], *v.t.* gouverner.—*v.i.* naviguer.
navigation [nævi'geiʃən], *n.* navigation, *f.*
navigator ['nævigeitə], *n.* navigateur, *m.*
navvy ['nævi], *n.* terrassier, *m.*
navy ['neivi], *n.* marine de guerre, *f.*; ***Merchant Navy***, marine marchande.
navy blue ['neivi'bluː], *a.* and *n.* bleu marine, *m.inv.*
*nay [nei], *adv.* non; bien plus; et même, qui plus est; ***to say nay***, refuser.
Neapolitan [niə'pɔlitən], *a.* napolitain, de Naples.—*n.* Napolitain (*personne*), *m.*
neap tide ['niːp'taid], *n.* marée de morte eau, *f.*

near [niə], *a.* proche, rapproché; chiche (*parcimonieux*); cher (*bien-aimé*); fidèle (*intime*); de gauche (*left*).—*adv.* près, de près; presque.—*prep.* près de, auprès de.—*v.t.*, *v.i.* s'approcher de.
nearby ['niəbai], *a.*, [niə'bai], *adv.* tout près, tout proche.
nearly ['niəli], *adv.* de près; à peu près; presque; ***he was nearly drowned***, il faillit se noyer.
nearness ['niənis], *n.* proximité; parcimonie (*avarice*), *f.*
neat [niːt], *a.* propre, soigné, net; simple et élégant; pur, sec (*sans mélange*).
neatly ['niːtli], *adv.* proprement; nettement; adroitement (*habilement*).
neatness ['niːtnis], *n.* propreté, netteté, *f.*
nebula ['nebjulə], *n.* (*Astron.*) nébuleuse, *f.*
nebulous ['nebjuləs], *a.* nébuleux.
necessaries ['nesəsəriz], *n.pl.* nécessaire, *m.*
necessarily ['nesəsərili], *adv.* nécessairement, forcément.
necessary ['nesəsri], *a.* nécessaire.
necessitate [ni'sesiteit], *v.t.* nécessiter.
necessitous [ni'sesitəs], *a.* nécessiteux, dans le besoin.
necessity [ni'sesiti], *n.* nécessité, *f.*; besoin (*indigence*), *m.*; ***of necessity***, nécessairement, forcément.
neck [nek], *n.* cou; goulot (*de bouteille etc.*); manche (*de violon*); collet (*de viande*), *m.*; encolure (*d'une robe*), langue (*de terre*), *f.*; ***stiff neck***, torticolis, *m.*
neckerchief ['nekətʃif], *n.* foulard (*d'homme*), fichu (*de femme*), *m.*
necklace ['neklis], *n.* collier, *m.*
neck-tie ['nektai], *n.* cravate, *f.*
necromancy ['nekrəmænsi], *n.* nécromancie, *f.*
necropolis [ni'krɔpəlis], *n.* nécropole, *f.*
nectar ['nektə], *n.* nectar, *m.*
nectarine ['nektərin], *n.* brugnon, *m.*
need [niːd], *n.* besoin, *m.*; nécessité; indigence, *f.*; ***if need be***, le cas échéant; ***in case of need***, au besoin; ***to be in need***, être dans la misère; ***to be in need of*** or ***to have need of***, avoir besoin de.—*v.t.* avoir besoin de; exiger.—*v.i.* avoir besoin; devoir, avoir (à); (*impers.*) falloir, être nécessaire.
needful ['niːdful], *a.* nécessaire; ***the needful***, le nécessaire, *m.*
needle ['niːdl], *n.* aiguille, *f.*
needless ['niːdlis], *a.* inutile.
needlework ['niːdlwəːk], *n.* ouvrage à l'aiguille, *m.*; (*Sch.*) couture, *f.*
*needs [niːdz], *adv.* (*used only with must*) nécessairement, absolument; ***I must needs***, il faut absolument que je (*with subj.*).
needy ['niːdi], *a.* indigent, nécessiteux.
ne'er [nɛə], (*poet.*) [NEVER].
nefarious [ni'fɛəriəs], *a.* abominable, infâme.
negation [ni'geiʃən], *n.* négation, *f.*
negative ['negativ], *a.* négatif.—*n.* négative, *f.*; (*Phot.*) cliché, négatif, *m.*—*v.t.* rejeter.
neglect [ni'glekt], *n.* négligence, *f.*; oubli, *m.*—*v.t.* négliger.
neglected [ni'glektid], *a.* négligé.
neglectful [ni'glektful], *a.* négligent.
negligence ['neglidʒəns], *n.* négligence, *f.*
negligent ['neglidʒənt], *a.* négligent.

493

negligible ['neglidʒibl], *a.* négligeable.
negotiable [ni'gouʃiabl], *a.* négociable.
negotiate [ni'gouʃieit], *v.t.*, *v.i.* négocier.
negotiation [nigouʃi'eiʃən], *n.* négociation, *f.*
negotiator [ni'gouʃieitə], *n.* négociateur, *m.*
Negress ['ni:gres], *n.* (*pej.*) noire, *f.*
Negro ['ni:grou], *n.* noir, *m.,* noire, *f.*
neigh [nei], *v.i.* hennir.—*n.* hennissement, *m.*
neighbor ['neibə], *n.* voisin, *m.*; (*Bibl.*) prochain, *m.*
neighborhood ['neibəhud], *n.* voisinage, *m.*; alentours, environs, *m.pl.*; quartier, *m.*
neighboring ['neibəriŋ], *a.* voisin.
neighborly ['neibəli], *a.* de voisin, de bon voisin.
neighing ['neiiŋ], *n.* hennissement, *m.*
neither ['naiðə, 'ni:ðə], *a.* and *pron.* ni l'un ni l'autre, *m.*—*conj.* ni; non plus; *neither ... nor,* ni ... ni.—*adv.* du reste, d'ailleurs.
nemesis ['nemisis]. némésis, *f.*
neolithic [ni:ə'liθik], *a.* néolithique.
neon ['ni:ɔn], *a. neon light,* lampe au néon, *f.*—*n.* (*Chem.*) néon, *m.*
Nepal [nə'pɔːl], le Népal, *m.*
Nepalese [nepə'li:z], *a.* népalais.—*n.* Népalais (*personne*), *m.*
nephew ['nefju, 'nevju], *n.* neveu, *m.*
nepotism ['nepətizm], *n.* népotisme, *m.*
Nero ['niərou]. Néron, *m.*
nerve [nəːv], *n.* nerf; (*fig.*) courage, *m.*; audace, *f.*; (*pop.*) toupet, *m.*
nerve cell ['nəːvsel], *n.* cellule nerveuse, *f.*
nerveless ['nəːvlis], *a.* sans nerf; (*fig.*) sans vigueur.
nerve-racking ['nəːvrækiŋ], *a.* horripilant, énervant.
nervous ['nəːvəs], *a.* nerveux (*physiquement*); timide, craintif (*moralement*); *nervous breakdown,* dépression nerveuse, *f.*
nervousness ['nəːvəsnis], *n.* inquiétude, timidité; nervosité, *f.*
nest [nest], *n.* nid, *m.*; nichée (*couvée d'oiseaux*), *f.*; (*fig.*) repaire, *m.*; *nest of tables,* table gigogne, *f.*—*v.i.* nicher, faire un nid.
nestle [nesl], *v.i.* nicher, se nicher.
nestling ['nesliŋ], *n.* petit oiseau encore au nid, béjaune, *m.*
net [net], *a.* net; pur.—*n.* filet, rets, *m.*; résille (*à cheveux*), *f.*; tulle (*tissu*), *m.*—*v.t.* prendre dans un filet; (*Comm.*) rapporter net.
nether ['neðə], *a.* bas, inférieur.
Netherlands ['neðələndz], **the.** les Pays-Bas, *m.pl.*
nethermost ['neðəmoust], *a.* le plus bas.
netting ['netiŋ], *n.* filet, réseau; grillage (*de fil de fer*), *m.*
nettle [netl], *n.* ortie, *f.*—*v.t.* piquer, agacer, irriter.
nettlerash ['netlræʃ], *n.* urticaire, *f.*
network ['netwəːk], *n.* réseau, enchevêtrement, *m.*
neuralgia [nju'rældʒə], *n.* névralgie, *f.*
neuritis [nju'raitis], *n.* névrite, *f.*
neurosis [nju'rousis], *n.* névrose, *f.*
neurotic [nju'rɔtik], *a.* and *n.* névrosé, *m.,* neurotique, *m., f.*
neuter ['njuːtə], *a.* and *n.* neutre, *m.*
neutral ['njuːtrəl], *a.* neutre; indifférent.—*n.* (*Motor.*) point-mort, *m.*
neutrality [nju'træliti], *n.* neutralité; indifférence, *f.*

neutralize ['njuːtrəlaiz], *v.t.* neutraliser.
neutron ['njuːtrɔn], *n.* neutron, *m.*
never ['nevə], *adv.* jamais; ne . . . jamais; *never mind!* peu importe!
nevermore [nevə'mɔː], *adv.* ne . . . jamais plus, ne . . . plus jamais.
nevertheless [nevəðə'les], *conj.* néanmoins, cependant, pourtant.
new [njuː], *a.* neuf (*qui n'a pas servi*); nouveau (*récemment acquis, différent*); frais, récent (*arrivé depuis peu*); *brand-new,* flambant neuf, tout battant neuf; *New Year's Day,* le jour de l'an, *m.*
new-born ['njuːbɔːn], *a.* nouveau-né; *new-born daughters,* filles nouveau-nées, *f.pl.*
new-comer ['njuːkʌmə], *n.* nouveau venu, *m.*
Newfoundland ['njuːfəndlænd, njuː'faundlənd]. la Terre-Neuve, *f.*—*n.* terre-neuve (*chien*), *m.*
New Guinea [njuː'gini]. la Nouvelle-Guinée, *f.*
new-laid ['njuːleid], *a.* frais (*œuf*).
newly ['njuːli], *adv.* nouvellement, fraîchement, récemment, de nouveau.
newness ['njuːnis], *n.* nouveauté, *f.*
New Orleans [njuː'ɔːliənz]. la Nouvelle-Orléans, *f.*
news [njuːz], *n.* nouvelle, *f.,* nouvelles, *f.pl.*; (*Rad., Tel.*) bulletin d'informations, *m.*
news-agent ['njuːzeidʒənt], *n.* marchand de journaux, *m.*
newspaper ['njuːspeipə], *n.* journal, *m.*
newt [njuːt], *n.* triton, *m.,* salamandre, *f.*
New Zealand [njuː'ziːlənd]. la Nouvelle-Zélande, *f.*—*a.* néo-zélandais.
New Zealander [njuː'ziːləndə], *n.* Néo-Zélandais, *m.*
next [nekst], *a.* voisin, le plus voisin; le plus près; de côté; prochain (*dans l'avenir*); suivant (*dans le passé*); premier (*à la suite de*).—*adv.* après, ensuite, puis; *what next?* et après ? ensuite ?—*prep. next to,* à côté de.
nib [nib], *n.* bec (*de stylo*), *m.*; pointe (*d'outil*), *f.*
nibble [nibl], *v.t.* mordiller, grignoter; mordre à (*l'hameçon*); brouter (*l'herbe etc.*). —*n.* grignotement, *m.*; touche (*du poisson*), *f.*
Nicaragua [nikə'rægjuə]. le Nicaragua, *m.*
Nicaraguan [nikə'rægjuən], *a.* nicaraguayen. —*n.* Nicaraguayen (*personne*), *m.*
nice [nais], *a.* bon, agréable, friand; (*colloq.*) délicat, gentil, aimable, charmant, propre; exact, difficile, exigeant (*délicat*); *a nice child,* un enfant gentil, *m.*
nicely ['naisli], *adv.* bien, agréablement; délicatement; gentiment, aimablement; joliment; d'une manière recherchée.
nicety ['naisəti], *n.* (*pl.* **niceties** ['naisətiz]) délicatesse, finesse, *f.*; soin scrupuleux, *m.*; précision; exactitude, *f.*; (*pl.*) subtilités, finesses, *f.pl.*
niche [nitʃ], *n.* niche, *f.*
Nicholas ['nikələs]. Nicolas, *m.*
nick [nik], *n.* moment précis, *m.*; encoche, entaille (*coupure*), *f.*; (*Print.*) cran, *m.*; *in the nick of time,* fort à propos, à point nommé.
nickel [nikl], *n.* nickel, *m.*; (*Am.*) pièce de cinq cents, *f.*
nickname ['nikneim], *n.* sobriquet, surnom, *m.*—*v.t.* donner un sobriquet à.
nicotine ['nikəti:n], *n.* nicotine, *f.*

niece [ni:s], *n.* nièce, *f.*
nifty ['nifti], *a.* (*fam.*) pimpant.
Niger ['naidʒə], **the.** le Niger, *m.*
Nigeria [nai'dʒiəriə]. le Nigéria, *m.*
Nigerian [nai'dʒiəriən], *a.* nigérien.—*n.* Nigérien (*personne*), *m.*
niggard ['nigəd], *a.* and *n.* avare, ladre, *m.*
niggardliness ['nigədlinis], *n.* mesquinerie, ladrerie, *f.*
niggardly ['nigədli], *a.* mesquin, ladre, chiche.—*adv.* avec avarice, en avare.
niggle [nigl], *v.i.* tatillonner; fignoler.
nigh [nai], *adv.* près; presque; *to draw nigh,* approcher, s'approcher (*de*).
night [nait], *n.* nuit, *f.;* soir, *m.; first night,* première, *f.*
night-club ['naitklʌb], *n.* boîte de nuit, *f.*
night-dress ['naitdres], *n.* chemise de nuit, *f.*
night-fall ['naitfɔ:l], *n.* tombée de la nuit, *f.*
nightie ['naiti], *colloq. abbr.* [NIGHT-DRESS].
nightingale ['naitiŋgeil], *n.* rossignol, *m.*
night-light ['naitlait], *n.* veilleuse, *f.*
nightly ['naitli], *a.* nocturne de nuit.—*adv.* chaque nuit, toutes les nuits; tous les soirs.
nightmare ['naitmɛə], *n.* cauchemar, *m.*
night-time ['naittaim], *n.* nuit, *f.; in the night-time,* pendant la nuit.
night-watchman ['nait'wɔtʃmən], *n.* (*pl.* **-men** [men]) veilleur de nuit, *m.*
nihilism ['naiilizm], *n.* nihilisme, *m.*
nil [nil], *n.* rien, néant, zéro, *m.*
Nile [nail], **the.** le Nil, *m.*
nimble [nimbl], *a.* agile, léger, leste.
nimbly ['nimbli], *adv.* agilement, lestement.
nine [nain], *a.* and *n.* neuf, *m.*
ninefold ['nainfould], *a.* neuf fois autant.
ninepins ['nainpinz], *n.pl.* quilles, *f.pl.;* jeu de quilles, *m.*
nineteen [nain'ti:n], *a.* and *n.* dix-neuf, *m.*
nineteenth [nain'ti:nθ], *a.* dix-neuvième; dix-neuf (*du mois ou souverains*).—*n.* dix-neuvième (*fraction*), *m.*
ninetieth ['naintiiθ], *a.* quatre-vingt-dixième. —*n.* quatre-vingt-dixième (*fraction*), *m.*
ninety ['nainti], *a.* and *n.* quatre-vingt-dix, *m.*
ninny ['nini], *n.* nigaud, niais, *m.*
ninth [nainθ], *a.* neuvième; neuf (*du mois ou souverains*).—*n.* neuvième (*fraction*), *m.*
nip [nip], *n.* pincement, *m.,* pince, *f.,* serrement, *m.;* morsure; (*Hort.*) brûlure (par le froid), *f.*—*v.t.* pincer; mordre; (*Hort.*) brûler (par le froid); *to nip off,* couper, enlever le bout de.
nipper ['nipə], *n.* pince, *f.;* (*colloq.*) gamin, gosse, *m.;* (*pl.*) pincettes, pinces, *f.pl.*
nipple [nipl], *n.* mamelon, bout de sein, *m.*
nippy ['nipi], *a.* preste, rapide; perçant (*froid*).
nit [nit], *n.* lente, *f.*
nitrate ['naitreit], *n.* nitrate, *m.*
nitre ['naitə], *n.* nitre, *m.*
nitric ['naitrik], *a.* nitrique, azotique.
nitrogen ['naitrədʒən], *n.* azote, *m.*
nitwit ['nitwit], *n.* imbécile, *m., f.*
no [nou], *a.* and *adv.* non, pas, ne . . . pas de, ne . . . point de; pas un, nul, aucun.—*n.* non, *m.*
Noah ['nouə]. Noé, *m.*
nob [nɔb], *n.* (*colloq.*) caboche, *f.;* gros bonnet, *m.*
nobility [no'biliti], *n.* noblesse, *f.*
noble [noubl], *a.* noble; illustre, grand; généreux.—*n.* noble, *m.*

nobleman ['noublmən], *n.* (*pl.* **-men** [men]) noble, gentilhomme, *m.*
nobly ['noubli], *adv.* noblement; superbement.
nobody ['noubədi], *pron.* personne, *m.; I know nobody,* je ne connais personne; *nobody else,* personne d'autre.—*n.* zéro, inconnu, *m.*
nocturnal [nɔk'tə:nl], *a.* nocturne, de nuit.
nod [nɔd], *n.* signe de tête, *m.;* inclination de tête, *f.*—*v.i.* faire un signe de tête; s'incliner; sommeiller (*s'assoupir*).
noggin ['nɔgin], *n.* petit pot (*en étain*), *m.*
noise [nɔiz], *n.* bruit; tapage, fracas, vacarme; tintement (*de cloche*), bourdonnement (*d'insectes etc.*); (fig.) éclat, *m.*—*v.t.* ébruiter, publier, répandre.
noiseless ['nɔizlis], *a.* sans bruit; silencieux.
noiselessly ['nɔizlisli], *adv.* sans bruit.
noisily ['nɔizili], *adv.* bruyamment.
noisome ['nɔisəm], *a.* malsain, infect, nuisible.
noisy ['nɔizi], *a.* bruyant; turbulent (*enfants*).
nomad ['noumæd], *n.* nomade, *m.*
nomadic [no'mædik], *a.* nomade.
nominal ['nɔminl], *a.* nominal; de nom; *nominal roll,* état nominatif, *m.*
nominally ['nɔminəli], *adv.* de nom; nominalement.
nominate ['nɔmineit], *v.t.* nommer; désigner; présenter, proposer (*un candidat etc.*).
nomination [nɔmi'neiʃən], *n.* nomination; présentation, *f.*
nominative ['nɔminətiv], *a.* au nominatif, nominatif.—*n.* (*Gram.*) nominatif, *m.*
nominee [nɔmi'ni:], *n.* personne nommée, *f.*
nonagenarian [nounədʒi'nɛəriən], *a.* and *n.* nonagénaire, *m., f.*
non-aggression [nɔnə'greʃən], *n.* non-agression, *f.*
non-alcoholic [nɔnælkə'hɔlik], *a.* non-alcoolique.
non-attendance [nɔnə'tendəns], *n.* absence, *f.*
nonchalance ['nɔnʃələns], *n.* nonchalance, *f.*
non-combatant [nɔn'kʌmbətənt, nɔn'kɔmbətənt], *a.* and *n.* non-combattant, *m.*
non-commissioned [nɔnkə'miʃənd], *a.* sans brevet; *non-commissioned officer,* sous-officier, *m.*
non-committal [nɔnkə'mitl], *a.* qui n'engage à rien, diplomatique.
nonconformist [nɔnkən'fɔ:mist], *a.* and *n.* dissident, *m.,* nonconformiste, *m., f.*
nondescript ['nɔndiskript], *a.* indéfinissable, quelconque.—*n.* chose sans nom, chose indéfinissable, *f.*
none [nʌn], *a.* and *pron.* nul, *m.,* nulle, *f.,* aucun, *m.,* aucune, *f.,* pas un, *m.,* pas une, *f.,* personne, *m.*—*adv.* pas, point; néant (*sur des bordereaux*).
nonentity [nɔ'nentiti], *n.* néant, *m.;* (fig.) nullité, *f.,* zéro, *m.*
nonesuch ['nʌnsʌtʃ], *a.* sans pareil, nonpareil.
non-existent ['nɔnig'zistənt], *a.* qui n'existe pas.
non-intervention ['nɔnintə'venʃən], *n.* non-intervention, *f.*
non-observance ['nɔnəb'zə:vəns], *n.* inobservation, *f.*
non-payment ['nɔn'peimənt], *n.* non-payement, *m.*

nonplussed ['nɔn'plʌst], *a.* embarrassé, dérouté.

nonsense ['nɔnsəns], *n.* non-sens, *m.*; sottise, absurdité, *f.*; **nonsense!** allons donc! quelle sottise!

nonsensical [nɔn'sensikl], *a.* vide de sens, absurde.

non-skid ['nɔn'skid], *a.* antidérapant.

non-stop ['nɔn'stɔp], *a.* and *adv.* sans arrêt.

noodle [nu:dl], *n.* nigaud, benêt, sot, *m.*; (*pl.*) (*Cook.*) nouilles, *f.pl.*

nook [nuk], *n.* recoin, réduit, *m.*

noon [nu:n], *n.* midi, *m.*

noonday ['nu:ndei], *a.* de midi.—*n.* midi, *m.*

noontide ['nu:ntaid], *n.* heure de midi, *f.*, midi, *m.*

noose [nu:s], *n.* nœud coulant, lacet, *m.*

nor [nɔ:], *conj.* ni; ni . . . ne.

norm [nɔ:m], *n.* norme, *f.*

normal [nɔ:ml], *a.* normal.

normally ['nɔ:məli], *adv.* normalement.

Norman ['nɔ:mən], *a.* normand.—*n.* Normand (*personne*), *m.*

Normandy ['nɔ:məndi], la Normandie, *f.*

north [nɔ:θ], *a.* du nord, septentrional.—*n.* nord, septentrion, *m.*—*adv.* au nord.

north-east [nɔ:θ'i:st], *n.* nord-est, *m.*

northerly ['nɔ:ðəli], *a.* septentrional, du nord.—*adv.* au nord, vers le nord.

northern ['nɔ:ðən], *a.* du nord; **northern lights**, aurore boréale, *f.*

northerner ['nɔ:ðənə], *n.* habitant du nord, *m.*

north-west [nɔ:θ'west], *n.* nord-ouest, *m.*

Norway ['nɔ:wei], la Norvège, *f.*

Norwegian [nɔ:'wi:dʒən], *a.* norvégien.—*n.* norvégien (*langue*); Norvégien (*personne*), *m.*

nose [nouz], *n.* nez; museau (*d'animal*); odorat (*flair*), *m.*; **Roman nose**, nez aquilin; *to blow one's nose*, se moucher; *to put someone's nose out of joint*, supplanter quelqu'un; *to turn up one's nose at*, faire fi de; *turned-up nose*, nez retroussé.—*v.t.* flairer.—*v.i.* to **nose about**, fureter.

nose-bag ['nouzbæg], *n.* musette (*de cheval etc.*), *f.*

nose-dive ['nouzdaiv], *v.i.* (*Av.*) piquer du nez.—*n.* piqué, *m.*

nosegay ['nouzgei], *n.* bouquet, *m.*

nostalgia [nɔs'tældʒiə], *n.* nostalgie, *f.*, mal du pays, *m.*

nostril ['nɔstril], *n.* narine, *f.*; naseau (*de cheval etc.*), *m.*

nosy ['nouzi], *a.* (*pop.*) fouinard.

not [nɔt], *adv.* non; ne . . . pas, ne . . . point, pas, non pas; *not at all*, point du tout; *why not?* pourquoi pas?

notability [noutə'biliti], *n.* notabilité, *f.*

notable ['noutəbl], *a.* notable, insigne; remarquable.—*n.* notable, *m.*, *f.*

notably ['noutəbli], *adv.* notamment (*particulièrement*)

notary ['noutəri], *n.* notaire, *m.*

notation [no'teiʃən], *n.* notation, *f.*

notch [nɔtʃ], *n.* encoche, entaille, brèche, *f.*—*v.t.* entailler, ébrécher.

note [nout], *n.* note, marque, *f.*, signe, *m.*; lettre, *f.*, billet, *m.*; marque (*distinction*), *f.*; *bank note*, billet de banque; *to take a note of*, prendre note de.—*v.t.* noter; remarquer.

notebook ['noutbuk], *n.* carnet, *m.*

noted ['noutid], *a.* distingué (*personne*); célèbre (*chose*).

notepaper ['noutpeipə], *n.* papier à lettres, *m.*

noteworthy ['noutwə:ði], *a.* remarquable.

nothing ['nʌθiŋ], *n.* rien, néant, *m.*; *a mere nothing*, (*fig.*) un zéro.—*pron.* (ne) rien; *good-for-nothing*, bon à rien, *m.*; *nothing at all*, rien du tout; *to do nothing but*, ne faire que.—*adv.* en rien, nullement, aucunement.

nothingness ['nʌθiŋnis], *n.* néant, rien, *m.*

notice ['noutis], *n.* connaissance; attention, *f.*; préavis, *m.*; notice (*article dans un journal*); (*Law*) notification; annonce (*dans un journal*); affiche (*avis placardé*), *f.*; *a week's notice*, un préavis de huit jours; *at short notice*, à court délai; *to give notice*, avertir, donner congé; *to take notice of*, faire attention à, remarquer; *until further notice*, jusqu'à nouvel ordre.—*v.t.* prendre connaissance de, remarquer, s'apercevoir de.

noticeable ['noutisəbl], *a.* perceptible.

noticeably ['noutisəbli], *adv.* perceptiblement, sensiblement.

notice-board ['noutisbɔ:d], *n.* écriteau, *m.*

notification [noutifi'keiʃən], *n.* notification, *f.*, avis, avertissement, *m.*

notify ['noutifai], *v.t.* faire savoir, notifier.

notion ['nouʃən], *n.* notion, idée, *f.*

notoriety [noutə'raiəti], *n.* notoriété, *f.*

notorious [no'tɔ:riəs], *a.* notoire.

notwithstanding [nɔtwið'stændiŋ], *prep.* malgré, nonobstant.—*adv.* néanmoins.

noun [naun], *n.* nom, substantif, *m.*

nourish ['nʌriʃ], *v.t.* nourrir; (*fig.*) entretenir.

nourishing ['nʌriʃiŋ], *a.* nourrissant, nutritif.

nourishment ['nʌriʃmənt], *n.* nourriture, alimentation, *f.*

Nova Scotia ['nouvə'skouʃə]. la Nouvelle-Écosse, *f.*

novel [nɔvl], *a.* nouveau, original.—*n.* roman, *m.*

novelist ['nɔvəlist], *n.* romancier, *m.*

novelty ['nɔvəlti], *n.* nouveauté, *f.*

November [no'vembə], *n.* novembre, *m.*

novercal [no'və:kl], *a.* de marâtre.

novice ['nɔvis], *n.* novice, *m.*, *f.*

novitiate [nə'viʃiit], *n.* noviciat, *m.*

now [nau], *adv.* maintenant, à présent, actuellement; alors, or, donc (*raisonnement*); *now and then*, de temps en temps; *now . . . now*, tantôt . . . tantôt; *now then!* eh bien!

nowadays ['nauədeiz], *adv.* aujourd'hui, de nos jours.

nowhere ['nouwɛə], *adv.* nulle part.

nowise ['nouwaiz], *adv.* en aucune manière.

noxious ['nɔkʃəs], *a.* nuisible.

nozzle [nɔzl], *n.* nez; bec, bout; (*Motor. etc.*) ajutage, *m.*; lance (*de tuyau*), *f.*

nuclear ['nju:klia], *a.* nucléaire; *nuclear fission*, fission de l'atome, *f.*; *nuclear war*, guerre atomique, *f.*

nucleus ['nju:kliəs], *n.* noyau, *m.*

nude [nju:d], *a.* and *n.* nu, *m.*

nudge [nʌdʒ], *n.* coup de coude, *m.*—*v.t.* donner un coup de coude à, pousser du coude.

nugget ['nʌgit], *n.* pépite (*d'or*), *f.*

nuisance ['nju:səns], *n.* peste, plaie, *f.*, fléau, *m.* (*Law*) dommage, *m.*

null [nʌl], *a.* nul; *null and void*, nul et non avenu.
nullify ['nʌlifai], *v.t.* annuler.
nullity ['nʌliti], *n.* nullité, *f.*
numb [nʌm], *a.* engourdi, transi.—*v.t.* engourdir (*par*).
number ['nʌmbə], *n.* nombre; chiffre (*de 0 à 9*); numéro (*d'une série*), *m.*; livraison (*de publications*), *f.*; (*fig., pl.*) nombres, *m.pl.*; *a number of*, plusieurs, une foule de (*gens*); *cardinal, ordinal, odd, or even number*, nombre cardinal, ordinal, impair *ou* pair.—*v.A.* compter; numéroter (*en série*).
numberless ['nʌmbəlis], *a.* innombrable.
number-plate ['nʌmbəpleit], *n.* (*Motor.*) plaque d'immatriculation, *f.*
numbness ['nʌmnis], *n.* engourdissement, *m.*
numeral ['nju:mərəl], *a.* numéral.—*n.* lettre numérale, *f.*, chiffre, *m.*
numerical [nju'merikl], *a.* numérique.
numerous ['nju:mərəs], *a.* nombreux.
numskull ['nʌmskʌl], *n.* benêt, idiot, *m.*
nun [nʌn], *n.* religieuse, (*fam.*) nonne, *f.*
nunnery ['nʌnəri], *n.* couvent (*de religieuses*), *m.*
nuptial ['nʌpʃəl], *a.* nuptial, de noces.
nuptials ['nʌpʃəlz], *n.pl.* noces, *f.pl.*
nurse [nə:s], *n.* bonne d'enfant, *f.*; garde-malade, *m., f.*; infirmier, *m.*, infirmière, *f.* (*à l'hôpital*); *wet nurse*, nourrice, *f.*—*v.t.* nourrir, élever; soigner, garder (*les malades*).
nurse-maid ['nə:smeid], *n.* bonne d'enfant, *f.*
nursery ['nə:səri], *n.* chambre d'enfants, *f.*; (*Hort.*) pépinière, *f.*; *nursery rhyme*, chanson d'enfants, *f.*
nursery-man ['nə:sərimən], *n.* (*pl.* -men [men]) pépiniériste, *m.*
nursery school ['nə:sərisku:l], *n.* école maternelle, *f.*
nursing home ['nə:siŋhoum], *n.* clinique, maison de santé, *f.*
nurture ['nə:tʃə], *n.* nourriture; éducation, *f.* —*v.t.* nourrir; élever.
nut [nʌt], *n.* noix (*du noyer etc.*); noisette (*du noisetier*), *f.*; (*Tech.*) écrou, *m.*
nut-brown ['nʌtbraun], *a.* châtain.
nut-cracker ['nʌtkrækə], *n.* casse-noix (*oiseau*), *m.*; (*pl.*) casse-noisettes, *m.pl.*
nutmeg ['nʌtmeg], *n.* muscade, *f.*
nutrient ['nju:triənt], *a.* nourrissant.
nutrition [nju'triʃən], *n.* nutrition; alimentation, *f.*
nutritious [nju'triʃəs], *a.* nourrissant, nutritif.
nutshell ['nʌtʃel], *n.* coquille de noix, *f.*
nut tree ['nʌtri:], *n.* noisetier, *m.*
nutty ['nʌti], *a.* qui a un goût de noisette; (*pop.*) fêlé, toqué.
nylon ['nailɔn], *n.* nylon, *m.*
nymph [nimf], *n.* nymphe, *f.*

O

O, o [ou]. quinzième lettre de l'alphabet, *m.*
oaf [ouf], *n.* idiot, *m.*
oafish ['oufiʃ], *a.* stupide, idiot.

oak [ouk], *n.* chêne; bois de chêne, *m.*
oak apple ['oukæpl], *n.* pomme de chêne, *f.*
oak tree ['ouktri:], *n.* chêne, *m.*
oar [ɔ:], *n.* aviron, *m.*, rame, *f.*
oarlock, see **rowlock**
oarsman ['ɔ:zmən], *n.* (*pl.* -men [men]) rameur, *m.*
oasis [ou'eisis], *n.* (*pl.* **oases** [ou'eisi:z]) oasis, *f.*
oatcake ['outkeik], *n.* galette d'avoine, *f.*
oaten [outn], *a.* d'avoine.
oath [ouθ], *n.* serment; juron, *m.*; *on oath*, sous serment; *to take an oath*, prêter serment.
oatmeal ['outmi:l], *n.* farine d'avoine, *f.*
oats [outs], *n.pl.* avoine, *f.*
obduracy ['ɔbdjurəsi], *n.* endurcissement, entêtement, *m.*
obdurate ['ɔbdjurit], *a.* endurci; obstiné, opiniâtre; impénitent.
obedience [o'bi:djəns], *n.* obéissance, soumission, *f.*
obedient [o'bi:djənt], *a.* obéissant, soumis.
obediently [o'bi:djəntli], *adv.* avec obéissance.
obeisance [o'beisəns], *n.* révérence, *f.*
obelisk ['ɔbəlisk], *n.* obélisque, *m.*
obese [o'bi:s], *a.* obèse.
obesity [o'bi:siti], *n.* obésité, *f.*
obey [o'bei], *v.t.* obéir à.—*v.i.* obéir.
obfuscate ['ɔbfʌskeit], *v.t.* offusquer, obscurcir.
obituary [ɔ'bitjuəri], *a.* obituaire; nécrologique.—*n.* nécrologie, *f.*
object (1) ['ɔbdʒikt], *n.* objet; but (*fin*), *m.*; considération, *f.*; (*Gram.*) régime, *m.*
object (2) [əb'dʒekt], *v.t.* objecter.—*v.i.* s'opposer (à).
objection [əb'dʒekʃən], *n.* objection, *f.*; obstacle, *m.*; (*Racing*) contestation, *f.*
objectionable [əb'dʒekʃənəbl], *a.* déplaisant; inadmissible.
objective [əb'dʒektiv], *a.* objectif.—*n.* objectif, but, *m.*
objectively [əb'dʒektivli], *adv.* objectivement.
oblation [o'bleiʃən], *n.* oblation, offrande, *f.*
obligation [ɔbli'geiʃən], *n.* obligation, *f.*; engagement, *m.*
obligatory [ə'bligətəri], *a.* obligatoire.
oblige [ə'blaidʒ], *v.t.* obliger; faire plaisir à.
obliging [ə'blaidʒiŋ], *a.* obligeant.
oblique [o'bli:k], *a.* oblique; indirect.
obliterate [ə'blitəreit], *v.t.* effacer, oblitérer.
obliteration [əblitə'reiʃən], *n.* oblitération, *f.*
oblivion [ə'bliviən], *n.* oubli, *m.*; *act of oblivion*, loi d'amnistie, *f.*
oblivious [ə'bliviəs], *a.* oublieux (*de*).
oblong ['ɔblɔŋ], *a.* oblong.—*n.* rectangle, *m.*
obnoxious [ɔb'nɔkʃəs], *a.* odieux, désagréable, déplaisant.
oboe ['oubou], *n.* hautbois, *m.*
obscene [əb'si:n], *a.* obscène, sale.
obscenity [əb'seniti], *n.* obscénité, *f.*
obscure [əb'skjuə], *a.* obscur; (*fig.*) caché.—*v.t.* obscurcir; voiler (*lumière*).
obscurely [əb'skjuəli], *adv.* obscurément.
obscurity [əb'skjuəriti], *n.* obscurité, *f.*
obsequies ['ɔbsikwiz], *n.pl.* obsèques, *f.pl.*
obsequious [əb'si:kwiəs], *a.* obséquieux.
obsequiousness [əb'si:kwiəsnis], *n.* soumission obséquieuse, *f.*

observance [əb'zə:vəns], *n.* observance;
pratique, observation, *f.*
observant [əb'zə:vənt], *a.* observateur.
observation [ɔbzə'veiʃən], *n.* observation, *f.*
observatory [əb'zə:vətri], *n.* observatoire, *m.*
observe [əb'zə:v], *v.t.* observer; remarquer;
faire remarquer.
observer [əb'zə:və], *n.* observateur, *m.*
obsess [əb'ses], *v.t.* obséder.
obsessed [əb'sest], *a.* obsédé.
obsession [əb'seʃən], *n.* obsession, *f.*
obsolete ['ɔbsəli:t], *a.* vieilli, suranné; tombé
en désuétude.
obstacle ['ɔbstəkl], *n.* obstacle, *m.*
obstetrics [ɔb'stetriks], *n.pl.* obstétrique, *f.*
obstinacy ['ɔbstinəsi], *n.* obstination, opiniâtreté, *f.*; entêtement (*de caractère*), *m.*
obstinate ['ɔbstinit], *a.* obstiné, opiniâtre,
entêté; têtu (*enfant*).
obstinately ['ɔbstinitli], *adv.* obstinément.
obstreperous [əb'strepərəs], *a.* turbulent,
tapageur; récalcitrant.
obstruct [əb'strakt], *v.t.* empêcher, retarder;
obstruer, encombrer, boucher.
obstruction [əb'strakʃən], *n.* empêchement,
obstacle, *m.*; (*Med., Polit.*) obstruction, *f.*;
encombrement (*circulation*), *m.*
obstructive [əb'straktiv], *a.* qui empêche;
(*Med.*) obstructif.
obtain [əb'tein], *v.t.* obtenir, gagner; se
procurer.—*v.i.* prévaloir.
obtainable [əb'teinəbl], *a.* qu'on peut
obtenir, procurable.
obtrude [əb'tru:d], *v.t.* imposer.—*v.i.* s'introduire de force; être importun.
obtrusive [əb'tru:siv], *a.* importun.
obtuse [əb'tju:s], *a.* obtus; émoussé; stupide.
obtuseness [əb'tju:snis], *n.* (*fig.*) stupidité, *f.*
obverse ['ɔbvə:s], *n.* face, *f.*, avers, obvers (*de
médaille etc.*), *m.*
obviate ['ɔbvieit], *v.t.* éviter, obvier à.
obvious ['ɔbviəs], *a.* évident, clair.
obviously ['ɔbviəsli], *adv.* évidemment.
occasion [ə'keiʒən], *n.* occasion, rencontre;
raison, cause, *f.*; besoin (*nécessité*), *m.*—*v.t.*
occasionner, causer.
occasional [ə'keiʒənəl], *a.* occasionnel,
fortuit.
occasionally [ə'keiʒənəli], *adv.* quelquefois,
de temps en temps.
occident ['ɔksidənt], *n.* occident, *m.*
occidental [ɔksi'dentl], *a.* occidental.
occult [ə'kʌlt], *a.* occulte.
occupant ['ɔkjupənt], *n.* occupant, *m.*; locataire (*de chambre louée*); titulaire (*d'un poste*),
m., *f.*
occupation [ɔkju'peiʃən], *n.* occupation, *f.*;
emploi, métier, *m.*; possession, *f.*
occupier ['ɔkjupaiə], *n.* occupant, *m.*; locataire (*de chambre louée*), *m.*, *f.*, habitant, *m.*
occupy ['ɔkjupai], *v.t.* occuper; employer;
habiter (*une maison*).
occur [ə'kə:], *v.i.* arriver, avoir lieu, se produire; venir à l'esprit; *it occurred to me
that*, l'idée m'est venue que.
occurrence [ə'kʌrəns], *n.* occurrence, rencontre, *f.*, événement, *m.*
ocean ['ouʃən], *a.* de l'océan.—*n.* océan, *m.*
oceanic [ouʃi'ænik], *a.* océanique.
ochre ['oukə], *n.* ocre, *f.*
o'clock [ə'klɔk], [CLOCK].
octagon ['ɔktəgən], *n.* octogone, *m.*

octagonal [ɔk'tægənəl], *a.* octogone, octo-
gonal.
octane ['ɔktein], *n.* octane, *m.*; **high-octane
fuel**, supercarburant, *m.*
octave ['ɔktiv], *n.* (*Mus., Eccles.*) octave, *f.*
octavo [ɔk'teivou], *n.* in-octavo, *m.*
octet(te) [ɔk'tet], *n.* (*Mus.*) octuor, *m.*
October [ɔk'toubə], octobre, *m.*
octogenarian [ɔktoudʒi'nɛəriən], *a.* and *n.*
octogénaire, *m.*, *f.*
octopus ['ɔktəpəs], *n.* pieuvre, *f.*
ocular ['ɔkjulə], *a.* oculaire.
oculist ['ɔkjulist], *n.* oculiste, *m.*
odd [ɔd], *a.* impair; de surplus; d'appoint
(*argent*); dépareillé (*article isolé d'une collection*); étrange, singulier, bizarre; **odd
moments**, moments perdus, *m.pl.*; **odd
number**, nombre impair, *m.*
oddity ['ɔditi], *n.* bizarrerie, *f.*; original
(*personne*), *m.*
odd-looking ['ɔdlukiŋ], *a.* à la mine bizarre.
oddly ['ɔdli], *adv.* étrangement; bizarrement.
oddments ['ɔdmənts], *n.pl.* bric-à-brac, *m.*,
fins de séries, *f.pl.*
odds [ɔdz], *n.pl.* inégalité, *f.*; (*fig.*) avantage,
m., supériorité, *f.*; chances, *f.pl.*; **it makes
no odds**, cela ne fait rien; **odds and ends**,
petits bouts, *m.pl.*; **to be at odds with**,
être mal avec.
ode [oud], *n.* ode, *f.*
odious ['oudiəs], *a.* odieux.
odium ['oudiəm], *n.* détestation, *f.*
odor ['oudə], *n.* odeur, *f.*, parfum, *m.*; **in
bad odor**, en mauvaise odeur.
odorless ['oudəlis], *a.* sans odeur.
odorous ['oudərəs], *a.* odorant.
o'er ['ɔ:ə], (*poet.*) [OVER].
of [ɔv], *prep.* de; d'entre.
off [ɔf, ɔ:f], *adv.* au loin, à distance; d'ici;
rompu, enlevé; fini; fermé (*électricité etc.*);
qui n'est plus frais (*aliments*); **day off**,
jour de congé, *m.*; **fifty yards off**, à cinquante pas; *I am off*, je m'en vais; **off and
on**, de temps à autre; **time off**, temps libre,
m.; **to be well off**, être dans l'aisance.—*a.*
off day, jour de congé, *m.*; **off side**, côté
droit, hors montoir; (*Ftb.*) hors-jeu; **off
white**, blanc teinté.—*prep.* de, de dessus;
éloigné de; (*Naut.*) au large de.
offal [ɔfl], *n.* issues, *f.pl.*; abats, *m.pl.*; rebut,
m.
offence [ə'fens], *n.* agression; offense; injure;
violation (*d'une loi etc.*), *f.*, délit, crime, *m.*
offend [ə'fend], *v.t.* offenser, outrager,
blesser; violer (*transgresser*).—*v.i.* déplaire
(à); commettre une offense.
offender [ə'fendə], *n.* offenseur; (*Law*)
délinquant, *m.*
offensive [ə'fensiv], *a.* offensant, désagréable;
choquant; offensif (*attaquant*).—*n.* offensive,
f.
offensively [ə'fensivli], *adv.* d'une manière
offensante; offensivement.
offensiveness [ə'fensivnis], *n.* nature offensante, *f.*
offer ['ɔfə], *v.t.* offrir, présenter, proposer à.—
v.i. s'offrir, se présenter à; essayer de.—*n.*
offre, *f.*
offering ['ɔfəriŋ], *n.* offrande, *f.*; sacrifice, *m.*
off-hand ['ɔf'hænd], *adv.* au premier abord;
sans réflexion, sur-le-champ; cavalière-

ment.—*a.* brusque, cavalier; impromptu, improvisé.

off-handed [ˈɔfˈhændid], *a.* sans façon, sans gêne.

off-handedness [ˈɔfˈhændidnis], *n.* sans-façon, sans-gêne, *m.*

office [ˈɔfis], *n.* bureau (*immeuble*), *m.*, agence, *f.*; cabinet (*du directeur*), *m.*; étude (*d'avoué etc.*), *f.*; office, emploi; ministère, *m.*, charge, *f.*, fonctions, *f.pl.*; (*pl.*) devoirs (*services*), *m.pl.*; place, *f.*; cabinet (of physician, dentist, lawyer), *m.*

officer [ˈɔfisə], *n.* officier; fonctionnaire (*du gouvernement*); agent (*de police*), *m.*; **non-commissioned officer**, sous-officier, *m.*—*v.t.* fournir des officiers à; encadrer.

official [əˈfiʃəl], *a.* officiel.—*n.* fonctionnaire; employé, *m.*

officialdom [əˈfiʃəldəm], *n.* bureaucratie, *f.*

officially [əˈfiʃəli], *adv.* officiellement.

officiate [əˈfiʃieit], *v.i.* officier, desservir.

officious [əˈfiʃəs], *a.* officieux; importun.

officiousness [əˈfiʃəsnis], *n.* zèle officieux, *m.*

offing [ˈɔfiŋ], *n.* (*Naut.*) **in the offing**, au large; (*fig.*) en perspective.

offset [ˈɔfset], *v.t.* (*Comm.*) compenser; (*Tech.*) désaxer, décaler.

offshoot [ˈɔfʃuːt], *n.* rejeton, *m.*

offspring [ˈɔfspriŋ], *n.* enfants, descendants, *m.pl.*; (*fig.*) fruit, produit, *m.*

often [ɔfn], ***oft** [ɔft], ***oftentimes** [ˈɔfn taimz], ***oft-times** [ˈɔfttaimz], *adv.* souvent, maintes fois.

ogle [ougl], *v.t.* lorgner; lancer des œillades à. —*n.* œillade, *f.*

ogler [ˈouglə], *n.* lorgneur, *m.*

ogling [ˈougliŋ], *n.* lorgnerie, *f.*, œillades, *f.pl.*

ogre [ˈougə], *n.* ogre, *m.*

ogress [ˈougris], *n.* ogresse, *f.*

oh! [ou], *int.* oh! hélas!

ohm [oum], *n.* (*Elec.*) ohm, *m.*

oil [ɔil], *n.* huile, *f.*; (*crude*) **oil**, pétrole (brut), *m.*; **fuel oil**, mazout, *m.*; **coal oil**, pétrole (lampant), *m.*—*v.t.* huiler; graisser; (*fig.*) délier (*la langue*).

oilcake [ˈɔilkeik], *n.* tourteau, *m.*

oil-can [ˈɔilkæn], *n.* burette, *f.*

oil-cloth [ˈɔilklɔθ], *n.* toile cirée, *f.*

oil field [ˈɔilfiːld], *n.* gisement pétrolifère, *m.*

oiliness [ˈɔilinis], *n.* onctuosité, nature huileuse, *f.*

oil lamp [ˈɔillæmp], *n.* lampe à huile *ou* à pétrole, *f.*

oil painting [ˈɔilpeintiŋ], *n.* peinture à l'huile, *f.*

oilskin [ˈɔilskin], *n.* toile cirée vernie, *f.*

oil stove [ˈɔilstouv], *n.* réchaud à pétrole, *m.*

oil tanker [ˈɔiltæŋkə], *n.* (*Naut.*) pétrolier; (*Motor.*) camion-citerne, *m.*

oil well [ˈɔilwel], *n.* puits de pétrole, *m.*

oily [ˈɔili], *a.* huileux; (*fig.*) oléagineux, onctueux.

ointment [ˈɔintmənt], *n.* onguent, *m.*, pommade, *f.*

old [ould], *a.* vieux; âgé; ancien, antique; **how old are you?** quel âge avez-vous? **old man** (*chap, boy*), mon vieux, mon brave; **to grow old**, vieillir.

olden [ˈouldən], *a.* vieux, ancien; **in olden times**, au temps jadis.

old-fashioned [ould ˈfæʃənd] *a.* démodé, suranné.

oldish [ˈouldiʃ], *a.* un peu vieux, vieillot.

old maid [ˈouldmeid], *n.* vieille fille, *f.*

oleaginous [ouliˈædʒinəs], *a.* oléagineux.

oleander [ouliˈændə], *n.* (*Bot.*) laurier-rose, oléandre, *m.*

oligarchy [ˈɔligaːki], *n.* oligarchie, *f.*

olive [ˈɔliv], *n.* olive, *f.*, olivier (*arbre*), *m.*

Oliver [ˈɔlivə]. Olivier, *m.*

Olympian [oˈlimpiən], *a.* olympien.

Olympic [oˈlimpik], *a.* olympique; **the Olympic Games**, les jeux olympiques, *m.pl.*

Olympus [oˈlimpəs]. Olympe, *m.*

omega [ˈoumigə], *n.* oméga, *m.*

omelet(te) [ˈɔmlit], *n.* omelette, *f.*

omen [ˈoumən], *n.* augure, *m.*

ominous [ˈɔminəs], *a.* de mauvais augure, sinistre; menaçant.

ominously [ˈɔminəsli], *adv.* de mauvais augure.

omission [oˈmiʃən], *n.* omission, *f.*

omit [oˈmit], *v.t.* omettre; oublier.

omnipotence [ɔmˈnipətəns], *n.* omnipotence, toute-puissance, *f.*

omnipotent [ɔmˈnipətənt], *a.* tout-puissant, omnipotent.

omniscient [ɔmˈnisiənt], *a.* omniscient.

omnivorous [ɔmˈnivərəs], *a.* omnivore.

on [ɔn], *prep.* sur, dessus; à; de; en, dans; lors de, après; **on foot**, à pied; **on Monday**, lundi; **on purpose**, à dessein, exprès; **on the whole**, en somme.—*adv.* dessus; en avant, avant, avancé; toujours (*continuation*); de suite (*succession*); **and so on**, et ainsi de suite; **on and on**, sans cesse, interminablement; **play on**, continuez de jouer; **read on**, lisez toujours.

once [wʌns], *adv.* une fois, une seule fois; autrefois, jadis (*anciennement*); **at once**, sur-le-champ, tout de suite; **once upon a time there was**, il était une fois.

one [wʌn], *a.* un; seul, unique; un certain.— *n.* un, *m.*, une, *f.*—*pron.* on, l'on; vous (*accusatif*); celui, *m.*, celle, *f.*; quelqu'un; un homme, *m.*, une femme, *f.*

one-armed [ˈwʌnaːmd], *a.* manchot.

one-eyed [ˈwʌnaid], *a.* borgne.

onerous [ˈɔnərəs], *a.* onéreux.

onerousness [ˈɔnərəsnis], *n.* poids, *m.*, charge, *f.*

oneself [wʌnˈself], *pron.* soi, soi-même; (*reflexive*) se.

one-sided [ˈwʌnˈsaidid], *a.* à un côté, à une face; (*fig.*) partial, unilatéral.

one-sidedness [ˈwʌnˈsaididnis], *n.* partialité, *f.*

one-way [ˈwʌnwei], *a.* **one-way street**, rue à sens unique, *f.*; **one-way ticket**, billet simple, *m.*

onion [ˈʌnjən], *n.* oignon, *m.*; **spring onion**, ciboule, *f.*

onion bed [ˈʌnjənbed], *n.* oignonnière, *f.*

onlooker [ˈɔnlukə], *n.* spectateur, *m.*

only [ˈounli], *a.* seul; unique; **only child**, enfant unique, *m., f.*—*adv.* seulement; rien que; uniquement; ne . . . que.—*conj.* mais.

onset [ˈɔnset], *n.* assaut, *m.*, attaque, charge, *f.*

onslaught [ˈɔnslɔːt], *n.* attaque, *f.*; assaut, *m.*

onus [ˈounəs], *n.* charge, responsabilité, obligation, *f.*

onward ['ɔnwəd], *a.* en avant; avancé, progressif.—*adv.* or **onwards** ['ɔnwədz], en avant.

onyx ['ɔniks], *n.* onyx, *m.*

ooze [u:z], *n.* limon, *m.*—*v.i.* suinter, filtrer; (*fig.*) s'ébruiter.

oozing ['u:ziŋ], *n.* suintement; (*fig.*) ébruitement, *m.*

oozy ['u:zi], *a.* vaseux, limoneux.

opal [oupl], *n.* opale, *f.*

opaque [o'peik], *a.* opaque; (*fig.*) épais.

opaqueness [o'peiknis], *n.* opacité, *f.*

open ['oupən], *v.t.* ouvrir; déboucher (*une bouteille*); (*fig.*) expliquer; commencer, entamer; révéler; décacheter (*une lettre*); défaire (*un colis*); inaugurer.—*v.i.* s'ouvrir; commencer.—*a.* ouvert, découvert, à découvert, nu, à nu; franc, sincère; libre; (*fig.*) clair; **in the open** (*air*), en plein air; **on the open sea**, en pleine mer.

opener ['oupənə], *n.* ouvreur, *m.*; **tin-opener**, ouvre-boîte, *m.*

open-handed ['oupən'hændid], *a.* libéral, généreux.

open-hearted ['oupən'hɑːtid], *a.* franc.

opening ['oupniŋ], *a.* qui commence, d'inauguration; **the opening chapter**, le premier chapitre.—*n.* ouverture, embrasure, *f.*; commencement, début, *m.*; chance; éclaircie (*dans une forêt etc.*), *f.*

openly ['oupənli], *adv.* ouvertement; franchement.

open-minded ['oupən'maindid], *a.* sans parti pris, libéral, à l'esprit ouvert.

open-mouthed ['oupən'mauðd], *a.* bouche béante, bouche bée.

openness ['oupənnis], *n.* franchise, sincérité, candeur, *f.*

opera ['ɔpərə], *n.* opéra, *m.*

opera glass ['ɔprəglɑːs], *n.* lorgnette, *f.*; (*pl.*) jumelles, *f.pl.*

opera hat ['ɔprəhæt], *n.* claque, *m.*

opera house ['ɔprəhaus], *n.* opéra, *m.*

operate ['ɔpəreit], *v.t.* opérer, effectuer.—*v.i.* opérer, agir; (*Fin.*) spéculer; **to operate on someone for appendicitis**, opérer quelqu'un de l'appendicite.

operatic [ɔpə'rætik], *a.* d'opéra.

operation [ɔpə'reiʃən], *n.* opération, action, *f.*

operative ['ɔpərətiv], *a.* actif, efficace; des ouvriers.—*n.* artisan, ouvrier, *m.*

operator ['ɔpəreitə], *n.* opérateur, *m.* **telephone operator** téléphoniste, *m.,* *f.*; **radio operator**, radio, *m.*

operetta [ɔpə'retə], *n.* opérette, *f.*

opiate ['oupiit], *a.* opiacé.—*n.* opiat, *m.*

opinion [ə'pinjən], *n.* opinion, *f.*, avis, sentiment, *m.*; idée, pensée; (*Law*) consultation, *f.*; **in my opinion**, à mon avis.

opinionated [ə'pinjəneitid], *a.* opiniâtre, têtu, imbu de ses opinions.

opium ['oupjəm], *n.* opium, *m.*

opossum [o'pɔsəm], *n.* opossum, *m.*; sarigue, *f.*

opponent [ə'pounənt], *n.* opposant, *m.*, adversaire, *m.,* *f.*

opportune ['ɔpətjuːn], *a.* opportun, à propos.

opportunely ['ɔpətjuːnli], *adv.* à propos.

opportunity [ɔpə'tjuːniti], *n.* occasion, *f.*

oppose [ə'pouz], *v.t.* opposer; s'opposer à.

opposite ['ɔpəzit], *a.* opposé; vis-à-vis, contraire (*à*), en face.—*n.* opposé, contre-pied,

m.—*adv.* vis-à-vis, en face.—*prep.* en face de, vis-à-vis de.

opposition [ɔpə'ziʃən], *n.* opposition, résistance; concurrence (*rivalité*), *f.*; obstacle, *m.*

oppress [ə'pres], *v.t.* opprimer; accabler.

oppression [ə'preʃən], *n.* oppression, *f.*

oppressive [ə'presiv], *a.* accablant, oppressif; lourd.

oppressiveness [ə'presivnis], *n.* caractère oppressif, *m.*, lourdeur, *f.*

oppressor [ə'presə], *n.* oppresseur, *m.*

opprobrious [ə'proubriəs], *a.* infamant; injurieux.

opprobrium [ə'proubriəm], *n.* opprobre, *m.*

opt [ɔpt], *v.i.* opter.

optic ['ɔptik], **optical** ['ɔptikəl], *a.* optique; d'optique.

optician [ɔp'tiʃən], *n.* opticien, *m.*

optimism ['ɔptimizm], *n.* optimisme, *m.*

optimist ['ɔptimist], *n.* optimiste, *m.,* *f.*

optimistic [ɔpti'mistik], *a.* optimiste.

option ['ɔpʃən], *n.* option, *f.*, choix, *m.*

optional ['ɔpʃənəl], *a.* facultatif.

opulence ['ɔpjuləns], *n.* opulence, *f.*

opulent ['ɔpjulənt], *a.* opulent.

or [ɔː], *conj.* ou; (*negatively*) ni; **or else**, ou bien, autrement.

oracle ['ɔrəkl], *n.* oracle, *m.*

oracular [ə'rækjulə], *a.* d'oracle; (*fig.*) dogmatique.

oral ['ɔːrəl], *a.* oral.

orally ['ɔːrəli], *adv.* oralement; par la bouche.

orange ['ɔrindʒ], *n.* orange; couleur orange, *f.*

orangery ['ɔrindʒəri], *n.* orangerie, *f.*

orange-tree ['ɔrindʒtriː], *n.* oranger, *m.*

orang-outang [o'ræŋu'tæŋ], *n.* orang-outang, *m.*

oration [o'reiʃən], *n.* allocution, *f.*, discours, *m.*; **funeral oration**, oraison funèbre, *f.*

orator ['ɔrətə], *n.* orateur, *m.*

oratorical [ɔrə'tɔrikəl], *a.* oratoire.

oratorio [ɔrə'tɔːriou], *n.* oratorio, *m.*

oratory ['ɔrətri], *n.* art oratoire, *m.*, éloquence, *f.*; oratoire (*chapelle*), *m.*

orb [ɔːb], *n.* globe; corps sphérique; orbe, *m.*

orbit ['ɔːbit], *n.* orbe, *m.*; (*Anat., Astron.*) orbite, *f.*

orchard ['ɔːtʃəd], *n.* verger, *m.*

orchestra ['ɔːkistrə], *n.* orchestre, *m.* [see stall]

orchestral [ɔː'kestrəl], *a.* d'orchestre, orchestral.

orchid ['ɔːkid], *n.* orchidée, *f.*

ordain [ɔː'dein], *v.t.* ordonner, décréter.

ordeal [ɔː'diːəl], *n.* dure épreuve, *f.*

order ['ɔːdə], *n.* ordre; règlement, *m.*; décoration (*insigne*), (*Mil.*) consigne; classe, *f.*, rang, *m.*; commande (*de marchandises*), *f.*; mandat (*de payer*), *m.*; **in order that**, afin que; **in order to**, afin de; **money order**, mandat-poste, *m.*—*v.t.* ordonner; régler; diriger (*administrer*); commander; prescrire (*médecine*).

ordering ['ɔːdəriŋ], *n.* disposition, *f.*, arrangement, *m.*

orderliness ['ɔːdəlinis], *n.* bon ordre, *m.*, méthode, *f.*

orderly ['ɔːdəli], *a.* en bon ordre, méthodique, rangé.—*n.* (*Mil.*) planton, *m.*

ordinal ['ɔːdinl], *a.* ordinal.

ordinance ['ɔːdinəns], *n.* ordonnance, *f.*

ordinarily ['ɔ:dinrili], *adv.* ordinairement, d'ordinaire.

ordinary ['ɔ:dinri], *a.* ordinaire; moyen.— *n.* ordinaire, *m.*; table d'hôte, *f.*

ordination [ɔ:di'neiʃən], *n.* ordination, *f.*

ordnance ['ɔ:dnəns], *n.* artillerie, *f.*; *ordnance map*, carte d'état major, *f.*

ore [ɔ:], *n.* minerai, *m.*

organ ['ɔ:gən], *n.* (*Anat. etc.*) organe; (*Mus.*) orgue, *m.*

organic [ɔ:'gænik], *a.* organique; des organes.

organism ['ɔ:gənizm], *n.* organisme, *m.*

organist ['ɔ:gənist], *n.* organiste, *m.*, *f.*

organization [ɔ:gənai'zeiʃən], *n.* organisation; œuvre, *f.*

organize ['ɔ:gənaiz], *v.t.* organiser; aménager.

organizer ['ɔ:gənaizə], *n.* organisateur, *m.*

orgy ['ɔ:dʒi], *n.* orgie, *f.*

orient ['ɔriənt], *n.* orient, *m.*

Oriental [ɔ:ri'entl], *a.* oriental, d'Orient.—*n.* natif de l'Orient, oriental, *m.*

orifice ['ɔrifis], *n.* orifice, *m.*, ouverture, *f.*

origin ['ɔridʒin], *n.* origine, source; provenance, *f.*

original [ə'ridʒinl], *a.* original, inédit (*nouveau*); primitif (*sens des mots etc.*).—*n.* original, *m.*

originality [əridʒi'næliti], *n.* originalité, *f.*

originally [ə'ridʒinali], *adv.* originairement; originellement.

originate [ə'ridʒineit], *v.t.* faire naître, produire; (*fig.*) inventer.—*v.i.* tirer son origine (*de*), provenir de.

originator [ə'ridʒineitə], *n.* initiateur, auteur, *m.*

oriole ['ɔ:rioul], *n.* (*Orn.*) loriot, *m.*

orison ['ɔrizn], *n.* oraison, prière, *f.*

Orkneys ['ɔ:kniz], the. les Orcades, *f.pl.*

ornament ['ɔ:nəmənt], *n.* ornement, *m.*—*v.t.* orner, décorer (*de*).

ornamental [ɔ:nə'mentl], *a.* ornemental, d'ornement; d'agrément.

ornate [ɔ:'neit], *a.* orné, élégant, paré.

ornately [ɔ:'neitli], *adv.* avec ornement.

ornithologist [ɔ:ni'θɔlədʒist], *n.* ornithologiste, ornithologue, *m.*, *f.*

ornithology [ɔ:ni'θɔlədʒi], *n.* ornithologie, *f.*

orphan ['ɔ:fən], *a.* and *n.* orphelin, *m.*

orphanage ['ɔ:fənidʒ], *n.* état d'orphelin; orphelinat, *m.*

orthodox ['ɔ:θədɔks], *a.* orthodoxe.

orthodoxy ['ɔ:θədɔksi], *n.* orthodoxie, *f.*

orthographic [ɔ:θə'græfik], *a.* orthographique.

orthography [ɔ:'θɔgrəfi], *n.* orthographe, orthographie, *f.*

orthop(a)edic [ɔ:θə'pi:dik], *a.* orthopédique.

orthop(a)edist [ɔ:θə'pi:dist], *n.* orthopédiste, *m.*

orthop(a)edy ['ɔ:θəpi:di], *n.* orthopédie, *f.*

oscillate ['ɔsileit], *v.i.* osciller; (*fig.*) balancer, vaciller.

oscillation [ɔsi'leiʃən], *n.* oscillation, *f.*

oscillatory ['ɔsileitəri], *a.* oscillatoire.

osier ['ouʒiə], *n.* osier, *m.*

osier bed [ou'ʒiəbed], *n.* oseraie, *f.*

osprey ['ɔsprei], *n.* (*Orn.*) orfraie, *f.*

osseous ['ɔsiəs], *a.* osseux.

ossicle ['ɔsikl], *n.* ossicule, osselet, *f.*

ossification [ɔsifi'keiʃən], *n.* ossification, *f.*

ossify ['ɔsifai], *v.t.* ossifier.—*v.i.* s'ossifier.

ostensible [ɔs'tensibl], *a.* prétendu.

ostensibly [ɔs'tensibli], *adv.* en apparence.

ostentation [ɔsten'teiʃən], *n.* ostentation, *f.*, faste, *m.*

ostentatious [ɔsten'teiʃəs], *a.* pompeux, fastueux.

osteopath ['ɔstiopæθ], *n.* ostéopathe, *m.*

ostler ['ɔslə], *n.* garçon d'écurie, *m.*

ostracism ['ɔstrəsizm], *n.* ostracisme, *m.*

ostracize ['ɔstrəsaiz], *v.t.* frapper d'ostracisme, exiler.

ostrich ['ɔstritʃ], *n.* autruche, *f.*

other ['ʌðə], *a.* autre; *every other day*, tous les deux jours; *other people*, d'autres, autrui.—*pron.* autre; autrui; *all the others*, tous les autres.

otherwise ['ʌðəwaiz], *adv.* autrement; sans quoi.

otter ['ɔtə], *n.* loutre, *f.*

ought [ɔ:t], *v.aux.* devoir; falloir; *you ought to do it*, vous devriez le faire; *you ought to have seen*, il aurait fallu voir.

ounce (1) [auns], *n.* once (*poids*), *f.*

ounce (2) [auns], *n.* (*Zool.*) once, *f.*

our ['auə], *a.poss.* notre, *sing.*, nos, *pl.*

ours ['auəz], *pron.* le nôtre, *m.*, la nôtre, *f.*, les nôtres, *pl.*; à nous.

ourselves [auə'selvz], *pron.* nous-mêmes; nous.

oust [aust], *v.t.* évincer, déloger.

out [aut], *adv.* hors, dehors; sorti (*pas chez soi*); découvert, exposé (*dévoilé*); éteint (*feu etc.*); épuisé, fini (*tout vendu* ou *tout consumé*), jusqu'au bout; haut, à haute voix (*parler*); dans l'erreur (*pas exact*); paru (*livre*); épanoui (*fleur*).—*a.* externe.

outbid [aut'bid], *v.t.* *irr.* (*conjug. like* BID) enchérir sur, surenchérir.

outboard [aut'bɔ:d], *a.* outboard *motorboat*, hors-bord, *m.*

outbreak ['autbreik], *n.* éruption, explosion; épidémie, *f.*

outburst ['autbə:st], *n.* explosion, *f.*, transport, éclat, *m.*

outcast ['autkɑ:st], *a.* expulsé, proscrit, rejeté.—*n.* proscrit, banni, paria, *m.*

outcome ['autkʌm], *n.* résultat, *m.*

outcry ['autkrai], *n.* clameur, *f.*, tollé, *m.*

outdated [aut'deitid], *a.* démodé.

outdo [aut'du:], *v.t. irr.* (*conjug. like* DO) surpasser, exceller.

outdoor ['autdɔ:], *a.* en plein air; externe.

outdoors [aut'dɔ:z], *adv.* en plein air; hors de la maison.

outer ['autə], *a.* extérieur, du dehors, externe.

outermost ['autəmoust], *a.* le plus extérieur.

outfit ['autfit], *n.* attirail, équipement; trousseau, *m.*

outfitter ['autfitə], *n.* confectionneur et chemisier, *m.*

outflank [aut'flæŋk], *v.t.* déborder, tourner.

outgoing ['autgouiŋ], *a.* sortant, qui sort.— *n.* (*pl.*) dépenses, *f.pl.*

outgrow [aut'grou], *v.t. irr.* (*conjug. like* GROW) dépasser, surpasser.

outgrowth ['autgrouθ], *n.* excroissance; conséquence, *f.*

outhouse ['authaus], *n.* hangar, *m.*; dépendance, *f.*

outing ['autiŋ], *n.* excursion, promenade, *f.*

outlandish [aut'lændiʃ], *a.* étranger; bizarre; retiré.

outlast [aut'lɑ:st], *v.t.* survivre à.

outlaw ['autlɔ:], *n.* proscrit, *m.*—*v.t.* mettre hors la loi, proscrire.

outlay ['autlei], *n.* dépense, *f.*, débours, *m.pl.*

outlet ['autlit], *n.* issue, sortie, *f.*; (*Comm.*) débouché, *m.*

outline ['autlain], *n.* contour; profil, *m.*, ébauche, *f.*—*v.t.* esquisser.

outlive [aut'liv], *v.t.* survivre à.

outlook ['autluk], *n.* vue, perspective, *f.*

outlying ['autlaiiŋ], *a.* éloigné, détaché.

outnumber [aut'nʌmbə], *v.t.* surpasser en nombre.

out-of-date [autəv'deit], *a.* démodé, dépassé.

outpost ['autpoust], *n.* avant-poste, *m.*

outpour [aut'pɔ:], *v.t.* épancher, verser à flots.

outpouring ['autpɔːriŋ], *n.* effusion, *f.*, épanchement, *m.*

outrage ['autreidʒ], *n.* outrage, *m.*—*v.t.* outrager.

outrageous [aut'reidʒəs], *a.* outrageux, outrageant.

outrageousness [aut'reidʒəsnis], *n.* nature outrageante, énormité, *f.*

outright ['autrait], *adv.* complètement; carrément (*à cœur ouvert*).

outrun [aut'rʌn], *v.t. irr.* (*conjug. like* RUN) dépasser à la course, gagner de vitesse.

outset ['autset], *n.* début, commencement, *m.*; *at the very outset*, dès l'origine.

outshine [aut'ʃain], *v.t. irr.* (*conjug. like* SHINE) surpasser en éclat, éclipser.

outside [aut'said], *a.* extérieur, externe, du dehors.—*n.* dehors, extérieur, *m.*—[aut 'said], *adv.* en dehors, à l'extérieur.—[aut'said], *prep.* hors de, à l'extérieur de.

outsider [aut'saidə], *n.* étranger; (*Racing*) outsider, *m.*

outsize ['autsaiz], *a.* de grande taille, hors série.

outskirts ['autskə:ts], *n.pl.* bords, *m.pl.*; lisière (*d'un bois*), banlieue, *f.*, faubourg (*d'une ville*), *m.*

outspoken [aut'spoukən], *a.* franc, clair, carré.

outstanding [aut'stændiŋ], *a.* saillant, remarquable, excellent; non payé; en suspens (*affaires*).

outstretched [aut'stretʃt], *a.* étendu, déployé, tendu.

outstrip [aut'strip], *v.t.* devancer, distancer.

outward ['autwəd], *a.* extérieur, du dehors, externe; superficiel.—*adv.* or **outwards** ['autwədz], *à* l'extérieur; au dehors, extérieurement; *outward bound*, en partance.

outwardly ['autwədli], *adv.* extérieurement, à l'extérieur; (*fig.*) en apparence.

outweigh [aut'wei], *v.t.* peser plus que; l'emporter sur.

outwit [aut'wit], *v.t.* surpasser en finesse, duper.

oval [ouvl], *a.* and *n.* ovale, *m.*

ovary ['ouvəri], *n.* ovaire, *m.*

ovation [o'veiʃən], *n.* ovation, *f.*

oven [ʌvn], *n.* four, *m.*

over ['ouvə], *prep.* sur; par-dessus; au-dessus de; de l'autre côté de (*en face*); pendant (*au cours de*); *over there*, là-bas.—*adv.* d'un côté à l'autre; par-dessus, au-dessus; trop (*à l'excès*); plus de (*excédant*);

de reste (*surplus inemployé*); fini, terminé, fait; passé.

overact [ouvər'ækt], *v.t.* outrer, exagérer.

overall ['ouvərɔ:l], *a.* total.—*n.* blouse, *f.*; tablier, *m.*; (*pl.*) salopette, combinaison, *f.*

overawe [ouvər'ɔ:], *v.t.* intimider, imposer à.

overbalance [ouvə'bæləns], *v.t.* l'emporter sur.—*v.i.* perdre l'équilibre.

overbearing [ouvə'bεəriŋ], *a.* impérieux, autoritaire.

overboard ['ouvəbɔ:d], *adv.* par-dessus bord.

overburden [ouvə'bə:dn], *v.t.* surcharger; accabler (*de*).

overcast ['ouvəka:st], *a.* couvert, nuageux.

overcharge [ouvə'tʃɑːdʒ], *v.t.* surcharger; faire payer trop cher.—*n.* prix excessif, *m.*

overcoat ['ouvəkout], *n.* pardessus, *m.*

overcome [ouvə'kʌm], *v.t. irr.* (*conjug. like* COME) surmonter, vaincre, accabler.—*v.i.* l'emporter.

over-confident ['ouvə'kɔnfidənt], *a.* trop confiant; présomptueux, téméraire.

overcrowd [ouvə'kraud], *v.t.* encombrer à l'excès, trop remplir.

overcrowding [ouvə'kraudiŋ], *n.* surpeuplement, *m.*

overdo [ouvə'du:], *v.t. irr.* (*conjug. like* DO) exagérer, outrer; faire trop cuire; harasser.

overdone [ouvə'dʌn], *a.* trop cuit; (*fig.*) exagéré.

overdose ['ouvədous], *n.* dose trop forte, *f.*

overdraw [ouvə'drɔ:], *v.t. irr.* (*conjug. like* DRAW) excéder; *to overdraw one's account*, tirer à découvert; tirer un chèque sans provision.

overdue [ouvə'dju:], *a.* en retard.

overestimate [ouvər'estimit], *v.t.* évaluer trop haut.

overflow [ouvə'flou], *v.t.* inonder.—*v.i.* déborder, se déborder.—['ouvəflou], *n.* inondation, *f.*, débordement, *m.*

overflowing [ouvə'flouiŋ], *a.* qui déborde, trop plein.—*n.* débordement, *m.*

overgrown [ouvə'groun], *a.* couvert (*d'herbes, ronces*); trop grand, énorme.

overhang ['ouvəhæŋ], *n.* surplomb, *m.*—[ouvə'hæŋ], *v.t. irr.* (*conjug. like* HANG) pencher sur, surplomber; faire saillie.

overhanging ['ouvəhæŋiŋ], *a.* en surplomb.

overhaul [ouvə'hɔ:l], *v.t.* examiner, revoir; réviser, vérifier, démonter.—['ouvəhɔ:l], *n.* examen détaillé, *m.*

overhead [ouvə'hed], *adv.* par-dessus la tête, en haut.—*a.* aérien (*fil etc.*).—['ouvə hedz], *n.* (*pl.*) (*Comm.*) frais généraux, *m.pl.*

overhear [ouvə'hiə], *v.t. irr.* (*conjug. like* HEAR) entendre par hasard.

overheat [ouvə'hi:t], *v.t.* surchauffer.

overjoyed [ouvə'dʒɔid], *a.* transporté de joie, ravi.

overland ['ouvəlænd], *a.* and *adv.* par voie de terre.

overlap [ouvə'læp], *v.t.* recouvrir.—['ouvə læp], *n.* recouvrement, *m.*

overlapping [ouvə'læpiŋ], *n.* recouvrement, chevauchement, *m.*

overload [ouvə'loud], *v.t.* surcharger, surmener.

overlook [ouvə'luk], *v.t.* donner sur, dominer; surveiller (*diriger*); fermer les yeux sur (*passer sur*); oublier, négliger.

overlooking [ouvə'lukiŋ], *a.* donnant (*sur*).
overmuch ['ouvəmʌtʃ], *a.* excessif.—*n.* trop, *m.*—*adv.* par trop, excessivement.
overnight [ouvə'nait], *adv.* durant la nuit; hier soir; du jour au lendemain.
overpay [ouvə'pei], *v.t. irr.* (*conjug. like* PAY) payer trop.
overpower [ouvə'pauə], *v.t.* vaincre; accabler (*de*).
overpowering [ouvə'pauəriŋ], *a.* accablant, écrasant.
overproduction [ouvəprə'dʌkʃən], *n.* surproduction, *f.*
overrate [ouvə'reit], *v.t.* estimer trop haut.
overreach [ouvə'ri:tʃ], *v.t.* tromper.—*v.i.* forger (*chevaux*); **to overreach oneself**, trop présumer de ses forces.
override [ouvə'raid], *v.t. irr.* (*conjug. like* RIDE) surmener, outrepasser.
overrule [ouvə'ru:l], *v.t.* dominer; (*Law*) rejeter.
overrun [ouvə'rʌn], *v.t. irr.* (*conjug. like* RUN) envahir, faire une irruption dans; infester (*de*).—*v.i.* déborder.
oversea ['ouvəsi:], **overseas** ['ouvəsi:z], ouvə'si:z], *a.* and *adv.* d'outre-mer.
oversee [ouvə'si:], *v.t. irr.* (*conjug. like* SEE) surveiller.
overseer ['ouvəsiə], *n.* surveillant; contremaître (*d'usine etc.*), *m.*
overshadow [ouvə'ʃædou], *v.t.* ombrager; éclipser.
overshoes ['ouvəʃu:z], *n.pl.* caoutchoucs, *m.pl.*
overshoot [ouvə'ʃu:t], *v.t. irr.* (*conjug. like* SHOOT) dépasser.
oversight ['ouvəsait], *n.* inadvertance, *f.*, oubli, *m.*
oversleep [ouvə'sli:p], *v.i. irr.* (*conjug. like* SLEEP) dormir au delà de son heure.
overstate [ouvə'steit], *v.t.* exagérer.
overstatement [ouvə'steitmənt], *n.* exagération, *f.*
overstep [ouvə'step], *v.t.* dépasser.
overt ['ouvə:t], *a.* ouvert, manifeste.
overtake [ouvə'teik], *v.t. irr.* (*conjug. like* TAKE) rattraper; doubler, dépasser.
overtax [ouvə'tæks], *v.t.* surtaxer, surcharger.
overthrow [ouvə'θrou], *v.t. irr.* (*conjug. like* THROW) renverser; défaire, détruire.— ['ouvəθrou], *n.* renversement, *m.*, défaite; destruction, *f.*
overtime ['ouvətaim], *n.* heures supplémentaires, *f.pl.*
overtop [ouvə'tɔp], *v.t.* s'élever au-dessus de, dépasser.
overture ['ouvətjuə], *n.* ouverture; offre, *f.*
overturn [ouvə'tə:n], *v.t.* renverser; bouleverser.—*v.i.* verser.
overweening [ouvə'wi:niŋ], *a.* présomptueux, outrecuidant.
overweight ['ouvəweit], *n.* excédent, *m.*
overwhelm [ouvə'welm], *v.t.* accabler (*de*); combler de (*bontés etc.*).
overwhelming [ouvə'welmiŋ], *a.* accablant, écrasant.
overwork [ouvə'wə:k], *v.t.* surcharger de travail, surmener.—*n.* travail excessif; surmenage, *m.*
ovoid ['ouvoid], *a.* ovoïde.
owe [ou], *v.t.* devoir; être redevable à . . . de.

owing ['ouiŋ], *a.* dû (à); **owing to**, à cause de grâce à.
owl [aul], *n.* hibou, *m.*; chouette, *f.*
owlet ['aulit], *n.* jeune hibou, *m.*
own (1) [oun], *a.* propre (à soi); **my own money**, mon propre argent; **to hold one's own**, se maintenir.—*v.t.* posséder, être propriétaire de (*avoir*).
own (2) [oun], *v.t.* avouer, confesser.
owner ['ounə], *n.* possesseur, *m.*, propriétaire, *m.*, *f.*
ownership ['ounəʃip], *n.* propriété, *f.*
ox [ɔks], *n.* (*pl.* oxen ['ɔksən]) bœuf, *m.*
oxalic [ɔk'sælik], *a.* oxalique.
ox-fly ['ɔksflai], *n.* taon, *m.*
oxide ['ɔksaid], *n.* oxyde, *m.*
oxidization [ɔksidai'zeiʃən], *n.* oxydation, calcination, *f.*
oxidize ['ɔksidaiz], *v.t.* oxyder; calciner.
oxyacetylene [ɔksiə'setili:n], *a.* oxyacétylénique.
oxygen ['ɔksidʒən], *n.* oxygène, *m.*
oxygenate ['ɔksidʒəneit], *v.t.* oxygéner.
oxygenous [ɔk'sidʒənəs], *a.* d'oxygène.
oyster ['ɔistə], *n.* huître, *f.*
oyster bed ['ɔistəbed], *n.* banc d'huîtres, *m.*
ozone [ou'zoun], *n.* ozone, *m.*

P

P, p [pi:]. seizième lettre de l'alphabet, *m.*
pabulum ['pæbjuləm], *n.* aliment, *m.*, nourriture, *f.*
pace [peis], *n.* pas, *m.*; allure (*do cheval*), *f.*; train, *m.*; vitesse, *f.*; **to put someone through his paces**, mettre quelqu'un à l'épreuve; arpenter; (*Spt.*) entraîner.—*v.i.* aller au pas, marcher.
pacific [pə'sifik], *a.* pacifique, paisible.—*n.* **the Pacific** (*Ocean*), le Pacifique, l'océan Pacifique, *m.*
pacification [pæsifi'keiʃən], *n.* pacification, *f.*
pacifier ['pæsifaiə], *n.* pacificateur, *m.*
pacifism ['pæsifizm], *n.* pacifisme, *m.*
pacifist ['pæsifist], *n.*-pacifiste, *m.*, *f.*
pacify ['pæsifai], *v.t.* pacifier, apaiser.
pack [pæk], *n.* paquet, ballot, *m.*; meute (*chiens de chasse*), *f.*; jeu (*de cartes*), *m.*—*v.t.* emballer, empaqueter.—*v.i.* s'assembler; se grouper; faire sa malle.
package ['pækidʒ], *n.* colis, paquet, *m.*
packer ['pækə], *n.* emballeur, *m.*
packet ['pækit], *n.* paquet; paquebot (*bateau*), *m.*
pack horse ['pækhɔ:s], *n.* cheval de bât, *m.*
pack-ice ['pækais], *n.* glace de banquise, *f.*, pack, *m.*
packing ['pækiŋ], *n.* emballage, *m.*
pact [pækt], *n.* pacte, *m.*
pad [pæd], *n.* tampon; coussinet, *m.*; **writing pad**, sous-main, bloc de papier, *m.*—*v.t.* ouater; rembourrer.—*v.i.* aller à pied.

padding ['pædiŋ], *n.* ouate, bourre, *f.*

paddle ['pædl], *n.* pagaie; aube (*de roue*), *f.* —*v.t.* pagayer.—*v.i.* patauger.
paddle boat ['pædlbout], *n.* bateau à aubes, *m.*
paddock ['pædək], *n.* enclos, pré, pâturage, *m.*
padlock ['pædlɔk], *n.* cadenas, *m.*—*v.t.* cadenasser, fermer au cadenas.
paean ['pi:ən], *n.* péan, *m.*
pagan ['peigən], *a.* and *n.* païen, *m.*
paganism ['peigənizm], *n.* paganisme, *m.*
page (1) [peidʒ], *n.* page (*garçon*), *m.*
page (2) [peidʒ], *n.* page (*de livre*), *f.*
pageant ['pædʒənt], *n.* spectacle pompeux, cortège *ou* spectacle historique, *m.*
pageantry ['pædʒəntri], *n.* pompe, *f.*, faste, apparat, *m.*
pagoda [pə'goudə], *n.* pagode, *f.*
paid [peid], *a.* payé, acquitté; affranchi (*lettres*).
pail [peil], *n.* seau, *m.*
pailful ['peilful], *n.* (plein) seau, *m.*
pain [pein], *n.* douleur; peine (*effort*), *f.*; **on pain of**, sous peine de; **to take pains**, se donner de la peine.—*v.t.* faire mal à; (*fig.*) faire de la peine à; affliger.
painful ['peinful], *a.* douloureux, pénible.
painless ['peinlis], *a.* sans douleur, indolore.
painstaking ['peinzteikiŋ], *a.* soigneux, assidu.
paint [peint], *n.* couleur; peinture, *f.*; fard (*pour le visage*), *m.*—*v.t.* peindre; farder (*le visage*).—*v.i.* peindre; se farder.
painter (1) ['peintə], *n.* peintre, *m.*
painter (2) ['peintə], *n.* (*Naut.*) amarre, *f.*
painting ['peintiŋ], *n.* peinture, *f.*; tableau (*picture*), *m.*
pair [pɛə], *n.* paire, *f.*; couple (*époux etc.*), *m.*—*v.t.* accoupler.—*v.i.* s'accoupler.
pajamas [pi'dʒa:məz], *n.pl.* pyjama, *m.*
Pakistan [pɑ:ki'stɑ:n], le Pakistan, *m.*
Pakistani [pɑ:ki'stɑ:ni], *a.* pakistanais.—*n.* Pakistanais (*personne*), *m.*
pal [pæl], *n.* (*colloq.*) camarade, copain, *m.*
palace ['pælis], *n.* palais, *m.*; **archbishop's palace**, archevêché, *m.*; **bishop's palace**, évêché, *m.*
palatable ['pælətəbl], *a.* agréable au goût.
palate ['pælit], *n.* palais (*fig.*) goût, *m.*
palatial [pə'leiʃl], *a.* du palais, palatial; grandiose.
palaver [pə'lɑ:və], *n.* palabre (*chez certains peuples primitifs*), *f.*; verbiage, *m.*; flagornerie, *f.*—*v.i.* palabrer, faire des phrases.
pale (1) [peil], *a.* pâle, blême; (*fig.*) blafard (*lumière*).—*v.i.* pâlir; (*fig.*) s'éclipser.
pale (2) [peil], *n.* pieu, palis, *m.*; limites (*bornes*), *f.pl.*; **beyond the pale**, au ban de la société.
pale-faced ['peilfeist], *a.* au teint pâle.
paleness ['peilnis], *n.* pâleur, *f.*
Palestine ['pælistain], la Palestine, *f.*
Palestinian [pælis'tinian], *a.* palestinien.
palette ['pælit], *n.* palette, *f.*
palfrey ['pɔ:lfri], *n.* palefroi, *m.*
paling ['peiliŋ], *n.* palissade, *f.*
palisade [pæli'seid], *n.* palissade, *f.*—*v.t.* palissader.
palish ['peiliʃ], *a.* un peu pâle, pâlot.
pall [pɔ:l], *n.* poêle; (*fig.*) drap mortuaire;

voile (*de fumée etc.*), *m.*—*v.i.* devenir fade, s'affadir.
pallet ['pælit], *n.* grabat, *m.*, paillasse, *f.*
palliate ['pælieit], *v.t.* pallier.
palliation [pæli'eiʃən], *n.* palliation, *f.*
palliative ['pæliətiv], *a.* and *n.* palliatif, *m.*
pallid ['pælid], *a.* pâle, blême, blafard.
pallor ['pælə], *n.* pâleur, *f.*
palm (1) [pɑ:m], *n.* paume (*de main*), *f.*—*v.t.* **to palm off** (*something on someone*), passer, refiler (*quelque chose à quelqu'un*).
palm (2) [pɑ:m], *n.* palmier (*arbre*), *m.*; palme (*rameau*), *f.*; **Palm Sunday**, dimanche des Rameaux, *m.*
palmist ['pɑ:mist], *n.* chiromancien, *m.*
palmistry [pɑ:mistri], *n.* chiromancie, *f.*
palmy ['pɑ:mi], *a.* beau, glorieux, heureux.
palpable ['pælpəbl], *a.* palpable; manifeste.
palpitate ['pælpiteit], *v.i.* palpiter.
palpitation [pælpi'teiʃən], *n.* palpitation, *f.*
palsied ['pɔ:lzid], *a.* frappé de paralysie, paralytique.
palsy ['pɔ:lzi], *n.* paralysie, *f.*
palter ['pɔ:ltə], *v.i.* tergiverser, biaiser.
paltriness ['pɔ:ltrinis], *n.* mesquinerie, *f.*
paltry ['pɔ:ltri], *a.* mesquin, misérable.
pamper ['pæmpə], *v.t.* choyer, dorloter.
pamphlet ['pæmflit], *n.* brochure, *f.*; (*pej.*) pamphlet, *m.*
pamphleteer [pæmfli'tiə], *n.* auteur de brochures, *m.*; (*pej.*) pamphlétaire, *m.*, *f.*
pan [pæn], *n.* casserole, *f.*; poêlon, *m.*; **frying pan**, poêle, *f.*
panacea [pænə'si:ə], *n.* panacée, *f.*
Panama ['pænəmɑ:], le Panama, *m.*
Panamanian [pænə'meiniən], *a.* panamanien. —*n.* Panamanien (*personne*), *m.*
pancake ['pænkeik], *n.* crêpe, *f.*
pancreas ['pænkriəs], *n.* (*Anat.*) pancréas, *m.*
pandemonium [pændi'mouniəm], *n.* pandémonium, *m.*
pander ['pændə], *v.i.* se prêter à, se faire complaisant pour.
pane [pein], *n.* carreau, *m.*, vitre, *f.*
panegyric [pæni'dʒirik], *a.* de panégyrique.— *n.* panégyrique, *m.*
panegyrist [pæni'dʒirist], *n.* panégyriste, *m.*,*f.*
panel [pænl], *n.* panneau, *m.*; liste (*de juré etc.*), *f.*; **instrument panel**, tableau de manœuvre, *m.*—*v.t.* diviser en panneaux; lambrisser.
panelling ['pænliŋ], *n.* panneaux, *m.pl.*, lambrissage, *m.*
pang [pæŋ], *n.* angoisse, vive douleur, *f.*; serrement de cœur, *m.*
panic ['pænik], *a.* panique.—*n.* panique; terreur panique, *f.*—*v.i.* s'affoler.
pannier ['pæniə], *n.* panier, *m.*, hotte, *f.*
panoply ['pænəpli], *n.* panoplie, armure complète, *f.*
panorama [pænə'rɑ:mə], *n.* panorama, *f.*
panoramic [pænə'ræmik], *a.* panoramique.
pansy ['pænzi], *n.* (*Bot.*) pensée, *f.*
pant [pænt], *n.* palpitation, *f.*, halètement, *m.* —*v.i.* haleter, palpiter, panteler.
pantechnicon [pæn'teknikn], *n.* garde-meuble, *m.*; voiture de déménagement, *f.*
pantheism ['pænθiizm], *n.* panthéisme, *m.*
pantheist ['pænθiist], *n.* panthéiste, *m.*, *f.*
pantheistic [pænθi'istik], *a.* panthéistique.
panther ['pænθə], *n.* panthère, *f.*

pantile ['pæntail], *n.* tuile faîtière *ou* flamande, *f.*

pantomime ['pæntəmaim], *n.* pantomime, *f.*

pantomimic [pæntə'mimik], *a.* pantomime.

pantry ['pæntri], *n.* office, *f.*, garde-manger, *m.*

pants [pænts], *n.pl.* (*collog.*) caleçon; (*Am.*) pantalon, *m.* [**panties,** see **knickers**]

pap [pæp], *n.* mamelle; bouillie (*aliment*), *f.*

papacy ['peipəsi], *n.* papauté, *f.*

papal ['peipəl], *a.* papal, du pape.

paper ['peipə], *a.* de papier.—*n.* papier, *m.*; feuille de papier, *f.*; journal; papier-monnaie, *m.*; billets, *m.pl.*; mémoire, *m.*; *étude* (*article*); composition (*d'examen*), *f.*; (*pl.*) papiers, *m.pl.*; dossier, *m.*; *blotting paper*, papier buvard; *kraft paper*, papier gris.—*v.t.* tapisser (*de papier*).

paper-back ['peipəbæk], *n.* livre broché, *m.*

paper clip ['peipəklip], *n.* attache, *f.*, trombone (*de fil*), *m.*

paper-hanger ['peipəhæŋə], *n.* colleur de papier, *m.*

paper-knife ['peipənaif], *n.* coupe-papier, *m.*

paper maker ['peipəmeikə], *n.* fabricant de papier, *m.*

paper mill ['peipəmil], *n.* papeterie, *f.*

paper trade ['peipətreid], *n.* papeterie, *f.*

papism ['peipizm], *n.* papisme, *m.*

papist ['peipist], *n.* papiste, *m.*, *f.*

Papua [pə'puə]. la Papouasie, *f.*

Papuan [pə'puən], *a.* papou.—*n.* Papou (*personne*), *m.*

papyrus [pə'paiərəs], *n.* (*pl.* **papyri** [pə'paiərai]) papyrus, *m.*

par [pɑː], *n.* pair, *m.*, égalité, (*Golf*) normale, *f.*; *at par*, au pair.

parable ['pærəbl], *n.* parabole, *f.*

parabola [pə'ræbələ], *n.* (*Math.*) parabole, *f.*

parachute ['pærəʃuːt], *n.* parachute, *m.*—*v.t.*, *v.i.* parachuter.

parachutist ['pærə'ʃuːtist], *n.* parachutiste, *m.*, *f.*

parade [pə'reid], *n.* parade, *f.*; étalage, *m.*; esplanade, *f.*; (*Mil.*) rassemblement, *m.*; procession, *f.*—*v.t.* faire parade de.—*v.i.* faire de la parade; (*Mil.*) parader.

paradise ['pærədais], *n.* paradis, *m.*

paradox ['pærədɔks], *n.* paradoxe, *m.*

paradoxical [pærə'dɔksikl], *a.* paradoxal.

paraffin ['pærəfin], *n.* (*Chem.*) paraffine, *f.*; *paraffin* (*oil*), pétrole (lampant), *m.*

paragon ['pærəgən], *n.* parangon; modèle, *m.*

paragraph ['pærəgrɑːf], *n.* paragraphe; alinéa, *m.*—*v.t.* diviser en paragraphes.

Paraguay ['pærəgwai]. le Paraguay, *m.*

Paraguayan [pærə'gwaiən], *a.* paraguayen.—*n.* Paraguayen (*personne*), *m.*

parakeet ['pærəkiːt], *n.* (*Orn.*) perruche, *f.*

parallel ['pærəlel], *a.* parallèle; (*fig.*) semblable, pareil.—*n.* ligne parallèle, *f.*, parallèle, *m.*; (*fig.*) comparaison, *f.*—*v.t.* mettre en parallèle, *f.*; (*fig.*) comparer (*à*); être pareil (*à*).

parallelism ['pærəlelizm], *n.* parallélisme, *m.*; (*fig.*) comparaison, *f.*

parallelogram [pærə'leləgræm], *n.* parallélogramme, *m.*

paralysis [pə'rælisis], *n.* paralysie, *f.*

paralytic [pærə'litik], *a.* and *n.* paralytique, *m.*, *f.*

paralyze ['pærəlaiz], *v.t.* paralyser.

paramount ['pærəmaunt], *a.* souverain, suprême; *of paramount importance*, d'une importance capitale.—*n.* souverain, seigneur, *m.*

paramour ['pærəmuə], *n.* amant, *m.*, maîtresse, *f.*

parapet ['pærəpit], *n.* (*Fort.*) parapet; garde-fou (*sur un pont etc.*), *m.*

paraphernalia [pærəfə'neiliə], *n.pl.* (*Law*) biens paraphernaux, *m.pl.*; équipage, attirail, *m.*

paraphrase ['pærəfreiz], *n.* paraphrase, *f.*—*v.t.* paraphraser.

parasite ['pærəsait], *n.* parasite, *m.*

parasitic [pærə'sitik], **parasitical** [pærə'sitikl], *a.* parasite, parasitique.

parasol ['pærə'sɔl], *n.* ombrelle, *f.*, parasol, *m.*

paratrooper ['pærətruːpə], *n.* (soldat) parachutiste, *m.*

parcel [pɑːsl], *n.* colis, paquet; lot, *m.*—*v.t.* morceler, diviser, partager; empaqueter.

parch [pɑːtʃ], *v.t.* brûler, dessécher (*par la chaleur*).—*v.i.* se brûler; se dessécher.

parchment ['pɑːtʃmənt], *n.* parchemin, *m.*

pardon [pɑːdn], *n.* pardon, *m.*; (*Law*) grâce, *f.*; *I beg your pardon?* plait-il? pardon? comment?—*v.t.* pardonner (*quelque chose à quelqu'un*); *pardon me!* pardon! permettez!

pardonable ['pɑːdnəbl], *a.* excusable, pardonnable (*acte*); digne de pardon (*personne*).

pare [pɛə], *v.t.* peler (*fruits etc.*); éplucher, rogner (*ongles etc.*).

parent ['pɛərənt], *a.* mère.—*n.* père, *m.*, mère, *f.*; (*pl.*) parents, les père et mère, *m.pl.*

parentage ['pɛərəntidʒ], *n.* parentage, *m.*; extraction, *f.*

parental [pə'rentl], *a.* des parents, du père, de la mère; paternel, maternel.

parenthesis [pə'renθisis], *n.* (*pl.* **parentheses** [pə'renθisiːz]) parenthèse, *f.*

parenthetic [pærən'θetik], **parenthetical** [pærən'θetikl], *a.* entre parenthèses.

pariah ['pæriə], *n.* paria, *m.*

paring ['pɛəriŋ], *n.* rognage; épluchage, *m.*

paring knife ['pɛəriŋ'naif], *n.* tranchet, *m.*

parish ['pæriʃ], *a.* de la commune; communal, vicinal (*routes, impôts etc.*); (*Eccles.*) de la paroisse, paroissial.—*n.* (*Eccles.*) paroisse; (*civil*) commune, *f.*

parishioner [pə'riʃənə], *n.* paroissien, *m.*

Parisian [pə'riziən], *a.* de Paris, parisien.—*n.* Parisien (*personne*), *m.*

parity ['pæriti], *n.* parité; égalité (*de rang etc.*), *f.*

park [pɑːk], *n.* parc, *m.*—*v.t.* parquer, garer.—*v.i.* stationner.

parking ['pɑːkiŋ], *n.* stationnement, parcage, *m.* [see **car-park**]

parlance ['pɑːləns], *n.* parler, langage, *m.*; *in common parlance*, dans le langage ordinaire.

parley ['pɑːli], *n.* pourparlers, *m.pl.*—*v.i.* être *ou* entrer en pourparlers (*avec*); (*Mil.*) parlementer.

parliament ['pɑːləmənt], *n.* parlement, *m.*; (*France*) les Chambres, *f.pl.*

parliamentary [pɑːlə'mentəri], *a.* parlementaire, du parlement.

parlor ['pɑːlə], *n.* petit salon; parloir (*de couvent ou école*), *m.*

parlous ['pɑːləs], *a.* alarmant, précaire.

505

parochial [pə'roukiəl], *a.* communal; (*Eccles.*) paroissial.
parody ['pærədi], *n.* parodie, *f.*—*v.t.* parodier.
parole [pə'roul], *n.* parole (d'honneur), *f.*
paroxysm ['pærəksizm], *n.* paroxysme, accès, *m.*
parquet [pa:'kei, pa:'ket], *n.* parquet, *m.*—*v.t.* parqueter.
parquetry ['pa:kitri], *n.* parqueterie, *f.*
parricidal [pæri'saidl], *a.* parricide.
parricide ['pærisaid], *n.* parricide (*crime*), *m.*; parricide (*personne*), *m.*, *f.*
parrot ['pærət], *n.* (*Orn.*) perroquet, *m.*
parry ['pæri], *v.t.* parer, détourner; (*fig.*) éviter.
parse [pa:z], *v.t.* analyser (grammaticalement).
parsimonious [pa:si'mouniəs], *a.* parcimonieux; pingre.
parsimony ['pa:siməni], *n.* parcimonie, épargne, *f.*
parsley ['pa:sli], *n.* (*Bot.*) persil, *m.*
parsnip ['pa:snip], *n.* (*Bot.*) panais, *m.*
parson [pa:sn], *n.* curé; (*Protestant*) pasteur, *m.*
parsonage ['pa:snidʒ], *n.* presbytère, *m.*, cure, *f.*
part [pa:t], *n.* partie; part, portion, *f.*; (*Theat.*) rôle; parti (*dans une dispute etc.*), *m.*; région (*de ville, pays etc.*), *f.*, quartier (*de ville*); (*pl.*) talent, *m.*; *spare parts*, pièces de rechange, *f.pl.*—*v.t.* partager; séparer (*de*).—*v.i.* se séparer (*de*); se quitter; se rompre (*câble*).
partake [pa:'teik], *v.t.*, *v.i. irr.* (*conjug. like* TAKE) prendre (*part à*, participer à.
partaker [pa:'teikə], *n.* participant, *m.*
partial [pa:ʃl], *a.* partial (*prévenu*), injuste; partiel (*en partie*).
partiality [pa:ʃi'æliti], *n.* partialité (*favoritisme*), *f.*; (*fig.*) goût, *m.*
partially [pa:'ʃəli], *adv.* partialement (*injustement*); en partie.
participant [pa:'tisipənt], *a.* and *n.* participant, *m.*
participate [pa:'tisipeit], *v.i.* participer (à).
participation [pa:tisi'peiʃən], *n.* participation, *f.*
participle ['pa:tisipl], *n.* participe, *m.*
particle [pa:'tikl], *n.* particule, molécule, parcelle, *f.*; atome, *m.*
particular [pa:'tikjulə], *a.* particulier, spécial; méticuleux; pointilleux; exigeant (*difficile*).—*n.* particularité, *f.*, détail, *m.*; (*pl.*) renseignements, *m.pl.*; signalement, *m.*
particularity [pətikju'læriti], *n.* particularité, *f.*; détail, *m.*
particularize [pə'tikjuləraiz], *v.t.* particulariser.—*v.i.* préciser.
particularly [pə'tikjuləli], *adv.* particulièrement; principalement, surtout.
parting ['pa:tiŋ], *a.* de séparation; d'adieu; dernier.—*n.* séparation; raie (*cheveux*), *f.*
partisan [pa:ti'zæn], *n.* partisan, *m.*
partition [pa:'tiʃən], *n.* partage (*division*), *m.*; cloison (*dans une pièce etc.*), *f.*—*v.t.* partager, diviser.
partitive ['pa:titiv], *a.* and *n.* partitif, *m.*
partly ['pa:tli], *adv.* en partie, partiellement.
partner ['pa:tnə], *n.* (*Comm.*) associé; (*Dancing*) danseur, cavalier, *m.*; (*Cards, Spt.*) partenaire, *m.*, *f.*—*v.t.* s'associer à;

(*Spt.*) être le partenaire de.
partnership ['pa:tnəʃip], *n.* association, *f.*
partridge ['pa:tridʒ], *n.* (*Orn.*) perdrix, *f.*; *young partridge*, perdreau, *m.*
part-time ['pa:ttaim], *a.* and *n.* (emploi) à temps partiel, *m.*; *to be on part-time*, être en chômage partiel.
party ['pa:ti], *n.* parti (*politique*), *m.*; partie (*de plaisir*), *f.*; (*fig.*) réunion; réception, *f.*, groupe, *m.*; *to give a party*, recevoir du monde, donner une soirée.
party wall ['pa:tiwɔ:l], *n.* mur mitoyen, *m.*
pasha ['pa:ʃə], *n.* pacha, *m.*
pass [pa:s], *v.t.* (*Motor.*) doubler.
pass [pa:s], *v.t.* passer; passer par, passer devant; dépasser; devancer; faire passer; prononcer (*sur*); voter (*un projet de loi etc.*); *to pass an examination*, être reçu *ou* réussir à un examen.—*v.i.* passer, se passer, s'écouler (*temps*); mourir; (*Exam.*) être reçu; (*Ftb.*) faire une passe; (*fig.*) arriver; *to pass away*, disparaître, mourir; *to pass out*, sortir; (*fig.*) s'évanouir.—*n.* passage, défilé, *m.*; gorge, *f.*, col; permis; laissez-passer, *m.*, permission; (*Ftb.*) passe, *f.*; (*fig.*) point, état, *m.*, extrémité, *f.*
passable ['pa:səbl], *a.* praticable; navigable (*fleuve etc.*); passable.
passage ['pæsidʒ], *n.* passage, *m.*, traversée, *f.*; (*Arch.*) couloir, corridor, *m.*
pass-book ['pa:sbuk], *n.* livre de compte, carnet de banque, *m.*
passenger ['pæsindʒə], *n.* voyageur; passager (*par mer ou avion*), *m.*
passer-by [pa:sə'bai], *n.* (*pl.* **passers-by** ['pa:səz'bai]) passant, *m.*
passing ['pa:siŋ], *a.* passager, éphémère, fugitif.—*adv.* extrêmement, éminemment.—*n.* passage; écoulement (*de temps*); (*fig.*) trépas (*mort*), *m.*
passion ['pæʃən], *n.* passion; colère, *f.*, emportement, *m.*
passionate ['pæʃənit], *a.* passionné, ardent; irascible.
passionately ['pæʃənitli], *adv.* à la passion; à la folie, passionnément.
passion-flower ['pæʃənflauə], *n.* passiflore, fleur de la passion, *f.*
passion play ['pæʃənplei], *n.* mystère (de la Passion), *m.*
Passion Week ['pæʃənwi:k], *n.* semaine de la Passion, *f.*
passive ['pæsiv], *a.* and *n.* passif, *m.*
passiveness ['pæsivnis], *n.* passivité, inertie, *f.*
pass-key ['pa:ski:], *n.* passe-partout, *m.*
Passover ['pa:souvə], *n.* la Pâque, *f.*
passport ['pa:spɔ:t], *n.* passeport, *m.*
password ['pa:swɔ:d], *n.* mot de passe; mot d'ordre, *m.*
past [pa:st], *a.* passé; ancien; dernier (*récent*).—*prep.* au-delà de; près de; sans, hors de; plus de (*âge*); *past three o'clock*, trois heures passées.—*n.* passé, *m.*
paste [peist], *n.* colle (*glu*); pâte (*pour pâtisseries*), *f.*; stras (*faux diamant*), *m.*—*v.t.* coller; *to paste up*, afficher.
pastel ['pæstəl], *n.* pastel, *m.*
pastern ['pæstə:n], *n.* paturon, *m.*
pasteurize ['pa:stjuəraiz], *v.t.* pasteuriser (*lait*).
pastille [pæs'ti:l], *n.* pastille, *f.*

pastime ['pɑːstaim], *n.* passe-temps, amusement, *m.*, distraction, *f.*
pastor ['pɑːstə], *n.* (*literal and fig.*) pasteur; (*literal*) berger, *m.*
pastoral ['pɑːstərəl], *a.* pastoral.—*n.* pastorale, églogue, *f.*
pastry ['peistri], *n.* pâtisserie, *f.*
pastry cook ['peistrikuk], *n.* pâtissier, *m.*
pasture ['pɑːstʃə], *n.* pâture, *f.,* herbage; pâturage (*champ etc.*), *m.*—*v.t.* faire paître. —*v.i.* paître.
pasty ['peisti], *a.* pâteux.—['pɑːsti], *n.* pâté, *m.*
pat [pæt], *a.* and *adv.* à propos, tout juste.—*n.* petite tape, caresse, *f.*; rond de beurre, *m.*—*v.t.* taper, tapoter, caresser.
patch [pætʃ], *n.* pièce, *f.*; mouche (*pour le visage*), *f.*; morceau (*de terre*); pan (*de ciel*), *m.*; tache (*de couleur*), *f.*—*v.t.* rapiécer, raccommoder; arranger.
patching ['pætʃiŋ], *n.* rapiéçage, ravaudage, *m.*
patchwork ['pætʃwəːk], *n.* mélange, *m.*, mosaïque, *f.*
patchy ['pætʃi], *a.* inégal.
pate [peit], *n.* (*colloq.*) caboche, tête, *f.*
patent ['peitənt, 'pætənt], *a.* breveté; (*fig.*) patent, apparent, évident.—*n.* lettres patentes, *f.pl.*, brevet d'invention, *m.*—*v.t.* breveter.
patentee [peitən'tiː], *n.* breveté, *m.*
paternal [pə'təːnl], *a.* paternel.
paternally [pə'təːnəli], *adv.* paternellement.
paternity [pə'təːniti], *n.* paternité, *f.*
paternoster ['pætə'nɔstə], *n.* patenôtre, *f.*, pater, *m.*
path [pɑːθ], *n.* sentier, chemin, *m.*; allée (*dans un jardin*), *f.*
pathless ['pɑːθlis], *a.* sans chemin frayé; (*fig.*) inconnu.
pathetic [pə'θetik], *a.* and *n.* pathétique, *m.*
pathfinder ['pɑːθfaində], *n.* pionnier, éclaireur, *m.*
pathological [pæθə'lɔdʒikl], *a.* pathologique.
pathologist [pə'θɔlədʒist], *n.* pathologiste, *f.*
pathology [pə'θɔlədʒi], *n.* pathologie, *f.*
pathos ['peiθɔs], *n.* pathétique, *m.*
pathway ['pɑːθwei], *n.* sentier; trottoir (*de rue*); accotement (*de route*), *m.*
patience ['peiʃəns], *n.* patience; (*Cards*) réussite, *f.*
patient ['peiʃənt], *a.* patient, endurant.—*n.* malade, *m.,f.*; patient; client (*de médecin*), *m.*
patiently ['peiʃəntli], *adv.* patiemment.
patriarch ['peitriɑːk], *n.* patriarche, *m.*
patriarchal [peitri'ɑːkl], *a.* patriarcal.
Patrick ['pætrik]. Patrice, *m.*
patrimony ['pætriməni], *n.* patrimoine, *m.*
patriot ['peitriət, 'pætriət], *n.* patriote, *m.*, *f.*
patriotic [peitri'ɔtik], *a.* patriotique (*chose*); patriote (*personne*).
patriotism ['peitriətizm], *n.* patriotisme, *m.*
patrol [pə'troul], *n.* patrouille, ronde, *f.*—*v.t.* faire la patrouille dans.—*v.i.* patrouiller; faire une ronde. [*see* **prison-van**]
patron ['peitrən], *n.* patron; protecteur; (*Comm.*) client, *m.*; pratique, *f.*
patronage ['pætrənidʒ], *n.* patronage, *m.*, protection, *f.*
patroness ['peitrənəs], *n.* patronne, protectrice; dame patronnesse (*d'œuvre de bienfaisance*), *f.*
patronize ['pætrənaiz], *v.t.* protéger, patronner; fréquenter (*un magasin*); traiter avec condescendance.
patronizing ['pætrənaiziŋ], *a.* protecteur; **patronizing tone**, ton de condescendance, *m.*
patronymic [pætrə'nimik], *a.* patronymique. —*n.* nom patronymique, *m.*
patten ['pætən], *n.* patin, socque; (*Arch.*) soubassement, *m.*
patter ['pætə], *v.i.* frapper à petits coups, crépiter; trottiner.
pattering ['pætəriŋ], *n.* grésillement; bruit de petits coups, *m.*
pattern ['pætən], *n.* modèle (*pour*); patron (*à couper*); échantillon (*morceau de tissu etc.*); dessin (*de décoration*); exemple, *m.*
patty ['pæti], *n.* petit pâté, *m.*; bouchée (à la reine), *f.*
paucity ['pɔːsiti], *n.* petit nombre, *m.*, disette (*de*), *f.*
Paul [pɔːl]. Paul, *m.*
Paula ['pɔːlə]. Paule, *f.*
paunch [pɔːntʃ], *n.* panse, *f.*, ventre, *m.*
paunchy ['pɔːntʃi], *a.* pansu.
pauper ['pɔːpə], *n.* indigent, *m.*
pauperism ['pɔːpərizm], *n.* paupérisme, *m.*
pauperize ['pɔːpəraiz], *v.t.* réduire à l'indigence.
pause [pɔːz], *n.* pause, *f.*; moment de silence; intervalle, *m.*—*v.i.* faire une pause, s'arrêter.
pave [peiv], *v.t.* paver (*de*); **to pave the way for**, frayer le chemin à ou pour.
pavement ['peivmənt], *n.* trottoir (*bord de rue*), dallage; pavé (*de marbre etc.*), *m.*
paver ['peivə], **pavior** ['peivjə], *n.* paveur, *m.*
pavilion [pə'viliən], *n.* pavillon, *m.*, tente, *f.*
paving ['peiviŋ], *n.* pavage, *m.*
paw [pɔː], *n.* patte; (*facet.*) main, *f.*—*v.t.* manier, tripoter (*manier*); **to paw the ground**, piaffer.
pawn (1) [pɔːn], *n.* (*Chess*) pion, *m.*
pawn (2) [pɔːn], *v.t.* engager, mettre en gage. —*n.* gage, *m.*
pawnbroker ['pɔːnbroukə], *n.* prêteur sur gage, *m.*
pawnshop ['pɔːnʃɔp], *n.* mont-de-piété, *m.*
pay [pei], *n.* paie, *f.*; salaire (*ouvrier*), traitement (*fonctionnaire*), *m.*, gages (*domestique*), *m.pl.*; solde (*officier*), *f.*, prêt (*soldat*), *m.*—*v.t. irr.* payer, acquitter, s'acquitter de; faire (*compliments etc.*); rendre (*honneur*); **carriage paid**, port payé; **to pay a visit to**, faire une visite à.—*v.i.* payer; rapporter.
payable ['peiəbl], *a.* payable; **payable to bearer**, au porteur; **payable to order**, à l'ordre de.
payee [pei'iː], *n.* porteur, *m.*, bénéficiaire, *m.*, *f.*
payer ['peiə], *n.* payeur, *m.*
pay-load ['peiloud], *n.* (*Av.*) poids utile, *m.*
paymaster ['peimɑːstə], *n.* payeur; trésorier, *m.*
payment ['peimənt], *n.* payement, paiement, versement, *m.*
pea [piː], *n.* pois, *m.*; **green peas**, petits pois, *m.pl.*; **sweet pea**, pois de senteur, *m.*
peace [piːs], *n.* paix, *f.*

peaceable ['pi:səbl], *a.* pacifique.
peaceably ['pi:səbli], *adv.* en paix; avec calme.
peaceful ['pi:sful], *a.* paisible; tranquille, calme.
peacefully ['pi:sfuli], *adv.* paisiblement, tranquillement.
peacefulness ['pi:sfulnis], *n.* tranquillité, *f.*, calme, *m.*
peaceless ['pi:slis], *a.* sans paix, agité.
peacemaker ['pi:smeikə], *n.* pacificateur, *m.*
peach [pi:tʃ], *n.* pêche, *f.*
peach tree ['pi:tʃtri:], *n.* pêcher, *m.*
peacock ['pi:kɔk], *n.* paon, *m.*
pea-green [pi:gri:n], *a.* and *n.* vert pois.
pea-hen ['pi:hen], *n.* paonne, *f.*
peak [pi:k], *n.* cime (*de montagne*), *f.*; pic, sommet, *m.*; visière (*d'une casquette*), *f.*
peaked [pi:kt], *a.* à pic, à pointe; à visière.
peal [pi:l], *n.* carillon (*de cloches*); coup, bruit, grondement (*de tonnerre etc.*); éclat (*de rire*), *m.*—*v.i.* carillonner; retentir, résonner; gronder.
peanut ['pi:nʌt], *n.* arachide, cacahuète, *f.*
pea pod ['pi:pɔd], *n.* cosse de pois, *f.*
pear [pɛə], *n.* poire, *f.*
pearl [pə:l], *n.* perle, *f.*; ***mother-of-pearl***, nacre, *f.*—*v.t.*, *v.i.* perler.
pearl oyster ['pə:lʹɔistə], *n.* huître perlière, *f.*
pearly ['pə:li], *a.* de perle, perlé.
pear tree ['pɛətri:], *n.* poirier, *m.*
peasant ['pezənt], *n.* paysan, *m.*
peasantry ['pezəntri], *n.* paysans, *m.pl.*
pea soup [pi:'su:p], *n.* purée de pois, *f.*
peat [pi:t], *n.* tourbe, *f.*
peat bog ['pi:tbɔg], *n.* tourbière, *f.*
pebble [pebl], *n.* caillou, galet (*de plage*), *m.*
pebbly ['pebli], *a.* caillouteux.
peccadillo [pekə'dilou], *n.* peccadille, *f.*
peck (1) [pek], *n.* picotin (*d'avoine etc.*), *m.*
peck (2) [pek], *n.* coup de bec (*d'oiseau*), *m.*—*v.t.* becqueter; ***a hen-pecked husband***, un mari mené par sa femme.
pectoral ['pektərəl], *a.* and *n.* pectoral, *m.*
peculation [pekju'leiʃən], *n.* péculat, *m.*
peculator ['pekjuleitə], *n.* concussionnaire, *m.*, *f.*
peculiar [pi'kju:liə], *a.* particulier, propre; singulier, bizarre.
peculiarity [pikjuli'æriti], *n.* singularité, particularité, *f.*
peculiarly [pi'kju:liəli], *adv.* particulièrement, singulièrement.
pecuniary [pi'kju:niəri], *a.* pécuniaire.
pedagogic(al) [pedə'gɔdʒik(l)], *a.* pédagogique.
pedagogue ['pedəgɔg], *n.* pédagogue, *m.*, *f.*
pedal [pedl], *n.* pédale, *f.*—*v.i.* pédaler.
pedant ['pedənt], *n.* pédant, *m.*
pedantic [pi'dæntik], *a.* pédant (*personne*), pédantesque (*choses*).
pedantry ['pedəntri], *n.* pédantisme, *m.*, pédanterie, *f.*
peddle [pedl], *v.t.* colporter.—*v.i.* faire le colportage.
peddler [PEDLAR].
pedestal ['pedistl], *n.* piédestal, socle, *m.*
pedestrian [pə'destriən], *a.* à pied, pédestre; (*fig.*) prosaïque.—*n.* piéton, marcheur, *m.*
pedigree ['pedigri:], *n.* généalogie; origine, *f.*; arbre généalogique, *m.*
pediment ['pedimənt], *n.* (*Arch.*) fronton, *m.*

pedlar ['pedlə], *n.* colporteur, *m.*
pedometer [pə'dɔmitə], *n.* podomètre, *m.*
peel [pi:l], *n.* pelure; écorce (*d'orange etc.*), *f.*—*v.t.* peler; éplucher.—*v.i.* se peler; s'écailler.
peep [pi:p], *n.* coup d'œil furtif, *m.*; pointe (*du jour*), *f.*—*v.i.* regarder à la dérobée; paraître, poindre.
peeper ['pi:pə], *n.* curieux, *m.*
peep-hole ['pi:phoul], *n.* judas, *m.*
peeping-Tom ['pi:piŋ'tɔm], *n.* voyeur, *m.*
peer (1) [piə], *v.i.* scruter du regard.
peer (2) [piə], *n.* pair; (*fig.*) égal, pareil, *m.*
peerage ['piəridʒ], *n.* pairie, *f.*; les pairs, *m.pl.*
peeress ['piəris], *n.* pairesse, *f.*
peerless ['piəlis], *a.* incomparable; **sans** pareil.
peerlessly ['piəlisli], *adv.* incomparablement.
peerlessness ['piəlisnis], *n.* supériorité incomparable, *f.*
peevish ['pi:viʃ], *a.* irritable, maussade.
peevishly ['pi:viʃli], *adv.* maussadement, avec mauvaise humeur.
peevishness ['pi:viʃnis], *n.* maussaderie, humeur acariâtre, *f.*
peewit [PEWIT].
peg [peg], *n.* cheville; patère (*à chapeau etc.*), *f.*; fausset (*de tonneaux*), piquet (*de tente*), *m.*—*v.t.*, *v.i.* cheviller.
pejorative [pə'dʒɔrətiv, 'pi:dʒərətiv], *a.* péjoratif.
Pekinese [pi:ki'ni:z], *a.* pékinois.—*n.* (épagneul) pékinois; Pékinois (*personne*), *m.*
Peking [pi:'kiŋ] Pékin, *m.*
Pekingese [pi:kiŋ'i:z], [PEKINESE].
pelican ['pelikən], *n.* pélican, *m.*
pellet ['pelit], *n.* boulette, *f.*; grain de plomb, *m.*
pellicle ['pelikl], *n.* pellicule, *f.*
pell-mell ['pel'mel], *adv.* pêle-mêle.
pellucid [pə'lju:sid], *a.* transparent, clair, pellucide.
pelmet ['pelmit], *n.* lambrequin, *m.*
pelt (1) [pelt], *v.t.* assaillir, battre.
pelt (2) [pelt], *n.* peau, *f.*—*v.t.* écorcher.
pelting ['peltiŋ], *a.* battant (*pluie*).—*n.* attaque, *f.*, assaut, *m.*; grêle (*de pierres*), *f.*
pelvic ['pelvik], *a.* pelvien.
pelvis ['pelvis], *n.* bassin, *m.*
pemmican ['pemikən], *n.* conserve de viande, *f.*; pemmican, *m.*
pen [pen], *n.* plume, *f.*; parc, enclos (*bestiaux etc.*); poulailler (*pour volaille*), *m.*; ***fountain pen***, stylo, *m.*—*v.t.* écrire; rédiger; parquer, enfermer (*bétail*).
penal [pi:nl], *a.* pénal, passible d'une amende; ***penal servitude***, travaux forcés, *m.pl.*
penalize ['pi:nəlaiz], *v.t.* infliger une peine à (*quelqu'un*); (*Spt.*) pénaliser.
penalty ['penəlti], *n.* peine; pénalité, amende, *f.*; (*Ftb.*) penalty, *m.*
penance ['penəns], *n.* pénitence, *f.*
pence [PENNY].
pencil [pensl], *n.* crayon, *m.*—*v.t.* dessiner *ou* écrire au crayon.
pencil case ['penslkeis], *n.* porte-crayon, *m.*
pencil sharpener ['pensl'ʃɑ:pnə], *n.* taille-crayon, *m.*
pendant ['pendənt], *n.* pendant, *m.*; pendeloque, *f.*; pendentif, *m.*

periodical

pendent ['pendənt], a. pendant; suspendu.

pending ['pendiŋ], a. pendant, non décidé; en cours.—*prep.* en attendant.

pendulum ['pendjuləm], n. pendule, balancier, m.

penetrable ['penitrəbl], a. pénétrable, sensible.

penetrate ['penitreit], v.t., v.i. pénétrer (dans).

penetrating ['penitreitiŋ], a. pénétrant, perçant; clairvoyant, perspicace.

penetration [peni'treiʃən], n. pénétration, f.

penguin ['peŋgwin], n. manchot, m.

pen-holder ['penhouldə], n. porte-plume, m.

penicillin [peni'silin], n. pénicilline, f.

peninsula [pi'ninsjulə], n. péninsule, presqu'île, f.

peninsular [pi'ninsjulə], a. péninsulaire.

penitence ['penitəns], n. pénitence, f., repentir, m.

penitent ['penitənt], a. pénitent, repentant.

penitentiary [peni'tenʃəri], a. pénitentiaire. —n. pénitencier, m.; (Am.) prison, f.

penknife ['pennaif], n. canif, m.

pennant ['penənt], n. (Naut.) flamme, f.

penniless ['penilis], a. sans le sou, sans ressources.

penny ['peni], n. (pl. pence [pens], of a sum, or pennies ['peniz], of a number of coins) penny, m.

pension ['penʃən], n. pension; pension de retraite, retraite (d'officiers etc.), f.—v.t. to pension off, mettre à la retraite.

pensioner ['penʃənə], n. pensionnaire, m., f.; (Mil.) invalide, m.

pensive ['pensiv], a. pensif, préoccupé, rêveur.

pensively ['pensivli], adv. d'un air pensif.

pensiveness ['pensivnis], n. air pensif, air préoccupé, m.

pent [pent], a. pent up, enfermé, (fig.) étouffé, refoulé.

pentagon ['pentəgən], n. pentagone, m.

Pentecost ['pentikɔst], n. Pentecôte, f.

penthouse ['penthaus], n. appartement sur toit; appentis, m.

penultimate [pe'nʌltimit], a. pénultième, avant-dernier.

penurious [pi'njuəriəs], a. avare; ladre; pauvre (choses).

penury ['penjuəri], n. pénurie, f.

peony ['piːəni], n. pivoine, f.

people [piːpl], n. peuple, m., nation, f., gens, m.pl.; on, monde, m., personnes (en général), f.pl.—v.t. peupler (de).

pepper ['pepə], n. poivre, m.—v.t. poivrer; (fig.) cribler de coups.

pepper caster ['pepə'kɑːstə], n. poivrière, f.

peppercorn ['pepəkɔːn], n. grain de poivre, m.

peppermint ['pepəmint], n. menthe poivrée, f.

peppery ['pepəri], a. poivré; (fig.) irritable.

per [pəː], prep. par; le, m., la, f., les, pl.; three francs per pound, trois francs la livre.

perambulate [pə'ræmbjuleit], v.t. parcourir.

perambulation [pəræmbju'leiʃən], n. parcours, m.; promenade, f.

perambulator [pə'ræmbjuleitə], n. voiture d'enfant, f.

perceive [pə'siːv], v.t. apercevoir (visuellement), s'apercevoir de (se rendre compte de).

percentage [pə'sentidʒ], n. pourcentage, m.

perceptibility [pəsepti'biliti], n. perceptibilité, f.

perceptible [pə'septibl], a. perceptible, sensible.

perceptibly [pə'septibli], adv. perceptiblement, sensiblement.

perception [pə'sepʃən], n. perception, sensibilité; découverte, f.

perceptive [pə'septiv], a. perceptif.

perch (1) [pəːtʃ], n. perche (poisson), f.

perch (2) [pəːtʃ], n. perchoir (à poules etc.) m. —v.t., v.i. percher.

percolate ['pəːkəleit], v.t., v.i. filtrer, passer.

percolation [pəːkə'leiʃən], n. filtration, infiltration, f.

percolator ['pəːkəleitə], filtre (à café), m.

percussion [pə'kʌʃən], n. percussion, f.

percussion cap [pə'kʌʃənkæp], n. capsule, f.

perdition [pə'diʃən], n. perdition, ruine, f.

peregrinate ['perigrineit], v.i. voyager.

peregrination [perigri'neiʃən], n. pérégrination, f., voyage à l'étranger, m.

peremptorily [pə'remptərili], adv. péremptoirement, absolument, formellement.

peremptory [pə'remptəri], a. péremptoire, absolu.

perennial [pə'renial], a. vivace (plantes); (fig.) éternel.—n. plante vivace, f.

perfect (1) ['pəːfikt], a. parfait; achevé.— [pə'fekt], v.t. rendre parfait, perfectionner; achever.

perfect (2) ['pəːfikt], n. (Gram.) parfait, m.

perfection [pə'fekʃən], n. perfection, f.

perfectly ['pəːfiktli], adv. parfaitement, m.

perfidious [pə'fidiəs], a. perfide.

perfidiousness [pə'fidiəsnis], perfidy ['pəːfidi], n. perfidie, f.

perforate ['pəːtəreit], v.t. perforer, percer.

perforation [pəːfə'reiʃən], n. percement, m., perforation; dentelure (de timbre-poste), f.

perforce [pə'fɔːs], adv. forcément, de force.

perform [pə'fɔːm], v.t. exécuter, accomplir; (Theat.) jouer.—v.i. jouer un rôle.

performance [pə'fɔːməns], n. accomplissement; ouvrage, m., œuvre (chose achevée), f.; (Mach.) fonctionnement, m.; (Theat.) représentation, f.; (Mus.) exécution; (Spt.) performance, f.

performer [pə'fɔːmə], n. (Theat.) acteur, m., actrice, f.; (Mus.) artiste, m., f.

perfume ['pəːfjum], n. parfum, m.—[pə'fjuːm], v.t. parfumer (de).

perfumery [pə'fjuːməri], n. parfumerie, f.

perfunctorily [pə'fʌŋktərili], adv. par manière d'acquit; tant bien que mal.

perfunctory [pə'fʌŋktəri], a. de pure forme; négligent.

perhaps [pə'hæps], adv. peut-être; perhaps not, peut-être que non; perhaps so, peut-être que oui.

peril ['peril], n. péril, danger, m.

perilous ['periləs], a. périlleux, dangereux.

perilously ['periləsli], adv. périlleusement.

perimeter [pə'rimitə], n. périmètre, m.

period ['piəriəd], n. période, f., temps, m., durée; époque; fin, f., terme (conclusion); (Am.) point (ponctuation), m.; (Rhet. etc.) phrase, f.; (pl.) (Physiol.) règles, f.pl.

periodic [piəri'ɔdik], a. périodique.

periodical [piəri'ɔdikl], a. and n. périodique, m.

509

periodically [piəri'ɔdikli], *adv.* périodiquement.
peripatetic [peripə'tetik], *a.* péripatéticien.
periphery [pə'rifəri], *n.* périphérie, *f.*
periphrasis [pə'rifrəsis], *n.* (*pl.* **periphrases** [pə'rifrəsi:z]) périphrase, *f.*
periscope ['periskoup], *n.* périscope, *m.*
perish ['periʃ], *v.i.* périr (*de*), mourir; dépérir.
perishable ['periʃəbl], *a.* périssable.
peritonitis [peritə'naitis], *n.* péritonite, *f.*
***periwig** ['periwig], *n.* perruque, *f.*
periwinkle ['periwiŋkl], *n.* (*Bot.*) pervenche, *f.*; bigorneau (*mollusque*), *m.*
perjure ['pə:dʒə], *v.t.* **to perjure oneself**, se parjurer.
perjurer ['pə:dʒərə], *n.* parjure, *m.*, *f.*
perjury ['pə:dʒəri], *n.* parjure; (*Law*) faux témoignage, faux serment, *m.*; **wilful perjury**, parjure prémédité.
perk [pə:k], *v.i.* **to perk up**, se ranimer, se raviver.—*n.* (*pl.*) (*fam.*) [PERQUISITE].
perky ['pə:ki], *a.* déluré; outrecuidant.
permanency ['pə:mənənsi], **permanence** ['pə:mənəns], *n.* permanence, *f.*
permanent ['pə:mənənt], *a.* permanent; en permanence.
permanently ['pə:mənəntli], *adv.* en permanence.
permeable ['pə:miəbl], *a.* perméable.
permeate ['pə:mieit], *v.t.* pénétrer.
permissible [pə'misibl], *a.* permis.
permission [pə'miʃən], *n.* permission, *f.*, permis, *m.*
permissive [pə'misiv], *a.* qui permet; toléré.
permit [pə'mit], *v.t.* permettre (*à quelqu'un de* . . .).—['pə:mit], *n.* permis, *m.*
permutation [pə:mju'teiʃən], *n.* permutation, *f.*
pernicious [pə'niʃəs], *a.* pernicieux.
perniciously [pə'niʃəsli], *adv.* pernicieusement.
peroration [perə'reiʃən], *n.* péroraison, *f.*
peroxide [pə'rɔksaid], *n.* peroxyde, *m.*—*v.t.* oxygéner (*cheveux*).
perpendicular [pə:pən'dikjulə], *a.* and *n.* perpendiculaire, *f.*
perpendicularly [pə:pən'dikjuləli], *adv.* perpendiculairement.
perpetrate ['pə:pitreit], *v.t.* commettre; (*Law*) perpétrer.
perpetration [pə:pi'treiʃən], *n.* exécution, (*Law*) perpétration, *f.*
perpetrator ['pə:pitreitə], *n.* auteur (*d'un crime*), *m.*
perpetual [pə'petjuəl], *a.* perpétuel.
perpetually [pə'petjuəli], *adv.* perpétuellement.
perpetuate [pə'petjueit], *v.t.* perpétuer.
perpetuation [pəpetju'eiʃən], *n.* perpétuation, *f.*
perpetuity [pə:pi'tju:iti], *n.* perpétuité, *f.*
perplex [pə'pleks], *v.t.* embarrasser.
perplexed [pə'plekst], *a.* perplexe, embarrassé.
perplexing [pə'pleksiŋ], *a.* embarrassant.
perplexity [pə'pleksiti], *n.* perplexité, *f.*
perquisite ['pə:kwizit], *n.* émolument casuel, *m.*
perry ['peri], *n.* poiré, *m.*
persecute ['pə:sikju:t], *v.t.* persécuter.
persecuting ['pə:sikju:tiŋ], *a.* persécuteur.
persecution [pə:si'kju:ʃən], *n.* persécution, *f.*

persecutor ['pə:sikjutə], *n.* persécuteur, *m.*
perseverance [pə:si'viərəns], *n.* persévérance, *f.*
persevere [pə:si'viə], *v.i.* persévérer (*à* ou *dans*).
persevering [pə:si'viəriŋ], *a.* persévérant.
perseveringly [pə:si'viəriŋli], *adv.* avec persévérance.
Persia ['pə:ʃə]. la Perse, *f.*
Persian ['pə:ʃən], *a.* de Perse, persan.—*n.* perse (*langue*); Persan (*personne*), *m.*; **the Persian Gulf**, le Golfe Persique.
persist [pə'sist], *v.i.* persister (*dans* ou *à*); continuer.
persistence [pə'sistəns], *n.* persistance, *f.*
persistent [pə'sistənt], *a.* persistant; opiniâtre.
person ['pə:sən], *n.* personne, *f.*; personnage, caractère, *m.*; (*pl.*) personnes, *f.pl.*, gens, *m.pl.*, *f.pl.*; **young persons**, les jeunes gens.
personage ['pə:sənidʒ], *n.* personnage, *m.*
personal ['pə:sənl], *a.* personnel.
personality [pə:sə'næliti], *n.* personnalité, *f.*
personally ['pə:sənli], *adv.* personnellement.
personate ['pə:səneit], *v.t.* se faire passer pour; représenter, contrefaire.
personification [pə:sɔnifi'keiʃən], *n.* personnification, *f.*
personify [pə'sɔnifai], *v.t.* personnifier.
personnel [pə:sə'nel], *n.* personnel, *m.*
perspective [pə'spektiv], *a.* perspectif.—*n.* perspective, *f.*
perspicacious [pə:spi'keiʃəs], *a.* pénétrant, perspicace; perçant (*la vision*).
perspicacity [pə:spi'kæsiti], *n.* perspicacité, *f.*
perspicuity [pə:spi'kju:iti], *n.* clarté, *f.*
perspicuous [pə'spikjuəs], *a.* clair, net.
perspiration [pə:spi'reiʃən], *n.* transpiration, sueur, *f.*
perspire [pə'spaiə], *v.i.* transpirer, suer.
persuade [pə'sweid], *v.t.* persuader; **to persuade from**, dissuader de.
persuasion [pə'sweiʒən], *n.* persuasion, *f.*
persuasive [pə'sweisiv], *a.* persuasif.
persuasiveness [pə'sweisivnis], *n.* force persuasive, *f.*
pert [pə:t], *a.* mutin, hardi; impertinent, insolent (*effronté*).
pertain [pə'tein], *v.i.* appartenir.
pertinacious [pə:ti'neiʃəs], *a.* obstiné, opiniâtre.
pertinacity [pə:ti'næsiti], *n.* obstination, *f.*
pertinence ['pə:tinəns], *n.* convenance, *f.*
pertinent ['pə:tinənt], *a.* pertinent, convenable.
pertly ['pə:tli], *adv.* impertinemment, insolemment.
pertness ['pə:tnis], *n.* impertinence, *f.*
perturb [pə'tə:b], *v.t.* agiter, troubler.
perturbation [pə:tə'beiʃən], *n.* agitation, *f.*
perturbed [pə'tə:bd], *a.* troublé, inquiet.
Peru [pə'ru:]. le Pérou, *m.*
perusal [pə'ru:zl], *n.* lecture, *f.*
peruse [pə'ru:z], *v.t.* lire attentivement.
Peruvian [pə'ru:vian], *a.* péruvien, du Pérou.—*n.* Péruvien (*personne*), *m.*
pervade [pə'veid], *v.t.* pénétrer dans; se répandre dans, remplir.
pervading [pə'veidiŋ], *a.* **all-pervading**, dominant.
perverse [pə'və:s], *a.* pervers.

perversely [pə'və:sli], *adv.* avec perversité.
perverseness [pə'və:snis], **perversity** [pə'və:siti], *n.* perversité, *f.*
perversion [pə'və:ʃən], *n.* perversion, *f.*
pervert [pə'və:t], *v.t.* pervertir; fausser, dénaturer.—['pə:və:t], *n.* perverti, *m.*
perverted [pə'və:tid], *a.* perverti.
pervious ['pə:viəs], *a.* perméable, pénétrable.
pessimism ['pesimizm], *n.* pessimisme, *m.*
pessimist ['pesimist], *n.* pessimiste, *m.,f.*
pessimistic [pesi'mistik], *a.* pessimiste.
pest [pest], *n.* peste, *f.*
pester ['pestə], *v.t.* tourmenter, ennuyer.
pestilence ['pestilans], *n.* peste, pestilence, *f.*
pestilent ['pestilant], *a.* pestilentiel, contagieux.
pestilential [pesti'lenʃl], *a.* pestilentiel.
pet (1) [pet], *a.* favori; *pet aversion,* bête noire, *f.*—*n.* chéri, *m.,* chérie, *f.,* favori, *m.,* favorite, *f.;* animal familier; enfant gaté, *m.*—*v.t.* choyer, dorloter; *(Am.)* caresser.
pet (2) [pet], *n.* accès d'humeur, *m.*
petal [petl], *n.* pétale, *m.*
Peter ['pi:tə]. Pierre, *m.*
peter out [pi:tə'raut], *v.i. (colloq.)* s'épuiser; tomber à l'eau *(projet),* flancher *(machine).*
petition [pi'tiʃən], *n.* pétition, *f.*—*v.t.* pétitionner.
petitioner [pi'tiʃənə], *n. (Law)* requérant, *m.;* pétitionnaire, *m.,f.*
petrel ['petrəl], *n. (Orn.)* pétrel, *m.*
petrifaction [petri'fækʃən], *n.* pétrification, *f.*
petrify ['petrifai], *v.t.* pétrifier.—*v.i.* se pétrifier.
petrol ['petrəl], *n.* essence, *f.; petrol station,* poste d'essence, *m.*
petrol can ['petrəlkæn], *n.* bidon d'essence, *m.*
petroleum [pi'trouliəm], *n.* pétrole, *m.,* huile de pétrole, *f.*
petticoat ['petikout], *n.* jupon, *m.*
pettifogging ['petifogiŋ], *a.* avocassier, chicaneur; chicanier *(méthodes etc.).*
pettiness ['petinis], *n.* petitesse, mesquinerie, *f.*
petty ['peti], *a.* petit; mesquin, chétif; *(Law)* inférieur.
petty officer ['peti'ofisə], *n. (Navy)* officier marinier, *m.*
petulance ['petjulans], *n.* irritabilité, *f.*
petulant ['petjulant], *a.* irritable.
pew [pju:], *n.* banc d'église, *m.*
pewit ['pi:wit], *n. (Orn.)* vanneau, *m.*
pewter ['pju:tə], *n.* étain, potin, *m.;* vaisselle d'étain, *f.*
phalanx ['fælænks], *n. (pl.* **phalanges** [fə'lændʒi:z]) phalange, *f.*
phantom ['fæntəm], *n.* fantôme, *m.*
Pharaoh ['fɛərou], *n.* Pharaon, *m.*
Pharisee ['færisi], *n.* Pharisien, *m.*
pharmaceutical [fa:mə'sju:tikəl], *a.* pharmaceutique.
pharmacy ['fɑ:məsi], *n.* pharmacie, *f.*
phase [feiz], *n.* phase, *f.*
pheasant ['fezənt], *n.* faisan, *m.*
phenomenal [fi'nəmənəl], *a.* phénoménal.
phenomenon [fi'nəmənən], *n. (pl.* **phenomena** [fi'nəmənə]) phénomène, *m.*
phew! [fju:], *int.* pouf!
phial ['faiəl], *n.* fiole, *f.*
philanthropic [filən'θrɔpik], *a.* philanthropique.

philanthropist [fi'lænθrəpist], *n.* philanthrope, *m.,f.*
philanthropy [fi'lænθrɔpi], *n.* philanthropie, *f.*
philatelist [fi'lætəlist], *n.* philatéliste, *m.,f.*
philharmonic [filha:'mɔnik], *a.* philharmonique.
Philip ['filip]. Philippe, *m.*
Philippine ['filipi:n], *a.* philippine.
Philippines ['filipi:nz], **the,** les Philippines, *f.pl.*
Philistine ['filistain], *a.* philistin.—*n.* Philistin *(personne).*
philologist [fi'lɔlədʒist], *n.* philologue, *m.,f.*
philology [fi'lɔlədʒi], *n.* philologie, *f.*
philosopher [fi'lɔsəfə], *n.* philosophe, *m.,f.*
philosophical [filə'sɔfikl], *a.* philosophique; philosophe *(personnes).*
philosophize [fi'lɔsəfaiz], *v.i.* philosopher.
philosophy [fi'lɔsəfi], *n.* philosophie, *f.; natural philosophy,* la physique, *f.*
philter, philtre ['filtə], *n.* philtre, *m.*
phlegm [flem], *n.* flegme, *m.*
phlegmatic [fleg'mætik], *a.* flegmatique.
phobia ['foubiə], *n.* phobie, *f.*
Phoebe ['fi:bi]. Phébé, *f.*
Phoenician [fi'ni:ʃən], *a.* phénicien.—*n.* Phénicien *(personne).*
phoenix ['fi:niks], *n.* phénix, *m.*
phone [foun], *n. (colloq.)* [TELEPHONE].
phonetic [fə'netik], *a.* phonétique.
phonetics [fə'netiks], *n.pl.* phonétique, *f.*
phoney ['founi], *a. (colloq.)* faux, factice.—*n.* charlatan, *m.*
phonograph, see **gramophone.**
phosphate ['fɔsfeit], *n.* phosphate, *m.*
phosphor ['fɔsfə], *n.* phosphore, *m.*
phosphoric [fɔs'fɔrik], *a.* phosphorique.
phosphorus ['fɔsfərəs], *n.* phosphore, *m.*
photo ['foutou], *n. (colloq.)* [PHOTOGRAPH].
photogenic [foutə'dʒenik], *a.* photogénique.
photograph ['foutəgra:f, 'foutəgræf], *n.* photographie, *(colloq.)* photo, *f.*—*v.t.* photographier.
photographer [fə'tɔgrəfə], *n.* photographe, *m.,f.*
photographic [foutə'græfik], *a.* photographique.
photography [fə'tɔgrəfi], *n.* photographie, *f.*
photostat ['foutəstæt], *n.* appareil photostat, *m.*
phrase [freiz], *n.* phrase, locution, *f.*—*v.t.* exprimer, nommer; *(Mus.)* phraser.
phraseology [freizi'ɔlədʒi], *n.* phraséologie, *f.*
phrenetic [fre'netik], *a.* fou, frénétique.
phrenologist [fre'nɔlədʒist], *n.* phrénologiste, phrénologue, *m.,f.*
phrenology [fre'nɔlədʒi], *n.* phrénologie, *f.*
physic ['fizik], *n.* médecine, *f.*—*v.t.* médicamenter; purger.
physical ['fizikl], *a.* physique; *physical training,* éducation physique, *f.*
physically ['fizikəli], *adv.* physiquement.
physician [fi'ziʃən], *n.* médecin, *m.*
physicist ['fizisist], *n.* physicien, *m.*
physics ['fiziks], *n.pl.* physique, *f.*
physiognomy [fizi'ɔnəmi, fizi'ɔgnəmi], *n.* physionomie, *f.*
physiological [fiziə'lɔdʒikl], *a.* physiologique.
physiology [fizi'ɔlədʒi], *n.* physiologie, *f.*

511

physiotherapy [fizio'θerəpi], *n.* physio-thérapie, *f.*

physique [fi'zi:k], *n.* physique, *m.*

pianist ['piənist], *n.* pianiste, *m., f.*

piano ['pjænou, 'pjɑː'nou], **pianoforte** [-'fɔːti], *n.* piano, *m.; grand piano*, piano à queue; *to play (on) the piano*, jouer du piano. [see **music-stool**]

pick [pik], *n.* pic, *m.*, pioche (*outil*), *f.*; choix, *m.—v.t.* piquer; cueillir; choisir, trier; ronger (*un os*); chercher (*querelle*); voler à la tire (*dans une poche*); crocheter (*une serrure*); *to pick up*, ramasser, relever.

pickaback ['pikəbæk], *adv.* sur le dos.

pickaxe ['pikæks], *n.* pioche, *f.*

picked [pikt], *a.* d'élite, choisi.

picker ['pikə], *n.* cueilleur, *m.*

picket ['pikit], *n.* piquet, jalon; petit poste, *m.—v.t.* former en piquet; guetter (*grévistes etc.*).

pickle [pikl], *n.* saumure, marinade, *f.; (pl.)* conserves au vinaigre, *f.pl.—v.t.* conserver au vinaigre, mariner; saler.

pickled [pikld], *a.* mariné, conservé au vinaigre; (*pop.*) ivre.

pickpocket ['pikpɔkit], *n.* voleur à la tire, *m.*

pick-up ['pikʌp], *n.* ramassage, *m.*; reprise (*de machine, des affaires*), *f.*; pick-up (*tourne-disque*), *m.*

picnic ['piknik], *n.* pique-nique, *m.—v.i.* faire un pique-nique.

pictorial [pik'tɔːriəl], *a.* illustré; de peintre.

pictorially [pik'tɔːriəli], *adv.* avec illustra-tions.

picture ['piktʃə], *n.* tableau, *m.*; peinture; (*fig.*) image, *f.; the pictures*, le cinéma.—*v.t.* peindre; (*fig.*) dépeindre, représenter.

picturesque [piktʃə'resk], *a.* pittoresque.

pie [pai], *n.* pâté (*de viande*), *m.*; tourte (*de fruit*), *f.; (colloq.) as easy as pie*, simple comme bonjour; *to eat humble pie*, avaler des couleuvres.

piebald ['paibɔːld], *a.* pie (*cheval*).

piece [piːs], *n.* pièce (*grand*), *f.*; morceau (*petit*); fragment, bout, *m.; a piece of furniture*, un meuble; *a piece of news*, une nouvelle; *to break to pieces*, mettre en pièces; *to take to pieces*, démonter.—*v.t.* rapiécer.

piecemeal ['piːsmiːl], *adv.* par morceaux, peu à peu.

pied [paid], *a.* bariolé, bigarré; pie (*cheval*).

pie dish ['paidiʃ], *n.* tourtière, terrine, *f.*

pier [piə], *n.* jetée, *f.*; ponton (*de rivière*), *m.*; pile (*d'un pont*), *f.*

pierce [piəs], *v.t.* percer, pénétrer.

pierced [piəst], *a.* à jour (*ouvrage*), *m.*

piercing ['piəsiŋ], *a.* perçant; pénétrant.

pier glass ['piəglɑːs], *n.* trumeau, *m.*

piety ['paiəti], *n.* piété, *f.*

pig [pig], *n.* cochon, porc, pourceau, *m.; to buy a pig in a poke*, acheter chat en poche.

pigeon ['pidʒin], *a.* timide, craintif.—*n.* pigeon, *m.; carrier pigeon*, pigeon voya-geur.

pigeon-hole ['pidʒinhoul], *n.* boulin, *m.*; case (*à papiers etc.*), *f.; set of pigeon-holes*, casier, *m.—v.t.* classer.

piggery ['pigəri], *n.* étable à cochons, *f.*

piggy ['pigi], **piglet** ['piglit], *n.* porcelet, goret, *m.*

pigheaded ['pighedid], *a.* têtu, stupide.

pig iron ['pigaiən], *n.* gueuse, *f.*

pigment ['pigmənt], *n.* couleur, *f.*, pigment, *m.*

pigmy [PYGMY].

pigsty ['pigstai], *n.* porcherie, *f.*

pigtail ['pigteil], *n.* queue (*de cheveux*), *f.*

pigtailed ['pigteild], *a.* à queue.

pike [paik], *n.* pique (*arme*), *f.*; brochet (*poisson*), *m.*

pilchard ['piltʃəd], *n.* (*Ichth.*) pilchard, *m.*

pile [pail], *n.* tas, monceau; (*fig.*) (*Build.*) édifice, bâtiment; pieu (*poteau*); poil (*de tissu*), *m.; atomic pile*, pile atomique, *f.; funeral pile*, bûcher, *m.—v.t.* entasser, empiler, amonceler.—*v.i. to pile up*, s'empiler, s'entasser.

piles [pailz], *n.pl.* (*Path.*) hémorroïdes, *f.pl.*

pilfer ['pilfə], *v.t.* dérober, chiper.—*v.i.* dérober.

pilferer ['pilfərə], *n.* chapardeur, chipeur, *m.*

pilfering ['pilfəriŋ], *n.* petit vol, larcin, *m.*

pilgrim ['pilgrim], *n.* pèlerin, *m.*

pilgrimage ['pilgrimidʒ], *n.* pèlerinage, *m.*

pill [pil], *n.* pilule, *f.*

pillage ['pilidʒ], *n.* pillage, saccagement, *m.—v.t.* saccager, piller.

pillar ['pilə], *n.* pilier, *m.*, colonne, *f.*; (*fig.*) soutien, *m.*

pillar-box ['piləbɔks], *n.* boîte aux lettres, *f.*

pillion ['piljən], *n.* coussinet (*de cheval*), *m.*; siège, *m.* (ou selle, *f.*) arrière (*de moto-cyclette*); *to ride pillion*, monter en croupe, monter derrière.

pillory ['piləri], *n.* pilori, *m.—v.t.* pilorier, mettre au pilori.

pillow ['pilou], *n.* oreiller, *m.—v.t.* reposer, coucher.

pillow-case ['piloukeis], **pillow slip** ['pilou slip], *n.* taie d'oreiller, *f.*

pilot ['pailət], *n.* pilote, *m.; test pilot*, pilote d'essais.—*v.t.* piloter, servir de pilote à.

pilotage ['pailətidʒ], *n.* pilotage, *m.*

pimpernel ['pimpənel], *n.* pimprenelle, *f.*, mouron, *m.*

pimple [pimpl], *n.* bouton, *m.*

pimply ['pimpli], *a.* bourgeonné, pustuleux.

pin [pin], *n.* épingle; cheville (*de bois*), *f.*; (*fig.*) rien, *m.—v.t.* épingler, attacher; cheviller.

pinafore ['pinəfɔː], *n.* tablier (d'enfant), *m.*

pincers ['pinsəz], *n.pl.* pince, *f.*, tenailles, *f.pl.*

pinch [pintʃ], *n.* pincée (*de sel etc.*); prise (*de tabac*), *f.; (fig.)* embarras, *m.; at a pinch*, à la rigueur, au besoin.—*v.t.* pincer; serrer, gêner (*habits*); (*pop.*) chiper (*voler*); pincer (*arrêter*).—*v.i.* pincer; se gêner.

pinching ['pintʃiŋ], *a.* pressant, piquant (*froid*).—*n.* pincement, *m.*

pin-cushion ['pinkuʃən], *n.* pelote, *f.*

pine (1) [pain], *n.* pin (*arbre*); bois de pin, *m.*

pine (2) [pain], *v.i.* languir; *to pine after*, soupirer après.

pineapple ['painæpl], *n.* ananas, *m.*

ping [piŋ], *n.* sifflement (*de balle de fusil*), *m.—v.i.* siffler.

ping-pong ['piŋpɔŋ], *n.* ping-pong, *m.*

pinion ['pinjən], *n.* aileron, bout d'aile, *m.—v.t.* couper le bout de l'aile à; lier.

pink (1) [piŋk], *a.* couleur de rose, rose.—*n.* œillet (*fleur*); rose (*couleur*), *m.; in the pink of condition*, en excellente condition;

(*colloq.*) *to be in the pink*, se porter à merveille.

pink (2) [piŋk], *v.i.* cliqueter (*moteur*).

pinnace ['pinəs], *n.* pinasse, *f.*

pinnacle ['pinəkl], *n.* pinacle, *m.*

pin-point ['pinpoint], *v.t.* indiquer exactement.

pin pricks ['pinpriks], *n.pl.* coups d'épingles, *m.pl.*

pint [paint], *n.* pinte (*un demi-litre*), *f.*

pintail ['pinteil], *n.* (*Orn.*) pilet, *m.*

pioneer [paiə'niə], *n.* pionnier, *m.*

pious ['paiəs], *a.* pieux.

piously ['paiəsli], *adv.* pieusement.

pip [pip], *n.* pépin (*de fruit*); (*Rad.*) top, *m.—v.i.* piauler (*oiseaux*).

pipe [paip], *n.* tuyau, conduit, *m.*; pipe (*à fumer, à vin etc.*), *f.*; (*Mus.*) pipeau, chalumeau, *m.—v.i.* jouer du chalumeau, siffler; (*pop.*) *pipe down!* boucle-la!

pipe-line ['paiplain], *n.* canalisation, *f.*, oléoduc, pipe-line, *m.*

piper ['paipə], *n.* joueur de flûte etc., *m.*

piping ['paipiŋ], *a.* qui joue du chalumeau, sifflant; flûté (*la voix*).*—n.* tubulure, *f.*, tuyautage, *m.*

pipit ['pipit], *n.* (*Orn.*) pipit, *m.*

pippin ['pipin], *n.* reinette, *f.*

piquancy [pi'kænsi], *n.* goût piquant, *m.*

piquant ['pi:kənt], *a.* piquant.

pique [pi:k], *n.* pique, brouillerie, *f.*

piquet [pi'ket], *n.* (*Cards*) piquet, *f.*

piracy ['paiərəsi], *n.* piraterie; (*fig.*) contrefaçon, *f.*, plagiat, *m.*

pirate ['paiərit], *n.* pirate; (*fig.*) contrefacteur, *m.*

piratical [pai'rætikl], *a.* de pirate; (*fig.*) de contrefaçon.

pirouette [piru'et], *n.* pirouette, *f.*

pish! [piʃ], *int.* bah!

piss [pis], *v.i.* (*vulg.*) pisser.*—n.* urine, *f.*

pistol [pistl], *n.* pistolet, *m.*

piston ['pistən], *n.* piston, *m.*

piston ring ['pistənriŋ], *n.* segment de piston, *m.*

piston rod ['pistənrəd], *n.* tige de piston, *f.*

pit [pit], *n.* fosse, *f.*; (*fig.*) cavité, *f.*; (*Theat.*) parterre; (*Mining*) puits; creux (*de l'estomac*), *m.*; aisselle (*du bras*), *f.—v.t.* creuser; marquer de petits creux.

pitch (1) [pitʃ], *n.* jet, lancement (*de caillou, balle*); (*Naut.*) tangage; point, degré, *m.*; pente (*de toit etc.*), *f.*; (*Mus.*) ton, diapason, *m.*; *to play pitch-and-toss*, jouer à pile ou face.*—v.t.* jeter, lancer; établir (*fixer*); dresser (*une tente*).*—v.i.* (*Naut.*) tanguer, plonger; tomber, se jeter.

pitch (2) [pitʃ], *n.* poix, *f.*; *pitch dark*, noir comme dans un four.

pitched [pitʃt], *a.* rangé; *pitched battle*, bataille rangée, *f.*

pitcher ['pitʃə], *n.* cruche, *f.*

pitchfork ['pitʃfɔ:k], *n.* fourche, *f.*

pitching ['pitʃiŋ], *n.* plongement (*de véhicules*); (*Naut.*) tangage, *m.*

pitch pine ['pitʃpain], *n.* pin à trochets, pitchpin, *m.*

piteous ['pitiəs], *a.* piteux; pitoyable (*digne de pitié*).

piteously ['pitiəsli], *adv.* piteusement.

piteousness ['pitiəsnis], *n.* état piteux, *m.*; tristesse, *f.*

pitfall ['pitfɔ:l], *n.* trappe, *f.*, piège, *m.*

pith [piθ], *n.* moelle; vigueur, énergie, *f.*; essentiel, *m.*

pithily ['piθili], *adv.* fortement, vigoureusement.

pithy ['piθi], *a.* plein de moelle; (*fig.*) substantiel, concis.

pitiable ['pitiəbl], *a.* pitoyable, à faire pitié.

pitiful ['pitiful], *a.* pitoyable.

pitifully ['pitifuli], *adv.* pitoyablement.

pitiless ['pitilis], *a.* impitoyable, sans pitié.

pitilessly ['pitilisli], *adv.* impitoyablement, sans pitié.

pitman ['pitmən], *n.* (*pl.* -men [men]) mineur, *m.*

pittance ['pitəns], *n.* pitance, *f.*

pitted ['pitid], *a.* grêlé (*de petite vérole*).

pity ['piti], *n.* pitié, *f.*; dommage (*regret*), *m.*; *what a pity!* quel dommage!*—v.t.* avoir pitié de, plaindre.

pityingly ['pitiiŋli], *adv.* avec pitié.

pivot ['pivət], *n.* pivot, *m.*

placable ['plækəbl], *a.* facile à apaiser.

placard ['plækɑ:d], *n.* placard, *m.*, affiche, pancarte, *f.—v.t.* afficher, placarder (*de*).

placate [plə'keit], *v.t.* apaiser.

place [pleis], *n.* lieu, endroit, *m.*, localité; place (*siège etc.*); position, *f.*, rang (*classe*), *m.*; demeure, résidence (*chez soi*), *f.*; emploi (*profession*), *m.*; *come to my place*, venez chez moi; *to take place*, avoir lieu; *out of place*, déplacé, inopportun.*—v.t.* placer, mettre.

placid ['plæsid], *a.* placide, tranquille, calme.

plagiarism ['pleidʒiərizm], *n.* plagiat, *m.*

plagiarist ['pleidʒiərist], *n.* plagiaire, *m.*, *f.*

plagiarize ['pleidʒiəraiz], *v.t.* plagier.

plague [pleig], *n.* peste, *f.*; (*fig.*) plaie, *f.*, fléau, *m.—v.t.* (*fig.*) tourmenter.

plaice [pleis], *n.* carrelet, *m.*; plie franche, *f.*

plaid [plæd], *n.* (*Sc.*) plaid; tartan, *m.*

plain [plein], *a.* uni, plat; simple, sans façon; ordinaire; sans attraits (*mine*); évident (*qui saute aux yeux*); franc (*sincère*); *in plain clothes*, en civil; *plain cooking*, cuisine bourgeoise *ou* au naturel, *f.—n.* plaine, *f.—adv.* simplement; franchement.

plainly ['pleinli], *adv.* bonnement; distinctement; franchement.

plainness ['pleinnis], *n.* simplicité; clarté; sincérité, *f.*

plain speaking ['plein'spi:kiŋ], *n.* franchise, *f.*

plain-spoken ['plein'spoukn], *a.* franc, clair, explicite.

plaint [pleint], *n.* plainte, *f.*

plaintiff ['pleintif], *n.* plaignant, *m.*

plaintive ['pleintiv], *a.* plaintif.

plaintively ['pleintivli], *adv.* d'une voix plaintive.

plaintiveness ['pleintivnis], *n.* ton plaintif, *m.*

plait [plæt], *n.* natte, tresse (*de cheveux*), *f.*; pli, *m.—v.t.* tresser, natter (*cheveux*); plisser.

plaited ['plætid], *a.* tressé (*cheveux*); plissé.

plan [plæn], *n.* plan; dessein, projet; système, *m.—v.t.* tracer un plan de; (*fig.*) projeter.

plane (1) [plein], *n.* (*Geom.*) plan; (*Carp.*) rabot, *f.*; (*colloq.*) avion, *m.—v.t.* raboter, aplanir.

plane (2) [plein], **plane tree** ['pleintri:], *n.* platane, *m.*

planet ['plænit], *n.* planète, *f.*

planetarium [plæni'tɛəriəm], *n.* planéta-
rium, *m.*
planetary ['plænitəri], *a.* planétaire.
planing ['pleiniŋ], *n.* rabotage, *m.*
plank [plæŋk], *n.* planche, *f.*, madrier; (*Naut.*)
bordage, *m.*—*v.t.* planchéier; (*Naut.*)
border.
plankton ['plæŋktən], *n.* plancton, *m.*
planner ['plænə], *n.* auteur d'un plan, *m.*;
town planner, urbaniste, *m.*
planning ['plæniŋ], *n.* tracé d'un plan, *m.*;
planification, *f.*; (*fig.*) invention, *f.*; *town
planning*, urbanisme, *m.*
plant [plɑ:nt], *n.* plante, *f.*; (*Tech.*) matériel,
m.—*v.t.* planter; (*fig.*) poser.
plantain ['plæntin], *n.* plantain, *m.*
plantation [plɑ:n'teiʃən], *n.* plantation, *f.*
planter ['plɑ:ntə], *n.* planteur, colon, *m.*
planting ['plɑ:ntiŋ], *n.* plantage, *m.*, plantation, *f.*
plasma ['plæzmə], *n.* plasma (du sang), *m.*
plaster ['plɑ:stə], *n.* plâtre; (*Pharm.*) emplâtre, *m.*; *sticking plaster*, sparadrap, *m.*
—*v.t.* plâtrer.
plasterer ['plɑ:stərə], *n.* plâtrier, *m.*
plastering ['plɑ:stəriŋ], *n.* plâtrage, *m.*
plastic ['plæstik], *a.* plastique.—*n.* (*pl.*) plas-
tiques, *m.pl.*
plat [PLAIT].
Plate [pleit], **the River.** le Rio de la Plata, *m.*
plate [pleit], *n.* assiette; (*Metal., Phot.*)
plaque, *f.*—*v.t.* plaquer (*de*); laminer;
étamer (*une glace*).
plateau ['plætou, plə'tou], *n.* plateau, *m.*
plated ['pleitid], *a.* plaqué.
plateful ['pleitful], *n.* assiettée, *f.*
plate glass ['pleitglɑ:s], *n.* glace sans tain, *f.*
plate-layer ['pleitleiə], *n.* (*Rail.*) poseur de
rails, *m.*
plate rack ['pleitræk], *n.* porte-assiettes, *m.*
platform ['plætfɔ:m], *n.* plateforme; estrade,
f.; (*Rail.*) quai, *m.*
plating ['pleitiŋ], *n.* placage, *m.*; *armor-
plating*, blindage, *m.*
platinum ['plætinəm], *n.* platine, *m.*
platitude ['plætitju:d], *n.* platitude, *f.*
Plato ['pleitou]. Platon, *m.*
platoon [plə'tu:n], *n.* (*Mil.*) section, *f.*
platter ['plætə], *n.* écuelle, *f.*; (*Am.*) plat, *m.*
platypus ['plætipəs], *n.* ornithor(h)ynque, *m.*
plaudit ['plɔ:dit], *n.* applaudissement, *m.*
plausible ['plɔ:zibl], *a.* plausible; spécieux.
play [plei], *n.* jeu, *m.*; récréation (*d'enfants*),
f.; essor (*champ libre*); badinage, *m.*; (*Mus.*)
exécution; (*Theat.*) comédie, pièce, *f.*; *fair
play*, franc jeu.—*v.t.* jouer, jouer à; faire
jouer (*une machine etc.*); représenter, faire
(*une pièce, un rôle etc.*); (*Mus.*) jouer de.—
v.i. jouer; folâtrer (*s'amuser*).
play-bill ['pleibil], *n.* affiche de théâtre, *f.*
player ['pleiə], *n.* joueur, *f.*; (*Theat.*) acteur, *m.*,
actrice, *f.*; artiste, *m.*, *f.*
playfellow ['pleifelou], **playmate** ['plei
meit], *n.* camarade de jeu, *m.*
playful ['pleiful], *a.* folâtre, badin.
playfully ['pleifuli], *adv.* en badinant.
playfulness ['pleifulnis], *n.* badinage, enjouement, *m.*
playground ['pleigraund], *n.* cour de récréation, *f.*
playhouse ['pleihaus], *n.* théâtre, *m.*
plaything ['pleiθiŋ], *n.* jouet, joujou, *m.*

playtime ['pleitaim], *n.* récréation, *f.*
playwright ['pleirait], *n.* auteur dramatique,
m., dramaturge, *m.*, *f.*
plea [pli:], *n.* procès, *m.*, cause, *f.*; prétexte,
m., excuse, *f.*
plead [pli:d], *v.t.*, *v.i.* plaider.
pleasant ['plezənt], *a.* agréable, charmant.
pleasantly ['plezəntli], *adv.* agréablement.
pleasantness ['plezəntnis], *n.* agrément,
charme, *m.*
pleasantry ['plezəntri], *n.* plaisanterie, *f.*
please [pli:z], *v.t.* plaire à; *to be pleased*,
être content; (*impers.*) il plait; *as you please*, comme vous voudrez;
if I please, si cela me plaît; (*if you*)
please, s'il vous plaît.
pleased [pli:zd], *a.* charmé, content (*de*);
satisfait (*de choses*).
pleasing ['pli:ziŋ], *a.* agréable, charmant.
pleasurable ['pleʒərəbl], *a.* agréable.
pleasure ['pleʒə], *n.* plaisir; gré (*will*), *m.*
pleasure ground ['pleʒəgraund], *n.* parc,
jardin d'agrément, *m.*
pleat [pli:t], *n.* plissé, *f.*—*v.t.* plisser.
plebeian [plə'bi:ən], *a.* and *n.* plébéien, *m.*
pledge [pledʒ], *n.* gage; nantissement, *m.*;
(*Law*) caution, *f.*—*v.t.* engager; garantir.
plenary ['pli:nəri], *a.* plein, complet, entier.
plenipotentiary [plenipo'tenʃəri], *a.* and *n.*
plénipotentiaire, *m.*, *f.*
plenitude ['plenitju:d], *n.* plénitude, *f.*
plenteous ['plentiəs], *a.* abondant.
plenteously ['plentiəsli], *adv.* abondamment.
plentiful ['plentiful], *a.* abondant.
plenty ['plenti], *n.* abondance, *f.*; *plenty
of*, beaucoup de.
plethora ['pleθərə], *n.* pléthore, *f.*
pleurisy ['pluərəsi], *n.* pleurésie, *f.*
pliable ['plaiəbl], *a.* pliable, flexible.
pliancy ['plaiənsi], *n.* flexibilité, *f.*
pliant ['plaiənt], *a.* pliant, flexible.
pliers ['plaiəz], *n.pl.* pinces, *f.pl.*
plight [plait], *n.* état, *m.*, condition; situation
difficile, *f.*—*v.t.* engager.
plinth [plinθ], *n.* plinthe, *f.*
plod [plɔd], *v.i.* marcher péniblement; (*fig.*)
peiner, travailler assidûment.
plodder ['plɔdə], *n.* piocheur, *m.*
plodding ['plɔdiŋ], *a.* laborieux, piocheur.—
n. travail pénible, *m.*
plop [plɔp], *adv.*, *n.*, *int.* plouf, flac, pouf, *m.*
plot [plɔt], *n.* complot; petit terrain, *m.*;
intrigue (*d'une pièce etc.*), *f.*; *building-
plot*, lotissement, *m.*—*v.t.* comploter;
(*Surv.*) faire le plan de.—*v.i.* comploter.
plotter ['plɔtə], *n.* conspirateur, comploteur,
m.
plotting ['plɔtiŋ], *n.* complots, *m.pl.*; (*Surv.*)
action de rapporter, *f.*
plough [plau], *n.* charrue, *f.*; *the Plough*, le
Chariot, *m.*, la Grande-Ourse, *f.*—*v.t.*
labourer; (*fig.*) sillonner.—*v.i.* labourer.
ploughing ['plauiŋ], *n.* labourage, *m.*
ploughman ['plaumən], *n.* (*pl.* **-men** [men])
laboureur, *m.*
ploughshare ['plauʃɛə], *n.* soc de charrue, *m.*
plover ['plʌvə], *n.* (*Orn.*) pluvier, vanneau, *m.*
plow, see **plough**.
pluck [plʌk], *v.t.* cueillir (*fleurs, fruits etc.*);
plumer (*volaille*); épiler (*sourcils*).—*n.* cœur,
courage, *m.*
pluckily ['plʌkili], *adv.* courageusement.

plucky ['plʌki], a. courageux.
plug [plʌg], n. tampon, bouchon, m.; bonde (de tonneau); (Elec.) prise de courant; (Teleph.) fiche, f.; **spark plug**, bougie (d'allumage), f.—v.t. tamponner, boucher.
plum [plʌm], n. prune, f.
plumage ['plu:midʒ], n. plumage, m.
plumb [plʌm], a. droit, vertical.—adv. à plomb; (Am., colloq.) complètement.—v.t. plomber; (Naut.) sonder.—n. plomb, m.
plumber ['plʌmə], n. plombier, m.
plumbing ['plʌmiŋ], n. plomberie; tuyauterie, f.
plumb line ['plʌmlain], n. fil à plomb, m.
plume [plu:m], n. plume, f; plumet, m.—v.t. plumer.
plummet ['plʌmit], n. plomb, m.
plump (1) [plʌmp], a. dodu, potelé, gras.
plump (2) [plʌmp], adv. tout d'un coup; droit—v.i. **to plump for**, donner tous ses votes pour.
plumpness ['plʌmpnis], n. embonpoint, m., rondeur, f.
plum tree ['plʌmtri:], n. prunier, m.
plunder ['plʌndə], v.t. piller, dépouiller.—n. butin (chose pillée); pillage (acte de piller), m.
plunderer ['plʌndərə], n. pillard, m.
plunge [plʌndʒ], v.t. plonger, précipiter.—v.i. plonger; se précipiter.—n. plongeon, m.
plural ['pluərəl], a. and n. pluriel, m.
plus [plʌs], prep. (Math.) plus.—a. positif.—n. plus, m.—adv. et davantage.
plush [plʌʃ], n. peluche, f.
plutocrat ['plu:tokræt], n. ploutocrate, m., f.
plutocratic [plu:to'krætik], a. ploutocratique.
plutonium [plu'tounjəm], n. plutonium, m.
pluvial ['plu:viəl], a. pluvial.
ply (1) [plai], v.t. manier (fortement); exercer, employer; presser (quelqu'un de prendre quelque chose).—v.i. travailler; faire le service.
ply (2) [plai], n. pli (de tissu); fil (de laine); toron (de corde), m.
plywood ['plaiwud], n. contre-plaqué, m.
pneumatic [nju'mætik], a. pneumatique.
pneumonia [nju'mounia], n. pneumonie, f.
poach (1) [poutʃ], v.t. braconner, voler.—v.i. braconner.
poach (2) [poutʃ], v.t. pocher (œufs).
poacher ['poutʃə], n. braconnier, m.
poaching ['poutʃiŋ], n. braconnage, m.
pock [pɔk], n. pustule (de petite vérole), f.
pocket ['pɔkit], n. poche, f.; gousset (de gilet), m.; blouse (de billard), f.—v.t. empocher, mettre en poche.
pocket-book ['pɔkitbuk], n. portefeuille (pour l'argent); livre de poche; calepin (carnet), m.
pocketful ['pɔkitful], n. pleine poche, f.
pocket-knife ['pɔkitnaif], n. couteau de poche, canif, m.
pocket money ['pɔkitmʌni], n. argent de poche, m.
pod [pɔd], n. cosse, gousse, f.—v.t. écosser.
podgy ['pɔdʒi], a. gras, potelé.
poem ['pouim], n. poème, m.
***poesy** ['pouizi], n. poésie, f.
poet ['pouit], n. poète, m.
poetaster ['pouitæstə], n. rimailleur, m.
poetess [poui'tes], n. poétesse, f.
poetic [pou'etik], **poetical** [pou'etikəl], a. poétique.

poetry ['pouitri], n. poésie, f.
poignancy ['pɔinjənsi], n. piquant, m.; nature poignante, f.
poignant ['pɔinjənt], a. piquant, vif, poignant.
poignantly ['pɔinjəntli], adv. d'une manière piquante.
point [pɔint], n. point (endroit), m.; pointe (bout aiguisé etc.), f.; (Compass) quart de vent; (Spt.) point; (fig.) but; (pl.) (Rail.) aiguillage, m.; **decimal point**, virgule, f.; **in point of fact**, en effet; **not to the point**, hors de propos; **that is not the point**, ce n'est pas là la question; **to make a point of**, se faire un devoir de; **to the point**, à propos.—v.t. aiguiser, tailler (affiler); indiquer; pointer (fusils etc.); (Build.) jointoyer; **to point out**, signaler; faire remarquer.—v.i. se tourner (vers); tomber en arrêt (chiens); **to point at**, montrer du doigt, indiquer.
point-blank ['pɔint'blæŋk], adv. à bout portant; à brûle-pourpoint, carrément.
pointed ['pɔintid], a. pointu; (fig.) mordant.
pointedly ['pɔintidli], adv. d'une manière piquante.
pointer ['pɔintə], n. index; chien d'arrêt, m.
pointing ['pɔintiŋ], n. (Build.) jointoiement, m.
pointless ['pɔintlis], a. sans pointe; (fig.) inutile, plat.
pointsman ['pɔintsmən], n. (pl. -men [men]) (Rail.) aiguilleur, m.
poise [pɔiz], n. poids, équilibre, m.—v.t. balancer, tenir en équilibre.
poison [pɔizn], n. poison, m.—v.t. empoisonner.
poisoner ['pɔiznə], n. empoisonneur, m.
poisoning ['pɔizniŋ], n. empoisonnement, m.
poisonous ['pɔiznəs], a. vénéneux (plante); venimeux (serpent etc.); toxique (gaz).
poke (1) [pouk], n. coup de coude ou de poing, m.—v.t. fourrer; pousser (des doigts); remuer, fourgonner (le feu); **to poke fun at**, se moquer de.—v.i. **to poke about**, tâtonner.
poke (2) [pouk], n. *sac, m.; poche, f.
poker ['poukə], n. tisonnier; (Cards) poker, m.
poky ['pouki], a. (colloq.) petit, mesquin.
Poland ['pouland], la Pologne, f.
polar ['poulə], a. polaire.
Pole [poul], n. Polonais (personne), m.
pole (1) [poul], n. perche, f.; bâton (de rideau); timon (d'une voiture); échalas (de vignes etc.); mât (de drapeau etc.); poteau (télégraphique), m.
pole (2) [poul], n. (Astron., Geog.) pôle, m.
poleaxe ['poulæks], n. hache d'armes, f.; assommoir, merlin, m.—v.t. assommer.
polecat ['poulkæt], n. putois, m.
polemics [pə'lemiks], n.pl. polémique, f.
pole-star ['poulsta:], n. étoile polaire, f.
pole vault ['poulvo:lt], n. saut à la perche, m.
police [pə'li:s], n. police, f.; **county police**, gendarmerie, f.; **police court**, tribunal de simple police, m.; **police station**, commissariat ou poste de police, m.—v.t. policer.
policeman [pə'li:smən], n. (pl. -men [men]) agent de police, gardien de la paix, m.
policewoman [pə'li:swumən], n. (pl. -women [wimin]) femme agent, f.
policy ['pɔlisi], n. politique, f.; plan, m.; **insurance policy**, police d'assurance, f.

poliomyelitis ['pouliomaia'laitis], (*fam.*) **pollo** ['pouliou], *n.* poliomyélite, *f.*

Polish ['pouliʃ], *a.* polonais.—*n.* polonais (*langue*), *m.*

polish ['poliʃ], *v.t.* polir; vernir (*meubles*); cirer (*chaussures*).—*v.i.* se polir.—*n.* poli, *m.*; (*fig.*) élégance, *f.*; *floor polish*, cire à parquet, *f. shoe polish*, cirage, *m.*

polished ['poliʃt], *a.* poli.

polisher ['poliʃə], *n.* polisseur; polissoir (*outil*), *m.*; *floor polisher*, cireur de parquet, *m.*

polite [pə'lait], *a.* poli, élégant, complaisant (*pour*).

politely [pə'laitli], *adv.* poliment.

politeness [pə'laitnis], *n.* politesse, *f.*

politic ['politik], *a.* politique.

political [pə'litikl], *a.* politique.

politically [pə'litikli], *adv.* politiquement.

politician [poli'tiʃən], *n.* homme politique; (*pej.*) politicien, *m.*

politics ['politiks], *n.pl.* politique, *f.*

poll [poul], *n.* (*Anat.*) *tête; liste électorale; élection, *f.*, scrutin; sondage (*de l'opinion publique*), *m.*—*v.t.* étêter (*arbres*); voter; obtenir (*un certain nombre de votes*).

pollen ['polən], *n.* pollen, *m.*

pollination [poli'neiʃən], *n.* pollination, *f.*

polling ['poulin], *n.* élection, *f.*; *polling booth*, bureau de scrutin, *m.*

pollute [pə'lju:t], *v.t.* polluer, souiller (*de*).

pollution [pə'lju:ʃən], *n.* pollution, souillure, *f.*

polo ['poulou], *n.* polo, *m.*

polygamist [pə'ligəmist], *n.* polygame, *m.,f.*

polygamy [pə'ligəmi], *n.* polygamie, *f.*

polyglot ['poliglot], *a.* and *n.* polyglotte, *m.,f.*

polygon ['poligən], *n.* polygone, *m.*

Polynesia [poli'ni:ziə], la Polynésie, *f.*

polypus ['polipəs], *n.* polype, *m.*

polytechnic [poli'teknik], *a.* polytechnique. —*n.* école d'arts et métiers, *f.*

pomade [pə'meid], *n.* pommade, *f.*

pomegranate ['pomgrænit], *n.* grenade, *f.*; *pomegranate tree*, grenadier, *m.*

pommel [pʌml], *v.t.* battre, rosser.—*n.* pommeau (*d'une selle, d'une epée etc.*), *m.*

pomp [pomp], *n.* pompe, *f.*, éclat, faste, *m.*

Pompey ['pompi]. Pompée, *f.*

pompon ['pompon], *n.* pompon, *m.*

pomposity [pom'positi], *n.* pompe, *f.*

pompous ['pompəs], *a.* pompeux, fastueux.

pompously ['pompəsli], *adv.* pompeusement.

pond [pond], *n.* étang, vivier, *m.*; mare (*pool*), *f.*

ponder ['pondə], *v.t.* peser, considérer, réfléchir à.—*v.i.* méditer.

ponderous ['pondərəs], *a.* lourd, pesant.

ponderously ['pondərəsli], *adv.* pesamment.

pontiff ['pontif], *n.* pontife, *m.*

pontificate [pon'tifikeit], *n.* pontificat, *m.*—*v.i.* pontifier.

Pontius Pilate ['pontʃəs'pailət]. Ponce Pilate, *m.*

pontoon [pon'tu:n], *n.* ponton, *m.*; (*Cards*) vingt-et-un, *m.*

pony ['pouni], *n.* poney, petit cheval, *m.*

poodle [pu:dl], *n.* caniche, *m.*

pooh! [pu:], *int.* bah! allons donc!

pooh-pooh ['pu:'pu:], *v.t.* tourner en ridicule.

pool [pu:l], *n.* étang, *m.*, mare; piscine (*pour nager*); (*Cards, Billiards etc.*) poule; mise en commun, *f.*—*v.t.* mettre en commun.

poop [pu:p], *n.* dunette, poupe, *f.*

poor [puə], *a.* pauvre, indigent; malheureux (*sans joie*); triste (*de pauvre qualité*); mauvais (*pas bon*).

poor-box ['puəboks], *n.* tronc des pauvres, *m.*

poor-house ['puəhaus], *n.* asile des indigents, *m.*

***poor-law** ['puələ:], *n.* loi sur l'assistance publique, *f.*

poorly ['puəli], *a.* indisposé, souffrant.—*adv.* pauvrement, mal, tristement.

poorness ['puənis], *n.* pauvreté; médiocrité, *f.*

pop (1) [pop], *n.* petit bruit vif et sec, *m.*; (*colloq.*) boisson pétillante, *f.*—*v.t.* pousser, fourrer *ou* mettre subitement.—*v.i.* entrer *ou* sortir subitement.—*int.* crac! pan!

pop (2) [pop], *n.* (*Am.colloq.*) papa, *m.*

pop (3) [pop], *a.* and *n.* (*colloq.*) (musique) populaire, *f.*; *the pops*, les chansons en vogue, *f.pl.*

Pope [Poup], *n.* Pape, *m.*

popedom ['poupdəm], *n.* papauté, *f.*

popery ['poupəri], *n.* papisme, *m.*

popish ['poupiʃ], *a.* papiste; de papiste (*choses*).

poplar ['poplə], *n.* (*Bot.*) peuplier, *m.*

poplin ['poplin], *n.* popeline, *f.*

poppet ['popit], *n.* poupée, marionnette, *f.*

poppy ['popi], *n.* pavot (*cultivé*); coquelicot (*sauvage*), *m.*

populace ['popjuləs], *n.* populace, *f.*

popular ['popjulə], *a.* populaire; en vogue.

popularity [popju'læriti], *n.* popularité, *f.*

popularize ['popjuləraiz], *v.t.* populariser.

popularly ['popjuləli], *adv.* populairement.

populate ['popjuleit], *v.t.* peupler.

population [popju'leiʃən], *n.* population, *f.*

populous ['popjuləs], *a.* populeux.

porcelain ['po:slin], *n.* porcelaine, *f.*

porch [po:tʃ], *n.* porche, *m.*

porcupine ['po:kjupain], *n.* porc-épic, *m.*

pore (1) [po:], *n.* pore, *m.*

pore (2) [po:], *v.i.* regarder avec grande attention; *to pore over*, dévorer (*un livre*).

pork [po:k], *n.* porc, *m.*

pork-butcher ['po:kbutʃə], *n.* charcutier, *m.*; *pork-butcher's shop*, charcuterie, *f.*

porker ['po:kə], *n.* porc d'engrais, cochon, *m.*

pork pie ['po:k'pai], *n.* pâté de porc, *m.*

pornography [po:'nogrəfi], *n.* pornographie, *f.*

porous ['po:rəs], *a.* poreux.

porphyry ['po:firi], *n.* porphyre, *m.*

porpoise ['po:pəs], *n.* marsouin, *m.*

porridge ['poridʒ], *n.* bouillie, *f.*

porringer ['porindʒə], *n.* bol à bouillie, *m.*

port (1) [po:t], *n.* port (*ville maritime*), *m.*

port (2) [po:t], *n.* (*Naut.*) bâbord, *m.*

port (3) [po:t], *n.* porto (*vin*), *m.*

portable ['po:təbl], *a.* portatif, transportable.

portal ['po:tl], *n.* portail, *m.*

portcullis [po:t'kalis], *n.* herse, *f.*

portend [po:'tend], *v.t.* présager, augurer.

portent ['po:tənt], *n.* mauvais augure, *m.*

portentous [po:'tentəs], *a.* de mauvais augure.

porter ['po:tə], *n.* commissionnaire; concierge (*de maison*); porteur (*de rue*); (*Rail.*) porteur, *m.*

porterage ['po:təridʒ], *n.* port; factage, *m.*

portfolio [pɔːtˈfouliou], n. carton, m.; serviette, f.; (Polit.) portefeuille, m.

port-hole [ˈpɔːthoul], n. sabord, m.

portico [ˈpɔːtikou], n. portique, m.

portion [ˈpɔːʃən], n. partie, part; dot (de mariage), f.—v.t. partager; doter (pour le mariage).

portliness [ˈpɔːtlinis], n. corpulence, f.

portly [ˈpɔːtli], a. d'un port majestueux; corpulent.

portmanteau [pɔːtˈmæntou], n. valise, f.

portrait [ˈpɔːtrit], n. portrait, m.

portray [pɔːˈtrei], v.t. peindre; (fig.) dépeindre, décrire.

Portugal [ˈpɔːtʃug(ə)l]. le Portugal, m.

Portuguese [pɔːtʃuˈgiːz], a. portugais.—n. portugais (langue); Portugais (personne), m.

pose [pouz], v.t. embarrasser, confondre; poser (une question).—v.i. poser (avec affectation).—n. pose, f.

poser [ˈpouzə], n. question embarrassante, f.

poseur [pouˈzə:], n. poseur, m.

position [pəˈziʃən], n. situation, position, f.

positive [ˈpozitiv], a. positif; absolu, sûr; décisif.—n. positif, m.

positively [ˈpozitivli], adv. positivement; absolument.

positiveness [ˈpozitivnis], n. nature positive, f.

posse [ˈposi], n. détachement (d'agents de police), m.

possess [pəˈzes], v.t. posséder; avoir; jouir de.

possession [pəˈzeʃən], n. possession, f.

possessive [pəˈzesiv], a. possessif.

possessor [pəˈzesə], n. possesseur, m.

*posset [ˈposit], n. lait caillé au vin, m.

possibility [posiˈbiliti], n. possibilité, f.; moyen (façon), m.

possible [ˈposibl], a. possible.

possibly [ˈposibli], adv. peut-être.

post (1) [poust], n. emploi; (Mil.) poste; courrier (livraison de lettres), m.; (Post office) poste, f.—v.t. mettre à la poste; (Mil. etc.) poster, affecter.

post (2) [poust], n. poteau (en bois); montant (de porte), m.—v.t. afficher.

postage [ˈpoustidʒ], n. port de lettre, port, affranchissement, f.

postage stamp [ˈpoustidʒstæmp], n. timbre-poste, m.

postal [ˈpoustəl], a. postal; postal order, mandat-poste, m.

postcard [ˈpoustkɑːd], n. carte postale, f.

postdate [poustˈdeit], v.t. postdater.

poster [ˈpoustə], n. affiche, f., placard, m.

posterior [posˈtiəriə], a. postérieur.

posterity [posˈteriti], n. postérité, f.

postern [ˈpoustəːn], a. de derrière.—n. poterne, f.

post-haste [poustˈheist], adv. en grande hâte.

posthumous [ˈpostjuməs], a. posthume.

posthumously [ˈpostjuməsli], adv. après décès.

postilion [posˈtiliən], n. postillon, m.

postman [ˈpoustmən], n. (pl. -men [men]) facteur, m.

postmark [ˈpoustmɑːk], n. cachet de la poste, m.

postmaster [ˈpoustmɑːstə], n. receveur des postes, m.

post meridiem [ˈpoustməˈridiəm], (abbr.

p.m. [ˈpiːˈem]) adv. de l'après-midi, du soir.

post-mortem [poustˈmɔːtəm], adv. après décès.—n. autopsie, f.

post office [ˈpoustɔfis], n. bureau de poste, m., poste, f.

postpone [poustˈpoun], v.t. ajourner, différer, remettre.

postponement [poustˈpounmənt], n. ajournement, m., remise, f.

postscript [ˈpoustskript], (abbr. P.S. [ˈpiːˈes]) n. post-scriptum, m.

postulate [ˈpostjuleit], v.t. postuler.

posture [ˈpostʃə], n. posture, pose, f.

post-war [poustˈwɔː], a. d'après guerre.

posy [ˈpouzi], n. petit bouquet, m.

pot [pot], n. pot, m.; marmite, f.; pots and pans, batterie de cuisine, f.—v.t. empoter, mettre en pot.

potable [ˈpoutəbl], a. potable.

potash [ˈpotæʃ], n. potasse, f.

potassium [pəˈtæsiəm], n. potassium, m.

potato [pəˈteitou], n. (pl. potatoes [pəˈtei touz]) pomme de terre, f.

pot-bellied [ˈpotbelid], a. pansu, ventru.

potency [ˈpoutənsi], n. puissance, force, f.

potent [ˈpoutənt], a. puissant, fort; (fig.) efficace.

potentate [ˈpoutənteit], n. potentat, m.

potential [pəˈtenʃəl], a. potentiel, latent.—n. (Elec. etc.) potentiel, m.

potful [ˈpotful], n. potée, f.

*pother [ˈpoðə], n. tumulte; bruit, m.

pot-hole [ˈpothoul], n. (Geol.) marmite torrentielle; (Motor.) flache, f.

pot-holer [ˈpothoulə], n. spéléologue, m., f.

pot-holing [ˈpothoulin], n. spéléologie, f.

pothook [ˈpothuk], n. crémaillère, f.

potion [ˈpouʃən], n. potion, f.; breuvage, m.

pot-luck [ˈpotˈlʌk], n. fortune du pot, f.

pot shot [ˈpotʃot], n. coup tiré au petit bonheur, m.

*pottage [ˈpotidʒ], n. potage (épais), m.

potted [ˈpotid], a. en pot, en terrine; potted meat, conserve de viande, f.

potter [ˈpotə], n. potier, m.—v.i. to potter about, s'amuser à des riens.

pottery [ˈpotəri], n. poterie, f.

potting [ˈpotin], a. potting shed, serre, resserre, f.—n. (Hort.) mise en pot, f.

pouch [pautʃ], n. poche, f., petit sac, m.; blague (à tabac), f.

poulterer [ˈpoultərə], n. marchand de volailles, m.

poultice [ˈpoultis], n. cataplasme, m.—v.t. mettre un cataplasme à.

poultry [ˈpoultri], n. volaille, f.

pounce [pauns], v.i. fondre (sur).

pound [paund], n. livre; livre sterling; fourrière (clôture), f.—v.t. broyer; (Metal.) bocarder.

poundage [ˈpaundidʒ], n. commission de tant par livre, f.

pounding [ˈpaundiŋ], n. broiement; (Metal.) bocardage, m.

pour [pɔː], v.t. verser.—v.i. couler; pleuvoir à verse (pluie).

pouring [ˈpɔːriŋ], a. torrentiel (pluie).

pout [paut], v.i. bouder, faire la moue.—n. bouderie, moue, f.

pouting [ˈpautiŋ], a. qui fait la moue; boudeur.

517

poverty ['povəti], *n.* pauvreté, misère, indigence, *f.*
poverty-stricken ['povətistrikn], *a.* réduit à la misère, indigent.
powder ['paudə], *n.* poudre, *f.*; *face powder*, poudre de riz; *gunpowder*, poudre à canon; *tooth powder*, poudre dentifrice.—*v.t.* réduire en poudre; poudrer (*les cheveux*); (*Cook.*) saupoudrer; *to powder one's face*, se poudrer.
powder compact ['paudəkompækt], *n.* poudrier (*de dame*), *m.*
powdered ['paudəd], *a.* pulvérisé; poudré (*cheveux*).
powder puff ['paudəpʌf], *n.* houppe, *f.*, pompon, *m.*
powdery ['paudəri], *a.* poudreux; friable.
power ['pauə], *n.* pouvoir, *m.*; force (*physique*); autorité, puissance (*morale*), *f.*; *the Great Powers*, les grandes puissances, *f.pl.*; *to be in power*, être au pouvoir.
powerful ['pauəful], *a.* puissant, fort.
powerfully ['pauəfuli], *adv.* puissamment, fortement.
powerless ['pauəlis], *a.* impuissant, faible.
power station ['pauəsteiʃən], *n.* usine génératrice, centrale électrique, *f.*
pox [poks], *n.* vérole, *f.*; *chicken pox*, varicelle, *f.*; *small-pox*, petite vérole, variole, *f.*
practicability [præktikə'biliti], *n.* possibilité, praticabilité, *f.*
practicable ['præktikəbl], *a.* praticable.
practical ['præktikl], *a.* pratique; *practical joke*, mauvaise farce, *f.*
practically ['præktikli], *adv.* en pratique; à peu près.
practice ['præktis], *n.* pratique, habitude, *f.*, usage, exercice, *m.*; clientèle (*de médecin, d'avocat etc.*); intrigue, *f.*
practice ['præktis], *v.t.* pratiquer, mettre en pratique; exercer, pratiquer (*une profession etc.*); (*Mus.*) étudier.—*v.i.* (*Mus.*) étudier; s'exercer (*à*); exercer, faire de la clientèle (*médecin*).
practised ['præktist], *a.* exercé (*à*); versé (*dans*); habile.
practising ['præktisiŋ], *a.* praticien, exerçant.
practitioner [præk'tiʃənə], *n.* praticien, *m.*; *general practitioner*, médecin ordinaire, *m.*; *medical practitioner*, médecin, *m.*
pragmatic [præg'mætik], **pragmatical** [præg'mætikəl], *a.* pragmatique; officieux; infatué de soi.
pragmatism ['prægmətizm], *n.* pragmatisme, *m.*
prairie ['prɛəri], *n.* prairie, savane, *f.*
praise [preiz], *n.* louange, *f.*, éloge, *m.*—*v.t.* louer, faire l'éloge de; vanter.
praiseworthy ['preizwə:ði], *a.* louable, digne d'éloges.
pram [præm], *n.* voiture d'enfant, *f.*
prance [prɑːns], *v.i.* fringuer (*cheval*).
prancing ['prɑːnsiŋ], *a.* fringant.
prank [præŋk], *n.* escapade, niche, *f.*, tour, *m.*
prate [preit], *v.i.* jaser, babiller, bavarder (*de*).
prating ['preitiŋ], *a.* bavard, babillard.
pratingly ['preitiŋli], *adv.* en bavard, en babillard.
prattle [prætl], *v.i.* babiller, jaser, caqueter.—*n.* babil, caquetage, bavardage, *m.*

prattler ['prætlə], *n.* bavard, babillard, *m.*
prattling ['prætliŋ], *n.* bavardage, caquet, *m.*
prawn [prɔːn], *n.* crevette rouge; salicoque, *f.*
pray [prei], *v.t.* prier, supplier.—*v.i.* prier.
prayer [prɛə], *n.* prière, supplication; (*Law*) demande, *f.*; *the Lord's Prayer*, l'oraison dominicale, *f.*
prayer book ['prɛəbuk], *n.* livre de prières, *m.*; liturgie, *f.*
preach [priːtʃ], *v.t.*, *v.i.* prêcher.
preacher ['priːtʃə], *n.* prédicateur, *m.*
preaching ['priːtʃiŋ], *n.* prédication, *f.*
preamble [priː'æmbl], *n.* préambule, *m.*
prearrange [priːə'reindʒ], *v.t.* arranger d'avance.
prebendary ['prebəndəri], *n.* chanoine, prébendier, *m.*
precarious [pri'kɛəriəs], *a.* précaire.
precariously [pri'kɛəriəsli], *adv.* précairement.
precariousness [pri'kɛəriəsnis], *n.* nature précaire; incertitude, *f.*
precaution [pri'kɔːʃən], *n.* précaution, *f.*
precautionary [pri'kɔːʃənri], *a.* de précaution.
precede [pri'siːd], *v.t.* précéder.
precedence ['presidəns], *n.* préséance, *f.*; *to have* or *take precedence over*, avoir le pas sur.
precedent (1) [pri'siːdənt], **preceding** [pri'siːdiŋ], *a.* précédent.
precedent (2) ['presidənt], *n.* précédent, *m.*
precept ['priːsept], *n.* précepte, *m.*
precinct ['priːsiŋkt], *n.* limite, borne, enceinte, *f.*
precious ['preʃəs], *a.* précieux; affecté; (*fam.*) fameux, fichu.
preciously ['preʃəsli], *adv.* précieusement; (*fam.*) fameusement, diablement.
preciousness ['preʃəsnis], *n.* haute valeur, *f.*
precipice ['presipis], *n.* précipice, *m.*
precipitate (1) [pri'sipitit], *a.* précipité.—*n.* (*Chem.*) précipité, *m.*
precipitate (2) [pri'sipiteit], *v.t.* précipiter.—*v.i.* se précipiter.
precipitation [prisipi'teiʃən], *n.* précipitation, *f.*
precipitous [pri'sipitəs], *a.* escarpé, abrupt.
precipitously [pri'sipitəsli], *adv.* à pic, en précipice; (*fig.*) précipitamment.
precise [pri'sais], *a.* précis, exact; formaliste, pointilleux, scrupuleux.
precisely [pri'saisli], *adv.* précisément.
precision [pri'siʒən], *n.* précision, exactitude, *f.*
preclude [pri'kluːd], *v.t.* exclure; empêcher (*mettre obstacle à*).
preclusion [pri'kluːʒən], *n.* exclusion, *f.*
precocious [pri'kouʃəs], *a.* précoce.
precociousness [pri'kouʃəsnis], *n.* précocité, *f.*
preconceived ['priːkən'siːvd], *a.* formé d'avance; *preconceived idea*, idée préconçue, *f.*
precursor [pri'kə:sə], *n.* précurseur, avant-coureur, *m.*
predatory ['predətəri], *a.* de rapine, de proie, pillard, rapace.
predecease ['priːdi'siːs], *v.t.* prédécéder.
predestinate [pri'destineit], **predestine** [pri'destin], *v.t.* prédestiner.

predestination [priːˈdestiˈneiʃən], n. prédestination, f.
predetermine [priːdiˈtəːmin], v.t. prédéterminer, arrêter d'avance.
predicament [priˈdikəmənt], n. état, m., position difficile, situation fâcheuse; catégorie, f., ordre, m.
predicate [ˈpredikit], n. prédicat, attribut, m.
predict [priˈdikt], v.t. prédire.
prediction [priˈdikʃən], n. prédiction, prévision, f.
predilection [priːdiˈlekʃən], n. prédilection, f.
predispose [priːdisˈpouz], v.t. prédisposer.
predisposition [priːdispəˈziʃən], n. prédisposition, f.
predominance [priˈdɔminəns], n. prédominance, f., ascendant, m.
predominant [priˈdɔminənt], a. prédominant.
predominantly [priˈdɔminəntli], adv. d'une manière prédominante.
predominate [priˈdɔmineit], v.i. prédominer, prévaloir.
pre-eminence [priːˈeminəns], n. prééminence, supériorité, f.
pre-eminent [priːˈeminənt], a. prééminent.
pre-eminently [priːˈeminəntli], adv. par excellence.
preen [priːn], v.t lisser, nettoyer (ses plumes); *to preen oneself*, se piquer.
pre-engage [priːinˈgeidʒ], v.t. engager d'avance.
pre-exist [priːigˈzist], v.i. préexister.
pre-existence [priːigˈzistəns], n. préexistence, f.
prefabricate [priːˈfæbrikeit], v.t. préfabriquer.
preface [ˈprefis], n. préface, f.; avant-propos, m.—v.t. faire une préface à.
prefect [ˈpriːfekt], n. préfet; (Sch.) surveillant, m.
prefer [priˈfəː], v.t. préférer, aimer mieux; avancer, élever (aux honneurs); porter (une accusation).
preferable [ˈprefərəbl], a. préférable (à).
preferably [ˈprefərəbli], adv. préférablement, de préférence.
preference [ˈprefərəns], n. préférence, f.
preferential [prefəˈrenʃl], a. préférentiel.
preferment [priˈfəːmənt], n. avancement, m., promotion, f.
prefix [ˈpriːfiks], n. (Gram.) préfixe, m.
pregnancy [ˈpregnənsi], n. grossesse, f.
pregnant [ˈpregnənt], a. enceinte, grosse; (fig.) gros, plein (de); fertile, fécond (en).
prehensile [priˈhensail], a. préhensile.
prehistoric [priːhisˈtɔrik], a. préhistorique.
prejudge [priːˈdʒʌdʒ], v.t. juger d'avance.
prejudice [ˈpredʒudis], v.t. prévenir, nuire à (faire du tort à).—n. prévention, f., préjugé; préjudice, tort (détriment), m.
prejudiced [ˈpredʒudist], a. prévenu.
prejudicial [predʒuˈdiʃl], a. préjudiciable, nuisible (à).
prelate [ˈprelit], n. prélat, m.
preliminary [priˈliminəri], a. and n. préliminaire, m.
prelude [ˈpreljuːd], n. prélude, m.
premature [ˈpremətjuə], a. prématuré.

prematurely [preməˈtjuəli], adv. prématurément.
premeditate [priˈmediteit], v.t. préméditer.
premeditated [priˈmediteitid], a. prémédité.
premeditation [primediˈteiʃən], n. préméditation, f.
premier [ˈpriːmiə, ˈpremiə], a. premier (de rang).—n. premier ministre, m.
premise [ˈpremis], n. (Log.) prémisse, f.
premises [ˈpremisiz], n.pl. lieux, m.pl.; établissement, local, m.
premium [ˈpriːmiəm], n. prime, f.; prix, m.
premonition [priːməˈniʃən], n. avertissement; pressentiment, m.
prenatal [priːˈneitl], a. prénatal.
preoccupied [priːˈɔkjupaid], a. préoccupé.
preordain [priːɔːˈdein], v.t. ordonner ou arranger d'avance.
prep [prep], a. (Sch. fam. abbr. preparatory) préparatoire.
prepaid [priːˈpeid], a. affranchi, franc de port.—adv. franco.
preparation [prepəˈreiʃən], n. préparation, f.; préparatifs, apprêts (de voyage etc.), m.pl.
preparatory [priˈpærətri], a. préparatoire.
prepare [priˈpeə], v.t. préparer.—v.i. se préparer, s'apprêter (à).
preparedness [priˈpeə(ri)dnis], n. état de préparation, f.
prepay [priːˈpei], v.t. irr (conjug. like PAY) payer d'avance; affranchir (lettres).
prepayment [priːˈpeimənt], n. payement d'avance; affranchissement (de lettres), m.
preponderance [priˈpɔndərəns], n. prépondérance, f.
preponderant [priˈpɔndərənt], a. prépondérant.
preponderate [priˈpɔndəreit], v.i. avoir la prépondérance, l'emporter (sur).
preposition [prepəˈziʃən], n. préposition, f.
prepossessing [priːpəˈzesiŋ], a. prévenant, engageant.
preposterous [priˈpɔstərəs], a. absurde, déraisonnable.
preposterously [priˈpɔstərəsli], adv. absurdement, déraisonnablement.
prerogative [priˈrɔgətiv], n. prérogative, f.
Presbyterian [prezbiˈtiəriən], a. and n. presbytérien, m.
Presbyterianism [prezbiˈtiəriənizm], n. presbytérianisme, m.
presbytery [ˈprezbitəri], n. presbytère, m.
prescience [ˈpreʃəns], n. prescience, f.
prescribe [priˈskraib], v.t. prescrire; (Med.) ordonner.—v.i. (Med.) faire une ordonnance.
prescription [priˈskripʃən], n. (Law) prescription; (Med.) ordonnance, f.
presence [ˈprezəns], n. présence, f.; air, maintien, m., mine (aspect); personnage supérieur, m.; *presence of mind*, présence d'esprit.
present [ˈprezənt], a. présent; actuel; *at the present moment*, à présent, actuellement; *to be present at*, assister à.—n. présent; cadeau, don, m.; *for the present*, pour le moment.—[priˈzent], v.t. présenter, offrir (à).
presentable [priˈzentəbl], a. présentable.
presentation [prezənˈteiʃən], n. présentation, f.; don, m.

519

presentiment [pri'zentimənt], *n.* pressentiment, *m.*

presently ['prezntli], *adv.* tout à l'heure, bientôt; à présent, actuellement.

preservation [prezə'veiʃən], *n.* salut, *m.*, conservation; préservation (*de*), *f.*

preservative [pri'zə:vətiv], *a.* and *n.* préservateur, préservatif, *m.*

preserve [pri'zə:v], *n.* confiture, *f.*, conserves, *f.pl.*; réserve, chasse réservée, *f.*—*v.t.* préserver (*de*); conserver; confire (*fruits etc.*); *preserved fruits*, fruits confits, *m.pl.*; *preserved meat*, conserves de viande, *f.pl.*

preserver [pri'zə:və], *n.* sauveur; conservateur, *m.*; *life preserver*, see **life-belt**.

preside [pri'zaid], *v.i.* présider (à).

presidency ['prezidənsi], *n.* présidence, *f.*

president ['prezidənt], *n.* président, *m.*; *vice president*, vice-président, *m.*

presidential [prezi'denʃəl], *a.* présidentiel; de président.

presiding [pri'zaidiŋ], *a.* présidant.

press (1) [pres], *v.t.* presser; serrer, étreindre; satiner (*papier*); pressurer (*fruits*); repasser (*vêtements*); (*fig.*) insister sur.—*v.i.* presser, pousser; avancer; se presser.—*n.* presse, pression, *f.*; pressoir (*à fruits etc.*), *m.*; armoire à linge, *f.*; *the press*, la presse, *f.*

press (2) [pres], *v.t.* enrôler (*marins*) de force.

press agency ['presidʒənsi], *n.* agence de presse, *f.*

press clipping ['presklipiŋ], *n.* coupure de journal, *f.*

pressed [prest], *a.* satiné; *hard pressed*, serré de près; aux abois; *pressed for time*, très pressé.

*press gang ['presgæŋ], *n.* (*Naut.*) presse, *f.*

pressing ['presiŋ], *a.* urgent, pressant.

pressman ['presmən], *n.* (*pl.* **-men** [men]) journaliste, reporter, *m.*

pressure ['preʃə], *n.* pression; tension; urgence, *f.*; poids (*lourdeur*), *m.*; *blood pressure*, tension artérielle.

pressure cooker ['preʃəkukə], *n.* autoclave; auto-cuiseur, *m.*, cocotte-minute, *f.*

pressure gauge ['preʃəgeidʒ], *n.* manomètre, *m.*

pressurize ['preʃəraiz], *v.t.* pressuriser.

prestige [pres'ti:ʒ], *n.* prestige, *m.*

presumably [pri'zju:məbli], *adv.* probablement.

presume [pri'zju:m], *v.t.* présumer; supposer.—*v.i.* présumer se permettre, avoir l'audace (*de*), prendre la liberté (*de*); *to presume upon*, présumer trop de.

presuming [pri'zju:miŋ], *a.* présomptueux, indiscret.

presumption [pri'zʌmpʃən], *n.* présomption, *f.*

presumptive [pri'zʌmptiv], *a.* présumé; (*Law*) présomptif.

presumptuous [pri'zʌmptjuəs], *a.* présomptueux.

presumptuousness [pri'zʌmptjuəsnis], *n.* présomption, *f.*

presuppose [pri:sə'pouz], *v.t.* présupposer.

pretend [pri'tend], *v.t.* prétexter; feindre.—*v.i.* prétendre (à); feindre (*de*), faire semblant (*de*).

pretended [pri'tendid], *a.* prétendu, soi-disant.

520

pretender [pri'tendə], *n.* prétendant, *m.*

pretense [pri'tens], *n.* prétexte, *m.*, simulation; prétention, *f.*; *to make a pretense of*, faire semblant de; *under false pretenses*, par des moyens frauduleux.

pretension [pri'tenʃən], *n.* prétention, *f.*

pretentious [pri'tenʃəs], *a.* prétentieux, ambitieux.

pretentiousness [pri'tenʃəsnis], *n.* air prétentieux, *m.*, prétention, *f.*

preternatural [pri:tə'nætʃərəl], *a.* surnaturel, contre nature.

pretext ['pri:tekst], *n.* prétexte, faux semblant, *m.*; *under the pretext of*, sous prétexte de.

prettily ['pritili], *adv.* joliment, gentiment.

prettiness ['pritinis], *n.* gentillesse, *f.*, agrément, *m.*

pretty ['priti], *a.* joli, gentil.—*adv.* assez; passablement; *pretty much*, presque, à peu près.

prevail [pri'veil], *v.i.* prévaloir, l'emporter (*sur*); réussir (*avoir du succès*); dominer.

prevailing [pri'veiliŋ], *a.* dominant, régnant, général.

prevalence ['prevələns], *n.* influence, prédominance; fréquence, durée (*de temps, maladie etc.*), *f.*

prevalent ['prevələnt], *a.* régnant, dominant; général.

prevaricate [pri'værikeit], *v.i.* équivoquer; tergiverser, mentir.

prevarication [priværi'keiʃən], *n.* tergiversation, *f.*

prevaricator [pri'værikeitə], *n.* chicaneur, menteur, *m.*

prevent [pri'vent], *v.t.* empêcher, détourner (*de*); prévenir.

preventable [pri'ventəbl], *a.* évitable.

prevention [pri'venʃən], *n.* empêchement, *m.*

preventive [pri'ventiv], *a.* préventif.—*n.* préservatif, *m.*

preview ['pri:vju:], *n.* avant-première, *f.*

previous ['pri:viəs], *a.* antérieur, préalable.

previously ['pri:viəsli], *adv.* antérieurement, auparavant.

previousness ['pri:viəsnis], *n.* antériorité, priorité; (*colloq.*) anticipation, *f.*

prey [prei], *n.* proie, *f.*; *to be a prey to*, être en proie à.—*v.i.* *to prey on*, faire sa proie de; tourmenter, obséder (*l'esprit*).

price [prais], *n.* prix, *m.*; *at any price*, à tout prix; *cost price*, prix coûtant; *market price*, prix courant.—*v.t.* tarifer, mettre un prix à.

priceless ['praislis], *a.* sans prix, inappréciable; impayable (*plaisanterie etc.*).

price list ['praislist], *n.* tarif, *m.*

prick [prik], *n.* piqûre; pointe, *f.*; (*fig.*) aiguillon (*stimulant*); remords, *m.*—*v.t.* piquer; dresser (*les oreilles*); aiguillonner (*stimuler*); (*fig.*) exciter, tourmenter de remords.

pricker ['prikə], *n.* poinçon, *m.*, pointe, *f.*

pricking ['prikiŋ], *a.* qui pique, piquant.—*n.* piqûre, *f.*; picotement (*sensation*), *m.*

prickle [prikl], *n.* aiguillon, piquant, *m.*; épine, *f.*—*v.t.* piquer.

prickly ['prikli], *a.* piquant, épineux, hérissé.

pride [praid], *n.* orgueil, *m.*, fierté; bande (*de lions*), *f.*—*v.r.* *to pride oneself on*, se piquer de, s'enorgueillir de.

prier ['praiə], *n.* curieux, *m.*

priest [priːst], *n.* prêtre, *m.*

priestess ['priːstes], *n.* prêtresse, *f.*

priesthood ['priːsthuːd], *n.* prêtrise, *f.*, sacerdoce, clergé, *m.*

priestly ['priːstli], *a.* de prêtre, sacerdotal.

prig [prig], *n.* faquin, fat; pédant, *m.*

priggish ['prigiʃ], *a.* suffisant, pédant.

priggishly ['prigiʃli], *adv.* avec suffisance.

prim [prim], *a.* affecté, précieux, collet monté.

primacy ['praiməsi], *n.* primauté, *f.*

primal ['praiməl], *a.* primitif; principal.

primarily ['praimərili], *adv.* dans le principe.

primary ['praiməri], *a.* primitif, premier; principal; (*Sch.*) primaire, élémentaire.

primate ['praimit], *n.* primat, *m.*

prime [praim], *a.* premier, principal; de premier rang, de première qualité; *prime minister*, premier ministre, *m.*—*n.* aube, *f.*; commencement; printemps, *m.*; fleur, élite, *f.*, choix (*mieux*), *m.*; première jeunesse, *f.*; *prime of life*, fleur de l'âge, *f.* —*v.t.* amorcer (*fusils*); (*Paint.*) imprimer.

primer [['prima], *n.* premier livre (*de lecture etc.*); (*R.-C. Ch.*) livre d'heures, *m.*

primeval [prai'miːvəl], *a.* primitif, primordial.

priming ['praimiŋ], *n.* amorçage, *m.*; amorce (*d'un fusil*); (*Paint.*) impression, *f.*

primitive ['primitiv], *a.* and *n.* primitif, *m.*

primitiveness ['primitivnis], *n.* caractère primitif, *m.*

primly ['primli], *adv.* d'un air collet monté.

primness ['primnis], *n.* afféterie, *f.*

primogeniture [praimou'dʒenitjuə], *n.* primogéniture, *f.*

primordial [prai'mɔːdiəl], *a.* primordial.

primrose ['primrouz], *n.* primevère, *f.*

prince [prins], *n.* prince, *m.*

princeliness ['prinslinis], *n.* caractère de prince, *m.*

princely ['prinsli], *a.* de prince, princier; magnifique.—*adv.* en prince, en princesse, magnifiquement.

princess [prin'ses], *n.* princesse, *f.*

principal ['prinsipl], *a.* principal, premier, en chef.—*n.* partie principale, *f.*, chef; directeur, patron; proviseur (*d'un lycée*), *m.*; directrice, *f.*

principality [prinsi'pæliti], *n.* principauté, *f.*

principally ['prinsipli], *adv.* principalement, surtout.

principle ['prinsipl], *n.* principe, *m.*

principled ['prinsipld], *a.* qui a des principes.

print [print], *v.t.* imprimer; faire une empreinte sur; (*Phot. etc.*) tirer; *printed matter*, imprimé(s), *m.* (*pl.*).—*n.* empreinte (*de pas etc.*), impression; estampe, gravure; indienne (*tissu*); (*Phot.*) épreuve, *f.*; (*Print.*) caractère, *m.*

printer ['printə], *n.* imprimeur, typographe, *m.*

printing ['printiŋ], *n.* impression (*tirage*); imprimerie (*art etc.*), *f.*

printing machine ['printiŋmə'ʃiːn], *n.* presse mécanique, *f.*

printing press ['printiŋpres], *n.* presse à imprimer, *f.*

prior ['praiə], *a.* antérieur.—*adv.* antérieurement (*à*), avant.—*n.* prieur, *m.*

prioress ['praiəris], *n.* prieure, *f.*

priority [prai'ɔriti], *n.* priorité, *f.*

priory ['praiəri], *n.* prieuré, *m.*

prise [praiz], *n.* levier, *m.*—*v.t.* *to prise open*, ouvrir avec un levier.

prism [prizm], *n.* prisme, *m.*

prismatic [priz'mætik], **prismatical** [priz'mætikəl], *a.* prismatique.

prison [prizn], *n.* prison, *f.*

prisoner ['priznə], *n.* prisonnier, *m.*; (*Law*) *prisoner (at the bar)*, accusé, prévenu, *m.*

prison-van ['priznvæn], *n.* voiture cellulaire, *f.*

pristine ['pristain], *a.* primitif, premier.

privacy ['praivəsi, 'privəsi], *n.* retraite, solitude, intimité, *f.*

private ['praivit], *a.* particulier, personnel, privé; confidentiel, secret; (*Law*) à huis clos.—*n.* (*Mil.*) simple soldat, *m.*

privateer [praivə'tiə], *n.* corsaire, *m.*

privately ['praivitli], *adv.* en particulier; en secret; (*Law*) à huis clos.

privation [prai'veiʃən], *n.* privation, *f.*

privet ['privit], *n.* (*Bot.*) troène, *m.*

privilege ['privilidʒ], *n.* privilège, *m.*, (*Law*) immunité, *f.*—*v.t.* privilégier.

privileged ['privilidʒd], *a.* privilégié.

privily ['privili], *adv.* secrètement, en secret.

privy ['privi], *a.* privé, secret; caché; *Privy Council*, conseil privé, *m.*

prize [praiz], *n.* prise (*ce qu'on prend*), *f.*; prix (*récompense*); lot (*dans une loterie*), *m.*—*v.t.* priser, estimer.

prize-giving ['praizgiviŋ], *n.* distribution des prix, *f.*

prize-winner ['praizwinə], *n.* lauréat, gagnant, *m.*

pro [prou], *prep.* pour; *pros and cons*, le pour et le contre.

probability [probə'biliti], *n.* probabilité, vraisemblance, *f.*

probable ['probəbl], *a.* probable; vraisemblable.

probably ['probəbli], *adv.* probablement.

probate ['proubeit], *n.* vérification (*d'un testament*), *f.*

probation [prə'beiʃən], *n.* probation, épreuve, *f.*; (*Univ. etc.*) examen, stage, *m.*; *on probation*, (*Law*) sous surveillance de la police.

probationary [prə'beiʃənəri], *a.* d'épreuve; de probation.

probationer [prə'beiʃənə], *n.* aspirant, *m.*, stagiaire; novice, *m.*, *f.*

probe [proub], *n.* sonde, *f.*, stylet, *m.*—*v.t.* sonder; (*fig.*) examiner à fond.

probing ['proubiŋ], *a.* pénétrant (*question*).

probity ['proubiti], *n.* probité, *f.*

problem ['probləm], *n.* problème, *m.*

problematic [probli'mætik], **problematical** [probli'mætikəl], *a.* problématique.

proboscis [prə'bosis], *n.* (*pl.* **probosces** [prə'bosiːz]) trompe, *f.*, (*facet.*) nez, *m.*

procedure [prə'siːdʒə], *n.* procédé, *m.*, procédure, *f.*

proceed [prə'siːd], *v.i.* procéder, avancer, continuer son chemin; provenir (*de*); se mettre (*à*).

proceeding [prə'siːdiŋ], *n.* procédé, *m.*; manière d'agir, *f.*; (*pl.*) démarches, *f.pl.*, faits, actes, *m.pl.*

proceeds ['prousiːdz], *n.pl.* produit, montant, *m.*

521

process ['prouses], *n.* procédé; processus; cours, *m.*, marche, suite (*du temps*), *f.*—*v.t.* (*Ind.*) traiter.
procession [prə'seʃən], *n.* procession, *f.*, cortège, *m.*
processional [prə'seʃənəl], *a.* processionnel. —*n.* hymne processionnel, *m.*
proclaim [prə'kleim], *v.t.* proclamer, déclarer, publier.
proclamation [prəklə'meiʃən], *n.* proclamation, publication, déclaration; ordonnance, *f.*
proclivity [prə'kliviti], *n.* penchant, *m.*, inclination (à), *f.*
procrastinate [pro'kræstineit], *v.t.* remettre. —*v.i.* retarder.
procrastination [prokræsti'neiʃən], *n.* retardement, délai, *m.*
procrastinator [pro'kræstineitə], *n.* temporiseur, *m.*
procreate ['proukrieit], *v.t.* procréer.
procreation [proukri'eiʃən], *n.* procréation, *f.*
procreative ['proukrieitiv], *a.* procréateur, productif.
proctor ['proktə], *n.* (*Univ.*) censeur; (*Law*) procureur, *m.*
procurable [prə'kjuərəbl], *a.* qu'on peut se procurer.
procuration [prokju'reiʃən], *n.* gestion des affaires d'autrui; (*Law*) procuration, *f.*
procurator [pro'kjureitə], *n.* agent d'affaires; (*Law*) procurateur, *m.*
procure [prə'kjuə], *v.t.* procurer, faire avoir, se procurer.
prod [prod], *v.t.* pousser du doigt *ou* du bout d'un bâton; piquer; (*fig.*) aiguillonner.—*n.* coup de pointe, *m.*
prodigal ['prodigl], *a.* and *n.* prodigue, *m.*, *f.*
prodigality [prodi'gæliti], *n.* prodigalité, *f.*
prodigious [prə'didʒəs], *a.* prodigieux.
prodigy ['prodidʒi], *n.* prodige, *m.*, *f.*
produce [prə'dju:s], *n.* produit, *m.*—[prə'dju:s], *v.t.* produire; exhiber, montrer; (*Geom.*) prolonger.
producer [prə'dju:sə], *n.* producteur; (*Theat.*) producteur, *m.*
producible [prə'dju:sibl], *a.* productible.
product ['prodʌkt], *n.* produit, *m.*; *by-product*, sous-produit, *m.*
production [prə'dʌkʃən], *n.* production, *f.*; (*Chem. etc.*) produit, *m.*; (*Theat.*) mise en scène, *f.*
productive [prə'dʌktiv], *a.* productif; fécond.
productivity [prodʌk'tiviti], *n.* productivité, *f.*
profanation [profə'neiʃən], *n.* profanation, *f.*
profane [prə'fein], *a.* profane.—*v.t.* profaner.
profanely [prə'feinli], *adv.* d'une manière profane.
profaner [prə'feinə], *n.* profanateur, *m.*
profanity [prə'fæniti], *n.* conduite profane, impiété, *f.*; langage profane, *m.*
profess [prə'fes], *v.t.* professer, faire profession de, déclarer.
professed [prə'fest], *a.* déclaré, de profession.
professedly [prə'fesidli], *adv.* ouvertement; de profession.
profession [prə'feʃən], *n.* profession, *f.*; état, métier (*emploi*), *m.*
professional [prə'feʃənəl], *a.* de sa profession, professionnel; *professional man*, homme qui exerce une carrière libérale, *m.*—*n.*

homme du métier, homme de l'art; (*Spt.*) professionnel, *m.*
professionalism [prə'feʃənəlizm], *n.* caractère professionnel; (*Spt.*) professionnalisme, *m.*
professionally [prə'feʃənəli], *adv.* par profession; en homme du métier.
professor [prə'fesə], *n.* professeur (d'université), *m.*
professorial [profe'sɔ:riəl], *a.* de professeur, professoral.
professorship [prə'fesəʃip], *n.* professorat, *m.*, chaire, *f.*
proffer ['profə], *n.* offre, *f.*—*v.t.* offrir, proposer.
proficiency [prə'fiʃənsi], *n.* capacité, *f.*; talent, *m.*, compétence, *f.*
proficient [prə'fiʃənt], *a.* versé, fort, compétent.
profile ['proufail], *n.* profil, *m.*; *in profile*, de profil.
profit ['profit], *n.* profit, bénéfice, rapport; (*fig.*) avantage, *m.*—*v.t.* profiter à, faire du bien à; avantager.—*v.i.* profiter (*de*).
profitable ['profitəbl], *a.* profitable, avantageux.
profitably ['profitəbli], *adv.* avantageusement, avec profit.
profiteer [profi'tiə], *n.* profiteur, *m.*—*v.i.* faire des bénéfices excessifs.
profitless ['profitlis], *a.* sans profit, inutile.
profligacy ['profligəsi], *n.* dérèglement, *m.*, dissolution, *f.*, libertinage, *m.*
profligate ['profligit], *a.* débauché, dissolu, libertin.—*n.* libertin, mauvais sujet, *m.*
profound [prə'faund], *a.* profond; approfondi.
profoundly [prə'faundli], *adv.* profondément.
profundity [prə'fʌnditi], *n.* profondeur, *f.*
profuse [prə'fju:s], *a.* prodigue; abondant, excessif (*choses*).
profusely [prə'fju:sli], *adv.* profusément, à profusion.
profuseness [prə'fju:snis], **profusion** [prə'fju:ʒən], *n.* profusion, prodigalité, abondance, *f.*
progenitor [prou'dʒenitə], *n.* aïeul, ancêtre, *m.*
progeny ['prodʒəni], *n.* postérité, *f.*, descendants, *m.pl.*
prognostic [prog'nostik], *a.* pronostique.—*n.* pronostic, *m.*
prognosticate [prog'nostikeit], *v.t.* pronostiquer.
prognostication [prognosti'keiʃən], *n.* pronostic, *m.*
program ['prougræm], *n.* programme, *m.*
progress ['prougres], *n.* progrès, avancement, cours, *m.*; marche, *f.*; voyage (*de cérémonie*), *m.*—[prə'gres], *v.i.* s'avancer, faire des progrès, avancer.
progression [prə'greʃən], *n.* progression, *f.*
progressive [prə'gresiv], *a.* and *n.* progressif, *m.*; (*Polit.*) progressiste, *m.*, *f.*
progressiveness [prə'gresivnis], *n.* marche progressive, *f.*
prohibit [prə'hibit], *v.t.* prohiber, défendre, interdire (à); *smoking prohibited*, défense de fumer.
prohibition [prouhi'biʃən], *n.* prohibition, défense, *f.*

prohibitive [prə'hibitiv], **prohibitory** [prə'hibitri], *a.* prohibitif (*mœurs*); **prohibitive price**, prix exorbitant, *m.*

project ['prɔdʒekt], *n.* projet, dessein, *m.*—[prə'dʒekt], *v.t.* projeter.—*v.i.* avancer, faire saillie.

projectile [prə'dʒektail], *n.* projectile, *m.*

projecting [prə'dʒektiŋ], *a.* saillant, en saillie.

projection [prə'dʒekʃən], *n.* projection, saillie, *f.*; (*Arch.*) ressaut, *m.*

projector [prə'dʒektə], *n.* homme à projets, projeteur; projecteur (*lumière*); (*Cine.*) appareil de projection, *m.*

proletarian [prouli'tɛəriən], *a.* and *n,* prolétaire, *m., f.*

proletariat [prouli'tɛəriət], *n.* prolétariat, *m.*

prolific [prə'lifik], *a.* prolifique; fécond, fertile.

prolix ['prouliks], *a.* prolixe.

prolixity [prə'liksiti], **prolixness** ['prouliksnis], *n.* prolixité, *f.*

prologue ['proulɔg], *n.* prologue, *m.*

prolong [prə'lɔŋ], *v.t.* prolonger; retarder, différer (*remettre*); **to be prolonged**, se prolonger.

prolongation [proulɔŋ'geiʃən], *n.* prolongement, *m.*; prolongation (*du temps etc.*), *f.*

promenade [prɔmə'nɑːd], *n.* promenade; esplanade (*au bord de la mer*), *f.*—*v.i.* se promener, se faire voir.

promenader [prɔmə'nɑːdə], *n.* promeneur, *m.*

prominence ['prɔminəns], *n.* proéminence, *f.* (*fig.*) distinction, *f.*

prominent ['prɔminənt], *a.* proéminent, saillant; prononcé (*remarquable*); (*fig.*) éminent, distingué.

prominently ['prɔminəntli], *adv.* en saillie; d'une manière frappante.

promiscuity [prɔmis'kjuːiti], **promiscuousness** [prə'miskjuəsnis], *n.* mélange confus, *m.*; promiscuité, *f.*

promiscuous [prə'miskjuəs], *a.* sans distinction de sexe, promiscu; mêlé, confus, sans ordre.

promiscuously [prə'miskjuəsli], *adv.* confusément; en commun, en promiscuité.

promise ['prɔmis], *n.* promesse; (*fig.*) espérance, *f.*—*v.t., v.i.* promettre.

promising ['prɔmisiŋ], *a.* prometteur, qui promet; qui donne des espérances.

promissory ['prɔmisəri], *a.* qui contient une promesse; **promissory note**, billet à ordre, *m.*

promontory ['prɔməntri], *n.* promontoire, *m.*

promote [prə'mout], *v.t.* servir, avancer; promouvoir; encourager; **to promote a company**, lancer une société anonyme.

promoter [prə'moutə], *n.* promoteur, protecteur, instigateur; (*Comm.*) lanceur d'affaires, *m.*

promotion [prə'mouʃən], *n.* promotion, *f.*, avancement, *m.*

prompt [prɔmpt], *v.t.* exciter, porter, pousser; inspirer, suggérer; (*Theat.*) souffler.—*a.* prompt, empressé.

prompter ['prɔmptə], *n.* souffleur, *m.*; **prompter's box**, trou du souffleur, *m.*

promptitude ['prɔmptitjuːd], **promptness** ['prɔmptnis], *n.* promptitude, *f.*, empressement, *m.*

promptly ['prɔmptli], *adv.* promptement, avec empressement.

promptness [PROMPTITUDE].

promulgate ['prɔmʌlgeit], *v.t.* promulguer.

promulgation [prɔmʌl'geiʃən], *n.* promulgation, *f.*

promulgator ['prɔmʌlgeitə], *n.* promulgateur, *m.*

prone [proun], *a.* penché, incliné; couché, étendu; (*fig.*) disposé, porté (à).

proneness ['prounnis], *n.* disposition, inclination, *f.*, penchant, *m.*

prong [prɔŋ], *n.* fourchon, *m.*, dent, *f.*

pronged [prɔŋd], *a.* à fourchons, à dents.

pronoun ['prounaun], *n.* pronom, *m.*

pronounce [prə'nauns], *v.t.* prononcer; déclarer, annoncer, dire.

pronounceable [prə'naunsəbl], *a.* prononçable.

pronouncement [prə'naunsmənt], *n.* prononcement, *m.*, déclaration, *f.*

pronunciation [prənʌnsi'ciʃən], *n.* prononciation, *f.*, accent, *m.*

proof [pruːf], *n.* **a proof against**, résistant à, à l'épreuve de; **waterproof**, imperméable. —*n.* preuve; épreuve, *f.*

proofless ['pruːflis], *a.* sans preuve.

proof sheet ['pruːfʃiːt], *n.* (*Print.*) épreuve, *f.*

prop [prɔp], *n.* étai, étançon; (*Hort.*) tuteur, échalas; (*fig.*) appui, soutien; (*Theat.*) (*fam.*) accessoire, *m.*—*v.t.* étayer; appuyer, soutenir; (*Hort.*) échalasser.

propaganda [prɔpə'gændə], *n.* propagande, *f.*

propagandist [prɔpə'gændist], *n.* propagandiste, *m., f.*

propagate ['prɔpəgeit], *v.t.* propager; (*fig.*) répandre; créer, enfanter (*des êtres*).—*v.i.* se propager.

propagation [prɔpə'geiʃən], *n.* propagation, *f.*

propagator ['prɔpəgeitə], *n.* propagateur, *m.*

propel [prə'pel], *v.t.* pousser en avant, faire marcher, propulser.

propeller [prə'pelə], *n.* hélice, *f.*; propulseur, moteur, *m.*

propelling [prə'peliŋ], *a.* propulseur, moteur; **propelling force**, force motrice, *f.*

propensity [prə'pensiti], *n.* penchant, *m.*, tendance, *f.*

proper ['prɔpə], *a.* propre, particulier; convenable, à propos (*comme il faut*); juste, exact (*correct*).

properly ['prɔpəli], *adv.* proprement, comme il faut.

property ['prɔpəti], *n.* propriété, *f.*; bien, *m.*, biens, *m.pl.*; qualité, *f.*; (*Theat., Cine.*) accessoire, *m.*

property tax ['prɔpətitæks], *n.* impôt foncier, *m.*

prophecy ['prɔfəsi], *n.* prophétie, *f.*

prophesy ['prɔfəsai], *v.t.* prophétiser, prédire.

prophet ['prɔfit], *n.* prophète, *m.*

prophetess ['prɔfites], *n.* prophétesse, *f.*

prophetic [prə'fetik], **prophetical** [prə'fetikəl], *a.* prophétique.

propinquity [prə'piŋkwiti], *n.* proximité, parenté (*de personnes*), *f.*

propitiate [prə'piʃieit], *v.t.* rendre propice.

propitiation [prəpiʃi'eiʃən], *n.* propitiation, *f.*

propitiator [prə'piʃieitə], *n.* propitiateur, *m.*

propitiatory [prə'piʃiətri], *a.* and *n.* propitiatoire, *m.*

propitious [prə'piʃəs], *a.* propice, favorable.

propitiousness [prə'piʃəsnis], *n.* nature propice, *f.*

proportion [prə'pɔːʃən], *n.* proportion; partie; portion, *f.*; *in proportion as*, à mesure que.—*v.t.* proportionner.

proportional [prə'pɔːʃənəl], *a.* en proportion; proportionnel.

proportionate [prə'pɔːʃənlt], *a.* proportionné.

proposal [prə'pouzl], *n.* proposition; demande en mariage, *f.*

propose [prə'pouz], *v.t.* proposer; offrir; *to propose a toast*, porter un toast.—*v.i.* se proposer; faire une demande en mariage.

proposer [prə'pouzə], *n.* auteur d'une proposition, *m.*

proposition [prɔpə'ziʃən], *n.* proposition; affaire, *f.*

propound [prə'paund], *v.t.* proposer, exposer, mettre en avant.

proprietary [prə'praiətri], *a.* de propriété.—*n.* actionnaire, *m.pl.*

proprietor [prə'praiətə], *n.* propriétaire, *m.*

proprietress [prə'praiətris], *n.* propriétaire, maîtresse, *f.*

propriety [prə'praiəti], *n.* convenance, propriété, *f.*

propulsion [prə'pʌlʃən], *n.* propulsion, *f.*; *jet propulsion*, propulsion à réaction.

prorogation [prouro'geiʃən], *n.* prorogation, *f.*

prorogue [prə'roug], *v.t.* proroger.

prosaic [pro'zeiik], *a.* prosaïque.

proscenium [prə'siːniəm], *n.* proscenium, *m.*, avant-scène, *f.*

proscribe [pro'skraib], *v.t.* proscrire.

proscription [pro'skripʃən], *n.* proscription, *f.*

prose [prouz], *n.* prose, *f.*

prosecute ['prɔsikjuːt], *v.t.* poursuivre; revendiquer (*ses droits etc.*).

prosecution [prɔsi'kjuːʃən], *n.* poursuite, *f.*, procès criminel, *m.*; *witness for the prosecution*, témoin à charge, *m.*

prosecutor ['prɔsikjuːtə], *n.* poursuivant, plaignant, *m.*; *public prosecutor*, procureur de la république, *m.*

prosecutrix ['prɔsikjuːtriks], *n.* poursuivante, plaignante, *f.*

proselyte ['prɔsəlait], *n.* prosélyte, *m.*, *f.*

proselytism ['prɔsəlitizm], *n.* prosélytisme, *m.*

proselytize ['prɔsəlitaiz], *v.t.* convertir.—*v.i.* faire des prosélytes.

prose writer ['prouzraitə], *n.* prosateur, *m.*

prosily ['prouzili], *adv.* prosaïquement, ennuyeusement.

prosiness ['prouzinis], *n.* prosaïsme, *m.*; verbosité, *f.*

prosody ['prɔsədi], *n.* prosodie, *f.*

prospect ['prɔspekt], *n.* vue; perspective, *f.*; (*fig.*) espoir; avenir, *m.*—[prə'spekt], *v.i.* faire des recherches (*minerai, pétrole etc.*), prospecter.

prospective [prə'spektiv], *a.* en perspective; à venir.

prospectively [prə'spektivli], *adv.* pour l'avenir.

prospector [prə'spektə], *n.* explorateur, *orpailleur, *m.*

prospectus [prə'spektəs], *n.* prospectus, *m.*

prosper ['prɔspə], *v.t.* faire prospérer, favoriser.—*v.i.* prospérer, réussir.

prosperity [prɔs'periti], *n.* prospérité, *f.*

prosperous ['prɔspərəs], *a.* prospère; florissant (*affaires*); (*fig.*) heureux; favorable.

prostitute ['prɔstitjuːt], *n.* prostituée, *f.*—*v.t.* prostituer.

prostitution [prɔsti'tjuːʃən], *n.* prostitution, *f.*

prostrate ['prɔstreit], *v.t.* coucher, prosterner; (*fig.*) renverser; *to prostrate oneself before*, se prosterner devant.—*a.* prosterné; (*fig.*) abattu.

prostration [prɔs'treiʃən], *n.* prosternation, *f.*; (*fig.*) abattement, *m.*

prosy ['prouzi], *a.* ennuyeux, fastidieux.

protagonist [prou'tægənist], *n.* protagoniste, *m.*

protect [prə'tekt], *v.t.* protéger, défendre; garantir, abriter (*contre le temps etc.*); sauvegarder (*intérêts*).

protection [prə'tekʃən], *n.* protection, défense; garantie, *f.*, abri (*contre le temps etc.*), *m.*; (*Law*) sauvegarde, *f.*

protectionism [prə'tekʃənizm], *n.* protectionnisme, *m.*

protectionist [prə'tekʃənist], *a.* and *n.* protectionniste, *m.*, *f.*

protective [prə'tektiv], *a.* protecteur.

protector [prə'tektə], *n.* protecteur, *m.*

protectorate [prə'tektərit], *n.* protectorat, *m.*

protectress [prə'tektris], *n.* protectrice, *f.*

protein ['proutiːn], *n.* protéine, *f.*

protest ['proutest], *n.* protestation, *f.*; (*Comm.*) protêt, *m.*—[prə'test], *v.t.*, *v.i.* protester.

Protestant ['prɔtistənt], *a.* and *n.* protestant, *m.*

Protestantism ['prɔtistəntizm], *n.* protestantisme, *m.*

protestation [prɔtes'teiʃən], *n.* protestation, *f.*

protester [prə'testə], *n.* personne qui fait faire un protêt, *f.*

protocol ['proutəkɔl], *n.* protocole, *m.*

proton ['prouton], *n.* proton, *m.*

prototype ['proutətaip], *n.* prototype, *m.*

protract [prə'trækt], *v.t.* prolonger, traîner en longueur.

protraction [prə'trækʃən], *n.* prolongation, *f.*

protractor [prə'træktə], *n.* rapporteur (*instrument*), *m.*

protrude [prə'truːd], *v.t.* pousser en avant, faire sortir.—*v.i.* s'avancer, faire saillie.

protruding [prə'truːdiŋ], *a.* en saillie, saillant.

protrusion [prə'truːʒən], *n.* saillie, *f.*

protuberance [prə'tjuːbərəns], *n.* protubérance, *f.*

protuberant [prə'tjuːbərənt], *a.* protubérant.

proud [praud], *a.* fier (*de*); orgueilleux.

proudly ['praudli], *adv.* fièrement, orgueilleusement.

provable ['pruːvəbl], *a.* prouvable, démontrable.

prove [pruːv], *v.t.* prouver, démontrer; mettre à l'épreuve, éprouver (*la qualité de*); vérifier (*testament etc.*).—*v.i.* se montrer, se révéler.

proved [pruːvd], *a.* prouvé, démontré, reconnu.

provender ['prɔvəndə], *n.* fourrage, *m.*, nourriture (*d'animaux*), *f.*

proverb ['prɔvə:b], *n.* proverbe, *m.*
proverbial [prɔ'və:biəl], *a.* proverbial.
provide [prə'vaid], *v.t.* pourvoir, fournir, munir; préparer (à); stipuler.—*v.i.* pourvoir.
provided [prə'vaidid], *a.* pourvu.—*conj.* *provided that,* pourvu que (*with subj.*).
providence ['prɔvidəns], *n.* providence (*divine*); prévoyance (*humaine*), *f.*
provident ['prɔvidənt], *a.* prévoyant; économe.
providential [prɔvi'denʃəl], *a.* providentiel, de la providence.
providently ['prɔvidəntli], *adv.* avec prévoyance.
provider [prə'vaidə], *n.* pourvoyeur, fournisseur, *m.*
province ['prɔvins], *n.* province, *f.*; (*fig.*) département, ressort, *m.*
provincial [prə'vinʃəl], *a.* provincial, de province.—*n.* provincial, *m.*
provincialism [prə'vinʃəlizm], *n.* provincialisme, *m.*
proving ['pru:viŋ], *n.* vérification, mise à l'épreuve, *f.*
provision [prə'viʒən], *n.* action de pourvoir; stipulation; (*Law*) disposition (*d'un projet de loi etc.*), *f.*; (*pl.*) vivres, comestibles, *m.pl.*—*v.t.* approvisionner.
provisional [prə'viʒənəl], *a.* provisoire.
provision dealer [prə'viʒəndi:lə], *n.* marchand de comestibles, *m.*
proviso [prə'vaizou], *n.* condition, clause conditionnelle, *f.*
provisory [prə'vaizəri], *a.* provisoire, conditionnel.
provocation [prɔvə'keiʃən], *n.* provocation, *f.*
provocative [prɔ'vɔkətiv], *a.* provocant, provocateur.
provoke [prə'vouk], *v.t.* provoquer; inciter; fâcher, irriter.
provoker [prə'voukə], *n.* provocateur, *m.*
provoking [prə'voukiŋ], *a.* provocant; ennuyeux, fâcheux, agaçant.
provokingly [prə'voukiŋli], *adv.* d'une manière provocante *ou* contrariante.
provost ['prɔvəst], *n.* prévôt, *f.*; (*Univ.*) principal; (*Sc.*) maire, *m.*
prow [prau], *n.* proue, *f.*
prowess ['prauis], *n.* bravoure, prouesse, *f.*
prowl [praul], *n.* action de rôder, *f.*—*v.i.* rôder.
prowler ['praulə], *n.* rôdeur, *m.*
proximate ['prɔksimit], *a.* proche, immédiat.
proximity [prɔk'simiti], *n.* proximité, *f.*
proximo ['prɔksimou], *adv.* du mois prochain.
proxy ['prɔksi], *n.* mandataire, *m.*, *f.*, délégué, *m.*; procuration (*chose*), *f.*; *by proxy,* par procuration.
prude [pru:d], *n.* prude, mijaurée, *f.*
prudence ['pru:dəns], *n.* prudence, *f.*
prudent ['pru:dənt], *a.* prudent, sage.
prudential [pru'denʃəl], *a.* de prudence, dicté par la prudence.
prudently ['pru:dəntli], *adv.* prudemment, sagement.
prudery ['pru:dəri], *n.* pruderie, *f.*
prudish ['pru:diʃ], *a.* prude, de prude.
prudishly ['pru:diʃli], *adv.* avec pruderie.
prune [pru:n], *n.* pruneau, *m.*—*v.t.* élaguer, tailler, émonder.
prunella [pru'nelə], *n.* prunelle, *f.*

pruning ['pru:niŋ], *n.* taille, *f.*, élagage, *m.*
pruning shears ['pru:niŋʃiəz], *n.pl.* sécateur, *m.*, cisailles, *f.pl.*
prurience ['pruəriəns], **pruriency** ['pruəriənsi], *n.* démangeaison, *f.*
prurient ['pruəriənt], *a.* qui démange.
Prussia ['prʌʃə]. la Prusse, *f.*
Prussian ['prʌʃən], *a.* prussien.—*n.* Prussien (*personne*), *m.*
prussic ['prʌsik], *a.* prussique.
pry [prai], *v.t.* soulever avec un levier.—*v.i.* fureter; fouiller (*dans*); *to pry into,* se mêler de.—*n.* regard scrutateur, regard indiscret, *m.*
prying ['praiiŋ], *a.* scrutateur, curieux.—*n.* curiosité, *f.*
psalm [sɑ:m], *n.* psaume, *m.*
psalmist ['sɑ:mist], *n.* psalmiste, *m.*
psalmody ['sɑ:mədi], *n.* psalmodie, *f.*
psalter ['sɔ:ltə], *n.* psautier, *m.*
pseudonym ['sju:dənim], *n.* pseudonyme, *m.*
pshaw! [pʃɔ:], *int.* bah! fi donc!
psychiatric [saiki'ætrik], *a.* psychiatrique.
psychiatrist [sai'kaiətrist], *n.* psychiatre, *m.*, *f.*
psychiatry [sai'kaiətri], *n.* psychiatrie, *f.*
psychic(al) ['saikik(l)], *a.* psychique.
psycho-analysis [saikouə'nælisis], *n.* psychanalyse, *f.*
psycho-analyst [saikou'ænəlist], *n.* psychanalyste, *m.*, *f.*
psycho-analyze [saikou'ænəlaiz], *v.t.* psychanalyser.
psychological [saikə'lɔdʒikl], *a.* psychologique.
psychologist [sai'kɔlədʒist], *n.* psychologiste, psychologue, *m.*
psychology [sai'kɔlədʒi], *n.* psychologie, *f.*
psychopath ['saikopæθ], *n.* psychopathe, *m.*, *f.*
psychosis [sai'kousis], *n.* psychose, *f.*
ptarmigan ['tɑ:migən], *n.* lagopède, *m.*
ptomaine ['toumein], *n.* ptomaïne, *f.*; *ptomaine poisoning,* intoxication alimentaire, *f.*
puberty ['pju:bəti], *n.* puberté, *f.*
pubescence [pju'besəns], *n.* pubescence, *f.*
pubescent [pju'besənt], *a.* pubescent.
public ['pʌblik], *a.* and *n.* public, *m.*
publican ['pʌblikən], *n.* cafetier, patron de bistro(t); (*Bibl.*) publicain, *m.*
publication [pʌbli'keiʃən], *n.* publication, *f.*
public-house ['pʌblikhaus], *n.* café, *m.*, brasserie, *f.*, bistro(t), *m.*
publicist ['pʌblisist], *n.* publiciste, journaliste; publicitaire, *m.*, *f.*
publicity [pʌb'lisiti], *n.* publicité; réclame, *f.*
publicize ['pʌblisaiz], *v.t.* faire connaître au public.
publicly ['pʌblikli], *adv.* publiquement; en public.
publish ['pʌbliʃ], *v.t.* publier; éditer.
publisher ['pʌbliʃə], *n.* éditeur, *m.*; *bookseller and publisher,* libraire-éditeur, *m.*
puce [pju:s], *a.* puce.
puck (1) [pʌk], *n.* lutin, *m.*
puck (2) [pʌk], *n.* (*Spt.*) palet de hockey (sur glace), *m.*
pucker ['pʌkə], *v.t.* rider, plisser; (*Dress.*) faire goder.—*v.i.* goder.—*n.* ride; (*Dress.*) poche, *f.*; mauvais pli, *m.*
puckering ['pʌkəriŋ], *n.* froncement, *m.*
puckish ['pʌkiʃ], *a.* malicieux; de lutin.

pudding

pudding ['pudiŋ], *n.* pudding, pouding, *m.*;
puddle [pʌdl], *n.* flaque (d'eau), mare, *f.*—
v.t. troubler, rendre bourbeux.
puerile ['pjuəraíl], *a.* puéril.
puerility [pjuə'riliti], *n.* puérilité, *f.*
puff [pʌf], *n.* souffle (*d'haleine*), *m.*; bouffée (*de vent, fumée etc.*), *f.*; feuilleté (*pâtisserie*), *m.*; houppe à poudrer (*de dames*), *f.*; bouillon (*de robes*); puff, *m.*, réclame tapageuse, *f.*—*v.t.* souffler, bouffir (*les joues*), gonfler; (*fig.*) faire mousser (*publicité*).—*v.i.* souffler, boursoufler, bouffir, bouffer, se gonfler; haleter.
puffin ['pʌfin], *n.* (*Orn.*) macareux, *m.*
puffiness ['pʌfinis], *n.* boursouflure, enflure, *f.*
puff pastry ['pʌfpeistri], *n.* pâte feuilletée, *f.*
puffy ['pʌfi], *a.* bouffi, gonflé.
pug [pʌg], *n.* carlin (*chien*), *m.*
pugilism ['pjuːdʒilizm], *n.* pugilat, *m.*, boxe, *f.*
pugilist ['pjuːdʒilist], *n.* boxeur, pugiliste, *m.*
pugilistic [pjuːdʒi'listik], *a.* de pugilat.
pugnacious [pʌg'neiʃəs], *a.* querelleur, batailleur.
pugnaciously [pʌg'neiʃəsli], *adv.* d'un air batailleur.
pugnacity [pʌg'næsiti], *n.* pugnacité, *f.*
pug nose ['pʌgnouz], *n.* nez épaté, *m.*
puke [pjuːk], *v.i.* vomir.
pule [pjuːl], *v.i.* piauler.
puling ['pjuːliŋ], *n.* cri; piaulement, *m.*
pull [pul], *v.t.* tirer; arracher; presser (*la détente*); **to pull a wry face**, faire la grimace; **to pull down**, abattre, démolir; **to pull off**, arracher, enlever; **to pull up**, hisser; déraciner; arrêter.—*v.i.* ramer (*tirer la rame*); **to pull in**, s'arrêter; **to pull round**, se remettre; **to pull through**, guérir, s'en tirer; **to pull up**, s'arrêter.—*n.* action de tirer, traction, *f.*; coup (*d'aviron*), effort, *m.*; secousse, *f.*; (*fig.*) avantage, *m.*; **hard pull**, rude effort.
pullet ['pulit], *n.* poulette, *f.*
pulley ['puli], *n.* poulie, *f.*
pullover ['pulouvə], *n.* pull-over, *m.*
pulmonary ['pʌlmənəri], *a.* pulmonaire.
pulp [pʌlp], *n.* pulpe; pâte (*papier*), *f.*—*v.t.* réduire en pâte.
pulpiness ['pʌlpinis], *n.* nature pulpeuse, *f.*
pulpit ['pulpit], *n.* chaire, *f.*
pulpous ['pʌlpəs], **pulpy** ['pʌlpi], *a.* pulpeux.
pulsate [pʌl'seit], *v.i.* battre; palpiter.
pulsation [pʌl'seiʃən], *n.* pulsation, *f.*
pulsatory ['pʌlsətri], *a.* pulsatoire.
pulse [pʌls], *n.* pouls, *m.*; pulsation, *f.*; plantes légumineuses, *f.pl.*
pulverization [pʌlvərai'zeiʃən], *n.* pulvérisation, *f.*
pulverize ['pʌlvəraiz], *v.t.* pulvériser.
puma ['pjuːmə], *n.* puma, couguar, *m.*
pumice ['pʌmis], *n.* pierre ponce, *f.*
pump [pʌmp], *n.* pompe, *f.*; escarpin (*chaussure*), *m.*—*v.t.* pomper; (*fig.*) sonder; **to pump up**, gonfler (*pneu*).—*v.i.* pomper.
pumpkin ['pʌmpkin], *n.* citrouille, courge, *f.*, potiron, *m.*
pump room ['pʌmpruːm], *n.* buvette, *f.*
pun [pʌn], *n.* calembour, jeu de mots, *m.*—*v.i.* faire des calembours.
punch (1) [pʌntʃ], *n.* emporte-pièce; (*Print.*) poinçon, *m.*—*v.t.* percer, poinçonner.

punch (2) [pʌntʃ], *n.* coup de poing, *m.*—*v.t.* donner un coup de poing à.
punch (3) [pʌntʃ], *n.* punch (*boisson*), *m.*
punch bowl ['pʌntʃboul], *n.* bol à punch, *m.*
puncheon ['pʌntʃən], *n.* poinçon, *m.*, pièce (de vin), *f.*
punctilio [pʌŋk'tiliou], *n.* exactitude scrupuleuse, *f.*, point d'étiquette, *m.*
punctilious [pʌŋk'tiliəs], *a.* pointilleux.
punctiliousness [pʌŋk'tiliəsnis], *n.* exactitude scrupuleuse, pointillerie, *f.*
punctual ['pʌŋktjuəl], *a.* ponctuel, exact.
punctuality [pʌŋktju'æliti], *n.* ponctualité, exactitude, *f.*
punctually ['pʌŋktjuəli], *adv.* ponctuellement, exactement.
punctuate ['pʌŋktjueit], *v.t.* ponctuer.
punctuation [pʌŋktju'eiʃən], *n.* ponctuation, *f.*
puncture ['pʌŋktʃə], *n.* piqûre; crevaison (*d'un pneu*), *f.*—*v.t.* piquer; crever (*pneu*).
pundit ['pʌndit], *n.* pandit, *m.*
pungency ['pʌndʒənsi], *n.* âcreté; aigreur, *f.*
pungent ['pʌndʒənt], *a.* âcre; piquant, mordant.
pungently ['pʌndʒəntli], *adv.* avec causticité.
puniness ['pjuːninis], *n.* petitesse, nature chétive, *f.*
punish ['pʌniʃ], *v.t.* punir, corriger; malmener.
punishable ['pʌniʃəbl], *a.* punissable.
punishment ['pʌniʃmənt], *n.* punition; peine, *f.*, châtiment, *m.*; **capital punishment**, peine capitale.
punitive ['pjuːnitiv], *a.* punitif.
punt [pʌnt], *n.* bachot, *m.*—*v.i.* conduire un bachot (*à la perche*).
puny ['pjuːni], *a.* petit, chétif.
pup [pʌp], *n.* petit chien, petit; (*pej.*) freluquet, fat, *m.*
pupil (1) ['pjuːpil], *n.* élève, *m.*, *f.*
pupil (2) ['pjuːpil], *n.* pupille (de l'œil), *f.*
pupilary ['pjuːpiləri], *a.* pupillaire.
puppet ['pʌpit], *n.* marionnette, *f.*; **glove puppet**, marionnette à gaine; **puppet government**, gouvernement fantoche, *m.*
puppet show ['pʌpitʃou], *n.* (spectacle de) marionnettes, *f.pl.*
puppy ['pʌpi], *n.* petit chien; (*fig.*) fat, freluquet, *m.*
purblind ['pəːblaind], *a.* myope.
purchase ['pəːtʃis], *n.* achat, *m.*, acquisition, emplette; (*Mech.*) prise, *f.*—*v.t.* acheter, acquérir.
purchase deed ['pəːtʃisdiːd], *n.* contrat d'achat, *m.*
purchaser ['pəːtʃisə], *n.* acquéreur, acheteur, *m.*
purchasing ['pəːtʃisiŋ], *n.* achat, *m.*; **purchasing power**, pouvoir d'achat, *m.*
pure [pjuə], *a.* pur; **pure-bred**, de race.
purely ['pjuəli], *adv.* purement.
pureness ['pjuənis], *n.* pureté, *f.*
purgation [pəː'geiʃən], *n.* purgation, *f.*
purgative ['pəːgətiv], *a.* and *n.* purgatif, *m.*
purgatorial [pəːgə'tɔːriəl], *a.* du purgatoire.
purgatory ['pəːgətəri], *n.* purgatoire, *m.*
purge [pəːdʒ], *v.t.* purger; purifier, épurer.—*n.* purgation, purge, *f.*; (*Polit.*) nettoyage, *m.*

purification [pjuərifi'keiʃən], *n.* purification; épuration, *f.*

purifier ['pjuərifaiə], *n.* purificateur, *m.*

purify ['pjuərifai], *v.t.* purifier.—*v.i.* se purifier.

purist ['pjuərist], *n.* puriste, *m., f.*

puritan ['pjuəritən], *n.* puritain, *m.*

puritan ['pjuəritən], *a.* puritain.

puritanical [pjuəri'tæn:kl], *a.* de puritain, puritain.

puritanism ['pjuəritənizm], *n.* puritanisme, *m.*

purity ['pjuəriti], *n.* pureté, *f.*

purl [pə:l], *v.t.* engrêler (*dentelle*).—*v.i.* murmurer, gazouiller.—*n.* engrêlure (*de dentelle*), *f.*; doux murmure, gazouillement, *m.*

purlieu ['pə:lju:], *n.* alentours, environs, *m.pl.*

purloin [pə'lɔin], *v.t.* dérober, voler.

purple [pə:pl], *a.* violet, mauve; pourpre.—*n.* pourpre, mauve (*couleur*), *m.*; pourpre (*teinture etc.*), *f.*—*v.i.* teindre en pourpre, empourprer, rougir.

purport ['pə:pət], *n.* sens, *m.*, teneur, portée, *f.*—[pə'pɔ:t], *v.t.* tendre à montrer, signifier, vouloir dire.

purpose ['pə:pəs], *n.* but, objet, *m.*, fin, *f.*, dessein, *m.*, intention, *f.*; **on purpose,** exprès, à dessein; **to answer one's purpose,** faire son affaire.—*v.t., v.i.* se proposer, avoir l'intention (*de*).

purposely ['pə:pəsli], *adv.* à dessein, exprès.

purr [pə:], *v.i.* ronronner.

purring ['pə:riŋ], *a.* qui fait ronron.—*n.* ronron, *m.*

purse [pə:s], *n.* porte-monnaie, *m.*; bourse, *f.*; (*Am.*) sac à main, *m.*—*v.t.* plisser, froncer (*les sourcils etc.*).

purser ['pə:sə], *n.* commissaire (*de navire*); (*Mining*) agent comptable, *m.*

pursuance [pə'sju:əns], *n.* poursuite, conséquence, *f.*; **in pursuance of,** conformément à.

pursuant [pə'sju:ənt], *a.* en conséquence (*de*), conforme (*à*).

pursue [pə'sju:], *v.t.* poursuivre; suivre, chercher.

pursuer [pə'sju:ə], *n.* poursuivant, *m.*

pursuit [pə'sju:t], *n.* poursuite, recherche; occupation, *f.*; (*pl.*) travaux, *m.pl.*

purulence ['pjuəruləns], **purulency** ['pjuərulənsi], *n.* purulence, *f.*

purulent ['pjuərulənt], *a.* purulent.

purvey [pə'vei], *v.t.* fournir, approvisionner, procurer.

purveyor [pə'veiə], *n.* pourvoyeur, fournisseur, *m.*

pus [pʌs], *n.* pus, *m.*

push [puʃ], *v.t.* pousser; (*fig.*) presser, importuner; **to push back,** repousser, faire reculer; **to push down,** faire tomber, renverser.—*v.i.* pousser; faire un effort; **to push off,** pousser au large; **to push on,** pousser en avant.—*n.* impulsion, poussée, *f.*; effort, *m.*; extrémité, *f.*

pushing ['puʃiŋ], *a.* entreprenant.

pusillanimity [pju:silə'nimiti], *n.* pusillanimité, *f.*

pusillanimous [pju:si'læniməs], *a.* pusillanime.

puss [pus], *n.* (*colloq.*) minet, *m.*, minette, *f.*

pustule ['pʌstju:l], *n.* pustule, *f.*

put [put], *v.t. irr.* mettre, poser, placer; proposer (*solution etc.*); lancer (*poids etc.*); **to put about,** gêner; **to put aside,** mettre de côté; **to put back,** replacer, remettre; **to put by,** mettre de côté; **to put forward,** mettre en avant; **to put off,** ôter; remettre; **to put on,** mettre (*vêtements*); **to put on the light,** allumer; **to put out,** mettre dehors; éteindre (*feu etc.*); **to put up,** installer; loger, caser (*dans un hôtel etc.*).—*v.i.* aller; germer, pousser; (*Naut.*) se mettre; **to put in,** entrer au port; **to put up,** loger (à ou chez), descendre (à); **to put up with,** supporter.

putrefaction [pju:tri'fækʃən], *n.* putréfaction, *f.*

putrefy ['pju:trifai], *v.t.* putréfier.—*v.i.* se putréfier.

putrid ['pju:trid], *a.* putride.

putridity [pju:'triditi], *n.* putridité, *f.*

putt [pʌt], *v.t.* (*Golf*) poter.

putter ['pʌtə], *n.* (*Golf*) poteur, *m.*

putting ['putiŋ], *n.* action du mettre, mise, *f.*

putty ['pʌti], *n.* mastic, *m.*

puzzle [pʌzl], *n.* (*fig.*) énigme, *f.*; jeu de patience, casse-tête (*jouet*), *m.*; **crossword puzzle,** mots croisés, *m.pl.*—*v.t.* intriguer, embarrasser; **to puzzle one's brains,** creuser la tête.

pygmean [pig'miən], *a.* de pygmée.

pygmy ['pigmi], *n.* pygmée, *m., f.*

pyjamas [pi'dʒɑːməz], *n.pl.* pyjama, *m.*

pylon ['pailən], *n.* pylône, *m.*

pyramid ['pirəmid], *n.* pyramide, *f.*

pyramidal [pi'ræmidl], *a.* pyramidal.

pyre ['paiə], *n.* bûcher, *m.*

Pyrenees [pirə'ni:z], the. les Pyrénées, *f.pl.*

pyrethrum [pai'ri:θrəm], *n.* (*Bot.*) pyrèthre, *m.*

pyrotechnic [paiərou'teknik], **pyrotechnical** [paiərou'teknikəl], *a.* pyrotechnique, pyrique.

pyrotechnics [paiərou'tekniks], *n.pl.* pyrotechnie, *f.*

pyrotechnist [paiərou'teknist], *n.* artificier, *m.*

python ['paiθən], *n.* python, *m.*

pyx [piks], *n.* ciboire, *m.*

Q

Q, q [kju:]. dix-septième lettre de l'alphabet, *m.*

quack [kwæk], *a.* de charlatan.—*n.* charlatan; couac, cri du canard, *m.*—*v.i.* crier (*comme les canards etc.*).

quackery ['kwækəri], *n.* charlatanisme, *m.*

Quadragesima [kwɔdrə'dʒesimə]. Quadragésime, *f.*

quadrangle ['kwɔdræŋgl], *n.* quadrilatère carré, *m.*; (*Univ.*) cour d'honneur, *f.*

quadrant ['kwɔdrənt], *n.* quart de cercle, *m.*

quadratic [kwɔd'rætik], *a.* du second degré.

quadrennial [kwɔd'reniəl], *a.* quadriennal.

quadrennially [kwɔd'reniəli], *adv.* tous les quatre ans.

quadrilateral [kwɔdri'lætərəl], *a.* quadrilatéral.—*n.* quadrilatère, *m.*

quadrille [kwə'dril], *n.* quadrille, *m.*; contredanse, *f.*

quadroon [kwə'dru:n], *n.* quarteron, *m.*

quadruped ['kwɔdruped], *n.* quadrupède, *m.*

quadruple ['kwɔdrupl], *a.* and *n.* quadruple, *m.*—*v.t.* quadrupler.

quadruplet ['kwɔdruplit], *n.* quadruplette, *f.*; (*pl.*) (*colloq.*) **quads** [kwɔdz], quadruplés, *m.pl.*

quaff [kwæf], *v.t.* boire à grands traits.

quaffer ['kwæfə], *n.* buveur, *m.*

quagmire ['kwægmaiə], *n.* fondrière, *f.*

quail (1) [kweil], *v.i.* perdre courage, fléchir.

quail (2) [kweil], *n.* (*Orn.*) caille, *f.*

quaint [kweint], *a.* singulier, bizarre; pittoresque.

quaintly ['kweintli], *adv.* singulièrement, bizarrement.

quaintness ['kweintnis], *n.* bizarrerie, originalité, *f.*

quake [kweik], *v.i.* trembler; branler.—*n.* tremblement, *m.*

Quaker ['kweikə], *n.* Quaker, *m.*

Quakerism ['kweikərizm], *n.* Quakerisme, *m.*

quaking ['kweikiŋ], *a.* tremblant.—*n.* tremblement, *m.*; terreur, *f.*

qualifiable ['kwɔlifaiəbl], *a.* qualifiable.

qualification [kwɔlifi'keiʃən], *n.* qualification, qualité; aptitude, *f.*, talent, *m.*; réserve, restriction, *f.*; (*pl.*) qualités, *f.pl.*, titres, *m.pl.*

qualified ['kwɔlifaid], *a.* qui a les qualités requises (*pour*), propre (*à*); *qualified teacher*, professeur diplômé, *m.*

qualify ['kwɔlifai], *v.t.* rendre capable (*de*); autoriser (*à*); modérer.—*v.i.* se préparer (*à*).

qualifying ['kwɔlifaiiŋ], *a.* qualificatif.

quality ['kwɔliti], *n.* qualité, *f.*; (*colloq.*) talent, *m.*

qualm [kwɑːm], *n.* nausée, *f.*; (*fig.*) scrupule, *m.*

qualmish ['kwɑːmiʃ], *a.* qui a mal au cœur.

quandary ['kwɔndəri], *n.* embarras, *m.*, impasse, *f.*

quantitative ['kwɔntitətiv], *a.* quantitatif.

quantity ['kwɔntiti], *n.* quantité, *f.*; grand nombre, *m.*

quantum ['kwɔntəm], *n.* montant, quantum, *m.*

quarantine ['kwɔrənti:n], *n.* quarantaine, *f.* —*v.t.* mettre en quarantaine.

quarrel ['kwɔrəl], *n.* querelle, dispute, brouille, *f.*—*v.i.* se quereller, se brouiller.

quarreller ['kwɔrələ], *n.* querelleur, *m.*

quarrelling ['kwɔrəliŋ], *n.* querelle; dispute, *f.*

quarrelsome ['kwɔrəlsəm], *a.* querelleur.

quarrelsomeness ['kwɔrəlsəmnis], *n.* humeur querelleuse, *f.*

quarry (1) ['kwɔri], *n.* carrière, *f.*—*v.t.* tirer d'une carrière.

quarry (2) ['kwɔri], *n.* (*Hunt.*) curée; proie, *f.*

quarrying ['kwɔriiŋ], *n.* extraction d'une carrière, *f.*

quarryman ['kwɔrimən], *n.* (*pl.* -**men** [men]) carrier, *m.*

quart [kwɔːt], *n.* quart de gallon (*1,14 litre*), *m.*

quarter ['kwɔːtə], *n.* quart; quart de quintal (*12,70 kg.*); quartier (*de ville, de la lune, de mouton etc.*), *m.*; partie, région (*d'un pays*), *f.*; côté (*direction*); trimestre (*de l'année*), *m.*; hanche (*de navire*), *f.*; (*pl.*) logement; (*Mil.*) quartier, *m.*; *to come to close quarters* en venir aux mains.—*v.t.* diviser en quatre; (*Mil.*) caserner; loger (*dans une maison*); (*Her.*) écarteler.

quarter day ['kwɔːtə'dei], *n.* jour du terme, *m.*

quarter-deck ['kwɔːtədek], *n.* gaillard d'arrière, *m.*

quartering ['kwɔːtəriŋ], *n.* division en quatre parties, *f.*; (*Mil.*) logement; (*Her.*) écartèlement, *m.*

quarterly ['kwɔːtəli], *a.* trimestriel.—*adv.* par trimestre, tous les trois mois.

quartermaster ['kwɔːtəmɑːstə], *n.* (*Navy*) maître timonier; (*Mil.*) officier d'approvisionnement, *m.*

quartet [kwɔː'tet], *n.* quatuor, *m.*

quarto ['kwɔːtou], *a.* and *n.* in-quarto, *m.*

quartz [kwɔːts], *n.* quartz, *m.*

quash [kwɔʃ], *v.t.* écraser; (*fig.*) dompter; (*Law*) annuler, casser.

quasi ['kweisai], *adv.* quasi.

quatrain ['kwɔtrein], *n.* quatrain, *m.*

quaver ['kweivə], *n.* tremblement de la voix, trille, *m.*; (*Mus.*) croche, *f.*—*v.i.* trembler; (*Mus.*) faire des trilles.

quavering ['kweivəriŋ], *a.* tremblant, chevrotant.—*n.* trille, tremolo; tremblement de voix, *m.*

quay [ki:], *n.* quai, *m.*

quayage ['ki:idʒ], *n.* quayage, *m.*

queen [kwi:n], *n.* reine; (*Cards etc.*) dame, *f.*

queen bee ['kwi:nbi:], *n.* reine-abeille, *f.*

queen like ['kwi:nlaik], **queenly** ['kwi:nli], *adv.* de reine, digne d'une reine.

queen-mother [kwi:n'mʌðə], *n.* reine-mère, *f.*

queer [kwiə], *a.* bizarre, étrange, drôle.

queerly ['kwiəli], *adv.* étrangement, bizarrement.

queerness ['kwiənis], *n.* étrangeté, bizarrerie, *f.*; malaise, *m.*

quell [kwel], *v.t.* réprimer, dompter.

quench [kwentʃ], *v.t.* éteindre; étancher; étouffer (*élan etc.*); *to quench one's thirst*, étancher sa soif, se désaltérer.

quenchable ['kwentʃəbl], *a.* extinguible.

quenchless ['kwentʃlis], *a.* inextinguible.

querulous ['kweruləs], *a.* plaintif, maussade.

querulousness ['kweruləsnis], *n.* humeur chagrine, *f.*

query ['kwiəri], *n.* question, *f.*; point d'interrogation, *m.*—*v.t.* mettre en doute.—*v.i.* questionner.

quest [kwest], *n.* enquête; recherche, *f.*; *in quest of*, à la recherche de.

question ['kwestʃən], *n.* question, interrogation, demande, *f.*; sujet (*problème*), *m.*; (*Parl.*) interpellation, *f.*; *out of the question*, absolument impossible; *that is not the question*, il ne s'agit pas de cela; *to ask a question*, poser une question.—*v.t.* questionner, interroger; mettre en doute.—*v.i.* se demander (*si*).

questionable ['kwestʃənəbl], *a.* contestable, douteux, incertain; suspect, équivoque.

questioner ['kwestʃənə], *n.* questionneur, *m.*

questioning ['kwestʃəniŋ], *n.* questions, *f.pl.*, interrogation, *f.*

question master ['kwestʃənmɑːstə], *n.* (*Rad.*, *Tel.*) meneur de débats, *m.*

questionnaire [kwestʃə'nɛə], *n.* questionnaire, *m.*

queue [kjuː], *n.* queue, *f.*—*v.i.* faire la queue.

quibble [kwibl], *n.* argutie, chicane, *f.*—*v.i.* ergoter, chicaner.

quibbler ['kwiblə], *n.* ergoteur, chicaneur, *m.*

quick [kwik], *a.* vite, rapide, prompt; agile, leste; vif (*vivant*); (*fig.*) fin.—*adv.* vite, promptement, lestement.—*n.* vif, *m.*; chair vive, *f.*; **stung to the quick**, piqué au vif; (*collect.*) **the quick**, les vivants, *m.pl.*

quicken ['kwikən], *v.t.* animer, vivifier; raviver, accélérer, hâter.—*v.i.* prendre vie, s'animer.

quickening ['kwikəniŋ], *a.* vivifiant, qui ranime.

quicklime ['kwiklaim], *n.* chaux vive, *f.*

quickly ['kwikli], *adv.* vite; promptement; bientôt.

quickness ['kwiknis], *n.* vitesse; promptitude; activité; pénétration; fréquence (*du pouls*), *f.*

quicksand ['kwiksænd], *n.* sable mouvant, *m.*

quickset ['kwikset], *a.* vive; **quickset hedge**, haie vive, *f.*—*n.* plante vive, *f.*

quicksilver ['kwiksilvə], *n.* vif-argent, mercure, *m.*

quicksilvered ['kwiksilvəd], *a.* étamé.

quicksilvering ['kwiksilvəriŋ], *n.* étamage, *m.*

quick-tempered ['kwik'tempəd], *a.* emporté, vif, colérique.

quick-witted ['kwik'witid], *a.* à l'esprit vif.

quid [kwid], *n.* chique; (*slang*) livre sterling, *f.*

quidnunc ['kwidnʌŋk], *n.* curieux, colporteur de nouvelles, *m.*

quiescence [kwi'esəns], *n.* quiétude, tranquillité, *f.*, repos, *m.*

quiescent [kwi'esənt], *a.* paisible, en repos, tranquille.

quiet ['kwaiət], *a.* tranquille, calme; paisible, silencieux; (*fig.*) modeste; **be quiet!** silence! taisez-vous! **to keep quiet**, se tenir tranquille, rester tranquille.—*n.* tranquillité, quiétude, *f.*; repos, calme, *m.*—*v.t.* (*also* **quieten** ['kwaiətn]) tranquilliser, apaiser, calmer.—*v.i.* **to quiet(en) down**, s'apaiser, se calmer.

quieten, *v.t.*, *v.i.* [QUIET].

quieting ['kwaiətiŋ], *a.* calmant, tranquillisant.

quietly ['kwaiətli], *adv.* tranquillement; doucement; en silence, sans bruit, discrètement, sans éclat.

quietness ['kwaiətnis], *n.* tranquillité, *f.*; calme, repos, *m.*

quietude ['kwaiitjuːd], *n.* quiétude, tranquillité, *f.*

quietus [kwai'iːtəs], *n.* repos, *m.*; mort, *f.*; (*fig.*) coup de grâce, *m.*; décharge, quittance, *f.*

quill [kwil], *n.* (tuyau de) plume; plume d'oie (*pour écrire*), *f.*; piquant (*de porc-épic*), *m.*—*v.t.* tuyauter, rucher.

quilling ['kwiliŋ], *n.* tuyautage, *m.*, ruche, *f.*

quilt [kwilt], *n.* édredon, *m.*, courtepointe, *f.*—*v.t.* piquer.

quilting ['kwiltiŋ], *n.* piqué; piquage, *m.*

quince [kwins], *n.* coing; cognassier (*arbre*), *m.*

quinine ['kwainain], *n.* quinine, *f.*

Quinquagesima [kwiŋkwə'dʒesimə]. Quinquagésime, *f.*

quinquennial [kwiŋ'kweniəl], *a.* quinquennial.

quinquina [kiŋ'kiːnə], *n.* quinquina, *m.*

quinsy ['kwinzi], *n.* angine, *f.*

quint [kwint], *n.* quinte, *f.*

quintal [kwintl], *n.* quintal, *m.*

quintessence [kwin'tesəns], *n.* quintessence, *f.*

quintet [kwin'tet], *n.* quintette, *m.*

quintuple ['kwintjupl], *a.* quintuple.—*v.t.* quintupler.

quintuplets ['kwintjuplits], (*colloq.*) **quins** [kwinz], *n.pl.* quintuplés, *m.pl.*

quip [kwip], *n.* mot piquant, sarcasme, *m.*—*v.t.* railler.

quire ['kwaiə], *n.* main (*de papier*), *f.*

quirk [kwəːk], *n.* sarcasme, *m.*, pointe; subtilité (*chicane*), *f.*

quit [kwit], *v.t. irr.* quitter, abandonner; **notice to quit**, congé, *m.*—*a.* quitte; **to get quit of**, se débarrasser de.

quite [kwait], *adv.* tout à fait, entièrement, complètement, tout; bien, parfaitement; assez.

quits [kwits], *a.* quitte.

quiver ['kwivə], *n.* carquois, *m.*—*v.i.* trembler, frissonner; palpiter (*la chair*); frémir.

quivering ['kwivəriŋ], *n.* tremblement, frissonnement; battement des paupières, *m.*

Quixote ['kwiksət], Don. Don Quichotte, *m.*

quixotic [kwik'sotik], *a.* de Don Quichotte; extravagant, exalté.

quiz [kwiz], *n.* plaisanterie, devinette, *f.*; examen oral, *m.*, colle, *f.*; **radio quiz**, jeu radiophonique, *m.*—*v.t.* questionner, interroger; [see **question master**]

quizzical ['kwizikəl], *a.* douteur.

quodlibet ['kwodlibet], *n.* quolibet, *m.*, subtilité, *f.*

quoin [koin], *n.* coin, *m.*

quoit [koit], *n.* palet, *m.*

quondam ['kwondəm], *a.* ci-devant, ancien.

quorum ['kwoːrəm], *n.* nombre suffisant, quorum, *m.*

quota ['kwoutə], *n.* quote-part, *f.*

quotable ['kwoutəbl], *a.* citable.

quotation [kwo'teiʃən], *n.* citation; (*Comm.*) cote, *f.*; (*St. Exch.*) cours, *m.* [see **comma**]

quote [kwout], *v.t.* citer; alléguer; (*Comm.*) coter.

quotidian [kwo'tidiən], *a.* quotidien, journalier.

quotient ['kwouʃənt], *n.* quotient, *m.*

R

R, r [ɑː]. dix-huitième lettre de l'alphabet, *m.*

rabbet ['ræbət], *n.* feuillure, rainure, *f.*—*v.t.* faire une rainure à.

rabbet-plane ['ræbətplein], *n.* guillaume, *m.*

rabbi ['ræbai], n. rabbin, m.; *chief rabbi*, grand rabbin.

rabbit ['ræbit], n. lapin, m.; *young rabbit*, lapereau, m.

rabble [ræbl], n. foule; populace, canaille, f.

rabid ['ræbid], a. féroce, furieux; enragé (*chien*).

rabies ['reibi:z], n. rage, hydrophobie, f.

raccoon [rə'ku:n], n. raton laveur, m.

race (1) [reis], n. (*Biol.*) race, f.

race (2) [reis], n. (*Spt.*) course, f.; raz, raz de marée (*courant*), m.—v.i. courir vite, courir, lutter de vitesse; *to go to the races*, aller aux courses.

race-course ['reiskɔ:s], n. champ de courses, hippodrome, m.

race-horse ['reishɔ:s], n. cheval de course, m.

racer ['reisə], n. coureur; cheval de course, m.

race-track ['reistræk], n. piste, f.

racial ['reiʃəl], a. de (la) race, ethnique.

raciness ['reisinis], n. piquant, m., verve, f.

racing ['reisiŋ], a. de course.—n. les courses, f.pl.

racing car ['reisiŋka:], n. automobile de course, f.

racism ['reisizm], n. racisme, m.

rack [ræk], n. râtelier (*dans une écurie etc.*); chevalet (*instrument de tension*), m.; roue (*instrument de supplice*) (*Tech.*) crémaillère, f.; *luggage rack*, (*Rail.*) filet, m.—v.t. mettre à la torture; (*fig.*) tourmenter; *to rack one's brains*, se creuser la cervelle.

racket ['rækit], n. fracas, tapage, tintamarre, caquet, m.; (*Ten.*) raquette; escroquerie, supercherie, combine, f.

rackety ['rækiti], a. tapageur.

racking ['rækiŋ], a. de torture; atroce (*douleur*).

racy ['reisi], a. (*fig.*) vif, piquant, plein de verve (*style etc.*).

radar ['reida:], n. radar, m.

radiance ['reidiəns], **radiancy** ['reidiənsi], n. rayonnement, éclat, m., splendeur, f.

radiant ['reidiənt], a. rayonnant (*de*); radieux, éclatant.

radiantly ['reidiəntli], adv. en rayonnant, splendidement.

radiate ['reidieit], v.t. émettre comme des rayons.—v.i. rayonner (*de*).

radiation [reidi'eiʃən], n. rayonnement, m., radiation, f.

radiator ['reidieitə], n. radiateur, m.

radical ['rædikəl], a. radical; fondamental.—n. radical, m.

radicalism ['rædikəlizm], n. radicalisme, m.

radically ['rædikəli], adv. radicalement, essentiellement.

radio ['reidiou], n. radio, la T.S.F., f. [see **wireless**]

radioactive [reidiou'æktiv], a. radio-actif.

radioactivity ['reidiouæk'tiviti], n. radio-activité, f.

radio control ['reidioukən'troul], n. téléguidage, m.—v.t. téléguider.

radiogram ['reidiougræm], n. radio-gramme, m.

radiography [reidi'ɔgrəfi], n. radiographie, f.

radish ['rædiʃ], n. radis, m.; *horse-radish*, raifort, m.

radium ['reidiəm], n. radium, m.

radius ['reidiəs], n. rayon, m.

radix ['reidiks], n. (*pl.* **radices** ['reidisi:z]) racine; base, f.

raffle [ræfl], n. loterie, tombola, f.—v.t. mettre en tombola.

raft [ra:ft], n. radeau; train de bois, m.

rafter ['ra:ftə], n. chevron, m.

raftered ['ra:ftəd], a. à chevrons.

rafting ['ra:ftiŋ], n. flottage en train, m.

raftsman ['ra:ftsmən], n. flotteur, m.

rag [ræg], n. chiffon (*nettoyage etc.*); haillon, m.; guenille, loque (*de vêtement*), f.; (*Sch.*) chahut, m.; brimade, f.—v.t. (*Sch.*) chahuter.

ragamuffin ['rægəmʌfin], n. gueux, polisson, va-nu-pieds, m.

rage [reidʒ], n. rage, fureur, f., emportement, m.; furie, manie, f.; *it's all the rage*, cela fait fureur.—v.i. être furieux, être en fureur, s'emporter; (*fig.*) sévir.

ragged ['rægid], a. en haillons, déguenillé (*personnes*); en lambeaux, déchiré (*choses*).

raggedness ['rægidnis], n. délabrement, déguenillement, m.; guenilles, f.pl.

raging ['reidʒiŋ], a. furieux, en fureur; déchaîné, acharné, violent (*tempête, guerre etc.*).—n. fureur, violence, f.

ragman ['rægmən], n. (*pl.* **-men** [men]) chiffonnier, m.

rag-time ['rægtaim], n. (*Mus.*) musique syncopée, f.

raid [reid], n. incursion, f.; raid, coup de main, m.; *air raid*, raid aérien.—v.t. faire une incursion dans; piller; bombarder.

raider ['reidə], n. maraudeur; commando, m.

rail (1) [reil], n. barre, f., barreau (*bois, métal etc.*), m.; rampe (*d'escalier*), f.; parapet (*de pont etc.*), (*Rail.*) rail, m.—v.t. enclore, griller.

rail (2) [reil], v.i. *to rail at*, criailler, invectiver.

railer ['reilə], n. criailleur, médisant, m.

railing (1) ['reiliŋ], n. grille, f., garde-fou, m.

railing (2) ['reiliŋ], n. injures, invectives, f.pl.

raillery ['reiləri], n. raillerie, f.

railway ['reilwei], n. chemin de fer, m., voie ferrée, f.

railwayman ['reilweimən], n. (*pl.* **-men** [men]) employé des chemins de fer, cheminot, m.

raiment ['reimənt], n. vêtement, m.

rain [rein], n. pluie, f.—v.t. faire pleuvoir.—v.i. pleuvoir; *it is pouring with rain*, il pleut à verse.

rainbow ['reinbou], n. arc-en-ciel, m.

raincoat ['reinkout], n. imperméable, m.

rainfall ['reinfɔ:l], n. pluie annuelle, pluie tombée, f.

rain gauge ['reingeidʒ], n. pluviomètre, m.

rainy ['reini], a. pluvieux.

raise [reiz], v.t. lever; élever; hausser (*prix etc.*); soulever (*élever à une petite hauteur etc.*); cultiver (*légumes*); augmenter, accroître (*ajouter à*); faire naître (*soupçons*); pousser (*un cri*); faire lever (*pâte*); se procurer (*argent*); faire (*un emprunt etc.*).—n. augmentation (*de gages*), f.

raised [reizd], a. levé; en relief.

raisin [reizn], n. raisin sec, m.

raising ['reiziŋ], n. augmentation, f., accroissement, m.; levée (*d'impôts, de troupes, de sièges etc.*), f.; élevage (*de bestiaux*), m.; culture (*de plantes etc.*), f.

rake (1) [reik], *n.* (*Hort.*) râteau.—*v.t.* (*Agric.*) râteler; (*Hort.*) ratisser; ramasser (*rassembler*); (*Mil.*) enfiler.
rake (2) [reik], *n.* roué (*libertin*), *m.*
raking ['reikiŋ], *a.* d'enfilade.—*n.* (*Hort.*) ratissage; (*Agric.*) râtelage, *m.*
rakish ['reikiʃ], *a.* dissolu; élancé (*navire*).
rakishness ['reikiʃnis], *n.* libertinage; air crâne, *m.*
rally ['ræli], *v.t.* rallier, rassembler.—*v.i.* se rallier, se rassembler; (*fig.*) se remettre.—*n.* ralliement, *m.*
Ralph [reif, rælf] Raoul, *m.*
ram [ræm], *n.* bélier; mouton, *m.*—*v.t.* enfoncer; pilonner, tasser (*terre etc.*); bourrer (*dans un canon*).
ramble ['ræmbl], *n.* excursion à pied, grande promenade; (*fig.*) divagation, *f.*—*v.i.* errer, se promener; errer çà et là; (*fig.*) divaguer.
rambler ['ræmblə], *n.* excursionniste (à pied), *m., f.*; (*Hort.*) rosier grimpant, *m.*
rambling ['ræmbliŋ], *a.* errant, vagabond; (*fig.*) décousu, incohérent.—*n.* excursions, promenades à l'aventure; (*fig.*) divagations, *f.pl.*
ramification [ræmifi'keiʃən], *n.* ramification, *f.*
ramify ['ræmifai], *v.i.* se ramifier.
rammer ['ræmə], *n.* pilon, *m.*
ramp [ræmp], *n.* rampe, montée; (*fam.*) escroquerie, *f.*
rampant ['ræmpənt], *a.* dominant, violent; effréné; (*Her.*) rampant.
rampart ['ræmpɑ:t], *n.* rempart, *m.*
ramrod ['ræmrɔd], *n.* baguette (*de fusil*), *f.*; écouvillon (*de canon*), *m.*; **stiff as a ramrod**, droit comme un piquet.
ramshackle ['ræmʃækl], *a.* qui tombe en ruines, délabré.
rancid ['rænsid], *a.* rance.
rancidity [ræn'siditi], **rancidness** ['rænsidnis], *n.* rancidité, *f.*
rancor ['ræŋkə], *n.* haine, rancune, *f.*
rancorous ['ræŋkərəs], *a.* rancunier, haineux.
Randolph ['rændɔlf], Rodolphe, *m.*
random ['rændəm], *a.* fait au hasard.—*n.* hasard, *m.*; **at random**, au hasard.
range [reindʒ], *n.* rangée, *f.*, rang (*file*), *m.*; chaîne (*de montagnes etc.*); étendue, portée, *f.*, fourneau; tir (*armes à feu*), *m.*; gamme (*de couleurs*), *f.*—*v.t.* ranger, arranger; aligner (*avec*); parcourir.—*v.i.* s'aligner; être rangé.
range finder [reindʒfaində], *n.* télémètre, *m.*
ranger ['reindʒə], *n.* garde-forestier, *m.*
rank (1) [ræŋk], *n.* rang, ordre, *m.*, classe, *f.*; (*Mil.*) grade; (*fig.*) haut rang, *m.*; station de taxis, *f.*—*v.t.* classer.—*v.i.* se ranger, être classé; occuper un rang.
rank (2) [ræŋk], *a.* luxuriant; (*fig.*) rude; extrême; fétide (*odeur*).
rankle [ræŋkl], *v.i.* s'envenimer, s'enflammer.
rankness ['ræŋknis], *n.* surabondance; grossièreté; rancidité, *f.*
ransack ['rænsæk], *v.t.* saccager, piller, fouiller.
ransacking ['rænsækiŋ], *n.* pillage, *m.*
ransom ['rænsəm], *n.* rançon, *f.*—*v.t.* rançonner.
rant [rænt], *n.* déclamation extravagante, *f.*—*v.i.* extravaguer; tempêter.

ranter ['ræntə], *n.* déclamateur, énergumène, *m.*
ranting ['ræntiŋ], *a.* d'énergumène, extravagant.
ranunculus [rə'nʌŋkjuləs], *n.* (*Bot.*) renoncule, *f.*
rap [ræp], *n.* tape, *f.*, petit coup sec, *m.*—*v.t.* *v.i.* frapper.
rapacious [rə'peiʃəs], *a.* rapace.
rapaciously [rə'peiʃəsli], *adv.* avec rapacité.
rapaciousness [rə'peiʃəsnis], **rapacity** [rə'pæsiti], *n.* rapacité, *f.*
rape (1) [reip], *n.* (*Poet.*) rapt, enlèvement; (*Law*) viol, *m.*—*v.t.* enlever de force; violer.
rape (2) [reip], *n.* (*Agric.*) colza, *m.*, navette, *f.*
rapid ['ræpid], *a.* and *n.* rapide, *m.*
rapidity [rə'piditi], **rapidness** ['ræpidnis], *n.* rapidité, *f.*
rapidly ['ræpidli], *adv.* rapidement.
rapier ['reipiə], *n.* rapière, *f.*
rapine ['ræpain], *n.* rapine, *f.*
rapt [ræpt], *a.* ravi, extasié; profond (*attention*).
rapture ['ræptʃə], *n.* ravissement, transport, *m.*, extase, *f.*
rapturous ['ræptʃərəs], *a.* ravissant; joyeux.
rapturously ['ræptʃərəsli], *adv.* avec transport.
rare [rɛə], *a.* rare; clairsemé; à moitié cru (*viande*).
rarefaction [rɛəri'fækʃən], *n.* raréfaction, *f.*
rarefy ['rɛərifai], *v.t.* raréfier.—*v.i.* se raréfier.
rarely ['rɛəli], *adv.* rarement.
rareness ['rɛənis], **rarity** ['rɛəriti], *n.* rareté, *f.*
rascal ['rɑ:skl], *n.* coquin, fripon, gredin, *m.*
rascality [rɑ:s'kæliti], *n.* friponnerie, gredinerie, coquinerie, *f.*
rascally ['rɑ:skəli], *a.* coquin, fripon.
rase [RAZE].
rash (1) [ræʃ], *a.* téméraire; irréfléchi, imprudent.
rash (2) [ræʃ], *n.* éruption, *f.*
rasher ['ræʃə], *n.* tranche, *f.*
rashly ['ræʃli], *adv.* témérairement; imprudemment.
rashness ['ræʃnis], *n.* témérité; précipitation, imprudence, *f.*
rasp [rɑ:sp], *n.* râpe, *f.*—*v.t.* râper; râcler, écorcher (*surface, peau*).—*v.i.* grincer, crisser.
raspberry ['rɑ:zbəri], *n.* framboise, *f.*
raspberry bush ['rɑ:zbəribuʃ], *n.* framboisier, *m.*
rasping ['rɑ:spiŋ], *a.* grinçant, âpre, rauque (*voix*).—*n.* râpage; crissement, *m.*
rat [ræt], *n.* rat, *m.*; **to smell a rat**, se douter de quelque chose.
ratchet ['rætʃit], *n.* cliquet, *m.*, dent d'engrenage, *f.*
ratchet-brace ['rætʃitbreis], **ratchet-jack** ['rætʃitdʒæk], *n.* vilbrequin à cliquet, *m.*
rate (1) [reit], *n.* prix, *m.*; raison, proportion, *f.*; taux (*argent, population*); cours (*de change*); degré, rang, ordre, *m.*; vitesse; taxe, *f.*, impôt (*taxe municipale*), *m.*; **at any rate**, en tout cas; **first-rate**, de première classe.—*v.t.* évaluer; classer; taxer; faire une estimation; regarder (*comme*).—*v.i.* **to rate as**, être classé comme.
rate (2) [reit], *v.t.* gronder.

531

rateable ['reitəbl], *a.* imposable; *rateable value,* valeur locative imposable (*d'un immeuble*), *f.*

rate-payer ['reitpeiə], *n.* contribuable, *m.,f.*

rather ['rɑːðə], *adv.* plutôt; un peu, quelque peu (*légèrement*); assez, passablement (*suffisamment*).

ratification [rætifi'keiʃən], *n.* ratification, *f.*

ratify ['rætifai], *v.t.* ratifier, approuver.

ratifying ['rætifaiiŋ], *a.* ratificatif.

rating (1) ['reitiŋ], *n.* estimation, évaluation; répartition d'impôt, *f.;* (*Navy*) matelot, *m.*

rating (2) ['reitiŋ], *n.* gronderie, *f.*

ratio ['reiʃiou], *n.* proportion, raison, *f.,* rapport, *m.*

ration ['ræʃən], *n.* ration, *f.*—*v.t.* rationner.

ration book ['ræʃənbuk], *n.* carte d'alimentation, *f.*

rationing ['ræʃəniŋ], *n.* rationnement, *m.*

rational ['ræʃənl], *a.* raisonnable, rationnel.

rationalism ['ræʃnəlizm], *n.* rationalisme, *m.*

rationalist ['ræʃnəlist], *n.* rationaliste, *m., f.*

rationalize ['ræʃnəlaiz], *v.t.* rationaliser.

rationally ['ræʃnəli], *adv.* raisonnablement, rationnellement.

rattan [rə'tæn], *n.* rotin, *m.*

ratten ['rætn], *v.t.* intimider; saboter.

rattle [rætl], *v.t.* faire claquer, faire sonner; secouer (*chaînes etc.*).—*v.i.* faire un bruit sec, cliqueter, crépiter.—*n.* bruit; cliquetis (*de métaux*); râle (*à la gorge*); hochet (*jouet*), *m.;* crécelle, *f.*

rattlesnake ['rætlsneik], *n.* serpent à sonnettes, crotale, *m.*

rattling ['rætliŋ], *a.* bruyant; (*fig.*) excellent. —*n.* bruit, cliquetis, *m.*

rat-trap ['rættræp], *n.* ratière, *f.*

raucous ['rɔːkəs], *a.* rauque.

ravage ['rævidʒ], *n.* ravage, *m.*—*v.t.* ravager.

ravager ['rævidʒə], *n.* ravageur, dévastateur, *m.*

rave [reiv], *v.i.* être en délire; (*fig.*) extravaguer.

ravel [rævl], *v.t.* embrouiller, entortiller.— *v.i.* s'embrouiller, s'entortiller.

raven (1) [reivn], *n.* (*Orn.*) corbeau, *m.*

raven (2) [rævn], *v.t.* dévorer.

ravenous ['rævənəs], *a.* dévorant, vorace.

ravenously ['rævənəsli], *adv.* avec voracité.

ravenousness ['rævənəsnis], *n.* voracité, rapacité, *f.*

ravine [rə'viːn], *n.* ravin, *m.*

raving ['reiviŋ], *a.* en délire, délirant; furieux, fou.—*n.* délire, *m.*

ravish ['ræviʃ], *v.t.* ravir; enlever; (*fig.*) transporter.

ravisher ['ræviʃə], *n.* ravisseur, *m.*

ravishing ['ræviʃiŋ], *a.* ravissant.

raw [rɔː], *a.* cru; vif, écorché (*égratigné etc.*); (*fig.*) sans expérience, novice; pur (*alcool*); brut (*cuir etc.*); froid et humide (*temps*); *raw materials,* matières premières, *f.pl.*

raw-boned ['rɔːbound], *a.* maigre, décharné.

rawness ['rɔːnis], *n.* crudité, *f.;* froid humide (*du temps*), *m.;* (*fig.*) inexpérience, *f.*

ray (1) [rei], *n.* rayon, *m.*

ray (2) [rei], *n.* (*Ichth.*) raie, *f.*

rayless ['reilis], *a.* sans rayon, sans lumière.

Raymond ['reimənd], Raymond, *m.*

rayon ['reiən], *n.* rayonne, *f.*

raze [reiz], *v.t.* raser, effleurer; rayer, effacer (*supprimer*); abattre, détruire (*édifice*).

razor ['reizə], *n.* rasoir, *m.;* *safety razor,* rasoir de sûreté.

re [riː, rei], *prep.* au sujet de, à propos de.

reach [riːtʃ], *n.* portée, atteinte; étendue (*capacité*), *f.;* bief (*de canal*), *m.*—*v.t.* atteindre, toucher; passer, donner (*rendre*); arriver à, parvenir à (*accomplir*).—*v.i.* s'étendre de . . . à.

reachable [riːtʃəbl], *a.* qu'on peut atteindre.

react [riː'ækt], *v.i.* réagir (*sur*).

reaction [riː'ækʃən], *n.* réaction, *f.*

reactionary [riː'ækʃənəri], *a.* and *n.* réactionnaire, *m., f.*

reactor [riː'æktə], *n.* réacteur, *m.*

read [riːd], *v.t. irr.* lire; faire la lecture de; (*fig.*) étudier.—*v.i.* lire; faire la lecture; se lire.

readable ['riːdəbl], *a.* lisible; qui se lit avec plaisir.

readableness ['riːdəblnis], *n.* lisibilité, *f.*

readdress [riːə'dres], *v.t.* faire suivre (*lettre*).

reader ['riːdə], *n.* lecteur; (*Print.*) correcteur; liseur (*amateur de lecture*); (*Sch.*) livre de lecture, *m.*

readily ['redili], *adv.* tout de suite, promptement; volontiers (*de bon gré*), avec plaisir.

readiness ['redinis], *n.* empressement, *m.,* promptitude; facilité; bonne volonté (*complaisance*), *f.*

reading ['riːdiŋ], *n.* lecture; variante (*textuelle*), leçon; hauteur (*de baromètre*), *f.*

reading book ['riːdiŋbuk], *n.* livre de lecture, *m.*

reading desk ['riːdiŋdesk], *n.* pupitre, *m.*

reading lamp ['riːdiŋlæmp], *n.* lampe de travail, *f.*

reading room ['riːdiŋruːm], *n.* salle de lecture, *f.*

readjust [riːə'dʒʌst], *v.t.* rajuster, rectifier.

readjustment [riːə'dʒʌstmənt], *n.* rajustement, *m.*

ready ['redi], *a.* prêt, prompt; facile; vif (*qui comprend vite*); *ready money,* argent comptant, *m.*

ready-made ['redimeid], *a.* tout fait, confectionné.

ready-reckoner ['redi'reknə], *n.* barème, *m.*

ready-witted ['redi'witid], *a.* à l'esprit vif.

reaffirm [riːə'fəːm], *v.t.* réaffirmer.

reafforestation [riːəforis'teiʃən], *n.* reboisement, *m.*

real ['riːəl], *a.* réel; vrai, véritable; effectif; (*Law*) immeuble, immobilier. [see **realty; estate-agent; house-agent**]

realism ['riːəlizm], *n.* réalisme, *m.*

realist ['riːəlist], *n.* réaliste, *m., f.*

realistic [riːə'listik], *a.* réaliste.

reality [riː'æliti], *n.* réalité, *f.;* réel, *m.*

realizable ['riːəlaizəbl], *a.* réalisable.

realization [riːəlai'zeiʃən], *n.* réalisation; conception nette, *f.*

realize ['riːəlaiz], *v.t.* réaliser; effectuer; se rendre compte de, bien comprendre; se figurer; rapporter (*somme*).

really ['riːəli], *adv.* réellement, en effet, effectivement; vraiment.—*int.* en vérité! à vrai dire!

realm [relm], *n.* royaume, *f.*, (*fig.*) domaine, *m.*

realty ['riːəlti], *n.* biens immeubles, *m.pl.*

ream [riːm], *n.* rame (*de papier*), *f.*

reap [ri:p], *v.t., v.i.* moissonner; (*fig.*) recueillir.

reaper ['ri:pə], *n.* moissonneur, *m.*

reaping ['ri:piŋ], *n.* moisson, *f.*

reaping machine ['ri:piŋməʃi:n], *n.* moissonneuse, *f.*

reappear [ri:ə'piə], *v.i.* reparaître, réapparaître.

reappearance [ri:ə'piərəns], *n.* réapparition; rentrée (*d'acteur*), *f.*

reappoint [ri:ə'point], *v.t.* réintégrer; renommer.

reappointment [ri:ə'pointmənt], *n.* réintégration, *f.*

rear (1) [riə], *a.* situé à l'arrière, postérieur; **rear wheel**, roue arrière, *f.—n.* dernier rang, *m.*; arrière-garde, *f.*; derrière (*d'édifice etc.*), *m.*; **to bring up the rear**, fermer la marche.

rear (2) [riə], *v.t.* élever.—*v.i.* se cabrer.

rear admiral ['riərædmərəl], *n.* contre-amiral, *m.*

re-arm [ri:'a:m], *v.t., v.i.* réarmer.

re-armament [ri:'a:məmənt], *n.* réarmement, *m.*

rearwards ['riəwədz], *adv.* à l'arrière.

reascend [ri:ə'send], *v.t., v.i.* remonter.

reason [ri:zn], *n.* raison, *f.*; raisonnement, *m.*; **the reason why**, la raison pour laquelle; **that stands to reason**, cela va sans dire; **to have reason to believe**, avoir lieu de croire.—*v.t., v.i.* raisonner.

reasonable ['ri:znəbl], *a.* raisonnable; modéré.

reasonableness ['ri:znəblnis], *n.* raison, modération, *f.*

reasonably ['ri:znəbli], *adv.* raisonnablement.

reasoner ['ri:zənə], *n.* raisonneur, logicien, *m.*

reasoning ['ri:zəniŋ], *n.* raisonnement, *m.*

reassemble [ri:ə'sembl], *v.t.* rassembler.—*v.i.* se rassembler.

reassert [ri:ə'sə:t], *v.t.* affirmer de nouveau.

reassess [ri:ə'ses], *v.t.* réévaluer.

reassessment [ri:ə'sesmənt], *n.* réimposition; réévaluation, *f.*

reassign [ri:ə'sain], *v.t.* réassigner.

reassignment [ri:ə'sainmənt], *n.* réassignation, *f.*

reassume [ri:ə'sju:m], *v.t.* réassumer; reprendre (*position*).

reassurance [ri:ə'ʃuərəns], *n.* action de rassurer; (*Comm.*) réassurance, *f.*

reassure [ri:ə'ʃuə], *v.t.* rassurer; (*Comm.*) réassurer.

rebate ['ri:beit], *n.* rabais, *m.*, remise, *f.*—[ri'beit], *v.t.* diminuer, rabattre.

rebel [rebl], *n.* rebelle, *m., f.*, révolté, *m.*—[ri'bel], *v.i.* se révolter, se soulever (*contre*).

rebellion [ri'beljən], *n.* rébellion, *f.*

rebellious [ri'beljəs], *a.* rebelle.

rebelliously [ri'beljəsli], *adv.* en rebelle.

rebelliousness [ri'beljəsnis], *n.* rébellion, *f.*

rebirth [ri:'bə:θ], *n.* renaissance, *f.*

reborn [ri:'bo:n], *a.* né de nouveau; réincarné.

rebound ['ri:baund], *n.* rebondissement, contre-coup, *m.*—[ri'baund], *v.i.* rebondir.

rebuff [ri'bʌf], *n.* rebuffade, *f.*, échec, *m.*—*v.t.* rebuter, repousser.

rebuild [ri:'bild], *v.t. irr.* (*conjug. like* BUILD) rebâtir, reconstruire.

rebuke [ri'bju:k], *n.* réprimande, *f.*, reproche, *m.*—*v.t.* réprimander, reprendre, censurer.

rebus ['ri:bəs], *n.* rébus, *m.*

rebut [ri'bʌt], *v.t.* rebuter, repousser, réfuter.

recalcitrant [ri'kælsitrənt], *a.* récalcitrant, insoumis, réfractaire.

recall [ri'ko:l], *n.* rappel, *m.*; révocation, *f.*; **beyond recall**, irrévocablement.—*v.t.* rappeler; se rappeler (*se souvenir de*).

recant [ri'kænt], *v.t.* rétracter, désavouer, abjurer.—*v.i.* se rétracter.

recantation [ri:kæn'teiʃən], *n.* rétractation, palinodie, *f.*

recapitulate [ri:kə'pitjuleit], *v.t.* récapituler.

recapitulation [ri:kəpitju'leiʃən], *n.* récapitulation, *f.*

recapture [ri:'kæptʃə], *n.* reprise, *f.—v.t.* reprendre.

recast [ri:'ka:st], *v.t. irr.* (*conjug. like* CAST) refondre; (*Theat.*) faire une nouvelle distribution des rôles.

recede [ri'si:d], *v.i.* se retirer (*de*); s'éloigner.

receding [ri'si:diŋ], *a.* fuyant (*le front*), effacé (*menton*).

receipt [ri'si:t], *n.* reçu, *m.*, quittance, *f.*, acquit, *m.*; réception (*le fait de recevoir*); (*pl.*) recette, *f.*, recettes, *f.pl.*; récépissé, *m.* —*v.t.* acquitter.

receive [ri'si:v], *v.t.* recevoir, accepter; accueillir; receler (*biens volés*).

receiver [ri'si:və], *n.* receveur; receleur (*d'objets volés*); liquidateur (*faillite*); (*Teleph.*) récepteur, *m.*

receiving [ri'si:viŋ], *n.* réception, *f.*; recel (*d'objets volés*), *m.*

recent ['ri:sənt], *a.* récent, frais, nouveau.

recently ['ri:səntli], *adv.* récemment, depuis peu.

receptacle [ri'septəkl], *n.* réceptacle; récipient, *m.*

reception [ri'sepʃən], *n.* réception, *f.*; accueil, *m.*

receptionist [ri'sepʃənist], *n.* réceptionniste, *m., f.*

receptive [ri'septiv], *a.* réceptif (*esprit*).

recess [ri'ses], *n.* enfoncement, *m.*, niche, *f.*; recoin, *m.*; vacances, *f.pl.*

recession [ri'seʃən], *n.* retraite, *f.*; désistement (*d'une revendication*), *m.*; (*St. Exch.*) baisse, *f.*

recidivist [ri'sidivist], *n.* récidiviste, *m., f.*

recipe ['resipi], *n.* (*Cook.*) recette, *f.*

recipient [ri'sipiənt], *n.* personne qui reçoit, *f.*, destinataire (*de lettre*), *m., f.*; (*Chem.*) récipient, *m.*

reciprocal [ri'siprəkl], *a.* réciproque.

reciprocate [ri'siprəkeit], *v.t.* échanger; répondre à.—*v.i.* alterner, se succéder.

reciprocation [risiprə'keiʃən], **reciprocity** [resi'prositi], *n.* réciprocité, *f.*

recital [ri'saitl], *n.* récit, *m.*; narration, énumération, *f.*; (*Mus.*) récital, *m.*

recitation [resi'teiʃən], *n.* récitation, *f.*

recitative [resitə'ti:v], *n.* récitatif, *m.*

recite [ri'sait], *v.t.* réciter, faire le récit de; raconter.

reciter [ri'saitə], *n.* récitateur; diseur, narrateur, *m.*

reck [rek], *v.i.* se soucier de.

reckless ['reklis], *a.* insouciant (*de*); téméraire, insensé.

recklessly ['reklisli], *adv.* témérairement, avec insouciance.

recklessness ['reklisnis], *n.* insouciance, témérité, *f.*

reckon [rekn], *v.t.* compter, calculer; regarder, évaluer (*comme*).—*v.i.* compter; *to reckon on*, compter sur; *to reckon with*, tenir compte de.

reckoner ['reknə], *n.* calculateur, chiffreur, *m.*; *ready-reckoner*, barème, *m.*

reckoning ['reknin], *n.* compte, calcul; écot, *m.*, note (*dans un hôtel*); addition (*dans un restaurant*) (*Naut.*) estime, *f.*

reclaim [ri:'kleim], *v.t.* réformer, corriger; ramener (*de*); réclamer, revendiquer (*ses droits*); défricher (*terre*).

reclaimable [ri:'kleiməbl], *a.* corrigible; cultivable, défrichable (*terre*).

reclaiming [ri:'kleimin], **reclamation** [reklə'meiʃən], *n.* défrichement (*de terre*), *m.*; réforme, correction (*de criminels*), *f.*

recline [ri'klain], *v.i.* s'appuyer, se reposer, se coucher.

reclining [ri'klainin], *a.* incliné, appuyé, couché.

reclothe [ri:'klouð], *v.t.* rhabiller.

recluse [ri:'klu:s], *a.* reclus; solitaire, retiré.— *n.* reclus, *m.*

reclusion [ri'klu:ʒən], *n.* réclusion, *f.*

recognition [rekəg'niʃən], *n.* reconnaissance, *f.*

recognizable [rekəg'naizəbl], *a.* reconnaissable.

recognizance [ri'kɔgnizəns], *n.* reconnaissance; (*Law*) obligation contractée, *f.*

recognize ['rekəgnaiz], *v.t.* reconnaître.

recoil [ri'kɔil], *n.* recul; contre-coup, *m.*; (*fig.*) répugnance, *f.*—*v.i.* reculer; retomber.

recollect [rekə'lekt], *v.t.* se souvenir de, se rappeler.

recollection [rekə'lekʃən], *n.* souvenir, *m.*; mémoire, *f.*

recommence [ri:kə'mens], *v.t.*, *v.i.* recommencer.

recommend [rekə'mend], *v.t.* recommander.

recommendation [rekəmen'deiʃən], *n.* recommandation; apostille (*d'une pétition*), *f.*

recompense ['rekəmpens], *n.* récompense, *f.*; dédommagement, *m.*—*v.t.* récompenser (*de*); dédommager (*de*); compenser, réparer.

reconcilable [rekən'sailəbl], *a.* réconciliable; conciliable (*avec*).(*choses*).

reconcile ['rekənsail], *v.t.* réconcilier (*avec*); habituer, accoutumer (*familiariser*) (*to*); *reconcile oneself to*, se résigner à.

reconciliation [rekənsili'eiʃən], *n.* réconciliation; conciliation (*de choses*); (*Bibl.*) expiation, *f.*

recondite [ri'kɔndait, 'rekəndait], *a.* secret, abstrus, profond, mystérieux.

recondition [ri:kən'diʃən], *v.t.* remettre à neuf, refaire.

reconnaissance [ri'kɔnisəns], *n.* reconnaissance, *f.*

reconnoiter [rekə'nɔitə], *v.t.* reconnaître.— *v.i.* faire une reconnaissance.

reconsider [ri:kən'sidə], *v.t.* considérer de nouveau; revenir sur (*une décision*).

reconsideration [ri:kənsidə'reiʃən], *n.* reconsidération, *f.*

reconstitute [ri:'kɔnstitju:t], *v.t.* reconstituer.

reconstruct [ri:kən'strʌkt], *v.t.* reconstruire.

reconstruction [ri:kən'strʌkʃən], *n.* reconstruction, *f.*

record ['rekɔ:d], *n.* registre, *m.*, archives, *f.pl.*; disque (*de phonographe*); (*Spt.*) record; dossier, *m.*; *keeper of the records*, archiviste, *m.*, *f.*; *long-playing record*, disque longue durée, *m*; *public records*, archives, *f.pl.*; *record library*, discothèque, *f.*; greffe, *m.*—[ri'kɔ:d], *v.t.* enregistrer; graver, imprimer (*dans l'esprit etc.*); mentionner (*fait historique*).

recorder [ri'kɔ:də], *n.* enregistreur, archiviste; greffier; (*Law*) officier judiciaire d'une ville; (*Mus.*) flageolet, *m.*; *tape recorder*, magnétophone, *m.*

recording [ri'kɔ:din], *n.* enregistrement, *m.*

recount (1) [ri'kaunt], *v.t.* raconter.

recount (2) [ri:'kaunt], *v.t.* recompter.— ['ri:kaunt], *n.* nouvelle addition des voix (*aux élections*), *f.*

recoup [ri'ku:p], *v.t.* rembourser, dédommager (*de*).

recourse [ri'kɔ:s], *n.* recours, *m.*

recover (1) [ri'kʌvə], *v.t.* recouvrer, retrouver; réparer (*perte*).—*v.i.* se rétablir, guérir; se remettre (*d'une maladie*); se relever (*d'une perte*).

recover (2) [ri:'kʌvə], *v.t.* recouvrir; regarnir.

recovery [ri'kʌvəri], *n.* recouvrement, *m.*; guérison, *f.*; rétablissement, *m.*; (*Econ.*) reprise, *f.*; *past recovery*, incurable, sans remède.

recreant ['rekriənt], *a. and n.* lâche, infidèle, *m.*, *f.*, apostat, *m.*

re-create [ri:kri'eit], *v.t.* recréer.

recreation [rekri'eiʃən], *n.* récréation, *f.*, divertissement, *m.*

recriminate [ri'krimineit], *v.i.* récriminer (*contre*).

recrimination [rikrimi'neiʃən], *n.* récrimination, *f.*

recriminatory [ri'kriminətri], *a.* récriminatoire.

recrudescence [ri:kru'desəns], *n.* recrudescence, *f.*

recruit [ri'kru:t], *n.* recrue, *f.*, conscrit, *m.*— *v.t.* rétablir, réparer (*restaurer*); (*Mil.*) recruter.—*v.i.* se recruter, se remettre.

recruiting [ri'kru:tin], **recruitment** [ri'kru:t mənt], *n.* recrutement, *m.*; *recruiting officer*, officier de recrutement, *m.*

rectangle ['rektæŋgl], *n.* rectangle, *m.*

rectangular [rek'tæŋgjulə], *a.* rectangulaire, rectangle, à angle droit.

rectifiable ['rektifaiəbl], *a.* rectifiable.

rectification [rektifi'keiʃən], *n.* rectification, *f.*

rectifier ['rektifaiə], *n.* rectificateur; (*Elec.*) redresseur, *m.*

rectify ['rektifai], *v.t.* rectifier; redresser.

rectilineal [rekti'liniəl], *a.* rectiligne.

rectitude ['rektitju:d], *n.* rectitude, droiture, *f.*

rector ['rektə], *n.* (*Ch. of England*) prêtre; (*R.-C.*) curé; (*Univ. etc.*) recteur, principal, *m.*

rectorial [rek'tɔ:riəl], *a.* rectoral.

rectorship ['rektəʃip], *n.* rectorat, *m.*

rectory ['rektəri], *n.* cure, *f.*, presbytère, *m.*

recumbent [ri'kʌmbənt], *a.* couché, étendu; appuyé (*sur*).

534

recuperate [ri'ku:pəreit], *v.t.* recouvrer, récupérer.—*v.i.* se rétablir, se remettre, reprendre ses forces.

recuperation [riku:pə'reiʃən], *n.* recouvrement; rétablissement (*personne*), *m.*

recur [ri'kə:], *v.i.* revenir; se reproduire.

recurrence [ri'kʌrəns], *n.* retour, *m.*

recurrent [ri'kʌrənt], **recurring** [ri'kə:riŋ], *a.* périodique; (*Anat. etc.*) récurrent.

red [red], *a.* rouge; roux (*cheveux*); vermeil (*lèvres etc.*); **red lead**, minium, *m.*; **red-letter day**, jour de fête, *m.*—*n.* rouge, *m.*

redbreast ['redbrest], *n.* rouge-gorge, *m.*

redden [redn], *v.t., v.i.* rougir.

reddish ['rediʃ], *a.* rougeâtre, roussâtre.

redeem [ri'di:m], *v.t.* racheter; (*Fin.*) rembourser, amortir; retirer (*objets mis en gage*); (*fig.*) réparer.

redeemable [ri'di:məbl], *a.* rachetable.

redeemer [ri'di:mə], *n.* rédempteur, *m.*

redeeming [ri'di:miŋ], *a.* qui rachète.

redemption [ri'dempʃən], *n.* rédemption, *f.*; (*Fin.*) amortissement; rachat (*de billets*), *m.*

red-hot ['redhot], *a.* tout rouge, chauffé au rouge, ardent (*charbon*).

redirect [ri:di'rekt], *v.t.* faire suivre (*lettre*).

rediscover [ri:dis'kʌvə], *v.t.* redécouvrir.

redistribution [ri:distri'bju:ʃən], *n.* nouvelle distribution, répartition, *f.*

redness ['rednis], *n.* rougeur; rousseur (*de cheveux*), *f.*

redolence ['redoləns], *n.* parfum, *m.*; senteur, *f.*

redolent ['redolənt], *a.* qui a un parfum de; **redolent of . . .**, qui sent le . . .

redouble [ri'dʌbl], *v.t., v.i.* redoubler.

redoubt [ri'daut], *n.* redoute, *f.*

redoubtable [ri'dautəbl], *a.* redoutable.

redound [ri'daund], *v.i.* contribuer (*à, en*), résulter (*pour*), rejaillir (*sur*).

redpole, redpoll ['redpoul], *n.* (*pop.*) linotte, *f.*

redraft [ri'dra:ft], *n.* nouveau dessin, *m.*; (*Comm.*) retraite, *f.*—*v.t.* rédiger de nouveau.

redress [ri'dres], *v.t.* redresser, corriger, réparer.—*n.* redressement, *m.*, réparation, *f.*, remède, *m.*

redshank ['redʃæŋk], *n.* (*Orn.*) chevalier, *m.*, gambette, *f.*

redskin ['redskin], *n.* Peau-Rouge, *m., f.*

red tape ['red'teip], *n.* bolduc, *m.*; (*fig.*) routine administrative, *f.*

reduce [ri'dju:s], *v.t.* réduire (*à ou en*); maigrir (*chair*); dégrader (*abaisser*); **a person in reduced circumstances**, une personne tombée dans la gêne.—*v.i.* maigrir.

reduction [ri'dʌkʃən], *n.* réduction, *f.*; **a reduction in prices**, une baisse des prix, *f.*; **reduction to the ranks**, cassation, *f.*

redundance [ri'dʌndəns], **redundancy** [ri'dʌndənsi], *n.* redondance, *f.*

redundant [ri'dʌndənt], *a.* redondant, superflu.

re-echo [ri:'ekou], *v.t.* répéter.—*v.i.* retentir.—*n.* écho répété, *m.*

reed [ri:d], *n.* roseau; chalumeau, *m.*; (*Mus.*) anche, *f.*

reed pipe ['ri:dpaip], *n.* chalumeau, pipeau, *m.*

reedy ['ri:di], *a.* couvert de roseaux; flûtée (*voix*).

reef (1) [ri:f], *n.* récif, écueil, *m.*

reef (2) [ri:f], *n.* ris (*de voile*), *m.*—*v.t.* prendre un ris dans.

reef knot ['ri:fnot], *n.* nœud plat, *m.*

reek [ri:k], *n.* fumée, *f.*, relent, *m.*—*v.i.* fumer; exhaler; **reeking with**, tout fumant de; **to reek of**, puer, empester.

reel (1) [ri:l], *n.* dévidoir, *m.*; bobine (*de coton*), *f.*; (*Angling*) moulinet, *m.*; (*Cine.*) bobine, bande, *f.*; **newsreel**, les actualités, *f.pl.*—*v.t.* dévider, débiter.—*v.i.* tournoyer, chanceler, trébucher.

reel (2) [ri:l], *n.* branle écossais (*danse*), *m.*

re-elect [ri:i'lekt], *v.t.* réélire.

re-election [ri:i'lekʃən], *n.* réélection, *f.*

re-embark [ri:əm'ba:k], *v.t.* rembarquer.—*v.i.* se rembarquer.

re-embarkation [ri:emba:'keiʃən], *n.* rembarquement, *m.*

re-embody [ri:əm'bodi], *v.t.* réincorporer.

re-enact [ri:i'nækt], *v.t.* remettre en vigueur (*une loi*); reconstituer (*un crime*).

re-enactment [ri:i'næktmənt], *n.* remise en vigueur; reconstitution, *f.*

re-engage [ri:in'geidʒ], *v.t.* rengager.

re-enlist [ri:in'list], *v.t., v.i.* (se) rengager.

re-enter [ri:'entə], *v.t., v.i.* rentrer.

re-entrant [ri:'entrənt], *a.* and *n.* rentrant, *m.*

re-establish [[ri:is'tæbliʃ], *v.t.* rétablir.

re-establishment [ri:is'tæbliʃmənt], *n.* rétablissement, *m.*

re-examine [ri:ig'zæmin], *v.t.* examiner de nouveau, revoir.

re-export [ri:iks'po:t], *v.t.* réexporter.

refashion [ri:'fæʃən], *v.t.* refaçonner.

refasten [ri:'fa:sn], *v.t.* rattacher; ragrafer.

refection [ri'fekʃən], *n.* repas, *m.*, collation, *f.*

refectory [ri'fektəri], *n.* réfectoire, *m.*

refer [ri'fə:], *v.t.* renvoyer, rapporter; adresser (*à*); remettre à la décision de.—*v.i.* se référer, se rapporter, avoir rapport (*à*); s'en rapporter, se référer (*personnes*); s'adresser (*à*).

referee [refə'ri:], *n.* arbitre, *m., f.*—*v.t., v.i.* (*Spt.*) arbitrer.

reference ['refərəns], *n.* renvoi; rapport (*respect*), *m.*; allusion, *f.*; renseignements, *m.pl.*, références (*de bonne vie et mœurs*), *f.pl.*; (*person*) référence, *f.*; **book of reference**, ouvrage à consulter, *m.*; **with reference to**, au sujet de; **to make reference to**, faire allusion à.

referendum [refə'rendəm], *n.* référendum, *m.*

refill [ri:'fil], *v.t.* remplir.—*v.i.* (*Motor.*) faire le plein (*d'essence*).—['ri:fil], *n.* objet (*feuilles, pile, ampoule*) de rechange; (*Motor.*) plein (*d'essence*), *m.*

refine [ri'fain], *v.t.* épurer (*liquides*); (*Metal.*) affiner; raffiner (*sucre etc.*); (*fig.*) purifier.

refined [ri'faind], *a.* raffiné; pur, délicat (*goût*).

refinement [ri'fainmənt], *n.* raffinage (*de sucre*); (*Metal.*) affinage, *m.*; épuration (*de liquides*); (*fig.*) délicatesse, *f.*

refinery [ri'fainəri], *n.* raffinerie (*de sucre*); (*Metal.*) affinerie, *f.*

refit [ri:'fit], *v.t.* réparer; (*Naut.*) radouber.—['ri:fit], *n.* réparation; (*Naut.*) refonte, *f.*

reflect [ri'flekt], *v.t.* réfléchir; faire rejaillir sur; refléter.—*v.i.* réfléchir; **to reflect upon**, réfléchir à, méditer sur.

reflected [ri'flektid], *a.* réfléchi.

reflection [REFLEXION].
reflective [ri'flektiv], *a.* réfléchissant; méditatif.
reflector [ri'flektə], *n.* réflecteur; (*Cycl., Motor.*) catadioptre, *m.*
reflex ['ri:fleks], *a.* réfléchi; (*Paint.*) reflété; (*Physiol. etc.*) réflexe.—*n.* (*Paint.*) reflet; (*Physiol.*) réflexe, *m.*
reflexion [ri'flekʃən], *n.* réflexion, *f.*; reflet (*lumière etc.*), *m.*; censure, *f.*; blâme, *m.*
reflexive [ri'fleksiv], *a.* réfléchi.
reform [ri'fɔ:m], *n.* réforme, *f.*—*v.t.* réformer; corriger.—*v.i.* se réformer, se corriger.
re-form [ri:'fɔ:m], *v.t.* reformer.—*v.i.* se reformer.
reformation [refɔ:'meiʃən], *n.* réformation; réforme, *f.*; **the Reformation,** (*Hist.*) la Réforme.
re-formation [ri:fɔ:'meiʃən], *n.* formation nouvelle, *f.*
reformer [ri'fɔ:mə], *n.* réformateur, *m.*
refract [ri'frækt], *v.t.* réfracter.
refraction [ri'frækʃən], *n.* réfraction, *f.*
refractive [ri'fræktiv], *a.* réfractif; réfringent.
refractory [ri'fræktri], *a.* indocile, récalcitrant, intraitable, rebelle; (*Chem. etc.*) réfractaire; rétif (*cheval*).
refrain [ri'frein], *v.i.* se retenir, s'abstenir (*de*).—*n.* refrain, *m.*
refresh [ri'freʃ], *v.t.* rafraîchir; délasser, restaurer; **to refresh oneself,** se rafraîchir.
refreshing [ri'freʃiŋ], *a.* rafraîchissant; réparateur, qui repose.
refreshment [ri'freʃmənt], *n.* rafraîchissement, *m.*; **refreshment bar,** buvette, *f.*; **refreshment car,** wagon-restaurant, *m.*; **refreshment room,** buffet, *m.*
refrigerate [ri'fridʒəreit], *v.t.* réfrigérer, frigorifier.
refrigeration [rifridʒə'reiʃən], *n.* réfrigération, *f.*
refrigerator [ri'fridʒəreitə], *n.* réfrigérateur; (*fam.*) Frigidaire (*marque déposée*), *m.*
refuel [ri:'fjuəl], *v.i.* (*Av.*) faire le plein (d'essence).
refuge ['refju:dʒ], *n.* refuge (*contre*), *m.*; **to take refuge,** se réfugier.
refugee [refju'dʒi:], *n.* réfugié, *m.*
refulgence [ri'fʌldʒəns], *n.* éclat, *m.*, splendeur, *f.*
refulgent [ri'fʌldʒənt], *a.* éclatant.
refund [ri'fʌnd], *v.t.* rembourser, rendre.—['ri:fʌnd], *n.* remboursement, *m.*
refurnish [ri:'fə:niʃ], *v.t.* remeubler.
refusal [ri'fju:zl], *n.* refus, *m.*
refuse ['refju:s], *n.* rebut, *m.*, ordures (*ménagères, de marché*), *f.pl.*; **refuse dump,** voirie, *f.*—[ri'fju:z], *v.t.* refuser; rejeter.—*v.i.* refuser.
refute [ri'fju:t], *v.t.* réfuter.
regain [ri'gein], *v.t.* regagner, reprendre.
regal [ri:gl], *a.* royal.
regale [ri'geil], *v.t.* régaler.—*v.i.* se régaler.
regally ['ri:gəli], *adv.* royalement, en roi.
regard [ri'ga:d], *n.* égard, *m.*; considération, *f.*; respect (*estime*), *m.*; (*pl.*) amitiés, *f.pl.*, compliments, *m.pl.*; **out of regard for,** par égard pour; **with regard to,** quant à.—*v.t.* regarder; considérer; **as regards,** quant à.

regarding [ri'ga:diŋ], *prep.* quant à, concernant.
regardless [ri'ga:dlis], *a.* peu soigneux (*de*); sans égard (*pour*); **regardless of,** sans se soucier de.
regatta [ri'gætə], *n.* régate(s), *f.*(*pl.*).
regency [ri:dʒənsi], *n.* régence, *f.*
regenerate [ri'dʒenərət], *a.* régénéré.—[ri:'dʒenəreit], *v.t.* régénérer.
regenerating [ri'dʒenəreitiŋ], *a.* régénérateur.
regeneration [ri:dʒenə'reiʃən], *n.* régénération, *f.*
regent ['ri:dʒənt], *n.* régent, *m.*
regicide ['redʒisaid], *n.* régicide (*crime*), *m.*; régicide (*personne*), *m., f.*
régime [rei'ʒi:m], *n.* (*Polit.*) régime, *m.*
regimen ['redʒimən], *n.* (*Gram., Med.*) régime, *m.*
regiment ['redʒimənt], *n.* régiment, *m.*
regimental [redʒi'mentl], *a.* du régiment, de régiment.
regimentation [redʒimen'teiʃən], *n.* enrégimentation, *f.*
Reginald ['redʒinəld]. Renaud, *m.*
region ['ri:dʒən], *n.* région, *f.*
regional ['ri:dʒənl], *a.* régional.
register ['redʒistə], *n.* registre, *m.*; liste électorale (*de votants*), *f.*—*v.t.* enregistrer; recommander (*lettre, paquet*); déclarer (*naissance*); immatriculer (*voiture*); déposer (*marque de fabrique etc.*).
registrar ['redʒistra:], *n.* (*Law*) greffier; (*Univ.*) secrétaire et archiviste; officier de l'état civil (*de naissances etc.*), *m.*
registration [redʒis'treiʃən], *n.* enregistrement; chargement (*de lettres*); dépôt (*d'une marque de fabrique etc.*), *m.*; immatriculation (*de véhicule*); inscription (*des bagages*), *f.*; **registration number,** (*Motor.*) numéro minéralogique, *m.*
registry ['redʒistri], *n.* enregistrement; (*Law*) greffe, *m.*
registry office ['redʒistri'ɔfis], *n.* bureau de l'état civil, *m.*
regret [ri'gret], *n.* regret, *m.*—*v.t.* regretter (*de*), avoir du regret (*à*).
regretful [ri'gretful], *a.* plein de regrets; regrettable.
regretfully [ri'gretfuli], *adv.* avec regret, à regret.
regrettable [ri'gretəbl], *a.* fâcheux, regrettable.
regular ['regjulə], *a.* régulier; réglé; en règle; ordinaire (*normal*); (*fig.*) franc, fieffé.
regularity [regju'læriti], *n.* régularité, *f.*
regularly ['regjuləli], *adv.* régulièrement.
regulate ['regjuleit], *v.t.* régler; diriger.
regulation [regju'leiʃən], *a.* réglementaire.—*n.* règlement, *m.*
regulator ['regjuleitə], *n.* régulateur, *m.*
rehabilitate [ri:hə'biliteit], *v.t.* réhabiliter.
rehabilitation [ri:həbili'teiʃən], *n.* réhabilitation, *f.*
rehearsal [ri'hə:sl], *n.* récit, *m.*; (*Theat.*) répétition, *f.*; **dress rehearsal,** répétition générale.
rehearse [ri'hə:s], *v.t.* (*Theat.*) répéter; (*fig.*) raconter (*narrer*).
rehouse [ri:'hauz], *v.t.* reloger.
reign [rein], *n.* règne, *m.*—*v.i.* régner.

reigning ['reiniŋ], *a.* régnant; (*fig.*) dominant (*prevailing*).
reimburse [ri:im'bə:s], *v.t.* rembourser.
reimbursement [ri:im'bə:smənt], *n.* remboursement, *m.*
rein [rein], *n.* rêne, *f.*—*v.t.* conduire à la bride, gouverner, brider; contenir.
reincarnation [ri:inka:'neiʃən], *n.* réincarnation, *f.*
reindeer ['reindiə], *n.* renne, *m.*
reinforce [ri:in'fɔ:s], *v.t.* renforcer; **reinforced concrete**, béton armé, *m.*
reinforcement [ri:in'fɔ:smənt], *n.* renforcement; (*Mil.*) renfort, *m.*
reinstall [ri:in'stɔ:l], *v.t.* réinstaller.
reinstate [ri:in'steit], *v.t.* rétablir.
reinstatement [ri:in'steitmənt], *n.* rétablissement, *m.*
reintroduce [ri:intrə'dju:s], *v.t.* introduire de nouveau, réintroduire.
reinvest [ri:in'vest], *v.t.* replacer.
reinvigorate [ri:in'vigəreit], *v.t.* ranimer.
reissue [ri:'isju:], *v.t.* émettre de nouveau, rééditer (*livre*).—*n.* nouvelle émission; nouvelle édition, *f.*
reiterate [ri:'itəreit], *v.t.* réitérer.
reiteration [ri:itə'reiʃən], *n.* réitération, *f.*
reiterative [ri:'itərətiv], *a.* réitératif.
reject [ri'dʒekt], *v.t.* rejeter.—['ri:dʒekt], *n.* pièce de rebut, *f.*
rejection [ri'dʒekʃən], *n.* rejet, *m.*
rejoice [ri'dʒɔis], *v.t.* réjouir.—*v.i.* se réjouir (*de*).
rejoicing [ri'dʒɔisiŋ], *n.* réjouissance, joie, *f.*
rejoin [ri:'dʒɔin], *v.t.* rejoindre.—[ri'dʒɔin], *v.i.* répliquer, répondre.
rejoinder [ri'dʒɔində], *n.* repartie; (*Law*) réplique, *f.*
rejuvenate [ri'dʒu:vəneit], *v.t.* rajeunir.
rejuvenation [ridʒu:və'neiʃən], *n.* rajeunissement, *m.*
rekindle [ri:'kindl], *v.t.* rallumer.
relapse [ri'læps], *n.* rechute, *f.*—*v.i.* retomber (*dans*); récidiver (*criminel*).
relate [ri'leit], *v.t.* raconter; rapporter.—*v.i.* se rapporter, avoir rapport (*à*).
related [ri'leitid], *a.* ayant rapport; parent (*de*); allié (*à*) (*par mariage etc.*).
relating [ri'leitiŋ], *a.* relatif, qui se rapporte (*à*).
relation [ri'leiʃən], *n.* relation, *f.*, rapport, récit (*narration*); parent (*de la famille*); allié (*par mariage*), *m.*; (*pl.*) relations, *f.pl.*, rapports (*contact*), *m.pl.*
relationship [ri'leiʃənʃip], *n.* parenté, *f.*; rapport, *m.*
relative ['relətiv], *a.* relatif (*à*).—*n.* parent; (*Gram.*) relatif, *m.*
relatively ['relətivli], *adv.* relativement.
relativity [relə'tiviti], *n.* relativité, *f.*
relax [ri'læks], *v.t.* relâcher, détendre.—*v.i.* se relâcher; se détendre; se délasser.
relaxation [ri:læk'seiʃən], *n.* relâchement, relâche, *m.*, détente, *f.*; (*Med.*) repos, *m.*
relaxing [ri'læksiŋ], *a.* relâchant; énervant, débilitant (*climat*).
relay ['ri:lei], *n.* relais, *m.*—*v.t.* relayer.
re-lay [ri:'lei], *v.t.* poser de nouveau.
release [ri'li:s], *v.t.* relâcher, élargir (*un prisonnier*); décharger (*de*); déclencher.—*n.* élargissement, *m.*; délivrance; décharge

(*d'une obligation*); (*Cine.*) sortie (*d'un film*), *f.*; déclenchement (*de ressort etc.*), *m.*
relegate ['reləgeit], *v.t.* reléguer.
relegation [relə'geiʃən], *n.* relégation, *f.*
relent [ri'lent], *v.i.* s'amollir, s'attendrir; se repentir (*regretter*).
relenting [ri'lentiŋ], *n.* attendrissement, *m.*
relentless [ri'lentlis], *a.* inflexible, impitoyable.
relentlessly [ri'lentlisli], *adv.* impitoyablement.
relentlessness [ri'lentlisnis], *n.* rigueur, dureté, *f.*
relevance ['relevəns], **relevancy** ['relevənsi], *n.* relation, *f.*, rapport, *m.*; pertinence, convenance, *f.*, à-propos, *m.*
relevant ['relevənt], *a.* relatif, applicable (*à*); à propos, pertinent.
reliable [ri'laiəbl], *a.* digne de confiance; sûr, exact, bien fondé (*renseignement*).
reliability [rilaiə'biliti], *n.* crédibilité, véracité; sûreté, *f.*
reliance [ri'laiəns], *n.* confiance, *f.*
relic ['relik], *n.* relique (*de saint ou martyr*), *f.*; (*pl.*) restes (*d'un être*); vestiges (*du passé*), *m.pl.*
relief [ri'li:f], *n.* soulagement (*de douleur etc.*); secours (*aide*), *m.*; (*Mil.*) relève, *f.*; (*Sculp. etc.*) relief, *m.*; **relief train**, train supplémentaire, *m.*
relieve [ri'li:v], *v.t.* soulager, adoucir; délivrer (*de*); secourir, aider (*assister*); (*Mil.*) relever (*sentinelle*).
religion [ri'lidʒən], *n.* religion, *f.*
religious [ri'lidʒəs], *a.* religieux; de religion.
religiously [ri'lidʒəsli], *adv.* religieusement.
relinquish [ri'liŋkwiʃ], *v.t.* abandonner; renoncer à.
relinquishment [ri'liŋkwiʃmənt], *n.* abandon, *m.*; renonciation, *f.*
reliquary ['relikwəri], *n.* reliquaire, *m.*
relish ['reliʃ], *n.* goût, *m.*, saveur, *f.*; (*Cook.*) assaisonnement, *m.*; (*fig.*) charme; appétit, *m.*—*v.t.* goûter, savourer; relever le goût de.
relive [ri:'liv], *v.t.* revivre.
reload [ri:'loud], *v.t.* recharger.
reluctance [ri'lʌktəns], *n.* répugnance, *f.*
reluctant [ri'lʌktənt], *a.* qui a de la répugnance à, qui agit à contre-cœur; peu disposé (*à*).
reluctantly [ri'lʌktəntli], *adv.* à contre-cœur.
rely [ri'lai], *v.i.* compter (*sur*), avoir confiance (*en*).
remain [ri'mein], *v.i.* rester, demeurer.
remainder [ri'meində], *n.* reste, *m.*
remaining [ri'meiniŋ], *a.* de reste, restant.
remains [ri'meinz], *n.pl.* restes; débris, *m.pl.*; **mortal remains**, dépouille mortelle, *f.*
remake [ri:'meik], *v.t. irr.* (*conjug. like* MAKE) refaire.
remand [ri'mɑ:nd], *v.t.* renvoyer à une autre audience.—*n.* renvoi à une autre audience, *m.*
remark [ri'mɑ:k], *n.* remarque, *f.*—*v.t.* remarquer, observer; faire remarquer, faire observer (*à une personne*).
remarkable [ri'mɑ:kəbl], *a.* remarquable.
remarkably [ri'mɑ:kəbli], *adv.* remarquablement.
remarriage [ri:'mæridʒ], *n.* remariage, *m.*
remarry [ri:'mæri], *v.t.* épouser de nouveau.—*v.i.* se remarier.

537

remedial

remedial [ri'mi:djəl], *a.* réparateur; *(Med.)* curatif.

remedy ['remədi], *n.* remède; *(Law)* recours, *m.*—*v.t.* remédier à, porter remède à.

remember [ri'membə], *v.t.* se souvenir de, se rappeler; reconnaître *(de vue).*

remembrance [ri'membrəns], *n.* souvenir, *m.*, mémoire, *f.*

remind [ri'maind], *v.t.* rappeler à, faire souvenir *(à . . . de),* faire penser à.

reminder [ri'maində], *n.* mémento, *m.*

reminisce [remi'nis], *v.i.* raconter ses souvenirs.

reminiscence [remi'nisəns], *n.* réminiscence, *f.*

reminiscent [remi'nisənt], *a.* qui rappelle.

remiss [ri'mis], *a.* négligent.

remission [ri'miʃən], *n.* rémission, *f.*, pardon; relâchement *(détente),* *m.*; remise *(de dette, peine),* *f.*

remit [ri'mit], *v.t.* relâcher *(détendre);* remettre *(amende etc.).*—*v.i.* se relâcher, se calmer; diminuer.

remittance [ri'mitəns], *n.* remise, *f.*; envoi de fonds, *m.*

remittent [ri'mitənt], *a. (Path.)* rémittent.

remnant ['remnənt], *n.* reste, coupon, bout *(de tissu),* *m.*; *(pl.)* restes, débris, *m.pl.*

remodel [ri:'mɔdl], *v.t.* remodeler.

remold [ri:'mould], *v.t.* mouler de nouveau.

remonstrance [ri'mɔnstrəns], *n.* remonstrance, *f.*

remonstrate ['remənstreit], *v.i.* remontrer.

remorse [ri'mɔ:s], *n.* remords, *m.*

remorseful [ri'mɔ:sful], *a.* rempli de remords.

remorseless [ri'mɔ:slis], *a.* sans remords, impitoyable.

remorselessness [ri'mɔ:slisnis], *n.* cruauté, inhumanité, *f.*

remote [ri'mout], *a.* éloigné, lointain, reculé *(époque);* distant *(personne).*

remotely [ri'moutli], *adv.* de loin; faiblement.

remoteness [ri'moutnis], *n.* éloignement, *m.*; réserve *(attitude),* *f.*

remount [ri:'maunt], *v.t., v.i.* remonter.—*n.* remonte, *f.*

removable [ri'mu:vəbl], *a.* transportable; *(fig.)* amovible *(fonctionnaire etc.).*

removal [ri'mu:vl], *n.* éloignement, départ; transport; déménagement *(de meubles);* déplacement, *m.*; révocation *(de ses fonctions),* *f.*

remove [ri'mu:v], *n.* degré *(parenté),* *m.*; distance, *f.*—*v.t.* éloigner; déplacer *(bouger);* transporter; déménager *(meubles),* ôter, enlever *(emporter);* renvoyer *(de ses fonctions).*—*v.i.* s'éloigner, se déplacer; déménager *(changer de domicile).*

removed [ri'mu:vd], *a.* éloigné; *first cousin once removed,* cousin issu de germains, *m.*

remover [ri'mu:və], *n.* déménageur, *m.*; *nail polish remover,* dissolvant (pour ongles), *m.*

remunerate [ri'mju:nəreit], *v.t.* rémunérer.

remuneration [rimju:nə'reiʃən], *n.* rétribution, rémunération, *f.*

remunerative [ri'mju:nərətiv], *a.* rémunérateur; *(Law)* rémunératoire.

rename [ri:'neim], *v.t.* renommer.

rend [rend], *v.t. irr.* déchirer; *(fig.)* fendre.

render ['rendə], *v.t.* rendre; interpréter, traduire; *(Cook.)* fondre *(graisse etc.).*

rendering ['rendəriŋ], *n.* traduction, interprétation, *f.*

renegade ['renigeid], *n.* renégat, *m.*

renew [ri'nju:], *v.t.* renouveler; renouer *(connaissance).*

renewal [ri'nju:əl], *n.* renouvellement, *m.*; *renewal of subscription,* réabonnement, *m.*

renounce [ri'nauns], *v.t.* renoncer *(à);* renier.

renouncement [ri'naunsmənt], *n.* renoncement, *m.*, renonciation, *f.*

renovate ['renəveit], *v.t.* renouveler; rajeunir.

renovation [renə'veiʃən], *n.* rénovation, *f.*

renovator ['renəveitə], *n.* rénovateur, *m.*

renown [ri'naun], *n.* renommée, *f.*, renom, *m.*

renowned [ri'naund], *a.* renommé.

rent (1) [rent], *n.* déchirure, fente, *f.*; accroc *(de vêtements),* *m.*

rent (2) [rent], *n.* loyer *(de maison ou d'appartement);* fermage *(de ferme),* *m.*; *(pl.)* rentes; *f.pl.*, revenu, *m.*; *ground rent,* rente foncière, *f.*—*v.t.* louer, prendre à ferme, donner à ferme.—*v.i.* se louer.

rent (3) [rent], *past and p.p.* [REND].

rental [rentl], *n.* valeur locative, *f.*

rent-free ['rentfri:], *a.* exempt de loyer.

renunciation [rinansi'eiʃən], *n.* renonciation, *f.*, renoncement, *m.*

reoccupation [ri:ɔkju'peiʃən], *n.* réoccupation, *f.*

reoccupy [ri:'ɔkjupai], *v.t.* réoccuper.

reopen [ri:'oupən], *v.t.* rouvrir.—*v.i.* rentrer *(écoles, tribunaux etc.).*

reopening [ri:'oupniŋ], *n.* réouverture; rentrée *(d'écoles etc.),* *f.*

reorganization [ri:ɔ:gənai'zeiʃən], *n.* réorganisation, *f.*

reorganize [ri:'ɔ:gənaiz], *v.t.* réorganiser.

rep (1) [rep], *a.* de reps.—*n.* reps *(tissu),* *m.*

rep (2) [rep], [REPERTORY].

rep (3) [rep], [REPRESENTATIVE].

repaint [ri:'peint], *v.t.* repeindre.

repair (1) [ri'pɛə], *v.t.* réparer; raccommoder *(vêtements etc.);* *(fig.)* rétablir.—*n.* réparation, *f.*; raccommodage *(de vêtements etc.);* *to keep in repair,* entretenir.

repair (2) [ri'pɛə], *n.* séjour *(retraite),* *m.*—*v.i.* aller; se rendre *(à).*

repairer [ri'pɛərə], *n.* réparateur; raccommodeur *(de vêtements),* *m.*

reparable ['repərəbl], *a.* réparable.

reparation [repə'reiʃən], *n.* réparation *(d'une offense),* *f.*

repartee [repa:'ti:], *n.* repartie, riposte, *f.*

repast [ri'pa:st], *n.* repas, *m.*

repatriate [ri:'pætrieit], *v.t.* rapatrier.

repay [ri'pei], *v.t. irr. (conjug. like* PAY*)* rembourser; *(fig.)* valoir la peine *(de).*

repayment [ri:'peimənt], *n.* remboursement, *m.*

repeal [ri'pi:l], *v.t.* révoquer; abroger *(loi etc.).*—*n.* révocation; abrogation *(de loi),* *f.*

repeat [ri'pi:t], *v.t.* répéter, réitérer; réciter *(par cœur);* bis *(après vers de chanson etc.).*—*n.* répétition; *(Mus.)* reprise, *f.*

repeated [ri'pi:tid], *a.* répété, réitéré.

repeatedly [ri'pi:tidli], *adv.* à plusieurs reprises; souvent, bien des fois.

repeating [ri'pi:tiŋ], *a.* qui répète; à répétition.

repel [ri'pel], *v.t.* repousser; combattre.
repellent [ri'pelənt], *a.* répulsif, répugnant.—
n. répulsif; (*Med.*) révulsif, *m.*
repent [ri'pent], *v.t.* se repentir de.—*v.i.* se
repentir.
repentance [ri'pentəns], *n.* repentir, *m.*
repentant [ri'pentənt], *a.* repentant.
repercussion [ri:pə'kʌʃən], *n.* répercussion, *f.*
repertory ['repətri], *n.* répertoire, *m.*;
repertory theatre, (*fam.*) *rep*, troupe à
demeure, *f.*
repetition [repi'tiʃən], *n.* répétition; (*Mus.*)
reprise, *f.*
repetitive [ri'petitiv], *a.* qui se répète.
repine [ri'pain], *v.i.* murmurer (*contre*); se
plaindre (*de*).
repining [ri'painiŋ], *a.* disposé à se plaindre,
mécontent.—*n.* plainte, *f.*, regret, *m.*
replace [ri:'pleis], *v.t.* replacer; remplacer
(*substituer*).
replacement [ri:'pleismənt], *n.* remplacement, *m.*
replant [ri:'plɑ:nt], *v.t.* replanter.
replay ['ri:plei], *n.* match rejoué, *m.*—
[ri:'plei], *v.t.*, *v.i.* rejouer.
replenish [ri'pleniʃ], *v.t.* remplir (*de*).—*v.i.*
se remplir.
replenishment [ri'pleniʃmənt], *n.* remplissage, *m.*
replete [ri'pli:t], *a.* plein, rempli (*de*).
repletion [ri'pli:ʃən], *n.* plénitude; (*Med.*)
réplétion, *f.*
replica ['replikə], *n.* double, *m.*, copie, *f.*
reply [ri'plai], *n.* réponse; (*Law*) réplique, *f.*
—*v.t.*, *v.i.* répondre, répliquer.
repopulate [ri:'pɔpjuleit], *v.t.* repeupler.
report [ri'pɔ:t], *v.t.* rapporter, raconter, dire;
rendre compte de; signaler; dénoncer (*à la
police*); *to report oneself*, se présenter à.—
n. rapport; bruit, ouï-dire (*rumeur*); compte
rendu, procès-verbal (*de réunion etc.*); (*Sch.*)
bulletin; coup (*de fusil*), *m.*; réputation
(*renom*), *f.*
reporter [ri'pɔ:tə], *n.* rapporteur; reporter
(*journaliste*), *m.*
reporting [ri'pɔ:tiŋ], *n.* reportage, *m.*
repose [ri'pouz], *v.t.* reposer.—*v.i.* se reposer.
—*n.* repos, *m.*
repository [ri'pɔzitri], *n.* dépôt, *m.*
repossess [ri:pə'zes], *v.t.* rentrer en possession de.
reprehend [repri'hend], *v.t.* réprimander,
censurer, blâmer.
reprehensible [repri'hensibl], *a.* répréhensible, blâmable.
represent [repri'zent], *v.t.* représenter.
representation [reprizen'teiʃən], *n.* représentation, *f.*
representative [repri'zentativ], *a.* représentatif, qui représente.—*n.* représentant;
(*Comm.*) (*fam. abbr.* **rep**) agent, *m.*
repress [ri'pres], *v.t.* réprimer.
repression [ri'preʃən], *n.* répression, *f.*
repressive [ri'presiv], *a.* répressif.
reprieve [ri'pri:v], *n.* sursis; répit, *m.*—*v.t.*
accorder un sursis à; commuer (*une peine*),
gracier.
reprimand ['reprimɑ:nd], *n.* réprimande, *f.*
—*v.t.* réprimander.
reprint ['ri:print], *n.* réimpression, *f.*—
[ri:'print], *v.t.* réimprimer.
reprisal [ri'praizl], *n.* représailles, *f.pl.*

reproach [ri'proutʃ], *n.* reproche; opprobre
(*honte*), *m.*; *above reproach*, irréprochable.
—*v.t.* reprocher.
reprobate ['reprəbit], *n.* vaurien, *m.*
reprobation [reprə'beiʃən], *n.* réprobation, *f.*
reproduce [ri:prə'dju:s], *v.t.* reproduire.—
v.i. se reproduire.
reproduction [ri:prə'dʌkʃən], *n.* reproduction, *f.*
reproductive [ri:prə'dʌktiv], *a.* reproducteur.
reproof [ri'pru:f], *n.* reproche, *m.*, réprimande, *f.*
reprove [ri'pru:v], *v.t.* blâmer; censurer.
reproving [ri'pru:viŋ], *a.* réprobateur.
reprovingly [ri'pru:viŋli], *adv.* d'un air ou
ton réprobateur.
reptile ['reptail], *a.* reptile; (*fig.*) rampant,
vil.—*n.* reptile, *m.*
reptilian [rep'tiliən], *a.* reptilien.
republic [ri'pʌblik], *n.* république, *f.*
republican [ri'pʌblikən], *a.* and *n.* républicain, *m.*
republication [ri:pʌbli'keiʃən], *n.* nouvelle
édition, réimpression (*de livre*), *f.*
republish [ri:'pʌbliʃ], *v.t.* republier, rééditer.
repudiate [ri'pju:dieit], *v.t.* répudier.
repudiation [ripju:di'eiʃən], *n.* répudiation, *f.*
repugnance [ri'pʌgnəns], *n.* répugnance, *f.*
repugnant [ri'pʌgnənt], *a.* répugnant.
repulse [ri'pʌls], *v.t.* repousser, rebuter.—*n.*
échec, refus, *m.*, rebuffade, *f.*; *to meet with
a repulse*, essuyer un échec.
repulsion [ri'pʌlʃən], *n.* répulsion, *f.*
repulsive [ri'pʌlsiv], *a.* rebutant; repoussant
(*forbidding*).
repulsiveness [ri'pʌlsivnis], *n.* caractère
repoussant, *m.*
repurchase [ri:'pə:tʃis], *v.t.* racheter.—*n.*
rachat; (*Law*) réméré, *m.*
reputable ['repjutəbl], *a.* honorable, de bonne
réputation, considéré.
reputably ['repjutəbli], *adv.* honorablement.
reputation [repju'teiʃən], *n.* réputation, *f.*
repute [ri'pju:t], *v.t.* (*usu. pass.*) réputer,
estimer.—*n.* réputation, *f.*, renom, *m.*
reputed [ri'pju:tid], *a.* réputé, censé, qui
passe pour.
request [ri'kwest], *n.* demande, prière; (*Law*)
requête, *f.*; *request stop*, arrêt facultatif
(*autobus*), *m.*—*v.t.* demander; prier.
requiem ['rekwiem], *n.* requiem, *m.*
require [ri'kwaiə], *v.t.* exiger, requérir; avoir
besoin de (*manquer de*); (*impers.*) falloir.
requirement [ri'kwaiəmənt], *n.* exigence,
nécessité, *f.*, besoin, *m.*; condition requise, *f.*
requisite ['rekwizit], *a.* requis, exigé, nécessaire.—*n.* qualité *ou* condition requise;
chose requise, *f.*
requisition [rekwi'ziʃən], *n.* réquisition, *f.*—
v.t. réquisitionner.
requital [ri'kwaitl], *n.* récompense, *f.*
requite [ri'kwait], *v.t.* récompenser; rendre la
pareille à; payer de retour.
reredos ['riədɔs], *n.* retable, *m.*
rescind [ri'sind], *v.t.* rescinder, annuler.
rescue ['reskju:], *n.* délivrance, *f.*; sauvetage,
m.; *to the rescue*, au secours!—*v.t.*
sauver, délivrer (*de*).
rescuer ['reskju:ə], *n.* sauveteur, libérateur, *m.*
research [ri'sə:tʃ], *n.* recherche, *f.*—*v.i.* faire
des recherches.

reseat [ri:'si:t], *v.t.* rasseoir.
resemblance [ri'zembləns], *n.* ressemblance, *f.*; (*fig.*) rapport, *m.*
resemble [ri'zembl], *v.t.* ressembler (*à*); *to resemble each other*, se ressembler.
resent [ri'zent], *v.t.* ressentir, se ressentir de; s'offenser de; prendre en mauvaise part.
resentful [ri'zentful], *a.* rancunier.
resentfully [ri'zentfuli], *adv.* avec ressentiment.
resentment [ri'zentmənt], *n.* ressentiment, *m.*, rancœur, *f.*
reservation [rezə'veiʃən], *n.* réserve, restriction, arrière-pensée, *f.*; (*Am.*) terrain réservé, *m.*; réservation, location (*place assise*), *f.*
reserve [ri'zə:v], *n.* réserve; retenue, prudence; arrière-pensée, *f.*—*v.t.* réserver.
reserved [ri'zə:vd], *a.* réservé.
reservedly [ri'zə:vidli], *adv.* avec réserve.
reservist [ri'zə:vist], *n.* réserviste, *m.*, *f.*
reservoir ['rezəvwa:], *n.* réservoir, *m.*
reset [ri:'set], *v.t. irr.* (*conjug. like* SET) poser *ou* fixer de nouveau; (*Print.*) composer de nouveau; (*Surg.*) remettre.
resetting [ri:'setiŋ], *n.* remontage (*de pierre précieuse*), *m.*; (*Print.*) recomposition, *f.*
resettle [ri:'setl], *v.t.* rétablir.—*v.i.* s'établir de nouveau.
resettlement [ri:'setlmənt], *n.* rétablissement, *m.*
reshape [ri:'ʃeip], *v.t.* reformer; remanier.
reside [ri'zaid], *v.i.* résider, demeurer.
residence ['rezidəns], *n.* résidence, demeure, *f.*; *board* (*and*) *residence*, la table et le logement.
resident ['rezidənt], *a.* résidant; interne (*de la maison*).—*n.* habitant; résident, *m.*
residential [rezi'denʃl], *a.* résidentiel.
residual [ri'zidjuəl], *a.* résiduel.
residuary [ri'zidjuəri], *a.* de résidu, de reste; universel (*légataire*).
residue ['rezidju:], *n.* reste, (*Chem.*) résidu; reliquat (*de dette*), *m.*
resign [ri'zain], *v.t.* donner sa démission de; renoncer à; *to be resigned to* or *resign oneself to*, se résigner à.—*v.i.* donner sa démission, démissionner (*de*).
resignation [rezig'neiʃən], *n.* résignation; cession; démission (*de ses fonctions*), *f.*
resigned [ri'zaind], *a.* résigné; démissionnaire (*d'un poste*).
resilience [ri'ziliəns], **resiliency** [ri'ziliənsi], *n.* rebondissement, *m.*; élasticité, *f.*
resilient [ri'ziliənt], *a.* rebondissant.
resin ['rezin], *n.* résine; colophane (*pour violons*), *f.*
resist [ri'zist], *v.t.* résister à.—*v.i.* résister.
resistance [ri'zistəns], *n.* résistance, *f.*
resistant [ri'zistənt], *a.* résistant.
re-sole [ri:'soul], *v.t.* ressemeler.
resolute ['rezəlju:t], *a.* déterminé, résolu.
resolutely ['rezəlju:tli], *adv.* résolument.
resoluteness ['rezəlju:tnis], *n.* résolution, fermeté, *f.*
resolution [rezə'lju:ʃən], *n.* résolution; décision (*d'assemblée*), *f.*
resolve [ri'zɔlv], *n.* résolution, *f.*—*v.t.* résoudre; fondre (*liquéfier*); éclaircir, dissiper (*doutes etc.*); déterminer, décider (*assemblée*).—*v.i.* se résoudre, se décider; se fondre (*se dissoudre*).

resolved [ri'zɔlvd], *a.* résolu.
resolvent [ri'zɔlvənt], *n.* (*Med.*) résolvant, *m.*
resonance ['rezənəns], *n.* résonance, *f.*
resonant ['rezənənt], *a.* résonnant, sonore.
resort [ri'zɔ:t], *n.* ressource, *f.*, recours; séjour, rendezvous (*endroit*); (*Law*) ressort, *m.*; *seaside resort*, station balnéaire, plage, *f.*—*v.i.* recourir, avoir recours (*à*); se rendre, aller (*à*).
resound [ri'zaund], *v.i.* résonner, retentir.
resounding [ri'zaundiŋ], *a.* retentissant.—*n.* retentissement, *m.*
resource [ri'sɔ:s], *n.* ressource, *f.*
resourceful [ri'sɔ:sful], *a.* plein de ressources.
respect [ri'spekt], *n.* respect, *m.*, estime, *f.*; égard, *m.*; (*pl.*) respects, hommages, *m.pl.*; *in every respect*, sous tous les rapports; *in respect to*, à l'égard de.—*v.t.* respecter, considérer, avoir égard à.
respectability [rispektə'biliti], *n.* honorabilité, *f.*; convenances, *f.pl.*; bienséance, *f.*
respectable [ri'spektəbl], *a.* respectable, honorable; comme il faut, convenable.
respectably [ri'spektəbli], *adv.* comme il faut, très bien.
respectful [ri'spektful], *a.* respectueux.
respectfully [ri'spektfuli], *adv.* avec respect; *yours respectfully* (*à un supérieur hiérarchique*), veuillez agréer, Monsieur, l'assurance de mes sentiments respectueux.
respecting [ri'spektiŋ], *prep.* à l'égard de, quant à, touchant.
respective [ri'spektiv], *a.* respectif, relatif.
respectively [ri'spektivli], *adv.* respectivement.
respiration [respi'reiʃən], *n.* respiration, *f.*
respirator ['respireitə], *n.* respirateur, *m.*
respiratory ['respirətri], *a.* respiratoire.
respire [ri'spaiə], *v.t.*, *v.i.* respirer.
respite [ri'spit], *n.* répit, relâche; (*Law*) sursis, *m.*
resplendence [ri'splendəns], *n.* éclat, *m.*, splendeur, *f.*
resplendent [ri'splendənt], *a.* resplendissant (*de*).
respond [ri'spɔnd], *v.i.* répondre (*à*).
respondent [ri'spɔndənt], *n.* répondant; (*Law*) défendeur, *m.*
response [ri'spɔns], *n.* réponse, *f.*; (*fig.*) écho; (*Eccles.*) répons, *m.*
responsibility [rispɔnsi'biliti], *n.* responsabilité, *f.*
responsible [ri'spɔnsibl], *a.* chargé (*de*), responsable (*de*); digne de confiance.
responsive [ri'spɔnsiv], *a.* sensible, facile à émouvoir.
rest (1) [rest], *n.* repos, *m.*; (*Mus.*) pause, *f.*; appui (*soutien*), *m.*; *at rest*, en repos.—*v.t.* reposer; faire reposer; (*fig.*) fonder.—*v.i.* se reposer; s'appuyer; *it rests with me to* . . ., c'est à moi de . . .; *to rest assured*, être assuré.
rest (2) [rest], *n.* reste, restant, *m.*; les autres, *m.pl.*—*v.i.* demeurer, rester.
restart [ri:'sta:t], *v.t.*, *v.i.* recommencer.
restaurant ['restərɔ̃:], *n.* restaurant, *m.*
restful ['restful], *a.* qui donne du repos, paisible.
resting ['restiŋ], *a.* couché, se reposant; appuyé, s'appuyant.—*n.* repos, *m.*
resting place ['restiŋpleis], *n.* lieu de repos, gîte, *m.*

restitution [resti'tju:ʃən], *n*. restitution, *f*.
restive ['restiv], *a*. rétif; inquiet.
restiveness ['restivnis], *n*. naturel rétif, *m*.; nervosité, *f*.
restless ['restlis], *a*. sans repos; inquiet; agité.
restlessly ['restlisli], *adv*. sans repos.
restlessness ['restlisnis], *n*. agitation; insomnie, *f*.
restock [ri:'stɔk], *v.t.* repeupler (*chasse réservée*); regarnir (*boutique*), réassortir.
restoration [restə'reiʃən], *n*. restauration, *f*.; rétablissement, *m*.; restitution (*après une perte injuste*), *f*.
restorative [ri'stɔ:rətiv], *a*. and *n*. fortifiant, *m*.
restore [ri'stɔ:], *v.t.* restituer, rendre (*redonner*); ramener (*personne*); restaurer (*bâtiment etc.*); remettre (*replacer*); rétablir.
restorer [ri'stɔ:rə], *n*. restaurateur, *m*.
restrain [ri'strein], *v.t.* retenir, contenir; **to restrain from**, empêcher de; **to restrain oneself**, se contraindre, se contenir.
restraining [ri'streiniŋ], *a*. qui restreint, restrictif.
restraint [ri'streint], *n*. contrainte; gêne, *f*.
restrict [ri'strikt], *v.t.* restreindre.
restriction [ri'strikʃən], *n*. restriction, *f*.
restrictive [ri'striktiv], *a*. restrictif.
result [ri'zʌlt], *n*. résultat, *m*.; **as a result of**, par suite de.—*v.i.* résulter; **to result in**, aboutir à.
resultant [ri'zʌltənt], *a*. résultant.—*n*. résultante, *f*.
resume [ri'zju:m], *v.t.* reprendre, renouer, continuer.
resumption [ri'zʌmpʃən], *n*. reprise, *f*.
resurface [ri:'sə:fis], *v.t.* remettre en état (*route*).—*v.i.* remonter à la surface.
resurgence [ri:'sə:dʒəns], *n*. résurrection, *f*.
resurrect [rezə'rekt], *v.t.* ranimer, ressusciter.
resurrection [rezə'rekʃən], *n*. résurrection, *f*.
resuscitate [ri'sʌsiteit], *v.t.* ressusciter.
resuscitation [risʌsi'teiʃən], *n*. résurrection; renaissance (*des arts etc.*); (*Med.*) ressuscitation, *f*.
retail ['ri:teil], *a*. en détail; **retail price**, prix de détail *m*.—*n*. détail, *m*., vente au détail, *f*.—[ri'teil], *v.t.* vendre en détail, détailler; (*fig.*) débiter; colporter (*nouvelles*).
retailer [ri'teilə], *n*. détaillant; colporteur (*de nouvelles*), *m*.
retain [ri'tein], *v.t.* retenir; engager (*en payant des arrhes*).
retainer [ri'teinə], *n*. serviteur, dépendant, *m*.; honoraires donnés d'avance (*acompte*), *m.pl.*
retaining [ri'teiniŋ], *a*. qui retient; **retaining wall**, mur de soutènement, *m*.
retake [ri:'teik], *v.t. irr. (conjug. like TAKE)* reprendre; (*Cine.*) retourner (*un plan*).
retaking [ri:'teikiŋ], *n*. reprise, *f*.
retaliate [ri'tælieit], *v.i.* rendre la pareille à.
retaliation [ritæli'eiʃən], *n*. représailles, *f.pl.*
retaliatory [ri'tæliətəri], *a*. de représailles.
retard [ri'ta:d], *v.t.* retarder.
retch [ri:tʃ], *v.i.* avoir des haut-le-cœur.
retching [ri:tʃiŋ], *n*. haut-le-cœur, *m*.
retell [ri:'tel], *v.t. irr. (conjug. like TELL)* redire, répéter.
retention [ri'tenʃən], *n*. conservation; (*Med.*) rétention, *f*.

retentive [ri'tentiv], *a*. qui retient; tenace, fidèle (*la mémoire*).
retentiveness [ri'tentivnis], *n*. pouvoir de rétention, *m*.; fidélité (*de la mémoire*), *f*.
reticence ['retisəns], *n*. réticence, *f*.
reticent ['retisənt], *a*. réservé, taciturne.
reticular [re'tikjulə], *a*. réticulaire.
reticulate [re'tikjulit], *a*. réticulé.
retina ['retinə], *n*. rétine, *f*.
retinue ['retinju:], *n*. suite, *f*.; cortège, *m*.
retire [ri'taiə], *v.t.* retirer.—*v.i.* se retirer, prendre sa retraite.
retired [ri'taiəd], *a*. retiré, retraité (*qui a pris sa retraite*); ancien (*qui n'exerce plus cette profession*); **on the retired list**, en retraite.
retirement [ri'taiəmənt], *n*. retraite; (*fig.*) solitude, *f*.
retiring [ri'taiəriŋ], *a*. réservé, timide, modeste; sortant (*d'un emploi*).
retort (1) [ri'tɔ:t], *n*. réplique, riposte, *f*.—*v.i.* riposter, répliquer.
retort (2) [ri'tɔ:t], *n*. (*Chem.*) cornue, *f*.
retouch [ri:'tʌtʃ], *v.t.* retoucher.
retrace [ri'treis], *v.t.* (*Paint.*) retracer; **to retrace one's steps**, revenir sur ses pas, rebrousser chemin.
retract [ri'trækt], *v.t.* rétracter.—*v.i.* se rétracter, se dédire.
retractable [ri'træktebl], *a.* (*Av.*) escamotable.
retransmit [ri:trɑ:ns'mit], *v.t.* retransmettre.
retread [ri:'tred], *v.t.* (*Motor.*) rechaper (*pneu*).—[ri:'tred], *n.* pneu rechapé, *m*.
retreat [ri'tri:t], *n*. retraite, *f*.—*v.i.* se retirer (*à ou dans*); (*Mil.*) battre en retraite.
retreating [ri'tri:tiŋ], *a*. qui bat en retraite; fuyant (*le front*).
retrench [ri'trentʃ], *v.t.* retrancher.—*v.i.* se retrancher.
retrenchment [ri'trentʃmənt], *n*. retranchement, *m*.
retribution [retri'bju:ʃən], *n*. récompense, rétribution, *f*.; (*fig.*) châtiment, *m*., vengeance, *f*.
retrievable [ri'tri:vəbl], *a*. recouvrable (*argent*); réparable (*perte*).
retrieve [ri'tri:v], *v.t.* rétablir; réparer (*chose brisée*); recouvrer (*chose perdue*); rapporter (*chien*).
retriever [ri'tri:və], *n*. chien rapporteur, *m*.
retroaction [ri:trou'ækʃən], *n*. rétroaction, *f*.
retroactive [ri:trou'æktiv], *a*. rétroactif.
retrograde ['retrougreid], *a*. rétrograde.
retrogression [retrou'greʃən], *n*. rétrogression, rétrogradation, *f*.
retrogressive [retrou'gresiv], *a*. rétrogressif.
retrospect ['retrospekt], *n*. regard jeté en arrière, *m*.; revue, *f*.; **in retrospect**, en rétrospective.
retrospective [retro'spektiv], *a*. rétrospectif; (*Law*) rétroactif.
retrospectively [retro'spektivli], *adv*. rétrospectivement; (*Law*) rétroactivement.
retroversion [retro'və:ʃən], *n*. renversement, *m*.
retrovert [retro'və:t], *v.t.* renverser.
return [ri'tə:n], *v.t.* rendre; renvoyer; rembourser (*argent etc.*); rapporter (*intérêt*); (*Comm.*) rendre compte; élire (*candidat*); **he was returned**, il fut élu.—*v.i.* revenir; retourner; rentrer.—*n*. retour, *m*.; rentrée, *f*.; renvoi, *m*.; remise en place (*chose déplacée*), *f*.; profit, *m*.; restitution, *f*.; remboursement,

m.; élection, f.; rapport, relevé, état (*impôts etc.*); bilan (*de banque*); (*pl.*) produit, m.; *by return mail*, par retour du courrier; *in return for*, en retour de; *nil return*, état néant; *on sale or return*, en dépôt; *return journey*, retour; *return match*, revanche, f.; *return ticket*, billet d'aller et retour, m.

returnable [ri'tə:nəbl], a. restituable.

reunion [ri:'ju:niən], n. réunion, f.

reunite [ri:ju'nait], v.t. réunir.—v.i. se réunir.

rev [rev], n. (*colloq.*, *Motor.*) tour, m.—v.t. *to rev the engine*, faire s'emballer le moteur. —v.i. s'emballer.

reveal [ri'vi:l], v.t. révéler.

reveille [ri'væli], n. réveil, m.

revel [revl], n. (*pl.*) divertissements, m.pl.— v.i. se réjouir, se divertir; *to revel in*, se délecter à.

revelation [revə'leiʃən], n. révélation, f.; *Book of Revelation*, Apocalypse, f.

reveller ['revələ], n. joyeux convive, m.

revelry ['revlri], n. réjouissances, f.pl., joyeux ébats, m.pl.

revenge [ri'vendʒ], n. vengeance; (*Spt.*) revanche, f.—v.t. venger; se venger de; *to revenge oneself on*, se venger de.

revengeful [ri'vendʒful], a. vindicatif.

revengefully [ri'vendʒfuli], adv. par vengeance.

revenue ['revənju:], n. revenu; (*State*) fisc, trésor, m.; *revenue officer*, officier de la douane, m.

reverberate [ri'və:bəreit], v.t. réverbérer; renvoyer (*son, chaleur etc.*).—v.i. se répercuter.

reverberation [rivə:bə'reiʃən], n. réverbération (*de chaleur*); répercussion, f.

revere [ri'viə], v.t. révérer, vénérer.

reverence ['revərəns], n. révérence, f.

reverend ['revərənd], a. révérend (*titre ecclésiastique*).

reverent ['revərənt], a. révérencieux.

reverently ['revərəntli], adv. avec révérence.

reverie ['revəri], n. rêverie, f.

reversal [ri'və:sl], n. annulation; cassation, f.

reverse [ri'və:s], a. contraire, opposé.—n. revers, m.; défaite, f.; *quite the reverse*, tout le contraire (*de*); *the reverse way*, en sens inverse.—v.t. renverser; appliquer en sens inverse; (*Law*) infirmer, casser.—v.i. (*Motor.*) faire marche ou machine en arrière.

reversed [ri'və:st], a. renversé; inverse.

reversible [ri'və:sibl], a. révocable, réversible, à double face (*tissu*).

reversion [ri'və:ʃən], n. réversion, f.

revert [ri'və:t], v.i. revenir (*sur*).

revertible [ri'və:tibl], a. réversible.

revetment [ri'vetmənt], n. revêtement, m.

revictual [ri:'vitl], v.t. ravitailler.

revictualling [ri:'vitliŋ], n. ravitaillement, m.

review [ri'vju:], n. revue, revision; critique, revue, f., périodique, m.—v.t. revoir, reviser; passer en revue; analyser, critiquer (*livre etc.*).

reviewer [ri'vju:ə], n. critique, m., f.

revile [ri'vail], v.t. injurier, insulter, outrager.

revilement [ri'vailmənt], n. injure, insulte, f.

reviling [ri'vailiŋ], a. diffamatoire, outrageant. —n. insultes, injures, f.pl.

revisal [ri'vaizl], n. revision, f.

revise [ri'vaiz], v.t. revoir, reviser, réviser.

reviser [ri'vaizə], n. personne qui revoit, f., réviseur, m.

revision [ri'viʒən], n. revision, révision, f.

revisit [ri:'vizit], v.t. revisiter, retourner voir.

revitalize [ri:'vaitəlaiz], v.t. revivifier.

revival [ri'vaivl], n. rétablissement, m.; renaissance (*des arts*); reprise (*d'une pièce*), f.; réveil (*religieux*), m.

revive [ri'vaiv], v.t. ressusciter; raviver.—v.i. se ranimer; renaître (*arts etc.*).

revivify [ri'vivifai], v.t. revivifier.

revocable ['revəkəbl], a. révocable.

revocation [revə'keiʃən], n. révocation, f.

revoke [ri'vouk], v.t. révoquer.—v.i. (*Cards*) renoncer.—n. (*Cards*) renonce, f.

revolt [ri'voult], n. révolte, f.—v.i. se révolter, se soulever.

revolting [ri'voultiŋ], a. révoltant.

revolution [revə'lju:ʃən], n. révolution, f.; tour (*de roue*), m.

revolutionary [revə'lju:ʃənəri], a. and n. révolutionnaire, m., f.

revolve [ri'vəlv], v.t. tourner; retourner; repasser, rouler (*dans l'esprit*).—v.i. tourner; (*fig.*) retourner, revenir.

revolver [ri'vəlvə], n. revolver, m.

revolving [ri'vəlviŋ], a. tournant.

revue [ri'vju:], n. (*Theat.*) revue, f.

revulsion [ri'vʌlʃən], n. révulsion, f.

reward [ri'wo:d], n. récompense, f.; prix, m. —v.t. récompenser (*de*).

rewind [ri:'waind], v.t. irr. (*conjug. like* WIND) rebobiner (*soie etc.*); remonter (*montre, horloge*); rembobiner (*film*).

rewrite [ri:'rait], v.t. irr. (*conjug. like* WRITE) récrire.

rhapsody ['ræpsədi], n. rapsodie, f.

Rheims [ri:mz]. Reims, m.

Rhenish ['reniʃ], a. du Rhin.—n. vin du Rhin, m.

rheostat ['ri:ostæt], n. rhéostat, m.

rhesus ['ri:səs], a. (*Med.*) rhésus.

rhetoric ['retərik], n. rhétorique, f.

rhetorical [ri'tərikl], a. de rhétorique; *rhetorical question*, question de pure forme, f.

rheum [ru:m], n. rhume, catarrhe, m.

rheumatic [ru:'mætik], a. rhumatismal; *rheumatic fever*, rhumatisme articulaire aigu, m.

rheumatism ['ru:mətizm], n. rhumatisme, m.

rheumatoid ['ru:mətoid], a. rhumatoide; *rheumatoid arthritis*, rhumatisme articulaire, m.

Rhine [rain], **the**. le Rhin, m.

Rhineland ['rainlænd]. la Rhénanie, f.

Rhinelander ['rainlændə], n. Rhénan, m.

rhinoceros [rai'nosərəs], n. rhinocéros, m.

Rhodesia [rou'di:zia]. la Rhodésie, f.

Rhodesian [rou'di:zian], a. rhodésien.—n. Rhodésien (*personne*), m.

rhododendron [roudə'dendrən], n. rhododendron, m.

rhombus ['rombəs], n. losange, m.

Rhone [roun]. le Rhône, m.

rhubarb ['ru:ba:b], n. rhubarbe, f.

rhyme [raim], n. rime, f.; (*pl.*) vers, m.pl.— v.t., v.i. rimer; rimailler.

rhythm [riðm], n. rythme, m.; cadence, f.

rhythmical ['riðmikl], a. rythmique.

rhythmically ['riðmikli], adv. avec rythme.

rib [rib], n. côte; baleine (*de parapluie*), f.

ribald ['ribəld], *a.* grossier, obscène.

ribaldry ['ribəldri], *n.* obscénités, *f.pl.*

ribbed [ribd], *a.* à côtes.

ribbon ['ribən], *n.* ruban; cordon (*de médaille*); lambeau (*morceau de tissu déchiré*), *m.*

rice [rais], *n.* riz, *m.*; *rice field*, rizière, *f.*

rich [ritʃ], *a.* riche; fertile, fécond (*terre*); de haut goût (*fort assaisonné*); voyant (*couleur*); (*fig.*) délicieux, généreux (*vin*); *the rich*, les riches, *m.pl.*; *to grow rich*, s'enrichir.

riches ['ritʃiz], *n.pl.* richesse, *f.*

richly ['ritʃli], *adv.* richement; grandement; (*fam.*) joliment.

richness ['ritʃnis], *n.* richesse; fécondité, *f.*; haut goût, *m.*

rick [rik], *n.* meule, *f.*

rickets ['rikits], *n.pl.* rachitis, rachitisme, *m.*

rickety ['rikiti], *a.* (*fig.*) boiteux (*meuble*).

rickshaw ['rikʃɔː], *n.* pousse-pousse, *m.*

ricochet ['rikəʃei], *n.* ricochet, *m.—v.i.* ricocher.

rid [rid], *v.t. irr.* délivrer, débarrasser; *to get rid of*, se débarrasser de.

riddance ['ridəns], *n.* débarras, *f.*

riddle (1) [ridl], *n.* énigme, *f.*

riddle (2) [ridl], *v.t.* cribler.—*n.* crible, *m.*

ride [raid], *v.t. irr.* monter, être monté sur; mener, conduire; faire (*une distance précise*). —*v.i.* monter (*à cheval, à bicyclette etc.*), aller, venir, être se promener (*à cheval, à bicyclette, en voiture etc.*); être monté (*sur*); flotter, voguer (*sur*); être (à l'ancre); *to ride away*, partir, s'en aller; *to ride back*, revenir, s'en retourner.—*n.* promenade, course (*à cheval, en voiture, à bicyclette etc.*), *f.*; trajet, *m.*; allée cavalière (*sentier dans un bois etc.*), *f.*

rider ['raidə], *n.* cavalier, *m.*, cavalière, *f.*; écuyer, *m.*, écuyère (*de cirque*), *f.*; jockey; codicille (*document*), *m.*

riderless ['raidəlis], *a.* sans cavalier.

ridge [ridʒ], *n.* sommet (*pic*), *m.*, cime; chaîne (*de montagnes*); arête, crête (*d'une montagne*) *f.*; faîte (*de toit*); (*Agric.*) sillon, billon, *m.—v.t.* sillonner.

ridicule ['ridikjuːl], *n.* ridicule, *m.—v.t.* tourner en ridicule, ridiculiser.

ridiculous [ri'dikjuləs], *a.* ridicule.

ridiculously [ri'dikjuləsli], *adv.* ridiculement.

riding (1) ['raidiŋ], *n.* promenade à cheval, *f.*, exercice à cheval, *m.*, équitation, *f.*; (*Naut.*) mouillage, *m.*

riding (2) ['raidiŋ], *n.* (*Yorkshire*) arrondissement, *m.*

riding habit ['raidiŋhæbit], *n.* amazone, *f.*

riding hood ['raidiŋhud], *n.* capuchon, *m.*; *Little Red Riding Hood*, le petit Chaperon rouge.

rife [raif], *a.* abondant, répandu; *to be rife*, régner (*tumulte etc.*), courir (*bruit*).

riff-raff ['rifræf], *n.* racaille, canaille, *f.*

rifle (1) [raifl], *v.t.* piller, dévaliser.

rifle (2) [raifl], *v.t.* rayer (*armes à feu*).—*n.* fusil (rayé), *m.*, carabine, *f.*; *rifle gallery* or *range*, tir, *m.*; *rifle practice* or *shooting*, tir au fusil, tir à la carabine, *m.*; *rifle shot*, coup de fusil, *m.*

rifleman ['raiflmən], *n.* (*pl.* -men [men]) carabinier, *m.*

rifling (1) ['raifliŋ], *n.* pillage.

rifling (2) ['raifliŋ], *n.* rayage (*de fusils*), *m.*

rift [rift], *n.* fente; éclaircie (*aux nuages*), *f.*

rig [rig], *n.* gréement; accoutrement (*vêtements*), *m.—v.t.* équiper, gréer; (*fig.*) accoutrer, attifer.

rigged [rigd], *a.* gréé.

rigging ['rigiŋ], *n.* gréement, *m.*, agrès, *m.pl.*

right [rait], *a.* droit; direct, en ligne droite; vrai, véritable; bon, propre, convenable; juste, correct; en règle; *all right!* c'est bien! *that is right*, c'est cela; *the right man*, l'homme qu'il faut; *the right road*, le bon chemin; *to be right*, avoir raison; être juste (*compte*); *to put right*, mettre en bon ordre, arranger.—*adv.* droit, tout droit; justement (*avec justice*); comme il faut, bien (*correctement*); tout à fait (*entièrement*); fort (*beaucoup*); très.—*n.* droit, *m.*, justice, raison, *f.*; côté droit, *m.*, droite, *f.*; *on* or *to the right*, à droite; *right of way*, droit de passage; *to put* or *set to rights*, arranger, mettre en ordre.—*v.t.* redresser, corriger (*choses*).—*v.i.* se redresser, se relever.

righteous ['raitʃəs], *a.* juste, droit.

righteously ['raitʃəsli], *adv.* justement.

righteousness ['raitʃəsnis], *n.* droiture, vertu, *f.*

rightful ['raitful], *a.* légitime, véritable.

right-handed ['raithændid], *a.* droitier.

rightly ['raitli], *adv.* bien; à juste titre; comme il faut (*convenablement*); juste (*exactement*).

rightness ['raitnis], *n.* rectitude; droiture; justesse, *f.*

rigid ['ridʒid], *a.* rigide, raide.

rigidity [ri'dʒiditi], *n.* rigidité; raideur, *f.*

rigidly ['ridʒidli], *adv.* rigidement; avec raideur.

rigmarole ['rigməroul], *n.* galimatias, *m.*

rigor ['rigə, 'raigə], *n.* (*Path.*) rigidité, *f.*

rigor ['rigə], *n.* rigueur, *f.*

rigorous ['rigərəs], *a.* rigoureux.

rigorously ['rigərəsli], *adv.* rigoureusement, avec rigueur, à la rigueur.

rile [rail], *v.t.* (*colloq.*) faire enrager, agacer.

rill [ril], *n.* petit ruisseau, *m.*

rim [rim], *n.* bord, rebord, *m.*; jante (*de roue*), *f.*

rime [raim], *n.* givre, *m.*; gelée blanche, *f.*

rimless ['rimlis], *a.* sans monture (*lunettes*).

rind [raind], *n.* écorce, peau, pelure; croûte (*de fromage*); couenne (*de lard*), *f.*

ring (1) [riŋ], *n.* anneau, *m.*, bague (*pour le doigt etc.*), *f.*; cercle, rond, *m.*; arène (*pour se battre*), *f.*; ring (*pour la boxe*), *m.*; (*fig.*) bande, clique, *f.*; (*Comm.*) syndicat, *m.—v.t.* mettre un anneau à; entourer.

ring (2) [riŋ], *v.t. irr.* sonner, faire sonner; *to ring someone up*, téléphoner à quelqu'un. —*v.i.* sonner; retentir (*de*); tinter (*aux oreilles*).—*n.* son, tintement, coup de sonnette, *m.*; sonnerie, *f.*; *there's a ring at the door*, on sonne.

ring-dove ['riŋdʌv], *n.* pigeon ramier, *m.*

ringer ['riŋə], *n.* sonneur, *m.*

ringing ['riŋiŋ], *n.* son (*de cloche*), *m.*; sonnerie, *f.*, tintement, retentissement, *m.*

ringleader ['riŋliːdə], *n.* meneur, chef de bande, *m.*

ringlet ['riŋlit], *n.* boucle (*de cheveux*), *f.*

ring-road ['riŋroud], *n.* route de ceinture, *f.*

ringworm ['riŋwəːm], *n.* herpès tonsurant, *m.*

rink [riŋk], *n.* patinoire (*de glace*), *f.*; skating (*pour patinage à roulettes*), *m.*

rinse [rins], *v.t.* rincer.

riot ['raiət], *n.* émeute, *f.*; vacarme, tumulte (*bruit*), *m.*; (*fig.*) festins, *m.pl.*—*v.i.* faire une émeute.

rioter ['raiətə], *n.* émeutier; tapageur, *m.*

riotous ['raiətəs], *a.* séditieux, tumultueux.

rip (1) [rip], *v.t.* fendre, déchirer; **to rip open,** ouvrir.—*n.* déchirure, *f.*

rip (2) [rip], *n.* (*slang*) vaurien, polisson, *m.*

ripe [raip], *a.* mûr.

ripen ['raipən], *v.t.* mûrir, faire mûrir.—*v.i.* mûrir, venir à maturité.

ripeness ['raipnis], *n.* maturité, *f.*

ripening ['raipniŋ], *n.* maturation, *f.*

ripple [ripl], *v.t.* rider.—*v.i.* se rider; onduler. —*n.* ride (*d'eau*), *f.*

rippling ['ripliŋ], *n.* clapotis, murmure, *m.*

rip-roaring ['rip'rɔːriŋ], *a.* tumultueux; robuste; épatant.

rise [raiz], *v.i. irr.* se lever, se relever (*après une chute, un malheur etc.*); s'élever, monter; se dresser (*montagne etc.*); s'augmenter, hausser (*prix*); aller en montant (*rue*); se soulever (*rébellion*); ressusciter (*les morts*); prendre sa source (*en ou dans*).—*n.* lever, *m.*; montée (*de colline etc.*); crue (*des eaux*); hausse (*de prix*), augmentation, *f.*; source, origine, *f.*

riser ['raizə], *n.* marche (*d'escalier*), *f.*; **early riser,** personne matinale, *f.*

risible ['rizibl], *a.* rieur.

rising ['raiziŋ], *a.* levant; montant (*marée*); (*fig.*) naissant; qui a de l'avenir (*qui promet*). —*n.* lever (*du lit, du soleil*), *m.*; montée (*de colline*); crue (*des eaux*); clôture (*d'assemblée*); résurrection, *f.*; soulèvement, *m.*, insurrection, *f.*

risk [risk], *n.* risque, *m.*—*v.t.* risquer.

risky ['riski], *a.* risqué, hasardeux.

rite [rait], *n.* rite, *m.*, cérémonie, *f.*

ritual ['ritjuəl], *a.* du rite.—*n.* rituel, *m.*

rival [raivl], *a.* and *n.* rival, *m.*—*v.t.* rivaliser avec.

rivalry ['raivlri], *n.* rivalité, *f.*

rive [raiv], *v.t. irr.* fendre.—*v.i.* se fendre.

river ['rivə], *a.* de rivière, fluvial.—*n.* fleuve (*qui débouche dans la mer*), *m.*; (*autrement*) rivière, *f.*; **down the river,** en aval; **up the river,** en amont.

riverside ['rivəsaid], *a.* au bord de l'eau.—*n.* bord de l'eau, *m.*

rivet ['rivit], *n.* rivet, *m.*; attache (*de porcelaine*), *f.*—*v.t.* river, riveter; (*fig.*) fixer.

riveting ['rivitiŋ], *n.* rivetage, *m.*

rivulet ['rivjulit], *n.* ruisseau, *m.*

roach [routʃ], *n.* (*Ichth.*) gardon, *m.*

road [roud], *n.* route, *f.*, chemin, *m.*; chaussée; rue (*en ville*); (*Naut.*) rade, *f.*; **by-road,** chemin détourné; **carriage road,** route carrossable; **cross-roads,** carrefour, *m.*; **high road,** grand-route, *f.*; **roads and bridges,** ponts et chaussées, *m.pl.*

road hog ['roudhɔg], *n.* (*Motor.*) chauffard, *m.*

road-house ['roudhaus], *n.* auberge, hôtellerie, *f.*

road map ['roudmæp], *n.* carte routière, *f.*

road mender ['roudmendə], *n.* cantonnier, *m.*

road metal ['roudmetl], *n.* cailloutis, empierrement, *m.*

roadside ['roudsaid], *n.* bord de la route, *m.*; **by the roadside,** au bord de la route.

roadstead ['roudsted], *n.* rade, *f.*

roadway ['roudwei], *n.* chaussée; voie (*de pont*), *f.*

roadworthy ['roudwəːði], *a.* (*Motor.*) en état de marche.

roam [roum], *v.t.* rôder dans *ou* parmi.—*v.i.* errer, rôder.

roan [roun], *a.* rouan.

roar [rɔː], *n.* rugissement (*de lion etc.*); mugissement (*de la mer etc.*); éclat (*de rire*); grondement (*de tonnerre etc.*), *m.*—*v.i.* rugir (*lion etc.*); mugir (*mer etc.*); gronder (*tonnerre, canon etc.*); (*colloq.*) vociférer; **to roar with laughter,** rire aux éclats.

roaring ['rɔːriŋ], *a.* rugissant, mugissant; **to do a roaring trade,** faire des affaires d'or.

roast [roust], *v.t.* rôtir; faire rôtir; torréfier (*café*); (*Metal.*) griller.—*v.i.* rôtir; griller. —*a.* rôti; **roast beef,** rosbif, *m.*; **roast pork,** rôti de porc, *m.*

roaster ['roustə], *n.* rôtisseur (*personne*), *m.*; rôtissoire (*chose*), *f.*

roasting ['roustiŋ], *a.* brûlant.—*n.* (*Metal.*) grillage, *m.*; torréfaction (*de café*), *f.*

rob [rɔb], *v.t.* voler; piller; priver (*de*).

robber ['rɔbə], *n.* voleur, *m.*

robbery ['rɔbəri], *n.* vol, *m.*

robe [roub], *n.* robe, *f.*—*v.t.* vêtir (*d'une robe*); revêtir (*de*).

robin ['rɔbin], *n.*, **robin redbreast** [rɔbin'red brest], *n.* (*Orn.*) rouge-gorge, *m.*

robot ['roubɔt], *n.* automate, robot, *m.*

robust [ro'bʌst], *a.* robuste, vigoureux.

robustness [ro'bʌstnis], *n.* robustesse, vigueur, *f.*

rock (1) [rɔk], *n.* rocher, roc, *m.*; (*Geol.*) roche, *f.*; sucre d'orge (*bonbon*), *m.*

rock (2) [rɔk], *v.t.* balancer; bercer, remuer.—*v.i.* se balancer; branler, trembler.

rockery ['rɔkəri], *n.* jardin de rocaille, *m.*

rocket ['rɔkit], *n.* fusée, *f.*; **rocket launcher,** lance-fusée, *m.*—*v.i.* monter en flèche (*prix*).

rockiness ['rɔkinis], *n.* nature rocailleuse, *f.*

rocking ['rɔkiŋ], *n.* balancement; bercement, *m.*

rocking chair ['rɔkintʃeə], *n.* chaise à bascule, *f.*

rocking horse ['rɔkinhɔːs], *n.* cheval à bascule, *m.*

rock salt ['rɔksɔːlt], *n.* sel gemme, *m.*

rocky ['rɔki], *a.* rocailleux, rocheux.

rod [rɔd], *n.* verge; baguette; tringle (*à rideaux etc.*); canne à pêche; perche (= 5,0291 *metres*); bielle (*de piston*), *f.*

rodent ['roudənt], *n.* (*Zool.*) rongeur, *m.*

rodeo [ro'deiou], *n.* rodéo, *m.*

roe (1) [rou], *n.* œufs (*de poisson*), *m.pl.*

roe (2) [rou], *n.* chevreuil, *m.*; chevrette, *f.*

roebuck ['roubʌk], *n.* chevreuil, *m.*

Roger ['rɔdʒə], *n.* Roger, *m.*

rogue [roug], *n.* coquin, fripon, fourbe, *m.*

roguery ['rougəri], *n.* coquinerie, friponnerie, fourberie, *f.*

roguish ['rougiʃ], *a.* coquin, fripon; (*facet.*) espiègle.

roguishly ['rougiʃli], *adv.* en fripon, en fourbe; (*facet.*) avec espièglerie.

roister ['rɔistə], *v.i.* faire du tapage.
roisterer ['rɔistərə], *n.* tapageur, *m.*
roistering ['rɔistəriŋ], *a.* tapageur, bruyant.
—*n.* tapage, *m.*
role [roul], *n.* rôle, *m.*
roll [roul], *n.* rouleau; roulement (*acte de rouler quelque chose*); roulis (*de navire*); petit pain; roulement (*de tambour*); rôle (*liste*), *m.*; (*pl.*) rôles, *m.pl.*; annales, archives, *f.pl.*—*v.t.* rouler; passer au rouleau (*gazon, gravier etc.*); (*Metal.*) laminer.—*v.i.* rouler, se rouler; tourner; (*Naut.*) avoir du roulis.
roll call ['roulkɔ:l], *n.* appel, *m.*
roller ['roulə], *n.* rouleau; cylindre, *m.*
roller skate ['rouləskeit], *n.* patin à roulettes, *m.*
rollicking ['rɔlikiŋ], *a.* folâtre, joyeux.
rolling ['rouliŋ], *n.* roulement; roulis (*de navire*); (*Metal.*) laminage, *m.*; **rolling stock**, matériel roulant, *m.*
rolling pin ['rouliŋpin], *n.* rouleau, *m.*
Roman ['roumən], *a.* romain; aquilin (*nez*).—*n.* Romain (*personne*), *m.*
Romance [ro'mæns], *a.* roman; **Romance languages**, langues romanes, *f.pl.*
romance [ro'mæns], *n.* roman de chevalerie, *m.*; histoire romanesque; (*Mus.*) romance; (*fam.*) amourette, aventure, *f.*—*v.i.* inventer à plaisir, exagérer, broder.
romanesque [roumə'nesk], *a.* (*Arch.*) roman.
Romania [ro'meiniə], [RUMANIA].
romantic [ro'mæntik], *a.* romanesque; romantique (*paysage, style etc.*).
romanticism [ro'mæntisizm], *n.* romantisme, *m.*
romanticist [ro'mæntisist], *n.* romantique, *m., f.*
Rome [roum]. Rome, *f.*
romp [rɔmp], *n.* gamine, garçonnière (*jeune fille*), *f.*; jeu violent, tapage, *m.*—*v.i.* jouer rudement, folâtrer.
rompers ['rɔmpəz], *n.pl.* barboteuse, *f.*
romping ['rɔmpiŋ], *n.* jeux rudes, *m.pl.*
roof [ru:f], *n.* toit; palais (*de la bouche*), *m.*—*v.t.* couvrir d'un toit; couvrir.
roofing ['ru:fiŋ], *n.* toiture, *f.*
roof rack ['ru:fræk], *n.* (*Motor.*) galerie, *f.*
rook (1) [ruk], *n.* freux, *m.*, (*pop.*) corneille, *f.*; (*slang*) tricheur, *m.*—*v.t., v.i.* (*slang*) friponner, filouter.
rook (2) [ruk], *n.* (*Chess*) tour, *f.*
rookery ['rukəri], *n.* colonie de freux, *f.*
rookie ['ruki], *n.* (*slang*) bleu, *m.*
room [ru:m], *n.* place, *f.*, espace, *m.*; chambre, salle, pièce(*d'appartement*),*f.*[see **residence**]
roomful ['ru:mful], *n.* chambrée, *f.*
roominess ['ru:minis], *n.* nature spacieuse, grandeur, *f.*
roomy ['ru:mi], *a.* spacieux, vaste.
roost [ru:st], *n.* juchoir, perchoir, *m.*—*v.i.* se jucher.
rooster ['ru:stə], *n.* coq, *m.*
root [ru:t], *n.* racine; (*fig.*) source, *f.*—*v.t.* **to root out**, déraciner, extirper.
rooted ['ru:tid], *a.* enraciné; (*fig.*) invétéré.
rooting ['ru:tiŋ], *n.* enracinement, *m.*; **rooting out**, arrachement, *m.*, extirpation, *f.*
rope [roup], *n.* corde, *f.*; cordage, *m.*; (*Mount.*) cordée, *f.*; **a piece of rope**, un bout de filin.—*v.t.* attacher avec une

corde; lier.—*v.i.* filer (*vin etc.*); (*Mount.*) s'encorder.
rope-walker ['roupwɔ:kə], *n.* funambule, *m., f.*
ropiness ['roupinis], *n.* viscosité, *f.*
ropy ['roupi], *a.* qui file, filant, visqueux.
rosary ['rouzəri], *n.* chapelet, *m.*
rose (1) [rouz], *n.* rose; (*Tech.*) pomme d'arrosoir; (*Arch.*) rosace, *f.*
rose (2) [rouz], *past* [RISE].
roseate ['rouziit], *a.* rosé.
rose bed ['rouzbed], *n.* massif de rosiers, *m.*
rosebud ['rouzbʌd], *n.* bouton de rose, *m.*
rose-bush ['rouzbuʃ], *n.* rosier, *m.*
rose garden ['rouzgɑ:dn], *n.* roseraie, *f.*
rosemary ['rouzməri], *n.* romarin, *m.*
rosette [ro'zet], *n.* rosette, *f.*
rose window ['rouzwindou], *n.* rosace, *f.*
rosin ['rɔzin], *n.* colophane, *f.*
rosiness ['rouzinis], *n.* couleur rose, *f.*
rostrum ['rɔstrəm], *n.* (*Rom. Hist.*) rostres, *m.pl.*; tribune (*estrade*), *f.*
rosy ['rouzi], *a.* de rose, rose, rosé, vermeil.
rot [rɔt], *n.* pourriture; (*colloq.*) blague, *f.*—*v.t.* pourrir, faire pourrir; carier (*dent*).—*v.i.* pourrir, se pourrir; se carier (*dent*).
rota ['routə], *n.* **by rota**, à tour de rôle.
rotary ['routəri], *a.* rotatif, rotatoire.
rotate [ro'teit], *v.t., v.i.* tourner.
rotation [ro'teiʃən], *n.* rotation, succession, *f.*; **rotation of crops**, assolement, *m.*
rote [rout], *n.* routine, *f.*; **by rote**, par cœur.
rotten [rɔtn], *a.* pourri; carié (*dent*); gâté (*œuf*).
rottenness ['rɔtnnis], *n.* pourriture; carie (*des dents*), *f.*
rotter ['rɔtə], *n.* (*fam.*) sale type, *m.*
rotting ['rɔtiŋ], *a.* qui pourrit; qui se carie.—*n.* putréfaction, *f.*
rotund [ro'tʌnd], *a.* rond, arrondi.
rotundity [ro'tʌnditi], *n.* rondeur, rotondité, *f.*
rouble [ru:bl], *n.* rouble, *m.*
rouge [ru:ʒ], *n.* rouge, fard, *m.*
rough [rʌf], *a.* rude; hérissé; raboteux (*chemin*); grosse, houleuse (*mer*); orageux (*temps*); âpre (*goût*); dépoli (*verre*); grossier (*manières*); approximatif (*pas exact*); **rough-and-ready**, fait à la va-vite; **rough copy** or **draft**, brouillon, *m.*; **rough estimate**, appréciation en gros, *f.*—*adv.* brutalement, rudement.—*n.* voyou, polisson, *m.*; **rough-and-tumble**, mêlée, bousculade, *f.*
roughcast ['rʌfkɑ:st], *v.t.* ébaucher; (*Build.*) crépir.—*n.* ébauche, *f.*; (*Build.*) crépi, *m.*
roughen [rʌfn], *v.t.* rendre rude.
rough-hewn ['rʌfhju:n], *a.* ébauché.
rough-house ['rʌfhaus], *n.* (*fam.*) chahut, *m.*
roughly ['rʌfli], *adv.* rudement; grossièrement; à peu près.
roughness ['rʌfnis], *n.* aspérité, rudesse; âpreté (*au goût*); agitation (*de la mer*); grossièreté (*de manières*), *f.*; mauvais état (*de rue*), *m.*
round [raund], *a.* rond; circulaire; en rond.—*adv.* en rond; à la ronde; tout autour, à l'entour; **to go round**, faire le tour de.—*prep.* autour de.—*n.* rond, cercle; tour (*petite promenade*), *m.*; ruelle (*de bœuf etc.*); salve (*d'applaudissements*), *f.*; (*Artill.*) coup de canon, *m.*; ronde (*de veilleurs, police etc.*); (*Golf*) tournée, *f.*; (*Box.*) round, *m.*; **round**

of ammunition, cartouche, *f.*—*v.t.* arrondir; entourer, faire le tour de (*faire un cercle*); doubler (*cap*); *to round off*, arrondir, finir, compléter; *to round up*, rassembler (*bestiaux etc.*); faire une rafle.—*v.i.* s'arrondir.

roundabout ['raundəbaut], *a.* détourné; indirect.—*n.* manège; (*Motor.*) rondpoint, *m.*

rounded ['raundid], *a.* arrondi.

*roundelay ['raundəlei], *n.* rondeau, *m.*

rounders ['raundəz], *n.pl.* balle au camp, *f.*

roundish ['raundiʃ], *a.* arrondi; rondelet (*personne*).

roundly ['raundli], *adv.* en rond; (*fig.*) rondement.

roundness ['raundnis], *n.* rondeur, *f.*; (*fig.*) franchise, *f.*

round trip, see **return**.

round-up ['raundʌp], *n.* rassemblement (*de bétail*), *m.*; rafle (*de criminels*), *f.*

roup [ru:p], *n.* pépie (*maladie de volaille*), *f.*

rouse [rauz], *v.t.* éveiller, (*fig.*) réveiller, exciter.

rout [raut], *n.* cohue; déroute (*d'une armée*), *f.*—*v.t.* mettre en déroute.

route [ru:t], *n.* itinéraire, parcours, *m.*—*v.t.* router (*circulation, colis etc.*).

route map [ru:tmæp], *n.* carte routière, *f.*

routine [ru:'ti:n], *n.* routine, *f.*

rove [rouv], *v.i.* rôder, courir.

rover ['rouvə], *n.* rôdeur, vagabond; pirate; (*Scouting*) éclaireur chevalier, *m.*

roving ['rouviŋ], *a.* errant, vagabond.

row (1) [rau], *n.* tapage, vacarme, *m.*; querelle, scène, *f.*

row (2) [rou], *n.* rang, rangée, file; colonne (*de chiffres*), *f.*

row (3) [rou], *n.* promenade en bateau, *f.*—*v.t.* (*Naut.*) faire aller à la rame.—*v.i.* ramer; (*Naut.*) nager.

rowan ['rauən], *n.* (*Sc.*) sorbier des oiseaux, *m.*

rowdy ['raudi], *a.* tapageur.—*n.* voyou, gredin, *m.*

rowdyism ['raudiizm], **rowdiness** ['raudinis], *n.* tapage, *m.*

rower ['rouə], *n.* rameur; (*Naut.*) nageur, *m.*

rowing ['rouiŋ], *n.* canotage, *m.*

rowing-boat ['rouiŋbout], *n.* bateau à rames, *m.*

rowlock ['rʌlək], *n.* tolet, *m.*, dame, *f.*

royal ['rɔiəl], *a.* royal, de roi.

royalist ['rɔiəlist], *a.* and *n.* royaliste, *m.*, *f.*

royally ['rɔiəli], *adv.* royalement, en roi.

royalty ['rɔiəlti], *n.* royauté; (*usu. pl.*) commission, *f.*, droit d'auteur, *m.*

rub [rʌb], *v.t.*, *v.i.* frotter; (*Med.*) frictionner.—*n.* frottement; coup de brosse, *m.*; (*fig.*) difficulté, *f.*, obstacle, *m.*

rubber (1) ['rʌbə], *n.* frotteur; frottoir (*chose*), *m.*; (*pl.*) (*Am.*) caoutchoucs (*chaussures*), *m.pl.*; **India rubber**, caoutchouc, *m.*, gomme (à effacer), *f.*

rubber (2) ['rʌbə], *n.* (*Cards*) rob, *m.*

rubber-stamp ['rʌbəstæmp], *n.* tampon; (*fig.*) béni-oui-oui, *m.*—*v.t.* ratifier.

rubbing ['rʌbiŋ], *n.* frottement; frottage, *m.*; (*Med.*) friction, *f.*

rubbish ['rʌbiʃ], *n.* débris, *m.pl.*; ordures, *f.pl.*; fatras (*sottises*), *m.*

rubbish bin ['rʌbiʃbin], *n.* poubelle, *f.*

rubbish cart ['rʌbiʃkɑːt], *n.* tombereau, *m.*

rubbish dump ['rʌbiʃdʌmp], *n.* dépotoir, *m.*

rubbishy ['rʌbiʃi], *a.* de rebut, sans valeur.

rubble ['rʌbl], *n.* blocaille, *f.*, moellons; décombres, *m.pl.*

rubicund ['ru:bikand], *a.* rubicond.

rubric ['ru:brik], *n.* rubrique, *f.*

ruby ['ru:bi], *a.* de rubis, vermeil.—*n.* rubis, *m.*; teinte rouge, *f.*, incarnat, *m.*

ruck [rʌk], *n.* peloton (*de coureurs, cyclistes*), *m.*

rucksack ['rʌksæk], *n.* sac à dos, *m.*

ruction ['rʌkʃən], *n.* (*colloq.*) bagarre, dispute, *f.*

rudder ['rʌdə], *n.* gouvernail, *m.*

ruddiness ['rʌdinis], *n.* rougeur, *f.*

ruddy ['rʌdi], *a.* rouge, au teint vermeil.

rude [ru:d], *a.* grossier, impoli; (*fig.*) rude, violent.

rudely ['ru:dli], *adv.* grossièrement; rudement.

rudeness ['ru:dnis], *n.* rudesse; grossièreté; insolence; violence, *f.*

rudiment ['ru:dimənt], *n.* rudiment, *m.*

rudimentary [ru:di'mentri], *a.* rudimentaire.

rue [ru:], *v.t.* se repentir de, regretter.

rueful ['ru:ful], *a.* triste; lamentable.

ruefully ['ru:fuli], *adv.* tristement, déplorablement.

ruff [rʌf], *n.* fraise, collerette, *f.*

ruffian ['rʌfiən], *n.* bandit, *m.*; brute, *f.*

ruffianism ['rʌfiənizm], *n.* brutalité, *f.*

ruffianly ['rʌfiənli], *a.* de brigand, brutal.

ruffle [rʌfl], *n.* manchette, ruche, *f.*—*v.t.* froncer (*le front etc.*); froisser (*sentiments*); ébouriffer (*les cheveux*).

rug [rʌg], *n.* couverture, *f.*; tapis, *m.*

rugby ['rʌgbi], *n.* (*Spt.*) rugby, *m.*

rugged ['rʌgid], *a.* rude; raboteux; âpre; bourru (*personne*).

ruggedness ['rʌgidnis], *n.* rudesse, âpreté, *f.*

ruin ['ru:in], *n.* ruine; perte, *f.*—*v.t.* ruiner.

ruination [ru:i'neiʃən], *n.* perte, *f.*

ruinous ['ru:inəs], *a.* ruineux; en ruine.

ruinously ['ru:inəsli], *adv.* ruineusement.

rule [ru:l], *n.* règle, *f.*; règlement; gouvernement, empire (*domination*), *m.*; (*Law*) ordonnance, *f.*; *as a rule*, en général, d'ordinaire.—*v.t.* régler, diriger; gouverner; régir; (*Law*) décider.—*v.i.* gouverner; (*Law*) décider; *to rule over*, régner sur.

ruler ['ru:lə], *n.* gouvernant, souverain, *m.*; règle (*instrument*), *f.*

ruling ['ru:liŋ], *a.* dominant, régnant, dirigeant.—*n.* (*Law*) ordonnance de juge, décision, *f.*

rum (1) [rʌm], *a.* drôle; (*colloq.*) cocasse.

rum (2) [rʌm], *n.* rhum, *m.*

Rumania [ru:'meinjə], la Roumanie, *f.*

Rumanian [ru:'meinjən], *a.* roumain.—*n.* roumain (*langue*); Roumain (*personne*), *m.*

rumba ['rʌmbə], *n.* rumba, *f.*

rumble [rʌmbl], *v.i.* gronder, gargouiller.

rumbling ['rʌmbliŋ], *a.* qui gronde; qui gargouille.—*n.* grondement; gargouillement, *m.*

rumbustious [rʌm'bʌstʃəs], *a.* (*fam.*) turbulent, tapageur.

ruminant ['ru:minənt], *a.* and *n.* ruminant, *m.*

ruminate ['ru:mineit], *v.i.* ruminer.

rumination [ru:mi'neiʃən], *n.* rumination, *f.*

rummage ['rʌmidʒ], *v.t.*, *v.i.* fouiller.—*n.* remue-ménage, *m.*

rummage sale ['rʌmidʒseil], *n.* vente d'objets usagés, *f.*

rumor ['ru:mə], *n.* rumeur, *f.*; bruit, *m.*—*v.t.* faire courir le bruit de.

rump [rʌmp], *n.* croupe; culotte (*de viande*), *f.*; croupion (*de volaille*), *m.*

rumple ['rʌmpl], *v.t.* chiffonner, froisser.—*n.* pli, *m.*, froissure, *f.*

rumpus ['rʌmpəs], *n.* (*colloq.*) tapage, *m.*

run [rʌn] (stocking), see **ladder**.

run [rʌn], *v.t.* *irr.* courir; encourir; faire courir, faire marcher, conduire (*machines*); poussei, enfoncer; diriger, exploiter, tenir; *to run down*, dénigrer (*décrier*); (*Hunt.*) forcer; *to run for*, courir chercher; *to run in*, enfoncer; arrêter, coffrer; (*Motor.*) roder; *to run out*, faire sortir; épuiser; *to run over*, (*Motor.*) écraser (*personne, animal*); *to run up*, monter en courant.—*v.i.* courir; accourir (*s'approcher*); se sauver (*s'échapper*); s'étendre; fuir (*bateau*); couler (*liquide*); se fondre (*couleurs*); fondre (*se dissoudre*); être (*exister*); courir, circuler; faire le service (*autobus etc.*); marcher, être en marche (*mécanisme*); s'écouler (*temps*); pleurer (*les yeux*); rouler (*avancer en tournant*); devenir; filer (*navire etc.*); suppurer (*ulcère etc.*); monter (*somme*); (*Am.*) se présenter (*aux élections*); *to run about*, courir çà et là; *to run after*, chercher; *to run against*, courir contre; *to run aground*, échouer; *to run at*, attaquer; *to run away*, se sauver, s'emballer (*cheval*); s'écouler (*liquide etc.*); *to run down*, descendre en courant, aller, venir, couler (*liquide*); s'arrêter (*mécanisme*); *to run from*, s'enfuir de; *to run for office*, see **stand**; *to run out*, courir dehors; couler; fuir; se terminer, expirer, tirer à sa fin; descendre (*marée*); *to run over*, déborder (*liquide etc.*); *to run through*, passer à travers de, parcourir; gaspiller; *to run up*, courir en haut, monter; *to run up to*, s'élever à, monter à.—*n.* course (*action de courir*), *f.*; cours (*série*); trajet, voyage, *m.*; durée, *f.*; succès (*vogue*), *m.*; irruption (*dans une banque etc.*), *f.*; commun (*généralité*), *m.*; *in the long run*, à la longue, à la fin.

runaway ['rʌnəwei], *a.* emballé (*cheval*).—*n.* fuyard; fugitif, déserteur, *m.*

rung (1) [rʌŋ], *n.* échelon (*d'échelle*); bâton (*de chaise etc.*), *m.*

rung (2) [rʌŋ], *p.p.* [RING (2)].

runner ['rʌnə], *n.* coureur; messager, courrier; (*Bot.*) rejeton, *m.*; *scarlet runner*, haricot d'Espagne, *m.*

running ['rʌniŋ], *a.* courant; de suite (*consécutivement*).—*n.* course, *f.*; écoulement (*d'eau*), *m.*

runt [rʌnt], *n.* bétail petit *ou* chétif; (*fig.*) avorton, nain, *m.*

runway ['rʌnwei], *n.* (*Av.*) piste d'envol, *f.*

rupee [ru:'pi:], *n.* roupie, *f.*

rupture ['rʌptʃə], *n.* rupture; (*Med.*) hernie, *f.*—*v.t.* rompre.—*v.i.* se rompre.

rural ['ruərəl], *a.* champêtre, rural, rustique.

ruse [ru:z], *n.* ruse, *f.*, stratagème, *m.*

rush (1) [rʌʃ], *n.* (*Bot.*) jonc, *m.*

rush (2) [rʌʃ], *n.* ruée, *f.*, mouvement précipité, *m.*; foule, presse (*gens*), *f.*—*v.t.* en-

traîner brusquement; dépêcher; envahir.—*v.i.* se jeter, se ruer, se précipiter (*sur*).

rushing ['rʌʃiŋ], *a.* impétueux.—*n.* élan, *m.*, précipitation, *f.*

rusk [rʌsk], *n.* biscotte, *f.*

russet ['rʌsit], *a.* roussâtre.—*n.* roux, *m.*; reinette grise (*pomme*), *f.*

Russia ['rʌʃə], la Russie, *f.*

Russian ['rʌʃən], *a.* russe, de Russie.—*n.* russe (*langue*), *m.*; Russe (*personne*), *m.*, *f.*

rust [rʌst], *n.* rouille, *f.*—*v.i.* se rouiller.

rustic ['rʌstik], *a.* rustique, champêtre.—*n.* rustre, paysan, *m.*

rusticate ['rʌstikeit], *v.t.* reléguer à la campagne; (*Univ.*) renvoyer temporairement.—*v.i.* se retirer à *ou* habiter la campagne.

rustication [rʌsti'keiʃən], *n.* villégiature, *f.*; (*Univ.*) renvoi temporaire, *m.*

rusticity [rʌs'tisiti], *n.* simplicité, rusticité, *f.*

rustiness ['rʌstinis], *n.* rouille, *f.*

rustle [rʌsl], *v.t.* (*Am.*) voler (*du bétail*).—*v.i.* bruire, frémir; faire frou-frou (*robe*); *to rustle against*, frôler.—*n.* frôlement; bruissement; frou-frou (*de robe*), *m.*

rustler ['rʌslə], *n.* (*Am.*) voleur de bétail, *m.*

rustless ['rʌstlis], *a.* inoxydable.

rustling ['rʌsliŋ], *a.* qui fait frou-frou, frémissant.—*n.* (*Am.*) vol de bétail, *m.*

rusty ['rʌsti], *a.* rouillé; roux (*couleur*).

rut [rʌt], *n.* ornière (*de route*), *f.*—*v.t.* sillonner d'ornières.

ruthless ['ru:θlis], *a.* impitoyable, insensible.

ruthlessly ['ru:θlisli], *adv.* sans pitié, sans merci.

ruthlessness ['ru:θlisnis], *n.* cruauté, inhumanité, *f.*

Rwanda ['rwɑ:ndə], le Rwanda, le Ruanda, *m.*

rye [rai], *n.* seigle, *m.*

rye grass ['raigrɑ:s], *n.* ivraie, *f.*, ray-grass, *m.*

S

S, s [es]. dix-neuvième lettre de l'alphabet, *m.*

Saar [sɑ:]. la Sarre, *f.*

Sabbath ['sæbəθ], *n.* (*Jews*) sabbat; dimanche; (*fig.*) repos, *m.*

sabbatic [sə'bætik], **sabbatical** [sə'bætikəl], *a.* sabbatique, du sabbat.

saber ['seibə], *n.* sabre, *m.*—*v.t.* sabrer.

sable [seibl], *a.* de zibeline, de martre; (*Her.*) de sable.—*n.* martre, zibeline, *f.*; (*Her.*) sable, *m.*

sabot ['sæbou], *n.* sabot, *m.*

sabotage ['sæbətɑ:ʒ], *n.* sabotage, *m.*—*v.t.* saboter.

saboteur [sæbə'tə:], *n.* saboteur, *m.*

sac [sæk], *n.* (*Anat.*) sac, *m.*; bourse, *f.*

saccharine ['sækərin], *n.* saccharine, *f.*

sacerdotal [sæsə'doutl], *a.* sacerdotal.

sack (1) [sæk], *n.* sac, *m.*; *to get the sack*, (*colloq.*) être renvoyé; *to give the sack to*, renvoyer, congédier.—*v.t.* (*colloq.*) congédier.

sack (2) [sæk], *n.* sac, saccagement (*d'une ville*), *m.*—*v.t.* saccager, mettre à sac.

sackcloth ['sækkləθ], *n.* toile à sac, *f.*
sackful ['sækful], *n.* sac plein, *m.*, sachée, *f.*
sacking (1) ['sækiŋ], *n.* toile à sac, *f.*
sacking (2) ['sækiŋ], *n.* sac, saccagement (*de ville*), *m.*
sacrament ['sækrəmənt], *n.* sacrement, *m.*
sacramental [sækrə'mentl], *a.* sacramentel.
sacred ['seikrid], *a.* sacré; saint (*histoire etc.*); (*fig.*) inviolable.
sacredly ['seikridli], *adv.* saintement; religieusement.
sacredness ['seikridnis], *n.* sainteté, *f.*, caractère sacré, *m.*
sacrifice ['sækrifais], *v.t.*, *v.i.* sacrifier.—*n.* sacrifice, *m.*; victime, *f.*
sacrificer ['sækrifaisə], *n.* sacrificateur, *m.*
sacrificial [sækri'fiʃl], *a.* des sacrifices, sacrificatoire.
sacrilege ['sækrilidʒ], *n.* sacrilège, *m.*
sacrilegious [sækri'lidʒəs], *a.* sacrilège.
sacrilegiously [sækri'lidʒəsli], *adv.* d'une manière sacrilège.
sacrilegiousness [sækri'lidʒəsnis], *n.* caractère sacrilège, *m.*
sacristy ['sækristi], *n.* sacristie, *f.*
sacrosanct ['sækrosæŋkt], *a.* sacro-saint.
sad [sæd], *a.* triste; pitoyable, déplorable; cruel (*perte*)
sadden ['sædn], *v.t.* attrister.—*v.i.* s'attrister.
saddle ['sædl], *n.* selle, *f.*; *pack-saddle*, bât, *m.*; *side-saddle*, selle d'amazone.—*v.t.* seller; charger, accabler.
saddle-bag ['sædlbæg], *n.* sacoche, *f.*
saddle-bow ['sædlbou], *n.* arçon, *m.*
saddler ['sædlə], *n.* sellier, *m.*
saddle room ['sædlru:m], *n.* sellerie, *f.*
saddlery ['sædləri], *n.* sellerie, *f.*
sadism ['seidizm], *n.* sadisme, *m.*
sadist ['seidist] *n.* sadique, *m.*, *f.*
sadistic [sə'distik], *a.* sadique.
sadly ['sædli], *adv.* tristement; mal, beaucoup, grandement.
sadness ['sædnis], *n.* tristesse, *f.*
safe [seif], *a.* sauf, en sûreté; à l'abri (*de*); sûr; *safe and sound*, sain et sauf.—*n.* coffrefort (*pour l'argent*); garde-manger (*pour aliments*), *m.*
safe-conduct ['seif'kɔndʌkt], *n.* sauf-conduit, *m.*
safeguard ['seifgɑ:d], *n.* sauvegarde, *f.*—*v.t.* sauvegarder.
safe-keeping ['seif'ki:piŋ], *n.* bonne garde, sûreté, *f.*
safely ['seifli], *adv.* sain et sauf; en sûreté.
safety ['seifti], *a.* de sûreté.—*n.* sûreté, *f.*, salut, *m.*
safety catch ['seiftikætʃ], *n.* cran de sûreté, cran d'arrêt, *m.*
safety lamp ['seiftilæmp], *n.* lampe de sûreté, *f.*
safety match ['seiftimætʃ], *n.* allumette suédoise, *f.*
safety pin ['seiftipin], *n.* épingle de sûreté, *f.*
safety valve ['seiftivælv], *n.* soupape de sûreté, *f.*
saffron ['sæfrən], *a.* couleur safran; de safran.—*n.* safran, *m.*
saffrony ['sæfrəni], *a.* safrané.
sag [sæg], *v.i.* plier, ployer, s'affaisser; se relâcher (*câble*).
saga ['sɑ:gə], *n.* saga, *f.*

sagacious [sə'geiʃəs], *a.* sagace; intelligent (*animal*).
sagaciously [sə'geiʃəsli], *adv.* avec sagacité.
sagaciousness [sə'geiʃəsnis], **sagacity** [sə'gæsiti], *n.* sagacité, *f.*
sage (1) [seidʒ], *a.* sage, prudent.—*n.* sage, *m.*
sage (2) [seidʒ], *n.* sauge (*herbes*), *f.*
sagely ['seidʒli], *adv.* sagement, prudemment.
sagging ['sægiŋ], *a.* affaissé, fléchi, ployé.—*n.* courbure, *f.*, affaissement, *m.*; baisse (*de prix*), *f.*
sago ['seigou], *n.* sagou; sagouier, sagoutier (*arbre*), *m.*
sagy ['seidʒi], *a.* qui a un goût de sauge.
Sahara [sə'hɑ:rə], the. le Sahara, *m.*
said [sed], *a.* dit, susdit [SAY].
sail [seil], *n.* voile, *f.*; (*collect.*) voiles, *f.pl.*, voilure; aile (*de moulin à vent*); course ou promenade à la voile (*sur l'eau*), *f.*—*v.t.* naviguer (*sur*), voguer (*sur ou dans*).—*v.i.* faire voile; cingler, naviguer; mettre à la voile, appareiller.
sailable ['seiləbl], *a.* navigable.
sail-cloth ['seilkləθ], *n.* toile à voiles, *f.*
sailing ['seiliŋ], *a.* à voiles.—*n.* navigation, *f.*; appareillage, *m.*; partance (*départ*), *f.*
sailing boat ['seilŋbout], *n.* bateau à voiles, *m.*
sailing ship ['seiliŋʃip], *n.* bâtiment à voiles voilier, *m.*
sail-maker ['seilmeikə], *n.* voilier, *m.*
sailor ['seilə], *n.* marin, matelot, *m.*
saint [seint] *strong form*, [sənt] *weak form*, *n.* saint, *m.*, sainte, *f.*; *All Saints' Day*, la Toussaint, *f.*
saintliness ['seintlinis], *n.* sainteté, *f.*
saintly ['seintli], *a.* saint; de saint, vénérable.
sake [seik], *n.* (*used only with* FOR); *art for art's sake*, l'art pour l'art; *for God's sake*, pour l'amour de Dieu; *for the sake of appearances*, pour sauver les apparences; *for the sake of health*, pour cause de santé; *for your sake*, par égard pour vous.
sal [sæl], *n.* sel, *m.*
salaam [sə'lɑ:m], *n.* salamalec, *m.*
salad ['sæləd], *n.* salade, *f.*
salad bowl ['sælədboul], *n.* saladier, *m.*
salad oil ['sælədɔil], *n.* huile de table, *f.*
salamander ['sæləmændə], *n.* salamandre, *f.*
salaried ['sælərid], *a.* qui touche des appointements.
salary ['sæləri], *n.* appointements, *m.pl.*; traitement (*de fonctionnaire*), *m.*
sale [seil], *n.* vente; mise en vente, *f.*; *for sale*, à vendre; *on sale*, en vente; *private sale*, vente à l'amiable; *sale by auction*, vente aux enchères; *to put up for sale*, mettre en vente.
saleable ['seiləbl], *a.* vendable; de bonne vente.
sale-room ['seilru:m], *n.* salle des ventes, *f.*
salesman ['seilzmən], *n.* (*pl.* -men [men]) vendeur, marchand; courtier de commerce, *m.*
Salic ['sælik], *a.* salique.
salient ['seiliənt], *a.* and *n.* saillant, *m.*
saliently ['seiliəntli], *adv.* d'une manière saillante.
salify ['sælifai], *v.t.* salifier.
saline ['seilain], *a.* salin.
saliva [sə'laivə], *n.* salive, *f.*

salivate ['sæliveit], *v.t.* faire saliver.
sallow ['sælou], *a.* jaunâtre, jaune, blême.
sallowness ['sælounis], *n.* teint blême, *m.*
sally ['sæli], *n.* sortie; (*fig.*) excursion; saillie (*d'esprit*), *f.—v.i.* sortir, faire une sortie.
salmon ['sæmən], *n.* saumon, *m.*
salmon trout ['sæməntraut], *n.* truite saumonée, *f.*
saloon [sə'lu:n], *n.* (grand) salon, *m.*, salle; (*Am.*) buvette, *f.*, bar, *m.*; conduite-intérieure (*voiture*), *f.*
salsify ['sælsifi], *n.* (*Bot.*) salsifis, *m.*
salt [sɔ:lt], *a.* salé; de sel.—*n.* sel, *m.*; *Epsom salts*, sels anglais, *m.pl.—v.t.* saler.
salt-cellar [' sɔ:ltselə], *n.* salière, *f.*
salted ['sɔ:ltid], *a.* salé; (*fig.*) aguerri.
salter ['sɔ:ltə], *n.* saunier; saleur, *m.*
salting ['sɔ:ltiŋ], *n.* salaison, *f.*, salage, *m.*
saltish ['sɔ:ltiʃ], *a.* un peu salé, saumâtre.
saltless ['sɔ:ltlis], *a.* sans sel; (*fig.*) insipide.
salt marsh ['sɔ:ltmɑ:ʃ], *n.* marais salant, *m.*
salt mine ['sɔ:ltmain], *n.* mine de sel, *f.*
saltness ['sɔ:ltnis], *n.* salure, *f.*
saltpeter [sɔ:lt'pi:tə], *n.* salpêtre, *m.*
saltpeter-works [sɔ:lt'pi:təwɑ:ks], *n.pl.* salpêtrière, *f.*
saltpetrous [sɔ:lt'petrəs], *a.* salpêtreux.
salt water ['sɔ:ltwɔ:tə], *n.* eau de mer, *f.*
salty ['sɔ:lti], *a.* salé; qui a un goût de sel.
salubrious [sə'lju:briəs], *a.* salubre, sain.
salubriously [sə'lju:briəsli], *adv.* d'une manière salubre.
salubrity [sə'lju:briti], *n.* salubrité, *f.*
salutary ['sæljutəri], *a.* salutaire.
salutation [sælju'teiʃən], *n.* salut, *m.*, salutation, *f.*
salute [sə'lju:t], *n.* salut, *m.*, salutation, salve (*de fusils*), *f.—v.t.* saluer, sauveter.
Salvador ['sælvədɔ:], El. le Salvador, *m.*
Salvadorean [sælvə'dɔ:riən], *a.* salvadorègne. —*n.* Salvadorègne (*personne*), *m.*, *f.*
salvage ['sælvidʒ], *n.* sauvetage, *m.*, objets sauvés, *m.pl.*; (*Ind.*) récupération, *f.—v.t.* récupérer; relever (*navire*).
salvage money ['sælvidʒmʌni], *n.* prix *ou* droit de sauvetage, *m.*
salvage vessel ['sælvidʒvesl], *n.* navire de relevage, *m.*
salvation [sæl'veiʃən], *n.* salut, *m.*; *Salvation Army*, Armée du Salut, *f.*
salve [sælv, sɑ:v], *n.* onguent, *m.*; (*fig.*) remède, baume, *m.*—[sælv], *v.t.* remédier à; (*Naut.*) sauver, sauveter.
salver ['sælvə], *n.* plateau, *m.*
salvo ['sælvou], *n.* réserve, restriction; salve (*d'artillerie*), *f.*
Samaritan [sə'mæritən], *a.* samaritain.—*n.* Samaritain (*personne*), *m.*
same [seim], *a.* même.—*n.* le même, *m.*, la même; même chose, *f.*; ledit, *m.*, ladite, *f.*, lesdits, *m.pl.*, lesdites, *f.pl.*; *all the same*, néanmoins, quand même; *it is all the same*, c'est égal; *just the same*, tout de même; *much about the same*, à peu près de même; *the same to you*, et vous de même.
sameness ['seimnis], *n.* identité; uniformité, *f.*
sample [sɑ:mpl], *n.* échantillon, *m.—v.t.* échantillonner; déguster (*vin*).
sampler ['sɑ:mplə], *n.* modèle; (*Needlework*) canevas, *m.*

sampling ['sɑ:mpliŋ], *n.* échantillonnage, *m.*; gustation (*des mets*), *f.*
sanatorium [sænə'tɔ:riəm], *n.* sanatorium, *m.*
sanctification [sæŋktifi'keiʃən], *n.* sanctification, *f.*
sanctified ['sæŋktifaid], *a.* sanctifié, saint.
sanctify ['sæŋktifai], *v.t.* sanctifier.
sanctimonious [sæŋkti'mouniəs], *a.* papelard, béat, hypocrite.
sanctimoniously [sæŋkti'mouniəsli], *adv.* d'un air béat.
sanctimoniousness [sæŋkti'mouniəsnis], *n.* dévotion affectée; cagoterie, *f.*
sanction ['sæŋkʃən], *n.* sanction, autorité, *f.— v.t.* sanctionner, autoriser.
sanctity [' sæŋktiti], *n.* sainteté, *f.*
sanctuary ['sæŋktjuəri], *n.* sanctuaire, asile, refuge, *m.*
sanctum ['sæŋktəm], *n.* sanctuaire; (*colloq.*) cabinet de travail, *m.*, retraite, *f.*
sand [sænd], *n.* sable; sablon (*sable fin*), *m.*; (*pl.*) plage, *f.*, bord de la mer, *m.—v.t.* sabler.
sandal [sændl], *n.* sandale, *f.*; santal, *m.*
sandbag ['sændbæg], *n.* sac de terre, *m.*
sand bank ['sændbæŋk], *n.* banc de sable, *m.*
sand drift ['sænddrift], *n.* amas de sable, *m.*
sand eel ['sændi:l], *n.* lançon, *m.*, équille, *f.*
sand glass ['sændglɑ:s], *n.* sablier, *m.*
sand martin ['sændmɑ:tin], *n.* hirondelle de rivage, *f.*
sand-paper ['sændpeipə], *n.* papier de verre, *m.—v.t.* passer au papier de verre.
sand pit ['sændpit], *n.* sablière, sablonnière, *f.*
sand shoes ['sændʃu:z], *n.pl.* espadrilles, *f.pl.*
sandstone ['sændstoun], *n.* grès, *m.*
sand-storm ['sændstɔ:m], *n.* ouragan de sable, *m.*
sandwich ['sændwitʃ], *n.* sandwich, *m.*
sandwich man ['sændwitʃmən], *n.* (*pl.* men [men]) homme-sandwich, homme-affiche, *m.*
sandy ['sændi], *a.* sablonneux, de sable; d'un blond ardent, roux (*couleur*).
sane [sein], *a.* sain, sain d'esprit.
sanguinary ['sæŋgwinəri], *a.* sanguinaire.
sanguine ['sæŋgwin], *a.* sanguin; plein de confiance, confiant.
sanguineness ['sæŋgwinnis], *n.* confiance, assurance, *f.*
sanitary ['sænitəri], *a.* sanitaire, hygiénique; *sanitary napkin*, serviette hygiénique, *f.*
sanitation [sæni'teiʃən], *n.* assainissement, *m.*
sanity ['sæniti], *n.* état sain, jugement sain, *m.*
Sanskrit ['sænskrit], *a.* and *n.* sanscrit, *m.*
Santa Claus ['sæntə'klɔ:z]. Père Noël, *m.*
sap (1) [sæp], *n.* sève, *f.*
sap (2) [sæp], *n.* (*Mil.*) sapé, *f.—v.t.* saper.
sapience ['seipiəns], *n.* sagesse, *f.*
sapient ['seipiənt], *a.* sage.
sapless ['sæplis], *a.* sans sève; sec, desséché.
sapling ['sæpliŋ], *n.* jeune arbre, baliveau, *m.*
saponaceous ['sæpə'neiʃəs], *a.* saponacé.
saponify [sə'pɔnifai], *v.t.* saponifier.—*v.i.* se saponifier.
sapper ['sæpə], *n.* sapeur, *m.*
sapphic ['sæfik], *a.* and *n.* (*Pros.*) saphique, *m.*
sapphire ['sæfaiə], *n.* saphir, *m.*
sappiness ['sæpinis], *n.* abondance de sève, *f.*
sappy ['sæpi], *a.* plein de sève.
saraband ['særəbænd], *n.* sarabande, *f.*

Saracen

Saracen ['særəsn], a. sarrasin.—n. Sarrasin, m.
sarcasm ['sɑːkæzm], n. sarcasme, m.
sarcastic [sɑː'kæstik], a. sarcastique.
sarcastically [sɑː'kæstikəli], adv. d'une manière ou d'un ton sarcastique.
sarcophagus [sɑː'kɔfəgəs], n. sarcophage, m.
sardine [sɑː'diːn], n. sardine, f.
Sardinia [sɑː'dinjə], la Sardaigne, f.
Sardinian [sɑː'dinjən], a. sarde.—n. Sarde (personne), m., f.
sardonic [sɑː'dɔnik], a. sardonique.
sarong [sə'rɔŋ], n. pagne, m., jupe (malaisien), f.
sarsaparilla [sɑːsəpə'rilə], n. salsepareille, f.
sash (1) [sæʃ], n. ceinture; écharpe (décoration), f.
sash (2) [sæʃ], n. châssis (de fenêtre), m.
sash window ['sæʃwindou], n. fenêtre à guillotine, f.
sassafras ['sæsəfræs], n. (Bot.) sassafras, m.
Satan ['seitən]. Satan, m.
satanic [sə'tænik], satanical [sə'tænikəl], a. satanique.
satchel [sætʃl], n. sacoche, f.; sac d'écolier, cartable, m.
sate [seit], v.t. rassasier (de), assouvir.
satellite ['sætəlait], n. satellite, m.
satiate ['seiʃieit], v.t. rassasier (de).
satiated ['seiʃieitid], a. rassasié (de); gorgé.
satiety [sə'taiəti], n. satiété, f.
satin ['sætin], a. de satin.—n. satin, m.
satin-wood ['sætinwuːd], n. bois de citronnier, m.
satire ['sætaiə], n. satire, f.
satiric [sə'tirik], satirical [sə'tirikəl], a. satirique.
satirist ['sætirist], n. satirique, m., f.
satirize ['sætiraiz], v.t. satiriser.
satisfaction [sætis'fækʃən], n. satisfaction; réparation (récompense), f.
satisfactorily [sætis'fæktərili], adv. d'une manière satisfaisante.
satisfactory [sætis'fæktri], a. satisfaisant.
satisfy ['sætisfai], v.t. satisfaire; satisfaire à; acquitter (dette); assouvir (passion); rassasier (de) (appétit); to be satisfied that, être persuadé, être convaincu que; to be satisfied with, être satisfait de, être content de.—v.i. satisfaire, donner satisfaction.
satisfying ['sætisfaiiŋ], a. satisfaisant; nourrissant (nourriture).
saturate ['sætʃureit], v.t. saturer.
saturation [sætʃu'reiʃən], n. saturation, f.
Saturday ['sætədei]. samedi, m.
Saturn ['sætən]. Saturne, m.
Saturnalia [sætə'neiliə]. saturnales, f.pl.
saturnine ['sætənain], a. sombre, taciturne.
satyr ['sætə], n. satyre, m.
sauce [sɔːs], n. sauce; (fig.) insolence, impertinence, f.—v.t. assaisonner; flatter (le goût); (fig.) dire des impertinences à.
sauce boat ['sɔːsbout], n. saucière, f.
saucer ['sɔːsə], n. soucoupe, f.; flying saucer, soucoupe volante.
saucepan ['sɔːspən], n. casserole, f.
saucily ['sɔːsili], adv. insolemment.
sauciness ['sɔːsinis], n. insolence, impertinence, f.
saucy ['sɔːsi], a. insolent, impertinent.
Saudi Arabia ['saudiə'reibiə]. l'Arabie Séoudite, f.
sauerkraut ['sauəkraut], n. choucroute, f.

saunter ['sɔːntə], v.i. flâner.—n. flânerie, f.
saunterer ['sɔːntərə], n. flâneur, m.
sauntering ['sɔːntəriŋ], a. de flâneur.—n. flânerie, f.
sausage ['sɔsidʒ], n. saucisse (à cuire), f.; saucisson (salami etc.), m.
sausage meat ['sɔsidʒmiːt], n. chair à saucisse, f.
sausage-roll ['sɔsidʒ'roul], n. friand, m.
savage ['sævidʒ], a. sauvage; féroce.—n. sauvage, m., f.—v.t. attaquer, mordre (bête).
savagely ['sævidʒli], adv. sauvagement, en sauvage; d'une manière féroce.
savageness ['sævidʒnis], n. férocité, brutalité; sauvagerie, f.
savagery ['sævidʒəri], n. férocité, barbarie, f.
savannah ['sævænə], n. savane, prairie, f.
save [seiv], v.t. sauver (de); épargner (argent etc.); mettre de côté, économiser.—v.i. économiser, faire des économies.—n. (Spt.) arrêt, m.—prep. hormis, excepté, sauf.
saver ['seivə], n. sauveur, libérateur, m.; économe (ménager), m., f.
saving ['seiviŋ], a. économe, ménager.—n. épargne; économie, f.; salut, m.
savings bank ['seiviŋzbæŋk], n. caisse d'épargne, f.
savior ['seivjə], n. sauveur, m.
savor ['seivə], n. saveur, f.; goût, m., odeur, f.—v.t. goûter, savourer.—v.i. avoir du goût; sentir.
savoriness ['seivərinis], n. goût agréable, m., saveur, f.
savory ['seivəri], a. savoureux, appétissant.—n. plat épicé, m.
saw (1) [sɔː], past [SEE].
saw (2) [sɔː], n. scie, f.—v.t., v.i. irr. scier.
saw (3) [sɔː], n. adage, dicton (proverbe), m.
sawdust [sɔː'dʌst], n. sciure (de bois), f.
saw-mill ['sɔːmil], n. scierie, f.
sawyer ['sɔːjə], n. scieur, scieur de long, m.
saxifrage ['sæksifreidʒ], n. (Bot.) saxifrage, f.
Saxon ['sæksən], a. saxon, de Saxe.—n. saxon (langue); Saxon (personne), m.
saxophone ['sæksəfoun], n. saxophone, m.
say [sei], v.t. irr. dire; parler, répéter, réciter; I say! dites donc! that is to say, c'est-à-dire; they say, on dit.—n. dire, mot, ce qu'on a à dire, m.
saying ['seiiŋ], n. mot, proverbe, dicton, m.; sentence, maxime, f.
scab [skæb], n. croûte (sur blessure etc.); gale (de mouton etc.), f.; [see BLACKLEG]
scabbard ['skæbəd], n. fourreau, m.
scabbiness ['skæbinis], n. état galeux, m.
scabby ['skæbi], a. couvert de croûtes; galeux.
scabious ['skeibiəs], a. scabieux.—n. scabieuse (plante), f.
scaffold ['skæfəld], n. échafaud, m.—v.t. échafauder.
scaffolding ['skæfəldiŋ], n. échafaudage, m.
scald [skɔːld], n. brûlure, f.—v.t. échauder, ébouillanter.
scalding ['skɔːldiŋ], n. échaudage, m.
scalding-hot ['skɔːldiŋ'hɔt], a. tout bouillant.
scale (1) [skeil], n. échelle, f.; (Mus.) gamme, f.—v.t. escalader.
scale (2) [skeil], n. écaille (de poisson), f.
scale (3) [skeil], n. bassin, plateau (balance), m.; scales or pair of scales, balance, f.

550

scale-maker ['skeilmeikə], n. balancier, m.
scalene ['skeili:n], a. scalène.
scaliness ['skeilinis], n. nature écailleuse, f.
scaling (1) ['skeilin], n. escalade (montagnes), f.

scaling (2) ['skeilin], n. écaillage (peintures), m.
scallop ['skoləp], n. coquille Saint-Jacques; coquille; dentelure, f., feston, m.—v.t. denteler; (Needlework) festonner.
scalp [skælp], n. cuir chevelu, m., chevelure, f., scalpe; (fig.) front, m., tête, f.—v.t. scalper.
scalpel ['skælpəl], n. (Surg.) scalpel, m.
scaly ['skeili], a. écaillé; (Bot.) écailleux.
scamp [skæmp], n. chenapan, vaurien, m.; young scamp, petit polisson, m.—v.t. bâcler.
scamper ['skæmpə], v.i. courir, s'enfuir.—n. course rapide, f.
scampi ['skæmpi], n.pl. langoustine, f.
scan [skæn], v.t. scruter; (Pros.) scander; (Rad.) balayer.
scandal [skændl], n. scandale, m.; honte; médisance, f.
scandalize ['skændəlaiz], v.t. scandaliser, choquer; calomnier.
scandal-monger ['skændlmʌngə], n. médisant, m.
scandalous ['skændələs], a. scandaleux; honteux.
Scandinavia [skændi'neivjə]. la Scandinavie, f.

Scandinavian [skændl'neivjən], a. scandinave.—n. Scandinave (personne), m., f.
scanner ['skænə], n. scrutateur, m.; radar scanner, déchiffreur de radar, m.
scanning ['skæniŋ], n. examen minutieux, m.; (Pros.) scansion, f.; (Rad.) balayage, m.
scansion ['skænʃən], n. scansion, f.
scant [skænt], a. rare; rétréci; faible; peu de.
scantily ['skæntili], adv. faiblement, d'une manière insuffisante.
scantiness ['skæntinis], n. insuffisance (de vivres etc.); faiblesse (de poids), f.
scantling ['skæntliŋ], n. échantillon, m.; (Carp.) volige, f., équarrissage, m.
scanty ['skænti], a. rétréci, faible, peu abondant, insuffisant (cheveux).
scapegoat ['skeipgout], n. bouc émissaire, (fig.) souffre-douleur, m.
scapegrace ['skeipgreis], n. vaurien, mauvais sujet, m.
scapement ['skeipmənt], n. échappement, m.
scapula ['skæpjulə], n. (Anat.) omoplate, f.
scapular ['skæpjulə], n. scapulaire.
scapulary ['skæpjuləri], n. (R.-C. Ch.) scapulaire, m.
scar [skɑ:], n. cicatrice, balafre, f.—v.t. cicatriser; balafrer.
scarab ['skærəb], **scarabaeus** [skærə'bi:əs], n. scarabée, m.
scaramouch ['skærəmu:ʃ], n. scaramouche, m.
scarce [skɛəs], a. rare; to make oneself scarce, disparaître, décamper, filer.
scarcely ['skɛəsli], adv. à peine, presque pas, guère.
scarcity ['skɛəsiti], n. rareté; disette (famine), f.
scare [skɛə], n. panique, frayeur subite, f.—v.t. effrayer, épouvanter, effaroucher.

scarecrow ['skɛəkrou], n. épouvantail, m.
scarf [skɑ:f], n. (pl. **scarfs** [skɑ:fs], **scarves** [skɑ:vz]) écharpe, f.; cache-nez, m.inv.; foulard, m.
scarifier ['skærifaiə], n. scarificateur, m.
scarify ['skærifai], v.t. scarifier (peau), ameublir (terre).
scarlatina [skɑ:lə'ti:nə], n. (fièvre) scarlatine, f.
scarlet ['skɑ:lit], a. and n. écarlate, f.; scarlet fever, fièvre scarlatine, f.; scarlet runner, haricot d'Espagne, m.
scarp [skɑ:p], n. (Fort.) escarpe, f.—v.t. escarper.
scarves [SCARF].
scathless ['skeiθlis], a. sans dommage, sain et sauf.
scathing ['skeiðiŋ], a. acerbe, cinglant, cassant.
scatter ['skætə], v.t. disperser, dissiper; répandre, éparpiller.—v.i. se disperser, se répandre.
scattered ['skætəd], a. dispersé, éparpillé, épars.
scattering ['skætəriŋ], n. éparpillement; petit nombre, m.
scavenge ['skævindʒ], v.t. ébouer, balayer.
scavenger ['skævindʒə], n. boueur; balayeur, m.
scavenging ['skævindʒiŋ], n. ébouage, balayage, m.
scene [si:n], n. scène; (Theat.) scène, décoration, f.; décor; (fig.) théâtre, m.; behind the scenes, dans la coulisse; scene shifter, machiniste, m.
scenery ['si:nəri], n. scène; (fig.) vue, perspective, f., paysage, m.; (Theat.) décors, m.pl.
scenic ['si:nik], a. scénique.
scent [sent], n. odeur, senteur, f., parfum; odorat; flair, nez (de chien), m.; voie (de cerf); (fig.) piste (traces), f.—v.t. parfumer (de); sentir, flairer (animal).
scent bottle ['sentbotl], n. flacon de parfum, m.
scentless ['sentlis], a. sans odeur, inodore.
scent spray ['sentsprei], n. vaporisateur, m.
sceptic ['skeptik], n. sceptique, m., f.
sceptical ['skeptikl], a. sceptique.
scepticism ['skeptisizm], n. scepticisme, m.
sceptre ['septə], n. sceptre, m.
sceptred ['septəd], a. portant le sceptre.
schedule ['ʃedju:l, (Am.) 'skedju:l], n. liste, f., inventaire; (Comm.) bilan; (Law) bordereau, m.—v.t. enregistrer, inventorier.
scheme [ski:m], n. arrangement, m., combinaison, f.; projet, système, m.—v.t. projeter, combiner.—v.i. faire des projets; (fig.) intriguer.
schemer ['ski:mə], n. faiseur de projets; (fig.) intrigant, m.
scheming ['ski:miŋ], a. à projets; intrigant.—n. projets m.pl., intrigues, f.pl.
schism [sizm], n. schisme, m.
schismatic [siz'mætik], n. schismatique, m., f.
schizophrenia [skitso'fri:niə], n. (Med.) schizophrénie, f.
schizophrenic [skitso'fri:nik], a. and n. schizophrène, m., f.
scholar ['skolə], n. écolier; érudit, savant (learned person), m.; day scholar, externe, m., f.

scholarly

scholarly ['skɔləli], *a.* d'érudit, savant.
scholarship ['skɔləʃip], *n.* érudition, *f.*, savoir, *m.*; (*Univ. etc.*) bourse, *f.*
scholastic [skɔ'læstik], *a.* and *n.* scolastique, *m.*, *f.*
scholasticism [skɔ'læstisizm], *n.* scolastique, *f.*
school [sku:l], *n.* école; bande, troupe (*de baleines etc.*), *f.*; *at school*, en classe, à l'école; *boarding school*, pension, *f.*, pensionnat, *m.*; *primary school*, école primaire; *grammar school*, collège, lycée, *m.*; *nursery school*, école maternelle.—*v.t.* instruire, enseigner; réprimander.
schooled [sku:ld], *a.* formé, entraîné, dressé.
schooling ['sku:liŋ], *n.* instruction; réprimande, *f.*
schoolmaster ['sku:lmɑːstə], *n.* instituteur, professeur, *m.*
schoolmistress ['sku:lmistris], *n.* maîtresse d'école, institutrice, *f.*
schooner ['sku:nə], *n.* (*Naut.*) goélette, *f.*
sciatic [sai'ætik], *a.* sciatique.
sciatica [sai'ætikə], *n.* sciatique, *f.*
science ['saiəns], *n.* science, *f.*
scientific [saiən'tifik], *a.* scientifique.
scientist ['saiəntist], *n.* homme de science, savant, *m.*
Scilly Isles ['siliailz], *the,* les Sorlingues, *f.pl.*
scimitar ['simitə], *n.* cimeterre, *m.*
scintillant ['sintilənt], *a.* scintillant.
scintillate ['sintileit], *v.i.* scintiller.
scintillation [sinti'leiʃən], *n.* scintillation, *f.*, scintillement, *m.*
scion ['saiən], *n.* (*Bot.*) scion; (*fig.*) rejeton, *m.*
scission ['siʃən], *n.* scission, *f.*
scissors ['sizəz], *n.pl.* ciseaux, *m.pl.*
scoff [skɔf], *n.* moquerie, *f.*, sarcasme, *m.*—*v.t.* se moquer de, bafouer.—*v.i.* railler.
scoffer ['skɔfə], *n.* moqueur, railleur, *m.*
scoffing ['skɔfiŋ], *n.* moqueur.—*n.* moquerie, dérision, *f.*
scoffingly ['skɔfiŋli], *adv.* par moquerie, en dérision.
scold [skould], *v.t.* gronder, criailler (*après*).—*v.i.* gronder.
scolding ['skouldiŋ], *a.* bougon.—*n.* semonce, *f.*
sconce [skɔns], *n.* candélabre (*fixé au mur*), *m.*; bobèche (*de bougeoir*), *f.*
scone [skɔn, skoun], *n.* petite galette (ronde), *f.*
scoop [sku:p], *n.* grande cuiller; (*Naut.*) écope; (*Journ. slang*) nouvelle à sensation, *f.*—*v.t.* vider, creuser; (*Naut.*) écoper.
scooter ['sku:tə], *n.* patinette, *f.*; scooter, *m.*
scope [skoup], *n.* portée, étendue; visée; liberté, *f.*
scorch [skɔːtʃ], *v.t.* brûler, roussir, griller.—*v.i.* se brûler.
scorching ['skɔːtʃiŋ], *a.* brûlant, très chaud.
score [skɔː], *n.* entaille, coche, *f.*; compte; vingt, *m.*, vingtaine, *f.*; (*Games*) nombre de points; (*fig.*) motif, *m.*, raison, cause; (*Mus.*) partition, *f.*; *on what score?* à quel titre?—*v.t.* entailler, marquer; rayer; (*Mus.*) orchestrer; *to score out*, rayer, biffer (*texte*).—*v.i.* marquer des points.
scorer ['skɔːrə], *n.* marqueur, *m.*
scoring ['skɔːriŋ], *n.* (*Games etc.*) marque; (*Mus.*) orchestration, *f.*
scorn [skɔːn], *v.t.* mépriser; dédaigner.—*v.i.* mépriser; dédaigner (*de*); *to scorn to fly,*

dédaigner de fuir.—*n.* mépris, dédain, *m.* dérision, *f.*
scornful ['skɔːnful], *a.* méprisant, dédaigneux.
scornfully ['skɔːnfuli], *adv.* dédaigneusement, avec dédain.
scornfulness ['skɔːnfulnis], *n.* caractère dédaigneux, *m.*
scorpion ['skɔːpjən], *n.* scorpion, *m.*
Scot [skɔt], *n.* Écossais, *m.*
Scotch [skɔtʃ], *a.* écossais (*but used* ONLY *in certain fixed expressions, which include the following*) *Scotch terrier,* terrier griffon, *m.*; *Scotch* (*whisky*), whisky écossais, *m.*; [SCOTS].
scotch [skɔtʃ], *v.t.* entailler; enrayer (*roue*); (*fig.*) annuler.
scot-free [skɔt'friː], *a.* sans frais; (*fig.*) sain et sauf, indemne.
Scotland ['skɔtlənd], *n.* l'Écosse, *f.*
Scots [skɔts], **Scottish** ['skɔtiʃ], *a.* écossais; *Scots Law,* droit écossais, *m.*
Scotsman ['skɔtsmən], *n.* (*pl.* **-men** [men]) Écossais, *m.*
Scotswoman ['skɔtswumən], *n.* (*pl.* **-women** [wimin]) Écossaise, *f.*
Scottish [SCOTS].
scoundrel ['skaundrəl], *n.* gredin, coquin, scélérat, *m.*
scour (1) ['skauə], *v.t.* nettoyer, récurer, purger, écurer.—*v.i.* écurer; nettoyer.
scour (2) ['skauə], *v.t.* parcourir.—*v.i.* courir.
scourer ['skauərə], *n.* récureur, nettoyeur, *m.*
scourge [skɔːdʒ], *n.* fouet; (*fig.*) fléau, *m.*—*v.t.* fouetter, flageller; (*fig.*) châtier.
scourger ['skɔːdʒə], *n.* châtieur; (*Eccles. Hist.*) flagellant, *m.*
scourging ['skɔːdʒiŋ], *n.* flagellation, *f.*
scouring ['skauəriŋ], *n.* récurage; nettoyage, *m.*
scout [skaut], *n.* éclaireur; scout, *m.*; (*Naut.*) vedette, *f.*; (*Av.*) avion de chasse, *m.*—*v.t.* repousser avec mépris.—*v.i.* aller en éclaireur.
scowl [skaul], *v.i.* se re(n)frogner, froncer le sourcil.—*n.* re(n)frognement, froncement de sourcil, *m.*
scowling ['skauliŋ], *a.* re(n)frogné, menaçant.
scrag [skræg], *n.* corps décharné, squelette, *m.*; *scrag-end,* bout saigneux (*de viande*), *m.*
scragginess ['skræginis], *n.* état raboteux, *m.*; maigreur, *f.*
scraggy ['skrægi], *a.* noueux, rugueux, rabougri.
scramble [skræmbl], *v.t.* (*Teleg.*) brouiller (*message*); *scrambled eggs,* œufs brouillés, *m.pl.*—*v.i.* grimper; se battre, se disputer.—*n.* mêlée, lutte, *f.*
scrap (1) [skræp], *n.* morceau, fragment, bout, *m.*; (*pl.*) bribes, *f.pl.*; restes, *m.pl.*—*v.t.* mettre au rebut.
scrap (2) [skræp], *n.* (*slang*) bagarre, rixe, *f.*
scrap-book ['skræpbuk], *n.* album, *m.*
scrape [skreip], *v.t.* gratter, érafler, râcler; décrotter (*bottes etc.*); (*Cook.*) ratisser; *to scrape together,* amasser petit à petit.—*v.i.* gratter; (*fam.*) râcler (*jouer du violon*); *to scrape through,* passer de justesse; *to bow and scrape,* faire des salamalecs.—*n.* grattage, *m.*; (*fig.*) difficulté, mauvaise affaire, *f.*

scraper ['skreipə], *n.* grattoir; râcloir, *m.*; (*Agric.*) ratissoire, *f.*; décrottoir (*pour chaussures*), *m.*

scrap heap ['skræphi:p], *n.* tas de ferraille, *m.*

scraping ['skreipiŋ], *n.* grattage, *m.*; ratissure (*de légumes*), *f.*; *with much bowing and scraping*, avec force révérences.

scrap iron ['skræpaiən], *n.* ferraille, *f.*

scratch [skrætʃ], *n.* égratignure, *f.*; coup de griffe ou d'ongle, *m.*; raie, rayure (*sur une surface polie*), *f.*—*v.t.* gratter; rayer (*surface polie*).—*v.i.* gratter; (*Spt.*) renoncer à concourir.

scratcher ['skrætʃə], *n.* égratigneur; grattoir (*instrument*), *m.*

scratching ['skrætʃiŋ], *n.* grattage, *m.*; égratignure; rayure, *f.*

scrawl [skrɔːl], *n.* griffonnage, *m.*, pattes de mouche, *f.pl.*—*v.t.*, *v.i.* griffonner.

scrawler ['skrɔːlə], *n.* griffonneur, *m.*

scrawny ['skrɔːni], *a.* décharné, émacié.

scream [skriːm], *n.* cri perçant, *m.*—*v.i.* crier, pousser des cris.

screamer ['skriːmə], *n.* crieur, *m.*

screaming ['skriːmiŋ], *a.* perçant; qui crie.—*n.* cris, *m.pl.*

screech [skriːtʃ], *n.* cri perçant, *m.*—*v.i.* crier.

screech owl ['skriːtʃaul], *n.* effraie, chouette, *f.*

screen [skriːn], *n.* écran; paravent (*pliant*); rideau (*d'arbres etc.*), *m.*; (*fig.*) voile, *f.*, abri, *m.*; défense, *f.*—*v.t.* mettre à couvert; abriter (*contre*).

screw [skruː], *a.* à hélice.—*n.* vis; hélice (*de navire etc.*), *f.*—*v.t.* visser; (*fig.*) serrer (*presser*); pressurer (*opprimer*).—*v.i.* se visser.

screw bolt ['skruːboult], *n.* boulon à vis, *m.*

screw cap ['skruːkæp], *n.* couvercle à vis, *m.*

screw-driver ['skruːdraivə], *n.* tournevis, *m.*

screw nail ['skruːneil], *n.* vis à bois, *f.*

screw nut ['skruːnʌt], *n.* écrou, *m.*

screw-wrench ['skruːrentʃ], *n.* clef anglaise, *f.*

scribble [skribl], *n.* griffonnage; barbouillage, *m.*—*v.t.*, *v.i.* griffonner.

scribbler ['skriblə], *n.* griffonneur; grattepapier, *m.*

scribe [skraib], *n.* scribe; écrivain, *m.*; (*Carp.*) tracer.

scrimmage ['skrimidʒ], *n.* lutte, rixe; (*Ftb.*) mêlée, *f.*

scrip [skrip], *n.* petit sac; (*Comm.*) titre ou certificat provisoire, *m.*

script [skript], *n.* manuscrit; (*Cine.*) scénario, *m.*

scriptural ['skriptʃuərəl], *a.* de l'Écriture Sainte, biblique, scriptural.

Scripture ['skriptʃə], *n.* l'Écriture Sainte, *f.*

script-writer ['skriptraitə], *n.* (*Cine.*) scénariste, *m.*, *f.*

scrofula ['skrɔfjulə], *n.* scrofule, *f.*

scrofulous ['skrɔfjuləs], *a.* scrofuleux.

scroll [skroul], *n.* rouleau, *m.*

scrounge [skraundʒ], *v.t.*, *v.i.* (*slang*) chiper, chaparder, grapiller; *to scrounge on someone*, vivre aux crochets de quelqu'un.

scrounger ['skraundʒə], *n.* chapardeur, *m.*

scrub [skrʌb], *v.t.*, *v.i.* frotter fort; laver, récurer.—*n.* broussailles, *f.pl.*; maquis, *m.*

scrubbing ['skrʌbiŋ], *n.* frottage, récurage, *m.*

scrubbing brush ['skrʌbiŋbrʌʃ], *n.* brosse de cuisine, *f.*

scrubby ['skrʌbi], *a.* rabougri, chétif, mal rasé.

scruff [skrʌf], *n.* nuque, *f.*

scruple [skruːpl], *n.* scrupule, *m.*—*v.i.* se faire scrupule (*de*), hésiter (*à*).

scrupulous ['skruːpjuləs], *a.* scrupuleux.

scrupulously ['skruːpjuləsli], *adv.* scrupuleusement.

scrupulousness ['skruːpjuləsnis], *n.* scrupule, doute, *m.*

scrutator [skruː'teitə], *n.* scrutateur, *m.*

scrutineer [skruːti'niə], *n.* pointeur (*de votes*); scrutateur, *m.*

scrutinize ['skruːtinaiz], *v.t.* scruter, examiner à fond.

scrutinizing ['skruːtinaiziŋ], *a.* scrutateur, inquisiteur.

scrutiny ['skruːtini], *n.* enquête rigoureuse, vérification, *f.*

scud [skʌd], *n.* léger nuage, *m.*; course rapide, *f.*—*v.i.* s'enfuir; courir (*nuages*).

scuffle [skʌfl], *n.* bagarre, rixe, mêlée, *f.*—*v.i.* se battre; traîner les pieds.

scull [skʌl], *n.* rame; godille, *f.*—*v.t.* ramer.

scullery ['skʌləri], *n.* arrière-cuisine, laverie, *f.*; *scullery maid*, laveuse de vaisselle, *f.*

sculptor ['skʌlptə], *n.* sculpteur, *m.*

sculpture ['skʌlptʃə], *n.* sculpture, *f.*—*v.t.* sculpter.

scum [skʌm], *n.* écume, *f.*; (*fig.*) rebut (*ordures*), *m.*; lie, *f.*—*v.t.* écumer.

scupper ['skʌpə], *n.* (*Naut.*) dalot, *m.*—*v.t.* saborder.

scurf [skəːf], *n.* pellicules (*des cheveux*), *f.pl.*

scurfy ['skəːfi], *a.* pelliculeux (*cheveux*).

scurrility [skʌ'riliti], **scurrilousness** ['skʌriləsnis], *n.* grossièreté, *f.*

scurrilous ['skʌriləs], *a.* grossier, ordurier.

scurry ['skʌri], *n.* débandade, *f.*; tourbillon (*de poussière, de neige etc.*), *m.*—*v.i.* se hâter.

scurvily ['skəːvili], *adv.* bassement, vilement.

scurviness ['skəːvinis], *n.* état scorbutique, *m.*; (*fig.*) bassesse; mesquinerie (*avarice*), *f.*

scurvy ['skəːvi], *a.* scorbutique; (*fig.*) vil, vilain.—*n.* scorbut, *m.*

scut [skʌt], *n.* couette de (*lièvre etc.*), *f.*

scutcheon ['skʌtʃən], *n.* [ESCUTCHEON].

scuttle (1) [skʌtl], *n.* panier; seau à charbon, *m.*

scuttle (2) [skʌtl], *n.* (*Naut.*) hublot, *m.*; écoutille, *f.*—*v.t.* saborder.

scuttle (3) [skʌtl], *v.i.* aller à pas précipités.

scuttling ['skʌtliŋ], *a.* en fuite, qui détale.—*n.* sabordage, *m.*

scythe [saið], *n.* faux, *f.*—*v.t.* faucher.

sea [siː], *a.* de mer, marin, maritime.—*n.* mer; lame; (*fig.*) multitude, *f.*, déluge, *m.*; *at sea*, en mer; *heavy sea*, mer houleuse; *in the open sea*, en pleine mer, au grand large.

seaboard ['siːbɔːd], *n.* littoral, rivage, *m.*, côte, *f.*

sea-borne ['siːbɔːn], *a.* transporté par mer.

sea calf ['siːkɑːf], *n.* veau marin, *m.*

sea cow ['siːkau], *n.* lamantin, *m.*

sea dog ['siːdɔg], *n.* loup de mer (*marin*), *m.*

seafarer ['siːfɛərə], *n.* homme de mer, marin, *m.*

seafaring ['siːfɛəriŋ], *a.* marin; *seafaring man*, marin, *m.*

sea-front ['siːfrʌnt], *n.* esplanade, *f.*, bord de mer, *m.*

sea-gauge ['si:geidʒ], *n.* tirant d'eau, *m.*
sea-going ['si:gouiŋ], *a.* de haute mer.
sea gull ['si:gʌl], *n.* mouette, *f.*, goéland, *m.*
sea horse ['si:hɔːs], *n.* morse, *m.*
sea kale ['si:keil], *n.* chou marin, *m.*
seal (1) [si:l], *n.* cachet; sceau (*officiel*), *m.*; (*Law*) scellés, *m.pl.*; **Privy Seal,** petit sceau.—*v.t.* cacheter; (*Law*) sceller; (*Customs*) plomber.
seal (2) [si:l], *n.* phoque, *m.*
sea legs ['si:legz], *n.pl.* pied marin, *m.*
sea level ['si:levəl], *n.* niveau de la mer, *m.*
sealing ['si:liŋ], *n.* action de sceller, *f.*
sealing wax ['si:liŋwæks], *n.* cire à cacheter, *f.*
sea lion ['si:laiən], *n.* lion de mer, *m.*, otarie, *f.*
seam [si:m], *n.* (*Dress.*) couture; (*Mining*) couche; (*Geol.*) veine, *f.*—*v.t.* coudre; couturer.
seaman ['si:mən], *n.* (*pl.* **-men** [men]) marin, matelot, homme de mer, *m.*
seamanship ['si:mənʃip], *n.* matelotage, *m.*
seamless ['si:mlis], *a.* sans couture.
seamstress ['si:mstris], [SEMPSTRESS].
seamy ['si:mi], *a.* plein de coutures; **the seamy side of life,** les dessous de la vie, *m.pl.*
sea nymph ['si:nimf], *n.* néréide, *f.*
seaplane ['si:plein], *n.* hydravion, *m.*
seaport ['si:pɔːt], *n.* port de mer, *m.*
sear [siə], *a.* séché, fané, flétri.—*v.t.* brûler; cautériser; faner.
search [səːtʃ], *n.* recherche; (*Law*) perquisition; (*Customs*) visite, *f.*—*v.t.* chercher, examiner; fouiller; (*Law*) faire une perquisition chez; (*Customs*) visiter.—*v.i.* chercher; fouiller.
searcher ['səːtʃə], *n.* chercheur, *m.*
searching ['səːtʃiŋ], *a.* scrutateur, pénétrant; vif, perçant (*vent*).
searchingly ['səːtʃiŋli], *adv.* minutieusement.
searchlight ['səːtʃlait], *n.* projecteur, *m.*
search party ['səːtʃpaːti], *n.* expédition de secours, *f.*
search warrant ['səːtʃwɔrənt], *n.* mandat de perquisition, *m.*
sea route ['si:ruːt], *n.* voie de mer, *f.*
seascape ['si:skeip], *n.* (*Paint.*) marine, *f.*
Sea Scout ['si:skaut], *n.* (boy-)scout marin, *m.*
sea-shell ['si:ʃel], *n.* coquillage, *m.*
seashore ['si:ʃɔː], *n.* bord de la mer, rivage, *m.*, côte, *f.*
sea-sick ['si:sik], *a.* qui a le mal de mer.
sea-sickness ['si:siknis], *n.* mal de mer, *m.*
seaside ['si:said], *n.* bord de la mer, *m.*
season [si:zn], *n.* saison, *f.*; (*fig.*) temps, moment opportun, *m.*—*v.t.* assaisonner (*de*); sécher (*bois*); (*fig.*) accoutumer (*à*).—*v.i.* s'acclimater; se sécher (*bois*).
seasonable ['si:znəbl], *a.* de saison; (*fig.*) à propos, opportun, convenable.
seasonably ['si:znəbli], *adv.* à propos.
seasonal ['si:znəl], *a.* des saisons; saisonnier.
seasoned ['si:znd], *a.* assaisonné (*viande*); (*fig.*) endurci, aguerri, acclimaté.
seasoning ['si:zniŋ], *n.* assaisonnement; séchage (*du bois*), *m.*
season ticket ['si:zn'tikit], *n.* carte d'abonnement, *f.*
seat [si:t], *n.* siège; banc, *m.*; banquette (*dans un véhicule*); (*fig.*) place; demeure (*château*), *f.*; théâtre (*de guerre*); fond (*de pantalon*), *m.*;

take your seats, please! en voiture!—*v.t.* asseoir; faire asseoir; placer.
seated ['si:tid], *a.* assis, placé.
sea wall ['si:wɔːl], *n.* digue, chaussée, *f.*
seaward ['si:wəd], *a.* tourné vers la mer.—*adv.* vers la mer.
seaweed ['si:wiːd], *n.* algue, *f.*, goémon, varech, *m.*
seaworthiness ['si:wəːðinis], *n.* navigabilité (*navire*), *f.*
seaworthy ['si:wəːði], *a.* en bon état (de navigation).
secant ['si:kənt], *a.* sécant.—*n.* sécante, *f.*
secede [si'si:d], *v.i.* se séparer (*de*).
seceder [si'si:də], *n.* scissionnaire, *m.*, *f.*; dissident, *m.*
secession [si'seʃən], *n.* sécession, séparation, *f.*
seclude [si'klu:d], *v.t.* séparer; éloigner.
secluded [si'klu:did], *a.* retiré, isolé, solitaire.
seclusion [si'klu:ʒən], *n.* retraite, solitude, *f.*
second ['sekənd], *a.* second, deuxième; deux (*du mois*); inférieur; **on second thoughts,** à la réflexion.—*n.* témoin, second (*dans un duel*), *m.*; seconde (*temps*), *f.*—*v.t.* seconder, aider; appuyer (*une motion*); [si'kɔnd] détacher (*fonctionnaire*).
secondary ['sekəndri], *a.* secondaire; accessoire.
seconder ['sekəndə], *n.* personne qui appuie, *f.*
second-hand ['sekənd'hænd], *a.* and *adv.* d'occasion.
secondly ['sekəndli], *adv.* secondement; en second lieu.
second-rate ['sekənd'reit], *a.* de second ordre.
secrecy ['si:krəsi], *n.* secret, *m.*; discrétion, *f.*
secret ['si:krit], *a.* secret; retiré (*maison etc.*). —*n.* secret, *m.*
secretarial [sekrə'teəriəl], *a.* de secrétaire.
secretariat [sekrə'teəriæt], *n.* secrétariat, *m.*
secretary ['sekrətri], *n.* secrétaire, *m.*, *f.*
secretaryship ['sekrətriʃip], *n.* secrétariat, *m.*
secrete [si'kri:t], *v.t.* cacher; (*Physiol.*) sécréter.
secretion [si'kri:ʃən], *n.* sécrétion, *f.*
secretive ['si:krətiv], *a.* réservé; dissimulé.
secretiveness ['si:krətivnis], *n.* caractère cachottier, *m.*
secretly ['si:krətli], *adv.* en secret; intérieurement.
sect [sekt], *n.* secte, *f.*
sectarian [sek'teəriən], *a.* de sectaire.—*n.* sectaire, *m.*, *f.*
sectarianism [sek'teəriənizm], *n.* esprit de secte, sectarisme, *m.*
section ['sekʃən], *n.* section; coupe, *f.*, profil; (*Mil.*) groupe de combat, *m.*
sectional ['sekʃənəl], *a.* en coupe; en sections.
sector ['sektə], *n.* secteur, *m.*
secular ['sekjulə], *a.* temporel; laïque; séculaire (*année*).
secularity [sekju'læriti], **secularness** ['sekjulənis], *n.* sécularité, mondanité, *f.*
secularization [sekjulərai'zeiʃən], *n.* sécularisation, *f.*
secularize ['sekjuləraiz], *v.t.* séculariser.
secure [si'kjuə], *a.* dans la sécurité, en sûreté; sûr, assuré (*chose*); bien fermé.—*v.t.* mettre en sûreté; assurer (*garantir*); s'assurer de; fermer; barrer (*attacher fortement*); (*fig.*) affermir.
securely [si'kjuəli], *adv.* en sûreté; sûrement; fortement.

secureness [si'kjuənis], *n.* sécurité, *f.*

security [si'kjuəriti], *n.* sécurité, sûreté; garantie, *f.*; (*pl.*) titres, *m.pl.*, valeurs, *f.pl.*; (*Law*) caution, *f.*

sedan [si'dæn] (*Motor.*), see **saloon**.

sedate [si'deit], *a.* posé, calme, rassis.

sedately [si'deitli], *adv.* posément, avec calme.

sedateness [si'deitnis], *n.* calme, *m.*

sedative ['sedətiv], *a.* and *n.* sédatif, *m.*

sedentary ['sedntri], *a.* sédentaire; inactif.

sedge [sedʒ], *n.* laîche, *f.*, jonc, *m.*

sediment ['sedimənt], *n.* sédiment, dépôt, *m.*

sedition [si'diʃən], *n.* sédition, *f.*

seditious [si'diʃəs], *a.* séditieux.

seditiousness [si'diʃəsnis], *n.* esprit séditieux, *m.*

seduce [si'djuːs], *v.t.* séduire.

seducer [si'djuːsə], *n.* séducteur, *m.*

seducing [si'djuːsiŋ], *a.* séduisant.

seduction [si'dakʃən], *n.* séduction, *f.*

seductive [si'daktiv], *a.* séducteur, séduisant.

sedulity [si'djuːliti], **sedulousness** ['sedjuləsnis], *n.* assiduité, diligence, *f.*

sedulous ['sedjuləs], *a.* assidu, diligent, zélé.

sedulously ['sedjuləsli], *adv.* assidûment, diligemment, avec application.

sedulousness [SEDULITY].

see (1) [siː], *n.* siège épiscopal, évêché; archevêché (*d'un archevêque*), *m.*; *the Holy See*, le Saint-Siège, *m.*

see (2) [siː], *v.t. irr.* voir; comprendre; accompagner, conduire.—*v.i.* voir; s'occuper (*de*); *I will see to it*, j'y veillerai.

seed [siːd], *n.* semence; graine (*de légumes*), (*fig.*) race, *f.*; *to run to seed*, monter en graine.—*v.t.* ensemencer; (*Spt.*) trier.—*v.i.* grener.

seed bed ['siːdbed], *n.* semis, *m.*

seed cake ['siːdkeik], *n.* gâteau à l'anis, *m.*

seedling ['siːdliŋ], *n.* semis, sauvageon, *m.*

seedsman ['siːdzmən], *n.* (*pl.* -men [men]) grainetier, *m.*

seed-time ['siːdtaim], *n.* semailles, *f.pl.*

seedy ['siːdi], *a.* râpé, usé (*vêtement*); souffrant; miteux.

seeing ['siːiŋ], *n.* vue; vision, *f.*—*conj. phr. seeing that*, vu que, puisque.

seek [siːk], *v.t. irr.* chercher; poursuivre, en vouloir à (*la vie etc.*).—*v.i.* chercher.

seeker ['siːkə], *n.* chercheur, *m.*

seeking [si'kiŋ], *n.* recherche, poursuite, *f.*

seem [siːm], *v.i.* sembler, paraître, avoir l'air (*de*).

seeming ['siːmiŋ], *a.* apparent, spécieux.—*n.* semblant, *m.*, apparence, *f.*, dehors, *m.*

seemingly ['siːmiŋli], *adv.* en apparence, apparemment.

seemliness ['siːmlinis], *n.* bienséance; convenance, *f.*

seemly ['siːmli], *a.* bienséant, convenable; joli.—*adv.* convenablement.

seep [siːp], *v.i.* s'infiltrer, suinter.

seer [siːə], *n.* prophète, voyant, *m.*

seesaw ['siːsɔː], *n.* bascule, balançoire, *f.*, va-et-vient, *m.*—*v.i.* faire la bascule.

seethe [siːð], *v.t.* faire bouillir.—*v.i.* bouillir, bouillonner.

segment ['segmənt], *n.* segment, *m.*

segregate ['segrigeit], *v.t.* séparer.—*v.i.* se diviser.

segregation [segri'geiʃən], *n.* séparation, ségrégation, *f.*

seize [siːz], *v.t.* saisir; se saisir de, s'emparer de; (*Naut.*) amarrer.—*v.i.* (*Mech.*) gripper, caler; se coincer.

seizure ['siːʒə], *n.* saisie, prise de possession; (*Path.*) attaque, *f.*

seldom ['seldəm], *adv.* rarement.

select [si'lekt], *a.* choisi; d'élite.—*v.t.* choisir.

selection [si'lekʃən], *n.* choix, *m.*

selectness [si'lektnis], *n.* excellence, *f.*

self [self], *pron.* (*pl.* **selves** [selvz]) même, soi-même; (*reflexively*) se.—*n.* le moi, individu, *m.*, personne, *f.*

self-assertion ['selfə'səːʃən], *n.* caractère impérieux, *m.*, outrecuidance, *f.*

self-assertive ['selfə'səːtiv], *a.* autoritaire, outrecuidant.

self-centered ['self'sentəd], *a.* égocentrique.

self-confidence ['self'kɔnfidəns], *n.* confiance en soi-même, assurance, *f.*

self-confident ['self'kɔnfidənt], *a.* sûr de soi-même.

self-conscious ['self'kɔnʃəs], *a.* embarrassé, intimidé; gêné.

self-consciousness ['self'kɔnʃəsnis], *n.* embarras, *m.*, gêne, *f.*

self-contained ['selfkən'teind], *a.* indépendant; avec entrée particulière (*appartement*).

self-control ['selfkən'troul], *n.* sang-froid, *m.*; maîtrise de soi, *f.*

self-defense ['selfdi'fens], *n.* défense personnelle; légitime défense, *f.*

self-denial ['selfdi'naiəl], *n.* abnégation, *f.*; désintéressement, *m.*

self-denying ['selfdi'naiiŋ], *a.* qui fait abnégation de soi.

self-educated ['self'edjukeitid], *a.* autodidacte.

self-esteem ['selfi'stiːm], *n.* amour-propre, *m.*

self-evident ['self'evidənt], *a.* évident en soi, qui saute aux yeux.

self-governed ['self'gavənd], *a.* indépendant, autonome.

self-government ['self'gavənmənt], *n.* autonomie, *f.*

self-help ['self'help], *n.* efforts personnels, *m.pl.*

self-importance ['selfim'pɔːtəns], *n.* suffisance, vanité, *f.*

self-important ['selfim'pɔːtənt], *a.* plein de soi, suffisant.

self-inflicted ['selfin'fliktid], *a.* volontaire.

selfish ['selfiʃ], *a.* égoïste.

selfishly ['selfiʃli], *adv.* en égoïste, d'une manière égoïste.

selfishness ['selfiʃnis], *n.* égoïsme, *m.*

selfless ['selflis], *a.* désintéressé.

self-made ['self'meid], *a.* qui s'est fait ce qu'il est; *he is a self-made man*, il est fils de ses œuvres.

self-opinioned ['self'pinjənd], **self-opinionated** ['selfə'pinjəneitid], *a.* entêté.

self-possessed ['selfpə'zest], *a.* calme; maître de soi.

self-possession ['selfpə'zeʃən], *n.* sang-froid, aplomb, *m.*

self-praise ['self'preiz], *n.* éloge de soi-même, *m.*

self-preservation ['selfprezə'veiʃən], *n.* conservation de soi-même, *f.*

self-propelled ['selfprə'peld], *a.* autopropulsé.

self-registering ['self'redʒistriŋ], *a.* à registre, enregistreur.

self-reliance ['selfri'laiəns], *n.* confiance en soi, indépendance, *f.*

self-respect ['selfris'pekt], *n.* respect de soi-même, amour-propre, *m.*; dignité, *f.*

self-righteous ['self'raitʃəs], *a.* pharisaïque.

self-sacrifice ['self'sækrifais], *n.* sacrifice de soi-même, *m.*, abnégation, *f.*

self-same ['selfseim], *a.* absolument le même.

self-satisfied ['self'sætisfaid], *a.* content de soi.

self-seeking ['self'si:kiŋ], *a.* égoïste.

self-service ['self'sə:vis], *n.* libre service, self-service, *m.*

self-starter ['self'sta:tə], *n.* démarreur automatique, *m.*

self-styled ['self'staild], *a.* soi-disant, prétendu.

self-sufficiency ['selfsə'fiʃənsi], *n.* suffisance; indépendance, *f.*

self-sufficient ['selfsə'fiʃənt], *a.* suffisant; indépendant.

self-supporting ['selfsə'pɔ:tiŋ], *a.* qui subsiste par ses propres moyens.

self-taught ['self'tɔ:t], *a.* autodidacte.

self-will ['self'wil], *n.* obstination, opiniâtreté, *f.*

self-willed ['self'wild], *a.* obstiné, opiniâtre.

sell [sel], *v.t. irr.* vendre.—*v.i.* se vendre; *to be sold out of an article,* avoir tout vendu, ne plus avoir d'un article.—*n.* attrape, *f.*

seller ['selə], *n.* vendeur, *m.*, vendeuse, *f.*

selling ['seliŋ], *n.* vente, *f.*; *selling off,* liquidation, *f.*

seltzer ['seltsə], **seltzer water** ['seltsə'wɔ:tə], *n.* eau de Seltz, *f.*

selvedge ['selvidʒ], *n.* lisière, *f.*

selves [SELF].

semaphore ['seməfɔ:], *n.* sémaphore, *m.*

semblance ['sembləns], *n.* semblant, *m.*, apparence, *f.*

semi ['semi], *pref.* semi, demi, à demi, à moitié.

semibreve ['semibri:v], *n. (Mus.)* ronde, *f.*

semi-circle ['semisə:kl], *n.* demi-cercle, *m.*

semicolon ['semi'koulən], *n.* point-virgule, *m.*

semi-detached ['semidi'tætʃt], *a. semi-detached houses,* maisons jumelles, *f.pl.*

semi-final ['semifainl], *n.* demi-finale, *f.*

seminary ['seminəri], *n.* séminaire, *m.*; institution *(école), f.*

semi-official ['semiə'fiʃl], *a.* demi-officiel, officieux.

semiquaver ['semikweivə], *n. (Mus.)* double croche, *f.*

semitone ['semitoun], *n. (Mus.)* demi-ton, semi-ton, *m.*

semolina [semə'li:nə], *n.* semoule, *f.*

sempstress ['sempstris, 'semstris], *n.* couturière, *f.*

senate ['senit], *n.* sénat, *m.*

senator ['senitə], *n.* sénateur, *m.*

senatorial [seni'tɔ:riəl], *a.* sénatorial.

send [send], *v.t. irr.* envoyer, faire parvenir; expédier *(marchandises); to send away,* renvoyer, congédier; *to send back,* renvoyer; *to send for,* envoyer chercher, faire venir; *to send forth,* lancer, émettre; *to*

send in, faire entrer; *to send on,* faire suivre *(lettres etc.).*—*v.i.* envoyer.

sender ['sendə], *n.* envoyeur; *(Comm.)* expéditeur, *m.*

Senegal [senigɔ:l]. le Sénégal, *m.*

Senegalese [senigə'li:z], *a.* sénégalais.—*n.* Sénégalais *(personne), m.*

senile ['si:nail], *a.* de vieillard, sénile.

senility [sə'niliti], *n.* sénilité, *f.*

senior ['si:njə], *a.* aîné; ancien; plus ancien, supérieur.—*n.* aîné; ancien; doyen, *m.*

seniority [si:ni'ɔriti], *n.* priorité d'âge; ancienneté, *f.*

senna ['senə], *n.* séné, *m.*

sensation [sen'seiʃən], *n.* sensation, *f.*

sensational [sen'seiʃənl], *a.* à sensation, à effet.

sensationalism [sen'seiʃənlizm], *n.* recherche du sensationnel, *f.*

sense [sens], *n.* sens; bon sens, sens commun; sentiment, *m.*; signification, *f.*

senseless ['senslis], *a.* sans connaissance, insensible; insensé, absurde *(pas raisonnable).*

senselessly ['senslisli], *adv.* d'une manière insensée; sottement.

senselessness ['senslisnis], *n.* sottise, absurdité, *f.*

sensibility [sensi'biliti], *n.* sensibilité, *f.*; sentiment, *m.*

sensible ['sensibl], *a.* sensé, raisonnable *(intelligent);* sensible *(de);* en pleine connaissance.

sensibly ['sensibli], *adv.* sensiblement; sensément, sagement *(avec intelligence).*

sensitive ['sensitiv], *a.* sensible *(à);* sensitif, impressionnable; susceptible *(ombrageux).*

sensitiveness ['sensitivnis], **sensitivity** [sensi'tiviti], *n.* sensibilité; susceptibilité *(facilité à se vexer etc.), f.*

sensitized ['sensitaizd], *a. (Phot.)* sensible *(papier).*

sensory ['sensəri], *a.* sensoriel, des sens.

sensual ['sensjuəl], *a.* sensuel; des sens.

sensualist ['sensjuəlist], *n.* sensualiste, *m., f.,* sensuel, *m.*

sensuality [sensju'æliti], *n.* sensualité, *f.*

sentence ['sentəns], *n.* phrase; maxime, *f.*; jugement, arrêt, *m.*, sentence, *f.*—*v.t.* prononcer une sentence *ou* un jugement *(contre),* condamner.

sententious [sen'tenʃəs], *a.* sentencieux.

sententiousness [sen'tenʃəsnis], *n.* caractère sentencieux, *m.*

sentient ['senʃənt], *a.* sensible.

sentiment ['sentimənt], *n.* sentiment; avis, *m.*, pensée, *f.*

sentimental [senti'mentl], *a.* sentimental.

sentimentality [sentimen'tæliti], *n.* sensiblerie, sentimentalité, *f.*

sentinel ['sentinl], **sentry** ['sentri], *n.* sentinelle, *f.*, factionnaire, *m.*

sentry box ['sentriboks], *n.* guérite, *f.*

separable ['sepərəbl], *a.* séparable, divisible.

separate ['sepərit], *a.* séparé; disjoint, désuni.—['sepəreit], *v.t.* séparer; disjoindre, désunir.—*v.i.* se séparer; se disjoindre.

separately ['sepəritli], *adv.* séparément, à part.

separation [sepə'reiʃən], *n.* séparation; désunion, *f.*

sepia ['si:pjə], *n.* sépia *(couleur);* seiche *(poisson), f.*

sepoy ['si:pɔi], *n.* cipaye, *m.*
September [sep'tembə]. septembre, *m.*
septennial [sep'teniəl], *a.* septennal.
septennially [sep'teniəli], *adv.* tous les sept ans.
septic ['septik], *a.* septique; infecté (*blessure*).
septuagenarian [septjuədʒə'neəriən], *a.* and *n.* septuagénaire, *m., f.*
Septuagesima [septjuə'dʒesimə]. Septuagésime, *f.*
sepulchral [si'pʌlkrəl], *a.* sépulcral.
sepulchre ['sepəlkə], *n.* sépulcre, *m.*
sepulture ['sepəltʃə], *n.* sépulture; inhumation, *f.*
sequel ['si:kwəl], *n.* suite, conséquence, *f.*
sequence ['si:kwəns], *n.* suite, série; succession; (*Cine.*) séquence, *f.*
sequester [si'kwestə], *v.t.* séquestrer.
sequestered [si'kwestəd], *a.* retiré, écarté; (*Law*) en séquestre.
sequestrate ['si:kwəstreit, si'kwestreit], *v.t.* séquestrer.
sequestration [si:kwəs'treiʃən], *n.* séquestre, *m.*; retraite, *f.*, isolement (*personne*), *m.*
sequestrator ['si:kwəstreitə], *n.* (*Law*) séquestre, *m.*
sequin ['si:kwin], *n.* sequin, *m.*
seraglio [se'rɑ:ljou], *n.* sérail, *m.*
seraph ['serəf], *n.* (*pl.* **seraphim** ['serəfim]) séraphin, *m.*
seraphic [sə'ræfik], *a.* séraphique.
Serbia ['sə:biə]. la Serbie, *f.*
Serbian ['sə:biən], *a.* serbe.—*n.* serbe (*langue*), *m.*; Serbe (*personne*), *m., f.*
sere [SEAR].
serenade [serə'neid], *n.* sérénade, *f.*—*v.t.* donner une sérénade à.
serene [si'ri:n], *a.* serein, calme; sérénissime (*titre*).
serenely [si'ri:nli], *adv.* avec sérénité.
sereneness [si'ri:nnis], **serenity** [si'reniti], *n.* sérénité, *f.*, calme, *m.*
serf [sə:f], *n.* serf, *m.*
serfdom ['sə:fdəm], *n.* servage, *m.*
serge [sə:dʒ], *n.* serge, *f.*
sergeant, serjeant ['sɑ:dʒənt], *n.* sergent (*infanterie*); maréchal des logis (*cavalerie, artillerie*); brigadier (*police*), *m.*
sergeant major ['sɑ:dʒənt'meidʒə], *n.* adjudant, *m.*
serial ['siəriəl], *a.* paraissant par numéros *ou* par livraisons; **serial** (**story**), (roman-) feuilleton, *m.*
serially ['siəriəli], *adv.* par numéros.
seriatim [siəri'eitim], *adv.* par série; successivement.
series ['siəri:z], *n.* série, suite, succession, *f.*
serious ['siəriəs], *a.* sérieux; grave.
seriously ['siəriəsli], *adv.* sérieusement; gravement.
seriousness ['siəriəsnis], *n.* sérieux, *m.*; gravité, *f.*
serjeant [SERGEANT].
sermon ['sə:mən], *n.* sermon, *m.*
sermonize ['sə:mənaiz], *v.t.* prêcher; sermonner.
sermonizer ['sə:mənaizə], *n.* sermonneur, *m.*
serpent ['sə:pənt], *n.* serpent, *m.*
serpentine ['sə:pəntain], *a.* serpentin, sinueux.—*n.* (*Min.*) serpentine, *f.*
serrate ['sereit], *a.* en scie, dentelé; serraté.

serration [se'reiʃən], *n.* dentelure, *f.*
serried ['serid], *a.* compact, serré.
serum ['siərəm], *n.* sérum, *m.*
servant ['sə:vənt], *n.* serviteur, *m.*, servante, *f.*; employé (*de compagnies etc.*), *m.*; domestique, *m.*; ordonnance (*d'officier*), *m., f.*; **civil servant**, fonctionnaire, *m., f.*
serve [sə:v], *v.t.* servir; servir à, être bon à; faire (*apprentissage*); desservir (*localité*); signifier (*une assignation*); **it serves him right**, c'est bien fait.—*v.i.* servir; être au service; suffire.—*n.* (*fam.*) (*Ten.*) service, *m.*
server ['sə:və], *n.* servant; (*Ten.*) serveur; (*Eccles.*) acolyte, *m.*
service ['sə:vis], *n.* service; (*fig.*) avantage, *m.*; utilité, signification (*d'assignation*); (*Mil.*) arme, *f.*—*v.t.* (*Motor.*) entretenir, réparer.
serviceable ['sə:visəbl], *a.* utile (à), avantageux, de bon usage.
serviceableness ['sə:visəblnis], *n.* utilité, *f.*
service station ['sə:vissteiʃən], *n.* station-service, *f.*
serviette [sə:vi'et], *n.* serviette de table, *f.*
servile ['sə:vail], *a.* servile; asservi.
servility [sə:'viliti], *n.* servilité, bassesse, *f.*
serving ['sə:viŋ], *a.* servant, qui sert.
servitude ['sə:vitju:d], *n.* servitude, *f.*, asservissement, *m.*; **penal servitude**, travaux forcés, *m.pl.*
sesame ['sesəmi], *n.* sésame, *m.*
session ['seʃən], *n.* session, séance, *f.*; (*pl.*) assises, *f.pl.*
set [set], *v.t.* *irr.* poser, opposer (*sceau, signature*), mettre, placer, poster; planter (*fleurs*); fixer; ajuster, arranger (*régler*); affûter (*outil*); donner (*exemple*); (*Mus.*) mettre en musique; remettre (*os*); sertir (*pierre précieuse*); dresser, tendre (*piège*); déployer (*voiles*); (*Print.*) composer; **to set aside**, mettre de côté; **to set at ease**, mettre à l'aise; **to set back**, reculer; **to set forth**, énoncer; **to set forward**, avancer; **to set off**, faire ressortir (*faire valoir*); **to set up**, ériger, établir (*fonder*).—*v.i.* se fixer; diriger, porter (*vers ou à*); se coucher (*soleil*); prendre (*confitures etc.*); **to set about**, commencer, se mettre à; **to set out**, partir, se mettre en route; **to set up** (*dans un commerce etc.*), s'établir.—*a.* mis, posé, placé; serti (*pierre précieuse*); prêt, arrêté, fixe; réglé; d'apparat, préparé (*discours*); **all set?** ça y est?—*n.* collection, *f.*, ensemble, assortiment, *m.*, série, *f.*, jeu; service (*de porcelaine etc.*), *m.*; parure (*de pierres précieuses*); mise en plis (*cheveux*), *f.*; (*Theat.*) décor; groupe, *m.*
set-back ['setbæk], *n.* recul, échec, *m.*
set-square ['setskweə], *n.* équerre, *f.*
settee [se'ti:], *n.* canapé, *m.*, causeuse, *f.*
setter ['setə], *n.* chien d'arrêt, *m.*; **bonesetter**, rebouteur, rebouteux, *m.*
setting ['setiŋ], *n.* mise, pose, *f.*; coucher (*du soleil etc.*); décor (*naturel ou de théâtre*), *m.* (*Mus.*) mise en musique, *f.*; remboîtement (*d'os*), *m.*; monture (*de pierre précieuse*), *f.*
settle (1) [setl], *v.t.* fixer; établir; décider, arrêter; assigner (*des biens à*); coloniser (*un pays*); accommoder; payer, régler (*dettes*).—*v.i.* s'établir; se fixer; se marier; se calmer (*devenir tranquille*); se poser (*oiseau*); s'ar-

ranger (avec); **to settle down,** se fixer, s'établir; **to settle down to,** s'appliquer à.
settle (2) [setl], n. banc (à dossier), f.
settled [setld], a. établi; calme, tranquille.
settlement ['setlmənt], **settling** ['setliŋ], n. établissement, arrangement; dépôt (au fond des liquides); accord, contrat, m.; colonisation; colonie, f.; règlement, solde (des comptes); (Build.) tassement, m.
settler ['setlə], n. colon, immigrant, m.
set-up ['setʌp], n. organisation, f.
seven ['sevən], a. and n. sept, m.
sevenfold ['sevənfould], a. septuple.—adv. sept fois.
seventeen [sevən'ti:n], a. and n. dix-sept, m.
seventeenth ['sevənti:nθ], a. dix-septième; dix-sept (des rois etc.).—n. dix-septième (fraction), m.
seventh ['sevənθ], a. septième; sept (des rois etc.).—n. septième (fraction), m.; (Mus.) septième, f.
seventieth ['sevəntiiθ], a. soixante-dixième. —n. soixante-dixième (fraction), m.
seventy ['sevənti], a. and n. soixante-dix, m.
sever ['sevə], v.t. séparer, diviser (de); disjoindre; couper.—v.i. se séparer (de).
several ['sevrəl], a. plusieurs, divers; distinct, respectif.
severally ['sevrəli], adv. séparément, individuellement.
severance ['sevərəns], n. séparation, disjonction; rupture, f.
severe [si'viə], a. sévère; rigoureux, rude (temps etc.); violent, aigu, vif (douleur etc.).
severity [si'veriti], n. sévérité; rigueur, f.
sew [sou], v.t. irr. coudre; brocher (livre).
sewage ['sju:idʒ], n. eaux d'égout, f.pl.
sewer (1) ['souə], n. couseur, m.
sewer (2) ['sju:ə], n. égout, m.
sewerage ['sju:əridʒ], n. système d'égouts, m., égouts, m.pl.
sewing ['souiŋ], n. couture, f.; **sewing machine,** machine à coudre, f.
sex [seks], n. sexe, m.
sexagenarian [seksədʒə'nɛəriən], a. and n. sexagénaire, m., f.
Sexagesima [seksə'dʒesimə]. Sexagésime, f.
sexennial [sek'seniəl], a. sexennal.
sexennially [sek'seniəli], adv. tous les six ans.
sextant ['sekstənt], n. sextant, m.
sextet [seks'tet], n. (Mus.) sextuor, m.
sexton ['sɛkstən], n. sacristain; fossoyeur, m.
sextuple ['sekstjupl], a. and n. sextuple, m.
sexual ['seksjuəl], a. sexuel.
sexuality [seksju'æliti], n. sexualité, f.
shabbily ['ʃæbili], adv. mal, pauvrement (mis ou vêtu); (fig.) mesquinement.
shabbiness ['ʃæbinis], n. état râpé (de vêtements), m.; (fig.) mesquinerie, f.
shabby ['ʃæbi], a. râpé; mal vêtu, mal mis; (fig.) mesquin, ignoble.
shackle [ʃækl], v.t. enchaîner; (fig.) entraver.
shackles [ʃæklz], n.pl. fers, m.pl., chaînes; (fig.) entraves, f.pl.
shad [ʃæd], n. alose (poisson), f.
shade [ʃeid], n. ombre, f.; ombrage (d'arbre etc.); abat-jour (de lampe etc.); garde-vue (pour les yeux), m.; nuance (couleur), f.; (pl.) enfers (où vivent les immortels), m.pl.; **in the shade,** à l'ombre.—v.t. ombrager (de); obscurcir; abriter (protéger); (Paint.) ombrer, nuancer; hachurer (une carte).

shaded ['ʃeidid], a. à l'ombre; ombragé (de); (Paint.) ombré.
shadiness ['ʃeidinis], n. ombrage, m., ombre; (fig.) nature suspecte, f.
shading ['ʃeidiŋ], n. ombres, nuances; hachures, f.pl.
shadow ['ʃædou], n. ombre, f.—v.t. ombrager; filer, espionner (suivre de près).
shadowing ['ʃædouiŋ], n. espionnage, m., filature, f.
shadowy ['ʃædoui], a. ombragé; sombre (morne); vague, chimérique (irréel).
shady ['ʃeidi], a. ombragé, ombreux; sombre (noir); (colloq.) louche (malhonnête).
shaft [ʃɑ:ft], n. flèche, f., dard, trait; brancard (de charette); manche (d'outil, d'arme); puits (de mine); (Mach.) arbre, m.
shag [ʃæg], n. poil rude; caporal (tabac); cormoran huppé (oiseau), m.
shagginess ['ʃæginis], n. état poilu, état hérissé, m.
shaggy ['ʃægi], a. poilu, velu; raboteux (pays).
shagreen [ʃə'gri:n], a. de peau de chagrin.— n. peau de chagrin, f.
shah [ʃɑ:], n. shah, m.
shake [ʃeik], n. secousse, f.; serrement, m.; poignée (de main), f.; hochement (de tête), m.—v.t. irr. secouer, branler, agiter; ébranler, faire trembler; **to shake hands with,** serrer la main à.—v.i. trembler (de); s'agiter, branler; chanceler (sur ses jambes).
shakedown ['ʃeikdaun], n. lit improvisé, m.
shakily ['ʃeikili], adv. en branlant; à pas chancelants.
shaking ['ʃeikiŋ], n. secousse, f., ébranlement, tremblement; ballottement (à cheval), m.
shako ['ʃækou], n. shako, m.
shaky ['ʃeiki], a. branlant; (fig.) peu solide; faible, chancelant (personne).
shale [ʃeil], n. argile schisteuse, f.
shall [ʃæl], v.aux. irr. (used as sign of the future) **I shall go,** j'irai; devoir; vouloir; **shall I go?** dois-je aller? voulez-vous que j'aille? **but he shall,** mais je l'y forcerai; **but I shall not,** mais je n'en ferai rien.
shallop ['ʃæləp], n. chaloupe, péniche, pinasse, f.
shallot [ʃə'lɔt], n. échalote, f.
shallow ['ʃælou], a. peu profond; (fig.) superficiel, léger, borné.
shallowness ['ʃælounis], n. peu de profondeur; esprit borné, m.
sham [ʃæm], a. feint, simulé; faux, factice.— n. feinte, f., prétexte, m.; imposture, frime, f.—v.t. feindre, simuler; faire le, la ou les.—v.i. feindre, faire semblant; jouer la comédie.
shamble [ʃæmbl], v.i. marcher en traînant les pieds.
shambles [ʃæmblz], n.pl. abattoir, m.; (fig.) scène de carnage; une belle pagaille, f.
shambling ['ʃæmbliŋ], a. traînant.
shame [ʃeim], n. honte; ignominie (déshonneur), f.; opprobre, m.; **what a shame!** quel dommage!—v.t. faire honte à.
shamefaced ['ʃeimfeist], a. honteux, confus.
shamefacedly ['ʃeim'feisidli], adv. d'un air penaud.
shamefacedness ['ʃeimfeistnis], n. mauvaise honte; timidité, f.
shameful ['ʃeimful], a. honteux; déshonnête.

shamefulness ['ʃeimfulnis], *n.* honte, ignominie, *f.*

shameless ['ʃeimlis], *a.* éhonté, effronté, impudent.

shamelessly ['ʃeimlisli], *adv.* sans honte, effrontément.

shamelessness ['ʃeimlisnis], *n.* effronterie, impudence, *f.*

shammer ['ʃæmə], *n.* simulateur, *m.*

shampoo [ʃæm'puː], *v.t.* frictionner; nettoyer (*la tête*).—*n.* shampooing, *m.*

shamrock ['ʃæmrɔk], *n.* trèfle (d'Irlande), *m.*

shank [ʃæŋk], *n.* jambe, *f.*

shanty (1) ['ʃænti], *n.* cabane, bicoque, hutte, *f.*

shanty-town ['ʃæntitaun], *n.* bidonville, *m.*

shape [ʃeip], *n.* forme, figure; tournure, taille (*de personne*); façon, coupe (*de vêtement*), *f.*—*v.t.* former, façonner; modeler (*sur*).

shapeless ['ʃeiplis], *a.* informe, sans forme.

shapelessness ['ʃeiplisnis], *n.* absence de forme, difformité, *f.*

shapeliness ['ʃeiplinis], *n.* beauté de forme, *f.*, galbe, *m.*

shapely ['ʃeipli], *a.* bien fait, beau.

share (1) [ʃɛə], *n.* soc (*de charrue*), *m.*

share (2) [ʃɛə], *n.* part, portion; (*St. Exch.*) action, *f.*; **preferred share**, action privilégiée.—*v.t., v.i.* partager; prendre part à; avoir part à.

shareholder ['ʃɛəhouldə], *n.* actionnaire, *m., f.*

sharer ['ʃɛərə], *n.* participant; (*Law*) partageant, *m.*

sharing ['ʃɛəriŋ], *n.* partage, *m.*

shark [ʃɑːk], *n.* requin; (*fig.*) escroc, filou (*personne*), *m.*

sharp [ʃɑːp], *a.* tranchant, affilé, qui coupe bien; pointu, aigu; saillant (*angle*); (*fig.*) vif, intelligent, pénétrant, perçant; anguleux (*traits*); piquant, aigre (*goût etc.*); rusé (*astucieux*); (*Mus.*) dièse; **sharp practice**, filouterie, rouerie, *f.*—*adv.* précise (*l'heure*); **at four o'clock sharp**, à quatre heures précises; **look sharp!** faites vite!—*n.* (*Mus.*) dièse, *m.*

sharpen ['ʃɑːpən], *v.t.* affiler, aiguiser; tailler en pointe, tailler (*crayon etc.*); (*fig.*) rendre vif.

sharper ['ʃɑːpə], *n.* aigrefin, escroc, chevalier d'industrie, *m.*

sharply ['ʃɑːpli], *adv.* rudement, vivement; nettement.

sharpness ['ʃɑːpnis], *n.* tranchant (*d'une lame*), *m.*; pointe (*acuité*); acidité (*de fruit*); violence (*de douleur etc.*); âpreté (*de langage etc.*); netteté (*de contour etc.*), *f.*; esprit éveillé (*d'enfants etc.*), *m.*

sharp-sighted ['ʃɑːp'saitid], *a.* à la vue perçante.

sharp-witted ['ʃɑːp'witid], *a.* à l'esprit délié.

shatter ['ʃætə], *v.t.* fracasser, briser en pièces. —*v.i.* se briser, se fracasser.

shave [ʃeiv], *v.t.* raser; faire la barbe à; effleurer (*friser*); (*Tech.*) planer.—*v.i.* se raser, se faire la barbe; **to have a close shave**, l'échapper belle; **to have a shave**, se raser, se faire raser.

shaving ['ʃeiviŋ], *n.* action de raser, *f.*; copeau (*de bois*), *m.*

shaving brush ['ʃeiviŋbrʌʃ], *n.* blaireau, *m.*

shaving cream ['ʃeiviŋkriːm], *n.* crème à raser, *f.*

shaving soap ['ʃeiviŋsoup], *n.* savon pour la barbe, *m.*

shawl [ʃɔːl], *n.* châle, *m.*

she [ʃiː], *pron.* elle; femelle (*de certains animaux*), *f.*

sheaf [ʃiːf], *n.* (*pl.* **sheaves** [ʃiːvz]) gerbe, *f.*; faisceau (*de flèches*), *m.*—*v.t.* engerber, mettre en gerbe.

shear [ʃiə], *v.t. irr.* tondre.

shearer ['ʃiərə], *n.* tondeur, *m.*; tondeuse (*machine*), *f.*

shearing ['ʃiəriŋ], *n.* tonte, tondaison, *f.*

shears [ʃiəz], *n.pl.* grands ciseaux, *m.pl.*; cisailles (*pour haie, pour métal*), *f.pl.*

she-ass ['ʃiːæs], *n.* ânesse, *f.*

sheath [ʃiːθ], *n.* (*pl.* **sheaths** [ʃiːðz]) gaine, *f.*; fourreau (*à épée*); étui (*à ciseaux etc.*); (*Ent.*) élytre, *m.*

sheathe [ʃiːð], *v.t.* mettre dans le fourreau, rengainer; envelopper; revêtir (*de*).

sheaves [SHEAF].

she-cat ['ʃiːkæt], *n.* chatte, *f.*

shed (1) [ʃed], *n.* hangar; (*Build.*) atelier, *m.*; **cow-shed**, étable (à vaches), *f.*; **lean-to shed**, appentis, *m.*

shed (2) [ʃed], *v.t. irr.* répandre, verser; se dépouiller de, perdre (*feuilles etc.*); jeter (*animal*).

shedding ['ʃediŋ], *n.* effusion (*de sang*); perte (*feuilles etc.*), *f.*

sheen [ʃiːn], *n.* éclat, lustre, brillant, *m.*

sheep [ʃiːp], *n.inv.* mouton; (*pl.*) brebis, *f.*; **black sheep**, brebis galeuse; **lost sheep**, brebis égarée.

sheep dip ['ʃiːpdip], *n.* bain parasiticide, *m.*

sheep dog ['ʃiːpdɔg], *n.* chien de berger, *m.*

sheep-fold ['ʃiːpfould], *n.* bergerie, *f.*, bercail, *m.*

sheepish ['ʃiːpiʃ], *a.* penaud, bête, niais.

sheepishly ['ʃiːpiʃli], *adv.* d'un air penaud.

sheep pen ['ʃiːppen], *n.* parc à moutons, *m.*

sheep-shearing ['ʃiːpʃiəriŋ], *n.* tonte, *f.*

sheepskin ['ʃiːpskin], *n.* peau de mouton, basane (*cuir*), *f.*

sheer (1) [ʃiə], *a.* pur; escarpé, à pic (*rocher*); **sheer force**, pure force, *f.*; **sheer nonsense**, pure sottise, *f.*—*adv.* tout droit; tout à fait.

sheer (2) [ʃiə], *n.* (*Naut.*) tonture; embardée, *f.*—*v.i.* faire des embardées; **to sheer off**, pousser au large, s'esquiver.

sheet [ʃiːt], *n.* drap, *m.*; feuille (*de papier ou métal*); nappe (*d'eau etc.*); (*Naut.*) écoute (*corde*), *f.*; **winding sheet**, linceul, *m.*

sheet anchor ['ʃiːtæŋkə], *n.* ancre de miséricorde; (*fig.*) ancre de salut, *f.*

sheet iron ['ʃiːtaiən], *n.* tôle, *f.*

sheet lightning ['ʃiːt'laitniŋ], *n.* éclair en nappe, *m.*

sheikh [ʃeik], *n.* cheik, *m.*

shelf [ʃelf], *n.* (*pl.* **shelves** [ʃelvz]) planche, *f.*; rayon (*de bibliothèque*), *m.*; tablette, *f.*; écueil (*dans la mer*), *m.*; **set of shelves**, étagères, *f.pl.*

shell [ʃel], *n.* coque (*d'œuf, fruits etc.*); coquille (*œuf vide*); cosse (*de petits pois etc.*); écaille (*d'huître, de tortue*); carapace (*de homard*), *f.*; (*Artill.*) obus; (*fig.*) extérieur, *m.* —*v.t.* écaler (*noisette etc.*); écosser (*petits pois etc.*); égrener (*graine*); (*Mil.*) bombarder.

shell-fish ['ʃelfiʃ], *n.* coquillage, mollusque, *m.*, crustacés, *m.pl.*

shelling ['ʃeliŋ], *n.* écossage; égrenage; (*Mil.*) bombardement, *m.*

shell-proof ['ʃelpru:f], *a.* blindé.

shelter ['ʃeltə], *n.* abri, couvert; (*fig.*) asile, *m.*; *to take shelter,* s'abriter.—*v.t.* abriter; protéger.—*v.i.* s'abriter.

sheltered ['ʃeltəd], *a.* abrité.

shelve [ʃelv], *v.t.* mettre sur un rayon; (*fig.*) enterrer.—*v.i.* aller en pente.

shelves [SHELF].

shelving ['ʃelviŋ], *a.* en pente, incliné.

shepherd ['ʃepəd], *n.* berger, pâtre; (*fig.*) pasteur, *m.*—*v.t.* piloter, guider.

shepherdess ['ʃepədes], *n.* bergère, *f.*

sherbet ['ʃə:bət], *n.* sorbet, *m.*

sheriff ['ʃerif], *n.* shérif; (*Am.*) chef de police (*d'un comté*), *m.*

sherry ['ʃeri], *n.* vin de Xérès, *m.*

shield [ʃi:ld], *n.* bouclier; écran protecteur; (*Her.*) écu, écusson, *m.*—*v.t.* défendre de, protéger contre.

shift [ʃift], *n.* changement; expédient, *m.*, ressource, *f.*; détour, faux-fuyant (*artifice*), *m.*; *chemise de femme; équipe, journée (d'ouvriers), f.*—*v.t.* changer; changer de place; (*fig.*) trouver des expédients; *to shift for oneself,* se débrouiller.

shiftiness ['ʃiftinis], *n.* manque de franchise, *m.*

shifting ['ʃiftiŋ], *a.* changeant; *shifting sand,* sable mouvant, *m.*—*n.* changement, déplacement (*de cargaison etc.*), *m.*

shiftless ['ʃiftlis], *a.* sans initiative; sans énergie; paresseux.

shifty ['ʃifti], *a.* plein d'expédients; *he is a shifty customer,* c'est un roublard.

shilling ['ʃiliŋ], *n.* shilling, *m.*

shilly-shally ['ʃili'ʃeli], *n.* irrésolution, *f.*—*v.i.* hésiter, être irrésolu.

shimmer ['ʃimə], *n.* lueur, *f.*—*v.i.* miroiter.

shin [ʃin], *n.* devant de la jambe; jarret (*de bœuf*), *m.*

shin-bone ['ʃinboun], *n.* tibia, *m.*

shindy ['ʃindi], *n.* tapage, *m.*

shine [ʃain], *v.i. irr.* luire; reluire; briller.—*n.* brillant, éclat, lustre, *m.*

shingle (1) [ʃiŋgl], *n.* bardeau (*pour toiture*), *m.*; coiffure à la garçonne, *f.*

shingle (2) [ʃiŋgl], *n.* galets, cailloux (*au bord de la mer*), *m.*

shingles [ʃiŋglz], *n.pl.* (*Med.*) zona, *m.*

shiningly ['ʃiŋgli], *a.* couvert de galets.

shining ['ʃainiŋ], *a.* luisant, brillant.

shiny ['ʃaini], *a.* luisant, reluisant.

ship [ʃip], *n.* navire; vaisseau, bâtiment, *m.*—*v.t.* embarquer; expédier (*marchandises*); armer (*avirons*).—*v.i.* s'embarquer.

shipboard ['ʃipbɔ:d], *n.* bord de navire, *m.*

shipbuilder ['ʃipbildə], *n.* constructeur de navires, *m.*

shipbuilding ['ʃipbildiŋ], *n.* construction navale, *f.*

ship chandler ['ʃip'tʃɑ:ndlə], *n.* fournisseur de navires, *m.*

shipmate ['ʃipmeit], *n.* camarade de bord, *m.*

shipment ['ʃipmənt], *n.* chargement, *m.*

shipowner ['ʃipounə], *n.* armateur, *m.*

shipper ['ʃipə], *n.* expéditeur, *m.*

shipping ['ʃipiŋ], *a.* maritime.—*n.* vaisseaux, navires, *m.pl.*; navigation; marine marchande; mise à bord (*chargement*), *f.*

ship's boat ['ʃips'bout], *n.* chaloupe, *f.*

ship's carpenter ['ʃips'kɑ:pintə], *n.* charpentier du bord, *m.*

shipshape ['ʃipʃeip], *a.* en ordre, bien arrangé.

shipwreck ['ʃiprek], *n.* naufrage, *m.*—*v.t.* faire faire naufrage à; *to be shipwrecked,* faire naufrage.

shipwrecked ['ʃiprekt], *a.* naufragé.

shipwright ['ʃiprait], *n.* constructeur de navires, *m.*

shipyard ['ʃipjɑ:d], *n.* chantier naval, *m.*

shire ['ʃaiə], *n.* comté, *m.*

shirk [ʃə:k], *v.t.* éviter, éluder.—*v.i.* finasser; tirer au flanc.

shirker ['ʃə:kə], *n.* carotteur, flanchard, *m.*

shirt [ʃə:t], *n.* chemise (*d'homme*), *f.*; *shirt collar,* col de chemise, *m.*; *shirt front,* devant de chemise, plastron, *m.*

shiver (1) ['ʃivə], *v.t.* briser en morceaux, fracasser.—*v.i.* se briser en morceaux.—*n.* fragment, morceau, éclat, *m.*

shiver (2) ['ʃivə], *v.i.* grelotter (*de froid*); frissonner (*de peur*).—*n.* frisson, tremblement, *m.*

shivering ['ʃivəriŋ], *a.* frissonnant.—*n.* frissonnement, frisson, *m.*

shoal [ʃoul], *n.* banc (*de poissons*), *m.*; foule, *f.*; bas-fond, haut-fond (*de la mer*), *m.*; *in shoals,* en foule.

shock (1) [ʃɔk], *n.* choc, *m.*; (*Elec.*) secousse, *f.*—*v.t.* choquer, heurter; scandaliser.

shock (2) [ʃɔk], *n.* moyette (*de blé*); tignasse (*de cheveux*), *f.*

shock absorber ['ʃɔkəbsɔ:bə], *n.* (*Motor.*) amortisseur, *m.*

shocking ['ʃɔkiŋ], *a.* choquant, affreux, dégoûtant.

shockingly ['ʃɔkiŋli], *adv.* affreusement.

shod [ʃɔd], *a.* ferré (*cheval*); chaussé (*personne*).

shoddy ['ʃɔdi], *a.* d'effilochage; de pacotille.—*n.* drap de laine d'effilochage, *m.*

shoe [ʃu:], *n.* soulier, *m.*; chaussure, *f.*; fer (*à cheval*); sabot (*en bois*), *m.*—*v.t. irr.* chausser; ferrer (*cheval etc.*).

shoe-black ['ʃu:blæk], *n.* cireur, *m.*

shoe-horn ['ʃu:hɔ:n], *n.* chausse-pied, *m.*

shoeing ['ʃu:iŋ], *n.* ferrage, *m.*

shoeing-smith ['ʃu:iŋsmiθ], *n.* maréchal ferrant, *m.*

shoe-lace ['ʃu:leis], *n.* lacet de chaussure, *m.*

shoemaker ['ʃu:meikə], *n.* cordonnier, *m.*

shoe-making ['ʃu:meikiŋ], *n.* cordonnerie, *f.*

shoe polish ['ʃu:pɔliʃ], *n.* cirage, *m.*

shoot [ʃu:t], *v.t. irr.* tirer, lancer, darder; décharger, tirer un coup (*de fusil etc.*); atteindre (*une cible*); tuer (*faire mourir*); fusiller; descendre (*rapides etc.*); *to shoot a film,* tourner un film; *to shoot oneself,* se tuer.—*v.i.* tirer; chasser (*gibier*); (*fig.*) s'élancer; filer (*étoile etc.*); pousser (*plante etc.*).—*n.* rejeton, *m.*, pousse (*plante*), *f.*; sarment (*de vigne*); dépôt de décombres (*ordures*), *m.*

shooter ['ʃu:tə], *n.* tireur, *m.*

shooting ['ʃu:tiŋ], *a.* lancinant (*douleur*); *shooting star,* étoile filante, *f.*—*n.* tir (*de fusil*), *m.*; chasse au fusil, *f.*; élancement (*de douleur*), *m.*; pousse (*de plante*); décharge (*des ordures*), *f.*; (*Cine.*) tournage (*de film*), *m.*

shooting-brake ['ʃu:tiŋbreik], *n.* (*Motor.*) canadienne, *f.*

shrinkage

shooting gallery ['ʃuːtiŋgæləri], *n.* tir, stand, *m.*
shop [ʃɔp], *n.* boutique (*petit*), *f.*; magasin (*grand*); atelier (*de fabrication*), *m.*—*v.i.* faire des emplettes; **to go shopping,** aller faire les courses.
shop-assistant ['ʃɔpəsistənt], *n.* vendeur, *m.*, vendeuse, commise, *f.*
shopkeeper ['ʃɔpkiːpə], *n.* marchand, *m.*
shoplifter ['ʃɔpliftə], *n.* voleur à l'étalage, *m.*
shoplifting ['ʃɔpliftiŋ], *n.* vol à l'étalage, *m.*
shopper ['ʃɔpə], *n.* acheteur, client, *m.*
shopping center ['ʃɔpiŋsentə], *n.* quartier commerçant, *m.*
shop steward ['ʃɔpstjuəd], *n.* responsable syndical, délégué ouvrier, *m.*
shop-walker ['ʃɔpwɔːkə], *n.* chef de rayon, inspecteur de magasin, *m.*
shop window ['ʃɔp'windou], *n.* devanture, vitrine, *f.*, étalage, *m.*
shopworn ['ʃɔpwɔːn], *a.* défraîchi.
shore [ʃɔː], *n.* rivage, bord, *m.*, plage, côte, *f.* —*v.t.* étayer, étançonner.
short [ʃɔːt], *a.* court; bref; passager (*temps*); petit (*taille*); insuffisant; croquant (*pâte*); brusque (*bourru*); **short circuit,** court-circuit, *m.*; **short story,** conte, *m.*, nouvelle, *f.*; **to cut the matter short,** pour en finir. —*adv.* court, vivement, brusquement; **it falls far short of it,** il s'en faut de beaucoup.
shortbread ['ʃɔːtbred], *n.* (gâteau) sablé, *m.*
short-circuit ['ʃɔːt'səːkit], *v.t.* mettre en court-circuit.
shortcoming ['ʃɔːtkʌmiŋ], *n.* défaut, *m.*, insuffisance, *f.*
shorten [ʃɔːtn], *v.t.* raccourcir; abréger.— *v.i.* (se) raccourcir.
shortening ['ʃɔːtniŋ], *n.* raccourcissement, *m.*
shorthand ['ʃɔːthænd], *n.* sténographie, *f.*
short-handed ['ʃɔːt'hændid], *a.* à court de personnel.
shorthand-typist ['ʃɔːt'hænd'taipist], *n.* sténodactylographe, (*fam.*) sténodactylo, *f.*
short-lived ['ʃɔːt'livd], *a.* qui vit peu de temps, éphémère.
shortly ['ʃɔːtli], *adv.* bientôt, sous peu; brièvement.
shortness ['ʃɔːtnis], *n.* courte durée, *f.*; peu d'étendue, *m.*; petitesse (*de taille*), *f.*
shorts [ʃɔːts], *n.pl.* culotte courte, *f.*, caleçon court, slip; short, *m.*
short-sighted ['ʃɔːt'saitid], *a.* myope; (*fig.*) peu prévoyant.
short-sightedness ['ʃɔːt'saitidnis], *n.* myopie, *f.*; (*fig.*) manque de prévoyance, *m.*
short-tempered ['ʃɔːt'tempəd], *a.* vif, pétulant, brusque.
short-winded ['ʃɔːt'windid], *a.* à l'haleine courte; poussif (*cheval*).
shot (1) [ʃɔt], *past* and *p.p.* [SHOOT].
shot (2) [ʃɔt], *n.* chatoyant; **shot silk,** soie gorge-de-pigeon, *f.*—*n.* coup de fusil, coup; trait (*d'arc*), *m.*; balle (*de fusil*), *f.*, boulet (*de canon*); plomb (*de fusil de chasse*), *m.*; (*Artill.*) charge; portée (*étendue*), *f.*; tireur (*personne*); (*Ftb.*) coup au but, *m.*; (*Med.*) injection; (*Cine.*) prise, *f.*; **at a shot,** d'un seul coup; **like a shot,** comme un trait; **to be a good shot,** être bon tireur; **to fire a shot,** tirer un coup de feu. [see **shy**]
shot-gun ['ʃɔtgʌn], *n.* fusil de chasse, *m.*

should [ʃud], *v.aux.* (*past of* **shall,** *used as sign of the conditional*) **I should speak,** je parlerais; (=**ought to,** *conditional tense of* **devoir**) **you should see it,** vous devriez le voir.
shoulder ['ʃouldə], *n.* épaule; (*Tech.*) languette, *f.*; **round shoulders,** dos rond, *m.*—*v.t.* charger sur les épaules; se charger de; porter (*armes*).
shoulder blade ['ʃouldəbleid], *n.* omoplate, *f.*
shout [ʃaut], *v.t.*, *v.i.* crier, huer, pousser des cris; vociférer.—*n.* cri, *m.*; acclamations, *f.pl.*; éclat (*de rire*), *m.*
shouting ['ʃautiŋ], *n.* acclamation, *f.*, cris, *m.pl.*
shove [ʃʌv], *v.t.* pousser; **to shove away,** repousser, éloigner.—*v.i.* pousser.—*n.* coup, *m.*, poussée, *f.*
shovel ['ʃʌvl], *n.* pelle, *f.*—*v.t.* ramasser avec la pelle, pelleter.
shovelful ['ʃʌvlful], *n.* pelletée, *f.*
show [ʃou], *v.t. irr.* montrer, faire voir, exposer à la vue; manifester, témoigner, démontrer; indiquer; expliquer; **to show in,** faire entrer; **to show off,** faire valoir.— *v.i.* paraître, se montrer; se faire remarquer; **to show off,** poser, se donner des airs.— *n.* apparence, *f.*; étalage, *m.*, parade, *f.*; spectacle, concours, *m.*; exposition, *f.*
show-case ['ʃoukeis], *n.* montre, vitrine, *f.*
shower ['ʃauə], *n.* ondée (*légère*); averse (*grosse*); pluie, grêle (*de coups, pierres etc.*); douche, *f.*—*v.t.* inonder (*de pluie*); (*fig.*) verser.
shower bath ['ʃauəbɑːθ], *n.* douche, *f.*, bain-douche, *m.*
showery ['ʃauəri], *a.* pluvieux.
show-ring ['ʃouriŋ], *n.* arène de vente, *f.*
show room ['ʃouruːm], *n.* salle d'exposition, *f.*
showy ['ʃoui], *a.* voyant, prétentieux, criard.
shrapnel ['ʃræpnəl], *n.* éclats d'obus, *m.pl.*
shred [ʃred], *n.* lambeau, bout, brin, *m.*; **to tear to shreds,** déchirer en lambeaux.— *v.t.* déchiqueter; râper grossièrement.
shrew [ʃruː], *n.* mégère, femme acariâtre, *f.*
shrewd [ʃruːd], *a.* sagace, fin, perspicace.
shrewdly ['ʃruːdli], *adv.* avec sagacité, avec pénétration, finement.
shrewdness ['ʃruːdnis], *n.* sagacité, pénétration, finesse, *f.*
shrewish ['ʃruːiʃ], *a.* acariâtre.
shrewishly ['ʃruːiʃli], *adv.* en mégère.
shrewishness ['ʃruːiʃnis], *n.* humeur acariâtre, *f.*
shriek [ʃriːk], *n.* cri perçant, *m.*—*v.t.* crier.— *v.i.* jeter un cri aigu.
shrieking ['ʃriːkiŋ], *n.* cris stridents, *m.pl.*
shrift [ʃrift], *n.* confession, *f.*; (*fig.*) **short shrift,** très court délai, *m.*
shrill [ʃril], *a.* aigu, perçant; aigre (*voix*).
shrillness ['ʃrilnis], *n.* son aigu, ton aigu, *m.*
shrilly ['ʃrilli], *adv.* d'un ton aigu.
shrimp [ʃrimp], *n.* crevette (*grise*), *f.*
shrine [ʃrain], *n.* châsse, *f.*; tombeau, *m.*, chapelle (*d'un saint*), *f.*
shrink [ʃriŋk], *v.t. irr.* rétrécir, faire rétrécir. —*v.i.* rétrécir, se rétrécir; se retirer; reculer; se tasser (*en vieillissant*).
shrinkage ['ʃriŋkidʒ], *n.* rétrécissement, *m.*, contraction, *f.*

shrinking ['ʃriŋkiŋ], n. rétrécissement, m.; action de reculer, f.

*****shrive** [ʃraiv], v.t. irr. confesser.

shrivel [ʃrivl], v.t. faire ratatiner, faire recroqueviller, rider, racornir.—v.i. se ratatiner, se recroqueviller.

shroud [ʃraud], n. linceul, suaire, m.; (Naut., pl.) haubans, m.pl.—v.t. (fig.) abriter, couvrir.

Shrovetide ['ʃrouvtaid]. les jours gras, m.pl.; Shrove Tuesday, mardi-gras, m.

shrub [ʃrʌb], n. arbuste, arbrisseau, m.

shrubbery ['ʃrʌbəri], n. plantation d'arbrisseaux, f.

shrubby ['ʃrʌbi], a. plein d'arbrisseaux, touffu.

shrug [ʃrʌg], n. haussement d'épaules, m.—v.t. hausser; to shrug one's shoulders, hausser les épaules.

shudder ['ʃʌdə], v.i. frissonner, frémir (de).—n. frissonnement, frémissement, m.

shuffle [ʃʌfl], v.t. mêler; (Cards) battre.—v.i. traîner les pieds; battre les cartes; tergiverser (équivoquer).

shuffling ['ʃʌfliŋ], a. chicaneur, biaiseur; traînant (allure).—n. marche traînante, f.; (Cards) battement des cartes, m.; (fig.) chicane, f.

shun [ʃʌn], v.t. éviter, fuir.

shunt [ʃʌnt], v.t. garer (train); détourner.

shunting ['ʃʌntiŋ], n. changement de voie, garage, m.

shut [ʃʌt], v.t. irr. fermer; enfermer; to shut off, intercepter, couper (vapeur etc.); to shut out, exclure; to shut up, fermer, enfermer; condamner (porte etc.); faire taire.—v.i. fermer, se fermer; shut up! taisez-vous!

shutter ['ʃʌtə], n. volet, contrevent (à l'extérieur de la fenêtre), m.

shuttle [ʃʌtl], n. navette; vanne, f.

shuttle-cock ['ʃʌtlkɔk], n. volant, m.

shuttle service ['ʃʌtlsəvis], n. navette, f.

shy (1) [ʃai], a. réservé, timide, honteux.—v.i. être ombrageux, faire un écart (cheval).

shy (2) [ʃai], v.t. jeter, lancer.—n. coup (de pierre etc.); essai, m.; to have a shy at, s'essayer à (faire quelque chose).

shyly ['ʃaili], adv. timidement, avec réserve.

shyness ['ʃainis], n. timidité, retenue, réserve; fausse honte, f.

Siam [sai'æm]. le Siam, m.

Siamese [saiə'miːz], a. siamois.—n. siamois (langue); Siamois (personne), m.

Siberia [sai'biəriə]. la Sibérie, f.

Siberian [sai'biəriən], a. sibérien.—n. Sibérien (personne), m.

sibilant ['sibilənt], a. sifflant.—n. lettre sifflante, f.

siccative ['sikətiv], a. and n. siccatif, m.

Sicilian [si'siliən], a. sicilien.—n. Sicilien (personne), m.

Sicily ['sisili]. la Sicile, f.

sick [sik], a. malade; qui a des nausées, qui a mal au cœur; sick headache, migraine, f.; sick man or woman, malade, m., f.; sick of, dégoûté de; to be sea-sick, avoir le mal de mer; to be sick, vomir.

sick-bed ['sikbed], n. lit de douleur, m.

sicken [sikn], v.t. rendre malade; (fig.) lasser, dégoûter.—v.i. tomber malade.

sickening ['sikniŋ], a. écœurant; (fig.) dégoûtant.

sickle [sikl], n. faucille, f.

sick leave ['sikliːv], n. congé de convalescence, m.

sickliness ['siklinis], n. mauvaise santé, f.

sick list ['siklist], n. rôle des malades, m.

sickly ['sikli], a. maladif; affadissant, affadi (goût etc.).

sickness ['siknis], n. maladie, f.; nausées, f.pl.

sick-nurse ['siknəːs], n. garde-malade, f.

sick-room ['sikruːm], n. chambre de malade, f.

side [said], a. de côté; latéral; indirect.—n. côté; flanc; bord; versant (de montagne); parti; (Spt.) camp, m.; by his side, à côté de lui; side by side, côte à côte; this side up (caisses), dessus; to take sides, prendre parti; wrong side out, à l'envers.—v.i. to side with, se ranger du côté de.

sideboard ['saidbɔːd], n. buffet, m.

sided ['saidid], a. à côtés, à faces; two-sided, à deux faces.

side door ['saiddɔː], n. porte latérale, f.

side-line ['saidlain], n. occupation secondaire, f.

sidelong ['saidlɔŋ], a. and adv. de côté.

side show ['saidʃou], n. spectacle forain, m.

sidesman ['saidzmən], n. (pl. -men [men]) (Eccles.) marguillier, m.

side-track ['saidtræk], v.t. garer (train); (fig.) semer (quelqu'un).

sidewalk ['saidwɔːk], n. (Am.) trottoir (de rue), m.

sideways ['saidweiz], adv. de côté; obliquement.

siding ['saidiŋ], n. voie d'évitement, voie de garage, f.

sidle [saidl], v.i. marcher de côté; s'insinuer.

siege [siːdʒ], n. siège, m.; to lay siege to, mettre le siège devant, faire le siège de, assiéger.

Sienna [si'enə]. Sienne, f.

sierra [si'eərə], n. sierra, f.

Sierra Leone [si'eərəli'oun]. le Sierra-Leone, m.

siesta [si'estə], n. sieste, f.

sieve [siv], n. tamis (fin); crible (grand), m.

sift [sift], v.t. tamiser; cribler; sasser (farine); (fig.) examiner.

sifting ['siftiŋ], n. tamisage; (fig.) examen minutieux, m.

sigh [sai], n. soupir, m.—v.i. soupirer; to sigh after, soupirer après; to sigh over, gémir sur.

sighing ['saiiŋ], n. soupirs, m.pl.

sight [sait], n. vue, vision, f.; regard, m., yeux, m.pl.; guidon, m., hausse (armes à feu), f.; spectacle, m.; a sight better, beaucoup mieux; at first sight, à première vue; by sight, de vue; in sight, en vue; out of sight, hors de vue; second sight, clairvoyance, f.; to catch sight of, apercevoir; to come in sight, apparaître.—v.t. apercevoir.

sighted ['saitid], a. en vue; qui voit, voyant; long-sighted, presbyte; short-sighted, myope; (fig.) peu clairvoyant.

sightliness ['saitlinis], n. beauté, f.

sight-reading ['saitriːdiŋ], n. (Mus.) déchiffrement, m.

sight-seeing ['saitsi:iŋ], *n.* **to go sight-seeing**, aller voir les curiosités.

sight-seer ['saitsi:ə], *n.* touriste, *m.*, *f.*, visiteur (*d'une ville*), *m.*

sign [sain], *n.* signe; indice, *m.*; enseigne (*panneau*), *f.*—*v.t.*, *v.i.* signer.

signal ['signəl], *a.* signalé, insigne.—*n.* signal; signe; (*Rail.*) sémaphore, *m.*; (*pl.*) (*Mil.*) les transmissions, *f.pl.*—*v.t.* signaler, faire signe à.—*v.i.* signaler; donner un signal.

signal-box ['signəlbɔks], *n.* poste à signaux, *m.*

signalman ['signəlmən], *n.* (*pl.* **-men** [men]) (*Rail.*) signaleur, *m.*

signaller ['signələ], *n.* signaleur, *m.*

signally ['signəli], *adv.* remarquablement.

signatory ['signətəri], *a.* and *n.* signataire, *m.*, *f.*

signature ['signətʃə], *n.* signature, *f.*

sign-board ['sainbɔːd], *n.* enseigne, *f.*

signet ['signit], *n.* sceau; cachet, *m.*

signet ring ['signitriŋ], *n.* chevalière, *f.*

significance [sig'nifikəns], *n.* signification, *f.*, sens, *m.*; importance, *f.*

significant [sig'nifikənt], *a.* significatif.

signification [signifi'keiʃən], *n.* signification, *f.*

signify ['signifai], *v.t.* vouloir dire, signifier; faire connaître; importer.

sign-post ['sainpoust], *n.* poteau indicateur, *m.*

silence ['sailəns], *n.* silence, *m.*; *silence !* (*notice*), défense de parler.—*v.t.* réduire au silence, faire taire.

silent ['sailənt], *a.* silencieux; peu loquace (*qui ne parle pas beaucoup*); muet (*lettre, film*).

silently ['sailəntli], *adv.* silencieusement, en silence; sans bruit.

silent partner ['sailənt'pɑːtnə], *n.* associé commanditaire, *m.*

Silesia [sai'liːʒə, sai'liːsiə]. la Silésie, *f.*

silex ['saileks], *n.* silex, *m.*

silhouette [silu'et], *n.* silhouette, *f.*

silica ['silikə], *n.* silice, *f.*

silicon ['silikən], *n.* silicium, *m.*

silicosis [sili'kousis], *n.* (*Med.*) silicose, *f.*

silk [silk], *a.* de soie, en soie.—*n.* soie, *f.*; (*pl.*) soieries, *f.pl.*

silken ['silkən], *a.* de soie; soyeux.

silkiness ['silkinis], *n.* nature soyeuse, *f.*

silkworm ['silkwəːm], *n.* ver à soie, *m.*

silky ['silki], *a.* de soie, soyeux.

sill [sil], *n.* seuil (*d'une porte*); rebord (*d'une fenêtre*), *m.*

silliness ['silinis], *n.* sottise, niaiserie, *f.*

silly ['sili], *a.* and *n.* sot, nigaud, niais, *m.*; *silly ass*, imbécile, *m.*; *silly thing*, sottise, *f.*; nigaud (*personne*).

silt [silt], *v.t.* envaser.—*v.i.* s'envaser.—*n.* vase, *f.*, limon, *m.*

silting ['siltiŋ], *n.* envasement, *m.*

silver ['silvə], *a.* d'argent; argenté (*couleur*); argentin (*son*).—*n.* argent, *m.*; monnaie d'argent; argenterie (*vaisselle*), *f.*—*v.t.* argenter; étamer (*miroir*).

silvering ['silvəriŋ], *n.* argenture, *f.*; étamage (*de miroirs*), *m.*

silver-plated ['silvə'pleitid], *a.* argenté, en plaqué.

silversmith ['silvəsmiθ], *n.* orfèvre, *m.*

silvery ['silvəri], *a.* d'argent; argenté (*couleur*); argentin (*son*).

similar ['similə], *a.* semblable, pareil; similaire (*de nature*).

similarity [simi'læriti], *n.* ressemblance, similitude; similarité (*de nature*), *f.*

similarly ['similəli], *adv.* pareillement, d'une manière semblable.

simile ['simili], *n.* comparaison, *f.*

similitude [si'militjuːd], *n.* similitude, *f.*

simmer ['simə], *v.i.* bouillir lentement, mijoter.

simmering ['siməriŋ], *n.* mijotement, *m.*

simnel ['simnəl], *n.* gâteau de Pâques *ou* de la mi-carême, *m.*

simper ['simpə], *n.* sourire niais, *m.*—*v.i.* sourire niaisement, minauder.

simpering ['simpəriŋ], *a.* minaudier.—*n.* minauderie, *f.*

simperingly ['simpəriŋli], *adv.* en minaudant.

simple [simpl], *a.* simple; *as simple as ABC*, simple comme bonjour.—*n.* simple, *m.*

simple-hearted ['simpl'hɑːtid], **simple-minded** ['simplmaindid], *a.* simple, ingénu, naïf.

simpleness ['simplnis], *n.* simplicité, *f.*

simpleton ['simpltən], *n.* niais, nigaud, *m.*

simplicity [sim'plisiti], *n.* simplicité, *f.*

simplification [simplifi'keiʃən], *n.* simplification, *f.*

simplify ['simplifai], *v.t.* simplifier.

simply ['simpli], *adv.* simplement (*sans complexité*); tout bonnement (*et rien de plus*).

simulate ['simjuleit], *v.t.* feindre, simuler.

simulation [simju'leiʃən], *n.* simulation, *f.*

simulator ['simjuleitə], *n.* simulateur, *m.*

simultaneous [siməl'teinjəs], *a.* simultané.

simultaneously [siməl'teinjəsli], *adv.* simultanément.

sin [sin], *n.* péché, *m.*; (*fig.*) offense, *f.*—*v.i.* pécher.

since [sins], *conj.* puisque (*parce que*); depuis que (*temps*).—*prep.* depuis; *since then*, depuis lors.—*adv.* depuis; *ever since*, depuis ce temps-là; *long since*, il y a longtemps.

sincere [sin'siə], *a.* sincère.

sincerely [sin'siəli], *adv.* sincèrement; *yours sincerely* (*lettre amicale mais sans intimité*), veuillez croire, cher Monsieur, à mes sentiments les meilleurs.

sincerity [sin'seriti], *n.* sincérité, bonne foi, *f.*

sine [sain], *n.* (*Trig.*) sinus, *m.*

sinecure ['sainəkjuə], *n.* sinécure, *f.*

sinew ['sinjuː], *n.* tendon, (*colloq.*) nerf, *m.*

sinewy ['sinjuːi], *a.* tendineux; (*fig.*) nerveux, vigoureux.

sinful ['sinful], *a.* pécheur, coupable.

sinfully ['sinfuli], *adv.* d'une manière coupable, en pécheur.

sinfulness ['sinfulnis], *n.* culpabilité, iniquité, *f.*

sing [siŋ], *v.t.*, *v.i. irr.* chanter, célébrer (*louer*); siffler (*vent*); *to make someone sing small*, rabattre le caquet à quelqu'un.

Singapore [siŋə'pɔː]. Singapour, *m.*

singe [sindʒ], *v.t.* flamber; roussir (*vêtements etc.*); (*Tech.*) griller.—*n.* légère brûlure, *f.*

singeing ['sindʒiŋ], *n.* flambage, (*Tech.*) grillage, *m.*

singer ['siŋə], *n.* chanteur, *m.*; cantatrice (*professionnelle*), *f.*

singing

singing ['siŋiŋ], *a.* qui chante; chanteur (*oiseau*).—*n.* chant; bourdonnement (*dans les oreilles*), *m.*

single [siŋgl], *a.* seul, simple, unique; particulier (*individuel*); singulier (*combat*); non marié, célibataire; **single bedroom,** chambre à un lit, *f.*; **single man,** célibataire, garçon, *m.*; **single** (*ticket*), billet simple, *m.*; **single woman,** femme non mariée, fille, *f.*—*n.* (*pl.*) (*Ten.*) partie simple, *f.*—*v.t.* choisir; *to* **single out,** choisir, distinguer de la foule.

single-handed ['siŋgl'hændid], *adv.* tout seul, sans aide.

single-hearted ['siŋgl'hɑːtid], *a.* sincère, honnête.

singleness ['siŋglnis], *n.* sincérité, simplicité, *f.*

singlet ['siŋglit], *n.* maillot fin, *m.*

single-track ['siŋgltræk], *a.* (*Rail.*) à voie unique; (*Cine.*) à simple piste.

singly ['siŋgli], *adv.* seulement; séparément; individuellement, un à un.

singsong ['siŋsɔŋ], *n.* chant monotone, *m.*

singular ['siŋgjulə], *a.* singulier; étrange (*bizarre*); simple (*pas complexe*), (*Gram.*)—*n.* singulier, *m.*

singularity [siŋgju'læriti], *n.* singularité, *f.*

singularly ['siŋgjuləli], *adv.* singulièrement.

sinister ['sinistə], *a.* sinistre; (*Her.*) sénestre.

sink [siŋk], *n.* évier (*de cuisine*); égout (*conduit*), *m.*; *a* **sink of iniquity,** un cloaque d'iniquité.—*v.t. irr.* faire tomber au fond, enfoncer; couler (*navire*); creuser (*puits etc.*); placer (*argent*) à fonds perdu; amortir (*dette*).—*v.i.* aller au fond, tomber au fond; s'enfoncer, sombrer, couler (*navire*); décliner; s'affaiblir (*santé etc.*); baisser (*prix etc.*); être abattu (*âme, cœur etc.*); descendre, se coucher (*soleil etc.*); dégénérer (*en*).

sinker ['siŋkə], *n.* plomb (*de ligne de pêche*), *m.*

sinking ['siŋkiŋ], *a.* qui coule (*navire*).—*n.* foncement (*de puits etc.*); tassement (*de fondements*); affaissement (*santé*); placement à fonds perdu (*d'argent*); amortissement (*d'une dette*); engloutissement (*de navire*), *m.*

sinking fund ['siŋkiŋfʌnd], *n.* fonds, *m.,* ou caisse d'amortissement (*d'une dette etc.*), *f.*

sinless ['sinlis], *a.* sans péché, innocent; pur.

sinner ['sinə], *n.* pécheur, *m.,* pécheresse, *f.*

sinuous ['sinjuəs], *a.* sinueux.

sinus ['sainəs], *n.* (*Anat.*) sinus, *m.*

sip [sip], *n.* petit coup, *m.,* petite gorgée, *f.*—*v.t., v.i.* boire à petit coups, siroter.

siphon ['saifən], *n.* siphon, *m.*—*v.t.* siphonner.

sir [səː], *n.* monsieur, *m.*

sire ['saiə], *n.* père; sire (*à un roi*), *m.*; (*pl.*) pères, aïeux, *m.pl.*; **grand-sire,** grand-père, *m.*

siren ['saiərən], *n.* sirène, *f.*

Sirius ['siriəs], (*Astron.*) Sirius, *m.*

sirloin ['səːloin], *n.* aloyau; faux-filet, *m.*

sirocco [si'rokou], *n.* siroco, *m.*

siskin ['siskin], *n.* (*Orn.*) tarin, *m.*

sissy ['sisi], *n.* (*colloq.*) poule mouillée, *f.*

sister ['sistə], *a.* sœur; du même gabarit (*navire*).—*n.* sœur; (*Med.*) infirmière-major, *f.*

sisterhood ['sistəhud], *n.* communauté de sœurs, *f.,* sœurs, *f.pl.*

sister-in-law ['sistərinlɔː], *n.* belle-sœur, *f.*

sisterly ['sistəli], *a.* de sœur, en sœur.

sit [sit], *v.t. irr.* asseoir; se tenir sur (*cheval*).—*v.i.* s'asseoir (*acte*); être assis (*attitude*); siéger, tenir séance, se réunir (*assemblée, cour, juge etc.*); couver (*poule etc.*), percher (*oiseau*); poser (*pour un portrait*); *to* **sit down,** s'asseoir; *to* **sit up,** se tenir droit; veiller (*s'abstenir du sommeil*).

sit-down strike ['sitdaunstraik], *n.* grève sur le tas, *f.*

site [sait], *n.* situation, *f.,* emplacement (*de bâtiment*); site (*paysage*), *m.*—*v.t.* placer.

sitfast ['sitfɑːst], *n.* (*Vet.*) cor, durillon, *m.*

sitter ['sitə], *n.* personne assise, *f.*; (*Paint.*) modèle, *m.*

sitting ['sitiŋ], *a.* assis; en séance (*cour etc.*); perché (*oiseau*); qui couve (*poule*).—*n.* séance; audience (*d'une cour*); couvaison (*des œufs*); place (*réservée*); (*Paint.*) séance, *f.*

sitting room ['sitiŋruːm], *n.* petit salon, *m.*

situate (1) ['sitjueit], *v.t.* situer.

situate (2) ['sitjuit], **situated** ['sitjueitid], *a.* situé; (*Law*) sis.

situation [sitju'eiʃən], *n.* situation, position, *f.,* état, *m.*; place, *f.,* emploi, *m.*

six [siks], *a.* and *n.* six, *m.*

sixteen ['siks'tiːn], *a.* and *n.* seize, *m.*

sixteenth ['siks'tiːnθ], *a.* seizième; seize (*rois etc.*).—*n.* seizième (*fraction*), *m.*

sixth [siksθ], *a.* sixième; six (*rois etc.*).—*n.* sixième (*fraction*), *m.*; (*Mus.*) sixte, *f.*

sixthly ['siksθli], *adv.* sixièmement.

sixtieth ['sikstiiθ], *a.* soixantième.—*n.* soixantième (*fraction*), *m.*

sixty ['siksti], *a.* and *n.* soixante, *m.*; *about* **sixty,** une soixantaine (*de*), *f.*

sizable ['saizəbl], *a.* d'une bonne grosseur.

size (1) [saiz], *n.* grandeur, dimension, taille (*physique*); grosseur, *f.,* volume (*espace occupé*); calibre (*de cartouche*); format (*de livre ou de papier*), *m.*; encolure (*de chemise*); pointure (*de gant, de chaussure etc.*), *f.*; effectif (*d'école, de classe etc.*); (*Comm.*) numéro, *m.*—*v.t.* classer, ranger (*par grosseur, par taille*); *to size up,* juger.

size (2) [saiz], *n.* colle, *f.,* encollage, *m.*—*v.t.* coller, encoller.

sized [saizd], *a.* de grosseur; de taille.

sizzle [sizl], *n.* grésillement, *m.*—*v.i.* grésiller.

skate (1) [skeit], *n.* (*Ichth.*) raie, *f.*

skate (2) [skeit], *n.* patin, *m.*; *roller skate,* patin à roulettes.—*v.i.* patiner.

skater ['skeitə], *n.* patineur, *m.*

skating ['skeitiŋ], *n.* patinage, *m.*

skating rink ['skeitiŋriŋk], *n.* patinoire, *f.*

skein [skein], *n.* écheveau, *m.*

skeleton ['skelətən], *n.* squelette, *m.*; (*Tech.*) charpente, carcasse, *f.*

skeleton key ['skelətən'kiː], *n.* passe-partout, *m.inv.*; crochet, *m.*

sketch [sketʃ], *n.* esquisse, *f.,* croquis, *m.,* ébauche; (*Theat.*) saynète, *f.*; (*fig.*) aperçu, *m.*—*v.t.* esquisser, ébaucher.

sketch-book ['sketʃbuk], *n.* cahier de croquis, *m.*

sketchily ['sketʃili], *adv.* incomplètement.

sketchy ['sketʃi], *a.* d'esquisse, ébauché; rudimentaire.

skew [skjuː], *a.* oblique, en biais.

skewer ['skjuə], *n.* brochette, *f.*—*v.t.* embrocher.

ski [skiː], *n.* ski, *m.*—*v.i.* faire du ski.

skid [skid], *n.* (*Motor.*) dérapage (*de*), *m.*, embardée, *f.*; (*Av.*) patin, *m.*—*v.i.* déraper (*bicyclette* ou *véhicule*).

skier ['ski:ə], *n.* skieur, *m.*

skiff [skif], *n.* esquif, *m.*

ski-ing ['ski:iŋ], *n.* le ski, *m.*

ski-lift ['ski:lift], *n.* remonte-pentes, *m.inv.*

skill [skil], *n.* habileté, dextérité, adresse, *f.*

skilled [skild], *a.* habile, adroit; *skilled labor*, main-d'œuvre spécialisée, *f.*; *skilled workman*, ouvrier qualifié, *m.*

skillful ['skilful], *a.* adroit, habile.

skillfully ['skilfuli], *adv.* adroitement, habilement.

skim [skim], *v.t.* écumer; écrémer (*lait*); (*fig.*) raser, effleurer.

skimp [skimp], *v.t.* lésiner; bâcler (*travail*).

skimpy ['skimpi], *a.* mesquin, chiche; étriqué.

skin [skin], *n.* peau, *f.*; *banana skin*, pelure de banane, *f.*; *to escape by the skin of one's teeth*, l'échapper belle; *wet to the skin*, trempé jusqu'aux os.—*v.t.* écorcher (*personne* ou *animal*); peler, éplucher (*fruits* etc.); (*fig.*) écorcher, plumer.

skin-deep ['skindi:p], *a.* superficiel, peu profond.

skinflint ['skinflint], *n.* pince-maille, grigou, ladre, *m.*

skinless ['skinlis], *a.* sans peau.

skinner ['skinə], *n.* écorcheur; pelletier (*marchand*), *m.*

skinny ['skini], *a.* maigre, décharné.

skip [skip], *n.* saut, bond, *m.*—*v.t.* sauter; passer (*en lisant*).—*v.i.* sauter, sautiller, gambader.

skipper ['skipə], *n.* patron (*de navire marchand*); (*Spt.*) chef d'équipe, *m.*

skipping ['skipiŋ], *n.* action de sauter, *f.*; saut à la corde, *m.*

skipping-rope ['skipiŋroup], *n.* corde à sauter, *f.*

skirmish ['skə:miʃ], *n.* escarmouche, *f.*—*v.i.* escarmoucher.

skirmisher ['skə:miʃə], *n.* tirailleur, *m.*

skirmishing ['skə:miʃiŋ], *n.* escarmouches, *f.pl.*

skirt [skə:t], *n.* pan (*d'un habit*), *m.*; jupe (*de robe*); (*pl.*) lisière, extrémité, *f.*, bord (*de forêt* etc.), *m.*; *outskirts*, bords, faubourgs, *m.pl.*—*v.t.* border; longer (*rivière* etc.).

skirting ['skə:tiŋ], **skirting-board** ['skə:tiŋbo:d], *n.* bord, *m.*, bordure; (*Arch.*) plinthe, *f.*

skit [skit], *n.* parodie, *f.*

skittish ['skitiʃ], *a.* capricieux, volage.

skittishly ['skitiʃli], *adv.* capricieusement.

skittishness ['skitiʃnis], *n.* légèreté, inconstance, *f.*

skittle ['skitl], *n.* quille, *f.*

skittle alley ['skitl'æli], *n.* jeu de quilles, *m.*

skulk [skʌlk], *v.i.* se cacher; rôder (*autour de*).

skull [skʌl], *n.* crâne, *m.*

skull-cap ['skʌlkæp], *n.* calotte, *f.*

skunk [skʌŋk], *n.* putois d'Amérique, *m.*

sky [skai], *n.* ciel, *m.*

sky-blue ['skaiblu:], *a.* bleu ciel, azuré.

sky-high ['skai'hai], *a.* qui touche aux cieux; *to blow up sky-high*, faire sauter jusqu'aux cieux; (*fig.*) tancer vertement.

skylark ['skailɑ:k], *n.* alouette (*des champs*), *f.*—*v.i.* (*fig.*) faire des farces.

skylarking ['skailɑ:kiŋ], *n.* farces, *f.pl.*

skylight ['skailait], *n.* châssis vitré, *m.*, lucarne faitière, *f.*

sky-line ['skailain], *n.* horizon, *m.*

sky-scraper ['skaiskreipə], *n.* gratte-ciel, *m.*

slab [slæb], *n.* dalle, plaque, table; tablette (*de chocolat*); dosse, *f.*

slack [slæk], *a.* lâche; faible, mou; détendu (*corde*); négligent; *business is slack*, les affaires ne vont pas; *the slack season*, la morte-saison, *f.*—*n.* menu charbon; mou (*de corde*); (*Eng.*) jeu; (*pl.*) pantalon, *m.*

slacken ['slækən], *v.t.* relâcher, détendre; affaiblir (*la rigueur*); ralentir (*vitesse*).—*v.i.* se relâcher, se détendre; se ralentir; diminuer; tomber.

slackening ['slækniŋ], *n.* relâchement, *m.*

slacker ['slækə], *n.* paresseux, *m.*

slacking ['slækiŋ], *n.* paresse, *f.*

slackly ['slækli], *adv.* mollement, lâchement; négligemment.

slackness ['slæknis], *n.* relâchement, *m.*; négligence, nonchalance (*morale*), *f.*

slag [slæg], *n.* scorie, *f.*; mâchefer, *m.*

slag-heap ['slæghi:p], *n.* crassier, *m.*

slake [sleik], *v.t.* éteindre (*chaux*); *to slake one's thirst*, se désaltérer.

slam [slæm], *v.t.* fermer avec violence, claquer.—*v.i.* se fermer avec bruit.—*n.* (*Cards*) vole, *f.*, chelem, *m.*

slander ['slɑ:ndə], *n.* calomnie; (*Law*) diffamation, *f.*—*v.t.* calomnier; (*Law*) diffamer.

slanderer ['slɑ:ndərə], *n.* calomniateur; (*Law*) diffamateur, *m.*

slanderous ['slɑ:ndərəs], *a.* calomnieux; (*Law*) diffamatoire.

slang [slæŋ], *n.* argot, *m.*, langue verte, *f.*

slangy ['slæŋi], *a.* d'argot, argotique.

slant [slɑ:nt], *v.t.* incliner.—*v.i.* incliner; être de biais, biaiser.—*n.* inclinaison, pente, *f.*; *on the slant*, en écharpe, en biais.

slanting ['slɑ:ntiŋ], *a.* oblique, en écharpe (*coup d'épée* etc.).

slantingly ['slɑ:ntiŋli], **slantwise** ['slɑ:ntwaiz], *adv.* obliquement, en biais.

slap [slæp], *n.* tape, *f.*; soufflet (*sur la figure*), *m.*—*v.t.* souffleter, donner une fessée à (*un enfant*).—*adv.* tout droit, en plein.

slapdash ['slæpdæʃ], *adv.* à la six-quatre-deux, n'importe comment.—*a.* fait à la hâte.

slap-happy ['slæp'hæpi], *a.* toqué.

slapstick ['slæpstik], *n.* (*Theat., Cine.*) *slapstick comedy* (*fam.*), tarte à la crème, *f.*

slash [slæʃ], *n.* taillade; balafre (*sur la figure*), *f.*—*v.t.* taillader; balafrer (*la figure*).—*v.i.* frapper.

slashing ['slæʃiŋ], *a.* mordant, cinglant.

slate [sleit], *n.* ardoise, *f.*—*v.t.* couvrir d'ardoises; (*colloq.*) tancer.

slate-colored ['sleitkʌləd], *a.* ardoisé, gris d'ardoise.

slate pencil ['sleitpensl], *n.* crayon d'ardoise, *m.*

slater ['sleitə], *n.* couvreur en ardoise, *m.*

slating ['sleitiŋ], *n.* toiture en ardoise; (*colloq.*) semonce, *f.*

slattern ['slætən], *n.* femme malpropre, souillon, *f.*

slatternly ['slætənli], *a.* négligent, malpropre, mal soigné.

slaty ['sleiti], *a.* schisteux, d'ardoise; ardoisé (*couleur*).

slaughter ['slɔːtə], *n.* tuerie, boucherie, *f.*, massacre; abattage (*des animaux*), *m.*—*v.t.* massacrer; abattre (*animaux*).

slaughterer ['slɔːtərə], *n.* abatteur, *m.*

slaughter-house ['slɔːtəhaus], *n.* abattoir, *m.*

Slav [slɑːv], *a.* slave.—*n.* Slave (*personne*), *m.*, *f.*

slave [sleiv], *n.* esclave, *m.*, *f.*—*v.i.* travailler comme un esclave, peiner.

slave driver ['sleivdraivə], *n.* (*fig.*) maître sévère et cruel, *m.*

slaver (1) ['sleivə], *n.* négrier, bâtiment négrier, *m.*

slaver (2) ['slævə], *v.i.* baver (*sur*).—*n.* bave, salive, *f.*

slavery ['sleivəri], *n.* esclavage, *m.*

slave trade ['sleivtreid], *n.* traite des noirs, *f.*

slavish ['sleiviʃ], *a.* d'esclave; servile (*imitation etc.*).

slavishly ['sleiviʃli], *adv.* en esclave; servilement.

slavishness ['sleiviʃnis], *n.* servilité, *f.*

Slavonic [slə'vɔnik], *a.* slave.—*n.* slave (*langues*), *m.*

slay [slei], *v.t. irr.* tuer.

slayer ['sleiə], *n.* tueur (*de*), meurtrier, *m.*

slaying ['sleiiŋ], *n.* tuerie, *f.*

sledge [sledʒ], *n.* traineau, *m.*—*v.i.* (*also to go sledging*) se promener en traineau.

sledge hammer ['sledʒhæmə], *n.* marteau à deux mains, *m.*

sleek [sliːk], *a.* lisse, luisant, poli; (*fig.*) doucereux, onctueux.

sleekness ['sliːknis], *n.* luisant, *m.*; (*fig.*) douceur, onctuosité, *f.*

sleep [sliːp], *n.* sommeil, *m.*; *beauty sleep*, sommeil avant minuit; *sound sleep*, profond sommeil; *to go to sleep*, s'endormir; *to put a dog to sleep*, tuer un chien.—*v.t. irr.* dormir.—*v.i.* dormir, coucher (*à, chez* ou *dans*).

sleeper ['sliːpə], *n.* dormeur, *m.*; (*Rail.*) traverse, *f.*; (*colloq.*) wagon-lit, *m.*

sleepily ['sliːpili], *adv.* d'un air endormi.

sleepiness ['sliːpinis], *n.* assoupissement, *m.*

sleeping ['sliːpiŋ], *a.* endormi; dormant.—*n.* sommeil, repos, *m.*; *sleeping pills* or *tablets*, somnifère, *m.*

sleeping bag ['sliːpiŋbæg], *n.* sac de couchage, *m.*

sleeping berth ['sliːpiŋbəːθ], *n.* couchette, *f.*

sleeping car ['sliːpiŋkɑː], *n.* wagon-lit, *m.*

sleeping draft ['sliːpiŋdrɑːft], *n.* somnifère, *m.*

sleeping partner ['sliːpiŋpɑːtnə], *n.* associé commanditaire, *m.*

sleepless ['sliːplis], *a.* sans sommeil.

sleeplessness ['sliːplisnis], *n.* insomnie, *f.*

sleep-walker ['sliːpwɔːkə], *n.* somnambule, *m.*, *f.*

sleepy ['sliːpi], *a.* qui a envie de dormir; soporifique (*somnifère*); *to feel sleepy*, avoir sommeil.

sleepy-head ['sliːpihed], *n.* paresseux, *m.*

sleet [sliːt], *n.* neige fondue, *f.*; grésil, *m.*

sleeve [sliːv], *n.* manche, *f.*

sleeveless ['sliːvlis], *a.* sans manches.

sleigh [slei], *n.* traineau, *m.*

sleight [slait], *n.* habileté, *f.*, escamotage, *m.*; *sleight of hand*, tour de passe-passe, *m.*

slender ['slendə], *a.* mince; élancé; svelte (*taille*); (*fig.*) léger; chétif, maigre.

slenderness ['slendənis], *n.* minceur, légèreté; modicité, *f.*

sleuth(-hound) ['sluːθ(haund)], *n.* (chien) limier; (*fig.*) détective, *m.*

slice [slais], *n.* tranche; écumoire (*ustensile*), *f.*; *fish-slice*, truelle, *f.*; *slice of bread and jam*, tartine de confiture, *f.*—*v.t.* couper en tranches.

slick [slik], *a.* adroit.

slickness ['sliknis], *n.* adresse, habileté, *f.*

slide [slaid], *n.* glissoire, glissade, *f.*; *lantern slide*, diapositive, vue, *f.*; (*fig.*) glisser; tirer (*de*).—*v.i.* glisser; couler.

slide rule ['slaidruːl], *n.* règle à calcul, *f.*

sliding ['slaidiŋ], *a.* glissant; à coulisse.—*n.* glissade, *f.*, glissement, *m.*

sliding door ['slaidiŋdɔː], *n.* porte à coulisse, *f.*

sliding scale ['slaidiŋskeil], *n.* (*Econ.*) échelle mobile, *f.*

slight [slait], *a.* mince, léger; insignifiant; *not in the slightest*, pas le moins du monde.—*n.* manque d'égards; affront, *m.*, insulte, *f.*—*v.t.* traiter sans égards; mépriser.

slightingly ['slaitiŋli], *adv.* avec mépris, avec dédain.

slightly ['slaitli], *adv.* légèrement, un peu.

slightness ['slaitnis], *n.* minceur; légèreté, *f.*

slim [slim], *a.* svelte, mince; (*colloq.*) rusé.—*v.i.* s'amincir.

slime [slaim], *n.* vase, *f.*, limon, *m.*, bave (*de colimaçon*), *f.*

sliminess ['slaiminis], *n.* viscosité, *f.*

slimness ['slimnis], *n.* sveltesse, taille mince, *f.*

slimy ['slaimi], *a.* vaseux, limoneux; visqueux, gluant; (*fam.*) obséquieux.

sling [sliŋ], *n.* fronde; bretelle (*de fusil*), écharpe (*pour un membre cassé*), *f.*—*v.t. irr.* lancer (*avec une fronde*); suspendre (*fusil etc.*).

slinger ['sliŋə], *n.* frondeur, *m.*

slink [sliŋk], *v.i. irr.* s'esquiver, se dérober.

slip [slip], *v.t.* glisser, couler; perdre; lâcher; filer (*câble*); pousser (*verrou*); *to slip in*, introduire; *to slip off*, enlever, ôter; *to slip on*, passer, mettre.—*v.i.* glisser, couler (*nœud*); patiner (*roues*); (*fig.*) faire un faux pas; *to slip away*, s'esquiver; *to slip down*, tomber; *to slip in*, se faufiler, entrer furtivement; *to slip up*, (*fam.*) se tromper.—*n.* glissade; combinaison (*sous-vêtement*), laisse (*à chien*), *f.*; engobe (*céramique*); (*Hort.*) scion, *m.*; cale (*de port etc.*), faute d'étourderie, *f.*, lapsus, *m.*; *pillow slip*, taie d'oreiller, *f.*; *slip of paper*, bout de papier, *m.*; *slip of the pen*, erreur de plume, *f.*; *to give someone the slip*, planter quelqu'un là; *to make a slip*, faire un faux pas.

slip-knot ['slipnɔt], *n.* nœud coulant, *m.*

slipper ['slipə], *n.* pantoufle, *f.*

slippered ['slipəd], *a.* en pantoufles.

slipperiness ['slipərinis], *n.* nature glissante; volubilité (*de la langue*), *f.*

slippery ['slipəri], *a.* glissant; incertain, peu sûr; peu stable; matois, rusé; *slippery customer*, rusé compère, *m.*

slipshod ['slipʃɔd], *a.* (*fig.*) négligé; décousu (*style*).

slipstream ['slipstri:m], *n.* sillage, *m.*
slipway ['slipwei], *n.* cale, *f.*
slit [slit], *v.t. irr.* fendre.—*v.i.* se fendre.—*n.* fente, fissure, *f.*
slither ['sliðə], *v.i.* glisser; ramper (*reptile*).
sliver ['slivə, 'slaivə], *n.* éclat, *m.*, tranche, *f.*, ruban, *m.*
slobber ['slɔbə], *v.i.* baver.
sloe [slou], *n.* (*Bot.*) prunelle, *f.*
sloe tree ['sloutri:], *n.* prunellier, *m.*
slogan ['slougən], *n.* mot d'ordre, *m.*, devise, *f.*, slogan, *m.*
sloop [slu:p], *n.* sloop, aviso, *m.*
slop [slɔp], *n.* (*usu. in pl.*) rinçures, *f.pl.*—*v.t.* répandre, renverser.
slop basin ['slɔpbeisn], **slop bowl** ['slɔp boul], *n.* bol à rinçures (*de thé*), *m.*
slope [sloup], *n.* pente, *f.*; talus, versant, *m.*—*v.t.* couper en biais; taluter.—*v.i.* pencher, aller en pente, incliner.
sloping ['sloupiŋ], *a.* de biais, en pente.
sloppiness ['slɔpinis], *n.* état détrempé, *m.*; mollesse (*personne*), *f.*
sloppy ['slɔpi], *a.* bourbeux, humide; (*fig.*) mou.
slot [slɔt], *n.* rainure, mortaise, fente; barre de bois, *f.*
sloth (1) [slouθ], *n.* paresse, fainéantise, *f.*
sloth (2) [slouθ], *n.* (*Zool.*) parcsseux, aï, *m.*
slothful ['slouθful], *a.* paresseux, fainéant.
slot machine ['slɔtməʃi:n], *n.* distributeur automatique, *m.*
slouch [slautʃ], *n.* démarche molle *ou* lourde, *f.*; lourdaud (*personne*), *m.*—*v.i.* marcher lourdement; **to slouch along**, marcher d'un pas traînant.
slouching ['slautʃiŋ], *a.* lourd et gauche.
slough [slau], *n.* bourbier, *m.*, fondrière (*dépouille (de serpent*), *f.*
Slovak ['slouvæk], *a.* slovaque.—*n.* Slovaque (*personne*), *m.,f.*
sloven [slʌvn], *n.* sans-soin, mal-soigné, *m.*
Slovene ['slouvi:n], *n.* Slovène (*personne*), *m.,f.*
Slovenian [slo'vi:niən], *a.* slovène.
slovenliness ['slʌvnlinis], *n.* malpropreté, saleté, négligence, *f.*
slovenly ['slʌvnli], *a.* mal soigné, mal peigné, débraillé.
slow [slou], *a.* lent, tardif; lourd (*pesant*); en retard (*montre etc.*).—*adv.* lentement.—*v.t.* ralentir.—*v.i.* se ralentir.
slowly ['slouli], *adv.* lentement, tardivement.
slowness ['slounis], *n.* lenteur; paresse; lourdeur (*pesanteur*), *f.*; retard (*de montre etc.*), *m.*
slow-worm ['slouwə:m], *n.* orvet, *m.*
sludge [slʌdʒ], *n.* boue, vase, *f.*; cambouis, *m.*
slug [slʌg], *n.* limace, *f.*; lingot (*de fusil*), *m.*
sluggard ['slʌgəd], *n.* paresseux, *m.*
sluggish ['slʌgiʃ], *a.* paresseux, indolent, lourd; lent (*ruisseau*).
sluggishly ['slʌgiʃli], *adv.* paresseusement, lourdement.
sluggishness ['slʌgiʃnis], *n.* paresse; lenteur (*de ruisseau*), *f.*
sluice [slu:s], *n.* écluse; bonde (*dans un étang*), *f.*—*v.t.* lâcher par une écluse; inonder d'eau.
sluice-gate ['slu:sgeit], *n.* vanne, *f.*
slum [slʌm], *n.* taudis, *m.*, (*pl.*) bas quartiers, *m.pl.*; **slum clearance**, lutte contre les taudis, *f.*

slumber ['slʌmbə], *n.* sommeil, *m.*—*v.i.* sommeiller, dormir.
slumberer ['slʌmbərə], *n.* dormeur, *m.*
slumbering ['slʌmbəriŋ], *a.* endormi, assoupi.—*n.* sommeil, assoupissement, *m.*
slump [slʌmp], *v.i.* s'enfoncer soudainement.—*n.* baisse subite; crise, *f.*
slur [slə:], *n.* tache; (*Mus.*) liaison, *f.*; **to cast a slur upon**, flétrir, dénigrer.—*v.t.* tacher, salir; (*Mus.*) lier; **to slur over**, glisser sur.
slurred [slə:d], *a.* (*Mus.*) coulé; brouillé (*paroles*).
slurring ['slə:riŋ], *n.* (*Mus.*) liaison, *f.*
slush [slʌʃ], *n.* boue, fange; neige à moitié fondue, *f.*
slut [slʌt], *n.* saligaude, souillon, *f.*
sly [slai], *a.* sournois, rusé; **on the sly**, en sourdine; **sly dog**, fin matois, *m.*
slyly ['slaili], *adv.* avec ruse, sournoisement.
slyness ['slainis], *n.* ruse, finesse, nature sournoise, *f.*
smack (1) [smæk], *n.* claquement (*de fouet*), *m.*; claque (*de la main*); gifle (*sur la figure*), *f.*; gros baiser, *m.*—*adv.* **smack in the middle**, en plein milieu.—*v.t.* faire claquer (*fouet, les lèvres*); donner une claque à.
smack (2) [smæk], *n.* (*fig.*) saveur, *f.*—*v.i.* **to smack of**, sentir (*le, la etc.*).
smack (3) [smæk], *n.* bateau de pêche, *m.*
smacking ['smækiŋ], *n.* claquement, *m.*; fessée, *f.*
small [smɔ:l], *a.* petit; fin, menu; (*fig.*) chétif, mince, pauvre; modeste, peu considérable; **small arms**, armes portatives, *f.pl.*; **small fry**, menu fretin, *m.*; **small letters**, minuscules, *f.pl.*—*n.* partie mince, *f.*; **small of the back**, chute des reins, *f.*
smallish ['smɔ:liʃ], *a.* un peu petit, un peu menu.
smallness ['smɔ:lnis], *n.* petitesse, *f.*; peu d'importance, *m.*
smallpox ['smɔ:lpɔks], *n.* petite vérole, *f.*
smarmy ['sma:mi], *a.* (*pop.*) mielleux.
smart [sma:t], *a.* piquant, cuisant, vif; vigoureux, rude; intelligent, éveillé; beau, élégant, pimpant, chic; **look smart!** dépêchez-vous! **smart Aleck**, finaud, *m.*—*n.* douleur aiguë, vive douleur, cuisson, *f.*—*v.i.* cuire, éprouver une vive douleur.
smarten [sma:tn] (**up**), *v.t.* animer; **to smarten oneself up**, se faire beau, s'attifer.
smarting ['sma:tiŋ], *a.* cuisant, poignant.—*n.* douleur cuisante, *f.*
smartly ['sma:tli], *adv.* lestement, vivement; habilement; vigoureusement, rudement; élégamment.
smartness ['sma:tnis], *n.* force, vigueur, élégance, *f.*, éclat (*de vêtements*), *m.*; finesse (*astuce*), *f.*
smash [smæʃ], *v.t.* briser, écraser; (*fig.*) ruiner.—*v.i.* se briser.—*n.* fracas, *m.*; (*Fin.*) déconfiture, faillite, banqueroute; (*Rail.*) catastrophe, *f.*—*adv.* **to go smash**, faire faillite.
smashing ['smæʃiŋ], *a.* (*pop.*) formidable, épatant.
smattering ['smætəriŋ], *n.* connaissances superficielles, *f.pl.*
smear [smiə], *v.t.* enduire, (*fig.*) salir.—*n.* tache, *f.*; (*fig.*) calomnie, atteinte à la réputation, *f.*

smell

smell [smel], *n.* odeur, *f.*; odorat (*sens*); flair (*de chien*), *m.*—*v.t., v.i. irr.* sentir; flairer (*chien*).

smelly ['smeli], *a.* malodorant.

smelt (1) [smelt], *n.* (*Ichth.*) éperlan, *m.*

smelt (2) [smelt], *v.t.* fondre.

smelting ['smeltiŋ], *n.* fonte, *f.*

smile [smail], *n.* sourire, *m.*—*v.i.* sourire.

smiling ['smailiŋ], *a.* souriant; riant (*paysage etc.*).

smilingly ['smailiŋli], *adv.* en souriant.

smirch [smə:tʃ], *v.t.* souiller, salir.—*n.* tache, *f.*

smirk [smə:k], *v.i.* minauder.—*n.* sourire affecté, *m.*

smirking ['smə:kiŋ], *a.* affecté, minauder.

smite [smait], *v.t. irr.* frapper; détruire; châtier; (*fig.*) charmer.

smith [smiθ], *n.* forgeron, *m.*

smithereens [smiðə'ri:nz], *n.pl.* **to smash to smithereens**, mettre en miettes.

smithy ['smiði], *n.* forge, *f.*

smock [smɔk], *n.* blouse, *f.*

smog [smɔg], *n.* brouillard épais et enfumé, *m.*

smoke [smouk], *n.* fumée, *f.*—*v.t., v.i.* fumer.

smokeless ['smouklis], *a.* sans fumée.

smoker ['smoukə], *n.* fumeur (*personne*), *m.*

smoke-stack ['smoukstæk], *n.* cheminée, *f.*

smokiness ['smoukinis], *n.* état enfumé, *m.*

smoking ['smoukiŋ], *a.* fumant.—*n.* habitude de fumer, *f.*; **no smoking**, défense de fumer.

smoky ['smouki], *a.* qui fume, plein de fumée.

smooth [smu:ð], *a.* uni; égal (*régulier*); doux (*non âpre*); poli, lisse (*verni*); plat (*mer*); doucereux (*personne*).—*v.t.* polir; adoucir; aplanir, unir; dérider (*le front*); lisser (*les cheveux*).

smooth-faced ['smu:ðfeist], *a.* imberbe.

smoothing-iron ['smu:ðiŋaiən], *n.* fer à repasser, *m.*

smoothly ['smu:ðli], *adv.* uniment; sans difficulté; doucement.

smoothness ['smu:ðnis], *n.* égalité; douceur, *f.*; calme (*de la mer*), *m.*

smooth-tongued ['smu:ð'tʌŋd], *a.* mielleux, doucereux.

smother ['smʌðə], *v.t.* suffoquer, étouffer.

smothering ['smʌðəriŋ], *a.* étouffant, suffocant.—*n.* étouffement, *m.*

smoulder ['smouldə], *v.i.* brûler sans fumée ni flamme; (*fig.*) couver.

smouldering ['smoulдəriŋ], *a.* qui couve.

smudge [smʌdʒ], *v.t.* barbouiller, noircir.—*n.* barbouillage, *m.*; tache, *f.*

smudgy ['smʌdʒi], *a.* barbouillé; taché.

smug [smʌg], *a.* suffisant, content de soi.

smuggle ['smʌgl], *v.t.* passer en contrebande —*v.i.* faire la contrebande.

smuggled ['smʌgld], *a.* de contrebande.

smuggler ['smʌglə], *n.* contrebandier, *m.*

smuggling ['smʌgliŋ], *n.* contrebande, fraude, *f.*

smugness ['smʌgnis], *n.* suffisance, *f.*

smut [smʌt], *n.* tache de suie; (*fig.*) saleté (*grivoiserie*), *f.*—*v.t.* noircir.

smuttiness ['smʌtinis], *n.* noirceur; (*fig.*) saleté, *f.*

smutty ['smʌti], *a.* noir; (*fig.*) obscène, grivois.

snack [snæk], *n.* morceau; casse-croûte, *m.*

snack-bar ['snækba:], *n.* snack-bar, *m.*

snaffle [snæfl], *n.* mors de bridon, filet, *m.*—

snag [snæg], *n.* (*fig.*) obstacle caché, *m.*

snail [sneil], *n.* escargot, limaçon, colimaçon, *m.*

snail's pace ['sneilzpeis], *n.* pas de tortue, *m.*

snake [sneik], *n.* serpent, *m.*—*v.i.* (*Naut.*) serpenter.

snap [snæp], *v.t.* saisir, happer; casser, rompre, éclater; faire claquer (*fouet etc.*); fermer avec un bruit sec; dire d'un ton sec. —*v.i.* tâcher de mordre *ou* de happer; se casser, se rompre; craquer; **to snap at**, (*fam.*) brusquer.—*n.* coup de dent, *m.*; cassure, *f.*; claquement (*de fouet etc.*); bruit sec; fermoir (*de sac à main*); biscuit craquant, *m.*; vivacité, *f.*

snapdragon ['snæpdrægən], *n.* muflier, *m.*

snappy ['snæpi], *a.* vif; **make it snappy!** dépêchez-vous!

snapshot ['snæpʃɔt], *n.* (*colloq.* **snap** [snæp]) instantané, *m.*

snare [snɛə], *n.* lacet, collet; (*fig.*) piège, *m.*—*v.t.* prendre (au piège).

snarl [sna:l], *v.i.* grogner; montrer les dents. —*n.* grognement, *m.*

snarling ['sna:liŋ], *a.* hargneux.—*n.* grognement, *m.*

snatch [snætʃ], *v.t.* saisir; **to snatch at**, chercher à saisir; **to snatch from**, arracher à; **to snatch up**, empoigner.—*n.* **by snatches**, à bâtons rompus; **snatches of conversation**, des bribes de conversation, *f.pl.*

sneak [sni:k], *v.t.* chiper.—*v.i.* s'en aller furtivement; (*Sch.*) cafarder, moucharder.—*n.* pleutre, pied-plat; cafard, *m.*

sneaking ['sni:kiŋ], *a.* rampant, servile; furtif, inavoué.

sneer [sniə], *n.* rire *ou* sourire moqueur, sarcasme, ricanement, *m.*—*v.i.* ricaner, se moquer (*de*).

sneering ['sniəriŋ], *a.* ricaneur, moqueur.—*n.* ricanement, *m.*

sneeringly ['sniəriŋli], *adv.* en ricanant.

sneeze [sni:z], *n.* éternuement, *m.*—*v.i.* éternuer.

sneezing ['sni:ziŋ], *n.* éternuement, *m.*

sniff [snif], *v.t.* flairer.—*v.i.* renifler.—*n.* reniflement, *m.*

snigger ['snigə], *v.i.* rire du bout des lèvres, ricaner.—*n.* rire en dessous, *m.*

snip [snip], *n.* coup de ciseaux, *m.*; (*pop.*) certitude, *f.*—*v.t.* couper (*d'un coup de ciseaux*).

snipe [snaip], *n.* bécassine, *f.*—*v.i.* (*Shooting*) canarder.

sniper ['snaipə], *n.* tireur embusqué, franc-tireur, *m.*

snippet ['snipit], *n.* petit morceau, *m.*

snivel [snivl], *v.i.* être morveux; (*fig.*) pleurnicher.

sniveller ['snivlə], *n.* pleurnicheur, *m.*

snivelling ['snivliŋ], *a.* morveux; (*fig.*) pleurnicheur.—*n.* pleurnicherie, *f.*

snob [snɔb], *n.* poseur; fat, snob, *m.*

snobbery ['snɔbəri], *n.* snobisme, *m.*

snobbish ['snɔbiʃ], *a.* affecté, poseur, prétentieux.

snobbishness ['snɔbiʃnis], *n.* snobisme, *m.*

snoop [snu:p], *v.i.* fureter.

snooper ['snu:pə], *n.* fureteur, *m.*

snooze [snu:z], *n.* somme, *m.*—*v.i.* sommeiller.

snore [snɔ:], *v.i.* ronfler.—*n.* ronflement, *m.*

snorkel [snɔ:rkl], *n.* schnorkel, *m.*

snort [snɔ:t], *v.i.* renâcler, s'ébrouer (*cheval*); ronfler.

snorting [snɔ:tiŋ], *n.* ronflement, *m.*

snot [snɔt], *n.* (*vulg.*) morve, *f.*

snotty [snɔti], *a.* (*vulg.*) morveux.

snout [snaut], *n.* museau; mufle (*de taureau*); groin (*de cochon*), *m.*

snow [snou], *n.* neige, *f.*—*v.i.* neiger, tomber de la neige.

snowball [snoubɔ:l], *n.* boule de neige, *f.*

snow-capped [snoukæpt], *a.* couronné de neige.

snow-drift [snoudrift], *n.* congère, *f.*, amas de neige, *m.*

snowdrop [snoudrɔp], *n.* perce-neige, *m.*

snowflake [snoufleik], *n.* flocon de neige, *m.*

snow-man [snoumæn], *n.* (*pl.* -men [men]) bonhomme de neige, *m.*

snowplow [snouplau], *n.* chasse-neige, *m.*

snow-shoe [snouʃu:], *n.* raquette, *f.*

snow-storm [snoustɔ:m], *n.* tempête de neige, *f.*

Snow White [snou'wait]. Blanche-Neige, *f.*

snow-white [snouwait], *a.* blanc comme la neige.

snowy [snoui], *a.* de neige; neigeux.

snub [snʌb], *n.* rebuffade, *f.*; affront, *m.*—*v.t.* rabrouer, rembarrer.

snub-nosed [snʌbnouzd], *a.* au nez camus.

snuff (1) [snʌf], *n.* tabac (à priser), *m.*; *pinch of snuff*, prise de tabac, *f.*

snuff (2) [snʌf], *n.* lumignon (*de mèche*), *m.*—*v.i.* moucher (*chandelle*).

snuff-box [snʌfbɔks], *n.* tabatière, *f.*

snuffle [snʌfl], *n.* reniflement, *m.*—*v.i.* nasiller, renifler.

snuffling [snʌfliŋ], *a.* nasillard.—*n.* nasillement, *m.*

snug [snʌg], *a.* confortable, commode et agréable, où l'on est bien; gentil; serré, compact; *we are very snug here*, nous sommes on ne peut mieux ici.

snuggery [snʌgəri], *n.* endroit petit et commode (*où l'on se sent chez soi*), *m.*

snuggle [snʌgl], *v.t.* serrer.—*v.i.* se serrer.

snugly [snʌgli], *adv.* commodément, à son aise.

snugness [snʌgnis], *n.* confort, bien-être, *m.*

so [sou], *adv.* and *conj.* ainsi, de cette manière, comme cela, comme ça (*de cette façon*); de même, de la même manière, tel (*pareillement*); si, tellement, tant (*à tel point*); aussi, donc (*alors*); and so on, et ainsi de suite; *be it so*, soit! *how so?* comment cela? *is that so?* vraiment? *just so!* parfaitement! *Mr. So-and-So*, Monsieur un tel; *or so*, environ, à peu près; *so as to*, de manière à; *so that*, de sorte que.

soak [souk], *v.t.* tremper; (*colloq.*) estamper.—*v.i.* tremper, s'infiltrer.

soaking [soukiŋ], *a.* qui trempe.—*n.* trempée (*de pluie*), *f.*

soap [soup], *n.* savon, *m.*—*v.t.* savonner.

soap bubble [soupbʌbl], *n.* bulle de savon, *f.*

soap flakes [soupfleiks], *n.pl.* savon en paillettes, *m.*

soap-suds [soupsʌdz], *n.pl.* eau de savon, *f.*

soar [sɔ:], *v.i.* prendre l'essor, s'élever; *to soar over*, planer sur.

soaring [sɔ:riŋ], *a.* qui s'élève; (*fig.*) élevé.—*n.* essor, élan, *m.*

sob [sɔb], *v.i.* sangloter.—*n.* sanglot, *m.*

sobbing [sɔbiŋ], *n.* sanglots, *m.pl.*

sober [soubə], *a.* qui n'a pas bu, qui n'est pas ivre; sobre, tempéré; grave, sérieux; sensé; calme, posé, rassis.—*v.t.* dégriser; (*fig.*) calmer.—*v.i.* *to sober up*, se désenivrer.

soberly [soubəli], *adv.* sobrement; raisonnablement.

soberness [soubənis], **sobriety** [sə'braiəti], *n.* sobriété, tempérance; gravité, *f.*

so-called [soukɔ:ld], *a.* soi-disant, prétendu.

soccer [sɔkə], *n.* (*fam.*) football, *m.*

sociability [souʃə'biliti], *n.* sociabilité, *f.*

sociable [souʃəbl], *a.* sociable.

social [souʃəl], *a.* social.

socialism [souʃəlizm], *n.* socialisme, *m.*

socialist [souʃəlist], *a.* and *n.* socialiste, *m.*, *f.*

socially [souʃəli], *adv.* socialement.

society [sə'saiəti], *n.* société; la société, *f.*; le monde, *m.*

sociology [sousi'ɔlədʒi], *n.* sociologie, *f.*

sock [sɔk], *n.* chaussette; semelle (*intérieure*), *f.*

socket [sɔkit], *n.* emboîture; orbite (*de l'œil*), *f.*; trou, *m.*, cavité; douille (*d'outil etc.*), *f.*

Socrates [sɔkrəti:z]. Socrate, *m.*

sod [sɔd], *n.* gazon, *m.*; motte de gazon, *f.*

soda [soudə], *n.* soude, *f.*; *baking soda*, bicarbonate de soude, *m.*

soda water [soudəwɔ:tə], *n.* eau de Seltz, *f.*, soda, *m.*

sodden [sɔdn], *a.* imprégné d'eau, détrempé; pâteux (*pain*); abruti (*d'alcool*).

sodium [soudiəm], *n.* (*Chem.*) sodium, *m.*

sodomy [sɔdəmi], *n.* sodomie, *f.*

sofa [soufə], *n.* canapé, *m.*

soft [sɔft], *a.* mou, mol, mollet; délicat, doux, facile, pas résistant; tendre; efféminé; faible; sot, niais; (*Gram.*) doux; *soft fruits*, fruits rouges, *m.pl.*—*adv.* mollement, doucement.—*int.* doucement! tout doux!

soften [sɔfn], *v.t.* amollir, ramollir; adoucir, apaiser; affaiblir; attendrir (*cœur*).—*v.i.* s'amollir, se ramollir; s'affaiblir; s'attendrir (*cœur*).

softener [sɔfnə], *n.* chose qui amollit, *f.*

softening [sɔfniŋ], *n.* amollissement; affaiblissement; attendrissement (*du cœur*), *m.*

soft-headed [sɔft'hedid], *a.* niais; sot.

soft-hearted [sɔft'hɑ:tid], *a.* tendre, compatissant.

softly [sɔftli], *adv.* mollement; doucement; tendrement.

softness [sɔftnis], *n.* mollesse; faiblesse; niaiserie; douceur, *f.*

soggy [sɔgi], *a.* détrempé; pâteux (*pain*).

soil (1) [sɔil], *n.* sol, terrain, terroir, *m.*, terre, *f.*

soil (2) [sɔil], *n.* tache, souillure, *f.*—*v.t.* salir, souiller.

sojourn [sɔdʒən], *n.* séjour, *m.*—*v.i.* séjourner.

sojourning [sɔdʒəniŋ], *n.* séjour, *m.*

solace [sɔlis], *n.* consolation, *f.*, soulagement, *m.*—*v.t.* consoler (*de*).

solar [soulə], *a.* solaire, du soleil.

solder [sɔ(l)də], *n.* soudure, *f.*—*v.t.* souder.

soldering [sɔ(l)dəriŋ], *n.* soudure, *f.*; soudage (*action*), *m.*; *soldering iron*, fer à souder, *m.*

soldier ['souldʒə], *n.* soldat, militaire, *m.*; **foot soldier**, fantassin, *m.*; *private soldier*, simple soldat.—*v.i.* servir comme soldat.

soldierly ['souldʒəli], *a.* de soldat, militaire, martial.

soldiery ['souldʒəri], *n.* troupes, *f.pl.*, soldats, *m.pl.*

sole (1) [soul], *a.* seul, unique.

sole (2) [soul], *n.* plante (*du pied*); semelle (*de soulier, d'outil etc.*), *f.*—*v.t.* ressemeler.

sole (3) [soul], *n.* (*Ichth.*) sole, *f.*

solecism ['sɔlisizm], *n.* solécisme, *f.*

solely ['soulli], *adv.* seulement, uniquement.

solemn ['sɔləm], *a.* solennel.

solemnity [sə'lemniti], *n.* solennité, *f.*

solemnization [sɔləmnai'zeiʃən], *n.* solennisation; célébration solennelle, *f.*

solemnize ['sɔləmnaiz], *v.t.* solenniser, célébrer.

solemnly ['sɔləmli], *adv.* solennellement.

solenoid ['sɔlinɔid], *n.* (*Elec.*) solénoïde, *m.*

solicit [sə'lisit], *v.t.* solliciter.

solicitation [səlisi'teiʃən], *n.* sollicitation, *f.*

solicitous [sə'lisitəs], *a.* désireux; *solicitous about*, soigneux, attentif à.

solicitude [sə'lisitju:d], *n.* sollicitude, *f.*

solid ['sɔlid], *a.* solide, massif.—*n.* solide, *m.*

solidarity [sɔli'dæriti], *n.* solidarité, *f.*

solidification [səlidifi'keiʃən], *n.* solidification, *f.*

solidify [sə'lidifai], *v.t.* solidifier.—*v.i.* se solidifier.

solidity [sə'liditi], **solidness** ['sɔlidnis], *n.* solidité, *f.*

solidly ['sɔlidli], *adv.* solidement.

soliloquize [sə'liləkwaiz], *v.i.* faire un soliloque.

soliloquy [sə'liləkwi], *n.* soliloque, *m.*

soling ['souliŋ], *n.* ressemelage, *m.*

solitary ['sɔlitəri], *a.* solitaire, retiré, isolé; seul.

solitude ['sɔlitju:d], *n.* solitude, *f.*

solo ['soulou], *n.* solo, *m.*

soloist ['soulouist], *n.* soliste, *m.*, *f.*

Solomon ['sɔləmən], Salomon, *m.*

solstice ['sɔlstis], *n.* solstice, *m.*

solubility [sɔlju'biliti], *n.* solubilité, *f.*

soluble ['sɔljubl], *a.* soluble.

solution [sə'lju:ʃən], *n.* solution, *f.*

solvable ['sɔlvəbl], *a.* soluble.

solve [sɔlv], *v.t.* résoudre, expliquer, éclaircir.

solvency ['sɔlvənsi], *n.* (*Fin.*) solvabilité, *f.*

solvent ['sɔlvənt], *a.* dissolvant; (*Comm.*) solvable.—*n.* dissolvant, *m.*

Somali [so'mɑ:li], *a.* somali.—*n.* somali (*langue*); Somali (*personne*), *m.*

Somalia [so'mɑ:liə], la Somalie, *f.*

Somaliland [so'mɑ:lilænd], la Somalie, *f.*

somber ['sɔmbə], *a.* sombre.

somberly ['sɔmbəli], *adv.* sombrement.

some [sʌm], *a.* quelque, *m.*, *f.*, quelques, *pl.*; un certain, *m.*, certains, *m.pl.*, plusieurs, *pl.*; du, *m.*, de la, *f.*, de l', *m.*, *f.*, des, *pl.*, de; quelconque; un certain nombre de, un peu de, une partie de.—*adv.* à peu près, environ, quelque.—*pron.* quelques-uns, *m.pl.*, quelques-unes, *f.pl.*; les uns, *m.pl.*, les unes, *f.pl.*, . . . les autres, *pl.*; en.

somebody ['sʌmbədi], **someone** ['sʌmwʌn], *pron.* quelqu'un, *m.*, quelqu'une, *f.*; *somebody else*, quelqu'un d'autre, quelque autre, un autre.

somehow ['sʌmhau], *adv.* d'une manière ou d'une autre, de façon ou d'autre.

someone [SOMEBODY].

somersault ['sʌməsɔ:lt], *n.* saut périlleux, *m.*, culbute, *f.*

something ['sʌmθiŋ], *n.* and *pron.* quelque chose (de), *m.*; *something else*, autre chose, *f.*—*adv.* un peu, quelque peu, tant soit peu.

sometime ['sʌmtaim], *adv.* autrefois, jadis; *sometime or other*, tôt ou tard.—*a.* ancien.

sometimes ['sʌmtaimz], *adv.* quelquefois, parfois; tantôt.

somewhat ['sʌmwɔt], *adv.* quelque peu, un peu; assez.—*n.* un peu, quelque peu, tant soit peu, *m.*

somewhere ['sʌmwɛə], *adv.* quelque part; *somewhere else*, ailleurs.

somnambulist [sɔm'næmbjulist], *n.* somnambule, *m.*, *f.*

somniferous [sɔm'nifərəs], *a.* somnifère.

somnolence ['sɔmnələns], *n.* somnolence, *f.*

somnolent ['sɔmnələnt], *a.* somnolent.

son [sʌn], *n.* fils; (*fig.*) descendant, *m.*

sonata [sə'nɑ:tə], *n.* sonate, *f.*

song [sɔŋ], *n.* chanson, *f.*; chant, *m.*; (*fig.*) ballade, *f.*; *a mere song*, un rien, *m.*, une bagatelle, *f.*

songster ['sɔŋstə], *n.* chanteur; oiseau chanteur, *m.*

songstress ['sɔŋstris], *n.* chanteuse, *f.*

song thrush ['sɔŋθrʌʃ], *n.* grive chanteuse, *f.*

song-writer ['sɔŋraitə], *n.* chansonnier, *m.*

son-in-law ['sʌninlɔ:], *n.* gendre, *m.*

sonnet ['sɔnit], *n.* sonnet, *m.*

sonorous ['sɔnərəs], *a.* sonore.

soon [su:n], *adv.* bientôt; tôt (*de bonne heure*); *as soon as*, aussitôt que, dès que; *how soon?* quand ? *see you soon!* à bientôt; *so soon*, si tôt; *too soon*, trop tôt.

sooner ['su:nə], *adv.* plus tôt (*de meilleure heure*); plutôt (*mieux*); *no sooner said than done*, aussitôt dit, aussitôt fait; *sooner or later*, tôt ou tard, *sooner than*, plutôt que.

soonest ['su:nist], *adv.* le plus tôt.

soothe [su:ð], *v.t.* apaiser, calmer; (*fig.*) charmer.

soothing ['su:ðiŋ], *a.* calmant, consolant; flatteur.

soothingly ['su:ðiŋli], *adv.* d'un ton doux.

soothsay ['su:θsei], *v.i.* prophétiser, prédire.

soothsayer ['su:θseiə], *n.* devin, *m.*, devineresse, *f.*, prophète, *m.*

sooty ['suti], *a.* de suie, fuligineux; plein *ou* couvert de suie.

sop [sɔp], *n.* morceau (de pain) trempé; (*fig.*) pot-de-vin (*pourboire*), *f.*—*v.t.* tremper.

Sophia [sə'faiə], Sophie, *f.*

sophism ['sɔfizm], *n.* sophisme, *m.*

sophist ['sɔfist], *n.* sophiste, *m.*, *f.*

sophisticate [sə'fistikeit], *v.t.* sophistiquer, falsifier.

sophisticated [sə'fistikeitid], *a.* falsifié; blasé (*personne*).
sophistication [səfisti'keiʃən], *n.* sophistication, falsification, *f.*
sophistry ['sofistri], *n.* sophismes, *m.pl.*
Sophocles ['sofəkli:z]. Sophocle, *m.*
soporific [sopə'rifik], *a.* and *n.* soporifique, *m.*
sopping ['sopiŋ] (wet), *a.* trempé.
soprano [sə'prɑ:nou], *n.* soprano, *m.*, *f.*
sorcerer ['so:sərə], *n.* sorcier, magicien, *m.*
sorceress ['so:səris], *n.* sorcière, magicienne, *f.*
sorcery ['so:səri], *n.* sorcellerie, magie, *f.*
sordid ['so:did], *a.* sordide, sale; bas, vil.
sordidly ['so:didli], *adv.* sordidement.
sordidness ['so:didnis], *n.* sordidité, *f.*
sore [so:], *a.* douloureux, endolori, sensible; (*fig.*) rude; fâché; **sore throat**, mal à la gorge, *m.*—*n.* plaie, *f.*
sorely ['so:li], *adv.* gravement, fortement, cruellement, rudement.
soreness ['so:nis], *n.* douleur; sensation pénible, *f.*
sorrel ['sorəl], *a.* saure; alezan.—*n.* oseille, *f.*; alezan (*cheval*), *m.*
sorrily ['sorili], *adv.* misérablement, pauvrement.
sorrow ['sorou], *n.* chagrin, *m.*, douleur; peine, tristesse, *f.*—*v.i.* être affligé.
sorrowful ['soroful], *a.* triste, affligé.
sorrowfully ['sorofuli], *adv.* tristement.
sorrowing ['sorouiŋ], *a.* affligé.
sorry ['sori], *a.* fâché, désolé (*de*); triste, pauvre, méchant, pitoyable; **I am sorry for you**, je vous plains; **I am sorry to say that . . .**, je regrette d'avoir à dire que . . .; **sorry!** pardon!
sort [so:t], *n.* sorte, *f.*, genre, *m.*, espèce; manière, façon, *f.*; **nothing of the sort**, pas du tout.
sort (2) [so:t], *v.t.* assortir, classer, distribuer; trier (*lettres etc.*).
sorted ['so:tid], *a.* assorti; trié, arrangé, séparé.
sorter ['so:tə], *n.* trieur, *m.*
sortie ['so:ti], *n.* (*Mil.*) sortie, *f.*; (*Av.*) vol, *m.*
sorting ['so:tiŋ], *n.* triage, tri; assortiment (*classement*), *m.*
so-so ['sou'sou], *a.* comme ci comme ça, (*fam.*) couci-couça.
sot [sot], *n.* ivrogne, *m.*, *f.*
sottish ['sotiʃ], *a.* hébété, abruti.
sough [sau, sʌf], *v.i.* murmurer, soupirer (*vent*).
soughing ['sauiŋ], *n.* bruissement, murmure, *m.*
soul [soul], *n.* âme, *f.*; (*fig.*) être; principe (*essence*), *m.*; **All Souls' Day**, le jour des morts, *m.*
soulful ['soulful], *a.* sentimental.
soulfully ['soulfuli], *adv.* avec expression; avec sentiment.
soulless ['soullis], *a.* sans âme; abrutissant.
sound (1) [saund], *n.* détroit (*goulet*), *m.*; (*Surg.*) sonde, *f.*—*v.t.* sonder (*les profondeurs etc.*); (*Surg.*) ausculter.
sound (2) [saund], *a.* en bon état, sain; (*fig.*) solide; profond (*sommeil*), valide, bien fondé; **safe and sound**, sain et sauf.
sound (3) [saund], *v.t.* faire sonner; proclamer.—*v.i.* sonner; retentir, résonner (*de*); sembler.—*n.* son, bruit, *m.*; **to break the**

sound barrier, (*Av.*) franchir le mur du son.
sounding (1) ['saundiŋ], *n.* sondage, *m.*; (*Surg.*) auscultation, *f.*
sounding (2) ['saundiŋ], *a.* résonnant, retentissant; (*fig.*) pompeux.—*n.* retentissement, résonnement, *m.*
sounding balloon ['saundiŋbə'lu:n], *n.* (*Meteor.*) ballon sonde, *m.*
sounding-lead ['saundiŋled], *n.* plomb de sonde, *m.*
sounding line ['saundiŋlain], *n.* ligne de sonde, *f.*
soundless ['saundlis], *a.* sans bruit, muet.
soundly ['saundli], *adv.* vigoureusement, rudement, ferme, bien; sainement, solidement; profondément (*sommeil*).
soundness ['saundnis], *n.* bon état, *m.*; force, vigueur (*physique*); droiture (*morale*), *f.*
sound-proof ['saundpru:f], *a.* insonore.
sound track ['saundtræk], *n.* (*Cine.*) piste sonore, *f.*
sound wave ['saundweiv], *n.* onde sonore, *f.*
soup [su:p], *n.* potage, *m.*, soupe, *f.*; (*colloq.*) **to be in the soup**, être dans le pétrin.
soup ladle ['su:pleidl], *n.* louche, *f.*
soup tureen ['su:ptju'ri:n], *n.* soupière, *f.*
sour ['sauə], *a.* aigre, acide; tourné (*lait*); (*fig.*) âpre.—*v.t.* aigrir; (*fig.*) empoisonner.—*v.i.* s'aigrir.
source [so:s], *n.* source, *f.*
souring ['sauəriŋ], *n.* aigrissement, *m.*
sourish ['sauəriʃ], *a.* suret, aigrelet.
sourly ['sauəli], *adv.* avec aigreur; (*fig.*) aigrement, âprement.
sourness ['sauənis], *n.* aigreur, acidité; (*fig.*) âpreté, *f.*
souse [saus], *v.t.* tremper; faire mariner.—*n.* marinade, *f.*
south [sauθ], *a.* au sud, du sud, du midi, méridional.—*n.* sud, midi, *m.*—*adv.* vers le midi, vers le sud, au sud; **South Africa**, l'Afrique du Sud; **South America**, l'Amérique du Sud, *f.*
south-east [sauθ'i:st], *a.* sud-est, du sud-est.—*n.* sud-est, *m.*—*adv.* vers le sud-est.
south-easter [sauθ'i:stə], *n.* vent du sud-est, *m.*
south-easterly [sauθ'i:stəli], **south-eastern** [sauθ'i:stn], *a.* du sud-est.
southerly ['sʌðəli], **southern** [sʌðən], *a.* du sud, du midi, méridional.
southerner ['sʌðənə], *n.* méridional, *m.*; (*Am.*) sudiste, *m.*, *f.*
southernmost ['sʌðənmost], *a.* à l'extrême sud.
southward ['sauθwəd], *adv.* vers le sud, au sud.
south-west ['sauθ'west], *a.* sud-ouest, du sud-ouest.—*n.* sud-ouest, *m.*—*adv.* vers le sud-ouest.
southwester [sau'westə], [SOU'WESTER].
south-westerly ['sauθ'westəli], **south-western** ['sauθ'westən], *a.* du sud-ouest, sud-ouest.
souvenir ['su:vəniə], *n.* souvenir, *m.*
sou'wester, southwester [sau'westə], *n.* vent du sud-ouest; suroît (*coiffure*), *m.*
sovereign ['sovrin], *a.* and *n.* souverain, *m.*
sovereignty ['sovrinti], *n.* souveraineté, *f.*
Soviet ['souviet], *n.* Soviet, *m.*; **the Soviet Union**, l'Union Soviétique, *f.*

sow (1) [sau], *n.* truie; gueuse (*de fer*), *f.*
sow (2) [sou], *v.t. irr.* semer.—*v.i.* semer, faire les semailles.
sower ['souə], *n.* semeur, *m.*
sowing ['souiŋ], *n.* semailles, *f.pl.*, ensemencement, *m.*
soya-bean ['sɔiə'bi:n], *n.* soya, soja, *m.*
spa [spɑ:], *n.* source minérale; ville d'eaux, *f.*
space [speis], *n.* espace, *m.*, étendue; place, *f.*; intervalle, *m.*—*v.t.* (*Print.*) espacer.
space ship ['speiʃip], *n.* astronef, *m.*
space suit ['speissju:t], *n.* combinaison spatiale, *f.*
space travel ['speistrævl], *n.* astronautique, *f.*, voyages interplanétaires, *m.pl.*
space traveller ['speistrævlə], *n.* astronaute, cosmonaute, *m., f.*
spacing ['speisiŋ], *n.* espacement; (*Print.*) interligne, *m.*
spacious ['speiʃəs], *a.* spacieux, vaste.
spaciously ['speiʃəsli], *adv.* spacieusement; amplement.
spaciousness ['speiʃəsnis], *n.* vaste étendue, *f.*
spade [speid], *n.* bêche, pelle (*d'enfant*), *f.*; (*Cards*) pique, *m.*
spadeful ['speidful], *n.* pelletée, *f.*
Spain [spein]. l'Espagne, *f.*
span [spæn], *n.* empan, *m.*; envergure (*d'ailes*), *f.*; moment, instant, *m.*—*v.t.* mesurer; embrasser; traverser.
spangle ['spæŋgl], *n.* paillette, *f.*—*v.t.* pailleter (*de*).
Spaniard ['spænjəd], *n.* Espagnol, *m.*
spaniel ['spænjəl], *n.* épagneul, *m.*
Spanish ['spæniʃ], *a.* espagnol, d'Espagne.—*n.* espagnol (*langue*), *m.*
spank [spæŋk], *v.t.* fesser.—*n.* (*also* spanking (1) ['spæŋkiŋ]) fessée, *f.*
spanking (2) ['spæŋkiŋ], *a.* vigoureux; rapide (*pas*).
spanner ['spænə], *n.* clef à écrous, *f.*; adjustable spanner, clef anglaise, *f.*
spar [spɑ:], *n.* perche, *f.*, poteau (*Naut.*) espar; (*Box.*) combat d'entraînement, *m.*—*v.i.* faire un assaut amical (*de boxe* ou *de paroles*); se disputer.
spare [speə], *v.t.* épargner; ménager; économiser (*dépenser avec précaution*); se passer de (*se priver de*); donner, céder; prêter.—*a.* disponible, de reste (*superflu*); libre (*temps*); (*Motor, etc.*) de rechange; modique, faible, pauvre; maigre, sec (*taille*).
spareness ['speənis], *n.* maigreur, *f.*
spare-rib ['speə'rib], *n.* côte de porc, *f.*
sparing ['speəriŋ], *a.* économe, ménager, frugal, sobre (*de*); parcimonieux.
sparingly ['speəriŋli], *adv.* frugalement, avec parcimonie; économiquement.
sparingness ['speəriŋnis], *n.* frugalité, épargne, parcimonie, *f.*
spark [spɑ:k], *n.* étincelle; (*fig.*) lueur, *f.*—*v.i.* produire des étincelles.
spark plug ['spɑ:kiŋplʌg], *n.* (*Motor.*) bougie (d'allumage), *f.*
sparkle ['spɑ:kl], *n.* étincellement, éclat, *m.*; vivacité (*d'esprit*), *f.*—*v.i.* étinceler, scintiller; pétiller (*boisson*).
sparkling ['spɑ:kliŋ], *a.* étincelant; mousseux (*boisson*).
sparling ['spɑ:liŋ], *n.* (*Ichth.*) éperlan, *m.*
sparrow ['spærou], *n.* moineau, passereau, *m.*
sparrow hawk ['spærouhɔ:k], *n.* épervier, *m.*

sparse [spɑ:s], *a.* épars; éparpillé, clairsemé.
sparsely ['spɑ:sli], *adv.* d'une manière éparse, de loin en loin.
sparseness ['spɑ:snis], *n.* rareté, *f.*; éparpillement, *m.*
Sparta ['spɑ:tə]. Sparte, *f.*
Spartan ['spɑ:tən], *a.* spartiate.—*n.* Spartiate (*personne*), *m., f.*
spasm [spæzm], *n.* spasme, accès, *m.*
spasmodic [spæz'mɔdik], spasmodical [spæz'mɔdikəl], *a.* spasmodique.
spasmodically [spæz'mɔdikəli], *adv.* par à-coups.
spastic ['spæstik], *a.* spasmodique.—*n.* paraplégique, *m., f.*
spat (1) [spæt], *past and p.p.* [SPIT].
spat (2) [spæt], *n.* guêtre de ville, *f.*
spate [speit], *n.* crue (*de rivière*); (*fig.*) affluence, *f.*
spatter ['spætə], *v.t.* éclabousser (*de*).
spatula ['spætjulə], *n.* spatule, *f.*
spavin ['spævin], *n.* éparvin, *m.*
spawn [spɔ:n], *n.* frai, *m.*; (*fig.*) race, engeance, *f.*—*v.t.* (*fig.*) engendrer.—*v.i.* frayer; (*fig.*) naître.
spawning ground ['spɔ:niŋgraund], *n.* frayère, *f.*
speak [spi:k], *v.t. irr.* parler; dire; (*Naut.*) héler; to speak one's mind, dire sa pensée.—*v.i.* parler; causer (*avec*); faire un discours (*en public*); dire; so to speak, pour ainsi dire; to speak out, parler à haute voix; to speak up, parler plus fort.
speaker ['spi:kə], *n.* personne qui parle, *f.*; orateur, (*Parl.*) président; (*Rad.* – loudspeaker) haut-parleur, *m.*
speaking ['spi:kiŋ], *a.* parlant, qui parle.—*n.* parole, *f.*, langage, discours, *m.*
speaking-tube ['spi:kiŋtju:b], *n.* tuyau *ou* tube acoustique, *m.*
spear [spiə], *n.* lance, *f.*—*v.t.* percer d'un coup de lance; harponner (*poisson etc.*).
spear-head ['spiəhed], *n.* fer de lance, *m.*; (*Mil.*) avancée, pointe, *f.*
spearman ['spiəmən], *n.* (*pl.* -men [men]) lancier, *m.*
spearmint ['spiəmint], *n.* menthe verte, *f.*
special ['speʃl], *a.* spécial, exprès; extraordinaire. [special delivery, see express]
specialist ['speʃəlist], *n.* spécialiste, *m., f.*
speciality [speʃi'æliti], specialty ['speʃəlti], *n.* spécialité, *f.*
specialization [speʃəlai'zeiʃən], *n.* spécialisation, *f.*
specialize ['speʃəlaiz], *v.i.* se spécialiser.
specially ['speʃəli], *adv.* particulièrement, surtout.
specie ['spi:ʃi], *n.* espèces, *f.pl.*, numéraire, *m.*
species ['spi:ʃi:z], *n.* espèce, *f.*; (*fig.*) genre, *m.*, sorte, *f.*
specific [spi'sifik], *a.* spécifique; précis.
specification [spesifi'keiʃən], *n.* spécification; description précise (*de brevet d'invention*), *f.*
specify ['spesifai], *v.t.* spécifier, déterminer; fixer d'avance (*une heure*).
specimen ['spesimən], *n.* spécimen, modèle, échantillon, *m.*
specious ['spi:ʃəs], *a.* spécieux, captieux.
speciousness ['spi:ʃəsnis], *n.* spéciosité, apparence plausible, *f.*

speck [spek], *n.* petite tache, marque, *f.*, point; grain (*de poussière*), *m.—v.t.* tacher, marquer.

speckle ['spekl], *v.t.* tacheter, marqueter, moucheter (*de*).—*n.* moucheture (*peau d'animal*), *f.*

speckled ['spekld], *a.* tacheté, marqueté, moucheté.

spectacle ['spektəkl], *n.* spectacle, *m.*; (*pl.*) lunettes, *f.pl.*

spectacle case ['spektəklkeis], *n.* étui à lunettes, *m.*

spectacle maker ['spektəklmeikə], *n.* lunetier, *m.*

spectacular [spek'tækjulə], *a.* théâtral, impressionnant.

spectator [spek'teitə], *n.* spectateur, *m.*; (*pl.*) assistants, *m.pl.*

specter ['spektə], *n.* spectre, fantôme, *m.*

spectral ['spektrəl], *a.* de spectre, spectral.

spectroscope ['spektrəskoup], *n.* spectroscope, *m.*

spectrum ['spektrəm], *n.* (*pl.* spectra ['spektrə]) spectre, *m.*

speculate ['spekjuleit], *v.i.* spéculer (*sur*), méditer (*sur*).

speculation [spekju'leiʃən], *n.* spéculation, méditation, *f.*

speculative ['spekjulətiv], *a.* spéculatif, contemplatif; (*Comm.*) spéculateur.

speculatively ['spekjulətivli], *adv.* en théorie.

speculator ['spekjuleitə], *n.* spéculateur, *m.*

speech [spi:tʃ], *n.* parole, *f.*; discours, *m.*, allocution (*public*); langue (*parler*), *f.*; **extempore speech**, improvisation, *f.*; (*Parl.*) **maiden speech**, discours de début.

speech-day ['spi:tʃdei], *n.* (*Sch.*) distribution des prix, *f.*

speechless ['spi:tʃlis], *a.* sans voix; muet, interdit.

speechlessness ['spi:tʃlisnis], *n.* mutisme, *m.*

speed [spi:d], *n.* vitesse, rapidité, célérité; hâte, diligence, promptitude, *f.*; (*fig.*) succès, *m.*; **God-speed!** bon succès! bonne chance!—*v.t. irr.* expédier, hâter; faire réussir (*faciliter*).—*v.i.* se hâter, se dépêcher.

speed-boat ['spi:dbout], *n.* motoglisseur, *m.*; hors-bord, *m.inv.*

speedily ['spi:dili], *adv.* vite, en toute hâte.

speediness ['spi:dinis], *n.* célérité, hâte, *f.*

speed limit ['spi:dlimit], *n.* limitation de vitesse, *f.*

speedometer [spi:'dɔmitə], *n.* indicateur de vitesse, tachymètre, *m.*

speedwell ['spi:dwel], *n.* (*Bot.*) véronique, *f.*

speedy ['spi:di], *a.* rapide, vite, prompt.

spell (1) [spel], *n.* temps, *m.*, période, *f.*; tour (*de service*), *m.*

spell (2) [spel], *n.* charme, *m.—v.t., v.i. irr.* épeler (*nommer les lettres*); orthographier (*écrire correctement*); signifier.

spell-bound ['spelbaund], *a.* charmé, fasciné.

speller ['spelə], *n.* personne qui orthographie *ou* qui épèle, *f.*

spelling ['speliŋ], *n.* orthographe; épellation, *f.*

spelling bee ['speliŋbi:], *n.* concours orthographique, *m.*

spelling book ['speliŋbuk], *n.* abécédaire, syllabaire, *m.*

spelter ['speltə], *n.* zinc, *m.*

spend [spend], *v.t. irr.* dépenser; gaspiller, perdre (*prodiguer*); passer (*temps*).—*v.i.* dépenser; se perdre (*se dissiper*); se consumer.

spending ['spendiŋ], *n.* action de dépenser, dépense, *f.*

spendthrift ['spendθrift], *n.* prodigue, *m.*, *f.*, dissipateur, *m.*

spent [spent], *a.* épuisé; mort (*balle etc.*).

sperm [spə:m], *n.* sperme; frai (*poisson etc.*); blanc de baleine, *m.*

spew [spju:], *v.t., v.i.* vomir.

spewing ['spju:iŋ], *n.* vomissement, *m.*

sphere [sfiə], *n.* sphère, *f.*

spherical ['sferikl], *a.* sphérique.

spherics ['sferiks], *n.pl.* théorie de la sphère, *f.*

spheroid ['sfiərɔid], *n.* sphéroïde, *m.*

sphinx [sfiŋks], *n.* (*pl.* sphinxes ['sfiŋksiz]) sphinx, *m.*

spice [spais], *n.* épice, *f.—v.t.* épicer (*de*).

spiciness ['spaisinis], *n.* goût épicé, *m.*

spick-and-span ['spikənd'spæn], *a.* tiré à quatre épingles; bien astiqué.

spicy ['spaisi], *a.* épicé, aromatique, parfumé.

spider ['spaidə], *n.* araignée, *f.*

spigot ['spigət], *n.* fausset; (*Am., Sc.*) robinet, *m.*

spike [spaik], *n.* pointe, *f.*; clou à grosse tête (*de métal*), *m.*; cheville (*de bois*), *f.*; **marline-spike**, épissoir, *m.—v.t.* clouer; hérisser. [see **stiletto heels**]

spiked [spaikt], *a.* à pointes, barbelé.

spikenard ['spaiknɑ:d], *n.* nard indien, *m.*

spiky ['spaiki], *a.* à pointe aiguë; armé de pointes.

spill (1) [spil], *v.t. irr.* répandre, verser; renverser.—*v.i.* se verser, se répandre.—*n.* culbute (*renversement*), *f.*

spill (2) [spil], *n.* allumette de papier, allumette en copeau, *f.*

spin [spin], *v.t. irr.* filer; faire tourner.—*v.i.* filer (*aller vite*); tourner.—*n.* tournoiement, *m.*; (*Av.*) vrille, *f.*; (*Motor.*) tour, *m.*; promenade, *f.*

spinach ['spinidʒ], *n.* épinards, *m.pl.*

spinal ['spainl], *a.* spinal; **spinal column**, colonne vertébrale, *f.*

spindle [spindl], *n.* fuseau; pivot; (*Mach.*) essieu; (*Tech.*) axe, *m.*

spindleful ['spindlful], *n.* fusée, *f.*

spindle-legs ['spindllegz], **spindle-shanks** ['spindlʃæŋks], *n.pl.* jambes de fuseau, *f.pl.*

spindrift ['spindrift], *n.* embrun, *m.*

spine [spain], *n.* épine dorsale; (*Bot.*) épine, *f.*

spineless ['spainlis], *a.* sans épines; (*fig.*) mou, flasque, invertébré.

spinet ['spinit, spi'net], *n.* épinette, *f.*

spinner ['spinə], *n.* fileur, *m.*

spinney ['spini], *n.* petit bois, bosquet, *m.*

spinning ['spiniŋ], *a.* tournoyant, tournant.—*n.* filage (*processus*), *m.*; filature (*art*), *f.*; tournoiement, *m.*

spinning machine ['spiniŋmə'ʃi:n], *n.* machine à filer, *f.*

spinning mill ['spiniŋmil], *n.* filature, *f.*

spinning top ['spiniŋtɔp], *n.* toupie, *f.*

spinning wheel ['spiniŋwi:l], *n.* rouet, *m.*

spinous ['spainəs], *a.* épineux.

spinster ['spinstə], *n.* fille non mariée, célibataire, *f.*

spinsterhood ['spinstəhud], *n.* célibat, *m.*

spiny ['spaini], *a.* épineux, couvert d'épines; (*fig.*) difficile.

spiraea

spiraea [spai'ri:ə], *n.* (*Bot.*) spirée, *f.*
spiral ['spaiərəl], *a.* spiral; en colimaçon
(*escalier*).—*n.* spirale, *f.*—*v.i.* monter en
spirale.
spirally ['spaiərəli], *adv.* en spirale.
spire ['spaiə], *n.* aiguille, flèche, *f.*
spirit (1) ['spirit], *n.* esprit, *m.*, âme, *f.*, fantôme, spectre (*apparition*), *m.*—*v.t.* **to
spirit away**, faire disparaître.
spirit (2) ['spirit], **spiritedness** ['spiritidnis],
n. (*fig.*) ardeur, force, vigueur, *f.*, feu, élan,
entrain, *m.*; fougue (*d'un cheval*); verve,
bonne humeur, *f.*, entrain, courage, *m.*—*v.t.*
animer, encourager.
spirit (3) ['spirit], *n.* (*sing.* ou *pl.*) spiritueux,
m. inv.; liqueur spiritueuse ou alcoolique, *f.*;
esprit (*de vin etc.*), *m.*; **methylated spirit**,
alcool à brûler, *m.*
spirited ['spiritid], *a.* animé, plein de cœur,
plein de vivacité; vif, plein de verve; fougueux (*cheval*).
spiritedly ['spiritidli], *adv.* avec ardeur,
chaleureusement, avec force, avec entrain.
spiritedness [SPIRIT (2)].
spirit lamp ['spiritlæmp], *n.* lampe à alcool,
f.
spiritless ['spiritlis], *a.* sans vigueur, mou,
énervé; sans courage; abattu (*découragé*).
spirit level ['spiritlevl], *n.* niveau à bulle
d'air, *m.*
spiritual ['spiritjuəl], *a.* spirituel.—*n.* chant
religieux (des Noirs), *m.*
spiritualism ['spiritjuəlizm], *n.* spiritisme
(*communication avec les esprits*), *m.*
spiritualist ['spiritjuəlist], *n.* spirite (*adepte
du spiritisme*), *m.*, *f.*
spiritualize ['spiritjuəlaiz], *v.t.* spiritualiser.
spirituous ['spiritjuəs], *a.* spiritueux.
spiry ['spaiəri], *a.* en flèche, élancé.
spit (1) [spit], *n.* broche; profondeur de
bêche (*plongée dans la terre*), *f.*—*v.t.* embrocher, mettre à la broche.
spit (2) [spit], *n.* crachat, *m.*, salive, *f.*—*v.t.
irr.* cracher.—*v.i.* cracher (*sur* ou *à*).
spite [spait], **spitefulness** ['spaitfulnis], *n.*
dépit, *m.*; rancune, malveillance, *f.*; **in
spite of**, en dépit de, malgré; **out of spite**,
par dépit; **to have a spite against**, en
vouloir à.—*v.t.* vexer, blesser, contrarier.
spiteful ['spaitful], *a.* rancunier, malveillant,
vindicatif.
spitefully ['spaitfuli], *adv.* par dépit, par
rancune.
spitefulness [SPITE].
spitfire ['spitfaiə], *n.* rageur, *m.*
spitter ['spitə], *n.* cracheur, *m.*
spitting ['spitiŋ], *n.* crachement, *m.*
spittle [spitl], *n.* salive, *f.*; (*colloq.*) crachat, *m.*
splash [splæʃ], *v.t.* éclabousser.—*v.i.* éclabousser; clapoter (*vagues*); patauger.—*n.*
éclaboussure, *f.*; clapotement, clapotis (*des
vagues*); flac (*bruit*), *m.*
splashing ['splæʃiŋ], *n.* éclaboussement (*acte*),
m.; éclaboussure (*ce qui rejaillit*), *f.*
splashy ['splæʃi], *a.* éclaboussé, bourbeux.
splay [splei], *v.t.* évaser; (*Arch.*) ébraser;
épauler (*cheval*).—*n.* écartement, (*Arch.*)
ébrasement, *m.*
splay-footed ['spleifutid], *a.* aux pieds plats
et tournés en dehors.
spleen [spli:n], *n.* rate, *f.*; (*fig.*) fiel, *m.*,
animosité, *f.*; spleen, *m.*, mélancolie, *f.*

splendid ['splendid], *a.* resplendissant,
somptueux, magnifique.
splendidly ['splendidli], *adv.* avec éclat,
magnifiquement.
splendor ['splendə], *n.* splendeur, *f.*, éclat,
m.
splenetic [splə'netik], *a.* splénétique, atrabilaire.
splice [splais], *n.* épissure, *f.*, raccordement,
m.—*v.t.* épisser; (*Carp.*) joindre.
splint [splint], *n.* éclisse, attelle, *f.*—*v.t.*
éclisser.
splinter ['splintə], *n.* éclat, éclat de bois, *m.*—
v.t. briser en éclats.—*v.i.* voler en éclats.
splintery ['splintəri], *a.* plein d'éclats, esquil-
leux.
split [split], *a.* fendu; **split personality**,
dédoublement de la personnalité, *m.*; **split
pin**, goupille, *f.*—*n.* fente; (*fig.*) scission, *f.*
—*v.t. irr.* fendre; diviser, partager.—*v.i.* se
fendre; se quereller.
split-second ['splitsekənd], *a.* ultra-rapide.
splitting ['splitiŋ], *n.* fendage, *m.*; **splitting
of the atom**, fission de l'atome, *f.*
splotch [splɔtʃ], *n.* grosse tache, *f.*, barbouillage, *m.*
splutter ['splʌtə], *v.i.* bredouiller, cracher
(*plume* ou *graisse*).—*n.* or **spluttering**
['splʌtəriŋ], bredouillement, crachage, *m.*
spoil [spɔil], *v.t. irr.* gâter, abimer; dépouiller
(*de*); ravager (*piller*).—*v.i.* se gâter, s'abimer.
—*n.* butin, *m.*, dépouille, *f.*, pillage, *m.*
spoiled [spɔild], *a.* gâté.
spoiler ['spɔilə], *n.* personne qui gâte, *f.*;
spoliateur (*pilleur*), *m.*
spoiling ['spɔiliŋ], *n.* action de gâter; avarie, *f.*
spoil-sport ['spɔilspɔːt], *n.* trouble-fête, *m.*
spoke [spouk], *n.* rais, rayon, *m.*
spoke-shave ['spoukʃeiv], *n.* (*Carp.*) plane, *f.*
spokesman ['spouksmən] (*pl.* **-men** [men]),
spokeswoman ['spoukswumən] (*pl.*
-women [wimin]), *n.* porte-parole, *m.inv.*
spoliate ['spoulieit], *v.t.* spolier, piller.
spoliation [spouli'eiʃən], *n.* spoliation, *f.*
sponge [spʌndʒ], *n.* éponge, *f.*; (*Artill.*)
écouvillon, *m.*—*v.t.* éponger; (*Artill.*)
écouvillonner.—*v.i.* **to sponge on**, vivre
aux dépens de.
sponge cake ['spʌndʒkeik], *n.* gâteau de
Savoie, *m.*
sponger ['spʌndʒə], *n.* pique-assiette, parasite, *m.*
sponginess ['spʌndʒinis], *n.* nature spon-
gieuse, *f.*
sponging ['spʌndʒiŋ], *n.* épongement, *m.*;
(*fig.*) corniflerie, *f.*
spongy ['spʌndʒi], *a.* spongieux.
sponsor ['spɔnsə], *n.* parrain, *m.*, marraine, *f.*;
garant (*qui cautionne*), *f.*—*v.t.* répondre
pour; parrainer.
sponsorship ['spɔnsəʃip], *n.* parrainage, *m.*
spontaneity [spɔntə'ni:iti], *n.* spontanéité, *f.*
spontaneous [spɔn'teiniəs], *a.* spontané.
spontaneously [spɔn'teiniəsli], *adv.* spontanément.
spool [spu:l], *n.* bobine, *f.*
spoon [spu:n], *n.* cuiller, cuillère, *f.*
spoonbill ['spu:nbil], *n.* (*Orn.*) palette, *f.*
spoonful ['spu:nful], *n.* cuillerée, *f.*
spoor [spuə], *n.* trace, *f.*, empreintes, *f.pl.*
sporadic [spə'rædik], *a.* sporadique.
spore [spɔː], *n.* spore, *f.*

sport [spɔːt], n. jeu, divertissement, amusement, m.; moquerie, raillerie, f.; jouet; sport, m.—v.t. faire parade de.—v.i. se divertir, s'amuser.

sporting ['spɔːtiŋ], a. de sport; sportif.

sportive ['spɔːtiv], a. badin, folâtre.

sportively ['spɔːtivli], adv. en badinant.

sportiveness ['spɔːtivnis], n. folâtrerie, f.

sportsman ['spɔːtsmən], n. (pl. -men [men]) sportif, sportsman, m.

sportsmanship ['spɔːtsmənʃip], n. sportivité, f.

spot [spɔt], n. tache, f.; endroit, lieu, m.; on the spot, sur place, sur-le-champ.—v.t. tacheter, moucheter; tacher; (fam.) repérer; (colloq.) observer.

spot-check ['spɔt'tʃek], n. contrôle-surprise, m.

spotless ['spɔtlis], a. sans tache; (fig.) immaculé, pur, irréprochable.

spotlessness ['spɔtlisnis], n. pureté, f.

spotted ['spɔtid], a. tacheté, moucheté; truité.

spotter ['spɔtə], n. (Mil. Av.) observateur, m.

spotty ['spɔti], a. couvert de taches, moucheté, tacheté.

spouse [spauz], n. époux, m., épouse, f.; mari, m., femme, f.

spout [spaut], n. tuyau, m.; gouttière (de maison), f.; bec (de cruche etc.), m.—v.i. jaillir; (fam.) déclamer.

spouter ['spautə], n. (fam.) déclamateur, m.

spouting ['spautiŋ], n. jaillissement, m.; déclamation, f.

sprain [sprein], n. entorse, foulure, f.—v.t. fouler; se faire une entorse à.

sprat [spræt], n. esprot, sprat, m.

sprawl [sprɔːl], v.i. s'étendre, s'étaler.

spray [sprei], n. branche, ramille (d'arbrisseau etc.), f.; embrun, m.; poussière (d'eau), f.; vaporisateur, m.—v.t. pulvériser, vaporiser, asperger.

spread [spred], v.t. irr. étendre, déployer; répandre; couvrir (table); mettre (nappe); tendre (voiles etc.).—v.i. s'étendre, se déployer; se répandre, se propager.—n. étendue, envergure (ailes), f.; (fam.) festin (banquet), m.

spreading ['sprediŋ], a. étendu, qui se répand.

spree [spriː], n. (colloq.) bamboche, bombe, f.

sprig [sprig], n. brin, m., brindille; pointe (clou), f.

sprightliness ['spraitlinis], n. vivacité, f., entrain, m.

sprightly ['spraitli], a. enjoué, vif, animé, gai.

spring [spriŋ], v.t. irr. to spring a leak, faire une voie d'eau; to spring upon, présenter à l'improviste . . . à.—v.i. bondir, s'élancer; jaillir (sourdre); pousser, naître (se développer); paraître, poindre (jour); provenir, découler, descendre (avoir pour ancêtres).—n. saut, bond, élan; ressort (élasticité), m.; source; cause, origine, f.; printemps, m.; (pl.) suspension (de voiture), f.

spring-board ['spriŋbɔːd], n. tremplin, m.

springiness ['spriŋinis], n. élasticité, f.

springlike ['spriŋlaik], a. printanier.

spring tide ['spriŋtaid], n. grande marée, f.

springy ['spriŋi], a. élastique.

sprinkle [spriŋkl], v.t. répandre; arroser (de), asperger (de) (eau bénite); saupoudrer (de).

sprinkler ['spriŋklə], n. (Eccles.) aspersoir, m.; (Hort.) arroseuse à jet tournant, f.

sprinkling ['spriŋkliŋ], n. arrosage, m.; (Eccles.) aspersion, f.; (fig.) petit nombre, m.

sprint [sprint], n. sprint, m.—v.i. courir à toute vitesse.

sprinter ['sprintə], n. coureur de vitesse, sprinter, m.

sprite [sprait], n. esprit follet, lutin, m.

sprout [spraut], n. pousse, f., jet, rejeton, m.; Brussels sprouts, choux de Bruxelles, m.pl.—v.i. pousser, bourgeonner (plantes).

sprouting ['sprautiŋ], n. germination, f.

spruce (1) [spruːs], a. paré, bien mis, pimpant.—v.t. attifer.

spruce (2) [spruːs], n. sapin (arbre), m.

spry [sprai], a. alerte, plein d'entrain.

spunk [spʌŋk], n. amadou; (colloq.) cœur, courage, m.

spur [spəː], n. éperon; ergot (de coq etc.); (fig.) aiguillon, stimulant, m.—v.t. éperonner; stimuler.

spurious ['spjuəriəs], a. faux, falsifié.

spuriousness ['spjuəriəsnis], n. fausseté, f.

spurn [spəːn], v.t. repousser, écarter (du pied); mépriser.—n. mépris, dédain, m.

spurred [spəːd], a. éperonné.

spurt [spəːt], v.t. faire jaillir.—v.i. s'élancer; (Spt.) démarrer.—n. jaillissement; (fig.) effort soudain; (Spt.) démarrage, m.

sputnik ['spʌtnik, 'sputnik], n. spoutnik, m.

sputter ['spʌtə], v.i. cracher; bredouiller.—n. salive, f.

sputtering ['spʌtəriŋ], n. bredouillement, m.

sputum ['spjuːtəm], n. crachat, m.

spy [spai], n. espion, m.—v.t. scruter; apercevoir.—v.i. épier, espionner.

spy-glass ['spaiglɑːs], n. longue-vue, f.

spying ['spaiiŋ], n. espionnage, m.

spy ring ['spairiŋ], spy system ['spaisistəm], n. espionnage, m.

squabble [skwɔbl], n. dispute, querelle, f.—v.i. se chamailler.

squabbler ['skwɔblə], n. querelleur, m.

squad [skwɔd], n. (Mil.) peloton, m.; (Rail.) brigade; équipe (de sauvetage etc.), f.

squadron ['skwɔdrən], n. (Mil.) escadron, m.; (Av.) escadrille; (Naut.) escadre, f.

squadron leader ['skwɔdrənliːdə], n. (Av.) commandant, m.

squalid ['skwɔlid], a. malpropre, sale.

squalidness [SQUALOR].

squall [skwɔːl], n. cri; coup de vent, m., bourrasque, rafale (de vent), f.—v.i. crier, brailler.

squalling ['skwɔːliŋ], a. criard, braillard.—n. criaillerie, f.

squally ['skwɔːli], a. à grains, à rafales.

squalor ['skwɔlə], squalidness ['skwɔlidnis], n. malpropreté, f.

squamous ['skweiməs], a. squameux; écailleux.

squander ['skwɔndə], v.t. dissiper, gaspiller.

squanderer ['skwɔndərə], n. gaspilleur, m., prodigue, m., f.

squandering ['skwɔndəriŋ], n. gaspillage, m.

square [skweə], a. carré; soldé (comptes etc.); (fig.) équitable, juste; de superficie (mesure). —n. carré; carreau (de verre etc.), m.; case (d'échiquier); place (dans une ville); place d'armes (de ville de garnison), f., parvis (devant une église), m.—v.t. carrer; (Carp.)

équarrir; balancer (comptes); (fig.) régler, ajuster.—v.i. cadrer, s'accorder (avec).

square-built ['skweəbilt], a. aux épaules carrées.

squarely ['skweəli], adv. carrément; (fig.) justement.

squareness ['skweənis], n. forme carrée, f.

squaring ['skweəriŋ], n. équarrissage, m.; *squaring of the circle*, quadrature du cercle, f.

squarish ['skweəriʃ], a. à peu près carré.

squash [skwɔʃ], v.t. écraser, aplatir; (fig.) rembarrer (personne).—n. écrasement (aplatissement), m.; foule serrée (de gens), f.; *lemon squash*, citronnade, f.

squashy ['skwɔʃi], a. mou et humide.

squat [skwɔt], a. accroupi, blotti; trapu, ramassé (courtaud).—v.i. s'accroupir; se blottir; (Am.) s'établir (sans droit).

squatter ['skwɔtə], n. personne accroupie, f.; colon (sans droit), m.

squatting ['skwɔtiŋ], n. accroupissement, m.

squaw [skwɔ:], n. femme peau-rouge, f.

squawk [skwɔ:k], n. cri rauque; couac, m.—v.i. pousser des cris rauques.

squeak [skwi:k], n. petit cri aigu, m.—v.i. pousser des cris aigus; jurer (instrument de musique).

squeaking ['skwi:kiŋ], a. criard; qui jure (instrument de musique).

squeal [skwi:l], v.i. pousser des cris perçants.—n. cri perçant, m.

squeamish ['skwi:miʃ], a. qui se soulève (l'estomac); trop délicat, difficile (scrupuleux).

squeamishly ['skwi:miʃli], adv. avec dégoût.

squeamishness ['skwi:miʃnis], n. délicatesse exagérée, f., goût difficile, m.

squeeze [skwi:z], n. compression; cohue, f.—v.t. serrer, presser; *to squeeze money out of*, extorquer de l'argent à; *to squeeze out*, exprimer; *to squeeze through*, forcer à travers.—v.i. *to squeeze through*, se forcer à travers.

squeezing ['skwi:ziŋ], n. étreinte, compression, f.; serrement (de la main), m.

squelch [skweltʃ], v.t. écraser, aplatir.

squib [skwib], n. pétard, m.; (fig.) satire, f.

squill [skwil], n. scille (plante), f.

squint [skwint], a. louche.—n. regard louche, m.—v.i. loucher.

squinting ['skwintiŋ], a. louche.—n. action de loucher, f., strabisme, m.

squire ['skwaiə], n. écuyer; châtelain; cavalier servant (d'une dame), m.—v.t. escorter (une dame).

squireen [skwaiə'ri:n], n. hobereau, m.

squirm [skwə:m], v.i. se tortiller, se tordre (de douleur ou d'embarras).

squirrel ['skwirəl], n. écureuil, m.

squirt [skwə:t], n. seringue, f.—v.t. seringuer, faire jaillir.—v.i. jaillir.

stab [stæb], n. coup de poignard, de couteau etc., m.—v.t. poignarder.

stabbing ['stæbiŋ], a. lancinant.—n. coup de poignard, m.

stability [stə'biliti], n. stabilité, solidité; (fig.) fermeté, f.

stabilization [steibilai'zeiʃən], n. stabilisation, f. [see **tail-plane**]

stabilize ['steibilaiz], v.t. stabiliser.

stable (1) [steibl], a. stable, fixe, solide; (fig.) constant.

stable (2) [steibl], n. écurie, f.—v.t. loger (chevaux); établer (bétail).

stable-boy ['steiblbɔi], **stableman** ['steiblmən] (pl. -men [men]), n. garçon d'écurie, m.

stabling ['steibliŋ], n. écuries (pour chevaux) étables (pour bétail), f.pl.

staccato [stə'kɑ:tou], a. saccadé.—adv. en staccato.

stack [stæk], n. souche (d'une cheminée); pile, f., tas (de charbon, de bois), m.; meule (de foin etc.), f.—v.t. empiler (bois); emmeuler (foin etc.).

stacking ['stækiŋ], n. emmeulage, empilage, entassement, m.

stack-yard ['stækjɑ:d], n. cour de ferme, f.

stadium ['steidiəm], n. stade, m.

staff [stɑ:f], n. (pl. **staves** [steivz]) bâton, bourdon (de pèlerin), m.; hampe (à drapeau), f.; (pl. **staffs**) corps, personnel; (Mil.) état-major, m.; *to be on the staff*, être attaché à, faire partie du personnel de.—v.t. fournir le personnel de.

staff officer ['stɑ:fɔfisə], n. officier d'état-major, m.

stag [stæg], n. cerf, m.

stag beetle ['stægbi:tl], n. (Ent.) cerf-volant, lucane, m.

stage [steidʒ], n. estrade (dans une salle); (Theat.) scène, f.; (fig.) théâtre, m.; étape (voyage), f.; (fig.) degré, m., phase, période, f.—v.t. *to stage a play*, monter une pièce.

stage-coach ['steidʒkoutʃ], n. diligence, f.

stage door ['steidʒ'dɔ:], n. entrée des artistes, f.

stage effect ['steidʒifekt], n. effet scénique, m.

stage-hand ['steidʒhænd], n. machiniste, m.

stage manager ['steidʒ'mænidʒə], n. régisseur, m.

stage properties ['steidʒ'prɔpətiz], n.pl. accessoires de théâtre, m.pl.

stage set ['steidʒset], n. décor, m.

stagger ['stægə], v.t. faire chanceler; (fig.) étonner; échelonner (heures, vacances etc.).—v.i. chanceler.

staggering ['stægəriŋ], a. chancelant; incertain.—n. chancellement; échelonnage, m.

stagnancy ['stægnənsi], n. stagnation, f.

stagnant ['stægnənt], a. stagnant; (fig.) inactif, mort.

stagnate [stæg'neit], v.i. être stagnant.

stagnation [STAGNANCY].

staid [steid], a. posé, sérieux, grave.

staidness ['steidnis], n. gravité, f.

stain [stein], n. tache; (Paint.) teinte; (fig.) honte, f., opprobre (disgrâce), m.—v.t. tacher (de); (fig.) souiller; (Dyeing) teindre.—v.i. se tacher.

stained [steind], a. taché; (fig.) souillé; (Dyeing) teint; *stained glass*, vitrail, m.

stainer ['steinə], n. teinturier, m.

staining ['steiniŋ], n. teinture, f.

stainless ['steinlis], a. sans tache; inoxydable (acier).

stair [steə], n. marche, f.; degré; (pl.) escalier, m.

staircase ['steəkeis], n. escalier, m.; cage d'escalier, f.; *back staircase*, escalier de service; *moving staircase*, escalier roulant.

stair-rod ['stɛərɔd], *n.* tringle (de tapis) d'escalier, *f.*

stake [steik], *n.* pieu, poteau, bûcher (de martyre); (*Cards etc.*) enjeu, *m.*, mise, *f.* —*v.t.* parier, gager; hasarder (*risquer*); **to stake out**, jalonner.

stalactite ['stælæktait], *n.* stalactite, *f.*

stalagmite ['stæləgmait], *n.* stalagmite, *f.*

stale [steil], *a.* vieux, rassis (*pain*); (*fig.*) suranné, passé, usé.

stalemate ['steilmeit], *v.t.* (*Chess*) faire pat.— *n.* pat, *m.*; (*fig.*) impasse, *f.*

staleness ['steilnis], *n.* vieillesse, *f.*; état rassis (*pain*), *m.*; banalité, *f.*

stalk [stɔːk], *n.* tige; queue (de fleur), *f.* trognon (de chou), *m.*; démarche fière (*allure*), *f.*—*v.t.* chasser à l'affût.—*v.i.* marcher fièrement.

stalker ['stɔːkə], *n.* chasseur à l'affût, *m.*

stalking ['stɔːkiŋ], *n.* (*Hunt.*) chasse à l'affût, *f.*

stall (1) [stɔːl], *n.* stalle (d'église ou d'écurie), étable (à bétail); écurie (à chevaux); échoppe, boutique, *f.*, étalage; (*Theat.*) fauteuil d'orchestre, *m.*

stall (2) [stɔːl], *v.t., v.i.* caler (*machine*).

stallion ['stæljən], *n.* étalon, *m.*

stalwart ['stɔːlwət], *a.* vigoureux, robuste, vaillant.

stamen ['steimen], *n.* étamine, *f.*

stamina ['stæminə], *n.* vigueur, résistance, *f.*

stammer ['stæmə], *v.t., v.i.* bégayer, balbutier.—*n.* bégaiement, *m.*

stammerer ['stæmərə], *n.* bègue, *m., f.*

stammering ['stæməriŋ], *a.* bègue.—*n.* bégaiement, *m.*

stamp [stæmp], *v.t.* frapper du pied; piétiner, empreindre, imprimer; contrôler (*garantir*); estamper (*pièce de monnaie*); timbrer (*documents, lettres etc.*); (*Metal.*) bocarder; estampiller (*marchandises*); affranchir (*payer d'avance*); poinçonner (*billet*).—*v.i.* trépigner, frapper du pied.—*n.* estampe (*outil*), *f.*; coin, poinçon, *m.*; empreinte, marque (*impression*), *f.*; poinçon de contrôle (*sur l'or*); timbre (*sur documents*); (*Metal.*) bocard, *m.*; (*Comm.*) estampille (*sur marchandises*), *f.*; (*fig.*) caractère, *m.*, trempe, *f.*; coup de pied, trépignement; timbre-poste, *m.*; **rubber stamp**, tampon, *m.*

stamp collecting ['stæmpkəlektiŋ], *n.* philatélie, *f.*

stamp collector ['stæmpkə'lektə], *n.* philatéliste, *m., f.*

stamp duty ['stæmp'djuːti], *n.* droit de timbre, *m.*

stampede [stæm'piːd], *n.* débandade, panique, *f.*—*v.i.* fuir en désordre.

stamping ['stæmpiŋ], *n.* contrôlage (*garantie*); timbrage (*Metal.*) bocardage; piétinement, trépignement (*des pieds*), *m.*

stamp machine ['stæmpmə'ʃiːn], *n.* distributeur automatique de timbres-poste, *m.*

stanch [stɑːntʃ], **staunch** [stɔːntʃ], *a.* solide, ferme; (*fig.*) sûr, dévoué.—*v.t.* étancher.

stauchion ['stɑːnʃən], *n.* étançon, étai, *m.*

stanchness [stɑːntʃnis], **staunchness** ['stɔːntʃnis], *n.* fermeté; constance, dévotion, *f.*

stand [stænd], *v.t. irr.* mettre debout, placer, poser; endurer, souffrir, supporter, soutenir; subir; résister à; payer (à boire).—*v.i.* se tenir; rester debout; se soutenir (*difficilement*); se placer, se mettre (*prendre place*);

être debout; se trouver, être (*bâtiment*); se maintenir (*ne pas lâcher pied*); se présenter (*comme candidat*); **stand by!** attention! **to stand aside**, se tenir à l'écart; **to stand by**, assister à (*être présent*); défendre, s'en tenir à (*un avis etc.*); se tenir prêt; **to stand down**, se retirer; **to stand firm**, tenir ferme, tenir bon; **to stand for**, soutenir; signifier; **to stand in for someone**, remplacer quelqu'un; **to stand out**, se dessiner (*être en relief*); résister; **to stand still**, s'arrêter, se tenir tranquille; **to stand up**, se lever.—*n.* arrêt, *m.*, halte, pause, *f.*; stand, étalage (*exposition etc.*); socle (à vases etc.), *m.*; (*fig.*) cessation, résistance, *f.*

standard ['stændəd], *a.* type, standard, normal; étalon; au titre (*argent*); classique (*livre*); (*Hort.*) en plein vent (*arbre*), sur tige (*roses*); régulateur (*prix*).—*n.* étendard, (*Naut.*) pavillon; étalon (de poids et mesures); titre (d'or et d'argent); (*fig.*) type, modèle; (*Hort.*) arbre en plein vent, *m.*

standard-bearer ['stændədbɛərə], *n.* porte-étendard, *m.*

standardization [stændədai'zeiʃən], *n.* étalonnage, *m.*; (*Comm.*) standardisation, *f.*

standardize ['stændədaiz], *v.t.* étalonner, standardiser.

stand-by ['stændbai], *n.* appui, soutien, *m.*, ressource, *f.*

stand-in ['stændin], *n.* remplaçant, *m.*

standing ['stændiŋ], *a.* stagnant; fixe; debout, sur pied (*non abattu*); (*fig.*) invariable.—*n.* position, *f.*; rang, *m.*; durée, date, *f.*, service, *m.*

stand-offish ['stænd'ɔfiʃ], *a.* réservé, distant.

stand-point ['stændpɔint], *n.* point de vue, *m.*

standstill ['stændstil], *n.* arrêt, *m.*

stand-to ['stænd'tuː], *n.* (*Mil.*) alerte, *f.*

stanza ['stænzə], *n.* stance, strophe, *f.*

staple (1) [steipl], *a.* établi; principal.—*n.* denrée principale (*marchandises*), *f.*; (*fig.*) fond, *m.*

staple (2) [steipl], *n.* agrafe; gâche (de serrure), *f.*—*v.t.* agrafer.

stapler ['steiplə], *n.* agrafeuse (*machine*), *f.*

star [stɑː], *n.* étoile, *f.*, astre, *m.*; (*Theat., Cine.*) vedette, *f.*—*v.t.* étoiler, parsemer d'étoiles; avoir comme vedettes.—*v.i.* tenir le premier rôle.

starboard ['stɑːbəd], *n.* tribord, *m.*

starch [stɑːtʃ], *n.* amidon, *m.*; fécule (*aliment*); (*fig.*) raideur, *f.*—*v.t.* empeser.

starchiness ['stɑːtʃinis], *n.* raideur, *f.*

starchy ['stɑːtʃi], *a.* féculent; empesé; (*fig.*) guindé.

stare [stɛə], *v.t.* dévisager.—*v.i.* regarder fixement; ouvrir de grands yeux (*être ébahi*).—*n.* regard fixe; regard ébahi, *m.*

starfish ['stɑːfiʃ], *n.* étoile de mer, *f.*

star-gazer ['stɑːgeizə], *n.* astrologue, *m., f.*; rêveur, *m.*

staring ['stɛəriŋ], *a.* voyant, tranchant (*couleur etc.*).

stark [stɑːk], *adv.* tout, tout à fait.—*a.* raide; stérile (*paysage*).

starless ['stɑːlis], *a.* sans étoiles.

starling ['stɑːliŋ], *n.* étourneau, sansonnet, *m.*

starlit ['stɑːlit], *a.* étoilé.

starry ['stɑːri], *a.* étoilé; (*fig.*) étincelant; **starry-eyed**, peu pratique.

start [stɑːt], *v.t.* commencer; faire lever (*gibier*); faire partir; mettre en marche (*machine*).—*v.i.* tressaillir (*de* ou *à*); partir (*s'en aller*); commencer, débuter; sursauter (*faire un bond*).—*n.* tressaillement; saut, bond; commencement, début; départ, *m.*; **to wake with a start**, se réveiller en sursaut.

starter ['stɑːtə], *n.* starter (*de course*); (*Motor.*) démarreur, *m.*

starting ['stɑːtiŋ], *n.* tressaillement; départ; commencement, début, *m.*; mise en marche (*de moteur etc.*), *f.*

starting-handle ['stɑːtiŋhændl], *n.* (*Motor.*) manivelle, *f.*

starting point ['stɑːtiŋpoint], *n.* point de départ, *m.*

starting post ['stɑːtiŋpoust], *n.* poteau de départ, *m.*

startle [stɑːtl], *v.t.* faire tressaillir, effrayer.

startling ['stɑːtliŋ], *a.* étonnant, saisissant.

starvation [stɑːˈveiʃən], *n.* inanition, faim, *f.*

starve [stɑːv], *v.t.* faire mourir de faim; affamer.—*v.i.* mourir de faim.

starveling ['stɑːvliŋ], *n.* affamé, meurt-de-faim, *m.*

starving ['stɑːviŋ], *a.* affamé, mourant de faim.

state [steit], *n.* état, *m.*, condition, *f.*; état (*organisme politique*); rang (*classe*), *m.*; pompe, *f.*, apparat (*pompe*), *m.*; **the United States**, les États-Unis, *m.pl.*—*v.t.* énoncer, déclarer.

state-controlled ['steitkənˈtrould], *a.* étatisé.

statecraft ['steitkrɑːft], *n.* politique, *f.*

stated ['steitid], *a.* réglé, fixe.

stateless ['steitlis], *a.* **stateless person**, apatride, *m.*, *f.*

stateliness ['steitlinis], *n.* majesté, grandeur, *f.*

stately ['steitli], *a.* imposant, majestueux, noble.—*adv.* majestueusement, avec dignité.

statement ['steitmənt], *n.* exposé, énoncé, rapport, *m.*; déclaration, *f.*

statesman ['steitsmən], *n.* (*pl.* **-men** [men]) homme d'État, *m.*

statesmanlike ['steitsmənlaik], *a.* d'homme d'État.

statesmanship ['steitsmənʃip], *n.* science du gouvernement, politique, *f.*

static ['stætik], **statical** ['stætikəl], *a.* statique.

station ['steiʃən], *n.* station, *f.*; rang (*classe*), *m.*; position; (*Rail.*) gare, *f.*; (*Mil.*) poste, *m.*, garnison, *f.*—*v.t.* placer; (*Mil.*) poster.

stationary ['steiʃənəri], *a.* stationnaire; fixe.

stationer ['steiʃənə], *n.* papetier, *m.*

stationery ['steiʃənəri], *n.* papeterie, *f.*

station wagon ['steiʃənwægən], *n.* (*Motor.*) canadienne, *f.*

statistic [stəˈtistik], **statistical** [stəˈtistikəl], *a.* statistique.

statistician [stætisˈtiʃən], *n.* statisticien, *m.*

statistics [stəˈtistiks], *n.pl.* statistique, *f.*

statuary ['stætjuəri], *n.* statuaire, *f.*

statue ['stætjuː], *n.* statue, *f.*

statuesque [stætjuˈesk], *a.* plastique.

stature ['stætʃə], *n.* stature, taille, *f.*

status ['steitəs], *n.* statut légal, *m.*; condition, *f.*, rang, *m.*

statute ['stætjuːt], *n.* statut, *m.*, loi, *f.*

statutory ['stætjutəri], *a.* réglementaire, statutaire.

staunch [STANCH].

stave [steiv], *n.* douve (*de baril*); (*Mus.*) portée, *f.*; verset (*de psaume*), *m.*—*v.t.* *irr.* crever; défoncer (*baril*); **to stave off**, chasser, repousser, éloigner, écarter, prévenir (*danger*).

staves [STAFF].

stay [stei], *v.t.* arrêter; apaiser (*sa faim*); étayer, accoter (*appuyer*).—*v.i.* rester; demeurer (*séjourner*); descendre; attendre.—*n.* séjour; (*Law*) sursis; soutien, appui (*aide*), *m.*

stay-at-home ['steiəthoum], *a.* and *n.* casanier, *m.*

stead [sted], *n.* lieu, *m.*, place, *f.*

steadfast ['stedfəst], *a.* ferme, constant, stable.

steadfastly ['stedfəstli], *adv.* fermement, avec constance.

steadfastness ['stedfəstnis], *n.* fermeté, constance, *f.*

steadily ['stedili], *adv.* fermement, avec persistance.

steadiness ['stedinis], *n.* fermeté; assurance, *f.*

steady ['stedi], *a.* ferme, assuré; posé (*sérieux*); régulier.—*adv.* doucement.—*v.t.* affermir; assujettir (*fixer*); calmer.

steak [steik], *n.* tranche (*de viande*), *f.*; entrecôte, *m.*; **fillet steak**, bifteck dans le filet, *m.*

steal [stiːl], *v.t.* *irr.* voler, dérober.—*v.i.* se dérober, se glisser furtivement, aller *ou* venir à la dérobée.

stealer ['stiːlə], *n.* voleur, *m.*

stealing ['stiːliŋ], *n.* vol, *m.*

stealth [stelθ], *n.* **by stealth**, à la dérobée, furtivement.

stealthily ['stelθili], *adv.* à la dérobée, furtivement, à pas de loup.

stealthy ['stelθi], *a.* dérobé, furtif.

steam [stiːm], *n.* vapeur, *f.*—*v.t.* (*Cook.*) cuire à la vapeur.—*v.i.* jeter de la vapeur; fumer.

steamboat ['stiːmbout], *n.* bateau à vapeur, *m.*

steam engine ['stiːmendʒin], *n.* machine à vapeur, *f.*

steamer ['stiːmə], *n.* vapeur, steamer, *m.*

steam gauge ['stiːmgeidʒ], *n.* manomètre, *m.*

steaming ['stiːmiŋ], *a.* fumant.

steam pipe ['stiːmpaip], *n.* tuyau de vapeur, *m.*

steam-roller ['stiːmroulə], *n.* rouleau compresseur, *m.*—*v.t.* (*fig.*) écraser.

steamship ['stiːmʃip], *n.* vapeur, *m.*

steam whistle ['stiːmwisl], *n.* sifflet à vapeur, *m.*

steamy ['stiːmi], *a.* humide.

steed [stiːd], *n.* (*poet*) coursier, *m.*

steel [stiːl], *a.* d'acier, en acier.—*n.* acier; fusil (*pour aiguiser un couteau*); (*fig.*) fer, *m.*—*v.t.* acérer, garnir d'acier; (*fig.*) fortifier.

steel-clad ['stiːlklæd], *a.* revêtu d'acier, bardé de fer.

steeliness ['stiːlinis], *n.* dureté d'acier; (*fig.*) dureté, *f.*

steel-plated ['stiːlpleitid], *a.* cuirassé.

steel-works ['stiːlwəːks], *n.pl.* aciérie, *f.*

steely ['stiːli], *a.* d'acier; (*fig.*) dur, de fer.

steelyard ['sti:lja:d], *n.* romaine, *f.*
steep (1) [sti:p], *a.* escarpé, à pic; raide (*escalier*).—*n.* pente rapide, *f.*; escarpement, *m.*
steep (2) [sti:p], *v.t.* tremper; (*fig.*) saturer (*de*).
steeping ['sti:piŋ], *n.* trempage, *m.*
steeple [sti:pl], *n.* clocher, *m.*
steeplechase [sti:pltʃeis], *n.* course au clocher, *f.*, steeplechase, *m.*
steepled [sti:pld], *a.* à clocher.
steeple-jack ['sti:pldʒæk], *n.* réparateur de clochers *ou* de cheminées, *m.*
steeply ['sti:pli], *adv.* en pente rapide.
steepness ['sti:pnis], *n.* raideur, pente rapide, *f.*
steer [stiə], *n.* bouvillon, jeune bœuf, *m.*—*v.t.* gouverner; diriger; (*Motor. etc.*) conduire. —*v.i.* se diriger.
steerage ['stiəridʒ], *n.* timonerie, *f.*; l'avant logement des passagers de troisième classe, *m.*
steering ['stiəriŋ], *n.* direction; (*Motor.*) conduite, *f.*
steering wheel ['stiəriŋwi:l], *n.* volant, *m.*
steersman ['stiəzmən], *n.* (*pl.* -men [men]) timonier, *m.*
stellar [stelə], *a.* stellaire.
stem [stem], *n.* tige; queue (*d'une fleur etc.*); (*fig.*) souche (*d'une famille*), *f.*—*v.t.* refouler (*courant*); (*fig.*) résister à.—*v.i.* **to stem from**, être issu de.
stench [stentʃ], *n.* puanteur, *f.*
stencil ['stensil], *n.* patron, pochoir, stencil, *m.*—*v.t.* tracer au patron, tirer au stencil.
sten gun ['stengʌn], *n.* fusil mitrailleur, *m.*
stenographer ['stenɔgrəfə], *n.* sténographe, *m.*, *f.*
stenography [ste'nɔgrəfi], *n.* sténographie, *f.*
stentorian [sten'tɔ:riən], *a.* de stentor.
step [step], *v.t.* mesurer en comptant les pas, arpenter.—*v.i.* faire un pas, marcher pas à pas; marcher, aller; monter (*dans*); descendre (*de*); **to step aside**, s'écarter; **to step back**, reculer; **to step forward**, s'avancer; **to step on**, fouler; **to step over**, enjamber.—*n.* pas; degré, *m.*, marche (*d'escalier*), *f.*; échelon (*d'échelle*); marchepied (*de voiture ou de bicyclette*), *m.*; (*fig.*) démarche; (*pl.*) échelle, *f.*
stepbrother ['stepbrʌðə], *n.* beau-frère, *m.*
stepchild ['steptʃaild], *n.* beau-fils, *m.*, belle-fille, *f.*
stepfather ['stepfɑ:ðə], *n.* beau-père, *m.*
Stephen [sti:vn], Étienne, *m.*
stepmother ['stepmʌðə], *n.* belle-mère, marâtre, *f.*
steppe [step], *n.* steppe (*plaine*), *f.*
stepping ['stepiŋ], *n.* marche, allure, *f.*
stepping-stone ['stepiŋstoun], *n.* (*pl.*) pierres de gué, *f.pl.*; (*fig.*) introduction, *f.*
stepsister ['stepsistə], *n.* belle-sœur, *f.*
stereoscopic [stiəriə'skɔpik], *a.* stéréoscopique.
stereotype ['stiəriətaip], *a.* stéréotypé; cliché. —*n.* stéréotypage; (*fig.*) cliché, *m.*—*v.t.* clicher; stéréotyper.
stereotyped ['stiəriətaipt], *a.* (*usu. fig.*) stéréotypé.
sterile ['sterail], *a.* stérile.
sterility [stə'riliti], *n.* stérilité, *f.*

sterilization [sterilai'zeiʃən], *n.* stérilisation, *f.*
sterilize ['sterilaiz], *v.t.* stériliser.
sterling ['stə:liŋ], *a.* sterling; (*fig.*) vrai, de bon aloi.
stern (1) [stə:n], *a.* sévère, dur; rigoureux.
stern (2) [stə:n], *n.* (*Naut.*) arrière, *m.*
sternly ['stə:nli], *adv.* sévèrement, durement.
sternmost ['stə:nmoust], *a.* le dernier.
sternness ['stə:nnis], *n.* sévérité, austérité, *f.*
stethoscope ['steθəskoup], *n.* stéthoscope, *m.*
stevedore ['sti:vədɔ:], *n.* arrimeur; déchargeur, *m.*
stew [stju:], *n.* étuvée, *f.*, ragoût (*de viande*); (*fig.*) embarras, *m.*, confusion, *f.*; **Irish stew**, ragoût de mouton.—*v.t.* étuver; mettre en ragoût, faire un ragoût de.—*v.i.* cuire à l'étuvée; (*fig.*) cuire dans sa peau.
steward ['stju:əd], *n.* intendant, régisseur (*d'une propriété*); économe (*de collège*); commissaire (*de bal etc.*); (*Naut.*) steward, *m.*; **steward's room**, cambuse, *f.*
stewardess ['stju:ədis], *n.* femme de chambre (de bord), stewardesse, *f.*
stewardship ['stju:ədʃip], *n.* intendance; (*fig.*) administration, *f.*
stewed [stju:d], *a.* étuvé, en ragoût; en compote.
stew-pan ['stju:pæn], *n.* casserole, *f.*
stew-pot ['stju:pɔt], *n.* cocotte, *f.*, faitout, *m.*
stick (1) [stik], *n.* bâton, *m.*; canne (*pour marcher*), *f.*; (*Av.*) manche; chapelet (*de bombes*), *m.*
stick (2) [stik], *v.t. irr.* percer, piquer; enfoncer; coller; **stick no bills**, défense d'afficher.—*v.i.* se coller, s'attacher; rester (*demeurer*); **to stick close**, ne pas quitter; **to stick out**, faire saillie; persister; **to stick to**, s'en tenir à; **to stick up**, se dresser.
stickiness ['stikinis], *n.* viscosité, *f.*
sticking plaster ['stikiŋ'plɑ:stə], *n.* taffetas d'Angleterre, *m.*
stickle [stikl], *v.i.* tenir beaucoup (à); se disputer.
stickleback ['stiklbæk], *n.* épinoche, *f.*
stickler ['stiklə], *n.* partisan, *m.*; rigoriste, *m.*, *f.*
sticky ['stiki], *a.* gluant, collant; (*fig.*) difficile (*personne*).
stiff [stif], *a.* raide, rigide, tenace; dur, ferme (*non fluide*); opiniâtre (*entêté*); gêné (*contraint*); courbatu (*muscles*); affecté, guindé (*style*).
stiffen [stifn], *v.t.* raidir; (*fig.*) endurcir.— *v.i.* se raidir; (*fig.*) s'endurcir.
stiffening ['stifniŋ], *n.* raidissement; soutien (*appui*), *m.*
stiffly ['stifli], *adv.* avec raideur; obstinément.
stiff neck ['stifnek], *n.* torticolis, *m.*
stiff-necked ['stifnekt], *a.* opiniâtre, entêté.
stiffness ['stifnis], *n.* raideur; gêne (*contrainte*); opiniâtreté (*entêtement*), *f.*; (*fig.*) air guindé, *m.*
stifle [staifl], *v.t.*, *v.i.* étouffer, suffoquer.—*n.* (*Vet.*) grasset, *m.*
stifling ['staifliŋ], *a.* étouffant, suffocant. —*n.* suffocation, *f.*
stigma ['stigmə], *n.* stigmate, *m.*, flétrissure, *f.*
stigmatize ['stigmətaiz], *v.t.* stigmatiser, flétrir.

579

stile

stile [stail], *n.* échallier, échalis, *m.*

stiletto [sti'letou], *n.* stylet, *m.*; **stiletto heels**, talons aiguille, *m.pl.*

still (1) [stil], *a.* silencieux; tranquille, calme, paisible, en repos; immobile; non mousseux (*vin*).—*adv.* encore, toujours; cependant, néanmoins (*malgré tout*).—*v.t.* calmer, apaiser.

still (2) [stil], *n.* alambic, *m.*

still-born ['stilbɔːn], *a.* mort-né.

stillness ['stilnis], *n.* tranquillité, *f.*, calme, *m.*

still room ['stilruːm], *n.* distillerie, *f.*, laboratoire, *m.*

stilt [stilt], *n.* échasse, *f.*; pilotis, pieu (*de pont etc.*), *m.*

stilted ['stiltid], *a.* guindé, pompeux.

stimulant ['stimjulənt], *n.* stimulant, *m.*

stimulate ['stimjuleit], *v.t.* stimuler; (*fig.*) exciter.

stimulating ['stimjuleitiŋ], *a.* stimulant.

stimulation [stimju'leiʃən], *n.* stimulation, *f.*

stimulus ['stimjuləs], *n.* stimulant, aiguillon, stimulus, *m.*

sting [stiŋ], *n.* aiguillon; dard (*d'ortie etc.*), *m.*; piqûre; (*fig.*) pointe, *f.*—*v.t. irr.* piquer; (*fig.*) irriter.

stingily ['stindʒili], *adv.* chichement, mesquinement.

stinginess ['stindʒinis], *n.* mesquinerie, ladrerie, *f.*

stinging ['stiŋiŋ], *a.* piquant; cinglant.—*n.* piqûre, *f.*

stingy ['stindʒi], *a.* avare, mesquin, ladre, chiche.

stink [stiŋk], *n.* puanteur, mauvaise odeur, *f.*—*v.i. irr.* puer; sentir mauvais.

stinking ['stiŋkiŋ], *a.* puant.

stint [stint], *v.t.* limiter, restreindre; **to stint oneself**, se priver (*de*).—*n.* limite, borne; portion; besogne, *f.*

stipend ['staipend], *n.* traitement (*d'ecclésiastique ou de magistrat*), *m.*

stipendiary [sti'pendiəri], *a.* appointé.

stipple [stipl], *v.t.* pointiller.

stippling ['stipliŋ], *n.* pointillage (*processus*); pointillé (*résultat*), *m.*

stipulate ['stipjuleit], *v.i.* stipuler (*de ou que*).

stipulation [stipju'leiʃən], *n.* stipulation, condition, *f.*

stipulator ['stipjuleitə], *n.* partie stipulante, *f.*

stir [stəː], *v.t.* remuer; (*fig.*) agiter; **to stir the fire**, attiser le feu.—*v.i.* remuer, se remuer, bouger.—*n.* remuement, bruit, *m.*; agitation, *f.*

stirring ['stəːriŋ], *a.* remuant; émouvant (*histoire etc.*).—*n.* agitation, *f.*

stirrup ['stirəp], *n.* étrier, *m.*

stirrup cup ['stirəpkʌp], *n.* coup de l'étrier, *m.*

stirrup leather ['stirəp'leðə], *n.* étrivière, *f.*

stitch [stitʃ], *n.* point, *m.*; maille (*en tricot*), *f.*; (*Med.*) point de suture, *m.*; **a stitch in time saves nine**, un point à temps en épargne cent.—*v.t.* piquer, coudre; brocher (*livres*); (*Med.*) suturer.

stitched [stitʃt], *a.* piqué, broché (*livre*).

stitching ['stitʃiŋ], *n.* couture, *f.*; brochage (*de livre*), *m.*; (*Med.*) suture, *f.*

stoat [stout], *n.* hermine d'été, *f.*

stock (1) [stɔk], *a.* courant, habituel.—*n.* souche (*d'arbre, famille etc.*), *f.*; cep (*de vigne*); bloc (*de bois etc.*), *m.*; monture (*de fusil*); (*Hort.*) ente (*pour greffer*), *f.*; (*Cook.*) consommé, *m.*; (*fig.*) race, famille, *f.*; approvisionnement, stock (*réserve*), assortiment (*sélection*), *m.*; (*pl.*) fonds publics, *m.pl.*, rentes, actions, *f.pl.*; (*Shipbuilding*) chantier, *m.*, cale de construction, *f.*; ceps (*punition*), *m.pl.*; **rolling stock**, matériel roulant, *m.*; **to take stock of**, faire l'inventaire de.—*v.t.* pourvoir (*de*); stocker (*magasin*); meubler (*ferme*); empoissonner (*vivier*).

stock (2) [stɔk], *n.* (*St. Exch.*), see **share** (2).

stockade [stɔ'keid], *n.* palissade, *f.*—*v.t.* palissader.

stock book ['stɔkbuk], *n.* livre de magasin, magasinier, *m.*

stock-breeder ['stɔkbriːdə], *n.* éleveur, *m.*

stock-breeding ['stɔkbriːdiŋ], *n.* élevage, *m.*

stockbroker ['stɔkbroukə], *n.* agent de change, *m.*

stock exchange ['stɔkikstʃeindʒ], *n.* bourse; compagnie des agents de change, *f.*

stockholder ['stɔkhouldə], *n.* actionnaire, *m.*, *f.*, rentier, *m.*

stocking ['stɔkiŋ], *n.* bas, *m.*

stockpile ['stɔkpail], *n.* stocks de réserve, *m.pl.*—*v.t.*, *v.i.* stocker.

stock-still ['stɔk'stil], *a.* immobile.—*adv.* sans bouger.

stock-taking ['stɔkteikiŋ], *n.* inventaire, *m.*

stocky ['stɔki], *a.* trapu.

stodgy ['stɔdʒi], *a.* pâteux, lourd.

stoic ['stouik], *n.* stoïcien, *m.*

stoic ['stouik], **stoical** ['stouikəl], *a.* stoïcien; (*fig.*) stoïque.

stoicism ['stouisizm], *n.* stoïcisme, *m.*

stoke [stouk], *v.t.* chauffer; tisonner (*le feu*).

stoker ['stoukə], *n.* chauffeur, *m.*

stoking ['stoukiŋ], *n.* chauffage, *m.*, chauffe, *f.*

stole (1) [stoul], *n.* étole; (*Cost.*) écharpe, *f.*

stole (2) [stoul], *past* [STEAL].

stolen ['stoulən], *a.* volé, dérobé.

stolid ['stɔlid], *a.* lourd, impassible.

stolidity [stɔ'liditi], **stolidness** ['stɔlidnis], *n.* flegme, *m.*

stomach ['stʌmək], *n.* estomac; (*euph.*) ventre; appétit, *m.*—*v.t.* avaler; endurer.

stomach ache ['stʌməkeik], *n.* mal à l'estomac, *m.*, colique, *f.*

stone [stoun], *a.* de pierre, en pierre; de grès (*céramique*).—*n.* pierre, *f.*; caillou (*galet*); noyau (*de fruits*); pépin (*de raisins*), *m.*; (*Path.*) calcul; (*Weight*) stone (*kg. 6,348*), *m.*—*v.t.* lapider; ôter les noyaux de (*fruits*).

stone-blind ['stounblaind], *a.* complètement aveugle.

stone-cold ['stounkould], *a.* complètement froid.—*adv.* complètement.

stone-dead ['stoun'ded], *a.* raide mort.

stone-deaf ['stoundef], *a.* complètement sourd.

stone fruit ['stounfruːt], *n.* fruit à noyau, *m.*

stone-mason ['stounmeisən], *n.* maçon, marbrier (*pour tombes*), *m.*

stone's throw ['stounzθrou], *n.* jet de pierre, *m.*

stoneware ['stounwɛə], *n.* grès, *m.*, poterie de grès, *f.*

stonework ['stounwəːk], *n.* maçonnerie, *f.*

stoniness ['stouninis], *n.* nature pierreuse; (*fig.*) dureté, *f.*

stoning ['stouniŋ], *n.* lapidation, *f.*

stony ['stouni], *a.* de pierre; pierreux (*plein de pierres*); (*fig.*) insensible; **stony-hearted**, au cœur de pierre.

stook [stu:k], *n.* tas de gerbes, *m.—v.t.* mettre en gerbes.

stool [stu:l], *n.* tabouret; escabeau, *m.*

stoop [stu:p], *v.i.* se pencher, se baisser; se voûter; (*fig.*) s'abaisser.—*n.* inclination, *f.*; (*fig.*) abaissement, *m.*

stooping ['stu:piŋ], *a.* penché, courbé.

stop [stop], *n.* halte; pause, *f.*; obstacle; (*Organ*) jeu, registre; arrêt (*de trains etc.*), *m.*; (*Gram.*) **full stop**, point, *m.—v.t.* arrêter, empêcher; couper (*le souffle*); suspendre (*paiement etc.*); retenir (*la paye*); (*Mus.*) presser; (*Gram.*) ponctuer; boucher (*trou etc.*); stopper (*machine*); plomber (*dent*).—*v.i.* s'arrêter; stopper.

stopcock ['stopkok], *n.* robinet d'arrêt, *m.*

stop-gap ['stopgæp], *n.* bouche-trou, *m.*

stoppage ['stopidʒ], *n.* interruption, halte, *f.*; arrêt (*d'un train etc.*), *m.*; obstruction; retenue (*de salaire*), *f.*; chômage (*arrêt de travail*); plombage (*de dent*), *m.*

stopper ['stopa], *n.* bouchon (*en verre*), *m.—v.t.* boucher.

stopping ['stopiŋ], *n.* arrêt; plombage (*de dent*), *m.*; matière à plomber, *f.*

stop-watch ['stopwotʃ], *n.* chronomètre, *m.*

storage ['sto:ridʒ], *n.* emmagasinage, *m.*, accumulation, *f.*

store [sto:], *n.* provision, *f.*; approvisionnement, *m.*, réserve, *f.*; magasin, *m.*, boutique, *f.*; (*fig.*) fonds, trésor, *m.*; **in store**, en réserve; **to lay in a store of**, faire une provision de.—*v.t.* pourvoir, munir, approvisionner (*de*); enrichir (*l'esprit*).

store-house ['sto:haus], *n.* magasin, entrepôt, dépôt, *m.*

store-keeper ['sto:ki:pə], *n.* garde-magasin, marchand (*boutiquier*), *m.*

store-room ['sto:ru:m], *n.* dépôt, office, *m.*; réserve, *f.*

storey, story (1) ['sto:ri], *n.* étage, *m.*

storied (1) ['sto:rid], *a.* à étage.

storied (2) ['sto:rid], *a.* historié.

stork [sto:k], *n.* cigogne, *f.*

storm [sto:m], *n.* orage, *m.*, tempête, *f.—v.t.* donner l'assaut à, prendre d'assaut.—*v.i.* faire de l'orage; (*fig.*) tempêter, s'emporter.

storm bell ['sto:mbel], *n.* tocsin, *m.*

storm cloud ['sto:mklaud], *n.* nuée, *f.*

storminess ['sto:minis], *n.* état orageux, *m.*

storming ['sto:miŋ], *n.* assaut, *m.*, prise d'assaut; (*fig.*) rage, *f.*

stormy ['sto:mi], *a.* orageux, à l'orage; **stormy petrel**, pétrel, *m.*

story (1) [STOREY].

story (2) ['sto:ri], *n.* histoire, *f.*, récit; conte (*littéraire*); mensonge (*tromperie*), *m.*

story-book ['sto:ribuk], *n.* livre de contes, *m.*

story-teller ['sto:ritelə], *n.* conteur (*narrateur*); menteur (*trompeur*), *m.*

stout [staut], *a.* fort; gros, corpulent; (*fig.*) brave, courageux.—*n.* stout, *m.*, bière brune forte (*boisson*), *f.*

stoutly ['stautli], *adv.* vigoureusement, fort et ferme.

stoutness ['stautnis], *n.* embonpoint, *m.*, corpulence; (*fig.*) fermeté, *f.*

stove (1) [stouv], *past and p.p.* [STAVE].

stove (2) [stouv], *n.* poêle; fourneau (*de cuisine*), *m.*

stow [stou], *v.t.* mettre en place; (*Naut.*) arrimer; **to stow away**, emmagasiner.

stowage ['stouidʒ], *n.* mise en place, *f.*, (*Naut.*) arrimage, *m.*

stowaway ['stouawei], *n.* passager clandestin, *m.—v.i.* s'embarquer clandestinement.

straddle [strædl], *v.t.* enfourcher.—*v.i.* écarter les jambes, marcher les jambes écartées.

strafe [stra:f], *v.t.* mitrailler, bombarder.

straggle [strægl], *v.i.* s'écarter; marcher à la débandade.

straggler ['stræglə], *n.* rôdeur; (*Mil.*) traînard, *m.*

straggling ['strægliŋ], *a.* séparé; éparpillé (*disséminé*).

straight [streit], *a.* droit; (*fig.*) équitable, juste.—*adv.* droit, tout droit, directement; **straight away**, sur-le-champ, tout de suite.

straight-edge ['streitedʒ], *n.* règle à araser, *f.*

straighten [streitn], *v.t.* rendre droit, redresser; ajuster (*habits*); mettre en ordre (*affaires, maison*).

straight-faced ['streit'feisd], *a.* imperturbable.

straightforward [streit'fo:wəd], *a.* droit, direct; (*fig.*) franc; simple (*problème*).

straightforwardly [streit'fo:wədli], *adv.* avec droiture; (*colloq.*) carrément.

straightforwardness [streit'fo:wədnis], *n.* droiture, franchise, *f.*

straightness ['streitnis], *n.* ligne directe; droiture, *f.*

straightway ['streitwei], *adv.* sur-le-champ, à l'instant.

strain (1) [strein], *v.t.* tendre; forcer (*contraindre*); se fouler (*muscles*); filtrer, passer (*liquide*).—*v.i.* s'efforcer; se filtrer (*liquide*).—*n.* grand effort, *m.*, tension; entorse, foulure (*de muscles*), *f.*; ton; chant, *m.*

strain (2) [strein], *n.* race, lignée, *f.*

strained [streind], *a.* forcé, pas naturel (*langage etc.*); tendu.

strainer ['streinə], *n.* passoire, *f.*

straining ['streiniŋ], *n.* tension, *f.*, grand effort, *m.*, exagération, *f.*; filtrage (*d'un liquide*), *m.*

strait [streit], *a.* étroit, serré; strict.—*n.* (*usu. pl.*) (*Geog.*) détroit, *m.*; (*pl.*) gêne, difficulté, *f.*, embarras, *m.*

straiten [streitn], *v.t.* rétrécir (*resserrer*); (*fig.*) gêner.

strait-laced ['streitleist], *a.* lacé étroitement; (*fig.*) sévère, prude.

straitness ['streitnis], *n.* étroitesse, *f.*

strait-waistcoat ['streitweiskout], **strait-jacket** ['streitdʒækit], *n.* camisole de force, *f.*

strand (1) [strænd], *n.* plage, grève, *f.—v.t.* jeter à la côte, échouer.—*v.i.* échouer.

strand (2) [strænd], *n.* cordon (*de corde*), *m.*

stranded ['strændid], *a.* échoué; (*fig.*) dans l'embarras.

stranding ['strændiŋ], *n.* échouement, échouage, *m.*

strange [streindʒ], *a.* étrange, singulier, bizarre.

strangely ['streindʒli], *adv.* étrangement, singulièrement.

strangeness ['streindʒnis], *n.* étrangeté, bizarrerie, *f.*

stranger ['streindʒə], *n.* étranger, inconnu, *m.*

strangle [stræŋgl], *v.t.* étrangler.

strangler ['stræŋglə], *n.* étrangleur, *m.*

strangling ['stræŋgliŋ], *n.* étranglement, *m.*

strangulation [stræŋgju'leiʃən], *n.* strangulation, *f.*

strap [stræp], *n.* courroie, *f.*; lien, *m.*, bande (*de fer*), *f.*—*v.t.* attacher avec une courroie; lier.

strapper ['stræpə], *n.* grand gaillard, *m.*

strapping ['stræpiŋ], *a.* bien découplé, bien bâti.

stratagem ['strætədʒəm], *n.* stratagème, *m.*

strategic [strə'ti:dʒik], **strategical** [strə'ti:dʒikəl], *a.* stratégique.

strategist ['strætədʒist], *n.* stratégiste, *m.*, *f.*

strategy ['strætədʒi], *n.* stratégie, *f.*

stratify ['strætifai], *v.t.* stratifier.

stratocruiser ['stræto'kru:zə], *n.* avion stratosphérique, *m.*

stratosphere ['strætəsfiə], *n.* stratosphère, *f.*

stratum ['stra:təm], *n.* (*pl.* **strata** ['stra:tə]) couche, *f.*

straw [strɔ:], *a.* de paille.—*n.* paille, *f.*; *it's the last straw,* c'est le comble.—*v.t.* rempailler (*chaise*).

strawberry ['strɔ:bəri], *n.* fraise, *f.*; fraisier (*plante*), *m.*

straw-colored ['strɔ:kʌləd], *a.* jaune-paille.

straw mat ['strɔ:'mæt], *n.* paillasson, *m.*

stray [strei], *v.i.* s'égarer, errer, vaguer; s'écarter (*de*).—*a.* égaré; (*fig.*) fortuit.—*n.* épave, *f.*; *waifs and strays,* des épaves, *f.pl.*

straying ['streiiŋ], *n.* égarement, *m.*

streak [stri:k], *n.* raie, bande, *f.*; *streak of lightning,* éclair, *m.*—*v.t.* rayer, strier; barioler, bigarrer.—*v.i.* filer.

streaked ['stri:kt], *a.* rayé (*de*); bariolé, bigarré.

streaky ['stri:ki], *a.* rayé; veiné (*marbre*); entrelardé (*viande*).

stream [stri:m], *n.* courant; cours d'eau, *m.*, rivière, *f.*; ruisseau; (*fig.*) cours; jet (*de lumière etc.*); torrent (*de paroles etc.*), *m.*; *to go down stream,* aller en aval; *to go up stream,* aller en amont.—*v.i.* couler; ruisseler (*sang etc.*); rayonner (*lumière*).

streamer ['stri:mə], *n.* banderole; (*Naut.*) flamme, *f.*; (*pl.*) serpentins (*de papier*), *m.pl.*

streamlet ['stri:mlit], *n.* petit ruisseau; ru, *m.*

stream-line ['stri:mlain], *n.* fil de l'eau, *m.*—*v.t.* caréner; (*fig.*) moderniser.

stream-lined ['stri:mlaind], *a.* **stream-lined body,** carrosserie carénée, *f.*; **stream-lined car,** voiture aérodynamique, *f.*

street [stri:t], *n.* rue, *f.*

street door ['stri:t'dɔ:], *n.* porte sur la rue, *f.*

street lamp ['stri:tlæmp], *n.* réverbère, *m.*

street sweeper ['stri:tswi:pə], *n.* balayeur de rue (*personne*), *m.*; balayeuse (*machine*), *f.*

strength [streŋθ], *n.* force, *f.*, forces, *f.pl.*; (*Build.*) solidité, *f.*; (*Mil.*) effectif, *m.*

strengthen [streŋθn], *v.t.* fortifier, affermir, raffermir; (*Mil.*) renforcer.—*v.i.* se fortifier, s'affermir, se raffermir.

strengthener ['streŋθnə], *n.* (*Med.*) fortifiant, *m.*

strengthening ['streŋθniŋ], *a.* fortifiant.

strenuous ['strenjuəs], *a.* énergique, vif, ardent, vigoureux.

strenuously ['strenjuəsli], *adv.* avec zèle, ardemment; vigoureusement.

strenuousness ['strenjuəsnis], *n.* zèle, *m.*, ardeur; vigueur, *f.*

streptococcus [strepto'kɒkəs], *n.* streptocoque, *m.*

streptomycin [strepto'maisin], *n.* streptomycine, *f.*

stress [stres], *n.* force, emphase, *f.*, poids; (*Gram.*) accent, *m.*; violence (*du temps*); (*Mech.*) tension, *f.*—*v.t.* appuyer sur, accentuer.

stretch [stretʃ], *v.t.* tendre (*un élastique*); étendre; déployer (*ailes*); élargir; forcer (*faire violence à*); (*fig.*) exagérer.—*v.i.* s'étendre; s'étirer; se déployer; s'élargir; prêter (*gants, tissu*).—*n.* étendue, tension, extension; section (*de route*), *f.*; (*fig.*) effort, *m.*; *at a stretch,* d'un trait.

stretcher ['stretʃə], *n.* brancard, *m.*, civière, baguette (*à gants*), *f.*, tendeur (*à chaussures*), *m.*

stretcher-bearer ['stretʃəbeərə], *n.* brancardier, *m.*

stretching ['stretʃiŋ], *n.* élargissement, *m.*; tension, *f.*

strew [stru:], *v.t. irr.* répandre, parsemer, semer.

strewing ['stru:iŋ], *n.* jonchée, *f.*

striate ['straiit], **striated** [strai'eitid], *a.* strié.

striation [strai'eiʃən], *n.* striure, *f.*

stricken [strikn], *p.p.* [STRIKE].—*a.* affligé; (*Med.*) atteint (*de*).

strict [strikt], *a.* exact, strict, précis; rigide; sévère.

strictly ['striktli], *adv.* strictement, formellement; *strictly speaking,* rigoureusement parlant.

strictness ['striktnis], *n.* exactitude, rigueur; sévérité, *f.*

stricture ['striktʃə], *n.* censure, critique, *f.*; (*Med.*) étranglement, *m.*

stride [straid], *n.* grand pas, *m.*, enjambée, *f.*—*v.i. irr.* marcher à grands pas *ou* à grandes enjambées.

strident ['straidənt], *a.* strident.

strife [straif], *n.* lutte, querelle, dispute, *f.*

strike [straik], *v.t. irr.* frapper; battre, cogner; asséner, porter (*un coup*); sonner (*l'heure*); rendre (*muet etc.*); établir (*l'équilibre*); allumer (*allumette*); faire (*marché etc.*); amener (*drapeau*); plier (*tente*); *to strike down,* abattre; *to strike off,* retrancher, effacer.—*v.i.* frapper; toucher; échouer (*heurter un écueil etc.*); heurter, donner (*contre*); sonner (*pendule etc.*); (*Hort.*) prendre racine; faire grève, se mettre en grève (*ouvriers*); *to strike out,* se lancer; (*Mus.*) *to strike up,* commencer à jouer.—*n.* grève (*d'ouvriers*), *f.*; *sit-down strike,* débrayage, *m.*; *stay-in-strike,* grève sur le tas.

striker ['straikə], *n.* frappeur, *m.*; gréviste (*ouvrier en grève*), *m.*, *f.*; percuteur (*de fusil*), *m.*

striking ['straikiŋ], *a.* frappant, saisissant; remarquable.—*n.* frappement, *m.*; frappe; sonnerie (*de pendule*), *f.*

strikingly ['straikiŋli], *adv.* d'une manière frappante.

582

string [striŋ], *n.* ficelle, corde, *f.*; fil; cordon, lacet (*de chaussures etc.*); chapelet (*d'oignons etc.*), *m.*; corde (*de violon*); bride (*de bonnet etc.*); (*fig.*) suite, série, *f.*; **the strings,** les instruments à cordes (*d'un orchestre*), *m.pl.*—*v.t. irr.* garnir de cordes; enfiler (*grains etc.*); (*Mus.*) accorder.

stringed [striŋd], *a.* à cordes (*instrument de musique*).

stringency ['strindʒənsi], *n.* rigueur, *f.*

stringent ['strindʒənt], *a.* rigoureux, strict.

stringy ['striŋi], *a.* fibreux; filandreux (*viande*).

strip [strip], *n.* bande, *f.*, ruban; lambeau, *m.*, langue (*de terre*), *f.*—*v.t.* dépouiller (*de*); dévaliser (*voler*); déshabiller (*dévêtir*); **to strip off,** se dépouiller de.—*v.i.* se déshabiller.

stripe [straip], *n.* raie; barre, bande; marque (*cicatrice*), *f.*; (*Mil.*) chevron, galon, *m.*—*v.t.* rayer, barrer.

striped [straipt], **stripy** ['straipi], *a.* rayé, à raies, zébré.

stripling ['striplin], *n.* adolescent, *m.*

strive [straiv], *v.i. irr.* s'efforcer (*de*), faire des efforts (*pour*), se débattre; se disputer (*rivaliser*).

striving ['straivin], *n.* lutte, *f.*, efforts, *m.pl.*

stroke [strouk], *n.* coup; trait; trait de plume; coup d'aviron, *m.*; brassée (*de la nage*), course (*de piston*), *f.*; (*Med.*) coup de sang, *m.*, attaque, *f.*; chef de nage (*de bateau à rames*), *m.*; **at a stroke,** d'un coup, d'un trait.—*v.t.* caresser.

stroking ['stroukiŋ], *n.* caresses, *f.pl.*

stroll [stroul], *n.* (courte) promenade, *f.*, tour, *m.*, flânerie, *f.*—*v.i.* errer, flâner.

stroller ['stroulə], *n.* flâneur, *m.*

strong [strɔŋ], *a.* fort, solide; (*fig.*) vigoureux, résolu; **strong light,** vive lumière, *f.*

strong-box ['strɔŋbɔks], *n.* coffre-fort, *m.*

stronghold ['strɔŋhould], *n.* forteresse, *f.*, fort, *m.*

strongly ['strɔŋli], *adv.* fortement, fermement.

strong-room ['strɔŋru:m], *n.* cave aux coffres-forts, *f.*

strontium ['strɔnʃiəm], *n.* strontium, *m.*

strop [strɔp], *n.* cuir à rasoir, *m.*—*v.t.* repasser, affiler.

strophe ['stroufi, 'strɔfi], *n.* stance, strophe, *f.*

structural ['strʌktʃərəl], *a.* de structure, structural.

structure ['strʌktʃə], *n.* construction, structure, *f.*; édifice, *m.*; facture (*de pièce, de poème*), *f.*

struggle [strʌgl], *n.* lutte, *f.*, effort, *m.*—*v.i.* lutter, se débattre.

struggling ['strʌgliŋ], *n.* lutte, *f.*; effort, *m.*

strum [strʌm], *v.i.* tapoter, taper (*sur*).

strumming ['strʌmiŋ], *n.* tapotage, *m.*

strut [strʌt], *n.* démarche fière, *f.*; (*Carp. etc.*) étai, *m.*—*v.i.* se pavaner, se carrer.

strychnine ['strikni:n], *n.* strychnine, *f.*

stub [stʌb], *n.* souche, *f.*; bout, *m.*

stubble [stʌbl], *n.* chaume, *m.*

stubborn ['stʌbən], *a.* obstiné, opiniâtre.

stubbornness ['stʌbənnis], *n.* opiniâtreté, *f.*

stubby ['stʌbi], *a.* trapu (*taille*).

stucco ['stʌkou], *n.* stuc, *m.*

stud (1) [stʌd], *n.* bouton de chemise; clou, *m.*—*v.t.* clouter; parsemer (*de*).

stud (2) [stʌd], *n.* écurie, *f.*; **stud farm,** haras, *m.*

student ['stju:dənt], *n.* étudiant, *m.*, élève, *m.*, *f.*

studied ['stʌdid], *a.* étudié (*style etc.*); prémédité (*calculé*).

studio ['stju:diou], *n.* atelier; (*Cine., Rad.*) studio, *m.*

studious ['stju:diəs], *a.* studieux; diligent.

studiously ['stju:diəsli], *adv.* studieusement.

studiousness ['stju:diəsnis], *n.* application, *f.*

study ['stʌdi], *n.* étude, *f.*; soin, *m.*, application (*attention*), *f.*; cabinet d'étude (*pièce*), *m.*; **to be in a brown study,** être dans la lune.—*v.t.* étudier, s'occuper de.—*v.i.* étudier, travailler.

stuff [stʌf], *n.* étoffe, *f.*, tissu, *m.*; (*fig.*) matière, *f.*; fatras (*bêtises*), *m.*—*v.t.* rembourrer; bourrer (*remplir*); boucher (*trou*); (*Taxidermy*) empailler; (*Cook.*) farcir.—*v.i.* se bourrer; se gorger.

stuffing ['stʌfiŋ], *n.* bourre (*substances*), *f.*; rembourrage (*opération*), *n.*; (*Cook.*) farce, *f.*; (*Taxidermy*) empaillage, *m.*

stuffy ['stʌfi], *a.* privé d'air, renfermé; **to be stuffy,** sentir le renfermé; (*fig.*) avoir des préjugés.

stultify ['stʌltifai], *v.t.* rendre nul; contredire (*démentir*); **to stultify oneself,** se rendre ridicule.

stumble [stʌmbl], *v.i.* trébucher, broncher; (*fig.*) faire un faux pas, faillir.—*n.* faux pas, *m.*

stumbling ['stʌmbliŋ], *a.* trébuchant.—*n.* trébuchement, *m.*

stumbling block ['stʌmbliŋblɔk], *n.* pierre d'achoppement, *f.*

stump [stʌmp], *n.* tronçon, *m.*, souche, *f.*; chicot (*de dent*); trognon (*de chou*), moignon (*de membre*), *m.*; (*Drawing*) estompe, *f.*

stumpy ['stʌmpi], *a.* trapu (*personne*).

stun [stʌn], *v.t.* étourdir.

stunning ['stʌniŋ], *a.* étourdissant; (*slang*) épatant.

stunt (1) [stʌnt], *v.t.* rabougrir.

stunt (2) [stʌnt], *n.* tour de force, *m.*; réclame, *f.*

stunted ['stʌntid], *a.* rabougri.

stupefaction [stju:pi'fækʃən], *n.* stupéfaction, *f.*

stupefy ['stju:pifai], *v.t.* hébéter, abrutir; stupéfier.

stupefying ['stju:pifaiiŋ], *a.* stupéfiant.

stupendous [stju'pendəs], *a.* prodigieux, foudroyant.

stupid ['stju:pid], *a.* stupide, sot, bête.

stupidity [stju'piditi], *n.* stupidité, bêtise, *f.*

stupidly ['stju:pidli], *adv.* stupidement.

stupor ['stju:pə], *n.* stupeur, *f.*

sturdy ['stə:di], *a.* vigoureux, fort, robuste; hardi.

sturgeon ['stə:dʒən], *n.* esturgeon, *m.*

stutter ['stʌtə], *v.t.*, *v.i.* bégayer.

stutterer ['stʌtərə], *n.* bègue, *m.*, *f.*

stuttering ['stʌtəriŋ], *n.* bégaiement, *m.*

sty (1) [stai], *n.* étable (à cochons), *f.*

sty (2), **stye** [stai], *n.* orgelet (à l'œil), *m.*

Stygian ['stidʒiən], *a.* stygien.

style [stail], *n.* style; (*fig.*) genre, *m.*, manière, *f.*; titre, *m.*; raison sociale (*d'une compagnie*), *f.*; **to live in style,** avoir un train de maison.—*v.t.* appeler, qualifier de.

stylish [ˈstailiʃ], *a.* élégant, de bon ton.

stylus [ˈstailəs], *n.* style, *m.*

styptic [ˈstiptik], *a.* and *n.* (*Med.*) styptique, *m.*

suave [swɑːv], *a.* suave.

suavity [ˈswɑːviti], *n.* suavité, *f.*

subaltern [ˈsʌbəltən], *a.* subalterne.—*n.* (sous-)lieutenant, *m.*

subconscious [sʌbˈkɒnʃəs], *a.* and *n.* (*Psych.*) subconscient, *m.*

subconsciously [sʌbˈkɒnʃəsli], *adv.* inconsciemment.

subdivide [sʌbdiˈvaid], *v.t.* subdiviser.

subdue [səbˈdjuː], *v.t.* subjuguer; dompter, étouffer; **subdued light**, demi-jour, *m.*

sub-editor [sʌbˈeditə], *n.* secrétaire de la rédaction, *m., f.*

subject [ˈsʌbdʒikt], *a.* assujetti, soumis; sujet (à), exposé (à).—*n.* sujet, *m.*; (*Sch.*) matière, *f.*; particulier, *m.*, personne, *f.*; [səbˈdʒekt], *v.t.* assujettir, soumettre; rendre sujet (à), exposer (à).

subjection [səbˈdʒekʃən], *n.* sujétion, *f.*

subjective [səbˈdʒektiv], *a.* subjectif.

subjectively [səbˈdʒektivli], *adv.* subjectivement.

subject matter [ˈsʌbdʒiktmætə], *n.* sujet, *m.* matière, *f.*

subjugate [ˈsʌbdʒugeit], *v.t.* subjuguer.

subjunctive [səbˈdʒʌŋktiv], *a.* and *n.* (*Gram.*) subjonctif, *m.*

sublet [sʌbˈlet], *v.t.* irr. (*conjug. like* LET) sous-louer.

sub-lieutenant [sʌblefˈtenənt], *n.* (*Navy*) enseigne, *m.*

sublimate [ˈsʌblimeit], *v.t.* sublimer.

sublime [səˈblaim], *a.* and *n.* sublime, *m.*

sublimeness [səˈblaimnis], *n.* sublimité, *f.*, sublime, *m.*

sub-machine gun [sʌbməˈʃiːngʌn], *n.* mitraillette, *f.*

submarine [ˈsʌbməriːn], *a.* and *n.* sous-marin, *m.*

submerge [səbˈmɜːdʒ], *v.t.* submerger.—*v.i.* plonger.

submission [səbˈmiʃən], *n.* soumission, résignation, déférence, *f.*

submissive [səbˈmisiv], *a.* soumis (à); docile.

submit [səbˈmit], *v.t.* soumettre (à).—*v.i.* se soumettre (à).

subnormal [sʌbˈnɔːml], *a.* sous-normal.

subordinate [səˈbɔːdinit], *a.* subordonné (à).—*n.* subordonné, *m.*—[səˈbɔːdineit], *v.t.* subordonner (à).

subordination [səbɔːdiˈneiʃən], *n.* subordination, *f.*; rang inférieur, *m.*

suborn [səˈbɔːn], *v.t.* suborner.

subpoena [sʌbˈpiːnə], *n.* (*Law*) citation, assignation, *f.*—*v.t.* citer, assigner.

subscribe [səbˈskraib], *v.t.* souscrire.—*v.i.* souscrire (à ou pour); s'abonner (à un journal).

subscriber [səbˈskraibə], *n.* abonné (à un journal), *m.*

subscription [səbˈskripʃən], *n.* souscription, *f.*; abonnement (à un journal etc.), *m.*

subsection [ˈsʌbsekʃən], *n.* subdivision, *f.*

subsequent [ˈsʌbsikwənt], *a.* subséquent, postérieur.

subsequently [ˈsʌbsikwəntli], *adv.* ensuite, après.

subservient [səbˈsɜːvjənt], *a.* subordonné (à); qui contribue à; obséquieux.

subserviently [səbˈsɜːviəntli], *adv.* en sousordre, utilement; servilement.

subside [səbˈsaid], *v.i.* s'affaisser (être accablé); baisser, s'abaisser, se calmer, s'apaiser (s'adoucir); se taire (personne); **to subside into**, se changer en.

subsidence [ˈsʌbsidəns, səbˈsaidəns], *n.* affaissement, *m.*; (*fig.*) baisse (rivière), *f.*

subsidiary [səbˈsidjəri], *a.* subsidiaire (à).—*n.* auxiliaire, *m.*; filiale (compagnie), *f.*

subsidize [ˈsʌbsidaiz], *v.t.* subventionner.

subsidy [ˈsʌbsidi], *n.* subvention, *f.*

subsist [səbˈsist], *v.i.* subsister, exister.

subsistence [səbˈsistəns], *n.* subsistance, *f.*; entretien, *m.*; existence, *f.*

subsistent [səbˈsistənt], *a.* existant, qui existe.

subsoil [ˈsʌbsɔil], *n.* sous-sol, *m.*

sub-species [ˈsʌbspiːʃiːz], *n.* sous-espèce, *f.*

substance [ˈsʌbstəns], *n.* substance, *f.*; fond (l'essentiel), *m.*; biens (richesses), *m.pl.*

substantial [səbˈstænʃl], *a.* substantiel, réel, solide; aisé (riche).

substantially [səbˈstænʃəli], *adv.* solidement, fortement, considérablement.

substantiate [səbˈstænʃieit], *v.t.* établir, confirmer.

substantive [ˈsʌbstəntiv], *a.* indépendant; (*Gram.*) substantif.—*n.* (*Gram.*) substantif, *m.*

substitute [ˈsʌbstitjuːt], *v.t.* substituer (à).—*n.* substitut, remplaçant, *m.*

substitution [sʌbstiˈtjuːʃən], *n.* substitution, *f.*

substratum [sʌbˈstrɑːtəm], *n.* (*pl.* **substrata** [sʌbˈstrɑːtə]) substratum, substrat, *m.*, couche inférieure, *f.*; (*Agric.*) sous-sol, *m.*

subtenant [ˈsʌbtenənt], *n.* sous-locataire, *m.*, *f.*

subterfuge [ˈsʌbtəfjuːdʒ], *n.* subterfuge, faux-fuyant, *m.*

subterranean [sʌbtəˈreiniən], *a.* souterrain.

sub-title [ˈsʌbtaitl], *n.* sous-titre, *m.*

subtle [sʌtl], *a.* subtil, rusé; fin.

subtlety [ˈsʌtlti], *n.* subtilité, finesse, *f.*

subtly [ˈsʌtli], *adv.* subtilement.

subtract [səbˈtrækt], *v.t.* défalquer; (*Arith.*) soustraire.

subtraction [səbˈtrækʃən], *n.* (*Arith.*) soustraction, *f.*

suburb [ˈsʌbəːb], *n.* faubourg, *m.*, (*pl.*) alentours, environs, *m.pl.*, banlieue, *f.*; **garden suburb**, cité-jardin, *f.*

suburban [səˈbɜːbən], *a.* de la banlieue, suburbain.

subvention [səbˈvenʃən], *n.* subvention, *f.*

subversive [səbˈvɜːsiv], *a.* subversif.

subway [ˈsʌbwei], *n.* passage souterrain; (*Am.*) métro, *m.*

succeed [səkˈsiːd], *v.t.* succéder à, suivre; **to succeed each other**, se succéder.—*v.i.* succéder (à); hériter (une propriété); parvenir (à), réussir (avoir du succès).

succeeding [səkˈsiːdiŋ], *a.* suivant (dans le passé); à venir, futur (à l'avenir); successif (consécutif).

success [səkˈses], *n.* succès, *m.*; **I wish you success!** bonne chance!

successful [səkˈsesful], *a.* heureux; couronné de succès, réussi, victorieux; **to be successful**, réussir.

successfully [sək'sesfuli], *adv.* heureusement, avec succès.
succession [sək'seʃən], *n.* succession, suite, *f.*;
avènement (*au trône etc.*), *m.*; postérité
(*descendance*), *f.*; *in succession*, successivement, de suite.
successive [sək'sesiv], *a.* successif, consécutif.
successor [sək'sesə], *n.* successeur, *m.*
succinct [sək'siŋkt], *a.* succinct, concis.
succinctly [sək'siŋktli], *adv.* avec concision.
succinctness [sək'siŋktnis], *n.* concision,
brièveté, *f.*
succor ['sʌkə], *v.t.* secourir, aider.—*n.*
secours, *m.*, aide, *f.*
succulent ['sʌkjulənt], *a.* succulent, plein de
jus.
succumb [sə'kʌm], *v.i.* succomber (à).
such [sʌtʃ], *a.* tel, pareil, semblable; *he is
such a bore*, il est si ennuyeux; *such a
one*, un tel, *m.*, une telle, *f.*; *such a one as*,
tel que; *such as it is*, tel quel, *m.*, telle
quelle, *f.*; *such as you*, tel que vous.
suchlike ['sʌtʃlaik], *a.* semblable, pareil; de
ce genre.
suck [sʌk], *v.t., v.i.* sucer; têter (*à la mamelle*);
aspirer.
sucker ['sʌkə], *n.* suceur, *m.*; (*fig.*) gobeur, *m.*
sucking ['sʌkiŋ], *a.* qui suce, aspirant.—*n.*
sucement, *m.*, succion, *f.*
sucking pig ['sʌkiŋpig], *n.* cochon de lait, *m.*
suckle ['sʌkl], *v.t.* allaiter, nourrir.
suction ['sʌkʃən], *n.* succion, aspiration, *f.*
Sudan [su'dæn, su'dɑ:n]. le Soudan, *m.*
Sudanese [sudə'niːz], *a.* soudanais.—*n.*
Soudanais (*personne*), *m.*
sudden [sʌdn], *a.* subit, soudain; (*fam.*) *all
of a sudden*, tout à coup.
suddenly ['sʌdnli], *adv.* subitement, soudain,
tout à coup.
suddenness ['sʌdnnis], *n.* soudaineté, *f.*
Sudetenland [su'deitnlænd]. les Sudètes,
m.pl.
suds [sʌdz], *soap-suds* ['soupsʌdz], *n.pl.* eau
de savon, lessive, *f.*
sue [sju:], *v.t.* poursuivre (en justice).—*v.i.*
implorer.
suède [sweid], *n.* daim (*chaussures*); suède
(*gants*), *m.*
suet ['sju:it], *n.* graisse de bœuf, *f.*
suffer ['sʌfə], *v.t.* souffrir; supporter, endurer,
subir (*éprouver*); laisser, permettre (*autoriser*).—*v.i.* souffrir (*de*); *to suffer for*,
porter la peine de.
sufferable ['sʌfərəbl], *a.* supportable, tolérable.
sufferance ['sʌfərəns], *n.* tolérance, *f.*
sufferer ['sʌfərə], *n.* victime (*de*), *f.*; patient,
m.
suffering ['sʌfəriŋ], *a.* souffrant.—*n.* souffrance, douleur, *f.*
suffice [sə'fais], *v.t.* suffire à, satisfaire.—*v.i.*
suffire.
sufficiency [sə'fiʃənsi], *n.* suffisance; aisance
(*financière*), *f.*
sufficient [sə'fiʃənt], *a.* suffisant, assez.
sufficiently [sə'fiʃəntli], *adv.* suffisamment,
assez.
suffix ['sʌfiks], *n.* suffixe, *m.*
suffocate ['sʌfəkeit], *v.t., v.i.* suffoquer,
étouffer, asphyxier.
suffocating ['sʌfəkeitiŋ], *a.* suffocant, étouffant, asphyxiant.

suffocation [sʌfə'keiʃən], *n.* suffocation,
asphyxie, *f.*
suffrage ['sʌfridʒ], *n.* suffrage, *m.*
suffuse [sə'fju:z], *v.t.* répandre, couvrir (*de*);
répandre sur; se répandre sur.
suffusion [sə'fju:ʒən], *n.* épanchement, *m.*,
suffusion, *f.*
sugar ['ʃugə], *n.* sucre, *m.*; *barley sugar*,
sucre d'orge; *brown(unrefined)sugar*,
cassonade, *f.*; *powdered sugar*, sucre
en poudre; *granulated sugar*, sucre
cristallisé; *lump sugar*, sucre cassé.—*v.t.*
sucrer; (*fig.*) adoucir.
sugar beet ['ʃugəbiːt], *n.* betterave à sucre, *f.*
sugar bowl ['ʃugəboul], *n.* sucrier, *m.*
sugar cane ['ʃugəkein], *n.* canne à sucre, *f.*
sugared ['ʃugəd], *a.* sucré; (*fig.*) doux.
sugar loaf ['ʃugəlouf], *n.* pain de sucre, *m.*
sugar refinery ['ʃugərifainəri], *n.* raffinerie
de sucre, *f.*
sugary ['ʃugəri], *a.* sucré; trop sucré.
suggest [sə'dʒest], *v.t.* suggérer; inspirer.
suggestion [sə'dʒestʃən], *n.* suggestion; proposition, idée; nuance, *f.*
suggestive [sə'dʒestiv], *a.* suggestif.
suicidal [sjuːi'saidl], *a.* de suicide; fatal.
suicide ['sjuːisaid], *n.* suicide (*acte*); suicidé
(*personne*), *m.*; *to commit suicide*, se
suicider.
suit [sjuːt], *n.* suite, collection complète, *f.*,
assortiment, *m.*; (*Cards*) couleur; sollicitation, prière; recherche en mariage; (*Law*)
instance, *f.*, procès, *m.*; *suit (of clothes)*,
complet (*d'homme*), tailleur (*de femme*), *m.*—
v.t. adapter; convenir à, aller à; plaire à
—*v.i.* s'accorder (*à*).
suitability [sjuːtə'biliti], *n.* convenance, *f.*
suitable ['sjuːtəbl], *a.* convenable (*à*); à
propos.
suitably ['sjuːtəbli], *adv.* convenablement.
suite [swiːt], *n.* suite, *f.*, ensemble, *m.*; *suite
of rooms*, appartement, *m.*; *suite of
furniture*, ameublement complet, *m.*
suitor ['sjuːtə], *n.* prétendant (*amoureux*);
(*Law*) plaideur, *m.*
sulk [sʌlk], *v.i.* bouder, faire la mine.
sulkily ['sʌlkili], *adv.* en boudant, en faisant
la mine.
sulkiness ['sʌlkinis], **sulking** ['sʌlkiŋ], *n.*
bouderie, *f.*
sulks [sʌlks], *n.pl.* mauvaise humeur, bouderie, *f.*
sulky ['sʌlki], *a.* boudeur.
sullen ['sʌlən], *a.* maussade, morose, renfrogné.
sullenly ['sʌlənli], *adv.* maussadement, d'un
air renfrogné.
sullenness ['sʌlənnis], *n.* air maussade, *m.*
sully ['sʌli], *v.t.* souiller, ternir (*de*).
sulphate ['sʌlfeit], *n.* sulfate, *m.*
sulphide ['sʌlfaid], *n.* sulfure, *m.*
sulphite ['sʌlfait], *n.* sulfite, *m.*
sulphonamide [sʌl'founəmaid], *n.* sulfa-
mide, *f.*
sulphur ['sʌlfə], *n.* soufre, *m.*
sulphuric [sʌl'fjuərik], *a.* sulfurique.
sulphurous ['sʌlfjurəs], *a.* sulfureux.
sultan ['sʌltən], *n.* sultan, *m.*
sultana [sʌl'tɑːnə], *n.* sultane, *f.*; (*pl.*) raisins
de Smyrne, *m.pl.*
sultriness ['sʌltrinis], *n.* chaleur étouffante, *f.*

sultry ['sʌltri], *a.* d'une chaleur étouffante, étouffant, suffocant; (*fam.*) épicé, salé (*histoire etc.*); *it is very sultry*, il fait très lourd.

sum [sʌm], *n.* somme (*d'argent*), *f.*; (*Arith.*) problème, calcul, *m.*; *the four sums*, les quatre opérations, *f.pl.—v.t. to sum up*, additionner, faire l'addition de; (*fig.*) récapituler.

summarily ['sʌmərili], *adv.* sommairement.

summarize ['sʌməraiz], *v.t.* résumer sommairement.

summary ['sʌməri], *a.* sommaire, prompt.— *n.* sommaire, résumé, *m.*

summer ['sʌmə], *a.* d'été, estival—*n.* été, *m.*; *in summer*, en été.

summer-house ['sʌməhaus], *n.* pavillon, *m.*

summing-up ['sʌmiŋ'ʌp], *n.* résumé, *m.*

summit ['sʌmit], *n.* sommet *m.*, cime, *f.*; (*fig.*) comble, *m.*

summon ['sʌmən], *v.t.* convoquer (*un rassemblement etc.*); sommer (*ordonner*); (*Law*) citer en justice; assigner (*témoins*).

summons ['sʌmənz], *n.* sommation (*commandement*); convocation, *f.*; appel (*invitation*), *m.*; (*Law*) citation, *f.*, mandat de comparution, *m.—v.t.* assigner, citer (en justice), appeler à comparaître.

sump [sʌmp], *n.* (*Mining*) puisard; (fond de) carter (*de voiture*), *m.*

sumptuous ['sʌmptjuəs], *a.* somptueux.

sumptuously ['sʌmptjuəsli], *adv.* somptueusement.

sun [sʌn], *n.* soleil, *m.—v.t.* exposer au soleil.

sun bath ['sʌnba:θ], *n.* bain de soleil, *m.*

sun-blind ['sʌnblaind], *n.* store, *m.*

sunburn ['sʌnbə:n], *n.* hâle; coup de soleil, *m.*

sunburnt ['sʌnbə:nt], *a.* hâlé; basané.

Sunday ['sʌndi], *n.* dimanche, *m.*

sunder ['sʌndə], *v.t.* séparer; couper en deux.

sundial ['sʌndaiəl], *n.* cadran solaire, *m.*

sundries ['sʌndriz], *n.pl.* choses diverses, *f.pl.*

sundry ['sʌndri], *a.* divers.

sun-flower ['sʌnflauə], *n.* tournesol, *m.*

sunken ['sʌŋkən], *a.* enfoncé; cave (*joues*); creux (*yeux*).

sunless ['sʌnlis], *a.* sans soleil.

sunlight ['sʌnlait], *n.* lumière du soleil, *f.*

sunlit ['sʌnlit], *a.* ensoleillé.

sunny ['sʌni], *a.* ensoleillé; (*fig.*) heureux; *it is sunny*, il fait du soleil.

sunrise ['sʌnraiz], *n.* lever du soleil, *m.*

sunset ['sʌnset], *n.* coucher du soleil, *m.*

sunshade ['sʌnʃeid], *n.* parasol, *m.*, ombrelle, *f.*

sunshine ['sʌnʃain], *n.* soleil, *m.*, clarté du soleil, *f.*

sunstroke ['sʌnstrouk], *n.* coup de soleil, *m.*, insolation, *f.*

sup [sʌp], *n.* (*Sc.*) petit coup, *m.*, gorgée, *f.—v.t.* boire à petits coups.—*v.i.* souper.

super ['sju:pə], *a.* (*slang*) *it is super*, c'est sensass (*sensationnel*).

superable ['sju:pərəbl], *a.* surmontable.

superabundance [sju:pərə'bʌndəns], *n.* surabondance, *f.*

superannuate [sju:pər'ænjueit], *v.t.* mettre à la retraite.

superannuated [sju:pər'ænjueitid], *a.* mis à la retraite, en retraite (*personne*); démodé.

superannuation [sju:pərænju'eiʃən], *n.* mise à la retraite, retraite, *f.*; *superannuation fund*, caisse de retraites, *f.*

superb [sju:'pə:b], *a.* superbe.

superbly [sju:'pə:bli], *adv.* superbement.

supercilious [sju:pə'siliəs], *a.* hautain, arrogant.

superciliously [sju:pə'siliəsli], *adv.* avec hauteur.

superciliousness [sju:pə'siliəsnis], *n.* hauteur; arrogance, *f.*

superficial [sju:pə'fiʃl], *a.* superficiel; de superficie (*mesure*).

superficiality [sju:pəfiʃi'æliti], *n.* caractère superficiel, *m.*

superficially [sju:pə'fiʃəli], *adv.* superficiellement.

superfine ['sju:pəfain], *a.* superfin; (*Comm.*) surfin.

superfluity [sju:pə'flu:iti], *n.* superfluité, *f.*; superflu, *m.*

superfluous [sju'pə:fluəs], *a.* superflu, inutile.

superhuman [sju:pə'hju:mən], *a.* surhumain.

superimpose [sju:pərim'pouz], *v.t.* superposer, surimposer.

superintend [sju:pərin'tend], *v.t.* surveiller.

superintendent [sju:pərin'tendənt], *n.* chef; directeur, inspecteur, surintendant; commissaire de police, *m.*

superior [sju'piəriə], *a.* and *n.* supérieur, *m.*

superiority [sjupiəri'oriti], *n.* supériorité, *f.*

superlative [sju'pə:lətiv], *a.* suprême; (*Gram.*) superlatif.—*n.* (*Gram.*) superlatif, *m.*

superman ['sju:pəmæn], *n.* (*pl.* -men [men]) surhomme, *m.*

supernatural [sju:pə'nætʃərəl], *a.* and *n.* surnaturel, *m.*

supernumerary [sju:pə'nju:mərəri], *a.* surnuméraire.—*n.* surnuméraire; (*Theat.*) figurant, *m.*

superscribe [sju:pə'skraib], *v.t.* mettre une adresse, une suscription *ou* une inscription à.

superscription [sju:pə'skripʃən], *n.* suscription; inscription; (*Coin.*) légende, *f.*; entête (*de lettre*), *m.*

supersede [sju:pə'si:d], *v.t.* remplacer.

superseded [sju:pə'si:did], *a.* démodé, périmé.

supersonic [sju:pə'sonik], *a.* (*onde*) ultrasonore; (*Av.*) supersonique.

superstition [sju:pə'stiʃən], *n.* superstition, *f.*

superstitious [sju:pə'stiʃəs], *a.* superstitieux.

superstructure ['sju:pəstrʌktʃə], *n.* superstructure, *f.*

super-tax ['sju:pətæks], *n.* surtaxe, *f.*

supervene [sju:pə'vi:n], *v.i.* survenir.

supervention [sju:pə'venʃən], *n.* survenance, *f.*

supervise ['sju:pəvaiz], *v.t.* surveiller.

supervision [sju:pə'viʒən], *n.* surveillance, inspection, *f.*

supervisor ['sju:pəvaizə], *n.* surveillant, *m.*

supine [sju'pain], *a.* couché sur le dos; (*fig.*) nonchalant.—['sju:pain], *n.* (*Gram.*) supin, *m.*

supper ['sʌpə], *n.* souper, *m.*; *supper time*, heure du souper, *f.*

supplant [sə'pla:nt], *v.t.* supplanter.

supple [sʌpl], *a.* souple, flexible.
supplement [sʌpli'ment], *v.t.* suppléer à; compléter.—['sʌpliment], *n.* supplément, *m.*
supplementary [sʌpli'mentəri], *a.* supplémentaire.
suppleness ['sʌplnis], *n.* souplesse, *f.*
suppliant ['sʌpliant], *a.* and *n.* suppliant, *m.*
supplicate ['sʌplikeit], *v.t.* supplier, implorer.
supplication [sʌpli'keiʃən], *n.* supplication, prière, *f.*
supplier [sə'plaiə], *n.* pourvoyeur; fournisseur, *m.*
supply [sə'plai], *n.* fourniture; provision, *f.,* approvisionnement (*réserve*), *m.*; (*Elec.*) alimentation, *f.*; (*Mil.*, *pl.*) vivres (*ravitaillement*); (*Parl.*) subsides, *m.pl.*—*v.t.* fournir; pourvoir à, subvenir à (*besoins*), ravitailler.
support [sə'pɔːt], *v.t.* soutenir, supporter; entretenir (*faire vivre*); appuyer (*aider*).—*n.* appui, soutien; support (*physique*); entretien (*des dépendants*), *m.*
supportable [sə'pɔːtəbl], *a.* supportable.
supporter [sə'pɔːtə], *n.* adhérent, partisan; appui, soutien; (*Spt.*) supporter; (*Her.*) support, *m.*
suppose [sə'pouz], *v.t.* supposer, s'imaginer; *to be supposed to* (*know*), être censé (*savoir*); *suppose we go,* si nous y allions.
supposed [sə'pouzd], *a.* présumé; prétendu, soi-disant; censé.
supposedly [sə'pouzidli], *adv.* censément.
supposing [sə'pouziŋ], *conj.* supposons, supposé (*que*).
supposition [sʌpə'ziʃən], *n.* supposition, *f.*
suppress [sə'pres], *v.t.* supprimer; réprimer (*révolte etc.*); étouffer; *a suppressed laugh,* un rire étouffé.
suppression [sə'preʃən], *n.* suppression; répression; dissimulation (*de la vérité*), *f.*
suppressor [sə'presə], *n.* (*Rad.*, *Tel.*) dispositif anti-parasites, *m.*
suppurate ['sʌpjureit], *v.i.* suppurer.
suppuration [sʌpju'reiʃən], *n.* suppuration, *f.*
supremacy [sju'preməsi], *n.* suprématie, *f.*
supreme [sju'priːm], *a.* suprême.
supremely [sju'priːmli], *adv.* suprêmement.
surcharge ['səːtʃɑːdʒ], *n.* surcharge, surtaxe, *f.*
sure [ʃuə], *a.* sûr, certain; assuré; *to be sure!* certainement! bien sûr! *to be sure to,* ne pas manquer de.—*adv.* sûrement, à coup sûr.
sure-footed [ʃuə'futid], *a.* au pied sûr.
surely ['ʃuəli], *adv.* sûrement, assurément, à coup sûr.
sureness ['ʃuənis], *n.* certitude, sûreté, *f.*
surety ['ʃuəti], *n.* certitude (*véracité*); sûreté, sécurité (*garantie*), *f.*; (*Law*) garant, *m.*
surf [səːf], *n.* ressac, *m.*; brisants sur la plage, *m.pl.*
surface ['səːfis], *n.* surface, *f.*
surfeit ['səːfit], *n.* rassasiement, *m.*; *to have a surfeit of,* être rassasié de.
surf-riding ['səːfraidiŋ], *n.* sport de l'aquaplane, planking, surf, *m.*
surge [səːdʒ], *n.* houle, lame de fond, *f.*—*v.i.* s'enfler, s'élever.
surgeon ['səːdʒən], *n.* chirurgien, *m.*
surgery ['səːdʒəri], *n.* chirurgie (*art*), *f.*
surgical ['səːdʒikl], *a.* chirurgical.
surliness ['səːlinis], *n.* morosité, *f.*

surly ['səːli], *a.* morose; hargneux (*chien*).
surmise ['səːmaiz], *n.* soupçon, *m.*, conjecture, *f.*—[sə'maiz], *v.t.* soupçonner, conjecturer.
surmount [sə'maunt], *v.t.* surmonter.
surmountable [sə'mauntəbl], *a.* surmontable.
surname ['səːneim], *n.* nom de famille, *m.*
surpass [sə'pɑːs], *v.t.* surpasser, l'emporter sur.
surpassable [sə'pɑːsəbl], *a.* qu'on peut surpasser.
surpassing [sə'pɑːsiŋ], *a.* éminent, supérieur, rare.
surplice ['səːplis], *n.* surplis, *m.*
surplus ['səːpləs], *a.* de surplus.—*n.* surplus, *m.*; *surplus stock,* solde, *m.*
surprise [sə'praiz], *n.* surprise, *f.*; étonnement, *m.*—*v.t.* surprendre, étonner.
surprising [sə'praiziŋ], *a.* surprenant, étonnant.
surrealism [sə'riːəlizm], *n.* surréalisme, *m.*
surrender [sə'rendə], *n.* reddition, capitulation, *f.*; abandon (*d'un titre, d'un droit*), *m.*; (*Law*) cession, *f.*—*v.t.* rendre; (*fig.*) abandonner, livrer (*personne etc.*); (*Law*) céder.—*v.i.* se rendre.
surreptitious [sʌrəp'tiʃəs], *a.* subreptice, clandestin; frauduleux.
surreptitiously [sʌrəp'tiʃəsli], *adv.* subrepticement.
surround [sə'raund], *v.t.* entourer, environner (*de*), (*Mil.*) cerner.
surrounding [sə'raundiŋ], *a.* environnant, d'alentour.—*n.* (*pl.*) alentours, environs, *m.pl.*, entourage, milieu, *m.*
surtax ['səːtæks], *n.* surtaxe, *f.*
survey ['səːvei], *n.* vue, *f.*, coup d'œil, *m.*; inspection (*examen*); expertise (*évaluation*), *f.*; arpentage (*de terrain etc*); (*Ordnance*) levé topographique, *m.*; *aerial survey,* levé aérophotogrammétrique, *m.*—[sə'vei], *v.t.* arpenter (*terrain*); (*Ordnance*) lever le plan de; (*fig.*) examiner, contempler.
surveying [sə'veiiŋ], *n.* arpentage, levé de plans, *m.*
surveyor [sə'veiə], *n.* inspecteur; arpenteur (*de terrain*); agent voyer (*ponts et chaussées*), *m.*
survival [sə'vaivl], *n.* survivance; survie, *f.*
survive [sə'vaiv], *v.t.* survivre à.—*v.i.* survivre.
surviving [sə'vaiviŋ], *a.* survivant.
survivor [sə'vaivə], *n.* survivant, *m.*
Susan [suːzn]. Suzanne, *f.*
susceptibility [səsepti'biliti], *n.* susceptibilité; sensibilité, *f.*
susceptible [sə'septibl], *a.* susceptible (*de*).
suspect ['sʌspekt], *a.* and *n.* suspect, *m.*—[sə'spekt], *v.t.*, *v.i.* soupçonner.
suspend [sə'spend], *v.t.* suspendre; cesser (*payements*).
suspender [sə'spendə], *n.* (*pl.*) jarretelles (*pour bas*); (*Am.*) bretelles (*pour pantalon*), *f.pl.*
suspense [sə'spens], *n.* suspens, doute, *m.*
suspension [sə'spenʃən], *n.* suspension, *f.*
suspicion [sə'spiʃən], *n.* soupçon, *m.*
suspicious [sə'spiʃəs], *a.* soupçonneux; suspect, louche (*équivoque*).
suspiciously [sə'spiʃəsli], *adv.* avec méfiance; d'une manière suspecte.

suspiciousness [sə'spiʃəsnis], *n.* caractère soupçonneux, *m.*, défiance, méfiance, *f.*

sustain [sə'stein], *v.t.* soutenir, supporter; éprouver, essuyer (*perte*).

sustaining [sə'steiniŋ], *a.* fortifiant, nourrissant.

sustenance ['sʌstinəns], *n.* nourriture, *f.*, aliments, *m.pl.*; entretien, *m.*, subsistance, *f.*

suzerain ['sju:zərein], *a.* and *n.* suzerain, *m.*

suzerainty ['sju:zəreinti], *n.* suzeraineté, *f.*

swab [swɔb], *n.* torchon; (*Naut.*) faubert; tampon (*de coton hydrophile*), *m.*—*v.t.* fauberter; nettoyer.

swaddle [swɔdl], *v.t.* emmailloter.

swaddling ['swɔdliŋ], *n.* emmaillotement, *m.*; *swaddling clothes*, maillot, *m.*

swag [swæg], *n.* (*slang*) butin; (*Australia*) baluchon, *m.*

swagger ['swægə], *v.i.* faire le rodomont; se donner des airs, se vanter.

swaggerer ['swægərə], *n.* fanfaron, *m.*

swaggering ['swægəriŋ], *a.* de fanfaron.—*n.* fanfaronnade, *f.*

swagman ['swægmən], *n.* (*pl.* -**men** [men]) (*Australia*) chemineau, *m.*

swain [swein], *n.* (*poet.*) berger, jeune paysan, *m.*

swallow (1) ['swɔlou], *v.t.* avaler; engloutir (*faire disparaître*); consumer; (*fig.*) gober.—*n.* (*pop.*) avaloir, gosier (*gorge*), *m.*; gorgée (*ce qu'on avale*), *f.*

swallow (2) ['swɔlou], *n.* hirondelle (*oiseau*), *f.*

swallow dive ['swɔloudaiv], *n.* (*Swim.*) saut de l'ange, *m.*

swallower ['swɔlouə], *n.* avaleur, *m.*

swallow-tail ['swɔloulteil], *a.* en queue d'aronde.—*n.* habit à queue de morue, *m.*

swamp [swɔmp], *n.* marais, marécage, *m.*—*v.t.* submerger; faire couler (*bateau*).

swampy ['swɔmpi], *a.* marécageux.

swan [swɔn], *n.* cygne, *m.* [see **swallow dive**]

swank [swæŋk], *n.* pose; (*pop.*) épate, *f.*—*v.i.* (*pop.*) crâner, poser; faire du chiqué.

swanky ['swæŋki], *a.* chic, rupin.

swap [swɔp], *v.t.* (*colloq.*) échanger, troquer.—*n.* troc, échange, *m.*

sward [swɔ:d], *n.* (*poet.*) gazon, *m.*, pelouse, *f.*

swarm [swɔ:m], *n.* essaim (*d'abeilles*), *m.*—*v.i.* essaimer; (*fig.*) accourir en foule.

swarming ['swɔ:miŋ], *n.* essaimage, *m.*

swarthiness ['swɔ:ðinis], *n.* teint basané, *m.*

swarthy ['swɔ:ði], *a.* basané, hâlé.

swashbuckler ['swɔʃbʌklə], *n.* fanfaron, matamore, *m.*

swastika ['swɔstikə], *n.* croix gammée, *f.*

swat [swɔt], *v.t.* écraser, tuer (*mouche*).

swath [swɔ:θ], *n.* andain, *m.*, fauchée, *f.*

swathe [sweið], *v.t.* emmailloter.

sway [swei], *v.t.* manier, porter; balancer (*agiter*); (*fig.*) diriger (*gouverner*); influencer (*l'opinion*).—*v.i.* se balancer.—*n.* empire, *m.*; domination (*règne*), *f.*

swaying ['sweiiŋ], *n.* balancement, *m.*; oscillation, *f.*

swear [swɛə], *v.t. irr.* faire prêter serment à (*témoins etc.*); prêter (*serment*); *to swear at*, injurier.—*v.i.* jurer; prêter serment.

swearer ['swɛərə], *n.* jureur, *m.*

swearing ['swɛəriŋ], *n.* serments; jurons (*gros mots*), *m.pl.*; *swearing in*, prestation de serment, assermentation (*de juges etc.*), *f.*

swear-word ['swɛəwə:d], *n.* juron, gros mot, *m.*

sweat [swet], *n.* sueur, transpiration, *f.*—*v.t.* faire suer.—*v.i.* suer, transpirer.

sweater ['swetə], *n.* chandail, tricot, pullover (*vêtement*), *m.*

sweatiness ['swetinis], *n.* sueur, *f.*, état de sueur, *m.*

sweating ['swetiŋ], *a.* en sueur; tout en sueur.—*n.* moiteur; fatigue, *f.*

sweaty ['sweti], *a.* en sueur.

Swede [swi:d], *n.* Suédois (*personne*), *m.*

swede [swi:d], *n.* (*Bot.*) rutabaga, *m.*

Sweden [swi:dn], la Suède, *f.*

Swedish ['swi:diʃ], *a.* suédois, de Suède,—*n.* suédois (*langue*), *m.*

sweep [swi:p], *v.t. irr.* balayer; ramoner (*cheminée*); draguer (*rivière*).—*v.i.* passer rapidement.—*n.* coup de balai; ramoneur (*de cheminées*), *m.*; étendue, portée (*distance*), courbe, *f.*; (*fig.*) sweepstake, *m.*; *to make a clean sweep of*, faire table rase de.

sweeper ['swi:pə], *n.* balayeur; ramoneur (*de cheminées*), *m.*

sweeping ['swi:piŋ], *a.* rapide, irrésistible; (*fig.*) général; balayage; ramonage (*de cheminées*), *m.*; (*pl.*) balayures, ordures, *f.pl.*

sweepstake ['swi:psteik], *n.* poule, *f.*; sweepstake, *m.*

sweet [swi:t], *a.* doux, sucré; parfumé (*odeur*); (*Mus.*) suave, mélodieux; frais (*poisson etc.*); (*fig.*) joli, charmant.—*n.* chose douce, *f.*; (*pl.*) entremets, sucreries, *f.pl.*; chéri, *m.*

sweetbread ['swi:tbred], *n.* ris de veau *ou* d'agneau, *m.*

sweeten [swi:tn], *v.t.* sucrer; purifier (*salle, l'air etc.*); (*fig.*) adoucir.

sweetener ['swi:tnə], *n.* adoucissant, *m.*

sweetening ['swi:tniŋ], *n.* adoucissement, *m.*

sweetheart ['swi:thɑ:t], *n.* amoureux; amant; bon ami, *m.*

sweetly ['swi:tli], *adv.* doucement, gentiment; mélodieusement.

sweetmeat ['swi:tmi:t], *n.* sucrerie, *f.*, bon-bon, *m.*

sweetness ['swi:tnis], *n.* douceur; fraîcheur; mélodie, *f.*; (*fig.*) charme, *m.*

sweet pea ['swi:t'pi:], *n.* pois de senteur, *m.*

sweet shop ['swi:tʃɔp], *n.* confiserie, *f.*

sweet william ['swi:t'wiljəm], *n.* œillet de poète, *m.*

swell [swel], *v.t. irr.* enfler, gonfler; aggraver; augmenter (*ajouter à*).—*v.i.* enfler, s'enfler, se gonfler; grossir, croître (*multiplier*); (*fig.*) bouffir (*d'orgueil, de colère etc.*).—*a.* (*colloq.*) à la mode, chic; épatant.—*n.* élévation, montée, *f.*; renflement (*de son*), *m.*; houle (*de mer*), *f.*; (*colloq.*) rupin, élégant, *m.*

swelling ['sweliŋ], *n.* grandissure (*qui augmente*).—*n.* enflure; bouffissure (*pathologique*), *f.*; gonflement (*protubérance*), *m.*, crue (*de rivière*), *f.*; soulèvement (*des vagues*); (*fig.*) mouvement, transport (*de colère etc.*), *m.*

swelter ['sweltə], *v.i.* étouffer de chaleur; *it is sweltering hot*, il fait une chaleur étouffante.

swerve [swə:v], *v.i.* s'écarter, se détourner, faire un écart (*cheval*), faire une embardée (*voiture*).

swerving ['swə:viŋ], *n.* écart, *m.*, déviation, embardée (*de voiture*), *f.*

swift [swift], *a.* vite; rapide, prompt.—*n.* (*Orn.*) martinet, *m.*

swift-footed ['swift'futid], *a.* rapide à la course; au pied léger.

swiftly ['swiftli], *adv.* vite, rapidement.

swiftness ['swiftnis], *n.* rapidité, vitesse, *f.*

swig [swig], *v.t., v.i.* (*pop.*) boire à longs traits.—*n.* long trait (*d'alcool*), *m.*

swill [swil], *v.t.* laver, rincer; boire avidement.—*v.i.* boire; (*colloq.*) s'enivrer.—*n.* lavure de vaisselle, lavure, *f.*; grand coup (*d'alcool*), *m.*

swim [swim], *v.t. irr.* traverser à la nage.—*v.i.* nager; flotter, surnager; (*fam.*) tourner (*la tête*); être inondé (de) (*être submergé*).—*n.* nage, *f.*; *in the swim*, à la page.

swimmer ['swimə], *n.* nageur, *m.*

swimming ['swimiŋ], *n.* natation (*sport*); nage (*action*), *f.*; (*fam.*) étourdissement (*de tête*), *m.*; *by swimming*, à la nage.

swimming baths ['swimiŋbɑːθz], **swimming pool** ['swimiŋpuːl], *n.* piscine, *f.*

swimmingly ['swimiŋli], *adv.* à merveille.

swim-suit ['swimsjuːt], *n.* maillot de bain, *m.*

swindle [swindl], *v.t.* escroquer.—*n.* escroquerie, *f.*

swindler ['swindlə], *n.* escroc, filou, *m.*

swindling ['swindliŋ], *n.* escroquerie, *f.*

swine [swain], *n.inv.* cochon, pourceau, porc; (*pop.*) salaud, *m.*

swing [swiŋ], *v.t. irr.* balancer; brandir (*une arme etc.*).—*v.i.* se balancer; osciller; pendiller, être suspendu.—*n.* oscillation (*mouvement*), *f.*; balancement, *m.*; balançoire (*siège*), *f.*; (*Mus.*) swing, *m.*; *in full swing*, en pleine activité.

swing-door ['swiŋ'dɔː], *n.* porte battante, *f.*

swinging ['swiŋiŋ], *n.* balancement, *m.*, oscillation, *f.*

swipe [swaip], *n.* taloche, *f.*—*v.t.* donner une taloche à; (*fam.*) chiper.

swirl [swəːl], *v.i.* tourbillonner.—*n.* remous, *m.*

swish [swiʃ], *v.t.* cingler, fouetter.—*v.i.* siffler, bruire.

Swiss [swis], *a.* helvétique, suisse.—*n.* Suisse (*personne*), *m.*, Suissesse, *f.*

switch [switʃ], *n.* badine, houssine, gaule; (*Rail.*) aiguille, *f.*; (*Elec.*) commutateur, interrupteur, *m.*—*v.t.* houspiller, cingler; (*Rail.*) aiguiller; changer (*de*); *to switch off*, couper; *to switch on*, ouvrir.—*v.i. to switch off*, couper le courant; *to switch on*, mettre le courant. [see **pointsman**]

switchboard ['switʃbɔːd], *n.* standard (téléphonique), *m.*; *switchboard operator*, standardiste, *m., f.*

Switzerland ['switsələnd]. la Suisse, *f.*

swivel [swivl], *n.* émerillon; pivot, *m.*—*v.i.* pivoter.

swoon [swuːn], *v.i.* s'évanouir.—*n.* evanouissement, *m.*

swoop [swuːp], *v.i.* fondre (*sur*).—*n. at one (fell) swoop*, d'un seul coup (*fatal*).

sword [sɔːd], *n.* épée, *f.*

sword bearer ['sɔːdbɛərə], *n.* porte-épée, *m.*

sword-fish ['sɔːdfiʃ], *n.* espadon, *m.*

swordsman ['sɔːdzmən], *n.* (*pl.* **-men** [men]) tireur, homme d'épée, *m.*

swordstick ['sɔːdstik], *n.* canne à épée, *f.*

sworn [swɔːn], *a.* juré; (*Law*) assermenté; acharné (*ennemi*).

swot [swɔt], *v.i.* (*Sch. slang*) piocher, bûcher.—*n.* bûcheur, *m.*

sycamore ['sikəmɔː], *n.* sycomore, *m.*

sycophancy ['sikəfənsi], *n.* adulation, *f.*

sycophant ['sikəfənt], *n.* adulateur, *m.*

sycophantic [sikə'fæntik], *a.* adulateur.

syllabic [si'læbik], *a.* syllabique.

syllable ['siləbl], *n.* syllabe, *f.*

syllabus ['siləbəs], *n.* résumé; sommaire, programme (*surtout d'études scolaires*), *m.*

syllogism ['silədʒizm], *n.* syllogisme, *m.*

sylph [silf], *n.* sylphe, *m.*

sylvan ['silvən], *a.* sylvestre, des bois, champêtre, agreste.

symbol [simbl], *n.* symbole, *m.*

symbolic [sim'bɔlik], **symbolical** [sim'bɔlikl], *a.* symbolique.

symbolism ['simbəlizm], *n.* symbolisme, *m.*

symbolize ['simbəlaiz], *v.t., v.i.* symboliser.

symmetrical [si'metrikl], *a.* symétrique.

symmetry ['simitri], *n.* symétrie, *f.*

sympathetic [simpə'θetik], *a.* sympathique (*nerf*); compatissant.

sympathize ['simpəθaiz], *v.i.* sympathiser (*avec*); compatir (*à*).

sympathizer ['simpəθaizə], *n.* sympathisant, *m.*

sympathy ['simpəθi], *n.* sympathie; compréhension, *f.*; condoléances, *f.pl.*

symphony ['simfəni], *n.* symphonie, *f.*

symposium [sim'pouzjəm], *n.* (*fig.*) recueil d'articles (*sur un seul sujet*), *m.*

symptom ['simptəm], *n.* symptôme, *m.*

symptomatic [simptə'mætik], *a.* symptomatique.

synagogue ['sinəgɔg], *n.* synagogue, *f.*

synchromesh ['siŋkromeʃ], *n.* and *n.* synchromesh, *m.*

synchronize ['siŋkrənaiz], *v.i.* synchroniser (*avec*).

syncopate ['siŋkəpeit], *v.t.* syncoper.

syndic ['sindik], *n.* syndic, *m.*

syndicate ['sindikit], *n.* syndicat, *f.*—['sindikeit], *v.t.* syndiquer.—*v.i.* se syndiquer.

synod ['sinəd], *n.* synode, *m.*

synonym ['sinənim], *n.* synonyme, *m.*

synonymous [si'nɔniməs], *a.* synonyme.

synopsis [si'nɔpsis], *n.* (*pl.* **synopses** [si'nɔpsiːz]) sommaire, *f.*

syntax ['sintæks], *n.* syntaxe, *f.*

synthesis ['sinθisis], *n.* (*pl.* **syntheses** ['sinθisiːz]) synthèse, *f.*

synthesize ['sinθisaiz], *v.t.* synthétiser.

synthetic [sin'θetik], *a.* synthétique.

synthetically [sin'θetikli], *adv.* synthétiquement.

Syria ['siriə]. la Syrie, *f.*

Syriac ['siriæk], *a.* syriaque.—*n.* syriaque (*langue*), *m.*

Syrian ['siriən], *a.* syrien.—*n.* syrien (*langue*); Syrien (*personne*), *m.*

syringe ['sirindʒ], *n.* seringue, *f.*—*v.t.* seringuer.

syrup ['sirəp], *n.* sirop, *m.*

syrupy ['sirəpi], *a.* sirupeux.

system ['sistəm], *n.* système, régime; réseau (*ferroviaire*), *m.*

systematic [sistə'mætik], *a.* systématique.
systematically [sistə'mætikli], *adv.* systématiquement.
systematize ['sistəmətaiz], *v.t.* systématiser.

T

T, t [ti:]. vingtième lettre de l'alphabet, *m.*;
  T-square, té à dessin, *m.*
tab [tæb], *n.* étiquette; patte, *f.*, écusson, *m.*
tabby ['tæbi], *a.* tacheté, moucheté.—*n.* chat
  moucheté, rayé *ou* tigré, *m.*
tabernacle ['tæbənækl], *n.* tabernacle, *m.*
table [teibl], *n.* table, *f.*; *to be seated at
  table*, être attablé; *to clear the table*,
  desservir; *to lay the table*, mettre le
  couvert; *to sit down to table*, se mettre à
  table.—*v.t.* déposer (*un projet de loi*).
table-cloth ['teiblklɔθ], *n.* nappe, *f.*
table linen ['teibllinin], *n.* linge de table, *m.*
tablespoon ['teiblspu:n], *n.* cuiller à soupe,
  f.
tablespoonful ['teiblspu:nful], *n.* grande
  cuillerée, *f.*
tablet ['tæblit], *n.* tablette, *f.*; (*Med.*) com
  primé, *m.*
taboo [tə'bu:], *a.* and *n.* tabou, *m.*
tabulate ['tæbjuleit], *v.t.* cataloguer.
tacit ['tæsit], *a.* tacite, implicite.
tacitly ['tæsitli], *adv.* tacitement, implicite
  ment.
taciturn ['tæsitə:n], *a.* taciturne.
Tacitus ['tæsitəs]. (*L. Lit.*) Tacite, *m.*
tack [tæk], *n.* petit clou, *m.*, broquette; (*Naut.*)
  amure, *f.*—*v.t.* clouer; (*Needlework*) bâtir,
  faufiler.—*v.i.* (*Naut.*) virer vent devant.
tackiness ['tækinis], *n.* viscosité, *f.*
tacking ['tækiŋ], *n.* cloutage, *m.*; (*Needlework*)
  faufilure, *f.*; (*Naut.*) virement de bord, lou
  voyage, *m.*
tackle [tækl], *n.* attirail, (*Naut.*) palan; (*Spt.*)
  plaquage, *m.*; (*fig.*) ustensiles, *m.pl.*;
  fishing tackle, articles de pêche, *m.pl.*—
  v.t. empoigner; (*Ftb.*) plaquer; (*fig.*)
  attaquer (*travail etc.*).
tacky ['tæki], *a.* collant, visqueux, gluant.
tact [tækt], *n.* toucher; (*fig.*) tact, savoir-faire,
  m.
tactful ['tæktful], *a.* plein de tact.
tactical ['tæktikl], *a.* tactique.
tactician [tæk'tiʃən], *n.* tacticien, *m.*
tactics ['tæktiks], *n.pl.* tactique, *f.*
tactile ['tæktail], *a.* tactile.
tactless ['tæktlis], *a.* sans tact, sans savoir-
  faire.
tadpole ['tædpoul], *n.* têtard, *m.*
taffeta ['tæfitə], *n.* taffetas, *m.*
taffrail ['tæfreil], *n.* couronnement (*de la
  poupe*), *m.*
tag [tæg], *n.* ferret, fer, bout ferré, *m.*; éti
  quette (*fiche*), *f.*; dicton, *m.*—*v.t.* ferrer
  (*cordon*); (*fig.*) coudre (à).
tail [teil], *n.* queue; (*fig.*) extrémité, *f.*; bout,
  pan (*d'habit*), *m.*; pile (*de pièce de monnaie*),
  f.; empennage (*d'avion*), *m.*—*v.t.* couper la

queue (*d'un animal*); ôter les queues (*de
  fruits*); (*fam.*) filer (*criminels etc.*).
tail coat ['teilkout], *n.* habit, *m.*
tailed [teild], *a.* à queue.
tailless ['teillis], *a.* sans queue, anoure.
tail-light ['teillait], *n.* feu arrière, *m.*
tailor ['teilə], *n.* tailleur, *m.*
tailor-made ['teilə'meid], *a.* and *n.* tailleur,
  m.
tail-plane ['teilplein], *n.* (*Av.*) stabilisateur, *m.*
taint [teint], *v.t.* corrompre, gâter.—*v.i.* se
  corrompre; se gâter (*viande*).—*n.* souillure,
  corruption; tache (*du péché*), *f.*
take [teik], *v.t. irr.* prendre; mener (*quel
  qu'un*); conduire (*personne en voiture*);
  porter (*chose*); emmener (*quelqu'un*); enlever
  (*voler*); soustraire (*retrancher*); saisir; ac
  cepter; (*fig.*) supposer; profiter de (*une
  occasion*); contenir (*avoir de la place pour*);
  faire (*une promenade etc.*); avoir (*vengeance
  etc.*); retenir (*chambre etc.*); suivre (*une
  route etc.*); mettre (*temps*); *to take advan
  tage of*, profiter de; *to take away*, em
  mener (*personne*), emporter (*choses*), ôter
  (*retirer*); desservir (*le couvert etc.*); dérober
  (*voler*); *to take back*, reprendre, rem
  porter; *to take down*, descendre; rabattre
  (*humilier*); démolir (*maison*); prendre note
  de (*inscrire*); *to take heed*, prendre garde
  (à); *to take in*, faire entrer; comprendre
  (*consister etc.*); recevoir, recevoir chez soi
  (*loger*); tromper, duper; faire sa provision de
  (*vivres etc.*); *to take off*, enlever, ôter,
  retirer (*vêtement*); caricaturer (*imiter*); *to
  take out*, faire sortir, sortir (*chose*); pro
  mener (*personne*); arracher (*dents*); ôter,
  enlever (*taches etc.*); *to take over*, se
  charger de, prendre la succession de
  (*affaires*); *to take up*, monter, faire monter,
  soulever (*lever*); ramasser (*relever*); com
  mencer, entamer, aborder (*des études etc.*);
  occuper (*temps*).—*v.i.* réussir (*avoir du
  succès*); prendre (*feu etc.*); *to take after*,
  ressembler à; (*Av.*) *to take off*, décoller;
  (*fam.*) *to take on*, se lamenter, s'affliger; *to
  take up with*, s'associer à.—*n.* prise,
  pêche, quantité (*de poissons*); (*Cine.*) prise de
  vue, *f.*
take-in ['teikin], *n.* duperie, attrape, *f.*
take-off ['teiko:f], *n.* caricature, charge, *f.*;
  (*Av.*) décollage, *m.*
take-over ['teikouvə], *n.* (*Fin.*) rachat (*d'entre
  prise*), *m.*; *take-over bid*, offre de rachat, *f.*
taking ['teikiŋ], *a.* attrayant, séduisant;
  (*collog.*) contagieux (*maladie*).—*n.* prise;
  arrestation, *f.*; (*pl.*) recettes (*argent*), *f.pl.*
talc [tælk], *n.* talc, *m.*
talcum powder ['tælkəm'paudə], *n.* talc, *m.*
tale [teil], *n.* conte, récit, *m.*; histoire, *f.*
talent ['tælənt], *n.* talent, *m.*
talented ['tæləntid], *a.* de talent, habile, bien
  doué.
talisman ['tælizmən], *n.* talisman, *m.*
talk [tɔ:k], *v.t.* parler, dire; *to talk over*,
  cajoler (*quelqu'un*); discuter (*quelque chose*).
  —*v.i.* parler (*de*); converser, causer;
  bavarder, jaser (*babiller*); *to talk at*, haran
  guer.—*n.* entretien, *m.*, propos, *m.pl.*, con
  versation; causerie (*intime*), *f.*; bavardage,
  bruit (*racontar*), *m.*; *small talk*, banalités,
  f.pl.
talkative ['tɔ:kətiv], *a.* causeur, bavard.

talker ['tɔːkə], n. causeur, parleur, m.
talking ['tɔːkiŋ], a. causeur, bavard.—n. conversation, causerie, f.
tall [tɔːl], a. grand (personne); haut (chose).
tallboy ['tɔːlbɔi], n. chiffonnier, m.; (haute) commode-secrétaire, f.
tallness ['tɔːlnis], n. grande taille, hauteur, f.
tallow ['tælou], n. suif, m.
tallow-candle ['tælou'kændl], n. chandelle, f.
tally ['tæli], n. taille; entaille, marque; étiquette (à bagages), f.—v.i. s'accorder; to tally with, s'accorder avec, correspondre à.
tally-ho! ['tæli'hou], int. (Hunt.) taïaut!
Talmud ['tælmʌd], n. talmud, m.
talon ['tælən], n. serre, griffe, f.
tambourine [tæmbə'riːn], n. tambour de basque, m.
tame [teim], a. apprivoisé; domestique; (fig.) insipide.—v.t. apprivoiser; dompter (dominer).
tamely ['teimli], adv. avec soumission; sans cœur.
tameness ['teimnis], n. apprivoisement, m., domesticité; soumission; (fig.) faiblesse (de style etc.), f.
tamer ['teimə], n. dompteur (de bête sauvage) m.
taming ['teimiŋ], n. apprivoisement, m.
tamp [tæmp], v.t. bourrer, tamponner.
tamper ['tæmpə], v.i. to tamper with, se mêler (de); expérimenter (avec); jouer avec; fausser (serrure etc.).
tampering ['tæmpəriŋ], n. menées secrètes, f.pl.
tan [tæn], n. tan; tanné (couleur); hâle (de la peau), m.—v.t. tanner; bronzer (la peau).
tandem ['tændəm], n. tandem (bicyclette), m.
tang [tæŋ], n. goût, m., saveur, f.
tangent ['tændʒənt], n. tangente, f.
tangerine [tændʒə'riːn], n. mandarine, f.
tangible ['tændʒibl], a. tangible, palpable.
Tangier(s) [tæn'dʒiə(z)]. Tanger, m.
tangle [tæŋgl], n. enchevêtrement, m.—v.t. embrouiller, enchevêtrer.
tangled [tæŋgld], a. embrouillé.
tango ['tæŋgou], n. tango, m.
tank [tæŋk], n. réservoir; (Mil.) char (d'assaut), m.
tankard ['tæŋkəd], n. chope, f.
tanker ['tæŋkə], n. bateau citerne, m.
tanner ['tænə], n. tanneur, m.
tannery ['tænəri], n. tannerie, f.
tanning ['tæniŋ], n. tannage, m.; (fam.) rossée, f.
tantalize ['tæntəlaiz], v.t. tantaliser, tourmenter.
tantalizing ['tæntəlaiziŋ], a. tentant, torturant.
tantamount ['tæntəmaunt], a. équivalent (à).
tantrum ['tæntrəm], n. mauvaise humeur, f.
Tanzania [tænzə'niːə]. la Tanzanie, f.
tap (1) [tæp], n. robinet (bain); comptoir (bar), m.; cannelle (de baril), f.; taraud (outil), m.; on tap, en perce.—v.t. tirer (liquide); mettre en perce (baril); inciser (arbre); tarauder (vis etc.); (Surg.) faire la ponction à.
tap (2) [tæp], n. tape, f., petit coup (à la porte etc.), m.—v.t. taper, frapper doucement.—v.i. taper, frapper.
tape [teip], n. ruban (de fil), m.; ganse (sur habit); bande (magnétique), f.; red tape, (fig.) routine administrative, f.

tape measure ['teipmeʒə], n. mètre ruban, m.
taper ['teipə], n. bougie effilée, f.; (Eccles.) cierge, m.
tape recorder ['teiprikɔːdə], n. magnétophone, m.
tape recording ['teiprikɔːdiŋ], n. enregistrement magnétique, m.
tapering ['teipəriŋ], a. effilé.
tapestry ['tæpistri], n. tapisserie, f.
tape-worm ['teipwəːm], n. ver solitaire, m.
tapioca [tæpi'oukə], n. tapioca, m.
tapir ['teipiə], n. tapir, m.
tappet ['tæpit], n. taquet (de soupape), m.
tapping (1) ['tæpiŋ], n. taraudage (de vis), m.; mise en perce (de baril); incision (d'arbre); (Surg.) ponction, f.
tapping (2) ['tæpiŋ], n. tapotement, m.
tar [tɑː], n. goudron; loup de mer (matelot), m. —v.t. goudronner.
tarantella [tærən'telə], n. tarentelle (danse), f.
tarantula [tə'ræntjulə], n. tarentule, f.
tardily ['tɑːdili], adv. tardivement, lentement.
tardiness ['tɑːdinis], n. lenteur; tardiveté (de fruit), f.
tardy ['tɑːdi], a. lent; en retard, tardif.
tare (1) [tɛə], n. tare (poids), f.
tare (2) [tɛə], n. (Script.) ivraie; (pl.) (Agric.) vesce, f.
target ['tɑːgit], n. cible, f.; but, objectif, m.
tariff ['tærif], n. tarif, m.
tarmac ['tɑːmæk], n. macadam, m.; (Av.) piste d'envol, f.—v.t. goudronner.
tarn [tɑːn], n. petit lac (de montagne), m.
tarnish ['tɑːniʃ], v.t. ternir; (fig.) souiller, flétrir.—v.i. se ternir.
tarpaulin [tɑː'pɔːlin], n. (Naut.) prélart, m., bâche, toile goudronnée, f.
tarry (1) ['tɑːri], a. goudronneux, bitumeux.
tarry (2) ['tæri], v.i. rester, tarder.
tart (1) [tɑːt], n. tarte, tourte, f.
tart (2) [tɑːt], a. acide, âcre; (fig.) aigre.
tartan ['tɑːtən], n. tartan, m.
tartar ['tɑːtə], n. (Chem.) tartre, m.
tartaric [tɑː'tærik], a. tartrique.
tartish ['tɑːtiʃ], a. aigrelet.
tartly ['tɑːtli], adv. avec aigreur, (fig.) vertement, sévèrement.
tartness ['tɑːtnis], n. acidité; (fig.) aigreur, f.
task [tɑːsk], n. tâche, f.; devoir (leçon); pensum (punition), m.; to take to task, réprimander, semoncer.
taskmaster ['tɑːskmɑːstə], n. chef de corvée, m.
Tasmania [tæz'meinjə]. la Tasmanie, f.
Tasmanian [tæz'meinjən], a. tasmanien.—n. Tasmanien (personne), m.
tassel [tæsl], n. gland, m.
taste [teist], v.t. goûter; (fig.) savourer, éprouver.—v.i. goûter (de); avoir un goût (de).—n. goût; soupçon (trace), m.
tasteful ['teistful], a. de bon goût.
tastefully ['teistfuli], adv. avec goût.
tasteless ['teistlis], a. fade, insipide.
tastelessly ['teistlisli], adv. insipidement, fadement.
taster ['teistə], n. dégustateur, m.
tasting ['teistiŋ], n. dégustation, f.
tasty ['teisti], a. (colloq.) de bon goût; savoureux.

tatter ['tætə], *n.* haillon, lambeau, *m.*, guenille, *f.*

tattered ['tætəd], *a.* déguenillé, en haillons (*personne*); en lambeaux, tout déchiré (*vêtements etc.*).

tatting ['tætiŋ], *n.* frivolité (*dentelle*), *f.*

tattle [tætl], *n.* babil, caquet, *m.*—*v.i.* bavarder.

tattler ['tætlə], *n.* babillard, bavard, *m.*

tattling ['tætliŋ], *a.* babillard, bavard.

tattoo [tə'tu:], *v.t.* tatouer.—*n.* tatouage, *m.*; (*Mil.*) fête militaire, *f.*

taunt [tɔ:nt], *n.* injure, *f.*, reproche amer, *m.* —*v.t.* tancer, reprocher à, injurier.

tauntingly ['tɔ:ntiŋli], *adv.* injurieusement.

Taurus ['tɔ:rəs], (*Astron.*) le Taureau, *m.*

taut [tɔ:t], *a.* raide, tendu; enflé (*voile*).

tautology [tɔ:'tɔlədʒi], *n.* tautologie, *f.*

tavern ['tævən], *n.* taverne, *f.*; cabaret, *m.*

tawdry ['tɔ:dri], *a.* criard, de mauvais goût, prétentieux.

tawny ['tɔ:ni], *a.* fauve.

tawse [tɔ:z], *n.* martinet, *m.*

tax [tæks], *n.* impôt, *m.*, taxe; (*fig.*) contribution, *f.*; *income tax*, impôt sur le revenu; *purchase tax*, taxe de luxe; *tax evasion*, fraude fiscale, *f.*; *surtax*, surtaxe, *f.*—*v.t.* imposer, taxer; (*fig.*) accuser (*de*).

taxable ['tæksəbl], *a.* imposable.

taxation [tæk'seiʃən], *n.* taxation, *f.*

tax-free ['tæks'fri:], *a.* exempt d'impôts.

taxi ['tæksi], *n.* taxi, *m.*

tax-payer ['tækspeiə], *n.* contribuable, *m.*, *f.*

tea [ti:], *n.* thé, *m.*; tisane (*infusion*), *f.*; goûter (*repas*), *m.*

tea caddy ['ti:kædi], *n.* boîte à thé, *f.*

tea cake ['ti:keik], *n.* brioche, *f.*

teach [ti:tʃ], *v.t. irr.* enseigner, instruire; apprendre (*à*).—*v.i.* enseigner, professer.

teachable ['ti:tʃəbl], *a.* disposé à apprendre, docile; enseignable (*chose*).

teacher ['ti:tʃə], *n.* maître, instituteur; professeur (*de lycée*), *m.*

tea chest ['ti:tʃest], *n.* caisse à thé, *f.*

teaching ['ti:tʃiŋ], *n.* enseignement, *m.*

tea-cup ['ti:kʌp], *n.* tasse à thé, *f.*

teak [ti:k], *n.* (*Bot.*) teck, tek, *m.*

teal [ti:l], *n.* (*Orn.*) sarcelle, *f.*

team [ti:m], *n.* attelage, *m.*, (*Spt.*) équipe, *f.*

teapot ['ti:pot], *n.* théière, *f.*

tear (1) [tiə], *n.* larme, *f.*, pleur, *m.*

tear (2) [tɛə], *v.t. irr.* déchirer; (*fig.*) arracher; *to tear asunder*, déchirer en deux.—*v.i.* se déchirer.—*n.* déchirure, *f.*; *wear and tear*, usure, *f.*

tear-drop ['tiədrop], *n.* larme, *f.*

tearful ['tiəful], *a.* tout en larmes.

tearfully ['tiəfuli], *adv.* les larmes aux yeux.

tearing ['tɛəriŋ], *n.* déchirement, *m.*

tease [ti:z], *v.t.* taquiner, tourmenter; carder (*laine*).—*n.* taquin, *m.*

tea service ['ti:sə:vis], *n.* service à thé, *m.*

teasing ['ti:ziŋ], *a.* taquin.—*n.* taquinerie, *f.*

teaspoon ['ti:spu:n], *n.* cuiller à thé, *f.*

teaspoonful ['ti:spu:nful], *n.* petite cuillerée, *f.*

tea strainer ['ti:streinə], *n.* passe-thé, *m.*

teat [ti:t], *n.* mamelon, tétin, *m.*; tette, *f.*

tea table ['ti:teibl], *n.* table à thé, *f.*

tea time ['ti:taim], *n.* l'heure du thé, *f.*

tea tray ['ti:trei], *n.* plateau à thé, *m.*

tea urn ['ti:ə:n], *n.* fontaine à thé, *f.*

technical ['teknikl], *a.* technique, de l'art; *technical school*, école professionnelle, *f.*

technicality [tekni'kæliti], *n.* caractère technique; terme technique (*mot*), *m.*; (*fig.*) formalité, *f.*

technically ['teknikli], *adv.* techniquement.

technician [tek'niʃən], *n.* technicien, *m.*

technique [tek'ni:k], *n.* technique, *f.*

technologist [tek'nɔlədʒist], *n.* technologue, *m.*, *f.*

technology [tek'nɔlədʒi], *n.* technologie, *f.*

teddy ['tedi], *n.* *teddy bear*, ours en peluche, *m.*

tedious ['ti:diəs], *a.* ennuyeux, fatigant.

tedium ['ti:diəm], *n.* ennui, *m.*

tee [ti:], *n.* dé (*au golf*), *m.*

teem [ti:m], *v.i.* être fécond (*en*); *to teem with*, abonder en.

teeming ['ti:miŋ], *a.* fécond, fertile, surabondant (*de*).

teenager ['ti:neidʒə], *n.* adolescent, *m.*

teens [ti:nz], *n.pl.* l'âge de treize à dix-neuf ans, *m.*; *to be in one's teens*, n'avoir pas vingt ans.

teeth [TOOTH].

teethe [ti:ð], *v.i.* faire ses dents.

teething ['ti:ðiŋ], *n.* dentition, *f.*

teetotal [ti:'toutl], *a.* de tempérance.

teetotal(l)er [ti:'toutlə], *n.* buveur d'eau, *m.*

teetotalism [ti:'toutəlizm], *n.* abstinence de boissons alcooliques, *f.*

telegram ['teligræm], *n.* télégramme, *m.*, dépêche, *f.*

telegraph ['teligra:f, -græf], *n.* télégraphe, *m.*; *telegraph office*, bureau télégraphique, *m.*—*v.t.*, *v.i.* télégraphier.

telegraphic [teli'græfik], *a.* télégraphique.

telegraphist [ti'legrəfist], *n.* télégraphiste, *m.*, *f.*

telegraph post ['teligra:fpoust], **telegraph pole** ['teligra:fpoul], *n.* poteau télégraphique, *m.*

telegraph wire ['teligra:fwaiə], *n.* fil télégraphique, *m.*

telegraphy [ti'legrəfi], *n.* télégraphie, *f.*; *wireless telegraphy*, télégraphie sans fil.

telepathy [ti'lepəθi], *n.* télépathie, *f.*

telephone ['telifoun], *n.* téléphone, *m.*; *telephone exchange*, central téléphonique, *m.*; *telephone booth*, cabine téléphonique, *f.*; *telephone operator*, téléphoniste, *m.*, *f.* —*v.t.*, *v.i.* téléphoner.

telephonic [teli'fonik], *a.* téléphonique.

teleprinter ['teliprintə], *n.* téléimprimeur, télétype, *m.*

telescope ['teliskoup], *n.* (*Astron.*) télescope, *m.*; longue vue, *f.*

telescopic [teli'skopik], *a.* télescopique.

televiewer ['telivju:ə], *n.* téléspectateur, *m.*

televise ['telivaiz], *v.t.* téléviser.

television [teli'viʒən], *n.* télévision, *f.*; *television set*, téléviseur, appareil de télévision, *m.*

tell [tel], *v.t. irr.* dire; faire part de; raconter (*réciter*); montrer, indiquer (*expliquer*); révéler, dévoiler; énumérer (*compter*); avouer (*confesser*); reconnaître (*à*); savoir (*deviner*).—*v.i.* dire; faire son effet, porter (*influer*); juger (*interpréter*).

teller ['telə], *n.* diseur; raconteur; (*Am.*, *Sc.*) caissier (*de banque*); (*Parl.*) scrutateur, *m.*

tessellated

telling ['teliŋ], a. qui porte; expressif.—n. récit, m., narration, f.
tell-tale ['telteil], n. rapporteur; (fig.) révélateur.—n. rapporteur, m.
temerity [ti'meriti], n. témérité, f.
temper ['tempə], n. tempérament, m., disposition; humeur; colère (rage), f.; sangfroid (équanimité), m.; trempe (d'acier etc.), f.; to lose one's temper, se mettre en colère.—v.t. tempérer (de); détremper (couleurs); tremper (acier etc.); (fig.) adoucir.
temperament ['tempərəmənt], n. tempérament, m.
temperamental [tempərə'mentl], a. capricieux, instable.
temperance ['tempərəns], n. tempérance, f.
temperate ['tempərit], a. modéré; tempéré (climat).
temperature ['temprit∫ə], n. température, f.
tempest ['tempist], n. tempête, f.
tempestuous [tem'pestjuəs], a. orageux, tempétueux.
templar ['templə], n. templier, m.
temple ['templ], n. temple, m.; (Anat.) tempe, f.
templet ['templit], n. patron, gabarit, m.
temporal ['tempərəl], a. temporel; (Anat.) temporal.
temporarily ['tempərərili], adv. temporairement.
temporary ['tempərəri], a. temporaire, provisoire.
temporization [tempərai'zeiʃən], n. temporisation, f.
temporize ['tempəraiz], v.i. temporiser.
tempt [tempt], v.t. tenter (de); pousser (à).
temptation [temp'teiʃən], n. tentation, f.
tempter ['temptə], n. tentateur, m.
tempting ['temptiŋ], a. tentant, séduisant, attrayant; appétissant (nourriture).
temptress ['temptris], n. tentatrice, f.
ten [ten], a. dix.—n. dix, m.; une dizaine (dix environ), f.
tenable ['tenəbl], a. soutenable.
tenacious [ti'neiʃəs], a. tenace.
tenaciously [ti'neiʃəsli], adv. d'une manière tenace, obstinément.
tenacity [ti'næsiti], n. ténacité, f.
tenancy ['tenənsi], n. location, f.
tenant ['tenənt], n. locataire, m., f.
tench [tentʃ], n. (Ichth.) tanche, f.
tend [tend], v.t. garder, soigner.—v.i. tendre (à); se diriger vers.
tendency ['tendənsi], n. tendance, disposition, f.
tender (1) ['tendə], n. offre (proposition); (Comm.) soumission, f.; legal tender, monnaie légale, f.—v.t. offrir.—v.i. to tender for, soumissionner pour.
tender (2) ['tendə], n. (Naut.) allège, f.; (Rail.) tender, m.
tender (3) ['tendə], a. tendre; sensible (vulnérable).
tender-hearted ['tendə'hɑ:tid], a. sensible, au cœur tendre.
tenderly ['tendəli], adv. tendrement.
tenderness ['tendənis], n. tendresse; sensibilité (vulnérabilité); sollicitude, f.
tendon ['tendən], n. tendon, m.
tendril ['tendril], n. (Bot.) vrille, f.
tenement ['tenimənt], n. habitation, maison,

tenet ['ti:nit, 'tenit], n. principe, m.
tenfold ['tenfould], a. décuple.—adv. dix fois.
tennis ['tenis], n. tennis; *jeu de paume, m.
tennis court ['tenisko:t], n. court de tennis, tennis; *jeu de paume, m.
tennis racket ['tenisrækit], n. raquette de tennis, f.
tenor ['tenə], n. (Mus.) ténor, m.
tense (1) [tens], n. (Gram.) temps, m.
tense (2) [tens], a. tendu, raide.
tensile ['tensail], a. ductile (métal).
tension ['tenʃən], n. tension, f.
tent [tent], n. tente, f.; bell tent, tente conique.
tentacle ['tentəkl], n. tentacule, m.
tentative ['tentətiv], a. tentatif, d'essai.
tentatively ['tentətivli], adv. en guise d'essai.
tenter-hook ['tentəhuk], n. clou à crochet, m.; to be on tenter-hooks, être sur des épines.
tenth [tenθ], a. dixième; dix (du mois, roi etc.). —n. dixième (fraction), m.; (Eccles.) dîme, f.
tenuous ['tenjuəs], a. délié, mince, ténu.
tenure ['tenjuə], n. tenure, f.
tepid ['tepid], a. tiède.
tercentenary [tə:sen'ti:nəri], a. de trois siècles.—n. tricentenaire, m.
term [tə:m], n. terme, m.; limite; (Law) session, f.; (Sch.) trimestre, m.; (pl.) conditions, f.pl.; prix, m.—v.t. nommer, appeler.
termagant ['tə:məgənt], n. mégère, f.
terminable ['tə:minəbl], a. terminable.
terminal ['tə:minl], a. terminal.—n. (Elec.) borne, f.; air terminal, gare aérienne, aérogare, f.
terminate ['tə:mineit], v.t. terminer, finir.
termination [tə:mi'neiʃən], n. fin, terminaison, f.
terminology [tə:mi'nɔlədʒi], n. terminologie, f.
terminus ['tə:minəs], n. terminus (gare), m.; tête de ligne, f.
tern [tə:n], n. sterne, m., hirondelle de mer, f.
ternary ['tə:nəri], a. ternaire, f.
terrace ['teris], n. terrasse, f.
terraced ['terist], a. étagé en terrasse.
terra cotta ['terə'kɔtə], n. terre cuite, f.
terra firma ['terə'fə:mə], n. terre ferme, f.
terrestrial [tə'restriəl], a. terrestre.
terrible ['teribl], a. terrible.
terribly ['teribli], adv. terriblement; (colloq.) diablement.
terrier ['teriə], n. terrier, chien terrier, m.
terrific [tə'rifik], a. terrible, épouvantable; (fam.) formidable.
terrify ['terifai], v.t. terrifier.
territorial [teri'tɔ:riəl], a. territorial.
territory ['teritəri], n. territoire, m.
terror ['terə], n. terreur, f.; effroi, m.
terrorism ['terizm], n. terrorisme, m.
terrorist ['terərist], n. terroriste, m., f.
terrorize ['terəraiz], v.t. terroriser.
terse [tə:s], a. net, concis; bien tourné, élégant.
tersely ['tə:sli], adv. nettement; d'une manière concise.
terseness ['tə:snis], n. netteté, f.
tertian ['tə:ʃən], a. tierce.
tertiary ['tə:ʃəri], a. tertiaire.
tessellated ['tesə'leitid], a. tessellé.

593

test

test [test], *n.* épreuve, *f.*; test; essai, *m.*; pierre de touche, *f.*—*v.t.* éprouver, mettre à l'épreuve, tester; (*Metal.*) coupeller.
testament ['testəmənt], *n.* testament, *m.*
testator [tes'teitə], *n.* testateur, *m.*
testicle ['testikl], *n.* testicule, *m.*
testify ['testifai], *v.t.* témoigner; (*Law*) déposer (*de*).—*v.i.* (*Law*) déposer.
testimonial [testi'mouniəl], *n.* témoignage; certificat, témoignage d'estime, *m.*
testimony ['testiməni], *n.* témoignage, *m.*
testiness ['testinis], *n.* humeur, irritabilité, *f.*
testing ['testiŋ], *n.* épreuve, *f.*, essai, *m.*
test tube ['testtju:b], *n.* éprouvette, *f.*
testy ['testi], *a.* irritable, susceptible.
tetanus ['tetənəs], *n.* tétanos, *m.*
tether ['teðə], *n.* longe, *f.*; *to be at the end of one's tether*, être à bout de forces.—*v.t.* mettre à l'attache, attacher (*à*).
tetrahedron [tetrə'hi:drən], *n.* tétraèdre, *m.*
tetrarch ['tetrɑ:k], *n.* tétrarque, *m.*
Teuton ['tju:tən], *a.* teuton.—*n.* Teuton (*personne*), *m.*
Teutonic [tju:'tɔnik], *a.* teutonique.
text [tekst], *n.* texte, *m.*
text-book ['tekstbuk], *n.* manuel, livre de classe, *m.*
textile ['tekstail], *a.* textile.—*n.* tissu, textile, *m.*, étoffe, *f.*
textual ['tekstjuəl], *a.* textuel.
texture ['tekstʃə], *n.* tissu, *m.*; contexture (*d'écrits etc.*), *f.*
Thai [tai], *a.* thaïlandais.—*n.* thaïlandais (*langue*); Thaïlandais (*personne*), *m.*
Thailand ['tailænd], *n.* la Thaïlande, *f.*, le Siam, *m.*
Thames [temz], *the.* la Tamise, *f.*
than [ðæn], *conj.* que; de (*between* more *or* less *and a* number); que de (*before an infinitive*).
thank [θæŋk], *v.t.* remercier (*de*); rendre grâces à.
thankful ['θæŋkful], *a.* reconnaissant (*de*).
thankfully ['θæŋkfuli], *adv.* avec reconnaissance.
thankfulness ['θæŋkfulnis], *n.* reconnaissance, *f.*
thankless ['θæŋklis], *a.* ingrat; oublié (*non reconnu*).
thanklessness ['θæŋklisnis], *n.* ingratitude, *f.*
thank offering ['θæŋkɔfəriŋ], *n.* sacrifice d'actions de grâces, *m.*
thanks [θæŋks], *n.pl.* remercîments, remercîments, *m.pl.*, grâces, *f.pl.*—*int.* merci.
thanksgiving ['θæŋksgiviŋ], *n.* actions de grâces, *f.pl.*
that [ðæt], *dem.a.* (*pl. those* [ðouz]) ce, cet, *m.*, cette, *f.*; (*emphatically*) ce . . . -là, cet . . . -là, *m.*, cette . . . -là, *f.*—*dem.pron.* celui-là, *m.*, celle-là (*that one*), *f.*; cela, (*colloq.*) ça, *m.*—*rel.pron.* qui, que, lequel, *m.*, laquelle, *f.*, lesquels, *m.pl.*, lesquelles, *f.pl.*—*conj.* que.
thatch [θætʃ], *n.* chaume, *m.*—*v.t.* couvrir de chaume.
thatcher ['θætʃə], *n.* couvreur en chaume, *m.*
thaw [θɔ:], *n.* dégel, *m.*—*v.t.* dégeler; (*fig.*) fondre, attendrir.—*v.i.* dégeler, se dégeler; (*fig.*) fondre, s'attendrir.
the [ðə], *before vowel* [ði], *def. art.* le, l', *m.*, la, l', *f.*, les, *pl.*
theater ['θiətə], *n.* théâtre, *m.*
theatrical [θi'ætrikl], *a.* de théâtre, théâtral.
theatricals [θi'ætriklz], *n.pl.* spectacle, *m.*

*thee** [ði:], *pron.* (*also Poet.*) toi; te.
theft [θeft], *n.* vol, *m.*; *petty theft*, larcin, *m.*
their [ðɛə], *poss.a.* leur, leurs, *pl.*
theirs [ðɛəz], *poss.pron.* le leur, *m.*, la leur, *f.*, les leurs, *pl.*, à eux, *m.pl.*, à elles, *f.pl.*
theism ['θi:izm], *n.* théisme, *m.*
theist ['θi:ist], *n.* théiste, *m.*, *f.*
theistic [θi:'istik], *a.* théiste.
them [ðem], *pron.* eux, *m.pl.*, elles, *f.pl.*; (*obj.*) les; (*dat.*) leur, *pl.*
theme [θi:m], *n.* thème, sujet, *m.*
theme song ['θi:msɔŋ], *n.* chanson leit-motif, *f.*
themselves [ðem'selvz], *pron.* eux-mêmes, *m.pl.*, elles-mêmes, *f.pl.*; (*reflexive*) se, *pl.*
then [ðen], *adv.* alors; ensuite, puis (*après*); dans ce cas (*puisqu'il en est ainsi*); donc; *but then*, par contre; *by then*, alors, déjà; *now and then*, de temps en temps.—*conj.* donc.
thence [ðens], *adv.* de là, en; dès lors.
thenceforth [ðens'fɔ:θ], **thenceforward** [ðens'fɔ:wəd], *adv.* dès lors, depuis lors, à partir de ce moment-là.
theocracy [θi:'ɔkrəsi], *n.* théocratie, *f.*
theocratic [θi:ə'krætik], *a.* théocratique.
theodolite [θi:'ɔdəlait], *n.* théodolite, *m.*
theologian [θi:ə'loudʒiən], *n.* théologien, *m.*
theological [θi:ə'lɔdʒikl], *a.* théologique.
theology [θi:'ɔlədʒi], *n.* théologie, *f.*
theorem ['θi:ərəm], *n.* théorème, *m.*
theoretic [θi:ə'retik], **theoretical** [θi:ə'retikəl], *a.* théorique.
theorist ['θi:ərist], **theorizer** ['θi:əraizə], *n.* théoricien, *m.*
theorize ['θi:əraiz], *v.i.* théoriser.
theory ['θi:əri], *n.* théorie, *f.*
therapeutic [θerə'pju:tik], *a.* thérapeutique.
therapeutics [θerə'pju:tiks], *n.pl.* thérapeutique, *f.*
therapist ['θerəpist], *n.* praticien, *m.*
therapy ['θerəpi], *n.* thérapie, *f.*
there [ðɛə], *adv.* là, y; (*impers.*) il; en cela; voilà; *here and there*, çà et là; *over there*, là-bas; *there and then*, séance tenante; *there he comes!* le voilà qui vient! *there is* or *there are*, il y a.
thereabout [ðɛərə'baut], **thereabouts** [ðɛərə'bauts], *adv.* par là, près de là; à peu près, environ (*plus ou moins*).
thereafter [ðɛər'ɑ:ftə], *adv.* après, d'après cela, ensuite.
thereat [ðɛər'æt], *adv.* par là, à cet endroit; (*fig.*) là-dessus, à cela.
thereby [ðɛə'bai], *adv.* par là, par ce moyen.
therefore ['ðɛəfɔ:], *adv.* donc, par conséquent.
therefrom [ðɛə'frɔm], *adv.* de là, en.
therein [ðɛər'in], *adv.* là-dedans, en cela; y.
thereof [ðɛər'ɔv], *adv.* en, de cela.
thereon [ðɛər'ɔn], *adv.* là-dessus.
Theresa [tə'ri:zə], *n.* Thérèse, *f.*
thereto [ðɛə'tu:], **thereunto** [ðɛər'ʌntu], *adv.* y, à cela; à quoi.
thereupon [ðɛərə'pɔn], *adv.* là-dessus, sur cela, sur ce.
therewith [ðɛə'wið], *adv.* avec cela, de cela, en.
therm [θə:m], *n.* thermie, *f.*
thermal [θə:məl], *a.* thermal.
thermometer [θə'mɔmitə], *n.* thermomètre, *m.*

thermometrical [θə:moˈmetrikl], *a.* thermo-métrique.

thermonuclear [θə:moˈnjuːkliə], *a.* thermo-nucléaire.

thermos [ˈθə:mɔs], *a.* (*reg. trade mark*) *thermos flask*, bouteille Thermos *ou* isolante, *f.*

thermostat [ˈθə:məstæt], *n.* thermostat, *m.*

these [ðiːz], *a.* ces, ces . . . -ci, *pl.*—*pron.* ceux-ci, *m.pl.*, celles-ci, *f.pl.*

thesis [ˈθiːsis], *n.* thèse, *f.*

Thespian [ˈθespiən], *a.* tragique, de la tragédie.

thew [θjuː], *n.* tendon, muscle, nerf, *m.*

they [ðei], *pron.* Ils, eux, *m.pl.*, elles, *f.pl.* ; (*followed by a relative*) ceux, *m.pl.*, celles, *f.pl.* ; (*impers.*) on (*les gens*); *they say*, on dit.

thick [θik], *a.* épais; gros (*tuyau*); fort, solide (*porte etc.*); trouble (*boisson*); dru, serré (*touffu*); indistinct (*prononciation*); (*fam.*) intime.—*n.* fort, *m.*; *in the thick of*, au (plus) fort de.—*adv.* (*also* **thickly** [ˈθikli]) épais; dru (*vite*); en foule (*l'un après l'autre*).

thicken [ˈθikn], *v.t.* épaissir; lier (*sauce*).—*v.i.* s'épaissir; augmenter; se lier (*sauce*).

thickening [ˈθikniŋ], *n.* épaississement, *m.*; liaison (*d'une sauce*), *f.*

thicket [ˈθikit], *n.* fourré, hallier, taillis, *m.*

thick-headed [ˈθikˈhedid], *a.* sot, bête, stupide.

thickly [THICK].

thickness [ˈθiknis], *n.* épaisseur; consistance (*composition*), *f.*

thick-set [ˈθikset], *a.* touffu; trapu (*personne*).

thick-skinned [ˈθikˈskind], *a.* (*fig.*) peu sensible.

thief [θiːf], *n.* (*pl.* **thieves** [θiːvz]) voleur, larron, *m.*

thieve [θiːv], *v.i.* voler.

thieving [ˈθiːviŋ], *n.* vol, larcin, *m.*, rapine, *f.*

thievish [ˈθiːviʃ], *a.* adonné au vol; voleur.

thievishly [ˈθiːviʃli], *adv.* en voleur; par le vol.

thievishness [ˈθiːviʃnis], *n.* penchant au vol, *m.*, habitude du vol, *f.*

thigh [θai], *n.* cuisse, *f.*

thigh-bone [ˈθaiboun], *n.* fémur, *m.*

thimble [θimbl], *n.* dé, *m.*

thimbleful [ˈθimblful], *n.* un plein dé, *m.*

thin [θin], *a.* mince; maigre (*décharné*); élancé, délié (*svelte*); peu nombreux (*gens*); clair; clairsemé, rare (*arbres etc.*); grêle, faible (*son etc.*).—*adv.* d'une manière éparse, clair.—*v.t.* amincir, allonger (*sauce etc.*); éclaircir; raréfier.

*****thine** [ðain], *pron.* le tien, *m.*, la tienne, *f.*, les tiens, *m.pl.*, les tiennes, *f.pl.*; à toi.

thing [θiŋ], *n.* chose, *f.*, objet, *m.*, affaire, *f.*; être, *m.*; (*pl.*) affaires, *f.pl.*, effets, *m.pl.*

think [θiŋk], *v.t. irr.* penser; croire (*tenir pour vrai*); imaginer, songer (*avoir l'idée*); trouver, juger (*considérer*).—*v.i.* penser; croire; s'imaginer; songer (*à*); s'aviser (*de*); avoir une idée *ou* opinion (*de*); *to think over*, à; *to think up*, inventer.

thinker [ˈθiŋkə], *n.* penseur, *m.*

thinking [ˈθiŋkiŋ], *a.* pensant, qui pense, réfléchi.—*n.* pensée, *f.*; jugement, avis, *m.*

thinly [ˈθinli], *adv.* légèrement (*vêtu*); clairsemé, de loin en loin (*répandu*).

thinness [ˈθinnis], *n.* ténuité; fluidité; rareté,

f., petit nombre (*quantité*), *m.*; maigreur (*du corps*), *f.*

thin-skinned [ˈθinˈskind], *a.* à la peau mince; (*fig.*) irritable, chatouilleux, susceptible.

third [θə:d], *a.* troisième; trois (*mois, roi etc.*).—*n.* tiers (*fraction*), *m.*; (*Mus.*) tierce, *f.*

thirdly [ˈθə:dli], *adv.* troisièmement.

thirst [θə:st], *n.* soif, *f.*; *to quench one's thirst*, se désaltérer.—*v.i.* avoir soif (*de*).

thirstily [ˈθə:stili], *adv.* avidement.

thirstiness [ˈθə:stinis], *n.* soif, *f.*

thirsty [ˈθə:sti], *a.* qui a soif; altéré.

thirteen [θə:ˈtiːn], *a.* and *n.* treize, *m.*

thirteenth [θə:ˈtiːnθ], *a.* treizième; treize (*rois etc.*).—*n.* treizième (*fraction*), *m.*

thirtieth [ˈθə:ræsik], *a.* trentième; trente (*du mois*).—*n.* trentième (*fraction*), *m.*

thirty [ˈθə:ti], *a.* and *n.* trente, *m.*

this [ðis], *a.* (*pl.* **these** [ðiːz]) ce, cet, *m.*, cette, *f.*; ce . . . -ci, cet . . . -ci, *m.*; cette . . . -ci, *f.*—*pron.* celui-ci, *m.*, celle-ci (*this one*), *f.*; ceci, *m.*

thistle [θisl], *n.* (*Bot.*) chardon, *m.*

thistly [ˈθisli], *a.* plein de chardons.

thither [ˈðiðə], *adv.* là, y; *hither and thither*, çà et là.

thong [θɔŋ], *n.* courroie, lanière, sangle, *f.*

thoracic [θɔˈræsik], *a.* thoracique.

thorax [ˈθɔːræks], *n.* thorax, *m.*

thorn [θɔːn], *n.* épine, *f.*

thorn bush [ˈθɔːnbuʃ], *n.* buisson épineux, *m.*

thorny [ˈθɔːni], *a.* épineux.

thorough [ˈθʌrə], *a.* entier, complet; achevé, parfait; vrai (*véritable*).

thoroughbred [ˈθʌrəbred], *a.* pur sang (*cheval*); (*colloq.*) consommé.

thoroughfare [ˈθʌrəfɛə], *n.* voie de passage, *f.*, passage, *m.*; artère, *f.*; *no thoroughfare*, passage interdit.

thoroughgoing [ˈθʌrəgouiŋ], *a.* résolu; achevé, consommé.

thoroughly [ˈθʌrəli], *adv.* tout à fait, entièrement; à fond.

thoroughness [ˈθʌrənis], *n.* caractère achevé, *m.*, perfection, *f.*

thorough-paced [ˈθʌrəpeist], *a.* achevé, franc, fieffé.

those [ðouz], *a.* ces; ces . . . -là, *pl.*—*pron.* ceux-là, *m.pl.*, celles-là, *f.pl.*

*****thou** [ðau], *pron.* tu; *than thou*, que toi.

though [ðou], *conj.* quoique, bien que (*with subj.*); quand même (*même si*).—*adv.* cependant, pourtant.

thought (1) [θɔːt], *past* and *p.p.* [THINK].

thought (2) [θɔːt], *n.* pensée; idée, *f.*; sentiment (*opinion*), *m.*

thoughtful [ˈθɔːtful], *a.* pensif, réfléchi; rêveur, méditatif; inquiet (*troublé*); attentif, soucieux (*prévenant*).

thoughtfully [ˈθɔːtfuli], *adv.* pensivement, avec attention.

thoughtfulness [ˈθɔːtfulnis], *n.* méditation, *f.*, recueillement, *m.*; sollicitude, prévenance (*attentions*), *f.*

thoughtless [ˈθɔːtlis], *a.* irréfléchi, insouciant.

thoughtlessly [ˈθɔːtlisli], *a.* avec insouciance; sans réflexion.

thoughtlessness [ˈθɔːtlisnis], *n.* insouciance, négligence, *f.*

thousand [ˈθauzənd], *a.* mille; mil (*dates*).—*n.* mille; millier, *m.*, (*pl.*) milliers, *m.pl.*

thousandth

thousandth ['θauzəndθ], *a.* millième.—*n.* millième (*fraction*), *m.*

thraldom ['θrɔːldəm], *n.* esclavage, asservissement, *m.*

thrall [θrɔːl], *n.* esclave, *m.*, *f.*; esclavage, *m.* [THRESH].

thrash [θræʃ], *v.t.* battre, rosser (*quelqu'un*); [THRESH].

thrasher ['θræʃə], [THRESHER].

thrashing ['θræʃiŋ], *n.* rossée, *f.*; [THRESHING].

thrashing machine [THRESHING MACHINE].

thread [θred], *n.* fil; filet (*de vis*), *m.*—*v.t.* enfiler; traverser (*faire son chemin à travers*).

threadbare ['θredbɛə], *a.* râpé; (*fig.*) rebattu.

threat [θret], *n.* menace, *f.*

threaten [θretn], *v.t.* menacer (*de*).

threatening ['θretniŋ], *a.* menaçant; de menaces.—*n.* menaces, *f.pl.*

threateningly ['θretniŋli], *adv.* avec menaces; d'un air menaçant.

three [θriː], *a.* and *n.* trois, *m.*

three-cornered ['θriːkɔːnəd], *a.* à trois cornes; **three-cornered hat**, tricorne, *m.*

threefold ['θriːfould], *a.* triple.

three-master ['θriːmɑːstə], *n.* trois-mâts, *m.*

three-ply ['θriːplai], *a.* à trois épaisseurs; **three-ply wood**, contreplaqué, *m.*

threescore ['θriːskɔː], *a.* soixante.—*n.* soixantaine, *f.*

thresh [θreʃ], *v.t.* (*Agric.*) battre (*en grange*).

thresher ['θreʃə], *n.* batteur en grange, *m.*

threshing ['θreʃiŋ], *n.* (*Agric.*) battage, *m.*

threshing machine ['θreʃiŋmə'ʃiːn], *n.* batteuse, *f.*

threshold ['θreʃould], *n.* seuil; (*fig.*) début, *m.*

thrift [θrift], **thriftiness** ['θriftinis], *n.* épargne, économie, *f.*

thriftily ['θriftili], *adv.* avec économie.

thriftiness [THRIFT].

thriftless ['θriftlis], *a.* dépensier, prodigue.

thriftlessly ['θriftlisli], *adv.* en prodigue, follement.

thriftlessness ['θriftlisnis], *n.* prodigalité, *f.*, gaspillage, *m.*

thrifty ['θrifti], *a.* ménager, économe, frugal.

thrill [θril], *v.t.* faire frissonner, faire tressaillir (*de*).—*v.i.* frémir, tressaillir (*de*).—*n.* tressaillement, frisson, *m.*

thriller ['θrilə], *n.* (*fam.*) roman *ou* film à sensation, *m.*

thrilling ['θriliŋ], *a.* saisissant, poignant, palpitant.

thrive [θraiv], *v.i. irr.* prospérer; réussir.

thriving ['θraiviŋ], *a.* florissant, vigoureux.

throat [θrout], *n.* gorge, *f.*; gosier, *m.*

throaty ['θrouti], *a.* guttural (*voix*).

throb [θrɔb], *v.i.* battre; palpiter.—*n.* battement, *m.*

throbbing ['θrɔbiŋ], *a.* palpitant, vibrant; lancinant (*douleur*).—*n.* battement; ronflement (*de moteur*), *m.*

throes [θrouz], *n. pl.* douleurs, angoisses, *f.pl.*

thrombosis [θrɔm'bousis], *n.* thrombose, *f.*

throne [θroun], *n.* trône, *m.*

throng [θrɔŋ], *n.* foule, multitude, *f.*—*v.t.* remplir.—*v.i.* accourir en foule, se presser.

thronged [θrɔŋd], *a.* serré (*personnes*); comble (*salle*).

throstle [θrɔsl], *n.* (*Orn.*) grive chanteuse, *f.*

throttle [θrɔtl], *v.t.* étrangler; étouffer.—*n.* gosier; (*Motor. etc.*) papillon, *m.*

through [θruː], *prep.* à travers; au travers de;

par; dans; par suite de (*à cause de*).—*a.* direct (*train, billet etc.*).—*adv.* directement, droit (*sans s'arrêter*); par tant en part; d'un bout à l'autre (*dans toute sa longueur*); jusqu'à la fin, jusqu'au bout; complètement; **to be wet through**, être trempé jusqu'aux os; **to fall through**, manquer, échouer (*projet*); **to go through with** (*something*), **to see** (*something*) **through**, mener (quelque chose) à bonne fin.

throughout [θruː'aut], *prep.* dans tout, par tout.—*adv.* d'un bout à l'autre; entièrement.

throw [θrou], *v.t. irr.* jeter; lancer; renverser; tordre (*soie*); démonter, désarçonner (*cavalier*); **to throw aside**, jeter de côté; **to throw away**, jeter, rejeter; gaspiller; **to throw off**, se défaire de, ôter (*vêtements*). —*n.* jet, coup; (*fig.*) élan, *m.*

thrower ['θrouə], *n.* jeteur, lanceur, *m.*

thrush [θrʌʃ], *n.* (*Orn.*) grive, *f.*

thrust [θrʌst], *v.t. irr.* pousser, enfoncer, fourrer; presser.—*v.i.* porter une botte *ou* un coup (*à*); se fourrer.—*n.* coup, *m.*; (*Fenc.*) botte; (*Arch. etc.*) poussée, *f.*

thud [θʌd], *n.* bruit sourd; son mat, *m.*—*v.i.* faire un bruit sourd.

thug [θʌg], *n.* bandit, *m.*

thumb [θʌm], *n.* pouce, *m.*—*v.t.* manier gauchement; feuilleter; salir (*avec les pouces*).

thumbnail ['θʌmneil], *a.* en raccourci, minuscule.

thumb-screw ['θʌmskruː], *n.* vis à ailettes, *f.*; poucettes (*supplice*), *f.pl.*

thumbstall ['θʌmstɔːl], *n.* poucier, doigtier, *m.*

thump [θʌmp], *v.t.* frapper du poing, cogner. —*n.* coup, *m.*, bourrade, *f.*

thunder ['θʌndə], *n.* tonnerre, *m.*; (*fig.*) foudre, *f.*—*v.i.* tonner; (*fig.*) fulminer.

thunderbolt ['θʌndəboult], *n.* foudre, *f.*

thunder-clap ['θʌndəklæp], *n.* coup de tonnerre, *m.*

thundering ['θʌndəriŋ], *a.* tonnant, foudroyant; (*colloq.*) énorme.

thunderous ['θʌndərəs], *a.* orageux; à tout rompre (*applaudissements*).

thunderstorm ['θʌndəstɔːm], *n.* orage (accompagné de tonnerre), *m.*

thunderstruck ['θʌndəstrʌk], *a.* foudroyé; (*fig.*) atterré.

thundery ['θʌndəri], *a.* orageux.

Thursday ['θəːzd(e)i], jeudi, *m.*

thus [ðʌs], *adv.* ainsi; **thus far**, jusqu'ici.

thwack [θwæk], *n.* coup, *m.*—*v.t.* frapper, rosser, battre.

thwacking ['θwækiŋ], *n.* roulée de coups, raclée, *f.*

thwart [θwɔːt], *v.t.* traverser; (*fig.*) contrarier.—*adv.* en travers.—*n.* banc de rameurs, *m.*

***thy** [ðai], *poss.a.* (*also poet.*) ton, *m.*, ta, *f.*, tes, *pl.*

thyme [taim], *n.* thym, *m.*

thyroid ['θairoid], *a.* thyroïde.

***thyself** [ðai'self], *pron.* (*also poet.*) toi-même, toi; (*reflexive*) te.

tiara [ti'ɑːrə], *n.* tiare, *f.*

Tibet [ti'bet], le Tibet, *m.*

Tibetan [ti'betn], *a.* tibétain.—*n.* tibétain (*langue*); Tibétain (*personne*), *m.*

tibia ['tibiə], *n.* (*Anat.*) tibia (*os de la jambe*), *m.*

tic [tik], *n.* tic, *m.*

tick (1) [tik], *n.* tic-tac (*bruit*), *m.*; marque, *f.* —*v.t.* marquer; **to tick off,** pointer.—*v.i.* faire tic-tac, battre (*horloges etc.*).

tick (2) [tik], *n.* coutil (*de matelas*), *m.*

ticket ['tikit], *n.* billet; ticket, *m.*; étiquette, *f.*; **return ticket,** billet d'aller et retour; **season ticket,** carte d'abonnement, *f.*; **single ticket,** billet simple.—*v.t.* étiqueter, numéroter.

ticket collector ['tikitkəlektə], *n.* contrôleur, *m.*

ticket office ['tikitɔfis], *n.* bureau des billets, guichet, *m.*

ticking (1) ['tikiŋ], *n.* tic-tac, battement (*de montre etc.*), *m.*

ticking (2) ['tikiŋ], *n.* coutil, *m.*, toile à matelas, *f.*

tickle [tikl], *v.t., v.i.* chatouiller.

tickling ['tikliŋ], *n.* chatouillement, *m.*

ticklish ['tikliʃ], *a.* chatouilleux; critique, délicat.

tidal [taidl], *a.* de marée; **tidal harbor,** port à marée, *m.*; **tidal wave,** raz de marée, *m.*

tide [taid], *n.* marée, *f.*; courant (*flot*), *m.*; (*fig.*) époque, *f.*

tidily ['taidili], *adv.* proprement, en bon ordre.

tidiness ['taidinis], *n.* propreté, netteté, *f.*, bon ordre, *m.*

tidings ['taidiŋz], *n.pl.* nouvelles, *f.pl.*

tidy ['taidi], *a.* rangé, bien arrangé, en ordre, propre, net.—*v.t.* mettre en ordre; ranger; arranger (*papiers etc.*).

tie [tai], *v.t.* lier, attacher; nouer, faire (*un nœud*).—*v.i.* se lier, se nouer; être à égalité. —*n.* lien; nœud (*knot*); cordon (*de chaussure*), *m.*; cravate; (*Mus.*) liaison; (*Games*) partie nulle, *f.*

tier [tiə], *n.* rang, *m.*; rangée, *f.*

tierce [tiəs], *n.* (*Cards*) tierce, *f.*

tiff [tif], *n.* petite querelle, pique, *f.*

tiffany ['tifəni], *n.* gaze de soie (*tissu*), *f.*

tiger ['taigə], *n.* tigre, *m.*

tiger lily ['taigəlili], *n.* (*Bot.*) lis tigré, *m.*

tiger moth ['taigəmɔθ], *n.* arctie, *f.*

tight [tait], *a.* serré; raide, tendu (*corde*); trop étroit (*vêtements*); imperméable; **air-tight** or **water-tight,** imperméable à l'air ou à l'eau.

tighten [taitn], *v.t.* serrer; tendre (*contraindre*); (*fig.*) resserrer.

tight-fisted ['tait'fistid], *a.* serré, ladre.

tightly ['taitli], *adv.* ferme, fortement; étroitement serré.

tightness ['taitnis], *n.* raideur; étroitesse (*des vêtements*), *f.*

tight-rope ['taitroup], *n.* corde raide, *f.*; **tight-rope walker,** funambule, danseur de corde, *m.*

tights [taits], *n.pl.* collant, maillot, *m.*

tigress ['taigris], *n.* tigresse, *f.*

tile [tail], *n.* tuile, *f.*; carreau (*for flooring*), *m.* —*v.t.* couvrir de tuiles; carreler (*une pièce*).

tiler ['tailə], *n.* couvreur (en tuiles) *m.*

tile works ['tailwə:ks], *n.* tuilerie, *f.*

till (1) [til], *prep.* jusqu'à.—*conj.* jusqu'à ce que (*with subj.*).

till (2) [til], *n.* caisse, *f.*

till (3) [til], *v.t.* labourer, cultiver.

tillable ['tiləbl], *a.* labourable.

tillage ['tilidʒ], *n.* labourage, *m.*

tiller (1) ['tilə], *n.* laboureur, *m.*

tiller (2) ['tilə], *n.* (*Naut.*) barre du gouvernail, *f.*

tilt (1) [tilt], *n.* bâche, banne (*toile*), *f.*

tilt (2) [tilt], *n.* joute; inclinaison, *f.*—*v.t.* incliner, faire pencher.—*v.i.* jouter; incliner, pencher.

tilth [tilθ], *n.* labourage, *m.*, culture, *f.*

timber ['timbə], *n.* bois de construction, *m.*— *v.t.* boiser.

timbering ['timbəriŋ], *n.* boisage, *m.*

timber-work ['timbəwə:k], *n.* charpente, *f.*

timbrel ['timbrəl], *n.* tambour de basque, tambourin, *m.*

time [taim], *n.* temps, *m.*; saison, époque, *f.*; terme (*période*), *m.*; heure (*de la journée*), *f.*; moment, *m.*; occasion; fois (*répétition*); époque, *f.*, siècle (*d'histoire*), *m.*; mesure, *f.*; (*Drilling*) pas, *m.*; **at times,** parfois, de temps à autre; **in no time,** en un clin d'œil; **in time,** à temps; (*Mus.*) en mesure.—*v.t.* faire à propos; fixer l'heure de; (*Spt.*) chronométrer; **ill-timed,** inopportun; **well-timed,** opportun, à propos.

time bomb ['taimbɔm], *n.* bombe à retardement, *f.*

time fuse ['taimfju:z], *n.* fusée à temps, *f.*

time-honored ['taimɔnəd], *a.* vénérable; séculaire.

time-keeper ['taimki:pə], *n.* surveillant, contrôleur, *m.*

time lag ['taimlæ:g], *n.* décalage, retard, *m.*

timeliness ['taimlinis], *n.* opportunité, *f.*, à-propos, *m.*

timely ['taimli], *a.* opportun, à propos.

time-piece ['taimpi:s], *n.* pendule, *f.*

time sheet ['taimʃi:t], *n.* feuille de présence, *f.*

timetable ['taimteibl], *n.* indicateur, horaire; (*Sch.*) emploi du temps, *m.*

time-worn ['taimwɔ:n], *a.* usé par le temps.

timid ['timid], *a.* timide, craintif, peureux.

timidity [ti'miditi], *n.* timidité, *f.*

timing ['taimiŋ], *n.* ajustement, règlement; réglage (*de montre etc.*), *m.*

timorous ['timərəs], *a.* timoré, timide.

timorously ['timərəsli], *adv.* craintivement.

timorousness ['timərəsnis], *n.* timidité, *f.*

tin [tin], *n.* étain, *m.*; boîte (*de conserve*), *f.*— *v.t.* étamer.

tincture ['tiŋktʃə], *n.* teinture, *f.*, extrait, *m.*; (*fig.*) nuance, *f.*—*v.t.* teindre (*de*).

tinder ['tində], *n.* amadou, *m.*

tinder-box ['tindəbɔks], *n.* boîte à amadou, *f.*, briquet à silex, *m.*

tinfoil ['tinfoil], *n.* feuille d'étain, *f.*

tinge [tindʒ], *n.* teinte, nuance, *f.*; soupçon (*goût*), *m.*—*v.t.* teindre.

tingle [tiŋgl], *v.i.* tinter; picoter, cuire (*douleur*).

tingling ['tiŋgliŋ], *n.* tintement (*son*); picotement, *m.*

tinker ['tiŋkə], *n.* rétameur, *m.*—*v.t.* rétamer; raccommoder.

tinkle [tiŋkl], *v.t.* faire tinter.—*v.i.* tinter.—*n.* tintement, *m.*

tinkling ['tiŋkliŋ], *n.* tintement, *m.*

tinny ['tini], *a.* qui abonde en étain; grêle (*son*).

tin plate ['tinpleit], *n.* fer-blanc, *m.*

tinsel

tinsel ['tinsəl], *a.* de clinquant; (*fig.*) faux.—*n.* clinquant; (*fig.*) faux éclat, *m.*

tinsmith ['tinsmiθ], *n.* ferblantier, *m.*

tint [tint], *n.* teinte, nuance, *f.*—*v.t.* teinter, nuancer (*de*).

tin-tack ['tintæk], *n.* semence étamée, *f.*

tinware ['tinwɛə], *n.* ferblanterie, *f.*

tiny ['tainɪ], *a.* tout petit, minuscule.

tip (1) [tip], *n.* bout, *m.*; extrémité, pointe, *f.*—*v.t.* garnir le bout.

tip (2) [tip], *n.* tape (*coup léger*), *f.*; pourboire (*gratuity*); dépotoir (*débris*) (*Spt.*) tuyau, *m.*—*v.t.* donner un pourboire à; décharger (*véhicule*) (*Spt.*) tuyauter.

tippet ['tipit], *n.* pèlerine, palatine (*fourrure*), *f.*

tipple [tipl], *v.i.* boire, pinter.—*n.* boisson, *f.*

tippler ['tiplə], *n.* buveur, *m.*

tippling ['tiplɪŋ], *n.* ivrognerie, *f.*

tipstaff ['tipstɑːf], *n.* huissier, *m.*

tipster ['tipstə], *n.* (*Spt.*) tuyauteur, *m.*

tipsy ['tipsi], *a.* gris, ivre.

tiptoe ['tiptou], *n.* pointe du pied, *f.*; **on tip-toe**, sur la pointe des pieds.

tip-top ['tiptɒp], *a.* (*colloq.*) excellent.—*n.* comble, sommet, *m.*

tirade [ti'reid, tai'reid], *n.* tirade, diatribe, *f.*

tire ['taiə], *n.* pneu (*de roue*), *m.*

tire ['taiə], *v.t.* lasser, fatiguer; ennuyer (*moralement*).—*v.i.* se fatiguer, se lasser.

tired ['taiəd], *a.* las, fatigué; ennuyé.

tiredness ['taiədnis], *n.* fatigue, lassitude, *f.*

tiresome ['taiəsəm], *a.* fatigant; ennuyeux (*assommant*).

tiresomeness ['taiəsəmnis], *n.* nature fatigante, *f.*; ennui, *m.*

tissue ['tiʃuː, 'tisjuː], *n.* tissu, *m.*—*v.t.* tisser, broder.

tissue paper ['tiʃjuːpeipə], *n.* papier de soie, *m.*

tit (1) [tit], *n.* mésange (*oiseau*), *f.*

tit (2) [tit], *n.* **tit for tat**, un prêté pour un rendu.

titanic [tai'tænik], *a.* titanique, titanesque.

titbit ['titbit], *n.* morceau friand, *m.*

tithe [taið], *n.* dîme, *f.*, dixième, *m.*—*v.t.* dîmer.

titillate ['titileit], *v.t., v.i.* chatouiller, titiller.

titillation [titi'leiʃən], *n.* titillation, *f.*, chatouillement, *m.*

titlark ['titlɑːk], *n.* alouette des prés, *f.*

title [taitl], *n.* titre; (*fig.*) droit, document, *m.*—*v.t.* titrer, qualifier (*de*).

titled [taitld], *a.* titré.

title deed ['taitldiːd], *n.* titre (de propriété), *m.*

title page ['taitlpeidʒ], *n.* titre, *m.*

titmouse ['titmaus], *n.* (*pl.* **titmice** ['titmais]) mésange, *f.*

titter ['titə], *v.i.* rire tout bas.—*n.* petit rire étouffé, *m.*

tittle [titl], *n.* point, iota, *m.*

tittle-tattle ['titltætl], *n.* caquetage, bavardage, *m.*—*v.i.* jaser, bavarder.

titular ['titjulə], *a.* de titre.—*n.* titulaire, *m., f.*

titulary ['titjuləri], *a.* de titre.—*n.* titulaire, *m., f.*

to [tu], *prep.* à, de (*before infinitive*); pour, afin de (*dans le but de*); à (*un endroit*); en (*before names of countries of the feminine gender and those of the masculine gender beginning with a vowel*); dans (*followed by* le, la, *etc.*); vers (*un endroit*); contre (*pari*); près de (*cour royale etc.*); outre, en addition à (*en plus de*);

pour (*faire quelque chose*); en comparaison de, auprès de (*à côté de*); jusqu'à (*telle ou telle limite*); envers (*à l'égard de*).

toad [toud], *n.* crapaud, *m.*

toadish ['toudiʃ], *a.* de crapaud.

toadstool ['toudstuːl], *n.* champignon vénéneux, *m.*

toady ['toudi], *n.* flagorneur, *m.*—*v.t.* flagorner, aduler.

toadyism ['toudiizm], *n.* flagornerie, servilité, *f.*

toast [toust], *n.* rôtie, tranche de pain grillée, *f.*; toast (*bu à la santé de quelqu'un*), *m.*—*v.t.* rôtir, griller; porter un toast à.

toaster ['toustə], *n.* grille-pain, *m.inv.*

toasting fork ['toustinfɔːk], *n.* fourchette à rôties, *f.*

toast-master ['toustmɑːstə], *n.* préposé aux toasts, *m.*

toast rack ['toustræk], *n.* porte-rôties, porte-toasts, *m.inv.*

tobacco [tə'bækou], *n.* tabac, *m.*

tobacco box [tə'bækoubɒks], *n.* boîte à tabac, *f.*

tobacco jar [tə'bækoudʒɑː], *n.* pot à tabac, *m.*

tobacconist [tə'bækənist], *n.* marchand de tabac, *m.*; **tobacconist's shop**, bureau de tabac, *m.*

tobacco pouch [tə'bækoupautʃ], *n.* blague à tabac, *f.*

toboggan [tə'bɒgən], *n.* toboggan, *m.*; luge, *f.*—*v.i.* luger.

tocsin ['tɒksin], *n.* tocsin, *m.*

today [tə'dei], *adv.* aujourd'hui.

toddle [tɒdl], *v.i.* trottiner.

toddler ['tɒdlə], *n.* tout petit enfant, *m.*

to-do [tə'duː], *n.* tapage, éclat, *m.*, (*fam.*) histoire, *f.*

toe [tou], *n.* orteil, doigt de pied; devant du sabot, *m.*, pince (*de cheval*), *f.*; bout (*de bas*), *m.*

toe-nail ['touneil], *n.* ongle de pied, *m.*

toffee, toffy ['tɒfi], *n.* caramel au beurre, *m.*

toga ['tougə], *n.* toge, *f.*

together [tə'geðə], *adv.* ensemble, à la fois, en même temps (*simultanément*); de concert (*entre eux*); de suite (*consécutivement*).

Togo ['tougou], le Togo, *m.*

Togolese [tougo'liːz], *a.* togolais.—*n.* Togolais (*personne*), *m.*

toil [tɒil], *n.* travail dur, labeur, *m.*; peine, *f.*; (*pl.*) piège, *m.*—*v.i.* travailler fort, se fatiguer.

toiler ['tɒilə], *n.* travailleur, *m.*

toilet ['tɒilit], *n.* toilette, *f.*; les toilettes (*dans les hôtels etc.*), *f.pl.*, cabinet d'aisances, *m.*

toiling ['tɒiliŋ], *n.* travail, labeur, *m.*, peine, *f.*

toilsome ['tɒilsəm], *a.* pénible, laborieux, fatigant.

toilsomeness ['tɒilsəmnis], *n.* difficulté, *f.*

token ['toukən], *n.* marque, *f.*; gage (*témoignage*); jeton (*jeux de cartes, téléphone etc.*), *m.*; **book token**, bon de livre, *m.*; **token strike**, grève d'avertissement, *f.*

tolerable ['tɒlərəbl], *a.* tolérable, passable (*assez bon*).

tolerably ['tɒlərəbli], *adv.* passablement, assez.

tolerance ['tɒlərəns], *n.* tolérance, *f.*

tolerant ['tɒlərənt], *a.* tolérant.

tolerate ['tɔləreit], v.t. tolérer; supporter.
toleration [tɔlə'reiʃən], n. tolérance, f.
toll (1) [toul], n. péage; droit; octroi (*impôt municipal*), m.
toll (2) [toul], n. tintement, glas (*de cloche*), m. —v.t., v.i. sonner, tinter (*cloche*).
toll-bar ['toulbɑ:], **toll-gate** ['toulgeit], n. barrière de péage, f.
toll bridge ['toulbridʒ], n. pont à péage, m.
toll call, see **trunk-call**.
toll-house ['toulhaus], n. bureau de péage, m.
tolling ['touliŋ], n. tintement, m.
tomahawk ['tɔməhɔ:k], n. tomahawk, m.; hache de guerre, f.
tomato [tə'mɑ:tou], n. tomate, f.
tomb [tu:m], n. tombeau, m.; tombe, f.
tomboy ['tɔmbɔi], n. garçon manqué, m.
tombstone ['tu:mstoun], n. pierre tombale, f.
tom-cat ['tɔmkæt], n. matou, m.
tome [toum], n. tome, volume, m.
tomfool [tɔm'fu:l], n. sot, bête, niais, m.
tomfoolery [tɔm'fu:ləri], n. sottise, bêtise, niaiserie, f.
Tommy gun ['tɔmigʌn], n. mitraillette, f.
tomorrow [tə'mɔrou], adv. demain.
tomtit ['tɔmtit], n. (*Orn.*) mésange bleue, f.
tom-tom ['tɔmtɔm], n. tam-tam, m.
ton [tʌn], n. tonne (*1016,04 kg.* (*U.K.*), 907 *kg.* (*U.S.*)), f.
tone [toun], n. ton; accent, timbre (*de voix*), m.—v.t. donner le ton à, régler; (*Mus.*) accorder; (*Phot.*) virer; **to tone down**, adoucir, pallier.
toneless ['tounlis], a. sans éclat, sans chaleur (*voix*).
tongs [tɔŋz], n.pl. pincettes; (*Tech.*) tenailles, pinces, f.pl.
tongue [tʌŋ], n. langue, f.; **to hold one's tongue**, se taire.
tongued [tʌŋd], a. à langue.
tongue-tied ['tʌŋtaid], a. qui a la langue liée; (*fig.*) réduit au silence, muet.
tonic ['tɔnik], a. and n. (*Med.*) tonique, fortifiant, m.
tonight [tə'nait], n. cette nuit, f., ce soir, m.
tonnage ['tʌnidʒ], n. tonnage, m.
tonsil ['tɔnsl], n. (*Anat.*) amygdale, f.
tonsil(l)itis [tɔnsi'laitis], n. amygdalite, f.
tonsure ['tɔnʃə], n. tonsure, f.—v.t. tonsurer.
too [tu:], adv. trop, par trop; aussi, de même, également (*pareillement*); d'ailleurs, de plus; **too much** or **too many**, trop.
tool [tu:l], n. outil, instrument; (*fig.*) agent, m.
tool chest ['tu:ltʃest], n. boîte à outils, f.
tooth [tu:θ], n. (*pl.* **teeth** [ti:θ]) dent, f.; **set of teeth**, râtelier, m.; **wisdom tooth**, dent de sagesse.—v.t. denteler.
toothache ['tu:θeik], n. mal de dents, m.
toothbrush ['tu:θbrʌʃ], n. brosse à dents, f.
toothed ['tu:θt], a. à dents; (*Tech.*) denté.
toothless ['tu:θlis], a. sans dents, édenté.
tooth-paste ['tu:θpeist], n. pâte dentifrice, f., dentifrice, m.
tooth-pick ['tu:θpik], n. cure-dents, m.inv.
tooth-powder ['tu:θpaudə], n. poudre dentifrice, f.
toothsome ['tu:θsəm], a. agréable au goût, savoureux, friand.
toothsomeness ['tu:θsəmnis], n. goût agréable, m.
top (1) [tɔp], a. premier, principal, extrême.—n. haut, sommet, m.; cime (*de montagne etc.*),

f.; faîte (*d'édifice*), m.; (*Naut.*) hune, f.; dessus (*de table*), m.—v.t. couronner, surmonter (*de*).
top (2) [tɔp], n. toupie (*jouet*), f.
topaz ['toupæz], n. topaze, f.
top boots ['tɔpbu:ts], n.pl. bottes à revers, f.pl.
top-coat ['tɔpkout], n. pardessus, m.
tope (1) [toup], v.i. (*colloq.*) pinter, boire.
tope (2) [toup], n. chien de mer, m.
toper ['toupə], n. ivrogne, m., f.
top hat ['tɔp'hæt], n. chapeau haut de forme, m.
topic ['tɔpik], n. matière, f., sujet, m.
topical ['tɔpikl], a. d'actualité; (*Med.*) topique.
topmast ['tɔpmɑ:st], n. mât de hune, m.
topmost ['tɔpmoust], a. le plus haut, le plus élevé.
top-sail ['tɔpsl], n. hunier, m.
topographer [tə'pɔgrəfə], n. topographe, m.
topographic [tɔpə'græfik], **topographical** [tɔpə'græfikəl], a. topographique.
topography [tə'pɔgrəfi], n. topographie, f.
topple [tɔpl], v.i. tomber, dégringoler.
topsy-turvy ['tɔpsi'tə:vi], adv. sens dessus dessous.
torch [tɔ:tʃ], n. torche, f., flambeau, m., lampe de poche, f.
torch-bearer ['tɔ:tʃbɛərə], n. porte-flambeau, m.
toreador [tɔriə'dɔ:], n. toréador, m.
torment (1) ['tɔ:ment], n. tourment, m., torture, f.; supplice, m.
torment (2) [tɔ:'ment], v.t. tourmenter, torturer.
tormentor [tɔ:'mentə], n. tourmenteur, bourreau, m.
tornado [tɔ:'neidou], n. tornade, f., ouragan, cyclone, m.
torpedo [tɔ:'pi:dou], n. torpille, f.—v.t. torpiller.
torpedo boat [tɔ:'pi:doubout], n. torpilleur, m.
torpid ['tɔ:pid], a. engourdi, torpide, inerte.
torpor ['tɔ:pə], n. torpeur, apathie, f.
torrefaction [tɔri'fækʃən], n. torréfaction, f.
torrefy ['tɔrifai], v.t. torréfier.
torrent ['tɔrənt], n. torrent, m.
torrential [tɔ'renʃl], a. torrentiel.
torrid ['tɔrid], a. brûlant, torride.
torridness ['tɔridnis], **torridity** [tɔ'riditi], n. chaleur brûlante, f.
torsion ['tɔ:ʃən], n. torsion, f.
torso ['tɔ:sou], n. torse, m.
tortoise ['tɔ:təs], n. tortue, f.
tortoise-shell ['tɔ:təsʃel], a. d'écaille.—n. écaille de tortue, écaille, f.
tortuous ['tɔ:tjuəs], a. tortueux, sinueux.
tortuousness ['tɔ:tjuəsnis], n. tortuosité, f.
torture ['tɔ:tʃə], n. torture, f.; supplice, m.—v.t. torturer; (*fig.*) faire souffrir.
torturer ['tɔ:tʃərə], n. bourreau, m.
toss [tɔs], n. jet, lancement, m.; **to win the toss**, gagner (à pile *ou* face).—v.t. lancer ou jeter (*en l'air*); ballotter; secouer.—v.i. s'agiter.
tossing ['tɔsiŋ], n. secousse, f.; ballottement; hochement, m.
toss-up ['tɔsʌp], n. coup de pile ou face, m.
total [toutl], a. total, complet, entier.—n. total, montant, m., somme, f.—v.t. se monter à.

totalitarian

totalitarian [toutæli'tɛəriən], *a.* (*Polit.*) totalitaire.

totalitarianism [toutæli'tɛəriənizm], *n.* totalitarisme, *m.*

totality [tou'tæliti], *n.* totalité, *f.*, montant, tout, *m.*

totalizator ['toutəlaizeitə], *n.* totalisateur, *m.*

totally ['toutəli], *adv.* totalement, tout à fait, entièrement.

totem ['toutəm], *n.* totem, *m.*

totter ['tɔtə], *v.i.* chanceler; (*fig.*) vaciller, trembler.

tottering ['tɔtəriŋ], *a.* chancelant, tremblant. —*n.* chancellement, *m.*

tottery ['tɔtəri], *a.* chancelant.

touch [tʌtʃ], *v.t.* toucher; toucher à (*s'ingérer dans*); émouvoir (*attendrir*); **to touch up**, retoucher.—*v.i.* toucher; se toucher; **to touch at**, aborder à (*navire*); **to touch upon**, effleurer, (*fig.*) faire allusion à.—*n.* le toucher (*sens tactile*); attouchement (*contact*), *m.*; légère attaque (*d'une maladie*), *f.*; (*fig.*) soupçon (*trace*), *m.*; **it was touch and go**, il s'en est fallu de bien peu; **to get in touch with**, se mettre en rapports, entrer en contact avec; **to keep in touch with**, garder le contact avec.

touchiness ['tʌtʃinis], *n.* irascibilité, *f.*

touching ['tʌtʃiŋ], *a.* touchant, émouvant.— *prep.* concernant, au sujet de.

touch-line ['tʌtʃlain], *n.* (*Ftb.*) ligne de touche, *f.*

touchstone ['tʌtʃstoun], *n.* pierre de touche, *f.*

touch-wood ['tʌtʃwud], *n.* amadou, *m.*

touchy ['tʌtʃi], *a.* irritable, susceptible.

tough [tʌf], *a.* dur, raide, résistant; coriace (*viande*); fort (*solide*); difficile.

toughen [tʌfn], *v.t.* durcir.—*v.i.* s'endurcir.

toughish ['tʌfiʃ], *a.* un peu dur.

toughly ['tʌfli], *adv.* durement; vigoureusement.

toughness ['tʌfnis], *n.* raideur; dureté, nature coriace (*viande etc.*); (*fig.*) difficulté, *f.*

tour ['tuə], *n.* tour, voyage, *m.*; randonnée, tournée, *f.*—*v.i.* visiter (*un pays*); voyager dans (*un pays*); excursionner.

tourism ['tuərizm], *n.* tourisme, *m.*

tourist ['tuərist], *n.* touriste, *m.*, *f.*, voyageur, *m.*; **tourist agency**, bureau de tourisme, *m.*

tournament ['tuənəmənt], *n.* tournoi; concours, *m.*

tourniquet ['tuənikei], *n.* garrot, *m.*

tousle [tauzl], *v.t.* tirailler, chiffonner; **tousled hair**, cheveux ébouriffés, *m.pl.*

tout [taut], *v.i.* racoler.—*n.* racoleur, *m.*

touting ['tautiŋ], *n.* racolage, *m.*

tow [tou], *n.* filasse, étoupe (*chanvre*); remorque, *f.*; **in tow**, à la remorque.—*v.t.* remorquer, touer, haler.

towage ['touidʒ], *n.* remorquage, touage, halage, *m.*

toward, towards [tu'wɔ:d(z)], *prep.* vers, envers; du côté de; à l'égard de (*par respect pour*); sur, environ, vers (*l'heure*).

tow-boat [toubout], *n.* remorqueur, *m.*

towel ['tauəl], *n.* essuie-mains, *m.inv.*, serviette, *f.*

towelling ['tauəliŋ], *n.* toile pour serviettes, *f.*; tissu-éponge, *m.*

tower ['tauə], *n.* tour, *f.*—*v.i.* s'élever (*au-dessus de*), dominer.

towering ['tauəriŋ], *a.* élevé; dominant; violent.

towing ['touiŋ], *n.* remorque, *f.*; halage (*sur canal*), *m.*

towing-boat ['touiŋbout], [TOW-BOAT].

tow(ing)-line ['tou(iŋ)lain], **tow(ing)-rope** ['tou(iŋ)roup], *n.* cable de remorque, *m.*, remorque, *f.*

tow(ing)-path ['tou(iŋ)pɑ:θ], *n.* chemin de halage, *m.*

town [taun], *n.* ville, *f.*

town clerk ['taun'klɑ:k], *n.* secrétaire de, mairie, *m.*

town council ['taun'kaunsl], *n.* conseil municipal, *m.*

town councilor ['taun'kaunsilə], *n.* conseiller municipal, *m.*

town hall ['taun'hɔ:l], *n.* hôtel de ville, *m.*, mairie, *f.*

town planning ['taun plæniŋ], *n.* urbanisme, *m.*

townsfolk [TOWNSPEOPLE].

township ['taunʃip], *n.* commune, *f.*

townsman ['taunzmən], *n.* (*pl.* -men [men]) habitant de la ville, bourgeois, *m.*

townspeople ['taunzpi:pl], **townsfolk** ['taunzfouk], *n.* habitants (de la ville), citadins, *m.pl.*

tow-rope [TOW(ING)-LINE].

toxic ['tɔksik], *a.* toxique.

toxicology [tɔksi'kɔlədʒi], *n.* toxicologie, *f.*

toy [tɔi], *n.* jouet, joujou, *m.*—*v.i.* jouer; folâtrer, s'amuser (*avec*).

trace (1) [treis], *n.* trace, *f.*; tracé (*calque*), *m.*—*v.t.* tracer; calquer (*dessin*); suivre la trace de (*to track*); (*fig.*) remonter à l'origine de.

trace (2) [treis], *n.* (*usu. pl.*) traits (*harnais*), *m.pl.*

traceable ['treisəbl], *a.* que l'on peut tracer.

tracer ['treisə], *n.* traceur; traçoir (*instrument*), *m.*

tracery ['treisəri], *n.* (*Arch.*) réseau, *m.*

trachea [trə'ki:ə], *n.* (*Anat.*) trachée-artère, *f.*

tracing ['treisiŋ], *n.* tracé, tracement; calque, *m.*; **tracing paper**, papier à calquer, *m.*

track [træk], *n.* (*Spt.*) piste, *f.*, chemin (*route*), *m.*; (*Hunt.*) piste (*Rail.*) voie; (*Astron.*) orbite, *f.*, sillage (*de bateau*), *m.*; **beaten track**, sentier battu, *m.*; (*Cine.*) **sound track**, bande sonore, *f.*—*v.t.* suivre à la piste; haler, remorquer.

tracker ['trækə], *n.* traqueur, *m.*

tracking ['trækiŋ], *n.* action de suivre à la trace, *f.*

trackless ['træklis], *a.* sans trace; sans chemins.

tract [trækt], *n.* étendue; contrée; brochure (*petit livre*), *f.*

tractable ['træktəbl], *a.* traitable, maniable.

tractile ['træktail], *a.* ductile.

traction ['trækʃən], *n.* traction, tension, *f.*

traction engine ['trækʃənendʒin], *n.* locomotive routière, *f.*

tractor ['træktə], *n.* tracteur, *m.*

trade [treid], *n.* commerce, trafic, négoce; métier, *m.*, profession (*vocation*), *f.*; **Board of Trade**, Ministère du Commerce, *m.*; **free trade**, libre-échange, *m.*; (*Comm.*) **trade name**, marque déposée, *f.*—*v.i.* trafiquer, faire le commerce (*de*).

trade-mark ['treidmɑ:k], *n.* marque de fabrique, *f.*
trader ['treidə], *n.* négociant, *m.*
tradesman ['treidzmən], *n.* (*pl.* -**men** [men]) marchand, boutiquier (*détaillant*); fournisseur, *m.*
trade union ['treid 'ju:njən], *n.* syndicat ouvrier, *m.*
trade unionism ['treid'ju:njənizm], *n.* syndicalisme, *m.*
trade unionist ['treid'ju:njənist], *n.* syndicaliste, *m., f.*
trade winds ['treidwindz], *n.pl.* vents alizés, *m.pl.*
trading ['treidiŋ], *a.* marchand, de commerce.—*n.* négoce, commerce, *m.*
tradition [trə'diʃən], *n.* tradition, *f.*
traditional [trə'diʃənəl], *a.* traditionnel.
traduce [trə'dju:s], *v.t.* diffamer, calomnier.
traducer [trə'dju:sə], *n.* calomniateur, *m.*
traffic ['træfik], *n.* trafic; commerce, négoce, *m.*; circulation (*de voitures*), *f.*; (*Rail.*) mouvement, *m.*; **traffic jam**, embouteillage; **traffic light**, feu de signalisation. *m.*—*v.i.* trafiquer, commercer.
trafficker ['træfikə], *n.* trafiquant, *m.*
tragedian [trə'dʒi:diən], *n.* auteur tragique, tragédien, *m.*
tragedy ['trædʒədi], *n.* tragédie, *f.*
tragic ['trædʒik], **tragical** ['trædʒikəl], *a.* tragique.
tragi-comedy ['trædʒi'komidi], *n.* tragi-comédie, *f.*
tragi-comical ['trædʒi'komikəl], *a.* tragi-comique.
trail [treil], *n.* traînée (*Hunt.*) piste, *f.*—*v.t.* suivre à la piste; traîner (*tirer après soi*).—*v.i.* traîner.
trailer ['treilə], *n.* remorque (*bicyclette, camion etc.*); (*Am.*) roulotte, caravane; (*Cine.*) bande de lancement, *f.*
train [trein], *n.* (*Rail.*) train, *m.*; suite, *f.*, cortège (*personnel*), *m.*; série, *f.*, enchaînement (*succession*), *m.*; traînée (*de poudre à canon*); queue, traîne (*de robe*), *f.*; **breakdown train**, train de secours; **freight train**, train de marchandises, *m.*—*v.t.* exercer, instruire; dresser, entraîner (*cheval etc.*); former.—*v.i.* s'entraîner.
train bearer ['treinbɛərə], *n.* porte-queue, *m.*
trainee [trei'ni:], *n.* stagiaire, *m., f.*
trainer ['treinə], *n.* dresseur; entraîneur, *m.*
training ['treiniŋ], *n.* éducation, instruction, *f.*; dressage (*de cheval*); entraînement (*de cheval de course*), *m.*
training ship ['treiniŋʃip], *n.* vaisseau-école, *m.*
trait [trei, treit], *n.* trait, *m.*
traitor ['treitə], *n.* traître, *m.*
traitorous ['treitərəs], *a.* traître, perfide.
traitorously ['treitərəsli], *adv.* en traître, perfidement.
traitress ['treitris], *n.* traîtresse, *f.*
trajectory [trə'dʒektəri], *n.* trajectoire, *f.*
tram(-car) ['træm(kɑ:)], *n.* tramway, *m.*
trammel ['træml], *n.* tramail (*filet*), *m.*; entrave (*de cheval*), *f.*—*v.t.* entraver, empêtrer (*de*).
tramp [træmp], *v.t.* faire à pied, faire.—*v.i.* aller à pied, marcher lourdement.—*n.* randonnée (*à pied*), *f.*; bruit de pas (*marche pesante*); vagabond, *m.*

trample ['træmpl], *v.t.* fouler (*aux pieds*).
trampling ['træmpliŋ], *n.* piétinement, bruit de pas, *m.*
trance [trɑ:ns], *n.* extase; (*Path.*) catalepsie, *f.*
tranquil ['træŋkwil], *a.* tranquille.
tranquillity [træŋ'kwiliti], *n.* tranquillité, *f.*, calme, *m.*
tranquillize ['træŋkwilaiz], *v.t.* tranquilliser, calmer.
tranquillizer ['træŋkwilaizə], *n.* calmant, *m.*
transact [træn'zækt], *v.t.* traiter, expédier.
transaction [træn'zækʃən], *n.* transaction, affaire, *f.*
transactor [træn'zæktə], *n.* négociateur, *m.*
transalpine [træn'zælpain], *a.* transalpin.
transatlantic [trænzət'læntik], *a.* transatlantique.
transcend [træn'send], *v.t.* dépasser, surpasser.
transcendence [træn'sendəns], **transcendency** [træn'sendənsi], *n.* excellence, transcendance, *f.*
transcendent [træn'sendənt], *a.* transcendant.
transcendental [trænsen'dentl], *a.* transcendantal.
transcribe [træn'skraib], *v.t.* transcrire, copier.
transcriber [træn'skraibə], *n.* copiste, *m., f.*, transcripteur, *m.*
transcript ['trænskript], *n.* copie, *f.*
transcription [træn'skripʃən], *n.* transcription, *f.*
transept ['trænsept], *n.* transept, *m.*
transfer [træns'fə:], *v.t.* transporter; (*Law*) transférer.—['trænsfə:], *n.* copie, *f.*; (*Law*) transfert, *m.*
transferable ['trænsfərəbl], *a.* transférable, transmissible.
transference ['trænsfərəns], *n.* transfert, *m.*
transfiguration [trænsfigju'reiʃən], *n.* transfiguration, transformation, *f.*
transfigure [træns'figə], *v.t.* transfigurer.
transfix [træns'fiks], *v.t.* transpercer.
transform [træns'fɔ:m], *v.t.* transformer, changer (*en*).—*v.i.* se transformer (*en*).
transformation [trænsfə'meiʃən], *n.* transformation, *f.*, changement, *m.*; **transformation scene**, changement à vue, *m.*
transformer [træns'fɔ:mə], *n.* transformateur, *m.*
transfuse [træns'fju:z], *v.t.* transfuser.
transfusion [træns'fju:ʒən], *n.* transfusion, *f.*
transgress [træns'gres, trænz'gres], *v.t.* transgresser, enfreindre.—*v.i.* transgresser, pécher.
transgression [træns'greʃən], *n.* transgression, infraction, *f.*
transgressor [træns'gresə], *n.* pécheur, *m.*, pécheresse, *f.*
tranship [træn'ʃip] *v.t.* transborder.
transience ['trænziəns], *n.* nature transitoire, courte durée, *f.*
transient ['trænziənt], *a.* passager, transitoire.
transistor [træn'zistə], *n.* transistor, transistron, *m.*
transit ['trænzit], *n.* passage, *m.*; *in transit*, en transit.
transition [træn'ziʃən], *n.* transition, *f.*
transitional [træn'ziʃənəl], *a.* de transition.
transitive ['trænzitiv], *a.* qui passe; (*Gram.*) transitif.

transitoriness

transitoriness ['trænzitərinis], *n.* nature transitoire, courte durée, *f.*
transitory ['trænzitəri], *a.* transitoire, passager.
translatable [træns'leitəbl], *a.* traduisible.
translate [træns'leit], *v.t.* traduire; transférer (*évêque*).
translation [træns'leiʃən], *n.* traduction; translation (*d'un évêque*), *f.*
translator [træns'leitə], *n.* traducteur, *m.*
translucent [trænz'lju:sənt], *a.* translucide.
transmarine [trænzmə'ri:n], *a.* d'outremer.
transmigrate ['trænzmaigreit], *v.i.* passer d'un corps dans un autre; émigrer.
transmigration [trænzmai'greiʃən], *n.* transmigration; métempsyc(h)ose (*des âmes*), *f.*
transmissible [trænz'misibl], *a.* transmissible.
transmission [trænz'miʃən], *n.* transmission, *f.* [(*Motor.*) see **gear-box**]
transmit [trænz'mit], *v.t.* transmettre, envoyer; (*Rad.*) émettre.
transmitter [trænz'mitə], *n.* (*Rad.*) émetteur, *m.*
transmutable [trænz'mju:təbl], *a.* transmuable.
transmutation [trænzmju'teiʃən], *n.* transmutation, *f.*; changement (*de couleur*), *m.*
transmute [trænz'mju:t], *v.t.* transmuer, convertir.
transom ['trænsəm], *n.* traverse (*de fenêtre*), imposte, *f.*
transparency [træns'pɛərənsi], *n.* transparence; (*Phot.*) diapositive, *f.*
transparent [træns'pɛərənt], *a.* transparent.
transparently [træns'pɛərəntli], *adv.* avec transparence; évidemment.
transpire [træns'paiə, trænz'paiə], *v.i.* transpirer; (*fig.*) avoir lieu, arriver.
transplant [træns'pla:nt, trænz'pla:nt], *v.t.* transplanter; (*fig.*) déplacer.
transplanting [træns'pla:ntiŋ, trænz'pla:ntiŋ], *n.* transplantation, *f.*
transport ['trænspɔ:t], *n.* transport, *m.*— [træns'pɔ:t], *v.t.* transporter; déporter (*forçat*).
transportation [trænspɔ:'teiʃən], *n.* transport, *m.*; déportation (*des forçats*), *f.*
transporter [træns'pɔ:tə], *n.* entrepreneur de transports; (*pont*) transbordeur, *m.*
transporting [træns'pɔ:tiŋ], *a.* ravissant, transportant.
transposal [træns'pouzl], *n.* transposition, *f.*
transpose [træns'pouz], *v.t.* transposer.
transubstantiation [trænsəbstænʃi'eiʃən], *n.* transsubstantiation, *f.*
Transvaal ['trænzvɑ:l], **the.** le Transvaal, *m.*
transversal [trænz'və:sl], *a.* transversal.
transversely [trænz'və:sli], *adv.* en travers.
transverse [trænz'və:s], *a.* transverse, transversal.
trap [træp], *n.* trappe, *f.*, piège, *m.*; carriole (*véhicule*), *f.*—*v.t.* prendre au piège, attraper.
trap door ['træpdɔ:], *n.* trappe, *f.*
trapeze [trə'pi:z], *n.* trapèze, *m.*
trapper ['træpə], *n.* trappeur, *m.*
trappings ['træpiŋz], *n.pl.* harnais, *m.*; (*fig.*) parure, *f.*, atours, *m.pl.*
traps [træps], *n.pl.* bagages, *m.pl.*
trash [træʃ], *n.* rebut, *m.*; camelote, *f.*; fatras (*écrits*), *m.*

trashy ['træʃi], *a.* de rebut, sans valeur.
travel [trævl], *v.t.* parcourir; faire (*distance etc.*).—*v.i.* voyager, être en voyage.—*n.* voyage, *m.*
traveller ['trævlə], *n.* voyageur; (*Comm.*) commis voyageur, *m.*; *traveller's check*, chèque de voyage, *m.*
travelling ['trævliŋ], *a.* voyageur, de voyage; ambulant (*itinérant*); *travelling expenses*, frais de déplacement, *m.pl.*; *travelling-case*, nécessaire de voyage, *m.*—*n.* voyage, *m.*, voyages, *m.pl.*
travelogue ['trævəlɔg], *n.* film de tourisme, *m.*
traverse ['trævəs], *a.* oblique.—*n.* traverse, *f.* —*v.t.* traverser; (*Law*) nier.
travesty ['trævəsti], *n.* travestissement, *m.*; parodie, *f.*—*v.t.* travestir, parodier.
trawl [trɔ:l], *n.* chalut (*filet*), *m.*—*v.i.* pêcher au chalut.
trawler ['trɔ:lə], *n.* chalutier, *m.*
trawling ['trɔ:liŋ], *n.* pêche au chalut, *f.*
tray [trei], *n.* plateau, *m.*
treacherous ['tretʃərəs], *a.* traître, perfide.
treacherously ['tretʃərəsli], *adv.* en traître.
treachery ['tretʃəri], *n.* trahison, perfidie, *f.*
treacle ['tri:kl], *n.* mélasse, *f.*
tread [tred], *v.t. irr.* fouler, écraser.—*v.i.* mettre le pied, marcher (*sur*); se poser (*pieds*).—*n.* pas, *m.*; marche (*d'escalier*); chape (*d'un pneu*), *f.*
treading ['trediŋ], *n.* pas, *m.*; marche, *f.*; foulage (*de raisins etc.*), *m.*
treadle [tredl], *n.* marche; pédale, *f.*
treadmill ['tredmil], *n.* trépigneuse, *f.*
treason [tri:zn], *n.* trahison, *f.*; *high treason*, lèse-majesté, *f.*
treasonable ['tri:znəbl], *a.* de trahison.
treasonably ['tri:znəbli], *adv.* par trahison, traîtreusement.
treasure ['treʒə], *n.* trésor, *m.*—*v.t.* garder, priser.
treasurer ['treʒərə], *n.* trésorier, *m.*
treasure-trove ['treʒətrouv], *n.* trésor trouvé, *m.*
treasury ['treʒəri], *n.* trésor, trésor public, *m.*, finances, *f.pl.*, trésorerie, *f.*
treat [tri:t], *n.* régal, festin, (*fig.*) plaisir, *m.*— *v.t.* traiter; régaler (*de*).—*v.i.* traiter (*de*); négocier.
treatise ['tri:tis], *n.* traité (*de ou sur*), *m.*
treatment ['tri:tmənt], *n.* traitement, *m.*
treaty ['tri:ti], *n.* traité, *m.*
treble [trebl], *a.* triple; (*Mus.*) de dessus, soprano.—*n.* triple; (*Mus.*) dessus, soprano, *m.*—*v.t.*, *v.i.* tripler.
trebling ['trebliŋ], *n.* triplement, *m.*
trebly ['trebli], *adv.* triplement, trois fois.
tree [tri:], *n.* arbre; embauchoir (*pour botte*), *m.*; (*fig.*) croix, *f.*
trefoil ['tri:fɔil], *n.* trèfle, *m.*
trellis ['trelis], *n.* treillis, treillage, *m.*
trellised ['trelist], *a.* treillissé.
tremble [trembl], *v.i.* trembler.
trembling ['trembliŋ], *a.* tremblant, tremblotant.—*n.* tremblement, *m.*
tremendous [tri'mendəs], *a.* terrible, épouvantable.
tremendously [tri'mendəsli], *adv.* terriblement.
tremor ['tremə], *n.* tremblement, *m.*; secousse, *f.*

tremulous ['tremjuləs], *a.* tremblant, (*fig.*) craintif.
tremulously ['tremjuləsli], *adv.* en tremblant, en tremblotant.
tremulousness ['tremjuləsnis], *n.* tremblotement, *m.*
trench [trentʃ], *n.* fossé, *m.*, tranchée; rigole (*entre sillons etc.*), *f.*—*v.t.* creuser.
trenchancy ['trentʃənsi], *n.* causticité, *f.*
trenchant ['trentʃənt], *a.* tranchant, caustique.
trencher ['trentʃə], *n.* tranchoir, tailloir, *m.*
trencherman ['trentʃəmən], *n.* (*pl.* -men [mɛn]) gros mangeur, *m.*
trend [trend], *n.* direction, tendance, *f.*—*v.i.* se diriger, tendre (*vers*).
trepan [trə'pæn], *n.* (*Surg.*) trépan, *m.*—*v.t.* trépaner.
trepanning [trə'pæniŋ], *n.* trépanation, *f.*
trepidation [trepi'deiʃən], *n.* trépidation, *f.*
trespass ['trespəs], *n.* violation de propriété, *f.*, délit, *m.*; (*Scripture*) offense, *f.*—*v.i.* violer la propriété, empiéter (*sur*); (*Scripture*) pécher; transgresser.
trespasser ['trespəsə], *n.* violateur du droit de propriété; (*Scripture*) pécheur, *m.*, pécheresse, *f.*
tress [tres], *n.* tresse, boucle, *f.*
trestle [tresl], *n.* tréteau, *m.*
trestle bed ['treslbed], *n.* lit de sangle, *m.*
triad ['traiæd], *n.* triade, *f.*
trial ['traiəl], *a.* d'essai.—*n.* expérience, épreuve, *f.*, essai; (*Law*) procès, *m.*
triangle ['traiæŋgl], *n.* triangle, *m.*
triangular [trai'æŋgjulə], *a.* triangulaire.
tribal ['traibl], *a.* tribal.
tribe [traib], *n.* tribu, peuplade; (*fig.*) race, *f.*
tribulation [tribju'leiʃən], *n.* tribulation, *f.*
tribunal [trai'bju:nl], *n.* tribunal, *m.*
tribune ['tribju:n], *n.* (*Rom. Hist.*) tribun, *m.*; tribune (*estrade*), *f.*
tributary ['tribjutəri], *a.* tributaire.—*n.* tributaire; affluent (*rivière*), *m.*
tribute ['tribju:t], *n.* tribut; (*fig.*) hommage, *m.*
trice (1) [trais], *n. in a trice*, en un clin d'œil.
trice (2) [trais], *v.t.* (*Naut.*) hisser.
trick [trik], *n.* tour, artifice, *m.*; (*Cards*) levée; ruse, finesse, *f.*; tic (*habitude*), *m.*; *nasty trick*, vilain tour; *to play someone a trick*, faire une niche *ou* jouer un tour à quelqu'un.—*v.t.* duper; tricher (*en jouant*); *to trick out*, parer, orner.
trickery ['trikəri], *n.* tromperie, fourberie, tricherie, *f.*
trickish ['trikiʃ], *a.* trompeur, fourbe, fin.
trickle [trikl], *v.i.* suinter, dégoutter.
trickling ['trikliŋ], *n.* écoulement, *m.*
trickster ['trikstə], *n.* fourbe, escroc, *m.*
tricky ['triki], *a.* fourbe, rusé; (*fig.*) compliqué; délicat (*à manier*).
tricolor ['traikʌlə], *n.* drapeau tricolore, *m.*
tricolored ['traikʌləd], *a.* tricolore.
tricycle ['traisikl], *n.* tricycle, *m.*
trident ['traidənt], *n.* trident, *m.*
tried [traid], *a.* éprouvé.
triennial [trai'eniəl], *a.* triennal.—*n.* (*Bot.*) plante triennale, *f.*
triennially [trai'eniəli], *adv.* tous les trois ans.
trier ['traiə], *n.* (*Law*) juge; arbitre, *m.*; (*fig.*) épreuve, pierre de touche, *f.*

trifle [traifl], *n.* bagatelle; (*Cook.*) sorte de charlotte russe, *f.*—*v.i.* badiner; *to trifle with*, plaisanter avec, se moquer de.
trifler ['traiflə], *n.* personne frivole, *f.*
trifling ['traifliŋ], *a.* de rien, insignifiant, frivole.—*n.* frivolité, *f.*, badinage, *m.*
trigamy ['trigəmi], *n.* trigamie, *f.*
trigger ['trigə], *n.* détente, *f.*
trigonometry [trigə'nɔmətri], *n.* trigonométrie, *f.*
trilateral [trai'lætərəl], *a.* trilatéral.
trill [tril], *n.* trille, *m.*—*v.i.* triller.
trillion ['triljən], *n.* (*since 1948*) trillion; (*before 1948*) quintillion, *m.*
trilogy ['trilədʒi], *n.* trilogie, *f.*
trim [trim], *a.* soigné, coquet, bien mis, bien arrangé.—*n.* bon ordre, *m.*; assiette (*de bateau*), *f.*; orientement (*des voiles*); arrimage (*de cale*), *m.*—*v.t.* arranger, mettre en ordre; garnir, parer (*de*); émonder, tailler (*couper*); (*Naut.*) arrimer (*cargaison*); orienter (*voiles*). —*v.i.* (*Polit. slang*) balancer entre deux partis.
trimly ['trimli], *adv.* bien, gentiment, proprement.
trimmer ['trimə], *n.* (*Polit.*) opportuniste, *m.*, *f.*; (*Naut.*) soutier, *m.*
trimming ['trimiŋ], *n.* garniture; semonce; (*pl.*) parure (*de viande*), *f.*
trimness ['trimnis], *n.* air soigné, bon ordre, *m.*
Trinidad ['trinidæd]. (Île de la) Trinité, *f.*
Trinity ['triniti], *n.* Trinité, *f.*
trinket ['triŋkit], *n.* petit bijou, *m.*, breloque, *f.*
trinomial [trai'noumiəl], *a. and n.* trinôme, *m.*
trio ['tri:ou], *n.* trio, *m.*
trip [trip], *v.t.* renverser, faire tomber.—*v.i.* trébucher, faire un faux pas; foucher (*la langue*); courir légèrement.—*n.* croc-enjambe, faux pas, *m.*; excursion, *f.*, tour, voyage, *m.*
tripe [traip], *n.* tripes, *f.pl.*
triple [tripl], *a.* triple.—*v.t.* tripler.
triplet ['triplit], *n.* (*Pros.*) tercet; (*Mus.*) triolet, *m.*; (*pl.*) triplés, *m.pl.*
triplicate ['triplikit], *a.* triplé.—*n.* triplicata (*copie*), *m.*
tripod ['traipɔd], *n.* trépied, *m.*
tripper ['tripə], *n.* (*colloq.*) excursionniste, *m.*, *f.*
tripping ['tripiŋ], *a.* agile, léger.—*n.* croc en jambe, faux pas, *m.*; erreur, *f.*; pas léger, *m.*
trireme ['trairi:m], *n.* trirème, *f.*
trisect [trai'sekt], *v.t.* couper en trois.
trisyllabic [traisi'læbik], *a.* trissyllabe.
trisyllable [trai'siləbl], *n.* trissyllabe, *m.*
trite [trait], *a.* usé, banal, rebattu.
triteness ['traitnis], *n.* nature banale, trivialité, *f.*
Triton ['traitən]. Triton, *m.*
triumph ['traiəmf], *n.* triomphe, *m.*—*v.i.* triompher.
triumphal [trai'ʌmfl], *a.* triomphal.
triumphant [trai'ʌmfənt], *a.* triomphant.
triumphantly [trai'ʌmfəntli], *adv.* en triomphe.
triumvir [trai'ʌmvə], *n.* triumvir, *m.*
triumvirate [trai'ʌmvərit], *n.* triumvirat, *m.*
trivet ['trivit], *n.* trépied, *m.*

trivial ['triviəl], *a.* banal, insignifiant, sans importance.
triviality [trivi'æliti], *n.* insignifiance; banalité, *f.*
troat [trout], *n.* bramement, *m.*—*v.t.* bramer, raire (*cerf*).
trochaic [tro'keiik], *a.* trochaïque.
trochee ['trouki], *n.* trochée, *m.*
Trojan ['troudʒən], *a.* troyen.—*n.* Troyen, *m.*
troll [troul], *v.t.* rouler, tourner.
trolley, trolly ['troli], *n.* fardier, chariot; (*Elec.*) trolley, *m.*; *dinner trolley*, table roulante, *f.* [see **tram(-car)**]
trolley bus ['trolibʌs], *n.* trolleybus, *m.*
trollop ['trolǝp], *n.* souillon, *f.*
trombone [trom'boun], *n.* trombone, *m.*
troop [tru:p], *n.* troupe, bande, *f.*—*v.i.* s'attrouper, s'assembler.
trooper ['tru:pǝ], *n.* (*Mil.*) soldat à cheval, cavalier, *m.*
trophy ['troufi], *n.* trophée, *m.*
tropic ['tropik], *n.* tropique, *m.*
tropical ['tropikǝl], *a.* tropical, des tropiques.
trot [trot], *n.* trot, *m.*—*v.i.* trotter, aller au trot; trottiner (*enfant*).
troth [trouθ], *n.* foi, *f.*; *by my troth!* ma foi!
trotter ['trotǝ], *n.* cheval de trot, trotteur, *m.*; (*pl.*) pieds de mouton, pieds de cochon, *m.pl.*
trotting ['trotiŋ], *a.* trotteur.—*n.* trot, *m.*
troubadour ['tru:bǝduǝ], *n.* troubadour, *m.*
trouble [trʌbl], *v.t.* agiter; troubler, déranger (*gêner*); tourmenter, affliger (*faire souffrir*); inquiéter (*préoccuper*).—*v.i.* s'inquiéter, se donner la peine (*de*).—*n.* trouble, *m.*; peine (*effort*); affliction, *f.*, souci, chagrin (*tristesse*); ennui (*difficulté*), *m.*; *it is not worth the trouble*, ce n'est pas la peine.
troubled [trʌbld], *a.* inquiet, agité; trouble (*eau etc.*).
troublesome ['trʌblsǝm], *a.* ennuyeux, incommode; fatigant, fâcheux.
troublesomeness ['trʌblsǝmnis], *n.* ennui, embarras, *m.*, gêne, *f.*
***troublous** ['trʌblǝs], *a.* troublé, agité, orageux.
trough [trof], *n.* auge, huche, *f.*; (*Cook.*) pétrin; auget, abreuvoir (*pour boire*), *m.*
trounce [trauns], *v.t.* rosser, étriller.
trouncing ['traunsiŋ], *n.* raclée, *f.*, étrillage, *m.*
trouser-press ['trauzǝpres], *n.* presse-pantalon, *m.*
trousers ['trauzǝz], *n.pl.* pantalon, *m.*
trousseau ['tru:sou], *n.* trousseau, *m.*
trout [traut], *n.* truite, *f.*
trowel ['trauǝl], *n.* truelle, *f.*
Troy [troi], Troie, *f.*
troy weight ['troiweit], *n.* troy (*poids de douze onces à la livre*).
truant ['tru:ǝnt], *n.* fainéant, vagabond, *m.*; *to play truant*, faire l'école buissonnière.
truce [tru:s], *n.* trêve, *f.*
truck [trʌk], *n.* fardier, chariot (*charrette*); (*Am.*) camion; (*Rail.*) wagon, *m.*—*v.i.* troquer.
truckle [trʌkl], *n.* roulette, *f.*—*v.i.* ramper, s'abaisser (*devant*).
truckle bed ['trʌklbed], *n.* grabat, *m.*
truckling ['trʌkliŋ], *n.* soumission, *f.*, abaissement, *m.*

truculence ['trʌkjulǝns], *n.* férocité, truculence, *f.*
truculent ['trʌkjulǝnt], *a.* brutal, féroce, farouche.
trudge [trʌdʒ], *n.* marche pénible, *f.*—*v.i.* clopiner, marcher péniblement.
true [tru:], *a.* vrai, véritable; fidèle (*véridique*); exact (*juste*); loyal (*honnête*); droit (*vertueux*); *to come true*, se réaliser.—*int.* c'est vrai! c'est juste!—*adv.* juste (*précisément*).—*v.t.* ajuster.
true-bred ['tru:bred], *a.* de bonne race, pur sang; (*fig.*) accompli.
true-hearted ['tru:'ha:tid], *a.* au cœur sincère.
trueness ['tru:nis], *n.* fidélité; justesse, *f.*
truffle [trʌfl], *n.* truffe, *f.*; *to stuff with truffles*, truffer.
truism ['tru:izm], *n.* truisme, *m.*
truly ['tru:li], *adv.* vraiment, véritablement.
trump [trʌmp], *n.* trompe, trompette, *f.*; (*Cards.*) atout, *m.*—*v.t.* jouer atout, couper.
trumpery ['trʌmpǝri], *a.* sans valeur, mesquin.—*n.* rebut, *m.*, blague, *f.*
trumpet ['trʌmpit], *n.* trompette, *f.*—*v.t.* proclamer.—*v.i.* barrir (*éléphant*).
trumpet call ['trʌmpitkɔ:l], *n.* coup de trompette, *m.*
trumpeter ['trʌmpitǝ], *n.* trompette, *m.*
truncate [trʌŋ'keit], *v.t.* tronquer.
truncheon ['trʌntʃǝn], *n.* bâton, *m.*; matraque, *f.*
trundle [trʌndl], *v.t.* rouler.
trunk [trʌŋk], *n.* tronc, *m.*; malle (*boîte*); trompe (*d'éléphant*), *f.*; coffre (*d'auto*), *m.*
trunk call ['trʌŋkkɔ:l], *n.* (*Teleph.*) appel interurbain, *m.*
trunk road ['trʌŋkroud], *n.* route à grande circulation, *f.*
trunnion ['trʌnjǝn], *n.* tourillon, *m.*
truss [trʌs], *n.* botte (*de foin etc.*), *f.*; paquet; (*Surg.*) bandage herniaire, *m.*—*v.t.* trousser (*une poule*); lier (*foin*).
trust [trʌst], *n.* confiance (*en*), *f.*; dépôt, *m.*; garde (*charge*), *f.*; crédit; (*Law*) fidéicommis; (*Comm.*) trust, syndicat, *m.*—*v.t.* se fier à, se confier à; faire crédit à (*en matière d'argent*).—*v.i.* avoir confiance (*en* ou *dans*); s'attendre (*à*).
trust deed ['trʌstdi:d], *n.* acte fiduciaire, *m.*
trusted ['trʌstid], *a.* de confiance.
trustee [trʌs'ti:], *n.* gardien, *m.*, dépositaire; (*Law*) fidéicommissaire, *m.*, *f.*
trusteeship [trʌs'ti:ʃip], *n.* administration; tutelle, *f.*, (*Law*) fidéicommis, *m.*
trustiness ['trʌstinis], *n.* fidélité, loyauté, *f.*
trusting ['trʌstiŋ], *a.* plein de confiance.
trustworthiness ['trʌstwǝ:ðinis], *n.* fidélité (*personne*); exactitude (*des nouvelles etc.*), *f.*
trustworthy ['trʌstwǝ:ði], *a.* digne de confiance; exact (*nouvelles*).
trusty ['trʌsti], *a.* sûr, fidèle, loyal.
truth [tru:θ], *n.* vérité, *f.*, vrai, *m.*; *to tell the truth . . .*, à vrai dire . . . .
truthful ['tru:θful], *a.* véridique, vrai.
truthfully ['tru:θfuli], *adv.* véridiquement, avec vérité.
truthfulness ['tru:θfulnis], *n.* véracité, *f.*
try [trai], *v.t.* essayer; éprouver, mettre à l'épreuve; tenter (*se prêter à*); (*Law*) juger.—*v.i.* essayer, tâcher (*de*).—*n.* essai, *m.*

trying ['traiiŋ], *a.* difficile, pénible.

*****tryst** [traist], *n.* rendez-vous, *m.*

Tsar [zɑː], *n.* Tsar, *m.*

Tsarina [zɑːˈriːnə], *n.* Tsarine, *f.*

tsetse ['tsetsi], *n.* mouche tsé-tsé, *f.*

tub [tʌb], *n.* cuve, *f.*, baquet; bain (*moderne*), *m.*—*v.t.* encuver; (*Gard.*) encaisser.

tuba ['tjuːbə], *n.* tuba, *m.*; contrebasse à vent, *f.*

tubby ['tʌbi], *a.* gros, obèse.

tube [tjuːb], *n.* tube; (*Anat.*) conduit, canal; (*Rail.*) métro, *m.*; *inner tube*, chambre à air, *f.*; (*Rad.*) lampe, *f.*

tuber ['tjuːbə], *n.* tubercule, *m.*

tubercular [tjuːˈbəːkjulə], *a.* tuberculeux.

tuberculosis [tjuːbəːkjuˈlousis], *n.* tuberculose, *f.*

tuberose ['tjuːbərous], *a.* tubéreux.—*n.* tubéreuse, *f.*

tuberous ['tjuːbərəs], *a.* tubéreux.

tubular ['tjuːbjulə], *a.* tubulaire.

tuck [tʌk], *n.* pli, *m.*—*v.t.* plisser; serrer; retrousser.

tucker ['tʌkə], *n.* chemisette, collerette, *f.*

Tuesday ['tjuːzd(e)i], mardi, *m.*; *Shrove Tuesday*, mardi gras.

tuft [tʌft], *n.* touffe (*d'herbe* ou *de cheveux*); huppe (*d'oiseau*), *f.*

tufted ['tʌftid], *a.* touffu; huppé (*oiseau*).

tug [tʌg], *v.t.* tirer avec effort; remorquer (*to tow*).—*n.* tiraillement; remorqueur (*bateau*), *m.*

tuition [tjuˈiʃən], *n.* instruction, *f.*, enseignement, *m.*; frais d'inscription, *m.*

tulip ['tjuːlip], *n.* tulipe, *f.*

tulle [tjuːl], *n.* tulle, *m.*

tumble ['tʌmbl], *n.* culbute, chute, *f.*—*v.t.* culbuter.—*v.i.* tomber; rouler (*descendre en roulant*); dégringoler (*se tourner*).

tumbledown ['tʌmbldaun], *a.* croulant, délabré.

tumbler ['tʌmblə], *n.* verre sans pied; gobelet; culbutant (*pigeon*), *m.*

tumblerful ['tʌmbləful], *n.* plein un grand verre, *m.*

tumbril ['tʌmbril], **tumbrel** ['tʌmbrəl], *n.* tombereau, *m.*

tumefaction [tjuːmiˈfækʃən], *n.* tuméfaction, *f.*

tumefy ['tjuːmifai], *v.t.* tuméfier.—*v.i.* se tuméfier.

tumid ['tjuːmid], *a.* enflé, gonflé; (*fig.*) boursouflé.

tumidity [tjuˈmiditi], **tumidness** ['tjuːmidnis], *n.* enflure; (*fig.*) turgescence, *f.*

tumor ['tjuːmə], *n.* tumeur, *f.*

tumular ['tjuːmjulə], *a.* en monticule.

tumult ['tjuːmʌlt], *n.* tumulte; trouble, *m.*

tumultuous [tjuˈmʌltjuəs], *a.* tumultueux, turbulent, agité.

tumultuousness [tjuˈmʌltjuəsnis], *n.* turbulence, *f.*

tun [tʌn], *n.* tonneau, fût, *m.*; cuve, *f.*

tunable ['tjuːnəbl], *a.* accordable.

tundra ['tʌndrə], *n.* toundra, *f.*

tune [tjuːn], *n.* air; accord, *m.*; (*fig.*) harmonie, humeur, *f.*; *in tune*, d'accord; *out of tune*, faux.—*v.t.* accorder, mettre d'accord.—*v.i.* (*Rad.*) *to tune in*, accrocher (*un poste*).

tuneful ['tjuːnful], *a.* harmonieux, mélodieux.

tuneless ['tjuːnlis], *a.* discordant.

tuner ['tjuːnə], *n.* accordeur, *m.*

tungsten ['tʌŋstən], *n.* tungstène, *m.*

tunic ['tjuːnik], *n.* tunique, *f.*

tuning ['tjuːniŋ], *n.* accord, *m.*, action d'accorder, *f.*

tuning fork ['tjuːniŋfɔːk], *n.* diapason, *m.*

tuning hammer ['tjuːniŋhæmə], *n.* accordoir, *m.*

Tunisia [tjuˈniziə], la Tunisie, *f.*

Tunisian [tjuˈniziən], *a.* tunisien.—*n.* Tunisien (*personne*), *m.*

tunnel [tʌnl], *n.* tunnel, passage souterrain, *m.*—*v.t.* percer un tunnel dans.

tunnelling ['tʌnəliŋ], *n.* construction de tunnels, *f.*

tunny ['tʌni], *n.* (*Ichth.*) thon, *m.*

turban ['təːbən], *n.* turban, *m.*

turbid ['təːbid], *a.* trouble, bourbeux.

turbidity [təːˈbiditi], **turbidness** ['təːbidnis], *n.* état bourbeux, état trouble, *m.*

turbine ['təːbin, 'təːbain], *n.* turbine, *f.*

turbo-prop ['təːboprɔp], *a.* (*Av.*) à turbopropulseur.

turbot ['təːbət], *n.* turbot, *m.*

turbulence ['təːbjuləns], **turbulency** ['təːbjulənsi], *n.* turbulence, *f.*, tumulte, *m.*

turbulent ['təːbjulənt], *a.* tumultueux, turbulent.

turbulently ['təːbjuləntli], *adv.* tumultueusement.

tureen [tjuˈriːn], *n.* soupière, *f.*

turf [təːf], *n.* gazon, *m.*; motte de gazon; tourbe (*combustible*), *f.*; (*fig.*) turf, *m.*—*v.t.* gazonner.

turfing ['təːfiŋ], *n.* gazonnement, *m.*

turf-moss ['təːfmɔs], **turf-pit** ['təːfpit], *n.* tourbière, *f.*

turfy ['təːfi], *a.* gazonné; tourbeux.

turgid ['təːdʒid], *a.* gonflé; boursouflé.

turgidity [təːˈdʒiditi], **turgidness** ['təːdʒidnis], *n.* turgescence; (*fig.*) emphase (*de style*), *f.*

Turk [təːk], *n.* Turc (*personne*), *m.*

Turkey ['təːki], la Turquie, *f.*

turkey ['təːki], *n.* dindon, *m.*; *hen turkey*, dinde, *f.*

Turkish ['təːkiʃ], *a.* de Turquie, turc.—*n.* turc (*langue*), *m.*

turmoil ['təːmɔil], *n.* tumulte, *m.*, agitation, *f.*

turn [təːn], *v.t.* tourner; faire tourner; faire pencher (*la balance*); retourner (*vêtement etc.*); changer, convertir (*transformer*); traduire (*en une autre langue*); soulever (*l'estomac*); émousser (*le tranchant*); (*fig.*) rouler (*dans la tête*); *to turn aside*, détourner, écarter (*de*); *to turn away*, renvoyer, congédier; *to turn back*, faire retourner; *to turn down*, rabattre (*un col*); refuser; *to turn in*, tourner en dedans; *to turn into*, changer en; *to turn off*, couper (*vapeur*), fermer (*robinet*); *to turn on*, donner (*vapeur*), ouvrir (*robinet*); *to turn out*, mettre dehors; éteindre (*lumière*); *to turn over*, retourner, feuilleter (*pages d'un livre*); *to turn tail*, prendre la fuite; *to turn up*, retrousser.—*v.i.* tourner, se tourner; se retourner (*vers*); se détourner (*s'écarter*); se changer (*en*); devenir, se faire; *to turn back*, rebrousser chemin; *to turn from*, s'éloigner de; *to turn in*, se coucher (*aller au lit*); *to turn round*, tourner, se

tourner, se retourner; *to turn to*, s'adresser
à; *to turn up*, se retrousser; arriver (*se
passer*).—*n.* tour; coude, détour (*tournant*);
service; changement, *m.*; occasion; tournure
(*d'esprit*), *f.*; trait (*de balance*), *m.*; *a bad
turn*, un mauvais tour; *a good turn*, un
service; *by turns, in turns*, à tour de
rôle.

turncoat ['tə:nkout], *n.* renégat, *m.*
turn-cock ['tə:nkɔk], *n.* fontainier, *m.*
turner ['tə:nə], *n.* tourneur, *m.*
turnery ['tə:nəri], *n.* art du tourneur, *m.*
turning ['tə:niŋ], *n.* tournant (*de route etc.*);
(*Carp.*) tournage, *m.*
turning-lathe ['tə:niŋleið], *n.* tour, *m.*
turning point ['tə:niŋpɔint], *n.* point décisif,
moment critique, *m.*
turnip ['tə:nip], *n.* navet, *m.*
turnkey ['tə:nki:], *n.* guichetier, porte-clefs,
m.
turn-out ['tə:naut], *n.* équipage, *m.*; tenue, *f.*
turn-over ['tə:nouvə], *n.* chiffre d'affaires;
chausson (*pâte*), *m.*
turnpike ['tə:npaik], *n.* barrière de péage, *f.*;
autoroute, *f.*
turnspit ['tə:nspit], *n.* tournebroche, *m.*
turnstile ['tə:nstail], *n.* tourniquet, *m.*
turn-table ['tə:nteibl], *n.* plaque tournante;
platine, *f.*
turn-up ['tə:nʌp], *n.* revers (*de pantalon*), *m.*
turpentine ['tə:pəntain], *n.* térébenthine, *f.*
turpitude ['tə:pitju:d], *n.* turpitude, *f.*
turquoise ['tə:kwɔiz], *n.* turquoise, *f.*
turret ['tʌrit], *n.* tourelle, *f.*
turreted ['tʌritid], *a.* garni de tourelles.
turtle ['tə:tl], *n.* tortue de mer, *f.*; *to turn
turtle*, chavirer (*bateau*), capoter (*voiture*).
turtle-dove ['tə:tldʌv], *n.* tourterelle, *f.*
Tuscan ['tʌskən], *a.* toscan.—*n.* Toscan
(*personne*), *m.*
Tuscany ['tʌskəni]. la Toscane, *f.*
tush! [tʌʃ], *int.* bah! fi donc!
tusk [tʌsk], *n.* défense (*d'éléphant*), *f.*; croc
(*dent*), *m.*
tussle [tʌsl], *n.* lutte, bagarre, *f.*
tut! [tʌt], *int.* bah! allons donc!
tutelage ['tju:tilidʒ], *n.* tutelle, *f.*
tutor ['tju:tə], *n.* précepteur (*dans une
famille*); (*Univ.*) maître-assistant, *m.*—*v.t.*
instruire, enseigner.
tutorial [tju:'tɔ:riəl], *a.* de précepteur.
tutoring ['tju:təriŋ], *n.* instruction, *f.*
tutorship ['tju:təʃip], *n.* préceptorat, *m.*
twaddle [twɔdl], *n.* bavardage, caquetage, *m.*
***twain** [twein], *a.* and *n.* deux, *m.*
twang [twæŋ], *n.* son sec (*d'une corde qui
vibre*); accent nasillard (*voix*), *m.*—*v.t.* faire
résonner, faire vibrer.—*v.i.* résonner,
nasiller.
tweak [twi:k], *v.t.* pincer (*en tordant*).
tweezers ['twi:zəz], *n.pl.* pinces à épiler (*pour
poils*), *f.pl.*
twelfth [twelfθ], *a.* douzième; douze (*du mois,
des rois etc.*), *m.*; *Twelfth Night*, jour des
Rois, *m.*—*n.* douzième (*fraction*), *m.*
twelve [twelv], *a.* and *n.* douze, *m.*; *twelve
o'clock*, midi (*noon*), minuit (*midnight*), *m.*
twelvemonth ['twelvmʌnθ], *n.* an, *m.*, année,
f.
twentieth ['twentiθ], *a.* vingtième; vingt
(*du mois etc.*).—*n.* vingtième (*fraction*), *m.*

twenty ['twenti], *a.* and *n.* vingt, *m.*
twenty-first ['twenti'fə:st], *a.* vingt et unième,
vingt et un (*du mois etc.*).
twice [twais], *adv.* deux fois.
twig [twig], *n.* brindille, ramille, *f.*
twilight ['twailait], *a.* crépusculaire.—*n.*
crépuscule, *m.*
twill [twil], *n.* étoffe croisée, *f.*
twin [twin], *a.* jumeau; jumelé; (*Bot.*) double,
géminé.—*n.* jumeau, *m.*, jumelle, *f.*
twine [twain], *n.* ficelle, *f.*—*v.t.* retordre;
enlacer.—*v.i.* s'entrelacer, s'enrouler.
twinge [twindʒ], *n.* élancement; remords (*de
conscience*), *m.*—*v.i.* élancer; (*fig.*) torturer.
twinkle [twiŋkl], *v.i.* étinceler.
twinkling ['twiŋkliŋ], *a.* scintillant, scintillant.
—*n.* scintillement, clignotement (*des yeux*),
m.; *in the twinkling of an eye*, en un
clin d'œil.
twirl [twə:l], *v.t.* faire tournoyer; friser
(*favoris*).—*v.i.* tournoyer, tourner rapidement.—*n.* tournoiement, *m.*; pirouette, *f.*
twist [twist], *v.t.* tordre; tortiller, retordre;
cercler, entourer; enlacer (*entortiller*); (*fig.*)
pervertir (*dénaturer*).—*v.i.* se tordre, s'entrelacer, s'enlacer, s'enrouler.—*n.* cordon, *m.*,
corde, *f.*; tortillon (*de papier*), *m.*; carotte
(*de tabac*), *f.*
twisted ['twistid], *a.* tordu; (*fig.*) perverti,
défiguré, dénaturé.
twisting ['twistiŋ], *a.* tortueux.—*n.* tordage;
tortillement, *m.*
twitch [twitʃ], *n.* saccade, *f.*; tic (*contraction
spasmodique*); tiraillement (*de douleur*), *m.*—
v.t. tirer brusquement; crisper.—*v.i.* se
contracter nerveusement.
twitching ['twitʃiŋ], *n.* saccade, crispation
(*des muscles etc.*), *f.*; tiraillement (*de douleur*),
m.
twitter ['twitə], *v.t.*, *v.i.* gazouiller.—*n.* gazouillement, *m.*
two [tu:], *a.* and *n.* deux, *m.*
two-edged ['tu:edʒd], *a.* à deux tranchants.
twofold ['tu:fould], *a.* double.—*adv.* doublement, deux fois.
two-stroke ['tu:strouk], *a.* à deux temps.
tycoon [tai'ku:n], *n.* taïcoun; (*fam.*) brasseur
d'affaires, manitou, *m.*
type [taip], *n.* type; (*Print.*) caractère; (*pop.*)
type, *m.*—*v.t.* [TYPEWRITE].
typewrite ['taiprait], *v.t.* écrire à la machine,
dactylographier, taper.
typewriter ['taipraitə], *n.* machine à écrire, *f.*
typewritten ['taipritn], *a.* tapé à la machine.
typhoid ['taifɔid], *a.* typhoïde.
typhoon [tai'fu:n], *n.* typhon, *m.*, trombe, *f.*
typhus ['taifəs], *n.* typhus, *m.*
typical ['tipikl], *a.* typique.
typically ['tipikli], *adv.* d'une manière
typique.
typify ['tipifai], *v.t.* symboliser.
typing ['taipiŋ], *n.* dactylographie, (*fam.*)
dactylo, *f.*
typist ['taipist], *n.* dactylographe, (*fam.*)
dactylo, *m.*, *f.*
typography [tai'pɔgrəfi], *n.* typographie, *f.*
tyrannical [ti'rænikl], *a.* tyrannique.
tyrannically [ti'rænikli], *adv.* tyrannique-
ment.
tyrannize ['tirənaiz], *v.i.* faire le tyran; *to
tyrannize over*, tyranniser.

tyranny ['tirəni], *n.* tyrannie, *f.*
tyrant ['taiərənt], *n.* tyran, *m.*
tyre ['taiə], *n.* pneu (*de roue*), *m.*
tyro ['taiərou], *n.* novice, débutant, *m.*
Tzar [TSAR].

U

U, u [ju:]. vingt et unième lettre de l'alphabet, *m.*
ubiquitous [ju'bikwitəs], *a.* omniprésent.
ubiquity [ju'bikwiti], *n.* ubiquité, *f.*
udder ['ʌdə], *n.* mamelle, *f.*, pis, *m.*
ugh! [u:x, u:h, ʌx, uf], *int.* pouah!
ugliness ['ʌglinis], *n.* laideur, *f.*
ugly ['ʌgli], *a.* laid, vilain.
Ukraine [ju'krein], the. l'Ukraine, *f.*
Ukrainian [ju'kreiniən], *a.* ukrainien.—*n.* Ukrainien (*personne*), *m.*
ukulele [ju:kə'leili], *n.* ukulélé, *m.*
ulcer ['ʌlsə], *n.* ulcère, *m.*
ulcerate ['ʌlsəreit], *v.t.* ulcérer.—*v.i.* s'ulcérer.
ulcerated ['ʌlsəreitid], *a.* ulcéré.
ulceration [ʌlsə'reiʃən], *n.* ulcération, *f.*
ulcerous ['ʌlsərəs], *a.* ulcéreux.
ullage ['ʌlidʒ], *n.* vidange, *f.*
ulterior [ʌl'tiəriə], *a.* ultérieur; *without ulterior motive*, sans arrière-pensée.
ultimate ['ʌltimit], *a.* dernier; extrême.
ultimately ['ʌltimitli], *adv.* finalement, à la fin.
ultimatum [ʌlti'meitəm], *n.* (*pl.* **ultimata** [ʌlti'meitə]) ultimatum, *m.*
ultimo ['ʌltimou], *adv.* (*abbr.* **ult.** [ʌlt]) du mois dernier.
ultra ['ʌltrə], *n.* ultra, *m.*
ultramarine [ʌltrəmə'ri:n], *a.* d'outremer.—*n.* outremer, *m.*
ululate ['ju:ljulət], *v.i.* ululer.
Ulysses [ju:'lisi:z]. Ulysse, *m.*
umber ['ʌmbə], *n.* (*Paint.*) terre d'ombre, *f.*
umbilical [ʌm'bilikl], *a.* ombilical.
umbrage ['ʌmbridʒ], *n.* ombrage, *m.*
umbrella [ʌm'brelə], *n.* parapluie, *m.*; *umbrella stand*, porte-parapluies, *m.inv.*
umpire ['ʌmpaiə], *n.* arbitre, *m.*—*v.t., v.i.* arbitrer.
unabashed [ʌnə'bæʃt], *a.* sans être confus.
unabated [ʌnə'beitid], *a.* sans diminution.
unable [ʌn'eibl], *a.* incapable (*de*); *to be unable to*, ne pas pouvoir.
unabridged [ʌnə'bridʒd], *a.* non abrégé; en entier.
unacceptable [ʌnək'septəbl], *a.* inacceptable.
unaccommodating [ʌnə'kɔmədeitiŋ], *a.* peu accommodant.
unaccompanied [ʌnə'kʌmpənid], *a.* seul, sans suite.
unaccountable [ʌnə'kauntəbl], *a.* inexplicable, inconcevable.
unaccountably [ʌnə'kauntəbli], *adv.* inconcevablement.
unaccustomed [ʌnə'kʌstəmd], *a.* inaccoutumé (*à*); peu habitué.

unacknowledged [ʌnək'nɔlidʒd], *a.* non reconnu; sans réponse (*lettre*).
unacquainted [ʌnə'kweintid], *a.* étranger (*à*); peu familier (*avec*).
unadopted [ʌnə'dɔptid], *a.* non adopté.
unadorned [ʌnə'dɔ:nd], *a.* sans ornement.
unadulterated [ʌnə'dʌltəreitid], *a.* pur, non frelaté.
unadvisable [ʌnəd'vaizəbl], *a.* peu sage, inopportun.
unadvised [ʌnəd'vaizd], *a.* malavisé; imprudent (*rash*).
unadvisedly [ʌnəd'vaizidli], *adv.* inconsidérément.
unaffected [ʌnə'fektid], *a.* sans affectation; insensible (*peu ému*).
unaffectedly [ʌnə'fektidli], *adv.* sans affectation.
unafraid [ʌnə'freid], *a.* sans peur.
unaided [ʌn'eidid], *a.* seul, sans aide.
unallayed [ʌnə'leid], *a.* non apaisé.
unallowable [ʌnə'lauəbl], *a.* non permis; inadmissible.
unalloyed [ʌnə'lɔid], *a.* pur, sans alliage, sans mélange.
unalterable [ʌn'ɔ:ltərəbl], *a.* inaltérable, invariable.
unalterably [ʌn'ɔ:ltərəbli], *adv.* immuablement.
unambitious [ʌnæm'biʃəs], *a.* sans ambition.
unanimity [ju:nə'nimiti], *n.* unanimité, *f.*
unanimous [ju'næniməs], *a.* unanime.
unanimously [ju'næniməsli], *adv.* unanimement, à l'unanimité.
unanswerable [ʌn'ɑ:nsərəbl], *a.* incontestable.
unanswered [ʌn'ɑ:nsəd], *a.* sans réponse.
unappeasable [ʌnə'pi:zəbl], *a.* implacable.
unappetizing [ʌn'æpitaiziŋ], *a.* peu appétissant.
unappreciated [ʌnə'pri:ʃieitid], *a.* inapprécié.
unapproachable [ʌnə'proutʃəbl], *a.* inaccessible, inabordable.
unarmed [ʌn'ɑ:md], *a.* sans armes.
unascertainable [ʌnæsə'teinəbl], *a.* qu'on ne peut constater.
unashamed [ʌnə'ʃeimd], *a.* sans honte.
unasked [ʌn'ɑ:skt], *a.* sans être invité; spontané.—*adv.* spontanément.
unaspiring [ʌnə'spaiəriŋ], *a.* sans ambition.
unassailable [ʌnə'seiləbl], *a.* hors d'atteinte; inattaquable, irréfutable.
unassisted [ʌnə'sistid], *a.* sans aide.
unassuming [ʌnə'sju:miŋ], *a.* sans prétention, modeste.
unattached [ʌnə'tætʃt], *a.* sans être attaché (*à*); en disponibilité.
unattainable [ʌnə'teinəbl], *a.* inaccessible.
unattended [ʌnə'tendid], *a.* seul, sans suite.
unattested [ʌnə'testid], *a.* non attesté.
unattractive [ʌnə'træktiv], *a.* peu attrayant, sans attrait.
unauthenticated [ʌnɔ:'θentikeitid], *a.* dont l'authenticité n'est pas prouvée.
unauthorized [ʌn'ɔ:θəraizd], *a.* sans autorisation; illicite, illégal (*chose*).
unavailable [ʌnə'veiləbl], *a.* non valable; inutilisable (*billet*); indisponible (*fonds, personne*); qu'on ne peut se procurer (*chose*).
unavailing [ʌnə'veiliŋ], *a.* inutile, inefficace.
unavenged [ʌnə'vendʒd], *a.* impuni, non vengé.

unavoidable [ʌnə'vɔidebl], *a.* inévitable.
unavoidably [ʌnə'vɔidəbli], *adv.* inévitablement.
unaware [ʌnə'wɛə], *a.* ignorant; *to be unaware of*, ignorer.
unawares [ʌnə'wɛəz], *adv.* à l'improviste; à son insu (*sans s'en rendre compte*); *to be taken unawares*, être pris au dépourvu.
unbalanced [ʌn'bælənst], *a.* mal équilibré.
unbearable [ʌn'bɛərəbl], *a.* insupportable, intolérable.
unbearably [ʌn'bɛərəbli], *adv.* insupportablement.
unbeatable [ʌn'bi:təbl], *a.* invincible.
unbeaten [ʌn'bi:tn], *a.* invaincu.
unbecoming [ʌnbi'kʌmiŋ], *a.* peu convenable, malséant; qui ne va pas bien (*vêtement*).
unbecomingly [ʌnbi'kʌmiŋli], *adv.* d'une manière peu séante.
unbefitting [ʌnbi'fitiŋ], *a.* qui ne convient pas, peu propre.
unbeknown [ʌnbi'noun], *a.* inconnu; *unbeknown to me*, à mon insu.
unbelief [ʌnbi'li:f], *n.* incrédulité, incroyance, *f.*
unbelievable [ʌnbi'li:vəbl], *a.* incroyable.
unbeliever [ʌnbi'li:və], *n.* incrédule; sceptique, *m., f.*
unbelieving [ʌnbi'li:viŋ], *a.* incrédule; sceptique.
unbend [ʌn'bend], *v.t. irr.* (*conjug. like* BEND) détendre, relâcher; débander (*l'arc*); (*fig.*) délasser (*l'esprit*).—*v.i.* se détendre.
unbending [ʌn'bendiŋ], *a.* inflexible.
unbiased [ʌn'baiəst], *a.* sans prévention, impartial.
unbidden [ʌn'bidn], *a.* sans être invité.
unbind [ʌn'baind], *v.t. irr.* (*conjug. like* BIND) délier, détacher.
unbleached [ʌn'bli:tʃt], *a.* écru.
unblemished [ʌn'blemiʃt], *a.* sans tache.
unblushing [ʌn'blʌʃiŋ], *a.* qui ne rougit point, éhonté, sans vergogne.
unblushingly [ʌn'blʌʃiŋli], *adv.* sans rougir.
unbolt [ʌn'boult], *v.t.* tirer les verrous de, ouvrir.
unborn [ʌn'bɔ:n], *a.* encore à naître; futur, à venir (*chose*).
unbosom [ʌn'buzm], *v.t. to unbosom oneself*, ouvrir son cœur.
unbound [ʌn'baund], *a.* délié; non relié (*livre*).
unbounded [ʌn'baundid], *a.* illimité, infini.
unbreakable [ʌn'breikəbl], *a.* incassable.
unbridled [ʌn'braidld], *a.* débridé; (*fig.*) effréné.
unbroken [ʌn'broukn], *a.* non rompu; continu (*ininterrompu*); indompté (*non vaincu*); intact (*non violé*); non dressé (*animal*).
unbrotherly [ʌn'brʌðəli], *a.* peu fraternel.
unbuckle [ʌn'bʌkl], *v.t.* déboucler.
unburden [ʌn'bə:dn], *v.t.* décharger; *to unburden oneself*, ouvrir son cœur.
unburied [ʌn'berid], *a.* sans sépulture.
unbusinesslike [ʌn'biznislaik], *a.* peu pratique.
unbutton [ʌn'bʌtn], *v.t.* déboutonner.
uncalled [ʌn'kɔ:ld], *a.* sans être appelé; *uncalled for*, sans être demandé; gratuit (*superflu*); peu convenable (*mal élevé*); non mérité (*injuste*).

uncanny [ʌn'kæni], *a.* mystérieux, surnaturel.
uncared-for [ʌn'kɛədfɔ:], *a.* négligé.
unceasing [ʌn'si:siŋ], *a.* incessant, sans cesse.
unceasingly [ʌn'si:siŋli], *adv.* continuellement, sans cesse.
uncensored [ʌn'sensəd], *a.* non expurgé.
unceremonious [ʌnseri'mouniəs], *a.* peu cérémonieux; sans façon.
unceremoniously [ʌnseri'mouniəsli], *adv.* sans cérémonie, sans façon.
uncertain [ʌn'sə:tin], *a.* incertain, peu sûr.
uncertainty [ʌn'sə:tinti], *n.* incertitude, *f.*
uncertificated [ʌnsə'tifikətid], *a.* non diplômé (*instituteur*).
unchain [ʌn'tʃein], *v.t.* déchaîner.
unchallenged [ʌn'tʃælindʒd], *a.* indisputé.
unchangeable [ʌn'tʃeindʒəbl], *a.* inaltérable, immuable.
unchanged [ʌn'tʃeindʒd], *a.* inchangé, toujours le même.
unchanging [ʌn'tʃeindʒiŋ], *a.* invariable, constant.
uncharitable [ʌn'tʃæritəbl], *a.* peu charitable.
uncharitableness [ʌn'tʃæritəblnis], *n.* manque de charité, *m.*
uncharitably [ʌn'tʃæritəbli], *adv.* sans charité.
uncharted [ʌn'tʃɑ:tid], *a.* inexploré.
unchaste [ʌn'tʃeist], *a.* incontinent, impudique.
unchecked [ʌn'tʃekt], *a.* non réprimé, sans frein; non vérifié.
unchivalrous [ʌn'ʃivlrəs], *a.* peu chevaleresque.
unchristian [ʌn'kristiən], *a.* peu chrétien.
uncircumcised [ʌn'sə:kəmsaizd], *a.* incirconcis.
uncivil [ʌn'sivil], *a.* malhonnête, impoli.
uncivilized [ʌn'sivilaizd], *a.* peu civilisé, barbare.
uncivilly [ʌn'sivili], *adv.* malhonnêtement, impoliment.
unclaimed [ʌn'kleimd], *a.* non réclamé.
unclasp [ʌn'klɑ:sp], *v.t.* dégrafer, défaire.
unclassified [ʌn'klæsifaid], *a.* non classé.
uncle [ʌŋkl], *n.* oncle, *m.*; (*slang*) *at uncle's*, chez ma tante (*le prêteur sur gage*).
unclean [ʌn'kli:n], *a.* malpropre, sale; impudique (*obscène*); impur.
uncleanliness [ʌn'klenlinis], **uncleanness** [ʌn'kli:nnis], *n.* saleté; (*fig.*) impureté, *f.*
unclench [ʌn'klentʃ], *v.t.* ouvrir, desserrer.
uncloak [ʌn'klouk], *v.t.* dévoiler.
unclose [ʌn'klouz], *v.t.* ouvrir.
unclosed [ʌn'klouzd], *a.* non fermé, ouvert.
unclothe [ʌn'klouð], *v.t.* déshabiller.
unclothed [ʌn'klouðd], *a.* déshabillé, nu.
unclouded [ʌn'klaudid], *a.* sans nuage, serein.
uncock [ʌn'kɔk], *v.t.* désarmer (*fusil etc.*).
uncoil [ʌn'kɔil], *v.t.* dérouler.—*v.i.* se dérouler.
uncombed [ʌn'koumd], *a.* mal peigné, ébouriffé.
uncomfortable [ʌn'kʌmftəbl], *a.* peu confortable, incommode; gêné (*personne*).
uncomfortably [ʌn'kʌmftəbli], *adv.* peu confortablement; mal à l'aise.
uncommitted [ʌnkə'mitid], *a.* non commis; non engagé, libre.

uncommon [ʌnˈkɔmən], *a.* peu commun; rare.

uncommonly [ʌnˈkɔmənli], *adv.* rarement; infiniment (*singulièrement*).

uncommunicative [ʌnkəˈmjuːnikətiv], *a.* peu communicatif, réservé.

uncomplaining [ʌnkəmˈpleiniŋ], *a.* sans plainte, résigné.

uncomplainingly [ʌnkəmˈpleiniŋli], *adv.* sans se plaindre, sans plainte.

uncompleted [ʌnkəmˈpliːtid], *a.* inachevé, incomplet.

uncomplimentary [ʌnkɔmpliˈmentəri], *a.* peu flatteur.

uncompromising [ʌnˈkɔmprəmaiziŋ], *a.* peu accommodant, intransigeant.

unconcern [ʌnkənˈsəːn], *n.* insouciance, indifférence, *f.*

unconcerned [ʌnkənˈsəːnd], *a.* indifférent, insouciant.

unconcernedly [ʌnkənˈsəːnidli], *adv.* avec indifférence.

unconditional [ʌnkənˈdiʃənl], *a.* sans conditions, absolu.

unconditionally [ʌnkənˈdiʃənəli], *adv.* sans condition.

unconfined [ʌnkənˈfaind], *a.* libre; illimité.

unconfinedly [ʌnkənˈfainidli], *adv.* sans limite.

unconfirmed [ʌnkənˈfəːmd], *a.* non confirmé.

uncongenial [ʌnkənˈdʒiːniəl], *a.* désagréable; peu sympathique.

unconnected [ʌnkəˈnektid], *a.* détaché, sans rapport (*avec*); décousu (*style*).

unconquerable [ʌnˈkɔŋkərəbl], *a.* invincible.

unconquered [ʌnˈkɔŋkəd], *a.* insoumis.

unconscionable [ʌnˈkɔnʃənəbl], *a.* déraisonnable.

unconscionably [ʌnˈkɔnʃənəbli], *adv.* déraisonnablement.

unconscious [ʌnˈkɔnʃəs], *a.* ignorant (*de*); sans connaissance, insensible.—*n.* inconscient, *m.*

unconsciously [ʌnˈkɔnʃəsli], *adv.* à son insu.

unconsciousness [ʌnˈkɔnʃəsnis], *n.* inconscience, *f.*; évanouissement, *m.*

unconsecrated [ʌnˈkɔnsikreitid], *a.* non consacré.

unconsidered [ʌnkənˈsidəd], *a.* inconsidéré.

unconstitutional [ʌnkɔnstiˈtjuːʃənl], *a.* inconstitutionnel.

unconstrained [ʌnkənˈstreind], *a.* sans contrainte; aisé (*style*).

unconstraint [ʌnkənˈstreint], *n.* aisance, *f.*

uncontaminated [ʌnkənˈtæmineitid], *a.* sans souillure.

uncontested [ʌnkənˈtestid], *a.* incontesté.

uncontrollable [ʌnkənˈtrouləbl], *a.* irrésistible; fou (*rire*).

uncontrollably [ʌnkənˈtrouləbli], *adv.* irrésistiblement.

uncontrolled [ʌnkənˈtrould], *a.* irrésistible.

unconventional [ʌnkənˈvenʃənl], *a.* peu conventionnel.

unconverted [ʌnkənˈvəːtid], *a.* inconverti.

unconvinced [ʌnkənˈvinst], *a.* non convaincu.

unconvincing [ʌnkənˈvinsiŋ], *a.* peu convaincant.

uncooked [ʌnˈkukt], *a.* non cuit, cru.

uncork [ʌnˈkɔːk], *v.t.* déboucher.

uncorrupted [ʌnkəˈrʌptid], *a.* non corrompu (*par*); intègre.

uncouple [ʌnˈkʌpl], *v.t.* découpler; débrayer.

uncouth [ʌnˈkuːθ], *a.* bizarre; grossier; gauche.

uncouthly [ʌnˈkuːθli], *adv.* rudement; gauchement.

uncover [ʌnˈkʌvə], *v.t.* découvrir.

uncovered [ʌnˈkʌvəd], *a.* découvert.

uncreasable [ʌnˈkriːsəbl], *a.* infroissable.

uncritical [ʌnˈkritikl], *a.* sans discernement.

uncrowned [ʌnˈkraund], *a.* non couronné.

unction [ˈʌŋkʃən], *n.* onction, *f.*

unctuous [ˈʌŋktjuəs], *a.* onctueux.

unctuously [ˈʌŋktjuəsli], *adv.* onctueusement.

uncultivated [ʌnˈkʌltiveitid], *a.* inculte.

uncultured [ʌnˈkʌltʃəd], *a.* sans culture.

uncurl [ʌnˈkəːl], *v.t.* dérouler; défriser (*cheveux*).—*v.i.* se dérouler; se défriser (*cheveux*).

uncustomary [ʌnˈkʌstəməri], *a.* inaccoutumé.

uncut [ʌnˈkʌt], *a.* non coupé; entier; non entamé (*pain etc.*).

undamaged [ʌnˈdæmidʒd], *a.* non endommagé; intact (*réputation*).

undated [ʌnˈdeitid], *a.* sans date.

undaunted [ʌnˈdɔːntid], *a.* intrépide.

undeceive [ʌndiˈsiːv], *v.t.* désabuser, détromper.

undecided [ʌndiˈsaidid], *a.* indécis.

undecipherable [ʌndiˈsaifərəbl], *a.* indéchiffrable.

undefeated [ʌndiˈfiːtid], *a.* invaincu.

undefended [ʌndiˈfendid], *a.* sans défense, non défendu; sans défenseur (*accusé*).

undefiled [ʌndiˈfaild], *a.* sans tache, immaculé.

undefinable [ʌndiˈfainəbl], *a.* indéfinissable.

undefined [ʌndiˈfaind], *a.* indéfini.

undelivered [ʌndiˈlivəd], *a.* non délivré.

undemonstrative [ʌndiˈmɔnstrətiv], *a.* peu démonstratif, réservé.

undeniable [ʌndiˈnaiəbl], *a.* incontestable.

undenominational [ʌndinɔmiˈneiʃənl], *a.* laïque (*école*).

under [ˈʌndə], *a.* de dessous, inférieur; sous, subalterne, subordonné (*rang*).—*prep.* sous; au-dessous de (*inférieur à etc.*); dans, en (*en état de*); avec, à (*ayant*); *to be under obligations to*, avoir des obligations à; *to be under way* (*ship*), être en marche; *under age*, mineur; *under consideration*, à l'examen; *under cover of*, sous prétexte de; *under discussion*, en discussion; *under the breath*, à demi-voix; *under these circumstances*, dans ces circonstances.—*adv.* dessous, au-dessous; *see under*, voyez ci-dessous.

under-carriage [ˈʌndəkæridʒ], *n.* (*Av.*) train d'atterrissage, *m.*

underclothes [ˈʌndəklouðz], *n.pl.* sous-vêtements, *m.pl.*

undercurrent [ˈʌndəkʌrənt], *n.* courant inférieur, *m.*

undercut (1) [ˈʌndəkʌt], *n.* filet (*de bœuf*), *m.*

undercut (2) [ʌndəˈkʌt], *v.t. irr.* (*conjug. like* CUT) vendre meilleur marché.

under-developed [ʌndədiˈveləpt], *a.* sous-développé.

under-dog [ˈʌndədɔg], *n.* opprimé, *m.*

underdone [ʌndəˈdʌn], *a.* peu cuit, saignant.

609

under-estimate [ʌndər'estimeit], *v.t.* sous-estimer.

under-exposed [ʌndəriks'pouzd], *a.* (*Phot.*) sous-exposé.

underfelt ['ʌndəfelt], *n.* thibaude, *f.*

underfoot [ʌndə'fut], *adv.* sous les pieds.

undergo [ʌndə'gou], *v.t. irr.* (*conjug. like* GO) subir; supporter, endurer.

undergraduate [ʌndə'grædjuət], *n.* étudiant, *m.*

underground ['ʌndəgraund], *a.* souterrain; clandestin.—*n.* (*Rail.*) métro, *m.*—[ʌndə 'graund], *adv.* sous terre.

undergrowth ['ʌndəgrouθ], *n.* broussailles, *f.pl.*

underhand ['ʌndəhænd], *a.* clandestin; sournois (*personne*).—[ʌndə'hænd], *adv.* sous main; en cachette.

underline [ʌndə'lain], *v.t.* souligner.

underling ['ʌndəliŋ], *n.* subalterne, *m., f.*

underlying [ʌndə'laiiŋ], *a.* fondamental.

under-manned [ʌndə'mænd], *a.* à court de personnel.

undermentioned [ʌndə'menʃənd], *a.* ci-dessous.

undermine [ʌndə'main], *v.t.* miner; (*fig.*) détruire.

undermost ['ʌndəmoust], *a.* le plus bas.

underneath [ʌndə'ni:θ], *prep.* sous, au-dessous de.—*adv.* dessous, au-dessous, par-dessous, en dessous.

under-nourished [ʌndə'nʌriʃt], *a.* sous-alimenté.

underpaid [ʌndə'peid], *a.* mal payé.

underpants ['ʌndəpænts], *n.pl.* caleçons, *m.pl.*

under-privileged [ʌndə'privilidʒd], *a.* non privilégié.

under-production [ʌndəprə'dʌkʃən], *n.* sous-production, *f.*

underrate [ʌndə'reit], *v.t.* sous-estimer, déprécier.

under-ripe [ʌndə'raip], *a.* pas assez mûr, vert.

under-secretary ['ʌndəsekrətəri], *n.* sous-secrétaire, *m., f.*

under-side ['ʌndəsaid], *n.* dessous, *m.*

undersigned ['ʌndəsaind], *a. and n.* sous-signé, *m.*

undersized [ʌndə'saizd], *a.* au-dessous de la moyenne.

understand [ʌndə'stænd], *v.t. irr.* (*conjug. like* STAND) entendre, comprendre; apprendre, entendre dire (*être informé de*); s'entendre (*à ou en*) (*savoir faire*).—*v.i.* comprendre.

understandable [ʌndə'stændəbl], *a.* intelligible; compréhensible.

understanding [ʌndə'stændiŋ], *n.* entendement, *m.*, intelligence; compréhension; entente (*accord*), *f.*

understudy ['ʌndəstʌdi], *n.* doublure, *f.*

undertake [ʌndə'teik], *v.t. irr.* (*conjug. like* TAKE) entreprendre, se charger (*de*); s'engager (*à*); promettre (*de*).

undertaker ['ʌndəteikə], *n.* entrepreneur des pompes funèbres, *m.*

undertaking [ʌndə'teikiŋ], *n.* entreprise, *f.*

undertone ['ʌndətoun], *n.* ton bas, *m.*; *in an undertone*, à voix basse.

underwear ['ʌndəwɛə], *n.* sous-vêtements, *m.pl.*

underworld ['ʌndəwə:ld], *n.* enfer, *m.*; (*fig.*) bas-fonds (*des criminels*), *m.pl.*

underwrite [ʌndə'rait], *v.t. irr.* (*conjug. like* WRITE) souscrire; (*Insurance*) assurer.

underwriter ['ʌndəraitə], *n.* assureur, *m.*

undeserved [ʌndi'zə:vd], *a.* immérité, non mérité.

undeservedly [ʌndi'zə:vidli], *adv.* à tort, injustement.

undesirable [ʌndi'zaiərəbl], *a.* peu désirable.

undetected [ʌndi'tektid], *a.* non découvert, inaperçu.

undetermined [ʌndi'tə:mind], *a.* indéterminé, indéfini.

undeterred [ʌndi'tə:d], *a.* sans être découragé.

undeveloped [ʌndi'veləpt], *a.* non développé.

undies ['ʌndiz], *n.pl.* (*fam.*) lingerie, *f.*

undigested [ʌndi'dʒestid], *a.* non digéré.

undignified [ʌn'dignifaid], *a.* sans dignité.

undiluted [ʌndai'lju:tid], *a.* non dilué.

undiminished [ʌndi'miniʃt], *a.* non diminué.

undiplomatic [ʌndiplo'mætik], *a.* peu diplomatique.

undisciplined [ʌn'disiplind], *a.* indiscipliné.

undisclosed [ʌndis'klouzd], *a.* non révélé, caché.

undiscovered [ʌndis'kʌvəd], *a.* non découvert.

undisguised [ʌndis'gaizd], *a.* sans déguisement.

undismayed [ʌndis'meid], *a.* sans peur, sans terreur.

undisputed [ʌndis'pju:tid], *a.* incontesté.

undistinguished [ʌndis'tiŋgwiʃt], *a.* (*fig.*) sans distinction.

undisturbed [ʌndis'tə:bd], *a.* tranquille, calme.

undivided [ʌndi'vaidid], *a.* sans partage, tout entier.

undo [ʌn'du:], *v.t. irr.* (*conjug. like* DO) défaire; délier, détacher (*dénouer*); ruiner, perdre (*détruire*).

undoing [ʌn'du:iŋ], *n.* ruine, perte, *f.*

undone [ʌn'dʌn], *a.* ruiné, perdu; défait, délié.

undoubted [ʌn'dautid], *a.* incontestable, certain.

undoubtedly [ʌn'dautidli], *adv.* sans aucun doute.

undress [ʌn'dres], *v.t.* déshabiller.—*v.i.* se déshabiller.—*n.* (*Mil.*) petite tenue, *f.*

undressed [ʌn'drest], *a.* déshabillé.

undrinkable [ʌn'driŋkəbl], *a.* imbuvable, non potable.

undue [ʌn'dju:], *a.* non dû; excessif.

undulate ['ʌndjuleit], *v.i.* onduler, ondoyer.

undulating ['ʌndjuleitiŋ], *a.* accidenté (*terrain*).

undulation [ʌndju'leiʃən], *n.* ondulation, *f.*

unduly [ʌn'dju:li], *adv.* indûment; à tort; trop.

undying [ʌn'daiiŋ], *a.* impérissable, immortel.

unearned [ʌn'ə:nd], *a.* qu'on n'a pas gagné; immérité; *unearned income*, rentes, *f.pl.*

unearth [ʌn'ə:θ], *v.t.* déterrer.

unearthly [ʌn'ə:θli], *a.* surnaturel; (*colloq.*) infernal.

uneasily [ʌn'i:zili], *adv.* mal à son aise; difficilement, péniblement, avec gêne.

uneasiness [ʌn'iːzinis], *n.* malaise, *m.*, peine; inquiétude (*d'esprit*), *f.*
uneasy [ʌn'iːzi], *a.* inquiet, gêné.
uneatable [ʌn'iːtəbl], *a.* immangeable.
uneconomical [ʌniːkə'nɔmikl], *a.* non économique.
uneducated [ʌn'edjukeitid], *a.* sans éducation.
unemotional [ʌni'mouʃənl], *a.* peu impressionnable; peu émotif.
unemployed [ʌnim'plɔid], *a.* sans travail, inoccupé; (*fig.*) inactif, oisif.—*n.pl.* the *unemployed*, les sans-travail, les chômeurs, *m.pl.*
unemployment [ʌnim'plɔimənt], *n.* manque de travail, chômage, *m.*
unencumbered [ʌnin'kʌmbəd], *a.* non embarrassé (*de*); non hypothéqué (*biens*).
unending [ʌn'endiŋ], *a.* interminable.
unendurable [ʌnin'djuərəbl], *a.* insupportable, intolérable.
un-English [ʌn'iŋgliʃ], *a.* non anglais; indigne d'un Anglais.
unenlightened [ʌnin'laitnd], *a.* peu éclairé.
unenterprising [ʌn'entəpraiziŋ], *a.* peu entreprenant.
unenthusiastic [ʌninθjuːzi'æstik], *a.* peu enthousiaste.
unenviable [ʌn'enviəbl], *a.* peu enviable.
unequal [ʌn'iːkwəl], *a.* inégal; au-dessous (*de*); *unequal to the task*, pas à la hauteur de la tâche.
unequalled [ʌn'iːkwəld], *a.* sans égal, sans pareil.
unequivocal [ʌni'kwivəkl], *a.* non équivoque.
unequivocally [ʌni'kwivəkli], *adv.* sans équivoque.
unerring [ʌn'əːriŋ], *a.* infaillible, sûr.
uneven [ʌn'iːvn], *a.* inégal; raboteux (*terrain*).
unevenly [ʌn'iːvinli], *adv.* inégalement.
unevenness [ʌn'iːvinnis], *n.* inégalité, *f.*
uneventful [ʌni'ventful], *a.* sans incidents, monotone.
unexaggerated [ʌnig'zædʒəreitid], *a.* nullement exagéré.
unexciting [ʌnik'saitiŋ], *a.* peu intéressant.
unexpected [ʌniks'pektid], *a.* inopiné, inattendu; imprévu.
unexpectedly [ʌniks'pektidli], *adv.* à l'improviste.
unexpired [ʌniks'paiəd], *a.* non expiré.
unexplained [ʌniks'pleind], *a.* sans explication, inexpliqué.
unexploded [ʌniks'ploudid], *a.* non éclaté.
unexplored [ʌniks'plɔːd], *a.* inexploré.
unexposed [ʌniks'pouzd], *a.* non exposé.
unextinguished [ʌniks'tiŋgwiʃt], *a.* non éteint.
unfading [ʌn'feidiŋ], *a.* (*fig.*) impérissable, immortel.
unfailing [ʌn'feiliŋ], *a.* inépuisable; infaillible (*certain*).
unfair [ʌn'fɛə], *a.* injuste; (*Spt.*) pas de jeu.
unfairly [ʌn'fɛəli], *adv.* injustement.
unfairness [ʌn'fɛənis], *n.* injustice, *f.*
unfaithful [ʌn'feiθful], *a.* infidèle.
unfaithfulness [ʌn'feiθfulnis], *n.* infidélité, *f.*
unfaltering [ʌn'fɔːltəriŋ], *a.* ferme, assuré; résolu (*actions etc.*).
unfamiliar [ʌnfə'miljə], *a.* peu familier (*avec*); peu connu.
unfashionable [ʌn'fæʃənəbl], *a.* démodé.

unfasten [ʌn'fɑːsn], *v.t.* ouvrir, détacher, défaire.
unfathomable [ʌn'fæðəməbl], *a.* insondable.
unfavorable [ʌn'feivərəbl], *a.* peu favorable.
unfed [ʌn'fed], *a.* mal nourri.
unfeeling [ʌn'fiːliŋ], *a.* insensible, dur, cruel.
unfeigned [ʌn'feind], *a.* vrai, sincère.
unfeignedly [ʌn'feinidli], *adv.* sincèrement.
unfelt [ʌn'felt], *a.* qu'on ne sent pas.
unfenced [ʌn'fenst], *a.* sans clôture.
unfetter [ʌn'fetə], *v.t.* ôter les fers à; (*fig.*) délivrer.
unfettered [ʌn'fetəd], *a.* libre, sans entraves.
unfilial [ʌn'filiəl], *a.* peu filial.
unfinished [ʌn'finiʃt], *a.* inachevé.
unfit [ʌn'fit], *a.* peu propre; impropre (*à*); incapable (*de*); en mauvaise santé.
unfitting [ʌn'fitiŋ], *a.* inconvenant.
unfix [ʌn'fiks], *v.t.* détacher.
unfixed [ʌn'fikst], *a.* mobile; indécis.
unflagging [ʌn'flægiŋ], *a.* infatigable.
unfledged [ʌn'fledʒd], *a.* sans plumes; (*fig.*) novice.
unflinching [ʌn'flintʃiŋ], *a.* ferme, déterminé.
unfold [ʌn'fould], *v.t.* déplier, déployer; révéler.—*v.i.* se déployer, se dévoiler.
unforeseen [ʌnfɔː'siːn], *a.* imprévu.
unforgettable [ʌnfə'getəbl], *a.* inoubliable.
unforgiving [ʌnfə'giviŋ], *a.* implacable.
unforgotten [ʌnfə'gɔtn], *a.* pas oublié.
unfortified [ʌn'fɔːtifaid], *a.* non fortifié, ouvert.
unfortunate [ʌn'fɔːtʃənit], *a.* infortuné, malheureux.
unfortunately [ʌn'fɔːtʃənitli], *adv.* malheureusement.
unfounded [ʌn'faundid], *a.* sans fondement.
unframed [ʌn'freimd], *a.* sans cadre.
unfrequented [ʌnfri'kwentid], *a.* peu fréquenté, solitaire.
unfriendliness [ʌn'frendlinis], *n.* disposition peu amicale, *f.*
unfriendly [ʌn'frendli], *a.* peu amical (*personne*); malveillant (*chose*).
unfrock [ʌn'frɔk], *v.t.* défroquer.
unfruitful [ʌn'fruːtful], *a.* infertile, stérile.
unfulfilled [ʌnful'fild], *a.* non accompli.
unfurl [ʌn'fɔːl], *v.t.* déferler, déployer.
unfurnished [ʌn'fɔːniʃt], *a.* non meublé.
ungainly [ʌn'geinli], *a.* maladroit.
ungenerous [ʌn'dʒenərəs], *a.* peu généreux.
ungentlemanliness [ʌn'dʒentlmənlinis], *n.* impolitesse, *f.*
ungentlemanly [ʌn'dʒentlmənli], *a.* de mauvais ton.
ungodliness [ʌn'gɔdlinis], *n.* impiété, *f.*
ungodly [ʌn'gɔdli], *a.* impie.
ungovernable [ʌn'gʌvənəbl], *a.* ingouvernable; effréné.
ungraceful [ʌn'greisful], *a.* peu gracieux.
ungracious [ʌn'greiʃəs], *a.* peu gracieux, déplaisant.
ungrammatical [ʌngrə'mætikl], *a.* incorrect.
ungrateful [ʌn'greitful], *a.* ingrat (*envers*).
ungratefully [ʌn'greitfuli], *adv.* avec ingratitude.
ungrudging [ʌn'grʌdʒiŋ], *a.* de bon cœur.
ungrudgingly [ʌn'grʌdʒiŋli], *adv.* volontiers, de bon cœur.
unguarded [ʌn'gɑːdid], *a.* sans défense; imprudent, irréfléchi (*inconsidéré*).

unguardedly [ʌn'gɑ:didli], *adv.* imprudemment.

unguent ['ʌŋgwənt], *n.* onguent, *m.*

unhallowed [ʌn'hæloud], *a.* non sanctifié.

unhampered [ʌn'hæmpəd], *a.* non embarrassé (*par*).

†unhand [ʌn'hænd], *v.t.* lâcher.

unhappily [ʌn'hæpili], *adv.* malheureusement.

unhappiness [ʌn'hæpinis], *n.* malheur, *m.*

unhappy [ʌn'hæpi], *a.* malheureux.

unharmed [ʌn'hɑ:md], *a.* sain et sauf.

unharness [ʌn'hɑ:nis], *v.t.* déharnacher; dételer (*d'une charrette*).

unhatched [ʌn'hætʃt], *a.* non éclos.

unhealthy [ʌn'helθi], *a.* insalubre, malsain; maladif (*personne*).

unheard [ʌn'hɑ:d], *a.* sans être entendu; **unheard of**, inconnu, inouï (*extraordinaire*).

unheeded [ʌn'hi:did], *a.* inaperçu, négligé.

unheedful [ʌn'hi:dful], **unheeding** [ʌn'hi:diŋ], *a.* insouciant; inattentif.

unhesitating [ʌn'heziteitiŋ], *a.* sans hésitation; résolu.

unhesitatingly [ʌn'heziteitiŋli], *adv.* sans hésiter.

unhewn [ʌn'hju:n], *a.* brut; non taillé.

unhinge [ʌn'hindʒ], *v.t.* démonter.

unhitch [ʌn'hitʃ], *v.t.* décrocher; dételer (*cheval*).

unholy [ʌn'houli], *a.* profane, impie.

unhook [ʌn'huk], *v.t.* décrocher; dégrafer (*vêtements*).

unhoped [ʌn'houpt], *a.* inattendu; **unhoped for**, inespéré.

unhorse [ʌn'hɔ:s], *v.t.* désarçonner, démonter.

unhurried [ʌn'hʌrid], *a.* lent, sans précipitation.

unhurt [ʌn'hɑ:t], *a.* sain et sauf, sans blessures.

unhygienic [ʌnhai'dʒi:nik], *a.* peu hygiénique.

unicorn ['ju:nikɔ:n], *n.* licorne, *f.*

unidentified [ʌnai'dentifaid], *a.* non identifié.

unification [ju:nifi'keiʃən], *n.* unification, *f.*

uniform ['ju:nifɔ:m], *a.* and *n.* uniforme, *m.*

uniformity [ju:ni'fɔ:miti], *n.* uniformité, *f.*

uniformly ['ju:nifɔ:mli], *adv.* uniformément.

unify ['ju:nifai], *v.t.* unifier.

unilateral [ju:ni'lætərəl], *a.* unilatéral.

unimaginable [ʌni'mædʒinəbl], *a.* inimaginable, inconcevable.

unimaginative [ʌni'mædʒinətiv], *a.* peu imaginatif.

unimpaired [ʌnim'pɛəd], *a.* inaltéré, intact.

unimpeachable [ʌnim'pi:tʃəbl], *a.* irréprochable.

unimpeded [ʌnim'pi:did], *a.* sans empêchement.

unimportance [ʌnim'pɔ:təns], *n.* peu d'importance, *m.*, insignifiance, *f.*

unimportant [ʌnim'pɔ:tənt], *a.* sans importance, insignifiant.

unimpressed [ʌnim'prest], *a.* sans être ému.

unimpressive [ʌnim'presiv], *a.* peu frappant.

uninformed [ʌnin'fɔ:md], *a.* non informé; ignorant.

uninhabitable [ʌnin'hæbitəbl], *a.* inhabitable.

uninhabited [ʌnin'hæbitid], *a.* inhabité.

uninitiated [ʌni'niʃieitid], *a.* non initié.

uninjured [ʌn'indʒəd], *a.* sain et sauf, sans blessures.

uninspired [ʌnin'spaiəd], *a.* non inspiré, terne.

uninspiring [ʌnin'spaiəriŋ], *a.* banal.

unintelligible [ʌnin'telidʒibl], *a.* inintelligible.

unintentional [ʌnin'tenʃənl], *a.* sans intention, involontaire.

unintentionally [ʌnin'tenʃənli], *adv.* fait sans le vouloir, sans intention.

uninterested [ʌn'intristid], *a.* non intéressé, indifférent.

uninteresting [ʌn'intristiŋ], *a.* peu intéressant.

uninterrupted [ʌnintə'rʌptid], *a.* ininterrompu.

uninvited [ʌnin'vaitid], *a.* sans invitation.

uninviting [ʌnin'vaitiŋ], *a.* peu attrayant; peu appétissant (*nourriture*).

union ['ju:niən], *n.* union, *f.*; **trade union**, syndicat ouvrier, syndicat (corporatif), *m.*

unique [ju'ni:k], *a.* unique.

uniquely [ju'ni:kli], *adv.* d'une manière unique.

unison ['ju:nizn], *n.* unisson, *m.*; **in unison**, à l'unisson.

unit ['ju:nit], *n.* unité, *f.*, bloc, élément, *m.*

unite [ju'nait], *v.t.* unir (à ou *avec*); réunir (*efforts etc.*).—*v.i.* s'unir, se réunir; se joindre (à ou *avec*).

united [ju'naitid], *a.* uni; réuni; joint; **the United Kingdom**, le Royaume-Uni, *m.*; **the United States**, les États-Unis, *m.pl.*

unity ['ju:niti], *n.* unité; union, *f.*

universal [ju:ni'və:sl], *a.* universel.

universally [ju:ni'və:səli], *adv.* universellement.

universe ['ju:nivə:s], *n.* univers, *m.*

university [ju:ni'və:siti], *n.* université, *f.*; **university degree**, grade universitaire, *m.*

unjust [ʌn'dʒʌst], *a.* injuste, inique.

unjustly [ʌn'dʒʌstli], *adv.* injustement.

unjustifiable [ʌn'dʒʌstifaiəbl], *a.* injustifiable.

unjustified [ʌn'dʒʌstifaid], *a.* sans justification.

unkind [ʌn'kaind], *a.* désobligeant; peu aimable; cruel.

unkindliness [ʌn'kaindlinis], *n.* désobligeance; malveillance, *f.*

unkindly [ʌn'kaindli], *a.* peu propice, défavorable.—*adv.* sans bienveillance; cruellement, mal.

unkindness [ʌn'kaindnis], *n.* manque d'amabilité, *m.*, désobligeance; cruauté, dureté, *f.*

unknowingly [ʌn'nouiŋli], *adv.* sans le savoir, à son insu.

unknown [ʌn'noun], *a.* inconnu; **unknown to me** (*without my knowledge*), à mon insu.

unlace [ʌn'leis], *v.t.* délacer, détacher.

unladylike [ʌn'leidilaik], *a.* peu digne d'une dame, de mauvais ton.

unlatch [ʌn'lætʃ], *v.t.* lever le loquet de, ouvrir.

unlawful [ʌn'lɔ:ful], *a.* illégal; illicite.

unlawfully [ʌn'lɔ:fuli], *adv.* illégalement; illicitement.

unleash [ʌn'li:ʃ], *v.t.* lâcher (*chien*).

unleavened [ʌn'levənd], *a.* sans levain; (*Scripture*) azyme.

unless [ʌn'les], *conj.* à moins que . . . ne (*with subjunctive*); à moins de (*followed by infinitive*); si . . . ne . . . pas (*followed by indicative*); si ce n'est, excepté que.

unlicensed [ʌn'laisənst], *a.* non autorisé; (*Comm.*) non patenté.

unlike [ʌn'laik], *a.* différent (*de*); qui ne ressemble pas (*à*).

unlikelihood [ʌn'laiklihud], *n.* invraisemblance, improbabilité, *f.*

unlikely [ʌn'laikli], *a.* improbable, invraisemblable, peu sûr.

unlimited [ʌn'limitid], *a.* illimité.

unlined [ʌn'laind], *a.* non doublé.

unlink [ʌn'liŋk], *v.t.* défaire, détacher.

unload [ʌn'loud], *v.t.* décharger; désarmer (*fusil*).

unlock [ʌn'lɔk], *v.t.* ouvrir.

unlooked-for [ʌn'luktfɔ:], *a.* inattendu, imprévu.

unloose [ʌn'lu:s], *v.t.* délier, détacher.

unloved [ʌn'lʌvd], *a.* pas aimé.

unluckily [ʌn'lʌkili], *adv.* malheureusement, par malheur.

unlucky [ʌn'lʌki], *a.* malheureux, infortuné; sinistre, de mauvais augure, de mauvais présage.

unmade [ʌn'meid], *a.* défait; pas fait (*lit*); non empierré (*route*).

unmanageable [ʌn'mænidʒəbl], *a.* ingouvernable; rebelle.

unmanliness [ʌn'mænlinis], *n.* conduite indigne d'un homme, lâcheté, *f.*

unmanly [ʌn'mænli], *a.* indigne d'un homme, lâche; mou, efféminé.

unmannerliness [ʌn'mænəlinis], *n.* grossièreté, impolitesse, *f.*

unmannerly [ʌn'mænəli], *a.* grossier, mal appris, impoli.

unmarked [ʌn'mɑ:kt], *a.* non marqué (*de*); inaperçu.

unmarketable [ʌn'mɑ:kitəbl], *a.* invendable.

unmarried [ʌn'mærid], *a.* célibataire; *unmarried man*, célibataire, *m.*; *unmarried woman*, demoiselle; vieille fille, *f.*

unmask [ʌn'mɑ:sk], *v.t.* démasquer; (*fig.*) dévoiler.

unmastered [ʌn'mɑ:stəd], *a.* indompté.

unmatched [ʌn'mætʃt], *a.* dépareillé; (*fig.*) sans pareil.

unmentionable [ʌn'menʃənəbl], *a.* dont on ne parle pas.

unmerciful [ʌn'mə:siful], *a.* impitoyable, cruel.

unmercifully [ʌn'mə:sifuli], *adv.* impitoyablement, sans pitié.

unmerited [ʌn'meritid], *a.* immérité.

unmindful [ʌn'maindful], *a.* peu soucieux (*de*).

unmistakable [ʌnmis'teikəbl], *a.* évident, clair.

unmistakably [ʌnmis'teikəbli], *adv.* évidemment, clairement.

unmitigated [ʌn'mitigeitid], *a.* non adouci; (*colloq.*) fieffé (*gredin etc.*).

unmolested [ʌnmə'lestid], *a.* sans être molesté.

unmotherly [ʌn'mʌðəli], *a.* peu maternel.

unmounted [ʌn'mauntid], *a.* à pied (*sans cheval*); non collé (*photographie etc.*).

unmourned [ʌn'mɔ:nd], *a.* sans être pleuré.

unmoved [ʌn'mu:vd], *a.* immobile; (*fig.*) non ému.

unmusical [ʌn'mju:zikl], *a.* peu harmonieux; pas musicien (*personne*).

unmuzzle [ʌn'mʌzl], *v.t.* démuseler.

unnamed [ʌn'neimd], *a.* innommé; anonyme.

unnatural [ʌn'nætʃrəl], *a.* contre nature; dénaturé (*personne*).

unnavigable [ʌn'nævigəbl], *a.* innavigable.

unnecessarily [ʌn'nesəsərili], *adv.* sans nécessité, inutilement; par trop.

unnecessary [ʌn'nesəsəri], *a.* peu nécessaire, inutile.

unneighborly [ʌn'neibəli], *a.* peu obligeant; de mauvais voisin.

unnerve [ʌn'nə:v], *v.t.* énerver; (*fig.*) décourager.

unnoticed [ʌn'noutist], *a.* inaperçu, inobservé.

unnumbered [ʌn'nʌmbəd], *a.* innombrable.

unobjectionable [ʌnəb'dʒekʃənəbl], *a.* irrécusable.

unobliging [ʌnə'blaidʒiŋ], *a.* désobligeant.

unobservant [ʌnəb'zə:vənt], *a.* peu observateur.

unobserved [ʌnəb'zə:vd], *a.* inaperçu.

unobtainable [ʌnəb'teinəbl], *a.* impossible à obtenir.

unobtrusive [ʌnəb'tru:siv], *a.* réservé, discret.

unobtrusively [ʌnəb'tru:sivli], *adv.* sans importunité, avec modestie.

unoccupied [ʌn'ɔkjupaid], *a.* inoccupé; libre, disponible (*temps etc.*); inhabité (*maison*).

unofficial [ʌnə'fiʃl], *a.* non officiel.

unofficially [ʌnə'fiʃəli], *adv.* non officiellement.

unopened [ʌn'oupənd], *a.* fermé; non décacheté (*lettre etc.*).

unopposed [ʌnə'pouzd], *a.* sans opposition.

unorganized [ʌn'ɔ:gənaizd], *a.* non organisé.

unoriginal [ʌnə'ridʒinəl], *a.* peu original.

unorthodox [ʌn'ɔ:θədɔks], *a.* peu orthodoxe.

unostentatious [ʌnɔsten'teiʃəs], *a.* sans faste; modeste.

unostentatiously [ʌnɔsten'teiʃəsli], *adv.* sans ostentation.

unpack [ʌn'pæk], *v.t.* déballer (*marchandises*); dépaqueter (*paquets*).

unpacking [ʌn'pækiŋ], *n.* déballage; dépaquetage (*de petits paquets*), *m.*

unpaid [ʌn'peid], *a.* non payé, sans paye.

unpalatable [ʌn'pælətəbl], *a.* désagréable (au goût).

unparalleled [ʌn'pærəleld], *a.* sans pareil; sans précédent.

unpardonable [ʌn'pɑ:dnəbl], *a.* impardonnable.

unparliamentary [ʌnpɑ:li'mentəri], *a.* peu parlementaire.

unpatriotic [ʌnpætri'ɔtik], *a.* peu patriotique (*sentiment*); peu patriote (*personne*).

unpaved [ʌn'peivd], *a.* non pavé. [see **unmade**]

unperturbed [ʌnpə'tə:bd], *a.* peu ému, impassible.

unphilosophical [ʌnfilə'sɔfikl], *a.* peu philosophique.

unpick [ʌn'pik], *v.t.* découdre.

unpicked [ʌn'pikt], *a.* non cueilli; décousu (*couture*).

unpin

unpin [ʌnˈpin], *v.t.* défaire.

unpitied [ʌnˈpitid], *a.* qu'on ne plaint pas.

unpitying [ʌnˈpitiiŋ], *a.* sans pitié, impitoyable.

unplayable [ʌnˈpleiəbl], *a.* injouable.

unpleasant [ʌnˈplezənt], *a.* déplaisant, fâcheux.

unpleasantly [ʌnˈplezntli], *adv.* désagréablement.

unpleasantness [ʌnˈplezntnis], *n.* désagrément, *m.*

unplowed [ʌnˈplaud], *a.* non labouré.

unpoetical [ʌnpoˈetikl], *a.* peu poétique.

unpolished [ʌnˈpoliʃt], *a.* non poli; mat (*or etc.*); non ciré (*chaussures*); dépoli (*verre*); (*fig.*) grossier.

unpolluted [ʌnpəˈljuːtid], *a.* non souillé; pur.

unpopular [ʌnˈpɔpjulə], *a.* impopulaire.

unpopularity [ʌnpɔpjuˈlæriti], *n.* impopularité, *f.*

unpractical [ʌnˈpræktikl], *a.* peu pratique.

unpractised [ʌnˈpræktist], *a.* inexpérimenté.

unprecedented [ʌnˈpresidəntid], *a.* sans précédent.

unprejudiced [ʌnˈpredʒudist], *a.* sans préjugés, impartial.

unpremeditated [ʌnpriˈmediteitid], *a.* inopiné, improvisé, sans préméditation.

unprepared [ʌnpriˈpɛəd], *a.* non préparé; *to be unprepared for*, ne pas s'attendre à.

unpreparedness [ʌnpriˈpɛəridnis], *n.* manque de préparation, *m.*

unprepossessing [ʌnpriːpəˈzesiŋ], *a.* peu engageant.

unprincipled [ʌnˈprinsipld], *a.* sans principes, sans mœurs.

unproductive [ʌnprəˈdʌktiv], *a.* improductif; stérile (*terre*).

unproductiveness [ʌnprəˈdʌktivnis], *n.* stérilité, *f.*

unprofessional [ʌnprəˈfeʃənəl], *a.* contraire aux règles d'une profession.

unprofitable [ʌnˈprɔfitəbl], *a.* peu lucratif, sans profit; inutile.

unprofitably [ʌnˈprɔfitəbli], *adv.* inutilement, sans profit.

unpronounceable [ʌnprəˈnaunsəbl], *a.* imprononçable.

unpropitious [ʌnprəˈpiʃəs], *a.* peu propice (*à*).

unprotected [ʌnprəˈtektid], *a.* sans protection, sans défense; à découvert.

unprovided [ʌnprəˈvaidid], *a.* dépourvu, dénué (*de*); *we were unprovided for that*, nous ne nous attendions pas à cela.

unprovoked [ʌnprəˈvoukt], *a.* sans provocation; *an unprovoked insult*, une insulte gratuite.

unpublished [ʌnˈpʌbliʃt], *a.* inédit.

unpunished [ʌnˈpʌniʃt], *a.* impuni.

unqualified [ʌnˈkwɔlifaid], *a.* incapable (*de*), incompétent; sans réserve; (*Law*) inhabile (*à*); non autorisé (*médecins etc.*).

unquenchable [ʌnˈkwentʃəbl], *a.* inextinguible.

unquestionable [ʌnˈkwestʃənəbl], *a.* incontestable, indubitable.

unquestionably [ʌnˈkwestʃənəbli], *adv.* incontestablement; sans contredit.

unravel [ʌnˈrævl], *v.t.* démêler, débrouiller. —*v.i.* se démêler, se débrouiller, s'effiler.

unreadable [ʌnˈriːdəbl], *a.* illisible.

unreadily [ʌnˈredili], *adv.* lentement, à contre-cœur.

unreadiness [ʌnˈredinis], *n.* manque de préparation *ou* de bonne volonté, *m.*

unready [ʌnˈredi], *a.* mal préparé; lent.

unreal [ʌnˈriːəl], *a.* irréel; chimérique, imaginaire.

unrealistic [ʌnriːəˈlistik], *a.* peu réaliste.

unreality [ʌnriˈæliti], *n.* défaut de réalité, *m.*

unrealizable [ʌnˈriːəlaizəbl], *a.* irréalisable.

unreasonable [ʌnˈriːznəbl], *a.* déraisonnable; exorbitant.

unreasonableness [ʌnˈriːznəblnis], *n.* déraison; absurdité, extravagance (*de demande*), *f.*

unreasonably [ʌnˈriːznəbli], *adv.* sans raison, à l'excès.

unrecognizable [ʌnˈrekəgnaizəbl], *a.* méconnaissable.

unrecognized [ʌnˈrekəgnaizd], *a.* sans être reconnu, (*fig.*) méconnu (*non apprécié*).

unrecompensed [ʌnˈrekəmpenst], *a.* sans récompense.

unreconciled [ʌnˈrekənsaild], *a.* irréconcilié.

unrecorded [ʌnriˈkɔːdid], *a.* non enregistré.

unredeemable [ʌnriˈdiːməbl], *a.* irrachetable.

unredeemed [ʌnriˈdiːmd], *a.* non racheté.

unrefined [ʌnriˈfaind], *a.* non raffiné, brut; (*fig.*) grossier.

unregistered [ʌnˈredʒistəd], *a.* non enregistré; non recommandé (*lettre etc.*).

unrelated [ʌnriˈleitid], *a.* sans rapport (*avec*); *who is unrelated to*, qui n'est pas parent de.

unrelenting [ʌnriˈlentiŋ], *a.* inflexible, implacable.

unreliable [ʌnriˈlaiəbl], *a.* peu sûr; sur qui *ou* sur quoi l'on ne peut compter.

unrelieved [ʌnriˈliːvd], *a.* non soulagé; sans relief.

unremitting [ʌnriˈmitiŋ], *a.* incessant, infatigable.

unremunerative [ʌnriˈmjuːnərətiv], *a.* peu rémunérateur, peu lucratif.

unrepentant [ʌnriˈpentənt], *a.* impénitent.

unrepresented [ʌnrepriˈzentid], *a.* non représenté.

unrequited [ʌnriˈkwaitid], *a.* sans être récompensé; qui n'est pas payé de retour (*amour*).

unreserved [ʌnriˈzəːvd], *a.* sans réserve; absolu (*total*).

unreservedly [ʌnriˈzəːvidli], *adv.* sans réserve.

unresisting [ʌnriˈzistiŋ], *a.* qui ne résiste pas, soumis.

unresolved [ʌnriˈzɔlvd], *a.* non résolu; irrésolu, indécis (*personne*).

unresponsive [ʌnrisˈpɔnsiv], *a.* peu sensible; froid.

unrest [ʌnˈrest], *n.* inquiétude, agitation, *f.*

unrestrained [ʌnriˈstreind], *a.* non restreint; non réprimé; effréné, déréglé.

unrestricted [ʌnriˈstriktid], *a.* sans restriction.

unretentive [ʌnriˈtentiv], *a.* peu tenace; peu fidèle (*la mémoire*).

unrevenged [ʌnriˈvendʒd], *a.* non vengé.

unrevised [ʌnriˈvaizd], *a.* non revu, non revisé.

unrewarded [ʌnriˈwɔːdid], *a.* sans récompense.

unrewarding [ʌnri'wɔ:diŋ], a. peu rémunérateur.

unrig [ʌn'rig], v.t. dégréer.

unrighteous [ʌn'raitʃəs], a. injuste, inique.

unrighteousness [ʌn'raitʃəsnis], n. injustice, iniquité, f.

unripe [ʌn'raip], a. pas mûr, vert; (fig.) prématuré.

unrivaled [ʌn'raivəld], a. sans rival, sans égal.

unroll [ʌn'roul], v.t. dérouler, déployer.—v.i. se dérouler, se déployer.

unruffled [ʌn'rʌfld], a. tranquille, calme.

unruly [ʌn'ru:li], a. indiscipliné, insoumis, turbulent.

unsaddle [ʌn'sædl], v.t. desseller; débâter (âne); désarçonner (cavalier).

unsafe [ʌn'seif], a. peu sûr, dangereux, hasardeux.

unsaleable [ʌn'seiləbl], a. invendable.

unsalted [ʌn'sɔ:ltid], a. non salé, sans sel.

unsanctified [ʌn'sæŋktifaid], a. non consacré, profane.

unsatisfactorily [ʌnsætis'fæktərili], adv. d'une manière peu satisfaisante.

unsatisfactory [ʌnsætis'fæktəri], a. peu satisfaisant.

unsatisfied [ʌn'sætisfaid], a. peu satisfait.

unsavoriness [ʌn'seivərinis], n. insipidité, fadeur, f.; mauvais goût, m.

unsavory [ʌn'seivəri], a. sans saveur, insipide; repoussant (désagréable).

unscarred [ʌn'skɑ:d], a. sans cicatrices.

unscathed [ʌn'skeiðd], a. sans blessures, sain et sauf.

unscholarly [ʌn'skɔləli], a. illettré, ignorant.

unscientific [ʌnsaiən'tifik], a. peu scientifique.

unscientifically [ʌnsaiən'tifikli], adv. peu scientifiquement.

unscrew [ʌn'skru:], v.t. dévisser.

unscrupulous [ʌn'skru:pjuləs], a. peu scrupuleux.

unscrupulously [ʌn'skru:pjuləsli], adv. sans scrupule.

unscrupulousness [ʌn'skru:pjuləsnis], n. manque de scrupule, m.

unseal [ʌn'si:l], v.t. décacheter; desceller.

unsealed [ʌn'si:ld], a. décacheté, ouvert.

unseasonable [ʌn'si:znəbl], a. mal à propos; indu (heure); pas de saison (temps).

unseat [ʌn'si:t], v.t. renverser; désarçonner (d'un cheval); (Polit.) invalider.

unseaworthy [ʌn'si:wə:ði], a. incapable de tenir la mer, innavigable.

unsecured [ʌnsi'kjuəd], a. sans garantie; mal fermé (porte).

unseeing [ʌn'si:iŋ], a. aveugle.

unseemliness [ʌn'si:mlinis], n. inconvenance, f.

unseemly [ʌn'si:mli], a. inconvenant, indécent.

unseen [ʌn'si:n], a. sans être vu, invisible.

unselfish [ʌn'selfiʃ], a. désintéressé.

unserviceable [ʌn'sə:visəbl], a. inutile, bon à rien.

unsettle [ʌn'setl], v.t. déranger; (fig.) troubler.

unsettled [ʌn'setld], a. mal fixé, mal établi; incertain (temps etc.); irrésolu (personne); dérangé, troublé (esprit); variable, changeant (inconstant).

unshackled [ʌn'ʃækld], a. sans entraves, libre.

unshaken [ʌn'ʃeikn], a. inébranlable, ferme.

unshapely [ʌn'ʃeipli], a. difforme, informe.

unshaved [ʌn'ʃeivd], **unshaven** [ʌn'ʃeivn], a. non rasé.

unsheathe [ʌn'ʃi:ð], v.t. dégainer.

unship [ʌn'ʃip], v.t. débarquer; démonter (gouvernail etc.); désarmer (avirons).

unshod [ʌn'ʃɔd], a. sans chaussures; déferré (cheval).

unshorn [ʌn'ʃɔ:n], a. non tondu.

unshrinkable [ʌn'ʃriŋkəbl], a. irrétrécissable.

unsightliness [ʌn'saitlinis], n. laideur, f.

unsightly [ʌn'saitli], a. laid, déplaisant.

unsigned [ʌn'saind], a. non signé.

unsisterly [ʌn'sistəli], a. peu digne d'une sœur.

unskilled [ʌn'skild], a. inexpérimenté (dans); non qualifié; **unskilled labor**, travail de manœuvre, m.; main-d'œuvre non spécialisée, f.

unskillful [ʌn'skilful], a. inhabile, maladroit.

unsociable [ʌn'souʃəbl], a. insociable.

unsoiled [ʌn'sɔild], a. sans tache.

unsold [ʌn'sould], a. invendu.

unsoldierly [ʌn'sould3əli], a. indigne d'un soldat.

unsolicited [ʌnsə'lisitid], a. sans être sollicité.

unsolved [ʌn'sɔlvd], a. non résolu.

unsophisticated [ʌnsə'fistikeitid], a. qui n'est pas frelaté; pur, vrai.

unsought [ʌn'sɔ:t], a. non recherché; spontané.

unsound [ʌn'saund], a. défectueux, malsain; faux, erroné; mal établi (crédit); vicieux, pas sain (cheval); **of unsound mind**, non sain d'esprit.

unsparing [ʌn'spɛəriŋ], a. libéral, prodigue; impitoyable (sans pitié).

unsparingly [ʌn'spɛəriŋli], adv. avec prodigalité; impitoyablement.

unspeakable [ʌn'spi:kəbl], a. inexprimable; indicible; ignoble, sans nom.

unspecified [ʌn'spesifaid], a. non spécifié.

unspoiled [ʌn'spɔild], a. non corrompu; bien élevé (enfant).

unspoken [ʌn'spoukn], a. non prononcé; tacite.

unsportsmanlike [ʌn'spɔ:tsmənlaik], a. indigne d'un chasseur ou d'un sportsman.

unspotted [ʌn'spɔtid], a. sans tache.

unstable [ʌn'steibl], a. irrésolu; inconstant; (Mech.) instable.

unstained [ʌn'steind], a. sans tache.

unstamped [ʌn'stæmpt], a. non timbré, sans timbre.

unsteadily [ʌn'stedili], adv. en chancelant; d'une manière irrégulière.

unsteadiness [ʌn'stedinis], n. instabilité, irrésolution, f.

unsteady [ʌn'stedi], a. chancelant; mal assuré, irrésolu, inconstant, irrégulier (conduite).

unstinted [ʌn'stintid], a. non restreint, abondant.

unstop [ʌn'stɔp], v.t. déboucher, ouvrir.

unstrengthened [ʌn'streŋθənd], a. non renforcé.

unstressed [ʌn'strest], a. inaccentué, atone.

unsubdued [ʌnsəb'dju:d], a. indompté.

unsubmissive [ʌnsəb'misiv], a. insoumis.

unsubmissiveness [ʌnsəbˈmisivnis], *n.* insoumission, *f.*

unsubstantial [ʌnsəbˈstænʃl], *a.* peu substantiel; peu solide; (*fig.*) immatériel; chimérique.

unsuccessful [ʌnsəkˈsesful], *a.* qui n'a pas réussi, sans succès.

unsuccessfully [ʌnsəkˈsesfuli] *adv.* sans succès.

unsuitable [ʌnˈsju:təbl], *a.* peu convenable, peu propre (*à*).

unsuited [ʌnˈsju:tid], *a.* peu fait (*pour*), peu convenable (*à*).

unsullied [ʌnˈsʌlid], *a.* sans souillure, sans tache.

unsung [ʌnˈsʌŋ], *a.* non célébré.

unsupervised [ʌnˈsju:pəvaizd], *a.* non surveillé.

unsupported [ʌnsəˈpɔ:tid], *a.* non soutenu; (*fig.*) sans appui.

unsuppressed [ʌnsəˈprest], *a.* mal contenu.

unsure [ʌnˈʃuə], *a.* peu sûr.

unsurpassed [ʌnsəˈpɑ:st], *a.* non surpassé, sans égal.

unsuspected [ʌnsəˈspektid], *a.* insoupçonné; non suspect.

unsuspecting [ʌnsəˈspektiŋ], sans soupçon, confiant.

unsuspicious [ʌnsəˈspiʃəs], *a.* sans méfiance, confiant.

unsustained [ʌnsəˈsteind], *a.* non soutenu.

unswayed [ʌnˈsweid], *a.* qui ne se laisse pas influencer.

unswerving [ʌnˈswə:viŋ], *a.* qui ne s'écarte pas, inébranlable.

unsymmetrical [ʌnsiˈmetrikl], *a.* asymétrique.

unsympathetic [ʌnsimpəˈθetik], *a.* froid, peu compatissant.

unsystematic [ʌnsistiˈmætik], *a.* peu systématique.

untainted [ʌnˈteintid], *a.* non corrompu; frais (*viande*).

untamable [ʌnˈteiməbl], *a.* indomptable.

untamed [ʌnˈteimd], *a.* indompté, non apprivoisé.

untapped [ʌnˈtæpt], *a.* inexploité (*ressources*).

untarnished [ʌnˈtɑ:niʃt], *a.* non terni.

untaught [ʌnˈtɔ:t], *a.* ignorant, illettré.

untaxed [ʌnˈtækst], *a.* exempt d'impôts.

unteachable [ʌnˈti:tʃəbl], *a.* incapable d'apprendre.

untearable [ʌnˈtɛərəbl], *a.* indéchirable.

untempered [ʌnˈtempəd], *a.* non trempé (*métal*).

untenable [ʌnˈtenəbl], *a.* insoutenable.

untended [ʌnˈtendid], *a.* non gardé.

untested [ʌnˈtestid], *a.* inessayé.

unthanked [ʌnˈθæŋkt], *a.* sans être remercié.

unthinking [ʌnˈθiŋkiŋ], *a.* inconsidéré, étourdi.

unthinkingly [ʌnˈθiŋkiŋli], *adv.* sans y penser.

untidily [ʌnˈtaidili], *adv.* sans ordre, sans soin.

untidiness [ʌnˈtaidinis], *n.* désordre, *m.*

untidy [ʌnˈtaidi], *a.* en désordre; négligé.

untie [ʌnˈtai], *v.t.* délier, dénouer; défaire (*nœud*).

until [ənˈtil], *prep.* jusqu'à; avant.—*conj.* jusqu'à ce que, avant que.

untilled [ʌnˈtild], *a.* inculte, en friche.

untimeliness [ʌnˈtaimlinis], *n.* inopportunité, *f.*

untimely [ʌnˈtaimli], *a.* prématuré, inopportun.—*adv.* avant terme, prématurément.

untiring [ʌnˈtaiəriŋ], *a.* infatigable.

untiringly [ʌnˈtaiəriŋli], *adv.* sans relâche.

***unto** [ˈʌntu], *prep.* [TO].

untold [ʌnˈtould], *a.* non raconté, non exprimé; sans nombre; inouï.

untouchable [ʌnˈtʌtʃəbl], *a. and n.* hors caste, paria, intouchable, *m., f.*

untouched [ʌnˈtʌtʃt], *a.* non touché; (*fig.*) non ému (*de*).

untoward [ʌnˈtɔ:d, ʌnˈtouəd], *a.* insoumis, indocile (*rebelle*); fâcheux.

untraceable [ʌnˈtreisəbl], *a.* introuvable.

untrained [ʌnˈtreind], *a.* inexpérimenté (*inexpert*); indiscipliné; non dressé (*animal*).

untrammelled [ʌnˈtræməld], *a.* sans entraves.

untranslatable [ʌntrɑ:nsˈleitəbl], *a.* intraduisible.

untravelled [ʌnˈtrævld], *a.* peu connu (*terre*); qui n'a pas voyagé (*personne*).

untried [ʌnˈtraid], *a.* non essayé; qui n'a pas encore été jugé.

untrimmed [ʌnˈtrimd], *a.* sans garniture; non émondé (*arbre*).

untrodden [ʌnˈtrɔdn], *a.* non frayé; immaculé (*neige*).

untroubled [ʌnˈtrʌbld], *a.* calme, tranquille.

untrue [ʌnˈtru:], *a.* faux; inexact (*nouvelle etc.*); déloyal (*à*).

untrustworthiness [ʌnˈtrʌstwə:ðinis], *n.* inexactitude, fausseté, *f.*

untrustworthy [ʌnˈtrʌstwə:ði], *a.* indigne de confiance; inexact, mensonger (*nouvelle etc.*).

untruth [ʌnˈtru:θ], *n.* contre-vérité, fausseté, *f.*

untruthful [ʌnˈtru:ful], *a.* menteur; mensonger (*nouvelle etc.*); perfide, faux, déloyal (*traître*).

untruthfulness [ʌnˈtru:θfulnis], *n.* fausseté, *f.*

untutored [ʌnˈtju:təd], *a.* peu instruit, ignorant.

untwine [ʌnˈtwain], *v.t.* détordre; dérouler.

untwist [ʌnˈtwist], *v.t.* détordre, détortiller, défaire.

unused (1) [ʌnˈju:zd], *a.* non employé, inutilisé; inusité (*mot*).

unused (2) [ʌnˈju:st], *a.* inaccoutumé; *unused to*, inaccoutumé à.

unusual [ʌnˈju:ʒuəl], *a.* peu commun, rare.

unusually [ʌnˈju:ʒuəli], *adv.* rarement, extraordinairement.

unutterable [ʌnˈʌtərəbl], *a.* inexprimable, indicible.

unuttered [ʌnˈʌtəd], *a.* non prononcé.

unvanquished [ʌnˈvæŋkwiʃt], *a.* indompté.

unvaried [ʌnˈvɛərid], *a.* uniforme.

unvarnished [ʌnˈvɑ:niʃt], *a.* non verni; (*fig.*) simple, naturel.

unvarying [ʌnˈvɛəriiŋ], *a.* invariable, uniforme.

unveil [ʌnˈveil], *v.t.* dévoiler; découvrir.

unventilated [ʌnˈventileitid], *a.* mal aéré.

unversed [ʌnˈvə:st], *a.* peu versé (*dans*).

unvisited [ʌnˈvizitid], *a.* non visité, peu fréquenté.

unwarily [ʌnˈwɛərili], *adv.* sans précaution, imprudemment.

unwariness [ʌn'wɛərinis], *n.* imprévoyance, imprudence, *f.*

unwarlike [ʌn'wɔːlaik], *a.* pacifique, peu belliqueux.

unwarrantable [ʌn'wɔrəntəbl], *a.* injustifiable.

unwarrantably [ʌn'wɔrəntəbli], *adv.* inexcusablement.

unwarranted [ʌn'wɔrəntid], *a.* non garanti; *an unwarranted insult*, une insulte gratuite.

unwary [ʌn'wɛəri], *a.* inconsidéré, imprudent.

unwashed [ʌn'wɔʃt], *a.* non lavé, sale, malpropre.

unwavering [ʌn'weivəriŋ], *a.* résolu, inébranlable.

unwearable [ʌn'wɛərəbl], *a.* qu'on ne peut plus porter.

unwearied [ʌn'wiərid], *a.* non lassé, infatigable.

unwelcome [ʌn'welkəm], *a.* importun; fâcheux.

unwell [ʌn'wel], *a.* indisposé, souffrant, mal portant.

unwept [ʌn'wept], *a.* non pleuré, non regretté.

unwholesome [ʌn'houlsəm], *a.* malsain, insalubre.

unwieldy [ʌn'wiːldi], *a.* lourd, pesant, difficile à manier.

unwilling [ʌn'wiliŋ], *a.* peu disposé, mal disposé; *to be unwilling to*, n'être pas disposé à.

unwillingly [ʌn'wiliŋli], *adv.* à contre-cœur, sans le vouloir.

unwillingness [ʌn'wiliŋnis], *n.* mauvaise volonté, *f.*

unwind [ʌn'waind], *v.t. irr. (conjug. like* WIND) dévider; dérouler; *(fig.)* débrouiller. —*v.i.* se dévider.

unwise [ʌn'waiz], *a.* peu sage, malavisé, insensé.

unwisely [ʌn'waizli], *adv.* peu sagement, imprudemment.

unwished (for) [ʌn'wiʃt(fɔː)], *a.* non souhaité.

unwitnessed [ʌn'witnist], *a.* sans témoin, non certifié.

unwitting [ʌn'witiŋ], *a.* inconscient.

unwittingly [ʌn'witiŋli], *adv.* sans le savoir, inconsciemment.

unwomanly [ʌn'wumənli], *a.* indigne d'une femme.

unwonted [ʌn'wountid], *a.* inaccoutumé, rare.

unworkable [ʌn'wəːkəbl], *a.* impraticable.

unworked [ʌn'wəːkt], *a.* inexploité *(mine etc.)*.

unworn [ʌn'wɔːn], *a.* non usé, non usagé.

unworthily [ʌn'wəːðili], *adv.* indignement, sans le mériter.

unworthiness [ʌn'wəːðinis], *n.* indignité, *f.*

unworthy [ʌn'wəːði], *a.* indigne *(de)*, sans mérite.

unwrap [ʌn'ræp], *v.t.* défaire, désenvelopper.

unwrinkle [ʌn'riŋkl], *v.t.* dérider.

unwrinkled [ʌn'riŋkld], *a.* sans rides, uni.

unwritten [ʌn'ritn], *a.* non écrit; *(fig.)* oral, traditionnel.

unyielding [ʌn'jiːldiŋ], *a.* qui ne cède pas, inflexible.

unyoke [ʌn'jouk], *v.t.* ôter le joug à, dételer.

up [ʌp], *adv.* au haut, en haut; haut; en l'air; levé, sur pied *(pas au lit)*; sur l'horizon; debout *(pas assis)*; en révolte, en insurrection; fini *(expiré)*; élevé *(prix)*; en hausse *(valeurs de Bourse)*; *it is up to us to do it*, c'est à nous de le faire; *road up*, rue barrée; *to be up to*, être au courant de; *to make up to*, faire des avances à; *up and down*, en haut et en bas, çà et là, de long en large, de haut en bas; *up there*, là-haut; *up to*, jusqu'à la hauteur de; *up to date*, à la dernière mode; à jour; *up to now*, jusqu'ici; *up to then*, jusque-là; *what's up? (colloq.)* qu'est-ce qu'il y a donc?—*prep.* en haut de, au haut de; en montant; *up hill* or *up stream*, en amont. —*n.* haut, *m.*; *the ups and downs*, les hauts et les bas, *m.pl.*

upbraid [ʌp'breid], *v.t.* reprocher à; réprouver.

upbraiding [ʌp'breidiŋ], *n.* reproche, *m.*

upcast ['ʌpkaːst], *n.* jet; coup, *m.*

upheaval [ʌp'hiːvl], *n.* soulèvement, *m.*

uphill ['ʌphil], *a.* *(fig.)* ardu, pénible.—[ʌp'hil], *adv.* en côte, en montant.

uphold [ʌp'hould], *v.t. irr. (conjug. like* HOLD) soutenir, maintenir.

upholster [ʌp'houlstə], *v.t.* tapisser.

upholsterer [ʌp'houlstərə], *n.* tapissier, *m.*

upholstery [ʌp'houlstəri], *n.* tapisserie, *f.*

upkeep ['ʌpkiːp], *n.* entretien, *m.*

upland ['ʌplənd], *a.* élevé, des hautes terres.

uplands ['ʌpləndz], *n.pl.* terrain élevé, haut pays, *m.*, hautes terres, *f.pl.*

uplift [ʌp'lift], *v.t.* lever, élever, soulever. —['ʌplift], *n. (fig.)* inspiration, *f.*

uplifting [ʌp'liftiŋ], *n.* soulèvement, *m.*

upon [ə'pɔn], *prep.* sur; *upon pain of*, sous peine de.

upper ['ʌpə], *a.* supérieur, d'en haut, de dessus, au-dessus; haut; *the Upper House* la Chambre Haute; *upper circle*, troisièmes loges, *f.pl.*; *upper deck*, pont supérieur, *m.*; *upper hand*, dessus, *m.*, supériorité, *f.*

uppermost ['ʌpəmoust], *a.* le plus élevé; *(fig.)* le plus fort.

uppers ['ʌpəz], *n.pl.* empeignes *(de chaussures)*, *f.pl.*; *(fam.)* *to be on one's uppers*, être dans la débine.

Upper Volta ['ʌpə'vɔltə]. la Haute Volta, *f.*

uppish ['ʌpiʃ], *a.* fier, arrogant.

uppishness ['ʌpiʃnis], *n.* fierté, arrogance, *f.*

upraise [ʌp'reiz], *v.t.* soulever, élever.

upright ['ʌprait], *a.* droit, debout; d'aplomb, vertical; *(fig.)* honnête *(intègre)*.—*adv.* tout droit.—*n.* montant, *m.*

uprightness ['ʌpraitnis], *n.* droiture, intégrité, *f.*

uprising [ʌp'raiziŋ], *n.* lever; soulèvement, *m.*

uproar ['ʌprɔː], *n.* tumulte, désordre; tapage, *m.*

uproarious [ʌp'rɔːriəs], *a.* bruyant; tumultueux.

uproariously [ʌp'rɔːriəsli], *adv.* avec un grand vacarme.

uproot [ʌp'ruːt], *v.t.* déraciner, extirper.

uprooting [ʌp'ruːtiŋ], *n.* déracinement, *m.*

upset [ʌp'set], *v.t. irr. (conjug. like* SET) renverser; *(fig.)* bouleverser.—*v.i.* se renverser;

617

verser (*véhicules*).—['ʌpset], *n.* bouleversement, *m.*

upshot ['ʌpʃɔt], *n.* résultat, *m.*, fin, *f.*, fin mot, *m.*

upside-down ['ʌpsaid'daun], *adv.* sens dessus dessous.

upstairs ['ʌpstɛəz], *a.* d'en haut.—[ʌp'stɛəz], *adv.* en haut.

upstanding [ʌp'stændiŋ], *a.* droit, debout.

upstart ['ʌpstɑːt], *n.* parvenu, nouveau riche, *m.*

upsurge [ʌp'səːdʒ], *n.* poussée, *f.*

upward ['ʌpwəd], *a.* dirigé en haut; ascendant.—*adv.* or **upwards** ['ʌpwədz], en haut; en montant; *upwards of*, plus de.

Ural ['juərəl] **Mountains.** les Monts Ourals, *m.pl.*

uranium [ju'reiniəm], *n.* uranium, *m.*

urban ['əːbən], *a.* urbain.

urbane [əː'bein], *a.* qui a de l'urbanité, poli.

urbanely [əː'beinli], *adv.* avec urbanité.

urbanity [əː'bæniti], *n.* urbanité, *f.*

urbanize ['əːbənaiz], *v.t.* urbaniser.

urchin ['əːtʃin], *n.* gamin, polisson; (*colloq.*) mioche, gosse, *m.*; *sea urchin*, oursin, *m.*

urge [əːdʒ], *v.t.* presser; pousser, exciter, porter (à); alléguer (*insister sur*); *to urge on*, pousser en avant.—*n.* impulsion, poussée, *f.*

urgency ['əːdʒənsi], *n.* urgence, *f.*

urgent ['əːdʒənt], *a.* urgent, instant.

urgently ['əːdʒəntli], *adv.* avec urgence, instamment.

urging ['əːdʒiŋ], *n.* sollicitation, *f.*

uric ['juərik], *a.* urique.

urinal ['juərinl], *n.* urinoir; (*Med.*) urinal, *m.*; vespasienne (*urinoir public*), *f.*

urinate ['juərineit], *v.i.* uriner.

urine ['juərin], *n.* urine, *f.*

urn [əːn], *n.* urne; fontaine (*à thé, à café etc.*), *f.*

Ursula ['əːsjulə], Ursule, *f.*

Uruguay ['juərugwai], l'Uruguay, *m.*

Uruguayan [juəru'gwaiən], *a.* uruguayen.—*n.* Uruguayen (*personne*), *m.*

us [ʌs], *pron.* nous; *for us Frenchmen*, pour nous autres Français.

usable ['juːzəbl], *a.* utilisable, employable.

usage ['juːzidʒ], *n.* usage, *m.*

use [juːs], *n.* usage, emploi, *m.*; utilité, *f.*, avantage, profit, *m.*; habitude, *f.*; (*Law*) usufruit, *m.*; *it is of no use*, cela ne sert à rien; *of use*, utile; *to make use of*, se servir de; *what is the use of that?* à quoi sert cela?—[juːz], *v.t.* user de, faire usage de, employer, se servir de; utiliser; consommer.

used [juːzd], *a.* usité (*mot etc.*), d'occasion (*voiture*); *very little used*, qui a peu servi, presque neuf (*vêtement etc.*).—[juːst] *to be* or *get used to*, s'accoutumer à, s'habituer à.—[juːst], *v. aux. in the expression used to* (*followed by inf.*) *usu. translated by the Imp. Tense in French*; *he used to admire*, il admirait.

useful ['juːsful], *a.* utile.

usefully ['juːsfuli], *adv.* utilement, avec profit.

usefulness ['juːsfulnis], *n.* utilité, *f.*

useless ['juːslis], *a.* inutile; vain.

uselessly ['juːslisli], *adv.* inutilement.

uselessness ['juːslisnis], *n.* inutilité, *f.*

usher ['ʌʃə], *n.* huissier (*de cour de justice*);

sous-maître, *m.*—*v.t.* faire entrer, introduire (*dans*); (*fig.*) annoncer.

usherette [ʌʃə'ret], *n.* (*Cine.*) ouvreuse, *f.*

usual ['juːʒuəl], *a.* usuel, ordinaire, habituel, accoutumé; d'usage; *as usual*, comme d'habitude.

usually ['juːʒuəli], *adv.* ordinairement, d'ordinaire, d'habitude.

usurer ['juːʒərə], *n.* usurier, *m.*

usurious [ju'zjuəriəs], *a.* usuraire.

usurp [ju'zəːp], *v.t.* usurper.

usurpation [juːzə'peiʃən], *n.* usurpation, *f.*

usurper [ju'zəːpə], *n.* usurpateur, *m.*

usury ['juːʒəri], *n.* usure, *f.*

utensil [ju'tensil], *n.* ustensile, *m.*

uterine ['juːtərain], *a.* utérin.

uterus ['juːtərəs], *n.* utérus, *m.*

utilitarian [juːtili'tɛəriən], *a.* utilitaire.

utilitarianism [juːtili'tɛəriənizm], *n.* utilitarisme, *m.*

utility [juː'tiliti], *n.* utilité, *f.*

utilizable ['juːtilaizəbl], *a.* utilisable.

utilization [juːtilai'zeiʃən], *n.* utilisation, *f.*

utilize ['juːtilaiz], *v.t.* utiliser.

utmost ['ʌtmoust], *a.* extrême, le dernier, le plus haut, le plus grand; le plus élevé (*prix etc.*).—*n.* extrême, comble, *m.*; *to do one's utmost*, faire tout son possible (*pour*).

Utopia [juː'toupiə], Utopie, *f.*

Utopian [juː'toupiən], *a.* d'utopie, utopique.

utter (1) ['ʌtə], *a.* entier, complet; absolu; le plus profond (*extrême*); vrai; fieffé (*véritable*).

utter (2) ['ʌtə], *v.t.* pousser; proférer, prononcer; dire; émettre (*fausse monnaie*).

utterable ['ʌtərəbl], *a.* exprimable.

utterance ['ʌtərəns], *n.* énonciation, prononciation, parole, expression, *f.*

utterer ['ʌtərə], *n.* personne qui prononce, *f.*; émetteur (*de fausse monnaie*), *m.*

utterly ['ʌtəli], *adv.* tout à fait, entièrement.

uttermost ['ʌtəmoust], *a.* extrême; le plus reculé.

uvula ['juːvjulə], *n.* (*Anat.*) luette, uvule, *f.*

uvular ['juːvjulə], *a.* uvulaire.

uxorious [ʌk'sɔːriəs], *a.* uxorieux, esclave de sa femme.

uxoriousness [ʌk'sɔːriəsnis], *n.* complaisance excessive pour sa femme, *f.*

V

V, v [viː]. vingt-deuxième lettre de l'alphabet, *m.*

vacancy ['veikənsi], *n.* vacance, place vacante, *f.*; vide, *m.*; lacune (*trou*), *f.*

vacant ['veikənt], *a.* vacant, vide; libre (*inoccupé*); vide d'expression (*regard perdu*).

vacate [və'keit], *v.t.* laisser vacant, quitter.

vacation [və'keiʃən], *n.* vacation, *f.*, vacances, *f.pl.*

vaccinate ['væksineit], *v.t.* vacciner.

vaccination [væksi'neiʃən], *n.* vaccination, vaccine, *f.*

vaccine ['væksiːn], *a.* de vache.—*n.* vaccin, *m.*

vacillate ['væsileit], *v.i.* vaciller; (*fig.*) hésiter.
vacillating ['væsileitiŋ], *a.* vacillant, indécis.
vacillation [væsi'leiʃən], *n.* vacillation, indécision, *f.*
vacuity [və'kju:iti], *n.* vide, *m.*; vacuité, *f.*
vacuous ['vækjuəs], *a.* vide; (*fig.*) bête.
vacuum ['vækjuəm], *n.* vide, *m.*
vacuum cleaner ['vækjuəm'kli:nə], *n.* aspirateur, *m.*
vade-mecum ['veidi'mi:kəm], *n.* vademecum, *m.*
vagabond ['vægəbɔnd], *a.* errant, vagabond.
—*n.* vagabond, *m.*
vagary ['veigəri], *n.* caprice, *m.*, lubie, boutade, *f.*
vagina [və'dʒainə], *n.* (*Anat.*) vagin, *m.*
vagrancy ['veigrənsi], *n.* vagabondage, *m.*
vagrant ['veigrənt], *a.* vagabond, errant.—*n.* vagabond, mendiant, *m.*
vague [veig], *a.* vague.
vaguely ['veigli], *adv.* vaguement.
vagueness ['veignis], *n.* vague, *m.*
vain [vein], *a.* vain; faux (*creux*); vaniteux, glorieux (*fier*); *in vain*, en vain.
vainglorious [vein'glɔ:riəs], *a.* vain, vaniteux.
vainglory [vein'glɔ:ri], *n.* vaine gloire, gloriole, *f.*
vainly ['veinli], *adv.* en vain, vainement.
vainness ['veinnis], *n.* vanité, *f.*
valance ['vælons], *n.* frange de lit, *f.*
vale [veil], *n.* (*poet.*) vallon, *m.*, vallée, *f.*
valedictory [væli'diktəri], *a.* d'adieu.—*n.* discours d'adieu, *m.*
valet ['vælit], *n.* valet de chambre, *m.*
valetudinarian [vælitju:di'nɛəriən], *a.* and *n.* valétudinaire, *m.,f.*
valiant ['væliənt], *a.* vaillant, valeureux.
valiantly ['væliəntli], *adv.* vaillamment.
valid ['vælid], *a.* valide, valable.
validate ['vælideit], *v.t.* valider, rendre valable.
validity [və'liditi], validness ['vælidnis], *n.* validité, *f.*
validly ['vælidli], *adv.* validement.
validness [VALIDITY].
valise [və'li:z], *n.* valise, *f.*; sac de voyage, *m.*
valley ['væli], *n.* vallée, *f.*, vallon, *m.*
valor ['vælə], *n.* valeur, vaillance, *f.*
valorous ['vælərəs], *a.* valeureux.
valuable ['væljuəbl], *a.* précieux.
valuation [vælju'eiʃən], *n.* évaluation, *f.*
valuator ['væljueitə], *n.* estimateur, *m.*
value ['vælju:], *n.* valeur, *f.*; prix, *m.*—*v.t.* évaluer, estimer.
valued ['vælju:d], *a.* estimé, apprécié.
valueless ['væljulis], *a.* sans valeur.
valuer ['væljuə], *n.* estimateur, commissaire-priseur, *m.*
valve [vælv], *n.* soupape; valve; (*Rad.*) lampe, *f.*
valved [vælvd], *a.* à soupape; (*Bot.*) valvé, à valves.
valvular ['vælvjulə], *a.* (*Med.*) valvulaire.
vamp [væmp], *n.* empeigne; (*fig.*) enjôleuse, femme fatale, *f.*—*v.t.* (*fig.*) raccommoder, rapiécer; (*Mus.*) improviser.
vampire ['væmpais], *n.* vampire, *m.*
van [væn], *n.* camionnette, voiture (*de déménagement*), *f.*; (*Rail. etc.*) fourgon, *m.*; avant-garde (*précurseur*), *f.*

vandal [vændl], *n.* vandale, *m.,f.*
vandalism ['vændəlizm], *n.* vandalisme, *m.*
vane [vein], *n.* girouette, *f.*
vanguard ['vænga:d], *n.* avant-garde, *f.*
vanilla [və'nilə], *n.* vanille, *f.*
vanish ['væniʃ], *v.i.* s'évanouir, disparaître.
vanishing point ['væniʃiŋpoint], *n.* point de fuite, *m.*
vanity ['væniti], *n.* vanité, *f.*
vanquish ['væŋkwiʃ], *v.t.* vaincre.
vanquisher ['væŋkwiʃə], *n.* vainqueur, *m.*
vantage ['va:ntidʒ], *n.* avantage, *m.*, supériorité, *f.*
vapid ['væpid], *a.* fade, insipide; éventé (*boisson alcoolique*).
vapidity [væ'piditi], vapidness ['væpidnis], *n.* fadeur, insipidité, *f.*
vapor ['veipə], *n.* vapeur; (*fig.*) fumée, *f.*
vaporish ['veipəriʃ], vapory ['veipəri], *a.* vaporeux.
vaporization [veipərai'zeiʃən], *n.* vaporisation, *f.*
vaporize ['veipəraiz], *v.t.* vaporiser.—*v.i.* se vaporiser.
vaporous ['veipərəs], *a.* vaporeux.
variability [vɛəriə'biliti], variableness ['vɛəriəblnis], *n.* variabilité; inconstance, *f.*
variable ['vɛəriəbl], *a.* variable; inconstant.
variance ['vɛəriəns], *n.* désaccord, *m.*
variation [vɛəri'eiʃən], *n.* variation, *f.*, changement, *m.*
varicose ['værikous], *a.* variqueux; *varicose vein*, varice, *f.*
varied ['vɛərid], *a.* varié, divers.
variegate ['vɛərigeit], *v.t.* varier; nuancer.
variegated ['vɛərigeitid], *a.* varié, bigarré; (*Bot.*) panaché.
variegation [vɛəri'geiʃən], *n.* bigarrure, *f.*
variety [və'raiəti], *n.* variété, diversité, *f.*
various ['vɛəriəs], *a.* divers, différent.
variously ['vɛəriəsli], *adv.* diversement.
varnish ['va:niʃ], *n.* vernis, *m.*—*v.t.* vernir; vernisser (*poterie etc.*).
varnisher ['va:niʃə], *n.* vernisseur, *m.*
varnishing ['va:niʃiŋ], *n.* vernissure, *f.*; vernissage, *m.*
vary ['vɛəri], *v.t.* varier; diversifier.—*v.i.* varier, changer.
varying ['vɛəriiŋ], *a.* changeant, qui varie, divers.
vascular ['væskjulə], *a.* vasculaire.
vase [va:z], *n.* vase, *m.*
vaseline ['væsəli:n], *n.* (*reg. trade mark*) vaseline, *f.*
vassal ['væsəl], *n.* vassal, *m.*
vassalage ['væsəlidʒ], *n.* vasselage, *m.*; (*fig.*) servitude, *f.*
vast [va:st], *a.* vaste, immense.—*n.* immensité, *f.*
vastly ['va:stli], *adv.* immensément, excessivement.
vastness ['va:stnis], *n.* vaste étendue, grandeur, *f.*
vat [væt], *n.* cuve, *f.*
vatful ['vætful], *n.* cuvée, *f.*
Vatican ['vætikən]. le Vatican, *m.*
vaudeville ['voudəvil], *n.* vaudeville, *m.*
vault [vɔ:lt], *n.* voûte, cave, *f.*; caveau (*lieu de sépulture*); saut (*bond*), *m.*—*v.t.* voûter.—*v.i.* sauter.
vaulted ['vɔ:ltid], *a.* voûté, en voûte.

619

vaulter ['vɔ:ltə], *n.* voltigeur, sauteur, *m.*, acrobate, *m.*, *f.*

vaulting ['vɔ:ltɪŋ], *n.* construction de voûtes, *f.*; voûtes, *f.pl.*; voltige (*acrobatie*), *f.*

vaunt [vɔ:nt], *n.* vanterie, *f.—v.t.* vanter, élever jusqu'aux nues.

vaunter ['vɔ:ntə], *n.* vantard, *m.*

vaunting ['vɔ:ntɪŋ], *a.* plein de jactance.

vauntingly ['vɔ:ntɪŋlɪ], *adv.* avec jactance.

veal [vi:l], *n.* veau, *m.*

vedette [və'det], *n.* vedette, *f.*

veer [vɪə], *v.t.* virer (*bateau*).—*v.i.* tourner, changer de direction; virer (*bateau*).

vegetable ['vedʒɪtəbl], *a.* végétal.—*n.* végétal, légume, *m.*

vegetal ['vedʒɪtl], *a.* végétal.

vegetarian [vedʒɪ'teərɪən], *a.* and *n.* végétarien, *m.*

vegetate ['vedʒɪteɪt], *v.i.* végéter.

vegetation [vedʒɪ'teɪʃən], *n.* végétation, *f.*

vegetative ['vedʒɪtətɪv], *a.* végétatif, végétant.

vehemence ['vi:ɪməns], *n.* véhémence; (*fig.*) ardeur, *f.*

vehement ['vi:ɪmənt], *a.* véhément, impétueux.

vehemently ['vi:ɪməntlɪ], *adv.* avec véhémence, impétueusement.

vehicle ['vi:ɪkl], *n.* véhicule, *m.*, voiture, *f.*

veil [veɪl], *n.* voile, *m.*; voilette (*de dame*), *f.—v.t.* voiler; (*fig.*) déguiser.

vein [veɪn], *n.* veine; (*fig.*) humeur, *f.—v.t.* veiner.

veined [veɪnd], **veiny** ['veɪnɪ], *a.* veiné.

vellum ['veləm], *n.* vélin, *m.*

velocity [və'lɒsɪtɪ], *n.* vélocité, vitesse, rapidité, *f.*

velvet ['velvɪt], *a.* de velours; (*Bot.*) velouté.—*n.* velours, *m.*

velveteen [velvə'ti:n], *n.* velours de coton, *m.*

velvety ['velvɪtɪ], *a.* velouté.

venal [vi:nl], *a.* vénal.

venality [vi:'nælɪtɪ], *n.* vénalité, *f.*

vend [vend], *v.t.* vendre (*petits articles*).

vending machine, see **slot-machine.**

vendetta [ven'detə], *n.* vendetta, *f.*

vendible ['vendɪbl], *a.* vendable.

vendor ['vendə], *n.* vendeur, *m.*

veneer [və'nɪə], *n.* feuille (*de bois etc.*); plaque, *f.*; (*fig.*) vernis, *m.—v.t.* plaquer (*de*).

veneering [və'nɪərɪŋ], *n.* placage, *m.*

venerable ['venərəbl], *a.* vénérable.

venerableness ['venərəblnɪs], *n.* caractère vénérable, *m.*

venerate ['venəreɪt], *v.t.* vénérer.

veneration [venə'reɪʃən], *n.* vénération, *f.*

venerator ['venəreɪtə], *n.* vénérateur, *m.*

venery ['venərɪ], *n.* chasse, vénerie, *f.*

Venetian [və'ni:ʃən], *a.* vénitien, de Venise; **Venetian blind,** jalousie, *f.*; **Venetian shutter,** persienne, *f.—n.* Vénitien (*personne*), *m.*

Venezuela [venə'zweɪlə]. le Vénézuéla, *m.*

Venezuelan [venə'zweɪlən], *a.* vénézuélien.—*n.* Vénézuélien (*personne*), *m.*

vengeance ['vendʒəns], *n.* vengeance, *f.*; **with a vengeance,** furieusement, à outrance.

vengeful ['vendʒful], *a.* vindicatif.

venial ['vi:nɪəl], *a.* véniel, pardonnable.

veniality [vi:nɪ'ælɪtɪ], *n.* vénialité, *f.*

Venice ['venɪs]. Venise, *f.*

venison ['venɪzn], *n.* venaison, *f.*

venom ['venəm], *n.* venin, *m.*

venomous ['venəməs], *a.* venimeux (*animal*); vénéneux (*plante*); (*fig.*) méchant.

venous ['vi:nəs], *a.* veineux.

vent [vent], *v.t.* donner issue à, exhaler, décharger.—*n.* issue, *f.*, passage, cours; trou de fausse (*de baril*); soupirail (*pour l'air*), *m.*; **to give vent to,** donner libre cours à.

ventilate ['ventɪleɪt], *v.t.* ventiler; aérer, (*fig.*) discuter.

ventilation [ventɪ'leɪʃən], *n.* ventilation, *f.*; **ventilation shaft,** puits d'aérage, *m.*

ventilator ['ventɪleɪtə], *n.* ventilateur, *m.*

ventral ['ventrəl], *a.* ventral.

ventricle ['ventrɪkl], *n.* ventricule, *m.*

ventriloquism [ven'trɪləkwɪzm], *n.* ventriloquie, *f.*

ventriloquist [ven'trɪləkwɪst], *n.* ventriloque, *m.*, *f.*

venture ['ventʃə], *n.* aventure, entreprise, *f.*—*v.t.* aventurer, risquer.—*v.i.* oser, se hasarder, s'aventurer; s'aviser de (*se permettre*).

venturer ['ventʃərə], *n.* personne aventureuse, *f.*

venturesome ['ventʃəsəm], *a.* aventureux, audacieux.

venue ['venju:], *n.* juridiction, *f.*; lieu de réunion, *f.*

Venus ['vi:nəs]. Vénus, *f.*

veracious [və'reɪʃəs], *a.* véridique.

veracity [və'ræsɪtɪ], *n.* véracité, *f.*

veranda, verandah [və'rændə], *n.* véranda, *f.*

verb [və:b], *n.* verbe, *m.*

verbal ['və:bəl], *a.* verbal, littéral.

verbally ['və:bəlɪ], *adv.* verbalement, mot à mot.

verbatim [və:'beɪtɪm], *adv.* mot pour mot.

verbena [və:'bi:nə], *n.* verveine, *f.*

verbiage ['və:bɪɪdʒ], *n.* verbiage, *m.*

verbose [və:'bəʊs], *a.* verbeux, diffus, prolixe.

verbosity [və:'bɒsɪtɪ], *n.* verbosité, *f.*

verdant ['və:dənt], *a.* verdoyant, vert.

verdict ['və:dɪkt], *n.* verdict; (*fig.*) arrêt, *m.*

verdigris ['və:dɪgrɪs], *n.* vert-de-gris, *m.*

verdure ['və:djə], *n.* verdure, *f.*

verge (1) [və:dʒ], *n.* bord, *m.*, bordure; lisière (*de forêt etc.*); verge (*baguette*), *f.*; **on the verge of setting out,** à la veille de partir.—*v.i.* pencher (*vers*); **to verge on,** toucher à.

verger ['və:dʒə], *n.* bedeau, huissier à verge, *m.*

verification [verɪfɪ'keɪʃən], *n.* vérification, *f.*

verifier ['verɪfaɪə], *n.* vérificateur, *m.*

verify ['verɪfaɪ], *v.t.* vérifier.

*verily ['verɪlɪ], *adv.* en vérité, vraiment.

verisimilar [verɪ'sɪmɪlə], *a.* vraisemblable.

verisimilitude [verɪsɪ'mɪlɪtju:d], *n.* vraisemblance, *f.*

veritable ['verɪtəbl], *a.* véritable.

verity ['verɪtɪ], *n.* vérité, *f.*

vermicelli [və:mɪ'selɪ], *n.* vermicelle, *m.*

vermicule ['və:mɪkju:l], *n.* vermisseau, *m.*

vermilion [və'mɪljən], *a.* vermeil.—*n.* vermillon, *m.*

vermin ['və:mɪn], *n.* vermine, *f.*

verminous ['və:mɪnəs], *a.* vermineux.

vernacular [vəˈnækjulə], *a.* du pays, indigène.
—*n.* langue vernaculaire, *f.*
vernal [ˈvəːnəl], *a.* printanier.
veronica [vəˈrɒnikə], *n.* véronique, *f.*
versatile [ˈvəːsətail], *a.* qui a des connaissances variées; qui se plie à tout.
versatility [vəːsəˈtiliti], *n.* souplesse, faculté
d'adaptation, *f.*
verse [vəːs], *n.* vers, *m.*, poésie; strophe
(*stance*), *f.*
versed [vəːst], *a.* versé (*dans*).
versification [vəːsifiˈkeiʃən], *n.* versification,
f.
versifier [ˈvəːsifaiə], *n.* versificateur, rimailleur, *m.*
versify [ˈvəːsifai], *v.t.* mettre en vers.—*v.i.*
versifier.
version [ˈvəːʃən], *n.* version, *f.*
versus [ˈvəːsəs], *prep.* contre.
vertebra [ˈvəːtibrə], *n.* (*pl.* **vertebræ** [ˈvəːti
briː]) vertèbre, *f.*
vertebral [ˈvəːtibrəl], *a.* vertébral.
vertebrate [ˈvəːtibrit], *a.* and *n.* vertébré, *m.*
vertex [ˈvəːteks], *n.* (*pl.* **vertices** [ˈvəːtisiːz])
sommet, zénith, *m.*
vertical [ˈvəːtikl], *a.* vertical.
vertically [ˈvəːtikli], *adv.* verticalement.
vertiginous [vəːˈtidʒinəs], *a.* vertigineux.
vertigo [ˈvəːtigou], *n.* vertige, *m.*
verve [vəːv], *n.* verve, *f.*
very [ˈveri], *a.* vrai, même, véritable.—*adv.*
fort, bien, très.
vesper [ˈvespə], *n.* étoile du soir, *f.*; soir
m.; (*pl.*) vêpres, *f.pl.*
vessel [vesl], *n.* vase; vaisseau, bâtiment,
navire, *m.*
vest [vest], *n.* tricot de corps; (*Am.*) gilet, *m.*—
v.t. vêtir, revêtir; investir (*de*).—*v.i.* échoir
(à).
vestal [vestl], *a.* vestale, de Vesta; (*fig.*)
chaste.—*n.* vestale, *f.*
vestibule [ˈvestibjuːl], *n.* vestibule, *m.*
vestige [ˈvestidʒ], *n.* vestige, *m.*, trace, *f.*
vestment [ˈvestmənt], *n.* vêtement (de cérémonie), *m.*; chasuble, *f.*
vestry [ˈvestri], *n.* sacristie, *f.*
vesture [ˈvestʃə], *n.* vêtements, *m.pl.*
Vesuvius [viˈsuːvjəs], le Vésuve, *m.*
vetch [vetʃ], *n.* vesce, *f.*
veteran [ˈvetərən], *a.* vieux, ancien, expérimenté.—*n.* vétéran, *m.*
veterinary [ˈvetərinri], *a.* vétérinaire;
veterinary surgeon, vétérinaire, *m.*, *f.*
veto [ˈviːtou], *n.* veto, *m.*—*v.t.* mettre son veto
à, interdire.
vex [veks], *v.t.* fâcher, vexer, contrarier.
vexation [vekˈseiʃən], *n.* vexation, contrariété,
f., chagrin, *m.*
vexatious [vekˈseiʃəs], *a.* vexatoire; irritant,
fâcheux, ennuyeux.
vexatiousness [vekˈseiʃəsnis], *n.* caractère
vexatoire, *m.*
vexed [vekst], *a.* vexé, fâché; (*fig.*) épineux
(*question*).
vexing [ˈveksiŋ], *a.* contrariant, vexant, ennuyeux.
via [ˈvaiə], *prep.* par, par voie de, via.
viability [vaiəˈbiliti], *n.* viabilité, *f.*
viable [ˈvaiəbl], *a.* viable.
viaduct [ˈvaiədʌkt], *n.* viaduc, *m.*
vial [ˈvaiəl], *n.* fiole, *f.*

viands [ˈvaiəndz], *n. pl.* aliments, *m.pl.*; mets,
m.
viaticum [vaiˈætikəm], *n.* viatique, *m.*
vibrate [vaiˈbreit], *v.t.* faire vibrer.—*v.i.*
vibrer, osciller.
vibration [vaiˈbreiʃən], *n.* vibration, oscillation, *f.*
vibrating [vaiˈbreitiŋ], **vibratory** [ˈvaibrə
təri], *a.* vibrant, vibratoire.
vicar [ˈvikə], *n.* (*Engl. Ch.*) pasteur; (*R.-C.
Ch.*) curé (*de paroisse*), *m.*; *vicar general*,
vicaire, *m.*
vicarage [ˈvikəridʒ], *n.* cure, *f.*, presbytère, *m.*
vicarial [viˈkɛəriəl], *a.* de la cure, du curé.
vicarious [viˈkɛəriəs], *a.* vicarial, de vicaire;
(*fig.*) de substitution.
vicariously [viˈkɛəriəsli], *adv.* par délégation, par substitution.
vice (1) [vais], *n.* vice, défaut, *m.*; *vice squad*,
brigade de mœurs, *f.*
vice (2) [vais], *n.* (*Tech.*) étau, *m.*
vice admiral [ˈvaisˈædmirəl], *n.* vice-amiral,
m.
vice chancellor [ˈvaistʃɑːnsələ], *n.* vice-
chancelier; (*Univ.*) recteur, *m.*
vice president [ˈvaisˈprezidənt], *n.* vice-
président, *m.*
viceroy [ˈvaisrɔi], *n.* vice-roi, *m.*
vicinity [viˈsiniti], *n.* voisinage, *m.*, proximité,
f., alentours, *m.pl.*
vicious [ˈviʃəs], *a.* vicieux; haineux.
viciously [ˈviʃəsli], *adv.* vicieusement;
rageusement.
viciousness [ˈviʃəsnis], *n.* nature vicieuse, *f.*,
vice, *m.*
vicissitude [viˈsisitjuːd], *n.* vicissitude, *f.*
victim [ˈviktim], *n.* victime, *f.*
victimization [viktimaiˈzeiʃən], *n.* tyrannisa-
tion, *f.*
victimize [ˈviktimaiz], *v.t.* exercer des
représailles contre, tromper.
victor [ˈviktə], *n.* vainqueur, *m.*
victorious [vikˈtɔːriəs], *a.* victorieux, de
victoire.
victoriously [vikˈtɔːriəsli], *adv.* victorieuse-
ment, en vainqueur.
victory [ˈviktəri], *n.* victoire, *f.*
victual [vitl], *v.t.* approvisionner, ravitailler.
victualler [ˈvitlə], *n.* pourvoyeur, fournisseur
(de vivres), *m.*; *licensed victualler*,
débitant de boissons, *m.*
victualling [ˈvitliŋ], *n.* ravitaillement, *m.*
victuals [vitlz], *n.pl.* vivres, *m.pl.*, provisions,
f.pl.
vie [vai], *v.i.* rivaliser, lutter (*de*); le disputer
(à).
Vienna [viˈenə]. Vienne, *f.*
Viennese [viːəˈniːz], *a.* viennois.—*n.* Viennois
(*personne*), *m.*
Vietnam [vjetˈnæm]. le Vietnam, *m.*
Vietnamese [vjetnəˈmiːz], *a.* vietnamien.—*n.*
Vietnamien (*personne*), *m.*
view [vjuː], *n.* vue, perspective, scène, *f.*;
regard (*coup d'œil*); aperçu, examen (*exposé*),
m.; intention, *f.*; dessein, *m.*; opinion,
pensée, *f.*; *in view of*, en considération de;
on view, ouvert au public; *with a view
to*, en vue de.—*v.t.* regarder; considérer;
examiner, inspecter; explorer.
viewer [ˈvjuːə], *n.* spectateur; téléspectateur,
m.
viewing [ˈvjuːiŋ], *n.* examen, *m.*, inspection, *f.*

view-point ['vju:point], *n.* point de vue, *m.*

vigil ['vidʒil], *n.* veille, veillée, (*Eccles.*) vigile, *f.*

vigilance ['vidʒiləns], *n.* vigilance, *f.*

vigilant ['vidʒilənt], *a.* vigilant, éveillé.

vigilantly ['vidʒiləntli], *adv.* avec vigilance.

vigorous ['vigərəs], *a.* vigoureux.

vigorously ['vigərəsli], *adv.* vigoureusement.

vigorousness ['vigərəsnis], *n.* (also **vigor** ['vigə], *n.* vigueur, *f.*

vile [vail], *a.* vil, abject, bas; détestable.

vileness ['vailnis], *n.* bassesse, *f.*

vilification [vilifi'keiʃən], *n.* diffamation, *f.*

vilifier ['vilifaiə], *n.* diffamateur, *m.*

vilify ['vilifai], *v.t.* vilipender, dénigrer.

villa ['vilə], *n.* villa, maison de campagne, *f.*

village ['vilidʒ], *n.* village, *m.*

villager ['vilidʒə], *n.* villageois, *m.*

villain ['vilən], *n.* scélérat, gredin; (*Theat.*) traître, *m.*

villainous ['vilənəs], *a.* vil, infâme.

villainy ['viləni], *n.* scélératesse, vilenie, *f.*

vindicate ['vindikeit], *v.t.* soutenir, défendre, justifier; venger.

vindication [vindi'keiʃən], *n.* défense, justification, *f.*

vindicator ['vindikeitə], *n.* défenseur, *m.*

vindictive [vin'diktiv], *a.* vindicatif.

vindictively [vin'diktivli], *adv.* d'une manière vindicative.

vindictiveness [vin'diktivnis], *n.* esprit de vengeance, *m.*

vine [vain], *n.* vigne, *f.*

vine-dresser [vaindresə], *n.* vigneron, *m.*

vinegar ['vinigə], *n.* vinaigre, *m.*

vine grower ['vaingrouə], *n.* viticulteur, *m.*

vine-growing ['vaingrouiŋ], *n.* viticulture, *f.*

vine harvest [vainhɑːvist], *n.* vendange, *f.*

vine prop ['vainprɔp], *n.* échalas, *m.*

vinery ['vainəri], *n.* serre à vignes, *f.*

vineyard ['vinjəd], *n.* vigne, *f.*; vignoble, *m.*

viniculture ['vinikʌltʃər], *a.* vinicole.

viniculture ['vinikʌltʃə], *n.* viniculture, *f.*

vinous ['vainous], *a.* vineux.

vintage ['vintidʒ], *n.* vendange; vinée, récolte de vin (*cueillette*), *f.*; vendanges (*temps de la récolte*), *f.pl.*; **a vintage wine**, un vin de marque, *m.*

vintager ['vintidʒə], *n.* vendangeur, *m.*

vintner ['vintnə], *n.* négociant en vins, *m.*

viny ['vaini], *a.* de vigne, de raisin; de vignoble.

viola (1) [vi'oulə], *n.* (*Mus.*) alto, *m.*; **viola player**, altiste, *m., f.*

viola (2) ['vaiələ], *n.* (*Bot.*) violette, *f.*

violate ['vaiəleit], *v.t.* violer, faire violence à; outrager.

violation [vaiə'leiʃən], *n.* violation, infraction, *f.*, viol (*d'une femme*), *m.*

violator ['vaiəleitə], *n.* violateur, *m.*

violence ['vaiələns], *n.* violence, *f.*; **with violence** (*of robbery*), à main armée.

violent ['vaiələnt], *a.* violent; atroce (*douleur*).

violently ['vaiələntli], *adv.* violemment, avec violence.

violet ['vaiəlit], *n.* violette (*plante*), *f.*; violet (*couleur*), *m.*

violin [vaiə'lin], *n.* violon, *m.*

violinist [vaiə'linist], *n.* violoniste, *m., f.*

violist [vi'oulist], *n.* altiste, violiste, *m., f.*

violoncellist [vaiələn'tʃelist], *n.* violoncelliste, *m., f.*

violoncello [vaiələn'tʃelou], *n.* violoncelle, *m.*

viper ['vaipə], *n.* vipère, *f.*

viperish ['vaipəriʃ], **viperous** ['vaipərəs], *a.* de vipère; (*fig.*) venimeux.

virago [vi'rɑːgou], *n.* virago, mégère, *f.*

virgin ['vəːdʒin], *a.* vierge; virginal, de vierge.—*n.* vierge, *f.*

virginal ['vəːdʒinəl], *a.* virginal, de vierge.

Virginia creeper [və'dʒinjə'kriːpə], *n.* vigne vierge, *f.*

virginity [və'dʒiniti], *n.* virginité, *f.*

viridity [vi'riditi], *n.* verdeur, fraîcheur, *f.*

virile [vi'rilti], *a.* viril, mâle.

virility [vi'riliti], *n.* virilité, nature virile, *f.*

virtual ['vəːtjuəl], *a.* virtuel; de fait.

virtually ['vəːtjuəli], *adv.* virtuellement, de fait.

virtue ['vəːtjuː], *n.* vertu; (*fig.*) valeur, *f.*, mérite, *m.*

virtuosity [vəːtju'ositi], *n.* virtuosité, *f.*

virtuoso [vəːtju'ousou], *n.* (*pl.* **virtuosi** [vəːtju'ousi]) virtuose, *m., f.*

virtuous ['vəːtjuəs], *a.* vertueux.

virtuously ['vəːtjuəsli], *adv.* vertueusement.

virtuousness ['vəːtjuəsnis], *n.* vertu, *f.*

virulence ['viruləns], *n.* virulence, *f.*

virulent ['virulənt], *a.* virulent.

virus ['vaiərəs], *n.* virus, *m.*

visa ['viːzə], *n.* visa, *m.*—*v.t.* viser.

visage ['vizidʒ], *n.* visage, *m.*, figure, *f.*

viscera ['visərə], *n.pl.* viscères, *m.pl.*

viscid ['visid], *a.* visqueux.

viscosity [vis'kositi], *n.* viscosité, *f.*

viscount ['vaikaunt], *n.* vicomte, *m.*

viscountess ['vaikauntis], *n.* vicomtesse, *f.*

viscountship ['vaikauntʃip], *n.* vicomté, *f.*

viscous ['viskəs], *a.* visqueux, glutineux.

vise [vais], *n.* (*Tech.*) étau, *m.*

visibility [vizi'biliti], *n.* visibilité, *f.*

visible ['vizibl], *a.* visible; clair.

visibly ['vizibli], *adv.* visiblement, à vue d'œil.

vision ['viʒən], *n.* vision, vue, *f.*

visionary ['viʒənəri], *a.* et *n.* visionnaire, *m., f.*

visit ['vizit], *n.* visite, *f.*; séjour (*a stay*), *m.*—*v.t.* visiter, aller, rendre visite à; **I visit the theatre twice a week**, je vais au théâtre deux fois par semaine.—*v.i.* faire des visites.

visitant ['vizitənt], *n.* visiteur, *m.*

visitation [vizi'teiʃən], *n.* inspection; épreuve, *f.*

visiting ['vizitiŋ], *a.* en visite, de visite.—*n.* visites, *f.pl.*

visitor ['vizitə], *n.* visiteur; (*official*) inspecteur, *m.*; **she has visitors**, elle a du monde.

visor ['vaizə], *n.* visière, *f.*

vista ['vistə], *n.* vue, perspective, *f.*

Vistula ['vistjulə], **the**, la Vistule, *f.*

visual ['viʒuəl], *a.* visuel.

visualize ['viʒjuəlaiz], *v.t.* se représenter.

vital [vaitl], *a.* vital, de vie; (*fig.*) essentiel.

vitality [vai'tæliti], *n.* vitalité, *f.*

vitalize ['vaitəlaiz], *v.t.* vivifier; (*fig.*) animer.

vitally ['vaitəli], *adv.* vitalement.

vitals [vaitlz], *n.pl.* parties vitales, *f.pl.*

vitamin ['vitəmin], *n.* vitamine, *f.*

vitiate ['viʃieit], *v.t.* vicier; (*fig.*) corrompre.
vitiation [viʃi'eiʃən], *n.* viciation; (*fig.*) corruption, *f.*
vitreous ['vitriəs], *a.* vitreux; (*Anat.*) vitré.
vitrify ['vitrifai], *v.t.* vitrifier.—*v.i.* se vitrifier.
vitriol ['vitriəl], *n.* vitriol, *m.*
vitriolic [vitri'olik], *a.* vitriolique.
vituperate [vi'tju:pəreit], *v.t.* vilipender, injurier.
vituperation [vitju:pə'reiʃən], *n.* reproches, *m.pl.*, invectives, *f.pl.*
vituperative [vi'tju:pərətiv], *a.* injurieux, hargneux.
vivacious [vi'veiʃəs], *a.* vif, vivace, animé.
vivaciously [vi'veiʃəsli], *adv.* vivement, avec vivacité.
vivaciousness [vi'veiʃəsnis], **vivacity** [vi'væsiti], *n.* vivacité, *f.*
vivary ['vivəri], *n.* vivier, *m.*
vivid ['vivid], *a.* vif, frappant.
vividly ['vividli], *adv.* d'une manière frappante, avec éclat.
vividness ['vividnis], *n.* vivacité, *f.*, éclat, *m.*
vivification [vivifi'keiʃən], *n.* vivification, *f.*
vivify ['vivifai], *v.t.* vivifier.
vivifying ['vivifaiiŋ], *a.* vivifiant.
viviparous [vi'vipərəs], *a.* vivipare.
vivisection [vivi'sekʃən], *n.* vivisection, *f.*
vivisector [vivi'sektə], *n.* vivisecteur, *m.*
vixen ['viksən], *n.* renarde (*bête*); mégère (*femme*), *f.*
vixenish ['viksəniʃ], *a.* de mégère, méchante.
viz. [viz] (*usu. read* namely), *adv.* à savoir.
vizier [vi'ziə], *n.* vizir, *m.*
vocabulary [vo'kæbjulari], *n.* vocabulaire, *m.*
vocal [voukl], *a.* vocal, de la voix.
vocalist ['voukəlist], *n.* chanteur, *m.*, chanteuse, *f.*
vocalize ['voukəlaiz], *v.t.*, *v.i.* vocaliser.
vocally ['voukəli], *adv.* par la voix, vocalement.
vocation [vo'keiʃən], *n.* vocation; profession, *f.*
vocational [vo'keiʃənəl], *a.* professionnel.
vocative ['vokətiv], *n.* vocatif, *m.*
vociferate [və'sifəreit], *v.t.*, *v.i.* vociférer.
vociferation [vəsifə'reiʃən], *n.* vociferation, *f.*
vociferous [və'sifərəs], *a.* qui vocifère, bruyant.
vociferously [və'sifərəsli], *adv.* en vociférant.
vodka ['vodkə], *n.* vodka, *f.*
vogue [voug], *n.* vogue, *f.*
voice [vois], *n.* voix, *f.*; *at the top of one's voice*, à tue-tête.—*v.t.* publier; exprimer.
void [void], *a.* vide, vacant; (*Law*) nul, de nul effet.—*n.* vide, espace vide, *m.*—*v.t.* vider; (*Law*) annuler.
voidable ['voidəbl], *a.* annulable.
volatile ['volətail], *a.* volatil; qui vole, volant; inconstant (*volage*).
volatility [volə'tiliti], *n.* volatilité, *f.*
volcanic [vol'kænik], *a.* volcanique.
volcano [vol'keinou], *n.* volcan, *m.*
vole [voul], *n.* campagnol, *m.*
volition [vo'liʃən], *n.* volition, volonté, *f.*
volley ['voli], *n.* décharge, salve (*de mousqueterie*); volée (*de canon*), *f.*—*v.t.* (*Ten.*) renvoyer (*la balle*) de volée.
volt [voult], *n.* (*Elec.*) volt, *m.*

voltage ['voultidʒ], *n.* voltage, *m.*
volte-face ['voltfa:s], *n.* volte-face, *f.*
volubility [volju'biliti], *n.* volubilité, *f.*
voluble ['voljubl], *a.* délié (*langue*); facile (*débit*).
volubly ['voljubli], *adv.* avec volubilité.
volume ['voljum], *n.* volume; tome (*livre*), *m.*
voluminous [və'lju:minəs], *a.* volumineux.
voluminously [və'lju:minəsli], *adv.* d'une manière volumineuse.
voluminousness [və'lju:minəsnis], *n.* grosseur, *f.*
voluntarily ['volantərili], *adv.* volontairement, spontanément.
voluntariness ['volantərinis], *n.* spontanéité, *f.*
voluntary ['volantəri], *a.* volontaire, spontané; libre; intentionnel.—*n.* (*Mus.*) improvisation, *f.*
volunteer [volan'tiə], *n.* volontaire, *m.*, *f.*—*v.t.* offrir volontairement.—*v.i.* offrir ses services; s'engager comme volontaire.
voluptuary [və'lʌptjuəri], *n.* voluptueux, épicurien, *m.*
voluptuous [və'lʌptjuəs], *a.* voluptueux.
voluptuously [və'lʌptjuəsli], *adv.* voluptueusement.
voluptuousness [və'lʌptjuəsnis], *n.* volupté, *f.*
volute [və'lju:t], *n.* volute, *f.*
voluted [və'lju:tid], *a.* voluté.
volution [və'lju:ʃən], *n.* spirale, *f.*
vomit ['vomit], *v.t.*, *v.i.* vomir.—*n.* vomissement, *m.*
voodoo ['vu:du:], *n.* vaudou, *m.*
voracious [və'reiʃəs], *a.* vorace.
voraciously [və'reiʃəsli], *adv.* avec voracité.
voraciousness [və'reiʃəsnis], **voracity** [və'ræsiti], *n.* voracité, *f.*
vortex ['vo:teks], *n.* (*pl.* **vortices** ['vo:tisi:z]) tourbillon, *m.*
vortical ['vo:tikl], *a.* tourbillonnant, en tourbillon.
votaress ['voutəris], *n.* adoratrice, *f.*
votary ['voutəri], *n.* adorateur; (*fig.*) admirateur, *m.*
vote [vout], *n.* vote, *m.*; voix, *f.*—*v.t.*, *v.i.* voter.
voter ['voutə], *n.* votant, *m.*
voting ['voutiŋ], *n.* vote, *m.*; *voting-paper*, bulletin de vote, *m.*
votive ['voutiv], *a.* votif, voué.
vouch [vautʃ], *v.t.* attester; affirmer.—*v.i.* témoigner (*de*); répondre (*de*).
voucher ['vautʃə], *n.* garant, *m.*, garantie; pièce justificative, *f.*; *luncheon voucher*, bon de repas, *m.*
vouchsafe [vautʃ'seif], *v.t.* daigner, accorder.
vow [vau], *n.* vœu, *m.*—*v.t.* vouer.—*v.i.* faire un vœu; jurer.
vowel ['vauəl], *n.* voyelle, *f.*
voyage ['voiidʒ], *n.* voyage (*par mer*), *m.*
voyager ['voiidʒə], *n.* voyageur, passager, *m.*
vulcanite ['vʌlkənait], *n.* caoutchouc vulcanisé, *m.*, ébonite, *f.*
vulcanize ['vʌlkənaiz], *v.t.* vulcaniser.
vulgar ['vʌlgə], *a.* vulgaire, commun.
vulgarism ['vʌlgərizm], *n.* expression vulgaire, *f.*
vulgarity [vʌl'gæriti], *n.* vulgarité, grossièreté, *f.*; mauvais goût, *m.*
vulgarize ['vʌlgəraiz], *v.t.* vulgariser.

vulnerability [vʌlnərə'biliti], *n.* vulnérabilité, *f.*
vulnerable ['vʌlnərəbl], *a.* vulnérable.
vulpine ['vʌlpain], *a.* de renard; (*fig.*) rusé.
vulture ['vʌltʃə], *n.* vautour, *m.*

W

W, w ['dʌbəlju:]. vingt-troisième lettre de l'alphabet, *m.*
wad [wɒd], *n.* bourre (*armes à feu etc.*), *f.*; tampon, paquet (*faisceau*), *m.*—*v.t.* bourrer (*armes à feu etc.*); ouater (*vêtement etc.*).
wadded ['wɒdid], *a.* ouaté (*de*).
wadding ['wɒdiŋ], *n.* bourre (*armes à feu*); ouate (*rembourrage*), *f.*
waddle [wɒdl], *v.i.* se dandiner.
waddling ['wɒdliŋ], *n.* dandinement, *m.*
wade [weid], *v.t.* traverser à gué.—*v.i.* marcher (*dans l'eau ou dans la vase*).
wafer ['weifə], *n.* pain à cacheter, *m.*; gaufrette; (*R.-C. Ch.*) hostie, *f.*
waffle [wɒfl], *n.* gaufre, *f.*
waffle iron ['wɒflaiən], *n.* gaufrier, *m.*
waft [wɒft], *v.t.* porter, transporter; faire flotter.
wag [wæg], *n.* badin, plaisant, farceur, *m.*—*v.t.* remuer, agiter.—*v.i.* s'agiter, remuer, se mouvoir.
wage [weidʒ], *v.t.* faire.—*n.* [WAGES].
wager ['weidʒə], *n.* gageure, *f.*, pari, *m.*—*v.t.* gager, parier.
wages ['weidʒiz], *n.pl.* gages (*de serviteur*), *m.pl.*; salaire, *m.*, paye (*d'ouvrier*), *f.*
waggery ['wægəri], *n.* espièglerie, plaisanterie, *f.*
waggish ['wægiʃ], *a.* badin, malin, facétieux.
waggishness ['wægiʃnis], *n.* badinage, *m.*, espièglerie, *f.*
waggle [wægl], *v.t.* remuer.—*v.i.* frétiller.
wagon ['wægən], *n.* charrette, *f.*, chariot, (*Mil.*) caisson, fourgon; (*Rail.*) wagon, *m.*
wagtail ['wægteil], *n.* hochequeue, *m.*
waif [weif], *n.* épave, *f.*
wail [weil], *v.t.* pleurer, lamenter.—*v.i.* pleurer, gémir, se lamenter.—*n.* (*also* **wailing** ['weiliŋ]) cri, *m.*, lamentation, plainte, *f.*
wain [wein], *n.* charrette, *f.*
wainscot ['weinzkət], *n.* lambris, *m.*, boiserie, *f.*
waist [weist], *n.* ceinture, taille, *f.*
waistband ['weistbænd], *n.* ceinture (*de pantalon etc.*), *f.*
waistcoat ['weis(t)kout], *n.* gilet, *m.*
wait [weit], *v.t.* attendre.—*v.i.* attendre; servir (*à table etc.*).—*n.* embuscade, *f.*, guet-apens, *m.*; attente, *f.*
waiter ['weitə], *n.* garçon, *m.*
waiting ['weitiŋ], *n.* attente, *f.*; service (*attentions*), *m.*; **no waiting**, stationnement interdit, *m.*
waiting-maid ['weitiŋmeid], **waiting-woman** ['weitiŋwumən] (*pl.* **-women**

[wimin]), *n.* femme de chambre; camériste (*de princesse etc.*), *f.*
waiting room ['weitiŋru:m], *n.* salle d'attente, *f.*.
waitress ['weitris], *n.* servante, fille de service, *f.*
waits [weits], *n.pl.* chanteurs de noëls, *m.pl.*
waive [weiv], *v.t.* écarter, mettre de côté; abandonner, renoncer.
wake (1) [weik], *v.t. irr.* éveiller, réveiller.—*v.i.* veiller (*ne pas se coucher*); se réveiller (*de sommeil*).—*n.* fête de village, *f.*
wake (2) [weik], *n.* sillage (*de navire*), *m.*; (*fig.*) suite, *f.*
wakeful ['weikful], *a.* éveillé; vigilant.
wakefulness ['weikfulnis], *n.* insomnie, *f.*
waken ['weikən], *v.t.* éveiller, réveiller.—*v.i.* s'éveiller, se réveiller.
waking ['weikiŋ], **wakening** ['weikniŋ], *a.* éveillé.—*n.* réveil, *m.*
wale [weil], *n.* marque (*de fouet*); côte (*de tissu*); (*pl.*) (*Naut.*) préceinte, *f.*
Wales [weilz]. le Pays de Galles, *m.*
walk [wɔ:k], *v.t.* parcourir, traverser à pied; faire à pied (*distance etc.*); mettre au pas (*cheval*).—*v.i.* marcher; aller à pied; se promener (*pour le plaisir*); aller au pas (*cheval*); **to walk over**, traverser *ou* parcourir à pied.—*n.* marche; promenade, *f.*, tour, *m.*; allée (*sentier*); démarche, allure, *f.*; pas (*de cheval*), *m.*; (*fig.*) sphère, *f.*, chemin, *m.*; **at a walk**, au pas.
walker ['wɔ:kə], *n.* promeneur, marcheur; piéton, *m.*
walkie-talkie ['wɔ:ki'tɔ:ki], *n.* (*fam.*) émetteur-récepteur portatif, *m.*
walking ['wɔ:kiŋ], *a.* ambulant; de marche.—*n.* la marche; promenade à pied, *f.*
walking stick ['wɔ:kiŋstik], *n.* canne, *f.*
walk-over ['wɔ:kouvə], *n.* (*Spt.*) **to have a walk-over**, remporter une victoire facile, gagner sans concurrent.
wall [wɔ:l], *n.* muraille, *f.*, mur, *m.*, paroi, *f.*, espalier (*à fruits*), *m.*—*v.t.* entourer de murailles; **to wall up**, murer.
wallet ['wɔlit], *n.* portefeuille, *m.*
wall-eye ['wɔ:lai], *n.* œil vairon, *m.*
wallflower ['wɔ:lflauə], *n.* giroflée jaune, ravenelle, *f.*
wall fruit ['wɔ:lfru:t], *n.* fruit d'espalier, *m.*
walling ['wɔ:liŋ], *n.* muraillement, *m.*; murs, *m.pl.*
wallop ['wɔləp], *v.t.* rosser.
walloping ['wɔləpiŋ], *n.* rossée, volée de coups, roulée, *f.*
wallow ['wɔlou], *v.i.* se vautrer, se rouler.
wall-paper ['wɔ:lpeipə], *n.* papier peint, *m.*
walnut ['wɔ:lnʌt], *n.* noix, *f.*; noyer (*bois*), *m.*
walnut tree ['wɔ:lnʌttri:], *n.* noyer, *m.*
walrus ['wɔ:lrəs], *n.* morse, cheval marin, *m.*
Walter ['wɔ:ltə]. Gauthier, *m.*
waltz [wɔ:l(t)s], *n.* valse, *f.*—*v.i.* valser.
waltzer ['wɔ:l(t)sə], *n.* valseur, *m.*
waltzing ['wɔ:l(t)siŋ], *n.* valse, *f.*
wan [wɔn], *a.* blême, pâle, pâlot.
wand [wɔnd], *n.* baguette, *f.*
wander ['wɔndə], *v.i.* errer; divaguer (*l'esprit*); délirer.
wanderer ['wɔndərə], *n.* vagabond, *m.*
wandering ['wɔndəriŋ], *a.* errant, vagabond; nomade (*tribu etc.*); (*fig.*) distrait.—*n.* course errante, divagation, *f.*; délire, *m.*

wanderlust ['wɔndəlʌst], *n.* manie des voyages, *f.*

wane [wein], *n.* déclin, *m.*; (*fig.*) décadence, *f.* —*v.i.* décroître (*lune*); (*fig.*) décliner.

wanly ['wɔnli], *adv.* avec pâleur.

wanness ['wɔnnis], *n.* pâleur, *f.*

want [wɔnt], *n.* besoin; manque; défaut (*absence*), *m.*; indigence, misère (*pauvreté*), *f.*; **for want of**, faute de.—*v.t.* avoir besoin de; manquer de; vouloir, désirer (*avoir envie de*); demander (*réclamer*).—*v.i.* manquer (*de*).

wanting ['wɔntiŋ], *a.* qui manque, manquant.

wanton ['wɔntən], *a.* folâtre (*capricieux*); licencieux, libertin (*impudique*); gratuit (*sans cause*).—*n.* débauchée, *f.*—*v.i.* folâtrer.

wantonly ['wɔntənli], *adv.* en folâtrant; gratuitement.

wantonness ['wɔntənnis], *n.* légèreté, *f.*; libertinage, *m.*

war [wɔ:], *n.* guerre, *f.*—*v.i.* faire la guerre (*à*), lutter (*contre*).

warble [wɔ:bl], *v.t., v.i.* gazouiller; (*fig.*) chanter.

warbler ['wɔ:blə], *n.* oiseau chanteur, *m.*; fauvette (*oiseau*), *f.*

warbling ['wɔ:bliŋ], *a.* mélodieux.—*n.* gazouillement, *m.*

ward [wɔ:d], *n.* pupille, *m., f.*; tutelle (*protection*); garde (*de serrure*); salle (*d'hôpital*), *f.*; arrondissement (*de ville*), *m.*—*v.i.* to **ward off**, parer, détourner.

warden [wɔ:dn], *n.* gardien; gouverneur, recteur (*d'université*); directeur (*de collège*), conservateur (*de jardin public*), *m.*

warder ['wɔ:də], *n.* gardien de prison, *m.*

wardress ['wɔ:dris], *n.* gardienne de prison, *f.*

wardrobe ['wɔ:droub], *n.* garde-robe; armoire (*meuble*), *f.*

ward-room ['wɔ:dru:m], *n.* (*Naut.*) carré des officiers, *m.*

ware [wɛə], *n.* (*collect.*) articles fabriqués, *m.pl.*; (*pl.*) marchandises, *f.pl.*

warehouse ['wɛəhaus], *n.* magasin; entrepôt, *m.*—*v.t.* emmagasiner.

warehousing ['wɛəhauziŋ], *n.* emmagasinage, *m.*

warfare ['wɔ:fɛə], *n.* la guerre, *f.*; les opérations, *f.pl.*

warily ['wɛərili], *adv.* prudemment, avec circonspection.

wariness ['wɛərinis], *n.* prudence, circonspection, *f.*

warlike ['wɔ:laik], *a.* guerrier, martial, belliqueux.

warlock ['wɔ:lɔk], *n.* sorcier, *m.*

warm [wɔ:m], *a.* chaud; (*fig.*) zélé, ardent; chaleureux (*accueil*).—*v.t.* chauffer; réchauffer (*ce qui s'était refroidi*); (*fig.*) échauffer.—*v.i.* chauffer, se chauffer, (*fig.*) s'animer.

warming ['wɔ:miŋ], *n.* chauffage, *m.*

warming pan ['wɔ:miŋpæn], *n.* bassinoire, *f.*

warmly ['wɔ:mli], *adv.* chaudement; (*fig.*) vivement.

war-monger ['wɔ:mʌŋgə], *n.* belliciste, *m., f.*

warmth [wɔ:mθ], *n.* chaleur; (*fig.*) ardeur, *f.*

war-office ['wɔ:rɔfis], *n.* ministère de la guerre, *m.*

warn [wɔ:n], *v.t.* avertir, prévenir (*de*); to **warn against**, mettre en garde contre.

warning ['wɔ:niŋ], *n.* avertissement, avis, *m.*

warp [wɔ:p], *n.* chaîne (*tissage*), *f.*—*v.t.* ourdir (*tissage*); faire déjeter (*bois*); (*Naut.*) touer; (*fig.*) fausser, pervertir.—*v.i.* se déjeter, se déformer (*gauchir*); (*fig.*) dévier (*de*).

warping ['wɔ:piŋ], *n.* ourdissage (*tissage*); déjettement, gauchissement (*de bois*), *m.*

warrant ['wɔrənt], *n.* autorisation, garantie, *f.*; ordre, mandat; mandat d'amener, *m.*; (*fig.*) justification, *f.*—*v.t.* garantir, autoriser.

warrant officer ['wɔrəntɔfisə], *n.* (*Mil.*) adjudant; (*Naut.*) premier maître, *m.*

warrantor ['wɔrəntə], *n.* (*Law*) garant, *m.*

warranty ['wɔrənti], *n.* garantie, *f.*

warren ['wɔrən], *n.* garenne, *f.*

warrior ['wɔriə], *n.* guerrier, soldat, *m.*

Warsaw ['wɔ:sɔ:], Varsovie, *f.*

wart [wɔ:t], *n.* verrue, *f.*, durillon, *m.*

warted ['wɔ:tid], **warty** ['wɔ:ti], *a.* couvert de verrues; (*Bot.*) verruqueux.

wary ['wɛəri], *a.* avisé, prudent; défiant.

wash [wɔʃ], *n.* blanchissage, *m.*, lessive (*de linge*), *f.*; (*Paint.*) lavis; sillage (*de navire*), *m.*—*v.t.* blanchir (*linge*); (*fig.*) mouiller, laver.—*v.i.* se laver; faire la lessive (*blanchisseuse etc.*); to **wash up**, faire la vaisselle.

washable ['wɔʃəbl], *a.* lavable.

washbasin ['wɔʃbeisn], *n.* lavabo, *m.*, cuvette, *f.*

washer ['wɔʃə], *n.* laveur, *m.*; machine à laver; (*Tech.*) rondelle, *f.*

washer-woman ['wɔʃəwumən], *n.* (*pl.* -**women** [wimin]) blanchisseuse, *f.*

wash-house ['wɔʃhaus], *n.* lavoir, *m.*, buanderie, *f.*

washing ['wɔʃiŋ], *n.* lavage; blanchissage (*du linge*), *m.*

washing machine ['wɔʃiŋməʃi:n], *n.* machine à laver, *f.*

wash-leather ['wɔʃleðə], *n.* peau de chamois, *f.*

wash-stand ['wɔʃstænd], *n.* toilette, *f.*; lavabo (*petit*), *m.*

wash-tub ['wɔʃtʌb], *n.* baquet, *m.*

washy ['wɔʃi], *a.* humide, mouillé; (*fig.*) fade.

wasp [wɔsp], *n.* guêpe, *f.*; **wasps' nest**, guêpier, *m.*

waspish ['wɔspiʃ], *a.* irascible, irritable.

waspishness ['wɔspiʃnis], *n.* humeur irascible, *f.*

wastage ['weistidʒ], *n.* gaspillage, *m.*

waste [weist], *a.* de rebut; sans valeur; perdu (*inemployé*); inculte (*terre*).—*n.* perte (*mauvais emploi*), *f.*; déchet (*à nettoyer*); gaspillage; rebut, *m.*; terre inculte, *f.*—*v.t.* gaspiller; perdre (*employer mal*); gâcher (*faire sans soin*); ravager, dévaster (*piller*).—*v.i.* s'user, s'épuiser; to **waste away**, dépérir, maigrir.

waste-book ['weistbuk], *n.* brouillard, *m.*

wasteful ['weistful], *a.* dissipateur, prodigue.

wastefulness ['weistfulnis], *n.* prodigalité, perte, *f.*, gaspillage, *m.*

waste paper ['weist'peipə], *n.* papier de rebut, *f.*

waste-paper basket ['weistpeipə'bɑ:skit], *n.* corbeille à papier, *f.*

waste-pipe ['weistpaip], *n.* tuyau de dégagement; écoulement, *m.*

waster ['weistə], **wastrel** ['weistril], *n.* prodigue, *m., f.*, gaspilleur, *m.*

wasting ['weistiŋ], a. qui épuise.—n. dépérissement, m., consumption (du corps), f.
watch [wotʃ], n. montre; veille (nocturne); vigilance (attention); garde, f.; (Naut.) quart, m.—v.t. veiller sur, surveiller, regarder, épier.—v.i. veiller (ne pas dormir); prendre, garde (faire attention); monter la garde; (Naut.) faire le quart.
watch-dog ['wotʃdɔg], n. chien de garde, m.
watcher ['wotʃə], n. surveillant, veilleur, m.
watch fire ['wotʃfaiə], n. feu de bivouac, m.
watchful ['wotʃful], a. vigilant, attentif.
watchfulness ['wotʃfulnis], n. vigilance, f.
watching ['wotʃiŋ], n. surveillance, f.
watch-maker ['wotʃmeikə], n. horloger, m.
watch-making ['wotʃmeikiŋ], n. horlogerie, f.
watchman ['wotʃmən], n. (pl. -men [men]) gardien; veilleur de nuit, m.
watch-tower ['wotʃtauə], n. tour de guet, f.
watchword ['wotʃwəːd], n. mot d'ordre, m.
water ['wɔːtə], a. d'eau, à eau; aquatique. —n. eau; marée (flux), f., (fig.) ordre, rang, m.; **drinking water**, eau potable; **fresh water**, eau douce (pas salée).—v.t. arroser; donner à boire à, abreuver (animal); mettre de l'eau dans, couper (diluer); moirer (étoffe).
water bottle ['wɔːtəbɔtl], n. carafe, f.; (Mil. etc.) bidon, m.; bouillotte (pour chauffer le lit), f.
water carrier ['wɔːtəkæriə], n. porteur d'eau; broc (à eau), m.
water cart ['wɔːtəkaːt], n. voiture d'arrosage, f.
water closet ['wɔːtəklɔzit], n. toilettes, f.pl.; cabinet d'aisances, m.
water color ['wɔːtəkʌlə], n. aquarelle, f.
watercress ['wɔːtəkres], n. cresson, cresson de fontaine, m.
water cure ['wɔːtəkjuə], n. hydrothérapie, f.
watered ['wɔːtəd], a. arrosé; moiré (étoffe).
waterfall ['wɔːtəfɔːl], n. cascade; chute d'eau, f.
water-fowl ['wɔːtəfaul], n. oiseau aquatique, m.
waterfront ['wɔːtəfrʌnt], n. les quais, m.pl., port, m.
water hen ['wɔːtəhen], n. poule d'eau, f.
wateriness ['wɔːtərinis], n. aquosité, f.
watering ['wɔːtəriŋ], n. arrosage (plantes), m.; irrigation (terre), f.; abreuvage (animaux); moirage (étoffe), m.
watering can ['wɔːtəriŋkæn], n. arrosoir, m.
watering place ['wɔːtəriŋpleis], n. ville d'eaux, station thermale, f.; abreuvoir (pour animaux), m.
water jug ['wɔːtədʒʌg], n. pot à eau, m.
water level ['wɔːtəlevl], n. niveau d'eau, m.
water lily ['wɔːtəlili], n. nénuphar, m.
water line ['wɔːtəlain], n. ligne de flottaison, f.
water-logged ['wɔːtəlɔgd], a. envahi par les eaux.
watermark ['wɔːtəmaːk], n. étiage (de rivière); filigrane (sur papier), m.
water-melon ['wɔːtəmelən], n. melon d'eau, m., pastèque, f.
water mill ['wɔːtəmil], n. moulin à eau, m.
water pipe ['wɔːtəpaip], n. tuyau d'eau, m.
water plant ['wɔːtəplaːnt], n. plante aquatique, f.

water polo ['wɔːtəpoulou], n. polo nautique, m.
water-power ['wɔːtəpauə], n. force hydraulique, f.
water pressure ['wɔːtəpreʃə], n. pression d'eau, f.
waterproof ['wɔːtəpruːf], a. and n. imperméable, m.—v.t. rendre imperméable, cirer (un tissu).
water rat ['wɔːtəræt], n. rat d'eau, m.
water-rate ['wɔːtəreit], n. taux d'abonnement aux eaux de la ville, m.
watershed ['wɔːtəʃed], n. versant, m.
waterspout ['wɔːtəspaut], n. trombe, f.; tuyau de descente, m.
water tank ['wɔːtətæŋk], n. réservoir à eau, m., citerne, f.
water-tight ['wɔːtətait], a. étanche.
water-works ['wɔːtəwəːks], n.pl. établissement pour la distribution des eaux, m., machine hydraulique, f.
watery ['wɔːtəri], a. aqueux; mouillé, plein d'eau; (poet.) humide.
watt [wot], n. (Elec.) watt, m.
wattage ['wotidʒ], n. (Elec.) wattage, m.
wattle [wotl], n. claie (d'osier etc.), f.—v.t. clayonner.
wave [weiv], n. vague, f., flot, m., lame, ondulation; (poet.) onde, f.; signe (de la main), m.; **permanent wave**, permanente, indéfrisable, f.; **long waves**, (Rad.) grandes ondes, f.; **short waves**, petites ondes, ondes courtes, f.pl.—v.t. agiter, faire signe de (la main); onduler (cheveux).—v.i. ondoyer, onduler, flotter; faire signe (à).
waved [weivd], a. ondulé.
wave-length ['weivleŋθ], n. longueur d'onde, f.
waver ['weivə], v.i. hésiter, vaciller, balancer.
waverer ['weivərə], n. personne indécise, f., esprit vacillant, m.
wavering ['weivəriŋ], a. indécis, vacillant, irrésolu.—n. hésitation, indécision, f.
waving ['weiviŋ], n. ondoiement, m., ondulation (blé etc.), f.; geste (de la main), m.
wavy ['weivi], a. ondoyant, onduleux.
wax [wæks], n. cire; poix (de cordonnier); (colloq.) colère, f.—v.t. cirer, enduire de cire. —v.i. croître (lune), s'accroître; devenir.
wax candle ['wæks'kændl], n. bougie, f.
waxen ['wæksn], a. de cire; cireux.
wax taper ['wæks'teipə], n. rat de cave; (Eccles.) cierge, m.
waxwing ['wækswiŋ], n. (Orn.) jaseur, m.
waxwork ['wækswəːk], n. ouvrage de cire, m.; (pl.) figures de cire, f., pl.
waxy ['wæksi], a. cireux.
way [wei], n. chemin, m., route, voie, f.; passage; côté, sens, m., direction; manière, façon, mode, f.; moyen, m., méthode, f.; état (condition), m.; **a long way off**, loin, très loin; **a long way** (by far), de beaucoup; **by the way**, à propos.
way-bill ['weibil], n. feuille de route, f.
wayfarer ['weifɛərə], n. voyageur, m.
wayfaring ['weifɛəriŋ], a. qui voyage.
waylay [wei'lei], v.t. guetter, guetter au passage.
wayside ['weisaid], a. au bord de la route.— n. bord de la route, m.
wayward ['weiwəd], a. capricieux, entêté.

waywardness ['weiwədnis], *n.* humeur capricieuse, *f.*

we [wi:], *pron.* nous; (*indef.*) on; *we Frenchmen*, nous autres Français.

weak [wi:k], *a.* faible, infirme, débile.

weaken [wi:kn], *v.t.* affaiblir; atténuer.—*v.i.* s'affaiblir.

weakening ['wi:kniŋ], *n.* affaiblissement, *m.*

weakling ['wi:kliŋ], *n.* être faible, faiblard, *m.*

weakly ['wi:kli], *a.* faible; infirme, débile.—*adv.* faiblement, sans force.

weak-minded ['wi:k'maindid], *a.* d'esprit faible.

weakness ['wi:knis], *n.* faiblesse; débilité, *f.*; (*fig.*) faible, *m.*

weak-spirited ['wi:k'spiritid], *a.* mou, sans courage.

weal [wiːl], *n.* bien, bien-être, bonheur, *m.*; marque (*sur la peau*), *f.*

wealth [welθ], *n.* richesse, *f.*, richesses, *f.pl.*; profusion, *f.*

wealthy ['welθi], *a.* riche, opulent.

wean [wi:n], *v.t.* sevrer; (*fig.*) détacher.

weaning ['wi:niŋ], *n.* sevrage, *m.*

weanling ['wi:nliŋ], *n.* enfant *ou* animal en sevrage, *m.*

weapon [wepn], *n.* arme, *f.*

wear [wɛə], *v.t. irr.* porter (*habits*); mettre (*enfiler*); *to wear out*, user, (*fig.*) épuiser, lasser.—*v.i.* s'user (*s'élimer*); se porter (*habits*); (*fig.*) se conserver.—*n.* usage (*port*), *m.*; usure (*élimage*), *f.*

wearable ['wɛərəbl], *a.* mettable.

wearied ['wiərid], *a.* fatigué, las; (*fig.*) ennuyé.

wearily ['wiərili], *adv.* péniblement, d'un air las.

weariness ['wiərinis], *n.* fatigue, lassitude, *f.*; (*fig.*) ennui, *m.*

wearisome ['wiərisəm], *a.* ennuyeux, lassant.

wearisomeness ['wiərisəmnis], *n.* nature ennuyeuse, *f.*

weary ['wiəri], *a.* fatigué, las, ennuyé; ennuyeux (*chose*).—*v.t.* lasser, fatiguer; ennuyer.

weasel [wi:zl], *n.* belette, *f.*

weather ['weðə], *a.* du côté du vent.—*n.* temps, *m.*; (*fig.*) tempête, *f.*—*v.t.* résister à (*tempête etc.*); (*fig.*) tenir tête à.

weather-beaten ['weðəbi:tn], *a.* battu par la tempête; (*fig.*) fatigué; hâlé.

weathercock ['weðəkɔk], *n.* girouette, *f.*

weather-glass ['weðəgla:s], *n.* baromètre, *m.*

weather-proof ['weðəpru:f], *a.* à l'épreuve du (*mauvais*) temps, imperméable.

weather report ['weðəripɔːt], *n.* bulletin météorologique, *m.*

weather ship ['weðəʃip], *n.* navire météorologique, *m.*

weave [wi:v], *n.* (*Tex.*) tissage, *m.*—*v.t., v.i. irr.* tisser; tresser (*entrelacer*).

weaver ['wi:və], *n.* tisserand, *m.*

weaving ['wi:viŋ], *n.* tissage, *m.*

web [web], *n.* tissu, *m.*; sangle (*pour selle*); toile (*d'araignée*), *f.*

webbed [webd], **webby** ['webi], *a.* palmé.

webbing ['webiŋ], *n.* sangles (*de chaise, lit etc.*), *f.pl.*

web-footed ['webfutid], *a.* palmipède.

wed [wed], *v.t.* épouser, se marier avec.—*v.i.* se marier.

wedded ['wedid], *a.* marié (*à*); conjugal.

wedding ['wediŋ], *a.* de noces, de mariage.—*n.* noce, *f.*, noces, *f.pl.*, mariage, *m.*

wedding ring ['wediŋriŋ], *n.* alliance, *f.*

wedge [wedʒ], *n.* coin, *m.*; cale (*pour tenir immobile*), *f.*—*v.t.* serrer; caler; coincer.

wedge-shaped ['wedʒʃeipt], *a.* en forme de coin, cunéiforme.

wedlock ['wedlɔk], *n.* mariage, *m.*

Wednesday ['wenzd(e)i]. mercredi, *m.*; *Ash Wednesday*, mercredi des Cendres.

weed [wi:d], *n.* mauvaise herbe, *f.*; *widow's weeds*, vêtements de deuil, *m.pl.*—*v.t.* sarcler; (*fig.*) nettoyer; *to weed out*, extirper.

weeder ['wi:də], *n.* sarcleur (*personne*); sarcloir (*outil*), *m.*

weeding ['wi:diŋ], *n.* sarclage, *m.*

weed killer ['wi:dkilə], *n.* herbicide, *m.*

weedy ['wi:di], *a.* plein de mauvaises herbes.

week [wi:k], *n.* semaine, *f.*; *this day week*, d'aujourd'hui en huit (*avenir*); il y a huit jours (*passé*).

weekday ['wi:kdei], *n.* jour ouvrable, jour de semaine, *m.*

week-end ['wi:k'end], *n.* fin de la semaine, *f.*, week-end, *m.*

weekly ['wi:kli], *a.* de la semaine; hebdomadaire (*revue*).—*n.* hebdomadaire, *m.*—*adv.* par semaine, tous les huit jours.

weep [wi:p], *v.t., v.i. irr.* pleurer; *to weep bitterly*, pleurer à chaudes larmes.

weeping ['wi:piŋ], *a.* qui pleure, éploré; (*Bot.*) pleureur; *weeping willow*, saule pleureur, *m.*—*n.* pleurs, *m.pl.*, larmes, *f.pl.*

weever ['wi:və], *n.* (*Ichth.*) vive, *f.*

weft [weft], *n.* trame, *f.*

weigh [wei], *v.t.* peser; (*fig.*) juger; (*Naut.*) lever (*l'ancre*).—*v.i.* peser.

weigh-bridge ['weibridʒ], *n.* pont à bascule, *m.*

weighing ['weiiŋ], *n.* pesage, *m.*; *weighing machine*, bascule, *f.*

weight [weit], *n.* poids, *m.*; *atomic weight*, masse atomique, *f.*

weighted ['weitid], *a.* chargé (*de*).

weightily ['weitili], *adv.* pesamment.

weightless ['weitlis], *a.* sans poids.

weightlessness ['weitlisnis], *n.* apesanteur, *f.*

weighty ['weiti], *a.* pesant, lourd; (*fig.*) important.

weir [wiə], *n.* barrage, déversoir, *m.*

weird [wiəd], *a.* fantastique, étrange.

weirdness ['wiədnis], *n.* étrangeté, magie, *f.*

welcome ['welkəm], *a.* bienvenu, agréable (*chose*); libre (*à profiter de quelque chose*).—*n.* bienvenue, *f.*, accueil, *m.*; *to bid (someone) welcome*, souhaiter la bienvenue à (quelqu'un).—*int.* soyez le bienvenu.—*v.t.* souhaiter la bienvenue à.   bien accueillir. *you are welcome*, see **mention**.

weld [weld], *v.t.* souder; (*fig.*) unir.—*n.* soudure, *f.*

welder ['weldə], *n.* soudeur, *m.*

welding ['weldiŋ], *n.* soudure, *f.*

welfare ['welfɛə], *n.* bien-être, bien, *m.*; *Welfare State*, état providence, *m.*

well (1) [wel], *n.* puits, *m.*; (*fig.*) source, *f.*; *ink-well*, encrier, *m.*—*v.i.* jaillir (*de*).

well (2) [wel], *a.* bien, en bonne santé; bon, heureux (*fortuné*); utile, profitable; *to get well*, se rétablir; *well off*, aisé (*riche*).—

adv. bien; très, fort; comme il faut; *well!* eh bien! *well done!* très bien! bravo! *well, I never!* pas possible!

well-being ['wel'bi:iŋ], *n.* bien-être, *m.*

well-informed ['welin'fɔ:md], *a.* instruit; bien renseigné.

wellingtons ['weliŋtənz], *n.pl.* demi-bottes, *f.pl.*

well-known ['welnoun], *a.* bien connu, célèbre.

well-meaning ['wel'mi:niŋ], *a.* bien intentionné.

well-meant ['wel'ment], *a.* fait à bonne intention.

well-nigh ['welnai], *adv.* presque.

well-timed ['wel'taimd], *a.* à propos, fait à propos.

well-to-do ['weltə'du:], *a.* très aisé, cossu.

well-wisher ['welwiʃə], *n.* ami, partisan, *m.*

Welsh [welʃ], *a.* gallois, du pays de Galles.—*n.* gallois (*langue*), *m.*; *the Welsh,* les Gallois, *m.pl.*

Welshman ['welʃmən], *n.* (*pl.* **-men** [men]) Gallois, *m.*

welt [welt], *n.* bordure (*de gant*); trépointe (*de semelle*), *f.*

welter ['weltə], *n.* confusion, *f.*—*v.i.* se vautrer, se rouler.

wen [wen], *n.* loupe, *f.*; goitre, *m.*

wench [wentʃ], *n.* donzelle; (*pej.*) souillon, *f.*

wend [wend], *v.t., v.i.* aller; *to wend one's way,* se diriger (*vers*).

wer(e)wolf ['wɑ:wulf], *n.* loup-garou, *m.*

west [west], *a.* de l'ouest, occidental.—*n.* ouest, occident, couchant, *m.*—*adv.* à l'ouest.

westerly ['westəli], *a.* d'ouest.—*adv.* vers l'ouest.

western ['westən], *a.* de l'ouest, occidental, ouest, d'occident; à l'ouest (*vue*).—*n.* (*Cine.*) western, *m.*

westward ['westwəd], *adv.* à l'ouest.

wet [wet], *a.* mouillé, humide; pluvieux (*temps*); *it is wet,* il pleut; *to get wet,* se mouiller; *wet through,* mouillé jusqu'aux os, trempé.—*n.* humidité; pluie, *f.*—*v.t. irr.* mouiller, humecter; arroser.

wetness ['wetnis], *n.* humidité, *f.*; état pluvieux, *m.*

wetting ['wetiŋ], *n.* trempage, *m.*

whack [hwæk], *n.* grand coup, *m.*; (*fam.*) part, *f.*—*v.t.* frapper, battre.

whale [hweil], *n.* baleine, *f.*

whalebone ['hweilboun], *n.* baleine, *f.*

whale oil ['hweiloil], *n.* huile de baleine, *f.*

whaler ['hweilə], *n.* baleinier, *m.*

wharf [hwɔ:f], *n.* (*pl.* **wharfs** [hwɔ:fs], **wharves** [hwɔ:vz]) quai, embarcadère, débarcadère; entrepôt (*pour marchandises*), *m.*

what [hwɔt], *a.* quel, *m.*, quelle, *f.*, quels, *m.pl.*, quelles, *f.pl.*—*pron.rel.* ce qui, ce que; qui, que; quoi.—*inter. pron.* qu'est-ce qui? que? qu'est-ce ,que? quoi? *what!* comment!

whatever [hwɔt'evə], **whatsoever** [hwɔtsou'evə], *pron.* and *a.* quoi que ce soit; quelque . . . que; tout ce qui, tout ce que (*all that*).

whatnot ['hwɔtnɔt], *n.* étagère, *f.*

whatsoever [WHATEVER].

wheat [hwi:t], *n.* blé, froment, *m.*

wheaten [hwi:tn], *a.* de froment.

wheedle [hwi:dl], *v.t.* cajoler, câliner.

wheedling ['hwi:dliŋ], *a.* cajoleur, câlin.—*n.* cajolerie, câlinerie, *f.*

wheel [hwi:l], *n.* roue, *f.*; volant (*pour conduire*); rouet (*pour filer*), *m.*; révolution, *f.*; tour, cercle (*rotation*); soleil (*feu d'artifice*), *m.*; *driving wheel,* roue motrice, *f.*; *flywheel,* volant, *m.*—*v.t.* rouler, faire tourner; brouetter; voiturer.—*v.i.* rouler (*sur des roues*); tourner, se tourner (*en cercle*); tournoyer (*pirouetter*); (*Mil.*) faire une conversion; *to wheel round,* faire volte-face.

wheel-barrow ['hwi:lbærou], *n.* brouette, *f.*

wheel-chair ['hwi:ltʃɛə], *n.* voiture de malade, *f.*, fauteuil roulant, *m.*

wheeled [hwi:ld], *a.* à roues.

wheeling ['hwi:liŋ], *n.* (*Mil.*) conversion, *f.*; tournoiement (*d'oiseau*), *m.*

wheelwright ['hwi:lrait], *n.* charron, *m.*

wheeze [hwi:z], *v.i.* siffler en respirant.

wheezing ['hwi:ziŋ], *n.* sifflement, *m.*

wheezy ['hwi:zi], *a.* poussif, asthmatique.

whelk [hwelk], *n.* buccin, *m.*

whelp [hwelp], *n.* petit (d'un fauve), *m.*—*v.i.* mettre bas.

when [hwen], *conj.* quand, lorsque; que, où; *the day when I saw him,* le jour où je l'ai vu.—*inter. adv.* quand est-ce que? quand?

whence [hwens], *adv.* d'où.

whenever [hwen'evə], **whensoever** [hwensou'evə], *adv.* toutes les fois que, quand, à n'importe quel moment que.

where [hwɛə], *adv.* où; là où.

whereabouts ['hwɛərəbauts], *adv.* où à peu près.—*n.* to know someone's *whereabouts,* savoir où est quelqu'un.

whereas [hwɛər'æz], *adv.* au lieu que, tandis que; (*Law*) vu que.

whereat [hwɛər'æt], *adv.* à quoi, de quoi; sur quoi.

whereby [hwɛə'bai], *adv.* par lequel, par où.

wherefore ['hwɛəfɔ:], *adv.* pourquoi, c'est pourquoi.

wherein [hwɛər'in], *adv.* en quoi, dans lequel, où.

whereof [hwɛər'ɔv], *adv.* dont, de quoi, duquel.

whereon [hwɛər'ɔn], **whereupon** ['hwɛərə'pɔn], *adv.* sur quoi, sur lequel; là-dessus.

wheresoever [hwɛəsou'evə], [WHEREVER].

wherever [hwɛər'evə], *adv.* partout où, n'importe où.

wherewith [hwɛə'wið], *adv.* avec quoi; de quoi.

wherewithal [hwɛəwið'ɔ:l], *n. to find the wherewithal to . . .,* trouver les moyens de . . . *ou* l'argent pour . . . .

wherry ['hweri], *n.* bachot, *m.*

whet [hwet], *v.t.* aiguiser, affiler; (*fig.*) stimuler.—*n.* aiguisement, repassage; (*fig.*) stimulant, *m.*

whether ['hweðə], *conj.* soit que; si, que; *whether . . . or,* soit . . . soit; si . . . ou, que . . . ou.

whetstone ['hwetstoun], *n.* pierre à aiguiser, *f.*

whey [hwei], *n.* petit lait, *m.*

which [hwitʃ], *a.* quel, *m.*, quelle, *f.*, quels, *m.pl.*, quelles, *f.pl.*; lequel, *m.*, laquelle, *f.*, lesquels, *m.pl.*, lesquelles, *f.pl.*—*rel. pron.*

qui, que, lequel, *m.*, laquelle, *f.*, lesquels, *m.pl.*, lesquelles, *f.pl.* ; ce qui, ce que (*that which*), *m.*

whichever [hwitʃ'evə], *pron.* lequel, *m.*, laquelle, *f.*, lesquels, *m.pl.*, lesquelles, *f.pl.* ; quelque . . . que ; *whichever you buy*, n'importe lequel que vous achetiez.

whiff [hwif], *n.* bouffée, haleine, *f.*—*v.t.* lancer en bouffées.

while [hwail], *n.* temps, *m.* ; *a little while ago*, il y a peu de temps ; *it is not worth while*, cela n'en vaut pas la peine.—*v.t.* passer, faire passer ; *to while away the time*, tuer le temps.—(*also* **whilst** [hwailst]), *conj.* pendant que (*au cours de*) ; tandis que (*par contraste*) ; tant que (*tout le temps que*) ; en, tout en (*suivi d'un participe présent*).

whilst [WHILE].

whim [hwim], *n.* caprice, *m.*

whimper ['hwimpə], *v.i.* pleurnicher.

whimpering ['hwimpəriŋ], *a.* pleurnicheur, geignard.—*n.* pleurnichement, *m.*

whimsical ['hwimzikl], *a.* fantasque ; capricieux.

whimsically ['hwimzikli], *adv.* capricieusement, fantasquement.

whin [hwin], *n.* ajonc, genêt épineux, *m.*

whine [hwain], *v.i.* se plaindre, geindre, pleurnicher.—*n.* pleurnichement, *m.*

whining ['hwainiŋ], *a.* plaintif, dolent.—*n.* gémissement, geignement, *m.* ; (*fig.*) plaintes, *f.pl.*

whinny ['hwini], *v.i.* hennir.—*n.* hennissement, *m.*

whip [hwip], *n.* fouet, *m.* ; cravache (*de cavalier*), *f.* ; (*Parl.*) secrétaire d'un parti, appel fait aux membres d'un parti, *m.*—*v.t.* fouetter ; (*fig.*) battre.

whip-cord ['hwipkɔːd], *n.* fouet ; (*Tex.*) fil à fouet, *m.*

whip hand ['hwiphænd], *n.* dessus, avantage, *m.*

whip-lash ['hwiplæʃ], *n.* mèche (de fouet), *f.*

whipper-in ['hwipər'in], *n.* piqueur, *m.*

whipper-snapper ['hwipəsnæpə], *n.* petit bout d'homme, *m.*

whippet ['hwipit], *n.* lévrier (de course), *m.*

whipping ['hwipiŋ], *n.* coups de fouet, *m.pl.*

whipping-top ['hwipiŋtɔp], *n.* sabot, *m.*

whir [hwəː], *v.i.* tourner avec bruit ; vrombir.—(*also* **whirring** ['hwəːriŋ]), *n.* bruissement, ronronnement, *m.*

whirl [hwəːl], *v.t.* faire tourner, faire tournoyer.—*v.i.* tournoyer, tourbillonner, pirouetter.—*n.* tournoiement ; tourbillon (*de poussière etc.*), *m.*

whirligig ['hwəːligig], *n.* tourniquet, *m.* ; pirouette, *f.*

whirlpool ['hwəːlpuːl], *n.* tourbillon (d'eau), *m.*

whirlwind ['hwəːlwind], *n.* tourbillon, cyclone, *m.*

whirring [WHIR]

whisk [hwisk], *n.* vergette, époussette, verge (*à œufs etc.*), *f.*—*v.t.* épousseter ; fouetter (*crème*) ; battre (*œufs*).—*v.i.* passer rapidement.

whiskered ['hwiskəd], *a.* à favoris ; à moustaches (*animal*).

whiskers ['hwiskəz], *n.* favoris, *m.pl.* ; moustache (*de chat etc.*), *f.*

whisky, whiskey ['hwiski], *n.* whisky, *m.*

whisper ['hwispə], *n.* chuchotement, *m.*—*v.t.* chuchoter, dire à l'oreille.—*v.i.* chuchoter, parler tout bas.

whispering ['hwispəriŋ], *n.* chuchotement, *m.*

whist [hwist], *n.* whist, *m.*

whistle [hwisl], *n.* sifflet ; coup de sifflet ; sifflement (*du vent*) ; (*colloq.*) gosier, bec (*gorge*), *m.*—*v.t.*, *v.i.* siffler.

whistler ['hwislə], *n.* siffleur, *m.*

whistling ['hwisliŋ], *a.* sifflant.—*n.* sifflement, coup de sifflet, *m.*

whit [hwit], *n.* iota, point, atome, brin, *m.*

white [hwait], *a.* blanc ; (*fig.*) sans tache, pur.—*n.* blanc ; aubier (*de bois*), *m.*

whitebait ['hwaitbeit], *n.* blanchaille, *f.*

whiten [hwaitn], *v.t.* blanchir ; (*Build.*) badigeonner.—*v.i.* blanchir.

whiteness ['hwaitnis], *n.* blancheur ; pâleur, *f.*

whitening ['hwaitniŋ], *n.* action de blanchir, *f.* ; [WHITING (I)].

whitewash ['hwaitwɔʃ], *n.* blanc de chaux, *m.*—*v.t.* blanchir à la chaux ; badigeonner.

whither ['hwiðə], *adv.* où, par où.

whithersoever [hwiðəsou'evə], *adv.* n'importe où.

whiting (I) ['hwaitiŋ], **whitening** ['hwaitniŋ], *n.* blanc d'Espagne, *m.*

whiting (2) ['hwaitiŋ], *n.* (*Ichth.*) merlan, *m.*

whitish ['hwaitiʃ], *a.* blanchâtre.

whitlow ['hwitlou], *n.* panaris, *m.*

Whitsun ['hwitsən], *a.* de la Pentecôte ; *Whitsunday*, le dimanche de la Pentecôte.

Whitsuntide ['hwitsəntaid]. Pentecôte, *f.*

whiz(z) [hwiz], *v.t.* siffler.

whizzing ['hwiziŋ], *n.* sifflement, *m.*

who [huː], *pron.* (*rel.*) qui ; lequel ; (*inter.*) qui ? qui est-ce qui ?

whodunit ['huː'dʌnit], *n.* (*colloq.*) roman policier, *m.*

whoever [hu'evə], *pron.* qui, quiconque ; qui que ce soit ; celui qui.

whole [houl], *a.* tout, entier, tout entier, complet ; intégral ; bien portant ; en grains (*non moulu*).—*n.* tout, ensemble ; total, montant, *m.* ; somme, totalité, *f.* ; *on the whole*, en somme, dans l'ensemble.

whole-hearted [houl'haːtid], *a.* sincère.

whole-heartedly [houl'haːtidli], *adv.* sincèrement.

wholesale ['houlseil], *a.* en gros.—*n.* vente en gros, *f.*

wholesome ['houlsəm], *a.* sain, salubre ; salutaire ; utile.

wholesomeness ['houlsəmnis], *n.* salubrité, nature salutaire, *f.*

wholly ['houlli], *adv.* entièrement, complètement, tout à fait.

whom [huːm], *pron.* (*rel.*) que, lequel ; (*inter.*) qui ? qui est-ce que ?

whomsoever [huːmsou'evə], *pron.* qui que ce soit que.

whoop [huːp], *n.* huée, *f.* ; cri (*de guerre*), *m.*—*v.t.*, *v.i.* huer, crier.

whooping ['huːpiŋ], *n.* huées, *f.pl.*

whooping cough ['huːpiŋkɔf], *n.* coqueluche, *f.*

whopper ['hwɔpə], *n.* (*slang*) chose énorme, *f.* ; mensonge énorme, *m.* ; bourde, *f.*

whose [huːz], *pron.* (*rel.*) dont, de qui ; duquel, *m.*, de laquelle, *f.*, desquels, *m.pl.*, desquelles, *f.pl.* ; (*inter.*) à qui ?

whosoever [hu:souˈevə], *pron.* qui que ce soit qui.

why [hwai], *adv.* pourquoi ?—*int.* eh bien, mais! tiens!

wick [wik], *n.* mèche, *f.*

wicked [ˈwikid], *a.* méchant, malin.

wickedly [ˈwikidli], *adv.* méchamment.

wickedness [ˈwikidnis], *n.* méchanceté, perversité, *f.*

wicker [ˈwikə], *a.* d'osier, en osier.—*n.* osier, *m.*

wicker-work [ˈwikəwə:k], *n.* clayonnage, *m.*; vannerie, *f.*

wicket [ˈwikit], *n.* guichet, *m.*

wide [waid], *a.* large, grand, ample, vaste, immense (*d'étendue*); **three feet wide**, large de trois pieds; **to open wide**, ouvrir tout grand.—*adv.* loin, au loin, largement; **far and wide**, partout; **wide apart**, écarté, espacé.

wide-awake [ˈwaidəˈweik], *a.* bien éveillé.

widely [ˈwaidli], *adv.* au loin, loin; grandement; largement; **widely known**, bien connu.

widen [waidn], *v.t.* élargir, étendre.—*v.i.* s'élargir, s'étendre.

wideness [ˈwaidnis], *n.* largeur, étendue, *f.*

widening [ˈwaidniŋ], *n.* élargissement, *m.*

wide-spread [ˈwaidspred], *a.* répandu; général, universel.

widow [ˈwidou], *n.* veuve, *f.*

widowed [ˈwidoud], *a.* veuf, veuve; (*fig.*) privé (*de*).—*n.* tressaillement, *m.*

widower [ˈwidouə], *n.* veuf, *m.*

widowhood [ˈwidouhud], *n.* veuvage, *m.*

width [widθ], *n.* largeur, étendue, *f.*

wield [wi:ld], *v.t.* manier, tenir.

wife [waif], *n.* (*pl.* **wives** [waivz]) femme, épouse, *f.*

wifely [ˈwaifli], **wife-like** [ˈwaiflaik], *a.* de femme, d'épouse, conjugal.

wig [wig], *n.* perruque, *f.*

wig-maker [ˈwigmeikə], *n.* perruquier, *m.*

wigged [wigd], *a.* à perruque, portant perruque.

wigging [ˈwigiŋ], *n.* (*colloq.*) savon, *m.*, semonce, *f.*

wiggle [wigl], *v.t.* agiter.—*v.i.* se dandiner.

wild [waild], *a.* sauvage; farouche (*non apprivoisé*); effaré, déréglé (*désordonné*); furieux (*de rage*); insensé, extravagant (*fou*); étrange, bizarre (*baroque*); **wild beast**, fauve, *m.*; **wild boar**, sanglier, *m.*; **wildcat**, chat sauvage, *m.*—*n.*(*pl.*) désert, lieu sauvage, *m.*

wilderness [ˈwildənis], *n.* lieu désert, *m.*

wildfire [ˈwaildfaiə], *n.* feu grégeois, *m.*; **like wildfire**, comme l'éclair.

wildly [ˈwaildli], *adv.* d'une manière farouche, d'un air effaré; étourdiment, follement; à tort et à travers.

wildness [ˈwaildnis], *n.* état sauvage; dérèglement, désordre, *m.*, turbulence, licence, *f.*

wile [wail], *n.* (*usu. pl.*) artifice, *m.*, ruse, *f.*

wilful [ˈwilful], *a.* opiniâtre; obstiné, volontaire, prémédité.

wilfully [ˈwilfuli], *adv.* opiniâtrement; à dessein.

wilfulness [ˈwilfulnis], *n.* obstination, opiniâtreté, *f.*

will [wil], *n.* volonté, *f.*; vouloir; bon plaisir, gré (*inclination*); (*Law*) testament, *m.*—*v.t.* vouloir, ordonner; léguer (*par testament*).—*v. aux. irr.*, *when used to indicate the future it is not translated; he will come*, il viendra; *when used emphatically it is translated by vouloir; I will not do it*, je ne veux pas le faire.

William [ˈwiljəm]. Guillaume, *m.*

willing [ˈwiliŋ], *a.* bien disposé; de bonne volonté; *to be willing*, vouloir bien, être disposé (*à*).

willingly [ˈwiliŋli], *adv.* volontiers.

willingness [ˈwiliŋnis], *n.* bonne volonté, *f.*, bon vouloir, *m.*; complaisance, *f.*

will-o'-the-wisp [wiləðəˈwisp], *n.* feu follet, *m.*

willow [ˈwilou], *n.* saule, *m.*

willy-nilly [ˈwiliˈnili], *adv.* bon gré mal gré.

wily [ˈwaili], *a.* rusé, fin, astucieux.

win [win], *v.t. irr.* gagner (*bataille, argent etc.*); remporter (*prix, victoire etc.*).—*v.i.* gagner; remporter la victoire, triompher.

wince [wins], *v.i.* sourciller, tressaillir (*de douleur*).—*n.* tressaillement, *m.*

winch [wintʃ], *n.* manivelle, *f.*, treuil (*cabestan*), *m.*

wind (1) [wind], *n.* vent; souffle, *m.*, respiration, haleine (*breath*), *f.*; (*Med.*) vents, *m.pl.* flatuosité, *f.*—*v.t.* faire perdre haleine à essouffler (*cheval*).

wind (2) [waind], *v.t. irr.* enrouler (*en peloton*); dévider (*soie etc.*); *to wind up*, remonter (*pendule etc.*), terminer (*négociation*); (*Comm.*) liquider.—*v.i.* tourner; se rouler, s'enrouler, s'enlacer; faire un détour; serpenter (*route, rivière*).

wind-bag [ˈwindbæg], *n.* (*fig.*) moulin à paroles, *m.*

winded [ˈwindid], *a.* hors d'haleine, essoufflé; *long-winded*, de longue haleine.

winder [ˈwaində], *n.* dévidoir (*appareil*); remontoir (*de montre*), *m.*

windfall [ˈwindfɔ:l], *n.* (*fig.*) bonne aubaine, *f.*

wind gauge [ˈwindgeidʒ], *n.* anémomètre, *m.*

winding [ˈwaindiŋ], *a.* sinueux, tortueux; en spirale (*escalier*).—*n.* sinuosité, *f.*; (*Elec.*) enroulement, *m.*

winding sheet [ˈwaindiŋʃi:t], *n.* linceul, *m.*

wind-jammer [ˈwinddʒæmə], *n.* (*Naut.*) voilier, *m.*

windlass [ˈwindləs], *n.* treuil, *m.*; (*Naut.*) guindeau, cabestan, *m.*

windmill [ˈwindmil], *n.* moulin à vent, *m.*

window [ˈwindou], *n.* fenêtre; glace (*de train, voiture etc.*); montre, vitrine, *f.*; étalage (*de magasin*), *m.*; (*pl.*) vitraux (*d'église*), *m.pl.*

window box [ˈwindouboks], *n.* jardinière, *f.*

window cleaner [ˈwindoukli:nə], *n.* laveur de carreaux, *m.*

window-dresser [ˈwindoudresə], *n.* étalagiste, *m.*, *f.*

window-dressing [ˈwindoudresiŋ], *n.* art de l'étalage; (*fam.*) trompe-l'œil, *m.*

window frame [ˈwindoufreim], *n.* châssis de fenêtre, *m.*

window pane [ˈwindoupein], *n.* carreau, *m.*

window-shopping [ˈwindouʃopiŋ], *n.* lèche-vitrine, *m.*

window shutter [ˈwindouʃʌtə], *n.* volet; contrevent, *m.*

window sill [ˈwindousil], *n.* rebord *ou* appui de fenêtre, *m.*

windpipe [ˈwindpaip], *n.* trachée-artère, *m.*

windshield ['windʃiːld], n. (Motor.) pare-brise, m.

wind-sock ['windsɔk], n. (Av.) manche à air, f.

wind tunnel ['windtʌnl], n. (Av.) tunnel aérodynamique, m.

windward ['windwəd], adv. au vent.—n. côté du vent, m.

windy ['windi], a. du vent; venteux; it is windy, il fait du vent.

wine [wain], n. vin, m.—v.t. to wine and dine, il fait du vent.

wine-bibber ['wainbibə], n. buveur, m., ivrogne, m., f.

wine bin ['wainbin], n. porte-bouteilles, m.

wine cellar ['wainselə], n. cave, f.

wineglass ['wainglɑːs], n. verre à vin, m.

wine-growing ['waingrouin], a. viticole—, viticulture, f.

wine merchant ['wainməːtʃənt], n. négo-ciant en vins, m.

wine-press ['wainpres], n. pressoir, m.

wine-tasting ['wainteistin], n. dégustation de vins, f.

wine waiter ['wainweitə], n. sommelier, m.

wing [win], n. aile; (Av.) escadre; (Theat.) (pl.) coulisse, f.; on the wing, au vol.—v.t. blesser à l'aile.

winged [wind], a. ailé; (fig.) rapide; blessé à l'aile.

winger ['winə], n. (Ftb.) ailier, m.

wing span ['winspæn], n. envergure, f.

wink [wink], n. clin d'œil, m., œillade, f.—v.i. cligner de l'œil; clignoter (lumière).

winking ['winkin], a. clignotant.—n. clignote-ment; clignement d'œil, m.

winkle [winkl], n. (Ichth.) bigorneau, m.

winner ['winə], n. gagnant; vainqueur (d'une course etc.), m.

winning ['winin], a. gagnant; (fig.) attrayant, séduisant.—n. (pl.) gain, m.

winning post ['wininpoust], n. poteau d'arrivée, but, m.

winnow ['winou], v.t. vanner.

winter ['wintə], a. d'hiver.—n. hiver, m.; in winter, en hiver.—v.i. hiverner, passer l'hiver (à).

wintry ['wintri], a. d'hiver, hivernal; (fig.) glacial.

wipe [waip], v.t. essuyer; to wipe off, effacer; to wipe up, nettoyer.

wiper ['waipə], n. windshield wiper, essuie-glace, m.

wire [waiə], n. fil métallique, fil de fer, m.; dépêche (télégramme), f.; barbed wire, fil de fer barbelé.—v.t. attacher ou lier avec du fil de métal; griller; (fig.) télégraphier.

wire cutters ['waiəkʌtəz], n.pl. cisailles coupe-fil, f.pl.

wire-haired ['waiəhɛəd], a. à poil dur (chien).

wireless ['waiəlis], a. sans fil.—n. radio, T.S.F., f.; wireless set, poste de T.S.F., m., radio, f.

wire netting ['waiə'netin], n. grillage, treillis métallique, m.

wire rope ['waiə'roup], n. câble métallique, m.

wiring ['waiərin], n. (Elec.) canalisation, f.; câblage, m.

wiry ['waiəri], a. (fig.) nerveux, souple.

wisdom ['wizdəm], n. sagesse; prudence, f.

wise [waiz], a. sage; discret, prudent.—n. manière, façon, sorte, guise, f.

wise-crack ['waizkræk], n. bon mot, m.

wisely ['waizli], adv. sagement; prudemment.

wish [wiʃ], n. souhait, désir, m., envie, f.—v.t., v.i. souhaiter, désirer, vouloir; I wish I could, je voudrais pouvoir; I wish I were . . ., je voudrais être . . .; to wish well to, vouloir du bien à.

wish-bone ['wiʃboun], n. lunette, fourchette, f.

wishful ['wiʃful], a. désireux (de).

wishy-washy ['wiʃi'wɔʃi], a. faible, pauvre.

wisp [wisp], n. bouchon de paille etc., m.; mèche (de cheveux), f.

wisteria [wis'tɛəriə], n. glycine, f.

wistful ['wistful], a. désireux; d'envie, de regret, pensif (air, regard, sourire).

wistfully ['wistfuli], adv. d'un air de vague regret.

wit [wit], n. esprit; entendement, jugement; (fig.) bel esprit; (pl.) esprit, m., raison, tête, f., sens, bon sens, m.; to be at one's wits' end, ne savoir que faire.—v.t. savoir; to wit, c'est-à-dire.

witch [witʃ], n. sorcière, magicienne, f.

witchcraft ['witʃkrɑːft], n. sorcellerie, magie noire, f.

witch hazel ['witʃheizl], n. (Bot.) hamamélis, m.

with [wið], prep. avec; de, par (au moyen de); à, au, à la, aux (in descriptive phrases); chez, parmi (in compagnie de); auprès de (de l'avis de); malgré (en dépit de); angry with, fâché contre.

withal [wið'ɔːl], adv. avec tout cela, en outre.

withdraw [wið'drɔː], v.t. irr. (conjug. like DRAW) retirer; rappeler; éloigner (de).—v.i. se retirer, s'éloigner (de).

withdrawal [wið'drɔːəl] n. retraite (des vaincus), f.; retrait (enlèvement), m.

wither ['wiðə], v.i. se flétrir, se faner.

withering ['wiðərin], a. écrasant (sarcas-tique).

withers ['wiðəz], n.pl. garrot (de cheval), m.

withhold [wið'hould], v.t. irr. (conjug. like HOLD) retenir; refuser.

within [wið'in], prep. dans, en; à moins de (pas plus de); within a pound or so, à une livre près; within reach of, à portée de.—adv. en dedans, à l'intérieur; à la maison, chez soi.

without [wið'aut], prep. sans (manquant de).—conj. à moins que, sans que (unless).—adv. en dehors, au dehors.

withstand [wið'stænd], v.t. irr. (conjug. like STAND) résister à, combattre.

withy ['wiði], a. d'osier.—n. osier, m.

witless ['witlis], a. sans esprit; sot.

witness ['witnis], n. témoin; témoignage (preuve), m.—v.t. témoigner; être témoin de.—v.i. témoigner, porter témoignage.

witticism ['witisizm], n. bon mot, m.

wittily ['witili], adv. spirituellement, avec esprit.

wittiness ['witinis], n. esprit, caractère spirituel, m.

wittingly ['witinli], adv. sciemment, à dessein.

witty ['witi], a. spirituel; plaisant (facétieux).

wives [WIFE].

wizard ['wizəd], n. sorcier, magicien, m.

wizened ['wizənd], a. ratatiné, ridé.

wobble [wɔbl], v.i. vaciller, ballotter.

wobbling ['wɔbliŋ], *a.* vacillant, branlant.—
n. vacillation, *f.*; dandinement, *m.*

wobbly ['wɔbli], *a.* branlant, vacillant.

woe [wou], *n.* (*fig.*) peine, douleur, *f.*; malheur, *m.*

woebegone ['woubigɔn], **woeful** ['wouful], *a.* triste, malheureux, abattu.

woefully ['woufuli], *adv.* tristement.

wolf [wulf], *n.* (*pl.* **wolves** [wulvz]) loup, *m.*; *she-wolf*, louve, *f.*

wolf cub ['wulfkʌb], *n.* louveteau, *m.*

wolf dog ['wulfdɔg], *n.* chien-loup, *m.*

wolfish ['wulfiʃ], *a.* de loup; (*fig.*) rapace.

wolves [WOLF].

woman ['wumən], *n.* (*pl.* **women** ['wimin]) femme, *f.*

woman hater ['wumənheitə], *n.* misogyne, *m.*

womanhood ['wumənhud], *n.* état de femme, *m.*

womankind ['wumənkaind], *n.* le sexe féminin, *m.*; les femmes, *f.pl.*

womanly ['wumənli], *a.* de femme.

womanliness ['wumənlinis], *n.* fémininité, *f.*

womb [wu:m], *n.* (*Anat.*) matrice, *f.*; (*fig.*) sein, *m.*, flancs, *m.pl.*

women [WOMAN].

wonder ['wandə], *n.* étonnement *m.*, surprise; merveille (*spectacle etc.*), *f.*, miracle, prodige, *m.*—*v.i.* s'étonner, être étonné; se demander; *to wonder whether*, se demander si.

wonderful ['wandəful], *a.* étonnant, merveilleux.

wonderfully ['wandəfuli], *adv.* étonnamment, merveilleusement.

wonderment ['wandəmənt], *n.* étonnement, *m.*

wondrous ['wandrəs], *a.* merveilleux.

wondrously ['wandrəsli], *adv.* merveilleusement.

wont [wount], *a.* *to be wont to*, avoir l'habitude de.—*n.* coutume, habitude, *f.*

wonted ['wountid], *a.* accoutumé, habituel.

woo [wu:], *v.t.* faire la cour à; courtiser.

wood [wud], *n.* bois (*matériel ou forêt*), *m.*

woodbine ['wudbain], *n.* chèvrefeuille, *m.*

woodcock ['wudkɔk], *n.* bécasse, *f.*

woodcut ['wudkʌt], *n.* gravure sur bois, *f.*

wood-cutter ['wudkʌtə], *n.* bûcheron, *m.*

wooded ['wudid], *a.* boisé.

wooden [wudn], *a.* de bois, en bois; (*fig.*) gauche (*mouvement etc.*).

woodland ['wudlənd], *a.* des bois, sylvestre. —*n.* pays boisé, bois, *m.*

woodman ['wudmən], *n.* (*pl.* -men [men]) garde forestier; bûcheron, *m.*

wood nymph ['wudnimf], *n.* nymphe des bois, dryade, *f.*

woodpecker ['wudpekə], *n.* pic, *m.*; *green woodpecker*, pivert, *m.*

wood pigeon ['wudpidʒin], *n.* pigeon ramier, *m.*

wood pulp ['wudpʌlp], *n.* pâte de bois, *f.*

wood-winds ['wudwindz], *n.pl.* (*Mus.*) les bois, *m.pl.*

woodwork ['wudwə:k], *n.* boiserie; menuiserie; charpente, *f.*

wood-worm ['wudwə:m], *n.* artison, *m.*

woody ['wudi], *a.* boisé; ligneux.

wood yard ['wudjɑ:d], *n.* chantier, *m.*

wooer ['wu:ə], *n.* amoureux, prétendant, *m.*

woof [wu:f], *n.* trame, *f.*; tissu (*texture*), *m.*

wooing ['wu:iŋ], *n.* cour, *f.*

wool [wul], *n.* laine, *f.*

woollen ['wulən], *a.* de laine, à laine.—*n.*(*pl.*) tissus de laine, *m.pl.*, laines, *f.pl.*, lainages, *m.pl.*; *woollen cloth*, drap, *m.*; *wool dealer*, marchand de draps, *m.*; *woollen goods*, (*fam.*) *woollies*, lainages, *m.pl.*

woolliness ['wulinis], *n.* nature laineuse; (*fig.*) imprécision, *f.*

woolly ['wuli], *a.* laineux.

Woolsack ['wulsæk], *n.* sac de laine (*siège du Lord Chancellor*), *m.*

word [wə:d], *n.* mot, *m.*; parole (*prononcée*), *f.*; avis, *m.*, nouvelle (*communication*), *f.*; *by word of mouth*, de vive voix; *in a word*, en un mot; *not a word!* bouche close!— *v.t.* exprimer; énoncer; rédiger (*télégramme*).

word-book ['wə:dbuk], *n.* vocabulaire, lexique, *m.*

wordiness ['wə:dinis], *n.* prolixité, verbosité, *f.*

wording ['wə:diŋ], *n.* expression, *f.*; énoncé (*d'un problème*), *m.*

wordy ['wə:di], *a.* verbeux, diffus.

work [wə:k], *v.t.* travailler; façonner (*ouvrager*); se frayer (*un chemin*); payer (*son passage*) en travaillant; broder (*coudre*); faire aller, manœuvrer (*machine etc.*); exploiter (*mine etc.*); *to work off*, user; *to work oneself up*, s'exciter; *to work out*, résoudre (*problème*).—*v.i.* travailler; fonctionner, marcher, aller, jouer; opérer, avoir de l'effet (*agir*); *to work loose*, se desserrer.— *n.* travail; ouvrage, *m.*, besogne (*tâche*); (*fig.*) affaire; (*Lit.*) œuvre, *f.*; (*pl.*) mécanisme (*de moteur*), *m.*; manœuvres (*d'une machine*), *f.pl.*; (*Ind.*) fabrique, usine, *f.*; (*Fort.*) travaux, *m.pl.*; mouvement (*de montre*), *m.*; *road works ahead*, attention, travaux! *to be out of work*, chômer.

workable ['wə:kəbl], *a.* réalisable; exploitable (*mine etc.*).

workaday ['wə:kədei], *a.* de tous les jours.

work-bench ['wə:kbentʃ], *n.* établi, *m.*

work-box ['wə:kbɔks], *n.* boîte à ouvrage, *f.*

worker ['wə:kə], *n.* travailleur; ouvrier; employé, *m.*

workhouse ['wə:khaus], *n.* maison des pauvres, *f.*; hospice, *m.*

working ['wə:kiŋ], *a.* qui travaille, ouvrier; de travail (*vêtements*); *hard-working*, laborieux; *in working order*, en état de fonctionnement; *working capital*, capital d'exploitation, *m.*; *working man*, ouvrier, *m.*—*n.* travail, *m.*; marche, *f.*; fonctionnement, jeu (*de machine*), *m.*; opération; exploitation (*de mine etc.*), *f.*

working class ['wə:kiŋklɑːs], *n.* classe ouvrière, *f.*

working day ['wə:kiŋdei], *n.* jour ouvrable, *m.*

workman ['wə:kmən], *n.* (*pl.* -men [men]) ouvrier, artisan, *m.*

workmanlike ['wə:kmənlaik], *a.* bien fait, bien travaillé.

workmanship ['wə:kmənʃip], *n.* ouvrage, travail, *m.*

work-room ['wə:kru:m], **work-shop** ['wə:kʃɔp], *n.* atelier, *m.*

world [wə:ld], *n.* monde; l'univers; (*fig.*) monde, *m.*, vie, *f.*; *all the world over*, dans le monde entier; *a world of good*, un bien infini; *the first world war*, la première guerre mondiale.

worldliness ['wə:ldlinis], *n.* mondanité; frivolité, *f.*

worldly ['wə:ldli], *a.* mondain, du monde.

worldwide ['wə:ldwaid], *a.* universel, répandu partout.

worm [wə:m], *n.* ver, *m.*; chenille, larve, *f.*; filet (*de vis*), *m.*—*v.t.* miner; *to worm oneself into*, s'insinuer, se faufiler dans.

worm cast ['wə:mka:st], *n.* déjection de ver (de terre), *f.*

worm-eaten ['wə:mi:tn], *a.* rongé des vers, vermoulu.

worm screw ['wə:mskru:], *n.* tire-bourre, *m.*

wormwood ['wə:mwud], *n.* armoise amère, *f.*; (*fig.*) fiel, *m.*

worried ['wʌrid], *a.* tourmenté, harassé, ennuyé.

worry ['wʌri], *n.* ennui, tracas, souci, *m.*—*v.t.* tourmenter, tracasser.—*v.i.* tracasser; *don't worry!* soyez tranquille!

worse [wə:s], *a.* pire; plus mauvais; plus malade, plus mal (*santé*).—*n.* pire; plus mauvais, *m.*—*adv.* plus mal, pis; *far worse*, bien pis, bien pire; *so much the worse*, tant pis.

worsen [wə:sn], *v.i.* empirer.

worsening ['wə:snin], *n.* aggravation, *f.*

worship ['wə:ʃip], *n.* culte, *m.*, adoration, *f.*; honneur (*titre*), *m.*—*v.t.*, *v.i.* adorer.

worshipful ['wə:ʃipful], *a.* honorable.

worshipper ['wə:ʃipə], *n.* adorateur, *m.*

worst [wə:st], *a.* le plus mauvais, le pire.—*adv.* le pis, le plus mal.—*n.* le plus mauvais, le pire, le pis.—*v.t.* battre, vaincre, défaire.

worsted ['wustid], *a.* de laine peignée.—*n.* laine peignée, *f.*

worth [wə:θ], *a.* qui vaut, valant; qui mérite (*digne*); qui est riche de (*qui possède*); *to be worth doing*, valoir la peine de faire.—*n.* valeur, *f.*; prix, *m.*; *for all one's worth*, de toutes ses forces.

worthily ['wə:ðili], *adv.* dignement.

worthiness ['wə:ðinis], *n.* mérite, *m.*

worthless ['wə:θlis], *a.* sans valeur, qui ne vaut rien; *worthless fellow*, vaurien, *m.*

worth-while ['wə:θ'hwail], *a.* qui vaut la peine (*de*).

worthy ['wə:ði], *a.* digne, honorable; (*colloq.*) brave.—*n.* (*colloq.*) brave homme; homme illustre, *m.*

would [wud], *v.aux. past* and *cond.* [WILL]. *When used emphatically would is translated by* vouloir.

would-be ['wudbi:], *a.* prétendu, soi-disant.

wound (1) [waund], *past* and *p.p.* [WIND (2)].

wound (2) [wu:nd], *n.* blessure; plaie, *f.*—*v.t.* blesser.

wounded ['wu:ndid], *a.* blessé.

woven ['wouvn], *a.* tissé.

wrack [ræk], *n.* varech, *m.*; ruine, *f.*, débris, *m.*

wraith [reiθ], *n.* revenant, *m.*

wrangle ['ræŋgl], *n.* dispute, querelle, *f.*—*v.i.* se disputer, se quereller.

wrangling ['ræŋgliŋ], *n.* dispute, *f.*, chamailleries, *f.pl.*

wrap [ræp], *v.t.* enrouler, envelopper.—*n.* châle, peignoir, *m.*

wrapper ['ræpə], *n.* enveloppe; toile d'emballage (*pour paquets*); bande (*pour journal*); couverture (*de livre*), *f.*

wrapping ['ræpiŋ], *n.* enveloppe, couverture, *f.*; *wrapping-paper*, papier d'emballage, *m.*

wrath [rɔ:θ], *n.* courroux, *m.*, colère, *f.*

wrathful ['rɔ:θful], *a.* courroucé.

wreak [ri:k], *v.t.* exécuter, satisfaire.

wreath [ri:θ], *n.* guirlande, *f.*, feston, *m.*; couronne (*d'épouse etc.*), *f.*

wreathe [ri:ð], *v.t.* entrelacer, tresser (*de*).—*v.i.* s'entrelacer, s'enrouler.

wreathed [ri:ðd], *a.* entrelacé.

wreck [rek], *n.* naufrage; navire naufragé, *m.*, épave (*fig.*) ruine, *f.*—*v.t.* faire faire naufrage à; (*fig.*) ruiner.

wreckage ['rekidʒ], *n.* débris de naufrage, *m.*, épaves, *f.pl.*

wrecked [rekt], *a.* naufragé; ruiné.

wrecker ['rekə], *n.* pilleur d'épaves, naufrageur, *m.*; (*Motor.*) dépanneuse, *f.* [see *house-breaker*; *train*]

wren [ren], *n.* (*Orn.*) roitelet, *m.*

wrench [rentʃ], *n.* torsion, *f.*, arrachement, *m.*; entorse (*des muscles*); clef (*outil*), *f.*—*v.t.* arracher (*à* ou *de*); se fouler (*cheville etc.*).

wrest [rest], *v.t.* arracher (*à*).

wrestle [resl], *v.i.* lutter.

wrestler ['reslə], *n.* lutteur, *m.*

wrestling ['resliŋ], *n.* lutte, *f.*; catch, *m.*; *all-in wrestling*, lutte libre.

wretch [retʃ], *n.* malheureux, *m.*; misérable (*scélérat*), *m.*, *f.*; *poor wretch*, pauvre diable, *m.*

wretched ['retʃid], *a.* malheureux, misérable; vilain, triste; pitoyable, à faire pitié.

wretchedly ['retʃidli], *adv.* malheureusement, misérablement; d'une manière pitoyable.

wretchedness ['retʃidnis], *n.* misère, pauvreté, *f.*

wriggle [rigl], *v.i.* se tortiller, se remuer.

wriggling ['rigliŋ], *n.* tortillement, *m.*

wring [riŋ], *v.t. irr.* tordre; arracher (*à*); presser, serrer (*étreindre*).

wringer ['riŋə], *n.* essoreuse (*à linge*), *f.*

wringing ['riŋiŋ], *a.* *wringing wet*, trempé jusqu'aux os (*personne*); mouillé à tordre (*vêtement*).

wrinkle [riŋkl], *n.* ride (*à la figure etc.*), *f.*, pli, faux pli (*de vêtement*); (*slang*) tuyau (*renseignement*), *m.*—*v.t.* rider; plisser; *to wrinkle one's brow*, froncer les sourcils.—*v.i.* se rider.

wrinkled [riŋkld], *a.* ridé; (*Bot.*) plissé.

wrist [rist], *n.* poignet, *m.*

wristband ['ristbænd], *n.* poignet, *m.*

wrist watch ['ristwɔtʃ], *n.* montre-bracelet, *f.*

writ [rit], *n.* exploit, mandat, *m.*, ordonnance, *f.*; (*Parl.*) lettre de convocation, *f.*

write [rait], *v.t.*, *v.i. irr.* écrire; *to write off*, (*Comm.*) passer au compte des profits et pertes.

write-off ['raitɔf], *n.* annulation; non-valeur (*personne*), *f.*

writer ['raitə], *n.* écrivain.

writhe [raið], *v.i.* se tordre (*de douleur*); se crisper.

writing ['raitiŋ], *n.* écriture (*calligraphie*), *f.*; écrit (*chose écrite*); (*fig.*) ouvrage, document, *m.*; inscription, *f.*; *in writing*, par écrit.

writing case ['raitiŋkeis], *n.* papeterie, *f.*

writing desk ['raitiŋdesk], *n.* pupitre, bureau, secrétaire, *m.*

writing paper ['raitiŋpeipǝ], n. papier à écrire, m.
writing table ['raitiŋteibl], n. table à écrire, f.
written [ritn], a. écrit, par écrit.
wrong [roŋ], a. faux, erroné, inexact (pas vrai); mal, mauvais; to be wrong, avoir tort (personne), n'être pas à l'heure, aller mal (montre); what's wrong with you? qu'avez-vous? wrong number, (Teleph.) mauvais numéro, m.; wrong side, envers, m.; wrong side up, sens dessus dessous.— adv. mal, à tort, à faux.—n. mal, m., injustice, f., tort; dommage, m.—v.t. faire du tort à, nuire à.
wrongdoer ['roŋduǝ], n. pervers, méchant, m.
wrongdoing ['roŋduiŋ], n. le mal, m.
wrongful ['roŋful], a. injuste.
wrongfully ['roŋfuli], adv. à tort, injustement.
wrongly ['roŋli], adv. à tort; rightly or wrongly, à tort ou à raison.
wroth [rouθ], a. (poet.) en colère, irrité, courroucé.
wrought [rɔ:t], a. travaillé; façonné; ouvré (tissu); wrought iron, fer forgé, m.
wry [rai], a. de travers, tordu, tors; to pull a wry face, faire la grimace.

X

X, x [eks]. vingt-quatrième lettre de l'alphabet; X, dix, m.
Xerxes ['zǝ:ksi:z]. Xerxès, m.
Xmas ['krismǝs]. (abbr. CHRISTMAS) Noël, m.
X-ray ['eksrei], a. radiographique; X-ray photograph, radiographie, f.—n. (pl.) rayons X, m.pl.—v.t. radiographier.
xylophone ['zailǝfoun], n. xylophone; (slang) claquebois, m.

Y

Y, y [wai]. vingt-cinquième lettre de l'alphabet; (l')i grec, m.
yacht [jot], n. yacht, m.
yacht club ['jotklʌb], n. cercle nautique, m.
yachting ['jotiŋ], n. yachting, m.
yachtsman ['jotsmǝn], n. (pl. -men [men]) yachtman, m.
yak [jæk], n. (Zool.) ya(c)k, m.
yam [jæm], n. igname, f.
yank [jæŋk], v.t. (fam.) tirer brusquement.
Yankee ['jæŋki], n. Yankee, Américain, m.
yap [jæp], v.i. japper, aboyer.—n. jappement, m.
yard (1) [ja:d], n. cour, f., préau, m.
yard (2) [ja:d], n. (Naut.) vergue, f.; (Measure) yard (mètre o,914383), m.
yard-arm ['ja:da:m], n. bout de vergue, m.
yarn [ja:n], n. fil; (Naut.) fil de caret; récit, conte (histoire), m.

yawl [jɔ:l], n. (Naut.) sloop, m.; (Row.) yole de mer, f.
yawn [jɔ:n], n. bâillement, m.—v.i. bâiller.
yawning ['jɔ:niŋ], a. qui bâille; (fig.) béant.
***ye** [ji:], pron.pl. vous.
yea [jei], adv. oui; vraiment, en vérité.—n. vote affirmatif, m.
year [jiǝ], n. an (unité de temps), m.; année (particulière), f.; every year, tous les ans; four times a year, quatre fois par an; new year, nouvel an; next year, l'an prochain.
year-book ['jiǝbuk], n. annuaire, m.
yearling ['jiǝliŋ], a. âgé d'un an.—n. poulain, m., ou pouliche, f., d'un an.
yearly ['jiǝli], a. annuel.—adv. tous les ans.
yearn [jǝ:n], v.i. to yearn after, soupirer après; to yearn to do something, brûler de faire quelque chose.
yearning ['jǝ:niŋ], n. désir ardent, m.
yeast [ji:st], n. levure, f.
yell [jel], n. hurlement, m.—v.i. hurler, pousser des hurlements.
yelling ['jeliŋ], n. hurlements, m.pl.
yellow ['jelou], a. jaune; (slang) poltron.—n. jaune, m.—v.t., v.i. jaunir.
yellow-hammer ['jelouhæmǝ], n. (Orn.) bruant jaune, m.
yellowish ['jelouiʃ], a. jaunâtre.
yellowness ['jelounis], n. couleur jaune, f.
yelp [jelp], v.i. glapir, japper.
yelping ['jelpiŋ], n. glapissement, jappement, m.
Yemen ['jemǝn]. le Yémen, m.
Yemeni ['jemeni], a. yémenite.—n. Yémenite (personne), m., f.
yeoman ['joumǝn], n. (pl. -men [men]) fermier-propriétaire, m.
yeomanry ['joumǝnri], n. fermiers-propriétaires, m.pl.
yes [jes], adv. oui; si (in reply to a negative).
yes-man ['jesmæn], n. (pl. men [men]) (pop.) Béni-oui-oui, m.
yesterday ['jestǝd(e)i], adv. and n. hier, m.; the day before yesterday, avant-hier; yesterday evening, hier soir.
yet [jet], conj. pourtant, cependant, tout de même.—adv. encore, déjà; as yet, jusqu'ici; not yet, pas encore.
yew [ju:], n. (Bot.) if, m.
yield [ji:ld], v.t. produire, rapporter; livrer, céder (au vainqueur); to yield up, rendre.— v.i. se rendre, céder (à); consentir (à).—n. rendement, produit, rapport, m.
yielding ['ji:ldiŋ], a. complaisant, facile.—n. reddition, soumission, f.
yoke [jouk], n. joug; attelage, m., paire; palanche (pour seaux), f.; (Dress.) empièce-ment, m.—v.t. atteler, accoupler.
yokel ['joukl], n. rustre, campagnard, m.
yolk [jouk], n. jaune (d'œuf), m.
yonder ['jondǝ], adv. là, là-bas.—a. yonder castle, ce château-là.
***yore** [jɔ:], adv. autrefois, jadis.
you [ju:], pron. vous; (to a child, relative, pet etc.) tu, te, toi; (indef.) on.
young [jʌŋ], a. jeune; novice, neuf, inexpéri-menté (non éprouvé); (fig.) naissant; young folks or young people, jeunes gens, m.pl.; young lady, demoiselle, f.—n.pl. les jeunes, les jeunes gens; les petits, m.pl.; with young, pleine (animal).

younger ['jʌŋgə], *a.* plus jeune; cadet (*de deux frères etc.*).
youngest ['jʌŋgist], *a.* le plus jeune.
youngish ['jʌŋiʃ], *a.* assez jeune.
youngster ['jʌŋstə], *n.* jeune homme; gamin, mioche, *m.*, gosse, *m.*, *f.*
your [jɔː], *a.* votre, (*pl.*) vos; (*to a child, relative, pet etc.*) ton, ta, tes; (*indef.*) son, sa, ses.
yours [jɔːz], *pron.* le vôtre, *m.*, la vôtre, *f.*, les vôtres, *pl.*; à vous (*your property*); de vous (*by you*); (*to a child, relative, pet etc.*) le tien, la tienne, les tiens, les tiennes; à toi (*your property*); de toi (*by you*).
yourself [jɔː'self], *pron.* (*pl.* **yourselves** [jɔː'selvz]) vous-même, toi-même; (*pl.*) vous-mêmes; (*reflexive*) vous, te.
youth [juːθ], *n.* jeunesse, adolescence, *f.*; jeune homme, adolescent (*personne*), *m.*; (*fig.*) jeunes gens, *m.pl.*
youthful ['juːθful], *a.* jeune; de jeunesse.
youthfulness ['juːθfulnis], *n.* jeunesse, *f.*
Yugoslav ['juːgo'slɑːv], *a.* yougoslave.—*n.* Yougoslave (*personne*), *m.*, *f.*
Yugoslavia [juːgo'slɑːvjə]. la Yougoslavie, *f.*
*****Yule** [juːl], **Yule-tide** ['juːltaid], *n.* Noël, *m.*, fête de Noël, *f.*
Yule log ['juːllɔg], *n.* bûche de Noël, *f.*

Z

Z. z [zed, (*Am.*) ziː]. vingt-sixième lettre de l'alphabet, *m.*

Zambesi [zæm'biːzi]. le Zambèze, *m.*
Zambia ['zæmbjə]. la Zambie, *f.*
zany ['zeini], *n.* zani, bouffon, *m.*
zeal [ziːl], *n.* zèle, *m.*
zealot ['zelət], *n.* zélateur, *m.*, fanatique, *m.*, *f.*
zealous ['zeləs], *a.* zélé, zélateur.
zealously ['zeləsli], *adv.* avec zèle.
zebra ['ziːbrə], *n.* zèbre, *m.*; *zebra crossing* (*pedestrian crossing*), passage clouté, *m.*
zenith ['zeniθ], *n.* zénith; (*fig.*) apogée, *m.*
zephyr ['zefə], *n.* zéphyr, zéphire, Zéphyre, *m.*
zero ['ziərou], *n.* zéro; (*fig.*) rien, *m.*; *zero hour*, l'heure H, *f.*
zest [zest], *n.* goût, *m.*, saveur, *f.*; zeste (*d'orange, de citron*); (*fig.*) entrain, *m.*, verve, *f.*
Zeus [zjuːs]. (*Myth.*) Zeus, *m.*
zigzag ['zigzæg], *a.* en zigzag.—*n.* zigzag, *m.*—*v.i.* aller en zigzag, zigzaguer.
zinc [ziŋk], *n.* zinc, *m.*—*v.t.* zinguer.
zinnia ['zinjə], *n.* (*Bot.*) zinnia, *m.*
Zion ['zaiən]. Sion, *m.*
zip [zip], *n.* sifflement (*de balle*), *m.*; énergie, verve, *f.*—*v.t.* siffler; *zip fastener*, fermeture à glissière, *f.*
zither ['ziðə], *n.* cithare, *f.*
zodiac ['zoudiæk], *n.* zodiaque, *m.*
zone [zoun], *n.* zone, *f.*
zoo [zuː], *n.* jardin zoologique, (*fam.*) zoo, *m.*
zoological [zouə'lɔdʒikl], *a.* zoologique; *zoological gardens*, jardin zoologique, *m.*
zoologist [zou'ɔlədʒist], *n.* zoologiste, zoologue, *m.*, *f.*
zoology [zou'ɔlədʒi], *n.* zoologie, *f.*
zoom [zuːm], *n.* bourdonnement, ronflement, *m.*—*v.i.* vrombir.
Zulu ['zuːluː], *a.* zoulou.—*n.* Zoulou, *m.*

French Verbs

1. All verbs not marked *irr.* in the French-English section of the Dictionary are either
   (a) regular, and conjugated like AIMER, FINIR or VENDRE according to their ending (see below) or
   (b) anomalous, and conjugated like the verb in that group to which the user is referred.
2. The Imperfect Indicative, Conditional, Imperative, and Imperfect Subjunctive are not given and may be assumed to be formed as follows:
   Imperfect Indicative: by substituting for the final *-ons* of 1st Person Plural, Present Indicative the endings *-ais, -ais, -ait, -ions, -iez, -aient* (except *être: j'étais*).
   Conditional: by substituting for the endings of the Future those of the Imperfect Indicative given above.
   Imperative: (a) 2nd Person Singular, 1st and 2nd Person Plural, by using these forms of

Infinitive	Participles	Present Indicative	Past Historic
REGULAR VERBS First Conjugation Infinitive in *-er*			
aim-*er*	aim-*ant* aim-*é*	aim-*e* aim-*es* aim-*e* aim-*ons* aim-*ez* aim-*ent*	aim-*ai* aim-*as* aim-*a* aim-*âmes* aim-*âtes* aim-*èrent*
Second Conjugation Infinitive in *-ir*			
fin-*ir*	fin-*issant* fin-*i*	fin-*is* fin-*is* fin-*it* fin-*issons* fin-*issez* fin-*issent*	fin-*is* fin-*is* fin-*it* fin-*îmes* fin-*îtes* fin-*irent*
Third Conjugation Infinitive in *-re*			
vend-*re*	vend-*ant* vend-*u*	vend-*s* vend-*s* vend vend-*ons* vend-*ez* vend-*ent*	vend-*is* vend-*is* vend-*it* vend-*îmes* vend-*îtes* vend-*irent*
ANOMALOUS VERBS			
amener	amenant amené	amène amènes amène amenons amenez amènent	amenai . . . amenâmes . . .
appeler	appelant appelé	appelle appelles appelle appelons appelez appellent	appelai . . . appelâmes . . .
assiéger	assiégeant assiégé	assiège assièges assiège assiégeons assiégez assiègent	assiégeai . . . assiégeâmes . . .

the Present Indicative without pronouns (-*er* verbs drop the final *s* of the 2nd Person Singular).

    (*b*) 3rd Person Singular and Plural by using these forms of the Present Subjunctive.

Imperfect Subjunctive: from the 2nd Person Singular of the Past Historic by adding -*se*, -*ses*, -*ˆt*, -*sions*, -*siez*, -*sent*.

3. Exceptions to the above rules are indicated in footnotes.
4. Compound verbs (e.g. DEVENIR, REVENIR, etc.) are given only where they differ from the simple form (e.g. VENIR).
5. Defective verbs are marked † and all existing forms are given.

Future	Present Subjunctive	English
aimer-*ai*	aim-*e*	to like, to love
aimer-*as*	aim-*es*	
aimer-*a*	aim-*e*	
aimer-*ons*	aim-*ions*	
aimer-*ez*	aim-*iez*	
aimer-*ont*	aim-*ent*	
finir-*ai*	fini-*sse*	to finish
finir-*as*	fini-*sses*	
finir-*a*	fini-*sse*	
finir-*ons*	fini-*ssions*	
finir-*ez*	fini-*ssiez*	
finir-*ont*	fini-*ssent*	
vendr-*ai*	vend-*e*	to sell
vendr-*as*	vend-*es*	
vendr-*a*	vend-*e*	
vendr-*ons*	vend-*ions*	
vendr-*ez*	vend-*iez*	
vendr-*ont*	vend-*ent*	
amènerai...	amène	to bring
amènerons...	amènes	
	amène	
	amenions	
	ameniez	
	amènent	
appellerai...	appelle	to call
appellerons...	appelles	
	appelle	
	appelions	
	appeliez	
	appellent	
assiégerai...	assiège	to besiege
assiégerons...	assièges	
	assiège	
	assiégions	
	assiégiez	
	assiègent	

French Verbs

Infinitive	Participles	Present Indicative	Past Historic
battre	battant battu	bats bats bat battons battez battent	battis . . . battîmes . . .
céder	cédant cédé	cède cèdes cède cédons cédez cèdent	cédai . . . cédâmes . . .
commencer	commençant commencé	commence commences commence commençons commencez commencent	commençai commenças commença commençâmes commençâtes commencèrent
dépecer	dépeçant dépecé	dépèce dépèces dépèce dépeçons dépecez dépècent	dépeçai dépeças dépeça dépeçâmes dépeçâtes dépecèrent
employer[1]	employant employé	emploie emploies emploie employons employez emploient	employai . . . employâmes . . .
manger	mangeant mangé	mange manges mange mangeons mangez mangent	mangeai mangeas mangea mangeâmes mangeâtes mangèrent
payer[1]	(See footnote)		
rapiécer	rapiéçant rapiécé	rapièce rapièces rapièce rapiéçons rapiécez rapiècent	rapiéçai rapiéças rapiéça rapiéçâmes rapiéçâtes rapiécèrent
rompre	rompant rompu	romps romps rompt rompons rompez rompent	rompis . . . rompîmes . . .

IRREGULAR VERBS

† absoudre	absolvant absous, m., absoute, f.	absous absous absout absolvons absolvez absolvent	

---

[1] All verbs in -oyer and -uyer change y to i before a mute e.   With verbs in -ayer, y or i may

Future	Present Subjunctive	English
battrai . . . battrons . . .	batte . . . battions . . .	to beat
céderai . . . céderons . . .	cède cèdes cède cédions cédiez cèdent	to yield
commencerai . . . commencerons . . .	commence . . . commencions . . .	to begin
dépècerai . . . dépècerons . . .	dépèce dépèces dépèce dépecions dépeciez dépècent	to cut up
emploierai . . . emploierons . . .	emploie emploies emploie employions employiez emploient	to employ, to use
mangerai . . . mangerons . . .	mange . . . mangions . . .	to eat
		to pay (for)
rapiécerai . . . rapiécerons . . .	rapièce rapièces rapièce rapiécions rapiéciez rapiècent	to patch
romprai . . . romprons . . .	rompe . . . rompions . . .	to break
absoudrai . . . absoudrons . . .	absolve . . . absolvions . . .	to absolve

be used. With *grasseyer*, *y* is always used.

French Verbs

[1] 2nd pers. sing. Imperative: *va*.
[2] The forms in *-oi* (or *-eoi*) (same conjugation as *prévoir*) are accepted by the Académie Française but considered as familiar or even vulgar.

Future	Present Subjunctive	English
believe)		
acquerrai... acquerrons...	acquière acquières acquière acquérions acquériez acquièrent	to acquire
il adviendra	il advienne	to happen
irai... irons...	aille ailles aille allions alliez aillent	to go
assaillirai... assaillirons...	assaille... assaillions...	to assault
assiérai... *or* assoirai... assiérons... *or* assoirons...	asseye[2]... asseyions...	to set to seat
aurai... aurons...	aie aies ait ayons ayez aient	to have
boirai... boirons...	boive boives boive buvions buviez boivent	to drink
bouillirai... bouillirons...	bouille... bouillions...	to boil
il braira ils brairont		to bray
		to rustle
cherrai... *or* choirai... cherrons... *or* choirons...		to fall
clorai... clorons...	close... closions...	to close

---

[2] Imperative: *aie, ayons, ayez.*
[4] Imperfect Indicative: *il brayait, ils brayaient.*
[5] Imperfect Indicative: *il bruissait, ils bruissaient* or *il bruyait, ils bruyaient.*

French Verbs

Infinitive	Participles	Present Indicative	Past Historic
conclure	concluant conclu	conclus, -s, -t concluons...	conclus... conclûmes...
conduire	conduisant conduit	conduis, -s, -t conduisons...	conduisis... conduisimes...
confire	confisant confit	confis, -s, -t confisons...	confis... confimes...
connaître	connaissant connu	connais connais connaît connaissons connaissez connaissent	connus... connûmes...
coudre	cousant cousu	couds... cousons...	cousis... cousimes...
courir	courant couru	cours,-s,-t courons...	courus... courûmes...
craindre	craignant craint	crains,-s,-t craignons...	craignis... craignimes...
croire	croyant cru	crois crois croît croyons croyez croient	crus... crûmes...
croître	croissant [1] crû, *m.*, crue, *f.*,	crois crois croit croissons croissez croissent	crûs... crûmes...
cueillir	cueillant cueilli	cueille... cueillons...	cueillis... cueillimes...
† déchoir [2]	déchu	déchois déchois déchoit déchoyons déchoyez déchoient	déchus... déchûmes...
devoir	devant dû, *m.*, due, *f.*, dus, *m.pl.*	dois dois doit devons devez doivent	dus... dûmes...
dire	disant dit	dis dis dit disons dites disent	dis... dîmes...
† échoir	échéant échu	il échoit ils échoient	il échut ils échurent

[1] The past part. of **accroître** is **accru**, and of **décroître**, **décru** (no circumflex on the *u* of the masculine sing.).   [2] No Imperfect Indicative.

Future	Present Subjunctive	English
conclurai... conclurons...	conclue... concluions...	to conclude
conduirai... conduirons...	conduise... conduisions...	to lead to drive
confirai... confirons...	confise... confisions...	to preserve
connaîtrai... connaîtrons...	connaisse... connaissions...	to know
coudrai... coudrons...	couse... cousions...	to sew
courrai... courrons...	coure... courions...	to run
craindrai... craindrons...	craigne... craignions...	to fear
croirai... croirons...	croie croies croie croyions croyiez croient	to believe
croîtrai... croîtrons...	croisse... croissions...	to grow
cueillerai... cueillerons...	cueille... cueillions...	to gather
décherrai... décherrons...	déchoie déchoies déchoie déchoyions déchoyiez déchoient	to fall to lose
devrai... devrons...	doive doives doive devions deviez doivent	to owe to have to
dirai... dirons...	dise... disions...	to say
il échoira *or* écherra ils échoiront *or* écherront	il échoie *or* échée ils échéent	to fall due

French Verbs

Infinitive	Participles	Present Indicative	Past Historic
écrire	écrivant écrit	écris,-s,-t écrivons...	écrivis... écrivîmes...
envoyer	envoyant envoyé	envoie envoies envoie envoyons envoyez envoient	envoyai... envoyâmes...
être[1]	étant été	suis es est sommes êtes sont	fus... fûmes...
† faillir	faillant failli	faut[2]	faillis[3]... faillîmes...
faire	faisant fait	fais fais fait faisons faites font	fis... fîmes...
† falloir[4]	fallu	il faut	il fallut
† férir[5]	féru		
† forfaire (à)	forfait		
† frire	frit	fris fris frit	
fuir	fuyant fui	fuis fuis fuit fuyons fuyez fuient	fuis... fuîmes...
† gésir[6]	gisant	gît gisons gisez gisent	
haïr	haïssant haï	hais,-s,-t haïssons...	haïs... haïmes[7]...
lire	lisant lu	lis,-s,-t lisons...	lus... lûmes...
luire	luisant lui	luis,-s,-t luisons...	luis... luîmes...
maudire	conjugated like the regular verbs in -ir, e.g. finir, except for the past		
médire (de)	médisant médit	médis... médisons...	médis... médîmes...

[1] Imperfect Indic.: *j'étais*; Imperative: *sois, soyons, soyez*.
[2] Only in the phrase *le cœur me faut*.
[3] In current usage followed by an infinitive, *e.g. il faillit tomber*, he nearly fell.
[4] Imperfect Indic.: *il fallait*.

Future	Present Subjunctive	English
écrirai... écrirons...	écrive... écrivions...	to write
enverrai... enverrons...	envoie envoies envoie envoyions envoyiez envoient	to send
serai... serons...	sois sois soit soyons soyez soient	to be
faudrai *or* faillirai		to fail
ferai... ferons...	fasse... fassions...	to make, to do
il faudra	il faille	to be necessary
		to strike
		to be false (to)
frirai... frirons...		to fry
fuirai... fuirons...	fuie... fuyions...	to flee
		to lie
haïrai... haïrons...	haïsse... haïssions...	to hate
lirai... lirons...	lise... lisions...	to read
luirai... luirons...	luise... luisions...	to gleam
participle (*maudit*).		to curse
médirai... médirons...	médise... médisions...	to speak ill of

[5] The infinitive is used only in the phrase *sans coup férir*, without striking a blow. *Féru* is adjectival only (*féru d'amour*, lovesick).
[6] The Imperfect Indic., *je gisais*, etc., is used.
[7] The plural is written without a circumflex: *haimes, haïtes.*

French Verbs

Infinitive	Participles	Present Indicative	Past Historic
mettre	mettant mis	mets,-s,-t mettons...	mis... mîmes...
moudre	moulant moulu	mouds mouds moud moulons moulez moulent	moulus... moulûmes...
mourir	mourant mort	meurs meurs meurt mourons mourez meurent	mourus... mourûmes...
mouvoir	mouvant [1]mû, m., mue, f., mus, m.pl.	meus meus meut mouvons mouvez meuvent	mus... mûmes...
naître	naissant né	nais nais naît naissons naissez naissent	naquis... naquîmes...
nuire (à)	nuisant nui	nuis,-s,-t nuisons...	nuisis... nuisîmes...
† oindre[2]	oint		
† ouïr[3]	oyant ouï		ouïs... ouïmes...
ouvrir	ouvrant ouvert	ouvre... ouvrons...	ouvris... ouvrîmes...
† paître	paissant	pais pais paît paissons paissez paissent	
plaire	plaisant plu	plais plais plaît plaisons plaisez plaisent	plus... plûmes..
† pleuvoir	pleuvant plu	il pleut	il plut
† poindre	poignant point	il point	
pourvoir	pourvoyant pourvu	pourvois,-s,-t pourvoyons,-yez,-ient	pourvus... pourvûmes...

[1] The past part. of *émouvoir* is *ému*, and of *promouvoir*, *promu* (no circumflex on the *u* of the masculine sing.).

Future	Present Subjunctive	English
mettrai... mettrons...	mette... mettions...	to put
moudrai... moudrons...	moule... moulions...	to grind
mourrai... mourrons...	meure meures meure mourions mouriez meurent	to die
mouvrai... mouvrons...	meuve meuves meuve mouvions mouviez meuvent	to move
naîtrai... naîtrons...	naisse... naissions...	to be born
nuirai... nuirons...	nuise... nuisions...	to harm
oindrai...		to anoint
ouïrai... ouïrons...		to hear
ouvrirai... ouvrirons...	ouvre... ouvrions...	to open
paîtrai... paîtrons...	paisse... paissions...	to graze
plairai... plairons...	plaise... plaisions...	to please
il pleuvra	il pleuve	to rain
il poindra ils poindront		to dawn to sting
pourvoirai... pourvoirons...	pourvoie... pourvoyions...	to provide

¹ Imperfect Indic.: *je oignais.*
² This verb is seldom used other than in the infinitive and in the compound tenses.

French Verbs

Infinitive	Participles	Present Indicative	Past Historic
pouvoir	pouvant pu	peux *or* puis peux peut pouvons pouvez peuvent	pus... pûmes...
prendre	prenant pris	prends prends prend prenons prenez prennent	pris... prîmes...
prévoir	prévoyant prévu	prévois,-s,-t prévoyons, -yez, -ient	prévis... prévîmes...
recevoir	recevant reçu	reçois reçois reçoit recevons recevez reçoivent	reçus... reçûmes...
résoudre	résolvant résolu *or* résous	résous résous résout résolvons résolvez résolvent	résolus... résolûmes...
rire	riant ri	ris,-s,-t rions...	ris... rîmes...
savoir[1]	sachant su	sais,-s,-t savons...	sus... sûmes...
sentir	sentant senti	sens,-s,-t sentons...	sentis... sentîmes...
† seoir	seyant	il sied ils siéent	
suffire	suffisant suffi	suffis,-s,-t suffisons...	suffis... suffîmes...
suivre	suivant suivi	suis,-s,-t suivons...	suivis... suivîmes...
surseoir[2]	sursoyant sursis	sursois,-s,-t sursoyons, -yez, -ient	sursis... sursîmes...
taire	conjug. like *plaire* except that there is no circumflex on the *i* of the 3rd		
tenir[3]	tenant tenu	tiens tiens tient tenons tenez tiennent	tins tins tint tînmes tîntes tinrent
† traire	trayant trait	trais,-s,-t trayons...	

[1] Imperative: *sache, sachons, sachez.*
[2] The Past Historic and the Imperfect Indicative are seldom used.

Future	Present Subjunctive	English
pourrai... pourrons...	puisse... puissions...	to be able
prendrai... prendrons...	prenne... prenions...	to take
prévoirai... prévoirons...	prévoie... prévoyions...	to foresee
recevrai... recevrons...	reçoive reçoives reçoive recevions receviez reçoivent	to receive
résoudrai... résoudrons...	résolve... résolvions...	to resolve
rirai... rirons...	rie... riions...	to laugh
saurai... saurons...	sache... sachions...	to know
sentirai... sentirons...	sente... sentions...	to feel to smell
il siéra ils siéront	il siée ils siéent	to become to suit
suffirai... suffirons...	suffise... suffisions...	to suffice
suivrai... suivrons...	suive... suivions...	to follow
surseoirai... surseoirons...	sursoie... sursoyions...	to delay to suspend
Pers. Sing. Pres. Indic.: *il tait.*		to keep silent about
tiendrai... tiendrons...	tienne tiennes tienne tenions teniez tiennent	to hold
trairai... trairons...	traie... trayions...	to milk

a Imperfect Subjunctive: *tinsse, -es, tint, tinssions, -iez, -ent.*

French Verbs

Infinitive	Participles	Present Indicative	Past Historic
vaincre	vainquant vaincu	vaincs vaincs vainc vainquons vainquez vainquent	vainquis... vainquîmes...
valoir	valant valu	vaux, -x, -t valons...	valus... valûmes...
vêtir	vêtant vêtu	vêts, vêts, vêt vêtons...	vêtis... vêtîmes...
vivre	vivant vécu	vis,-s,-t vivons...	vécus... vécûmes...
voir	voyant vu	vois,-s,-t voyons, -yez, -ient	vis... vîmes...
vouloir[1]	voulant voulu	veux veux veut voulons voulez veulent	voulus... voulûmes...

[1] Imperative: *veuille, veuillons, veuillez.*

Future	Present Subjunctive	English
vaincrai... vaincrons...	vainque... vainquions...	to conquer
vaudrai... vaudrons...	[2]vaille... valions...	to be worth
vêtirai... vêtirons...	vête... vêtions...	to clothe
vivrai... vivrons...	vive... vivions...	to live
verrai... verrons...	voie... voyions...	to see
voudrai... voudrons...	veuille... voulions...	to be willing to want, to wish

[2] *prévaloir: prévale, prévalions.*

English Verbs

All verbs not marked *irr.* in the English-French section of the Dictionary come in one of the following categories:

(*a*) Regular verbs, conjugated like WORK or LIVE.

(*b*) Verbs ending in -*y* preceded by one or more consonants, e.g. DENY, REPLY, IMPLY, conjugated like CARRY (i.e. the *y* changes to *i* in the Past Tense and Past Participle).

(*c*) Verbs ending in a single consonant preceded by one or more vowels (but not a diphthong, e.g. WAIT, or a double vowel, e.g. SEEM), which are monosyllabic or in which the stress falls on the last syllable, conjugated like DROP and PREFER (i.e. the final consonant is doubled in the Past Tense and Past Participle).

N.B. Apart from those which are irregular, all verbs ending in -*l* preceded by one or more vowels (but not a diphthong, e.g. SAIL, or a double vowel, e.g. PEEL) may double the *l* in the Past and Past Participle even if the stress does not fall on the last syllable, e.g. IMPERIL, DIAL.

* – obsolete.   *A – obsolete, but still used adjectivally.   † – becoming obsolete.
†A – becoming obsolete, but still used adjectivally.

Infinitive	Past Tense	Past Participle	French
REGULAR VERBS (*a*)			
work	worked	worked	travailler
live	lived	lived	vivre
REGULAR VERBS (*b*)			
carry	carried	carried	porter
REGULAR VERBS (*c*)			
drop	dropped	dropped	laisser tomber
prefer	preferred	preferred	préférer
imperil	imperilled	imperilled	hasarder
dial	dialled	dialled	composer un numéro
IRREGULAR VERBS			
abide	abode	abode	demeurer
awake	awoke	awoken *or* awakened	éveiller
be *Pres. Indic.* am, art, is, are	was, were	been	être
bear	bore	borne *or* born[1]	porter
beat	beat	beaten	battre
beget	begot *begat	begotten	engendrer
begin	began	begun	commencer
bend	bent	bent	courber
bereave	bereaved *or* bereft	bereaved *or* bereft	priver (de)
beseech	besought	besought	supplier
bid	bade *or* bid	bidden *or* bid	ordonner

[1] *born* – né; *borne* – porté.

Infinitive	Past Tense	Past Participle	French
bind	bound	bound *A bounden[1]	lier
bite	bit	bitten	mordre
bleed	bled	bled	saigner
blow	blew	blown	souffler
break	broke	broken	casser
breed	bred	bred	élever
bring	brought	brought	apporter
build	built	built	construire
burn	burnt or burned	burnt or burned	brûler
burst	burst	burst	éclater
buy	bought	bought	acheter
Pres. Indic. can	could	——	pouvoir
cast	cast	cast	jeter
catch	caught	caught	attraper
choose	chose	chosen	choisir
cleave (*v.t.*)	cleft *clove	cleft *A cloven[2]	fendre
cling	clung	clung	s'attacher
come	came	come	venir
cost	cost	cost	coûter
creep	crept	crept	ramper
crow	crowed or †crew	crowed	chanter (coq)
cut	cut	cut	couper
deal	dealt	dealt	distribuer
dig	dug	dug	creuser
do	did	done	faire
draw	drew	drawn	tirer, dessiner
dream	dreamt or dreamed	dreamt or dreamed	rêver
drink	drank	drunk *A drunken[3]	boire
drive	drove	driven	conduire

[1] It is his *bounden* duty.   [2] *Cloven* hoof.   [3] A *drunken* brawl.

English Verbs

Infinitive	Past Tense	Past Participle	French
dwell	dwelt	dwelt	demeurer
eat	ate	eaten	manger
fall	fell	fallen	tomber
feed	fed	fed	nourrir
feel	felt	felt	sentir
fight	fought	fought	combattre
find	found	found	trouver
flee	fled	fled	fuir
fling	flung	flung	lancer
fly	flew	flown	voler
forbear	forbore	forborne	s'abstenir
forbid	forbade *or* forbad	forbidden	interdire
forget	forgot	forgotten	oublier
forsake	forsook	forsaken	abandonner
freeze	froze	frozen	geler
get	got	got *A* gotten[1]	obtenir, devenir
gird	girded *or* girt	girded *or* girt	ceindre
give	gave	given	donner
go	went	gone	aller
grind	ground	ground	moudre
grow	grew	grown	croître, devenir
hang[2]	hung	hung	pendre
have *Pres. Indic.* have,*hast, has	had	had	avoir
hear	heard	heard	entendre
heave	heaved *or* hove	heaved *or* hove	soulever
hew	hewed	hewn *or* hewed	tailler
hide	hid	hidden	cacher
hit	hit	hit	frapper

[1] Ill-*gotten* gains; but in America *gotten* is often standard usage as an alternative Past Participle.
[2] To suspend. In the meaning 'to execute by hanging', the verb is regular.

654

Infinitive	Past Tense	Past Participle	French
hold	held	held	tenir
hurt	hurt	hurt	blesser
keep	kept	kept	garder
kneel	knelt	knelt	s'agenouiller
know	knew	known	savoir
lay	laid	laid	poser
lead	led	led	conduire
lean	leant *or* leaned	leant *or* leaned	pencher
leap	leapt *or* leaped	leapt *or* leaped	sauter
learn	learnt *or* learned	learnt *or* learned	apprendre
leave	left	left	laisser, quitter
lend	lent	lent	prêter
let	let	let	laisser
lie[1]	lay	lain	être couché
light	lit *or* lighted	lit *or* lighted	allumer
lose	lost	lost	perdre
make	made	made	faire
Pres. Indic. may	might	——	pouvoir (permission, probabilité)
mean	meant	meant	signifier
meet	met	met	rencontrer
mow	mowed	mowed *or* mown	faucher
pay	paid	paid	payer
put	put	put	mettre
quit	quitted *or* quit	quitted *or* quit	quitter
read	read	read	lire
rend	rent	rent	déchirer
rid	rid	rid	débarrasser
ride	rode	ridden	aller à cheval *etc.*
ring[2]	rang	rung	sonner

[1] To recline. In the meaning 'to be untruthful', the verb is regular.
[2] (Of a bell). In the meaning 'to put a ring round', the verb is regular.

English Verbs

Infinitive	Past Tense	Past Participle	French
rise	rose	risen	se lever
rive	rived	riven *or* rived	fendre
run	ran	run	courir
saw	sawed	sawn	scier
say	said	said	dire
see	saw	seen	voir
seek	sought	sought	chercher
sell	sold	sold	vendre
send	sent	sent	envoyer
set	set	set	placer
sew	sewed	sewn *or* sewed	coudre
shake	shook	shaken	secouer
Pres. Indic. shall[1]	should[1]	——	——
shear	sheared	shorn *or* sheared	tondre
shed	shed	shed	verser
shine	shone	shone	briller
shoe	shod	shod	chausser
shoot	shot	shot	tirer (au fusil)
show	showed	shown *or* showed	montrer
shrink	shrank	shrunk *A shrunken	rétrécir
shrive	shrove	shriven	se confesser
shut	shut	shut	fermer
sing	sang	sung	chanter
sink	sank	sunk *A sunken[2]	sombrer
sit	sat	sat	être assis
slay	slew	slain	tuer
sleep	slept	slept	dormir
slide	slid	slid	glisser
sling	slung	slung	lancer

[1] Used as auxiliaries only.   [2] *Sunken* cheeks.

Infinitive	Past Tense	Past Participle	French
slink	slunk	slunk	s'esquiver
slit	slit	slit	fendre
smell	smelt *or* smelled	smelt *or* smelled	sentir
smite	smote	smitten	frapper
sow	sowed	sown *or* sowed	semer
speak	spoke *spake	spoken	parler
speed	sped *or* speeded	sped *or* speeded	se hâter
spell	spelt *or* spelled	spelt *or* spelled	épeler
spend	spent	spent	dépenser
spill	spilt *or* spilled	spilt *or* spilled	verser
spin	spun	spun	filer
spit[1]	spat *or* spit	spat *or* spit	cracher
split	split	split	fendre
spoil	spoilt *or* spoiled	spoilt *or* spoiled	gâter
spread	spread	spread	s'étendre
spring	sprang	sprung	s'élancer
stand	stood	stood	être debout
stave	staved *or* stove	staved *or* stove	crever
steal	stole	stolen	voler
stick	stuck	stuck	coller
sting	stung	stung	piquer
stink	stank	stunk	puer
strew	strewed	strewed *or* strewn	répandre
stride	strode	stridden	marcher à grands pas
strike	struck	struck †A stricken[2]	frapper
string	strung	strung	ficeler
strive	strove	striven	s'efforcer
swear	swore	sworn	jurer
sweep	swept	swept	balayer

[1] To expectorate. In the meaning 'to put on a spit', the verb is regular.
[2] *Stricken* in years.

English Verbs

Infinitive	Past Tense	Past Participle	French
swell	swelled	swollen *or* swelled	enfler
swim	swam	swum	nager
swing	swung	swung	se balancer
take	took	taken	prendre
teach	taught	taught	enseigner
tear	tore	torn	déchirer
tell	told	told	dire
think	thought	thought	penser
thrive	thrived *or* throve	thrived *or* thriven	prospérer
throw	threw	thrown	jeter
thrust	thrust	thrust	lancer
tread	trod	trodden	fouler
wake	woke *or* waked	waked	éveiller
wear	wore	worn	porter (vêtements)
weave	wove	woven	tisser
weep	wept	wept	pleurer
wet	wetted *or* wet	wetted *or* wet	mouiller
will	would	——	vouloir
win	won	won	gagner
wind	wound	wound	enrouler
wring	wrung	wrung	tordre
write	wrote	written	écrire